Fundamentals of Mathematics

Algebra II

Sanjay Mishra

B.Tech.
Indian Institute of Technology, Varanasi

G K Publications (P) Ltd

Title : Fundamentals of Mathematics Algebra II

Language : English

Author : Sanjay Mishra

Typeset & Published by :

Career Launcher Infrastructure (P) Ltd.

A-45, Mohan Cooperative Industrial Area, Near Mohan Estate Metro Station, New Delhi - 110044

Marketed by :

G.K. Publications (P) Ltd.

Plot No. 63, Sector-27A, Near Sector - 28 Metro Station, Faridabad, Haryana-121003

ISBN : **978-81-93975-88-6**

Printer's Details : Printed in India, New Delhi.

Preface

The word Mathematics is from the word *'mathesis'*, meaning 'learning'. Plato, an eminent philosopher, said, "It means realization of eternal truth present and embedded in the mind". Therefore, Mathematics is a set of skills and laws that are eternally and universally true. In my yesteryears, during my high school days, as an IIT-JEE aspirant, and later as a tutor of Mathematics for the last fifteen years, I always felt the need of a comprehensive text-book for this subject. I, therefore, always had an insatiable desire to write one.

This book has been written with the objective of providing a text book as well as an exercise book, focussing on problem solving. I feel this will not only fulfil the need of a beginner, pre-college student (i.e., students of Std XI and XII), but also meet the requirements of advanced level students who are preparing for various entrance examinations like the JEE, BIT-SAT, and other engineering entrance examinations. This book gives deep insights intc topics like Matrices, Determinants, Complex Numbers, Vectors, Three Dimensional Geometry and Probability. These are the six scariest but highly scoring topics of Mathematics. The well-arranged content list will help students and teachers both to access conveniently the chapters and sub-topics of their interest. Each chapter is divided into several topics. Each topic contains theory and sometimes subtopics with sufficient number of worked out illustrative problems. Students can develop applicative ability of the concepts learned. This is followed by a textual exercise of both objective and subjective problems, as per the requirements. At the end of the theory of each chapter, a large set of solved examples of both objective and subjective type is given. This will involve application of all the concepts learnt in the chapter so that students can develop mastery over the chapter. The tutorial exercise given at the end contains a large number of multiple choice problems of single and multiple correct answers, comprehension passages, column matching problems, numerical integer type questions to facilitate the students to do the thorough revision of the entire chapter and to enhance their level of understanding of the topics. For teachers, this text book will be quite helpful as it will provide a set of well graded problems and well arranged topics, that can be used to give home assignments to their students.

All suggestions for improvement are welcome and shall be gratefully acknowledged.

Sanjay Mishra, B. Tech (IIT-Varanasi)

Acknowledgements

I am really grateful to GK Publications, for showing faith in me and for providing me with an opportunity to transform my yearning, my vast experience of years of teaching and my knowledge into the present comprehensive text book, *Fundamentals of Mathematics—Algebra II*. I would like to thank all my friends and teachers for their valuable criticism, support and advice that was really helpful to carve out this work. I am pleased to award special acknowledgements to all my pupils. During my interactions with my students, I have got much of the inspiration of writing this text book. I feel that by interacting with them, I have learnt much more than I could have ever taught them. I wish to thank my parents and all my family members, for their patience and support in bringing out this book and donating their valuable share of time for such cause. I extend my special thanks to my team, including my assisting teachers, managers and computer operators, for their hard work and dedication in completing this task.

Sanjay Mishra, B. Tech (IIT-Varanasi)

Contents

1

Matrices

■ INTRODUCTION

The theory of matrices finds its origin in different kind of linear problems. The most important of them concerns the nature of solutions of any given system of linear equations and the various linear transformations in geometry. Initially, the subject was related to determinants and it was thought that matrices and determinants are inseparably related. But with the passage of time, the subject matter of matrices developed as an independent theory which has far greater importance than determinant. Infact, the theory of determinant was reduced to merely a tool to study and apply the square matrices to solve various types of problems.

Arthour Cayley (1825 – 1895), a British mathematician is given credit for the formulation of the general theory of matrices, which was proposed in 1857. Another famous mathematician, Hamilton in association with Cayley, developed the properties of matrices as a pure algebraic structure. Caley-Hamilton theorem is very useful in finding out inverse of a given matrix and study of nature of various matrix polynomials.

We cannot think of solving the system of linear equations having large number of unknown variables without the help of matrices. The theory of matrices do not constitute any divine revelation but they only constitute the formation of what has been found useful in several situation.

The subject of matrices has found its applications not only in algebra but also to a very large number of disciplines, such as Geometry, Statistics, Chemistry, Physics, Psychology, Education, etc. Cryptography is an art of encoding the messages to insure the security of the sensitive information. A cryptographer often uses matrix operations to encode sensitive messages.

During the World War–II, Allied analysts such as Alan Turing (1921 – 1954) were able to break German codes produced by the Enigme machine using sophisticated decoding techniques.

In the present chapter, we will study definition and detailed properties of matrices and Algebra of matrices along with application of matrices in Algebra and Geometry.

■ MATRIX

A matrix is a *rectangular array* of symbols (which could be real or complex numbers) arranged in a *row* and *column.* If a matrix has m rows and n columns, then the order of matrix is $m \times n$. The order of matrix represents the number of elements in the arrangement. Matrix A of order $m \times n$ is usually written as:

$$A = \begin{bmatrix} a_{11} & a_{12} & \cdots & a_{1n} \\ a_{21} & a_{22} & \cdots & a_{2n} \\ \cdots & \cdots & \cdots & \cdots \\ a_{m1} & a_{m2} & \cdots & a_{mn} \end{bmatrix}$$

(*Matrices are represented* by [ ], (), || ||)

Here the symbols a_{ij} represents the general element of matrix and it is an element lying in the ith row (*from the top*) and jth column (*from the left*). Obviously there is no blank place (i.e., without an element) at any entry.

NOTES

If two matrices A and B are of the same order, then only their addition and subtraction is possible and these matrices are said to be **conformable** *for addition or subtraction (or comparable). On the other hand, if the matrices A and B are of different orders, then their addition and subtraction is not possible and these matrices are called* **non-conformable** *for addition and subtraction (or non-comparable).*

ILLUSTRATION 1: In a given matrix A, find the following whenever they exist $A = \begin{bmatrix} 4 & 2-i & 2+i & 3 \\ 2+i & 3 & -2i & 3i \\ 2-i & 2i & 2 & 5 \\ 3 & -3i & 5 & 1 \end{bmatrix}$

(a) $a_{11}, a_{22}, a_{33}, a_{44}, a_{34}, a_{45}$ (b) second row and third column

SOLUTION: (a) Clearly, the element lying in first row and first column (a_{11}) is 4, similarly, one can observe that $a_{22} = 3$, $a_{33} = 2$, $a_{44} = 1$, $a_{34} = 5$ and a_{45} does not exist.

(b) Second row of the matrix is $2 + i$, 3, $-2i$, $3i$, and the third column is $2 + i$, $-2i$, 2 and 5.

TEXTUAL EXERCISE 1: (SUBJECTIVE)

1. Construct a 2 × 3 matrix whose elements a_{ij} are given by

(a) $a_{ij} = 2i - j$ (b) $a_{ij} = \dfrac{i-j}{i+j}$

(c) $a_{ij} = \dfrac{(i-2j)^2}{2}$ (d) $a_{ij} = 2ij + i + j$

2. Construct a 3 × 2 matrix A, whose elements are given

(i) $a_{ij} = \dfrac{(i-2j)^2}{2}$

(ii) $a_{ij} = i - j$

Answer Key

1. (a) $\begin{bmatrix} 1 & 0 & -1 \\ 3 & 2 & 1 \end{bmatrix}$ (b) $\begin{bmatrix} 0 & -1/3 & -1/2 \\ 1/3 & 0 & -1/5 \end{bmatrix}$ (c) $\begin{bmatrix} 1/2 & 9/2 & 25/2 \\ 0 & 2 & 8 \end{bmatrix}$ (d) $\begin{bmatrix} 4 & 7 & 10 \\ 7 & 12 & 17 \end{bmatrix}$

2. (i) $\begin{bmatrix} 1/2 & 9/2 \\ 0 & 2 \\ 1/2 & 1/2 \end{bmatrix}$ (ii) $\begin{bmatrix} 0 & -1 \\ 1 & 0 \\ 2 & 1 \end{bmatrix}$

■ VARIOUS KINDS OF MATRICES

Horizontal/Vertical Matrix

A matrix is called a horizontal matrix if there are less number of rows than columns and a matrix is called vertical if there are more number of rows than colums.

i.e., $A = [a_{ij}]_{m \times n}$ is a horizontal matrix if $m < n$.

and $A = [a_{ij}]_{m \times n}$ is a vertical matrix if $m > n$. (*where m is number of rows and n is number of columns*) e.g., $\begin{bmatrix} x_1 & y_1 & z_1 \\ x_2 & y_2 & z_2 \end{bmatrix}, \begin{bmatrix} 2 & 5 \\ 3 & 6 \\ 4 & 7 \end{bmatrix}$, are respectively horizontal and vertical matrices.

Row Matrix/Column Matrix

A matrix having just *one row/one column* is known as *row matrix/column matrix* (*or row vector/column vector*). $A = [a_{11}, a_{12}, ...a_{1n}]$ having one row is a $(1 \times n)$ row matrix (or row vectors). and

$A = \begin{bmatrix} a_{11} \\ a_{21} \\ ..... \\ a_{m1} \end{bmatrix}$ having one column is a $(m \times 1)$ column matrix. (or column vectors).

e.g., $A = [x\, y\, z]$, $B = [3\ 5\ 7\ 9\ 11]$, $C = \begin{bmatrix} x \\ y \\ z \end{bmatrix}$, A and B are row matrices but C is column matrix.

Square Matrix

If in a matrix, number of rows (m) = number of columns (n), then it is said to be a square matrix and the elements $a_{11}, a_{22}, ..., a_{mm}$ are called diagonal elements and the line passing through them is known as *principal or leading diagonal.* The other diagonal is known as *off diagonal.*

e.g., $[1]_{1 \times 1}$, $\begin{bmatrix} x_1 & x_2 & z_1 \\ y_1 & y_2 & z_2 \\ z_1 & z_2 & z_3 \end{bmatrix}$ Principal Diagonal

NOTES

(i) Determinant is a numerical value assigned to matrix and it is defined only for square matrices.

(ii) Determinant of a matrix A is denoted by |A| and it will be discussed in chapter 2 of present volume.

Caution: *|A| should not be confused with modulus of A.*

(iii) A square matrix is called singular matrix if its determinant is zero otherwise it is non-singular.

(iv) In a square matrix, the pair of elements a_{ij} and a_{ji} are called conjugate elements.

(v) In plane geometry every square is a rectangle, but this is not the case with matrices, so a square matrix is (never) a rectangular matrix.

Trace of a matrix The sum of all the elements of a square matrix A lying along the principal diagonal is called the trace of A, i.e., $tr(A)$. Thus if $A = [a_{ij}]_{n \times n}$, then

$$tr(A) = \sum_{i=1}^{n} a_{ii} = a_{11} + a_{22} + ... + a_{nn}$$

Properties of trace of a matrix Let $A = [a_{ij}]_{n \times n}$ and $B = [b_{ij}]_{n \times n}$ and λ be a scalar, then

(i) $tr(\lambda A) = \lambda\, tr(A)$

(ii) $tr\,(A + B) = tr(A) + tr\,(B)$

(iii) $tr\,(AB) = tr(BA)$

Diagonal Matrix/Scalar Matrix

A square matrix, in which all the non-diagonal elements, are zeros, is called a ***diagonal matrix***. If in a diagonal matrix all the elements in the principal diagonal are equal, then it is known as *scalar matrix*.

i.e., $A = [a_{ij}]_{m \times m}$; $a_{ij} = 0$ when $i \neq j$ is a diagonal matrix

$[a_{ij}]_{m \times m}$ is scalar marix iff $a_{ij} = 0$ when $i \neq j$

& $[a_{ij}]_{m \times m} = k$ for all $i = j$

e.g., $\begin{bmatrix} a & 0 & 0 \\ 0 & b & 0 \\ 0 & 0 & c \end{bmatrix}, \begin{bmatrix} k & 0 & 0 \\ 0 & k & 0 \\ 0 & 0 & k \end{bmatrix}$ *etc., they are also denoted as diag (a, b, c) and diag(k, k, k) respectively.*

NOTES

1. Minimum number of zeros in a diagonal matrix of order n = n(n – 1)

2. Matrix of order 1 × 1 is always considered to be a diagonal matrix.

Unit Matrix (Identity matrix)

A square matrix in which all the elements in the *leading diagonal* are *1* and remaining elements are *zeros*, is called a *unit matrix* or *identity matrix*. A unit matrix of order n ususally denoted by I_n. Thus, for an identity matrix

$$a_{ij} = \begin{cases} 0 & \text{if } i \neq j \\ 1 & \text{if } i = j \end{cases}$$

e.g., $\begin{bmatrix} 1 & 0 & 0 \\ 0 & 1 & 0 \\ 0 & 0 & 1 \end{bmatrix}$, so identity matrix I_n of order n is a scalar matrix with each diagonal element equal to 1.

NOTES

1. *By interchanging rows/columns of an identity matrix, the matrix is transformed to an elementary matrix. The operation E_{13} for an identity matrix (I_3) implies interchanging first and third row and the resulting elementary matrix is* $\begin{bmatrix} 0 & 0 & 1 \\ 0 & 1 & 0 \\ 1 & 0 & 0 \end{bmatrix}$.
2. *Unitary matrix is not a unit matrix.*

Upper/lower Triangular Matrix

A square matrix whose all the elements below principal diagonal are zeros i.e., $a_{ij} = 0$ for all $i > j$ is called upper triangular matrix. e.g., $\begin{bmatrix} 1 & 6 & 5 \\ 0 & 2 & 4 \\ 0 & 0 & 3 \end{bmatrix}$.

And a square matrix whose all the elements *above* principal diagonal are zeros i.e., $a_{ij} = 0$ for all $i < j$ is called lower triangular matrix. e.g., $\begin{bmatrix} 1 & 0 & 0 \\ 3 & 2 & 0 \\ 5 & 6 & 3 \end{bmatrix}$.

NOTES

(i) A triangular matrix is called strictly triangular iff $a_{ii} = 0$ for all $1 \leq i \leq n$.
(ii) Diagonal matrix is both upper as well as lower triangular.
(iii) Minimum number of zeros in an upper triangular matrix of order $n = n(n-1)/2$.

Null Matrix or Zero Matrix

A matrix, all of whose elements are zeros is said to be a *null matrix* or zero matrix and is denoted by O. e.g., $\begin{bmatrix} 0 & 0 \\ 0 & 0 \end{bmatrix}_{2\times 2}, \begin{bmatrix} 0 & 0 & 0 \\ 0 & 0 & 0 \end{bmatrix}_{2\times 3}$, are null matrices of the order 2×2, 2×3 respectively.

Real Matrix

If all the elements of a matrix are real, the matrix is called a real matrix.

Complex Matrix

If at least one of the elements of a matrix contains an imaginary number, then the matrix is called a complex matrix.

Complex Conjugate of a Matrix

If a matrix A is having complex numbers as its elements, then the matrix obtained from A by replacing each element of A by its conjugate $(\overline{a \pm ib} = a \mp ib)$ is called the conjugate of matrix A. Conjugate of a matrix A is denoted by $\overline{A}$: $\overline{A} = [\overline{a}_{ij}]_{m\times n}$ where $A = [a_{ij}]_{m\times n}$

Properties

(i) $\overline{\overline{A}} = A$

(ii) $\overline{A+B} = \overline{A} + \overline{B}$ or $\overline{AB} = \overline{A}\,\overline{B}$

(iii) If a_{ij} are purely real, then $A = \overline{A}$ and $\overline{A} = -A$ if a_{ij} are purely *imaginary*.

(iv) $(\overline{A^n}) = (\overline{A})^n$

ILLUSTRATION 2: Find the conjugate of matrix $A = \begin{bmatrix} 2+3i & 1+i \\ 2 & 5i \end{bmatrix}$.

SOLUTION: $A = \begin{bmatrix} 2+3i & 1+i \\ 2 & 5i \end{bmatrix} \Rightarrow \overline{A} = \begin{bmatrix} 2-3i & 1-i \\ 2 & -5i \end{bmatrix}$

Sub Matrix

Let A be an $m \times n$ matrix. Then a matrix obtained by leaving some rows and columns or both of A is called submatrix of A.

e.g., $A = \begin{bmatrix} 2 & 2 & 5 & 6 \\ 5 & 7 & 1 & 0 \\ 2 & 1 & 1 & 7 \end{bmatrix}$

$\Rightarrow \begin{bmatrix} \not{2} & \not{2} & \not{5} & \not{6} \\ 5 & 7 & \not{1} & 0 \\ 2 & 1 & \not{1} & 7 \end{bmatrix} = \text{(sub matrix of } A) = \begin{bmatrix} 5 & 7 & 0 \\ 2 & 1 & 7 \end{bmatrix}$

Also $\begin{bmatrix} - & - & \not{5} & \not{6} \\ \not{5} & \not{7} & \not{1} & \not{0} \\ 2 & 1 & \not{1} & 7 \end{bmatrix} = \text{(sub matrix of } A) = [2\ 1\ 7]$

Singular Matrix

A square matrix A is said to be *singular* if $|A| = 0$. A square matrix is said to be non-singular if $|A| \neq 0$.
(where $|A|$ denotes the determinant of matrix A, to evaluate it students are adviced to see the expansion of determinant given in chapter 2 of present volume).

Equal Matrices

Two matrices $A = [a_{ij}]_{m \times n}$ and $B = [b_{ij}]_{r \times p}$ are said to be equal (written as $A = B$) if

(i) they are of same order i.e., $m = r$ and $n = p$

(ii) The elements at the corresponding positions of the two matrices are equal. i.e., $a_{ij} = b_{ij}$ for all i and j

ILLUSTRATION 3: If $\begin{bmatrix} l+5 & 2m+1 \\ n-2 & 4p-6 \end{bmatrix} = \begin{bmatrix} -l-3 & 0 \\ 5 & 3p \end{bmatrix}$ then find l, m, n, p.

SOLUTION: Two matrices are equal

$\therefore\ l+5 = -l-3 \quad \Rightarrow 2l = -8 \quad \Rightarrow l = -4$

$\therefore\ 2m+1 = 0 \quad \Rightarrow 2m = -1 \quad \Rightarrow m = -1/2$

$n-2 = 5 \quad \Rightarrow n = 5+2 \quad \Rightarrow n = 7$

$4p-6 = 3p \quad \Rightarrow 4p - 3p = 6 \quad \Rightarrow p = 6$

$\therefore\ (l, m, n, p) = (-4, -1/2, 7, 6)$

ILLUSTRATION 4: Which of the following matrices is/are singular?

(i) $\begin{bmatrix} 1 & 2 & 3 \\ 1 & 1 & 2 \\ 1 & 3 & 4 \end{bmatrix}$ (ii) $\begin{bmatrix} 1 & 0 & 0 \\ 0 & 1 & 0 \\ 0 & 0 & 1 \end{bmatrix}$ (iii) $\begin{bmatrix} 3 & 3 & 2 \\ 1 & 2 & 4 \\ 2 & 5 & 6 \end{bmatrix}$

SOLUTION: (i) Given matrix is $\begin{bmatrix} 1 & 2 & 3 \\ 1 & 1 & 2 \\ 1 & 3 & 4 \end{bmatrix}$. Its determinant $= 1(4-6) - 2(4-2) + 3(3-1)$

$= -2 - 4 + 6 = 0$. Hence, it is singular.

(ii) Given matrix is $\begin{bmatrix} 1 & 0 & 0 \\ 0 & 1 & 0 \\ 0 & 0 & 1 \end{bmatrix}$. Its determinant $= 1(1-0) - 0\,(0-0) + 0\,(0-1)$

$= 1$. Hence, it is not singular, i.e. non-singular

(iii) Given matrix is $\begin{bmatrix} 3 & 3 & 2 \\ 1 & 2 & 4 \\ 2 & 5 & 6 \end{bmatrix}$ Its determinant $= 3\,(12-20) - 3\,(6-8) + 2\,(5-4)$

$= -24 + 6 + 2 = -16$. Hence, it is not singular.

ILLUSTRATION 5: Express $\begin{bmatrix} 2 & 5 & -7 \\ -9 & 12 & 4 \\ 15 & -13 & 6 \end{bmatrix}$ as the sum of a lower triangular matrix and a strictly upper triangular matrix.

SOLUTION: Let $L = \begin{bmatrix} a & 0 & 0 \\ b & c & 0 \\ d & e & f \end{bmatrix}$ be the lower triangular matrix and $U = \begin{bmatrix} 0 & p & q \\ 0 & 0 & r \\ 0 & 0 & 0 \end{bmatrix}$ the strictly upper triangular matrix such that $\begin{bmatrix} 2 & 5 & -7 \\ -9 & 12 & 4 \\ 15 & -13 & 6 \end{bmatrix} = \begin{bmatrix} a & 0 & 0 \\ b & c & 0 \\ d & e & f \end{bmatrix} + \begin{bmatrix} 0 & p & q \\ 0 & 0 & r \\ 0 & 0 & 0 \end{bmatrix}$.

$$\Rightarrow \begin{bmatrix} 2 & 5 & -7 \\ -9 & 12 & 4 \\ 15 & -13 & 6 \end{bmatrix} = \begin{bmatrix} a+0 & 0+p & 0+q \\ b+0 & c+0 & 0+r \\ d+0 & e+0 & f+0 \end{bmatrix}$$

Equating the corresponding elements on the two sides, we get

$2 = a,\ 5 = p,\ -7 = q,\ -9 = b,\ 12 = c,\ 4 = r,\ 15 = d,\ -13 = e,\ 6 = f$

$$\therefore\ L = \begin{bmatrix} 2 & 0 & 0 \\ -9 & 12 & 0 \\ 15 & -13 & 6 \end{bmatrix} \text{ and } U = \begin{bmatrix} 0 & 5 & -7 \\ 0 & 0 & 4 \\ 0 & 0 & 0 \end{bmatrix}$$

TEXTUAL EXERCISE 2: (SUBJECTIVE)

1. Given the following matrices

(i) $\begin{bmatrix} 3 & 4 & 2 & 8 \\ 3 & 5 & 4 & 2 \\ -3 & -8 & 0 & 5 \end{bmatrix}$ (ii) $\begin{bmatrix} 2 \\ 4 \\ 6 \end{bmatrix}$

(iii) $\begin{bmatrix} 2 & 4 & 6 \\ 1 & 3 & 5 \\ 5 & 7 & 9 \end{bmatrix}$ (iv) $\begin{bmatrix} 0 & 0 & 0 \\ 0 & 0 & 0 \\ 0 & 0 & 0 \end{bmatrix}$

(v) $[1\ 4\ 7\ 9]$ (vi) $\begin{bmatrix} 1 & 0 & 0 \\ 2 & 3 & 0 \\ 4 & 6 & 5 \end{bmatrix}$

(vii) $\begin{bmatrix} 3 & 2 & 4 \\ 0 & 5 & 6 \\ 0 & 0 & 7 \end{bmatrix}$ (viii) $\begin{bmatrix} 3 & 5 & 7 \\ 2 & 4 & 6 \\ 1 & 3 & 5 \\ 3 & 8 & 13 \end{bmatrix}$

(ix) $\begin{bmatrix} 1 & 0 & 0 & 0 \\ 0 & 1 & 0 & 0 \\ 0 & 0 & 1 & 0 \\ 0 & 0 & 0 & 1 \end{bmatrix}$ (x) $\begin{bmatrix} a & 0 & 0 \\ 0 & a & 0 \\ 0 & 0 & a \end{bmatrix}$

(xi) $\begin{bmatrix} 2 & 0 & 0 \\ 0 & 2 & 0 \\ 0 & 0 & 4 \end{bmatrix}$

For each of the following terms, give the number of matrix above that corresponds to it.

(a) Square (b) Row
(c) Column (d) Diagonal
(e) Scalar (f) Identity
(g) Null (h) Horizontal
(i) Vertical (j) Upper triangular
(k) Lower triangular

2. For what values of x and y; matrices $A = \begin{bmatrix} 2x+1 & y^2+2 \\ 5 & y^2-5y \end{bmatrix}, B = \begin{bmatrix} x+3 & 3y \\ 5 & -6 \end{bmatrix}$ are equal?

3. For what values of x, the matrix $\begin{bmatrix} 3-x & 2 & 2 \\ 2 & 4-x & 1 \\ -2 & -4 & -1-x \end{bmatrix}$ is singular?

Answer Key

1. (i) h (ii) c, i (iii) a (iv) a, d, e, g, j, k (v) b, h (vi) a, k (vii) a, j (viii) i
(ix) a, d, e, f, j, k (x) a, d, e, j, k (xi) a, d, j, k

2. $A = B$ if $x = 2$ and $y = 2$

3. $x = 0, 3$

■ ADDITION OF MATRICES

If $A(a_{ij})$ and B (b_{ij}) are two matrices each of the order $m \times n$, then their sum $A + B$ is a matrix C of the same order $m \times n$ such that every element of C is the sum of the corresponding elements of the given matrices A and B. Thus if A and B are two matrices defined by $\begin{bmatrix} a_1 & a_2 & a_3 \\ a_4 & a_5 & a_6 \end{bmatrix}$ and $\begin{bmatrix} b_1 & b_2 & b_3 \\ b_4 & b_5 & b_6 \end{bmatrix}$,

then $C = A + B = [a_{ij} + b_{ij}] = \begin{bmatrix} a_1+b_1 & a_2+b_2 & a_3+b_3 \\ a_4+b_4 & a_5+b_5 & a_6+b_6 \end{bmatrix}$.

ILLUSTRATION 6: If $A = \begin{bmatrix} l & n & p \\ m & o & q \end{bmatrix}$ and $B = \begin{bmatrix} 10 & 12 & 14 \\ 11 & 13 & 15 \end{bmatrix}$, then find $A + B$.

SOLUTION: $A + B = \begin{bmatrix} l+10 & n+12 & p+14 \\ m+11 & o+13 & q+15 \end{bmatrix}$

Properties of Matrix Addition

If A, B, C are three matrices of same order $m \times n$ and $A = [a_{ij}]$, $B = [b_{ij}]$, $C = [c_{ij}]$, then following properties hold in matrix addition:

1. Commutative law i.e., $A + B = B + A$

Proof: Let $A = [a_{ij}]_{m \times n}$, $B = [b_{ij}]_{m \times n}$ be two matrices of the same order $m \times n$, then

$A + B = [a_{ij}]_{m \times n} + [b_{ij}]_{m \times n} = [a_{ij} + b_{ij}]_{m \times n}$ (*by definition of sum*)

$= [b_{ij} + a_{ij}]_{m \times n}$ ($\because$ *addition of numbers is commutative*)

$= [b_{ij}]_{m \times n} + [a_{ij}]_{m \times n} = B - A$

2. Associative law i.e., $A + (B + C) = (A + B) + C$

Proof: Let $A = [a_{ij}]_{m \times n}$, $B = [b_{ij}]_{m \times n}$, $C = [c_{ij}]_{m \times n}$ be three matrices of the same order, then

$(A + B) + C = ([a_{ij}]_{m \times n} + [b_{ij}]_{m \times n}) + [c_{ij}]_{m \times n}$

$= [a_{ij} + b_{ij}]_{m \times n} + [c_{ij}]_{m \times n} = [(a_{ij} + b_{ij}) + c_{ij}]_{m \times n}$

$= [a_{ij} + (b_{ij} + c_{ij})]_{m \times n}$ ($\because$ *addition of numbers is associative*)

$= [a_{ij}]_{m \times n} + [b_{ij} + c_{ij}]_{m \times n}$

$= [a_{ij}]_{m \times n} + ([b_{ij}]_{m \times n} + [c_{ij}]_{m \times n}) = A + (B + C)$

3. Additive Identity Any matrix which when added to the matrix A gives the resultant as A is called the additive identity for A. i.e., $A + O = A = O + A$ (*where null matrix O is additive identity*)

Proof: Let $A = [a_{ij}]_{m \times n}$, be any matrix and O be the null matrix of the same order $m \times n$, then

$O = [0_{ij}]_{m \times n}$, where $0_{ij} = 0$ for all i, j.

$A + O = [a_{ij}]_{m \times n} + [0_{ij}]_{m \times n} = [a_{ij} + 0_{ij}]_{m \times n}$

$= [a_{ij} + 0_{ij}]_{m \times n} = [a_{ij}]_{m \times n}$ ($\because a + 0 = a$ *for all* real *number a*)

$= A$

Also $A + O = O + A$ ($\because$ *addition of matrices* is *commutative*)

$\therefore\ A + O = A = O + A$

4. Additive inverse Any matrix B is the additive inverse for A iff it follow $A + B = O = B + A$. Since we already know that $A + (-A) = O = A + (-A)$

$\therefore\ B = -A$

(*Here B is the additive inverse of the matrix A or the negative of A*)

Proof: For any matrix $A = [a_{ij}]_{m \times n}$, there exists a matrix $-A = [-a_{ij}]_{m \times n}$, such that

$A + (-A) = O = (-A) + A$

$A + (-A) = [a_{ij}]_{m \times n} + [-a_{ij}]_{m \times n}$

$= [a_{ij} + (-a_{ij})]_{m \times n} = [0_{ij}]_{m \times n} = O_{m \times n}$

$\because\ A + (-A) = (-A) + (A)$ ($\because$ *addition of matrices is commutative*)

$\therefore\ A + (-A) = O = (-A) + A$

5. Left cancellation law i.e., $A + B = A + C \Leftrightarrow B = C$

6. Right cancellation law i.e., $B + A = C + A \Leftrightarrow B = C$

7. The equation $A + X = 0$ has a unique solution i.e., $X = -A$; where X has order $m \times n$. (if A has order $m \times n$)

ILLUSTRATION 7: If $A = \begin{bmatrix} 1 & 2 \\ 3 & 4 \\ 5 & 6 \end{bmatrix}$ and $B = \begin{bmatrix} -3 & -2 \\ 1 & -5 \\ 4 & 3 \end{bmatrix}$, find $D = \begin{bmatrix} p & q \\ r & s \\ t & u \end{bmatrix}$ such that $A + B - D =$ 'O'

SOLUTION: Here $A + B - D = O \Rightarrow D = A + B$

$$\Rightarrow \begin{bmatrix} p & q \\ r & s \\ t & u \end{bmatrix} = \begin{bmatrix} 1 & 2 \\ 3 & 4 \\ 5 & 6 \end{bmatrix} + \begin{bmatrix} -3 & -2 \\ 1 & -5 \\ 4 & 3 \end{bmatrix} = \begin{bmatrix} 1-3 & 2-2 \\ 3+1 & 4-5 \\ 5+4 & 6+3 \end{bmatrix} = \begin{bmatrix} -2 & 0 \\ 4 & -1 \\ 9 & 9 \end{bmatrix}$$

On comparing the corresponding elements, $p = -2$, $q = 0$, $r = 4$, $s = -1$, $t = 9$ and $u = 9$

$$\therefore\ D = \begin{bmatrix} -2 & 0 \\ 4 & -1 \\ 9 & 9 \end{bmatrix}$$

ILLUSTRATION 8: If A, B and C are three matrices of the same order, then prove $B = C \Leftrightarrow A + B = A + C$

SOLUTION: To prove : $B = C \Rightarrow A + B = A + C$

Since A, B and C are of the same order, $A + B$ and $A + C$ are also of the same order.

Now $B = C \Rightarrow$ corresponding elements of B and C are equal.

$\Rightarrow$ (i, j) th element of $B = (i, j)$th element of C

$\Rightarrow b_{ij} = c_{ij} \Rightarrow a_{ij} + b_{ij} = a_{ij} + c_{ij}$ ($\because b = c \Rightarrow a + b = a + c$)

$\Rightarrow$ (i, j)th element of $(A + B) = (i, j)$th element of $(A + C)$

$\Rightarrow$ corresponding elements of $(A + B)$ and $(A + C)$ are equal.

$\Rightarrow$ $A + B = A + C$; To prove: $A + B = A + C \Rightarrow B = C$

Since $A + B = A + C \Rightarrow A, B$ and C are of the same order.

$\Rightarrow$ $-A, A, B$ and C are of the same order.

Now $A + B = A + C$ *(given)*.

$\Rightarrow$ $(-A) + (A + B) = (-A) + (A + C)$

$\Rightarrow$ $(-A + A) + B = (-A + A) + C$ *(using associative law)*

$\Rightarrow$ $O + B = O + C \Rightarrow B = C$

■ SUBTRACTION OF MATRICES

If $A(a_{ij})$ and $B(b_{ij})$ are two matrices of same order, then $A - B$ is a matrix each of whose elements is the difference of the corresponding elements of A and B. i.e., $A - B = [a_{ij} - b_{ij}]$.

ILLUSTRATION 9: Solve the following equations for X and Y. $X - Y = \begin{bmatrix} 3 & -3 & 0 \\ 3 & 3 & 2 \end{bmatrix}$ and $Y + X = \begin{bmatrix} 4 & 1 & 5 \\ -1 & 4 & -4 \end{bmatrix}$

SOLUTION: Given $X - Y = \begin{bmatrix} 3 & -3 & 0 \\ 3 & 3 & 2 \end{bmatrix}$ ......(i)

and $Y + X = \begin{bmatrix} 4 & 1 & 5 \\ -1 & 4 & -4 \end{bmatrix}$ ......(ii)

Adding (i) and (ii), we get $2X = \begin{bmatrix} 3 & -3 & 0 \\ 3 & 3 & 2 \end{bmatrix} + \begin{bmatrix} 4 & 1 & 5 \\ -1 & 4 & -4 \end{bmatrix} = \begin{bmatrix} 7 & -2 & 5 \\ 2 & 7 & -2 \end{bmatrix}$

$\Rightarrow \quad X = \begin{bmatrix} 7/2 & -1 & 5/2 \\ 1 & 7/2 & -1 \end{bmatrix}$

$\therefore \quad Y = \begin{bmatrix} 4 & 1 & 5 \\ -1 & 4 & -1 \end{bmatrix} - \begin{bmatrix} 7/2 & 1 & 5/2 \\ 1 & 7/2 & -1 \end{bmatrix} = \begin{bmatrix} 1/2 & 2 & 5/2 \\ -2 & 1/2 & -3 \end{bmatrix}$

Thus $X = \begin{bmatrix} 7/2 & -1 & 5/2 \\ 1 & 7/2 & -1 \end{bmatrix}$ and $Y = \begin{bmatrix} 1/2 & 2 & 5/2 \\ -2 & 1/2 & -3 \end{bmatrix}$

TEXTUAL EXERCISE 3: (SUBJECTIVE)

1. Show with the help of an example, taking three suitable matrices A, B and C that $(A - B) - C \neq A - (B - C)$

2. Find x, y, z and w, given that $\begin{bmatrix} 3x & 3y \\ 3z & 3w \end{bmatrix} = \begin{bmatrix} x & 6 \\ -1 & 2w \end{bmatrix} + \begin{bmatrix} 4 & x+y \\ x+w & 3 \end{bmatrix}$

3. If $A + B = \begin{bmatrix} 1 & -1 \\ 3 & 0 \end{bmatrix}$ and $A - B = \begin{bmatrix} 3 & 1 \\ 1 & 4 \end{bmatrix}$, find the matrices A and B.

4. If $A = \begin{bmatrix} 2 & 3-i & 2+i \\ 6-i & 5 & 4-2i \end{bmatrix}$ and $B = \begin{bmatrix} 2 & -2i & 3-i \\ 3+i & 2-3i & 6+i \end{bmatrix}$; then evaluate
(i) $A + \bar{A}$ (ii) $B - \bar{B}$ (iii) $\bar{A} + \bar{B}$

5. If $A=\begin{bmatrix}2+i & 5 & 9+i\\ 3 & 6-i & 2\\ 8-i & 7 & 5+2i\end{bmatrix}$; $B=\begin{bmatrix}3-i & 2 & 6+i\\ -1 & 0 & 8-2i\\ 2 & 5 & 4+2i\end{bmatrix}$; verify

(i) $T_r(A+B) = T_r(A) + T_r(B)$
(ii) $T_r(A-B) = T_r(A) - T_r(B)$
(iii) $T_r(\overline{A \pm B}) = T_r(\bar{A}) \pm T_r(\bar{B})$; where $T_r(A)$ stands for trace of matrix A.

Answer Key

2. $x = 2, y = 4, z = 4/3, w = 3$

3. $A = \begin{bmatrix}2 & 0\\ 2 & 2\end{bmatrix}$ and $B = \begin{bmatrix}-1 & -1\\ 1 & -2\end{bmatrix}$

4. (i) $\begin{bmatrix}4 & 6 & 4\\ 12 & 10 & 8\end{bmatrix}$ (ii) $\begin{bmatrix}0 & -4i & -2i\\ 2i & -6i & 2i\end{bmatrix}$ (iii) $\begin{bmatrix}4 & 3+3i & 5\\ 9 & 7+3i & 10+i\end{bmatrix}$

■ MULTIPLICATION OF A MATRIX BY NUMBERS

The matrix obtained by multiplying every element of the matrix A by k (*where k is a constant, real or complex*) is called the product of A by k and is denoted by kA or Ak, defined as a matrix whose order is the same as that of A. If matrix $A = [a_{ij}]$, then $kA = k\,[a_{ij}]$

e.g., **1.** If $A = \begin{bmatrix}a & b & c\\ b & c & a\\ c & a & b\end{bmatrix} \Rightarrow kA = \begin{bmatrix}ka & kb & kc\\ kb & kc & ka\\ kc & ka & kb\end{bmatrix}$

2. If $A = \begin{bmatrix}2 & 3 & 2\\ 4 & 5 & 1\\ 5 & 6 & 3\end{bmatrix} \Rightarrow 2A = \begin{bmatrix}4 & 6 & 4\\ 8 & 10 & 2\\ 10 & 12 & 6\end{bmatrix}$

Properties *Distributive laws:*

1. $k(A+B) = kA + kB$; where $k \in \mathbb{R}$

Proof: $k(A+B) = k\,[a_{ij} + b_{ij}]_{m\times n} = [k\,(a_{ij} + b_{ij})]_{m\times n}$
$= [k\,a_{ij} + k\,b_{ij}]_{m\times n}$
($\because$ $(a+b)\,c = ac + bc$ *for all scalars a, b, c*)
$= [k\,a_{ij}]_{m\times n} + [k\,b_{ij}]_{m\times n} = kA + kB$

(ii) $(k+l)A = kA + lA$ (*where k and l are both scalars*)

Proof: $(k+l)A = (k+l)\,[a_{ij}]_{m\times n}$
$= [k\,a_{ij} + l\,a_{ij}]_{m\times n} = [k\,a_{ij}]_{m\times n} + [l\,a_{ij}]_{m\times n} = k\,A + l\,A$

(iii) $(kl)A = k(lA) = l(kA)$

Proof: $k\,(l\,A) = k\,(l\,[a_{ij}]_{m\times n}) = k\,[l\,a_{ij}]_{m\times n})$
$= [k\,(l\,a_{ij})]_{m\times n} = [(kl)\,a_{ij}]_{m\times n}$
$= k\,l\,[a_{ij}]_{m\times n} = (kl)\,A$ ...(i)
Similarly, we get $l(kA) = (lk)\,A = (kl)\,A$ ...(ii)
From (i) and (ii), we get $k\,(lA) = (kl)\,A = l\,(kA)$

ILLUSTRATION 10: If $A = \begin{bmatrix}2 & 3\\ 5 & 2\\ 8 & 9\end{bmatrix}$, $B = \begin{bmatrix}2 & 1\\ 5 & 2\\ 1 & 9\end{bmatrix}$ and $A + B - 2D = 0$ find D.

SOLUTION: Given $A + B - 2D = 0$

$$\Rightarrow D = \frac{1}{2}(A+B);\ \text{Let } D = \frac{1}{2}A + \frac{1}{2}B \Rightarrow D = \frac{1}{2}\begin{bmatrix}2 & 3\\ 5 & 2\\ 8 & 9\end{bmatrix} + \frac{1}{2}\begin{bmatrix}2 & 1\\ 5 & 2\\ 1 & 9\end{bmatrix} \Rightarrow \frac{1}{2}\begin{bmatrix}4 & 4\\ 10 & 4\\ 9 & 18\end{bmatrix} = \begin{bmatrix}2 & 2\\ 5 & 2\\ 9/2 & 9\end{bmatrix}$$

■ MULTIPLICATION OF MATRICES

Two matrices A and B are said to be conformable for the product AB, if $A = (a_{ij})$ is of the order $m \times n$ and $B = (b_{ij})$ is of the order $n \times p$, the resulting matrix is of the order $m \times p$. and $AB = (C_{ij})$ where $(C_{ij}) = \sum_{k=1}^{n} a_{ik}b_{kj} = a_{i1}\,b_{1j} + a_{i2}\,b_{2j} + ...a_{in}b_{nj}$ for $i = 1,2,3,......m$ and $j = 1,2,3,........p$

As an aid to memory, denote the rows of matrix A by R_1, R_2, R_3 and columns of B by C_1, C_2 and C_3.

$$\text{Also, } A \times B = \begin{bmatrix} R_1 \\ R_2 \\ R_3 \end{bmatrix} \times (C_1 C_2 C_3) = \begin{bmatrix} R_1C_1 & R_1C_2 & R_1C_3 \\ R_2C_1 & R_2C_2 & R_2C_3 \\ R_3C_1 & R_3C_2 & R_3C_3 \end{bmatrix}$$

where R_iC_j is the scalar product of R_i and C_j.

The diagrammatical working of product of two matrices is shown as

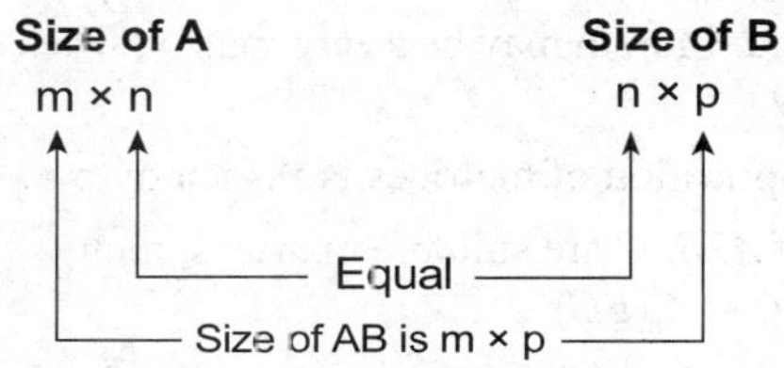

FIGURE 1.1

NOTES

1. *In the product AB, A = prefactor; B = postfactor*

2. $A = [a_1\ a_2 \ldots\ldots a_n]$ *and* $B = \begin{bmatrix} b_1 \\ b_2 \\ \vdots \\ b_n \end{bmatrix}$;

$\Rightarrow AB = [a_1 b_1 + a_2 b_2 + \ldots\ldots + a_n b_n]$

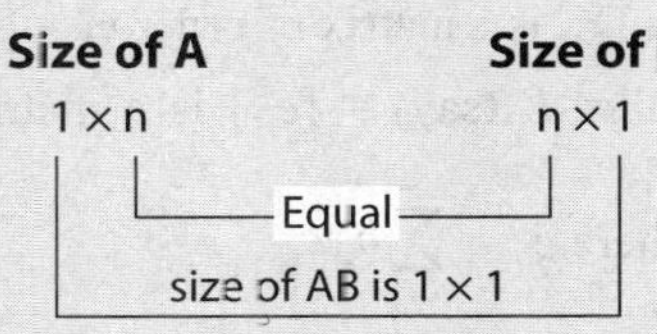

FIGURE 1.2

ILLUSTRATION 11: If $A = \begin{bmatrix} a & b \\ c & d \\ e & f \end{bmatrix}$, $B = \begin{bmatrix} x & y & z \\ l & m & n \end{bmatrix}$, then show that $AB \neq BA$.

SOLUTION: A is of order 3×2 and B is of the order 2×3.

So, AB as well as BA can be found. The rule for finding the product is as:

$$AB = \begin{bmatrix} a & b \\ c & d \\ e & f \end{bmatrix} \times \begin{bmatrix} x & y & z \\ l & m & n \end{bmatrix} = \begin{bmatrix} ax + bl & ay + bm & az + bn \\ cx + dl & cy + dm & cz + dn \\ ex + fl & ey + fm & ez + fn \end{bmatrix}$$

$$\text{and } BA = \begin{bmatrix} x & y & z \\ l & m & n \end{bmatrix} \times \begin{bmatrix} a & b \\ c & d \\ e & f \end{bmatrix} = \begin{bmatrix} xa + yc + ze & xb + yd + zf \\ la + mc + ne & lb + md + nf \end{bmatrix}$$

Observe that AB is a 3×3 matrix while BA is a 2×3 matrix. So $AB \neq BA$.

Post-Multiplication and Pre-Multiplication

In the product AB, the matrix A is said to be post-multiplied by the matrix B. Whereas, the matrix B is said to be pre-multiplied by A.

Properties of Matrix Multiplication

If A, B, C are different matrices, then in general $AB \neq BA$. However, in some particular cases.

1. AB and BA both may be defined yet $AB \neq BA$.
2. AB and BA both may be defined and $AB = BA$.
3. One of the product AB or BA may not be defined.
4. If A be a square matrix of the same order as I, then $IA = AI = A$ and $OA = AO = O$ where O is a null matrix i.e., multiplication by identity and null matrix is commutative.
5. AB may be a zero matrix and BA may be a non-zero matrix or vice versa when $A \neq O$, $B \neq O$.

6. AB and BA both may be a zero matrix, when $A \neq O$ and $B \neq O$.

7. Multiplication of matrices is associative:
i.e., if A, B, C are suitable matrices, then
$(AB)\,C = A\,(BC)$

Proof: As $(AB)C$ is defined, let $A = [a_{ij}]$, $B = [b_{jk}]$, $C = [c_{kl}]$ be three matrices of orders $m \times n$ and $n \times p$ and $p \times q$ respectively, where $1 \le i \le m$, $1 \le j \le n$, $1 \le k \le p$, $1 \le l \le q$.

Then, $AB = D$ (say) $= [d_{ik}]$ is a matrix of order $m \times p$

where $d_{ik} = \sum_{j=1}^{n} a_{ij} b_{jk}$

$\Rightarrow$ $(AB)C = DC$ is a matrix of order $m \times q$.

Also $BC = E$ (say) $= [e_{jl}]$ is a matrix of order

$n \times q$ where $e_{jl} = \sum_{k=1}^{p} b_{jk} c_{kl}$

$\Rightarrow$ $A(BC) = AE$ is a matrix of order $m \times q$.

Thus $(AB)C$ and $A(BC)$ are both matrices of order $m \times q$.

Now (i, l)th element of $(AB)C$ = (i, l)th element of DC

$$= \sum_{k=1}^{p} d_{ik} c_{kl} = \sum_{k=1}^{p}\left(\sum_{j=1}^{n} a_{ij}\, b_{jk}\right) c_{kl} = \sum_{j=1}^{n} a_{ij}\left(\sum_{k=1}^{p} b_{jk} c_{kl}\right)$$

$= \sum_{j=1}^{n} a_{ij} e_{jl}$ = (i, l)th element of AE = (i, l)th element of $A(BC)$

$\Rightarrow$ Corresponding elements of $(AB)C$ and $A(BC)$ are equal. $\Rightarrow$ $(AB)C = A(BC)$

8. Multiplication is distributive over addition i.e., if A, B, C are sutaible matrices, then
(i) $A(B + C) = AB + AC$ (ii) $(A + B)C = AC + BC$

Proof: As $A\,(B + C)$, let $A = [a_{ij}]$, $B = [b_{jk}]$, $C = [c_{jk}]$ be three matrices of orders $m \times n$, $n \times p$ and $n \times p$ respectively, $1 \le i \le m$, $1 \le j \le n$, $1 \le k \le p$,

Then, $B + C = [b_{jk} + c_{jk}]$ is a matrix of order $n \times p$
$\Rightarrow$ $A\,(B + C)$ is a matrix of order $m \times p$

Also AB, AC are both matrices of order $m \times p$
$\Rightarrow$ $AB + AC$ is a matrix of order $m \times p$

Thus $A(B + C)$, $AB + AC$ are both matrices of order $m \times p$

Now (i, k)th element of $A(B + C)$

$$= \sum_{j=1}^{n} a_{ij}(b_{jk} + c_{jk})$$

$$= \sum_{j=1}^{n}(a_{ij}b_{jk} + a_{ij}c_{jk}) = \sum_{j=1}^{n} a_{ij}b_{jk} + \sum_{j=1}^{n} a_{ij}c_{jk}$$

= (i, k)th elements of $A(B + C)$ and $AB + AC$ are equal = (i, k)th element of $(AB + AC)$

$\Rightarrow$ corresponding elements of $A(B + C)$ and $AB + AC$ are equal

$\Rightarrow$ $A(B + C) = AB + AC$

Similarly, in (ii) part, we can proceed in same way as in (i) part by taking $A = [a_{ij}]$, $B = [b_{ij}]$, $C = [c_{jk}]$ be three matrices of orders $m \times n$, $m \times n$ and $n \times p$ respectively.

NOTES

The matrix AB is the matrix B pre-multiplied by A and the matrix BA is the B post multiplied by A.

9. If A, B are suitable matrices and λ is a scalar, then $\lambda\,(AB) = (\lambda\,A)B = A(\lambda B)$.

Proof: As AB is defined, let $A = [a_{ij}]$, $B = [b_{jk}]$ be two matrices of order $m \times n$ and $n \times p$ respectively, λ is any scalar.

Then $AB = [c_{ik}]$ is a matrix of order $m \times p \Rightarrow \lambda(AB)$ is a matrix of order $m \times p$.

Also $\lambda A = [\lambda\, a_{ij}]$, $\lambda B = [\lambda\, b_{jk}]$ are matrices of orders $m \times n$ and $n \times p$ respectively.

$\Rightarrow$ $\lambda\,(AB)$, $(\lambda\,A)B$ are both matrices of order $m \times p$.

Thus $\lambda\,(AB)$, $(\lambda\,A)B$ and $A(\lambda B)$. are all matrices of order $m \times p$.

Now (i, k)th element of $\lambda\,(AB) = \lambda c_{ik} = \lambda \sum_{j=1}^{n} a_{ij} b_{jk}$

(i, k)th element of $(\lambda\,A)B = \sum_{j=1}^{n} (\lambda a_{ij}) c_{jk} = \lambda \sum_{j=1}^{n} a_{ij} b_{jk}$

(i, k)th element of $A\,(\lambda\,B) = \sum_{j=1}^{n} a_{ij} (\lambda b_{jk}) = \lambda \sum_{j=1}^{n} a_{ij} b_{jk}$

$\Rightarrow$ Corresponding elements $\lambda\,(AB)$, $(\lambda\,A)B$ and $A(\lambda B)$ are equal.

$\Rightarrow$ $\lambda\,(AB) = (\lambda\,A)B = A(\lambda B)$.

10. Existence of multiplicative Identity: If $A = [a_{ij}]$ is an $m \times n$ matrix, then $I_m A = A = AI_n$.

Proof: As I_m and I_n are identity matrices of orders m and n respectively, it follows that $I_m A$, A and $A I_n$ are all matrices of order $m \times n$.

Now (i, j)th element of $I_m A = 0.a_{1j} + 0.a_{2j} + \ldots + 1.a_{ij} + \ldots + 0.a_{mj}$

$\Rightarrow a_{ij} = (i, j)$th element of A

($\because$ In I_m each diagonal element is 1 and every other element = 0)

Also (i, j)th element of $AI_n = a_{i1}.0 + a_{i2}.0 + \ldots + a_{ij}.1 + \ldots + a_{in}.0$

$\Rightarrow a_{ij} = (i, j)$th element of A

$\Rightarrow$ Corresponding elements of $I_m A$, A and AI_n are equal.

$\Rightarrow I_m A = A = AI_n$

11. The product of any matrix and null matrix of a suitable order is a null matrix.

If $A = [a_{ij}]$ is an $m \times n$ matrix, then $O_{p \times m} A = O_{p \times n}$ and $AO_{n \times q} = O_{m \times q}$.

Proof: As $O_{p \times m}$ is a null matrix of order $p \times m$ and A is of order $m \times n$, $O_{p \times m} A$ is of order $p \times n$.

$\Rightarrow O_{p \times m} A$ and $O_{p \times n}$ are both matrices of order $p \times n$

Now (k, j)th element of $O_{p \times m} A = 0.a_{1j} + 0.a_{2j} + \ldots + 0.a_{mj}$

($\because$ *every element of* $O_{p \times m}$ *is zero*)

$= 0 = (k, j)$th element of $O_{p \times m}$

$\Rightarrow$ Corresponding elements of $O_{p \times m} A$ and $O_{p \times n}$ are equal.

$\Rightarrow O_{p \times m} A = O_{p \times n}$. Similarly, $AO_{n \times q} = O_{m \times q}$

12. Powers of a square matrix: Let A be a square matrix of order n, then AA makes sense and it is also a square matrix of order n. We define:

$A^1 = A;\ A^2 = AA, \ldots \ldots A^m = A^{m-1} A = AA^{m-1}$ for all positive integers m.

ILLUSTRATION 12: If $A = \begin{bmatrix} 1 & 2 \\ 3 & 0 \\ 4 & 1 \end{bmatrix}$ and $B = \begin{bmatrix} 0 & 1 & 0 \\ 0 & 2 & 1 \\ 2 & 3 & 0 \end{bmatrix}$, find BA. Can we find AB also?

SOLUTION: The matrix B has 3 columns and matrix A has 3 rows, therefore the product BA is defined. By the row by column rule of multiplication, we have

$$BA = \begin{bmatrix} 0 & 1 & 0 \\ 0 & 2 & 1 \\ 2 & 3 & 0 \end{bmatrix} \times \begin{bmatrix} 1 & 2 \\ 3 & 0 \\ 4 & 1 \end{bmatrix} = \begin{bmatrix} 0.1+1.3+0.4 & 0.2+1.0+0.1 \\ 0.1+2.3+1.4 & 0.2+2.0+1.1 \\ 2.1+3.3+0.4 & 2.2+3.0+0.1 \end{bmatrix} = \begin{bmatrix} 3 & 0 \\ 10 & 1 \\ 11 & 4 \end{bmatrix}$$

It should be noted that here we cannot find AB, since the number of columns of A is 2 and number of rows of B is 3 i.e., they are not equal.

ILLUSTRATION 13: Find the product matrix of the matrices $A = \begin{bmatrix} 2 & 1 & 2 & 1 \\ 1 & 1 & 1 & 1 \end{bmatrix}$ and $B = \begin{bmatrix} 2 & -1 & 0 \\ 0 & 4 & 1 \\ -2 & 1 & 0 \\ 1 & -3 & 2 \end{bmatrix}$.

SOLUTION: The matrix A is of the type 2×4 and the matrix B is of the type 4×3. Therefore the product AB is defined and it will be a matrix of the type 2×3.

$$\text{Now, } AB = \begin{bmatrix} 2 & 1 & 2 & 1 \\ 1 & 1 & 1 & 1 \end{bmatrix} \times \begin{bmatrix} 2 & -1 & 0 \\ 0 & 4 & 1 \\ -2 & 1 & 0 \\ 1 & -3 & 2 \end{bmatrix}$$

$$= \begin{bmatrix} 2.2+1.0+2.(-2)+1.1 & 2.(-1)+1.4+2.1+1.(-3) & 2.0+1.1+2.0+1.2 \\ 1.2+1.0+1.(-2)+1.1 & 1.(-1)+1.4+1.1+1.(-3) & 1.0+1.1+1.0+1.2 \end{bmatrix} = \begin{bmatrix} 1 & 1 & 3 \\ 1 & 1 & 3 \end{bmatrix}$$

ILLUSTRATION 14: If $A = \begin{bmatrix} 0 & 1 \\ -1 & 0 \end{bmatrix}$; find x and y such that $(xI + yA)^2 = A$.

SOLUTION: $xI + yA = x\begin{bmatrix} 1 & 0 \\ 0 & 1 \end{bmatrix} + y\begin{bmatrix} 0 & 1 \\ -1 & 0 \end{bmatrix} = \begin{bmatrix} x & 0 \\ 0 & x \end{bmatrix} + \begin{bmatrix} 0 & y \\ -y & 0 \end{bmatrix} = \begin{bmatrix} x & y \\ -y & x \end{bmatrix}$

Given $(xI + yA)^2 = A \quad \Rightarrow \quad \begin{bmatrix} x & y \\ -y & x \end{bmatrix}\begin{bmatrix} x & y \\ -y & x \end{bmatrix} = \begin{bmatrix} 0 & 1 \\ -1 & 0 \end{bmatrix}$

$\Rightarrow \begin{bmatrix} x^2 - y^2 & 2xy \\ -2xy & x^2 - y^2 \end{bmatrix} = \begin{bmatrix} 0 & 1 \\ -1 & 0 \end{bmatrix} \qquad \Rightarrow \begin{cases} x^2 - y^2 = 0, & 2xy = 1 \\ -2xy = -1, & x^2 - y^2 = 0 \end{cases}$

$\Rightarrow x^2 - y^2 = 0,\ 2xy = 1 \qquad \Rightarrow x = \pm y,\ 2xy = 1$

Two cases arise:

Case I: Let $x = y$, then $2xy = 1 \qquad \Rightarrow 2x^2 = 1 \qquad \Rightarrow x = \pm 1/\sqrt{2}$

Solutions are (i) $x = \frac{1}{\sqrt{2}}, y = \frac{1}{\sqrt{2}}$; (ii) $x = -\frac{1}{\sqrt{2}}, y = -\frac{1}{\sqrt{2}}$

Case II: Let $x = -y$, then $2xy = 1 \qquad \Rightarrow -2x^2 = 1 \qquad \Rightarrow x = \pm i/\sqrt{2}$

Solutions are (iii) $x = \frac{i}{\sqrt{2}}, y = -\frac{i}{\sqrt{2}}$; (iv) $x = -\frac{i}{\sqrt{2}}, y = \frac{i}{\sqrt{2}}$

ILLUSTRATION 15: Give examples of matrices:

(i) A and B such that $AB \neq BA$

(ii) A and B such that $AB = O = BA$, $A \neq O$, $B \neq O$

(iii) A and B such that $AB = O$ but $BA \neq O$

(iv) A, B and C such that $AB = AC$ but $B \neq C$, $A \neq O$

SOLUTION: (i) Let $A = \begin{bmatrix} 1 & 1 \\ 0 & 0 \end{bmatrix}$ and $B = \begin{bmatrix} 1 & 0 \\ 1 & 0 \end{bmatrix}$

$AB = \begin{bmatrix} 1 & 1 \\ 0 & 0 \end{bmatrix}\begin{bmatrix} 1 & 0 \\ 1 & 0 \end{bmatrix} = \begin{bmatrix} 1.1 + 1.1 & 1.0 + 1.0 \\ 0.1 + 0.1 & 0.0 + 0.0 \end{bmatrix} = \begin{bmatrix} 2 & 0 \\ 0 & 0 \end{bmatrix}$ and

$BA = \begin{bmatrix} 1 & 0 \\ 1 & 0 \end{bmatrix}\begin{bmatrix} 1 & 1 \\ 0 & 0 \end{bmatrix} = \begin{bmatrix} 1.1 + 0.0 & 1.1 + 0.0 \\ 1.1 + 0.0 & 1.1 + 0.0 \end{bmatrix} = \begin{bmatrix} 1 & 1 \\ 1 & 1 \end{bmatrix}$

$\Rightarrow AB \neq BA$

(ii) Let $A = \begin{bmatrix} 1 & 0 \\ 0 & 0 \end{bmatrix}$ and $B = \begin{bmatrix} 0 & 0 \\ 0 & 1 \end{bmatrix}$, then

$A \neq O, B \neq O$

$AB = \begin{bmatrix} 1 & 0 \\ 0 & 0 \end{bmatrix}\begin{bmatrix} 0 & 0 \\ 0 & 1 \end{bmatrix} = \begin{bmatrix} 1.0 + 0.0 & 1.0 + 0.1 \\ 0.0 + 0.0 & 0.0 + 0.1 \end{bmatrix} = \begin{bmatrix} 0 & 0 \\ 0 & 0 \end{bmatrix} = O$

$BA = \begin{bmatrix} 0 & 0 \\ 0 & 1 \end{bmatrix}\begin{bmatrix} 1 & 0 \\ 0 & 0 \end{bmatrix} = \begin{bmatrix} 0.1 + 0.0 & 0.0 + 0.0 \\ 0.1 + 1.0 & 0.0 + 1.0 \end{bmatrix} = \begin{bmatrix} 0 & 0 \\ 0 & 0 \end{bmatrix} = O$

$\Rightarrow AB = O = BA, A \neq O, B \neq O$

(iii) Let $A = \begin{bmatrix} 1 & 0 \\ 0 & 0 \end{bmatrix}$ and $B = \begin{bmatrix} 0 & 0 \\ 1 & 0 \end{bmatrix}$, then

$$AB = \begin{bmatrix} 1 & 0 \\ 0 & 0 \end{bmatrix}\begin{bmatrix} 0 & 0 \\ 1 & 0 \end{bmatrix} = \begin{bmatrix} 1.0+0.1 & 1.0+0.0 \\ 0.0+0.1 & 0.0+0.0 \end{bmatrix} = \begin{bmatrix} 0 & 0 \\ 0 & 0 \end{bmatrix} = 0$$

$$\text{and } BA = \begin{bmatrix} 0 & 0 \\ 1 & 0 \end{bmatrix}\begin{bmatrix} 1 & 0 \\ 0 & 0 \end{bmatrix} = \begin{bmatrix} 0.1+0.0 & 0.0+0.0 \\ 1.1+0.0 & 1.0+0.0 \end{bmatrix} = \begin{bmatrix} 0 & 0 \\ 1 & 0 \end{bmatrix} \neq 0$$

Thus $AB = O$ but $BA \neq O$

(iv) Let $A = \begin{bmatrix} 1 & 0 \\ 0 & 0 \end{bmatrix}$, $B = \begin{bmatrix} 0 & 0 \\ 1 & 0 \end{bmatrix}$ and $C = \begin{bmatrix} 0 & 0 \\ 0 & 1 \end{bmatrix}$, then $A \neq O, B \neq C$

$$AB = \begin{bmatrix} 1 & 0 \\ 0 & 0 \end{bmatrix}\begin{bmatrix} 0 & 0 \\ 1 & 0 \end{bmatrix} = \begin{bmatrix} 1.0+0.1 & 1.0+0.0 \\ 0.0+0.1 & 0.0+0.0 \end{bmatrix} = \begin{bmatrix} 0 & 0 \\ 0 & 0 \end{bmatrix} \text{ and}$$

$$AC = \begin{bmatrix} 1 & 0 \\ 0 & 0 \end{bmatrix}\begin{bmatrix} 0 & 0 \\ 0 & 1 \end{bmatrix} = \begin{bmatrix} 1.0+0.0 & 1.0+0.1 \\ 0.0+0.0 & 0.0+0.1 \end{bmatrix} = \begin{bmatrix} 0 & 0 \\ 0 & 0 \end{bmatrix} \Rightarrow AB = AC, B \neq C, A \neq O.$$

ILLUSTRATION 16: Given $A = \begin{bmatrix} 1 & 4 \\ 0 & 0 \end{bmatrix}$, $B = \begin{bmatrix} 1 & 5 \\ 2 & 1 \end{bmatrix}$, $C = \begin{bmatrix} 1 & 1 \\ 2 & 2 \end{bmatrix}$. Prove that $AB = AC$, $\not\Rightarrow$ B = C

SOLUTION: $AB = \begin{bmatrix} 1 & 4 \\ 0 & 0 \end{bmatrix}\begin{bmatrix} 1 & 5 \\ 2 & 1 \end{bmatrix} = \begin{bmatrix} 1(1)+4(2) & 1(5)+4(1) \\ 0(1)+0(2) & 0(5)+0(1) \end{bmatrix} = \begin{bmatrix} 9 & 9 \\ 0 & 0 \end{bmatrix}$

$$AC = \begin{bmatrix} 1 & 4 \\ 0 & 0 \end{bmatrix}\begin{bmatrix} 1 & 1 \\ 2 & 2 \end{bmatrix} = \begin{bmatrix} 1(1)+4(2) & 1(1)+4(2) \\ 0(1)+0(2) & 0(1)+0(2) \end{bmatrix} = \begin{bmatrix} 9 & 9 \\ 0 & 0 \end{bmatrix}$$

Clearly, $B \neq C$ but $AB = AC$

ILLUSTRATION 17: Matrix A has x rows and $x + 5$ columns. Matrix B has y rows and $11 - y$ columns. Both AB and BA exist. Find x and y.

SOLUTION: Since both AB and BA exist, so number of rows of A is equal to the number of columns of B and number or rows of B is equal to the number of columns of A.

$\therefore \quad x = 11 - y \quad$ or $\quad x + y = 11 \quad$ ...(i)

and $\quad x + 5 = y \quad$ or $\quad x - y = -5 \quad$ ...(ii)

$\therefore \quad x + y = 11 \quad$ and $\quad x - y = -5$

$\Rightarrow \quad x = 3 \quad$ and $\quad y = 8$

ILLUSTRATION 18: If $A = \begin{bmatrix} 1 & 2 \\ -2 & 3 \end{bmatrix}$, $B = \begin{bmatrix} 2 & 1 \\ 2 & 3 \end{bmatrix}$ and $C = \begin{bmatrix} -3 & 1 \\ 2 & 0 \end{bmatrix}$, verify that $(AB)C = A(BC)$.

SOLUTION: $AB = \begin{bmatrix} 1 & 2 \\ -2 & 3 \end{bmatrix}\begin{bmatrix} 2 & 1 \\ 2 & 3 \end{bmatrix} = \begin{bmatrix} 6 & 7 \\ 2 & 7 \end{bmatrix}$ and $(AB)\,C = \begin{bmatrix} 6 & 7 \\ 2 & 7 \end{bmatrix}\begin{bmatrix} -3 & 1 \\ 2 & 0 \end{bmatrix} = \begin{bmatrix} -4 & 6 \\ 8 & 2 \end{bmatrix}$

and also $A(BC) = \begin{bmatrix} 1 & 2 \\ -2 & 3 \end{bmatrix} \times \begin{bmatrix} 2 & 1 \\ 2 & 3 \end{bmatrix} \times \begin{bmatrix} -3 & 1 \\ 2 & 0 \end{bmatrix}$

$= \begin{bmatrix} 1 & 2 \\ -2 & 3 \end{bmatrix} \times \begin{bmatrix} -4 & 2 \\ 0 & 2 \end{bmatrix} = \begin{bmatrix} -4 & 6 \\ 8 & 2 \end{bmatrix}$. Hence $(AB)\,C = A(BC)$

TEXTUAL EXERCISE 4: (SUBJECTIVE)

1. Evaluate the matrix product,

$$\begin{bmatrix}1\\-2\\3\end{bmatrix}\times[4\ 5\ 2]\times\begin{bmatrix}2\\-3\\5\end{bmatrix}\times[3\ 2].$$

2. If $A=\begin{bmatrix}1&-2&3\\2&3&-1\\-3&1&2\end{bmatrix}$ and $B=\begin{bmatrix}1&0&2\\0&1&2\\1&2&0\end{bmatrix}$ then find the product AB and BA, and show that $AB \neq BA$.

3. Prove that the product of two matrices

$$\begin{bmatrix}\cos^2\theta & \cos\theta\sin\theta\\ \cos\theta\sin\theta & \sin^2\theta\end{bmatrix} \text{ and } \begin{bmatrix}\cos^2\phi & \cos\phi\sin\phi\\ \cos\phi\sin\phi & \sin^2\phi\end{bmatrix}$$

is a null matrix when θ and ϕ differ by an odd multiple of $\pi/2$.

4. If $A=\begin{bmatrix}1&-2&3\\2&3&-1\\-3&1&2\end{bmatrix}$ and I is the unit matrix of order 3, evaluate $A^2 - 3A + 9I$.

5. Evaluate $\begin{bmatrix}\cos\theta+\sin\theta & \sqrt{2}\sin\theta\\ -\sqrt{2}\sin\theta & \cos\theta-\sin\theta\end{bmatrix}^n$

6. If $A=\begin{bmatrix}1&1&1\\0&1&1\\0&0&1\end{bmatrix}$; then find A^n.

Answer Key

1. $\begin{bmatrix}9&6\\-18&-12\\27&18\end{bmatrix}$

4. $\begin{bmatrix}-6&1&2\\5&4&4\\2&8&-3\end{bmatrix}$

5. $\begin{bmatrix}\cos n\theta+\sin n\theta & \sqrt{2}\sin n\theta\\ -\sqrt{2}\sin n\theta & \cos n\theta-\sin n\theta\end{bmatrix}$

6. $\begin{bmatrix}1 & n & \frac{n(n+1)}{2}\\ 0&1&n\\0&0&1\end{bmatrix}$

TEXTUAL EXERCISE 1: (OBJECTIVE)

1. Matrix theory was introduced by
   (a) Cauchy-Riemann
   (b) Cayley-Hamilton
   (c) Newton
   (d) Cauchy Schwarz

2. The matrix (2 × 3) whose elements in the jth row and the kth column are $a_{jk} = 3j - 2k$, is
   (a) $\begin{bmatrix}1&-1&-3\\4&2&0\end{bmatrix}$ (b) $\begin{bmatrix}1&1&3\\0&4&2\end{bmatrix}$
   (c) $\begin{bmatrix}-1&1&3\\4&2&0\end{bmatrix}$ (d) None of these

3. If $A = (a_{ij})_{2\times2}$ where $a_{ij} = i + j$, then A is equal to
   (a) $\begin{bmatrix}1&1\\2&2\end{bmatrix}$ (b) $\begin{bmatrix}1&2\\1&2\end{bmatrix}$
   (c) $\begin{bmatrix}1&2\\3&4\end{bmatrix}$ (d) $\begin{bmatrix}2&3\\3&4\end{bmatrix}$

4. The values of x, y, z and a in the statement $\begin{bmatrix}x&y\\z&a\end{bmatrix}=\begin{bmatrix}1&-1\\0&3\end{bmatrix}$ are
   (a) $x = 1, y = -1, z = 0, a = 3$
   (b) $x = y = z = 1, a = 3$
   (c) $x = y = -1, z = 0, a = 3$
   (d) None of these

5. If $A = [a_{ij}]$ is a scalar matrix of order $n \times n$ such that $a_{ii} = k$ for all i, then trace of A is
   (a) k^n (b) n/k
   (c) nk (d) None of these

6. If A and B are two matrices such that $A + B$ and AB both are defined, then
   (a) A, B are square matrices of same order
   (b) number of columns of A = number of rows of B
   (c) A and B can be any matrices
   (d) None of these

7. If $A = \begin{bmatrix} 1 & 2 \\ 3 & 0 \\ 4 & 1 \end{bmatrix}_{3\times2}$ and $B = \begin{bmatrix} 0 & 1 & 0 \\ 0 & 2 & 1 \\ 2 & 3 & 0 \end{bmatrix}_{3\times3}$, then BA is

(a) $\begin{bmatrix} 4 & 0 \\ 1 & 10 \\ 11 & 6 \end{bmatrix}$ (b) $\begin{bmatrix} 6 & 0 \\ 1 & 10 \\ 11 & 4 \end{bmatrix}$

(c) $\begin{bmatrix} 3 & 0 \\ 10 & 1 \\ 11 & 4 \end{bmatrix}$ (d) None of these

8. The value of x such that $[1\ x\ 1]\begin{bmatrix} 1 & 3 & 2 \\ 2 & 5 & 1 \\ 15 & 3 & 2 \end{bmatrix}\begin{bmatrix} 1 \\ 2 \\ x \end{bmatrix} = O$, is

(a) $x = 2, 14$
(b) $x = -2, 14$
(c) $x = -2, -14$
(d) None of these

9. Given $A = \begin{bmatrix} 1 & 1 \\ 2 & -1 \end{bmatrix}$, which of the following results is true?

(a) $A^2 = I$ (b) $A^2 = 3I$
(c) $A^2 = 2I$ (d) None of these

10. If $A = \begin{bmatrix} a & b \\ b & a \end{bmatrix}$, $A^2 = \begin{bmatrix} \alpha & \beta \\ \beta & \alpha \end{bmatrix}$, then

(a) $\alpha = 2ab$, $\beta = \alpha^2 + \beta^2$
(b) $\alpha = a^2 + b^2$, $\beta = a^2 - b^2$
(c) $\alpha = a^2 + b^2$, $\beta = 2ab$
(d) $\alpha = a^2 + b^2$, $\beta = ab$

11. If $A = \begin{bmatrix} 1 & 0 & 0 \\ 0 & 1 & 0 \\ 0 & 0 & 1 \end{bmatrix}$, then $A^2 + 2A$ equals

(a) $4A$ (b) $3A$
(c) $2A$ (d) A

12. Choose the correct answer:
(a) Every scalar matrix is an identity matrix
(b) Every identity matrix is a scalar matrix
(c) Every diagonal matrix is an identity matrix
(d) A square matrix whose each element is 1 is an identity matrix.

13. If $A = \begin{bmatrix} i & 0 \\ 0 & i \end{bmatrix}$, $n \in N$, then A^{4n} equals

(a) $\begin{bmatrix} 0 & i \\ i & 0 \end{bmatrix}$ (b) $\begin{bmatrix} 0 & 0 \\ 0 & 0 \end{bmatrix}$

(c) $\begin{bmatrix} 1 & 0 \\ 0 & 1 \end{bmatrix}$ (d) $\begin{bmatrix} 0 & -i \\ i & 0 \end{bmatrix}$

14. If $A = \begin{bmatrix} 0 & c & -b \\ -c & 0 & a \\ b & -a & 0 \end{bmatrix}$ and $B = \begin{bmatrix} a^2 & ab & ac \\ ab & b^2 & bc \\ ac & bc & c^2 \end{bmatrix}$, then AB is equal to

(a) B (b) A
(c) O (d) I

15. If $A = \begin{bmatrix} a & b \\ b & a \end{bmatrix}$, $A^2 = \begin{bmatrix} \alpha & \beta \\ \beta & \alpha \end{bmatrix}$, then $(a + b)^2$ is equal to

(a) $\alpha^2 + \beta^2$ (b) $\alpha - \beta$
(c) $\alpha - \beta$ (d) $\alpha^2 - \beta^2$

Answer Key

1. (b)	**2.** (a)	**3.** (d)	**4.** (a)	**5.** (c)	**6.** (a)	**7.** (c)	**8.** (c)	**9.** (b)	**10.** (c)
11. (b)	**12.** (b)	**13.** (c)	**14.** (c)	**15.** (c)					

■ TRANSPOSE OF A MATRIX

A matrix obtained by interchanging rows and columns of a matrix A is called the *transpose* of a matrix. If A is a matrix, then its transpose is denoted by A' or A^T. e.g., If

$$A = \begin{bmatrix} 2 & 3 & 5 \\ 5 & 6 & 8 \end{bmatrix}, \text{ then } A^T = \begin{bmatrix} 2 & 5 \\ 3 & 6 \\ 5 & 8 \end{bmatrix}$$

Properties

(i) $(A^T)^T = A$ i.e., the transpose of the transpose of a matrix is the matrix itself.

Proof: Let $A = [a_{ij}]$ be an $m \times n$ matrix
$\Rightarrow A^T$ is an $n \times m$ matrix $\Rightarrow (A^T)^T$ is an $m \times n$ matrix
Thus $(A^T)^T$ and A are both $m \times n$ matrices
Now (i, j)th element of $(A^T)^T = (j, i)$th element of A^T
$= (i, j)$th element of A

$\Rightarrow$ corresponding elements of $(A^T)^T$ and A are equal

$\Rightarrow (A^T)^T = A$

(ii) $(A + B)^T = A^T + B^T$ i.e., the transpose of the sum of two matrices is the sum of their transposes.

Proof: As $A + B$ is defined, let $A = [a_{ij}]$ and $B = [b_{jk}]$ be two $m \times n$ matrices.

$\Rightarrow A + B$ is an $m \times n$ matrix $\Rightarrow (A + B)^T$ is an $n \times m$ matrix

Also A^T, B^T are both $n \times m$ matrices $\Rightarrow A^T + B^T$ is an $n \times m$ matrix

Thus $(A + B)^T$ and $B^T + A^T$ are both $n \times m$ matrices

Now (j, i) th element of $(A + B)^T = (i, j)$th element of $A + B$

$= (i, j)$ th element of $A + (i, j)$ th element of B

$= (j, i)$ th element of $A^T + (j, i)$ th element of B^T

$= (j, i)$ th element of $(A^T + B^T)$

$\Rightarrow$ Corresponding elements of $(A + B)^T$ and $(A^T + B^T)$ are equal

$\Rightarrow (A + B)^T = A^T + B^T$

(iii) $(kA)^T = kA^T$ (where k is a *scalar*)

Proof: Let $A = [a_{ij}]$ be an $m \times n$ matrix

$\Rightarrow$ kA is an $m \times n$ matrix (*where k is any scalar*)

$\Rightarrow (kA)^T$ is an $n \times m$ matrix

Also A^T is an $n \times m$ matrix

$\Rightarrow kA^T$ is an $n \times m$ matrix

Thus $(kA)^T$ and kA^T are both $n \times m$ matrices

Now (j, i) th element of $(kA)^T = (i, j)$ th element of $kA = ka_{ij}$

$= k$ times (i, j) th element of $A = k$ times (j, i) th element of A^T

$= (j, i)$ th element of kA^T

$\Rightarrow$ corresponding elements of $(kA)^T$ and kA^T are equal

$\Rightarrow (kA)^T = kA^T$

(iv) $(AB)^T = B^TA^T$ i.e., the transpose of the product of two matrices is the product in reverse order of their transposes.

Proof: As AB is defined, let $A = [a_{ij}]$ and $B = [b_{jk}]$ be two $m \times n$ and $n \times p$ matrices respectively.

$A^T = [c_{ji}]$ where $c_{ji} = a_{ij}$

and $B^T = [d_{kj}]$ where $d_{kj} = b_{jk}$ are $n \times m$ and $p \times n$ matrices respectively

$\Rightarrow AB$ is a $m \times p$ matrix

$\Rightarrow (AB)^T$ is a $p \times m$ matrix

Also B^T is a $p \times n$ matrix and A^T is $n \times m$ matrix

$\Rightarrow B^TA^T$ is a $p \times m$ matrix

Thus $(AB)^T$ and B^TA^T are both $p \times m$ matrices

Now (k, i)th element of $(AB)^T = (i, k)$th element of AB

$$= \sum_{j=1}^{n} a_{ij}b_{jk} = \sum_{j=1}^{n} c_{ji}\, d_{kj} = \sum_{j=1}^{n} d_{kj}c_{ji} \quad (\because ab = ba \text{ for all real numbers})$$

$= (k, i)$th element of B^TA^T

$\Rightarrow$ Corresponding elements of $(AB)^T$ and B^TA^T are equal

$\Rightarrow (AB)^T = B^TA^T$

This is called reversal law for transposes.

(iv) $(-A)^T = ((-1)\, A)^T = (-1)A^T = -A^T$

(v) $(A - B)^T = (A + (-B))^T = A^T + (-B)^T = A^T + (-B^T) = (A^T - B^T)$

NOTES

If A is an $m \times n$ matrix, then A^T is an $n \times m$ matrix.

■ SYMMETRIC AND SKEW SYMMETRIC MATRICES

Symmetric Matrix

A square matrix will be called *symmetric* if the elements across principal diagonal are symmetrically equal, *i.e.*, $a_{ij} = a_{ji}$ or $A' = A$. e.g., $\begin{bmatrix} 1 & 5 & 6 \\ 5 & 2 & 7 \\ 6 & 7 & 3 \end{bmatrix}$.

Skew Symmetric Matrix

A square matrix is called *skew symmetric matrix* if $a_{ij} = -a_{ji}$ for all values of i and j so all the diagonal elements will be zero. i.e., $A = -A'$ or $A' = -A$; e.g., $\begin{bmatrix} 0 & -7 \\ 7 & 0 \end{bmatrix}, \begin{bmatrix} 0 & i+1 & 3 \\ -1-i & 0 & -2 \\ -3 & 2 & 0 \end{bmatrix}$

Hence if A is skew symmetric, then $a_{ii} = -a_{ii} \Rightarrow a_{ii} = 0$ for all i.

Thus the diagonal elements of a skew symmetric square matrix are all zero, but not the converse.

Properties

1. A symmetric/skew symmetric matrix is necessarily a square matrix.
2. Symmetric matrix does not change by interchanging the rows and columns.

   i.e., symmetric matrices are transpose of themselves.
3. A is symmetric if $A^T = A$ and A is skew symmetric if $A^T = -A$
4. $A + A^T$ is a symmetric matrix and $A - A^T$ is a skew symmetric matrix.

   Consider $(A + A^T)^T = A^T + (A^T)^T = A^T + A = A + A^T$ $\Rightarrow A + A^T$ is symmetric.

   Similarly, we can prove that $A - A^T$ is skew symmetric.
5. The sum of two symmetric matrices is a symmetric matrix and the sum of two skew symmetric matrices is a skew symmetric matrix.

   Let $A^T = A$; $B^T = B$ *where A and B have the same order.*

   Then $(A + B)^T = A^T - B^T = A + B$ Similarly we can prove the other.
6. If A and B are symmetric matrices, then $AB + BA$ is a symmetric matrix and $AB - BA$ is a skew symmetric matrix.

NOTES

1. *Every square matrix can be uniquely expressed as the sum of symmetric and skew symmetric matrix. i.e.,* $A = \frac{1}{2}(A + A') + \frac{1}{2}(A - A')$, *where* $\frac{1}{2}(A + A')$ *and* $\frac{1}{2}(A - A')$ *respectively are the symmetric and skew symmetric parts of A.*
2. *Maximum number of distinct entries in a symmetric matrix of order n is* $\frac{n(n+1)}{2}$.
3. *The matrix* (B^TAB) *is symmetric or non-symmetric according as A is symmetric or non-symmetric respectively.*
4. *The determinant of any skew symmetric matrix of odd order always* **vanishes.**
5. *The determinant of skew symmetric matrix with even order is always a* **perfect square, i.e.** of the form $\left[\sum \pm(\alpha\beta\gamma....)\right]^2$; where α, β, γ ....are elements of matrix.

ILLUSTRATION 19: If A is any square matrix prove that AA^T is symmetric.

SOLUTION: $(AA^T)^T = (A^T)^T A^T$ $\quad [\because (AB)^T = B^T A^T)]$

$= AA^T$ $\quad$ as $(A^T)^T = A^T$

$\Rightarrow AA^T$ is a symmetric matrix

ILLUSTRATION 20: If A, B are skew symmetric matrices of the same order, prove that AB is symmetric iff A and B commute.

SOLUTION: As A and B are skew symmetric matrices, therefore, $A^T = -A$ and $B^T = -B$.

Since A and B are square matrices of same order AB and BA are both defined.

Now, AB is symmetric iff $(AB)^T = AB$

i.e., iff $B^TA^T = AB$ (reversal law of transpose)

i.e., iff $(-B)(-A) = AB$ i.e., iff $BA = AB$

i.e., iff A and B commute

ILLUSTRATION 21: Show that all positive integral powers of a symmetric matrix are symmetric.

SOLUTION: Let A be a symmeric matrix $\Rightarrow A^T = A$ ...(i)

Let m be any positive integer, then $A^m = AAA....$up to m times

$$(A^m)^T = (AAA....\text{up to } m \text{ times})^T = (A^T A^T A^T....\text{up to } m \text{ times})$$
$$= (A^T)^m = A^m$$

$\Rightarrow A^m$ is symmetric, for all $m \in N$

ILLUSTRATION 22: Every square matrix, can be uniquely expressed as a sum of symmetric and skew symmetric matrix.

SOLUTION: Let A be a square matrix then we can express $A = \frac{1}{2}(A + A') + \frac{1}{2}(A - A')$

Let $B = \frac{1}{2}(A + A')$ and $C = \frac{1}{2}(A + A')$

$$B' = \left[\frac{1}{2}(A + A')\right]' = \left[\frac{1}{2}(A + A')'\right] = \frac{1}{2}(A' - A) = B$$. So B is symmetric matrix.

Again $C' = \left[\frac{1}{2}(A - A')\right]' = \left[\frac{1}{2}(A' - A)\right] = -C$. So C is skew symmetric.

Hence A can be expressed as the sum of a symmetric and a skew symmetric matrix.

To prove the uniqueness, assume that P is a symmetric matrix and Q is a skew symmetric matrix such that $A = P + Q$.

Then $A' = P' + Q' = P - Q$.Thus $P = \frac{1}{2}(A+A')$ and $Q = \frac{1}{2}(A-A')$

which shows that there is one and only one way of expressing A as the sum of a symmetric and skew symmetric matrix.

ILLUSTRATION 23: Express the matrix $A = \begin{bmatrix} 1 & 2 & 4 \\ -2 & 5 & 3 \\ -1 & 6 & 3 \end{bmatrix}$ as the sum of a symmetric and a skew symmetric matrix:

SOLUTION: Given $A = \begin{bmatrix} 1 & 2 & 4 \\ -2 & 5 & 3 \\ -1 & 6 & 3 \end{bmatrix}$. By Transposing, we get $A' = \begin{bmatrix} 1 & -2 & -1 \\ 2 & 5 & 6 \\ 4 & 3 & 3 \end{bmatrix}$

Adding A and A', we have $A+A' = \begin{bmatrix} 1 & 2 & 4 \\ -2 & 5 & 3 \\ -1 & 6 & 3 \end{bmatrix} + \begin{bmatrix} 1 & -2 & -1 \\ 2 & 5 & 6 \\ 4 & 3 & 3 \end{bmatrix} = \begin{bmatrix} 2 & 0 & 3 \\ 0 & 10 & 9 \\ 3 & 9 & 6 \end{bmatrix}$ ...(i)

Subtracting A' from A, we get $A-A'=\begin{bmatrix}1&2&4\\-2&5&3\\-1&6&3\end{bmatrix}-\begin{bmatrix}1&-2&-1\\2&5&6\\4&3&3\end{bmatrix}=\begin{bmatrix}0&4&5\\-4&0&-3\\-5&3&0\end{bmatrix}$ ...(ii)

Addding equations (i) and (ii), we have $2A=\begin{bmatrix}2&0&3\\0&10&9\\3&9&6\end{bmatrix}+\begin{bmatrix}0&4&5\\-4&0&-3\\-5&3&0\end{bmatrix}$

$$\Rightarrow\ A=\begin{bmatrix}1&0&3/2\\0&5&9/2\\3/2&9/2&3\end{bmatrix}+\begin{bmatrix}0&2&5/2\\-2&0&-3/2\\-5/2&3/2&0\end{bmatrix}=\text{Symmetric matrix + skew Symmetric matrix}$$

ILLUSTRATION 24: If $A=\begin{bmatrix}\cos\alpha&\sin\alpha\\-\sin\alpha&\cos\alpha\end{bmatrix}$, verify that $AA'=I=A'A$ where I is the unit matrix.

SOLUTION: Given $A=\begin{bmatrix}\cos\alpha&\sin\alpha\\-\sin\alpha&\cos\alpha\end{bmatrix}$, $A'=\begin{bmatrix}\cos\alpha&-\sin\alpha\\\sin\alpha&\cos\alpha\end{bmatrix}$

$$AA'=\begin{bmatrix}\cos\alpha&\sin\alpha\\-\sin\alpha&\cos\alpha\end{bmatrix}\begin{bmatrix}\cos\alpha&-\sin\alpha\\\sin\alpha&\cos\alpha\end{bmatrix}$$

$$=\begin{bmatrix}\cos^2\alpha+\sin^2\alpha&-\sin\alpha\cos\alpha+\cos\alpha\sin\alpha\\-\sin\alpha\cos\alpha+\cos\alpha\sin\alpha&\sin^2\alpha+\cos^2\alpha\end{bmatrix}=\begin{bmatrix}1&0\\0&1\end{bmatrix}=I$$

and $$A'A=\begin{bmatrix}\cos\alpha&-\sin\alpha\\\sin\alpha&\cos\alpha\end{bmatrix}\begin{bmatrix}\cos\alpha&\sin\alpha\\-\sin\alpha&\cos\alpha\end{bmatrix}$$

$$=\begin{bmatrix}\cos^2\alpha+\sin^2\alpha&-\sin\alpha\cos\alpha+\cos\alpha\sin\alpha\\-\sin\alpha\cos\alpha+\cos\alpha\sin\alpha&\sin^2\alpha+\cos^2\alpha\end{bmatrix}=\begin{bmatrix}1&0\\0&1\end{bmatrix}=I$$

$\therefore\ AA'=I=A'A$

HERMITIAN AND SKEW HERMITIAN MATRICES

Hermitian Matrix

If transpose of the conjugate matrix is equal to the matrix itself $(\bar{A})^T=A$.

A square matrix A such that $\overline{A'}=A$ is called *hermitian matrix*, provided $a_{ij}=\bar{a}_{ji}$ for all values of i and j or $\left[\bar{a}_{ji}\right]=A$. e.g., $\begin{bmatrix}2&3+2i\\3-2i&7\end{bmatrix}$

Properties

Diagonal elements are purely real.

$$a_{ii}=\overline{a_{ii}}\ \Rightarrow\ a_{ii}-\bar{a}_{ii}=0\Rightarrow 2I_m(a_{ii})=0$$

Skew-Hermitian Matrix

A square matrix A such that $\overline{A'}=-A$ is called *skew-hermitian matrix*, i.e., $a_{ij}=-\overline{a_{ji}}$ for all values of i and j or $A^\theta=-A$.

Example:

Let $A=\begin{bmatrix}3i&1-3i&2\\-1-3i&0&4+i\\-2&-4+i&2i\end{bmatrix}$

$$\Rightarrow\ A^T=\begin{bmatrix}3i&-1-3i&-2\\1-3i&0&-4+i\\2&4+i&2i\end{bmatrix}$$

$$\Rightarrow\ (\overline{A^T}) = A^\theta = \begin{bmatrix} -3i & -1+3i & -2 \\ 1+3i & 0 & -4-i \\ 2 & 4-i & -2i \end{bmatrix}$$

$$= -\begin{bmatrix} 3i & 1-3i & 2 \\ -1-3i & 0 & 4+i \\ -2 & -4+i & 2i \end{bmatrix} = -A$$

Properties

1. Elements on principal diagonal are either purely imaginary or zero. $\because\ a_{ii} = -\overline{a_{ii}}$ for $i = j$

   $a_{ii} = -\overline{a_{ii}} \quad \Rightarrow \quad \mathbb{R}(a_{ii}) = 0$

   $\Rightarrow\ a_{ii}$ is purly imaginary
2. Every skew-symmetric matrix with real numbers as elements is skew-Hermitian.
3. Every square matrix can be uniquely represented as the sum of a hermitian and skew-hermitian matrices
4. If A is any matrix, then $A = \frac{1}{2}\{A + A^\theta\} + \frac{1}{2}\{A - A^\theta\}$

   = hermitian + skew-hermitian.

TEXTUAL EXERCISE 5: (SUBJECTIVE)

1. Write the transpose of a matrix $A = \begin{bmatrix} a & b & c \\ d & e & f \end{bmatrix}$ and hence show that $(A')' = A$.
2. (a) If $a_{ij} = ij$, show that $A = [a_{ij}]$ is a symmetric matrix.

   (b) If $a_{ij} = i^2 - j^2$, show that $A = [a_{ij}]$ is a skew symmetric matrix.
3. Is there a matrix which is symmetric as well as skew symmetric?
4. Show that the determinant of a Hermitian matrix is real.
5. Show that $D = \text{Diag.}\ (d_1, d_2,..,d_n) \Rightarrow |D| = d_1 . d_2 ... d_n$
6. If B is a real $m \times n$ matrix, show that $B'B$ as well as BB' is a symmetric matrix.
7. Show that positive odd integral powers of a skew symmetric matrix are skew symmetric and positive even integral power are symmetric.

Answer Key

3. Yes; A Square Null Matrix

■ SPECIAL KINDS OF MATRICES

Orthogonal Matrix

A square matrix A is called an *orthogonal matrix* if the product of the matrix A and its transpose A' is an identity matrix. *i.e.*, $AA' = A'A = I$.

ILLUSTRATION 25: Verify that $A = \frac{1}{3}\begin{bmatrix} 1 & 2 & 2 \\ 2 & 1 & -2 \\ -2 & 2 & -1 \end{bmatrix}$ is orthogonal.

SOLUTION: $A = \frac{1}{3}\begin{bmatrix} 1 & 2 & 2 \\ 2 & 1 & -2 \\ -2 & 2 & -1 \end{bmatrix} \Rightarrow A' = \frac{1}{3}\begin{bmatrix} 1 & 2 & -2 \\ 2 & 1 & 2 \\ 2 & -2 & -1 \end{bmatrix}$ $AA' = \frac{1}{9}\begin{bmatrix} 1 & 2 & 2 \\ 2 & 1 & -2 \\ -2 & 2 & -1 \end{bmatrix}\begin{bmatrix} 1 & 2 & -2 \\ 2 & 1 & 2 \\ 2 & -2 & -1 \end{bmatrix}$

$= \frac{1}{9}\begin{bmatrix} 9 & 0 & 0 \\ 0 & 9 & 0 \\ 0 & 0 & 9 \end{bmatrix} = \begin{bmatrix} 1 & 0 & 0 \\ 0 & 1 & 0 \\ 0 & 0 & 1 \end{bmatrix} = I$. Hence A is an orthogonal matrix.

Properties

(i) If $AA' = I$, then $A^{-1} = A'$ i.e. inverse of A equals A'.
(ii) If A and B are orthogonal, then AB is also orthogonal.
(iii) Value of corresponding determinant of orthogonal matrix is ± 1.

ILLUSTRATION 26: Show that the matrix $\begin{bmatrix} l_1 & m_1 & n_1 \\ l_2 & m_2 & n_2 \\ l_3 & m_3 & n_3 \end{bmatrix}$ is orthogonal if

$$l_1^2 + m_1^2 + n_1^2 = \sum l_1^2 = 1 = \sum l_2^2 = \sum l_3^2 \text{ and } l_1 l_2 + m_1 m_2 + n_1 n_2 = \sum l_1 l_2 = 0 = \sum l_2 l_3 = \sum l_3 l_1$$

SOLUTION: Let $A = \begin{bmatrix} l_1 & m_1 & n_1 \\ l_2 & m_2 & n_2 \\ l_3 & m_3 & n_3 \end{bmatrix} \Rightarrow A' = \begin{bmatrix} l_1 & l_2 & l_3 \\ m_1 & m_2 & m_3 \\ n_1 & n_2 & n_3 \end{bmatrix}$

Now $AA' = \begin{bmatrix} l_1 & m_1 & n_1 \\ l_2 & m_2 & n_2 \\ l_3 & m_3 & n_3 \end{bmatrix} \times \begin{bmatrix} l_1 & l_2 & l_3 \\ m_1 & m_2 & m_3 \\ n_1 & n_2 & n_3 \end{bmatrix} = \begin{bmatrix} \sum l_1^2 & \sum l_1 l_2 & \sum l_3 l_1 \\ \sum l_1 l_2 & \sum l_2^2 & \sum l_2 l_3 \\ \sum l_3 l_1 & \sum l_2 l_3 & \sum l_3^2 \end{bmatrix} = \begin{bmatrix} 1 & 0 & 0 \\ 0 & 1 & 0 \\ 0 & 0 & 1 \end{bmatrix} = I.$

Hence matrix A is orthogonal.

ILLUSTRATION 27: If M is a 3×3 matrix, where $M'M = I$ and $\det M = 1$, then prove that $\det(M - I) = 0$

SOLUTION: $\det M = 1 \Rightarrow \det M' = 1$

Now $\det(M - I)$ $= \det(M - I)\det M'$

$= \det(MM' - IM')$ $\quad(\det A \det B = \det(AB))$

$= \det(I - M') = -\det(M' - I) = -\det(M - I)$

Thus $\det(M - I) = -\det(M - I)$ $\Rightarrow \det(M - I) = 0$

Idempotent Matrix

A square matrix A is called idempotent provided it satisfies the relation $A^2 = A$.

Properties

(i) If A and B are idempotent matrices, then AB is an idempotent matrix, if $AB = BA$
(ii) If A and B are idempotent matrices, then $A + B$ is an idempotent if $AB + BA = O$.
(iii) A is idempotent and $A + B = I$, then B is also idempotent and $AB = BA = O$.

ILLUSTRATION 28: Show that the matrix $A = \begin{bmatrix} 2 & -2 & -4 \\ -1 & 3 & 4 \\ 1 & -2 & -3 \end{bmatrix}$ is idempotent.

SOLUTION: $A^2 = A.A = \begin{bmatrix} 2 & -2 & -4 \\ -1 & 3 & 4 \\ 1 & -2 & -3 \end{bmatrix} \times \begin{bmatrix} 2 & -2 & -4 \\ -1 & 3 & 4 \\ 1 & -2 & -3 \end{bmatrix} = \begin{bmatrix} 2 & -2 & -4 \\ -1 & 3 & 4 \\ 1 & -2 & -3 \end{bmatrix} = A$. So, A is idempotent.

Periodic Matrix

A square matrix A is called *periodic*, if $A^{k+1} = A$, where k is a positive integer. If k is the least positive integer for which $A^{k+1} = A$, then k is said to be period of A. For $k = 1$, we get $A^2 = A$ and hence is *idempotent matrix.*

Nilpotent Matrix

A square matrix A is called *Nilpotent matrix* of order k provided it satisfies the relation $A^k = O$ and $A^{k-1} \neq O$, where k is positive integer and O is null matrix and k is the order of the nilpotent matrix A.

ILLUSTRATION 29: Show that $\begin{bmatrix} 1 & 1 & 3 \\ 5 & 2 & 6 \\ -2 & -1 & -3 \end{bmatrix}$ is nilpotent matrix of order 3.

SOLUTION: Let $A = \begin{bmatrix} 1 & 1 & 3 \\ 5 & 2 & 6 \\ -2 & -1 & -3 \end{bmatrix}$ $\therefore A^2 = A.A = \begin{bmatrix} 1 & 1 & 3 \\ 5 & 2 & 6 \\ -2 & -1 & -3 \end{bmatrix} \times \begin{bmatrix} 1 & 1 & 3 \\ 5 & 2 & 6 \\ -2 & -1 & -3 \end{bmatrix} = \begin{bmatrix} 0 & 0 & 0 \\ 3 & 3 & 9 \\ -1 & -1 & -3 \end{bmatrix}$

$$A^3 = A^2.A = \begin{bmatrix} 0 & 0 & 0 \\ 3 & 3 & 9 \\ -1 & -1 & -3 \end{bmatrix} \times \begin{bmatrix} 1 & 1 & 3 \\ 5 & 2 & 6 \\ -2 & -1 & -3 \end{bmatrix} = \begin{bmatrix} 0 & 0 & 0 \\ 0 & 0 & 0 \\ 0 & 0 & 0 \end{bmatrix}$$

$\therefore A^3 = O$ i.e., $A^k = O$

Hence $k = 3$, therefore k is nilpotent of order 3.

Involutory Matrix

A square matrix A is called ***involutory*** matrix provided it satisfies the relation $A^2 = \boldsymbol{I}$, where I is identity matrix.

e.g., $A = \begin{bmatrix} 1 & 0 \\ 0 & -1 \end{bmatrix}$ and $A^2 = \begin{bmatrix} 1 & 0 \\ 0 & 1 \end{bmatrix} = I$

Properties

(i) A is involutory iff $(A + I)(A - I) = O$

(ii) Identity matrix is a trivial example of involutory matrix.

ILLUSTRATION 30: Show that the matrix $A = \begin{bmatrix} -5 & -8 & 0 \\ 3 & 5 & 0 \\ 1 & 2 & -1 \end{bmatrix}$ is an involutory matrix.

SOLUTION: $A^2 = A.A = \begin{bmatrix} -5 & -8 & 0 \\ 3 & 5 & 0 \\ 1 & 2 & -1 \end{bmatrix} \times \begin{bmatrix} -5 & -8 & 0 \\ 3 & 5 & 0 \\ 1 & 2 & -1 \end{bmatrix} = \begin{bmatrix} 1 & 0 & 0 \\ 0 & 1 & 0 \\ 0 & 0 & 1 \end{bmatrix}$

$= \boldsymbol{I}$. Hence the given matrix A is involutory.

Unitary Matrix

A square matrix A is called a *unitary matrix* if $A.\, A^{\theta} = \mathrm{I}$, where I is an identity matrix and A^{θ} is the transposed conjugate of A. If the entries of matrix are real numbers, then orthogonal matrix and unitary matrix are same.

Properties of Unitary Matrix

(i) If A is unitary matrix, then A' is also unitary.

(ii) If A is unitary matrix, then A^{-1} is also unitary.

(iii) If A and B are unitary matrices, then $\boldsymbol{AB}$ is also unitary.

LLUSTRATION 31: Prove that $\begin{bmatrix} \frac{1}{2} & \frac{\sqrt{3}}{2}i \\ -\frac{\sqrt{3}}{2}i & -\frac{1}{2} \end{bmatrix}$ is a unitary matrix.

SOLUTION: $\overline{A^T} = \begin{bmatrix} \frac{1}{2} & \frac{\sqrt{3}}{2}i \\ -\frac{\sqrt{3}}{2}i & -\frac{1}{2} \end{bmatrix}$

$$\therefore\ A.\overline{A^T} = \begin{bmatrix} \frac{1}{2} & \frac{\sqrt{3}}{2}i \\ -\frac{\sqrt{3}}{2}i & -\frac{1}{2} \end{bmatrix}\begin{bmatrix} \frac{1}{2} & \frac{\sqrt{3}}{2}i \\ -\frac{\sqrt{3}}{2}i & -\frac{1}{2} \end{bmatrix} = \begin{bmatrix} \frac{1}{4}-\frac{3}{4} & \frac{\sqrt{3}}{4}i-\frac{\sqrt{3}}{4}i \\ -\frac{\sqrt{3}}{4}i+\frac{\sqrt{3}}{4}i & \frac{3}{4}+\frac{1}{4} \end{bmatrix}$$

$$= \begin{bmatrix} 1 & 0 \\ 0 & 1 \end{bmatrix} = I \quad \Rightarrow \text{ I is a unitary matrix.}$$

TEXTUAL EXERCISE 6: (SUBJECTIVE)

1. If $A = \frac{1}{9}\begin{bmatrix} -8 & 1 & 4 \\ 4 & 4 & 7 \\ 1 & -8 & 4 \end{bmatrix}$, prove that $A^{-1} = A'$; A' being the transpose of A.

2. Show that $A = \begin{bmatrix} \cos\theta & 0 & \sin\theta \\ 0 & 1 & 0 \\ -\sin\theta & 0 & \cos\theta \end{bmatrix}$ is orthogonal. Find the value of $|A|$.

3. If $A^n = O$, then evaluate
(a) $I + A + A^2 + A^3 + ... + A^{n-1}$ for odd 'n'
(b) $I - A + A^2 - A^3 + ... + (-1)^{n-1} A^{n-1}$

4. If A is non identity non-singular square matrix and B is a square matrix such that $AB = BA^2$ and $B^3 = I$, then find k_{min} if $A^k = I$.

5. Show that $A = \begin{bmatrix} 2 & -3 & -5 \\ -1 & 4 & 5 \\ 1 & -3 & -4 \end{bmatrix}$ is idempotent.

6. Show that the matrix $\begin{bmatrix} 2 & -2 & -4 \\ -1 & 3 & 4 \\ 1 & -2 & -3 \end{bmatrix}$ is periodic. Is the matrix idempotent?

7. Show that $\begin{bmatrix} 0 & 4 & 3 \\ 1 & -3 & -3 \\ -1 & 4 & 4 \end{bmatrix}$ is involutory.

8. If A and B are two matrices such that $AB = A$ and $BA = B$, then prove that A^T and B^T are idempotent matrices.

9. If A is nilpotent matrix of index 2, then show that $A(I \pm A)^n = A\ \forall\ n \in \mathbb{N}$.

10. If A is idempotent, then show that $(A + I)^n = I + (2n - 1)A\ \forall\ n \in \mathbb{N}$.

Answer Key

2. (1) **3.** (a) $(I - A)^{-1}$ (b) $(I + A)^{-1}$ **4.** 7

TEXTUAL EXERCISE 2: (OBJECTIVE)

1. If $AB = A$ and $BA = B$, then B^2 is equal to
(a) B (b) A
(c) I (d) O

2. If A, B are two square matrices such that $AB = A$ and $BA = B$, then
(a) only B is idempotent
(b) A, B are idempotent
(c) only A is idempotent
(d) None of these

3. If B is an idempotent matrix and $A = I - B$, then
(a) $A^2 = A$ (b) $A^2 = I$
(c) $AB = O$ (d) $BA = O$

4. If the matrix $\begin{bmatrix} 0 & 2\beta & \gamma \\ \alpha & \beta & -\gamma \\ \alpha & -\beta & \gamma \end{bmatrix}$ is orthogonal, then
(a) $\alpha = \pm\frac{1}{\sqrt{2}}$ (b) $\beta = \pm\frac{1}{\sqrt{6}}$
(c) $\gamma = \pm\frac{1}{\sqrt{3}}$ (d) All of these

5. If A is an orthogonal matrix, then A^{-1} equals
(a) A (b) A^T
(c) A^2 (d) None of these

6. If A is an orthogonal matrix, then
(a) det $A = 1$ (b) det $A = 0$
(c) det $A = -1$ (d) None of these

7. The matrix $\begin{bmatrix} 0 & 5 & -7 \\ -5 & 0 & 11 \\ 7 & -11 & 0 \end{bmatrix}$ is known as
(a) skew symmetric matrix
(b) symmetric matrix
(c) diagonal matrix
(d) upper triangular matrix

8. If A is a skew-symmetric matrix, then trace of A is
(a) 1 (b) –1
(c) 0 (d) None of these

9. If A is a skew-symmetric matrix of order 3, then matrix A^3 is:
(a) skew-symmetric matrix
(b) symmetric matrix
(c) diagonal matrix
(d) None of these

10. For every square matrix A, $AA^T - A^TA$ is
(a) a symmetric matrix (b) a skew-symmetric matrix
(c) a null matrix (d) None of these

11. If A and B be symmetric matrices of the same order then
(a) $A + B$ is symmetric matrix.
(b) $AB - BA$ is a skew-symmetric matrix
(c) $AB + BA$ is a symmetric matrix
(d) None of these

Answer Key

1. (a) **2.** (b) **3.** (a, c, d) **4.** (d) **5.** (b) **6.** (a, c) **7.** (a) **8.** (c) **9.** (a) **10.** (a)
11. (a, b, c)

■ MINORS AND CO FACTORS

Minor: The determinant obtained by deleting the ith row and j^{th} column through the element a_{ij} is called the minor of element a_{ij} in the determimant and is denoted by M_{ij}.

Co factor: The cofactors of the element a_{ij} is $(-1)^{i+j}$ times the determinant obtained by deleting the ith row and j^{th} column passing through a_{ij}. We shall denote the cofactor of an element by the corresponding capital letter $C_{ij} \Rightarrow C_{ij} = (-1)^{i+j} M_{ij}$ If $\Delta = \begin{vmatrix} a_{11} & a_{12} & a_{13} \\ a_{21} & a_{22} & a_{23} \\ a_{31} & a_{32} & a_{33} \end{vmatrix}$ *(So, we will get 9 minors corresponding to 9 elements of the above determinant).*

e.g., The minor of element $a_{21} = M_{21} = \begin{vmatrix} a_{12} & a_{13} \\ a_{32} & a_{33} \end{vmatrix}$

ADJOINT OF A SQUARE MATRIX

Let $A = [a_{ij}] = \begin{bmatrix} a_{11} & a_{12} & a_{13} \\ a_{21} & a_{22} & a_{23} \\ a_{31} & a_{32} & a_{33} \end{bmatrix}$ be a square matrix of order n and let C_{ij} be co-factor of a_{ij} in A. Then the transpose of the matrix of co-factors of elements of A is called the adjoint of A and denoted by $adj(A)$.

$$[C_{ij}] = \begin{bmatrix} C_{11} & C_{12} & C_{13} \\ C_{21} & C_{22} & C_{23} \\ C_{31} & C_{32} & C_{33} \end{bmatrix} \text{ therefore } adj(A) = [C_{ij}]^T.$$

$$\text{Then } (adj\ A) = \begin{bmatrix} C_{11} & C_{21} & C_{31} \\ C_{12} & C_{22} & C_{32} \\ C_{13} & C_{23} & C_{33} \end{bmatrix}$$

e.g., Let $A = \begin{bmatrix} a_1 & b_1 & c_1 \\ a_2 & b_2 & c_2 \\ a_3 & b_3 & c_3 \end{bmatrix}$. If A_1, B_1 etc., represent the co-factors of a_1, b_1 etc., respectively in A, then

$$adj\ A = \begin{bmatrix} A_1 & A_2 & A_3 \\ B_1 & B_2 & B_3 \\ C_1 & C_2 & C_3 \end{bmatrix}.$$

ILLUSTRATION 32: Find the adjoint of matrix $A = \begin{bmatrix} 1 & 1 & 1 \\ 2 & 1 & -3 \\ -1 & 2 & 3 \end{bmatrix}$.

SOLUTION: Let C_{ij} be a co-factor of a_{ij} in A. Then co-factors of elements of A are given by

$$C_{11} = \begin{vmatrix} 1 & -3 \\ 2 & 3 \end{vmatrix} = 9;\ C_{12} = -\begin{vmatrix} 2 & -3 \\ -1 & 3 \end{vmatrix} = -3;\ C_{13} = \begin{vmatrix} 2 & 1 \\ -1 & 2 \end{vmatrix} = 5$$

$$C_{21} = -\begin{vmatrix} 1 & 1 \\ 2 & 3 \end{vmatrix} = -1;\ C_{22} = \begin{vmatrix} 1 & 1 \\ -1 & 3 \end{vmatrix} = 4;\ C_{23} = -\begin{vmatrix} 1 & 1 \\ -1 & 2 \end{vmatrix} = -3$$

$$C_{31} = \begin{vmatrix} 1 & 1 \\ 1 & -3 \end{vmatrix} = -4;\ C_{32} = -\begin{vmatrix} 1 & 1 \\ 2 & -3 \end{vmatrix} = 5;\ C_{33} = \begin{vmatrix} 1 & 1 \\ 2 & 1 \end{vmatrix} = -1$$

$$\therefore\ adj\ A = \begin{bmatrix} 9 & -3 & 5 \\ -1 & 4 & -3 \\ -4 & 5 & -1 \end{bmatrix}' = \begin{bmatrix} 9 & -1 & -4 \\ -3 & 4 & 5 \\ 5 & -3 & -1 \end{bmatrix}$$

ILLUSTRATION 33: Prove that $A.\ Adj(A) = |A|\ I$ for a 3×3 matrix.

SOLUTION: $A.\ (Adj.\ A) = \begin{bmatrix} a_{11} & a_{12} & a_{13} \\ a_{21} & a_{22} & a_{23} \\ a_{31} & a_{32} & a_{33} \end{bmatrix} \begin{bmatrix} C_{11} & C_{21} & C_{31} \\ C_{12} & C_{22} & C_{32} \\ C_{13} & C_{23} & C_{33} \end{bmatrix}$

$$= \begin{bmatrix} a_{11}C_{11} + a_{12}C_{12} + a_{13}C_{13} & a_{11}C_{21} + a_{12}C_{22} + a_{13}C_{23} & a_{11}C_{31} + a_{12}C_{32} + a_{13}C_{33} \\ a_{21}C_{11} + a_{22}C_{12} + a_{23}C_{13} & a_{21}C_{21} + a_{22}C_{22} + a_{23}C_{23} & a_{21}C_{31} + a_{22}C_{32} + a_{23}C_{33} \\ a_{31}C_{11} + a_{32}C_{12} + a_{33}C_{13} & a_{31}C_{21} + a_{32}C_{22} + a_{33}C_{23} & a_{31}C_{31} + a_{32}C_{32} + a_{33}C_{33} \end{bmatrix}$$

$$= \begin{bmatrix} |A| & 0 & 0 \\ 0 & |A| & 0 \\ 0 & 0 & |A| \end{bmatrix} = |A|\,I$$

Similarly $(Adj.\ A)\ .\ A = |A|\ I$ for any matrix A of order $n \times n$

Properties of adjoint A

1. If A be n rowed square matrix, then $(adj\ A)\ A = A\ (adj\ A) = |A|.I_n$

   i.e., the product of a matrix and its adjoint is commutative and equals the |A| multiple of identity matrix.

   Deductions from above property:

   (a) If A is n rowed square singular matrix, then $(adj\ A)\ A = A\ (adj\ A) = O$ (null matrix) since for singular matrix, $|A| = 0$

   (b) If A is n rowed square non-singular matrix, then $|adj\ A| = |A|^{n-1}$ since for non-singular matrix, $|A| \neq 0$

   Proof Taking determinant on both sides of the equations A adj. $A = |A|\ I$, we get $|\text{adj. } A| = |A|^{n-1}$.

2. $Adj\ (AB) = (Adj\ B).\ (Adj\ A)$

   Proof Pre multiplying both sides by $A\ B$.

   LHS: $AB\ (adj\ AB) = |AB|\ I = |A| \times |B| I$

   RHS: $AB\ (adj B)\ (adj A) = A\ (B\ adj\ B)\ (adj\ A)$

   $= A\ |B| I\ (adj\ A)$

   $= A\ (adj\ A)\ |B| = |A|\ |B| I$

   $\therefore$ LHS = RHS

3. $(adj\ A)' = adj\ A'$

4. $adj\ (adj\ A) = |A|^{n-2} A$, where A is a non-singular matrix.

   Proof Let $Adj.\ (Adj.\ A) = X$.

   Post multiplying both sides by Adj A

   $(Adj.\ Adj.\ A)\ (Adj\ A) = X.\ (Adj.\ A)$

   $|Adj.\ A|\ I = X\ .\ Adj.\ A$

   Post multiplying both sides by A

   $|Adj.\ A|\ A = X\ .\ (Adj.\ A).\ A = X\ |A|\ I$

   $\Rightarrow\ X = Adj.\ (Adj.\ A) = \dfrac{|Adj. A|\ A}{|A|} = |A|^{n-2} A$

5. $|Adj\ (Adj\ A)| = |A|^{(n-1)^2}$, where A is a non-singular matrix.

   Proof $|X| = |Adj.\ Adj.\ A| = ||A|^{n-2} A|$

   $= |A|^{n(n-2)}\ |A| = |A|^{n^2-2n+1} = |A|^{(n-1)^2}$.

6. Adjoint of a diagonal matrix is a diagonal matrix.

7. $adj\ (kA) = k^{n-1}\ (adj\ A)$, k is a scalar

   Proof: Post multiplying both sides by kA, we get

   LHS = $Adj\ (kA) \times (kA) = |k\ A|\ I$

   RHS = $k^n\ (Adj\ A)\ A = k^n\ |A|\ I = |kA|\ I$.

ILLUSTRATION 34: To find $|Adj\ (Adj\ (Adj\ A))|$

SOLUTION: Let $Adj\ (Adj\ Adj\ A) = Y$

Post multiplying with $Adj\ Adj\ A$, we get $Adj\ (Adj\ Adj\ A)\ .\ (Adj\ Adj\ A) = Y\ .\ Adj\ (Adj\ A)$

$|Adj\ Adj\ A|\ I = Y.\ (Adj\ Adj\ A)$

Post multiplying with $Adj\ A$; $|Adj\ Adj\ A|\ (Adj\ A) = Y.(Adj\ Adj\ A)\ .\ (Adj\ A)$

$|A|^{(n-1)^2}\ (Adj A) = Y.|\ Adj A|\ I$

$$Y = Adj\ (Adj\ (Adj\ A)) = \frac{|A|^{(n-1)^2}}{|Adj\ A|}(Adj\ A) = \frac{|A|^{(n-1)^2}}{|A|^{n-1}}(Adj\ A)$$

$$= |A|^{(n-1)^2-(n-1)}\ (Adj\ A) = |A|^{(n-1)(n-2)}\ (Adj\ A)$$

$\therefore\ |Y| = |Adj\ Adj\ Adj\ A| = ||A|^{(n-1)(n-2)}\ (Adj\ A)| = |A|^{n(n-1)(n-2)}\ |A|^{n-1} = |A|^{(n-1)^3}$

Note: In general, we can conclude $\left|\underbrace{Adj\ Adj....Adj}_{r\text{ times }Adj}\ A\right| = |A|^{(n-1)^r}$.

■ INVERSE OF A MATRIX

A square matrix A (*non-singular*) of order n is said to be invertible iff there exists a matrix B such that $AB = I_n = BA$, then B is called the inverse of A and denoted by A^{-1}. (read "as A inverse")

$\therefore\ A^{-1} = B \Leftrightarrow AB = I = BA$

We have $A(adj\ A) = |A| I_n \Rightarrow A^{-1}A(adj\ A) = A^{-1}I_n|A|$

$\Rightarrow\ I_n(adj\ A) = A^{-1}|A|\ I_n$

$\Rightarrow\ A^{-1} = \dfrac{(adj\ A)}{|A|}$; provided $|A| \neq 0$.

NOTES

1. *The necessary and sufficient condition for a square matrix A to be invertible is that* $|A| \neq 0$.
2. *Inverse of a non-singular diagonal matrix*

If $A = \begin{bmatrix} a & 0 & 0 \\ 0 & b & 0 \\ 0 & 0 & c \end{bmatrix}$ *such that* $|A| \neq 0$ **i.e. abc ≠ 0** $\therefore\ A^{-1} = \begin{bmatrix} 1/a & 0 & 0 \\ 0 & 1/b & 0 \\ 0 & 0 & 1/c \end{bmatrix}$

Theorems Related to Invertible Matrix

1. Every invertible matrix possesses a unique inverse

Proof: Let A be an invertible matrix of order $n \times n$

Let B and C be two inverse of A

Then $AB = BA = I_n$ .....(i)

and $AC = CA = I_n$ .....(ii)

Now $AB = I_n$

$\Rightarrow C(AB) = CI_n$ *(pre-multiplying by C)*

$\Rightarrow (CA)B = CI_n$ *(by associativity)*

$\Rightarrow I_n B = C I_n$ $[\because CA = I_n$ by (ii)$]$

$\Rightarrow B = C$ $[\because I_n B = B,\ CI_n = C]$

Hence an invertible matrix possesses a unique inverse.

2. A square matrix is invertible if and only if it is non-singular

Proof: Let A be an invertible matrix. Then there exists a matrix B such that $AB = I_n = BA$

$\Rightarrow |AB| = |I_n|$

$\Rightarrow |A||B| = 1$ $(\because |AB| = |A||B|)$

$\Rightarrow |A| \neq 0$

$\Rightarrow$ A is non-singular matrix.

Conversely, if A is non-singular, then $A.\dfrac{(adjA)}{|A|} = I_n$

$\Rightarrow A^{-1} = \dfrac{adjA}{|A|}$

3. If *A, B* be two non-singular matrices of the same order then *AB* is also non-singular and $(AB)^{-1} = B^{-1}A^{-1}$ (reversal law of inverse)

Proof: The first part easily follows from $|AB| = |A||B|$. To prove the other part, we note that

$(AB)(B^{-1}A^{-1}) = A(BB^{-1})A^{-1} = AIA^{-1} = (AI)A^{-1} = AA^{-1} = I$

Similarly, $(B^{-1}A^{-1})AB = I$.

Thus $B^{-1}A^{-1}$ is the inverse of AB.

Properties

If *A, B, C* are non-singular square matrices

1. (i) $AB = AC \Rightarrow B = C$

(ii) $BA = CA \Rightarrow B = C$

Proof: (i) Pre multiplying both sides by A^{-1}

$A^{-1}AB = A^{-1}AC \Rightarrow IB = IC \Rightarrow B = C$

(ii) Post multiplying both sides by A^{-1}

$BAA^{-1} = CAA^{-1} \Rightarrow BI = CI \Rightarrow B = C$

2. Since, we already know that $(AB)^{-1} = B^{-1}A^{-1}$, therefore, in general we can say that $(ABC.......Z)^{-1} = Z^{-1}Y^{-1}....B^{-1}A^{-1}$

3. If A is an invertible square matrix, then $adj\,(A') = (adj\,A)'$

Proof Premultiplying both sides by A'

LHS: $(Adj\,A')(A') = |A'|I = |A|I$

RHS: $(Adj\,A)'A' = (A\,Adj\,A)' = (|A|I)' = |A|I =$ RHS

4. $(A^T)^{-1} = (A^{-1})^T$

Proof Premultiplying both sides by A^T

LHS: $(A^T)^{-1}A^T = I$

RHS: $(A^{-1})^T A^T = (AA^{-1})^T = I^T = I =$ LHS

5. $\left(\overline{A^T}\right)^{-1} = \left(\overline{A^{-1}}\right)^T$

Proof Premultiplying both sides by $\overline{(A^T)}$

$LHS: (\overline{A^T})^{-1}(\overline{A^T}) = |\overline{A^T}|I = |A|I$

$RHS: (\overline{A^{-1}})^T(\overline{A^T}) = (\overline{A^{-1}})^T(\overline{A})^T$

$= (\overline{A}\,\overline{A^{-1}})^T = (\overline{A\,A^{-1}})^T$

$= (\overline{|A|I})^T = (|A|I)^T$

$= |A|I = LHS$

7. $AA^{-1} = A^{-1}A = I$

8. $(A^{-1})^{-1} = A$

A method to find inverse of a matrix

Let A be non-singular square matrix of order n. Then $A\,(adj\,A) = |A|I_n = (adj\,A)\,A$

$$\Rightarrow A\left(\frac{1}{|A|}adj\ A\right) = I_n = \left(\frac{1}{|A|}adj\ A\right)A$$

$$\Rightarrow \boldsymbol{A^{-1} = \frac{1}{|A|}adj\ A}\ \textit{\textbf{(by definition of inverse)}}$$

MATRIX POLYNOMIAL

Let $f(x) = a_0 x^m + a_1 x^{m-1} + ... a_{m-1} x + a_m$ be a polynomial in x and A be a square matrix of order n, then $f(A) = a_0 A^m + a_1 A^{m-1} + .. + a_{m-1} A + a_m I_n$ is called a matrix polynomial in A. Thus, to obtain $f(A)$, replace x by A in $f(x)$ and the constant term is multiplied by the identity matrix of the order equal to that of A.

The polynomial equation $f(x) = 0$ is said to be satisfied by the matrix A iff $f(A) = O$.

e. g., if $f(x) = 2x^2 - 3x + 7$ and A is a square matrix of order 3 then $f(A) = 2A^2 - 3A + 7I_3$.

Characteristic Polynomial/Equation of Matrix A:

$|A - xI|$ is called characteristic polynomial of square matrix A and $|A - xI| = 0$ is called characteristic equation. If a square matrix B satisfies the equation $a_0 x^n + a_1 x^{n-1} + ... + a_n = 0$, then $a_0 B^n + a_1 B^{n-1} + ... + a_n I = O$. Roots of characteristic equation are called characteristic roots.

Cayley Hamilton Theorem

Every square matrix satisfies its characteristics equation $|A - xI| = 0$, because $|A - AI| = |A - A| = 0$

so $a_0 A^n + a_1 A^{n-1} + a_2 A^{n-2} + ... + a_n I = O$

$$\Rightarrow A^{-1} = -\left[\frac{a_0}{a_n} A^{n-1} + \frac{a_1}{a_n} A^{n-2} + ...\right]$$

ILLUSTRATION 35: Find the inverse of matrix $A = \begin{bmatrix} 0 & 1 & 2 \\ 1 & 2 & 3 \\ 3 & 1 & 1 \end{bmatrix}$.

SOLUTION: $|A| = 0(2-3) - 1(1-9) + 2(1-6) = 0 + 8 - 10 = -2 \neq 0$

If C be the matrix of co-factors of the elements in $|A|$

$$C_{11} = \begin{vmatrix} 2 & 3 \\ 1 & 1 \end{vmatrix} = -1; \quad C_{12} = -\begin{vmatrix} 1 & 3 \\ 3 & 1 \end{vmatrix} = 8; \quad C_{13} = \begin{vmatrix} 1 & 2 \\ 3 & 1 \end{vmatrix} = -5$$

$$C_{21} = -\begin{vmatrix} 1 & 2 \\ 1 & 1 \end{vmatrix} = 1; \quad C_{22} = \begin{vmatrix} 0 & 2 \\ 3 & 1 \end{vmatrix} = -6; \quad C_{23} = -\begin{vmatrix} 0 & 1 \\ 3 & 1 \end{vmatrix} = 3$$

$$C_{31} = \begin{vmatrix} 1 & 2 \\ 2 & 3 \end{vmatrix} = -1; \quad C_{32} = -\begin{vmatrix} 0 & 2 \\ 1 & 3 \end{vmatrix} = 2; \quad C_{33} = \begin{vmatrix} 0 & 1 \\ 1 & 2 \end{vmatrix} = -1$$

$$\therefore C = \begin{bmatrix} -1 & 8 & -5 \\ 1 & -6 & 3 \\ -1 & 2 & -1 \end{bmatrix}. \text{ Now } adj\, A = C^T = \begin{bmatrix} -1 & 1 & -1 \\ 8 & -6 & 2 \\ -5 & 3 & -1 \end{bmatrix}$$

$$\therefore A^{-1} = \frac{adj\, A}{|A|} = \frac{1}{-2}\begin{bmatrix} -1 & 1 & -1 \\ 8 & -6 & 2 \\ -5 & 3 & -1 \end{bmatrix} = -\begin{bmatrix} -1/2 & 1/2 & -1/2 \\ 4 & -3 & 1 \\ -5/2 & 3/2 & -1/2 \end{bmatrix} = \begin{bmatrix} 1/2 & -1/2 & 1/2 \\ -4 & 3 & -1 \\ 5/2 & -3/2 & 1/2 \end{bmatrix}$$

ILLUSTRATION 36: Show that inverse of a symmetric matrix is symmetric.

SOLUTION: If A is symmetric, then $A' = A$. To show that A^{-1} is symmetric we must show that $(A^{-1})' = A^{-1}$.

By definition of inverse $AA^{-1} = I$, on taking transpose $(AA^{-1})' = I'$

On applying reversal law of transpose $(A^{-1})' A' = I$ ($\because I' = I$)

$\Rightarrow (A^{-1})'A$ $\quad$ ($\because A' = A$) $\quad \Rightarrow CA = I$ where $C = (A^{-1})'$

$\Rightarrow C = A^{-1}$ $\quad \Rightarrow (A^{-1})' = A^{-1}$ $\quad \Rightarrow A^{-1}$ is symmetric

ILLUSTRATION 37: Find out the matrix polynomial for the matrix $\begin{bmatrix} 2 & 1 \\ 3 & 2 \end{bmatrix}$ and hence find its inverse using Cayley Hamilton theorem.

SOLUTION: $A = \begin{bmatrix} 2 & 1 \\ 3 & 2 \end{bmatrix}$ $\Rightarrow |A - xI| = \begin{vmatrix} 2-x & 1 \\ 3 & 2-x \end{vmatrix} = 0$

$\Rightarrow (2 - x)^2 - 3 = 0$

$\Rightarrow x^2 - 4x + 1 = 0$

$\because$ matrix satisfies its characterstic equation $A^2 - 4A - 1 = 0 \Rightarrow I = 4A - A^2$

Multiplying by A^{-1}, we get $A^{-1} = 4AA^{-1} - A^{-1}AA = 4I - A$

$$\Rightarrow A^{-1} = 4I - A = \begin{bmatrix} 4 & 0 \\ 0 & 4 \end{bmatrix} - \begin{bmatrix} 2 & 1 \\ 3 & 2 \end{bmatrix} = \begin{bmatrix} 2 & -1 \\ -3 & 2 \end{bmatrix}$$

TEXTUAL EXERCISE 7: (SUBJECTIVE)

1. Find A^{-1}, when

(a) $A = \begin{bmatrix} 1 & 3 & 3 \\ 1 & 4 & 3 \\ 1 & 3 & 4 \end{bmatrix}$ (b) $A = \begin{bmatrix} 2 & 5 & 3 \\ 3 & 1 & 2 \\ 1 & 2 & 1 \end{bmatrix}$

2. If $A = \begin{bmatrix} 1 & 1 & 3 \\ 1 & 3 & -3 \\ -2 & -4 & -4 \end{bmatrix}$, show that $A^{-1} = \frac{1}{8}(20I - A^2)$.

3. Given that $A = \begin{bmatrix} 1 & -1 \\ 2 & 3 \end{bmatrix}$, verify that $A^2 - 4A + 5I = O$ and hence prove that $A^{-1} = \dfrac{4I - A}{5}$

4. Write the characteristic equation for following matrices and get their inverses.

(a) $\begin{bmatrix} 2 & 5 \\ 1 & 4 \end{bmatrix}$

(b) $\begin{bmatrix} 1 & 1 & 2 \\ 2 & 1 & 3 \\ 3 & 2 & 1 \end{bmatrix}$

5. Express $2A^5 - 3A^4 + A^2 - 4I$ as a linear polynomial in A, by using Cayley Hamilton Theorem, where $A = \begin{bmatrix} 3 & 1 \\ -1 & 2 \end{bmatrix}$.

Answer Key

1. (a) $\begin{bmatrix} 7 & -3 & -3 \\ -1 & 1 & 0 \\ -1 & 0 & 1 \end{bmatrix}$ (b) $\begin{bmatrix} \frac{-3}{4} & \frac{1}{4} & \frac{7}{4} \\ \frac{-1}{4} & \frac{-1}{4} & \frac{5}{4} \\ \frac{5}{4} & \frac{1}{4} & \frac{-13}{4} \end{bmatrix}$

4. (a) $x^2 - 6x + 3$; $\frac{1}{3}\begin{bmatrix} 4 & -5 \\ -1 & 2 \end{bmatrix}$ (b) $-x^3 + 3x^2 + 11x + 4$; $\frac{1}{4}\begin{bmatrix} -5 & 3 & 1 \\ 7 & -5 & 1 \\ 1 & 1 & 1 \end{bmatrix}$

5. $138A - 403I$

TEXTUAL EXERCISE 3: (OBJECTIVE)

1. If $A = \begin{bmatrix} a & 0 & 0 \\ 0 & a & 0 \\ 0 & 0 & a \end{bmatrix}$, then the value of $|adj\ A|$ is

(a) a^{27} (b) a^9
(c) a^6 (d) a^2

2. If A is singular matrix, then $adj\ A$ is
(a) non-singular
(b) singular
(c) symmetric
(d) not defined

3. If $A = \begin{bmatrix} 1 & 2 & -1 \\ -1 & 1 & 2 \\ 2 & -1 & 1 \end{bmatrix}$, then det.$(adj(adj\ A))$ is

(a) $(14)^4$ (b) $(14)^3$
(c) $(14)^2$ (d) $(14)^1$

4. If A is 3×4 matrix and B is a matrix such that A^TB and BA^T are both defined. Then B is of the order
(a) 3×4 (b) 3×3
(c) 4×4 (d) 4×3

5. If $A = \begin{bmatrix} 3 & 8 \\ 2 & 1 \end{bmatrix}$, then A^{-1} is

(a) $\begin{bmatrix} -1/13 & 8/13 \\ 2/13 & -3/13 \end{bmatrix}$ (b) $\begin{bmatrix} 1/13 & -8/13 \\ 2/13 & -3/13 \end{bmatrix}$

(c) $\begin{bmatrix} 1/13 & -8/13 \\ -2/13 & 3/13 \end{bmatrix}$ (d) None of these

6. With 1, ω, ω^2 as cube roots of unity, inverse of which of the following matrices exists?

(a) $\begin{bmatrix} 1 & \omega \\ \omega & \omega^2 \end{bmatrix}$ (b) $\begin{bmatrix} \omega^2 & 1 \\ 1 & \omega^2 \end{bmatrix}$

(c) $\begin{bmatrix} \omega & \omega^2 \\ \omega^2 & 1 \end{bmatrix}$ (d) None of these

7. The multiplictive inverse of $A = \begin{bmatrix} \cos\theta & -\sin\theta \\ \sin\theta & \cos\theta \end{bmatrix}$ is equal to

(a) $\begin{bmatrix} \cos\theta & \sin\theta \\ \sin\theta & -\cos\theta \end{bmatrix}$ (b) $\begin{bmatrix} -\cos\theta & -\sin\theta \\ \sin\theta & -\cos\theta \end{bmatrix}$

(c) $\begin{bmatrix} \cos\theta & \sin\theta \\ -\sin\theta & \cos\theta \end{bmatrix}$ (d) $\begin{bmatrix} -\cos\theta & -\sin\theta \\ -\sin\theta & \cos\theta \end{bmatrix}$

8. If $A = \begin{bmatrix} \cos x & \sin x & 0 \\ -\sin x & \cos x & 0 \\ 0 & 0 & 1 \end{bmatrix} = f(x)$, then A^{-1} is

(a) $f(-x)$ (b) $f(x)$
(c) $-f(x)$ (d) $-f(-x)$

9. If B is a non-singular matrix and A is a square matrix, then det $(B^{-1}AB)$ is equal to
(a) det(A^{-1}) (b) det(B^{-1})
(c) det(A) (d) det(B)

10. If D = diag $(d_1\ d_2\ d_3 \ldots\ldots d_n)$, where $d_i \neq 0$ for all $i = 1,2,\ldots,n$, then D^{-1} is equal to
(a) D (b) diag $(d_1^{-1}, d_2^{-1}, \ldots. d_n^{-1})$
(c) I_n (d) None of these

11. If A is a non-singular matrix, then
(a) A^{-1} is symmetric if A is symmetric
(b) A^{-1} is skew-symmetric if A is symmetric
(c) $|A^{-1}| = |A|$
(d) $|A^{-1}| = |A|^{-1}$

Answer Key

1. (c) 2. (b) 3. (a) 4. (a) 5. (a) 6. (b) 7. (c) 8. (a) 9. (c) 10. (b)
11. (a, d)

■ ELEMENTARY TRANSFORMATION

1. Interchange of any two rows or columns: Denoted by $R_i \leftrightarrow R_j$ or $C_i \leftrightarrow C_j$

e.g., $\begin{bmatrix} 3 & 0 & 3 \\ -3 & 1 & 2 \\ 1 & 5 & 4 \end{bmatrix} \xrightarrow[T_1]{C_1 \leftrightarrow C_3} \begin{bmatrix} 3 & 0 & 3 \\ 2 & 1 & -3 \\ 4 & 5 & 1 \end{bmatrix}$

Similarly $\begin{bmatrix} 3 & 0 & 3 \\ -3 & 1 & 2 \\ 1 & 5 & 4 \end{bmatrix} \xrightarrow[T_2]{R_1 \leftrightarrow R_3} \begin{bmatrix} 1 & 5 & 4 \\ -3 & 1 & 2 \\ 3 & 0 & 3 \end{bmatrix}$

2. Multiplication by non-zero scalar: Denoted $R_i \to kR_i$ or $C_j \to kC_j$

e.g. $\begin{bmatrix} 3 & 0 & 3 \\ -3 & 1 & 2 \\ 1 & 5 & 4 \end{bmatrix} \xrightarrow[T]{R_2 \to 3R_2} \begin{bmatrix} 3 & 0 & 3 \\ -9 & 3 & 6 \\ 1 & 5 & 4 \end{bmatrix}$

3. Replacing i^{th} row (or column) by the sum of its elements and scalar multiplication of corresponding elements of any other row (or column)

Denoted: $R_i \to R_i + kR_j$

or $C_i \to C_i + k\,C_j$

e.g. $\begin{bmatrix} 3 & 0 & 3 \\ -3 & 1 & 2 \\ 1 & 5 & 4 \end{bmatrix} \xrightarrow{R_1 \to R_1 - 2R_3} \begin{bmatrix} 1 & -10 & -5 \\ -3 & 1 & 2 \\ 1 & 5 & 4 \end{bmatrix}$

NOTE

Transformed matrix using sequence of elementary transformations (one or more) is known as equivalent matrix of A.

Elementary Matrix

Elementary matix is a matrix obtained from identity matrix by single elementary transformation:

e.g., $\begin{bmatrix} 1 & 0 & 0 \\ 0 & 1 & 0 \\ 0 & 0 & 1 \end{bmatrix} \xrightarrow{R_1 \leftrightarrow R_3} \begin{bmatrix} 0 & 0 & 1 \\ 0 & 1 & 0 \\ 1 & 0 & 0 \end{bmatrix}$

then $B = \begin{bmatrix} 3 & 0 & 3 \\ -3 & 5 & 2 \\ 2 & 1 & 3 \end{bmatrix}$

Equivalent Matrices

Two matrices A and B are equivalent if one can be obtained from the other by a sequence of elementary transformations denoted by $A \sim B$. e.g., If $A = \begin{bmatrix} 1 & 2 \\ 3 & 5 \end{bmatrix}$ and $B = \begin{bmatrix} 1 & 2 \\ 2 & 3 \end{bmatrix}$, then A and B are equivalent matrices.

$\because \quad A = \begin{bmatrix} 1 & 2 \\ 3 & 5 \end{bmatrix} \xrightarrow{R_2 \to R_2 - R_1} B = \begin{bmatrix} 1 & 2 \\ 2 & 3 \end{bmatrix}$

Theorem 1: (Gauss Jordan Theorem): Elementary row (column) transformation of $m \times n$ matrix (not identity matrix) can be obtained by pre (post) multiplication of A with corresponding elementary matrix obtained by I_m (I_n) subjecting to same transformation.

e.g., if $A = \begin{bmatrix} 1 & -1 & 0 \\ -3 & 5 & 2 \\ 2 & 1 & 3 \end{bmatrix} \xrightarrow{R_1 \to R_1 + R_3} \begin{bmatrix} 3 & 0 & 3 \\ -3 & 5 & 2 \\ 2 & 1 & 3 \end{bmatrix} = B \text{ (say)}$

Now, Elementary matrix E obtained from I_3 by $R_1 \to R_1 + R_3$ is $E = \begin{bmatrix} 1 & 0 & 1 \\ 0 & 1 & 0 \\ 0 & 0 & 1 \end{bmatrix}$; then

$$EA = \begin{bmatrix} 1 & 0 & 1 \\ 0 & 1 & 0 \\ 0 & 0 & 1 \end{bmatrix} \begin{bmatrix} 1 & -1 & 0 \\ -3 & 5 & 2 \\ 2 & 1 & 3 \end{bmatrix} = \begin{bmatrix} 3 & 0 & 3 \\ -3 & 5 & 2 \\ 2 & 1 & 3 \end{bmatrix} = B$$

Theorem 2: If $C = AB$, then any elementary row/column transfer of AB can be further obtained by the above theorem

Gauss Jordan Method to find inverse of a non-singular matrix

- $A = [a_{ij}]_{m\times n} \xrightarrow[T_1]{R_i \leftrightarrow R_j} [b_{ij}]_{m\times n} = B$

  $B = E_1 A$

- If A is non-singular matrix of order n, then A can be reduced to I_n by a finite sequence of elementary transformation only and using above theorem $(E_k E_{k-1} E_{k-2} \ldots E_3 E_2 E_1) A = I_n$, post multiplying by A^{-1}

  $\Rightarrow (E_k E_{k-1} \ldots E_2 E_1) A.\, A^{-1} = I_n . A^{-1}$

- $A^{-1} = (E_k E_{k-1} \ldots E_2 E_1)\, I_n$

  So if same series of transformations are performed on I_n, it will convert to A^{-1}.

Steps to proceed

(i) Write $A = I_n A$

(ii) Apply sequence of E transformation on A on LHS which becomes I_n, then RHS become $B.A$.

$\Rightarrow B = A^{-1}$ becuase $I_r = BA \Rightarrow B$ is A^{-1}

e.g., $A = \begin{bmatrix} 1 & 2 \\ 3 & 7 \end{bmatrix} \quad \Rightarrow \quad \begin{bmatrix} 1 & 2 \\ 3 & 7 \end{bmatrix} = \begin{bmatrix} 1 & 0 \\ 0 & 1 \end{bmatrix} \begin{bmatrix} 1 & 2 \\ 3 & 7 \end{bmatrix}$

$\Rightarrow \begin{bmatrix} 1 & 2 \\ 3 & 7 \end{bmatrix} = \begin{bmatrix} 1 & 0 \\ 0 & 1 \end{bmatrix} A$

$\Rightarrow \begin{bmatrix} 1 & 2 \\ 0 & 1 \end{bmatrix} = \begin{bmatrix} 1 & 0 \\ -3 & 1 \end{bmatrix} A \qquad (e_1 = R_2 \to R_2 - 3R_1)$

$$\Rightarrow \begin{bmatrix} 1 & 0 \\ 0 & 1 \end{bmatrix} = \begin{bmatrix} 7 & -2 \\ -3 & 1 \end{bmatrix} A \qquad (e_2 = R_1 \to R_1 - 2R_2)$$

$$\Rightarrow A^{-1} = \begin{bmatrix} 7 & -2 \\ -3 & 1 \end{bmatrix}.$$

These elementrary transformations reduce a given square matrix A to the unit matrix and when applied to unit matrix I gives A^{-1}.

ILLUSTRATION 38: Use elementary transformations to find the inverse of $\begin{bmatrix} 1 & 2 & -2 \\ -1 & 3 & 0 \\ 0 & -2 & 1 \end{bmatrix}$.

SOLUTION: $A = IA \Rightarrow \begin{bmatrix} 1 & 2 & -2 \\ -1 & 3 & 0 \\ 0 & -2 & 1 \end{bmatrix} = \begin{bmatrix} 1 & 0 & 0 \\ 0 & 1 & 0 \\ 0 & 0 & 1 \end{bmatrix} A$

$$\begin{bmatrix} 1 & 2 & -2 \\ 0 & 5 & -2 \\ 0 & -2 & 1 \end{bmatrix} = \begin{bmatrix} 1 & 0 & 0 \\ 1 & 1 & 0 \\ 0 & 0 & 1 \end{bmatrix} A \qquad [Applying\ R_2 \to R_2 + R_1]$$

$$\begin{bmatrix} 1 & 0 & -1 \\ 0 & 1 & 0 \\ 0 & -2 & 1 \end{bmatrix} = \begin{bmatrix} 1 & 0 & 1 \\ 1 & 1 & 2 \\ 0 & 0 & 1 \end{bmatrix} A \qquad [Applying\ R_2 \to R_2 + 2R_3]$$

$$\begin{bmatrix} 1 & 0 & -1 \\ 0 & 1 & 0 \\ 0 & 0 & 1 \end{bmatrix} = \begin{bmatrix} 1 & 0 & 1 \\ 1 & 1 & 2 \\ 2 & 2 & 5 \end{bmatrix} A \qquad [Applying\ R_3 \to R_3 + 2R_2]$$

$$\begin{bmatrix} 1 & 0 & 0 \\ 0 & 1 & 0 \\ 0 & 0 & 1 \end{bmatrix} = \begin{bmatrix} 3 & 2 & 6 \\ 1 & 1 & 2 \\ 2 & 2 & 5 \end{bmatrix} A \quad \Rightarrow \quad A^{-1} = \begin{bmatrix} 3 & 2 & 6 \\ 1 & 1 & 2 \\ 2 & 2 & 5 \end{bmatrix} \qquad [Applying\ R_1 \to R_1 + R_3]$$

ILLUSTRATION 39: If $A = \begin{bmatrix} 3 & -3 & 4 \\ 2 & -3 & 4 \\ 0 & -1 & 1 \end{bmatrix}$, find A^{-1}. Also if two non-singular matrices P and Q such that $PAQ = I$ where I is the unit matrix then show that $A^{-1} = QP$.

SOLUTION: By Gauss-Jorden reduction method $\begin{bmatrix} 3 & -3 & 4 & : & 1 & 0 & 0 \\ 2 & -3 & 4 & : & 0 & 1 & 0 \\ 0 & -1 & 1 & : & 0 & 0 & 1 \end{bmatrix}$

Applying transformations $R_1 \to R_1 - R_2$ and then $R_2 \to R_2 - 2R_1$, we get

$$\begin{bmatrix} 1 & 0 & 0 & : & 1 & -1 & 0 \\ 0 & -3 & 4 & : & -2 & 3 & 0 \\ 0 & -1 & 1 & : & 0 & 0 & 1 \end{bmatrix}$$

$R_2 \to R_2 - 4R_3$, we get $\begin{bmatrix} 1 & 0 & 0 & : & 1 & -1 & 0 \\ 0 & 1 & 0 & : & -2 & 3 & -4 \\ 0 & -1 & 1 & : & 0 & 0 & 1 \end{bmatrix}$

$R_3 \to R_3 + R_2$, we get $\left[\begin{array}{ccc:ccc} 1 & 0 & 0 & 1 & -1 & 0 \\ 0 & 1 & 0 & -2 & 3 & -4 \\ 0 & 0 & 1 & -2 & 3 & -3 \end{array}\right] \Rightarrow A^{-1} = \begin{bmatrix} 1 & -1 & 0 \\ -2 & 3 & -4 \\ -2 & 3 & -3 \end{bmatrix}$

$PAQ = I$ as P is non-singular P^{-1} exist.

$P^{-1}PAQ = P^{-1} \Rightarrow AQ = P^{-1}$

Post multiplying by Q^{-1}, we get $A = P^{-1}Q^{-1} \Rightarrow A^{-1} = (P^{-1}.Q^{-1})^{-1} = (Q^{-1})^{-1}(P^{-1})^{-1} = QP$

TEXTUAL EXERCISE 8: (SUBJECTIVE)

1. Determine the inverse of the following matrix by using elementary transformations.

   (i) $\begin{bmatrix} 1 & 3 & 3 \\ 1 & 4 & 3 \\ 1 & 3 & 4 \end{bmatrix}$ (ii) $\begin{bmatrix} 0 & 4 & 3 \\ 1 & -3 & -3 \\ -1 & 4 & 4 \end{bmatrix}$

2. Using the Gauss Jordan reduction method, find the inverse of the matrix $\begin{bmatrix} 1 & 1 & 2 \\ 1 & 2 & 3 \\ 2 & 3 & 1 \end{bmatrix}$.

3. Verify Gauss Jordan Theorem for matrix

   (i) $\begin{bmatrix} 2 & 3 & 6 \\ -1 & 2 & 3 \end{bmatrix}$ by using the transformations

   (a) $R_1 \to R_1 + 2R_2$

   (b) $C_1 \leftrightarrow C_3$

   (ii) $\begin{bmatrix} 2 & 3 \\ 6 & -3 \\ 2 & -1 \end{bmatrix}$ by using the transformations

   (a) $R_1 \to R_1 + R_3$ (b) $R_2 \leftrightarrow R_3$

   (c) $C_2 \to C_2 - C_1$

4. Obtain the elementary matrix of order 3 × 3 by using the row transformation $R_2 \to R_2 + 2R_2$ and hence verify Gauss Jordan Theorem for the same transformation for the matrix $A = \begin{bmatrix} 5 & -3 & 2 \\ 6 & 4 & 1 \\ 3 & 2 & 4 \end{bmatrix}$.

5. Obtain the elementary matrix of order 3 × 3 by using the column transformation $C_3 \to C_3 - 2C_1$ and hence verify Gauss Jordan Theorem for the same transformation for the matrix $A = \begin{bmatrix} 3 & 2 & -1 \\ 6 & -4 & 2 \\ 5 & 3 & 1 \end{bmatrix}$.

Answer Key

1. (i) $\begin{bmatrix} 7 & -3 & -3 \\ -1 & 1 & 0 \\ -1 & 0 & 1 \end{bmatrix}$ (ii) $A^{-1} = A$ i.e. $A^{-1} = \begin{bmatrix} 0 & 4 & 3 \\ 1 & -3 & -3 \\ -1 & 4 & 4 \end{bmatrix}$

2. $\frac{1}{4}\begin{bmatrix} 7 & -5 & 1 \\ -5 & 3 & 1 \\ 1 & 1 & -1 \end{bmatrix}$

■ SYSTEM OF SIMULTANEOUS EQUATIONS

When System of Equations is Non-Homogeneous

Consider the following system of m linear equation (non-homogenous) in n unknowns $x_1, x_2, \ldots x_n$

$$a_{11}x_1 + a_{22}x_2 + \ldots + a_{1n}x_m = b_1$$
$$a_{22}x_1 + a_{22}x_2 + \ldots + a_{2n}x_m = b_2$$
$$\ldots\ldots\ldots\ldots\ldots\ldots\ldots\ldots$$
$$a_{m1}x_1 + c_{m2}x_2 + \ldots + a_{mr}x_n = b_n$$

This system of equation can be written in matrix form, as follows

$$\begin{bmatrix} a_{11} & a_{12} \ldots\ldots & a_{1n} \\ a_{21} & a_{22} & a_{2n} \\ \vdots & \vdots & \vdots \\ a_{n1} & a_{n2} \ldots\ldots & a_{nn} \end{bmatrix} \begin{bmatrix} x_1 \\ x_2 \\ \vdots \\ x_n \end{bmatrix} = \begin{bmatrix} b_1 \\ b_2 \\ \vdots \\ b_n \end{bmatrix}$$

$AX = B$. Here A is square matrix. A system is said to be consistent if it has atleast one set of solution otherwise known as inconsistent equation.

$AX = B$ is called homogenous if $B = O$, otherwise it is called a nonhomogenous system of equations.

System of Linear Equations in Three Unknowns

Consider the system of equations $a_1 x + b_1 y + c_1 z = d_1$ ..(i)

$$a_2 x + b_2 y + c_2 z = d_2 \quad \text{....(ii)}$$
$$a_3 x + b_3 y + c_3 z = d_3 \quad \text{....(iii)}$$

There are three methods of solving non-homogenous equation in three variables:

(a) Determinant method (Cramer' s Rule) which has already been dealt with in the chapter on Determinants

(b) Matrix method

The given system of equations can be written as:

$$AX = B \text{ where } A = \begin{bmatrix} a_1 & b_1 & c_1 \\ a_2 & b_2 & c_2 \\ a_3 & b_3 & c_3 \end{bmatrix}, X = \begin{bmatrix} x \\ y \\ z \end{bmatrix}, B = \begin{bmatrix} d_1 \\ d_2 \\ d_3 \end{bmatrix}$$

$Ax = B$

Premultiplying by $adj\ A$ $(adj\ A)\ A\ X = (adj\ A)B$

$|A|\ IX = (adj\ A)B$

Criterian for Consistency

1. Matrix method

1. If $|A| \neq 0$, System is consistent having unique solution
2. If $|A| \neq 0$, and $(adj\ A).B \neq$ Null matrix

   System is consistent having unique non-trivial solution
3. If $|A| \neq 0$, and $(adj\ A).\ B = 0$ (Null matrix)

   System is consistent having trivial solution
4. If $|A| = 0$, Matrix method fails; then the system of equation given by $AX = B$ can be consistent with infinitely many solutions or it can be inconsistent also.

Case I: if $(adj\ A).\ B =$ null matrix $\Rightarrow$ Infinitely many solutions

Case II: If $(adj\ A).\ B \neq 0$ Inconsistent $\Rightarrow$ (**no** solution)

e.g., $2x + y = 3$ and $4x + 2y = 6$

$\Rightarrow$ $|A| = 0$ so A^{-1} does not exist but system has infinitely many solutions.

i.e., $x = m$ and $y = 3 - 2m$ is solution

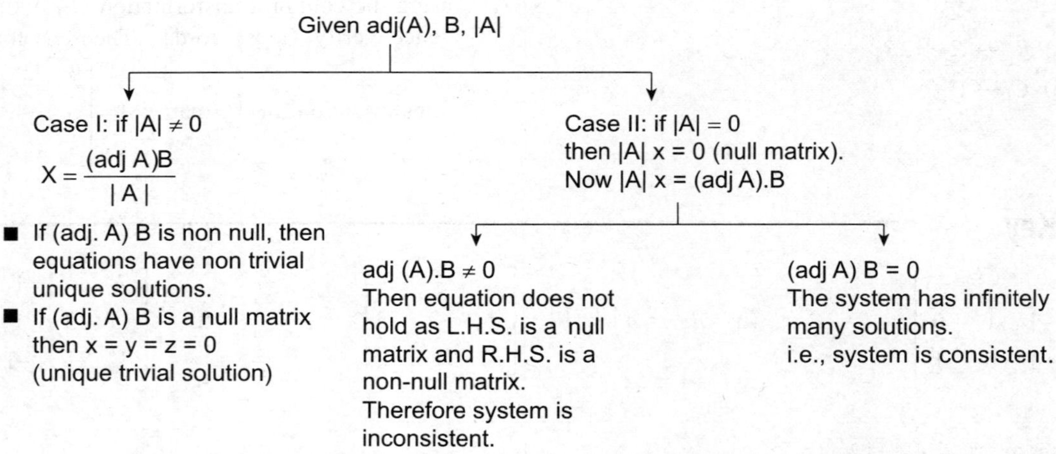

FIGURE 1.3

When System of Equations is Homogeneous and Linear Equations

Consider the following system of homogenous linear equation in n unknowns $x_1, x_2, \ldots x_n$

$$a_{11}x_1 + a_{22}x_2 + \ldots + a_{1n}x_m = 0$$
$$a_{22}x_1 + a_{22}x_2 + \ldots + a_{2n}x_m = 0$$
$$\ldots\ldots\ldots\ldots\ldots\ldots\ldots\ldots\ldots\ldots$$
$$a_{m1}x_1 + a_{m2}x_2 + \ldots + a_{mn}x_n = 0$$

This system of equation can be written in matrix form, as follows:

$$\begin{bmatrix} a_{11} & a_{12} \,\ldots\ldots & a_{1n} \\ a_{21} & a_{22} & a_{2n} \\ \vdots & \vdots & \vdots \\ a_{n1} & a_{n2} \,\ldots\ldots & a_{nn} \end{bmatrix} \begin{bmatrix} x_1 \\ x_2 \\ \vdots \\ x_n \end{bmatrix} = \begin{bmatrix} 0 \\ 0 \\ \vdots \\ 0 \end{bmatrix} \Rightarrow AX = O$$

(i) If $|A| \neq 0$, the system of equations has only trivial solution and that will be the only solution.

(ii) If $|A| = 0$, the system of equations has non-trivial solution and it has infinite solutions.

(iii) If No. of equations < No. of unknowns, then it has non trivial solution.

Given [B] = 0, A
(adj. A).AX = (ajd A).B
|A|IX = 0

Case I:
⇒ If |A| = 0
⇒ X = 0
only one trival solution

Case II:
If |A| = 0
⇒ 0X = 0
⇒ Infinitely many solutions

FIGURE 1.4

NOTES

Non-homogeneous linear equations are also solved by Cramer's rule. This method has been discussed in the chapter on determinants.

ILLUSTRATION 40: Find the solution of the equations $x + y + z = 6, x + 2y + 3z = 14. x + 4y + 7z = 30$.

SOLUTION: The given system is written in from $AX = B$ ...(i)

$$\Rightarrow |A| = \begin{vmatrix} 1 & 1 & 1 \\ 4 & 2 & 3 \\ 1 & 4 & 7 \end{vmatrix} = 1(14 - 12) - 1(7 - 3) + 1\,(4 - 2) = 0$$

So equation has no solution or infinite number of solutions.

Now decide about this we have to find $(Adj\ A)\ B$

Let C be the matrix of co-factors of elements in $|A|$

$$\text{Such that } C = \begin{bmatrix} C_{11} & C_{12} & C_{13} \\ C_{21} & C_{22} & C_{23} \\ C_{31} & C_{32} & C_{33} \end{bmatrix}$$

After calculating $C_{11}, C_{12}\ldots\ldots C_{33}$ we write

$$Adj\ A = C^T = \begin{bmatrix} 2 & -4 & 2 \\ -3 & 6 & -3 \\ 1 & -2 & 1 \end{bmatrix} = \begin{bmatrix} 2 & -3 & 1 \\ -4 & 6 & -2 \\ 2 & -3 & 1 \end{bmatrix}$$

$$\text{then, } (Adj\ A)\ B = \begin{bmatrix} 2 & -3 & 1 \\ -4 & 6 & -2 \\ 2 & -3 & 1 \end{bmatrix} \begin{bmatrix} 6 \\ 14 \\ 30 \end{bmatrix} = \begin{bmatrix} 0 \\ 0 \\ 0 \end{bmatrix} = O$$

So system of equations is consistent and has an infinite number of solutions.

Let us taken any two of the given equations, say (1) and (2), i.e. $x + y + z = 6$ and $x + 2y + 3z = 14$. Substitute $z = k \in \mathbb{R}$

$x + y = 6 - k$ and $x + 2y = 14 - 3k$

Solving, we get $x = k - 2, y = 8 - 2k, z = k$; where $k \in \mathbb{R}$

ILLUSTRATION 41: Determine the value of λ so that the equations $2x + y + 2z = 0$, $x + y + 3z = 0$, $4x + 3y + \lambda z = 0$ have a non-zero solution.

SOLUTION: We have $\begin{bmatrix} 2 & 1 & 2 \\ 1 & 1 & 3 \\ 4 & 3 & \lambda \end{bmatrix}\begin{bmatrix} x \\ y \\ z \end{bmatrix} = \begin{bmatrix} 0 \\ 0 \\ 0 \end{bmatrix}$ or $\begin{vmatrix} 2 & 1 & 2 \\ 1 & 1 & 3 \\ 4 & 3 & \lambda \end{vmatrix} = 0 \Rightarrow 2(\lambda - 9) + (-1)[\lambda - 12] + 2[3 - 4] = 0$

$\Rightarrow 2\lambda - 18 - \lambda + 12 - 2 = 0 \qquad \Rightarrow \lambda - 8 = 0 \qquad \therefore \lambda = 8$

Hence system has a non-zero solution.

TEXTUAL EXERCISE 9: (SUBJECTIVE)

1. Using matrix method find the values of λ and μ so that the system of equations $2x - 3y + 5z = 12$; $3x + y + \lambda z = \mu$; $x - 7y + 8z = 17$ has
   (i) a unique solution (ii) infinite solutions
   (iii) no solution
2. Determine for what values of λ and μ the following equations $x + y + z = 6$, $x + 2y + 3z = 10$, $x + 2y + \lambda z = \mu$ have
   (i) no solution
   (ii) a unique solution
   (iii) infinite number of solutions
3. Let λ and α be real. Find the set of all values of λ for which the system of linear equations $\lambda x + \sin\alpha.y + \cos\alpha.z = 0$, $x + \cos\alpha.y + \sin\alpha.z = 0$, $-x + \sin\alpha.y - \cos\alpha.z = 0$ has a non-tivial solution. For $\lambda = 1$, find all the values of α.

Answer Key

1. (i) $\lambda \neq 2$ (ii) $\lambda = 2$ and $\mu = 7$ (iii) $\lambda = 2$ and $\mu \neq 7$
2. (i) $\lambda = 3$ and $\mu \neq 10$ (ii) $\lambda \neq 3$ and μ may have any value (iii) $\lambda = 3$ and $\mu = 10$
3. $2\alpha = 2n\pi \pm \pi/4 + \pi/4$. $n \in \mathbb{Z}$ and $\lambda \in \left[-\sqrt{2}, \sqrt{2}\right]$

TEXTUAL EXERCISE 4: (OBJECTIVE)

1. The system of homogeneous equations: $2x + 3y - z = 0$; $x - y - 2z = 0$;$3x + y - 2z = 0$ has
   (a) only trivial solution $x = y = z = 0$
   (b) infinitely many solutions
   (c) can't be said
   (d) None of these
2. The equation $2x - 3y + 6z = 4$, $5x + 7y + 4z = 1$, $3x + 2y - 4z = 0$ have
   (a) unique solution
   (b) no solution
   (c) infinitely many solutions
   (d) None of these
3. If the system of equations $ax + y = 1$, $x + 2y = 3$, $2x + 3y = 5$ are consistent, a is given by
   (a) 0 (b) 1
   (c) 2 (d) None of these
4. If the system of equations $\lambda x + 2y - 2z = 1$, $4x + 2\lambda y - z = 2$, $6x + 6y + \lambda z = 3$ has a unique solution, then
   (a) λ can't be 1 (b) λ can't be 2
   (c) λ can't be 3 (d) None of these
5. The system of linear equations $x + y + z = 2$, $2x + y - z = 3$, $3x + 2y + kz = 4$ has unique solution if
   (a) $k \neq 0$ (b) $-1 < k < 1$
   (c) $-2 < k < 2$ (d) $k = 0$
6. The value of 'a' for which the following system of equations has a non-trivial solution:
   $a^3x + (a + 1)^3y + (a + 2)^3z = 0$; $ax + (a + 1)y + (a + 2)z = 0$; $x + y + z = 0$, is equal to

(a) 0 (b) 1
(c) –1 (d) None of these

7. The real value of r for which the system of equation $2rx - 2y + 3z = 0$, $x + ry + 2z = 0$, $2x + rz = 0$ has non-trivial solutions is
(a) $r = 2$ (b) $r = -2$
(c) $r = 0$ (d) None of these

8. If $2x + py + 6z = 8$; $x + 2y + qz = 5$; $x + y + 3z = 4$, then the values of p and q, when the system of equations have
(i) no solution
(a) $p = 2, q = 3$ (b) $p \neq 2, q = 3$
(c) $p = 3, q = 2$ (d) None of these
(ii) a unique solution
(a) $p = q = 2$ (b) $p \neq 2, q = 3$
(c) $p \neq 2, q \neq 3$ (d) None of these
(iii) infinitely many solutions
(a) $p = 3, q = 1$ (b) $p = 2, q \in R$
(c) $p \neq 2, q \neq 3$ (d) None of these

9. The system of linear equations $ax + by = 0$, $cx + dy = 0$ has a non-trivial solution if
(a) $ad - bc = 0$ (b) $ac + bd = 0$
(c) $ad - bc < 0$ (d) $ad - bc > 0$

10. The value of λ for which the equations $x + y - 3 = 0$, $(1 + \lambda) x + (2 + \lambda) y - 8 = 0$, $x - (1 + \lambda)y + (2 + \lambda) = 0$ are consistent is
(a) 1 (b) 5/3
(c) –5/3 (d) None of these

11. The equations $x + 2y + 3z = 1$, $x - y + 4z = 0$, $2x + y + 7z = 1$ have
(a) only two solutions (b) only one solutions
(c) no solution (d) infinitely many solutions

12. The system of equations $x + y + z = 8$, $x - y + 2z = 6$, $3x + 5y - 7z = 14$ has
(a) a unique solution
(b) infinitely many solutions
(c) no solution
(d) None of these

13. The system of equations $x + 2y + 3z = 4$; $2x + 3y + 4z = 5$; $3x + 4y + 5z = 5$ has
(a) infinitely many solutions
(b) no solution
(c) unique solution
(d) None of these

14. If $a > b > c$ and the system of equations $ax + by + cz = 0$, $bx + cy + az = 0$ and $cx + ay + bz = 0$ has a non-trivial solution, then both the roots of the quadratic equation $at^2 + bt - c = 0$ are
(a) at least one positive root
(b) opposite in sign
(c) positive
(d) imaginary

Answer Key

1. (a)	2. (a)	3. (a)	4. (b)	5. (a)	6. (c)	7. (a)	8. (i) (b) (ii) (c) (iii) (b)
9. (a)	10. (a, c)	11. (d)	12. (a)	13. (a)	14. (a)		

■ LINEAR TRANSFORMATION

The transformation in which the straight line remains straight and origin does not change its position. We represent point (x, y) by column matrix $\begin{bmatrix} x \\ y \end{bmatrix}$ and transformation mapping is denoted by a matrix operation which transform $\begin{bmatrix} x \\ y \end{bmatrix}$ to $\begin{bmatrix} X \\ Y \end{bmatrix}$

Definition: Any transformation of $\begin{bmatrix} x \\ y \end{bmatrix}$ to $\begin{bmatrix} X \\ Y \end{bmatrix}$ that can be expressed by the linear equation $a_1x + b_1y = X$ and $a_2x + b_2y = Y$ is called linear transformation.

$\begin{bmatrix} a_1 & b_1 \\ a_2 & b_2 \end{bmatrix}\begin{bmatrix} x \\ y \end{bmatrix} = \begin{bmatrix} X \\ Y \end{bmatrix}$. Operator $M = \begin{bmatrix} a_1 & b_1 \\ a_2 & b_2 \end{bmatrix}$ is matrix of transformation.

Origin remains invariant of such transformation. Some common linear transformations are

1. Drag by a factor k along x-axis
2. Enlargment or reduction
3. Reflection in any line through origin
4. Rotation through any angle about origin
5. Shearing parallel to x-axis/y-axis

Compound Transformation

When a transformation (2) is carried out after (1) the compound transformation is denoted by a matrix operator $M_2 \, o \, M_1 = M_2$

M_1 where M_2 and M_1 are respective matrix operators for (i) and (ii) operation. $M_2 \, o \, M_1$ is known as composition of M_2 with M_1 (order of performance of operations must be mentioned)

■ THE REFLECTION MATRIX

The Reflection in the *x-axis*

Let $P(x, y)$ be any point $P'(x_1, y_1)$ be its image after reflection in the x-axis, then $\begin{cases} x_1 = x \\ y_1 = -y \end{cases}$ (O' is the midpoint of PP')

These may be rewritten as $\begin{cases} x_1 = 1.x + 0.y \\ y_1 = 0.x + (-1).y \end{cases}$

These systems of equations in the matrix form are written as: $\begin{bmatrix} x_1 \\ y_1 \end{bmatrix} = \begin{bmatrix} 1 & 0 \\ 0 & -1 \end{bmatrix} \cdot \begin{bmatrix} x \\ y \end{bmatrix}$

Thus the matrix $\begin{bmatrix} 1 & 0 \\ 0 & -1 \end{bmatrix}$ describes the reflection of a point $P(x, y)$ in the x-axis.

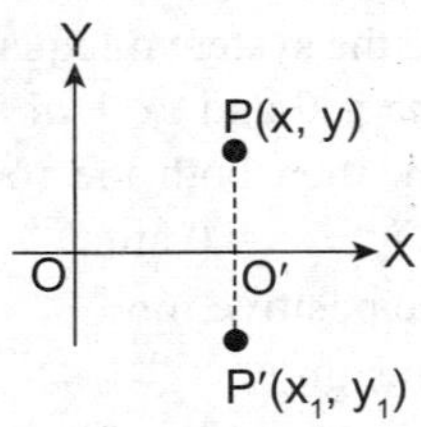

FIGURE 1.5

Reflection in the y-axis

Let $P(x, y)$ be any point $P'(x_1, y_1)$ be its image after reflection in the y-axis, then

$\begin{cases} x_1 = -x \\ y_1 = y \end{cases}$ (O' is the midpoint of PP')

These may be rewritten as $\begin{cases} x_1 = (-1).x + 0.y \\ y_1 = 0.x + 1.y \end{cases}$

These systems of equations in the matrix form can be written as $\begin{bmatrix} x_1 \\ y_1 \end{bmatrix} = \begin{bmatrix} -1 & 0 \\ 0 & 1 \end{bmatrix} \cdot \begin{bmatrix} x \\ y \end{bmatrix}$

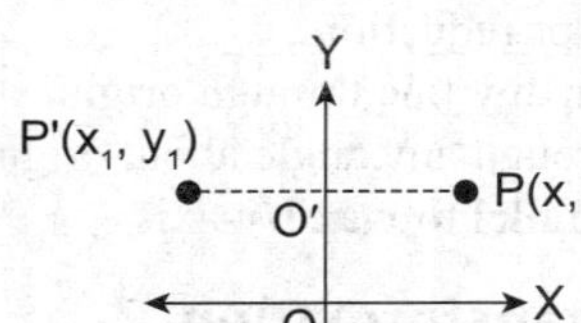

FIGURE 1.6

Thus the matrix $\begin{bmatrix} -1 & 0 \\ 0 & 1 \end{bmatrix}$ describes the reflection of a point $P(x, y)$ in the y-axis.

Reflection Through the Origin

Let $P(x, y)$ be any point and $P'(x_1, y_1)$ be its image after reflection through the origin, then

$\begin{cases} x_1 = -x \\ y_1 = -y \end{cases}$ (O' is the midpoint of PP').

These may be rewritten as $\begin{cases} x_1 = (-1).\,x + 0.y \\ y_1 = 0.x + (-1).y \end{cases}$

These systems of equations in the matrix form can be written as $\begin{bmatrix} x_1 \\ y_1 \end{bmatrix} = \begin{bmatrix} -1 & 0 \\ 0 & -1 \end{bmatrix} \cdot \begin{bmatrix} x \\ y \end{bmatrix}$

Thus the matrix $\begin{bmatrix} -1 & 0 \\ 0 & -1 \end{bmatrix}$ describes the reflection of a point $P(x, y)$ in the origin.

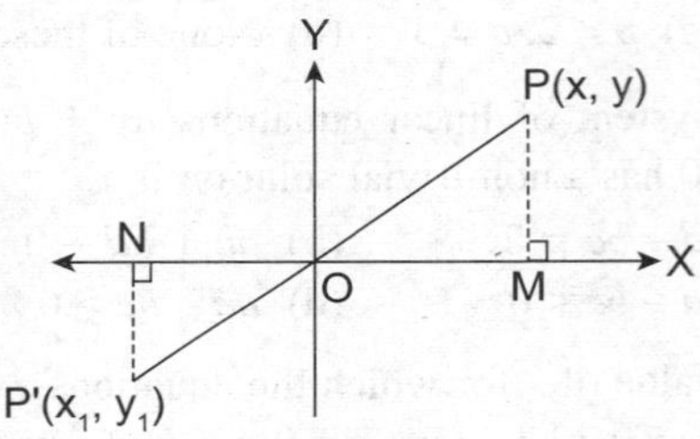

FIGURE 1.7

Reflection in the Line *y* = *x*

Let $P(x, y)$ be any point $P'(x_1, y_1)$ be its image after reflection in the line $y = x$, then $\begin{cases} x_1 = y \\ y_1 = x \end{cases}$ (O' is the midpoint of PP')

These may be rewritten as $\begin{cases} x_1 = 0.x + 1.y \\ y_1 = 1.x + 0.y \end{cases}$

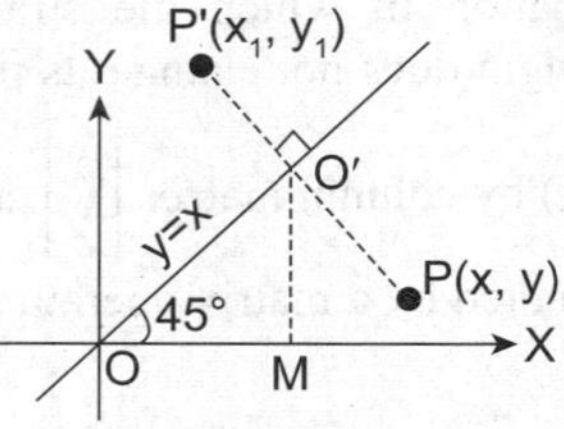

FIGURE 1.8

These systems of equations in the matrix form can be written as $\begin{bmatrix} x_1 \\ y_1 \end{bmatrix} = \begin{bmatrix} 0 & 1 \\ 1 & 0 \end{bmatrix} \begin{bmatrix} x \\ y \end{bmatrix}$

Thus the matrix $\begin{bmatrix} 0 & 1 \\ 1 & 0 \end{bmatrix}$ describes the reflection of a point $P(x, y)$ in the line $y = x$

Reflection in the Line $y = x \tan \theta$

Let $P(x, y)$ be any point and $P'(x_1, y_1)$ be its image after reflection in the line $y = x \tan \theta$, then $\begin{cases} x_1 = x\cos 2\theta + y\sin 2\theta \\ y_1 = x\sin 2\theta - y\cos 2\theta \end{cases}$

(O′ is the midpoint of PP')

These may be rewritten as $\begin{cases} x_1 = x\cos 2\theta + y\sin 2\theta \\ y_1 = x\sin 2\theta + y(-\cos 2\theta) \end{cases}$

These systems of equations in the matrix form can be written as: $\begin{bmatrix} x_1 \\ y_1 \end{bmatrix} = \begin{bmatrix} \cos 2\theta & \sin 2\theta \\ \sin 2\theta & -\cos 2\theta \end{bmatrix} \begin{bmatrix} x \\ y \end{bmatrix}$

Thus the matrix $\begin{bmatrix} \cos 2\theta & \sin 2\theta \\ \sin 2\theta & -\cos 2\theta \end{bmatrix}$ describes the reflection of a point $P(x, y)$ in the line $y = x \tan\theta$.

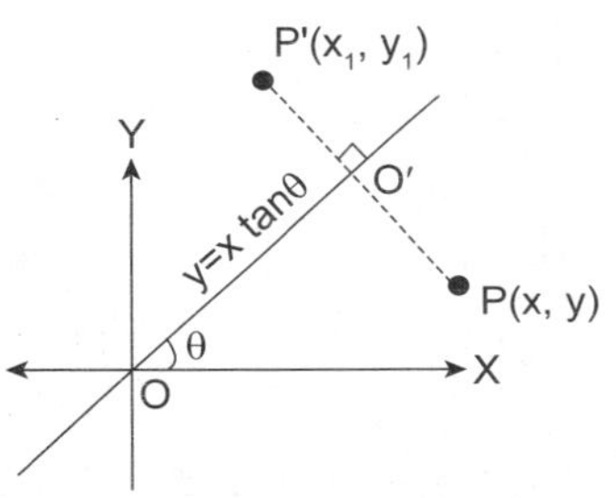

FIGURE 1.9

Rotation of a line passing through origin by an Angle θ

Let $P(x, y)$ be any point such that $OP = r$ and $\angle POX = \phi$. Let OP rotate through an angle θ in the anti-clockwise direction such that $P'(x_1, y_1)$ is the new position

$$\therefore \quad OP' = r\ (\because OP = OP'); \text{ then } \begin{cases} x_1 = x\cos\theta - y\sin\theta \\ y_1 = x\sin\theta + y\cos\theta \end{cases}$$

These systems of equations in the matrix form can be written as below: $\begin{bmatrix} x_1 \\ y_1 \end{bmatrix} = \begin{bmatrix} \cos\theta & -\sin\theta \\ \sin\theta & \cos\theta \end{bmatrix} \begin{bmatrix} x \\ y \end{bmatrix}$

Thus the matrix $\begin{bmatrix} \cos\theta & -\sin\theta \\ \sin\theta & \cos\theta \end{bmatrix}$ describes a rotation of a line segment through the origin by an angle θ.

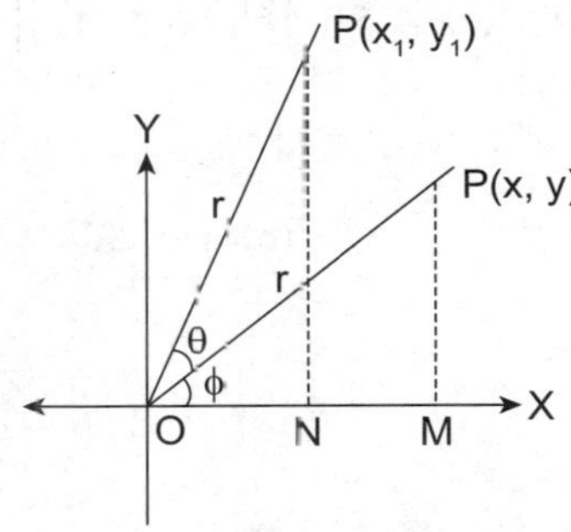

FIGURE 1.10

Shearing by Angle θ Parallel to x-axis

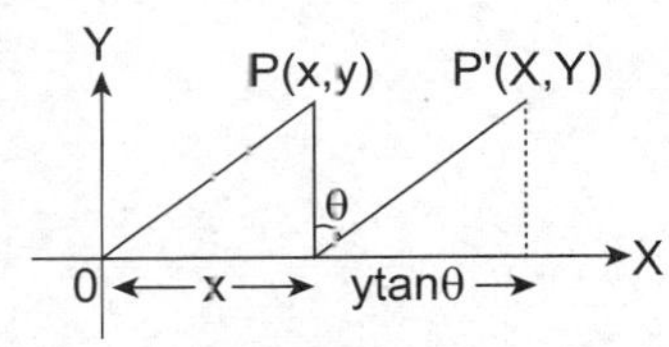

FIGURE 1.11

Clearly $X = x + y \tan \theta$; $Y = y \Rightarrow \begin{bmatrix} x_1 \\ y_1 \end{bmatrix} = \begin{bmatrix} 1 & \tan\theta \\ 0 & 1 \end{bmatrix} \begin{bmatrix} x \\ y \end{bmatrix}$

TEXTUAL EXERCISE 10: (SUBJECTIVE)

1. Obtain the matrix of transformation for the following transformations:
   (a) reflection in the x-axis
   (b) a stretch by a factor of 2 parallel to OY
   (c) an enlargement by a factor of $k > 0$
   (d) reflection in the x-axis combined with a stretch by a factor of 2 parallel to OX
   (e) reflection in the line $y = x$
   (f) rotation through an angle θ about O
   (g) shear by angle θ parallel to x-axis
   (h) reflection in the origin O
2. Describe the transformation represented by $\begin{bmatrix} 1 & 1 \\ 1 & 1 \end{bmatrix}$.
3. Write the following transformation in matrix form $x_1 = \frac{\sqrt{3}}{2} y_1 + \frac{1}{2} y_2$ and $x_2 = -\frac{1}{2} y_1 + \frac{\sqrt{3}}{2} y_2$

Hence find the transformation in matrix form which expresses y_1, y_2 in terms of x_1, x_2.

4. Find the equation of the image of the line $y = 2x - 1$ under the transformation $\begin{bmatrix} 2 & -1 \\ 0 & 2 \end{bmatrix}$.

5. Using transformation $\begin{bmatrix} 0 & -1 \\ -1 & 0 \end{bmatrix}\begin{bmatrix} x \\ y \end{bmatrix} = \begin{bmatrix} X \\ Y \end{bmatrix}$, find the equation of the images of the lines.
(a) $x = 2$ (b) $2y = x$
(c) $x + y + 2 = 0$

Answer Key

1. (a) $\begin{bmatrix} 1 & 0 \\ 0 & -1 \end{bmatrix}$ (b) $\begin{bmatrix} 1 & 0 \\ 0 & 2 \end{bmatrix}$ (c) $\begin{bmatrix} k & 0 \\ 0 & k \end{bmatrix}$ (d) $\begin{bmatrix} 2 & 0 \\ 0 & -1 \end{bmatrix}$ (e) $\begin{bmatrix} 0 & 1 \\ 1 & 0 \end{bmatrix}$

(f) $\begin{bmatrix} \cos\theta & -\sin\theta \\ \sin\theta & \cos\theta \end{bmatrix}$ (g) $\begin{bmatrix} 1 & \tan \\ 0 & 1 \end{bmatrix}$ (h) $\begin{bmatrix} -1 & 0 \\ 0 & -1 \end{bmatrix}$

2. $P(x, y) \rightarrow P(x + y, x + y)$

3. $y_1 = \frac{\sqrt{3}}{2}x_1 - \frac{1}{2}x_2$ and $y_2 = \frac{1}{2}x_1 + \frac{\sqrt{3}}{2}x_2$

4. $x = 1$

5. (a) $Y = -2$ (b) $y = 2X$ (c) $X + Y - 2 = 0$

MULTIPLE CHOICE QUESTIONS

SECTION–I

SUBJECTIVE SOLVED EXAMPLES

1. Show that pre multiplication (post multiplication) of a square matrix A by a diagonal matrix D multiplies each row (column) of A by the corresponding diagonal element of D. Deduce that the only matrices commutative with a diagonal matrix with distinct diagonal elements are diagonal matrices. Also, show that if a diagonal matrix is commutative with every matrix of the same type (with all non-zero entries) for multiplication, then it is necessarily a scalar matrix.

Solution: Let $A = [a_{ij}]$ be $n \times n$ matrix commutative with every $n \times n$ diagonal matrix B.

We take B = Diag. $[b_1 ... b_n]$ with diagonal elements all distinct.

The $(i, j)$the element of $BA = b_i a_{ij}$ and the (i, j)th element of $AB = b_j a_{ij}$

As $AB = BA$

We have $b_i a_{ij} = b_j a_{ij} = a_{ij} = 0$ when $i \neq j$ (for $b_i \neq b_j$ when $i \neq j$)

Thus A is a diagonal matrix. Let A = Diag. $[a_{11}, a_{22}, ..., a_{nn}]$

We take now $B = [b_{ij}]$ which is any matrix none of whose elements is zero

The (i, j)th elements of AB and BA being $a_{ii} b_{ij}$ and $a_{jj} b_{ij}$

We have $a_{ii} b_{ij} = a_{jj} b_{ij}$

$\Rightarrow a_{ii} = a_{jj}$ (for $b_{ij} \neq 0$)

Thus A is a scalar matrix

2. If $A = \begin{bmatrix} 0 & -\tan(\alpha/2) \\ \tan(\alpha/2) & 0 \end{bmatrix}$ and I is a 2×2 unit matrix, then prove that $I + A = (I - A)\begin{bmatrix} \cos\alpha & -\sin\alpha \\ \sin\alpha & \cos\alpha \end{bmatrix}$

Solution: Since $I = \begin{bmatrix} 1 & 0 \\ 0 & 1 \end{bmatrix}$

and given $A = \begin{bmatrix} 0 & -\tan\alpha/2 \\ \tan\alpha/2 & 0 \end{bmatrix}$

$$\therefore \quad I + A = \begin{bmatrix} 1 & -\tan\alpha/2 \\ \tan\alpha/2 & 1 \end{bmatrix}$$

$$\text{R.H.S} = (I - A)\begin{bmatrix} \cos\alpha & -\sin\alpha \\ \sin\alpha & \cos\alpha \end{bmatrix}$$

$$= \begin{bmatrix} 1 & \tan\alpha/2 \\ -\tan\alpha/2 & 1 \end{bmatrix}\begin{bmatrix} \cos\alpha & -\sin\alpha \\ \sin\alpha & \cos\alpha \end{bmatrix}$$

$$= \begin{bmatrix} 1 & \tan\alpha/2 \\ -\tan\alpha/2 & 1 \end{bmatrix}\begin{bmatrix} \frac{1-\tan^2\alpha/2}{1+\tan^2\alpha/2} & \frac{-2\tan\alpha/2}{1+\tan^2\alpha/2} \\ \frac{2\tan\alpha/2}{1+\tan^2\alpha/2} & \frac{1-\tan^2\alpha/2}{1+\tan^2\alpha/2} \end{bmatrix}$$

$$= \begin{bmatrix} \frac{(1+\tan^2\alpha/2)}{(1+\tan^2\alpha/2)} & -\frac{\tan\alpha/2(1+\tan^2\alpha/2)}{1+\tan^2\alpha/2} \\ \frac{\tan\alpha/2(1+\tan^2\alpha/2)}{1+\tan^2\alpha/2} & \frac{(1+\tan^2\alpha/2)}{(1+\tan^2\alpha/2)} \end{bmatrix}$$

$$= \begin{bmatrix} 1 & -\tan\alpha/2 \\ \tan\alpha/2 & 1 \end{bmatrix} = I + A = \text{L.H.S}$$

3. Find x so that $[1\ x\ 1]\begin{bmatrix} 1 & 3 & 2 \\ 0 & 5 & 1 \\ 0 & 3 & 2 \end{bmatrix}\begin{bmatrix} 1 \\ 1 \\ x \end{bmatrix} = O$

Solution: $[1\ x\ 1]\begin{bmatrix} 1 & 3 & 2 \\ 0 & 5 & 1 \\ 0 & 3 & 2 \end{bmatrix}\begin{bmatrix} 1 \\ 1 \\ x \end{bmatrix} = O$

$$\Rightarrow [1\ \ 5x + 6\ \ x + 4]\begin{bmatrix} 1 \\ 1 \\ x \end{bmatrix} = O$$

$$\Rightarrow [1 + 5x + 6 + x^2 + 4x] = O \text{ or } x^2 + 9x + 7 = 0$$

$$\therefore \quad x = \frac{-9 \pm \sqrt{(81-28)}}{2} \quad \therefore x = \frac{-9 \pm \sqrt{53}}{2}$$

4. If A and B are square matrices of order n, then prove that A and B will commute if and only if $A - \lambda I$ and $B - \lambda I$ commute for every scalar λ.

Solution: Suppose the matrices A and B commute, i.e., $AB = BA$

Then to prove that the matrices $A - \lambda I$ and $B - \lambda I$ commute for every scalar λ, we have

$(A - \lambda I)(B - \lambda I) = AB - \lambda AI - \lambda IB + \lambda^2 I^2 = AB - \lambda A - \lambda B + \lambda^2 I = AB - \lambda(A + B) + \lambda^2 I$

Similarly, $(B - \lambda I)(A - \lambda I) = BA - \lambda(A + B) + \lambda^2 I$.
But it is given that $AB = BA$.
Therefore $(A - \lambda I)(B - \lambda I) = (B - \lambda I)(A - \lambda I)$ for every scalar λ.
Conversely, suppose that $A - \lambda I$ and $B - \lambda I$ commute for every scalar λ. Then $(A - \lambda I)(B - \lambda I) = (B - \lambda I)(A - \lambda I)$

$\therefore\ AB - \lambda(A + B) + \lambda^2 I = BA - \lambda(A + B) + \lambda^2 I$

or $AB = BA$ and hence A and B commute.

5. If $A_\alpha = \begin{bmatrix} \cos\alpha & \sin\alpha \\ -\sin\alpha & \cos\alpha \end{bmatrix}$, then show that

(i) $(A_\alpha)^n = \begin{bmatrix} \cos n\alpha & \sin n\alpha \\ -\sin n\alpha & \cos n\alpha \end{bmatrix}$, where n is a positive integer.

(ii) $A_\alpha A_\beta = A_{\alpha+\beta}$

Solution: (i) We shall prove the result by induction on n.

$$\Rightarrow (A_\alpha)^1 = \begin{bmatrix} \cos 1\alpha & \sin 1\alpha \\ -\sin 1\alpha & \cos 1\alpha \end{bmatrix}$$

Thus the result is true when $n = 1$. now suppose that the result is true for any positive integer n,

i.e., $\begin{bmatrix} \cos n\alpha & \sin n\alpha \\ -\sin n\alpha & \cos n\alpha \end{bmatrix}$

We shall prove that the result is true for $n + 1$ if it is true for n. We have $(A_\alpha)^{n+1} = (A_\alpha)^n . A_\alpha$

$$= \begin{bmatrix} \cos n\alpha & \sin n\alpha \\ -\sin n\alpha & \cos n\alpha \end{bmatrix}\begin{bmatrix} \cos\alpha & \sin\alpha \\ -\sin\alpha & \cos\alpha \end{bmatrix}$$

$$\begin{bmatrix} \cos n\alpha\cos\alpha - \sin n\alpha\sin\alpha & -\cos n\alpha\sin\alpha + \sin n\alpha\cos\alpha \\ -\sin n\alpha\cos\alpha - \cos n\alpha\sin\alpha & -\sin n\alpha\sin\alpha + \cos\alpha\cos\alpha \end{bmatrix}$$

$$= \begin{bmatrix} \cos(n+1)\alpha & \sin(n+1)\alpha \\ -\sin(n+1)\alpha & \cos(n+1)\alpha \end{bmatrix}$$

Thus the result is true for $n + 1$ if it is true for n. Now the proof is completed by induction.

(ii) $A_\alpha A_\beta = \begin{bmatrix} \cos\alpha & \sin\alpha \\ -\sin\alpha & \cos\alpha \end{bmatrix}\begin{bmatrix} \cos\beta & \sin\beta \\ -\sin\beta & \cos\beta \end{bmatrix}$

$$= \begin{bmatrix} \cos\alpha\cos\beta - \sin\alpha\sin\beta & \cos\alpha\sin\beta + \sin\alpha\cos\beta \\ -\sin\alpha\cos\beta - \cos\alpha\sin\beta & -\sin\alpha\sin\beta + \cos\alpha\cos\beta \end{bmatrix}$$

$$= \begin{bmatrix} \cos(\alpha+\beta) & \sin(\alpha+\beta) \\ -\sin(\alpha+\beta) & \cos(\alpha+\beta) \end{bmatrix} = A_{\alpha+\beta}$$

6. If A and B are matrices such that $AB = BA$, then show that for every positive integer n

(i) $AB^n = B^n A$ (ii) $(AB)^n = A^n B^n$

Solution: (i) We shall prove the result by induction on n.
To start the induction, we see that the result is true when $n = 1$.
For $AB^1 = AB = BA = B^1A$
Now suppose that the result is true for any positive integer n.
Then $AB^{n+1} = (AB^n)B = (B^nA)B = B^n(AB)$
$= B^n(BA) = (B^nB)A = B^{n+1}A$, showing that the result is true for $n + 1$
Now the proof is complete by induction.

(ii) We shall prove the result by induction on n. To start the induction, we see that the result is true when $n = 1$. For $(AB)^1 = AB = A^1B^1$
Now suppose that the result is true for any positive integer n. i.e., $(AB)^n = A^n B^n$, then
$(AB)^{n+1} = (AB)^n(AB) = (A^nB^n)(AB) = A^n(B^nA)B$
$= A^n(AB^n)B$ [*by part* (i) *of the question*]
$= A^{n+1}B^{n+1}$, showing that the result is the for $n + 1$.
The proof is now complete by induction.

7. If A and B be m-rowed square matrices which commute and n be a positive integer, prove the binomial theorem $(A + B)^n = {}^nC_0 A^n + {}^nC_1 A^{n-1} B + ... + {}^nC_r A^{n-r} B^r + ... + {}^nC_n B^n$

Solution: We have $A + B = A^1 + B^1$
Now $(A + B)^2 = (A + B)(A + B)$
$= A^2 + AB + BA + B^2$ by distributive law
$= A^2 + 2AB + B^2$, since $AB = BA$
$= {}^2C_0 A^2 + {}^2C_1 AB + {}^2C_2 B^2$.
Thus the thoerem is true for $n = 2$.
Now assume that the theorem is true for n i.e.,
$(A + B)^n = {}^nC_0 A^n + {}^nC_1 A^{n-1} B + ... + {}^nC_r A^{n-r} B^r + ... + {}^nC_n B^n$
Then $(A + B)^{n+1} = (A + B)(A + B)^n$
$= (A + B)({}^nC_0 A^n + {}^nC_1 A^{n-1} B + ... + {}^nC_r A^{n-r} B^r + {}^nC_{r+1} A^{n-r-1} B^{r+1} + ... + {}^nC_n B^n)$
$= {}^nC_0 A^{n+1} + ({}^nC_0 BA^n + {}^nC_1 A^n B) + ... + ({}^nC_r BA^{n-r} B^r + {}^nC_{r+1} A^{n-r} B^{r+1}) + ... + {}^nC_n B^{n+1})$
Now $AB = BA$. We can prove by induction that for every positive integer n, $BA^n = A^n B$.
Again $BA^{n-r} B^r = (BA^{n-r}) B^r = (A^{n-r}B) B^r = A^{n-r} BB^r = A^{n-r} B^{r+1}$
Also ${}^nC_0 = {}^{n+1}C_0 = 1$ ${}^nC_n = {}^{n+1}C_{n+1} = 1$ and ${}^nC_r + {}^nC_{r+1} = {}^{n+1}C_{r+1}$
Hence $(A + B)^{n+1} = {}^{n+1}C_0 A^{n+1} + ({}^nC_0 + {}^nC_1)A^n B + ... + ({}^nC_r + {}^nC_{r+1}) A^{n-r} B^{r+1} + ... + {}^{n+1}C_{n+1} B^{n+1}$
$= {}^{n+1}C_0 A^{n+1} + {}^{n+1}C_1 A^n B + ... + {}^{n+1}C_{r+1} A^{n-r} B^{r+1} + ... + {}^{n+1}C_{n+1} B^{n+1}$ Thus the theorem is true for

$n + 1$, if it is true for n. But it is true for $n = 2$. Hence it is true for all positive integral values of n.

8. Show that the Matrix $A = \begin{bmatrix} ab & b^2 \\ -a^2 & -ab \end{bmatrix}$ is nilpotent such that $A^2 = O$. Conversely, show that all 2-rowed nilpotent matrices such that $A^2 = O$ are of the above form.

Solution: If $A = \begin{bmatrix} ab & b^2 \\ -a^2 & -ab \end{bmatrix}$,

$$A^2 = AA = \begin{bmatrix} ab & b^2 \\ -a^2 & -ab \end{bmatrix}\begin{bmatrix} ab & b^2 \\ -a^2 & -ab \end{bmatrix}$$

$$= \begin{bmatrix} a^2b^2 - b^2a^2 & ab^3 - ab^3 \\ -a^3b + a^3b & -a^2b^2 + a^2b^2 \end{bmatrix} = \begin{bmatrix} 0 & 0 \\ 0 & 0 \end{bmatrix}$$

Hence the matrix A is nilpotent of the index 2.

Conversely, suppose $A = \begin{bmatrix} \alpha & \beta \\ \gamma & \delta \end{bmatrix}$ is a two rowed nilpotent matrix such that $A^2 = O$ i.e.,

$$\begin{bmatrix} \alpha^2 + \beta\gamma & \alpha\beta + \beta\delta \\ \alpha\gamma + \gamma\delta & \gamma\beta + \delta^2 \end{bmatrix} = \begin{bmatrix} 0 & 0 \\ 0 & 0 \end{bmatrix}$$

If the above equation holds,

$\alpha^2 + \beta\gamma = 0$ ....(i)

$\alpha\beta + \beta\delta = 0$ ....(ii)

$\alpha\gamma + \gamma\delta = 0$ ....(iii)

$\gamma\beta + \delta^2 = 0$ ...(iv)

must hold simultaneously.

From (i) and (iv), it is obvious that the above four equations will hold simultaneously if $\alpha^2 = \delta^2$ i.e., $\alpha = \pm\, \delta$. If $\alpha = -\delta$ the above four equations will hold simultaneously for all values of the numbers α, β, γ proveided thay are related by the condition $\alpha^2 + \beta\gamma = 0$.

If $\alpha = \delta$ and either of them is not equal to 0, we have from (ii) and (iii) $\beta = 0$ and $\gamma = 0$. Then from (i) and (iv), we shall have $\alpha = \delta = 0$. Hence if $\alpha = \delta \neq 0$, then above four equations cannot hold simultaneously.

If $\alpha = \delta = 0$, then equations can hold simultaneously, but this solution can be included in the solution $\alpha = -\delta$, $\alpha^2 + \beta\gamma = 0$.

Thus the matrix A is nilpotent if $A = \begin{bmatrix} \alpha & \beta \\ \gamma & -\alpha \end{bmatrix}$ and α, β, γ are any numbers related by the condition $\alpha^2 + \beta\gamma = 0$. Obviously the matrix A is of the given form.

11. Discuss for all values of k the system of equations $2x + 3ky + (3k + 4)z = 0$; $x + (k + 4)y + (4k + 2)z = 0$; $x + 2(k + 1)y + (3k + 4)z = 0$.

Solution: The given system of equations is equivalent to the single matrix equation.

$$AX = \begin{bmatrix} 2 & 3k & 3k+4 \\ 1 & k+4 & 4k+2 \\ 1 & 2k+2 & 3k+4 \end{bmatrix}\begin{bmatrix} x \\ y \\ z \end{bmatrix} = O$$

Performing $R_1 \leftrightarrow R_2$, we have

$$\begin{bmatrix} 1 & k+4 & 4k+2 \\ 2 & 3k & 3k+4 \\ 1 & 2k+2 & 3k+4 \end{bmatrix}\begin{bmatrix} x \\ y \\ z \end{bmatrix} = O$$

Performing $R_2 \to R_2 - 2R_1$, $R_3 \to R_3 - R_1$, we have

$$\begin{bmatrix} 1 & k+4 & 4k+2 \\ 0 & k-8 & -5k \\ 0 & k-2 & -k+2 \end{bmatrix}\begin{bmatrix} x \\ y \\ z \end{bmatrix} = O$$

If the given system of equations is to possess any linearly independent solution, the coefficient matrix A must be of rank less than 3. For the matrix A to be of rank than 3, we must have $(k - 8)(-k + 2) + 5k(k - 2) \neq 0$.

i.e., $-k^2 + 2k + 8k - 16 - 5k^2 - 10k \neq 0$.

i.e., $4k^2 - 16 \neq 0$. i.e., $k \neq \pm 2$

Now two cases arises:

Case I: When $k \neq \pm 2$, the given system of equations possesses no linearly independent solution and $x = y = z = 0$ is the only solution.

Case II: If $k = 2$, the equation (i) reduces to $\begin{bmatrix} 1 & 6 & 10 \\ 0 & -6 & -10 \\ 0 & 0 & 0 \end{bmatrix}\begin{bmatrix} x \\ y \\ z \end{bmatrix} = O$. The coefficient matrix being of rank 2, the given system of equations now possesses $3 - 2 = 1$ linearly independent solution. The given system of equations is now equivalent to $-6y - 10z = 0$, $x + 6y + 10z = 0$. Thus $y = -\frac{5}{3}z$, $x = 0$.

Hence, $x = 0, y = -\frac{5}{3}c, z = c$.

13. Let A be a 3×3 matrix given by $A = (a_{ij})_{3\times3}$. If for every column vector X, $X^TAX = O$ and $a_{23} = -2006$, then sum of digits of element a_{32} must be equal to.

Solution: Let $X = \begin{pmatrix} x_1 \\ x_2 \\ x_3 \end{pmatrix}$; $X'AX = O$ [Null matrix]

$$\Rightarrow (x_1\ x_2\ x_3)\begin{pmatrix} a_{11} & a_{12} & a_{13} \\ a_{21} & a_{22} & a_{23} \\ a_{31} & a_{32} & a_{33} \end{pmatrix}\begin{pmatrix} x_1 \\ x_2 \\ x_3 \end{pmatrix} = O$$

$$\Rightarrow a_{11}x_1^2 + a_{22}x_2^2 + a_{33}x_3^2 + (a_{12} + a_{21})x_1x_2 + (a_{13} + a_{31})$$

$x_1x_3 + (a_{23} + a_{32})x_2x_3 = 0$

If this is true for every x_1, x_2, x_3,

then $a_{11} = a_{22} = a_{33} = 0$

and $a_{12} = -a_{21}$, $a_{13} = -a_{31}$, $a_{23} = -a_{32}$

Now as $a_{23} = -2006$; $a_{32} = 2006$.

$\therefore$ sum of digits of 2006 = **8**

14. If $\begin{bmatrix} 1 & 2 & a \\ 0 & 1 & 4 \\ 0 & 0 & 1 \end{bmatrix}^n = \begin{bmatrix} 1 & 18 & 2007 \\ 0 & 1 & 36 \\ 0 & 0 & 1 \end{bmatrix}$, then evaluate $(n + a)$.

Solution: $A = \begin{bmatrix} 1 & 2 & a \\ 0 & 1 & 4 \\ 0 & 0 & 1 \end{bmatrix}$

$$\therefore A^2 = \begin{bmatrix} 1 & 2 & a \\ 0 & 1 & 4 \\ 0 & 0 & 1 \end{bmatrix}\begin{bmatrix} 1 & 2 & a \\ 0 & 1 & 4 \\ 0 & 0 & 1 \end{bmatrix} = \begin{bmatrix} 1 & 4 & 2a+8 \\ 0 & 1 & 8 \\ 0 & 0 & 1 \end{bmatrix}$$

$$A^3 = \begin{bmatrix} 1 & 4 & 2a+8 \\ 0 & 1 & 8 \\ 0 & 0 & 1 \end{bmatrix}\begin{bmatrix} 1 & 2 & a \\ 0 & 1 & 4 \\ 0 & 0 & 1 \end{bmatrix} = \begin{bmatrix} 1 & 6 & 3a+24 \\ 0 & 1 & 12 \\ 0 & 0 & 1 \end{bmatrix}$$

Generalizing the result, we get

$$A^n = \begin{bmatrix} 1 & 2n & na + 8\sum_{k=0}^{n-1} k \\ 0 & 1 & 4n \\ 0 & 0 & 1 \end{bmatrix} = \begin{bmatrix} 1 & 18 & 2007 \\ 0 & 1 & 36 \\ 0 & 0 & 1 \end{bmatrix}$$

$$\Rightarrow 2n = 18 \Rightarrow n = 9 \quad \therefore \quad 9a + 8\sum_{k=0}^{8} k = 2007$$

$$\Rightarrow 9a + 8\left[\frac{8 \times 9}{2}\right] = 2007 \Rightarrow 9a = 2007 - 288$$

$$\Rightarrow 9a = 1719;\ a = 191 \quad \therefore \quad n + a = 9 + 191 = 200.$$

SECTION–II

OBJECTIVE SOLVED EXAMPLES

1. What is wrong in the following computation?

$$\begin{bmatrix} 1 & 0.01 \\ 1 & 1 \end{bmatrix}^n = \left\{\begin{bmatrix} 1 & 0 \\ 1 & 1 \end{bmatrix} + 10^{-2}\begin{bmatrix} 0 & 1 \\ 0 & 0 \end{bmatrix}\right\}^n$$

$$= \begin{bmatrix} 1 & 0 \\ 1 & 1 \end{bmatrix}^n + n \times 10^{-2}\begin{bmatrix} 1 & 0 \\ 1 & 1 \end{bmatrix}^{n-1}\begin{bmatrix} 0 & 1 \\ 0 & 0 \end{bmatrix}$$

Since $\begin{bmatrix} 0 & 1 \\ 0 & 0 \end{bmatrix}^k = \begin{bmatrix} 0 & 0 \\ 0 & 0 \end{bmatrix}$ for $k \geq 2$

(a) $\begin{bmatrix} 0 & 1 \\ 0 & 0 \end{bmatrix}^k = \begin{bmatrix} 0 & 0 \\ 0 & 0 \end{bmatrix}$ for $k \geq 2$ is not true

(b) computation of second term on R.H.S. is not valid

(c) first term should be calculated completely

(d) None of these

Solution: (d) $(A + B)^n$ can be expanded using binomial theorem if A and B commute. Since $\begin{bmatrix} 1 & 0 \\ 1 & 1 \end{bmatrix}$ and $\begin{bmatrix} 0 & 1 \\ 0 & 0 \end{bmatrix}$ do not commute, we cannot use binomial theorem.

2. If $A = \begin{bmatrix} \cos\theta & \sin\theta \\ -\sin\theta & \cos\theta \end{bmatrix}$, then $\lim_{n \to \infty} \frac{1}{n} A^n$ is

(a) a zero matrix (b) an identity matrix

(c) $\begin{bmatrix} 0 & 1 \\ -1 & 0 \end{bmatrix}$ (d) None of these

Solution: (a) If $A^n = [b_{ij}]$, then $\lim_{n \to \infty} \frac{1}{n} A^n = \left[\lim_{n \to \infty} b_{ij}\right]$

$$A^n = \begin{bmatrix} \cos(n\theta) & \sin(n\theta) \\ -\sin(n\theta) & \cos(n\theta) \end{bmatrix}$$

Now,

$$\frac{1}{n}.A^n = \begin{bmatrix} \cos(n\theta)/n & \sin(n\theta)/n \\ -\sin(n\theta)/n & \cos(n\theta)/n \end{bmatrix}$$

Since $-1 \leq \cos(n\theta), \sin(n\theta) \leq 1$,

$$\lim_{n\to\infty} \frac{\cos(n\theta)}{n} = 0 = \lim_{n\to\infty} \frac{\sin(n\theta)}{n}$$

Thus, $\lim_{n\to\infty} \frac{1}{n} A^n = \begin{bmatrix} 0 & 0 \\ 0 & 0 \end{bmatrix}$.

3. If $A = \begin{bmatrix} 1 & 0 \\ 1/2 & 1 \end{bmatrix}$, then A^{50} is

(a) $\begin{bmatrix} 1 & 0 \\ 0 & 50 \end{bmatrix}$ (b) $\begin{bmatrix} 1 & 0 \\ 50 & 1 \end{bmatrix}$

(c) $\begin{bmatrix} 1 & 25 \\ 0 & 1 \end{bmatrix}$ (d) None of these

Solution: (d) We have

$$A^2 = \begin{bmatrix} 1 & 0 \\ 1/2 & 1 \end{bmatrix}\begin{bmatrix} 1 & 0 \\ 1/2 & 1 \end{bmatrix} = \begin{bmatrix} 1 & 0 \\ 2(1/2) & 1 \end{bmatrix} = \begin{bmatrix} 1 & 0 \\ 1 & 1 \end{bmatrix}$$

$$A^4 = \begin{bmatrix} 1 & 0 \\ 1 & 1 \end{bmatrix}\begin{bmatrix} 1 & 0 \\ 1 & 1 \end{bmatrix} = \begin{bmatrix} 1 & 0 \\ 2 & 1 \end{bmatrix};$$

$$A^8 = \begin{bmatrix} 1 & 0 \\ 2 & 1 \end{bmatrix}\begin{bmatrix} 1 & 0 \\ 2 & 1 \end{bmatrix} = \begin{bmatrix} 1 & 0 \\ 4 & 1 \end{bmatrix}$$

In general, by induction $A^n = \begin{bmatrix} 1 & 0 \\ n/2 & 1 \end{bmatrix}$

$$\Rightarrow A^{50} = \begin{bmatrix} 1 & 0 \\ 25 & 1 \end{bmatrix}$$

4. The matrices $\begin{bmatrix} \cos\theta & -\sin\theta \\ \sin\theta & \cos\theta \end{bmatrix}$ and $\begin{bmatrix} a & 0 \\ 0 & b \end{bmatrix}$ commute under multiplication

(a) if $a = b$ or $\theta = n\pi$, where n is an integer

(b) always

(c) never

(d) if $a \cos\theta \neq b \sin\theta$

Solution: (a) $\begin{bmatrix} \cos\theta & -\sin\theta \\ \sin\theta & \cos\theta \end{bmatrix}\begin{bmatrix} a & 0 \\ 0 & b \end{bmatrix} = \begin{bmatrix} a\cos\theta & -b\sin\theta \\ a\sin\theta & b\cos\theta \end{bmatrix}$

and $\begin{bmatrix} a & 0 \\ 0 & b \end{bmatrix}\begin{bmatrix} \cos\theta & -\sin\theta \\ \sin\theta & \cos\theta \end{bmatrix} = \begin{bmatrix} a\cos\theta & -a\sin\theta \\ b\sin\theta & b\cos\theta \end{bmatrix}$

$a \sin\theta = b \sin\theta$

$\Rightarrow (a - b) \sin\theta = 0$

either $a = b$ or $\sin\theta = 0$

$\Rightarrow \theta = n\pi;\ n \in \mathbb{Z}$

5. Let $A = [\alpha_{ij}]$ be n-rowed square matrix and I_{12} be the matrix obtained by interchanging the first and second rows of the n-rowed identity matrix. Then AI_{12} is such that its first:

(a) row is the same as its second row

(b) row is the same as the second row of A

(c) column is the same as the second column of A

(d) row is all zero.

Solution: (c) $AI_{12} = \begin{bmatrix} a_{11} & a_{12} & \cdots & a_{1n} \\ a_{21} & a_{22} & \cdots & a_{2n} \\ \cdots & \cdots & \cdots & \cdots \\ a_{n1} & a_{n2} & \cdots & a_{nn} \end{bmatrix}\begin{bmatrix} 0 & 1 & \cdots & 0 \\ 1 & 0 & \cdots & 0 \\ \cdots & \cdots & \cdots & \cdots \\ 0 & 0 & \cdots & 1 \end{bmatrix}$

$$\begin{bmatrix} a_{12} & a_{11} & a_{13}\cdots & a_{1n} \\ a_{22} & a_{21} & a_{23}\cdots & a_{2n} \\ \cdots & \cdots & \cdots & \cdots \\ a_{n2} & a_{n1} & a_{n3}\cdots & a_{nn} \end{bmatrix}$$

$\Rightarrow$ First column is identical to second column of A.

6. Let $P = \begin{bmatrix} \frac{\sqrt{3}+1}{2\sqrt{2}} & \frac{\sqrt{3}-1}{2\sqrt{2}} \\ \frac{1-\sqrt{3}}{2\sqrt{2}} & \frac{\sqrt{3}+1}{2\sqrt{2}} \end{bmatrix}$, $A = \begin{bmatrix} i & 0 \\ 0 & i \end{bmatrix}$, and

$Q = P^TAP$, then $PQ^{2010}P^T$ is equal to

(a) $\begin{bmatrix} 2010 & 0 \\ 0 & 2010 \end{bmatrix}$ (b) $\begin{bmatrix} 0 & 2010 \\ 1 & 1 \end{bmatrix}$

(c) $\begin{bmatrix} i & 0 \\ 0 & i \end{bmatrix}$ (d) None of these

Solution: (d) Consider the product

$$PP^T = \begin{bmatrix} \frac{\sqrt{3}+1}{2\sqrt{2}} & \frac{\sqrt{3}-1}{2\sqrt{2}} \\ \frac{1-\sqrt{3}}{2\sqrt{2}} & \frac{\sqrt{3}+1}{2\sqrt{2}} \end{bmatrix}\begin{bmatrix} \frac{\sqrt{3}+1}{2\sqrt{2}} & \frac{1-\sqrt{3}}{2\sqrt{2}} \\ \frac{\sqrt{3}-1}{2\sqrt{2}} & \frac{\sqrt{3}+1}{2\sqrt{2}} \end{bmatrix}$$

$$= \begin{bmatrix} 1 & 0 \\ 0 & 1 \end{bmatrix} = I \qquad \text{......}(i)$$

Now, $Q = P^TAP$

$\Rightarrow Q^2 = (P^TAP)(P^TAP) = P^TA^2P$ $(\because$ of (i))

$\Rightarrow Q^3 = (P^TA^2P)(P^TAP) = P^TA^3P$ $(\because$ of (i))

$\Rightarrow Q^{2010} = P^TA^{2010}P$

$\Rightarrow P\,.\,Q^{2010}P^T = P.\,P^TA^{2010}P\,.\,P^T = A^{2010}$

$\Rightarrow [\because PP^T = I] \quad \Rightarrow \begin{bmatrix} i^{2010} & 0 \\ 0 & i^{2010} \end{bmatrix} = \begin{bmatrix} -1 & 0 \\ 0 & -1 \end{bmatrix}$

7. Let A be an $n \times n$ matrix such that $A^n = \alpha A$, where α is a real number different from 1 and –1. Then, the matrix $A + I_n$ is

(a) Singular

(b) non-singular, i.e., invertible

(c) Scalar matrix

(d) None of these

Solution: (b) Let $B = A + I_n$. Since $A = B - I_n$, the condition $A^n = \alpha A$ can be written in the form $(B-I_n)^n = \alpha(B - I_n)$

$\Rightarrow B^n - {}^nC_1B^{n-1} + {}^nC_2B^{n-2} + ... + (-1)^n I_n = \alpha B - \alpha I_n$

$\Rightarrow B^n - {}^nC_1B^{n-1} + {}^nC_2B^{n-2} + ... + (-1)^{n-1} B - \alpha B = -\alpha I_n - (-1)^n I_n$.

$\Rightarrow B(B^{n-1} - {}^nC_1 B^{n-2} + {}^nC_2B^{n-3} + ... + (-1)^{n-1} I_n - \alpha I_n) = [(-1)^{n+1} - \alpha]I_n$.

Since $(-1)^{n+1} - \alpha \neq 0$, $[\because \alpha \neq \pm 1]$

$\therefore$ B is invertible

8. If $A^k = O$ for some value of k and $B = I + A + A^2 + ... + A^{k-1}$, then B^{-1} equals

(a) $I - A$ (b) $I + A$

(c) $I - A^{k-1}$ (d) None of these

Solution: (a) Let $B = I + A + A^2 + A^3 + ... + A^{k-1}$

$\therefore$ $B(I - A) = (I + A + A^2 + ... + A^{k-1})(I - A)$

$= I - A + A - A^2 + A^2 + ... + A^{k-1} - A^k = I - A^k = I$

$(\because A^k = O)$

Hence, $(I - A)^{-1} = I + A + A^2 + ... + A^k - 1 = B$

$\Rightarrow B^{-1} = I - A$

9. If $a = \cos\theta + i \sin\theta$, $b = \cos 2\theta - i \sin 2\theta$, $c = \cos 3\theta + i \sin 3\theta$ and if $A = \begin{bmatrix} a & b & c \\ b & c & a \\ c & a & b \end{bmatrix}$, then find the values of θ if matrix A is non invertible

(a) $n\pi$; $n \in \mathbb{Z}$ (b) $2n\pi$; $n \in \mathbb{Z}$

(c) $(2n + 1)\pi/2$; $n \in \mathbb{Z}$ (d) None of these

Solution: (b) We have, $\begin{vmatrix} a & b & c \\ b & c & a \\ c & a & b \end{vmatrix} = 0$

$\Rightarrow -1/2\,(a + b + c)\,[(a - b)^2 + (b - c)^2 + (c - a)^2] = 0$

$\Rightarrow$ Either $a + b + c = 0$ or $a = b = c$

If $a + b + c = 0$, then we must have

$\Rightarrow \cos\theta + \cos 3\theta + \cos 2\theta = 0$ & $\sin\theta + \sin 3\theta - \sin 2\theta = 0$

or, $\cos 2\theta(2\cos\theta + 1) = 0$ &, $\sin 2\theta\,(2\cos\theta - 1) = 0$

The above equations do not hold simultaneously

$\Rightarrow$ As $\cos 2\theta = 0$. $\Rightarrow \sin 2\theta = \pm 1$.

$\Rightarrow 2\cos^2\theta - 1 = 0$ $\Rightarrow \cos^2\theta = 1/2$

$\Rightarrow \cos\theta = \pm 1/\sqrt{2}$

$\Rightarrow \cos\theta \neq 1/2$ and $\cos\theta = -1/2$

$\Rightarrow \cos\theta = -1/2$ $\Rightarrow \sin 2\theta \neq 0$

Therefore, the only possibilitiy is $a = b = c$.

or, $e^{i\theta} = e^{-2i\theta} = e^{3i\theta}$ which is satisfied only when

$e^{i\theta} = 1$, i.e., $\cos\theta + i \sin\theta = 1$

$\therefore$ $\cos\theta = 1$ and $\sin\theta = 0$

$\therefore$ $\theta = 2n\pi$; $n \in \mathbb{Z}$

10. For $A = \begin{bmatrix} a & b & c \\ d & e & f \\ g & h & i \end{bmatrix}$, $a, b, c, d, e, f, g, h, i \in C$,

we say $A^\theta = \begin{bmatrix} \bar{a} & \bar{d} & \bar{g} \\ \bar{b} & \bar{e} & \bar{h} \\ \bar{c} & \bar{f} & \bar{i} \end{bmatrix}$ and we say that A is the Hermitian matrix if $A = A^\theta$.

Suppose A is the Hermitian matrix such that $A^2 = O$ then

(a) $A = -A'$ (b) $A = A'$

(c) $A = O$ (d) $A = I$

Solution: $A = \begin{bmatrix} a & b & c \\ d & e & f \\ g & h & i \end{bmatrix}$

$A^2 = A\,.\,A = A\,A^\theta$ [$\because$ Given that $A = A^\theta$]

$\Rightarrow A^2 = \begin{bmatrix} a & b & c \\ d & e & f \\ g & h & i \end{bmatrix}\begin{bmatrix} \bar{a} & \bar{d} & \bar{g} \\ \bar{b} & \bar{e} & \bar{h} \\ \bar{c} & \bar{f} & \bar{i} \end{bmatrix}$

$$\Rightarrow \begin{bmatrix} |a|^2 + |b|^2 + |c|^2 & a\bar{d} + b\bar{e} + c\bar{f} & a\bar{g} + b\bar{h} + c\bar{i} \\ d\bar{a} + e\bar{b} + f\bar{c} & |d|^2 + |e|^2 + |f|^2 & d\bar{g} + e\bar{h} + f\bar{i} \\ g\bar{a} + h\bar{b} + i\bar{c} & g\bar{d} + h\bar{e} + i\bar{f} & |g|^2 + |h|^2 + |i|^2 \end{bmatrix} = \begin{bmatrix} 0 & 0 & 0 \\ 0 & 0 & 0 \\ 0 & 0 & 0 \end{bmatrix}$$

$(\because$ Given $A^2 = O)$

$\Rightarrow |a|^2 + |b|^2 + |c|^2 = 0$

$\Rightarrow Re(a) = Re(b) = Re(c) = Im(a) = Im(b) = Im(c) = 0$

Similarly

$Re(d) = Re(e) = Re(f) = Im(d) = Im(e) = Im(f) = 0$

and

$Re(g) = Re(h) = Re(i) = Im(g) = Im(h) = Im(i) = 0$

$\therefore$ $A = \begin{bmatrix} 0+0i & 0+0i & 0+0i \\ 0+0i & 0+0i & 0+0i \\ 0+0i & 0+0i & 0+0i \end{bmatrix}$

= Null matrix of order 3×3

11. Let A be a square matrix such that $A^2 = A$ and $|A| \neq 0$, then

(a) $A = -A'$ (b) $A = A'$

(c) $A' = -I$ (d) $AA' = I$

Solution: (b), (d) $A^2 = A$

$\because$ $|A| \neq 0$;

$\therefore$ Pre multiplying above equation by A^{-1} we get
$A^{-1}AA = A^{-1}A = I$ or $A = I$
Now If $A = I$
$\Rightarrow A^{-1} = AA^{-1} = I$
$\Rightarrow$ option (b) and (d) are correct.

12. Let A be as in above problem and $B = 4A - 2I$, where I is the identity matrix, then

(a) $B^2 = 4I$ (b) $B^2 = 2B$
(c) $B^2 = 4B$ (d) $B^2 = O$

Solution: (a), (b) $B = 4A - 2I = 4I - 2I = 2I$
$\Rightarrow B^2 = 4I^2 = 4I = 2B \quad \therefore \quad B^2 = 2B = 4I.$

13. Let A be a square matrix of order $n \times n$ and let P be a non-singular matrix, then which of the following matrices have the same characteristic roots.

(a) A and PA (b) A and AP
(c) A and $P^{-1}AP$ (d) None of these

Solution: (c) Let the characteristic root of A be λ.
$\Rightarrow |A - \lambda I| = 0$
For $P^{-1}AP$; $|P^{-1}AP - \lambda I| = |P^{-1}AP - \lambda P^{-1}PI|$
$= |P^{-1}|\,|A - \lambda I|\,|P| = |A - \lambda I|$.
$\Rightarrow \lambda$ is also characteristic roots of matrix $P^{-1}AP$

14. Let $C_k = {}^nC_k$ for $0 \le k \le n$ and $A_k = \begin{bmatrix} C_{k-1} & 0 \\ 0 & C_k \end{bmatrix}$ for $k \ge$ 1and $A_1A_2 + A_2A_3 + A_3A_4 + ..+A_{n-1}A_n = \begin{bmatrix} a & 0 \\ 0 & b \end{bmatrix}$, then

(a) $a = b$ (b) $a + b = 2 \times ({}^{2n}C_{n-1} - n)$
(c) $a = 2b$ (d) All of these

Solution: (a), (b) $A_k = \begin{bmatrix} C_{k-1} & 0 \\ 0 & C_k \end{bmatrix}$; $A_{k+1} = \begin{bmatrix} C_k & 0 \\ 0 & C_{k+1} \end{bmatrix}$

$$\Rightarrow A_kA_{k+1} = \begin{bmatrix} C_{k-1}C_k & 0 \\ 0 & C_kC_{k+1} \end{bmatrix}$$

$$\Rightarrow \sum_{k=1}^{n-1} A_kA_{k+1} = \begin{bmatrix} \sum_{k=1}^{n-1} C_{k-1}C_k & 0 \\ 0 & \sum_{k=1}^{n-1} C_kC_{k+1} \end{bmatrix}$$

Therefore $a = \sum_{k=1}^{n-1} C_{k-1}C_k$ and $b = \sum_{k=1}^{n-1} C_kC_{k+1}$
$\Rightarrow a = C_0C_1 + C_1C_2 + \ldots + C_{n-2}C_{n-1}$
and $b = C_1C_2 + C_2C_3 + \ldots + C_{n-2}C_{n-1} + C_{n-1}C_n$
Now, $C_0C_1 = C_{n-1}C_n$ [$\because C_0 = C_n$ and $C_{n-1} = C_1$]
$\therefore a = b$
To find 'a'

$(1 + x)^n = C_0x^0 + C_1x^1 + C_2x^2 + \ldots\ldots + C_{n-1}x^{n-1} + C_nx^n$
$(x + 1)^n = C_0x^n + C_1x^{n-1} + C_2x^{n-2} + \ldots\ldots + C_{n-1}x + C_nx^0$
Multiplying and equating coefficient of x^{n-1} on both sides ${}^{2n}C_{n-1} = C_0C_1 + C_1C_2 + \ldots\ldots + C_{n-1}C_n$
$\therefore C_1C_2 + C_2C_3 + \ldots\ldots + C_{n-1}C_n = a = b = {}^{2n}C_{n-1} - C_0C_1 = {}^{2n}C_{n-1} - n.$
$\Rightarrow a = b$ and $a + b = 2 \times ({}^{2n}C_{n-1} - n)$

Direction: The questions given below consist of an assertion (A) and the reason (R). Use the following key to choose the appropriate answer.

(a) If both assertion and reason are correct and reason is the correct explanation of the assertion.
(b) If both assertion and reason are correct but reason is not correct explanation of the assertion.
(c) If assertion is correct, but reason is incorrect
(d) If assertion is incorrect, but reason is correct

Now consider the following statements:

15. A: The possible dimensions of a matrix containing 32 elements is 6.
R: The number of ways of expressing 32 as a pro-duct of two positive integers is 6.

Solution: (c) $32 = 2^5$; Number of ways of expressing 32 as product of two positive integers $= \dfrac{5+1}{2} = 3$.
Possible dimensions of a matrix are $\{1 \times 32, 32 \times 1, 2 \times 16, 16 \times 2, 4 \times 8, 8 \times 4\} = 6$
$\Rightarrow A$ is true R is false

16. A : If $f_1(x), f_2(x), \ldots, f_9(x)$ are polynomials whose degree ≥ 1, where $f_1(\alpha) = f_2(\alpha) = f_3(\alpha) \ldots = f_9(\alpha) = 0$ and $A(x) = \begin{bmatrix} f_1(x) & f_2(x) & f_3(x) \\ f_4(x) & f_5(x) & f_6(x) \\ f_7(x) & f_8(x) & f_9(x) \end{bmatrix}$, then $\dfrac{A(x)}{x-\alpha}$ is also a matrix of 3×3 whose entries are also polynomials
R : $x - \alpha$ is a factor of polynomial $f(x)$ if $f(\alpha) = 0$.

Solution: (a) $f_1(\alpha) = f_2(\alpha) = \ldots = f_9(\alpha) = 0$
$\Rightarrow x - \alpha$ is a factor of $f_i(x)\ \forall\ i$

$$\Rightarrow A(x) = (x - \alpha)\begin{bmatrix} g_1(x) & g_2(x) & g_3(x) \\ g_4(x) & g_5(x) & g_6(x) \\ g_7(x) & g_8(x) & g_9(x) \end{bmatrix}$$

$\Rightarrow \dfrac{A(x)}{(x-\alpha)}$ is a 3×3 matrix having its entries as polynomials.

17. A: There are only finitely many 2×2 matrices which commute with the matrix $\begin{bmatrix} 1 & 2 \\ -1 & -1 \end{bmatrix}$

R: If A is non-singular, then it commutes with I, $Adj\ A$ and A^{-1}.

Solution: (d) The reason R is true since $AI = IA$, $AA^{-1} = A^{-1}A = I$, $A\ (adj\ A) = (adj.\ A)\ A = |A|\ I_n$

But a matrix can commute with general order matrices which may be infinite in number.

Let $B = \begin{bmatrix} a & b \\ c & d \end{bmatrix}$ be a matrix which commute with A,

then $AB = BA$.

$$\Rightarrow \begin{bmatrix} 1 & 2 \\ -1 & -1 \end{bmatrix}\begin{bmatrix} a & b \\ c & d \end{bmatrix} = \begin{bmatrix} a & b \\ c & d \end{bmatrix}\begin{bmatrix} 1 & 2 \\ -1 & -1 \end{bmatrix}$$

$$\Rightarrow \begin{bmatrix} a+2c & b+2d \\ -a-c & -b-d \end{bmatrix} = \begin{bmatrix} a-b & 2a-b \\ c-d & 2c-d \end{bmatrix}$$

$\Rightarrow a + 2c = a - b,\ b + 2d = 2a - b - a - c = c - d,$ $-b - d = 2c - d$

The above four relations are equivalent to only two independent relations $a - d = b$, $b + 2c = 0$

If $d = \lambda$, then $a = b + \lambda$, $b = -2c$

Thus, $\begin{bmatrix} \lambda - 2c & -2c \\ c & \lambda \end{bmatrix}$ are all possible 2×2 matrices which commute with given matrix $A = \begin{bmatrix} 1 & 2 \\ -1 & -1 \end{bmatrix}$

λ & c being any arbitrary complex numbers. Thus assertion is therefore false.

COLUMAN MATCHING TYPE

1. Match the matrix in column I with the equations satisfied by them in column II.

Column I	Column II
(i) $\begin{bmatrix} 0 & r & \beta \\ r & 0 & \alpha \\ \beta & \alpha & 0 \end{bmatrix}$	(a) $x^3 - (\alpha^2 + \beta^2 + r^2)x - 2\alpha\beta r = 0$
(ii) $\begin{bmatrix} 0 & \alpha & r \\ \alpha & 0 & \beta \\ r & \beta & 0 \end{bmatrix}$	(b) $x^3 + (\alpha^2 + \beta^2 + r^2)x = 0$
(iii) $\begin{bmatrix} 0 & \beta & \alpha \\ r & 0 & r \\ \alpha & \beta & 0 \end{bmatrix}$	(c) $x^2 + (\alpha^2 + \beta^2 + r^2) = 0$
(iv) $\begin{bmatrix} 0 & r & -\beta \\ -r & 0 & \alpha \\ \beta & -\alpha & 0 \end{bmatrix}$	(d) $x^4 - (\alpha^2 + \beta^2 + r^2)x^2 - 2\alpha\beta rx = 0$
	(e) None of these

Answers:

(i) → (a,d); (ii) → (a,d); (iii) → (e); (iv) → (b)

Solution: To find the characteristic equation of A

(i) $A = \begin{bmatrix} 0 & r & \beta \\ r & 0 & \alpha \\ \beta & \alpha & 0 \end{bmatrix}$

$$|A - \lambda I| = 0 \Rightarrow \begin{vmatrix} -\lambda & r & \beta \\ r & -\lambda & \alpha \\ \beta & \alpha & -\lambda \end{vmatrix} = 0$$

$\Rightarrow \lambda^3 - (\alpha^2 + \beta^2 + r^2)\lambda - 2\alpha\beta r = 0$

$\because$ A satisfies this equation i.e.,

$x^3 - (\alpha^2 + \beta^2 + r^2)x - 2\ \alpha\beta r = 0$ $\therefore$ option (a)

$\Rightarrow x^4 - (\alpha^2 + \beta^2 + r^2)x^2 - 2\ \alpha\beta rx = 0$ $\therefore$ option (d)

(ii) $A = \begin{bmatrix} 0 & \alpha & r \\ \alpha & 0 & \beta \\ r & \beta & 0 \end{bmatrix}$

$$|A - \lambda I| = 0 \Rightarrow \begin{vmatrix} -\lambda & \alpha & r \\ \alpha & -\lambda & \beta \\ r & \beta & -\lambda \end{vmatrix} = 0$$

$\Rightarrow \lambda^3 - (\alpha^2 + \beta^2 + r^2)\ \lambda - 2\alpha\beta r = 0$ $\therefore$ option (a)

$\Rightarrow x^3 - (\alpha^2 + \beta^2 + r^2)\ x - 2\alpha\beta r = 0$

$\Rightarrow x^4 - (\alpha^2 + \beta^2 + r^2)\ x^2 - 2\alpha\beta rx = 0$ $\therefore$ option (d)

(iii) $A = \begin{bmatrix} 0 & \beta & \alpha \\ r & 0 & r \\ \alpha & \beta & 0 \end{bmatrix}$

$$|A - \lambda I| = \begin{vmatrix} -\lambda & \beta & \alpha \\ r & -\lambda & r \\ \alpha & \beta & -\lambda \end{vmatrix} = 0$$

$\Rightarrow -\lambda^3 + 2\alpha\beta r + \lambda\alpha^2 + \lambda\beta r + \lambda\beta r = 0$

$\Rightarrow x^3 - (\alpha^2 + 2\beta r)x - 2\alpha\beta r = 0$ $\therefore$ option (e)

(iv) $A = \begin{bmatrix} 0 & r & -\beta \\ -r & 0 & \alpha \\ \beta & -\alpha & 0 \end{bmatrix}$

$$|A - \lambda I| = \begin{vmatrix} -\lambda & r & -\beta \\ -r & -\lambda & \alpha \\ \beta & -\alpha & -\lambda \end{vmatrix} = 0$$

$\Rightarrow \lambda^3 + (\alpha^2 + \beta^2 + r^2)\lambda = 0$

$\because$ A is skew symmetric matrix of odd order, $|A| = 0$

$\therefore$ A^{-1} does not exist and hence A satisfy $x^3 + (\alpha^2 + \beta^2 + r^2)x = 0$ and x cannot be factored out.

$\therefore$ option (b)

2. Suppose a, b, c, d are three distinct real numbers and $f(x)$ is a real cubic polynomial such that

$$\begin{bmatrix} a^3 & a^2 & a & 1 \\ b^3 & b^2 & b & 1 \\ c^3 & c^2 & c & 1 \\ d^3 & d^2 & d & 1 \end{bmatrix}\begin{bmatrix} f(0) \\ f(2) \\ f(3) \\ f(1) \end{bmatrix} = 3\begin{bmatrix} -a^3+5a^2+16a \\ -b^3+5b^2+16b \\ -c^3+5c^2+16c \\ -d^3+5d^2+16d \end{bmatrix}$$

Then based on the above information; match the entries from column I to their respective answers in column II

Column I

(i) If the difference in the value of x where $f(x)$ achieves its local maxima and local minima is given by k; then the value of $3k^2$ is.

(ii) If the area bounded by $f(x)$ in quadrant II is given by K then the value of K is

(iii) If the area bounded by $f(x)$ in quadrant III is given by k, then the value of $|4k|$ is

(iv) If the area bounded by f(x) in fourth quadrant is λ, then $|4\lambda|$ equals

(v) If α, β, γ are the roots of $f(x) = 0$; then find the value of $|\alpha\beta| + |\beta\gamma| + |\gamma\delta|$.

Column II

(a) 4

(b) 7

(c) 9

(d) 16

Answers: (i) – d, (ii) – a, (iii) – b, (iv) – c, (v) – b

Solution : From the information provided to us, we can conclude that $a^3(f(0)) + a^2(f(2)) + a(f(3)) + f(1) = -3a^3 + 15a^2 + 48a$

Similarly for b, c and d

$\therefore$ $x^3[f(0) + 3] + x^2[f(2) - 15] + x[f(3) - 48] + [f(1)] = 0$ is satisfy by a, b, c and d ....(i)

$\therefore$ The equation (i) being a cubic is being satisfied by 4 distinct real no.'s a,b,c & d and hence equation (i) must be an identity.

$\therefore$ We can get that $f(0) = -3$, $f(2) = 15$, $f(3) = 48$ & $f(1) = 0$

$\because$ $f(1) = 0$

$\therefore$ $(x - 1)$ must be a factor of $f(x)$

Let $f(x) = (x - 1)(Ax^2 + Bx + C)$

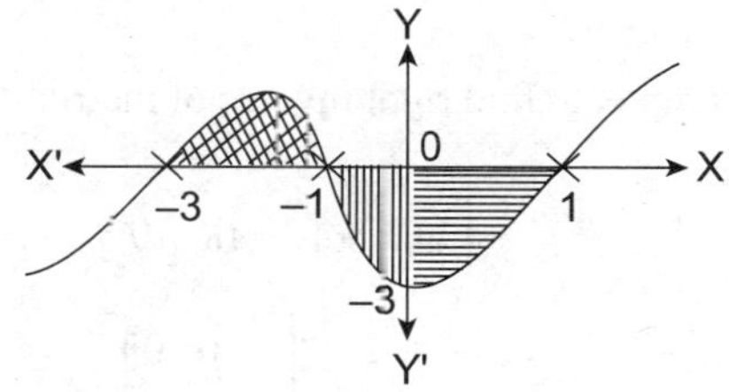

Solving for f(0)

$\Rightarrow (0 - 1)(C) = -3$

$\Rightarrow C = 3$

Similarly $A = 1$ and $B = 4$

$\therefore$ $f(x)$ is given by $(x - 1)(x^2 + 4x + 3)$

$\therefore$ $f(x) = (x - 1)(x + 1)(x + 3) = x^3 + 3x^2 - x - 3$

(i) $f'(x) = 0$

$\Rightarrow 3x^2 + 6x - 1 = 0$

Let θ, ϕ be the roots of this equation

$\therefore$ $|\theta - \phi| = \dfrac{\sqrt{D}}{|a|} = \dfrac{\sqrt{48}}{3} = k$

$\Rightarrow 3k^2 = 16$

(ii) $\displaystyle\int_{-3}^{-1} f(x)\,dx = \left[\left(\frac{x^4}{4} + x^3 - \frac{x^2}{2} - 3x\right)\right]_{-3}^{-1}$

$= \left(\frac{1}{4} - 1 - \frac{1}{2} + 3\right) - \left(\frac{81}{4} - 27 - \frac{9}{2} + 9\right) = 4$

(iii) $\displaystyle\int_{-1}^{0} f(x)\,dx = \left[\frac{x^4}{4} + x^3 - \frac{x^2}{2} - 3x\right]_{-1}^{0} = -\frac{7}{4} \Rightarrow |4k| = 7$

(iv) $\displaystyle\int_{0}^{1} f(x)\,dx = \left[\frac{x^4}{4} + x^3 - \frac{x^2}{2} - 3x\right]_{0}^{1}$

$= \frac{1}{4} + 1 - \frac{1}{2} - 3 = \frac{-9}{4}$

$\Rightarrow |4\lambda| = 9$

(v) Let $\alpha = -3$; $\beta = -1$; $\gamma = 1$

Then $|\alpha\beta| + |\beta\gamma| + |\alpha\gamma| = 7$

COMPREHENSION TYPE

Paragraph for questions 1–3

(A): Let A be an $m \times n$ matrix. If there exists a matrix L of type $n \times m$ such that $LA = I_n$, then L is called left inverse of A. Similarly, if there exists a matrix R of type $n \times m$ such that $AR = I_m$, then R is called right inverse of A.

For example, to find right inverse of matrix $A = \begin{bmatrix} 1 & -1 \\ 1 & 1 \\ 2 & 3 \end{bmatrix}$

we take $R = \begin{bmatrix} x & y & z \\ u & v & w \end{bmatrix}$ and solve $AR = I_3$

i.e., $\begin{bmatrix} 1 & -1 \\ 1 & 1 \\ 2 & 3 \end{bmatrix} \begin{bmatrix} x & y & z \\ u & v & w \end{bmatrix} = \begin{bmatrix} 1 & 0 & 0 \\ 0 & 1 & 0 \\ 0 & 0 & 1 \end{bmatrix}$

$\Rightarrow x - u = 1 \qquad y - v = 0 \qquad z - w = 0$

$x + u = 0 \qquad y + v = 1 \qquad z + w = 0$

$2x + 3u = 0 \qquad 2y + 3v = 0 \qquad 2z + 3w = 1$

As this system of equations is inconsistent, we say there is no right inverse for matrix A.

1. Which of the following matrices is NOT left inverse of matrix $\begin{bmatrix} 1 & -1 \\ 1 & 1 \\ 2 & 3 \end{bmatrix}$?

(a) $\begin{bmatrix} \frac{1}{2} & \frac{1}{2} & 0 \\ -\frac{1}{2} & \frac{1}{2} & 0 \end{bmatrix}$ (b) $\begin{bmatrix} 2 & -7 & 3 \\ -\frac{1}{2} & \frac{1}{2} & 0 \end{bmatrix}$

(c) $\begin{bmatrix} -\frac{1}{2} & \frac{1}{2} & 0 \\ -\frac{1}{2} & \frac{1}{2} & 0 \end{bmatrix}$ (d) $\begin{bmatrix} 0 & 3 & -1 \\ -\frac{1}{2} & \frac{1}{2} & 0 \end{bmatrix}$

2. The number of right inverses for the matrix $\begin{bmatrix} 1 & -1 & 2 \\ 2 & -1 & 1 \end{bmatrix}$

(a) 0 (b) 1
(c) 2 (d) infinite

3. For which of the following matrices number of left inverses is greater than the number of right inverses?

(a) $\begin{bmatrix} 1 & 2 & 4 \\ -3 & 2 & 1 \end{bmatrix}$ (b) $\begin{bmatrix} 3 & 2 & 1 \\ 3 & 2 & 1 \end{bmatrix}$

(c) $\begin{bmatrix} 1 & 4 \\ 2 & -3 \\ 5 & 4 \end{bmatrix}$ (d) $\begin{bmatrix} 3 & 3 \\ 1 & 1 \\ 4 & 4 \end{bmatrix}$

Solution:

1. (c) As 2nd row of all the options is same, we are to look at the elements of the first row. let left inverse be $\begin{bmatrix} a & b & c \\ d & e & f \end{bmatrix}$, then $\begin{bmatrix} a & b & c \\ d & e & f \end{bmatrix} \begin{bmatrix} 1 & -1 \\ 1 & 1 \\ 2 & 3 \end{bmatrix} = \begin{bmatrix} 1 & 0 \\ 0 & 1 \end{bmatrix}$

$\therefore\ a + b + 2c = 1, -a + b + 3c = 0$

i.e. $b = \dfrac{1-5c}{2},\ a = \dfrac{1+c}{2}$

Thus matrices in the options (a), (b) and (d) are the inverses and matrix in option (c) is not the left inverse.

2. (d) Let right inverse be $\begin{bmatrix} a & b \\ c & d \\ e & f \end{bmatrix}$

Now $a - c + 2e = 1 \quad \Rightarrow b - d + 2f = 0$

$\Rightarrow 2a - c + e = 0 \quad \Rightarrow 2b - d + f = 1$

$\therefore$ **infinite solution**

($\because$ a,c,e have two equations and b,d,f have two equations)

3. (c) By observation there cannot be any left inverse for (b) and (d) so we will check for (a) and (c) only.

For (a) let left inverse be $\begin{bmatrix} a & b \\ c & d \\ e & f \end{bmatrix}$, then

$\begin{bmatrix} a & b \\ c & d \\ e & f \end{bmatrix} \begin{bmatrix} 1 & 2 & 4 \\ -3 & 2 & 1 \end{bmatrix} = \begin{bmatrix} 1 & 0 & 0 \\ 0 & 1 & 0 \\ 0 & 0 & 1 \end{bmatrix}$

Now $a - 3b = 1$, $2a + 2b = 0$ and $4a + b = 0$ which is not possible

For (c) $\begin{bmatrix} a & b & c \\ d & e & f \end{bmatrix} \begin{bmatrix} 1 & 4 \\ 2 & -3 \\ 5 & 4 \end{bmatrix} = \begin{bmatrix} 1 & 0 \\ 0 & 1 \end{bmatrix}$

$\Rightarrow a + 2b + 5c = 1,\ 4a - 3b + 4c = 0,\ d + 2e + 5f = 0,\ 4d - 3e + 4f = 1$

$\therefore$ there are infinite number of left inverses.

$\begin{bmatrix} 1 & 4 \\ 2 & -3 \\ 5 & 4 \end{bmatrix} \begin{bmatrix} a & b & c \\ d & e & f \end{bmatrix} = \begin{bmatrix} 1 & 0 & 0 \\ 0 & 1 & 0 \\ 0 & 0 & 1 \end{bmatrix}$

$\Rightarrow a + 4d = 1$, $2a - 3d = 0$ and $5a + 4d = 0$. Which is not possible.

$\therefore$ There is no right inverse.

Paragraph for question 4-6

(B): There exists a matrix A satisfying $(A^{-1})^T = \lambda^2 A$ and B matrix satisfying $BB^T + (A^{-1})^T A^{-1} = O$. If C is a matrix such that $\lambda CA = AB$ where A, B and C are non singular square matrices of same odd order and $\lambda \neq 0$.

4. Value of CC^T is

(a) I (b) $\lambda^2 I$
(c) $-I$ (d) $-\lambda^2 I$

5. The value of $B^{-1} AA^T(B^{-1})^T$ is

(a) $-\lambda^2 I$ (b) $\lambda^2 I$

(c) $\frac{1}{\lambda^2}(-I)$ (d) $\frac{1}{\lambda^4}(-I)$

6. $|C|^2$ is equal to

(a) $|B|^2$ (b) $|AB|^2$

(c) $|A|^2$ (d) 1

Solution:

4. **(c)** $CA = \frac{AB}{\lambda} \Rightarrow C = \frac{ABA^{-1}}{\lambda} \Rightarrow C^T = \frac{(ABA^{-1})^T}{\lambda}$

$$\Rightarrow C.C^T = \frac{(ABA^{-1})(ABA^{-1})^T}{\lambda^2}$$

$$= (A\,B\,A^{-1} \cdot (A^{-1})^T B^T A^T)\,\frac{1}{\lambda^2}$$

$$= AB\,A^{-1}(A^T)^{-1}B^T A^T.\,\frac{1}{\lambda^2}$$

$$\left[\begin{array}{ll} \because & (A^{-1})^T = \lambda^2 A \\ \Rightarrow & A^{-1}(A^{-1})^T = \lambda^2 I \\ \Rightarrow & A^{-1}(AT)^{-1} = \lambda^2 I \\ \Rightarrow & (A^T.A)^{-1} = \lambda^2 I \\ \multicolumn{2}{l}{\text{Similarly}\,(A.A^T)^{-1} = \lambda^2 I} \end{array}\right]$$

$$= AB\,(A^TA)^{-1} B^T A^T \frac{1}{\lambda^2} = (AB(A^TA)^{-1} B^TA^T)\,\frac{1}{\lambda^2}$$

$$= (AB(\lambda^2 I)^{-1} B^TA^T)\,\frac{1}{\lambda^2}$$

$$= ABB^TA^T = A(BB^T)A^T = A(-\lambda^2 I)A^T$$

$$= (AA^T)(-\lambda^2) = \left(\frac{1}{\lambda^2} I\right)(-\lambda^2) = -I.$$

5. **(d)** $(A^{-1})^T.A^T = \lambda^2 AA^T \quad \Rightarrow (AA^{-1})^T = \lambda^2 AA^T$

$\Rightarrow AA^T = \frac{I}{\lambda^2}$ ....(i) $\quad \Rightarrow A^T(A^{-1})^T = \lambda^2 A^TA$

$\Rightarrow (A^{-1}A)^T = \lambda^2 A^TA$

$\Rightarrow A^TA = \frac{I}{\lambda^2}$ ....(ii); from (i) and (ii) $AA^T = A^TA$

Also $BB^T = -(AA^T)^{-1} = -\lambda^2 I$ ... (iii)

Now $B^{-1}AA^T(B^{-1})^T$

$$= B^{-1}\frac{I}{\lambda^2}(B^{-1})^T = \frac{1}{\lambda^2} B^{-1}(B^{-1})^T = \frac{1}{\lambda^2}(B^TB)^{-1}$$

$$\left[\begin{array}{ll} \because BB^T = -\lambda^2 I & \Rightarrow B^{-1}BB^T = -\lambda^2 B^{-1} \\ \Rightarrow B^T = -\lambda^2 B^{-1} & \Rightarrow B^T B = -\lambda^2 I \end{array}\right]$$

$$= \frac{1}{\lambda^2}(-\lambda^2 I)^{-1} = -\frac{}{}(I) = -\frac{1}{\lambda^4}(I)$$

6. **(b)** $|C|\,|A| = \frac{|AB|}{\lambda^{2n-1}}$ ....(i)

Let A and B are of $(2n + 1) \times (2n + 1)$ order

Also $|A||A^T| = \frac{1}{\lambda^{4n+2}} \left[\because AA^T = \frac{I}{\lambda^2}\right]$

$|A| = \frac{\pm 1}{\lambda^{2n+1}}$ ....(ii); $\therefore$ from (i) and (ii)

$|C| = \pm\,|AB| \Rightarrow |C|^2 = |AB|^2$

Paragraph for questions 7-9

(C): Let A be the set of all 3 x 3 symmetric matrices all of whose entries are either 0 or 1. Five of these entries are 1 and four of them are 0.

7. The number of matrices of A is :

(a) 12 (b) 6

(c) 9 (d) 3

8. The number of matrices in A for which the sytem of linear equation $A\begin{bmatrix} x \\ y \\ z \end{bmatrix} = \begin{bmatrix} 1 \\ 0 \\ 0 \end{bmatrix}$ has a unique solution is:

(a) less than 4

(b) at least 4 but less than 7

(c) at least 7 but less than 10

(d) at least 10

9. The number of matrices in A for which the system of linear equation A$\begin{bmatrix} x \\ y \\ z \end{bmatrix} = \begin{bmatrix} 1 \\ 0 \\ 0 \end{bmatrix}$ is inconsistent, is

(a) 0 (b) more than 2

(c) 2 (d) 1

Solution:

7. **(a)** Diagonal entries may be all one or two zero's and a one. If the diagonal entries are all 1, then two places for remaining two 1 can be selected in ${}^3C_1$ ways from one side of diagonal. If two of diagonal entries are 0, which can be seleted in ${}^3C_2$ ways, then one place for a zero can be selected in ${}^3C_1$ ways. Total number of possible matrices $= {}^3C_1 + {}^3C_2 \times {}^3C_1 = 12$.

8. **(b)** Let $A = \begin{bmatrix} a_{11} & a_{12} & a_{13} \\ a_{21} & a_{22} & a_{23} \\ a_{31} & a_{32} & a_{33} \end{bmatrix}$, then the system of equations is

$a_{11}x + a_{12}y + a_{13}z = 1$
$a_{21}x + a_{22}y + a_{23}z = 0$
$a_{31}x + a_{32}y + a_{33}z = 0$

For unique solution, $\Delta = \begin{bmatrix} a_{11} & a_{12} & a_{13} \\ a_{21} & a_{22} & a_{23} \\ a_{31} & a_{32} & a_{33} \end{bmatrix} \neq 0$

$\Rightarrow a_{11}a_{22}a_{33} - a_{11}(a_{23})^3 - a_{22}(a_{13})^2 - a_{33}(a_{12})^2 + 2a_{12}a_{13}$
$a_{23} \neq 0$ $(\because a_{ij} = a_{ji})$

Case I: Let all diagonal entries be 1,then
$\Delta = 1-(a_{23})^2 - (a_{13})^2 - (a_{12})^2 + 2a_{23}a_{13}a_{12}$
Now out of a_{23}, a_{13}, a_{12} exactly one is 1 and other two are zeros, so $\Delta = 0$.

Case II: Let two of the diagonal entries be 0.
Let $a_{11} = a_{22} = 0$, then $\Delta = a_{33}(a_{12})^2 + 2a_{23}a_{12}a_{13} \neq 0$
Provided $a_{12} \neq 0 \Rightarrow 2$ possibilities
Similarly for $a_{22} = a_{33} = 0$; $a_{11} \neq 0$ and $a_{11} = a_{33} = 0$; $a_{22} \neq 0$, we get total 6 cases for which $\Delta \neq 0$.

9. **(b)** The six matrix A of which $|A| = 0$ are

$\begin{vmatrix} 0 & 0 & 1 \\ 0 & 0 & 1 \\ 1 & 1 & 1 \end{vmatrix} \Rightarrow$ in consistent

$\begin{vmatrix} 0 & 1 & 0 \\ 1 & 1 & 1 \\ 0 & 1 & 0 \end{vmatrix} \Rightarrow$ in consistent

$\begin{vmatrix} 1 & 1 & 1 \\ 1 & 0 & 0 \\ 1 & 0 & 0 \end{vmatrix} \Rightarrow$ infinite solution

$\begin{vmatrix} 1 & 1 & 0 \\ 1 & 1 & 0 \\ 0 & 0 & 1 \end{vmatrix} \Rightarrow$ in consistent

$\begin{vmatrix} 1 & 0 & 1 \\ 0 & 1 & 0 \\ 1 & 0 & 1 \end{vmatrix} \Rightarrow$ in consistent

$\begin{vmatrix} 1 & 0 & 0 \\ 0 & 1 & 1 \\ 0 & 1 & 1 \end{vmatrix} \Rightarrow$ infinite solution

Paragraph for Questions 10 to 12

(D): Let p be an odd prime number and T_p be the following set of 2×2 matrices:

$$T_p = \left\{ A = \begin{bmatrix} a & b \\ c & a \end{bmatrix}; a, b, c \in \{0, 1, 2, \ldots, p-1\} \right\}$$

10. The number of A in T_p such that A is either symmetric or skew-symmetric or both, and det(A) divisible by p is
(a) $(p-1)^2$ (b) $2(p-1)$
(c) $(p-1)^2 + 1$ (d) $2p - 1$

11. The number of A in T_p such that the trace of A is not divisible by p but det(A) is divisible by p is
(a) $(p-1)(p^2 - p + 1)$ (b) $p^3 - (p-1)^2$
(c) $(p-1)^2$ (d) $(p-1)(p^2-2)$

12. The number of A in T_p such that det (A) is not divisible by p is
(a) $2p^2$ (b) $p^3 - 5p$
(c) $p^3 - 3p$ (d) $p^3 - p^2$

Solution:

10. (d) $A = \begin{bmatrix} a & b \\ c & a \end{bmatrix}$ where $a, b, c \in \{0, 1, 2, \ldots, p-1\}$

Case I: A is symmetric matrix $\Rightarrow b = c$
$\Rightarrow$ det(A) $= a^2 - b^2$ is divisible by p
$\Leftrightarrow (a - b)(a + b)$ is divisible by p
(a) $a - b$ is divisible by p if $a = b$, then 'p' cases are possible.
(b) $a + b$ is divisible by p if $a + b = p$, then $\frac{p-1}{2}$

$x^2 = (p-1)$ cases are possible.

Case II: A is skew symmetric matrix
If $a = 0$, $b + c = 0$, then det(A) $= b^2$
$\Rightarrow b^2$ can never be divisible by p. Except for $b = 0$
$\Rightarrow a = b = c = 0$, but this case is included in sub case(a) of case I
So no case is possible.
Total number of A is possible $= 2p - 1$.

11. (c) $a^2 - bc$ divisible by p; $2a$ is not divisible by p
$\Rightarrow a \neq 0$
Now, a can be chosen in $p - 1$ ways $(a \neq 0)$
$\because T_r(A) = 2a$ which is not divisible by 'p'
$\Rightarrow p \nmid 2a$ and p is odd prime
$\Rightarrow p \nmid a$ but $a \in \{0, 1, 2, \ldots, (p-1)\} \Rightarrow a \neq 0$
$\Rightarrow a$ has $(p-1)$ choices i.e., $1, 2, 3, \ldots (p-1)$
Now since $p \nmid$ det (A) $\Rightarrow p \nmid a^2 - bc$
However $p \nmid a$ thus $p \nmid a^2$. Hence $c, b \neq 0$ (otherwise p/a^2)
Leading to the fact that for b we are left with $(p-1)$ choices.
Now fixing a and b for $p/a^2 - bc$
a^2 and bc must leave same remainder when divided by p.

Let $a^2 = pq + r$ where r $\in \{1, 2,\ldots, P-1\}$

$$\left\{\begin{array}{l} if\ bc = mp + r\ \&\ bc_1 = m_1p + r \\ \Rightarrow bc - mp = bc_1 - m_1p \\ \Rightarrow c - \dfrac{mp}{b} = c_1 - \dfrac{m_1p}{b} \\ \Rightarrow c - c_1 = \dfrac{p}{b}(m - m_1) \end{array}\right\}$$

$\Rightarrow$ there will be unique choice of $c \in \{1,2,\ldots p-1\}$ for which bc when divided by p leave remainder r (i.e., same as of a^2) i.e., for different values of $c \in \{1, 2,\ldots, p-1\}$ after fixing b, bc gives different remainder

$\Rightarrow$ $\{1, 2,\ldots, p-1\}$ and there is unique c for which $bc = p.q_0 + r$

$\Rightarrow$ a and b can be chosen in $(p-1)(p-1) = (p-1)^2$ ways and corresponding to each pair of (a, b) there always exist unique choice of c

$\Rightarrow$ No of total matrices in $T_p = (p-1)^2$ so $(p-1)^2$.

12. (d) As = Total cases – ($a \neq 0$ and $|A|$ is divisible by p) – ($a = 0$ and $|A|$ is divisible by p) $= p^3 - (p-1)^2 - (2p-1) = p^3 - p^2$, since b and c both are coprime to p

$\Rightarrow$ one of them must be zero

If $b = 0$

$\Rightarrow$ c can be chosen from $\{0, 1, \ldots, p-1\}$

and If $c = 0$

$\Rightarrow$ b can be chosen from $\{0, 1, \ldots, p-1)$

Paragraph for Questions 13 to 16

Suppose A and B be two non-singular matrices, such that $AB = BA^m$ and $B^n = I$ and $A^p = I$, then answer the questions that follows.

13. If $m = 2$, $n = 5$, then p can be

(a) 32 (b) 31
(c) 62 (d) 91

Solution: (b, c) $B = A^{-1}BAA$

$B^5 = (A^{-1}BAA)(A^{-1}BAA)(A^{-1}BAA)(A^{-1}BAA)(A^{-1}BAA)$

$\Rightarrow I = A^{-1}B(AB)(AB)(AB)(AB)AA$

$\Rightarrow I = A^{-1}B(BA^2)(AB)(AB)(AB)AA$

$\Rightarrow I = A^{-1}B^2A^3\ BA\ BA\ BAA$

$\Rightarrow I = A^{-1}B^2(BA^7)\ BA\ BAA$

$\Rightarrow I = A^{-1}B^3(BA^{15})\ BAA$ $\Rightarrow I = A^{-1}B^4BA^{32}$

$\Rightarrow I = A^{-1}B^5A^{32}$ $\Rightarrow I = A^{-1}IA^{32}$

$\Rightarrow I = A^{-1}A^{32} = A^{31}$. and $A^{31}\ A^{31} = I$

$\Rightarrow A^{62} = I$

(Here we use $AB = BA^2 \Rightarrow A^2B = (AB)A^2 = BA^2$. $A^2 = BA^4$, in general $A^kB = BA^{2k}$)

14. If $m = 3$ and $n = 4$, then $p = ?$

(a) 80 (b) 81
(c) 83 (d) 127

Solution: (a) $B = A^{-1}B\ A\ A\ A$

$B^4 = (A^{-1}BAAA)(A^{-1}BAAA)(A^{-1}BAAA)(A^{-1}BAAA)$

$\Rightarrow I = A^{-1}BA(AB)AA\ BAA\ BAAA$

$\Rightarrow I = A^{-1}BA(BA^3)AA\ BAA\ BAAA$

$\Rightarrow I = A^{-1}BBA^8\ BA^2\ BA^3$

$\Rightarrow I = A^{-1}B^2\ BA^{24}\ A^2\ B\ A^3 \Rightarrow I = A^{-1}B^3\ B\ A^{78}\ A^3$

$\Rightarrow I = A^{-1}B^4BA^{81} = A^{-1}I\ A^{81} \Rightarrow I = A^{80}$.

(Here we use $AB = BA^3 \Rightarrow A^2B = (AB)A^3 = BA^3$. $A^3 = BA^6$ in general $A^kB = BA^{3k}$)

15. Which of the following represents the correct relation between m, n, p?

(a) $mn^2 = p$ (b) $p = m^n - 1$
(c) $p = n^m - 1$ (d) $p = m^{n-1}$.

Solution: (b) $B = A^{-1}B\ A^m$

$$B^n = \underbrace{A^{-1}BA^m\ A^{-1}BA^m \ldots\ldots A^{-1}BA^m}_{n\ times}$$

$$\Rightarrow \quad B^n = A^{-1}\underbrace{BA^{m-1}\ BA^{m-1}\ \ldots\ BA^{m-1}\ BA^{m-1}}_{(n)\ times}A \quad \text{and}$$

we know $AB = BA^m$

$\Rightarrow AAB = ABA^m = BA^{2m}$ $\Rightarrow AAAB = BA^{3m}$

Similarly: $A^xB = BA^{mx}$

$$\Rightarrow \quad B^n = I = A^{-1}BB\,(A)^{(m-1)m}\,A^{m-1}\underbrace{BA^{m-1}\ BA^{m-1}\ldots\ BA^{m-1}}_{(n-2)\ times}A$$

$$\Rightarrow \quad B^n = I = A^{-1}B^2\ (A)^{(m^2-1)}\underbrace{BA^{m-1}\ BA^{m-1}\ldots\ldots BA^{m-1}}_{(n-2)\ times}A$$

$$\Rightarrow \quad B^n = I = A^{-1}B^2\ (A)^{(m^2-1)m}\,A^{m-1}\underbrace{BA^{m-1}\ BA^{m-1}\ldots\ BA^{m-1}}_{(n-3)\ times}A$$

$$\Rightarrow \quad B^n = I = A^{-1}B^3\ (A)^{(m^3-1)}\underbrace{BA^{m-1}\ BA^{m-1}\ldots\ BA^{m-1}}_{(n-3)\ times}A$$

and similarly, we get $I = A^{-1}\ B^n\ (A)^{(m^n-1)}\ A$

$\Rightarrow I = A^{-1}A^{m^n}$ $(\because B^n = I)$

$\Rightarrow I = (A)^{(m^n-1)}$ $\Rightarrow p = m^n - 1$.

16. Which of the following ordered triplet (m, n, p) is false?

(a) (7, 4, 2400) (b) (5, 6, 15624)
(c) (13, 3, 2197) (d) (11, 4, 14640)

Solution: (c) Clearly $2197 \neq 13^3 - 1$.

TUTORIAL EXERCISE

SECTION–III

OBJECTIVE TYPE: (ONLY ONE CORRECT ANSWER)

1. If A and B are symmetric matrices, then ABA is
(a) symmetric matrix (b) skew symmetric
(c) diagonal matrix (d) scalar matrix

2. If the product of n matrices $\begin{bmatrix}1 & 1\\0 & 1\end{bmatrix}\begin{bmatrix}1 & 2\\0 & 1\end{bmatrix}\begin{bmatrix}1 & 3\\0 & 1\end{bmatrix}\cdots\cdots\begin{bmatrix}1 & n\\0 & 1\end{bmatrix}$ is equal to the matrix $\begin{bmatrix}1 & 378\\0 & 1\end{bmatrix}$, then the value of n is equal to
(a) 26 (b) 27
(c) 337 (d) 378

3. If $A = \begin{bmatrix}a & b\\c & d\end{bmatrix}$ satisfies the equation $x^2 - (a + b)x + k = 0$, then
(a) $k = bc$ (b) $k = a\,d$
(c) $k = a^2 + b^2 + c^2 + d^2$ (d) $cd = bc = 0$

4. Identify the incorrect statement in respect of two square matrices A and B conformable for sum and product.
(a) $t_r(A+B) = t_r(A) + t_r(B)$
(b) $t_r(\alpha A) = \alpha t_r(A)$
(c) $t_r(A^T) = t_r(A)$
(d) $t_r(AB) \neq t_r(BA)$

5. A and B are two given matrices such that the order of A is 3×4, if $A'B$ and BA' are both defined, then
(a) order of B' is 3×4 (b) order of $B'A$ is 4×4
(c) order of $B'A$ is 3×3 (d) $B'A$ is undefined

6. Matrix $A = \begin{bmatrix}x & 3 & 2\\1 & y & 4\\2 & 2 & z\end{bmatrix}$, if $x\,y\,z = 60$ and $8x + 4y + 3z = 20$, then $A(\text{adj } A)$ is equal to

(a) $\begin{bmatrix}64 & 0 & 0\\0 & 64 & 0\\0 & 0 & 64\end{bmatrix}$ (b) $\begin{bmatrix}88 & 0 & 0\\0 & 88 & 0\\0 & 0 & 88\end{bmatrix}$

(c) $\begin{bmatrix}68 & 0 & 0\\0 & 68 & 0\\0 & 0 & 68\end{bmatrix}$ (d) $\begin{bmatrix}34 & 0 & 0\\0 & 34 & 0\\0 & 0 & 34\end{bmatrix}$

7. Let $A + 2B = \begin{bmatrix}1 & 2 & 0\\6 & -3 & 3\\-5 & 3 & 1\end{bmatrix}$ and $2A - B = \begin{bmatrix}2 & -1 & 5\\2 & -1 & 6\\0 & 1 & 2\end{bmatrix}$, then $Tr\,(A) - Tr\,(B)$ has the value equal to
(a) 0 (b) 1
(c) 2 (d) None of these

8. The number of solutions of the matrix equation $X^2 = I$, other than I is
(a) 0 (b) 1
(c) 2 (d) more than 2

9. There are two possible values of A in the solution of the matrix equation $\begin{bmatrix}2A+1 & -5\\-4 & A\end{bmatrix}^{-1}\begin{bmatrix}A-5 & B\\2A-2 & C\end{bmatrix} = \begin{bmatrix}14 & D\\E & F\end{bmatrix}$ where A, B, C, D, E, F are real numbers. The absolute value of the difference of these two solutions is
(a) $\frac{8}{3}$ (b) $\frac{11}{3}$
(c) $\frac{1}{3}$ (d) $\frac{19}{3}$

10. Number of real values of λ for which the matrix $A = \begin{bmatrix}\lambda-1 & \lambda & \lambda+1\\2 & -1 & 3\\\lambda+3 & \lambda-2 & \lambda+7\end{bmatrix}$ has no inverse is
(a) 0 (b) 1
(c) 2 (d) infinite

11. Let three matrices $A = \begin{bmatrix}2 & 1\\4 & 1\end{bmatrix}$; $B = \begin{bmatrix}3 & 4\\2 & 3\end{bmatrix}$ and $C = \begin{bmatrix}3 & -4\\-2 & 3\end{bmatrix}$, then

$$t_r(A) + t_r\left(\frac{ABC}{2}\right) + t_r\left(\frac{A(BC)^2}{4}\right) + t_r\left(\frac{A(BC)^3}{8}\right) + \ldots + \infty =$$

(a) 6 (b) 9
(c) 12 (d) None of these

12. If A and B are different matrices satisfying $A^3 = B^3$ and $A^2B = B^2A$, then
(a) $\det(A^2 + B^2)$ must be zero
(b) $\det(A - B)$ must be zero

(c) $\det(A^2 + B^2)$ as well as $\det(A - B)$ must be zero

(d) At least one of $\det(A^2 + B^2)$ and $\det(A - B)$ must be zero.

13. Let the matrix A and B be defined as $A = \begin{bmatrix} 3 & 2 \\ 2 & 1 \end{bmatrix}$ and $B = \begin{bmatrix} 3 & 1 \\ 7 & 3 \end{bmatrix}$, then the value of Det. $(2A^9B^{-1})$, is

(a) 2 (b) 1

(c) – 1 (d) – 2

14. For a matrix $A = \begin{bmatrix} 1 & 2r-1 \\ 0 & 1 \end{bmatrix}$, the values of $\prod_{r=1}^{50} \begin{bmatrix} 1 & 2r-1 \\ 0 & 1 \end{bmatrix}$ is equal to

(a) $\begin{bmatrix} 1 & 100 \\ 0 & 1 \end{bmatrix}$ (b) $\begin{bmatrix} 1 & 4950 \\ 0 & 1 \end{bmatrix}$

(c) $\begin{bmatrix} 1 & 5050 \\ 0 & 1 \end{bmatrix}$ (d) $\begin{bmatrix} 1 & 2500 \\ 0 & 1 \end{bmatrix}$

15. Let $A = \begin{bmatrix} a & b & c \\ p & q & r \\ x & y & z \end{bmatrix}$ and suppose that det. $(A) = 2$, then the det. (B) equals, where $B = \begin{bmatrix} 4x & 2a & -p \\ 4y & 2b & -q \\ 4z & 2c & -r \end{bmatrix}$

(a) $\det(B) = -2$ (b) $\det(B) = -8$

(c) $\det(B) = -16$ (d) $\det(B) = 8$

16. If $A = \begin{bmatrix} a & 1 \\ -1 & b \end{bmatrix}$; where a and b are real numbers and A^2 is null matrix, then the product ab equals

(a) 0 (b) 1

(c) –1 (d) ±1

17. Let $\Delta_0 = \begin{vmatrix} a_{11} & a_{12} & a_{13} \\ a_{21} & a_{22} & a_{23} \\ a_{31} & a_{32} & a_{33} \end{vmatrix}$ and let Δ_1 denotes the determinant formed by the cofactors of elements of Δ_0 and Δ_2 denotes the determinant formed by the cofactors of Δ_1 and so on Δ_n denotes deteminatnt formed by the cofactors of Δ_{n-1}, then the determinant value of Δ_n is

(a) Δ_0^{2n} (b) $\Delta_0^{2^n}$

(c) $\Delta_0^{n^2}$ (d) Δ_0^2

18. If $A = \begin{bmatrix} 1 & \tan x \\ -\tan x & 1 \end{bmatrix}$, then the value of $|A^T A^{-1}|$ is

(a) $\cos 4x$ (b) $\sec^2 x$

(c) $-\cos 4x$ (d) 1

19. If $A = \begin{bmatrix} 1 & 0 & 0 \\ 0 & 1 & 0 \\ a & b & -1 \end{bmatrix}$, then A^2 is equal to

(a) unit matrix (b) null matrix

(c) A (d) $-A$

20. If $A = \begin{bmatrix} a & 0 & 0 \\ 0 & a & 0 \\ 0 & 0 & a \end{bmatrix}$, then $|A|\,|Adj\,A|$ is equal to

(a) a^{25} (b) A^{27}

(c) a^{81} (d) None of these

21. If A and B are two square matrices of the same order and m is a positive integer, then $(A + B)^m = {}^mC_0A^m + {}^mC_1A^{m-1}B + {}^mC_2A^{m-2}B^2 + ... + {}^mC_{m-1}A\,B^{m-1} + {}^mC_mB^m$ if

(a) $AB = BA$ (b) $AB + BA = O$

(c) $A^m = O, B^m = O$ (d) None of these

22. If $A = (a_{ij})_{3\times 3}$ is a skew symmetric matrix, then

(a) $a_{ii} = 0, \forall i$ (b) $A-A'$ is null matrix

(c) $|A| \neq 0$ (d) None of these

23. If a matrix A is symmetric as well as skew symmetric, then A is a

(a) diagonal matrix (b) null matrix

(c) unit matrix (d) None of these

24. If A and B are symmetric matrices of the same order, then

(a) AB is a symmetric matrix

(b) $A - B$ is skew -symmetric matrix

(c) $AB + BA$ is a symmetric matrix

(d) $AB - BA$ is symmetric matrix

25. Matrix A has m rows and $n + 5$ columns; matrix B has m rows and $11 - n$ columns. If both AB and BA exist, then

(a) AB and BA are square matrices

(b) AB and BA are of order 8×8 and 3×13 respectively

(c) $AB = BA$

(d) None of these

26. Let A,B be two square matrices of the same dimension and let $[A, B] = AB - BA$, then for three 2×2 matrices A,B,C, $[\,[A, B],C] + [\,[\,B, C], A] + [\,[C,A], B]$ is equal to

(a) 1 (b) 0
(c) $ABC - CBA$ (d) None of these

27. If the matrices $A, B, (A + B)$ are non-singular, then $\left[A(A+B)^{-1}B\right]^{-1}$ is equal to
(a) $A + B$ (b) $A^{-1} + B^{-1}$
(c) $(A + B)^{-1}$ (d) None of these

28. If A and B matrices commute (given that A and B are non-singular), then
(a) A^{-1} and B also commute
(b) B^{-1} and A also commute
(c) A^{-1} and B^{-1} also commute
(d) All the above

29. Trace of a skew symmetric matrix is always equal to
(a) $\sum a_{ij}$ (b) $\sum a_{ii}$
(c) zero (d) None of these

30. The number of non-zero diagonal matrices of order 4 satisfying $A^2 = A$ is
(a) 2 (b) 4
(c) 16 (d) 15

31. If $A = \begin{bmatrix} 0 & c & -b \\ -c & 0 & a \\ b & -a & 0 \end{bmatrix}$ and $B = \begin{bmatrix} a^2 & ab & ac \\ ab & b^2 & bc \\ ac & bc & c^2 \end{bmatrix}$, then AB is equal to
(a) A^3 (b) B^2
(c) O (d) I

32. Let A be a square matrix of order 3 such that transpose of inverse of A is A itself, then $|adj\ (adj\ A)|$ is equal to
(a) 9 (b) 27
(c) 4 (d) 1

33. If $A = \begin{bmatrix} \alpha & a \\ \beta & b \\ \gamma & c \end{bmatrix}$, then AA^T is
(a) a non-singular matrix
(b) a symmetric matrix
(c) an identity matrix
(d) None of these

34. If A and B are two square matrices, such that $AB = O$, then which of the following is possible?
(a) A and B both can be non-singular matrices
(b) Neither A nor B can be null matrix
(c) If A be a non-singular matrix, then B cannot be a null matrix
(d) det $B = 0$

35. Let $C_k = {}^nC_k$ for $0 \le k \le n$ and $A_k = \begin{bmatrix} C_{k-1}^2 & 0 \\ 0 & C_k^2 \end{bmatrix}$ for $k \ge 1$ and $A_1 + A_2 + ... + A_n = \begin{bmatrix} k_1 & 0 \\ 0 & k_2 \end{bmatrix}$, then
(a) $k_1 = k_2$ (b) $k_1 + k_2 = {}^{2n}C_{2n} + 1$
(c) $k_1 = {}^{2n}C_{n-1}$ (d) $k_2 = {}^{2n}C_{n+1}$

36. If A and B are two square matrices such that $B = -A^{-1}BA$, then $(A + B)^2$ is equal to
(a) O (b) $A^2 + B^2$
(c) $A^2 + 2AB + B^2$ (d) $A + B$

37. If $A = \begin{bmatrix} x & 2 & -1 \\ -1 & 1 & 2 \\ 2 & -1 & 1 \end{bmatrix}$; $\left(x \ne \frac{-11}{3}\right)$ and det $(adj\ (adj\ A)) = (14)^4$. Then the value of x is
(a) 2 (b) –2
(c) 0 (d) None of these

38. Let A and B be two 2×2 matrices, consider the statements:
(i) $AB = O \Rightarrow A = O$ or $B = O$
(ii) $AB = I_2 \Rightarrow A = B^{-1}$; provided B is non-singular
(iii) $(A + B)^2 = A^2 + 2AB + B^2$, then
(a) (i) is false, (ii) and (iii) are true
(b) (i) and (iii) are false, (ii) is true
(c) (i) and (ii) are false, (iii) is true
(d) (ii) and (iii) are false, (i) is ture

39. The inverse of a skew symmetric matrix of odd order is
(a) a symmetric matrix (b) a skew symmetric matrix
(c) diagonal matrix (d) does not exist

40. Give the correct order of initials T or F for the following statemtnts. Use T if statement is true and F if it is false.
Statement - 1 : If A is an invertible 3×3 matrix and B is a 3×4 marix, then $A^{-1}B$ is defined.
Statement - 2 : It is never true that $A + B$, $A - B$, and AB are all defined.
Statement - 3 : Every matrix none of whose entries are zero is invertible.
Statement - 4 : Every invertible matrix is square and has no two rows the same.
(a) TFFF
(b) TTFF
(c) TFFT
(d) TTTF

SECTION–IV

OBJECTIVE TYPE (MORE THAN ONE CORRECT ANSWERS)

1. If matrix $A = \begin{bmatrix} a & b & c \\ b & c & a \\ c & a & b \end{bmatrix}$, where a, b, c are real number, $abc = 1$ and $A^TA = I$, then which of the following is/are possible.

(a) $a + b + c = 1$ (b) $a^2 + b^2 + c^2 = 1$
(c) $ab + bc + ca = 0$ (d) $a^3 + b^3 + c^3 = 4$

2. If A and B are 3×3 matrices and $|A| \neq 0$, then which of the following are true ?

(a) $|AB| = 0 \Rightarrow |B| = 0$
(b) $|AB| = 0 \Rightarrow B = O$
(c) $|A^{-1}| = |A|^{-1}$
(d) $|A + A| = 2|A|$

3. If D_1 and D_2 are two 3×3 diagonal matrices where none of the diagonal elements is zero, then

(a) D_1D_2 is a diagonal matrix
(b) $D_1D_2 = D_2D_1$
(c) $D_1^2 + D_2^2$ is a diagonal matrix
(d) None of these

4. If A and B are two matrices such that their product AB is a null matrix, then

(a) det $A \neq 0 \Rightarrow B$ must be a null matrix.
(b) det $B \neq 0 \Rightarrow A$ must be a null matrix.
(c) Atleast one of the two matrices must be singular.
(d) If neither det. A nor det. B is zero, then the given statement is not possible.

5. If a,b and c are all different from zero, such that $\frac{1}{a}+\frac{1}{b}+\frac{1}{c}=0$, then the matrix $A = \begin{bmatrix} 1+a & 1 & 1 \\ 1 & 1+b & 1 \\ 1 & 1 & 1+c \end{bmatrix}$ is

(a) symmetric
(b) non -singular
(c) can be written as sum of a symmetric and a skew symmetric matrix
(d) None of these

6. The system $AX = B$ of n equations in n unknowns has infinitely many solutions if

(a) det $A \neq 0$ (b) (adj$A$)$B \neq O$
(c) det $A = 0$ (d) (adj$A$)$B = O$

7. If, for a square matrix, $A = [a_{ij}]$ of even order, $a_{ij} = i^2 - j^2$, then

(a) A is skew - symmetric
(b) $|A|$ is a perfect square
(c) A is symmetric and $|A| = 0$
(d) A is neither symmetric nor skew symmetric

8. If A,B and C are three square matrices of the same order, then $AB = AC \Rightarrow B = C$ if

(a) $|A| \neq 0$ (b) A is invertible
(c) A is orthogonal (d) A is symmetric

SECTION–V

ASSERTION AND REASON TYPE

The questions given below consist of an assersion (A) and the reason (R). Use the following key to choose the appropriate answer.

(a) If both assertion and reason are correct and reason is the correct explanation of the assertion.
(b) If both assertion and reason are correct but reason is not correct explanation of the assertion.
(c) If assertion is correct, but reason is incorrect.
(d) If assertion is incorrect, but reason is correct.

Now consider the following statements:

1. A : If a 2×2 matrix A is such that $AB = BA$ for every 2×2 matrix B, then A must be a scalar matrix.
R : Every 2×2 matrix is conformable for multiplication with every 2×2 matrix.

2. A : If D = diag$[d_1, d_2, d_3 \ldots d_n]$; $d_j \neq 0\ \forall\ i$, then $D^{-1} = diag\ [d_1^{-1}, d_2^{-1} \ldots, d_n^{-1}]$
R : If $D = diag[d_1, d_2, d_3, \ldots, d_n]$, then D^n = diag $[d_1^n, d_2^n, d_3^n, \ldots, d_n^n]$

3. **A :** If a,b,c are real numbers with $abc = 1$ and $AA^T = I$, where $A = \begin{bmatrix} a & b & c \\ b & c & a \\ c & a & b \end{bmatrix}$, then $a^3 + b^3 + c^3 = 4$ or 2.

R : $\frac{1}{a}+\frac{1}{b}+\frac{1}{c}=0$.

4. Let X be any matrix of order $m \times n$, where $n < m$ and not all elements of X are zeros, then

A: $|XX^T|$ will be a singular matrix

R: $|XX^T|$ will be the product of two determinants, where each one of them is zero.

5. **A :** A matrix $[a_{ij}]_{3\times 3}$, $a_{ij} = \frac{i-j}{i+2j}$ can not be expressed as sum of symmetric and skew symmetric

R : A matrix $[a_{ij}]_{3\times 3}$, $a_{ij} = \frac{i-j}{i+2j}$ is neither symmetric nor skew symmetric.

SECTION–VI

LINKED COMPREHENSION TYPE

A: Consider a system of linear equations in three variables x,y,z

$a_1x + b_1y + c_1z = d_1$; $a_2x + b_2y + c_2z = d_2$;
$a_3x + b_3y + c_3z = d_3$;
which can be expressed by the matrix equation

$$\begin{bmatrix} a_1 & b_1 & c_1 \\ a_2 & b_2 & c_2 \\ a_3 & b_3 & c_3 \end{bmatrix}\begin{bmatrix} x \\ y \\ z \end{bmatrix} = \begin{bmatrix} d_1 \\ d_2 \\ d_3 \end{bmatrix} \text{ or } AX = B$$

If A is non -singular matrix then the unique solution of above system can be found by $X = A^{-1}B$.
If A is a singular matrix i.e. $|A| = 0$, then the system will have infinite number of solutions, if $(Adj\ A)\ B = O$ and the system has no solution (i.e., it is inconsistent) if $(Adj\ A)\ B \neq O$, where $(Adj\ A)$ is the adjoint of the matrix A,
which is obtained by taking transpose of the matrix obtained by replacing each element of matrix A with corresponding co-factors.
Now, consider the following matrices $A = \begin{bmatrix} a & 1 & 0 \\ 1 & b & d \\ 1 & b & c \end{bmatrix}; B = \begin{bmatrix} a & 1 & 1 \\ 0 & d & c \\ f & g & h \end{bmatrix}; U = \begin{bmatrix} f \\ g \\ h \end{bmatrix}; V = \begin{bmatrix} a^2 \\ 0 \\ 0 \end{bmatrix}; X = \begin{bmatrix} x \\ y \\ z \end{bmatrix}$

1. The system $AX = U$ has infinitely many solutions if
(a) $c = d$; $ab = 1$ (b) $c = d, h = g$
(c) $ab = 1, h = g$ (d) $c = d, h = g, ab = 1$

2. If $AX = U$ has infinitely many solutions, then the equation $BX = V$ has
(a) unique solution
(b) infinitely many solutions
(c) no solution
(d) either infinitely many or no solution

3. If $AX = U$ has infinitely many solutions, then the equation $BX = V$ is consistent if
(a) $a = 0$ (b) $d = 0$
(c) $f = 0$ (d) $adf \neq 0$

B: If $A = \begin{bmatrix} 1 & 0 & 0 \\ 2 & 1 & 0 \\ 3 & 2 & 1 \end{bmatrix}$ and U_1, U_2, U_3 are column matrices satisfying

$AU_1 = \begin{bmatrix} 1 \\ 0 \\ 0 \end{bmatrix}, AU_2 = \begin{bmatrix} 2 \\ 3 \\ 0 \end{bmatrix}, AU_3 = \begin{bmatrix} 2 \\ 3 \\ 1 \end{bmatrix}$ and U is 3×3 matrix whose coloumns are U_1, U_2, U_3, then answer the following questions based on above passage

4. The value of $|U|$ is
(a) 3 (b) –3
(c) 3/2 (d) 2

5. The sum of the elements of U^{-1} is
(a) –1 (b) 0
(c) –1 (d) 3

6. The value of $[3, 20]\ U \begin{bmatrix} 3 \\ 2 \\ 0 \end{bmatrix}$ is
(a) [5] (b) [5/2]
(c) [4] (d) [3/2]

C: There exists a matrix B such that $ABA^T = N$, where $A = \begin{bmatrix} 1 & 2 & 0 \\ 2 & 1 & 0 \\ 0 & 0 & 1 \end{bmatrix}$ and N is a diagonal matrix of the form N = diagonal (n_1, n_2, n_3); n_1, n_2, n_3 are three values of n satisfying $\det(A - nI) = 0; (n_1 > n_2 > n_3)$

7. Three roots of n are
(a) 0, 1, 2 (b) –1, 1, 3
(c) –2, 2, 3 (d) –3, 1, 5

8. Matrix A satisfies
(a) $A^2-(n_1+n_2)A+n_1n_2I=O$
(b) $A^2-(n_1+n_2)A+n_1n_3I=O$
(c) $A^2-(n_1+n_2)A+n_2n_3I=O$
(d) None of these

9. The matrix B is
(a) symmetric (b) scalar
(c) skew Hermitian (d) skew-symmetric

10. Trace of matrix A^k is
(a) $3^k+1+(-1)^k$ (b) 2^k+3^k-2
(c) 3^k-2^k+2 (d) 2^k+1

11. The value of det B is
(a) –9 (b) –1/3
(c) –81 (d) –1/243

12. Consider the principle diagonal elements of B as (b_1, b_2, b_3) such that $b_1>b_2>b_3$, then the value of λ for which $b_1, b_2, (b_3\lambda)$ are in G.P.
(a) 3 (b) 1
(c) –1/3 (d) 81/91

SECTION–VII

MATRIX MATCH TYPE

1. If A is non-singular matrix of order $n \times n$, then

Column I	Column II
(i) $\text{adj}(A^{-1})$ is equals	(a) $\|A\|^{n-1}(adj\ A)$
(ii) $\|\text{adj}(A)^{-1}\|$ is equals	(b) $\frac{A}{\|A\|}$
(iii) $adj(\|A\|A)$ is equals	(c) $\|A\|^{n-2}A$
(iv) $adj(\text{adj}A)$ is equals	(d) $\frac{adj(adjA)}{\|A\|^{n-1}}$
	(e) $\|A\|^{1-n}$

2. A is a square matrix such that

Column - I	Column - II
(i) $A^2=A$	(a) involutary matrix
(ii) $A^m=O$	(b) idempotent matrix
(iii) $A^2=I$	(c) symmetric matrix
(iv) $A^T=A$	(d) nilpotent matrix

3. **Column I**
(i) If A, B and C be 2 × 2 matrices with entries from the set of real numbers. Define * as follows $A*B=\frac{1}{2}(AB+BA)$, then
(ii) If A, B and C be 2 × 2 matrices with entries from the set of real numbers. Define * as follows $A*B=\frac{1}{2}(AB'+A'B)$, then
(iii) If A, B and C be 2 × 2 matrices with entries from the set of real numbers. Define * as follows $A*B=\frac{1}{2}(AB-BA)$, then

Column II
(a) $A*B=B*A$
(b) $A*(B+C)=A*B+A*C$
(c) $A*A=A^2$
(d) $A*I=A$
(e) $A*I=O$

SECTION–VIII

INTEGER TYPE

1. If $\alpha, \beta, \gamma \in (0, \pi/2)$ and $\begin{bmatrix} 0 & 2\sin\beta & \tan\gamma \\ \cos\alpha & \sin\beta & \tan\gamma \\ \cos\alpha & -\sin\beta & \tan\gamma \end{bmatrix}$ is orthogonal, then find $\frac{\alpha+\gamma}{5\pi}$

2. Let $A=[a_{ij}]_{3\times3}$ be a square matrix whose elements are distinct integers from 1, 2,....,9. The matrix is formed so that the sum of numbers in every row, column and each diagonal is a multiple of 9. Find the number of all such possible matrices.

3. Let X be the solution set of the equation $A^x=I$; where $A=\begin{bmatrix} 2 & -1 \\ 3 & -2 \end{bmatrix}$ and I is the corresponding unit matrix and $x \in \mathbb{N}$, then find the minimum value of $\Sigma(\cos^x\theta+\sin^x\theta),\ \theta \in \mathbb{R}-\left\{\frac{n\pi}{2}; n \in \mathbb{Z}\right\}$.

4. The matrix $A = \begin{bmatrix} a & b & c \\ b & c & a \\ c & a & b \end{bmatrix}$ where a, b, c are real positive numbers, $abc = 1$ and $A^TA = I$, then find the sum of all possible values of $a^3 + b^3 + c^3$.

5. Let a, b, c, d be real numbers in G.P. If u, v, w satisfy the system of equations, $u + 2v + 3w = 6$, $4u + 5v + 6w = 12$, $6u + 9v = 4$. Also, if it is known that the roots of the equation $\left(\frac{1}{u}+\frac{1}{v}+\frac{1}{w}\right)x^2 + [(b-c)^2 + (c-a)^2 + (d-b)^2]x + u + v + w = 0$ and $20x^2 + k(a-d)^2x - 9 = 0$ are reciprocals of each other. Then find the of value of k.

6. $A = \begin{bmatrix} \sin\theta & \cos\theta & \sin 2\theta \\ \sin(\theta+2\pi/3) & \cos(\theta+2\pi/3) & \sin(2\theta+4\pi/3) \\ \sin(\theta-2\pi/3) & \cos(\theta-2\pi/3) & \sin(2\theta-4\pi/3) \end{bmatrix}$, then find $|A|$ for all values of θ.

7. Consider the system of linear equations in x, y, z : $(\sin 3\theta)x - y + z = 0$, $(\cos 2\theta)\, x + 4y + 3z = 0$, $2x + 7y + 7z = 0$. If the values of θ for which this system has nontrivial solutions are given by $n\pi$, $n\pi + (-1)^n \pi/k$, then find the value of k.

8. If the system of equations $2x - 3y + 5z = 12$, $3x + y + \lambda z = \mu$, $x - 7y + 8z = 17$ has infinitely many real solutions, then evaluate $\lambda + \mu$

9. Let (x, y, z) be points with integer coordinates satisfying the system of homogeneous equations: $3x - y - z = 0$, $-3x + z = 0$, $-3x + 2y + z = 0$. Then find the number of such points for which $x^2 + y^2 + z^2 \le 100$.

10. Find the number of 3×3 matrices A whose entries are either 0 or 1 and for which the system:

$$A\begin{bmatrix} x \\ y \\ x \end{bmatrix} = \begin{bmatrix} 1 \\ 0 \\ 0 \end{bmatrix}$$ has exactly two distinct solutions.

11. Let k be positive real number and let

$$A = \begin{bmatrix} 2k-1 & 2\sqrt{k} & 2\sqrt{k} \\ 2\sqrt{k} & 1 & -2k \\ -2\sqrt{k} & 2k & -1 \end{bmatrix} \ \&\ B = \begin{bmatrix} 0 & 2k-1 & \sqrt{k} \\ 1-2k & 0 & 2\sqrt{k} \\ -\sqrt{k} & -2\sqrt{k} & 0 \end{bmatrix}$$

If det (Adj. A) + det (Adj. B) = 10^6, then find $[k]$,.

12. Let $a, b, c \in \mathbb{R}^+$ and the system of equations $(1-a)x + y + z = 0$, $x + (1-b)y + z = 0$, $x + y\,(1-c)z = 0$ has infinitely many solutions, then find the minimum value of 'abc'.

13. Find the number of values of k for which the system of equations $(k+1)x + 8y = 4k$, $kx + (k+3)y = 3k - 1$ has infinitely many solutions.

Answer Key

SECTION III

1. (a) **2.** (b) **3.** (d) **4.** (d) **5.** (b) **6.** (c) **7.** (c) **8.** (d) **9.** (d) **10.** (d)
11. (a) **12.** (d) **13.** (d) **14.** (d) **15.** (c) **16.** (c) **17.** (b) **18.** (d) **19.** (a) 20 (d)
21. (a) **22.** (a) **23.** (b) **24.** (c) **25.** (a) **26.** (b) **27.** (b) **28.** (d) **29.** (c) **30.** (d)
31. (c) **32.** (d) **33.** (b) **34.** (d) **35.** (a) **36.** (b) **37.** (d) **38.** (b) **39.** (d) **40.** (c)

SECTION IV

1. (a,b,c,d) **2.** (a,c) **3.** (a,b,c) **4.** (c,d) **5.** (a,b,c) **6.** (c,d) **7.** (a,b) **8.** (a,b)

SECTION V

1. (b) **2.** (b) **3.** (b) **4.** (a) **5.** (d)

SECTION VI

1. (b,d) **2.** (b) **3.** (a,b,c) **4.** (a) **5.** (b) **6.** (a) **7.** (b) **8.** (d) **9.** (a) **10.** (a)
11. (b) **12.** (d)

SECTION VII

1. (i) → (b,d), (ii) → (e), (iii) → (a), (iv) → (c)
2. (i) → (b), (ii) → (d), (iii) → (a), (iv) → (c)
3. (i) → (a,b,c,d), (ii) → (b), (iii) → (b,e)

SECTION VIII

1. 12 **2.** 48 **3.** 2 **4.** 6 **5.** 10 **6.** 0 **7.** 6 **8.** 9 **9.** 7 **10.** 0
11. 4 **12.** 27 **13.** 1

HINTS AND SOLUTIONS

TEXTUAL EXERCISE 3: (SUBJECTIVE)

1. Let $A=\begin{bmatrix}3&5&8\\2&1&4\end{bmatrix}; B=\begin{bmatrix}7&1&3\\6&5&1\end{bmatrix}$ and $C=\begin{bmatrix}7&1&3\\6&5&1\end{bmatrix}$

$\Rightarrow\quad A-B=\begin{bmatrix}-4&4&5\\-4&-4&3\end{bmatrix}$

so $(A-B)-C=\begin{bmatrix}-16&-4&1\\-11&-13&-1\end{bmatrix}$

Now $B-C=\begin{bmatrix}-5&-7&-1\\-1&-4&-3\end{bmatrix}$ so $A-(B-C)=\begin{bmatrix}8&12&9\\3&5&7\end{bmatrix}$

Clearly $(A-B)-C \neq A-(B-C)$

2. Solving $\begin{bmatrix}3x&3y\\3z&3w\end{bmatrix}=\begin{bmatrix}x+4&x+y+6\\x+w-1&2w+3\end{bmatrix}$ gives $x=2$, $y=4$, $z=4/3$, $w=3$

3. $(A+B)+(A-B)=2A=\begin{bmatrix}4&0\\4&4\end{bmatrix}\quad\Rightarrow\quad A=\begin{bmatrix}2&0\\2&2\end{bmatrix}$

Similarly $(A+B)-(A-B)=2B=\begin{bmatrix}-2&-2\\2&-4\end{bmatrix}$

$\Rightarrow\quad B=\begin{bmatrix}-1&-1\\1&-2\end{bmatrix}$

4. (i) $A+\bar{A}=\begin{bmatrix}2&3-i&2+i\\6-i&5&4-2i\end{bmatrix}+\begin{bmatrix}2&3+i&2-i\\6+i&5&4+2i\end{bmatrix}$

$=\begin{bmatrix}4&6&4\\12&10&8\end{bmatrix}$

(ii) $B-\bar{B}=\begin{bmatrix}2&-2i&3-i\\3+i&2-3i&6+i\end{bmatrix}-\begin{bmatrix}2&2i&3+i\\3-i&2+3i&6-i\end{bmatrix}$

$=\begin{bmatrix}0&-4i&-2i\\2i&-6i&2i\end{bmatrix}$

(iii) $\bar{A}+\bar{B}=\begin{bmatrix}2&3+i&2-i\\6+i&5&4+2i\end{bmatrix}+\begin{bmatrix}2&2i&3+i\\3-i&2+3i&6-i\end{bmatrix}$

$=\begin{bmatrix}4&3+3i&5\\9&7+3i&10+i\end{bmatrix}$

5. $A=\begin{bmatrix}2+i&5&9+i\\3&6-i&2\\8-i&7&5+2i\end{bmatrix}; B=\begin{bmatrix}3-i&2&6+i\\-1&0&8-2i\\2&5&4+2i\end{bmatrix}$

(i) $(A+B)=\begin{bmatrix}5&7&15+2i\\2&6-i&10-2i\\10-i&12&9+4i\end{bmatrix}$;

$\overline{(A+B)}=\begin{bmatrix}5&7&15-2i\\2&6+i&10+2i\\10+i&12&9-4i\end{bmatrix}$

$\therefore\quad Tr.(A+B)=5+6-i+9+4i=20+3i$

$Tr.(A)=2+i+6-i+5+2i=13+2i$ and

$Tr(B)=3-i+0+4+2i=7+i$

$\Rightarrow\quad Tr(A)+Tr(B)=20+3i$

Clearly $Tr(A+B)=Tr.(A)+Tr.(B)=20+3i$

(ii) $A-B=\begin{bmatrix}-1+2i&3&3\\4&6-i&-6+2i\\6-i&2&1\end{bmatrix}$;

$\overline{(A-B)}=\begin{bmatrix}-1-2i&3&3\\4&6+i&-6-2i\\6+i&2&1\end{bmatrix}$

$\therefore\quad T_r(A-B)=-1+2i+6-i+1=6+i$ and

$Tr(A)-Tr(B)=13+2i-7-i=6+i$

Clearly $Tr(A-B)=T_r(A)-Tr(B)$

(iii) $T_r(\overline{A+B})=5+6+i+9-4i=20-3i$;

$T_r(\bar{A})=2-i+6+i+5-2i=13-2i$

And $T_r(\bar{B})=3+i+0+4-2i=7-i$

$\Rightarrow\quad Tr.(\bar{A})+Tr(\bar{B})=20-3i$

Clearly $Tr(\overline{A+B})=T_r(\bar{A})+Tr(\bar{B})$

(iv) $T_r(\overline{A-B})=-1-2i+6+i+1=6-i$;

Also $T_r(\bar{A})-T_r(\bar{B})=13-2i-7+i=6-i$

Clearly $T_r(\overline{A-B})=T_r.(\bar{A})-T_r.(\bar{B})$

TEXTUAL EXERCISE 4: (SUBJECTIVE)

1. $\begin{bmatrix}1\\-2\\3\end{bmatrix}\times[4\ 5\ 2]\times\begin{bmatrix}2\\-3\\5\end{bmatrix}\times[3\ 2]=\begin{bmatrix}1\\-2\\3\end{bmatrix}\times[452]\times\begin{bmatrix}6&4\\-9&-6\\15&10\end{bmatrix}$

$=\begin{bmatrix}1\\-2\\3\end{bmatrix}\times[9\ 6]=\begin{bmatrix}9&6\\-18&-12\\27&18\end{bmatrix}$

2. $AB=\begin{bmatrix}1&-2&3\\2&3&-1\\-3&1&2\end{bmatrix}\times\begin{bmatrix}1&0&2\\0&1&2\\1&2&0\end{bmatrix}=\begin{bmatrix}4&4&-2\\1&1&10\\-1&5&-4\end{bmatrix}$

$BA=\begin{bmatrix}1&0&2\\0&1&2\\1&2&0\end{bmatrix}\times\begin{bmatrix}1&-2&3\\2&3&-1\\-3&1&2\end{bmatrix}=\begin{bmatrix}-5&0&7\\-4&5&3\\5&4&1\end{bmatrix}$

So $AB \neq BA$

3. $\begin{bmatrix} \cos^2\theta & \cos\theta\sin\theta \\ \cos\theta\sin\theta & \sin^2\theta \end{bmatrix}\begin{bmatrix} \cos^2\phi & \cos\phi\sin\phi \\ \cos\phi\sin\phi & \sin^2\phi \end{bmatrix}$

$= \cos(\theta-\phi)\begin{bmatrix} \cos\theta\cos\phi & \cos\theta\sin\phi \\ \sin\theta\cos\phi & \sin\theta\sin\phi \end{bmatrix}$

When even $\theta = \left\{(2k+1)\frac{\pi}{2}+\phi\right\}$ then $\cos(\theta - \phi) = 0$ which makes it a null matrix

4. $A^2 = \begin{bmatrix} 1 & -2 & 3 \\ 2 & 3 & -1 \\ -3 & 1 & 2 \end{bmatrix}\begin{bmatrix} 1 & -2 & 3 \\ 2 & 3 & -1 \\ -3 & 1 & 2 \end{bmatrix} = \begin{bmatrix} -12 & -5 & 11 \\ 11 & 4 & 1 \\ -7 & 11 & -6 \end{bmatrix}$

and $(-3)(A-3I) = (-3)\begin{bmatrix} -2 & -2 & 3 \\ 2 & 0 & -1 \\ -3 & 1 & -1 \end{bmatrix} = \begin{bmatrix} 6 & 6 & -9 \\ -6 & 0 & 3 \\ 9 & -3 & 3 \end{bmatrix}$

so $A^2 - 3A + 9I = \begin{bmatrix} -6 & 1 & 2 \\ 5 & 4 & 4 \\ 2 & 8 & -3 \end{bmatrix}$

5. $A' = \begin{bmatrix} \cos\theta+\sin\theta & \sqrt{2}\sin\theta \\ -\sqrt{2}\sin\theta & \cos\theta-\sin\theta \end{bmatrix}$

$A^2 = \begin{bmatrix} \cos\theta+\sin\theta & \sqrt{2}\sin\theta \\ -\sqrt{2}\sin\theta & \cos\theta-\sin\theta \end{bmatrix}\begin{bmatrix} \cos\theta+\sin\theta & \sqrt{2}\sin\theta \\ -\sqrt{2}\sin\theta & \cos\theta-\sin\theta \end{bmatrix}$

$= \begin{bmatrix} 1+\sin 2\theta - 2\sin^2\theta & \sqrt{2}\sin\theta\cos\theta + \sqrt{2}\sin\theta\cos\theta \\ -\sqrt{2}\sin\theta\cos\theta - \sqrt{2}\sin\theta\cos\theta & -2\sin^2\theta + 1 - \sin 2\theta \end{bmatrix}$

$\therefore \quad A^2 = \begin{bmatrix} \sin 2\theta + \cos 2\theta & \sqrt{2}\sin 2\theta \\ -\sqrt{2}\sin 2\theta & \cos 2\theta - \sin 2\theta \end{bmatrix}$

Thus by induction, it can be verified that

$A^n = \begin{bmatrix} \sin n\theta + \cos n\theta & \sqrt{2}\sin n\theta \\ -\sqrt{2}\sin n\theta & \cos n\theta - \sin n\theta \end{bmatrix}$

6. $A = \begin{bmatrix} 1 & 1 & 1 \\ 0 & 1 & 1 \\ 0 & 0 & 1 \end{bmatrix} \Rightarrow A^2 \begin{bmatrix} 1 & 1 & 1 \\ 0 & 1 & 1 \\ 0 & 0 & 1 \end{bmatrix}\begin{bmatrix} 1 & 1 & 1 \\ 0 & 1 & 1 \\ 0 & 0 & 1 \end{bmatrix} = \begin{bmatrix} 1 & 2 & 3 \\ 0 & 1 & 2 \\ 0 & 0 & 1 \end{bmatrix}$

Further $A^3 = \begin{bmatrix} 1 & 2 & 3 \\ 0 & 1 & 2 \\ 0 & 0 & 1 \end{bmatrix}\begin{bmatrix} 1 & 1 & 1 \\ 0 & 1 & 1 \\ 0 & 0 & 1 \end{bmatrix} = \begin{bmatrix} 1 & 1+2 & 1+2+3 \\ 0 & 1 & 1+2 \\ 0 & 0 & 1 \end{bmatrix}$

$\therefore \quad A^3 = \begin{bmatrix} 1 & 3 & (1+2+3) \\ 0 & 1 & 3 \\ 0 & 0 & 1 \end{bmatrix}$

$\therefore$ By induction; $A^n = \begin{bmatrix} 1 & n & \frac{n(n+1)}{2} \\ 0 & 1 & n \\ 0 & 0 & 1 \end{bmatrix}$

TEXTUAL EXERCISE 1: (OBJECTIVE)

1. (b) Cayley Hamilton
2. (a) $[a_{jk}]_{2\times 3} = [(3j - 2k)] = \begin{bmatrix} 1 & -1 & -3 \\ 4 & 2 & 0 \end{bmatrix}$
3. (d) $[a_{ij}]_{2\times 2} = [(i + j)]_{2\times 2} = \begin{bmatrix} 2 & 3 \\ 3 & 4 \end{bmatrix}$
4. (a) $\begin{bmatrix} x & y \\ z & a \end{bmatrix} = \begin{bmatrix} 1 & -1 \\ 0 & 3 \end{bmatrix} \Rightarrow x = 1, y = -1, z = 0, a = 3$
5. (c) $a_{ii} = k$ for all $1 \le i \le n \Rightarrow TrA = nk$
6. (a) $A + B$ defined $\Rightarrow A$ and B are of same order.
   AB defined $\Rightarrow$ no. of column in A
   = No. of rows in B
   $\Rightarrow$ Both are square matrices of the same order.
7. (c) $BA = \begin{bmatrix} 0 & 1 & 0 \\ 0 & 2 & 1 \\ 2 & 3 & 0 \end{bmatrix}\begin{bmatrix} 1 & 2 \\ 3 & 0 \\ 4 & 1 \end{bmatrix} = \begin{bmatrix} 3 & 0 \\ 10 & 1 \\ 11 & 4 \end{bmatrix}$
8. (c) $[1\ x\ 1]\begin{bmatrix} 1 & 3 & 2 \\ 2 & 5 & 1 \\ 15 & 3 & 2 \end{bmatrix}\begin{bmatrix} 1 \\ 2 \\ x \end{bmatrix} = [1\ x\ 1]\begin{bmatrix} (7+2x) \\ (12+x) \\ (21+2x) \end{bmatrix}$
   $= [(x^2 + 16x + 28)] = [0]$ (given) so $x = -2, -14$
9. (b) $A^2 = \begin{bmatrix} 1 & 1 \\ 2 & -1 \end{bmatrix}\begin{bmatrix} 1 & 1 \\ 2 & -1 \end{bmatrix} = \begin{bmatrix} 3 & 0 \\ 0 & 3 \end{bmatrix} = 3I$
10. (c) $A^2 = \begin{bmatrix} a & b \\ b & a \end{bmatrix}\begin{bmatrix} a & b \\ b & a \end{bmatrix} = \begin{bmatrix} (a^2+b^2) & 2ab \\ 2ab & (a^2+b^2) \end{bmatrix} = \begin{bmatrix} \alpha & \beta \\ \beta & \alpha \end{bmatrix}$
    (given)
    $\Rightarrow \alpha = a^2 + b^2$ and $\beta = 2ab$
11. (b) $A = I_{3\times 3} \Rightarrow A^2 = I_3$ hence $A^2 + 2A = 3A$ (or $3I_3$)
12. (b) A scalar matrix is diagonal $\{k, k, \ldots, k\}$ which become identity matrix if and only if $k = 1$
13. (c) $A^2 = \begin{bmatrix} i & 0 \\ 0 & i \end{bmatrix}\begin{bmatrix} i & 0 \\ 0 & i \end{bmatrix} = \begin{bmatrix} -1 & 0 \\ 0 & -1 \end{bmatrix}$
    And $A^4 = A^2 . A^2 = \begin{bmatrix} -1 & 0 \\ 0 & -1 \end{bmatrix}\begin{bmatrix} -1 & 0 \\ 0 & -1 \end{bmatrix} = \begin{bmatrix} 1 & 0 \\ 0 & 1 \end{bmatrix} = I_2$
    $\Rightarrow A^4 . A^4 \ldots\ldots A^4$ (n times) $= A^{4n} = I_2$
14. (c) $\begin{bmatrix} 0 & c & -b \\ -c & 0 & a \\ b & -a & 0 \end{bmatrix}\begin{bmatrix} a^2 & ab & ac \\ ab & b^2 & bc \\ ac & bc & c^2 \end{bmatrix} = \begin{bmatrix} 0 & 0 & 0 \\ 0 & 0 & 0 \\ 0 & 0 & 0 \end{bmatrix}$
15. (c) $\alpha = a^2 + b^2$; $\beta = 2ab$
    $\Rightarrow (a + b)^2 = \alpha + \beta$

TEXTUAL EXERCISE 5: SUBJECTIVE

1. $A' = \begin{bmatrix} a & d \\ b & e \\ c & f \end{bmatrix} \Rightarrow (A')' = \begin{bmatrix} a & b & c \\ d & e & f \end{bmatrix} = A$

2. (a) $a_{ij} = i.j = ji = a_{ji} \Rightarrow [a_{ij}]$ is symmetric
   (b) $a_{ij} = i^2 - j^2 = -(j^2 - i^2) = -(a_{ji}) \Rightarrow [a_{ij}]$ is skew symmetric

3. Yes a square null matrix

4. Let if possible in the case of a hermitian matrix the det(A) = $a + ib$, then det $A^T = a + ib$

   $\Rightarrow \left|\overline{(A^T)}\right| = a - ib$

   But $|A| = \left|\overline{(A^T)}\right| \Rightarrow a + ib = a - ib \Rightarrow b = 0 \Rightarrow |A| = a \in \mathbb{R}$

5. $D = \text{diag}\,(d_1 d_2 \ldots d_n) = \begin{bmatrix} d_1 & 0 & 0 \ldots\ldots\ldots 0 \\ 0 & d_2 & 0 \ldots\ldots\ldots 0 \\ 0 & 0 & d_3 \ldots\ldots\ldots 0 \\ 0 & 0 & 0 \ldots\ldots\ldots d_n \end{bmatrix}$

   $|D| = d_1 \begin{vmatrix} d_2 & 0 & 0 & 0 \ldots\ldots 0 \\ 0 & d_3 & 0 & 0 \ldots\ldots 0 \\ \ldots\ldots \\ \ldots\ldots \\ 0 & 0 & 0 & 0 \ldots\ldots d_n \end{vmatrix} = d_1 d_2 \begin{vmatrix} d_3 & 0 & 0 \ldots\ldots 0 \\ 0 & d_4 & 0 \ldots\ldots 0 \\ 0 & 0 & d_5 \ldots\ldots 0 \\ \ldots\ldots \\ \ldots\ldots \\ 0 & 0 & 0 \ldots\ldots d_n \end{vmatrix}$

   Continuing gives $|D| = d_1 d_2 d_3 \ldots\ldots d_n$

6. Let $B_{m\times n} = \begin{bmatrix} a_{11} & a_{12} \ldots\ldots & a_{1n} \\ a_{21} & a_{22} \ldots\ldots & a_{2n} \\ & \ldots\ldots\ldots & \\ & \ldots\ldots\ldots & \\ a_{m1} & a_{m2} \ldots\ldots & a_{mn} \end{bmatrix}$ and

   $B' = \begin{bmatrix} a_{11} & a_{21} \ldots\ldots & a_{m1} \\ a_{12} & a_{22} \ldots\ldots & a_{m2} \\ & \ldots\ldots\ldots & \\ & \ldots\ldots\ldots & \\ a_{1n} & a_{2n} \ldots\ldots & a_{mn} \end{bmatrix}_{n\times m}$

   For clarity write $B' = \begin{bmatrix} b_{11} & b_{12} \ldots\ldots & b_{1m} \\ b_{21} & b_{22} \ldots\ldots & b_{2m} \\ & \ldots\ldots\ldots & \\ & \ldots\ldots\ldots & \\ b_{n1} & b_{n2} \ldots\ldots & b_{nm} \end{bmatrix}$

   If $C = BB'$ then $C = (BB')_{m\times m} \Rightarrow [c_{ik}]_{m\times m} = \left[\sum_{j=1}^{n} a_{ij}.b_{jk}\right]$

   Since $b_{pq} = a_{qp} \Rightarrow [c_{ij}]_{m\times m} = \left[\sum_{j=1}^{n} a_{ij}.a_{kj}\right]$

   To show symmetry $[c_{kj}]_{m\times m} = \left[\sum_{j=1}^{n} a_{kj}.b_{ji}\right] = \left[\sum_{j=1}^{n} a_{kj}.a_{ij}\right]$

   $\therefore\ [c_{ik}]_{m\times m} = [c_{ki}]_{m\times n}$ hence symmetric. Similarly for $B'B$

7. Let A be a skew symmetric matrix

   $\Rightarrow\ A^T = A$

   Let n be any positive integer, then

   $(A^n)^T = (A.A.A\ldots\ldots A)^T = (A^T.A^T.A^T \ldots\ldots A^T) = (A^T)^n$

   $= (-A)^n \begin{cases} (-A)^n \text{ if } n \text{ is odd} \\ A^n \text{ if } n \text{ is even} \end{cases}$

   Thus $(A^n)^T = \begin{cases} -(A^n) \text{ if } n \text{ is odd} \\ A^n \text{ if } n \text{ is even} \end{cases}$

   $\Rightarrow \begin{cases} A^n \text{ is skew-symmetric for n = odd} \\ A^n \text{ is symmetric for n = even} \end{cases}$

TEXTUAL EXERCISE 6: SUBJECTIVE

1. $AA' = \frac{1}{81}\begin{bmatrix} -8 & 1 & 4 \\ 4 & 4 & 7 \\ 1 & -8 & 4 \end{bmatrix}\begin{bmatrix} -8 & 4 & 1 \\ 1 & 4 & -8 \\ 4 & 7 & 4 \end{bmatrix}$

   $= \frac{1}{81}\begin{bmatrix} 81 & 0 & 0 \\ 0 & 81 & 0 \\ 0 & 0 & 81 \end{bmatrix} = I_3$

   Since $AA' = I \Rightarrow (A^{-1}A)\,A' = A^{-1}I$ so $A' = A^{-1}$

2. $AA' = \begin{bmatrix} \cos\theta & 0 & \sin\theta \\ 0 & 1 & 0 \\ -\sin\theta & 0 & \cos\theta \end{bmatrix}\begin{bmatrix} \cos\theta & 0 & -\sin\theta \\ 0 & 1 & 0 \\ \sin\theta & 0 & \cos\theta \end{bmatrix}$

   $= \begin{bmatrix} 1 & 0 & 0 \\ 0 & 1 & 0 \\ 0 & 0 & 1 \end{bmatrix} = I_3$

3. (a) $A^n = O \Rightarrow A^n - I = -I$ so $(A - I)\,\{A^{n-1} + A^{n-2} + \ldots + I\} = A^n - I = -I$
   $\Rightarrow\ (I + A + A^2 + \ldots\ldots + A^{n-1}) = -I\,(A - I)^{-1}$ or $(I - A)^{-1}$
   (b) Since n is odd, $(A + I)\,\{I - A + A^2 - A^3 + \ldots\ldots + (-1)^{n-1} A^{n-1}\} = A^n + I = I$
   So $I - A + A^2 - A^3 + A^4 + \ldots\ldots + (-1)^{n-1} A^{n-1} = (A + I)^{-1}$

4. Given $B^3 = I$ and $AB = BA^2$
   $\Rightarrow\ B = A^{-1}BA^2 = A^{-1}BAA$
   $\therefore\ B^3 = I \Rightarrow (A^{-1}BAA)\,(A^{-1}BAA)\,(A^{-1}BAA)$
   $\Rightarrow\ I = (A^{-1}BA)\,(BA)\,(BAA)$
   $\Rightarrow\ I = A^{-1}B\,(AB)\,(AB)AA$
   $\Rightarrow\ I = A^{-1}B(BA^2)(BA^2)\,AA$ $\quad (\because AB = BA^2)$
   $\Rightarrow\ I = A^{-1}\,BBA(A-B)A^4$
   $\Rightarrow\ I = A^{-1}BBA(BA^2)A^4 = A^{-1}B^2\,(AB)\,A^6 = A^{-1}B^2(BA^2)A^6$
   $\Rightarrow\ I = A^{-1}B^3A^8 = A^{-1}IA^8 = A^7$
   Thus $k_{min} = 7$ for $A^k = I$
   $\therefore\ 7$

5. $A = \begin{bmatrix} 2 & -3 & -5 \\ -1 & 4 & 5 \\ 1 & -3 & -4 \end{bmatrix}$

$\Rightarrow A^2 = \begin{bmatrix} 2 & -3 & -5 \\ -1 & 4 & 5 \\ 1 & -3 & -4 \end{bmatrix}\begin{bmatrix} 2 & -3 & -5 \\ -1 & 4 & 5 \\ 1 & -3 & -4 \end{bmatrix} = \begin{bmatrix} 2 & -3 & -5 \\ -1 & 4 & 5 \\ 1 & -3 & -4 \end{bmatrix} = A$

$\Rightarrow$ A is idempotent

6. Let $A = \begin{bmatrix} 2 & -2 & -4 \\ -1 & 3 & 4 \\ 1 & -2 & -3 \end{bmatrix}$

$\Rightarrow A^2 \begin{bmatrix} 2 & -2 & -4 \\ -1 & 3 & 4 \\ 1 & -2 & -3 \end{bmatrix}\begin{bmatrix} 2 & -2 & -4 \\ -1 & 3 & 4 \\ 1 & -2 & -3 \end{bmatrix} = \begin{bmatrix} 2 & -2 & -4 \\ -1 & 3 & 4 \\ 1 & -2 & -3 \end{bmatrix} = A$

$\Rightarrow$ A is periodic with period 1, also it is idempotent

7. Let $A = \begin{bmatrix} 0 & 4 & 3 \\ 1 & -3 & -3 \\ -1 & 4 & 4 \end{bmatrix}$

$\Rightarrow A^2 = \begin{bmatrix} 0 & 4 & 3 \\ 1 & -3 & -3 \\ -1 & 4 & 4 \end{bmatrix}\begin{bmatrix} 0 & 4 & 3 \\ 1 & -3 & -3 \\ -1 & 4 & 4 \end{bmatrix} = \begin{bmatrix} 1 & 0 & 0 \\ 0 & 1 & 0 \\ 0 & 0 & 1 \end{bmatrix} = I_3$

$\Rightarrow$ A is involuntary Matrix.

8. Given $AB = A$ and $BA = B$ ....(i)

Now $A^2 = A.A. = (A).\ A = (AB).A$ ($\because A = AB$)
$= A(BA) = AB$ ($\because BA = B$) $= A$ $\therefore A^2 = A \Rightarrow (A^2)^T = A^T$
$\Rightarrow$ $(AT)^2 = A^T \Rightarrow A^T$ is idempotent matrix
Similarly B^T is idempotent

9. $\because$ A is nilpotent matrix of index 2, $A^2 = 0$; For $n = 1$; $A(I \pm A) = A \pm A^2 = A \pm 0$
Now, for $n \geq 2$, $A(I \pm A)^n = A[I \pm {}^nC_1A + {}^nC_2A^2 \pm {}^nC_3A^3 + ... + {}^nC_nA^n]$
$= A + A^2[\pm {}^nC_1 + {}^nC_2A \pm {}^nC_3^2 + ... + {}^nC_nA^{n-2}]$
$= A + O = A$; Thus $A(I \pm A)^n = A\ \forall\ n \in \mathbb{N}$

10. $\because$ A is idempotent, $A^2 = A$; for $n = 1$; $(A + I)^1 = I + (2^1 - 1)A$
For $n \geq 2$; $(A + I)^n = (I + A)^n$
$= I + {}^nC_1A + {}^nC_2A^2 + {}^nC_3A^3 + ...+ {}^nC_nA^n$
$= I + {}^nC_1A + {}^nC_2A + {}^nC_3A + ...+ {}^nC_nA$
($\because A^2 = A,\ A^3 = A^2.A = A.A = A^2 = A,\ A^4 = A^2.A^2 = A.A = A^2 = A...$)
$= I + A\,({}^nC_1 + {}^nC_2 + {}^nC_3 + ..{}^nC_n) = I + (2n - 1)A$

TEXTUAL EXERCISE 2: (OBJECTIVE)

1. **(a)** $B^2 = B.B = BA(B) = BA = B$

2. **(b)** $B = BA \Rightarrow B(B) = BA(B) = B(AB) = BA = B \Rightarrow B^2 = B$
Also, $A = AB \Rightarrow A(A) = AB(A) = A\,(BA) = AB = A \Rightarrow A^2 = A$
Both are idempotent

3. **(a,c,d)** $A = I - B \Rightarrow A^2 = I + B^2 - 2B = I + B - 2B = I - B = A$
$A = I - B \Rightarrow AB = B - B^2 = B - B = O$ (null matrix)
$A = I - B \Rightarrow BA = B - B^2 = B - B = O$

4. **(d)** $AA^T = \begin{bmatrix} 0 & 2\beta & \gamma \\ \alpha & \beta & -\gamma \\ \alpha & -\beta & \gamma \end{bmatrix}\begin{bmatrix} 0 & \alpha & \alpha \\ 2\beta & \beta & -\beta \\ \gamma & -\gamma & \gamma \end{bmatrix} = I$

$= \begin{bmatrix} (4\beta^2+\gamma^2) & (2\beta^2-\gamma^2) & (-2\beta^2+\gamma^2) \\ (2\beta^2-\gamma^2) & (\alpha^2+\beta^2+\gamma^2) & (\alpha^2-\beta^2-\gamma^2) \\ (\gamma^2-2\beta^2) & (\alpha^2-\beta^2-\gamma^2) & (\alpha^2+\beta^2+\gamma^2) \end{bmatrix} = I$

$\Rightarrow 4\beta^2 + \gamma^2 = \alpha^2 + \beta^2 + \gamma^2 = 1$ and $\alpha^2 - \beta^2 - \gamma^2 = 2\beta^2 = \gamma^2 = 0$
Gives $2\alpha^2 = 1$, so $\alpha = \pm\frac{1}{\sqrt{2}}$ and $\beta^2 = \frac{1}{6}; \gamma^2 = \frac{1}{3}$

$\Rightarrow \beta = \pm\frac{1}{\sqrt{6}}$ and $\gamma = \pm\frac{1}{\sqrt{3}}$

5. **(b)** A is orthogonal
$\Rightarrow AA^T = I \Rightarrow A^{-1}AA^T = A^{-1}I$, so $A^T = A^{-1}$

6. **(a,c)** A is orthogonal $\therefore AA^T = I$
$\Rightarrow$ det (AA^T) = (det A) (det A^T)
$\Rightarrow$ det $A = \pm 1$ as det A = det A^T

7. **(a)** Matrix $\begin{bmatrix} 0 & 5 & -7 \\ -5 & 0 & 11 \\ 7 & -11 & 0 \end{bmatrix}$ is skew symmetric

8. **(c)** $a_{ii} = 0$ for a symmetric matrix $\Rightarrow TrA = 0$

9. **(a)** A is skew symmetric $\Rightarrow A^T = -A$
So $(A.A.A)^T = A^TA^TA^T = (-A)(-A)(-A) = -A^3$
$\Rightarrow$ A^3 is skew symmetric

10. **(a)** $(AA^T - A^TA)^T = (AA^T)^T - (A^TA)^T = AA^T - A^TA$
$\Rightarrow$ Symmetric matrix

11. **(a,b,c)** A and B are symmetric
$\Rightarrow$ $A' = A$ and $B' = B$
$\Rightarrow$ $(A + B)' = B' + A' = B + A = A + B \Rightarrow (A + B)$ is symmetric
$(AB + BA)' = (AB)' + (BA)' = B'A' + A'B' = BA + AB = AB + BA$
So $(AB + BA)$ is symmetric
Now, $(AB - BA)' = (AB)' - (BA)' = B'A' - A'B' = BA - AB = -(AB - BA)$
Hence $(AB - BA)$ is skew symmetric

TEXTUAL EXERCISE 7: (SUBJECTIVE)

1. (a) $A = \begin{bmatrix} 1 & 3 & 3 \\ 1 & 4 & 3 \\ 1 & 3 & 4 \end{bmatrix}$ and $|A| = 1$

$C_{11} = 7, C_{12} = -1, C_{13} = -1, C_{21} = -3, C_{22} = 1,$

$C_{23} = 0, C_{31} = -3, C_{32} = 0, C_{33} = 1$

$$\Rightarrow A^{-1} = \begin{bmatrix} 7 & -3 & -3 \\ -1 & 1 & 0 \\ -1 & 0 & 1 \end{bmatrix}$$

(b) $A = \begin{bmatrix} 2 & 5 & 3 \\ 3 & 1 & 2 \\ 1 & 2 & 1 \end{bmatrix}$ and $|A| = 4$

$C_{11} = -3, C_{12} = -1, C_{13} = 5, C_{21} = 1, C_{22} = -1,$
$C_{23} = 1, C_{31} = 7, C_{32} = 5, C_{33} = -13$

$$\Rightarrow A^{-1} = \frac{1}{4}\begin{bmatrix} -3 & 1 & 7 \\ -1 & -1 & 5 \\ 5 & 1 & -13 \end{bmatrix}$$

2. $A = \begin{bmatrix} 1 & 1 & 3 \\ 1 & 3 & -3 \\ -2 & -4 & -4 \end{bmatrix}$

$$\Rightarrow |A| = \begin{vmatrix} 1 & 1 & 3 \\ 1 & 3 & -3 \\ -2 & -4 & -4 \end{vmatrix} = 1\,(-24) - (-10) + 3\,(2) = -8 \neq 0$$

$\Rightarrow A^{-1}$ exists

$$\text{Now } A^2 = \begin{bmatrix} 1 & 1 & 3 \\ 1 & 3 & -3 \\ -2 & -4 & -4 \end{bmatrix}\begin{bmatrix} 1 & 1 & 3 \\ 1 & 3 & -3 \\ -2 & -4 & -4 \end{bmatrix} = \begin{bmatrix} -4 & -8 & -12 \\ 10 & 22 & 6 \\ 2 & 2 & 22 \end{bmatrix}$$

$$A^3 = \begin{bmatrix} -4 & -8 & -12 \\ 10 & 22 & 6 \\ 2 & 2 & 22 \end{bmatrix}\begin{bmatrix} 1 & 1 & 3 \\ 1 & 3 & -3 \\ -2 & -4 & -4 \end{bmatrix} = \begin{bmatrix} 12 & 20 & 60 \\ 20 & 52 & -60 \\ -40 & -80 & -88 \end{bmatrix}$$

Now $A^3 - 20A =$

$$\begin{bmatrix} 12 & 20 & 60 \\ 20 & 52 & -60 \\ -40 & -80 & -88 \end{bmatrix} - 20\begin{bmatrix} 1 & 1 & 3 \\ 1 & 3 & -3 \\ -2 & -4 & -4 \end{bmatrix} = \begin{bmatrix} -8 & 0 & 0 \\ 0 & -8 & 0 \\ 0 & 0 & -8 \end{bmatrix} = -8I$$

$\therefore\ A^3 - 20A = -8I \quad \Rightarrow\ (A^3 - 20A)A^{-1} = -8A^{-1}$

$\Rightarrow\ A^2 - 20I = -8A^{-1} \quad \Rightarrow\ A^{-1} = \frac{1}{8}(20I - A^2)$

3. $|A - xI| = 0 \Rightarrow \begin{vmatrix} 1-x & -1 \\ 2 & 3-x \end{vmatrix} = 0$ so $x^2 - 4x + 5 = 0$

$\Rightarrow A^2 - 4A + 5I = O \Rightarrow 5I = 4A - A^2$

Multiplication by A^{-1} gives $5A^{-1} = 4I - A$, so $A^{-1} = \dfrac{4I - A}{5}$

4. (a) $\begin{vmatrix} 2-x & 5 \\ 1 & 4-x \end{vmatrix} = 0 \Rightarrow x^2 - 6x + 3 = 0$

$\Rightarrow A^2 - 6A + 3I = O$

$$\Rightarrow A^{-1} = \frac{6I - A}{3} = \frac{1}{3}\begin{bmatrix} (6-2) & (0-5) \\ (0-1) & (6-4) \end{bmatrix} = \frac{1}{3}\begin{bmatrix} 4 & -5 \\ -1 & 2 \end{bmatrix}$$

(b) $\begin{vmatrix} 1-x & 1 & 2 \\ 2 & 1-x & 3 \\ 3 & 2 & 1-x \end{vmatrix} = 0$ gives

$(1 - x)\{x^2 + 1 - 2x - 6\} - \{2 - 2x - 9\} + 2\{4 - 3 + 3x\} = 0$

$\Rightarrow 3x^2 + 11x + 4 - x^3 = 0$; So $A^{-1} = \frac{1}{4}\{A^2 - 3A - 11I\}$

$$= \frac{1}{4}\left(\begin{bmatrix} 9 & 6 & 7 \\ 13 & 9 & 10 \\ 10 & 7 & 13 \end{bmatrix} - \begin{bmatrix} 14 & 3 & 6 \\ 6 & 14 & 9 \\ 9 & 6 & 14 \end{bmatrix}\right) = \frac{1}{4}\begin{bmatrix} -5 & 3 & 1 \\ 7 & -5 & 1 \\ 1 & 1 & -1 \end{bmatrix}$$

5. $A = \begin{bmatrix} 3 & 1 \\ -1 & 2 \end{bmatrix}$

$\therefore\ |A - xI| = 0 \Rightarrow \begin{vmatrix} 3-x & 1 \\ -1 & 2-x \end{vmatrix} = (3 - x)(2 - x) + 1 = 0$

$\Rightarrow x^2 - 5x + 7 = 0$

$\therefore$ By Cayley Himation theorem

$A^2 - 5A + 7I = 0$ .....(i)

Now $2A^5 - 3A^4 + A^2 - 4I = (A^2 - 5A + 7I)(2A^3 + 7A^2 + 21A + 57I) + (138A - 403I) = 0 + 138A - 403I$

(∵ of (1))

$\therefore\ 2A^5 - 3A^4 + A^2 - 4I = 138A - 403I$

TEXTUAL EXERCISE 3: (OBJECTIVE)

1. (c) $A = \begin{bmatrix} a & 0 & 0 \\ 0 & a & 0 \\ 0 & 0 & a \end{bmatrix} \Rightarrow |A| = a^3,\ |Adj\ A| = |A|^{n-1} = (a^3)^2 = a^6$

2. (b) $\because\ |AdjA| = |A|^{n-1}$

$\therefore\ |A| = 0 \Rightarrow |AdjA| = 0$

$\Rightarrow$ $AdjA$ is also singular matrix

3. **(a)** $A = \begin{bmatrix} 1 & 2 & -1 \\ -1 & 1 & 2 \\ 2 & -1 & 1 \end{bmatrix} \Rightarrow |A| = 14$ det. $Adj(Adj\ A)$

$= |A|^{(n-1)^2} = (14)^4$

4. **(a)** Let order of B be $m \times n$

$\Rightarrow$ For A^TB to be defined $m = 3$ and for BA^T to be defined $n = 4$

$\therefore$ order of $B = 3 \times 4$

5. **(a)** $A = \begin{bmatrix} 3 & 8 \\ 2 & 1 \end{bmatrix} \Rightarrow |A| = -13 \Rightarrow A^{-1} = \begin{Bmatrix} \frac{-1}{13} & \frac{8}{13} \\ \frac{2}{13} & \frac{-3}{13} \end{Bmatrix}$

6. **(b)** As $\omega^4 = \omega$, so $\omega^4 - 1 \neq 0 \quad \Rightarrow \begin{vmatrix} \omega^2 & 1 \\ 1 & \omega^2 \end{vmatrix} \neq 0$

7. **(c)** $A = \begin{bmatrix} \cos\theta & -\sin\theta \\ \sin\theta & \cos\theta \end{bmatrix} \Rightarrow |A| = 1 \therefore A^{-1} = \begin{bmatrix} \cos x & \sin x \\ -\sin x & \cos x \end{bmatrix}$

8. (a) $A^{-1} = \begin{bmatrix} \cos x & -\sin x & 0 \\ \sin x & \cos x & 0 \\ 0 & 0 & 1 \end{bmatrix} = f(-x)$

9. (c) Let $B^{-1}AB = X$

$\Rightarrow BB^{-1}AB = BX$ or $AB = BX$

$\Rightarrow$ (det A) (det B) = (det B) (det X) since det $B \neq 0$

det X = det $(B^{-1}AB)$ = det A

10. (b) $D = \text{Diag}(d_1\ d_2\ d_3, \ldots d_n) \Rightarrow |D| = d_1 d_2 d_3 \ldots d_n \neq 0$

$C_{ii} = d_1 d_2 \ldots\ldots d_{i-1}, d_{i+1}, \ldots\ldots, d_n$ and $C_{ij} = 0$ for $i \neq j$

$\Rightarrow \quad D^{-1} = \text{diag}\left\{\frac{1}{d_1}, \frac{1}{d_2}, \frac{1}{d_3}, \ldots \frac{1}{d_n}\right\}$

11. (a,d) A^{-1} is also symmetric

$A^{-1} = \frac{1}{|A|}\{AdjA\}$ now $|Adj\ A| = |A|^{n-1}$

$|A^{-1}| = \{|A|^{-1}\}^n . |A|^{n-1} = |A|^{-1}$

TEXTUAL EXERCISE 8: (SUBJECTIVE)

1. (a) $\begin{bmatrix} 1 & 3 & 3 \\ 1 & 4 & 3 \\ 1 & 3 & 4 \end{bmatrix} = \begin{bmatrix} 1 & 0 & 0 \\ 0 & 1 & 0 \\ 0 & 0 & 1 \end{bmatrix} A$

$R_2 \to R_2 - R_1$ and $R_3 \to R_3 - R_1$ gives

$\begin{bmatrix} 1 & 3 & 3 \\ 0 & 1 & 0 \\ 0 & 0 & 1 \end{bmatrix} = \begin{bmatrix} 1 & 0 & 0 \\ -1 & 1 & 0 \\ -1 & 0 & 1 \end{bmatrix} A$

$R_1 \to R_1 - 3R_2$ gives , $\begin{bmatrix} 1 & 0 & 3 \\ 0 & 1 & 0 \\ 0 & 0 & 1 \end{bmatrix} = \begin{bmatrix} 4 & -3 & 0 \\ -1 & 1 & 0 \\ -1 & 0 & 1 \end{bmatrix} .A$

$R_1 \to R_1 - 3R_3$ gives $\begin{bmatrix} 1 & 0 & 0 \\ 0 & 1 & 0 \\ 0 & 0 & 1 \end{bmatrix} = \begin{bmatrix} 7 & -3 & -3 \\ -1 & 1 & 0 \\ -1 & 0 & 1 \end{bmatrix} .A$

$\Rightarrow A^{-1} = \begin{bmatrix} 1 & -3 & -3 \\ -1 & 1 & 0 \\ -1 & 0 & 1 \end{bmatrix}$

(b) $\begin{bmatrix} 0 & 4 & 3 \\ 1 & -3 & -3 \\ -1 & 4 & 4 \end{bmatrix} = \begin{bmatrix} 1 & 0 & 0 \\ 0 & 1 & 0 \\ 0 & 0 & 1 \end{bmatrix} A$

$R_1 \leftrightarrow R_2$ (interchange) $\begin{bmatrix} 1 & -3 & -3 \\ 0 & 4 & 3 \\ -1 & 4 & 4 \end{bmatrix} = \begin{bmatrix} 0 & 1 & 0 \\ 1 & 0 & 0 \\ 0 & 0 & 1 \end{bmatrix} A$

$R_3 \to R_3 + R_1$ gives $\begin{bmatrix} 1 & -3 & -3 \\ 0 & 4 & 3 \\ 0 & 1 & 1 \end{bmatrix} = \begin{bmatrix} 0 & 1 & 0 \\ 1 & 0 & 0 \\ 0 & 1 & 1 \end{bmatrix} A$

$R_1 \to R_1 + 3R_3$ gives $\begin{bmatrix} 1 & 0 & 0 \\ 0 & 4 & 3 \\ 0 & 1 & 1 \end{bmatrix} = \begin{bmatrix} 0 & 4 & 3 \\ 1 & 0 & 0 \\ 0 & 1 & 1 \end{bmatrix} A$

$R_2 \to R_2 - 3R_3$ gives $\begin{bmatrix} 1 & 0 & 0 \\ 0 & 1 & 0 \\ 0 & 1 & 1 \end{bmatrix} = \begin{bmatrix} 0 & 4 & 3 \\ 1 & -3 & -3 \\ 0 & 1 & 1 \end{bmatrix} A$

$R_3 \to R_3 - R_2$ gives $\begin{bmatrix} 1 & 0 & 0 \\ 0 & 1 & 0 \\ 0 & 0 & 1 \end{bmatrix} = \begin{bmatrix} 0 & 4 & 3 \\ 1 & -3 & -3 \\ -1 & 4 & 4 \end{bmatrix} A$

We observe that $A^{-1} = A$

2. $\begin{bmatrix} 1 & 1 & 2 & : & 1 & 0 & 0 \\ 1 & 2 & 3 & : & 0 & 1 & 0 \\ 2 & 3 & 1 & : & 0 & 0 & 1 \end{bmatrix}$

$R_2 \to R_2 - R_1$ and $R_3 \to R_3 \to 2R_1$

$\Rightarrow \begin{bmatrix} 1 & 1 & 2 & : & 1 & 0 & 0 \\ 0 & 1 & 1 & : & -1 & 1 & 0 \\ 0 & 1 & -3 & : & -2 & 0 & 1 \end{bmatrix}$

$R_1 \to R_1 - R_2$ and $R_3 \to R_3 \to R_2$

$\Rightarrow \begin{bmatrix} 1 & 0 & 1 & : & 2 & -1 & 0 \\ 0 & 1 & 1 & : & -1 & 1 & 0 \\ 0 & 0 & -4 & : & -1 & -1 & 1 \end{bmatrix}$

$R_3 \to (-1/4)\ R_3$

$\Rightarrow \begin{bmatrix} 1 & 0 & 1 & : & 2 & -1 & 0 \\ 0 & 1 & 1 & : & -1 & 1 & 0 \\ 0 & 0 & 1 & : & 1/4 & 1/4 & -1/4 \end{bmatrix}$

$R_2 \to R_2 - R_3$ and $R_1 \to R_1 - R_3$

$\Rightarrow \begin{bmatrix} 1 & 0 & 0 & : & \frac{7}{4} & \frac{-5}{4} & \frac{1}{4} \\ 0 & 1 & 0 & : & \frac{-5}{4} & \frac{3}{4} & \frac{1}{4} \\ 0 & 0 & 1 & : & \frac{1}{4} & \frac{1}{4} & \frac{-1}{4} \end{bmatrix}$

$\Rightarrow \quad A^{-1} = \frac{1}{4}\begin{bmatrix} 7 & -5 & 1 \\ -5 & 3 & 1 \\ 1 & 1 & -1 \end{bmatrix}$

3. (i) $A = \begin{bmatrix} 2 & 3 & 6 \\ -1 & 2 & 3 \end{bmatrix}$

Matrix obtained by using the transformation

$R_1 \to R_1 + 2R_2 = B(say) = \begin{bmatrix} 0 & 7 & 12 \\ -1 & 2 & 3 \end{bmatrix}$

Let us operate the same elementary transformation to I_2 to obtained matrix $C = \begin{bmatrix} 1 & 2 \\ 0 & 1 \end{bmatrix}$

Now, $CA = \begin{bmatrix} 1 & 2 \\ 0 & 1 \end{bmatrix}\begin{bmatrix} 2 & 3 & 6 \\ -1 & 2 & 3 \end{bmatrix} = \begin{bmatrix} 0 & 7 & 12 \\ -1 & 2 & 3 \end{bmatrix}$

Clearly $B = CA$

(b) $A = \begin{bmatrix} 2 & 3 & 6 \\ -1 & 2 & 3 \end{bmatrix}$

Matrix obtained by using the column transformation $C_1 \Leftrightarrow C_3$ is $B(say) = \begin{bmatrix} 6 & 3 & 2 \\ 3 & 2 & -1 \end{bmatrix}$

Matrix obtained by operating same transformations to I_3 is $C = \begin{bmatrix} 0 & 0 & 1 \\ 0 & 1 & 0 \\ 1 & 0 & 0 \end{bmatrix}$

Now $AC = \begin{bmatrix} 2 & 3 & 6 \\ -1 & 2 & 3 \end{bmatrix}\begin{bmatrix} 0 & 0 & 1 \\ 0 & 1 & 0 \\ 1 & 0 & 0 \end{bmatrix} = \begin{bmatrix} 6 & 3 & 2 \\ 3 & 2 & -1 \end{bmatrix}$

Clearly $B = A - C$

(ii) Let $A = \begin{bmatrix} 2 & 3 \\ 6 & -3 \\ 2 & -1 \end{bmatrix}$

(a) $R_1 \to R_1 + R_3$, gives the elementary matrix

$\begin{bmatrix} 1 & 0 & 1 \\ 0 & 1 & 0 \\ 0 & 0 & 1 \end{bmatrix} = C(say)$

Matrix obtained using the same transformation on Matrix A, is $B = \begin{bmatrix} 4 & 2 \\ 6 & -3 \\ 2 & -1 \end{bmatrix}$

Now, by jordan's theorem $B = CA$

Now $CA = \begin{bmatrix} 1 & 0 & 1 \\ 0 & 1 & 0 \\ 0 & 0 & 1 \end{bmatrix}\begin{bmatrix} 2 & 3 \\ 6 & -3 \\ 2 & -1 \end{bmatrix} = \begin{bmatrix} 4 & 2 \\ 6 & -3 \\ 2 & -1 \end{bmatrix} = B$

(b) $R_2 \leftrightarrow R_3$

Elementary matrix obtained $= \begin{bmatrix} 1 & 0 & 0 \\ 0 & 0 & 1 \\ 0 & 1 & 0 \end{bmatrix} = C(say)$

Now equivalent matrix obtained by using same transformation to matrix

$A = \begin{bmatrix} 2 & 3 \\ 2 & -1 \\ 6 & -3 \end{bmatrix} = B(say)$

Now, $CA = \begin{bmatrix} 1 & 0 & 0 \\ 0 & 0 & 1 \\ 0 & 1 & 0 \end{bmatrix}\begin{bmatrix} 2 & 3 \\ 6 & -3 \\ 2 & -1 \end{bmatrix} = \begin{bmatrix} 2 & 3 \\ 2 & -1 \\ 6 & -3 \end{bmatrix} = B$

(c) $C_2 \leftrightarrow C_2 - C_1$

Elementary matrix obtained $= \begin{bmatrix} 1 & -1 \\ 0 & 1 \end{bmatrix} = C(say)$

Now equivalent matrix obtained by using same transformation to matrix A $= \begin{bmatrix} 2 & 1 \\ 6 & -9 \\ 2 & -3 \end{bmatrix} = B(say)$

Now AC $= \begin{bmatrix} 2 & 3 \\ 6 & -3 \\ 2 & -1 \end{bmatrix}\begin{bmatrix} 1 & -1 \\ 0 & 1 \end{bmatrix} = \begin{bmatrix} 2 & -1 \\ 6 & -9 \\ 2 & -3 \end{bmatrix} = B$

4. Elementary matrix of order 3 × 3 obtained by using the elementary row transformation

$R_2 \to R_2 + 2R_3 = C(say) = \begin{bmatrix} 1 & 0 & 0 \\ 0 & 1 & 2 \\ 0 & 0 & 1 \end{bmatrix}$

Now $A = \begin{bmatrix} 5 & -3 & 2 \\ 6 & 4 & 1 \\ 3 & 2 & 4 \end{bmatrix}$

$R_2 \to R_3 + 2R_3$ gives $B = \begin{bmatrix} 5 & -3 & 2 \\ 12 & 8 & 9 \\ 3 & 2 & 4 \end{bmatrix}$

Now, $CA = \begin{bmatrix} 1 & 0 & 0 \\ 0 & 1 & 2 \\ 0 & 0 & 1 \end{bmatrix}\begin{bmatrix} 5 & -3 & 2 \\ 6 & 4 & 1 \\ 3 & 2 & 4 \end{bmatrix} = \begin{bmatrix} 5 & -3 & 2 \\ 12 & 8 & 9 \\ 3 & 2 & 4 \end{bmatrix} = B$

Hence Gauss Jordan theorem is verified.

5. Elementary matrix of order 3 × 3 obtained by using the elementary column – transformation

$C_3 \to C_3 - 2C_1 = C(say) = \begin{bmatrix} 1 & 0 & -2 \\ 0 & 1 & 0 \\ 0 & 0 & 1 \end{bmatrix}$

Now $A = \begin{bmatrix} 3 & 2 & -1 \\ 6 & -4 & 2 \\ 5 & 3 & 1 \end{bmatrix}$

$C_3 \to C_3 - 2C_1$ gives $B = \begin{bmatrix} 3 & 2 & -7 \\ 6 & -4 & -10 \\ 5 & 3 & -9 \end{bmatrix}$

Now, $AC = \begin{bmatrix} 3 & 2 & -1 \\ 6 & -4 & 2 \\ 5 & 3 & 1 \end{bmatrix}\begin{bmatrix} 1 & 0 & -2 \\ 0 & 1 & 0 \\ 0 & 0 & 1 \end{bmatrix} = \begin{bmatrix} 3 & 2 & -7 \\ 6 & -4 & -10 \\ 5 & 3 & -9 \end{bmatrix} = B$

Hence Gauss –Jordan theorem is verified ...

TEXTUAL EXERCISE 9: (SUBJECTIVE)

1. $AX = B \Rightarrow \begin{bmatrix} 2 & -3 & 5 \\ 3 & 1 & \lambda \\ 1 & -7 & 8 \end{bmatrix}\begin{bmatrix} x \\ y \\ z \end{bmatrix} = \begin{bmatrix} 12 \\ \mu \\ 17 \end{bmatrix}$

$\therefore$ $|A| = 2(8 + 7\lambda) + 3(24 - \lambda) + 5(-21 - 1) = 11\lambda - 22$

(i) For unique solution $|A| \neq 0 \Rightarrow \lambda \neq 2$

(ii) For infinite solutions $\lambda = 2$ and (adj A) $B = O$

$$AdjA = \begin{bmatrix} (8+7\lambda) & (\lambda-24) & -22 \\ -11 & 11 & 11 \\ (-3\lambda-5) & (15-2\lambda) & 11 \end{bmatrix}^T$$

(For $\lambda = 2$) : $(Adj\,A)B = \begin{bmatrix} 22 & -11 & -11 \\ -22 & 11 & 11 \\ -22 & 11 & 11 \end{bmatrix}\begin{bmatrix} 12 \\ \mu \\ 17 \end{bmatrix} = \begin{bmatrix} 0 \\ 0 \\ 0 \end{bmatrix}$

gives $22 \times 12 - 11\mu - 11 \times 17 = 0 \Rightarrow \mu = 7$

(iii) For no solutions (Adj A) . $B \neq O$

$\Rightarrow$ $\lambda = 2$ $\mu \neq 7$

2. $A \times B \Rightarrow \begin{bmatrix} 1 & 1 & 1 \\ 1 & 2 & 3 \\ 1 & 2 & \lambda \end{bmatrix}\begin{bmatrix} 6 \\ 10 \\ \mu \end{bmatrix}$

$|A| = (2\lambda - 6) + (3 - \lambda) + 0 = \lambda - 3$

(i) For no solution $|A| = 0 \Rightarrow \lambda = 3$ and (Adj A) $B \neq O$

$$\Rightarrow (Adj)B = \begin{bmatrix} (2\lambda-6) & (2-\lambda) & 1 \\ (3-\lambda) & (\lambda-1) & -2 \\ 0 & -1 & 1 \end{bmatrix}\begin{bmatrix} 6 \\ 10 \\ \mu \end{bmatrix} \neq \begin{bmatrix} 0 \\ 0 \\ 0 \end{bmatrix}$$

$$(\text{For } \lambda = 3) \begin{bmatrix} 0 & -1 & 1 \\ 0 & 2 & -2 \\ 0 & -1 & 1 \end{bmatrix}\begin{bmatrix} 6 \\ 10 \\ \mu \end{bmatrix} = \begin{bmatrix} (\mu-10) \\ (20-2\mu) \\ (\mu-10) \end{bmatrix} \neq \begin{bmatrix} 0 \\ 0 \\ 0 \end{bmatrix}$$

$\Rightarrow$ $\mu \neq 10$ so $\lambda = 3$ and $\mu \neq 10$

(ii) For a unique solutions $|A| \neq 0 \Rightarrow \lambda \neq 3$ (now μ can have any value)

(iii) For infinite number of solutions $|A| = 0$ And (Adj A) $B = O \Rightarrow \lambda = 3$, $\mu = 10$

3. $AX = \begin{bmatrix} \lambda & \sin\alpha & \cos\alpha \\ 1 & \cos\alpha & \sin\alpha \\ -1 & \sin\alpha & -\cos\alpha \end{bmatrix}\begin{bmatrix} x \\ y \\ z \end{bmatrix} = \begin{bmatrix} 0 \\ 0 \\ 0 \end{bmatrix}$

For non-trivial solution of this homogenous system; $|A| = 0$; ($|A| \neq 0$ gives trivial solutions $x = y = z = 0$)

Now, $|A| = \cos 2\alpha + \sin 2\alpha - \lambda = 0$

$$\lambda = \sqrt{2}\sin\left(\frac{\pi}{4} + 2\alpha\right)$$

$\Rightarrow$ $\lambda \in [-\sqrt{2}, \sqrt{2}]$ For $\lambda = 1 \Rightarrow \sqrt{2}\sin\left(\frac{\pi}{4} + 2\alpha\right) = 1$

Gives $2\alpha = \left(2n\pi + \frac{\pi}{4}\right) \pm \frac{\pi}{4}$

TEXTUAL EXERCISE 4: (OBJECTIVE)

1. (a) $AX = \begin{bmatrix} 2 & 3 & -1 \\ 1 & -1 & -2 \\ 3 & 1 & -2 \end{bmatrix}\begin{bmatrix} x \\ y \\ z \end{bmatrix} = \begin{bmatrix} 0 \\ 0 \\ 0 \end{bmatrix}$

$|A| = 2(4) - 3(-2 + 6) - 1(1 + 3) = -8 \neq 0$

So only trivial solution $x = y = z = 0$

2. (a) $AX = \begin{bmatrix} 2 & -3 & 6 \\ 5 & 7 & 4 \\ 3 & 2 & -4 \end{bmatrix}\begin{bmatrix} x \\ y \\ z \end{bmatrix} = \begin{bmatrix} 4 \\ 1 \\ 0 \end{bmatrix}$

$\therefore$ $|A| = 2(-28 - 8) + 3(-20 - 12) + 6(10 - 21) = -234 \neq 0$

$\therefore$ Unique solution

3. (a) $AX = \begin{bmatrix} 1 & 2 \\ 2 & 3 \end{bmatrix}\begin{bmatrix} x \\ y \end{bmatrix} = \begin{bmatrix} 3 \\ 5 \end{bmatrix}$

$|A| = -1, X = \begin{bmatrix} x \\ y \end{bmatrix} = (-1)\begin{bmatrix} 3 & -2 \\ -2 & 1 \end{bmatrix}\begin{bmatrix} 3 \\ 5 \end{bmatrix} = \begin{bmatrix} 1 \\ 1 \end{bmatrix}$

$\Rightarrow$ $ax + y = 1 \Rightarrow a = 0$

4. (b) $AX = \begin{bmatrix} \lambda & 2 & -2 \\ 4 & 2\lambda & -1 \\ 6 & 6 & \lambda \end{bmatrix}\begin{bmatrix} x \\ y \\ z \end{bmatrix} = \begin{bmatrix} 1 \\ 2 \\ 3 \end{bmatrix}$

For unique Solution

$|A| = \lambda(2\lambda^2 + 6) - 2(4\lambda + 6) - 2(24 - 12\lambda) \neq 0$

$\Rightarrow$ $2\lambda^3 + 22\lambda - 60 \neq 0$

Or $\lambda^3 + 11\lambda - 30 \neq 0$ or $(\lambda - 2)\{(\lambda^2 + 2\lambda + 1) + 14\} \neq 0$

$\lambda \neq 2$

5. (a) $AX = \begin{bmatrix} 1 & 1 & 1 \\ 2 & 1 & -1 \\ 3 & 2 & k \end{bmatrix}\begin{bmatrix} x \\ y \\ z \end{bmatrix} = \begin{bmatrix} 2 \\ 3 \\ 4 \end{bmatrix}$

$|A| = 1(k + 2) - (2k + 3) + (4 - 3) = 0 - k \neq 0$

$\Rightarrow k \neq 0$

6. (c) $AX = \begin{bmatrix} 1 & 1 & 1 \\ a & a+1 & (a+2) \\ a^3 & (a+1)^3 & (a+2)^3 \end{bmatrix}\begin{bmatrix} x \\ y \\ z \end{bmatrix} = \begin{bmatrix} 0 \\ 0 \\ 0 \end{bmatrix}$

For non-trivial solution $|A| = 0$

$|A| = \{6a + 6\} = 0$

$a = -1$

7. (a) $AX = \begin{bmatrix} 2r & -2 & 3 \\ 1 & r & 2 \\ 2 & 0 & r \end{bmatrix}\begin{bmatrix} x \\ y \\ z \end{bmatrix} = \begin{bmatrix} 0 \\ 0 \\ 0 \end{bmatrix}$

For non trivial solution $|A| = 0$

$|A| = 2\{-4 - 3r\} + r\{2r^2 + 2\} = 2(r^3 - 2r - 4)$

$\Rightarrow$ $2(r - 2)\{r^2 + 2r + 2\} = 0$ gives $r = 2$

$\{\because r^2 + 2r + 2 = (r + 1)^2 + 1 \neq 0$

8. (i) (b) $AX = \begin{bmatrix} 2 & p & 6 \\ 1 & 2 & q \\ 1 & 1 & 3 \end{bmatrix}\begin{bmatrix} x \\ y \\ z \end{bmatrix} = \begin{bmatrix} 8 \\ 5 \\ 4 \end{bmatrix}$

$|A| = (p-2)(q-3)$

For no solution $|A| = 0$ and (Adj A) $B \neq O$

$|A| = 0 \Rightarrow p = 2$ or $q = 3$

For $p = 2$, (Adj$A$) $B = O$ and $q \in \mathbb{R}$. So consider $q = 3$

and $p \neq 2$, then $\begin{bmatrix} 3 & (6-3p) & (3p-12) \\ 0 & 0 & 0 \\ -1 & (p-2) & (4-p) \end{bmatrix}\begin{bmatrix} 8 \\ 5 \\ 4 \end{bmatrix} \neq \begin{bmatrix} 0 \\ 0 \\ 0 \end{bmatrix}$

$\Rightarrow \begin{bmatrix} 6-3p \\ 0 \\ p-2 \end{bmatrix} \neq \begin{bmatrix} 0 \\ 0 \\ 0 \end{bmatrix}$ gives $p \neq 2$

$\therefore \; q = 3, p \neq 2$

(ii) For unique solutions $|A| \neq 0 \Rightarrow p \neq 2, q \neq 3$

(iii) For infinite solutions $|A| = 0$ and (Adj A) $B = O$

$\because \; p = 2, q \in \mathbb{R} \Rightarrow |A| = 0$ and (Adj$A$)$.B = 0$

$\Rightarrow$ there will be infinitely many solutions

9. (a) $AX = \begin{bmatrix} a & b \\ c & d \end{bmatrix}\begin{bmatrix} x \\ y \end{bmatrix} = \begin{bmatrix} 0 \\ 0 \end{bmatrix}$ homogeneous equations will have non-trivial solutions if $|A| = 0$

$\Rightarrow ad - bc = 0$

10. (a, c) $\begin{bmatrix} 1 & 1 \\ (1+\lambda) & (2+\lambda) \end{bmatrix}\begin{bmatrix} x \\ y \end{bmatrix} = \begin{bmatrix} 3 \\ 8 \end{bmatrix}$

$|A| = 1 \neq 0$ and $A^{-1}B = X$ gives

$\begin{bmatrix} x \\ y \end{bmatrix} = \begin{bmatrix} (2+\lambda) & -1 \\ -(\lambda+1) & 1 \end{bmatrix}\begin{bmatrix} 3 \\ 8 \end{bmatrix} = \begin{bmatrix} 3\lambda-2 \\ 5-3\lambda \end{bmatrix}$

Putting in the 3rd equation

$(3\lambda - 2) - (1 + \lambda)(5 - 3\lambda) + (\lambda + 2) = 0$

Gives $3\lambda^2 + 2\lambda - 5 = 0$

$(\lambda - 1)\{3\lambda + 5\} = 0 \quad \Rightarrow \lambda = 1; \lambda = -5/3$

11. (d) $AX = B \Rightarrow \begin{bmatrix} 1 & 2 & 3 \\ 1 & -1 & 4 \\ 2 & 1 & 7 \end{bmatrix}\begin{bmatrix} x \\ y \\ z \end{bmatrix} = \begin{bmatrix} 1 \\ 0 \\ 1 \end{bmatrix}$

$|A| = 0$, (Adj A)$B = O$, So infinite solutions for non-homologous equation

As$(Adj\ A)B = \begin{bmatrix} -11 & -11 & 11 \\ 1 & 1 & -1 \\ 3 & 3 & -3 \end{bmatrix}\begin{bmatrix} 1 \\ 0 \\ 1 \end{bmatrix} = \begin{bmatrix} 0 \\ 0 \\ 0 \end{bmatrix}$

12. (a) $AX = \begin{bmatrix} 1 & 1 & 1 \\ 1 & -1 & 2 \\ 3 & 5 & -7 \end{bmatrix}\begin{bmatrix} x \\ y \\ z \end{bmatrix} = \begin{bmatrix} 8 \\ 6 \\ 14 \end{bmatrix}$

$|A| = (7 - 10) - 1(-7 - 6) + 1(5 + 3) = 18 \neq 0$ (unique solution)

13. (a) $AX = \begin{bmatrix} 1 & 2 & 3 \\ 2 & 3 & 4 \\ 3 & 4 & 5 \end{bmatrix}\begin{bmatrix} x \\ y \\ z \end{bmatrix} = \begin{bmatrix} 4 \\ 5 \\ 6 \end{bmatrix}$

$|A| = 0;\ Adj\ A = \begin{bmatrix} -1 & 2 & -1 \\ 2 & -4 & 2 \\ -1 & 2 & -1 \end{bmatrix}^T$

$(Adj\ A)'B = \begin{bmatrix} -1 & 2 & -1 \\ 2 & -4 & 2 \\ -1 & 2 & -1 \end{bmatrix}\begin{bmatrix} 4 \\ 5 \\ 6 \end{bmatrix} = \begin{bmatrix} 0 \\ 0 \\ 0 \end{bmatrix}$

So, infinite number of solutions

14. (a) $AX = \begin{bmatrix} a & b & c \\ b & c & a \\ c & a & b \end{bmatrix}\begin{bmatrix} x \\ y \\ z \end{bmatrix} = \begin{bmatrix} 0 \\ 0 \\ 0 \end{bmatrix}$

$|A| = 0$ gives $a(bc - a^2) - b(b^2 - ac) + c(ab - b^2) = 0$

or $a^3 + b^3 + c^3 - 3abc = 0$

$\Rightarrow \frac{1}{2}(a+b+c)\{a^2 + b^2 + c^2 - ab - bc - ca\} = 0$

Since $a > b > c$

$\Rightarrow \frac{1}{2}(a+b+c)\{(a-b)^2 + (b-c)^2 + (c-a)^2\} = 0$

has only solution $a + b + c = 0$ i.e. $-b = (a + c)$

Now for $t = 1$; $at^2 + bt + c = 0$ gives $a + b + c = 0$

$t = 1, t = c/a$ or $t = \left(\frac{-b}{a} - 1\right)$

TEXTUAL EXERCISE 10: (SUBJECTIVE)

1. **(a)** $x_1 = x = 1.x + 0.Y$

$y_1 = -y = 0.x + (-1)y$

$\Rightarrow \begin{bmatrix} x_1 \\ y_1 \end{bmatrix} = \begin{bmatrix} 1 & 0 \\ 0 & -1 \end{bmatrix}\begin{bmatrix} x \\ y \end{bmatrix}$

$\therefore$ matrix of transformation is $\begin{bmatrix} 1 & 0 \\ 0 & -1 \end{bmatrix}$

(b) $x_1 = 1.x + 0.y$

$y_1 = 0.x + 2.y \quad \Rightarrow \begin{bmatrix} x_1 \\ y_1 \end{bmatrix} = \begin{bmatrix} 1 & 0 \\ 0 & 2 \end{bmatrix}\begin{bmatrix} x \\ y \end{bmatrix}$

$\Rightarrow$ Matrix of transformation is $\begin{bmatrix} 1 & 0 \\ 0 & 2 \end{bmatrix}$

(c) $x_1 = kx = kx + 0y$

$y_1 = ky = 0x + ky$

$\Rightarrow \begin{bmatrix} x_1 \\ y_1 \end{bmatrix} = \begin{bmatrix} k & 0 \\ 0 & k \end{bmatrix}\begin{bmatrix} x \\ y \end{bmatrix}$

$\Rightarrow$ Matrix of transformation is $\begin{bmatrix} k & 0 \\ 0 & k \end{bmatrix}$

(d) $P'(x_1, y_1)$ so $x_1 = x = 1x + 0y$

$y_1 = -y = 0.x + (-1)y$

P″(x_2, y_2) so $x_2 = 2x_1 = 2.x + 0.y$

$y_2 = y_1 = 0.x + (-1)y$

$$\begin{bmatrix} x_2 \\ y_2 \end{bmatrix} = \begin{bmatrix} 2 & 0 \\ 0 & -1 \end{bmatrix}\begin{bmatrix} x \\ y \end{bmatrix}$$

$\Rightarrow$ Matrix of transformation is $\begin{bmatrix} 2 & 0 \\ 0 & -1 \end{bmatrix}$

(e) $x_1 = y = 0x + (1)y \quad y_1 = x = 1x + 0.y$

$$\begin{bmatrix} x_1 \\ y_1 \end{bmatrix} = \begin{bmatrix} 0 & 1 \\ 1 & 0 \end{bmatrix}\begin{bmatrix} x \\ y \end{bmatrix}$$

$\Rightarrow$ Matrix of transformation is $\begin{bmatrix} 0 & 1 \\ 1 & 0 \end{bmatrix}$

(f) $x_1 = x\cos\theta - y\sin\theta \quad y_1 = x\sin\theta + y\cos\theta$

$$\begin{bmatrix} x_1 \\ y_1 \end{bmatrix} = \begin{bmatrix} \cos\theta & -\sin\theta \\ \sin\theta & \cos\theta \end{bmatrix}\begin{bmatrix} x \\ y \end{bmatrix}$$

$\Rightarrow$ Matrix of transformation is $\begin{bmatrix} \cos\theta & -\sin\theta \\ \sin\theta & \cos\theta \end{bmatrix}$

(g) $x'/y = \tan\theta; \quad x' = y\tan\theta$

$$\left.\begin{matrix} x_1 = 1x + y\tan\theta \\ y_1 = 0.x + 1y \end{matrix}\right] \Rightarrow \begin{bmatrix} 1 & \tan\theta \\ 0 & 1 \end{bmatrix}\begin{bmatrix} x \\ y \end{bmatrix}$$

(h) Reflection is origin: $P'(-x, -y)$

$$\left.\begin{matrix} x_1 = -x = (-1)x + 0.y \\ y_1 = -y = 0.x + (-1)y \end{matrix}\right] \Rightarrow \begin{bmatrix} x_1 \\ y_1 \end{bmatrix} = \begin{bmatrix} -1 & 0 \\ 0 & -1 \end{bmatrix}\begin{bmatrix} x \\ y \end{bmatrix}$$

$\Rightarrow$ Matrix of transformation $= \begin{bmatrix} -1 & 0 \\ 0 & -1 \end{bmatrix}$

2. $\begin{bmatrix} x_1 \\ y_1 \end{bmatrix} = \begin{bmatrix} 1 & 1 \\ 1 & 1 \end{bmatrix}\begin{bmatrix} x \\ y \end{bmatrix} \Rightarrow x_1 = x + y, y_1 = x + y$

This transforms a point (x, y) to a point p' on the line $y = x$ such that the distance of p' from both x-axis and y-axis is the (combined) sum of the distances of original point P from x-axis and y-axis. i.e., $P(x, y) \to P'(x + y, x + y)$

3. $x_1 = \frac{\sqrt{3}}{2}y_1 + \frac{1}{2}y_2$ and $x_2 = \frac{-1}{2}y_1 + \frac{\sqrt{3}}{2}y_2$

We observe $\frac{\sqrt{3}}{2}x_1 - \frac{1}{2}x_2 = \frac{3}{4}y_1 + \frac{\sqrt{3}}{2}.\frac{1}{2}y_2 + \frac{1}{4}y_1 - \frac{\sqrt{3}}{2}\frac{1}{2}y_2$

$\Rightarrow \frac{\sqrt{3}}{2}x_1 - \frac{1}{2}x_2 = y_1$

Similarly $\frac{1}{2}x_1 + \frac{\sqrt{3}}{2}x_2 = \frac{1}{4}y_2 + \frac{3}{4}y_2 = y_2$

$\therefore \quad y_1 = \frac{\sqrt{3}}{2}x_1 - \frac{1}{2}x_2;\ y_2 = \frac{1}{2}x_1 + \frac{\sqrt{3}}{2}x_2$

4. $y = 2x - 1$ or $2x - y = 1$

$$\begin{bmatrix} x_1 \\ y_1 \end{bmatrix} = \begin{bmatrix} 2 & -1 \\ 0 & 2 \end{bmatrix}\begin{bmatrix} x \\ y \end{bmatrix} = \begin{bmatrix} (2x - y) \\ 2y \end{bmatrix} = \begin{bmatrix} 1 \\ 2y \end{bmatrix}$$

$\Rightarrow$ Image become the vertical line $x = 1$ with $P(x, y) \to P'(1, 2y)$

5. (a) $\left.\begin{matrix} x = 2, & X = -y \\ & Y = -x = -2 \end{matrix}\right]$

Gives horizontal line $Y = -2$

(b) $\left.\begin{matrix} y = \frac{x}{2}, X = -y = -\frac{x}{2} \\ Y = -x \end{matrix}\right] \Rightarrow Y = 2X$

(c) $\left.\begin{matrix} y = -x - 2, X = -y = x + 2 \\ Y = -x \end{matrix}\right] \Rightarrow X + Y - 2 = 0$

SECTION III: (OBJECTIVE TYPE)

1. (a) $A^T = A$ and $B^T = B \Rightarrow (ABA)^T = A^T(AB)^T = ABA$ so ABA is symmetric

2. (b) Observe $A_1A_2 = \begin{bmatrix} 1 & 1 \\ 0 & 1 \end{bmatrix}\begin{bmatrix} 1 & 2 \\ 0 & 1 \end{bmatrix} = \begin{bmatrix} 1 & 3 \\ 0 & 1 \end{bmatrix} = \begin{bmatrix} 1 & (2+1) \\ 0 & 1 \end{bmatrix}$

and $A_1A_2A_3 = \begin{bmatrix} 1 & 3 \\ 0 & 1 \end{bmatrix}\begin{bmatrix} 1 & 3 \\ 0 & 1 \end{bmatrix} = \begin{bmatrix} 1 & (3+2+1) \\ 0 & 1 \end{bmatrix}$

So, in general $A_1A_2A_3 \ldots\ldots A_n$

$$= \begin{bmatrix} 1 & n + (n-1) + (n-2) + \ldots + 3 + 2 + 1 \\ 0 & 1 \end{bmatrix}$$

So $\frac{n(n+1)}{2} = 378 \Rightarrow n = 27$

3. (d) $x^2 - (a + b)x + k = 0 \Rightarrow k = ab$

$$KI = \begin{bmatrix} ab & 0 \\ 0 & ab \end{bmatrix} = (a+b)A - A^2$$

$$\begin{bmatrix} ab & 0 \\ 0 & ab \end{bmatrix} = \begin{bmatrix} (a+b)a & (a+b)b \\ (a+b)c & (a+b)d \end{bmatrix} - \begin{bmatrix} (a^2+bc) & (ab+bd) \\ (ac+cd) & (bc+d^2) \end{bmatrix}$$

$ab = a^2 + ab - a^2 - bc \Rightarrow bc = 0$ and $b^2 - bd = b(b - d) = 0$ and $ac + bc - ac - cd = 0 \Rightarrow cd = 0$ (as $bc = 0$)

4. (d) If A and B are conformable for product then AB need not be equal to BA. Hence tr (AB) need not be equal to tr(BA)

5. (b) Let B be $m \times n$, A is 3×4 so A' is 4×3

$A'B = [A']_{4\times3} \times [B]_{m\times n} \Rightarrow m = 3$

$BA' = [B]_{m\times n} \times [A']_{4\times3} \Rightarrow n = 3$

$B'A = [B]_{4\times3}\,[A]_{3\times4} \Rightarrow B'A$ is 4×4

6. (c) $A(\text{Adj}A) = |A|I_n$; $|A| = xyz - (8x + 4y + 3z) + 28$

$$= 60 - 20 + 28 = 68 \Rightarrow A(Adj\ A) = \begin{bmatrix} 68 & 0 & 0 \\ 0 & 68 & 0 \\ 0 & 0 & 68 \end{bmatrix}$$

7. (c) $(A + 2B) + (4A - 2B) = 5A = \begin{bmatrix} 5 & 0 & 10 \\ 10 & -5 & 15 \\ -5 & 5 & 5 \end{bmatrix}$

$$\Rightarrow A = \begin{bmatrix} 1 & 0 & 2 \\ 2 & -1 & 3 \\ -1 & 1 & 1 \end{bmatrix}$$

$$\Rightarrow\quad B = 2A - \begin{bmatrix} 2 & -1 & 5 \\ 2 & -1 & 6 \\ 0 & 1 & 2 \end{bmatrix} \quad \Rightarrow \quad B = \begin{bmatrix} 0 & 1 & -1 \\ 2 & -1 & 0 \\ -2 & 1 & 0 \end{bmatrix}$$

$\therefore\; Tr(A) = 1;\; Tr(B) = 1 \quad \Rightarrow \quad Tr(A) - Tr(B) = 2$

8. (d) $X^2 = I \Rightarrow X^{-1}(XX) = X = X^{-1}I = X^{-1}$
$X \equiv \pm I$ or $X = X^{-1}$
Self invertible involuntary matrices.
There are many such matrices which are inverse of their own

9. (d) $\begin{bmatrix} (A-5) & B \\ (2A-2) & C \end{bmatrix} = \begin{bmatrix} 2A+1 & -5 \\ -4 & A \end{bmatrix}\begin{bmatrix} 14 & D \\ E & F \end{bmatrix}$

$\Rightarrow A - 5 = 28A + 14 - 5E \Rightarrow 5E = 27A + 19$
$2A - 2 = AE - 56 \Rightarrow AE = 2A + 54$
$5AE = 27A^2 + 19A$ and $5AE = 10A + 270$
$\Rightarrow 27A^2 + 9A - 270 = 0 \Rightarrow 9(A-3)(3A+10) = 0$

$A = 3, A = -10/3 \Rightarrow$ Absolute value of difference $= \dfrac{19}{3}$

10. (d) $A = \begin{vmatrix} \lambda-1 & \lambda & \lambda+1 \\ 2 & -1 & 3 \\ \lambda+3 & \lambda-2 & \lambda+7 \end{vmatrix} = \begin{vmatrix} \lambda-1 & \lambda & \lambda+1 \\ 2 & -1 & 3 \\ 0 & 0 & 0 \end{vmatrix} = 0$

$R_3 \to R_3 - (2R_2 + R_1)$. Independent of λ
$\Rightarrow \lambda$ can have any value

11. (a) Observe that $BC = \begin{bmatrix} 3 & 4 \\ 2 & 3 \end{bmatrix}\begin{bmatrix} 3 & -4 \\ -2 & 3 \end{bmatrix} = \begin{bmatrix} 1 & 0 \\ 0 & 1 \end{bmatrix} = I$

$\Rightarrow BC = (BC)^2 = (BC)^3 = \ldots\ldots\ldots\ldots = I$ and $A(BC)^n = A$
So the series boils down to

becomes, $tr(A) + \dfrac{tr(A)}{2} + \dfrac{tr(A)}{2^2} + \dfrac{tr(A)}{2^3} + \ldots..$

$= 3 + \dfrac{3}{2} + \dfrac{3}{4} + \dfrac{3}{8} + \ldots.. = 3\{2\} = 6$

12. (d) $A^3 - A^2B = B^3 - B^2A$ gives
$A^2(A - B) = B^2(B - A)$ or $(A^2 + B^2)(A - B) = O$
Either det $(A^2 + B^2) = 0$ det $(A - B) = 0$

13. (d) $A^{-9}B^{-1}$ is a 2 × 2 matrix

$\Rightarrow \det(2A^9B^{-1}) = 2^2(\det A)^9 \dfrac{1}{(\det B)} = \dfrac{4\times(-1)^9}{2} = -2$

14. (d) Let $B = \prod_{r=1}^{r=50} \begin{bmatrix} 1 & 2r-1 \\ 0 & 1 \end{bmatrix} = \begin{bmatrix} 1 & 1 \\ 0 & 1 \end{bmatrix}\begin{bmatrix} 1 & 3 \\ 0 & 1 \end{bmatrix}\begin{bmatrix} 1 & 5 \\ 0 & 1 \end{bmatrix}\ldots$

Observe that $\begin{bmatrix} 1 & 1 \\ 0 & 1 \end{bmatrix}\begin{bmatrix} 1 & 3 \\ 0 & 1 \end{bmatrix} = \begin{bmatrix} 1 & 4 \\ 0 & 1 \end{bmatrix} = \begin{bmatrix} 1 & (3+1) \\ 0 & 1 \end{bmatrix}$

And $\begin{bmatrix} 1 & 4 \\ 0 & 1 \end{bmatrix}\begin{bmatrix} 1 & 5 \\ 0 & 1 \end{bmatrix} = \begin{bmatrix} 1 & 9 \\ 0 & 1 \end{bmatrix} = \begin{bmatrix} 1 & 5+3+1 \\ 0 & 1 \end{bmatrix}$

And so on $\Rightarrow B = \begin{bmatrix} 1 & (1+3+5+\ldots 99 \text{ i.e. } 50 \text{ terms}) \\ 0 & 1 \end{bmatrix}$

$$B = \begin{bmatrix} 1 & 2500 \\ 0 & 1 \end{bmatrix}$$

15. (c) $B^T = \begin{bmatrix} 4x & 4y & 4z \\ 2a & 2b & 2c \\ -p & -q & -r \end{bmatrix} \Rightarrow |B| = (-8)\begin{vmatrix} x & y & z \\ a & b & c \\ p & q & r \end{vmatrix}$

Interchange R_1 and R_2 and then interchange R_2 and R_3

$\Rightarrow |B| = (-8)(-1)(-1)\begin{vmatrix} a & b & c \\ p & q & r \\ x & y & z \end{vmatrix} = (-8)(2) = -16$

16. (c) $A^2 = \begin{bmatrix} a & 1 \\ -1 & b \end{bmatrix}\begin{bmatrix} a & 1 \\ -1 & b \end{bmatrix} = \begin{bmatrix} (a^2-1) & (a+b) \\ -(a+b) & (b^2-1) \end{bmatrix} = \begin{bmatrix} 0 & 0 \\ 0 & 0 \end{bmatrix}$

$a + b = 0 \Rightarrow a = -b$ and $a^2 - 1 = b^2 - 1 = 0$
$\Rightarrow a = 1;\, b = -1$ or $a = -1,\, b = 1 \Rightarrow ab = -1$

17. (b) Using $A.\text{Adj}A = |A|I_n$ and $\det(A.(\text{Adj}A)) = |A|^n$
$\Rightarrow |\text{Adj}A| = |A|^{n-1}$ so $\Delta_1 = \Delta_0^2$ and similarly
$\Delta_2 = \Delta_1^2 = \Delta_0^4;\ \Delta_3 = \Delta_2^2 = \Delta_1^4\ \Delta_0^8$; and so on
$\Rightarrow \Delta_n = \Delta_0^{2^n}$

18. (d) $|A| = 1 + \tan^2 x = \sec^2 x$
$\det(A^TA^{-1}) = \det(A^T).\det(A^{-1}) = \det(A)\dfrac{1}{\det(A)} = 1$

19. (a) $A^2 = \begin{bmatrix} 1 & 0 & 0 \\ 0 & 1 & 0 \\ a & b & -1 \end{bmatrix}\begin{bmatrix} 1 & 0 & 0 \\ 0 & 1 & 0 \\ a & b & -1 \end{bmatrix} = \begin{bmatrix} 1 & 0 & 0 \\ 0 & 1 & 0 \\ 0 & 0 & 1 \end{bmatrix} = I_3$

20. (d) $|A| = a^3$; using $A(\text{Adj}A) = |A|\,I_n$
$\Rightarrow \det(A).\det(\text{Adj}A) = |A|^n = |A|^3 = a^3.a^3.a^3 = a^9$

21. (a) $(A + B)^m = {}^mC_c\,A^m + {}^mC_1\,A^{m-1}B + {}^mC_2\,A^{m-2}B^2 + \ldots.$ is possible only when $A^pB^q = B^qA^p$ i.e $AB = BA$

22. (a) $A = [a_{ij}]_{3\times3}$ is a skew –symmetric matrix of odd $(n = 3)$ order $\Rightarrow a_{ii} = 0$ and $|A| = 0$; $A + A^T = O$

23 (b) $\left.\begin{matrix} \text{For symmetric} & a_{ij} = a_{ji} \\ \text{and for skew-symmetric} & a_{ij} = -a_{ji} \end{matrix}\right] \Rightarrow a_{ij} = a_{ji} = -a_{ji}$

Possible only when $a_{ij} = 0$. Hence a null matrix.

24. (c) $(AB)^T = B^TA^T = BA$ unless the matrices commute, they will not be symmetric
$(A - B)^T = A^T - B^T = A - B \Rightarrow A - B$ is symmetric
$(AB + BA)^T = (AB)^T + (BA)^T = B^TA^T + A^TB^T$
$= BA + AB = AB + BA \therefore$ symmetric
$(AB - BA)^T = (AB)^T - (BA)^T = B^TA^T - A^TB^T = BA - AB$
$= -(AB - BA)$ hence skew symmetric

25. (a) $[A]_{m\times(n+5)}\,[B]_{m\times(11-n)}$
$[B]_{m\times(11-n)}\,[A]_{m\times(n+5)}$
$\Rightarrow n + 5 = m$ and $11 - n = m$
$\Rightarrow n = 3;\, m = 8$
$\Rightarrow A$ is of order 8 × 8 and B is of order 8 × 8
$\Rightarrow [AB]_{8\times8}$ and $[BA]_{8\times8}$

26. (b) $[[A, B], C] = (ABC - BAC - CAB + CBA)$
$[[B, C], A] = (BCA - CBA - ABC + ACB)$
$[[C, A], B] = \{CAB - ACB - BCA + BAC\}$ Sum $= O$

27. (b) Let $A + B = C$ and $(A + B)^{-1} = D$ then by reversal law
$(ADB)^{-1} = B^{-1}D^{-1}A^{-1} = B^{-1}\,C\,A^{-1}$
$= B^{-1}(A + B)A^{-1} = B^{-1}AA^{-1} + B^{-1}BA^{-1}$
$= B^{-1}I + IA^{-1} = A^{-1} + B^{-1}$

28. (d) Given $AB = BA$
Pre-multiplication by A^{-1} gives $IB = A^{-1}BA$
Post multiplication by A^{-1} gives $BA^{-1} = A^{-1}BI = A^{-1}B$
$\Rightarrow$ A^{-1} and B commute similarly B^{-1} and A commute as well as A^{-1} and B^{-1} commute

29. (c) In skew symmetric matrix $a_{ii} = 0\ \forall\ i$
$\Rightarrow T_r(A) = 0$

30. (d) A is a non-zero diagonal matrix where $A^2 = A$

$$\Rightarrow \text{diag. } A^2 = \begin{bmatrix} \sin 2\theta + \cos 2\theta & \sqrt{2}\sin 2\theta \\ -\sqrt{2}\sin 2\theta & \cos 2\theta - \sin 2\theta \end{bmatrix}$$

$\Rightarrow a_{ii}^2 = a_{ii}\ \forall\ i \in \{1,2,3,4\} \Rightarrow a_{ii} = 1$ or o $\forall\ i$
$\Rightarrow$ Total (16 – 1) = 15 non-zero diagonal matrices are possible.

31. (c) $$AB = \begin{bmatrix} 0 & c & -b \\ -c & 0 & a \\ b & -a & 0 \end{bmatrix}\begin{bmatrix} a^2 & ab & ac \\ ab & b^2 & bc \\ ac & bc & c^2 \end{bmatrix} = \begin{bmatrix} 0 & 0 & 0 \\ 0 & 0 & 0 \\ 0 & 0 & 0 \end{bmatrix} = O$$

32. (d) $(A^{-1})^T = A$ given $\Rightarrow A^{-1} = A^T$
$AA^{-1} = I = AA^T$ (Orthogonal matrix) $\Rightarrow |A| = |A^T| = \pm 1$
$\Rightarrow |\text{Adj}A| = |A|^{n-1} = (\pm 1)^2 = 1$
$\Rightarrow |\text{Adj}(\text{Adj}A)| = (1)^2 = 1$

33. (b) $$AA^T = \begin{bmatrix} \alpha & a \\ \beta & b \\ \gamma & c \end{bmatrix}\begin{bmatrix} \alpha & \beta & \gamma \\ a & b & c \end{bmatrix}$$

$$= \begin{bmatrix} (\alpha^2 + \alpha^2) & (\alpha\beta + ab) & (\alpha\gamma + ac) \\ (\alpha\beta + ab) & (\beta^2 + b^2) & (\beta\gamma + bc) \\ (\alpha\gamma + ac) & (\beta\gamma + bc) & (\gamma^2 + c^2) \end{bmatrix}$$

34. (d) $AB = O$ gives $(\det A)(\det B) = A$
Either $\det(A) = 0$ or $\det(B) = 0$

35. (a) $$A_k = \begin{bmatrix} \left({}^nC_{k-1}\right)^2 & 0 \\ 0 & \left({}^nC_k\right)^2 \end{bmatrix}$$

$$\Rightarrow \sum_{p=1}^{n} A_p = \begin{bmatrix} \sum_0^{n-1}\left({}^nC_r\right)^2 & 0 \\ 0 & \sum_1^{n}\left({}^nC_r\right)^2 \end{bmatrix}$$

$$= \begin{bmatrix} {}^{2n}C_n - 1 & 0 \\ 0 & {}^{2n}C_n - 1 \end{bmatrix} = \begin{bmatrix} k_1 & 0 \\ 0 & k_2 \end{bmatrix} \text{ (given)}$$

$\Rightarrow k_1 = k_2 = {}^{2n}C_n - 1$

36. (b) Given $B = -A^{-1}BA$ or $-AB = BA$
So $AB + BA = O \Rightarrow (A + B)^2 = A^2 + B^2$

37. (d) $\det\{\text{Adj}(\text{Adj } A)\} = (14)^4 = |A|^{(n-1)2}$
$\Rightarrow |A| = 14 = 3x + 11 \Rightarrow x = 1$

38. (b) (i) $AB = O \Rightarrow A = O$ or $B = O$ is false
(ii) $AB = I_2 \Rightarrow A = B^{-1}$ is true, B is non-singular
(iii) $(A + B)^2 = A^2 + 2AB + B^2$ is true only if A and B commute (i.e $AB = BA$)

39. (d) The determinant of skew –symmetric matrix of odd order vanishes so inverse does not exist

40. (c) **Statement –1:** $[A]_{3\times 3}$ is invertible and B is 3×4
$\Rightarrow A^{-1}B$ is defined so true
Statement –2: It is never true that $A + B$, $A - B$ and AB are all defined, is false as they are defined for A and B square matrices of same order
Statement – 3 ; Every matrix none of whose entries is zero is invertible is false as there are matrices having all non-zero elements, still are singular.e.g. $\begin{bmatrix} 1 & 2 & 3 \\ 4 & 5 & 6 \\ 7 & 8 & 9 \end{bmatrix}$

Statement – 4 : true

SECTION IV: (MORE THAN ONE CORRECT ANSWER)

1. (a, b, c, d) $abc = 1$; $A = \begin{bmatrix} a & b & c \\ b & c & a \\ c & a & b \end{bmatrix}$

$|A| = 3bc - (a^3 + b^3 + c^3)$
$A^TA = I \Rightarrow A^T = A^{-1} \Rightarrow |A| = |A^T| = \pm 1$ (orthogonal)
$\Rightarrow 3abc - (a^3 + b^3 + c^3) = \pm 1$
or $a^3 + b^3 + c^3 = 3abc \pm 1 = 2,4$

$$\text{Now } A^TA = \begin{bmatrix} a & b & c \\ b & c & a \\ c & a & b \end{bmatrix}\begin{bmatrix} a & b & c \\ b & c & a \\ c & a & b \end{bmatrix}$$

$$= \begin{bmatrix} a^2+b^2+c^2 & ab+bc+ca & ab+bc+ca \\ ab+bc+ca & a^2+b^2+c^2 & ab+bc+ca \\ ab+bc+ca & ab+bc+ca & a^2+b^2+c^2 \end{bmatrix}$$

Clearly $(a^2 + b^2 + c^2) = 1$ and $(ab + bc + ca) = 0$
So $(a^3 + b^3 + c^3 - 3abc) = (a + b + c)\{(a^2 + b^2 + c^2) - (ab + bc + ca)\} = (a + b + c) = \pm 1$
$(a + b + c)^2 = (a^2 + b^2 + c^2) + 2(ab + bc + ca) = 1$
So $(a + b + c) = \pm 1$
If $(a + b + c) = 1$, then $a^3 + b^3 + c^3 = 4$

2. (a, c) $[A]_{3\times 3}$ and $[B]_{3\times 3}$ $(|A| \neq 0)$
$\Rightarrow |AB| = 0 \Rightarrow (\det A)(\det B) = 0$
$\Rightarrow \det B = 0$ (as $|A| \neq 0$) Also $|A^{-1}| = |A|^{-1}$

3. (a,b,c) Let $D_1 = \begin{bmatrix} d_1 & 0 & 0 \\ 0 & d_2 & 0 \\ 0 & 0 & d_3 \end{bmatrix}$ and $D_2 = \begin{bmatrix} d_4 & 0 & 0 \\ 0 & d_5 & 0 \\ 0 & 0 & d_6 \end{bmatrix}$

$$D_1D_2 = \begin{bmatrix} d_1d_4 & 0 & 0 \\ 0 & d_2d_5 & 0 \\ 0 & 0 & d_3d_6 \end{bmatrix} = D_2D_1$$

$\therefore$ D_1D_2 is a diagonal matrix

$$D_1^2 = \begin{bmatrix} d_1^2 & 0 & 0 \\ 0 & d_2^2 & 0 \\ 0 & 0 & d_3^2 \end{bmatrix} \text{ and } D_2^2 = \begin{bmatrix} d_4^2 & 0 & 0 \\ 0 & d_5^2 & 0 \\ 0 & 0 & d_6^2 \end{bmatrix} \text{ and}$$

sum gives a diagonal matrix

4. (c, d) $AB = O \Rightarrow \det(AB) = (\det A)(\det B) = 0$

$\Rightarrow$ either $\det A = 0$ or $\det B = 0$

$\therefore$ At least one of the two matrices must be singular otherwise this statements is not possible

5. (a,b,c) We observe that $a_{ij} = a_{ji} \Rightarrow$ symmetric

$\Rightarrow$ A is symmetric

$$|A| = abc + ab + bc + ca = abc\left\{1+\left(\frac{1}{a}+\frac{1}{b}+\frac{1}{c}\right)\right\}$$

Since a,b,c are non zero and $\frac{1}{a}+\frac{1}{b}+\frac{1}{c}=0$

$\therefore$ $|A| = abc \neq 0$

Now $\frac{1}{2}\{(A+A^T)\}$ is symmetric since $A^T = A$

$\therefore$ For a symmetric matrix $\Rightarrow A = A + O$ (null matrix)

Here the null matrix will serve as a skew symmetric matrix

6. (c, d) The system will have infinitely many solutions if det $A = 0$ and (Adj A). $B = O$

7. (a, b) $[a_{ij}] = i^2 - j^2$ (given) $\Rightarrow a_{kk} = 0$ and $a_{ij} = -(j^2 - i^2) = -a_{ji}$

Hence a skew symmetric matrix, since the order is even

Det A will be a perfect square

8. (a, b) $AB = AC \Rightarrow B = C$. If A is invertible i.e. $|A| \neq 0$

$\{$As $A^{-1}(AB) = A^{-1}(AC) \Rightarrow IB = IC$ or $B = C\}$

SECTION V: (ASSERTION AND REASON TYPE)

1. (b) Clearly reason is correct. Let $A = \begin{bmatrix} a & b \\ c & d \end{bmatrix}$

Since $AB = BA$ holds for every 2×2 matrix B. So, in particular let $B = \begin{bmatrix} 0 & 1 \\ 1 & 0 \end{bmatrix}$

Thus $\begin{bmatrix} a & b \\ c & d \end{bmatrix}\begin{bmatrix} 0 & 1 \\ 1 & 0 \end{bmatrix} = \begin{bmatrix} 0 & 1 \\ 1 & 0 \end{bmatrix}\begin{bmatrix} a & b \\ c & d \end{bmatrix}$

$$\Rightarrow \begin{bmatrix} b & a \\ d & c \end{bmatrix}\begin{bmatrix} c & d \\ a & b \end{bmatrix} \Rightarrow a = d, b = c$$

$$\therefore \quad A = \begin{bmatrix} a & b \\ b & a \end{bmatrix}$$

Further let $B = \begin{bmatrix} 1 & 1 \\ 0 & 0 \end{bmatrix}$ then $\begin{bmatrix} a & b \\ b & a \end{bmatrix}\begin{bmatrix} 1 & 1 \\ 0 & 0 \end{bmatrix} = \begin{bmatrix} 1 & 1 \\ 0 & 0 \end{bmatrix}\begin{bmatrix} a & b \\ b & a \end{bmatrix}$

$$\Rightarrow \begin{bmatrix} a & a \\ b & b \end{bmatrix} = \begin{bmatrix} a+b & b+a \\ 0 & 0 \end{bmatrix} \Rightarrow b = 0$$

$$\therefore \quad A = \begin{bmatrix} a & 0 \\ 0 & a \end{bmatrix} \Rightarrow A \text{ is a scalar matrix}$$

But assertion does not follow from reason.

2. (b) Let $D = \text{diag}(d_1, d_2, d_3, \ldots d_n)$

$|D| = d_1.d_2.d_3$

$\therefore$ $d_n \neq 0$ as each $d \neq 0$

Now Adj$(D) = [(-1)^{i+i}\, d_1.d_2 \ldots d_{i-1}.d_{i+1} \ldots d_n]$

$$\Rightarrow D^{-1} = \frac{1}{d_1.d_2....d_n}[d_1\, d_2\, d_3 \ldots d_{i-1}.d_{i+1}..d_n]$$

$$\Rightarrow D^{-1} = [k_{ij}]; k_{ij} = \begin{cases} \frac{1}{d_i} \text{for } i = j \\ 0 \text{ for } i \neq j \end{cases}$$

$\Rightarrow$ D^{-1} diag. $(d_1^{-1} d_2^{-1} d_3^{-1}.....d_n^{-1})$

$\Rightarrow$ Assertion is correct, reason is also correct but not correct explanation.

3 (b) **A:** given $abc = 1$ and $AA^T = I \Rightarrow |A^T| = |A| = \pm 1$

$$AA^T = \begin{bmatrix} a & b & c \\ b & c & a \\ c & a & b \end{bmatrix}\begin{bmatrix} a & b & c \\ b & c & a \\ c & a & b \end{bmatrix}$$

$$= \begin{bmatrix} a^2+b^2+c^2 & ab+bc+ca & ab+bc+ca \\ ab+bc+ca & a^2+b^2+c^2 & ab+bc+ca \\ ab+bc+ca & ab+bc+ca & a^2+b^2+c^2 \end{bmatrix} = \begin{bmatrix} 1 & 0 & 0 \\ 0 & 1 & 0 \\ 0 & 0 & 1 \end{bmatrix}$$

gives $a^2 + b^2 + c^2 = 1$ and $ab + bc + ca = 0$

$abc = 1 \Rightarrow \frac{1}{a}+\frac{1}{b}+\frac{1}{c}=0$

$(a + b + c)^2 = a^2 + b^2 + c^2 - 2\,(ab + bc + ca) = 1$

$\Rightarrow$ $(a + b + c) = \pm 1$

$|A| = -(a^3 + b^3 + c^3) + 3abc = 3 - (a^3 + b^3 + c^3) = \pm 1$

For $|A| = -1$, $a^3 + b^3 + c^3 = 4$ and for $|A| = 1$, $a^3 + b^3 + c^3 = 2$

We observe that R : $\frac{1}{a}+\frac{1}{b}+\frac{1}{c}=0$ is true, but without using this result assertion can be derived i.e., by using $\Sigma a^2 = 1$ and $\Sigma ab = 0$

$\therefore$ Reason is not true correct explanation of assertion.

4. Let $X = \begin{bmatrix} a & b \\ c & d \\ e & f \end{bmatrix}_{3\times 2}$; $X^T = \begin{bmatrix} a & c & e \\ b & d & f \end{bmatrix}$

$$\therefore \quad XX^T = \begin{bmatrix} a & b \\ c & d \\ e & f \end{bmatrix}\begin{bmatrix} a & c & e \\ b & d & f \end{bmatrix}$$

$$= \begin{bmatrix} a^2+b^2 & ac+bd & ac+bf \\ ca+bd & c^2+d^2 & ce+df \\ ae+bf & ce+df & e^2+f^2 \end{bmatrix}$$

$$= \begin{bmatrix} a & b & 0 \\ c & d & 0 \\ e & f & 0 \end{bmatrix}\begin{bmatrix} a & c & e \\ b & d & f \\ 0 & 0 & 0 \end{bmatrix} = AB(say)$$

Clearly $|A| = |B| = 0 \Rightarrow |XX^T| = |AB| = |A|\,|B|$

$\therefore$ XX^T is a singular matrix.

Similarly XX^T is a singular matrix when X is of any order $m \times n$; $m > n$. Thus assertion as well as reason both are correct and reason is the correct explanation of reason

5. **(d)** R :3 × 3 matrix $a_{ij} = \dfrac{i-j}{i+2j}$

$$A = \begin{bmatrix} 0 & \frac{-1}{5} & \frac{-2}{7} \\ \frac{1}{4} & 0 & -\frac{1}{8} \\ \frac{2}{5} & \frac{1}{7} & 0 \end{bmatrix}$$ which is neither symmetric nor skew symmetric

$\therefore$ R is true statement that $\left[a_{ij}\right]_{3\times 3} = \dfrac{i-j}{i+2j}$ cannot be expressed as sum of a symmetric and a skew symmetric matrix, is not true as every square matrix can be expressed as the sum of a symmetric matrix $P(=1/2(A + A^T))$ and skew symmetric matrix $Q(=1/2(A - A^T)$

SECTION VI: (LINKED COMPREHENSION TYPE)

Comprehension A:

1. (b,d) $AX = U \Rightarrow \begin{bmatrix} a & 1 & 0 \\ 1 & b & d \\ 1 & b & c \end{bmatrix}\begin{bmatrix} x \\ y \\ z \end{bmatrix} = \begin{bmatrix} f \\ g \\ h \end{bmatrix}$

$\Rightarrow \begin{bmatrix} (ax+y) \\ (x+by+dz) \\ (x+by+cz) \end{bmatrix} = \begin{bmatrix} f \\ g \\ h \end{bmatrix}$; Now $|A| = (c - d)\,(ab - 1) = 0$

Gives $c = d$ or $ab = 1$

$$(\text{Adj } A)U = \begin{bmatrix} (bc-bd) & -c & d \\ (d-c) & ac & -ad \\ 0 & (1-ab) & (ab-1) \end{bmatrix}\begin{bmatrix} f \\ g \\ h \end{bmatrix} = O$$

$\Rightarrow \begin{bmatrix} bf(c-d)-cg+dh \\ f(d-c)+acg-adh \\ 0+(1-ab)g+(ab-1)h \end{bmatrix} = \begin{bmatrix} 0 \\ 0 \\ 0 \end{bmatrix}$; If $c = d \Rightarrow g = h$;

Which is minimum and overall $c = d$, $h = g$, $ab = 1$

2. (b) $BX = V \Rightarrow \begin{bmatrix} a & 1 & 1 \\ 0 & d & c \\ f & g & h \end{bmatrix}\begin{bmatrix} x \\ y \\ z \end{bmatrix} = \begin{bmatrix} a^2 \\ 0 \\ 0 \end{bmatrix}$

$\Rightarrow \begin{bmatrix} (ax+y+z) \\ (dy+cz) \\ fx+gy+hz \end{bmatrix} = \begin{bmatrix} a^2 \\ 0 \\ 0 \end{bmatrix}$

Now $c = d$ $\qquad \Rightarrow y = -z$

$\Rightarrow x = a, f.x = 0$, so either $f = 0$ or $x = 0$

Now, $|B| = a\,(dh - gc) + f(c - d) = 0$

As $c = d, h = g$; $(\text{Adj}B).V = \begin{bmatrix} dh-gc & g-h & c-d \\ fc & ah-f & -ac \\ -df & f-ag & ad \end{bmatrix}\begin{bmatrix} a^2 \\ 0 \\ 0 \end{bmatrix}$

$= \begin{bmatrix} a^2(dh-gc) \\ a^2 fc \\ -a^2 fd \end{bmatrix} = \begin{bmatrix} 0 \\ a^2 fc \\ -a^2 fd \end{bmatrix}$ (Adj B) V will be a null matrix

($\because f = 0$ or $x = 0 \Rightarrow a = x = 0 \Rightarrow$ (Adj B).$V = O$)

$\therefore$ Infinite number of solutions

3. (a, b, c) For $BX = V$ to be consistent (Adj B) . $V = O$ i.e. $a^2fc = 0$; $a^2fd = 0$

Which is possible if $a = 0$ or $f = 0$ or $d = 0$

Comprehension B:

$AU_1 = \begin{bmatrix} 1 \\ 0 \\ 0 \end{bmatrix}$ (given) $\Rightarrow \begin{bmatrix} 1 & 0 & 0 \\ 2 & 1 & 0 \\ 3 & 2 & 1 \end{bmatrix}\begin{bmatrix} x \\ y \\ z \end{bmatrix} = \begin{bmatrix} 1 \\ 0 \\ 0 \end{bmatrix}$

Gives $x = 1$, $2x + y = 0 \Rightarrow y = -2$

$3x + 2y + z = 0 \qquad \Rightarrow z = 1$; Hence $U_1 = \begin{bmatrix} 1 \\ -2 \\ 1 \end{bmatrix}$

Similarly $U_2 = \begin{bmatrix} 2 \\ -1 \\ -4 \end{bmatrix}$ and $U_3 = \begin{bmatrix} 2 \\ -1 \\ -3 \end{bmatrix}$

4. (a) $|U| = \begin{vmatrix} 1 & 2 & 2 \\ -2 & -1 & -1 \\ 1 & -4 & -3 \end{vmatrix} = 3$

5. (b) $Adj\,U = \begin{bmatrix} -1 & -2 & 0 \\ -7 & -5 & -3 \\ 9 & 6 & 3 \end{bmatrix}$

$$U^{-1} = \frac{Adj\,U}{|U|} = \frac{1}{3}\begin{bmatrix} -1 & -2 & 0 \\ -7 & -5 & -3 \\ 9 & 6 & 3 \end{bmatrix}$$

Sum of the elements = 0

6. (a) The value of $[3\ 2\ 0]\begin{bmatrix} 1 & 2 & 2 \\ -2 & -1 & -1 \\ 1 & -4 & -3 \end{bmatrix}\begin{bmatrix} 3 \\ 2 \\ 0 \end{bmatrix}$

$= [-1\ 4\ 4]\begin{bmatrix} 3 \\ 2 \\ 0 \end{bmatrix} = [8 - 3] = [5]$

Comprehension C:

7. (b) Solving $|A - nI| = 0$, we get

$$\begin{vmatrix} (1-n) & 2 & 0 \\ 2 & (1-n) & 0 \\ 0 & 0 & (1-n) \end{vmatrix} = (1-n)\{n^2 + 1 - 2n - 4\} = 0$$

$\Rightarrow (1-n)\{(n-3)(n+1)\} = 0$, so $n = -1, 1, 3$

As $n_1 > n_2 > n_3$, so $n_1 = 3$, $n_2 = 1$, $n_3 = -1$

$$\therefore \quad N = \begin{bmatrix} 3 & 0 & 0 \\ 0 & 1 & 0 \\ 0 & 0 & -1 \end{bmatrix}$$

8. (d) The equation must be in A^3

9. (a) A is symmetric

$\therefore$ $(A^T)^{-1} = A^{-1}$ and inverse is also symmetric

$$A^{-1} = \frac{1}{3}\begin{bmatrix} -1 & 2 & 0 \\ 2 & -1 & 0 \\ 0 & 0 & 3 \end{bmatrix}$$

$B = A^{-1} N (A^{-1})^T = A^{-1}\, N\, A^{-1}$

$$= \frac{1}{3}\begin{bmatrix} -1 & 2 & 0 \\ 2 & -1 & 0 \\ 0 & 0 & 3 \end{bmatrix}\begin{bmatrix} 3 & 0 & 0 \\ 0 & 1 & 0 \\ 0 & 0 & -1 \end{bmatrix}\begin{bmatrix} A^{-1} \end{bmatrix}$$

$$\begin{bmatrix} -1 & \frac{2}{3} & 0 \\ 2 & \frac{-1}{3} & 0 \\ 0 & 0 & -1 \end{bmatrix}\begin{bmatrix} -\frac{1}{3} & \frac{2}{3} & 0 \\ \frac{2}{3} & -\frac{1}{3} & 0 \\ 0 & 0 & 1 \end{bmatrix} = \begin{bmatrix} \frac{7}{9} & \frac{-8}{9} & 0 \\ -\frac{8}{9} & \frac{13}{9} & 0 \\ 0 & 0 & -1 \end{bmatrix}$$

$\Rightarrow$ B is either Symmetric or Hermitian

10. (a) $A^2 = \begin{bmatrix} 1 & 2 & 0 \\ 2 & 1 & 0 \\ 0 & 0 & 1 \end{bmatrix}\begin{bmatrix} 1 & 2 & 0 \\ 2 & 1 & 0 \\ 0 & 0 & 1 \end{bmatrix}$

$$= \begin{bmatrix} (1\times1+2\times2+0\times0) & (1\times2+2\times1+0\times0) & 0 \\ (1\times2+2\times1+0\times0) & (2\times2+1\times1+0\times0) & 0 \\ 0 & 0 & 1 \end{bmatrix}$$

$$A^3 = \begin{bmatrix} (1^2+2^2) & (1\times2+2\times1) & 0 \\ (1\times2+2\times1) & (1^2+2^2) & 0 \\ 0 & 0 & 1 \end{bmatrix}\begin{bmatrix} 1 & 2 & 0 \\ 2 & 1 & 0 \\ 0 & 0 & 1 \end{bmatrix}$$

$$= \begin{bmatrix} 13 & 14 & 0 \\ 14 & 13 & 0 \\ 0 & 0 & 1 \end{bmatrix}$$

Trace $(A^2) = 11$, *Trace* $(A^3) = 27$ $Tr = 27; (A^4) = 83$

$3^k + 1 + (-1)^k$ gives (for $k = 2$) $3^2 + 1 + 1 = 11$

$k = 3 \Rightarrow 3^3 + 1 - 1 = 27$

$k = 4 \Rightarrow 3^4 + 1 + 1 = 83$

11. (b) $|B| = \begin{vmatrix} \frac{7}{9} & -\frac{8}{9} & 0 \\ -\frac{8}{9} & \frac{13}{9} & 0 \\ 0 & 0 & 1 \end{vmatrix} = \frac{91-64}{81} = \frac{27}{81} = \frac{1}{3}$

12. (d) According to the given now $b_1 = \frac{13}{9}, b_2 = 1, b_3 = \frac{7}{9}$

$b_1, b_2, b_3\, \lambda$ are in G.P $\Rightarrow$ $b_1 b_3 \lambda = b_2^2$ i.e., $\frac{13}{9}\cdot\frac{7}{9}\lambda = 1$

$\Rightarrow \lambda = \frac{81}{91}$.

SECTION VII: (COLUMN MATCHING)

1. (i) → (b,d) (ii) → (e) (iii) → (a) (iv) → (c)

(i) $A(\text{Adj } A) = |A|\, I_n$

$\Rightarrow A^{-1}\,\text{Adj}(A^{-1}) = |A^{-1}|\, I_n$ (as $A^{-1}A = I$)

$\Rightarrow \text{Adj } (A^{-1}) = |A^{-1}|\, A = \frac{A}{|A|}\left(\because |A^{-1}| = \frac{1}{|A|}\right)$

Also $Adj(A^{-1}) = \frac{Adj(Adj\ A)}{|A|^{n-1}}$

(ii) $|A^{-1}|\,|\text{Adj } A^{-1}| = |A^{-1}|^n$ $\quad$ $|\text{Adj } A^{-1}| = |A^{-1}|^{n-1}$ or $|A|^{1-n}$

(iii) (Adj kA) where $k = |A|$

(kA). (Adj kA) $= |kA|\, I_n = k^n |A|\, I_n$

Now, $k = |A| \Rightarrow A(Adj\ kA) = \frac{|A|^n}{|A|}.|A|\, I_n = |A^n|\, I_n$

Now pre-multiply by A^{-1}; so (Adj kA) $= |A|^n A^{-1} I_n$

Substitution of $A^{-1} = \frac{AdjA}{|A|}$ gives $(Adj\ KA) = \frac{|A|^n\,(AdjA)}{|A|} I_n$

$= |A|^{n-1}\,\text{Adj}A$

(iv) Adj (Adj A) $= |A|^{n-2} A$ (standard result)

2. (i) → (b) (ii) → (d) (iii) → (a) (iv) → (c)

(i) $A^2 = A \rightarrow$ (b) idempotent

(ii) $A^m = O \rightarrow$ (d) nilpotent

(iii) $A^2 = I \rightarrow$ (a) Involuntary

(iv) $A^T = A \rightarrow$ (c) Symmetric

3. (i) → (a,b,c,d) (ii) → (b) (iii) → (b,e)

(i) $A * B = (1/2)(AB + BA)$

(a) $A * B = \frac{1}{2}(AB + BA) = \frac{1}{2}(BA + AB) = B * A$

(b) $A * (B + C) = \frac{1}{2}\{A(B - C) + (B + C)A\}$

$= \frac{1}{2}\{AB + AC + BA + CA\}$

$= \frac{1}{2}\{AB + BA\} + \frac{1}{2}\{AC + CA\} = A * B + A * C$

(c) $A*A=\frac{1}{2}\{AA+AA\}=AA=A^2$

(d) $A*I=\frac{1}{2}\{AI+IA\}=\frac{1}{2}\{A+A\}=A$

e. $A*I=O$ (since $A\times I=A$)
So this statement is not true

(ii) $A*B=\frac{1}{2}\{AB'+A'B\}=\frac{1}{2}\{A'B+AB'\}$

(a) $B*A=-\{BA'+B'A\}\neq A*B$ False

(b) $A*(B+C)=\frac{1}{2}\{A(B+C)'+A'(B+C)\}$

$=\frac{1}{2}\{AB'+AC'+A'C+A'B\}$

$=\frac{1}{2}\{AB'+A'B\}+\frac{1}{2}\{AC'+A'C\}$

$=A*B+A*C$

$\Rightarrow$ $A*(B+C)=A*B+A*C$. Hence true

(c) To Check $A*A=A^2$;

$A*A=\frac{1}{2}\{AA'+A'A\}\neq A^2$ False

(d) To check $A*I=A$;

$A*I=\frac{1}{2}\{AI'+A'I\}=\frac{1}{2}\{A+A'\}\neq A$.

Hence not true

(e) $A*I=O$ will not hold as $A*I=\frac{1}{2}\{A+A'\}$

(iii) $A*B=\frac{1}{2}\{AB-BA\}=-\frac{1}{2}\{BA-AB\}$

(a) $B*A=\frac{1}{2}\{BA-AB\}=-A*B$ so not true

(b) $A*(B+C)=\frac{1}{2}\{A(B+C)-(B+C)A\}$

$=-\{AB-BA+AC-CA\}$

$=\frac{1}{2}\{AB-BA\}+\frac{1}{2}\{AC-CA\}=A*B+A*C$

$\Rightarrow$ $A*(B+C)=A*B+A*C$ is true

(c) $A*A=1/2(A^2-A^2)=O\neq A^2$ False

(d) $A*I=\frac{1}{2}\{AI-IA\}=O\neq A$ so not true

(e) $A*I=O$ as worked in d option. Hence true

SECTION VIII: (INTEGER TYPE)

1. Let $A=\begin{bmatrix}\theta & 2\sin\beta & \tan\gamma\\ \cos\alpha & \sin\beta & -\tan\gamma\\ \cos\alpha & -\sin\beta & \tan\gamma\end{bmatrix}$ $\therefore$ **A is orthogonal** $\Rightarrow$ $AA^T=I=A^TA$

$$\Rightarrow \begin{bmatrix}0 & 2\sin\beta & \tan\gamma\\ \cos\alpha & \sin\beta & -\tan\gamma\\ \cos\alpha & -\sin\beta & \tan\gamma\end{bmatrix}\begin{bmatrix}0 & \cos\alpha & \cos\alpha\\ 2\sin\beta & \sin\beta & -\sin\beta\\ \tan\gamma & -\tan\gamma & \tan\gamma\end{bmatrix}=I_3$$

$$\Rightarrow \begin{bmatrix}4\sin^2\beta+\tan^2\gamma & 2\sin^2\beta-\tan^2\gamma & -2\sin^2\beta+\tan^2\gamma\\ 2\sin^2\beta-\tan^2\gamma & \cos^2\alpha+\sin^2\beta+\tan^2\gamma & \cos^2\alpha-\sin^2\beta-\tan^2\gamma\\ -2\sin^2\beta+\tan^2\gamma & \cos^2\alpha-\sin^2\beta-\tan^2\gamma & \cos^2\alpha+\sin^2\beta+\tan^2\gamma\end{bmatrix}=I_3$$

$\Rightarrow$ $4\sin^2\beta+\tan^2\gamma=\cos^2\alpha+\sin^2\beta+\tan^2\gamma=1$ ...(1)

and $2\sin^2\beta-\tan^2\gamma=-2\sin^2\beta+\tan^2\gamma=\cos^2\alpha-\sin^2\beta-\tan^2\gamma=0$ ....(2)

$\Rightarrow$ $2\sin^2\beta=\tan^2\gamma;\cos^2\alpha=\frac{3}{2}\tan^2\gamma$; $3\tan^2\gamma=1$ $\Rightarrow$ $\tan\gamma=\frac{1}{\sqrt{3}}$; $\cos\alpha=\frac{1}{\sqrt{2}};\sin\beta=\frac{1}{\sqrt{6}}$ as α, β, $\gamma\in(0,\pi/2)$

$\Rightarrow$ $\gamma=\frac{\pi}{6};\alpha=\frac{\pi}{4};\beta=\sin^{-1}\left(\frac{1}{\sqrt{6}}\right)$ $\therefore$ $\left(\frac{\alpha+\gamma}{5\pi}\right)^{-1}=\left(\frac{\frac{\pi}{4}+\frac{\pi}{6}}{5\pi}\right)^{-1}=\left(\frac{5\pi}{12}\times\frac{1}{5\pi}\right)^{-1}=\left(\frac{1}{12}\right)^{-1}=12$

2. Let $A=\begin{bmatrix}a_{11} & a_{12} & a_{13}\\ a_{21} & a_{22} & a_{23}\\ a_{31} & a_{32} & a_{33}\end{bmatrix}$

Given; $a_{ij}\in\{1, 2, 3, \ldots, 9\}$ and all a_{ij}'s are different

$\Rightarrow$ A contains all the elements from 1 to 9 such that

$\sum_{k=1}^{3}a_{ik}=9\lambda i$ for each $i\in\{1, 2, 3\}$; $\sum_{k=1}^{3}a_{kj}=9\mu j$ for each $j\in\{1, 2, 3\}$

And $a_{11}+a_{22}+a_{33}=9\nu$; where λi, μj, $\nu\in\{1, 2\}$. Now we can get a sum = 9 as follows

$1+2+3=9$; $1+3+5=9$ and $2+3+4=9$

Next we can get a sum = 18 as follow
1+ 8 + 9 = 18; 2 + 7 + 9 = 18;
3 + 7 + 8 = 18; 3 + 6 + 9 = 18;
4 + 5 + 9 = 18; 4 + 6 + 8 = 18
and 5 + 6 + 7 = 18

Now if we desire to find the number of matrices having sum in each row, each column and each of the two diagonals a multiple of 9, then the require in position a_{22} an element occurring 4 times in above triplets

$\Rightarrow$ $a_{22} \in \{3, 6, 9\}$

$\therefore$ Following types of matrices are possible

$$A=\begin{bmatrix}1 & & \\ & 3 & \\ & & 5\end{bmatrix}; B=\begin{bmatrix}2 & & \\ & 3 & \\ & & 4\end{bmatrix}; C=\begin{bmatrix}7 & & \\ & 3 & \\ & & 8\end{bmatrix};$$

$$D=\begin{bmatrix}6 & & \\ & 3 & \\ & & 9\end{bmatrix}; E=\begin{bmatrix}1 & & \\ & 6 & \\ & & 2\end{bmatrix}; F=\begin{bmatrix}3 & & \\ & 6 & \\ & & 9\end{bmatrix};$$

$$G=\begin{bmatrix}4 & & \\ & 6 & \\ & & 8\end{bmatrix}; H=\begin{bmatrix}5 & & \\ & 6 & \\ & & 7\end{bmatrix}; I=\begin{bmatrix}1 & & \\ & 9 & \\ & & 8\end{bmatrix};$$

$$J=\begin{bmatrix}2 & & \\ & 9 & \\ & & 7\end{bmatrix}; K=\begin{bmatrix}3 & & \\ & 9 & \\ & & 6\end{bmatrix}; L=\begin{bmatrix}4 & & \\ & 9 & \\ & & 5\end{bmatrix}$$

Now consider $A=\begin{bmatrix}1 & & \\ & 3 & \\ & & 5\end{bmatrix}$

Now, at position a_{12} we are to locate the element which appear with both 1 as well as with 3, which are 2, 6, 8, 9 except for 5 as elements of A must be different.

Let us take $2 = a_{12}$

$\therefore$ $A=\begin{bmatrix}1 & 2 & \\ & 3 & \\ & & 5\end{bmatrix}$, then clearly completing A, we get

$A=\begin{bmatrix}1 & 2 & 6\\ 8 & 3 & 7\\ 9 & 4 & 5\end{bmatrix}$ (Choosing other elements to form triplets as formed in starting)

If we interchange 1 and 5 to obtain $A_1=\begin{bmatrix}5 & 4 & 9\\ 7 & 3 & 8\\ 6 & 2 & 1\end{bmatrix}$

Also $A^T=\begin{bmatrix}1 & 8 & 9\\ 2 & 3 & 4\\ 6 & 7 & 5\end{bmatrix}$ and $A_1^T=\begin{bmatrix}5 & 7 & 6\\ 4 & 3 & 2\\ 9 & 5 & 1\end{bmatrix}$

Thus from A we get 4 matrices A, A_1, A^T, A_1^T.
Similarly from $B, C, D, \ldots, K, L$ we get 4 matrices
Thus, total 12 × 4 = 48 such matrices

3. $A^2=\begin{bmatrix}2 & -1\\ 3 & -2\end{bmatrix}\begin{bmatrix}2 & -1\\ 3 & -2\end{bmatrix}=\begin{bmatrix}1 & 0\\ 0 & 1\end{bmatrix}=I; x = 2, 4, 6, 8.....$

$\Rightarrow$ $\Sigma(\cos^x\theta + \sin^x\theta) = (\cos^2\theta + \sin^2\theta) + (\cos^4\theta + \sin^4\theta) + (\cos^6\theta + \sin^6\theta) + \ldots + \ldots.$

$$= \frac{\cos^2\theta}{1-\cos^2\theta}+\frac{\sin^2\theta}{1-\sin^2\theta}=\cot^2\theta+\tan^2\theta$$

Using $AM \geq GM$, $\frac{1}{2}(\cot^2\theta+\tan^2\theta)\geq\sqrt{\cot^2\theta\tan^2\theta}$

$\Rightarrow$ $(\cot^2\theta + \tan^2\theta) \geq 2$ $\Rightarrow$ So, minimum value = 2

4. $A=\begin{bmatrix}a & b & c\\ b & c & a\\ c & a & b\end{bmatrix}=\{a^3+b^3+c^3-3abc\}$

from $AA^T = I$, $a^2 + b^2 + c^2 = 0$ and $ab + bc + ca = 0$
$|A| = |A^T| = 1 \Rightarrow a^3 + b^3 + c^3 - 3abc = a + b + c = \pm1$
$a^3 + b^3 + c^3 = 2,4$ {if $a + b + c = 1$ then $a^3 + b^3 + c^3 = 4$}
$\Rightarrow$ Sum of all posible values = 2 + 4 = 6

5. $AX=\begin{bmatrix}1 & 2 & 3\\ 4 & 5 & 6\\ 6 & 9 & 0\end{bmatrix}\begin{bmatrix}u\\ v\\ w\end{bmatrix}=\begin{bmatrix}6\\ 12\\ 4\end{bmatrix}, |A|=36$

$$X=A^{-1}B=\begin{bmatrix}\frac{-54}{36} & \frac{3}{4} & \frac{-1}{12}\\ 1 & \frac{-1}{2} & \frac{1}{6}\\ \frac{1}{6} & \frac{1}{12} & -\frac{1}{12}\end{bmatrix}\begin{bmatrix}6\\ 12\\ 4\end{bmatrix}=\begin{bmatrix}\frac{-1}{3}\\ \frac{2}{3}\\ \frac{5}{3}\end{bmatrix}$$

$\Rightarrow$ $u = -1/3, v = 2/3, w = 5/3 \Rightarrow \frac{1}{u}+\frac{1}{v}+\frac{1}{w}=-\frac{9}{10}$

and $(u - v + w) = 2$

As a result the given equations are

$$-\frac{9}{10}x^2+\left[(b-c)^2+(c-a)^2+(d-b)^2\right]x+2=0$$

and $20x^2 + k[(a - d)^2]x - 9 = 0$

Now, $x^2-\frac{10}{9}\left[(b-c)^2+(c-a)^2+(d-b)^2\right]x-\frac{20}{9}=0$ ...(i)

$x^2+\frac{k}{20}\left[(a-d)^2\right]x-\frac{9}{20}=0$ ...(ii)

Equating we get $k = 10$ as shown below

From (i) equation, $\alpha+\beta=\frac{10}{9}\left[\sum(b-c)^2\right]$; $\alpha\beta=\frac{-20}{9}$;

From (ii) equation, $\frac{1}{\alpha}+\frac{1}{\beta}=\frac{\alpha+\beta}{\alpha\beta}$

$$=-\frac{K}{20}\left[\sum(b-c)^2\right]; \frac{1}{\alpha\beta}=\frac{-9}{20}$$

$$\Rightarrow \frac{10}{9}\left(\frac{-9}{20}\right)\left[\sum(b-c)^2\right]=-\frac{k}{20}\left[\sum(b-c)^2\right]\Rightarrow k=10$$

($\because$ When a,b,c,d are in G.P then $(a - d)^2 = [(b - c)^2 + (c - a)^2 + (d - b)^2]$)

6. $$|A| = \begin{vmatrix} \sin\theta & \cos\theta & \sin 2\theta \\ \sin(\theta + 2\pi/3) & \cos\left(\theta + \frac{2\pi}{3}\right) & \sin\left(2\theta + \frac{4\pi}{3}\right) \\ \sin\left(\theta - \frac{2\pi}{3}\right) & \cos\left(\theta - \frac{2\pi}{3}\right) & \sin\left(2\theta - \frac{4\pi}{3}\right) \end{vmatrix}$$

Observe that in R_2 and R_3 the $(A + B)$ and $(A - B)$ form is there

$\therefore$ Operate $R_1 \to R_1 + R_2 + R_3$

$$\Rightarrow |A| = \begin{vmatrix} \sin\theta - \sin\theta & \cos\theta - \cos\theta & \sin 2\theta - \sin 2\theta \\ \sin\left(\theta + \frac{2\pi}{3}\right) & \cos\left(\theta + \frac{2\pi}{3}\right) & \sin\left(2\theta + \frac{4\pi}{3}\right) \\ \sin\left(\theta - \frac{2\pi}{3}\right) & \cos\left(\theta - \frac{2\pi}{3}\right) & \sin\left(2\theta - \frac{4\pi}{3}\right) \end{vmatrix}$$

$\Rightarrow$ $|A| = 0$ using $\sin(A + B) + \sin(A - B) = 2\sin A \cos B$

And $\cos(A + B) + \cos(A - B) = 2\cos A \cos B = 0$

7. $$|A| = \begin{vmatrix} \sin 3\theta & -1 & 1 \\ \cos 2\theta & 4 & 3 \\ 2 & 7 & 7 \end{vmatrix} = \begin{vmatrix} \sin 3\theta & 0 & 1 \\ \cos 2\theta & 7 & 3 \\ 2 & 14 & 7 \end{vmatrix}$$

$\Rightarrow \Delta = \sin 3\theta\,\{49 - 42\} + 14\cos 2\theta - 14 = 0$

Or $\sin 3\theta + 2\cos 2\theta = 2$

$3\sin\theta - 4\sin^3\theta + 2(1 - 2\sin^2\theta) - 2 = 0$

$3\sin\theta - 4\sin^3\theta - 4\sin^2\theta = 0$

gives $\sin\theta\,\{2\sin\theta + 3\}\,\{2\sin\theta - 1\} = 0$

so $\sin\theta = 0 \Rightarrow \theta = n\pi$, $\sin\theta = 1/2 \Rightarrow \theta = n\pi + (-1)^n.\frac{\pi}{6}$

$\sin\theta = -3/2$ is impossible , so $k = 6$

8. $$AX = \begin{bmatrix} 2 & -3 & 5 \\ 3 & 1 & \lambda \\ 1 & -7 & 8 \end{bmatrix}\begin{bmatrix} x \\ y \\ z \end{bmatrix} = \begin{bmatrix} 12 \\ \mu \\ 17 \end{bmatrix}$$

Gives $|A| = -22 + 11\lambda = 0 \Rightarrow \lambda = 2$; $(\text{Adj } A).B = O$

$$\Rightarrow \begin{vmatrix} 22 & -11 & -11 \\ -22 & 11 & 11 \\ -22 & 11 & 11 \end{vmatrix}\begin{bmatrix} 12 \\ \mu \\ 17 \end{bmatrix} = \begin{bmatrix} 0 \\ 0 \\ 0 \end{bmatrix} \Rightarrow \mu = 7. \text{ So } \lambda + \mu = 9$$

9. $(3x - z) - y = 0$, $(-3x + z) = 0$; $(-3x + z) + 2y = 0$

So $y = 0$ and $3x = z$

$\therefore$ $x^2 + y^2 + z^2 \le 100$ gives $10x^2 \le 100$

So $x^2 \le 10 \Rightarrow x = 0, \pm 1, \pm 2, \pm 3$

Hence 7 such points are possible.

10. Let $$A = \begin{vmatrix} a_1 & a_2 & a_3 \\ a_4 & a_5 & a_6 \\ a_7 & a_8 & a_9 \end{vmatrix}\begin{bmatrix} x \\ y \\ z \end{bmatrix} = \begin{bmatrix} 1 \\ 0 \\ 0 \end{bmatrix}$$

$\Rightarrow a_4 = a_5 = a_6 = a_7 = a_8 = a_9 = 0$

and $a_1x + a_2y + a_3z = 1$ has exactly two distinct solutions, which is not possible

Under the given conditions $(a_1, a_2, a_3 = 0, 1)$ and $x, y, z \in$, $\mathbb{R}$. So there is no unique $A_{3\times 3}$ matrix. $\Rightarrow 0$

11. $$|A| = \begin{vmatrix} 2k-1 & 2\sqrt{k} & 2\sqrt{k} \\ 2\sqrt{k} & 1 & -2k \\ -2\sqrt{k} & 2k & -1 \end{vmatrix}$$

Operate $R_2 \to R_2 + R_3$ and take $(2k + 1)$ out from R_2

$$|A| = (2k+1)\begin{vmatrix} 2k-1 & 2\sqrt{k} & 2\sqrt{k} \\ 0 & 1 & -1 \\ -2\sqrt{k} & 2k & -1 \end{vmatrix}$$

Operate $C_2 \to C_2 + C_3$

$$|A| = \begin{vmatrix} 2k-1 & 4\sqrt{k} & 2\sqrt{k} \\ 0 & 0 & -1 \\ -2\sqrt{k} & 2k-1 & -1 \end{vmatrix}(2k+1)$$

$= (2k + 1)\,\{(2k - 1)^2 + 8k\} = (2k + 1)\,\{2k + 1\}^2 = (2k + 1)^3$

and $|B| = 0$ (Skew symmetric determinant of odd order)

$|A| = (2k + 1)^3 \Rightarrow |\text{Adj}A| = (|A|)^{n-1} \Rightarrow (2k + 1)^3 (2k + 1)^3$ for $n = 3$; $|\text{Adj } B| = |B|^2 = 0$

$\Rightarrow (2k + 1)^6 = 10^6 \Rightarrow 2k + 1 = 10$

$k = 9/2 \Rightarrow [k] = 4$

12. $$\begin{vmatrix} 1-a & 1 & 1 \\ 1 & 1-b & 1 \\ 1 & 1 & 1-c \end{vmatrix} = \begin{vmatrix} -a & b & 0 \\ 0 & -b & c \\ 1 & 1 & 1-c \end{vmatrix}$$

$= (-a)\,\{bc - b - c\} - b\,(-c) = -abc + ab + ac + bc$

$= ab + bc + ca - abc = 0$ or $ab + bc + ca = abc$

$\because$ a, b, c are real and positive so $\frac{1}{a} + \frac{1}{b} + \frac{1}{c} = 1$

$$AM \ge GM \Rightarrow \frac{1}{3}\left\{\frac{1}{a} + \frac{1}{b} + \frac{1}{c}\right\} \ge \left(\frac{1}{abc}\right)^{1/3}$$

or $$\frac{1}{27}\left\{\frac{1}{a} + \frac{1}{b} + \frac{1}{c}\right\}^3 \ge \frac{1}{abc}$$

so $$\frac{1}{abc} \le \frac{1}{27} \Rightarrow abc \ge 27$$

$\therefore$ Minimum value of $abc = 27$

13. $(k + 1)x + 8y - 4k = 0$

$kx + (k + 3)y - (3k - 1) = 0$

[Super imposition of two straight lines]

For infinite solutions $\frac{a_1}{a_2} = \frac{b_1}{b_2} = \frac{c_1}{c_2}$

$$\Rightarrow \frac{k+1}{k} = \frac{8}{k+3} = \frac{4k}{3k-1}$$

From first two parts, we get $(k + 1)(k + 3) = 8k$;

$k^2 - 4k + 3 = 0$; $(k - 3)(k - 1) = 0$; .....(i)

From last two parts $4k^2 + 12k = 24k - 8$;

$\Rightarrow$ $4k^2 - 12k + 8 = 0$ or $(k - 2)(k - 1) = 0$ ......(ii)

From (i) and (ii), we get $k = 1$ is the solution.

$\therefore$ number of values (of k) = 1

2

Determinants

■ INTRODUCTION

We are familiar with simultaneous linear equations. The equations in two variables can be easily solved. But if the number of variables are three, then our task becomes lengthier because now we have to first eliminate one unknown by using any two equations, and then again eliminate the same unknown from a different set of two equations. We thus get two equations in two variables which can be easily solved. We can solve a system of equations of 3, 4, 5,... upto n variables by attempting same method as explained above. But imagine how tedious it is going to be.

Mathematicians observed that whatsoever be the number of variables, the steps involved in solving the system of equations follow a certain sequence of algebraic operations being performed on these equations. To carry out these operations readily and simultaneously, the terms of the equations were sought to be arranged in a convenient manner, which therefore developed the tool of the determinant and it was propagated by Leibnitz in the concluding portion of the 17th century and further developed by Cramer, Lagrange, Laplace, Lapha, Cauchy, Tacobi etc. With the result of this a number of properties of determinants were identified and made applicable.

The knowledge of determinants is also very useful for almost all the topics of mathematics especially in the vectors, coordinate geometry and calculus. Some of the formulae are easy to remember in determinant form as compared to their other style. Determinants are also used in eliminating certain variables out of given equations to obtain the eliminant. Usually, it is used to write the eliminant expressions and other conditions in compact form.

This chapter deals with the evaluation of 3rd order determinants mainly by application of properties with proper technique for speedy results. All theoretical aspects are supported with adequate number of illustrations and of different levels of application.

■ DEFINITION

Consider the two homogeneous linear equations $a_1x + b_1y = 0$...(i) and $a_2x + b_2y = 0$ ...(ii) Multiplying the first equation by b_2 and the second equation by b_1, then subtracting and dividing by x, we get $a_1b_2 - a_2b_1 = 0$. This result is sometimes written as $\Delta = \begin{vmatrix} a_1 & b_1 \\ a_2 & b_2 \end{vmatrix} = 0$. The expression on the left side is called a determinant. It is denoted by Δ. So determinant can be precisely defined as below:

"Determinant is a square array of elements which is associated with some definite numerical value (Remember, the matrix is a rectangular arrangement of numbers and has no numerical value)." If $A = [a_{ij}]$ be a square matrix, it can be associated with a determinant formed by the same array of elements of the square matrix A, and is denoted by the symbol ***det*** *A or* | *A* |.

Basic Properties of Determinant

For any given determinant, the following points are to be noted.

(a) **Number of rows = Number of columns** (*i.e., defined only corresponding to square matrices*)

(b) It is not simply a systematic arrangement of numbers (*as matrix*) but it also has some **numerical value.**

(c) The number of rows (or of columns) of a determinant is called **order of determinant.**

Expansion of Determinant

Determinant of order 2 Let $a_{11}, a_{12}, a_{21}, a_{22}$ be any four real (or complex) numbers, then symbol $\Delta = \begin{vmatrix} a_{11} & a_{12} \\ a_{21} & a_{22} \end{vmatrix}$

represents the number $(a_{11}\, a_{22} - a_{21}a_{12})$ and is known as determinant of order two and above numbers (a_{11}, a_{12} etc.) are known as elements of determinant. *Value of determinant of order two = (product of elements of principal diagonal) – (product of elements of off diagonal)*

e.g., Let a matrix $A = \begin{bmatrix} 5 & 2 \\ 7 & 3 \end{bmatrix}$ so that $|\ \ |$ $\begin{vmatrix} 5 & 2 \\ 7 & 3 \end{vmatrix}$,

then $|A| = 5 \times 3 - 7 \times 2 = 15 - 14 = 1$

Determinant of order 3

$A = \begin{vmatrix} a_{11} & a_{12} & a_{13} \\ a_{21} & a_{22} & a_{23} \\ a_{31} & a_{32} & a_{33} \end{vmatrix}$; $a_{ij} \in \mathbb{R}$ or C represents determinant of order 3×3.

The elements a_{11}, a_{22}, a_{33} are called the principal diagonal elements and the elements a_{13}, a_{22}, a_{31} are called the off diagonal elements.

To understand the expansion of higher order determinant we should learn the concept of minors and cofactors.

■ MINORS AND CO-FACTORS

Minor

The determinant obtained by deleting the ith *row* and j^{th} *column* through the element a_{ij} is called the minor of element a_{ij} in the determimant ($|a_{ij}|$) of order n and is denoted by M_{ij}.

For example:

(i) The minor of a_{12} in $\begin{vmatrix} a_{11} & a_{12} \\ a_{21} & a_{22} \end{vmatrix} = a_{21}$ (denoted by M_{21})

(ii) The minor of element a_{21} of A of 3×3 order $= M_{21} = \begin{vmatrix} a_{12} & a_{13} \\ a_{32} & a_{33} \end{vmatrix}$. (the determinant obtained by deleting the elements of row and column passing through a_{21}).

Co-factor

The co-factors of the element a_{ij} is $(-1)^{i+j}$ times the determinant obtained by deleting the ith row and j^{th} column passing through a_{ij}. We shall denote the co-factor of an element by the corresponding capital letter C_{ij}. The minor M_{ij} multiplied by $(-1)^{i+j}$ is called the co-factors of the element a_{ij}. If we denote the co-factor of the element a_{ij}, by C_{ij}, then co-factor of a_{ij} is $C_{ij} = (-1)^{i+j} M_{ij}$

$\therefore\ C_{ij} = (-1)^{i+j} M_{ij}$

If $\Delta = \begin{vmatrix} a_{11} & a_{12} & a_{13} \\ a_{21} & a_{22} & a_{23} \\ a_{31} & a_{32} & a_{33} \end{vmatrix}$ (So, we will get 9 minors /cofactors corresponding to 9 elements of the above determinant).

NOTE

Thus co-factor of the element $a_{21} = C_{21} = (-1)^{2+1} M_{21} = -\begin{vmatrix} a_{12} & a_{13} \\ a_{32} & a_{33} \end{vmatrix}$

ILLUSTRATION 1: Find the mentioned minors and cofactors of the elements of the following determinant

$$|A| = \begin{vmatrix} a & b & c \\ d & e & f \\ g & h & i \end{vmatrix}$$

(a) M_{11}, C_{11} (b) M_{23}, C_{23} (c) M_{31}, C_{31}

SOLUTION: (a) $M_{11} = \begin{vmatrix} e & f \\ h & i \end{vmatrix} = ei - fh \Rightarrow C_{11} = (-1)^{1+1}\begin{vmatrix} e & f \\ h & i \end{vmatrix} = ei - fh$

(b) $M_{23} = \begin{vmatrix} a & b \\ g & h \end{vmatrix} = ah - bg \Rightarrow C_{23} = (-1)^{2+3}\begin{vmatrix} a & b \\ g & h \end{vmatrix} = bg - ah$

(c) $M_{31} = \begin{vmatrix} b & c \\ e & f \end{vmatrix} = bf - ec \Rightarrow C_{31} = (-1)^{3+1}\begin{vmatrix} b & c \\ e & f \end{vmatrix} = bf - ec$

ILLUSTRATION 2: Find the minors and co-factors of determinant $\begin{vmatrix} 1 & 2 & 3 \\ 4 & 5 & 6 \\ 7 & 8 & 9 \end{vmatrix}$ along second column.

SOLUTION: Minors along second column, i.e., elements 2, 5, and 8 are

$$M_{12} = \begin{vmatrix} 4 & 6 \\ 7 & 9 \end{vmatrix} = 36 - 42 = -6; \; M_{22} = \begin{vmatrix} 1 & 3 \\ 7 & 9 \end{vmatrix} = 9 - 21 = -12;$$

$$M_{32} = \begin{vmatrix} 1 & 3 \\ 4 & 6 \end{vmatrix} = 6 - 12 = -6$$

And co-factors of the corresponding elements are $C_{12} = (-1)^{1+2}(-6) = 6$;

$C_{22} = (-1)^{2+2}(-12) = -12$ and $C_{32} = (-1)^{3+2}(-6) = 6$

Expansion of Determinant Using Minors/Co-factors

The value of determinant is defined as the sum of the product of elements of any row (column) by their corresponding co-factors.

$$\text{Let } \Delta = \begin{vmatrix} a_{11} & a_{12} & a_{13} \\ a_{21} & a_{22} & a_{23} \\ a_{31} & a_{32} & a_{33} \end{vmatrix}$$

$$= a_{11}\begin{vmatrix} a_{22} & a_{23} \\ a_{32} & a_{33} \end{vmatrix} - a_{12}\begin{vmatrix} a_{21} & a_{23} \\ a_{31} & a_{33} \end{vmatrix} + a_{13}\begin{vmatrix} a_{21} & a_{22} \\ a_{31} & a_{32} \end{vmatrix}$$

$$= \underbrace{a_{11}C_{11} + a_{12}C_{12} + a_{13}C_{13}}_{\text{expanding along } R_1}$$

$$= a_{11}a_{22}a_{33} - a_{11}a_{32}a_{23} + a_{12}a_{31}a_{23} - a_{12}a_{21}a_{33} + a_{13}a_{21}a_{32} - a_{13}a_{31}a_{22}$$

Therefore the value of the determinant can be obtained

as $\Delta = a_{11}C_{11} + a_{12}C_{12} + a_{13}C_{13}$ (expanding along R_1)

or $\Delta = a_{12}C_{12} + a_{22}C_{22} + a_{32}C_{33}$ (expanding along C_2)

or $\Delta = a_{31}C_{31} + a_{32}C_{32} + a_{33}C_{33}$ (expanding along R_3)

In general, expanding along i^{th} row we get

$\Delta = a_{i1}C_{i1} + a_{i2}C_{i2} + \ldots + a_{in}C_{in} = \sum_{k=1}^{n} a_{ik}C_{ik}$ (for all $i = 1, 2, \ldots, n$)

And expanding along j^{th} coulmn, we get

or $\Delta = a_{1j}C_{1j} + a_{2j}C_{2j} + \ldots\ldots + a_{nj}C_{nj} = \sum_{k=1}^{n} a_{kj}C_{kj}$ (for all $j = 1, 2, \ldots$ or n)

NOTE

1. *The expansion generates same value irrespective of its performance through any row or column.*
2. *The determinant can be expanded along any row or any column. If a_{ij} is the element occuring in the ith row and the jth column; then to fix the positive or negative sign before it, we should multiply it by $(-1)^{i+j}$*
3. *The expansion contains 3! i.e., 6 terms which is the number of permutations of 1, 2, 3 in a line.*

$$\text{i.e., } \begin{vmatrix} a_1 & b_1 & c_1 \\ a_2 & b_2 & c_2 \\ a_3 & b_3 & c_3 \end{vmatrix} = \underbrace{(a_1b_2c_3 + b_1c_2a_3 + c_1a_2b_3)}_{\text{positive zone}} - \underbrace{(a_1b_3c_2 + b_1a_2c_3 + c_1a_3b_2)}_{\text{negative zone}}.$$

4. *Each term is product of three entries of the determinant.*
5. *3 terms are positive, 3 other are negative (even and odd permutations).*
6. *Each entry of the determinant Δ once appears in the positive zone and once in the negative zone. For instance a_1 appears as in the first and fourth term.*

Sarrus rule of expanding a determinant of third order Sarrus gave a rule for evaluating a determinant of the order three mentioned as below

Rule: Write down the three rows of the determinant, and rewrite the first two rows just below them. The three diagonals sloping down to the right give the three positive terms and the three diagonals sloping down to the left give the three negative terms.

If $\Delta = \begin{vmatrix} a_{11} & a_{12} & a_{13} \\ a_{21} & a_{22} & a_{23} \\ a_{31} & a_{32} & a_{33} \end{vmatrix}$, then

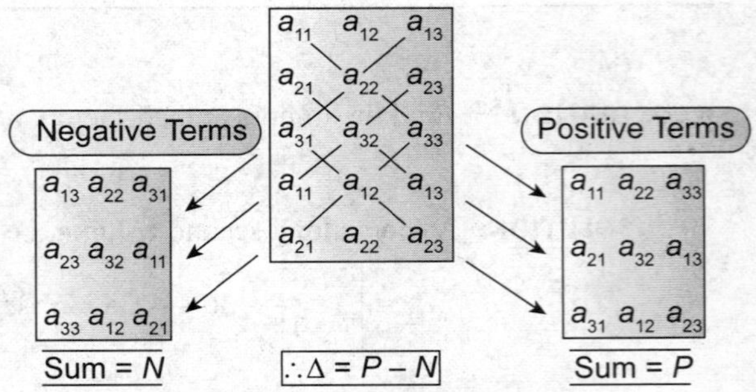

FIGURE 2.1

ILLUSTRATION 3: For $|A| = \begin{vmatrix} 2 & 5 & -3 \\ 0 & 4 & 2 \\ -1 & 3 & 9 \end{vmatrix}$ Find

(a) The sum of the minors of the principal diagonal

(b) The sum of the cofactors of the off diagonal

SOLUTION: (a) $M_{11} = \begin{vmatrix} 4 & 2 \\ 3 & 9 \end{vmatrix} = 30;\ M_{22} = \begin{vmatrix} 2 & -3 \\ -1 & 9 \end{vmatrix} = 15;\ M_{33} = \begin{vmatrix} 2 & 5 \\ 0 & 4 \end{vmatrix} = 8$; Sum = 53

(b) $M_{13} = \begin{vmatrix} 0 & 4 \\ -1 & 3 \end{vmatrix} = 4 \Rightarrow C_{13} = (-1)^{1+3} M_{13} = 4 \quad M_{22} = \begin{vmatrix} 2 & -3 \\ -1 & 9 \end{vmatrix} = 15$

$\Rightarrow C_{22} = (-1)^{2+2} M_{22} = 15 \quad M_{31} = \begin{vmatrix} 5 & -3 \\ 4 & 2 \end{vmatrix} = 22 \Rightarrow C_{31} = (-1)^{3+1} M_{31} = 22$; Sum = 41

ILLUSTRATION 4: Find values of Determinant by expanding them

(i) $\begin{vmatrix} 1 & 3 & 4 \\ 2 & -1 & 3 \\ 2 & 1 & 2 \end{vmatrix}$ along 1st row. (ii) $\begin{vmatrix} 1 & 0 & 2 \\ 2 & 4 & 3 \\ 1 & 0 & 0 \end{vmatrix}$ along 3rd row

SOLUTION: (i) $\Delta = a_{11}C_{11} + a_{12}C_{12} + a_{13}C_{13} = 1(-2-3) - 3(4-6) + 4(2-(-2)) = -5 + 6 + 16 = 17$

(ii) $\Delta = a_{31}C_{31} + a_{32}C_{32} + a_{33}C_{33} = 1(0-8) - 0(3-4) + 0(4-0) = -8$

ILLUSTRATION 5: Expand the determinant $\begin{vmatrix} 1 & 2 & 3 \\ 3 & 2 & 1 \\ 2 & 1 & 3 \end{vmatrix}$ along R_1 as well as C_2 and show that both expansions yield same result.

SOLUTION: Given determinant is $\begin{vmatrix} 1 & 2 & 3 \\ 3 & 2 & 1 \\ 2 & 1 & 3 \end{vmatrix}$

Expanding along R_1: $1(6-1) - 2(9-2) + 3(3-4) = -12$

Expanding along C_2: $-2(9-2) + 2(3-6) - 1(1-9) = -12$

APPLICATION OF DETERMINANT

Out of wide applications of determinants; a few are given below.

- **Area of Δ with vertices $A(x_1, y_1)$, $B(x_2, y_2)$, $C(x_3, y_3)$**

  is given by $\Delta = \left\| \frac{1}{2}\begin{vmatrix} x_1 & y_1 & 1 \\ x_2 & y_2 & 1 \\ x_3 & y_3 & 1 \end{vmatrix} \right\|$

  where $|x|$ denotes absolute value of x

- **Cross product of vectors**

  $\vec{a} = a_x\hat{i} + a_y\hat{j} + a_z\hat{k}; \vec{b} = b_x\hat{i} + b_y\hat{j} + b_z\hat{k}$

$$\Rightarrow \vec{a} \times \vec{b} = \begin{vmatrix} \hat{i} & \hat{j} & \hat{k} \\ a_x & a_y & a_z \\ b_x & b_y & b_z \end{vmatrix}$$

It is also used to find the scalar triple product (S.T.P.) of three vectors $\vec{a}.(\vec{b} \times \vec{c})$ is S.T.P. of $[\vec{a}\vec{b}\vec{c}] = \begin{vmatrix} a_x & a_y & a_z \\ b_x & b_y & b_z \\ c_x & c_y & c_z \end{vmatrix}$

(Detailed explanation would be given in the chapter of vectors)

TEXTUAL EXERCISE 1: (SUBJECTIVE)

1. The co-factor and minor of any element of determinant will be equal when sum of the row number and column number is .... for that particular element.

2. If we have n order determinant, then how many co-factors are possible for such determinant?

3. Evalulate the following determinants

(a) $\begin{vmatrix} 2^2 & 3^2 & 4^2 \\ 3^2 & 4^2 & 5^2 \\ 4^2 & 5^2 & 6^2 \end{vmatrix}$ (b) $\begin{vmatrix} b+c & a+b & a \\ c+a & b+c & b \\ a+b & c+a & c \end{vmatrix}$

(c) $\begin{vmatrix} a & b & 0 \\ 0 & a & b \\ b & 0 & a \end{vmatrix}$ (d) $\begin{vmatrix} 2ab & a^2 & b^2 \\ a^2 & b^2 & 2ab \\ b^2 & 2ab & a^2 \end{vmatrix}$

(e) $\begin{vmatrix} 7 & 11 & 13 \\ 17 & 19 & 23 \\ 29 & 31 & 37 \end{vmatrix}$ (f) $\begin{vmatrix} 0 & x & y \\ -x & 0 & z \\ -y & -z & 0 \end{vmatrix}$

4. Find the value of b for which the points (2, 5);(4, 5) and (6, b) are collinear

5. Find the area of triangle having its vertices A(2,5); B(4,8) and C(3,4).

6. If $|C|$ be the determinant formed by replacing the elements of $|A|$ by their respective co-factors and $|\ | = \begin{vmatrix} 3 & 2 & 9 \\ -5 & 7 & 2 \\ 0 & 1 & 1 \end{vmatrix}$; then find the value of $|C|$

7. If α, β, γ, are the roots of a cubic equation $f(x) = 0$, then evaluate $\begin{vmatrix} f(\alpha) & \alpha & \alpha^2 \\ f(\beta) & \beta & \beta^2 \\ f(\gamma) & \gamma & \gamma^2 \end{vmatrix}$

8. Show that the value of determinant $\begin{vmatrix} u & v & w \\ v & w & u \\ 1 & 1 & 1 \end{vmatrix}$ is always non-positive.

Answer Key

1. even **2.** n^2 **3.** (a) -8 (b) $a^3 + b^3 + c^3 - 3abc$ (c) $a^3 + b^3$ (d) $-(a^3 + b^3)^2$ (e) 36 (f) zero
4. 5 **5.** 5/2 square units **6.** 4900 **7.** 0

PROPERTIES OF DETERMINANTS

Property 1. The value of determinant remains unaltered if the rows and columns are interchanged

e.g., If $\Delta = \begin{vmatrix} a_1 & b_1 \\ a_2 & b_2 \end{vmatrix} = (a_1 b_2 - b_1 a_2)$ and $\Delta' = \begin{vmatrix} a_1 & a_2 \\ b_1 & b_2 \end{vmatrix}$

$= (a_1 b_2 - a_2 b\,) \Rightarrow \Delta = \Delta'$

Property 2. If all the elements of a row/column are zero, then the value of determinant will be zero.

e.g., $\begin{vmatrix} a & 0 & -a \\ b & 0 & b \\ c & 0 & -c \end{vmatrix} = 0$ *(expanding along second column)*

Property 3. Reduction and increase of order of determinant

(a) If all the elements in a row (or a column) except one element, are zeros the determinant reduces to a determinant of an order less by one. e.g.,

$$\begin{vmatrix} 3 & 0 & 0 \\ 2 & 5 & 7 \\ 4 & 5 & 1 \end{vmatrix} = 3\begin{vmatrix} 5 & 7 \\ 5 & 1 \end{vmatrix}$$ *(expanding along first rows)*

(b) A determinant can be replaced by a determinant of a higher order by one as per the requirment.

e.g., $\begin{vmatrix} 2 & 3 \\ -5 & 4 \end{vmatrix} = \begin{vmatrix} 1 & 0 & 0 \\ 0 & 2 & 3 \\ 0 & -5 & 4 \end{vmatrix}$ or $\begin{vmatrix} 2 & 3 & 0 \\ -5 & 4 & 0 \\ 0 & 0 & 1 \end{vmatrix}$

or $\begin{vmatrix} 0 & 0 & 1 \\ 2 & 3 & 0 \\ -5 & 4 & 0 \end{vmatrix}$ or $\begin{vmatrix} 1 & 0 & 0 \\ 1 & 2 & 3 \\ 2 & -5 & 4 \end{vmatrix}$

Property 4. If any two rows or two columns of a determinant are interchanged, the determinant retains its absolute value but changes its sign and symbolically the interchange of ith and j^{th} rows or i^{th} and j^{th} columns is written as $\Delta = -\Delta_{R_i \rightleftarrows R_j}$ (or $-\Delta_{C_i \rightleftarrows C_j}$)

e.g., $\Delta_1 = \begin{vmatrix} 1 & 2 & 3 \\ 2 & 3 & 4 \\ 0 & 1 & 5 \end{vmatrix}$

$= 1(15-4) - 2(10-0) + 3(2-0) = -3$

Interchanging Ist row and IInd row, we get

$\Delta_2 = \begin{vmatrix} 2 & 3 & 4 \\ 1 & 2 & 3 \\ 0 & 1 & 5 \end{vmatrix} = 2(10-3) - 3(5-0) + 4(1-0) = 3.$

Clearly $\Delta_1 = -\Delta_2$

Property 5. The value of a determinant is zero if any two rows or columns are identical. Symbolically, it is written as $\Delta_{R_i \equiv R_j} = 0$ or $\Delta_{C_i \equiv C_j} = 0$

Let $\Delta = |a_{ij}|_{n\times n}$ such that R_1 and R_3 are identical.

Then $\Delta = -\Delta$ (By $R_1 \leftrightarrow R_3$ i.e., interchanging 1st and 3rd row)

$\Rightarrow \Delta + \Delta = 0 \Rightarrow 2\Delta = 0 \Rightarrow \Delta = 0$

Property 6(a): If every element of a given row of matrix A is multiplied by a number λ, the matrix thus obtained has determinant equal to λ (det A). As a consequence, if every element in a row of a determinant has the same factor this can be factored out of the determinant.

Symbolically, it is written as $\Delta = m.\Delta_{R_i \to \frac{1}{m} R_i}$.

e.g., $\begin{bmatrix} 32 & 24 & 16 \\ 8 & 3 & 5 \\ 4 & 5 & 3 \end{bmatrix}$ *[Taking out 8 as a factor common from 1st row.]*

$= 8\begin{bmatrix} 4 & 3 & 2 \\ 8 & 3 & 5 \\ 4 & 5 & 3 \end{bmatrix} = 8\times 4\begin{vmatrix} 1 & 3 & 2 \\ 2 & 3 & 5 \\ 1 & 5 & 3 \end{vmatrix}$ *[by taking 4 common from the 1st column]*

Proof: Let $A = \begin{pmatrix} a_1 & a_2 & a_3 \\ b_1 & b_2 & b_3 \\ c_1 & c_2 & c_3 \end{pmatrix}$ and B be the matrix obtained from A by multiplying the 2nd row of A by α.

Then $B = \begin{pmatrix} a_1 & a_2 & a_3 \\ \alpha b_1 & \alpha b_2 & \alpha b_3 \\ c_1 & c_2 & c_3 \end{pmatrix}$. By expanding det B in terms of the 2nd row,

det (B) $= \alpha.b_1C_{21} + \alpha b_2C_{22} + \alpha\, b_3C_{23}$

where C_{21}, C_{22} and C_{23} are co-factors of corresponding elements of row of det(A) as well as det(B).

$= \alpha\,[b_1\,C_{21} + b_2\,C_{22} + b_3\,C_{23}] = \alpha$ det A

(b) If all the elements of a row (column) of a determinant are multiplied by a constant (k), then the determinant gets multiplied by that constant.

$$\begin{vmatrix} a_1 & kb_1 & c_1 \\ a_2 & kb_2 & c_2 \\ a_3 & kb_3 & c_3 \end{vmatrix} = k\begin{vmatrix} a_1 & b_1 & c_1 \\ a_2 & b_2 & c_2 \\ a_3 & b_3 & c_3 \end{vmatrix}$$ and

$$k\begin{vmatrix} a_1 & b_1 & c_1 \\ a_2 & b_2 & c_2 \\ a_3 & b_3 & c_3 \end{vmatrix} = \begin{vmatrix} ka_1 & kb_1 & kc_1 \\ a_2 & b_2 & c_2 \\ a_3 & b_3 & c_3 \end{vmatrix}$$

NOTES

(a) *If the elements in any row (or column) are multiple of the corresponding elements in any other row (or column), then the determinant vanishes.*

e.g., $\begin{vmatrix} 2 & 3 & 5 \\ 220 & 330 & 550 \\ 7 & 9 & 11 \end{vmatrix} = 0 \quad \left[\because \begin{array}{c} a_{21} = 110 \times a_{11} \\ a_{22} = 110 \times a_{12} \\ a_{23} = 110 \times a_{13} \end{array}\right]$

(b) *If the signs of all the elements in any row (or column) be changed the sign of the determinant is changed, because this is equivalent to multiplying the determinant by the factor – 1.*

(c) *If A be an n-rowed square matrix and k be any scalar, then* $|kA| = k^n |A$

Property 7. The value of the determinant corresponding to a triangular determinant is equal to product of its principal diagonal elements. e.g., $\begin{vmatrix} a & b & c \\ 0 & c & a \\ 0 & 0 & b \end{vmatrix} =$ abc (expanding along C_1)

Property 8. If any row or column of a determinant be passed over n rows or columns, the resulting determinant will be $(-1)^n$ times the original determinant.

ILLUSTRATION 6: Show that the determinant $|A|$ vanishes when

(a) $|A| = \begin{vmatrix} 15 & 20 & 25 \\ 2 & 4 & 6 \\ 6 & 8 & 10 \end{vmatrix}$ (b) $|A| = \begin{vmatrix} 1/2 & 1/3 & 5/7 \\ 21 & 14 & 30 \\ 7 & 3 & 2 \end{vmatrix}$

SOLUTION: (a) $|A| = \begin{vmatrix} 15 & 20 & 25 \\ 2 & 4 & 6 \\ 6 & 8 & 10 \end{vmatrix}$; $R_1 \to \frac{R_1}{5}; |A| = 5\begin{vmatrix} 3 & 4 & 5 \\ 2 & 4 & 6 \\ 6 & 8 & 10 \end{vmatrix}$; $R_3 \to \frac{R_3}{2}; |A| = 10\begin{vmatrix} 3 & 4 & 5 \\ 2 & 4 & 6 \\ 3 & 4 & 5 \end{vmatrix}$

$\because R_1 = R_3 \qquad \Rightarrow |A| = 0$

(b) $|A| = \begin{vmatrix} 1/2 & 1/3 & 5/7 \\ 21 & 14 & 30 \\ 7 & 3 & 2 \end{vmatrix}$;

$R_1 \to 42R_1; |A| = \frac{1}{42}\begin{vmatrix} 21 & 14 & 30 \\ 21 & 14 & 30 \\ 7 & 3 & 2 \end{vmatrix} \quad \because R_1 = R_2 \Rightarrow |A| = 0$

ILLUSTRATION 7: For positive numbers x, y and z (not equal to 1), show that the numerical value of the determinant $\begin{vmatrix} 1 & \log_x y & \log_x z \\ \log_y x & 1 & \log_y z \\ \log_z x & \log_z y & 1 \end{vmatrix}$ is zero.

SOLUTION: Let $\Delta = \begin{vmatrix} 1 & \log_x y & \log_x z \\ \log_y x & 1 & \log_y z \\ \log_z x & \log_z y & 1 \end{vmatrix} = \frac{1}{\log x . \log y . \log z}\begin{vmatrix} \log x & \log y & \log z \\ \log x & \log y & \log z \\ \log x & \log y & \log z \end{vmatrix} = 0$

ILLUSTRATION 8: Show that $\begin{vmatrix} \alpha & \beta & \gamma \\ \theta & \varphi & \psi \\ \lambda & \mu & \nu \end{vmatrix} = \begin{vmatrix} \beta & \mu & \varphi \\ \alpha & \lambda & \theta \\ \gamma & \nu & \psi \end{vmatrix}$

SOLUTION: $L.H.S = \begin{vmatrix} \alpha & \beta & \gamma \\ \theta & \varphi & \psi \\ \lambda & \mu & \nu \end{vmatrix} = \begin{vmatrix} \alpha & \theta & \lambda \\ \beta & \varphi & \mu \\ \gamma & \psi & \nu \end{vmatrix}$ (interchanging rows and columns)

$$= (-1)\begin{vmatrix} \alpha & \lambda & \theta \\ \beta & \mu & \varphi \\ \gamma & \nu & \psi \end{vmatrix} (C_2 \leftrightarrow C_3) = (-1)^2 \begin{vmatrix} \beta & \mu & \varphi \\ \alpha & \lambda & \theta \\ \gamma & \nu & \psi \end{vmatrix} (R_1 \leftrightarrow R_2) = \begin{vmatrix} \beta & \mu & \varphi \\ \alpha & \lambda & \theta \\ \gamma & \nu & \psi \end{vmatrix} = R.H.S$$

ILLUSTRATION 9: If $|A| = 3$; then find $|\lambda A|$ (where $|A|$ is a determinant of order 4×4)

SOLUTION: Let $|A| = \begin{vmatrix} a & b & c & d \\ e & f & g & h \\ i & j & k & l \\ m & n & o & p \end{vmatrix} = 3$, then $|\lambda A| = \begin{vmatrix} \lambda a & \lambda b & \lambda c & \lambda d \\ \lambda e & \lambda f & \lambda g & \lambda h \\ \lambda i & \lambda j & \lambda k & \lambda l \\ \lambda m & \lambda n & \lambda o & \lambda p \end{vmatrix}$

Taking out λ common from C_1, C_2, C_3 and C_4; we get

$$|\lambda A| = \lambda^4 \begin{vmatrix} a & b & c & d \\ e & f & g & h \\ i & j & k & l \\ m & n & o & p \end{vmatrix} = \lambda^4 \times |A| = 3 \times \lambda^4 = 3\lambda^4$$

ILLUSTRATION 10: Identify the transformations T_i; $i \in \{1,2,3,.........\}$

$$\begin{vmatrix} 6 & 18 \\ 12 & 24 \end{vmatrix} \xrightarrow{T_1} \begin{vmatrix} 24 & 12 \\ 18 & 6 \end{vmatrix} \xrightarrow{T_2} \begin{vmatrix} 8 & 36 \\ 6 & 18 \end{vmatrix} \xrightarrow{T_3} \begin{vmatrix} 4 & 18 \\ 12 & 36 \end{vmatrix} \xrightarrow{T_4} \begin{vmatrix} 4 & 54 \\ 4 & 36 \end{vmatrix}$$

SOLUTION: $T_1 : R_1 \leftrightarrow R_2 \; \& \; C_1 \leftrightarrow C_2$; $\quad T_2 : C_1 \to \frac{C_1}{3} \; \& \; C_2 \to 3C_2$;

$T_3 : R_1 \to \frac{R_1}{2} \; \& \; R_2 \to 2R_2$; $\quad T_4 : C_2 \to 3C_2 \; \& \; R_2 \to \frac{R_2}{3}$

TEXTUAL EXERCISE 2: (SUBJECTIVE)

1. Mention the property/properties and their sequence to obtain the following transformations

$$\begin{vmatrix} a & b \\ c & d \end{vmatrix} \xrightarrow{T_1} \begin{vmatrix} d & c \\ b & a \end{vmatrix} \xrightarrow{T_2} \begin{vmatrix} d & b \\ c & a \end{vmatrix} \xrightarrow{T_3}$$

$$\frac{1}{6}\begin{vmatrix} 3d & 6b \\ c & 2a \end{vmatrix} \xrightarrow{T_4} -\frac{1}{2}\begin{vmatrix} c & 2a \\ d & 2b \end{vmatrix}$$

2. Evaluate the determinants without expansion $\begin{vmatrix} 2 & 4 & 6 \\ 3 & 1 & 5 \\ 4 & 8 & 12 \end{vmatrix}$

3. Show that the determinant $\begin{vmatrix} a & b & c \\ x & y & z \\ l & m & n \end{vmatrix} = \begin{vmatrix} y & z & x \\ m & n & l \\ b & c & a \end{vmatrix}$

4. If $|A| = 5$; where A is a square matrix of order n, then find $|m A|$ where $m \in \mathbb{R}$

5. Identify the transformations T_i; $i \in \{1,2,3.......\}$

$$\begin{vmatrix} 2 & 4 & 6 \\ 1 & 3 & 5 \\ 12 & 8 & 16 \end{vmatrix} \xrightarrow{T_1} 8\begin{vmatrix} 1 & 2 & 3 \\ 1 & 3 & 5 \\ 3 & 2 & 4 \end{vmatrix} \xrightarrow{T_2} \begin{vmatrix} 4 & 2 & 6 \\ 4 & 3 & 10 \\ 12 & 2 & 8 \end{vmatrix} \xrightarrow{T_3}$$

$$\begin{vmatrix} 4 & 3 & 10 \\ 4 & 2 & 6 \\ 12 & 2 & 8 \end{vmatrix} \xrightarrow{T_4} \begin{vmatrix} 4 & 3 & 10 \\ 12 & 2 & 8 \\ 4 & 2 & 6 \end{vmatrix}$$

6. Identify the transformations T_i; $i \in \{1,2,3........\}$

$$\begin{vmatrix} 5 & 10 & 25 \\ 9 & 6 & 3 \\ 2 & 4 & 8 \end{vmatrix} \xrightarrow{T_1} 30\begin{vmatrix} 1 & 3 & 1 \\ 2 & 2 & 2 \\ 5 & 1 & 4 \end{vmatrix} \xrightarrow{T_2}$$

$$\begin{vmatrix} 2 & 6 & 2 \\ 6 & 6 & 6 \\ 25 & 5 & 20 \end{vmatrix} \xrightarrow{T_3} \begin{vmatrix} 6 & 6 & 6 \\ 25 & 5 & 20 \\ 2 & 6 & 2 \end{vmatrix}$$

Answer Key

1. $T_1 : R_1 \leftrightarrow R_2$ and $C_1 \leftrightarrow C_2$; T_2: Transpose is taken, i.e $R \leftrightarrow C$; $T_3 : R_1 \to 1/3(3R_1)$ and $C_2 \to 1/2\ (2C_2)$; $T_4 : R_1 \leftrightarrow R_2$ and $R_2 \to 3(1/3\ R_2)$ **2.** 0 **4.** $5(m)^n$

5. $T_1 : R_1 \to \frac{1}{2}R_1$ and $R_3 \to \frac{1}{4}R_3$; $T_2 : C_1 \to 4C_1$ and $C_3 \to 2C_3$; $T_3 : R_1 \leftrightarrow R_2$; $T_4 : R_2 \leftrightarrow R_3$

6. $T_1 : R \to C$ and then taking 5,3,2 common respectively from C_1, C_2, C_3 i.e., $C_1 \to \frac{C_1}{5}$; $C_2 \to \frac{C_2}{3}$; $C_3 \to \frac{C_3}{2}$
$T_2 : R_1 \to 2R_1$; $R_2 \to 3R_2$; $R_3 \to 5R_3$; $T_3 : R_1$ rolling over two rows R_2 and R_3

Property 9. (a) If every element of a column or (row) is the sum (difference) of two terms, then the determinant is equal to the sum (difference) of two determinants of same order; one containing only the first term in place of each sum, the other only the second term. The remaining elements of both determinants are the same as in the given determinant.

Let $\Delta_1 = \begin{vmatrix} a_1 & b_1 & c_1 \\ a_2 & b_2 & c_2 \\ a_3 & b_3 & c_3 \end{vmatrix}$, $\Delta_2 = \begin{vmatrix} d_1 & b_1 & c_1 \\ d_2 & b_2 & c_2 \\ d_3 & b_3 & c_3 \end{vmatrix}$ be two third order determinants which have 3 – 1= 2 (one less than the 'order') columns identical. Then their addition is also a determinant of the third order given by $\Delta_1 + \Delta_2 = \begin{vmatrix} a_1+d_1 & b_1 & c_1 \\ a_2+d_2 & b_2 & c_2 \\ a_3+d_3 & b_3 & c_3 \end{vmatrix}$.

Similarly, if $\Delta_3 = \begin{vmatrix} a_1 & b_1 & c_1 \\ d_2 & e_2 & f_2 \\ a_3 & b_3 & c_3 \end{vmatrix}$, then

$$\Delta_1 + \Delta_3 = \begin{vmatrix} a_1 & b_1 & c_1 \\ a_2+d_2 & b_2+e_2 & c_2+f_2 \\ a_3 & b_3 & c_3 \end{vmatrix}$$

But $\Delta_2 + \Delta_3$ cannot be found like this.
The above process can be generalized as given below:

i.e., $\sum_{r=1}^{n} \begin{vmatrix} f(r) & g(r) & h(r) \\ a_2 & b_2 & c_2 \\ a_3 & b_3 & c_3 \end{vmatrix}$

$$= \begin{vmatrix} \sum_{r=1}^{n} f(r) & \sum_{r=1}^{n} g(r) & \sum_{r=1}^{n} h(r) \\ a_2 & b_2 & c_2 \\ a_3 & b_3 & c_3 \end{vmatrix}$$

(b) A determinant having two or more terms in the elements of a row (or column) can be written as the sum of two or more determinants.

Proof: Let $\Delta = \begin{pmatrix} a_1 & a_2 & a_3 \\ \alpha_1+\beta_1 & \alpha_2+\beta_2 & \alpha_3+\beta_3 \\ c_1 & c_2 & c_3 \end{pmatrix}$ and

$$\Delta_0 = \begin{pmatrix} a_1 & a_2 & a_3 \\ x_1 & x_2 & x_3 \\ c_1 & c_2 & c_3 \end{pmatrix}$$

The truth of the above property can be established based on following crucial facts.

- Co-factors of x_i in Δ_0 is the same as co-factor of $(\alpha_i + \beta_i)$ in Δ. First note that the minors in the respective determinants are the same, by having a look at the following pictorial representation of the minors of x_2 and $\alpha_2 + \beta_2$

$$= \begin{pmatrix} a_1 & \cancel{a_2} & a_3 \\ \cancel{x_1} & \cancel{x_2} & \cancel{x_3} \\ c_1 & \cancel{c_2} & c_3 \end{pmatrix} = \begin{pmatrix} a_1 & \cancel{a_2} & a_3 \\ \cancel{\alpha_1+\beta_1} & \cancel{\alpha_2+\beta_2} & \cancel{\alpha_3+\beta_3} \\ c_1 & \cancel{c_2} & c_3 \end{pmatrix}$$

- Secondly, check that the same signs get prefixed to the minors of x_2 and $\alpha_2 + \beta_2$ because they occupy the same position in the respective determinants. Therefore, expanding the determinant in terms of its 2nd row, we get $\Delta = (\alpha_1 + \beta_1) \times$ co-factor of x_1 in $\Delta_0 + (\alpha_2 + \beta_2) \times$ co-factor of x_2 in $\Delta_0 + (\alpha_3 + \beta_3) \times$ co-factor of x_3 in Δ_0

$$= \sum_{i=1}^{3} \alpha_i \times \text{cofactor of } x_i \text{ in } \Delta_0 + \sum_{i=1}^{3} \beta_i \times \text{cofactor of } x_i \text{ in } \Delta_0$$

$$= \begin{vmatrix} a_1 & a_2 & a_3 \\ \alpha_1 & \alpha_2 & \alpha_3 \\ c_1 & c_2 & c_3 \end{vmatrix} + \begin{vmatrix} a_1 & a_2 & a_3 \\ \beta_1 & \beta_2 & \beta_3 \\ c_1 & c_2 & c_3 \end{vmatrix}$$

This last step being true because one can expand these determinants in term of their 2nd rows and also the co-factors of the α_i's and β_i's in these determinants are just those of x_i's in Δ's.

Property 10. The value Δ of a determinant A remains unchanged if all the elements of one row (column) are multiplied by a scalar and added or subtracted to the corresponding elements of another row(column). Symbolically, it is written as $\Delta = \Delta_{R_i \to R_i + mR_j}$ (or $\Delta_{C_j \to C_j + mC_i}$) and operation is also symbolically written as $R_i \to R_i + mR_j$ or $C_j \to C_j + mC_i$.

Proof: Let $|A| = \begin{vmatrix} a_1 & a_2 & a_3 \\ b_1 & b_2 & b_3 \\ c_1 & c_2 & c_3 \end{vmatrix}$ and if $R_2 \to R_2 + \alpha R_3$ we get det B; $|B| = \begin{vmatrix} a_1 & a_2 & a_3 \\ b_1+\alpha c_1 & b_2+\alpha c_2 & b_3+\alpha c_3 \\ c_1 & c_2 & c_3 \end{vmatrix}$

The theorem says $|B| = |A|$ which can be verified as

$$|B| = \begin{vmatrix} a_1 & a_2 & a_3 \\ b_1+\alpha c_1 & b_2+\alpha c_2 & b_3+\alpha c_3 \\ c_1 & c_2 & c_3 \end{vmatrix}$$

$$= \begin{vmatrix} a_1 & a_2 & a_3 \\ b_1 & b_2 & b_3 \\ c_1 & c_2 & c_3 \end{vmatrix} + \begin{vmatrix} a_1 & a_2 & a_3 \\ \alpha c_1 & \alpha c_2 & \alpha c_3 \\ c_1 & c_2 & c_3 \end{vmatrix}$$

$$= |A| + \alpha \begin{vmatrix} a_1 & a_2 & a_3 \\ c_1 & c_2 & c_3 \\ c_1 & c_2 & c_3 \end{vmatrix} \quad (R_2 \text{ and } R_3 \text{ are identical})$$

$$= |A| + \text{zero} = |A|$$

e.g., Let $\Delta = \begin{vmatrix} 1 & 2 & 3 \\ 2 & 3 & 4 \\ 2 & 0 & 5 \end{vmatrix} = -7$; and $\Delta_1 = \begin{vmatrix} 5 & 2 & 13 \\ 2 & 3 & 4 \\ 2 & 0 & 5 \end{vmatrix}$

$[R_1 \to R_1 + 2R_3]$, gives $5(15-0) - 2(10-8) + 13(0-6) = 75 - 4 - 78 = -7$. Hence $\Delta = \Delta_1$

NOTES

If any row or column which is changed is multiplied by a number, then the determinant will have to be divided by that number so that its value remains unaltered.

$$\text{e.g., } \Delta = \begin{vmatrix} a_1 & a_2 & a_3 \\ b_1 & b_2 & b_3 \\ c_1 & c_2 & c_3 \end{vmatrix} = \frac{1}{k}\begin{vmatrix} ka_1 & ka_2 & ka_3 \\ b_1 & b_2 & b_3 \\ c_1 & c_2 & c_3 \end{vmatrix} = \frac{1}{k}\begin{vmatrix} a_1 & ka_2 & a_3 \\ b_1 & kb_2 & b_3 \\ c_1 & kc_2 & c_3 \end{vmatrix} = \frac{1}{k}\begin{vmatrix} ka_1 & a_2 & a_3 \\ kb_1 & b_2 & b_3 \\ kc_1 & c_2 & c_3 \end{vmatrix} \text{ etc.}$$

ILLUSTRATION 11: Evaluate without expanding $\begin{vmatrix} b^2-ab & b-c & bc-ca \\ ab-a^2 & a-b & b^2-ab \\ bc-ca & c-a & ab-a^2 \end{vmatrix}$.

SOLUTION: Let $\Delta = \begin{vmatrix} b^2-ab & b-c & bc-ca \\ ab-a^2 & a-b & b^2-ab \\ bc-ca & c-a & ab-a^2 \end{vmatrix} = (b-a)^2 \begin{vmatrix} b & b-c & c \\ a & a-b & b \\ c & c-a & a \end{vmatrix}$ $(C_2 \to C_2 + C_3)$

$$= (b-a)^2 \begin{vmatrix} b & b & c \\ a & a & b \\ c & c & a \end{vmatrix} = (b-a)^2.0 = 0$$

Property 11. (a) The sum of the products of elements of a row (or column) with their corresponding co-factors is equal to the value of the determinant. e.g., $a_{11}C_{11} + a_{12}C_{12} + a_{13}C_{13} = a_{21}C_{21} + a_{22}C_{22} + a_{23}C_{23} = \Delta$

(b) Sum of the products of elements of any row (or column) with the co-factors of the corres sponding elements of a parallel row (or column) is always zero. e.g., $a_{11}C_{21} + a_{12}C_{22} + a_{13}C_{23} = 0$

Proof: $\Delta = \begin{vmatrix} a_{11} & a_{12} & a_{13} \\ a_{21} & a_{22} & a_{23} \\ a_{31} & a_{32} & a_{33} \end{vmatrix}; R_2 \to R_2 + R_1$

$$\Delta = \begin{vmatrix} a_{11} & a_{12} & a_{13} \\ a_{21}+a_{11} & a_{22}+a_{12} & a_{23}+a_{13} \\ a_{31} & a_{32} & a_{33} \end{vmatrix}$$

Now expanding along R_2

$\Delta = (a_{21} + a_{11})C_{21} + (a_{22} + a_{12})C_{22} + (a_{23} + a_{13})C_{23}$

$\Rightarrow \Delta = (a_{21}C_{21} + a_{22}C_{22} + a_{23}C_{23}) + (a_{11}C_{21} + a_{12}C_{22} + a_{13}C_{23})$

$\Rightarrow \Delta = \Delta + a_{11}C_{21} + a_{12}C_{22} + a_{13}C_{23}$

$\Rightarrow a_{11}C_{21} + a_{12}C_{22} + a_{13}C_{23} = 0$

The same argument will prove the facts: $a_{11}C_{31} + a_{12}C_{32} + a_{13}C_{33} = a_{21}C_{11} + a_{22}C_{12} + a_{23}C_{13} = a_{21}C_{31} + a_{22}C_{32} + a_{23}C_{33} = 0$

Concluding the argument, we may note that, in any determinant, if the elements of any row (or column) are multiplied by their respective co-factors and the results added, we get the value of the determinant. Contrary to which, if these elements are multiplied by the co-factors of the corresponding elements in a parallel row (or column) and the results added, we obtain zero.

Property 12. If the elements of a Determinant Δ involve x, i.e., the determinant is a polynomial in x and if it vanishes for $x = a$, then $(x - a)$ must be a factor of Δ. In other words, if two rows (or two column) become identical for $x = a$, then $(x - a)$ is a factor of Δ.

Generalizing this result, we can say if r rows (or r columns) become identical when a is substituted for x, then $(x - a)^{r-1}$ should be a factor of Δ. e.g., If $\Delta = \begin{vmatrix} x & 5 & 2 \\ x^2 & 9 & 4 \\ x^3 & 16 & 8 \end{vmatrix}$

at $x = 2$, $\Delta = 0$ ($\because C_1$ and C_2 become identical at $x = 2$)

CAUTION

While applying all the above properties from propery 1 to property 10 at least one row (or column) must remain unchanged.

ILLUSTRATION 12: Solve the equation $\begin{vmatrix} a & a & x \\ a & a & a \\ b & x & b \end{vmatrix} = 0$

SOLUTION: The given equation is $\begin{vmatrix} a & a & x \\ a & a & a \\ b & x & b \end{vmatrix} = 0 \Rightarrow \begin{vmatrix} 0 & 0 & x-a \\ a & a & a \\ b & x & b \end{vmatrix} = 0$ $(R_1 \to R_1 - R_2)$

$\Rightarrow (x - a)(ax - ab) = 0 \Rightarrow x = a$ or $x = b \Rightarrow x = a$ or b.

ILLUSTRATION 13: Show that $\begin{vmatrix} 1 & a & a^2 \\ 1 & b & b^2 \\ 1 & c & c^2 \end{vmatrix} = (a - b)(b - c)(c - a)$

SOLUTION: Given determinant is $\Delta = \begin{vmatrix} 1 & a & a^2 \\ 1 & b & b^2 \\ 1 & c & c^2 \end{vmatrix}$

Applying the transformation $R_2 \to R_2 - R_1$, $R_3 \to R_3 - R_2$, we get

$$\Delta = \begin{vmatrix} 1 & a & a^2 \\ 0 & b-a & b^2-a^2 \\ 0 & c-b & c^2-b^2 \end{vmatrix}$$; Taking $(b-a)$ common from R_2 and $(c-b)$ from R_3 we get

$$\Delta = (b-a)(c-b)\begin{vmatrix} 1 & a & a^2 \\ 0 & 1 & b+a \\ 0 & 1 & c+b \end{vmatrix}$$. Apply $R_3 \to R_3 - R_2$; $\Delta = (a-b)(b-c)(c-a)$

Aliter: $\begin{vmatrix} 1 & a & a^2 \\ 1 & b & b^2 \\ 1 & c & c^2 \end{vmatrix} = \begin{vmatrix} 1 & 1 & 1 \\ a & b & c \\ a^2 & b^2 & c^2 \end{vmatrix}$ $(R \leftrightarrow C)$. Substituting $a = b$, we can see that

First and second columns are identical which implies that $(a - b)$ must be a factor of Δ. Similarly, putting $b = c$, $c =$ a we can show $(b - c)$ and $(c - a)$ must be a factor of Δ. And as we know that the product of the diagonal elements of given determinant (Δ) is $1.\ b.c^2$, which is a third degree expression, so Δ is a polynomial of degree 3. And $(a - b)(b - c)(c - a)$ is a factor of Δ which is a polynomial of degree 3 itself in a, b, c. Therefore, the only other factor of Δ that can be a constant, say k.

$$\Delta = \begin{vmatrix} 1 & 1 & 1 \\ a & b & c \\ a^2 & b^2 & c^2 \end{vmatrix} = k(a-b)(b-c)(c-a)$$

In order to find the value of k, give arbitrary values to a, b and c such that calculations remain simple and the two sides do not vanish. e.g., assuming $a = 0, b = 1, c = 2$

we get, $\begin{vmatrix} 1 & 1 & 1 \\ 0 & 1 & 2 \\ 0 & 1 & 4 \end{vmatrix} = k(0-1)(1-2)(2-0)$

or $2 = 2k \Rightarrow k = 1$ (on solving the determinant along first coulmn)

Hence, $\begin{vmatrix} 1 & 1 & 1 \\ a & b & c \\ a^2 & b^2 & c^2 \end{vmatrix} = (a-b)(b-c)(c-a)$

ILLUSTRATION 14: Prove that $\begin{vmatrix} a^2+1 & ab & ac \\ ab & b^2+1 & bc \\ ac & bc & c^2+1 \end{vmatrix} = 1 + a^2 + b^2 + c^2$

SOLUTION: L.H.S = $\begin{vmatrix} a^2+1 & ab & ac \\ ab & b^2+1 & bc \\ ac & bc & c^2+1 \end{vmatrix}$ (Multiplying C_1, C_2, C_3 by a, b, c respectively)

i.e., $\Delta = \frac{1}{abc}.\Delta_{C_1 \to aC_1;\ C_2 \to bC_2;\ C_3 \to cC_3}$ $\Rightarrow \Delta = \frac{1}{abc}\begin{vmatrix} a(a^2+1) & ab^2 & ac^2 \\ a^2b & b(b^2+1) & bc^2 \\ a^2c & b^2c & c(c^2+1) \end{vmatrix}$

Now taking common a, b, c from R_1, R_2, R_3 respectively, the determinant transforms to

$$\Rightarrow \Delta = \frac{abc}{abc}\begin{vmatrix} (a^2+1) & b^2 & c^2 \\ a^2 & (b^2+1) & c^2 \\ a^2 & b^2 & (c^2+1) \end{vmatrix} = \begin{vmatrix} 1+a^2+b^2+c^2 & b^2 & c^2 \\ 1+a^2+b^2+c^2 & (b^2+1) & c^2 \\ 1+a^2+b^2+c^2 & b^2 & (c^2+1) \end{vmatrix};$$

(Applying $C_1 \to C_1 + C_2 + C_3$); Taking $(1 + a^2 + b^2 + c^2)$ common from C_1.

$$\Rightarrow \Delta = (1+a^2+b^2+c^2)\begin{vmatrix} 1 & b^2 & c^2 \\ 1 & (b^2+1) & c^2 \\ 1 & b^2 & (c^2+1) \end{vmatrix}$$

Applying the transformation $[R_2 \to R_2 - R_1$ and $R_3 \to R_3 - R_1]$

$$\Rightarrow \Delta = (1+a^2+b^2+c^2)\begin{vmatrix} 1 & b^2 & c^2 \\ 0 & 1 & 0 \\ 0 & 0 & 1 \end{vmatrix};$$

Since the above determinant is upper triangular, therefore,

$\Rightarrow \Delta = (1 + a^2 + b^2 + c^2)(1.1.1) = (1 + a^2 + b^2 + c^2) =$ R.H.S

ILLUSTRATION 15: Show that the roots of the equation $\begin{vmatrix} x & m & n & 1 \\ a & x & b & 1 \\ a & b & x & 1 \\ a & b & c & 1 \end{vmatrix} = 0$ are independent of m and n.

SOLUTION: Let $\Delta = \begin{vmatrix} x-a & m-x & n-b & 0 \\ 0 & x-b & b-x & 0 \\ 0 & 0 & x-c & 0 \\ a & b & c & 1 \end{vmatrix}$; $\begin{matrix} R_1 \to R_1 - R_2 \\ R_2 \to R_2 - R_3 \\ R_3 \to R_3 - R_4 \end{matrix}$

$$\Rightarrow \Delta = \begin{vmatrix} x-a & m-x & n-b \\ 0 & x-b & b-x \\ 0 & 0 & x-c \end{vmatrix} = (x-a)(x-b)(x-c) \therefore \Delta = 0 \Rightarrow (x-a)(x-b)(x-c) = 0$$

$\Rightarrow x = a, b, c$ which are independent of m and n

Aliter: *Using method of factorization:*

Putting $x = a$ and taking 'a' common from first column, the first and fourth coulmn of the determinant become identical, therefore $x - a$ is a factor. Now putting $x = b$, second and third row become identical. Similarly putting $x = c$, third and fourth row become identical.

Therefore the *LHS* expression has $(x - a)(x - b)(x - c)$ as a factor since it is cubic in x because the product of the diagonal elements is x^3. Therefore when equated to 0, it will have three roots. i.e., $x = a, b, c$ which are obviously independent of m and n.

ILLUSTRATION 16: Evaluate the determinant $\begin{vmatrix} 1 & bc & bc(b+c) \\ 1 & ca & ca(c+a) \\ 1 & ab & ab(a+b) \end{vmatrix}$.

SOLUTION: Let the given determinant $\Delta = \begin{vmatrix} 1 & bc & bc(b+c) \\ 1 & ca & ca(c+a) \\ 1 & ab & ab(a+b) \end{vmatrix}$

Transforming $(R_1 \to aR_1, R_2 \to bR_2, R_3 \to cR_3)$ and dividing the determinant by abc.

$$\Rightarrow \Delta = \frac{1}{abc}\begin{vmatrix} a & abc & abc(b+c) \\ b & abc & cba(c+a) \\ c & abc & abc(a+b) \end{vmatrix}$$

Taking $(abc)^2$ common from C_2 and C_3 both, we get

$$\Rightarrow \Delta = \frac{(abc)^2}{abc}\begin{vmatrix} a & 1 & (b+c) \\ b & 1 & (c+a) \\ c & 1 & (a+b) \end{vmatrix}$$

Applying $(C_1 \to C_1 + C_3)$ and taking $(a+b+c)$ common from C_1 we get

$$\Rightarrow \Delta = abc(a+b+c)\begin{vmatrix} 1 & 1 & (b+c) \\ 1 & 1 & (c+a) \\ 1 & 1 & (a+b) \end{vmatrix}$$

$\Rightarrow \Delta = abc(a+b+c).0 = 0$ ($\because$ C_1 and C_1 are identical) $\Rightarrow \Delta = 0$

ILLUSTRATION 17: Let $\Delta_a = \begin{vmatrix} (a-1) & n & 6 \\ (a-1)^2 & 2n^2 & 4n-2 \\ (a-1)^3 & 3n^3 & 3n^2-3n \end{vmatrix}$, show that $\sum_{a=1}^{n} \Delta_a = C$ a constant *w.r.t* variable *a*.

SOLUTION: Given $\Delta_a = \begin{vmatrix} (a-1) & n & 6 \\ (a-1)^2 & 2n^2 & 4n-2 \\ (a-1)^3 & 3n^3 & 3n^2-3n \end{vmatrix}$

$\because$ C_2 and C_3 are identical for all determinants, therefore applying the property of summation of determinants.

$$\Rightarrow \sum_{a=1}^{n}\Delta_a = \begin{vmatrix} \sum_{a=1}^{n}(a-1) & n & 6 \\ \sum_{a=1}^{n}(a-1)^2 & 2n^2 & 4n-2 \\ \sum_{a=1}^{n}(a-1)^3 & 3n^3 & 3n^2-3n \end{vmatrix} = \begin{vmatrix} \frac{n(n-1)}{2} & n & 6 \\ \frac{n(n-1)(2n-1)}{6} & 2n^2 & 4n-2 \\ \frac{n^2(n-1)^2}{4} & 3n^3 & 3n^2-3n \end{vmatrix}$$

Taking $\frac{n(n-1)}{12}$ common from Ist column of the determinants

$$= \frac{n(n-1)}{12}\begin{vmatrix} 6 & n & 6 \\ 4n-2 & 2n^2 & 4n-2 \\ 3n^2-3n & 3n^3 & 3n^2-3n \end{vmatrix} = \frac{n(n-1)}{12}.0 = 0$$ (Since C_1 and C_3 are identical)

ILLUSTRATION 18: If *a*, *b*, *c* be positive and not all equal, then show that the value of the determinant $\begin{vmatrix} a & b & c \\ b & c & a \\ c & a & b \end{vmatrix}$ has negative sign.

SOLUTION: Let $\Delta = \begin{vmatrix} a & b & c \\ b & c & a \\ c & a & b \end{vmatrix} = \begin{vmatrix} a+b+c & b & c \\ a+b+c & c & a \\ a+b+c & a & b \end{vmatrix}$ [Applying transformation $C_1 \to C_1 + C_2 + C_3$]

$$= (a+b+c)\begin{vmatrix} 1 & b & c \\ 1 & c & a \\ 1 & a & b \end{vmatrix}$$ (Taking $(a+b+c)$ common from Ist column)

$$= (a+b+c)\begin{vmatrix} 1 & b & c \\ 0 & c-b & a-c \\ 0 & a-b & b-c \end{vmatrix} = (a+b+c)\begin{vmatrix} c-b & a-c \\ a-b & b-c \end{vmatrix} \ (R_2 \to R_2 - R_1 \text{ and } R_3 \to R_3 - R_1)$$

(expanding along Ist row)

$= (a + b + c)\ \{(c - b)(b - c) - (a - c)(a - b)\}$

$= (a + b + c)\ \{bc - c^2 - b^2 + bc - a^2 + ab + ac - bc\} = (a + b + c)\ (-a^2 - b^2 - c^2 + ab + bc + ca)$

$= -\frac{1}{2}(a+b+c)\ (2a^2 + 2b^2 + 2c^2 - 2ab - 2bc - 2ca)$

$\therefore\ \Delta = -\frac{1}{2}(a+b+c)\ [(a-b)^2 + (b-c)^2 + (c-a)^2]$

Since a, b, c are positve and unequal

$a + b + c > 0$ and $(a - b)^2 + (b - c)^2 + (c - a)^2 > C$. Hence, Δ has negative sign.

TEXTUAL EXERCISE 3: (SUBJECTIVE)

1. Without expanding the determinant, prove the following

(a) $\begin{vmatrix} 18 & 40 & 89 \\ 40 & 89 & 198 \\ 89 & 198 & 440 \end{vmatrix} = -1$

(b) $\begin{vmatrix} a^2 & b^2 & c^2 \\ (a+1)^2 & (b+1)^2 & (c+1)^2 \\ (a-1)^2 & (b-1)^2 & (c-1)^2 \end{vmatrix} = 4\begin{vmatrix} a^2 & b^2 & c^2 \\ a & b & c \\ 1 & 1 & 1 \end{vmatrix}$

(c) $\begin{vmatrix} 1 & a & a^2-bc \\ 1 & b & b^2-ca \\ 1 & c & c^2-ab \end{vmatrix} = 0$

(d) $\begin{vmatrix} ax & by & cz \\ x^2 & y^2 & z^2 \\ 1 & 1 & 1 \end{vmatrix} = \begin{vmatrix} a & b & c \\ x & y & z \\ yz & zx & xy \end{vmatrix}$

2. Solve for x and y

(i) $\begin{vmatrix} x+2 & 2x+3 & 3x+4 \\ 2x+3 & 3x+4 & 4x+5 \\ 3x+5 & 5x+8 & 10x+17 \end{vmatrix} = 0$

(ii) $\begin{vmatrix} 6i & -3i & 1 \\ 4 & 3i & -1 \\ 20 & 3 & i \end{vmatrix} = x + iy$

3. If $a + b + c = 0$, solve for x: $\begin{vmatrix} a-x & c & b \\ c & b-x & a \\ b & a & c-x \end{vmatrix} = 0$

4. Prove that

(i) $\begin{vmatrix} S-a_1 & S-a_2 & S-a_3 \\ S-a_3 & S-a_1 & S-a_2 \\ S-a_2 & S-a_3 & S-a_1 \end{vmatrix} = -2\begin{vmatrix} a_1 & a_2 & a_3 \\ a_3 & a_1 & a_2 \\ a_2 & a_3 & a_1 \end{vmatrix}$

where $S = a_1 + a_2 + a_3$

(ii) $\begin{vmatrix} a & b-c & c+b \\ a+c & b & c-a \\ a-b & a+b & c \end{vmatrix}$

$= (a+b+c)(a^2+b^2+c^2)$

(iii) $\begin{vmatrix} a & b & c \\ a^2 & b^2 & c^2 \\ b+c & c+a & a+b \end{vmatrix}$

$= (a+b+c)(a-b)(b-c)(c-a)$

5. Add the following determinants without expanding them:

(a) $\begin{vmatrix} a & b & c \\ x & y & z \\ 1 & 3 & 5 \end{vmatrix} + \begin{vmatrix} 2 & 4 & 6 \\ a & b & c \\ x & y & z \end{vmatrix} + \begin{vmatrix} x & y & z \\ 3 & 5 & 7 \\ a & b & c \end{vmatrix} + \begin{vmatrix} a & b & c \\ x & y & z \\ 4 & 6 & 8 \end{vmatrix}$

(b) $\begin{vmatrix} a & b \\ x & y \end{vmatrix} + \begin{vmatrix} x^2 & y^2 \\ a & b \end{vmatrix} + \begin{vmatrix} a & b \\ x^3 & y^3 \end{vmatrix} + \begin{vmatrix} x^4 & y^4 \\ a & b \end{vmatrix} + \ldots\infty$ if $|x|, |y| < 1$

(c) $\begin{vmatrix} a & b \\ x & y \end{vmatrix} + \begin{vmatrix} a & b \\ x^2 & y^2 \end{vmatrix} + \begin{vmatrix} a & b \\ x^3 & y^3 \end{vmatrix}$ $+ \ldots\infty$ if $|x|, |y| < 1$

6. By using the properties of determinants, prove that the determinant $\begin{vmatrix} 1005 & 1002 & 3 \\ 2006 & 2009 & -3 \\ 3008 & 2998 & 10 \end{vmatrix}$ vanish.

Answer Key

2. (i) $x = -1$ or -2 (ii) $x = 0$ and $y = 0$

3. $x = 0$ or $\pm\sqrt{\frac{3}{2}(a^2 + b^2 + c^2)}$ or $\pm\sqrt{-3(ab + bc + ca)}$

5. (a) $\begin{vmatrix} a & b & c \\ x & y & z \\ 10 & 18 & 26 \end{vmatrix}$ (b) $\begin{vmatrix} a & b \\ \dfrac{x}{1+x} & \dfrac{y}{1+y} \end{vmatrix}$ (c) $\begin{vmatrix} a & b \\ \dfrac{x}{1-x} & \dfrac{y}{1-y} \end{vmatrix}$

TEXTUAL EXERCISE 3: (OBJECTIVE)

1. The value of the determinant $\begin{vmatrix} 1 & a & b+c \\ 1 & b & c+a \\ 1 & c & a+b \end{vmatrix}$ is

(a) abc (b) $a + b + c$
(c) 0 (d) $(a + b + c)^2$

2. If $\Delta = \begin{vmatrix} a-b & b-c & c-a \\ b-c & c-a & a-b \\ c-a & a-b & b-c \end{vmatrix}$, then $\Delta =$

(a) $4abc$ (b) abc
(c) 0 (d) None of these

3. One root of the equation $\begin{vmatrix} 3x-8 & 3 & 3 \\ 3 & 3x-8 & 3 \\ 3 & 3 & 3x-8 \end{vmatrix} = 0$ is

(a) 8/3 (b) 2/3
(c) 1/3 (d) None of these

4. $\begin{vmatrix} 1 & 1 & 1 \\ {}^mC_1 & {}^{m+1}C_1 & {}^{m+2}C_1 \\ {}^mC_2 & {}^{m+1}C_2 & {}^{m+2}C_2 \end{vmatrix}$ is equal to

(a) $m(m + 1)$ (b) 0
(c) 1 (d) $m(m - 1)$

5. If α, β, γ are the roots of the equation $x^3 + px + q = 0$, then the value of the determinant $\begin{vmatrix} \alpha & \beta & \gamma \\ \beta & \gamma & \alpha \\ \gamma & \alpha & \beta \end{vmatrix}$ is

(a) 4 (b) 2
(c) 0 (d) -2

6. The value of $\begin{vmatrix} {}^{10}C_4 & {}^{10}C_5 & {}^{11}C_m \\ {}^{11}C_6 & {}^{11}C_7 & {}^{12}C_{m+2} \\ {}^{12}C_8 & {}^{12}C_9 & {}^{13}C_{m+4} \end{vmatrix}$ is equal to zero, when m is

(a) 6
(b) 4
(c) 5
(d) None of these

7. If $\Delta_1 = \begin{vmatrix} 10 & 4 & 3 \\ 17 & 7 & 4 \\ 4 & -5 & 7 \end{vmatrix}$, $\Delta_2 = \begin{vmatrix} 4 & x+5 & 3 \\ 7 & x+12 & 4 \\ -5 & x-1 & 7 \end{vmatrix}$ such that $\Delta_1 = -\Delta_2$; then

(a) $x = 5$
(b) x has no real value
(c) $x = 0$
(d) None of these

8. The value of $\begin{vmatrix} 1 & 0 & 0 & 0 & 0 \\ 2 & 2 & 0 & 0 & 0 \\ 4 & 4 & 3 & 0 & 0 \\ 5 & 5 & 5 & 4 & 0 \\ 6 & 6 & 6 & 6 & 5 \end{vmatrix}$ is equal to

(a) 6! (b) 5!
(c) $1.2^2.3.4^3.5^3.6^4$ (d) None of these

9. If $i = \sqrt{-1}$ and $i^{1/4} = \alpha, \beta, \gamma, \delta$ then $\begin{vmatrix} \alpha & \beta & \gamma & \delta \\ \beta & \gamma & \delta & \alpha \\ \gamma & \delta & \alpha & \beta \\ \delta & \alpha & \beta & \gamma \end{vmatrix}$ is equal to

(a) i (b) $-i$
(c) 1 (d) 0

10. If x, y, z are in $A.P.$, then the value of the determinant $\begin{vmatrix} a+2 & a+3 & a+2x \\ a+3 & a+4 & a+2y \\ a+4 & a+5 & a+2z \end{vmatrix}$ is

(a) 1
(b) 0
(c) $2a$
(d) a

11. If $\alpha, \beta, \gamma \in \mathbb{R}$, then the determinant $\Delta = \begin{vmatrix} (e^{i\alpha}+e^{-i\alpha})^2 & (e^{i\alpha}-e^{-i\alpha})^2 & 4 \\ (e^{i\beta}+e^{-i\beta})^2 & (e^{i\beta}-e^{-i\beta})^2 & 4 \\ (e^{i\gamma}+e^{-i\gamma})^2 & (e^{i\gamma}-e^{-i\gamma})^2 & 4 \end{vmatrix}$ is

(a) independent of α, β and γ
(b) dependent on α, β and γ
(c) independent of α, β only
(d) independent of α, γ only

12. The value of the determinant $\begin{vmatrix} 265 & 240 & 219 \\ 240 & 225 & 198 \\ 219 & 198 & 181 \end{vmatrix}$ is

(a) 779 (b) 679
(c) 0 (d) None of these

13. The value of the determinant $\begin{vmatrix} 3421 & 3422 & 3423 \\ 3424 & 3425 & 3426 \\ 3427 & 3428 & 3429 \end{vmatrix}$ is equal to

(a) 0 (b) 1
(c) 2 (d) None of these

14. If $\begin{vmatrix} b^2+c^2 & ab & ca \\ ab & c^2-a^2 & bc \\ ca & bc & a^2+b^2 \end{vmatrix} = 4k$, then $k =$

(a) $a^2b^2c^2$ (b) ab^2c^3
(c) bc^2a^3 (d) ca^2b^3

15 If $u_n = \begin{vmatrix} n & 1 & 5 \\ n^2 & 2N-1 & 2N+1 \\ n^3 & 3N^2 & 3N \end{vmatrix}$, then $\sum_{n=1}^{N} u_n =$

(a) $\dfrac{N(N+1)}{2}$ (b) N^2
(c) N^3 (d) 0

Answer Key

1. (c)	**2.** (c)	**3.** (b)	**4.** (c)	**5.** (c)	**6.** (c)	**7.** (a)	**8.** (b)	**9.** (d)	**10.** (b)
11. (a)	**12.** (c)	**13.** (a)	**14.** (a)	**15.** (d)					

■ SPECIAL DETERMINANTS

Symmetric Determinant

Symmetric determinant is a determinant in which the elements situated at equal distance (symmetrically) from the principle diagonal are equal both in magnitude and sign.

i.e., $(i, j)^{th}$ element $(a_{ij}) = (j, i)^{th}$ element (a_{ji}). e.g. $\begin{vmatrix} a & h & g \\ h & b & f \\ g & f & c \end{vmatrix}$

$= abc + 2fgh - af^2 - bg^2 - ch^2$.

Skew Symmetric Determinant

All the diagonal elements are zeros and the elements situated at equal distance from the diagonal are equal in magnitude but opposite in sign. i.e., $(i, j)^{th}$ element $= -(j, i)^{th}$ element. i.e., $a_{ij} = -a_{ji}$. The value of a skew symmetric determinant of odd order is zero.

e.g., $\Delta = \begin{vmatrix} 0 & b & -c \\ -b & 0 & a \\ c & -a & 0 \end{vmatrix} = 0$

Cyclic Determinants:

Determinants in which if a is replaced by b, b by c and c by a, then value of determinants remains unchanged are called cyclic determinants.

(i) $\begin{vmatrix} 1 & 1 & 1 \\ a & b & c \\ a^2 & b^2 & c^2 \end{vmatrix} = (a-b)(b-c)(c-a)$

(Already proved in previous article)

(ii) $\begin{vmatrix} 1 & 1 & 1 \\ a & b & c \\ a^3 & b^3 & c^3 \end{vmatrix} = (a-b)(b-c)(c-a)(a+b+c)$

(can be proved using factorization)

(iii) $\begin{vmatrix} 1 & 1 & 1 \\ a^2 & b^2 & c^2 \\ a^3 & b^3 & c^3 \end{vmatrix} = (a-b)(b-c)(c-a)(ab+bc+ca)$

(can be proved using factorization)

Circulants:

Circulants are those determinants in which the elements of rows (or columns) are cyclic arrangements of letters

(i) $\begin{vmatrix} x+a & x+b & x+c \\ x+b & x+c & x+a \\ x+c & x+a & x+b \end{vmatrix}$

(ii) $\begin{vmatrix} a & b & c & d \\ b & c & d & a \\ c & d & a & b \\ d & a & b & c \end{vmatrix}$; $\begin{vmatrix} a & b & c \\ b & c & a \\ c & a & b \end{vmatrix} = -(a+b+c-3abc)$

(iii) $\begin{vmatrix} a & b & c \\ b & c & a \\ c & a & b \end{vmatrix} = -(a^3+b^3+c^3-3abc)$

(iv) $\begin{vmatrix} a^2 & b^2 & c^2 \\ b^2 & c^2 & a^2 \\ a^2 & b^2 & c^2 \end{vmatrix}$; $\begin{vmatrix} x+a & y+b & z+c \\ y+b & z+c & x+a \\ z+c & x+a & y+b \end{vmatrix}$

REMARKS

1. *An expression is called cyclic in x, y, z iff cyclic replacement of variables does not change the expression.*
   e.g., $x+y+z$, $xy+yz+zx$ *etc.*
   Such expression can be abbreviated by cyclic sigma notation as below:
   $\sum x^2 = x^2+y^2+z^2$, $\sum xy = xy+yz+zx$, $\sum (x-y) = 0$;
   $x+y+z+x^2+y^2+z^2 = \sum x + \sum x^2$
2. *An expression is called symmetric in variable x and y iff interchanging x and y does not change the expression.*
   e.g. x^2+y^2, x^2+y^2-xy ; $x^3+y^3+x^2y+y^2x$ *where as* x^3-y^3 *is not symmetric.*

■ PRODUCT OF TWO DETERMINANTS

Two determinants are conformable to multiply iff they are of same size.

1. **Method of multiplication: (Row by Column)** The ij^{th} element p_{ij} of product determinant $[p_{ij}]$ is obtained by dot product of ith row vector of Ist determinant with j^{th} column vector of the IInd determinant.

e.g., Let $\Delta_1 = \begin{vmatrix} a_1 & b_1 & c_1 \\ a_2 & b_2 & c_2 \\ a_3 & b_3 & c_3 \end{vmatrix}$, $\Delta_2 = \begin{vmatrix} l_1 & l_2 & l_3 \\ m_1 & m_2 & m_3 \\ n_1 & n_2 & n_3 \end{vmatrix}$

$$\Rightarrow \Delta = \Delta_1\Delta_2 = \begin{vmatrix} a_1l_1+b_1m_1+c_1n_1 & a_1l_2+b_1m_2+c_1n_2 & a_1l_3+b_1m_3+c_1n_3 \\ a_2l_1+b_2m_1+c_2n_1 & a_2l_2+b_2m_2+c_2n_2 & a_2l_3+b_2m_3+c_2n_3 \\ a_3l_1+b_3m_1+c_3n_1 & a_3l_2+b_3m_2+c_3n_2 & a_3l_3+b_3m_3+c_3n_3 \end{vmatrix} \text{ (row by column)}$$

Since value does not change when rows and columns are interchanged, thus we can also find the product by row × row or column × column multiplication.

2. Method of multiplication: (Row by Row): Here p_{ij} is obtained as dot product of ith row vector of Ist determinant with j^{th} row vector of IInd determinant.

Therefore take the first row of Δ_1 and the first row of Δ_2 i.e., $a_1\ b_1\ c_1$ and $l_1\ l_2\ l_3$ multiplying the corresponding elements and add. The result $a_1l_1 + b_1\ l_2 + c_1\ l_3$ is the first element of first row of Δ.

Now similar product of first row of Δ_1 and second row of Δ_2 gives $a_1\ m_1 + b_1\ m_2 + c_1\ m_3$ as the second element of first row of Δ, and the product of first row of Δ_1 and third row of Δ_2 gives $a_1n_1 + b_1\ n_2 + c_1\ n_3$ as the third element of first row of Δ. Proceeding in the above manner, we get

$$\Rightarrow\ \Delta = \Delta_1\Delta_2 = \begin{vmatrix} a_1l_1 + b_1l_2 + c_1l_3 & a_1m_1 + b_1m_2 + c_1m_3 & a_1n_1 + b_1n_2 + c_1n_3 \\ a_2l_1 + b_2l_2 + c_2l_3 & a_2m_1 + b_2m_2 + c_2m_3 & a_2n_1 + b_2n_2 + c_2n_3 \\ a_3l_1 + b_3l_2 + c_3l_3 & a_3m_1 + b_3m_2 + c_3m_3 & a_3n_1 + b_3n_2 + c_3n_3 \end{vmatrix}$$

3. Method of multiplying: (column by Column) Take the first column of Δ_1 and the first column of Δ_2 i.e., $a_1\ a_2\ a_3$ and $l_1\ m_1\ n_1$ multiplying the corresponding elements and add. The result $a_1l_1 + a_2\ m_1 + a_3n_1$ is the first element of first column of Δ. i.e., $p_{ij} = C_i \times C_j$ (where C_i is ith column of Δ_1 and C_j is jth column of Δ_2)

Now similar product of first column of Δ_1 and second column of Δ_2 gives $a_1\ l_2 + a_2m_2 - a_3\ n_2$ as the second element of first row of Δ, and the product of first column of Δ_1 and third column of Δ_2 gives $a_1l_3 + a_2\ m_3 + a_3\ n_3$ as the third element of first row of Δ_1. Proceeding in the above manner, we get

$$\Rightarrow\ \Delta = \Delta_1\Delta_2 = \begin{vmatrix} a_1l_1 + a_2m_1 + a_3n_1 & a_1l_2 + a_2m_2 + a_3n_2 & a_1l_3 + a_2m_3 + a_3n_3 \\ a_1l_1 + b_2m_1 + b_3n_1 & b_1l_2 + b_2m_2 + b_3n_2 & b_1l_3 + b_2m_3 + b_3n_3 \\ a_1l_3 + c_2m_1 + c_3n_1 & c_1l_2 + c_2m_2 + c_3n_2 & c_1l_3 + c_2m_3 + c_3n_3 \end{vmatrix}$$

4. Method of multiplying : (Column by Row) $\Delta = [p_{ij}]$ where p_{ij} = dot product of C_i column vector of Δ_1 and R_j row vector of Δ_2.

NOTES

For the two determinants to be multiplied without expanding them, they must be of the same order.

■ ADJOINT OR ADJUGATE DETERMINANT:

The determinant $\Delta' = |C_{ij}|$ where C_{ij} is the cofactor of a_{ij} in $\Delta = |a_{ij}|$ is called the adjoint or adjugate of Δ.

Jacobi's Theorem:

If $\Delta = |a_{ij}|$ is a determinant of nth order and $\Delta' = |C_{ij}|$, the adjoint of Δ, then $\Delta' = \Delta^{n-1}$ when $\Delta \neq 0$. We have

$$\Delta.\Delta' = \begin{vmatrix} a_{11} & a_{12} & \cdots & a_{1n} \\ a_{21} & a_{22} & \cdots & a_{2n} \\ \cdots & \cdots & \cdots & \cdots \\ a_{n1} & a_{n2} & \cdots & a_{nn} \end{vmatrix} \times \begin{vmatrix} C_{11} & C_{12} & \cdots & C_{1n} \\ C_{21} & C_{22} & \cdots & C_{2n} \\ \cdots & \cdots & \cdots & \cdots \\ C_{n1} & C_{n2} & \cdots & C_{nn} \end{vmatrix} = \begin{vmatrix} \sum_{r=1}^{n} a_{1r}C_{1r} & \sum_{r=1}^{n} a_{1r}C_{2r} & \cdots & \sum_{r=1}^{n} a_{1r}C_{nr} \\ \sum_{r=1}^{n} a_{2r}C_{1r} & \sum_{r=1}^{n} a_{2r}C_{2r} & \cdots & \sum_{r=1}^{n} a_{2r}C_{nr} \\ \cdots & \cdots & \cdots & \cdots \\ \sum_{r=1}^{n} a_{nr}C_{1r} & \sum_{r=1}^{n} a_{nr}C_{2r} & \cdots & \sum_{r=1}^{n} a_{nr}C_{nr} \end{vmatrix}$$

(By product theorem, taking row by row multiplication)

$$= \begin{vmatrix} \Delta & 0 & \cdots & 0 \\ 0 & \Delta & \cdots & 0 \\ \cdots & \cdots & \cdots & \cdots \\ 0 & 0 & \cdots & \Delta \end{vmatrix} = \Delta^n$$

Since $\sum_{r=1}^{n} a_{ir}C_{jr} = \begin{cases} \Delta \text{ when } i = j \\ 0 \text{ when } i \neq j \end{cases}$

$\therefore \quad \Delta' = \Delta^{n-1}$ when $\Delta \neq 0$

Note that If $\Delta = 0$, then $\Delta' = 0$.

Reciprocal Determinant:

If $\Delta = |a_{ij}| \neq 0$, then $\Delta'' = \left|\dfrac{C_{ij}}{\Delta}\right|$ where C_{ij} is the cofactor of a_{ij} is called the reciprocal determinant of Δ.

$$\Delta'' = \left|\frac{C_{ij}}{\Delta}\right| = \frac{1}{\Delta^n}|C_{ij}| = \frac{\Delta'}{\Delta^n} = \frac{\Delta^{n-1}}{\Delta^n} = \frac{1}{\Delta}.$$

ILLUSTRATION 19: Express $\begin{vmatrix} 0 & c & b \\ c & 0 & a \\ b & a & 0 \end{vmatrix}^2$ as a single determinant.

SOLUTION: $\begin{vmatrix} 0 & c & b \\ c & 0 & a \\ b & a & 0 \end{vmatrix}^2 = \begin{vmatrix} 0 & c & b \\ c & 0 & a \\ b & a & 0 \end{vmatrix}\begin{vmatrix} 0 & c & b \\ c & 0 & a \\ b & a & 0 \end{vmatrix}$

By multiplying, we get determinant as required (row by column) $= \begin{vmatrix} b^2 + c^2 & ab & ac \\ ba & c^2 + a^2 & bc \\ ca & cb & a^2 + b^2 \end{vmatrix}$

Method to Break a Determinant as the Product of Two Determinants

Although the factorization of determinant as the product of two determinants is an arbitrary process, but if we observe the following points, then the process becomes simpler.

(a) Observe the diagonal symmetry of the elements and apply the following facts:

- The determinant of skew symmetric determinant with odd order always vanishes, therefore any odd order skew symmetric determinant can be broken into product of two matrices of which at least one is singular.
- The determinant of skew symmetric determinant with even order is a perfect square. Therefore an even ordered skew symmetric determinant can be written as a square of a determinant having symmetrical elements.

(b) Observe the symmetry of the elements and make sure whether $(i, j)^{th}$ element of the given determinant can be written as $R_i \cdot C_j$ where R_i is the ith row of the first factor (determinant) and C_j is the jth column of the second factor (determinant).

(c) While applying the approach (b) it is advised to choose the $(i, j)^{th}$ element to be diagonal elements

ILLUSTRATION 20: Express the determinant $\begin{vmatrix} (a-x)^2 & (b-x)^2 & (c-x)^2 \\ (a-y)^2 & (b-y)^2 & (c-y)^2 \\ (a-z)^2 & (b-z)^2 & (c-z)^2 \end{vmatrix}$ as product of two determinants and hence evaluate it.

SOLUTION: Given determinant Δ is $\begin{vmatrix} (a-x)^2 & (b-x)^2 & (c-x)^2 \\ (a-y)^2 & (b-y)^2 & (c-y)^2 \\ (a-z)^2 & (b-z)^2 & (c-z)^2 \end{vmatrix}$

$$\Rightarrow \Delta = \begin{vmatrix} a^2-2ax+x^2 & b^2-2bx+x^2 & c^2-2cx+x^2 \\ a^2-2ay+y^2 & b^2-2by+y^2 & c^2-2cy+y^2 \\ a^2-2az+z^2 & b^2-2bz+z^2 & c^2-2cz+z^2 \end{vmatrix}$$

Each element has expressed as sum of three elements, looking at column (i) a^2 is common factor in Ist term, $-2a$ in second term and 1 in third one and similarly looking C_2 and C_3 and therefore constructing diagonal elements we get,

$$= \begin{vmatrix} 1 & x & x^2 \\ 1 & y & y^2 \\ 1 & z & z^2 \end{vmatrix} \begin{vmatrix} a^2 & b^2 & c^2 \\ -2a & -2b & -2c \\ 1 & 1 & 1 \end{vmatrix}$$ (taking -2 common from R_2 interchanging R_1 and R_3)

$$= 2 \begin{vmatrix} 1 & x & x^2 \\ 1 & y & y^2 \\ 1 & z & z^2 \end{vmatrix} \begin{vmatrix} 1 & 1 & 1 \\ a & b & c \\ a^2 & b^2 & c^2 \end{vmatrix}$$ (using the method of factorization for two circulants)

$= 2\,(x-y)\,(y-z)\,(z-x)\,(a-b)\,(b-c)\,(c-a)$

ILLUSTRATION 21: Evaluate the determinant $\begin{vmatrix} \cos(A-P) & \cos(A-Q) & \cos(A-R) \\ \cos(B-P) & \cos(B-Q) & \cos(B-R) \\ \cos(C-P) & \cos(C-Q) & \cos(C-R) \end{vmatrix}$

SOLUTION: Given determinant Δ is $\begin{vmatrix} \cos(A-P) & \cos(A-Q) & \cos(A-R) \\ \cos(B-P) & \cos(B-Q) & \cos(B-R) \\ \cos(C-P) & \cos(C-Q) & \cos(C-R) \end{vmatrix}$

($\because \cos(A-P) = \cos A \cos P + \sin A \sin P$)

$[\cos A \;\; \sin A \;\; 0] \begin{bmatrix} \cos P \\ \sin P \\ 0 \end{bmatrix}$ and therefore breaking into two determinants, we get

$$\Rightarrow \begin{vmatrix} \cos A & \sin A & 0 \\ \cos B & \sin B & 0 \\ \cos C & \sin C & 0 \end{vmatrix} \begin{vmatrix} \cos P & \cos Q & \cos R \\ \sin P & \sin Q & \sin R \\ 0 & 0 & 0 \end{vmatrix} = 0$$

Theorem 1: *For a given matrix A if C be the co-factor matrix of A, then determinant of C is equal to* $|A|^{n-1}$ *where n is the order of the matrix A. (Its proof is given in the chapter of Matrices.)*

ILLUSTRATION 22: Prove that $\begin{vmatrix} a^2+\lambda^2 & ab+c\lambda & ca-b\lambda \\ ab-c\lambda & b^2+\lambda^2 & bc+a\lambda \\ ac+b\lambda & bc-a\lambda & c^2+\lambda^2 \end{vmatrix} \times \begin{vmatrix} \lambda & c & -b \\ -c & \lambda & a \\ b & -a & \lambda \end{vmatrix} = \lambda^3(\lambda^2+a^2+b^2+c^2)^3$

SOLUTION: Let $\Delta_1 = \begin{vmatrix} a^2+\lambda^2 & ab+c\lambda & ca-b\lambda \\ ab-c\lambda & b^2+\lambda^2 & bc+a\lambda \\ ac+b\lambda & bc-a\lambda & c^2+\lambda^2 \end{vmatrix}$ and $\Delta = \begin{vmatrix} & c & b \\ c & & a \\ b & a & \end{vmatrix}$

Since Δ_1 is determinant of co-factor matrix of Δ as the elements of Δ_1 are co-factors of corresponding elements of Δ, Therefore from the given theorem.

$$\Rightarrow \Delta_1 . \Delta = \Delta^3 = \begin{vmatrix} \lambda & c & -b \\ -c & \lambda & a \\ b & -a & \lambda \end{vmatrix}^3 \text{ (expanding the determinant)}$$

$$= (\lambda(\lambda^2 + a^2 + b^2 + c^2))^3 = \lambda^3(\lambda^2 + a^2 + b^2 + c^2)^3$$

ILLUSTRATION 23: Show that $\begin{vmatrix} 2bc-a^2 & c^2 & b^2 \\ c^2 & 2ca-b^2 & a^2 \\ b^2 & a^2 & 2ab-c^2 \end{vmatrix} = (a^3+b^3+c^3-3abc)^2 = \begin{vmatrix} bc-a^2 & ac-b^2 & ab-c^2 \\ ac-b^2 & ab-c^2 & bc-a^2 \\ ab-c^2 & bc-a^2 & ac-b^2 \end{vmatrix}$

SOLUTION: $\begin{vmatrix} 2bc-a^2 & c^2 & b^2 \\ c^2 & 2ca-b^2 & a^2 \\ b^2 & a^2 & 2ab-c^2 \end{vmatrix}$ (looking at diagonal elements)

$$\begin{vmatrix} a & b & c \\ b & c & a \\ c & a & b \end{vmatrix} \begin{vmatrix} -a & -b & -c \\ c & a & b \\ b & c & a \end{vmatrix} \text{ (operating } R_2 \leftrightarrow R_3 \text{ in 2nd determinant)}$$

$$\begin{vmatrix} a & b & c \\ b & c & a \\ c & a & b \end{vmatrix} \begin{vmatrix} a & b & c \\ b & c & a \\ c & a & b \end{vmatrix} = \begin{vmatrix} a & b & c \\ b & c & a \\ c & a & b \end{vmatrix}^2 = (a^3 + b^3 + c^3 - 3abc)^2$$

Further, if Δ is the given determinant of order n (i.e., of matrix $A_{n\times n}$) and Δ_1 is the determinant formed by the co-factor matrix of A, then $\Delta_1 = \Delta^{n-1}$

Let $\Delta = \begin{vmatrix} a & b & c \\ b & c & a \\ c & a & b \end{vmatrix}$ and co-factor $\Delta_1 = \begin{vmatrix} bc-a^2 & ac-b^2 & ab-c^2 \\ ac-b^2 & ab-c^2 & bc-a^2 \\ ab-c^2 & bc-a^2 & ac-b^2 \end{vmatrix}$

$$\Rightarrow \Delta.\Delta_1 = \begin{vmatrix} \Delta & 0 & 0 \\ 0 & \Delta & 0 \\ 0 & 0 & \Delta \end{vmatrix} = \Delta^3 \Rightarrow \Delta_1 = \Delta^2 \ (\because \Delta_1 = \Delta^{n-1}). \text{ Hence the result.}$$

Theorem 2: *The determinant of skew symmetric matrix with odd order always* **vanishes.**

$$\Delta = \begin{vmatrix} 0 & a_{12} & a_{13} & \cdots & \cdots & a_{1n} \\ -a_{12} & 0 & a_{23} & \cdots & \cdots & a_{2n} \\ -a_{13} & -a_{23} & 0 & \cdots & \cdots & \cdots \\ \vdots & \vdots & \vdots & \vdots & \vdots & \vdots \\ \vdots & \vdots & \vdots & \vdots & \vdots & a_{n-1.n} \\ -a_{1n} & \cdots & \cdots & \cdots & -a_{n-1,n} & 0 \end{vmatrix} = (-1)^n \begin{vmatrix} 0 & -a_{12} & -a_{13} & \cdots & \cdots & -a_{1n} \\ a_{12} & 0 & -a_{23} & \cdots & \cdots & -a_{2n} \\ a_{13} & \cdots & \cdots & \cdots & \cdots & \cdots \\ \vdots & \vdots & \vdots & \vdots & \vdots & \vdots \\ \vdots & \vdots & \vdots & \vdots & \vdots & -a_{n-1,n} \\ a_{1n} & \cdots & \cdots & \cdots & a_{n-1,n} & 0 \end{vmatrix} = -\Delta$$

$\therefore \quad 2\Delta = 0 \Rightarrow \Delta = 0$

Example: Let a skew symmetric determinant of third order be Δ given as

$$\Delta = \begin{vmatrix} 0 & b & c \\ -b & 0 & a \\ -c & -a & 0 \end{vmatrix}. \text{ Interchanging rows and columns, we get } \Delta = \begin{vmatrix} 0 & -b & -c \\ b & 0 & -a \\ c & a & 0 \end{vmatrix} = (-1)^3 \begin{vmatrix} 0 & b & c \\ -b & 0 & a \\ -c & -a & 0 \end{vmatrix} = -\Delta$$

(Taking – 1 common from each row)

$\Rightarrow\ 2\Delta = 0 \Rightarrow \Delta = 0$

ILLUSTRATION 24: Without expanding the determinant at any stage, prove that $\begin{vmatrix} 0 & \beta & -\gamma \\ -\beta & 0 & \alpha \\ \gamma & -\alpha & 0 \end{vmatrix} = 0$

SOLUTION: Let $\Delta = \begin{vmatrix} 0 & \beta & -\gamma \\ -\beta & 0 & \alpha \\ \gamma & -\alpha & 0 \end{vmatrix}$ interchanging rows and columns, we get

$$\Delta = \begin{vmatrix} 0 & -\beta & \gamma \\ \beta & 0 & -\alpha \\ -\gamma & \alpha & 0 \end{vmatrix} = (-1)^3 \begin{vmatrix} 0 & \beta & -\gamma \\ -\beta & 0 & \alpha \\ \gamma & -\alpha & 0 \end{vmatrix} = -\Delta \text{ (Taking – 1 common from each row)}$$

$\Rightarrow\ 2\Delta = 0 \Rightarrow \Delta = 0$

Theorem 3: *The determinant of skew symmetric matrix with even order is* ***perfect square.*** i.e., of the form $\left(\sum \pm (abc...)\right)^2$; where a, b, c …. are elements of determinant

Example: $\begin{vmatrix} 0 & a \\ -a & 0 \end{vmatrix} = a^2$; $\begin{vmatrix} 0 & a & b & c \\ -a & 0 & d & e \\ -b & -d & 0 & f \\ -c & -e & -f & 0 \end{vmatrix} = (af - be + cd)^2$

TEXTUAL EXERCISE 4: (SUBJECTIVE)

1. Without expanding the determinant, show that the value of the following determinant is real

(a) $\begin{vmatrix} -5 & 3+5i & (3/2)-4i \\ 3-5i & 8 & 4+5i \\ (3/2)+4i & 4-5i & 9 \end{vmatrix}$

(b) $\begin{vmatrix} 0 & p-q & p-r \\ q-p & 0 & q-r \\ r-p & r-q & 0 \end{vmatrix}$

2. Prove that

$$\begin{vmatrix} \sin(A+B+C) & \sin A & \sin B \\ \sin(\pi + A) & \sin(B+C+A) & \sin C \\ \sin(\pi + B) & \sin(\pi + C) & \sin(A+B+C) \end{vmatrix}$$

vanishes if sum of A, B, C is odd integral multiple of π.

3. Split the following determinant as product of two determinants and hence evaluate its value.

$$\begin{vmatrix} x^2+y^2+z^2 & xy+yz+zx & zx+xy+yz \\ yx+zy+xz & z^2+x^2+x^2 & yz+zx+xy \\ zx+xy+zy & zy+zx+xy & z^2+x^2+y^2 \end{vmatrix}$$

Answer Key

3. $(x^3 + y^3 + z^3 - 3xyz)^2$

TEXTUAL EXERCISE 4: (OBJECTIVE)

1. If $\Delta = \begin{vmatrix} 1 & a & a^2 & a^3+bcd \\ 1 & b & b^2 & b^3+cda \\ 1 & c & c^2 & c^3+abd \\ 1 & d & d^2 & d^3+abc \end{vmatrix}$; then Δ is equal to

(a) $a^3b^3c^3$ (b) $b^3c^3d^3$
(c) $c^3d^3a^3$ (d) 0

2. If $\begin{vmatrix} y+z & z & y \\ z & z+x & x \\ y & x & x+y \end{vmatrix} = k\,xyz$, then $k =$

(a) 1 (b) 2
(c) 3 (d) 4

3. The value of the determinant $\begin{vmatrix} a+b+2c & a & b \\ c & b+c+2a & b \\ c & a & c+a+2b \end{vmatrix}$ is

(a) $2(a+b+c)$ (b) $2(a+b+c)^3$
(c) $ab+bc+ca$ (d) $2bc(ab+bc+ca)$

4. If $\begin{vmatrix} x+a & a^2 & a^3 \\ x+b & b^2 & b^3 \\ x+c & c^2 & c^3 \end{vmatrix} = 0$, $a \neq b \neq c \neq a$, then $x =$

(a) $\dfrac{abc}{\sum ab}$ (b) $-\dfrac{abc}{\sum ab}$
(c) $\dfrac{\sum ab}{abc}$ (d) $-\dfrac{\sum ab}{abc}$

5. If a, b, c are non-zero real numbers such that $\begin{vmatrix} bc & ca & ab \\ ca & ab & bc \\ ab & bc & ca \end{vmatrix} = 0$, then

(a) $\dfrac{1}{a}+\dfrac{1}{b\omega}+\dfrac{1}{c\omega^2}=0$ (b) $\dfrac{1}{a}+\dfrac{1}{b\omega^2}+\dfrac{1}{c\omega}=0$
(c) $\dfrac{1}{a\omega}+\dfrac{1}{b\omega^2}+\dfrac{1}{c}=0$ (d) $\dfrac{1}{a}+\dfrac{1}{b}+\dfrac{1}{c}=0$

6. **(i)** The value of the determinant $\begin{vmatrix} 2a_1b_1 & a_1b_2+a_2b_1 & a_1b_3+a_3b_1 \\ a_1b_2+a_2b_1 & 2a_2b_2 & a_2b_3+a_3b_2 \\ a_1b_3+a_3b_1 & a_3b_2+a_2b_3 & 2a_3b_3 \end{vmatrix}$ is

(a) 1 (b) –1
(c) 0 (d) $a_1a_2a_3b_1b_2b_3$

(ii) If $\Delta = \begin{vmatrix} 1+\alpha & 1+\alpha x & 1+\alpha x^2 \\ 1+\beta & 1+\beta x & 1+\beta x^2 \\ 1+\gamma & 1+\gamma x & 1+\gamma x^2 \end{vmatrix}$, then $\Delta =$

(a) 0 (b) $(\alpha-\beta)(\beta-\gamma)(\gamma-\alpha)$
(c) $\alpha\beta\gamma$ (d) None of these

7. If $a \neq p$, $b \neq q$, $c \neq r$ and $\begin{vmatrix} p & b & c \\ a & q & c \\ a & b & r \end{vmatrix} = 0$, then $\dfrac{p}{p-a}+\dfrac{q}{q-b}+\dfrac{r}{r-c}$ is equal to

(a) 0 (b) 1
(c) –1 (d) 2

8. If $l_i^2+m_i^2+n_i^2=1$ etc. and $l_i l_j + m_i m_j + n_i n_j = 0$ for $i, j \in \{1, 2, 3\}$ and $i \neq j$ etc., then $\Delta = \begin{vmatrix} l_1 & m_1 & n_1 \\ l_2 & m_2 & n_2 \\ l_3 & m_3 & n_3 \end{vmatrix} =$

(a) 1 (b) 2
(c) 3 (d) ±1

Answer Key

1. (d) **2.** (d) **3.** (b) **4.** (b) **5.** (a,b,c,d) **6.** **(i)** (c), **(ii)** (a) **7.** (d) **8.** (d)

DIFFERENTIATION OF DETERMINANTS

Given a determinant $\Delta = \begin{vmatrix} f_1(x) & f_2(x) \\ g_1(x) & g_2(x) \end{vmatrix}$ of order 2, which is a function of x, then

$$\frac{d\Delta}{dx} = \frac{d}{dx}\begin{vmatrix} f_1(x) & f_2(x) \\ g_1(x) & g_2(x) \end{vmatrix} = \frac{d}{dx}(f_1(x)g_2(x) - g_1(x)f_2(x))$$

$$= (f_1(x)g_2'(x) + g_2(x)f_1'(x) - g_1(x)f_2'(x) - f_2(x)g_1'(x)$$

$$= \begin{vmatrix} f_1'(x) & f_2'(x) \\ g_1(x) & g_2(x) \end{vmatrix} - \begin{vmatrix} f_1(x) & f_2(x) \\ g_1'(x) & g_2'(x) \end{vmatrix}$$

Similarly, we can write for the determinant of order three:

Rule of Differentiation

The differentiation of a determinant can be obtained as the sum of as many determinants as the order. The process can be carried out along the row/column by differentiating one row/column at a time and retaining the others as they are.

NOTES

In order to find out the coefficient of x^r in any polynomial f(x), differentiate the given polynomial f(x) r times successively and then substitute x = 0. i.e., the coefficient of $x^r = \left[\frac{f^r(0)}{r!}\right]$, where $f^r(0) = \left(\frac{d^r f(x)}{dx^r}\right)$ at x = 0.

ILLUSTRATION 25: If $f(x) = \begin{vmatrix} x & x^2 & x^3 \\ x+a & x^2+a & x^3+a \\ a & a^2 & a^3 \end{vmatrix}$, then find $f^1(x)$.

SOLUTION: $f'(x) = \begin{vmatrix} 1 & 2x & 3x^2 \\ x+a & x^2+a & x^3+a \\ a & a^2 & a^3 \end{vmatrix} + \begin{vmatrix} x & x^2 & x^3 \\ 1 & 2x & 3x^2 \\ a & a^2 & a^3 \end{vmatrix} + \begin{vmatrix} x & x^2 & x^3 \\ x+a & x^2+a & x^3+a \\ 0 & 0 & 0 \end{vmatrix}$

ILLUSTRATION 26: Find $f'(0)$ if $f(x) = \begin{vmatrix} x & x^2 & x^3 \\ x+a & x^2+a & x^3+a \\ a & a^2 & a^3 \end{vmatrix}$

SOLUTION: $f(x) = \begin{vmatrix} x & x^2 & x^3 \\ x+a & x^2+a & x^3+a \\ a & a^2 & a^3 \end{vmatrix}$

$$\Rightarrow f'(x) = \begin{vmatrix} 1 & 2x & 3x^2 \\ x+a & x^2+a & x^3+a \\ a & a^2 & a^3 \end{vmatrix} + \begin{vmatrix} x & x^2 & x^3 \\ 1 & 2x & 3x^2 \\ a & a^2 & a^3 \end{vmatrix} - \begin{vmatrix} x & x^2 & x^3 \\ x+a & x^2+a & x^3+a \\ 0 & 0 & 0 \end{vmatrix}$$

$$\Rightarrow f'(0) = \begin{vmatrix} 1 & 0 & 0 \\ a & a & a \\ a & a^2 & a^3 \end{vmatrix} + \begin{vmatrix} 0 & 0 & 0 \\ 1 & 0 & 0 \\ a & a^2 & a^3 \end{vmatrix} + \begin{vmatrix} 0 & 0 & 0 \\ a & a & a \\ 0 & 0 & 0 \end{vmatrix} \Rightarrow f'(0) = a^4 - a^3$$

ILLUSTRATION 27: If $\begin{vmatrix} \lambda^2+3\lambda & \lambda-1 & \lambda+3 \\ \lambda+1 & 1-2\lambda & \lambda-4 \\ \lambda-2 & \lambda+4 & 3\lambda \end{vmatrix} = p\lambda^4 + q\lambda^3 + r\lambda^2 + s\lambda + t$ be an identity in λ, where p, q, r, s and t are constants, find the coefficient of λ.

SOLUTION: $\Delta = \begin{vmatrix} \lambda^2+3\lambda & \lambda-1 & \lambda+3 \\ \lambda+1 & 1-2\lambda & \lambda-4 \\ \lambda-2 & \lambda+4 & 3\lambda \end{vmatrix}$ (differentiating w.r.t λ once)

$$\frac{d\Delta}{d\lambda} = \begin{vmatrix} 2\lambda+3 & 1 & 1 \\ \lambda+1 & 1-2\lambda & \lambda-4 \\ \lambda-2 & \lambda+4 & 3\lambda \end{vmatrix} + \begin{vmatrix} \lambda^2+3\lambda & \lambda-1 & \lambda+3 \\ 1 & -2 & 1 \\ \lambda-2 & \lambda+4 & 3\lambda \end{vmatrix} + \begin{vmatrix} \lambda^2+3\lambda & \lambda-1 & \lambda+3 \\ \lambda+1 & 1-2\lambda & \lambda-4 \\ 1 & 1 & 3 \end{vmatrix}$$

$= 4p\lambda^3 + 3q\lambda^2 + 2r\lambda + s.$ So coefficient of $\lambda = s = \frac{d\Delta}{d\lambda}$ at $\lambda = 0$

$$\Rightarrow s = \begin{vmatrix} 3 & 1 & 1 \\ 1 & 1 & -4 \\ -2 & 4 & 0 \end{vmatrix} + \begin{vmatrix} 0 & -1 & 3 \\ 1 & -2 & 1 \\ -2 & 4 & 0 \end{vmatrix} + \begin{vmatrix} 0 & -1 & 3 \\ 1 & 1 & -4 \\ 1 & 1 & 3 \end{vmatrix} = 62 + 2 + 7 = 71$$

ILLUSTRATION 28: Find the coefficient of x in the expansion of $\begin{vmatrix} (1+x)^{22} & (1+x)^{44} & (1+x)^{66} \\ (1+x)^{33} & (1+x)^{66} & (1+x)^{99} \\ (1+x)^{44} & (1+x)^{88} & (1+x)^{144} \end{vmatrix}$.

SOLUTION: Let $f(x) = \begin{vmatrix} (1+x)^{22} & (1+x)^{44} & (1+x)^{66} \\ (1+x)^{33} & (1+x)^{66} & (1+x)^{99} \\ (1+x)^{44} & (1+x)^{88} & (1+x)^{144} \end{vmatrix}$

Since $f(x)$ is a polynomial, therefore $f(x) = A_0 + A_1x + A_2x^2 + ... + A_{232} . x^{232}$

Here, the coefficient of $x = f'(0) = A_1$

Now, differentiating both sides with respect to x and then putting $x = 0$ in both sides, we get

$$f'(0) = \begin{vmatrix} 22 & 44 & 66 \\ 1 & 1 & 1 \\ 1 & 1 & 1 \end{vmatrix} + \begin{vmatrix} 1 & 1 & 1 \\ 33 & 66 & 99 \\ 1 & 1 & 1 \end{vmatrix} + \begin{vmatrix} 1 & 1 & 1 \\ 1 & 1 & 1 \\ 44 & 88 & 144 \end{vmatrix}$$

$\Rightarrow f'(0) = 0 + 0 + 0.$ Hence, coefficient of x in the given determinant = 0.

■ INTEGRATION OF A DETERMINANT

Integration of a determinant: As determinant is a numerical value, so it can always be integrated by expanding but the integration of the determinant can be done without expansion, if it has only one variable row/column.

Given a determinant $\Delta(x) = \begin{vmatrix} f(x) & g(x) & h(x) \\ a & b & c \\ l & m & n \end{vmatrix}$

(*where a, b, c, l, m* and *n are constants*) as a function of x.

$$\text{So } \int_a^b \Delta(x)dx = \begin{vmatrix} \int_a^b f(x)dx & \int_a^b g(x)dx & \int_a^b h(x)dx \\ a & b & c \\ l & m & n \end{vmatrix}.$$

Proof: $\because \Delta(x) = \begin{vmatrix} f(x) & g(x) & h(x) \\ a & b & c \\ l & m & n \end{vmatrix}$

$= f(x).C_{11} + g(x).C_{12} + h(x).C_{13}$

where $C_{11} = bn - mc$; $C_{12} = cl - an$; $C_{13} = am - bl$

$\Rightarrow \int_a^b \Delta(x)dx = C_{11}\int_a^b f(x).dx +$

$C_{12}\int_a^b g(x)\,dx + C_{13}\int_a^b h(x)\,dx$

$$= \begin{vmatrix} \int_a^b f(x)dx & \int_a^b g(x)dx & \int_a^b h(x)dx \\ a & b & c \\ l & m & n \end{vmatrix}$$

ILLUSTRATION 29: If $f(x) = \begin{vmatrix} \sin^5 x & \ln \sin x & \dfrac{\sqrt{\sin x}}{\sqrt{\sin x}+\sqrt{\cos x}} \\ n & \sum_{k=1}^{n} k & \prod_{k=1}^{n} k \\ 8/15 & \dfrac{\pi}{2}\ln\left(\dfrac{1}{2}\right) & \dfrac{\pi}{4} \end{vmatrix}$, then find the value of $\int_0^{\pi/2} f(x)dx$.

SOLUTION: $$\int_0^{\pi/2} f(x)dx = \begin{vmatrix} \int_0^{\pi/2} \sin^5 xdx & \int_0^{\pi/2} \ln \sin xdx & \int_0^{\pi/2} \dfrac{\sqrt{\sin x}dx}{\sqrt{\sin x}+\sqrt{\cos x}} \\ n & \sum_{k=1}^{n} k & \prod_{k=1}^{n} k \\ 8/15 & \dfrac{\pi}{2}\ln\left(\dfrac{1}{2}\right) & \dfrac{\pi}{4} \end{vmatrix}$$

$$= \begin{vmatrix} \underset{\text{(by walli's farmula)}}{\dfrac{4}{5}.\dfrac{2}{3}} & -\dfrac{\pi}{2}\ln 2 & \dfrac{\pi}{4} \\ n & \sum_{k=1}^{n} k & \prod_{k=1}^{n} k \\ 8/15 & \dfrac{\pi}{2}\ln\left(\dfrac{1}{2}\right) & \dfrac{\pi}{4} \end{vmatrix} = \begin{vmatrix} \dfrac{8}{15} & \dfrac{\pi}{2}\ln\left(\dfrac{1}{2}\right) & \dfrac{\pi}{4} \\ n & \sum_{k=1}^{n} k & \prod_{k=1}^{n} k \\ 8/15 & \dfrac{\pi}{2}\ln\left(\dfrac{1}{2}\right) & \dfrac{\pi}{4} \end{vmatrix} = \mathbf{0} \ (P_1 \text{ and } R_3 \text{ are identical})$$

REMARK (WALLI'S FORMULA)

- *An easy way to evaluate* $\int_0^{\pi/2} \sin^m x \cos^n xdx$*, where m, n* $\in \mathbb{N}$

We have $$\int_0^{\pi/2} \sin^m x \cos^n xdx = \frac{\{(m-1)(m-3)...2 \text{ or } 1\}\{(n-1)(n-3)...2 \text{ or } 1\}}{\{(m+n)(m+n-2)(m+n-4)...2 \text{ or } 1\}}(p)$$

where p is π/2 if m and n both are even, otherwise p = 1.
(For more details on Walli's formula, refer to our book on calculus).

TEXTUAL EXERCISE 5: (SUBJECTIVE)

1. If $p(x)$, $q(x)$ and $r(x)$ are three polynomials of degree 2, then show that $\begin{vmatrix} p(x) & p'(x) & p''(x) \\ q(x) & q'(x) & q''(x) \\ r(x) & r'(x) & r''(x) \end{vmatrix}$ is independent of x.

2. If $F(x)$, $G(x)$ and $H(x)$ are three polynomials of degree 2. Then find the nature of polynomial $\phi(x)$ where $\phi(x) = \begin{vmatrix} F(x) & G(x) & H(x) \\ F'(x) & G'(x) & H'(x) \\ F''(x) & G''(x) & H''(x) \end{vmatrix}$

3. If $\Delta = \begin{vmatrix} e^{x^2} & \sin x & 1 \\ \sec x & \ln(1+x^2) & 1 \\ x^3 & x^2 & 1 \end{vmatrix} = a + bx + cx^2$, then find the values of a and b.

4. If $f(x) = \begin{vmatrix} \cos x & x & 1 \\ 2\sin x & x^2 & 2x \\ \tan x & x & 1 \end{vmatrix}$, then find $\lim_{x\to 0} \dfrac{f'(x)}{x}$

5. If $f(x)=\begin{vmatrix} 3 & 2 & 1 \\ 6x^2 & 2x^3 & x^4 \\ 1 & a & a^2 \end{vmatrix}$. Find the value of $f''(a)$.

6. If $f(x)=\begin{vmatrix} 2\cos^2 x & \sin 2x & \sin x \\ \sin 2x & 2\sin^2 x & -\cos x \\ \sin x & -\cos x & 0 \end{vmatrix}$, find $\int_0^{\pi/2}\{f'(x)+f(x)\}\,dx$.

Answer Key

2. $\phi(x)$ is a constant **3.** $a = 0, b = -1$ **4.** -2 **5.** 0 **6.** $-\pi$

TEXTUAL EXERCISE 5: (OBJECTIVE)

1. (i) If $\Delta=\begin{vmatrix} x^2-5x+3 & 2x-5 & 3 \\ 3x^2+x+4 & 6x+1 & 9 \\ 7x^2-6x+9 & 14x-6 & 21 \end{vmatrix} = ax^3+bx^2+cx + d$, then $\Delta'(0)$ i.e., $\frac{d}{dx}(\Delta)$ at $x =$

(a) 6 (b) 5
(c) 4 (d) 0

(ii) If $\Delta=\begin{vmatrix} x & x^2 & x^3 \\ 1 & 2x & 3x^2 \\ 0 & 2 & 6x \end{vmatrix}$, then $\frac{d}{dx}(\Delta)=$

(a) 6 (b) $6x$
(c) $6x^2$ (d) 0

(iii) If $f(x) = \begin{vmatrix} x+a^2 & x^4+1 & 3 \\ x+b^2 & 2x^4+2 & 3 \\ x+c^2 & 3x^4+7 & 3 \end{vmatrix}$, where $x \neq 0$ and $f'(x) = 0$, then a^2, b^2, c^2 are in:

(a) A.P (b) G.P
(c) H.P (d) None of these

2. If $\Delta(x)=\begin{vmatrix} e^{x^2} & \ln(1+x) \\ \tan x & \sin x \end{vmatrix}$, then $\lim_{x\to 0}\frac{\Delta(x)}{x}=$

(a) -1 (b) 0
(c) 1 (d) None of these

3. Let $f(x)=\begin{vmatrix} x^3 & \sin x & \cos x \\ 6 & -1 & 0 \\ p & p^2 & p^3 \end{vmatrix}$, where p is a constant, then $\frac{d^3}{dx^3}\left[f(x)\right]$ at x = 0 is

(a) p (b) $p + p^2$
(c) $p + p^3$ (d) Independent of p

4. Let $f(x)=\begin{vmatrix} x^n & \sin x & \cos x \\ n! & \sin\frac{n\pi}{2} & \cos\frac{n\pi}{2} \\ p & p^2 & p^3 \end{vmatrix}$, then $\frac{d^n}{dx^n}(f(x))$ at $x = 0$ is

(a) 0 (b) p
(c) p^3 (d) Independent of p

5. Let $f(x)=\begin{vmatrix} 1 & a & a^2 \\ \sin(n-1)x & \sin nx & \sin(n+1)x \\ \cos(n-1)x & \cos nx & \cos(n+1)x \end{vmatrix}$ then, $\int_0^{\pi/2} f(x)dx$ is equal to

(a) $a - (1 + a^2)$ (b) $1 + a + a^2$
(c) $-a + (1 + a^2)$ (d) $-(1 + a + a^2)$

Answer Key

1. (i) (d) **(ii)** (c) **(iii)** (a) **2.** (c) **3.** (d) **4.** (a, d) **5.** (a)

■ SYSTEM OF LINEAR EQUATION

A system of linear equation is said to be *consistent* ***if it has at least one solution.***

System of Equations in Two Variables

Let the given system of equations be $a_1x + b_1y = c_1$ and $a_2x + b_2y = c_2$ (where $\frac{a_1}{a_2} \neq \frac{b_1}{b_2}$)

Solving by Cramer's Rule for two variables, we have

$$\frac{x}{b_2c_1 - b_1c_2} = \frac{y}{a_1c_2 - a_2c_1} = \frac{1}{a_1b_2 - a_2b_1} \text{ OR,}$$

$$\frac{X}{\begin{vmatrix} b_1 & c_1 \\ b_2 & c_2 \end{vmatrix}} = \frac{y}{\begin{vmatrix} a_1 & c_1 \\ a_2 & c_2 \end{vmatrix}} = \frac{1}{\begin{vmatrix} a_1 & b_1 \\ a_2 & b_2 \end{vmatrix}}$$

$$\text{Thus } x = \frac{\begin{vmatrix} c_1 & b_1 \\ c_2 & b_2 \end{vmatrix}}{\begin{vmatrix} a_1 & b_1 \\ a_2 & b_2 \end{vmatrix}} = \frac{\Delta_1}{\Delta} \text{ and } y = \frac{\begin{vmatrix} a_1 & c_1 \\ a_2 & c_2 \end{vmatrix}}{\begin{vmatrix} a_1 & b_1 \\ a_2 & b_2 \end{vmatrix}} = \frac{\Delta_2}{\Delta};$$

This is known as Cramer's Rule. According to this rule, if

(i) Δ: the determinant of the coefficients

(ii) Δ_1: what becomes of Δ when the coefficients of x are replaced by c's.

(iii) Δ_2: what becomes of Δ when the coefficients of y are replaced by c's, then $x = \dfrac{\Delta_1}{\Delta}$ and $y = \dfrac{\Delta_2}{\Delta}$

System of Linear Equations in Three Variables

The given system of linear equations in three variables x, y and z is

$$a_1x + b_1y + c_1z = d_1$$
$$a_2x + b_2y + c_2z = d_2$$
$$a_3x + b_3y + c_3z = d_3$$

$$\text{Let } \Delta = \begin{vmatrix} a_1 & b_1 & c_1 \\ a_2 & b_2 & c_2 \\ a_3 & b_3 & c_3 \end{vmatrix}, \quad \Delta_1 = \begin{vmatrix} d_1 & b_1 & c_1 \\ d_2 & b_2 & c_2 \\ d_3 & b_3 & c_3 \end{vmatrix},$$

$$\Delta_2 = \begin{vmatrix} a_1 & d_1 & c_1 \\ a_2 & d_2 & c_2 \\ a_3 & d_3 & c_3 \end{vmatrix}, \quad \Delta_3 = \begin{vmatrix} a_1 & b_1 & d_1 \\ a_2 & b_2 & d_2 \\ a_3 & b_3 & d_3 \end{vmatrix}$$

Let us consider

$$\Delta_1, \Delta_1 = \begin{vmatrix} d_1 & b_1 & c_1 \\ d_2 & b_2 & c_2 \\ d_3 & b_3 & c_3 \end{vmatrix} = \begin{vmatrix} a_1x+b_1y+c_1z & b_1 & c_1 \\ a_2x+b_2y+c_2z & b_2 & c_2 \\ a_3x+b_3y+c_3z & b_3 & c_3 \end{vmatrix}$$

$$= \begin{vmatrix} a_1x & b_1 & c_1 \\ a_2x & b_2 & c_2 \\ a_3x & b_3 & c_3 \end{vmatrix} + \begin{vmatrix} b_1y & b_1 & c_1 \\ b_2y & b_2 & c_2 \\ b_3y & b_3 & c_3 \end{vmatrix} + \begin{vmatrix} c_1z & b_1 & c_1 \\ c_2z & b_2 & c_2 \\ c_3z & b_3 & c_3 \end{vmatrix}$$

$$= x\,\Delta + y.0 + z.0 = x\,\Delta \quad \text{.... (i)}$$

Similarly, we can prove the other two results.

$$y\,\Delta = \Delta_2 \quad \text{............ (ii)}$$

$$\text{and } z\,\Delta = \Delta_3 \quad \text{.......... (iii)}$$

$$\Rightarrow \quad x = \frac{\Delta_1}{\Delta}; y = \frac{\Delta_2}{\Delta}; z = \frac{\Delta_3}{\Delta}$$

Now there are two possibilities:

Case I: If $\Delta \neq 0$, then x, y, z will have one definite value. In this case, given system of equations will have a unique solution. $x = \dfrac{\Delta_1}{\Delta}; y = \dfrac{\Delta_2}{\Delta}; z = \dfrac{\Delta_3}{\Delta}$

Case II: If $\Delta = 0$, again there are two possibilities;

(i) **$\Delta = 0$ and at least one of Δ_1, Δ_2, Δ_3 is non zero.**
Let $\Delta_1 \neq 0$, then from (i), $\Delta_1 = x\,\Delta$ will not be satisfied for any value of x because $\Delta = 0$ and $\Delta_1 \neq 0$, hence no value of x is possible in this case. Similarly we can analyse for y and z.
Thus, if $\Delta = 0$ and any of Δ_1, Δ_2 and Δ_3 is non zero, then no solution is possible and hence, the system of equations will be inconsistent.

(ii) **$\Delta = 0$ and $\Delta_1 = \Delta_2 = \Delta_3 = 0$:**
In this case $\Delta_1 = x\Delta$; $\Delta_2 = y\Delta$; $\Delta_2 = z\Delta$ will be true for all values of x, y and z
But since $a_1x + b_1y + c_1z = d_1$, therefore only two of x, y, z will be independent and the third will be dependent on the other two.
Thus infinitely many values of x, y, z, are possible and out of x, y, z. only two can be given independent values. Hence if $\Delta = \Delta_1 = \Delta_2 = \Delta_3 = 0$, then the system of equations will be consistent and it will have infinitely many solutions.

Condition For Consistency of Three Linear Equations in two Unknowns

Consider the system of three linear equation in x and y:

$$a_1x + b_1y = c_1 \quad \text{...(i)}$$
$$a_2x + b_2y = c_2 \quad \text{....(ii)}$$
$$\text{and } a_3x + b_3y = c_3 \quad \text{....(iii)}$$

will be consistent if the values of x and y obtained from any two equations satisfy the third equation. Solving the first two by Cramer's rule, we have $x = \dfrac{\begin{vmatrix} c_1 & b_1 \\ c_2 & b_2 \end{vmatrix}}{\begin{vmatrix} a_1 & b_1 \\ a_2 & b_2 \end{vmatrix}}$ & $y = \dfrac{\begin{vmatrix} a_1 & c_1 \\ a_2 & c_2 \end{vmatrix}}{\begin{vmatrix} a_1 & b_1 \\ a_2 & b_2 \end{vmatrix}}$

These values of x and y will satisfy the third equation if

$$a_3\begin{vmatrix} c_1 & b_1 \\ c_2 & b_2 \end{vmatrix} + b_3\begin{vmatrix} a_1 & c_1 \\ a_2 & c_2 \end{vmatrix} = c_3\begin{vmatrix} a_1 & b_1 \\ a_2 & b_2 \end{vmatrix} \text{ or } \begin{vmatrix} a_1 & b_1 & c_1 \\ a_2 & b_2 & c_2 \\ a_3 & b_3 & c_3 \end{vmatrix} = 0$$

This is the required condition for consistency of three linear equations in two unknowns. If such system of equations is consistent, then the number of solutions is one and hence this system of equations give an unique solution.

Given out of Δ, Δ_1, Δ_2, Δ_3

- If $\Delta \neq 0$, then system is consistent and has unique set of finite solutions.
  $y=\frac{\Delta_1}{\Delta}$; $y=\frac{\Delta_2}{\Delta}$ and $y=\frac{\Delta_3}{\Delta}$
- If $\Delta = 0$
  - $\Delta_1 = \Delta_2 = \Delta_3 = 0$
    $\Rightarrow$ System is consistent with infinitely many solution. Because 0 = x.0 has infinite solutions
  - At least one of Δ_1, Δ_2, Δ_3 is non zero
    $\Rightarrow$ system becomes inconsistent and so has no solutions e.g., $\Delta_1 = 1$ then 1 = x.0 never possible.

FIGURE 2.2

■ SYSTEM OF HOMOGENEOUS LINEAR EQUATIONS

A system of linear equations is said to be homogeneous, if the sum of powers of the variables in each term is same and constant term as $RHS = 0$. Let the three homogeneous linear equations in three unknown

$$x, y, z, \text{ be } \left.\begin{array}{l} a_1x + b_1y + c_1z = 0 \ldots\ldots(i) \\ a_2x + b_2y + c_2z = 0 \ldots\ldots(ii) \\ a_3x + b_3y + c_3z = 0 \ldots\ldots(iii) \end{array}\right\} \ldots\ldots(A)$$

Clearly, $\Delta_1 = \Delta_2 = \Delta_3 = 0$

Now, if $\Delta = \begin{vmatrix} a_1 & b_1 & c_1 \\ a_2 & b_2 & c_2 \\ a_3 & b_3 & c_3 \end{vmatrix} \neq 0$,

$\Rightarrow$ then $x = \frac{\Delta_1}{\Delta} = y = \frac{\Delta_2}{\Delta} = z = \frac{\Delta_3}{\Delta} = 0$,

so $x = y = z = 0$ is a solution of system of equations (A). This solution is called a trivial solution. Any solution other than x = y = z = 0 if exist is called a non trivial solution. Non trivial solution exist iff, $\Delta = \Delta_1 = \Delta_2 = \Delta_3 = 0$, then all values of x, y, z satisfy the system of equation and thus system has infinitely many solutions.

Given out of Δ, & $\Delta_1 = \Delta_2 = \Delta_3 = 0$

- If $\Delta \neq 0$; then system has x = y = z = 0 as unique/trivial solution
  $x = \frac{\Delta_1}{\Delta} = 0$, $y = \frac{\Delta_2}{\Delta} = 0$ &
  $z = \frac{\Delta_3}{\Delta} = 0$
- If $\Delta = 0$
  If $\Delta = 0$, since $\Delta_1 = x.\,\Delta$ therefore 0 = x.0, there will be infinitely many solutions for x. Similarly for y and z.
  ► So condition that a homogeneous set of equation has non trivial solution is $\Delta = 0$

FIGURE 2.3

■ GEOMETRIC INTERPRETATION

Two Dimensions A system of linear equations in two variables represents lines in two dimensions. If the system has two equations, then it represents two lines in two dimensions. The system has either unique solution or infinite solutions or no solution according to the two lines being non-parallel, coincident, or parallel.

Three Dimensions: Three planes represent a system of three linear equations in three variables. If three planes have a common point the system has a unique solution (as in fig (i). If three planes are coincident or have a common line of intersection (fig (ii)), then the system has infinite solutions. Finally the system has no solutions, if either three planes are parallel or two are parallel and third is intersecting them or the three planes are forming a prismatic hut (fig (iii), (iv) and (v)).

(i)
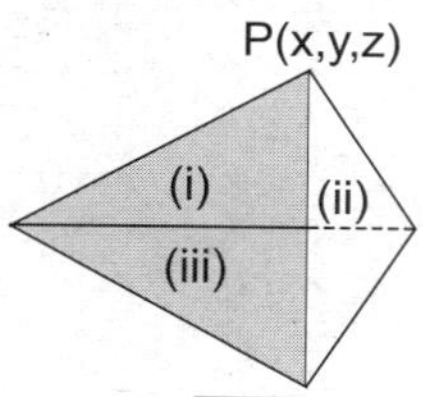

(ii)
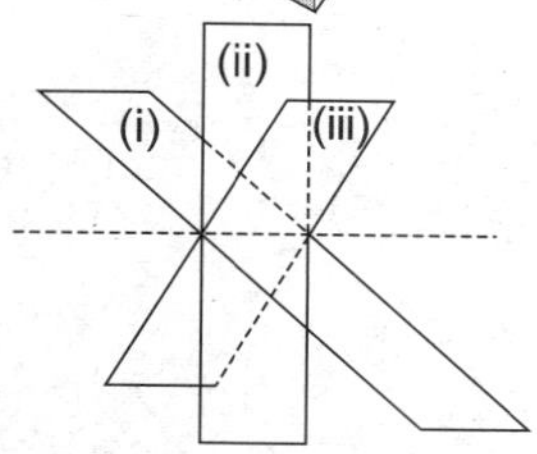

(iii)
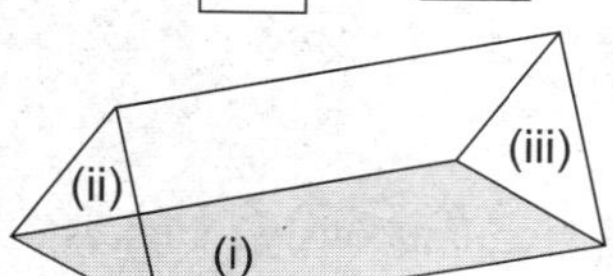

(iv)
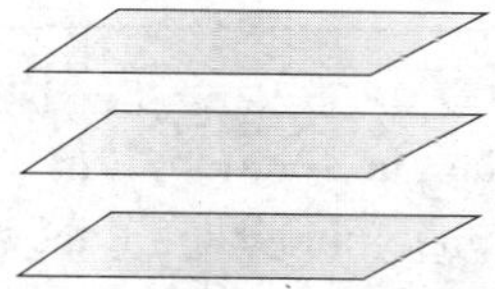

(v)
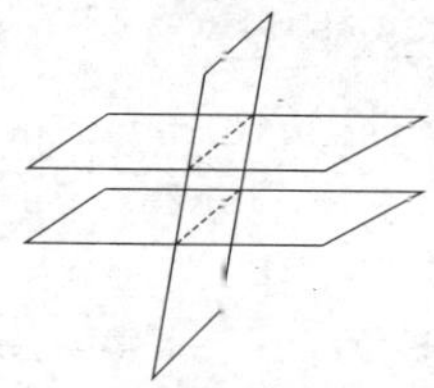

■ ELIMINANT

Eliminant of a given number of equations in some variables is an expression which is obtained by eliminating the variables out of these equations. e.g., if the equations $a_1x + b_1 = 0$ and $a_2 x - b_2 = 0$ is satisfied by same values of x, then $a_1b_2 - a_2 b_1 = 0$, i.e., the second order determinant $\begin{vmatrix} a_1 & b_1 \\ a_2 & b_2 \end{vmatrix} = 0$, which is called eliminant of the given two equations.

ILLUSTRATION 30: Obtain the eliminant of the given system of equations
$a_1x + b_1y + c_1 = 0$ ....(i); $a_2x + b_2y + c_2 = 0$ ....(ii) and $a_3x + b_3y + c_3 = 0$ ....(iii)

SOLUTION: Solving the equations (i) and (ii) using Cramer 's rule $a_1x + b_1y = -c_1$; $a_2x + b_2y = -c_2$

$$\Rightarrow x = \frac{\begin{vmatrix} c_1 & b_1 \\ c_2 & b_2 \end{vmatrix}}{\begin{vmatrix} a_1 & b_1 \\ a_2 & b_2 \end{vmatrix}} \text{ and } y = \frac{\begin{vmatrix} a_1 & -c_1 \\ a_2 & -c_2 \end{vmatrix}}{\begin{vmatrix} a_1 & b_1 \\ a_2 & b_2 \end{vmatrix}}$$

. Using the value of x and y in equtation (iii), we get

$$\Rightarrow a_3\begin{vmatrix} b_1 & c_1 \\ b_2 & c_2 \end{vmatrix} + b_3\begin{vmatrix} c_1 & a_1 \\ c_2 & a_2 \end{vmatrix} + c_3\begin{vmatrix} a_1 & b_1 \\ a_2 & b_2 \end{vmatrix} = 0 \Rightarrow \begin{vmatrix} a_3 & b_3 & c_3 \\ a_1 & b_1 & c_1 \\ a_2 & b_2 & c_2 \end{vmatrix} = 0 \Rightarrow \begin{vmatrix} a_1 & b_1 & c_1 \\ a_2 & b_2 & c_2 \\ a_3 & b_3 & c_3 \end{vmatrix} = 0$$

ILLUSTRATION 31: Eliminate x from the equations $ax^3 + bx^2 + cx + d = 0, fx^2 + gx + h = 0$.

SOLUTION: From these equations, we have $\frac{a}{f} = \frac{bx^2 + cx + d}{gx^2 + hx}$ and $\frac{ax + b}{fx + g} = \frac{cx + d}{hx}$

hence $(ag - bf)x^2 + (ah - cf)x - df = 0$ and $(ah - cf)x^2 + (bh - cg - df)x - dg = 0$

Combining these two equations with $fx^2 + gx + h = 0$

and regarding x^2 and x as distinct variables, we obtain a relation for the eliminant as

$$\begin{vmatrix} f & g & h \\ ag - bf & ah - cf & -df \\ ah - cf & bh - cg - df & -dg \end{vmatrix} = 0$$

ILLUSTRATION 32: Show that the system of equations $ax + 4y + z = 0$, $2y + 3z - 1 = 0$ and $3x - bz + 2 = 0$ has
(1) an unique solution, if $ab \neq 15$,
(2) infinitely many solutions if $ab = 15$ and $a = 3$, $b = 5$,
(3) no solutions if $ab = 15$, $a \neq 3$, $b \neq 5$.

SOLUTION: The given system of equations can be written as

$ax + 4y + z = 0$, $0.x + 2y + 3z = 1$ and $3x + 0.y - bz = -2$

$$\Rightarrow \Delta = \begin{vmatrix} a & 4 & 1 \\ 0 & 2 & 3 \\ 3 & 0 & -b \end{vmatrix} = 30 - 2ab; \qquad \Delta_x = \begin{vmatrix} 0 & 4 & 1 \\ 1 & 2 & 3 \\ -2 & 0 & -b \end{vmatrix} = 4b - 20;$$

$$\Delta_y = \begin{vmatrix} a & 0 & 1 \\ 0 & 1 & 3 \\ 3 & -2 & -b \end{vmatrix} = -ab + 6a - 3; \quad \Delta_z = \begin{vmatrix} a & 4 & 0 \\ 0 & 2 & 1 \\ 3 & 0 & -2 \end{vmatrix} = -4a + 12$$

Now the system will have unique solution if $\Delta \neq 0 \Rightarrow ab \neq 15$

If $ab = 15$; let us re-write $\Delta_x, \Delta_y, \Delta_z$, by substituting $b = \dfrac{15}{a}$.

$\therefore$ we get, $\Delta_x = \dfrac{60}{a} - 20$, $\Delta_y = 6a - 18$, $\Delta_z = -4a + 12$

We note that there is a value of a for which $\Delta_x, \Delta_y, \Delta_z$ vanish simultaneously which is obviously $a = 3$; Also for $a \neq 3$ all the determinants become non-zero.

Thus the system will have infinitely many solutions if $ab = 15$, $a = 3$ and will have no solutions if $ab = 15$, $a \neq 3$, $b \neq 5$

ILLUSTRATION 33: Show that the system $ax + y + z = a$, $x + by + z = b$ and $x + y + cz = c$ is inconsistent, if $abc - a - b - c + 2 = 0$ and atleast two of a, b, c are different from unity.

SOLUTION: We have $\Delta = \begin{vmatrix} a & 1 & 1 \\ 1 & b & 1 \\ 1 & 1 & c \end{vmatrix} = abc - a - b - c + 2$; $\Delta_x = \begin{vmatrix} a & 1 & 1 \\ b & b & 1 \\ c & 1 & c \end{vmatrix} = abc - a + b + c - 2bc$

$\Delta_y = abc - b + a + c - 2ac$ and $\Delta_z = abc - c + a + b - 2ab$

Now for a system to be inconsistent, it is necessary that $\Delta = 0$

$\Rightarrow abc - a - b - c + 2 = 0$

But for a system to be inconsistent, it is necessary that $\Delta = 0$ and at least one of $\Delta_x, \Delta_y, \Delta_z \neq 0$

$\Delta_x = abc - a - b - c + 2 + 2b + 2c - 2bc - 2$

$= 0 + 2b + 2c - 2bc - 2 = -2(1 - b)(1 - c)$. ($\because \Delta = 0$)

Similarly $\Delta_y = -2(1 - c)(1 - a)$, $\Delta_z = -2(1 - a)(1 - b)$

For Δ_x, Δ_y and Δ_z simultaneously not equal to 0, at least two of a, b, c, must be different from unity.

ILLUSTRATION 34: For what values of p and q the system of equations $2x + py + 6z = 8$; $x + 2y + qz = 5$ and $x + y + 3z = 4$ has

(i) unique solution (ii) no solution (iii) infinitely many solutions?

SOLUTION: Here the system of linear equations in x, y, z is

$2x + py + 6z = 8$; $x + 2y + qz = 5$ and $x + y + 3z = 4$

$$\therefore\ \Delta = \begin{vmatrix} 2 & p & 6 \\ 1 & 2 & q \\ 1 & 1 & 3 \end{vmatrix} = \begin{vmatrix} 2 & p-2 & 0 \\ 1 & 1 & q-3 \\ 1 & 0 & 0 \end{vmatrix} \ (C_2 \to C_2 - C_1,\ C_3 \to C_3 - 3 \times C_1)$$

$$= \begin{vmatrix} p-2 & 0 \\ 1 & q-3 \end{vmatrix} = (p-2)(q-3)$$

$\therefore$ if $p \neq 2$, $q \neq 3$ then $\Delta \neq 0$ and so the system will have unique solution, i.e.the system will be independently/solvable/consistent.

If $p = 2$ or $q = 3$ then $\Delta = 0$ and so the system cannot have unique solution. When $p = 2$

$$\Delta_x = \begin{vmatrix} 8 & p & 6 \\ 5 & 2 & q \\ 4 & 1 & 3 \end{vmatrix} = \begin{vmatrix} 8 & 2 & 6 \\ 5 & 2 & q \\ 4 & 1 & 3 \end{vmatrix} = 2\begin{vmatrix} 4 & 1 & 3 \\ 5 & 2 & q \\ 4 & 1 & 3 \end{vmatrix} = 0 \qquad (\because R_1 \equiv R_3)$$

$$\Delta_y = \begin{vmatrix} 2 & 8 & 6 \\ 1 & 5 & q \\ 1 & 4 & 3 \end{vmatrix} = 2\begin{vmatrix} 1 & 4 & 3 \\ 1 & 5 & q \\ 1 & 4 & 3 \end{vmatrix} = 0\ (\because R_1 \equiv R_3)$$

$$\Delta_z = \begin{vmatrix} 2 & 2 & 8 \\ 2 & 2 & 5 \\ 1 & 1 & 4 \end{vmatrix} = 2\begin{vmatrix} 1 & 1 & 4 \\ 1 & 2 & 5 \\ 1 & 1 & 4 \end{vmatrix} = 2(0) = 0 \quad (\because R_{\ } \equiv R_3)$$

$\therefore$ when $p = 2$, $\Delta = 0 = \Delta_x = \Delta_y = \Delta_z$

$\therefore$ the system of equations will have infinite number of solutions for $p = 2$ and for any real value of q.

When $q = 3$, $\Delta_x = \begin{vmatrix} 8 & p & 6 \\ 5 & 2 & 3 \\ 4 & 1 & 3 \end{vmatrix} = \begin{vmatrix} 0 & p-2 & 0 \\ 2 & 2 & 3 \\ 1 & 1 & 3 \end{vmatrix}$, $R_1 \to R_1 - 2R_3 = -(p-2)(3)$

$\therefore$ if $p \neq 2$, $\Delta_x \neq 0$ and so the system of equations will have no solutions, i.e., the system is unsolvable/inconsistent when $q = 3$ but $p \neq 2$.

Thus we find that the system of equations will have

(i) unique solution if $p \neq 2$ and $q \neq 3$ (ii) no solution if $p \neq 2$ and $q = 3$

(iii) infinite number of solutions if $p = 2$ and $q \in \mathbb{R}$

ILLUSTRATION 35: Using condition of consistency of equations, prove that $\begin{vmatrix} ap & a & p \\ bq & b & q \\ cr & c & r \end{vmatrix} = 0$ if $bc + qr = ca + rp = ap + pq = -1$

SOLUTION: We have $bc + qr = -1$; multiplying by ap, $abcp + apqr + ap = 0$ ..(i)

$ca + rp = -1$; multiplying by bq, $abcq + bpqr + bq = 0$ ...(ii)

$ab + pq = -1$; multiplying by cr, $abcr + cpqr + cr = 0$ ...(iii)

(i), (ii) and (iii) may be considered as three equations in (abc) and (pqr)

Hence, using consistency of equations, i.e., eliminating abc and pqr, we get

$$\begin{vmatrix} p & a & ap \\ q & b & bq \\ r & c & cr \end{vmatrix} = 0 \qquad \therefore \quad \begin{vmatrix} ap & a & p \\ bq & b & q \\ cr & c & r \end{vmatrix} = 0$$

ILLUSTRATION 36: For what value of k to the following system of equations possess a non-trivial solution over the set of rationals $x + ky + 3z = 0$; $3x + ky - 2z = 0$; $2x + 3y - 4z = 0$. For that value of k, find all the solutions of the system.

SOLUTION: For non-trivial solution $\Delta = 0$; $\begin{vmatrix} 1 & k & 3 \\ 3 & k & -2 \\ 2 & 3 & -4 \end{vmatrix} = 0$ (applying $R_2 \to R_2 - 3R_1$ and $R_3 \to R_3 - 2R_1$)

$$\therefore \begin{vmatrix} 1 & k & 3 \\ 0 & -2k & -11 \\ 0 & 3-2k & -10 \end{vmatrix} = 0 \Rightarrow \begin{vmatrix} -2k & -11 \\ 3-2k & -10 \end{vmatrix} = 0 \Rightarrow 20k + 33 - 22k = 0 \quad \therefore \quad k = 33/2$$

Putting the value of k in the given equations, the equations becomes $x + \frac{33}{2}y + 3z = 0$ ..(i)

and $3x + \frac{33}{2}y - 2z = 0$ ..(ii) and $2x + 3y - 4z = 0$ ...(iii)

Multiplying (i) by 3 and subtracting from (ii), we get $-33y - 11z = 0$ or $z = -3y$ ..(iv)

again multiplying (i) by 2 and subtracting from (iii) we get $-30y - 10z = 0$ or $z = -3y$ ..(v)

Now let $y = \lambda$, therefore $z = -3\lambda$

Substituting values of y and z in (iii), we get $2x + 3\lambda + 12\lambda = 0 \quad \Rightarrow x = -\frac{15\lambda}{2}$

$x : y : z :: -\frac{15}{2} : 1 : -3 \quad \Rightarrow x : y : z :: 15 : -2 : 6$

ILLUSTRATION 37: Find all values of k for which the following system possesses a non-trivial solution $x + ky + 3z = 0$; $kx + 2y + 2z = 0$; $2x + 3y + 4z = 0$.

SOLUTION: Let $\Delta = \begin{vmatrix} 1 & k & 3 \\ k & 2 & 2 \\ 2 & 3 & 4 \end{vmatrix} = 0 \quad \Rightarrow (8-6) - k(4k-4) + 3(3k-4) = 0$

$\Rightarrow 2 - 4k^2 + 4k + 9k - 12 = 0 \quad \Rightarrow 4k^2 - 13k + 10 = 0$

$\Rightarrow 4k^2 - 8k - 5k + 10 = 0 \quad \Rightarrow 4k(k-2) - 5(k-2) = 0$

$\Rightarrow (4k-5)(k-2) = 0 \quad \Rightarrow k = 2, 5/4$

TEXTUAL EXERCISE 6: (SUBJECTIVE)

1. Eliminate m from the equations $m^2x - my + a = 0$, $my + x = 0$.
2. Eliminate m, n from the equations $m^2x - my + a = 0$, $n^2x - ny + a = 0$ and $mn + 1 = 0$
3. Eliminate m, n between the equations $mx - ny = a(m^2 - n^2)$, $nx + my = 2amn$, $m^2 + n^2 = 1$
4. Eliminate m from the equations $y + mx = a(1 + m)$, $my - x = a(1 - m)$
5. Find the solution of system of equations $x + y = 4$ and $2x - 3y = 9$
6. Let the system of equation be $a_1 x + b_1 y + c_1 z = 0$; $a_2x + b_2y + c_2z = 0$; $a_1x + b_3y + c_3 z = 0$
   (a) If $\Delta \neq 0$, then given system of equations has only trivial solution and find the number of solutions in this case.
   (b) If $\Delta = 0$, then given system of equations has non-trivial solutions as well as trivial solution and find the number of solutions in this case.
   (c) Find Δ for non-trivial solutions of system of homogenous linear equations.
   (d) Homogenous system of equations is always consistent. (True/False)

7. If the system of equations in x, y; $ax + hy + g = 0$; $hx + by + f = 0$; $ax^2 + 2hxy + by^2 + 2gx + 2fy + c = t$ admits of a solution, then prove that $t = \begin{vmatrix} a & h & g \\ h & b & f \\ g & f & c \end{vmatrix} \div \begin{vmatrix} a & h \\ h & b \end{vmatrix}$

8. Test the consistency and solve them when consistent, the following system of equations for all values of λ : $x + y + z = 1$; $x + 3y - 2z = 1$; $3x + (\lambda + 2)y - 3z = 2\lambda + 1$

9. Find the values of c for which the equations $2x + 3y = 3$; $(c + 2)x + (c + 4)y = c + 6$; $(c + 2)^2 x + (c + 4)^2 y = (c + 6)^2$ are consistent. Also solve above equations for those values of c.

Answer Key

1. $x^3 + xy^2 + ay^2 = 0$ 2. $x + a = 0$ 3. $x^2 + y^2 = a^2$ 4. $x^2 + y^2 = 2a^2$ 5. $x = 4.2$ and $y = -0.2$

6. (a) one (b) infinite (c) $\Delta = 0$ (d) True 8. For $\lambda \neq 5$; $x = -\frac{5-7\lambda}{3(\lambda-5)}, y = \frac{2(\lambda-1)}{(\lambda-5)}, z = \frac{4(\lambda-1)}{3(\lambda-5)}$

9. $c = 0, -10$

TEXTUAL EXERCISE 6: (OBJECTIVE)

1. Find the values of λ and μ for which the equations $x + y + z = 3$, $x + 3y + 2z = 6$ and $x + \lambda y + 3z = \mu$ have a unique solution.
   (a) $\lambda = 5, \mu \neq 9$ (b) $\lambda \neq 5, \mu \in \mathbb{R}$
   (c) $\lambda = 5, \mu = 9$ (d) None of these

2. Find the values of λ and μ for which the equations $x + y + z = 3$, $x + 3y + 2z = 6$ and $x + \lambda y + 3z = \mu$ have no solution.
   (a) $\lambda = 5, \mu \neq 9$ (b) $\lambda \neq 5, \mu \in \mathbb{R}$
   (c) $\lambda = 5, \mu = 9$ (d) None of these

3. Find the values of λ and μ for which the equations $x + y + z = 3$, $x + 3y + 2z = 6$ and $x + \lambda y + 3z = \mu$ have infinitely many solutions.
   (a) $\lambda = 5, \mu \neq 9$ (b) $\lambda \neq 5, \mu \in \mathbb{R}$
   (c) $\lambda = 5, \mu = 9$ (d) None of these

4. The system of equations $2x - y + z = 0$; $x - 2y + z = 0$; $\lambda x - y + 2z = 0$ has infinite number of non trivial solutions for
   (a) $\lambda = 1$ (b) $\lambda = 5$
   (c) $\lambda = 5$ (d) no real value

5. If the system of equations $x + 4ay + az = 0$, $x + 3by + bz = 0$, $x + 2cy + cz = 0$ has a non-trivial solution, then a, b, c are in
   (a) AP (b) GP
   (c) HP (d) None of these

6. The equations $2x + y = 5$, $x + 3y = 5$, $x - 2y = 0$ have
   (a) no solution (b) one solution
   (c) two solution (d) infinitely many solutions

7. Let a, b, c, d, u, v be non-zero integers. If the system of equations $ax + by = u$ and $cx + dy = v$ has a unique solution, then
   (a) $ad - bc = 0$ (b) $ad - bc = -1$
   (c) $ad - bc \neq 0$ (d) None of these

8. If the system of equations $ax + by + c = 0$, $bx + cy + a = 0$, $cx + ay + b = 0$ has a unique solution, then the system of equations $(b + c)x + (c + a)y + (a + b)z = 0$; $(c + a)x + (a + b)y + (b + c)z = 0$ and $(a + b)x + (b + c)y + (c + a)z = 0$ has
   (a) only one solution (b) infinitely many solutions
   (c) no solution (d) None of these

9. The number of values of k for which the system of equations $(k + 1)x + 8y = 4k$ and $kx + (k + 3)y = 3k - 1$ has infinitely many solutions is
   (a) 0 (b) 1
   (c) 2 (d) infinite

Answer Key

1. (b) 2. (a) 3. (c) 4. (b) 5. (c) 6. (b) 7. (c) 8. (b) 9. (b)

MULTIPLE CHOICE QUESTIONS

SECTION–I

SUBJECTIVE SOLVED EXAMPLES

1. If $f(\theta)=\begin{vmatrix}\cos^2\theta & \cos\theta\sin\theta & -\sin\theta\\ \cos\theta\sin\theta & \sin^2\theta & \cos\theta\\ \sin\theta & -\cos\theta & 0\end{vmatrix}$, then find the value of $f\left(\frac{\pi}{6}\right)$.

Solution: $f(\theta)=\begin{vmatrix}\cos^2\theta & \cos\theta\sin\theta & -\sin\theta\\ \cos\theta\sin\theta & \sin^2\theta & \cos\theta\\ \sin\theta & -\cos\theta & 0\end{vmatrix}$

$$\Rightarrow f\left(\frac{\pi}{6}\right)=\begin{vmatrix}\cos^2\frac{\pi}{6} & \cos\frac{\pi}{6}\sin\frac{\pi}{6} & -\sin\frac{\pi}{6}\\ \cos\frac{\pi}{6}\sin\frac{\pi}{6} & \sin^2\frac{\pi}{6} & \cos\frac{\pi}{6}\\ \sin\frac{\pi}{6} & -\cos\frac{\pi}{6} & 0\end{vmatrix}$$

$$=\begin{vmatrix}\frac{3}{4} & \frac{\sqrt{3}}{4} & -\frac{1}{2}\\ \frac{\sqrt{3}}{4} & \frac{1}{4} & \frac{\sqrt{3}}{2}\\ \frac{1}{2} & -\frac{\sqrt{3}}{2} & 0\end{vmatrix}$$

$$=\frac{3}{4}\left(\frac{1}{4}.0+\frac{3}{4}\right)-\frac{\sqrt{3}}{4}\left(-\frac{\sqrt{3}}{4}\right)-\frac{1}{2}\left(-\frac{3}{8}-\frac{1}{8}\right)$$

(Expanding along first row)

$$\Rightarrow f\left(\frac{\pi}{6}\right)=\frac{9}{16}+\frac{3}{16}+\frac{4}{16}=1$$

2. Show that the determinant $\begin{vmatrix}a^2+x & ab & ac\\ ab & b^2+x & bc\\ ac & bc & c^2+x\end{vmatrix}$ is divisible by x^2.

Solution: Let $\Delta=\begin{vmatrix}a^2+x & ab & ac\\ ab & b^2+x & bc\\ ac & bc & c^2+x\end{vmatrix}$

Putting $x = 0$, we get, $\Delta=\begin{vmatrix}a^2 & ab & ac\\ ab & b^2 & bc\\ ac & bc & c^2\end{vmatrix}$

$$=abc\begin{vmatrix}a & a & a\\ b & b & b\\ c & c & c\end{vmatrix}=0$$

At $x = 0$, $\Delta = 0$ since three columns identical. Therefore $(x - 0)$ is a repeated root of the equation.

$\Rightarrow x^2$ is factor of determinant. $\Rightarrow \Delta$ is divisible by x^2

3. If m and p are positive $(m \geq p)$ and $\Delta\ (m, p)$ $=\begin{vmatrix}{}^mC_p & {}^mC_{p+1} & {}^mC_{p+2}\\ {}^{m+1}C_p & {}^{m+1}C_{p+1} & {}^{m+1}C_{p+2}\\ {}^{m+2}C_p & {}^{m+2}C_{p+1} & {}^{m+2}C_{p+2}\end{vmatrix}$, then prove that

$$\Delta\ (m, p)=\frac{{}^{m+2}C_3}{{}^{p+2}C_3}\Delta_{(m-1,\,p-1)}.$$

Solution: We know that, ${}^mC_p=\frac{m!}{(m-p)!\,p!}=\frac{m}{p}.{}^{m-1}C_{p-1}$

$\Rightarrow \Delta\ (m, p)$

$$=\begin{vmatrix}\frac{m}{p}\,{}^{m-1}C_{p-1} & \frac{m}{p+1}\,{}^{m-1}C_p & \frac{m}{p+2}\,{}^{m-1}C_{p+1}\\ \frac{m+1}{p}\,{}^{m}C_{p-1} & \frac{m+1}{p+1}\,{}^{m}C_p & \frac{m+1}{p+2}\,{}^{m}C_{p+1}\\ \frac{m+2}{p}\,{}^{m+1}C_{p-1} & \frac{m+2}{p+1}\,{}^{m+1}C_p & \frac{m+2}{p+2}\,{}^{m+1}C_{p+1}\end{vmatrix}$$

$$=\frac{m(m+1)(m+2)}{p(p+1)(p+2)}\Delta_{(m-1,\,p-1)}=\frac{{}^{m+2}C_3}{{}^{p+2}C_3}\Delta_{(m-1,\,p-1)}$$

4. Without expanding at any stage show that $\begin{vmatrix}x^3+x & x+1 & x-2\\ 2x^3+3x-1 & 3x & 3x-3\\ x^3+2x+3 & 2x-1 & 2x-1\end{vmatrix}=xA+B$ where A and B are determinants of order 3 not involving x

Solution: The given determinant

$$\Delta=\begin{vmatrix}x^3+x & x+1 & x-2\\ 2x^3+3x-1 & 3x & 3x-3\\ x^3+2x+3 & 2x-1 & 2x-1\end{vmatrix};\ (R_2\to R_2-R_1-R_3)$$

$$\Rightarrow \Delta = \begin{vmatrix} x^3+x & x+1 & x-2 \\ -4 & 0 & 0 \\ x^3+2x+3 & 2x-1 & 2x-1 \end{vmatrix}; (R_3 \to R_3 - R_1)$$

$$\Rightarrow \Delta = \begin{vmatrix} x^3+x & x+1 & x-2 \\ -4 & 0 & 0 \\ x+3 & x-2 & x+1 \end{vmatrix}; (C_3 \to C_3 - C_2)$$

$$\Rightarrow \Delta = 3\begin{vmatrix} x^3+x & x+1 & -1 \\ -4 & 0 & 0 \\ x+3 & x-2 & 1 \end{vmatrix} = 12\begin{vmatrix} x^3+x & x+1 & -1 \\ -1 & 0 & 0 \\ x+3 & x-2 & 1 \end{vmatrix}$$

Operating $(R_1 \to R_1 + x^3 R_2)$

$$= 12\begin{vmatrix} x & x+1 & -1 \\ -1 & 0 & 0 \\ x+3 & x-2 & 1 \end{vmatrix} \quad (R_3 \to R_3 - R_1)$$

$$\Rightarrow \Delta = 12\begin{vmatrix} x & x+1 & -1 \\ -1 & 0 & 0 \\ 3 & -3 & 2 \end{vmatrix}$$

$$= 12\begin{vmatrix} x & x & 0 \\ -1 & 0 & 0 \\ 3 & -3 & 2 \end{vmatrix} + 12\begin{vmatrix} 0 & 1 & -1 \\ -1 & 0 & 0 \\ 3 & -3 & 2 \end{vmatrix} = xA + B$$

5. Show that the following determinant is independent of x.

$$\begin{vmatrix} \sin(x+\alpha) & \cos(x+\alpha) & a+x\sin\alpha \\ \sin(x+\beta) & \cos(x+\beta) & b+x\sin\beta \\ \sin(x+\gamma) & \cos(x+\gamma) & c+x\sin\gamma \end{vmatrix}$$

Solution: $\Delta = \begin{vmatrix} \sin(x+\alpha) & \cos(x+\alpha) & a+x\sin\alpha \\ \sin(x+\beta) & \cos(x+\beta) & b+x\sin\beta \\ \sin(x+\gamma) & \cos(x+\gamma) & c+x\sin\gamma \end{vmatrix}$

Differentiating w.r.t. x (column-wise), we get

$$= \frac{d\Delta}{dx} = \begin{vmatrix} \cos(x+\alpha) & \cos(x+\alpha) & a+x\sin\alpha \\ \cos(x+\beta) & \cos(x+\beta) & b+x\sin\beta \\ \cos(x+\gamma) & \cos(x+\gamma) & c+x\sin\gamma \end{vmatrix} +$$

$$\begin{vmatrix} \sin(x+\alpha) & -\sin(x+\alpha) & a+x\sin\alpha \\ \sin(x+\beta) & -\sin(x+\beta) & b+x\sin\beta \\ \sin(x+\gamma) & -\sin(x+\gamma) & c+x\sin\gamma \end{vmatrix} +$$

$$\begin{vmatrix} \sin(x+\alpha) & \cos(x+\alpha) & \sin\alpha \\ \sin(x+\beta) & \cos(x+\beta) & \sin\beta \\ \sin(x+\gamma) & \cos(x+\gamma) & \sin\gamma \end{vmatrix}$$

First two determinants are vanishing. In the third determinant

$C_1 \to C_1 - \cos x.\ C_3$ and $C_2 \to C_2 + \sin xC_3$

$$\frac{d\Delta}{dx} = \begin{vmatrix} \sin x\cos\alpha & \cos x\cos\alpha & \sin\alpha \\ \sin x\cos\beta & \cos x\cos\beta & \sin\beta \\ \sin x\cos\gamma & \cos x\cos\gamma & \sin\gamma \end{vmatrix}$$

$$= \sin x\cos x \begin{vmatrix} \cos\alpha & \cos\alpha & \sin\alpha \\ \cos\beta & \cos\beta & \sin\beta \\ \cos\gamma & \cos\gamma & \sin\gamma \end{vmatrix} = 0$$

($\because$ two columns are identical)

Since $\frac{d\Delta}{dx} = 0$, Δ is independent of x.

6. Let $f(x) = \begin{vmatrix} 2\cos^2 x & \sin 2x & -\sin x \\ \sin 2x & 2\sin^2 x & \cos x \\ \sin x & -\cos x & 0 \end{vmatrix}$, then find the value of $\int_0^{\pi/2} \{f(x) + f'(x)\}\, dx$

Solution: Given $f(x) = \begin{vmatrix} 2\cos^2 x & \sin 2x & -\sin x \\ \sin 2x & 2\sin^2 x & \cos x \\ \sin x & -\cos x & 0 \end{vmatrix}$

$\left.\begin{matrix} C_1 \to C_1 + 2\sin x\, C_3 \\ C_2 \to C_2 - 2\cos x\, C_3 \end{matrix}\right\}$. Further operating,

$C_1 \to C_1 - 4\sin x\, C_3$; $C_2 \to C_2 + 4\cos x\, C_3$

$$f(x) = \begin{vmatrix} 2 & 0 & -\sin x \\ 0 & 2 & \cos x \\ \sin x & -\cos x & 0 \end{vmatrix} = 2\sin^2 x + 2\cos^2 x = 2$$

$$\Rightarrow \int_0^{\pi/2} (f(x) + f'(x)).dx = 2\int_0^{\pi/2} dx = \pi$$

7. In ΔABC, prove that $\begin{vmatrix} \sin 2A & \sin C & \sin B \\ \sin C & \sin 2B & \sin A \\ \sin B & \sin A & \sin 2C \end{vmatrix} = 0$

Solution: $\Delta = \begin{vmatrix} 2\sin A\cos A & \sin C & \sin B \\ \sin C & 2\sin B\cos B & \sin A \\ \sin B & \sin A & 2\sin C\cos C \end{vmatrix}$

$$= \begin{vmatrix} 2ka\left(\frac{b^2+c^2-a^2}{2bc}\right) & kc & kb \\ kc & 2kb\left(\frac{c^2+a^2-b^2}{2ca}\right) & ka \\ kb & ka & 2kc\left(\frac{a^2+b^2-c^2}{2ab}\right) \end{vmatrix}$$

$$= \frac{k^3}{bc.ca.ab}\begin{vmatrix} a(b^2+c^2-a^2) & bc^2 & cb^2 \\ ac^2 & b(c^2+a^2-b^2) & ca^2 \\ ab^2 & ba^2 & c(a^2+b^2-c^2) \end{vmatrix}$$

$$= \frac{k^3}{a^2b^2c^2}abc\begin{vmatrix} (b^2+c^2-a^2) & c^2 & b^2 \\ c^2 & (c^2+a^2-b^2) & a^2 \\ b^2 & a^2 & (a^2+b^2-c^2) \end{vmatrix}$$

Operating $\begin{bmatrix} C_2 \to C_2 - C_1 \\ C_3 \to C_3 - C_1 \end{bmatrix}$

$$= \frac{k^3}{abc}\begin{vmatrix} (b^2+c^2-a^2) & a^2-b^2 & a^2-c^2 \\ c^2 & a^2-b^2 & a^2-c^2 \\ b^2 & a^2-b^2 & a^2-c^2 \end{vmatrix} = 0$$

[$\because$ C_2 and C_3 are identical when $(a^2 - b^2)$ and $(a^2 - c^2)$ are taken common]

8. If $a, b, c \neq 0$ and $\begin{vmatrix} 1+a & 1 & 1 \\ 1 & 1+b & 1 \\ 1 & 1 & 1+c \end{vmatrix} = 0$, then find the value of $\frac{1}{a}+\frac{1}{b}+\frac{1}{c}$

Solution: Let $\Delta = \begin{vmatrix} 1+a & 1 & 1 \\ 1 & 1+b & 1 \\ 1 & 1 & 1+c \end{vmatrix}$

$$\Rightarrow \Delta = abc\begin{vmatrix} \frac{1}{a}+1 & \frac{1}{b} & \frac{1}{c} \\ \frac{1}{a} & \frac{1}{b}+1 & \frac{1}{c} \\ \frac{1}{a} & \frac{1}{b} & \frac{1}{c}+1 \end{vmatrix}$$

(taking a, b, c, common from C_1 C_2 C_3 respectively)

Operating $(C_1 \to C_1 + C_2 + C_3)$

$$= abc\begin{vmatrix} 1+\frac{1}{a}+\frac{1}{b}+\frac{1}{c} & \frac{1}{b} & \frac{1}{c} \\ 1+\frac{1}{a}+\frac{1}{b}+\frac{1}{c} & \frac{1}{b}+1 & \frac{1}{c} \\ 1+\frac{1}{a}+\frac{1}{b}+\frac{1}{c} & \frac{1}{b} & \frac{1}{c}+1 \end{vmatrix}$$

$$= (abc)\left(1+\frac{1}{a}+\frac{1}{b}+\frac{1}{c}\right)\begin{vmatrix} 1 & 1/b & 1/c \\ 1 & 1+1/b & 1/c \\ 1 & 1/b & 1+1/c \end{vmatrix}$$

$$= abc\left(1+\frac{1}{a}+\frac{1}{b}+\frac{1}{c}\right).\ 1$$

But given that $\Delta = 0$ $\therefore$ $abc\left(1+\frac{1}{a}+\frac{1}{b}+\frac{1}{c}\right) = 0$

But $a, b, c \neq 0$, therefore $\frac{1}{a}+\frac{1}{b}+\frac{1}{c} = -1$

9. If A, B and C are 3 distinct angles in the interval $(0, \pi/3)$ and $\Delta = \begin{vmatrix} \sin^3 A & \sin^3 B & \sin^3 C \\ \sin A & \sin B & \sin C \\ \cos A & \cos B & \cos C \end{vmatrix}$, then prove that $\Delta \neq 0$.

Solution: Let $\Delta = \begin{vmatrix} \sin^3 A & \sin^3 B & \sin^3 C \\ \sin A & \sin B & \sin C \\ \cos A & \cos B & \cos C \end{vmatrix}$

$$= \sin A \sin B \sin C\begin{vmatrix} \sin^2 A & \sin^2 B & \sin^2 C \\ 1 & 1 & 1 \\ \cot A & \cot B & \cot C \end{vmatrix}$$

(Applying $C_2 \to C_2 - C_1$ and $C_3 \to C_3 - C_1$)

$$\Delta = \begin{vmatrix} \sin^2 A & \sin^2 B - \sin^2 A & \sin^2 C - \sin^2 A \\ 1 & 0 & 0 \\ \cot A & \cot B - \cot A & \cot C - \cot A \end{vmatrix}$$

Expanding along R_2 and simplifying, we get
$\Delta = -\sin(A - B)\sin(B - C)\sin(C - A)\sin(A + B + C)$
Since A, B, $C \in (0, \pi/3)$ and are distinct, so none of these factors are zero. Hence $\Delta \neq 0$.

10. If a and x are real numbers and n is a positive integer, then show that

$$\begin{vmatrix} a^n - x & a^{n+1} - x & a^{n+2} - x \\ a^{n+3} - x & a^{n+4} - x & a^{n+5} - x \\ a^{n+6} - x & a^{n+7} - x & a^{n+8} - x \end{vmatrix} = 0, \text{ for any } x.$$

Solution: $\Delta = \begin{vmatrix} a^n - x & a^{n+1} - x & a^{n+2} - x \\ a^{n+3} - x & a^{n+4} - x & a^{n+5} - x \\ a^{n+6} - x & a^{n+7} - x & a^{n+8} - x \end{vmatrix} \begin{bmatrix} C_1 \to C_1 - C_3 \\ C_2 \to C_2 - C_3 \end{bmatrix}$

$$\Rightarrow \Delta = \begin{vmatrix} a^n - a^{n+2} & a^{n+1} - a^{n+2} & a^{n+2} - x \\ a^{n+3} - a^{n+5} & a^{n+4} - a^{n+5} & a^{n+5} - x \\ a^{n+6} - a^{n+8} & a^{n+7} - a^{n+8} & a^{n+8} - x \end{vmatrix}$$

$$= a^{2n+1}(1-a)^2(1+a)\begin{vmatrix} 1 & 1 & a^{n+2} - x \\ a^3 & a^3 & a^{n+5} - x \\ a^6 & a^6 & a^{n+8} - x \end{vmatrix}$$

Two columns are indentical, so $\Delta = 0$ for any x.

11. Let α be a repeated root of the quadratic equation $f(x) = 0$ with the leading coefficient as unity and $A(x)$, $B(x)$ and $C(x)$ are polynomials of degree 3, 4 and 5 respectively. Show that $\begin{vmatrix} A(x) & B(x) & C(x) \\ A(\alpha) & B(\alpha) & C(\alpha) \\ A'(\alpha) & B'(\alpha) & C'(\alpha) \end{vmatrix}$ is divisible by $f(x)$.

Solution: Since α is the repeated root of the quadratic equation $f(x) = 0$

Therefore $f(x)$ can be written as: $f(x) = (x - \alpha)^2$

Let, $g(x) = \begin{vmatrix} A(x) & B(x) & C(x) \\ A(\alpha) & B(\alpha) & C(\alpha) \\ A'(\alpha) & B'(\alpha) & C'(\alpha) \end{vmatrix}$

Since two rows are identical for $x = \alpha$, so $(x - \alpha)$ is root of $g(x)$; $g'(\alpha) = \begin{vmatrix} A'(\alpha) & B'(\alpha) & C'(\alpha) \\ A(\alpha) & B(\alpha) & C(\alpha) \\ A'(\alpha) & B'(\alpha) & C'(\alpha) \end{vmatrix} = 0$

Since in $g'(x)$ two rows are identical for $x = \alpha$, therefore $(x - \alpha)$ is a factor of $g'(x)$. Then $(x - \alpha)^2$ is a factor of $g(x)$, which completes the proof.

12. Prove that $\begin{vmatrix} 1 & \cos(\alpha-\beta) & \cos(\gamma-\alpha) \\ \cos(\alpha-\beta) & 1 & \cos(\beta-\gamma) \\ \cos(\gamma-\alpha) & \cos(\beta-\gamma) & 1 \end{vmatrix} = 0$

Solution: The above determinant can be expressed as product of two determinants.

$$= \begin{vmatrix} \cos^2\alpha+\sin^2\alpha & \cos\alpha\cos\beta+\sin\alpha\sin\beta & \cos\gamma\cos\alpha+\sin\gamma\sin\alpha \\ \cos\alpha\cos\beta+\sin\alpha\sin\beta & \cos^2\beta+\sin^2\beta & \cos\beta\cos\gamma+\sin\beta\sin\gamma \\ \cos\gamma\cos\alpha+\sin\gamma\sin\alpha & \cos\beta\cos\gamma+\sin\beta\sin\gamma & \cos^2\gamma+\sin^2\gamma \end{vmatrix}$$

$$= \begin{vmatrix} \cos\alpha & \sin\alpha & 0 \\ \cos\beta & \sin\beta & 0 \\ \cos\gamma & \sin\gamma & 0 \end{vmatrix} \times \begin{vmatrix} \cos\alpha & \cos\beta & \cos\gamma \\ \sin\alpha & \sin\beta & \sin\gamma \\ 0 & 0 & 0 \end{vmatrix} = 0 \times 0 = 0$$

13. If α, β are the roots of the equation $ax^2 + bx + c = 0$ and $S_n = \alpha^n + \beta^n$, then show that

$$\begin{vmatrix} 3 & 1+S_1 & 1+S_2 \\ 1+S_1 & 1+S_2 & 1+S_3 \\ 1+S_2 & 1+S_3 & 1+S_4 \end{vmatrix} = \frac{(a+b+c)^2}{a^4}(b^2-4ac)$$

Solution: The determinant

$$\begin{vmatrix} 3 & 1+\alpha+\beta & 1+\alpha^2+\beta^2 \\ 1+\alpha+\beta & 1+\alpha^2+\beta^2 & 1+\alpha^3+\beta^3 \\ 1+\alpha^2+\beta^2 & 1+\alpha^3+\beta^3 & 1+\alpha^4+\beta^4 \end{vmatrix}$$

can be written as $\begin{vmatrix} 1 & 1 & 1 \\ 1 & \alpha & \beta \\ 1 & \alpha^2 & \beta^2 \end{vmatrix} \times \begin{vmatrix} 1 & 1 & 1 \\ 1 & \alpha & \alpha^2 \\ 1 & \beta & \beta^2 \end{vmatrix}$

$$= \begin{vmatrix} 1 & 1 & 1 \\ 1 & \alpha & \beta \\ 1 & \alpha^2 & \beta^2 \end{vmatrix} \times \begin{vmatrix} 1 & 1 & 1 \\ 1 & \alpha & \beta \\ 1 & \alpha^2 & \beta^2 \end{vmatrix}$$

$$= \begin{vmatrix} 1 & 1 & 1 \\ 1 & \alpha & \beta \\ 1 & \alpha^2 & \beta^2 \end{vmatrix}^2 = (\alpha\beta^2 - \beta\alpha^2 + \beta - \beta^2 + \alpha^2 - \alpha)^2$$

$$= (\alpha\beta(\beta - \alpha) + \alpha^2 - \beta^2 + \beta - \alpha)^2 = [-(\alpha - \beta)(1 - (\alpha + \beta) + \alpha\beta)]^2 = \frac{(b^2-4ac)(a+b+c)^2}{a^4}$$

14. Let a, b, c be real numbers with $a^2 + b^2 + c^2 = 1$. Show that the equation

$$\begin{vmatrix} ax-by-c & bx+ay & cx+a \\ bx+ay & -ax+by-c & cy+b \\ cx+a & cy+b & -ax-by+c \end{vmatrix} = 0$$

represents a straight line.

Solution: Given

$$\begin{vmatrix} ax-by-c & bx+ay & cx+a \\ bx+ay & -ax+by-c & cy+b \\ cx+a & cy+b & -ax-by+c \end{vmatrix} = 0$$

$(C_1 \to aC_1 + bC_2 + cC_3)$

$$\Rightarrow \begin{vmatrix} (a^2+b^2+c^2)x & bx+ay & cx+a \\ (a^2+b^2+c^2)y & -ax+by-c & cy+b \\ (a^2+b^2+c^2) & cy+b & -ax-by+c \end{vmatrix} = 0$$

$$\Rightarrow \begin{vmatrix} x & bx+ay & cx+a \\ y & -ax+by-c & cy+b \\ 1 & cy+b & -ax-by+c \end{vmatrix} = 0$$

Applying $C_2 \to C_2 - b\,C_1$ and $C_3 \to C_3 - cC_1$

$$\Rightarrow \Delta = \begin{vmatrix} x & ay & a \\ y & -ax-c & b \\ 1 & cy & -ax-by \end{vmatrix} = 0$$

Applying $R_3 \to R_3 + x\,R_1 + y\,R_2$

$$\Rightarrow \Delta = \begin{vmatrix} x & ay & a \\ y & -ax-c & b \\ x^2+y^2+1 & 0 & 0 \end{vmatrix} = 0$$

$\Rightarrow (x^2 + y^2 + 1)(aby + a^2x + ac) = 0$

$\Rightarrow ax + by + c = 0$

$\because\ x^2 + y^2 + 1 \neq 0$ for any x and $y \in \mathbb{R}$

15. Find the coefficient of x in the determinant

$$\begin{vmatrix} (1+x)^{a_1b_1} & (1+x)^{a_1b_2} & (1+x)^{a_1b_3} \\ (1+x)^{a_2b_1} & (1+x)^{a_2b_2} & (1+x)^{a_2b_3} \\ (1+x)^{a_3b_1} & (1+x)^{a_3b_2} & (1+x)^{a_3b_3} \end{vmatrix}.$$

Solution: Since we have to find the coefficient of x, therefore we, after applying binomial expansion, will ignore the terms containing powers of x^2 onwards,

$$\begin{vmatrix} 1+a_1b_1x & 1+a_1b_2x & 1+a_1b_3x \\ 1+a_2b_1x & 1+a_2b_2x & 1+a_2b_3x \\ 1+a_3b_1x & 1+a_3b_2x & 1+a_3b_3x \end{vmatrix}$$

Now the above determinant can be written as the sum of 8 determinants as below:

$$= \begin{vmatrix} 1 & 1 & 1 \\ 1 & 1 & 1 \\ 1 & 1 & 1 \end{vmatrix} + \begin{vmatrix} 1 & 1 & a_1b_3x \\ 1 & 1 & a_2b_3x \\ 1 & 1 & a_3b_3x \end{vmatrix} + \begin{vmatrix} 1 & a_1b_2x & 1 \\ 1 & a_2b_2x & 1 \\ 1 & a_3b_2x & 1 \end{vmatrix}$$

$$+ \begin{vmatrix} 1 & a_1b_2x & a_1b_3x \\ 1 & a_2b_2x & a_2b_3x \\ 1 & a_3b_2x & a_3b_3x \end{vmatrix} + \begin{vmatrix} a_1b_1x & 1 & 1 \\ a_2b_1x & 1 & 1 \\ a_3b_1x & 1 & 1 \end{vmatrix}$$

$$+ \begin{vmatrix} a_1b_1x & 1 & a_1b_3x \\ a_2b_1x & 1 & a_2b_3x \\ a_3b_1x & 1 & a_3b_3x \end{vmatrix} + \begin{vmatrix} a_1b_1x & a_1b_2x & 1 \\ a_2b_1x & a_2b_2x & 1 \\ a_3b_1x & a_3b_2x & 1 \end{vmatrix}$$

$$+ \begin{vmatrix} a_1b_1x & a_1b_2x & a_1b_3x \\ a_2b_1x & a_2b_2x & a_2b_3x \\ a_3b_1x & a_3b_2x & a_3b_3x \end{vmatrix}$$

Observing the above determinants, we get that the value of some determinants is zero and the value of rest of the determinants, has the coefficient x^2 atleast. Therefore, no determinants whose coefficient is x.

$\Rightarrow$ Coefficient of x is zero.

16. If $2x + py + 6z = 8$; $x + 2y + qz = 5$; $x + y + 3z = 4$. Then for what values of p and q, the system of equations have (i) no solution (ii) a unique solution (iii) infinitely many solutions.

Solution: Here, $\Delta = \begin{vmatrix} 2 & p & 6 \\ 1 & 2 & q \\ 1 & 1 & 3 \end{vmatrix} = (p-2)(q-3)$

$$\Rightarrow \Delta_1 = \begin{vmatrix} 8 & p & 6 \\ 5 & 2 & q \\ 4 & 1 & 3 \end{vmatrix} = (4q-15)(p-2) \text{ and}$$

$$\Delta_2 = \begin{vmatrix} 2 & 8 & 6 \\ 1 & 5 & q \\ 1 & 4 & 3 \end{vmatrix} = 0 \Rightarrow \Delta_3 = \begin{vmatrix} 2 & p & 8 \\ 1 & 2 & 5 \\ 1 & 1 & 4 \end{vmatrix} = p-2$$

Case 1: When $\Delta \neq 0$ i.e., $p \neq 2$ and $q \neq 3$, then given system of equation has unique solution

Case 2: When $\Delta = 0$ i.e., $p = 2$ or $q = 3$

$\Rightarrow$ When $p = 2$, $\Delta = 0$, $\Delta_1 = 0$, $\Delta_2 = 0$, $\Delta_3 = 0$

Given system of equations has infinitely many solutions.

$\Rightarrow$ When $q = 3$; $p \neq 2$, $\Delta = 0$, $\Delta_3 \neq 0$

$\therefore$ Given system of equations has *no solution.*

Concluding above, we can say that

(i) unique solution when $p \neq 2$ and $q \neq 3$

(ii) infinitely many solutions when $p = 2$

(iii) no solution when $p \neq 2$. $q = 3$.

17. Prove without expansion that

$$\begin{vmatrix} ah+bg & g & ab+ch \\ bf+ba & f & hb+bc \\ af+bc & c & bg+fc \end{vmatrix} = a\begin{vmatrix} ah+bg & a & h \\ bf+ba & h & b \\ af+bc & g & f \end{vmatrix}$$

Solution: Rewriting the given determinant as mentioned below:

$$\frac{1}{c}\begin{vmatrix} ah+bg & gc & ab+ch \\ bf+ba & fc & hb+bc \\ af+bc & c^2 & bg+fc \end{vmatrix} - \frac{a}{c}\begin{vmatrix} ah+bg & a & ch \\ bf+ba & h & cb \\ af+bc & g & cf \end{vmatrix} = 0$$

By operating in second determinant $C_3 \to C_3 + bC_2$, we get

$$= \frac{1}{c}\Delta_1 - \frac{a}{c}\begin{vmatrix} ah+bg & a & ab+ch \\ bf+ba & h & hb+cb \\ af+bc & g & bg+cf \end{vmatrix}$$

$$= \frac{1}{c}\Delta_1 + \frac{1}{c}\begin{vmatrix} ah+bg & -a^2 & ab+ch \\ bf+ba & -ah & hb+cb \\ af+bc & -ag & bg+cf \end{vmatrix}$$

$$= \frac{1}{c}\begin{vmatrix} ah+bg & gc-a^2 & ab+ch \\ bf+ba & fc-ah & hb+cb \\ af+bc & c^2-ag & bg+cf \end{vmatrix}$$

$$= \frac{1}{c}\begin{vmatrix} a & h & g \\ h & b & f \\ g & f & c \end{vmatrix}\begin{vmatrix} 0 & a & b \\ -a & 0 & c \\ b & c & 0 \end{vmatrix}$$

$$= -\frac{1}{c}\begin{vmatrix} a & h & g \\ h & b & f \\ g & f & c \end{vmatrix} \times \begin{vmatrix} 0 & a & b \\ -a & 0 & c \\ -b & -c & 0 \end{vmatrix} = 0$$

18. Factorize the determinant

$$\Delta = \begin{vmatrix} 1 & bc+ad & b^2c^2+a^2d^2 \\ 1 & ca+bd & c^2a^2+b^2d^2 \\ 1 & ab+cd & a^2b^2+c^2d^2 \end{vmatrix}$$

Solution: Let $\left.\begin{matrix} bc+ad = x \\ ca+bd = y \\ ab+cd = z \end{matrix}\right]$ and using $C_3 \to C_3 + 2abcd.\, C_1$ in the given determinant

$$\Delta = \begin{vmatrix} 1 & x & x^2 \\ 1 & y & y^2 \\ 1 & z & z^2 \end{vmatrix} = (x-y)(y-z)(z-x).$$

By putting the values back and solving it, we get the required answer

$\Delta = -(a-b)(b-c)(c-d)(a-d)(b-d)(c-d)$

19. Show that $\begin{vmatrix} yz-x^2 & zx-y^2 & xy-z^2 \\ zx-y^2 & xy-z^2 & yz-x^2 \\ xy-z^2 & yz-x^2 & zx-y^2 \end{vmatrix}$

$$= \begin{vmatrix} r^2 & u^2 & u^2 \\ u^2 & r^2 & u^2 \\ u^2 & u^2 & r^2 \end{vmatrix}$$

where $r^2 = x^2 + y^2 + z^2$ and $u^2 = xy + yz + zx$.

Solution: Consider the determinant, $\Delta = \begin{vmatrix} x & y & z \\ y & z & x \\ z & x & y \end{vmatrix}$

We see that the *L.H.S.* determinant has its constituents which are the co-factors of Δ. Hence *L.H.S.* determinant = Δ^2

$$= \begin{vmatrix} x & y & z \\ y & z & x \\ z & x & y \end{vmatrix}\begin{vmatrix} x & y & z \\ y & z & x \\ z & x & y \end{vmatrix}$$

$$= \begin{vmatrix} x^2+y^2+z^2 & xy+yz+zx & xy+yz+zx \\ xy+yz+zx & y^2+z^2+x^2 & yz+zx+xy \\ zx+xy+yz & yz+xz+xy & z^2+x^2+y^2 \end{vmatrix}$$

$$= \begin{vmatrix} r^2 & u^2 & u^2 \\ u^2 & r^2 & u^2 \\ u^2 & u^2 & r^2 \end{vmatrix}$$

20. If α, β and γ are such that $\alpha + \beta + \gamma = 0$, then prove that $\begin{vmatrix} 1 & \cos\gamma & \cos\beta \\ \cos\gamma & 1 & \cos\alpha \\ \cos\beta & \cos\alpha & 1 \end{vmatrix} = 0$

Solution: Operating $C_2 \to C_2 - \cos\gamma\, C_1$, $C_3 \to C_3 - \cos\beta\, C_1$.

$$\Delta = \begin{vmatrix} 1 & 0 & 0 \\ \cos\gamma & \sin^2\gamma & \cos\alpha - \cos\beta\cos\gamma \\ \cos\beta & \cos\alpha - \cos\beta\cos\gamma & \sin^2\beta \end{vmatrix}$$

$$\Delta = \begin{vmatrix} 1 & 0 & 0 \\ \cos\gamma & \sin^2\gamma & -\sin\beta\sin\gamma \\ \cos\beta & -\sin\gamma\sin\beta & \sin^2\beta \end{vmatrix}$$

$$\left[\begin{matrix} \because \alpha = -(\beta+\gamma) \\ \because \cos\alpha = \cos(\beta+\gamma) \\ \cos\alpha = \cos\beta\cos\gamma - \sin\beta\sin\gamma \end{matrix}\right.$$

$= 1\,(\sin^2\gamma\sin^2\beta - \sin^2\gamma\sin^2\beta) = 0$

21. Given that $\alpha = \cos\theta + i\sin\theta$, $\beta = \cos2\theta - i\sin2\theta$, $\gamma = \cos3\theta + i\sin3\theta$ and if $\begin{vmatrix} \alpha & \beta & \gamma \\ \beta & \gamma & \alpha \\ \gamma & \alpha & \beta \end{vmatrix} = 0$, show that $\theta = 2n\pi$, $n \in Z$.

Solution: $\begin{vmatrix} \alpha & \beta & \gamma \\ \beta & \gamma & \alpha \\ \gamma & \alpha & \beta \end{vmatrix} = -\frac{1}{2}(\alpha+\beta+\gamma)((\alpha-\beta)^2 + (\beta-\gamma)^2 + (\gamma-\alpha)^2) = 0$

$\Rightarrow \alpha + \beta + \gamma = 0$ or $\alpha = \beta = \gamma$

If $\alpha + \beta + \gamma = 0$, we have $\cos\theta + \cos2\theta + \cos3\theta = 0$, $\sin\theta - \sin2\theta + \sin3\theta = 0$

$\therefore \cos2\theta\,(2\cos\theta + 1) = 0$ ...(i)

and $\sin2\theta\,(1 - 2\cos\theta) = 0$ ......(ii)

which is not possible as $\cos2\theta = 0$ gives $\sin2\theta \neq 0$, $\cos\theta \neq 1/2$

and $\cos\theta = -1/2$ gives $\sin 2\theta \neq 0$, $\cos\theta \neq 1/2$

$\therefore$ equation (i) and (ii) does not hold simultaneously

$\therefore$ $\alpha + \beta + \gamma \neq 0$

$\therefore$ $\alpha = \beta = \gamma$ or $e^{i\theta} = e^{-2\theta} = e^{3i\theta}$ which is satisfied only by $e^{i\theta} = 1$

i.e., $\cos\theta = 1$, $\sin\theta = 0$, so $\theta = 2n\pi$, $n \in Z$

22. If $A + B + C = \pi$, then find

$$\begin{vmatrix} \sin(A+B+C) & \sin B & \cos C \\ -\sin B & 0 & \tan A \\ \cos(A+B) & -\tan A & 0 \end{vmatrix}$$

Solution: $\Delta = \begin{vmatrix} 0 & \sin B & \cos C \\ -\sin B & 0 & \tan A \\ -\cos C & -\tan A & 0 \end{vmatrix}$

Apply $R \leftrightarrow C$ we get, $\begin{vmatrix} 0 & -\sin B & -\cos C \\ \sin B & 0 & -\tan A \\ \cos C & \tan A & 0 \end{vmatrix}$

taking -1 common from each row

$$= -\begin{vmatrix} 0 & \sin B & \cos C \\ -\sin B & 0 & \tan A \\ -\cos C & -\tan A & 0 \end{vmatrix} = -\Delta$$

$\Rightarrow 2\Delta = 0 \quad \Rightarrow \Delta = 0$

Note: Skew symmetric determinant of odd order is zero.

23. Using properties, prove that

$$\begin{vmatrix} a+x & y & z \\ x & a+y & z \\ x & y & a+z \end{vmatrix} = a^2(a+x+y+z)$$

Solution: Applying $R_3 \to R_3 - R_2$

$$\Delta = \begin{vmatrix} a+x & y & z \\ x & a+y & z \\ 0 & -a & a \end{vmatrix} = a\begin{vmatrix} a+x & y & z \\ x & a+y & z \\ 0 & -1 & 1 \end{vmatrix}$$

Applying $R_2 \to R_2 - R_1$

$$\Delta = a\begin{vmatrix} a+x & y & z \\ -a & a & 0 \\ 0 & -1 & 1 \end{vmatrix} = a^2\begin{vmatrix} a+x & y & z \\ -1 & 1 & 0 \\ 0 & -1 & 1 \end{vmatrix}$$

Applying $C_1 \to C_1 + C_2 + C_3$;

$$\Delta = a^2\begin{vmatrix} a+x+y+z & y & z \\ 0 & 1 & 1 \\ 0 & -1 & 1 \end{vmatrix}$$

$$= a^2\begin{vmatrix} a+x+y+z & y+z & z \\ 0 & 1 & 1 \\ 0 & 0 & 1 \end{vmatrix} = a^2(a+x+y+z)$$

24. Prove that $\begin{vmatrix} a^2+2a & 2a+1 & 1 \\ 2a+1 & a+2 & 1 \\ 3 & 3 & 1 \end{vmatrix}$ > or = or < 0 according as $a > 1$ or $a = 1$ or $a < 1$

Solution: Some times a determinant has all its elements = 1 (or equal) in a row (or column) {e.g., in the third column}. By transformation $R_1 \to R_1 - R_3$, etc., it is very easy to get at least two zeros in a particular row or column and which reduces the order of the determinant. Operating $R_1 \to R_1 - R_3$ and $R_2 \to R_2 - R_3$

$$\Rightarrow \Delta = \begin{vmatrix} a^2+2a-3 & 2a-2 & 0 \\ 2a-2 & a-1 & 0 \\ 3 & 3 & 1 \end{vmatrix}; R_1 \to R_1 - 2R_2$$

$$\Rightarrow \Delta = \begin{vmatrix} a^2+2a-1 & 0 & 0 \\ 2(a-1) & a-1 & 0 \\ 3 & 3 & 1 \end{vmatrix}$$

$$= \Delta = \begin{vmatrix} (a-1)^2 & 0 \\ 2(a-1) & a-1 \end{vmatrix} = (a-1)^3$$

$\therefore$ $\Delta > 0$ if $(a-1)^3 > 0$ i.e. $a > 1$; $\Delta = 0$ if $(a-1)^3 = 0$ i.e., $a = 1$ and $\Delta < 0$ if $(a-1)^3 < 0$ i.e. $a < 1$

25. Solve $\begin{vmatrix} a^2+\lambda & ab & ac \\ ab & b^2+\lambda & bc \\ ac & bc & c^2+\lambda \end{vmatrix} = 0$, $\lambda \in \mathbb{R}$

Solution: **Important:** Some determinants are such that there is a factor common between the elements in the first row and the first column but not necessarily at the junction of the row and column. Similar situation may exist for the other rows and columns. In the above problem those common factors are a, b, c respectively. In such problems, common factors are taken out row wise (or column wise) and re-entered columnwise (or row wise) respectively.

Here $\Delta = abc\begin{vmatrix} a+\lambda/a & b & c \\ a & b+\lambda/b & c \\ a & b & c+\lambda/c \end{vmatrix}$

$$= \begin{vmatrix} a^2+\lambda & b^2 & c^2 \\ a^2 & b^2+\lambda & c^2 \\ a^2 & b^2 & c^2+\lambda \end{vmatrix}; C_1 \to C_1 + C_2 + C_3$$

$$\Rightarrow \Delta = \begin{vmatrix} \lambda+(a^2+b^2+c^2) & b^2 & c^2 \\ \lambda+(a^2+b^2+c^2) & b^2+\lambda & c^2 \\ \lambda+(a^2+b^2+c^2) & b^2 & c^2+\lambda \end{vmatrix}$$

$$= [\lambda+(a^2+b^2+c^2)]\begin{vmatrix} 1 & b^2 & c^2 \\ 1 & b^2+\lambda & c^2 \\ 1 & b^2 & c^2+\lambda \end{vmatrix}$$

$R_2 \to R_2 - R_1,\ R_3 \to R_3 - R_1$

$$\Rightarrow \Delta = [\lambda+(a^2+b^2+c^2)]\begin{vmatrix} 1 & b^2 & c^2 \\ 0 & \lambda & 0 \\ 0 & 0 & \lambda \end{vmatrix}$$

$= \lambda^2(\lambda + a^2 + b^2 + c^2)$ (because the determinant is triangular)

$\therefore$ the equation is $\lambda^2(\lambda + a^2 + b^2 + c^2) = 0$

$\Rightarrow \lambda = 0, -(a^2 + b^2 + c^2)$

26. For a fixed positive integer n, if $\Delta = \begin{vmatrix} n! & (n+1)! & (n+2)! \\ (n+1)! & (n+2)! & (n+3)! \\ (n+2)! & (n+3)! & (n+4)! \end{vmatrix}$, then show that $\dfrac{\Delta}{(n!)^3} - 4$ is divisible by n.

Solution: $\Delta = n!.(n+1)!.(n+2)!\begin{vmatrix} 1 & (n+1) & (n+1)(n+2) \\ 1 & (n+2) & (n+2)(n+3) \\ 1 & (n+3) & (n+3)(n+4) \end{vmatrix}$

$$\Rightarrow \Delta = n!.(n+1)!.(n+2)!\begin{vmatrix} 1 & (n+1) & (n+1)(n+2) \\ 0 & 1 & 2(n+2) \\ 0 & 1 & 2(n+3) \end{vmatrix}$$

$\Rightarrow \Delta = (n!)^3\,(n + 1)^2.(n + 2).2$

$\Rightarrow \dfrac{\Delta}{(n!)^3} = 2(n^2+2n+1)(n+2) = 2(n^3+4n^2+5n)+4$

$\Rightarrow \dfrac{\Delta}{(n!)^3} - 4 = 2n(n^2+4n+5)$, which is divisible by n

$\Rightarrow \dfrac{\Delta}{(n!)^3} - 4$ is divisible by n

27. Evaluate the determinant $\begin{vmatrix} x & x(x^2+1) & x+1 \\ y & y(y^2+1) & y+1 \\ z & z(z^2+1) & z+1 \end{vmatrix}$.

Solution: Let $\Delta = \begin{vmatrix} x & x(x^2+1) & x+1 \\ y & y(y^2+1) & y+1 \\ z & z(z^2+1) & z+1 \end{vmatrix} = \begin{vmatrix} x & x^3 & 1 \\ y & y^3 & 1 \\ z & z^3 & 1 \end{vmatrix}$

$(C_2 \to C_2 - C_1,\ C_3 \to C_3 - C_1)$

$$= \begin{vmatrix} x & x^3 & 1 \\ y-x & y^3-x^3 & 0 \\ z-y & z^3-y^3 & 0 \end{vmatrix} \quad (R_2 \to R_2 - R_1,\ R_3 \to R_3 - R_2)$$

$= (y - x)\,(z^3 - y^3) - (z - y)\,(y^3 - x^3)$

$= (x - y)(y - z)(y^2 - z^2 + yz - z^2 - y^2 - xy)$

$= (x - y)(y - z)[z^2 - x^2 + y(z - x)] = (x - y)(y - z)(z - x)(x + y + z)$

28. Show that $\begin{vmatrix} a^2 & bc & ac+c^2 \\ a^2+ab & b^2 & ac \\ ab & b^2+bc & c^2 \end{vmatrix} = 4a^2b^2c^2$

Solution: L.H.S. $= \begin{vmatrix} a^2 & bc & ac+c^2 \\ a^2+ab & b^2 & ac \\ ab & b^2+bc & c^2 \end{vmatrix}$

$$= abc\begin{vmatrix} a & c & a+c \\ a+b & b & a \\ b & b+c & c \end{vmatrix}$$

$$= abc\begin{vmatrix} a & c & 0 \\ a+b & b & -2b \\ b & b+c & -2b \end{vmatrix}$$

(applying $C_3 \to C_3 - C_1 - C_2$)

Taking $2b$ common from column C_3.

$$= 2ab^2c\begin{vmatrix} a & c & 0 \\ a+b & b & -1 \\ b & b+c & -1 \end{vmatrix} \quad (\text{applying } R_2 \to R_2 - R_3)$$

$$= 2ab^2c\begin{vmatrix} a & c & 0 \\ a & -c & 0 \\ b & b+c & -1 \end{vmatrix} = 2ab^2c(-ac - ac) = 4a^2b^2c^2$$

29. Let

$$f(x) = \begin{vmatrix} \sec x & \cos x & \sec^2 x + \cot x \operatorname{cosec} x + \cos x \\ \cos^2 x & \cos^2 x & \operatorname{cosec}^2 x + \cos^4 x \\ 1 & \cos^2 x & \cos^2 x \end{vmatrix}$$

then, evaluate $\int_0^{\pi/2} f(x)\,dx$

Solution:

$$f(x) = \begin{vmatrix} 0 & 0 & \sec^2 x + \cot x \operatorname{cosec} x \\ 0 & \cos^2 x - \cos^4 x & \operatorname{cosec}^2 x \\ 1 & \cos^2 x & \cos^2 x \end{vmatrix}$$

$(R_1 \to R_1 - \sec x\, R_3,\ R_2 \to R_2 - \cos^2 x\, R_3)$

$\therefore\ \Delta = (\sec^2 x + \cot x.\operatorname{cosec} x)(-\cos^2 x + \cos^4 x)$

$= -\sin^2 x - \cos^3 x$

Now, $\int_0^{\pi/2} f(x)\,dx = \int_0^{\pi/2} (-\sin^2 x - \cos^3 x)dx$

Using Wallis thecrom $= -\dfrac{1}{2}.\dfrac{\pi}{2} - \dfrac{2}{3} = -\left(\dfrac{\pi}{4} + \dfrac{2}{3}\right)$

30. If $p, q \in \mathbb{R}$; and $p^2 + q^2 - pq - p - q + 1 \le 0$ and $a+b+c=0$, then evaluate $\Delta = \begin{vmatrix} 1 & \cos c & \cos b \\ \cos c & p & \cos a \\ \cos a & \cos b & q \end{vmatrix}$

Solution: Given $p^2 + q^2 - pq - p - q + 1 \le 0$

$\Rightarrow (p-1)^2 + (q-1)^2 + (p-1)(1-q) \le 0$

Dividing by $(q-1)^2$. (Assuming $(q-1) \neq 0$)

$\Rightarrow \left(\frac{p-1}{1-q}\right)^2 + \left(\frac{p-1}{1-q}\right) + 1 \le 0$ which is not possible.

$\therefore q = 1 \qquad \Rightarrow p^2 - 2p + 1 \le 0$

$\Rightarrow p = 1 \qquad \therefore \Delta = \begin{vmatrix} 1 & \cos c & \cos b \\ \cos c & 1 & \cos a \\ \cos a & \cos b & 1 \end{vmatrix}$

Let $a = B - C$; $b = C - A$; $c = A - B$

$(\because a + b + c = 0)$

$$\therefore \Delta = \begin{vmatrix} 1 & \cos(A-B) & \cos(C-A) \\ \cos(A-B) & 1 & \cos(B-C) \\ \cos(B-C) & \cos(C-A) & 1 \end{vmatrix}$$

$$= \begin{vmatrix} \cos A & \sin A & 0 \\ \cos B & \sin B & 0 \\ \cos C & \sin C & 0 \end{vmatrix} \times \begin{vmatrix} \cos A & \cos B & \cos C \\ \sin A & \sin B & \sin C \\ 0 & 0 & 0 \end{vmatrix} = 0$$

31. If all the entries of a 3×3 determinant are either 1 or -1, show that the only values the determinant can take are 0, ± 4.

Solution: We have $\Delta = \begin{vmatrix} a_1 & b_1 & c_1 \\ a_2 & b_2 & c_2 \\ a_3 & b_3 & c_3 \end{vmatrix} = a_1b_2c_3 + a_2b_3c_1 +$

$a_3b_1c_2 - a_1b_3c_2 - a_3b_2c_1 - a_2b_1c_3$ ....(i)

Since all the nine numbers in the determinant are either 1 or -1, each term in *RHS* of (i) is either 1 or -1. Therefore the maximum and minimum value of such a determinant may be 6 and -6 respectively. We will show that these values can never be attained. The determinant is equal to 6 if and only if

$a_1b_2c_3 = 1$, $a_2b_3c_1 = 1$, $a_3b_1c_2 = 1$,

and $a_1b_3c_2 = -1$, $a_3b_2c_1 = -1$, $a_2b_1c_3 = -1$

The above six equations cannot exist simultaneously. To show this let us multiply all the above equations to arrive at a contradiction $a_1^2\, b_1^2\, c_1^2\, a_2^2\, b_2^2\, c_2^2\, a_3^2\, b_3^2\, c_3^2 = -1$ which is impossible as square of a real number is ≥ 0. A similar proof can be given in order to show that the determinant cannot be equal to -6. Now we show that the determinant cannot be an odd number either. From (i)

$\Delta = x_1 + x_2 + x_3 - x_4 - x_5 - x_6$ (such that $x_1 = a_1b_2c_3$ etc) where each x_i is either 1 or -1

$= (x_1 - x_4) + (x_2 - x_5) + (x_3 - x_6) = y_1 + y_2 + y_3$ where $y_1 = x_1 - x_4$ etc.

Now since each x_i is either 1 or -1, each y_i is either 0 or 2 or -2. Consequently, $y_1 + y_2 + y_3$ is essentially even. Now, we show that there exists a determinant with entries 1 or -1 whose value is equal to 4 or (-4).

This determinant is $\begin{vmatrix} 1 & -1 & 1 \\ 1 & 1 & -1 \\ -1 & 1 & 1 \end{vmatrix}$

(interchange any two adjacent rows to make the value -4)

We finally show that the value of the determinant cannot be ± 2. It is sufficient to show that the value cannot be 2 (for if 2 is possible -2 is also possible and if 2 is not possible then -2 is also not possible)

Note that $\Delta = 2$ if and only if $y_1 = 2, y_2 = 2, y_3 = -2$ (or their permutations)

or $y_1 = 2, y_2 = 0, y_3 = 0$ (or their permutations)

Now $y_1 = 2 \Rightarrow a_1b_2c_3 = 1, a_1b_3c_2 = -1$

$y_2 = 2 \Rightarrow a_2b_3c_1 = 1, a_3b_2c_1 = -1,$

$y_3 = -2 \Rightarrow a_3b_1c_2 = -1, a_2b_1c_3 = 1$

On multiplying all the six relations, we get $1 = -1$, a contradiction

Again $y_1 = 2, y_2 = 0, y_3 = 0$

$\Rightarrow a_1b_2c_3 = 1, a_1b_3c_2 = -1;$

$a_2b_3c_1 = 1, a_3b_2c_1 = 1$ ....(ii)

$a_3b_1c_2 = 1, a_2b_1c_3 = 1$

which again yields $1 = -1$ a contradiction

(At (ii) $a_2b_3c_1 = -1, a_3b_2c_1 = -1$ is also possible but the final result is not affected)

32. Show that $\Delta(a, b, c)$

$$= \begin{vmatrix} (b+c)^2 & a^2 & a^2 \\ b^2 & (c+a)^2 & b^2 \\ c^2 & c^2 & (a+b)^2 \end{vmatrix} = 2abc(a+b+c)^3$$

Solution: Applying $C_2 \to C_2 - C_1$ and $C_3 \to C_3 - C_1$ we get $\Delta(a, b, c)$

$$= \begin{vmatrix} (b+c)^2 & (a+b+c)(a-b-c) & (a+b+c)(a-b-c) \\ b^2 & (c+a+b)(c+a-b) & 0 \\ c^2 & 0 & (a+b+c)(a+b-c) \end{vmatrix}$$

$$= (a+b+c)^2 \begin{vmatrix} (b+c)^2 & (a-b-c) & (a-b-c) \\ b^2 & (c+a-b) & 0 \\ c^2 & 0 & (a+b-c) \end{vmatrix}$$

On applying $R_1 \to R_1 - (R_2 + R_3)$, we get

$$\Delta = (a+b+c)^2 \begin{vmatrix} 2bc & -2c & -2b \\ b^2 & (c+a-b) & 0 \\ c^2 & 0 & (a+b-c) \end{vmatrix}$$

$= 2(a + b + c)^2\ [bc(c + a - b)(a + b - c) - 0 + c(a + b - c)b^2 + bc^2(c + a - b)]$

On expanding along Ist row after taking 2 as a common factor

$= 2(a + b + c)^2[abc^2 + bca^2 + cab^2] = 2abc(a + b + c)^3$

33. Prove without expanding and applying concept of factorization that

$$\begin{vmatrix} 1 & a^2 & a^3 \\ 1 & a^2 & a^3 \\ 1 & c^2 & c^3 \end{vmatrix} = (ab+bc+ac)(a-b)(b-c)(c-a)$$

Solution: The *LHS* is a homogeneous expression of degree 5 in *a*, *b*, *c*. If we replace *a* by *b*, *b* by *c* and *c* by *a*, then the expression does not change (interchange two rows twice). On putting $a = b$

$$\text{LHS} = \begin{vmatrix} 1 & a^2 & a^3 \\ 1 & a^2 & a^3 \\ 1 & c^2 & c^3 \end{vmatrix} = 0.$$

$\Rightarrow$ $(a - b)$ is factor of LHS. Similarly, $(b - c)$ and $(c - a)$ are also factors. Note that $(a - b)(b - c)(c - a)$ does not change if *a* is replaced by *b*, *b* by *c* and *c* by *a*. But the degree of expression is 5, therefore it must have a homogeneous symmetric expression of degree 2 as factor. The two degree symmetric expressions are only $a^2 + b^2 + c^2$, $ab + bc + ca$, $(a + b + c)^2$, $a^2 + b^2 + c^2 - ab - bc - ac$. Thus one of the following must be an identity.

$$\begin{vmatrix} 1 & a^2 & a^3 \\ 1 & b^2 & b^3 \\ 1 & c^2 & c^3 \end{vmatrix} = k(a-b)(b-c)(c-a)(a^2+b^2+c^2)$$

or

$$\begin{vmatrix} 1 & a^2 & a^3 \\ 1 & b^2 & b^3 \\ 1 & c^2 & c^3 \end{vmatrix} = k(a-b)(b-c)(c-a)(a+b+c)^2$$

or

$$\begin{vmatrix} 1 & a^2 & a^3 \\ 1 & b^2 & b^3 \\ 1 & c^2 & c^3 \end{vmatrix} = k(a-b)(b-c)(c-a)(a^2+b^2+c^2-ab-bc-ac)$$

or

$$\begin{vmatrix} 1 & a^2 & a^3 \\ 1 & b^2 & b^3 \\ 1 & c^2 & c^3 \end{vmatrix} = k(a-b)(b-c)(c-a)(ab+bc+ac)$$

(where *k* is a constant)

In the first assumption, put $a = 0$, $b = 1$, $c = -1$, we get,

$$\begin{vmatrix} 1 & 0 & 0 \\ 1 & 1 & 1 \\ 1 & 1 & -1 \end{vmatrix} = k\,(0-1)\,(1+1)\,(-1-0)\,(2)$$

$\Rightarrow -2 = 4k \quad \Rightarrow \quad k = -1/2$

Again putting $a = 0$, $b = 1$, $c = 2$, we get $k = 2/5$

Since the two values of *k* are different, the first of the above cannot be an identity. We can similarly show that second and third are not identities either. Thus the only possibility left is fourth. Thus $\begin{vmatrix} 1 & a^2 & a^3 \\ 1 & b^2 & b^3 \\ 1 & c^2 & c^3 \end{vmatrix} = k$

$(a - b)(b - c)(c - a)(ab + bc + ac)$

On putting $a = 0$, $b = 1$, $c = -1$ we get $k = 1$

(any other choice of values for *a*, *b*, *c* will yield same *k*)

34. Without expanding, show that $\begin{vmatrix} 1 & a^2 & a^3 \\ 1 & b^2 & b^3 \\ 1 & c^2 & c^3 \end{vmatrix}$

$$= (ab+bc+ac)\begin{vmatrix} 1 & a & a^2 \\ 1 & b & b^2 \\ 1 & c & c^2 \end{vmatrix}$$

Solution: Let $\Delta = \begin{vmatrix} 1 & a^2 & a^3 \\ 1 & b^2 & b^3 \\ 1 & c^2 & c^3 \end{vmatrix}$.

$$\text{Then } \Delta = abc\begin{vmatrix} 1/a & a & a^2 \\ 1/b & b & b^2 \\ 1/c & c & c^2 \end{vmatrix} = \begin{vmatrix} bc & a & a^2 \\ ac & b & b^2 \\ ab & c & c^2 \end{vmatrix}$$

$$= \begin{vmatrix} bc-a^2 & a & a^2 \\ ac-b^2 & b & b^2 \\ ab-c^2 & c & c^2 \end{vmatrix} \quad (C_1 \to C_1 - C_3)$$

$$= \begin{vmatrix} bc+ac-a^2 & a & a^2 \\ ac+bc-b^2 & b & b^2 \\ ab & c & c^2 \end{vmatrix} \quad (C_1 \to C_1 + c\,C_2)$$

$$= \begin{vmatrix} bc+ac & a & a^2 \\ ac+bc+ab-b^2 & b & b^2 \\ ab+ac & c & c^2 \end{vmatrix} \quad (C_1 \to C_1 + a\,C_2)$$

$$= \begin{vmatrix} ab+bc+ac & a & a^2 \\ ab+bc+ac & b & b^2 \\ ab+bc+ac & c & c^2 \end{vmatrix} \quad (C_1 \to C_1 + b\,C_2)$$

$$= (ab+bc+ac)\begin{vmatrix} 1 & a & a^2 \\ 1 & b & b^2 \\ 1 & c & c^2 \end{vmatrix} = \text{RHS}$$

35. Let p be the sum of all possible determinants of order 2 having 0, 1, 2 and 3 as their four elements. Then find the common root α of the equations $x^2 + ax + [m+1] = 0$; $x^2 + bx + [m+4] = 0$; $x^2 - cx + [m+15] = 0$ such that $\alpha > p$, where $a + b + c = 0$ and $m = \lim_{n\to\infty} \frac{1}{n}\sum_{r=1}^{2n} \frac{r}{\sqrt{n^2+r^2}}$ (where [.] denotes the greatest integer function)

Solution: Let α be the common root, then

$\alpha^2 + a\alpha + [m+1] = 0$ ...(i)

$\alpha^2 + b\alpha + [m+4] = 0$ ....(ii)

$\alpha^2 - c\alpha + [m+15] = 0$ ...(iii)

From (i) + (ii) – (iii), we get

$\alpha^2 + [m] - 10 = 0$ ....(iv)

But $m = \lim_{n\to\infty} \frac{1}{n}\sum_{r=1}^{2n} \frac{r}{\sqrt{n^2+r^2}}$

$$= \lim_{n\to\infty} \frac{1}{n}\sum_{r=1}^{2n} \frac{r/n}{\sqrt{1+(r/n)^2}} = \int_0^2 \frac{x}{\sqrt{1+x^2}}dx$$

$$= \sqrt{1+x^2}\Big|_0^2 = \sqrt{5}-1$$

Now $[m] = [\sqrt{5}-1] = 1$

From equation (iv) $\alpha^2 + 1 - 10 = 0$

$\Rightarrow \alpha = \pm 3$ ...(v)

Number of determinants of order 2 having 0,1, 2, 3 = 4! = 24

Let $\Delta_1 = \begin{vmatrix} a_1 & a_2 \\ a_3 & a_4 \end{vmatrix}$ be one such determinant and there exists another determinant.

$\Delta_2 = \begin{vmatrix} a_3 & a_4 \\ a_1 & a_2 \end{vmatrix}$ (obtained on interchanging R_1 and R_2) such that $\Delta_1 + \Delta_2 = 0$

p = sum of all the 24 determinants = 0

Since $\alpha > p$ $\Rightarrow \alpha > 0$

Therefore from the equation (v) we get $\alpha = 3$

36. Let λ and α be real. Find the set of all values of λ for which the system of linear equations $\lambda x + (\sin\alpha) y + (\cos\alpha)z = 0$ ....(i); $x + (\cos\alpha)y + (\sin\alpha)z = 0$...(ii) and $-x + (\sin\alpha)y - (\cos\alpha)z = 0$...(iii) has a trivial solution. For $\lambda = 1$ find all values of α.

Solution: For non-trivial solution

$$\Delta = \begin{vmatrix} \lambda & \sin\alpha & \cos\alpha \\ 1 & \cos\alpha & \sin\alpha \\ -1 & \sin\alpha & -\cos\alpha \end{vmatrix} = 0$$

Expanding we get $\lambda(-1) - 1(-2\sin\alpha\cos\alpha) - 1(\sin^2\alpha - \cos^2\alpha) = 0$

$\therefore$ $\lambda = \sin 2\alpha + \cos 2\alpha$

If $\lambda = 1$, then $\sin 2\alpha + \cos 2\alpha = 1$ or

$$\cos\left(2\alpha - \frac{\pi}{4}\right) = \frac{1}{\sqrt{2}} = \cos\frac{\pi}{4}$$

$$\therefore \quad 2\alpha - \frac{\pi}{4} = 2n\pi \pm \frac{\pi}{4}$$

$$\text{or} \quad 2\alpha = 2n\pi \pm \frac{\pi}{4} + \frac{\pi}{4}; n \in \mathbb{Z}$$

37. Prove that

$$\begin{vmatrix} 2 & \alpha+\beta+\gamma+\delta & \alpha\beta+\gamma\delta \\ \alpha+\beta+\gamma+\delta & 2(\alpha+\beta)(\gamma+\delta) & \alpha\beta(\gamma+\delta)+\gamma\delta(\alpha+\beta) \\ \alpha\beta+\gamma\delta & \alpha\beta(\gamma+\delta)+\gamma\delta(\alpha+\beta) & 2\alpha\beta\gamma\delta \end{vmatrix} = 0$$

Solution: $$\Delta = \begin{vmatrix} 2 & \gamma+\delta-\alpha-\beta & \alpha\beta+\gamma\delta \\ \alpha+\beta+\gamma+\delta & (\alpha+\beta)(\gamma+\delta-\alpha-\beta) & \alpha\beta(\gamma+\delta)+\gamma\delta(\alpha+\beta) \\ \alpha\beta+\gamma\delta & \alpha\beta(\gamma+\delta-\alpha-\beta) & 2\alpha\beta\gamma\delta \end{vmatrix}$$

On operating $C_2 \to C_2 - (\alpha+\beta).C_1$

$$= (\gamma+\delta-\alpha-\beta) \times \begin{vmatrix} 2 & 1 & \alpha\beta+\gamma\delta \\ \alpha+\beta+\gamma+\delta & (\alpha+\beta) & \alpha\beta(\gamma+\delta)+\gamma\delta(\alpha+\beta) \\ \alpha\beta+\gamma\delta & \alpha\beta & 2\alpha\beta\gamma\delta \end{vmatrix}$$

$$= (\gamma + \delta - \alpha - \beta)\begin{vmatrix} 1 & 1 & \alpha\beta + \gamma\delta \\ \gamma + \delta & (\alpha + \beta) & \alpha\beta(\gamma + \delta) + \gamma\delta(\alpha + \beta) \\ \gamma\delta & \alpha\beta & 2\alpha\beta\gamma\delta \end{vmatrix}$$

On operating $C_1 \to C_1 - C_1 = (\gamma + \delta - \alpha - \beta)\begin{vmatrix} 1 & 1 & 0 \\ \gamma+\delta & (\alpha+\beta) & 0 \\ \gamma\delta & \alpha\beta & 0 \end{vmatrix}$;

$C_3 \to C_3 - \alpha\beta.C_1 - \gamma\delta.C_2 = (\gamma + \delta - \alpha - \beta) \times 0 = 0$

Aliter: In this method, if you can observe the determinant, as product of two determinants then the solution becomes extremely simple. But for that the experience counts.As in the given determinant

$$\Delta = \begin{vmatrix} 2 & \alpha+\beta+\gamma+\delta & \alpha\beta+\gamma\delta \\ \alpha+\beta+\gamma+\delta & 2(\alpha+\beta)(\gamma+\delta) & \alpha\beta(\gamma+\delta)+\gamma\delta(\alpha+\beta) \\ \alpha\beta+\gamma\delta & \alpha\beta(\gamma+\delta)+\gamma\delta(\alpha+\beta) & 2\alpha\beta\gamma\delta \end{vmatrix} = 0$$

Looking at the diagonal symmetry of the elements, we can write above determinant as product of two determinants:

$$\begin{vmatrix} 1 & 1 & 0 \\ \gamma+\delta & (\alpha+\beta) & 0 \\ \gamma\delta & \alpha\beta & 0 \end{vmatrix} \times \begin{vmatrix} 1 & (\alpha+\beta) & \alpha\beta \\ 1 & (\gamma+\delta) & \gamma\delta \\ 0 & 0 & 0 \end{vmatrix} = 0 \times 0 = 0$$

38. If $p(x)$, $q(x)$ and $r(x)$ are the polynomial of degree 2 and if $f(x) = \begin{vmatrix} p(x) & q(x) & r(x) \\ p(x-\alpha) & q(x-\alpha) & r(x-\alpha) \\ p(x-\beta) & q(x-\beta) & r(x-\beta) \end{vmatrix}$; then show that $f''(x)$ is independent of x

Solution: Let $p(x) = a_1x^2 + b_1 x + c_1$; $q(x) = a_2x^2 + b_2 x + c_2$; $r(x) = a_3x^2 + b_3x + c_3$

$p(x - \alpha) = a_1 (x - \alpha)^2 + b_1 (x - \alpha) + c_1 = p(x) - 2\alpha a_1 x + d_1$; where $d_1 = a_1\alpha^2 - b_1 \alpha$

Similarly $p(x - \beta) = p(x) - 2\beta a_1 x + e_1$; where $e_1 = a_1 \beta^2 - b_1 \beta$

$$f(x) = \begin{vmatrix} p(x) & q(x) & r(x) \\ p(x) - 2\alpha a_1 x + d_1 & q(x) - 2\alpha a_2 x + d_2 & r(x) - 2\alpha a_3 x + d_3 \\ p(x) - 2\beta a_1 x + e_1 & q(x) - 2\beta a_2 x + e_2 & r(x) - 2\beta a_3 x + e_3 \end{vmatrix}$$

Applying $R_2 \to R_2 - R_1$ and $R_3 \to R_3 - R_1$

$$\begin{vmatrix} p(x) & q(x) & r(x) \\ d_1 - 2\alpha a_1 x & d_2 - 2\alpha a_2 x & d_3 - 2\alpha a_3 x \\ e_1 - 2\beta a_1 x & e_2 - 2\beta a_2 x & e_3 - 2\beta a_3 x \end{vmatrix} = \begin{vmatrix} p(x) & q(x) & r(x) \\ d_1 & d_2 & d_3 \\ e_1 & e_2 & e_3 \end{vmatrix} - 2\alpha x \begin{vmatrix} p(x) & q(x) & r(x) \\ a_1 & a_2 & a_3 \\ e_1 & e_2 & e_3 \end{vmatrix}$$

$$-2\beta x \begin{vmatrix} p(x) & q(x) & r(x) \\ d_1 & d_2 & d_3 \\ a_1 & a_2 & a_3 \end{vmatrix} + 0 ; f'(x) = \begin{vmatrix} p'(x) & q'(x) & r'(x) \\ d_1 & d_2 & d_3 \\ e_1 & e_2 & e_3 \end{vmatrix} - 2\alpha \begin{vmatrix} p(x) & q(x) & r(x) \\ a_1 & a_2 & a_3 \\ e_1 & e_2 & e_3 \end{vmatrix}$$

$$-2\beta \begin{vmatrix} p(x) & q(x) & r(x) \\ d_1 & d_2 & d_3 \\ a_1 & a_2 & a_3 \end{vmatrix} - 2\alpha x \begin{vmatrix} p'(x) & q'(x) & r'(x) \\ a_1 & a_2 & a_3 \\ e_1 & e_2 & e_3 \end{vmatrix} - 2\beta x \begin{vmatrix} p'(x) & q'(x) & r'(x) \\ d_1 & d_2 & d_3 \\ a_1 & a_2 & a_3 \end{vmatrix}$$

then $f''(x) = \Delta_1 + \Delta_2 + \Delta_3 + \Delta_4 + \Delta_5$ where $\Delta_1 = \begin{vmatrix} p''(x) & q''(x) & r''(x) \\ d_1 & d_2 & d_3 \\ e_1 & e_2 & e_3 \end{vmatrix}$; $\Delta_2 = -4\alpha \begin{vmatrix} p'(x) & q'(x) & r'(x) \\ a_1 & a_2 & a_3 \\ e_1 & e_2 & e_3 \end{vmatrix}$

$$\Delta_3 = -4\beta\begin{vmatrix} p'(x) & q'(x) & r'(x) \\ d_1 & d_2 & d_3 \\ a_1 & a_2 & a_3 \end{vmatrix};\ \Delta_4 = -2\alpha x\begin{vmatrix} p''(x) & q''(x) & r''(x) \\ a_1 & a_2 & a_3 \\ e_1 & e_2 & e_3 \end{vmatrix};\ \Delta_5 = -2\beta x\begin{vmatrix} p''(x) & q''(x) & r''(x) \\ d_1 & d_2 & d_3 \\ a_1 & a_2 & a_3 \end{vmatrix}$$

Since, $\begin{vmatrix} p''(x) & q''(x) & r''(x) \\ a_1 & a_2 & a_3 \\ e_1 & e_2 & e_3 \end{vmatrix} = 2\begin{vmatrix} a_1 & a_2 & a_3 \\ a_1 & a_2 & a_3 \\ e_1 & e_2 & e_3 \end{vmatrix}$ and $\begin{vmatrix} p''(x) & q''(x) & r''(x) \\ d_1 & d_2 & d_3 \\ a_1 & a_2 & a_3 \end{vmatrix} = 0$ (i.e., $\Delta_4 = \Delta_5 = 0$)

$$f'''(x) = \begin{vmatrix} p'''(x) & q'''(x) & r'''(x) \\ d_1 & d_2 & d_3 \\ e_1 & e_2 & e_3 \end{vmatrix} - 4\alpha\begin{vmatrix} p''(x) & q''(x) & r''(x) \\ a_1 & a_2 & a_3 \\ e_1 & e_2 & e_3 \end{vmatrix} - 4\beta\begin{vmatrix} p''(x) & q''(x) & r''(x) \\ d_1 & d_2 & d_3 \\ a_1 & a_2 & a_3 \end{vmatrix} = 0$$

since $f'''(x) = 0$. $\therefore f''(x)$ is a constant and hence independent of x.

39. Prove that $\begin{vmatrix} \cos\theta & \cos 2\theta & \cos 3\theta \\ \cos 3\theta & \cos\theta & \cos 2\theta \\ \cos 2\theta & \cos 3\theta & \cos\theta \end{vmatrix}$

$$= 2\sin\frac{3\theta}{2}\left(\sin^3\frac{5\theta}{2} - \sin^3\frac{3\theta}{2}\right)$$

Solution: Applying $C_1 \to C_1 + C_2 + C_3$ followed by $R_2 \to R_2 - R_1$ and $R_3 \to R_3 - R_1$ and expanding along C_1, so that the determinant is

$$\begin{vmatrix} \cos\theta + \cos 2\theta + \cos 3\theta & \cos 2\theta & \cos 3\theta \\ \cos\theta + \cos 2\theta + \cos 3\theta & \cos\theta & \cos 2\theta \\ \cos\theta + \cos 2\theta + \cos 3\theta & \cos 3\theta & \cos\theta \end{vmatrix}$$

$$= (\cos\theta + \cos 2\theta + \cos 3\theta)\begin{vmatrix} 1 & \cos 2\theta & \cos 3\theta \\ 1 & \cos\theta & \cos 2\theta \\ 1 & \cos 3\theta & \cos\theta \end{vmatrix}$$

$= (\cos\theta + \cos 2\theta + \cos 3\theta)$

$$\begin{vmatrix} 1 & \cos 2\theta & \cos 3\theta \\ 0 & \cos\theta - \cos 2\theta & \cos 2\theta - \cos 3\theta \\ 0 & \cos 3\theta - \cos 2\theta & \cos\theta - \cos 3\theta \end{vmatrix}$$

$= (\cos\theta + \cos 2\theta + \cos 3\theta) \times \{(\cos\theta - \cos 2\theta)(\cos\theta - \cos 3\theta) + (\cos 3\theta - \cos 2\theta)^2\}$

This can be simplified using the results.

$(\cos\theta + \cos 2\theta + \cos 3\theta) = 2\cos 2\theta\cos\theta + \cos 2\theta = \cos 2\theta(2\cos\theta + 1)$; Also, $(\cos\theta - \cos 2\theta)$

$$= 2\sin\frac{\theta + 2\theta}{2}\sin\frac{2\theta - \theta}{2} = 2\sin\frac{3\theta}{2}\sin\frac{\theta}{2} \text{ and}$$

$$\cos\theta - \cos 3\theta = 2\sin\frac{\theta + 3\theta}{2}\sin\frac{3\theta - \theta}{2} = 2\sin 2\theta\sin\theta$$

$$\text{and } \cos 3\theta - \cos 2\theta = -2\sin\frac{5\theta}{2}\sin\frac{\theta}{2}$$

Now, the determinant now be written as $\cos 2\theta(2\cos\theta + 1)\left(4\sin\frac{3\theta}{2}\sin\frac{\theta}{2}\sin 2\theta\sin\theta + 4\sin^2\frac{\theta}{2}\sin^2\frac{5\theta}{2}\right)$

$$= 4\sin^2\frac{\theta}{2}(\cos 2\theta)(2\cos\theta + 1)$$

$$\left(\sin\frac{3\theta}{2}\sin 2\theta\,(2\cos\theta/2) + \sin^2\frac{5\theta}{2}\right)$$

Further simplification follows after noting that

$$\sin\frac{\theta}{2}(2\cos\theta + 1) = \sin\frac{\theta}{2}\left[1 + 2(1 - 2\sin^2(\theta/2)\right]$$

$$= \sin\frac{\theta}{2}\left[3 - 4\sin^2\left(\frac{\theta}{2}\right)\right] = 3\sin\frac{\theta}{2} - 4\sin^3\left(\frac{\theta}{2}\right) = \sin\frac{3\theta}{2}$$

And $4\sin(\theta/2)\cos 2\theta = 2\left(2\sin\frac{\theta}{2}\cos 2\theta\right)$

$$= 2\left[\sin\left(2\theta + \frac{\theta}{2}\right) - \sin\left(2\theta - \frac{\theta}{2}\right)\right]$$

$$= 2\left[\sin\frac{5\theta}{2} - \sin\frac{3\theta}{2}\right]$$

$$\text{and } 2\cos\frac{\theta}{2}\sin 2\theta = \sin\left(2\theta + \frac{\theta}{2}\right) + \sin\left(2\theta - \frac{\theta}{2}\right)$$

$$= \sin\frac{5\theta}{2} + \sin\frac{3\theta}{2}$$

After substituting these results, the determinants become

$$2\sin\frac{3\theta}{2}\left[\sin\frac{5\theta}{2} - \sin\frac{3\theta}{2}\right]$$

$$\left[\sin\frac{3\theta}{2}\left(\sin\frac{5\theta}{2} + \sin\frac{3\theta}{2}\right) + \sin^2\frac{5\theta}{2}\right]$$

$$= 2\sin\frac{3\theta}{2}\left[\sin^3\frac{5\theta}{2} - \sin^3\frac{3\theta}{2}\right]$$

Using the identity $(a - b)(a^2 + ab + b^2) = (a^3 - b^3)$. This proves the result.

SECTION–II

OBJECTIVE SOLVED EXAMPLES

1. If x, y, z are integers in AP, lying between 1 and 9, and $x51$, $y41$, and $z31$ are three digit numbers, then the value of $\begin{vmatrix} 5 & 4 & 3 \\ x51 & y41 & z31 \\ x & y & z \end{vmatrix}$ is

(a) $x+y+z$ (b) $x-y+z$
(c) 0 (d) None of these

Solution: (c)

$$\Delta = \begin{vmatrix} 5 & 4 & 3 \\ 100x+50+1 & 100y+40+1 & 100z+30+1 \\ x & y & z \end{vmatrix}$$

$$= \begin{vmatrix} 5 & 4 & 3 \\ 1 & 1 & 1 \\ x & y & z \end{vmatrix} \quad (R_2 \to R_2 - 100R_3 - 10\,R_1)$$

$$= x - 2y + z = 0 \quad (\because x, y, z \text{ are in } A.P.)$$

2. If $f(x) = \begin{vmatrix} 1 & x & x+1 \\ 2x & x(x-1) & x(x+1) \\ 3x(x-1) & x(x-1)(x-2) & x(x^2-1) \end{vmatrix}$, then $f(100)$ is equal to

(a) 0 (b) 1
(c) 100 (d) –100

Solution: (a) $f(x) = x.\,x.\,(x-1)\begin{vmatrix} 1 & x & x+1 \\ 2 & (x-1) & x+1 \\ 3 & (x-2) & x+1 \end{vmatrix}$

(Taking x common from R_2 and $x\,(x-1)$ from R_3)

$$= x^2(x-1)\begin{vmatrix} 1 & x & 1 \\ 2 & (x-1) & 2 \\ 3 & (x-2) & 3 \end{vmatrix} = 0 \text{ for all } x$$

(operating $C_3 \to C_3 - C_2$) $\therefore\ f(100) = 0$

3. If the determinant $\begin{vmatrix} \cos 2x & \sin^2 x & \cos 4x \\ \sin^2 x & \cos 2x & \cos^2 x \\ \cos 4x & \cos^2 x & \cos 2x \end{vmatrix}$ is exapanded in terms of sinx, then the constant term in the expansion is

(a) 1 (b) 2
(c) –1 (d) None of these

Solution: (c) The constant term = value of the determinant at $x = 0$.

4. If the system of equations $ax + by + c = 0$; $bx + cy + a = 0$; $cx + ay + b = 0$ has a non–trivial solution, then the system of equations.
$(b+c)x + (c+a)y + (a-b)z = 0$; $(c+a)x + (a+b)y + (b+c)z = 0$, $(a+b)x + (b+c)y + (c+a)z = 0$ has;

(a) only one solution
(b) no solution
(c) infinite number of solutions
(d) None of these

Solution: (c) For existence of a non–trivial solution of the first system $\begin{vmatrix} a & b & c \\ b & c & a \\ c & a & b \end{vmatrix} = 0$

$$\Rightarrow (a+b+c)\begin{vmatrix} 1 & b & c \\ 1 & c & a \\ 1 & a & b \end{vmatrix} = 0$$

$$\Rightarrow \begin{vmatrix} 1 & b & c \\ 1 & c & a \\ 1 & a & b \end{vmatrix} = 0 \text{ or } (a+b+c) = 0$$

$$\Rightarrow \begin{vmatrix} 1 & b & c \\ 0 & c-b & a-c \\ 0 & a-b & b-c \end{vmatrix} = 0 \text{ or } (a+b+c) = 0$$

$$\Rightarrow \begin{vmatrix} c-b & a-c \\ a-b & b-c \end{vmatrix} = 0 \text{ or } (a+b+c) = 0 \quad \text{.... (i)}$$

The second system will have a non-trivial solution if we can prove that $\Delta = \begin{vmatrix} b+c & c+a & a+b \\ c+a & a+b & b+c \\ a+b & b+c & c+a \end{vmatrix} = 0$

Now, $\Delta = 2(a+b+c)\begin{vmatrix} 1 & c+a & a+b \\ 1 & a+b & b+c \\ 1 & b+c & c+a \end{vmatrix}$

$$= 2(a+b+c)\begin{vmatrix} 1 & c+a & a+b \\ 0 & b-c & c-a \\ 0 & b-a & c-b \end{vmatrix}$$

$$= 2(a+b+c)\begin{vmatrix} b-c & c-a \\ b-a & c-b \end{vmatrix}$$

$$= 2(a+b+c)\begin{vmatrix} c-b & a-c \\ a-b & b-c \end{vmatrix} = 0 \text{ (using equation (i))}$$

$\therefore$ The second system will have a non-trivial solution.

Note:

Remember that the existence of one nontrivial solution implies existence of infinite number of nontrivial solutions for homogeneous equations.

5. If $\begin{vmatrix} b^2+c^2 & ab & ac \\ ba & c^2+a^2 & bc \\ ca & cb & a^2+b^2 \end{vmatrix}$ = square of determinant Δ of the third order, then Δ is equal to

(a) $\begin{vmatrix} 0 & c & b \\ c & 0 & a \\ b & a & 0 \end{vmatrix}$ (b) $\begin{vmatrix} a & b & c \\ b & c & a \\ c & a & b \end{vmatrix}$

(c) $\begin{vmatrix} 0 & -c & b \\ c & 0 & -a \\ -b & -a & 0 \end{vmatrix}$ (d) None of these

Solution: (a) Check $\begin{vmatrix} 0 & c & b \\ c & 0 & a \\ b & a & 0 \end{vmatrix} \times \begin{vmatrix} 0 & c & b \\ c & 0 & a \\ b & a & 0 \end{vmatrix}$ = the given determinant

6. If $\Delta_1 = \begin{vmatrix} x & b & b \\ a & x & b \\ a & a & x \end{vmatrix}$ and $\Delta_2 = \begin{vmatrix} x & b \\ a & x \end{vmatrix}$ are the given determinants, then

(a) $\Delta_1 = 3(\Delta_2)^2$ (b) $(d/dx)\Delta_1 = 3\Delta_2$

(c) $\frac{d}{dx}\Delta_1 = 3(\Delta_2)^2$ (d) $\Delta_1 = 3(\Delta_2)^{3/2}$

Solution: (b) $\frac{d}{dx}\Delta_1 = \begin{vmatrix} 1 & 0 & 0 \\ a & x & b \\ a & a & x \end{vmatrix} + \begin{vmatrix} x & b & b \\ 0 & 1 & 0 \\ a & a & x \end{vmatrix} + \begin{vmatrix} x & b & b \\ a & x & b \\ 0 & 0 & 1 \end{vmatrix}$

$$= \begin{vmatrix} x & b \\ a & x \end{vmatrix} + \begin{vmatrix} x & b \\ a & x \end{vmatrix} + \begin{vmatrix} x & b \\ a & x \end{vmatrix} = 3\Delta_2$$

7. In a quadrilateral $ABCD$.

Let $\Delta = \begin{vmatrix} \cos A & \sin A & \cos(A+D) \\ \cos B & \sin B & \cos(B+D) \\ \cos C & \sin C & \cos(C+D) \end{vmatrix}$, then Δ is

(a) independent of A and B only
(b) independent of B and C only
(c) independent of A, B and C only
(d) independent of A, B, C and D all

Solution: (d) Applying $C_3 \to C_3 - C_1 \cos D + C_2 \sin D$
So $\Delta = 0$, hence Δ is independent of A, B, C and D all.

8. If $A + B + C = \pi$, then $\begin{vmatrix} \sin(A+B+C) & \sin B & \cos C \\ -\sin B & 0 & \tan A \\ \cos(A+B) & -\tan A & 0 \end{vmatrix}$ is equal to

(a) $\sin A \sin B \sin C$ (b) 0
(c) $\sin^2(A+B+C)$ (d) None of these

Solution: (b) Above is skew symmetric determinant of odd order because $\cos(A+B) = -\cos C$ and $\sin(A+B+C) = 0$, therefore its value is zero.

9. If ω is a cube root of unity, then a root of the equation $\begin{vmatrix} x+1 & \omega & \omega^2 \\ \omega & x+\omega^2 & 1 \\ \omega^2 & 1 & x+\omega \end{vmatrix} = 0$ is

(a) $x = 1$ (b) $x = \omega$
(c) $x = \omega^2$ (d) $x = 0$

Solution: (d) Let $\Delta = \begin{vmatrix} x+1 & \omega & \omega^2 \\ \omega & x+\omega^2 & 1 \\ \omega^2 & 1 & x+\omega \end{vmatrix}$

Apply $C_1 \to C_1 + C_2 + C_3$

$$\Delta = \begin{vmatrix} x+1+\omega+\omega^2 & \omega & \omega^2 \\ x+1+\omega+\omega^2 & x+\omega^2 & 1 \\ x+1+\omega+\omega^2 & 1 & x+\omega \end{vmatrix}$$

$\because [1+\omega+\omega^2 = 0]$

$$= x\begin{vmatrix} 1 & 1 & 1 \\ \omega & x+\omega^2 & 1 \\ \omega^2 & 1 & x+\omega \end{vmatrix} \quad \therefore x = 0 \Rightarrow \Delta = 0$$

Hence, $x = 0$ is one of the roots of the equation.

10. For $\begin{vmatrix} \cos^2\theta & \cos\theta\sin\theta & -\sin\theta \\ \cos\theta\sin\theta & \sin^2\theta & \cos\theta \\ \sin\theta & -\cos\theta & 0 \end{vmatrix}$, $f(\theta)$ is equal to

(a) 0 (b) 1
(c) 2 (d) None of these

Solution: Applying $C_1 \to C_1 - \sin\theta \,.\, C_3$; $C_2 \to C_2 + \cos\theta \,.\, C_3$

$$\Rightarrow f(\theta) = \begin{vmatrix} 1 & 0 & -\sin\theta \\ 0 & 1 & \cos\theta \\ \sin\theta & -\cos\theta & 0 \end{vmatrix}$$

Apply $R_3 \to R_3 - R_1 \sin\theta + R_2 \cos\theta$

$$\Rightarrow f(\theta) = \begin{vmatrix} 1 & 0 & -\sin\theta \\ 0 & 1 & \cos\theta \\ 0 & 0 & 1 \end{vmatrix} = 1$$

$\Rightarrow f(\theta) = 1$ for all θ, it is an identity.

11. The values of θ lying between $\theta = 0$ and $\theta = \dfrac{\pi}{2}$ and satisfying the equation,
$$\begin{vmatrix} 1+\sin^2\theta & \cos^2\theta & 4\sin 4\theta \\ \sin^2\theta & 1+\cos^2\theta & 4\sin 4\theta \\ \sin^2\theta & \cos^2\theta & 1+4\sin 4\theta \end{vmatrix} = 0 \text{ are:}$$

(a) $\dfrac{5\pi}{24}$ (b) $\dfrac{11\pi}{24}$

(c) $\dfrac{\pi}{24}$ (d) $\dfrac{7\pi}{24}$

Solution: (b) and (d) Using $R_1 \to R_1 - R_3$ and $R_2 \to R_2 - R_3$; we get $\Delta = \begin{vmatrix} 1 & 0 & -1 \\ 0 & 1 & -1 \\ \sin^2\theta & \cos^2\theta & 1+4\sin 4\theta \end{vmatrix}$

Apply $C_1 \to C_1 + C_2$

$$\Rightarrow \Delta = \begin{vmatrix} 1 & 0 & -1 \\ 1 & 1 & -1 \\ 1 & \cos^2\theta & 1+4\sin 4\theta \end{vmatrix}$$

Apply $C_1 \to C_1 + C_3$

$$\Rightarrow \Delta = \begin{vmatrix} 0 & 0 & -1 \\ 0 & 1 & -1 \\ 2+4\sin 4\theta & \cos^2\theta & 1+4\sin 4\theta \end{vmatrix}$$

Expanding along C_1 and solving $(2 + 4\sin 4\theta) = 0$

$\Rightarrow \sin 4\theta = -1/2$

$\Rightarrow 4\theta = \dfrac{7\pi}{6}, \dfrac{11\pi}{6} \quad \Rightarrow \theta = \dfrac{7\pi}{24}, \dfrac{11\pi}{24}$

12. If the system of the equation $ax + by + cz = 0$, $bx + cy + az = 0$ and $cx + ay + bz = 0$ has non-zero solution, then which of the following may be true?

(a) $a + b + c = 0$

(b) $a = b = c$

(c) $(a - b)^2 + (b - c)^2 + (c - a)^2 = 0$

(d) None of these

Solution: $\begin{vmatrix} a & b & c \\ b & c & a \\ c & a & b \end{vmatrix} = 0$

$\Rightarrow a(bc - a^2) + c(ab - c^2) - b(b^2 - ac) = 0$

$\Rightarrow -a^3 - c^3 - b^3 + 3abc = 0$

$\Rightarrow a^3 + b^3 + c^3 - 3abc = 0$

$\Rightarrow (a + b + c)(a^2 + b^2 + c^2 - ab - bc - ca) = 0$

Hence (a), (b), (c) follows.

13. The value of
$$\Delta = \begin{vmatrix} \cos(\pi/3) & \cos(2\pi/3) & 1 \\ -1 & \cos(\pi/3) & \cos(2\pi/3) \\ \cos(\pi/3) & -1 & \cos(\pi/3) \end{vmatrix}$$ is equal to:

(a) 2 (b) 1/2

(c) −1/2 (d) 1

Solution: (b) $\begin{vmatrix} 1/2 & -1/2 & 1 \\ -1 & 1/2 & -1/2 \\ 1/2 & -1 & 1/2 \end{vmatrix} = \dfrac{1}{8}\begin{vmatrix} 1 & -1 & 2 \\ -2 & 1 & -1 \\ 1 & -2 & 1 \end{vmatrix}$

$\Rightarrow \dfrac{1}{8}(4) = \dfrac{1}{2}$.

14. The value of the determinant $\begin{vmatrix} x & x+a & x+2a \\ x+1 & x+2a & x+4a \\ x+2 & x+3a & x+6a \end{vmatrix}$ is:

(a) 0 (b) $a^3 - x^3$

(c) $x^3 - a^3$ (d) $(x - a)^3$

Solution: Given $\Delta = \begin{vmatrix} x & x+a & x+2a \\ x+1 & x+2a & x+4a \\ x+2 & x+3a & x+6a \end{vmatrix}$

$R_3 \to R_3 - R_2$ and $R_2 \to R_2 - R_1$

$$\Rightarrow \Delta = \begin{vmatrix} x & x+a & x+2a \\ 1 & a & 2a \\ 1 & a & 2a \end{vmatrix} = 0$$

15. The value of a for which the system of equations, $a^3x + (a + 1)^3 y + (a + 2)^3 z = 0$; $ax + (a + 1)y + (a + 2)z = 0$; $x + y + z = 0$; has a non – zero solution is:

(a) 1 (b) 0

(c) −1 (d) None of these

Solution: $\begin{vmatrix} a^3 & (a+1)^3 & (a+2)^3 \\ a & (a+1) & (a+2) \\ 1 & 1 & 1 \end{vmatrix} = 0$

$C_3 \to C_3 - C_2$ and $C_2 \to C_2 - C_1$

$$\begin{vmatrix} a^3 & \begin{pmatrix} (a+1)^2 + a^2 + \\ a(a+1) \end{pmatrix} & \begin{pmatrix} (a+2)^2 + (a+1)^2 + \\ (a+1)(a+2) \end{pmatrix} \\ a & 1 & 1 \\ 1 & 0 & 0 \end{vmatrix}$$

$= a^2 + a(a+1) - (a+2)^2 - (a+1)(a+2) = 0$

$\Rightarrow a = -1$

16. If a, b and c are non – zero real numbers then $\Delta = \begin{vmatrix} b^2c^2 & bc & b+c \\ c^2a^2 & ca & c+a \\ a^2b^2 & ab & a+b \end{vmatrix}$ is equal to

(a) abc (b) $a^2b^2c^2$

(c) $bc + ca + ab$ (d) zero

Solution: (d) The given determinant is

$$\Delta = \begin{vmatrix} b^2c^2 & bc & b+c \\ c^2a^2 & ca & c+a \\ a^2b^2 & ab & a+b \end{vmatrix}$$

$$\Rightarrow \Delta = a^2b^2c^2 \begin{vmatrix} bc & 1 & 1/b + 1/c \\ ca & 1 & 1/c + 1/a \\ ab & 1 & 1/a + 1/b \end{vmatrix}$$

(Applying $R_1 \to R_1 - R_2$ and $R_2 \to R_2 - R_3$)

$$\Rightarrow \Delta = a^2b^2c^2 \begin{vmatrix} c(b-a) & 0 & 1/b - 1/a \\ a(c-b) & 0 & 1/c - 1/b \\ ab & 1 & 1/a + 1/b \end{vmatrix}$$

$$\Rightarrow \Delta = a^2b^2c^2 \begin{vmatrix} c(b-a) & 0 & -\frac{(b-a)}{ab} \\ a(c-b) & 0 & -\frac{(c-b)}{bc} \\ ab & 1 & \frac{1}{a}+\frac{1}{b} \end{vmatrix}$$

$$\Delta = a^2b^2c^2(b-a)(c-b) \begin{vmatrix} c & 0 & -\frac{1}{ab} \\ a & 0 & -\frac{1}{bc} \\ ab & 1 & \frac{1}{a}+\frac{1}{b} \end{vmatrix}$$

(expanding along C_2)

$\Rightarrow a^2b^2c^2(b-a)(c-b) \cdot \left(-\frac{1}{b}+\frac{1}{b}\right) = 0$. therefore (d) is correct answer.

17. If $A + B + C = \pi$, then the value of the determinant $\Delta = \begin{vmatrix} \sin^2 A & \cot A & 1 \\ \sin^2 B & \cot B & 1 \\ \sin^2 C & \cot C & 1 \end{vmatrix}$ is

(a) 1 (b) –1

(c) 0 (d) None of these

Solution: $\Delta = \begin{vmatrix} \sin^2 A & \cot A & 1 \\ \sin^2 B & \cot B & 1 \\ \sin^2 C & \cot C & 1 \end{vmatrix}$

Applying $R_2 \to R_2 - R_1$ and $R_3 \to R_3 - R_1$

$$\Rightarrow \Delta = \begin{vmatrix} \sin^2 A & \cot A & 1 \\ \sin(B+A)\sin(B-A) & \frac{\sin(A-B)}{\sin A \sin B} & 0 \\ \sin(C+A)\sin(C-A) & \frac{\sin(A-C)}{\sin A \sin C} & 0 \end{vmatrix}$$

Expanding along C_3, we get

$$\Delta = \frac{\sin(A-B)\sin(A-C)}{\sin A}\left[-\frac{1}{\sin A}+\frac{1}{\sin A}\right] = 0$$

18. The absolute value of the determinant $\begin{vmatrix} -1 & 2 & 1 \\ 3+2\sqrt{2} & 2+2\sqrt{2} & 1 \\ 3-2\sqrt{2} & 2-2\sqrt{2} & 1 \end{vmatrix}$ is:

(a) $16\sqrt{2}$ (b) $8\sqrt{2}$

(c) 8 (d) None of these

Solution: (a) $\begin{vmatrix} -1 & 2 & 1 \\ 3+2\sqrt{2} & 2+2\sqrt{2} & 1 \\ 3-2\sqrt{2} & 2-2\sqrt{2} & 1 \end{vmatrix}$

Operate $C_1 \to C_1 - (C_2 + C_3)$

$$= \Delta = \begin{vmatrix} -4 & 2 & 1 \\ 0 & 2+2\sqrt{2} & 1 \\ 0 & 2-2\sqrt{2} & 1 \end{vmatrix} = (-4)(4\sqrt{2})$$

$= 2[-4(2 + 2\sqrt{2} - 2)]$

$= -16\sqrt{2}$. Absolute value $= 16\sqrt{2}$.

19. If $\Delta_r = \begin{vmatrix} x & y & z \\ 2^r & 2 \times 3^r & 3 \times 4^r \\ 2(2^n - 1) & 3(3^n - 1) & 4(4^n - 1) \end{vmatrix}$, then the value of $\sum_{r=1}^{n} \Delta_r$

(a) $x + y + z$ (b) n

(c) 1 (d) 0

Solution: (d) $\Delta_r = \begin{vmatrix} x & y & z \\ 2^r & 2 \times 3^r & 3 \times 4^r \\ 2(2^n - 1) & 3(3^n - 1) & 4(4^n - 1) \end{vmatrix}$

$\therefore \quad x^2+y^2=\dfrac{a^2}{(m^2+1)^2}=\left[(m^2+2m-1)^2+(m^2-2m-1)^2\right]$

$\therefore \quad \dfrac{a^2}{(m^2+1)^2}[2m^4+8m^2+2-4m^2]$

$=\dfrac{2a^2}{(m^2+1)}(m^4+2m^2+1)=2a^2 \;\therefore\; x^2+y^2=2a^2$

5. $x+y-4=0;\; 2x-3y-9=0$

$$\frac{x}{\begin{vmatrix}1 & -4\\ -3 & -9\end{vmatrix}}=\frac{y}{\begin{vmatrix}-4 & 1\\ -9 & 2\end{vmatrix}}=\frac{1}{\begin{vmatrix}1 & 1\\ 2 & -3\end{vmatrix}}$$

Gives $x=\dfrac{21}{5}=4.2$ and $y=-\dfrac{1}{5}=-0.2$

6 Homogenous system

(a) $\Delta \neq 0$, number of trivial sol = 1
(b) $\Delta = 0$, number of solutions are infinite
(c) $\Delta = 0$, for non-trival sol of homogenous system
(d) Consistancy of homogenous system of equation is always there

7. Given: $ax+hy+g=0$ .... (i)
$hx+by+f=0$ ....(ii)
and $x(ax+hy+g)+y(hx+by+f)+gx+fy+c-t=0$
or $gx+fy+c-t=0$ ....(iii)
(i) and (ii) are linear in x and y so any solution to these will also solve (iii)

$$\therefore \begin{vmatrix}a & h & g\\ h & b & f\\ g & f & (c-t)\end{vmatrix}=0, \text{ i.e., } \begin{vmatrix}a & h & g\\ h & b & f\\ g & f & c\end{vmatrix}+\begin{vmatrix}a & h & 0\\ h & b & 0\\ g & f & -t\end{vmatrix}=0$$

$\Rightarrow \{abc+2fgh-af^2-bg^2-ch^2\}-t(ab-h^2)=0$

$$\text{Gives } t=\frac{(abc+2fgh-af^2-bg^2-ch^2)}{ab-h^2}=\frac{\begin{vmatrix}a & h & g\\ h & b & f\\ g & f & c\end{vmatrix}}{\begin{vmatrix}a & h\\ h & b\end{vmatrix}}$$

8. $x+y+z=1$ ..... (i)
$x+3y-2z=1$ ....(ii)
$3x+(\lambda+2)y-3z=2\lambda+1$ ....(iii)

$$|A|=\begin{vmatrix}1 & 1 & 1\\ 1 & 3 & -2\\ 3 & (\lambda+2) & -3\end{vmatrix}=\begin{vmatrix}1 & 0 & 0\\ 1 & 2 & -3\\ 3 & (\lambda-1) & -6\end{vmatrix}=3\lambda-15$$

If $|A|=0$ then $\lambda=5$
We observe (i) + 2 (ii), gives $3x+7y-3z=3$
And for $\lambda=5$ (iii) is $3x+7y-3z=11$. So inconsistent.
$\Rightarrow \lambda \neq 5$ i.e., $|A| \neq 0$ then
$3x+7y-3z=3$; $3x+(\lambda+2)y-3z=2\lambda+1$
Gives $(\lambda-5)y=2\lambda-2$

$\Rightarrow \quad y=\dfrac{2(\lambda-1)}{\lambda-5}$ where $\lambda \neq 5$

Putting in (i) and (ii) $x+\dfrac{2\lambda-2}{\lambda-5}+z=1$ i.e., $x+z=\dfrac{-(\lambda+3)}{\lambda-5}$

And $x+\dfrac{6\lambda-6}{\lambda-5}-2z=1$ i.e., $x-2z=\dfrac{-(5\lambda-1)}{\lambda-5}$

Subtraction gives $z=\dfrac{4\lambda-4}{3(\lambda-5)}$

Similarly $x=\dfrac{-7\lambda-5}{3(\lambda-5)}$ and $y=\dfrac{2\lambda-2}{\lambda-5}$

9. $2x+3y=3$
$(c+2)x+(c+4)y=(c+6)$
$(c+2)^2x+(c+4)^2y=(c+6)^2$
Will be consistent (the concurrent lines or three superimposed lines)

$$\text{i.e., } \begin{vmatrix}2 & 3 & 3\\ (c+2) & (c+4) & (c+6)\\ (c+2)^2 & (c+4)^2 & (c+6)^2\end{vmatrix}=0$$

$$\text{gives } \begin{vmatrix}2 & 1 & 0\\ c+2 & 2 & 2\\ (c-2)^2 & (4c+12) & (4c+20)\end{vmatrix}$$

$=2(8c+40-8c-24)-(2c^2+20c+32)=0$
Gives $(-2c)(c+10)=0$ gives $c=0,-10$

TEXTUAL EXERCISE 6: (OBJECTIVE)

1. (b) $\Delta=\begin{vmatrix}1 & 1 & 1\\ 1 & 3 & 2\\ 1 & \lambda & 3\end{vmatrix}=\begin{vmatrix}1 & 1 & 1\\ 0 & 2 & 1\\ 0 & \lambda-1 & 2\end{vmatrix}=5-\lambda\neq 0$

Gives $\lambda \neq 5$ (now $\mu \in \mathbb{R}$)

2 (a) $\Delta=\begin{vmatrix}1 & 1 & 1\\ 1 & 3 & 2\\ 1 & \lambda & 3\end{vmatrix}=0$ for no solution (i.e., $\lambda=5$)

Also at least one of $\Delta_x, \Delta_y, \Delta_z$ is non zero.

Consider $\Delta_x=\begin{vmatrix}3 & 1 & 1\\ 6 & 3 & 2\\ \mu & 5 & 3\end{vmatrix}=\begin{vmatrix}3 & 1 & 1\\ 0 & 1 & 0\\ \mu-9 & 2 & 0\end{vmatrix}=-\mu+9\neq 0$

$\Rightarrow \mu \neq 9;\; \Delta_y=\begin{vmatrix}1 & 3 & 1\\ 1 & 6 & 2\\ 1 & \mu & 3\end{vmatrix}=\begin{vmatrix}1 & 1 & 1\\ 0 & 3 & 1\\ 0 & (\mu-3) & 2\end{vmatrix}$

$=6+3-\mu\neq 0$, i.e., $\mu \neq 9$

3. (c) $x+y+z=3$ .... (i)
$x+3y+2z=6$ ....(ii)
$x+\lambda y+3z=\mu$ ....(iii)
2(ii) – (i) gives $x+5y+3z=9$
Comparing with (iii) $\lambda=5,\ \mu=9$
And it will give infinitely many solutions

(using $1 + \omega + \omega^2 = 0$)

$$\Delta = \begin{vmatrix} 1+\omega^2 & \omega & \omega \\ 1 & \omega+\omega^2 & 1 \\ \omega^2 & \omega^2 & 1+\omega \end{vmatrix}$$

$$\Rightarrow \Delta = \begin{vmatrix} 1+\omega^2 & (1+\omega+\omega^2=0) & \omega \\ 1 & 0 & 1 \\ \omega^2 & 2\omega^2 & \omega^2 \end{vmatrix}$$

$(-2\omega^2)(1 + \omega^2 - \omega) = (-2\omega^2)(-2\omega) = 4\omega^3 = 4$

$\Rightarrow \text{Im}(\Delta) = 0;\ \text{Re}(\Delta) + \text{Im}(\Delta) = 4$

32. (a) Column wise differentiation gives

$$f'(x) = \begin{vmatrix} 1 & x^2+1 & 1 \\ 1 & 2x^2-1 & 1 \\ 1 & 3x^2-2 & 1 \end{vmatrix} + \begin{vmatrix} x+a & 2x & 1 \\ x+b & 4x & 1 \\ x+c & 6x & 1 \end{vmatrix} + \begin{vmatrix} x+a & (x^2+1) & 0 \\ x+b & (2x^2-1) & 0 \\ x+c & (3x^2-2) & 0 \end{vmatrix}$$

Operating, $R_1 \to R_1 + R_3 - 2R_2$ gives zeroes in R_2 of middle determinant.

$\Rightarrow f'(x) = 0 + 0 + 0 = 0$

33. (c) $f(x) = \begin{vmatrix} \sin x & \sin 2x & \sin 3x \\ 0 & 3 & 4\sin x \\ 0 & \sin x & 1 \end{vmatrix}$

$= \sin x \{3 - 4\sin^2 x\} = \sin 3x$

$$\Rightarrow I = \int_0^{\pi/2} \sin 3x\, dx = \left.\frac{-\cos 3x}{3}\right|_0^{\pi/2} = \left(-\frac{1}{3}\right)\{0-1\} = \frac{1}{3}$$

34. (d) (a)

$$\Delta = \frac{1}{abc}\begin{vmatrix} a & abc & abc(b+c) \\ b & abc & abc(c+a) \\ c & abc & abc(a+b) \end{vmatrix} = \frac{(abc)^2}{(abc)}\begin{vmatrix} a & 1 & b+c \\ b & 1 & c+a \\ c & 1 & a+b \end{vmatrix}$$

$$= (abc)(a+b+c)\begin{vmatrix} 1 & 1 & (b+c) \\ 1 & 1 & (c+a) \\ 1 & 1 & (a+b) \end{vmatrix} = 0$$

$$\text{(ii) } \Delta = abc\begin{vmatrix} 1 & \frac{1}{c} & \frac{1}{a}+\frac{1}{b} \\ 1 & \frac{1}{a} & \frac{1}{b}+\frac{1}{c} \\ 1 & \frac{1}{b} & \frac{1}{a}+\frac{1}{c} \end{vmatrix}$$

Operate $C_3 \to C_2 + C_3$ and takeout $\left(\frac{1}{a}+\frac{1}{b}+\frac{1}{c}\right)$, then

$$\Delta = abc\left\{\frac{1}{a}+\frac{1}{b}+\frac{1}{c}\right\}\begin{vmatrix} 1 & 1/c & 1 \\ 1 & 1/a & 1 \\ 1 & 1/b & 1 \end{vmatrix} = 0$$

(c) $$\Delta = \begin{vmatrix} \frac{\ell n\, xyz}{\ell n\, x} & \frac{\ell n\, y}{\ell n\, x} & \frac{\ell n\, z}{\ell n\, x} \\ \frac{\ell n\, xyz}{\ell n\, y} & \frac{\ell n\, y}{\ell n\, y} & \frac{\ell n\, z}{\ell n\, y} \\ \frac{\ell n\, xyz}{\ell n\, z} & \frac{\ell n\, y}{\ell n\, z} & \frac{\ell n\, z}{\ell n\, z} \end{vmatrix}$$

$$= \frac{1}{\log_e x \log_e y \log_e z} \times \begin{vmatrix} \log_e x & \log_e y & \log_e z \\ \log_e x & \log_e y & \log_e z \\ \log_e x & \log_e y & \log_e z \end{vmatrix},$$

since $R_1 = R_2 = R_3$

$\therefore$ $\Delta = 0$ so all determinants are vanishing

35. (b) $\Delta = \begin{vmatrix} a & b & a\alpha+b \\ b & c & b\alpha+c \\ a\alpha+b & b\alpha+c & 0 \end{vmatrix}$

$C_3 \to C_3 - (\alpha C_1 + C_2)$ gives

$$\begin{vmatrix} a & b & 0 \\ b & c & 0 \\ a\alpha+b & b\alpha+c & -(a\alpha^2+2b\alpha+c) \end{vmatrix}$$

$= -(ac - b^2)(a\alpha^2 + 2b\alpha + c)$

$\therefore$ $\Delta = 0$ if a,b,c are in G.P.

36. (d) Since $a,b,c,d > 0$

$(a^2 + b^2 + c^2)x^2 - 2(ab + bc + cd)x + (b^2 + c^2 + d^2) \le 0$

$(ax - b)^2 + (bx - c)^2 + (cx - d)^2 \le 0$

$\Rightarrow x = \frac{b}{a} = \frac{c}{b} = \frac{d}{c}$ or a, b, c, d are in G.P. with common ratio x.

$$\text{Now } \Delta = \begin{vmatrix} 33 & 14 & \log_e a \\ 65 & 27 & \log_e b \\ 97 & 40 & \log_e c \end{vmatrix} = \begin{vmatrix} 33 & 14 & \log_e a \\ -1 & -1 & \log_e\left(\frac{b}{a}\right) \\ -2 & -2 & \log_e\left(\frac{c}{a}\right) \end{vmatrix}$$

(using $R_2 \to R_2 - 2R_1$ and $R_3 \to R_3 - 3R_1$)

$$= \begin{vmatrix} 33 & 14 & \ell n\, a \\ -1 & -1 & \ell n\left(\frac{b}{a}\right) \\ 0 & 0 & \ell n\left(\frac{ca}{b^2}\right) \end{vmatrix} = (-19)\ell n\left(\frac{ca}{b^2}\right)$$

Since $b^2 = ac \Rightarrow \Delta = -19\ ln 1 = 0$

37. (d) Let the determinant of 2×2 is $\begin{vmatrix} a_{11} & a_{12} \\ a_{21} & a_{22} \end{vmatrix}$.

$\therefore$ Total number of determinants under the given conditions $= 2^4 = 16$

Now $\begin{vmatrix}1 & 1\\ 1 & 0\end{vmatrix} = \begin{vmatrix}0 & 1\\ 1 & 0\end{vmatrix} = \begin{vmatrix}0 & 1\\ 1 & 1\end{vmatrix} = -1$ are the only determinants with –ve values

∴ number of non-negative determinants = 13

38. (a) $\Delta = \begin{vmatrix}\alpha & -\beta & 0\\ 0 & \alpha & \beta\\ \beta & 0 & \alpha\end{vmatrix} = \alpha^3 - \beta^3 = 0$

$\Rightarrow (\alpha - \beta)\{\alpha^2 + \beta^2 + \alpha\beta\} = 0$

$\Rightarrow \alpha = \beta$ or $\left(\dfrac{\alpha}{\beta}\right)^2 + \left(\dfrac{\alpha}{\beta}\right) + 1 = 0$ but $\alpha \neq \beta$ (given)

Which shows that $\dfrac{\alpha}{\beta}$ is one of the cube roots of unity

39. (a) $\Delta = \begin{vmatrix}\cos\alpha & -\sin\alpha & 1\\ \sin\alpha & \cos\alpha & 1\\ \cos(\alpha-\beta) & -\sin(\alpha-\beta) & 1\end{vmatrix}$

Operate $R_3 \to R_3 - \{R_1 \cos b\} + R_2 \sin b$

$\Delta = \begin{vmatrix}\cos\alpha & -\sin\alpha & 1\\ \sin\alpha & \cos\alpha & 1\\ 0 & 0 & 1+\sin\beta-\cos\beta\end{vmatrix}$

$= \{1 - (\sin\beta + \cos\beta)\}(\cos^2\alpha + \sin^2\alpha)$

Now $\sin\beta + \cos\beta = \sqrt{2}\left\{\sin\left(\beta + \dfrac{\pi}{4}\right)\right\} \in \left[-\sqrt{2}, \sqrt{2}\right]$

$\Rightarrow \Delta \in [1 - \sqrt{2} + 1 + \sqrt{2}]$

40. (a) $\begin{vmatrix}a & b & c\\ b & c & a\\ c & a & b\end{vmatrix} = 3abc - (a^3 + b^3 + c^3) = 0$

Gives $-(a + b + c)\{a^2 + b^2 + c^2 - (ab + bc + ca)\} = 0$

Since $a + b + c \neq 0$

∴ $\dfrac{1}{2}\{(a-b)^2 + (b-c)^2 + (c-a)^2\} = 0$

or a = b = c i.e., equilateral triangle so ∠A = ∠B = ∠C = 60°

$\Rightarrow \sin^3 A + \sin^3 B + \sin^3 C = 3\left(\dfrac{\sqrt{3}}{2}\right)^3 = 3\sin A \sin B \sin C$

41. (a) For non-zero /non –trivial solution

$\Delta = \begin{vmatrix}a & b & c\\ b & c & a\\ c & a & b\end{vmatrix} = 3abc - (a^3 + b^3 + c^3) = 0$

i.e., $-(a + b + c)\{(a-b)^2 + (b-c)^2 + (c-a)^2\} = 0$

Since $a > b > c$ ∴ $(a + b + c) = 0$

$\{$as $a - b \neq 0, b - c \neq 0, c - a \neq 0\}$

Now $at^2 + bt + c = 0$ is satisfied by $t = 1$

(As $a + b + c = 0$), the other root will be c/a

or $\left(-\dfrac{b}{a} - 1\right)$

∴ At least one positive root

42. (a) $x - 3y = 4$; $5x + y = 2$;

$15x + 3y = 6$

$16x = 10$ or $x = \dfrac{5}{8}$ and $y = -\dfrac{9}{8}$

∴ $[2\pi]x - [e]y = [2x]$

gives $6x - 2y = 6 = [2a]$

$\Rightarrow 6 \leq 2a < 7$; so $a \in [3, 3.5)$

43. (c) $\Delta = \begin{vmatrix}n! & (n+1)! & (n+2)!\\ (n+1)! & (n+2)! & (n+3)!\\ (n+2)! & (n+3)! & (n+4)!\end{vmatrix}$

$= \begin{vmatrix}n! & (n+1)! & (n+2)!\\ n.(n!) & (n+1).(n+1)! & (n+2).(n+2)!\\ (n+1).(n+1)! & (n+2).(n+2)! & (n+3).(n+3)!\end{vmatrix}$

(By $R_2 \to R_2 - R_1$ and $R_3 \to R_3 - R_2$)

$= \begin{vmatrix}n! & (n+1)! & (n+2)!\\ n(n!) & (n+1).(n+1)! & (n+2).(n+2)!\\ (n+1)^2.(n!) & (n-2)^2.(n+1)! & (n+3)^2.(n+2)!\end{vmatrix}$

(By $R_2 \to R_2 - R_1$)

$= (n!).(n+1)!.(n+2)!\begin{vmatrix}1 & 1 & 1\\ n & n+1 & n+2\\ (n+1)^2 & (n+2)^2 & (n+3)^2\end{vmatrix}$

$= 2(n!).(n + 1)!(n + 2)!$

44. (c) $\Delta = \begin{vmatrix}1 & 1 & 1\\ \cot\dfrac{A}{2} & \cot\dfrac{B}{2} & \cot\dfrac{C}{2}\\ \tan\dfrac{B}{2} + \tan\dfrac{C}{2} & \tan\dfrac{C}{2} + \tan\dfrac{A}{2} & \tan\dfrac{A}{2} + \tan\dfrac{B}{2}\end{vmatrix} = 0$

$= \begin{vmatrix}1 & 0 & 0\\ \cot\dfrac{A}{2} & \cot\dfrac{B}{2} - \cot\dfrac{A}{2} & \cot\dfrac{C}{2} - \cot\dfrac{A}{2}\\ \tan\dfrac{B}{2} + \tan\dfrac{C}{2} & \tan\dfrac{A}{2} - \tan\dfrac{B}{2} & \tan\dfrac{A}{2} - \tan\dfrac{C}{2}\end{vmatrix} = 0$

$\Rightarrow \left(\cot\dfrac{B}{2} - \cot\dfrac{A}{2}\right)\left(\tan\dfrac{A}{2} - \tan\dfrac{C}{2}\right)$

$= \left(\tan\dfrac{A}{2} - \tan\dfrac{B}{2}\right)\left(\cot\dfrac{C}{2} - \cot\dfrac{A}{2}\right)$

$\Rightarrow \dfrac{\tan\dfrac{A}{2} - \tan\dfrac{B}{2}.\tan\dfrac{B}{2} - \tan\dfrac{C}{2}.\tan\dfrac{C}{2} - \tan\dfrac{A}{2}}{\tan\dfrac{A}{2}.\tan\dfrac{B}{2}.\tan\dfrac{C}{2}} = 0$

Either $\tan\dfrac{A}{2} = \tan\dfrac{B}{2}$ or $\tan\dfrac{B}{2} = \tan\dfrac{C}{2}$ or $\tan\dfrac{C}{2} = \tan\dfrac{A}{2}$

∴ At least isosceles triangle (not necessarily an equilateral Δ)

HINTS AND SOLUTIONS

TEXTUAL EXERCISE 1: (SUBJECTIVE)

1. even

2. There will be n^2 entries $\therefore$ n^2 cofactors

3. (a) $\begin{vmatrix} 2^2 & 3^2 & 4^2 \\ 3^2 & 4^2 & 5^2 \\ 4^2 & 5^2 & 6^2 \end{vmatrix} = \begin{vmatrix} 4 & 9 & 16 \\ 9 & 16 & 25 \\ 16 & 25 & 36 \end{vmatrix} = \begin{vmatrix} 4 & 5 & 7 \\ 9 & 7 & 9 \\ 16 & 9 & 11 \end{vmatrix}$

$= \begin{vmatrix} 4 & 5 & 2 \\ 9 & 7 & 2 \\ 16 & 9 & 2 \end{vmatrix} = \begin{vmatrix} 4 & 5 & 2 \\ 5 & 2 & 0 \\ 7 & 2 & 0 \end{vmatrix} = 2(10 - 14) = -8$

(b) $\Delta = \begin{vmatrix} b+c & a+b & a \\ c+a & b+c & b \\ a+b & c+a & c \end{vmatrix}$

(**Note:** observe sum along the columns)

$R_1 \to R_1 + R_2 + R_3$

$\Rightarrow \Delta = \begin{vmatrix} 2(a+b+c) & 2(a+b+c) & (a+b+c) \\ c+a & b+c & b \\ a+b & c+a & c \end{vmatrix}$

$\Rightarrow \Delta = (a+b+c)\begin{vmatrix} 2 & 2 & 1 \\ c+a & b+c & b \\ a+b & c+a & c \end{vmatrix}$

operate $C_1 : C_1 - C_2$ and $C_2 : C_2 - 2C_3$

$= (a+b+c)\begin{vmatrix} 0 & 0 & 1 \\ (a-b) & (c-b) & b \\ (b-c) & (a-c) & c \end{vmatrix}$

$= (a + b + c) \{(a - b)(a - c) + (b - c)^2\}$

$(a + b + c) \{(a^2 + b^2 + c^2) - (ab + bc + ca)\}$

$= \frac{1}{2}(a+b+c)\{(a-b)^2 + (b-c)^2 + (c-a)^2\}$

or $a^3 + b^3 + c^3 - 3abc$

(c) $\begin{vmatrix} a & b & 0 \\ 0 & a & b \\ b & 0 & a \end{vmatrix} = \begin{vmatrix} (a+b) & b & 0 \\ (a+b) & a & b \\ (a+b) & 0 & a \end{vmatrix}$

$= \begin{vmatrix} (a+b) & b & 0 \\ 0 & (a-b) & b \\ 0 & -a & (a-b) \end{vmatrix} = (a + b) \{(a - b)^2 + ab\}$

$= (a + b) \{a^2 + b^2 - ab\} = a^3 + b^3$

(d) $\begin{vmatrix} 2ab & a^2 & b^2 \\ a^2 & b^2 & 2ab \\ b^2 & 2ab & a^2 \end{vmatrix} = \begin{vmatrix} (a^2+b^2+2ab) & a^2 & b^2 \\ (a^2+b^2+2ab) & b^2 & 2ab \\ (a^2+b^2+2ab) & 2ab & a^2 \end{vmatrix}$

$= (a+b)^2\begin{vmatrix} 1 & a^2 & b^2 \\ 1 & b^2 & 2ab \\ 1 & 2ab & a^2 \end{vmatrix}$

$= (a+b)^2\begin{vmatrix} 1 & a^2 & b^2 \\ 0 & (b^2-a^2) & (2ab-b^2) \\ 0 & (2ab-b^2) & (a^2-2ab) \end{vmatrix}$

$= (a + b)^2 \{(b^2 - a^2)(a^2 - 2ab) - (2ab - b^2)^2\}$

$= (a + b)^2 \{-a^4 + a^2b^2 + 2a^3b - 2ab^3 - b^4 - 4a^2b^2 + 4ab^3\}$

$= -(a + b)^2 \{(a^4 + b^4 + 2a^2b^2) + a^2b^2 - 2ab(a^2+b^2)\}$

$= -(a + b)^2\{(a^2 + b^2 - ab)^2\} = -\{(a^3 + b^3)^2\}$

(e) $\Delta = \begin{vmatrix} 7 & 11 & 13 \\ 17 & 19 & 23 \\ 29 & 31 & 37 \end{vmatrix} = \begin{vmatrix} 7 & 4 & 2 \\ 17 & 2 & 4 \\ 29 & 2 & 6 \end{vmatrix} \; (C_2 - C_1 ; C_3 - C_2)$

$= \begin{vmatrix} (7-34) & 0 & (2-8) \\ -12 & 0 & -2 \\ 29 & 2 & 6 \end{vmatrix} = (-2)\begin{vmatrix} -27 & -6 \\ -12 & -2 \end{vmatrix} = 36$

(f) $\begin{vmatrix} 0 & x & y \\ -x & 0 & z \\ -y & -z & 0 \end{vmatrix} = 0$

(Third order skew symmetric determinant)

$= 0 + x\{yz\} + (-y)\{xz\} = 0$

4 The points will be collinear where area of $\Delta = 0$

i.e., $\left|\frac{1}{2}\begin{vmatrix} 2 & 5 & 1 \\ 4 & 5 & 1 \\ 6 & b & 1 \end{vmatrix}\right| = 0 \Rightarrow \begin{vmatrix} 2 & 5 & 1 \\ 2 & 0 & 0 \\ 2 & (b-5) & 0 \end{vmatrix} = 0$

or $2(b - 5) = 0$ so $b = 5$

5. $\Delta = \left|\frac{1}{2}\begin{vmatrix} 2 & 5 & 1 \\ 4 & 8 & 1 \\ 3 & 4 & 1 \end{vmatrix}\right| = \left|\frac{1}{2}\begin{vmatrix} 2 & 5 & 1 \\ 2 & 3 & 0 \\ 1 & -1 & 0 \end{vmatrix}\right| = \frac{1}{2}|-2-3| = \frac{5}{2}$ square units

6. $|A| = \begin{vmatrix} 3 & 2 & -9 \\ -5 & 7 & 2 \\ 0 & 1 & 1 \end{vmatrix} = \begin{vmatrix} 3 & 11 & -9 \\ -5 & 5 & 2 \\ 0 & 0 & 1 \end{vmatrix}$

$\Rightarrow$ $|A| = 15 + 55 = 70$. We know that $|C| = |C^T|$

$\therefore$ $|C| = |\text{Adj}A| = |A|^{n-1} = 70^2 = 4900$

7. α, β, γ are the roots of $f(x) = 0$

$\therefore$ $f(x) = a(x - \alpha)(x - \beta)(x - \gamma) = ax^3 + bx^2 + cx + d$

$= a\{x^3 - (\alpha + \beta + \gamma)x^2 - (\alpha\beta + \beta\gamma + \gamma\alpha)x - \alpha\beta\gamma\}$

We observe that $f(\alpha) = f(\beta) = f(\gamma) = 0$

Hence $\begin{vmatrix} f(\alpha) & \alpha & \alpha^2 \\ f(\beta) & \beta & \beta^2 \\ f(\gamma) & \gamma & \gamma^2 \end{vmatrix} = \begin{vmatrix} 0 & \alpha & \alpha^2 \\ 0 & \beta & \beta^2 \\ 0 & \gamma & \gamma^2 \end{vmatrix} = 0$

8. $\Delta = \begin{vmatrix} u & (v-u) & (w-v) \\ v & (w-v) & (u-v) \\ 1 & 0 & 0 \end{vmatrix} = -(v-u)^2 - (w-v)^2 = -\{(v-u)^2$
$+ (w-v)^2\} \leq \mathbf{0}$

TEXTUAL EXERCISE 2: (SUBJECTIVE)

1. $\begin{vmatrix} a & b \\ c & d \end{vmatrix} \xrightarrow{T_1} \begin{vmatrix} d & c \\ b & a \end{vmatrix} \xrightarrow{T_2} \begin{vmatrix} d & b \\ c & a \end{vmatrix}$

$\xrightarrow{T_3} \dfrac{1}{6}\begin{vmatrix} 3d & 6b \\ c & 2a \end{vmatrix} \xrightarrow{T_4} \dfrac{1}{2}\begin{vmatrix} c & 2a \\ d & 2b \end{vmatrix}$

$T_1 : C_1 \leftrightarrow C_2$ and $R_1 \leftrightarrow R_2$; T_2 : Interchange rows and column (i.e., taking transpose) : rows $\leftrightarrow$ columns
$T_3 : R_1 \to 1/3(3R_1) + C_2 \to 1/2(2C_2)$
$T_4 : R_1 \leftrightarrow R_2$ and then $R_2 \to 3(1/3\ R_2)$

2. $\begin{vmatrix} 2 & 4 & 6 \\ 3 & 1 & 5 \\ 4 & 8 & 12 \end{vmatrix} = 0$ (as $R_3 = 2R_1$)

3. $\begin{vmatrix} a & b & c \\ x & y & z \\ l & m & n \end{vmatrix} = -\begin{vmatrix} b & a & c \\ y & x & z \\ m & l & n \end{vmatrix} (C_1 \leftrightarrow C_2)$

$= \begin{vmatrix} b & c & a \\ y & z & x \\ m & n & l \end{vmatrix} (C_2 \leftrightarrow C_3) = -\begin{vmatrix} y & z & x \\ b & c & a \\ m & n & l \end{vmatrix} = \begin{vmatrix} y & z & x \\ m & n & l \\ b & c & a \end{vmatrix}$

(By operating $R_1 \leftrightarrow R_2$ and $R_2 \leftrightarrow R_3$)

4. $|A| = 5$; $[A]_{n\times n} \Rightarrow |mA| = m^n\,|A| = 5m^n$; $m \in \mathbb{R}$

$T_1 : R_1 \to 2\left(\dfrac{1}{2}R_1\right)$ and $R_3 \to 4\left(\dfrac{1}{4}R_3\right)$

$T_2 : C_1 \to 1/4(4C_1)$ and $C_3 \to 1/2(2C_3)$
$T_3 : R_1 \leftrightarrow R_2$ $\qquad T_4 : R_2 \leftrightarrow R_3$

6 Interchange Rows and columns (Transpose)
$T_1 : R \leftrightarrow C$ and then taking 5, 3, 2 common from C_1, C_2 and C_3 respectively
$T_1 : C_1 \to 1/5$; C_1, $C_2 \to 1/3C_2$; $C_3 \to 1/2C_2$
$T_2 : R_1 \to 2R_1$, $R_2 \to 3R_2$ and $R_3 \to 5R_3$
$T_3 : R_1 \leftrightarrow R_2$ then $R_2 \leftrightarrow R_3$ or rolling R_1 over R_2 and R_3

TEXTUAL EXERCISE 3: (SUBJECTIVE)

1. (a) $\begin{vmatrix} 18 & 40 & 89 \\ 40 & 89 & 198 \\ 89 & 198 & 440 \end{vmatrix} = \begin{vmatrix} 18 & 40 & 89 \\ 40 & 89 & 198 \\ 9 & 20 & 44 \end{vmatrix}$

(By $R_3 \to R_3 - 2R_2$); next operate $R_1 \leftrightarrow R_1 - 2R_3$;

$= \begin{vmatrix} 0 & 0 & 1 \\ 40 & 89 & 198 \\ 9 & 20 & 44 \end{vmatrix} = 40 \times 20 - 9 \times 89 = 800 - 801 = -1$

(b) $\begin{vmatrix} a^2 & b^2 & c^2 \\ 2 & 2 & 2 \\ (a-1)^2 & (b-1)^2 & (c-1)^2 \end{vmatrix} (R_2 \to R_2 + R_3 - 2R_1)$

$= 2\begin{vmatrix} a^2 & b^2 & c^2 \\ 1 & 1 & 1 \\ (1-2a) & (1-2b) & (1-2c) \end{vmatrix} (R_3 \to R_3 - R_1)$

$= 2\begin{vmatrix} a^2 & b^2 & c^2 \\ 1 & 1 & 1 \\ -2a & -2b & -2c \end{vmatrix} (R_3 \to R_3 - R_2)$

$= 4\begin{vmatrix} a^2 & b^2 & c^2 \\ a & b & c \\ 1 & 1 & 1 \end{vmatrix} (R_3 \leftrightarrow R_2)$

(c) $\Delta = \begin{vmatrix} 1 & a & a^2 \\ 1 & b & b^2 \\ 1 & c & c^2 \end{vmatrix} - \begin{vmatrix} 1 & a & bc \\ 1 & b & ca \\ 1 & c & ab \end{vmatrix} = (\Delta_1 - \Delta_2)$

Now, $\Delta_2 = \begin{vmatrix} 1 & a & bc \\ 1 & b & ca \\ 1 & c & ab \end{vmatrix} = \dfrac{1}{abc}\begin{vmatrix} a & a^2 & abc \\ b & b^2 & abc \\ c & c^2 & abc \end{vmatrix}$

$= \dfrac{abc}{abc}\begin{vmatrix} a & a^2 & 1 \\ b & b^2 & 1 \\ c & c^2 & 1 \end{vmatrix} = -\begin{vmatrix} a & 1 & a^2 \\ b & 1 & b^2 \\ c & 1 & c^2 \end{vmatrix}$

$= \begin{vmatrix} 1 & a & a^2 \\ 1 & b & b^2 \\ 1 & c & c^2 \end{vmatrix} = \Delta_1 \Rightarrow \Delta = \Delta_1 - \Delta_2 = 0$

(d) $\begin{vmatrix} ax & by & cz \\ x^2 & y^2 & z^2 \\ 1 & 1 & 1 \end{vmatrix} = (xyz)\begin{vmatrix} a & b & c \\ x & y & z \\ \frac{1}{x} & \frac{1}{y} & \frac{1}{z} \end{vmatrix} = \begin{vmatrix} a & b & c \\ x & y & z \\ yz & xz & xy \end{vmatrix}$

2 (i) $\begin{vmatrix} (x+2) & (2x+3) & (3x+4) \\ (x+1) & (x+1) & (x+1) \\ (x+2) & 2(x+2) & 6(x+2) \end{vmatrix} = 0$

(By $R_3 \to (R_3 - R_2)$; $R_2 \to (R_2 - R_1)$)

$= \begin{vmatrix} (x+2) & (x+1) & (x+1) \\ (x+1) & 0 & 0 \\ (x+2) & (x+2) & 4(x+2) \end{vmatrix} = 0$;

$C_3 \to C_3 - C_2$; $C_2 \to C_2 - C_1$
$= -(x+1)\,\{4(x+1)(x+2) - (x+1)(x+2)\} = 0$
$= 3(x+1)\,\{(x+1)(x+2)\} = 0 \Rightarrow x = -1, -2$

(ii) $\begin{vmatrix} (4+6i) & 0 & 0 \\ 4 & 3i & -1 \\ 20 & 3 & i \end{vmatrix} = x + iy$

$(4+6i)\{-3+3\} = 0 \Rightarrow x = 0, y = 0$

3. $\begin{vmatrix}(a+b+c-x) & c & b\\(a+b+c-x) & (b-x) & a\\(a+b+c-x) & a & (c-x)\end{vmatrix}$ $(C_1 \to C_1 + C_2 + C_3)$

$$= (a+b+c-x)\begin{vmatrix}1 & c & b\\1 & (b-x) & a\\1 & a & c-x\end{vmatrix}$$

$$= (a+b+c-x)\begin{vmatrix}1 & c & b\\0 & (b-x-c) & (a-b)\\0 & (a-c) & (c-x-b)\end{vmatrix}$$

$= (a + b + c - x) [\{(-x) + (b - c)\} \{(-x) - (b - c)\} - (a - c)(a - b)]$

$= (a + b + c - x) \{x^2 - (a^2 + b^2 + c^2 - ab - bc - ac)\}$

$= \frac{1}{2}(a+b+c-x)\ [2x^2 - \{(a - b)^2 + (b - c)^2 + (c - a)^2\}]$

Either $x = 0$ or $x^2 = (a + b + c)^2 -3 (ab + bc + ca)$

$\Rightarrow x = 0$ or $x^2 = -3(ab + bc + ca)$

Now $(a + b + c)^2 = a^2 + b^2 + c^2 + 2ab + 2bc +2ca$

$\Rightarrow 0 = a^2 + b^2 + c^2 + 2 (ab + bc + ca)$

$\Rightarrow ab + bc + ca = -1/2 (a^2 + b^2 + c^2)$

$x^2 = \frac{3}{2} (a^2 + b^2 + c^2)$

$\Rightarrow x = \pm\sqrt{\frac{3}{2}(a^2+b^2+c^2)}$ or $x = \pm\sqrt{-3(ab+bc+ca)}$

$x = 0$ or $\pm\sqrt{\frac{3}{2}(a^2+b^2+c^2)}$ or $\pm\sqrt{-3(ab+bc+ca)}$

4. (i) $\begin{vmatrix}(a_2+a_3) & (a_1+a_3) & (a_1+a_2)\\(a_1+a_2) & (a_2+a_3) & (a_1+a_3)\\(a_1+a_3) & (a_1+a_2) & (a_2+a_3)\end{vmatrix}$

(By operating $C_1 \to C_1 + C_2 + C_3$), we get

$$2\begin{vmatrix}(a_1+a_2+a_3) & (a_1+a_3) & (a_1+a_2)\\(a_1+a_2+a_3) & (a_2+a_3) & (a_1+a_3)\\(a_1+a_2+a_3) & (a_1+a_2) & (a_2+a_3)\end{vmatrix}$$

Operate $C_2 \to C_2 - C_1$; $C_3 \to C_1$

$$2\begin{vmatrix}(a_1+a_2+a_3) & -a_2 & -a_3\\(a_1+a_2+a_3) & -a_1 & -a_2\\(a_1+a_2+a_3) & -a_3 & -a_1\end{vmatrix}$$

Operate $C_1 \to C_1 + C_2 + C_3$

$$= 2\begin{vmatrix}a_1 & -a_2 & -a_3\\a_3 & -a_1 & -a_2\\a_2 & -a_3 & -a_1\end{vmatrix} = 2(-1)^2\begin{vmatrix}a_1 & a_2 & a_3\\a_3 & a_1 & a_2\\a_2 & a_3 & a_1\end{vmatrix}$$

(ii) Multiplying C_1 by a ; C_2 by b ; C_3 by c and dividing the determinant by (abc), we get

$$\Delta = \frac{1}{abc}\begin{vmatrix}a^2 & b^2-bc & c^2+bc\\a^2+ac & b^2 & c^2-ac\\a^2-ab & ab+b^2 & c^2\end{vmatrix}$$

$= \frac{a^2+b^2+c^2}{abc}\begin{vmatrix}1 & b^2-bc & c^2+bc\\1 & b^2 & c^2-ac\\1 & ab+b^2 & c^2\end{vmatrix}$ (By $C_1 \to C_1 + C_2 +$ C_3 and taking $a^2 + b^2 + c^2$ common from C_1)

$= \frac{(a^2+b^2+c^2)}{abc}\begin{vmatrix}1 & b^2-bc & c^2+bc\\0 & bc & -bc-ac\\0 & ab+bc & -bc\end{vmatrix}$ (By $R_2 \to R_2 -$ R_1 and $R_3 \to R_3 - R_1 = (a + b + c)(a^2 + b^2 + c^2)$

(iii) Operate: $(R_3 \to R_3 + R_1)$, then

$$\Delta = \begin{vmatrix}a & b & c\\a^2 & b^2 & c^2\\(a+b+c) & (a+b+c) & (a+b+c)\end{vmatrix}$$

$$= (a+b+c)\begin{vmatrix}a & b & c\\a^2 & b^2 & c^2\\1 & 1 & 1\end{vmatrix}$$

$$= (a+b+c)\begin{vmatrix}(a-b) & (b-c) & c\\(a-b)(a+b) & (b-c)(b+c) & c^2\\0 & 0 & 1\end{vmatrix}$$

$$= (a + b + c)(a - b)(b - c)\begin{vmatrix}1 & 1 & c\\(a+b) & (b+c) & c^2\\0 & 0 & 1\end{vmatrix}$$

$= (a + b + c) (a - b) (b - c) (c - a)$

5. (a) Rearrange and get $\begin{vmatrix}a & b & c\\x & y & z\\1 & 3 & 5\end{vmatrix} + \begin{vmatrix}a & b & c\\x & y & z\\2 & 4 & 6\end{vmatrix} + \begin{vmatrix}a & b & c\\x & y & z\\3 & 5 & 7\end{vmatrix} +$

$$\begin{vmatrix}a & b & c\\x & y & z\\4 & 6 & 8\end{vmatrix} = \begin{vmatrix}a & b & c\\x & y & z\\10 & 18 & 26\end{vmatrix}$$

(b) Let $\Delta = \begin{vmatrix}a & b\\x & y\end{vmatrix} - \begin{vmatrix}a & b\\x^2 & y^2\end{vmatrix} + \begin{vmatrix}a & b\\x^3 & y^3\end{vmatrix} - \begin{vmatrix}a & b\\x^4 & y^4\end{vmatrix} + \ldots..$

Then

$$\Delta = \begin{vmatrix}a & b\\(x-x^2+x^3-x^4+\ldots\ldots.) & (y-y^2+y^3-y^4+\ldots\ldots.)\end{vmatrix}$$

$$= \begin{vmatrix}a & b\\\frac{x}{1-(-x)} & \frac{y}{1-(-y)}\end{vmatrix} = \begin{vmatrix}a & b\\\frac{x}{1+x} & \frac{y}{1+y}\end{vmatrix}$$

(c) Similarly Let $\Delta = \begin{vmatrix}a & b\\x & y\end{vmatrix} + \begin{vmatrix}a & b\\x^2 & y^2\end{vmatrix} + \begin{vmatrix}a & b\\x^3 & y^3\end{vmatrix} + \ldots\ldots.,$

then $\Delta = \begin{vmatrix}a & b\\(x+x^2+x^3+\ldots\ldots\ldots.) & (y+y^2+y^3+\ldots\ldots\ldots)\end{vmatrix}$

$$= \begin{vmatrix}a & b\\\frac{x}{1-x} & \frac{y}{1-y}\end{vmatrix}$$

6. Operate $C_1 \to C_1 - C_2 - C_3$,

we get $\Delta = \begin{vmatrix} 0 & 1002 & 3 \\ 0 & 2009 & -3 \\ 0 & 2998 & 10 \end{vmatrix} = 0$

TEXTUAL EXERCISE 3: (OBJECTIVE)

1. (c) $\begin{vmatrix} 1 & a & b+c \\ 1 & b & c+a \\ 1 & c & a+b \end{vmatrix} = \begin{vmatrix} 1 & a & b+c \\ 0 & (b-a) & (a-b) \\ 0 & (c-a) & (a-c) \end{vmatrix}$

Operate $R_2 \to R_2 - R_1$; $R_3 \to R_3 - R_1$
$= (b-a)(a-c) - (c-a)(a-b) = 0$

2. (c) Operate $C_1 \to C_1 + C_2 + C_3$ $\Delta = \begin{vmatrix} 0 & b-c & c-a \\ 0 & c-a & a-b \\ 0 & a-b & b-c \end{vmatrix} = 0$

3. (b) $\Delta = \begin{vmatrix} (3x-2) & 3 & 3 \\ (3x-2) & 3x-8 & 3 \\ (3x-2) & 3 & 3x-8 \end{vmatrix}$

By operate $(C_1 \to C_1 + C_2 + C_3)$

$= (3x-2)\begin{vmatrix} 1 & 3 & 3 \\ 1 & 3x-8 & 3 \\ 1 & 3 & 3x-8 \end{vmatrix}$

$= (3x-2)\begin{vmatrix} 1 & 3 & 3 \\ 0 & (3x-11) & 0 \\ 0 & 0 & (3x-11) \end{vmatrix}$

$= (3x-2)\{3x-11\}^2 = 0$

$\Rightarrow \quad x = \frac{2}{3}, \frac{11}{3}, \frac{11}{3} \qquad \Rightarrow \quad x = 2/3$

4. (c) $\Delta = \begin{vmatrix} 1 & 1 & 1 \\ {}^mC_1 & {}^{m+1}C_1 & {}^{m+2}C_1 \\ {}^mC_2 & {}^{m+1}C_2 & {}^{m+2}C_2 \end{vmatrix}$

$= \begin{vmatrix} 1 & 0 & 0 \\ {}^mC_1 & 1 & 1 \\ {}^mC_2 & {}^{m+1}C_2 - {}^mC_2 & {}^{m+2}C_2 - {}^{m+1}C_2 \end{vmatrix}$

Operated $C_2 \to C_2 - C_1$; $C_3 \to C_3 - C_2$
$\Rightarrow \Delta = ({}^{m+2}C_2 - {}^{m+1}C_2) - ({}^{m+1}C_2 - {}^mC_2)$
$= {}^{m+2}C_2 + {}^mC_2 - 2.\,{}^{m+1}C_2$
Using ${}^{n+1}C_r = {}^nC_{r-1} + {}^nC_r$ we get
$\Delta = {}^{m+1}C_1 - {}^mC_1 = (m+1) - m = 1$

5. (c) α, β, γ are the roots of $x^3 + px + q = 0$
So, $\alpha + \beta + \gamma = 0$; $\alpha\beta + \beta\gamma + \gamma\alpha = p$, $\alpha\beta\gamma = -q$

$\begin{vmatrix} \alpha & \beta & \gamma \\ \beta & \gamma & \alpha \\ \gamma & \alpha & \beta \end{vmatrix} = (\alpha+\beta+\gamma)\begin{vmatrix} 1 & \beta & \gamma \\ 1 & \gamma & \alpha \\ 1 & \alpha & \beta \end{vmatrix} = 0$

$(\because \alpha + \beta + \gamma) = 0$

6. (c) $\Delta = \begin{vmatrix} {}^{10}C_4 & {}^{10}C_5 & {}^{11}C_m \\ {}^{11}C_6 & {}^{11}C_7 & {}^{12}C_{m+2} \\ {}^{12}C_8 & {}^{12}C_9 & {}^{13}C_{m+4} \end{vmatrix} = 0$

We observe that operating $C_2 \to C_2 + C_1$ and using ${}^nC_{r-1} + {}^nC_r = {}^{n+1}C_r$ gives ${}^{10}C_4 + {}^{10}C_5 = {}^{11}C_5 = {}^{11}C_m$; ${}^{11}C_6 + {}^{11}C_7 = {}^{12}C_7 = {}^{12}C_{m+2}$ and ${}^{12}C_8 + {}^{12}C_9 = {}^{13}C_9 = {}^{13}C_{m+4} \Rightarrow m = 5$

7. (a) Rewriting $\Delta_1 = -\begin{vmatrix} 4 & 10 & 3 \\ 7 & 17 & 4 \\ -5 & 4 & 7 \end{vmatrix} = -\begin{vmatrix} 4 & x+5 & 3 \\ 7 & x+12 & 4 \\ -5 & x-1 & 7 \end{vmatrix}$

(Given $\Delta_1 = -\Delta_2$)
Comparing column # 2 of both gives $x = 5$

8. (b) The given determinant is triangular
$\therefore \quad \Delta$ = product of diagonal elements = 5!

9. (d) $\because (i)^{1/4} = \alpha, \beta, \gamma, \delta \Rightarrow \alpha, \beta, \gamma, \delta$ are 4 roots of $(i)^{1/4}$
i.e., of $x^4 - i = 0 \Rightarrow \alpha + \beta + \gamma + \delta = 0$
using $C_1 \to C_1 + C_2 + C_3 + C_4$ gives all elements of $C_1 = 0 \Rightarrow \Delta = 0$

10. (b) Observe that $2R_2 = R_1 + R_3$
$\Rightarrow \Delta = 0$ (as x, y, z are in A.P. so $x + z = 2y$)

11. (a) Operate $C_1 \to C_1 - C_2$, then $\Delta = \begin{vmatrix} 4 & (e^{i\alpha} - e^{-i\alpha})^2 & 4 \\ 4 & (e^{i\beta} - e^{-i\beta}) & 4 \\ 4 & (e^{i\gamma} - e^{-i\gamma})^2 & 4 \end{vmatrix} = 0$

So Δ is independent of α, β, γ

12. (c) $\Delta = \begin{vmatrix} 265 & 240 & 219 \\ 240 & 225 & 198 \\ 219 & 198 & 181 \end{vmatrix}$

Apply $C_1 \to C_1 - C_3$ and $C_2 \to C_2 - C_3$

$\Delta = \begin{vmatrix} 46 & 21 & 219 \\ 42 & 27 & 198 \\ 38 & 17 & 181 \end{vmatrix}$;

operate $C_1 \to C_1 - 2C_2$; $C_3 \to C_3 - 10C_2$

$\Delta = \begin{vmatrix} 4 & 21 & 9 \\ -12 & 27 & -72 \\ 4 & 17 & 11 \end{vmatrix}$;

Apply $R_1 \to R_1 - R_3$; $R_2 \to R_2 + 3R_3$

$\Delta = \begin{vmatrix} 0 & 4 & -2 \\ 0 & 78 & -39 \\ 4 & 17 & 11 \end{vmatrix} = 2 \times 39 \begin{vmatrix} 0 & 2 & -1 \\ 0 & 2 & -1 \\ 4 & 17 & 11 \end{vmatrix} = 0$ (as $R_1 = R_2$)

13. (a) Operate $C_3 \to C_3 - C_2$ and $C_2 \to C_2 - C_1$

$\Delta = \begin{vmatrix} 3421 & 1 & 1 \\ 3424 & 1 & 1 \\ 2427 & 1 & 1 \end{vmatrix} = 0$

14. (a) Writing Δ as the product we get,

$$\Delta = \begin{vmatrix} 0 & c & b \\ c & 0 & a \\ b & a & 0 \end{vmatrix} \times \begin{vmatrix} 0 & c & b \\ c & 0 & a \\ b & a & 0 \end{vmatrix} = (2abc)^2 = 4k \Rightarrow k = a^2b^2c^2$$

15. (d). $\sum_{n=1}^{n=N} u_n = \begin{vmatrix} 1 & 1 & 5 \\ 1^2 & 2N+1 & 2N+1 \\ 1^3 & 3N^2 & 3N \end{vmatrix} + \begin{vmatrix} 2 & 1 & 5 \\ 2^2 & 2N+1 & 2N+1 \\ 2^3 & 3N^2 & 3N \end{vmatrix} +$

$\begin{vmatrix} 3 & 1 & 5 \\ 3^2 & 2N+1 & 2N+1 \\ 3^3 & 3N^2 & 3N \end{vmatrix} + \ldots$ upto $n = N$

$$= \begin{vmatrix} \dfrac{N(N+1)}{2} & 1 & 5 \\ \dfrac{N(N+1)(2N+1)}{6} & (2N+1) & (2N+1) \\ \left\{\dfrac{N(N+1)}{2}\right\}^2 & 3N^2 & 3N \end{vmatrix}$$

$$\Delta = \frac{N(N+1)}{12} \begin{vmatrix} 6 & 1 & 5 \\ 2(2N+1) & 2N+1 & 2N+1 \\ 3(N)(N+1) & 3N^2 & 3N \end{vmatrix}$$

Observe that $C_1 = C_2 + C_3 \Rightarrow \Delta = 0$

TEXTUAL EXERCISE 4: (SUBJECTIVE)

1. (a) Let $\Delta = \begin{vmatrix} -5 & 3+5i & (3/2)-4i \\ 3-5i & 8 & 4+5i \\ (3/2)+4i & 4-5i & 9 \end{vmatrix} = A + iB$

We observe that $\bar{\Delta} = \begin{vmatrix} -5 & 3-5i & \dfrac{3}{2}+4i \\ 3+5i & 8 & 4-5i \\ \dfrac{3}{2}-4i & 4+5i & 9 \end{vmatrix} = \Delta^T$

$\Delta = A + iB = \Delta^T = \bar{\Delta} = A - iB \Rightarrow A + iB = A - iB$

$\because |A| = |A^T| \Rightarrow B = 0$, hence Δ is purely real

(b) $\Delta = \begin{vmatrix} 0 & p-q & p-r \\ q-p & 0 & q-r \\ r-p & r-q & 0 \end{vmatrix}$ Third order skew symmetric determinant $\Rightarrow \Delta = 0$

2. $\Delta = \begin{vmatrix} \sin(A+B+C) & \sin A & \sin B \\ -\sin A & \sin(A+B+C) & \sin C \\ -\sin B & -\sin C & \sin(A+B+C) \end{vmatrix}$

If $A + B + C = (2k + 1)\pi$, then it is a skew symmetric determinant of odd order $\therefore \Delta = 0$

3. $\Delta = \begin{vmatrix} x & y & z \\ y & z & x \\ z & x & y \end{vmatrix} \begin{vmatrix} x & y & z \\ y & z & x \\ z & x & y \end{vmatrix} = \begin{vmatrix} x & y & z \\ y & z & x \\ z & x & y \end{vmatrix}^2$

$= \{3xyz - (x^3 + y^3 + z^3)\}^2 = (x^3 + y^3 + z^3 - 3xyz)^2$

TEXTUAL EXERCISE 4: (OBJECTIVE)

1 (d) $\Delta = \begin{vmatrix} 1 & a & a^2 & a^3 \\ 1 & b & b^2 & b^3 \\ 1 & c & c^2 & c^3 \\ 1 & d & d^2 & d^3 \end{vmatrix} + \begin{vmatrix} 1 & a & a^2 & bcd \\ 1 & b & b^2 & cda \\ 1 & c & c^2 & abd \\ 1 & d & d^2 & abc \end{vmatrix}$ $\Delta_1 + \Delta_2$ (say)

Now, $\Delta_2 = \dfrac{1}{abcd} \begin{vmatrix} a & a^2 & a^3 & abcd \\ b & b^2 & b^3 & abcd \\ c & c^2 & c^3 & abcd \\ d & d^2 & d^3 & abcd \end{vmatrix}$

$= \dfrac{abcd}{abcd} \begin{vmatrix} a & a^2 & a^3 & 1 \\ b & b^2 & b^3 & 1 \\ c & c^2 & c^3 & 1 \\ d & d^2 & d^3 & 1 \end{vmatrix} = (-1)^3(\Delta_1) = -\Delta_1 \Rightarrow \Delta = \Delta_1 + \Delta_2$

2. (d) $\Delta = \begin{vmatrix} y+z & z & y \\ z & z+x & x \\ y & x & x-y \end{vmatrix} = kxyz$; Put $x = 1, y = 2, z = 3$

$\Delta = \begin{vmatrix} 5 & 3 & 2 \\ 3 & 4 & 1 \\ 2 & 1 & 3 \end{vmatrix}$ operate $R_1 \to R_1 - 2R_2$ and $R_3 \to R_3 - 3R_2$

$\Delta = \begin{vmatrix} -1 & -5 & 0 \\ 3 & 4 & 1 \\ -7 & -11 & 0 \end{vmatrix} = (-1)\ \{11 - 35) = 24$

So, $kxyz = 6k = 24$ gives $k = 4$

3. (b) Operate $C_1 \to C_1 + C_2 + C_3$ and take $2(a + b + c)$ common

$\Rightarrow \Delta = 2(a+b+c) \begin{vmatrix} 1 & a & b \\ 1 & b+c+2a & b \\ 1 & a & c+a+2b \end{vmatrix}$

$= 2(a+b+c) \begin{vmatrix} 1 & a & b \\ 0 & (a+b+c) & 0 \\ 0 & 0 & (a+b+c) \end{vmatrix}$

Which is a triangular determinant $\Rightarrow \Delta = 2\,(a + b + c)^3$

4. (b) $\Delta = \begin{vmatrix} x & a^2 & a^3 \\ x & b^2 & b^3 \\ x & c^2 & c^3 \end{vmatrix} + \begin{vmatrix} a & a^2 & a^3 \\ b & b^2 & b^3 \\ c & c^2 & c^3 \end{vmatrix}$

$= x \begin{vmatrix} 1 & a^2 & a^3 \\ 1 & b^2 & b^3 \\ 1 & c^2 & c^3 \end{vmatrix} + abc \begin{vmatrix} 1 & a & a^2 \\ 1 & b & b^2 \\ 1 & c & c^2 \end{vmatrix}$

$= x\,(a - b)(b - c)(c - a)\,(\Sigma ab) + abc\,(a - b)(b - c)(c - a)$

$= (a - b)\,(b - c)\,(c - a)\,\{x(ab + bc + ca) + abc\} = 0$

(given) $x = \dfrac{-abc}{\Sigma ab}$ $\qquad (\because a \neq b \neq c \neq a)$

5. (a,b,c,d) $\begin{vmatrix} bc & ca & ab \\ ca & ab & bc \\ ab & bc & ca \end{vmatrix} = -(\Sigma ab)\{\Sigma(ab)^2 - \Sigma(ab)(bc)\}$

$= -(ab + bc + ca)\{(a^2b^2 + b^2c^2 + c^2a^2) - (acb^2 + bca^2 + abc^2)\} = 0$

$ab + bc + ca = 0$ gives $\frac{1}{a}+\frac{1}{b}+\frac{1}{c}=0$

Using $x^2 + y^2 + z^2 - (xy + yz + zx) = (x + \omega y + \omega^2 z)(x + \omega^2 y + z\omega)$. So either

$ab + \omega bc + \omega^2 ca = 0$ dividing by $\omega^4 abc$ ($\omega^4 = \omega$),

we get $\frac{1}{a}+\frac{1}{b\omega^2}+\frac{1}{c\omega}=0$

or $(ab + \omega^2 bc + \omega ca) = 0$

Dividing by $\omega^2 abc$, we get $\frac{1}{a}+\frac{1}{b\omega}+\frac{1}{\omega^2 c}=0$

or $(ab + \omega^2 bc + \omega ca) = 0$

Dividing by $\omega^3 abc$, we get $\frac{1}{a\omega}+\frac{1}{b\omega^2}+\frac{1}{c}=0$

6. (i) (c) writing the determinant as product

$$\Delta = \begin{vmatrix} 0 & a_1 & b_1 \\ 0 & a_2 & b_2 \\ 0 & a_3 & b_3 \end{vmatrix}\begin{vmatrix} 0 & 0 & 0 \\ b_1 & b_2 & b_3 \\ a_1 & a_2 & a_3 \end{vmatrix} = 0 \text{ (row × column)}$$

(ii) $$\Delta = \begin{vmatrix} 1 & 1+\alpha x & 1+\alpha x^2 \\ 1 & 1+\beta x & 1+\beta x^2 \\ 1 & 1+\gamma x & 1+\gamma x^2 \end{vmatrix} + \begin{vmatrix} \alpha & 1+\alpha x & 1+\alpha x^2 \\ \beta & 1+\beta x & 1+\beta x^2 \\ \gamma & 1+\gamma x & 1+\gamma^2 x \end{vmatrix} = \Delta_1 + \Delta_2$$

Now $$\Delta_1 = \begin{vmatrix} 1 & \alpha x & \alpha x^2 \\ 1 & \beta x & \beta x^2 \\ 1 & \gamma x & \gamma x^2 \end{vmatrix} = x^3\begin{vmatrix} 1 & \alpha & \alpha \\ 1 & \beta & \beta \\ 1 & \gamma & \gamma \end{vmatrix} = 0$$

{Operated $C_2 \to C_2 - C_1 : C_3 \to C_3 - C_1$}

and $$\Delta_2 = \begin{vmatrix} \alpha & 1 & 1 \\ \beta & 1 & 1 \\ \gamma & 1 & 1 \end{vmatrix} = 0$$

{Operated $C_2 \to C_2 - xC_1 : C_3 \to C_2 - x^2C_1$}. Thus $\Delta = 0$

7. (d) $$\begin{vmatrix} p & b & c \\ a & q & c \\ a & b & r \end{vmatrix} = \begin{vmatrix} p-a & b-q & 0 \\ a & q & c \\ 0 & (b-q) & (r-c) \end{vmatrix}$$

Gives $(p - a)\cdot\{q(r - c) - c(b - q)\} - a\{(b - q)(r - c)\} = 0$

Dividing by $(p - a)(q - b)(r - c)$ gives,

$$\frac{q}{q-b}+\frac{C}{r-c}+\frac{a}{p-a}=0$$

So $$\left\{\frac{a}{p-a}+1\right\}+\frac{q}{q-b}+\left\{\frac{c}{r-c}+1\right\}=2$$

$$\frac{p}{p-a}+\frac{q}{q-b}+\frac{r}{r-c}=2$$

8. (d) Let $$\begin{vmatrix} \ell_1 & m_1 & n_1 \\ \ell_2 & m_2 & n_2 \\ \ell_3 & m_3 & n_3 \end{vmatrix}\begin{vmatrix} \ell_1 & \ell_2 & \ell_3 \\ m_1 & m_2 & m_3 \\ n_1 & n_2 & n_3 \end{vmatrix} = |I| = 1$$

Since, $\Sigma\ell_1^2 = 1$ and $\ell_1\ell_2 + m_1m_2 + n_1n_2 = 0$ etc.

$\Rightarrow \Delta^2 = 1 \Rightarrow \Delta = \pm 1$

TEXTUAL EXERCISE 5: (SUBEJCTIVE)

1. Let $\Delta = f(x) \Rightarrow \frac{d\Delta}{dx} = f'(x)$

$$= \begin{vmatrix} p'(x) & p'(x) & p''(x) \\ q'(x) & q'(x) & q''(x) \\ r'(x) & r'(x) & r''(x) \end{vmatrix} + \begin{vmatrix} p(x) & p''(x) & p''(x) \\ q(x) & q''(x) & q''(x) \\ r(x) & r''(x) & r''(x) \end{vmatrix} + \begin{vmatrix} q(x) & p'(x) & 0 \\ q(x) & q'(x) & 0 \\ r(x) & r'(x) & 0 \end{vmatrix} = 0+0+0=0$$

As $p(x)$, $q(x)$, $r(x)$ are polynomials of degree 2, implies $P'''(x) = q'''(x) = r'''(x) = 0$

Hence $f'(x) = 0 \Rightarrow f(x) = \Delta$ is independent of x.

2. $\phi(x) = \begin{vmatrix} F(x) & G(x) & H(x) \\ F'(x) & G'(x) & H'(x) \\ F''(x) & G''(x) & H''(x) \end{vmatrix}$ as in question # 1, $\phi(x)$ is independent of x and it is a constant function.

3. $$\Delta(x) = \begin{vmatrix} e^{x^2} & \sin x & 1 \\ \sec x & \log(1+x^2) & 1 \\ x^3 & x^2 & 1 \end{vmatrix} = a+bx+cx^2$$

$$\Delta(0) = \begin{vmatrix} 1 & 0 & 1 \\ 1 & 0 & 1 \\ 0 & 0 & 1 \end{vmatrix} = 0 \Rightarrow a = 0$$

$$\Delta'(x) = \begin{vmatrix} 2xe^{x^2} & \cos x & 0 \\ \sec x & \log(1+x^2) & 1 \\ x^3 & x^2 & 1 \end{vmatrix} + \begin{vmatrix} e^{x^2} & \sin x & 1 \\ \sec x\tan x & \frac{2x}{1+x^2} & 0 \\ x^3 & x^2 & 1 \end{vmatrix} + \begin{vmatrix} e^{x^2} & \sin x & 1 \\ \sec x & \log(1+x^2) & 1 \\ 3x^2 & 2x & 0 \end{vmatrix}$$

$\Delta'(0) = 0 = -1 + 0 + 0 = -1 = b$

4. $$f(x) = \begin{vmatrix} \cos x & x & 1 \\ 2\sin x & x^2 & 2x \\ \tan x & x & 1 \end{vmatrix}$$

$$f'(x) = \begin{vmatrix} -\sin x & 1 & 0 \\ 2\sin x & x^2 & 2x \\ \tan x & x & 1 \end{vmatrix} + \begin{vmatrix} \cos x & x & 1 \\ 2\cos x & 2x & 2 \\ \tan x & x & 1 \end{vmatrix} + \begin{vmatrix} \cos x & x & 1 \\ 2\sin x & x^2 & 2x \\ \sec^2 x & 1 & 0 \end{vmatrix}$$

$\Rightarrow$ f'(0) = 0 $\Rightarrow \lim_{x\to 0}\frac{f'(x)}{x} = \frac{f''(x)}{1} = f''(x)(at\, x=0)$

Now, f''(x) = (0 + 0 + 0) + (–2 + 0 + 0) + (0 + 0 + 0) = –2

$\therefore \lim_{x\to 0}\frac{f'(x)}{x} = f''(x)_{at\,x=0} = -2$

5. $f(x)=\begin{vmatrix}3&2&1\\6x^2&2x^3&x^4\\1&a&a^2\end{vmatrix}$; $f'(x)=|A|+\begin{vmatrix}3&2&1\\12x&6x^2&4x^3\\1&a&a^2\end{vmatrix}+|B|$

where |A| = 0 , |B| = 0 as one row is zero in both and

$f''(x)=\begin{vmatrix}3&2&1\\12&12x&12x^2\\1&a&a^2\end{vmatrix}$; $f''(a)=\begin{vmatrix}3&2&1\\12&12a&12a^2\\1&a&a^2\end{vmatrix}$

as $R_2 = 12R_3 \Rightarrow f''(a) = 0$

6. $f(x)=\begin{vmatrix}2\cos^2 x&\sin 2x&\sin x\\\sin 2x&2\sin^2 x&-\cos x\\\sin x&-\cos x&0\end{vmatrix}$

Observe that $C_1 \to 2\sin x.C_3 + C_1$ is useful

$\Rightarrow f(x)=\begin{vmatrix}2(\cos^2 x+\sin^2 x)&\sin 2x&\sin x\\2\sin x\cos x-2\sin x\cos x&2\sin^2 x&-\cos x\\\sin x&-\cos x&0\end{vmatrix}$

$f(x)=\begin{vmatrix}2&\sin 2x&\sin x\\0&2\sin^2 x&-\cos x\\\sin x&-\cos x&0\end{vmatrix}$;

Now $C_2 \to C_2 - 2\cos x\, C_3$, gives

$f(x)=\begin{vmatrix}2&0&\sin x\\0&2&-\cos x\\\sin x&-\cos x&0\end{vmatrix}$

= –2cos² x = 2sin²x – (–2)

So f'(x) = 0 $\Rightarrow \int_0^{\pi/2}\{f'(x)+f(x)\}dx = \int_0^{\pi/2}-2dx$

$= (-2)\frac{\pi}{2} = -\pi$

TEXTUAL EXERCISE 5: (OBJECTIVE)

1. (i) (d) $\Delta(x)=\begin{vmatrix}x^2-5x+3&2x-5&3\\3x^2+x+4&6x+1&9\\7x^2-6x+9&14x-6&21\end{vmatrix}$

$\Rightarrow \Delta'(x)=\begin{vmatrix}2x-5&2x-5&3\\6x+1&6x+1&9\\14x-6&14x-6&21\end{vmatrix}+$

$\begin{vmatrix}x^2-5x+3&2&3\\3x^2+x+4&6&9\\7x^2-6x+9&14&21\end{vmatrix}+0$

$\Delta'(x)_{at\,x=0}=0+\begin{vmatrix}3&2&3\\4&6&9\\9&14&21\end{vmatrix}+0 = 5\,(42-42)=0$

(ii) (c) $\Delta=\begin{vmatrix}x&x^2&x^3\\1&2x&3x^2\\0&2&6x\end{vmatrix}$

$\Delta'(x)=\begin{vmatrix}1&2x&3x^2\\1&2x&3x^2\\0&2&6x\end{vmatrix}+\begin{vmatrix}x&x^2&x^3\\0&2&6x\\0&2&6x\end{vmatrix}+\begin{vmatrix}x&x^2&x^3\\1&2x&3x^2\\0&0&6\end{vmatrix}=6x^2$

(iii) (a) $f'(x)=\begin{vmatrix}1&x^4+1&3\\1&2x^4+2&3\\1&3x^4+7&3\end{vmatrix}+\begin{vmatrix}(x+a^2)&4x^3&3\\(x+b^2)&8x^3&3\\(x+c^2)&12x^3&3\end{vmatrix}+0$

$\Rightarrow f'(x)=0+12x^3\begin{vmatrix}(x+a^2)&1&1\\(x+b^2)&2&1\\(x+c^2)&3&1\end{vmatrix} = 12x^3\begin{vmatrix}(x+a^2)&1&1\\(b^2-a^2)&1&0\\(c^2-b^2)&1&0\end{vmatrix}$

$= 12x^3\,\{b^2 - a^2 + b^2 - c^2\} = 0$

$\because\ x \neq 0 \Rightarrow 2b^2 = a^2 + c^2$

$\Rightarrow a^2, b^2, c^2$ are in AP.

2. (c) $\Delta(x)=\begin{vmatrix}e^{x^2}&\ln(1+x)\\\tan x&\sin x\end{vmatrix}$

$\Delta(0)=0 \Rightarrow \lim_{x\to 0}\frac{\Delta(x)}{x}=\frac{\Delta'(0)}{1}$

$\Delta'(x)=\begin{vmatrix}2xe^{x^2}&\frac{1}{1+x}\\\tan x&\sin x\end{vmatrix}+\begin{vmatrix}e^{x^2}&\ln(1+x)\\\sec^2 x&\cos x\end{vmatrix}$

$\Rightarrow \Delta'(0)=0+\begin{vmatrix}1&0\\1&1\end{vmatrix}=1 \Rightarrow \lim_{x\to 0}\frac{\Delta(x)}{x}=\frac{1}{1}=1$

3. (d) $f(x)=\begin{vmatrix}x^3&\sin x&\cos x\\6&-1&0\\p&p^2&p^3\end{vmatrix}$

$\Rightarrow f'(x)=\begin{vmatrix}3x^2&\cos x&-\sin x\\6&-1&0\\p&p^2&p^3\end{vmatrix}$

$\Rightarrow f''(x)=\begin{vmatrix}6x&-\sin x&-\cos x\\6&1&0\\p&p^2&p^3\end{vmatrix}$

$\Rightarrow f'''(x)=\begin{vmatrix}6&-\cos x&\sin x\\6&-1&0\\p&p^2&p^3\end{vmatrix}$

$\Rightarrow \frac{d^3}{dx^3}f(x)_{(at\,x=0)}=\begin{vmatrix}6&-1&0\\6&-1&0\\p&p^2&p^3\end{vmatrix}=0$

4. (a, d) $f(x)=\begin{vmatrix} x^n & \sin x & \cos x \\ n! & \sin\frac{n\pi}{2} & \cos\frac{n\pi}{2} \\ p & p^2 & p^3 \end{vmatrix}$

$$f^n(x)=\begin{vmatrix} n! & \sin\left(\frac{n\pi}{2}+x\right) & \cos\left(\frac{n\pi}{2}+x\right) \\ n! & \sin\frac{n\pi}{2} & \cos\frac{n\pi}{2} \\ p & p^2 & p^3 \end{vmatrix}$$

Thus $x=0, \frac{d^n f(x)}{dx^n}=0$

5. (a) $f(x)=\begin{vmatrix} 1 & a & a^2 \\ \sin(n-1)x & \sin nx & \sin(n+1)x \\ \cos(n-1)x & \cos nx & \cos(n+1)x \end{vmatrix}$

Operate $C_1 \to C_1 + C_3 - 2\cos x C_2$

$$\Rightarrow f(x)=\begin{vmatrix} 1+a^2-2a\cos x & a & a^2 \\ 0 & \sin nx & \sin(n+1)x \\ 0 & \cos nx & \cos(n+1)x \end{vmatrix}$$

$= (1 + a^2 - 2a \cos x) \{\sin nx \cos (n + 1)x - \cos nx \sin (n + 1)x\} = (1 + a^2 - 2a \cos x) \sin(-x) = a \sin 2x - (1 + a^2) \sin x$

$$\Rightarrow \int_0^{\pi/2} f(x)dx = \int_0^{\pi/2}\{a\sin 2x-(1+a^2)\sin x\}dx$$

$$= \frac{(-a)}{2}\cos 2x\Big|_0^{\pi/2}+(1+a^2)\cos x\Big|_0^{\pi/2}$$

$$= \left(\frac{-a}{2}\right)\{-1-1\}+(1+a^2)\{0-1\} = a-(1+a^2)$$

TEXTUAL EXERCISE 6: (SUBJECTIVE)

1. $m=-\frac{x}{y}\quad \left(-\frac{x}{y}\right)^2 x-\left(-\frac{x}{y}\right)y+a=0$

$\frac{x^3}{y^2}+x+a=0$ or $x^3 + xy^2 + ay^2 = 0$

Aliter: (using Matrices)

$$\begin{bmatrix} x & -y \\ 0 & y \end{bmatrix}\begin{bmatrix} m^2 \\ m \end{bmatrix}=\begin{bmatrix} -a \\ -x \end{bmatrix}\quad \Delta=\begin{vmatrix} x & -y \\ 0 & y \end{vmatrix}=xy$$

$$\Delta_1=\begin{vmatrix} -a & -y \\ -x & y \end{vmatrix}=-ay-xy\ ;\ \Delta_2=\begin{vmatrix} x & -a \\ 0 & -x \end{vmatrix}=-x^2$$

$\therefore\ m^2=\frac{\Delta_1}{\Delta}=\frac{-ay-xy}{xy}=-1-\frac{a}{x}$ .....(i)

And $m=\frac{\Delta_2}{\Delta}=\frac{-x^2}{xy}=-\frac{x}{y}$ .....(ii)

$\therefore$ from (i) and (ii) $-1-\frac{a}{x}=\frac{x^2}{y^2}$

$\Rightarrow -xy^2 - ay^2 = x^3 \qquad \Rightarrow x^3 + xy^2 + ay^2 = 0$

2. $mn + 1 = 0 \quad \Rightarrow mn = -1$ ...(i)

Given equations are $m^2x - my + a = 0$ ....(ii)

and $n^2x - ny + a = 0$ .....(iii)

(ii) × n and (iii) × m gives,

$m^2nx - mny + an = 0$ and $mn^2x - mny + am = 0$ or $- mx + y + an = 0$ and $-nx + y + am = 0$ (using $mn = -1$)

$$\Rightarrow \begin{bmatrix} -x & a \\ a & -x \end{bmatrix}\begin{bmatrix} m \\ n \end{bmatrix}=\begin{bmatrix} -y \\ -y \end{bmatrix}$$

Since there are infinitely many real m, n for which $mn = -1$

$$\Rightarrow \Delta=\begin{vmatrix} -x & a \\ a & -x \end{vmatrix}=\Rightarrow x^2-a^2=0\Rightarrow x=\pm a$$

Now $\Delta_1=\begin{vmatrix} -y & a \\ -y & -x \end{vmatrix}=xy+ay=y(x+a)$

$\Delta_2=\begin{vmatrix} -x & -y \\ a & -y \end{vmatrix}=xy+ay=y(x+a)$

$\therefore\ \Delta=\Delta_1=\Delta_2=0\Rightarrow x+a=0$

3. $\begin{bmatrix} m & -n \\ n & m \end{bmatrix}\begin{bmatrix} x \\ y \end{bmatrix}=\begin{bmatrix} a(m^2-n^2) \\ 2amn \end{bmatrix}$

Now $\Delta = m^2 + n^2 = 1 \neq 0$

$\Delta_1=\begin{vmatrix} a(m^2-n^2) & -n \\ 2amn & m \end{vmatrix}=a(m^2-n^2)m+2amn^2=am^3+amn^2=$ $am(m^2+n^2)=am$

$\Delta_2=\begin{vmatrix} m & a(m^2-n^2) \\ n & 2amn \end{vmatrix}=2am^2n-a(m^2-n^2)n=$ $am^2n+an^3=an(m^2+n^2)=an$

$\therefore\ x=\frac{\Delta_1}{\Delta}=am;\ y=\frac{\Delta_2}{\Delta}=an \quad \Rightarrow \quad m=\frac{x}{a};n=\frac{y}{a}$

$\therefore\ m^2+n^2=1\Rightarrow x^2+y^2=a^2$

4. $\begin{bmatrix} m & 1 \\ -1 & m \end{bmatrix}\begin{bmatrix} x \\ y \end{bmatrix}=\begin{bmatrix} a(1+m) \\ a(1-m) \end{bmatrix}$; Now, $\Delta=\begin{vmatrix} m & 1 \\ -1 & m \end{vmatrix}=m^2+1$

$\Delta_1=\begin{vmatrix} a(1+m) & 1 \\ a(1-m) & m \end{vmatrix}=am(1+m)-a(1-m)$

$= a[m + m^2 - 1 + m] = a (m^2 + 2m - 1)$

$\Rightarrow\ x=\frac{\Delta_1}{\Delta}=\frac{a(m^2+2m-1)}{m^2+1}$

$\Delta_2=\begin{vmatrix} m & a(1+m) \\ -1 & a(1-m) \end{vmatrix}$

$= a[m - m^2 + 1 + m] = -a [m^2 - 2m - 1]$

$\therefore\ y=\frac{\Delta^2}{\Delta}=\frac{-a(m^2-2m-1)}{(m^2-1)}$

$$\therefore \quad x^2 + y^2 = \frac{a^2}{(m^2+1)^2} = \left[(m^2+2m-1)^2 + (m^2-2m-1)^2\right]$$

$$\therefore \quad \frac{a^2}{(m^2+1)^2}[2m^4 + 8m^2 + 2 - 4m^2]$$

$$= \frac{2a^2}{(m^2+1)}(m^4 + 2m^2 + 1) = 2a^2 \quad \therefore x^2 + y^2 = 2a^2$$

5. $x + y - 4 = 0;\ 2x - 3y - 9 = 0$

$$\frac{x}{\begin{vmatrix} 1 & -4 \\ -3 & -9 \end{vmatrix}} = \frac{y}{\begin{vmatrix} -4 & 1 \\ -9 & 2 \end{vmatrix}} = \frac{1}{\begin{vmatrix} 1 & 1 \\ 2 & -3 \end{vmatrix}}$$

Gives $x = \frac{21}{5} = 4.2$ and $y = -\frac{1}{5} = -0.2$

6 Homogenous system

(a) $\Delta \neq 0$, number of trivial sol = 1
(b) $\Delta = 0$, number of solutions are infinite
(c) $\Delta = 0$, for non-trival sol of homogenous system
(d) Consistancy of homogenous system of equation is always there

7. Given: $ax + hy + g = 0$ .... (i)
$hx + by + f = 0$ ....(ii)
and $x(ax + hy + g) + y(hx + by + f) + gx + fy + c - t = 0$
or $gx + fy + c - t = 0$ ....(iii)
(i) and (ii) are linear in x and y so any solution to these will also solve (iii)

$$\therefore \begin{vmatrix} a & h & g \\ h & b & f \\ g & f & (c-t) \end{vmatrix} = 0, \text{ i.e., } \begin{vmatrix} a & h & g \\ h & b & f \\ g & f & c \end{vmatrix} + \begin{vmatrix} a & h & 0 \\ h & b & 0 \\ g & f & -t \end{vmatrix} = 0$$

$\Rightarrow \{abc + 2fgh - af^2 - bg^2 - ch^2\} - t(ab - h^2) = 0$

$$\text{Gives } t = \frac{(abc + 2fgh - af^2 - bg^2 - ch^2)}{ab - h^2} = \frac{\begin{vmatrix} a & h & g \\ h & b & f \\ g & f & c \end{vmatrix}}{\begin{vmatrix} a & h \\ h & b \end{vmatrix}}$$

8. $x + y + z = 1$ ..... (i)
$x + 3y - 2z = 1$ ....(ii)
$3x + (\lambda + 2)y - 3z = 2\lambda + 1$ ....(iii)

$$|A| = \begin{vmatrix} 1 & 1 & 1 \\ 1 & 3 & -2 \\ 3 & (\lambda+2) & -3 \end{vmatrix} = \begin{vmatrix} 1 & 0 & 0 \\ 1 & 2 & -3 \\ 3 & (\lambda-1) & -6 \end{vmatrix} = 3\lambda - 15$$

If $|A| = 0$ then $\lambda = 5$
We observe (i) + 2 (ii), gives $3x + 7y - 3z = 3$
And for $\lambda = 5$ (iii) is $3x + 7y - 3z = 11$. So inconsistent.
$\Rightarrow \lambda \neq 5$ i.e., $|A| \neq 0$ then
$3x + 7y - 3z = 3$; $3x + (\lambda + 2)y - 3z = 2\lambda + 1$
Gives $(\lambda - 5)y = 2\lambda - 2$

$\Rightarrow y = \frac{2(\lambda-1)}{\lambda-5}$ where $\lambda \neq 5$

Putting in (i) and (ii) $x + \frac{2\lambda-2}{\lambda-5} + z = 1$ i.e., $x + z = \frac{-(\lambda+3)}{\lambda-5}$

And $x + \frac{6\lambda-6}{\lambda-5} - 2z = 1$ i.e., $x - 2z = \frac{-(5\lambda-1)}{\lambda-5}$

Subtraction gives $z = \frac{4\lambda-4}{3(\lambda-5)}$

Similarly $x = \frac{-7\lambda-5}{3(\lambda-5)}$ and $y = \frac{2\lambda-2}{\lambda-5}$

9. $2x + 3y = 3$
$(c + 2)x + (c + 4)y = (c + 6)$
$(c + 2)^2x + (c + 4)^2y = (c + 6)^2$
Will be consistent (the concurrent lines or three superimposed lines)

$$\text{i.e., } \begin{vmatrix} 2 & 3 & 3 \\ (c+2) & (c+4) & (c+6) \\ (c+2)^2 & (c+4)^2 & (c+6)^2 \end{vmatrix} = 0$$

$$\text{gives } \begin{vmatrix} 2 & 1 & 0 \\ c+2 & 2 & 2 \\ (c+2)^2 & (4c+12) & (4c+20) \end{vmatrix}$$

$= 2(8c + 40 - 8c - 24) - (2c^2 + 20c + 32) = 0$
Gives $(-2c)(c + 10) = 0$ gives $c = 0, -10$

TEXTUAL EXERCISE 6: (OBJECTIVE)

1. (b) $\Delta = \begin{vmatrix} 1 & 1 & 1 \\ 1 & 3 & 2 \\ 1 & \lambda & 3 \end{vmatrix} = \begin{vmatrix} 1 & 1 & 1 \\ 0 & 2 & 1 \\ 0 & \lambda-1 & 2 \end{vmatrix} = 5 - \lambda \neq 0$

Gives $\lambda \neq 5$ (now $\mu \in \mathbb{R}$)

2 (a) $\Delta = \begin{vmatrix} 1 & 1 & 1 \\ 1 & 3 & 2 \\ 1 & \lambda & 3 \end{vmatrix} = 0$ for no solution (i.e., $\lambda = 5$)

Also at least one of $\Delta_x, \Delta_y, \Delta_z$ is non zero.

Consider $\Delta_x = \begin{vmatrix} 3 & 1 & 1 \\ 6 & 3 & 2 \\ \mu & 5 & 3 \end{vmatrix} = \begin{vmatrix} 3 & 1 & 1 \\ 0 & 1 & 0 \\ \mu-9 & 2 & 0 \end{vmatrix} = -\mu + 9 \neq 0$

$\Rightarrow \mu \neq 9;\ \Delta_y = \begin{vmatrix} 1 & 3 & 1 \\ 1 & 6 & 2 \\ 1 & \mu & 3 \end{vmatrix} = \begin{vmatrix} 1 & 1 & 1 \\ 0 & 3 & 1 \\ 0 & (\mu-3) & 2 \end{vmatrix}$

$= 6 + 3 - \mu \neq 0$, i.e., $\mu \neq 9$

3. (c) $x + y + z = 3$ .... (i)
$x + 3y + 2z = 6$ ....(ii)
$x + \lambda y + 3z = \mu$ ....(iii)
2(ii) – (i) gives $x + 5y + 3z = 9$
Comparing with (iii) $\lambda = 5$, $\mu = 9$
And it will give infinitely many solutions

4. (b) For infinite solutions of Homogenous system, $\Delta = 0$

So $\begin{vmatrix} 2 & -1 & 1 \\ 1 & -2 & 1 \\ \lambda & -1 & 2 \end{vmatrix} = \begin{vmatrix} 2 & -1 & 1 \\ -1 & -1 & 0 \\ \lambda-4 & 1 & 0 \end{vmatrix}$

$= -1 + (\lambda - 4) = 0$ gives $\lambda = 5$

5. (c) For non-trivial solution, $\Delta = 0$

i.e., $\begin{vmatrix} 1 & 4a & a \\ 1 & 3b & b \\ 1 & 2c & c \end{vmatrix} = \begin{vmatrix} 1 & 4a & a \\ 0 & (3b-4a) & (b-a) \\ 0 & (2c-4a) & (c-a) \end{vmatrix}$

$= (3b - 4a)(c - a) - (b - a)(2c - 4a)$

$= ab + bc - 2ac = 0$ gives $\frac{1}{c} + \frac{1}{a} = \frac{2}{b}$

So a,b,c are in H.P.

6. (b) $2x + y = 5$ ....(i)

$x + 3y = 5$ ....(ii)

$x - 2y = 0$ ....(iii)

From (iii), we get $x = 2y$ putting in (i), gives $y = 1$ so $x = 2$

(ii) is satisfied for $x = 2$, $y = 1$, so one solution.

7 (c) $ax + by = u$

$cx + dy = v$

(a, b, c, d, u, v are integers) has a unique solution.

Now, for unique solution $\frac{a}{c} \neq \frac{b}{d}$, i.e., $ad - bc \neq 0$

8. (c) $ax + by + c = 0$, $bx + cy + a = 0$, $cx + ay + b = 0$ has a unique solution (Three concurrent lines)

$\Rightarrow \begin{vmatrix} a & b & c \\ b & c & a \\ c & a & b \end{vmatrix} = 0$ The second system (3 planes)

$\begin{vmatrix} (b+c) & (c+a) & (a+b) \\ (a+c) & (a+b) & (b+c) \\ (a+b) & (b+c) & (c+a) \end{vmatrix} = 2\begin{vmatrix} (a+b+c) & (c+a) & (a+b) \\ (a+b+c) & (a+b) & (b+c) \\ (a+b+c) & (b+c) & (c+a) \end{vmatrix}$

$= 2\begin{vmatrix} b & (c+a) & a+b \\ c & (a+b) & (b+c) \\ a & (b+c) & (c+a) \end{vmatrix} = \begin{vmatrix} b & (c+a) & a \\ c & (a+b) & b \\ a & (b+c) & c \end{vmatrix} = \begin{vmatrix} b & c & a \\ c & a & b \\ a & b & c \end{vmatrix}$

$= \begin{vmatrix} a & b & c \\ b & c & a \\ c & a & b \end{vmatrix} = 0$

9. (b) $(k + 1)x + 8y = 4k$ and $kx + (k + 3)y = 3k - 1$

For infinite solutions $\frac{a_1}{a_2} = \frac{b_1}{b_2} = \frac{c_1}{c_2}$

So $\frac{k+1}{k} = \frac{8}{k+3} = \frac{4k}{3k-1}$

Solving first two, we get $k^2 + 4k + 3 = 8k$

$\Rightarrow k^2 - 4k + 3 = 0$

$\Rightarrow (k - 3)(k - 1) = 0$

$\therefore k = 1, 3$ and solving last two

$\Rightarrow 4k^2 + 12k = 24k - 8$

$\Rightarrow 4k^2 - 12k + 8 = 0$

$\Rightarrow k^2 - 3k + 2 = 0;$

$k = 1, 2$

$k = 1$ will satisfy all the requirements.

SECTION III: (SINGLE CORRECT ANSWER)

1. (d) $\Delta = \begin{vmatrix} 1+a & 1 & 1 \\ 1 & 1+b & 1 \\ 1 & 1 & 1+c \end{vmatrix} = abc\begin{vmatrix} \frac{1}{a}+1 & 1/b & 1/c \\ 1/a & 1+\frac{1}{b} & 1/c \\ 1/a & 1/b & 1+\frac{1}{c} \end{vmatrix};$

$abc\left(1+\frac{1}{a}+\frac{1}{b}+\frac{1}{c}\right)\begin{vmatrix} 1 & 1/b & 1/c \\ 1 & 1+1/b & 1/c \\ 1 & 1/b & 1+1/c \end{vmatrix} = abc\left(1+\frac{1}{a}+\frac{1}{b}+\frac{1}{c}\right)$

Since $abc \neq 0$

$\therefore 1+\frac{1}{a}+\frac{1}{b}+\frac{1}{c} = 0$ so $\frac{1}{a}+\frac{1}{b}+\frac{1}{c} = -1$

2. (c) $\Delta = \begin{vmatrix} 1+\sin^2 x & \cos^2 x & 4\sin 2x \\ \sin^2 x & 1+\cos^2 x & 4\sin 2x \\ \sin^2 x & \cos^2 x & 1+4\sin 2x \end{vmatrix}$

$= \begin{vmatrix} 1 & 0 & -1 \\ 0 & 1 & -1 \\ \sin^2 x & \cos^2 x & (1+4\sin 2x) \end{vmatrix}$

$1 + 4\sin 2x + \cos^2 x + \sin^2 x = 2 + 4\sin 2x$

$\therefore$ Maximum value of $\Delta = 6$

3. (c) Put $x = 0$, then $t = \begin{vmatrix} 0 & -1 & 3 \\ 1 & 2 & -3 \\ -3 & 4 & 0 \end{vmatrix} = 21$

4. (a) It is a skew symmetric det of odd order so it will vanish

$\Rightarrow |A|$ is independent of α and β

5. (c) $|A| = 6$ .....(i)

Now, $B = \begin{bmatrix} p+x & q+y & r+z \\ a+x & b+y & c+z \\ a+p & b+q & c+r \end{bmatrix}$

$\Rightarrow \det B = \begin{vmatrix} p & q & r \\ x & y & z \\ a & b & c \end{vmatrix} + \begin{vmatrix} x & y & z \\ a & b & c \\ p & q & r \end{vmatrix}$

$= (-1)^2\begin{vmatrix} a & b & c \\ p & q & r \\ x & y & z \end{vmatrix} + (-1)^2\begin{vmatrix} a & b & c \\ p & q & r \\ x & y & z \end{vmatrix} = 2|A| = 12$

6. $D_1 = \begin{vmatrix} a & b & a+b \\ c & d & c+d \\ a & b & a-b \end{vmatrix} = \begin{vmatrix} a & b & 0 \\ c & d & 0 \\ a & b & -2b \end{vmatrix} = (-2b)\{ad-bc\}$

$D_2 = \begin{vmatrix} a & c & a+c \\ b & d & b+d \\ a & c & a+b+c \end{vmatrix} = \begin{vmatrix} a & c & 0 \\ b & d & 0 \\ a & c & b \end{vmatrix} = b(ad-bc)$

$\therefore\ D_1/D_2 = (-2)$

7. **(a, b)** $a^2x - ay - 1 = -a$, for $x = y = 1$ gives

$\Rightarrow\ a^2 = 1 \Rightarrow a = \pm 1$; For $a = 1$

$\Rightarrow\ b + (3 - 2b) = 4$ gives $-b = 1$ or $b = -1$ and for $a = -1$

$\Rightarrow\ b + (3 - 2b) = 2 \Rightarrow b = 1$

$\therefore\ a = 1, b = -1$ or $a = -1, b = 1$

8. (d) $x = 1, y = 3$

Now, $ax - by = 2a - b$ gives $a - 3b = 2a - b$ or $a = -2b$;

$(c + 1)x + cy = 10 - a + 3b$ gives $c + 1 + 3c = 10 - a + 3b$

$\Rightarrow\ 4c + 1 = 10 + 5b$ or $b = \dfrac{4c-9}{5}$ so $a = \dfrac{18-8c}{5}$

$= a,b,c = \left(\dfrac{18-8c}{5}, \dfrac{4c-9}{5}, c\right); c \in \mathbb{R}$

Many such triplets are possible i.e. infinetly many

9. (c) For non-zero (non trivial solution)

$|A| = 0$, so $\begin{vmatrix} (k-1) & (3k+1) & 2k \\ (k-1) & (4k-2) & (k+3) \\ 2 & (3k+1) & 3(k-1) \end{vmatrix} = 0$

$\Rightarrow\ \begin{vmatrix} (k-1) & (3k+1) & 2k \\ 0 & (k-3) & (-k+3) \\ 2 & (3k+1) & 3(k-1) \end{vmatrix}$

$\Rightarrow\ (k-3)\begin{vmatrix} k-1 & 3k+1 & 2k \\ 0 & 1 & -1 \\ 2 & 3k+1 & 3k-3 \end{vmatrix} = 0$

$\Rightarrow\ (k-3)\begin{vmatrix} k-1 & 5k+1 & 2k \\ 0 & 0 & -1 \\ 2 & 6k-2 & 3k-3 \end{vmatrix} = 0$

$2(k - 3)[(k - 1)(3k - 1) - (5k - 1)] = 0$

$2(k - 3)(3k^2 - 9k) = 0$

$2(k - 3)3(k)(k - 3) = 0 \Rightarrow k = 0$ or 3

10. (d) $\Delta = \begin{vmatrix} \dfrac{1}{z} & \dfrac{1}{z} & \dfrac{-(x+y)}{z^2} \\ \dfrac{-(y+z)}{x^2} & \dfrac{1}{x} & \dfrac{1}{x} \\ \dfrac{y(y+z)}{x^2z} & \dfrac{x+2y+z}{xz} & \dfrac{-y(x+y)}{xz^2} \end{vmatrix}$

Multiply C_1, C_2 and C_3 respectively With x, y, z, then

$\Delta = \dfrac{1}{xyz}\begin{vmatrix} \dfrac{x}{z} & \dfrac{y}{z} & -\left(\dfrac{x+y}{z}\right) \\ -\left(\dfrac{y+z}{x}\right) & y/x & z/x \\ \dfrac{-y(y+z)}{xz} & \dfrac{y(x+2y+z)}{xz} & \dfrac{-y(x+y)}{xz} \end{vmatrix}$

Now $C_1 \to C_1 + C_2 + C_3$ gives,

$\Delta = \begin{vmatrix} 0 & y/z & -\dfrac{(x+y)}{z} \\ 0 & y/x & z/x \\ 0 & \dfrac{y(x+2y+z)}{xz} & \dfrac{-(x+y)y}{xz} \end{vmatrix} = 0$

$\therefore\ \Delta$ is independent of x, y, z

11. (d) (i) Consider an equilateral Δ with sides 0.99 cm, then its

area $= \Delta_1 = \dfrac{\sqrt{3}}{4}(0.99)^2$ sq cm

Consider an other Δ with sides $12m$, $12m$ and $24-h; h \to 0^+$, then

the area of second $\Delta_2 = \dfrac{1}{2}(24-h)\sqrt{144-\left(12-\dfrac{h}{2}\right)^2}; h \to 0^+$

$\Rightarrow\ \sqrt{144-\left(12-\dfrac{h}{2}\right)^2}; h \to 0^+$

$= \dfrac{1}{2}(24-h)\sqrt{12h-\dfrac{h^2}{4}}; h \to 0^+ \to 0$

$\therefore$ area = 0, so (i) is possible

(ii) Given $\dfrac{1}{(x-y)^2} + \dfrac{1}{(y-z)^2} + \dfrac{1}{(z-x)^2}$

$= \left\{\dfrac{1}{x-y} + \dfrac{1}{y-z} + \dfrac{1}{z-x}\right\}^2$ gives

$2\sum \dfrac{1}{(x-y)(y-z)} = 2\left\{\dfrac{(z-x)+(x-y)+(y-z)}{(x-y)(y-z)(z-x)}\right\} = 0$

$\Rightarrow$ for x, y, z are all different real numbers.

(iii) L.H.S $= \log_3 x . \log_4 x . \log_5 x = \dfrac{\ell n x . \ell n x . \ell n x}{\ell n 3 . \ell n 4 . \ell n 5}$

R.H.S $= (\ell n x)^2\left\{\dfrac{1}{\ell n 3 . \ell n 4} + \dfrac{1}{\ell n 4 . \ell n 5} + \dfrac{1}{\ell n 5 . \ell n 3}\right\}$

So $\dfrac{\ell n x}{\ell n 3 . \ell n 4 . \ell n 5} = \dfrac{\ell n 3 + \ell n 4 + \ell n 5}{\ell n 3 . \ell n 4 . \ell n 5}$; gives $x = 60$

(iii) $\to$ true

(iv) $12 = 1 \times 12 = 2 \times 6 = 3 \times 4$

So 1×12 ; 12×1 ; 2×6; 6×2 ; 3×4; 4×3 are six matrices of different order, hence (iv) true

12. (a) Observe that $C_2 \to C_2 + C_3 - 2C_1$ gives

$f'(x) = \begin{vmatrix} mx & 0 & mx+p \\ n & 0 & n-p \\ mx+2n & 0 & mx+2n-p \end{vmatrix} = 0$

$\Rightarrow$ $f(x)$ = constant

$\Rightarrow$ a horizontal line which will be parallel to x-axis

13. (a) $\Delta(x) = \begin{vmatrix} (x-1) & (x-1)^2 & x^3 \\ (x-1) & x^2 & (x+1)^3 \\ x & (x-1)^2 & (x+1)^3 \end{vmatrix}$

$$\Rightarrow \Delta'(x) = \begin{vmatrix} 1 & (x-1)^2 & x^3 \\ 1 & x^2 & (x+1)^3 \\ 1 & (x-1)^2 & (x+1)^3 \end{vmatrix} +$$

$$\begin{vmatrix} (x-1) & 2(x-1) & x^3 \\ (x-1) & 2x & (x+1)^3 \\ x & 2(x-1) & (x+1)^3 \end{vmatrix} + \begin{vmatrix} (x-1) & (x-1)^2 & 3x^2 \\ (x-1) & x^2 & 3(x+1)^2 \\ x & (x-1)^2 & 3(x+1)^2 \end{vmatrix}$$

Put $x = 0$

$$\Rightarrow \Delta'(0) = \begin{vmatrix} 1 & 1 & 0 \\ 1 & 0 & 1 \\ 1 & 1 & 1 \end{vmatrix} + \begin{vmatrix} -1 & -2 & 0 \\ -1 & 0 & 1 \\ 0 & -2 & 1 \end{vmatrix} + \begin{vmatrix} -1 & 1 & 0 \\ -1 & 0 & 3 \\ 0 & 1 & 3 \end{vmatrix}$$

$$= \begin{vmatrix} 0 & 1 & 0 \\ 1 & 0 & 1 \\ 0 & 1 & 1 \end{vmatrix} + \begin{vmatrix} -1 & -2 & 0 \\ -1 & 2 & 0 \\ 0 & -2 & 1 \end{vmatrix} + \begin{vmatrix} -1 & 1 & 0 \\ 0 & -1 & 3 \\ 0 & 1 & 3 \end{vmatrix}$$

$= (-1) + (-4) + 6 = 1$

14. (d) Under the given conditions the determinants

$|A| = \begin{vmatrix} (a+b) & ab & 0 \\ 1 & (a+b) & ab \\ 0 & 1 & a+b \end{vmatrix}$; gives $|A| = (a^2 + b^2)(a + b)$

15. (d) $\Delta = \dfrac{1}{abc}\begin{vmatrix} a(a^2+1) & ab^2 & ac^2 \\ a^2b & b(b^2+1) & bc^2 \\ a^2c & b^2c & c(c^2+1) \end{vmatrix}$

$$= \frac{abc}{abc}\begin{vmatrix} 1+a^2 & b^2 & c^2 \\ a^2 & (b^2+1) & c^2 \\ a^2 & b^2 & c^2+1 \end{vmatrix}$$

$$= (1+a^2+b^2+c^2)\begin{vmatrix} 1 & b^2 & c^2 \\ 1 & b^2+1 & c^2 \\ 1 & b^2 & c^2+1 \end{vmatrix}$$

$$= (1+a^2+b^2+c^2)\begin{vmatrix} 0 & 0 & -1 \\ 0 & 1 & -1 \\ 1 & b^2 & c^2+1 \end{vmatrix}$$

$= (a^2 + b^2 + c^2 + 1)(1) = 1$ (given)

$\Rightarrow$ $a^2 + b^2 + c^2 = 0$, so $a = b = c = 0$

16. (b) $\varDelta = \begin{vmatrix} 3a+3b & a+b & a+2b \\ 3a+3b & a & a+b \\ 3a+3b & a+2b & a \end{vmatrix}$

$$= 3(a+b)\begin{vmatrix} 1 & a+b & a+2b \\ 1 & a & a+b \\ 1 & a+2b & a \end{vmatrix}$$

$$= 3(a+b)\begin{vmatrix} 1 & (a+b) & (a+2b) \\ 0 & -b & -b \\ 0 & b & -2b \end{vmatrix}$$

$= 3(a + b)(3b^2) = 9b^2(a + b)$

17. (b) $\varDelta = \begin{vmatrix} (a+2b-x) & b & b \\ (a+2b-x) & (a-x) & b \\ (a+2b-x) & b & (a-x) \end{vmatrix} = 0$

$$\Rightarrow (a+2b-x)\begin{vmatrix} 1 & b & b \\ 0 & (a-b-x) & 0 \\ 0 & 0 & (a-b-x) \end{vmatrix} = 0$$

Gives $x = a - b$, $a - b$ so roots are real and coincident

18. (b) $\begin{vmatrix} 1 & 2a & a \\ 1 & 3b & b \\ 1 & 4c & c \end{vmatrix} = 0 \Rightarrow \begin{vmatrix} 1 & 2a & a \\ 0 & (3b-2a) & (b-a) \\ 0 & (4c-2a) & (c-a) \end{vmatrix} = 0$

Gives $3bc - 2ac - 3ab + 2a^2 + 4ac - 2a^2 - 4bc + 2ab = 0$

$\Rightarrow$ $2ac = ab + bc$ or $\dfrac{2}{b} = \dfrac{1}{c} + \dfrac{1}{a}$

$\Rightarrow$ a, b, c are in H.P.

19. (b) **Statement I:** is true, if lines are not parallel or coincidental then they will intersect in a unique point

Statement II: In homogenous system a non-zero (non-trival) solution means infinite number of solutions as the system is consistent. Statement II is true.

Statement III: False, $x = y = 2/3$ and $z = -1/3$ is the solution. System is consistent.

Statement IV: If two equations in a system are inconsistent then obviously the whole system will be inconsistent.

20. (a) $\varDelta = \begin{vmatrix} 1 & -2 & 5 \\ 0 & (x+4) & -11 \\ 0 & 4 & 2x \end{vmatrix} = 86 \quad \Rightarrow 2x^2 + 8x + 4 = 86$

$\Rightarrow$ $x^2 + 4x - 21 = 0$

$\Rightarrow$ Sum of roots = –4

21. (a) $\varDelta = \begin{vmatrix} pa & qb & rc \\ qc & ra & pb \\ rb & pc & qa \end{vmatrix}$

$= pqr(a^3 + b^3 + c^3) - abc(p^3 + q^3 + r^3)$

From $p + q + r = 0 \Rightarrow p + q = -r$ so $(p + q)^3 = -r^3$;

$p^3 + q^3 + 3pq(p + q) + r^3 = 0$ or $p^3 + q^3 + r^3 = 3pqr$

Similarly $a^3 + b^3 + c^3 = 3abc$

$\therefore$ $\Delta = pqr(3abc) - abc(3pqr) = 0$

22. (b) $\varDelta = \begin{vmatrix} \tan A & 1 & 0 \\ 1 & \tan B & 1-\tan B \\ 1 & 1 & \tan C - 1 \end{vmatrix} = \tan A(\tan B.\tan C - 1)$

$- 1(\tan C - 1 - 1 + \tan B)$

$= \tan A \tan B \tan C - \tan A - \tan B - \tan C + 2 = 2$

(Using $\tan A \tan B \tan C = \tan A + \tan B + \tan C$ in a Δ)

23. (d) $\Delta=\begin{vmatrix}(a-1) & a & (a+1)\\(b-1) & b & (b+1)\\(c-1) & c & (c+1)\end{vmatrix}$; we observe that $2C_2 = C_1 + C_3$

$\therefore$ Operation $C_1 \to C_1 + C_3 - 2C_2$ $\Delta=\begin{vmatrix}0 & a & a+1\\0 & b & b+1\\0 & c & c+1\end{vmatrix}=0$

24. (a) $A = a^2 + b^2 + c^2$, $B = ab + bc + ca$

we know that $-(a^3 + b^3 - c^3 - 3abc) = \begin{vmatrix}a & b & c\\b & c & a\\c & a & b\end{vmatrix}$

$\therefore$ $(a^3 + b^3 + c^3 - 3abc)^2 = \begin{vmatrix}a & b & c\\b & c & a\\c & a & b\end{vmatrix}\begin{vmatrix}a & b & c\\b & c & a\\c & a & b\end{vmatrix}$

$=\begin{vmatrix}a^2+b^2+c^2 & ab+bc+ca & ac+ab+bc\\ab+bc+ca & a^2+b^2+c^2 & ab+bc+ca\\ab+bc+ca & ab+bc+ca & a^2+b^2+c^2\end{vmatrix}$

$=\begin{vmatrix}A & B & B\\B & A & B\\B & B & A\end{vmatrix}=(-1)^2\begin{vmatrix}B & A & B\\B & B & A\\A & B & B\end{vmatrix}$

25. (c) $\Delta=\begin{vmatrix}\sin\frac{A}{2} & \sin\frac{B}{2} & \sin\frac{C}{2}\\0 & \sin\frac{B}{2} & \cos\frac{A}{2}\\0 & 0 & \sin\frac{C}{2}\end{vmatrix}$

Since this is a triangular matrix

$\therefore$ $\Delta = \sin A/2.\sin B/2.\sin C/2$

The maxima will be at $\angle A = \angle B = \angle C = 60^0$

i.e., equilateral triangle $\Rightarrow \Delta\le\left(\frac{1}{2}\right)^3=\frac{1}{8}$

26. (b) $\Delta=\begin{vmatrix}(x-5) & 2 & 5\\0 & x & 3\\(5-x) & 4 & x\end{vmatrix}=\begin{vmatrix}(x-5) & 2 & 5\\0 & x & 3\\0 & 6 & (x+5)\end{vmatrix}$

$= (x-5)\{x^2 + 5x - 18\} = 0$, sum of roots $= -5$

27. (a) $\Delta=(x+y+z+a+b+c)=\begin{vmatrix}1 & (y+b) & (z+c)\\1 & (z+c) & (x+a)\\1 & (x+a) & (y+b)\end{vmatrix}=0$

Since $a + b + c = 0$;

$\Delta=(x+y+z)\begin{vmatrix}1 & (y+b) & (z+c)\\0 & (z+c)-(y+b) & (x+a)-(z+c)\\0 & (x+a)-(z+c) & (y+b)-(x+a)\end{vmatrix}$

$\Rightarrow$ $(x + y + z)\{(z + c)(y + b) - (y + b)^2 - (x + a)(z + c) + (y + b)(x + a) - (z + c)^2 + (x + a)(z + c) - (x + a)^2 + (x + a)(z + c)\} = 0$

$-(x+y+z).\frac{1}{2}\left[\{(x+a)-(y+b)\}^2+\{(y+b)-(z+c)\}^2+\{(z+c)-(x+a)\}^2\right]=0$

$\Rightarrow$ $x+y+z=0$ or $x+a=y+b=z+c$ (impossible as line segment joining any two points is not equally inclined to axes

$\Rightarrow$ $2\left(\frac{-y}{2}\right)=x+z \Rightarrow x,\frac{-y}{2},z$ are in A.P.

28. (a) Operate $C_3 - C_2$ and $C_2 - C_1$ then

$\Delta=\begin{vmatrix}1 & 0 & 0\\m & 3 & 3\\{}^mC_2 & {}^{m+3}C_2-{}^mC_2 & {}^{m+6}C_2-{}^{m+3}C_2\end{vmatrix}$

$= 3\{{}^{m+6}C_2 - {}^{m+3}C_2 - {}^{m+3}C_2 + {}^mC_2\}$

$=3\left\{\frac{(m+6)(m+5)}{2}+\frac{m(m-1)}{2}-\frac{2(m+3)(m+2)}{2}\right\}$

$=3\left(\frac{18}{2}\right)=27=3^3=2^\alpha\,3^\beta\,5^\gamma \Rightarrow \alpha=0,\ \beta=3,\ \gamma=0$

$\alpha+\beta+\gamma=3$

29. (a) $\Delta(x)=\begin{vmatrix}e^x & \sin 2x & \tan x^2\\\ell n(1+x) & \cos x & \sin x\\\cos x^2 & e^x-1 & \sin x^2\end{vmatrix}$

$=A + Bx + Cx^2 + \ldots\ldots$ $\Rightarrow B = \Delta'(0)$

Now, $\Delta'(x)=\begin{vmatrix}e^x & \sin 2x & \tan x^2\\\frac{1}{1+x} & -\sin x & \cos x\\\cos x^2 & e^x-1 & \sin x^2\end{vmatrix}+$

$\begin{vmatrix}e^x & 2\cos 2x & 2x\sec^2 x^2\\\ell n(1+x) & \cos x & \sin x\\\cos x^2 & e^x-1 & \sin x^2\end{vmatrix}$

$+\begin{vmatrix}e^x & \sin 2x & \tan x^2\\\ell n(1+x) & \cos x & \sin x\\-2x\sin x^2 & e^x & 2x\cos x^2\end{vmatrix}$

$\Rightarrow$ $\Delta'(0)=\begin{vmatrix}1 & 0 & 0\\1 & 0 & 1\\1 & 0 & 0\end{vmatrix}+\begin{vmatrix}1 & 2 & 0\\0 & 1 & 0\\1 & 0 & 0\end{vmatrix}+\begin{vmatrix}1 & 0 & 0\\0 & 1 & 0\\0 & 1 & 0\end{vmatrix}=0 \Rightarrow B=0$

30. (d) $\Delta=\begin{vmatrix}\alpha & \beta & \gamma\\\beta & \gamma & \alpha\\\gamma & \alpha & \beta\end{vmatrix}=3\alpha\beta\gamma-\{\alpha^3+\beta^3+\gamma^3\}$

$\because$ α, β, γ are the roots of $x^3 + ax^2 + 0x + b = 0$

$\Rightarrow$ $\alpha + \beta + \gamma = -a$ and $\alpha\beta\gamma = -b$; $\Sigma\alpha\beta = 0$

$\Rightarrow$ $D = -(\alpha + \beta + \gamma)\{\alpha^2 + \beta^2 + \gamma^2 - \alpha\beta - \beta\gamma - \gamma\alpha\}$

$= -(-a)\{(\alpha + \beta + \gamma)^2 - 3\Sigma\alpha\beta\} = a\{(-a)^2 - 0] = a^3$

31. **(b, d)** Let $a = 1$, $b = \omega$ and $c = \omega^2$ then $a^2 = 1$, $b^2 = \omega^2$, $c^2 = \omega$

(using $1+\omega+\omega^2=0$)

$$\Delta=\begin{vmatrix}1+\omega^2 & \omega & \omega\\ 1 & \omega+\omega^2 & 1\\ \omega^2 & \omega^2 & 1+\omega\end{vmatrix}$$

$$\Rightarrow \Delta=\begin{vmatrix}1+\omega^2 & (1+\omega+\omega^2=0) & \omega\\ 1 & 0 & 1\\ \omega^2 & 2\omega^2 & \omega^2\end{vmatrix}$$

$(-2\omega^2)(1+\omega^2-\omega)=(-2\omega^2)(-2\omega)=4\omega^3=4$

$\Rightarrow$ Im $(\Delta)=0$; Re(Δ) + Im$(\Delta)=4$

32. (a) Column wise differentiation gives

$$f'(x)=\begin{vmatrix}1 & x^2+1 & 1\\ 1 & 2x^2-1 & 1\\ 1 & 3x^2-2 & 1\end{vmatrix}$$

$$+\begin{vmatrix}x+a & 2x & 1\\ x+b & 4x & 1\\ x+c & 6x & 1\end{vmatrix}+\begin{vmatrix}x+a & (x^2+1) & 0\\ x+b & (2x^2-1) & 0\\ x+c & (3x^2-2) & 0\end{vmatrix}$$

Operating, $R_1\to R_1+R_3-2R_2$ gives zeroes in R_2 of middle determinant.

$\Rightarrow f'(x)=0+0+0=0$

33. (c) $$f(x)=\begin{vmatrix}\sin x & \sin 2x & \sin 3x\\ 0 & 3 & 4\sin x\\ 0 & \sin x & 1\end{vmatrix}$$

$=\sin x\,\{3-4\sin^2 x\}=\sin 3x$

$$\Rightarrow I=\int_0^{\pi/2}\sin 3x\,dx=\left.\frac{-\cos 3x}{3}\right|_0^{\pi/2}=\left(-\frac{1}{3}\right)\{0-1\}=\frac{1}{3}$$

34. (d) (a)

$$\Delta=\frac{1}{abc}\begin{vmatrix}a & abc & abc(b+c)\\ b & abc & abc(c+a)\\ c & abc & abc(a+b)\end{vmatrix}=\frac{(abc)^2}{(abc)}\begin{vmatrix}a & 1 & b+c\\ b & 1 & c+a\\ c & 1 & a+b\end{vmatrix}$$

$$=(abc)(a+b+c)\begin{vmatrix}1 & 1 & (b+c)\\ 1 & 1 & (c+a)\\ 1 & 1 & (a+b)\end{vmatrix}=0$$

$$\text{(ii) }\Delta=abc\begin{vmatrix}1 & \frac{1}{c} & \frac{1}{a}+\frac{1}{b}\\ 1 & \frac{1}{a} & \frac{1}{b}+\frac{1}{c}\\ 1 & \frac{1}{b} & \frac{1}{a}+\frac{1}{c}\end{vmatrix}$$

Operate $C_3\to C_2+C_3$ and takeout $\left(\frac{1}{a}+\frac{1}{b}+\frac{1}{c}\right)$, then

$$\Delta=abc\left\{\frac{1}{a}+\frac{1}{b}+\frac{1}{c}\right\}\begin{vmatrix}1 & 1/c & 1\\ 1 & 1/a & 1\\ 1 & 1/b & 1\end{vmatrix}=0$$

(c) $$\Delta=\begin{vmatrix}\frac{\ell n\,xyz}{\ell n\,x} & \frac{\ell n\,y}{\ell n\,x} & \frac{\ell n\,z}{\ell n\,x}\\ \frac{\ell n\,xyz}{\ell n\,y} & \frac{\ell n\,y}{\ell n\,y} & \frac{\ell n\,z}{\ell n\,y}\\ \frac{\ell n\,xyz}{\ell n\,z} & \frac{\ell n\,y}{\ell n\,z} & \frac{\ell n\,z}{\ell n\,z}\end{vmatrix}$$

$$=\frac{1}{\log_e x\log_e y\log_e z}\times\begin{vmatrix}\log_e x & \log_e y & \log_e z\\ \log_e x & \log_e y & \log_e z\\ \log_e x & \log_e y & \log_e z\end{vmatrix},$$

since $R_1=R_2=R_3$

$\therefore\ \Delta=0$ so all determinants are vanishing

35. (b) $$\Delta=\begin{vmatrix}a & b & a\alpha+b\\ b & c & b\alpha+c\\ a\alpha+b & b\alpha+c & 0\end{vmatrix}$$

$C_3\to C_3-(\alpha C_1+C_2)$ gives

$$\begin{vmatrix}a & b & 0\\ b & c & 0\\ a\alpha+b & b\alpha+c & -(a\alpha^2+2b\alpha+c)\end{vmatrix}$$

$=-(ac-b^2)(a\alpha^2+2b\alpha+c)$

$\therefore\ \Delta=0$ if a,b,c are in G.P.

36. (d) Since $a,b,c,d>0$

$(a^2+b^2+c^2)x^2-2(ab+bc+cd)x+(b^2+c^2+d^2)\le 0$

$(ax-b)^2+(bx-c)^2+(cx-d)^2\le 0$

$\Rightarrow\ x=\frac{b}{a}=\frac{c}{b}=\frac{d}{c}$ or a, b, c, d are in G.P. with common ratio x.

$$\text{Now }\ \Delta=\begin{vmatrix}33 & 14 & \log_e a\\ 65 & 27 & \log_e b\\ 97 & 40 & \log_e c\end{vmatrix}=\begin{vmatrix}33 & 14 & \log_e a\\ -1 & -1 & \log_e\left(\frac{b}{a}\right)\\ -2 & -2 & \log_e\left(\frac{c}{a}\right)\end{vmatrix}$$

(using $R_2\to R_2-2R_1$ and $R_3\to R_3-3R_1$)

$$=\begin{vmatrix}33 & 14 & \ell n\,a\\ -1 & -1 & \ell n\left(\frac{b}{a}\right)\\ 0 & 0 & \ell n\left(\frac{ca}{b^2}\right)\end{vmatrix}=(-19)\ell n\left(\frac{ca}{b^2}\right)$$

Since $b^2=ac\Rightarrow\Delta=-19\ ln1=0$

37. (d) Let the determinant of 2×2 is $\begin{vmatrix}a_{11} & a_{12}\\ a_{21} & a_{22}\end{vmatrix}$.

$\therefore$ Total number of determinants under the given conditions $=2^4=16$

Now $\begin{vmatrix}1 & 1\\1 & 0\end{vmatrix} = \begin{vmatrix}0 & 1\\1 & 0\end{vmatrix} = \begin{vmatrix}0 & 1\\1 & 1\end{vmatrix} = -1$ are the only determinants with –ve values

$\therefore$ number of non-negative determinants = 13

38. (a) $\Delta = \begin{vmatrix}\alpha & -\beta & 0\\0 & \alpha & \beta\\\beta & 0 & \alpha\end{vmatrix} = \alpha^3 - \beta^3 = 0$

$\Rightarrow$ $(\alpha - \beta)\{\alpha^2 + \beta^2 + \alpha\beta\} = 0$

$\Rightarrow$ $\alpha = \beta$ or $\left(\frac{\alpha}{\beta}\right)^2 + \left(\frac{\alpha}{\beta}\right) + 1 = 0$ but $\alpha \neq \beta$ (given)

Which shows that $\frac{\alpha}{\beta}$ is one of the cube roots of unity

39. (a) $\Delta = \begin{vmatrix}\cos\alpha & -\sin\alpha & 1\\\sin\alpha & \cos\alpha & 1\\\cos(\alpha-\beta) & -\sin(\alpha-\beta) & 1\end{vmatrix}$

Operate $R_3 \to R_3 - \{R_1 \cos b\} + R_2 \sin b$

$\Delta = \begin{vmatrix}\cos\alpha & -\sin\alpha & 1\\\sin\alpha & \cos\alpha & 1\\0 & 0 & 1+\sin\beta-\cos\beta\end{vmatrix}$

$= \{1 - (\sin\beta + \cos\beta)\}(\cos^2\alpha + \sin^2\alpha)$

Now $\sin\beta + \cos\beta = \sqrt{2}\left\{\sin\left(\beta + \frac{\pi}{4}\right)\right\} \in \left[-\sqrt{2}, \sqrt{2}\right]$

$\Rightarrow$ $\Delta \in [1-\sqrt{2}+1+\sqrt{2}]$

40. (a) $\begin{vmatrix}a & b & c\\b & c & a\\c & a & b\end{vmatrix} = 3abc - (a^3 + b^3 + c^3) = 0$

Gives $-(a + b + c)\{a^2 + b^2 + c^2 - (ab + bc + ca)\} = 0$

Since $a + b + c \neq 0$

$\therefore$ $\frac{1}{2}\{(a - b)^2 + (b - c)^2 + (c - a)^2\} = 0$

or a = b = c i.e., equilateral triangle so $\angle A = \angle B = \angle C = 60°$

$\Rightarrow$ $\sin^3 A + \sin^3 B + \sin^3 C = 3\left(\frac{\sqrt{3}}{2}\right)^3 = 3\sin A \sin B \sin C$

41. (a) For non-zero /non –trivial solution

$\Delta = \begin{vmatrix}a & b & c\\b & c & a\\c & a & b\end{vmatrix} = 3abc - (a^3 + b^3 + c^3) = 0$

i.e., $-(a + b + c)\{(a - b)^2 + (b - c)^2 + (c - a)^2\} = 0$

Since $a > b > c$ $\therefore$ $(a + b + c) = 0$

$\{$as $a - b \neq 0,\ b - c \neq 0,\ c - a \neq 0\}$

Now $at^2 + bt + c = 0$ is satisfied by $t = 1$

(As $a + b + c = 0$), the other root will be c/a

or $\left(-\frac{b}{a} - 1\right)$

$\therefore$ At least one positive root

42. (a) $x - 3y = 4$; $5x + y = 2$;

$15x + 3y = 6$

$16x = 10$ or $x = \frac{5}{8}$ and $y = -\frac{9}{8}$

$\therefore$ $[2\pi]x - [e]y = [2x]$

gives $6x - 2y = 6 = [2a]$

$\Rightarrow$ $6 \leq 2a < 7$; so $a \in [3, 3.5)$

43. (c) $\Delta = \begin{vmatrix}n! & (n+1)! & (n+2)!\\(n+1)! & (n+2)! & (n+3)!\\(n+2)! & (n+3)! & (n+4)!\end{vmatrix}$

$= \begin{vmatrix}n! & (n+1)! & (n+2)!\\n.(n!) & (n+1).(n+1)! & (n+2).(n+2)!\\(n+1).(n+1)! & (n+2).(n+2)! & (n+3).(n+3)!\end{vmatrix}$

(By $R_2 \to R_2 - R_1$ and $R_3 \to R_3 - R_2$)

$= \begin{vmatrix}n! & (n+1)! & (n+2)!\\n(n!) & (n+1).(n+1)! & (n+2).(n+2)!\\(n+1)^2.(n!) & (n+2)^2.(n+1)! & (n+3)^2.(n+2)!\end{vmatrix}$

(By $R_2 \to R_2 - R_1$)

$= (n!).(n+1)!.(n+2)!\begin{vmatrix}1 & 1 & 1\\n & n+1 & n+2\\(n+1)^2 & (n+2)^2 & (n+3)^2\end{vmatrix}$

$= 2(n!).(n + 1)!(n + 2)!$

44. (c) $\Delta = \begin{vmatrix}1 & 1 & 1\\\cot\frac{A}{2} & \cot\frac{B}{2} & \cot\frac{C}{2}\\\tan\frac{B}{2}+\tan\frac{C}{2} & \tan\frac{C}{2}+\tan\frac{A}{2} & \tan\frac{A}{2}+\tan\frac{B}{2}\end{vmatrix} = 0$

$= \begin{vmatrix}1 & 0 & 0\\\cot\frac{A}{2} & \cot\frac{B}{2}-\cot\frac{A}{2} & \cot\frac{C}{2}-\cot\frac{A}{2}\\\tan\frac{B}{2}+\tan\frac{C}{2} & \tan\frac{A}{2}-\tan\frac{B}{2} & \tan\frac{A}{2}-\tan\frac{C}{2}\end{vmatrix} = 0$

$\Rightarrow$ $\left(\cot\frac{B}{2} - \cot\frac{A}{2}\right)\left(\tan\frac{A}{2} - \tan\frac{C}{2}\right)$

$= \left(\tan\frac{A}{2} - \tan\frac{B}{2}\right)\left(\cot\frac{C}{2} - \cot\frac{A}{2}\right)$

$\Rightarrow$ $\frac{\left(\tan\frac{A}{2} - \tan\frac{B}{2}\right).\left(\tan\frac{B}{2} - \tan\frac{C}{2}\right).\left(\tan\frac{C}{2} - \tan\frac{A}{2}\right)}{\tan\frac{A}{2}.\tan\frac{B}{2}.\tan\frac{C}{2}} = 0$

Either $\tan\frac{A}{2} = \tan\frac{B}{2}$ or $\tan\frac{B}{2} = \tan\frac{C}{2}$ or $\tan\frac{C}{2} = \tan\frac{A}{2}$

$\therefore$ At least isosceles triangle (not necessarily an equilateral Δ)

45. (c) Let $\Delta = \begin{vmatrix} a^2 & b^2 & c^2 \\ (a+1)^2 & (b+1)^2 & (c+1)^2 \\ (a-1)^2 & (b-1)^2 & (c-1)^2 \end{vmatrix}$

$$\Delta = \begin{vmatrix} a^2-b^2 & (b^2-c^2) & c^2 \\ (a-b)(a+b+2) & (b+c+2)(b-c) & (c+1)^2 \\ (a-b)(a+b-2) & (b-c)(b+c-2) & (c-1)^2 \end{vmatrix}$$

$$= (a-b)(b-c)\begin{vmatrix} (a+b) & (b+c) & c^2 \\ 2 & 2 & 1+2c \\ -2 & -2 & 1-2c \end{vmatrix}$$

$$= (a-b)(b-c)\begin{vmatrix} (a+b) & (b+c) & c^2 \\ 0 & 0 & 2 \\ -2 & -2 & 1-2c \end{vmatrix}$$

$= (-2)\ (a-b)\ (b-c)\ [2b + 2c - 2a - 2b]$
$= (-4)\ (a-b)\ (b-c)\ (c-a) = 0$ gives either $a = b$ or $b = c$ or $c = a$, so (at least) isosceles Δ

(Not necessarily an equilateral triangle)

SECTION IV: (MORETHEN ONE CORRECT)

1. **(a, b)** With $a_1, a_2, a_3, \ldots, a_9$ distinct numbers the number of 3×3 determinants formed $= 9!$ irrespective of their values. By interchanging two consecutive rows (or columns) the value of determinant become –ive so for this pair the sum = 0

$\Rightarrow$ Total sum = 0 for all the $\dfrac{9!}{2}$ pairs

2. **(a, c, d)** Operate $C_2 \to C_2 - 2C_3$ then

$$\Delta = \begin{vmatrix} x^2 & y^2+z^2 & yz \\ y^2 & x^2+z^2 & xz \\ z^2 & x^2+y^2 & xy \end{vmatrix} = (x^2+y^2+z^2)\begin{vmatrix} x^2 & 1 & yz \\ y^2 & 1 & xz \\ z^2 & 1 & xy \end{vmatrix}$$

$$= \frac{(x^2+y^2+z^2)}{xyz}\begin{vmatrix} x^3 & x & xyz \\ y^3 & y & xyz \\ z^3 & z & xyz \end{vmatrix} = -(x^2+y^2+z^2)\begin{vmatrix} 1 & x & x^3 \\ 1 & y & y^3 \\ 1 & z & z^3 \end{vmatrix}$$

$= -(x^2 + y^2 + z^2)\ (x - y)\ (y - z)\ (z - x)\ (x + y + z)$

3. (c) $\Delta(x) = \begin{vmatrix} x & x^2 & x \\ x & 1 & x^2 \\ x^2 & x & 1 \end{vmatrix} = x(1-x^3) - x^2(x-x^4)$

$= x(x^3 - 1)\ (x^2 - 1) = 0$ gives $x = 0, \pm 1, \omega, \omega^2$

4. (a, b, c) $\Delta(x) = \begin{vmatrix} \cos 2x & \sin^2 x & \cos 4x \\ \sin^2 x & \cos 2x & \cos^2 x \\ \cos 4x & \cos^2 x & \cos 2x \end{vmatrix}$

$$\Delta(0) = \begin{vmatrix} 1 & 0 & 1 \\ 0 & 1 & 1 \\ 1 & 1 & 1 \end{vmatrix} = \begin{vmatrix} 1 & 0 & 1 \\ 0 & 1 & 1 \\ 0 & 1 & 0 \end{vmatrix} = (-1) = a_0$$

Now, $\dfrac{d\Delta(x)}{d(\sin x)} = \dfrac{d(\Delta x)}{dx} \Big/ \left(\dfrac{d\sin x}{dx}\right) = \dfrac{1}{\cos x}\left\{\dfrac{d}{dx}(\Delta(x))\right\}$

At $x = 0$, $\cos x = 1$

$$\Delta(x) = \begin{vmatrix} 1-2\sin^2 x & \sin^2 x & 1+8\sin^4 x - 8\sin^2 x \\ \sin^2 x & 1-2\sin^2 x & 1-\sin^2 x \\ 1+8\sin^4 x - 8\sin^2 x & 1-\sin^2 x & 1-2\sin^2 x \end{vmatrix}$$

Diff. w.r.t to sinx ($\sin x = t$) at $x = 0$ gives

$$\begin{vmatrix} 0 & 0 & 0 \\ 0 & 1 & 1 \\ 1 & 1 & 1 \end{vmatrix} + \begin{vmatrix} 1 & 0 & 1 \\ 0 & 0 & 0 \\ 1 & 1 & 1 \end{vmatrix} + \begin{vmatrix} 1 & 0 & 1 \\ 0 & 1 & 1 \\ 0 & 0 & 0 \end{vmatrix} = 0 = a_1,$$

$$\frac{d}{dt}\{\Delta(x)\}_{(at\ x=0)} = \begin{vmatrix} -4t & 2t & 32t^3-16t \\ t^2 & 1-2t^2 & 1-t^2 \\ 1+8t^4-8t^2 & 1-t^2 & 1-2t^2 \end{vmatrix}$$

$$+\begin{vmatrix} 1-2t^2 & t^2 & 1+8t^4-8t^2 \\ 2t & -4t & -2t \\ 1+8t^4-8t^2 & 1-t^2 & (1-2t^2) \end{vmatrix}$$

$$+\begin{vmatrix} 1-2t^2 & t^2 & 1+8t^4-8t^2 \\ t^2 & 1-2t^2 & 1-t^2 \\ (32t^3-16t) & -2t & -4t \end{vmatrix}$$

$$\frac{d^2\{\Delta(x)\}}{dt^2(at\ x=0)} = \left\{\begin{vmatrix} -4 & 2 & -16 \\ 0 & 1 & 1 \\ 1 & 1 & 1 \end{vmatrix} + 0 + 0\right\}$$

$$\left\{0 + \begin{vmatrix} 1 & 0 & 1 \\ 2 & -4 & -2 \\ 1 & 1 & 1 \end{vmatrix} + 0\right\} + \left\{0 + 0 + \begin{vmatrix} 1 & 0 & 1 \\ 0 & 1 & 1 \\ -16 & -2 & -4 \end{vmatrix}\right\}$$

$= 18 + 4 + 14 = 36 \quad \Rightarrow \quad 2a_2 = 36 \Rightarrow a_2 = 18$

5. **(a, b, c, d)** $\Delta = \dfrac{xyz}{xyz}\begin{vmatrix} x^4 & y^4 & z^4 \\ 1 & 1 & 1 \\ x & y & z \end{vmatrix} = \begin{vmatrix} x^4-y^4 & y^4 & (z^4-y^4) \\ 0 & 1 & 0 \\ (x-y) & y & (z-y) \end{vmatrix}$

$\Delta = (x - y)(z - y)\{(x^2 + y^2)(x + y) - (z^2 + y^2)\ (y + z)\}$
$= (x - y)(y - z)\{(z^3 - x^3) + y^2 (z - x) + y\ (z^2 - x^2)\}$
$= (x - y)(y - z)(z - x)\{x^2 + y^2 + z^2 + xy + yz + zx\}$

6. **(b, d)** Operate $C_2 \to C_2 - \beta C_1$ and $C_3 \to C_3 - \gamma C_1$

$$\Delta = \begin{vmatrix} c & b\cos B & a\cos A + c\alpha \\ a & c\cos B & b\cos A + a\alpha \\ b & a\cos B & c\cos A + b\alpha \end{vmatrix}$$

Operate $C_3 \to C_3 - \alpha C_2$

$$= \cos B.\cos A\begin{vmatrix} c & b & a \\ a & c & b \\ b & a & c \end{vmatrix} = -\cos A\ \cos B\{c^3 + b^3 + a^3 - 3abc\} = 0$$

$$\Rightarrow \cos A.\cos B\frac{1}{2}(a+b+c)\{(a-b)^2 + (b-c)^2 + (c-a)^2\} = 0$$

$\Rightarrow$ Either $a = b = c$ or $\cos A = 0$ or $\cos B = 0$

$\therefore$ Δ may be equilateral or it may be right angled at A or B

7. (a, b, c) $\Delta = \begin{vmatrix} a & b & c \\ b & c & a \\ c & a & b \end{vmatrix} = 3abc - (a^3 + b^3 + c^3)$

$\Delta = -(a + b + c)\{a + b\omega + c\omega^2\}\{a + b\omega^2 + c\omega\}$

for $f(x) = a + bx + cx^2$

$f(1) = a + b + c; f(\omega) = a + b\omega + c\omega^2$

$f(\omega^2) = a + b\omega^2 + c\omega^4 = a + b\omega^2 + c\omega$

$f(1), f(\omega)$ and $f(\omega^2)$ are the factors of Δ

8. (a, d) $\Delta(x) = \begin{vmatrix} (1+x) & x & x^2 \\ x & 1+x & x^2 \\ x^2 & x & 1+x \end{vmatrix}$

$$\underset{(at\, x=0)}{\Delta(x)} = \begin{vmatrix} 1 & 0 & 0 \\ 0 & 1 & 0 \\ 0 & 0 & 1 \end{vmatrix} = 1 = z$$

$$\frac{d}{dx}\underset{(at\, x=0)}{\Delta(x)} = \begin{vmatrix} 1 & 1 & 0 \\ 0 & 1 & 0 \\ 0 & 0 & 1 \end{vmatrix} + \begin{vmatrix} 1 & 0 & 0 \\ 1 & 1 & 0 \\ 0 & 0 & 1 \end{vmatrix} + \begin{vmatrix} 1 & 0 & 0 \\ 0 & 1 & 0 \\ 0 & 1 & 1 \end{vmatrix} = 3$$

$\Rightarrow$ z = 1 and $n = 3$

9 (a, c, d) Operate $C_2 \to C_2 - (2C_1 + 2C_3)$

$$\Delta = \begin{vmatrix} a^2 - (b^2 + c^2 + a^2) & bc \\ b^2 - (c^2 + a^2 + b^2) & ac \\ c^2 - (a^2 + b^2 + c^2) & ab \end{vmatrix} = -(a^2 + b^2 + c^2)\begin{vmatrix} a^2 & 1 & bc \\ b^2 & 1 & ac \\ c^2 & 1 & ab \end{vmatrix}$$

$$= -(a^2 + b^2 + c^2)\begin{vmatrix} a^3 & a & 1 \\ b^3 & b & 1 \\ c^3 & c & 1 \end{vmatrix}$$

$= -(a^2 + b^2 + c^2)(a - b)(b - c)(c - a)(a + b + c)$

10. (a, b, c, d) Operate $C_3 \to C_1 + C_2 + C_3$

$$\Delta = \begin{vmatrix} 1+\sin^2 A & \cos^2 A & (2+2\sin 4\theta) \\ \sin^2 A & 1+\cos^2 A & (2+2\sin 4\theta) \\ \sin^2 A & \cos^2 A & (2+2\sin 4\theta) \end{vmatrix}$$

$$= 2(1+\sin 4\theta)\begin{vmatrix} 1+\sin^2 A & \cos^2 A & 1 \\ \sin^2 A & 1+\cos^2 A & 1 \\ \sin^2 A & \cos^2 A & 1 \end{vmatrix}$$

$$= \begin{vmatrix} 1 & -1 & 0 \\ 0 & 1 & 0 \\ \sin^2 A & \cos^2 A & 1 \end{vmatrix} 2(1+\sin 4\theta)$$

$\Delta = 2(1 + \sin 4\theta) = 0 \Rightarrow 4\theta = -\frac{\pi}{2}, \frac{3\pi}{2}$

Δ is independent of A and $\theta = -\frac{\pi}{8}, \frac{3\pi}{8}$

Hence all options are valid

11. (a, b, c, d)

$$\sum_{r=1}^{n} \Delta_r = \begin{vmatrix} 2(1+2+3+...+n) & x & n(n+1) \\ 6(1^2+2^2+3^2+....+n^2)-n & y & n^2(2n+3) \\ 4\sum n^3 - 2n(1+2+3+......+n) & z & n^3(n+1) \end{vmatrix}$$

$$= \begin{vmatrix} n(n+1) & x & n(n+1) \\ 2n^3+3n^2+n-n & y & n^2(2n+3) \\ n^2\{(n+1)^2-(n+1)\} & z & n^3(n+1) \end{vmatrix} \text{ as } C_1 = C_3$$

$\therefore$ $\Delta = 0$

12. (a,b,c,d)
$$\sum_{k=1}^{k=n} D_k = \begin{vmatrix} \sum_{r=0}^{n-1} 2^r & \sum_{r=1}^{n} \frac{1}{r(r+1)} & \sum_{k=1}^{n} \sin k\theta \\ x & y & z \\ 2^n - 1 & \frac{n}{n+1} & \frac{\sin\left(\frac{n+1}{2}\right)\theta \sin\frac{n}{2}\theta}{\sin\frac{\theta}{2}} \end{vmatrix}$$

We observe $1 + 2^1 + 2^2 + ...2^{n-1} = \frac{2^n - 1}{2-1} = 2^n - 1$

and $\frac{1}{1.2} + \frac{1}{2.3} + ... + \frac{1}{n(n+1)}$

$= \left(1 - \frac{1}{2}\right) + \left(\frac{1}{2} - \frac{1}{3}\right) + ... \left(\frac{1}{n} - \frac{1}{n+1}\right) = 1 - \frac{1}{n+1} = \frac{n}{n+1}$

$\{\sin\theta + \sin 2\theta + ... + \sin n\theta\} = \frac{\sin\left(\frac{n+1}{2}\right)\theta . \sin\frac{n\theta}{2}}{\sin\frac{\theta}{2}} = S \text{ (say)}$

$$\Rightarrow \Delta = \begin{vmatrix} 2^r - 1 & \frac{n}{n+1} & S \\ x & y & z \\ 2^r - 1 & \frac{n}{n+1} & S \end{vmatrix} = 0 \text{ as } R_1 = R_3$$

13. (a, b, c) Operate $R_3 \to 100R_1 + 10R_2 + R_3$

$$\Rightarrow \Delta = \begin{vmatrix} A & 6 & 8 \\ 8 & B & 6 \\ A38 & 6B8 & 86C \end{vmatrix}$$

Let $A88 = 72n_1$, $6B8 = 72.n_2$, $86C = 72.n_3$

$$\Rightarrow \Delta = 72\begin{vmatrix} A & 6 & 8 \\ 8 & B & 6 \\ n_1 & n_2 & n_3 \end{vmatrix}.$$

Further $A88 = 72n_1$, Also $288 = 72 \approx 4$

$\Rightarrow$ $n_1 = 4$, $A = 2$

Similarly $6B8 = 72\, n_2$, Also $648 = 72 \approx 9$

$\Rightarrow$ $n_2 = 9$, $B = 4$ and $86C = 72n_3$ and $864 = 72 \approx 12$

$\Rightarrow$ $n_3 = 12$, $C = 4$

Hence $\Delta = 72\begin{vmatrix} 2 & 6 & 8 \\ 8 & 4 & 6 \\ 4 & 9 & 12 \end{vmatrix} = 72 \times 2 \times 2\begin{vmatrix} 1 & 6 & 4 \\ 4 & 4 & 3 \\ 2 & 9 & 6 \end{vmatrix}$

$\Rightarrow \Delta = (288)$

SECTION V: (ASSERTION REASION TYPE)

1. (b) $\Delta = xyz\begin{vmatrix} \frac{a}{x} & \left(\frac{b}{y}-1\right) & \left(\frac{c}{z}-1\right) \\ \left(\frac{a}{x}-1\right) & b/y & \left(\frac{c}{z}-1\right) \\ \left(\frac{a}{x}-1\right) & \left(\frac{b}{y}-1\right) & (c/z) \end{vmatrix}$

$= \left(\frac{a}{x}+\frac{b}{y}+\frac{c}{z}-2\right)(xyz)\begin{vmatrix} 1 & \left(\frac{b}{y}-1\right) & \left(\frac{c}{z}-1\right) \\ 1 & b/y & \left(\frac{c}{z}-1\right) \\ 1 & (b/y-1) & \left(\frac{c}{z}\right) \end{vmatrix}$

$= \left(\frac{a}{x}+\frac{b}{y}+\frac{c}{z}-2\right)(xyz)\begin{vmatrix} 1 & \left(\frac{b}{y}-1\right) & \left(\frac{c}{z}-1\right) \\ 0 & 1 & 0 \\ 0 & 0 & 1 \end{vmatrix}$

$= \left(\frac{a}{x}+\frac{b}{y}+\frac{c}{z}-2\right)(xyz) = 0$ gives $\frac{a}{x}+\frac{b}{y}+\frac{c}{z} = 2$, since $x, y, z \neq 0$

A is true, similarly

$\begin{vmatrix} 1 & 3\cos x & 1 \\ \sin x & 1 & 3\cos x \\ 1 & \sin x & 1 \end{vmatrix} = \begin{vmatrix} 0 & 3\cos x - \sin x & 0 \\ \sin x & 1 & 3\cos x \\ 1 & \sin x & 1 \end{vmatrix}$

$= (3\cos x - \sin x)\ \{3\cos x - \sin x\}$

$= (10)\left\{\frac{3}{\sqrt{10}}\cos x - \frac{1}{\sqrt{10}}\sin x\right\}^2 = 10\cos(x + \phi)$

Where $\cos\phi = \frac{3}{\sqrt{10}}$ and $\sin\phi = \frac{1}{\sqrt{10}}$

$\Rightarrow$ Maximum value of $f(x) = 10$

But no where this statement (R) is supporting the statement A

2. (a) $\Delta = (a+b+c)\begin{vmatrix} a & 1 & a^2 \\ b & 1 & b^2 \\ c & 1 & c^2 \end{vmatrix}$

$= -(a + b + c)(a - b)(b - c)(c - a) = 0$

Since a,b,c are distinct

$\therefore\ a + b + c = 0 \Rightarrow (a + b) = c$

$\therefore\ ax + by + c = 0$

$\Rightarrow ax + by - a - b = 0$

$\Rightarrow a(x - 1) + b(y - 1) = 0$

$\Rightarrow (x - 1) + b/a\ (y - 1) = 0$

which is the equation of straight line passing through the point of intersection of $x - 1 = 0$ and $y - 1 = 0$ i.e.,(1, 1) a fixed point.

3. (a) Sum of the product of elements of any row/column with co-factor of some other row/column vanishes, is true

The statement that the value of determinant does not change when $R_i \to R_i + lR_j$ or $C_i \to C_i lC_j (i \neq j)$ is performed.

The statement is true and it is basis of the truth of statement A

4. (a) The statement R: that $|A^T| = |A|$ and $|kA| = k^n|A|$ where n is the order of matrix A is true

If we put $k = -1$ and $(n = 2m + 1)$ so that n is odd then $kA = A^T$ so $|kA| = (-1)^{2m+1}|A| = -|A|$

$\Rightarrow$ If there is a skew symmetric matrix of odd order then $|A^T| = |A| = -|A| \Rightarrow |A| = 0$

So statement assertion is true and it can be derived from statement R

5. (a) If $A = [a_{ij}]_{n\times n}$ is Hermitian, then $(\overline{A})^T = A$

$\Rightarrow \overline{a_{ij}} = a_{ji}$ and $|A^T| = |A|$ so $\overline{\Delta} = \Delta = |A|$

$\Rightarrow$ If $|A| = x + iy$ then $|\overline{A}| = x - iy$

Since $\Delta = \overline{\Delta} \Rightarrow x + iy = x - iy \Rightarrow \text{Im}(\Delta) = 0$

Hence R statement is true

This implies that the determinant of a Hermitian matrix will be real

$\Rightarrow$ Statement (A) is true and it is implied by (R)

SECTION VI: (LINKED COMPRIHENTION TYPE)

1. (b) $\begin{vmatrix} 1 & 1 & 1 \\ a^2 & b^2 & c^2 \\ bc & ca & ab \end{vmatrix} = \frac{abc}{abc}\begin{vmatrix} a & b & c \\ a^3 & b^3 & c^3 \\ 1 & 1 & 1 \end{vmatrix} = \begin{vmatrix} 1 & 1 & 1 \\ a & b & c \\ a^3 & b^3 & c^3 \end{vmatrix}$

$= (a - b)(b - c)(c - a)(a + b + c)$

2. (c) $\Delta = \begin{vmatrix} a & b & c \\ a^2 & b^2 & c^2 \\ bc & ca & ab \end{vmatrix} = \begin{vmatrix} a^2 & b^2 & c^2 \\ a^3 & b^3 & c^3 \\ 1 & 1 & 1 \end{vmatrix} = \begin{vmatrix} 1 & 1 & 1 \\ a^2 & b^2 & c^2 \\ a^3 & b^3 & c^3 \end{vmatrix}$

$= (a - b)(b - c)(c - a)(ab + bc + ca)$

3. (d) $\Delta = \begin{vmatrix} a & b & c \\ a^2 & b^2 & c^2 \\ a^3 & b^3 & c^3 \end{vmatrix} = abc\,(a - b)(b - c)(c - a)$

as $\Delta = abc\begin{vmatrix} 1 & 1 & 1 \\ a & b & c \\ a^2 & b^2 & c^2 \end{vmatrix} = abc\,(a - b)(b - c)(c - a)$

4. (a) $A_\theta(\alpha,\beta,\gamma)=\begin{vmatrix}\cos(\alpha+\theta) & \sin(\alpha+\theta) & 1\\ \cos(\beta+\theta) & \sin(\beta+\theta) & 1\\ \cos(\gamma+\theta) & \sin(\gamma+\theta) & 1\end{vmatrix}$

$$a=A_{\frac{\pi}{2}}(\alpha,\beta,\gamma)=\begin{vmatrix}-\sin\alpha & \cos\alpha & 1\\ -\sin\beta & \cos\beta & 1\\ -\sin\gamma & \cos\gamma & 1\end{vmatrix}$$

$$b=A_{\pi/3}(\alpha,\beta,\gamma)=\begin{vmatrix}\cos\left(\frac{\pi}{3}+\alpha\right) & \sin\left(\frac{\pi}{3}+\alpha\right) & 1\\ \cos\left(\frac{\pi}{3}+\beta\right) & \sin\left(\frac{\pi}{3}+\beta\right) & 1\\ \cos\left(\frac{\pi}{3}+\gamma\right) & \sin\left(\frac{\pi}{3}+\gamma\right) & 1\end{vmatrix}$$

Now $\cos\left(\frac{\pi}{3}+\alpha\right)=\frac{1}{2}\cos\alpha-\frac{\sqrt{3}}{2}\sin\alpha$

and $\sin\left(\frac{\pi}{3}+\alpha\right)=\frac{\sqrt{3}}{2}\cos\alpha+\frac{1}{2}\sin\alpha$

$$\Rightarrow \frac{\sqrt{3}}{2}\cos\left(\alpha+\frac{\pi}{3}\right)-\frac{1}{2}\sin\left(\alpha+\frac{\pi}{3}\right)=-\sin\alpha$$

$$\Rightarrow b=\frac{2}{\sqrt{3}}\begin{vmatrix}-\sin\alpha & \left(\frac{\sqrt{3}}{2}\cos\alpha+\frac{1}{2}\sin\alpha\right) & 1\\ -\sin\beta & \left(\frac{\sqrt{3}}{2}\cos\beta+\frac{1}{2}\sin\beta\right) & 1\\ -\sin\gamma & \left(\frac{\sqrt{3}}{2}\cos\gamma+\frac{1}{2}\sin\gamma\right) & 1\end{vmatrix}$$

Operate $C_2+\frac{C_1}{2}$ and the take out $\frac{\sqrt{3}}{2}$ common we will observe that $b = a$

5. (b) $\frac{d}{d\theta}=A_\theta(\alpha,\beta,\gamma)$ operate derivative (Column wise) and observe

For Ist column Derivative $C_1 = -C_2$

For IInd column Derivative $C_1 = C_2$

For IIIrd column Derivative $C_3 = 0$

$$\Rightarrow \frac{dA_{\pi/3}}{d\theta}(\alpha,\beta,\gamma)=0$$

6. (b) $A_\theta=\begin{vmatrix}\cos\left(\beta+\theta+\frac{2\pi}{3}\right) & \sin\left(\beta+\theta+\frac{2\pi}{3}\right) & 1\\ \cos(\beta+\theta) & \sin(\beta+\theta) & 1\\ \cos(\gamma+\theta) & \sin(\gamma+\theta) & 1\end{vmatrix}$ $R_1\to R_1-R_2$ and $R_2\to R_2-R_3$ gives

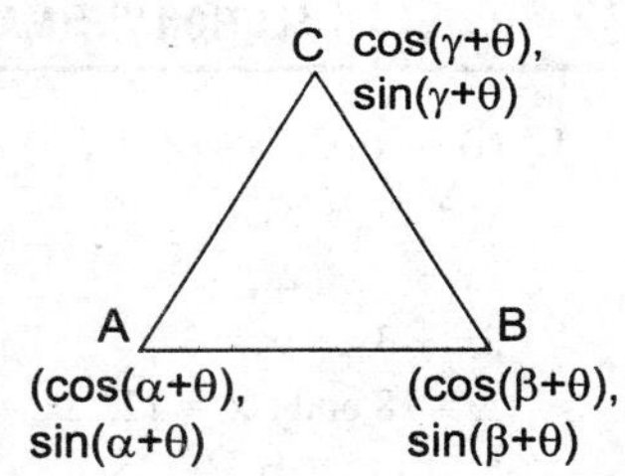

$$A_\theta=\begin{vmatrix}-2\sin\left(\beta+\theta+\frac{\pi}{3}\right)\sin\frac{\pi}{3} & 2\cos\left(\beta+\theta+\frac{\pi}{3}\right)\sin\frac{\pi}{3} & 0\\ -2\sin\left(\frac{\beta+\gamma}{2}+\theta\right)\sin\left(\frac{\beta-\gamma}{2}\right) & 2\cos\left(\frac{\beta+\gamma}{2}+\theta\right)\sin\left(\frac{\beta-\gamma}{2}\right) & 0\\ \cos(\gamma+\theta) & \sin(\gamma+\theta) & 1\end{vmatrix}$$

$$\begin{vmatrix}-\sqrt{3}\sin\left(\beta+\theta+\frac{\pi}{3}\right) & \sqrt{3}\cos\left(\beta+\theta+\frac{\pi}{3}\right)\\ -2\sin\left(\frac{\beta+\gamma}{2}+\theta\right) & 2\cos\left(\frac{\beta+\gamma}{2}+\theta\right)\end{vmatrix}=2\sqrt{3}\sin\left(\frac{\beta-\gamma}{2}\right)\sin\left[\frac{\beta+\gamma}{2}+\theta-\beta-\theta-\frac{\pi}{3}\right]=2\sqrt{3}\sin\left(\frac{\beta-\gamma}{2}\right)\sin\left(\frac{\gamma-\beta}{2}-\frac{\pi}{3}\right)$$

$$=\sqrt{3}\left[\cos\left(\beta-\gamma+\frac{\pi}{3}\right)-\cos\left(\frac{\pi}{3}\right)\right]=\sqrt{3}\left[\cos\left(\beta-\gamma+\frac{\pi}{3}\right)-\frac{1}{2}\right]=\sqrt{3}\left[\cos\left(\alpha-\frac{2\pi}{3}-\gamma+\frac{\pi}{3}\right)-\frac{1}{2}\right]=\sqrt{3}\left[\cos\left(\alpha-\gamma-\frac{\pi}{3}\right)-\frac{1}{2}\right]$$

Which is maximum for $\alpha-\gamma-\pi/3=2n\pi,\ n\in\mathbb{Z}$

$$\Rightarrow \gamma=\alpha-\left(2n\pi+\frac{\pi}{3}\right);n\in\mathbb{Z}\ \Rightarrow\ \gamma=\alpha-\frac{\pi}{3}\ for\ n=0$$

7. (c) $xyz = m$; det $A=\begin{vmatrix}x & y & z\\ z & x & y\\ y & z & x\end{vmatrix}$

Given $A^TA = I \Rightarrow |A| = |A^T| = \pm 1$

$|A| = x^3 + y^3 + z^3 - 3xyz$

$$=\frac{1}{2}(z+y+z)\{(x-y)^2+(y-z)^2+(z-x)^2\}$$

From $AA^T=\begin{vmatrix}x & y & z\\ z & x & y\\ y & z & x\end{vmatrix}\begin{vmatrix}x & z & y\\ y & x & z\\ z & y & x\end{vmatrix}$

$$= \begin{vmatrix} (x^2+y^2+z^2) & (\Sigma xy) & (\Sigma xy) \\ (\Sigma xy) & (\Sigma x^2) & (\Sigma xy) \\ \Sigma xy & \Sigma xy & \Sigma x^2 \end{vmatrix} = I_3$$

So $xy + yz + zx = 0$

$\Rightarrow \quad \frac{1}{x}+\frac{1}{y}+\frac{1}{z}=\frac{0}{m}=0$; $x^2 + y^2 + z^2 = 1$

8 (b) $x^3 + y^3 + z^3 - 3m = \pm 1$

So $x^3 + y^3 + z^3 = 3m \pm 1$

9 **(a, b)** Roots of cubic $\frac{1}{x},\frac{1}{y},\frac{1}{z}$

$|A| = (x + y + z)(x^2 + y^2 + z^2 - xy - yz - zx) = (x + y + z)(1 - 0) = x + y + z$

Now, $\frac{x+y+z}{xyz}=\frac{1}{xy}+\frac{1}{yz}+\frac{1}{zx}=\frac{\pm 1}{m}$ and

$\frac{1}{xyz}=\frac{1}{m},\frac{1}{x}+\frac{1}{y}+\frac{1}{z}=0$

$\therefore$ Equation will be $t^3 + 0t^2 + (\pm 1/m)t - 1/m = 0$ gives $mt^3 \pm t - 1 = 0$

SECTION VII: (MATRIX MATCH TYPE)

1. (i) → (a), (ii) → (b), (iii) → (c) , (iv) → (d)

$x_1 + 2x_2 + 3x_3 = 1$

$3x_1 + x_2 + 2x_3 = 2$

$2x_1 + 3x_2 + x_3 = 3$

$\Delta = 18$ and $\Delta x_1 = 12$; $\Delta x_2 = 12$; $\Delta x_3 = -6$

Gives $x_1=\frac{2}{3}; x_2=\frac{2}{3}; x_3=-\frac{1}{3}$

So $x_1 + x_2 = 4/3$; $x_1 + x_3 = 1/3$

2. (i) → (b) , (ii) → (c), (iii) → (a), (iv) → (d)

$$f(x)=\begin{vmatrix} \sec^2 x & 1 & 1 \\ \cos^2 x & \cos^2 x & \operatorname{cosec}^2 x \\ 1 & \cos^2 x & \cot^2 x \end{vmatrix}$$

. Operate $C_2 \to C_2 - C_1 \cos^2 x$

$$f(x)=\begin{vmatrix} \sec^2 x & 0 & 1 \\ \cos^2 x & \cos^2 x - \cos^4 x & \operatorname{cosec}^2 x \\ 1 & 0 & \cot^2 x \end{vmatrix}$$

$= \cos^2 x(1 - \cos^2 x)\{\sec^2 x \cot^2 x - 1\} = \cos^4 x$

$\Rightarrow \quad f(x)=\cos^4 x=\frac{1}{8}\{3+4\cos 2x+\cos 4x\}$

Period of $f(x) = \pi$ as $\cos^4 x = \cos^4(\pi + x)$

max value of $f(x) = 1$ at $x = n\pi$

minimum value of $f(x) = 0$ at $x = (2k + 1)\pi/2$

$$\int_0^{\pi/4} f(x)\,dx=\int_0^{\pi/4}\left(\frac{3}{8}+\frac{\cos 2x}{2}+\frac{1}{8}\cos 4x\right)dx$$

$$=\left.\frac{3}{8}x+\frac{\sin 2x}{4}+\frac{1}{32}\sin 4x\right|_0^{\pi/4}=\frac{3\pi}{32}+\frac{1}{4}$$

$$=\int_0^{\pi/4} f(x)\,dx-\frac{1}{4}=\frac{3\pi}{32}$$

3. (i) → (a),(c),(d) (ii) (a), (b) (iii) → (b)(iv) → (b)

(i) $a, b, c \in \mathbb{R} - \{0\}, a \neq b \neq c$

$\frac{1}{a}+\frac{1}{b}+\frac{1}{c}=0$

$$\Delta = abc\begin{vmatrix} \frac{1}{a}+1 & \frac{1}{b} & \frac{1}{c} \\ \frac{1}{a} & \frac{1}{b}+1 & \frac{1}{c} \\ \frac{1}{a} & \frac{1}{b} & \frac{1}{c}+1 \end{vmatrix}$$

$$=\left(\frac{1}{a}+\frac{1}{b}+\frac{1}{c}+1\right)abc\begin{vmatrix} 1 & \frac{1}{b} & \frac{1}{c} \\ 1 & \frac{1}{b}+1 & \frac{1}{c} \\ 1 & \frac{1}{b} & \frac{1}{c}+1 \end{vmatrix}$$

$$= abc\left(1+\frac{1}{a}+\frac{1}{b}+\frac{1}{c}\right)\begin{vmatrix} 1 & 1/b & 1/c \\ 0 & 1 & 0 \\ 0 & 0 & 1 \end{vmatrix} = abc \neq 0$$

$\therefore$ Non-singular so invertible

Also it is symmetric as $a_{ij} = a_{ji}$

(ii) $$\begin{vmatrix} 1 & \cos(\alpha-\beta) & \cos(\alpha-\gamma) \\ \cos(\beta-\alpha) & 1 & \cos(\beta-\gamma) \\ \cos(\gamma-\alpha) & \cos(\gamma-\beta) & 1 \end{vmatrix}$$

(Determinant of symmetric matrix)

$$=\begin{vmatrix} \cos\alpha & \sin\alpha & 0 \\ \cos\beta & \sin\beta & 0 \\ \cos\gamma & \sin\gamma & 0 \end{vmatrix}\begin{vmatrix} \cos\alpha & \cos\beta & \cos\gamma \\ \sin\alpha & \sin\beta & \sin\gamma \\ 0 & 0 & 0 \end{vmatrix} = 0 \times 0 = 0$$

$\Rightarrow$ singular

(iii) $$\begin{vmatrix} 1+2\omega+\omega^2 & \omega^2 & 1 \\ 1 & 1+\omega^2+2\omega & \omega \\ \omega & \omega^2 & 2+\omega+2\omega^2 \end{vmatrix}$$

$$=\begin{vmatrix} \omega & \omega^2 & 1 \\ 1 & \omega & \omega \\ \omega & \omega^2 & -\omega \end{vmatrix}=\begin{vmatrix} 0 & 0 & 1+\omega \\ 1 & \omega & \omega \\ \omega & \omega^2 & -\omega \end{vmatrix} \quad (\text{using } R_1 \to R_1 - R_2)$$

$= (1 + \omega)(0) = 0$

$\Rightarrow$ Singular

(iv) This is a skew symmetric matrix of odd order

$\Rightarrow$ Singular

SECTION VIII: (INTEGER TYPE)

1. $$xyz\begin{vmatrix} \frac{p}{x} & \left(\frac{q}{y}-1\right) & \left(\frac{r}{z}-1\right) \\ \left(\frac{p}{x}-1\right) & q/y & \left(\frac{r}{z}-1\right) \\ \left(\frac{p}{x}-1\right) & \left(\frac{q}{y}-1\right) & \left(\frac{r}{z}\right) \end{vmatrix}$$

$$= xyz\left(\frac{p}{x}+\frac{q}{y}+\frac{r}{z}-2\right)\begin{vmatrix} 1 & (q/y-1) & \left(\frac{r}{z}-1\right) \\ 1 & q/y & \left(\frac{r}{z}-1\right) \\ 1 & \left(\frac{q}{y}-1\right) & \frac{r}{z} \end{vmatrix}$$

$$= xyz\left(\frac{p}{x}+\frac{q}{x}+\frac{r}{z}-2\right)\begin{vmatrix} 1 & \left(\frac{q}{y}-1\right) & \left(\frac{r}{z}-1\right) \\ 0 & 1 & 0 \\ 0 & 0 & 1 \end{vmatrix} = 0$$

For $x, y, z \neq 0$ $\quad\therefore\quad \frac{p}{x}+\frac{q}{y}+\frac{r}{z}=2$

2. $$\Delta = abc\begin{vmatrix} 1 & 1 & 1 \\ \frac{1}{a} & \frac{1}{b} & \frac{1}{c} \\ p & q & r \\ 1 & 1 & 1 \end{vmatrix} = abc\begin{vmatrix} 1 & \left(\frac{1}{b}-\frac{1}{a}\right) & \left(\frac{1}{c}-\frac{1}{a}\right) \\ p & (q-p) & (r-p) \\ 1 & 0 & 0 \end{vmatrix}$$

$$= abc\left\{(q-p)\left\{\frac{1}{a}-\frac{1}{c}\right\}+\left(\frac{1}{b}-\frac{1}{a}\right)(r-p)\right\}$$

Consider $\frac{1}{a} = A_0 + (p-1)d; \frac{1}{b}$

$= A_0 + (q-1)d; \frac{1}{c} = A_0 + (r-1)d$

$\Rightarrow \frac{1}{a}-\frac{1}{c} = (p-r)d$

and $\frac{1}{b}-\frac{1}{a} = (p-q)d$

$\Rightarrow \Delta = \{(q-p)(p-r)d + (q-p)(r-p)d\}abc = 0$

3. $$\Sigma\Delta = \begin{vmatrix} \left(1+\frac{1}{2}+\frac{1}{4}+\frac{1}{8}+..\right) & 4 \\ \left(1+\frac{1}{3}+\frac{1}{9}+\frac{1}{27}+...\right) & 3 \end{vmatrix}$$

$$= \begin{vmatrix} 2 & 4 \\ \frac{3}{2} & 3 \end{vmatrix} = 0$$

4. $$x^n y^n z^n\begin{vmatrix} 1 & x^2 & x^3 \\ 1 & y^2 & y^3 \\ 1 & z^2 & z^3 \end{vmatrix}$$

$= (x-y)(y-z)(z-x)\{(xy+yz+zx)\, x^n y^n z^n\}$

$= (x-y)(y-z)(z-x)\left(\frac{1}{x}+\frac{1}{y}+\frac{1}{z}\right)$ (given)

This is possible only when $(xy + yz + zx)(x^n y^n z^n)$

$= \frac{1}{x}+\frac{1}{y}+\frac{1}{z} \quad \Rightarrow \quad n = -1$

Aliter: Degree on L.H.S $= n + (n + 2) + (n + 3) = 5 + 3n$
Degree on R.H.S. $= 3 - 1 = 2$, so $n = -1$

5. $$\begin{vmatrix} a & 1 & 1 \\ 1 & b & 1 \\ 1 & 1 & c \end{vmatrix} = +2-(a+b+c)+abc > 0$$

$\Rightarrow abc + 2 > a + b + c$

Using $\frac{a+b+c}{3} \geq (abc)^{1/3}$ gives $(a + b + c) \geq 3(abc)^{1/3}$

So $abc + 2 > 3(abc)^{1/3}$ put $(abc)^{1/3} = x$

So $x^3 + 2 > 3x$ or $x^3 - 3x + 2 > 0$

$\Rightarrow (x - 1)(x^2 + x - 2) > 0$

$\Rightarrow (x - 1)^2 (x + 2) > 0$

$\Rightarrow x + 2 > 0 \Rightarrow x > -2$ i.e., $abc > -8$

$\therefore k = 8$

6. Applying $R_3 \to R_3 - R_1$ and $R_2 - R_1$

$$\Delta = \begin{vmatrix} 1+\sin^2\theta & \cos^2\theta & 4\sin 4\theta \\ -1 & 1 & 0 \\ -1 & 0 & 1 \end{vmatrix}$$

$$= \begin{vmatrix} 2 & \cos^2\theta & 4\sin 4\theta \\ 0 & 1 & 0 \\ -1 & 0 & 1 \end{vmatrix}$$

$= 2 + 4\sin^4\theta = 0$ gives $\sin 4\theta = -1/2$

i.e., $4\theta = m\pi + (-1)^m\left(-\frac{\pi}{6}\right)$

or $\theta = \frac{m\pi}{4} + (-1)^{m+1}\frac{\pi}{24}$

For $\theta \in [0, \pi/2]$, put $m = 1$, then $\theta = \frac{7\pi}{24}$

put $m = 2$, then $\theta = \frac{11\pi}{24}$; $\theta = \frac{n\pi}{k}$; HCF$(n,k) = 1$

$\Rightarrow k = 24$

7. Operate $C_3 \to C_3 + C_2 - C_1$

$$\Delta(x) = \begin{vmatrix} 1 & \cos x & 0 \\ 1+\sin x & \cos x & 0 \\ \sin x & \sin x & 1 \end{vmatrix}$$

$= -\sin x \cos x = -\frac{1}{2}\sin 2x$

$= \left(-\frac{1}{2}\right)\int_0^{\pi/2} \sin 2x\,dx = \frac{1}{4}\cos 2x\Big|_0^{\pi/2} = \frac{1}{4}\{-1-1\} = -\frac{1}{2}$

$= -\frac{1}{2} = -\frac{1}{k} \Rightarrow k = 2$

8. $f(x) = \begin{vmatrix} \cos x & 1 & 0 \\ 1 & 2\cos x & 1 \\ 0 & 1 & 2\cos x \end{vmatrix} = 4\cos^3 x - 3\cos x = \cos 3x$

$\therefore \int_0^{\pi/2} f(x)dx = \int_0^{\pi/2} \cos 3x dx = \frac{\sin 3x}{3}\Big|_0^{\pi/2} = -\frac{1}{3} = -\frac{1}{k}$

$\Rightarrow k = 3$

9. $f(\theta) = \begin{vmatrix} 1 & 1 & 0 \\ 1 & e^{i\theta} & 0 \\ 1 & -1 & (e^{-i\theta}-1) \end{vmatrix} = (e^{-i\theta}-1)(e^{i\theta}-1)$

$= -\{e^{i\theta} + e^{-i\theta} - 2\} = -\{2\cos\theta - 2\}$

$\Rightarrow f\left(\frac{\pi}{3}\right) = 2 - 1 = 1$

10. Observe that $f(x)$ is an odd function as $f(-x) = -f(x)$

$\Rightarrow \int_{-\pi/2}^{\pi/2} f(x)dx = 0$

11. Operate $C_1 \to C_1 + C_2 + C_3$ and take $(\sin x + 2\cos x)$ common

$\Delta(x) = (\sin x + 2\cos x)\begin{vmatrix} 1 & \cos x & \cos x \\ 1 & \sin x & \cos x \\ 1 & \cos x & \sin x \end{vmatrix}$

$= (\sin x + 2\cos x)\begin{vmatrix} 1 & \cos x & \cos x \\ 1 & \sin x & \cos x \\ 0 & 0 & (\sin x - \cos x) \end{vmatrix}$

$= (\sin x + 2\cos x)(\sin x - \cos x)^2 = 0$

for $-\frac{\pi}{4} \le x \le \frac{\pi}{4}$

$\Rightarrow$ Number of solutions = 1 *i.e.,* $x = \frac{\pi}{4}$ is the only solution

12. For more than one solutions of linear equations they must coincide

$\Rightarrow \frac{k+1}{k} = \frac{8}{k+3} = \frac{4k}{3k-1}$ ....(i)

From first two members

$k^2 - 4k + 3 = 0$

$\Rightarrow k = 1$ or 3, $k = 1$ satisfied (i) and $k = 3$ does not

$\therefore k = 1$

13. Operate $R_1 \to R_1 - R_2$

$\Delta(x) = \begin{vmatrix} 1 & 1 & 1 \\ x & 3x+1 & 5x+3 \\ x^2 & (3x+1)^2 & (5x+3)^2 \end{vmatrix}$

$= \begin{vmatrix} 1 & 0 & 0 \\ x & (2x+1) & (4x+3) \\ x^2 & (4x+1)(2x+1) & (4x+3)(6x+3) \end{vmatrix}$

$= (2x+1)(4x+3)\begin{vmatrix} 1 & 0 & 0 \\ x & 1 & 1 \\ x^2 & (4x+1) & (6x+3) \end{vmatrix}$

$= (2x+1)(4x+3)(2x+2) = 2(x+1)(2x+1)(4x+3)$

Observe that for $\Delta_x \ge 0$; $x \ge -\frac{1}{2} = -\frac{1}{k}$ gives $k = 2$

14. $\begin{vmatrix} (1+a_1+b_1) & (a_1+b_2) & (a_1+b_3) \\ (a_2+b_1) & (1+a_2+b_2) & (a_2+b_3) \\ (a_3+b_1) & (a_3+b_2) & (1+a_3+b_3) \end{vmatrix}$

$= k + \sum_{i=1}^{3}(a_i+b_i) + \sum_{1\le i<j\le 3}\sum (a_i-a_j)(b_j-b_i)$

To get k put a_i's = 0 and b_i's = 0 then

$\Delta = \begin{vmatrix} 1 & 0 & 0 \\ 0 & 1 & 0 \\ 0 & 1 & 0 \end{vmatrix} = 1 \Rightarrow k = 1$

15. Put $\alpha = e^{-iA}$, $\beta = e^{-ib}$ and $\gamma = e^{-ic}$

$\Rightarrow \alpha\beta\gamma = e^{-i(A+B+C)} = e^{-i\pi} = -1$

The determinant $= \begin{vmatrix} \frac{1}{\alpha^2} & \gamma & \beta \\ \gamma & \frac{1}{\beta^2} & \alpha \\ \beta & \alpha & \frac{1}{\gamma^2} \end{vmatrix}$

Multiplying by $\alpha^2\beta^2\gamma^2 = (-1)^2 = 1$

$\Delta = \begin{vmatrix} 1 & \alpha^2\gamma & \alpha^2\beta \\ \beta^2\gamma & 1 & \beta^2\alpha \\ \beta\gamma^2 & \alpha\gamma^2 & 1 \end{vmatrix}$

Using $\beta\gamma = -1/\alpha$, $\alpha\gamma = -1/\beta$, $\alpha\beta = -1/\gamma$

Multiply C_1, C_2, and C_3 respectively by α, β and γ

$= \frac{1}{(-1)}\begin{vmatrix} \alpha & -\alpha & -\alpha \\ -\beta & \beta & -\beta \\ -\gamma & -\gamma & \gamma \end{vmatrix} = \begin{vmatrix} 1 & -1 & -1 \\ -1 & 1 & -1 \\ -1 & -1 & 1 \end{vmatrix}$

$= \begin{vmatrix} 0 & 0 & -2 \\ -1 & 1 & -1 \\ -1 & -1 & 1 \end{vmatrix} = -4$

16. $$\frac{d^n}{dx^n} f(x) = \begin{vmatrix} n! & \sin\left(x + \frac{n\pi}{2}\right) & \cos\left(x + \frac{n\pi}{2}\right) \\ n! & \sin\left(\frac{n\pi}{2}\right) & \cos\frac{n\pi}{2} \\ a & a^2 & a^3 \end{vmatrix}$$

at $x = 0$; $R_1 = R_2$

So $\frac{d^n}{dx^n} f(x) = 0$ at $x = 0$

17. $$a_k = \int_0^{\pi/2} (k + \sin\theta)^2 \cos\theta d\theta$$

$$= \left|\frac{(k + \sin\theta)^3}{3}\right|_0^{\pi/2} = \frac{(k+1)^3}{3} - \frac{k^3}{3} = \frac{k^2 + (k+1)^2 + k(k+1)}{}$$

Operate $R_2 \to R_2 \to R_1$ and $R_3 \to R_3 - R_2$ then

$$\Delta = \begin{vmatrix} \frac{(k+1)^3 - k^3}{3} & k & k^2 \\ \frac{(k+2)^3 - (k+1)^3}{3} & k+1 & (k+1)^2 \\ \frac{(k+3)^3 - (k+2)^3}{3} & k+2 & (k+2)^2 \end{vmatrix} = \frac{2}{k} \text{ (Given)}$$

Observe that $(k + 1)^3 - k^3 = (k + 1)^2 + 2k^2 + k$

Using $x^3 - y^3 = (x - y) \{x^2 + y^2 + xy\}$ and $x^2 - y^2 = (x - y)(x + y)$

$\Rightarrow$ Operate $C_1 - 1/3\ (2C_3 + C_2)$ and we get

$$= \Delta = \frac{1}{3}\begin{vmatrix} (k+1)^2 & k & k^2 \\ (k+2)^2 & k+1 & (k+1)^2 \\ (k+2)^2 & (k+2) & (k+2)^2 \end{vmatrix}$$

$$= \frac{1}{3}\begin{vmatrix} 2k+1 & (k) & k^2 \\ 2k+3 & (k+1) & (k+1)^2 \\ 2k+5 & (k+2) & (k+2)^2 \end{vmatrix}$$

Operate $C_1 \to C_1 - 2C_2$ then

$$\Delta = \frac{1}{3}\begin{vmatrix} 1 & k & k^2 \\ 1 & k+1 & (k+1)^2 \\ 1 & k+2 & (k+2)^2 \end{vmatrix}$$

$$= \frac{1}{3}\begin{vmatrix} 1 & k & k^2 \\ 0 & 1 & (2k+1) \\ 0 & 1 & (2k+3) \end{vmatrix} = \frac{1}{3}(2) = \frac{2}{3} = \frac{2}{k} \Rightarrow k = 3$$

18. $R_1 \to R_1 + R_2 + R_3$ and take out (2 + 4 sin2x)

$$\Delta = (2 + 4\sin 2x)\begin{vmatrix} 1 & 1 & 1 \\ \cos^2 x & 1+\cos^2 x & \cos^2 x \\ 4\sin 2x & 4\sin 2x & 1+4\sin 2x \end{vmatrix}$$

$$= (2 + 4\sin 2x)\begin{vmatrix} 0 & 0 & 1 \\ 0 & 1 & \cos^2 x \\ -1 & -1 & 1+4\sin 2x \end{vmatrix}$$

$= 2 + 4 \sin 2x$

Since $\sin 2x$ has a maximum value of 1 at $x = \pi/4$

$\therefore\ D \le 6$

(as $0 < x < \pi/2$)

19. Operate $C_2 \to C_2 - 2C_1$; $C_3 \to C_3 - 3C_1$

$$\begin{vmatrix} x^2 - 4x + 6 & (12x - 2) & 10x - 2 \\ x - 2 & 6 & 5 \\ 1 & 0 & 0 \end{vmatrix}$$

$= 60x - 10 - 60x + 12 = 2$

$$\int_{-2}^{2} 2x^2 dx = \left.\frac{2x^3}{3}\right|_{-2}^{2} = \frac{32}{3}$$

Now $\left\{\frac{32}{3}\right\} = \frac{2}{3}$ (where{} denotes fractional part function)

$\Rightarrow\ \frac{2}{3} = \frac{2}{k} \Rightarrow k = 3$

3

Vector

■ INTRODUCTION

The method of studying vector quantities using algebra of vectors by resolving vectors into three orthogonal components was initiated because of the introduction of cartesian co-ordinate system by French philosopher Rene Descartes (1596 to 1650), which led to study of geometry with the help of Algebra. This process attracted attention of the future mathematicians, and in 1679, Leibnitz made an attempt to apply calculus over vectors, although his attempt was a partial success. Mathematicians William Rowan Hamilton (Quaternions theory) and H. G Grass mann (Concept of 'Ausdelmungslehre') made a remarkable improvement for the development of Algebra of vectors although it could not be called as vector analysis but it can be regarded as the parent of modern vector analysis of today.

An investigator in mathematical physics Prof. W. Gibbs (American) feeling the need of simplest form of vector analysis did admissible work to adapt to his requirement the best and simplest parts of both the system of Hamilton and Grassman and therefore developing an analysis (1881 – 1884).

The application to geometry of vector algebra so far developed is called affine geometry. The relation which involved the comparison of distances lying along the same or parallel lines only or the relation which deals with the comparision of direction only, so far as parallelism is concerned, are called affine.

During the last sixty or seventy years, there has appeared a broad generalization of vector analysis under the name of Tensor Analysis, which sprang from the study of differential geometry of multidimentional space. The history of differential geometry of spaces of more than three dimensions may be said to have begun with a paper by Bernhard Riemann (1826-1866). Riemannian geometry is based on the assumption that the square of a linear element is represented by a quadratic differential form, usually called a Riemannian metric, the corresponding Riemannian space, which may be of any number of dimensions.

Einstein assumed a Riemannian space of four dimensions as the basis of his general theory and found in the absolute differential calculus the best instrument for formuating his ideas. Since then the tensor calculus has been used extensively by mathematicians and physicists and has proved itself to be a useful and powerful instrument of research.

■ PHYSICAL QUANTITY

It is a property of a phenomenon, body or substance, where the property has a magnitude that can be expressed as a number and a reference. For example, the phenomenon of movement of a body has the property distance which can be expressed in k number of meters, where k is a real number.

Physical quantities are of two types:

1. Scalars **2.** vectors

■ SCALARS

Scalars are those physical quantities which have *only magnitude* but do not have a *direction* in the space, e.g., time, mass, length, volume, temperature, distance and specific gravity etc. are scalars.

■ VECTORS

Vectors are those physical quanttities which have magnitude as well as *direction* and follow the vector addition laws of triangle and parallelogram (described below), e.g., displacement, force, velocity, momentum, electric and magnetic field intensity, acceleration etc. are vectors.

Triangle law of vector addition: If two vectors are represented by two adjacent sides of a triangle taken in the same order, then the closing side of triangle taken in the opposite order represents the sum of the first two vectors.

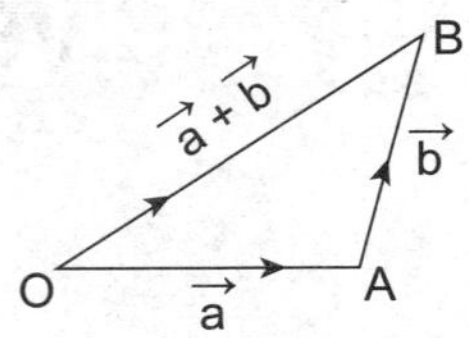

FIGURE 3.1

■ PARALLELOGRAM LAW OF VECTOR ADDITION

If two vectors are represented by the two adjacent sides of a parallelogram both in magnitude and direction, then their resultant will be given by the diagonal through the intersection of these sides (in both senses i.e., magnitude and direction).

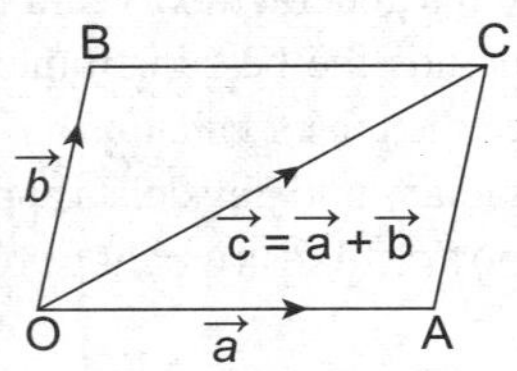

FIGURE 3.2

We can use Δ law of vector addition and parallelogram law of vector addition both simultaneously or seperately depending upon the location of vectors as illustrated below while finding $\overrightarrow{AD}$.

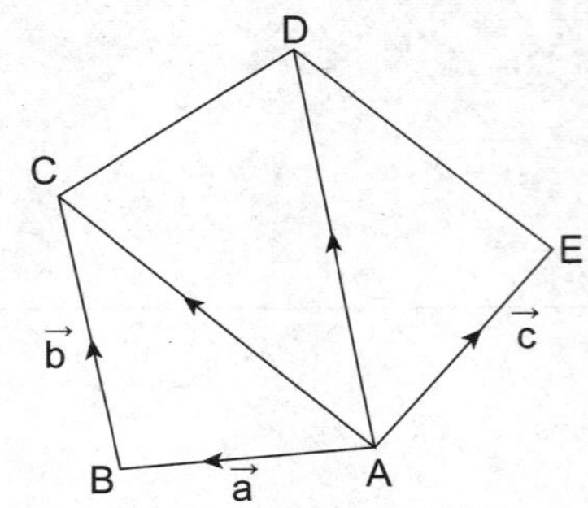

FIGURE 3.3

If $\overrightarrow{AB}=\vec{a}$, $\overrightarrow{BC}=\vec{b}$ and $\overrightarrow{AE}=\vec{c}$, then we can find $\overrightarrow{AD}$ as follows: by Δ law of vector addition.

$$\overrightarrow{AB}+\overrightarrow{BC}=\overrightarrow{AC}$$

$$\Rightarrow \overrightarrow{AC}=\vec{a}+\vec{b}$$

Also, by parallelogram law of vector addition

$$\overrightarrow{AD}=\overrightarrow{AC}+\overrightarrow{AE}=\vec{a}+\vec{b}+\vec{c} \text{ (using (i))}$$

NOTE

Electric current flowing through a wire has both magnitude and direction, but no question of applying triangle rule arises. So electric current is not a vector quantity.

Directed Line Segment

A directed line segment OA is defined as a segment cut by points O and A from a given line containing points O *and* A with a sense from O to A. Clearly, for every directed line segment, three terms can be defined as given below

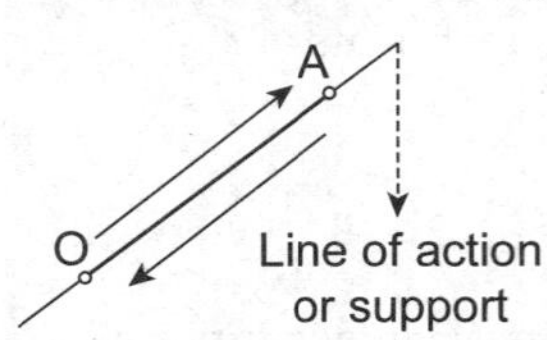

FIGURE 3.4

(i) ***Length:*** The length of $\overrightarrow{OA}$ will be denoted by the symbol $|\overrightarrow{OA}|$. Obviously, we have $|\overrightarrow{OA}|=|\overrightarrow{AO}|$.

(ii) ***Support:*** The line of unlimited length of which a directed line segment is a part is called its line of support or simply the support or line of action of given vector.

(iii) ***Sense:*** The sense of $\overrightarrow{OA}$ is from O to A and that of $\overrightarrow{AO}$ from A to O so that sense of directed line segment is from its initial to the terminal point. The directed line segments $\overrightarrow{OA}$ and $\overrightarrow{AO}$ have the same lengths and support but different senses.

Representation of a Vector

A vector quantity is geometrically represented by a directed line segment OA as shown in the figure; where O is called initial point of the vector and A is called terminal point or final point of the vector.The length OA is known as magnitude of the vector and arrow gives direction of this vector. It is also denoted by $\vec{a}$ or $\overrightarrow{OA}$.

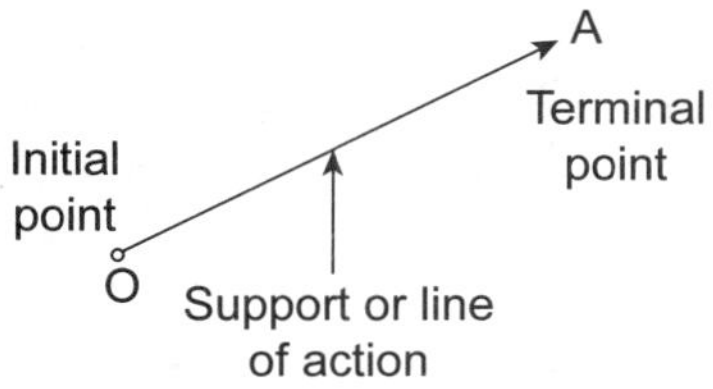

FIGURE 3.5

Notation of Vector

A vector is also denoted by a single letter under an arrow such as $\vec{a}, \vec{b}, \vec{c}$ or bold face type letters ***a***, ***b***, ***c*** etc. The symbol $|\vec{a}|$ denotes the length of the vector $\vec{a}$ and is called modulus of the vector or magnitude of $\vec{a}$.

ILLUSTRATION 1: Find the number of line segments and maximum number of vectors (non null) that can be formed by joining the vertices of a given convex.

(a) Pentagon (b) Hexagon

SOLUTION: **(a)** Number of line segments that can be formed by joining the vertices of pentagon $= {}^nC_2 = {}^5C_2 = 10$

Maxmium number of vectors that can be formed $= 2 \times {}^nC_2 = 2 \times {}^5C_2 = 20$ ($\because$ from every segment *AB*, we can draw two vectors i.e., $\overrightarrow{AB}$ & $\overrightarrow{BA}$

(b) Number of line segments that can be formed by joining the vertices of hexagon $= {}^nC_2 = {}^6C_2 = 15$. Maximum number of vectors that can be formed $= 2 \times {}^nC_2 = 2 \times {}^6C_2 = 30$

ILLUSTRATION 2: Find the maximum number of diagonals and diagonal vectors and vectors (non null) that can be formed by joining the vertices of a given convex

(a) Octagon (b) Duodecagon

SOLUTION: (a) Number of diagonals $= {}^8C_2 - 8 = 20$

Maximum number of diagonal vectors $= 2({}^8C_2 - 8) = 40$

(b) Number of diagonals $= {}^{12}C_2 - 12 = 54$

Maximum number of diagonal vectors $= 2({}^{12}C_2 - 12) = 108$

ILLUSTRATION 3: Find the number of line segments and maximum number of vectors (non null) that can be formed by joining the 10 points out of which 4 are collinear.

SOLUTION: No. of line segments $= {}^{10}C_2 = 45$

No. of vectors $= {}^{10}P_2 = 90$. Since every pair of points from non-collinear or collinear points gives rise to a unique vector, those formed from non collinear points would have different directions, whereas those from collinear points would have same or opposite directions but have different magnitudes.

Equality of Two Vectors and Equal Vectors

Two vectors are said to be equal if and only if they have

(a) equal magnitudes (*same length*)

(b) same direction i.e., (*same or parallel support, their lines of action may be different.*)

(c) same sense.

NOTES

1. *It may thus be seen that two different directed line segments may correspond to the same vector. Thus the vectors $\overrightarrow{AB}, \overrightarrow{CD}, \overrightarrow{EF}$ are equal.*

2. *Two vectors will not be equal if they have different lengths or inclined supports or again, they will not be equal even if they have the same lengths and parallel supports but different senses.*

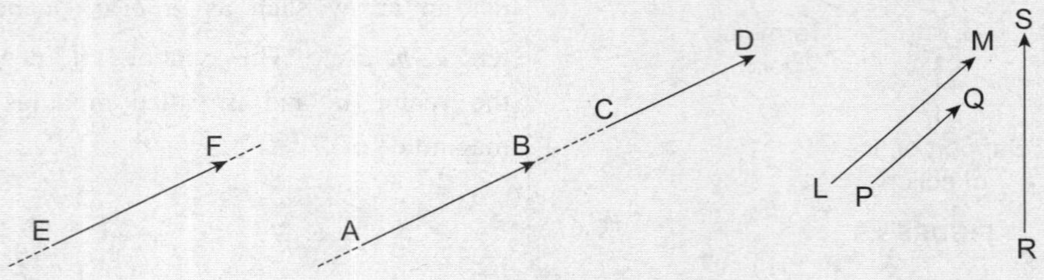

FIGURE 3.6

ILLUSTRATION 4: Find the number of line segments and different vectors (non-null) that can be formed by joining the vertices of a given convex
(a) Regular pentagon (b) Regular hexagon

SOLUTION: **(a)** Number of line segments = ${}^5C_2 = 10$

Number of non null vectors = ${}^5P_2 = 20$, since number of vectors obtained are unequal (either non-parallel, or have unequal magnitude).

(b) Number of line segments = ${}^6C_2 = 15$

Number of non-null vectors = $\frac{6P_2 - 6}{2} + 6 = 18$, since every vector except for $\overrightarrow{AD}, \overrightarrow{DA}, \overrightarrow{BE}, \overrightarrow{EB}, \overrightarrow{CF}, \overrightarrow{FC}$ are repeated twice in ${}^6P_2$ number of vectors e.g., $\overrightarrow{AB} = \overrightarrow{ED}$ etc. because of having equal magnitude and same direction.

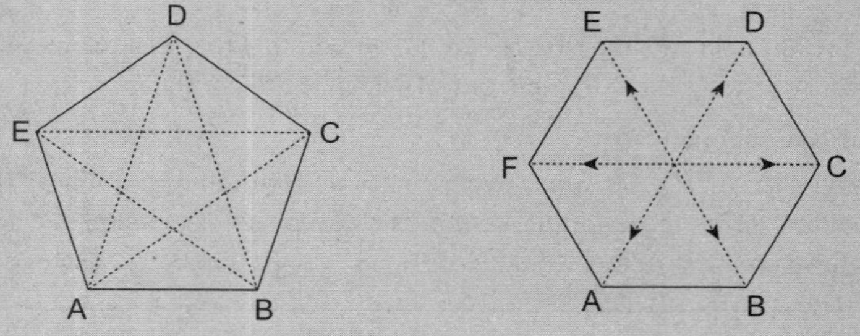

FIGURE 3.7

■ TYPES OF VECTORS

Opposite Vectors (Negative Vectors)

The negative of a vector $\vec{a}$ is defined as a vector having same magnitude that of $\vec{a}$ and the direction opposite to $\vec{a}$. It is denoted as $-\vec{a}$.

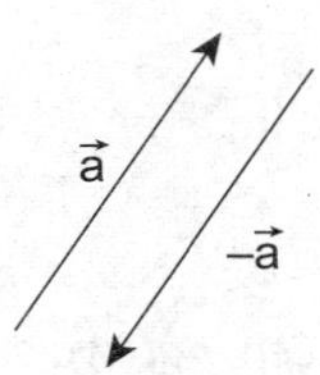

FIGURE 3.8

Zero Vector (Null Vector)

A vector whose initial and terminal points are same is called null vector. e.g., $\overrightarrow{AA}$. Such vector has zero magnitude and arbitrary (indefinite) direction. It is denoted by $\vec{O}$.

$$\overrightarrow{AB}+\overrightarrow{BC}+\overrightarrow{CA}=\overrightarrow{AA}$$

or $$\overrightarrow{AB}+\overrightarrow{BC}+\overrightarrow{CA}=\vec{O}$$

Like and Unlike Parallel Vectors

Two vectors are said to be *like* when they have same direction in the same sense irrespective of their magnitude. Thus all vectors drawn in the same direction, whatever their magnitude may be called like vectors, e.g., $\vec{a}$ and $\vec{b}$ shown below are like vectors.

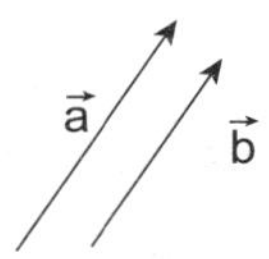

FIGURE 3.9

Two vectors of any magnitude are said to be *Unlike* if they are in opposite directions. e.g., $\vec{a}$ *and* $-\vec{b}$ are two unlike vectors as their directions are opposite, $\vec{a}$ and -3$\vec{a}$ are unlike vectors.

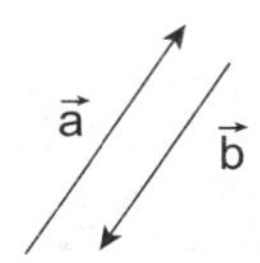

FIGURE 3.10

Unit Vector

A unit vector is a vector whose mangitude is unity. We write a unit vector in the direction of $\vec{a}$ as $\hat{a}$ given by $\dfrac{\vec{a}}{|\vec{a}|}$

The unit vector always represents direction of any vector. For example the vector $\vec{a}$ may be represented as $\vec{a}=|\vec{a}|\ \hat{a}$; where $\hat{a}$ is the unit vector in the direction of vector $\vec{a}$.

Collinear/Parallel Vectors

Vectors which are parallel to the same line are called collinear vectors whatever be their magnitude and sense of direction. Hence $\vec{a}, \vec{b}, \vec{c}$, $\vec{d}$ are representing collinear vectors and for collinear vectors the line of actions is either coincident or parallel.

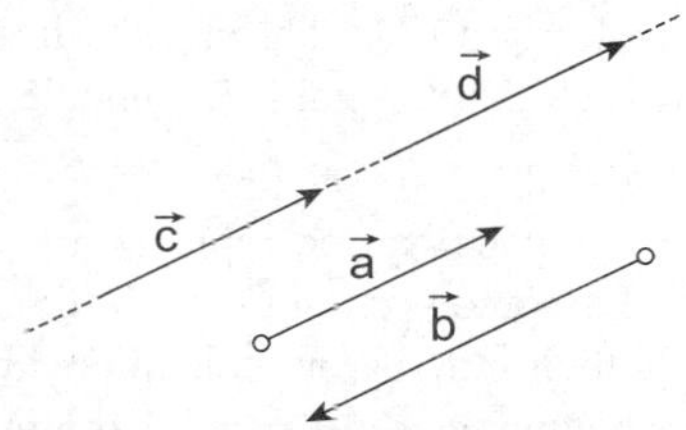

FIGURE 3.11

Co-planar Vectors

If the directed line segments representing various vectors are parallel or lie on the same plane,or parallel plane, then these vectors are called co-planar vectors. Any plane which is parallel to this plane is called the plane of vectors.

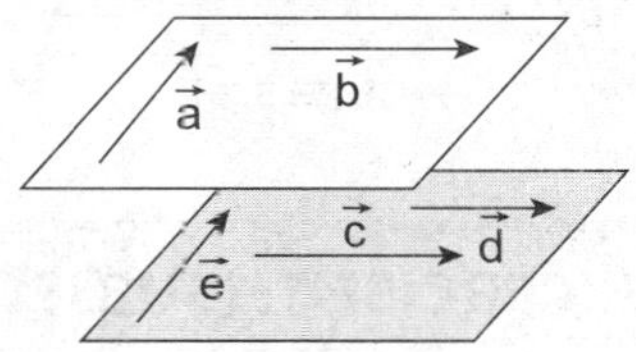

FIGURE 3.12

Thus $\vec{a},\vec{b},\vec{c},\vec{d},\vec{e}$ as shown in above figure are coplanar.

Free and localized Vectors

Free Vector A vector $\vec{a}$ which can be represented by any one of the two directed line segments $\overrightarrow{AB}$ and $\overrightarrow{PQ}$ whose lengths are equal and are in the same direction is known as a free vector. Thus we find that a vector which is not restricted to pass through some fixed point in space is a free vector, i.e., vectors whose initial points are not fixed are called free vectors that is the reason why by keeping the magnitude and directions fixed, the initial points of free vectors can be shifted.

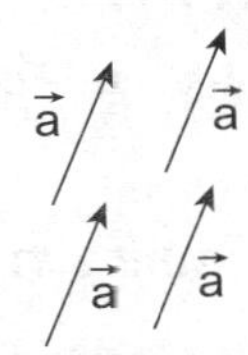

FIGURE 3.13

Localized Vector If a vector is restricted to pass through a specified point (i.e., a fixed point), then it is called localized vector. An example of a localized vector is a force, as its effect depends on the point of its application. Coterminus vectors, position vectors etc., are examples of localized vectors.

Coinitial Vectors or Coterminus Vectors

Since a free vector remains unaltered if it is shifted in space parallel to itself, so any vector $\vec{a}=\overrightarrow{PQ}$ (say) may be drawn from any assigned origin O by shifting the line segment PQ parallel to itself such that the point P coincide with O and Q coincide with other point A, So that $\vec{a} = \overrightarrow{PQ} = \overrightarrow{OA}$. In this way, all vectors in space can be replaced by vectors drawn from the some of assigned origin O by shifting them parallel to themselves till their initial point coincide with the origin O. All such vectors having the same point as origin are called co-initial vectors.

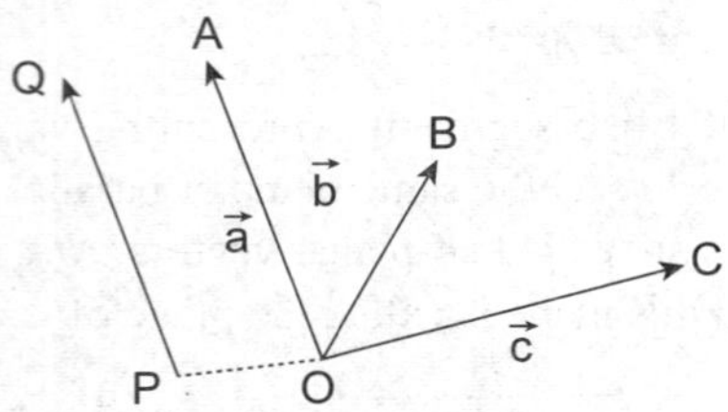

FIGURE 3.14

Position Vector

Let O be a fixed origin, then the position vector of a point P is the vector $\overrightarrow{OP}$. If $\vec{a}$ and $\vec{b}$ be the position vectors of two points A and B, then $\overrightarrow{AB} = \vec{b} - \vec{a}$

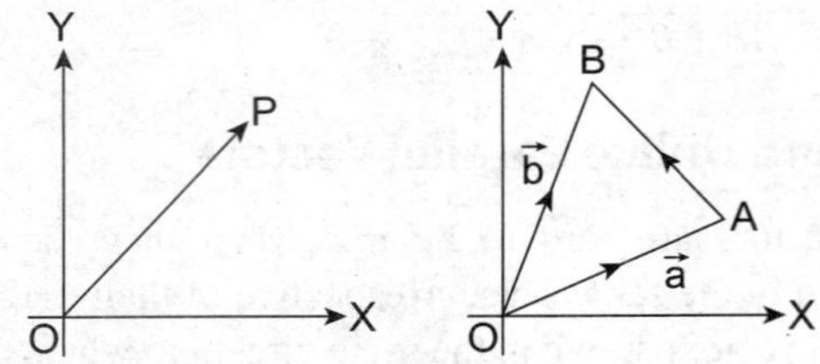

FIGURE 3.15

= Position Vector of B – Position Vector of A

TEXTUAL EXCERCISE 1: (SUBJECTIVE)

1. If $ABCD$ and $AEFC$ are two parallelograms, then find $\overrightarrow{AF}$ and $\overrightarrow{FA}$ ·

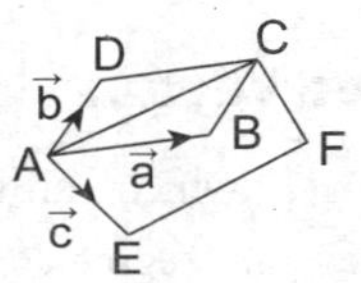

FIGURE 3.16

2. If $ABCD$ is a parallelogram, then find $\overrightarrow{AE}$ and $\overrightarrow{EA}$

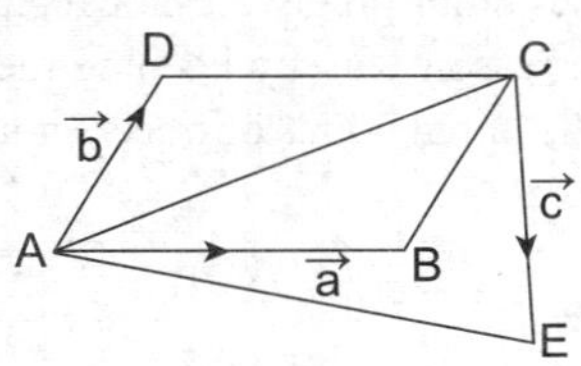

FIGURE 3.17

3. In the figure given below, find the number of non-null different free vectors (free vectors having different non-zero magnitudes) that can be formed by joining some the points A, B, C, D and O; where A, O, C and B, O, D are collinear points, when
   (i) $OA \neq OC$ (ii) $OA = OC$

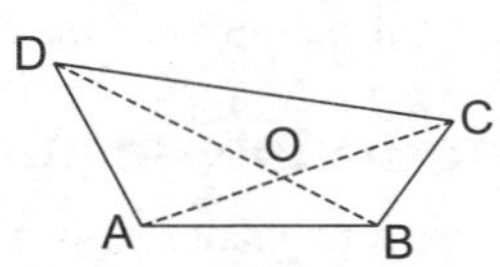

FIGURE 3.18

4. In the figure given below, find the number of non-null different free vectors (free vectors having different non-zero magnitudes) that can be formed by joining the points A, B, C, D and O; where $OC \parallel AB$, $OB = OD$ and $OC = AB$ and B, O, D are collinear.

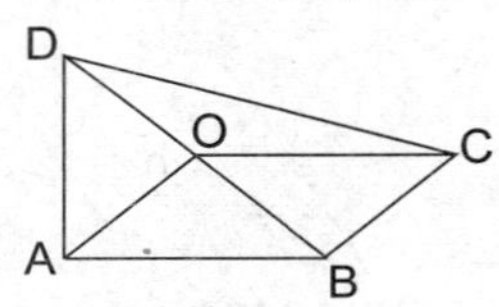

FIGURE 3.19

5. Find the number of different non-null free vectors (free vectors having different non-zero magnitudes) obtained by joining the vertices of given cuboid.

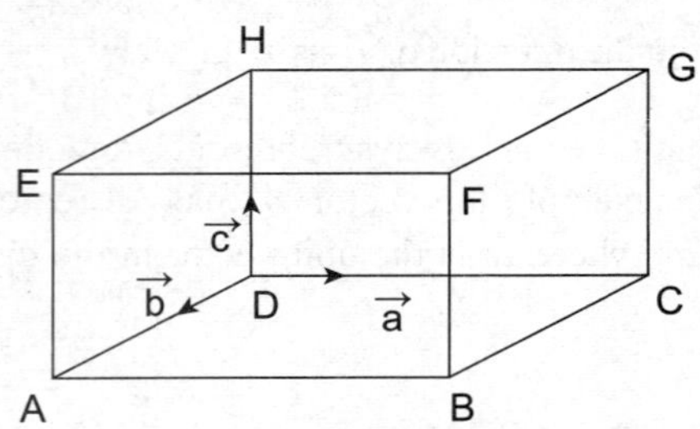

FIGURE 3.20

Also find among those vectors,
(i) the number of pairs of collinear vectors having different lines of actions
(ii) the number of different coplanar vectors with the plane $EFGH$, also name them.

Answer Key

1. $\vec{a}+\vec{b}+\vec{c}; -(\vec{a}+\vec{b}+\vec{c})$ **2.** $\vec{a}+\vec{b}+\vec{c}; -(\vec{a}+\vec{b}+\vec{c})$ **3.** (i) 20 (ii) 18 **4.** 14

5. 26 (i) 96 (ii) 8; $\vec{a},-\vec{a},\vec{b},-\vec{b},(\vec{a}+\vec{b}),-(\vec{a}+\vec{b}),(\vec{a}-\vec{b}),-(\vec{a}-\vec{b})$

■ POSITION VECTOR IN COMPONENT FORM

Let P be a point having co-ordinates (x,y,z) having position vector $\overrightarrow{OP}$. Let $\hat{i},\hat{j},\hat{k}$ be unit vectors along the direction of x-axis, y-axis and z-axis respectively

Draw a $\perp PM$ from P to $M(x,y,0)$ on x-y plane.

From M draw lines $MA \parallel$ to x-axis and $MB \parallel$ to y-axis such that $B(x,0,0)$, $A(0,y,0)$.

From P draw a line $\parallel$ to OM which meets z-axis at $C(0, 0, z)$.

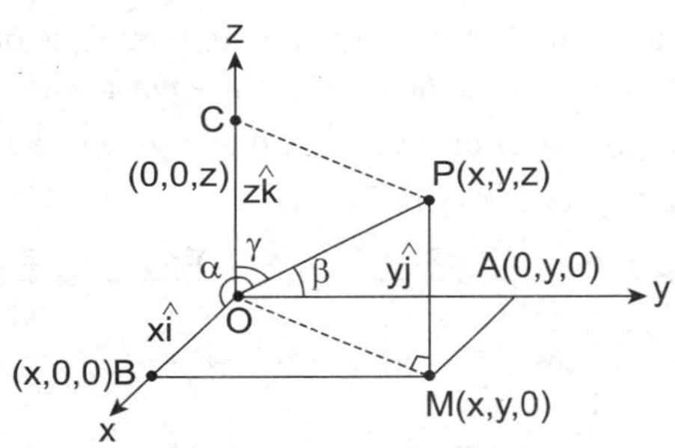

FIGURE 3.21

$$\Rightarrow \overrightarrow{OB} = \left|\overrightarrow{OB}\right|\hat{i} = x\hat{i},\ \overrightarrow{OA} = \left|\overrightarrow{OA}\right|\hat{j} = y\hat{j} \text{ and } \overrightarrow{OC} = \left|\overrightarrow{OC}\right|\hat{k} = z\hat{k}$$

$$\because \quad \overrightarrow{MP} = \overrightarrow{OC} = z\hat{k},$$

$$\therefore \overrightarrow{OP} = (\overrightarrow{OM} + \overrightarrow{MP}) = \overrightarrow{OA} + \overrightarrow{OB} + \overrightarrow{MP}$$

$$\Rightarrow \vec{r}_P = x\hat{i} + y\hat{j} + z\hat{k} \qquad \because \ OP^2 = OM^2 + MP^2$$

$$\Rightarrow |\vec{r}_P|^2 = x^2 + y^2 + z^2$$

$$\Rightarrow \left|\vec{r}_P\right| = \sqrt{x^2+y^2+z^2} = r$$

■ REPRESENTATION OF A FREE VECTOR IN COMPONENT FORM

Let $\vec{a} = \overrightarrow{PQ}$ be any free vector in space having its initial and terminal points P and Q respectively.

We can shift $\overrightarrow{PQ}$ parallely so that P coincides with origin O and Q coincides with point A.

Thus $\overrightarrow{PQ} = \overrightarrow{OA} = x\hat{i} + y\hat{j} + z\hat{k}$; where (x, y, z) are coordiantes of point A as shown in figure below.

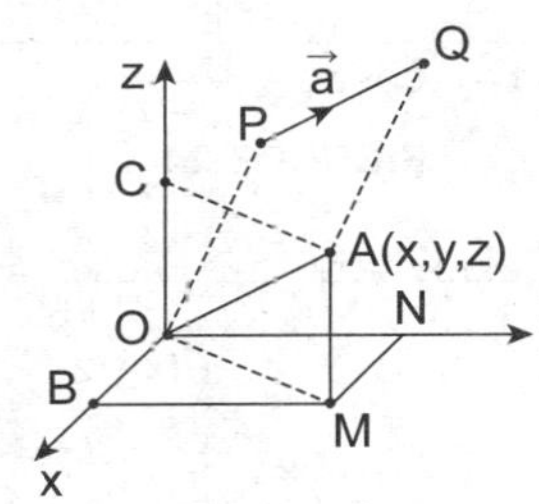

FIGURE 3.22

Thus $\overrightarrow{PQ} = x\hat{i} + y\hat{j} + z\hat{k}$, i.e., every vector in space can be represented in component form. It can be verified that if coordinates of P and Q are respectively (x_1, y_1, z_1) and (x_2, y_2, z_2), then $x = (x_2 - x_1)$; $y = (y_2 - y_1)$; $z = (z_2 - z_1)$ as by triangle law of vector addition $\overrightarrow{OP} + \overrightarrow{PQ} = \overrightarrow{OQ} \Rightarrow \overrightarrow{PQ} = \overrightarrow{OQ} - \overrightarrow{OP}$

i.e., $x\hat{i} + y\hat{j} + z\hat{k} = (x_2 - x_1)\hat{i} + (y_2 - y_1)\hat{j} + (z_2 - z_1)\hat{k}$

Thus

$$\overrightarrow{PQ} = x\hat{i} + y\hat{j} + z\hat{k} = (x_2 - x_1)\hat{i} + (y_2 - y_1)\hat{j} + (z_2 - z_1)\hat{k}$$

■ DIRECTION COSINES AND RATIOS OF VECTORS

Directions of a vector $\overrightarrow{OP}$ is defined as the smallest angle which the vector $\overrightarrow{OP}$ makes with the positive direction of co-ordinate axes x, y, z respectively.

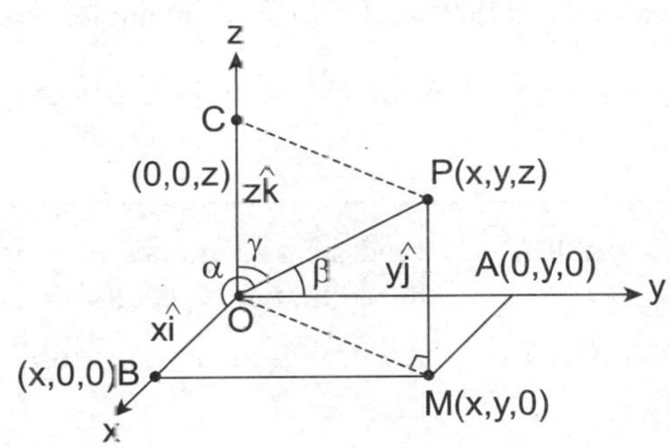

FIGURE 3.23

i.e., α with x-axis; β with y-axis and γ with z-axis ($\alpha, \beta, \gamma \in [0,\pi]$). The cosines of these angles are called direction cosines ($D.C$'s).

Direction of Cosine w.r.t. $x \to \cos\alpha = l$

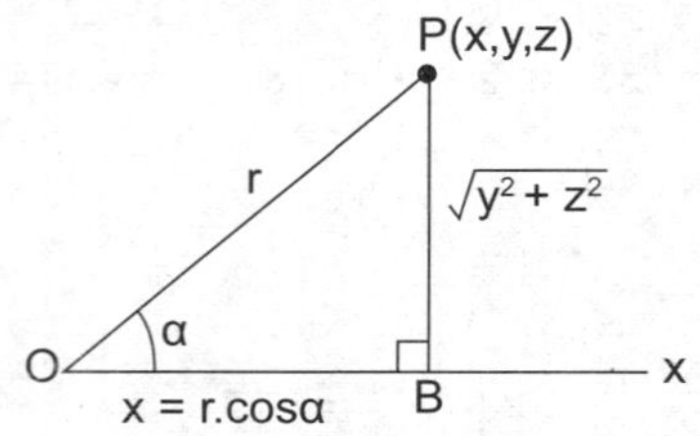

FIGURE 3.24

Direction of Cosine w.r.t. $y \to \cos\beta = m$

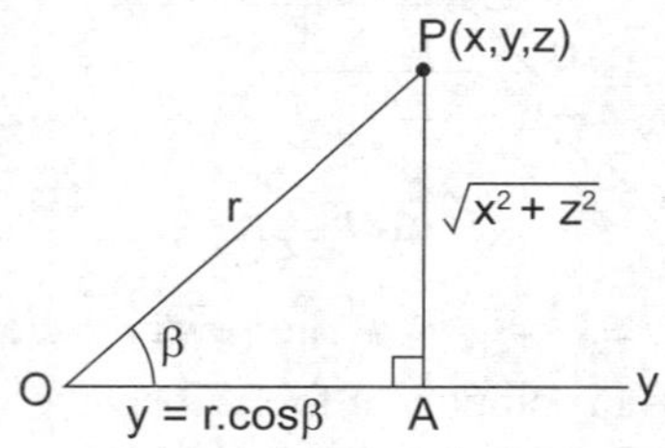

FIGURE 3.25

Direction of Cosine w.r.t. $z \to \cos\gamma = n$

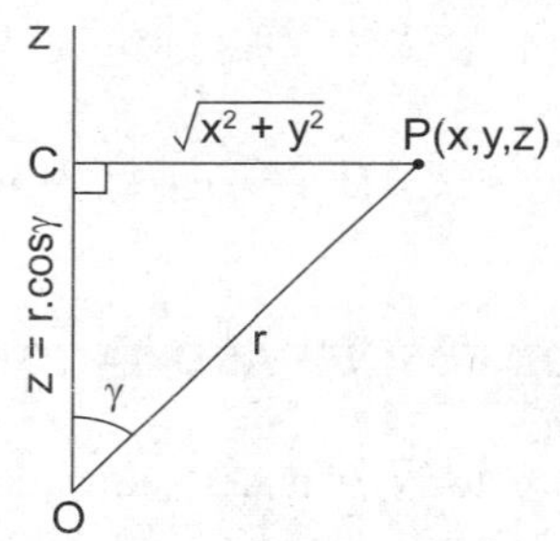

FIGURE 3.26

Because in ΔOBP, angle at B is right angle.

$\Rightarrow \frac{x}{r} = \cos\alpha$ *Similarly* $\frac{y}{r} = \cos\beta$ & $\frac{z}{r} = \cos\gamma$

Direction Ratios: Any non zero constant multiples of direction cosines are called direction ratios of vectors.

i.e., $\langle \lambda l, \lambda m, \lambda n \rangle$ *where* $\lambda \neq 0$; and $\lambda \in \mathbb{R}$ are called direction ratios of the vector whose D.C.'s are $\langle l, m, n \rangle$.

Properties of Direction cosines and Ratios:

1. Direction cosines of a given vector being the values of cosine of angles lie in interval [-1, 1], where as direction ratios may assume any real values.
2. Summation of square of direction cosines of any vector in the space is equal to one.
   Proof: $\because x = r\cos\alpha \Rightarrow \cos\alpha = x/r = l;$
   $\&\ y = r\cos\beta \Rightarrow \cos\beta = y/r = m;$
   $z = r\cos\gamma \Rightarrow \cos\gamma = z/r = n;$
   $\therefore l^2 + m^2 + n^2 = \cos^2\alpha + \cos^2\beta + \cos^2\gamma$
   $= \frac{x^2 + y^2 + z^2}{r^2} = \frac{r^2}{r^2} = 1$
3. Component of a vector is nothing, but it is one of the direction ratios, since $x = l.r, y = m.r$ and $z = n.r$
4. Component of unit vector along a given vector $\vec{r}$ are direction cosines of $\vec{r}$.
   Proof: $\hat{r} = \frac{\vec{r}}{r} = \frac{x\hat{i} + y\hat{j} + z\hat{k}}{r} = \frac{x}{r}\hat{i} + \frac{y}{r}\hat{j} + \frac{z}{r}\hat{k}$
   $\cos\alpha\hat{i} + \cos\beta\hat{j} + \cos\gamma\hat{k} = l\hat{i} + m\hat{j} + n\hat{k}$
   e.g. if $a = \frac{2}{\sqrt{29}}\hat{i} + \frac{3}{\sqrt{29}}\hat{j} - \frac{4}{\sqrt{29}}\hat{k},$
   then direction cosines of $\vec{a}$ are $\left\langle \frac{2}{\sqrt{29}}, \frac{3}{\sqrt{29}}, -\frac{4}{\sqrt{29}} \right\rangle$
5. Direction cosines of like vectors are same, e.g., direction cosines of $\vec{a}$ & $3\vec{a}$ are same.
6. Direction cosines of unlike vectors are numerically same but opposite in sign, e.g., direction cosines of $\vec{a}$ & $-3\vec{a}$ are same in magnitude but opposite in sign.

ILLUSTRATION 5: Find the direction cosines of the vectors that makes equal angles with co-ordinate axes and hence find unit vectors along those vectors.

SOLUTION: According to question cosα = cosβ = cosγ = k (say); we know that $\cos^2\alpha + \cos^2\beta + \cos^2\gamma = 1$

$\Rightarrow 3k^2 = 1 \qquad \Rightarrow k = \pm\frac{1}{\sqrt{3}}$

$\therefore$ Direction cosines along the required vectors are $\left\langle \frac{1}{\sqrt{3}}, \frac{1}{\sqrt{3}}, \frac{1}{\sqrt{3}} \right\rangle$ and $\left\langle \frac{-1}{\sqrt{3}}, \frac{-1}{\sqrt{3}}, \frac{-1}{\sqrt{3}} \right\rangle$ and

unit vectors along those vectors are $\frac{1}{\sqrt{3}}\hat{i} + \frac{1}{\sqrt{3}}\hat{j} + \frac{1}{\sqrt{3}}\hat{k}$ and $\frac{-1}{\sqrt{3}}\hat{i} - \frac{1}{\sqrt{3}}\hat{j} - \frac{1}{3}\hat{k}$

ILLUSTRATION 6: Find the unit vector along the vector $\vec{a} = 5\hat{i} - 4\hat{j} + 2\hat{k}$ and hence find direction cosines of $\vec{a}$.

SOLUTION: $a = 5\hat{i} - 4\hat{j} + 2\hat{k}$ and unit vector along $\vec{a} = \hat{a} = \frac{\vec{a}}{|\vec{a}|}$

$$= \frac{5\hat{i} - 4\hat{j} + 2\hat{k}}{\sqrt{25+16+4}} = \frac{5\hat{i} - 4\hat{j} + 2\hat{k}}{\sqrt{45}} = \frac{5}{3\sqrt{5}}\hat{i} - \frac{4}{3\sqrt{5}}\hat{j} + \frac{2}{3\sqrt{5}}\hat{k}$$

$\therefore$ Direction cosines along $\vec{a}$ are $\left\langle \frac{5}{3\sqrt{5}}, \frac{-4}{3\sqrt{5}}, \frac{2}{3\sqrt{5}} \right\rangle$ and direction ratios are <5, –4, 2>

ILLUSTRATION 7: Direction cosines of a vector along x-axis and y-axis are respectively $\frac{1}{\sqrt{2}}$ and $\frac{\sqrt{7}}{4}$, then find the direction cosine of vector along z-axis.

SOLUTION: Given $l = \frac{1}{\sqrt{2}}, m = \frac{\sqrt{7}}{4}$; To find : n. We know that $l^2 + m^2 + n^2 = 1$

$$\Rightarrow \frac{1}{2} + \frac{7}{16} + n^2 = 1 \quad \Rightarrow \quad n^2 = 1 - \frac{1}{2} - \frac{7}{16} = \frac{1}{16} \quad \Rightarrow \quad n = \pm\frac{1}{4}$$

$\therefore$ Direction cosines of vector along z-axis are $\pm\frac{1}{4}$.

ILLUSTRATION 8: If $\sin\theta$, $\sin\phi$, $\sin\psi$ are the direction cosines of a vector, then evaluate $\cos 2\theta + \cos 2\phi + \cos 2\psi$

SOLUTION: $\cos 2\theta + \cos 2\phi + \cos 2\psi = (1 - 2\sin^2\theta) + (1 - 2\sin^2\phi) + (1 - 2\sin^2\psi)$
$= 3 - 2[\sin^2\theta + \sin^2\phi + \sin^2\psi] = 3 - 2[l^2 + m^2 + n^2] = 3 - 2(1) = 1$

ILLUSTRATION 9: In the figure given below if
$\vec{a} = \overrightarrow{AB} = 2\hat{i} - 3\hat{j} + 5\hat{k}$; $\vec{b} = \overrightarrow{AE} = 3\hat{i} + 5\hat{j} + \hat{k}$; and $\vec{c} = \overrightarrow{DC} = 10\hat{i} + 4\hat{j} + 12\hat{k}$, then find unit vector along $\overrightarrow{BC}$ and hence direction cosines along $\overrightarrow{BC}$.

SOLUTION: $\overrightarrow{AD} = \vec{a} + \vec{b} = (2\hat{i} - 3\hat{j} + 5\hat{k}) + (3\hat{i} + 5\hat{j} + \hat{k}) = 5\hat{i} + 2\hat{j} + 6\hat{k}$

Now $\overrightarrow{AC} = \overrightarrow{AD} + \overrightarrow{DC} = (5\hat{i} + 2\hat{j} + 6\hat{k}) + (10\hat{i} + 4\hat{j} + 12\hat{k})$

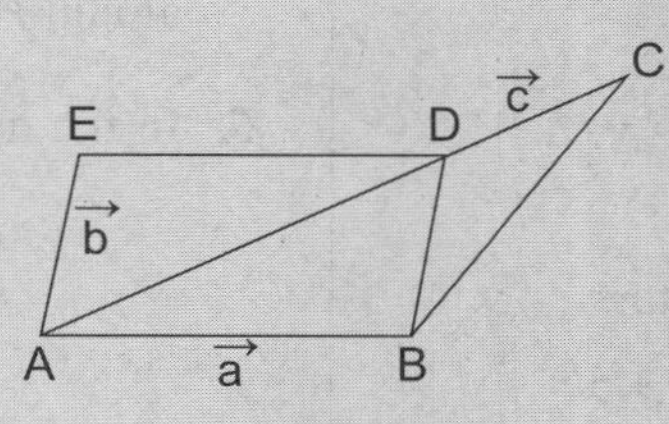

FIGURE 3.27

$$\left[\begin{array}{l} \because \overrightarrow{DC} = 2\overrightarrow{AD} \\ \Rightarrow A, C, D \text{ are collinear} \\ \Rightarrow \overrightarrow{AC} = \overrightarrow{AD} + \overrightarrow{DC} \end{array}\right] = 15\hat{i} + 6\hat{j} + 18\hat{k}$$

Now in ΔABC, $\overrightarrow{AB} + \overrightarrow{BC} = \overrightarrow{AC}$ (By Δ law of vectors addition)

$$\Rightarrow \overrightarrow{BC} = \overrightarrow{AC} - \overrightarrow{AB} = (15\hat{i} + 6\hat{j} + 18\hat{k}) - (2\hat{i} - 3\hat{j} + 5\hat{k}) = 13\hat{i} + 9\hat{j} + 13\hat{k}$$

$\therefore$ Unit vector along the direction of $\overrightarrow{BC} = \dfrac{13}{\sqrt{419}}\hat{i} + \dfrac{9}{\sqrt{419}}\hat{j} + \dfrac{13}{\sqrt{419}}\hat{k}$

Hence direction cosines of $\overrightarrow{BC} = \dfrac{13}{\sqrt{419}}, \dfrac{9}{\sqrt{419}}, \dfrac{13}{\sqrt{419}}$

ILLUSTRATION 10: Find the angles that the vectors $\vec{r}$ makes with the co-ordinate axes, if the direction cosines of the vector are given by

(a) $\left(\dfrac{-\sqrt{3}}{2}, \dfrac{-1}{2}, 0\right)$ (b) $\left(\dfrac{-1}{\sqrt{3}}, \dfrac{1}{\sqrt{3}}, \dfrac{-1}{\sqrt{3}}\right)$ (c) $\left\langle \dfrac{1}{2}, \dfrac{1}{3}, \dfrac{1}{2} \right\rangle$

SOLUTION: (a) $l = \dfrac{-\sqrt{3}}{2}, m = \dfrac{-1}{2}, n = 0 \Rightarrow \cos\alpha = \dfrac{-\sqrt{3}}{2}, \cos\beta = \dfrac{-1}{2}, \cos\gamma = 0$

$\Rightarrow \alpha = 150^\circ, \beta = 120^\circ, \gamma = 90^\circ)$

(b) $l = \dfrac{-1}{\sqrt{3}}, m = \dfrac{1}{\sqrt{3}}, n = \dfrac{-1}{\sqrt{3}} \Rightarrow \cos\alpha = \dfrac{-1}{\sqrt{3}}, \cos\beta = \dfrac{1}{\sqrt{3}}, \cos\gamma = \dfrac{-1}{\sqrt{3}}$

$\Rightarrow \alpha = \pi - \cos^{-1}\left(\dfrac{1}{\sqrt{3}}\right); \beta = \cos^{-1}\left(\dfrac{1}{\sqrt{3}}\right), \gamma = \pi - \cos^{-1}\left(\dfrac{1}{\sqrt{3}}\right)$

(c) $l = \dfrac{1}{2}, m = \dfrac{1}{3}, n = \dfrac{1}{2}$ $\because l^2 + m^2 + n^2 = \dfrac{1}{4} + \dfrac{1}{9} + \dfrac{1}{4} = \dfrac{22}{36} = \dfrac{11}{18} \neq 1$

$\therefore \left\langle \dfrac{1}{2}, \dfrac{1}{3}, \dfrac{1}{2} \right\rangle$ can't be the direction cosines of a vector.

TEXTUAL EXERCISE 2: (SUBJECTIVE)

1. Find the angle subtended by $\vec{r}$ with the +ve direction of axes, having their direction cosines as given below

   (a) $\left\langle \dfrac{1}{\sqrt{2}}, \dfrac{1}{\sqrt{2}}, 0 \right\rangle$ (b) $\left\langle \dfrac{-1}{2}, 0, \dfrac{\sqrt{3}}{2} \right\rangle$

   (c) $\left\langle \dfrac{1}{\sqrt{3}}, \dfrac{-1}{\sqrt{3}}, \dfrac{1}{\sqrt{3}} \right\rangle$

2. Find the direction cosines of given vectors

   (a) $\vec{a} = 2\hat{i} - \hat{j} - 3\hat{k}$ (b) $\vec{a} = 5\hat{i} - 4\hat{j} + 6\hat{k}$

   (c) $\vec{a} = \hat{i} - \hat{j} + \hat{k}$

3. Given direction cosines along two axes; find that along other axis for a given vector.

   (a) $\left\langle \dfrac{1}{\sqrt{3}}, \sqrt{\dfrac{2}{3}}, n \right\rangle$ (b) $\left\langle \dfrac{\sqrt{3}}{4}, m, \dfrac{\sqrt{3}}{8} \right\rangle$

   (c) $\left\langle l, \dfrac{\sqrt{3}}{4}, \dfrac{1}{4} \right\rangle$

4. If co-ordinates of point P and Q are respectively (2, 5, 7) and (–3, –1, 2), then find unit vector along $\overrightarrow{PQ}$ and hence direction cosines along $\overrightarrow{PQ}$.

5. In the figure given below

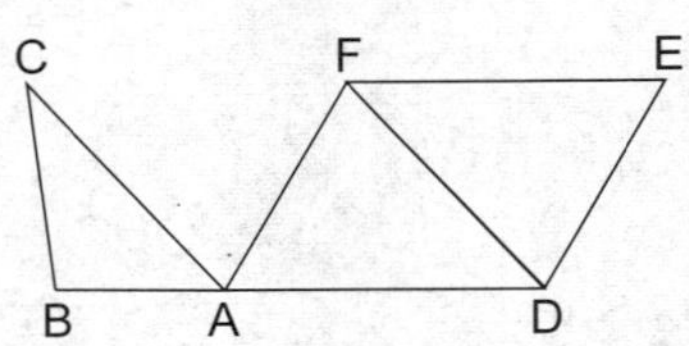

FIGURE 3.28

$\overrightarrow{AB} = 3\hat{i} - \hat{j} + 4\hat{k}; \overrightarrow{BC} = \hat{i} - 2\hat{j} + 2\hat{k}$ $AC \parallel DF$ and $AC = DF$; $AD = 2(AB)$, and $ADEF$ is a parallelogram, then find a unit vector along $\overrightarrow{AE}$ and direction cosines of $\overrightarrow{AE}$. Given that B, A, D are collinear points.

Answer Key

1. (a) 45°, 45°, 90° (b) 120°, 90°, 30° (c) $\cos^{-1}\left(\frac{1}{\sqrt{3}}\right), \pi - \cos^{-1}\left(\frac{1}{\sqrt{3}}\right), \cos^{-1}\left(\frac{1}{\sqrt{3}}\right)$

2. (a) $\left\langle \frac{2}{\sqrt{14}}, \frac{-1}{\sqrt{14}}, \frac{-3}{\sqrt{14}} \right\rangle$ (b) $\left\langle \frac{5}{\sqrt{77}}, \frac{-4}{\sqrt{77}}, \frac{6}{\sqrt{77}} \right\rangle$ (c) $\left\langle \frac{1}{\sqrt{3}}, \frac{-1}{\sqrt{3}}, \frac{1}{\sqrt{3}} \right\rangle$

3. (a) n = ± 0 (b) m = ± 7/8 (c) $l = \pm\frac{\sqrt{3}}{2}$

4. $\frac{-5}{\sqrt{86}}\hat{i} - \frac{6}{\sqrt{86}}\hat{j} - \frac{5}{\sqrt{86}}\hat{k}$ $\left\langle \frac{-5}{\sqrt{86}}, \frac{-6}{\sqrt{86}}, \frac{-5}{\sqrt{86}} \right\rangle$

5. $\frac{-8}{\sqrt{165}}\hat{i} + \frac{1}{\sqrt{165}}\hat{j} - \frac{10}{\sqrt{165}}\hat{k}; \left\langle \frac{-8}{\sqrt{165}}, \frac{1}{\sqrt{165}}, -\frac{10}{\sqrt{165}} \right\rangle$

■ ALGEBRA OF VECTORS

ADDITION OF TWO VECTORS

Let there be two vectors $\vec{a}$ and $\vec{b}$ represented by $\overrightarrow{OA}$ and $\overrightarrow{AB}$ respectively. Then the vector $\overrightarrow{OB}$ obtained by joining the initial point O of $\vec{a}$ (or $\overrightarrow{OA}$) and the terminal point B of $\vec{b}$ (or $\overrightarrow{AB}$) is defined as the sum of vector $\vec{a}$ and $\vec{b}$ i.e., $\vec{c} = \vec{a} + \vec{b}$ or $\overrightarrow{OB} = \overrightarrow{OA} + \overrightarrow{AB}$

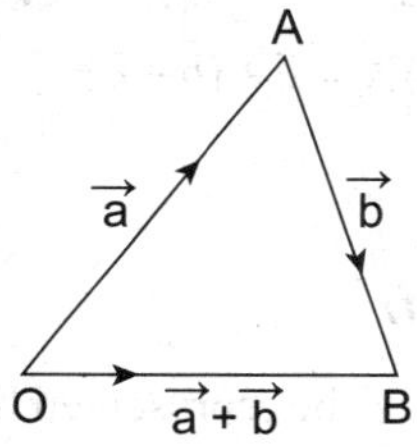

FIGURE 3.29

This law is called the *triangle law of vector addition* which states that if two vectors are represented by two adjacent sides of a Δ both in the sense of magnitude and direction, the third side of the triangle taken in opposite order represents the sum of first two vectors.

If two vectors $\vec{a}$ and $\vec{b}$ are represented by two adjacent sides of a parallelogram having same initial point, then their sum is represented by the diagonal of parallelogram passing through the point of intersection of given vectors.

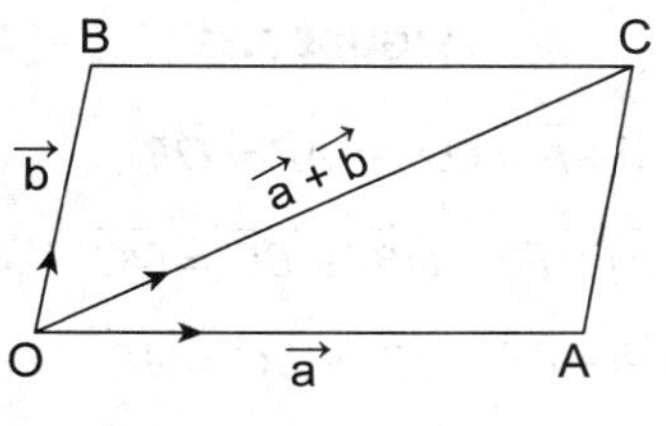

FIGURE 3.30

Thus if $\overrightarrow{OA} = \vec{a}$ and $\overrightarrow{OB} = \vec{b}$, then $\overrightarrow{OC} = \vec{a} + \vec{b}$

For adding more than two vectors, we have a Polygon Law of addition which is just an extension of the triangle law.

$\overrightarrow{OA} + \overrightarrow{AB} + \overrightarrow{BC} + \overrightarrow{CD} + \overrightarrow{DE} + \overrightarrow{EF} = \overrightarrow{OF}$.

As a consequence of this result we conclude that, if the terminal point of the last vector coincides with the initial point of the first vector, then the sum of the vectors is $\vec{O}$.

In general if $\vec{a}$ and $\vec{b}$ are vectors in *x-y* plane, and

$\vec{a} = x_1\hat{i} + x_2\hat{j}$ and $\vec{b} = y_1\hat{i} + y_2\hat{j}$,

then $\vec{a} + \vec{b} = (x_1 + y_1)\hat{i} + (x_2 + y_2)\hat{j}$

and if $\vec{a}$ and $\vec{b}$ are vectors in space and

$\vec{a} = x_1\hat{i} + x_2\hat{j} + x_3\hat{k}$ and $\vec{b} = y_1\hat{i} + y_2\hat{j} + y_3\hat{k}$,

then $\vec{a} + \vec{b} = (x_1 + y_1)\hat{i} + (x_2 + y_2)\hat{j} + (x_3 + y_3)\hat{k}$

Subtraction of Vectors

Let there be two vectors $\vec{a}$ and $\vec{b}$, then the difference of $\vec{a}$ and $\vec{b}$ is defined as the addition of $\vec{a}$ and $-\vec{b}$. Thus $\vec{a} - \vec{b} = \vec{a} - (-\vec{b})$.

Geometrical Representation

We take any point O in space, $\overrightarrow{OA} = \vec{a}$ and $\overrightarrow{OB} = \vec{b}$

Then $\vec{a} - \vec{b} = \vec{a} + (-\vec{b}) = \overrightarrow{OA} - \overrightarrow{OB} = \overrightarrow{BO} + \overrightarrow{OA} = \overrightarrow{BA}$

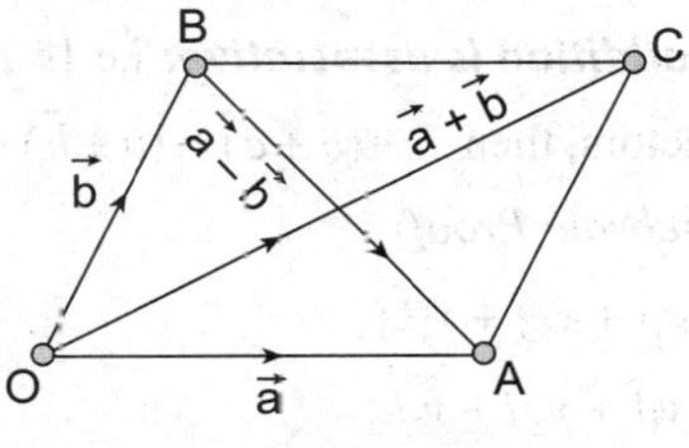

FIGURE 3.31

In general if $\vec{a}$ and $\vec{b}$ are vectors in $x-y$ plane, and

$\vec{a}=x_1\hat{i}+x_2\hat{j}$ and $\vec{b}=y_1\hat{i}+y_2\hat{j}$,

then $\vec{a}-\vec{b}=(x_1-y_1)\hat{i}+(x_2-y_2)\hat{j}$

and if $\vec{a}$ and $\vec{b}$ are vectors in space and

$\vec{a}=x_1\hat{i}+x_2\hat{j}+x_3\hat{k}$ and $\vec{b}=y_1\hat{i}+y_2\hat{j}+y_3\hat{k}$,

then $\vec{a}-\vec{b}=(x_1-y_1)\hat{i}+(x_2-y_2)\hat{j}+(x_3-y_3)\hat{k}$

NOTES

1. *Hence we conclude that to subtract $\vec{b}$ from $\vec{a}$, we reverse the direction of $\vec{b}$ and add it to $\vec{a}$.*
2. *When $\vec{b}=\vec{a}$, $\vec{b}-\vec{a}=\vec{a}-\vec{a}=\overrightarrow{OB}-\overrightarrow{BO}=\overrightarrow{OO}=\vec{0}$, where $\overline{OO}$ is degenerate vector of zero length called as null/zero vector. All zero vector regarded as equal irrespective of direction.*
3. *Direction of zero vector is arbitrary.*
4. *Vectors other than zero vector are called proper vectors.*

Properties of Vector Addition

(a) ***Vector addition is commutative:*** i.e., $\vec{a}+\vec{b}=\vec{b}+\vec{a}$

Proof: *(Algebraic Proof)* If $\vec{a}$ and $\vec{b}$ are vectors in space and $\vec{a}=x_1\hat{i}+x_2\hat{j}+x_3\hat{k}$ and $\vec{b}=y_1\hat{i}+y_2\hat{j}+y_3\hat{k}$,

then $\vec{a}+\vec{b}=(x_1+y_1)\hat{i}+(x_2+y_2)\hat{j}+(x_3+y_3)\hat{k}$

$=(y_1+x_1)\hat{i}+(y_2+x_2)\hat{j}+(y_3+x_3)\hat{k}=\vec{b}+\vec{a}$

(Geometrical Proof)

Let the vectors $\vec{a}$ and $\vec{b}$ be represented by $\overline{OA}$ and $\overline{AB}$ so that $\overrightarrow{OB}=\overrightarrow{OA}+\overrightarrow{AB}=\vec{a}+\vec{b}$ ....(i)

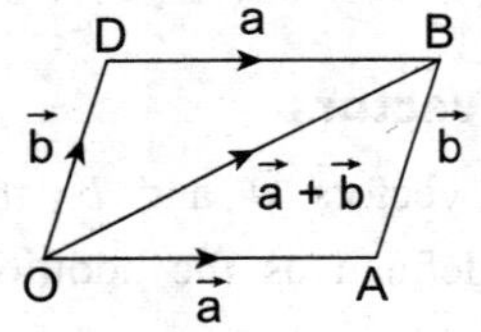

FIGURE 3.32

Complete the parallelogram *OABD* as shown in the figure. Obviously $\overrightarrow{OD}=\vec{b}=\overrightarrow{AB}$ and $\overrightarrow{DB}=\overrightarrow{OA}=\vec{a}$

Hence $\overrightarrow{OB}=\overrightarrow{OD}+\overrightarrow{DB}=\vec{b}+\vec{a}$ ....(ii)

Hence from (i) and (ii) we get, $\vec{a}+\vec{b}=\vec{b}+\vec{a}$

(b) ***Vector addition is associative:*** i.e If $\vec{a},\vec{b},\vec{c}$ be any three vectors, then $\vec{a}+(\vec{b}+\vec{c})=(\vec{a}+\vec{b})+\vec{c}$

Proof: *(Algebraic Proof)*

Let $\vec{a}=x_1\hat{i}+x_2\hat{j}+x_3\hat{k}$;

$\vec{b}=y_1\hat{i}+y_2\hat{j}+y_3\hat{k}$;

$\vec{c}=z_1\hat{i}+z_2\hat{j}+z_3\hat{k}$,

then $(\vec{a}+\vec{b})+\vec{c}=\left[(x_1+y_1)\hat{i}+(x_2+y_2)\hat{j}+(x_3+y_3)\hat{k}\right]$

$+(z_1\hat{i}+z_2\hat{j}+z_3\hat{k})=(x_1+y_1+z_1)\hat{i}+(x_2+y_2+z_2)\hat{j}+$

$(x_3+y_3+z_3)\hat{k}$

$=[x_1+(y_1+z_1)]\hat{i}+[x_2+(y_2+z_2)]\hat{j}+$

$[x_3+(y_3+z_3)]\hat{k}=\vec{a}+(\vec{b}+\vec{c})$

$=\vec{a}+(\vec{b}+\vec{c})$

(Geometrical Proof)

Let the vectors $\vec{a},\vec{b},\vec{c}$ be represented by $\overline{OA}$, $\overline{AB}$ and $\overline{BC}$ respectively

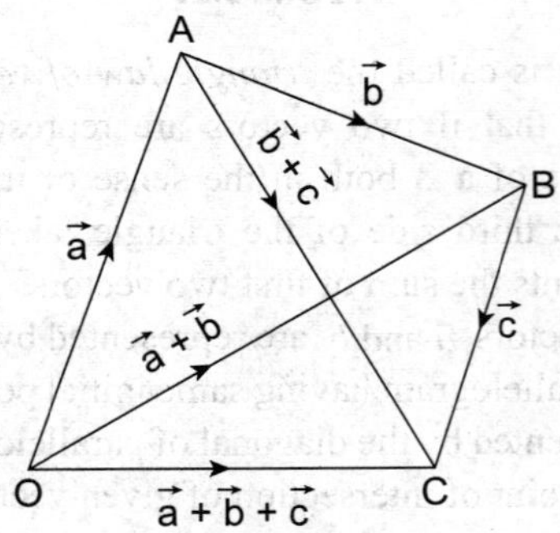

FIGURE 3.33

We have $\vec{a}+\vec{b}=\overrightarrow{OA}+\overrightarrow{AB}=\overrightarrow{OB}$

$\therefore\quad (\vec{a}+\vec{b})+\vec{c}=\overrightarrow{OB}+\overrightarrow{BC}=\overrightarrow{OC}$ .....(i)

Also $\vec{b}+\vec{c}=\overrightarrow{AB}+\overrightarrow{BC}=\overrightarrow{AC}$

$\therefore\quad \vec{a}+(\vec{b}+\vec{c})=\overrightarrow{OA}+\overrightarrow{AC}=\overrightarrow{OC}$ ....(ii)

NOTES

The associative law holds for the addition of any number of vectors and the summation is independent of order and grouping of the vectors.

(c) ***Additive identity Vector:*** If $\vec{a}$ be any vector and $\vec{0}$ be zero vector, then $\vec{a}+\vec{0}=\vec{0}+\vec{a}=\vec{a}$; $\vec{0}$ is callled additive identity vector.

(d) ***Additive inverse Vector:*** If $\vec{a}$ be any vector, then there exists a vector $-\vec{a}$ such that $\vec{a}+(-\vec{a})=\vec{0}=(-\vec{a})+\vec{a}$ Here $-\vec{a}$ is called the additive inverse vector of $\vec{a}$.

(e) ***Triangle Inequalities:***

(i) $|\vec{a}+\vec{b}| \le |\vec{a}| + |\vec{b}|$

(ii) $|\vec{a}+\vec{b}| \ge ||\vec{a}| - |\vec{b}||$

(iii) $||\vec{a}|-|\vec{b}|| \le |\vec{a}+\vec{b}| \le |\vec{a}|+|\vec{b}|$.

(f) The sum and difference of two vectors always lie in the plane containing $\vec{a}$ & $\vec{b}$. i.e. $\pm\vec{a}, \pm\vec{b}, \pm(\vec{a}\pm\vec{b})$ are coplanar.

MULTIPLICATION OF VECTORS BY A SCALAR

The product of a vector $\vec{a}$ and a real number m, denoted by $m\vec{a}$ or $\vec{a}\,m$, is defined as a vector whose length is $|m|$ times that of $\vec{a}$, and whose direction is the same as that of $\vec{a}$ or the opposite direction, according as m is positive or negative.

Division of a vector by a non-zero real number m is defined as multiplication of the vector by $1/m$. Thus if $\hat{a}$ is the unit vector in the direction of $\vec{a}$, then $\hat{a}=\frac{\vec{a}}{|\vec{a}|}$, and if $\vec{b}$ is parallel to $\vec{a}$, then $\vec{b} = \pm b\left(\frac{\vec{a}}{a}\right)$, according as the two vectors have the same direction or opposite directions. The multiplication of a vector by a scalar satisfies the commutative, associative and distributive laws, i.e., $m\vec{a} = \vec{a}m$ ....(i) (commutative)

$m(n\vec{a}) = n(m\vec{a}) = (mn)\vec{a}$ ....(ii) (associative)

$(m+n)\vec{a} = m\vec{a} + n\vec{a}$ and $m(\vec{a}+\vec{b}) = m\vec{a} + m\vec{b}$ ....(iii) (distributive)

Where m and n are any two scalars and $\vec{a}$ and $\vec{b}$ are any two vectors

The first three results can be obtained directly from the definition.

Proof: $m(\vec{a}+\vec{b}) = m\vec{a} + m\vec{b}$. Let $\overrightarrow{OA}=\vec{a}$ and $\overrightarrow{AB}=\vec{b}$, then $\overrightarrow{OB}=\vec{a}+\vec{b}$

Case I: *If m is a positive number* Choose A′ and B′ on OA and OB produced such that $OA' = mOA$ and $OB' = m.OB$

$\therefore$ $\overrightarrow{OA'} = m\vec{a}$ and $\overrightarrow{OB'} = m(\vec{a}+\vec{b})$ ....(i)

Also as $A'B'$ is parallel to AB

$\therefore$ and $A'B' = m\,AB$; $\overrightarrow{A'B'} = m\overrightarrow{AB} = m\vec{b}$ .....(ii)

Also $\overrightarrow{OA'} + \overrightarrow{A'B'} = \overrightarrow{OB'}$

i.e., $m\vec{a} + m\vec{b} = m(\vec{a}+\vec{b})$ (from (i) and (ii))

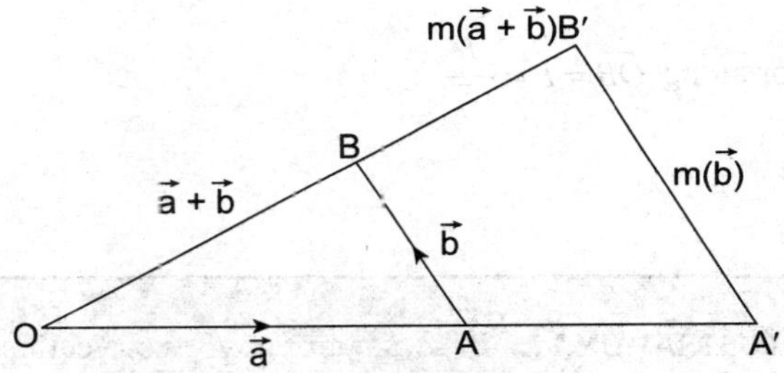

FIGURE 3.34

Case II: *If m is a negative number*:

We choose A' on AO produced (*and not OA produced as above*) such that $OA' = |m|.\,OA$ but in the direction oppostie to that of OA. The result in this case can be proved with the help of diagram given below.

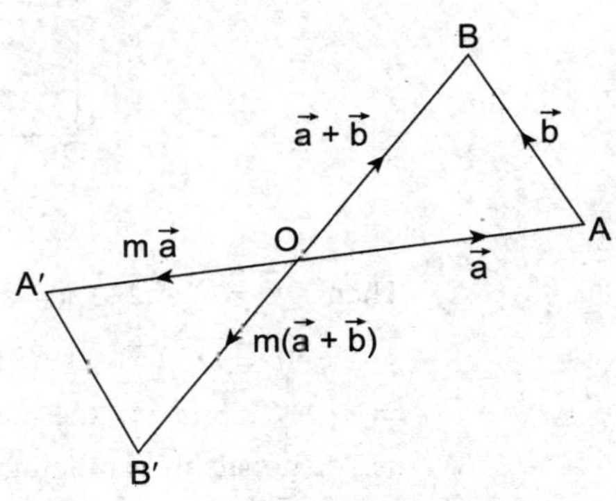

FIGURE 3.35

$\overrightarrow{OA'} = |m|(-\vec{a}) = -|m|\vec{a} = m\vec{a}\ (\because m = -|m|)$

Also $\overrightarrow{OB'} = |m|[-(\vec{a}+\vec{b})]$

$= -|m|(\vec{a}+\vec{b}) = m(\vec{a}+\vec{b})$

and $\overrightarrow{A'B'} = |m|(-\vec{b}) = -|m|\vec{b} = m\vec{b}$

[From similar Δs OAB and $OA'B'$]

Therefore from triangle law of vector addition

$\overrightarrow{OA'} + \overrightarrow{A'B'} = \overrightarrow{OB'}$

$\Rightarrow m\vec{a} + m\vec{b} = m(\vec{a}+\vec{b})$

Unit Vector Along Diagonal/Angle Bisector of a Parallelogram

Vector along the diagonal $OC = \vec{a}+\vec{b}$; unit vector along $\overrightarrow{OC} = \hat{n} = \dfrac{\vec{a}+\vec{b}}{|\vec{a}+\vec{b}|}$; unit vector along $\overrightarrow{OA} = \hat{a} = \dfrac{\vec{a}}{|\vec{a}|}$; unit vector along $\overrightarrow{OB} = \hat{b} = \dfrac{\vec{b}}{|\vec{b}|}$

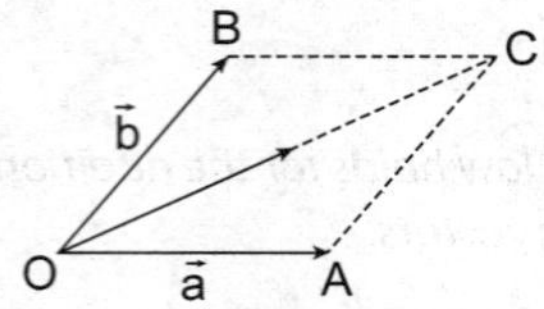

FIGURE 3.36

Therefore the vector along the angle bisector is given by $\hat{a}+\hat{b}$ and so the unit vector along the angle bisector will be given by $\dfrac{\hat{a}+\hat{b}}{|\hat{a}+\hat{b}|}$ ($\because$ $OLNM$ is a rhombus having side length unity, and in rhombus diagonal coincides with internal angle bisector)

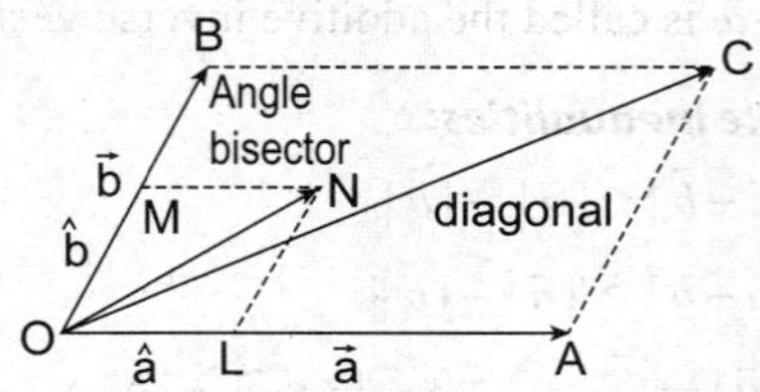

FIGURE 3.37

Thus unit vector along diagonal $= \dfrac{\vec{a}+\vec{b}}{|\vec{a}+\vec{b}|}$

and unit vector along internal angle bisector $= \dfrac{\hat{a}+\hat{b}}{|\hat{a}+\hat{b}|}$

ILLUSTRATION 11: If $\vec{a}, \vec{b}$ are any two vectors, then give the geometrical interpretation of the relation; $|\vec{a}+\vec{b}| = |\vec{a}-\vec{b}|$

SOLUTION: Let $\overrightarrow{OA} = \vec{a}$ and $\overrightarrow{AB} = \vec{b}$. Completing the parallelogram $OABC$

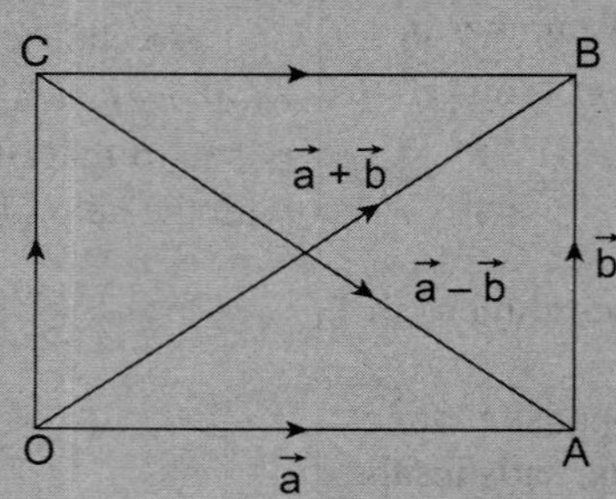

FIGURE 3.38

Then $\overrightarrow{OC} = \vec{b}$ and $\overrightarrow{CB} = \vec{a}$; From ΔOAB, we have $\overrightarrow{OA} + \overrightarrow{AB} = \overrightarrow{OB}$

$\Rightarrow$ $\vec{a}+\vec{b} = \overrightarrow{OB}$; From ΔOCA, we have $\overrightarrow{OC} + \overrightarrow{CA} = \overrightarrow{OA}$

$\Rightarrow$ $\vec{b} + \overrightarrow{CA} = \vec{a} \Rightarrow \overrightarrow{CA} = \vec{a}-\vec{b}$ $\therefore$ $|\vec{a}+\vec{b}| = |\vec{a}-\vec{b}|$ (Given), i.e., $|\overrightarrow{OB}| = |\overrightarrow{CA}|$

$\Rightarrow$ diagonals of parallelogram $OABC$ are equal

$\Rightarrow$ $OABC$ is a rectangle $\Rightarrow$ $\overrightarrow{OA} \perp \overrightarrow{AB} \Rightarrow \vec{a} \perp \vec{b}$

ILLUSTRATION 12: If the sum of two unit vectors is a unit vector, prove that the magnitude of their difference is $\sqrt{3}$.

SOLUTION: Let $\hat{a}$ and $\hat{b}$ be two unit vectors represented by sides OA and AB of a triangle OAB.

Then $\overrightarrow{OA} = \hat{a}$, $\overrightarrow{AB} = \hat{b}$, $\overrightarrow{OB} = \overrightarrow{OA} + \overrightarrow{AB} = \hat{a} + \hat{b}$ {*using triangle law of addition*}

It is given that; $|\hat{a}| = |\hat{b}| = |\hat{a}+\hat{b}| = 1$ $\Rightarrow |\overrightarrow{OA}| = |\overrightarrow{AB}| = |\overrightarrow{OB}| = 1$

$\Rightarrow$ ΔOAB is an equilateral triangle; Since $|\overrightarrow{OA}| = |\hat{a}| = 1 = |-\hat{b}| = |\overrightarrow{AB'}|$

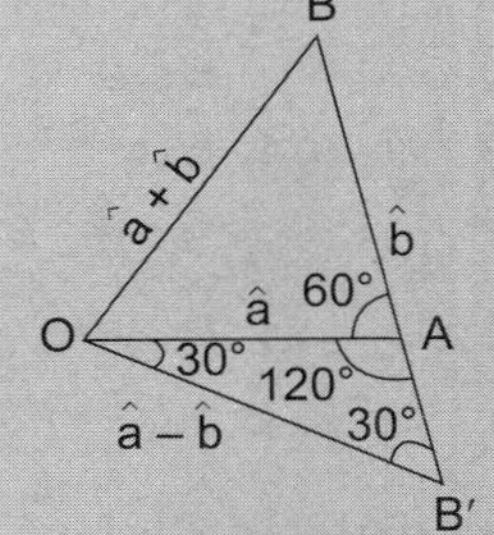

FIGURE 3.39

Therefore $\Delta OAB'$, is an isosceles triangle. $\Rightarrow \angle AB'O = \angle AOB' = 30°$

$\Rightarrow \angle BOB' = \angle BOA + \angle AOB' = 60° + 30° = 90° \Rightarrow \Delta BOB'$ is right angled

$\therefore$ In $\Delta BOB'$, we have $|OB|^2 + |OB'|^2 = |BB'|^2$

$\Rightarrow |\hat{a}+\hat{b}|^2 + |\hat{a}-\hat{b}|^2 = 2^2 \Rightarrow 1^2 + |\hat{a}-\hat{b}|^2 = 2^2 \Rightarrow |\hat{a}-\hat{b}| = \sqrt{3}$

ILLUSTRATION 13: If $\vec{a}, \vec{b}, \vec{c}, \vec{d}$ represent the consecutive sides of a quadrilateral. Show that the necessary and sufficient condition for the quadrilateral to be a parallelogram is $\vec{a}+\vec{c}=\vec{0}$ and this implies $\vec{b}+\vec{d}=\vec{0}$.

SOLUTION: Let $\vec{a}, \vec{b}, \vec{c}, \vec{d}$ represent the sides AB, BC, CD and DA of the quadrilateral $ABCD$. Then, the origin of the first vector $\vec{a}$ coincides with the terminal point of the last vector $\vec{d}$, so we get $\overrightarrow{AB} + \overrightarrow{BC} + \overrightarrow{CD} + \overrightarrow{DA} = \vec{0}$ $\Rightarrow \vec{a}+\vec{b}+\vec{c}+\vec{d} = \vec{0}$.

If the quadrilateral $ABCD$ be a parallelogram, then AB and CD are parallel and equal.

$\therefore$ $\overrightarrow{AB} = -\overrightarrow{CD}$, since they are in opposite direction, i.e., $\vec{a} = -\vec{c}$ or $\vec{a}+\vec{c} = \vec{0}$

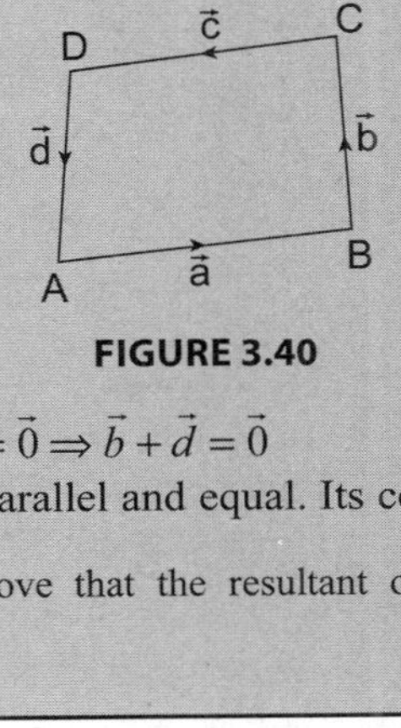

FIGURE 3.40

Hence $\vec{a}+\vec{b}+\vec{c}+\vec{d} = \vec{0} \Rightarrow \vec{b}+\vec{d} = \vec{0}$ $\Rightarrow \vec{b} = -\vec{d}$ $\Rightarrow \overrightarrow{BC} = -\overrightarrow{DA}$

i.e., BC and DA are parallel and equal. Its converse can be proved similarly.

ILLUSTRATION 14: *ABCDE* is a pentagon. Prove that the resultant of the forces $\overrightarrow{AB}$, $\overrightarrow{AE}$, $\overrightarrow{BC}$, $\overrightarrow{DC}$, $\overrightarrow{ED}$ and $\overrightarrow{AC}$ is $3\overrightarrow{AC}$.

SOLUTION: Let $\vec{R}$ be the resultant force

$\therefore \quad \vec{R} = \overrightarrow{AB} + \overrightarrow{AE} + \overrightarrow{BC} + \overrightarrow{DC} + \overrightarrow{ED} + \overrightarrow{AC}$

$\Rightarrow \quad \vec{R} = (\overrightarrow{AB} + \overrightarrow{BC}) + (\overrightarrow{AE} + \overrightarrow{DC} + \overrightarrow{ED}) + \overrightarrow{AC} = \overrightarrow{AC} + \overrightarrow{AC} + \overrightarrow{AC} = 3\,\overrightarrow{AC}$

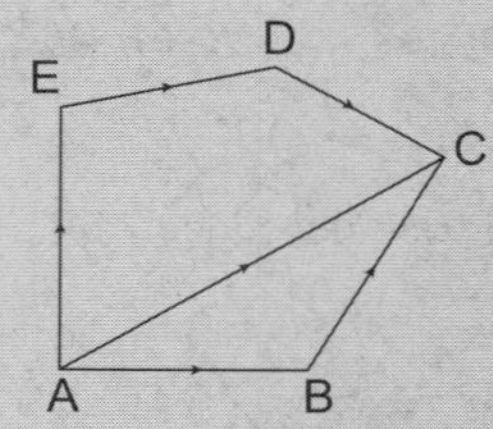

FIGURE 3.41

ILLUSTRATION 15: *ABC* is a triangle and *P* be any point on *BC*. If $\overrightarrow{PQ}$ is the resultant of $\overrightarrow{AP}, \overrightarrow{PB}, \overrightarrow{PC}$, show that *ABQC* is a parallelogram and *Q* therefore is a fixed point for all positions of *P*.

SOLUTION: Given $\overrightarrow{AP} + \overrightarrow{PB} + \overrightarrow{PC} = \overrightarrow{PQ}$ .....(i)

Since $\overrightarrow{AP} + \overrightarrow{PB} = \overrightarrow{AB}$ from (i), we get $\overrightarrow{AB} + \overrightarrow{PC} = \overrightarrow{PQ}$ or $\overrightarrow{AB} = \overrightarrow{PQ} - \overrightarrow{PC} = \overrightarrow{CQ}$

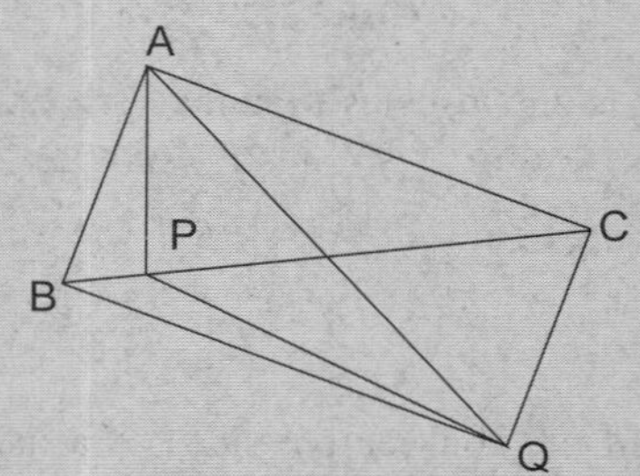

FIGURE 3.42

Hence *AB* and *CQ* are equal and parallel and hence *AB*QC is a parallelogram.

Again $\overrightarrow{AQ} = \overrightarrow{AB} + \overrightarrow{BQ} = \overrightarrow{AB} + \overrightarrow{AC}$ and hence position vector of *Q* remains unaltered for all positions of P.

ILLUSTRATION 16: *ABCDEF* is a regular hexagon; express the vector $\overrightarrow{AC}, \overrightarrow{AD}, \overrightarrow{AF}$ in terms of $\overrightarrow{AB}, \overrightarrow{BC}$.

SOLUTION: Let $\overrightarrow{AB} = \vec{a}$ and $\overrightarrow{BC} = \vec{b}$ $\qquad \therefore \quad \overrightarrow{AC} = \vec{a} + \vec{b}$

Since *AD* is parallel to *BC* and double in length of *BC*, we get $\overrightarrow{AD} = 2\vec{b}$

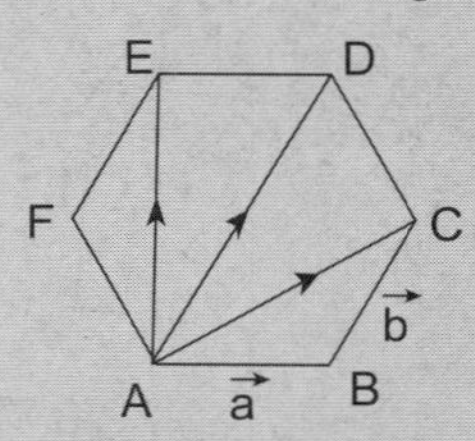

FIGURE 3.43

$\therefore \quad \overrightarrow{AE} = \overrightarrow{AD} + \overrightarrow{DE} = \overrightarrow{AD} + \overrightarrow{BA} \qquad \Rightarrow \quad \overrightarrow{AE} = \overrightarrow{AD} - \overrightarrow{AB} = 2\vec{b} - \vec{a}$

and $\overrightarrow{AF} = \overrightarrow{AE} + \overrightarrow{EF} = \overrightarrow{AE} + \overrightarrow{CB} = \overrightarrow{AE} + (-\overrightarrow{BC}) = 2\vec{b} - \vec{a} - \vec{b} = \vec{b} - \vec{a}$

ILLUSTRATION 17: Show that the sum of three vectors determined by the medians of triangle directed from the vertices is zero vector.

SOLUTION: Let AD, BE and CF be the three medians of the triangle ABC. Then by law of vector addition,

$\overrightarrow{AD} = \overrightarrow{AB} + \overrightarrow{BD} = \overrightarrow{AB} + \frac{1}{2}\overrightarrow{BC}$; Similarly, $\overrightarrow{BE} = \overrightarrow{BC} + \frac{1}{2}\overrightarrow{CA}$ and $\overrightarrow{CF} = \overrightarrow{CA} + \frac{1}{2}\overrightarrow{AB}$

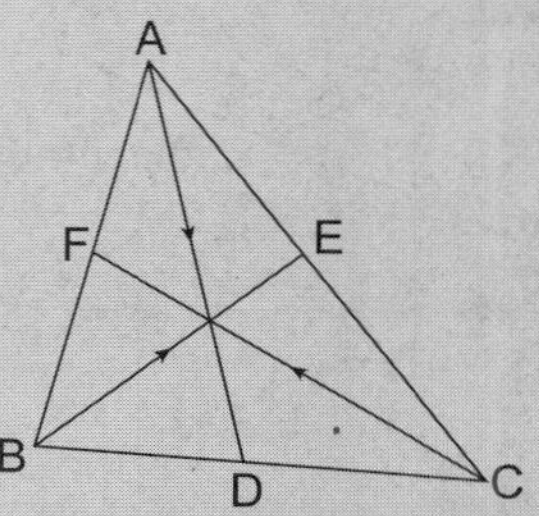

FIGURE 3.44

Adding these, we get

$$\overrightarrow{AD} + \overrightarrow{BE} + \overrightarrow{CF} = \overrightarrow{AB} + \overrightarrow{BC} + \overrightarrow{CA} + \frac{1}{2}\overrightarrow{AB} + \frac{1}{2}\overrightarrow{BC} + \frac{1}{2}\overrightarrow{CA} = \frac{3}{2}(\overrightarrow{AB} + \overrightarrow{BC} + \overrightarrow{CA}) = \vec{0}$$

ILLUSTRATION 18: If P, Q, R be the mid-points of the sides AB, BC, CA of triangle ABC and O be a point with in the ΔABC, then prove that $\overrightarrow{OA} + \overrightarrow{OB} + \overrightarrow{OC} = \overrightarrow{OP} + \overrightarrow{OQ} + \overrightarrow{OR}$.

SOLUTION: From triangle law of addition, we get $\overrightarrow{OA} = \overrightarrow{OP} + \overrightarrow{PA} = \overrightarrow{OP} + \frac{1}{2}\overrightarrow{BA}$ ...(i)

$\overrightarrow{OB} = \overrightarrow{OQ} + \frac{1}{2}\overrightarrow{CB}$ ...(ii)

$\overrightarrow{OC} = \overrightarrow{OR} + \frac{1}{2}\overrightarrow{AC}$ ...(iii)

Adding (i), (ii) and (iii), we get $\overrightarrow{OA} + \overrightarrow{OB} + \overrightarrow{OC} = \overrightarrow{OP} + \overrightarrow{OQ} + \overrightarrow{OR} + \frac{1}{2}(\overrightarrow{BA} + \overrightarrow{CB} + \overrightarrow{AC})$

$= \overrightarrow{OP} + \overrightarrow{OQ} + \overrightarrow{OR}$ [$\because$ $\overrightarrow{AB} + \overrightarrow{BC} + \overrightarrow{CA} = \vec{0}$]

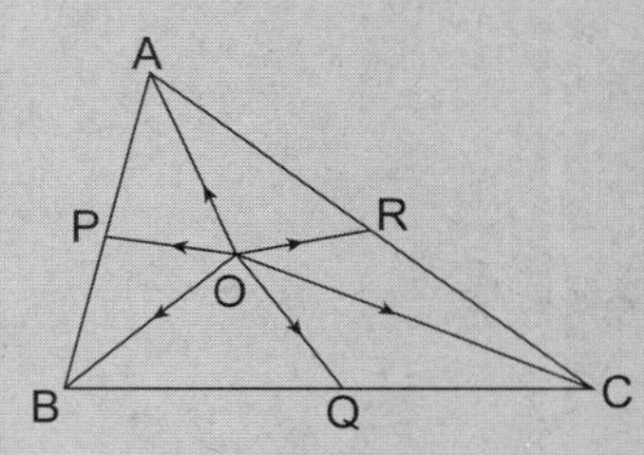

FIGURE 3.45

ILLUSTRATION 19: Find the unit vector along the diagonals of the parallelogram with adjacent sides given by vectors $\vec{a} = \hat{i} + 2\hat{j} + 2\hat{k}$ and $\vec{b} = 3\hat{i} + 4\hat{j}$.

SOLUTION: Vector along the diagonal $OC = \vec{a} + \vec{b}$

Therefore the unit vector along the diagonal OC is given as $\frac{\vec{a} + \vec{b}}{|\vec{a} + \vec{b}|}$

i.e., same as $\frac{4\hat{i} + 6\hat{j} + 2\hat{k}}{2\sqrt{14}} = \frac{2\hat{i} + 3\hat{j} + \hat{k}}{\sqrt{14}}$

Similarly, Vector along the diagonal BA = $\vec{a}-\vec{b}$

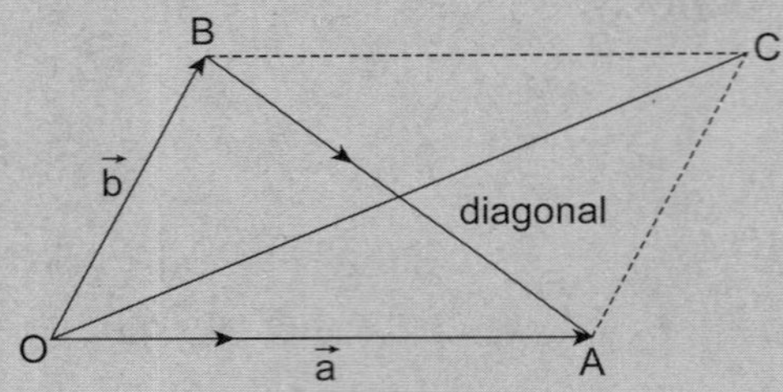

FIGURE 3.46

Therefore the unit vector along the diagonal $B\,A$ is given by $\dfrac{\vec{a}-\vec{b}}{|\vec{a}-\vec{b}|}$

i.e., same as $\dfrac{-2\hat{i}-2\hat{j}+2\hat{k}}{2\sqrt{3}}=\dfrac{-\hat{i}-\hat{j}+\hat{k}}{\sqrt{3}}$

ILLUSTRATION 20: Find a unit vector in the direction of the internal as well as external bisector of the angle between the vectors $\vec{a}=\vec{i}+2\vec{j}+2\vec{k}$ and $\vec{b}=2\vec{i}-2\vec{j}-\vec{k}$.

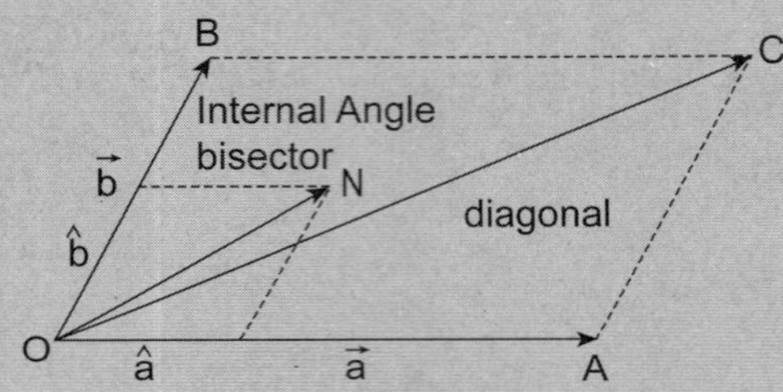

FIGURE 3.47

SOLUTION: Vector along internal bisector is given by $\vec{c}=\dfrac{\vec{a}}{|\vec{a}|}+\dfrac{\vec{b}}{|\vec{b}|}=\dfrac{\vec{i}+2\vec{j}+2\vec{k}}{3}+\dfrac{2\vec{i}-2\vec{j}-k}{3}=\vec{i}+\dfrac{\vec{k}}{3}$

$$\Rightarrow\ |\vec{c}|=\sqrt{1+\frac{1}{9}}=\frac{\sqrt{10}}{3}$$

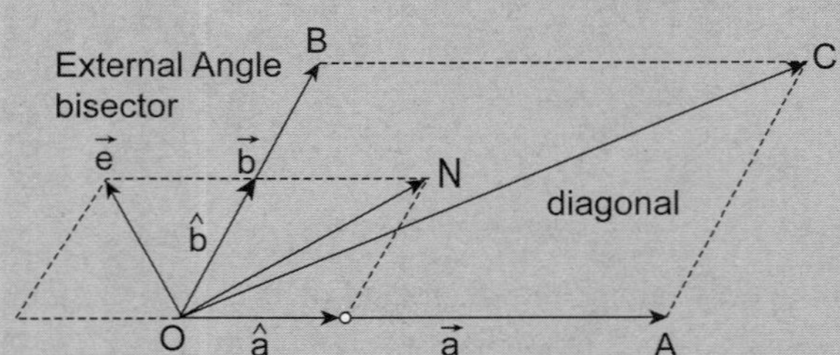

FIGURE 3.48

$\therefore$ the unit vector is given by $\pm\dfrac{3}{\sqrt{10}}\left(\vec{i}+\dfrac{\vec{k}}{3}\right)$. Vector along the external bisector is given

by: $\vec{e}=-\dfrac{\vec{a}}{|\vec{a}|}+\dfrac{\vec{b}}{|\vec{b}|}=-\dfrac{\vec{i}+2\vec{j}+2\vec{k}}{3}+\dfrac{2\vec{i}-2\vec{j}-\vec{k}}{3}=\dfrac{\hat{i}}{3}-\dfrac{4}{3}\hat{j}-\hat{k}$

TEXTUAL EXERCISE 3: (SUBJECTIVE)

1. $ABCD$ is a parallelogram and AC, BD are its diagonals. Express
   (a) $\overrightarrow{AC}$ and $\overrightarrow{BD}$ in terms of $\overrightarrow{AB}$ and $\overrightarrow{AD}$
   (b) $\overrightarrow{AB}$ and $\overrightarrow{AD}$ in terms of $\overrightarrow{AC}$ and $\overrightarrow{BD}$
   (c) $\overrightarrow{AB}$ and $\overrightarrow{AC}$ in terms of $\overrightarrow{AD}$ and $\overrightarrow{BD}$.
   Show that $\overrightarrow{AC}+\overrightarrow{DB}=2\overrightarrow{DC}, \overrightarrow{AC}+\overrightarrow{BD}=2\overrightarrow{AD}$

2. If $\vec{a}$ and $\vec{b}$ represent the sides $\overrightarrow{AB}$ and $\overrightarrow{BC}$ of a regular hexagon $ABCDEF$, then find the vector $\overrightarrow{FA}$.

3. If $ABCDEF$ is a regular hexagon, then prove
   (a) $\overrightarrow{AC}+\overrightarrow{AD}+\overrightarrow{EA}+\overrightarrow{FA}=3\overrightarrow{AB}$
   (b) $\overrightarrow{AB}+\overrightarrow{AD}+\overrightarrow{AF}=4\overrightarrow{AO}$
   where O is the centre of hexagon.

4. A vector A has components A_1, A_2, A_3 in a right handed rectangular cartesian system OX, OY, OZ. The coordinate system is rotated about the z-axis through an angle $\pi/2$ radians in anti-clockwise, when viewed from the positive direction of z-axis towards origin. Find the components of $\vec{A}$ in new co-ordinate system in terms of A_1, A_2, A_3.

5. If $\vec{a},\vec{b},\vec{c}$ be the vectors representing three coterminus edges of parallelopiped, then find what does the following vectors represent in relation to the above parallelepiped?
   (a) $\vec{a}-\vec{b}-\vec{c}$ (b) $\vec{a}\pm\vec{c}$
   (c) $\vec{a}+\vec{b}+\vec{c}$

Answer Key

1. (a) $\overrightarrow{AC}=\overrightarrow{AB}+\overrightarrow{AD}$; $\overrightarrow{BD}=\overrightarrow{AD}-\overrightarrow{AB}$ (b) $\overrightarrow{AB}=\dfrac{\overrightarrow{AC}-\overrightarrow{BD}}{2}$; $\overrightarrow{AD}=\dfrac{\overrightarrow{AC}+\overrightarrow{BD}}{2}$
   (c) $\overrightarrow{AB}=\overrightarrow{AD}-\overrightarrow{BD}$; $\overrightarrow{AC}=2\overrightarrow{AD}-\overrightarrow{BD}$
2. $\vec{a}-\vec{b}$ 4. $A_2, -A_1, A_3$
5. (a) Body diagonal (b) face diagonal (c) A body diagonal

■ SECTION FORMULA

If a point C is said to divide the line segment AB in the ratio $n: m$, then following two things must hold good:

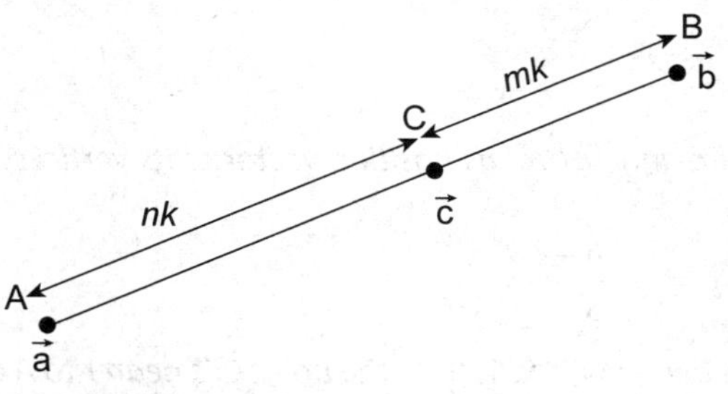

FIGURE 3.49

(i) C must lie on the line passing through A and B

(ii) $\dfrac{CA}{CB}=\dfrac{n}{m}$

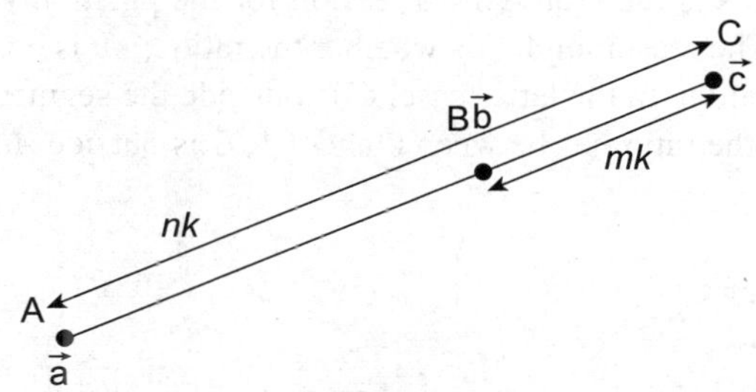

FIGURE 3.50

Subjected to the above two conditions, if C lies on the line segment AB, then it is called internal division and if C lies outside of line segment AB, then it is called external division.

The position vector of a point C dividing the line segment joining points A and B having position vector $\vec{a}$, $\vec{b}$ respectively in the ratio $n: m$ is given by $\vec{r}=\dfrac{m\vec{a}+n\vec{b}}{m+n}$. For internal division we take n/m as positive and for external division take n/m as negative.

Proof: If the points $A(\vec{a}), B(\vec{b}), C(\vec{c})$ are collinear means the point C will divide the line segment AB in certain ratio, say $n: m$.

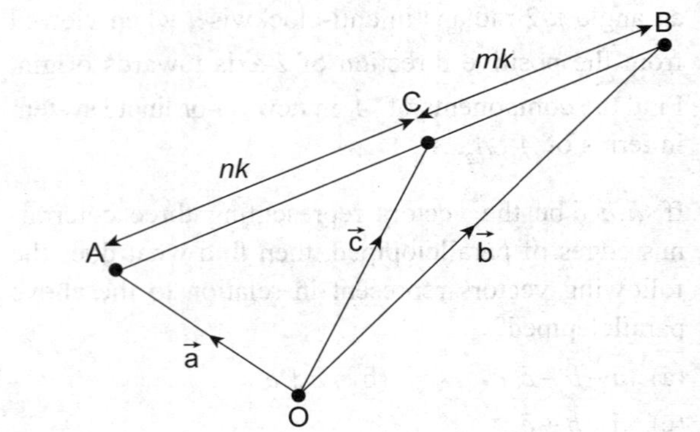

FIGURE 3.51

Let A, B be the two points and $\vec{a}, \vec{b}$ their position vectors relative to the origin O. Then the position vector of the point C which divides AB in the ratio $n: m$, may be found in terms of $\vec{a}$ and $\vec{b}$. For since $m\overrightarrow{AC} = n\overrightarrow{CB}$, it follows that

$$m(\vec{c} - \vec{a}) = n(\vec{b} - \vec{c})$$

$$\text{whence } \vec{c} = \frac{m\vec{a} + n\vec{b}}{n+m} \quad (n + m \neq 0) \qquad \text{...(i)}$$

This is the required expression for the position vector of C. The reasoning holds whether the ratio $n: m$ is positive or negative. In the latter case, C is out side the segment AB and if the ratio lies between 0 and -1, C is outside AB and nearer to A. If the ratio lies betwen -1 and $-\infty$, C is outside AB and nearer to B.

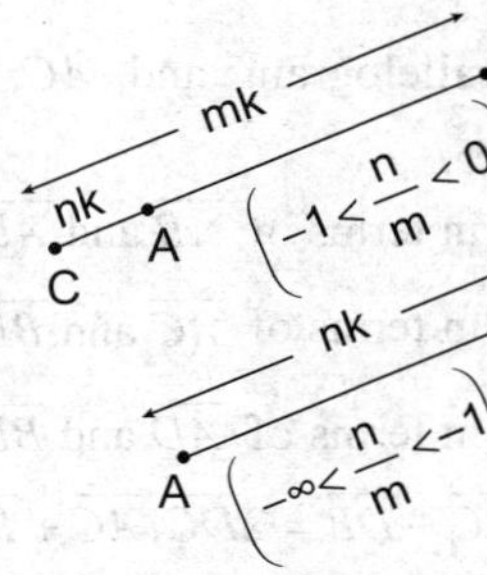

FIGURE 3.52

For the particular case in which $n = m$, the above formula gives $\frac{1}{2}(\vec{a} + \vec{b})$ for the position vector of the mid-point of AB. Also the equation (i) is equivalent to

$$m\overrightarrow{OA} + n\overrightarrow{OB} = (m+n)\overrightarrow{OC} \qquad \text{...(ii)}$$

where C is the point dividing AB in the ratio $n : m$. This form of the result is often useful.

Further, if the equation (i) is written in the form

$$(n+m)\vec{c} - m\vec{a} - n\vec{b} = 0. \qquad \text{...(iii)}$$

the sum of the coefficients of $\vec{c}, \vec{a}, \vec{b}$ is zero. If C is distinct from A and B, and at a finite distance from them, none of the coefficients in (iii) is zero.

Thus, for three distinct collinear points C, A, B there exist numbers l, m, n different from zero, such that lc + na + mb = 0, l + m + n = 0 ...(iv)

Conversely, when these relations hold the three points are collinear.

NOTE

1. *If $\vec{R}$ is the mid-point of PQ, then $\vec{R} = \frac{\vec{p} + \vec{q}}{2}$. For a triangle, having $\vec{a}, \vec{b}, \vec{c}$ as position vector of its vertices, the position vector of the centroid G($\vec{g}$) of the triangle is given by $\vec{g} = \frac{\vec{a} + \vec{b} + \vec{c}}{3}$.*
2. *If ratio is positive, then C lies between A and B.When ratio lies between 0 to 1, then the point C is nearer to A and when ratio lies between 1 to ∞, then it is nearer toB . If the ratio is negative, C is out side the segment AB and if the ratio lies between 0 and –1, C is outside of AB and nearer to A. If the ratio lies betwen -1 and -∞, C is outside AB and nearer to B.*

ILLUSTRATION 21: Find the position vectors of the points which divide the join of the points $2\vec{a} - 3\vec{b}$ and $3\vec{a} - 2\vec{b}$ internally and externally in the ratio 2: 3

SOLUTION: Let A and B be the given points with position vectors $2\vec{a} - 3\vec{b}$ and $3\vec{a} - 2\vec{b}$ respectively. Let P and Q be the points dividing AB in the ratio 2 : 3 internally and externally repectively. Then.

$$\text{Position vector of } P = \frac{3(2\vec{a}-3\vec{b})+2(3\vec{a}-2\vec{b})}{3+2} = \frac{12\vec{a}}{5} - \frac{13\vec{b}}{5}$$

$$\text{Position vector of } Q = \frac{3(2\vec{a}-3\vec{b})-2(3\vec{a}-2\vec{b})}{3-2} = -5\vec{b}$$

ILLUSTRATION 22: If $\vec{a}$ and $\vec{b}$ are position vectors of points A and B respectively, then find the position vector of points of trisection of AB.

SOLUTION: Let P and Q be points of trisection to AB. Then $AP = PQ = QB = \lambda$ (say). Since P divides AB in the ratio λ: 2λ i.e., 1 : 2. Therefore, position vector of P is $\dfrac{1\vec{b}+2.\vec{a}}{1+2} = \dfrac{\vec{b}+2\vec{a}}{3}$

Since Q is the mid-points of PB, therefore position vector of Q is $\dfrac{\dfrac{\vec{b}+2\vec{a}}{3}+\vec{b}}{2} = \dfrac{4\vec{b}+2\vec{a}}{6} = \dfrac{\vec{a}+2\vec{b}}{3}$

ILLUSTRATION 23: Show that the segments joining vertices to the centroid of opposite faces of a tetrahedron are concurrent. Hence find the position vector of the point of concurrence.

SOLUTION: Let $\vec{a}, \vec{b}, \vec{c}$ and $\vec{d}$ are the position vectors of vertices of the tetrahedron and P, Q, R and S are the centroid of faces opposite to A, B, C and D respectively.

$3\vec{p} = \vec{b}+\vec{c}+\vec{d} \Rightarrow \vec{p} = \dfrac{\vec{b}+\vec{c}+\vec{d}}{3}$, ||rly $\vec{q} = \dfrac{\vec{c}+\vec{d}+\vec{a}}{3}$, $\vec{r} = \dfrac{\vec{d}+\vec{a}+\vec{b}}{3}$, $\quad \overline{\vec{a}+\vec{b}+\vec{c}}$

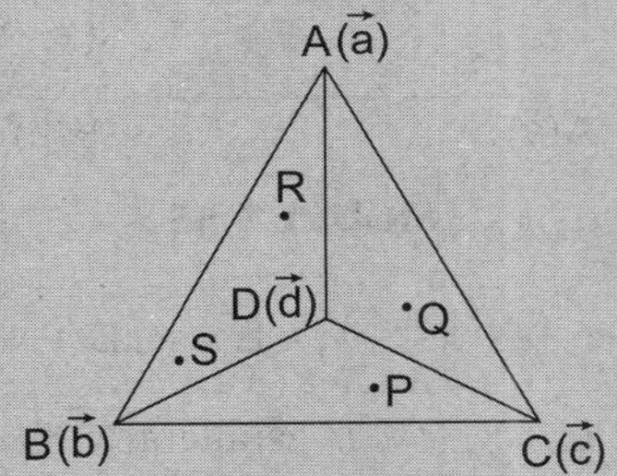

FIGURE 3.53

$$\Rightarrow 3\vec{q} = \vec{c}+\vec{d}+\vec{a} \quad \Rightarrow \quad 3\vec{r} = \vec{d}+\vec{a}+\vec{b} \quad \Rightarrow \quad 3\vec{s} = \vec{a}+\vec{b}+\vec{c}$$

$$\Rightarrow \frac{3\vec{p}+\vec{a}}{4} = \frac{3\vec{q}+\vec{b}}{4} = \frac{3\vec{r}+\vec{c}}{4} = \frac{3\vec{s}+\vec{d}}{4} = \frac{\vec{a}+\vec{b}+\vec{c}-\vec{d}}{4} \quad \Rightarrow \quad G = \left(\frac{\vec{a}+\vec{b}+\vec{c}+\vec{d}}{4}\right)$$

$\therefore$ G is the common point of intersection of AP, BQ, CR, DS dividing each in the ratio of 3: 1 internally.

ILLUSTRATION 24: Show that the diagonals of parallelogram bisect each other.

SOLUTION: Let $\vec{a}, \vec{b}, \vec{c}$ and $\vec{d}$ are the position vectors of A, B, C, D respectively.

Let $ABCD$ be a parallelogram $\Rightarrow$ $AB = CD$ and $AB \parallel DC \Rightarrow \overrightarrow{AB} = \overrightarrow{DC}$

$$\Rightarrow \vec{b}-\vec{a} = \vec{c}-\vec{d} \quad \Rightarrow \quad \vec{b}+\vec{d} = \vec{a}+\vec{c} \quad \Rightarrow \quad \frac{1}{2}(\vec{b}+\vec{d}) = \frac{1}{2}(\vec{a}+\vec{c})$$

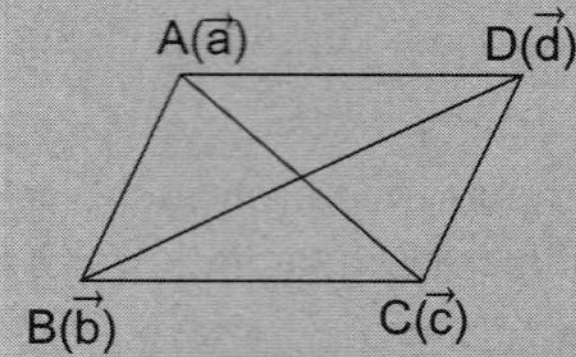

FIGURE 3.54

$\Rightarrow$ Position vector of mid-point of $\overline{BD}$ = Position vector of mid-point of $\overline{AC}$

$\Rightarrow$ mid-points of BD and AC coincide $\Rightarrow AC$ and BD bisect each other.

ILLUSTRATION 25: Prove that the segment joining mid-points of the diagonals of a trapezium is parallel to the parallel sides of the trapezium and is equal to half the difference of their lengths.

SOLUTION : Let $ABCD$ be a trapezium and M, N are the mid-points of the diagonals AC and BD. Let $\vec{a}$, $\vec{b}$, $\vec{c}$ and $\vec{d}$ are the position vectors of A, B, C, D respectively.

Let $\vec{m}$ and $\vec{n}$ be the position vectors of M and N respectively. $\Rightarrow \vec{m} = \dfrac{\vec{a}+\vec{c}}{2}$ and $\vec{n} = \dfrac{\vec{b}+\vec{d}}{2}$

Now $\overrightarrow{MN} = \vec{n} - \vec{m} = \dfrac{\vec{b}+\vec{d}}{2} - \dfrac{\vec{a}+\vec{c}}{2}$

$$\Rightarrow \overrightarrow{MN} = \frac{\vec{b}-\vec{a}}{2} + \frac{\vec{d}-\vec{c}}{2} = \frac{1}{2}(\overrightarrow{AB}+\overrightarrow{CD}) \Rightarrow \overrightarrow{MN} = \frac{1}{2}(\overrightarrow{AB}-\overrightarrow{DC})$$

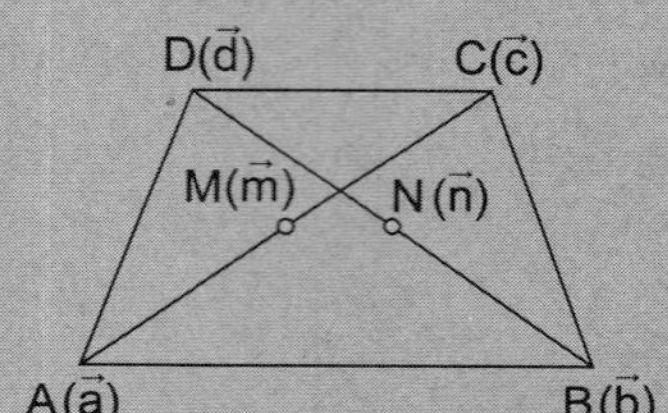

FIGURE 3.55

Let $\overrightarrow{AB} = k.\overrightarrow{DC}$ (Since $(\overrightarrow{AB} \parallel \overrightarrow{DC})$, k is a scalar)

$\therefore \overrightarrow{MN} = \dfrac{1}{2}(k-1)\overrightarrow{DC} \Rightarrow \overrightarrow{MN}$ is parallel to $\overrightarrow{DC}$

$\Rightarrow MN$ is parallel to DC and is half the difference of AB and DC.

ILLUSTRATION 26: Let $\vec{a}, \vec{b}, \vec{c}$ be the position vectors of three distinct points A,B,C. If there exist scalars x, y, z (not all zero) such that $x\,\vec{a} + y\vec{b} + z\vec{c} = \vec{0}$, then show that A,B and C lie on a line.

SOLUTION: It is given that x,y,z are not all zero. So let z be non-zero. Then,

$\Rightarrow x\vec{a} + y\vec{b} + z\vec{c} = \vec{0} \Rightarrow z\vec{c} = -\left(x\vec{a} + y\vec{b}\right)$

$\Rightarrow \vec{c} = -\dfrac{\left(x\vec{a}+y\vec{b}\right)}{z} \Rightarrow \vec{c} = \dfrac{x\vec{a}+y\vec{b}}{x+y}$ $[\because x+y+z=0 \Rightarrow z = -(x+y)]$

ILLUSTRATION 27: Four points A,B,C,D with position vectors $\vec{a},\vec{b},\vec{c},\vec{d}$ respectively are such that $3\vec{a} - \vec{b} + 2\vec{c} - 4\vec{d} = \vec{0}$. Show that the four points are co-planar. Also find the position vector of the point of intersection of lines AC and BD.

SOLUTION: We have $3\vec{a}-\vec{b}+2\vec{c}-4\vec{d}=\vec{0} \Rightarrow 3\vec{a}+2\vec{c}=\vec{b}+4\vec{d}$

We note that the sum of the coefficients on both sides of the above result is 5. We therefore divide both sides by 5 to get $\dfrac{3\vec{a}+2\vec{c}}{5}=\dfrac{\vec{b}+4\vec{d}}{5} \Rightarrow \dfrac{3\vec{a}+2\vec{c}}{3+2}=\dfrac{\vec{b}+4\vec{d}}{1+4}$.

This shows that the position vector of a point P dividing AC in the ratio 2 : 3 is same as that of a point dividing BD in the ratio 4: 1. Consequently, point P is common to AC and BD. Therefore AC and BD intersect. Hence points A,B,C and D are co-planar. Since P is the points of intersection of AC and BD, therefore the position vector of the point of intersection of AC and BD is $\dfrac{3\vec{a}+2\vec{c}}{5}$ or $\dfrac{\vec{b}+4\vec{d}}{5}$.

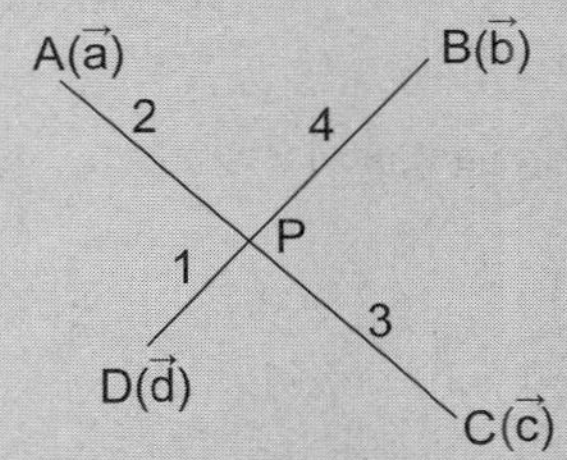

FIGURE 3.56

ILLUSTRATION 28: Show that the medians of the triangle are concurrent and point of concurrence divides each median in the ratio 2: 1.

SOLUTION: Let ABC be a triangle and $\vec{a}, \vec{b}, \vec{c}$ are the position vectors of A, B, C respectively.

Let D, E and F are the mid-points of AB, BC and AC respectively.

$\therefore\ 2\vec{d}=\vec{a}+\vec{b}$ as $\vec{d}=\dfrac{\vec{a}+\vec{b}}{2}$; ..... (i) ||rly $2\vec{e}=\vec{b}+\vec{c}$ ..... (ii) $2\vec{f}=\vec{a}+\vec{c}$ ...... (iii)

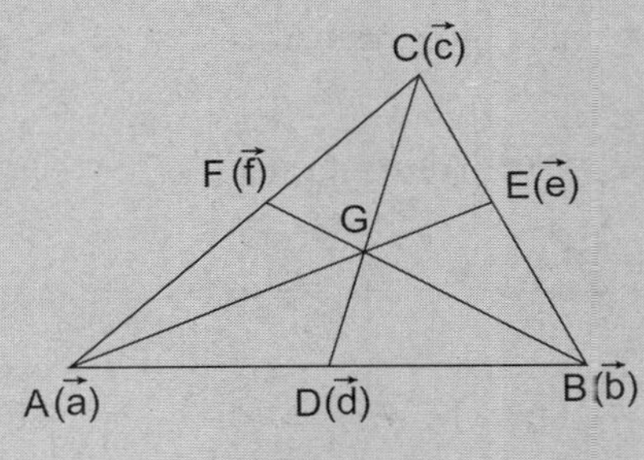

FIGURE 3.57

As any point on a line passing through two points $C(\vec{c})$ and $D(\vec{d})$ has its position vector $\lambda\vec{c}+\mu\vec{d}$ (: $\lambda+\mu=1$) and since we are looking for a point G lying on CD as well as on BF and AE, therefore adding vector $\vec{c}$ in both sides of equation (i), $\vec{a}$ on both sides of (ii) and $\vec{b}$ on both sides of (iii) respectively we have, $2\vec{d}+\vec{c}=\vec{a}+\vec{b}+\vec{c}$; $2\vec{e}+\vec{a}$ $=\vec{a}+\vec{b}+\vec{c}$; $2\vec{f}+\vec{b}=\vec{a}+\vec{b}+\vec{c}$

$\Rightarrow\ 2\vec{d}+\vec{c}=2\vec{e}+\vec{a}=2\vec{f}+\vec{b}=\vec{a}+\vec{b}+\vec{c}$

$\Rightarrow\ \dfrac{2\vec{d}+\vec{c}}{3}=\dfrac{2\vec{e}+\vec{a}}{3}=\dfrac{2\vec{f}+\vec{b}}{3}=\dfrac{\vec{a}+\vec{b}+\vec{c}}{3} \quad \Rightarrow\ \dfrac{2\vec{d}+\vec{c}}{2+1}=\dfrac{2\vec{e}+\vec{a}}{2+1}=\dfrac{2\vec{f}+\vec{b}}{2+1}=\dfrac{\vec{a}+\vec{b}+\vec{c}}{3}$

$\Rightarrow$ Point $G\left(\frac{\vec{a}+\vec{b}+\vec{c}}{3}\right)$ divides *AE*, *BF* and *CD* each internally in ratio 2: 1.

Hence G is the point of concurrence of all medians called centroid of Δ.

$\Rightarrow$ Medians are concurrent and centroid G divides each median internally in the ratio 2: 1.

and $\vec{g}=\left(\frac{\vec{a}+\vec{b}+\vec{c}}{3}\right)$ will be the position vector of centroid G.

ILLUSTRATION 29: Show that the angle bisectors of a triangle are concurrent and hence find the position vector of the incentre.

SOLUTION: Let ABC be a triangle and $\vec{a}, \vec{b}, \vec{c}$ are the position vectors of A, B and C respectively.

Let $BC = x$, $AC = y$ and $AB = z$

Let AD, BE and CF are the angle bisectors of $\angle A$, $\angle B$ and $\angle C$ respectively.

Since, AD bisects angle A.

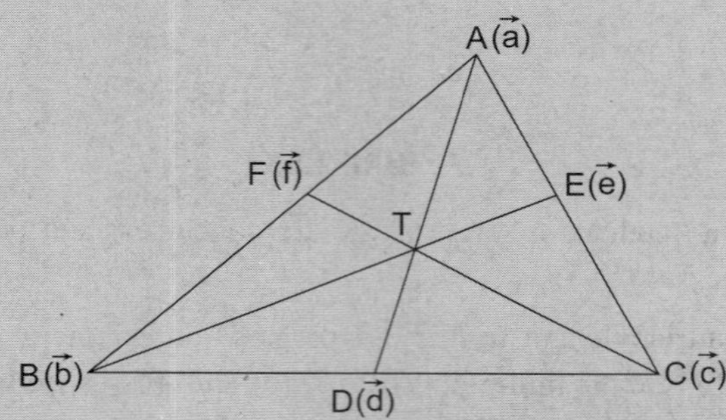

FIGURE 3.58

$\Rightarrow \quad \frac{BD}{DC}=\frac{AB}{AC}$ (By angle bisector theroem) $\quad \Rightarrow \quad \frac{BD}{DC}=\frac{z}{y}$

Now, $\vec{d}=\frac{z\vec{c}+y\vec{b}}{z+y} \Rightarrow (z+y)\vec{d}=z\vec{c}+y\vec{b}$ ....(i)

Similarly, $\vec{e}=\frac{x\vec{a}+z\vec{c}}{x+z} \Rightarrow (z+x)\vec{e}=x\vec{a}+z\vec{c}$ ...(ii)

and $\vec{f}=\frac{y\vec{b}+x\vec{a}}{y+x} \Rightarrow (y+x)\vec{f}=y\vec{b}+x\vec{a}$ ...(iii)

From equations (i), (ii) and (iii), we have

$$(z+y)\vec{d}+x\vec{a} = (x+z)\vec{e}+y\vec{b} = (x+y)\vec{f}+z\vec{c} = x\vec{a}+y\vec{b}+z\vec{c}$$

$$\Rightarrow \frac{(z+y)\vec{d}+x\vec{a}}{(y+z)+x}=\frac{(x+z)\vec{e}+y\vec{b}}{(x+z)+y}=\frac{(x+y)\vec{f}+z\vec{c}}{(x+y)+z}=\frac{x\vec{a}+y\vec{b}+z\vec{c}}{x+y+z}=\vec{I} \text{ (say)}$$

$\therefore$ The point T, $\vec{I}=\frac{x\vec{a}+y\vec{b}+z\vec{c}}{x+y+z}$ divides each internal bisector (AD, BE and CF) in the ratio $y+z: x$, $x+z: y$ and $x+y: z$ respectively.

$\Rightarrow$ T is the common point of intersection of all bisectors having its position vector $\vec{I}=\frac{x\vec{a}+y\vec{b}+z\vec{c}}{x+y+z}$

ILLUSTRATION 30: D and E divide sides BC and CA of a triangle ABC in the ratio 2: 3 respectively. Find the position vector of the point of intersection of AD and BE and the ratio in which this point divides AD and BE.

SOLUTION: Let ABC be a triangle.

Let $\vec{a}, \vec{b}, \vec{c}$ are the position vectors of A, B and C respectively and $\vec{d}$ and $\vec{e}$ are the position vector of D and E respectively.

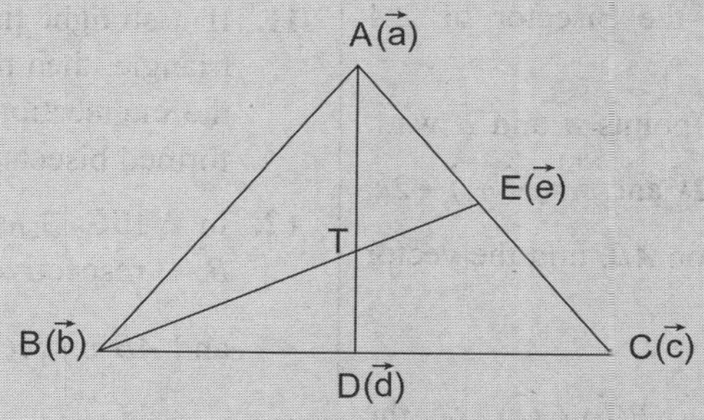

FIGURE 3.59

Since D and E divide sides BC and CA in the ratio 2: 3

$$\Rightarrow \vec{d} = \frac{3\vec{b}+2\vec{c}}{5} \Rightarrow 5\vec{d} = 3\vec{b}+2\vec{c} \quad \text{...(i)}$$

$$\text{and } \vec{e} = \frac{3\vec{c}+2\vec{a}}{5} \Rightarrow 5\vec{e} = 3\vec{c}+2\vec{a} \quad \text{....(ii)}$$

From equations (i) and (ii), we get $15\vec{d}+4\vec{a} = 10\vec{e}+9\vec{b} = 4\vec{a}+9\vec{b}+6\vec{c}$

We can write it, $\dfrac{15\vec{d}+4\vec{a}}{15+4} = \dfrac{10\vec{e}+9\vec{b}}{10+9} = \dfrac{4\vec{a}+9\vec{b}+6\vec{c}}{19}$ = position vector of T dividing

$\overrightarrow{AD}$ and $\overrightarrow{BE}$ in ratio 15 : 4 and 10 : 9 respectively.

TEXTUAL EXERCISE 4: (SUBJECTIVE)

1. (a) Let $ABCDEF$ be a regular hexagon. If $\overrightarrow{AD} = x\overrightarrow{BC}$ and $\overrightarrow{CF} = y\,\overrightarrow{AB}$, then evaluate xy.

   (b) If A, B, C, D be any four points and E and F be the middle points of AC and BD respectively, then prove that $\overrightarrow{AB}+\overrightarrow{CB}+\overrightarrow{CD}+\overrightarrow{AD} = 4\overrightarrow{EF}$.

2. Prove that the sum of the three vectors determined by the medians of a triangle directed from the vertices is zero.

3. The median AD of the triangle ABC is bisected at E, BE meets AC in F, then find the ratio $AF : AC$.

4. Show that the internal (external) bisector of any angle of a triangle divides the opposite side internally (externally) in the ratio of the sides containing the said angle.

5. Prove that the internal bisector of an angle of a triangle and the external bisectors of the other two are concurrent.

6. Median AD of a ΔABC is bisected at E and BE meets AC in F. Prove that $EF = BF/4$.

7. (a) If the vectors $\overrightarrow{AB} = -3\hat{i}+4\hat{k}$ and $\overrightarrow{AC} = 5\hat{i}-2\hat{j}+4\hat{k}$ represent the sides of a triangle ABC, then find the length of median through A, also find the unit vector along this median.

(b) The two sides of ΔABC are given by $\overline{AB} = 2\hat{i} + 4\hat{j} + 4\hat{k}$ & $\overline{AC} = 2\hat{i} + 2\hat{j} + \hat{k}$. Then find the length of median through A.

8. (a) If $4\hat{i} + 7\hat{j} + 8\hat{k}, 2\hat{i} + 3\hat{j} + 4\hat{k}$ and $2\hat{i} + 5\hat{j} + 7\hat{k}$ are the position vectors of the vertices A, B and C respectively of triangle ABC. Find the position vector of the point where the bisector of $\angle A$ meets BC.

(b) The position vectors of the points A and B w.r.t. origin O are $a = \hat{i} + 3\hat{j} - 2\hat{k}$ and $b = 3\hat{i} + \hat{j} - 2\hat{k}$ respectively. If P is a point on AB, find the vector $\overline{OP}$ which bisects $\angle AOB$.

9. In a triangle ABC where $A(\vec{a}), B(\vec{b}), C(\vec{c})$ be the position vectors of vertices A, B and C respectively and $D(\vec{d}), E(\vec{e})$ and $F(\vec{f})$ are middle points of the sides BC, CA and AB respectively, then prove the following statements

(a) FE is mid parallel to BC.

(b) $\overline{AD} + \overline{BE} + \overline{CF}$ is equal to null vector.

(c) $\overline{AD}, \overline{BE}$ and $\overline{CF}$ intersects at one point, also find the position vector of that point.

10. (a) If D is the mid point of side BC of ΔABC prove that $\overline{AB} + \overline{AC} = 2\overline{AD}$.

(b) Prove that the line segments joining mid point of adjacent sides of a quadrilateral form a parallelogram.

(c) $ABCD$ is a parallelogram. E, F are the mid points of BC and CD respectively. AE, AF meet the diagonal BD at Q and P respectively. Show that P and Q trisect DB.

11. If a straight line is drawn parallel to the base of a triangle, then prove that the line joining the vertex to the intersection of the diagonals of the trapezium so formed bisects the base of the triangle.

12. In ΔABC $\vec{a}, \vec{b}, \vec{c}$ be position vectors of vertices A, B, C respectively and D, E, F are points on BC, CA and AB respectively such that $\frac{BD}{DC} = \frac{CE}{EA} = \frac{AF}{FB} = \frac{2}{1}$ and $\vec{a} = (\hat{i} + \hat{j} + \hat{k}), \vec{b} = 4\hat{i} + 2\hat{k}, \vec{c} = 4\hat{i} + 2\hat{j} + 3\hat{k}$ and AD intersects BE at B_0 and CF at A_0, where as CF intersects BE at C_0, then answer the following problems.

(a) Find the position vector of the centroid of $\Delta A_0B_0C_0$

(b) Find the ratio of AB_0/B_0D

(c) Find the ratio $\frac{ar.\Delta ABC}{ar.\Delta A_0B_0C_0}$

(d) If $\frac{AB_0}{B_0D} = \lambda$ and $\frac{BC_0}{C_0E} = \mu$ and $\frac{CA_0}{A_0F} = \nu$, then evaluate $\frac{\lambda u + \mu\nu + \nu\lambda}{\lambda\mu\nu}$

Answer key

1. (a) –4 **3.** 1 : 3 **7.** unit vector along $AD = \frac{1}{3\sqrt{2}}\{\hat{i} - \hat{j} + 4\hat{k}\}$ (a) $3\sqrt{2}$ (b) $\frac{\sqrt{77}}{2}$

8. (a) $\frac{1}{3}(6\hat{i} + 13\hat{j} + 18\hat{k})$ (b) $2(\hat{i} + \hat{j} - \hat{k})$ **9.** (c) $\frac{\vec{a} + \vec{b} + \vec{c}}{3}$

12. (a) $3\hat{i} + \hat{j} + 2\hat{k}$ (b) 3 : 4 (c) 7 : 1 (d) 4

TEXTUAL EXERCISE 1: (OBJECTIVE)

1. P, Q have position vectors $\vec{b}$ and $\vec{b}$ relative to the origin 'O' and X, Y divide $\overrightarrow{PQ}$ internally and externally respectively in the ratio 2 : 1. Vector $\overrightarrow{XY}$ =

(a) $\frac{3}{2}(\vec{b} - \vec{a})$ (b) $\frac{4}{3}(\vec{a} - \vec{b})$

(c) $\frac{5}{6}(\vec{b} - \vec{a})$ (d) $\frac{4}{3}(\vec{b} - \vec{a})$

2. If G and G' be the centroids of the triangles ABC and $A'B'C'$ respectively, then $\overrightarrow{AA'} + \overrightarrow{BB'} + \overrightarrow{CC'} =$

(a) $\frac{2}{3}\overrightarrow{GG'}$ (b) $\overrightarrow{GG'}$

(c) $2\overrightarrow{GG'}$ (d) $3\overrightarrow{GG'}$

3. If $A(\vec{b})$, $B(\vec{b})$, $C(\vec{c})$ be the vertices of a triangle whose circumcentre is the origin, then orthocentre is given by

(a) $\frac{\vec{a}+\vec{b}+\vec{c}}{3}$ (b) $\frac{\vec{a}+\vec{b}+\vec{c}}{2}$

(c) $\vec{a}+\vec{b}+\vec{c}$ (d) None of these

4. If in the given figure $\overrightarrow{OA} = \vec{a}$, $\overrightarrow{OB} = \vec{b}$ and $AP : PB = m : n$, then $\overrightarrow{OP} =$

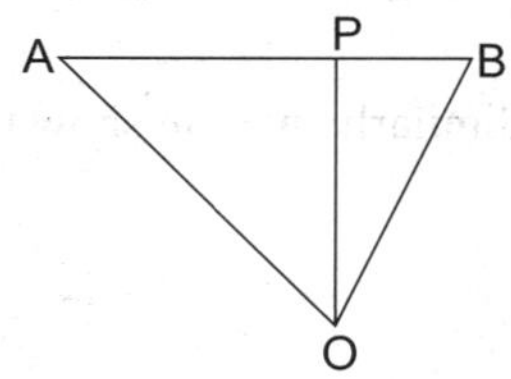

FIGURE 3.60

(a) $\frac{m\vec{a}+n\vec{b}}{m+n}$ (b) $\frac{n\vec{a}+m\vec{b}}{m+n}$

(c) $m\vec{a} - n\vec{b}$ (d) $\frac{m\vec{a}-n\vec{b}}{m-n}$

5. The position vectors of three consecutive vertices of a parallelogram are $i + j + k$, $i + 3j + 5k$ and $7i + 9j + 11k$. The position vector of the fourth vertex is

(a) $6(i + j + k)$

(b) $7(i + j + k)$

(c) $2j - 4k$

(d) $6i + 8j + 10k$

6. Let $\overrightarrow{AB} = 3\vec{i} + \vec{j} - \vec{k}$ and $\overrightarrow{AC} = \vec{i} - \vec{j} + 3\vec{k}$. If the point P on the line segment BC is equidistant from AB and AC, then $\vec{P}$ is

(a) $2\vec{i} - \vec{k}$ (b) $\vec{i} - \vec{k}$

(c) $2\vec{i} + \vec{k}$ (d) None of these

Answer Keys

1. (d) 2. (d) 3. (c) 4. (b) 5. (b) 6. (c)

■ COLLINEAR VECTORS

Vectors which are parallel to the same line are called collinear vectors irrespective of their magnitude and sense of direction.

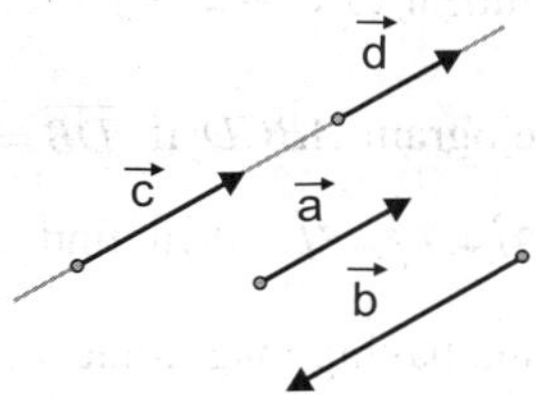

FIGURE 3.61

Hence, $\vec{a},\vec{b},\vec{c},\vec{d}$ are representing collinear vectors and for collinear vectors the line of action is either same or parallel. We know that the vectors $\vec{a}$ and $m\vec{a}$ are parallel to each other In view of this, we can conclude that if two vectors $\vec{a}$ and $\vec{b}$ are parallel (collinear), then there exists a scalar m (+ve or –ve) such that $\vec{a} = m\vec{b}$. Combined term for like and unlike or parallel is collinear in Vector's terminology.

■ CONDITIONS FOR VECTORS TO BE COLLINEAR

Two vectors are said to be collinear if any one of the following conditions is satisfied.

(a) There exists a relation $\vec{a} = m\vec{b}$ where m is a non-zero scalar.

(b) If $\vec{a}$ and $\vec{b}$ are non-zero collinear vectors, then there exists a set of x and y other than (0, 0), such that $x\vec{a} + y\vec{b} = \vec{0}$

Here converse is also true i.e., if $x\vec{a} + y\vec{b} = \vec{0}$ and x, y are non-zero scalars,then $\vec{a}$ and $\vec{b}$ are collinear vectors.

(c) For two vectors $\vec{a}$ and $\vec{b}$ to be collinear

$$\vec{a}\times\vec{b} = \vec{0}, \text{ i.e., } \begin{vmatrix} \hat{i} & \hat{j} & \hat{k} \\ a_1 & a_2 & a_3 \\ b_1 & b_2 & b_3 \end{vmatrix} = \vec{0}$$

NOTE:

1. *If $\vec{a}$ and $\vec{b}$ are non -zero and non-collinear, then $x\vec{a}+y\vec{b}=\vec{0} \Rightarrow x=0, y=0$ as proved in theorem given below.*
2. *If three points $A(\vec{a}), B(\vec{b}), C(\vec{c})$ are collinear, then $(\vec{b}-\vec{a})=\lambda(\vec{c}-\vec{b})$ or equivalently $(\vec{c}-\vec{a})=\lambda(\vec{c}-\vec{b})$ i.e. $(\vec{b}-\vec{a})$ and $(\vec{c}-\vec{b})$ are collinear vectors.*

Theorem: *If $\vec{a}$ and $\vec{b}$ are two non-collinear non-zero vectors, m and n are scalars such that $m\vec{a}+n\vec{b}=0$, then $m=0$ and $n=0$.*

Proof: Given $m\vec{a}+n\vec{b}=0$ ...(i)

Dividing both sides of (i) by scalar m (supposing $m \neq 0$) we get

$$\vec{a}+\left(\frac{n}{m}\right)\vec{b}=0 \text{ or } \vec{a}=-\left(\frac{n}{m}\right)\vec{b} \quad \text{...(ii)}$$

Since $\frac{n}{m}$ is a scalar, the equation (ii) shows that $\vec{a}$ and $\vec{b}$ are collinear vectors (i.e., vectors having the same or parallel line of action) which is against hypothesis that $\vec{a}$ and $\vec{b}$ are non-collinear vectors. Hence our supposition is wrong

$\therefore$ $m=0$. Similarly, we can show that $n=0$.

TEXTUAL EXERCISE 5: (SUBJECTIVE)

1. Find all $\lambda \in \mathbb{R}$ such that $(x, y, z) \neq (0, 0, 0)$ and $(\vec{i}+\vec{j}+3\vec{k})x+(3\vec{i}+3\vec{j}+\vec{k})y+(-4\vec{i}+5\vec{j})z=\lambda(x\vec{i}+y\vec{j}+z\vec{k})$
2. Find unit vectors parallel to the vector $\vec{a}=3\vec{i}+4\vec{j}-2\vec{k}$? Find the vector $\vec{b}$ such that $\hat{a}+\vec{b}$ becomes the unit vector $\vec{i}$.
3. Vectors $\vec{a}, \vec{b}$ are non-collinear. Find x so that the vectors $(x-1)\vec{a}+\vec{b}$ and $(2+3x)\vec{a}-2\vec{b}$, are collinear.
4. The position vectors of the points A, B and C are $\vec{a}, \vec{b}, \vec{c}$ respectively. If $3\vec{a}+2\vec{c}=5\vec{b}$, find whether the points A, B and C collinear if so, find $AB : BC$.
5. If the points A, B and C represented by the position vectors $\vec{a}, \vec{b}$ and $\vec{c}$ are collinear and $l\vec{a}+m\vec{b}+n\vec{c}=\vec{0}$ where l, m, n are scalars, then find the value of $\frac{l+n}{m}$.
6. Given that $\vec{a}, \vec{b}$ is a pair of non-collinear vectors such that $(1+2h-k)\vec{a}+(2-h+2k)\vec{b}=\vec{0}$, then find h and k.
7. Let $\vec{a}, \vec{b}$ and $\vec{c}$ be three non-zero vectors such that any two of them are non-collinear. If $\vec{a}+2\vec{b}$ is collinear with $\vec{c}$ and $\vec{b}+3\vec{c}$ is collinear with $\vec{a}$, then prove that $\vec{a}+2\vec{b}+6\vec{c}=\vec{0}$.
8. Find $\vec{\beta}$ collinear to $\vec{\alpha}=2\hat{i}-\hat{j}+\hat{k}$ *if* $|\vec{\beta}|=4$.
9. In a parallelogram $ABCD$ if $\overrightarrow{DB}=\vec{a}=\hat{i}-\hat{j}+\hat{k}$ and $\overrightarrow{AC}=\vec{b}=3\hat{i}+3\hat{j}-5\hat{k}$, then find a vector collinear with $\overrightarrow{BC}$ and having magnitude 4 units.

Answer Key

1. 0, –1 **2.** $\frac{\pm 1}{\sqrt{29}}(3\vec{i}+4\vec{j}-2\vec{k})$, $\vec{i}\mp\frac{1}{\sqrt{29}}(3\vec{i}+4\vec{j}-2\vec{k})$ **3.** 0 **4.** yes, 2: 3

5. –1 **6.** $h=-\frac{4}{3}, k=-\frac{5}{3}$ **8.** $\vec{\beta}=\pm\frac{4}{\sqrt{6}}(2\hat{i}-\hat{j}+\hat{k})$ **9.** $\pm\frac{4}{\sqrt{14}}(\hat{i}+2\hat{j}-3\hat{k})$

TEXTUAL EXERCISE 2: (OBJECTIVE)

1. The vector $\vec{a}$ and $\vec{b}$ are non-zero and non-collinear the value of x for which vector $\vec{c} = (x-2)\vec{a} + \vec{b}$ and $\vec{d} = (2x+1)\vec{a} - \vec{b}$ are collinear is
   (a) 1 (b) 1/2
   (c) 1/3 (d) 2
2. The vectors $\vec{a} = x\hat{i} + 2\hat{j} + 5\hat{k}$ and $\vec{b} = \hat{i} + y\hat{j} - 2\hat{k}$ are collinear if
   (a) $x = -5/2, y = -4/5$
   (b) $x = 5, y = -4$
   (c) $x = -5/2, y = -2/5$
   (d) None of these
3. The vectors $\vec{a} = x\hat{i} - 2\hat{j} + 5\hat{k}$ and $\vec{b} = \hat{i} + y\hat{j} - z\hat{k}$ are collinear if
   (a) $x = 1, y = -2, z = -5$
   (b) $x = 1/2, y = -4, z = -10$
   (c) $x = -1/2, y = 4, z = 10$
   (d) $x = -1, y = 2, z = 5$
4. The value of k for which the vectors $\vec{a} = \hat{i} - \hat{j}$ and $\vec{b} = -2\hat{i} - k\hat{j}$ are collinear is
   (a) 2 (b) $\frac{1}{2}$
   (c) $\frac{1}{3}$ (d) 3
5. If $\vec{a}$ and $\vec{b}$ are two non-zero non-collinear vectors and $x\vec{a} + x\vec{b} = \vec{0}$, then
   (a) $x = 0$, but y is not necessarily zero
   (b) $y = 0$, but x is not necessarily zero
   (c) $x = 0, y = 0$
   (d) None of these
6. In a trapezium, the vector $\overrightarrow{BC} = \lambda\overrightarrow{AD}$. We will then find that $\vec{p} = \overrightarrow{AC} + \overrightarrow{BD}$ is collinear with $\overrightarrow{AD}$, if $\vec{p} = \mu\overrightarrow{AD}$, then
   (a) $\mu = \lambda + 1$
   (b) $\lambda = \mu + 1$
   (c) $\lambda + \mu = 1$
   (d) $\mu = 2 + \lambda$
7. Let O be the point of intersection of diagonals of the paralleogram $ABCD$. The points M, N, K, P are the mid-points of the segments AO, BM, CN and DK respectively, then
   (a) O, N, P are collinear
   (b) O, N, P form a triangle of non-zero area
   (c) $\overrightarrow{ON} = \overrightarrow{OP}$
   (d) None of these

Answer Key

1. (c) 2. (a) 3. (a,b,c,d) 4. (a) 5. (c) 6. (a) 7. (a)

■ LINEAR COMBINATION OF VECTORS

Linear combination of vectors $\vec{a}_1, \vec{a}_2, \vec{a}_3, \ldots \vec{a}_n$ is a vector written as $\vec{r} = \lambda_1\vec{a}_1 + \lambda_2\vec{a}_2 + \lambda_3\vec{a}_3 + \ldots + \lambda_n\vec{a}_n$ where $\lambda_1, \lambda_2, \ldots\lambda_n$ are scalars, e.g., if $\vec{a}, \vec{b}, \vec{c}$ are any three vectors, then $l\vec{a} + m\vec{b} + n\vec{c}$ is called a linear combination of vectors and l, m, n are any three scalars.

Linearly Dependent Vectors

A system of vectors $\vec{a}_1, \vec{a}_2, \vec{a}_3, \ldots \vec{a}_n$ is said to be linearly dependent if there exist n scalars $\lambda_1, \lambda_2, \ldots\lambda_n$ (not all zero) such that $\lambda_1\vec{a}_1 + \lambda_2\vec{a}_2 + \lambda_3\vec{a}_3 + \ldots\lambda_n\vec{a}_n = \vec{0}$ (i.e., above system is linearly dependent if one or some of them can be written as linear combination of the remaining.)

Two collinear vectors are always linearly dependent.

Three co-planar vectors are always linearly dependent.

Linearly Independent Vectors

A system of n vectors $\vec{a}_1, \vec{a}_2, \vec{a}_3, \ldots \vec{a}_n$ is said to be linearly independent if none of them can be written as the linear combination of the remaining; therefore mathematically it means.

If $\lambda_1\vec{a}_1 + \lambda_2\vec{a}_2 + \lambda_3\vec{a}_3 + \ldots\lambda_n\vec{a}_n = \vec{0}$

$\Rightarrow \lambda_1 = \lambda_2 = \ldots\ldots = \lambda_n = 0$ where $\lambda_1, \lambda_2, \ldots\lambda_n$ are n scalars

e.g., two non-collinear vectors are always linearly independent and three non-coplanar vectors are always linearly independent.

ILLUSTRATION 31: If $\vec{a} = \vec{i} + \vec{j} + \vec{k}$, $\vec{b} = 4\vec{i} + 3\vec{j} + 4\vec{k}$ and $\vec{c} = \vec{i} + \alpha\vec{j} + \beta\vec{k}$ are linearly dependent vectors and $|\vec{c}| = \sqrt{3}$, then find α and β.

SOLUTION: Here $\vec{c} = t\vec{a} + s\vec{b}$ and $|\vec{c}| = \sqrt{3} = \sqrt{1+\alpha^2+\beta^2}$

Now $\vec{i} + \alpha\vec{j} + \beta\vec{k} = t(\vec{i} + \vec{j} + \vec{k}) + s(4\vec{i} + 3\vec{j} + 4\vec{k})$

$\Rightarrow 1 = t + 4s,\ \alpha = t + 3s,\ \beta = t + 4s \quad \therefore \quad$ we get $1 + \alpha^2 + \beta^2 = 3$

$\Rightarrow (t + 3s)^2 + (t + 4s)^2 = 2 \quad \Rightarrow \quad (1 - 4s + 3s)^2 + (1 - 4s + 4s)^2 = 2$ or $(1 - s)^2 = 1$

$\Rightarrow 1 - s = \pm 1 \Rightarrow s = 1 \pm 1 = 0, 2 \qquad \Rightarrow t = 1 - 4s = 1, -7$

$\Rightarrow \alpha = t + 3s = 1 + 3(0); -7 + 3(2) = 1, -1$ and $\beta = t + 4s = 1 + 4.\ 0, -7 + 4.2 = 1,1$

ILLUSTRATION 32: *A* transversal cuts the sides *OL*, *OM* and diagonal *ON* of a parallelogram at *A*, *B*, *C* respectively. Prove that $\frac{OL}{OA} + \frac{OM}{OB} = \frac{ON}{OC}$

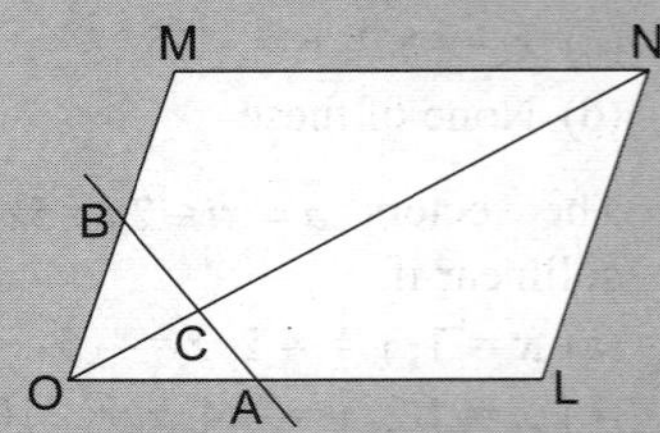

FIGURE 3.62

SOLUTION: We have $\overrightarrow{ON} = \overrightarrow{OL} + \overrightarrow{LN} = \overrightarrow{OL} + \overrightarrow{OM}$ .... (i)

Let, $\overrightarrow{OL} = x\overrightarrow{OA}$, $\overrightarrow{OM} = y\overrightarrow{OB}$ and $\overrightarrow{ON} = z\overrightarrow{OC}$

So, $|\overrightarrow{OL}| = x|\overrightarrow{OA}|$, $|\overrightarrow{OM}| = y|\overrightarrow{OB}|$ and $|\overrightarrow{ON}| = z|\overrightarrow{OC}|$

$\Rightarrow x = \frac{OL}{OA}, y = \frac{OM}{OB}$ and $z = \frac{ON}{OC}$ .... (ii)

$\therefore$ from (i) and (ii) we have $z\overrightarrow{OC} = x\overrightarrow{OA} + y\overrightarrow{OB}$ or $x\overrightarrow{OA} + y\overrightarrow{OB} - z\overrightarrow{OC} = \vec{0}$

$\because$ Points *A*, *B*, *C* are collinear, the sum of the coefficients of their *P.V.* must be zero

$\Rightarrow x + y - z = 0$ i.e., $\frac{OL}{OA} + \frac{OM}{OB} = \frac{ON}{OC}$

ILLUSTRATION 33: Prove that,

(i) If a subset of *n* vectors is linearly dependent, then the *n* vectors are also linearly dependent.

(ii) If *n* vectors are linearly independent, then any subset of these *n* vectors is linearly independent.

(iii) If *n* vectors are linearly independent, but $(n + 1)$ vectors are linearly dependent, then the $(n + 1)^{th}$ vector is a linear combination of the other *n* vectors.

SOLUTION: (i) Let $A = \{\vec{a}_1, \vec{a}_2, ..., \vec{a}_m\}$ be a subset of $B = \{\vec{a}_1, \vec{a}_2, ..., \vec{a}_m, \vec{a}_{m+1}, ..., \vec{a}_n\}$

Since $\vec{a}_1, \vec{a}_2, ..., \vec{a}_m$ are linearly dependent, we can determine scalars $\lambda_1, \lambda_2 ...... \lambda_m$ not all zero, such that $\lambda_1\vec{a}_1 + \lambda_2\vec{a}_2 + ..., \lambda_m\vec{a}_m = \vec{0}$ ....(i)

From (i) we have $\lambda_1\vec{a}_1 + \lambda_2\vec{a}_2 + ... + \lambda_m\vec{a}_m + 0\,\vec{a}_{m+1} + ... + 0\,.\,\vec{a}_n = \vec{0}$ ....(ii)

Since not all scalars $\lambda_1, \lambda_2, ..., \lambda_m$ are zero in (ii) hence *n* vectors $\vec{a}_1, \vec{a}_2, ..., \vec{a}_n$ are linearly dependent.

(ii) Let $A = \{\vec{a}_1, \vec{a}_2, \vec{a}_3, ..., \vec{a}_m\}$ be a subset of $B = \{\vec{a}_1, \vec{a}_2, ..., \vec{a}_m, \vec{a}_{m+1}, ..., \vec{a}_n\}$

Let the set *B* is linearly independent. If possible let the set *A* be linearly dependent.

So that the scalars $\lambda_1, \lambda_2, .., \lambda_m$ exist not all zero such that $\lambda_1\vec{a}_1 + \lambda_2\vec{a}_2 + ..., \lambda_m\vec{a}_m = \vec{0}$

$\Rightarrow \quad \lambda_1\vec{a}_1 + \lambda_2\vec{a}_2 + ..., \lambda_m\vec{a}_m + 0\,\vec{a}_{m+1} + ... + 0\,.\,\vec{a}_n = \vec{0}$

Showing that the set *B* is linearly dependent, which contradicts the given fact. Hence our assumption that the set *A* is linearly dependent is incorrect.

$\Rightarrow$ *A* must be linearly independent.

(iii) Let n vectors $\vec{a}_1, \vec{a}_2, \ldots\ldots, \vec{a}_n$ be linearly independent and let $\vec{a}_{n+1}$ be the $(n+1)^{th}$ vector such that $\vec{a}_1, \vec{a}_2, \ldots\ldots, \vec{a}_n, \vec{a}_{n+1}$ are linearly dependent. Hence, there exist scalars $\lambda_1, \lambda_2, \ldots\ldots, \lambda_{n+1}$ not all zero such that $\lambda_1\vec{a}_1 + \lambda_2\vec{a}_2 + \ldots\ldots + \lambda_n\vec{a}_n + \lambda_{n+1}\vec{a}_{n+1} = \vec{0}$ ......(1)

Now let $\lambda_{n+1} = 0$ then (1) reduces to $\lambda_1\vec{a} + \lambda_2\vec{a} + \ldots\ldots, \lambda_n\vec{a} = \vec{0}$

Showing that $\vec{a}_1, \vec{a}_2, \ldots\ldots, \vec{a}_n$ are linearly dependent since not all scalars $\lambda_1, \lambda_2, \ldots\ldots, \lambda_n$ are zero. Thus we arrive at a contradiction of the given fact that $\vec{a}_1, \vec{a}_2, \ldots\ldots, \vec{a}_n$ are linearly independent. Hence we cannot assume that $\lambda_{n+1} = 0$

Let $\lambda_{n+1} \neq 0$, then from (1) $\vec{a}_{n+1} = -\dfrac{1}{\lambda_{n+1}}\left[\lambda_1\vec{a}_1 + \lambda_2\vec{a}_2 + \ldots\ldots + \lambda_n\vec{a}_n\right]$.

Showing that $\vec{a}_{n+1}$ is a linear combination of $\vec{a}_1, \vec{a}_2, \ldots\ldots, \vec{a}_n$

■ COLLINEARITY OF THREE POINTS

The necessary and sufficient condition for three points with position vector $\vec{a}, \vec{b}, \vec{c}$ to be collinear is that there exist three scalars x, y, z not all zero, such that $x\vec{a} + y\vec{b} + z\vec{c} = \vec{0}$ where $x + y + z = 0$.

Proof: If the points $A(\vec{a}), B(\vec{b}), C(\vec{c})$ are collinear means the point C will divide the line segment AB in certain ratio, say $n : m$.

Let A, B be the two points and $\vec{a}, \vec{b}$ their position vectors relative to the origin O. Then the position vector of the point C which divides AB in the ratio $n : m$, may be found in terms of $\vec{a}$ and $\vec{b}$.

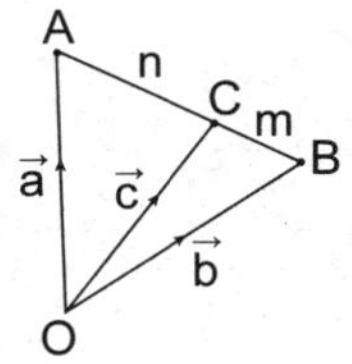

FIGURE 3.63

Since $AC : BC = n : m$ and AC and BC are collinear

Therefore $\overrightarrow{AC} = \dfrac{n}{m+n}\overrightarrow{AB} \Rightarrow \overrightarrow{AC} = \dfrac{n}{m+n}(\vec{b} - \vec{a})$

but $\vec{c} = \overrightarrow{OA} + \overrightarrow{AC} = \vec{a} + \overrightarrow{AC} = \vec{a} + \dfrac{n(\vec{b} - \vec{a})}{m+n}$

$= \dfrac{m\vec{a} + n\vec{b}}{m+n}$ $(n + m \neq 0)$ ...(i)

$\Rightarrow (n+m)\vec{c} - m\vec{a} - n\vec{b} = 0$ ...(ii)

i.e., the sum of the coefficients of $\vec{c}, \vec{a}, \vec{b}$ is zero. If C is distinct from A and B, and at a finite distance from them, none of the coefficients in (ii) is zero.

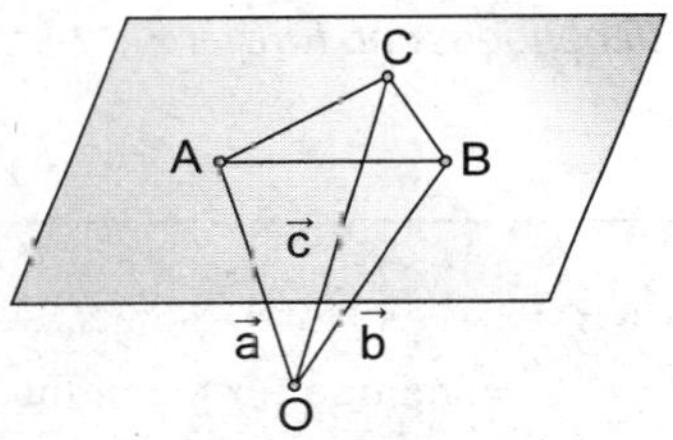

FIGURE 3.64

If $\vec{a}, \vec{b}, \vec{c}$ do not lie in a plane (i.e., non-coplanar), then points A, B, C will be necessarily co-planar

For three distinct collinear points C, A, B there exist real numbers (scalars) x, y, z different from zero, such that $x\vec{a} + y\vec{b} + z\vec{c} = \vec{0}$ where $x + y + z = 0$

Conversely, when these relations hold the three points are collinear.

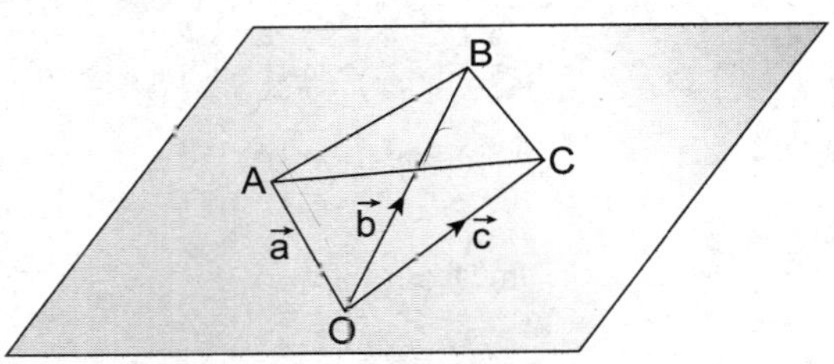

FIGURE 3.65

When $\vec{a}, \vec{b}, \vec{c}$ are co-planar but the points A, B, C form a triangle of non-zero area. Then $x\vec{a} + y\vec{b} + z\vec{c} = \vec{0}$ but $x + y + z \neq 0$

Proof: ***(Sufficient conditions):***

Suppose $x\vec{a}+y\vec{b}+z\vec{c}=\vec{0}$, where $x+y+z=0$ is true. Now assume that $z \neq 0$, then $x+y=-z\neq 0$

Then $x\vec{a}+y\vec{b}+z\vec{c}=\vec{0}$ gives $x\vec{a}+y\vec{b}=-z\vec{c}$

or, $\dfrac{x\vec{a}+y\vec{b}}{-z}=\dfrac{-z\vec{c}}{-z}$ or $\dfrac{x\vec{a}+y\vec{b}}{x+y}=\vec{c}$ $[\because -z=x+y]$

$\Rightarrow$ $A(\vec{a}), B(\vec{b})$ & $C(\vec{c})$ are collinear

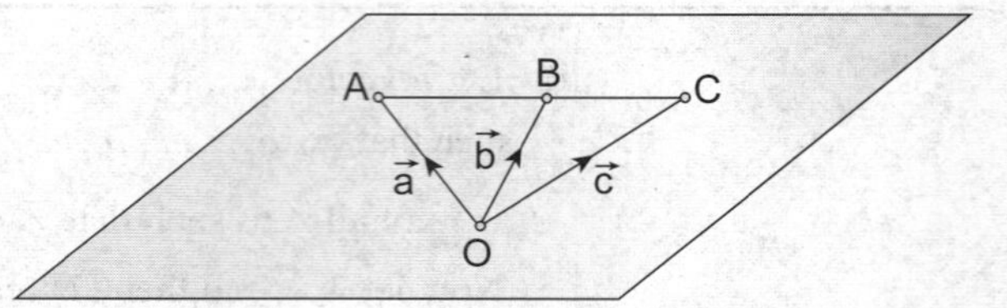

FIGURE 3.66

When $\vec{a},\vec{b},\vec{c}$ are co-planar but the points A, B, C form a triangle of zero area. Then $x\vec{a}+y\vec{b}+z\vec{c}=\vec{0}$ and $x+y+z=0$

NOTES

1. *If the points $A(\vec{a}), B(\vec{b}), C(\vec{c})$ are collinear, then $\overrightarrow{AB}=\lambda\overrightarrow{BC}$ where λ is a scalar.*
2. *If three points A ($\vec{a}$), B ($\vec{b}$), C ($\vec{c}$) are collinear, then $(\vec{b}-\vec{a})=\lambda(\vec{c}-\vec{b})$ or equivalently area of triangle ABC is zero, i.e., $(\vec{b}-\vec{a})\times(\vec{c}-\vec{b})=\vec{0}$.*
3. *If $x\vec{a}+y\vec{b}+z\vec{c}=\vec{0}$ and $x+y+z=0$ has non-trivial solution for x, y, z means co-planarity of $\vec{a},\vec{b},\vec{c}$ i.e., they are linearly dependent and further $x+y+z=0$ means points having position vectors $\vec{a},\vec{b},\vec{c}$ are also collinear.*

ILLUSTRATION 34: Given three points whose position vectors are $x\vec{i}+y\vec{j}+z\vec{k}$, $\vec{i}+z\vec{j}$ and $-\vec{i}-\vec{j}$. Find the condition for the points to be collinear.

SOLUTION: Let the points be A, B and C respectively. Then $\overrightarrow{OA}=x\vec{i}+y\vec{j}+z\vec{k}$; $\overrightarrow{OB}=\vec{i}+z\vec{j}$ and $\overrightarrow{OC}=-\vec{i}-\vec{j}$

Now $\overrightarrow{AB}=\overrightarrow{AO}+\overrightarrow{OB}=\overrightarrow{OB}-\overrightarrow{OA}=(\vec{i}+z\vec{j})-(x\vec{i}+y\vec{j}+z\vec{k})=(1-x)\vec{i}+(z-y)\vec{j}-z\vec{k}$

$\overrightarrow{AC}=\overrightarrow{AO}+\overrightarrow{OC}=\overrightarrow{OC}-\overrightarrow{OA}=-\vec{i}-\vec{j}-(x\vec{i}+y\vec{j}+z\vec{k})=-(1+x)\vec{i}-(1+y)\vec{j}-z\vec{k}$

A, B, C are collinear if $\overrightarrow{AB}=\lambda\overrightarrow{AC}$

or $(1-x)\vec{i}+(z-y)\vec{j}-z\vec{k}=\lambda\{-(1+x)\vec{i}-(1+y)\vec{j}-z\vec{k}\}$

$\Rightarrow 1-x=-\lambda(1+x)$ ....(i)

$z-y=-\lambda(1+y)$ ....(ii)

$-z=-\lambda z$ ....(iii)

Clearly $\lambda\neq 1$, for otherwise B and C are coincident, from equation (iii) we get $z=0$

from equation (ii) we get $-y=-\lambda(1+y)$ or $\lambda=\dfrac{y}{1+y}$

and from (i) we get $\lambda=\dfrac{x-1}{x+1}\Rightarrow\dfrac{y}{1+y}=\dfrac{x-1}{x+1}$,

$\Rightarrow xy+y=x-1+xy-y\Rightarrow y=\dfrac{x-1}{2}, z=0$

ILLUSTRATION 35: The position vectors of three points are $2\vec{a}-\vec{b}+3\vec{c}$, $\vec{a}-2\vec{b}+\lambda\vec{c}$ and $\mu\vec{a}-5\vec{b}$ where $\vec{a},\vec{b},\vec{c}$ are non-coplanar vectors. Find the value of λ and μ so that the points are collinear.

SOLUTION: If the points be A, B and C respectively, then $\overrightarrow{AB} = \overrightarrow{OB} - \overrightarrow{OA} = \vec{a} - 2\vec{b} + \lambda\vec{c} - (2\vec{a} - \vec{b} + 3\vec{c})$
$= -\vec{a} - \vec{b} + (\lambda - 3)\vec{c}$ $\overrightarrow{AC} = \overrightarrow{OC} - \overrightarrow{OA} = \mu\vec{a} - 5\vec{b} - (2\vec{a} - \vec{b} + 3\vec{c}) = (\mu - 2)\vec{a} - 4\vec{b} - 3\vec{c}$

The points are collinear if $\overrightarrow{AB} = t\overrightarrow{AC}$ $\Rightarrow -1 = t(\mu - 2), -1 = -4t, \lambda - 3 = -3t$

$\Rightarrow t = \frac{1}{4}$ and $-1 = \frac{1}{4}(\mu - 2), \lambda - 3 = -\frac{3}{4}$ $\Rightarrow \mu = -2$ and $\lambda = 9/4$

■ COPLANAR AND NON-COPLANAR VECTORS

A set of vectors is said to be coplanar if they lie on same or parallel plane i.e., their line of action are parallel to same plane or lie on same plane. A set of vectors is said to be non-coplanar when it contains atleast one vector whose line of action is not parallel to the plane of remaining vectors of the set.Two intersecting vectors, two collinear vectors are always coplanar. Three vectors $\vec{a}, \vec{b}, \vec{c}$ are coplanar means they are lying in the same plane or their line of action are parallel to same plane.

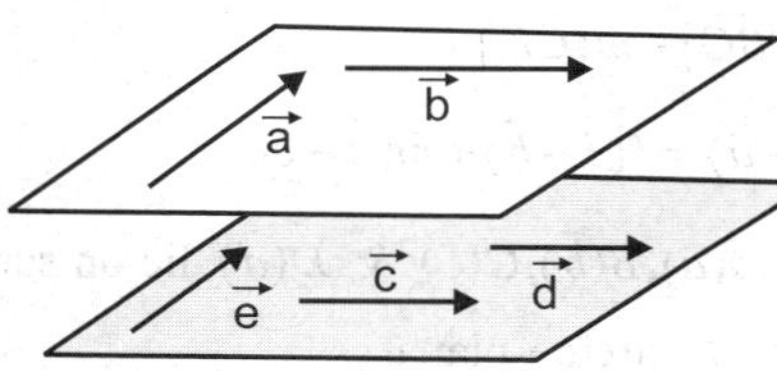

FIGURE 3.67

Theorm 1: **(Resolution of copalanar vectors)**

If $\vec{a}, \vec{b}$ be two given non-collinear vectors, then every vectors $\vec{r}$ co-planar with $\vec{a}$ and $\vec{b}$ can be expressed uniquely as a linear combination $x\vec{a} + y\vec{b}$, x, y being scalars or three different vectors (no two vectors are collinear) $\vec{a}, \vec{b}, \vec{c}$ are coplanar if and only if there exists scalars l,m such that $\vec{c} = l\vec{a} + m\vec{b}$ i.e., one can be expressed as a linear combination of the other two vectors.

Proof:

Take any point O.

Let $\overrightarrow{OA} = \vec{a}$, $\overrightarrow{OB} = \vec{b}$ and $\overrightarrow{OP} = \vec{r}$

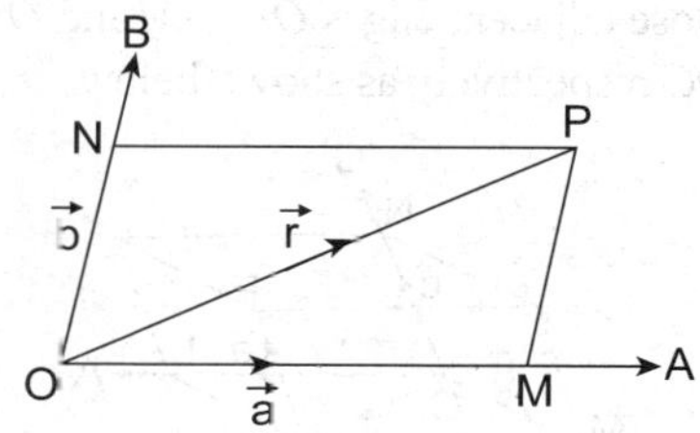

FIGURE 3.68

Clearly OA, OB and OP are co-planar. Through P, draw lines PM and PN, parallel to OB and OA respectively meeting them at M and N

We have $\overrightarrow{OP} = \overrightarrow{OM} + \overrightarrow{MP} = \overrightarrow{OM} + \overrightarrow{ON}$

Now $\overrightarrow{OM}$ and $\overrightarrow{OA}$ are collinear vectors

$\therefore$ $\overrightarrow{OM} = x\overrightarrow{OA} = x\vec{a}$ where x is a scalar

Similarly, $\overrightarrow{ON} = y\overrightarrow{OB} = y\vec{b}$ where y is a scalar

Hence from (i) we get $\overrightarrow{OP} = x\vec{a} + y\vec{b}$ or $\vec{r} = x\vec{a} + y\vec{b}$

Uniqueness:

If possible, let $\vec{r} = x\vec{a} + y\vec{b}$ and $x'\vec{a} + y'\vec{b}$ be two different ways of representing $\vec{r}$; Hence $x\vec{a} + y\vec{b} = x'\vec{a} + y'\vec{b}$

$\Rightarrow (x - x')\vec{a} + (y - y')\vec{b} = \vec{0}$

But $\vec{a}$ and $\vec{b}$ are non-collinear vectors

$\therefore (x - x') = 0$ and $(y - y') = 0$

$\Rightarrow x = x'$ and $y = y'$. Thus uniqueness is established

Conversely, let each of $\vec{a}, \vec{b}$ and $\vec{c}$ can be expressed as the linear combination of other two vectors. Let $\vec{c} = x\vec{a} + y\vec{b}; x, y \neq 0$ (as every two vectors are non-collinear). $x\vec{a} + y\vec{b}$ represents a vector in the plane of $\vec{a}$ and $\vec{b}$, but it is $\vec{c}$, thus $\vec{a}, \vec{b}, \vec{c}$ are coplanar.

NOTES

In this relation $\vec{r} = x\vec{a} + y\vec{b}$, $\vec{r}$ is called the resultant of two vectors $x\vec{a}$ and $y\vec{b}$ and vectors $x\vec{a}$ and $y\vec{b}$ are called the components of the vector $\vec{r}$.

Theorm 2: **(Resolution of non-copalanar vectors)**

If $\vec{a}, \vec{b}, \vec{c}$ are any three non-coplanar vectors (no two are collinear), then any vector $\vec{r}$ can be expressed as a linear combination of $\vec{a}, \vec{b}, \vec{c}$ i.e., $l\vec{a}+m\vec{b}+n\vec{c}$ where l, m, n are any three scalars.

Proof: Let OA, OB, OC be the three non-coplanar lines (i.e., no two lines are parallel). If taken in pair these lines determine three planes BOC, COA and AOB. Construct a parallelopiped whose adjacent edges OL, OM and ON are along OA, OB and OC respectively as shown below.

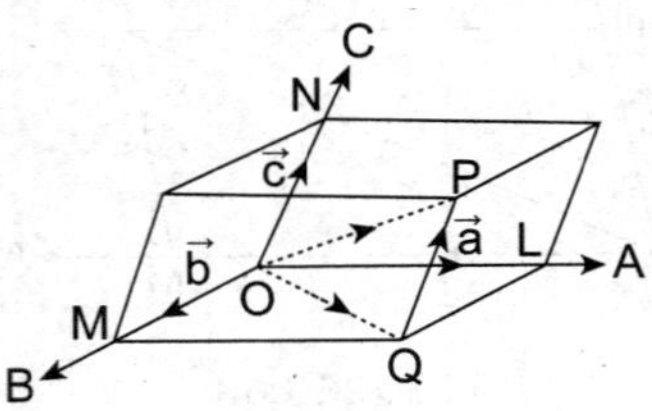

FIGURE 3.69

Let $\overline{OA}=\vec{a}, \overline{OB}=\vec{b}, \overline{OC}=\vec{c}$ and $\overline{OP}=\vec{r}$

Evidently, $\overline{OL}=l\vec{a}$, $\overline{OM}=m\vec{b}$, $\overline{ON}=n\vec{c}$

Now $\vec{r} = \overline{OP}=\overline{OQ}+\overline{QP} = (\overline{OL}+\overline{LQ})+\overline{QP}$

$=\overline{OL}+\overline{OM}+\overline{ON}$

$\therefore\ \vec{r} = l\vec{a}+m\vec{b}+n\vec{c}$

Therefore any vector $\vec{r}$ (say) can be represented as a linear combination of three non-coplanar vectors $\vec{a}, \vec{b}, \vec{c}$. Now, since $\vec{r} = l\vec{a}+m\vec{b}+n\vec{c}$

Let $\vec{r}$ can be expressed in another way say $\vec{r} = l'\vec{a}+m'\vec{b}+n'\vec{c}$ where l, m and n are another scalars different from l, m, n and hence $l\vec{a}+m\vec{b}+n\vec{c} = l'\vec{a}+m'\vec{b}+n'\vec{c}$

$\Rightarrow\ (l-l')\vec{a}+(m-m')\vec{b}+(n-n')\vec{c}=\vec{0}$

$\Rightarrow\ (l-l')=0; (m-m')=0; (n-n')=0$ as $\vec{a}, \vec{b}, \vec{c}$ are non-co-planar vectors $\Rightarrow l=l', m=m', n=n'$

Hence linear combination $\vec{r}=l\vec{a}+m\vec{b}+n\vec{c}$ is unique '

Theorm 3: **The necessary and sufficient condition for three vectors $\vec{a}, \vec{b}, \vec{c}$ to be coplanar is $[\vec{a}\vec{b}\vec{c}]=0$** {where $\left[\vec{a}\,\vec{b}\,\vec{c}\right]$ is called scalar triple product of $\vec{a}, \vec{b}, \vec{c} = \vec{a}.\left(\vec{b}\times\vec{c}\right)$

i.e., $\begin{vmatrix} a_1 & a_2 & a_3 \\ b_1 & b_2 & b_3 \\ c_1 & c_2 & c_3 \end{vmatrix}=0$

Proof: Let $\vec{a}, \vec{b}, \vec{c}$ be coplanar vectors then there exists scalars l, m such that

$$\vec{a}=l\vec{b}+m\vec{c}=(lb_1+mc_1)\hat{i}+(lb_2+mc_2)\hat{j}+(lb_3+mc_3)\hat{k}$$

$\Rightarrow\ a_1=lb_1+mc_1, a_2=lb_2+mc_2, a_3=lb_3+mc_3$

$$\Rightarrow \begin{vmatrix} a_1 & a_2 & a_3 \\ b_1 & b_2 & b_3 \\ c_1 & c_2 & c_3 \end{vmatrix} = \begin{vmatrix} lb_1+mc_1 & lb_2+mc_2 & lb_3+mc_3 \\ b_1 & b_2 & b_3 \\ c_1 & c_2 & c_3 \end{vmatrix}$$

$$= l\begin{vmatrix} b_1 & b_2 & b_3 \\ b_1 & b_2 & b_3 \\ c_1 & c_2 & c_3 \end{vmatrix} + m\begin{vmatrix} b_1 & b_2 & b_3 \\ b_1 & b_2 & b_3 \\ c_1 & c_2 & c_3 \end{vmatrix} = l(0)+m(0)=0$$

Conversely, let $\begin{vmatrix} a_1 & a_2 & a_3 \\ b_1 & b_2 & b_3 \\ c_1 & c_2 & c_3 \end{vmatrix}=0 \Rightarrow \vec{a}.\left(\vec{b}\times\vec{c}\right)=0$

$\Rightarrow\ \vec{a}$ is perpendicular to $\vec{b}\times\vec{c}$

$\Rightarrow\ \vec{a}$ is parallel to plane containing $\vec{b}$ and $\vec{c}$

$\Rightarrow\ \vec{a}, \vec{b}, \vec{c}$ are coplanar.

Corollary:

(1) Four points $A(\vec{a}), B(\vec{b}), C(\vec{c})$ & $D(\vec{d})$ lie in the same plane if there exist ℓ, $m \in \mathbb{R}$ such that $\overline{AB}=\ell\left(\overline{BC}\right)+m\left(\overline{CD}\right)$

i.e., $(\vec{b}-\vec{a})=\ell(\vec{c}-\vec{b})+m(\vec{d}-\vec{c})$

Proof: Let $A(\vec{a}), B(\vec{b}), C(\vec{c})$ & $D(\vec{d})$ lie on same plane

$\Rightarrow\ \overline{AB}, \overline{BC}, \overline{CD}$ are co-planar

$\Rightarrow\ \left(\vec{b}-\vec{a}\right), \left(\vec{c}-\vec{b}\right), \left(\vec{d}-\vec{c}\right)$ are co-planar

$\Rightarrow$ there exist scalars ℓ, m

such that $(\vec{b}-\vec{a})=\ell(\vec{c}-\vec{b})+m(\vec{d}-\vec{c})$

(2) A, B, C, D are coplanar if there exist scalars k, l, m, n (not all zero), such that $k\vec{a}+\ell\vec{b}+m\vec{c}+n\vec{d}=\vec{0}$; where $k+l+m+n=0$

Proof: From above corollary we have $(\vec{b}-\vec{a})=p(\vec{c}-\vec{b})+q(\vec{d}-\vec{c})$

$\Rightarrow\ 1(\vec{a})+(-1-p)\vec{b}+(p-q)\vec{c}+q\vec{d}=\vec{0}$

$\Rightarrow\ k\vec{a}+\ell\vec{b}+m\vec{c}+n\vec{d}=\vec{0}$; where $k=1$, $l=-1-p$, $m=p-q$, $n=q$ and $k+l+m+n=0$

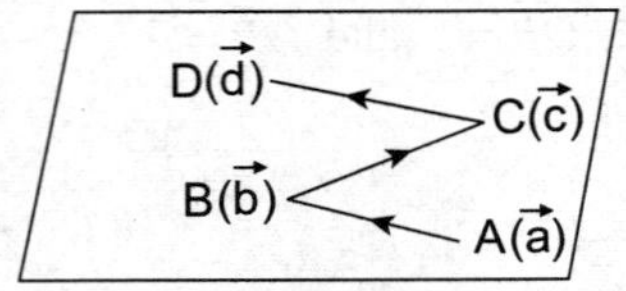

FIGURE 3.70

Theorem 4 : Any two non-zero collinear vectors are linearly dependent.

Proof: Let $\vec{a}$ and $\vec{b}$ be non-zero collinear vectors

$\Rightarrow \vec{a} = \lambda\vec{b}$ for $\lambda \in \mathbb{R}$ and $\lambda \neq 0$

$\Rightarrow \vec{a} + (-\lambda)\vec{b} = \vec{0}$ $\Rightarrow (1)\vec{a} + (-\lambda)\vec{b} = \vec{0}$

$\Rightarrow x\vec{a} + y\vec{b} = \vec{0}$; where $x = 1, y = -\lambda$ (both non-zero scalars)

$\therefore$ $\vec{a}$ and $\vec{b}$ are linearly dependent vectors

Theorem 5: Two non-collinear vectors are linearly independent.

Proof: Let $\vec{a}$ and $\vec{b}$ be two non-collinear vectors then there exist scalars l and m such that $l\vec{a} + m\vec{b} = \vec{0} \Rightarrow l\vec{a} = -m\vec{b}$
$l\vec{a}$ is vector in the direction of $\vec{a}$, $-m\vec{b}$ is vector collinear to $\vec{b}$ but opposite to direction of $\vec{b}$. Since $\vec{a}$ and $\vec{b}$ have different directions. Therefore equality can hold iff $l = 0$, $m = 0$. Hence $\vec{a}$ and $\vec{b}$ are linearly independent.

Theorem 6: Three coplanar vectors are linearly dependent.

Proof: Let $\vec{a}$, $\vec{b}$ and $\vec{c}$ be three co-planar vectors

$\therefore$ $\vec{a} = l\vec{b} + m\vec{c}$ where l, m are scalars

$\Rightarrow (1)\vec{a} + (-l)\vec{b} + (-m)\vec{c} = \vec{0}$

Hence $\vec{a}$, $\vec{b}$ and $\vec{c}$ are linearly dependent.

Theorem 7: Three non coplanar vectors are linearly independent.

Proof: Let $\vec{a}$, $\vec{b}$ and $\vec{c}$ be three non-coplanar vectors. Let there exist scalars l, m, n such that $l\vec{a} + m\vec{b} + n\vec{c} = \vec{0}$

$\Rightarrow (-l)\vec{a} = m\vec{b} + n\vec{c}$. Right side is vector in plane of $\vec{b}$ and $\vec{c}$ but $\vec{a}$ does not lie in the plane of $\vec{b}$ and $\vec{c}$.

$\Rightarrow$ $l = m = n = 0$

Hence $\vec{a}$, $\vec{b}$ and $\vec{c}$ are linearly independent.

Aliter: It is given that $x\vec{a} + y\vec{b} + z\vec{c} = \vec{0}$ ...(i)

Let $x \neq 0$, then (i) can be written as

$x\vec{a} = -y\vec{b} - z\vec{c} \Rightarrow \vec{a} = -\frac{y}{x}\vec{b} - \frac{z}{x}\vec{c}$ ....(ii)

Since y/x and z/x are scalar, thus (ii) expresses $\vec{a}$ as a linear combination of $\vec{b}$ and $\vec{c}$ Hence $\vec{a}$ is co-planar with $\vec{b}$ and $\vec{c}$, but we are given that $\vec{a}, \vec{b}, \vec{c}$ are non-coplanar vectors. Thus our supposition that $x \neq 0$ is wrong. Hence $x = 0$. Similarly we can prove that $y = 0$ and $z = 0$.

ILLUSTRATION 36: If the vectors $x\vec{i} + \vec{j} + \vec{k}$, $\vec{i} + y\vec{j} + \vec{k}$ and $\vec{i} + \vec{j} + z\vec{k}$ are co-planar where $x \neq 1, y \neq 1, z \neq 1$, then prove that $\frac{1}{1-x} + \frac{1}{1-y} + \frac{1}{1-z} = 1$.

SOLUTION: The vectors are co-planar if we can find two scalars λ, μ such that $x\vec{i} + \vec{j} + \vec{k} = \lambda(\vec{i} + y\vec{j} + \vec{k}) + \mu(\vec{i} + \vec{j} + z\vec{k})$

$\Rightarrow x = \lambda + \mu, 1 = \lambda y + \mu, 1 = \lambda + \mu z$ $\Rightarrow 1 - x = 1 - \lambda - \mu,\ y = \frac{1-\mu}{\lambda}, z = \frac{1-\lambda}{\mu}$

$\Rightarrow (1-y) = \frac{\lambda - 1 + \mu}{\lambda}$ and $1 - z = \frac{\mu - 1 + \lambda}{\mu}$

$\Rightarrow \frac{1}{1-x} + \frac{1}{1-y} + \frac{1}{1-z} = \frac{1}{1-\lambda-\mu} + \frac{\lambda}{\lambda+\mu-1} + \frac{\mu}{\lambda+\mu-1} = \frac{1-\lambda-\mu}{1-\lambda-\mu} = 1$

ILLUSTRATION 37: Show that the vectors $\vec{i} - \vec{j} - 2\vec{k}$, $2\vec{i} + 3\vec{j} + \vec{k}$ and $7\vec{i} + 3\vec{j} - 4\vec{k}$ are co-planar.

SOLUTION: Let $\vec{a} = \vec{i} - \vec{j} - 2\vec{k}$, $\vec{b} = 2\vec{i} + 3\vec{j} + \vec{k}$ and $\vec{c} = 7\vec{i} + 3\vec{j} - 4\vec{k}$

Let $\vec{a} = k_1\vec{b} + k_2\vec{c}$ where k_1 and k_2 are scalars $\Rightarrow \vec{a} = k_1(2\vec{i} + 3\vec{j} + \vec{k}) + k_2(7\vec{i} + 3\vec{j} - 4\vec{k})$

$\Rightarrow \vec{i} - \vec{j} - 2\vec{k} = (2k_1 + 7k_2)\vec{i} + (3k_1 + 3k_2)\vec{j} + (k_1 - 4k_2)\vec{k}$

$\Rightarrow 2k_1 + 7k_2 = 1$ ....(i)

$3k_1 + 3k_2 = -1$ ...(ii)

and $k_1 - 4k_2 = -2$ ...(iii)

Solving the above equation $k_1 = -2/3$ and $k_2 = 1/3$

$\therefore \quad \vec{a} = -\frac{2}{3}\vec{b} + \frac{1}{3}\vec{c}$

$\Rightarrow$ $\vec{a}$ can be uniquely expressed as a linear combination of $\vec{b}$ and $\vec{c}$.

So vectors $\vec{a}$, $\vec{b}$ and $\vec{c}$ are co-planar

ILLUSTRATION 38: Show that the points $P(\vec{a}+2\vec{b}+\vec{c})$, $Q(\vec{a}-\vec{b}-\vec{c})$, $R(3\vec{a}+\vec{b}+2\vec{c})$ and $S(5\vec{a}+3\vec{b}+5\vec{c})$ are co-planar given that $\vec{a}$, $\vec{b}$ and $\vec{c}$ are non-coplanar.

SOLUTION: $\overrightarrow{PQ} = -3\vec{b}-2\vec{c}$; $\overrightarrow{PR} = 2\vec{a}-\vec{b}+\vec{c}$

$\overrightarrow{PS} = 4\vec{a}+\vec{b}+4\vec{c}$ and $\overrightarrow{PQ} = k_1\overrightarrow{PR} + k_2\overrightarrow{PS}$

$\Rightarrow \; -3\vec{b}-2\vec{c} = k_1(2\vec{a}-\vec{b}+\vec{c}) + k_2(4\vec{a}+\vec{b}+4\vec{c})$

$\Rightarrow \; -3\vec{b}-2\vec{c} = (2k_1+4k_2)\vec{a} + (-k_1+k_2)\vec{b} + (k_1+4k_2)\vec{c}$

$\Rightarrow \; 2k_1 + 4k_2 = 0$ ...(i)

$-k_1 + k_2 = -3$ ...(ii)

$k_1 + 4k_2 = -2$ ....(iii)

Solving the above equations $k_1 = 2$, $k_2 = -1 \Rightarrow \overrightarrow{PQ} = 2\overrightarrow{PR} - \overrightarrow{PS}$

$\therefore$ $\overrightarrow{PQ}, \overrightarrow{PR}, \overrightarrow{PS}$ are co-planar because $\overrightarrow{PQ}$ is a linear combination of $\overrightarrow{PR}$ and $\overrightarrow{PS}$

ILLUSTRATION 39: Show that points with position vectors $\vec{a}-2\vec{b}+3\vec{c}$, $-2\vec{a}+3\vec{b}-\vec{c}$, $4\vec{a}-7\vec{b}+7\vec{c}$ are collinear. It is given that vectors $\vec{a}, \vec{b}, \vec{c}$ are non-coplanar.

SOLUTION: The three points are collinear, if we can find $\lambda_1, \lambda_2, \lambda_3$ such that

$\lambda_1(\vec{a}-2\vec{b}+3\vec{c}) + \lambda_2(-2\vec{a}+3\vec{b}-\vec{c}) + \lambda_3(4\vec{a}-7\vec{b}+7\vec{c}) = \vec{0}$ with $\lambda_1 + \lambda_2 + \lambda_3 = 0$

Since $\vec{a}$, $\vec{b}$, $\vec{c}$ are non-coplanar i.e., linearly independent.

equating the coefficients $\vec{a}$, $\vec{b}$, $\vec{c}$ seperately to zero, we get

$\lambda_1 - 2\lambda_2 + 4\lambda_3 = 0$, $-2\lambda_1 + 3\lambda_2 - 7\lambda_3 = 0$ and $3\lambda_1 - \lambda_2 + 7\lambda_3 = 0$

On solving we get $\lambda_1 = -2$, $\lambda_2 = 1$, $\lambda_3 = 1$ so that $\lambda_1 + \lambda_2 + \lambda_3 = 0$

Hence the given vectors are collinear.

ILLUSTRATION 40: If $\vec{a}, \vec{b}, \vec{c}$ are non-coplanar vectors such that $x_1\vec{a} + y_1\vec{b} + z_1\vec{c} = x_2\vec{a} + y_2\vec{b} + z_2\vec{c}$, then prove that $x_1 = x_2$, $y_1 = y_2$ and $z_1 = z_2$.

SOLUTION: We have $x_1\vec{a} + y_1\vec{b} + z_1\vec{c} = x_2\vec{a} + y_2\vec{b} + z_2\vec{c}$ $\Rightarrow (x_1-x_2)\vec{a} + (y_1-y_2)\vec{b} + (z_1-z_2)\vec{c} = \vec{0}$

$\Rightarrow (x_1 - x_2) = 0, (y_1 - y_2) = 0, (z_1 - z_2) = 0$ $\Rightarrow x_1 = x_2, y_1 = y_2$ and $z_1 = z_2$

ILLUSTRATION 41: Show the vectors $\hat{i}+\hat{j}, \hat{j}+\hat{k}, \hat{k}+\hat{i}$ are linearly independent.

SOLUTION: Consider the equation $x(\hat{i}+\hat{j}) + y(\hat{j}+\hat{k}) + z(\hat{k}+\hat{i}) = \vec{0}$ where x, y, z are scalars

$\Rightarrow (x+z)\hat{i} + (y+x)\hat{j} + (y+z)\hat{k} = \vec{0}$

$\Rightarrow (x+z) = 0, (y+x) = 0, (y+z) = 0$ ....(i)

and $2(x+y+z) = 0$ ...(ii)

$\Rightarrow x = 0, y = 0, z = 0$

Hence the vectors $\hat{i}+\hat{j}, \hat{j}+\hat{k}, \hat{k}+\hat{i}$ are linearly independent.

TEXTUAL EXERCISE 6: (SUBJECTIVE)

1. Test the coplanarity of given set of points: $2\vec{a}+3\vec{b}-\vec{c}$, $\vec{a}-2\vec{b}+3\vec{c}$, $3\vec{a}+4\vec{b}-2\vec{c}$, $\vec{a}-6\vec{b}+6\vec{c}$; where $\vec{a},\vec{b},\vec{c}$ are linearly independent.
2. Check the following set of vectors for linear depedence/independence
   (a) $\hat{i}-\hat{j}+2\hat{k},\ 4\hat{i}-\hat{j}+7\hat{k},\ 2\hat{i}+\hat{j}+3\hat{k}$
   (b) $\hat{i}+2\hat{j}+3\hat{k},\ \hat{i}-\hat{j}+4\hat{k},\ 2\hat{i}+7\hat{j}-\hat{k}$
3. Let α, β, γ be distinct real numbers, then show that the points with position vectors $\alpha\hat{i}+\beta\hat{j}+\gamma\hat{k}$, $\beta\hat{i}+\gamma\hat{j}+\alpha\hat{k}$, $\gamma\hat{i}+\alpha\hat{j}+\beta\hat{k}$ form1 an equilateral triangle and hence find the condition of collinearity of these points.
4. If $\vec{a},\vec{b},\vec{c}$ are three non-zero vectors, no two of which are collinear and the vector $\vec{a}+\vec{b}$ is collinear with $\vec{c}$, $\vec{b}+\vec{c}$ is collinear with $\vec{a}$, then find the value of $\vec{a}+\vec{b}+\vec{c}$.
5. Given the following vectors $\vec{r}_1=2\hat{i}-\hat{j}+\hat{k}$, $\vec{r}_2=\hat{i}+3\hat{j}-2\hat{k}$, $\vec{r}_3=-2\hat{i}+\hat{j}-3\hat{k}$, $\vec{r}_4=3\hat{i}-2\hat{j}+5\hat{k}$. If $\vec{r}_4=a\vec{r}_1+b\vec{r}_2+c\vec{r}_3$, then prove that $a=c-11b$.
6. If $\vec{a}=\hat{i}+\hat{j}+\hat{k}, \vec{b}=4\hat{i}+3\hat{j}+4\hat{k}$ and $c=\hat{i}+\alpha\hat{j}+\beta\hat{k}$ are linearly dependent vectors and $|\vec{c}|=\sqrt{3}$,then find the value of α and β.
7. If the points A, B, C and D have position vectors $\vec{a}$, $2\vec{a}+\vec{b}$, $4\vec{a}+2\vec{b}$ and $5\vec{a}+4\vec{b}$ respectively, then find the three collinear points out of these.

Answer Key

1. coplaner **2.** (a) linearly dependent (b) linearly independent **3.** α = β = γ
4. 0 **6.** $\alpha=\pm1, \beta=1$ **7.** B, A and D

TEXTUAL EXERCISE 3: (OBJECTIVE)

1 If the position vectors of the points A, B, C and D are $2\hat{i}+3\hat{j}$, $\hat{i}-\hat{j}-\hat{k}$, $3\hat{i}+2\hat{j}-\hat{k}$ and $\hat{i}-6\hat{j}-3\hat{k}$ respectively, then
   (a) AB || CD (b) AD || BC
   (c) AC || BD (d) |AB| = 1/2 |CD|
2 The points A(1, –2, 3); B(2, –3, 4); C(6, –7, 8)
   (a) are non-collinear
   (b) are collinear
   (c) forms a triangle of non-zero area
   (d) are linearly dependent.
3 The points A(–1, 2, 1); B(2, –3, 1) and C(2, 1, 3)
   (a) are collinear
   (b) non-collinear
   (c) form an equilateral triangle
   (d) linearly independent
4 The vectors $\vec{a}=\hat{i}+2\hat{j}-3\hat{k}$; $\vec{b}=2\hat{i}-\hat{j}+\hat{k}$; $\vec{c}=3\hat{i}+2\hat{j}+\lambda\hat{k}$ are
   (a) collinear for λ = –27/5
   (b) linearly dependent for λ = –17/5
   (c) non-collinear for λ = –27/5
   (d) linearly independent for λ = –27/5
5 A vectors $\vec{a}$ of magnitude 5 units is collinear with $\vec{b}=2\hat{i}-\hat{j}+4\hat{k}$ and makes an obtuse angle with +ve direction of z-axis, then $\vec{a}$ = .
   (a) $5\sqrt{21}\vec{b}$ (b) $\frac{5}{\sqrt{21}}\vec{b}$
   (c) $\frac{-5}{\sqrt{21}}\vec{b}$ (d) None of these
6. If $A(\vec{a}), B(\vec{b}), C(\vec{c})$ are collinear, then
   (a) $\vec{a}, \vec{b}$ & $\vec{c}$ are coplanar
   (b) $\vec{a}, \vec{b}$ & $\vec{c}$ need not be coplanar
   (c) $\vec{a}, \vec{b}, \vec{c}$ are linearly dependent
   (d) $\vec{a}, \vec{b}, \vec{c}$ are linearly independent

Answer Key

1. (a, d) **2.** (b, d) **3.** (b, d) **4.** (b, c, d) **5.** (c) **6.** (a, c)

■ PRODUCT OF TWO VECTORS

The two vector quantities appear in geometry, physics and mechanics in two distinct type of products out of them one is a scalar (· dot product) and other one is a vector (× cross product). And they are described as below:

Scalar Product of Two Vectors (Dot Product)

Quantitative Definition The scalar product of $\vec{b}$ and $\vec{b}$ written as $\vec{a}.\vec{b}$, is defined as $|\vec{b}|.|\vec{b}|.\cos\theta$.

(Where θ is the angle between the two vectors when drawn from the same initial point here the angle θ is restricted to the interval $0 \le \theta \le \pi$). It is also known as *inner product* or *dot product.*

Geometrical interpretation

$\vec{a}.\vec{b}$ is the product of length of one vector and length of the projection of the other vector in the direction of the former.

$$\vec{a}.\vec{b} = |\vec{a}|.(|\vec{b}|\cos\theta)$$
$$= |\vec{a}|.\text{ Projection of } |\vec{b}| \text{ in direction of } \vec{a}$$
$$= OA.ON$$
$$\vec{a}.\vec{b} = |\vec{b}|.(|\vec{a}|\cos\theta)$$
$$= |\vec{b}|.\text{ Projection of } |\vec{a}| \text{ in direction of } \vec{b}$$
$$= OB.OM$$

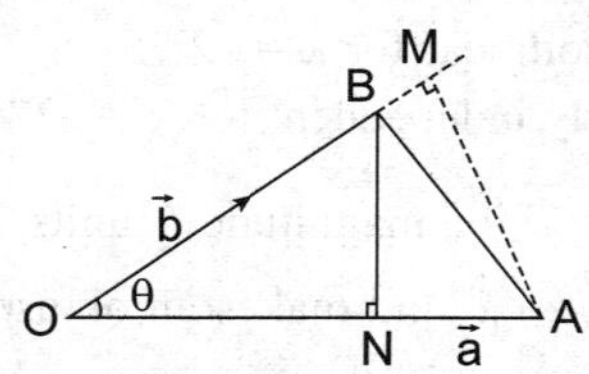

FIGURE 3.71

Conclusions:

1. If θ is acute angle

$\Rightarrow \cos\theta > 0 \Rightarrow \vec{a}.\vec{b} > 0$

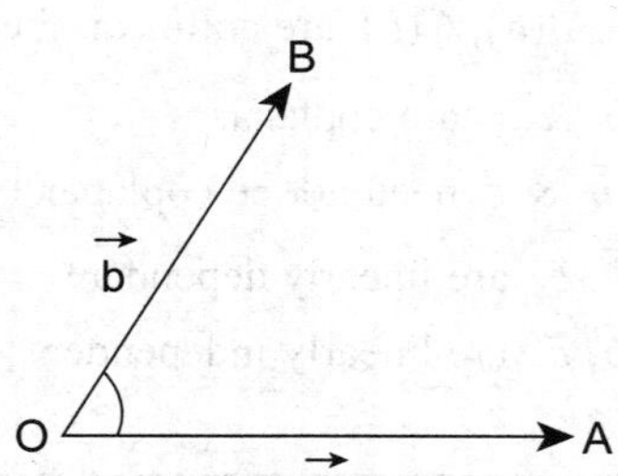

FIGURE 3.72

2. If θ is right angle

$\Rightarrow \cos\theta = 0 \Rightarrow \vec{a}.\vec{b} = 0$

Thus $\vec{a}.\vec{b} = 0 \Rightarrow \vec{a} = 0$

or $\vec{b} = 0$ or $\theta = 90°$

Thus the scalar product of two non-zero vectors is zero iff they are at right angles to each other.

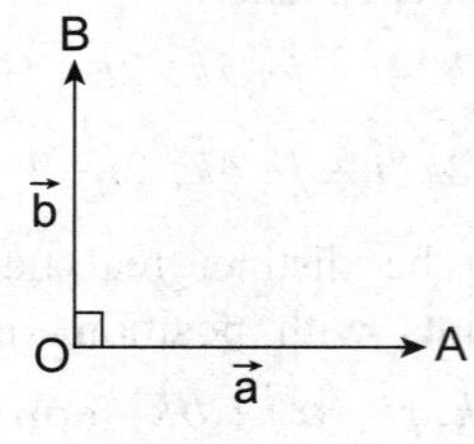

FIGURE 3.73

3. If θ is obtuse angle

$\Rightarrow \cos\theta < 0 \Rightarrow \vec{a}.\vec{b} < 0$

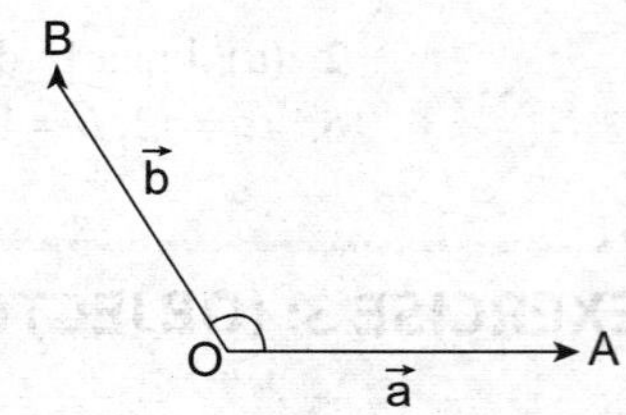

FIGURE 3.74

Properties of scalar product

1. ***Commutativity:*** Dot product of two vectors is commutative, i.e., $\vec{a}.\vec{b} = \vec{b}.\vec{a}$

This property is obvious from the definition of dot product itself. Since $\vec{a}.\vec{b} = ab\cos\theta = ba\cos\theta = \vec{b}.\vec{a}$

[*since a, b are real numbers so they commute ab* = *ba*]

2. $\vec{a}.(-\vec{b}) = -(\vec{a}.\vec{b})$

$\Rightarrow (-\vec{a}).(-\vec{b}) = \vec{a}.\vec{b}$ for every pair of vectors $\vec{a}, \vec{b}$

The proof is obvious from the figure

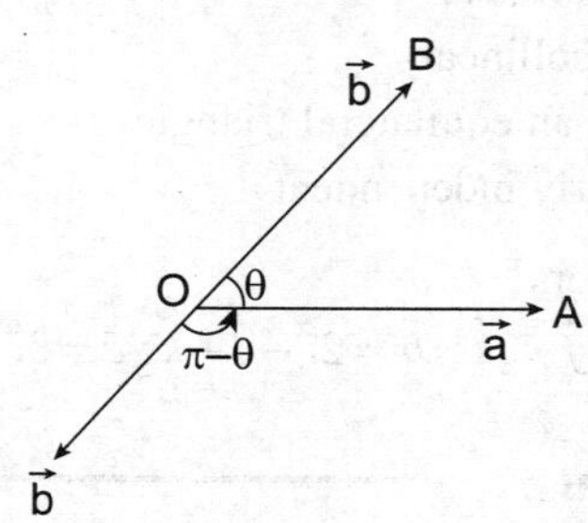

FIGURE 3.75

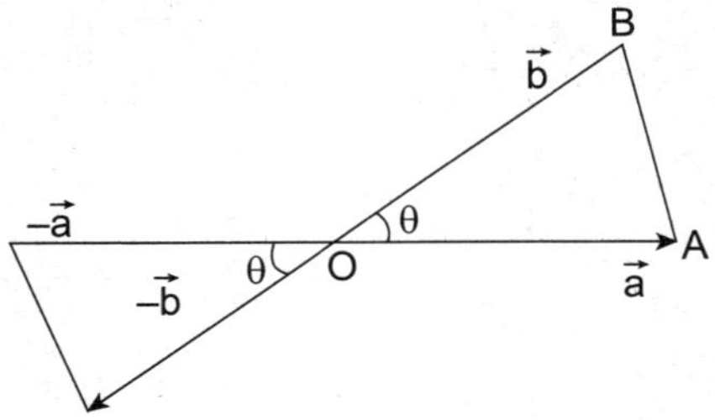

FIGURE 3.76

3. Dot product of two vectors is *associative* with a scalar. Let l be a scalar, then $(l\vec{a})\cdot\vec{b}=l(\vec{a}.\vec{b})=(\vec{a}.l\vec{b})$

Case I: When $l>0$

$l\vec{a}$ has the same direction as $\vec{a}$.

Let the angle between $\vec{a}$ and $\vec{b}$ be θ, so is the angle between $\vec{a}$ and $\vec{b}$.

Hence $(l\vec{a}).\vec{b}=l\ ab\cos\theta\ =l(\vec{a}.\vec{b})$

Case II: When $l<0$

$l\vec{a}$ has the opposite direction to $\vec{a}$.

Hence angle between $l\vec{a}$ and $\vec{b}$ $=\pi-\theta$

$\vec{a}$ and $\vec{b}$ be θ, so is the angle between $l\vec{a}$ and $\vec{b}$.

$\therefore\ \ (l\vec{a}).\vec{b}=-l\,ab\cos(\pi-\theta)\ =l\,ab\cos\theta\ =l(\vec{a}.\vec{b})$

Hence in both cases $\vec{a}(l\vec{b})=l(\vec{a}.\vec{b})$

In similar way, we can also prove that $\vec{a}(l\vec{b})=l(\vec{a}.\vec{b})$

Although the dot prouct of three vectors is not associative

$\Rightarrow\ \vec{a}.(\vec{b}.\vec{c})\neq(\vec{a}.\vec{b}).\vec{c}$ i.e., $\lambda\vec{a}\neq\mu\vec{c}$ (which is obviously true)

4. ***Distributive law:*** Scalar multiplication of vectors is distributive over the addition/subtraction of vectors, that means $\vec{a}.(\vec{b}+\vec{c})=\vec{a}.\vec{b}+\vec{a}.\vec{c}$ holds good for all vectors $\vec{a},\vec{b},\vec{c}$.

Proof: Let $\overline{OB}$ and $\overline{BC}$ represent the vectors $\vec{b}$ and $\vec{c}$.

Hence $\overline{OC}=\vec{b}+\vec{c}$.

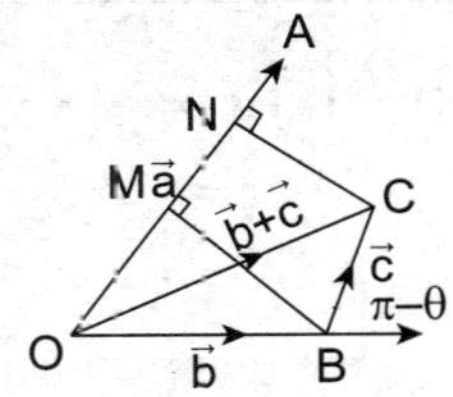

FIGURE 3.77

Let $\overline{OA}$ represent the vector $\vec{a}$ and $\overline{ON}$ be the scalar component of $\overline{OC}$ along $\vec{a}$ and OM the scalar component of $\overline{OB}$ along $\vec{a}$. MN is the scalar component of $\overline{BC}$ along $\vec{a}$.

Consequently: $\vec{a}.(\vec{b}+\vec{c})=a(ON)$

$=a\,(OM+MN)$

$=a\,(OM)+a(MN)$

= a (scalar component of $\vec{b}$ along $\vec{a}$) + a (scalar component of $\vec{c}$ along $\vec{a}$)

$=\vec{a}.\vec{b}+\vec{a}.\vec{c}$

5. The scalar product of a vector with itself is often written as square of the vector.

i.e., $\vec{a}^2=\vec{a}.\vec{a}=|\vec{a}|^2$, but no other powers of a vector are defined.

Therefore $\hat{i}.\hat{i}=\hat{j}.\hat{j}=\hat{k}.\hat{k}=1$

6. $\cos\theta=\dfrac{\vec{a}.\vec{b}}{|\vec{a}|.|\vec{b}|}=\dfrac{a_1b_1+a_2b_2+a_3b_3}{\sqrt{a_1^2+a_2^2+a_3^2}\sqrt{b_1^2+b_2^2+b_3^2}}$

i.e., $\theta=\cos^{-1}\hat{a}.\hat{b}$

7. $\vec{a}.\vec{b}=0$, therefore $\hat{i}.\hat{j}=\hat{j}.\hat{k}=\hat{k}.\hat{i}=0$

(*Vector* $\vec{a}$ *and* $\vec{b}$ *are perpendicular to each other, provided* $\vec{a}$ *and* $\vec{b}$ *are non-zero vectors*)

8. Let $\vec{a}=a_1\hat{i}+a_2\hat{j}+a_3\hat{k}$, $\vec{b}=b_1\hat{i}+b_2\hat{j}+b_3\hat{k}$

$\vec{a}.\vec{b}=(a_1\hat{i}+a_2\hat{j}+a_3\hat{k}).(b_1\hat{i}+b_2\hat{j}+b_3\hat{k})=a_1b_1+a_2b_2+a_3b_3$

9. $\vec{a}=a_1\hat{i}+a_2\hat{j}+a_3\hat{k}=(\vec{a}.\hat{i})\hat{i}+(\vec{a}.\hat{j})\hat{j}+(\vec{a}.\hat{k})\hat{k}$

10. $(\vec{a}\pm\vec{b})^2=(\vec{a}\pm\vec{b}).(\vec{a}\pm\vec{b})=\vec{a}^2+\vec{b}^2\pm2\vec{a}.\vec{b}$

LLUSTRATION 42: The vectors $\vec{a},\vec{b},\vec{c}$ are of the same length and pairwise form equal angles. If $\vec{a}=\hat{i}+\hat{j}$ and $\vec{b}=\hat{j}+\hat{k}$, then find the position vectors of $\vec{c}$.

SOLUTION: Let $\vec{c} = x\hat{i} + y\hat{j} + z\hat{k}$ $\Rightarrow x^2 + y^2 + z^2 = 2$ $(\because |\vec{c}| = |\vec{a}| = |\vec{b}| = \sqrt{2})$ .....(i)

now $\vec{a}\,.\,\vec{b} = \vec{b}\,.\,\vec{c} = \vec{c}\,.\,\vec{a}$ $\Rightarrow 1 = y + z = x + y$ .....(ii)

$\therefore\ z = x;\quad y = 1 - x$

put z and y in terms of x in (1) to get x and then get y and z as (1, 0, 1) and $\left(-\frac{1}{3}, \frac{4}{3}, -\frac{1}{3}\right)$ respectively.

ILLUSTRATION 43: The resultant of two vectors $\vec{a}$ and $\vec{b}$ is perpendicular to $\vec{a}$. If $|\vec{b}| = |\sqrt{2}\,\vec{a}|$, show that the resultant of $2\vec{a}$ and $\vec{b}$ is perpendicular to $\vec{b}$.

SOLUTION: The resultant of $\vec{a}$ and $\vec{b}$ is $\vec{a}+\vec{b}$; Since $\vec{a}+\vec{b}$ is perpendicular to $\vec{a}$

$(\vec{a}+\vec{b}).\vec{a} = 0 \Rightarrow \vec{a}.\vec{a} + \vec{b}.\vec{a} = 0$; Hence $\vec{b}.\vec{a} = -|\vec{a}|^2$

Now resultant of $2\vec{a}$ and $\vec{b} = 2\vec{a}+\vec{b}$

$\therefore\ (2\vec{a}+\vec{b}).\vec{b} = 2(\vec{a}.\vec{b}) + \vec{b}.\vec{b}$ $\Rightarrow -2|\vec{a}|^2 + 2|\vec{a}|^2 = 0$ as $|\vec{b}| = |\sqrt{2}\,\vec{a}|$

$\therefore\ (2\vec{a}+\vec{b}).\vec{b} = 0$ $\Rightarrow 2\vec{a}+\vec{b}$ is perpendicular to $\vec{b}$

ILLUSTRATION 44: Find the values of x for which the angle between the vectors $\vec{a} = x\hat{i} - 3\hat{j} - \hat{k}$ and $\vec{b} = 2x\hat{i} + x\hat{j} - \hat{k}$ is obtuse.

SOLUTION: Since angle between $\vec{a}$ and $\vec{b}$ is obtuse, $\vec{a}.\vec{b} < 0$

$\Rightarrow 2x^2 - 3x + 1 < 0$ $\Rightarrow \frac{1}{2} < x < 1$

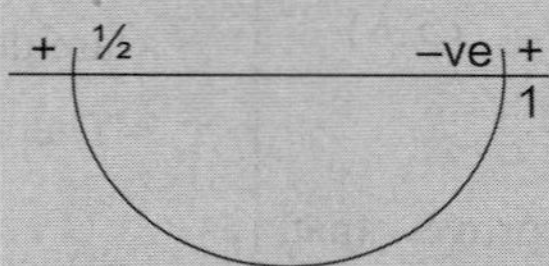

FIGURE 3.78

ILLUSTRATION 45: Let $\vec{a}$ and $\vec{b}$ be two non parallel unit vectors in a plane. If $(\alpha\vec{a} + \vec{b})$ bisects the internal angle between $\vec{a}$ and $\vec{b}$, then find α.

SOLUTION: $\vec{a}\,.\,(\alpha\vec{a} + \vec{b}) = \vec{b}\,.\,(\alpha\vec{a} + \vec{b})$

$\Rightarrow \alpha + \vec{a}\,.\,\vec{b} = \alpha\,\vec{a}\,.\,\vec{b} + 1$ $\Rightarrow (\alpha - 1)\vec{a}.\vec{b}(\alpha - 1) = 0$

$\Rightarrow (\alpha - 1)\{1 - \vec{a}.\vec{b}\} = 0$ as $\vec{a}.\vec{b} \neq 1$ $(\because |\vec{a}| = |\vec{b}| = 1$ but $\vec{a} \neq \vec{b}) \Rightarrow$ so $\alpha = 1$

ILLUSTRATION 46: The position vectors of the foci of an ellipse are $\vec{b}$ and $-\vec{b}$ and the length of major axis is $2a$. Prove that the equation of the ellipse is $a^4 - a^2(r^2 + b^2) + (\vec{b}.\vec{r})^2 = 0$.

SOLUTION: Since in an ellipse the sum of the focal distances of any point on it is equal to $2a$, the length of major axis.

$\therefore$ If $\vec{r}$ be any point on ellipse, then $|\vec{r}+\vec{b}| + |\vec{r}-\vec{b}| = 2a$

$\Rightarrow (\vec{r}+\vec{b})^2 = [2a - |\vec{r}-\vec{b}|]^2 \Rightarrow r^2 + 2\vec{r}.\vec{b} + b^2 = 4a^2 - 4a|\vec{r}-\vec{b}| + r^2 + b^2 - 2\vec{r}.\vec{b}$

$\Rightarrow a^2 - \vec{r}.\vec{b} = a|\vec{r}-\vec{b}|$; Squaring both sides, we get

$\Rightarrow a^4 + (\vec{r}.\vec{b})^2 - 2a^2(\vec{r}.\vec{b}) = a^2(r^2 + b^2 - 2\vec{r}.\vec{b}) \Rightarrow a^4 - a^2(r^2 + b^2) + (\vec{r}.\vec{b})^2 = 0$

APPLICATION OF DOT PRODUCTS

(a) Scalar and Vector Projection of vector on some other vector:

Scalar projection of $\vec{a}$ on $\vec{b}$

$= |\overrightarrow{OM}| = OM = |OA\cos\theta|$

$= ||\vec{a}|\cos\theta|$

$= \dfrac{|\vec{a}|.|\vec{b}||\cos\theta|}{|\vec{b}|} = |\vec{a}.\hat{b}|$

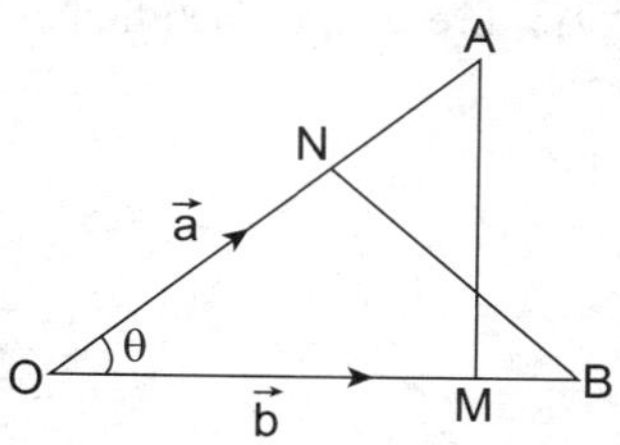

FIGURE 3.79

Scalar projection of $\vec{b}$ on $\vec{a}$

$ON = |OB\cos\theta| = ||\vec{b}|\cos\theta| = |\hat{a}.\vec{b}|$

Therefore Vector projection of $\vec{a}$ on $\vec{b} = \overrightarrow{OM} = (\vec{a}.\hat{b})\hat{b}$

and Vector projection of $\vec{b}$ on $\vec{a} = \overrightarrow{ON} = (\hat{a}.\vec{b})\hat{a}$

(b) Scalar and Vector Projections Normal to a given vector: Scalar projection of $\vec{a}$ perpendicular to $\vec{b}$

$MA = ||\vec{a}|\sin\theta|$

$= \dfrac{|\vec{a}\times\vec{b}|}{|\vec{b}|} = |\vec{a}\times\hat{b}|$

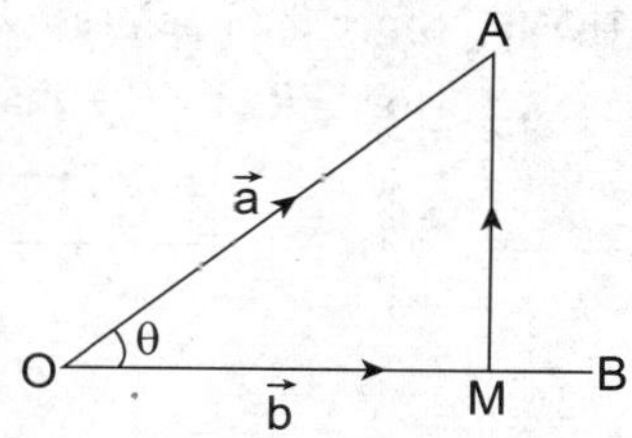

FIGURE 3.80

Vector projection of $\vec{a}$ perpendicular to $\vec{b}$

$\overrightarrow{MA} = \overrightarrow{OA} - \overrightarrow{OM} = \vec{a} - (\vec{a}.\hat{b})\hat{b}$

$\vec{a}-$(vector projection of $\vec{a}$ on $\vec{b}$)

ILLUSTRATION 47: Find the vector projection of $\vec{B} = 6\hat{i}+3\hat{j}+2\hat{k}$ on $\vec{A} = \hat{i}-2\hat{j}-2\hat{k}$ and the scalar component of $\vec{B}$ on $\vec{A}$.

SOLUTION: Since projection of B on A ($\text{proj}_A B$) $= (\vec{b}.\hat{a})\hat{a} = \dfrac{\vec{b}.\vec{a}}{|\vec{a}|^2}.\vec{a}$

$$= \frac{6-6-4}{1+4+4}(\hat{i}-2\hat{j}-2\hat{k}) = -\frac{4}{9}(\hat{i}-2\hat{j}-2\hat{k}) = -\frac{4}{9}\hat{i}+\frac{8}{9}\hat{j}-\frac{8}{9}\hat{k}$$

We find the scalar component of $\vec{B}$ on $\vec{A}$

$$= |\vec{B}|\cos\theta = \vec{B}.\frac{\vec{A}}{|\vec{A}|} = (6\hat{i}+3\hat{j}+2\hat{k})\left(\frac{1}{3}\hat{i}-\frac{2}{3}\hat{j}-\frac{2}{3}\hat{k}\right) = 2-2-\frac{4}{3} = -\frac{4}{3}$$

ILLUSTRATION 48: Express $\vec{b} = 2\hat{i}+\hat{j}-3\hat{k}$ as the sum of a vector parallel to $\vec{a} = 3\hat{i}-\hat{j}$ and a vector orthogonal to $\vec{a}$.

SOLUTION: $\vec{a}.\vec{b} = 6-1 = 5$ and $\vec{a}.\vec{a} = 9+1 = 10$

$$\vec{b} = \frac{\vec{b}.\vec{a}}{\vec{a}.\vec{a}}\vec{a} + \left(\vec{b} - \frac{\vec{b}.\vec{a}}{\vec{a}.\vec{a}}\vec{a}\right)$$

$$= \frac{5}{10}(3\hat{i}-\hat{j}) + \left(2\hat{i}+\hat{j}-3\hat{k} - \frac{5}{10}(3\hat{i}-\hat{j})\right) = \left(\frac{3}{2}\hat{i}-\frac{1}{2}\hat{j}\right)+\left(\frac{1}{2}\hat{i}+\frac{3}{2}\hat{j}-3\hat{k}\right)$$

Check: The first vector in the sum is parallel to $\vec{a}$ because it is $\frac{1}{2}\vec{a}$. The second vector in the sum is orthogonal to $\vec{a}$ becuase $\left(\frac{1}{2}\hat{i}+\frac{3}{2}\hat{j}-3\hat{k}\right).(3\hat{i}-\hat{j})=\frac{3}{2}-\frac{3}{2}=0$

ILLUSTRATION 49: Show that the perpendicular distance of a point with position vector $\vec{a}$ from the line $\vec{r}=\vec{b}+t\vec{c}$ is $\left|\vec{b}+\frac{(\vec{a}-\vec{b}).\vec{c}}{c^2}\vec{c}-\vec{a}\right|$

SOLUTION: Since the line passes through the point $R(\vec{b})$ and is parallel to vector $\vec{c}$; $\overrightarrow{QP}=\vec{a}-\vec{b}$

Now PR or RP = magnitude of the resolved part of $\overrightarrow{PQ}$ in direction perpendicular to $\vec{c}$

$$=\left|(\vec{a}-\vec{b})-\frac{(\vec{a}-\vec{b}).\vec{c}}{|\vec{c}|^2}\vec{c}\right|$$

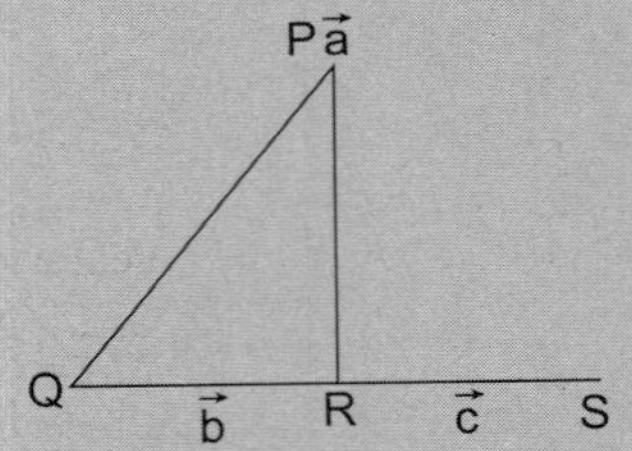

FIGURE 3.81

ILLUSTRATION 50: Prove by vector method that the middle point of the hypotenuse of a right angle triangle is equidistant from its vertices.

SOLUTION: Let ABC be a right angled triangle in which $\angle B = 90°$. Let E be the middle point by AC.

Let position vector of A and C be $\vec{b}$ and $\vec{c}$ with respect to B as origin of reference.

Hence $\vec{c}=\overrightarrow{BC}=\overrightarrow{BE}+\overrightarrow{EC}$ and $\vec{a}=\overrightarrow{BA}=\overrightarrow{BE}+\overrightarrow{EA}=\overrightarrow{BE}-\overrightarrow{AE}$

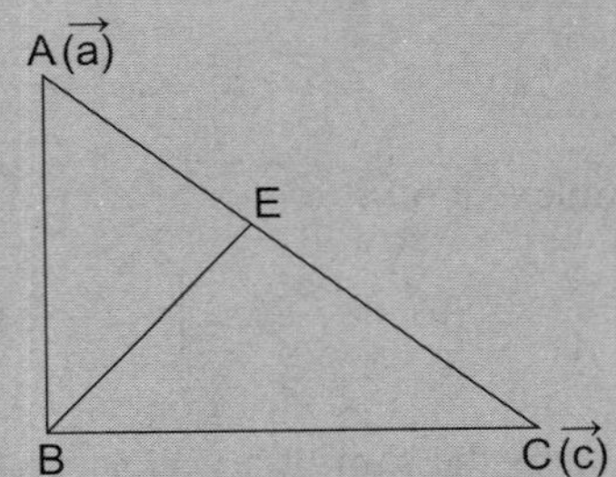

FIGURE 3.82

$\Rightarrow$ $\vec{a}=\overrightarrow{BE}-\overrightarrow{EC}$ [$\because$ $\overrightarrow{AE}=\overrightarrow{EC}$] $\Rightarrow$ $\vec{a}.\vec{c}=0=(\overrightarrow{BE}+\overrightarrow{EC}).(\overrightarrow{BE}-\overrightarrow{EC})=BE^2=EC^2$

$\Rightarrow$ $BE=EC=AE$ as E is mid-point of AC.

ILLUSTRATION 51: Prove that the sum of the squares of the diagonals of a paralleogram is equal to the sum of the squares of the sides.

SOLUTION: Let position vector of B and D be $\vec{b}$ and $\vec{d}$ with A as origin of refrence.

$\therefore$ $\overrightarrow{AC}=\vec{b}+\vec{d}$, $\overrightarrow{BD}=\vec{d}-\vec{b}$

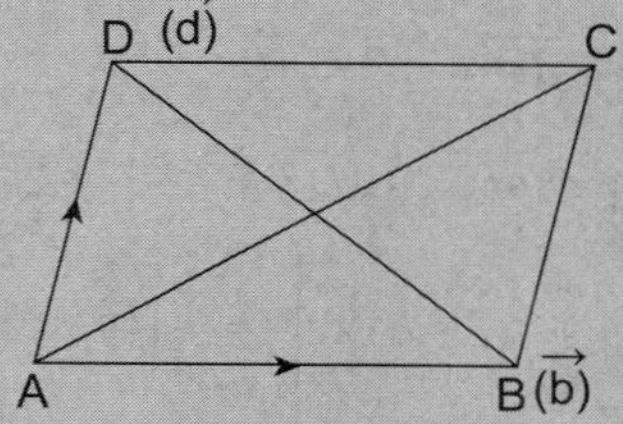

FIGURE 3.83

$$\therefore\ AC^2 + BD^2 = \overrightarrow{AC}^2 + \overrightarrow{BD}^2 = \vec{b}^2 + \vec{d}^2 + 2\vec{b}.\vec{d} + \vec{d}^2 + \vec{b}^2 - 2\vec{b}.\vec{d} = 2\,(b^2 + d^2)$$

$$= \overrightarrow{AB}^2 + \overrightarrow{BC}^2 + \overrightarrow{CD}^2 + \overrightarrow{DA}^2$$

ILLUSTRATION 52: For any triangle *ABC*, show that the perpendiculars from the vertices to the opposite sides are concurrent.

SOLUTION: Let *AD* and *BE* be the perpendicular from *A* and *B* to *BC* and *AC* respectively. Let *AD* and *BE* meet in *O*. Join *CO* and produce to meet *AB* in *F*. We have to prove that *CF* is perpendicular to *AB*. Let position vector of *A*, *B* and *C* with *O* as origin of reference be $\vec{a}, \vec{b}, \vec{c}$ is respectively.

Now $\overrightarrow{BC} = \vec{c} - \vec{b}$, $\overrightarrow{CA} = \vec{a} - \vec{c}$ Since $AD \perp BC$

$\therefore\ \vec{a}.(\vec{c} - \vec{b}) = 0 \Rightarrow \vec{a}.\vec{c} = \vec{a}.\vec{b}$ .... (i)

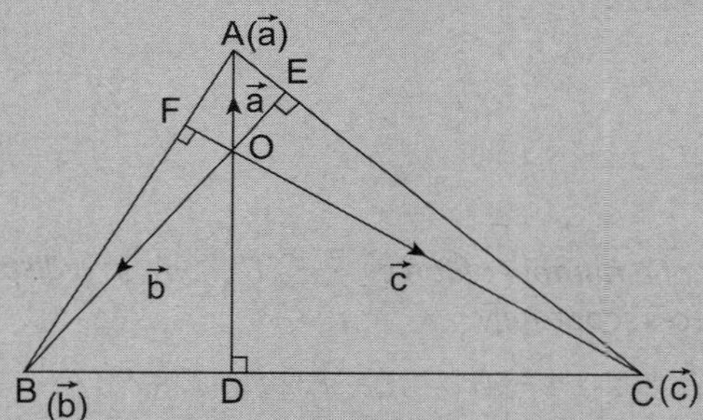

FIGURE 3.84

Similarly $\vec{b}.(\vec{a} - \vec{c}) \Rightarrow \vec{a}.\vec{c} = \vec{b}.\vec{c}$ .... (i)

From (i) and (ii) $\vec{a}.\vec{c} = \vec{b}.\vec{c} \Rightarrow (\vec{a} - \vec{b}).\,\vec{c} = 0 \Rightarrow BA \perp OC$, i.e., $BA \perp CF$

ILLUSTRATION 53: If *D* be the mid-point of the side *BC* of triangle *ABC*, show that $AB^2 + AC^2 = 2(AD^2 + BD^2)$

SOLUTION: Let *D* be the mid-point of *BC* and position vectors of points *B* and *C* be $\vec{b}$ and $\vec{c}$ with respect to *A* as origin of reference.

position vector of *D* is $\dfrac{\vec{b} + \vec{c}}{2}$

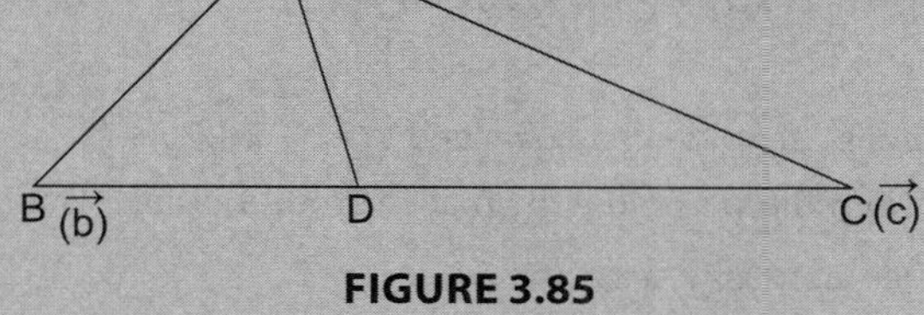

FIGURE 3.85

$\therefore\ \overrightarrow{AD} = \dfrac{\vec{b}+\vec{c}}{2}$; Again $\overrightarrow{BD} = \overrightarrow{AD} - \overrightarrow{AB} = \dfrac{\vec{b}+\vec{c}}{2} - \vec{b} = \dfrac{1}{2}(\vec{c}-\vec{b})$

Now $AB^2 + AC^2 = b^2 + c^2$ and $2\,(AD^2 + BD^2) = 2\,(\overrightarrow{AD}^2 + \overrightarrow{BD}^2)$

$$= 2\left[\left\{\frac{1}{2}(\vec{b}+\vec{c})\right\}^2 + \left\{\frac{1}{2}(\vec{c}-\vec{b})\right\}^2\right] = \frac{2}{4}[b^2 + c^2 + 2\vec{b}.\vec{c} + c^2 + b^2 - 2\vec{b}.\vec{c}] = b^2 + c^2$$

(c) Work Done: In day to day life, work means any activity that required muscular and mental effort. But in science this term refer to specifically to a force acting on a body and a subsequent displacement of the body. If a body moves a distance D in a straight line as a result of being acted upon upon by a force of fixed magnitude F in the direction of motion and the work W done by the force over the body is defined as

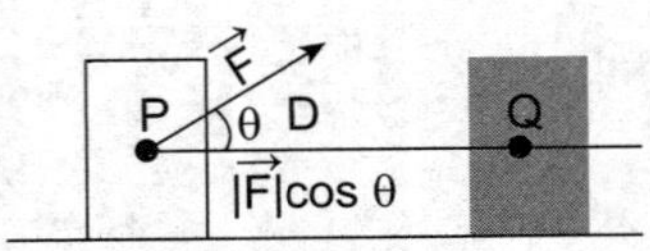

FIGURE 3.86

$W = FD$, but this formula holds only if the force is acting along the line of motion but if force F makes an object to move through a displacement $D\ (\overrightarrow{PQ})$ other than in the direction of the force, then the work is performed by the component of force in the direction of D and it can be defined as below:

Work = (scalar component of $\vec{F}$ in the direction of $\vec{D}$) (length of $\vec{D}$) $= (|\vec{F}|\cos\theta)\,|\vec{D}| = \vec{F}.\vec{D}$

It is also equal to $|\vec{F}|$ multiplied by component of displacement along the force.

NOTES

1. *The work done by the resultant of a number of forces $\vec{F}_1, \vec{F}_2, \vec{F}_3, \ldots, \vec{F}_n$ in a displacement $\vec{D}$ of a particle is equal to the sum of work done by the forces separately.*

   i.e., work done $= \vec{F}_1.\vec{D} + \vec{F}_2.\vec{D} + \vec{F}_3.\vec{D} + \ldots + \vec{F}_n.\vec{D} = (\vec{F}_1 + \vec{F}_2 + \vec{F}_3 + \ldots + \vec{F}_n).\vec{D} = \vec{R}.\vec{D}$; *where* $\vec{R} = \vec{F}_1 + \vec{F}_2 + \vec{F}_3 + \ldots + \vec{F}_n$

2. *The work done by a force $\vec{F}$ when its point of application experiences a number of consecutive displacements $\vec{D}_1, \vec{D}_2, \vec{D}_3, \ldots, \vec{D}_n$ is equal to the work done by the force in single displacement from the beginning to end.*

   i.e., work done $= \vec{F}.(\vec{D}_1 + \vec{D}_2 + \vec{D}_3 + \ldots + \vec{D}_n)$

   = The work done by the force $\vec{F}$ in the single displacement from the beginning to end.

ILLUSTRATION 54: If $|\vec{F}| = 40N$ (newtons), $|\vec{D}| = 3 = |\overrightarrow{PQ}|$ and $\theta = 60°$, then what will be the work done by $\vec{F}$ in acting from P to Q.

SOLULTION: Work $= |\vec{F}||\vec{D}|\cos\theta = (40)(3)\cos 60° = (120)\dfrac{1}{2} = 60\ J$ (joules)

ILLUSTRATION 55: Constant forces $\vec{P} = 2\hat{i} - 5\hat{j} + 6\hat{k}$ and $\vec{Q} = -\hat{i} + 2\hat{j} - \hat{k}$ act on a particle. Determine the work done when the particle is displaced from a point A with position vector $4\hat{i} - 3\hat{j} + 2\hat{k}$ to the point B having position vector $6\hat{i} + \hat{j} - 3\hat{k}$.

SOLUTION: Let $\vec{F}$ be the resultant force of $\vec{P}$ and $\vec{Q}$

$\therefore\ \vec{F} = \vec{P} + \vec{Q} = \hat{i} - 3\hat{j} + 5\hat{k}$

$\vec{d}$ = displacement $= 6\hat{i} + \hat{j} - 3\hat{k} - 4\hat{i} + 3\hat{j} - 2\hat{k} = 2\hat{i} + 4\hat{j} - 5\hat{k}$

$\therefore$ Work done $= \vec{F}.\vec{d} = (\hat{i} - 3\hat{j} + 5\hat{k})\cdot(2\hat{i} + 4\hat{j} - 5\hat{k}) = 2 - 12 - 25 = -35$ units

TEXTUAL EXERCISE 7: (SUBJECTIVE)

1. If $\vec{a} = \hat{i} + 2\hat{j} + \hat{k}$, $\vec{b} = -\hat{i} - 3\hat{j} + \hat{k}$ and $\vec{c} = 2\hat{i} + 3\hat{j}$, then find λ such that $(\vec{a} + \lambda\vec{b}) \perp \vec{c}$.
2. Find the angle between the vectors $2\hat{i} + \hat{j} - 3\hat{k}$ and $3\hat{i} - 2\hat{j} - \hat{k}$.
3. Find the vector $\vec{V}$ which is collinear with the vector $\vec{a} = 2\hat{i} + \hat{j} - \hat{k}$ and satisfies the condition $\vec{a}\,.\,\vec{V} = 3$.
4. Let $\vec{A} = \hat{i} + 2\hat{j} + 3\hat{k}$; $\vec{B} = -\hat{i} + 2\hat{j} + \hat{k}$ and $\vec{C} = 3\hat{i} + \hat{j}$. If $\vec{A} + t\vec{B}$ is perpendicular to $\vec{C}$, then find the value of t.
5. If the vectors $\hat{i} - 2x\hat{j} - 3y\hat{k}$ and $\hat{i} + 3x\hat{j} + 2y\hat{k}$ are orthogonal to each other, then find the locus of the point (x, y).
6. A vector $\vec{x}$ is co-planar with vectors $\vec{a} = -\hat{i} + \hat{j} + \hat{k}$ and $\vec{b} = 2\hat{i} + \hat{k}$ and is orthogonal to the vector $\vec{b}$. If $\vec{x}.\vec{a} = 7$ then find the vector $\vec{x}$.
7. Given a vector $\vec{A} = 3\hat{i} - \hat{j} + 5\hat{k}$ and $\vec{B} = \hat{i} + 2\hat{j} - 3\hat{k}$. If the vector $\vec{C}$ is perpendicular to the z-axis and satisfies the condition $\vec{C}\,.\,\vec{A} = 9$ and $\vec{C}\,.\,\vec{B} = -4$, then find vector $\vec{C}$
8. The three successive vertices of a parallelogram have the position vectors as, $A(-3, -2, 0)$; $B(3, -3, 1)$ and $C(5, 0, 2)$. Find the position vector of the fourth vertex D and the angle between $\overrightarrow{AC}$ and $\overrightarrow{BD}$
9. If e_1 and e_2 are two unit vectors such that $e_1 - e_2$ is also a unit vector, then find the angle θ between e_1 and e_2.
10. Find the scalar projection of $\hat{i} - 2\hat{j} + \hat{k}$ on $4\hat{i} - 4\hat{j} + 7\hat{k}$.
11. Find the work done in moving an object along the full lenghth of vector $2\hat{i} + 4\hat{j} - \hat{k}$ if the force applied is $\hat{i} + 3\hat{j} + 5\hat{k}$

Answer Key

1. 8/11 **2.** 60° **3.** $\hat{i} + \frac{\hat{j}}{2} - \frac{\hat{k}}{2}$ **4.** 5 **5.** a circle **6.** $-\frac{3}{2}\hat{i} + \frac{5}{2}\hat{j} + 3\hat{k}$ **7.** $2\hat{i} - 3\hat{j}$

8. $(-1, 1, 1)$; $\frac{2\pi}{3}$ **9.** 60° **10.** 19/9 **11.** 9 units

TEXTUAL EXERCISE 4: (OBJECTIVE)

1. If $|\vec{a}| = 5, |\vec{a} - \vec{b}| = 8$ and $|\vec{a} + \vec{b}| = 10$, then $|\vec{b}|$ is
   (a) 1 (b) $\sqrt{57}$
   (c) 3 (d) None of these
2. If $\vec{a} = 4\hat{i} + 6\hat{j}$ and $\vec{b} = 3\hat{j} + 4\hat{k}$, then the component of $\vec{a}$ along $\vec{b}$ is
   (a) $\frac{10}{10\sqrt{3}}(3\hat{j} + 4\hat{k})$ (b) $\frac{18}{25}(3\hat{j} + 4\hat{k})$
   (c) $\frac{9}{25}(3\hat{j} + 4\hat{k})$ (d) $(3\hat{j} + 4\hat{k})$

3. If vector $\vec{a} = 2\hat{i} - 3\hat{j} + 6\hat{k}$ and vector $\vec{b} = -2\hat{i} + 2\hat{j} - \hat{k}$, then $\dfrac{\text{projection of vector } \vec{a} \text{ on vector } \vec{b}}{\text{projection of vector } \vec{b} \text{ on vector } \vec{a}} =$

(a) $\dfrac{3}{7}$ (b) $\dfrac{7}{3}$

(c) 3 (d) 7

4. The vector $(\vec{a} + 3\vec{b})$ is perpendicular to $(7\vec{a} - 5\vec{b})$ and $(\vec{a} - 4\vec{b})$ is perpendicular to $(7\vec{a} - 2\vec{b})$. The angle between $\vec{a}$ and $\vec{b}$ is:

(a) 30° (b) 45°

(c) 60° (d) None of these

5. If $\vec{a}.\vec{b} = 0$ and $\vec{a} + \vec{b}$ makes an angle of 30° with $\vec{a}$, then

(a) $|\vec{b}| = 2|\vec{a}|$ (b) $|\vec{a}| = 2|\vec{b}|$

(c) $|\vec{a}| = |\vec{b}|$ (d) None of these

6. If force of magnitudes 6 and 7 units acting in the directions $\hat{i} - 2\hat{j} + 2\hat{k}$ and $2\hat{i} - 3\hat{j} - 6\hat{k}$ respectively act on a particle which is displaced from the point $P(2, -1, -3)$ to $Q(5, -1, 1)$, then the work done by the force is

(a) 4 units (b) – 4 units

(c) 7 units (d) –7 units

7. Let $\vec{a} = \hat{i} + \hat{j} + \hat{k}$, $\vec{c}$ is a vector such that $\vec{a}.\vec{c} = |\vec{c}|$ and $|\vec{a} + \vec{c}| = \sqrt{6}$, then $\vec{a} \cdot \vec{c}$ is equal to

(a) 1 (b) 5

(c) 3 (d) None of these

8. The position vectors of the vertices A, B and C of a triangle are three unit vectors $\hat{a}$, $\hat{b}$ and $\hat{c}$. A vector $\vec{d}$ is such that $\vec{d}.\hat{a} = \vec{d}.\hat{b} = \vec{d}.\hat{c}$ and $\vec{d} = \lambda(\hat{b} + \hat{c})$, then triangle ABC is

(a) acute angled (b) obtuse angled

(c) right angled (d) None of these

9. Angles between any two opposite edges of a regular tetrahedron are

(a) acute angle (b) obtuse angle

(c) right angle (d) reflexive angle

10. The value of c so that for all real x, the vectors $cx\hat{i} - 6\hat{j} + 3\hat{k}$, $x\hat{i} + 2\hat{j} + 2cx\hat{k}$ make an obtuse angle are

(a) $c < 0$ (b) $0 < c < \dfrac{4}{3}$

(c) $-\dfrac{4}{3} < c < 0$ (d) $c > 0$

11. The vector $\vec{v}$ is co-planar with the vectors $\hat{i} + \hat{j} - 2\hat{k}$ and $\hat{i} - 2\hat{j} + \hat{k}$ and is orthogonal to the vector $-2\hat{i} + \hat{j} + \hat{k}$ and it is given that the projection of $\vec{v}$ along the vector $\hat{i} - \hat{j} + \hat{k}$ is equal to $6\sqrt{3}$, then it is

(a) $9(-\hat{j} + \hat{k})$ (b) $3(-\hat{j} + \hat{k})$

(c) $6(-\hat{j} + \hat{k})$ (d) None of these

12. The two vectors $(x^2 - 1)\hat{i} + (x + 2)\hat{j} + x^2\hat{k}$ and $2\hat{i} - x\hat{j} + 3\hat{k}$ are orthogonal:

(a) for no real value of x

(b) for $x = -1$

(c) for $x = 1/2$

(d) for $x = -1/2$ and $x = 1$

13. If $\hat{a}, \hat{b}$ and $\hat{c}$ are unit vectors, then $|\hat{a} - \hat{b}|^2 + |\hat{b} - \hat{c}|^2 + |\hat{c} - \hat{a}|^2$ does not exceed

(a) 4 (b) 9

(c) 8 (d) 6

14. The values of x for which the angle between the vectors $\vec{a} = x\hat{i} - 3\hat{j} - \hat{k}$ and $\vec{b} = 2x\hat{i} + x\hat{j} - \hat{k}$ is acute, and the angle between the vector $\vec{b}$ and the axis of ordinates is obtuse, are

(a) 1, 2 (b) –2, –3

(c) all $x < 0$ (d) all $x > 0$

15. If a line has a vector equation $\vec{r} = 2\hat{i} + 6\hat{j} + \lambda(\hat{i} - 3\hat{j})$ then which of the following statements holds good?

(a) the line is parallel to $2\hat{i} + 6\hat{j}$

(b) the line passes through the point $3\hat{i} + 3\hat{j}$

(c) the line passes through the point $\hat{i} + 9\hat{j}$

(d) the line is parallel to xy plane

16. The vectors $\overrightarrow{AB} = 3\hat{i} - 2\hat{j} + 2\hat{k}$ and $\overrightarrow{BC} = -\hat{i} - 2\hat{k}$ are the adjacent sides of a parallelogram. The angle between its diagonals is

(a) $\pi/4$ (b) $\pi/3$

(c) $3\pi/4$ (d) $2\pi/3$

17. Let $\vec{a}, \vec{b}$ and $\vec{c}$ be three vectors such that $\vec{a} + \vec{b} + \vec{c} = 0$ and $|\vec{a}| = 3$, $|\vec{b}| = 5$, $|\vec{c}| = 7$. Then an angle between $\vec{a}$ and $\vec{b}$ is

(a) 15° (b) $\cos^{-1}\frac{2}{3}$

(c) 30° (d) 60°

18. One of the value of x for which the angle between $\vec{c}=x\hat{i}+\hat{j}+\hat{k}$ and $\vec{d}=i+x\hat{j}+\hat{k}$ is $\pi/3$ is

(a) $x = 1, 2$ (b) $x = 0, 4$

(c) $x = 3, 1$ (d) None of these

19. A vector of length $\sqrt{7}$ which is perpendicular to $2j - k$ and $-i + 2j - 3k$ and makes an obtuse angle with y-axis is

(a) $(1/\sqrt{5})(4i + j + k)$

(b) $(1/\sqrt{3})(4i - j - 2k)$

(c) $(1/\sqrt{3})(-4i + j + 2k)$

(d) $(1/\sqrt{3})(-4i - j + 2k)$

20. The angle between two diagonals of a cube is

(a) $\cos^{-1}\frac{1}{\sqrt{3}}$ (b) $\cos^{-1}\frac{2}{\sqrt{3}}$

(c) $\cos^{-1}\frac{1}{3}$ (d) $\cos^{-1}\frac{2}{3}$

21. If $\vec{a}$ and $\vec{b}$ are mutually perpendicular vectors, then $(\vec{a}+\vec{b})^2 =$

(a) $\vec{a}+\vec{b}$ (b) $\vec{a}-\vec{b}$

(c) $a^2 - b^2$ (d) $\left(\vec{a}-\vec{b}\right)^2$

22. If the vectors $\hat{i}-2x\hat{j}+3y\hat{k}$ and $\hat{i}+2x\hat{j}+3y\hat{k}$ are perpendicular, then the locus of (x, y) is

(a) a circle (b) an ellipse

(c) a hyperbola (d) None of these

23. $\left(\vec{a}.\vec{b}\right)\vec{c}$ and $\left(\vec{a}.\vec{c}\right)\vec{b}$ are

(a) Two like vectors

(b) Two equal vectors

(c) Two vectors in direction of $\vec{a}$

(d) None of these

24. Let $\vec{a}, \vec{b}$ and $\vec{c}$ be vectors with magnitudes 3, 4 and 5 respectively and $\vec{a}+\vec{b}+\vec{c}=\vec{o}$, then the values $\vec{a}.\vec{b}+\vec{b}.\vec{c}+\vec{c}.\vec{a}$ is

(a) 47 (b) 25

(c) 50 (d) –25

25. A particle acted on by constant forces $4\hat{i}+\hat{j}-3\hat{k}$ and $3\hat{i}+\hat{j}-\hat{k}$ is displaced from the point $\hat{i}+2\hat{j}+3\hat{k}$ to the point $5i + 4j + k$. The total work done by the force is

(a) 20 unit (b) 30 unit

(c) 40 unit (d) 50 unit

26. The number of vectors of unit length perpendicular to the vectors $\vec{a}=\hat{i}-\hat{j}$ and $\vec{b}=\hat{j}+\hat{k}$ is

(a) one (b) two

(c) three (d) infinite

27. Given the vectors $\vec{a}$ and $\vec{b}$, the angle between these equals 120°. If $|\vec{a}| = 3$ and $|\vec{b}| = 4$, then the length of the vector, $2\vec{a} - (3/2)\vec{b}$ is

(a) $6\sqrt{3}$ (b) $7\sqrt{2}$

(c) $4\sqrt{5}$ (d) None of these

28. If $|\vec{a}| = 11, |\vec{b}| = 23$, $\left|\vec{a}-\vec{b}\right| = 30$, then $\left|\vec{a}+\vec{b}\right|$ is:

(a) 10 (b) 20

(c) 30 (d) 40

29. The lengths of the diagonals of a parallelogram constructed on the vectors $\vec{p} = 2\vec{a} + \vec{b}$ and $\vec{q} = \vec{a} - 2\vec{b}$, where $\vec{a}$ and $\vec{b}$ are unit vectors forming an angle of 60° are:

(a) 3 and 4 (b) $\sqrt{7}$ and $\sqrt{13}$

(c) $\sqrt{5}$ and $\sqrt{11}$ (d) None of these

30. If $\vec{a}$ is perpendicular to $\vec{b}+\vec{c}$, $\vec{b}$ is perpendicular to $\vec{c}+\vec{a}$ and $\vec{c}$ is perpendicular to $\vec{a}+\vec{b}$ and $|\vec{a}| = |\vec{b}| = |2\vec{c}| = 3$, then $|\vec{a}+\vec{b}+\vec{c}|$ is

(a) 9/2 (b) $2\sqrt{3}$

(c) $\sqrt{14}$ (d) None of these

31. If $|\vec{a}| = 3$ and $|\vec{b}| = 4$. The value of l for which $(\vec{a} + l\vec{b})$ and $(\vec{a} - l\vec{b})$ are perpendicular is given by

(a) 3/4 (b) –2/3

(c) 2/3 (d) –3/4

32. A unit vector in $x - y$ plane which makes an angle of 45° with the vector $\hat{i}+\hat{j}$ and an angle of 60° with the vector $3\hat{i}-4\hat{j}$ is

(a) $\hat{i}$ (b) $\frac{\hat{i}+\hat{j}}{\sqrt{2}}$

(c) $\frac{\hat{i}-\hat{j}}{\sqrt{2}}$ (d) None of these

33. If $\hat{a}, \hat{b}, \hat{c}$ are three unit vectors such that $\hat{a}+\hat{b}+\hat{c}=\vec{0}$, then $\hat{a}.\hat{b}+\hat{b}.\hat{c}+\hat{c}.\hat{a}$ is equal to
(a) –3/2 (b) –1
(c) 0 (d) 3

34. If $\hat{x}$ and $\hat{y}$ are two unit vectors and ϕ is the angle between them, then $\frac{1}{2}|\hat{x}-\hat{y}|$ is
(a) 0 (b) $\frac{\phi}{2}$
(c) $\left|\sin\frac{\phi}{2}\right|$ (d) $\left|\cos\frac{\phi}{2}\right|$

Answer Key

1. (b)	**2.** (b)	**3.** (b)	**4.** (c)	**5.** (d)	**6.** (a)	**7.** (a)	**8.** (c)	**9.** (c)	**10.** (c)
11. (a)	**12.** (d)	**13.** (b)	**14.** (b, c)	**15.** (b,c,d)	**16.** (a, c)	**17.** (d)	**18.** (b)	**19.** (b)	**20.** (c)
21. (d)	**22.** (c)	**23.** (d)	**24.** (d)	**25.** (c)	**26.** (b)	**27.** (a)	**28.** (b)	**29.** (b)	**30.** (a)
31. (a,d)	**32.** (d)	**33.** (a)	**34.** (c)						

■ VECTOR PRODUCT (CROSS PRODUCT)

The cross product of two vectors is a vector quantity and it is also known as *vector product or skew product or outer product*. These are widely used to describe the tilt (inclination) of plane containing two vectors and effect of forces in study of electricity, magnetism, flow of fluids and orbital mechanics etc.

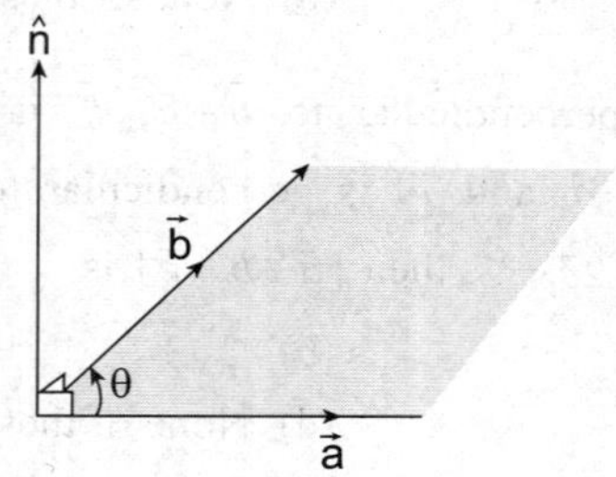

FIGURE 3.87

The vector product of two vectors $\vec{a}$ and $\vec{b}$, whose moduli are $|\vec{a}|$ and $|\vec{b}|$ respectively, is the vector whose modulus is $ab\sin\theta$, where θ $(0<\theta<\pi)$ is angle between vectors $\vec{a}$ and $\vec{b}$. And the direction is that of a unit vector $\hat{n}$ perpendicular to both $\vec{a}$ and $\vec{b}$ such that $\vec{a}$, $\vec{b}$, $\hat{n}$ are in right handed orientation.By the right handed orientation we mean that if we turn the vector $\vec{a}$ into the vector $\vec{b}$ through the angle θ, then $\hat{n}$ points in the direction in which a right handed screw would move if turned in the same manner.

$$\vec{a}\times\vec{b}=|\vec{a}||\vec{b}|\sin\theta\,\hat{n}$$

$$\Rightarrow |\vec{a}\times\vec{b}|=|\vec{a}||\vec{b}|\sin\theta$$

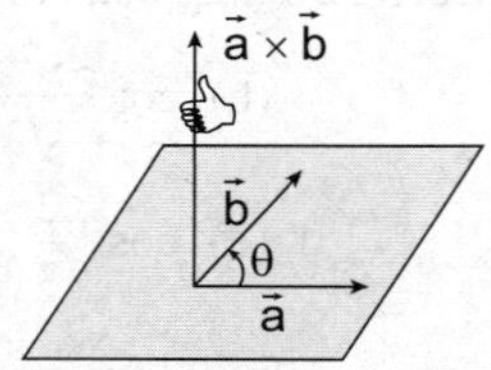

Construction of ā × b

FIGURE 3.88

$$\Rightarrow \quad \vec{a}\times\vec{b}=\vec{0} \quad \Rightarrow \vec{a}=\vec{0}, \text{ or } \vec{b}=\vec{0} \text{ or } \vec{a}\parallel\vec{b}$$

Construction of $\vec{a}\times\vec{b}$

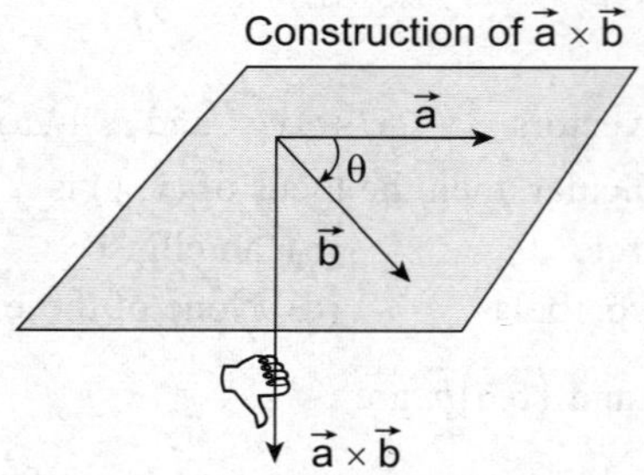

FIGURE 3.89

■ PROPERTIES OF VECTOR PRODUCT

1. Anticommutative: $\vec{a}\times\vec{b}=-(\vec{b}\times\vec{a})$
2. $(m\vec{a})\times\vec{b}=m(\vec{a}\times\vec{b})=\vec{a}\times(m\vec{b})$;(*where m is a scalar*)
3. If two vectors $\vec{a}$ and $\vec{b}$ are parallel, we have $\vec{a}\times\vec{b}=\vec{0}$
4. $\vec{a}\times\vec{b}=\vec{0}\Rightarrow\vec{a}$ and $\vec{b}$ are parallel vectors (*provided $\vec{a}$ and $\vec{b}$ are both non-zero vectors*)
5. $\vec{a}\times\vec{b}=|\vec{a}||\vec{b}|\hat{n}\Rightarrow\vec{a}\perp\vec{b}$

6. $\hat{i}\times\hat{i}=\hat{j}\times\hat{j}=\hat{k}\times\hat{k}=\vec{0}$

7. $\hat{i}\times\hat{j}=\hat{k}=-(\hat{j}\times\hat{i})$

8. $\hat{j}\times\hat{k}=\hat{i}=-(\hat{k}\times\hat{j})$

9. $(\hat{k}\times\hat{i})=\hat{j}=-(\hat{i}\times\hat{k})$

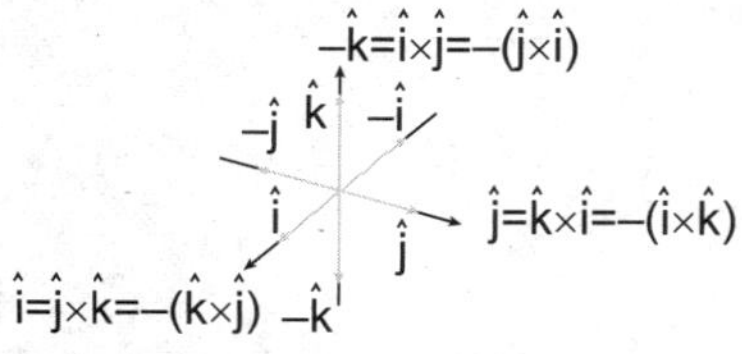

FIGURE 3.90

10. Cross product is distributive over addition or substraction i.e., $\vec{a}\times(\vec{b}\pm\vec{c})=(\vec{a}\times\vec{b})\pm(\vec{a}\times\vec{c})$

11. Cross product of three vectors is not associative

12. Let $\vec{a}=a_1\hat{i}+a_2\hat{j}+a_3\hat{k}$ and $\vec{b}=b_1\hat{i}+b_2\hat{j}+b_3\hat{k}$

$$\Rightarrow \vec{a}\times\vec{b}=\begin{vmatrix}\hat{i} & \hat{j} & \hat{k}\\ a_1 & a_2 & a_3\\ b_1 & b_2 & b_3\end{vmatrix}$$

$$=\hat{i}\,(a_2b_3-a_3b_2)+\hat{j}\,(a_3b_1-a_1b_3)+\hat{k}\,(a_1b_2-a_2b_1)$$

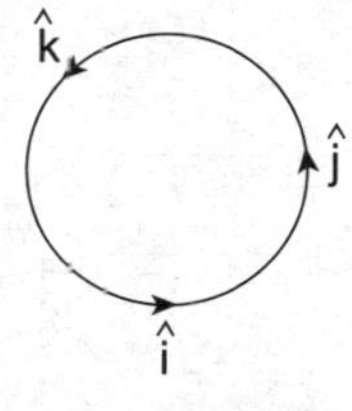

FIGURE 3.91

13. $\sin\theta=\dfrac{|\vec{a}\times\vec{b}|}{|\vec{a}||\vec{b}|}$

NOTES

We can't find the value of θ by using cross product, but we can find the value of sin θ give, by $\sin\theta=\dfrac{|\vec{a}\times\vec{b}|}{|\vec{a}||\vec{b}|}$ *as θ may be* $\sin^{-1}\dfrac{|\vec{a}\times\vec{b}|}{|\vec{a}||\vec{b}|}$ *or* $\pi-\sin^{-1}\dfrac{|\vec{a}\times\vec{b}|}{|\vec{a}||\vec{b}|}$

Geometrical interpretation

The magnitude of the vector product of two vectors is the area of a parallelogram whose adjacent sides are represented by two vectors $\vec{a}$ and $\vec{b}$.

$$|\vec{a}\times\vec{b}|=|\vec{a}||\vec{b}|\sin\theta$$

$$=(OA)\,(OB)\sin\theta$$

= area of the parallelogram $OACB$

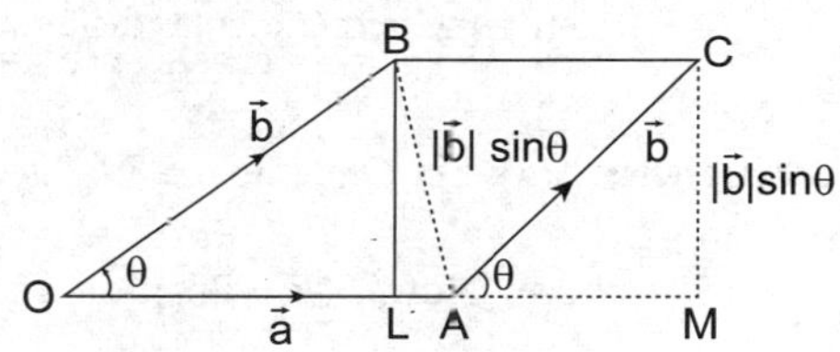

FIGURE 3.92

$\therefore$ Area of $\Delta\, OAB=\dfrac{1}{2}|\vec{a}\times\vec{b}|$

ILLUSTRATION 56: Find a unit vector perpendicular to the plane through the points $P(1, -1, 0)$, $Q(2, 1, -1)$ and $R(-1, 1, 2)$.

SOLUTION: The vector $\overrightarrow{PQ}\times\overrightarrow{PR}$ is perpendicular to the plane because it is perpendicular to both vectors. In terms of components

$$\overrightarrow{PQ}=(2-1)\,\hat{i}+(1+1)\,\hat{j}+(-1-0)\,\hat{k}=\hat{i}+2\hat{j}-\hat{k}$$

$$\overrightarrow{PR}=(-1-1)\,\hat{i}+(1+1)\,\hat{j}+(2-0)\,\hat{k}=-2\hat{i}+2\hat{j}+2\hat{k}$$

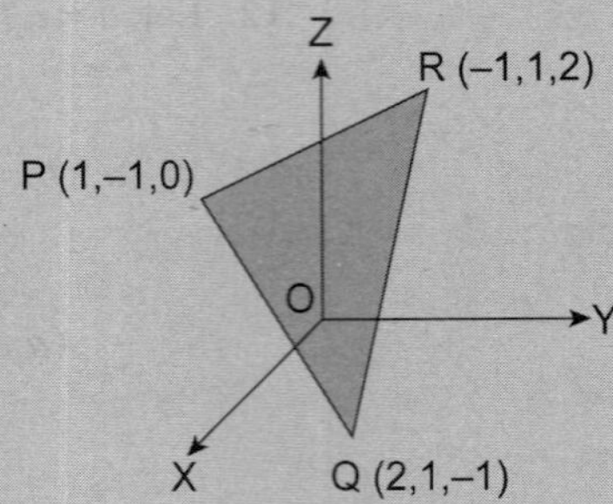

FIGURE 3.93

$$\overrightarrow{PQ}\times\overrightarrow{PR} = \begin{vmatrix} \hat{i} & \hat{j} & \hat{k} \\ 1 & 2 & -1 \\ -2 & 2 & 2 \end{vmatrix} = \begin{vmatrix} 2 & -1 \\ 2 & 2 \end{vmatrix}\hat{i} - \begin{vmatrix} 1 & -1 \\ -2 & 2 \end{vmatrix}\hat{j} + \begin{vmatrix} 1 & 2 \\ -2 & 2 \end{vmatrix}\hat{k} = 6\hat{i}+6\hat{k}$$

$\Rightarrow$ Unit vector perpendicular to plane $= \dfrac{1}{6\sqrt{2}}(6\hat{i}+6\hat{k}) = \dfrac{1}{\sqrt{2}}(\hat{i}+\hat{k})$

ILLUSTRATION 57: Find the area of the triangle with vertices $P(1, -1, 0)$, $Q(2, 1, -1)$ and $R(-1, 1, 2)$.

SOLUTION: The area of the parallelogram determined by P, Q, R is $\overrightarrow{PQ}\times\overrightarrow{PR} = |6\hat{i}+6\hat{k}| = \sqrt{(6)^2+(6)^2}$ $= 6\sqrt{2}$ square units. The triangle area is half of this or $3\sqrt{2}$ square units

ILLUSTRATION 58: $\vec{a}, \vec{b}, \vec{c}$ be the position vectors of vertices A, B, and C of ΔABC respectively then, prove that:

(a) area of the $\Delta ABC = \dfrac{1}{2}\left|(\vec{a}\times\vec{b})+(\vec{b}\times\vec{c})+(\vec{c}\times\vec{a})\right|$

(b) condition that point A lies on the base BC of $\Delta\, ABC$ is $(\vec{a}\times\vec{b})+(\vec{b}\times\vec{c})+(\vec{c}\times\vec{a}) = \overrightarrow{0}$

(c) the perpendicular distance of the point C from the line joining A and B is $\dfrac{|\vec{a}\times\vec{b}+\vec{b}\times\vec{c}+\vec{c}\times\vec{a}|}{|\vec{b}-\vec{a}|}$

SOLUTION: (a) Let O be the origin. Area of $\Delta ABC = \dfrac{1}{2}|\overrightarrow{AB}\times\overrightarrow{AC}|$

Now, $\overrightarrow{AB}$ = Position vector of B – Position vector of $A \Rightarrow \overrightarrow{AB} = \vec{b}-\vec{a}$

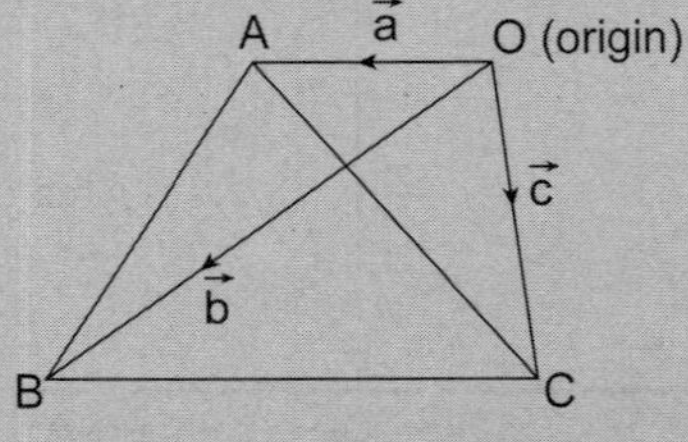

FIGURE 3.94

$\overrightarrow{AC}$ = Position vector of C – Position vector of A

$\Rightarrow \overrightarrow{AC} = \vec{c}-\vec{a}$ $\qquad\Rightarrow \overrightarrow{AB}\times\overrightarrow{AC} = (\vec{b}-\vec{a})\times(\vec{c}-\vec{a})$

$= \vec{b}\times\vec{c}-\vec{b}\times\vec{a}-\vec{a}\times\vec{c}+\vec{a}\times\vec{a} = \vec{a}\times\vec{b}+\vec{b}\times\vec{c}+\vec{c}\times\vec{a} \qquad (\because\ \vec{a}\times\vec{a}=\vec{0})$

Hence, area of $\Delta ABC = \dfrac{1}{2}|\overrightarrow{AB}\times\overrightarrow{AC}| = \dfrac{1}{2}|\vec{a}\times\vec{b}+\vec{b}\times\vec{c}+\vec{c}\times\vec{a}|$

(b) If the points A, B, C are collinear, then area of $\Delta ABC = 0$

$$\Rightarrow -|\vec{a}\times\vec{b}+\vec{b}\times\vec{c}+\vec{c}\times\vec{a}|=0$$

$$\Rightarrow |\vec{a}\times\vec{b}+\vec{b}\times\vec{c}+\vec{c}\times\vec{a}|=\vec{0} \quad \Rightarrow \vec{a}\times\vec{b}+\vec{b}\times\vec{c}-\vec{c}\times\vec{a}=\vec{0}$$

Thus $\vec{a}\times\vec{b}+\vec{b}\times\vec{c}+\vec{c}\times\vec{a}=\vec{0}$ is the required condition for collinearity of three points with position vectors $\vec{a}$, $\vec{b}$ and $\vec{c}$

(c) Let ABC be a triangle and let $\vec{a}$, $\vec{b}$ and $\vec{c}$ be the position vector of its vertices A, B and C respectively. Let CM be the perpendicular from C on AB.

Then, area of $\Delta ABC = \frac{1}{2}(AB).(CM) = \frac{1}{2}|\overrightarrow{AB}||\overrightarrow{CM}|$

Also, area of $\Delta ABC = \frac{1}{2}|\vec{a}\times\vec{b}+\vec{b}\times\vec{c}+\vec{c}\times\vec{a}|$

$$\therefore \quad \frac{1}{2}|\overrightarrow{AB}||\overrightarrow{CM}| = \frac{1}{2}|\vec{a}\times\vec{b}+\vec{b}\times\vec{c}+\vec{c}\times\vec{a}| \quad \Rightarrow CM = \frac{|\vec{a}\times\vec{b}+\vec{b}\times\vec{c}+\vec{c}\times\vec{a}|}{|\vec{b}-\vec{a}|}$$

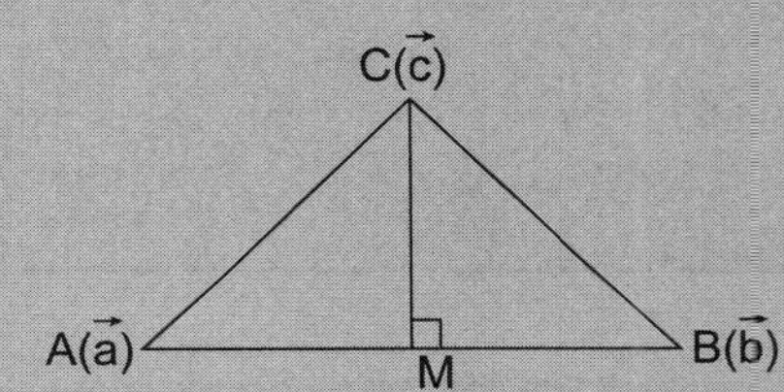

FIGURE 3.95

ILLUSTRATION 59: Show that $(\vec{a}-\vec{b})\times(\vec{a}+\vec{b}) = 2(\vec{a}\times\vec{b})$ and interpret the result geometrically.

SOLUTION: $(\vec{a}-\vec{b})\times(\vec{a}+\vec{b}) = \vec{a}\times\vec{a}+\vec{a}\times\vec{b}-\vec{b}\times\vec{a}-\vec{b}\times\vec{b} = \vec{0}+\vec{a}\times\vec{b}-(-\vec{a}\times\vec{b})-\vec{0} = 2(\vec{a}\times\vec{b})$

Interpretation: Let $ABCD$ be a parallelogram whose diagonals intersect at O.

Let $\overrightarrow{AO}=\vec{a}=\overrightarrow{OC}$ and $\overrightarrow{OD}=\vec{b}$ $\qquad \therefore \quad \overrightarrow{OB}=-\vec{b}$

Now $\overrightarrow{AB}=\vec{a}-\vec{b}$; $\overrightarrow{AD}=\vec{a}+\vec{b}$; $\overrightarrow{AB}\times\overrightarrow{AD}=(\vec{a}-\vec{b})\times(\vec{a}+\vec{b})$

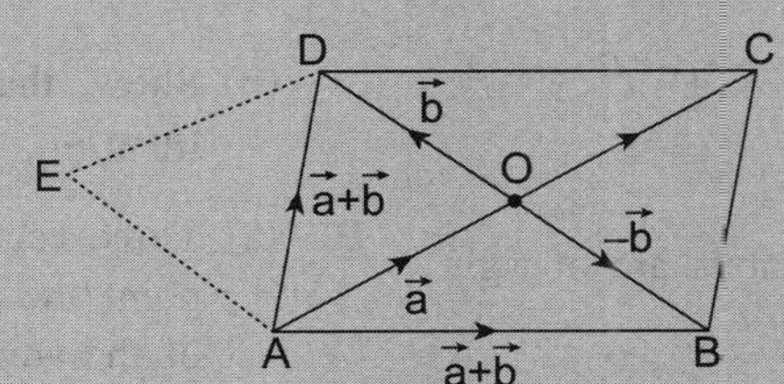

FIGURE 3.96

= area of parallelogram $ABCD$

Fuctor, $\vec{a}\times\vec{b}$ = area of parallelogram whose adjacent sides are $\vec{a}$ and $\vec{b}$

Hence, area of parallelogram $ABCD$ is equal to twice the area of the parallelogram whose adjacent sides are semi diagonals of palallelogram $ABCD$, i.e., as $(ABCD) = 2ar\,.\,(AODE)$.

ILLUSTRATION 60: If $\vec{a}$, $\vec{b}$ and $\vec{c}$ are three non-zero vectors such that $\vec{a}\times\vec{b}=\vec{c}$ and $\vec{b}\times\vec{c}=\vec{a}$, prove that $\vec{a}$, $\vec{b}$ and $\vec{c}$ are mutually at right angles and $|\vec{b}|=1$ and $|\vec{c}|=|\vec{a}|$.

SOLUTION: $\vec{a}\times\vec{b}=\vec{c}$ and $\vec{b}\times\vec{c}=\vec{a} \Rightarrow \vec{c}\perp\vec{a}, \vec{c}\perp\vec{b}$ and $\vec{a}\perp\vec{b}, \vec{a}\perp\vec{c}$

$\Rightarrow \vec{a}\perp\vec{b}, \vec{b}\perp\vec{c}$ and $\vec{c}\perp\vec{a}$

$\Rightarrow \vec{a}, \vec{b}$ and $\vec{c}$ are mutually perpendicular vectors

Again $\vec{a}\times\vec{b}=\vec{c}$ and $\vec{b}\times\vec{c}=\vec{a}$ $\Rightarrow |\vec{a}\times\vec{b}|=|\vec{c}|$ and $|\vec{b}\times\vec{c}|=|\vec{a}|$

$\Rightarrow |\vec{a}||\vec{b}|\sin\frac{\pi}{2}=|\vec{c}|$ and $|\vec{b}||\vec{c}|\sin\frac{\pi}{2}=|\vec{a}| \Rightarrow |\vec{a}||\vec{b}|=|\vec{c}|$ and $|\vec{b}||\vec{c}|=|\vec{a}|$

$\Rightarrow |\vec{b}|^2|\vec{c}|=|\vec{c}| \Rightarrow |\vec{b}|^2=1 \Rightarrow |\vec{b}|=1$ putting in $|\vec{a}||\vec{b}|=|\vec{c}| \Rightarrow |\vec{a}|=|\vec{c}|$

ILLUSTRATION 61: Find the moment of the couple consisting of the force $\vec{F}=3\hat{i}+2\hat{j}-\hat{k}$ acting through the point $\hat{i}-\hat{j}+\hat{k}$ and force $-\vec{F}$ acting through the point $2\hat{i}-3\hat{j}-\hat{k}$

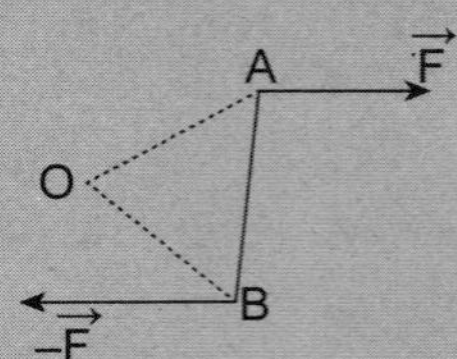

FIGURE 3.97

SOLUTION: Let $\overline{OA}=\hat{i}-\hat{j}+\hat{k}$ and $\overline{OB}=2\hat{i}-3\hat{j}-\hat{k}$,

then $\overline{BA}=\overline{OA}-\overline{OB}=(\hat{i}-\hat{j}+\hat{k})-(2\hat{i}-3\hat{j}-\hat{k})=-\hat{i}+2\hat{j}+2\hat{k}$

$\therefore$ Moment of the couple $=\overline{BA}\times\vec{F}=\begin{vmatrix}\hat{i} & \hat{j} & \hat{k}\\ -1 & 2 & 2\\ 3 & 2 & -1\end{vmatrix}=-6\hat{i}+5\hat{j}-8\hat{k}$

TEXTUAL EXERCISE 8: (SUBJECTIVE)

1. Find a unit vector perpendicular to both $6\hat{i}+2\hat{j}+3\hat{k}$ and $3\hat{i}-2\hat{k}$

2. Find the area of parallelogram whose diagonals are $3\hat{i}+\hat{j}-2\hat{k}$ and $\hat{i}-3\hat{j}+4\hat{k}$

3. Let $\vec{A},\vec{B}$ and $\vec{C}$ be unit vectors. Suppose that $\vec{A}.\vec{B}=\vec{A}.\vec{C}=0$ and that the angle between $\vec{B}$ and $\vec{C}$ is $\frac{\pi}{6}$, then prove that $\vec{A}=\pm 2(\vec{B}\times\vec{C})$

4. Show that the diagonals of a rhombus are at right angles using vector method.

5. Show that the angle in a semi-circle is a right angle.

6. Prove that in any parallelogram the difference of squares of the diagonals is four times the rectangle constructed by either of these sides and projection of the other upon it.

7. In any triangle, show that the perpendicular bisectors of the sides are concurrent.

8. If $\vec{a}$ and $\vec{b}$ are diagonals of a parallelogram, then find its adjacent sides and hence show that its area is equal to $(\vec{a}\times\vec{b})/2$ and that the result of area is also valid for general quadrilateral.

9. (a) *ABCD* is a quadrilateral such that $\overline{AB}=\vec{b}$, $\overline{AD}=\vec{d}$ and $\overline{AC}=m\vec{b}+n\vec{d}$. Show that the area of the quadrilateral *ABCD* is $1/2\,|(m+n)|\,|\vec{b}\times\vec{d}|$

   (b) Show that $(\vec{a}\times\vec{b})^2=\vec{a}^2\vec{b}^2-(\vec{a}.\vec{b})^2$ (Lagrange's Identity)

10. (a) Three vectors of magnitudes *a*, 2*a*, 3*a* meet in a point and their directions are along the diagonals of the adjacent faces of a cube. Determine their resultant and its direction cosines.

    (b) Use the unit vectors
    $\vec{p}=\cos\theta\hat{i}+\sin\theta\hat{j}$ and $\vec{q}=\cos\phi\hat{i}+\sin\phi\hat{j}$
    to prove the identities
    $\sin(\theta\pm\phi)=\sin\theta\cos\phi\pm\cos\theta\sin\phi$

11. (a) For non-collinear, non-zero vectors, if $\vec{a}+\vec{b}+\vec{c}=\vec{0}$, then show that $\vec{b}\times\vec{c}=\vec{c}\times\vec{a}=\vec{a}\times\vec{b}$ and show that $\frac{\sin A}{a}=\frac{\sin B}{b}=\frac{\sin C}{c}$

(b) If $\vec{a},\vec{b},\vec{c}$ are the position vectors of the vertices of a triangle *ABC*, show that $\frac{1}{2}\left[\vec{b}\times\vec{c}+\vec{c}\times\vec{a}+\vec{a}\times\vec{b}\right]$ gives the vector perpendicular to the plane of triangle and represents the area (vectorial) of the triangle. Hence deduce the condition that the three points are collinear if $\vec{b}\times\vec{c}+\vec{c}\times\vec{a}+\vec{a}\times\vec{b}=\vec{0}$. Also find the unit vector normal to the plane of the triangle with vertices (1, 1, 1) (0, 0, 0) and (0, 1, 1,).

Answer Key

1. $\pm\frac{4\hat{i}-21\hat{j}+6\hat{k}}{\sqrt{493}}$ **2.** $5\sqrt{3}$ **8.** $\frac{\vec{a}+\vec{b}}{2},\frac{\vec{a}-\vec{b}}{2}$ **10. (a)** $\frac{a}{\sqrt{2}}\left(5\hat{i}+4\hat{j}+3\hat{k}\right)$ **11. (b)** $\pm\frac{\hat{j}-\hat{k}}{\sqrt{2}}$

TEXTUAL EXERCISE 5: (OBJECTIVE)

1. If $\vec{u}=\vec{a}-\vec{b}$, $\vec{v}=\vec{a}+\vec{b}$ and $|\vec{a}|=|\vec{b}|=2$, then $|\vec{u}\times\vec{v}|$ is

(a) $2\sqrt{16-(\vec{a}\cdot\vec{b})^2}$ (b) $2\sqrt{4-(\vec{a}\cdot\vec{b})^2}$

(c) $\sqrt{16-(\vec{a}\cdot\vec{b})^2}$ (d) $\sqrt{4-(\vec{a}\cdot\vec{b})^2}$

2. If $\vec{a}=2\hat{i}+3\hat{j}-\hat{k}$, $\vec{b}=-\hat{i}+2\hat{j}-4\hat{k}$ and $\vec{c}=\hat{i}+\hat{j}+\hat{k}$, then $(\vec{a}\times\vec{b})\,.\,(\vec{a}\times\vec{c})$

(a) 60 (b) 64

(c) 74 (d) –74

3. If $|\vec{a}.\vec{b}|=|\vec{a}\times\vec{b}|$, then the angle between $\vec{a}$ and $\vec{b}$ is:

(a) 0° (b) 180°

(c) 135° (d) 45°

4. $(\vec{a}\times\vec{b})^2$ + $(\vec{a}.\vec{b})^2$ is equal to

(a) 0 (b) $(\vec{a}^2\vec{b}^2)$

(c) $(|\vec{a}|+|\vec{b}|)^2$ (d) 1

5. If the position vectors of three points *A*, *B*, *C* are respectively $\hat{i}+\hat{j}+\hat{k}$, $2\hat{i}+3\hat{j}-4\hat{k}$ and $7\hat{i}+4\hat{j}+9\hat{k}$, then the unit vector perpendicular to the plane of triangle *ABC* is

(a) $31\hat{i}-18\hat{j}-9\hat{k}$ (b) $\frac{31\hat{i}-38\hat{j}-9\hat{k}}{\sqrt{2486}}$

(c) $\frac{31\hat{i}+18\hat{j}+9\hat{k}}{\sqrt{2486}}$ (d) None of these.

6. If $\vec{a}\times\vec{b}=\vec{c}\times\vec{d}$ and $\vec{a}\times\vec{c}=\vec{b}\times\vec{d}$, then the vectors $\vec{a}-\vec{d}$ and $\vec{b}-\vec{c}$ are:

(a) collinear (b) linearly independent

(c) perpendicular (d) parallel

7. $\vec{c},\vec{a}\neq\vec{0}$ if $\vec{a}.\vec{b}=\vec{a}.\vec{c}$ and $\vec{a}\times\vec{b}=\vec{a}\times\vec{c}$, then

(a) $\vec{b}=\vec{c}$ (b) $\vec{b}=\vec{0}$

(c) $\vec{b}+\vec{c}=\vec{0}$ (d) None of these

8. The value of $\left|\vec{a}\times\hat{i}\right|^2+\left|\vec{a}\times\hat{j}\right|^2+\left|\vec{a}\times\hat{k}\right|^2$ equals

(a) $|\vec{a}|^2$ (b) $2|\vec{a}|^2$

(c) $3|\vec{a}|^2$ (d) $6|\vec{a}|^2$

9. If $|\vec{a}|=4$, $|\vec{b}|=2$ and the angle between $\vec{a}$ and $\vec{b}$ is $\pi/6$, then $(\vec{a}\times\vec{b})^2$ is

(a) 48 (b) $(\vec{a})^2$

(c) 16 (d) 32

10. Let $\hat{a}$ and $\hat{b}$ be two non-collinear unit vectors. If $\vec{u}=\hat{a}-(\hat{a}.\hat{b})\hat{b}$ and $\vec{v}=\hat{a}\times\vec{b}$, then $|\vec{v}|$ is

(a) $|\vec{u}|$ (b) $|\vec{u}|+\vec{v}.\hat{a}$

(c) $|\vec{u}|-\vec{u}.\hat{b}$ (d) $|\vec{u}|+\vec{u}.(\hat{a}+\hat{b})$

11. In the adjacent figure, *AB*, *DE* and *GF* are parallel to each other and *AD*, *BG* and *EF* are parallel to each other. If *CD*: *CE* = *CG*: *CB* = 2 : 1, then the value of area (ΔAEG): area (ΔABD) is equal to

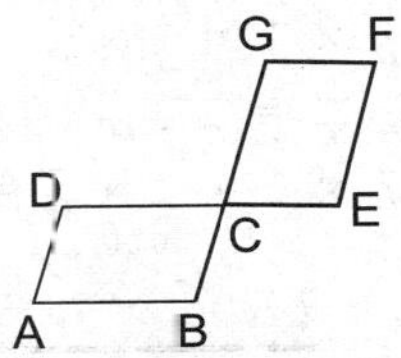

FIGURE 3.98

(a) 7/2 (b) 3

(c) 4 (d) 9/2

12. A rigid body rotates with constant angular velocity ω about the line whose vector equation is, $\vec{r} = \lambda(\hat{i} + 2\hat{j} + 2\hat{k})$. The speed of the particle at the instant it passes through the point with position vector $2\hat{i} + 3\hat{j} + 2\hat{k}$ is
(a) $\omega\sqrt{2}$ (b) 2ω
(c) $\frac{\omega}{\sqrt{2}}$ (d) None of these

13. If $\vec{a}, \vec{b}, \vec{c}$ are three mutually perpendicular vectors, then the projection of the vector $\left(\ell\frac{\vec{a}}{|\vec{a}|} + m\frac{\vec{b}}{|\vec{b}|} + n\frac{(\vec{a}\times\vec{b})}{|\vec{a}\times\vec{b}|}\right)$ along bisector of the vectors $\vec{a}$ and $\vec{b}$ may be given by
(a) $\frac{l^2+m^2}{\sqrt{l^2+m^2+n^2}}$ (b) $\sqrt{l^2+m^2+n^2}$
(c) $\frac{\sqrt{l^2+m^2}}{\sqrt{l^2+m^2+n^2}}$ (d) $\frac{l+m}{\sqrt{2}}$

14. Let $\vec{a}$ and $\vec{b}$ be non-collinear vectors of which $\vec{a}$ is a unit vector. The angles of the triangle whose two sides are represented by $\sqrt{3}(\vec{a}\times\vec{b})$ and $\vec{b} - (\vec{a}.\vec{b})\vec{a}$ by
(a) $\frac{\pi}{2}, \frac{\pi}{3}, \frac{\pi}{6}$ (b) $\frac{\pi}{2}, \frac{\pi}{4}, \frac{\pi}{4}$
(c) $\frac{\pi}{3}, \frac{\pi}{3}, \frac{\pi}{3}$ (d) data insufficient

15. If $\vec{a}$ and $\vec{b}$ are two vectors such that $\vec{a}.\vec{b} = \vec{0}$ and $\vec{a}\times\vec{b} = \vec{0}$, then
(a) $\vec{a}$ is parallel to $\vec{b}$
(b) $\vec{a}$ is perpendicular to $\vec{b}$
(c) either $\vec{a}$ or $\vec{b}$ is a null vector
(d) None of these

16. If the vector $\vec{a}, \vec{b}$ and $\vec{c}$ form the sides BC, CA and AB respectively of a triangle ABC, then
(a) $\vec{a}\cdot\vec{b} + \vec{b}\cdot\vec{c} + \vec{c}\cdot\vec{a} = \vec{0}$
(b) $\vec{a}\times\vec{b} = \vec{b}\times\vec{c} = \vec{c}\times\vec{a}$
(c) $\vec{a}\cdot\vec{b} = \vec{b}\cdot\vec{c} = \vec{c}\cdot\vec{a}$
(d) $\vec{a}\times\vec{b} + \vec{b}\times\vec{c} + \vec{c}\times\vec{a} = \vec{0}$

17. For non-zero distinct a, b, c, $\hat{x}$ and $\hat{y}$ are two mutually perpendicular unit vectors. If the vectors $a\hat{x} + a\hat{y} + c(\hat{x}\times\hat{y})$, $\hat{x} + (\hat{x}\times\hat{y})$ and $c\hat{x} + c\hat{y} + b(\hat{x}\times\hat{y})$ lie in a plane, then c is
(a) arithmetic mean of a and b
(b) geometric mean of a and b
(c) harmonic mean of a and b
(d) None of these

18. If $\vec{a} = \hat{i} - \hat{j} + \hat{k}, \vec{a}.\vec{b} = 0, \vec{a}\times\vec{b} = \vec{c}$, where $\vec{c} = -2\hat{i} - \hat{j} + \hat{k}$, then $\vec{b}$ =
(a) (1, 0, –1) (b) (0, 1, 1)
(c) (–1, –1, 0) (d) (–1, 0, 1)

19. Let $\vec{a}$, $\vec{b}$ and $\vec{c}$ be three non-zero vectors, no two of which are collinear and the vector $\vec{a}+\vec{b}$ is collinear with $\vec{c}$ while $\vec{b}+\vec{c}$ is collinear with $\vec{a}$, then $\vec{a}+\vec{b}+\vec{c} =$
(a) $\vec{a}$ (b) $\vec{b}$
(c) $\vec{0}$ (d) None of these

20. If the magnitude of moment about the point $\vec{j}+\vec{k}$ of a force $\vec{i} + a\vec{j} - \vec{k}$ acting through the point $\vec{i}+\vec{j}$ is $\sqrt{8}$, then the value of a is
(a) 1 (b) 2
(c) 3 (d) 4

21. If $\vec{a}, \vec{b}$ and $\vec{c}$ are three vectors such that $\vec{a}\times\vec{b} = \vec{c}$ and $\vec{b}\times\vec{c} = \vec{a}$, then
(a) $\vec{a}, \vec{b}$ and $\vec{c}$ are mutually orthogonal
(b) $|\vec{a}| = |\vec{b}| = |\vec{c}|$
(c) $|\vec{a}| = |\vec{b}| = |\vec{c}| \neq 1$
(d) None of these

22. The value of k for which the points $A(1, 0, 3)$, $B(-1, 3, 4)$, $C(1, 2, 1)$ and $D(k, 2, 5)$ are co-planar is
(a) 1 (b) 13
(c) 0 (d) –1

Answer Key

1. (a)	2. (d)	3. (c,d)	4. (b)	5. (b)	6. (a,d)	7. (a)	8. (b)	9. (b,c)	10. (a,b,c)
11. (a)	12. (a)	13. (d)	14. (a)	15. (c)	16. (b)	17. (b)	18. (b)	19. (d)	20. (b)
21. (a)	22. (b)								

■ MULTIPLE PRODUCT

Scalar Triple Product

The scalar triple product of three vectors $\vec{a},\vec{b}$ and $\vec{c}$ is defined as $(\vec{a}\times\vec{b}).\vec{c}$. We denote it by $[\vec{a}\ \vec{b}\ \vec{c}]$. Here we have both cross and dot sign. But first we take vector product and get a vector quantity and then it's dot is taken with the third vector and a scalar quantity is obtained.

$$(\vec{a}\times\vec{b}).\vec{c} = (\vec{b}\times\vec{c}).\vec{a} = (\vec{c}\times\vec{a}).\vec{b}$$

i.e., $[\vec{a}\,\vec{b}\,\vec{c}] = [\vec{b}\,\vec{c}\,\vec{a}] = [\vec{c}\,\vec{a}\,\vec{b}]$

Let $\vec{a} = a_1\hat{i} + a_2\hat{j} + a_3\hat{k}$; $\vec{b} = b_1\hat{i} + b_2\hat{j} + b_3\hat{k}$;

$\vec{c} = c_1\hat{i} + c_2\hat{j} + c_3\hat{k}$

$$\Rightarrow \quad \vec{a}\times\vec{b} = \begin{vmatrix} \hat{i} & \hat{j} & \hat{k} \\ a_1 & a_2 & a_3 \\ b_1 & b_2 & b_3 \end{vmatrix}$$

$$= \hat{i}\begin{vmatrix} a_2 & a_3 \\ b_2 & b_3 \end{vmatrix} - \hat{j}\begin{vmatrix} a_1 & a_3 \\ b_1 & b_3 \end{vmatrix} + \hat{k}\begin{vmatrix} a_1 & a_2 \\ b_1 & b_2 \end{vmatrix}$$

$$\Rightarrow \quad (\vec{a}\times\vec{b}).\vec{c} = c_1\begin{vmatrix} a_2 & a_3 \\ b_2 & b_3 \end{vmatrix} - c_2\begin{vmatrix} a_1 & a_3 \\ b_1 & b_3 \end{vmatrix} + c_3\begin{vmatrix} a_1 & a_2 \\ b_1 & b_2 \end{vmatrix}$$

$$= \begin{vmatrix} c_1 & c_2 & c_3 \\ a_1 & a_2 & a_3 \\ b_1 & b_2 & b_3 \end{vmatrix}$$

R_1 rolling over R_2 and R_3

$$= (-1)^2\begin{vmatrix} a_1 & a_2 & a_3 \\ b_1 & b_2 & b_3 \\ c_1 & c_2 & c_3 \end{vmatrix} = \vec{a}.(\vec{b}\times\vec{c})$$

Geometrical interpretation of scalar triple product

Consider a parallelopiped whose coterminus edges OA, OB, OC have the lengths and directions of the vectors $\vec{a}$, $\vec{b}$, $\vec{c}$ respectively. Let $\vec{a}\times\vec{b} = \vec{n}$, then from our definition of vector product, the vector $\vec{n}$ is perpendicular to the face $OADB$ and its modulus n is the measure of the area of the parallelogram $OADB$. Also, by definition, the vector $\vec{a}$, $\vec{b}$ and $\vec{n}$ form a right handed triad. If ϕ is angle between direction $\overrightarrow{OC}$ and $\vec{n}$. Then the vectors $\vec{a}$, $\vec{b}$ and $\vec{c}$ will form a right hand or a left handed triad accordingly as ϕ acute or obtuse

Now $(\vec{a}\times\vec{b}).\vec{c} = |(\vec{a}\times\vec{b})||\vec{c}|\cos\phi = |\vec{n}||\vec{c}|\cos\phi$

$= |\vec{a}\times\vec{b}|\,|\overrightarrow{OC}|\cos\phi$

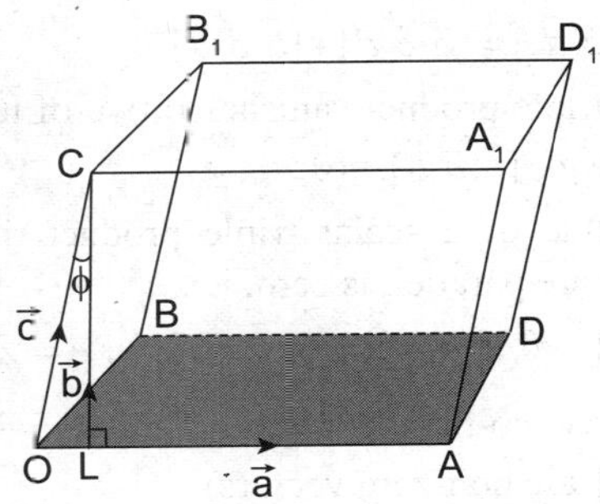

FIGURE 3.99

Now $|\overrightarrow{OC}|\cos\phi$ will be positive or negative according as ϕ is acute or obtuse. Its absolute value will give us the length of the perpendicular from C to the plane of the parallelogram $OADB$. Now the volume V of the parallelopiped

= (Area of the parallelogram $OADB$) × (length of the perpendicular from C on this parallelogram)

$= |(\vec{a}\times\vec{b}).\vec{c}|$

∴ $(\vec{a}\times\vec{b}).\vec{c} = +V$; if ϕ is acute, i.e., if $\vec{a}$, $\vec{b}$, $\vec{c}$ form a right handed triad

and $(\vec{a}\times\vec{b}).\vec{c} = -V$; if ϕ is obtuse, i.e., if $\vec{a}$, $\vec{b}$, $\vec{c}$ form a left handed triadtc.

Properties of scalar triple product

(a) $|(a\times\vec{b}).\vec{c}|$ represents the volume of the ***parallelopiped*** whose *co-terminus edges* are represented by the vectors $\vec{a},\vec{b}$ and $\vec{c}$.

(b) Volume of tetrahedron $= \dfrac{1}{6}[\vec{a}\ \vec{b}\ \vec{c}]$

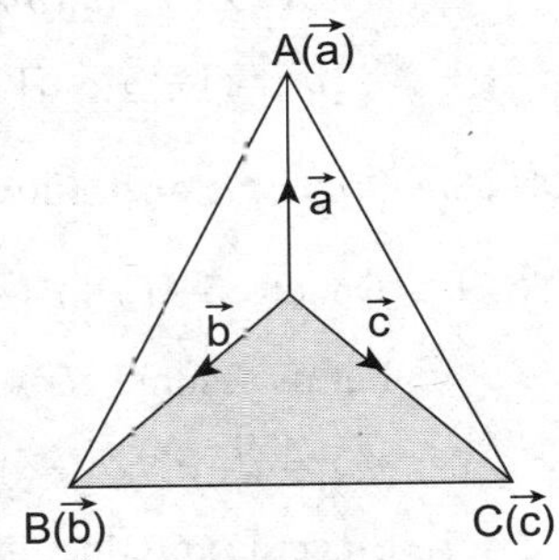

FIGURE 3.100

(c) Dot and cross can be interchange without changing the value of scalar triple proudct $\vec{a}.(\vec{b}\times\vec{c}) = (\vec{a}\times\vec{b}).\vec{c}$

(d) Scalar triple product remains same if cyclic order of three vectors is maintained

i.e., $[\vec{a}\ \vec{b}\ \vec{c}] = [\vec{b}\ \vec{c}\ \vec{a}] = [\vec{c}\ \vec{a}\ \vec{b}]$

(e) $[\vec{a}+\vec{b}\ \vec{c}\ \vec{d}\,]=[\vec{a}\ \vec{c}\ \vec{d}]+[\vec{b}\ \vec{c}\ \vec{d}]$.

(f) Scalar triple product vanishes if two of its vectors are equal, e.g., $[\vec{a}\ \vec{a}\ \vec{b}]=0$

(g) The value of a scalar triple product, if two of its vectors are parallel, is zero. i.e.,
$[\vec{a}\ \vec{b}\ \vec{c}]=0$ if $\vec{a}=\lambda\vec{b}$ or $\vec{b}=\lambda\vec{c}$ or $\vec{c}=\lambda\vec{a}$

(h) For three co-planar vectors $[\vec{a}\ \vec{b}\ \vec{c}]=0$ (even if $[\vec{a}\ \vec{b}\ \vec{c}]$ are non-zero vectors)

(i) If $[\vec{a}\ \vec{b}\ \vec{c}]=[\vec{d}\ \vec{a}\ \vec{b}]+[\vec{d}\ \vec{b}\ \vec{c}]+[\vec{d}\ \vec{c}\ \vec{a}]$
$\Rightarrow \vec{a},\vec{b},\vec{c}$ and $\vec{d}$ are co-planar

(j) If λ is a scalar then $[\lambda\vec{a}\ \vec{b}\ \vec{c}]=\lambda[\vec{a}\ \vec{b}\ \vec{c}]$

(k) The volume of the ***triangular prism*** whose adjacent sides are represented by the vectors $\vec{a},\vec{b},\vec{c}$ is $\frac{1}{2}[\vec{a}\ \vec{b}\ \vec{c}]$.

ILLUSTRATION 62: Show that the vectors $\vec{a}=2\hat{i}-3\hat{j}+4\hat{k}$, $\vec{b}=\hat{i}+2\hat{j}-\hat{k}$ and $\vec{c}=3\hat{i}-\hat{j}+2\hat{k}$ are co-planars.

SOLUTION: $[\vec{a}\ \vec{b}\ \vec{c}]=\begin{vmatrix}-1 & 2 & -1\\ 2 & -1 & -1\\ -1 & -1 & 2\end{vmatrix}=-1(-3)-2(3)-1(-3)=0$. Hence $\vec{a},\vec{b},\vec{c}$ are co-planar.

ILLUSTRATION 63: Find the volume of the parallelopiped whose edges are represented by $\vec{a}=2\hat{i}-3\hat{j}+4\hat{k}$, $\vec{b}=\hat{i}+2\hat{j}-\hat{k}$ and $\vec{c}=3\hat{i}-\hat{j}+2\hat{k}$

SOLUTION: $\vec{a}.(\vec{b}\times\vec{c})=\begin{vmatrix}2 & -3 & 4\\ 1 & 2 & -1\\ 3 & -1 & 2\end{vmatrix}=2(3)+3(5)+4(-7)=6+15-28=-7$

$\Rightarrow |\vec{a}.(\vec{b}\times\vec{c})|=7$. Therefore the required volume $V=7$ cubic units

ILLUSTRATION 64: For any three vectors $\vec{a},\vec{b},\vec{c}$ prove that $[\vec{a}+\vec{b}\ \ \vec{b}+\vec{c}\ \ \vec{c}+\vec{a}]=2[\vec{a}\ \vec{b}\ \vec{c}]$

SOLUTION: By definition of scalar triple product

$[\vec{a}+\vec{b}\ \ \vec{b}+\vec{c}\ \ \vec{c}+\vec{a}]=(\vec{a}+\vec{b}).[(\vec{b}+\vec{c})\times(\vec{c}+\vec{a})]$

$=(\vec{a}+\vec{b}).[\vec{b}\times\vec{c}+\vec{b}\times\vec{a}+\vec{c}\times\vec{c}+\vec{c}\times\vec{a}]$

$=\vec{a}.(\vec{b}\times\vec{c})+\vec{a}.(\vec{b}\times\vec{a})+\vec{a}.(\vec{c}\times\vec{a})+\vec{b}.(\vec{b}\times\vec{c})+\vec{b}.(\vec{b}\times\vec{a})+\vec{b}.(\vec{c}\times\vec{a})$

$=[\vec{a}\ \vec{b}\ \vec{c}]+[\vec{b}\ \vec{c}\ \vec{a}]=[\vec{a}\ \vec{b}\ \vec{c}\,]+[\vec{a}\ \vec{b}\ \vec{c}]=2[\vec{a}\ \vec{b}\ \vec{c}]$

ILLUSTRATION 65: Prove the distributive law $\vec{a}\times(\vec{b}+\vec{c})=\vec{a}\times\vec{b}+\vec{a}\times\vec{c}$ using scalar triple product

SOLUTION: Denote $\vec{a}\times(\vec{b}+\vec{c})-(\vec{a}\times\vec{b}+\vec{a}\times\vec{c})=\vec{p}$

Let us assume $\vec{d}$ to be arbitrary vector and consider

$\vec{d}.\vec{p}=\vec{d}.[\vec{a}\times(\vec{b}+\vec{c})-(\vec{a}\times\vec{b}+\vec{a}\times\vec{c})]=\vec{d}.[\vec{a}\times(\vec{b}+\vec{c})]-\vec{d}.(\vec{a}\times\vec{b})-\vec{d}.(\vec{a}\times\vec{c})$

Since dot product is distributive and in scalar triple product, the position of dot and cross can be interchanged hence, we get

$\Rightarrow \vec{d}.\vec{p}=(\vec{d}\times\vec{a}).(\vec{b}+\vec{c})-(\vec{d}\times\vec{a}).\vec{b}-(\vec{d}\times\vec{a}).\vec{c}=(\vec{d}\times\vec{a}).(\vec{b}+\vec{c}-\vec{b}-\vec{c})\Rightarrow \vec{d}\cdot\vec{p}=\vec{0}$

Since $\vec{d}$ is any arbitrary vector and $\vec{d}.\vec{p}=\vec{0}\Rightarrow \vec{p}=\vec{0}$

It is not necessary that $\vec{d}\perp\vec{p}$ or $\vec{d}=0$, i.e., $\vec{a}\times(\vec{b}+\vec{c})-\vec{a}\times\vec{b}-\vec{a}\times\vec{c}=\vec{0}$

$\Rightarrow \vec{a}\times(\vec{b}+\vec{c})=\vec{a}\times\vec{b}+\vec{a}\times\vec{c}$

ILLUSTRATION 66: Prove that $(\vec{a}+2\vec{b}-\vec{c}).\{(\vec{a}-\vec{b})\times(\vec{a}-\vec{b}-\vec{c})\} = 3[\vec{a}\,\vec{b}\,\vec{c}]$

SOLUTION: $(\vec{a}+2\vec{b}-\vec{c}).\{(\vec{a}-\vec{b})\times(\vec{a}-\vec{b}-\vec{c})\}$

$= (\vec{a}+2\vec{b}-\vec{c}).\{\vec{a}\times\vec{a}-\vec{a}\times\vec{b}-\vec{a}\times\vec{c}-\vec{b}\times\vec{a}+\vec{b}\times\vec{b}+\vec{b}\times\vec{c}\}$

$= (\vec{a}+2\vec{b}-\vec{c}).\{\vec{c}\times\vec{a}+\vec{b}\times\vec{c}\} = [\vec{a}\,\vec{b}\,\vec{c}]+2[\vec{a}\,\vec{b}\,\vec{c}] = 3[\vec{a}\,\vec{b}\,\vec{c}]$

ILLUSTRATION 67: Show that $\vec{a}.(2\vec{b}+2\vec{c})\times(3\vec{a}+3\vec{b}+3\vec{c}) = 0$

SOLUTION: Let $\vec{a}.(2\vec{b}+2\vec{c})\times(3\vec{a}+3\vec{b}+3\vec{c})$

$= \vec{a}.2(\vec{b}+\vec{c})\times 3(\vec{a}+\vec{b}+\vec{c}) = 6\vec{a}.(\vec{b}+\vec{c})\times(\vec{a}+\vec{b}+\vec{c})$

$= 6\{\vec{a}.[\vec{b}\times\vec{a}+\vec{b}\times\vec{b}+\vec{b}\times\vec{c}+\vec{c}\times\vec{a}+\vec{c}\times\vec{b}+\vec{c}\times\vec{c}]\}$

$= 6\{\vec{a}.[\vec{b}\times\vec{a}+\vec{b}\times\vec{c}+\vec{c}\times\vec{a}+\vec{c}\times\vec{b}]\} = 6\{[\vec{a}\,\vec{b}\,\vec{a}]+[\vec{a}\,\vec{b}\,\vec{c}]+[\vec{a}\,\vec{c}\,\vec{a}]+[\vec{a}\,\vec{c}\,\vec{b}]\}$

$= 6\{0+[\vec{a}\,\vec{b}\,\vec{c}]+0-[\vec{a}\,\vec{b}\,\vec{c}]\} = 0$

ILLUSTRATION 68: If $\vec{x}.\vec{a} = \vec{x}.\vec{b} = \vec{x}.\vec{c} = 0$ for some non-zero vector $\vec{x}$, then show that $[\vec{a}\,\vec{b}\,\vec{c}] = 0$

SOLUTION: Given $\vec{x}.\vec{a} = 0$, $\vec{x}.\vec{b} = 0$, $\vec{x}.\vec{c} = 0$

Therefore $\vec{x}$ is perpendicular to vector $\vec{a}$, $\vec{b}$ and $\vec{c}$ and hence $\vec{a}$, $\vec{b}$ and $\vec{c}$ are co-planar

$\therefore\ [\vec{a}\,\vec{b}\,\vec{c}] = 0$

ILLUSTRATION 69: Find out the volume of a prism on triangular base, the three sides of the prism meeting on a vertex are given below $\overline{OA} = 3\hat{i}+4\hat{j}+12\hat{k}$, $\overline{OB} = 12\hat{i}+3\hat{j}+4\hat{k}$, $\overline{OC} = 4\hat{i}+12\hat{j}+3\hat{k}$

SOLUTION: Volume $= 1/2 \begin{vmatrix} 3 & 4 & 12 \\ 12 & 3 & 4 \\ 4 & 12 & 3 \end{vmatrix} = 1/2\,[3(9-48)-4(36-16)+12\,(144-12)] = \dfrac{1387}{2} = 693.5$

$\therefore$ Volume of triangular base prism = 693.5 cusic units.

ILLUSTRATION 70: If $\vec{p} = p_1\hat{i}+p_2\hat{j}+p_3\hat{k}$; $\vec{q} = q_1\hat{i}+q_2\hat{j}+q_3\hat{k}$ and $\vec{r} = r_1\hat{i}+r_2\hat{j}+r_3\hat{k}$, then show that the value of the scalar triple product $[n\vec{p}+\vec{q}\ \ n\vec{q}+\vec{r}\ \ n\vec{r}+\vec{p}]$ is $(n^3+1)\begin{vmatrix} \vec{p}.\hat{i} & \vec{p}.\hat{j} & \vec{p}.\hat{k} \\ \vec{p}.\hat{i} & \vec{q}.\hat{j} & b.\hat{k} \\ \vec{p}.\hat{i} & \vec{r}.\hat{j} & b.\hat{k} \end{vmatrix}$

SOLUTION: $[n\vec{p}+\vec{q}\ \ n\vec{q}+\vec{r}\ \ n\vec{r}+\vec{p}] = (n\vec{p}+\vec{q}).[(n\vec{q}+\vec{r})\times(n\vec{r}+\vec{p})]$

$= (n\vec{p}+\vec{q}).\left[n^2(\vec{q}\times\vec{r})+n(\vec{q}\times\vec{p})+(\vec{r}\times\vec{p})\right]$

$= (n^3+1)[\vec{p}\,\vec{q}\,\vec{r}]$

$= (n^3+1)\begin{vmatrix} \vec{p}_1 & \vec{p}_2 & \vec{p}_3 \\ \vec{q}_1 & \vec{q}_2 & \vec{q}_3 \\ \vec{r}_1 & \vec{r}_2 & \vec{r}_3 \end{vmatrix} = (n^3+1)\begin{vmatrix} \vec{p}.\hat{i} & \vec{p}_2.\hat{j} & \vec{p}.\hat{k} \\ \vec{q}.\hat{i} & \vec{q}.\hat{j} & \vec{q}.\hat{k} \\ \vec{r}.\hat{i} & \vec{r}.\hat{j} & \vec{r}.\hat{k} \end{vmatrix}$. Hence proved.

TEXTUAL EXERCISE 9: (SUBJECTIVE)

1. The volume of a parallelopiped is 4 whose three co-terminus edges are represented by the vectors $\hat{i}+x\hat{j}-x^2\hat{k}$, $\hat{i}+\hat{j}-\hat{k}$ and $\hat{i}-\hat{j}+\hat{k}$. Find the possible real values of x.

2. If $\vec{A}=x_1\vec{a}+y_1\vec{b}+z_1\vec{c}$, $\vec{B}=x_2\vec{a}+y_2\vec{b}+z_2\vec{c}$ and $\vec{C}=x_3\vec{a}+y_3\vec{b}+z_3\vec{c}$, then prove that

$$[\vec{A}\vec{B}\vec{C}]=\begin{vmatrix} x_1 & y_1 & z_1 \\ x_2 & y_2 & z_2 \\ x_3 & y_3 & z_3 \end{vmatrix}[\vec{a}\ \vec{b}\ \vec{c}]$$

3. V_1 is the volume of a parallelopiped and V_2 is the volume of the parallelopiped formed with three concurrent diagonals of the three faces of the original parallelopiped. Find the relation between V_1 and V_2.

4. If $\begin{vmatrix} a & a^2 & 1+a^3 \\ b & b^2 & 1+b^3 \\ c & c^2 & 1+c^3 \end{vmatrix}=0$ and the vectors $\vec{A}=(1,a,a^2)$, $\vec{B}=(1,b,b^2)$ and $\vec{C}=(1,c,c^2)$ are non-copalanar, then find abc.

Answer Key

1. –1, 2 3. $V_2 = 2V_1$ 4. –1

TEXTUAL EXERCISE 6: (OBJECTIVE)

1. $(\vec{a}+2\vec{b}-\vec{c}).\{(\vec{a}-\vec{b})\times(\vec{a}-\vec{b}-\vec{c})\}$ is equal to

(a) $[\vec{a}\ \vec{b}\ \vec{c}]$ (b) $2[\vec{a}\ \vec{b}\ \vec{c}]$
(c) $3\ [\vec{a}\ \vec{b}\ \vec{c}]$ (d) 0

2. The volume of the parallelopiped whose edges are represented by $-12\hat{i}+a\hat{k}$, $3\hat{j}-\hat{k}$ and $2\hat{i}+\hat{j}-15\hat{k}$ is 546, then a is

(a) 3 (b) 2
(c) –3 (d) –2

3. For non-zero vectors $\vec{a}, \vec{b}$ and $\vec{c}$, $|\vec{a}\times\vec{b}\ .\ \vec{c}| = |\vec{a}||\vec{b}||\vec{c}|$ holds if and only if

(a) $\vec{a}.\vec{b}=0,\ \vec{b}.\vec{c}=0$ (b) $\vec{c}.\vec{a}=0,\ \vec{a}.\vec{b}=0$
(c) $\vec{a}=3\hat{i}-\hat{k}$ (d) $\vec{a}.\vec{b}=\vec{b}.\vec{c}=\vec{c}.\vec{a}=0$

4. If $\hat{a}$, $\hat{b}$ and $\hat{c}$ be unit co-planar vectors, then the scalar triple product $[\,2\hat{a}-\hat{b},\ 2\hat{b}-\hat{c},\ 2\hat{c}-\hat{a}\,]$ is equal to

(a) 0 (b) 1
(c) $-\sqrt{3}$ (d) $\sqrt{3}$

5. If $\vec{e}_1$ and $\vec{e}_2$ are two unit vectors and θ is the angle between them, then sin $\left(\frac{\theta}{2}\right)$ is:

(a) $\frac{1}{2}|\vec{e}_1+\vec{e}_2|$ (b) $\frac{|\vec{e}_1.(\vec{e}_1-\vec{e}_2)|}{|\vec{e}_1-e_2|}$
(c) $\frac{\vec{e}_1.\vec{e}_2}{2}$ (d) $\frac{|\vec{e}_1\times\vec{e}_2|}{|\vec{e}_1+\vec{e}_2|}$

6. Which of the following expression is meaningful?

(a) $\vec{u}.(\vec{v}\times\vec{w})$ (b) $(\vec{u}.\vec{v}).\vec{w}$
(c) $(\vec{u}+\vec{v})\times\vec{w}$ (d) $\vec{u}\times(\vec{v}.\vec{w})$

7. The value of b, such that the scalar product of the vectors $\hat{i}+\hat{j}+\hat{k}$ with the unit vector parallel to the sum of the vectors $2\hat{i}+4\hat{j}-5\hat{k}$ and $b\hat{i}+2\hat{j}+3\hat{k}$ is one, is

(a) –2 (b) –1
(c) 0 (d) 1

8. Let A_r (r = 1, 2, 3, 4) be the area of four faces of a tetrahedron with co-terminus edges $\vec{a}, \vec{b}$ and $\vec{c}$. Let $\vec{n}_r$ be the outwards drawn normals to the rth face with magnitudes equal to corresponding areas. Prove that $\vec{n}_1+\vec{n}_2+\vec{n}_3+\vec{n}_4$ is equal to

(a) $6[\vec{a}\times\vec{b}+\vec{b}\times\vec{c}+\vec{c}\times\vec{a}]$
(b) $3[\vec{a}\times\vec{b}+\vec{b}\times\vec{c}+\vec{c}\times\vec{a}]$
(c) zero
(d) None of these

9. The volume of a right triangular prism $ABCA_1B_1C_1$ is equal to 3. If the position vectors of the vertices of the base ABC are $A(1, 0, 1)$; $B(2,0, 0)$ and $C(0, 1, 0)$, the position vectors of the vertex A_1 can be:
   (a) (2, 2, 2) (b) (0, 2, 0)
   (c) (0, −2, 2) (d) (0, −2, 0)

10. The value of $[\vec{a}-\vec{b}, \vec{b}-\vec{c}, \vec{c}-\vec{a}]$ is
   (a) 0 (b) 1
   (c) 2 (d) None of these

11. The three vectors $\hat{i}+\hat{j}$, $\hat{j}+\hat{k}$, $\hat{k}+\hat{i}$ taken two at a time form three planes. The three unit vectors drawn perpendicular to these three planes form a parallelopiped of volume
   (a) 1/3 (b) 4
   (c) $\frac{3\sqrt{3}}{4}$ (d) $\frac{4}{3\sqrt{3}}$

12. Let $\vec{\alpha}=a_1\hat{i}+a_2\hat{j}+a_3\hat{k}$, $\vec{\beta}=b_1\hat{i}+b_2\hat{j}+b_3\hat{k}$ and $\vec{\gamma}=c_1\hat{i}+c_2\hat{j}+c_3\hat{k}$, $|\vec{\alpha}|=2$, $\vec{\alpha}$ makes angle $\pi/6$ with the plane of $\vec{\beta}$ and $\vec{\gamma}$ and angle between $\vec{\beta}$ and $\vec{\gamma}$ is $\pi/4$, then $\begin{vmatrix} a_1 & a_2 & a_3 \\ b_1 & b_2 & b_3 \\ c_1 & c_2 & c_3 \end{vmatrix}^n$ is equal to (n is even natural number)
   (a) $\left(\frac{|\vec{\beta}||\vec{\gamma}|}{2}\right)^{\frac{n}{2}}$ (b) $\frac{(|\vec{\beta}||\vec{\gamma}|)^n}{2^{n/2}}$
   (c) $\frac{(|\vec{\beta}||\vec{\gamma}|)^{n/2}}{2^n}$ (d) None of these

13. If $\vec{x}.\vec{a}=1$, $\vec{y}.\vec{b}=1$, $\vec{z}.\vec{c}=1$ and $\vec{x}$ is perpendicular to $\vec{b}$ and $\vec{c}$, $\vec{y}$ is perpendicular to $\vec{c}$ and $\vec{a}$ and $\vec{z}$ is perpendicular $\vec{a}$ and $\vec{b}$ (where $\vec{a}$, $\vec{b}$, $\vec{c}$ are non-zero, non-coplanar), then $[\vec{x}\,\vec{y}\,\vec{z}]$ equals
   (a) $[\vec{a}\,\vec{b}\,\vec{c}]$ (b) $\frac{1}{[\vec{a}\,\vec{b}\,\vec{c}]}$
   (c) $[\vec{a}\,\vec{b}\,\vec{c}]^2$ (d) None of these

14. A vector of magnitude $5\sqrt{5}$ co-planar with vectors $\hat{i}+2\hat{j}$ and $\hat{j}-2\hat{k}$ perpendicular to the vector $2\hat{i}+\hat{j}+2\hat{k}$ is
   (a) $\pm 5\,(5\hat{i}+6\hat{j}-8\hat{k})$
   (b) $\pm\sqrt{5}\,(5\hat{i}+6\hat{j}-8\hat{k})$
   (c) $\pm 5\sqrt{5}\,(5\hat{i}+6\hat{j}-8\hat{k})$
   (d) $\pm(5\hat{i}+6\hat{j}-8\hat{k})$

15. The value of a for which the volume of parallelopiped formed by the vectors $\hat{i}+a\hat{j}+\hat{k}$, $\hat{j}+a\hat{k}$ and $a\hat{i}+\hat{k}$ is minimum is
   (a) −3 (b) 3
   (c) $1/\sqrt{3}$ (d) $-\sqrt{3}$

16. Let $\vec{V}=2\hat{i}+\hat{j}-\hat{k}$ and $\vec{W}=\hat{i}+3\hat{k}$. If $\vec{U}$ is a unit vector, then the maximum value of the scalar triple product $[\vec{U}\,\vec{V}\,\vec{W}]$ is
   (a) −1 (b) $\sqrt{10}+\sqrt{6}$
   (c) $\sqrt{59}$ (d) $\sqrt{60}$

17. Let $\vec{a}=\hat{i}-\hat{k}$, $\vec{b}=x\hat{i}+\hat{j}+(1-x)\hat{k}$ and $\vec{c}=y\hat{i}+x\hat{j}+(1+x-y)\hat{k}$. Then $[\vec{a}\,\vec{b}\,\vec{c}]$ depends on
   (a) only x (b) only y
   (c) neither x nor y (d) both x and y

18. The vectors $\lambda\hat{i}+\hat{j}+2\hat{k}$, $\hat{i}+\lambda\hat{j}-\hat{k}$ and $2\hat{i}-\hat{j}+\lambda\hat{k}$ are co-planar if
   (a) $\lambda=-2$ (b) $\lambda=1+\sqrt{3}$
   (c) $\lambda=1-\sqrt{3}$ (d) $\lambda=0$

Answer Key

1. (c)	2. (c)	3. (d)	4. (a)	5. (b, d)	6. (a, c)	7. (d)	8. (c)	9. (a)	10. (a)
11. (d)	12. (b)	13. (b)	14. (d)	15. (c)	16. (c)	17. (c)	18. (a, b, c)		

■ VECTOR TRIPLE PRODUCT

The vector product of two vectors one of which is itself the vector product of two vectors is a vector quantity, called a Vector Triple Product. Thus if $\vec{a}$, $\vec{b}$ and $\vec{c}$ be three vectors, the product of the form $(\vec{a}\times\vec{b})\times\vec{c}$ and $\vec{a}\times(\vec{b}\times\vec{c})$ is called a Vector Triple Product of Vectors $\vec{a}, \vec{b}$ and $\vec{c}$.

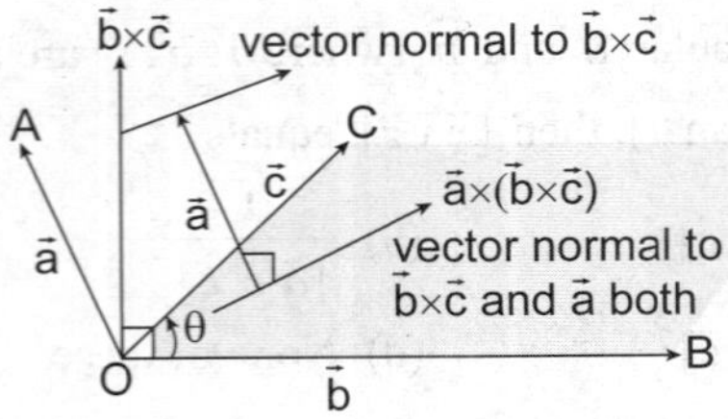

FIGURE 3.101

Since $\vec{a}\times(\vec{b}\times\vec{c})$ is a vector normal to both $\vec{a}$ and $\vec{b}\times\vec{c}$ and being normal to $\vec{b}\times\vec{c}$ it must lie in the plane coplanar with that containing $\vec{b}$ and $\vec{c}$. Therefore it can be written as the linear combination of and $\vec{c}$.

So let $\vec{a}\times(\vec{b}\times\vec{c}) = \lambda_1\vec{b}+\lambda_2\vec{c}$

but since it is also perpendicular to $\vec{a}$ so dot product of $\vec{a}\times(\vec{b}\times\vec{c})$ with $\vec{a}$ must vanish.

$\Rightarrow \ (\vec{a}\times(\vec{b}\times\vec{c})).\vec{a} = 0 = \lambda_1\vec{b}.\vec{a}+\lambda_2\vec{c}.\vec{a}$

$\Rightarrow \ \lambda_1\vec{b}.\vec{a} = -\lambda_2\vec{c}.\vec{a} = k$

$\Rightarrow \ \dfrac{\lambda_1}{\vec{c}.\vec{a}} = \dfrac{-\lambda_2}{\vec{b}.\vec{a}} = k \Rightarrow \lambda_1 = k\,\vec{c}.\vec{a}$ and $\lambda_2 = -k\,\vec{b}.\vec{a}$

therefore, $\vec{a}\times(\vec{b}\times\vec{c}) = k\{(\vec{a}.\vec{c})\vec{b}-(\vec{a}.\vec{b})\vec{c}\}$ ...(i)

The value of k in equation (i) can be obtained by analysing the magnitude of vectors involved as illustrated below.

Let $\vec{a} = a_1\hat{i}+a_2\hat{j}+a_3\hat{k}$; $\vec{b} = b_1\hat{i}+b_2\hat{j}$; $\vec{c} = c_1\hat{i}$

$\vec{b}\times\vec{c} = -b_2c_1\hat{k}$

$\vec{a}\times(\vec{b}\times\vec{c}) = -(a_1\hat{i}+a_2\hat{j}+a_3\hat{k})\times b_2c_1\hat{k}$

$= a_1\,b_2c_1\hat{j} - a_2b_2c_1\hat{i}$ ...(ii)

Also, $(\vec{a}.\vec{c})\vec{b}-(\vec{a}.\vec{b})\vec{c} = a_1\,b_2c_1\hat{j} - a_2b_2c_1\hat{i}$ ....(iii)

which is same as from (ii)

Therefore the given identity (i) holds when $k = 1$

Properties of vector triple product

1. $\vec{a}\times(\vec{b}\times\vec{c}) = -(\vec{b}\times\vec{c})\times\vec{a} = -[(\vec{b}.\vec{a})\,\vec{c} - (\vec{c}.\vec{a})\vec{b}]$
$= (\vec{c}.\vec{a})\vec{b}-(\vec{b}.\vec{a})\,\vec{c} = (\vec{a}.\vec{c})\vec{b}-(\vec{a}.\vec{b})\vec{c}$

   Aid to memory: $\vec{a}\times(\vec{b}\times\vec{c}) = (\vec{a}.\vec{c})\vec{b}-(\vec{a}\,.\,\vec{b})\,\vec{c}$ *outer × (adjacent × remote)*
   = *(outer. remote) adjacent - (outer. adjacent) remote*
2. $(\vec{a}\times\vec{b})\times\vec{c} \neq \vec{a}\times(\vec{b}\times\vec{c})$
   The equality holds only when $\vec{a}$ and $\vec{c}$ are collinear
3. $\hat{i}\times(\hat{j}\times\hat{k}) = \vec{0}$
4. $\vec{a}\times(\vec{b}\times\vec{c})$ is a linear combination of those two vectors which are with in brackets
5. If $\vec{r} = \vec{a}\times(\vec{b}\times\vec{c})$, then $\vec{r}$ is perpendicular to $\vec{a}$ and lie in the plane parallel to that of of $\vec{b}$ and $\vec{c}$

ILLUSTRATION 71: Find the unit vector which is orthogonal to the vector $3\hat{i}+2\hat{j}+6\hat{k}$ and is co-planar with the vectors $2\hat{i}+\hat{j}+\hat{k}$ and $\hat{i}-\hat{j}+\hat{k}$.

SOLUTION: Let $\vec{a} = 3\hat{i}+2\hat{j}+6\hat{k}$, $\vec{b} = 2\hat{i}+\hat{j}+\hat{k}$, $\vec{c} = \hat{i}-\hat{j}+\hat{k}$

Then by definition, a vector orthogonal to $\vec{a}$ and co-planar to $\vec{b}$ and $\vec{c}$ is given by

$\Rightarrow \ \vec{a}\times(\vec{b}\times\vec{c}) = (\vec{a}.\vec{c})\vec{b}-(\vec{a}.\vec{b})\vec{c}$

$$= 7(2\hat{i}+\hat{j}+\hat{k})-14(\hat{i}-\hat{j}+\hat{k}) = 21\hat{j}-7\hat{k} = \frac{\vec{a}\times(\vec{b}\times\vec{c})}{|\vec{a}\times(\vec{b}\times\vec{c})|} = \frac{3\hat{j}-\hat{k}}{\sqrt{10}}$$

ILLUSTRATION 72: Prove that $\vec{a}\times(\vec{b}\times\vec{c})+\vec{b}\times(\vec{c}\times\vec{a})+\vec{c}\times(\vec{a}\times\vec{b}) = \vec{0}$

SOLUTION: Since $\vec{a}\times(\vec{b}\times\vec{c}) = (\vec{a}.\vec{c})\vec{b}-(\vec{a}.\vec{b})\vec{c}$ ...(i)

$\vec{b}\times(\vec{c}\times\vec{a}) = (\vec{b}.\vec{a}).\vec{c}-(\vec{b}.\vec{c}).\vec{a}$ ...(ii)

$\vec{c}\times(\vec{a}\times\vec{b}) = (\vec{c}.\vec{b})\vec{a}-(\vec{c}.\vec{a})\vec{b}$ ...(iii)

Adding (i), (ii) and (iii),we get the result.

ILLUSTRATION 73: Prove that $[\vec{a}\times\vec{b}\ \vec{b}\times\vec{c}\ \vec{c}\times\vec{a}]=[\vec{a}\ \vec{b}\ \vec{c}]^2$

SOLUTION: Let $[\vec{a}\times\vec{b}\ \vec{b}\times\vec{c}\ \vec{c}\times\vec{a}] = [(\vec{a}\times\vec{b})\times(\vec{b}\times\vec{c})].(\vec{c}\times\vec{a})$. Let $\vec{a}\times\vec{b} = \vec{\lambda}$

hence $[\vec{\lambda}\times(\vec{b}\times\vec{c})].(\vec{c}\times\vec{a}) = [(\vec{\lambda}.\vec{c})\vec{b}-(\lambda.\vec{b})\vec{c}].(\vec{c}\times\vec{a}) = [\vec{a}\ \vec{b}\ \vec{c}]\ \vec{b}.(\vec{c}\times\vec{a})=[\vec{a}\ \vec{b}\ \vec{c}]^2$

ILLUSTRATION 74: If $\vec{a}=(\hat{i}+\hat{j}+\hat{k}),\ \vec{a}.\vec{b}=1$ and $\vec{a}\times\vec{b}=\hat{j}-\hat{k}$, then evaluate $\vec{b}$.

SOLUTION: As we know $\vec{a}\times(\vec{a}\times\vec{b})=(\vec{a}.\vec{b})\vec{a}-(\vec{a}.\vec{a})\vec{b}$

$\Rightarrow\ (\hat{i}+\hat{j}+\hat{k})\times(\hat{j}-\hat{k}) = (1)\ \vec{a}-|\vec{a}|^2\vec{b}$ $\qquad \Rightarrow\ 3\vec{b}=-(-2\hat{i}+\hat{j}+\hat{k})+(\hat{i}+\hat{j}+\hat{k})$

where $(\hat{i}+\hat{j}+\hat{k})\times(\hat{j}-\hat{k}) = -2\hat{i}+\hat{j}+\hat{k}$ and $\vec{a}=\hat{i}+\hat{j}+\hat{k}\Rightarrow 3\vec{b}=3\hat{i}$ or $\vec{b}=\hat{i}$

ILLUSTRATION 75: Prove that $[(\vec{a}\times\vec{b})\times(\vec{a}\times\vec{c})].\vec{d}=(\vec{a}.\vec{d})[\vec{a}\ \vec{b}\ \vec{c}]$

SOLUTION: Let $\vec{a}\times\vec{b}=\vec{\lambda}$ $\qquad \therefore\ [(\vec{a}\times\vec{b})\times(\vec{a}\times\vec{c})].\vec{d} = [\vec{\lambda}\times(\vec{a}\times\vec{c})].\vec{d} = [(\vec{\lambda}.\vec{c})\vec{a}-(\vec{\lambda}.\vec{a})\vec{c}].\vec{d}$

$= [\{(\vec{a}\times\vec{b}).\vec{c}\}\vec{a}-\{(\vec{a}\times\vec{b}).\vec{a}\}\vec{c}].\vec{d} = (\vec{a}.\vec{d})[\vec{a}\ \vec{b}\ \vec{c}]$

ILLUSTRATION 76: Show that $(\vec{a}\times\vec{b})\times\vec{c}=\vec{a}\times(\vec{b}\times\vec{c})$ if and only if $\vec{a}$ and $\vec{c}$ are collinear.

SOLUTION: Let $(\vec{a}\times\vec{b})\times\vec{c}=\vec{a}\times(\vec{b}\times\vec{c})$ $\qquad \Rightarrow\ (\vec{a}.\vec{c})\vec{b}-(\vec{b}.\vec{c})\vec{a}=(\vec{a}.\vec{c})\vec{b}-(\vec{a}.\vec{b})\vec{c}$

$\Rightarrow\ \vec{a}=\dfrac{(\vec{a}.\vec{b})\vec{c}}{\vec{b}.\vec{c}}$ $\quad \Rightarrow\ \vec{a}=\lambda\vec{c}\Rightarrow\vec{a}$ and $\vec{c}$ are collinear vector

Conversely if $\vec{a}=\lambda\vec{c}$; $(\vec{a}\times\vec{b})\times\vec{c} = (\lambda\vec{c}\times\vec{b})\times\vec{c}$

$= (\lambda\vec{c}.\vec{c})\vec{b}-(\vec{b}.\vec{c})\lambda\vec{c} = \lambda[(\vec{c}.\vec{c})\vec{b}-(\vec{b}.\vec{c})\vec{c}]$

Again $\vec{a}\times(\vec{b}\times\vec{c}) = \lambda\vec{c}\times(\vec{b}\times\vec{c}) = (\lambda\vec{c}.\vec{c})\vec{b}-(\lambda\vec{c}.\vec{b})\vec{c} = \lambda[(\vec{c}.\vec{c})\vec{b}-(\vec{c}.\vec{b})\vec{c}]$

From (i) and (ii), we get $(\vec{a}\times\vec{b})\times\vec{c} = \vec{a}\times(\vec{b}\times\vec{c})$

ILLUSTRATION 77: Prove that $\vec{a}\times(\vec{b}\times\vec{c}),\ \vec{b}\times(\vec{c}\times\vec{a}),\ \vec{c}\times(\vec{a}\times\vec{b})$ are co-planar

SOLUTION: We have to show that $[\vec{a}\times(\vec{b}\times\vec{c})\vec{b}\times(\vec{c}\times\vec{a})\vec{c}\times(\vec{a}\times\vec{b})]=0$

We have $\{\vec{a}\times(\vec{b}\times\vec{c})\}.[\{\vec{b}\times(\vec{c}\times\vec{a})\}\times\{\vec{c}\times(\vec{a}\times\vec{b})\}]$

$= \{(\vec{a}.\vec{c})\vec{b}-(\vec{a}.\vec{b})\vec{c}\}.[\{(\vec{b}.\vec{a})\vec{c}-(\vec{b}.\vec{c})\vec{a}\}\times\{(\vec{c}.\vec{b})\vec{a}-(\vec{c}.\vec{a})\vec{b}\}] = \{(\vec{a}.\vec{c})\vec{b}-(\vec{a}.\vec{b})\vec{c}\}.$

$\left\{(\vec{a}.\vec{b})(\vec{b}.\vec{c})(\vec{c}\times\vec{a})+(\vec{a}.\vec{b})(\vec{c}.\vec{a})(\vec{b}\times\vec{c})+(\vec{b}.\vec{c})(\vec{c}.\vec{a})(\vec{a}\times\vec{b})\right\}$

$= (\vec{a}.\vec{b})(\vec{b}.\vec{c})(\vec{c}.\vec{a})[\vec{b}\ \vec{c}\ \vec{a}]-(\vec{a}.\vec{b})(\vec{b}.\vec{c})(\vec{c}.\vec{a})[\vec{c}\ \vec{a}\ \vec{b}]=0$

ILLUSTRATION 78: If $\vec{p},\vec{q},\vec{r}$ are non-coplanar vectors and $\vec{s}$ is a unit vector, then find the value of $|\vec{A}|$ $= |(\vec{p}.\vec{s})(\vec{q}\times\vec{r})+(\vec{q}.\vec{s})(\vec{r}\times\vec{p})+(\vec{r}.\vec{s})(\vec{p}\times\vec{q})|$ independent of $\vec{s}$, where $(\vec{p}+\vec{q}+\vec{r})$ is not $\perp r$ to $(k\vec{s}-\vec{A})$ for any scalar k.

SOLUTION: Given $[\vec{p}\vec{q}\vec{r}]\neq 0$ [$\vec{p},\vec{q},\vec{r}$ are non-coplanar or there does not exist any linear relation between them]

Also, $\vec{s}^2=1$. Let $\vec{A}=x(\vec{q}\times\vec{r})+y(\vec{r}\times\vec{p})+z(\vec{p}\times\vec{q})$ where $x=\vec{p}.\vec{s},\ y=\vec{q}.\vec{s},\ z=\vec{r}.\vec{s}$

Multiplying both sides scalarly by $\vec{p}, \vec{q}, \vec{r}$ and we know that scalar triple product is zero when two vectors are equal, $\vec{A}.\vec{p} = x[\vec{p}\ \vec{q}\ \vec{r}] + 0$

Putting for x, we get $(\vec{p}.\vec{s})[\vec{p}\ \vec{q}\ \vec{r}] = \vec{A}.\vec{p}$

Similarly we have. $(\vec{q}.\vec{s})[\vec{p}\ \vec{q}\ \vec{r}] = \vec{A}.\vec{q}$

$(\vec{r}.\vec{s})[\vec{p}\ \vec{q}\ \vec{r}] = \vec{A}.\vec{r}$ adding the above relations,

we get $[(\vec{p}+\vec{q}+\vec{r}).\vec{s}][\vec{p}\ \vec{q}\ \vec{r}] = \vec{A}.(\vec{p}+\vec{q}+\vec{r})$

or $(\vec{p}+\vec{q}+\vec{r}).[\vec{s}[\vec{p}\ \vec{q}\ \vec{r}] - \vec{A}] = 0$.

As $(\vec{p}+\vec{q}+\vec{r})$ is not perpendicular to $(k\vec{s} - \vec{A})$ for any scalar k and since $\vec{p}, \vec{q}, \vec{r}$ are non-coplanar, i.e., $\vec{p}+\vec{q}+\vec{r} \neq 0$.

Hence, $[\vec{p}\ \vec{q}\ \vec{r}]\vec{s} = \vec{A}$. Taking modulus of both sides, $|\vec{A}| = \|[\vec{p}\ \vec{q}\ \vec{r}]\|$ as $|\vec{s}| = 1$

It is independent of $\vec{s}$.

Scalar Product of Four Vectors

$$(\vec{a}\times\vec{b}).(\vec{c}\times\vec{d})$$

Let $(\vec{a}\times\vec{b}) = \vec{n}$, therefore

$= \vec{n}.(\vec{c}\times\vec{d}) = (\vec{n}\times\vec{c}).\vec{d} = ((\vec{a}\times\vec{b})\times\vec{c}).\vec{d}$

$= -(\vec{c}\times(\vec{a}\times\vec{b})).\vec{d} = -((\vec{c}.\vec{b})\vec{a} - (\vec{c}.\vec{a})\,\vec{b}).\vec{d}$

$$= (\vec{c}.\vec{a})(\vec{b}.\vec{d}) - (\vec{b}.\vec{c})(\vec{a}.\vec{d}) = \begin{vmatrix} \vec{a}.\vec{c} & \vec{b}.\vec{c} \\ \vec{a}.\vec{d} & \vec{b}.\vec{d} \end{vmatrix}$$

It is also called as Lagrange's Identity;

Vector Product of Four Vectors

If $\vec{a}, \vec{b}, \vec{c}, \vec{d}$ are four vectors, the product $(\vec{a}\times\vec{b}) \times (\vec{c}\times\vec{d})$ is called vector product of four vectors.

i.e., $(\vec{a}\times\vec{b}) \times (\vec{c}\times\vec{d}) = [\vec{a}\ \vec{b}\ \vec{d}]\vec{c} - [\vec{a}\ \vec{b}\ \vec{c}]\vec{d}$

Also, $(\vec{a}\times\vec{b}) \times (\vec{c}\times\vec{d}) = [\vec{a}\ \vec{c}\ \vec{d}]\vec{b} - [\vec{b}\ \vec{c}\ \vec{d}]\vec{a}$

Proof: $(\vec{a}\times\vec{b}) \times (\vec{c}\times\vec{d}) = \vec{n}\times(\vec{c}\times\vec{d})$

$= (\vec{n}.\vec{d})\vec{c} - (\vec{n}.\vec{c})\,\vec{d} = ((\vec{a}\times\vec{b}).\vec{d})\vec{c} - ((\vec{a}\times\vec{b}).\vec{c})\vec{d}$

$= [\vec{a}\ \vec{b}\ \vec{d}]\vec{c} - [\vec{a}\ \vec{b}\ \vec{c}]\vec{d}$ lies in the plane coplanar with that of $\vec{c}$ and $\vec{d}$

NOTES

We can look upon the above product as vector product in two ways i.e., $(\vec{a}\times\vec{b})\times(\vec{c}\times\vec{d}) = [\vec{a}\ \vec{b}\ \vec{d}]\vec{c} - [\vec{a}\ \vec{b}\ \vec{c}]\vec{d}$

and $(\vec{a}\times\vec{b})\times(\vec{c}\times\vec{d}) = [\vec{a}\ \vec{c}\ \vec{d}]\vec{b} - [\vec{b}\ \vec{c}\ \vec{d}]\vec{a}$

So it can be defined either as linear combination of $\vec{a}$ *and* $\vec{b}$ *or as linear combination of* $\vec{c}$ *and* $\vec{d}$

■ RECIPROCAL SYSTEM OF VECTORS

Let $\vec{a}, \vec{b}, \vec{c}$ be a system of, three non-coplanar vectors. Then the system of vectors $\vec{a}', \vec{b}', \vec{c}'$ which satisfies $\vec{a}.\vec{a}' = \vec{b}.\vec{b}' = \vec{c}.\vec{c}' = 1$ and $\vec{a}.\vec{b}' = \vec{a}.\vec{c}' = \vec{b}.\vec{c}' = \vec{b}.\vec{a}' = \vec{c}.\vec{a}' = \vec{c}.\vec{b}' = 0$, is called the reciprocal system to the vector $\vec{a}, \vec{b}, \vec{c}$ in term $\vec{a}, \vec{b}, \vec{c}$ the vector $\vec{a}', \vec{b}', \vec{c}'$ are given by

$$\vec{a}' = \frac{\vec{b}\times\vec{c}}{[\vec{a}\ \vec{b}\ \vec{c}]},\ \vec{b}' = \frac{\vec{c}\times\vec{a}}{[\vec{a}\ \vec{b}\ \vec{c}]},\ \vec{c}' = \frac{\vec{a}\times\vec{b}}{[\vec{a}\ \vec{b}\ \vec{c}]}$$

Properties of the Reciprocal System

1. $\vec{a}.\vec{a}' = \vec{b}.\vec{b}' = \vec{c}.\vec{c}' = 1$

2. $\vec{a}.\vec{b}' = \vec{b}.\vec{c}' = \vec{c}.\vec{a}' = 0$

3. $[\vec{a}\ \vec{b}\ \vec{c}] = \dfrac{1}{[\vec{a}'\ \vec{b}'\ \vec{c}']}$

4. $\vec{a} = \dfrac{\vec{b}' \times \vec{c}'}{[\vec{a}'\ \vec{b}'\ \vec{c}']}$

5. $\vec{a}.\vec{b}' = \vec{a}.\vec{c}' = \vec{b}.\vec{a}' = \vec{b}.\vec{c}' = \vec{c}.\vec{a}' = \vec{c}.\vec{b}' = 0$

6. $[\vec{a}\ \vec{b}\ \vec{c}]\times[\vec{a}'\ \vec{b}'\ \vec{c}'] = 1$

7. System of unit vectors $\hat{i}, \hat{j}, \hat{k}$ is its own reciprocal $\hat{i}' = \hat{i}, \hat{j}' = \hat{j}, \hat{k}' = \hat{k}$

8. The orthogonal triad of vectors $\hat{i}, \hat{j}, \hat{k}$ is self reciprocal.

9. $\vec{a}, \vec{b}$ and $\vec{c}$ are non-copalnar iff $\vec{a}', \vec{b}'$ and $\vec{c}'$ are non-coplanar.

ILLUSTRATION 79: If $\vec{a}' = \dfrac{\vec{b}\times\vec{c}}{[\vec{a}\ \vec{b}\ \vec{c}]}, \vec{b}' = \dfrac{\vec{c}\times\vec{a}}{[\vec{a}\ \vec{b}\ \vec{c}]}, \vec{c}' = \dfrac{\vec{a}\times\vec{b}}{[\vec{a}\ \vec{b}\ \vec{c}]}$, then show that $\vec{a}\times\vec{a}' + \vec{b}\times\vec{b}' + \vec{c}\times\vec{c}' = \vec{0}$ where $\vec{a}', \vec{b}', \vec{c}'$ are non-coplanar.

SOLUTION: Here $\vec{a}\times\vec{a}' = \dfrac{\vec{a}\times(\vec{b}\times\vec{c})}{[\vec{a}\ \vec{b}\ \vec{c}]} = \dfrac{(\vec{a}.\vec{c})\vec{b} - (\vec{a}.\vec{b})\vec{c}}{[\vec{a}\ \vec{b}\ \vec{c}]}$ ...(i)

Similarly, $\vec{b}\times\vec{b}' = \dfrac{(\vec{b}.\vec{a})\vec{c} - (\vec{b}.\vec{c})\vec{a}}{[\vec{a}\ \vec{b}\ \vec{c}]}$ ...(ii)

and $\vec{c}\times\vec{c}' = \dfrac{(\vec{c}.\vec{b})\vec{a} - (\vec{c}.\vec{a})\vec{b}}{[\vec{a}\ \vec{b}\ \vec{c}]}$ ...(iii)

$\therefore\ \vec{a}\times\vec{a}' + \vec{b}\times\vec{b}' + \vec{c}\times\vec{c}'$

$= \dfrac{(\vec{a}.\vec{c})\vec{b} - (\vec{a}.\vec{b})\vec{c} + (\vec{b}.\vec{a})\vec{c} - (\vec{b}.\vec{c})\vec{a} + (\vec{c}.\vec{b})\vec{a} - (\vec{c}.\vec{a})\vec{b}}{[\vec{a}\ \vec{b}\ \vec{c}]} = \vec{0}$ $(\because [\vec{a}\ \vec{b}\ \vec{c}] \neq 0)$

ILLUSTRATION 80: Find a set of vectors reciprocal to the vectors $\vec{a}, \vec{b}$ and $\vec{a}\times\vec{b}$.

SOLUTION: Let the given vectors be denoted by $\vec{a}, \vec{b}, \vec{c}$ where $\vec{c} = \vec{a}\times\vec{b}$

$[\vec{a}\ \vec{b}\ \vec{c}] = (\vec{a}\times\vec{b}).\vec{c} = (\vec{a}\times\vec{b}).(\vec{a}\times\vec{b}) = (\vec{a}\times\vec{b})^2$

and let the reciprocal system of vectors be $\vec{a}', \vec{b}', \vec{c}'$

$\therefore\ \vec{a}' = \dfrac{(\vec{b}\times\vec{c})}{[\vec{a}\ \vec{b}\ \vec{c}]} = \dfrac{\vec{b}\times(\vec{a}\times\vec{b})}{|\vec{a}\times\vec{b}|^2}$; $\vec{b}' = \dfrac{\vec{c}\times\vec{a}}{[\vec{a}\ \vec{b}\ \vec{c}]} = \dfrac{(\vec{a}\times\vec{b})\times\vec{a}}{|\vec{a}\times\vec{b}|^2}$; $\vec{c}' = \dfrac{\vec{a}\times\vec{b}}{[\vec{a}\ \vec{b}\ \vec{c}]} = \dfrac{(\vec{a}\times\vec{b})}{|\vec{a}\times\vec{b}|^2}$

$\therefore\ \vec{a}', \vec{b}'$ and $\vec{c}'$ are required reciprocal system of vectors for $\vec{a}, \vec{b}$ and $\vec{a}\times\vec{b}$.

TEXTUAL EXERCISE 10: (SUBJECTIVE)

1. Find $\vec{a}\times(\vec{b}\times\vec{c})$ if

 (i) $\vec{a} = 2\hat{i} - 10\hat{j} + 2\hat{k}$, $\vec{b} = 3\hat{i} + \hat{j} + 2\hat{k}$ and $\vec{c} = 2\hat{i} + \hat{j} + 3\hat{k}$.

 (ii) $\vec{a} = 2\hat{i} + \hat{j} - 3\hat{k}$, $\vec{b} = \hat{i} - 2\hat{j} + \hat{k}$ and $\vec{c} = -\hat{i} + \hat{j} - 4\hat{k}$

2. Prove that $(\vec{a}\times\vec{b})\times\vec{c} = \vec{a}\times(\vec{b}\times\vec{c})$ if and only if $(\vec{c}\times\vec{a})\times\vec{b} = \vec{0}$.

3. Let $\vec{a}, \vec{b}, \vec{c}$ be three non-coplanar vectors and $\vec{p}, \vec{q}, \vec{r}$ are vectors defined by
$\vec{p} = \dfrac{\vec{b}\times\vec{c}}{[\vec{a}\ \vec{b}\ \vec{c}]}$, $\vec{q} = \dfrac{\vec{c}\times\vec{a}}{[\vec{a}\ \vec{b}\ \vec{c}]}$, $\vec{r} = \dfrac{\vec{a}\times\vec{b}}{[\vec{a}\ \vec{b}\ \vec{c}]}$ find the value of $(\vec{a}+\vec{b}).\vec{p}+(\vec{b}+\vec{c}).\vec{q}+(\vec{c}+\vec{a}).\vec{r}$

4. Show that the reciprocal system of vectors $\vec{u}, \vec{v}, \vec{n}$ is $\dfrac{\vec{l}}{\sin\theta}, \dfrac{\vec{m}}{\sin\theta}, \vec{n}$ where $\vec{n}$ is a unit vector perpendicular to plane of $\vec{u}$ and $\vec{v}$ such that $\vec{u}\times\vec{v} = \vec{n}\sin\theta$ and $\vec{l}$ is perpendicular to $\vec{v}$ and $\vec{n}$ and $\vec{m}$ is perpendicular to $\vec{u}$ and $\vec{v}$.

5. Prove that $\vec{a}.\vec{b}' = \vec{b}.\vec{c}' = \vec{a}.\vec{c}' = 0$.

6. Prove $[\vec{a}'\ \vec{b}'\ \vec{c}'] = \dfrac{1}{[\vec{a}\ \vec{b}\ \vec{c}]}$

7. Find the reciprocal systen of $\vec{a}, \vec{b}, \vec{c}$ where $\vec{a} = 2\hat{i}+3\hat{j}-\hat{k}$, $\vec{b} = \hat{i}-\hat{j}-2\hat{k}$, $\vec{c} = -\hat{i}+2\hat{j}+2\hat{k}$.

8. If the vectors $\vec{b}, \vec{c}, \vec{d}$ are not co-planar, then prove that the vector $(\vec{a}\times\vec{b})\times(\vec{c}\times\vec{d})+(\vec{a}\times\vec{c})\times(\vec{d}\times\vec{b})+(\vec{a}\times\vec{d})\times(\vec{b}\times\vec{c})$ is parallel to $\vec{b}$

9. Prove that (i) $(\vec{a}\times\vec{b})\times(\vec{c}\times\vec{d}) = [\vec{a}\,\vec{b}\,\vec{d}]\vec{c} - [\vec{a}\,\vec{b}\,\vec{c}]\vec{d}$
(ii) $(\vec{a}\times\vec{b})\times(\vec{c}\times\vec{d}) = [\vec{a}\,\vec{c}\,\vec{d}]\vec{b} - [\vec{b}\,\vec{c}\,\vec{d}]\vec{a}$.

10. If $\vec{a},\vec{b},\vec{c}$ and $\vec{a},\vec{b},\vec{c}$ be the reciprocal system of vecotrs, prove that
$\vec{a}' = \dfrac{\vec{b}\times\vec{c}}{[\vec{a}\ \vec{b}\ \vec{c}]}, \vec{b}' = \dfrac{\vec{c}\times\vec{a}}{[\vec{a},\vec{b},\vec{c}]}$ and $\vec{c}' = \dfrac{\vec{a}\times\vec{b}}{[\vec{a}\ \vec{b}\ \vec{c}]}$

Answer Key

1. (i) 0 (ii) $8\hat{i}-19\hat{j}-\hat{k}$ 3. 3 7. $\vec{a}' = \dfrac{2\hat{i}+\hat{k}}{3}$, similarly $\vec{b}'$ and $\vec{c}'$ can be obtained.

TEXTUAL EXERCISE 7: (OBJECTIVE)

1. For any vector $\vec{r}$, the value of $\hat{i}\times(\vec{r}\times\hat{i})+\hat{j}\times(\vec{r}\times\hat{j})+\hat{k}\times(\vec{r}\times\hat{k})$ is
(a) $\vec{0}$ (b) $2\vec{r}$
(c) $-2\vec{r}$ (d) None of these

2. If $\vec{a}, \vec{b}, \vec{c}$ are non-coplanar unit vectors such that $\vec{a}\times(\vec{b}\times\vec{c}) = \dfrac{\vec{b}+\vec{c}}{\sqrt{2}}$, then the angle between $\vec{a}$ and $\vec{b}$ is equal to
(a) $3\pi/4$ (b) $\pi/4$
(c) $\pi/2$ (d) π

3. If $\vec{a}, \vec{b}$ and $\vec{c}$ are non-coplanar vectors and $\vec{a}\times\vec{c}$ is perpendicular to $\vec{a}\times(\vec{b}\times\vec{c})$, then the value of $[\vec{a}\times(\vec{b}\times\vec{c})]\times\vec{c}$ is equal to
(a) $[\vec{a}\ \vec{b}\ \vec{c}]\,\vec{c}$ (b) $[\vec{a}\ \vec{b}\ \vec{c}]\,\vec{b}$
(c) $\vec{0}$ (d) None of these

4. If $\vec{a}, \vec{b}$ and $\vec{c}$ are three unit vectors such that $\vec{a}\times(\vec{b}\times\vec{c}) = \frac{1}{2}\vec{b}$ then
(a) $\vec{a}$ and $\vec{b}$ are perpendicular
(b) angle between $\vec{a}$ and $\vec{b}$ is $\pi/3$
(c) $\vec{a}$ and $\vec{c}$ are inclined at an angle $\pi/6$
(d) $\vec{a}, \vec{b}, \vec{c}$ are mutually an orthogonal

5. The scalars α and β if $\vec{a}\times(\vec{b}\times\vec{c})+(\vec{a}.\vec{b})\vec{b} = (4-2\beta-\sin\alpha)\,\vec{b}+(\beta^2-1)\vec{c}$ and $(\vec{a}.\vec{c})\vec{c} = \vec{c}$ where $\vec{b}$ and $\vec{c}$ are non-collinear, are
(a) $\beta = 1$, $\alpha = (4n+1)\pi/2$; $n \in \mathbb{Z}$
(b) $\beta = 1$, $\alpha = (4n-1)\pi/2$; $n \in \mathbb{Z}$
(c) $\beta = -1$, $\alpha = (4n+1)\pi/2$; $n \in \mathbb{Z}$
(d) $\beta = -1$, $\alpha = (4n-1)\pi/2$; $n \in \mathbb{Z}$

6. If $\vec{a} = \vec{p}+\vec{q}$, $\vec{p}\times\vec{b} = \vec{0}$ and $\vec{q}.\vec{b} = 0$, then $\dfrac{\vec{b}\times(\vec{a}\times\vec{b})}{\vec{b}.\vec{b}}$ is equal to

(a) $\vec{q}$ (b) $\vec{p}$
(c) $\vec{p}\times\vec{q}$ (d) None of these

7. If $\vec{a}$ and $\vec{b}$ are two unit vectors, then the vector $(\vec{a}+\vec{b})\times(\vec{a}\times\vec{b})$ is parallel to the vector

(a) $\vec{a}-\vec{b}$ (b) $\vec{a}+\vec{b}$
(c) $2\vec{a}-\vec{b}$ (d) $2\vec{a}+\vec{b}$

8. If $\vec{a},\vec{b}$ and $\vec{c}$ are any three vectors, then $\vec{a}\times(\vec{b}\times\vec{c}) = (\vec{a}\times\vec{b})\times\vec{c}$ if and only if

(a) $\vec{b}$ and $\vec{c}$ are collinear
(b) $\vec{a}$ and $\vec{c}$ are collinear
(c) $\vec{a}$ and $\vec{b}$ are collinear
(d) None of these

9. If $(\vec{a}\times\vec{b})\times(\vec{c}\times\vec{d})=[\vec{a}\vec{b}\vec{d}]\vec{c}+k\vec{d}$, then the value of k is

(a) $[\vec{b}\vec{a}\vec{c}]$ (b) $[\vec{a}\vec{b}\,\vec{c}]$
(c) $[\vec{b}\,\vec{c}\vec{d}]$ (d) $[\vec{c}\vec{b}\vec{d}]$

10. If $\vec{a},\vec{b},\vec{c}$ are three non-coplanar vectors, then the length of projection of vector $\vec{a}$ in the plane of the vector $\vec{b}$ and $\vec{c}$ may be given as

(a) $\dfrac{|\vec{a}.(\vec{b}\times\vec{c})|}{|(\vec{b}\times\vec{c})|}$ (b) $\dfrac{|\vec{a}\times(\vec{b}\times\vec{c})|}{|(\vec{b}\times\vec{c})|}$

(c) $\dfrac{|\vec{a}\ \vec{b}\ \vec{c})|}{(\vec{b}\times\vec{c})}$ (d) None of these

11. If $\vec{p}=\dfrac{\vec{b}\times\vec{c}}{[\vec{a}\ \vec{b}\ \vec{c}]}$, $\vec{q}=\dfrac{\vec{c}\times\vec{a}}{[\vec{a}\ \vec{b}\ \vec{c}]}$, $\vec{r}=\dfrac{\vec{a}\times\vec{b}}{[\vec{a}\ \vec{b}\ \vec{c}]}$ where $\vec{a},\vec{b},\vec{c}$ are three non-coplanar vectors, then the value of the expression $(\vec{a}+\vec{b}+\vec{c}).(\vec{p}+\vec{q}+\vec{r})$ is

(a) 3 (b) 2
(c) 1 (d) 0

12. Let $\vec{a}',\vec{b}',\vec{c}'$ be three non-coplanar vectors and let p, q and $\vec{r}$ be the vector defined by the relations $\vec{p}=\dfrac{\vec{b}\times\vec{c}}{[\vec{a}\vec{b}\vec{c}]}$, $q=\dfrac{\vec{c}\times\vec{a}}{[\vec{a}\vec{b}\vec{c}]}$ and $r=\dfrac{\vec{a}\times\vec{b}}{[\vec{a}\vec{b}\vec{c}]}$ then the value of expression $(\vec{a}+\vec{b}).\vec{p}+(\vec{b}+\vec{c}).\vec{q}+(\vec{c}+\vec{a}).\vec{r}$ is equal to

(a) 0 (b) 1
(c) 2 (d) 3

13. If $\vec{a},\vec{b},\vec{c},\vec{d}$ are any four vectors, then $(\vec{a}\times\vec{b})\times(\vec{c}\times\vec{d})$ is a vector

(a) perpendicular to $\vec{a},\vec{b},\vec{c},\vec{d}$
(b) along the line of intersection of two planes one containing $\vec{a},\vec{b}$ and the other containing $\vec{c},\vec{d}$
(c) equally inclined to both $\vec{a}\times\vec{b}$ and $\vec{c}\times\vec{d}$
(d) None of these

14. If $\vec{d}=\vec{a}\times(\vec{b}\times\vec{c})+\vec{b}\times(\vec{c}\times\vec{a})+\vec{c}\times(\vec{a}\times\vec{b})$, then

(a) $\vec{d}$ is a unit vector
(b) $\vec{d}=\vec{a}+\vec{b}+\vec{c}$
(c) $\vec{d}=\vec{0}$
(d) $\vec{a},\vec{b},\vec{c}$ and $\vec{d}$ are co-planar

15. If $\vec{a},\vec{b},\vec{c},\vec{d}$ lie in the same plane, then $(\vec{a}\times\vec{b})\times(\vec{c}\times\vec{d})$ is equal to

(a) $\vec{c}+\vec{d}$ (b) $\vec{0}$
(c) $[\vec{a}\vec{b}\vec{c}]\vec{a}+2\vec{b}$ (d) $[\vec{b}\vec{c}\vec{d}]\vec{c}+\vec{d}$

16. The value of $\left|\vec{a}\times(\hat{i}\times\hat{j})\right|^2+\left|\vec{a}\times(\hat{j}\times\hat{k})\right|^2+\left|\vec{a}\times(\hat{k}\times\hat{i})\right|^2$ is

(a) $|a|^2$ (b) $2|a|^2$
(c) $3|a|^2$ (d) None of these

17. Let $\vec{a}=2\hat{i}-\hat{j}+\hat{k}$, $\vec{b}=\hat{i}+2\hat{j}-\hat{k}$ and $\vec{c}=\hat{i}+\hat{j}-2\hat{k}$ be three vectors. A vector in the plane of $\vec{b}$ and $\vec{c}$ whose projection on $\vec{a}$ is of magnitude $\sqrt{\dfrac{2}{3}}$ is

(a) $2\hat{i}+3\hat{j}-3\hat{k}$ (b) $2\hat{i}+3\hat{j}+3\hat{k}$
(c) $-2\hat{i}-\hat{j}+5\hat{k}$ (d) $2\hat{i}+\hat{j}+5\hat{k}$

18. Let the vector $\vec{a},\vec{b},\vec{c}$ and $\vec{d}$ be such that $(\vec{a}\times\vec{b})\times\vec{c}\times\vec{d}=\vec{0}$. Let P_1 and P_2 be planes determined by the pairs of vectors $\vec{a},\vec{b},\vec{c}$ and respectively. Then the angle between P_1 and P_2 is

(a) 0 (b) $\pi/4$
(c) $\pi/3$ (d) $\pi/2$

Answer Key

1. (b)	**2.** (a)	**3.** (c)	**4.** (a)	**5.** (a)	**6.** (a)	**7.** (a)	**8.** (b)	**9.** (a)	**10.** (b)
11. (a)	**12.** (d)	**13.** (b,c)	**14.** (c)	**15.** (b)	**16.** (b)	**17.** (a,c)	**18.** (a)		

■ GEOMETRICAL APPLICATIONS

Parametric Vectorial Equations

It is possible to express the position vectors ($\vec{r}$) of points lying on a given curve (surface) in terms of some fixed vectors and some variable scalars (parameters) such that:

(i) For arbitrary values of the parameters, the resulting position vectors represent points on the locus in question

(ii) Conversely, the position vector of each point on the locus can be obtained for some suitable value of the parameters.

Such equations are called parameteric vectorial equation of the locus under consideration

Here we are discussing vector equations of straight line and planes in various forms.

Vector Equation of Straight Line

(a) Line passing through a point A with position vector $\vec{a}$ and parallel to another vector $\vec{b}$ is given by the equation $\vec{r}=\vec{a}+\lambda(\vec{b})$.

Proof: Let us consider an arbitrary point P with position vector $\vec{r}$ on the line AB as shown in the figure:

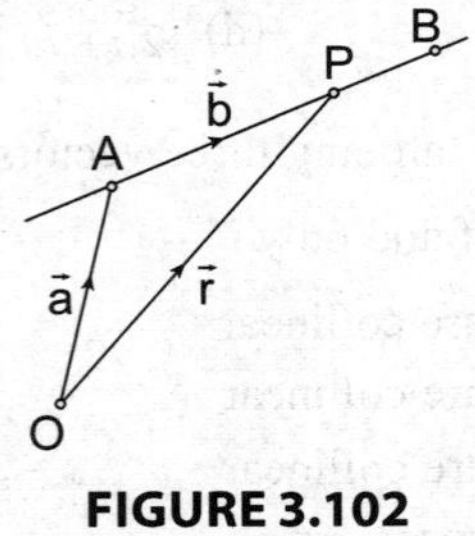

FIGURE 3.102

$$\overrightarrow{OP}=\overrightarrow{OA}+\overrightarrow{AP}=\overrightarrow{OA}+\lambda\,\overrightarrow{AB}$$

$\Rightarrow\ \vec{r}=\vec{a}+\lambda(\vec{b})$. (where λ is a parameter)

NOTES

If co-ordinates of point $A(x_1, y_1, z_1)$ and direction cosines of $\vec{b}$ is (l, m, n) respectively, then the cartesian equation of above line can also be derived as $(x\hat{i}+y\hat{j}+z\hat{k})=(x_1\hat{i}+y_1\hat{j}+z_1\hat{k})+\lambda(l\hat{i}+m\hat{j}+n\hat{k})$

Since i, j, k, are linearly independent.

Therefore $(x-x_1)-\lambda l=0$, $(y-y_1)-\lambda m=0$ and $(z-z_1)-\lambda n=0$

$$\Rightarrow\ \frac{(x-x_1)}{l}=\frac{(y-y_1)}{m}=\frac{(z-z_1)}{n}=\lambda$$

(b) Line passing through two points A with position vector $\vec{a}$ and b with position vector $\vec{b}$ is given by the equation $\vec{r}=\vec{a}+\lambda(\vec{b}-\vec{a})$, where λ is any real scalar parameter

or $\vec{r}=\vec{b}+\lambda(\vec{b}-\vec{a})$

$\Rightarrow\ \vec{r}=(1+\lambda)\vec{b}+(-\lambda)\vec{a}$

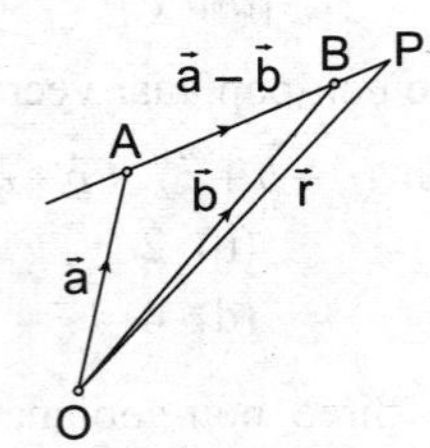

FIGURE 3.103

NOTES

If co-ordinate of point A are (x_1, y_1, z_1) and that of B are (x_2, y_2, z_2). Therefore direction ratios of line will be $<(x_2-x_1), (y_2-y_1), (z_2-z_1)>$.

The equation of line through A and B can also be writen as $\frac{(x-x_1)}{(x_2-x_1)}=\frac{(y-y_1)}{(y_2-y_1)}=\frac{(z-z_1)}{(z_2-z_1)}=\lambda$

ILLUSTRATION 82: In a ΔOAB, E is the mid-point of OB and D is a point on AB such that $AD : DB = 2: 1$. If OD and AE intersect at P, determine the ratio $OP : PD$ using vector methods:

SOLUTION: Let O be the origin. Let position vectors of the points A, B, D, E and P be $\vec{a}, \vec{b}, \vec{d}, \vec{e}$ and $\vec{p}$ respectively.

$\therefore \quad \vec{e} = \frac{\vec{b}}{2},\ \vec{d} = \frac{\vec{a}+2\vec{b}}{3}$ $\therefore$ Equation of $\overrightarrow{OD}$ is $\vec{r} = \lambda\left(\frac{\vec{a}+2\vec{b}}{3}\right)$ ...(i)

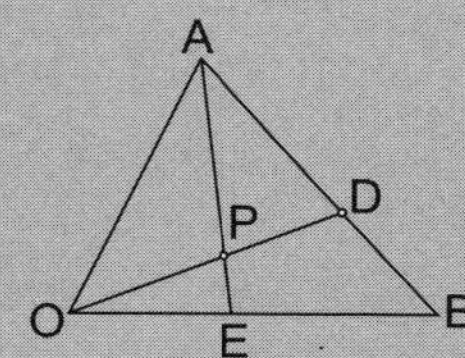

FIGURE 3.104

Equation of $\overrightarrow{AE}$ is $\vec{r} = \vec{a} + \mu(\vec{e} - \vec{a})$

i.e., $\vec{r} = \vec{a} + \mu\left(\frac{\vec{b}}{2} - \vec{a}\right)$ ...(ii)

$\therefore$ for point P, equating equations (i) and (ii), we get

$$\left(\frac{\lambda}{3}\right)\vec{a} + \left(\frac{2\lambda}{3}\right)\vec{b} = (1-\mu)\vec{a} + \left(\frac{\mu}{2}\right)\vec{b} \quad \left(\frac{\lambda}{3}\right) = (1-\mu) \text{ and } \frac{2\lambda}{3} = \frac{\mu}{2} \Rightarrow \lambda = 3/5 \text{ and } \mu = 4/5$$

$$\therefore \quad \vec{p} = \frac{3}{5}\left(\frac{\vec{a}+2\vec{b}}{3}\right) = \frac{3\left(\frac{\vec{a}+2\vec{b}}{3}\right) + 2.\vec{0}}{3+2}$$

$\therefore$ Point P divides $\overrightarrow{OD}$ in the ratio $3 : 2$ internally $\therefore$ $OP : PD = 3 : 2$

ILLUSTRATION 83: Find the equation of altitudes of the triangle ABC having its vertices $A(0,0,0)$; $B(2,2,1)$ and $C(0,0,1)$

SOLUTION: Clearly, ΔABC is right angled triangle. $\overrightarrow{AM} = \frac{1}{\lambda+1}(2\hat{i} + 2\hat{j} + \hat{k})$; $\overrightarrow{AC} = \hat{k}$

$$\overrightarrow{MC} = \frac{-2}{\lambda+1}\hat{i} - \frac{2}{\lambda+1}\hat{j} + \left(1 - \frac{1}{\lambda+1}\right)\hat{k} = \frac{-2\hat{i} - 2\hat{j} + \lambda\hat{k}}{\lambda+1}$$

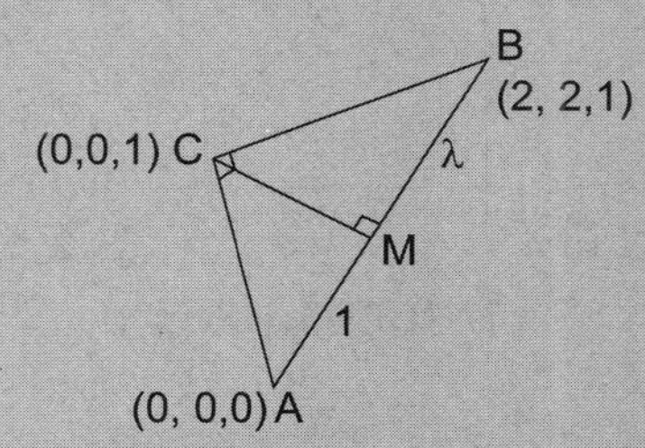

FIGURE 3.105

Now $\overrightarrow{MC} \perp \overrightarrow{AB}$ $\Rightarrow$ $-\frac{4}{\lambda+1} - \frac{4}{\lambda-1} + \frac{\lambda}{\lambda+1} = 0 \Rightarrow \lambda = 8$

Altitude through A: $\vec{r} = \lambda\hat{k}$ Altitude through B: $\vec{r} = \hat{k} + \lambda(2\hat{i} + 2\hat{j})$

or $\vec{r} = \hat{k} + \mu(\hat{i} + \hat{j})$; Altitude through C: $\vec{r} = \hat{k} + \lambda\left(\frac{8\hat{k} - 2\hat{i} - 2\hat{j}}{9} - \hat{k}\right)$

$\vec{r} = \hat{k} + \mu(\hat{k} + 2(\hat{i} + \hat{j}))$ where $\mu = \left(-\frac{\lambda}{9}\right)$

ILLUSTRATION 84: Find the equation of straight line parallel to $2\hat{i}-\hat{j}+3\hat{k}$ and passing through the point (5, –2, 4)

SOLUTION: ***Vector form:*** Let $P=(5,-2,4)$ and $\overrightarrow{OP}=5\hat{i}-2\hat{j}+4\hat{k}=\vec{a}$ also $\vec{b}=2\hat{i}-\hat{j}+3\hat{k}$

$\therefore$ equation of straight line passing through $\vec{a}$ and parallel to $\vec{b}$ is given by $\vec{r}=\vec{a}+\lambda\vec{b}$

or $\vec{r}=(5\hat{i}-2\hat{j}+4\hat{k})+\lambda(2\hat{i}-\hat{j}+3\hat{k})$

Cartesian form: Here $(x_1, y_1, z_1)=(5,-2,4)$ and parallel to straight line whose direction cosines are $(2,-1,3)$ is $\dfrac{x-5}{2}=\dfrac{y+2}{-1}=\dfrac{z-4}{3}$

INTERNAL AND EXTERNAL ANGLE BISECTORS OF A LINE

The internal bisector of angle between unit vectors $\hat{a}$ and $\hat{b}$ is along the vector $\hat{a}+\hat{b}$. The external bisector is along $\hat{a}-\hat{b}$. Equation of internal and external bisectors of the lines $\vec{r}=\vec{a}+\lambda\vec{b}_1$ and $\vec{r}=\vec{a}+\mu\vec{b}_2$; internally at A ($\vec{a}$) are given by $\vec{r}=\vec{a}+t\left(\dfrac{\vec{b}_1}{|\vec{b}_1|}\pm\dfrac{\vec{b}_2}{|\vec{b}_2|}\right)$

ILLUSTRATION 85: Find the vector equation of internal as well as external bisector of a triangle ABC through the vertex A and B where A is(0, 0, 0) B is (2,2,1) and C is (0, 0, 1).

SOLUTION: Internal bisector through A:

$$\vec{r}=\lambda\left(\frac{2}{3}\hat{i}+\frac{2}{3}\hat{j}+\frac{1}{3}\hat{k}+\hat{k}\right)=\frac{\lambda}{3}(2\hat{i}+2\hat{j}+4\hat{k})=\frac{2\lambda}{3}(\hat{i}+\hat{j}+2\hat{k});\ \vec{r}=\mu(\hat{i}+\hat{j}+2\hat{k})$$

External bisector through A:

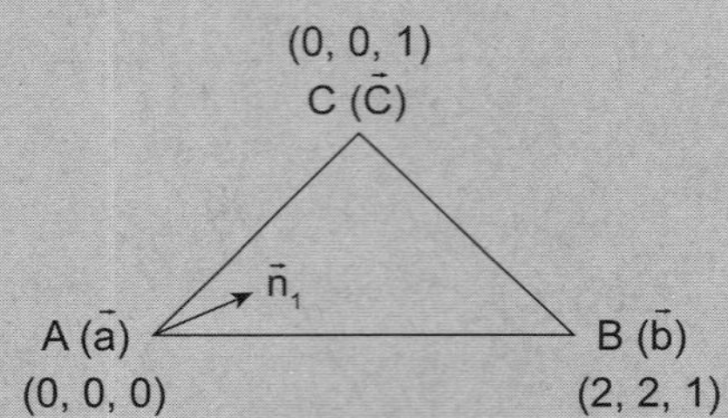

FIGURE 3.106

$$\vec{r}=\lambda\left(\frac{2\hat{i}+2\hat{j}+\hat{k}-3\hat{k}}{3}\right)\Rightarrow\vec{r}=\frac{2\lambda}{3}(\hat{i}+\hat{j}-\hat{k})\ \Rightarrow\vec{r}=\mu(\hat{i}+\hat{j}-\hat{k})$$

Internal bisector through B. Vector along internal bisector through

$$B=\left(\frac{-2\hat{i}-2\hat{j}-\hat{k}}{3}\right)-\left(\frac{2\hat{i}+2\hat{j}}{2\sqrt{2}}\right)=\frac{-2\hat{i}-2\hat{j}-\hat{k}}{3}-\left(\frac{\hat{i}+\hat{j}}{\sqrt{2}}\right)=-\left[\frac{(2\sqrt{2}+3)(\hat{i}+\hat{j})+(\sqrt{2})\hat{k}}{3\sqrt{2}}\right]$$

Therefore the equation of internal bisector through B

$$\vec{r}=2\hat{i}+2\hat{j}+\hat{k}+\lambda\left(\frac{(2\sqrt{2}+3)(\hat{i}+\hat{j})+(\sqrt{2})\hat{k}}{3\sqrt{2}}\right)$$

or $\vec{r}=2\hat{i}+2\hat{j}+\hat{k}+\mu\{(2\sqrt{2}+3)(\hat{i}+\hat{j})+(\sqrt{2})\hat{k}\}$ where μ is $\dfrac{\lambda}{3\sqrt{2}}$

External bisector through B. Vector along internal bisector through

$$B = \frac{-2\hat{i}-2\hat{j}-\hat{k}}{3} + \frac{2\hat{i}+2\hat{j}}{2\sqrt{2}} = -\left[\frac{(2\sqrt{2}-3)(\hat{i}+\hat{j})+(\sqrt{2})\hat{k}}{3\sqrt{2}}\right]$$

Therefore the equation of internal bisector through B

$$\vec{r} = 2\hat{i}+2\hat{j}+\hat{k}+\lambda\left(\frac{(2\sqrt{2}-3)(\hat{i}+\hat{j})+(\sqrt{2})\hat{k}}{3\sqrt{2}}\right)$$

or $\vec{r} = 2\hat{i}+2\hat{j}+\hat{k}+\mu\left\{(2\sqrt{2}-3)(\hat{i}+\hat{j})+(\sqrt{2})\hat{k}\right\}$ where μ is $\frac{\lambda}{3\sqrt{2}}$

Vector Equation of a Plane

(a) The vector equation of plane passing through origin and containing $\vec{a}$ and $\vec{b}$ is $\vec{r} = \lambda_1\vec{a}+\lambda_2\vec{b}$

$\Rightarrow \vec{r}.(\vec{a}\times\vec{b}) = 0$

Since any vector lying in the plane is perpendicular to $a\times b$

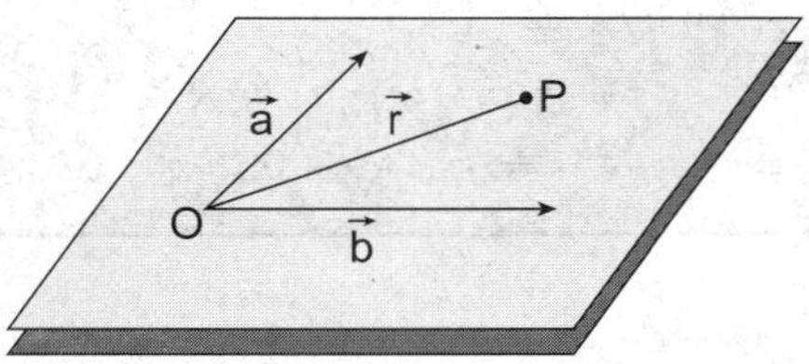

FIGURE 3.107

(b) Vector equation of plane passing through some other point $C(\vec{c})$ and co-planar with two vectors $\vec{a}$ and $\vec{b}$ is $\vec{r} = \vec{c}+\lambda_1\vec{a}+\lambda_2\vec{b}$

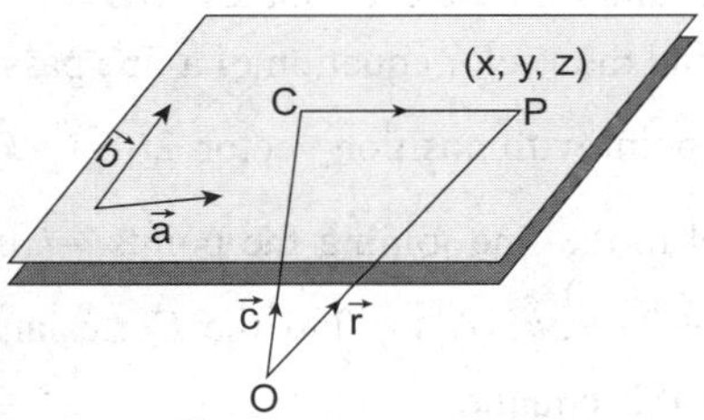

FIGURE 3.108

Taking dot product with $\vec{a}\times\vec{b}$,

$(\vec{r}-\vec{c}).(\vec{a}\times\vec{b}) = 0 \Rightarrow \vec{r}.(\vec{a}\times\vec{b}) = [\vec{a}\ \vec{b}\ \vec{c}]$

Aliter: Plane through a given point parallel to two given straight lines. Let $\vec{c}$ be the given point and $\vec{a}$, $\vec{b}$ two vectors parallel to the given lines. Then $\vec{a}\times\vec{b}$ is perpendicular to the plane and we have only to write down the equation of the plane through $\vec{c}$ perpendicular to $\vec{a}\times\vec{b}$. Since $\overline{CP}\perp(\vec{a}\times\vec{b})$, $(\vec{r}-\vec{c}).(\vec{a}\times\vec{b}) = 0$

i.e., $\vec{r}.(\vec{a}\times\vec{b}) = [\vec{a}\vec{b}\vec{c}]$

(c) Vector equation of a plane passing through three points A, B, C having position vectors $\vec{a}$, $\vec{b}$ and $\vec{c}$ respectively.

$\overline{AB} = \vec{b}-\vec{a}$; $\overline{AC} = \vec{c}-\vec{a}$

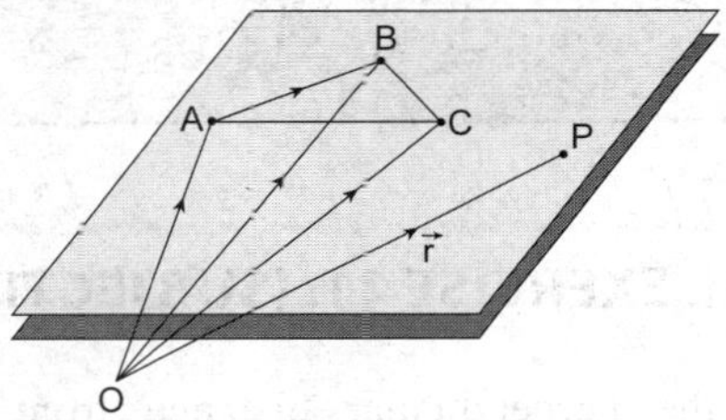

FIGURE 3.109

Therefore $\vec{r} = \lambda(\vec{b}-\vec{a})+\mu(\vec{c}-\vec{a})$

Aliter: Plane through three given points A, B, C. Let $\vec{a},\vec{b},\vec{c}$ be the position vectors of the points relative to an assigned origin O, $\vec{r}$ that of a variable point P on the plane. Since P, A, B, C all lie on the plane, the vector $\vec{r}-\vec{a}$, $\vec{a}-\vec{b}$, $\vec{b}-\vec{c}$ are co-planar and their scalar triple product is zero. Hence $(\vec{r}-\vec{a}).\left\{(\vec{a}-\vec{b})\times(\vec{b}-\vec{c})\right\} = 0$

If we expand this and neglect the triple prouducts in which any vector occurs twice, then equation becomes $\vec{r}.(\vec{b}\times\vec{c}+\vec{c}\times\vec{a}+\vec{a}\times\vec{b}) = [\vec{a}\vec{b}\vec{c}]$. Thus the plane is perpendicular to the vector $\vec{n} = \vec{b}\times\vec{c}+\vec{c}\times\vec{a}+\vec{a}\times\vec{b}$ which represents twice the vector area of the triangle ABC.

ILLUSTRATION 86: Find the vector and cartesian forms of the equation of the plane passing through the point (1, 2, –4) and parallel to the lines $\vec{r} = \hat{i} + 2\hat{j} - 4\hat{k} + \lambda(2\hat{i} + 3\hat{j} + 6\hat{k})$ and $\vec{r} = \hat{i} + 3\hat{j} + 5\hat{k} + \mu(\hat{i} + \hat{j} - \hat{k})$

SOLUTION: We have $\vec{a} = \hat{i} + 2\hat{j} - 4\hat{k}$, $\vec{b} = 2\hat{i} + 3\hat{j} + 6\hat{k}$ and $\vec{b}' = \hat{i} + \hat{j} - \hat{k}$

Then the vector equation of the plane is $[\vec{r} - (\hat{i} + 2\hat{j} - 4\hat{k})].[(2\hat{i} + 3\hat{j} + 6\hat{k}) \times (\hat{i} + \hat{j} - \hat{k})] = 0$

Therefore, the cartesian equation of the plane is given by $\begin{vmatrix} x-1 & y-2 & z+4 \\ 2 & 3 & 6 \\ 1 & 1 & -1 \end{vmatrix} = 0$

or $(x - 1)(-3 - 6) - (y - 2)(-2 - 6) + (z + 4)(2 - 3) = 0$

$\Rightarrow -9(x - 1) + 8(y - 2) - (z + 4) = 0 \Rightarrow -9x + 8y - z - 11 = 0 \Rightarrow 9x - 8y + z + 11 = 0$

ILLUSTRATION 87: Find the vector and cartesian forms of the equation of the plane containing two lines $\vec{r} = \hat{i} + 2\hat{j} - 4\hat{k} + \lambda(2\hat{i} + 3\hat{j} + 6\hat{k})$ and $\vec{r} = 3\hat{i} + 3\hat{j} - 5\hat{k} + \mu(-2\hat{i} + 3\hat{j} + 8\hat{k})$

SOLUTION: We have $\vec{a} = \hat{i} + 2\hat{j} - 4\hat{k}$, $\vec{a}' = 3\hat{i} + 3\hat{j} - 5\hat{k}$

$\vec{b} = 2\hat{i} + 3\hat{j} + 6\hat{k}$, $\vec{b}' = -2\hat{i} + 3\hat{j} + 8\hat{k}$

Then the vector equation of the plane is

$[\vec{r} - (\hat{i} + 2\hat{j} - 4\hat{k})].[(2\hat{i} + 3\hat{j} + 6\hat{k}) \times (-2\hat{i} + 3\hat{j} + 8\hat{k})] = 0$

Therefore, the cartesian equation of the plane is given by $\begin{vmatrix} x-1 & y-2 & z+4 \\ 2 & 3 & 6 \\ -2 & 3 & 8 \end{vmatrix} = 0$

$\Rightarrow 6(x - 1) - 28(y - 2) + 12(z + 4) = 0 \qquad \Rightarrow 3x - 14y + 6z + 49 = 0$

TEXTUAL EXERCISE 11: (SUBJECTIVE)

1. Find the perpendicular distance from the point P (–1, 2, 6) to the straight line through the points A(2, 3 – 4) and B(8,6, –8).

2. Find the plane through the point (1, 4, –2) perpendicular to the line of intersection of the planes $x + y + z = 10$, $2x - y + 3z = 18$.

3. Show that the plane through the point (2, –4, 5) perpendicular to the line of intersection of the planes $2x + 3y - 4z = 1$ and $3x + y - 2z = 2$ is $2x + 8y + 7z = 7$.

4. The plane through the points A(3, –5, –1), B(–1, 5, 7) and parallel to the vector (3, –1, 7) is $3x + 2y - z = 0$

5. Show that the perpendicular distance from C to the straight line through A and B is $\dfrac{|\vec{b} \times \vec{c} + \vec{c} \times \vec{a} + \vec{a} \times \vec{b}|}{|\vec{b} - \vec{a}|}$.

6. Show that if the vector area of each face of a tetrahedron has the direction of the outward normal, the sum of their vector areas is zero.

7. (a) The points A (4, 5, 10), B (2, 3, 4) and C (1, 2, –1) are three vertices of a parallelogram $ABCD$. Find vector and Cartesian equations of the sides AB and BC and find the coordinates of D.

   (b) Find the vector equation of a line passing through a point with position vector $2\hat{i} - \hat{j} + \hat{k}$ and parallel to the line joining the points $-\hat{i} + 4\hat{j} + \hat{k}$ and $\hat{i} + 2\hat{j} + 2\hat{k}$. Also, find the Cartesian equivalent of this equation.

8. (a) Find the equation of the plane through the points P(1, 1, 0), Q(1, 2, 1), R (–2, 2, –1).

   (b) Let $\vec{n}$ be a vector of magnitude $2\sqrt{3}$ such that it makes equal acute angles with the coordinate axes. Find the vector and cartesian forms of the equation of a plane passing through (1, –1, 2) and normal to the vector $\vec{n}$

Answer Key

1. 7 units **2.** $4x - y - 3z - 6 = 0$ **7.** (a) AB: $\vec{r} = 4\hat{i} + 5\hat{j} + 10\hat{k} + \mu(\hat{i} + \hat{j} + 3\hat{k})$, $\frac{x-4}{1} = \frac{y-5}{1} = \frac{z-10}{3}$

BC: $\vec{r} = 2\hat{i} + 3\hat{j} + 4\hat{k} + \nu(\hat{i} + \hat{j} + 5\hat{k})$ $\frac{x-2}{1} = \frac{y-3}{1} = \frac{z-4}{5}$ D: (3,4,5)

(b) $(2\hat{i} - \hat{j} + \hat{k}) + \lambda(2\hat{i} - 2\hat{j} + \hat{k})$ $\frac{x-2}{2} = \frac{y+1}{-2} = \frac{z-1}{1}$

8. (a) $2x + 3y - 3z - 5 = 0$ (d) V.Eq: $\vec{r}(\hat{i} + \hat{j} + \hat{k}) = 2$ C. Eq: $x + y + z = 2$

TEXTUAL EXERCISE 8: (OBJECTIVE)

1. The equation of plane coplanar with vectors $\vec{a} = 2\hat{i} + \hat{j} - 3\hat{k}$ and $\vec{b} = -\hat{i} + \hat{j} + \hat{k}$ is

(a) $4x - y - 3z + k_1 = 0; k_1 \in \mathbb{R}$
(b) $4x + y - 3z + k_1 = 0; k_1 \in \mathbb{R}$
(c) $4x + y + 3z + k_1 = 0; k_1 \in \mathbb{R}$
(d) None of these

2. The vector equation of plane coplanar with vectors $\vec{a} = \hat{i} - \hat{j} + \hat{k}$ and $\vec{b} = 4\hat{i} - 2\hat{j} + \hat{k}$ and passing through the point (1, 2, 5) is

(a) $\vec{r}.(\hat{i} + 3\hat{j} - 2\hat{k}) = 15$ (b) $\vec{r}.(\hat{i} + 3\hat{j} + 2\hat{k}) = 17$

(c) $\vec{r}.(3\hat{i} + \hat{j} - \hat{k}) = 17$ (d) None of these

3. The vector equation of plane containing three points A (2, 1, 5); B(0, –1, 6); C(–3, 4, 5) is

(a) $\vec{r}.(3\hat{i} - 5\hat{j} + 16\hat{k}) = 90$

(b) $\vec{r}.(2\hat{i} - \hat{j} + 5\hat{k}) = 80$

(c) $\vec{r}.(3\hat{i} + 5\hat{j} + 16\hat{k}) = 91$

(d) None of these

4. The equation of plane passing through points A(2,1,5); B(3, –1, 2) and parallel to vector $\hat{i} + \hat{j} - \hat{k}$ is

(a) $\vec{r}.(5\hat{i} - 2\hat{j} + 3\hat{k}) - 23 = 0$

(b) $\vec{r}.(5\hat{i} - 2\hat{j} + 3\hat{k}) + 23 = 0$

(c) $\vec{r}.(\hat{i} + 2\hat{j} - 3\hat{k}) + 11 = 0$

(d) None of these

5. The equation of a plane passing through points A(0,–1,–1); B(–4,4,4); C(4,5,1) is $5x - 7y + 11z + \lambda = 0$, then value of μ for which point $(\lambda - 1, \lambda + \mu, \lambda)$ lies on the plane containing points A, B and C is

(a) 4 (b) 3
(c) 2 (d) 5

Answer Key

1. (c) **2.** (b) **3.** (c) **4.** (a) **5.** (d)

■ VECTOR EQUATIONS AND METHOD OF SOLVING

A vector equation is a relation between some unknown vector/s and some known quantities and the values of the unknown vectors satisfying the equation is called the solution of equation. Solving a vector equation means determining an unknown vector (or a number of vectors satisfying the given conditions)

Methods to Solve Vector Equations

Generally, to solve vector equations, we express the unknown vector as the linear combination of three non-coplanar vectors as:

$\vec{r} = x\vec{a} + y\vec{b} + z(\vec{a} \times \vec{b})$; as $\vec{a}, \vec{b}$ and $\vec{a} \times \vec{b}$ are non-coplanar and find x, y, z using given conditions. Some times we can directly solve the given conditions also.

Type-I: To solve for $\vec{r}$, i.e., $\vec{r} \times \vec{b} = \vec{a} \times \vec{b}$ .....(i)
where $\vec{a}, \vec{b}$ are two given vectors

Let $\vec{r}$ be any solution of the equation

Rewriting the given equation as $(\vec{r}-\vec{a})\times\vec{b}=\vec{0}$

We see that $(\vec{r}-\vec{a})$ is parallel to $\vec{b}$, so that we must have $\vec{r}-\vec{a}=t\vec{b} \Rightarrow \vec{r}=\vec{a}+t\vec{b}$ ....(ii)

where t is a scalar. Also it may be seen that $\vec{r}=\vec{a}+t\vec{b}$ satisfies (i) for every value of the scalar t. Thus (ii) gives the general solution of the given equation.

Geometrically, we know that the points whose position vectors are given by (ii) for different values of the scalar t is on a straight line which passes through the point with position vector $\vec{a}$ and is parallel to the vector $\vec{b}$.

Type -II: To solve for $\vec{r}$, i.e., $\vec{r}\times\vec{b}=\vec{a}$ where a b are two given vectors such that $\vec{a}$ is perpendicular to $\vec{b}$.

Consider three non-co-planar vectors $\vec{a}, \vec{b}, \vec{a}\times\vec{b}$

So that every vector is expressible as a linear combinations of the same

Suppose that a solution of given equation is

$$\vec{r}=x\vec{a}+y\vec{b}+z(\vec{a}\times\vec{b})$$

Substituting in the given equation we obtain

$$(x\vec{a}+y\vec{b}+z(\vec{a}\times\vec{b}))\times\vec{b}=\vec{a}$$

$$\Rightarrow\ x\vec{a}\times\vec{b}+z\{(\vec{a}.\vec{b})\vec{b}-(\vec{b}.\vec{b})\vec{a}\}=\vec{a}$$

$$\Rightarrow\ -\{1+z(\vec{b}.\vec{b})\}\vec{a}+x\,\vec{a}\times\vec{b}=0 \text{ for } \vec{a}.\vec{b}=0$$

$$\Rightarrow\ 1+z(\vec{b}.\vec{b})=0,\ x=0$$

$\vec{a}$, $\vec{a}\times\vec{b}$ being non-collinear vectors. Thus we have

$$\vec{r}=y\vec{b}-\frac{1}{\vec{b}.\vec{b}}\vec{a}\times\vec{b} \quad \text{....(i)}$$

Substituting (i) in the given equation, we may verify that this is a solution for every value of the scalar y,

It follows that $\vec{r}=-\frac{1}{\vec{b}.\vec{b}}\vec{a}\times\vec{b}+y\vec{b}$ is the general solution of the eqaution; y being the parameter.

Geometrically the points whose position vectors satisfy the given equation lies on the straight line which passes through the point with position vector $-\frac{1}{\vec{b}.\vec{b}}\vec{a}\times\vec{b}$ and is parallel to the vector $\vec{b}$.

Type III: To solve simultaneously for $\vec{r}$

$$\vec{r}\times\vec{b}=\vec{c}\times\vec{b} \quad \text{....(i)}$$

$$\vec{r}.\vec{a}=0 \quad \text{....(ii)}$$

provided that $\vec{a}$ is not perpendicular to $\vec{b}$.

Suppose that $\vec{r}$ is a solution of the given equations. Rewriting (i) as $(\vec{r}-\vec{c})\times\vec{b}=\vec{0}$

We see that $(\vec{r}-\vec{c})$ and $\vec{b}$ are collinear so that

$$(\vec{r}-\vec{c})=t\vec{b} \Leftrightarrow \vec{r}=\vec{c}+t\vec{b}$$

where t is a scalar. Substituting in (ii)

we obtain $(\vec{c}+t\vec{b}).\vec{a}=0$

$$\Leftrightarrow\ \vec{c}.\vec{a}+t\vec{b}.\vec{a}=0$$

$$\Rightarrow\ t=\frac{\vec{c}.\vec{a}}{\vec{b}.\vec{a}} \text{ for } \vec{b}.\vec{a}\neq 0$$

$$\text{Thus } \vec{r}=\vec{c}-\left(\frac{\vec{c}.\vec{a}}{\vec{b}.\vec{a}}\right)\vec{b} \quad \text{...(iii)}$$

We may also easily verify that $\vec{r}$ given by (iii) does satisfy the given equations. Hence $\vec{r}=\vec{c}-\left(\frac{\vec{c}.\vec{a}}{\vec{b}.\vec{a}}\right)\vec{b}$ is a solution and the only solution of the given equations. It may be seen that $\vec{r}.\vec{a}=0$ represents the plane which passes through the origin and is normal to the vector $\vec{a}$. Thus the solution represents the point of intersection of a line and a plane.

Type -IV: To solve for $\vec{r}$: $k\vec{r}+\vec{r}\times\vec{a}=\vec{b}$ where k is a given non-zero scalar and $\vec{a}, \vec{b}$ are two given vectors. Suppose that $\vec{r}$ is a solution. Expressing, $\vec{r}$ as a linear combination of the non-coplanar vectors $\vec{a}, \vec{b}, \vec{a}\times\vec{b}$, we write $\vec{r}=x\vec{a}+y\vec{b}+z\vec{a}\times\vec{b}$

Substituting in the given equation, we obtain

$$k(x\vec{a}+y\vec{b}+z\vec{a}\times\vec{b})-y\vec{a}\times\vec{b}+$$
$$z\{\vec{a}.\vec{a})\vec{b}-(\vec{a}.\vec{b})\vec{a}\}=\vec{b}$$

$$\Rightarrow\ \{kx-z(\vec{a}.\vec{b})\}\vec{a}+(ky+z\vec{a}^2-1)\vec{b}+$$
$$(kz-y)\vec{a}\times\vec{b}=0$$

$$\Rightarrow\ kx-z(\vec{a}.\vec{b})=0,\ ky+z\vec{a}^2-1=0,\ kz-y=0$$

$\vec{a}, \vec{b}, \vec{a}\times\vec{b}$ being non-coplanar vectors. It follows that

$$x=\frac{\vec{a}.\vec{b}}{k(k^2+\vec{a}^2)},\ y=\frac{k}{k^2+\vec{a}^2},\ z=\frac{1}{k^2+\vec{a}^2}$$

It follows that $\vec{r}=\frac{1}{k^2+\vec{a}^2}\left[\frac{\vec{a}.\vec{b}}{k}\vec{a}+k\vec{b}+\vec{a}\times\vec{b}\right]$ ....(ii)

Also we may easily verifying that $\vec{r}$ given by (ii) satisfies the given equations. Hence this is a solution and the only solution.

ILLUSTRATION 88: Solve the equation $\vec{x}\times\vec{a}=\vec{b}$, $(\vec{a}.\vec{b}=0)$

SOLUTION: Form the vector product of each member with $\vec{a}$ and obtain $\vec{a}^2\,\vec{x}-(\vec{a}.\vec{x})\vec{a}=\vec{a}\times\vec{b}$

The general solution, with λ as parameter is $\vec{x}=\lambda\vec{a}+\vec{a}\times\dfrac{\vec{b}}{\vec{a}^2}$

ILLUSTRATION 89: Solve the simultaneous equations $p\vec{x}+q\vec{y}=\vec{a}$, $\vec{x}\times\vec{y}=\vec{b}$, $(\vec{a}.\vec{b}=0)$

SOLUTION: Multiply the first vectorially by $\vec{x}$ and substitute for $\vec{x}\times\vec{y}$ from the second.

Then $q\vec{b}=\vec{x}\times\vec{a}$. Thus $\vec{x}=\lambda\vec{a}+q\vec{a}\times\dfrac{\vec{b}}{\vec{a}^2}$; Substitution of this value in the first equation gives y.

ILLUSTRATION 90: Find $\vec{x}$ so as to satisfy both the equations $\vec{x}\times\vec{a}=\vec{b}$, $\vec{x}.\vec{c}=p$ $(\vec{a}.\vec{b}=0)$

SOLUTION: Multiply the first vectorically by $\vec{c}$, expand and use the second.

Thus $(\vec{c}.\vec{a})\vec{x}-p\vec{a}=\vec{c}\times\vec{b}$ or $\vec{x}=\dfrac{p\vec{a}+\vec{c}\times\vec{b}}{\vec{a}.\vec{c}}$

provided $\vec{a}.\vec{c}\neq 0$. If however, $\vec{a}.\vec{c}=0$ use the general solution of the first equation.

Thus $\vec{x}=\dfrac{\lambda\vec{a}+\vec{a}\times\vec{b}}{\vec{a}^2}$. This will satisfy the second equation for any value of λ provided $p\vec{a}=\vec{a}\times\vec{b}.\vec{c}$ which is a necessary condition when $\vec{a}.\vec{c}=0$

ILLUSTRATION 91: Solve $\vec{x}\times\vec{a}+(\vec{x}.\vec{b})\vec{c}=\vec{d}$

SOLUTION: Multiply scalarly by $\vec{a}$. Then $(\vec{x}.\vec{b})(\vec{a}.\vec{c})=\vec{a}.\vec{d}$.

Substitute for $\vec{x}.\vec{b}$ in given equation and obtain $\vec{x}\times\vec{a}=\dfrac{\vec{d}-(\vec{a}.\vec{d})\vec{c}}{\vec{a}.\vec{c}}=\vec{a}\times\dfrac{\vec{d}\times\vec{c}}{\vec{a}.\vec{c}}$

The solution is $\vec{x}=\dfrac{\lambda\vec{a}+\vec{a}\times(\vec{a}\times(\vec{d}\times\vec{c}))}{(\vec{a}.\vec{c})^2}$

ILLUSTRATION 92: Solve $p\vec{x}+\vec{x}\times\vec{a}=\vec{b}$ $(p\neq 0)$

SOLUTION: Given $p\vec{x}+\vec{x}\times\vec{a}=\vec{b}$ ....(i)

Multiply scalarly by $\vec{a}$. Then $p\vec{x}+\vec{a}=\vec{b}.\vec{a}$ ...(ii)

Multiply vectorically by $\vec{a}$, expand the triple product, and substitute for $\vec{x}.\vec{a}$ from (ii). Then $p^2\,\vec{x}\times\vec{a}+(\vec{b}.\vec{a})\vec{a}-p\vec{a}^2\vec{x}=p\vec{b}\times\vec{a}$

Eliminate $\vec{x}\times\vec{a}$ between this equation and (i) and find $\vec{x}=\dfrac{p^2\vec{b}+(\vec{b}.\vec{a})\vec{a}-p\vec{b}\times\vec{a}}{p(p^2+a^2)}$

TEXTUAL EXERCISE 12: (SUBJECTIVE)

1. If $\vec{a}=\hat{i}-\hat{j}+\hat{k}, \vec{b}=-\hat{i}+2\hat{j}-\hat{k}$ and $\vec{c}=(x-1)\hat{i}+(x+2)\hat{j}+\hat{k}$. If $\vec{c}.(\vec{a}\times\vec{b})=0$, then solve for x and give geometrical meaning of above problem.

2. Solve for $\vec{r}$; where $\vec{r}\times\vec{a}=\vec{b}\times\vec{a}$ and $\vec{r}\times\vec{b}=\vec{a}\times\vec{b}$. Give geometrical meaning.

3. If $\vec{a}.\vec{b}=\vec{a}.\vec{c}$ and $\vec{a}\times\vec{b}=\vec{c}\times\vec{a}$ $(\vec{a},\vec{b},\vec{c}\neq\vec{0}$ and $\vec{a},\vec{b},\vec{c}$ are different vectors), then solve for $\vec{a}$, giving geometrical meaning.

4. Solve for $\vec{r}$; $\vec{r}\times\vec{a}=\vec{r}\times\vec{b}$ and $\vec{a},\vec{b},\vec{r}$ are non-zero and non-collinear giving geometrical meaning.

5. Solve for $\vec{r}$ where $\vec{r}.\vec{a}=\vec{r}.\vec{b}$ and $\vec{r}.\vec{a}=-\vec{r}.\vec{b}$ and $\vec{a}$ and $\vec{b}$ are non collinear. Give geometrical interpretation.

Answer Key

1. $x = 2$, $\vec{c}=\hat{i}+3\hat{j}+\hat{k}$ is coplanar with a and b
2. $\vec{r}=\vec{a}+\vec{b}$ represents the position vector of the point of intersection of straight lines $\vec{r}=\vec{a}+\mu\vec{b}$ and $\vec{r}=\vec{b}+\lambda\vec{a}$ and it will be the extremity of diagonal passing through origin of parallelogram having its adjacent sides represented by vectors $\vec{a}$ and $\vec{b}$.
3. $\vec{a}=k\left(\vec{b}+\vec{c}\right);k\in\mathbb{R}\sim\{0\}$; $|\vec{b}|=|\vec{c}|$, geometrically $\vec{b}$ and $\vec{c}$ are two adjacent sides of a rhombus and $\vec{a}$ is parallel to diagonal through the point of intersection of $\vec{b}$ and $\vec{c}$.
4. $\vec{r}=\lambda(\vec{a}-\vec{b})\lambda\in\mathbb{R}-\{0\}$ $\vec{r}$ is along the diagnal of a ||gram through the point of intersection of $\vec{a}$ and $-\vec{b}$.
5. $\vec{r}=t(\vec{a}\times\vec{b});\vec{r}$ is perpendicular to plane containing $\vec{a}$ and $\vec{b}$.

TEXTUAL EXERCISE 9: (OBJECTIVE)

1. If the non-zero vectors $\vec{a}$ and $\vec{b}$ are perpendicular to each other and vector $\vec{r}$ satisfies the equation $\vec{r}\times\vec{a}=\vec{b}$, then which of the following is true about $\vec{r}$?
   (a) $\vec{r}$ is always parallel to $\vec{a}$
   (b) $\vec{r}$ is may be parallel to $\vec{a}\times\vec{b}$
   (c) $\vec{r}$ lies in plane of $\vec{a}$ and $\vec{b}$
   (d) None of these

2. If $\vec{x}$ and $\vec{y}$ are two non-collinear vectors and ABC is a triangle with sides a, b, c satisfying $(20a-15b)\vec{x}+(15b-12c)\vec{y}+(12c-20a)(\vec{x}\times\vec{y})=\vec{0}$, then the triangle ABC is
   (a) an acute angled triangle
   (b) an obtuse angled triangle
   (c) a right angled triangle
   (d) isosceles triangle

3. Angle between the line $\vec{r}=(2\hat{i}-\hat{j}+\hat{k})+\lambda(-\hat{i}+\hat{j}+\hat{k})$ and the plane $\vec{r}.(3\hat{i}+2\hat{j}-\hat{k})=4$ is
   (a) $\cos^{-1}\left(\frac{2}{\sqrt{45}}\right)$ (b) $\cos^{-1}\left(-\frac{2}{\sqrt{42}}\right)$
   (c) $\sin^{-1}\left(\frac{2}{\sqrt{42}}\right)$ (d) $\sin^{-1}\left(-\frac{2}{\sqrt{42}}\right)$

4. A line L_1 pases through the point $3\hat{i}$ and is parallel to the vector $-\hat{i}+\hat{j}+\hat{k}$ and another L_2 passes through the point $\hat{i}+\hat{j}$ and is parallel to the vector $\hat{i}+\hat{k}$, then P.V. of the point of intersection of the lines is
   (a) $\hat{i}+2\hat{j}+\hat{k}$ (b) $2\hat{i}+\hat{j}+\hat{k}$
   (c) $2\hat{i}-2\hat{j}-\hat{k}$ (d) $\hat{i}-2\hat{j}+\hat{k}$

5. Let $\vec{a}=\hat{i}+\hat{j}$ and $\vec{b}=2\hat{i}-\hat{k}$, then the point of intersection of the lines $\vec{r}\times\vec{a}=\vec{b}\times\vec{a}$ and $\vec{r}\times\vec{b}=\vec{a}\times\vec{b}$ is
   (a) (–1, 1, 1) (b) (3, –1, 1)
   (c) (3, 1, –1) (d) (1, –1, –1)

6. Let $\hat{\alpha},\hat{\beta},\hat{\gamma}$ be the unit vectors such that $\hat{\alpha}$ and $\hat{\beta}$ are mutually perpendicular and $\hat{\gamma}$ is equally inclined to $\hat{\alpha}$ and $\hat{\beta}$ at an angle θ. If $\vec{r}=x\hat{\alpha}+y\hat{\beta}+z(\hat{\alpha}\times\hat{\beta})$, then
   (a) $z^2 = 1 - 2x^2$ (b) $z^2 = 1 - 2y^2$
   (c) $z^2 = 1 - x^2 - y^2$ (d) $x^2 = y^2$

7. The vertices of a triangle have the position vectors $\vec{a},\vec{b},\vec{c}$ and $P(\vec{r})$ is a point in the plane of triangle such that $\vec{a}.\vec{b}+\vec{c}.\vec{r}=\vec{a}.\vec{c}+\vec{b}.\vec{r}=\vec{b}.\vec{c}+\vec{a}.\vec{r}$, then for the triangle, P is the
   (a) circumcentre (b) centroid
   (c) orthocentre (d) incentre

8. If $\vec{r}$ satisfies the equation $\vec{r}\times(\hat{i}+2\hat{j}+\hat{k})=\hat{i}-\hat{k}$, then for any scalar α, $\vec{r}$ is equal to

(a) $\hat{i}+\alpha(\hat{i}+2\hat{j}+\hat{k})$ (b) $\hat{j}+\alpha(\hat{i}+2\hat{j}+\hat{k})$

(c) $\hat{k}+\alpha(\hat{i}+2\hat{j}+\hat{k})$ (d) $\hat{i}-\hat{k}+\alpha(\hat{i}+2\hat{j}+\hat{k})$

9. If $\vec{a},\vec{b}$ are non-zero vectors and $\vec{a}$ is perpendicular to $\vec{b}$, then a nonzero vector $\vec{r}$ satisfying $\vec{r}.\vec{a}=\alpha$, for some scalar α, $\vec{a}\times\vec{r}=\vec{b}$ is

(a) $\dfrac{\alpha\vec{a}+(\vec{a}+\vec{b})}{|a|^2}$ (b) $\dfrac{\alpha\vec{a}+\vec{a}\times\vec{b}}{|b|^2}$

(c) $\dfrac{\alpha\vec{a}-(\vec{a}\times\vec{b})}{|a|^2}$ (d) $\dfrac{\alpha\vec{a}-(\vec{a}\times\vec{b})}{|b|^2}$

Answer Key

1. (b) **2.** (d) **3.** (d) **4.** (b) **5.** (c) **6.** (a,b,c,d) **7.** (c) **8.** (b) **9.** (c)

SOME MISCELLANEOUS THEOREMS

Ceva's Theorem

If *D, E, F* are three points on the sides *BC, CA, AB* respectively of a triangle *ABC* such that the lines *AD, BE* and *CF* are concurrent, then $\frac{BD}{CD}.\frac{CE}{AE}.\frac{AF}{BF}=-1$ and conversely.

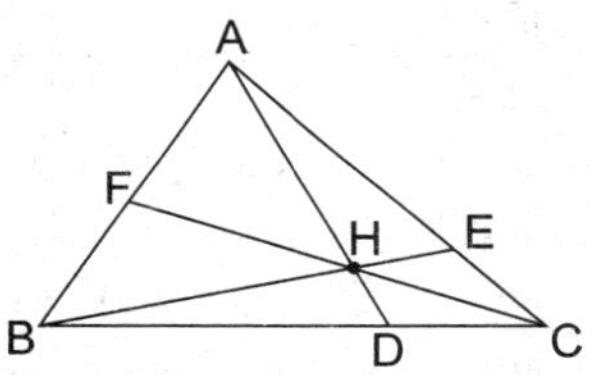

FIGURE 3.110

Let *AD, BE* and *CF* meet at H. Take any point *O*, as the origin of reference. Let $\vec{a},\vec{b},\vec{c},\vec{h}$ be the position vectors of the points *A, B, C, H* respectively.

These four points being co-planar, there exist four scalars *x, y, z, t* such that

$$x\vec{a}+y\vec{b}+z\vec{c}+t\vec{h}=\vec{0},\ x+y+z+t=0$$

These gives $\dfrac{x\vec{a}+y\vec{b}}{x+y}=\dfrac{z\vec{c}+t\vec{h}}{z+t}$

Now $\dfrac{x\vec{a}+y\vec{b}}{x+y}$ and $\dfrac{z\vec{c}+t\vec{h}}{z+t}$ are points of the lines *AB* and *CH* respectively. It follows that $\dfrac{x\vec{a}+y\vec{b}}{x+y}$ is the position vector of the point *F* of intersection of the lines *AB* and *CH* so that *F* divides *AB* in the ratio

$$\frac{AF}{FB}=\frac{y}{x}\Leftrightarrow\frac{AF}{BF}=-\frac{y}{x}$$

Similarly, $\dfrac{BD}{CD}=-\dfrac{z}{y},\ \dfrac{CE}{AE}=-\dfrac{x}{z}$

$$\therefore\quad \frac{BD}{CD}.\frac{CE}{AE}.\frac{AF}{BF}=\left(-\frac{z}{y}\right)\left(-\frac{x}{z}\right).\left(-\frac{y}{x}\right)=-1$$

Conversely, let *D, E, F* be three points on the sides *BC, CA* and *AB* respectively such that

$$\frac{BD}{CD}.\frac{CE}{AE}.\frac{AF}{BF}=-1 \quad \text{........ (i)}$$

Suppose that $\dfrac{BD}{CD}=-\dfrac{z}{y},\ \dfrac{CE}{AE}=-\dfrac{x}{z}$

so that by (i) $\dfrac{AF}{BF}=-\dfrac{y}{x}$

$$\therefore\quad \frac{BD}{DC}=\frac{z}{y},\ \frac{CE}{EA}=\frac{x}{z},\ \frac{AF}{FB}=\frac{y}{x}$$

If $\vec{a},\vec{b},\vec{c}$ be the position vectors of the points *A, B, C,* then the position vectors of the points *D, E, F* are $\dfrac{y\vec{b}+z\vec{c}}{y+z}$, $\dfrac{z\vec{c}+x\vec{a}}{z+x}$, $\dfrac{x\vec{a}+y\vec{b}}{x+y}$ respectively.

Therefore the position vetors of the points dividing *AD, BE, CF* in the ratios

$y+z: x, z+x: y, x+y: z$ are all equal to $\dfrac{x\vec{a}+y\vec{b}+z\vec{c}}{x+y+z}$

Thus the lines *AD, BE* and *CF* are concurrent.

Aliter: If the lines joining the vertices *A, B, C* of a triangle to a point *H*, in the plane of the triangle, cut the opposite sides in *D, E, F* respectively, then the product of the ratios in which these points divide *BC, CA, AB* is equal to unity. Since *A, B, C, H* are co-planar, their position vectors satisfy a linear relation of the form $x\vec{a}+y\vec{b}+z\vec{c}+t\vec{h}=\vec{0},\ x+y+z+t=0$

The four coefficients being different from zero. From these equations, it follows that

$$\frac{y\vec{b}+z\vec{c}}{y+z}=\frac{x\vec{a}+t\vec{h}}{x+t}=d$$

The first of these expressions is the position vector of a point dividing BC in the ratio $z: y$ and the second is that of a point dividing AH in the ratio $t: x$. Each therefore represents that of the point D in which the line AH intersect BC. Thus $BD: DC = z: y$. Similarly, E and F divide CA and AB in the ratios $x: z$ and $y: t$ respectively. The product of these three ratios is unity.

Menelau's Theorem

If D, E, F are three points on the sides BC, CA, AB respectively of a triangle ABC such that the points D, E, F are collinear, then $\frac{BD}{CD}\cdot\frac{CE}{AE}\cdot\frac{AF}{BF}=1$ and conversely.

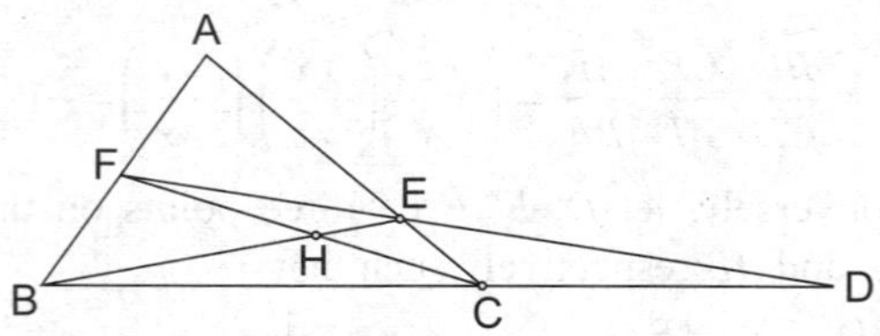

FIGURE 3.111

Let BE and CF meet at H. Let a, b, c, h be the position vectors of the points A, B, C, H relative to any origin O of the reference. These four points being co-planar, there exist four scalars x, y, z, t such that $x\vec{a}+y\vec{b}+z\vec{c}+t\vec{h}=\vec{0}$, $x+y+z+t=0$

The position vectors of the points E and F, therefore are

$$\frac{x\vec{a}+z\vec{c}}{x+z},\ \frac{x\vec{a}+y\vec{b}}{x+y}$$

Now we require the position vector of the point D.

Writing $e=\frac{x\vec{a}+z\vec{c}}{x+z}$ and $f=\frac{x\vec{a}+y\vec{b}}{x+y}$ and eliminating $\vec{b}$,

we have $(x+z)\vec{e}-(x-y)\vec{f}=z\vec{c}-y\vec{b}$

$$\Rightarrow\quad \frac{(x+z)\vec{e}-(x-y)\vec{f}}{(x+z)-(x+y)}=\frac{z\vec{c}-y\vec{b}}{z-y}$$

This equality shows that $\frac{z\vec{c}-y\vec{b}}{z-y}$ is the position vector of the point D. Thus

$$\frac{BD}{CD}=-\frac{z}{y},\ \frac{CE}{EA}=\frac{x}{z},\ \frac{AF}{FB}=\frac{y}{x}\Rightarrow\frac{BD}{CD}\cdot\frac{CE}{AE}\cdot\frac{AF}{BF}=1$$

Conversely, let D, E, F be three points on the sides BC, CA and AB respectively such that

$$\frac{BD}{CD}\cdot\frac{CE}{AE}\cdot\frac{AF}{BF}=1$$

Suppose that $\frac{BD}{CD}=\frac{z}{y},\ \frac{CE}{AE}=-\frac{x}{z}$ so that $\frac{AF}{BF}=-\frac{y}{x}$

$$\therefore\ \frac{BD}{DC}=-\frac{z}{y},\ \frac{CE}{EA}=\frac{x}{z},\ \frac{AF}{FB}=\frac{y}{x}$$

If $\vec{a},\vec{b},\vec{c}$ be the position vectors of the points A, B, C, then the position vectors of the points D, E, F are $\frac{z\vec{c}-y\vec{b}}{z-y}$, $\frac{x\vec{a}+z\vec{c}}{x+z}$, $\frac{x\vec{a}+y\vec{b}}{x+y}$ respectively

Denoting these by $\vec{d}$, $\vec{e}$, $\vec{f}$ respectively, we obtain

$$-(z-y)\vec{d}+(x+z)\vec{e}-(x+y)\vec{f}=\vec{0}$$

where $-(z-y)+(x+z)-(x+y)=0$

Thus the points D, E, F are collinear

Aliter: If a trasversal cuts the sides BC, CA, AB of a triangle at in the point D, E, F respectively, the product of the ratios in which D, E, F divide those sides is equal to -1. Let E divide CA in the ratio $y: z$. Then we can find a number x such that F divides AB in the ratio $x: y$.

Consequently, $(y+z)\vec{e}+z\vec{c}+y\vec{a}$, $(x+y)\vec{f}+y\vec{a}+x\vec{b}$

Eliminate $\vec{a}$ and write the result in the form

$$\frac{z\vec{c}-x\vec{b}}{z-x}=\frac{(y+z)\vec{e}-(x+y)\vec{f}}{z-x}=\vec{d}$$

Thus BC and FE intersect at D which divides BC in the ratio $-z:x$. Consequently, the product of the three ratios is -1.

Observing that $(z-x)\vec{d}-(y+z)\vec{e}+(x+y)\vec{f}=\vec{0}$, we can also show conversely that if the product of the above ratios is -1, then D, E, F are collinear.

Deasargue Theorem

If ABC and $A_1B_1C_1$ are two triangles such that the three lines AA_1, BB_1 and CC_1 are concurrent, then the points of intersection of the three pairs of sides. BC, B_1C_1; CA, C_1A_1; AB, A_1B_1 are collinear and conversely,

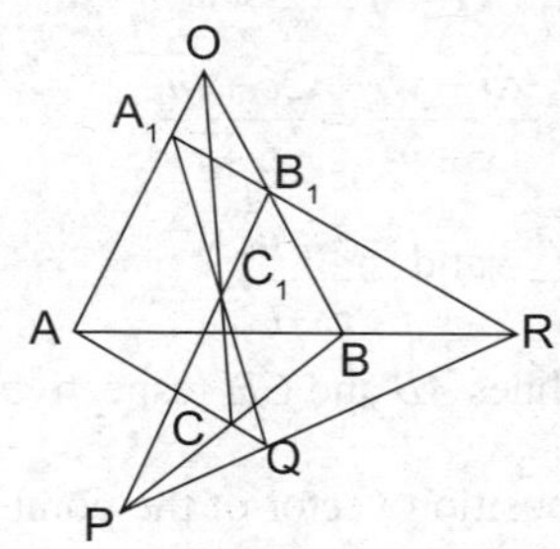

FIGURE 3.112

Let AA_1, BB_1 and CC_1 meet at O. Take O as the origin of reference.

Let $\overline{OA} = \vec{a}$, $\overline{OB} = \vec{b}$, $\overline{OC} = \vec{c}$

Then $\overline{OA_1} = \alpha\vec{a}$, $\overline{OB_1} = \beta\vec{b}$, $\overline{OC_1} = \gamma\vec{c}$

where α, β, γ are some scalars.

The equations of BC and $B_1\ C_1$ respectively are

$$\vec{r} = \vec{b} + t(\vec{b} - \vec{c}),\ r = \beta\vec{b} + p(\beta\vec{b} - \gamma\vec{c})$$

so that at the point of intersection P of BC and B_1C_1 we have

$$\vec{b} + t(\vec{b} - \vec{c}) = \beta b + p(\beta\vec{b} - \gamma\vec{c})$$

$$\Rightarrow\ (1 + t - \beta - p\beta)\vec{b} + (-t + p\gamma)\vec{c} = \vec{0}$$

$$\Rightarrow\ 1 + t - \beta - p\beta = 0,\ -t + p\gamma = 0$$

the vectors $\vec{b}$ and $\vec{c}$ being non-parallel. These give $p = \dfrac{1-\beta}{\beta-\gamma}$

Making substitution, we see that the position vector of the point P of intersection of BC, B_1C_1 is

$$\beta\vec{b} + \frac{1-\beta}{\beta-\gamma}(\beta\vec{b} - \gamma\vec{c}) = \frac{1-\gamma}{\mu-\gamma}\beta\vec{b} + \frac{1-\beta}{\gamma-\beta}\gamma\vec{c} = p$$

By considerations of symmetry the two other points of intersection Q and R are

$$\frac{1-\alpha}{\gamma-\alpha}\gamma\vec{c} + \frac{1-\gamma}{\alpha-\gamma}\alpha\vec{a} = q \text{ and}$$

$$\frac{1-\beta}{\gamma-\beta}\alpha\vec{a} + \frac{1-\alpha}{\beta-\alpha}\beta\vec{b} = r$$

We now see that $\sum(1-\alpha)(\beta-\gamma t)\vec{p} = \vec{0}$ where $\Sigma(1-\alpha)(\beta-\lambda) = 0$

Thus the three points of intersection whose position vectors are p, q, r are collinear.

Conversely: Let $a, b, c; a_1, b_1, c_1$ be the position vectors of the vertices of the triangle ABC and $A_1\ B_1\ C_1$ sespectively with respect to some origin O. Let P, Q, R be the points of intersection of the pairs of lines.

$BC, B_1C_1; CA, C_1A_1; AB, A_1B_1$ are collinear

Let P divides BC in the ratio $z: y$ so that the position vector of the position vector of the point P is $\dfrac{y\vec{b} - z\vec{c}}{y+z}$.

Let Q divide BC in the ratio $x: z$ so that the position vector of the point Q is $\dfrac{z\vec{c} + x\vec{a}}{z+x}$

The position vector of the point R of intersection of PQ and AB may now be easily seen to be $\dfrac{y\vec{b} - x\vec{a}}{y-x}$

Denoting these position vectors by p, q, r respectively, we have the relation

$$(y+z)\vec{p} - (z+x)\vec{q} - (y-x)\vec{r} = \vec{0} \quad \text{...(i)}$$

between the position vectors of the collinear points P, Q, R

Similarly, denoting by $z_1: y_1$ and $x_1: y_1$ the ratios in which the points P and Q divide B_1C_1 and $C_1\ A_1$ we obtain

$$\vec{p} = \frac{y_1\vec{b} - z_1\vec{c}}{y_1 + z_1},\ \vec{q} = \frac{z_1\vec{c} + x_1\vec{a}}{z_1 + x_1},\ \vec{r} = \frac{y_1\vec{b} - x_1\vec{a}}{y_1 - x_1} \quad \text{...(ii)}$$

From (i) and (ii) we obtain $\dfrac{y+z}{y_1+z_1} = \dfrac{z+x}{z_1+x_1} = \dfrac{y-x}{y_1-x_1} = k$

so that $y + z = k(y_1 + z_1)$, $z + x = k(z_1 + x_1)$,

$y - x = k(y_1 + x_1)$ ...(iii)

Also we have $\dfrac{y\vec{b} - z\vec{c}}{y+z} = \dfrac{y_1\vec{b} - z_1\vec{c}}{y_1 + z_1}$,

$$\frac{z\vec{c} + x\vec{a}}{z+x} = \frac{z_1\vec{c} + x_1\vec{a}}{z_1 + x_1},\ \frac{y\vec{b} - x\vec{a}}{y-x} = \frac{y_1\vec{b} - x_1\vec{a}}{y_1 - x_1} \quad \text{...(iv)}$$

So that with the help of (iii) we obtain

$$z\vec{c} - kz_1\vec{c}_1 = ky_1\vec{b}_1 - y\vec{b} = kx\vec{a}_1 - x\vec{a}$$

$$\Rightarrow\ \frac{z\vec{c} - kz_1\vec{c}_1}{z - kz_1} = \frac{ky_1\vec{b}_1 - y\vec{b}}{ky_1 - y} = \frac{kx\vec{a}_1 - x\vec{a}}{kx - x} \quad \text{..(v)}$$

The three equal vectors in (v) being the position vectors of points on CC_1, BB_1, AA_1, we see that these lines are concurrent.

Aliter: If the lines joining corresponding vertices of two triangles are concurrent, the points of intersection of corresponding sides are collinear.

Let A, B, C correspond to D, E, F respectively. Then BC and EF are corresponding sides. Given AD, BE, CF intersect at a point F, we have relations of the form

$$x\vec{a} + x'\vec{d} = y\vec{b} + y'\vec{e} = z\vec{c} + z'\vec{f} = \vec{h}$$

where $x + x' = y + y' = z + z' = 1$

Hence $\dfrac{y\vec{b} - z\vec{c}}{y-z} = \dfrac{y'\vec{e} - z'\vec{f}}{y' - z'} = \vec{p}$

Giving the position vector of the point P of intersection of BC and EF. Write down similar expressions for q and r the intersection of the other pairs of corresponding sides and verify that

$$(y-z)\vec{p} + (z-x)\vec{q} + (x-y)\vec{r} = \vec{0}$$

in which the sum of the coefficients is zero. Consequently P, Q, R are collinear.

MULTIPLE CHOICE QUESTIONS

SECTION–I

SUBJECTIVE SOLVED EXAMPLES

1. Given a regular tetrahedron $DABC$ with edge length 'a'. Points E and F are taken on the edges AD and BD respectively such that E divides $\overrightarrow{DA}$ and F divides $\overrightarrow{BD}$ in the ratio 2: 1 each. Then find the area of triangle CEF.

Solution: Considering D as origin, as tetrahedron is regular clearly, $|\vec{a}| = |\vec{b}| = |\vec{c}| = |\vec{b}-\vec{a}| = |\vec{c}-\vec{b}|$

$$|\vec{a}-\vec{c}| = a \qquad \dots (i)$$

$$\left|\overrightarrow{DE}\right| = \frac{2a}{3} \ \& \ \left|\overrightarrow{DF}\right| = \frac{a}{3}$$

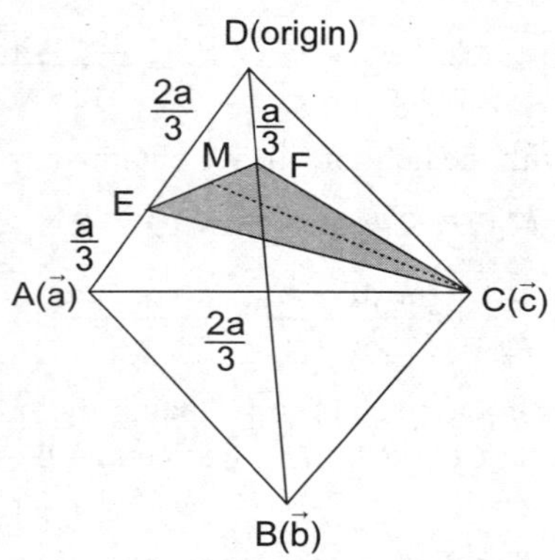

Also $CE = CF$ (As ΔCFD and ΔCEA are congruent)

$$\left|\overrightarrow{DE}\right| = \left|\overrightarrow{DF}\right| = k\ (say) \qquad \dots\dots (iii)$$

For k; consider ΔCAE

$$\cos C = \frac{a^2 + \left(\frac{a}{3}\right)^2 - k^2}{2a.\frac{a}{3}}; \ \angle C = 60^0$$

$$\Rightarrow \frac{a^2}{3} = a^2 + \frac{a^2}{9} - k^2 \ \Rightarrow k^2 = \frac{7a^2}{9} \ \Rightarrow k = \frac{a\sqrt{7}}{3}$$

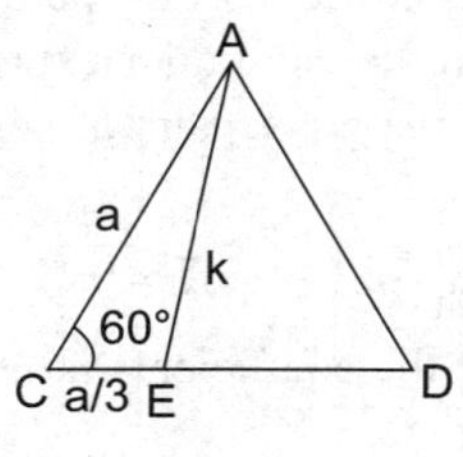

Also in ΔDEF;

$$\cos\frac{\pi}{3} = \frac{(DE)^2 + (DF)^2 - (EF)^2}{2(DE)(DF)} = \frac{\frac{4a^2}{9} + \frac{a^2}{9} - (EF)^2}{2\left(\frac{29}{3}\right)\left(\frac{a}{3}\right)}$$

$$\Rightarrow \frac{2a^2}{9} = \frac{a^2}{9} - (EF)^2 \ \Rightarrow \ (EF)^2 = \frac{a^2}{3}$$

$$\Rightarrow \left|\overrightarrow{EF}\right| = \frac{a}{\sqrt{3}} \qquad \dots. (iv)$$

$$\Rightarrow \left|\overrightarrow{CM}\right| = \frac{5a}{6} \quad (\because M \text{ is mid point of } EF)$$

$$\because \ Area\ of\ \Delta CEF = \frac{1}{2}\left|\overrightarrow{EF}\right|\left|\overrightarrow{CM}\right|$$

$$= \frac{1}{2}\left(\frac{a}{\sqrt{3}}\right)\left(\frac{5a}{6}\right) = \left(\frac{5a^2}{12\sqrt{3}}\right)$$

2. If $\vec{a}, \vec{b}, \vec{c}$ are mutually perpendicular vectors of equal magnitude show that $\vec{a}+\vec{b}+\vec{c}$ are equally inclined to $\vec{a}$, $\vec{b}$ and $\vec{c}$.

Solution: We have $|\vec{a}+\vec{b}+\vec{c}|^2 = (\vec{a}+\vec{b}+\vec{c}).(\vec{a}+\vec{b}+\vec{c})$

$= \vec{a}.\vec{a} + \vec{b}.\vec{b} + \vec{c}.\vec{c} + 2\vec{a}.\vec{b} + 2\vec{b}.\vec{c} + 2\vec{c}.\vec{a} = 3|\vec{a}|^2$

$\Rightarrow |\vec{a}+\vec{b}+\vec{c}| = \sqrt{3}|\vec{a}|$; Now $(\vec{a}+\vec{b}+\vec{c}).\vec{a}|$

$= |\vec{a}|^2 = |\vec{a}+\vec{b}+\vec{c}||\vec{a}|\cos\theta_1$

where θ_1 is the angle between $\vec{a}+\vec{b}+\vec{c}$ and $\vec{a}$

Hence $|\vec{a}|^2 = \sqrt{3}|\vec{a}|^2\cos\theta_1 \Rightarrow \cos\theta_1 = \frac{1}{\sqrt{3}}$

Similarly, if θ_2, θ_3 are the angles between $\vec{a}+\vec{b}+\vec{c}$ and $\vec{b}$, $\vec{a}+\vec{b}+\vec{c}$ and $\vec{c}$ respectively, then

$\cos\theta_2 = \frac{1}{\sqrt{3}}$, $\cos\theta_3 = \frac{1}{\sqrt{3}}$. Hence $\theta_1 = \theta_2 = \theta_3$

3. $\vec{a}, \vec{b}, \vec{c}$ are three co-planar vectors. If $\vec{a}$ is not parallel to $\vec{b}$, show that
$$\vec{c} = \frac{\begin{vmatrix} \vec{c}.\vec{a} & \vec{a}.\vec{b} \\ \vec{c}.\vec{b} & \vec{b}.\vec{b} \end{vmatrix}\vec{a} + \begin{vmatrix} \vec{a}.\vec{a} & \vec{c}.\vec{a} \\ \vec{a}.\vec{b} & \vec{c}.\vec{b} \end{vmatrix}\vec{b}}{\begin{vmatrix} \vec{a}.\vec{a} & \vec{a}.\vec{b} \\ \vec{a}.\vec{b} & \vec{b}.\vec{b} \end{vmatrix}}$$

Solution: Given $\vec{a},\vec{b},\vec{c}$ are co-planar, therefore L.D.

$\Rightarrow \ \vec{c} = x_1\vec{a} + y_2\vec{b}$ ....(i)

Taking dot product by vector $\vec{a}$ and $\vec{b}$, we get two linear equations in $\Rightarrow \ \vec{a}.\vec{c} = x_1\,\vec{a}.\vec{a} + y_2\vec{a}.\vec{b}$ .....(ii)

and $\vec{b}.\vec{c} = x_1\,\vec{b}.\vec{a} + y_2\,\vec{b}.\vec{b}$ ....(iii)

Solving (i) and (ii), by Cramer's rule, we find that

$$x_1 = \frac{\begin{vmatrix} \vec{a}.\vec{c} & \vec{a}.\vec{b} \\ \vec{b}.\vec{c} & \vec{b}.\vec{b} \end{vmatrix}}{\begin{vmatrix} \vec{a}.\vec{a} & \vec{a}.\vec{b} \\ \vec{b}.\vec{a} & \vec{b}.\vec{b} \end{vmatrix}} \text{ and } y_2 = \frac{\begin{vmatrix} \vec{a}.\vec{a} & \vec{a}.\vec{c} \\ \vec{b}.\vec{a} & \vec{b}.\vec{c} \end{vmatrix}}{\begin{vmatrix} \vec{a}.\vec{a} & \vec{a}.\vec{b} \\ \vec{b}.\vec{a} & \vec{b}.\vec{b} \end{vmatrix}}$$

Substituting for x_1 and y_2, we get the required expression for $\vec{c}$.

4. Show that the area of the triangle formed by joining the extremities of an oblique side of a trapezium to the mid-point of opposite side is half that of the trapezium.

Solution: Let $ABCD$ be the trapezium and E be the mid-point of BC. Let A be the initial point and let $\vec{b}$ be the p.v. of B and $\vec{d}$ that of D. Since DC is parallel to AB. $t\vec{b}$ is a vector along DC, so that the p.v. of C is $\vec{d} + t\vec{b}$.

$\Rightarrow$ the p.v. of E is $\dfrac{\vec{b}+\vec{d}+t\vec{b}}{2} = \dfrac{\vec{d}+(1+t)\vec{b}}{2}$

Area of

$$\Delta AED = \frac{1}{2}\left|\frac{\vec{d}+(1+t)\vec{b}}{2}\times\vec{d}\right| = \frac{1}{4}|(1+t)||\vec{b}\times\vec{d}\,|$$

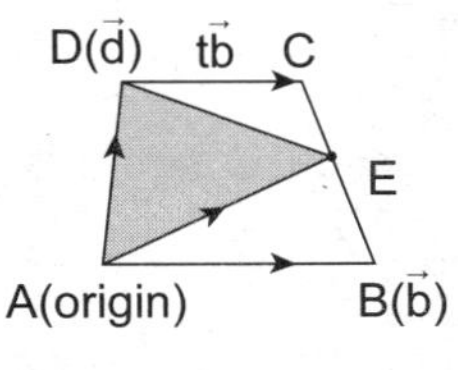

Area of the trapezium = Area ($\Delta\, ACD$) + Area ($\Delta\, ABC$)

$= \frac{1}{2}|\,\vec{b}\times(\vec{d}+t\vec{b})+(\vec{d}+t\vec{b})\times\vec{d}\,| = \frac{1}{2}|(1+t)|\,|\,\vec{b}\times\vec{d}\,|$

$= 2\ \Delta AED$

5. ABC is a triangle. A line is drawn parallel to BC to meet AB and AC in D and E respectively. Prove that the median through A bisects DE.

Solution: Take the vertex A of the triangle ABC as the origin. Let $\vec{b}$ and $\vec{c}$ be the p.v. of point B and C respectively. The mid-point (F) of BC has the position vector $= \vec{f} = \dfrac{\vec{b}+\vec{c}}{2}$.

The equation of the median is $\vec{r} = t\,\dfrac{\vec{b}+\vec{c}}{2}$.

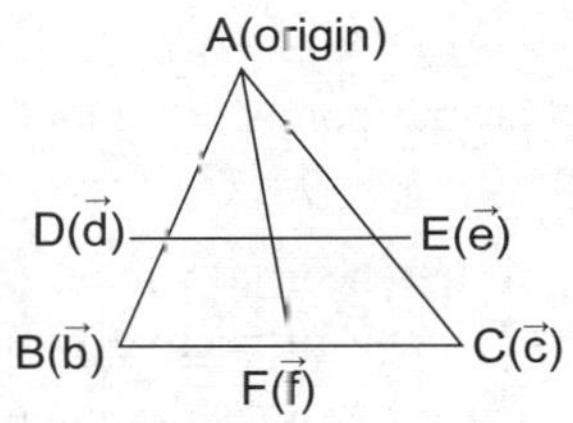

By B.P.T. (*Basic Proportionality Theorem*)

$\dfrac{AD}{AB} = \dfrac{AE}{AC} = \lambda \qquad \Rightarrow \ \vec{d} = \lambda\vec{b}$ and $\vec{e} = \lambda\vec{c}$

position vector of the mid-point of DE = $\dfrac{\lambda(\vec{b}+\vec{c})}{2}$

which evidently lies on the median, $\vec{r} = t\left(\dfrac{\vec{b}+\vec{c}}{2}\right)$.

Hence the median bisects DE.

6. Show that mid-point of three diagonals of a complete quadrilateral are collinear.

Solution: A complete quadrilateral is a figure made by four straight lines no three of which are concurrent.

Let $ABCD$ be a quadrailateral and let P, Q and R be the respective mid-points of the diagonals BD, CA and EF.

Let $\vec{a}, \vec{b}, \vec{c}, \vec{d}, \vec{e}, \vec{f}, \vec{p}, \vec{q}, \vec{r}$ be the position vectors of A, B, C, D, E, F, P, Q and R respectively.

then $\vec{p} = \dfrac{\vec{b}+\vec{d}}{2}$, $\vec{r} = \dfrac{\vec{e}+\vec{b}}{2}$ and $\vec{q} = \dfrac{\vec{c}+\vec{a}}{2}$

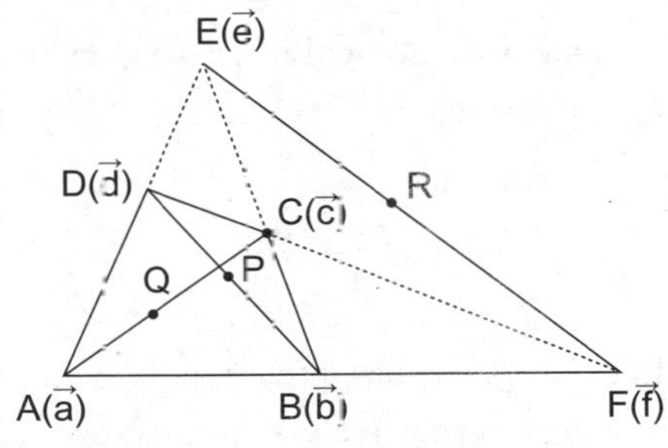

since E lies on the two lines BC and AD and F lies on the two lines BA and CD respectively, we have

$\vec{e} = (1-s)\vec{b} + s\vec{c}$ ....(i)

$\vec{e} = (1-t)\vec{a} + t\vec{d}$ ....(ii)

$\vec{f} = (1-u)\vec{b} + u\vec{a}$ ...(iii)

$\vec{f} = (1-v)\vec{c} + v\vec{d}$ .....(iv)

(where s, t, u and v are scalars)

adding (i), (ii), (iii) and (iv), we get

$(2-s-u)(\vec{b}+\vec{d})+(1-t+u)(\vec{c}+\vec{a})-2(\vec{e}+\vec{f})=0$

setting $1-t+u=1+s-v$ and $2-s-u=t+v$

so that $(2-s-u)+(1-t+u)-2=0$

This shows that the points P, Q and R are collinear since the sum $(2-s-u)+(1-t+u)-2=0$

7. If $OABC$ is a tetrahedron where O is the origin and A, B and C have respective position vectors as $\vec{a}, \vec{b}$ and $\vec{c}$, then prove that the circumcentre of the tetrahedron is $\dfrac{(\vec{a})^2(\vec{b}\times\vec{c})+(\vec{b})^2(\vec{c}\times\vec{a})+(\vec{c})^2(\vec{a}\times\vec{b})}{2[\vec{a}\ \vec{b}\ \vec{c}]}$

Solution: If $\vec{r}$ is the circumcentre of tetrahedron $OABC$, then $|\vec{r}-\vec{a}|=|\vec{r}-\vec{b}|=|\vec{r}-\vec{c}|=|\vec{r}|$ ....(1)

consider $|\vec{r}-\vec{a}|=|\vec{r}|\Rightarrow(\vec{r}-\vec{a})(\vec{r}-\vec{a})=\vec{r}.\vec{r}$

$\Rightarrow\ 2\vec{a}.\vec{r}=|\vec{a}|^2$; Similarly, $2\vec{b}.\vec{r}=|\vec{b}|^2$

$2\vec{c}.\vec{r}=|\vec{c}|^2$ Since $\vec{a}\times\vec{c}, \vec{b}\times\vec{c}, \vec{c}\times\vec{a}$ are three L.I vectors.

$\Rightarrow\ \vec{r}=x(\vec{b}\times\vec{c})+y(\vec{c}\times\vec{a})+z(\vec{a}\times\vec{b})$

Taking dot product with $\vec{a}, \vec{b}, \vec{c}$ respectively

$\therefore\ \vec{r}.\vec{a}=x\vec{a}.(\vec{b}\times\vec{c})\Rightarrow x=\dfrac{\vec{r}.\vec{a}}{[\vec{a}\ \vec{b}\ \vec{c}]}=\dfrac{|\vec{a}|^2}{2[\vec{a}\ \vec{b}\ \vec{c}]}$

Simillarly, $y=\dfrac{|\vec{b}|^2}{2[\vec{a}\vec{b}\vec{c}]}$ and $z=\dfrac{|\vec{c}|^2}{2[\vec{a}\ \vec{b}\ \vec{c}]}$

$\therefore\ \vec{r}=\dfrac{|\vec{a}|^2(\vec{b}\times\vec{c})+|\vec{b}|^2(\vec{c}\times\vec{a})+|\vec{c}|^2(\vec{a}\times\vec{b})}{2[\vec{a}\ \vec{b}\ \vec{c}]}.$

is the position vector of circumcentre of tetrahedron.

8. If $\vec{a}$, $\vec{b}$ are two non-collinear vectors, show that points $l_1\vec{a}+m_1\vec{b}$, $l_2\vec{a}+m_2\vec{b}$, $l_3\vec{a}+m_3\vec{b}$ are collinear if $\begin{vmatrix} l_1 & l_2 & l_3 \\ m_1 & m_2 & m_3 \\ 1 & 1 & 1 \end{vmatrix}=0$.

Solution: Let P, Q, R be three points with position vector $\vec{\alpha},\vec{\beta},\vec{\gamma}$ respectively such that $\vec{\alpha}=l_1\vec{a}+m_1\vec{b}$; $\vec{\beta}=l_2\vec{a}+m_2\vec{b}$; $\vec{\gamma}=l_3\vec{a}+m_3\vec{b}$ where $\vec{a}$ and $\vec{b}$ are L.I.

If $P(\vec{\alpha}), Q(\vec{\beta}), R(\vec{\gamma})$ are collinear, then

$x\vec{\alpha}+y\vec{\beta}+z\vec{\gamma}=0$ and $x+y+z=0$

Now, $x\vec{\alpha}+y\vec{\beta}+z\vec{\gamma}=0$

gives $x(l_1\vec{a}+m_1\vec{b})+y(l_2\vec{a}+m_2\ )+z(l_3\vec{a}+m_3\vec{b})=0$

or $(xl_1+yl_2+zl_3)\vec{a}+(xm_1+ym_2+zm_3)\vec{b}=0$

Since $\vec{a}$ and $\vec{b}$ are non-collinear vectors, it follows that

$xl_1+yl_2+zl_3=0$ ...(i)

and $xm_1+ym_2+zm_3=0$ ...(ii)

Also given $x+y+z=0$ ...(iii)

Eliminating x, y, z from the three equations (i), (ii) and (iii), we get, $\begin{vmatrix} l_1 & l_2 & l_3 \\ m_1 & m_2 & m_3 \\ 1 & 1 & 1 \end{vmatrix}=0$

9. The points D, E, F divide the sides BC, CA, AB of a triangle ABC in the ratio 1 : 2. The pairs of lines AD, BE; BE, CF; CF, AD meet at P, Q, R respectively. Show that the area of triangle $PQR=\dfrac{1}{7}$ (area of triangle ABC). Also find the ratios

(i) $\dfrac{PA}{PD}$ (ii) $\dfrac{BP}{PE}$ (iii) $\dfrac{CQ}{QF}$ (iv) $\dfrac{AR}{AD}$

Solution: To find the position vectors of P, Q, R; applying section formulae.

$\vec{d}=\dfrac{2\vec{b}+\vec{c}}{3}$, $\vec{e}=\dfrac{2\vec{c}+\vec{a}}{3}$, $\vec{f}=\dfrac{2\vec{a}+\vec{b}}{3}$

$\Rightarrow\ 3\vec{d}=2\vec{b}+\vec{c}$ ...(*i*)

$3\vec{e}=2\vec{c}+\vec{a}$ ...(*ii*)

$3\vec{f}=2\vec{a}+\vec{b}$ ...(*iii*)

From (i) and (ii)

$\Rightarrow\ \begin{cases} 6\vec{d}=4\vec{b}+2\vec{c} \\ 3\vec{e}=2\vec{c}+\vec{a} \end{cases}\ \Rightarrow\ \begin{cases} \vec{a}+6\vec{d}=4\vec{b}+2\vec{c}+\vec{a} \\ 4\vec{b}+3\vec{e}=2\vec{c}+\vec{a}+4\vec{b} \end{cases}$

$\Rightarrow\ \vec{p}=\dfrac{\vec{a}+4\vec{b}+2\vec{c}}{7}$ is P.V. of the point P that divides AD in ratio 6 : 1 and BE in ratio 3 : 4.

$\Rightarrow\ \dfrac{PA}{PD}=6$ & $\dfrac{PB}{PE}=\dfrac{3}{4}$

Similarly from (ii) and (iii) we get

$6\vec{e}=4\vec{c}+2\vec{a}\Rightarrow\vec{b}+6\vec{e}=2\vec{a}+4\vec{c}+\vec{b}$

$3\vec{f}=2\vec{a}+\vec{b}\Rightarrow 3\vec{f}+4\vec{c}=2\vec{a}+\vec{b}+4\vec{c}$

$\Rightarrow\ \vec{q}=\dfrac{\vec{b}+2\vec{a}+4\vec{c}}{7}=\dfrac{\vec{b}+6\vec{e}}{7}=\dfrac{4\vec{c}+3\vec{f}}{7}$

is the position vector of point of intersection Q.

$\Rightarrow\ \dfrac{CQ}{QF}=\dfrac{3}{4}$; From (i) and (iii)

$3\vec{d}=2\vec{b}+\vec{c}\Rightarrow 4\vec{a}+3\vec{d}=4\vec{a}+2\vec{b}+\vec{c}$

$6\vec{f}=4\vec{a}+2\vec{b}\Rightarrow 6\vec{f}+\vec{c}=4\vec{a}+2\vec{b}+\vec{c}$

$\Rightarrow\ \vec{r}=\dfrac{4\vec{a}+2\vec{b}+\vec{c}}{7}=\dfrac{4\vec{a}+3\vec{d}}{7}=\dfrac{\vec{c}+6\vec{f}}{7}$

is the position vector of R that divides AD in ratio 3 : 4 and CF in ratio 6 : 1.

$$\Rightarrow \frac{RA}{RD}=\frac{3}{4} \Rightarrow \frac{DR}{RA}=\frac{4}{3} \Rightarrow \frac{DR+RA}{RA}=\frac{7}{3}$$

$$\Rightarrow \frac{AD}{RA}=\frac{7}{3} \Rightarrow \frac{RA}{AD}=\frac{3}{7}.$$

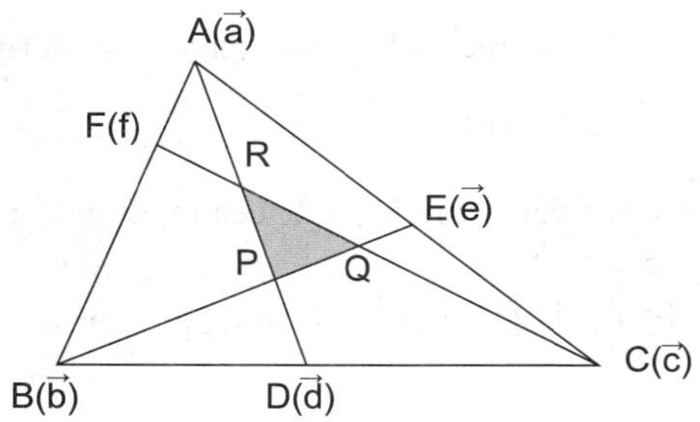

$\overrightarrow{PQ}$ = position vector of $\vec{Q}$ - position vector of $\vec{P}$

$= \frac{1}{7}(\vec{a}-3\vec{b}+2\vec{c}) \qquad \overrightarrow{PR}=\frac{1}{7}(3\vec{a}-2\vec{b}-\vec{c})$

area of $\Delta PQR = \frac{1}{2}|\overrightarrow{PQ}\times\overrightarrow{PR}|$

$$= \frac{1}{2}.\frac{1}{49}7(\vec{a}\times\vec{b}+\vec{b}\times\vec{c}+\vec{c}\times\vec{a})$$

$$= \frac{1}{2}.\frac{1}{7}(\vec{a}\times\vec{b}+\vec{b}\times\vec{c}+\vec{c}\times\vec{a})$$

area of $\Delta ABC = \frac{1}{2}(\vec{a}\times\vec{b}+\vec{b}\times\vec{c}+\vec{c}\times\vec{a})$

therefore, area of $\Delta PQR = \frac{1}{7}$ (area of ΔABC)

10. Prove that the line joining the centres of two intersecting circles is perpendicular to their common chord.

Solution: Considering the centre of one circle at origin 'O' and other circle's at $C(\vec{c})$; and their radii are a and b respectively.

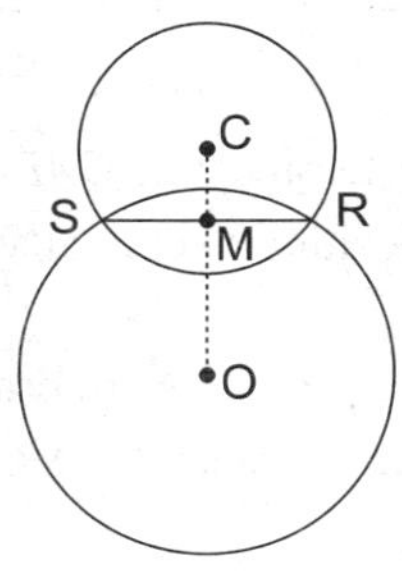

As shown in the figure circles intersect at $R(\vec{r})$ and M is the mid point of chord RS.

P. V. of C is $\vec{c}$, and that of R is $\vec{r}$

$\Rightarrow \overrightarrow{CR}=\vec{r}-\vec{c}$

$\Rightarrow \vec{r}\,.\,\vec{r}=a^2 \qquad ....(i)$

$\Rightarrow (\vec{r}-\vec{c}).(\vec{r}-\vec{c})=b^2 \qquad ....(ii)$

For the point of intersection, solving (i) and (ii)

$a^2-b^2-2(\vec{r}\,.\,\vec{c})+|\vec{c}|^2=0$

$\Rightarrow \vec{r}\,.\,\vec{c}=\frac{1}{2}(|\vec{c}|^2+a^2-b^2) \qquad ....(iii)$

To prove $OC \perp RS$ we try to prove $\overrightarrow{OC}\,.\,\overrightarrow{RS}=0$

$\because \overrightarrow{OR}=\overrightarrow{OM}+\overrightarrow{MR}=x\vec{c}+y\overrightarrow{RS} \qquad ....(iv)$

$\overrightarrow{OS}=\overrightarrow{OM}+\overrightarrow{MS}=x\vec{c}+z\overrightarrow{RS} \qquad ....(v)$

$\because$ P. V. of the point of intersection R and S given as $\vec{r}$ satisfies equation (iii)

$\Rightarrow \overrightarrow{OR}.\vec{c}=\vec{r}.\vec{c}=(x\vec{c}+y\overrightarrow{RS}).\vec{c}=\frac{1}{2}(|\vec{c}|^2+a^2-b^2)$

and $\overrightarrow{OS}.\vec{c}=\vec{r}.\vec{c}=(x\vec{c}+z\overrightarrow{RS}).\vec{c}=\frac{1}{2}.(|\vec{c}|^2+a^2-b^2)$

$\Rightarrow \left(x\vec{c}+y\overrightarrow{RS}\right).\vec{c}=\left(x\vec{c}+z\overrightarrow{RS}\right).\vec{c}$

$\Rightarrow \overrightarrow{RS}\,.\,\vec{c}=0 \Rightarrow \overrightarrow{RS}\perp\overrightarrow{OC}$

11. For any pair of vectors $\vec{a}$ and $\vec{b}$ and a positive scalar 'x' prove that $|\vec{a}+\vec{b}|^2 \le (1+x)|\vec{a}|^2+\left(1+\frac{1}{x}\right)|\vec{b}|^2$

Solution: Consider, $(1+x)|\vec{a}|^2+\left(1+\frac{1}{x}\right)|\vec{b}|^2$

$$=|\vec{a}|^2+|\vec{b}|^2-x|\vec{a}|^2+\frac{1}{x}|\vec{b}|^2 \qquad ....(i)$$

Applying inequality of mean AM ≥ GM, we have

$$\frac{x|\vec{a}|^2+\frac{|\vec{b}|^2}{x}}{2}\ge\sqrt{|\vec{a}^2|^2|\vec{b}|^2}$$

$$\Rightarrow x|\vec{a}|^2+\frac{|\vec{b}|^2}{x}\ge 2|\vec{a}||\vec{b}| \qquad ....(ii)$$

From (i) and (ii)

$$\Rightarrow (1+x)|\vec{a}|^2+\left(1+\frac{1}{x}\right)\vec{b}|^2 \ge |\vec{a}|^2+|\vec{b}|^2+2|\vec{a}||\vec{b}|$$

$$\Rightarrow (1+x)|\vec{a}|^2+\left(1+\frac{1}{x}\right)|\vec{b}|^2 \ge \left(|\vec{a}|+|\vec{b}|\right)^2$$

By triangle inequality $|\vec{a}|+|\vec{b}| \ge |\vec{a}+\vec{b}|$

$$\Rightarrow (1+x)|\vec{a}|^2+\left(1+\frac{1}{x}\right)|\vec{b}|^2 \ge |\vec{a}+\vec{b}|^2$$

12. A, B, C, D are four points in space. Using vector methods, prove that $AC^2 + BD^2 + AD^2 + BC^2 \ge AB^2 + CD^2$, what is the implication of the sign of equality

Solution: considering the position vector of *A*, *B*, *C*, *D* be $\vec{a}, \vec{b}, \vec{c}, \vec{d}$ respectively

$A \to P$ and $\vec{a} \to \vec{p}$

$B \to Q$ and $\vec{b} \to \vec{q}$

$C \to R$ and $\vec{c} \to \vec{r}$

$D \to S$ and $\vec{d} \to \vec{s}$

then $AC^2 + BD^2 + AD^2 + BC^2$

$$= (\vec{c}-\vec{a}).(\vec{c}-\vec{a})+(\vec{d}-\vec{b}).(\vec{d}-\vec{b})+ (\vec{d}-\vec{a}).(\vec{d}-\vec{a})+(\vec{c}-\vec{b}).(\vec{c}-\vec{b})$$

$$= |\vec{c}|^2 + |\vec{a}|^2 - 2\vec{a}.\vec{c} + |\vec{d}|^2 + |\vec{b}|^2 - 2\vec{d}.\vec{b} + |\vec{d}|^2 + |\vec{a}|^2 - 2\vec{d}.\vec{a} + |\vec{c}|^2 + |\vec{b}|^2 - 2\vec{c}.\vec{b}$$

$$= |\vec{a}|^2 + |\vec{b}|^2 - 2\vec{a}.\vec{b} + |\vec{c}|^2 + |\vec{d}|^2 - 2\vec{c}.\vec{d} + |\vec{a}|^2 + |\vec{b}|^2 + |\vec{c}|^2 + |\vec{d}|^2 + 2\vec{a}.\vec{b} + 2\vec{c}.\vec{d} - 2\vec{a}.\vec{c} - 2\vec{b}.\vec{d} - 2\vec{a}.\vec{d} - 2\vec{b}.\vec{c}$$

$$= (\vec{a}-\vec{b}).(\vec{a}-\vec{b})+(\vec{c}-\vec{d}).(\vec{c}-\vec{d})+ (\vec{a}+\vec{b}-\vec{c}-\vec{d}).(\vec{a}+\vec{b}-\vec{c}-\vec{d})$$

$$= \overline{AB}^2 + \overline{CD}^2 + (\vec{a}+\vec{b}-\vec{c}-\vec{d}).(\vec{a}+\vec{b}-\vec{c}-\vec{d})$$

$\Rightarrow AC^2 + BD^2 + AD^2 + BC^2 \geq AB^2 + CD^2$

for the sign of equality to hold

$\vec{a}+\vec{b}-\vec{c}-\vec{d} = 0 \quad \vec{a}-\vec{c} = \vec{d}-\vec{b}$

$\Rightarrow \vec{AC}$ and $\vec{BD}$ are collinear

$\Rightarrow$ the four points *A*, *B*, *C*, *D* are collinear.

13. Show that $x_1\hat{i}+y_1\hat{j}+z_1\hat{k}$, $x_2\hat{i}+y_2\hat{j}+z_2\hat{k}$ and $x_3\hat{i}+y_3\hat{j}+z_3\hat{k}$ are non-coplanar if $|x_1| > |y_1| + |z_1|$, $|y_2| > |x_2| + |z_2|$ and $|z_3| > |x_3| + |y_3|$.

Solution: If the vectors $x_1\hat{i}+y_1\hat{j}+z_1\hat{k}$, $x_2\hat{i}+y_2\hat{j}+z_2\hat{k}$ and $x_3\hat{i}+y_3\hat{j}+z_3\hat{k}$ are co-planar

$$\Rightarrow \begin{vmatrix} x_1 & y_1 & z_1 \\ x_2 & y_2 & z_2 \\ x_3 & y_3 & z_3 \end{vmatrix} = 0 \text{ or the set of equations}$$

$x_1x + y_1y + z_1z = 0$

$x_2x + y_2y + z_2z = 0$

$x_3x + y_3y + z_3z = 0$

have a non-trivial solution. Let the given set have a non-trivial solution for *x*, *y*, *z*.

Then without loss of generality we can assume $x \geq y \geq z$

For the given equation; $x_1x + y_1y + z_1z = 0$

We have $x_1x = -y_1y - z_1z$

$\Rightarrow |x_1x| = |y_1y + z_1z| \leq |y_1x + z_1x|$

$\Rightarrow |x_1x| \leq |y_1x + z_1x|$

$\Rightarrow |x_1| \leq |y_1| + |z_1|$

which is contradiction to given inequality

i.e., $|x_1| > |y_1| + |z_1|$

Similarly, the other inequalities can be ruled out the possibility of a non-trivial solution. Hence the given equation have only a trivial solution. Hence the given vectors are co-planar

14. Using vector method prove that in a ΔABC $\cos 2A + \cos 2B + \cos 2C \geq -\frac{3}{2}$.

Solution: Consider a circle with centre *O* and a ΔABC inscribed in it.

$\Rightarrow |\overline{OA}| = |\overline{OB}| = |\overline{OC}| = R$ (circum-radius)

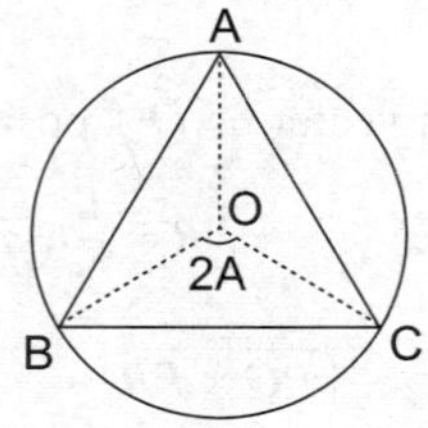

$\because |\overline{OA}+\overline{OB}+\overline{OC}|^2 \geq 0$

$\Rightarrow (\overline{OA}+\overline{OB}+\overline{OC}).(\overline{OA}+\overline{OB}+\overline{OC}) \geq 0$

$\Rightarrow |\overline{OA}|^2 + |\overline{OB}|^2 + |\overline{OC}|^2 + 2\left(\overline{OA}\,.\,\overline{OB} + \overline{OB}\,.\,\overline{OC} + \overline{OC}\,.\,\overline{OA}\right) \geq 0$

$\Rightarrow 3R^2 + 2R^2\left(\cos 2A + \cos 2B + \cos 2C\right) \geq 0$

$\Rightarrow 2\left(\cos 2A + \cos 2B + \cos 2C\right) + 3 \geq 0$

$\therefore \cos 2A + \cos 2B + \cos 2C \geq -\frac{3}{2}$

15. Prove that sum of the outward drawn normal vectors $\overline{N_1}, \overline{N_2}, \overline{N_3}, \overline{N_4}$ to the faces of tetrahedron whose magnitude is equal to the area of respective faces is a null vector.

Solution: Consider a tetrahedron *OABC* with *O* as origin and $\vec{a}, \vec{b}, \vec{c}$ as position vector of vertices *A*, *B* and *C* respectively.

$\overline{N_1}, \overline{N_2}, \overline{N_3}$ & $\overline{N_4}$ be outward drawn normal vectors respectively over the faces ΔOAB, ΔABC, ΔOBC and ΔOCA.

Let *O* be the origin and $\vec{a}$, $\vec{b}$ and $\vec{c}$ are the position vectors of *A*, *B* and *C* respectively.

$\overline{OA} = \vec{a}$, $\overline{OB} = \vec{b}$ and $\overline{OC} = \vec{c}$

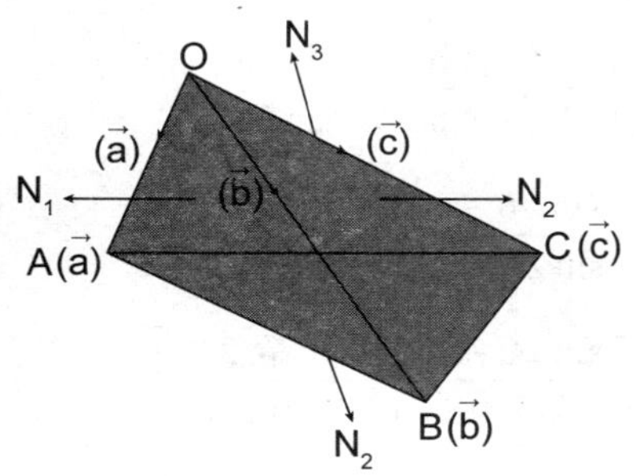

$\overrightarrow{N_1}$ = Area vector of (ΔOAB) = $\frac{1}{2}(\vec{a}\times\vec{b})$

$\overrightarrow{N_2}$ = Area vector of (ΔOBC) = $\frac{1}{2}(\vec{b}\times\vec{c})$

$\overrightarrow{N_3}$ = Area vector of (ΔOCA) = $\frac{1}{2}(\vec{c}\times\vec{a})$

$\overrightarrow{N_4}$ = Area vector of (ΔABC) = $\frac{1}{2}(\overrightarrow{AC}\times\overrightarrow{AB})$

$\Rightarrow\ \overrightarrow{N_4} = \frac{1}{2}[(\vec{c}-\vec{a})\times(\vec{b}-\vec{a})]$

$\Rightarrow\ \overrightarrow{N_4} = \frac{1}{2}[\vec{c}\times\vec{b}+\vec{b}\times\vec{a}+\vec{a}\times\vec{c}]$

$= -\frac{1}{2}(\vec{b}\times\vec{c})-\frac{1}{2}(\vec{a}\times\vec{b})-\frac{1}{2}(\vec{c}\times\vec{a})$

$\Rightarrow\ \overrightarrow{N_4} = -(\overrightarrow{N_2}+\overrightarrow{N_1}+\overrightarrow{N_3}) \Rightarrow \overrightarrow{N_1}+\overrightarrow{N_2}+\overrightarrow{N_3}+\overrightarrow{N_4}=\vec{O}$

16. If the median AD of $\Delta\ ABC$ is bisected at E and BE intersects AC in F, then evaluate AF/AC.

Solution: Let A be the origin and position vectors of B and C be $\vec{b}$ and $\vec{c}$ respectively. Now $\frac{BD}{DC} = 1, \frac{AE}{ED} = 1,$

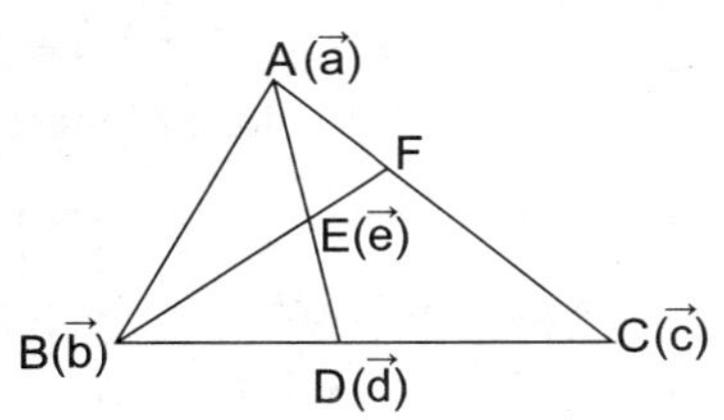

$\vec{d} = \frac{\vec{b}+\vec{c}}{2}$ and $\vec{e} = \frac{\vec{b}+\vec{c}}{4}$

Equation of $\overrightarrow{BF}$ is $\vec{r} = \vec{b} + \lambda\left(\frac{\vec{b}+\vec{c}}{4}-\vec{b}\right)$ ... (1)

Equation of $\overrightarrow{AC}$ is $\vec{r} = \mu\vec{c}$ ... (2)

For the point, F, $\vec{b} + \lambda\left(\frac{\vec{b}+\vec{c}}{4}-\vec{b}\right) = \mu\vec{c}$, for some particular λ and μ.

Since $\vec{b}$ and $\vec{c}$ are non-collinear

$1+\frac{\lambda}{4}-\lambda = 0,\ \frac{\lambda}{4} = \mu \Rightarrow \lambda = 4/3,\ \mu = 1/3$

$\Rightarrow$ Position vector of $F = \mu\vec{c} = (1/3)\ \vec{c}$

Thus $AF/AC = 1/3$

17. AD, BE, CF are altitudes of triangle ABC, Show that altitudes are concurrent and find point of concurrency.

Solution: $\frac{BD}{DC} = \frac{AD\cot B}{AD\cot C} = \frac{\tan C}{\tan B}$

$\therefore\ \vec{d} = \frac{\vec{b}\tan B+\vec{c}\tan C}{\tan B+\tan C}\ \therefore\ \vec{a}\tan A+\vec{d}(\tan B+\tan C)$

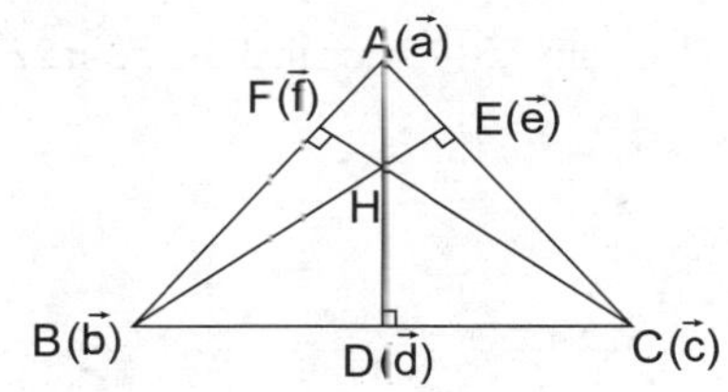

$= \vec{a}\tan A+\vec{b}\tan B+\vec{c}\tan C$

||rly, $\vec{b}\tan B+\vec{e}(\tan A+\tan C)$

$= \vec{a}\tan A+\vec{b}\tan B+\vec{c}\tan C$

and $\vec{c}\tan C+\vec{f}(\tan A+\tan B)$

$= \vec{a}\tan A+\vec{b}\tan B+\vec{c}\tan C$

$\Rightarrow\ \frac{\vec{a}\tan A+\vec{d}(\tan B+\tan C)}{\tan A+(\tan B+\tan C)}$

$= \frac{\vec{b}\tan B+\vec{e}(\tan A+\tan C)}{\tan B+(\tan A+\tan C)}$

$= \frac{\vec{c}\tan C+\vec{f}(\tan A+\tan B)}{\tan C+(\tan A+\tan B)}$

$= \frac{\vec{a}\tan A+\vec{b}\tan B+\vec{c}\tan C}{\tan A+\tan B+\tan C}$

$\Rightarrow$ point of concurrency $= \frac{\vec{a}\tan A+\vec{b}\tan B+\vec{c}\tan C}{\tan A+\tan B+\tan C}$

18. Show that perpendicular bisectors of a triangle are concurrent and hence find the circumcentre.

Solution: Let O be the circumcentre and let OD, OE and OF $\perp$rs on BC, CA and AB respetively

$\therefore\ \frac{BD}{DC} = \frac{A_{\Delta BDA}}{A_{\Delta ADC}} = \frac{A_{\Delta BDO}}{A_{\Delta ODC}} = \frac{A_{\Delta BDA}-A_{\Delta BDO}}{A_{\Delta ADC}-A_{\Delta ODC}}$

$= \frac{A_{\Delta BOA}}{A_{\Delta COA}} = \frac{\frac{1}{2}r^2\sin 2C}{\frac{1}{2}r^2\sin 2B}$

$\Rightarrow \dfrac{BD}{DC} = \dfrac{\sin 2C}{\sin 2B}$

$\Rightarrow (\sin 2B + \sin 2C)\vec{d} = (\vec{b}\sin 2B + \vec{c}\sin 2C)$

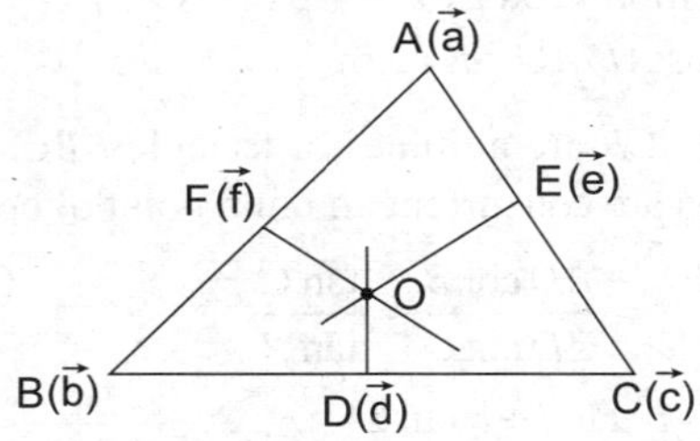

Similarly, $(\sin 2A + \sin 2C)\vec{e} = \vec{a}\sin 2A + \vec{c}\sin 2C$

and $(\sin 2A + \sin 2B)\vec{f} = \vec{a}\sin 2A + \vec{b}\sin 2B$

$\Rightarrow \dfrac{\vec{a}\sin 2A + (\sin 2B + \sin 2C)\vec{d}}{\sin 2A + (\sin 2B + \sin 2C)}$

$= \dfrac{\vec{b}\sin 2B + (\sin 2A + \sin 2C)\vec{e}}{\sin 2B + (\sin 2A + \sin 2C)}$

$= \dfrac{\vec{c}\sin 2C + (\sin 2A + \sin 2B)\vec{f}}{\sin 2A + \sin 2B + \sin 2C}$

$= \dfrac{\vec{a}\sin 2A + \vec{b}\sin 2B + \vec{c}\sin 2C}{\sin 2A + \sin 2B + \sin 2C}$

Three right bisectors of sides are concurrent and hence circumcentre is $\vec{O} = \dfrac{\vec{a}\sin 2A + \vec{b}\sin 2B + \vec{c}\sin 2C}{\sin 2A + \sin 2B + \sin 2C}$

SECTION–II

OBJECTIVE SOLVED EXAMPLES

1. Given that $(\vec{x} - \hat{a}).(\vec{x} + \hat{a}) = 8$ and $\vec{x} . \hat{a} = 2$, then the angle between $(\vec{x} - \hat{a})$ and $(\vec{x} + \hat{a})$ is:

(a) $\sec^{-1}\left(\dfrac{\sqrt{21}}{4}\right)$ (b) $\cos^{-1}\left(\dfrac{3}{\sqrt{21}}\right)$

(c) $\cos^{-1}\left(\dfrac{5}{\sqrt{21}}\right)$ (d) None of these

Solution: (a) $(\vec{x} - \hat{a}).(\vec{x} + \hat{a}) = 8 \Rightarrow |\vec{x}|^2 = 9 \Rightarrow |\vec{x}| = 3$

To determine $(\vec{x} - \hat{a})$, we have $(\vec{x} - \hat{a}) . (\vec{x} - \hat{a})$

$= |\vec{x}|^2 - 2(\vec{x}.\hat{a}) + \hat{a}.\hat{a} = 9 - 4 + 1 = 6 \Rightarrow |\vec{x} - \hat{a}|^2 = 6$

$\Rightarrow |(\vec{x} - \hat{a})| = \sqrt{6}$ and similarly, $|\vec{x} + \hat{a}| = \sqrt{14}$

Now let the angle between $(\vec{x} - \hat{a})$ and $(\vec{x} + \hat{a})$ be θ.

Then $(\vec{x} - \hat{a}) . (\vec{x} + \hat{a}) = \sqrt{14} \times \sqrt{6} \cos\theta$

$\Rightarrow 8 = \sqrt{14} \times \sqrt{6}\cos\theta \Rightarrow \cos\theta = \dfrac{4}{\sqrt{21}}$

2. The vector $(\vec{a} + 3\vec{b})$ is perpendicular to $(7\vec{a} - 5\vec{b})$ and $(\vec{a} - 4\vec{b})$ is perpendicular to $(7\vec{a} - 2\vec{b})$. The angle between $\vec{a}$ and $\vec{b}$ is:

(a) 30° (b) 45°

(c) 60° (d) None of these

Solution: (c) Given $(\vec{a} + 3\vec{b}).(7\vec{a} - 5\vec{b}) = 0$

$\Rightarrow 7\vec{a}^2 - 15\vec{b}^2 + 16\vec{a}.\vec{b} = 0$ ...... (i)

Also, $(\vec{a} - 4\vec{b}).(7\vec{a} - 2\vec{b}) = 0$

$\Rightarrow 7\vec{a}^2 + 8\vec{b}^2 - 30\vec{a}.\vec{b} = 0$ ...... (ii)

Subtracting, $-23\vec{b}^2 + 46\,\vec{a}.\vec{b} = 0 \Rightarrow \vec{a}.\vec{b} = \dfrac{\vec{b}^2}{2}$

Putting this in (i), $7\vec{a}^2 - 7\vec{b}^2 = 0 \Rightarrow |\vec{a}| = |\vec{b}|$

Thus $\vec{a}.\vec{b} = ab\cos\theta$

$\Rightarrow \dfrac{b^2}{2} = b^2\cos\theta \Rightarrow \cos\theta = \dfrac{1}{2}$ or $\theta = 60°$.

3. $\vec{a}, \vec{b}, \vec{c}$ are mutually perpendicular vectors of equal magnitude, then angle between $\vec{a} + \vec{b} + \vec{c}$ and $\vec{b}$ is:

(a) $\cos^{-1}(1/3)$ (b) $\cos^{-1}(1/\sqrt{3})$

(c) 0 (d) None of these

Solution: (b) Given $|\vec{a}| = |\vec{b}| = |\vec{c}| = a$ (say)

and $\vec{a}.\vec{b} = \vec{b}.\vec{c} = \vec{c}.\vec{a} = 0$. Now, $|\vec{a} + \vec{b} + \vec{c}|^2$

$= |\vec{a}|^2 + |\vec{b}|^2 + |\vec{c}|^2 + 2\sum \vec{a}.\vec{b} = 3a^2$

$\Rightarrow |\vec{a} + \vec{b} + \vec{c}| = a\sqrt{3}$

$\Rightarrow \vec{a}.(\vec{a} + \vec{b} + \vec{c}) = a.\,a\sqrt{3}\cos\theta$

$\Rightarrow a^2 = \sqrt{3}a^2\cos\theta \Rightarrow \cos\theta = \dfrac{1}{\sqrt{3}}$

$\Rightarrow \theta = \cos^{-1}\dfrac{1}{\sqrt{3}}$

4. If $\vec{a} + \vec{b}$ is along the angle bisector of $\vec{a}$ and $\vec{b}$, (given $\vec{a}$ and $\vec{b}$ are non collinear vector), then

(a) $\vec{a}$ and $\vec{b}$ are perpendicular

(b) $|\vec{a}| = |\vec{b}|$

(c) angle between $\vec{a}$ and $\vec{b}$ is 60°

(d) None of these

Solution: (b) Any vector along the angle bisector of $\vec{a}$ and $\vec{b}$ is $= \lambda\ (\hat{a} + \hat{b})$ where $\lambda \neq 0$

$\Rightarrow\ (\vec{a}+\vec{b}) = \lambda(\hat{a} + \hat{b}) = \lambda\left(\frac{\vec{a}}{|\vec{a}|} + \frac{\vec{b}}{|\vec{b}|}\right)$

$\Rightarrow\ \frac{\lambda}{|\vec{a}|} = 1 = \frac{\lambda}{|\vec{b}|}$. Which is possible when $|\vec{a}| = |\vec{b}|$

5. X-component of a vector $\vec{a}$ is twice its Y-component. If the magnitude of the vector is $5\sqrt{2}$ and it makes an angle of 135° with z-axis, then the components of vecor $\vec{a}$ may be

(a) $2\sqrt{3}, \sqrt{5}, -5$ (b) $2\sqrt{3}, \sqrt{3}, -5$

(c) $2\sqrt{5}, \sqrt{5}, -5$ (d) None of these

Solution: (c) Consider vector $\vec{a}$ as $\vec{a} = 2x\hat{i} + x\hat{j} + z\hat{k}$

$\Rightarrow \sqrt{5x^2 + z^2} = 5\sqrt{2}$ .....(i)

Also given that

$\cos 135° = \frac{z}{\sqrt{5x^2 + z^2}} = \frac{z}{5\sqrt{2}} = -\frac{1}{\sqrt{2}} \Rightarrow z = -5$

Substituting in (i), we get

$5x^2 + 25 = 50 \Rightarrow |x| = \sqrt{5} \Rightarrow x = \pm\sqrt{5}$

$\therefore$ The required vector $\vec{a} = 2\sqrt{5}\,\hat{i} + \sqrt{5}\,\hat{j} - 5\hat{k}$

or $-2\sqrt{5}\hat{i} - \sqrt{5}\hat{j} - 5\hat{k}$

6. Solve the vector equation for $\vec{x}$: $\vec{x} + \vec{x} \times \vec{a} = \vec{b}$

(a) $\frac{1}{1 + \vec{a}.\vec{a}}\{\vec{b} + (\vec{a}.\vec{b})\vec{a} + \vec{a} \times \vec{b}\}$

(b) $\frac{1}{1 - \vec{a}.\vec{a}}\{\vec{b} + (\vec{a}.\vec{b})\vec{a} + \vec{a} \times \vec{b}\}$

(c) $\frac{1}{1 + \vec{a}.\vec{a}}\{\vec{b} - (\vec{a}.\vec{b})\vec{a} - \vec{a} \times \vec{b}\}$

(d) None of these

Solution: (a) Taking dot product with $\vec{a}$, we get $\vec{x}.\vec{a} = \vec{b}.\vec{a}$ ....(i)

Now, taking cross product with $\vec{a}$, we get

$\vec{x} \times \vec{a} + (\vec{x} \times \vec{a}) \times \vec{a} = \vec{b} \times \vec{a}$ ....(ii)

$\Rightarrow \vec{x} \times \vec{a} + (\vec{x}.\vec{a})\vec{a} - (\vec{a}.\vec{a})\vec{x} = \vec{b} \times \vec{a}$

$\Rightarrow \vec{b} - \vec{x} + (\vec{x}.\vec{a})\vec{a} - (\vec{a}.\vec{a})\vec{x} = \vec{b} \times \vec{a}$

$\Rightarrow \vec{b} + \vec{a}(\vec{b}.\vec{a}) - \vec{b} \times \vec{a} = \vec{x}(1 + \vec{a}.\vec{a})$

$\Rightarrow \vec{x} = \frac{1}{1 + \vec{a}.\vec{a}}\{\vec{b} + (\vec{a}.\vec{b})\vec{a} + \vec{a} \times \vec{b}\}$

7. Let ABC be a triangle, the position vectors of whose vertices are respectively, $A(7\hat{j} + 10\hat{k})$, $B(-\hat{i} + 6\hat{j} + 6\hat{k})$ and $C(-4\hat{i} + 9\hat{j} + 6\hat{k})$. Then the triangle ABC is:

(a) isosceles (b) equilateral

(c) right angled (d) None of these

Solution: (a, c) We have, $\vec{AB}$ = P.V. of B – P.V. of $A = -\hat{i} - \hat{j} - 4\hat{k}$,

and $\vec{BC}$ = P.V of C – P.V. of $B = -3\hat{i} + 3\hat{j}$

Similarly, $\vec{CA} = 4\hat{i} - 2\hat{j} + 4\hat{k}$

$\therefore\ |\vec{AB}| = |\vec{BC}| = 3\sqrt{2}$ and $|\vec{CA}| = 6$

evidently, $|\vec{AB}|^2 + |\vec{BC}|^2 = |\vec{AC}|^2$

$\therefore$ the triangle is right angled isosceles triangle.

8. If $|\vec{a}.\vec{b}| = |\vec{a} \times \vec{b}|$, then the angle between $\vec{a}$ and $\vec{b}$ is:

(a) 0° (b) 180°

(c) 135° (d) 45°

Solution: (c, d) Given $|\vec{a} \times \vec{b}| = |\vec{a}.\vec{b}|$

$\Rightarrow \left||\vec{a}||\vec{b}|\cos\theta\right| = \left||\vec{a}||\vec{b}|\sin\theta\right|$

$\Rightarrow |\cos\theta| = |\sin\theta| \Rightarrow \theta = 45°, 135°$

9. If a vector $\vec{r}$ of magnitude $3\sqrt{6}$ is directed along the bisector of the angle between the vectors $\vec{a} = 7\hat{i} - 4\hat{j} - 4\hat{k}$ and $\vec{b} = -2\hat{i} - \hat{j} + 2\hat{k}$, then $\vec{r}$ is equal to

(a) $\hat{i} - 7\hat{j} + 2\hat{k}$ (b) $\hat{i} + 7\hat{j} - 2\hat{k}$

(c) $-\hat{i} + 7\hat{j} - 2\hat{k}$ (c) $\hat{i} - 7\hat{j} - 2\hat{k}$

Solution: (a, c) The required vector, $\vec{r} = \lambda(\hat{a} + \hat{b})$, λ is a scalar

or $\vec{r} = \lambda\left(\frac{1}{9}(7\hat{i} - 4\hat{j} - 4\hat{k}) + \frac{1}{3}(-2\hat{i} - \hat{j} + 2\hat{k})\right)$

$= \frac{\lambda}{9}(\hat{i} - 7\hat{j} + 2\hat{k})$

$\because |\vec{r}|^2 = 54 \Rightarrow \frac{\lambda^2}{81}(1 + 49 + 4) = 54 \Rightarrow \lambda = \pm 9$

10. Let $\vec{a}, \vec{b}, \vec{c}$ are three non-coplanar vectors such that, $\vec{r}_1 = \vec{a} - \vec{b} + \vec{c}$, $\vec{r}_2 = \vec{b} + \vec{c} - \vec{a}$, $\vec{r}_3 = \vec{c} + \vec{a} + \vec{b}$, $\vec{r} = 2\vec{a} - 3\vec{b} + 4\vec{c}$. If $\vec{r} = \lambda_1\vec{r}_1 + \lambda_2\vec{r}_2 + \lambda_3\vec{r}_3$, then:

(a) $\lambda_1 = 7$ (b) $\lambda_1 + \lambda_3 = 3$

(c) $\lambda_1 + \lambda_2 + \lambda_3 = 4$ (d) $\lambda_3 + \lambda_2 = 2$

Solution: (b,c) We have $\vec{r} = \lambda_1\vec{r}_1 + \lambda_2\vec{r}_2 + \lambda_3\vec{r}_3$

$\Rightarrow 2\vec{a} - 3\vec{b} + 4\vec{c} = (\lambda_1 - \lambda_2 + \lambda_3)\vec{a} + (\lambda_2 + \lambda_3 - \lambda_1)\vec{b} + (\lambda_1 + \lambda_2 + \lambda_3)\vec{c}$

($\because \vec{a}, \vec{b}, \vec{c}$ linearly independent as given as non co-planar vector)

$\Rightarrow \lambda_1 - \lambda_2 + \lambda_3 = 2, \lambda_3 + \lambda_2 - \lambda_1 = -3, \lambda_1 + \lambda_2 + \lambda_3 = 4$

$\Rightarrow \lambda_1 = \frac{7}{2}, \lambda_2 = 1, \lambda_3 = -\frac{1}{2}$

11. Given $\vec{p} = 3\hat{i} + 4\hat{j}$, $\vec{q} = 5\hat{i}$, $4\vec{r} = \vec{p} + \vec{q}$, and $2\vec{s} = \vec{p} - \vec{q}$; where $\hat{i}, \hat{j}, \hat{k}$ are mutually orthogonal unit vectors, then

(a) $|\vec{r} + k\vec{s}| = |\vec{r} - k\vec{s}|$ for all real k

(b) $\vec{s}$ is perpendicular to $\vec{s}$

(c) $\vec{r} + \vec{s}$ is perpendicular to $\vec{r} - \vec{s}$

(d) $|\vec{r}| = |\vec{s}| = |\vec{p}| = |\vec{q}|$

Solution: (a,b,c) we have, $\hat{i}.\hat{j} = \hat{j}.\hat{k} = \hat{k}.\hat{i} = 0$

given $\vec{p} = 3\hat{i} + 4\hat{j}$, $\vec{q} = 5\hat{i}$ $4\vec{r} = \vec{p} + \vec{q}$, $2\vec{s} = \vec{p} - \vec{q}$

$\Rightarrow \vec{r} = 2\vec{i} + \vec{j}$, $\vec{s} = -\vec{i} + 2\vec{j}$

For option (a): $|\vec{r} + k\vec{s}| = |(2-k)\,\hat{i} + (1+2k)\,\hat{j}|$

$= \sqrt{(2-k)^2 + (1+2k)^2} = \sqrt{5 + 5k^2}$ ...... (1)

and $|\vec{r} - k\vec{s}| = |(2+k)\,\hat{i} + (1-2k)\hat{j}|$

$= \sqrt{(2+k)^2 + (1-2k)^2} = \sqrt{(5 + 5k^2)}$ ...... (2)

from (1) and (2), $|\vec{r} + k\vec{s}| = |\vec{r} - k\vec{s}|$

For option (b): $\because$ $\vec{r}.\vec{s} = 0 \Rightarrow \vec{r} \perp \vec{s}$

For option (c): $\because$ $\vec{r} + \vec{s} = \hat{i} + 3\hat{j}$

and $\vec{r} - \vec{s} = 3\hat{i} - j \Rightarrow (\vec{r} + \vec{s}).(\vec{r} - \vec{s}) = 0$

Hence $(\vec{r} + \vec{s})$ is perpendicular to $(\vec{r} - \vec{s})$

For option (d): $|\vec{r}| = \sqrt{5}, |\vec{s}| = \sqrt{5}, |\vec{p}| = 5, |\vec{q}| = 5$

$\therefore$ $|\vec{r}| = |\vec{s}| \neq |\vec{p}| = |\vec{q}|$

12. If the non-zero vectors $\vec{a}$ and $\vec{b}$ are perpendicular to each other, then the solution of the equation, $\vec{r} \times \vec{a} = \vec{b}$ is:

(a) $\vec{r} = x\vec{a} + \frac{1}{\vec{a}.\vec{a}}(\vec{a} \times \vec{b})$

(b) $\vec{r} = x\vec{b} - \frac{1}{\vec{b}.\vec{b}}(\vec{a} \times \vec{b})$

(c) $\vec{r} = x\,(\vec{a} \times \vec{b})$

(d) None of these

Solution: (a) Since $\vec{a}, \vec{b}$ and $(\vec{b} \times \vec{b})$ are non-coplanar

$\therefore$ $\vec{r} = x\vec{a} + y\vec{b} + z(\vec{a} \times \vec{b})$ ...... (i)

for some scalars x, y, z; also given $\vec{b} = \vec{r} \times \vec{a}$

$\therefore$ $\vec{b} = \{x\vec{a} + y\vec{b} + z(\vec{a} \times \vec{b})\} \times \vec{a}$

$= x(\vec{a} \times \vec{a}) + y(\vec{b} \times \vec{a}) + z\{(\vec{a} \times \vec{b}) \times \vec{a}\}$

$= 0 + y(\vec{b} \times \vec{a}) + z\,\{(\vec{a}.\vec{a})\vec{b} - (\vec{a}.\vec{b})\vec{a}\}$

$\therefore$ $\vec{b} = y(\vec{b} \times \vec{a}) + z\,(\vec{a}\,.\,\vec{a})b$ $\{\because\ \vec{a}\,.\,\vec{b} = 0\}$

Comparing the coefficients, we get $y = 0$ and $z = \frac{1}{(\vec{a}.\vec{a})}$ Putting the values of y and z in (i),

we get $\vec{r} = x\vec{a} + \frac{1}{(\vec{a}.\vec{a})}(\vec{a} \times \vec{b})$

13. If $\vec{a}, \vec{b}$ and $\vec{c}$ are non-coplanar unit vectors such that $\vec{a} \times (\vec{b} \times \vec{c}) = \frac{(\vec{b} + \vec{c})\sqrt{3}}{2}$, then the angle between $\vec{a}$ and $\vec{b}$ is

(a) $\frac{\pi}{6}$ (b) $\frac{5\pi}{6}$

(c) $\frac{\pi}{2}$ (d) $\frac{2\pi}{3}$

Solution: (b) We have $\vec{a} \times (\vec{b} \times \vec{c}) = \frac{(\vec{b} + \vec{c})\sqrt{3}}{2}$

$\Rightarrow (\vec{a}.\vec{c})\vec{b} - (\vec{a}.\vec{b})\vec{c} = \frac{\sqrt{3}\vec{b}}{2} + \frac{\sqrt{3}\vec{c}}{2}$

$\Rightarrow \left(\vec{a}\,.\,\vec{c} - \frac{\sqrt{3}}{2}\right)\vec{b} - \left(\vec{a}.\vec{b} + \frac{\sqrt{3}}{2}\right)\vec{c} = 0$

then $\vec{a}.\vec{c} - \frac{\sqrt{3}}{2} = 0$ and $\vec{a}.\vec{b} + \frac{\sqrt{3}}{2} = 0$

($\because$ $\vec{a}, \vec{b}, \vec{c}$ are non coplanar)

Let the angle between $\vec{a}$ and $\vec{b}$ be θ, then $\vec{a}.\vec{b} = -\frac{\sqrt{3}}{2}$

$\Rightarrow |\vec{a}||\vec{b}|\cos\theta = -\frac{\sqrt{3}}{2} \Rightarrow 1.\,1\cos\theta = -\frac{\sqrt{3}}{2}$

$\Rightarrow \theta = \pi - \frac{\pi}{6} = \frac{5\pi}{6}$

14. Let $\vec{a}$ and $\vec{b}$ are two vectors making angle θ with each other, then which of the following represents unit vectors along bisector of $\vec{a}$ and $\vec{b}$ is:

(a) $\pm\dfrac{\hat{a}+\hat{b}}{2}$ (b) $\pm\dfrac{\hat{a}+\hat{b}}{2\cos\theta}$

(c) $\pm\dfrac{\hat{a}+\hat{b}}{2\cos\theta/2}$ (d) $\dfrac{(\hat{a}+\hat{b})}{|\hat{a}+\hat{b}|}$

Solution: (c) In ΔABC, Let AD is angle bisector of angle A.

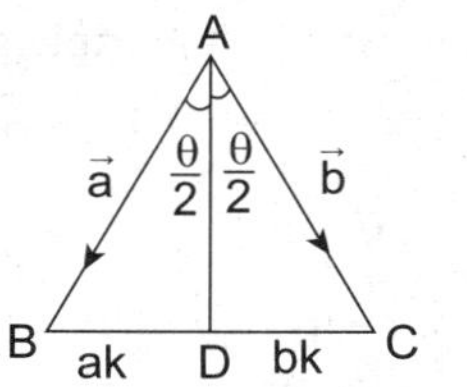

$\therefore\ BD = ak,\ DC = bk \quad \therefore\ BC = (a+b)k$

Applying cosine formula, we have

$$\cos\theta = \frac{(AB)^2+(AC)^2-(BC)^2}{2(AB)(AC)}$$

$$= \frac{a^2+b^2-(a+b)^2k^2}{2ab} \quad \text{..... (1)}$$

Also in ΔADC and ΔABD

$$\cos\frac{\theta}{2} = \frac{b^2+(AD)^2-b^2k^2}{2b\,AD} = \frac{a^2+(AD)^2-a^2k^2}{2a\,AD}$$

$$\Rightarrow (AD)^2 = ab\,(1-k^2)$$

$$= ab\left\{1-\frac{a^2+b^2-2ab\cos\theta}{(a+b)^2}\right\} \text{ [from (1)]}$$

$$= \frac{4a^2b^2\cos^2\theta/2}{(a+b)^2} \Rightarrow AD = \frac{2ab\cos\theta/2}{(a+b)}$$

$$\therefore\ \overrightarrow{AD} = \pm\frac{(\vec{a}b+\vec{b}a)}{(a+b)} = \pm\frac{ab}{(a+b)}\left(\frac{\vec{a}}{a}+\frac{\vec{b}}{b}\right)$$

$$= \pm\frac{ab}{(a+b)}(\hat{a}+\hat{b})$$

$$\therefore\ \hat{AD} = \frac{\overrightarrow{AD}}{AD} = \pm\frac{(\hat{a}+\hat{b})}{2\cos\theta/2}$$

15. Let $\vec{p},\ \vec{q},\ \vec{s}$ be three mutually perpendicular vectors of the same magnitude. If a vector $\vec{x}$ satisfies the equation

$\vec{p}\times((\vec{x}-\vec{q})\times\vec{p})+\vec{q}\times((\vec{x}-\vec{r})\times\vec{q})+$
$\vec{r}\times((\vec{x}-\vec{p})\times\vec{r})=0.$

Then $\vec{x}$ is given by:

(a) $\dfrac{1}{2}(\vec{p}+\vec{q}-2\vec{r})$ (b) $\dfrac{1}{3}(\vec{p}+\vec{q}+\vec{r})$

(c) $\dfrac{1}{2}(\vec{p}+\vec{q}+\vec{r})$ (d) $\dfrac{1}{3}(2\vec{p}+\vec{q}-\vec{r})$

Solution: (c) As $\vec{p},\vec{q},\vec{r}$ are mutually perpendicular,

$\vec{p}.\vec{q} = \vec{q}\ \vec{r} = \vec{r}.\vec{p} = 0$. Let $|\vec{p}| = |\vec{q}| = |\vec{r}| = k$ ....(i)

Now the given equation reduces to

$(3\vec{x}-\vec{p}-\vec{q}-\vec{r})k^2 = \vec{p}(\vec{p}.\vec{x})+\vec{q}(\vec{q}.\vec{x})+\vec{r}(\vec{r}.\vec{x})$ .....(i)

Also let $\vec{x} = A\vec{p}+B\vec{q}+C\vec{r}$

$\therefore\ \vec{p}.\vec{x} = Ak^2,\ \vec{q}.\vec{x} = Bk^2,\ \vec{r}.\vec{x} = Ck^2$

$$\Rightarrow A = \frac{\vec{p}.\vec{x}}{k^2},\ B = \frac{\vec{q}.\vec{x}}{k^2},\ C = \frac{\vec{r}.\vec{x}}{k^2}$$

$\therefore\ k^2\vec{x} = (\vec{p}.\vec{x})\vec{p}+\vec{q}(\vec{q}.\vec{x})+\vec{r}(\vec{r}.\vec{x})$ ....(ii)

$\therefore$ from (1) and (2) $\vec{x} = \dfrac{\vec{p}+\vec{q}+\vec{r}}{2}$

16. If $\cos\alpha\,\hat{i}+\hat{j}+\hat{k},\ \hat{i}+\cos\beta\,\hat{j}+\hat{k}$ and $\hat{i}+\hat{j}+\cos\gamma\,\hat{k}$, such that $(\alpha\neq\beta\neq\gamma\neq 2n\pi)$ are co-planar vectors then the value of $\left[\text{cosec}^2\dfrac{\alpha}{2}+\text{cosec}^2\dfrac{\beta}{2}+\text{cosec}^2\dfrac{\gamma}{2}\right]$ is equal to

(a) 1 (b) 2
(c) 3 (d) None of these

Solution: (b) $\because$ S.T.P of three coplaner vectors vanishes

$$\Rightarrow \begin{vmatrix}\cos\alpha & 1 & 1\\ 1 & \cos\beta & 1\\ 1 & 1 & \cos\gamma\end{vmatrix} = 0$$

$R_1 \to R_1 - R_2$ and $R_2 \to R_2 - R_3$

$$\Rightarrow \begin{vmatrix}\cos\alpha-1 & 1-\cos\beta & 0\\ 0 & \cos\beta-1 & 1-\cos\gamma\\ 1 & 1 & \cos\gamma\end{vmatrix} = 0$$

$$\Rightarrow \begin{vmatrix}-2\sin^2\alpha/2 & 2\sin^2\beta/2 & 0\\ 0 & -2\sin^2\beta/2 & 2\sin^2\gamma/2\\ 1 & 1 & \cos\gamma\end{vmatrix} = 0$$

$$\Rightarrow 2\sin^2\frac{\alpha}{2}\left(2\sin^2\frac{\beta}{2}\cos\gamma+2\sin^2\frac{\gamma}{2}\right)+2$$

$$\sin^2\frac{\beta}{2}\,2\sin^2\frac{\gamma}{2} = 0$$

$$\Rightarrow \sin^2\frac{\alpha}{2}\left[\sin^2\frac{\beta}{2}\left(1-2\sin^2\frac{\gamma}{2}\right)+\sin^2\frac{\gamma}{2}\right]+$$

$$\sin^2\frac{\beta}{2}\sin^2\frac{\gamma}{2} = 0$$

multiplying by $\text{cosec}^2\frac{\alpha}{2}\ \text{cosec}^2\frac{\beta}{2}\ \text{cosec}^2\frac{\gamma}{2}$,

we have $\text{cosec}^2\frac{\gamma}{2} - 2 + \text{cosec}^2\frac{\beta}{2} + \text{cosec}^2\frac{\alpha}{2} = 0$

$\Rightarrow\ \text{cosec}^2\frac{\alpha}{2} + \text{cosec}^2\frac{\beta}{2} + \text{cosec}^2\frac{\gamma}{2} = 2$

17. Let $\vec{\alpha} = a_1\hat{i} + a_2\hat{j} + a_3\hat{k}$, $\vec{\beta} = b_1\hat{i} + b_2\hat{j} + b_3\hat{k}$ and $\vec{\gamma} = c_1\hat{i} + c_2\hat{j} + c_3\hat{k}$, $|\vec{\alpha}| = 2$, $\vec{\alpha}$ makes angle $\pi/6$ with the plane of $\vec{\beta}$ and $\vec{\gamma}$ and angle between $\vec{\beta}$ and $\vec{\gamma}$ is $\pi/4$, then $\begin{vmatrix} a_1 & a_2 & a_3 \\ b_1 & b_2 & b_3 \\ c_1 & c_2 & c_3 \end{vmatrix}^n$ is equal to (*where n is even natural number*)

(a) $\left(\frac{|\vec{\beta}||\vec{\gamma}|}{2}\right)^{\frac{n}{2}}$ (b) $\frac{(|\vec{\beta}||\vec{\gamma}|)^n}{2^{n/2}}$

(c) $\frac{(|\vec{\beta}||\vec{\gamma}|)^{n/2}}{2^n}$ (d) None of these

Solution: (b) $\left\|\begin{matrix} a_1 & a_2 & a_3 \\ b_1 & b_2 & b_3 \\ c_1 & c_2 & c_3 \end{matrix}\right\|$ denotes the absoluate value of volume (v) of parallelopiped whose adjacent sides are given by $\vec{\alpha}$, $\vec{\beta}$, $\vec{\gamma}$.

$$V = |\vec{\beta} \times \vec{\gamma}||\vec{\alpha}|\ \sin\frac{\pi}{6}$$

$$= |\vec{\beta}||\vec{\gamma}|\frac{1}{\sqrt{2}}.\frac{1}{2}|\vec{\alpha}| = \frac{|\vec{\beta}||\vec{\gamma}|}{\sqrt{2}}$$

$$\therefore\ (\text{volume})^n = \left(\frac{|\vec{\beta}||\vec{\gamma}|}{\sqrt{2}}\right)^n = \frac{(|\vec{\beta}||\vec{\gamma}|)^n}{2^{n/2}}$$

18. If $A(\vec{a})$, $B(\vec{b})$ and $C(\vec{c})$ be vertices of a triangle whose circumcentre is the origin, then orthocentre is given by

(a) $\frac{\vec{a}+\vec{b}+\vec{c}}{3}$ (b) $\frac{\vec{a}+\vec{b}+\vec{c}}{2}$

(c) $\vec{a}+\vec{b}+\vec{c}$ (d) None of these

Solution: (c) Centroid of triangle will be $\frac{\vec{a}+\vec{b}+\vec{c}}{3}$ now line joining the orthocentre and the circumcentre is divided by centroid in 2 : 1 ratio internally, so orthocentre will be $\vec{a}+\vec{b}+\vec{c}$.

19. Find a vector $\vec{v}$ which is co-planar with the vectors $\vec{a} = \hat{i} - 2\hat{j} + \hat{k}$ and $\vec{b} = \hat{i} - \hat{j} + 2\hat{k}$ and is orthogonal to the vector $\vec{c} = -2\hat{i} + \hat{j} + \hat{k}$. It is given that the projection of $\vec{v}$ along the vector $\hat{i} - \hat{j} + \hat{k}$ is equal to $16\sqrt{3}$.

(a) $6\hat{j} - 12\hat{k}$ (b) $12\hat{i} - 6\hat{j} + 30\hat{k}$

(c) $9(\hat{i} - \hat{j} + \hat{k})$ (d) None of these

Solution: (b) *A* vector co-planar with $\vec{a}$ and $\vec{b}$ and orthogonal to $\vec{c}$ is parallel to the triple product $(\vec{a}\times\vec{b})\times\vec{c}$, given as $(\vec{a}\times\vec{b})\times\vec{c} = (\vec{a}.\vec{c})\ \vec{b} - (\vec{b}.\vec{c})\ \vec{a}$

$\vec{v} = \propto ((\vec{a}.\vec{c})\vec{b} - (\vec{b}.\vec{c})\vec{a})$

Hence $\vec{v} = \alpha\left[-3(\hat{i} - \hat{j} + 2\hat{k}) + (\hat{i} - 2\hat{j} + \hat{k})\right]$

$= \alpha[-2\hat{i} + \hat{j} - 5\hat{k}]$

Projection of $\vec{v}$ along

$$\hat{i} - \hat{j} + \hat{k} = \frac{\vec{v}.(\hat{i} - \hat{j} + \hat{k})}{|\hat{i} - \hat{j} + \hat{k}|} = 16\sqrt{3}$$

$\alpha[-2\hat{i} + \hat{j} - 5\hat{k}]\ .\ (\hat{i} - \hat{j} + \hat{k}) = 48$

$\alpha(-8) = 48 \Rightarrow \alpha = -6 \Rightarrow \vec{v} = 12\hat{i} - 6\hat{j} + 30\hat{k}$

20. Let *O* be the point of intersection of diagonals of the parallelogram *ABCD*. The points *M, N, K, P* are the mid-points of the segments *AO, BM, CN* and *DK* respectively, then which of the following is true.

(a) *O, N, P* collinear

(b) *O, N, P* form a triangle of non-zero area

(c) $\overline{ON} = \overline{OP}$

(d) None of these

Solution: (a) Let $O = \vec{0}, A(\vec{a}), B(\vec{b}), C(-\vec{a})$ and $D(-\vec{b})$

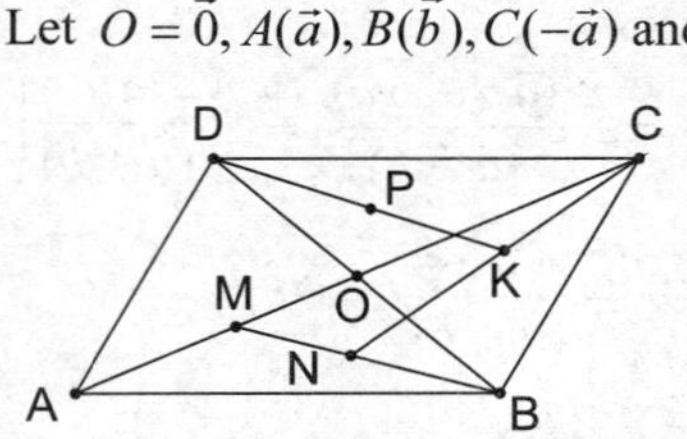

$$\Rightarrow\ M \equiv \frac{\vec{a}}{2}, N \equiv \frac{\vec{a}/2 + \vec{b}}{2} = \frac{\vec{a}+2\vec{b}}{4}$$

$$\text{Also } K \equiv \frac{\frac{\vec{a}+2\vec{b}}{4} - \vec{a}}{2} = \frac{2\vec{b}-3\vec{a}}{8};$$

$$\text{and } P \equiv \frac{-\vec{b} + \frac{2\vec{b}-3\vec{a}}{8}}{2} = \frac{-6\vec{b}-3\vec{a}}{2}$$

$\Rightarrow \ \overrightarrow{OP} = -\frac{3}{2}(2\vec{b}+\vec{a})$

and $\overrightarrow{ON} = \frac{1}{4}(\vec{a}+2\vec{b}) \ = -\frac{1}{6}\overrightarrow{OP}$

$\Rightarrow$ $\overrightarrow{ON}$ and $\overrightarrow{OP}$ are collinear

$\Rightarrow$ points O, N and P are collinear

21. If $\vec{a}$, $\vec{b}$ and $\vec{c}$ are non-coplanar vectors and $\vec{a}\times\vec{c}$ is perpendicular to $\vec{a}\times(\vec{b}\times\vec{c})$, then the value of $\left[\vec{a}\times(\vec{b}\times\vec{c})\right]\times\vec{c}$ is equal to

(a) $[\vec{a}\ \vec{b}\ \vec{c}]\vec{c}$ (b) $[\vec{a}\ \vec{b}\ \vec{c}]\vec{b}$

(c) $\vec{0}$ (d) $[\vec{a}\ \vec{b}\ \vec{c}]\ \vec{a}$

Solution: (c) Given that $\vec{a}$, $\vec{b}$ and $\vec{c}$ are non-coplanar

$\Rightarrow$ $[\vec{a}\ \vec{b}\ \vec{c}]\neq 0$. Again $(\vec{a}\times(\vec{b}\times\vec{c})).(\vec{a}\times\vec{c})=0$

$\Rightarrow$ $[(\vec{a}.\vec{c})\vec{b}-(\vec{a}.\vec{b})\vec{c}].(\vec{a}\times\vec{c})=0$

$\Rightarrow$ $(\vec{a}.\vec{c})[\vec{b}\ \vec{a}\ \vec{c}]=0$ $\quad(\because -[\vec{a}\vec{b}\vec{c}]=[\vec{b}\vec{a}\vec{c}]\neq 0)$

$\Rightarrow$ $(\vec{a}.\vec{c})=0 \Rightarrow \vec{a}$ and $\vec{c}$ are perpendicular

$\Rightarrow$ $[\vec{a}\times(\vec{b}\times\vec{c})]\times\vec{c}=(\vec{b}\times\vec{c})(\vec{a}.\vec{c})-\vec{a}\{(\vec{b}\times\vec{c}).\vec{c}\}$

22. If $\hat{a}+\hat{b}+\hat{c}=\vec{0}$, then the triangle whose sides $\overrightarrow{BC}$, $\overrightarrow{CA}$ and $\overrightarrow{AB}$ are respectively $\vec{a}$, $\vec{b}$ and $\vec{c}$ is

(a) isosceles (b) equilateral

(c) right angled (d) None of these

Solution: (b) $\because\ \hat{a}+\hat{b}+\hat{c}=\vec{0}$

$\Rightarrow\ \hat{a}=-(\hat{b}+\hat{c}) \qquad \Rightarrow\ |\hat{a}|=|\hat{b}+\hat{c}|$

squaring both sides, we get $1 = 1 + 1 + 2\cos(\pi - A)$

$\Rightarrow\ \cos A = \frac{1}{2} \Rightarrow A = 60°$

similarly we can show that $B = C = 60°$; hence ΔABC is equilateral.

23. Let $ABCD$ be a tetrahedron in which position vectors of A, B, C and D are $\hat{i}+\hat{j}+\hat{k}$, $2\hat{i}+\hat{j}+2\hat{k}$, $3\hat{i}+2\hat{j}+\hat{k}$ and $2\hat{i}+3\hat{j}+2\hat{k}$. If ABC be the base of tetrahedron, then height of tetrahedron is

(a) $\sqrt{\frac{3}{2}}$ (b) $\sqrt{\frac{3}{5}}$

(c) $\frac{1}{3}\sqrt{\frac{2}{3}}$ (d) None of these

Solution: (c) $\overrightarrow{AB}\times\overrightarrow{AC}=(\hat{i}+\hat{k})\times(2\hat{i}+\hat{j})=\hat{k}+2\hat{j}-\hat{i}$

Height of tetrahedron

$$=\frac{\left|\overrightarrow{AD}.\left(\overrightarrow{AB}\times\overrightarrow{AC}\right)\right|}{6\left|\overrightarrow{AB}\times\overrightarrow{AC}\right|}=\frac{\left|(\hat{i}+2\hat{j}+\hat{k}).(-\hat{i}+2\hat{j}+\hat{k})\right|}{6\left|-\hat{i}+2\hat{j}+\hat{k}\right|}$$

$$=\frac{|-1+4+1|}{|6\sqrt{6}|}=\frac{4}{6\sqrt{6}}=\frac{1}{3}\sqrt{\frac{2}{3}}$$

24. Let $\vec{a}=\hat{i}+\hat{j}+\hat{k}$, $\vec{c}$ is a vector such that $\vec{a}.\vec{c}=|\vec{c}|$, $|\vec{a}+\vec{c}|=\sqrt{6}$, then $\vec{a}.\vec{c}$ is equal to

(a) 1 (b) 5

(c) 3 (d) None of these

Solution: (a) Let $(\vec{a}+\vec{c}).(\vec{a}+\vec{c})=|\vec{a}|^2+|\vec{c}|^2+2\,\vec{a}.\vec{c}$

$\because$ Given $|\vec{a}+\vec{c}|^2=6$

$\Rightarrow\ |\vec{a}|^2+|\vec{c}|^2+2|\vec{c}|=6 \Rightarrow 3+|\vec{c}|^2+2|c|=6$

$\Rightarrow\ |\vec{c}|^2+2|\vec{c}|+3=6 \Rightarrow |\vec{c}|=1$

25. The position vectors of the vertices A, B and C of a triangle are three unit vectors $\hat{a}$, $\hat{b}$ and $\hat{c}$. A vector $\vec{d}$ is such that $\vec{d}.\hat{a}=\vec{d}.\hat{b}=\vec{d}.\hat{c}$ and $\vec{d}=\lambda(\hat{b}+\hat{c})$, then triangle ABC is

(a) acute angled (b) obtuse angled

(c) right angled (d) None of these

Solution: (c) $\vec{d}.\hat{a}=\vec{d}.\hat{b}=\vec{d}.\hat{c}$

$\Rightarrow\ \lambda(1+\hat{b}.\hat{c})=\lambda(1+\hat{b}.\hat{c})=\lambda(\hat{a}.\hat{b}+\hat{a}.\hat{c})$

$\Rightarrow\ 1+\hat{b}.\hat{c}=\hat{a}.\hat{b}+\hat{a}.\hat{c} \Rightarrow 1-\hat{a}.\hat{b}+\hat{b}.\hat{c}-\hat{a}.\hat{c}=0$

$\Rightarrow\ 1-\hat{a}.\hat{b}+(\hat{b}-\hat{a}).\hat{c}=0 \Rightarrow \hat{a}.(\hat{a}-\hat{b})+(\hat{b}-\hat{a}).\hat{c}=0$

$\Rightarrow\ (\hat{a}-\hat{c}).(\hat{a}-\hat{b})=0$

$\Rightarrow\ \hat{a}-\hat{c}$ is perpendicular to $(\hat{a}-\hat{b})$

$\Rightarrow\ \overrightarrow{CA}$ is perpendicular to $\overrightarrow{BA}$

$\Rightarrow$ The triangle is right angled

26. $\vec{a}$, $\vec{b}$ and $\vec{c}$ be three non-coplanar vectors and $\vec{d}$ be a non-zero vector, which is perpendicular to $(\vec{a}+\vec{b}+\vec{c})$. Now if $\vec{d}=\sin x(\vec{a}\times\vec{b})+\cos y(\vec{b}\times\vec{c})+2(\vec{c}\times\vec{a})$, then minimum value of x^2+y^2 is equal to

(a) π^2 (b) 0

(c) $\pi^2/4$ (d) $5\pi^2/4$

Solution: (d) Let $\vec{d}.\vec{a}=(\cos y)[\vec{a}\ \vec{b}\ \vec{c}] = -\vec{d}.(\vec{b}+\vec{c})$

[as $\vec{d}.(\vec{a}+\vec{b}+\vec{c})=0$]

$\Rightarrow\ \cos y=-\frac{\vec{d}.(\vec{b}+\vec{c})}{[\vec{a}\vec{b}\vec{c}]}$ ......(i)

similarly, $\sin x=-\frac{\vec{d}.(\vec{a}+\vec{b})}{[\vec{a}\vec{b}\vec{c}]}$ .....(ii)

$$2 = -\frac{\vec{d}.(\vec{a}+\vec{c})}{[\vec{a}\,\vec{b}\,\vec{c}]} \quad \text{.......(iii)}$$

Adding above equations, we get $\sin x + \cos y + 2 = 0$

$\Rightarrow \sin x + \cos y = -2$

$\Rightarrow \sin x = -1, \cos y = -1$

$\Rightarrow$ x = (4n – 1)π/2, y = (2n + 1); n ∈ $\mathbb{Z}$

$x = (4n-1)\pi/2, y = (2n+1)\pi$

since we want minimum value of $x^2 + y^2$,

so $x = -\frac{\pi}{2}, y = \pm\pi. \quad \Rightarrow x^2 + y^2 = \frac{5\pi^2}{4}$

27. If it is given that vectors $\vec{a},\vec{b},\vec{c}$ are non-coplanar, then the the points with p.v. $\vec{a}-2\vec{b}+3\vec{c},\ -2\vec{a}+3\vec{b}-\vec{c},\ 4\vec{a}-7\vec{b}+7\vec{c}$ are

(a) co-planar but non-collinear
(b) collinear
(c) non-coplanar
(d) None of these

Solution: (b) The three points are collinear, if we can find λ_1, λ_2, and λ_3, such that $\lambda_1(\vec{a}-2\vec{b}+3\vec{c})$ + $\lambda_2(-2\vec{a}+3\vec{b}-\vec{c})$ + $\lambda_3(4\vec{a}-7\vec{b}+7\vec{c}) = \vec{0}$

where $\lambda_1 + \lambda_2 + \lambda_3 = 0$

Equating the coefficients of $\vec{a},\vec{b},\vec{c}$ separately to zero, we get $\lambda_1 - 2\lambda_2 + 4\lambda_3 = 0$ .....(i)

$-2\lambda_1 + 3\lambda_2 - 7\lambda_3 = 0$ ......(ii)

$3\lambda_1 - \lambda_2 + 7\lambda_3 = 0$ ....(iii)

Solving the system of equations,

We find that $\lambda_1 = -2$, $\lambda_2 = 1$, $\lambda_3 = 1$ so that $\lambda_1 + \lambda_2 + \lambda_3 = 0$.

Hence the given vectors are collinear

28. Angles between any two opposite edges of a regular tetrahedron are

(a) acute angle (b) obtuse angle
(c) right angle (d) reflexive angle

Solution: (c) Take one of the vertices of the tetrahedron as the origin *O*. Then the position vectors of the points *A*, *B*, *C* of the tetrahedron *OABC* are $\vec{a},\vec{b},\vec{c}$, where $|\vec{a}| = |\vec{b}| = |\vec{c}|$. Since all the edges are of equal length, all the four faces of the tetrahedron are equilateral triangles.

$\Rightarrow \vec{a}.\vec{b} = \vec{a}.\vec{c} = \vec{b}.\vec{c} \Rightarrow \vec{a}.(\vec{b}-\vec{c}) = 0.$

Hence the opposite edges are perpendicular to each other.

29. If $\vec{a},\vec{b}$ and $\vec{c}$ are three unit vectors such that $\vec{a}\times(\vec{b}\times\vec{c}) = \frac{1}{2}\vec{b}$ and $\vec{b}$ is non-collinear to $\vec{c}$, then which of the following is true?

(a) $\vec{a}$ and $\vec{b}$ are perpendicular
(b) angle between $\vec{a}$ and $\vec{b}$ is π/3
(c) angle between $\vec{a}$ and $\vec{c}$ is π/3
(d) $\vec{a}, \vec{b}, \vec{c}$ are mutually orthogonal

Solution: (a, c) We are given that $\vec{a}\times(\vec{b}\times\vec{c}) = \frac{1}{2}\vec{b}$

Now definition of V.T.P., and non-collinearily of $\vec{b}$ and $\vec{c}$

$\Rightarrow (\vec{a}.\vec{c})\vec{b} - (\vec{a}.\vec{b})\vec{c} = \frac{1}{2}\vec{b}$

$\Rightarrow \vec{a}.\vec{c} = \frac{1}{2}$ and $\vec{a}.\vec{b} = 0$

Hence the angle between $\vec{a}$ and $\vec{c}$ is π/3 and that between $\vec{a}$ and $\vec{b}$ is π/2.

30. Line L_1 is parallel to a vector $\vec{\alpha} = -3\hat{i} - 2\hat{j} + 4\hat{k}$ and passes through a point *A*(7, 6, 2) and the line L_2 is parallel to a vector $\vec{\beta} = 2\hat{i} + \hat{j} + 3\hat{k}$ and passes through a point *B*(5, 3, 4). Now a line L_3 parallel to a vector $\vec{r} = 2\hat{i} - 2\hat{j} - \hat{k}$ intersects the lines L_1 and L_2 at points *C* and *D* respectively, then $|\overrightarrow{CD}|$ is

(a) 3 (b) 6
(c) 9 (d) None of these

Solution: (c) Position Vector of *C* is given by $\vec{r}_1 = (7\hat{i} + 6\hat{j} + 2\hat{k}) + a(-3\hat{i} + 2\hat{j} + 4\hat{k})$, $a \in \mathbb{R}$

Position Vector of *D* is given by

$\vec{r}_2 = (5\hat{i} + 3\hat{j} + 4\hat{k}) + b(2\hat{i} + \hat{j} + 3\hat{k})$, $b \in \mathbb{R}$

$\overrightarrow{CD} = \vec{r}_2 - \vec{r}_1$ and we know that $\overrightarrow{CD} \parallel \vec{r}$ (given)

$\Rightarrow \overrightarrow{CD} = c((2\hat{i} - 2\hat{j} - \hat{k}))$

Hence by comparing the coefficient of $\hat{i},\hat{j},\hat{k}$ for both values of vector $\overrightarrow{CD}$, we have

$3a + 2b - 2c = 2$ ......(i)

$-2a + b + 2c = 3$ .....(ii)

and $-4a + 3b + c = -2$ ....(iii)

$\Rightarrow a = 2, b = 1, c = 3 \Rightarrow |\overrightarrow{CD}| = 3\sqrt{2^2 + 2^2 + 1^2} = 9$

31. The value of $\vec{x}$ satisfying $\vec{x} + \vec{y} = \vec{a}$

(i) $\vec{x}\times\vec{y} = \vec{b}$ (ii) $\vec{x}.\vec{a} = 1$ is

(a) $\dfrac{\vec{a}-(\vec{a}\times\vec{b})}{|\vec{a}|^2}$

(b) $\dfrac{\vec{a}+(\vec{a}\times\vec{b})}{|\vec{a}|^2}$

(c) $\dfrac{\vec{a}(|\vec{a}|^2-1)-(\vec{a}\times\vec{b})}{|\vec{a}|^2}$

(d) None of these

Solution: (c) Taking dot product of equation (i) by $\vec{b}$

$\Rightarrow\ \vec{a}.\vec{x}+\vec{a}.\vec{y}=|\vec{a}|^2 \Rightarrow \vec{a}.\vec{y}=|\vec{a}|^2-1\ (\because \vec{a}.\vec{x}=1)$

Also taking cross product by $\vec{b}$ the second given equation $\vec{a}\times(\vec{x}\times\vec{y})=\vec{a}\times\vec{b}$

$\Rightarrow\ (\vec{a}.\vec{y})\vec{x}-(\vec{a}.\vec{x})\vec{y}=\vec{a}\times\vec{b}$

$\Rightarrow\ (|\vec{a}|^2-1)\vec{x}-\vec{y}=\vec{a}\times\vec{b}$

$\Rightarrow\ |\vec{a}|^2\vec{x}-(\vec{x}+\vec{y})=\vec{a}\times\vec{b}$

$\Rightarrow\ |\vec{a}|^2\vec{x}-\vec{a}=\vec{a}\times\vec{b}\qquad(\because \vec{x}+\vec{y}=\vec{a})$

$\therefore\ \vec{x}=\dfrac{\vec{a}+(\vec{a}\times\vec{b})}{|\vec{a}|^2}$ and

$\vec{y}=\vec{a}-\vec{x}=\dfrac{\vec{a}(|\vec{a}|^2-1)-(\vec{a}\times\vec{b})}{|\vec{a}|^2}$

32. The scalars α and β if $\vec{a}\times(\vec{b}\times\vec{c})+(\vec{a}.\vec{b})\vec{b}=(4-2\beta\text{-}\sin\alpha)\vec{b}+(\beta^2-1)\vec{c}$ and $(\vec{c}.\vec{c})\vec{a}=\vec{c}$ where $\vec{b}$ and $\vec{c}$ are non-collinear, are

(a) $\beta=1,\ \alpha=(4n+1)\dfrac{\pi}{2};n\in\mathbb{Z}$

(b) $\beta=1,\ \alpha=(4n-1)\dfrac{\pi}{2};n\in\mathbb{Z}$

(c) $\beta=-1,\ \alpha=(4n+1)\dfrac{\pi}{2};n\in\mathbb{Z}$

(d) $\beta=-1,\ \alpha=(4n-1)\dfrac{\pi}{2};n\in\mathbb{Z}$

Solution: (a)

$\vec{a}\times(\vec{b}\times\vec{c})+(\vec{a}.\vec{b})\vec{b}=(4-2\beta-\sin\alpha)\vec{b}+(\beta^2-1)\vec{c}$

$\Rightarrow\ (\vec{a}.\vec{c})\vec{b}-(\vec{a}.\vec{b})\vec{c}+(\vec{a}.\vec{b})\vec{b}=$

$(4-2\beta-\sin\alpha)\vec{b}+(\beta^2-1)\vec{c}$

Comparing we get $\vec{a}.\vec{c}+\vec{a}.\vec{b}=(4-2\beta-\sin\alpha)$ ....(i)

$\vec{a}.\vec{b}=1-\beta^2$ ...(ii)

or, $\vec{a}.\vec{c}=\beta^2-2\beta+3-\sin\alpha$ ...(iii)

now, it is also given that $(\vec{c}.\vec{c})\vec{a}=\vec{c}$

$\Rightarrow\ \vec{a}=\dfrac{\vec{c}}{\vec{c}.\vec{c}}$ or, $\vec{a}.\vec{c}=\dfrac{\vec{c}.\vec{c}}{\vec{c}.\vec{c}}=1$

Therefore from equation (iii), we have,

$\beta^2-2\beta+2-\sin\alpha=0$

$\Rightarrow\ \sin\alpha=1+(1-2\beta+\beta^2)=1+(1-\beta)^2$

Since $\sin\alpha\le 1\Rightarrow(1-\beta)^2=0$

$\therefore\ \beta=1$ and hence $\sin\alpha=1$

$\therefore\ \alpha=2n\pi+\pi/2$, where $n\in\mathbb{Z}$

33. If $\vec{a}$ and $\vec{b}$ are unit vectors and $|\vec{c}|=4$ with $\vec{a}\times\vec{c}=2\vec{a}\times\vec{b}$. The angle between $\vec{a}$ and $\vec{b}$ is $\cos^{-1}\left(\dfrac{1}{2}\right)$.

The values of λ which satisfies condition $\vec{c}-2\vec{b}=\lambda\vec{a}$

(a) $1+\sqrt{13}$ (b) $1-\sqrt{13}$

(c) $-1+\sqrt{13}$ (d) $-1-\sqrt{13}$

Solution: (c and d) Now $\vec{c}=\lambda\vec{a}+2\vec{b}$

$|\vec{c}|^2=\vec{c}.\vec{c}=\lambda^2|\vec{a}|+4|\vec{b}|^2+4\lambda(\vec{a}.\vec{b})$

$|\vec{c}|^2=\lambda^2(1)+4(1)+4\lambda|\vec{a}||\vec{b}|\left(\dfrac{1}{2}\right)$

$\Rightarrow\ 16=\lambda^2+4+2\lambda\ \Rightarrow\ \lambda^2+2\lambda-12=0$

$\Rightarrow\ \lambda=-1\pm\sqrt{13}$

34. Let $\vec{a}$ and $\vec{b}$ be two non-collinear unit vectors. If $\vec{A}=\vec{a}-(\vec{a}.\vec{b})\vec{b}$ and $\vec{B}=\vec{a}\times\vec{b}$, the value of $|\vec{B}|$ is equal to

(a) $|\vec{A}|$ (b) $|\vec{A}|+|\vec{A}.\vec{a}|$

(c) $|\vec{A}|+|\vec{A}.\vec{b}|$ (d) None of these

Solution: (a, c) $\because\ |\vec{A}|^2=\vec{A}.\vec{A}=\left(\vec{a}-(\vec{a}.\vec{b})\vec{b}\right).\left(\vec{a}-(\vec{a}.\vec{b})\vec{b}\right)$

$\Rightarrow\ |\vec{A}|=|\vec{a}|^2+(\vec{a}.\vec{b})^2|\vec{b}|^2-2(\vec{a}.\vec{b})^2$

$\Rightarrow\ |\vec{A}|^2=1+\cos^2\theta-2\cos^2\theta=1-\cos^2\theta=\sin^2\theta$

$\therefore\ |\vec{A}|=|\sin\theta|$ ..... (i)

$|\vec{B}|^2=|\vec{a}|^2|\vec{b}|^2\sin^2\theta|\hat{n}|^2=\sin^2\theta$

$\Rightarrow\ |\vec{B}|^2=\sin^2\theta\ \Rightarrow\ |\vec{B}|=|\sin\theta|$ .... (ii)

$\therefore\ |\vec{A}|=|\vec{B}|=|\sin\theta|$

Now, $\vec{A}.\vec{a}=\vec{a}.\vec{a}-(\vec{a}.\vec{b})^2=1-\cos^2\theta=\sin^2\theta$

$\therefore\ |\vec{A}.\vec{a}|=\sin^2\theta$

$\therefore\ |\vec{A}|+|\vec{A}.\vec{a}|=|\sin\theta|+\sin^2\theta\ne|\vec{B}|$

Now, $\vec{A}.\vec{b}=(\vec{a}.\vec{b})-(\vec{a}.\vec{b})|\vec{b}|^2=0$

$\therefore\ |\vec{A}|+|\vec{A}.\vec{b}|=|\sin\theta|=|\vec{B}|$

So options *a* and *c* are correct.

35. A parallelogram is constructed on the vectors $\overline{AB}=\vec{a}=2\vec{\alpha}-\vec{\beta}$ and $\overline{BC}=\vec{b}=\vec{\alpha}-2\vec{\beta}$. If value of

$|\vec{\alpha}|$ and $|\vec{\beta}| = 3$ and angle between $\vec{\alpha}$ and $\vec{\beta}$ is $\frac{\pi}{3}$, then length of diagonal of

(a) $|\overline{AC}| = 9$ (b) $|\overline{BD}| = \sqrt{27}$

(c) $|\overline{BD}| = \sqrt{28}$ (d) $|\overline{AC}| = \sqrt{34}$

Solution: (a, b); $\overline{AC} = \vec{a} + \vec{b}$

$\Rightarrow |\overline{AC}|^2 = |\vec{a}+\vec{b}|^2 = |\vec{a}|^2 + |\vec{b}|^2 + 2(\vec{a}.\vec{b})$

Now, $|\vec{a}| = \sqrt{4|\vec{\alpha}|^2 + |\vec{\beta}|^2 - 4(\vec{\alpha}.\vec{\beta})}$

$= \sqrt{4(9)+9-4(3)(3)\times\frac{1}{2}} = \sqrt{45-18} = \sqrt{27} = 3\sqrt{3}$

$|\vec{b}| = \sqrt{|\vec{\alpha}|^2 + 4|\vec{\beta}|^2 - 4\vec{\alpha}.\vec{\beta}}$

$= \sqrt{9+4(9)-4(3)(3)\times\frac{1}{2}}$

$= \sqrt{9+36-18} = \sqrt{27} = 3\sqrt{3}$

$\vec{a}.\vec{b} = (2\vec{\alpha}-\vec{\beta}).(\vec{\alpha}-2\vec{\beta})$

$= 2|\vec{\alpha}|^2 + 2|\vec{\beta}|^2 - 5(\vec{\alpha}.\vec{\beta})$

$= 2(3)^2 + 2(3)^2 - 5\left(3\times3\times\frac{1}{2}\right) = \frac{27}{2}$

$\therefore |\overline{AC}|^2 = 27+27+27 = 81 \therefore |\overline{AC}| = \sqrt{81} = 9$

Similarly, $|\overline{BD}|^2 = (\vec{b}-\vec{a})^2 = |\vec{b}|^2 + |\vec{a}|^2 - 2(\vec{b}.\vec{a})$

$= 27 + 27 - 27 = 27 \quad \therefore |\overline{BD}| = \sqrt{27}.$

36. If unit vectors $\hat{i}$ and $\hat{j}$ are at right angles to each other and $\vec{a} = 3\hat{i} + 4\hat{j}$ and $\vec{b} = 5\hat{i}$, $4\vec{A} = \vec{a}+\vec{b}$ and $2\vec{B} = \vec{a}-\vec{b}$ then which of the following is true?

(a) $|\vec{A}+k\vec{B}| \neq |\vec{A}-k\vec{B}| \; \forall k \in \mathbb{R}$

(b) $\vec{A}$ is perpendicular to $\vec{B}$

(c) $\vec{A}+\vec{B}$ is perpendicular to $\vec{A}-\vec{B}$

(d) $|\vec{A}| = |\vec{B}| \neq |\vec{a}| = |\vec{b}|$

Solution: (b, c) Here $\vec{A} = \frac{1}{4}(8\hat{i}+4\hat{j}) = 2\hat{i}+\hat{j}$

and $\vec{B} = \frac{1}{2}(-2\hat{i}+4\hat{j}) = -\hat{i}+2\hat{j}$

Now, $|\vec{A}+k\vec{B}| = (2-k)\hat{i} + (1+2k)\hat{j}$

$\therefore |\vec{A}+k\vec{B}| = (k^2+4-4k+1+4k^2+4k)^{1/2} = (5k^2+5)^{1/2}$

Now $|\vec{A}-k\vec{B}| = \left((k+2)^2+(1-2k)^2\right)^{1/2}$

$= \left(k^2+4+4k+1+4k^2-4k\right)^{1/2} = \left(5k^2+5\right)^{1/2}$

$\therefore |\vec{A}+k\vec{B}| = |\vec{A}-k\vec{B}|$

$\therefore$ (a) is false

Now, $\vec{A}.\vec{B} = (2\hat{i}+\hat{j}).(-\hat{i}+2\hat{j}) = -2+2 = 0$

$\therefore \vec{A} \perp \vec{B} \therefore$ (b) is true

Further $\vec{A}+\vec{B} = (\hat{i}+3\hat{j})$ and $\vec{A}-\vec{B} = (3\hat{i}-\hat{j})$

$\therefore (\vec{A}+\vec{B}).(\vec{A}-\vec{B}) = 0$

$\therefore$ (c) is true

Now $|\vec{A}| = \sqrt{5}$; $|\vec{B}| = \sqrt{5}$; $|\vec{a}| = 5$ and $|\vec{b}| = 5$

(d) is false

Passage:

Given a regular parallelopiped whose coterminous edges are given by vectors $\vec{a}, \vec{b}$ and $\vec{c}$ such that $|\vec{a}| = |\vec{b}| = |\vec{c}| = 2$ and the angle between $\vec{a}$ and $\vec{b}$ is $\frac{\pi}{3}$, $\vec{b}$ and $\vec{c}$ is $\frac{\pi}{3}$, $\vec{c}$ and $\vec{a}$ is $\frac{\pi}{3}$,

Answer the following three problems based on above facts.

37. The volume of the parallelopiped whose adjacent edge are represented by the vectors $\vec{a}, \vec{b}$ and $\vec{c}$ is

(a) $5-\sqrt{2}$ (b) $4\sqrt{2}$

(c) $2\sqrt{5}$ (d) 4

Solution: (c) $\left[\vec{a}\;\vec{b}\;\vec{c}\right]\left[\vec{a}\;\vec{b}\;\vec{c}\right] = \begin{vmatrix} \vec{a}.\vec{a} & \vec{a}.\vec{b} & \vec{a}.\vec{c} \\ \vec{b}.\vec{a} & \vec{b}.\vec{b} & \vec{b}.\vec{c} \\ \vec{c}.\vec{a} & \vec{c}.\vec{b} & \vec{c}.\vec{c} \end{vmatrix}$

Now $\vec{a}.\vec{a} = |\vec{a}|^2 = 4 = \vec{b}.\vec{b} = \vec{c}.\vec{c}$

$\vec{a}.\vec{b} = |\vec{a}||\vec{b}|\cos\frac{\pi}{3} = 2\times2\times\frac{1}{2} = 2.$

$\vec{a}.\vec{c} = |\vec{a}||\vec{c}|\cos\frac{\pi}{3} = 2 \qquad \vec{c}.\vec{b} = |\vec{c}||\vec{b}|\cos\frac{\pi}{3} = 2$

$= \begin{vmatrix} 4 & 2 & 2 \\ 2 & 4 & 2 \\ 2 & 2 & 4 \end{vmatrix} = 4(16-4) - 2(8-4) + 2(4-8)$

$= 4(12) - 2(4) + 2(-4) = 36 - 8 - 8 = 20$

$\Rightarrow (\vec{a}\;\vec{b}\;\vec{c})^2 = 20 \Rightarrow [\vec{a}\;\vec{b}\;\vec{c}] = 2\sqrt{5}$

38. The height of the parallelopiped whose adjacent edge are represented by the vectors $\vec{a}, \vec{b}, \vec{c}$ is

(a) $3\sqrt{\frac{5}{2}}$ (b) $\sqrt{\frac{5}{3}}$

(c) $2\sqrt{\frac{3}{5}}$ (d) $2\sqrt{\frac{5}{3}}$

Solution: (b) V = (base area) × (height)

$\Rightarrow V = |\vec{a}\times\vec{b}| \times h$

$\Rightarrow\ 2\sqrt{5} = (2)\times(2)\times\frac{\sqrt{3}}{2}\times h$

$\Rightarrow\ h = \sqrt{\frac{5}{3}}$

39. The height of regular tetrahedron whose adjacent edges are represented by the vectors $\vec{a}, \vec{b}$ & $\vec{c}$ is

(a) $h = \sqrt{\frac{3}{5}}$ (b) $h = \sqrt{\frac{5}{3}}$

(c) $h = \sqrt{\frac{2}{3}}$ (d) $h = \sqrt{\frac{3}{2}}$

Solution: (b) Volume of tetrahedron

$= \frac{1}{6}\left[\vec{a}\ \vec{b}\ \vec{c}\right] = \frac{1}{6}\times 2\sqrt{5} = \frac{\sqrt{5}}{3}$

Also, volume $= \frac{1}{3}\times(\text{base area})\times(\text{height})$

$\Rightarrow\ \frac{\sqrt{5}}{3} = \frac{1}{3}\times\left(\frac{\sqrt{3}}{4}\times 2^2\right)\times h \Rightarrow h = \sqrt{\frac{5}{3}}$

40. $\vec{a}, \vec{b}, \vec{c}$ and $\vec{d}$ are the position vectors of the points $A \equiv (x, y, z)$; $B \equiv (y, -2z, 3x)$; $C \equiv (2z, 3x, -y)$ and $D \equiv (1, -1, 2)$ respectively. If $|\vec{a}| = 2\sqrt{3}$ and angle between $\vec{a}$ and $\vec{b}$ = angle between $\vec{a}$ and $\vec{c}$ and angle between $\vec{a}$ & $\vec{d} = \frac{\pi}{2}$ and vector $\vec{a}$ makes obtuse angle with positive direction of y-axis. then find x, y and z.

Solution: $|\vec{a}| = 2\sqrt{3}$ squaring both sides

$(\because |\vec{a}| = \sqrt{x^2+y^2+z^2}) \Rightarrow x^2 + y^2 + z^2 = 12$ ...(i)

$\because\ \widehat{(\vec{a}\ \vec{b})} = \widehat{(\vec{a}\ \vec{c})} \Rightarrow \frac{\vec{a}.\vec{b}}{|\vec{a}||\vec{b}|} = \frac{\vec{a}.\vec{c}}{|\vec{a}||\vec{c}|}$

$\Rightarrow\ \vec{a}.\vec{b} = \vec{a}.\vec{c}\ \left[\because |\vec{b}| = |\vec{c}| = \sqrt{9x^2+y^2+4z^2}\right]$

$\Rightarrow$ xy – 2yz + 3zx = 2xz + 3yx – yz

$\Rightarrow$ 2xy + yz – zx = 0 ...(ii)

Also $\widehat{(\vec{a}\ \vec{d})} = \frac{\pi}{2} \Rightarrow \vec{a}.\vec{d} = 0 \Rightarrow x - y + 2z = 0$

$\Rightarrow$ y = x + 2z ...(iii)

put in (ii) we get, $2x(x + 2z) + z(x + 2z) - zx = 0$

$\Rightarrow\ 2(x^2 + z^2 + 2xz) = 0 \Rightarrow (x + z)^2 = 0 \Rightarrow x = -z$

$\Rightarrow\ y = z$ (using (iii)) Now put $y = z$, $x = -z$ in (i)

$\Rightarrow\ z = \pm 2$ we take only $z = -2$

because $\widehat{(\vec{a}.\hat{j})}$ is obtuse so $x = 2, y = -2, z = -2$.

41. Given three points on the xy plane as $O(0, 0)$; $A(1, 0)$ and $B(-1, 0)$. Point P is moving on the plane satisfying the condition $(\overrightarrow{PA}.\overrightarrow{PB}) + 3(\overrightarrow{OA}.\overrightarrow{OB}) = 0$ If the maximum and minimum values of $|\overrightarrow{PA}||\overrightarrow{PB}|$ are M and m respectively, then find the value of $M^2 + m^2$.

Solution: $O(0, 0)$; $A(1, 0)$; $B(-1, 0)$

$\overrightarrow{PA} = (1-x)\hat{i} - y\hat{j}$; $\overrightarrow{OA} = \hat{i}$;

$\overrightarrow{PB} = (-1-x)\hat{i} - y\hat{j}$; $\overrightarrow{OB} = -\hat{i}$

Now $\overrightarrow{PA}.\overrightarrow{PB} + 3(\overrightarrow{OA}.\overrightarrow{OB}) = 0$ (given)

$\Rightarrow\ (x^2 - 1) + y^2 - 3(1) = 0$

$\Rightarrow\ x^2 + y^2 = 4$ ...(i)

$\Rightarrow\ -2 \le x, y \le 2$

Now $|\overrightarrow{PA}||\overrightarrow{PB}| = \sqrt{(x-1)^2+y^2}\ \sqrt{(x+1)^2+y^2}$

$= \sqrt{x^2+y^2+1-2x}\ \sqrt{x^2+y^2+1+2x}$

$= \sqrt{5-2x}\ \sqrt{5+2x}$

$= \sqrt{25-4x^2}$

Now, M = Max $|\overrightarrow{PA}||\overrightarrow{PB}| = 5$ (when x = 0)

and m = Min. $|\overrightarrow{PA}||\overrightarrow{PB}| = 3$ (when x = ±2)

$M^2 + m^2 = 5^2 + 3^2 = 34$

42. Find the minimum area of the triangle whose vertices are $A(-1, 1, 2)$; $B(1, 2, 3)$ and $C(t, 1, 1)$; where t is a real number.

Solution: $\overrightarrow{AB} = 2\hat{i} + \hat{j} + \hat{k}$

$\overrightarrow{AC} = (t+1)\hat{i} + 0\hat{j} - \hat{k}$

Now, $\overrightarrow{AB}\times\overrightarrow{AC} = \begin{vmatrix} \hat{i} & \hat{j} & \hat{k} \\ 2 & 1 & 1 \\ t+1 & 0 & -1 \end{vmatrix}$

$= -\hat{i} + (t+3)\hat{j} - (t+1)\hat{k}$

$\Rightarrow\ |\overrightarrow{AB}\times\overrightarrow{AC}| = \sqrt{1+(t+3)^2+(t+1)^2}$

$= \sqrt{2t^2+8t+11}$

$\Rightarrow$ Area of $\Delta ABC = \frac{1}{2}|\overrightarrow{AB}\times\overrightarrow{AC}|$

$\Rightarrow\ \Delta = \frac{1}{2}\sqrt{2t^2+8t-1} = \frac{1}{\sqrt{2}}\sqrt{(t-2)^2+\frac{9}{2}} \ge \frac{3}{2}$

$\therefore$ Min. area of $\Delta = \frac{3}{2}$ sq. units.

TUTORIAL EXERCISE

SECTION–III

SINGLE CORRECT ANSWER

1. If $ABCD$ is a rhombus whose diagonals cut at the origin O, then $\overrightarrow{OA}+\overrightarrow{OB}+\overrightarrow{OC}+\overrightarrow{OD}$ equals

(a) $\overrightarrow{AB}+\overrightarrow{AC}$ (b) $\vec{0}$

(c) $2(\overrightarrow{AB}+\overrightarrow{BC})$ (d) $\overrightarrow{AC}+\overrightarrow{BD}$

2. If $|\vec{a}+\vec{b}|=|\vec{a}-\vec{b}|$, $\vec{a}\neq\vec{0}$, then

(a) $\vec{a}\parallel\vec{b}$ (b) $\vec{a}\perp\vec{b}$

(c) $|\vec{a}|=|\vec{b}|$ (d) None of these

3. If the vectors $\vec{a}=-4\hat{i}+3\hat{j}$ and $\vec{b}=14\hat{i}+2\hat{j}-5\hat{k}$ have same initial point then, the angle bisector of $\vec{a}$ and $\vec{b}$ of magnitude $\sqrt{6}$ is

(a) $\dfrac{2\hat{i}+11\hat{j}-5\hat{k}}{5}$ (b) $\hat{i}-\hat{j}+2\hat{k}$

(c) $\hat{i}-\hat{j}-2\hat{k}$ (d) None of these

4. If two vectors $\vec{b}$ and $\vec{c}$ are in the directions north-east and north-west respectively with $|\vec{b}|$ and $|\vec{c}|=4$, then $\vec{c}-\vec{b}$ is

(a) $4\sqrt{2}$ towards north

(b) $4\sqrt{2}$ towards west

(c) $4\sqrt{2}$ towards south

(d) $4\sqrt{2}$ towards east

5. P, Q have position vectors $\vec{a}$ and $\vec{b}$ relative to the origin 'O' and X, Y divide $\overline{PQ}$ internally and externally respectively in the ratio 2 : 1, vector $\overline{XY}$ =

(a) $\frac{3}{2}(\vec{b}-\vec{a})$ (b) $\frac{4}{3}(\vec{a}-\vec{b})$

(c) $\frac{5}{6}(\vec{b}-\vec{a})$ (d) $\frac{4}{3}(\vec{b}-\vec{a})$

6. The sides of a parallelogram are $2\hat{i}+4\hat{j}-5\hat{k}$ and $\hat{i}+2\hat{j}+3\hat{k}$, then the unit vector parallel to one of the diagonals is

(a) $\frac{1}{7}(3\hat{i}+6\hat{j}-2\hat{k})$ (b) $\frac{1}{7}(3\hat{i}-6\hat{j}-2\hat{k})$

(c) $\frac{1}{7}(-3\hat{i}+6\hat{j}-2\hat{k})$ (d) $\frac{1}{7}(3\hat{i}+6\hat{j}+2\hat{k})$

7. Let the position vectors of the points A, B, C be $\hat{i}+2\hat{j}+3\hat{k}$, $-\hat{i}-\hat{j}+8\hat{k}$ and $-4\hat{i}+4\hat{j}+6\hat{k}$ respectively. Then the $\Delta\, ABC$ is

(a) right angled

(b) equilateral

(c) isosceles (not equilateral)

(d) None of these

8. If $\vec{a}$ and $\vec{b}$ are two vectors of magnitude 2 units inclined at an angle 60°, then the angle between $\vec{a}$ and $\vec{a}+\vec{b}$ is

(a) 30° (b) 60°

(c) 45° (d) None of these

9. If $\vec{a}$ = 5, $|\vec{a}-\vec{b}|$ = 8 and $|\vec{a}+\vec{b}|$=10, then $|\vec{b}|$ is

(a) 1 (b) $\sqrt{57}$

(c) 3 (d) None of these

10. $(\vec{a}\times\vec{b})^2+(\vec{a}.\vec{b})^2$ is equal to

(a) 0 (b) $|\vec{a}|^2|\vec{b}|^2$

(c) $(|a|\ \ |b|)$ (d) 1

11. If $\vec{a}=4\hat{i}+6\hat{j}$ and $\vec{b}=3\hat{j}+4\hat{k}$, then the vector component of $\vec{a}$ along $\vec{b}$ is

(a) $\frac{18}{10\sqrt{3}}(3\hat{j}+4\hat{k})$ (b) $\frac{18}{25}(3\hat{j}+4\hat{k})$

(c) $\frac{18}{\sqrt{3}}(3\hat{j}+4\hat{k})$ (d) $3\hat{j}+4\hat{k}$

12. If $\vec{a}.\vec{b}$ = 0 and $\vec{a}+\vec{b}$ makes an angle of 30° with $\vec{a}$, then

(a) $|\vec{b}|=2|\vec{a}|$ (b) $|\vec{a}|=2|\vec{b}|$

(c) $|\vec{a}|=\sqrt{3}|\vec{b}|$ (d) None of these

13. If forces of magnitudes 6 and 7 units acting in the directions $\hat{i}-2\hat{j}+2\hat{k}$ and $2\hat{i}-3\hat{j}-6\hat{k}$ respectively act on a

particle which is displaced from the point $P(2, -1, -3)$ to $Q(5, -1, 1)$, then the work done by the force is

(a) 4 units (b) − 4 units
(c) 7 units (d) −7 units

14. If $\vec{a} = \hat{i} + \hat{j} - \hat{k}$, $\vec{b} = -\hat{i} + 2\hat{j} + \hat{k}$ and $\vec{c} = -\hat{i} + 2\hat{j} - \hat{k}$, then a unit vector ⊥ to both $\vec{a} + \vec{b}$ and $\vec{b} + \vec{c}$ is

(a) $\hat{i}$ (b) $\hat{j}$
(c) $\hat{k}$ (d) $\dfrac{\hat{i} + \hat{j} + \hat{k}}{\sqrt{3}}$

15. If the position vectors of three points A, B and C are respectively $\hat{i} + \hat{j} + \hat{k}$, $2\hat{i} + 3\hat{j} - 4\hat{k}$ and $7\hat{i} + 4\hat{j} + 9\hat{k}$, then the unit vector perpendicular to the plane of triangle ABC is

(a) $31\hat{i} - 18\hat{j} - 9\hat{k}$ (b) $\dfrac{31\hat{i} - 38\hat{j} - 9\hat{k}}{\sqrt{2486}}$
(c) $\dfrac{31\hat{i} + 18\hat{j} + 9\hat{k}}{\sqrt{2486}}$ (d) None of these

16. Let $\vec{\alpha} = (x + 4y)\vec{a} + (2x + y + 1)\vec{b}$ and $\vec{\beta} = (y - 2x + 2)\vec{a} + (2x - 3y - 1)\vec{b}$, where $\vec{a}$ and $\vec{b}$ are non-zero and non-collinear. If $3\vec{\alpha} = 2\vec{\beta}$, then

(a) $x = 1, y = 2$ (b) $x = 2, y = 1$
(c) $x = -1, y = 2$ (d) $x = 2, y = -1$

17. The points with position vectors $10\hat{i} + 3\hat{j}$, $12\hat{i} - 5\hat{j}$ and $a\hat{i} + 11\hat{j}$ are collinear if the value of a is

(a) −8 (b) 4
(c) 8 (d) 12

18. $[\vec{a} - \vec{b}\ \ \vec{b} - \vec{c}\ \ \vec{c} - \vec{a}]$ is equal to

(a) $2\,[\vec{a}\ \vec{b}\ \vec{c}]$ (b) $[\vec{a}\ \vec{b}\ \vec{c}]$
(c) 0 (d) None of these

19. For any vector $\vec{r}$, the value of $\hat{i} \times (\vec{r} \times \hat{i}) + \hat{j} \times (\vec{r} \times \hat{j}) + \hat{k} \times (\vec{r} \times \hat{k})$ is

(a) $\vec{0}$ (b) $2\vec{r}$
(c) $-2\vec{r}$ (d) None of these

20. The number of vectors of unit length perpendicular to the vectors $\vec{a} = \hat{i} + \hat{j}$ and $\vec{b} = \hat{j} + \hat{k}$ is

(a) one (b) two
(c) three (d) infinite

21. $(\vec{a} + 2\vec{b} - \vec{c}).\{(\vec{a} - \vec{b}) \times (\vec{a} - \vec{b} - \vec{c})\}$ is equal to

(a) $[\vec{a}\ \vec{b}\ \vec{c}]$ (b) $2[\vec{a}\ \vec{b}\ \vec{c}]$
(c) $3\,[\vec{a}\ \vec{b}\ \vec{c}]$ (d) 0

22. Given the vectors $\vec{a}$ and $\vec{b}$ the angle between which equals 120°. If $|\vec{a}| = 3$ and $|\vec{b}| = 4$, then the length of the vector. $2\vec{a} - \dfrac{3}{2}\vec{b}$ is

(a) $6\sqrt{3}$ (b) $7\sqrt{2}$
(c) $4\sqrt{5}$ (d) None of these

23. The value of $|\vec{a} \times \hat{i}|^2 + |\vec{a} \times \hat{j}|^2 + |\vec{a} \times \hat{k}|^2$ is equal to:

(a) $|\vec{a}|^2$ (b) $2\,|\vec{a}|^2$
(c) $3|\vec{a}|^2$ (d) $6|\vec{a}|^2$

24. A unit vector perpendicular to vectors $\vec{a} = 2\hat{i} + \hat{j} + \hat{k}$ and $\vec{b} = 3\hat{i} + 4\hat{j} - \hat{k}$ is:

(a) $\dfrac{-\hat{i} + \hat{j} + \hat{k}}{\sqrt{3}}$ (b) $\dfrac{\hat{i} + \hat{j} - \hat{k}}{\sqrt{3}}$
(c) $\dfrac{\hat{i} + \hat{j} + \hat{k}}{\sqrt{3}}$ (d) $\dfrac{-\hat{i} - \hat{j} - \hat{k}}{\sqrt{3}}$

25. The projection of the vector $\vec{a} = 4\hat{i} - 3\hat{j} + 2\hat{k}$ on the vector making equal acute angles with the co-ordinate axes is

(a) $\sqrt{3}$ (b) 3
(c) $\dfrac{1}{\sqrt{3}}$ (d) None of thesev

26. For non-zero vectors $\vec{a}, \vec{b}, \vec{c}$, $|(\vec{a} \times \vec{b}).\vec{c}| = |\vec{a}||\vec{b}||\vec{c}|$ holds if and only if

(a) $\vec{a}.\vec{b} = 0$, $\vec{b}.\vec{c} = 0$
(b) $\vec{c}.\vec{a} = 0$, $\vec{a}.\vec{b} = 0$
(c) $\vec{a} = 3\hat{i} - \hat{k}$
(d) $\vec{a}.\vec{b} = \vec{b}.\vec{c} = \vec{c}.\vec{a} = 0$

27. If $|\vec{a}| = 11$, $|\vec{b}| = 23$, $|\vec{a} - \vec{b}| = 30$, then $|\vec{a} + \vec{b}|$ is:

(a) 10 (b) 20
(c) 30 (d) 40

28. If $\vec{a} + \vec{b} + \vec{c} = \vec{0}$, $|\vec{a}| = 3$, $|\vec{b}| = 5$, $|\vec{c}| = 7$, then the angle between $\vec{a}$ and $\vec{b}$ is:

(a) $\dfrac{\pi}{6}$ (b) $\dfrac{2\pi}{3}$
(c) $\dfrac{5\pi}{3}$ (d) $\dfrac{\pi}{3}$

29. The lengths of the diagonals of a parallelogram constructed on the vectors $\vec{p} = 2\vec{a} + \vec{b}$ and $\vec{q} = \vec{a} - 2\vec{b}$, where $\vec{a}$ and $\vec{b}$ are unit vectors forming an angle of 60 ≡ are:

(a) 3 and 4 (b) $\sqrt{7}$ and $\sqrt{13}$
(c) $\sqrt{5}$ and $\sqrt{11}$ (d) None of these

30. If $\vec{u}, \vec{v}, \vec{w}$ be vectors such that $\vec{u}+\vec{v}+\vec{w}=\vec{0}$. If $|\vec{u}|=3, |\vec{v}|=4$ and $|\vec{w}|=5$, then $\vec{u}.\vec{v}+\vec{v}.\vec{w}+\vec{w}.\vec{u}$ is

(a) 47 (b) –25
(c) 0 (d) 25

31. If the vector $6\hat{i} - 3\hat{j} - 6\hat{k}$ is decomposed into vectors parallel and perpendicular to the vector $\hat{i} + \hat{j} + \hat{k}$, then the vectors are:

(a) $-(\hat{i} + \hat{j} + \hat{k})$ and $7\hat{i} - 2\hat{j} - 5\hat{k}$

(b) $-2(\hat{i} + \hat{j} + \hat{k})$ and $8\hat{i} - \hat{j} - 4\hat{k}$

(c) $2(\hat{i} + \hat{j} + \hat{k})$ and $4\hat{i} - 5\hat{j} - 8\hat{k}$

(d) None of the above

32. If $\hat{x}$ and $\hat{y}$ are two unit vectors and ϕ is the angle between them, then $\frac{1}{2}|\hat{x}-\hat{y}|$ is

(a) 0 (b) $\frac{\pi}{2}$

(c) $\left|\sin\frac{\phi}{2}\right|$ (d) $\left|\cos\frac{\phi}{2}\right|$

33. The value of b, such that the scalar product of the vectors $\hat{i}+\hat{j}+\hat{k}$ with the unit vector parallel to the sum of the vectors $2\hat{i}+4\hat{j}-5\hat{k}$ and $b\hat{i}+2\hat{j}+3\hat{k}$ is one, is

(a) –2 (b) –1
(c) 0 (d) 1

34. A parallelogram is constructed on the vectors $\vec{u}=3\vec{a}-\vec{b}, \vec{v}=\vec{d}$. If $|\vec{a}|=|\vec{b}|=2$ and the angle between $\vec{a}$ and $\vec{b}$ is $\pi/3$, then the length of a diagonal of the parallelogram is

(a) $4\sqrt{5}$ (b) $4\sqrt{3}$
(c) $4\sqrt{7}$ (d) None of these

35. If $\vec{a}$ and $\vec{b}$ be two vectors then, the equality $|\vec{a}+\vec{b}|=|\vec{a}|+|\vec{b}|$ holds

(a) only if $\vec{a} = \vec{b} = 0$

(b) for all $\vec{a}$, $\vec{b}$

(c) only if $\vec{a} = \lambda\vec{b}, \lambda > 0$ or $\vec{a} = 0$ or $\vec{b} = 0$

(d) None of these

36. If $\vec{a},\vec{b},\vec{c}$ are non-collinear vectors and the position vectors of three points are $\vec{a}-2\vec{b}+3\vec{c}$, $2\vec{a}+3\vec{b}-4\vec{c}$, $-7\vec{b}+9\vec{c}$, then the three points are

(a) collinear (b) co-planar
(c) non-collinear (d) None of these

37. The vectors $\vec{a}$ and $\vec{b}$ are non-zero and non-collinear, the value of x for which vector $\vec{c}=(x-2)\vec{a}+\vec{b}$ and $\vec{d}=(2x+1)\vec{a}-\vec{b}$ are collinear is

(a) 1 (b) $\frac{1}{2}$

(c) $\frac{1}{3}$ (d) 2

38. If $\vec{a} = \hat{i}+\hat{j}+\hat{k}$, $\vec{b} = 4\hat{i}+3\hat{j}+4\hat{k}$ and $c = \hat{i}+\alpha\hat{j}+\beta\hat{k}$ are linearly dependent vectors and $|\vec{c}| = \sqrt{3}$, then

(a) $\alpha = 1, \beta = -1$ (b) $\alpha = 1, \beta = \pm 1$
(c) $\alpha = -1, \beta = \pm 1$ (d) $\alpha = 1, \beta = 1$

39. The volume of the parallelopiped whose edges are represented by $-12\hat{i}+a\hat{k}$, $3\hat{j}-\hat{k}$ and $2\hat{i}+\hat{j}-15\hat{k}$ is 546, then a is

(a) 3 (b) 2
(c) –3 (d) –2

40. If $\hat{a}$, $\hat{b}$ and $\hat{c}$ are coplanar unit vectors, then the scalar triple product $[2\hat{a}-\hat{b}, 2\hat{b}-\hat{c}, 2\hat{c}-\hat{a}]$ is equal to

(a) 0 (b) 1
(c) $-\sqrt{3}$ (d) $\sqrt{3}$

41. Let $\vec{a}=2\hat{i}+\hat{j}-2\hat{k}$ and $\vec{b}=\hat{i}+\hat{j}$. If $\vec{c}$ is a vector such that $\vec{a}.\vec{b} = |\vec{c}|$, and the angle between $(\vec{a}\times\vec{b})$ and $\vec{c}$ is 30°, then $|(\vec{a}\times\vec{b})\times\vec{c}|$ is

(a) 2/3 (b) 9/2
(c) 2 (d) 3

42. Let $\vec{a}=2\hat{i}+\hat{j}+\hat{k}$ and $\vec{b}=\hat{i}+2\hat{j}-\hat{k}$ and a unit vector $\hat{c}$ be coplanar. If $\hat{c}$ is perpendicular to $\vec{a}$, then $\hat{c}$ is

(a) $\frac{1}{\sqrt{2}}(-\hat{j}+\hat{k})$ (b) $\frac{1}{\sqrt{3}}(-\hat{i}-\hat{j}-\hat{k})$

(c) $\frac{1}{\sqrt{5}}(\hat{i}-2\hat{j})$ (d) $\frac{1}{\sqrt{3}}(\hat{i}-\hat{j}-\hat{k})$

43. A non-zero vector $\vec{a}$ is such that its projections along the vectors $\frac{\hat{i}+\hat{j}}{\sqrt{2}}$ and $\frac{-\hat{i}+\hat{j}}{\sqrt{2}}$ and $\hat{k}$ are equal, then unit vector along $\vec{a}$ is

(a) $\sqrt{2}\hat{j}-\hat{k}$ (b) $\hat{j}+2\hat{k}$

(c) $\frac{\hat{j}-\hat{k}}{\sqrt{2}}$ (d) $\frac{\sqrt{2}\hat{j}+\hat{k}}{\sqrt{3}}$

44. If $\vec{a}, \vec{b}, \vec{c}$ represent the three concurrent edges of a rectangular parallelopiped whose lengths are 4, 3, 2 respectively, then the value of $(\vec{a}+\vec{b}+\vec{c}).(\vec{a}\times\vec{b}+\vec{b}\times\vec{c}+\vec{c}\times\vec{a})$ is

(a) 0 (b) 48

(c) 72 (d) None of these

45. If $\vec{a}=(-1, 1, 1)$ and $\vec{b}=(2, 0, 1)$, then the vector $\overrightarrow{X}$ satisfying the conditions:

(i) that it is coplanar with $\vec{a}$ and $\vec{b}$

(ii) that it is perpendicular to $\vec{b}$

(iii) that $\vec{a}.\vec{X}=7$ is

(a) $-3\hat{j}+4\hat{j}+6\hat{k}$ (b) $\frac{-3}{2}\hat{i}+\frac{5}{2}\hat{j}+3\hat{k}$

(c) $3\hat{i}+16\hat{j}-6\hat{k}$ (d) None of these

46. The vectors $2\hat{i}+3\hat{j}$, $5\hat{i}+6\hat{j}$ and $8\hat{i}+\lambda\hat{j}$ have their initial points at (1, 1). The value of λ so that vectors terminate on one straight line, is

(a) 0 (b) 3

(c) 6 (d) 9

47. Four coplanar forces are applied at a point *O*. Each of them is equal to *k*, and the angle between two consecutive forces equals 45°. Then the resultant is equal to

(a) $k\sqrt{2+2\sqrt{2}}$ (b) $k\sqrt{3+2\sqrt{2}}$

(c) $k\sqrt{4+2\sqrt{2}}$ (d) None of these

48. The values of *k* for which the points *A*(1, 0, 3), *B*(−1, 3, 4), *C*(1, 2, 1) and *D*(*k*, 2, 5) are co-planar are

(a) 1 (b) 2

(c) 0 (d) −1

49. If $\vec{a}$, $\vec{b}$ and $\vec{c}$ are three vectors, then $\vec{a}\times(\vec{b}\times\vec{c})=(\vec{a}\times\vec{b})\times\vec{c}$ if and only if

(a) $\vec{b}$ and $\vec{c}$ are collinear

(b) $\vec{a}$ and $\vec{c}$ are collinear

(c) $\vec{a}$ and $\vec{b}$ are collinear

(d) None of these

50. $\vec{A}$ is a vector with direction cosines, cos α, cos β and cos γ respectively. Assuming *yz* plane as a mirror the direction cosines of the reflected image of $\vec{A}$ in the *yz* plane is

(a) cos α, cos β, cos γ (b) cos α, – cos β, cos γ

(c) –cos α, cos β, cos γ (d) –cos α, –cos β, – cos γ

51. The two vectors $(x^2-1)\hat{i}+(x+2)\hat{j}+x^2\hat{k}$ and $2\hat{i}-x\hat{j}+3\hat{k}$ are orthogonal:

(a) for no real value of *x*

(b) for $x=-1$

(c) for $x=\frac{1}{2}$

(d) for $x=-\frac{1}{2}$ and $x=1$

52. If $\vec{a}=2\hat{i}+3\hat{j}-\hat{k}$, $\vec{b}=-\hat{i}+2\hat{j}-4\hat{k}$ and $\vec{c}=\hat{i}+\hat{j}+\hat{k}$ then $(\vec{a}\times\vec{b}).(\vec{a}\times\vec{c})$

(a) 60 (b) 64

(c) 74 (d) −74

53. If $\vec{u}=\vec{a}-\vec{b}$, $\vec{v}=\vec{a}+\vec{b}$ and $|\vec{a}|=|\vec{b}|=2$, then $|\vec{u}\times\vec{v}|$ is

(a) $2\sqrt{16-(\vec{a}.\vec{b})^2}$ (b) $2\sqrt{4-(\vec{a}.\vec{b})^2}$

(c) $\sqrt{16-(\vec{a}.\vec{b})^2}$ (d) $\sqrt{4-(\vec{a}.\vec{b})^2}$

54. Let $\vec{a}, \vec{b}, \vec{c}$ be three vectors such that $\vec{a}\neq\vec{0}$ and $\vec{a}\times\vec{b}=2\vec{a}\times\vec{c}$, $|\vec{a}|=|\vec{c}|=1$, $|\vec{b}|=4$ and $|\vec{b}\times\vec{c}|=\sqrt{15}$. If $\vec{b}-2\vec{c}=\lambda\vec{a}$ and ∠s are acute, then λ is

(a) ± 2 (b) ± 4

(c) ± 3 (d) None of these

55. The vector $\vec{b}=2\hat{i}+\hat{j}-3\hat{k}$ is to be written as the sum of a vector $\vec{\alpha}$ parallel to $\vec{a}=\hat{i}+\hat{j}$ and a vector $\vec{\beta}$ perpendicular to $\vec{a}$, then $\vec{\alpha}=$

(a) $\frac{3}{4}(\hat{i}+\hat{j})$ (b) $\frac{2}{3}(\hat{i}+\hat{j})$

(c) $\frac{1}{2}(\hat{i}+\hat{j})$ (d) $\frac{1}{3}(\hat{i}+\hat{j})$

56. Let $\vec{a}, \vec{b}, \vec{c}$ be three non-zero vectors, no two of which are collinear. If the vector $3\vec{a}+7\vec{b}$ is collinear with $\vec{c}$ and $2\vec{b}+2\vec{c}$ is collinear with $\vec{a}$ then $9\vec{a}+21\vec{b}+21\vec{c}=\vec{0}$ is equal to

(a) $\lambda\vec{a}$ (b) $\lambda\vec{c}$
(c) $\vec{0}$ (d) None of these

57. Let $\vec{A}, \vec{B}, \vec{C}$ be unit vectors. Suppose $\vec{A}\cdot\vec{B}=\vec{A}\cdot\vec{C}=0$ and the angle between $\vec{B}$ and $\vec{C}$ is $\frac{\pi}{4}$, then

(a) $\vec{A}=\pm 2(\vec{B}\times\vec{C})$ (b) $\vec{A}=\pm\sqrt{2}(\vec{B}\times\vec{C})$
(c) $\vec{A}=\pm 3(\vec{B}\times\vec{C})$ (d) $\vec{A}=\pm\sqrt{3}(\vec{B}\times\vec{C})$

58. If $\hat{a}, \hat{b}, \hat{c}$ are three non-coplanar unit vectors, then $[\hat{a}\,\vec{p}\,\vec{q}]\,\hat{a}+[\hat{b}\,\vec{p}\,\vec{q}]\hat{b}+[\hat{c}\,\vec{p}\,\vec{q}]\hat{c}$ is equal to

(a) $(\hat{a}+\hat{b}+\hat{c})\times(\vec{p}\times\vec{q})$
(b) $\hat{a}+\hat{b}+\hat{c}+\vec{p}+\vec{q}$
(c) $\vec{p}+\vec{q}$
(d) $\vec{p}\times\vec{q}$

59. If $\hat{a}$ & $\hat{b}$ are two unit vectors perpendicular to each other, then $[\vec{r}\cdot(\hat{b}\times(\hat{a}\times\hat{b})]\,\hat{a}+[\vec{r}\cdot(\hat{a}\times(\hat{b}\times\hat{a})]\,\hat{b}+[\vec{r}\cdot(\hat{a}\times\hat{b})]\,(\hat{a}\times\hat{b})$ is equal to

(a) 0 (b) $\vec{r}\times(\hat{a}\times\hat{b})$
(c) $\vec{r}$ (d) None of these

60. Locus of the point P for which $\vec{OP}$ represents a vector with direction cosine $\cos\alpha=\frac{1}{2}$ ('O' is the origin) is

(a) A circle parallel to y-z plane with centre on the x-axis.
(b) A cone concentric with positive x-axis having vertex at the origin and the slant height equal to the magnitude of the vector.
(c) A ray emanating from the origin and making an angle of 60° with x-axis
(d) A disc parallel to y-z plane with centre on x-axis and radius equal to $|\vec{OP}|\sin 60°$.

61. Let a, b, c be distinct non-negative numbers. If the vectors $a\hat{i}+a\hat{j}+c\hat{k}$, $\hat{i}+\hat{k}$ and $c\hat{i}+c\hat{j}+b\hat{k}$ lie in the plane, then c is

(a) the $A.M.$ between a and b
(b) the $G.M.$ between a and b
(c) the $H.M.$ between a and b
(d) equal to 0.

62. If $\vec{p}=\frac{\vec{b}\times\vec{c}}{[\vec{a}\,\vec{b}\,\vec{c}]}$, $\vec{q}=\frac{\vec{c}\times\vec{a}}{[\vec{a}\,\vec{b}\,\vec{c}]}$, $\vec{r}=\frac{\vec{a}\times\vec{b}}{[\vec{a}\,\vec{b}\,\vec{c}]}$ where $\vec{a},\vec{b},\vec{c}$ are three non-coplanar vectors, then the value of the expression $(\vec{a}+\vec{b}+\vec{c})\cdot(\vec{p}+\vec{q}+\vec{r})$ is

(a) 3 (b) 2
(c) 1 (d) 0

63. $[(\vec{a}\times\vec{b})\times(\vec{b}\times\vec{c})\;(\vec{b}\times\vec{c})\times(\vec{c}\times\vec{a})\;(\vec{c}\times\vec{a})\times(\vec{a}\times\vec{b})]$ is equal to

(a) $[\vec{a}\,\vec{b}\,\vec{c}]^2$ (b) $[\vec{a}\vec{b}\vec{c}]^3$
(c) $[\vec{a}\vec{b}\vec{c}]^4$ (d) None of these

64. In a quadrilateral $ABCD$, $\vec{AC}$ is the bisector of the $(\vec{AB},\vec{AD})$ which is $\frac{2\pi}{3}$ and $15|\vec{AC}|=3|\vec{AB}|=5|\vec{AD}|$, then $\cos(\vec{BA},\vec{CD})$ is equal to

(a) $-\frac{\sqrt{14}}{7\sqrt{2}}$ (b) $\frac{\sqrt{21}}{7\sqrt{3}}$
(c) $\frac{2}{\sqrt{7}}$ (d) $\frac{2\sqrt{7}}{14}$

65. If the unit vectors $\vec{a}$ and $\vec{b}$ are inclined at an angle 2θ such that $|\vec{a}-\vec{b}|<1$ and $0\le\theta\le\pi$, then θ lies in the interval

(a) $[0, \pi/6)$ (b) $(-5\pi/6, \pi)$
(c) $[\pi/6, \pi/2]$ (d) $[\pi/2, 5\pi/6]$

66. If the vectors $ax\hat{i}+3\hat{j}-5\hat{k}$ & $x\hat{i}+2\hat{j}+2ax\hat{k}$ make an acute angle with each other for all $x\in R$, then 'a' belongs to the interval

(a) $(-1/4, 0)$ (b) $(0, 6/25)$
(c) $[0, 6/25)$ (d) $(-3/25, 0)$

67. If the vectors $\vec{a}$ and $\vec{b}$ are mutually perpendicular, then $\vec{a}\times\{\vec{a}\times(\vec{a}\times(\vec{a}\times\vec{b}))\}$ is equal to

(a) $|\vec{a}|^2$ (b) $|\vec{a}|^3\,\vec{b}$
(c) $|\vec{a}|^4\,\vec{b}$ (d) None of these

68. If $\vec{r}\times\vec{b}=\vec{a}\times\vec{b}$, then $\vec{r}$ is equal to

(a) $\vec{a}$
(b) $\frac{\vec{a}\times\vec{b}}{\vec{b}}$
(c) $\vec{a}+t\vec{b}$, where t is any scalar
(d) None of these

69. Five points given by A,B,C,D,E are in a plane. Three forces $\overrightarrow{AC}$, $\overrightarrow{AD}$ and $\overrightarrow{AE}$ act at A and three forcess $\overrightarrow{CB}$, $\overrightarrow{EB}$, $\overrightarrow{DB}$ act at B. Then their resultant is

(a) $2\overrightarrow{AC}$ (b) $3\overrightarrow{AB}$
(c) $3\overrightarrow{DB}$ (d) $2\overrightarrow{BC}$

70. If $|\vec{a}+\vec{b}| > |\vec{a}-\vec{b}|$, then the angle between $\vec{a}$ and $\vec{b}$ is

(a) Acute (b) Obtuse
(c) 3 (d) π

71. If $\vec{A}, \vec{B}, \vec{C}$ are three non-colpanar vectors, then $\frac{\vec{A}.(\vec{B}\times\vec{C})}{(\vec{C}\times\vec{A}).\vec{B}} + \frac{\vec{B}.(\vec{A}\times\vec{C})}{\vec{C}.(\vec{A}\times\vec{B})} = ...$

(a) 0 (b) 2
(c) 1 (d) None of these

72. $\vec{A} = (1, 1, 1)$, $\vec{C} = (0, 1, -1)$ are given vectors, then a vector $\vec{B}$ satisfying the equations $\vec{A}\times\vec{B} = \vec{C}$ and $\vec{A}.\vec{B} = 3$ is....

(a) $\left(\frac{5}{3}, \frac{2}{3}, \frac{2}{3}\right)$ (b) $\left(-\frac{5}{3}, -\frac{2}{3}, \frac{2}{3}\right)$
(c) $\left(\frac{1}{3}, -\frac{2}{3}, \frac{2}{3}\right)$ (d) None of these

73. If the vectors $a\hat{i}+\hat{j}+\hat{k}, \hat{i}+b\hat{j}+\hat{k}$ and $\hat{i}+\hat{j}+c\hat{k}$, $(a \neq b,\ c \neq 1)$ are coplanar, then the value of $\frac{1}{1-a}+\frac{1}{1-b}+\frac{1}{1-c}$ is

(a) 1
(b) –1
(c) 2
(d) None of these

74. $\vec{\beta} = 4\hat{i}+3\hat{j}$ and $\vec{\gamma}$ are two vectors perpendicular to each other in the x–y plane. All the vectors in the same plane having projections 1 and 2 along β and γ respectively are given by

(a) $2\hat{i}-\hat{j}$, $1/5\,(-2\hat{i} + 11\hat{j})$
(b) $3\hat{i}-\hat{j}$, $1/5\,(-2\hat{i} + 11\hat{j})$
(c) $2\hat{i} + \hat{j}$, $1/5\,(2\hat{i} + 11\hat{j})$
(d) None of these

75. If A, B, C, D are any four points in space, then $|\overrightarrow{AB}\times\overrightarrow{CD}+\overrightarrow{BC}\times\overrightarrow{AD}-\overrightarrow{CA}\times\overrightarrow{BD}|$ equals

(a) ar. ΔABC
(b) 2ar. ΔABC
(c) 4ar. ΔABC
(d) 8ar. ΔABC

76. A unit vector in xy-plane that makes an angle of 45° with vector $\hat{i}+\hat{j}$ and an angle of 60° with the vector $3\hat{i}-4\hat{j}$ is

(a) i (b) $\frac{(\hat{i}+\hat{j})}{\sqrt{2}}$
(c) $\frac{(\hat{i}-\hat{j})}{\sqrt{2}}$ (d) None of these

SECTION–IV

MORE THEN ONE CORRECT ANSWERS

1. If $\vec{a} = x\hat{i} + y\hat{j} + z\hat{k}$, $\vec{b} = y\hat{i} + z\hat{j} + x\hat{k}$ and $\vec{c} = z\hat{i} + x\hat{j} + y\hat{k}$, then $\vec{a}\times(\vec{b}\times\vec{c})$ is:

(a) parallel to $(y-z)\,\hat{i} + (z-x)\,\hat{j} + (x-y)\,\hat{k}$
(b) orthogonal to $\hat{i}+\hat{j}+\hat{k}$
(c) orthogonal to $(y+z)\,\hat{i} + (z+x)\,\hat{j} + (x+y)\,\hat{k}$
(d) orthogonal to $x\hat{i}+y\hat{j}+z\hat{k}$

2. If $\vec{a}, \vec{b}, \vec{c}$ be three non-zero vectors satisfying the condition $\vec{a}\times\vec{b} = \vec{c}$ and $\vec{b}\times\vec{c} = \vec{a}$, then

(a) $\vec{a}, \vec{b}, \vec{c}$ are orthogonal in pairs
(b) $[\vec{a}, \vec{b}, \vec{c}] = |\vec{a}|^2$
(c) $[\vec{a}, \vec{b}, \vec{c}] = |\vec{c}|^2$
(d) $|\vec{b}| = |\vec{c}|$

3. If a line has a vector equation, $\vec{r} = 2\hat{i} + 6\hat{j} + \lambda(\hat{i} - 3\hat{j})$, then which of the following statements hold good?

(a) the line is parallel to $2\hat{i} + 6\hat{j}$
(b) the line passes through the point $3\hat{i} + 3\hat{j}$
(c) the line passes through the point $\hat{i} + 9\hat{j}$
(d) the line is parallel to xy plane

4. If a, b, c are different real numbers and $a\hat{i} + b\hat{j} + c\hat{k}$, $b\hat{i} + c\hat{j} + a\hat{k}$ and $c\hat{i} + a\hat{j} + b\hat{k}$ are position vectors of three non-collinear points A, B and C, then
(a) centroid of triangle ABC is $\frac{a+b+c}{3}(\hat{i} + \hat{j} + \hat{k})$
(b) $\hat{i} + \hat{j} + \hat{k}$ is equally inclined to the three vectors
(c) perpendicular from the origin to the plane of triangle ABC meet at centroid
(d) triangle ABC is an equilateral triangle.

5. If $\vec{z}_1 = a\hat{i} + b\hat{j}$ and $\vec{z}_2 = c\hat{i} + d\hat{j}$ are two vectors in $\hat{i}$ & $\hat{j}$ system where $|\vec{z}_1| = |\vec{z}_2| = r$ and $\vec{z}_1 . \vec{z}_2 = 0$, then $\vec{w}_1 = a\hat{i} + c\hat{j}$ and $\vec{w}_2 = b\hat{i} + d\hat{j}$ satisfy:
(a) $|\vec{w}_1| = r$ (b) $|\vec{w}_2| = r$
(c) $\vec{w}_1 . \vec{w}_2 = 0$ (d) None of these

6. The volume of the parallelopiped whose edges are represented by the vectors $a\hat{i} + b\hat{j} + c\hat{k}$, $b\hat{i} + c\hat{j} + a\hat{k}$ and $c\hat{i} + a\hat{j} + b\hat{k}$ is zero. This implies that:
(a) $a = b = c$
(b) $a^2 + b^2 + c^2 - ab - bc - ca = 0$
(c) $a + b + c = 0$
(d) $a^3 + b^3 + c^3 - 3abc = 0$

7. If three unit vectors $\ell_1\hat{i} + m_1\hat{j} + n_1\hat{k}$; $\ell_2\hat{i} + m_2\hat{j} + n_2\hat{k}$; $\ell_3\hat{i} + m_3\hat{j} + n_3\hat{k}$ are mutually perpendicular, then the value of the determinant $\begin{vmatrix} \ell_1 & m_1 & n_1 \\ \ell_2 & m_2 & n_2 \\ \ell_3 & m_3 & n_3 \end{vmatrix}$ is
(a) 1 (b) –1
(c) 3 (d) 0

8. Which of the following statement(s) is/are true?
(a) If $\vec{n} . \vec{a} = 0$, $\vec{n} . \vec{b} = 0$ and $\vec{n} . \vec{c} = 0$ for some non-zero vector $\vec{n}$, then $[\vec{a}\,\vec{b}\,\vec{c}] = 0$
(b) there exist a vector having direction angles $\alpha = 30°$ and $\beta = 45°$
(c) locus of a point for which $x = 3$ and $y = 4$ is a line parallel to the z-axis whose distance from the z-axis is 5
(d) the vertices of a regular tetrahedron are $OABC$ where 'O' is the origin. The vector $\overrightarrow{OA} + \overrightarrow{OB} + \overrightarrow{OC}$ is perpendicular to the plane ABC.

9. If $\vec{a}$, $\vec{b}$, $\vec{c}$ are non-zero, non-collinear vectors such that a vector $\vec{p} = ab\cos\{2\pi - \cos^{-1}(\hat{a}.\hat{b})\}$ and a vector $\vec{q} = ac\cos\{\pi - \cos^{-1}(\hat{a}.\hat{c})\}$, then $\vec{p} + \vec{q}$ is
(a) parallel to $\vec{a}$
(b) perpendicular to $\vec{a}$
(c) coplanar with $\vec{b}$ and $\vec{c}$
(d) None of these

10. If $\vec{a}$ and $\vec{b}$ are not perpendicular to each other and $\vec{r} \times \vec{a} = \vec{b} \times \vec{a}$ and $\vec{r} \times \vec{c} = \vec{0}$, then r is equal to
(a) $\vec{a} - \vec{c}$ (b) $\vec{b} + x\vec{a}$
(c) $\vec{b} - \frac{(\vec{b}.\vec{c})}{(\vec{a}.\vec{c})}\vec{a}$ (d) None of these

11. The vector $\hat{i} + p\hat{j} + 3\hat{k}$ is rotated through an angle θ and doubled in magnitude, then it becomes $4\hat{i} + (4p-2)\hat{j} + 2\hat{k}$. The value of p is
(a) $-\frac{2}{3}$ (b) $\frac{1}{3}$
(c) $\frac{2}{3}$ (d) 2

12. The vector $\frac{1}{3}(2\hat{\ } - 2\hat{j} + \hat{k})$ is
(a) A unit vector
(b) Makes an angle $\pi/3$ with the vector $2\hat{i} - 4\hat{j} + 3\hat{k}$
(c) Parallel to the vector $-\hat{i} + \hat{j} - \frac{1}{2}\hat{k}$
(d) Perpendicular to the vector $3\hat{i} + 2\hat{j} - 2\hat{k}$

SECTION–V

ASSERTION AND REASON TYPE QUESTIONS

The questions given below consist of an assertion (A) and the reason (R). Use the following key to choose the appropriate answer.

(a) If both assertion and reason are correct and reason is the correct explanation of the assertion.

(b) If both assertion and reason are correct but reason is not correct explanation of the assertion.

(c) If assertion is correct, but reason is incorrect

(d) If assertion is incorrect, but reason is correct

Now consider the following statements:

1. **A:** If three points P, Q and R have position vectors $\vec{a}, \vec{b}, \vec{c}$ respectively and $2\vec{a}+3\vec{b}-5\vec{c}=0$, then the points P, Q, R must be collinear.

   R: If for three points A, B, C, $\overrightarrow{AB} = \lambda\overrightarrow{AC}$, then the points A, B, C must be collinear.

2. **A:** If the vectors $\vec{a}$ and $\vec{c}$ are non-collinear, then the lines $\vec{r} = 6\vec{a}-\vec{c}+\lambda(2\vec{c}-\vec{a})$ and $\vec{r} = \vec{a}-\vec{c}+\mu(\vec{a}-3\vec{c})$ intersect in a point

   R: There exist λ and μ such that the two values of $\vec{r}$ become same.

3. **A:** If the vectors $\vec{a}$ and $\vec{c}$ are non-collinear, then the lines $\vec{r} = 6\vec{a}-\vec{c}+\lambda(2\vec{c}-\vec{a})$ and $\vec{r} = \vec{a}-\vec{c}+\mu(\vec{a}-3\vec{c})$ are coplanar.

   R: There exist λ and μ such that the two values of $\vec{r}$ becomes same.

4. **A:** If $\vec{u}$ and $\vec{v}$ are unit vectors inclined at an angle α and $\vec{x}$ is a unit vector bisecting then angle between them, then $\vec{x} = \dfrac{\vec{u}+\vec{v}}{\sqrt{2}}$

   R: If ABC be an isosceles triangle with $AB = AC$, then vector representing bisector of angle A is given by $\overrightarrow{AD} = \dfrac{\overrightarrow{AB}+\overrightarrow{AC}}{2}$.

5. **A :** Set of any four vectors is always linearly dependent

   R : If a subset of n vectors is L.D, then set of those n vectors is linearly dependent (L.D.).

6. **A :** Null vector has zero magnitude and indefinite direction.

   R : Null vector has both initial and terminal point coincident

7. **A :** If three vectors are Linearly dependent then their S.T.P. = 0

   R : Three Coplanar vectors from a parallelopiped (considered as coterminus edges) whose volume is zero).

8. **A :** Two non collinear vectors are always Linearly independent

   R : A set of vectors is called L.I iff vector of the set cannot be generated with the Linear combination of the remaining vectors

9. **A :** Three non coplaner vectors are always linearly independent

   R : If a set of n vectors are linearly independent, then any subset of the set of these n vectors is also linearly independent

10. **A :** Any vector $\vec{r}$ in a space can be written as $\vec{r} = x\vec{a}+y\vec{b}+z(\vec{a}\times\vec{b})$ where $\vec{a}$ and $\vec{b}$ are any two non zero non collinear vectors, x, y, z are suitably chosen scalars.

    R : Any vector in the 3 - D space can always be written as a linear combination of three non coplanar vectors.

SECTION–VI

COMPREHENSION TYPE QUESTIONS

A: Let ABC be a triangle, AD, BE and CF be the angular bisectors of its interior angles. These bisectors are concurrent at a point I called incentre of the triangle.

We know from geometry that $\dfrac{BD}{DC} = \dfrac{AB}{AC}$

If $BC = \alpha$, $CA = \beta$ and $AB = \gamma$ and with reference to some origin. Let $\vec{a}, \vec{b}, \vec{c}$ be position vectors of A, B and C respectively, then

1. The position vector of I must be

   (a) $\dfrac{\vec{a}+\vec{b}+\vec{c}}{3}$ (b) $\dfrac{\alpha\vec{a}+\beta\vec{b}+\gamma\vec{c}}{3}$

   (c) $\dfrac{\alpha\vec{a}+\beta\vec{b}+\gamma\vec{c}}{\alpha+\beta+\gamma}$ (d) None of these

2. If r is perpendicular distance of I from the side BC, then $\overrightarrow{IB}.\overrightarrow{IC}$ must be

   (a) $r^2 \operatorname{cosec}\dfrac{B}{2}\operatorname{cosec}\dfrac{C}{2}$

   (b) $r^2 \operatorname{cosec}\dfrac{B}{2}\operatorname{cosec}\dfrac{C}{2}\sin\dfrac{A}{2}$

(c) $-r^2 \text{cosec}\frac{B}{2}\text{cosec}\frac{C}{2}\sin\frac{A}{2}$

(d) None of these

3. If r is same as in above question, then value of $|\overrightarrow{IB} \times \overrightarrow{IC}|$ must be

(a) $r^2 \text{cosec}\frac{B}{2}\text{cosec}\frac{C}{2}$

(b) $r^2 \text{cosec}\frac{B}{2}\text{cosec}\frac{C}{2}\cos\frac{A}{2}$

(c) $r^2 \text{cosec}\frac{B}{2}\text{cosec}\frac{C}{2}\text{cosec}\frac{A}{2}$

(d) None of these

B: Let A,B,C be the vertices of a triangle ABC in which B is taken as origin of reference and position vectors of A and C are $\vec{a}$ and $\vec{c}$ respectively. A line AR parallel to BC is drawn from A. PR (P is mid-point of AB) meets AC at Q (where $QR < PR$) and area of triangle ACR is 2 times area of triangle ABC.

4. Position vector of R in terms of $\vec{a}$ and $\vec{c}$ is

(a) $\vec{a} + 2\vec{c}$ (b) $\vec{a} + 3\vec{c}$

(c) $+ \vec{c}$ (d) $\vec{a} + 4\vec{c}$

5. Position vector of Q is

(a) $\frac{2\vec{a}+3\vec{c}}{5}$ (b) $\frac{3\vec{a}+2\vec{c}}{5}$

(c) $\frac{\vec{a}+2\vec{c}}{3}$ (d) None of these

6. $\left(\frac{PQ}{QR}\right).\left(\frac{AQ}{QC}\right)$ is equal to

(a) 1/4 (b) 2/5

(c) 3/5 (d) 1/6

C. In triangle ABC; O, N,G and O' are the circumcentre, nine point centre,centroid and orthocentre of ΔABC respectively. AL and BM are perpendiculars from A and B on sides BC and CA respectively.

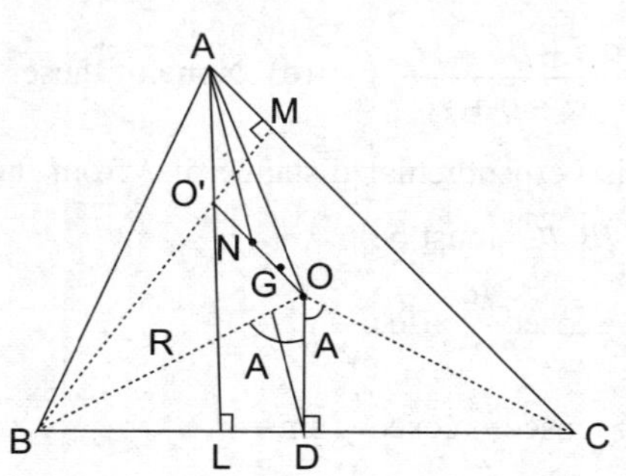

Let AD be the median and OD is perpendicular to side BC and R be the circumradius of ΔABC, then $OA = OB = OC = R$. Now, in ΔOBD, $OD = R \cos A$, in ΔABM, $AO' = AM \sec (90° - C)$

$[\because \angle O'AM = (90° - C)]$

$\Rightarrow AM \text{cosec } C = \frac{C \cos A}{\sin C}$; $2R \cos A$

$\therefore AO' = 2OD$

If AP is the diameter of the circum circle. Then answer the following questions

7. $\overrightarrow{OA} + \overrightarrow{OB} + \overrightarrow{OC}$ is equal to

(a) $\overrightarrow{OO'}$ (b) $2\overrightarrow{O'O}$

(c) $2\overrightarrow{AO}$ (d) $\vec{0}$

8. $\overrightarrow{O'A} + \overrightarrow{O'B} + \overrightarrow{O'C}$ is equal to

(a) $\overrightarrow{OO'}$ (b) $2\overrightarrow{O'O}$

(c) $2\overrightarrow{AO'}$ (d) null vector

9. $\overrightarrow{AO'} + \overrightarrow{O'B} + \overrightarrow{O'C}$ is equal to

(a) $\overrightarrow{OO'}$ (b) $2\overrightarrow{O'O}$

(c) $2\overrightarrow{AO}$ (d) $\frac{1}{2}\overrightarrow{OO'}$

D. Cross product of vectors finds its vast application in the field of science and technology specially in physics, e.g., to find moment of force; angular velocity and magnetic field intensity etc.

(i) Moment of force :

moment of force $\vec{F}$ about point O is defined as $\vec{M} = \vec{r} \times \vec{F} = |\vec{r}|.|\vec{F}|\sin\theta.\hat{n}$, where θ is the angle between $\vec{F}$ & $\vec{r}$

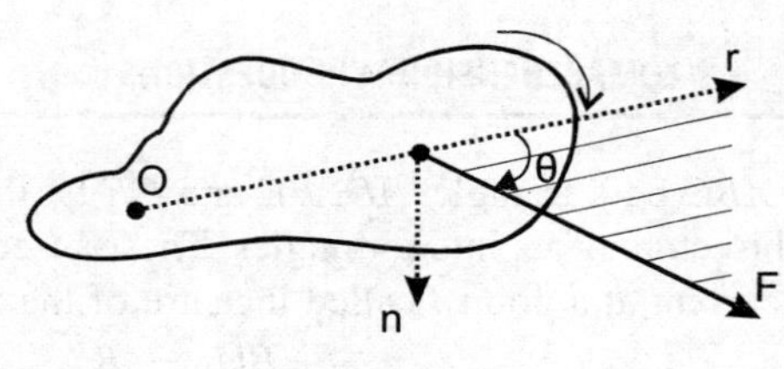

(ii) Angular velocity :

If a rigid of body is rotating about an axis passing through A the body and directed along vector $\hat{n}$ and the body is spining with angular velocity ω rad/sec, then tangential velocity of the point B on the body is $\vec{v} = \vec{\omega} \times \vec{r}$, where $\vec{r} = \overrightarrow{AB}$

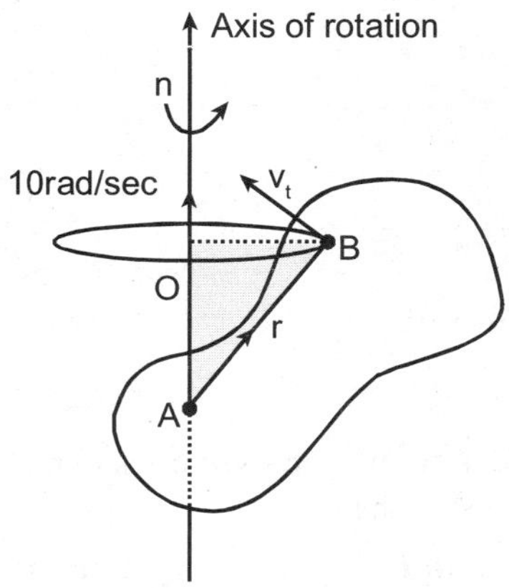

10. A Force $\vec{F}$ is acting at point P on a rigid body free to rotate about point O(0, 0, 0) and position vector of point P on the body is $(3\hat{i}+4\hat{k})$. If $\vec{F}=10\hat{i}+5\hat{j}+10\hat{k}$, then moment of force about O is

(a) $5(-4\hat{i}+2\hat{j}+3\hat{k})$ (b) $(-4\hat{i}+2\hat{j}+3\hat{k})$

(c) $5(4\hat{i}-2\hat{j}+3\hat{k})$ (d) $(4\hat{i}-2\hat{j}+3\hat{k})$

11. If co-ordinates of A be (2, 1, 2) and that of B be (4, 3, 3) and magnitude of angular velocity be 10 radians per second and $\hat{n}$ is unit vector along $3\hat{i}+4\hat{j}$, then the tangential velocity of point B must be

(a) $-8\hat{i}+6\hat{j}+4\hat{k}$ (b) $8\hat{i}-6\hat{j}-4\hat{k}$

(c) $8\hat{i}+6\hat{j}+4\hat{k}$ (d) $8\hat{i}+4\hat{j}+6\hat{k}$

E. Tetrahedron, is a pyramid with triangular base and its volume is one sixth of the volume of parallelopiped formed by any of its three coinitial edges denoted by vectors $\vec{a},\vec{b},\vec{c}$ respectively.

$$\because\ V=\frac{1}{3}(\text{Area of base})\cdot\text{height}=\frac{1}{3}\left(\frac{\vec{b}\times\vec{c}}{2}\right).|\vec{a}|\cos\theta$$

(where θ is angle between $\vec{a}\ \&\ \vec{b}\times\vec{c}$)

$$=\frac{1}{3}\times\frac{1}{2}\times[\vec{a}\,\vec{b}\,\vec{c}]=\frac{1}{6}[\vec{a}\ \vec{b}\ \vec{c}]$$

Regular Tetrahedron, is a tetrahedron length of whose edges are all equal is called regular tetrahedron.

$|\vec{a}|=|\vec{b}|=|\vec{c}|=|\vec{a}-\vec{b}|=|\vec{b}-\vec{c}|=|\vec{a}-\vec{c}|$

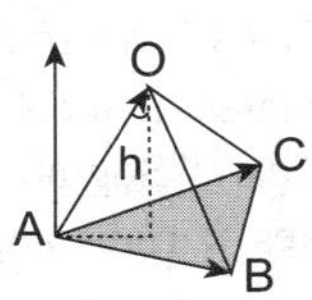

Answer the following questions based on the above facts:

12. Sum of 4 outwards drawn normal to four faces of tetrahedron with magnitude equal to area of respective face is equal to

(a) $2\{\vec{a}\times\vec{b}+\vec{b}\times\vec{c}+\vec{c}\times\vec{a}\}$

(b) $\vec{a}\times\vec{b}+\vec{b}\times\vec{c}+\vec{c}\times\vec{a}$

(c) zero

(d) None of the above

13. Line joining the vertices of a tetrahedron to centroid of opposite faces are concurrent and if G_1, G_2, G_3, G_4 be the centroid of the faces OBC, BCA, CAO, OAB respectively, then the point of concurrency of line AG_1, OG_2, BG_3, CG_4 divides these lines in the ratio

(a) 2 : 1 internally (b) 3 : 1 internally

(c) 2 : 3 internally (d) None of these

14. Which of the following statements are false?

(a) Six mid points of six edges of tetrahedron lie on a sphere.

(b) If pair of opposite edges are ⊥, then centre of such sphere is the centroid of tetrahedron.

(c) Volume of tetrahedron whose coterminus edges are represented by vectors $\hat{i}+\hat{j}$, $\hat{j}+\hat{k}$, $\hat{k}+\hat{i}$ respectively is 3 cubic units.

(d) None of these.

15. Which of the following is true about regular tetrahedron?

(a) All faces are equilateral Δ

(b) Angle between any two concurrent edges is 60°

(c) Any two opposite skew edges are ⊥ to each other

(d) None of these.

16. Angle between any two plane faces of the regular tetrahedron is given by:

(a) $\cos^{-1}\frac{1}{\sqrt{3}}$ (b) $\cos^{-1}\frac{1}{3}$

(c) 60° (d) None of these

17. Angle between any edge and a face not containing that edge is

(a) $\cos^{-1}\frac{1}{\sqrt{3}}$ (b) $\cos^{-1}\frac{1}{3}$

(c) 60° (d) None of these

18. Distance of any vertex from opposite face of regular tetrahedron (where λ is length of any edge) is

(a) $\sqrt{\frac{2}{3}}\,\lambda$ (b) $\frac{\lambda}{\sqrt{3}}$

(c) $\lambda\sqrt{3}$ (d) $2\sqrt{3}.\lambda$

SECTION–VII

COLUMN MATCHING TYPE QUESTIONS

1. Observe the following columns:

Column-I

(i) The value of $(\vec{a}\times\vec{b})\times(\vec{c}\times\vec{d})$ is

(ii) The value of $(\vec{a}\times\vec{c})\times(\vec{b}\times\vec{d})$ is

(iii) The value of $(\vec{a}\times\vec{d})\times(\vec{b}\times\vec{c})$ is

Column-II

(a) $[\vec{a}\vec{c}\vec{d}]\vec{b}+[\vec{a}\vec{b}\vec{c}]\vec{d}$

(b) $[\vec{a}\vec{b}\vec{c}]\vec{d}-[\vec{b}\vec{c}\vec{d}]\vec{a}$

(c) $[\vec{a}\vec{c}\vec{d}]\vec{b}-[\vec{b}\vec{c}\vec{d}]\vec{a}$

(d) $[\vec{a}\vec{b}\vec{d}]\vec{c}-[\vec{a}\vec{c}\vec{d}]\vec{b}$

(e) $[\vec{a}\vec{b}\vec{d}]\vec{c}+[\vec{b}\vec{c}\vec{d}]\vec{a}$

2. A parallelopiped whose co-terminus edges are represented by $\vec{a}=2\hat{i}+3\hat{j}+4\hat{k}$; $\vec{b}=\hat{i}+2\hat{j}-\hat{k}$; $\vec{c}=3\hat{i}-\hat{j}+2\hat{k}$.

Column - I

(i) Length of an edge

(ii) Area of a face is

(iii) Area of largest face is

(iv) Twice of the volume of parallelopiped

(v) Length of longest edge

Column - II

(a) $\sqrt{285}$

(b) $\sqrt{29}$

(c) $\sqrt{83}$

(d) $\sqrt{14}$, $\sqrt{6}$

(e) 74

3. If $\hat{a}$ and $\hat{b}$ are two unit vectors inclined at an angle α to each other, then

Column I	Column II
(i) $\vert\hat{a}+\hat{b}\vert<1$ if	(a) $\frac{2\pi}{3}<\alpha<\pi$
(ii) $\vert\hat{a}-\hat{b}\vert=\vert\hat{a}+\hat{b}\vert$	(b) $\frac{\pi}{2}<\theta\le\pi$
(iii) $\vert\hat{a}+\hat{b}\vert<\sqrt{2}$	(c) $\alpha=\pi/2$
(iv) $\vert\hat{a}-\hat{b}\vert<\sqrt{2}$	(d) $0\le\theta<\pi/2$

4. Column I

(i) $\vec{a}.\vec{b}=0$

(ii) $\vec{a}\times\vec{b}=\vec{0}$

(iii) $[\vec{c}\,\vec{a}\,\vec{b}]=0$

(iv) $[\vec{c}\vec{a}\vec{b}]=\vec{c}\,|\vec{a}\times\vec{b}|$

Column II

(a) either of vectors may be zero

(b) angle between vectors $\vec{a}$ and $\vec{b}$ is $\frac{\pi}{2}$; $\vec{a},\vec{b}\neq\vec{0}$

(c) vectors $\vec{a}$ and $\vec{b}$ are parallel; $\vec{a},\vec{b}\neq\vec{0}$

(d) $\vec{c}$ is ∥ to plane of vectors $\vec{a}$ and $\vec{b}$; $\vec{a},\vec{b}\neq\vec{0}$

(e) $\vec{c}$ is ∥ to $\vec{b}\times\vec{a}$ when $\vec{a}$ and $\vec{b}$ are non-collinear and non-zero

SECTION–VIII

INTEGER TYPE QUESTIONS

1. If $\vec{a}$ and $\vec{b}$ are vectors in space given by $\vec{a}=\frac{\hat{i}-2\hat{j}}{\sqrt{5}}$ and $\vec{b}=\frac{2\hat{i}+\hat{j}+3\hat{k}}{\sqrt{14}}$, then the value of $(2\vec{a}+\vec{b}).[(\vec{a}\times\vec{b})\times(\vec{a}+6\vec{b})]$ is

2. Two adjacent sides of a parallelogram *ABCD* are given by $\overline{AB}=2\hat{i}+10\hat{j}+11\hat{k}$ and $\overline{AD}=-\hat{i}+2\hat{j}+2\hat{k}$. The side *AD* is rotated about *A* by an acute angle α in the plane of the parallelogram, so that *AD* becomes *AD*'. If *AD*' makes a right angle with the side *AB*, cosine of angle α is given by $\frac{\sqrt{\lambda}}{\lambda-8}$. Then value of λ is

3. Non-zero vectors $\vec{a},\vec{b},\vec{c}$ satisfy $\vec{a}.\vec{b}=0,(\vec{b}-\vec{a}).(\vec{b}+\vec{c})=0$ and $2|\vec{b}+\vec{c}|=|\vec{b}-\vec{a}|$. If $\vec{a}=\mu\vec{b}+4\vec{c}$, then find the maximum possible value of μ.

4. Find the cosine of angle between the vectors $\vec{b}$ and $\vec{c}$ where $\vec{a},\vec{b}$ and $\vec{c}$ are unit vectors, satisfying $\vec{b}+\vec{c}+2\vec{a}=\vec{0}$

5. Let $\hat{x},\hat{y},\hat{z}$ be unit vectors such that $\hat{x}+\hat{y}+\hat{z}=\vec{a},\hat{x}\times(\hat{y}\times\hat{z})=\vec{b},(\hat{x}\times\hat{y})\times\hat{z}=\vec{c}$, $\vec{a}.\hat{x}=\frac{3}{2}$, $\vec{a}.\hat{y}=\frac{7}{4}$ and $|\vec{a}|=2$. If $\hat{x}=l_1\vec{a}+m_1\vec{b}+n_1\vec{c};\hat{y}=l_2\vec{a}+m_2\vec{b}+n_2\vec{c};\hat{z}=l_3\vec{a}+m_3\vec{b}+n_3\vec{c}$

then find the value of $|3\Delta|$ where $\Delta=\begin{vmatrix} l_1 & m_1 & n_1\\ l_2 & m_2 & n_2\\ l_3 & m_3 & n_3\end{vmatrix}$

6. Given a vector $\vec{A}$ defined as $\vec{A}=(\vec{a}\times\vec{b})\times(\vec{c}\times\vec{d})+(\vec{a}\times\vec{c})\times(\vec{b}\times\vec{d})+(\vec{a}\times\vec{d})\times(\vec{b}\times\vec{c})$ then find the value of $|\vec{A}\times\vec{a}|$.

7. The position vectors of the vertices A, B and C of tetrahedron $ABCD$ are $\hat{i}+\hat{j}+\hat{k}$, $\hat{i}$ and $3\hat{i}$ respectively. The altitude from vertex D to the opposite face ABC meets the median through A of the triangle ABC at point E. The length of the side AD is 4 and the volume of the tetrahedron is $\frac{2\sqrt{2}}{3}$. If the value of magnitude of position vector E be λ, then find the maximum value of $\frac{}{\sqrt{19}}$.

8. Let $\vec{b}=4\hat{i}+3\hat{j}$ and $\vec{c}$ (length of $\vec{c}$ does not matter) be two vectors perpendicular to each other in the xy-plane. If r_i, where = 1, 2, 3…, n are, then vectors in the same plane having projections 1 and 2 along $\vec{b}$ and $\vec{c}$ respectively, then evaluate $\sum_{r=1}^{n}|r_i|^2$.

9. Find the value of the constant S such that the scalar product of the vector $(\hat{i}+\hat{j}+\hat{k})$ with the unit vector parallel to the sum of vectors $2\hat{i}+4\hat{j}-5\hat{k}$ and $(S\hat{i}+2\hat{j}+3\hat{k})$ is equal to one

10. Let P, Q and R have position vectors $\vec{r}_1=3\hat{i}-2\hat{j}-\hat{k}:\vec{r}_2=\hat{i}+3\hat{j}+4\hat{k}$ and $\vec{r}_3=2\hat{i}+\hat{j}-2\hat{k}$ relative to an origin O, then find the distance of P from the plane OQR.

11. If vectors $\vec{a},\vec{b},\vec{c}$ are coplanar, then find the value of the determinant $\Delta=\begin{vmatrix}|\vec{a}| & |\vec{b}| & |\vec{c}|\\ \vec{a}.\vec{a} & \vec{a}.\vec{b} & \vec{a}.\vec{c}\\ \vec{b}.\vec{b} & \vec{b}.\vec{b} & \vec{b}.\vec{b}\end{vmatrix}$

12. It is given that $\vec{x}=\frac{\vec{b}\times\vec{c}}{[\vec{a}\,\vec{b}\,\vec{c}]};\vec{y}=\frac{\vec{c}\times\vec{a}}{[\vec{a}\,\vec{b}\,\vec{c}]};\vec{z}=\frac{\vec{a}\times\vec{b}}{[\vec{a}\,\vec{b}\,\vec{c}]}$; where a, b, c are non-coplanar vectors, then find the value of $\vec{x}\,(\vec{a}+\vec{b})+\vec{y}.(\vec{b}+\vec{c})+\vec{z}.(\vec{c}+\vec{a})$

13. A point $A(x_1, y_1)$ with abscissa x_1 = 1 and a point $B(x_2, y_2)$ with ordinate y_2 = 11 are given in a rectangular Cartesian system of co-ordinates OXY on the part of the curve $y = x^2 - 2x + 3$ which lies in the first quadrant, then the scalar product of $\overline{OA}$ and $\overline{OB}$

14. If $\vec{a}=\hat{i}+2\hat{j}-3\hat{k}$, $\vec{b}=2\hat{i}+\hat{j}-\hat{k}$ and $\vec{u}$ is satisfying the equations $\vec{u}\times\vec{a}=\vec{b}$ and $\vec{u}.\vec{a}=0$, then evaluate $28|\vec{u}|^2$.

15. If $\vec{d}=\lambda(\vec{a}\times\vec{b})+\mu(\vec{b}\times\vec{c})+v(\vec{c}\times\vec{a}),[\vec{a}\;\vec{b}\;\vec{c}]=\frac{1}{8}$ and $\vec{d}.(\vec{a}+\vec{b}-\vec{c})=8$ then find the value of $\lambda+\mu+v$.

16. In ΔABC, points D, E and F are taken on the sides BC, CA and AB respectively such that $BD : DC = CE : EA = AF : FB = 3 : 1$, given the ar(Δ DEF) = λ (ar (ΔABC)). Then find the value of [36 λ]. (*where [x] denotes greatest integer function of x*).

Answer Key

SECTION–III

1. (b)	**2.** (b)	**3.** (a)	**4.** (b)	**5.** (b)	**6.** (a)	**7.** (b)	**8.** (a)	**9.** (b)	**10.** (b)
11. (b)	**12.** (c)	**13.** (a)	**14.** (c)	**15.** (b)	**16.** (d)	**17.** (c)	**18.** (c)	**19.** (b)	**20.** (b)
21. (c)	**22.** (a)	**23.** (b)	**24.** (a)	**25.** (a)	**26.** (d)	**27.** (b)	**28.** (d)	**29.** (b)	**30.** (b)
31. (a)	**32.** (c)	**33.** (d)	**34.** (b)	**35.** (c)	**36.** (b)	**37.** (c)	**38.** (d)	**39.** (c)	**40.** (a)
41. (b)	**42.** (a)	**43.** (d)	**44.** (c)	**45.** (b)	**46.** (d)	**47.** (c)	**48.** (d)	**49.** (b)	**50.** (c)
51. (d)	**52.** (d)	**53.** (a)	**54.** (b)	**55.** (a)	**56.** (b)	**57.** (b)	**58.** (d)	**59.** (c)	**60.** (b)
61. (b)	**62.** (a)	**63.** (c)	**64.** (c)	**65.** (a)	**66.** (c)	**67.** (c)	**68.** (c)	**69.** (b)	**70.** (a)
71. (a)	**72.** (a)	**73.** (a)	**74.** (a)	**75.** (c)	**76.** (d)				

SECTION–IV

1. (a,b,c,d) **2.** (a,b,c) **3.** (b,c,d) **4.** (a,b,c,d) **5.** (a,b,c) **6.** (a,b,c,d) **7.** (a,b) **8.** (c,d) **9.** (b,c)
10. (b,c) **11.** (a,d) **12.** (a,c,d)

SECTION–V

1. (a)	**2.** (a)	**3.** (a)	**4.** (a)	**5.** (b)	**6.** (a)	**7.** (a)	**8.** (a)	**9.** (b)	**10.** (a)

SECTION–VI

1. (c)	**2.** (c)	**3.** (b)	**4.** (a)	**5.** (b)	**6.** (d)	**7.** (a)	**8.** (b)	**9.** (c)	**10.** (a)
11. (a)	**12.** (c)	**13.** (b)	**14.** (c)	**15.** (a,b,c)	**16.** (b)	**17.** (a)	**18.** (a)		

SECTION–VII

1. (i) → (c); (ii) (a,e); (iii) (b,d)
2. (i) → (b,d); (ii) → (a,c); (iii) → (a); (iv) → (e); (v) → (b)
3. (i) → (a); (ii) → (c); (iii) → (b); (iv) → (d)
4. (i) → (a,b); (ii) → (a,c); (iii) → (a,c,d); (iv) → (a,c,e)

SECTION–VIII

1. 5	**2.** 17	**3.** 5	**4.** 1	**5.** 16	**6.** 0	**7.** 2	**8.** 20	**9.** s = 1	**10.** 3
11. 0	**12.** 3	**13.** 26	**14.** 5	**15.** 64					

HINTS AND SOLUTIONS

1. *ABCD* and *AEFC* are || gms.

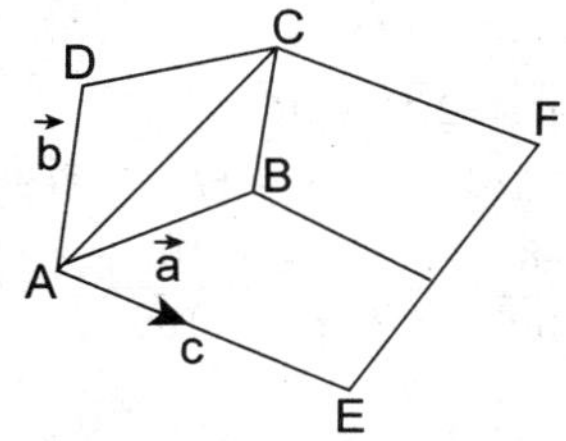

Given $\overrightarrow{AB}=\vec{a}$, $\overrightarrow{AD}=\vec{b}$ and $\Rightarrow \overrightarrow{AE}=\vec{c}$

As BC || AD $\therefore$ $BC=\vec{b} \Rightarrow \overrightarrow{AC}=\vec{a}+\vec{b}$ and $\overrightarrow{AE}=\overrightarrow{CF}=\vec{c}$

Now $\overrightarrow{AF}=\overrightarrow{AC}+\overrightarrow{CF}=\left(\vec{a}+\vec{b}\right)+\vec{c}=\vec{a}+\vec{b}+\vec{c}$

and $\overrightarrow{FA}=-\overrightarrow{AF}=-\left(\vec{a}+\vec{b}+\vec{c}\right)$

2. $\overrightarrow{AC}=\overrightarrow{AB}+\overrightarrow{BC}=\vec{a}+\vec{b}$

$\overrightarrow{AE}=\overrightarrow{AC}+\overrightarrow{CE}=(\vec{a}+\vec{b})+\vec{c} = \vec{a}+\vec{b}+\vec{c}$

And $\overrightarrow{EA}=-\overrightarrow{AE}=-\left(\vec{a}+\vec{b}+\vec{c}\right)$

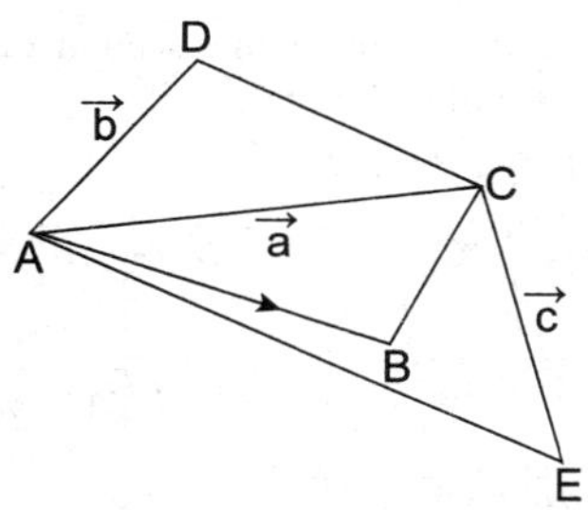

3. (i) $OA \neq OC$

Now we have free vectors as

$\overrightarrow{AB},\overrightarrow{AC},\overrightarrow{BC},\overrightarrow{AO},\overrightarrow{OC},\overrightarrow{OB},\overrightarrow{AD},\overrightarrow{CD},\overrightarrow{OD},\overrightarrow{DB}$

and their negative vectors $\Rightarrow$ 20 free vectors.

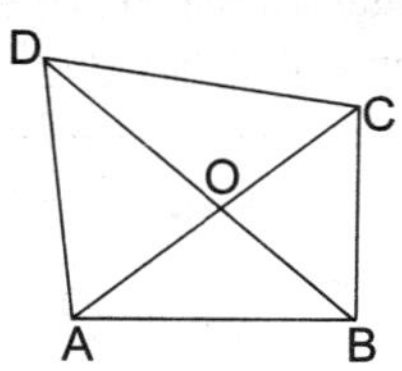

(ii) When OA = OC then $\overrightarrow{OA}=\overrightarrow{OC}$ as A, O, C are collinear so 9 free vectors and their negative vectors

$\Rightarrow$ 18 vectors.

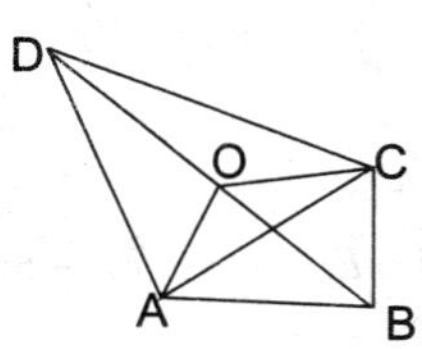

4. Given $OC = AB$, $OC \parallel AB$

$OB = OD$ and B, O, D are

Collinear $\left(\overrightarrow{AB}=\overrightarrow{OC}\right)$

and $\left(\overrightarrow{AO}=\overrightarrow{BC}\right),\left(\overrightarrow{OB}=\overrightarrow{DO}\right),\overrightarrow{AC},\overrightarrow{CD},\overrightarrow{AD},\overrightarrow{DB}$

Number of free vectors = 7 × 2 = 14 free vectors.

5. $\overrightarrow{DA}=\overrightarrow{CB}=\overrightarrow{GF}=\overrightarrow{HE}=\vec{b}$; $\overrightarrow{DC}=\overrightarrow{AB}=\overrightarrow{EF}=\overrightarrow{HG}=\vec{a}$;

$\overrightarrow{DH}=\overrightarrow{AE}=\overrightarrow{BF}=\overrightarrow{CG}=\vec{c}$; $\overrightarrow{AC}=\vec{a}-\vec{b}=\overrightarrow{EG}$

$\overrightarrow{DB}=\overrightarrow{HF}=\vec{a}+\vec{b}$; $\overrightarrow{AH}=\overrightarrow{BG}=\vec{c}-\vec{b}$, $DE=\vec{b}+\vec{c}=\overrightarrow{CF}$

$\overrightarrow{DG}=\overrightarrow{AF}=\vec{a}+\vec{c},\overrightarrow{CH}=\overrightarrow{BE}=\vec{c}-\vec{a}$

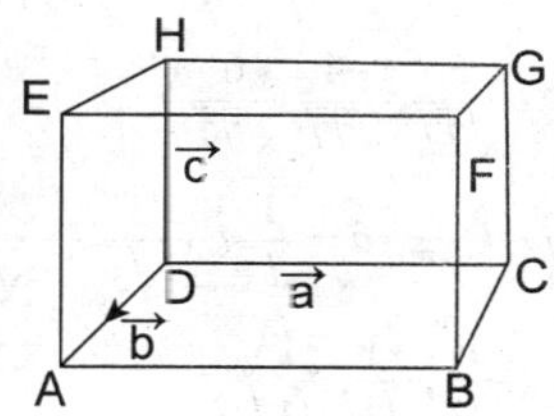

Body Diagonals: $\overrightarrow{AG}=\vec{a}+\vec{c}-\vec{b},\overrightarrow{BH}=\vec{c}-\vec{a}-\vec{b}$

$\overrightarrow{CE}=\vec{b}+\vec{c}-\vec{a},\overrightarrow{DF}=\vec{a}+\vec{b}+\vec{c}$

13 free vectors and their negative vectors

$\Rightarrow$ Total 26 vectors

(i) Consider side $\vec{a}=\overrightarrow{DC}$ it is collinear with $\overrightarrow{AB}=\overrightarrow{EF}=\overrightarrow{HG}$ and their negative vectors (with different lines of action) similarly $\overrightarrow{AB}$ $\overrightarrow{BA}$ will from

Similarly for $\vec{b}$ and $\vec{c}$ $\Rightarrow$ No of pairs formed by the sides = 72 pairs

Body diagonal will not form any collinear vectors

The surface diagonal $\overrightarrow{AF}$ and $\overrightarrow{FA}$ will form pairs with *DG* and *GD* and every surface has two surface diagonal (4 vectors) = 8 pairs

Formed by two parallel planes. Total 8 × 3 = 24 pairs

$\Rightarrow$ Total 96 vectors

(ii) Coplanar vectors with *EFGH* plane:

$\overrightarrow{EF}=\overrightarrow{AB}=\overrightarrow{CD}=\overrightarrow{HG}=\vec{a}$

and $\overrightarrow{DA}=\overrightarrow{HE}=\overrightarrow{CB}=\overrightarrow{GH}-\vec{b}$ and their negative vectors $\overrightarrow{DB}=\overrightarrow{HF}=\vec{a}-\vec{b}$ and their negative vectors, $\overrightarrow{AC}=\overrightarrow{EG}=\vec{a}-\vec{b}$ and their negative vectors. So total 8 vectors

TEXTUAL EXERCISE 2: (SUBJECTIVE)

1. (a) $\cos\alpha=\ell=\frac{1}{\sqrt{2}}$; $\cos\beta=m=\frac{1}{\sqrt{2}}$;$\cos\gamma=n=0$

so $\alpha=\beta=\frac{\pi}{4},\gamma=\frac{\pi}{2}$

(b) $\cos\alpha = \ell = -\frac{1}{2}, \cos\beta = 0 = m, \cos\gamma = n = \frac{\sqrt{3}}{2}$

$\alpha = \frac{2\pi}{3}, \beta = \frac{\pi}{2}, \gamma = \frac{\pi}{6}$ or $120°, 90°, 30°$

(c) $\cos\alpha = \ell = \frac{1}{\sqrt{3}}, \cos\beta = m = \frac{-1}{\sqrt{3}}, \cos\gamma = n = \frac{1}{\sqrt{3}}$

so $\alpha = \gamma = \cos^{-1}\left(\frac{1}{\sqrt{3}}\right)$ and $\beta = \pi - \cos^{-1}\left(\frac{1}{\sqrt{3}}\right)$

2. (a) $\vec{a} = 2\hat{i} - \hat{j} - 3\hat{k} \Rightarrow \hat{a} = \frac{2}{\sqrt{14}}\hat{i} - \frac{1}{\sqrt{14}}\hat{j} - \frac{3}{\sqrt{14}}\hat{k}$

$D.C's = \left\langle \frac{2}{\sqrt{14}}, \frac{-1}{\sqrt{14}}, \frac{-3}{\sqrt{14}} \right\rangle$

(b) $\vec{a} = 5\hat{i} - 4\hat{j} + 6\hat{k} \Rightarrow \hat{a} = \frac{5}{\sqrt{77}}\hat{i} - \frac{4}{\sqrt{77}}\hat{j} + \frac{6}{\sqrt{77}}$

$D.C,'s = \left\langle \frac{5}{\sqrt{77}}, \frac{-4}{\sqrt{77}}, \frac{6}{\sqrt{77}} \right\rangle$

(c) $\vec{a} = \hat{i} + \hat{j} - \hat{k} \Rightarrow \hat{a} = \frac{1}{\sqrt{3}}\hat{i} + \frac{1}{\sqrt{3}}\hat{j} - \frac{1}{\sqrt{3}}\hat{k}$

$D.C.'s = \left\langle \frac{1}{\sqrt{3}}, \frac{+1}{\sqrt{3}}, \frac{-1}{\sqrt{3}} \right\rangle$

3. (a) $\ell = \frac{1}{\sqrt{3}}, m = \sqrt{\frac{2}{3}}, n = ?$

$\ell^2 + m^2 + n^2 = 1 \Rightarrow \frac{1}{3} + \frac{2}{3} + n^2 = 1 \Rightarrow n = 0$

(b) $\ell = \frac{\sqrt{3}}{4}, m = ?, n = \frac{\sqrt{3}}{8}$

$\ell^2 + m^2 + n^2 = \frac{3}{16} + m^2 + \frac{3}{64} = \frac{15}{64} + m^2 = 1$

$m^2 = \frac{49}{64} \Rightarrow m = \pm\frac{7}{8}$

(c) $\ell = ?, m = \frac{\sqrt{3}}{4}, n = \frac{1}{4}$

Now $\ell^2 + m^2 + n^2 = \ell^2 + \frac{3}{16} + \frac{1}{16} = 1$

$\ell^2 = 1 - \frac{1}{4} = \frac{3}{4} \Rightarrow \ell = \pm\frac{\sqrt{3}}{2}$

4. $P(2,5,7)$ and $Q(-3,-1,2)$

$\overrightarrow{PQ} = (-3-2)\hat{i} + (-1-5)\hat{j} + (2-7)\hat{k}$

$= -5\hat{i} - 6\hat{j} - 5\hat{k} \Rightarrow \widehat{PQ} = \frac{5}{\sqrt{86}}\hat{i} - \frac{6}{\sqrt{86}}\hat{j} - \frac{5}{\sqrt{86}}$

5. $\overrightarrow{AB} = 3\hat{i} - \hat{j} + 4\hat{k}$; $\overrightarrow{BC} = \hat{i} - 2\hat{j} + 2\hat{k}$

$\overrightarrow{AC} = \overrightarrow{AB} + \overrightarrow{BC} = 4\hat{i} - 3\hat{j} + 6\hat{k}$

$\overrightarrow{AD} = (-2)\overrightarrow{AB} = -6\hat{i} + 2\hat{j} - 8\hat{k}$

Let G be the mid point of DF then

$\overrightarrow{AG} = \overrightarrow{AD} + \frac{1}{2}\overrightarrow{DF} = \overrightarrow{AD} + \frac{1}{2}\overrightarrow{AC}$

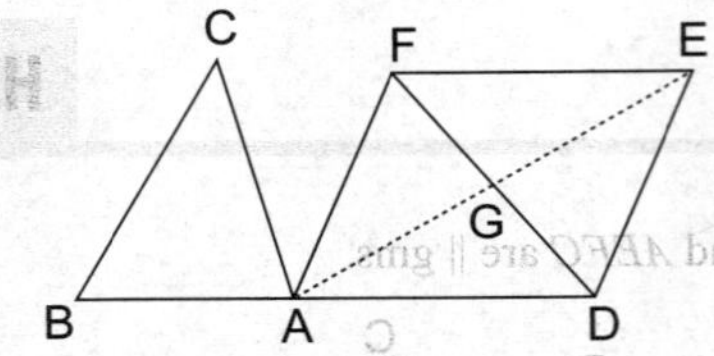

and $\overrightarrow{AE} = 2\overrightarrow{AG} = 2\overrightarrow{AD} + \overrightarrow{AC}$

$= -12\hat{i} + 4\hat{j} - 16\hat{k} + 4\hat{i} - 3\hat{j} + 6\hat{k} = -8\hat{i} + \hat{j} - 10\hat{k}$

$\Rightarrow \widehat{AE} = \frac{-8}{\sqrt{165}}\hat{i} + \frac{1}{\sqrt{165}}\hat{j} - \frac{10}{\sqrt{165}}\hat{k}$.

TEXTUAL EXERCISE 3: (SUBJECTIVE)

1. **(a)** $BC = AD$; Δ law of vector addition from $\overrightarrow{AB} + \overrightarrow{BC} = \overrightarrow{AC}$

So $\overrightarrow{AC} = \overrightarrow{AB} + \overrightarrow{AD} \Rightarrow \overrightarrow{BD} = \overrightarrow{AD} - \overrightarrow{AB}$

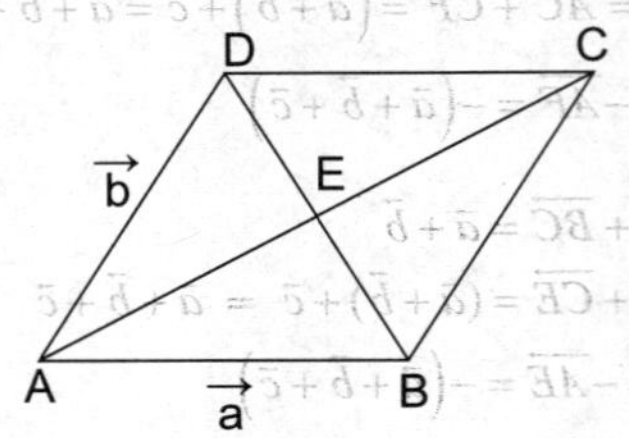

(b) Let E be the point of intersection of diagonals, then diagonals will be bisected at it

Now $\overrightarrow{AE} + \overrightarrow{EB} = \overrightarrow{AB}$

so $\overrightarrow{AB} = \frac{1}{2}\overrightarrow{AC} - \frac{1}{2}\overrightarrow{BD}$; $\overrightarrow{AB} = \frac{1}{2}\left\{\overrightarrow{AC} - \overrightarrow{BD}\right\}$

$\overrightarrow{AD} = \overrightarrow{AE} + \overrightarrow{ED} = \left\{\frac{1}{2}\overrightarrow{AC} + \frac{1}{2}\overrightarrow{BD}\right\} = \frac{1}{2}\left\{\overrightarrow{AC} + \overrightarrow{BD}\right\}$

(c) $\overrightarrow{AB} = \overrightarrow{AD} + \overrightarrow{DB} = \overrightarrow{AD} - \overrightarrow{BD}$ and

$\overrightarrow{AC} = \overrightarrow{AD} + \overrightarrow{DB} + \overrightarrow{BC} = \overrightarrow{AD} - \overrightarrow{BD} + \overrightarrow{AD} = 2\overrightarrow{AD} - \overrightarrow{BD}$

$\overrightarrow{AC} + \overrightarrow{DB} = \overrightarrow{AB} + \overrightarrow{BC} + \overrightarrow{DB} = \overrightarrow{AB} + \overrightarrow{DC} = 2\overrightarrow{DC}$

$\overrightarrow{AC} + \overrightarrow{BD} = 2\overrightarrow{EC} + 2\overrightarrow{BE} = 2\overrightarrow{BC} = 2\overrightarrow{AD}$

2. ABCDEF is a regular hexagon $\overrightarrow{AB} = \vec{a}, \overrightarrow{BC} = \vec{b}$

Let O be the centre of the hexagon

Then $\overrightarrow{AO} = \overrightarrow{BC} = \vec{b}$ and $\overrightarrow{OF} = \overrightarrow{BA} = -\vec{a}$

$\overrightarrow{FA} = \overrightarrow{OA} = \overrightarrow{FO} = -\vec{b} + \vec{a} = \vec{a} - \vec{b}$

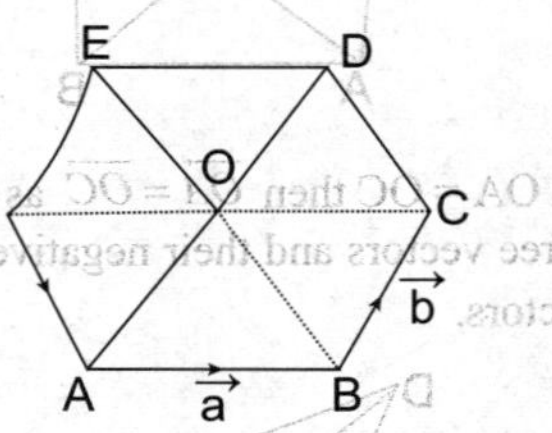

3. (a) $\overrightarrow{AC} = \overrightarrow{AB} + \overrightarrow{BC}$

$\overrightarrow{AD} = 2\overrightarrow{BC}$ $\overrightarrow{EA} = \overrightarrow{EF} + \overrightarrow{FA} = \overrightarrow{FA} - \overrightarrow{BC}$

Using and adding

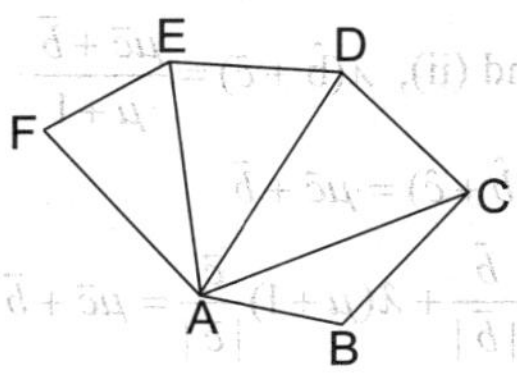

$\overrightarrow{AC}+\overrightarrow{AD}+\overrightarrow{EA}+\overrightarrow{FA} = \overrightarrow{AB}+2\overrightarrow{BC}+\overrightarrow{FA}+\overrightarrow{FA}$

Now $\overrightarrow{FA}+\overrightarrow{AB}+\overrightarrow{BC}=\overrightarrow{FC}=2\overrightarrow{AB}$ .....(I)

$\overrightarrow{AC}+\overrightarrow{AD}+\overrightarrow{EA}+\overrightarrow{FA}=2\overrightarrow{AB}+\overrightarrow{BC}+\overrightarrow{FA}$

From $\overrightarrow{FE}+\overrightarrow{ED}+\overrightarrow{DC}=\overrightarrow{FC}$

we get $\overrightarrow{BC}+\overrightarrow{AB}+\overrightarrow{DC}=2\overrightarrow{AB}$

So $\overrightarrow{FA}+\overrightarrow{BC}=\overrightarrow{AB}$ .....(II)

From (I) and (II) $\Rightarrow$ $\overrightarrow{AC}+\overrightarrow{AD}+\overrightarrow{EA}+\overrightarrow{FA}=3\overrightarrow{AB}$

(b) From the figure $\{\overrightarrow{CD}=\overrightarrow{AF}\}$

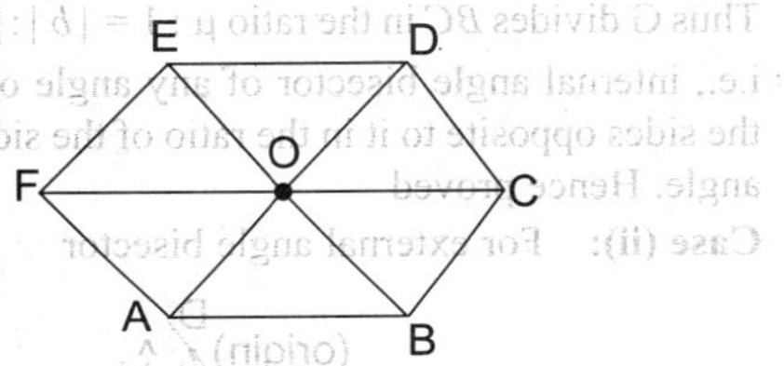

$\overrightarrow{AD}=\overrightarrow{AC}+\overrightarrow{CD}=\overrightarrow{AC}+\overrightarrow{AF}=2\overrightarrow{AO}$

$\overrightarrow{AC}+\overrightarrow{AD}+\overrightarrow{AF}=2\overrightarrow{AD}=4\overrightarrow{AO}$

4. By the figure, the vector $\vec{A}$ in terms of new axes can be given by $\vec{A}=A_2\hat{i}-A_1\hat{j}+A_3\hat{k}$

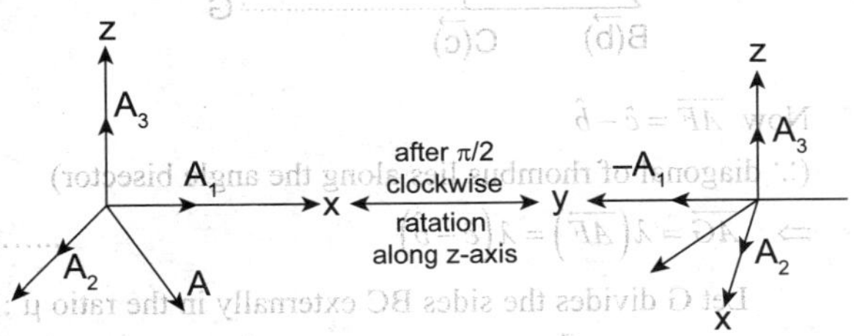

5. (a) $\vec{a}-\vec{b}-\vec{c}$ gives the body diagonal

(b) $(\vec{a}+\vec{c})$ gives the surface (or face)diagonal $(\vec{a}-\vec{c})$ gives the face diagonal

(c) $\vec{a}+\vec{b}+\vec{c}$ gives a body diagonal

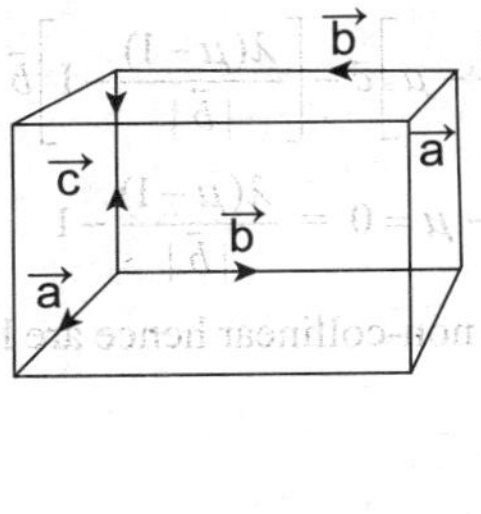

TEXTUAL EXERCISE 4: SUBJECTIVE

1. (a) since $ABCDEF$ is a regular hexagon $ABCO$ is a parallelogram and so is $BODC$.

$\Rightarrow$ $\overrightarrow{AO}=\overrightarrow{BC}$ and $\overrightarrow{OD}=\overrightarrow{BC}$

$\Rightarrow$ $\overrightarrow{AO}+\overrightarrow{OD}=2\overrightarrow{BC}=\overrightarrow{AD}\Rightarrow x=2$

for similar orgument $\overrightarrow{AB}=2\overrightarrow{FC}=2\overrightarrow{CF}\Rightarrow y=-2$

$\Rightarrow$ $xy=2\times-2=-4$

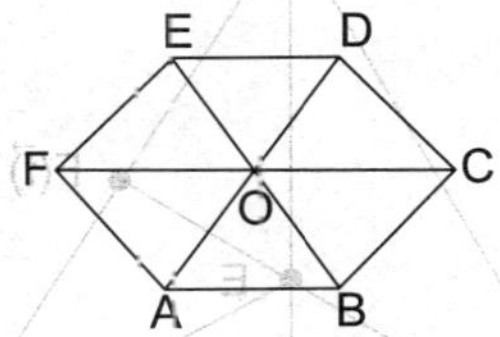

(b) Let $\vec{a},\vec{b},\vec{c},\vec{d}$

$\vec{e},\vec{f}$ be the respective position vectors

$\vec{e}=\dfrac{\vec{a}+\vec{c}}{2}$ and $\vec{f}=\dfrac{\vec{b}-\vec{d}}{2}$

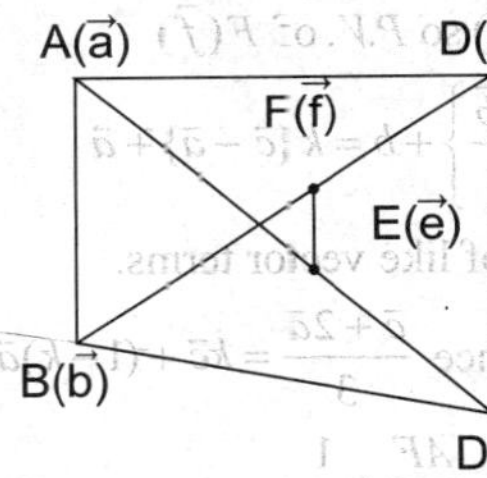

So $\overrightarrow{AB}+\overrightarrow{CB}+\overrightarrow{CD}+\overrightarrow{AD} = \vec{b}-\vec{a}+\vec{b}-\vec{c}+\vec{d}-\vec{c}+\vec{d}-\vec{a}$

$=2\vec{b}+2\vec{d}-2\vec{a}-2\vec{c}=4\left\{\dfrac{\vec{b}+\vec{d}}{2}-\dfrac{\vec{a}+\vec{c}}{2}\right\}$

$=4\{\vec{f}-\vec{e}\}=4\overrightarrow{EF}$ Hence proved

2. P.V of mid - point of $\overrightarrow{AC}=\vec{e}=\dfrac{\vec{b}+\vec{a}}{2}$

$\overrightarrow{BE}=\vec{e}-\vec{b}=\dfrac{\vec{c}+\vec{a}-2\vec{b}}{2}$

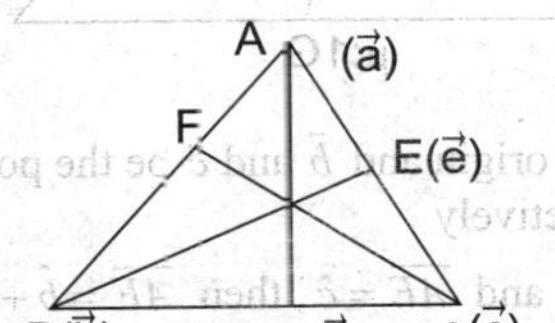

Similarly $\overrightarrow{AD}=\dfrac{\vec{b}+\vec{c}-2\vec{a}}{2}$ and $\overrightarrow{CF}=\dfrac{\vec{a}+\vec{b}-2\vec{c}}{2}$

$\overrightarrow{AD}+\overrightarrow{CF}+\overrightarrow{BE}=\dfrac{\vec{c}+\vec{a}-2\vec{b}+\vec{b}+\vec{c}-2\vec{a}+\vec{a}+\vec{b}-2c}{2}=\vec{O}$

3. $\vec{d} = \dfrac{\vec{b}+\vec{c}}{2}$ {AD is the median}

Mid pt of AD = E $\Rightarrow \vec{e} = \dfrac{\vec{b}+\vec{c}+2\vec{a}}{4}$

$\overline{BE} = \vec{e} - \vec{b} = \dfrac{\vec{c}+2\vec{a}-3\vec{b}}{4}$

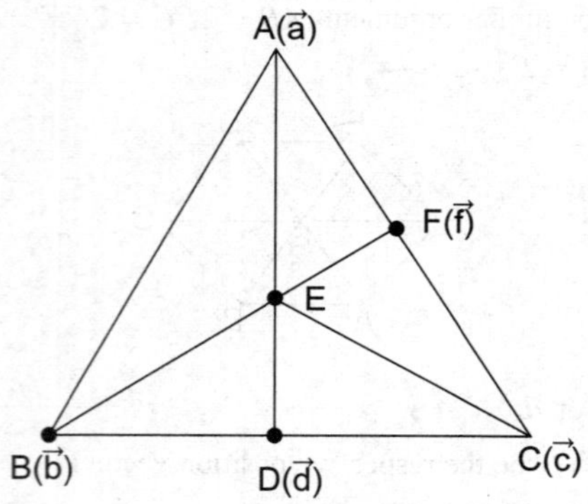

Let pt F divide AC such that $\dfrac{AF}{AC} = k \Rightarrow \overline{AF} = k(\vec{c}-\vec{a})$

Let $\overline{BF} = \mu(\overline{BE})$ so $P.V.$ of $F(\vec{f})$

$= \mu\left\{\dfrac{\vec{c}+2\vec{a}-3\vec{b}}{4}\right\} + b = k\{\vec{c}-\vec{a}\} + \vec{a}$

on comparison of like vector terms.

Gives $\mu = \dfrac{4}{3}$ hence $\dfrac{\vec{c}+2\vec{a}}{3} = k\vec{c} + (1-k)\vec{a}$

Gives k = 1/3 so $\dfrac{AF}{AC} = \dfrac{1}{3}$

4. Case (i): (for internal angle bisector)

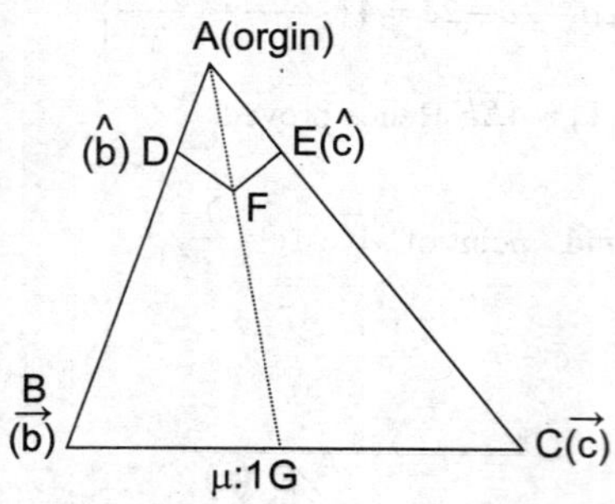

Let A be the origin and $\vec{b}$ and $\vec{c}$ be the position vectors of B and C respectively

Let $\overline{AD} = \hat{b}$ and $\overline{AE} = \hat{c}$, then $\overline{AF} = \hat{b} + \hat{c}$

($\because$ diagonal of rhombus *ADFE* lies along the angle bisector)

$\Rightarrow \overline{AG} = \lambda\overline{AF} \quad \Rightarrow \overline{AG} = \lambda(\hat{b}+\hat{c})$ ... (i)

Further let *G* divides *BC* in the ratio μ : 1

Internally, then $\overline{AG} = \dfrac{\mu\vec{c}+\vec{b}}{\mu+1}$ ......(ii)

$\therefore$ From (i) and (ii), $\lambda(\hat{b}+\hat{c}) = \dfrac{\mu\vec{c}+\vec{b}}{\mu+1}$

$\Rightarrow \lambda(\mu+1)(\hat{b}+\hat{c}) = \mu\vec{c}+\vec{b}$

$\Rightarrow \lambda(\mu+1)\dfrac{\vec{b}}{|\vec{b}|} + \lambda(\mu+1)\dfrac{\vec{c}}{|\vec{c}|} = \mu\vec{c}+\vec{b}$

$\Rightarrow \left[\dfrac{\lambda(\mu+1)}{|\vec{b}|} - 1\right]\vec{b} + \left[\dfrac{\lambda(\mu+1)}{|\vec{c}|} - \mu\right]\vec{c} = \vec{0}$

But $\vec{b}$ and $\vec{c}$ and non-collinear vectors (hence linearly independent)

$\Rightarrow \dfrac{\lambda(\mu+1)}{|\vec{b}|} - 1 = 0$ and $\dfrac{\lambda(\mu+1)}{|\vec{c}|} - \mu = 0$

$\Rightarrow \lambda(\mu+1) = |\vec{b}| = \mu(|\vec{c}|)$

$\Rightarrow \mu = \dfrac{|\vec{b}|}{|\vec{c}|}$ and $\lambda = \dfrac{|\vec{b}|}{\dfrac{|\vec{b}|}{|\vec{c}|}+1} = \dfrac{|\vec{b}|.|\vec{c}|}{|\vec{b}|+|\vec{c}|}$

Thus G divides *BC* in the ratio μ : 1 = $|\vec{b}| : |\vec{c}| = |\overline{AB}| : |\overline{AC}|$

i.e., internal angle bisector of any angle of triangle divides the sides opposite to it in the ratio of the sides containing the angle. Hence proved

Case (ii): For external angle bisector

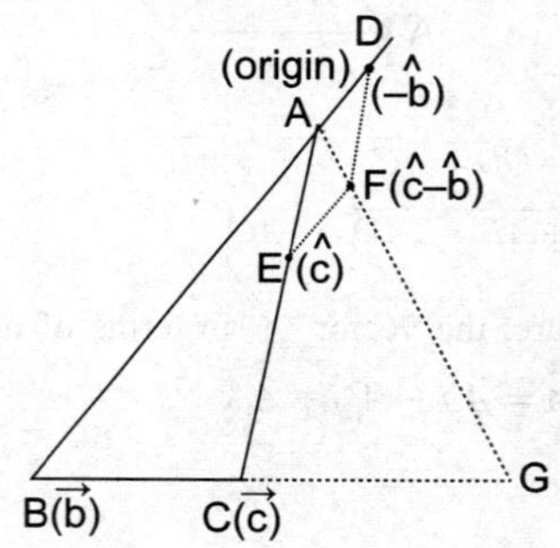

Now $\overline{AF} = \hat{c} - \hat{b}$

($\because$ diagonal of rhombus lies along the angle bisector)

$\Rightarrow \overline{AG} = \lambda(\overline{AF}) = \lambda(\hat{c}-\hat{b})$ ......(i)

Let G divides the sides BC externally in the ratio μ : 1

$\Rightarrow \overline{AG} = \dfrac{\mu\vec{c}-\vec{b}}{\mu-1}$ ......(ii)

$\therefore$ from (i) and (ii), we get $\lambda(\hat{c}-\hat{b}) = \dfrac{\mu\vec{c}-\vec{b}}{\mu-1}$

$\Rightarrow \lambda(\mu-1)\left[\dfrac{\vec{c}}{|\vec{c}|} - \dfrac{\vec{b}}{|\vec{b}|}\right] = \mu\vec{c}-\vec{b}$

$\Rightarrow \left[\dfrac{\lambda(\mu-1)}{|\vec{c}|} - \mu\right]\vec{c} - \left[\dfrac{\lambda(\mu-1)}{|\vec{b}|} - 1\right]\vec{b} = 0$

$\Rightarrow \dfrac{\lambda(\mu-1)}{|\vec{c}|} - \mu = 0 = \dfrac{\lambda(\mu-1)}{|\vec{b}|} - 1$

($\because \vec{c}$ and $\vec{b}$ are non-collinear hence are linearly independent)

$\Rightarrow \lambda(\mu-1)=\mu|\vec{c}|=|\vec{b}| \quad \Rightarrow \mu=\dfrac{|\vec{b}|}{|\vec{c}|}$

$\therefore$ G divides AC externally in the ratio

$\mu : 1 = |\vec{b}|:|\vec{c}| = |\overline{AB}|:|\overrightarrow{AC}|$

5. consider triangle *ABC*, *BD* is the internal bisector of $\angle A$ and *BE* is the external bisector of $\angle B$, join *CE*

Let $\angle A = a$ $\angle B = b$ $\angle C = c$

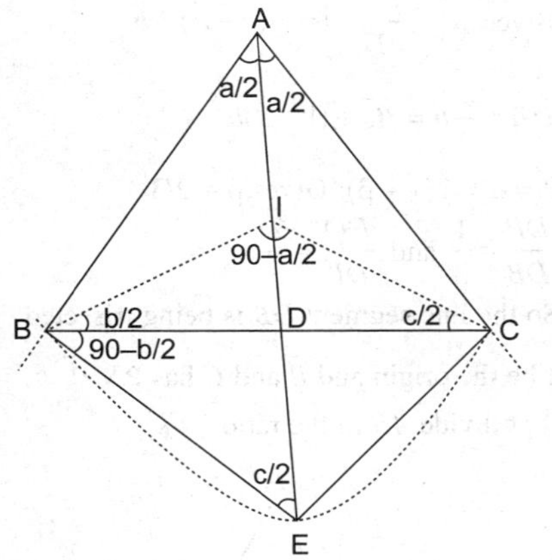

In ΔABE, by angle sum of property $\angle BED = c/2$

$\Rightarrow$ $\angle BED$ = *BCI* (which are angles in the same segment)

Thus for same reason $\angle CED$ = b/2

Now by angle sum property, $\angle ECD = 90 - c/2$

$\Rightarrow$ *CE* is th eexternal bisectro of $\angle c$

$\Rightarrow$ Hence *AE, CE, BE* are can correct

6. Let $A(\vec{a}), B(\vec{b}), c(\vec{c})$ be the P.V of these points then

$D(\vec{d})=\dfrac{\vec{b}+\vec{c}}{2}$

The mid pt of *AD* is *E* and it has P.V. as

$E(\vec{e})=\dfrac{1}{2}\left\{\vec{a}+\dfrac{\vec{b}+\vec{c}}{2}\right\}=\dfrac{\vec{b}+\vec{c}+2\vec{a}}{4}$

And $\overline{BE}=\vec{e}-\vec{b}=\dfrac{\vec{c}+2\vec{a}-3\vec{b}}{4}$

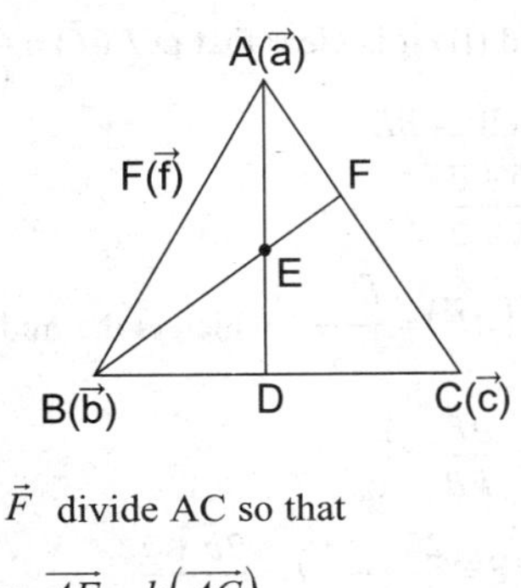

Let point $\vec{F}$ divide AC so that

$\dfrac{AF}{AC}=k$ or $\overline{AF}=k\left(\overline{AC}\right)$

Now let $\overline{BF}=\mu(\overline{BE})$ then $P.V.$ of $F(\vec{f})$ will be

$\mu\left\{\dfrac{\vec{c}+\vec{a}-3\vec{b}}{4}\right\}+\vec{b}=\kappa(\vec{c}-\vec{a})$; Comparing $\mu=\dfrac{4}{3}$

$\Rightarrow BF=\dfrac{4}{3}BE$; $EF=(BF-BE)=\dfrac{1}{3}BE$

$=\dfrac{3}{4}\cdot\dfrac{1}{3}BF=\dfrac{1}{4}BF$ so $BF = 4EF$; $\overline{BF}=\overline{4EF}$

7. (a) $\overline{AB}=-3\hat{i}+4\hat{k}$; $\overline{AC}=5\hat{i}-2\hat{j}+4\hat{k}$

AD is the median through *A*. Using the fact that diagonals of the || gm bisect each other. Hence form a || gm with *AB* and *AC* as adjacent sides.

$\Rightarrow \overline{AD}=\dfrac{\overline{AE}}{2}=\dfrac{1}{2}\{\overline{AC}+\overline{AB}\}=\dfrac{1}{2}\{2i-2\hat{j}+8\hat{k}\}$

$\overline{AD}=\hat{i}-\hat{j}+4\hat{k} \Rightarrow AD=\sqrt{18}=3\sqrt{2}$ units

Unit vector along $\overline{AD}=\dfrac{1}{3\sqrt{2}}\{\hat{i}-\hat{j}+4\hat{k}\}$

(b) $\overline{AB}=2\hat{i}+4\hat{j}+4\hat{k}$ and $\overline{AC}=2\hat{i}+2\hat{j}+\hat{k}$

Median $\overline{AD}=\dfrac{1}{2}\left(\overline{AB}+\overline{AC}\right)$

$=2\hat{i}+3\hat{j}+\dfrac{5}{2}k \Rightarrow AD=\sqrt{\dfrac{16+36+25}{4}}=\dfrac{\sqrt{77}}{2}$

8. **(a)** P.V. of $A=4\hat{i}+7\hat{j}+8\hat{k}$; P.V. of $B=2\hat{i}+3\hat{j}+4\hat{j}$

P.V. of $C=2\hat{i}+5\hat{j}+7\hat{k} \Rightarrow \left|\overline{AB}\right|=\left|-2\hat{i}-4\hat{j}-4\hat{k}\right|=6$ units

$\left|\overline{AC}\right|=\left|-2\hat{i}-2\hat{j}-\hat{k}\right|=3$ units

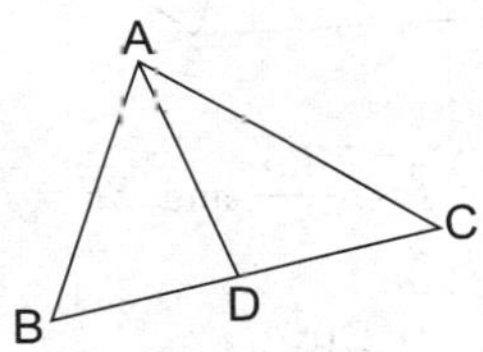

Let *D* be the point where angle bisector of $\angle A$ meets *BC*

P.V. of $D=\dfrac{|AC|\,PV\ of\ B+|AB|\,P.V\ of\ C}{|AB|+|AC|}$

{angle bisector theorem}

$=\dfrac{\left(6\hat{i}+9\hat{j}+12\hat{k}\right)+\left(12\hat{i}+30\hat{j}+42\hat{k}\right)}{9}$

$=\dfrac{18\hat{i}+39\hat{j}+54\hat{k}}{9}=\dfrac{1}{3}\{6\hat{i}+13\hat{j}+18k\}$

(b) $\vec{a}=\overline{OA}=\hat{i}+3\hat{j}-2\hat{k}$; $a=\sqrt{14}$ units

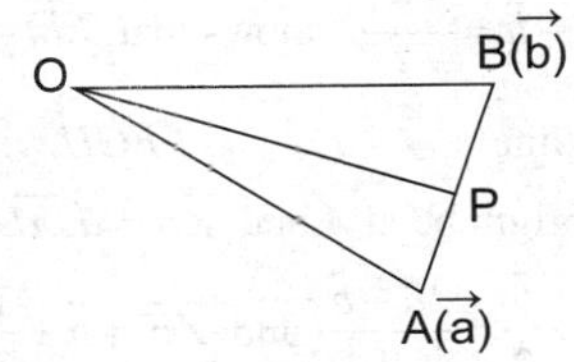

$\vec{b} = 3\hat{i} + \hat{j} - 2\hat{k} \Rightarrow |b| = \sqrt{14}$ units

P.V. of $P = \overrightarrow{OP} = \dfrac{|a|\vec{b} + |b|\vec{a}}{|a| + |b|}$ {angle bisector theorem}

$= \dfrac{1}{2}\{4\hat{i} + 4\hat{j} - 4\hat{k}\} = 2\hat{i} + 2\hat{j} - 2\hat{k} = 2(\hat{i} + \hat{j} - k)$

9. (a) $\overrightarrow{BC} = \overrightarrow{AC} - \overrightarrow{AB}$

$\Rightarrow \dfrac{1}{2}\overrightarrow{AC} - \dfrac{1}{2}\overrightarrow{AB} = \overrightarrow{FE} = \dfrac{1}{2}\overrightarrow{BC} = \overrightarrow{FE}$

$\therefore$ $\overrightarrow{FE}$ is mid parallel to $\overrightarrow{BC}$

(b) Refer to Q.1 (b)

(c) Since the medians have been provid to be conaennent hence proved.

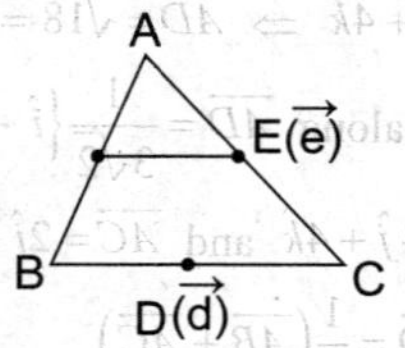

10. (a) $\overrightarrow{AB} + \overrightarrow{AC} = 2\overrightarrow{AD}$; Form a || gm with sides AB and AC

Since diagonals of a || gm bisect each other

$\therefore$ $2AD = AE = \overrightarrow{AB} + \overrightarrow{AC}$

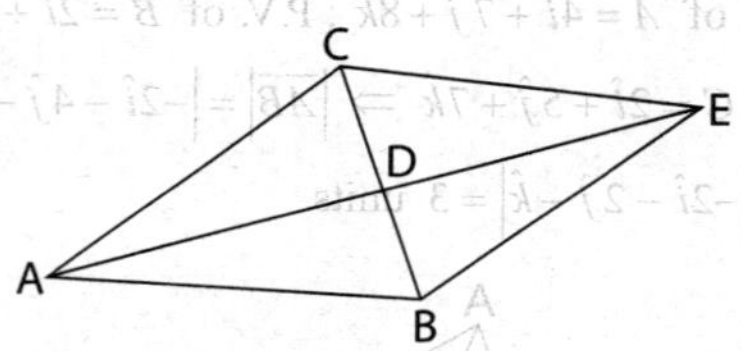

(b) $\vec{e} = \dfrac{\vec{b} + \vec{a}}{2}$, $\vec{f} = \dfrac{\vec{c} + \vec{b}}{2}$ and $\overrightarrow{EF} = \vec{f} - \vec{e} = \dfrac{\vec{c} - \vec{a}}{2}$

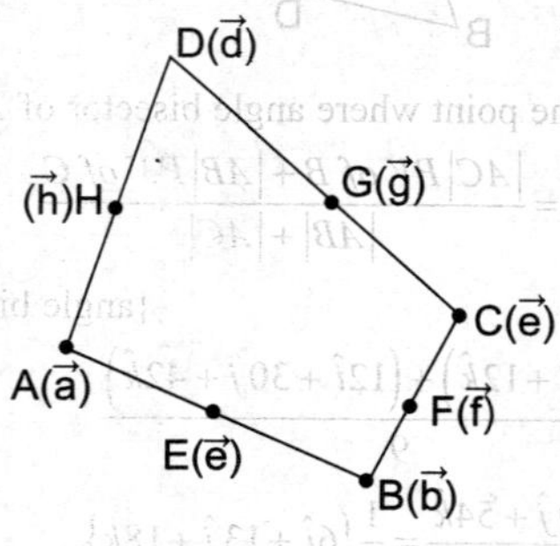

Similarly $\vec{g} = \dfrac{\vec{c} + \vec{d}}{2}$ and $\vec{h} = \dfrac{\vec{a} + \vec{d}}{2}$

and $\overrightarrow{HG} = \vec{g} - \vec{h} = \dfrac{\vec{c} - \vec{a}}{2}$ shows that $\overrightarrow{EF} = \overrightarrow{HG}$

On the same line $\overline{EH}$ $\overline{FG}$, so $EFGH$ will form a || gm

(c) Let the origin be at A and $\overrightarrow{AB} = \vec{a}, \overrightarrow{AD} = \vec{b}$,

$\overrightarrow{AE} = \vec{a} + \dfrac{\vec{b}}{2} = \dfrac{2\vec{a} + \vec{b}}{2}$ and $\overrightarrow{AF} = \vec{b} + \dfrac{\vec{a}}{2} = \dfrac{\vec{a} + 2\vec{b}}{2}$

$\overrightarrow{DB} = \vec{a} - \vec{b}$ now let $\overrightarrow{AP} = \mu\overrightarrow{AF}$ and $\overrightarrow{DP} = \lambda.\overrightarrow{DB}$

Hence $\mu\left(\dfrac{\vec{a} + 2\vec{b}}{2}\right) = \lambda(\vec{a} - \vec{b}) + \vec{b} = \lambda\vec{a} + (1 - \lambda)\vec{b}$

so $\dfrac{\mu}{2}\vec{a} + \mu\vec{b} = \lambda\vec{a} + (1 - \lambda)\vec{b} \Rightarrow 2\lambda = (1 - \lambda) = \mu$

$\Rightarrow$ $\lambda = 1/3$, similarly for $\overline{DQ}$; $\overrightarrow{AQ} = \alpha\overrightarrow{AF}$ and $\overrightarrow{DQ} = \beta\overrightarrow{DB}$

Gives $\alpha\left(\dfrac{2\vec{a} + \vec{b}}{2}\right) = \beta(\vec{a} - \vec{b}) + \vec{b}$

$\alpha\vec{a} + \dfrac{\alpha}{2}\vec{b} = \overline{\beta a} + (1 - \beta)\vec{b}$

$\Rightarrow$ $\beta = \alpha = 2(1 - \beta)$; Gives $\beta = 2/3$

$\therefore$ $\dfrac{DP}{DB} = \dfrac{1}{3}$ and $\dfrac{DQ}{DB} = \dfrac{2}{3}$

So the line segment DB is being trisected

11. Let A be the origin and B and C has P.V. $\vec{b}, \vec{c}$

Let D pt divide AB in the ratio $1 : k$

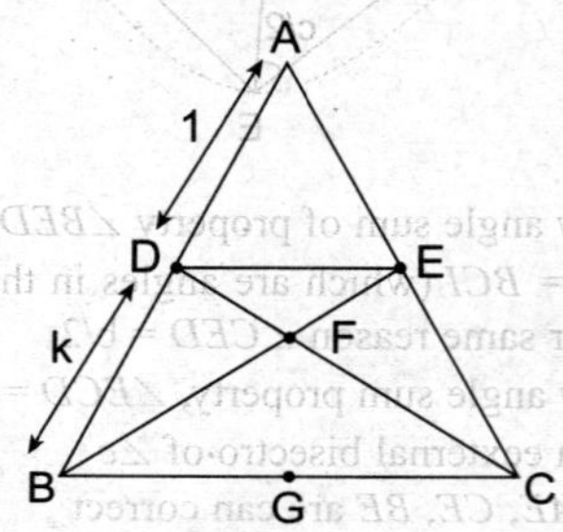

P.V of $D(\vec{d}) = \overrightarrow{AD} = \dfrac{\vec{b}}{1+k}$ P.V. of $E(\vec{e}) = \overrightarrow{AE} = \dfrac{\vec{c}}{1+k}$

Any point on DC will be given by

$\dfrac{\vec{c} + (k+1)\vec{d}}{(k+2)} = \dfrac{\vec{c} + \vec{b}}{k+2}$ ....(I)

Similarly a pt on BE will be give by

$\dfrac{\vec{e}(k+1) + \vec{b}}{k+2} = \dfrac{\vec{b} + \vec{c}}{k+2}$ ....(II)

From (I) and (II) it is clear that pt $F(\vec{f}) = \dfrac{\vec{b} + \vec{c}}{(k+2)}$ lies both on DC as well as BE.

$\Rightarrow$ $\overrightarrow{AF} = \dfrac{\vec{b} + \vec{c}}{k+2}$

$\Rightarrow$ $\dfrac{(k+2)}{2}(\overrightarrow{AF}) = \dfrac{\vec{b} + \vec{c}}{2}$ which is the mid pt of BC

12. $\dfrac{BD}{DC} = \dfrac{CE}{EA} = \dfrac{AF}{FB} = \dfrac{2}{1}$ ....(i)

$\vec{d} = \dfrac{2\vec{c} + \vec{b}}{3}$; $\vec{e} = \dfrac{2\vec{a} + \vec{c}}{3}$; $\vec{f} = \dfrac{2\vec{b} + \vec{a}}{3}$

$\Rightarrow$ $\vec{d} \equiv \left(4, \dfrac{4}{3}, \dfrac{8}{3}\right), \vec{e} \equiv \left(2, \dfrac{4}{3}, \dfrac{5}{3}\right) \vec{f} \equiv \left(3, \dfrac{1}{3}, \dfrac{5}{3}\right)$

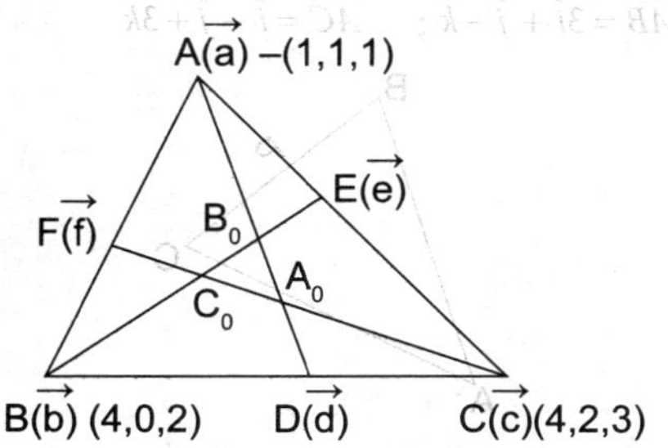

Now equation of $\overrightarrow{AD}$ will be $\vec{r}=\vec{a}+\lambda(\vec{d}-\vec{a})$ ....(ii)

Equation of $\overrightarrow{BE}$ will be $\vec{r}=\vec{b}+\mu(\vec{e}-\vec{b})$ ....(iii)

and equation of $\overrightarrow{CF}$ will be $\vec{r}=\vec{c}+t(\vec{f}-\vec{c})$ ....(iv)

For A_0, (point of intersection of $\overrightarrow{CF}$ and $\overrightarrow{AD}$)

$\therefore\ \vec{a}+\lambda(\vec{d}-\vec{a})=\vec{c}+t(\vec{f}-\vec{c})$

$\Rightarrow\ (1,1,1)+\lambda\left(3,\frac{1}{3},\frac{5}{3}\right)=(4,2,3)+t\left(-1,\frac{-5}{3},\frac{-4}{3}\right)$

$\Rightarrow$ $1+3\lambda = 4-t$, $1+\lambda/3 = 2-5/3t$, $1+5/3\lambda = 3-4/3t$

$\Rightarrow$ $t=3/7$, $\lambda=6/7$

$\Rightarrow\ A_o\equiv(1,1,1)+\frac{6}{7}\left(3,\frac{1}{3},\frac{5}{3}\right)\equiv\left(\frac{25}{7},\frac{9}{7},\frac{17}{7}\right)$

Similarly for B_o, (point intersection of $\overrightarrow{AD}$ and $\overrightarrow{BE}$)

$\Rightarrow\ \vec{a}+\lambda(\vec{d}-\vec{a})=\vec{b}+\mu(\vec{e}-\vec{b})$

$\Rightarrow\ (1,1,1)+\lambda\left(3,\frac{1}{3},\frac{5}{3}\right)=(4,0,2)+\mu\left(-2,\frac{4}{3},\frac{-1}{3}\right)$

$\Rightarrow\ 1+3\lambda=4-2\mu,\ 1+\frac{\lambda}{3}=\frac{4}{3}\mu, 1+\frac{5}{3}\lambda=2\frac{-1}{3}\mu$

$\Rightarrow\ \lambda=\frac{3}{7}, \mu=\frac{6}{7}\Rightarrow B_0=(1,1,1)+\frac{3}{7}\left(3,\frac{1}{3},\frac{5}{3}\right)=\left(\frac{16}{7},\frac{8}{7},\frac{12}{7}\right)$

For C_0 (Point of intersection of $\overrightarrow{BE}$ and $\overrightarrow{CF}$)

$\vec{b}+\mu(\vec{e}-\vec{b})\vec{c}+t(\vec{f}-\vec{c})$

$\Rightarrow\ (4,0,2)+\mu\left(-2,\frac{4}{3},\frac{-1}{3}\right)=(4,2,3)+t\left(-1,\frac{-5}{3},\frac{-4}{3}\right)$

$\Rightarrow$ $4-2\mu=4-t$; $4/3\mu=2-5/3t$; $2-1/3\mu = 3-4/3t$

$\Rightarrow\ \mu=\frac{3}{7}, t=\frac{6}{7}\quad\Rightarrow\quad C_0=\left(\frac{22}{7},\frac{4}{7},\frac{13}{7}\right)$

$\therefore$ (a) Centroid of

$$\Delta A_0B_0C_0\equiv\left(\frac{25+16+22}{21},\frac{9+8+4}{21},\frac{17+12+13}{21}\right)\equiv(3,1,2)$$

(b) $$\frac{AB_0}{B_0D}=\frac{\sqrt{\left(\frac{16}{7}-1\right)^2+\left(\frac{8}{7}-1\right)^2+\left(\frac{12}{7}-1\right)^2}}{\sqrt{\left(4-\frac{16}{7}\right)^2+\left(\frac{4}{3}-\frac{8}{7}\right)^2+\left(\frac{8}{3}-\frac{12}{7}\right)^2}}$$

$$=\frac{\sqrt{81+1+25}\times 3}{\sqrt{9\times144+(16)+400}}=\frac{3}{4}=3:4$$

(c) $$\frac{ar.\Delta ABC}{ar.\Delta A_oB_oC_o}=\frac{|\overrightarrow{AB}\times\overrightarrow{BC}|}{|\overrightarrow{A_oB_o}\times\overrightarrow{B_oC_o}|}$$

$$=\frac{|(3,-1,1)\times(0,2,1)|}{\left|\left(-\frac{9}{7},\frac{-1}{7},\frac{-5}{7}\right)\times\left(\frac{6}{7},\frac{-4}{7},\frac{1}{7}\right)\right|}$$

$$=\frac{|-3\hat{i}-3\hat{j}-6\hat{k}|}{\frac{1}{49}|-21\hat{i}-21\hat{j}+42\hat{k}|}=\frac{3|-\hat{i}-\hat{j}+2\hat{k}|\times 49}{21|-\hat{i}-\hat{j}+2\hat{k}|}=7:1$$

(d) $\frac{A_oB_o}{B_oD}=\lambda\Rightarrow\lambda=\frac{3}{4};\frac{BC_o}{C_oE}=\mu;\frac{CA_0}{A_0F}=V$

Now $$\frac{BC_0}{C_0E}=\frac{\sqrt{\left(\frac{22}{7}-4\right)^2\left(\frac{4}{7}-0\right)^2+\left(\frac{13}{7}-2\right)^2}}{\sqrt{\left(2-\frac{22}{7}\right)^2+\left(\frac{4}{3}-\frac{4}{7}\right)^2+\left(\frac{5}{3}-\frac{13}{7}\right)^2}}$$

$$=\frac{\sqrt{36+16+1}\times 3}{\sqrt{64\times9+256+16}}=\frac{3}{4}$$

$\Rightarrow$ $\mu = 3/4$

And $$\frac{CA_0}{A_0F}=\frac{\sqrt{\left(\frac{25}{7}-4\right)^2\left(\frac{9}{7}-2\right)^2+\left(\frac{17}{7}-3\right)^2}}{\sqrt{\left(3-\frac{25}{7}\right)^2+\left(\frac{1}{3}-\frac{9}{7}\right)^2+\left(\frac{5}{3}-\frac{17}{7}\right)^2}}$$

$$=\frac{\sqrt{9+25+16\times3}}{\sqrt{9\times16+400+256}}=\frac{3}{4}$$

$\Rightarrow$ $v = 3/4$

$$\therefore\ \frac{\lambda\mu+\mu v+v\lambda}{\lambda\mu v}=\frac{3\times(9/16)}{27/64}=\frac{27}{16}\times\frac{64}{27}=4$$

TEXTUAL EXERCISE 1: (OBJECTIVE)

1. (d) P.V. of $x=\frac{\vec{a}+2\vec{b}}{3}$ P.V of $y=\frac{2\vec{b}-\vec{a}}{1}$

$\overrightarrow{XY}=2\vec{b}-\vec{a}-\frac{a+2b}{3}=\frac{4\vec{b}}{3}-\frac{4}{3}\vec{a}=\frac{4}{3}(\vec{b}-\vec{a})$

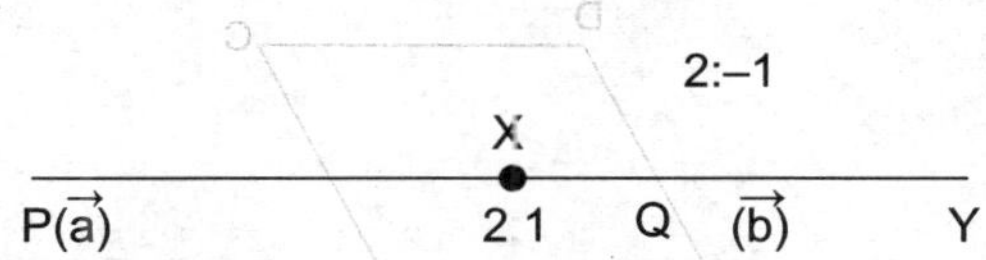

2. (d) Let P.V. of $A(\vec{a}), B(\vec{b}), C(\vec{c})$,

$A'(\vec{a}_1), B(\vec{b}_1), C(\vec{c}_1)$

Now P.V.of $G=\frac{\vec{a}+\vec{b}+\vec{c}}{3}$; Similarly $G'=\frac{\vec{a}_1+\vec{b}_1+\vec{c}_1}{3}$

Now $\overrightarrow{AA'}=\vec{a}_1-\vec{a}, \overrightarrow{BB'}=\vec{b}_1-\vec{b}, \overrightarrow{CC'}=\vec{c}_1-\vec{c}$

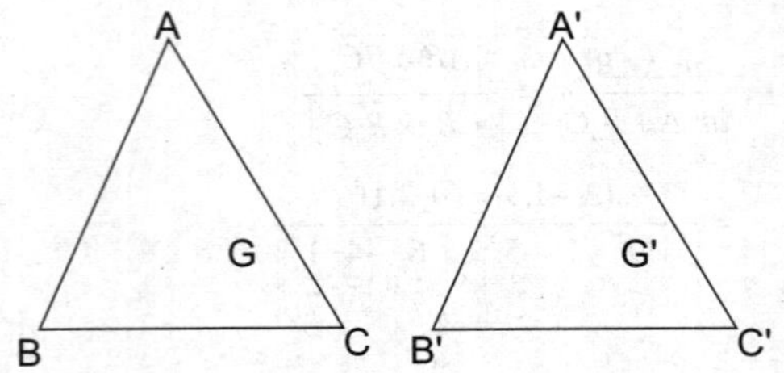

So $\overline{AA'}+\overline{BB'}+\overline{CC'}=(a_1+b_1+\vec{c}_1)-(\vec{a}+b+\vec{c})$

$$= 3\left\{\frac{a_1+b_1+c_1}{3}-\frac{a_1+b_1+c_1}{3}\right\}=3\overline{GG'}$$

3. (c) $A(\vec{a}), B(\vec{b}), C(\vec{c})$ are the vertices of the ΔABC. Circum-centre is at origin. $G(\vec{g})=\dfrac{\vec{a}+\vec{b}+\vec{c}}{3}$

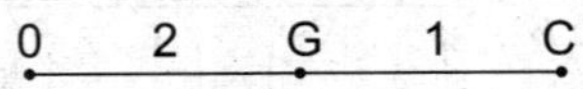

$$G=\frac{2\vec{c}+\vec{O}}{3}\Rightarrow \vec{O}=3\vec{G}$$

$$\Rightarrow \quad \vec{O}=3\left(\frac{\vec{a}+\vec{b}+\vec{c}}{3}\right)=\vec{a}+\vec{b}+\vec{c}$$

4. (b) $\overline{OP}=P.V.of\ P=\dfrac{m\vec{b}+n\vec{a}}{m+n}$

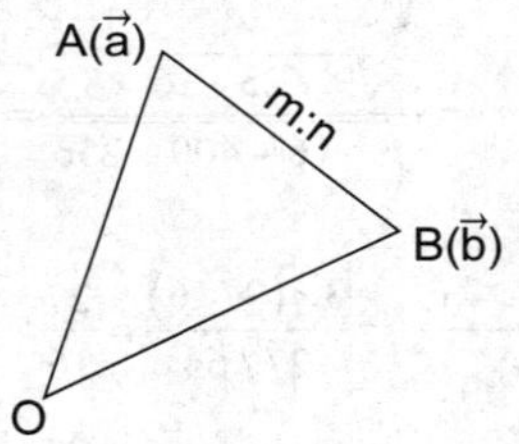

Remember, here O is assumed to be the origin

5. (b) Let $A(\vec{a})=\hat{i}+\hat{j}+\hat{k}$

$B(\vec{b})=\hat{i}+3\hat{j}+5\hat{k}$

$C(\vec{c})=7\hat{i}+9\hat{j}+11\hat{k}$

$D(\vec{d})$ is to be determined

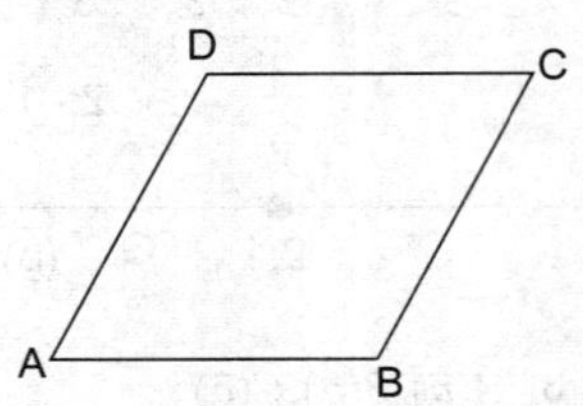

ABCD is a || gm so $\frac{1}{2}\{\vec{b}+\vec{d}\}=\frac{1}{2}\{\vec{a}+\vec{c}\}$

$\vec{d}=\vec{a}+\vec{c}-\vec{b}=8\hat{i}+10\hat{j}+12\hat{k}-(\hat{i}+3j+5\hat{k})$

$= 7\hat{j}+7\hat{j}+7\hat{k}=7(\hat{i}+\hat{j}+\hat{k})$

6. (c) $\overline{AB}=3\hat{i}+\hat{j}-\hat{k}$; $\overline{AC}=\hat{i}-\hat{j}+3\hat{k}$

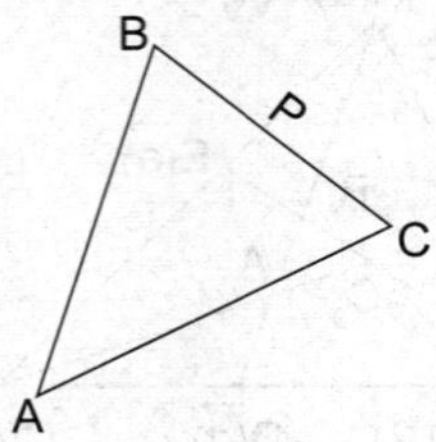

Observe that $AB=AC=\sqrt{11}$ units

$\therefore$ ΔABC is isosceles P is the mid pt of BC (treating A as origin) $\bar{p}=\frac{1}{2}\{4\hat{i}+2\hat{k}\}=2\hat{i}+\hat{k}$

TEXTUAL EXERCISE 5: SUBJECTIVE

1. $LHS=(x+3y-4z)\hat{i}+(x+3y+5z)\hat{j}+(3x+y)\hat{k}$

and $RHS=\lambda(x\hat{i}+y\hat{j}+z\hat{k})$

Now $\left.\begin{aligned} x+3y-4z&=\lambda x\\ x+3y+5z&=\lambda y\\ 3x+y\quad &=\lambda z\end{aligned}\right\}$

$\Rightarrow$ $-9z=\lambda(x-y)$ as $(x, y, z)\neq(0,0,0)$

So $\begin{vmatrix}(1-\lambda) & 3 & -4\\ 1 & 3-\lambda & 5\\ 3 & 1 & -\lambda\end{vmatrix}=0$

$\Rightarrow$ $(-\lambda^3+4\lambda^2+2\lambda-5)+(3\lambda+45)+(32-12\lambda)$

$=-\lambda^3+4\lambda^2-7\lambda+72=0$

2. $\vec{a}=3\hat{i}+4\hat{j}-2\hat{k}\Rightarrow \hat{a}=\frac{1}{\sqrt{29}}\{3\hat{i}+4\hat{j}-2\hat{k}\}$

Now $\hat{i}=\hat{a}+\vec{b}$ so $\vec{b}=\hat{i}-\hat{a}$

$\Rightarrow$ $\vec{b}=\hat{i}-\frac{1}{\sqrt{29}}\{3\hat{i}+4\hat{j}-2\hat{k}\}$

3. $(x-1)\,\vec{a}+\vec{b}$ and $(2+3x)\vec{a}-2\vec{b}$

are collinear $\Rightarrow \dfrac{x-1}{2+3x}=\dfrac{1}{-2}$; So $3x+2=2-2x\Rightarrow x=0$

4. Since $3\vec{a}+2\vec{c}-5\vec{b}=0$

$\Rightarrow$ $\vec{b}=\dfrac{3\vec{a}+2\vec{c}}{(3+2)}\Rightarrow B$ divides AC in the ratio 2 : 3

$\Rightarrow$ Points A, B, C are collinear and $AB : BC = 2 : 3$

5. $A(\vec{a}), B(\vec{b}), C(\vec{c})$ are collinear

And $\ell\vec{a}+m\vec{b}+n\vec{c}=\vec{o}\Rightarrow -m\vec{b}=\ell\vec{a}+n\vec{c}$

B divides AC in the ratio $n : \ell$

So $\vec{b}=\dfrac{\ell\vec{a}+n\vec{c}}{\ell+n}\Rightarrow -m=\ell+n$, so $\dfrac{\ell+n}{+m}=-1$

6. Since $\vec{a}$ and $\vec{b}$ are not collinear

$\therefore$ $(1+2h-k)\vec{a}+(2-h+2k)\vec{b}=\vec{o}$

Gives $1 + 2h - k = 0$ and $2 - h + 2k = 0 \Rightarrow 2k = h + 2$

$\therefore\ k = 2h + 1 \Rightarrow 2k = 4h + 2 = h - 2$

gives $h = -4/3$ and $k = -5/3$

7. $\vec{a} + 2\vec{b} = p\vec{c}$ and $\vec{b} + 3\vec{c} = q\vec{a}$ shows that these vectors are coplanar.

$\Rightarrow\ \vec{a} + 2\vec{b} - p\vec{c} = \vec{o}$ and $q\vec{a} - \vec{b} - 3\vec{c} = \vec{o}$

gives $\frac{q}{1} = \frac{-1}{2} = \frac{3}{p} \Rightarrow q = -\frac{1}{2}$ and $p = -6$ so $\vec{a} + 2\vec{b} + 6\vec{c} = \vec{o}$

8. $\vec{\alpha} = 2\hat{i} - \hat{j} + \hat{k}$ gives $|\vec{\alpha}| = \sqrt{6}$ since $|\vec{\beta}| = 4$

So $\beta = \pm\frac{4}{\sqrt{6}}\{2\hat{i} - \hat{j} + \hat{k}\}$

9. $\overline{DB} = \vec{a} = \hat{i} - j + \hat{k}$; $\overline{AC} = b = 3\hat{i} + 3\hat{j} - 5\hat{k}$

$\overline{BC} = \frac{1}{2}\left(\overline{AC} - \overline{DB}\right) = \hat{i} + 2\hat{j} - 3\hat{k}$

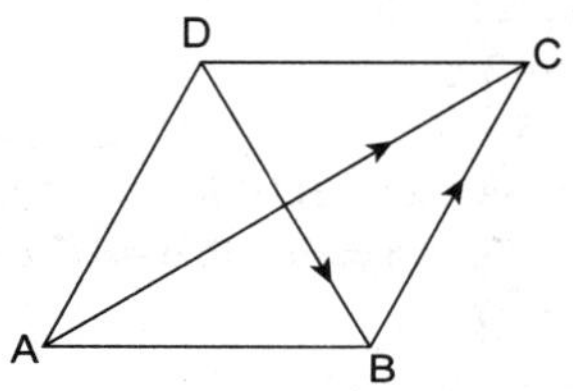

$\left|\overline{BC}\right| = \sqrt{14}$. Now a vector $\vec{\beta}$ collinear with $\overline{BC}$ and having a magnitude of 4 units is $\vec{\beta} = \frac{\pm 4}{\sqrt{14}}\{\hat{i} + 2\hat{j} - 3\hat{k}\}$

TEXTUAL EXERCISE 2: (OBJECTIVE)

1. (c) $\vec{a}$ and $\vec{b}$ are non-zero and non-collinear

$\vec{C} = (x-2)\vec{a} + \vec{b}$ and $\vec{d} = (2x+1)\vec{a} - \vec{b}$ are collinear

So $2x + 1 = 2 - x \Rightarrow x = 1/3$

2. (a) $\vec{a} = x\hat{i} - 2\hat{j} + 5\hat{k}$ and $\vec{b} = \hat{i} + y\hat{j} - 2\hat{k}$ are

Collinear $\Rightarrow \frac{x}{1} = \frac{2}{y} = \frac{5}{-2} \Rightarrow x = -\frac{5}{2}, y = -\frac{4}{5}$

3. (a,b,c,d) $\vec{a} = x\hat{i} - 2\hat{j} + 5\hat{k}$ and $\vec{b} = \hat{i} + y\hat{j} - z\hat{k}$

Are collinear $\frac{x}{1} = \frac{-2}{y} = \frac{5}{-z}$

$\Rightarrow$ for $x = k$, $y = -\frac{2}{k}$ and $z = \frac{-5}{k}$

for $x = 1, y = -2, z = -5$

for $x = 1/2, y = -4, z = -10$

for $x = -1/2$, $y = 4$, $z = 10$

for $x = -1, y = 2, z = 5$

4. (a) $\vec{a} = \hat{i} - \hat{j}$ and $\vec{b} = -2\hat{i} + kj$ are collinear

$\Rightarrow\ \frac{1}{-2} = \frac{-1}{k} \Rightarrow k = 2$

5. (c) $\vec{a}$ and $\vec{b}$ are two non-collinear vectors and $x\vec{a} + y\vec{b} = \vec{o}$

$\Rightarrow\ x = 0, y = 0$

6. (a) $\overline{BC} = \lambda\overline{AD}$; $\overline{AC} + \overline{BD} = \vec{p}$ is collinear with $\overline{AD} \Rightarrow \overline{AD} + \overline{DC} + \overline{BC} + \overline{CD} = p$

$\overline{AD} + \lambda\overline{AD} = \vec{p} \Rightarrow \vec{p} = (1+\lambda)\overline{AD} = \mu\overline{AD} \Rightarrow (1 + \lambda) = \mu$

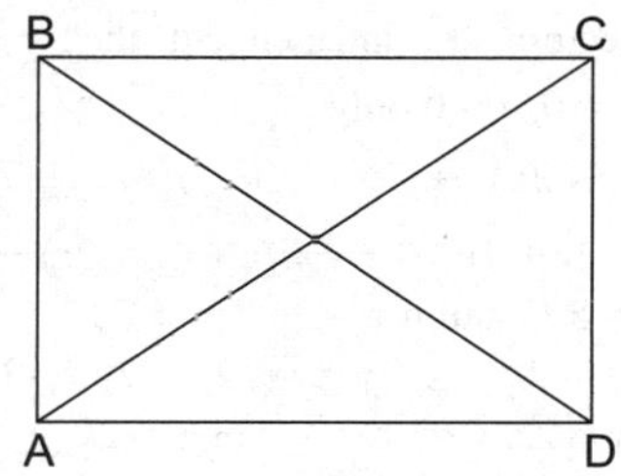

7. (a) Let A be the origin then $\overline{AO} = \frac{\vec{a} + \vec{b}}{2}$, So $\overline{AM} = \frac{\vec{a} + \vec{b}}{4}$

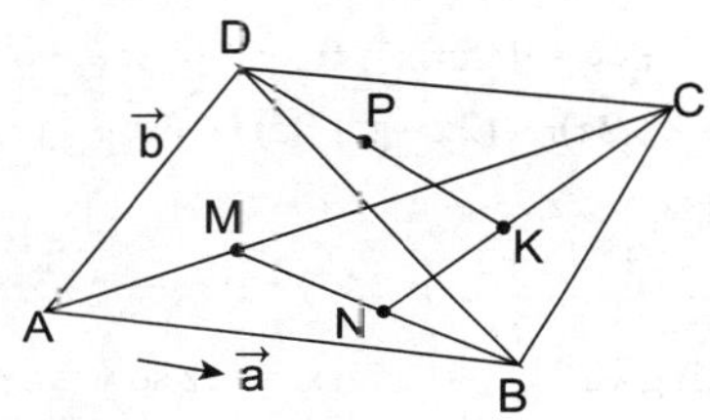

P.V. of $N = \frac{1}{2}\left\{\frac{\vec{a} + \vec{b}}{4} + \vec{a}\right\} = \frac{5\vec{a} + \vec{b}}{8}$

P.V. of $K = \frac{1}{2}\left\{\frac{5\vec{a} + \vec{b}}{8} + \vec{a} + \vec{b}\right\} = \frac{13\vec{a} + 9\vec{b}}{16}$

P.V. of $P = \frac{1}{2}\left\{\frac{13\vec{a} + 9\vec{b}}{16} + \vec{b}\right\} = \frac{13\vec{a} + 25\vec{b}}{32}$

Checking: $\overline{ON} = \frac{5\vec{a} - \vec{b}}{8} - \frac{\vec{a} + \vec{b}}{2} = \frac{\vec{a} - 3\vec{b}}{8}$

$\overline{OP} = \frac{13\vec{a} + 25\vec{b}}{32} - \frac{\vec{a} + \vec{b}}{2} = \frac{-3\vec{a} + 9\vec{b}}{32} = \left(\frac{-3}{32}\right)\{\vec{a} - 3\vec{b}\}$

Hence we can write $\frac{3}{4}[\overline{ON}] + \overline{OP} = O$:

$\Rightarrow\ \overline{ON}$ and $\overline{OP}$ are collinear.

TEXTUAL EXERCISE 6: SUBJECTIVE

1. Let Points A,B,C,D be the point given by these vectors

$\overline{AB} = (\vec{a} - 2\vec{b} + 3\vec{c}) - (2\vec{a} + 3\vec{b} - \vec{c}) = -\vec{a} - 5\vec{b} + 4\vec{c}$

$\overline{BC} = (3\vec{a} + 4\vec{b} - 2\vec{c}) - (\vec{a} - 2\vec{b} + 3\vec{c}) = 2\vec{a} + 6\vec{b} - 5\vec{c}$

$\overline{CD} = (\vec{a} - 6\vec{b} + 6\vec{c}) - (3\vec{a} + 4\vec{b} - 2\vec{c}) = -2\vec{a} - 10\vec{b} + 8\vec{c}$

(Observe that $\overline{CD} = 2\overline{AB}$ and two vectors are always in same plane

If these vectors are coplanar then

$$\begin{vmatrix} -1 & -5 & 4 \\ 2 & 6 & 5 \\ -2 & -10 & 8 \end{vmatrix} = 0 \text{ since } 2R_1 = R_2$$

Hence these points are coplanar

2. **(a)** Let $\vec{a} = \hat{i} - \hat{j} + 2\hat{k}, \vec{b} = 4\hat{i} - \hat{j} + 7\hat{k}$ and $\vec{c} = 2\hat{i} + \hat{j} + 3\hat{k}$

If these vectors are independent then $x\vec{a} + y\vec{b} + z\vec{c} = \vec{0}$ for x = 0, y = 0, z = 0 only

i.e., $(x + 4y + 2z)\,\hat{i} + (-x - y + z)\hat{j} + (2x + 7y + 3z)k = \vec{0}$

Solving for 2x + 7y + 3z = m(x + 4y + 2z) + n(–x – y + z)

We get m = 5 /3 and n = –1/3

$\Rightarrow$ x + 4y = –2z ; –x – y = –z; 2x + 7y = –3z

gives x = 2z, y = –z, z = z or x = 2k, y = –k, z = k

so these vectors are dependent linearly

(b) Let $\vec{a} = \hat{i} + 2\hat{j} + 3\hat{k}, \vec{b} = \hat{i} - \hat{j} + 4\hat{k}$,

$\vec{c} = 2\hat{i} + 7\hat{j} - \hat{k}$. These vector will be independent

If $x\vec{a} + y\vec{b} + z\vec{c} = \vec{0}$ for x = 0 , y = 0 , z = 0 only

i.e., $(x + y + 2z)\hat{i} + (2x - y + 7z)\hat{j} + (3x + 4y - z)\hat{k} = \vec{0}$

gives x + y = –2z ..... (I),

2x – y = – 7z ... (II)

3x + 4y = z ...(iii)

(i) and (ii) give 3x = – 9z i.e x = –3z so y = z putting in (iii)

LHS = –9z + 4z = 5z ≠ z ⇒ z = 0 so x = 0 , y = 0

Hence independent linearly

3. Let $A(\vec{a}) = \alpha\hat{i} + \beta\hat{j} + \gamma\hat{k}, B(\vec{b}) = \beta\hat{i} + \gamma\hat{j} + \alpha\hat{k}$

$C(\vec{c}) = \gamma\hat{i} + \alpha\hat{j} + \beta - \hat{k}$ where α,β,γ are distinct real numbers, consider $x\vec{a} + y\vec{b} + z\vec{c} = \vec{0}$

Which gives

$(x\alpha + y\beta + z\gamma)\hat{i} + (x\beta + y\gamma + z\alpha)\hat{j} + (x\gamma + y\alpha + z\beta)\hat{k} = \vec{0}$

$$\begin{vmatrix} \alpha & \beta & \gamma \\ \beta & \gamma & \alpha \\ \gamma & \alpha & \beta \end{vmatrix} = -\frac{1}{2}\{(\alpha-\beta)^2 + (\beta-\gamma)^2 + (\gamma-\alpha)^2\}(\alpha+\beta+\gamma)$$

Since α,β,γ are distinct so α + β + γ = 0 gives

$\vec{a} + \vec{b} + \vec{c} = \vec{0}$ which shows that these pts are coplanar (But not collinear).

In that case $|\vec{a}| = \sqrt{\alpha^2 + \beta^2 + (\alpha+\beta)^2}$

$= \sqrt{2(\alpha^2 + \beta^2 + \alpha\beta)} = |\vec{b}| = |\vec{c}|$

So an equilateral Δ is formed with side

$|a| = \sqrt{2(\alpha^2 + \beta^2 + \alpha\beta)}$

These points will be collinear when α = β = γ ≠ 0 then $\vec{a} = \vec{b} = \vec{c} \neq \vec{0}$ also when α = β = γ = 0 then $\vec{a} = \vec{b} = \vec{c} = \vec{0}$ and these points converge into one point.

4. $\vec{a}, \vec{b}, \vec{c}$ are non zero and non-collinear so let $\vec{a} + \vec{b} = p\vec{c}$ and $\vec{b} + \vec{c} = q\vec{a}$

$\Rightarrow$ $q\vec{a} + q\vec{b} = pq\vec{c}$ or $\vec{b} + \vec{c} + q\vec{b} = pq\vec{c}$

i.e., $(q+1)\vec{b} = (pq-1)\vec{c}$ Since $\vec{b}$ and $\vec{c}$ are not collinear

∴ q = –1, pq = 1 so p = –1, i.e., $\vec{a} + \vec{b} + \vec{c} = \vec{0}$

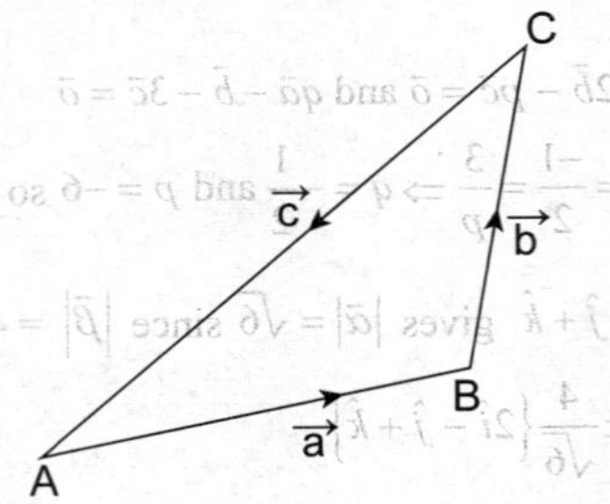

5. $\vec{r_4} = a\vec{r_1} + b\vec{r_2} + c\vec{r_3}$, Now $3\hat{i} - 2\hat{j} + 5\hat{k} = (2a + b - 2c)\hat{i} + (-a + 3b + c)\hat{j} + (a - 2b - 3c)\hat{k}$

Gives 2a + b – 2c = 3 ....(i)

–a + 3b + c = –2 ....(ii)

a – 2b – 3c = 5 ....(iii)

(i) – (ii) gives 3a – 2b – 3c = 5

(iii) is a – 2b – 3c = 5 ⇒ a = 0, b = 1/7 c = –11/7

(c – 11b = 0 = a)

6. $\vec{a} = \hat{i} + \hat{j} + \hat{k}, \vec{b} = 4\hat{i} + 3\hat{j} + 4\hat{i}$

$\vec{c} = \hat{i} + \alpha\hat{j} + \beta\hat{k}$ since $|\vec{c}| = \sqrt{3}$ i.e $\alpha^2 + \beta^2 + 1 = 3$

$\alpha^2 + \beta^2 = 2$ and $\ell\vec{a} + m\vec{b} = \vec{c}$

Gives $(\ell + 4m)\hat{i} + (\ell + 3m)\hat{j} + (\ell + 4m)\hat{k} = \hat{i} + \alpha\hat{j} + \beta\hat{k}$

so ℓ + 4m = 1

∴ β = 1 putting in $\alpha^2 + \beta^2 = 2$ gives α = ± 1 for β = 1

7. P.V. of $A = \vec{a}, B = 2\vec{a} + \vec{b}, C = 4\vec{a} + 2\vec{b}, D = 5\vec{a} + 4\vec{b}$

Note that $\overrightarrow{AB} = \vec{a} + \vec{b}$ and

$\overrightarrow{AB} = \vec{a} + \vec{b}, \overrightarrow{BC} = 2\vec{a} + \vec{b}, \overrightarrow{BD} = 3\vec{a} + 3\vec{b}$

$\overrightarrow{AC} = 3\vec{a} + 2\vec{b}, \overrightarrow{CD} = \vec{a} + 2\vec{b}$ $\overrightarrow{BD} = 3(\vec{a} + \vec{b}) = 3\overrightarrow{AB}$

So B, A, D are collinear

TEXTUAL EXERCISE 3: (OBJECTIVE)

1. **(a, d)** By the question,

$\overrightarrow{AB} = -\hat{i} - 4\hat{j} - \hat{k}, \overrightarrow{AC} = \hat{i} - \hat{j} - \hat{k}, \overrightarrow{BC} = 2\hat{i} + 3\hat{j}$

$\overrightarrow{AD} = -\hat{i} - 9\hat{j} - 3\hat{k}, \overrightarrow{BD} = -5\hat{j} - 2\hat{k}, \overrightarrow{CD} = -2\hat{i} - 8\hat{j} - 2\hat{k}$

We observe that $\overrightarrow{CD} = 2\overrightarrow{AB}$

$\Rightarrow$ $|AB| = \frac{1}{2}|CD|$ and $AB \parallel CD$

2. **(b, d)** A(1,–2,3), B(2–3,4), C(6–7,8)

so $\overrightarrow{AB} = \hat{i} - \hat{j} + \hat{k}$

and $\overrightarrow{BC} = 4\hat{i} - 4\hat{j} + 4\hat{k} = 4\overrightarrow{AB}$

∴ A, B, C are collinear hence are linearly dependent

3. (b, d) A(–1,2,1),B(2,–3,1), C(2,1,3)

$\overline{AB} = 3\hat i - 5\hat j$, $\overline{BC} = 4\hat j + 2\hat k$

$\overline{AC} = 3\hat i - \hat j + 2\hat k, |AB| = \sqrt{34}, BC = \sqrt{20}, |AC| = \sqrt{14}$

so $\overline{AB} \neq k\,\overline{BC}$

$\therefore$ These points are not collinear. Hence the vectors $\left(\overline{AB} \text{ and } \overline{BC}\right)$ are linearly independent vectors

4. (b, c, d) $\vec a = \hat i + 2\hat j - 3\hat k$; $\vec b = 2\hat i - \hat j + \hat k$; $\vec c = 3\hat i + 2\hat j + \lambda \hat k$

Consider $\vec c = \ell\vec a + m\vec b$

So $3\hat i + 2\hat j + \lambda\hat k = (\ell + 2m)\hat i + (2\ell - m)\hat j + (-3\ell + m)\hat k$

$\Rightarrow \ell + 2m = 3, 2\ell - m = 2$ or $4\ell - 2m = 4$

$\Rightarrow \ell = 7/5$, m = 4/5 and $\lambda = m - 3\ell = \frac{4}{5} - \frac{21}{5} = -\frac{17}{5}$

If $\lambda = -\frac{17}{15}$ then these vectors are linearly dependent

For $\lambda = \frac{-27}{5}$ these vectors will be linearly independent

obviously they are not collinear for $\lambda = -\frac{27}{5}$

5. (c) $\vec b = 2\hat i - \hat j + 4\hat k$ so $|\vec b| = \sqrt{21}$; $|\vec a| = 5 \Rightarrow \vec a = \frac{5}{21}(\vec b)$

Since $\vec a$ make obtuse $\angle$ with +ive direction of z axis

$\therefore \quad \vec a = -\frac{5}{\sqrt{21}}\vec b$

6. (a, c) $A(\vec a), B(\vec b), C(\vec c)$ are collinear point $\therefore\ \vec a, \vec b, \vec c$ a are coplanar vectors Hence they are linearly dependent also

TEXTUAL EXERCISE 7: (SUBJECTIVE)

1. $(\vec a + \lambda\vec b) = (\hat i + 2\hat j + \hat k) + \lambda(-\hat i - 3\hat j + \hat k)$

$= (1-\lambda)\hat i + (2 - 3\lambda)\hat j + (1+\lambda)\hat k$

$(\vec a + \lambda\vec b) \perp \vec c \Rightarrow (\vec a + \lambda\vec b).\vec c = 0$

i.e. $\{(1-\lambda)\hat i + (2 - 3\hat i)\hat j + (1+\lambda)\hat k\}.\{2\hat i + 3\hat j\} = 0$

$\Rightarrow$ 2 –2λ + 6 – 9λ = 0 gives λ = 8/11

2. $\vec a = 2\hat i + \hat j - 3\hat k$ and $\vec b = 3\hat i - 2\hat j - \hat k$

Let $\cos\theta = \frac{\vec a.\vec b}{|\vec a||\vec b|} = \frac{6 - 2 + 3}{\sqrt{14}\sqrt{14}} = \frac{7}{14} = \frac{1}{2} \Rightarrow \theta = \frac{\pi}{3} = 60^o$

3. $\vec a = 2\hat i + \hat j - \hat k \Rightarrow \vec a^2 = 6$

Let $\vec V = p\vec a$ and $\vec a.\vec v = 3$ so $p\vec a^2 = 6p = 3$ gives $p = \frac{1}{2}$

$\therefore \quad \vec v = \frac{1}{2}\vec a = \hat i + \frac{1}{2}j - \frac{1}{2}\hat k$

4. $\vec A + t\vec B = (1-t)\hat i + (2+2t)\hat j + (3+t)\hat k$

$\left(\vec A + t\vec B\right) \perp \vec C$ gives 3 – 3t + 2 + 2t = 0 ⇒ t = 5

5. $\vec a.\vec b = 1 - 6x^2 - 6y^2 = 0$ {orthogonal vectors}

Gives $6(x^2 + y^2) = 1$ or $x^2 + y^2 = 1/6$ which is circle centered at origin having radius = $\frac{1}{\sqrt 6}$

6. Let $\vec x = p\vec b + q\vec a$; $\vec x \perp \vec b = \vec b.(p\vec b + q\vec a) = p\vec b^2 + q\vec a.\vec b = 0$

Or $5p - q = 0$

Now $\vec x.\vec a = (p\vec b + q\vec a).\vec a = p\vec a.\vec b + q\vec a^2 = 7$

Or $3q - p = 7$ and $5p - q = 0 \Rightarrow p = 1/2, q = 5/2$

$\vec x = \frac{1}{2}\{2\hat i + \hat k\} + \frac{5}{2}\{-\hat i + \hat j + \hat k\} = -\frac{3}{2}\hat i + \frac{5}{2}\hat j + 3\hat k$

7. $\vec A = 3\hat i - \hat j + 5\hat k$, $\vec B = \hat i + 2\hat j - 3\hat k$

As stated $\vec C \perp z-axis \Rightarrow \vec c = x\hat i + y\hat j$

$\left.\begin{array}{l}\vec C.\vec A = 9 \Rightarrow 3x - y = 9\\ \vec C.\vec B = -4 \Rightarrow x + 2y = -4\end{array}\right]$ gives x = 2, y = –3

$\therefore \quad \vec c = 2\hat i - 3\hat j$

8. Let $D(x, y, z)$, then mid point of BD = mid pt of AC

$(1, -1, 1) = \left(\frac{3+x}{2}, \frac{-3+y}{2}, \frac{1+z}{2}\right)$

Gives $x = -1, y = 1, z = 1 \Rightarrow D(-1,1,1)$

$\overline{AC} = 8\hat i + 2\hat j + 2\hat k$, $\overline{BD} = -4\hat i + 4\hat j + 0\hat k$

$\cos\theta = \frac{\overline{AC}.\overline{BD}}{\left|\overline{AC}\right|\left|\overline{BD}\right|} = \frac{-32 + 8}{\sqrt{72}\sqrt{32}} = \frac{-24}{6.\sqrt2.4\sqrt2} = \frac{1}{2}$

$\therefore \quad \theta = 120^0$ or $\frac{2\pi}{3}$

9. Given $|\vec e_1| = |\vec e_2| = |\vec e_1 - \vec e_2| = 1$

Squaring $\vec e_1^2 = \vec e_2^2 = \vec e_1^2 + \vec e_2^2 - 2\vec e_1.\vec e_2 = 1$

$\Rightarrow \quad \vec e_1.\vec e_2 = \frac{1}{2} \Rightarrow \cos\theta = \frac{1}{2}$ hence $\theta = \frac{\pi}{3} = 60°$

10. Length of projection of $a = \hat i - 2\hat j + \hat k$ on $b = 4\hat i - 4\hat j + 7\hat k$

$= \left(\frac{\vec a.\vec b}{|\vec b|}\right) = \frac{4 + 8 + 7}{\sqrt{81}} = \frac{19}{\sqrt{81}} = \frac{19}{9}$ **Units**

11. $\vec F = \hat i + 3\hat j + 5\hat k$; $\vec D = 2\hat i + 4\hat j - \hat k$

$w = \vec F.\vec D = 2 + 12 - 5 = 9$ units of work

TEXTUAL EXERCISE 4: (OBJECTIVE)

1. (b) Given $|\vec a - \vec b| = 8$, $|\vec a + \vec b| = 10, |\vec a| = 5$

Squaring and adding $2(a^2 + b^2) = 164$

$2b^2 = 164 - 50 = 114 \Rightarrow |\vec b| = \sqrt{57}$

2. **(b)** Component of $\vec{a} = 4\hat{i} + 6\hat{j}$ along $\vec{b} = 3\hat{j} + 4\hat{k} = \{\hat{a}.\hat{b}\}.\hat{b}$

$$= \left(\frac{\vec{a}.\vec{b}}{b^2}\right)\vec{b} = \frac{18}{25}(3\hat{j} + 4\hat{k})$$

3. **(b)** $\vec{a} = 2\hat{i} - 3\hat{j} + 6\hat{k}, \vec{b} = -2\hat{i} + 2\hat{j} - \hat{k}$

Now $$\frac{\text{Projection vector } \vec{a} \text{ on } \vec{b}}{\text{Projection of } \vec{b} \text{ on } \vec{a}} = \frac{\dfrac{\vec{a}.\vec{b}}{|\vec{b}|}}{\dfrac{\vec{a}.\vec{b}}{|\vec{a}|}} = \frac{|\vec{a}|}{|\vec{b}|} = \frac{7}{3}$$

4. **(c)** $(\vec{a} + 3\vec{b}) \perp (7\vec{a} - 5\vec{b}) \Rightarrow 7a^2 - 15b^2 + 16\vec{a}.\vec{b} = 0$

$(\vec{a} - 4\vec{b}) \perp (7\vec{a} - 2\vec{b})$

$\Rightarrow \; 7a^2 + 8b^2 - 30\vec{a}.\vec{b} = 0$

Subtraction gives $-23b^2 + 46\vec{a}.\vec{b} = 0$ or $2\vec{a}.\vec{b}$

Putting in any one equation $a^2 = 2\vec{a}.\vec{b}$

So $|\vec{a}| = |\vec{b}| \Rightarrow |\vec{a}||\vec{a}| = 2\vec{a}.\vec{b}$ or $|\vec{a}||\vec{b}| = 2\vec{a}.\vec{b}$

Now $\cos\theta^o = \dfrac{\vec{a}.\vec{b}}{|\vec{a}||\vec{b}|} = \dfrac{1}{2} \Rightarrow \theta = \dfrac{\pi}{3} = 60^o$

5. **(d)** $\dfrac{|\vec{b}|}{|\vec{a}|} = \tan 30^\circ = \dfrac{1}{\sqrt{3}} \Rightarrow |\vec{a}| = \sqrt{3}|\vec{b}|$

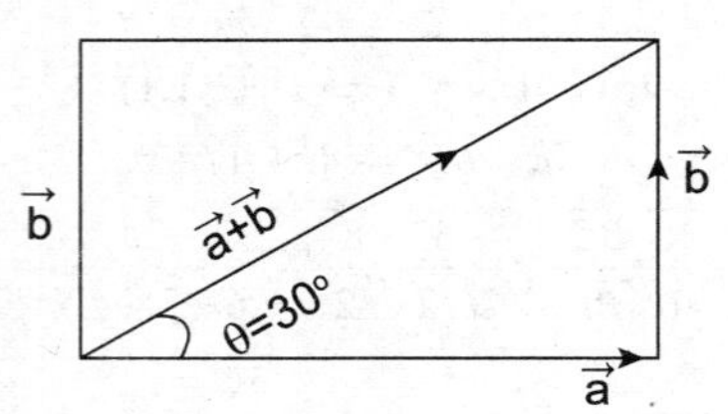

Aliter: $\vec{a}.\vec{b} = 0 \Rightarrow \vec{a} \perp \vec{b}$

$\cos\theta = \dfrac{(\vec{a} + \vec{b})}{|\vec{a} + \vec{b}||\vec{a}|} = \dfrac{\sqrt{3}}{2}$ so $\vec{a}^2 + \vec{a}.\vec{b} = \dfrac{\sqrt{3}}{2}|\vec{a} + \vec{b}||\vec{a}|$

$\Rightarrow \; |\vec{a}||\vec{a}| = |\vec{a}||\vec{a} + \vec{b}|\dfrac{\sqrt{3}}{2}$ squaring $a^2 = \dfrac{3}{4}(a^2 + b^2 + 2\vec{a}.\vec{b})$

$a^2 = 3b^2 \; |\vec{a}| = \sqrt{3}|\vec{b}|$

6. **(a)** $\vec{F}_1 = 6 \text{ units} = 2(\hat{i} - 2\hat{j} + 2\hat{k})$

$\vec{F}_2 = 7$ units $= 2\hat{i} - 3\hat{j} - 6\hat{k}$

$\vec{D} = \overrightarrow{PQ} = 3\hat{i} + 4\hat{k}$

Work Done $= \vec{F}_1.\vec{D} + \vec{F}_2\vec{D}$

$= (4\hat{i} - 7\hat{j} - 2\hat{k}).(3\hat{i} + 4\hat{k}) = 12 - 8 = 4$ units

7. **(a)** $a = \hat{i} + \hat{j} + \hat{k} = \sqrt{3}$ units $\vec{a}.\vec{c} = |\vec{c}|, |\vec{a} + \vec{c}| = \sqrt{6}$

Squaring $a^2 + c^2 + 2\vec{a}.\vec{c} = 6$

So $c^2 + 2\vec{a}.\vec{b} = 3 \Rightarrow (|\vec{c}| - 1)(|\vec{c}| + 3) = 0$

Gives $|\vec{c}| = 1 \; \therefore \; \vec{a}.\vec{c} = 1$

8. **(c)** Let (origin) O be the Circumcentre of ΔABC and $A(\vec{a}), B(\vec{b}), C(\vec{c})$ lie

On a unit circle, Since $\vec{d} = \lambda(\vec{b} + \vec{c})$

Then $\vec{d}$ will be along the $\angle$ bisectors of $\overline{OB}$ and $\overline{OC}$

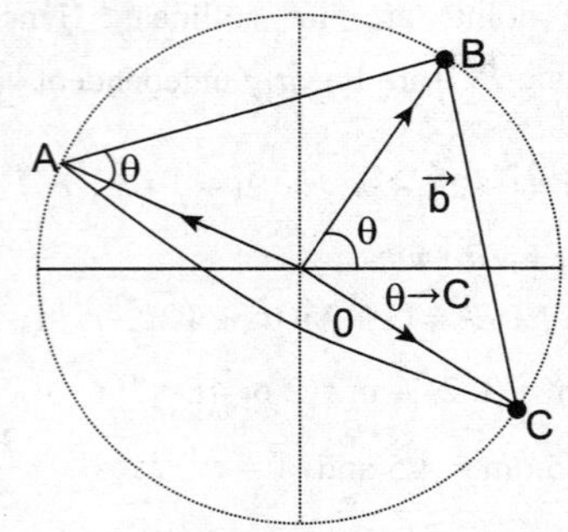

$\Rightarrow \; \vec{d}.\vec{b} = \vec{d}.\vec{c}$

But $\vec{d}.\vec{a}$ will vary depending upon the angle between $\vec{d}$ and $\vec{a}$ if $\vec{d} \neq \vec{O}$

$\Rightarrow \; \vec{d} = \vec{O}$ means $\vec{b} = -\vec{c}$ then $\vec{d}.\vec{a} = \vec{d}.\vec{b} = \vec{d}.\vec{c} = 0$

Now pt A may be anywhere on the circle {except pts B and C}

$\Rightarrow$ Right angled triangle

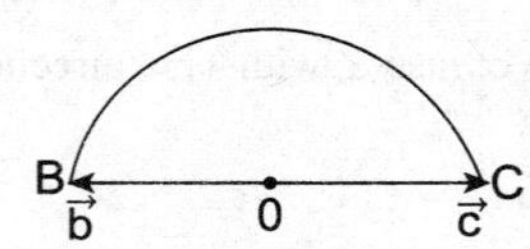

9. **(c)** Consider a regular tetrahedron of side √3

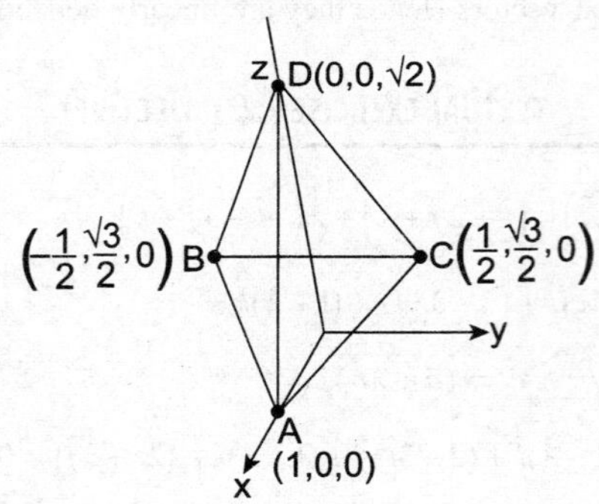

Top view

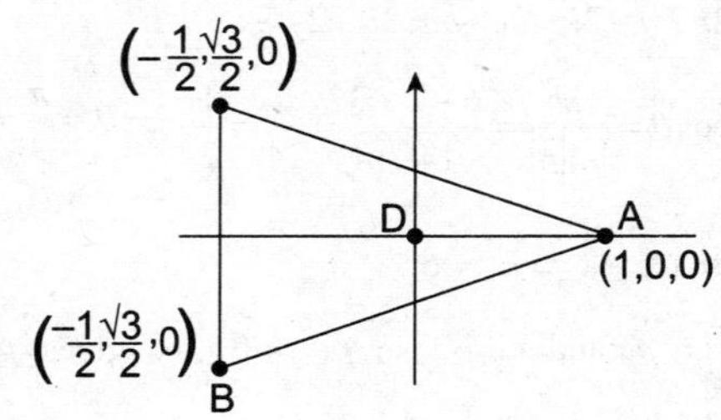

$\overline{BC} = \sqrt{3}\hat{j}, \; \overline{AD} = -\hat{i} + \sqrt{2}\hat{k},$

$\overrightarrow{BC}.\overrightarrow{AD} = (\sqrt{3}\hat{j}).(-\hat{i} + \sqrt{2}\hat{k}) = 0$,

$\overrightarrow{BC} \perp \overrightarrow{AD}$ Hence right $\angle$ ed

10. **(c)** For obtuse $\angle$ we get $(cx\hat{i} - 6\hat{j} + 3\hat{k}).(x\hat{i} + 2\hat{j} + 2cx\hat{k}) < 0$

i.e. $cx^2 - 12 + 6\,cx < 0$ for $x \in \mathbb{R}$

then $c < 0$ and $D < 0$ *i.e.*

$D = 36c^2 + 48c < 0 \Rightarrow 12c(3c + 4) < 0$

Since $c < 0$ so $3c + 4 > 0 \Rightarrow c > -4/3$

Hence $-4/3 < c < 0$

11. **(a)** Since all the options are of the form $p(-\hat{j} + \hat{k})$ so they are orthogonal to $\left(-2\hat{i} + \hat{j} + \hat{k}\right)$

Checking $p(-\hat{j} + \hat{k}).(\hat{i} - \hat{j} + \hat{k}) = 6\sqrt{3}$ gives $p_2 = 18$

$\Rightarrow$ p = 9 so $\vec{v} = 9(-\hat{j} + \hat{k})$

12. **(d)** The vectors will be orthogonal when $\{(x^2 - 1)\hat{i} + (x + 2)\hat{j} + x^2\hat{k}\}\ .\ \{2\hat{i} - x\hat{j} + 3\hat{k}\} = 0$

i.e. $2x^2 - 2 - x^2 - 2x + 3x^2 = 0$

Or $4x^2 - 2x - 2 = 0 \Rightarrow 2(x - 1)(2x + 1) = 0$, so $x = 1, -1/2$

13. (b)

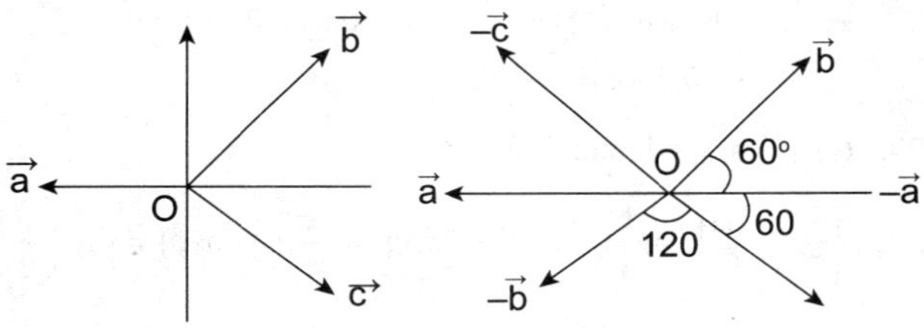

$|\hat{a} - \hat{b}|^2 + |\hat{b} - \hat{c}|^2 + |\hat{c} - \hat{a}|^2$ is

Maximum when they are at 120° to each other. Then

$|\hat{c} - \hat{a}| = |\hat{b} - \hat{c}| = |\hat{a} - \hat{b}| = \sqrt{3}$

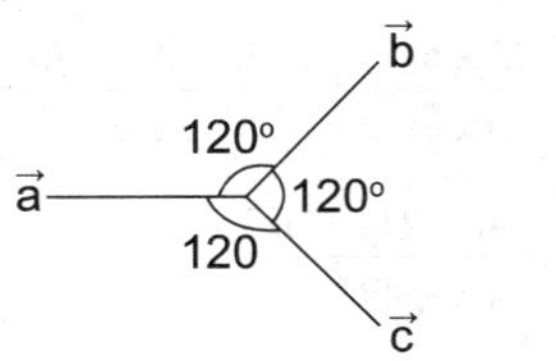

so maximum value = 3 + 3 + 3 = 9

14. **(b, c)** For acute $\angle$, $\vec{a}.\vec{b} > 0$

i.e. $2x^2 - 3x + 1 > 0$ or $(2x - 1)(x - 1) > 0$

So $x \in \left(-\infty, \frac{1}{2}\right) \cup (1, \infty)$

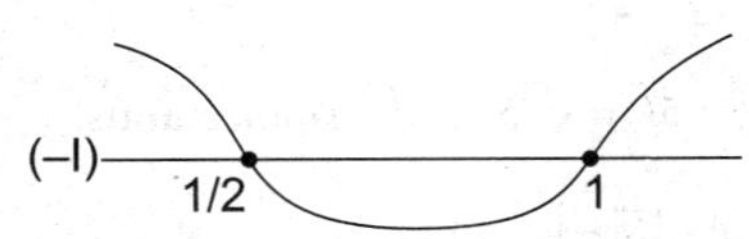

Axis of ordinates is y-axis

By the question $\vec{b}.\hat{j} < 0 \Rightarrow x < 0$

$x \in (-\infty, 0)$ i.e., $x < 0$

$-2, -3$ also belong to this interval

15. **(b, c, d)** The equation of line vector is

$\vec{r} = (2\hat{i} + 6\hat{j}) + \lambda(\hat{i} - 3\hat{j})$

Putting $\lambda = 1$, $\vec{r} = 3\hat{i} + 3\hat{j}$, Putting $\lambda = -1$ $\vec{r} = \hat{i} + 9\hat{j}$

Since $\vec{r}.\hat{k} = 0 \Rightarrow \hat{k} \perp xy$ plane so $\vec{r}$ is parallel to xy plane

16. **(a, c)** $\overrightarrow{AC} = \overrightarrow{AB} + \overrightarrow{BC} = 2\hat{i} - 2\hat{j}$

and $\overrightarrow{DB} = \overrightarrow{AB} - \overrightarrow{BC} = 4\hat{i} - 2\hat{j} + 4\hat{k}$ 6units

$\Rightarrow \quad |\cos\theta| = \left|\frac{\overrightarrow{AC}\,\overrightarrow{DB}}{|\overrightarrow{AC}||\overrightarrow{DB}|}\right| = \frac{12}{12\sqrt{2}} = \frac{1}{\sqrt{2}} \Rightarrow \theta = \frac{\pi}{4}\ or\ \frac{3\pi}{4}$

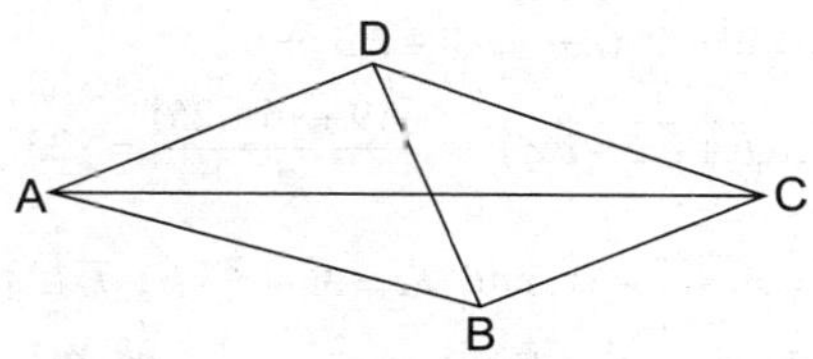

17. **(d)** $\vec{a} + \vec{b} = -\vec{c}$ squaring $a^2 + b^2 + 2\vec{a}.\vec{b} = c^2$

$9 + 25 + 2\vec{a}.\vec{b} = 49 \Rightarrow \vec{a}.\vec{b} = \frac{15}{2}$

$\cos\theta = \frac{\vec{a}.\vec{b}}{|\vec{a}|\,|\vec{b}|} = \frac{1}{2} \Rightarrow \theta = \frac{\pi}{3} = 60°$

18. **(b)** $\vec{c} = x\hat{i} + \hat{j} + 9\hat{k} \Rightarrow |\vec{c}| = \sqrt{2 + x^2}$

$\vec{d} = \hat{i} + x\hat{j} + \hat{k} \Rightarrow |\vec{d}| = \sqrt{x^2 + 2}$

$\cos\theta = \frac{\vec{c}.\vec{d}}{|\vec{c}|\,|\vec{b}|} = \frac{x + x + 1}{x^2 + 2} = \frac{1}{2} = 4x + 2 \Rightarrow x = 0, 4$

19. (b) Let the vector be $l\hat{i} + m\hat{j} + n\hat{k}$

By the question $2m - n = 0$, $-l + 2m - 3n = 0$, $l^2 + m^2 + n^2 = 1$ and since this vector makes an obtuse angle with y-axis

$\Rightarrow$ m < 0 $\quad \Rightarrow l\hat{i} - m\hat{j} + n\hat{k} = \frac{+4}{\sqrt{3}}\hat{i} - \frac{2}{\sqrt{3}}\hat{j} - \frac{2}{3}\hat{k}$

20. **(c)** $\overline{OC} = \hat{i} + \hat{j} + \hat{k}$; $\overline{AF} = -\hat{i} + \hat{j} + \hat{k}$

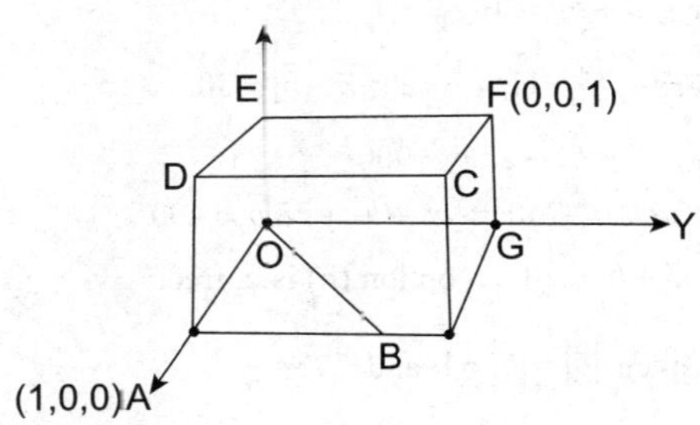

$\cos\theta = \frac{\overline{OC}\,\overline{AF}}{|\overline{OC}||\overline{AF}|} = \frac{1}{3}$; $\theta = \cos^{-1}\left(\frac{1}{3}\right)$

21. (d) $\vec{a} \perp \vec{b} \Rightarrow \vec{a}.\vec{b} = 0$

So $(\vec{a}+\vec{b})^2 = a^2 + b^2 = (\vec{a}-\vec{b})^2$

22. (c) $(\hat{i} - 2x\hat{j} + 3y\hat{k}).(\hat{i} + 2x\hat{j} + 3y\hat{k}) = 0$

$1 - 4x^2 + 9y^2 = 0$ or $4x^2 - 9y^2 = 1$

$\Rightarrow \dfrac{x^2}{\left(\frac{1}{2}\right)^2} - \dfrac{y^2}{\left(\frac{1}{3}\right)^2} = 1$ which is a hyperbola

23. (d) $(\vec{a}.\vec{b})\vec{c}$ is a vector in the direction $\vec{c}$ and $(\vec{a}.\vec{c})\vec{b}$ is a vector in the direction of $\vec{b}$

24. (d) $(\vec{a}+\vec{b}+\vec{c}) = \vec{0}$ squaring

$a^2 + b^2 + c^2 + 2\,(\vec{a}.\vec{b} + \vec{b}.\vec{c} + \vec{c}.\vec{a}) = 0$

gives $(\vec{a}.\vec{b} + \vec{b}.\vec{c} + \vec{c}.\vec{a}) = \dfrac{-(9+16+25)}{2} = -25$

25. (c) $\vec{F}_1 = 4\hat{i} + \hat{j} - 3\hat{k}$ **and** $\vec{F}_2 = 3\hat{i} + \hat{j} - \hat{k}$; $\vec{D} = 4\hat{i} + 2\hat{j} - 2\hat{k}$

Work done = $(\vec{F}_1 + \vec{F}_2).\vec{D} = (7\hat{i} + 2\hat{j} - 4\hat{k}).(4\hat{i} + 2\hat{j} - 2\hat{k})$

28 + 4 + 8 = 40 units

26. (b) $\vec{a}\times\vec{b} = \begin{vmatrix} \hat{i} & \hat{j} & \hat{k} \\ 1 & 1 & 0 \\ 0 & 1 & 1 \end{vmatrix} = \hat{i} - \hat{j} + \hat{k} = \sqrt{3}$

$\Rightarrow \pm\dfrac{1}{\sqrt{3}}(\vec{a}\times\vec{b})$ is perpendicular to both $\vec{a}$ and $\vec{b}$ hence

only two units vectors are possible $\pm\dfrac{1}{3}(\hat{i} - \hat{j} + \hat{k})$

27. (a) $\vec{a}.\vec{b} = |\vec{a}||\vec{b}|\cos\theta = -6$

$\left(2\vec{a} - \dfrac{3}{2}\vec{b}\right)^2 = 4a^2 + \dfrac{9}{4}b^2 - 6\vec{a}.\vec{b} = 36 + 36 - 6\,(-6) = 108$

Hence $\left|2\vec{a} - \dfrac{3}{2}\vec{b}\right| = 6\sqrt{3}$

28. (b) $|\vec{a}-\vec{b}|^2 + |\vec{a}+\vec{b}|^2 = 2(a^2 + b^2)$

So $(\vec{a}+\vec{b})^2 = 2[121 + 529] - 900 = 400$

Hence $|\vec{a}+\vec{b}| = 20$

Aliter: $|\vec{a}| = 11; |\vec{b}| = 23; |\vec{a}-\vec{b}| = 30$

Gives $a^2 + b^2 - 2\vec{a}.\vec{b} = 900$

$\therefore\ 2\vec{a}.\vec{b} = -250 \Rightarrow a^2 + b^2 + 2\vec{a}.\vec{b} = 400$

$|\vec{a}+\vec{b}| = 20 \Rightarrow$ option (b) is correct

29. (b) Given $|\vec{a}| = |\vec{b}| = 1$ and $\vec{a}.\vec{b} = \dfrac{1}{2}$

Now $|\vec{p}+\vec{q}| = |3\vec{a}-\vec{b}| = \sqrt{9+1-3} = \sqrt{7}$ units

and $|\vec{p}-\vec{q}| = |\vec{a}+3\vec{b}| = \sqrt{1+9+3} = \sqrt{13}$ units

30. (a) $|\vec{a}| = |\vec{b}| = |2\vec{c}| = 3$, $\vec{a}.(\vec{b}+\vec{c}) = \vec{a}.\vec{b} + \vec{c}.\vec{a} = 0$,

$\vec{b}(\vec{c}+\vec{a}) = \vec{b}.\vec{c} + \vec{a} + \vec{b} = 0$, $\vec{c}.(\vec{a}+\vec{b}) = \vec{a}.\vec{b} + \vec{b}.\vec{c} = 0$,

So $\vec{a}.\vec{b} + \vec{b}.\vec{c} + \vec{c}.\vec{a} = 0$,

Now $|\vec{a}+\vec{b}+\vec{c}|^2 = \{a^2 + b^2 + c^2 + 2(\vec{a}.\vec{b} + \vec{b}.\vec{c} + \vec{c}.\vec{a}\}$

$= 9 + 9 + \dfrac{9}{4} = \dfrac{81}{4} \Rightarrow |\vec{a}+\vec{b}+\vec{c}| = \dfrac{9}{2}$

31. (a and d) $|\vec{a}| = 3$ **and** $|\vec{b}| = 4$; $(\vec{a}+\ell\vec{b}) \perp (\vec{a}-\ell\vec{b})$

$\Rightarrow a^2 - \ell^2 b^2 = 0;\ 16\ell^2 = 9 \Rightarrow \ell = \pm\dfrac{3}{4}$

32. (d) Let $\vec{c} = x\hat{i} + y\hat{j}$ be such a vector where $x^2 + y^2 = 1$

$x + y = \sqrt{2}.\dfrac{1}{\sqrt{2}} = 1$; $3x - 4y = 5/2$

Gives $x = \dfrac{13}{14}$ and $y = \dfrac{1}{14}$ But $x^2 + y^2 = \left(\dfrac{13}{14}\right)^2 + \left(\dfrac{1}{14}\right)^2 \neq 1$

So no such vector is possible

33. (a) $|\hat{a}| = |\hat{b}| = |\hat{c}| = 1$ **and** $(\hat{a} + \hat{b} + \hat{c}) = \vec{O}$

$\Rightarrow a^2 + b^2 + c^2 + 2\,(\vec{a}+\vec{b} + \vec{b}.\vec{c} + \vec{c}.\vec{a}) = 0$

$\Rightarrow \vec{a}.\vec{b} + b.\vec{c} + \vec{c}.\vec{a} = -3/2$

34. (c) $|\vec{x}| = |\vec{y}| = 1$ and $\vec{x}.\vec{y} = \cos\phi$

$\left\{\dfrac{1}{2}|\vec{x}-\vec{y}|\right\}^2 = \dfrac{1}{4}\{x^2 + y^2 - 2\vec{x}.\vec{y}\} = \dfrac{2}{4}\{1 - \cos\phi\} = \sin^2\left(\dfrac{\phi}{2}\right)$

$\Rightarrow \dfrac{1}{2}|\vec{x}-\vec{y}| = \left|\sin\left(\dfrac{\phi}{2}\right)\right|$

TEXTUAL EXERCISE 8: (SUBJECTIVE)

1. $\vec{a} = 6\hat{i} + 2\hat{j} + 3\hat{k}, \vec{b} = 3\hat{i} - 2\hat{k}$

$\Rightarrow \hat{n} = \pm\dfrac{(\vec{a}\times\vec{b})}{|\vec{a}\times\vec{b}|} = \pm\dfrac{(-4\hat{i} + 21\hat{j} - 6\hat{k})}{\sqrt{493}}$

Or $\hat{n} = \pm\dfrac{(4\hat{i} - 21\hat{j} + 6\hat{k})}{\sqrt{493}}$

2. $\vec{D}_1 = 3\hat{i} + \hat{j} - 2\hat{k}$ **and** $\vec{D}_2 = \hat{i} - 3\hat{j} + 4\hat{k}$

Area the $\|\,gm = \dfrac{1}{2}|\vec{D}_1 \times \vec{D}_2|$

$= \dfrac{1}{2}\begin{vmatrix} \hat{i} & \hat{j} & \hat{k} \\ 3 & 1 & -2 \\ 1 & -3 & 4 \end{vmatrix} = \dfrac{1}{2}|-2\hat{i} - 14\hat{j} - 10\hat{k}|$

$= |\hat{i} + 7\hat{j} + 5\hat{k}| = \sqrt{75} = 5\sqrt{3}$ **square units.**

3. Given $|\vec{A}| = |\vec{B}| = |\vec{C}| = 1$

$\vec{A}.\vec{B} = 0 \Rightarrow A \perp B$ and $\vec{A}.\vec{C} = 0 \Rightarrow A \perp C$

$\Rightarrow \quad \vec{A} = m(\vec{B}\times\vec{C})$, Now $\vec{B}\times\vec{C} = |\vec{B}||\vec{C}|\sin\theta\hat{n} = \pm\frac{1}{2}A$

Hence $\Rightarrow \vec{A} = \pm 2(\vec{B}\times\vec{C})$ Proved

4. Consider a rhombus ABCD having its diagonals intersecting at O. Let $\overrightarrow{AO} = \vec{a}$ and $\overrightarrow{OD} = \vec{b}$ then $\overrightarrow{OB} = -\vec{b}$,

Now $\overrightarrow{AD} = \vec{a} + \vec{b}$ and $\overrightarrow{AB} = \vec{a} - \vec{b}$

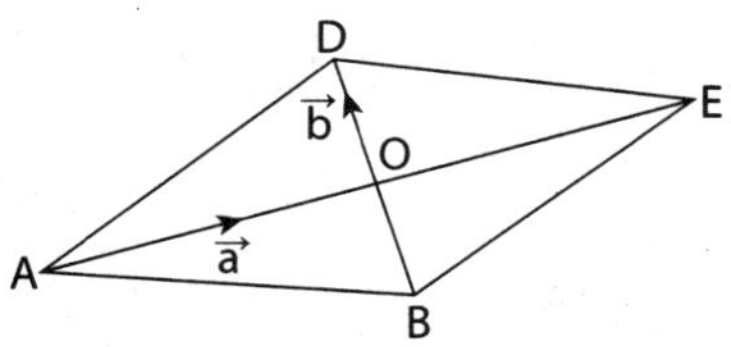

Since rhombus has equal sides $|\overrightarrow{AD}| = |\overrightarrow{AB}|$

$|\vec{a}+\vec{b}| = |\vec{a}-\vec{b}|$ squaring we get

i.e., $a^2 + b^2 + 2\ \vec{a}.\vec{b} = a^2 + b^2 - 2\vec{a}.\vec{b}$

$\Rightarrow \quad \vec{a}.\vec{b} = 0 \Rightarrow \vec{a} \perp \vec{b}$ **hence proved**

5. Consider a semicircle centered at O (origin), having AOB as one of diameter of the circle

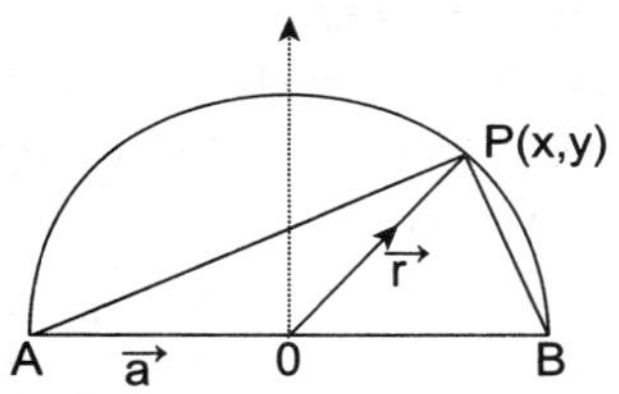

Let $\overrightarrow{OA} = \vec{a}$ then $\overrightarrow{OB} = -\vec{a}$ also $|\vec{a}| = |\vec{r}|$

Let P(x,y) be any point on the semi circle with P.V $\vec{r}$

$\overrightarrow{AP} = \vec{r} - \vec{a}$ and $\overrightarrow{BP} = \vec{r} - (-\vec{a}) = \vec{r} + \vec{a}$

Now $\overrightarrow{AP}.\overrightarrow{BP} = (\vec{r}-\vec{a}).(\vec{r}+\vec{a}) = r^2 - a^2 = 0$; Since $|\vec{a}| = |\vec{r}|$

$\Rightarrow \quad (\vec{r}-\vec{a}) \perp (\vec{r}+\vec{a})$; $\angle APB = 90^0$ **hence proved**

6. Consider a parallelogram $ABCD$ with $\overrightarrow{AB} = \vec{a}$, $\overrightarrow{BC} = \vec{b}$,

$\overrightarrow{AC} = \vec{a} + \vec{b}$ and $\overrightarrow{DB} = \vec{a} - \vec{b}$

Now $AC^2 - DB^2 = (\vec{a}+\vec{b})^2 - (\vec{a}-\vec{b})^2 = 4\vec{a}.\vec{b}$ ......(i)

$\overrightarrow{OB} = \vec{b}, \overrightarrow{OA} = \vec{a}$; Projection of $\vec{b}$ on $\vec{a} = \hat{a}.\vec{b}$

Area of rectangle with sides $|\vec{a}|$ and $\hat{a}.\vec{b}$ = $(|\vec{a}|)(\hat{a}.\vec{b}) = \vec{a}.\vec{b}$

Hence from (i)

$\therefore$ Difference of squares of diagonals = 4 Area of rectangle Hence Proved

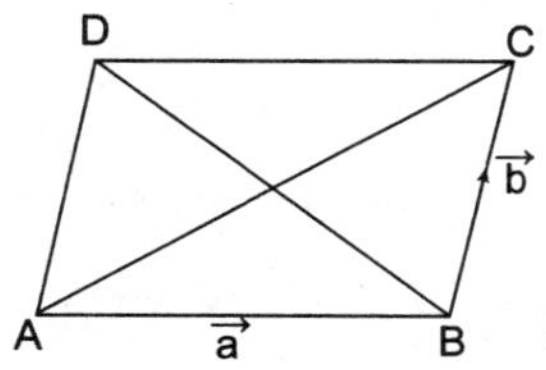

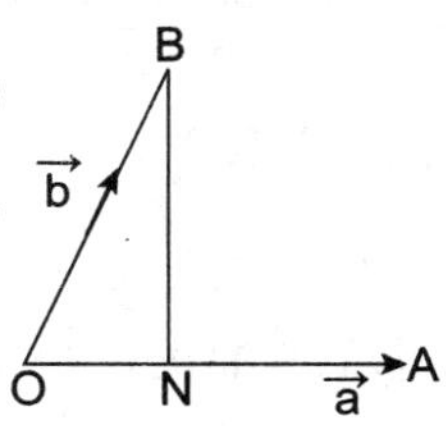

7. Consider a ΔLMN as shown in the figure

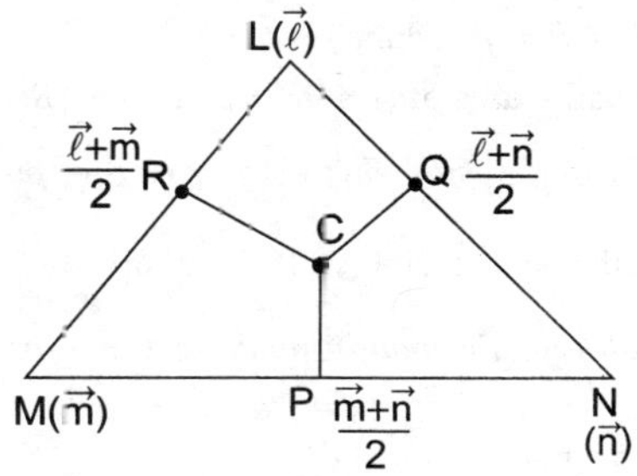

Let right bisectors of sides LM and MN intersect at $C(\vec{c})$

Then $(\vec{\ell} - \vec{m}) \perp \left(\vec{c} - \frac{\vec{\ell}+\vec{m}}{2}\right) \Rightarrow \vec{\ell}.\vec{c} - \vec{m}.\vec{c} - \frac{\ell^2 - m^2}{2} = 0$

Similarly $(\vec{m} - \vec{n}) \perp \left(\vec{c} - \frac{\vec{m}+\vec{n}}{2}\right)$

$\Rightarrow \quad \vec{m}.\vec{c} - \vec{n}.\vec{c} - \frac{m^2 - n^2}{2} = 0$. Adding $\vec{\ell}.\vec{c} - \vec{n}.\vec{c} - \frac{\ell^2 - n^2}{2} = 0$

or $\quad (\vec{\ell} - \vec{n}).\left(\vec{c} - \frac{\vec{\ell}+\vec{n}}{2}\right) = 0$; $(\vec{\ell} - \vec{n}) \perp \left(\vec{c} - \frac{\vec{\ell}+\vec{n}}{2}\right)$

so right bisectors are concurrent

Note: Here LMN is an accute angle triangle but the point of intersection does not necessary lie inside the triangle as in an obtuse triangle.

8. Let $ABCD$ be a ||gm with $\overrightarrow{AC} = \vec{a}$ and $\overrightarrow{DB} = \vec{b}$ its diagonals, Let these diagonals intersect at O then $\overrightarrow{OA} = \frac{-a}{2}, \overrightarrow{OC} = \frac{\vec{a}}{2}$, $\overrightarrow{OD} = \frac{-\vec{b}}{2}, \overrightarrow{OB} = \frac{\vec{b}}{2}$, $\overrightarrow{DA} = \frac{\vec{b}}{2} - \frac{\vec{a}}{2}$ or

$\overrightarrow{AD} = \frac{\vec{a}-\vec{b}}{2}$ Similarly $\overrightarrow{AB} = \frac{\vec{a}+\vec{b}}{2}$

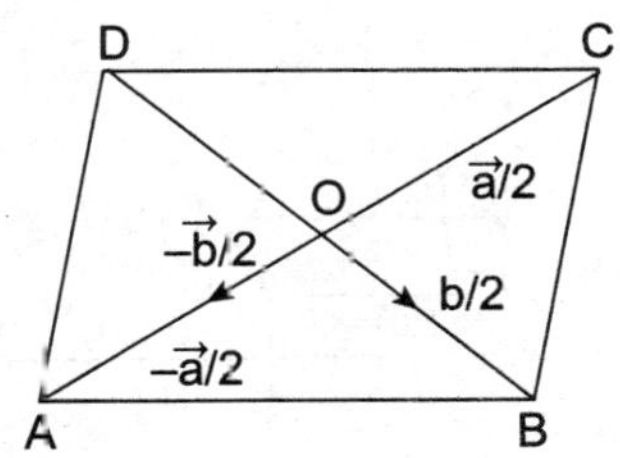

Now Area = $|\overrightarrow{AB} \times \overrightarrow{AD}| = \left|\left(\frac{\vec{a}+\vec{b}}{2} \times \frac{(\vec{a}-\vec{b}}{2}\right)\right|$

$= \frac{2}{4}|(\vec{a}\times\vec{b})| = \frac{1}{2}|(\vec{a}\times\vec{b})|$. In case of a general quadrilateral

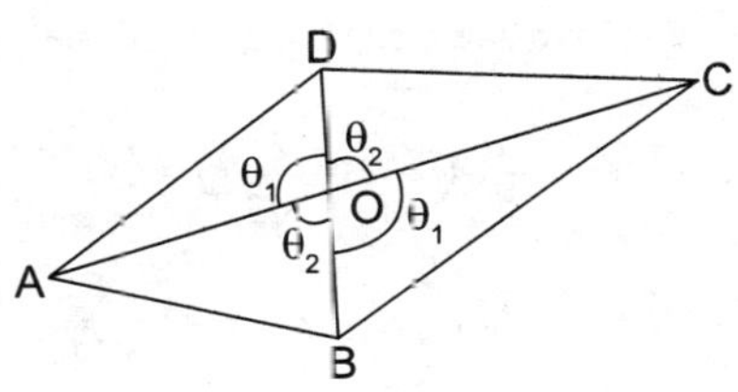

Let $\overrightarrow{AC} = \vec{a}$ and $\overrightarrow{DB} = \vec{b}$, $\overrightarrow{AO} = m\vec{a}, \overrightarrow{OC} = n\vec{a}$,

$\overrightarrow{DO} = p\vec{b}, \overrightarrow{OB} = q\vec{b}$ (where $p + q = 1$)

Area of quad = area of ($\Delta AOB + \Delta AOD + \Delta BOC + \Delta DOC$)

$= -\left\{|m\vec{a} \times q\vec{b}| + |m\vec{a} \times p\vec{b}| + |(q\vec{b} \times n\vec{a})| + |p\vec{b} \times n\vec{a}|\right\}$

{observe that $\sin\theta_1 = \sin\theta_2$ as $\theta_2 = \pi - \theta_1$}

$= \dfrac{1}{2}\{mqab + mpab + nqab + npab\}\sin\theta_1 = \dfrac{1}{2}ab\sin\theta_1$

$= \dfrac{1}{2}|\vec{a} \times \vec{b}|$ hence proved

9. $\overrightarrow{AB} = \vec{b}, \overrightarrow{AD} = \vec{d}$; $\overrightarrow{AC} = m\vec{b} + n\vec{d}$. Now $\overrightarrow{DB} = \vec{b} - \vec{d}$

Area of a quad = $\dfrac{1}{2}|\overrightarrow{AC} \times \overrightarrow{DB}| = \dfrac{1}{2}\left|\left(m\vec{b} + n\vec{d}\right) \times \left(\vec{b} - \vec{d}\right)\right|$

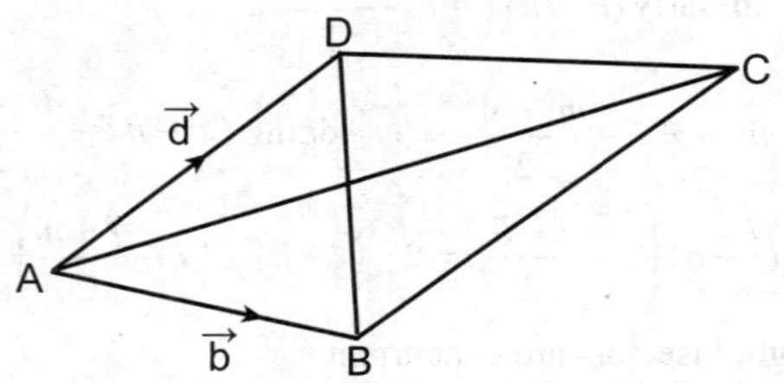

$= \dfrac{1}{2}\left|-m\vec{b} \times \vec{d} + n\vec{d} \times \vec{b}\right| = \dfrac{1}{2}|(m+n)|\left|\vec{b} \times \vec{d}\right|$ **Hence proved**

(b) Let $\vec{a} \times \vec{b} = \vec{c} = ab\sin\theta\hat{n}$

$= (\vec{a} \times \vec{b}) = c^2 = a^2b^2\sin^2\theta = a^2b^2(1 - \cos^2\theta)$

$= \vec{a}^2\vec{b}^2 - (ab\cos\theta)^2 = \vec{a}^2\vec{b}^2 - (\vec{a}.\vec{b})^2$

10. **(a)** Let $\vec{a}$ be in $x - y$ plane along $\hat{i} + \hat{j}$ so $\vec{a} = \dfrac{a}{\sqrt{2}}(\hat{i} + \hat{j})$,

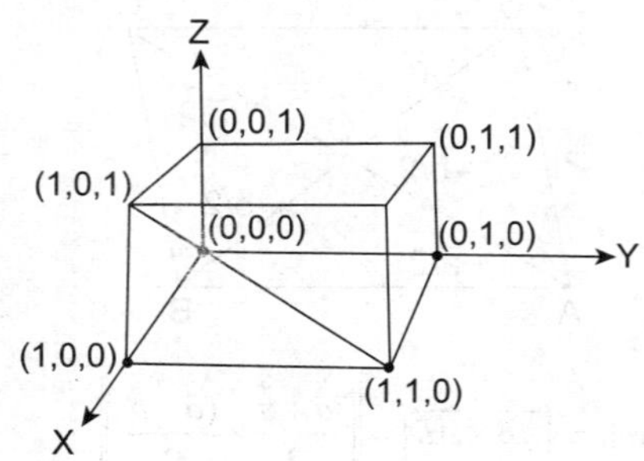

$|\vec{b}| = |2\vec{a}|$ be in *yz*-plane along $\hat{j} + \hat{k}$, so $\vec{b} = a\sqrt{2}(\hat{i} + \hat{j})$,

$|\vec{c}| = |3\vec{a}|$ be in *xy*-plane along $\hat{i} + \hat{k}$, so $\vec{c} = \dfrac{3a}{\sqrt{2}}\left(\hat{i} + \hat{k}\right)$

Let $\vec{d} = \vec{a} + \vec{b} + \vec{c} = \dfrac{a}{\sqrt{2}}(\hat{i} + \hat{j}) + \dfrac{2a}{\sqrt{2}}(\hat{j} + \hat{k}) + \dfrac{3a}{\sqrt{2}}(\hat{i} + \hat{k})$

$= \vec{d} = \dfrac{a}{\sqrt{2}}\{4\hat{i} + 3\hat{j} + 5\hat{k}\}$ $\qquad d.c's = \left\langle \dfrac{4}{5\sqrt{2}}, \dfrac{3}{5\sqrt{2}}, \dfrac{5}{5\sqrt{2}} \right\rangle$

(b) $\hat{p} = \cos\theta\hat{i} + \sin\theta\hat{j}$; $\hat{q} = \cos\phi\hat{i} + \sin\phi\hat{j}$

$\hat{q} \times \hat{p} = |\hat{q}||\hat{p}|\sin(\theta - \phi)$

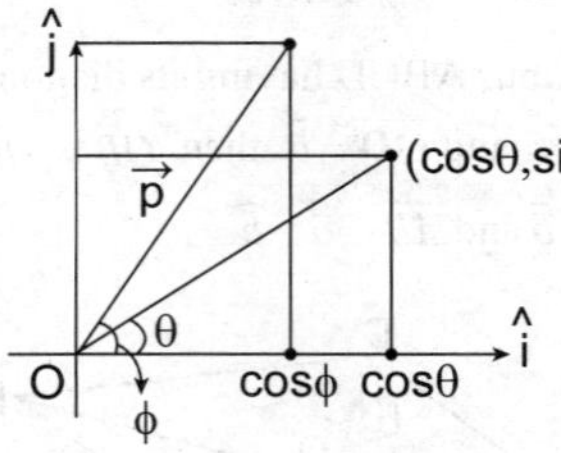

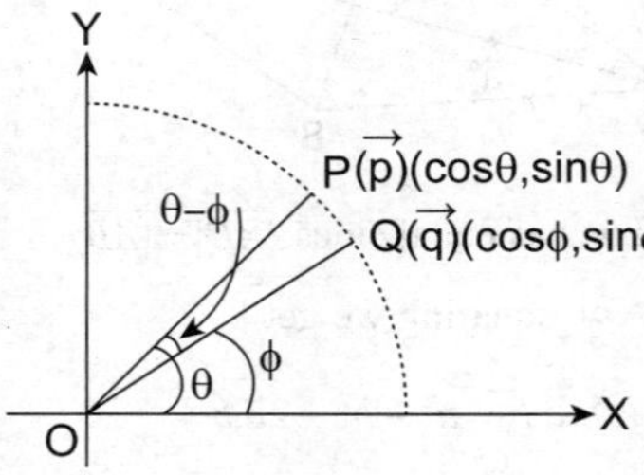

$\Rightarrow \quad \sin(\theta - \phi) = \dfrac{|\hat{p} \times \hat{q}|}{|\hat{p}||\hat{q}|} = |-\cos\theta\sin\phi\hat{k} + \cos\phi\sin\theta\hat{k}|$

$= \sin\theta\cos\phi - \cos\theta\sin\phi$

Replacing ϕ by $-\phi$ we get $\sin\{\theta - (-\phi)\}$

$= \sin(\theta + \phi) = |\cos(\phi)\hat{i} + \sin(-\phi)\hat{j}| \times |\cos\theta\hat{i} + \sin\theta\hat{j}|$

$= (\sin\theta\cos\phi + \sin\phi\cos\theta)$

11. (a) Given $\vec{a} + \vec{b} + \vec{c} = \vec{0} \Rightarrow \vec{b} + \vec{c} = -\vec{a}$

$\Rightarrow \quad \vec{b} \times (\vec{b} + \vec{c}) = \vec{b} \times (-\vec{a}) \Rightarrow \vec{b} \times \vec{c} = \vec{a} \times \vec{b}$

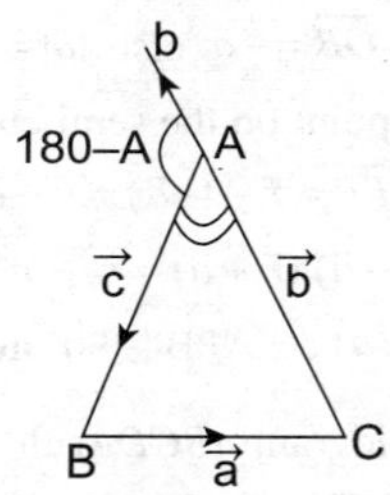

Similarly $\vec{c} \times (\vec{b} + \vec{c}) = \vec{c} \times (-\vec{a})$; $\vec{c} \times \vec{b} = -\vec{c} \times \vec{a}$

gives $\vec{b} \times \vec{c} = \vec{c} \times \vec{a}$. Hence prove that $\vec{a} \times \vec{b} = \vec{b} \times \vec{c} = \vec{c} \times \vec{a}$

$\dfrac{1}{2}|\vec{b} \times \vec{c}| = \dfrac{1}{2}|\vec{b}||\vec{c}|\sin(\pi - A) = 1/2\ bc\sin A = \Delta ABC$

Similarly $\dfrac{1}{2}ac\sin B = \dfrac{1}{2}ab\sin c = \Delta ABC$

$\dfrac{abc}{2}\dfrac{\sin A}{a} = \dfrac{abc}{2}\dfrac{\sin B}{b} = \dfrac{abc}{2}\dfrac{\sin C}{c} = \Delta ABC$ area

Hence $\dfrac{\sin A}{a} = \dfrac{\sin B}{b} = \dfrac{\sin C}{c}$

(b) $\overrightarrow{AB} = \vec{b} - \vec{a}$, $\overrightarrow{AC} = \vec{c} - \vec{a}$,

area of $\Delta ABC = \dfrac{1}{2}|\overrightarrow{AB} \times \overrightarrow{AC}| = \dfrac{1}{2}|(\vec{b} - \vec{a}) \times (\vec{c} - \vec{a})|$

$= \frac{1}{2}(\vec{b}\times\vec{c} - \vec{b}\times\vec{a} - \vec{a}\times\vec{c}) = \frac{1}{2}\left[\vec{b}\times\vec{c} + \vec{a}\times\vec{b} + \vec{c}\times\vec{a}\right]$

Now $\frac{1}{2}\left[\vec{b}\times\vec{c} + \vec{a}\times\vec{b} + \vec{c}\times\vec{a}\right]$ is a vector

Perpendicular to $\overrightarrow{AB}$ and $\overrightarrow{AC}$ (i.e., the plane of ΔABC) and it represents the area of ΔABC when ABC are collinear then $\vec{b}\times\vec{c} + \vec{c}\times\vec{a} + \vec{a}\times\vec{b} = \vec{0}$

To find the unit vector normal to a Δ triangle $A(1,1,1)$, $B(0,0,0)$, $C(0,1,1)$ $\overrightarrow{BA} = \hat{i} + \hat{j} + \hat{k}$ and $\overrightarrow{BC} = \hat{j} + \hat{k}; \vec{n} = \pm\left(\overrightarrow{BA}\times\overrightarrow{BC}\right) = \pm(\hat{j} - \hat{k})$

$\therefore$ unit vector $= \pm\left(\frac{\hat{j} - \hat{k}}{\sqrt{2}}\right)$

TEXTUAL EXERCISE 5: (OBJECTIVE)

1. (a) $\vec{u} = \vec{a} - \vec{b}, \vec{v} = \vec{a} + \vec{b}$, $|\vec{a}| = |\vec{b}| = 2$, $|\vec{u}\times\vec{v}| = 2|(\vec{a}\times\vec{b})|$

$= 2\left\{\sqrt{\vec{a}^2\vec{b}^2 - (\vec{a}.\vec{b})^2}\right\} = 2\sqrt{16 - (\vec{a}.\vec{b})^2}$

2. (d) $\vec{a} = 2\hat{i} + 3\hat{j} - \hat{k}$; $\vec{b} = -\hat{i} + 2\hat{j} - 4\hat{k}$; $\vec{c} = \hat{i} + \hat{j} + \hat{k}$

$\Rightarrow \vec{a}\times\vec{b} = \begin{vmatrix} \hat{i} & \hat{j} & \hat{k} \\ 2 & 3 & -1 \\ -1 & 2 & -4 \end{vmatrix} = -10\hat{i} + 9\hat{j} + 7\hat{k}$,

$\Rightarrow \vec{a}\times\vec{c} = \begin{vmatrix} \hat{i} & \hat{j} & \hat{k} \\ 2 & 3 & -1 \\ 1 & 1 & 1 \end{vmatrix} = 4\hat{i} - 3\hat{j} - \hat{k}$,

$so (\vec{a}\times\vec{b}).(\vec{a}\times\vec{c}) = -40 - 27 - 7 = 74$

3. (c, d) Given $|\vec{a}.\vec{b}| = |\vec{a}\times\vec{b}|$

$\Rightarrow$ $|ab\cos\theta| = |ab\sin\theta|$ $\Rightarrow$ $\cos\theta = \pm\sin\theta$

$\Rightarrow$ $\theta = \frac{\pi}{4}, \frac{3\pi}{4}$ $\Rightarrow$ $45^0, 135^0$

4. (b) $(\vec{a}\times\vec{b})^2 + (\vec{a}.\vec{b})^2 = a^2b^2$

5. (b) $A(\vec{a}) = (\hat{i} + \hat{j} + \hat{k})$, $B(\vec{b}) = 2\hat{i} + 3\hat{j} - 4\hat{k}$,

$C(\vec{c}) = 7\hat{i} + 4\hat{j} + 9\hat{k} \Rightarrow \overrightarrow{AB} = \hat{i} + 2\hat{j} - 5\hat{k}$,

$\Rightarrow$ $\overrightarrow{AC} = 6\hat{i} + 3\hat{j} + 8\hat{k}$,

Now $\overrightarrow{AB}\times\overrightarrow{AC} = \begin{vmatrix} \hat{i} & \hat{j} & -\hat{k} \\ 1 & 2 & -5 \\ 6 & 3 & 8 \end{vmatrix} = 31\hat{i} - 38\hat{j} - 9\hat{k}$

$\Rightarrow$ $|31\hat{i} - 38\hat{j} - 9\hat{k}| = \sqrt{2486}$, Unit vector $= \frac{31\hat{i} - 38\hat{j} - 9\hat{k}}{\sqrt{2486}}$

6. (a and d) Given $\vec{a}\times\vec{b} = \vec{c}\times\vec{d}$ and $\vec{a}\times\vec{c} = \vec{b}\times\vec{d}$

$\Rightarrow$ $\vec{a}\times\vec{b} + \vec{b}\times\vec{d} = \vec{a}\times\vec{c} + \vec{c}\times\vec{d}$

or $(\vec{a} - \vec{d})\times\vec{b} = (\vec{a} - \vec{d})\times\vec{c}$

$\Rightarrow$ $(\vec{a} - \vec{d})\times\vec{b} - (\vec{a} - \vec{d})\times\vec{c} = \vec{0}$ So $(\vec{a} - \vec{d})\times(\vec{b} - \vec{c}) = \vec{0}$

$(\vec{a} - \vec{d})$ is collinear or parallel to $(\vec{b} - \vec{c})$

7. (a) $\vec{a}.\vec{b} = \vec{a}.\vec{c}$, $\vec{a}\times\vec{b} = \vec{a}\times\vec{c}$; $\vec{a} \neq 0, \vec{c} \neq 0$ squaring and adding

Gives $\vec{a}^2\vec{b}^2 = \vec{a}^2\vec{c}^2$ or $|\vec{b}| = |\vec{c}|$

Since $\vec{c} \neq 0$ and $\vec{a}\times\vec{b} = \vec{a}\times\vec{c}$ so $\vec{b} = \vec{c}$

Aliter: $\vec{a}.(\vec{b} - \vec{c}) = 0$ **and** $\vec{a}\times(\vec{b} - \vec{c}) = \vec{O}$

Possible only if $\vec{b} - \vec{c} = \vec{O}$ i.e., $\vec{b} = \vec{c}$

8. (b) Let $\vec{a} = a_1\hat{i} + a_2\hat{j} + a_3\hat{k}$,

then $|(\vec{a}\times\hat{i})|^2 = |a_3\hat{j} - a_2\hat{k}|^2 = a_2^2 + a_3^2$

so $|\vec{a}\times\hat{i}|^2 + |\vec{a}\times\hat{j}|^2 + |\vec{a}\times\hat{k}|^2$

$= (a_2^2 + a_3^2) + (a_1^2 + a_3^2) + (a_1^2 + a_2^2)$

$= 2(a_1^2 + a_2^2 - a_3^2) = 2(|a|)^2$

9. (a, c) $|\vec{a}\times\vec{b}| = |\vec{a}||\vec{b}||\sin\theta| = 4$

$\Rightarrow$ $(\vec{a}\times\vec{b})^2 = (|\vec{a}\times\vec{b}|)^2 = 16$

10. (a, b, c) $\vec{u} = \hat{a} - (\hat{a}.\hat{b})\hat{b}$ so $\vec{u} = \hat{a} - \cos\theta\hat{b} \Rightarrow |\vec{u}| = \sin\theta$

Similarly $|\vec{v}| = |\vec{a}\times\vec{b}| = \sin\theta$

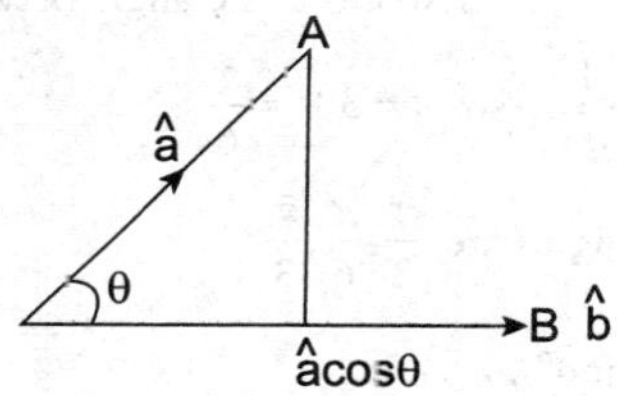

$\Rightarrow$ $|\vec{u}| = |\vec{v}|$; $|\vec{u}| + \vec{v}.\hat{c} = \vec{a}.(\hat{a}\times\hat{b}) = \sin\theta$

$|\vec{u}| + \vec{u}.\hat{b} = \sin\theta + |\hat{a}.\hat{b} - ab(1)\} = \sin\theta$

11. (a) Let $\overrightarrow{AB} = 2\vec{p}$ and $\overrightarrow{AD} = \vec{q}$

Let origin be A; $\overrightarrow{AE} = (3\vec{p} + \vec{q})$ and $\overrightarrow{AG} = (3\vec{q} + 2\vec{p})$

$\Delta ABD = \frac{1}{2}|2\vec{p}\times\vec{q}| = |\vec{p}\times\vec{q}| = pq\sin\theta$

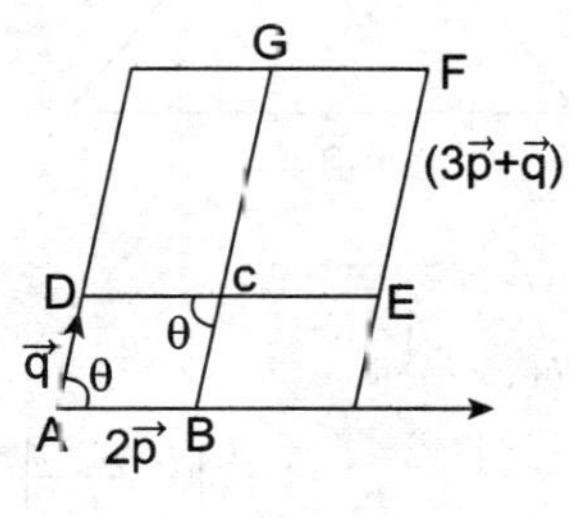

Area of $\Delta AEG = \frac{1}{2}|(3\vec{p} + \vec{q})\times(3\vec{q} + 2\vec{p})|$

$= \frac{1}{2}|(9\vec{p}\times\vec{q} - 2\vec{p}\times\vec{q})| = \frac{7}{2}|\vec{p}\times\vec{q}| = \frac{7}{2}\Delta ABD$

12. (a) $\therefore$ $v = r\omega$

$r = (2-1)\hat{i} + (3-2)\hat{j} = \hat{i} + \hat{j}$

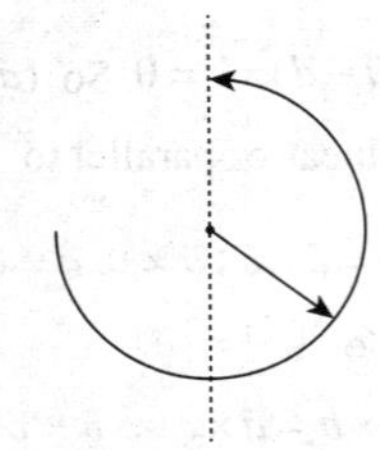

speed $= |\vec{v}| = |\vec{r}|\omega = \sqrt{2}\omega$

13. **(d)** Consider a unit vector along $\vec{a}, \vec{b}, \vec{c}$ (considering it a right-handed system) then $\vec{V} = (\ell\hat{a} + m\hat{b} + n\hat{c})$. Projection of $\vec{v}$ along the $\angle$bisector $\vec{a}$ and $\vec{b}$ $= \dfrac{\vec{v}(\hat{a}+\hat{b})}{\sqrt{2}} = \dfrac{\ell + m}{\sqrt{2}}$

14. **(a)** Given $|\vec{a}| = 1$, one side is $\overrightarrow{AB} = \sqrt{3}(\vec{a}\times\vec{b})$ and other is $\overrightarrow{BC} = \vec{b} - (\vec{b}.\vec{a})\vec{a}$. Observe that $\overrightarrow{AB} \perp \overrightarrow{BC}$

Since $(\vec{a}\times\vec{b}) \perp \vec{a}$ and $(\vec{a}\times\vec{b}) \perp \vec{b}$

$\therefore$ One angle $\angle B = 90^{\circ}$.

Now $|\overrightarrow{AB}| = \sqrt{3}b\sin\theta$ and $|\overrightarrow{BC}| = b\sin\theta$

{Note θ is the angle between $\vec{a}$ and $\vec{b}$ }

$\Rightarrow \tan A = \dfrac{1}{\sqrt{3}}$, So $A = 30^{\circ} = \dfrac{\pi}{6}$

Hence angles are $\dfrac{\pi}{2}, \dfrac{\pi}{6}, \dfrac{\pi}{3}$

15. (c) $\vec{a}.\vec{b} = 0$ and $\vec{a}\times\vec{b} = \vec{0}$

$\Rightarrow$ either $\vec{a}$ or $\vec{b}$ is a null vector

16. **(b)** Observe that $\vec{a} + \vec{b} + \vec{c} = \vec{0}$

$\vec{a}\times\vec{b} = \vec{b}\times\vec{c}\times\vec{a} = 2\Delta ABC$

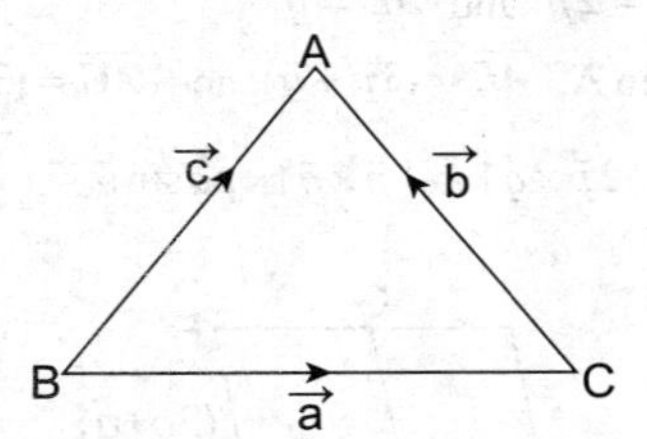

17. **(b)** $\vec{v}_1 = a\hat{x} + a\hat{y} + c(\hat{x}\times\hat{y})$; $\vec{v}_2 = \hat{x} + \hat{y} + (\hat{x}\times\hat{y})$;
$\vec{v}_3 = c\hat{x} + c\hat{y} + b(\hat{x}\times\hat{b})$

Vector will be coplanar when $= \begin{vmatrix} a & a & c \\ 1 & 0 & c \\ c & c & b \end{vmatrix} = 0$ i.e., $ab = c^2$

$\Rightarrow$ c is the G.M. between a and b

18. **(b)** $\vec{a} = \hat{i} - \hat{j} + \hat{k}$; $\vec{a}.\vec{b} = 0$

and $\vec{a}\times\vec{b} = \vec{c}$ where $c = -\ \hat{i} - \hat{j} + \hat{k}$

Let $\vec{b} = b_1\hat{i} + b_2\hat{j} + b_3\hat{k}$

where $b_1 + b_3 - b_2 = 0$ Now $\vec{a}\times\vec{b} = \begin{vmatrix} \hat{i} & \hat{j} & \hat{k} \\ 1 & -1 & 1 \\ b_1 & b_2 & b_3 \end{vmatrix}$

$= -(b_2 + b_3)\hat{i} - (b_3 - b_1)\hat{j} + (b_2 + b_1)\hat{k} = -2\hat{i} - \hat{j} + \hat{k}$

so $b_2 + b_3 = 2$, $b_3 - b_1 = 1$, $b_1 + b_2 = 1$

gives $b_1 = 0$, $b_2 = b_3 = 1 \Rightarrow \vec{b} = <0, 1, 1>$

19. **(c)** Given $\vec{a}, \vec{b}, \vec{c}$ are non-zero vectors such that $\vec{a} \neq k\vec{b}$, $\vec{b} \neq \lambda\vec{c}$; $\vec{c} \neq \mu\vec{a}$ for every real k,λ,μ

and $\vec{a} + \vec{b}$ is collinear with $\vec{c}$ ...(i)

$\vec{b} + \vec{c}$ is collinear with $\vec{a}$ ....(ii)

To find $\vec{a} + \vec{b} + \vec{c}$; $\vec{a} + \vec{b} = \lambda\vec{c}$ ...(iii)

and $\vec{b} + \vec{c} = \mu\vec{a}$ ...(iv)

(iii)...(iv) given

$\Rightarrow \vec{a} - \vec{c} = \lambda\vec{c} - \mu\vec{a} \quad \Rightarrow (\mu + 1)\vec{a} = (\lambda + 1)\vec{c}$

But $\vec{a}$ is non-collinear with $\vec{c}$

$\Rightarrow \mu + 1 = \lambda + 1 = 0 \quad \Rightarrow \mu = \lambda = -1$

$\Rightarrow \vec{a} + \vec{b} = -\vec{c}$ and $\vec{b} + \vec{c} = -\vec{a} \Rightarrow \vec{a} + \vec{b} + \vec{c} = \vec{0}$

20. **(b)** $\vec{F} = \hat{i} + a\hat{j} - \hat{k}$; $\vec{D} = (\hat{i} + \hat{j}) - (\hat{j} + \hat{k}) = \hat{i} - \hat{k}$

$|\vec{F}\times\vec{D}| = \begin{vmatrix} \hat{i} & \hat{j} & \hat{k} \\ 1 & a & -1 \\ 1 & 0 & -1 \end{vmatrix} = \sqrt{8}$

$\Rightarrow |(-a)\hat{i} + 0\hat{j} - a\hat{k}| = \sqrt{a^2 + a^2} = \sqrt{2a^2} = \sqrt{8}$

$a = \pm 2$ or $a = 2$

21. **(a)** $\vec{a}\times\vec{b} = \vec{c} \Rightarrow \vec{c} \perp \vec{a}$ and $\vec{c} \perp \vec{b}$

Also $\vec{b}\times\vec{c} = \vec{a} \quad \Rightarrow \quad \vec{a} \perp \vec{b}$ and $\vec{a} \perp \vec{c}$

$\Rightarrow$ $\vec{a}, \vec{b}, \vec{c}$ are mutually perpendicular

22. **(b)** A(1,0,3), B(–1,3,4), C(1,2,1), D(k,2,5)

Now $\overrightarrow{AB} = -2\hat{i} + 3\hat{j} + \hat{k}$; $\overrightarrow{BC} = 2\hat{i} - \hat{j} - 3\hat{k}$;

$\overrightarrow{CD} = (\hat{k} - 1)\hat{i} + 4\hat{j}$. Vectors will be coplanar if

$\begin{vmatrix} -2 & 3 & 1 \\ 2 & -1 & -3 \\ (k-1) & 0 & 4 \end{vmatrix} = 0$ or $\begin{vmatrix} -2 & 3 & 1 \\ -4 & 8 & 0 \\ (k+7) & -12 & 0 \end{vmatrix}$

$= -48 - 8(k + 7) = 0$ *i.e.* $(k + 7) = -6 \Rightarrow k = -13$

TEXTUAL EXERCISE 9: (SUBJECTIVE)

1. $\begin{vmatrix} 1 & x & -x^2 \\ 1 & 1 & -1 \\ 1 & -1 & 1 \end{vmatrix} = 2x^2 - 2x = 4$

$\Rightarrow x^2 - x - 2 = 0 \quad \Rightarrow (x - 2)(x + 1) = 0$

$\Rightarrow x = 2, -1$

2. $\left[\vec{a}\ \vec{b}\ \vec{c}\right]=\left[a\hat{a}\ b\hat{b}\ c\hat{c}\right]=abc\left[\hat{a}\ \hat{b}\ \hat{c}\right]$

$\vec{A}=x_1a\hat{a}+y_1bb+z_1c\hat{c}$

$$\text{Now }\left[\vec{A}\ \vec{B}\ \vec{C}\right]=\begin{vmatrix}x_1a(\hat{a}) & y_1b(\hat{b}) & z_1c(\hat{c})\\ x_2a(\hat{a}) & y_2b(\hat{b}) & z_2c(\hat{c})\\ x_3a(\hat{a}) & y_3b(\hat{b}) & z_3c(\hat{c})\end{vmatrix}$$

$$=abc\begin{vmatrix}x_1 & y_1 & z_1\\ x_2 & y_2 & z_2\\ x_3 & y_3 & z_3\end{vmatrix}\begin{vmatrix}\hat{a} & 0 & 0\\ 0 & \hat{b} & 0\\ 0 & 0 & \hat{c}\end{vmatrix}\quad \{\text{Row x column method}\}$$

$$=\begin{vmatrix}x_1 & y_1 & z_1\\ x_2 & y_2 & z_2\\ x_3 & y_3 & z_3\end{vmatrix}\begin{vmatrix}a\hat{a} & 0 & 0\\ 0 & b\hat{b} & 0\\ 0 & 0 & c\hat{c}\end{vmatrix}=\begin{vmatrix}x_1 & y_1 & z_1\\ x_2 & y_2 & z_2\\ z_1 & z_2 & z_3\end{vmatrix}\left[\vec{a}\ \vec{b}\ \vec{c}\right]$$

3. Let $\vec{a},\vec{b},\vec{c}$ represent the three co-terminus edges of a || piped $V_1=\left[\vec{a}\ \vec{b}\ \vec{c}\right]=\vec{a}.(\vec{b}\times\vec{c})$

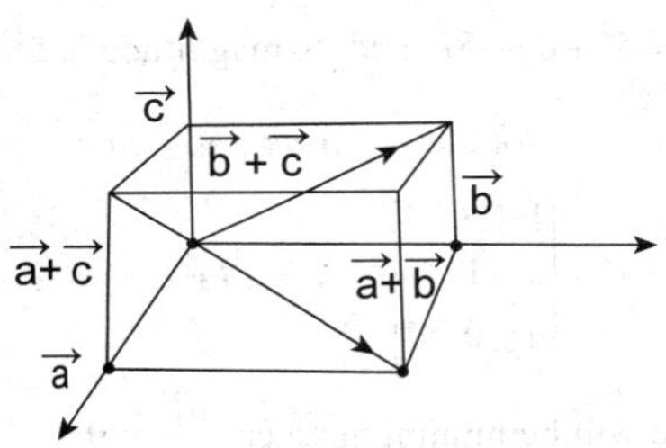

$V_2=\left[\vec{a}+\vec{b}\ \ \vec{b}+\vec{c}\ \ \vec{c}+\vec{a}\right]=(\vec{a}+\vec{b}).\left\{(\vec{b}+\vec{c})\times(\vec{c}+\vec{a})\right\}$

$=(\vec{a}+\vec{b})\left\{\vec{b}\times\vec{c}+\vec{c}\times\vec{a}+\vec{b}\times\vec{a}\right\}$

$=\vec{a}.(\vec{b}\times\vec{c})+\vec{a}.(\vec{c}\times\vec{a})+\vec{a}.(\vec{b}\times\vec{a})+$

$\vec{b}.(\vec{b}\times\vec{c})+\vec{b}.(\vec{c}\times\vec{a})+\vec{b}.(\vec{b}\times\vec{a})$

$=\left[\vec{a}\ \vec{b}\ \vec{c}\right]+0+0+0+\left[\vec{b}\ \vec{c}\ \vec{a}\right]+0\ =\ 2\left[\vec{a}\ \vec{b}\ \vec{c}\right]$

$\Rightarrow$ $V_2=2V_1$.

4. Given $\begin{vmatrix}a & a^2 & 1+a^3\\ b & b^2 & 1+b^3\\ c & c^2 & 1+c^3\end{vmatrix}=\begin{vmatrix}a & a^2 & a^3\\ b & b^2 & b^3\\ c & c^2 & c^3\end{vmatrix}+\begin{vmatrix}a & a^2 & 1\\ b & b^2 & 1\\ c & c^2 & 1\end{vmatrix}$

$=(abc+1)\begin{vmatrix}1 & a & a^2\\ 1 & b & b^2\\ 1 & c & c^2\end{vmatrix}=0$. Since $\vec{A},\vec{B},\vec{C}$ are not collinear.

$\therefore$ abc + 1 = 0 so abc = –1

TEXTUAL EXERCISE 6: (OBJECTIVE)

1. (c) $(\vec{a}+2\vec{b}-\vec{c}).\left\{(\vec{a}-\vec{b})\times(\vec{a}-\vec{b}-\vec{c})\right\}$

$=\left(\vec{a}+2\vec{b}-\vec{c}\right).\left[\left\{(\vec{a}-\vec{b}-\vec{c})+(\vec{c})\right\}\times(\vec{a}-\vec{b}-\vec{c})\right]$

$=(\vec{a}+2\vec{b}-\vec{c}).\{\vec{c}\times(\vec{a}-\vec{b}-\vec{c})\}$

$=\{(\vec{a}-\vec{b}-\vec{c})+3\vec{b}\}.\{\vec{c}\times(\vec{a}-\vec{b}-\vec{c})\}=0$

$=3\vec{b}.\{\vec{c}\times(\vec{a}-\vec{b}-\vec{c})\}=3\left[\vec{b}\ \vec{c}\ \vec{a}\right]$

$\left\{as\ 3\vec{b}.\{\vec{c}\times(-\vec{b})\}=3\vec{b}.\{(\vec{c}\times(-\vec{c})\}=0\right\}$

2. (c) Volume $=\begin{vmatrix}-12 & 0 & 2\\ 0 & 3 & -1\\ 2 & 1 & -15\end{vmatrix}=546$

Now 12 × 44 – 6a = 546 gives a = –3

3. (d) $|(\vec{a}\times\vec{b}).\vec{c}|=|\vec{a}||\vec{b}||\vec{c}|$ which is possible only if $\vec{a},\vec{b},\vec{c}$ are mutually perpendicular

i.e., $\vec{a}.\vec{b}=\vec{b}.\vec{c}=\vec{c}.\vec{a}=0$

4. (a) $\vec{a},\vec{b},\vec{c}$ are coplanar unit vectors

$\Rightarrow$ $\left[\vec{a}\ \vec{b}\ \vec{c}\right]=0$; So $\left[2\vec{a}-\vec{b}\ \ 2\vec{b}-\vec{c}\ \ 2\vec{c}-\vec{a}\right]$

$=(2\vec{a}-\vec{b}).\left\{4\vec{b}\times\vec{c}-2\vec{b}\times\vec{a}+\vec{c}\times\vec{a}\right\}$

$=8\left[\vec{a}\ \vec{b}\ \vec{c}\right]-\left[\vec{b}\ \vec{c}\ \vec{a}\right]=0\quad(\because[\vec{a}\vec{b}\vec{c}]=0)$

5. (b, d) $(\vec{e}_1+\vec{e}_2)$ will be a vector along the angle bisector

$\Rightarrow\ \sin\left(\dfrac{\theta}{2}\right)=\dfrac{|\vec{e}_1\times(\vec{e}_1+\vec{e}_2)|}{|\vec{e}_1||\vec{e}_1+\vec{e}_2|}=\dfrac{|\vec{e}_1\times\vec{e}_2|}{|\vec{e}_1+\vec{e}_2|}$

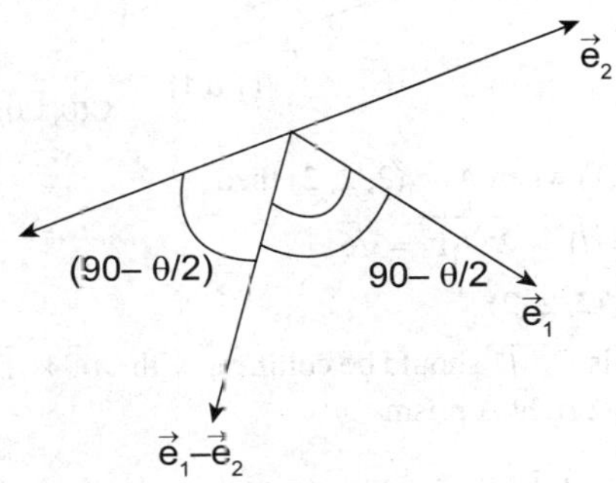

6. (a, c) Only $\vec{u}(\vec{v}\times\vec{w})$ is meaningful $(\vec{a}.\vec{v}).\vec{w}$ which is the dot product of a scalar and a vector which is not possible similarly (d) is not valid.

7. (d) Vector formed by sum $=(b+2)\hat{i}+6\hat{j}-2\hat{k}$

Now $\dfrac{(\hat{i}+\hat{j}+\hat{k}).\{(b+2)\hat{i}+6\hat{j}-2\hat{k}\}}{\sqrt{36+4+(b+2)^2}}=1$

$\Rightarrow\ (b+2)+6-2=\sqrt{(b+2)^2+40}$

On squaring $b^2+36+12b=b^2+44+4b$ gives 8b = 8

$\Rightarrow$ b = 1

8. **(c)** $\vec{n}_1=\left|\dfrac{(\vec{c}\times\vec{b})}{2}\right|,\ \vec{n}_2=\left|\dfrac{(\vec{a}\times\vec{c})}{2}\right|,\ \vec{n}_3=\left|\dfrac{(\vec{b}\times\vec{c})}{-2}\right|$

$=\vec{n}_4=\left|\dfrac{(\vec{b}-\vec{a})\times(\vec{c}-\vec{b})}{2}\right|=\vec{n}_1+\vec{n}_2+\vec{n}_3+\vec{n}_4$

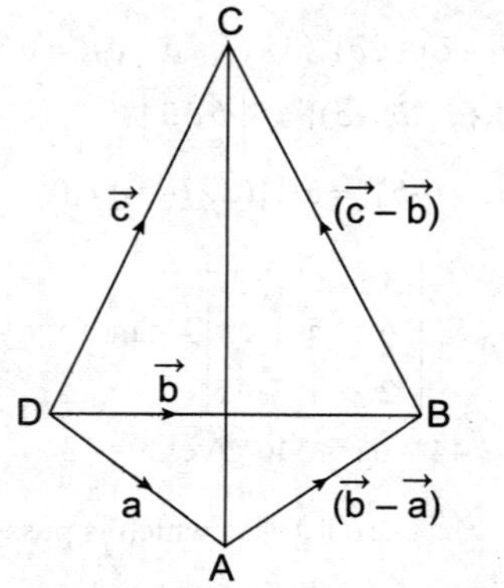

$$= \frac{1}{2}\{\vec{b}\times\vec{a}+\vec{a}\times\vec{c}+\vec{c}\times\vec{b}+\vec{b}+\vec{c}-\vec{a}\times\vec{c}+\vec{a}\times\vec{b}\} = \frac{1}{2}\{\vec{O}\} = \vec{O}$$

9. (a) Volume of prism $\frac{1}{2}|\overline{AA'}||\overline{AC}\times\overline{AB}| = 6$

$\Rightarrow \; |\overline{AA'}|\left|\{(-\hat{i}+\hat{j}-\hat{k})\times(\hat{i}-\hat{k})\}\right| = 6 \Rightarrow |AA'| = \sqrt{6}$

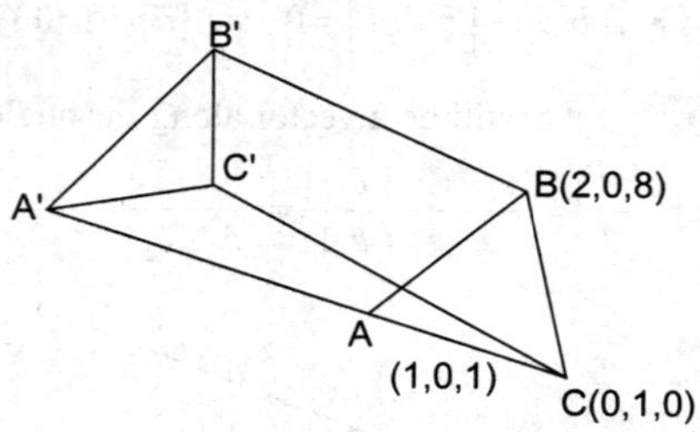

A(1,0,1) when A' = (2, 2, 2) then

$\overline{AA}' = \sqrt{1^2+2^2+1^2} = \sqrt{6}$

$\Rightarrow$ A'(2, 2, 2)

Also $\overline{AA}'$ should be collinear with $\overline{AC}\times\overline{AB}$ since this is a right Δ prism

10. (a) $\left[\vec{a}-\vec{b}\;\; \vec{b}-\vec{c}\;\; \vec{c}-\vec{a}\right]$ $(\vec{a}-\vec{b}).\{\vec{b}\times\vec{c}+\vec{c}\times\vec{a}+\vec{a}\times\vec{b}\}$

$= \vec{a}.(\vec{b}\times\vec{c}) - \vec{b}.(\vec{c}\times\vec{a}) = 0$

11. (d) Let $\vec{a} = \hat{i}+\hat{j}$, $\vec{b} = \hat{j}+\hat{k}$, $\vec{c} = \hat{k}+\hat{i}$

edge is $\vec{e}_1 = (\vec{a}\times\vec{b}) \Rightarrow \vec{e}_1 = \frac{\hat{i}-\hat{j}+\hat{k}}{\sqrt{3}}$,

$\vec{e}_2 = |\vec{b}\times\vec{c}| = \hat{i}-\hat{k}+\hat{j} \Rightarrow \hat{e}_2 = \frac{\hat{i}+\hat{j}-\hat{k}}{\sqrt{3}}$,

$\vec{e}_3 = (\vec{a}\times\vec{c}) \Rightarrow \hat{e}_3 = \frac{\hat{i}-\hat{j}-\hat{k}}{\sqrt{3}}$

Volume of parallelepiped with $\hat{e}_1, \hat{e}_2, \hat{e}_3$

$$= \left|\left(\frac{1}{\sqrt{3}}\right)^3 \begin{vmatrix} 1 & -1 & 1 \\ 1 & 1 & -1 \\ 1 & -1 & -1 \end{vmatrix}\right| = \frac{1}{3\sqrt{3}}|(-2)|(2) = \frac{4}{3\sqrt{3}}$$

12. (b) Volume of the parallelepiped $= \frac{2|\vec{\beta}||\vec{\gamma}|}{2\sqrt{2}} = \frac{|\vec{\beta}||\vec{\gamma}|}{2}$

$\Rightarrow \; \Delta^n = \frac{\{|\vec{\beta}||\vec{\gamma}|\}^n}{2^{n/2}}$

13. (b) $\vec{x}.\vec{a} = 1$, $\vec{y}.\vec{b} = 1$, $\vec{z}\vec{c} = 1$,

$\vec{x}.\vec{b} = 0$, $\vec{x}.\vec{c} = 0$, $\vec{y}.\vec{a} = 0$, $\vec{z}.\vec{b} = 0, \vec{z}.\vec{a} = 0$, $\vec{y}.\vec{a} = 0$

As a result $\vec{a}, \vec{b}, \vec{c}$ form a reciprocal system of vectors for $\vec{x}$, $\vec{y}$ and $\vec{z}$, i.e. $[\vec{x}\;\vec{y}\;\vec{z}] = \frac{1}{[\vec{a}\;\vec{b}\;\vec{c}]}$

14. (d) A vector coplanar with $(\hat{i}+2\hat{j})$ and $(\hat{j}+2\hat{k})$

Will be $\vec{V} = \ell(\hat{i}+2\hat{j}) + m(\hat{j}+2\hat{k})$

$= \ell\hat{i} + (2\ell+m)\hat{j} + 2m\hat{k}$

Since it is perpendicular to $2\hat{i}+\hat{j}+2\hat{k}$

$\Rightarrow \; 2\ell + 2\ell + m + 4m = 0$ or $4\ell = -5m$

Consider $\ell = 5$ and $m = -4$

$\Rightarrow \; \vec{v} = 5\hat{i} + 6\hat{j} - 8\hat{k}$ and its magnitude is $5\sqrt{5}$ units

15. (c) $v_1 = \hat{i} + a\hat{j} + \hat{k}$, $v_2 = \hat{j} + a\hat{k}$, $v_3 = a\hat{i} + \hat{k}$,

Volume $V = \begin{vmatrix} 1 & a & 1 \\ 0 & 1 & a \\ a & 0 & 1 \end{vmatrix} = 1 + a(a^2 - 1) = a^3 - a + 1$

Volume will be minimum when $\frac{dV}{da} = 0$

i.e., $3a^2 - 1 = 0$; so $a \pm \frac{1}{\sqrt{3}}$

16. (c) $[\vec{u}\;\vec{v}\;\vec{w}] = \vec{u}.[\vec{v}\times\vec{w}]$

$= \vec{u}\left[(2\hat{i}+\hat{j}-\hat{k})\times(\hat{i}+3\hat{k})\right] = \vec{u}(3\hat{i}-7\hat{j}-\hat{k})$

The value will be max when $\vec{u}$ and $(3\hat{i}-7\hat{j}-\hat{k})$ are collinear or parallel

So max value of $|\vec{u}|\left|3\hat{i}-7\hat{j}-\hat{k}\right| = 1\sqrt{59} = \sqrt{59}$

17. (c) $\vec{a} = \hat{i}-\hat{k}$, $\vec{b} = x\hat{i}+\hat{j}+(1-x)t$, $\vec{c} = y\hat{i}+x\hat{j}+(1+x-y)\hat{k}$

$\left[\vec{a}\;\vec{b}\;\vec{c}\right] = \begin{vmatrix} 1 & 0 & -1 \\ x & 1 & 1-x \\ y & x & x-y \end{vmatrix} = 0$ so independent of x and y

$[\vec{a}\;\vec{b}\;\vec{c}]$ does not depend on x and y

18. (a, b, c) Vector will be coplanar when $\left[\vec{a}\;\vec{b}\;\vec{c}\right] = 0$

i.e. $\begin{vmatrix} \lambda & 1 & 2 \\ 1 & \lambda & -1 \\ 2 & -1 & \lambda \end{vmatrix} = \lambda(\lambda^2 - 1) - (\lambda + 2) + 2(-1 - 2\lambda) = 0$

$\Rightarrow \; \lambda^3 - 6\lambda - 4 = 0$ or $(\lambda + 2)\{\lambda^2 - 2\lambda - 2\} = 0$

$\Rightarrow \; \lambda = -2, 1 \pm \sqrt{3}$

Now $\lambda = -2$ gives $-8 + 12 - 4 = 0$

i.e. $\lambda^2 - 2\lambda - 2 = 0$ gives $\lambda = \dfrac{2+\sqrt{4+8}}{2} = (1 \pm \sqrt{3})$

TEXTUAL EXERCISE 10: (SUBJECTIVE)

1. (i) $\vec{a} = 2\hat{i} - 10\hat{j} + 2\hat{k}, \vec{b} = 3\hat{i} + \hat{j} + 2\hat{k}, \vec{c} = 2\hat{i} + \hat{j} + 3\hat{k}$

$\vec{a}\times(\vec{b}\times\vec{c}) = (\vec{a}.\vec{c})\vec{b} - (\vec{a}.\vec{b})\vec{c} = \overline{ob} - \overline{oc} = \vec{0}$

(ii) $\vec{a} = 2\hat{i} + \hat{j} - 3\hat{k}, \vec{b} = \hat{i} - 2\hat{j} + \hat{k}, \vec{c} = -\hat{i} + \hat{j} - 4\hat{k}$

$\vec{a}\times(\vec{b}\times\vec{c}) = (\vec{a}.\vec{c})\vec{b} - (\vec{a}.\vec{b})\vec{c}$

$= 11(\hat{i} - 2\hat{j} + \hat{k}) + 3(-\hat{i} + \hat{j} - 4\hat{k}) = 8\hat{i} - 19\hat{j} - \hat{k}$

2. $(\vec{a}\times\vec{b})\times\vec{c} = \vec{a}\times(\vec{b}\times\vec{c})$

$\Rightarrow \quad (\vec{c}.\vec{a})\vec{b} - (\vec{c}.\vec{b})\vec{a} = (\vec{a}.\vec{c})\vec{b} - (\vec{a}.\vec{b})\vec{c}$

$\left\{-(\vec{a}.\vec{b}) + \vec{c} + (\vec{c}.\vec{b})\vec{a}\right\} = \vec{o}$

Also $\vec{a}\times(\vec{c}\times\vec{b}) = \vec{o}$ or $(\vec{c}\times\vec{a})\times\vec{b} = \vec{o}$

3. $\vec{p} = \dfrac{\vec{b}\times\vec{c}}{[\vec{a}\vec{b}\vec{c}]}, \vec{q} = \dfrac{\vec{c}\times\vec{a}}{[\vec{a}\vec{b}\vec{c}]}, \vec{\gamma} = \dfrac{\vec{a}\times\vec{b}}{[\vec{a}\vec{b}\vec{c}]}$

$(\vec{a}+\vec{b}).\vec{p} + (\vec{b}+\vec{c}).\vec{q} + (\vec{c}+\vec{a}).\vec{r}$

$\dfrac{(\vec{a}+\vec{b}).(\vec{b}\times\vec{c})}{[\vec{a}\vec{b}\vec{c}]} = (\vec{a}+\vec{b}).\vec{p} = \dfrac{[abc]}{[abc]} = 1$

Similarly others are equal to 1.

$\Rightarrow \quad (\vec{a}+\vec{b}).\ \vec{p}(\vec{b}+\vec{c}).\vec{q} + (\vec{c}+\vec{a}).\vec{r} = 3$

4. Given $\vec{u}\times\vec{v} = \vec{n}\ \sin\theta$, $\vec{v}\times\vec{n} = \ell$, $\vec{n}\times\vec{u} = m$

$\left([\vec{n}\ \vec{u}\ \vec{v}] = \vec{n}.(\vec{u}\times\vec{v})\right) = \vec{n}.\vec{n}\ \sin\theta = \sin\theta$

Let $\vec{u}, \vec{v}, \vec{n}$, be the reciprocal system of vectors

$\vec{u} = \dfrac{\vec{v}\times\vec{n}}{[\vec{n}\vec{u}\vec{v}]} = \dfrac{\ell}{\sin\theta}$, $n' = \dfrac{\vec{u}\times\vec{v}}{[\vec{n}\ \vec{u}\ \vec{v}]} = \dfrac{\sin\theta\vec{n}}{\sin\theta} = \vec{n}$

$\vec{V}' = \dfrac{\vec{n}\times\vec{u}}{[\vec{n}\vec{u}\vec{v}]} = \dfrac{m}{\sin\theta}$ hence proved

5. $\vec{a}' = \dfrac{\vec{b}\times\vec{c}}{[\vec{a}\ \vec{b}\ \vec{c}]} \Rightarrow \vec{a}'\vec{b} = \dfrac{\vec{b}.(\vec{b}\times\vec{c})}{[\vec{a}\vec{b}\vec{c}]} = 0$

Similarly other products

6. $\vec{a}' = \dfrac{\vec{b}\times\vec{c}}{[\vec{a}\vec{b}\vec{c}]}, \vec{b} = \dfrac{\vec{c}\times\vec{a}}{[\vec{a}\vec{b}\vec{c}]}, \vec{c}' = \dfrac{\vec{a}\times\vec{b}}{[\vec{a}\vec{b}\vec{c}]}$

$[\vec{a}'\vec{b}, \vec{c}] = \dfrac{(\vec{b}\times\vec{c})\left\{(\vec{c}\times\vec{a})\times(\vec{a}\times\vec{b})\right\}}{(\vec{a}\ \vec{b}\vec{c})^3}$

$= \dfrac{(b\times c)}{[\vec{a}b\vec{c}]}[\{(\vec{c}\times\vec{b}).\vec{b}\}\vec{a} = \dfrac{(\vec{b}\times\vec{c}).[\vec{c}\ \vec{a}\vec{b}]\vec{a}}{[\vec{a}\vec{b}\ \vec{c}]^3} = \dfrac{[\vec{a}\ \vec{b}\ \vec{c}]^2}{[\vec{a}\vec{b}\ \vec{c}]^3}$

$= \dfrac{1}{[\vec{a}\vec{b}\vec{c}]}$ **Hence proved**

7. $\vec{a} = 2\hat{i} + 3\hat{j} - \hat{k}$, $\vec{b} = \hat{i} - \hat{j} - 2\hat{k}$, $\vec{c} = -\hat{i} + 2\hat{j} + 2\hat{k}$

$$[\vec{a}\ \vec{b}\vec{c}] = \begin{vmatrix} 2 & 3 & -1 \\ 1 & -1 & -2 \\ -1 & 2 & 2 \end{vmatrix} = 3$$

$\vec{a}' = \dfrac{\vec{b}\times\vec{c}}{[\vec{a}\vec{b}\vec{c}]} = \dfrac{2\hat{i} + o\hat{j} + \hat{k}}{3} = \dfrac{2\hat{i} + \hat{k}}{3}$

$\vec{b}' = \dfrac{\vec{c}\times\vec{a}}{[\vec{a}\vec{b}\vec{c}]} = \dfrac{-8\hat{i} + 3\hat{j} - 7\hat{k}}{3}$

$\vec{c} = \dfrac{\vec{a}\times\vec{b}}{[\vec{a}\vec{b}\vec{c}]} = \dfrac{-7\hat{i} + 3\hat{j} - 5\hat{k}}{3}$; Verified by $\vec{a}.\vec{a}' = 1$

8. $[\vec{b}\ \vec{c}\ \vec{d}] \neq 0$

$(\vec{a}\times\vec{b})\times(\vec{c}\times\vec{d}) = [\vec{a}\ \vec{c}\ \vec{d}]\vec{b} - [\vec{b}\ \vec{c}\ \vec{d}]\vec{a}$

$(\vec{a}\times\vec{c})\times(\vec{d}\times\vec{b}) = [\vec{a}\vec{d}\vec{b}]\vec{c} - [\vec{c}\vec{d}\vec{b}]\vec{a}$

$(\vec{a}\times\vec{d})\times(\vec{b}\times\vec{c}) = [\vec{a}\vec{d}\vec{c}]\vec{b} - [\vec{a}\vec{d}\vec{b}]c$

Sum $= -2[\vec{b}\ \vec{c}\ \vec{d}]\vec{a}$; $[\vec{a}\ \vec{d}\ \vec{c}] = -[\vec{a}\vec{c}\vec{d}]$ row interchange

Since (-2) $[\vec{b}\ \vec{c}\ \vec{a}] \neq 0$ $\vec{a}$ is collinear with the sum

Hence proved

9. To prove $(\vec{a}\times\vec{b})\times(\vec{c}\times\vec{d}) = [\vec{a}\vec{c}\ \vec{d}]\vec{b} - [\vec{b}\ \vec{c}\ \vec{d}]\vec{a}$

Let $\vec{c}\times\vec{d} = \vec{\lambda} \Rightarrow (\vec{a}\times\vec{b})\times\vec{\lambda} = (\vec{\lambda}.\vec{a})\vec{b} - (\vec{\lambda}.\vec{b})\vec{a}$

$= \{(\vec{c}\times\vec{d}).\vec{a}\}\vec{b} - \{(\vec{c}\times\vec{d}).\vec{b}\}\vec{a} = [\vec{a}\ \vec{c}\ \vec{d}]\vec{b} - [\vec{b}\ \vec{c}\ \vec{d}]\vec{a}$

Similarly putting $\vec{a}\times\vec{b} = \vec{p}$ we can form the product other way

10. $\vec{a}, \vec{b}, \vec{c}$ *and* $\vec{a}, \vec{b}\ \vec{c}$ are the reciprocal system of vectors

$\vec{a}.\vec{a} = 1$ since $\vec{a}^2 = \dfrac{\vec{a}.(\vec{b}\times\vec{c})}{[\vec{a}\ \vec{b}\ \vec{c}]}$ or $\vec{a} = \dfrac{\vec{b}\times\vec{c}}{[\vec{a}\ \vec{b}\ \vec{c}]}$

TEXTUAL EXERCISE 7: (OBJECTIVE)

1. (b) Let r = $r = r_1\hat{i} - r_2\hat{j} + r_3\hat{k}$

Observe that $\hat{i}\times(\vec{r}\times\hat{i}) + \hat{j}\times(\vec{r}\times\hat{j}) + \hat{k}\times(\vec{r}\times\hat{k})$

$= (\vec{r} - r_1\hat{i}) + (\vec{r} - r_2\hat{j}) + (\vec{r} - r_3\hat{k}) = 3\vec{r} - \vec{r} = 2\vec{r}$

2. (a) $\vec{a}\times(\vec{b}\times\vec{c}) = (\vec{a}.\vec{c})\vec{b} - (\vec{a}.\vec{b})\vec{c} = \dfrac{\vec{b}+\vec{c}}{\sqrt{2}}$

$\vec{a}.\vec{c} = \dfrac{1}{\sqrt{2}}$ $\vec{a}.\vec{b} = -\dfrac{1}{\sqrt{2}}$; $\theta_1 = 45°$ $\theta_2 = 135°$

Angle between $\vec{a}\times\vec{b}$ is $\dfrac{3\pi}{4}$

3. (c) From the given $(\vec{a}\times\vec{c})$. $\{\vec{a}\times(\vec{b}\times\vec{c})\} = 0$

$\Rightarrow \quad (\vec{a}\times\vec{c}).\{(\vec{a}.\vec{c})\vec{b} - (\vec{a}.\vec{b}).\vec{c}\} = \vec{0} \Rightarrow (\vec{a}.\vec{c})[\vec{a}.\vec{c}.\vec{b}] - \vec{0} = \vec{0}$

$\vec{a}\times(\vec{b}\times\vec{c}) = -(\vec{a}.\vec{b})\vec{c}$.

Hence $\{\vec{c}\times(\vec{b}\times\vec{c})\}\times\vec{c} = \vec{o}$ as $\vec{c}\times\vec{c} = \vec{0} \Rightarrow [\vec{a}.\vec{c}] = \vec{0}$

4. **(a)** Given $\vec{a}(\vec{b}\times\vec{c})=\frac{\vec{b}}{2}$, $|\vec{a}|=|\vec{b}|=|\vec{c}|=1$

$\vec{a}\times(\vec{b}\times\vec{c})=(\vec{a}.\vec{c})\vec{b}-(\vec{a}.\vec{b})\vec{c}=\frac{\vec{b}}{2}$ given

$\Rightarrow$ $\vec{a}.\vec{c}=\frac{1}{2}$ angle between $\vec{a}\,\&\,\vec{b}$ is $\pi/3$

$\vec{a}.\vec{b}=0$ angle between $\vec{a}\,\&\,\vec{b}$ is $\pi/2$

5. **(a)** $\vec{a}\times(\vec{b}\times\vec{c})+(\vec{a}.\vec{b})\vec{b}=(\vec{a}.\vec{c}+\vec{a}.\vec{b})\vec{b}=(\vec{a}.\vec{b})\vec{c}$

$=(4-2\beta-\sin\alpha)\ \vec{b}+(\beta^2-1)\vec{c}$

Comparing $\vec{a}.\vec{c}$ $+(1-\beta^2)=4-2\beta-\sin\alpha$; $1-\beta^2=\vec{a}.\vec{b}$

$\vec{a}.\vec{c}=1$ and $\beta^2=1$ (from the values given In the options)

$\Rightarrow$ $1-\beta^2=0$ so $\vec{a}.\vec{c}=1=4-2\beta-\sin\alpha$

Possible only when $\beta=1$ & $\sin\alpha=1$ (i.e.$\alpha=2n\pi+\pi/2$)

$\Rightarrow$ $\beta=1\ \&\ \alpha=(4n+1)\frac{\pi}{2}$

6. $\vec{a}=\vec{p}+\vec{q},\vec{p}\times\vec{b}=\vec{o}\ \left(\Rightarrow\vec{p}=k\vec{b}\right),\vec{q}.\vec{b}=0$

Now $\frac{\vec{b}\times(\vec{a}\times\vec{b})}{b^2}=\frac{(b^2)\vec{a}-(\vec{a}.\vec{b})\vec{b}}{b^2}$

Using $\vec{a}=\vec{p}+\vec{q}=k\vec{b}+\vec{q}\Rightarrow\vec{a}.\vec{b}=kb^2+\vec{q}.\vec{b}=kb^2$

$\therefore$ $\frac{\vec{b}\times(\vec{a}\times\vec{b})}{b^2}=\vec{a}-k\vec{b}=\vec{p}+\vec{q}-\vec{p}=\vec{q}$

7. (a) $(\vec{a}+\vec{b})\times(\vec{a}\times\vec{b})$ $=\vec{a}\times(\vec{a}\times\vec{b})+\vec{b}\times(\vec{a}\times\vec{b})$

$=(\vec{a}.\vec{b})\vec{a}-(a^2)\vec{b}+(b^2)\vec{a}-(\vec{a}.\vec{b})\vec{b}$

$=(1+\vec{a}.\vec{b})\vec{a}-(1+\vec{a}.\vec{b})\vec{b}=(1+\vec{a}.\vec{b})(\vec{a}-\vec{b})$

$\Rightarrow$ $(\vec{a}+\vec{b})\times(\vec{a}\times\vec{b})$ is parallel to $\vec{a}-\vec{b}$

8. (b) $\vec{a}\times(\vec{b}\times\vec{c})=(\vec{a}\times\vec{b})\times\vec{c}$ $=(\vec{c})\times(\vec{a}\times\vec{b})$

$(\vec{b}.\vec{c})\vec{a}=(\vec{a}.\vec{b})\vec{c}$ i.e., $\vec{a}\parallel\vec{c}$

9. **(a)** $(\vec{a}\times\vec{b})\times(\vec{c}\times\vec{d})=[\vec{a}\,\vec{b}\,\vec{d}]\vec{c}$

$\Rightarrow$ $k=-[\vec{a}\ \vec{b}\ \vec{c}]=[\vec{b}\ \vec{a}\ \vec{c}]$

10. **(b)** length of projection of $\vec{a}$ on the plane of $\vec{b}\,\&\,\vec{c}$

$|\vec{a}||\cos\theta|=|\vec{a}|$ sin (90° – θ)

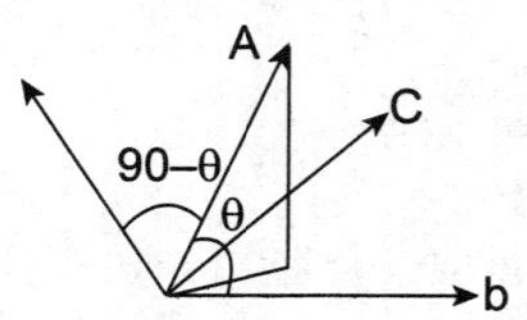

$=\frac{|\vec{a}\times(\vec{b}\times\vec{c})|}{|\vec{b}\times\vec{c}|}=\frac{|\vec{a}\times(\vec{b}\times\vec{c})|}{|\vec{b}\times\vec{c}|}$

11. **(a)** $\vec{p}=\frac{\vec{b}\times\vec{c}}{[\vec{a}\,\vec{b}\,\vec{c}]},\vec{q}=\frac{\vec{c}\times\vec{a}}{[\vec{a}\,\vec{b}\,\vec{c}]},\vec{r}=\frac{\vec{a}\times\vec{b}}{[\vec{a}\,\vec{b}\,\vec{c}]}$

$\Rightarrow$ $\vec{p},\vec{q},\vec{r}$ Represents the reciprocal vector system of $\vec{a},\vec{b},\vec{c}$

$\Rightarrow$ $\vec{a}.\vec{p}=\vec{b}.\vec{q}=\vec{c}.\vec{r}=1$ (Other products will vanish)

$\Rightarrow$ $(\vec{a}+\vec{b}+\vec{c}).(\vec{p}+\vec{q}+\vec{r})$ $=1+1+1=3$

12. **(d)** As in Q 11. $(\vec{a}+\vec{b}).\vec{p}+(\vec{b}+\vec{c}).\vec{q}+(\vec{c}+\vec{a})\vec{r}=3$

13. (b and c) $\vec{v}=(\vec{a}\times\vec{b})\times(\vec{c}\times\vec{d})=[\vec{a}\ \vec{b}\ \vec{d}]\vec{c}$

$=[\vec{a}\ \vec{c}\ \vec{d}]\vec{b}-[\vec{b}\ \vec{c}\ \vec{d}]\vec{a}-[\vec{a}\,\vec{b}\ \vec{c}]\vec{d}$

So the vector $\vec{V}$ is along the(line of) intersection of the two planes

Its inclination with both the planes is zero (it is in both the planes) $\Rightarrow$ equally inclined

14. **(c)** $\vec{d}=\vec{a}\times(\vec{b}\times\vec{c})+\vec{b}\times(\vec{c}\times\vec{a})+\vec{c}\times(\vec{a}\times\vec{b})$

$=(\vec{a}.\vec{c})\vec{b}-(\vec{a}.\vec{b})\vec{c}+(\vec{b}.\vec{a})\vec{c}-(\vec{b}.\vec{c})\vec{a}$ $+$ $(\vec{c}.\vec{b})\vec{a}-(\vec{c}.\vec{a})\vec{b}=\vec{o}$

15. **(b)** $\vec{a},\vec{b},\vec{c},\vec{d}$ lie in the same plane so $(\vec{a}\times\vec{b})\parallel(\vec{c}\times\vec{b})$

$\Rightarrow$ $(\vec{a}\times\vec{b})\times(\vec{c}\times\vec{d})=\vec{o}$

16. **(b)** $\{\vec{a}\times(\hat{i}\times\hat{j})\}^2+\{\vec{a}\times(\hat{j}\times\hat{k})\}^2+\{\vec{a}\times(\hat{k}\times\hat{i})\}^2$

$=\{\vec{a}\times\hat{k}\}^2+(\vec{a}\times\hat{j})^2+(\vec{a}\times\hat{j})^2$

$=\{a_2\hat{i}-a_1\hat{j}\}^2+(a_3\hat{j}-a_2\hat{k})+(a_1\hat{k}-a_3\hat{i})^2$

$=$ $a_2^2+a_1^2+a_3^2+a_2^2+a_1^2+a_3^2=2(a_1^2+a_2^2+a_3^2)$ $=$ $2|\vec{a}|^2$

17. **(a and c)** The product will lie in the plane of $\vec{b}\times\vec{c}$

Let $\left(\ell\vec{b}+m.\vec{c}\right)$ be such a vector then $\frac{\vec{a}.\vec{v}}{|\vec{a}|}=\sqrt{\frac{2}{3}}$ $\Rightarrow$ $\vec{v}.\vec{a}=2$

From the given option (a) and (c) satisfy the require condition

18. **(a)** $(\vec{a}\times\vec{b})\times(\vec{c}\times\vec{d})=\vec{o}$

$\Rightarrow$ either $\vec{a}\times\vec{b}=\vec{o}$

or $\vec{c}\times\vec{d}=\vec{o}\ or(\vec{a}\times\vec{b})\parallel$

when $(\vec{a}\times\vec{b})\parallel(\vec{c}\times\vec{d})$ then $\angle\theta=0$

TEXTUAL EXERCISE 11: (SUBJECTIVE)

1. $|\overline{PL}|=\frac{2\Delta ABC}{|\overline{BA}|}$

$=\frac{|\overline{AB}\times\overline{AP}|}{|\overline{AB}|}=\frac{|(6\hat{i}+3\hat{j}-4\hat{k})\times(3\hat{i}+\hat{j}-10\hat{k})|}{|6\hat{i}+3\hat{j}-4\hat{k}|}$

$=\frac{|-26\hat{i}+48\hat{j}-3\hat{k}|}{\sqrt{61}}$ $\frac{\sqrt{2989}}{\sqrt{61}}=\frac{\sqrt{49\times61}}{61}=7$ units

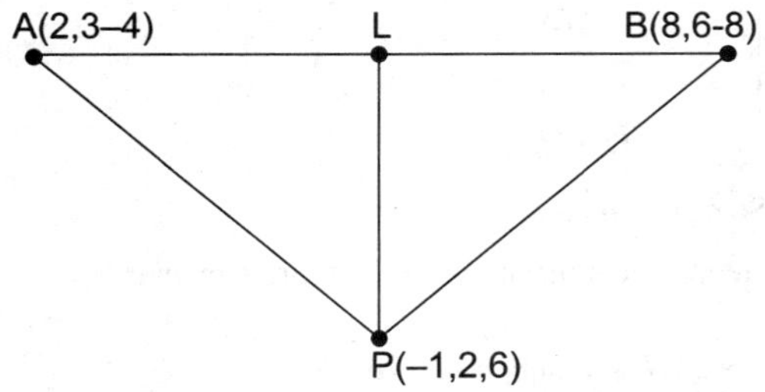

Aliter:

The equation $\overrightarrow{AB} = (2\hat{i} + 3\hat{j} - 4\hat{k}) + \lambda(6\hat{i} + 3\hat{j} - 4\hat{k})$

Using $\vec{r} = \vec{a} + \lambda\vec{b}$

Now $P(\vec{\alpha}) = (-1, 2, 6)$. Let L be the foot of perpendicular from P on $\overrightarrow{AB}$

$\therefore \quad \overrightarrow{PL} = (\vec{a} + \lambda\vec{b}) - \vec{\alpha} = (3 + 6\lambda)\hat{i} + (1 + 3\lambda)\hat{j} - (10 + 4\lambda)\hat{k}$

Since $\overrightarrow{PL} \perp \overrightarrow{AB} \quad \Rightarrow \quad \overrightarrow{PL}.\vec{b} = 0$

i.e. $(\vec{a} - \vec{\alpha})\vec{b} + \lambda\vec{b}^2 = 0$

So $18 + 36\lambda + 3 + 9\lambda + 40 + 16\lambda = 0$

Or $61\lambda + 61 = 0 \quad \Rightarrow \lambda = -1$

$\Rightarrow \quad \overrightarrow{PL} = -3\hat{i} - 2\hat{j} - 6\hat{k}$

So $|\overrightarrow{PL}|$ 7 units. Foot of perpendicular L = (–4,0,0)

2. A vector along the line of intersection of planes $x + y + z - 10 = 0$ and $2x - y + 3z - 18 = 0$.

is given by $\vec{n}_1 \times \vec{n}_2 = \begin{vmatrix} \hat{i} & \hat{j} & \hat{k} \\ 1 & 1 & 1 \\ 2 & -1 & 3 \end{vmatrix} = 4\hat{i} - \hat{j} - 3\hat{k}$

The vector $(\vec{n}_1 \times \vec{n}_2)$ is perpendicular (i.e. normal) to the plane 4x – y – 3x + d = 0. Since $P(\vec{a}) = <1, 4, -2>$ lies on it

$\therefore$ 4x – y – 3z – 6 = 0 is the required plane.

3. $\vec{n}_1 \times \vec{n}_2 = \begin{vmatrix} \hat{i} & \hat{j} & \hat{k} \\ 2 & 3 & -4 \\ 3 & 1 & -2 \end{vmatrix} = (-2\hat{i} - 8\hat{j} - 7\hat{k})$ or $2\hat{i} + 8\hat{j} + 7\hat{k}$

As (2 –4,5) lies on the plane

$\therefore$ 2x + 8y + 7z + d = 0 so d = –4 + 32 – 35 = –7

The plane is 2x + 8y + 7z = 8 Hence verified.

4. A(3,–5,–1), B = (–1, 5,7), $\vec{C} = 3\hat{i} - \hat{j} + 7\hat{k}$

$\overrightarrow{AB} = -4\hat{i} + 10\hat{j} + 8\hat{k}$

equation of the plane is $(\vec{\gamma} - \vec{a})\{\overrightarrow{AB} \times \vec{C}\} = 0$

So $\begin{vmatrix} (x-3) & (y+5) & (z+1) \\ -4 & 10 & 8 \\ 3 & -1 & 7 \end{vmatrix}$

= 78 (x–3)+ 52 (y + 5) – 26 (z + 1) = 0

Or 3x – 9 + 2y + 10 – z – 1 = 0, *i.e.* 3x + 2y – z = 0

5. equation of the line $\overrightarrow{AB} = \vec{r} = \vec{a} + \lambda\vec{b}$. Let L be the point of foot of perpendicular

$$|\overrightarrow{CL}| = \frac{2\Delta ABC}{|\overrightarrow{AB}|} = \frac{2 \times \frac{1}{2}\{\vec{a} \times \vec{b} + \vec{b} \times \vec{c} + \vec{c} \times \vec{a}\}}{|\vec{b} - \vec{a}|}$$

Hence the result

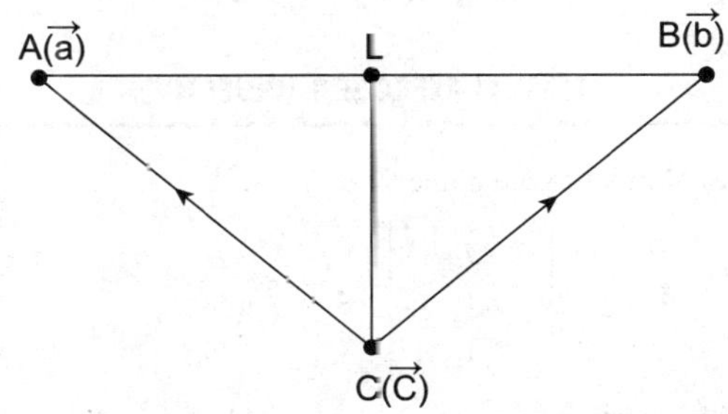

6. $\vec{n}_1 = \frac{1}{2}|(\vec{a} \times \vec{b})|$; $\vec{n}_2 = \frac{1}{2}|(\vec{c} \times \vec{c})|$; $\vec{n}_3 = \left|\frac{\vec{b} \times \vec{c}}{-2}\right|$;

$\vec{n}_4 = \left|\frac{(\vec{b} - \vec{a}) \times (\vec{c} - \vec{b})}{2}\right|$

$\vec{n}_1 + \vec{n}_2 + \vec{n}_3 + \vec{n}_4$

$= \frac{1}{2}\{(\vec{b} \times \vec{a}) + (\vec{a} \times \vec{c}) + (\vec{c} \times \vec{b}) + (\vec{b} \times \vec{c}) - (\vec{a} \times \vec{c}) + (\vec{a} \times \vec{b})\} = \vec{0}$

7. **(a)** D(x_4, y_4, z_4)

Vector equation of

$\overrightarrow{AB} : \vec{r} = (4\hat{i} + 5\hat{j} + 10\hat{k}) + \lambda(-2\hat{i} - 2\hat{j} - 6\hat{k})$

Or $\vec{r} = (4\hat{i} + 5\hat{j} + 10\hat{k}) + \mu(\hat{i} + \hat{j} + 3\hat{k})$

Cartesian form = $\frac{x-4}{-2} = \frac{y-5}{-2} = \frac{z-10}{-6} = \lambda$

Vector form of $BC : \vec{r} = (2\hat{i} + 3\hat{j} + 4\hat{k}) + \lambda(-\hat{i} - \hat{j} - 5\hat{k})$

Cartesian form = $\frac{x-2}{-1} = \frac{y-3}{-1} = \frac{z-4}{-5} = \lambda$

D = $(x_1 + x_3 - x_2, y_1 + y_3 - y_2, z_1 + z_3 - z_2)$ = (3,4,5)

(b) $\vec{b} = 2\hat{i} - 2\hat{j} + \hat{k}$

$\vec{\gamma} = (2\hat{i} - \hat{j} + \hat{k}) + \lambda(2\hat{i} - 2\hat{j} + \hat{k})$

Cartesian From : $\frac{x-2}{2} = \frac{y+1}{-2} = \frac{z-1}{1} = \lambda$

8. (a) equation of plane through P(1,10), Q(1,2,1), R(–2,2,–1) is

$\begin{vmatrix} x-1 & y-1 & z \\ 0 & 1 & 1 \\ -3 & 0 & -2 \end{vmatrix} = 0$

or 2–2x + 3 – 3y + 3z = 0

i.e. 2x + 3y + 3z – 5 = 0

(b) Let < a b c > be the d.c's of the vector then

$a = b = c = \dfrac{1}{\sqrt{3}}$

The vector with magnitude $2\sqrt{3}$ will be $\vec{n} = (2\hat{i} + 2\hat{j} + 2\hat{k})$

A plane normal to this vector will be x + y + z + d = 0

The plane passing though (1, –1,2) will be

$X + y + z - 2 = 0$ or $\vec{r}(\hat{i} + \hat{j} + \hat{k}) = 2$

TEXTUAL EXERCISE 8: (OBJECTIVE)

1. (c) Normal to the plane

$$\vec{n} = \vec{a} \times \vec{b} = \begin{vmatrix} \hat{i} & \hat{j} & \hat{k} \\ 2 & 1 & -3 \\ -1 & 1 & 11 \end{vmatrix} = 4\hat{i} + \hat{j} + 3\hat{k}$$

The equation of the plan: 4x + y + 3z + k = 0

2. (b) Equation of the plane is $\begin{vmatrix} (x-1) & (y-2) & (z-5) \\ 1 & -1 & 1 \\ 4 & -2 & 1 \end{vmatrix} = 0$

$\Rightarrow$ (x–1) + 3 (y –2) + 2 (z–5) = 0

X + 3y + 2z – 17 = 0 or $\vec{r}.(\hat{i} + 3\hat{j} + 2\hat{k}) = 17$

3. (c) A(2,1,5), B(0,–1,6), C (–3,4,5)

Equation of the plane = $\begin{vmatrix} (x-2) & (y-2) & (z-5) \\ 2 & 2 & -1 \\ 5 & -3 & 0 \end{vmatrix} = 0$

$\Rightarrow$ (x–2) (–3) –5(y–1) –16 (z –5) = 0

i.e. (–1) (3x – 6 + 5y – 5 + 16z –80) = 0

so $\vec{r}.(3\hat{i} + 5\hat{j} + 16\hat{k}) = 91$

4. (a) The equation of the plane

$$\begin{vmatrix} (x-2) & (y-1) & (z-5) \\ 1 & -2 & -3 \\ 1 & 1 & -1 \end{vmatrix} = 0$$

Or 5 (x–2) – 2(y –1) + 3 (z–5) = 0

i.e. 5x – 2y + 3z – 23 = 0

So $\vec{r}.(5\hat{i} - 2\hat{j} + 3\hat{k}) - 23 = 0$

5. (d) 5x –7y + 11z + λ = 0

Contains A(0,–1,–1) $\Rightarrow$ λ = 4

$\Rightarrow$ (λ –1, λ + μ, λ) = (3 , 4 + μ, 4) which lies on the plane

$\Rightarrow$ 15 –28 – 7μ + 44 + 4 = 0

35 – 7μ = so μ = 5

TEXTUAL EXERCISE 12: (SUBJECITVE)

1. $\vec{a} = (\hat{i} - \hat{j} + \hat{k}), \vec{b} = -\hat{i} + 2\hat{j} - \hat{k}$,

$\vec{c} = (x-1)\hat{i} + (x+2)\hat{j} + \hat{k}$

Now $\vec{c}.(\vec{a} \times \vec{b}) = 0$ gives

$$\begin{vmatrix} 1 & -1 & 1 \\ -1 & 2 & -1 \\ (x-1) & (x+2) & 1 \end{vmatrix} \Rightarrow 2 - x = 0 \Rightarrow x = 2$$

So $\vec{c} = \hat{i} + 4\hat{j} + \hat{k}$

Geometrical meaning: $\vec{a}, \vec{b}, \vec{c}$ are coplanar

2. $\vec{r} \times \vec{a} = \vec{b} \times \vec{a}$ and $\vec{r} \times \vec{b} = \vec{a} \times \vec{b}$

$(\vec{r} - \vec{b}) \times \vec{a} = \vec{0}$ and $(\vec{r} - \vec{a}) \times \vec{b} = \vec{0}$

$(\vec{r} - \vec{b})$ is collinear with $\vec{a}$ and $(\vec{\pi} - \vec{a})$ is collinear with $\vec{b}$

$\vec{r} = \vec{b} + \lambda\vec{a}$ and $\vec{r} = \vec{a} + \mu\vec{b}$

$\Rightarrow$ $\vec{r} = \vec{a} + \vec{b} \Rightarrow \vec{r}$ is along the diagonal of a ||gm with adjacent sides $\vec{a}$ and $\vec{b}$

alternatively $\vec{r}$ is the P.V. of the point of intersection of two lines $\vec{r}_1 = \vec{b} + \lambda\vec{a}$ and $\vec{r}_2 = \vec{a} + \mu\vec{b}$

3. $\vec{a}.\vec{b} = \vec{a}.\vec{c}$ and $\vec{a} \times \vec{b} = -\vec{a} \times \vec{c}$,

$\vec{a}.(\vec{b} - \vec{c}) = 0$ and $\vec{a} \times (\vec{b} + \vec{c}) = \vec{0}$

So $(\vec{b} - \vec{c}) \perp \vec{a}$ and $\vec{b} + \vec{c} = t\vec{a}$ or $\vec{a} = \lambda(\vec{b} + \vec{c})$;

(where λ ∈ **R** – {0})

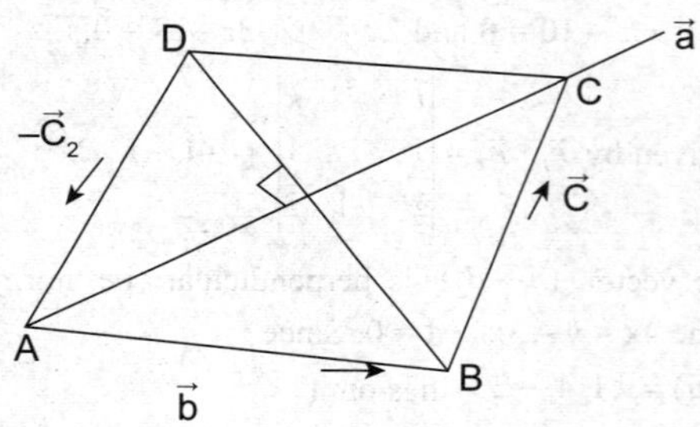

{We know that diagonals of a rhombus or a square intersect at 90°}

which gives $|\vec{b}| = |\vec{c}|$ and $\vec{a}$ is along the diagonal passing through the intersection of $\vec{b}$ and $\vec{e}$

4. $\vec{r} \times \vec{a} = \vec{r} \times \vec{b} \Rightarrow \vec{r} \times (\vec{a} - \vec{b}) = \vec{O}$

gives $\vec{r} = \lambda(\vec{a} - \vec{b})$

$\therefore$ Geometrically $\vec{r}$ is caplanar with $\vec{a}$ and $\vec{b}$.

5. given $\vec{r}.\vec{a} = \vec{r}.\vec{b} = -\vec{r}.\vec{b}$

$\Rightarrow$ $\vec{r}.\vec{b} = 0$ $\quad \Rightarrow \vec{r} \perp \vec{b} \Rightarrow \vec{r} \perp \vec{a}$

Since $\vec{a} \neq \vec{b}$

$\Rightarrow$ $\vec{r}$ is collinear with $\vec{a} \times \vec{b}$ i.e. $\vec{r}$ is normal vector to the plane of $\vec{a}$ and $\vec{b}$;

$\vec{r} = \lambda(\vec{a} \times \vec{b})$

TEXTUAL EXERCISE 9: (SUBJECITVE)

1. (b) Given $\vec{a}.\vec{b} = 0$ and $\vec{r} \times \vec{a} = \vec{b}$,

$\vec{b} \times (\vec{r} \times \vec{a}) = \vec{b} \times \vec{b} = \vec{O}$

and $(\vec{b}.\vec{a})\vec{r} - (\vec{b}.\vec{r})\vec{a} = \vec{O} \Rightarrow \vec{b} \perp \vec{r}$

since $(\vec{r} \times \vec{a})$ is perpendicular to both $\vec{a}$ and $\vec{r}$

Let $\vec{r} = x\vec{a} + y\vec{b} + z(\vec{a} \times \vec{b})$

$\vec{r} \times \vec{a} = +y(\vec{b} \times \vec{a}) + z(\vec{a} \times \vec{b}) \times \vec{a} = \vec{b}$

$\Rightarrow y(\vec{b} \times \vec{a}) + z(\vec{a})^2\vec{b} = \vec{b}$

Gives $z = \dfrac{1}{(|\vec{a}|)^2}\ y = 0$

So $\vec{r} = x\vec{a} + \dfrac{\vec{a} \times \vec{b}}{(|\vec{a}|)^2}$

$\therefore$ $\vec{r}$ and $\vec{a}$ are in a plane normal to $\vec{b}$.

If x = 0 only then $\vec{r} \parallel (\vec{a} \times \vec{b})$

2. (c) $(20a - 15b)\vec{x} + (15b - 12c)\vec{y} + (12c - 20a)\ (\vec{x} \times \vec{y}) = \vec{O}$

Gives 4a = 3b, 5b = 4c, 3c = 5a

$\Rightarrow$ a : b : c = 3 : 4 : 5 so ΔABC is right angled (at C point)

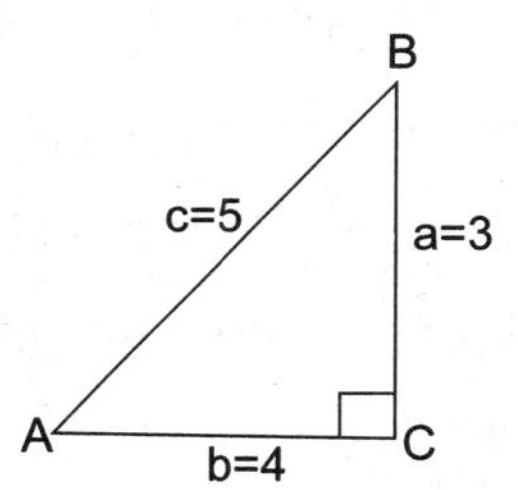

3. (c) Equation of line $\vec{r} = (2\hat{i} - \hat{j} + \hat{k}) + \lambda(-\hat{i} + \hat{j} + \hat{k})$ D.c.'s

of the line = $\left\langle -\dfrac{1}{\sqrt{3}}, \dfrac{1}{\sqrt{3}}, \dfrac{1}{\sqrt{3}} \right\rangle$

d.c of he plane $\left\langle \dfrac{3}{\sqrt{14}}, \dfrac{2}{\sqrt{14}}, -\dfrac{1}{\sqrt{14}} \right\rangle$

sinθ = |sum of the products of d.c.'s| = $\left|\dfrac{-3+2-1}{\sqrt{42}}\right| = \left|\dfrac{-2}{\sqrt{42}}\right|$

$\theta = \sin^{-1}\left(\dfrac{2}{\sqrt{42}}\right)$

4. (b) $L_1 : \vec{r}_1 = 3\hat{i} + \lambda(-\hat{i} + \hat{j} + \hat{k})$

$L_2 : \vec{r}_2 = (\hat{i} + \hat{j}) + \mu(\hat{i} + \hat{k})$

Now (3 – λ) = (1 + μ), gives λ = 1, μ = 1 and the point of intersection is $2\hat{i} + \hat{j} + \hat{k}$ i.e. (2,1,1)

5. (c) $\vec{r} \times \vec{a} = \vec{b} \times \vec{a}$ and $\vec{r} \times \vec{b} = \vec{a} \times \vec{b}$,

$(\vec{r} - \vec{b}) \times \vec{a} = \vec{O}$ and $(\vec{r} - \vec{a}) \times \vec{b} = \vec{O}$

$\vec{r} = \vec{b} + \lambda\vec{a}$ and $\vec{r} = \vec{a} + \mu\vec{\beta}$

Point of intersection will be at λ = μ = 1

$\Rightarrow \vec{r} = \vec{a} + \vec{b} = 3\hat{i} + \hat{j} - \hat{k}$ i.e. (3,1–1)

6. (a, b, c, d) $\hat{\alpha}.\hat{r} = \hat{\beta}.\hat{r}$ and $\hat{\alpha}.\hat{\beta} = 0$ -

So $\hat{r} = x\hat{\alpha} + y\hat{\beta} + z(\hat{\alpha} \times \hat{\beta})$ $\{|\hat{\alpha} \times \hat{p}| = 1$ as $\hat{\alpha} \perp \hat{\beta}\}$

Gives $x^2 + y^2 + z^2 = 1$

$\left.\begin{array}{l}\hat{r}.\hat{\alpha} = x\hat{\alpha}^2 = x \\ \hat{r}.\beta = x\beta^2 = y\end{array}\right\} \Rightarrow x = y \text{ or } x^2 = y^2$

$z^2 = 1 - x^2 - y^2 = 1 - 2y^2 = 1 - 2x^2$

7. (c) $P(\vec{r})$ is the P.V. of point P

$\vec{a}.\vec{b} + \vec{c}.\vec{r} = \vec{a}.\vec{c} + \vec{b}.\vec{r} = \vec{b}.\vec{c} + \vec{a}.\vec{r}$

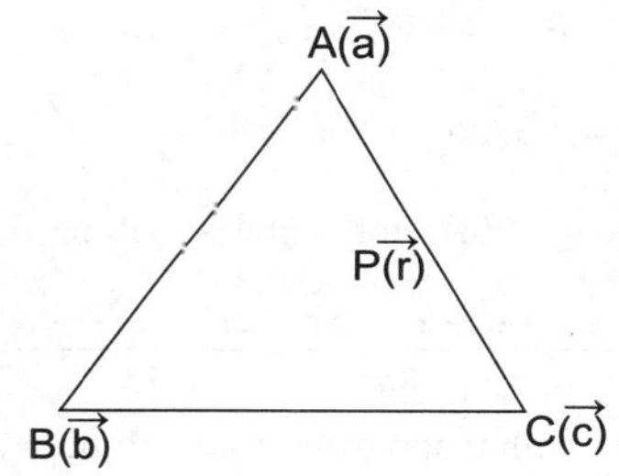

Take two (sides) parts

$\vec{a}.(\vec{b} - \vec{c}) + \vec{r}.(\vec{c} - \vec{b}) = 0$

Or $(\vec{r} - \vec{a}).(\vec{c} - \vec{b}) = 0 \Rightarrow (\vec{r} - \vec{a}) \perp (\vec{c} - \vec{b})$

i.e. $\overrightarrow{AP} \perp \overrightarrow{BC}$ Similarly $\overrightarrow{BP} \perp \overrightarrow{AC}$ and $\overrightarrow{CP} \perp \overrightarrow{AB}$. Hence P is orthocenter

8. (b) $\vec{r} \times (\hat{i} + 2\hat{j} + \hat{k}) = \hat{i} - \hat{k}$

Let $\vec{r} = \vec{a} + \alpha(\hat{i} + 2\hat{j} + \hat{k})$

$\Rightarrow \vec{r} \times (\hat{i} + 2\hat{j} + \hat{k}) = \vec{a} \times (\hat{i} + 2\hat{j} + \hat{k}) = \hat{i} - \hat{k}$

When $\vec{a} = \hat{j}$ then $\hat{j} \times \hat{i} = -\hat{k}$ and $\hat{j} \times \hat{k} = \hat{i}$

Hence $\vec{r} = \hat{j} + (\hat{i} + 2\hat{j} + \hat{k})$

9. (c) $\vec{a}.\vec{b} = 0, \vec{a} \times \vec{r} = \vec{b}, \vec{r}.\vec{a} = \alpha$

Let $\vec{r} = x\vec{a} + y\vec{b} + z(\vec{a} \times \vec{b})$

$\vec{r}, \vec{a} = x(a^2) + 0 + 0 \Rightarrow x = \dfrac{\alpha}{a^2}$

$\vec{a} \times \vec{r} = y(\vec{a} \times \vec{b}) + z(a^2)\vec{b} = \vec{b}$ gives $z = \dfrac{-1}{a^2} 1y = 0$

$\Rightarrow \vec{r} = \dfrac{\alpha}{|\vec{a}|^2}\vec{a} - \dfrac{1}{|\vec{a}|^2}(\vec{a} \times \vec{b})$

SECTION III: (ONLY ONE CORRECT ANSWER)

1. **(b)** Since diagonals bisect each other at 90°

So $\overline{OA} = -\overline{OC}$ and $\overline{OD} = -\overline{OB}$

$\Rightarrow \quad \overline{OA} + \overline{OB} + \overline{OC} + \overline{OD} = \vec{O}$

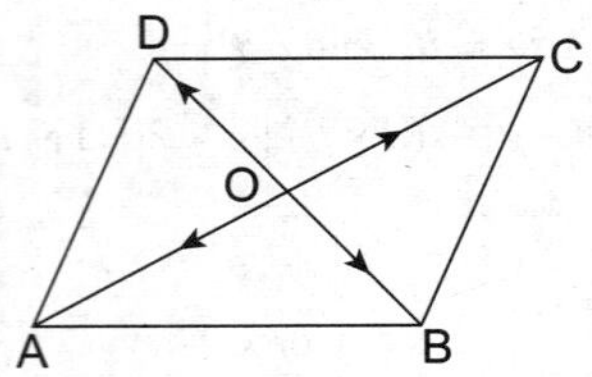

2. **(b)** $|\vec{a}+\vec{b}| = |\vec{a}-\vec{b}|$, $(\vec{a} \neq 0)$

Squaring we get

$= (\vec{a})^2 + (\vec{b})^2 + 2(\vec{a}\vec{b}) = (\vec{a})^2 + (\vec{b})^2 - 2\vec{a}\vec{b}$

$\Rightarrow \quad 4\vec{a}.\vec{b} = 0 \qquad \Rightarrow \quad a \perp b$

3. **(a)** $\vec{a} = -4\hat{i} + 3\hat{j}, \vec{b} = 14\hat{i} + 2\hat{j} - 5\hat{k}$

Vector along $\angle$ bisector $\vec{a}$ and $\vec{b}$ will be $\hat{a} + \hat{b}$

$= \dfrac{-4\hat{i}+3\hat{j}}{5} + \dfrac{14\hat{i}+2\hat{j}-5\hat{k}}{15} = \dfrac{2\hat{i}+11\hat{j}-5\hat{k}}{15}$

The vector with magnitude of √6 will be

$\frac{1}{5}\left\{2\hat{i}+11\hat{j}-5\hat{k}\right\}$

4. **(b)** $|\vec{b}| = |\vec{c}| = 4$ **units**

$\vec{c} - \vec{b} = 4\sqrt{2}$ units towards west

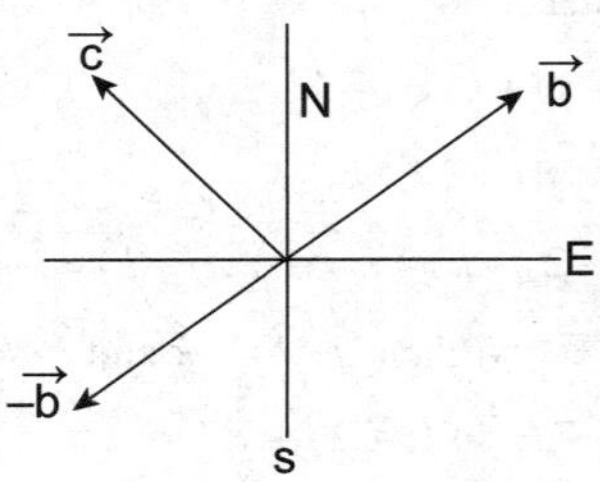

5. **(b)** P.V. of point $X(\vec{C}) = \dfrac{2\vec{b}+\vec{a}}{3}$

P.V. of Point Y $(\vec{d}) = \dfrac{2\vec{b}-\vec{a}}{1} = 2\vec{b} - \vec{a}$

$\therefore \quad \overline{XY} = \vec{d} - \vec{c} = \dfrac{6\vec{b} - 3\vec{a} - 2\vec{b} - \vec{a}}{3} = \dfrac{4\vec{a} - 4\vec{b}}{3}$

$= \frac{4}{3}(\vec{a} - \vec{b})$

6. **(a)** $\vec{a} = 2\hat{i} + 4\hat{j} - 5\hat{k}$ and $\vec{b} = \hat{i} + 2\hat{j} + 3\hat{k}$

Diagonal will be $(\vec{a} + \vec{b})$

$= 3\hat{i} + 6\hat{j} - 2\hat{k}, |3\hat{i} + 6\hat{j} - 2\hat{k}| = 7$

So unit vector $\frac{1}{7}\left\{3\hat{i} + 6\hat{j} - 2\hat{k}\right\}$

7. **(b)** $A(\vec{a}) = \hat{i} + 2\hat{j} + 3\hat{k}$, $B(\vec{b}) = -\hat{i} - \hat{j} + 8\hat{k}$

$\vec{C}(\vec{c}) = -4\hat{i} + 4\hat{j} + 5\hat{k}$, now

$\overline{AB} = -2\hat{i} - 3\hat{j} + 5\hat{k} = \sqrt{38}$ units

$\overline{AC} = -5\hat{i} + 2\hat{j} + 3\hat{k} = \sqrt{38}$ units

$\overline{BC} = 3\hat{i} + 5\hat{j} - 2\hat{k} = \sqrt{38}$ units

$\Rightarrow \Delta$ is (isosceles also) equilateral

8. **(a)** $|\vec{a}| = |\vec{b}| = 2$ units

$(\angle\theta = 60°)$ $|\vec{a} + \vec{b}| = 2\sqrt{3}$,

$\vec{a}.\vec{b} = 4.\frac{1}{2} = 2$

Now $\cos\theta = \dfrac{\vec{a}(\vec{a}+\vec{b})}{(2)2\sqrt{3}} = \dfrac{4+2}{4\sqrt{3}} = \dfrac{\sqrt{3}}{2} \Rightarrow \theta = 30°$

9. **(b)** $\vec{a} = 5, |\vec{a} - \vec{b}| = 8, |\vec{a} + \vec{b}| = 10$

$\Rightarrow \; 2(a^2 + b^2) = |(\vec{a}+\vec{b})|^2 + \left(|\vec{a}-\vec{b}|\right)^2 = 164$

So $b^2 = 82 - 25 = 57 \Rightarrow |\vec{b}| = \sqrt{57}$ units

10. **(b)** $(\vec{a} \times \vec{b})^2 + (\vec{a}.\vec{b})^2 = (|\vec{a}||\vec{b}|\sin\theta)^2 + (|\vec{a}||\vec{b}|\cos\theta)^2$

$= a^2b^2 = |\vec{a}|^2\,|\vec{b}|^2$

11. **(b)** $\vec{a} = 4\hat{i} + 6\hat{j}$, $\vec{b} = 3\hat{j} + 4\hat{k}$

Vector component of $\vec{a}$ along

$\vec{b} = \dfrac{(\vec{a}.\vec{b})}{|\vec{b}|^2}.\vec{b} = \dfrac{18}{25}(3\hat{j} + 4\hat{k})$

12. **(c)** Given $\vec{a}.\vec{b} = 0 \Rightarrow \quad \vec{a} \perp \vec{b}$, $\dfrac{\vec{a}.(\vec{a}+\vec{b})}{|\vec{a}||\vec{a}+\vec{b}|} = \cos 30°$

$\Rightarrow \; 2|\vec{a}| = \sqrt{3}|\vec{a}+\vec{b}|$ squaring $4(\vec{a})^2 = 3\left\{(\vec{a})^2 + (\vec{b})^2 + 0\right\}$

gives $3(\vec{b})^2 = (\vec{a})^2 \Rightarrow |\vec{a}| = \sqrt{3}|\vec{b}|$

13. **(a)** $\vec{F} = 2(\hat{i} - 2\hat{j} + 2\hat{k}) = \vec{F}_1 = 2(\hat{i} - 2\hat{j} + 2\hat{k}) = 6$ units

$\vec{F}_2 = 2\hat{i} - 3\hat{j} - 6\hat{k} = 7$ units

$\vec{D} = \overline{PQ} = 3\hat{i} + \hat{j} + 4\hat{k}$

Work done $(\vec{F}_1 + \vec{F}_2)\vec{D}$

$= (4\hat{i} - 7\hat{j} - 2\hat{k}).(3\hat{i} + 4\hat{k}) = 12 - 8 = 4$ units

14. (c) $\vec{a}=\hat{i}+\hat{j}-\hat{k}$,

$\vec{b}=-\hat{i}+2\hat{j}+\hat{k}$, $\vec{c}=-\hat{i}+2\hat{j}-\hat{k}$,

$(\vec{a}+\vec{b})=3\hat{j}$ and $(\vec{b}+\vec{c})=-2\hat{i}+4\hat{j}$,

A unit vector perpendicular to $(\vec{a}+\vec{b})$ and $(\vec{b}+\vec{c})$

$$\hat{n}=\frac{(\vec{a}+\vec{b})\times(\vec{b}+\vec{c})}{|(\vec{a}+\vec{b})\times(\vec{b}\times\vec{c})|}=\frac{6\hat{k}}{6}=\hat{k}$$

15. (b) P.V. of three points $A(\vec{a})$, $B(\vec{b})$, $C(\vec{c})$ where

$\vec{a}=\hat{i}+\hat{j}+\hat{k}$, $\vec{b}=2\hat{i}+3\hat{j}-4\hat{k}$, $\vec{c}=7\hat{i}+4\hat{j}+9\hat{k}$,

so $\overrightarrow{AB}=\hat{i}+2\hat{j}-5\hat{k}$, $\overrightarrow{AC}=6\hat{i}+3\hat{j}+8\hat{k}$

(A unit vector perpendicular to the plane of ΔABC)

Required vector = $\dfrac{\overrightarrow{AB}\times\overrightarrow{AC}}{|\overrightarrow{AB}\times\overrightarrow{AC}|}=\dfrac{31\hat{i}-38\hat{j}-9\hat{k}}{\sqrt{2486}}$

16. (d) $\vec{\alpha}=(x+4)\vec{a}+(2x+y+1)\vec{b}$,

$\vec{\beta}=(y-2x+2)\vec{a}+(2x-3y-1)\vec{b}$,

and $3\vec{\alpha}=2\vec{\beta}\Rightarrow$ 3x + 12y = 2y – 4x + 4 or 7x + 10y = 4

And 6x + 3y + 3 = 4x – 6y – 2 or 2x + 9y = –5

Solving we x = 2, y = –1

17. (c) Given $P(\vec{p})=10\hat{i}+3\hat{j}$,

$Q(\vec{q})=12\hat{i}-5\hat{j}$, $R(\vec{r})=a\hat{i}+11j$

So $\overrightarrow{PQ}=2\hat{i}-8\hat{j}$ and $\overrightarrow{PR}=\{(a-10)\hat{i}+8\hat{j}\}$

P,Q,R will be collinear when (a –10) = –2 ⇒ a = 8

18. (c) $\left[\vec{a}-\vec{b}\ \vec{b}-\vec{c}\ \vec{c}-\vec{a}\right]$

$=(\vec{a}-\vec{b}).((\vec{b}-\vec{c})\times(\vec{c}\times\vec{a}))=(\vec{a}-\vec{b}).\{\vec{b}\times\vec{c}+\vec{a}\times\vec{b}+\vec{c}\times\vec{a}\}$

$=\vec{a}.(\vec{b}\times\vec{c})-\vec{b}.(\vec{c}\times\vec{a})=0$

19. (b) Let $\vec{r}=r_1\hat{i}+r_2\hat{j}+r_3\hat{k}$

Now $\hat{i}\times(\vec{r}\times\hat{i})=\vec{r}-r_1\hat{i}$ similarly other parts

$\Rightarrow\ i\times(\vec{r}\times\hat{i})+\hat{j}\times(\vec{r}\times\hat{j})+\hat{k}\times(\vec{r}\times\hat{k})=3\vec{r}-\vec{r}=2\vec{r}$

20. (b) The unit vector ⊥ to $\vec{a}=\hat{i}+\hat{j}$ and $\vec{b}=\hat{j}+\hat{k}$

will be $\hat{n}=\pm\dfrac{\vec{a}\times\vec{b}}{|\vec{a}\times\vec{b}|}\Rightarrow$ Two vectors are possible

21. (c) $(\vec{a}+2\vec{b}-\vec{c})\{(\vec{a}-\vec{b})\times(\vec{a}-\vec{b}-\vec{c})\}$

$=(\vec{a}+2\vec{b}+\vec{c})\left[\{(\vec{a}-\vec{b}-\vec{c})+\vec{c}\}\times(\vec{a}-\vec{b}-\vec{c})\right]$

$=(\vec{a}+2\vec{b}-\vec{c}).\{\vec{c}\times\vec{a}-\vec{c}\times\vec{b}\}$

$=\left[\vec{a}\ \vec{b}\ \vec{c}\right]+2\left[\vec{b}\ \vec{c}\ \vec{a}\right]=3\left[\vec{a}\ \vec{b}\ \vec{c}\right]$

22. (a) $|\vec{a}|=3, |\vec{b}|=4$ and ; θ = 120° ⇒ $\vec{a}.\vec{b}=-6$

So $\left|2\vec{a}-\dfrac{3}{2}\vec{b}\right|=\sqrt{36+36+36}=6\sqrt{3}$ units

23. (b) Let $\vec{a}=a_1\hat{i}+a_2\hat{j}+a_3\hat{k}$

Now $|\vec{a}\times\hat{i}|^2=\left(-a_2\hat{k}+a_3\hat{j}\right)^2=a_2^2+a_3^2$ similarly other parts

$\Rightarrow\ |\vec{a}\times\hat{i}|^2+|\vec{a}\times\hat{j}|^2+|\vec{a}\times\hat{k}|^2=2\left(a_1^2+a_2^2+a_3^2\right)=2(\vec{a})^2$

24. (a) (Unit vector ⊥ to the given vectors)

The required unit vector $\hat{r}=\pm\dfrac{\vec{a}\times\vec{b}}{|\vec{a}\times\vec{b}|}$

$=\dfrac{\pm(-5\hat{i}+5\hat{j}+5\hat{k})}{5\sqrt{3}}=\dfrac{\hat{i}-\hat{j}-\hat{k}}{\sqrt{3}}$ or $\dfrac{-\hat{i}+\hat{j}+\hat{k}}{\sqrt{3}}$

25. (a) The required axis will be given by $\vec{b}=\hat{i}+\hat{j}+\hat{k}$,

Projection of $\vec{a}=4\hat{i}-3\hat{j}+2\hat{k}$ $\left(\text{on } \vec{b}=\hat{i}+\hat{j}+\hat{k}\right)$

$=\dfrac{\vec{a}.\vec{b}}{|\vec{b}|}=\dfrac{4-3+2}{\sqrt{3}}=\sqrt{3}$

26. (d) $\left|(\vec{a}\times\vec{b}).\vec{c}\right|=|\vec{a}||\vec{b}||\vec{c}|=\vec{a},\vec{b},\vec{c}$ are non-zero vectors

Possible only when sinθ = 1

⇒ cos θ = 0 for any two vectors

where $\vec{a}.\vec{b}=\vec{b}.\vec{c}=\vec{c}.\vec{a}=0$

27. (b) $|\vec{a}|=11, |\vec{b}|=23, |\vec{c}|=30$

Now $|\vec{a}+\vec{b}|^2=2\left(|\vec{a}|^2+|\vec{b}|^2\right)-\left(\vec{a}-\vec{b}\right)^2$

= 1300 – 900 ⇒ $|\vec{a}+\vec{b}|=20$

28. (d) $\vec{a}+\vec{b}=-\vec{c}$

$\Rightarrow\ (\vec{a})^2+(\vec{b})^2+2\vec{a}.\vec{b}=(\vec{c})^2$

$\Rightarrow\ 9+25+2\vec{a}.\vec{b}=49\ \Rightarrow\ \vec{a}.\vec{b}=\dfrac{15}{2}$

15cosθ = 15/2 ⇒ θ = π/3

29. (b) $|\vec{a}|=|\vec{b}|=1$ and $\vec{a}.\vec{b}=\dfrac{1}{2}\left\{\cos 60°=\dfrac{1}{2}\right\}$

$=|\vec{p}+\vec{q}|=|3\vec{a}-\vec{b}|=\sqrt{9+1-3}=\sqrt{7}$

$=|\vec{p}-\vec{q}|=|\vec{a}+3\vec{b}|=\sqrt{1-9+3}=\sqrt{13}$

30. (b) $|\vec{u}|=3, |\vec{v}|=4, |\vec{w}|=5$

Now $(\vec{u}+\vec{v}+\vec{w})^2=\vec{u}^2+\vec{v}^2+\vec{w}^2+2(\vec{u}\vec{v}+\vec{v}.\vec{w}+\vec{u}.\vec{w})$

$9+16+25+2(\vec{u}\vec{v}+\vec{v}\vec{w}+\vec{u}.\vec{w})=0$

$\Rightarrow\ \vec{u}.\vec{v}+\vec{v}.\vec{w}+\vec{u}.\vec{w}=-25$

31. **(a)** Component vector of projection of $\vec{a} = 6\hat{i} - 3\hat{j} - 6\hat{k}$

$(on\ \vec{b} = \hat{i} + \hat{j} + \hat{k}) = \frac{\vec{a}.\vec{b}}{(b)^2}\vec{b} = \frac{(-3)}{3}(\hat{i} + \hat{j} + \hat{k}) = -(\hat{i} + \hat{j} + \hat{k})$

The perpendicular component

$= \vec{a} + (\hat{i} + \hat{j} + \hat{k}) = 7\hat{i} - 2\hat{j} - 5\hat{k}$

32. **(c)** $|\hat{x}| = |\hat{y}| = 1$ at angle ϕ then

$\frac{1}{2}|\hat{x} - \hat{y}| = \frac{1}{2}\sqrt{1+1-2\cos\phi} = \left|\sin\frac{\phi}{2}\right|$

33. **(d)** Unit vector along the sum $= \frac{(b+2)\hat{i} + 6\hat{j} - 2\hat{k}}{\sqrt{b^2 + 4b + 44}}$

Scalar product (with $\hat{i} + \hat{j} + \hat{k}$) $= \frac{(b+2) + 6 - 2}{\sqrt{b^2 + 4b + 44}} = 1$

Squaring $b^2 + 36 + 12b = b^2 + 4b + 44 \Rightarrow b = 1$

34. **(b)** $\vec{u} = 3\vec{a} - \vec{b}$, $\vec{v} = \vec{a} - 3\vec{b}$;

where $|\vec{a}| = |\vec{b}| = 2$ **and** $\vec{a}.\vec{b} = 2$

$\Rightarrow |\vec{u} + \vec{v}| = |4\vec{a} - 4\vec{b}| = 4\sqrt{4+4-4} = 8$,

and $|\vec{u} - \vec{v}| = |2\vec{a} - 4\vec{b}| = \sqrt{16+64-32} = \sqrt{48} = 4\sqrt{3}$

35. **(c)** $|\vec{a} + \vec{b}| = |\vec{a}| + |\vec{b}|$

Squaring both sides $|\vec{a}|^2 + |\vec{b}|^2 + 2\vec{a}.\vec{b}$

$= |\vec{a}|^2 + |\vec{b}|^2 + 2|\vec{a}||\vec{b}|$ gives $\vec{a}.\vec{b} = |\vec{a}||\vec{b}|$

$\Rightarrow \cos\theta = 1$ or $|\vec{a}| = 0$ or $|\vec{b}| = 0$

i.e. $\vec{a} = \lambda\vec{b}$; where $\lambda > 0$

or at least one of $\vec{a}$ and $\vec{b}$ is a null vector

36. **(b)** P.V of $P(\vec{p}) = \vec{a} - 2\vec{b} + 3\vec{c}$,

$Q(\vec{q}) = 2\vec{a} + 3\vec{b} - 4\vec{c}$, $R(\vec{r}) = -7\vec{b} + 9\vec{c}$,

$\Rightarrow \overrightarrow{PQ} = \vec{a} + 5\vec{b} - 7\vec{c}$, $\overrightarrow{PR} = -\vec{a} - 5\vec{b} + 6\vec{c}$

Now $\overrightarrow{PQ} \neq \lambda\overrightarrow{PR}$ $\therefore$ The points are not collinear

But three non-collinear points are always coplanar

37. **(c)** $\vec{c} = (x-2)\vec{a} + \vec{b}$ and $\vec{d} = (2x-1)\vec{a} - \vec{b}$

as $\vec{c}$ and $\vec{d}$ are collinear

$\therefore$ $x - 2 = -2x - 1$

i.e. $3x = 1$ gives $x = 1/3$

38. **(d)** $|\vec{c}| = \sqrt{3} \Rightarrow \alpha^2 + \beta^2 + 1 = 3$ or $\alpha^2 + \beta^2 = 2$

Since vectors are linearly dependent

$\Rightarrow \vec{c} = \lambda\vec{a} + \mu\vec{b}$, Now $4\hat{i} + 3\hat{j} + 4\hat{k}$

$= (\lambda + \mu)\hat{i} + (\lambda + \mu\alpha)\hat{j} + (\alpha + \mu\beta)\hat{k}$

gives $\lambda + \mu = 4$, $\lambda + \mu\alpha = 3\lambda + \mu\beta = 4 = (\lambda + \mu)$

$\Rightarrow \beta = 1$, so $\alpha^2 = 1$

Case (i): $\alpha = 1$, then $\lambda + \mu = 4$ and $\lambda + \mu = 3$ (not possible)

Case (ii): $\alpha = -1$, then $\lambda + \mu = 4$, $\lambda - \mu = 3$

gives $\mu = 72$, $\mu = 1/2$

39. **(c)** Let $\vec{a} = -12\hat{i} + 0\hat{j} + a\hat{k}$, $\vec{b} = 3\hat{j} - \hat{k}$, $\vec{c} = 2\hat{i} + \hat{j} - 15\hat{k}$

Vol of parallelepiped $= [\vec{a}\ \vec{b}\ \vec{c}] = \left\|\begin{matrix} -12 & 0 & a \\ 0 & 3 & -1 \\ 2 & 1 & -15 \end{matrix}\right\|$

$= |(-12) \times (-44) - 6a| = 546$

So $-6a = 546 - 528 \Rightarrow a = -3$

40. **(a)** $\hat{a}, \hat{b}, \hat{c}$ are coplanar unit vector

$\Rightarrow [\hat{a}\ \hat{b}\ \hat{c}] = 0 \Rightarrow [2a - \hat{b}\ \ 2\hat{b} - \hat{c}\ \ 2\hat{c} - \hat{a}] = 0$

41. **(b)** $\vec{a} = 2\hat{i} + \hat{j} - 2\hat{k}, \vec{b} = \hat{i} + \hat{j}$

$\Rightarrow \vec{a}.\vec{b} = 2 + 1 = 3 = |\vec{c}| = \sqrt{c_1^2 + c_2^2 + c_3^2}$ so $|\vec{c}| = 3$

$(\vec{a} \times \vec{b}) = \begin{vmatrix} \hat{i} & \hat{j} & \hat{k} \\ 2 & 1 & -2 \\ 1 & 1 & 0 \end{vmatrix} = -2\hat{i} + 2\hat{j} + \hat{k} = 3$ units

Now $|(\vec{a} \times \vec{b}) \times \vec{c}| = |(\vec{a} \times \vec{b})||\vec{c}|\sin 30° = 3(3)\frac{1}{2} = \frac{9}{2}$

42. **(a)** Let $\vec{c} = \ell\hat{i} + m\hat{j} + n\hat{k}$

Since $\vec{c} \perp \vec{a}$

$\Rightarrow 2\ell + m + n = 0$ ...(i)

Since $\vec{c}$ coplanar with $\vec{a}$ and $\vec{b}$

$\therefore$ $\ell\hat{i} + m\hat{j} + n\hat{k} = \lambda\vec{a} + \mu\vec{b}$

$= (2\lambda + \mu)\hat{i} + (\lambda + 2\mu)\hat{j} + (\lambda - \mu)\hat{k}$

gives $2\lambda + \mu = \ell$; $\lambda + 2\mu = m$, $\lambda - \mu = n$

Now $2\lambda + \mu = m + n = \ell$

But from (I)$2\ell = -(m + n) = -\ell \Rightarrow \ell = 0$

$\Rightarrow m + n = 0$ $\Rightarrow m = -n$

Since $\vec{c}$ is a unit vector

$\therefore$ $\ell^2 + m^2 + n^2 = 1$

$|n| = |m| = \frac{1}{\sqrt{2}}$

$\Rightarrow c = \frac{1}{\sqrt{2}}(-\hat{j} + \hat{k})$ or $c = \frac{1}{2}(\hat{j} - \hat{k})$

43. **(d)** consider a unit vector $\hat{a} = \ell\hat{i} + m\hat{j} + n\hat{k}$

Now $\frac{\ell + m}{\sqrt{2}} = \frac{-\ell + m}{\sqrt{2}} = n$ where $\ell^2 + m^2 + n^2 = 1$

$\Rightarrow 1 = 0$, $m = \sqrt{2}\,n$, from $1^2 + m^2 + n^2 = 1$

we get $3n^2 = 1 \Rightarrow n \pm \frac{1}{\sqrt{3}}, m = \frac{\sqrt{2}}{\sqrt{3}}$

$\Rightarrow \quad \hat{a} = \pm\left\{\frac{\sqrt{2}}{\sqrt{3}}\hat{j} + \frac{1}{\sqrt{3}}\hat{k}\right\}$ or $\pm\left(\frac{\sqrt{2}\hat{j}+\hat{k}}{\sqrt{3}}\right)$

44. (c) According to the given $\left[\vec{a}, \vec{b}, \vec{c}\right] = 24$

So $(\vec{a}+\vec{b}+\vec{c}).\{\vec{a}\times\vec{b}+\vec{b}\times\vec{c}+\vec{c}\times\vec{a}\}$

$= \left[\vec{c}\ \vec{a}\ \vec{b}\right]+\left[\vec{a}\ \vec{b}\ \vec{c}\right]+\left[\vec{b}\ \vec{c}\ \vec{a}\right] = 3\left[\vec{a}\ \vec{b}\ \vec{c}\right] = 72$

45. (b) $\vec{a} = (-\hat{i}+\hat{j}+\hat{k}) = 2\hat{i}+0\hat{j}+\hat{k}$

Let $\vec{x} = x_1\hat{i}+x_2\hat{j}+x_3\hat{k} = (2\mu-\lambda)\hat{i}+\lambda\hat{j}+(\lambda+\mu)\hat{k}$

$\therefore \quad \vec{x}\perp\vec{b} \Rightarrow 4\mu - 2\lambda + \lambda + \mu = 5\mu - \lambda = 0 \Rightarrow \lambda = 5\mu$

$\therefore \quad \vec{X} = \mu\{-3\hat{i}+5\hat{j}+6\hat{k}\}$,

$\vec{a}.\vec{X} = \mu\{3+5+6\} = 14\mu = 7$

$\Rightarrow \quad \mu = 1/2$

$\therefore \quad x = 5/2$

$\vec{X} = \frac{1}{2}\{-3\hat{i}+5\hat{j}+6\hat{k}\}$

46. (d) P.V. of the terminating points will be respectively $3\hat{i}+4\hat{j}, 6\hat{i}+7\hat{j}, 8\hat{i}+\lambda\hat{j}$

Aliter: Since these points are collinear (as they are on the same straight line)

$\therefore \quad \overline{PQ} = m\overline{PR}$ i.e. $3\hat{i}+3\hat{j} = m\{5\hat{i}+(\lambda-4)\hat{j}\}$

so m = 3/5 and $\lambda - 4 = 5$

$\Rightarrow \lambda = 9$

47. (c) (Let $k > 0$). Resultant of $\overline{F}_2$ and $\overline{F}_4$ will be $\sqrt{2}k$ along $\vec{F}_3$ (*i.e.* y-axis)

$\therefore$ Along *y*-axis is $(\sqrt{2}+1)k$

Hence overall resultant force = $\overline{F_R} = k\left\{\sqrt{1+(1+\sqrt{2})^2}\right\}$

$= \hat{k}\left\{\sqrt{4+2\sqrt{2}}\right\}$

48. (d) As A(1,0,3), B(–1,3,4), C(1,2,1), D(k,2,5)

are coplanar $\Rightarrow \left[\overline{AB}\ \overline{BC}\ \overline{CD}\right] = 0$

so $\begin{vmatrix} -2 & 3 & 1 \\ 2 & -1 & -3 \\ (k-1) & 0 & 4 \end{vmatrix} = (-8)(k-1) + 4(-4) = 0$

or –8 – 8k = 0 hence k = –1

49. (b) Given $\vec{a}\times(\vec{b}\times\vec{c})+\vec{c}\times(\vec{a}\times\vec{b}) = 0$

So $(\vec{a}.\vec{c})\vec{b} - (\vec{a}.\vec{b})\vec{c} = (\vec{c}.\vec{b})\vec{b} - (\vec{b}.\vec{c})\vec{a}$

Gives $\vec{c} = \left(\frac{\vec{b}.\vec{c}}{\vec{a}.\vec{b}}\right)\vec{a} \Rightarrow \vec{a}$ and $\vec{c}$ are collinear

50. (c) The $\angle\alpha$ with (+ve direction of) x-axis after reflection will be with –ve direction x – axis. Other $\angle$s are not effected

$\Rightarrow$ d,c's will be – $\cos\alpha$, $\cos\beta$, $\cos\gamma$

51. (d) Given $\vec{a} = (x^2-1)\hat{i}+(x+2)\hat{j}+x^2\hat{k}$ and $\vec{b} = 2\hat{i}-x\hat{j}+3\hat{k}$ are orthogonal $\Rightarrow \vec{a}.\vec{b} = 0$

$\therefore \quad 2x^2 - 2 - x^2 - 2x + 3x^2 = 0 \Rightarrow 4x^2 - 2x - 2 = 0$

i.e., 2 {(2x + 1) (x –1)} 0 gives x = 1, –1/2

52. (d) $\vec{a}\times\vec{b} = \begin{vmatrix} \hat{i} & \hat{j} & \hat{k} \\ 2 & 3 & -1 \\ -1 & 2 & -4 \end{vmatrix} = (-10\hat{i}+9\hat{j}+7\hat{k})$

Gives $(\vec{a}\times\vec{b}).(\vec{a}\times\vec{c}) = \begin{vmatrix} -10 & 9 & 7 \\ 2 & 3 & -1 \\ 1 & 1 & 1 \end{vmatrix}$

$= (-7) + (-67) = -74$

53. (a) $|\vec{u}\times\vec{v}| = (\vec{a}-\vec{b})\times(\vec{a}+\vec{b})$

$= |\vec{a}\times\vec{b}+\vec{a}\times\vec{b}| = 2\{|a||b|\sin\theta\}$

$= 2.4\left\{\sqrt{1-\left(\frac{\vec{a}.\vec{b}}{|\vec{a}||\vec{b}|}\right)^2}\right\} = 2\sqrt{16-(\vec{a}.\vec{b})^2}$

54. (b) $|\vec{a}| = |\vec{c}|, |\vec{b}| = 4$

So $|\vec{b}\times\vec{c}| = |\vec{b}||\vec{c}|\sin\theta = \sqrt{15}$

$\Rightarrow \quad \sin\theta = \frac{\sqrt{15}}{4}, \cos\theta = \frac{1}{4}$

as $\vec{a}\times\vec{b} = 2, \vec{a}\times\vec{c}$

Now $\vec{b} - 2\vec{c} = \lambda\vec{a}$

Squaring $\vec{b}^2 + 4\vec{c}^2 - 4\vec{b}.\vec{c} = \lambda^2\vec{a}^2$

gives 16 + 4 – 4(4) (1/4) = $\lambda^2 \Rightarrow \lambda^2 = 16$ or $\lambda = \pm 4$

55. (a) $\vec{a} = \frac{(\vec{b}.\vec{a})}{|\vec{a}|^2}\vec{a} = \frac{3}{4}(\hat{i}+\hat{j})$

56. (b) $3\vec{a}+7\vec{b} = m\vec{c}$ **and** $(\vec{b}+\vec{c}) = \frac{n}{2}\vec{a} = (p\vec{a})$

{means $\vec{a}, \vec{b}, \vec{c}$ are coplanar and $\vec{a}$ is along the diagonal}

$\frac{3}{p}(\vec{b}+\vec{c})+7\vec{b} = m\vec{c}$

$\Rightarrow \left(\frac{3}{b}+7\right)\vec{b}+\left(\frac{3}{p}-m\right)\vec{c}=0$

$\Rightarrow p=-\frac{3}{7}$ and $\therefore$ m = –7

So we get $3\vec{a}+7\vec{b}=-7\vec{c}$

Or $9\vec{a}+21\vec{b}+2\vec{c}=\vec{0} \Rightarrow 9\vec{a}+21\vec{c}+14\vec{c}=-7\vec{c}$

57. **(b)** $\vec{A}.\vec{B}=\vec{A}\vec{C}=0$

A,B,C are the unit vectors. Angle between B and C is $\pi/4$

Unit vector $|B\times C|=\frac{1}{\sqrt{2}}$

$\Rightarrow \vec{A}=\pm\sqrt{2}\left(\vec{B}\times\vec{C}\right)$

58. **(d)** Since $\hat{a},\hat{b},\hat{c}$ are three non-coplanar unit vectors so they will form a system.

let $\vec{p}\times\vec{q}=\vec{d}=x\hat{a}+y\hat{b}+z\hat{c}$

Now $\hat{a}.\vec{d}=x$

$\Rightarrow (\hat{a}.\vec{d})\hat{a}=x\hat{a}$

Similarly $(\hat{b}.\vec{d})\hat{b}=y\hat{b}$ and $(\hat{c}.\vec{d})\hat{c}=z\hat{c}$

$\Rightarrow [\hat{a}\ \vec{p}\ \vec{q}]\hat{a}+[\hat{b}\ \vec{p}\ \vec{q}]\hat{b}+[\hat{c}\ \vec{p}\ \vec{q}]\vec{c}$

$=x\hat{a}+y\hat{b}+z\hat{c}=\vec{d}=\vec{p}\times\vec{q}$

59. (c) Consider a unit vector $\vec{c}$ perpendicular to both a and b we are concerned with $[\vec{r}.(\hat{b}\times(\hat{a}\times\hat{b}))]\hat{a}+[\vec{r}.(\hat{a}\times(\hat{b}\times\hat{a}))]\hat{b}+[\vec{r}.(\hat{a}\times\hat{b})](\hat{a}\times\hat{b})$

$\Rightarrow [\vec{r}.(\hat{b}\times\hat{c})]\hat{a}+[\vec{r}.(\hat{a}\times(\vec{c}))]\hat{b}+[\vec{r}.\vec{c}]\hat{c}$

$\Rightarrow [\vec{r}.\hat{a}]\hat{a}+(\vec{r}.\hat{b})\hat{b}+[\vec{r}.\hat{c}]\hat{c}$

Let $\vec{r}=x\hat{a}+y\hat{b}+2\hat{c}$

Hence the expression reduces to

$\Rightarrow \hat{a}x+y\hat{b}+z\hat{c}=\vec{r}$

Hence, the entire equation reduces $\vec{r}$

60. **(b)** Now we can rotate $\overrightarrow{OP}$ about x-axis by 360° by keeping 'O' point fixed.

This will generate a cone having its axis along +ive x-axis and vertx at 'O' and with slant height equal to the magnitude of the vector

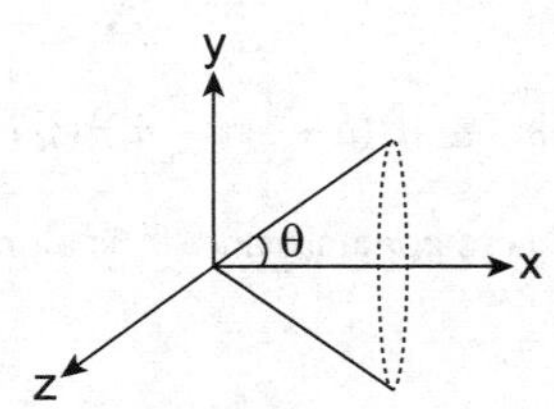

61. **(b)** Since vectors are coplanar $\therefore\ [\vec{p}\ \vec{q}\ \vec{r}]=0$

$\Rightarrow \begin{vmatrix} a & a & c \\ 1 & 0 & 1 \\ c & c & b \end{vmatrix}=(c^2-ab)=0$

$\Rightarrow$ **ab = c²**

So c is the G.M. between a and b

62. **(a)** $\vec{p}=\frac{\vec{b}\times\vec{c}}{[\vec{a}\ \vec{b}\ \vec{c}]},\vec{q}=\frac{\vec{c}\times\vec{a}}{[\vec{a}\ \vec{b}\ \vec{c}]},\ \vec{r}=\frac{\vec{a}\times\vec{b}}{[\vec{a}\ \vec{b}\ \vec{c}]}$

We know that $\vec{a}.\vec{p}=1,\ \vec{p}.\vec{b}=\vec{p}.\vec{c}=0$ similarly other parts

$\therefore\ (\vec{a}+\vec{b}+\vec{c})(\vec{p}+\vec{q}+\vec{r})=1+1+1=3$

63. **(c)** we know that $(\vec{a}\times\vec{b})\times(\vec{c}\times\vec{d})=[\vec{a}\ \vec{b}\ \vec{d}]\vec{c}-[\vec{a}\ \vec{b}\ \vec{c}]\vec{d}$

$\Rightarrow (\vec{a}\times\vec{b})\times(\vec{b}\times\vec{c})=[\vec{a}\ \vec{b}\ \vec{c}]\vec{b}-[\vec{a}\ \vec{b}\ \vec{b}]\vec{c}$

$=[\vec{a}\ \vec{b}\ \vec{c}]\vec{b}$, put $[\vec{a}\ \vec{b}\ \vec{c}]=m$

$\Rightarrow [(\vec{a}\times\vec{b})\times(\vec{b}\times\vec{c})\ \ (\vec{b}\times\vec{c})\times(\vec{c}\times\vec{a})\ \ (\vec{c}\times\vec{a})\times(\vec{a}\times\vec{b})]$

$=[m\vec{b}\ m\vec{c}\ m\vec{a}]=m^3[\vec{b}\ \vec{c}\ \vec{a}]=m^4=[\vec{a}\ \vec{b}\ \vec{c}]^4$

64. Let 'A' **be** the origin and AB be the x-axis (+ve part)

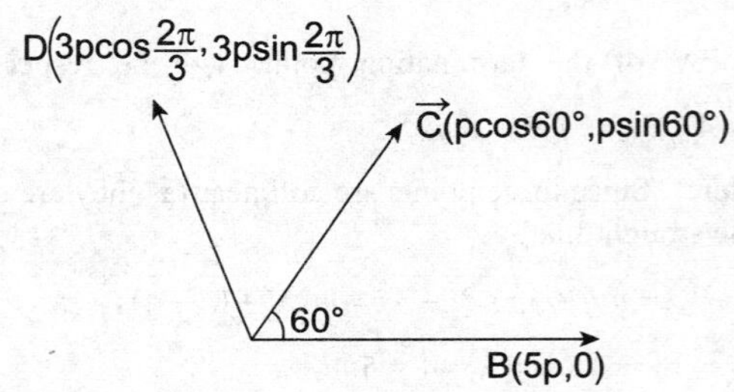

$\Rightarrow \overrightarrow{CD}=\left(\frac{3p}{2}-\frac{p}{2}\right)\hat{i}+\left(\frac{3\sqrt{3}}{2}p-\frac{\sqrt{3}}{2}p\right)\hat{j}$

$\overrightarrow{CD}=-2p\hat{i}+\sqrt{3}p\hat{j}$

cos θ = angle formed by

$\left\{(\overrightarrow{CD},\overrightarrow{BA})\right\}=\frac{2p}{\sqrt{4p^2+3p^2}}=\frac{2}{\sqrt{7}}$

65. **(a)** $|\vec{a}|=|\vec{b}|=1$

$0\le|\vec{a}-\vec{b}|<1 \qquad \Rightarrow \ 0<(a^2+\vec{b}-2\vec{a}.\vec{b})<1$

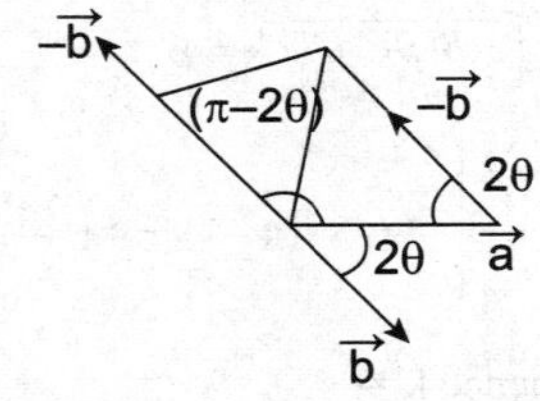

$-2 \le -2\vec{a}.\vec{b} < -1$

$\Rightarrow$ **2 ≥ 2cos2θ > 1 so** $0 \le 2\theta < \frac{\pi}{3}$

$\Rightarrow \theta \in \left[0, \frac{\pi}{6}\right)$

66. (c) Since vectors are at acute angle to each other

$\therefore (ax\hat{i} + 3\hat{j} - 5\hat{k}).(x\hat{i} + 2\hat{j} + 2ax\hat{k}) > 0$

$\Rightarrow ax^2 + 6 - 10ax > 0$ for all $x \in R$

{For a = 0, $ax^2 + 6 - 10ax = 6 > 0$}

For a > 0 and D < 0 we get $100a^2 - 24a < 0$

$\Rightarrow a \in [0, 6/25)$

since a = 0 also satisfies

$\therefore a \in [0, 6/25)$

67. **(c)** Given $\vec{a}.\vec{b} = 0$, Now $\vec{a} \times (a \times \vec{b}) = (\vec{a}.\vec{b})\vec{a} - (a)^2\vec{b}$

$\Rightarrow \{\vec{a} \times (\vec{a} \times (\vec{a} \times \vec{b})\} = \vec{a} \times \{(-\vec{a})^2\vec{b}\} = -(a)^2(\vec{a} \times \vec{b})$

$\Rightarrow \{\vec{a} \times (\vec{a} \times (a \times \vec{b}))\} = (-a^2)\vec{a} \times (\vec{a} \times \vec{b})$

$= (-a^2)\{0 - a^2\vec{b}\} = (|\vec{a}|^4)\vec{b}$

68. **(c)** $\vec{r} \times \vec{b} = \vec{a} \times \vec{b} \quad \Rightarrow (\vec{r} - \vec{a}) \times \vec{b} = \vec{0}$

$\Rightarrow \vec{r} - \vec{a} = t\vec{b}$ or $\vec{r} = \vec{a} + t\vec{b}$ **,** $t \in \mathbb{R}$

69. **(b)** Forces acting on point A are $\overrightarrow{AD}, \overrightarrow{AC}, \overrightarrow{AE}$ and on point B are $\overrightarrow{CB}, \overrightarrow{EB}, \overrightarrow{DB}$

Resultant $R = (\overrightarrow{AD} + \overrightarrow{DB}) + (\overrightarrow{AC} + \overrightarrow{CB}) + (\overrightarrow{AE} + \overrightarrow{EB})$

$= 3\overrightarrow{AB}$

70. **(a)** $|\vec{a} + \vec{b}| > |\vec{a} - \vec{b}|$ on squaring

$\vec{a}^2 + \vec{b}^2 + 2\vec{a}\vec{b} > \vec{a}^2 + \vec{b} - 2\vec{a}\vec{b}$

$\Rightarrow \vec{a}.\vec{b} > 0 \Rightarrow$ vectors are inclined at acute angle

71. **(a)** $\frac{\vec{A}.(\vec{B} \times \vec{C})}{(\vec{C} \times \vec{A})\vec{B}} + \frac{\vec{B}(\vec{A} \times \vec{C})}{\vec{C}(\vec{A} \times \vec{B})} = 1 - 1 = 0$

72. **(a)** $\vec{A} = \hat{i} + \hat{j} + \hat{k}, \vec{c} = \hat{j} - \hat{k}$

Let $\vec{B} = b_1\hat{i} + b_2\hat{j} + b_3\hat{k}$ $\vec{B} = b_1\hat{i} + b_2\hat{j} + b_3\hat{k}$.

Now $\vec{A}.\vec{B} = b_1 + b_2 + b_3 = 3$

Option (a) data satisfies as shown

$$\vec{A} \times \vec{B} = \begin{vmatrix} \hat{i} & \hat{j} & \hat{k} \\ 1 & 1 & 1 \\ 5/3 & 2/3 & 2/3 \end{vmatrix}$$

$= 0\hat{i} - \hat{k}\left\{\frac{2}{3} - \frac{5}{3}\right\} + \hat{k}\left\{\frac{2}{3} - \frac{5}{3}\right\} = \hat{j} - \hat{k}$ **so** $\vec{B} = \frac{1}{3}\{5\hat{i} + 2\hat{j} + 2\hat{k}\}$

73. **(a)** Vectors are coplanar

$$\Rightarrow \begin{vmatrix} a & 1 & 1 \\ 1 & b & 1 \\ 1 & 1 & c \end{vmatrix} = (ab - 1)(c - 1) + (a - 1)(b - 1) = 0$$

or $(1 - ab)(1 - c) + (1 - a)(1 - b) = 0$

$\Rightarrow \frac{1 - ab}{(1 - cb)(1 - b)} + \frac{1}{(1 - c)} = 0$

Observe that $\frac{1 - ab}{(1 - a)(1 - b)} + 1 = \frac{1 - ab + 1 - a - b}{(1 - a)(1 - b)}$

$= \frac{1}{(1 - b)} + \frac{1}{(1 - a)}$

$\Rightarrow \left(\frac{1}{1 - c} + \frac{1}{1 - b} - 1\right) + \frac{1}{(1 - c)} = 0$

So $\frac{1}{1 - a} + \frac{1}{1 - b} + \frac{1}{1 - c} = 1$

74. **(a)** $\vec{\beta} = 4\hat{i} + 3\hat{j}$ **and** $\vec{\gamma} = (3\hat{i} - 4\hat{j})\lambda$

(Let λ = 1 for easy work)

Since $\vec{\beta}.\vec{\gamma} = 0$ and both $\vec{\beta}$ and $\vec{\gamma}$ are in x –y plane

and $|\vec{\beta}| = |\vec{\gamma}| = 5$ units

Observe that vector in (a) option are

$(2\hat{i} - \hat{j})$ and $\frac{1}{5}(-2\hat{i} + 11\hat{j})$ so on checking

$(2\hat{i} - \hat{j})\left(\frac{4\hat{i} + 3\hat{j}}{5}\right) = 1$ and $\frac{1}{5}(-2\hat{i} + 11\hat{j}).\left(\frac{4\hat{i} + 3\hat{j}}{5}\right) = 1$

Also $(2\hat{i} - \hat{j})\left(\frac{3\hat{i} - 4\hat{j}}{5}\right) = 2$

and $\frac{1}{5}(-2\hat{i} + 11\hat{j}).\left(\frac{3\hat{i} - 4\hat{j}}{5}\right) = -2$

75. **(c)** $\overrightarrow{AB} \times \overrightarrow{CD}$

$= \overrightarrow{AB} \times (\overrightarrow{AD} - \overrightarrow{AC}) = \overrightarrow{AB} \times \overrightarrow{AD} - \overrightarrow{AB} \times \overrightarrow{AC}$

= – 2 Δ ADB (out wards) – 2 Δ ABC (out wards)

$\overrightarrow{CA} \times \overrightarrow{BD} = 2$ (quad ABCD inwards) = (–2) (quad ABCD outwards)

Now $\overrightarrow{BC} \times \overrightarrow{AD} = (\overrightarrow{AC} - \overrightarrow{AB}) \times \overrightarrow{AD}$

$= \overrightarrow{AC} \times \overrightarrow{AD} - \overrightarrow{AB} \times \overrightarrow{AD}$

So $\overrightarrow{AB} \times \overrightarrow{CD} + \overrightarrow{BC} \times \overrightarrow{AD}$

$= \{\overrightarrow{AB} \times \overrightarrow{AD} - \overrightarrow{AB} \times \overrightarrow{AC}\} + \{\overrightarrow{AC} \times \overrightarrow{AB} - \overrightarrow{AB} \times \overrightarrow{AD}\}$

$= \overrightarrow{AC} \times \overrightarrow{AD} - \overrightarrow{AB} \times \overrightarrow{AC} = 2\Delta ACD - 2\Delta ABC$

$\Rightarrow |\overrightarrow{AB} + \overrightarrow{CD} + \overrightarrow{AB} \times \overrightarrow{CD} + \overrightarrow{BC} \times \overrightarrow{AD}| = 4\Delta ABC$

76. (d) On Checking none of the vectors given in option (a),(b) and (c) satisfies the conditions

SECTION IV: (MORETHEN ONE CORRECT)

1. **(a, b, c and d)** $\vec{a} = x\hat{i} + y\hat{j} + z\hat{k}$, $\vec{b} = y\hat{i} + z\hat{j} + x\hat{k}$

and $\vec{c} = z\hat{i} + x\hat{j} + y\hat{k}$

So $\vec{a}\times(\vec{b}\times\vec{c}) = (\vec{a}.\vec{c})\vec{b} - (\vec{a}.\vec{b})\vec{c}$

$= (xz + xy + yz)\vec{b} - (xy + yz + zx)\vec{c}$

$= (xy + yz + zx)\{(y-z)\hat{i} + (z-x)\hat{j} + (x-y)\hat{k}\}$

Clearly $\vec{a}\times(\vec{b}\times\vec{c})$ is parallel to

$\{(y-z)\hat{i} + (z-x)\hat{j} + (x-y)\hat{k})\}$,

The vector is orthogonal to

$(\hat{i} + \hat{j} + \hat{k}), \{(y+z)\hat{i} + (z+x)\hat{j} + (x+y)\hat{k}\}$,

$(x\hat{i} + y\hat{j} + z\hat{k})$

2. **(a, b and c)** $\vec{a}\times\vec{b} = \vec{c}$ and $\vec{b}\times\vec{c} = \vec{a}$,

$\vec{a}.(\vec{a}\times\vec{b}) = \vec{a}.\vec{c} = 0$, $\vec{b}.(\vec{a}\times\vec{b}) = \vec{b}.\vec{c} = 0$

And $\vec{a}.\vec{c} = \vec{c}.(\vec{b}\times\vec{c}) = 0$; $\vec{a}.\vec{c} = \vec{c}(\vec{a}\times\vec{c}) = 0$

$\Rightarrow$ $\vec{a}, \vec{b}, \vec{c}$ are orthogonal in Pairs

So $\vec{c}.(\vec{a}\times\vec{b}) = \vec{c}^2$ and $\vec{a}.(\vec{b}\times\vec{c}) = \vec{a}^2$

$\therefore$ $|\vec{a}| = |\vec{c}|$

3. **(b, c and d)** Equation of the line

L : $\vec{r} = (2\hat{i} + 6\hat{j}) + \lambda(\hat{i} - 3\hat{j})$. For λ = 1, the line passing through the point $3\hat{i} + 3\hat{j}$

For λ = –1, the line passes through the point $(\hat{i} + 9\hat{j})$. .The line is in x-y plane so it is parallel to xy-plane

4. **(a, b, c and d)** $A(\vec{p}) = a\hat{i} + b\hat{j} + c\hat{k}$, $B(\vec{q}) = b\hat{i} + c\hat{j} + a\hat{k}$

and $C(\vec{r}) = c\hat{i} + a\hat{j} + b\hat{k}$

The centroid G of ΔABC = $\frac{(a+b+c)^2}{3}.\{\hat{i} + \hat{j} + \hat{k}\}$

Let $\overline{OG} = \vec{g}$

$\Rightarrow$ $\vec{p}.\vec{g} = \vec{q}.\vec{g} = \vec{r}.\vec{g} = \frac{(a+b+c)^2}{3}$ so equal inclination

Now $\overrightarrow{AB} = (b-a)\hat{i} + (c-b)\hat{j} + (a-c)\hat{k}$

and $\overrightarrow{AC} = (c-a)\hat{i} + (a-b)\hat{j} + (b-c)\hat{k}$

Observe that $\overline{AB}.\vec{g} = \overline{AC}.\vec{g} = \overline{BC}.\vec{g} = 0$

$\Rightarrow$ $\overrightarrow{OG} = \vec{g}$ is normal to the plane of ΔABC

So $|AB|^2 = |BC|^2 = |AC|^2 = 2\{a^2 + b^2 + c^2 - (ab + bc + ca)\}$

$\therefore$ ΔABC is equilateral

5. **(a, b, and c)** Given $a^2 + b^2 = c^2 + d^2 = r^2$ and $ac + bd = 0$

$\vec{w}_1 = a\hat{i} + c\hat{j}$ and $\vec{w}_2 = b\hat{i} + d\hat{j}$

$\vec{w}_1 . \vec{w}_2 = ab + cd$,

$|\vec{w}_1|^2 = a^2 + b^2 = r^2$,

$|\vec{w}_1|^2 = b^2 + d^2 = r^2$,

Let a = mb and d = –mc

$\Rightarrow$ $b^2(1 + m^2) = c^2(1 + m)^2 = r^2$

$\therefore$ |b| = |c| $\Rightarrow$ |a| = |d|

Let a = –d then b = c

$\therefore$ $\vec{w}_1 . \vec{w}_2 = 0$

6. **(a, b, c and d)** Vol of the parallel parallelopiped

$$= \begin{vmatrix} a & b & c \\ b & c & a \\ c & a & b \end{vmatrix} = 3abc - (a^3 + b^3 + c^3) = 0$$

$\Rightarrow$ $-\frac{1}{2}(a+b+c)\{(a-b)^2 + (b-c)^2 + (c-a)^2\} = 0$

Either (a + b + c) = 0 or a = b = c

7. **(a and b)** Since unit vectors $\hat{a}, \hat{b}, \hat{c}$ are orthogonal to each other

$\therefore$ $\left[\vec{a}\,\vec{b}\,\vec{c}\right] = +1$ or –1

8. **(a)** $\vec{n}.\vec{a} = \vec{n}.\vec{b} = \vec{n}.\vec{c} = 0$ $(\vec{n} \neq 0)$

$\Rightarrow$ $\vec{a}, \vec{b}, \vec{c}$ are coplanar $\Rightarrow \left[\vec{a}\,\vec{b}\,\vec{c}\right] = 0$

(b) min value **of** $|\alpha| + |\beta|$ **= 90°**

So α = 30° and β = 45° is not possible

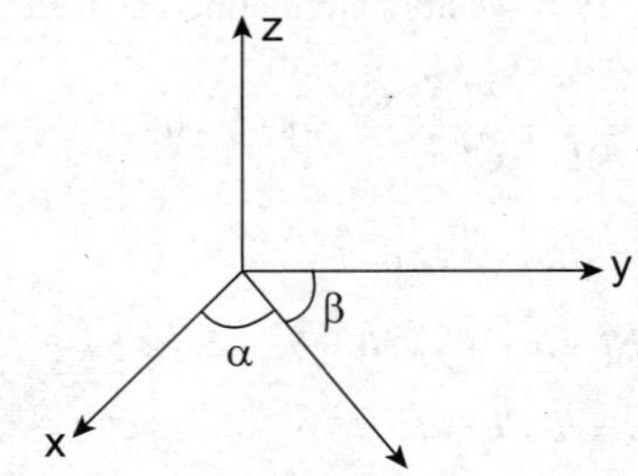

(c) The statement is true

(d) $|\overrightarrow{OA}| = |\overrightarrow{OB}| = |\overrightarrow{OC}|$

from the symmetry

$\overline{OD} = \left(\frac{\vec{a} + \vec{b} + \vec{c}}{3}\right)$ $\overline{OD} = \left(\frac{\vec{a} + \vec{b} + \vec{c}}{3}\right)$

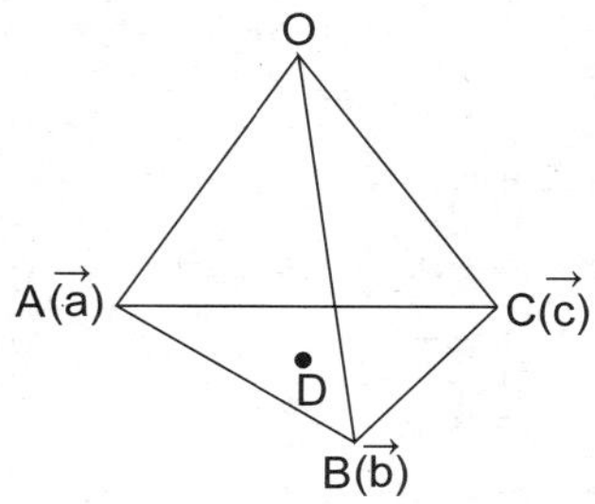

Where D is the centroid of ΔABC

9. (b and c) $\vec{a}.\vec{p} = |ab|(\vec{a}.\vec{c})\cos(2a - \cos^{-1}\hat{a}\hat{b})$

$= |a^2bc|\cos(\hat{a}.\hat{c})\cos(\hat{a}.\hat{b})$

and $\vec{a}.\vec{q} = |ac|\vec{a}.\vec{b}\cos\{\pi - \cos^{-1}(\hat{a}.\hat{c})\}$

$= -|a^2bc|\cos(\hat{a}.\hat{c})\cos(\hat{a}.\hat{b})$

so $\vec{a}(\vec{p}+\vec{q}) = 0$

$\Rightarrow \vec{a} \perp (\vec{p}+\vec{q})$

Obviously $(\vec{p}+\vec{q})$ is in the plane of $\vec{b}+\vec{c}$

10. (b and c) Let $\vec{r} = x\vec{a} + y\vec{b} + z\vec{c}$

so $\vec{r}\times\vec{a} = y\vec{b}\times\vec{a} + z\vec{c}\times\vec{a} = \vec{b}\times\vec{a} \Rightarrow$ **y = 1**

(either z = 0 or $\vec{c}\parallel\vec{a}$ **)**

$(\vec{r}-\vec{b})\times\vec{a} = \vec{0}\ (\vec{r}-\vec{b})\times\vec{a} = \vec{O} \Rightarrow \vec{r} = \lambda\vec{a} + \vec{b} + \overrightarrow{OC}$

Or $\vec{r} = \vec{b} + \lambda\vec{a}$ where $\lambda \in R$

11. (a and d) Since doubling (the magnitude) does not change the direction cosines of a vector

$\therefore$ Before doubling (the vector on rotation) = $2\hat{i} + (2p-1)\hat{j} + \hat{k}$

The length of vector remains the same

$\therefore$ $9 + 1 + p^2 = 4 + 1 + 4p^2 + 1 - 4p$

$\Rightarrow$ $3p^2 - 4p - 4 = 0 \therefore p = 2, -2/3$

12. (a, c, and d) $\vec{a} = \dfrac{2\hat{i} - 2\hat{j} + \hat{k}}{3}$ $\vec{a} = \dfrac{2\hat{i} - 2\hat{j} + \hat{k}}{3} \Rightarrow |\vec{a}| = 1$

Angle with $(2\hat{i} - 4\hat{j} + 3\hat{k}) : \cos\theta = \dfrac{|4+8+3|}{\sqrt{29}} = \dfrac{5}{\sqrt{29}} \neq \dfrac{1}{2}$,

$\vec{a}$ is parallel to $\left(-\hat{i} + \hat{j} - \dfrac{\hat{k}}{2}\right)$ as $\dfrac{-3}{2}\vec{a} = -\hat{i} + \hat{j} - \dfrac{\hat{k}}{2}$

so Angle with $(3\hat{i} + 2\hat{j} - 2\hat{i}) : \cos\theta = \dfrac{6-4-2}{3\sqrt{17}} = 0$

$\Rightarrow \theta = 90^\circ$

SECTION V: (ASSERTION AND REASON TYPE)

1. (a) R: For three point A,B,C if $\overrightarrow{AB} = \lambda\overrightarrow{AC}$, then the three points are collinear **(True)**

A: Since $2\vec{a} + 3\vec{b} = 5\vec{c} \Rightarrow \dfrac{2\vec{a}+3\vec{b}}{2+3} = \vec{c}$ hence assertion is true and it follows from R

As $\overrightarrow{AC} = \vec{c} - \vec{a} = \dfrac{3}{5}(\vec{b} - \vec{a})$ **and** $\overrightarrow{AB} = \vec{b} - \vec{a}$

So $\overrightarrow{AB} = \dfrac{5}{3}\overrightarrow{AC} = \lambda\overrightarrow{AC}$

2. (a) R: Since $\vec{r}_1 = (2\lambda - 1)\vec{c} + (6-\lambda)\vec{a}$

and $r_2 = -(1+3\mu)\vec{c} + (1+\mu)\vec{a}$ are not parallel

Two lines will intersect for some value of λ and μ (since they are not parallel) as only two vectors are involved

$\Rightarrow$ Reason is true

A: for λ = 15 , μ = –10,

$r_1 = 29\vec{c} - 9\vec{a}$ and $r_2 = 29\vec{c} - 9\vec{a}$

Hence they intersect and it follows from R

3. (a) R : Since $\vec{r}_1$ and $\vec{r}_2$ (the equations of lines) are formed with only two vectors they are in the plane of vectors $\vec{c}$ and $\vec{c}$.

$\Rightarrow$ Reason is true so they will intersect (as these are not parallel)

A: $\vec{r}_1$ and $\vec{r}_2$ are composed of only two vector $\vec{a}$ and $\vec{c}$. So they are in the plane of $\vec{a}$ and $\vec{c}$. hence copolnar

$\Rightarrow$ **Assertion is true and it follows from reason**

4. (a) R : $\overrightarrow{AD} = \dfrac{\overrightarrow{AB} + \overrightarrow{AC}}{2}$

$\Rightarrow$ Reason is true

{Although $|\overrightarrow{AB}| = |\overrightarrow{AC}| = 1\ |\overrightarrow{AB}| = |\overrightarrow{AC}| = 1$ but $|\overrightarrow{AD}| \neq 1$ }

A: Since $|\vec{u}| = |\vec{v}| = 1$

$\Rightarrow$ $\angle$ bisector is along $(\vec{u} + \vec{v})$

$\therefore$ a unit vector $\hat{x}$ along $(\vec{u} + \vec{v})$ will be

$\hat{x} = \dfrac{\vec{u} + \vec{v}}{\sqrt{2}}$ and it follows from R

5. (b) If a subset of *n* vectors is L.D. (Linearly dependent) then obviously the set of *n* vectors in L.D.

$\Rightarrow$ Reason is true

A: Set of any four vectors is always L.D. is true but it does not follow from Reason in any way

6. (a) Since point is a dimensionless quantity so a null vector has zero magnitude. Also its direction is indefinite

$\Rightarrow$ **Assertion is true**

And it follows from the reason that a null vector has both initial and terminal points coincident (*i.e.* not distinct)

7. **(a)** Since three vectors are L.D.

$\therefore$ They are in a single plane (*i.e.* coplanar)

$\Rightarrow$ scalar triple product will be zero

So Assertion (reason) is true and it follows from the fact that the parallelepiped formed by three coplanar vector has zero volume

8. (a) A set of vectors $\{\vec{v}_1, \vec{v}_2, \vec{v}_3, ..., \vec{v}_n\}$ will be L.I. when

$a_1\vec{v}_1 + a_2\vec{v}_2 + a_3\vec{v}_3 + ... + a_n\vec{v}_n = \vec{O}$ only

If $a_1 = a_2 = a_3 .... a_n = 0$

Otherwise we can express any vector as a linear combination of the remaining vectors

$\therefore$ Reason is true and it shows that if two vectors are not collinear (or parallel) then we can not express one vector in terms of the other

$\{a_1\vec{x}_1 + a_2\vec{x}_2 = \vec{0}$ only for $a_1 = a_2 = 0\}$ as $\vec{x}_1 \neq \vec{x}_2$.

9. **(b)** If a set of n vectors are L.I. then any of its subset will also be L.I. So **Reason is true**

(The fact that) three non – coplanar vectors are always L.I. as one can not be expressed in terms of the other two so **Assertion is true**

But this does not follow from the reason

$\Rightarrow$ **(B) option**

10. Any vector in 3D can be written as a linear combination of three non-zero non-coplanar vector

$\Rightarrow$ **Reason is true**

$\vec{r} = x\vec{a} + y\vec{b} + z(\vec{a}\times\vec{b})$ is true since $\vec{a} \neq \lambda\vec{b}$ and $(\vec{a}\times\vec{b}) \perp \vec{a}$ and $(\vec{a}\times\vec{b}) \perp \vec{b}$ hence $\vec{a}, \vec{b}, (\vec{a}\times\vec{b})$ form is system and it follow from **Reason**

SECTION VI: (COMPREHENSION)

Passage A:

1. **(c) |BC| = α, |CA| = β, |AB| = γ**

From the ∠ bisector theorem

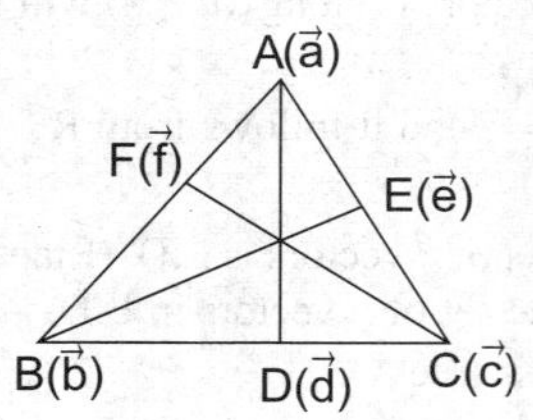

$$\frac{BD}{DC} = \frac{AB}{AC} = \frac{\gamma}{\beta}$$

P.V of D $D(d)$ $\dfrac{\beta b \quad \gamma c}{\beta \quad \gamma}$

Similarly P.V of $E(\vec{e}) = \dfrac{\gamma\vec{c} + \alpha\vec{a}}{\gamma + \alpha}$

and P.V. of $F(\vec{f}) = \dfrac{\alpha\vec{a} + \beta\vec{b}}{\alpha + \beta}$

$$\Rightarrow \alpha\vec{a} + \beta\vec{b} + \gamma\vec{c} = \vec{d}(\beta + \gamma) + \alpha\vec{a}$$

$$= \vec{e}(\gamma + \alpha) + \beta\vec{b} = \vec{f}(\alpha + \beta) + \gamma\vec{c}$$

$$\Rightarrow \frac{\vec{d}(\beta+\gamma) + \alpha\vec{a}}{(\beta+\gamma)+\alpha} = \frac{\vec{e}(\gamma+\alpha) + \beta\vec{b}}{(\gamma+\alpha)\beta} = \frac{\vec{f}(a+\beta) + \gamma\vec{c}}{(\alpha+\beta)\gamma}$$

$$= \frac{\alpha\vec{a} + \beta\vec{b} + \gamma\vec{c}}{\alpha + \beta + \gamma} = \vec{I} \ \textbf{(say)}$$

The common point is I(say) with $P.V. = \dfrac{\alpha\vec{a} + \beta\vec{b} + \gamma\vec{c}}{\alpha + \beta + \gamma}$

2. **(c)** $I = \dfrac{\alpha\vec{a} + \beta\vec{b} + \gamma\vec{c}}{\alpha + \beta + \gamma}$

$$|\vec{IB} \times \vec{IC}| = 2\Delta = r(BC) = r(r)\left\{\cot\frac{B}{2} + \cot\frac{C}{2}\right\}$$

$$\Rightarrow |\vec{IB}||\vec{IC}|\sin\left(\frac{B+C}{2}\right) = r^2\left(\cot\frac{B}{2} + \cot\frac{B}{2}\right)$$

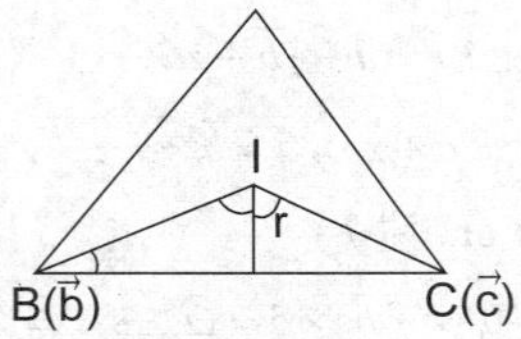

Now $\vec{IB} = -|\vec{IB}||\vec{IC}|\cos\left(\dfrac{B+C}{2}\right)$

$$= -r^2\left(\cot\frac{B}{2} + \cot\frac{C}{2}\right).\cot\left(\frac{B+C}{2}\right)$$

(convert into sin and cos)

$$= -r^2\left\{\frac{\sin\left(\frac{B+C}{2}\right)}{\sin\frac{B}{2}\sin\frac{C}{2}}\right\}\left\{\frac{\cos\left(\frac{B+C}{2}\right)}{\sin\left(\frac{B+C}{2}\right)}\right\}$$

$$= -r^2 \operatorname{cosec}\frac{B}{2}\operatorname{cosec}\frac{C}{2}\sin\frac{A}{2}$$

$$\left(Use \ \frac{B+C}{2} = \frac{\pi - A}{2}\right)$$

3. **(b)** $|\vec{IB} \times \vec{IC}| = \vec{IB}\,|\vec{IC}|\sin\left(\dfrac{B+C}{2}\right)$

$$= r^2\left(\cot\frac{B}{2} + \cot\frac{C}{2}\right)$$

$$= r^2\frac{\sin\left(\frac{B+C}{2}\right)}{\sin\frac{B}{2}\sin\frac{C}{2}} = r^2\operatorname{cosec}\frac{B}{2}\operatorname{cosec}\frac{C}{2}\cos\frac{A}{2}$$

Passage B:

4. (a) Area of ΔACR = 2ΔABC

$$\left|\frac{1}{2}\{\overrightarrow{AR}\times\overrightarrow{AC}\}\right| = \left|2\left\{\frac{1}{2}\overrightarrow{AC}\times\overrightarrow{BC}\right\}\right|$$

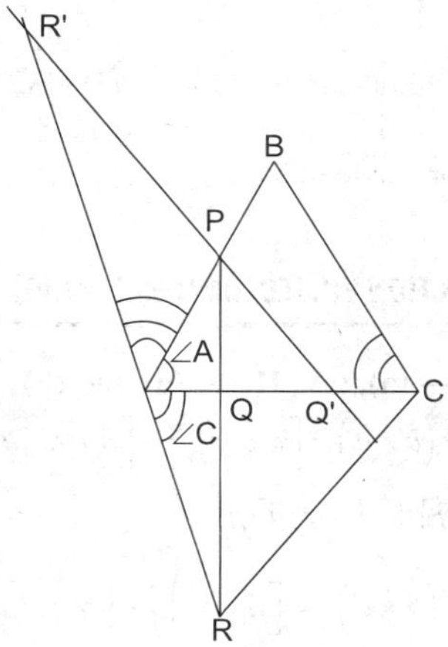

$\Rightarrow \sin C\,|\overrightarrow{AR}||\overrightarrow{AC}| = 2|\overrightarrow{AC}||\overrightarrow{BC}|\sin C$

$\Rightarrow |\overrightarrow{AR}| = 2|\overrightarrow{BC}|$

$\Rightarrow$ P.V of $R(\vec{r}) = \vec{a} + 2\vec{c}$

5. **(b)** Let $Q = \dfrac{m\vec{a}+\vec{c}}{1+m} = \dfrac{(\vec{a}+2\vec{c})+\frac{a}{2}.n}{(1+n)}$

$\Rightarrow$ **(m,n ≠ –1)**

$(m+mn)\,\vec{a} + (n+1)\vec{c}$

$= \left(\dfrac{2+n}{2}\right)\vec{a}(1+m) + (2+2m)\vec{c}$

$\Rightarrow \left(\dfrac{mn-n-2}{2}\right)\vec{a} + (n-1-2m)\vec{c} = \vec{0}$

$\Rightarrow$ n = 2m + 1

Gives m = –1, m = 3/2

so $2m^2 + m - 2m - 3 = 0$ {m = –1 rejected)

m = 3/2 and n = 4

$\Rightarrow Q = \dfrac{\frac{3}{2}\vec{a}+\vec{c}}{1+\frac{3}{2}} = \dfrac{3\vec{a}+2\vec{c}}{5}$

6. **(d)** $\dfrac{PQ}{QR}.\dfrac{AQ}{QC} = \dfrac{1}{n}.\dfrac{1}{m} = \dfrac{1}{4}\dfrac{1}{\left(\frac{3}{2}\right)} = \dfrac{1}{6}$

Passage C:

7. **(a)** Let origin be at the circumcentre 'O' (0, 0, 0) and P.V. of $A(\vec{a})$, $B(\vec{b})$, $C(\vec{c})$ and $|\vec{a}| = |\vec{b}| = |\vec{c}| = R$

Now $\overrightarrow{OA}+\overrightarrow{OB}+\overrightarrow{OC} = \vec{a}+\vec{b}+\vec{c}$

We know that orthocenter O = 3 (P.V of G the centroid –2 (P.V of circumcentre)

$= \vec{a}+\vec{b}+\vec{c}$

Hence $\overrightarrow{OO'} = \vec{a}+\vec{b}+\vec{c}$

$\therefore \quad \overrightarrow{OA}+\overrightarrow{OB}+\overrightarrow{OC} = \overrightarrow{OO'}$

8. **(b)** $\overrightarrow{O'A}+\overrightarrow{O'B}+\overrightarrow{O'C}$

$= \left(\overrightarrow{O'O}+\overrightarrow{OA}\right)+\left(\overrightarrow{O'O}+\overrightarrow{OB}\right)+\left(\overrightarrow{O'O}+\overrightarrow{OC}\right)$

$= 3\overrightarrow{O'O}+\overrightarrow{OO'} = 2\overrightarrow{O'O}$ **or** $-2\overrightarrow{OO'}$

9. **(c)** $\overrightarrow{AO'}+\overrightarrow{O'B}+\overrightarrow{O'C}$

$= 2\overrightarrow{AO}+\left\{\overrightarrow{O'A}+\overrightarrow{O'B}+\overrightarrow{O'C}\right\}$

$\overrightarrow{OD} = \dfrac{\vec{b}+\vec{c}}{2} \qquad \Rightarrow 2\overrightarrow{OD} = \overrightarrow{AO'}$

$= \overrightarrow{AO'}+\overrightarrow{O'B}+\overrightarrow{O'C} = 2\overrightarrow{AO'}+\overrightarrow{O'O}$

$= 2\overrightarrow{AO}$

10. Moment About

$$O = \vec{r}\times\vec{F} = \begin{vmatrix}\hat{i} & \hat{j} & \hat{k}\\ 3 & 0 & 4\\ 10 & 5 & 10\end{vmatrix}$$

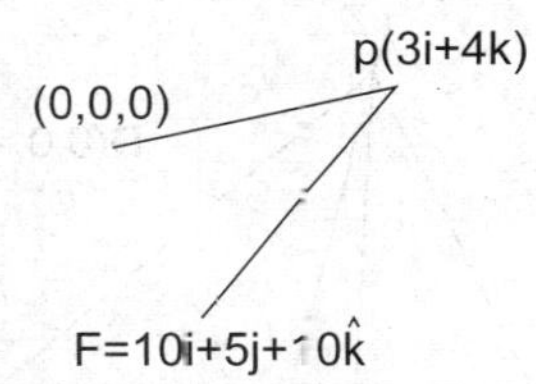

$= -20\hat{i}+10\hat{j}+15\hat{k} = 5\{-4\hat{i}+2\hat{j}+3\hat{k}\}$

11. **(c)** $\vec{n}_1 = \left(-\dfrac{1}{2}\right)\vec{a}\times\vec{b}$, $\vec{n}_2 = \dfrac{1}{2}(\vec{a}\times\vec{c})$, $\vec{n}_3 = \dfrac{-1}{2}(\vec{b}\times\vec{c})$,

$\vec{n}_4 = \dfrac{1}{2}(\vec{b}-\vec{a})\times(\vec{c}-\vec{b}) \Rightarrow \vec{r}_1+\vec{n}_2+\vec{n}_3+\vec{n}_4 = \vec{O}$

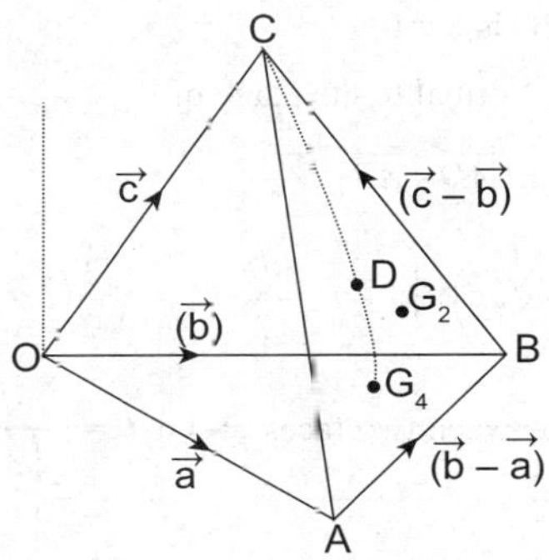

12. **(b)** $G_4(\vec{g}_4)=\dfrac{\vec{a}+\vec{b}}{3} \Rightarrow \overline{CG}=\dfrac{\vec{a}+\vec{b}-3\vec{c}}{3}$

Let $D(\vec{d})$ be the point of concurrency and $G_4D : CD = \lambda : 1$

$$\Rightarrow \quad D(\vec{d})=\frac{1}{(1+\lambda)}\left\{\lambda\vec{c}+\frac{\vec{a}+\vec{b}}{3}\right\} = \frac{\vec{a}+\vec{b}+\vec{c}}{3(1+\mu)},$$

$$\therefore \quad \frac{\vec{a}+\vec{b}+3\lambda\vec{c}}{3(1+\lambda)}=\frac{\vec{a}+\vec{b}+\vec{c}}{3(1+\mu)},$$

from $G_2=\dfrac{\vec{a}+\vec{b}+\vec{c}}{3}$; $\dfrac{OD}{DG_2}=\dfrac{1}{\mu}$

Since $\lambda = \mu$; $\lambda = 1/3$ so D divides CG_4 internally in the ratio 3 : 1

13. Observe that $\begin{vmatrix} 2 & 3 & 4 \\ 1 & 2 & -1 \\ 3 & -1 & 2 \end{vmatrix} = 37 \Rightarrow$ statement (c) is false.

Other statements are true.

14. Statements under option (a), (b) (c) are true

15. We know that $|\vec{a}\times\vec{b}|=|\vec{a}\times\vec{c}|$ {due to the structure being a regular one}

$$(\vec{a}\times\vec{b})\times(\vec{a}\times\vec{c}) = [\vec{a}\ \vec{b}\ \vec{c}]\vec{a}-[\vec{a}\ \vec{b}\ \vec{a}]\vec{c} = [\vec{a}\ \vec{b}\ \vec{c}]\vec{a}$$

16. (b) Consider a tetrahedron with side $\sqrt{3}$ units

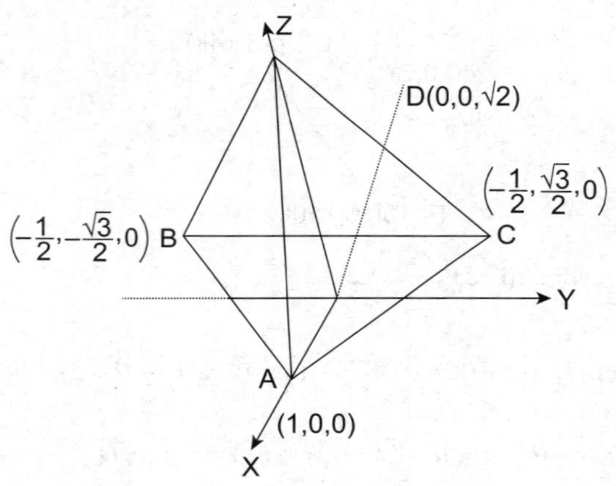

Plane of ABC is z = 0

$\therefore \quad n_1=\hat{k}$, Normal to the plane of

$$ABD=\pm\left(\overline{AD}\times\overline{AB}\right)$$

$$=\left(-\hat{i}+\sqrt{2}\hat{k}\right)\times\left(-\frac{3}{2}\hat{i}-\frac{\sqrt{3}}{2}\hat{j}\right) = \sqrt{\frac{3}{2}}\left(\hat{i}-\hat{j}+\hat{k}\right)$$

Angle between two faces $\Rightarrow \cos\theta=\dfrac{\sqrt{3}}{2\left\{\dfrac{3\sqrt{3}}{2}\right\}}=\dfrac{1}{3}$

17. **(a)** $\angle$ between edge $\overline{AD}$ and face ABC

$$\Rightarrow \quad \sin\theta=\frac{\hat{k}.(-\hat{c}+\sqrt{2}\hat{k})}{\sqrt{3}}$$

$$\sin\theta=\sqrt{\frac{2}{3}} \Rightarrow \cos\theta=\frac{1}{\sqrt{3}} \textbf{ so } \theta=\cos^{-1}\left(\frac{1}{\sqrt{3}}\right)$$

18. **(a)** Height of tetrahedron (for $\lambda_1 = \sqrt{3}$) = $\sqrt{2}$

$\therefore \quad$ height for a side of $\lambda=\sqrt{\dfrac{2}{3}}\,\lambda$

SECTION VII: (COLUMN MATCHING)

1. **I → (c) ; II → (a), (e) , III → (d) and (b)**

(i) $(\vec{a}\times\vec{b})\times(\vec{c}\times\vec{d})=[\vec{a}\ \vec{b}\ \vec{d}]\vec{c}-[\vec{a}\ \vec{b}\ \vec{c}]\vec{d}$

$=[\vec{a}\ \vec{c}\ \vec{d}]\vec{b}-[\vec{b}\ \vec{c}\ \vec{d}]\vec{a}$

(ii) $(\vec{a}\times\vec{c})\times(\vec{b}\times\vec{d}) = [\vec{a}\ \vec{c}\ \vec{d}]\vec{b}-[\vec{a}\ \vec{c}\ \vec{d}]\vec{d}$

$=[\vec{a}\ \vec{c}\ \vec{d}]\vec{b}+[\vec{a}\ \vec{b}\ \vec{c}]\vec{d}$

$=[\vec{a}\ \vec{b}\ \vec{d}]\vec{c}-[\vec{c}\ \vec{b}\ \vec{d}]\vec{a}$

(iii) $(\vec{a}\times\vec{b})\times(\vec{b}\times\vec{c})=[\vec{a}\ \vec{d}\ \vec{c}]\vec{b}-[\vec{a}\ \vec{d}\ \vec{b}]\vec{c}$

$=[\vec{a}\ \vec{b}\ \vec{d}]\vec{c}-[\vec{a}\ \vec{c}\ \vec{d}]\vec{b}$ **(d) option**

$=[\vec{a}\ \vec{b}\ \vec{c}]\vec{d}-[\vec{d}\ \vec{b}\ \vec{c}]\vec{a}$

$=[\vec{a}\ \vec{b}\ \vec{c}]\vec{d}-[\vec{b}\ \vec{c}\ \vec{d}]\vec{a}$ **(b) option**

2. I → (a) and (d); (II) → (a) and (e); (III) → (a); (IV) → (e) ; (V) → (b)

$\vec{a}=2\hat{i}+3\hat{j}+4\hat{k}=\sqrt{29}$ units

$\vec{b}=\hat{i}+2\hat{j}-\hat{k}=\sqrt{6}$ units , $\vec{c}=3\hat{i}-\hat{j}+2\hat{k}=\sqrt{14}$

(i) Length of an edge → (b) and (d)

(ii) Length of longest edge → (b)

Area of faces = $|\vec{a}\times\vec{b}|$, $|\vec{b}\times\vec{c}|$, $|\vec{c}\times\vec{a}|$ respectively gives

$=|-11\hat{i}+6\hat{j}+\hat{k}|=\sqrt{185}$; $|3\hat{i}-5\hat{j}-7\hat{k}|=\sqrt{83}$;

$|10\hat{i}+8\hat{j}-11\hat{k}|=\sqrt{285}$

Vol of the parallelepiped = $\begin{vmatrix} 2 & 3 & 4 \\ 1 & 2 & 1 \\ 3 & -1 & 2 \end{vmatrix} = 37$

Twice the volume = 74

(iv) → (e)

(ii) Area of a face → (a) and (c)

(iii) Area of the largest face → (a)

3. **I → (a) , (II) → (c), (III) → (b), (IV) → (d)**

$|\vec{a}| = |\vec{b}| = 1$

(i) $|\vec{a}+\vec{b}|<1 \Rightarrow a^2+b^2+2\hat{a}.\hat{b}<1$

$\Rightarrow \quad 2\hat{a}.\hat{b}<1 \Rightarrow \dfrac{2\pi}{3}<\alpha<\pi$

(ii) $|\hat{a}-\hat{b}|=|\hat{a}+\hat{b}|$ squaring

$a^2+b^2-2\hat{a}.\hat{b}=a^2+b^2+2\hat{a}.\hat{b}$

$\Rightarrow \quad \hat{a}.\hat{b}=0$

$\therefore \quad \alpha = 90^{\circ}$

(iii) $|\hat{a}+\hat{b}|<\sqrt{2}$

$\Rightarrow \quad a^2+b^2+2\hat{a}.\hat{b}<2$

Gives $\hat{a}.\hat{b}<\sqrt{2}$

$\Rightarrow \quad \dfrac{\pi}{2}<\alpha<\pi$

(iv) $|\hat{a}-\hat{b}|<\sqrt{2}$ squaring $a^2+b^2-2\hat{a}.\hat{b}<2$

$\hat{a}.\hat{b}>0 \qquad \Rightarrow \quad 0\le\alpha<\dfrac{\pi}{2}$

4. (I) → (a) and (b); (II) → (a) and (c); (iii) → (a, c, d)

(i) $\vec{a}.\vec{b}=0$

$\Rightarrow$ either of the vectors may be zero or $\vec{a}\perp\vec{b}$

(ii) $\vec{a}\times\vec{b}=\vec{0} \Rightarrow$ either of the vectors may be zero

Or $\vec{a}\,||\,\vec{b}$ gives

(iii) $[\vec{c}\ \vec{a}\ \vec{b}]=0 \Rightarrow$ either of the vectors may be zero

or $\vec{a}$ and $\vec{b}$ are parallel or $\vec{c}$ is || to plane of $\vec{a}\times\vec{b}$

SECTION VIII: (INTEGER TYPE)

1. Observe that $|\vec{a}|=|\vec{b}|=1$ and $\vec{a}.\vec{b}=0$

$|(2\vec{a}+\vec{b}).[(\vec{a}\times\vec{b})\times(\vec{a}+6\vec{b})]|$

$= |\{(\vec{a}+(\vec{a}+\vec{b})\}.[(\vec{a}\times\vec{b})\times\{(\vec{a}+\vec{b})+5\vec{b}\}]|$

$= |\vec{a}.\{(\vec{a}\times\vec{b})\times 5\vec{b}\}|$

$= |(-5\vec{a}).\{\vec{a}-0\}| = 5$

2. $\overrightarrow{AB} = 2\hat{i}+10\hat{j}+11\hat{k}$

and $\overrightarrow{AD}- = \hat{i}+2\hat{j}+2\hat{k} = 3$ units

Angle between sides $\dfrac{\overrightarrow{AB}.\overrightarrow{AD}}{|\overrightarrow{AB}||\overrightarrow{AD}|} = \dfrac{|-2+20+22|}{45} = \dfrac{40}{45} = \dfrac{8}{9}$

After rotation by α the angle is (θ + α) = 90°

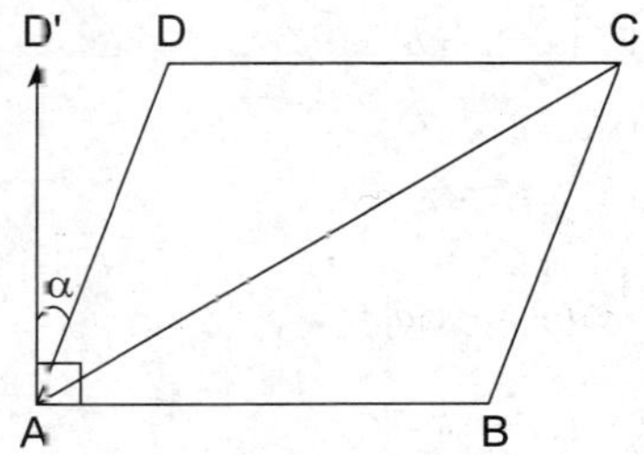

$\Rightarrow \cos\alpha = \cos(\pi/2-\theta) = \sin\theta = \dfrac{\sqrt{17}}{9} = \dfrac{\sqrt{\lambda}}{\lambda-8}$

So λ = 17

3. Given $\vec{a} = \mu\vec{b}+\mu\vec{c}$

$\Rightarrow \vec{c} = \dfrac{\vec{a}-\mu\vec{b}}{4}$; using in $(\vec{b}-\vec{a}).(\vec{b}+\vec{c})=0$

and $|\vec{b}+\vec{c}| = |\vec{b}-\vec{a}|$

We have , $(\vec{b}-\vec{a}).\left(\vec{b}+\dfrac{\vec{a}-\mu\vec{b}}{4}\right)=0;\ 2\left|\vec{b}+\dfrac{\vec{a}-\mu\vec{b}}{4}\right| = |\vec{b}-\vec{a}|$

$\Rightarrow \quad (\vec{b}-\vec{a}).\left(\left(1-\dfrac{\mu}{4}\right).\vec{b}+\dfrac{1}{4}\vec{a}\right)=0$;

$2\left|\left(1-\dfrac{\mu}{4}\right)\vec{b}+\dfrac{1}{4}\vec{a}\right| = |\vec{b}-\vec{a}|$

$\Rightarrow \quad \left(1-\dfrac{\mu}{4}\right)|\vec{b}|^2-\dfrac{1}{4}|\vec{a}|^2=0;$

$4\left[\left(1-\dfrac{\mu}{4}\right)^2|\vec{b}|^2+\dfrac{1}{16}|\vec{a}|^2\right] = |\vec{b}|^2+|\vec{a}|^2$

$\Rightarrow |\vec{a}|^2 = 4\left(1-\dfrac{\mu}{4}\right)|\vec{b}|^2$ and

$\left(\dfrac{(4-\mu)^2}{4}-1\right)\left(|\vec{b}|^2\right) = \dfrac{3}{4}\times4\left(1-\dfrac{\mu}{4}\right)\times\left(|\vec{b}|^2\right)$

$\Rightarrow \quad \dfrac{16+\mu^2-8\mu-4}{4} = 3\left(1-\dfrac{\mu}{4}\right)$

$\Rightarrow \mu^2-8\mu+12 = 12-3\mu$

$\Rightarrow \mu^2-5\mu = 0$

$\Rightarrow \mu(\mu-5)=0 \Rightarrow \mu=0$ or $\mu=5$

$\Rightarrow \mu_{max.} = 5$

4. $\vec{b}+\vec{c} = -2\vec{c}$

Clearly the magnitude on R.H.S = 2 units

$\therefore \quad \vec{b}=\vec{c}=-\vec{a}$, hence ∠θ between $\vec{b}$ and $\vec{c}$ is zero

$\Rightarrow \cos\theta = 1$

5. $\hat{x},\hat{y},\hat{z}$ are unit vectors and $\hat{x}+\hat{y}+\hat{z}=\vec{a}$ ...(i)

$\hat{x}\times(\hat{y}\times\hat{z}) = \vec{b}$

$\Rightarrow \quad (\hat{x}.\hat{z})\hat{y} - (\hat{x}.\hat{y})\hat{z} = \vec{b}$ ...(ii)

$(\hat{x} \times \hat{y}) \times \hat{z} = \vec{c}$

$\Rightarrow \quad (\hat{x}.\hat{z})\hat{y} - (\hat{y}.\hat{z})\hat{x} = \vec{c}$ ....(iii)

$\vec{a}.\hat{x} = \frac{3}{2},\ \vec{a}.\hat{y} = \frac{7}{4};\ |\vec{a}| = 2$

$\hat{x} = \ell_1\hat{i} + m_1\hat{j} + n_1\hat{k}$

$\hat{y} = \ell_2\hat{i} + m_2\hat{j} + n_2\hat{k}$

And $\hat{z} = \ell_3\hat{i} + m_3\hat{j} + n_3\hat{k}$

Let $\hat{x}.\hat{y} = r, \hat{y}.\hat{z} = p, \hat{z}.\hat{x} = q$

$\therefore$ from (ii) $q\hat{y} - r\hat{z} = \vec{b}$ ...(iv)

And $q\hat{y} - p\hat{x} = \vec{c}$ ...(v)

From (i); $1 + 1 + 1 + 2(\hat{x}.\hat{y} + \hat{y}.\hat{z} + \hat{z}.\hat{x}) = |\vec{a}|^2$ (squaring)

$\Rightarrow \quad r + p + q = \frac{1}{2}$ ....(vi)

Taking dot product (i) by $\hat{x}, \hat{y}$ we get

$1 + \hat{x}.\hat{y} + \hat{y}.\hat{z} = \vec{a}.\hat{x} = \frac{3}{2}$ (given)

$\Rightarrow \quad \ell + q = \frac{1}{2}$ ...(vii)

$\hat{x}.\hat{y} + 1 + \hat{y}.\hat{z} = \vec{a}.\hat{y} = \frac{7}{4}$

$\Rightarrow \quad r + p = \frac{3}{4}$ .....(viii)

Solving (vi), (vii), (viii), we get $p = 0, q = \frac{-1}{4}, \ell = \frac{3}{4}$

$\therefore$ from (iv) and (v), $-\frac{1}{4}\hat{y} - \frac{3}{4}\hat{z} = \vec{b}; -\frac{1}{4}\hat{y} = \vec{c}$ ..(ix)

From (i) $\hat{x} = \vec{a} - \hat{y} - \hat{z}$

$\Rightarrow \quad \hat{x} = \vec{a} + 4\vec{c} - \frac{4}{3}(\vec{c} - \vec{b})$

$\hat{x} = \vec{a} + \frac{4}{3}\vec{b} + \left(\frac{8}{3}\right)\vec{c}$

$\hat{y} = -4\vec{c}; \hat{z} = -\frac{4}{3}\vec{b} + \frac{4}{3}\vec{c}$

Now

$\because \hat{x} = \ell_1\vec{a} + m_1\vec{b} + n_1\vec{c}$

$\hat{y} = \ell_2\vec{a} + m_2\vec{b} + n_2\vec{c}$ and $\hat{z} = \ell_3\vec{a} + m_3\vec{b} + n_3\vec{c}$

$\Rightarrow \quad (\ell_1, m_1, n_1) \equiv \left(1, \frac{4}{3}, \frac{8}{3}\right); (\ell_2, m_2, n_2) \equiv (0, 0, -4);$

$(\ell_3, m_3, n_3) \equiv \left(0, \frac{-4}{3}, \frac{4}{3}\right)$

$$\therefore \quad \Delta = \begin{vmatrix} 1 & \frac{4}{3} & \frac{8}{3} \\ 0 & 0 & -4 \\ 0 & \frac{-4}{3} & \frac{4}{3} \end{vmatrix} = \left(-\frac{16}{3}\right)$$

$\Rightarrow \quad 3\Delta = -16$

$\Rightarrow \quad |3\Delta| = 16$

6. Let $\vec{V} = (\vec{a} \times \vec{b}) \times (\vec{c} \times \vec{d}) = (\vec{a} \times \vec{b}) \times \vec{p}$ (say)

$= (\vec{a}.\vec{p})\vec{b} - (\vec{b}.\vec{p})\vec{a}$

$= \vec{a}.(\vec{c} \times \vec{d})\vec{b} - \vec{b}.(\vec{c} \times \vec{d})\vec{a}$

$= [\vec{a}\ \vec{c}\ \vec{d}]\vec{b} - [\vec{b}\ \vec{c}\ \vec{d}]\vec{a}$ ...(i)

Similarly, $\vec{V_2} = (\vec{a} \times \vec{c}) \times (\vec{d} \times \vec{b}) = \vec{q} \times (\vec{d} \times \vec{b})$

$= [\vec{a}\ \vec{c}\ \vec{b}]\vec{d} - [\vec{a}\ \vec{c}\ \vec{d}]\vec{b}$ .... (ii)

And $\vec{V_3} = (\vec{a} \times \vec{d}) \times (\vec{b} \times \vec{c}) = (\vec{a} \times \vec{d}) \times \vec{r}$

$= [\vec{a}\ \vec{b}\ \vec{c}]\vec{d} - [\vec{d}\ \vec{b}\ \vec{c}]\vec{a}$ ....(iii)

$\therefore \quad \vec{A} = \vec{V_1} + \vec{V_2} + \vec{V_3} = -2[\vec{b}\ \vec{c}\ \vec{d}]\vec{a} \neq \vec{0}$ as $\vec{b}, \vec{c}, \vec{d}$ are non-coplanar and which is a vector parallel to $\vec{a}$

$\Rightarrow \quad \vec{A} \times \vec{a} = -2[\vec{b}\ \vec{c}\ \vec{d}](\vec{a} \times \vec{a}) = \vec{0}$

$\Rightarrow \quad |\vec{A} \times \vec{a}| = 0$

7. $\overline{BC} = 2\hat{i}, \overline{AB} = (\hat{j} + \hat{k})$

Normal to the plane of

$\Delta ABC = \pm\{2\hat{i} \times (\hat{j} + \hat{k})\} = \pm(j - k)(2)$

Observe that $\pm$ (y – z) = 0 is the plane of ΔABC as (0,0,0) lies on it

Vol of tetrahedron $= \frac{2\sqrt{2}}{3} = \frac{1}{3}(\Delta ABC) \times ht$

$\Rightarrow$ height of the tetrahedron = 2 units

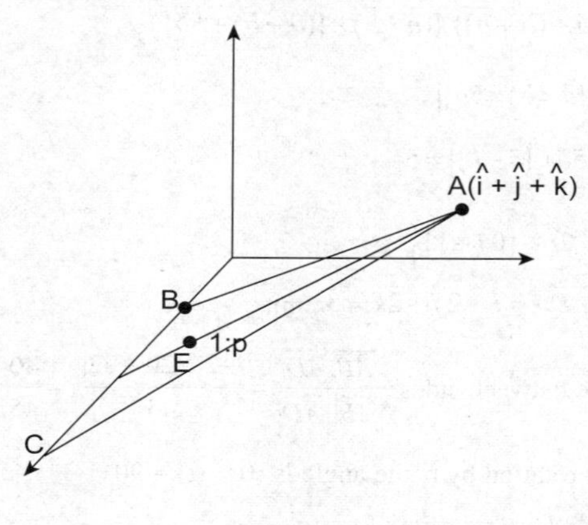

Let $\vec{E}(e)=\dfrac{2\hat{i}p+(\hat{i}+\hat{j}+\hat{k})}{1+p}$

P.V. of $D=\vec{e}+\sqrt{2}(\hat{j}-\hat{k})$

$\left|\overline{AD}\right|=4$ units $\left|\overline{AE}\right|=\sqrt{12}=2\sqrt{3}$ units

Median vector through A

i.e $\overline{AE}=\pm(\hat{i}-\hat{j}-\hat{k})=\sqrt{3}$ units

$\overline{AE}=\pm 2(\hat{i}-\hat{j}-\hat{k})$

$\Rightarrow \quad E(\vec{e})=3\hat{i}-\hat{j}-\hat{k} \text{ or } -\hat{i}+3\hat{j}+3\hat{k}$

So $\left|\overline{OE}\right|=\sqrt{19}=\lambda(\max)$

$\Rightarrow \quad \dfrac{2\lambda}{\sqrt{19}}=2$

8. Let $\vec{C}=\pm\lambda(3\hat{i}-4\hat{j})$

{consider λ = 1 for easy calculation},

$\vec{b}=4\hat{i}+3\hat{j}$

Vectors ± $(2\hat{i}-j)$

and $\pm\frac{1}{5}(2\hat{i}-11\hat{j})$

are the vectors which fulfill the requirements

$\Rightarrow \quad \Sigma|r_i|^2=2(5+5)=20$

9. Sum of vectors $(2+s)\,\hat{i}+6\hat{j}-2\hat{k}$

Prob of unit vector (along sum) with

$(\hat{i}+\hat{j}+\hat{k})=\dfrac{|(2+s)+6-2|}{\sqrt{36+4+(s+2)^2}}=1$

$\Rightarrow$ $(s+6)^2=(s+2)^2+40$ give s = 1

10. By the question $\vec{r}_1=\overline{OP}=3\hat{i}-2\hat{j}-\hat{k}$

$\vec{r}_2=\overline{PQ}=\hat{i}+3\hat{j}+4\hat{k}$

$r=\overline{OR}=2\hat{i}+\hat{j}-2\hat{k}$

If $\overline{OQ}\times\overline{QR}=\vec{n}\begin{vmatrix} i & j & k \\ 1 & 3 & 4 \\ 2 & 1 & -2 \end{vmatrix}$

$=-10\hat{i}+10\hat{j}-5\hat{k}$

The distance of p from OQR

= projection of $\overline{OP}$ on $\overline{QQ}\times\overline{OR}\Rightarrow\vec{n}$

$\Rightarrow \quad \dfrac{\overline{OP}.\vec{n}}{|\vec{n}|}$

$=\dfrac{|(3\hat{i}-2\hat{j}-\hat{k}).(-10\hat{i}+10\hat{j}-5k)|}{\sqrt{(10)^2+10^2+25}}$

$=\dfrac{|-30-20+5|}{15}=3$

11. $\vec{a},\vec{b},\vec{c}$ are copolnar as a result linear combination of thse vectors will also be copolnar

$$\Delta=\begin{vmatrix} a & b & c \\ \vec{a}.\vec{a} & \vec{a}.\vec{b} & \vec{a}.\vec{c} \\ \vec{b}.\vec{b} & \vec{b}.\vec{b} & \vec{b}.\vec{b} \end{vmatrix}=0$$

12. Given $\vec{x}=\dfrac{\vec{b}\times\vec{c}}{[\vec{a}\,\vec{b}\,\vec{c}]};\vec{y}=\dfrac{\vec{c}\times\vec{a}}{[\vec{a}\,\vec{b}\,\vec{c}]};z=\dfrac{\vec{a}\times\vec{b}}{[\vec{a}\vec{b}\vec{c}]}$

$\vec{x},\vec{y},\vec{z}$ are reciprocal vectors of $\vec{a},\vec{b},\vec{c}$ respectively

$\Rightarrow \quad \vec{x}.(\vec{a}+\vec{b})+\vec{y}.(\vec{b}+\vec{c})+\vec{z}.(\vec{c}+\vec{a})=3$

13. The curve is $y=x^2-2x+3$

$A(x_1,y_1)$ for $x_1=1$

$\Rightarrow$ $y_1=2$ **so** $\overline{OA}=\hat{i}-2\hat{j}$

Similarly $B(x_2,y_2)$ for $y_2=11$

$\Rightarrow$ $x^2-2x-8=0$ so $(x-4)(x+2)=0$

B(4,11) {In Ist quadrant} or $OB=4\hat{i}+11\hat{j}$

So $\overline{OA}.\overline{OB}=4+22=26$

14. We have $\vec{u}\times\vec{a}=\vec{b}$

$\Rightarrow \quad (\vec{u}\times\vec{a})\times\vec{a}=\vec{b}\times\vec{a}$

$\Rightarrow \quad \vec{a}(\vec{u}.\vec{a})-\vec{u}(\vec{a}.\vec{a})=\vec{b}\times\vec{a}$

$\Rightarrow \quad \vec{a}(0)-\vec{u}|\vec{a}|^2=\vec{b}\times\vec{a}$

$\Rightarrow \quad \vec{u}=\dfrac{\vec{a}\times\vec{b}}{|\vec{a}|^2}$

$\Rightarrow \quad |\vec{u}|=\dfrac{1}{|\vec{a}|^2}.|\vec{a}\times\vec{b}|$ .....(i)

Now $\vec{a}\times\vec{b}=\begin{vmatrix} \hat{i} & \hat{j} & \hat{k} \\ 1 & 2 & -3 \\ 2 & 1 & -1 \end{vmatrix}=\hat{i}(1)-\hat{j}(5)+\hat{k}(-3)$

$\Rightarrow \quad |\vec{a}\times\vec{b}|=\sqrt{1+25+9}=\sqrt{35}$ ....(ii)

And $|\vec{a}|^2=1+4+9=14$ .... (iii)

Using (ii) and (iii) in (i) we get

$|\vec{u}|=\frac{1}{14}(\sqrt{35})$

$\Rightarrow \quad |\vec{u}|^2=\dfrac{35}{196}=\dfrac{5}{28} \qquad \Rightarrow 28|\vec{u}|^2=5$

15. $\vec{d} = \lambda(\vec{a}\times\vec{b}) + \mu(\vec{b}\times\vec{c}) + \nu(\vec{c}\times\vec{a})$

$\Rightarrow \quad \vec{d}(\vec{a}+\vec{b}+\vec{c}) = (\lambda+\mu+\nu)[\vec{a}\,\vec{b}\,\vec{c}] = 8$

As $[\vec{a}\,\vec{b}\,\vec{c}] = 1/8$

$\Rightarrow$ **λ = 64**

16. $\dfrac{BD}{DC} = \dfrac{CE}{EA} = \dfrac{AF}{FB} = \dfrac{3}{1}$

$$\Delta AFE = \frac{1}{2}\left[\frac{3}{4}\overrightarrow{AB}\times\frac{1}{4}\overrightarrow{AC}\right] = \frac{3}{16}(\Delta ABC)$$

Similarly ΔBFD and ΔCED

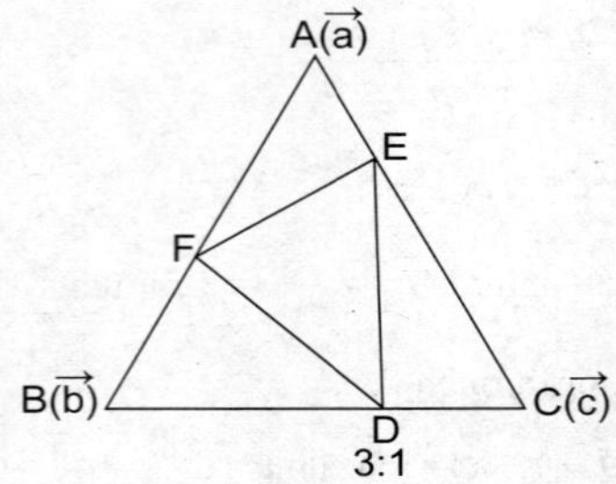

$\Rightarrow \quad \Delta DEF = \dfrac{7}{16}\Delta ABC$

$\Rightarrow \quad [36\lambda] = \left[36\times\dfrac{7}{16}\right] = 15$

4

3-D Geometry

■ INTRODUCTION

Since all points in a $3D$ space do not lie in a plane therefore to locate these points, two co-ordinates are not sufficient. Therefore to locate a point in a three dimensional space, we need three co-ordinates corresponding to three mutually perpendicular co-ordinate axes.

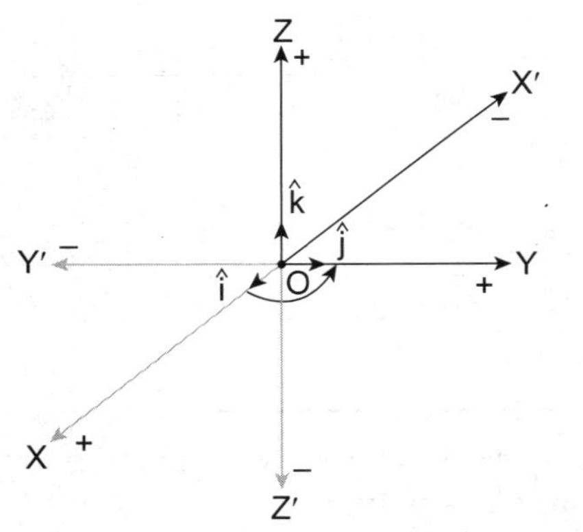

FIGURE 4.1

Three dimensional cartesian co-ordinate system is made of three mutually perpendicular axes XOX' (x-axis), YOY' (y-axis), ZOZ' (z-axis), and their point of intersection O is called the origin. These axes divide the complete three -dimensional space in eight octants. Let OX and OX' be the positive and negative directions of x-axis respectively. Let OY and OY' be the positive and negative directions of y-axis and OZ and OZ' be the postiive and negative directions of z-axis.

Therefore the sign convention of the co-ordinates of point in these octants can be given as below:

Octant		Sign Convention
$OXYZ$	(I)	(+, +, +)
$OX'YZ$	(II)	(–, +, +)
$OXY'Z$	(III)	(+, –, +)
$OXYZ'$	(IV)	(+, +, –)
$OX'Y'Z$	(V)	(–, –, +)
$OX'YZ'$	(VI)	(–, +, –)
$OXY'Z'$	(VII)	(+, –, –)
$OX'Y'Z'$	(VIII)	(–, –, –)

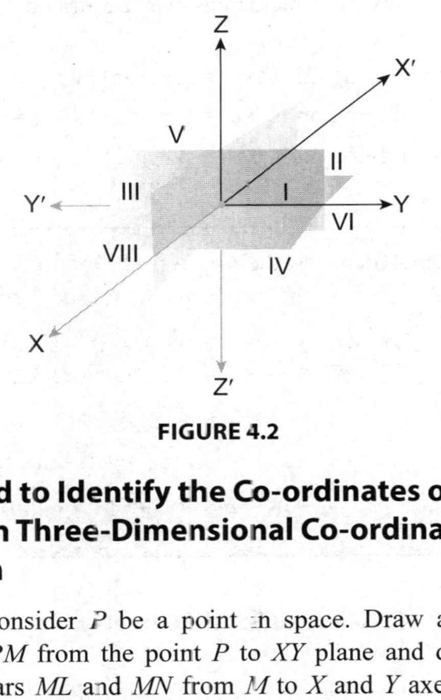

FIGURE 4.2

Method to Identify the Co-ordinates of a Point in Three-Dimensional Co-ordinate System

Let us consider P be a point in space. Draw a perpendicular PM from the point P to XY plane and draw perpendiculars ML and MN from M to X and Y axes respectively. Now the co-ordinates of point P can be defined as below:

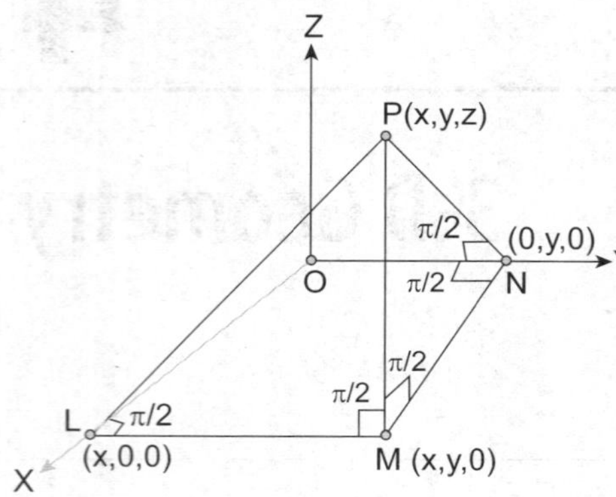

FIGURE 4.3

x-co-ordinate of a point *P* = length of perpendicular from *P* to *YZ* plane with proper sign

y-co-ordinate of a point *P* = length of perpendicular from *P* to *ZX* plane with proper sign

z-co-ordinate of a point *P* = length of perpendicular from *P* to *XY* plane with proper sign

If *L, M, N* be the feet of perpendiculars from *P* to *X, Y, Z* axes respectively, then

X-co-ordinate of *P* = length *OL* with proper sign

Y-co-ordinate of *P* = length *ON* with proper sign

Z-co-ordinate of *P* = length *PM* with proper sign

Therefore following conclusions can be drawn from the above:

- Any point lying on *x*-axis = $\{(x, y, z) \mid y = z = 0\}$
- Any point lying on *y*-axis = $\{(x, y, z) \mid x = z = 0\}$
- Any point lying on *z*-axis = $\{(x, y, z) \mid x = y = 0\}$
- Any point lying on *xy* plane = $\{(x, y, z) \mid z = 0\}$
- Any point lying on *yz* plane = $\{(x, y, z) \mid x = 0\}$
- Any point lying on *zx* plane = $\{(x, y, z) \mid y = 0\}$
- Distance of point *P* (*x, y, z*) from origin *O* is $OP = \sqrt{x^2 + y^2 + z^2}$

Shifting of Origin

Shifting the origin to another point without changing the directions of the axes is called the translation of axes. Let the origin *O* be shifted to another point $O'(\alpha, \beta, \gamma)$ without changing the direction of axes. Let the new co-ordinate frame be $O'X'Y'Z'$. Let *P* (*x, y, z*) be a point with respect to the co-ordinate frame *OXYZ*.

Then co-ordinate of point *P* w.r.t. new co-ordinate fram $O'X'Y'Z'$ is (x_1, y_1, z_1) where $x_1 = x - \alpha$, $y_1 = y - \beta$, $z_1 = z - \gamma$

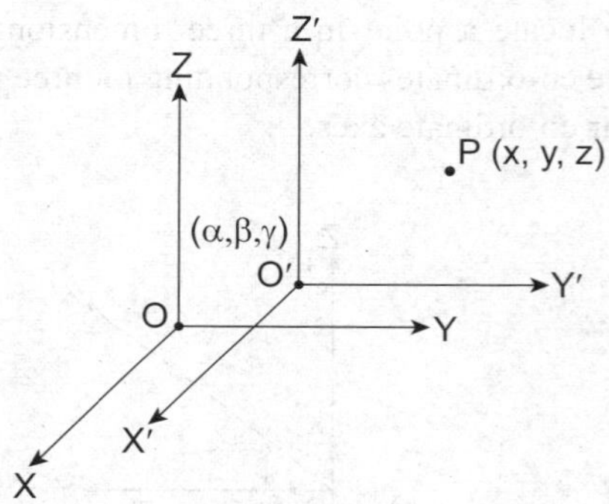

FIGURE 4.4

ILLUSTRATION 1: If the origin is shifted to (1, 2, – 3) without changing the directions of the axes, then find the new co-ordinates of the point (0, 4, 5) with respect to new frame.

SOLUTION: $x' = x - x_1 \Rightarrow x' = 0 - 1 = -1$

$y' = y - y_1 \Rightarrow y' = 4 - 2 = 2$

$z' = z - z_1 \Rightarrow z' = 5 + 3 = 8$

where (x_1, y_1, z_1) is the shifted origin

The co-ordinates of the point w.r.t to new co-ordinate frame is (–1, 2, 8)

Some Facts of Euclidean Solid Geometry

- Two intersecting lines are always co-planar and one and only one plane can be drawn through two intersecting lines in the space.

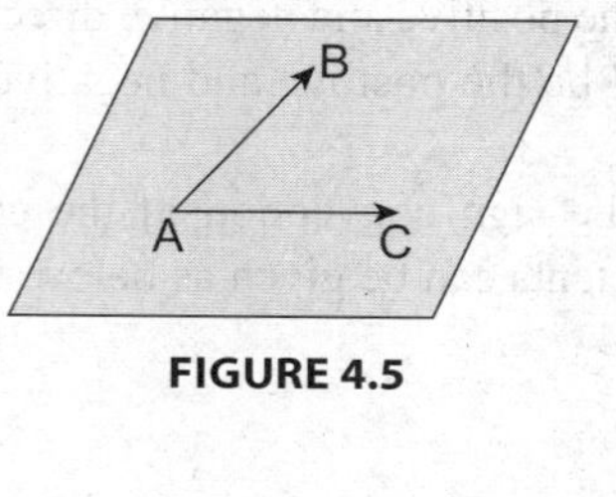

FIGURE 4.5

- One and only one plane can be drawn from three non-collinear points

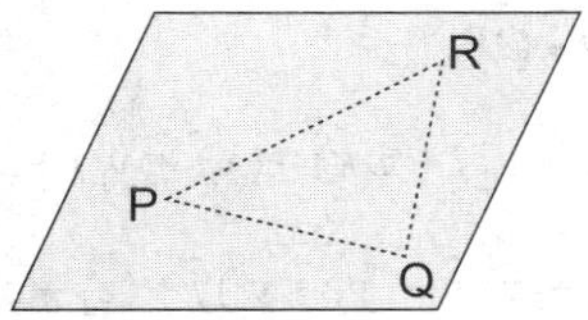

FIGURE 4.6

- One and only one plane can be drawn through given line and a point not lying on the line.

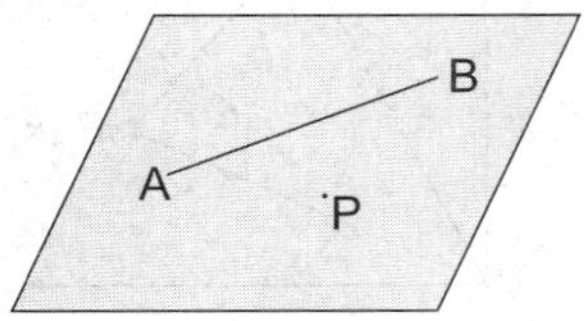

FIGURE 4.7

- Two parallel lines of space are always co-planar.

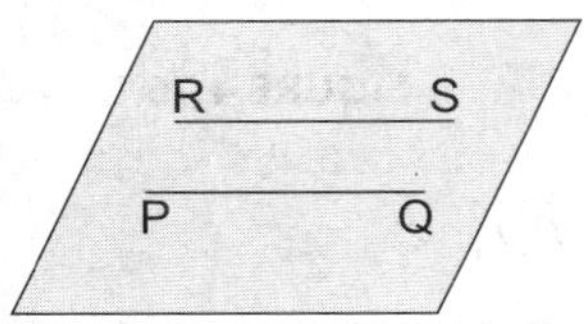

FIGURE 4.8

- Two lines in the space which are neither parallel nor intersecting are called skewlines. Since every pair of non-parallel co-planar lines are always intersecting, therefore skewlines are non-coplanar.

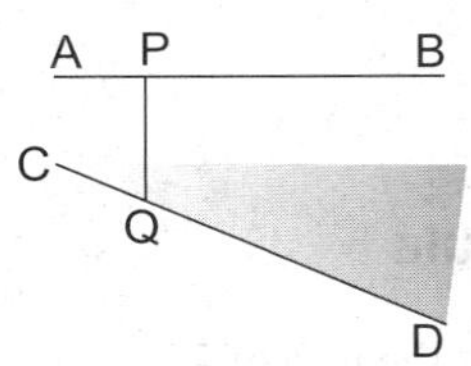

FIGURE 4.9

- A line perpendicular to two intersecting line is always perpendicular to the plane containing the two lines.

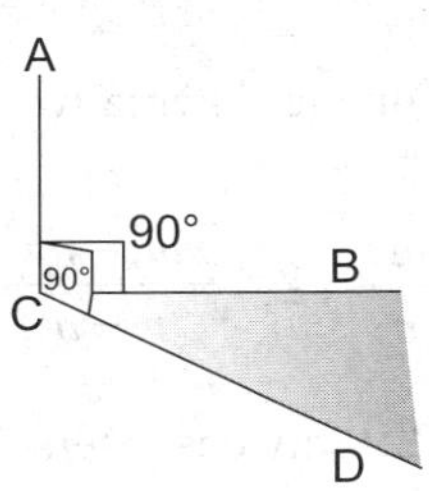

FIGURE 4.10

- Line perpendicular to a plane is always perpendicular to every line lying in that plane.

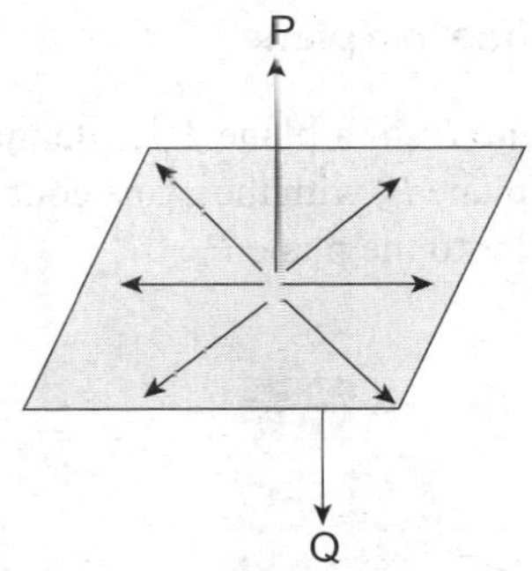

FIGURE 4.11

Angle between two lines

Angle between two lines in the space is defined as the angle between the lines drawn through any point of space parallel to these lines. Angle between any two lines in space is the angle between two co-initial vectors parallel to these lines.

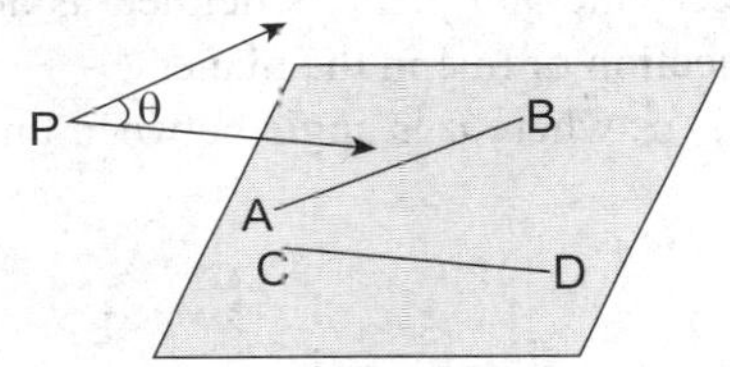

FIGURE 4.12

Angle between two planes

Angle between two planes in the space is defined as the angle between the lines lying in the respective planes perpendicular to the line of intersection. That can also be defined as the angle between their normals.

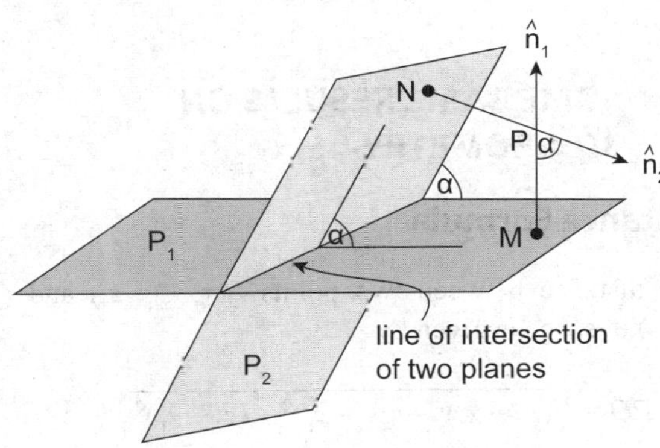

FIGURE 4.13

Therefore, the angle between planes P_1 and P_2 is equal to the angle between their normals $PM\ (\hat{n}_1)$ and $PN\ (\hat{n}_2)$ given as α. (as shown in the diagram).

Projection of line in a plane

Projection of line L_1 in a plane P_1 is defined as the line of intersection of plane P_1 with the plane containing the line L_1 but perpendicular to the plane P_1.

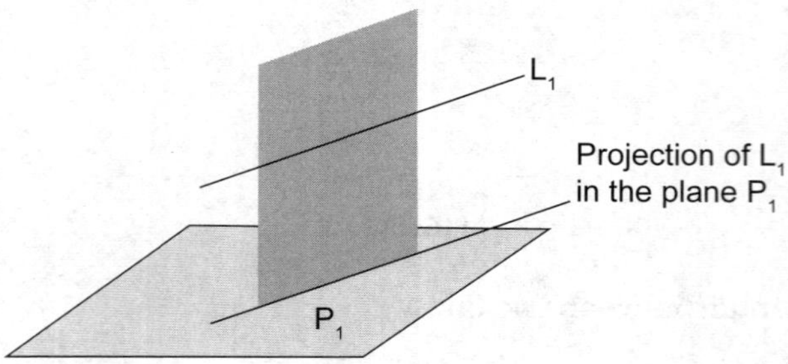

FIGURE 4.14

Angle between line and plane

Angle between line and plane is defined as angle between line and projection of line in the plane.

$\theta = 90° - \alpha$; where α is angle between line and normal to plane.

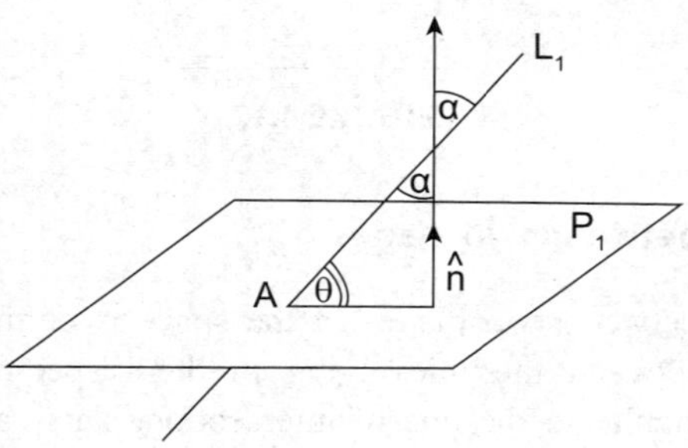

FIGURE 4.15

■ SOME BASIC RESULTS ON 3D-GEOMETRY

Distance Formula

The distance between two points $P(x_1, y_1, z_1)$ and $Q(x_2, y_2, z_2)$ in space is given by

$$PQ = \sqrt{(x_2 - x_1)^2 + (y_2 - y_1)^2 + (z_2 - z_1)^2}$$

Proof: Let O be the origin and let $P(x_1, y_1, z_1)$ and $Q(x_2, y_2, z_2)$ be two given points.

Then $\overrightarrow{OP} = x_1\hat{i} + y_1\hat{j} + z_1\hat{k}$, $\overrightarrow{OQ} = x_2\hat{i} + y_2\hat{j} + z_2\hat{k}$

Now $\overrightarrow{PQ}$ = position vector of Q-position vector of P

$$= \overrightarrow{OQ} - \overrightarrow{OP}$$

$$= (x_2\hat{i} + y_2\hat{j} + z_2\hat{k}) - (x_1\hat{i} + y_1\hat{j} + z_1\hat{k})$$

$$= (x_2 - x_1)\,\hat{i} + (y_2 - y_1)\hat{j} + (z_2 - z_1)\hat{k}$$

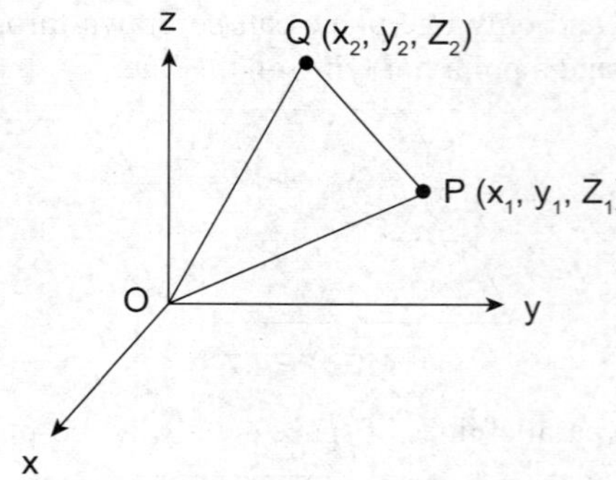

FIGURE 4.16

$$\therefore \quad PQ = |\overrightarrow{PQ}|$$

$$= \sqrt{(x_2 - x_1)^2 + (y_2 - y_1^2) + (z_2 - z_1)^2}$$

Hence, $PQ = \sqrt{(x_2 - x_1)^2 + (y_2 - y_1^2) + (z_2 - z_1)^2}$

Corollary: Distance of (x_1, y_1, z_1) from origin O = $\sqrt{(x_1^2 + y_1^2 + z_1^2)}$

Section Formula

If $R(x, y, z)$ divides the join of $P(x_1, y_1, z_1)$ and $Q(x_2, y_2, z_2)$ in ratio $m : n$ $(m, n > 0)$, then

$$x = \frac{mx_2 + nx_1}{m+n},\; y = \frac{my_2 + ny_1}{m+n},$$

$$z = \frac{mz_2 + nz_1}{m+n} \text{ divides internally}$$

$$\text{and } x = \frac{mx_2 - nx_1}{m-n};\; y = \frac{my_2 - ny_1}{m-n},$$

$$z = \frac{mz_2 - nz_1}{m-n} \text{ divides externally}$$

Proof: Let O be the origin. Then $\overrightarrow{OP} = \vec{r}_1$, $\overrightarrow{OQ} = \vec{r}_2$ and $\overrightarrow{OR} = \vec{r}$.

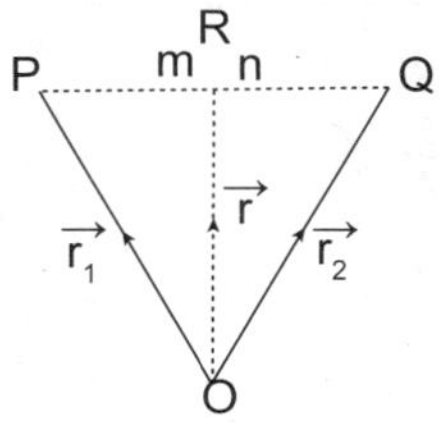

FIGURE 4.17

Now $\frac{PR}{RQ} = \frac{m}{n} \Rightarrow nPR = mRQ$

$\Rightarrow \quad n\overrightarrow{PR} = m\overrightarrow{RQ}$

$\Rightarrow \quad n(\overrightarrow{OR} - \overrightarrow{OP}) = m(\overrightarrow{OQ} - \overrightarrow{OR})$

$\Rightarrow \quad n(\vec{r} - \vec{r}_1) = m(\vec{r}_2 - \vec{r}) \Rightarrow (m+n)\vec{r} = m\vec{r}_2 + n\vec{r}_1$

$\Rightarrow \quad \vec{r} = \frac{m\vec{r}_2 + n\vec{r}_1}{m+n}$ (internal division)

Similarly for external division, we can prove that $\vec{r} = \frac{m\vec{r}_2 - n\vec{r}_1}{m-n}$; where $PR : PQ = m : n$

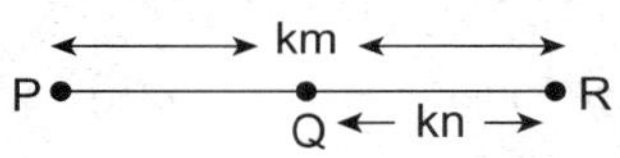

FIGURE 4.18

Corollary

(a) If $R(x, y, z)$ divides the join of $P(x_1, y_1, z_1)$ and $Q(x_2, y_2, z_2)$ in ratio λ: 1, then

$$x = \frac{\lambda x_2 \pm x_1}{\lambda \pm 1};\ y = \frac{\lambda y_2 \pm y_1}{\lambda \pm 1};\ z = \frac{\lambda z_2 \pm z_1}{\lambda \pm 1}$$

Positive sign is taken for internal division and negative for external division.

(b) The mid-point of PQ is $\left(\frac{x_1 + x_2}{2}, \frac{y_1 + y_2}{2}, \frac{z_1 + z_2}{2}\right)$

Centroid of a Triangle

The centroid of a triangle ABC whose vertices are A (x_1, y_1, z_1), $B(x_2, y_2, z_2)$ and $C(x_3, y_3, z_3)$ are

$$\left(\frac{x_1 + x_2 + x_3}{3}, \frac{y_1 + y_2 + y_3}{3}, \frac{z_1 + z_2 + z_3}{3}\right).$$

Centroid of a Tetrahedron

The centroid of a tetrahedron $ABCD$ whose vertices are A (x_1, y_1, z_1), $B(x_2, y_2, z_2)$, $C(x_3, y_3, z_3)$ and $D(x_4, y_4, z_4)$ are

$$\left(\frac{x_1 + x_2 + x_3 + x_4}{4}, \frac{y_1 + y_2 + y_3 + y_4}{4}, \frac{z_1 + z_2 + z_3 + z_4}{4}\right)$$

ILLUSTRATION 2: Planes are drawn parallel to the co-ordinate planes through the points (1, 2, 3) and (3, –4, –5). Find the lengths of the edges of the parallelopiped so formed.

SOLUTION: Let $P = (1, 2, 3)$, $Q = (3, -4, -5)$ through which planes are drawn parallel to the co-ordinate planes as shown below,

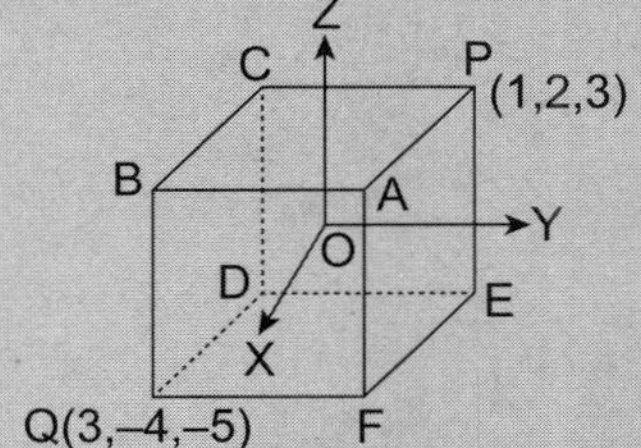

FIGURE 4.19

$\therefore$ PE = distance between parallel planes $ABCP$ and $FQDE$, i.e, (along z-axis) $= |-5 - 3| = 8$

PA = distance between parallel planes $ABQF$ and $PCDE = |3 - 1| = 2$

PC = distance between parallel planes $BCDQ$ and $APEF = |-4 - 2| = 6$

$\therefore$ lengths of edges of the parallelopiped are 2, 6, 8

ILLUSTRATION 3: Let O be the origin and $OP = r$, which makes an angle of θ with the positive direction of x-axis and lies in xy-plane. Find the coordinates of P.

SOLUTION: Let $P \equiv (\alpha, \beta, \gamma)$. Since, P lies in xy plane

$\therefore$ $\gamma = 0$; Also $\alpha = r\cos\theta$ and $\beta = r\sin\theta$; $P \equiv (r\cos\theta, r\sin\theta, 0)$

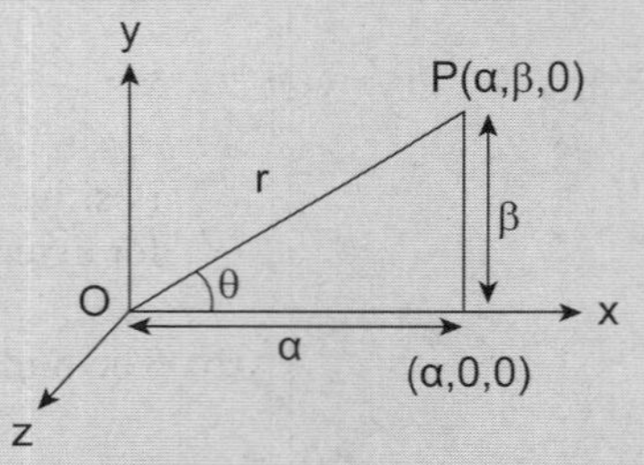

FIGURE 4.20

ILLUSTRATION 4: Find the locus of a point the sum of whose distances from (1, 0, 0) and (–1, 0, 0) is equal to 10.

SOLUTION: Let the points be A (1, 0, 0), B (– 1, 0, 0) and P (x, y, z). Given: $PA + PB = 10$

$\Rightarrow \sqrt{(x-1)^2+(y-0)^2+(z-0)^2}+\sqrt{(x+1)^2+(y-0)^2+(z-0)^2}=10$

$\Rightarrow \sqrt{(x-1)^2+y^2+z^2}=10-\sqrt{(x+1)^2+y^2+z^2}$. Squaring both sides, we get,

$\Rightarrow (x-1)^2+y^2+z^2=100+(x+1)^2+y^2+z^2-20\sqrt{(x+1)^2+y^2+z^2}$

$\Rightarrow -4x-100=-20\sqrt{(x+1)^2+y^2+z^2} \qquad \Rightarrow x+25=5\sqrt{(x+1)^2+y^2+z^2}$

Again squaring both sides, we get, $x^2 + 50x + 625 = 25\{(x^2 + 2x + 1) + y^2 + z^2\}$

$\Rightarrow 24x^2 + 25y^2 + 25z^2 - 600 = 0$. Which is the required equation of locus.

ILLUSTRATION 5: Show that the plane P: $ax + by + cz + d = 0$ divides the line joning (x_1, y_1, z_1) and (x_2, y_2, z_2) in the ratio of $\left(-\frac{ax_1+by_1+cz_1+d}{ax_2+by_2+cz_2+d}\right)=-\frac{P_1}{P_2}$; where $P_1 = ax_1 + by_1 + cz_1 + d$ and $P_2 = ax_2 + by_2 + cz_2 + d$.

SOLUTION: Let the plane $ax + by + cz + d = 0$ divides the line joining (x_1, y_1, z_1) and (x_2, y_2, z_2) in the ratio k: 1 as shown in figure;

$\therefore$ co-ordinates of $P\left(\frac{kx_2+x_1}{k+1},\frac{ky_2+y_1}{k+1},\frac{kz_2+z_1}{k+1}\right)$ must satisfy $ax + by + cz + d = 0$

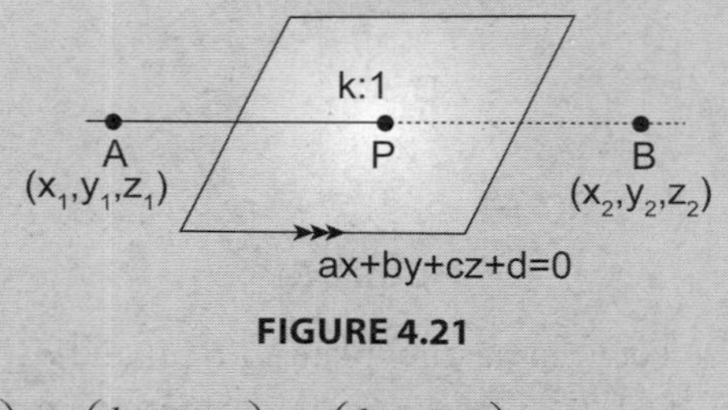

FIGURE 4.21

i.e., $a\left(\frac{kx_2+x_1}{k+1}\right)+b\left(\frac{ky_2+y_1}{k+1}\right)+c\left(\frac{kz_2+z_1}{k+1}\right)+d=0$

$\Rightarrow a(kx_2 + x_1) + b(ky_2 + y_1) + c(kz_2 + z_1) + d(k + 1) = 0$

$\Rightarrow k(ax_2 + by_2 + cz_2 + d) + (ax_1 + by_1 + cz_1 + d) = 0 \Rightarrow k=\left(-\frac{ax_1+by_1+cz_1+d}{ax_2+by_2+cz_2+d}\right)=-\frac{P_1}{P_2}$

■ RELATIVE POSITION OF POINT WITH RESPECT TO A PLANE.

Case I: If P and Q lie on opposite sides of plane.

$\Rightarrow$ Division is internal.

$\Rightarrow$ Ratio of division is positive.

$\lambda > 0$

$$\Rightarrow \frac{-P_1}{P_2} > 0 \Rightarrow \frac{P_1}{P_2} < 0$$

$\Rightarrow P_1$ & P_2 have opposite signs.

Case II: If P and Q lie on same side of plane.

$\Rightarrow$ Division is external.

$\Rightarrow$ Ratio of division is negative.

$\lambda < 0$

$$\Rightarrow \frac{-P_1}{P_2} < 0 \Rightarrow \frac{P_1}{P_2} > 0$$

$\Rightarrow P_1$ & P_2 have same signs.

ILLUSTRATION 6: Prove that the three points $A(3, -2, 4)$, $B(1, 1, 1)$ and $C(-1, 4, -2)$ are collinear.

SOLUTION: The general co-ordinates of a point R which divides the line joining A (3, –2, 4) and B (1, 1, 1) in the ratio μ: 1 are $\left(\frac{\mu+3}{\mu+1}, \frac{\mu-2}{\mu+1}, \frac{\mu+4}{\mu+1}\right)$ ...(i)

If $C(-1, 4, -2)$ lies on the line AB, then for some value of m the co-crdinates of the point R will be the same as those of C. Let x-co-ordinate of point R = x-co-ordinate of point C

Then $\frac{\mu+3}{\mu+1} = -1 \Rightarrow \mu = -2$

Putting $\mu = -2$ in (i), the co-ordinates of R are (–1, 4, –2) which are also the co-ordinates of C. Hence the points A, B, C are collinear.

ILLUSTRATION 7: Find the ratio in which (the plane) $2x + 3y + 5z = 1$ divides the line joining the points (1, 0, –3) and (1, –5, 7)

SOLUTION: Here, $2x + 3y + 5z = 1$ divides (1, 0, –3) and (1 – 5, 7) in the ratio of k: 1 at point P.

Then, $P = \left(\frac{k+1}{k+1}, \frac{-5k}{k+1}, \frac{7k-3}{k+1}\right)$ which must satisfy $2x + 3y + 5z = 1$

$$\Rightarrow 2\left(\frac{k+1}{k+1}\right) + 3\left(\frac{-5k}{k+1}\right) + 5\left(\frac{7k-3}{k+1}\right) = 1$$

$\Rightarrow 2k + 2 - 15k + 35k - 15 = k + 1 \Rightarrow 21k = 14$

$\Rightarrow k = 2/3 \therefore 2x + 3y + 5z = 1$

divides the joint of (1, 0 – 3) and (1, –5, 7) in the ratio of 2: 3.

TEXTUAL EXERCISE 1: (SUBJECTIVE)

1. Find the co-ordinates of the point on the x-axis that is equidistant from $P(4, 3, 1)$ and $Q(-2, -6, -2)$.
2. A cube of side 3 units has one vertex at point (1, 1, 1) and the three edges from this vertex are respectively parallel to positive x-axis and negative y-axis and z-axis. Find the co-ordinates of other vertices of the cube.
3. Find the ratio in which the surface $x^2 + y^2 + z^2 = 25$ divides the line joining (0, 1, 2) and (3, 4, 5).
4. Find the co-ordinates of the point where the line through (3, 4, 1) and (5, 1, 6) crosses xy-plane.
5. Find the co-ordinates of the point which divides the line joining points (2, 3, 4) and (3, –4, 7) in the ratio 5:3 internally.

6. Find the reflection of the point (α, β, γ) in the xy-plane.
7. Find the distance of point $P(a, b, c)$ from x-axis.
8. Show that the points (0, 7, 10), (–1, 6, 6) and (–4, 9, 6) form a right angled isosceles triangle.
9. Prove that the lines joining the mid-points of opposite edges of tetrahedron are concurrent.
10. Find the ratio in which the line joining the points (2, 4, 5), (3, 5, –4) is divided by the xy-plane and also find the co-ordinates of the dividing point.
11. Find the ratio in which the join of A (2, 1, 5) and B (3, 4, 3) is divided by the plane $2x + 2y - 2z = 1$. Also, find the co-ordinates of the point of division.
12. Find the co-ordinates of the foot of the perpendicular drawn from the point $A(1, 2, 1)$ to the line joining $B(1, 4, 6)$ and $C(5, 4, 4)$.

Answer Key

1. $\left(-\frac{3}{2}, 0, 0\right)$ **2.** (1, 1, –2)(1, –2, 1)(1, –2, –2)(4, 1, 1)(4, 1, –2) (4, –2, 1)(4, –2, –2)

3. $\frac{11 \pm \sqrt{621}}{25}$ **4.** $\left(\frac{13}{5}, \frac{23}{5}, 0\right)$ **5.** $\left(\frac{21}{8}, \frac{-11}{8}, \frac{47}{8}\right)$ **6.** $(\alpha, \beta, -\gamma)$

7. $\sqrt{b^2 + c^2}$ **10.** 5: 4; (23/9, 41/9, 0) **11.** $\left(\frac{29}{12}, \frac{9}{4}, \frac{25}{6}\right)$ and ratio 5 : 7 **12.** (3, 4, 5).

■ DIRECTION COSINES (DC'S)

If a line makes an angle α, β, γ with positive directions of x, y, z axes, then $\cos \alpha$, $\cos\beta$, $\cos\gamma$ are called the direction cosines (or d.c.'s) of the line. Generally, direction cosines are represented by l, m, n

Then angles α, β, γ are called the direction angles of directed the line OP and the direction cosines of PO are $\cos(\pi - \alpha)$, $\cos(\pi - \beta)$ and $\cos(\pi - \gamma)$ i.e., $-\cos\alpha, -\cos\beta, -\cos\gamma$.

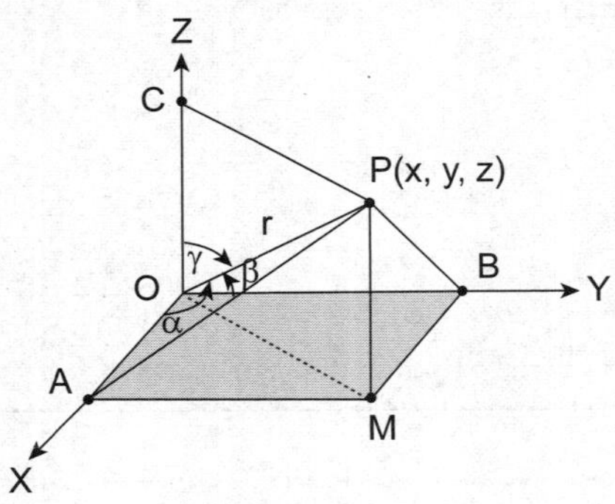

FIGURE 4.22

Deductions

(a) The direction cosines of the x-axis are $\cos 0$, $\cos \frac{\pi}{2}$, $\cos \frac{\pi}{2}$ i.e., 1, 0, 0. Similarly, the d.c's of y and z axis are (0, 1, 0) and (0, 0, 1) respectively.

(b) If l, m, n be the d.c's of a line OP and $OP = r$, then the co-ordinates of the point P are (lr, mr, nr)

(c) $l^2 + m^2 + n^2 = 1$ or $\cos^2 \alpha + \cos^2 \beta + \cos^2 \gamma = 1$

Let OP be any line through the origin O which has direction cosines l, m, n

Let $P = (x, y, z)$ and $OP = r$

Then $OP^2 = x^2 + y^2 + z^2 = r^2$ ...(i)

From P draw PA, PB, PC perpendicular on the coordinate axes, so that $OA = x$, $OB = y$, $OC = z$

Also, $\angle POA = \alpha$, $\angle POB = \beta$ and $\angle POC = \gamma$

From triangle AOP, $l = \cos \alpha = x/r \Rightarrow x = lr$

Similarly, $y = mr$ and $z = nr$

Hence from (i) we get, $r^2 (l^2 + m^2 + n^2) = x^2 + y^2 + z^2 = r^2$

$\Rightarrow l^2 + m^2 + n^2 = 1$

Direction Ratios (DR's)

Direction ratios of a line are numbers which are proportional to the d.c's of a line. Direction ratios of a line PQ (where P and Q are (x_1, y_1, z_1) and (x_2, y_2, z_2) respectively are $x_2 - x_1, y_2 - y_1, z_2 - z_1$)

Relation between the DC's and DR's

If a, b, c are the d.r's and l, m, n are the d.c's, then

$$l = \pm \frac{a}{\sqrt{a^2 + b^2 + c^2}}, \quad m = \pm \frac{b}{\sqrt{a^2 + b^2 + c^2}},$$

$$n = \pm \frac{c}{\sqrt{a^2 + b^2 + c^2}}$$

NOTES

1. *If a, b, c are the DR's of $\overrightarrow{AB}$ then DC's of $\overrightarrow{AB}$ are given by the +ve sign and those of $\overrightarrow{BA}$ by -ve sign.*
2. *The unit vector along $\overrightarrow{AB}$ the line can be written as $l\hat{i}+m\hat{j}+n\hat{k}$;* Where $<\ell, m, n>$ are direction. cosines of $\overrightarrow{AB}$
3. *If DC's of $\overrightarrow{AB}$ is (l, m, n), then direction cosine's of line $\overrightarrow{BA}$ will be <–ℓ, –m, –n>.*

Some important results

I. The direction ratios of the line segment joining points (x_1, y_1, z_1) and (x_2, y_2, z_2) are proportional to $x_2 - x_1$, $y_2 - y_1$, $z_2 - z_1$.

Proof: Let $P(x_1, y_1, z_1)$ and $Q(x_2, y_2, z_2)$ be two given points. Then,

$\overrightarrow{PQ}$ = Position vector of Q – Position vector of P

$$\Rightarrow \overrightarrow{PQ} = (x_2\hat{i}+y_2\hat{j}+z_2\hat{k})-(x_1\hat{i}+y_1\hat{j}+z_1\hat{k})$$

$$= (x_2-x_1)\hat{i}+(y_2-y_1)\hat{j}+(z_2-z_1)\hat{k}$$

So, direction ratios of $\overrightarrow{PQ}$ are proprotional to $x_2 - x_1$, $y_2 - y_1$, $z_2 - z_1$ and its direction cosines are

$$\frac{x_2-x_1}{|\overrightarrow{PQ}|}, \frac{y_2-y_1}{|\overrightarrow{PQ}|}, \frac{z_2-z_1}{|\overrightarrow{PQ}|}.$$

II. Two parallel vectors have proportional direction ratios.

Proof: Let $\vec{a}$ and $\vec{b}$ be two paralled vectors. Then $\vec{b} = \lambda\vec{a}$ for some scalar λ.

If $\vec{a} = a_1\hat{i}+a_2\hat{j}+a_3\hat{k}$, then

$$\vec{b} = \lambda\vec{a} \Rightarrow \vec{b} = (\lambda a_1)\hat{i}+(\lambda a_2)\hat{j}+(\lambda a_3)\hat{k}$$

This shows that the direction ratios of $\vec{b}$ are proportional to $\lambda a_1, \lambda a_2, \lambda a_3$ or a_1, a_2, a_3

$$\therefore \lambda a_1 : \lambda a_2 : \lambda a_3 = a_1 : a_2 : a_3.$$

Thus $\vec{a}$ and $\vec{b}$ have proportional direction ratios and hence same direction cosines also.

III. If a vector $\vec{r}$ has direction ratios proportional to a, b, c then $\vec{r} = \frac{|\vec{r}|}{\sqrt{a^2+b^2+c^2}}(a\hat{i}+b\hat{j}+c\hat{k})$

Proof: Since direction ratios of $\vec{r}$ are proportional to a, b, c, Therefore, its direction cosines are

$$l = \frac{a}{\sqrt{a^2+b^2+c^2}}, m = \frac{b}{\sqrt{a^2+b^2+c^2}},$$

$$n = \frac{c}{\sqrt{a^2+b^2+c^2}}$$

So, $\vec{r} = |\vec{r}|\,(l\hat{i}+m\hat{j}+n\hat{k})$

$$\Rightarrow \vec{r} = |\vec{r}|\left\{\frac{a}{\sqrt{a^2+b^2+c^2}}\hat{i}+\frac{b}{\sqrt{a^2+b^2+c^2}}\hat{j}+\frac{c}{\sqrt{a^2+b^2+c^2}}\hat{k}\right\}$$

$$\Rightarrow \vec{r} = \frac{|\vec{r}|}{\sqrt{a^2+b^2+c^2}}(a\hat{i}+b\hat{j}+c\hat{k})$$

LLUSTRATION 8: Find the direction ratios and direction cosines of the line joining the points $A(6, -7, -1)$ and $B(2, -3, 1)$.

SOLUTION: Direction ratios of AB are <4, –4, –2> = <2, –2, –1> ≡ <a, b, c> (say) $a^2 + b^2 + c^2 = 9$

$\Rightarrow$ Direction cosines are $\left(\pm\frac{2}{3}, \mp\frac{2}{3}, \mp\frac{1}{3}\right)$

ILLUSTRATION 9: If a straight line makes angles α, β, γ with x, y, z axes respectively, then show that $\sin^2\alpha+\sin^2\beta+\sin^2\gamma = 2$

SOLUTION: $\cos\alpha$, $\cos\beta$, $\cos\gamma$ are direction cosines of line

$\Rightarrow \cos^2\alpha + \cos^2\beta + \cos^2\gamma = 1$ $\qquad \Rightarrow 1 - \sin^2\alpha + 1 - \sin^2\beta + 1 - \sin^2\gamma = 1$

$\Rightarrow 2 = \sin^2\alpha + \sin^2\beta + \sin^2\gamma$

ILLUSTRATION 10: Can $\frac{1}{\sqrt{3}}, \frac{2}{\sqrt{3}}, \frac{-2}{\sqrt{3}}$ be the direction cosines of any directed line? Justify your answer.

SOLUTION: Given numbers are: $<l, m, n> \equiv \frac{1}{\sqrt{3}}, \frac{2}{\sqrt{3}}, \frac{-2}{\sqrt{3}}$, are direction cosines if they satisfy $l^2 + m^2 + n^2 = 1$

Now, $l^2 + m^2 + n^2 = \frac{9}{3} = 3 \neq 1$, $\quad \therefore \frac{1}{\sqrt{3}}, \frac{2}{\sqrt{3}}, \frac{-2}{\sqrt{3}}$ can not be *d.c*'s

ILLUSTRATION 11: A line passes through the points $A(10, -11, 1)$ and $B(2, -3, 5)$. Find direction ratios and direction cosines of the line so directed that the angle α is acute.

SOLUTION: The direction ratios of a line passing through $P\{x_1, y_1, z_1)$ and $Q(x_2, y_2, z_2)$ are proportional to $x_2 - x_1, y_2 - y_1, z_2 - z_1$. Therefore, direction ratios of AB are proportional to $-8, 8, 4$ or $-2, 2, 1$

We known that if the directions of a line are proportional to a, b, c, then its direction cosines are

$$\pm\frac{a}{\sqrt{a^2+b^2+c^2}}, \pm\frac{b}{\sqrt{a^2+b^2+c^2}}, \pm\frac{c}{\sqrt{a^2+b^2+c^2}}$$

Therefore, direction cosines of AB are

$$\pm\frac{-2}{\sqrt{(-2)^2+2^2+1^2}}, \pm\frac{2}{\sqrt{(-2)^2+2^2+1^2}}, \pm\frac{1}{\sqrt{(-2)^2+2^2+1^2}} \quad \text{i.e. } \pm-\frac{2}{3}, \pm\frac{2}{3}, \pm\frac{1}{3}$$

Since α is acute. Therefore $\cos\alpha > 0$; Hence direction cosines of AB are $\frac{2}{3}, -\frac{2}{3}, -\frac{1}{3}$.

IILLUSTRATION 12: Find the direction cosines of vector $\vec{r}$ which is equally inclined to OX, OY and OZ. Find total number of such vectors.

SOLUTION: Let l, m, n be the direction cosines of $\vec{r}$.

Since $\vec{r}$ is equally inclined with x, y and z-axis, $l = m = n$

$\therefore l^2 + m^2 + n^2 = 1 \quad \Rightarrow 3l^2 = 1$

$\Rightarrow l = \pm\frac{1}{\sqrt{3}} \quad \therefore$ direction cosines of $\vec{r}$ are $\pm\frac{1}{\sqrt{3}}, \pm\frac{1}{\sqrt{3}}, \pm\frac{1}{\sqrt{3}}$

Now, $\vec{r} = |\vec{r}|(l\hat{i} + m\hat{j} + n\hat{k}) \Rightarrow \vec{r} = |\vec{r}|\left(\pm\frac{1}{\sqrt{3}}\hat{i} \pm \frac{1}{\sqrt{3}}\hat{j} \pm \frac{1}{\sqrt{3}}\hat{k}\right)$

since + and – signs can be arranged at three places

$\Rightarrow$ there are eight vectors, i.e., $2 \times 2 \times 2$ which are equally inclined to axes.

ILLUSTRATION 13: Find the direction cosines of two lines which are connected by the relations $l - 5m + 3n = 0$ and $7l^2 + 5m^2 - 3n^2 = 0$.

SOLUTION: The given relations are $l - 5m + 3n = 0 \Rightarrow l = 5m - 3n$ ....(i)

and $7l^2 + 5m^2 - 3n^2 = 0$ ....(ii)

Putting the value of l from (i) in (ii), we get $7(5m - 3n)^2 + 5m^2 - 3n^2 = 0$

or, $(2m - n)(3m - 2n) = 0 \Rightarrow \frac{m}{n} = \frac{1}{2}$ or $\frac{2}{3}$

when $\frac{m}{n} = \frac{1}{2}$ i.e., $n = 2m \Rightarrow l = 5m - 3n = -m$ or $\frac{l}{m} = -1$

thus $\frac{m}{n} = \frac{1}{2}$ and $\frac{l}{m} = -1$ giving $\frac{l}{-1} = \frac{m}{1} = \frac{n}{2}$

or, $\frac{l}{-1}=\frac{m}{1}=\frac{n}{2}=\sqrt{\frac{(l^2+m^2+n^2)}{\{(-1)^2+1^2+2^2\}}}=\frac{1}{\sqrt{6}}$

So, direction cosines of one line are $-\frac{1}{\sqrt{6}},\frac{1}{\sqrt{6}},\frac{2}{\sqrt{6}}$

Again when $\frac{m}{n}=\frac{2}{3}\Rightarrow\frac{l}{m}=\frac{1}{2}$ giving $\frac{l}{1}=\frac{m}{2}=\frac{n}{3}=\frac{1}{\sqrt{1^2+2^2+3^2}}=\frac{1}{\sqrt{14}}$

$\therefore$ The direction cosines of the other line are $\frac{1}{\sqrt{14}},\frac{2}{\sqrt{14}},\frac{3}{\sqrt{14}}$

ILLUSTRATION 14: Find the *d*.c's l, m, n of a line which are connected by the relations $l+m-n=0$ and $2ml-2mn+nl=0$.

SOLUTION: Given $l+m-n=0$ .... (1)

$2ml-2mn+nl=0$ ....(2)

From (1), $n=m+l$

Putting this value of n in equation (2), we get $2ml-2m(m+l)+l(m+l)=0$

$\Rightarrow 2ml-2m^2-2ml+ml+l^2=0$ $\Rightarrow l^2+ml-2m^2=0$

$\Rightarrow (l-m)(l+2m)=0$

Either $l=m$ or $l=-2m$

Case I: $l=m$

$\Rightarrow n=m+l=2m$

$\therefore$ DR's are <1, 1, 2>

$\therefore$ DC's are $\pm\frac{1}{\sqrt{1^2+1^2+2^2}},\pm\frac{1}{\sqrt{1^2+1^2+2^2}},\pm\frac{2}{\sqrt{1^2+1^2+2^2}}$

$\therefore$ DC's are $<\frac{1}{\sqrt{6}},\frac{1}{\sqrt{6}},\frac{2}{\sqrt{6}}>$ or $<\frac{-1}{\sqrt{6}},\frac{-1}{\sqrt{6}},\frac{-2}{\sqrt{6}}>$

Case II: $l=-2m$ $\Rightarrow n=-m$

$\therefore$ DR's are $-2, 1, -1$

DC's are $\pm\frac{-2}{\sqrt{(-2)^2+1^2+(-1)^2}},\pm\frac{1}{\sqrt{(-2)^2+1^2+(-1)^2}},\pm\frac{-1}{\sqrt{(-2)^2+1^2+(-1)^2}}$

$\Rightarrow$ DC's are $<\frac{-2}{\sqrt{6}},\frac{1}{\sqrt{6}},\frac{-1}{\sqrt{6}}>$ or $<\frac{2}{\sqrt{6}},\frac{-1}{\sqrt{6}},\frac{1}{\sqrt{6}}>$

ILLUSTRATION 15: Find the conditions that the two lines whose *d*.c's are given by the relations $pl+qm+rn=0$ and $l^2+2m^2+3n^2=0$ are

(i) Perpendicular (ii) Parallel

SOLUTION: Given equations are $pl+qm+rn=0$ ..... (i)

and $l^2+2m^2+3n^2=0$ .... (ii)

Let l_1, m_1, n_1 and l_2, m_2, n_2 be the *d*.c.'s of the two lines.

Putting the value of n from (i) and (ii), we have $l^2+2m^2+3\left(\frac{pl+qm}{r}\right)^2=0$

or $r^2l^2+2r^2m^2+3p^2l^2+3q^2m^2+6pqlm=0$

or $(r^2 + 3p^2)l^2 + 6pqlm + (2r^2 + 3q^2)m^2 = 0$

or $(r^2+3p^2)\left(\frac{l}{m}\right)^2 + 6pq\left(\frac{l}{m}\right) + (2r^2+3q^2) = 0$

$\therefore \quad \frac{l_1}{m_1} \times \frac{l_2}{m_2} = \frac{2r^2+3q^2}{r^2+3p^2}$ .... (iii)

$\left[\text{where } \frac{l_1}{m_1} \;\&\; \frac{l_2}{m_2} \text{ are the roots of equation (iii)}\right]$

or $\frac{l_1 l_2}{2r^2+3q^2} = \frac{m_1 m_2}{r^2+3p^2}$; similarly, we get $\frac{\ell_1 \ell_2}{2\ell^2+3q^2} = \frac{n_1 n_2}{q^2+2p^2}$

$\Rightarrow \frac{l_1 l_2}{2r^2+3q^2} = \frac{m_1 m_2}{r^2+3p^2} = \frac{n_1 n_2}{q^2+2p^2} = k(say)$

For two lines to be perpendicular $l_1 l_2 + m_1 m_2 + n_1 n_2 = 0$

or $k(2r^2 + 3q^2) + k(r^2 + 3p^2) + k(q^2 + 2p^2) = 0$

or $5p^2 + 4q^2 + 3r^2 = 0$

For two lines to be parallel. Their *d.c.*'s must be equal or the roots of equation (iii) must be equal

$\Rightarrow 36p^2q^2 - 4(r^2 + 3p^2)(2r^2 + 3q^2) = 0$

$\Rightarrow 2r^4 + 3q^2r^2 + 6p^2r^2 = 0$

$\Rightarrow p^2 + \frac{q^2}{2} + \frac{r^2}{3} = 0$

TEXTUAL EXERCISE 2: (SUBJECTIVE)

1. Show that $A(-1, -3, 4)$, $B(5, -1, 1)$, $C(7, -4, 7)$, and $D(1, -6, 10)$ form a rhombus.

2. Find the direction cosines l, m, n of two lines which are connected by the relations $l + m + n = 0$ and $mn - 2nl - 2lm = 0$.

3. Find the direction cosine of two lines $<l, m, n>$ are given by $l + m + n = 0$ and $nl - 2mn - 2ml = 0$.

4. Lines OA, OB are drawn from O with direction cosines proportional to $(1, -2, -1)$, $(3, -2, 3)$. Find the direction cosines of the normal to the plane AOB

5. What are the direction cosines of a line which is equally inclined to axes?

6. A line OP through origin O is inclined at 30° and 45° to OX and OY respectively. Find the angle at which it is inclined to OZ.

7. A vector $\vec{r}$ has length 21 and direction ratios 2, –3, 6. Find the direction cosines and components of $\vec{r}$, given that $\vec{r}$ makes an obtuse angle with x-axis.

8. If $l_1, m_1, n_1; l_2, m_2, n_2$ be the *d.c*'s of two concurrent lines, show that the *d.c's* of the line bisecting the angles between them are proportional to $l_1 + l_2, m_1 + m_2, n_1 + n_2$.

9. Find the direction cosines l, m, n of two lines which are connected by the relations

(i) $l + m + n = 0$, $2lm + 2ln - mn = 0$.

(ii) $l - 5m + 3n = 0$, $7l^2 + 5m^2 - 3n^2 = 0$

10. Find whether a point (1, 3, 5) lies towards the origin side of plane $x + y - z + 3 = 0$ or non-origin side of plane.

11. The vertices of a triangle ABC are the points $(-1, 2, -3)$, $(5, 0, -6)$ and $(0, 4, -1)$ respectively. Determine the direction ratios of the bisector of the angle BAC.

Answer Key

2. $\left\langle \mp\frac{1}{\sqrt{6}}, \mp\frac{1}{\sqrt{6}}, \pm\sqrt{\frac{2}{3}} \right\rangle$ and $\left\langle \pm\frac{1}{\sqrt{6}}, \mp\frac{2}{\sqrt{6}}, \pm\frac{1}{\sqrt{6}} \right\rangle$ **3.** $\left\langle \mp\frac{2}{\sqrt{6}}, \pm\frac{1}{\sqrt{6}}, \pm\frac{1}{\sqrt{6}} \right\rangle$ and $\left\langle \mp\frac{1}{\sqrt{6}}, \mp\frac{1}{\sqrt{6}}, \pm\sqrt{\frac{2}{3}} \right\rangle$

4. $\left\langle \pm\frac{4}{\sqrt{29}}, \pm\frac{3}{\sqrt{29}}, \mp\frac{2}{\sqrt{29}} \right\rangle$ **5.** direction cosines are $\left(\frac{1}{\sqrt{3}}, \frac{1}{\sqrt{3}}, \frac{1}{\sqrt{3}}\right)$ or $\left(-\frac{1}{\sqrt{3}}, -\frac{1}{\sqrt{3}} - \frac{1}{\sqrt{3}}\right)$.

6. no such line is possible **7.** $\left(-\frac{2}{7}, \frac{3}{7} - \frac{6}{7}\right)$, $-6\hat{i}.+9\hat{j}$ and $-18\hat{k}$

9. (i) $\pm\left(\frac{1}{\sqrt{6}}, -\frac{2}{\sqrt{6}}, \frac{1}{\sqrt{6}}\right); \mp\left(\frac{1}{\sqrt{6}}, \frac{1}{\sqrt{6}}, -\frac{2}{\sqrt{6}}\right)$ (ii) $\pm\left(\frac{-1}{\sqrt{6}}, \frac{1}{\sqrt{6}}, \frac{2}{\sqrt{6}}\right); \pm\left(\frac{1}{\sqrt{14}}, \frac{2}{\sqrt{14}}, \frac{3}{\sqrt{14}}\right)$

10. same side **11.** (25, 8, 5)

■ THE ANGLE BETWEEN TWO LINES

Angle between two lines is defined as angle between their direction vectors. If (l_1, m_1, n_1) and (l_2, m_2, n_2) be the direction cosines of any two lines and θ be the angle between them then $\cos\theta = l_1l_2 + m_1m_2 + n_1n_2$

Corollary:

(a) If lines are perpendicular, then $l_1l_2 + m_1m_2 + n_1n_2 = 0$

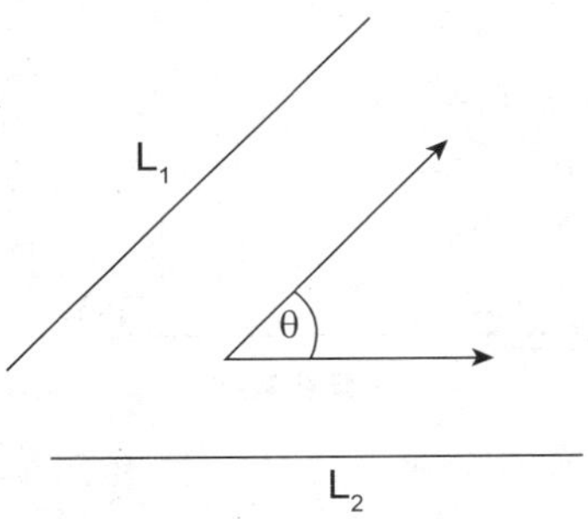

FIGURE 4.23

(b) If lines are parallel, then $\frac{l_1}{l_2} = \frac{m_1}{m_2} = \frac{n_1}{n_2}$

(c) If the *d.r*'s of the two lines are a_1, b_1, c_1 and a_2, b_2, c_2, then

$$\cos\theta = \frac{a_1a_2 + b_1b_2 + c_1c_2}{\sqrt{a_1^2 + b_1^2 + c_1^2}\sqrt{a_2^2 + b_2^2 + c_2^2}} \text{ and}$$

$$\sin\theta = \frac{\sqrt{\sum (b_1c_2 - b_2c_1)^2}}{\sqrt{a_1^2 + b_1^2 + c_1^2}\sqrt{a_2^2 + b_2^2 + c_2^2}}$$

so that the conditions for perpendicular and parallelism of two lines are respectively

$$a_1a_2 + b_1b_2 + c_1c_2 = 0 \text{ and } \frac{a_1}{a_2} = \frac{b_1}{b_2} = \frac{c_1}{c_2}$$

(d) If (l_1, m_1, n_1) and (l_2, m_2, n_2) are the *d.c's* of two lines, then *d.r's* of the line which are perpendicular to both of them are $m_1n_2 - m_2n_1, n_1l_2 - n_2l_1, l_1m_2 - l_2m_1$

ILLUSTRATION 16: Find the angle between the lines $\vec{r} = 3\hat{i} + 2\hat{j} - 4\hat{k} + \lambda(\hat{i} + 2\hat{j} + 2\hat{k})$ and $\vec{r} = (5\hat{j} - 2\hat{k}) + \mu(3\hat{i} + 2\hat{j} + 6\hat{k})$.

SOLUTION: Let θ be the angle between the given lines. The given lines are parallel to the vector $\vec{b_1} = \hat{i} + 2\hat{j} + 2\hat{k}$ and $\vec{b_2} = 3\hat{i} + 2\hat{j} + 6\hat{k}$ respectively. So, the angle θ between them is given by

$$\cos\theta = \frac{\vec{b_1}.\vec{b_2}}{|\vec{b_1}||\vec{b_2}|} = \frac{(\hat{i} + 2\hat{j} + 2\hat{k}).(3\hat{i} + 2\hat{j} + 6\hat{k})}{|\hat{i} + 2\hat{j} + 2\hat{k}||3\hat{i} + 2\hat{j} + 6\hat{k}|}$$

$$\cos\theta = \frac{3 + 4 + 12}{\sqrt{1 + 4 + 4}\sqrt{9 + 4 + 36}} = \frac{19}{21} \Rightarrow \theta = \cos^{-1}\left(\frac{19}{21}\right)$$

ILLUSTRATION 17: Find the angle between two lines having direction ratio <1, 1, 2> and $\langle (\sqrt{3}-1), (-\sqrt{3}-1), 4 \rangle$.

SOLUTION: Let $\vec{m}_1$ and $\vec{m}_2$ be vectors parallel to the two given lines. Then, angle between the two given lines is same as the angle between $\vec{m}_1$ and $\vec{m}_2$.

$\vec{m}_1$ = Vector parallel to the line with direction ratios <1, 1, 2> = $\hat{i}+\hat{j}+2\hat{k}$ and

$\vec{m}_2$ = Vector parallel to the line with direction ratio $<(\sqrt{3}-1), (-\sqrt{3}-1), 4>$ = $(\sqrt{3}-1)\hat{i}+(-\sqrt{3}-1)\hat{j}+4\hat{k}$

Let θ be the angle between the given lines. Then,

$$\cos\theta = \frac{\vec{m}_1.\vec{m}_2}{|\vec{m}_1||\vec{m}_2|} \Rightarrow \cos\theta = \frac{(\sqrt{3}-1)-(\sqrt{3}+1)+8}{\sqrt{1+1+4}\sqrt{(\sqrt{3}-1)^2+(\sqrt{3}+1)^2+16}}$$

$$\cos\theta = \frac{6}{\sqrt{6}\sqrt{24}} = \frac{1}{2} \Rightarrow \theta = \frac{\pi}{3}$$

■ PROJECTION OF A LINE

Projection of a line joining the points $P(x_1, y_1, z_1)$ and $Q(x_2, y_2, z_2)$ on another line whose direction cosines are $l, m, n = |(x_2-x_1)\,l + (y_2-y_1)\,m + (z_2-z_1)\,n|$

Corollary:

(a) If P is a point (x_1, y_1, z_1), then the projection of OP on a line whose direction cosines are (l_1, m_1, n_1) is $|l_1 x_1 + m_1 y_1 + n_1 z_1|$, where O is origin.

(b) The projections of PQ when P is (x_1, y_1, z_1) and Q is (x_2, y_2, z_2) on the co-ordinates axes are = (x_2-x_1), (y_2-y_1), (z_2-z_1).

(c) If Projections of PQ on AB is zero then PQ is perpendicular to AB.

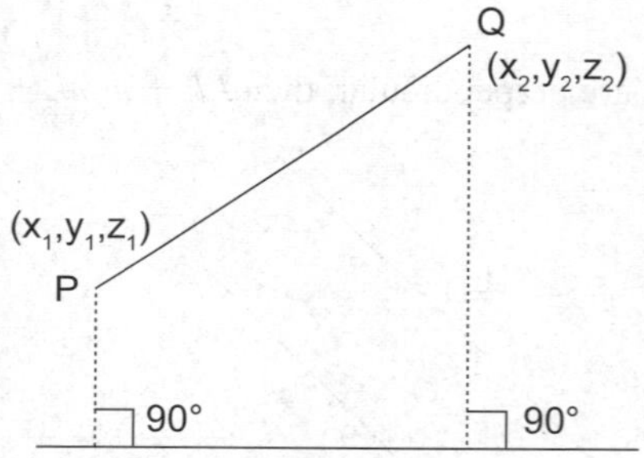

FIGURE 4.24

ILLUSTRATION 18: Find the projection of line segment AB, where $A(1, -2, 1)$ and $B(2, 1, 3)$ on the line with d.c's $(1, \sqrt{3}, 1)$

SOLUTION: Projection = $(x_2-x_1)l + (y_2-y_1)m + (z_2-z_1)n = 1+3\sqrt{3}+2 = 3(\sqrt{3}+1)$

TEXTUAL EXERCISE 3: (SUBJECTIVE)

1. Find the angles between the lines, whose direction cosines are given by the equation $l^2 - m^2 + n^2 = 0$, $l + m + n = 0$.
2. Find the acute angle between the lines in 3-dimesional space, whose direction ratios are proportional to 6, 9, 18 and 1, 2, 2.
3. Find the components of line vectors whose magnitude is given by 63 and direction ratios are 3, –2, 6.
4. If the foot of perpendicular from the origin on a plane is (11, 11, 11), then find the sum of the squares of the intercepts made by the plane on the coordinate axis.

5. If a line makes angles α, β, γ, ϕ with four diagonals of a cube, then find $\cos^2\alpha + \cos^2\beta + \cos^2\gamma + \cos^2\phi$.
6. Values of projections of a line on coordinate axis are 4, 12, 3. Then find the length and direction cosines of the line.
7. Show that the straight lines whose *d*.c's are given by $a^2l + b^2m + c^2n = 0$, $mn + nl + lm = 0$ will be parallel if $a + b + c = 0$.
8. Show that the points (3, 2, 2), (–1, 1, 3), (0, 5, 6), (2, 1, 6) lie on sphere whose centre is (1, 3, 4). Find also the radius of sphere.
9. Find the ratio in which sphere $x^2 + y^2 + z^2 = 350$ divides the line segment joining the points (3, –1, 2) and (9, –3, 6).
10. If l_1, m_1, n_1 ; l_2, m_2, n_2 ; l_3, m_3, n_3 are the direction cosines of 3-mutually ⊥ lines. Find the direction cosines of line which makes equal angles with them and find the angles.
11. Find the angle between the diagonals of a rectangular parallelopiped whose co-terminus edges are *a*, *b*, *c*.

Answer Key

1. π/3 **2.** $\cos^{-1}(20/21)$ **3.** 27, –18, 54 **4.** 3267 **5.** 4/3

6. 4/13, 12/13, 3/13 **8.** 3 units **9.** $\dfrac{-157 \pm \sqrt{5833}}{112}$

10. $\dfrac{l_1+l_2+l_3}{\sqrt{3}}, \dfrac{m_1+m_2+m_3}{\sqrt{3}}, \dfrac{n_1+n_2+n_3}{\sqrt{3}}$; $\cos^{-1}\left(\dfrac{1}{\sqrt{3}}\right)$ **11.** $\cos^{-1}\left(\dfrac{\pm a^2 \pm b^2 \pm c^2}{a^2+b^2+c^2}\right)$.

TEXTUAL EXERCISE 1: (OBJECTIVE)

1. Distance between the points (1, 3, 2) and (2, 1, 3) is
   (a) 12 (b) $\sqrt{12}$
   (c) $\sqrt{6}$ (d) 6
2. The direction cosines of any normal to the *xy*-plane are
   (a) 1, 0, 0 (b) 0, 1, 0
   (c) 1, 1, 0 (d) 0, 0, 1
3. Graph of the equation $y^2 + z^2 = 0$ in three-dimensional space is
   (a) *x*-axis (b) *y*-axis
   (c) *z*-axis (d) *yz*-plane
4. If $\left(\dfrac{1}{2}, \dfrac{1}{3}, n\right)$ are the direction cosines of a line, then the possible value of *n* is
   (a) $\dfrac{\sqrt{23}}{6}$ (b) $\dfrac{23}{6}$
   (c) $\dfrac{2}{3}$ (d) $\dfrac{3}{2}$
5. The nature of the locus of a point(*x*, *y*, *z*) is, when
   (i) $y = 0$
   (a) *xz* plane (b) *xy* plane
   (c) *yz* plane (d) None of these
   (ii) $z = c$
   (a) plane parallel to *yz* plane
   (b) plane parallel to *xy* plane
   (c) plane parallel to *xz* plane
   (d) None of these
   (iii) $y = 0, z = 0$
   (a) *x*-axis (b) *y*-axis
   (c) z -axis (d) None of these
   (iv) $y = b, z = c$
   (a) line parallel to *y*-axis passes through (0, *b*, *c*)
   (b) line parallel to *x*-axis passes through (0, *b*, *c*)
   (c) line parallel to *z*-axis passes through (0, *b*, *c*)
   (d) None of these
6. The projection of a line on a co-ordinate axes are 2, 3, 6. Then the length of the line is
   (a) 7 units (b) 5 units
   (c) 1 units (d) 11 units

7. A line makes angles α, β, γ with three dimensional co-ordinate axes respectively, then, $\cos 2\alpha + \cos 2\beta + \cos 2\gamma =$
(a) –2 (b) –1
(c) 1 (d) 2

8. *xy*-plane divides the line joining the points (2, 4, 5) and (–4, 3, –2) in the ratio
(a) 3: 5 (b) 5: 2
(c) 1: 3 (d) 3:4

9. Distance of the point (1, 2, 3) from the co-ordinate axes are
(a) 13, 10, 5 (b) $\sqrt{13}, \sqrt{10}, \sqrt{5}$
(c) $\sqrt{5}, \sqrt{13}, \sqrt{10}$ (d) $\frac{1}{\sqrt{13}}, \frac{1}{\sqrt{10}}, \frac{1}{\sqrt{5}}$

10. If the co-ordinates of the points *A*, *B*, *C*, *D* be (2, 3, –1), (3, 5, –3), (1, 2, 3) and (3, 5, 7) respectively, then the projection of *AB* on *CD* is
(a) 0 (b) 1
(c) 2 (d) $\sqrt{3}$

11. A point (*x*, *y*, *z*) moves parallel to *x*-axis. Which of the three variables *x*, *y*, *z* remain fixed?
(a) *x* (b) *y* and *z*
(c) *x* and *y* (d) z and *x*

12. The projection of the line segment joining the points (–1, 0, 3) and (2, 5, 1) on the line whose direction ratios are 6, 2, 3 is
(a) 22/7 (b) 15/7
(c) 9/7 (d) None of these

13. Which of the following set of points are non-collinear?
(a) (1, –1, 1), (–1, 1, 1), (0, 0, 1)
(b) (1, 2, 3), (3, 2, 1), (2, 2, 2)
(c) (–2, 4, –3), (4, –3, –2), (–3, –2, 4)
(d) (2, 0, –1), (3, 2, –2), (5, 6, –4)

14. Points (–2, 4, 7), (3, –6, –8) and (1, –2, –2) are:
(a) Collinear
(b) Vertices of an equilateral triangle
(c) Vertices of an isosceles triangle
(d) None of these

15. If θ is the angle between the lines *AB* and *CD*, then projection of line segment *AB* on line *CD*, is
(a) $AB \sin \theta$ (b) $AB \cos \theta$
(c) $AB \tan \theta$ (d) $CD \cos \theta$

16. If *A*(1, 2, –1) and *B*(–1, 0, 1) are given, then the co-ordinates of *P* which divides *AB* externally in the ratio 1: 2, are:
(a) $\frac{1}{3}$ (1, 4, –1) (b) (3, 4, –3)
(c) $\frac{1}{3}$ (3, 4, –3) (d) None of these

17. If the points (0, 1, 2), (2, –1, 3) and (1, –3, 1) are the vertices of a triangle, Then the triangle is
(a) Right angled scalene
(b) Isosceles right angled
(c) Equilateral
(d) None of these

18. If the sum of the squares of the distance of a point from the three co-ordinate axes be 36, then its distance from the origin is
(a) 6 (b) $3\sqrt{2}$
(c) $2\sqrt{3}$ (d) None of these

19. The ratio in which the line joining the points (2, 4, 5), (3, 5, –4) is divided by the *xy*-plane and the co-ordinates of the dividing point are
(a) 4: 5 ; (1, 2, 3)
(b) 2:3 ; (1, 2, 3)
(c) 5: 4 ; (23/9, 41/9, 0)
(d) None of these

20. The mid-points of the sides of a triangle are (1, 5, –1), (0, 4, –2) and (2, 3, 4), then its vertices are
(a) *A* (1, 2, 3), *B* (3, 4, 5), *C* (–1, 6, –7)
(b) *A* (1, 2, 3), *B* (3, 4, 5), *C* (1, 6, 7)
(c) *A* (1, 2, 3), *B* (1, 4, 5), *C* (1, 6, 7)
(d) None of these

21. The vertices of a ΔABC are the points (–1, 2, –3), (5, 0, –6) and (0, 4, –1) respectively. The direction ratios of the bisector of the angle *BAC* is
(a) (25, 8, 5) (b) (2, 8, 5)
(c) (1, 8, 5) (d) None of these

22. The perpendicular distances of a point (*x*, *y*, *z*) from the axes are
(a) $\sqrt{x^2+y^2+z^2}, \sqrt{x^2+y^2+z^2}, \sqrt{x^2+y^2+z^2}$
(b) $\sqrt{(y^2+z^2)}, \sqrt{(z^2+x^2)}, \sqrt{(x^2+y^2)}$
(c) (*x*, *y*, *z*)
(d) None of these

23. The co-ordinates of a point which is equidistant from the points (0, 0, 0), (*a*, 0, 0), (0, *b*, 0) and (0, 0, *c*) are given by

(a) $\left(\frac{a}{2},\frac{b}{2},\frac{c}{2}\right)$ (b) $\left(-\frac{a}{2},-\frac{b}{2},\frac{c}{2}\right)$

(c) $\left(\frac{a}{2},-\frac{b}{2},-\frac{c}{2}\right)$ (d) $\left(-\frac{a}{2},\frac{b}{2},-\frac{c}{2}\right)$

24. The direction cosines *l*, *m*, *n* of two lines which are connected by the relations $l + m + n = 0$, $2lm + 2ln - mn = 0$ are

(a) $\frac{1}{\sqrt{6}},\frac{-2}{\sqrt{5}},\frac{1}{\sqrt{6}}$ (b) $\frac{-2}{\sqrt{6}},\frac{1}{\sqrt{6}},\frac{1}{\sqrt{6}}$

(c) $\frac{1}{\sqrt{6}},\frac{1}{\sqrt{6}},\frac{1}{\sqrt{6}}$ (d) None of these

Answer Key

1. (c)	**2.** (d)	**3.** (a)	**4.** (a)	**5.** (i) (a)	(ii) (b)	(iii) (a)	(iv) (b)	**6.** (a)	**7.** (b)
8. (b)	**9.** (b)	**10.** (a)	**11.** (b)	**12.** (a)	**13.** (c)	**14.** (a)	**15.** (b)	**16.** (b)	**17.** (b)
18. (b)	**19.** (c)	**20.** (a)	**21.** (a)	**22.** (b)	**23.** (a)	**24.** (a)			

■ VECTOR EQUATION OF A CURVE

Vector equation of any curve is given by $f(\vec{r},\vec{a},\vec{b},\lambda)=0$ where $\vec{r}$ is position vector of a point moving on the curve and $\vec{a}\,\&\,\vec{b}$ are given vectors and λ is scalar parameter.

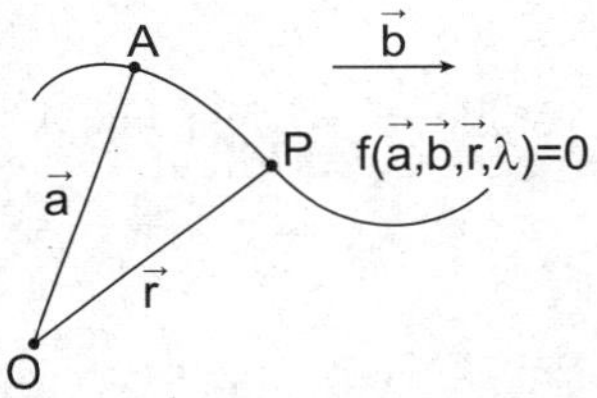

FIGURE 4.25

Cartesian Equation of a Curve

Replacing $\vec{r}$ by $x\hat{i}+y\hat{j}+z\hat{k}$ in the obtained vector equation and comparing scalar coefficients of $\hat{i},\hat{j},\hat{k}$ from both sides of the equation, we get an equation in *x*, *y*, *z* as F(*x*, *y*, *z*) = 0 called as Cartesian equation of curve.

■ THE STRAIGHT LINE

Straight line is the locus formed by the intersection of any two planes

1. One and only one line can be drawn through a given point in a given direction.

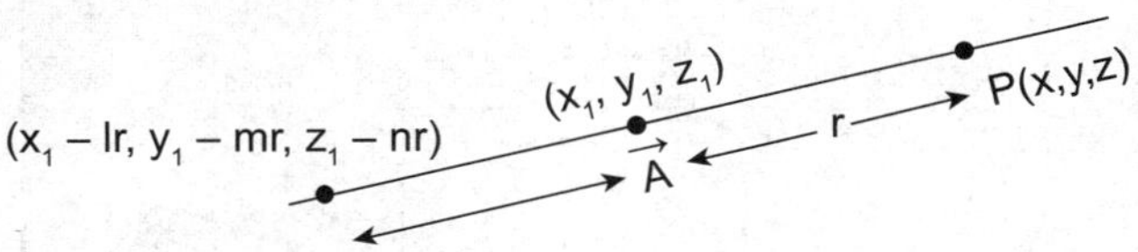

FIGURE 4.26

2. One and only one line can be drawn through two given points.
3. Intersection of two non-parallel planes is a unique line.

Thus to summarize, we can say that a straight line in space will be determined uniquely if

(i) it passes through a fixed point and is parallel to a fixed line.

(ii) it passes through two fixed points.

(iii) it is the intersection of two given non-parallel planes.

■ STRAIGHT LINES IN 3-D GEOMETRY

Vector equation

Vector equation of straight line passing through the point $A_{\vec{a}}(x_1, y_1, z_1)$

and parallel to a vector

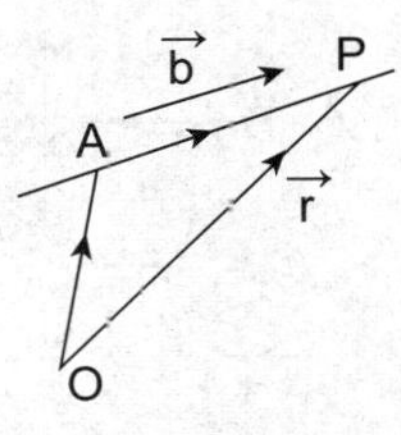

FIGURE 4.27

$\vec{b}=(l\hat{i}+m\hat{j}+n\hat{k})$ is given by : $\vec{r}=\vec{a}+\lambda\vec{b}$

$\Rightarrow\ \vec{r}=\vec{a}+\lambda\vec{b}$ as $\because\ \overrightarrow{OP}=\overrightarrow{OA}+\overrightarrow{AP}$

(where λ is a real parameter)

Cartesian Equation : $\because\ \vec{r}-\vec{a}=\lambda\vec{b}$

$\Rightarrow (x\hat{i}+y\hat{j}+z\hat{k})-(x_1\hat{i}+y_1\hat{j}+z_1\hat{k})=\lambda(l\hat{i}+m\hat{j}+n\hat{k})$

Comparing coefficients of linearly independent vectors $\hat{i},\hat{j},\hat{k}$, we have $\left.\begin{aligned}x-x_1&=\lambda l\\ y-y_1&=\lambda m\\ z-z_1&=\lambda n\end{aligned}\right\}$

$$\Rightarrow \frac{x-x_1}{l}=\frac{y-y_1}{m}=\frac{z-z_1}{n}=\lambda$$

Cartesian Equation of Straight Line (Symmetric form):

Let l, m, n are direction ratios of the straight line.

$$\Rightarrow \because \frac{x-x_1}{l}=\frac{y-y_1}{m}=\frac{z-z_1}{n}=\lambda$$

$$\Rightarrow \frac{x-x_1}{\cos\alpha}=\frac{y-y_1}{\cos\beta}=\frac{z-z_1}{\cos\gamma}=r;$$

where $\underbrace{r=\lambda\sqrt{l^2+m^2+n^2}}_{r \text{ is distance of } P(x,y,z) \text{ from } A(x_1,y_1,z_1)}$

ILLUSTRATION 19: Find the equation of straight line parallel to $2\hat{i}-\hat{j}+3\hat{k}$ and passing through the point (5, –2, 4)

SOLUTION: Vector form: Let $P\equiv(5,-2,4)$ and $\overrightarrow{OP}=5\hat{i}-2\hat{j}+4\hat{k}=\vec{a}$

Also $\vec{b}=2\hat{i}-\hat{j}+3\hat{k}$

$\therefore$ equation of straight line passing through $\vec{a}$ and parallel to straight line whose direction ratios are $\vec{b}$

$\Rightarrow \vec{r}=\vec{a}+\lambda\vec{b}$; $\vec{r}=(5\hat{i}-2\hat{j}+4\hat{k})+\lambda(2\hat{i}-\hat{j}+3\hat{k})$

Cartesian form: Here $(x_1, y_1, z_1)=(5,-2,4)$and parallel to straight line whose dr's are $(2,-1,3)$ is $\frac{x-5}{2}=\frac{y+2}{-1}=\frac{z-4}{3}$

ILLUSTRATION 20: Find the direction cosines of the line $\frac{x-2}{2}=\frac{2y-5}{-3}; z=-1$. Also find the vector equation of the line.

SOLUTION: The given line is $\frac{x-2}{2}=\frac{y-5/2}{-3/2}; z=-1 \quad\Rightarrow\quad \frac{x-2}{2}=\frac{y-5/2}{-3/2}=\frac{z+1}{0}$

This, shows that the given line passes through the point $\left(2,\frac{5}{2},-1\right)$ and has direction ratios $\left\langle 2,-\frac{3}{2},0\right\rangle$

$$\therefore \text{ Direction cosines: } \left(\frac{2}{\sqrt{2^2+\left(-\frac{3}{2}\right)^2+0^2}},\frac{-3/2}{\sqrt{2^2+\left(\frac{3}{2}\right)^2+0^2}},\frac{0}{\sqrt{2^2+\left(-\frac{3}{2}\right)^2+0^2}}\right)$$

or $\left(\frac{4}{5},\frac{3}{5},0\right)$

Thus, straight line is passing through $\vec{a}=2\hat{i}-\frac{5}{2}\hat{j}-\hat{k}$ and is parallel to $\left(\frac{4}{5}\hat{i}-\frac{3}{5}\hat{j}+0\hat{k}\right)$. Therefore, its vector equation is: $\vec{r}=\left(2\hat{i}-\frac{5}{2}\hat{j}-\hat{k}\right)+\lambda\left(\frac{4}{5}\hat{i}-\frac{3}{5}\hat{j}+0\hat{k}\right)$

Equation of Line Passing Through Two Points

The vector equation of a line passing through two points whose position vectors are $\vec{a}$ and $\vec{b}$ is: $\vec{r} = \vec{a} + \lambda(\vec{b} - \vec{a})$

The equations of line passing through (x_1, y_1, z_1) and (x_2, y_2, z_2) is $\frac{x - x_1}{x_2 - x_1} = \frac{y - y_1}{y_2 - y_1} = \frac{z - z_1}{z_2 - z_1}$.

Proof: Let O be the origin and A and B be the given points with position vectors $\vec{a}$ and $\vec{b}$ respectively.

Then $\overrightarrow{OP} = \vec{r}$, $\overrightarrow{OA} = \vec{a}$ and $\overrightarrow{OB} = \vec{b}$.

Since $\overrightarrow{AP}$ is collinear with $\overrightarrow{AB}; \overrightarrow{AP} = \lambda \overrightarrow{AB}$ for some scalar λ.

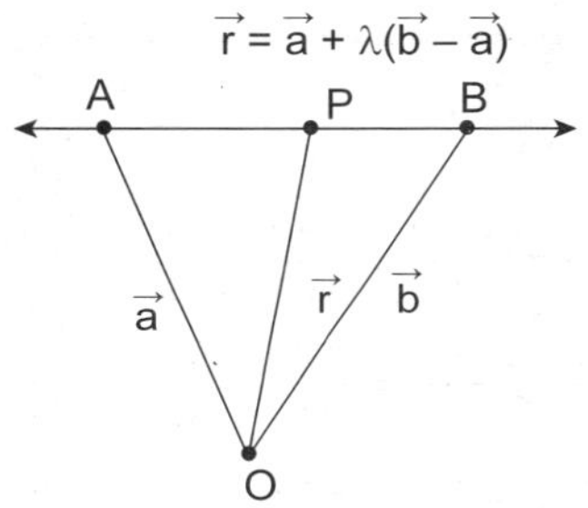

FIGURE 4.28

$\Rightarrow \overrightarrow{OP} - \overrightarrow{OA} = \lambda(\overrightarrow{OB} - \overrightarrow{OA})$

$\Rightarrow \vec{r} - \vec{a} = \lambda(\vec{b} - \vec{a})$

$\Rightarrow \vec{r} = \vec{a} + \lambda(\vec{b} - \vec{a})$

$\therefore$ Equation of straight line passing through $\vec{a}$ and $\vec{b}$ is given by $\vec{r} = \vec{a} + \lambda(\vec{b} - \vec{a})$

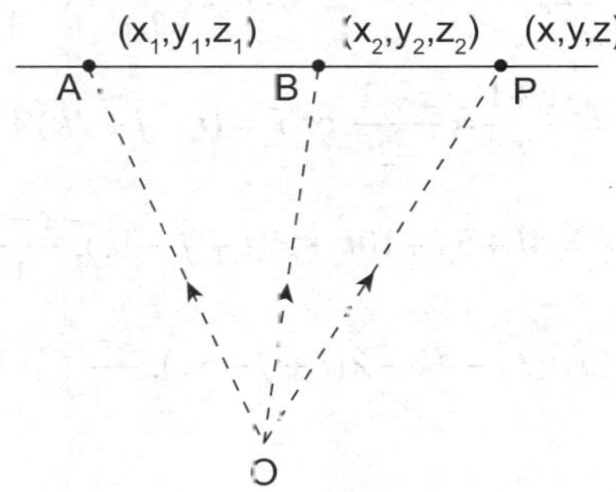

FIGURE 4.29

Equation of straight line passing through (x_1, y_1, z_1) and (x_2, y_2, z_2)

The direction ratios of AB are $(x_2 - x_1, y_2 - y_1, z_2 - z_1)$

The direction ratios of AP are $(x - x_1, y - y_1, z - z_1)$

Since they are proportional

$$\Rightarrow \frac{x - x_1}{x_2 - x_1} = \frac{y - y_1}{y_2 - y_1} = \frac{z - z_1}{z_2 - z_1}$$

NOTES

- *Any variable point on the line $\vec{r} = \vec{a} + \lambda\vec{b}$ has its position vector $(\vec{a} + \lambda'\vec{b})$, where λ' is scalar parameter.*
- *In cartesian from, a variable point on the line is takes as $(x_1 + \lambda l, y_1 + \lambda' m, z_1 + \lambda' n)$, where λ' is a parameter.*
- *Equation of the line passing through two points with position vectors $\vec{a}$ and $\vec{b}$ respectively is given by the equation $\vec{r} = \vec{a} + \lambda(\vec{b} - \vec{a})$*
- *The equation of line passing through two given points (x_1, y_1, z_1) and (x_2, y_2, z_2) is given by $\frac{x - x_1}{x_2 - x_1} = \frac{y - y_1}{y_2 - y_1} = \frac{z - z_1}{z_2 - z_1}$*
- *The points $A(x_1, y_1, z_1)$, $B(x_2, y_2, z_2)$ and $C(x_3, y_3, z_3)$ are said to be collinear if the third point satisfies the equation of line formed by 2 points. i.e. $\frac{x_3 - x_1}{x_2 - x_1} = \frac{y_3 - y_1}{y_2 - y_1} = \frac{z_3 - z_1}{z_2 - z_1}$*

TEXTUAL EXERCISE 4: (SUBJECTIVE)

1. Find in vector form as well as in cartesian form, the equation of the line passing through the points $A(1, 2, -1)$ and $B(2, 1, 1)$
2. Find the vector equation for the line which passes through the point (1, 2, 3) and parallel to the vector $\hat{i} - 2\hat{j} + 3\hat{k}$. Reduce the corresponding equation in cartesian form.

3. Find the cartesian equation of the line passing through (1, –1, 2) and parallel to the line whose D. R's are (1, 2, –2)

4. The points A (4, 5, 10), B (2, 3, 4) and C (1, 2, –1) are three vertices of a parallelogram $ABCD$. Find the vector and cartesian equations for the sides AB and BC. Also find the co-ordinates of D.

Answer Key

1. $\vec{r}=\hat{i}+2\hat{j}-\hat{k}+\lambda(\hat{i}-\hat{j}+2\hat{k}); \frac{x-1}{1}=\frac{y-2}{-1}=\frac{z+1}{2}$

2. $\vec{r}=\hat{i}+2\hat{j}+3\hat{k}+\lambda(\hat{i}-2\hat{j}+3\hat{k}); \frac{x-1}{1}=\frac{y-2}{-2}=\frac{z-3}{3}$

3. $\frac{x-1}{1}=\frac{y+1}{2}=\frac{z-2}{-2}$ or $\vec{r}=(\hat{i}-\hat{j}+2\hat{k})+\lambda(\hat{i}+2\hat{j}-2\hat{k})$

4. AB: $\vec{r}=4\hat{i}+5\hat{j}+10\hat{k}+\lambda(\hat{i}+\hat{j}+3\hat{k}), \frac{x-4}{1}=\frac{y-5}{1}=\frac{z-10}{3}$

   $BC: 2\hat{i}+3\hat{j}+4\hat{k}+\lambda(\hat{i}+\hat{j}+5\hat{k}), \frac{x-2}{1}=\frac{y-3}{1}=\frac{z-4}{5}$; Co-ordinates of D are (3, 4, 5)

TEXTUAL EXERCISE 2: (OBJECTIVE)

1. The equation of line passing through the point (1, –1, 1) and perpendicular to the line joining the points (4, 3, –2), (1, –1, 0) and (1, 2, –1), (2, 1, –3) is
   (a) $\frac{x-1}{10}=\frac{y+1}{-4}=\frac{z-1}{7}$
   (b) $\frac{x+1}{10}=\frac{y+1}{-4}=\frac{z+1}{7}$
   (c) $\frac{x+1}{-4}=\frac{y+1}{10}=\frac{z+1}{7}$
   (d) None of these

2. If the line through the points (4, 1, 2) and (5, k, 0) is parallel to the line through the points (2, 1, 1) and (3, 3, –1), then k is equal to
   (a) 3 (b) 2
   (c) 1 (d) None of these

3. The direction cosines of the line $x = y = z$ are:
   (a) $\frac{1}{\sqrt{3}}, \frac{1}{\sqrt{3}}, \frac{1}{\sqrt{3}}$ (b) $\frac{1}{3}, \frac{1}{3}, \frac{1}{3}$
   (c) $\sqrt{5}, \sqrt{13}, \sqrt{10}$ (d) $\frac{1}{\sqrt{13}}, \frac{1}{\sqrt{10}}, \frac{1}{\sqrt{5}}$

4. The number of straight lines that are equally inclined to the three dimensional co-ordinate axes, is:
   (a) 2 (b) 4
   (c) 6 (d) 8

5. The equation of straight line passing through the point (a, b, c) and parallel to z-axis, is
   (a) $\frac{x-a}{1}=\frac{y-b}{1}=\frac{z-c}{0}$
   (b) $\frac{x-a}{0}=\frac{y-b}{1}=\frac{z-c}{1}$
   (c) $\frac{x-a}{1}=\frac{y-b}{0}=\frac{z-c}{0}$
   (d) $\frac{x-a}{0}=\frac{y-b}{0}=\frac{z-c}{1}$

6. Equation of x-axis is
   (a) $\frac{x}{1}=\frac{y}{1}=\frac{z}{1}$ (b) $\frac{x}{0}=\frac{y}{1}=\frac{z}{1}$
   (c) $\frac{x}{1}=\frac{y}{0}=\frac{z}{0}$ (d) $\frac{x}{0}=\frac{y}{0}=\frac{z}{1}$

7. The straight line $\frac{x-3}{3}=\frac{y-2}{1}=\frac{z-1}{0}$ is
   (a) Parallel to x-axis (b) Parallel to y-axis
   (c) Parallel to z-axis (d) Perpendicular to z-axis

8. The projection of the line segment joining the points (–1, 0, 3) and (2, 5, 1) on the line whose direction ratios are 6, 2 and 3 is
   (a) $\frac{10}{7}$ (b) $\frac{22}{7}$
   (c) $\frac{18}{7}$ (d) None of these

9. The acute angle between the line $\frac{x+1}{3}=\frac{y-1}{2}=\frac{z-2}{4}$ and the plane $2x + y - 3z + 4 = 0$ is:

(a) $\sin^{-1}\left(\frac{4}{\sqrt{406}}\right)$ (b) $\sin^{-1}\left(\frac{-4}{\sqrt{406}}\right)$

(c) $\sin^{-1}\left(\frac{2}{7\sqrt{29}}\right)$ (d) None of these

10. The angle between the lines $2x = 3y = -z$ and $6x = -y = -4z$ is

(a) 0° (b) 30°

(c) 45° (d) 90°

11. If line $\frac{x-x_1}{\ell}=\frac{y-y_1}{m}=\frac{z-z_1}{n}$ is parallel to the plane $ax + by + cz + d = 0$, then

(a) $\frac{a}{\ell}=\frac{b}{m}=\frac{c}{n}$

(b) $al + bm + cn = 0$

(c) $\frac{a}{\ell}+\frac{b}{m}+\frac{c}{n}=0$

(d) None of these

12. The angle between two lines $\frac{x+1}{2}=\frac{y+3}{2}=\frac{z-4}{-1}$ and $\frac{x-4}{1}=\frac{y+4}{2}=\frac{z+1}{2}$ is:

(a) $\cos^{-1}\left(\frac{1}{9}\right)$ (b) $\cos^{-1}\left(\frac{2}{9}\right)$

(c) $\cos^{-1}\left(\frac{3}{9}\right)$ (d) $\cos^{-1}\left(\frac{4}{9}\right)$

Answer Key

1. (a)	**2.** (a)	**3.** (a)	**4.** (b)	**5.** (d)	**6.** (c)	**7.** (d)	**8.** (b)	**9.** (a)	**10.** (d)
11. (b)	**12.** (d)								

■ ANGLE BETWEEN A LINE AND A PLANE

Angle between line and plane is defined as angle between line and projection of line in the plane. $\theta = 90° - \alpha$, where α is angle between line and normal to plane.

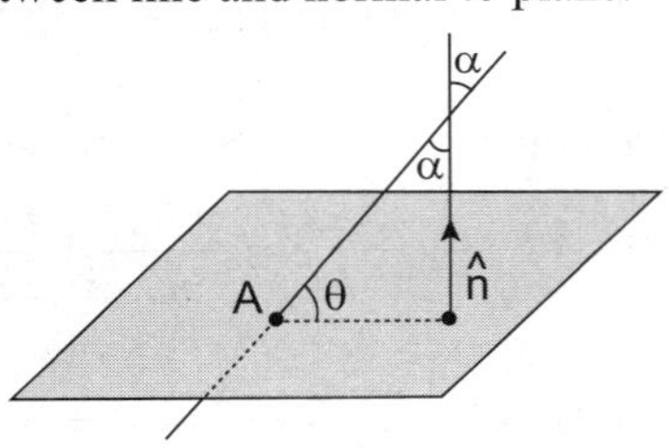

FIGURE 4.30

If angle between the line $\frac{x-x_1}{a}=\frac{y-y_1}{b}=\frac{z-z_1}{c}$ and the plane $a_1x + b_1y + c_1z + d_1 = 0$ is θ, then $90° - \theta$ is the angle between normal and the line

i.e., $$\cos(90° - \theta) = \frac{aa_1 + bb_1 + cc_1}{\sqrt{a^2+b^2+c^2}\sqrt{a_1^2+b_1^2+c_1^2}}$$

or $$\sin\theta = \frac{aa_1 + bb_1 + cc_1}{\sqrt{a^2+b^2+c^2}\sqrt{a_1^2+b_1^2+c_1^2}}$$

Corollary: If line is parallel to the plane, then $a_1a_2 + b_1b_2 + c_1c_2 = 0$

■ ANGLE BETWEEN TWO LINES

Let $L_1 = C : \vec{r} = \vec{a} + \lambda\vec{b}$ ... (i)

$L_2 = C : \vec{r} = \vec{c} + \mu\vec{d}$ ... (ii)

be two straight lines in space.

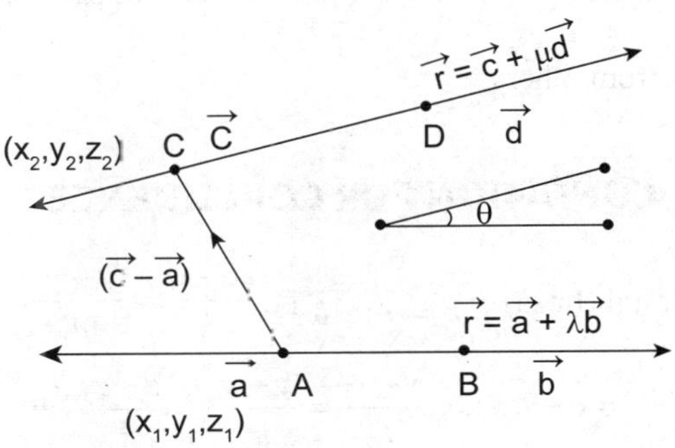

FIGURE 4.31

Clearly, (i) and (ii) are straight lines in the directions of $\vec{b}$ and $\vec{d}$ respectively. Let θ be the angle between the straight line (i) and (ii).

Then θ is the angle between the vectors $\vec{b}$ and $\vec{d}$ also $\vec{b}.\vec{d} = |\vec{b}||\vec{d}|\cos\theta$

$$\Rightarrow \cos\theta = \frac{\vec{b}.\vec{d}}{|\vec{b}||\vec{d}|}$$

Cartesian form:

Let $\dfrac{x-x_1}{l_1}=\dfrac{y-y_1}{m_1}=\dfrac{z-z_1}{n_1}$

and $\dfrac{x-x_2}{l_2}=\dfrac{y-y_2}{m_2}=\dfrac{z-z_2}{n_2}$ be the cartesian form of (i) and (ii), then $\theta=\cos^{-1}\left(\dfrac{l_1l_2+m_1m_2+n_1n_2}{\sqrt{l_1^2+m_1^2+n_1^2}\sqrt{l_2^2+m_2^2+n_2^2}}\right)$

■ CONDITION OF PARALLELISM AND COPLANARITY

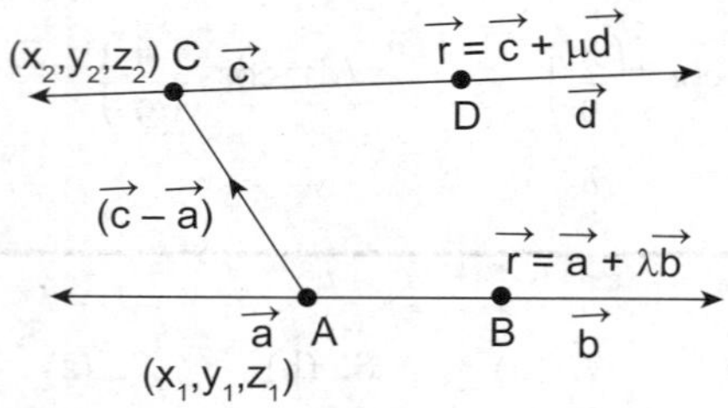

FIGURE 4.32

The above two lines will be parallel (but not coincident) when $\vec{b}=\lambda'\,\vec{d}\neq(\vec{c}-\vec{a})$ and $[(\vec{c}-\vec{a})\ \vec{b}\ \vec{d}]=0$

i.e. $\dfrac{l_1}{l_2}=\dfrac{m_1}{m_2}=\dfrac{n_1}{n_2}$

But out of $\dfrac{l_1}{x_2-x_1},\ \dfrac{m_1}{y_2-y_1},\ \dfrac{n_1}{z_2-z_1}$ atleast one is different from others.

■ CONDITION FOR COINCIDENCE

The straight lines $L_1:\vec{r}=\vec{a}+\lambda\vec{b}$ i.e. $\dfrac{x-x_1}{l_1}=\dfrac{y-y_1}{m_2}=\dfrac{z-z_1}{n_2}$

and $L_2:\vec{r}=\vec{c}+\mu\vec{d}$ i.e., $\dfrac{x-x_2}{l_2}=\dfrac{y-y_2}{m_2}=\dfrac{z-z_2}{n_2}$ are coincident, if they lie in same plane and the vector $\vec{b},\vec{d},\vec{c}-\vec{a}$ are collinear

$$\Rightarrow\ (\vec{c}-\vec{a})=\lambda\vec{d} \qquad \text{..... (i)}$$

and $\vec{b}=k\vec{d}$ .....(ii)

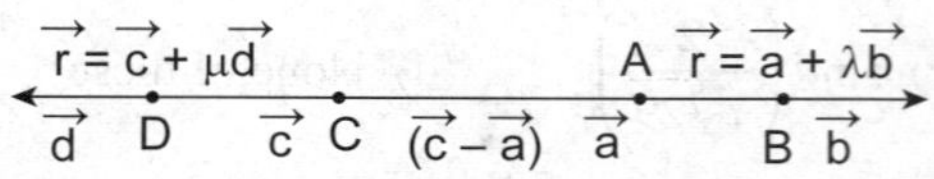

FIGURE 4.33

$\therefore$ For coincident $\vec{b}=k\vec{d}=\lambda(\vec{c}-\vec{a})$

i.e., $\dfrac{l_1}{l_2}=\dfrac{m_1}{m_2}=\dfrac{n_1}{n_2}$ and (x_1,y_1,z_1) satisfies $L_2=0$

■ CONDITION OF PERPENDICULARITY

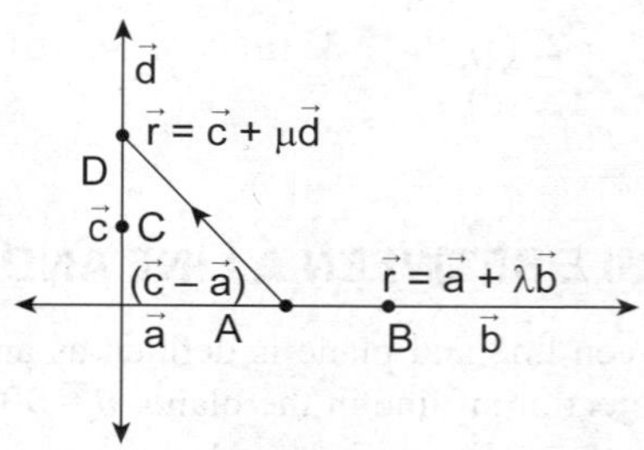

FIGURE 4.34

The straight line

$L_1:\ \vec{r}=\vec{a}+\lambda\vec{b}$ i.e., $\dfrac{x-x_1}{l_1}=\dfrac{y-y_1}{m_1}=\dfrac{z-z_1}{n_1}$ and,

$L_2:\ \vec{r}=\vec{c}+\mu\vec{d}$ i.e., $\dfrac{x-x_2}{l_2}=\dfrac{y-y_2}{m_2}=\dfrac{z-z_2}{n_2}$

are perpendicular iff $\vec{b}\,.\,\vec{d}=0$

$\Rightarrow l_1\,l_2+m_1\,m_2+n_1\,n_2=0$

ILLUSTRATION 22: Find the angle between the pair of lines $\vec{r}=3\hat{i}+2\hat{j}-4\hat{k}+\lambda(\hat{i}+2\hat{j}+2\hat{k})$ and $\vec{r}=5\hat{i}-2\hat{k}+\mu(3\hat{i}+2\hat{j}+6\hat{k})$

SOLUTION: Given lines are: $\vec{r}=(3\hat{i}+2\hat{j}-4\hat{k})+\lambda(\hat{i}+2\hat{j}+2\hat{k})$; $\vec{r}=(5\hat{i}-2\hat{k})+\mu(3\hat{i}+2\hat{j}+6\hat{k})$

We know, angle between $\vec{r}=\vec{a}_1+\lambda\vec{b}_1$ and $\vec{r}=\vec{a}_2+\mu\vec{b}_2$ is given by

$$\cos\theta = \frac{\vec{b_1}.\vec{b_2}}{|\vec{b_1}||\vec{b_2}|} \Rightarrow \cos\theta = \frac{(\hat{i}+2\hat{j}+2\hat{k}).(3\hat{i}+2\hat{j}+6\hat{k})}{\sqrt{1^2+2^2+2^2}\sqrt{3^2+2^2+6^2}}$$

$$= \frac{3+4+12}{\sqrt{9}\sqrt{49}} = \frac{19}{21} \Rightarrow \theta = \cos^{-1}\left(\frac{19}{21}\right)$$

ILLUSTRATION 23: To find the equation of a line which passes through (2, –1, 3) and is perpendicular to the line ;

$\vec{r} = (\hat{i}+\hat{j}-\hat{k}) + \lambda(2\hat{i}-2\hat{j}+\hat{k})$ and $\vec{r} = (2\hat{i}-\hat{j}+3\hat{k}) + \mu(\hat{i}+2\hat{j}+2\hat{k})$

SOLUTION: To find a straight line perpendicular to given lines, $\vec{r} = \vec{a_1} + \lambda\vec{b_1}$ and $\vec{r} = \vec{a_2} + \lambda\vec{b_2}$ has dr's proportional to $\vec{b} = \vec{b_1} \times \vec{b_2}$

$$\text{Now, } \vec{b} = \begin{vmatrix} \hat{i} & \hat{j} & \hat{k} \\ 2 & -2 & 1 \\ 1 & 2 & 2 \end{vmatrix} = -6\hat{i} - 3\hat{j} + 6\hat{k}$$

Thus, the required line passes through the point (2, –1, 3) and is parallel to the vector, $\vec{b} = -6\hat{i} - 3\hat{j} + 6\hat{k}$

$\therefore$ its equation is $\vec{r} = (2\hat{i}-\hat{j}+3\hat{k}) + \lambda(-6\hat{i}-3\hat{j}+6\hat{k})$

FOOT OF THE PERPENDICULAR/ IMAGE OF A POINT IN A LINE

Given a point P (x_1, y_1, z_1) with P.V. = $\vec{c}$ and the straight line $L_1 : \vec{r} = \vec{a} + \lambda\vec{b} =$ i.e. $\frac{x-\alpha}{l} = \frac{y-\beta}{m} = \frac{z-\gamma}{n}$. If the foot of perpendicular of P in the line be M and image be Q, then the position vector of the foot of perpendicular $M(\vec{r}_m)$ is given as $\vec{r}_m = \overrightarrow{OA} + \overrightarrow{AM}$

Now $\overrightarrow{AM}$ is the projection of $\overrightarrow{AP}$ on $\hat{b}$

$$\therefore \overrightarrow{AM} = \left((\vec{c}-\vec{a}).\hat{b}\right)\hat{b}$$

$$\Rightarrow \vec{r}_m = \vec{a} + ((\vec{c}-\vec{a}).\hat{b})\hat{b}$$

$$\Rightarrow \vec{r}_m = \vec{a} + \frac{[(\vec{c}-\vec{a}).(l\hat{i}+m\hat{j}+n\hat{k})]\,(l\hat{i}+m\hat{j}+n\hat{k})}{l^2+m^2+n^2}$$

where $\vec{a} = \alpha\hat{i} + \beta\hat{j} + \gamma\hat{k}$

and $\vec{c} = x_1\hat{i} + y_1\hat{j} + z_1\hat{k}$

The position vector of the image Q $(\vec{q})$ is given as $\vec{q} = 2\vec{r}_m - P.V. \text{of } p = 2\vec{r}_m - \vec{c}$

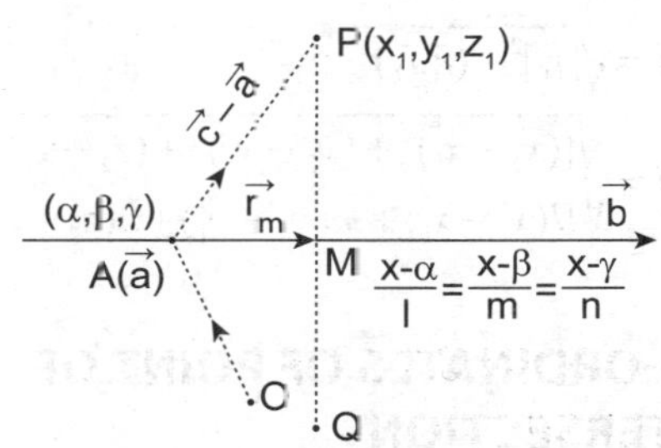

FIGURE 4.35

Cartesian method: let the foot of perpendicular M be $(\lambda l + \alpha, \lambda m + \beta, \lambda n + \gamma)$

Now, $PM \perp \vec{b} \Rightarrow \overrightarrow{PM}.\vec{b} = 0$

$$\Rightarrow (\lambda l + \alpha - x_1)l + (\lambda m + \beta - y_1)m + (\lambda n + \gamma - z_1)n = 0$$

$$\Rightarrow \lambda = \frac{l(x_1-\alpha) + m(y_1-\beta) + n(z_1-\gamma)}{l^2+m^2+n^2}$$

so the coordinate of M can be obtained and the coordinate of image Q is given by $Q_x = 2Mx - Px$; $Q_y = 2My - P_y$; $Q_z = 2M_z - P_z$ where $M(M_x, M_y, M_z)$.

- **The Distance of the Point $P(x_2, y_2, z_2)$ from the Line $\frac{x-x_1}{l} = \frac{y-y_1}{m} = \frac{z-z_1}{n}$, (where l, m and n are Direction Cosines of the Line), is**

$[(x_2-x_1)^2+(y_2-y_1)^2+(z_2-z_1)^2-\{l(x_2-x_1)+m(y_2-y_1)$
$+n(z_2-z_1)\}^2]^{1/2}$

Let $\vec{r}_1=(x_2-x_1)\hat{i}+(y_2-y_1)\hat{j}+(z_2-z_1)\hat{k}$

$\vec{r}_2=l\hat{i}+m\hat{j}+n\hat{k}$

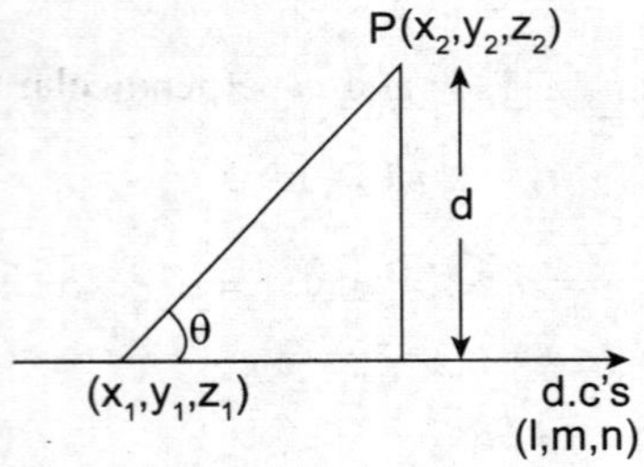

FIGURE 4.36

$\therefore \quad \cos\theta=\dfrac{\vec{r}_2.\vec{r}_1}{|\vec{r}_1||\vec{r}_2|}$

also $d=|\vec{r}_1|\sin\theta$, $d^2=|\vec{r}_1|^2\sin^2\theta$

$=|\vec{r}_1|^2(1-\cos^2\theta)=|\vec{r}_1|^2\left(1-\dfrac{(\vec{r}_1.\vec{r}_2)^2}{|\vec{r}_1|^2|\vec{r}_2|^2}\right)$

$\Rightarrow \; d^2=|\vec{r}_1|^2-(\vec{r}_1.\vec{r}_2)^2 \; \{\text{where }, |\vec{r}_2|=1\}$

$\Rightarrow \; d=\sqrt{|\vec{r}_1|^2-(\vec{r}_1.\vec{r}_2)^2}$

$$\Rightarrow \; d=\sqrt{\begin{aligned}&\{(x_2-x_1)^2+(y_2-y_1)^2+(z_2-z_1)^2\}-\\&\{l(x_2-x_1)+m(y_2-y_1)+n(z_2-z_1)\}^2\end{aligned}}$$

■ CO-ORDINATES OF POINT OF INTERSECTION

If the two lines are intersecting, the co-ordinates can be found as.

Method 1:

Step I: Compare the position vectors of both lines. i.e. let position vector of point of intersection be $\vec{r}=\vec{a}+\lambda\vec{b}=\vec{c}+\mu\vec{d}$.

Step II: Compare the scalar coefficient of linearly independent vectors to get three linear equations in λ and μ

Step III: Solving any two to get λ and μ and if the values obtained satisfy 3rd equation, then lines are intersecting and for the obtained value of λ, get the position vector of the point.

Method 2:

Step I: Take a general point of $L_1=0$. $(\lambda l_1+x_1, \lambda m_1+y_1, \lambda n_1+z_1)$.

Step II: Substitute in equation $L_2=0$, to get two equations in λ.

Step III: If the values of λ obtained from both equations are same, then the lines intersect otherwise they are parallel or skew.

Step IV: If the lines intersect, then the values of λ obtained generate point of intersection

Special Cases: If $[(\vec{c}-\vec{a})\vec{b}\;\vec{d}]=0$ and $\vec{b}\neq k\vec{d}$. lines intersect.

Case I: $\vec{c}-\vec{a}=\lambda\vec{b}$; Point of intersection is C.

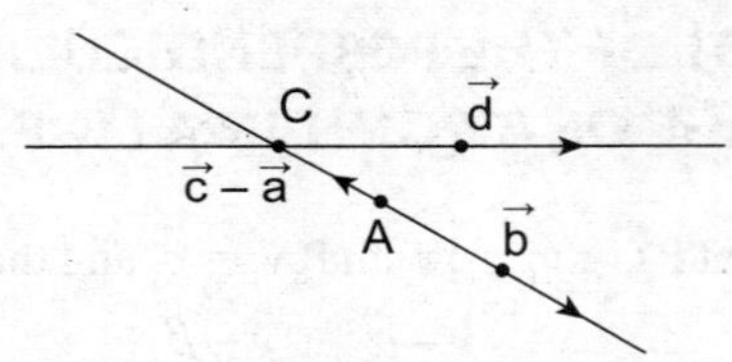

FIGURE 4.37

Case II: $\vec{c}-\vec{a}=\lambda\vec{d}$ Point of intersection is A

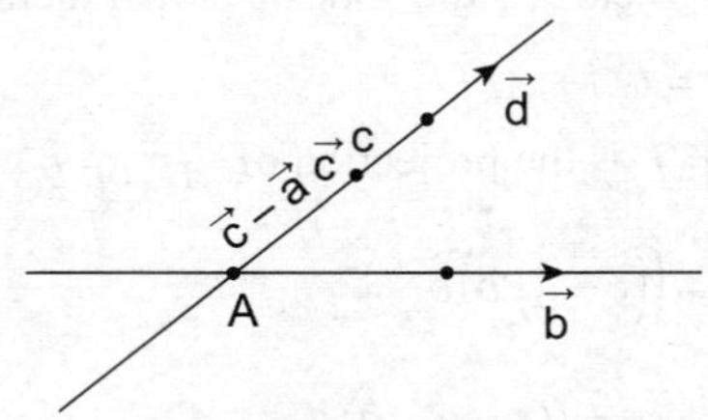

FIGURE 4.38

ILLUSTRATION 24: Find the coordinates of a point which is at a distance of √5 units from $A=\vec{a}=3\hat{i}+4\hat{j}+5\hat{k}$ measured along the vector $\sqrt{2}\hat{i}+\hat{j}+\sqrt{2}\hat{k}$

SOLUTION: Let $\vec{b}=\sqrt{2}\hat{i}+\hat{j}+\sqrt{2}\hat{k}$

$\Rightarrow \; \hat{b}=\dfrac{\sqrt{2}}{\sqrt{5}}\hat{i}+\dfrac{1}{\sqrt{5}}\hat{j}+\dfrac{1}{\sqrt{5}}\hat{k} \Rightarrow \vec{r}_1=\vec{a}+\sqrt{5}\hat{b}$

$$\Rightarrow \vec{r}_1 = \left(3\hat{i}+4\hat{j}+5\hat{k}\right)+\sqrt{5}\left(\frac{\sqrt{2}}{\sqrt{5}}\hat{i}+\frac{1}{\sqrt{5}}\hat{j}+\frac{\sqrt{2}}{\sqrt{5}}\hat{k}\right)$$

$$\Rightarrow \vec{r}_1 = \left(3+\sqrt{2}\right)\hat{i}+5\hat{j}+\left(5+\sqrt{2}\right)\hat{k}$$; Similarly $\vec{r}_2 = \vec{a}-\sqrt{5}\hat{b}$

$$= \left(3\hat{i}+4\hat{j}+5\hat{k}\right)-\sqrt{5}\left(\frac{\sqrt{2}}{\sqrt{5}}\hat{i}+\frac{1}{\sqrt{5}}\hat{j}+\frac{\sqrt{2}}{\sqrt{5}}\hat{k}\right) = \left(3-\sqrt{2}\right)\hat{i}+3\hat{j}+\left(5-\sqrt{2}\right)\hat{k}$$

Aliter: $\dfrac{x-x_1}{\cos\alpha}=\dfrac{y-y_1}{\cos\beta}=\dfrac{z-z_1}{\cos\gamma}=r$

Where (x, y, z) = (3, 4, 5) and $\cos\alpha=\dfrac{\sqrt{2}}{\sqrt{5}}; \cos\beta=\dfrac{1}{\sqrt{5}}; \cos\gamma=\dfrac{\sqrt{2}}{\sqrt{5}}$ & $r=\pm\sqrt{5}$

$\Rightarrow$ (x, y, z) = $(3+\sqrt{2}, 5, 5+\sqrt{2})$ or $(3-\sqrt{2}, 3, 5-\sqrt{2})$

ILLUSTRATION 25: Find the image of the point (1, 6, 3) in the line $\dfrac{x}{1}=\dfrac{y-1}{2}=\dfrac{z-2}{3}$

SOLUTION: Let P be the given point and let L be the foot of perpendicular from P to the given line.

The co-ordinates of a general point on the given line are given by $\dfrac{x-0}{1}=\dfrac{y-1}{2}=\dfrac{z-2}{3}=$

i.e., $x=\lambda$, $y=2\lambda+1$, $z=3\lambda+2$

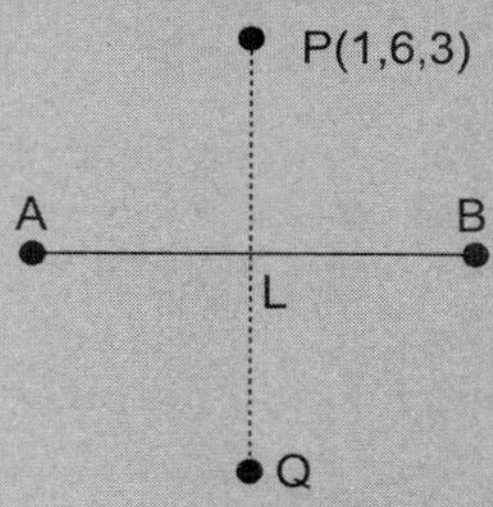

FIGURE 4.39

Let the co-ordinates of L be $(\lambda, 2\lambda+1, 3\lambda+2)$ ...(i)

So, direction ratios of PL are: $(\lambda-1, 2\lambda-5, 3\lambda-1)$

direction ratios of the given line are (1, 2, 3) which is perpendicular to PL

$\Rightarrow (\lambda-1).1+(2\lambda-5).2+(3\lambda-1).3=0, \Rightarrow \lambda=1$

So, co-ordinates of L are (1, 3, 5)

Let $Q(x_1, y_1, z_1)$ be the image of $P(1, 6, 3)$ on given line.

where L is mid-point of PQ

$\therefore\ 1=\dfrac{x_1+1}{2}, 3=\dfrac{y_1+6}{2}, 5=\dfrac{z_1+3}{2} \qquad \Rightarrow x_1=1, y_1=0, z_1=7$

ILLUSTRATION 26: Show that the two lines $\dfrac{x-1}{2}=\dfrac{y-2}{3}=\dfrac{z-3}{4}$ and $\dfrac{x-4}{5}=\dfrac{y-1}{2}=z$ intersect. Also find the point of intersection of these lines.

SOLUTION: Here $\dfrac{x-1}{2}=\dfrac{y-2}{3}=\dfrac{z-3}{4}=r\text{(say)}$ ....(i)

$\dfrac{x-4}{5}=\dfrac{y-1}{2}=\dfrac{z-0}{1}=\lambda\text{(say)}$ ...(ii)

Any point on line (i) is $P(2r + 1, 3r + 2, 4r + 3)$

and any point on the line (ii) is $Q(5\lambda + 4, 2\lambda + 1, \lambda)$.

They intersect if and only if $2r + 1 = 5\lambda + 4; 3r + 2 = 2\lambda + 1, 4r + 3 = \lambda$

Solving, $r = -1, \lambda = -1$

clearly for these values of λ and r $P(-1, -1, -1)$

Hence (i) and (ii) intersect at $(-1, -1, -1)$

LLUSTRATION 27: Show that the line $x = \frac{y-2}{2} = \frac{z+3}{3}$ & $\frac{x-2}{4} = \frac{y-6}{3} = \frac{z-3}{4}$ intersect each other and also find their point of intersection.

SOLUTION: $L_1 : \frac{x}{1} = \frac{y-2}{2} = \frac{z+3}{3} = \vec{a} + \lambda\vec{b}$ and $L_2 : \frac{x-2}{4} = \frac{y-6}{3} = \frac{z-3}{4} = \vec{c} + \mu\vec{d}$

$\Rightarrow \vec{a} = 2\hat{j} - 3\hat{k} \Rightarrow \vec{b} = \hat{i} + 2\hat{j} + 3\hat{k} \Rightarrow \vec{c} = 2\hat{i} + 6\hat{j} + 3\hat{k} \Rightarrow \vec{d} = 4\hat{i} + 3\hat{j} + 4\hat{k}$

$\Rightarrow \vec{c} - \vec{a} = 2\hat{i} + 4\hat{j} + 6\hat{k} = 2(\hat{i} + 2\hat{j} + 3\hat{k}) = 2\vec{b} \quad \because \vec{c} - \vec{a} = n\vec{b}$

$\therefore$ Point of intersection is $\vec{c} = 2\hat{i} + 6\hat{j} + 3\hat{k}$

ILLUSTRATION 28: Find the value of 'a' for which the lines

$L_1 : \frac{x-2}{1} = \frac{y-9}{2} = \frac{z-13}{3}; L_2 : \frac{x-a}{-1} = \frac{y-7}{2} = \frac{z+2}{-3}$ intersect

SOLUTION: Let $L_1 = \frac{x-2}{1} = \frac{y-9}{2} = \frac{z-13}{3} = \lambda(\text{say})$ and $L_2 = \frac{x-a}{-1} = \frac{y-7}{2} = \frac{z+2}{-3}$

Now any general point on L_1, will be given by $x = \lambda + 2, y = 2\lambda + 9, z = 3\lambda + 13$

$\because$ This point lies on L_2.

$$\therefore \quad \frac{(\lambda+2)-a}{-1} = \frac{(2\lambda+9)-7}{2} = \frac{(3\lambda+13)+2}{-3}$$

Solving for λ; $\frac{(2\lambda+9)-7}{2} = \frac{(3\lambda+13)+2}{-3}$

$$\Rightarrow \frac{2\lambda+2}{2} = \frac{3\lambda+15}{-3} \Rightarrow \lambda+1 = -\lambda-5 \Rightarrow 2\lambda = -6 \text{ or } \lambda = -3$$

$$\therefore \text{ Solving for } a : \frac{\lambda+2-a}{-1} = \frac{(2\lambda+9)-7}{2} \Rightarrow a = -3$$

Aliter: $L_1 : (2\hat{i} + 9\hat{j} + 13\hat{k}) + \lambda(\hat{i} + 2\hat{j} + 3\hat{k})$ .... (i)

and $L_2 : (a\hat{i} + 7\hat{j} - 2\hat{k}) + \mu(-\hat{i} + 2\hat{j} - 3\hat{k})$ .... (ii)

Now since, the two lines intersect each other, therefore vectors are same for some value of λ and μ

$\therefore$ comparing coefficients of $\hat{i}$ on both sides, we get $2 + \lambda = a - \mu$ ..... (iii)

Similarly, $9 + 2\lambda = 7 + 2\mu$ ..... (iv)

and $13 + 3\lambda = -2 - 3\mu$ .... (v)

Solving (iv) and (v) ; we get $\lambda = -3; \mu = -2$

Putting these values in equation (iii), we get $2 + (-3) = a - (-2)$

$\Rightarrow -1 = a + 2 \qquad \Rightarrow a = -3$

TEXTUAL EXERCISE 5: (SUBJECTIVE)

1. Find the angle between the following pairs of lines:
   (i) $\vec{r} = (4\hat{i} - \hat{j}) + \lambda(\hat{i} + 2\hat{j} - 2\hat{k})$ and
   $\vec{r} = \hat{i} - \hat{j} + 2\hat{k} - \mu(2\hat{i} + 4\hat{j} - 4\hat{k})$
   (ii) $\vec{r} = \lambda(\hat{i} + \hat{j} + 2\hat{k})$ and
   $\vec{r} = 2\hat{j} + \mu[(\sqrt{3} - 1)\hat{i} - (\sqrt{3} + 1)\hat{j} + 4\hat{k}]$
2. Find the angle between the pairs of lines with direction ratios proportional to 2, 2, 1 and 4, 1, 8.
3. Find the equation of the line passing through the point (1, 2, –4) and parallel to the line $\frac{x-3}{4} = \frac{y-5}{2} = \frac{z+1}{3}$.
4. Find the equation of the line passing through point (2, 1, 3) and perpendicular to the lines $\frac{x-1}{1} = \frac{y-2}{2} = \frac{z-3}{3}$ and $\frac{x}{-3} = \frac{y}{2} = \frac{z}{5}$.
5. Find the vector equation of the line passing through the point (2, –1, –1) which is parallel to the line $6x - 2 = 3y + 1 = 2z - 2$.
6. If the lines $\frac{x-1}{-3} = \frac{y-2}{2\lambda} = \frac{z-3}{2}$ and $\frac{x-1}{3\lambda} = \frac{y-1}{1} = \frac{z-6}{-5}$ are perpendicular, find the value of λ.
7. Find the perpendicular distance of the point (1, 0, 0) from the line $\frac{x-1}{2} = \frac{y+1}{-3} = \frac{z+10}{8}$. Also find the co-ordinates of the foot of the perpendicular.
8. Find the equation of the perpendicular drawn from the point P (2, 4, –1) to the line $\frac{x+5}{1} = \frac{y+3}{4} = \frac{z-6}{-9}$.
9. Find the image of the point (5, 9, 3) in the line $\frac{x-1}{2} = \frac{y-2}{3} = \frac{z-3}{4}$
10. Find the image of the point (2, –1, 5) in the line $\vec{r} = (11\hat{i} - 2\hat{j} - 8\hat{k}) + \lambda(10\hat{i} - 4\hat{j} - 11\hat{k})$.
12. (a) Find the co-ordinates of the point where the line through the points A(3, 4, 1) and B(5, 1, 6) crosses the XY plane.
    (b) Find the co-ordinates of the point where the line through (5, 1, 6) and (3, 4, 1) crosses the YZ plane.
    (c) Find the co-ordinates of the point where the line through (3, –4, –5) and (2, –3, 1) crosses the plane $2x + y + z = 7$.
13. Show that the line segments joining the points (4, 7, 8) (–1, –2, 1) and (2, 3, 4), (1, 2, 5) intersect. Also find the point of intersection.
14. (a) Find the image of the point (1, 6, 3) in the line $\frac{x}{1} = \frac{y-1}{2} = \frac{z-2}{3}$
    (b) Find the image of the point (1, 2, 3) in the line $\vec{r} = (6\hat{i} + 7\hat{j} + 7\hat{k}) + \lambda(3\hat{i} + 2\hat{j} - 2\hat{k})$
15. Show that the lines $\frac{x}{1} = \frac{y-2}{2} = \frac{z+3}{3}$ and $\frac{x-2}{2} = \frac{y-6}{3} = \frac{z-3}{4}$ intersect and find their point of intersection.
16. Show that the lines $\frac{x-1}{3} = \frac{y+1}{2} = \frac{z-1}{5}$ and $\frac{x+2}{4} = \frac{y-1}{3} = \frac{z+1}{-2}$ do not intersect.
17. Prove that the line $\vec{r} = (\hat{i} + \hat{j} - \hat{k}) + \lambda(3\hat{i} - \hat{j})$ and $\vec{r} = (4\hat{i} - \hat{k}) + \mu(2\hat{i} + 3\hat{k})$ intersect and find their point of intersection.

Answer Key

1. (i) 0° (ii) $\pi/3$
2. $\cos^{-1}\left(\frac{2}{3}\right)$
3. $\frac{x-1}{4} = \frac{y-2}{2} = \frac{z+4}{3}$
4. $\frac{x-2}{2} = \frac{y-1}{-7} = \frac{z-3}{4}$
5. $\vec{r} = (2\hat{i} - \hat{j} - \hat{k}) + \lambda(\hat{i} + 2\hat{j} + 3\hat{k})$
6. $\lambda = -\frac{10}{7}$
7. $2\sqrt{6}, (3, -4, -2)$
8. $(-4, 1 - 3), \frac{x-2}{-6} = \frac{y-4}{-3} = \frac{z+1}{-2}$
9. (1, 1, 11)

10. (0, 5, 1) **11.** (a) $\left(\frac{13}{5}, \frac{23}{5}, 0\right)$ (b) $\left(0, \frac{17}{2}, \frac{-13}{2}\right)$ (c) (1, –2, 7)

12. $P\left(\frac{3}{2}, \frac{5}{2}, \frac{9}{2}\right)$ **13.(a)** (1,0,7) **(b)** (5,8,15) **14.** (2, 6, 3) **16.** (4, 0, –1)

TEXTUAL EXERCISE 3: (OBJECTIVE)

1. The co-ordinates of the foot of the perpendiculars drawn from the point A (1, 2, 1) to the line joining B(1, 4, 6) and C(5, 4, 4), is
(a) (2, 3, 4) (b) (1, 2, 3)
(c) (3, 4, 5) (d) None of these

2. The foot of perpendicular from the point (0, 2, 3) on the line $\frac{x+3}{5} = \frac{y-1}{2} = \frac{z+4}{3}$ and the length of the perpendicular is
(a) (2, 3, –1), $\sqrt{21}$ units
(b) (1, 2, 3), $\sqrt{21}$ units
(c) (5, 2, 3), $\sqrt{21}$ units
(d) None of these

3. The image of the point (1, 6, 3) in the line $\frac{x}{1} = \frac{y-1}{2} = \frac{z-2}{3}$ is
(a) (1, 0, 7) (b) (7, 0, 1)
(c) (1, 2, 7) (d) None of these

4. The foot of the perpendicular from the point (1, 2, 3) to the line $\frac{x}{1} = \frac{y-1}{2} = \frac{z-2}{3}$ is
(a) $\left(\frac{3}{7}, \frac{13}{7}, \frac{23}{7}\right)$ (b) $\left(1, \frac{9}{4}, \frac{11}{4}\right)$
(c) (1, 3, 2) (d) (3, 1, 2)

5. The image of the point (1, 2, 3) in the line $\frac{x}{2} = \frac{y-1}{3} = \frac{z-1}{3}$ is
(a) $\left(1, \frac{5}{2}, \frac{5}{2}\right)$ (b) $\left(1, \frac{9}{4}, \frac{11}{4}\right)$
(c) (1, 3, 2) (d) (3, 1, 2)

6. Cosine of the acute angle between the lines
$\vec{r} = 5\hat{i} - \hat{j} + 4\hat{k} + \lambda(\hat{i} + 2\hat{j} + 2\hat{k})$ and
$\vec{r} = 7\hat{i} + 2\hat{j} + 2\hat{k} + \mu(3\hat{i} + 2\hat{j} + 6\hat{k})$ is
(a) 0 (b) 1/2
(c) 19/21 (d) None of these

7. The angle between the lines $\frac{x}{1} = \frac{y}{0} = \frac{z}{-1}$ and $\frac{x}{3} = \frac{y}{4} = \frac{z}{5}$ is
(a) $\cos^{-1}\frac{1}{5}$ (b) $\cos^{-1}\frac{1}{3}$
(c) $\cos^{-1}\frac{1}{2}$ (d) $\cos^{-1}\frac{1}{4}$

8. Direction ratios of two lines are a, b, c and $\frac{1}{bc}, \frac{1}{ca}, \frac{1}{ab}$. The lines are
(a) Mutually perpendicular
(b) Parallel
(c) Coincident
(d) None of these

9. The length of the perpendicular from point (1, 2, 3) to the line $\frac{x-6}{3} = \frac{y-7}{2} = \frac{z-7}{-2}$ is
(a) 5 (b) 6
(c) 7 (d) 8

10. If θ is the angle between the lines whose vector equations are $\vec{r} = 3\hat{i} + 2\hat{j} + 4\hat{k} + \lambda(\hat{i} + 2\hat{j} + 2\hat{k})$ and $\vec{r} = 5\hat{i} - 2\hat{j} + \mu(3\hat{i} + 2\hat{j} + 6\hat{k})$; λ and μ being parameters, then
(a) $\cos\theta = 19/21$ (b) $\sin\theta = 19/21$
(c) $\sin\theta = 4\sqrt{5}/21$ (d) $\cos\theta = 4\sqrt{5}/21$

11. The lines $\frac{x-1}{3} = \frac{y-1}{-1} = \frac{z+1}{0}$ and $\frac{x-4}{2} = \frac{y+0}{0} = \frac{z+1}{3}$
(a) do not intersect
(b) intersect at (4, 1, –2)
(c) intersect at (4, 0, –1)
(d) intersect at (1, 1, –1)

12. If the lines $\frac{x-1}{2}=\frac{y+1}{3}=\frac{z-1}{4}$ and $\frac{x-3}{1}=\frac{y-k}{1}=\frac{z}{1}$ intersect, then $k=$
(a) 2/9 (b) –1/2
(c) 0 (d) None of these

13. The point of intersection of lines, $\frac{x-3}{1}=\frac{y-k}{1}=\frac{z}{1}$ and $\frac{x-1}{2}=\frac{y-2}{3}=\frac{z-3}{4}$ is equal to
(a) $\left(-4,-\frac{11}{2},-7\right)$ (b) (–1, –1, 1)
(c) (1, –1, –1) (d) (–1, 1, –1)

14. The point where the line $\frac{x-1}{2}=\frac{y-2}{-3}=\frac{z+3}{4}$ meets the plane $2x+4y-z=1$, is
(a) (3, –1, 1) (b) (3, 1, 1)
(c) (1, 1, 3) (d) (1, 3, 1)

15. The length and foot of the perpendicular from the point (2, –1, 5) to the line, $\frac{x-11}{10}=\frac{y+2}{-4}=\frac{z+8}{-11}$ are
(a) $\sqrt{14}$, (1, 2, –3) (b) $\sqrt{14}$, (1, –2, 3)
(c) $\sqrt{14}$, (1, 2, 3) (d) None of these

16. The distance of the point (–1, –5, –10) from the point of intersection of the line $\frac{x-2}{3}=\frac{y+1}{4}=\frac{z-2}{12}$ and the plane $x-y+z=5$ is
(a) 10 (b) 11
(c) 12 (d) 13

17. The perpendicular distance of the point (2, 4, –1) from the line $\frac{x+5}{1}=\frac{y+3}{4}=\frac{x-6}{-9}$ is
(a) 3 (b) 5
(c) 7 (d) 9

18. The point of intersection of lines $\frac{x-4}{5}=\frac{y-1}{2}=\frac{z}{1}$ and $\frac{x-1}{2}=\frac{y-2}{3}=\frac{z-3}{4}$ is
(a) (–1, –1, –1) (b) (–1, –1, 1)
(c) (1, –1, –1) (d) (–1, 1, –1)

Answer Key

1. (c)	2. (a)	3. (a)	4. (a)	5. (a)	6. (c)	7. (a)	8. (b, c)	9. (c)
10. (a, c)	11. (c)	12. (b)	13. (a)	14. (a)	15. (c)	16. (d)	17. (c)	18. (a)

TWO LINES IN THREE DIMENSIONAL SPACE

As we are familiar with the fact (for 2 dimensional co-ordinate geometry) that if two objects move along straight path their loci must intersect at some point unless they are parallel straight lines but in three dimensional geometry it is not exactly the same

In 3-Dimensional geometry; the two point objects moving on straight paths can be such that their paths may be either parallel or intersecting or neither parallel nor intersecting (such straight paths are termed as skew lines)

Condition of Coplanarity

The two straight lines $\vec{r}=\vec{a}+\lambda\vec{b},\ \vec{r}=\vec{c}+\mu\vec{d}$ are coplanar or intersecting if $(\vec{a}-\vec{c}).(\vec{b}\times\vec{d})=0$. i.e. $\left[\vec{a}\ \vec{b}\ \vec{d}\right]=\left[\vec{c}\ \vec{b}\ \vec{d}\right]$

Proof : The line $\vec{r}=\vec{a}+\lambda\vec{b}$ passes through the point $A(\vec{a})$ and parallel to $\vec{b}$ and the line $\vec{r}=\vec{c}+\mu\vec{d}$ passes through point $C(\vec{c})$ and parallel to $\vec{d}$.

If these two lines are in the same plane, then $\overrightarrow{AC},\vec{b}$ and $\vec{d}$ lies in the same plane. Since $\vec{b}\times\vec{d}$ is normal to this plane.

$$\Rightarrow\ \overrightarrow{AC}.(\vec{b}\times\vec{d})=0\ \Rightarrow\ (\vec{c}-\vec{a}).(\vec{b}\times\vec{d})=0$$

$$\Rightarrow\ \left[\vec{c}\ \vec{b}\ \vec{d}\right]=\left[\vec{a}.\vec{b}\ \vec{d}\right]$$

Two coplanar lines can be

(i) Parallel
(ii) Non-parallel (intersecting)

PARALLEL LINES

If $L_1:\vec{r}_1=\vec{a}+\lambda\vec{b}$ *or* $\frac{x-x_1}{l_1}=\frac{y-y_1}{m_1}=\frac{z-z_1}{n_1}$

and $L_2:\vec{r}_2=\vec{c}+\mu\vec{d}$ *or* $\frac{x-x_2}{l_2}=\frac{y-y_2}{m_2}=\frac{z-z_2}{n_2}$

are parallel are proportional then

$\vec{b}=k\vec{d}$ *or* (l_1,m_1,n_1) and (l_2,m_2,n_2)

DISTANCE BETWEEN TWO PARALLEL LINES

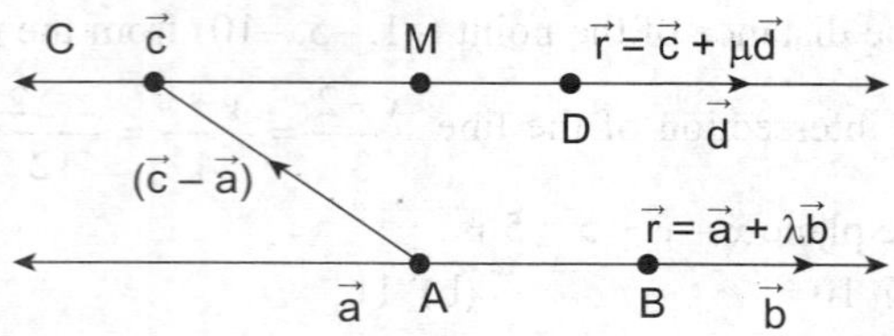

FIGURE 4.40

Vector Projection of $(\vec{c}-\vec{a})$ on $\vec{b}$ $=((\vec{c}-\vec{a}).\hat{b})\hat{b}$

Scalar Projection of $(\vec{c}-\vec{a}) \perp$ to $\vec{b}$ $=|(\vec{c}-\vec{a})-((\vec{c}-\vec{a}).\hat{b})\hat{b}|$

$$=\frac{|(\vec{c}-\vec{a})\times\vec{b}|}{|\vec{b}|}$$

INTERSECTING LINES

$L_1:\vec{r}_1=\vec{a}+\lambda\vec{b}$ or $\dfrac{x-x_1}{l_1}=\dfrac{y-y_1}{m_1}=\dfrac{z-z_1}{n_1}$ and

$L_2:\vec{r}_2=\vec{c}+\mu\vec{d}$ or $\dfrac{x-x_2}{l_2}=\dfrac{y-y_2}{m_2}=\dfrac{z-z_2}{n_2}$

are intersecting, if they are non-parallel, but coplanar.

$\Rightarrow$ $\vec{b}\ \vec{d},\ \vec{c}-\vec{a}$ are coplanar and $\vec{b}\neq k\vec{d}$ for $k\in\mathbb{R}$

$\Rightarrow$ $\vec{b}\neq k\vec{d};k\in\mathbb{R}$ and $[\vec{c}-\vec{a}\ \vec{b}\ \vec{d}]=0$

SKEW LINES

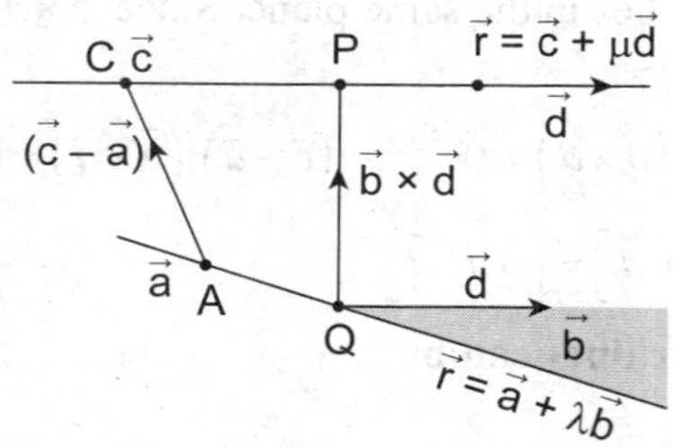

FIGURE 4.41

Skew lines are defined as " pair of lines in the space which are neither parallel nor intersecting".

Two straight lines in space are called skew lines, when they are non coplanar

CONDITION FOR NON COPLANARITY

Given Two straight lines

$$L_1=0:\vec{r}=\vec{a}+\lambda\vec{b}\ \Rightarrow\frac{x-x_1}{l_1}=\frac{y-y_1}{m_1}=\frac{z-z_1}{n_1}$$

$$L_2=0:\vec{r}=\vec{c}+\mu\vec{d}\Rightarrow\frac{x-x_2}{l_2}=\frac{y-y_2}{m_2}=\frac{z-z_2}{n_2}$$

are non coplanar iff $[\vec{c}-\vec{a}\ \vec{b}\ \vec{d}]\neq 0$

Condition in Cartesian form

$$\begin{vmatrix} x_2-x_1 & y_2-y_1 & z_2-z_1 \\ l_1 & m_1 & n_1 \\ l_2 & m_2 & n_2 \end{vmatrix}\neq 0$$

Proof: If two straight lines $\vec{r}=\vec{a}+\lambda\vec{b}$ and $\vec{r}=\vec{c}+\mu\vec{d}$ are non coplanar, then $\vec{b},\vec{c}-\vec{a},\vec{d}$ do not lie in the same plane

$\Rightarrow\ (\vec{c}-\vec{a}).(\vec{b}\times\vec{d})\neq 0 \qquad \Rightarrow\ \left[(\vec{c}-\vec{a})\ \vec{b}\ \vec{d}\right]\neq 0$

$$\Rightarrow\ \begin{vmatrix} x_2-x_1 & y_2-y_1 & z_2-z_1 \\ l_1 & m_1 & n_1 \\ l_2 & m_2 & n_2 \end{vmatrix}\neq 0$$

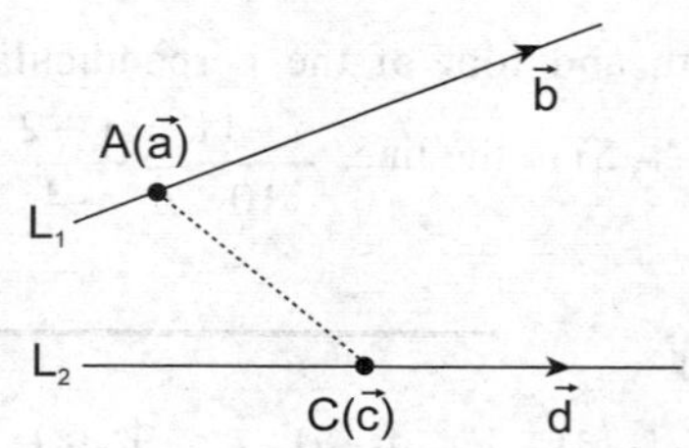

FIGURE 4.42

SKEW LINES AND THEIR SHORTEST DISTANCE

Two skew lines can be intersected by an infinite number of lines as a variable point on one can be joined to a variable point on the other. Of these intersecting lines there is one and only one which is shortest and intersects both the skew lines perpendicularly. By the shortest distance between two lines we mean the join of a point in one with one point on the other so that the length of the segment so obtained is the smallest. If the equation of two straight lines are given, one can always obtain the equation of shortest distance as well as the shortest distance between the given two straight lines.

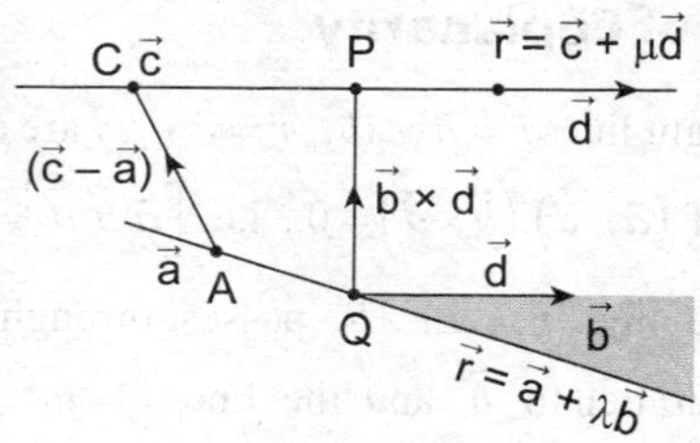

FIGURE 4.43

Shortest distance between them is the line segment perpendicular to both of them

Given two skew lines $\vec{r}=\vec{a}+\lambda\vec{b}$ and $\vec{r}=\vec{c}+\mu\vec{d}$. Vector along SD is $\vec{b}\times\vec{d}$

Let $\overline{SD}=\alpha(\vec{b}\times\vec{d})=\overline{QP}$

Length of shortest distance (SD): Position vector of any point on $\overline{QP}$ is given by $\vec{r}=\vec{a}+\lambda_1\vec{b}+\alpha(\vec{b}\times\vec{d})$

If this point represents

$\because$ PV of $P=\vec{c}+\mu\vec{d}$, taking dot product with $(\vec{b}\times\vec{d})$,

we have $\vec{a}.(\vec{b}\times\vec{d})+0+\alpha(\vec{b}\times\vec{d}).(\vec{b}\times\vec{d})=\vec{c}.(\vec{b}\times\vec{d})+0$

$$\Rightarrow \quad -(\vec{a}-\vec{c}).(\vec{b}\times\vec{d})=\alpha(\vec{b}\times\vec{d})^2$$

$$\Rightarrow \quad \alpha=\frac{(\vec{c}-\vec{a}).(\vec{b}\times\vec{d})}{|\vec{b}\times\vec{d}|^2}$$

$$\Rightarrow \quad \text{S.D.}=\left|\alpha(\vec{b}\times\vec{d})\right|=|\alpha|\left|\vec{b}\times\vec{d}\right|$$

$$\Rightarrow \quad \text{S.D}=\frac{(\vec{a}-\vec{c}).(\vec{b}\times\vec{d})}{|\vec{b}\times\vec{d}|}$$

Which is nothing but scalar projection of $\overline{AC}$ along $(\vec{b}\times\vec{d})$

$$\Rightarrow \quad SD=\frac{\left\|\begin{matrix} x_2-x_1 & y_2-y_1 & z_2-z_1 \\ l_1 & m_1 & n_1 \\ l_2 & m_2 & n_2 \end{matrix}\right\|}{\left\|\begin{matrix} \hat{i} & \hat{j} & \hat{k} \\ l_1 & m_1 & n_1 \\ l_2 & m_2 & n_2 \end{matrix}\right\|}$$

Equation of shortest distance (SD)

Let PQ and RS are two skew lines and a line which is perpendicular to both PQ and RS. Then the length of the line is called the shortest distance between PQ and RS.

Let equations of the given lines are

$$\frac{x-x_1}{l_1}=\frac{y-y_1}{m_1}=\frac{z-z_1}{n_1} \text{ and } \frac{x-x_2}{l_2}=\frac{y-y_2}{m_2}=\frac{z-z_2}{n_2}$$

Let $S.D$ lies along the line $\frac{x-\alpha}{l}=\frac{y-\beta}{m}=\frac{z-\gamma}{n}$, then

S.D. $=|l(x_2-x_1)+m(y_2-y_1)+n(z_2-z_1)|$ and equation of shortest distance is $\begin{vmatrix} x-x_1 & y-y_1 & z-z_1 \\ l_1 & m_1 & n_1 \\ l_2 & m_2 & n_2 \end{vmatrix}=0$

Equation of SD Line:

As intersection of plane PCS and PAD i.e., as $[\vec{r}-\vec{c}\ \vec{d}\ \vec{b}\times\vec{d}]=0$ and $[\vec{r}-\vec{a}\ \vec{b}\ \vec{b}\times\vec{d}]=0$

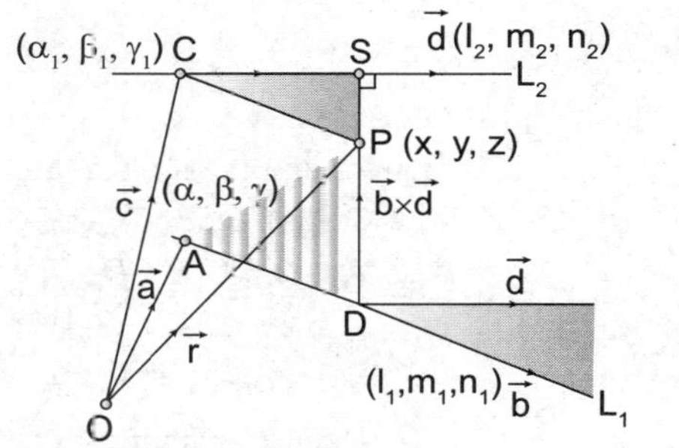

FIGURE 4.44

ILLUSTRATION 29: Find the shortest distance between the lines; $\vec{r}=(4\hat{i}-\hat{j})+\lambda(\hat{i}+2\hat{j}-3\hat{k})$ and $\vec{r}=(\hat{i}-\hat{j}+2\hat{k})+\mu(2\hat{i}+4\hat{j}-5\hat{k})$

SOLUTION: We know, the shortest distance between the lines $\vec{r}=\vec{a}_1+\ \vec{b}_1$ and $\vec{r}=\vec{a}_2+\lambda\vec{b}_2$ is given by

$$d=\left|\frac{(\vec{a}_2-\vec{a}_1).(\vec{b}_1\times\vec{b}_2)}{|\vec{b}_1\times\vec{b}_2|}\right|$$

Comparing the given equation with the equations $\vec{r}=\vec{a}_1+\lambda\vec{b}_1$ and $\vec{r}=\vec{a}_2+\lambda\vec{b}_2$ respectively, we have $\vec{a}_1=4\hat{i}-\hat{j}, \vec{a}_2=\hat{i}-\hat{j}+2\hat{k}, \vec{b}_1=\hat{i}+2\hat{j}-3\hat{k}$ and $\vec{b}_2=2\hat{i}+4\hat{j}-5\hat{k}$

Now, $\vec{a}_2-\vec{a}_1=-3\hat{i}+0\hat{j}+2\hat{k}$ and $\vec{b}_1\times\vec{b}_2=\begin{vmatrix} \hat{i} & \hat{j} & \hat{k} \\ 1 & 2 & -3 \\ 2 & 4 & -5 \end{vmatrix}=2\hat{i}-\hat{j}+0\hat{k}$

$$\therefore \quad (\vec{a}_2-\vec{a}_1).(\vec{b}_1\times\vec{b}_2)=(-3\hat{i}+0\hat{j}+2\hat{k}).(2\hat{i}-\hat{j}+0\hat{k})=-6$$

and $|\vec{b}_1 \times \vec{b}_2| = \sqrt{4+1+0} = \sqrt{5}$

$\therefore$ Shortest distance; $d = \left|\dfrac{(\vec{a}_2 - \vec{a}_1).(\vec{b}_1 \times \vec{b}_2)}{|\vec{b}_1 \times \vec{b}_2|}\right| = \left|\dfrac{-6}{\sqrt{5}}\right| = \dfrac{6}{\sqrt{5}}$

ILLUSTRATION 30: Find the shortest distance and the vector equation of the line of shortest distance between the lines given by $\vec{r} = (3\hat{i} + 8\hat{j} + 3\hat{k}) + \lambda(3\hat{i} - \hat{j} + \hat{k})$ and $\vec{r} = (-3\hat{i} - 7\hat{j} + 6\hat{k}) + \mu(-3\hat{i} + 2\hat{j} + 4\hat{k})$

SOLUTION: Given lines are $\vec{r} = (3\hat{i} + 8\hat{j} + 3\hat{k}) + \lambda(3\hat{i} - \hat{j} + \hat{k})$ ....(i)

and $\vec{r} = (-3\hat{i} - 7\hat{j} + 6\hat{k}) + \mu(-3\hat{i} + 2\hat{j} + 4\hat{k})$ ...(ii)

Equation of lines (i) and (ii) in cartesian form are $AB: \dfrac{x-3}{3} = \dfrac{y-8}{-1} = \dfrac{z-3}{1} = \lambda$ ...(iii)

and $CD: \dfrac{x+3}{-3} = \dfrac{y+7}{2} = \dfrac{z-6}{4} = \mu$

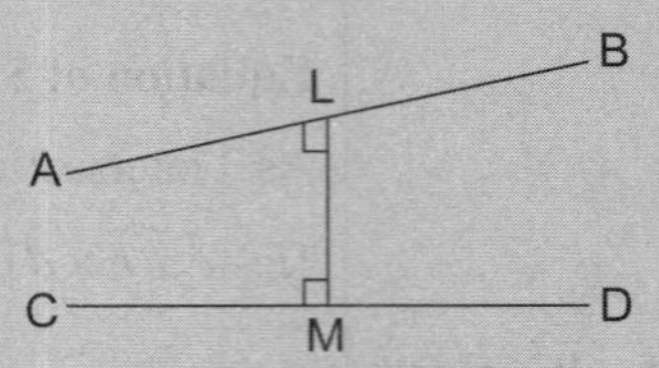

FIGURE 4.45

Let L$(3\lambda + 3, -\lambda + 8, \lambda + 3)$ and M$(-3\mu - 3, 2\mu - 7, 4\mu + 6)$

Direction ratios of ML are: $(3\lambda + 3\mu + 6, -\lambda - 2\mu + 15, \lambda - 4\mu - 3)$ since $ML \perp AB$

$\therefore$ $3(3\lambda + 3\mu + 6) - 1(-\lambda - 2\mu + 15) + 1(\lambda - 4\mu - 3) = 0$ or $11\lambda + 7\mu = 0$ ......(v)

Again $LM \perp CD$

$\Rightarrow$ $-3(3\lambda + 3\mu + 6) + 2(-\lambda - 2\mu + 15) + 4(\lambda - 4\mu - 3) = 0$ or $-7\lambda - 29\mu = 0$ ....(vi)

Solving (v) and (vi), we get: $\lambda = 0 = \mu$ $\Rightarrow$ $L \equiv (3, 8, 3)$ and $M \equiv (-3, -7, 6)$

Hence the shortest distance $LM = \sqrt{(3+3)^2 + (8+7)^2 + (3-6)^2} = 3\sqrt{30}$ units

$\therefore$ vector equation of LM is $\vec{r} = 3\hat{i} + 8\hat{j} + 3\hat{k} + t(6\hat{i} + 15\hat{j} - 3\hat{k})$

also the cartesian equation of LM is: $\dfrac{x-3}{6} = \dfrac{y-8}{15} = \dfrac{z-3}{-3}$

ILLUSTRATION 31: Find the shortest distance between the lines $\dfrac{x-1}{2} = \dfrac{y-2}{3} = \dfrac{z-3}{4}$ and $\dfrac{x-2}{3} = \dfrac{y-4}{4} = \dfrac{z-5}{5}$

SOLUTION: Given lines are $\dfrac{x-1}{2} = \dfrac{y-2}{3} = \dfrac{z-3}{4}$ ...(i)

and $\dfrac{x-2}{3} = \dfrac{y-4}{4} = \dfrac{z-5}{5}$ ...(ii)

Here, $x_1 = 1, y_1 = 2, z_1 = 3; x_2 = 2, y_2 = 4, z_2 = 5$

$l_1 = 2, m_1 = 3, n_1 = 4; l_2 = 3, m_2 = 4, n_2 = 5$

Shortest distance between the lines (i) and (ii) are: Modulus of

$$\frac{\begin{vmatrix} x_2 - x_1 & y_2 - y_1 & z_2 - z_1 \\ l_1 & m_1 & n_1 \\ l_2 & m_2 & n_2 \end{vmatrix}}{\sqrt{(l_1m_2 - l_2m_1)^2 + (m_1n_2 - m_2n_1)^2 + (l_1n_2 - l_2n_1)^2}} \quad ...(iii)$$

Now, $\begin{vmatrix} x_2-x_1 & y_2-y_1 & z_2-z_1 \\ l_1 & m_1 & n_1 \\ l_2 & m_2 & n_2 \end{vmatrix} = \begin{vmatrix} 1 & 2 & 2 \\ 2 & 3 & 4 \\ 3 & 4 & 5 \end{vmatrix} = 1(15-16)-2(10-12)+2(8-9) = -1$

also, $(l_1m_2 - l_2m_1)^2 + (m_1n_2 - m_2n_1)^2 + (n_1l_2 - n_2l_1)^2 = (8-9)^2 + (15-16)^2 + (10-12)^2 = 6$

from (iii) shortest distance between lines (i) and (ii) $= \left|-\frac{1}{\sqrt{6}}\right| = \frac{1}{\sqrt{6}}$

Aliter: Let $\vec{a} = \hat{i}+2\hat{j}+3\hat{k}, \vec{b} = 2\hat{i}+4\hat{j}+5\hat{k}$; $\vec{c} = 2\hat{i}+3\hat{j}+4\hat{k}, \vec{d} = 3\hat{i}+4\hat{j}+5\hat{k}$

Equations of two given lines in vector form is: $\vec{r} = \vec{a} + \lambda\vec{c}$ ...(i)

and $\vec{r} = \vec{b} + \mu\vec{d}$ ...(ii)

$\overrightarrow{AP} \parallel \vec{c}$ and $\overrightarrow{BQ} \parallel \vec{d}$

Shortest distance between AP and BQ = projection of $\overrightarrow{AB}$ on $\overrightarrow{LM}$.

= porjection of $\overrightarrow{AB}$ on $\vec{c}\times\vec{d}$ $(\because \overrightarrow{LM} \parallel \vec{c}\times\vec{d})$ $= \left|\frac{(\vec{b}-\vec{a}).(\vec{c}\times\vec{d})}{\vec{c}\times\vec{d}\,|}\right|$ ...(iii)

Now, $\vec{b}-\vec{a} = \hat{i}+2\hat{j}+2\hat{k}$ and $\vec{c}\times\vec{d} = -\hat{i}+2\hat{j}-\hat{k}$

$\therefore\ |\vec{c}\times\vec{d}| = \sqrt{6}, (\vec{b}-\vec{a}).(\vec{c}\times\vec{d}) = 1$ $\therefore$ from (iii), shortest distance $= \left|\frac{1}{\sqrt{6}}\right| = \frac{1}{\sqrt{6}}$

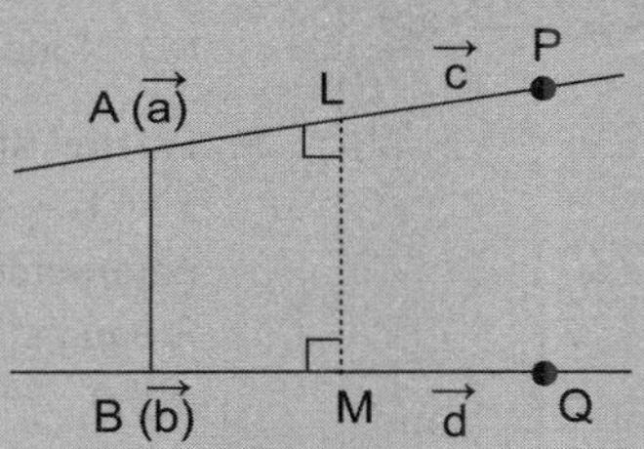

FIGURE 4.46

TEXTUAL EXERCISE 6: (SUBJECTIVE)

1. Find the shortest distance between the following pairs of lines whose vector equations are:

$\vec{r} = (1-t)\hat{i} + (t-2)\hat{j} + (3-t)\hat{k}$ and

$\vec{r} = (\lambda-1)\hat{i} + (\lambda+1)\hat{j} - (1+\lambda)\hat{k}$

2. Find the shortest distance between the following pairs of lines whose cartesian equations are:

(i) $\frac{x-1}{2} = \frac{y-2}{3} = \frac{z-3}{4}$ and $\frac{x-2}{3} = \frac{y-3}{4} = \frac{z-5}{5}$

(ii) $\frac{x-1}{-1} = \frac{y+2}{1} = \frac{z-3}{-2}$ and $\frac{x-1}{1} = \frac{y+1}{2} = \frac{z+1}{-2}$

3. By computing the shortest distance determine whether the following pairs of lines intersect or not:

(i) $\vec{r} = (\hat{i}+\hat{j}-\hat{k}) + \lambda(3\hat{i}-\hat{j})$;

$\vec{r} = (4\hat{i}-\hat{k}) + \mu(2\hat{i}+3\hat{k})$

(ii) $\frac{x-1}{2} = \frac{y+1}{3} = z$; $\frac{x+1}{5} = \frac{y-2}{1}$; $z = 2$

4. Find the shortest distance between the following pairs of parallel lines whose equations are:

$\vec{r} = (\hat{i}+\hat{j}) + \lambda(2\hat{i}-\hat{j}+\hat{k})$ and

$\vec{r} = (2\hat{i}+\hat{j}-\hat{k}) + \mu(4\hat{i}-2\hat{j}+2\hat{k})$

5. Find the shortest distance between the lines $\frac{x-1}{2} = \frac{y-2}{3} = \frac{z-3}{4}$ and $\frac{x-2}{3} = \frac{y-4}{4} = \frac{z-5}{5}$ Also find the equations of this line.

6. Obtain the co-ordinates of the points where the line of shortest distance between the lines

$\frac{x-23}{-6} = \frac{y-19}{-4} = \frac{z-25}{3}$ and $\frac{x-12}{-9} = \frac{y-1}{4} = \frac{z-5}{2}$

intersect the above lines.

7. Find the shortest distance and equation of the line of shortest distance between the lines:

$\vec{r}=(\lambda-1)\hat{i}+(\lambda+1)\hat{j}-(\lambda+1)\hat{k}$,

$\vec{r}=(1-\mu)\hat{i}+(2\mu-1)\hat{j}+(\mu+2)\hat{k}$

8. Define the line of shortest distance between two skew lines. Find the shortest distance and the vector equation of the line of shortest distance between the line given by

$\vec{r}=(2\hat{j}-3\hat{k}\sqrt{b^2-4ac})+\lambda(2\hat{i}-\hat{j})$

$\vec{r}=(4\hat{i}+3\hat{k})+\lambda(3\hat{i}+\hat{j}+\hat{k})$

Answer Key

1. $\frac{1}{\sqrt{2}}$ 2. (i) $\frac{1}{\sqrt{6}}$ (ii) $\frac{8}{\sqrt{29}}$ 3. (i) Yes (ii) No 4. $\frac{\sqrt{11}}{\sqrt{6}}$

5. $\frac{1}{\sqrt{6}}, \frac{3x-5}{3}=\frac{y-3}{-2}\frac{3z-13}{3}$ 6. (11,11,31), (3,5,7) 7. $\vec{r}=-2\hat{i}+\lambda(\hat{i}+\hat{k}), \frac{5}{\sqrt{2}}$ units 8. $\sqrt{30}$ units

TEXTUAL EXERCISE 4: (OBJECTIVE)

1. Two lines $\frac{x}{1}=\frac{y}{2}=\frac{z}{3}$ and $\frac{x+1}{1}=\frac{y+2}{2}=\frac{z+3}{3}$ are
   (a) Distinct parallel lines
   (b) Intersecting at one point
   (c) Skew lines
   (d) Coinciding lines

2. The straight lines $\frac{x-1}{1}=\frac{y-2}{2}=\frac{z-3}{3}$ and $\frac{x-1}{2}=\frac{y-2}{2}=\frac{z-3}{-2}$ are
   (a) Parallel lines (b) Intersecting at 60°
   (c) Skew lines (d) Intersecting at right angle

3. The line $\frac{x-2}{1}=\frac{y-3}{1}=\frac{z-4}{-k}$ and $\frac{x-1}{k}=\frac{y-4}{2}=\frac{z-5}{1}$ are co-planar, if
   (a) $k = 0$ or -1 (b) $k = 0$ or 1
   (c) $k = 0$ or -3 (d) $k = 3$ or -3

4. The direction cosines of three lines passing through the origin are l_1, m_1, n_1;, l_2, m_2, n_2 and l_3, m_3, n_3. The lines will be co-planar if

   (a) $\begin{vmatrix} l_1 & n_1 & m_1 \\ l_2 & n_2 & m_2 \\ l_3 & n_3 & m_3 \end{vmatrix}=0$

   (b) $\begin{vmatrix} l_1 & m_2 & n_3 \\ l_2 & m_3 & n_1 \\ l_3 & m_1 & n_2 \end{vmatrix}=0$

   (c) $l_1l_2l_3 + m_1m_2m_3 + n_1n_2n_3 = 0$
   (d) None of these

5. If the straight lines $x = 1 + s$, $y = -3 - \lambda s$, $z = 1 + \lambda s$ and $x = t/2$, $y = 1 + t$, $z = 2 - t$, with parameters s and t respectively, are co-planar, then λ equals
   (a) 0 (b) –1
   (c) –1/2 (d) –2

6. A line with direction cosines proportional to 2, 1, 2 meets each of the lines $x = y + a = z$ and $x + a = 2y = 2z$. The co-ordinates of each of the points of intersection are given by
   (a) (2a, a, 3a); (2a, a, a)
   (b) (3a, 2a, 3a); (a, a, a)
   (c) (3a, 2a, 3a); (a, a, 2a)
   (d) (3a, 3a, 3a); (a, a, a)

7. The equation of straight line passing through the point (a, b, c) and parallel to z-axis, is
   (a) $\frac{x-a}{1}=\frac{y-b}{1}=\frac{z-c}{0}$
   (b) $\frac{x-a}{0}=\frac{y-b}{1}=\frac{z-c}{1}$
   (c) $\frac{x-a}{1}=\frac{y-b}{0}=\frac{z-c}{0}$
   (d) $\frac{x-a}{0}=\frac{y-b}{0}=\frac{z-c}{1}$

Answer Key

1. (d) 2. (d) 3. (c) 4. (a) 5. (d) 6. (b) 7. (d)

■ PLANE

Plane is a locus of a point which moves so that any point on the line segment joining two position of moving point always lie on the same locus.

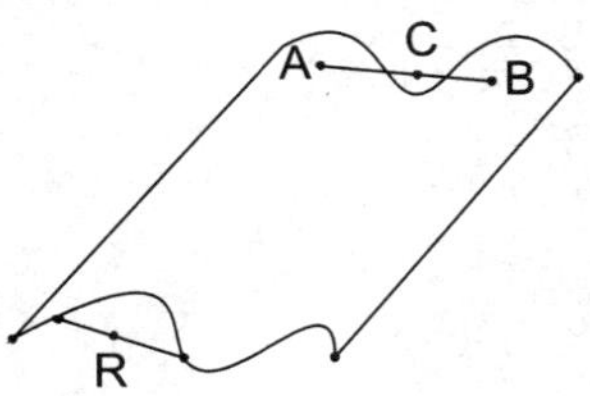

FIGURE 4.47

Here points C and R do not lie on the surface and hence given surface is not a plane.

Here every point on segment joining A and B (for every positin) lies on the surface and the above definition is true for this of surface and hence this surface is a plane.

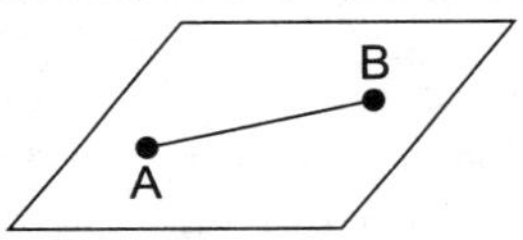

FIGURE 4.48

Properties of plane:

- It has a unique normal vector $\hat{n}$ defining its orientation in the space

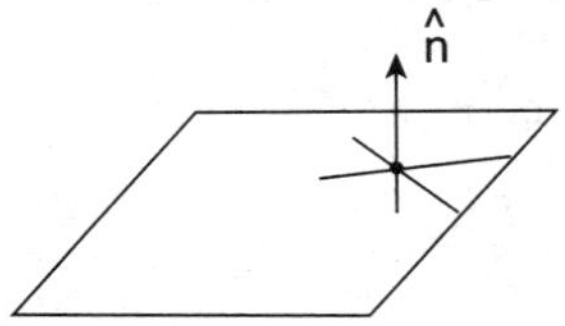

FIGURE 4.49

- The normal vector of the plane remains perpendicular to all the line lying in that plane

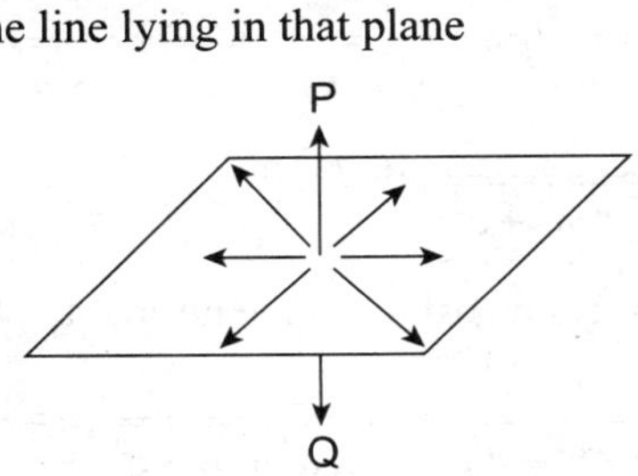

FIGURE 4.50

Equation of Plane

Any linear equation in 3 variables x, y, z of the form $ax + by + cz + d = 0$ ... (i) represents a plane surface.

Proof: Let $A(x_1, y_1, z_1)$ and $B(x_2, y_2, z_2)$ be any two points on (i),

then $ax_1 + by_1 + cz_1 + d = 0$ ... (ii)

and $ax_2 + by_2 + cz_2 + d = 0$ .... (iii)

Locus (i) will represent a plane if the line joining any two points on the surface fully lies on the surface. Let $C(x_3, y_3, z_3)$ be any point on the line AB.

$$\& \; x_3 = \frac{\lambda x_2 + x_1}{\lambda + 1}; \; y_3 = \frac{\lambda y_2 + y_1}{\lambda + 1} \; \& \; z_3 = \frac{\lambda z_2 + z_1}{\lambda + 1}$$

Putting coordinates of C in equation (i), we have

$$a\left(\frac{\lambda x_2 + x_1}{\lambda + 1}\right) + b\left(\frac{\lambda y_2 + y_1}{\lambda + 1}\right) + c\left(\frac{\lambda z_2 + z_1}{\lambda + 1}\right) + d = 0$$

$\Rightarrow \lambda(ax_2 + by_2 + cz_2 + d) + (ax_1 + by_1 + cz_1 + d) = 0$

$\therefore$ LHS = 0 = RHS

$\therefore$ C point satisfies equation (i) and hence all the points on line joining A and B lie on locus (i). Thus locus (i) is a plane.

Case I: Equation of a plane passing through a point $A_{\vec{a}'}(x_1, y_1, z_1)$ and normal to vector $\vec{n} = a\hat{i} + b\hat{j} + c\hat{k}$

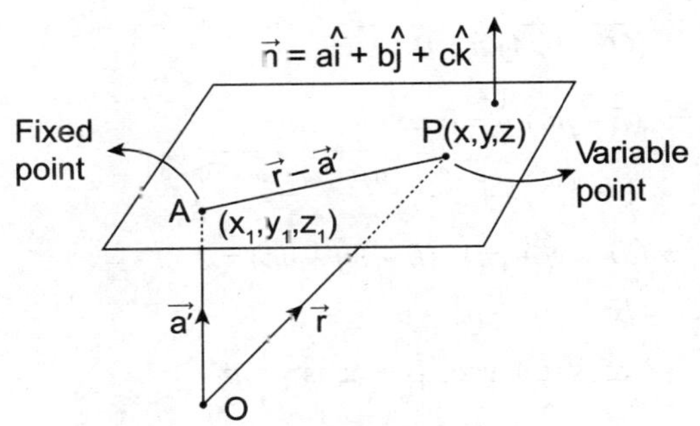

FIGURE 4.51

Vector Equation: Let $P_{\vec{r}}(x, y, z)$ be a point in the plane.

Since AP lies in the plane

$$\therefore \; \overrightarrow{AP} \cdot \vec{n} = 0 \Rightarrow \left(\overrightarrow{OP} - \overrightarrow{OA}\right) \cdot \vec{n} = 0 \Rightarrow (\vec{r} - \vec{a}') \cdot \vec{n} = 0$$

$\Rightarrow \vec{r} \cdot \vec{n} = \vec{a}' \cdot \vec{n} \Rightarrow \vec{r} \cdot \vec{n} = d$, where d is constant.

Cartesian Equation:

$\because\ \vec{r}.\vec{n} = \vec{a}'.\vec{n}$

$\Rightarrow (x\hat{i} + y\hat{j} + z\hat{k}).(a\hat{i} + b\hat{j} + c\hat{k}) = \vec{a}'.\vec{n}$

$\Rightarrow ax + by + cz = \underbrace{ax_1 + by_1 + cz_1}_{d}$

where *a, b, c* are direction ratios of normal vector to the plane.

ILLUSTRATION 32: Find the equation (vector as well as Cartesian) of the plane with direction ratios of normal as (2, 1, 2) and passing through

(a) (0, 0, 0) **(b)** (1, 2, –1)

SOLUTION: **(a)** $\vec{r}.\vec{n} = \vec{a}.\vec{n} \Rightarrow \vec{r} \Rightarrow \vec{r}.(2\hat{i} + \hat{j} + 2\hat{k}) = (0\hat{i} + 0\hat{j} + 0\hat{k}).(2\hat{i} + \hat{j} + 2\hat{k})$

$\therefore$ Vector equation : $\vec{r}.(2\hat{i} + \hat{j} + 2\hat{k}) = 0$

Cartesian equation: $(x\hat{i} + y\hat{j} + z\hat{k}).(2\hat{i} + \hat{j} + 2\hat{k}) = 0$

$\Rightarrow 2x + y + 2z = 0$

(b) $\vec{r}.\vec{n} = \vec{a}.\vec{n} \Rightarrow \vec{r}.(2\hat{i} + \hat{j} + 2\hat{k}) = (\hat{i} + 2\hat{j} - \hat{k}).(2\hat{i} + \hat{j} + 2\hat{k})$

$\therefore$ Vector equation : $\vec{r}.(2\hat{i} + \hat{j} + 2\hat{k}) = 2$

Cartesian equation : $(x\hat{i} + y\hat{j} + z\hat{k}).(2\hat{i} + \hat{j} + 2\hat{k}) = 2 \Rightarrow 2x + y + 2z = 2.$

Normal/Perpendicular form

Equation of plane upon which the length of ⊥r from origin is *p* and normal vector has direction cosines $\langle l, m, n \rangle$. is given by : $lx + my + nz = p$

Proof: $\because\ AP \perp \hat{u}$

$\Rightarrow (\overrightarrow{OP} - \overrightarrow{OA}).\hat{u} = 0$

$\Rightarrow (\vec{r} - p\hat{u}).\hat{u} = 0 \Rightarrow \underbrace{\vec{r}.\hat{u} = p}_{\text{vector equ}^n\text{. of plane}}$

$\Rightarrow (x\hat{i} + y\hat{j} + z\hat{k}).(l\hat{i} + m\hat{j} + n\hat{k}) = p$

$\Rightarrow\ lx + my + nz = p$

$\Rightarrow\ x\cos\alpha + y\cos\beta + z\cos\gamma = p$

cartesian equation of plane.

To convert general equation of plane $\vec{r}.\vec{n} = d$ or $ax + by + cz = d$ *to normal form*

We divide both sides by $\sqrt{a^2 + b^2 + c^2}$:

to get $ln + my + nz = p$.

Transformation of equation of the plane $ax + by + cz + d = 0$ to normal form :

Given equation is $ax + by + cz + d = 0$ ...(i)

From (1), $ax + by + cz = -d$

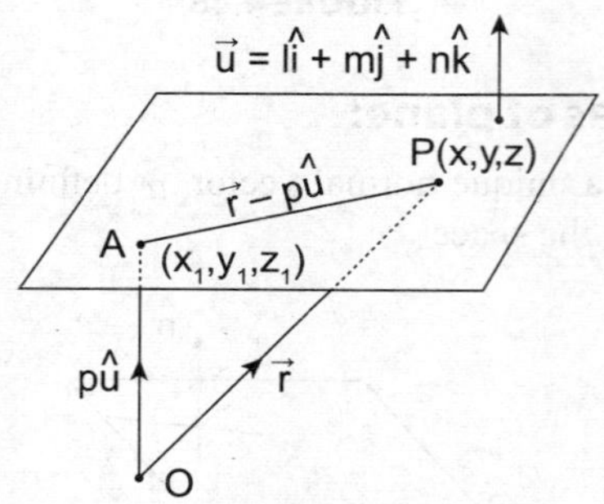

Normal form of equation (i) is

$$\frac{a}{\sqrt{a^2 + b^2 + c^2}}x + \frac{b}{\sqrt{a^2 + b^2 + c^2}}y + \frac{c}{\sqrt{a^2 + b^2 + c^2}}z$$

$$= -\frac{d}{\sqrt{a^2 + b^2 + c^2}}, \text{ if } d < 0$$

Here direction cosines of the normal to plane are

$$l = \frac{a}{\sqrt{a^2 + b^2 + c^2}}, m = \frac{b}{\sqrt{a^2 + b^2 + c^2}}, n = \frac{c}{\sqrt{a^2 + b^2 + c^2}}$$

or $-\frac{a}{\sqrt{a^2+b^2+c^2}}x-\frac{b}{\sqrt{a^2+b^2+c^2}}y-\frac{c}{\sqrt{a^2+b^2+c^2}}z=\frac{d}{\sqrt{a^2+b^2+c^2}}$, if $d>0$

Here direction cosines of the normal to plane are

$$l=-\frac{a}{\sqrt{a^2+b^2+c^2}}, m=-\frac{b}{\sqrt{a^2+b^2+c^2}},$$

$$m=-\frac{c}{\sqrt{a^2+b^2+c^2}}$$

In both cases, a,b,c are the direction ratios of the normal to the plane (i)

NOTES

1. *If $ax+by+cz+d=0$ be the equation of a plane, then a,b,c are the direction ratios of the normal to the plane and direction cosines of the normal to the plane are* $\frac{a}{\sqrt{a^2+b^2+c^2}}, \frac{b}{\sqrt{a^2+b^2+c^2}}, \frac{c}{\sqrt{a^2+b^2+c^2}}$
2. *Direction cosines of the z-axis which is normal to xy-plane are 0,0,1 therefore equation of xy-plane will be $z=0$ (Here $p=0$)*
3. *Equation of xz-plane is $y=0$*
4. *Equation of yz-plane is $x=0$*
5. *The normal forms of plane* $\vec{r}.\vec{n}=d \Rightarrow \vec{r}.\hat{n}=\frac{d}{|\vec{n}|}$
6. $\vec{r}.\vec{n}=d_1$ *and* $\vec{r}.\vec{n}=d_2$ *are two planes parallel to each other because their normal vectors are same.*
7. *Equation of a plane parallel to xy plane is $z=c$*
8. *Equation of a plane parallel to zx plane is $y=c$*
9. *Equation of a plane parallel to yz plane is $x=c$*

ILLUSTRATION 33: Find the vector equation of plane which is at a distance of 8 units from the origin and which is normal to the vector $2\hat{i}+\hat{j}+2\hat{k}$.

SOLUTION: Here, $d=8$ and $\vec{n}=2\hat{i}+\hat{j}+2\hat{k}$

$$\therefore \quad \hat{n}=\frac{\vec{n}}{|\vec{n}|}=\frac{2\hat{i}+\hat{j}+2\hat{k}}{\sqrt{2^2+1^2+2^2}}=\frac{2\hat{i}+\hat{j}+2\hat{k}}{3}$$

Hence, the required equation of plane is, $\vec{r}.\hat{n}=d$

$$\Rightarrow \vec{r}.\left(\frac{2\hat{i}+\hat{j}+2\hat{k}}{3}\right)=8 \text{ or } \vec{r}.\left(2\hat{i}+\hat{j}+2\hat{k}\right)=24$$

ILLUSTRATION 34: A vector $\vec{n}$ of magnitude 8 units is inclined to x-axis at 45°, y - axis at 60° and at an acute angle with z-axis. If a plane passes through a point $(\sqrt{2},-1,1)$ and is normal to $\vec{n}$, find its equation in vector form.

SOLUTION: Let γ be the angle made by $\vec{n}$ with z-axis, then direction cosines of $\vec{n}$ are

$$l=\cos 45^\circ=\frac{1}{\sqrt{2}}, m=\cos 60^\circ=\frac{1}{2} \text{ and } n=\cos\gamma$$

$\therefore\ l^2+m^2+n^2=1 \Rightarrow \frac{1}{2}+\frac{1}{4}+n^2=1$

$\Rightarrow\ n^2=\frac{1}{4};\ \Rightarrow n=\frac{1}{2}\left(\text{neglecting } n=-\frac{1}{2} \text{as } \gamma \text{ is acute, } \therefore n>0\right)$

we have $|\vec{n}|=8$

$\therefore\ \vec{n}=|\vec{n}|(l\hat{i}+m\hat{j}+n\hat{k})$

$\Rightarrow\ \vec{n}=8\left(\frac{1}{\sqrt{2}}\hat{i}+\frac{1}{2}\hat{j}+\frac{1}{2}\hat{k}\right)$

$\Rightarrow 4\sqrt{2}\ \hat{i}+4\hat{j}+4\hat{k}$

The required plane passes through the point $(\sqrt{2},-1,1)$ having position vector $\vec{a}=\sqrt{2}\ \hat{i}-\hat{j}+\hat{k}$

So, its vector equation is: $(\vec{r}-\vec{a}).\vec{n}=0$

or $\vec{r}\ .\ \vec{n}=\vec{a}\ .\ \vec{n}$

$\Rightarrow\ \vec{r}.(4\sqrt{2}\ \hat{i}+4\hat{j}+4\hat{k})=(\sqrt{2}\ \hat{i}-\hat{j}+\hat{k}).(4\sqrt{2}\ \hat{i}+4\hat{j}+4\hat{k})$

$\Rightarrow\ \vec{r}.(4\sqrt{2}\hat{i}+4\hat{j}+4\hat{k})=8$

$\Rightarrow\ \vec{r}.(\sqrt{2}\hat{i}+\hat{j}+\hat{k})=2.$

Intercept form of the plane

The equation of a plane which cuts on intercept a on x-axis; b on y-axis and c, on z-axis is given by $\frac{x}{a}+\frac{y}{b}+\frac{z}{c}=1$.

Proof: Let P be a general point on this plane, then $\overrightarrow{AB},\overrightarrow{AP}$ & $\overrightarrow{AC}$ are coplanar and hence $\left[\overrightarrow{AP}\,\overrightarrow{AB}\,\overrightarrow{AC}\right]=0$

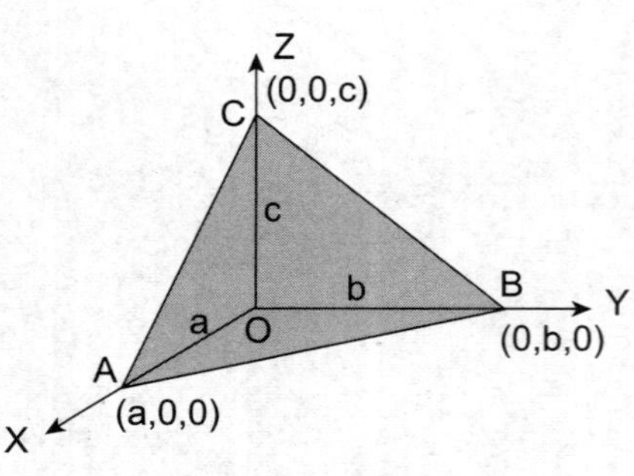

FIGURE 4.52

$\Rightarrow \left[(\vec{r}-\vec{a})(\vec{b}-\vec{a})(\vec{c}-\vec{a})\right]=0$

or $(\vec{r}-\vec{a}).\left((\vec{b}-\vec{a})\times(\vec{c}-\vec{a})\right)=0$

Cartesian Equation: we know that

$\vec{a}=a\hat{i}\ ;\ \vec{b}=b\hat{j}\ ;\ \vec{c}=c\hat{k}$

Now $\vec{b}-\vec{a}=b\hat{j}-a\hat{i}$ & $\vec{c}-\vec{a}=c\hat{k}-a\hat{i}$

$\Rightarrow\ (\vec{r}-\vec{a}).\left((\vec{b}-\vec{a})\times(\vec{c}-\vec{a})\right)=0$

$$\Rightarrow \begin{vmatrix} x-a & y-0 & z-0 \\ -a & b & 0 \\ a & & c \end{vmatrix}=0$$

$\Rightarrow\ bcx + acy + abz = abc$

Dividing both sides by abc; we get $\frac{x}{a}+\frac{y}{b}+\frac{z}{c}=1$

Aliter: Let the equation of plane $Ax + By + Cz = D$

Given that the plane passes through $(a, 0, 0)$; $(0, b, 0)$ and $(0, 0, c)$.

$\therefore$ we get $A=\frac{D}{a}, B=\frac{D}{b}, C=\frac{D}{c}$

$\Rightarrow$ Equation becomes $\frac{D}{a}x+\frac{D}{b}y+\frac{D}{c}z=D$

$\Rightarrow\ \frac{x}{a}+\frac{y}{b}+\frac{z}{c}=1$

ILLUSTRATION 35: If from a point $P(a, b, c)$ perpendiculars PA and PB are drawn to yz and zx planes, find the equation of the plane OAB.

SOLUTION: The co-ordinates of A and B are $(0, b, c)$ and $(a, 0, c)$ respectively.

The equation of the plane passing through $O(0, 0, 0)$, $A(0, b, c)$ and $B(a, 0, c)$ is given by

$$\begin{vmatrix} x-0 & y-0 & z-0 \\ 0-0 & b-0 & c-0 \\ a-0 & 0-0 & c-0 \end{vmatrix} = 0 \Rightarrow bcx + acy - abz = 0 \Rightarrow \frac{x}{a}+\frac{y}{b}-\frac{z}{c}=0$$

Equation of plane passing through three points

Considering three points $A(x_1, y_1, z_1)$ having position vector $\vec{a}$; $B(x_2, y_2, z_2)$ with position vector $\vec{b}$ and $C(x_3, y_3, z_3)$ with position vector $\vec{c}$.

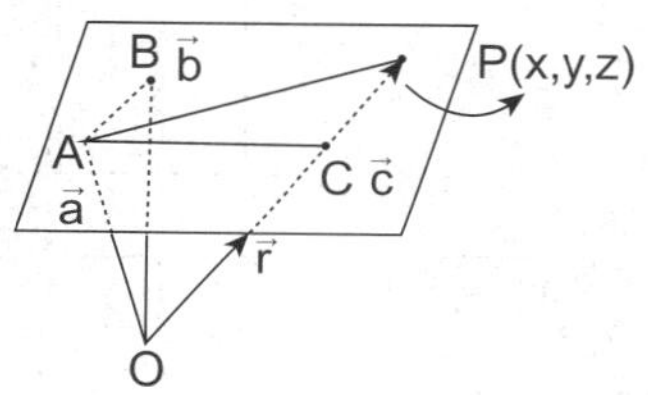

FIGURE 4.53

Equation : $\overrightarrow{AP}.\left(\overrightarrow{AB}\times\overrightarrow{AC}\right)=0$.

$$\Rightarrow \left[(\vec{r}-\vec{a})\,(\vec{b}-\vec{a})\,(\vec{c}-\vec{a})\right]=0$$

or $$\begin{vmatrix} x-x_1 & y-y_1 & z-z_1 \\ x_2-x_1 & y_2-y_1 & z_2-z_1 \\ x_3-x_1 & y_3-y_1 & z_3-z_1 \end{vmatrix}=0$$

Condition for four points to be coplanar

$A(x_1, y_1, z_1)$, $B(x_2, y_2, z_2)$, $C(x_3, y_3, z_3)$ and $D(x_4, y_4, z_4)$ to be co-planar: (x_4, y_4, z_4) must lies in plane ABC

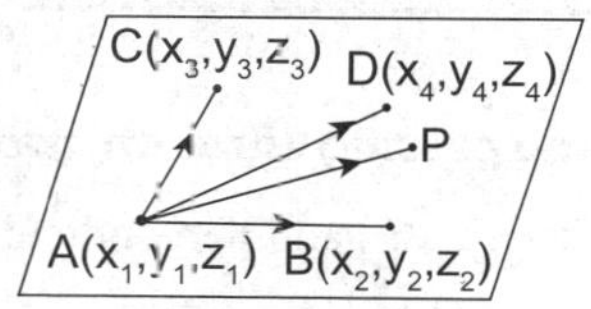

FIGURE 4.54

Equation of Plane ABC: $\overrightarrow{AP}.(\overrightarrow{AB}\times\overrightarrow{AC})=0$

$$\begin{vmatrix} x-x_1 & y-y_1 & z-z_1 \\ x_2-x_1 & y_2-y_1 & z_2-z_1 \\ x_3-x_1 & y_3-y_1 & z_3-z_1 \end{vmatrix}$$ is equation of plane

So condition is $$\begin{vmatrix} x_4-x_1 & y_4-y_1 & z_4-z_1 \\ x_2-x_1 & y_2-y_1 & z_2-z_1 \\ x_3-x_1 & y_3-y_1 & z_3-z_1 \end{vmatrix}=0$$

or $[\overrightarrow{AB}\,\overrightarrow{AC}\,\overrightarrow{AD}]=0$

ILLUSTRATION 36: Find the equation of the plane through the points $A(2. 2, -1)$, $B(3, 4. 2)$ and $C(7, 0, 6)$;

SOLUTION: The general equation of a plane passing through $(2, 2, -1)$ is

$a(x-2)+b(y-2)+c(z+1)=0$ ...(i)

It will pass through $B(3, 4, 2)$ and $C(7, 0, 6)$ if

$a(3-2)+b(4-2)+c(2+1)=0 \Rightarrow a+2b+3c=0$ ...(ii)

and $a(7-2)+b(0-2)+c(6+1)=0 \Rightarrow 5a-2b+7c=0$ ...(iii)

Solving (ii) and (iii) by cross-multiplication, we have

$$\frac{a}{14+6}=\frac{b}{15-7}=\frac{c}{-2-10}$$

$$\Rightarrow \frac{a}{5}=\frac{b}{2}=\frac{c}{-3}=\lambda(\text{say})$$

$\Rightarrow a = 5\lambda,\ b = 2\lambda$ and $c = -3\lambda$,

Substituting the values of a, b and c in (i), we get

$5\lambda(x-2) + 2\lambda(y-2) - 3\lambda(z+1) = 0$

$\Rightarrow 5(x-2) + 2(y-2) - 3(z+1) = 0$

$\Rightarrow 5x + 2y - 3z = 17$ which is the required equation of the plane.

Aliter: The equation of the plane passing through points (2, 2, –1), (3, 4, 2) and (7, 0, 6) is given by $\begin{vmatrix} x-2 & y-2 & z+1 \\ 3-2 & 4-2 & 2+1 \\ 7-2 & 0-2 & 6+1 \end{vmatrix} = 0$ or, $\begin{vmatrix} x-2 & y-2 & z+1 \\ 1 & 2 & 3 \\ 5 & -2 & 7 \end{vmatrix} = 0$

or $(x-2)(14+6) - (y-2)(7-15) + (z+1)(-2-10) = 0$

or $20(x-2) + 8(y-2) - 12(z+1) = 0$

or $5x + 2y - 3z = 17$

Equation of plane passing through two points

$A(x_1, y_1, z_1)$ and $B(x_2, y_2, z_2)$ and perpendicular to the plane $lx + my + nz = p$.

Proof : Let a variable point $P(x,y,z)$ lying in the plane, where $\vec{\alpha} = \ell\hat{i} + m\hat{j} + n\hat{k}$

$\Rightarrow (\overrightarrow{AB} \times \vec{\alpha})$ *is normal vector to the plane.*

$\Rightarrow \overrightarrow{AP}.(\overrightarrow{AB} \times \vec{\alpha}) = 0 \Rightarrow [\overrightarrow{AP}\ \ \overrightarrow{AB}\ \ \vec{\alpha}] = 0$

$\Rightarrow [(\vec{r} - \vec{a})(\vec{b} - \vec{a})\ \ \vec{\alpha}] = 0$

$$\Rightarrow \begin{vmatrix} x-x_1 & y-y_1 & z-z_1 \\ x_2-x_1 & y_2-y_1 & z_2-z_1 \\ l & m & n \end{vmatrix} = 0$$

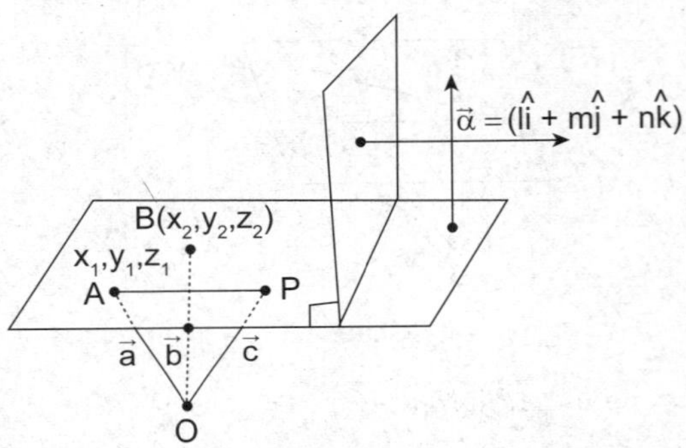

FIGURE 4.55

NOTE

This case is similar to the case of finding the equation of a plane passing through two points $A(x_1, y_1, z_1)$ *and* $B(x_2, y_2, z_2)$ *and parallel to a vector* $l\hat{i} + m\hat{j} + n\hat{k} = 0$.

ILLUSTRATION 37: Find the equation of the plane through the points (2, 2, 1), (9, 3, 6) ⊥ r to the plane $2x + 6y + 6z = 9$.

SOLUTION : $\begin{vmatrix} x-2 & y-2 & z-1 \\ 9-2 & 3-2 & 6-1 \\ 2 & 6 & 6 \end{vmatrix} = 0$

$\Rightarrow 3x + 4y - 5z = 9$

Equation of a plane passing through a point and parallel to two lines

The equation of the plane passing through a point $P(x_1, y_1, z_1)$ and parallel to two lines whose d.r.'s are $<\alpha_1, \beta_1, \gamma_1>$ and $<\alpha_2, \beta_2, \gamma_2>$ is $\begin{vmatrix} x-x_1 & y-y_1 & z-z_1 \\ \alpha_1 & \beta_1 & \gamma_1 \\ \alpha_2 & \beta_2 & \gamma_2 \end{vmatrix} = 0$

Proof: Direction ratios of normal is given by :

$$\begin{vmatrix} \hat{i} & \hat{j} & \hat{k} \\ \alpha_1 & \beta_1 & \gamma_1 \\ \alpha_2 & \beta_2 & \gamma_2 \end{vmatrix}$$

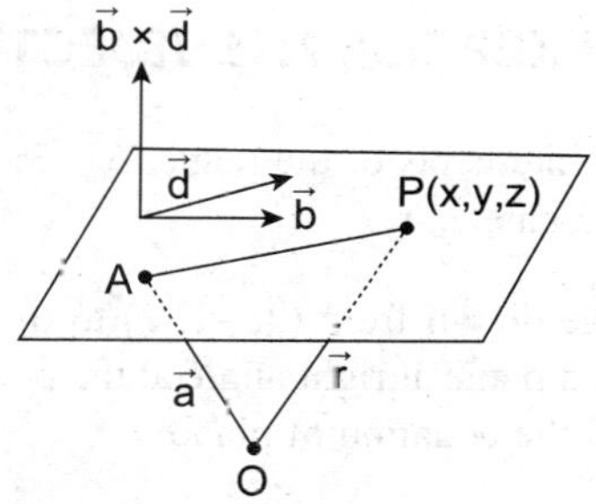

FIGURE 4.56

$\Rightarrow \begin{vmatrix} x-x_1 & y-y_1 & z-z_1 \\ \alpha_1 & \beta_1 & \gamma_1 \\ \alpha_2 & \beta_2 & \gamma_2 \end{vmatrix} = 0$ is equation of required plane

ILLUSTRATION 38: Find the equation of the plane through the points (2,-1,1) and || to the lines $\frac{x-1}{1} = \frac{y}{2} = \frac{z-2}{2}$ & $\frac{x}{1} = \frac{y-1}{-1} = \frac{z}{3}$.

SOLUTION: $\vec{a} : 2\hat{i} - \hat{j} + \hat{k}$ position vector of A.

$\vec{b} = \hat{i} + 2\hat{j} + 2\hat{k}$

$\vec{d} = \hat{i} - \hat{j} + 3\hat{k}$

Equation of plane : $\left[\overrightarrow{PA}\ \vec{b}\ \vec{d}\right] = 0$

$$\begin{vmatrix} (x-2) & (y+1) & (z-1) \\ 1 & 2 & 2 \\ 1 & -1 & 3 \end{vmatrix} = 0$$

i.e.

$8x - y - 3z = 14.$

■ AREA OF A TRIANGLE

If A_{yz}, A_{zx}, A_{xy} be the projections of an area A on the co-ordinate planes yz, zx and xy respectively, then $A = \sqrt{(A_{yz}^2 + A_{zx}^2 + A_{xy}^2)}$.

If vertices of a triangle are (x_1, y_1, z_1), (x_2, y_2, z_2) and (x_3, y_3, z_3), then

$$A_{yz} = \frac{1}{2}\left\|\begin{matrix} y_1 & z_1 & 1 \\ y_2 & z_2 & 1 \\ y_3 & z_3 & 1 \end{matrix}\right\| ;$$

$$A_{zx} = \frac{1}{2}\left\|\begin{matrix} z_1 & x_1 & 1 \\ z_2 & x_2 & 1 \\ z_3 & x_3 & 1 \end{matrix}\right\| \text{ and}$$

$$A_{xy} = \frac{1}{2}\left\|\begin{matrix} x_1 & y_1 & 1 \\ x_2 & y_2 & 1 \\ x_3 & y_3 & 1 \end{matrix}\right\|$$

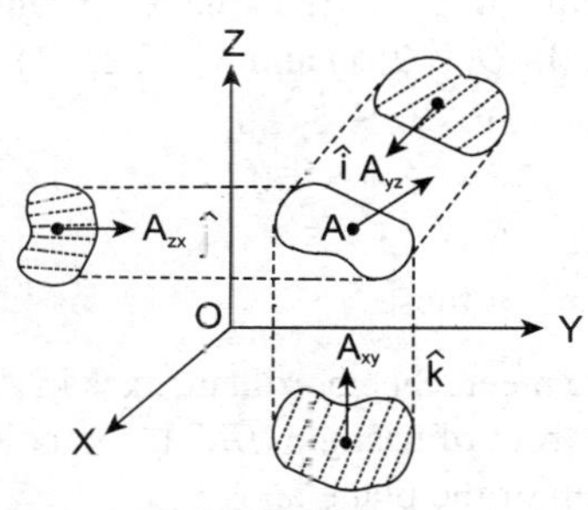

FIGURE 4.57

TEXTUAL EXERCISE 7: (SUBJECTIVE)

1. Find the intercepts of the plane $2x - 3y + 4z = 12$ on the coordinate axes.

2. If the line drawn from (4, –1, 2) to the point (–3, 2, 3) meets a plane at right angle at the point (–10, 5, 4), then find the equation of plane.

3. Find the equation to the plane through the points (2, 3, 1) and (4, –5, 3) and parallel to x-axis.

4. If a plane meets the coordinate axes at A, B and C in such a way that the centroid of ΔABC is at the point (1, 2, 3), then find the equation of the plane.

5. Find the equation of the plane passing through the mid point of the line of the points (1, 2, 3) and (3, 4, 5) and perpendicular to it.

6. A variable plane moves so that sum of the reciprocals of its intercepts on the coordinate axes is 1/2. Then, the plane passes through a fixed point, find that point

7. Foot of the perpendicular from B(–2, 1, 4) to a plane is (3, 1, 2). Then, find the equation of the plane.

8. Find the equation of plane passing through a point A(2, –1, 1) and parallel to the vector $\vec{a} = (3\hat{i} - \hat{k})$ & $\vec{b} = (-3\hat{i} + 2\hat{j} + 2\hat{k})$.

9. Prove that the points $A(4, 5, 1)$; $B(0, -1, -1)$; $C(3, 9, 4)$ and $D(-4, 4, 4)$ are coplanar.

10. A plane π makes intercepts 3 and 4 respectively on y-axis and x-axis. If π is parallel to y-axis, then find its equation.

11. Find the equation of the plane which passes through (1, 1, 1) and (1, –1, –1) and is perpendicular to $2x - y + z + 5 = 0$.

12. The plane $\frac{x}{2} + \frac{y}{3} + \frac{z}{4} = 1$ cuts the coordinate axes at A, B, C, then find the area of the ΔABC.

Answer Key

1. 6, –4, 3
2. $7x - 3y - z + 89 = 0$
3. $y + 4z = 7$
4. $\frac{x}{3} + \frac{y}{6} + \frac{z}{9} = 1$
5. $x + y + z = 9$
6. (2, 2, 2)
7. $5x - 2z = 11$
8. $2x - 3y + 6z - 25 = 0$
10. $3x + 4z = 12$
11. $x + y - z - 1 = 0$
12. $\sqrt{61}$ *sq. units*

TEXTUAL EXERCISE 5: (OBJECTIVE)

1. The equation of a plane which cuts equal intercepts of unit length on the axes is
(a) $x + y + z = 0$ (b) $x + y + z = 1$
(c) $x + y - z = 1$ (d) $x/a + y/a + z/a = 1$

2. The equation of the plane through the points $P(1, 1, 0)$, $Q(1, 2, 1)$ and $R(-2, 2, -1)$ is
(a) $-2x - 3y - 3z + 5 = 0$
(b) $2x + 3y - 3z + 5 = 0$
(c) $-2x - 3y + 3z + 5 = 0$
(d) None of these

3. A plane meets the coordinate axes in A, B, C such that the centroid of triangle ABC is the point (p, q, r). The equation of the plane is
(a) $x/p + y/q + z/r = 3$
(b) $x + y + z = 3$
(c) $x + y + z = 1$
(d) None of these

4. The equation of the plane through the points (2, 2, 1) and (9, 3, 6) and perpendicular to the plane $2x + 6y + 6z = 9$ is
(a) $3x + 4y + 5z = 9$ (b) $3x + 4y - 5z = 9$
(c) $-3x + 4y - 5z = 6$ (d) None of these

5. The equation to a plane through $P(a, b, c)$ and perpendicular to OP, (where O is the origin) is
(a) $ax + by + cz = 0$
(b) $ax - by + cz = 0$

(c) $ax + by + cz = a^2 + b^2 + c^2$
(d) None of these

6. The area of the triangle whose vertices are the points (1, 2, 3), (–2, 1, –4) and (3, 4, –2) is

(a) 0 (b) $\frac{\sqrt{1218}}{2}$
(c) $\sqrt{609}$ (d) None of these

7. The point of intersection of the line $\frac{x}{1} = \frac{y-1}{2} = \frac{z+2}{3}$ and the plane $2x + 3y + z = 0$ is:
(a) (0, 1, –2) (b) (1, 2, 3)
(c) (–1, 9, –25) (d) $\left(\frac{-1}{11}, \frac{9}{11}, \frac{-25}{11}\right)$

8. If $4x + 4y + kz = 0$ is the equation of the plane through the origin that contains the line $\frac{x-1}{2} = \frac{y+1}{3} = \frac{z}{4}$, then $k =$
(a) 1 (b) 3
(c) –5 (d) 7

9. The line $\frac{x-1}{-1} = \frac{y-1}{2} = \frac{z}{-1}$ lies in the plane
(a) $2x + 3y + 4z = 7$ (b) $2x + 4y + 2z = 6$
(c) $2x + 3y + 4z = 5$ (d) $3x + 4y + 2z = 7$

10. Equation of plane perpendicular to the line $\frac{x}{1} = \frac{y}{2} = \frac{z}{3}$ and passing through the point (2, 3, 4) is
(a) $x + 2y + 3z = 9$ (b) $x + 2y + 3z = 20$
(c) $2x + 3y + z = 17$ (d) $3x + 2y + z = 16$

11. Equation of the plane containing the lines $\vec{r} = \hat{i} + 2\hat{j} + \hat{k} + \lambda(\hat{i} + \hat{j} + \hat{k})$ and $\vec{r} = \hat{i} + 2\hat{j} + \hat{k} + \mu(\hat{i} + 2\hat{j} + 2\hat{k})$ will be
(a) $\vec{r} = \hat{i} + 2\hat{j} + \hat{k} + \lambda(\hat{i} + \hat{j} + 2\hat{k})$
(b) $\vec{r} = \hat{i} + \hat{j} + \hat{k} + \lambda(\hat{i} + 2\hat{j} + \hat{k}) + \mu(\hat{i} + 2\hat{j} + 2\hat{k})$
(c) $\vec{r} = \hat{i} + 2\hat{j} + 2\hat{k} + \lambda(\hat{i} + \hat{j} + \hat{k}) + \mu(\hat{i} + 2\hat{j} + \hat{k})$
(d) $\vec{r} = \hat{i} + 2\hat{j} + \hat{k} + \lambda(\hat{i} + \hat{j} + \hat{k}) + \mu(\hat{i} + 2\hat{j} + 2\hat{k})$

12. Equation of plane containing the line $\frac{x-x_1}{a_1} = \frac{y-y_1}{b_1} = \frac{z-z_1}{c_1}$ and parallel to the line $\frac{x-x_2}{a_2} = \frac{y-y_2}{b_2} = \frac{z-z_2}{c_2}$ is

(a) $\begin{vmatrix} x-x_1 & y-y_1 & z-z_1 \\ a_1 & b_1 & c_1 \\ x_2 & y_2 & z_2 \end{vmatrix} = 0$

(b) $\begin{vmatrix} x-x_2 & y-y_2 & z-z_2 \\ a_2 & b_2 & c_2 \\ x_1 & y_1 & z_1 \end{vmatrix} = 0$

(c) $\begin{vmatrix} x-x_1 & y-y_1 & z-z_1 \\ a_1 & b_1 & c_1 \\ a_2 & b_2 & c_2 \end{vmatrix} = 0$

(d) None of these

13. A point moves in such a way that the sum of its distance from *xy*-plane and *yz*-plane remains equal to its distance from *zx*-plane. The locus of the point is
(a) $x - y + z = 2$ (b) $x + y - z = 0$
(c) $x - y + z = 0$ (d) $x - y - z = 2$

14. The equation of the plane through the three points (1, 1, 1), (1, –1, 1) and (–7, –3, –5), is equal to
(a) $3x - 4z + 1 = 0$ (b) $3x - 4y + 1 = 0$
(c) $3x + 4y + 1 = 0$ (d) None of these

15. The equation of the perpendicular from the point (α, β, γ) to the plane $ax + by + cz + d = 0$ is
(a) $a(x - \alpha) + b(y - \beta) + c(z - \gamma) = 0$
(b) $\frac{x-\alpha}{a} = \frac{y-\beta}{b} = \frac{z-\gamma}{c}$
(c) $a(x - \alpha) + b(y - \beta) + c(z - \gamma) = abc$
(d) None of these

16. The co-ordinates of the foot of the perpendicular drawn from the origin to a plane is (2, 4, –3). The equation of the plane is
(a) $2x - 4y - 3z = 29$
(b) $2x - 4y + 3z = 29$
(c) $2x + 4y - 3z = 29$
(d) None of these

17. In three dimensional space, the equation $3y + 4z = 0$ represents
(a) A plane containing *x*-axis
(b) A plane containing *y*-axis
(c) A plane containing *z*-axis
(d) A line with direction ratios 0, 3, 4

18. If from a point $P(a, b, c)$ perpendiculars PA and PB are drawn to *yz* and *zx* planes, then the equation of the plane OAB

(a) $bcx + cay + abz = 0$
(b) $bcx + cay - abz = 0$
(c) $bcx - cay + abz = 0$
(d) $-bcx + cay + abz = 0$

19. The equation of a plane parallel to x-axis is
(a) $ax + by + cz + d = 0$
(b) $ax + by + d = 0$
(c) $by + cz + d = 0$
(d) $ax + cz + d = 0$

20. In the space, the equation $by + cz + d = 0$ represents a plane perpendicular to the plane
(a) YOZ (b) $Z = k$
(c) ZOX (d) XOY

22. The line $\frac{x-2}{3} = \frac{y-3}{4} = \frac{z-4}{0}$ is parallel to
(a) xy-plane (b) yz-plane
(c) zx-plane (d) None of these

23. Under what condition does a straight line $\frac{x-x_0}{l} = \frac{y-y_0}{m} = \frac{z-z_0}{n}$ is parallel to the xy-plane
(a) $l = 0$ (b) $m = 0$
(c) $n = 0$ (d) $l = 0, m = 0$

24. A plane which passes through the point (3, 2, 0) and containes the line $\frac{x-3}{1} = \frac{y-6}{5} = \frac{z-4}{4}$ is
(a) $x - y + z = 1$ (b) $x + y + z = 5$
(c) $x + 2y - z = 0$ (d) $2x - 2y + z = 0$

25. The point of intersection of the line $\frac{x-1}{3} = \frac{y+2}{4} = \frac{z-3}{-2}$ and plane $2x - y + 3z - 1 = 0$ is
(a) (10, –10, 3) (b) (10, 10, –3)
(c) (–10, 10, 3) (d) None of these

Answer Key

1. (b)	**2.** (c)	**3.** (a)	**4.** (b)	**5.** (c)	**6.** (b)	**7.** (d)	**8.** (c)	**9.** (c)	**10.** (b)
11. (d)	**12.** (c)	**13.** (c)	**14.** (a)	**15.** (b)	**16.** (c)	**17.** (a)	**18.** (b)	**19.** (c)	**20.** (a)
22. (a)	**23.** (c)	**24.** (a)	**25.** (b)						

■ ANGLE BETWEEN TWO PLANES

If $\left.\begin{array}{l}\vec{r}.\vec{n}_1 = d_1\\ \vec{r}.\vec{n}_2 = d_2\end{array}\right\}$ be vector equations of two planes, then angle between the planes is defined as the angle between their normals. *i.e.*, $\theta = \cos^{-1}\left(\frac{\vec{n}_1.\vec{n}_2}{|\vec{n}_1||\vec{n}_2|}\right)$

If θ be the angle between the planes $a_1x + b_1y + c_1z + d_1 = 0$ and $a_2x + b_2y + c_2z + d_2 = 0$, then

$$\theta = \cos^{-1}\left(\frac{a_1a_2 + b_1b_2 + c_1c_2}{\sqrt{a_1^2 + b_1^2 + c_1^2}\sqrt{a_2^2 + b_2^2 + c_2^2}}\right)$$

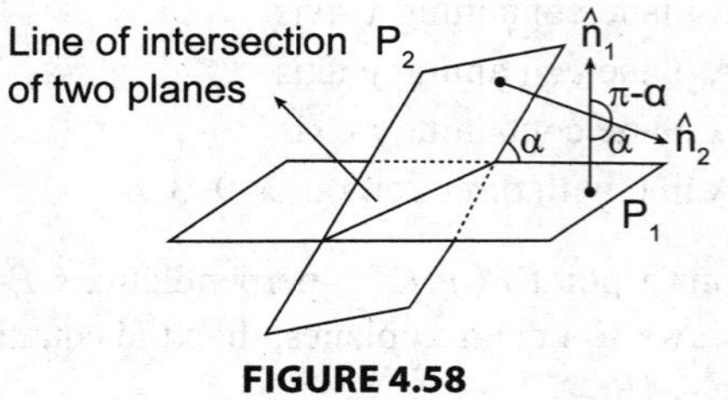

FIGURE 4.58

Corollaries:

1. If planes are perpendicular, then $\vec{n}_1.\vec{n}_2 = 0$ or $a_1a_2 + b_1b_2 + c_1c_2 = 0$
2. If planes are parallel, then $\vec{n}_1 = k\vec{n}_2$ or $\frac{a_1}{a_2} = \frac{b_1}{b_2} = \frac{c_1}{c_2}$
3. If planes are coincident, then $\frac{a_1}{a_2} = \frac{b_1}{b_2} = \frac{c_1}{c_2} = \frac{d_1}{d_2}$

■ ANGLE BETWEEN LINE AND PLANE

Angle between lines $L: \frac{x-\alpha}{l} = \frac{y-\beta}{m} = \frac{z-\gamma}{n}$ and the plane $\pi : ax + by + cz + d = 0$. Let θ be the acute angle between the line and the plane and α be that between line and normal to the plane.

$$\Rightarrow \quad \theta = \frac{\pi}{2} - \alpha$$

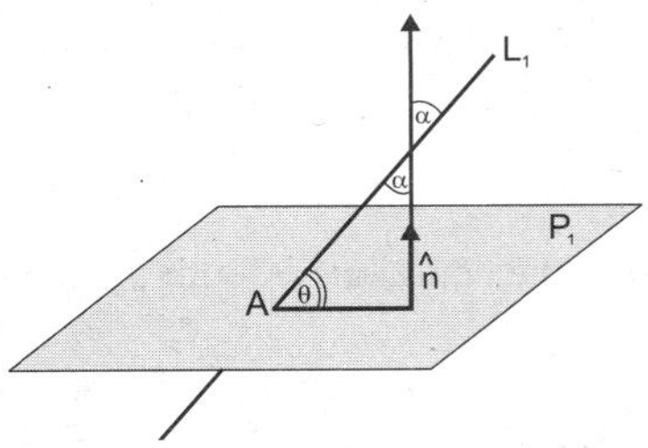

FIGURE 4.59

$$\Rightarrow \quad \sin\theta = \cos\alpha = \frac{\left|\left(l\hat{i}+m\hat{j}+n\hat{k}\right).\left(a\hat{i}+b\hat{j}+c\hat{k}\right)\right|}{\sqrt{l^2+m^2+n^2}\sqrt{a^2+b^2+c^2}}$$

$$\Rightarrow \quad \theta = \sin^{-1}\left(\frac{|al+bm+cn|}{\sqrt{a^2+b^2+c^2}\sqrt{l^2+m^2+n^2}}\right)$$

Corollaries:

1. Line is perpendicular to plane if $\frac{a}{l}=\frac{b}{m}=\frac{c}{n}$
2. Line is parallel to plane if $al + bm + cn = 0$
3. Line is coincident in the plane if $\begin{cases} al+bm+cn=0\ \& \\ a\alpha+b\beta+c\gamma+d=0 \end{cases}$

ILLUSTRATION 39: Find the angle between the plane $\vec{r}.(2\hat{i}-\hat{j}+\hat{k})=6$ and $\vec{r}.(\hat{i}+\hat{j}+2\hat{k})=5$.

SOLUTION: We know that the angle between the planes $\vec{r}.\vec{n}_1=d_1$ and $\vec{r}.\vec{n}_2=d_2$ is given by $\cos\theta=\frac{\vec{n}_1.\vec{n}_2}{|\vec{n}_1||\vec{n}_2|}$.

Here, $\vec{n}_1=2\hat{i}-\hat{j}+\hat{k}$ and $\vec{n}_2=\hat{i}+\hat{j}+2\hat{k}$.

$$\therefore \quad \cos\theta=\frac{(2\hat{i}-\hat{j}+\hat{k}).(\hat{i}+\hat{j}+2\hat{k})}{|2\hat{i}-\hat{j}+\hat{k}||\hat{i}+\hat{j}+2\hat{k}|}=\frac{2-1+2}{\sqrt{4+1+1}\sqrt{1+1+4}}=\frac{1}{2}\Rightarrow\lambda=-2\Rightarrow\theta=\pi/3.$$

ILLUSTRATION 40: If the planes $\vec{r}.(2\hat{i}-\hat{j}+\lambda\hat{k})=5$ and $\vec{r}.(3\hat{i}+2\hat{j}+2\hat{k})=4$ are perpendicular, find the value of λ.

SOLUTION: We know that the planes $\vec{r}.\vec{n}_1=d$ and $\vec{r}.\vec{n}_2=d_2$ are perpendicular, if $\vec{n}_1.\vec{n}_2=0$ therefore, given planes will be perpendicular to each other, if $(2\hat{i}-\hat{j}+\lambda\hat{k}).(3\hat{i}+2\hat{j}+2\hat{k})=0 \Rightarrow \lambda=-2$

ILLUSTRATION 41: Find the angle between the planes $-x+y+2z=9$ and $x+2y+z=5$.

SOLUTION: Given planes are $-x + y + 2z = 9$ ......(1)

$x + 2y + z = 5$ ......(2)

The direction cosines of the normal to the plane (1) are $\frac{-1}{\sqrt{6}},\frac{1}{\sqrt{6}},\frac{2}{\sqrt{6}}$

The direction cosines of the normal to the plane (2) are $\frac{1}{\sqrt{6}},\frac{2}{\sqrt{6}},\frac{1}{\sqrt{6}}$

If θ be the angle between the planes (1) and (2), then

$$\cos\theta=\left(\frac{-1}{\sqrt{6}}\right)\left(\frac{1}{\sqrt{6}}\right)+\left(\frac{1}{\sqrt{6}}\right)\left(\frac{2}{\sqrt{6}}\right)+\left(\frac{2}{\sqrt{6}}\right)\left(\frac{1}{\sqrt{6}}\right)=\frac{-1}{6}+\frac{2}{6}+\frac{2}{6}=\frac{1}{2} \text{ or, } \theta=60°.$$

[$\because$ angle between planes = angle between their normals]

ILLUSTRATION 42: Find the angle between the line $\frac{x+1}{3}=\frac{y-1}{2}=\frac{z-2}{4}$ and the plane $2x+y-3z+4=0$

SOLUTION: The given line is parallel to the vector $\vec{b}=3\hat{i}+2\hat{j}+4\hat{k}$ and the given plane is normal to the vector $\vec{n}=2\hat{i}+\hat{j}-3\hat{k}$. If θ is the acute angle between the line and plane, then

$$\sin\theta=\frac{|\vec{b}.\vec{n}|}{|\vec{b}||\vec{n}|}=\frac{|(3\hat{i}+2\hat{j}+4\hat{k}).(2\hat{i}+\hat{j}-3\hat{k})|}{\sqrt{3^2+2^2+4^2}\sqrt{2^2+1^2+3^2}}=\frac{|6+2-12|}{\sqrt{29}\sqrt{14}}=\frac{|-4|}{\sqrt{406}}\Rightarrow\theta=\sin^{-1}\left(\frac{4}{\sqrt{406}}\right)$$

■ EQUATION OF A PLANE PARALLEL TO A PLANE

Since the two parallel planes have the same normal, therefore equation of family of planes parallel to a plane $ax+by+cz+d=0$ or $\vec{r}.\vec{n}=d$ is given by $ax + by + cz + \lambda = 0$ or $\vec{r}.\vec{n}=\lambda$ represents family of planes parallel to given plane.

Distance Between two parallel planes

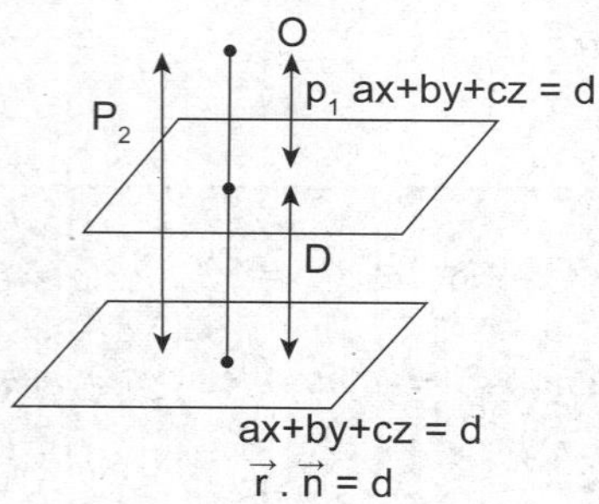

FIGURE 4.60

$ax + by + cz =$ d and $ax + by + cz =$ d' is given by $\dfrac{|d-d'|}{\sqrt{a^2+b^2+c^2}}$

Proof: Writing the equations of both the planes in normal form, we have

$$\frac{ax+by+cz}{\sqrt{a^2+b^2+c^2}}=\frac{d}{\sqrt{a^2+b^2+c^2}}$$

$$\& \ \frac{ax+by+cz}{\sqrt{a^2+b^2+c^2}}=\frac{d'}{\sqrt{a^2+b^2+c^2}}$$

The distance between the planes

$$=|d_1 - d_2| = \frac{|d-d'|}{\sqrt{a^2+b^2+c^2}}.$$

ILLUSTRATION 43: (a) Find the distance between the parallel planes given by the equation $\vec{r}.\left(2\hat{i}-2\hat{j}+\hat{k}\right)+3=0$ & $\vec{r}.\left(4\hat{i}-4\hat{j}+2\hat{k}\right)+5=0$.

(b) Find the distance between the parallel planes $x + y - z + 4 = 0$ and $x + y - z + 5 = 0$.

SOLUTION : (a) $P_1:\vec{r}.\left(2\hat{i}-2\hat{j}+\hat{k}\right)=-3 \quad P_2:\vec{r}.\left(4\hat{i}-4\hat{j}+2\hat{k}\right)=-5 \Rightarrow \vec{r}.\left(2\hat{i}-2\hat{j}+\hat{k}\right)=-5/2$

$$\text{Now distance} = \frac{|-3-(-5/2)|}{|2\hat{i}-2\hat{j}+\hat{k}|}=\frac{1/2}{\sqrt{9}}=\frac{1}{6}.$$

$$\text{(b) distance} = \frac{|-4-(-5)|}{\sqrt{1^2+1^2+1^2}}=\frac{1}{\sqrt{3}}.$$

■ DISTANCE OF A POINT FROM A GIVEN PLANE

Given plane π : $\vec{r}.\vec{n}$ = d or $ax+by+cz+d=0$

& a point $P_{(\vec{p})}(x_1, y_1, z_1)$

Let $M_{\vec{r}_M}(x_M, y_M, z_M)$ be the foot of perpendicular

Vector form:

Line PM $\parallel \vec{n} \Rightarrow \vec{r}_M-\vec{p}=\lambda\vec{n}$. Also $\vec{r}_M.\vec{n}=d$

$$\Rightarrow \vec{r}_M.\vec{n} - \vec{p}.\vec{n} = \lambda|\vec{n}|^2 \Rightarrow \frac{d-\vec{p}.\vec{n}}{|\vec{n}|^2}=\lambda$$

$$\Rightarrow \vec{r}_M=\vec{p}+\frac{d-\vec{p}.\vec{n}}{|\vec{n}|^2}\vec{n}$$

$$\Rightarrow \left|\vec{r}_M-\vec{p}\right|=\left|\frac{d-\vec{p}.\vec{n}}{|\vec{n}|^2}\vec{n}\right|=\left|\frac{d-\vec{p}.\vec{n}}{|\vec{n}|}\right|$$

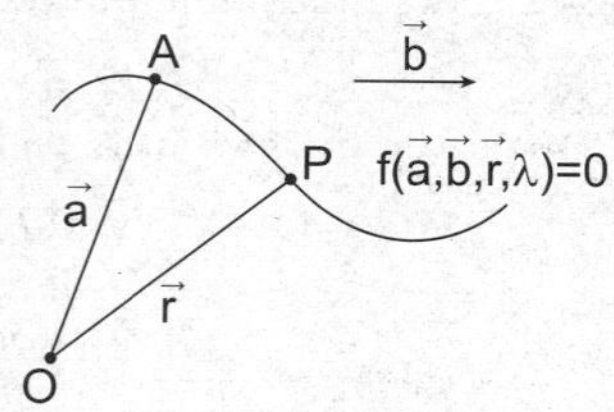

FIGURE 4.61

Cartesian form: Equation of family of planes parallel to a plane $ax + by + cz + d = 0$ and passing through point $P(x_1, y_1, z_1)$ is given by $ax + by + cz = ax_1 + by_1 + cz_1$

So distance of the point $P(x_1, y_1, z_1)$ is given by distance between the two planes. i.e.,

$$PM = \left|\frac{ax_1 + by_1 + cz_1}{\sqrt{a^2+b^2+c^2}} - \frac{-d}{\sqrt{a^2+b^2+c^2}}\right|$$

$$= \left|\frac{ax_1 + by_1 + cz_1 + d}{\sqrt{a^2+b^2+c^2}}\right|$$

ILLUSTRATION 44: Find the distance between the point P(1,-3,2) and the plane $2x - y + 2z + 6 = 0$.

SOLUTION: Distance $= \dfrac{|2x_1 - y_1 + 2z_1 + 6|}{\sqrt{2^2+(-1)^2+2^2}} = \dfrac{|2\times1 - 1.\times(-3) + 2\times2 + 6|}{\sqrt{9}} = \dfrac{15}{3} = 5\ units$.

ILLUSTRATION 45: Find the distance of the point P(1,-1,1) from the plane $x-2y + z + 3 = 0$ measured along the line $\dfrac{x}{2} = \dfrac{y}{1} = \dfrac{z}{-2}$

SOLUTION : Equation of line PM is given by $\vec{r} = \vec{p} + \lambda\vec{a} = (\hat{i} - \hat{j} + \hat{k}) + \lambda(2\hat{i} + \hat{j} - 2\hat{k})$

$= (1-2\lambda)\hat{i} + (-1+\lambda)\hat{j} + (1-2\lambda)\hat{k}$

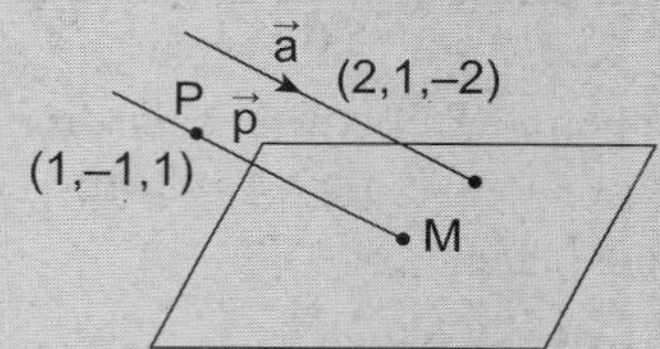

FIGURE 4.62

$\because$ This line meets the plane

$\therefore$ $(1 + 2\lambda, -1 + \lambda, 1 - 2\lambda)$ satisfies the equation of the plane.

$\Rightarrow$ $(1 + 2\lambda) - 2(-1 + \lambda) + (1 - 2\lambda) + 3 = 0 \Rightarrow \lambda = 7/2$

$\therefore$ coordinate of point M are $\left(1 + 2\times\frac{7}{2}; -1 + \frac{7}{2}, 1 - 2\times\frac{7}{2}\right) = \left(8, \frac{5}{2}, -6\right)$

$\therefore$ distance $PM = \sqrt{(8-1)^2 + (5/2+1)^2 + (-6-1)^2} = \dfrac{21}{2}$. units.

FOOT OF PERPENDICULAR/IMAGE OF A POINT IN A PLANE

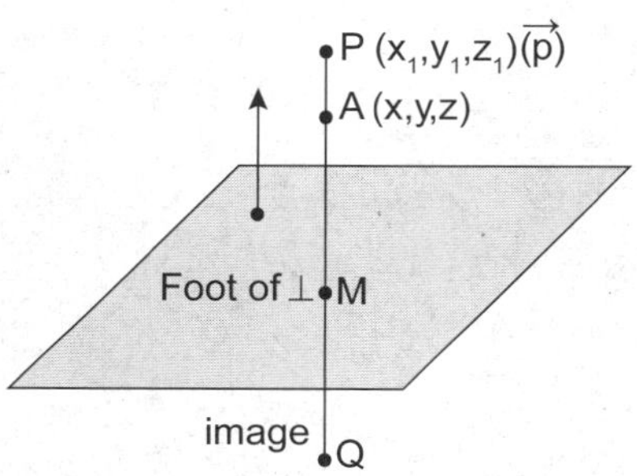

FIGURE 4.63

Given plane $\pi : \vec{r}.\vec{n} = d_0$ or $ax + by + cz + d = 0$

& a point $P_{(\vec{p})}(x_1, y_1, z_1)$

Let $M_{\vec{r}_M}(x_M, y_M, z_M)$ be the foot of ⊥r and $Q_{\vec{q}}(x_Q, y_Q, z_Q)$ be image of P in the plane π.

Consider a point $A(\vec{a}) \equiv (x, y, z)$ on the perpendicular from P to the plane π. Equation of line perpendicular to plane and through $P(x_1, y_1, z_1)$ is given by $\vec{r} = \vec{p} + \lambda\vec{n}$

$\because$ d.c.'s of $\overrightarrow{AP} : \langle x - x_1,\ y - y_1,\ z - z_1\rangle$

d.c.'s of $\vec{n} : \langle a,\ b,\ c\rangle$

$$\Rightarrow \frac{x - x_1}{a} = \frac{y - y_1}{b} = \frac{z - z_1}{c}$$

$$\Rightarrow \frac{x-x_1}{a}=\frac{y-y_1}{b}=\frac{z-z_1}{c}$$

$$=\frac{a(x-x_1)+b(y-y_1)+c(z-z_1)}{a^2+b^2+c^2}$$

$$=\frac{(ax+by+cz+d)-(ax_1+by_1+cz_1+d)}{a^2+b^2+c^2}$$

If (x, y, z) lies on A, then

$$\frac{x-x_1}{a}=\frac{y-y_1}{b}=\frac{z-z_1}{c}=-\frac{(ax_1+by_1+(z_1+d)}{a^2+b^2+c^2}$$

■ IMAGE OF A POINT

Since Q is the image of point P

$\therefore$ M is the mid point of segment PQ

Vector Form: $\vec{r}_q+\vec{r}_p=2\vec{r}_m$

$$\Rightarrow \vec{r}_q=2\vec{r}_m-\vec{r}_p$$

$$\Rightarrow \overrightarrow{rm}=\vec{p}+\frac{d-\vec{p}.\vec{n}}{|\vec{n}|^2}\vec{n} \text{ (proved earlier)}$$

Cartesian Form: For $A(x, y, z)$ to be the image of point P mid point of PA should lie on the plane therefore $-(ax_1 + by_1 + cz_1 + d) = (ax + by + cz + d)$

$$\Rightarrow \frac{x-x_1}{a}=\frac{y-y_1}{b}=\frac{z-z_1}{c}=-\frac{2(ax_1+by_1+cz_1+d)}{a^2+b^2+c^2}.$$

ILLUSTRATION 46: Find the length and foot of perpendicular from the point (7, 14, 5) to the plane $2x + 4y - z = 2$.

SOLUTION: The required length $=\dfrac{2(7)+4(14)-(5)-2}{\sqrt{2^2+4^2+1^2}}=\dfrac{14+56-5-2}{\sqrt{4+16+1}}=\dfrac{63}{\sqrt{21}}$

Let the co-ordinates of the foot of perpendicular from the point $P(7, 14, 5)$ be $M(\alpha, \beta, \gamma)$.

Then the direction ratios of PM are $(\alpha - 7, \beta - 14, \gamma - 5)$

i.e., d.r's of normal to the plane: $(\alpha - 7, \beta - 14, \gamma - 5)$

But the d.r's of normal to the given plane

$2x + 4y - z = 2$ are 2, 4. – 1

Hence, $\dfrac{\alpha-7}{2}=\dfrac{\beta-14}{4}=\dfrac{\gamma-5}{-1}=k(say)$

$\Rightarrow \alpha = 2k + 7, \beta - 4k + 14, \gamma = -k + 5$ ..... (i)

Since (α, β, γ) lies on the plane $2x + 4y - z = 2$

$\therefore$ $2\alpha + 4\beta - \gamma = 2 \Rightarrow 2(7 + 2k) + 4(14 + 4k) - (5 - k) = 2$

$\Rightarrow 14 + 4k + 56 + 16k - 5 + k = 2 \Rightarrow 21k + 65 = 2 \Rightarrow k = -3$

Now, putting $k = -3$ in (i), we get $\alpha = 1, \beta = 2, \gamma = 8$

Hence the co-ordinates of the foot of the perpendicular are (1, 2, 8)

ILLUSTRATION 47: Find the image of the point P (3, 5, 7) in the plane $2x + y + z = 0$

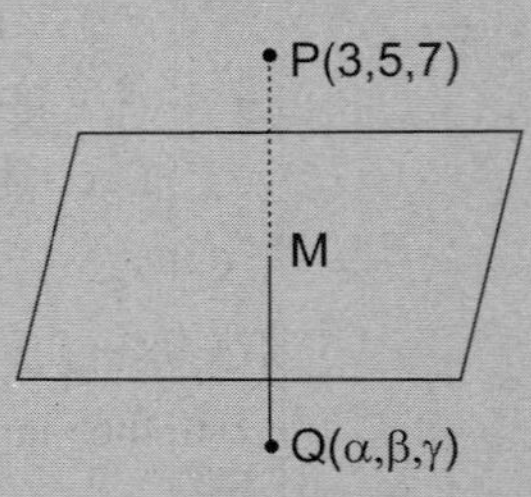

FIGURE 4.64

SOLUTION: Given plane is $2x + y + z = 0$ ....(i)

$P(3, 5, 7)$dr's of normal to the plane (i) are 2, 1, 1

Let Q be the image of a point P in plane (i)

$\therefore$ Equation of line PQ is, $\frac{x-3}{2}=\frac{y-5}{1}=\frac{z-7}{1}=r$,

Let $M=(2r+3, r+5, r+7)$

Since M lies on (i)

$\therefore$ $2(2r+3)+(r+5)+(r+7)=0$

$\Rightarrow$ $6r+18=0$ $\Rightarrow r=-3$

$\therefore$ $M\equiv(-3, 2, 4)$ Let $Q\equiv(\alpha, \beta, \gamma)$. Since M is mid-point of PQ

$\therefore$ $-3=\frac{\alpha+3}{2}\Rightarrow\alpha=-9$; $2=\frac{\beta+5}{2}\Rightarrow\beta=-1$; $4=\frac{\gamma+7}{2}\Rightarrow\gamma=1$. Thus $Q\equiv(-9, 1, 1)$

■ IMAGE OF A LINE IN A PLANE

Step I: Given a plane $ax+by+cz+d=0$ and a line $\frac{x-x_1}{l}=\frac{y-y_1}{m}=\frac{z-z_1}{n}$.

Step II: Find the point of intersection of line and plane *i.e* point A (say (x_0, y_0, z_0))

Setp III: Take a point $P(x_1, y_1, z_1)$ on line and find the image Q of P and foot M of perpendicular $P(x_1, y_1, z_1)$ in the given plane.

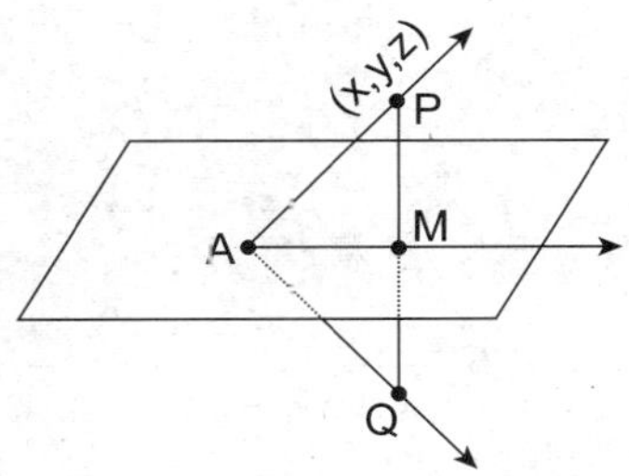

FIGURE 4.65

Step IV: Write the equation of line AQ (image of the line) and AM (line of projection)

ILLUSTRATION 48: Find equation of the image/line of projection of the line $\frac{x-1}{2}=\frac{y-2}{1}=\frac{z-3}{-2}$ in the plane $x+y+z-3=0$

SOLUTION: We find the point of intersection of line and plane:

Any general point on line is given by $(2r+1, r+2, 3-2r)$ and if this point is A (pt. of intersection), then $(2r+1)+(r+2)+(3-2r)-3=0\Rightarrow r=-3$

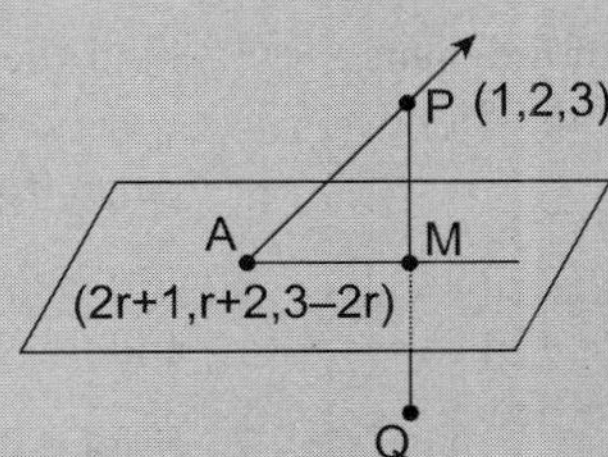

FIGURE 4.66

$\therefore$ $A=(-5, -1, 9)$

Also the image of point $P(1, 2, 3)$ of the line L on the plane is given by

$$\frac{x-1}{1}=\frac{y-2}{1}=\frac{z-3}{1}=\frac{-2(1+2+3-3)}{1^2+1^2+1^2}\Rightarrow Q\equiv(-1,0,1)$$

$\therefore$ Equation of line $AQ \equiv \dfrac{x+1}{4} = \dfrac{y}{1} = \dfrac{z-1}{-8}$

Also Coordinates of points M $\equiv$ mid point of segment $PQ \equiv (0, 1, 2)$

$\therefore$ Equation of projection of line L on plane π is $\dfrac{x}{5} = \dfrac{y-1}{2} = \dfrac{z-2}{-7}$

ILLUSTRATION 49: Find the equation of the image of the line $\dfrac{x-1}{2} = \dfrac{y-2}{-4} = \dfrac{z-3}{2}$

(a) in the plane $x + y + z - 3 = 0$ (b) in the plane $x + y + z - 6 = 0$

SOLUTION: (a) The dc's of line L are <2, –4, 2> The dc's of normal to the plane $x + y + z - 3 = 0$ are <1,1,1>

$\because$ $2 \times 1 - 4 \times 1 - 2 \times 1 = 0$

$\Rightarrow$ Line L is parallel to the plane. Now we find the image of any point (1,2,3) about the plane

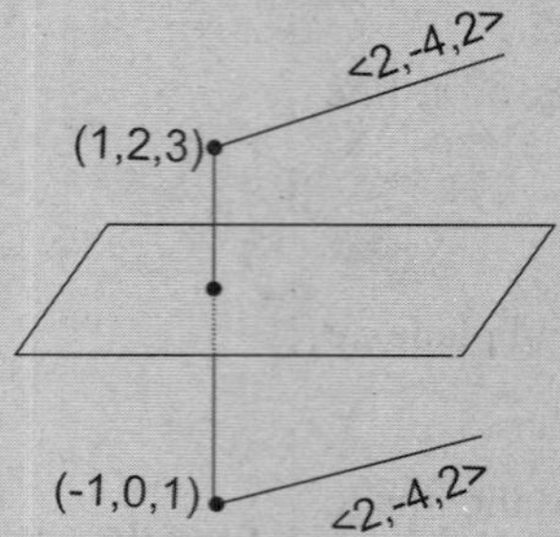

FIGURE 4.67

$$\Rightarrow \frac{x-1}{1} = \frac{y-2}{1} = \frac{z-3}{1} = \frac{-2(1+2+3-3)}{1^2+1^2+1^2} \qquad \Rightarrow Q \equiv (-1, 0, 1)$$

$\therefore$ image of line is $\dfrac{x+1}{2} = \dfrac{y}{-4} = \dfrac{z-1}{2}$

(b) Line is coincident with the plane so it is image of itself

TEXTUAL EXERCISE 8: (SUBJECTIVE)

1. If the distance of the point $P(1, -2, 1)$ from the plane $x + 2y - 2z = a$, where $a > 0$, is 5, then find the foot of the perpendicular from P to the plane.

2. Let a plane passes through the point $P(-1, -1, 1)$ and also contains a line joining the points $Q(0, 1, 1)$ and $R(0, 0, 2)$. Then find the distance of plane from the point (0, 0, 0).

3. Let L be the line of intersection of the planes $2x + 3y + z = 1$ and $x + 3y + 2z = 2$. If L makes an angle α, with the positive x-axis, then find $\cos \alpha$.

4. A plane π passing through (1, –2, 1) and is perpendicular to two planes $2x - 2y + z = 0$ and $x - y + 2z = 4$, then find the distance of the plane π from the point (1, 2, 2).

5. Find the equation of the plane parallel to the planes $x + 2y + 3z - 5 = 0$, $x + 2y + 3z - 7 = 0$ and equidistance from them.

6. If θ is the angle between the planes $2x - y + z - 1 = 0$ and $x - 2y + z + 2 = 0$, then find $\cos \theta$.

7. If for a plane, the intercepts on the coordinate axes are 8, 4, 4, then find the length of the perpendicular from the origin to the plane.

8. Find the equation of the plane through the point (1, 2, 3) and parallel to the plane $x + 2y + 5z = 0$.

9. Find the image of the point $P(1, 3, 4)$ in the plane $2x - y + z + 3 = 0$.

10. Find the angle between the planes $2x - y + z = 6$ and $x + y + 2z = 3$.

11. Find the value of k for which the planes $3x - 6y - 2z = 7$ and $2x + y - kz = 5$ are perpendicular to each other.

12. Find the distance of the point (2, 3, 4) from the plane, $3x - 6y + 2z + 11 = 0$.

13. If the given planes, $ax + by + cz + d = 0$ and $a'x + b'y + c'z + d' = 0$ be mutually perpendicular, then find $aa' + bb' + cc'$.

14. Find the angle between the planes, $3x - 4y + 5z = 0$ and $2x - y - 2z = 5$.

15. Find the angle θ between the plane $ax + by + cz + d = 0$ and a line whose direction cosines are l, m, n.

16. Find the distance between parallel planes, $2x - 2y + z + 3 = 0$ and $4x - 4y + 2z + 5 = 0$.

17. Find the necessary and sufficient condition, the line $\frac{x-x_1}{l} = \frac{y-y_1}{m} = \frac{z-z_1}{n}$ to be parallel to the plane $ax + by + cz + d = 0$.

Answer Key

1. $\left(\frac{8}{3}, \frac{4}{3}, -\frac{7}{3}\right)$ **2.** $\sqrt{2}$ units **3.** $1/\sqrt{3}$ **4.** $2\sqrt{2}$ **5.** $x + 2y + 3z - 6 = 0$ **6.** 5/6

7. 8/3 **8.** $x + 2y + 5z - 20 = 0$ **9.** (–3, 5, 2) **10.** π/3 **11.** 0

12. 1 **13.** $aa' + bb' + cc' = 0$ **14.** $\frac{\pi}{2}$ **15.** $\sin^{-1}\left(\frac{al + bm + cn}{\sqrt{a^2 + b^2 + c^2}}\right)$ **16.** 1/6

17. $al + bm + cn = 0$

■ FAMILY OF PLANES

Equation of family of planes parallel to a plane $ax + by + cz - d = 0$ or $\vec{r}.\vec{n} = d$ is given by $ax+by+cz = \lambda$ or $\vec{r}.\vec{n} = \lambda$; where λ is a parameter

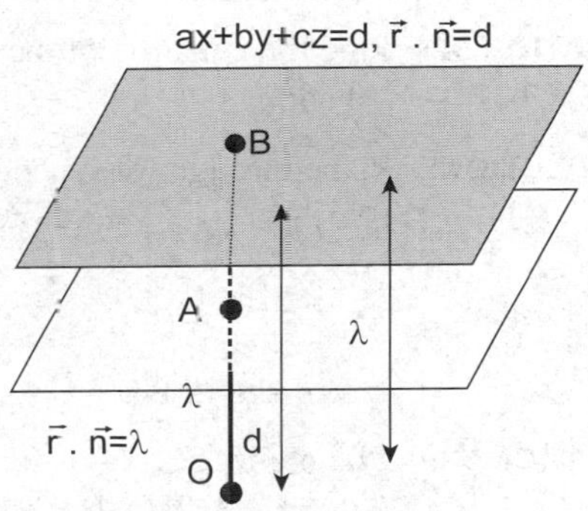

FIGURE 4.68

ILLUSTRATION 50: Find the equation of the plane through (2, 5, 4) and parallel to the plane $3x + 4y - 5z = 0$.

SOLUTION: The equation of any plane parallel to the plane $3x + 4y - 4y - 5z = 0$ may be taken as

$3x + 4y - 5z + k = 0$ ....(1)

If plane (1) passes through the point (2, 5, 4), we get, $3.2 + 4.5 - 5.4 + k = 0$

$\Rightarrow$ $6 + 20 - 20 + k = 0$ or, $k = -6$ ....(2)

From (1) and (2), the equation of required plane is $3x + 4y - 5z = 6$.

ILLUSTRATION 51: Find the equation of the plane which is parallel to the plane $x + 5y - 4z + 5 = 0$ and the sum of whose intercepts on the co-ordinate axes is 15 units.

SOLUTION: Equation of any plane parallel to the plane $x + 5y - 4z + 5 = 0$ may be taken as

$x + 5y - 4z + k = 0$ .....(1)

or $\frac{x}{-k}+\frac{y}{-\frac{k}{5}}+\frac{z}{\frac{k}{4}}=1$ $\Rightarrow$ Sum of intercepts on axes $= -k-\frac{k}{5}+\frac{k}{4}=\frac{-19}{20}k$

Given, $\frac{-19}{20}k=15$ $\Rightarrow$ $k=-15\times\frac{20}{19}=\frac{-300}{19}$ ....(2)

From (1) and (2), equation of required plane is $x + 5y - 4z = \frac{300}{19}$.

Equation of plane passing through the Intersection of two given planes

Since infinitely many planes can pass through the line of intersection of planes $P_1 = 0$ and $P_2 = 0$. Therefore the equation of family of these planes is given by $P_1 + \lambda P_2 = 0$.

Let $P_1 : a_1x + b_1y + c_1z = d_1$, i.e., $\vec{r}_1.\vec{n}_1 = d_1$ and

$P_2 : a_2x + b_2y + c_2z = d_2$, i.e., $\vec{r}.\vec{n}_2 = d_2$

$\Rightarrow$ Family of planes through line of intersection is

$$\vec{r}.(\vec{n_1}+\lambda\vec{n_2}) = d_1 + \lambda d_2$$

Or $(a_1x+b_1y+c_1z)+\lambda(a_2x+b_2y+c_2z)=d_1+\lambda d_2$

Since it is linear in (x, y, z) so it represents a plane because the equation contains a scalar parameter 'λ' so it represents a family of planes.The above equation is satisfied by all the points of the line of intersection so it is called Family of planes passing through intersection of planes $P_1 = 0$ and $P_2 = 0$

ILLUSTRATION 52: Find the equation of the plane passing through the intersection of the plane P_1: $2x - 3y + z - 4 = 0$ and $P_2 : x - y + z + 1 = 0$ and $\perp$ to the plane P_3: $x + 2y - 3z + 6 = 0$

SOLUTION: Plane through intersection of $P_1 = 0$ and $P_2 = 0$ is given by $P_1 + \lambda P_2 = 0$

i.e., $(2 + \lambda) x - (\lambda + 3)y + (1 + \lambda)z - 4 + \lambda = 0$ which is be $\perp$r to $P_3 = 0$

$\Rightarrow 2 + \lambda - 2\lambda - 6 - 3 - 3\lambda = 0$ $\Rightarrow \lambda = \frac{-7}{4}$

$\therefore$ Required plane is $x - 5y - 3z - 23 = 0$

ILLUSTRATION 53: The planes $P_1 : x - y - z = 4$ is rotated through 90° about its line of intersection with the plane $P_2 : x + y + 2z = 4$. Find the equation in the new position

SOLUTION: $P_1 + \lambda P_2 = 0$; $(x - y - z - 4) + \lambda (x + y + 2z - 4) = 0$

i.e., $(1 + \lambda) x + (\lambda - 1) y + (2\lambda - 1)z - (4\lambda + 4) = 0$ which is $\perp$r to $P_1 = 0$

$\Rightarrow (1 + \lambda) + (1 - \lambda) + 1 - 2\lambda = 0 \Rightarrow \lambda = 3/2$

$\Rightarrow$ Equation of the required plane is $5x + y + 4z = 20$

Equation of line of intersection of two planes

Given two planes $P_1 = ax + by + cz - d = 0$ i.e., $\vec{r}.\vec{n} = d$ and $P_2 = a_1x + b_1y + c_1z - d_1 = 0$ i.e., $\vec{r}.\vec{n}_1 = d_1$. Since the normal vectors of both the planes are perpendicular to the line of intersection. So the direction vector of the line of intersection of planes will be $\vec{n}\times\vec{n}_1$

i.e., $\begin{vmatrix} \hat{i} & \hat{j} & \hat{k} \\ a & b & c \\ a_1 & b_1 & c_1 \end{vmatrix} = \langle l, m, n \rangle$ (say)

Intersection of the planes $ax + by + cz = d$ and $a_1x + b_1y + c_1z = d_1$ with $x - y$ plane ($z = 0$) is given by pair of straight lines $ax + by = d$, $a_1x + b_1y = d_1$ and $(\alpha, \beta, 0)$ be the point of intersection

$\Rightarrow$ Equation of line of intersection of plane is

$$\frac{x-\alpha}{l}=\frac{y-\beta}{m}=\frac{z}{n}$$

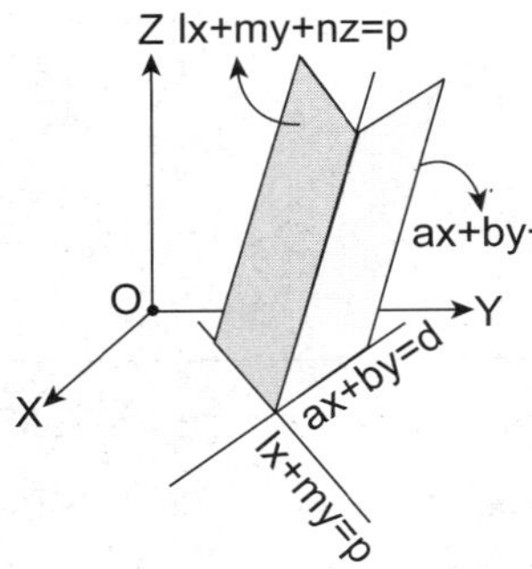

FIGURE 4.69

Algorithm to convert general equation of a line to symmetrical form

(a) **Point:** Put $x = 0$ (or $y = 0$ or $z = 0$) in the given equations and solve for y and z. The values of x, y and z are the co-ordinates of a point lying on the line

(b) **Direction cosines:** since line is perpendicular to the normals to the given planes, find direction cosines. Then write down the equation of line with the help of a point and direction cosines

Let the equation of the line in the general form be

$$a_1x + b_1y + c_1z + d_1 = 0 \quad \text{...(1) and}$$

$$a_2x + b_2y + c_2z + d_2 = 0 \quad \text{...(2)}$$

Let l, m, n be the direction ratios of the line of intersection of planes (1) and (2).

Direction ratios of normal to plane (1) are $\langle a_1, b_1, c_1\rangle$

Direction ratios of normal to plane (2) are $\langle a_2, b_2, c_2\rangle$

Direction ratios of the line of intersection AB be $\langle l, m, n\rangle$

Since AB lies in both the planes (1) and (2) therefore normal to planes (1) and (2) are perpendicular to AB.

$$\Rightarrow la_1 + mb_1 + nc_1 = 0 \quad \text{...(3)}$$

$$\text{and } la_2 + mb_2 + nc_2 = 0 \quad \text{...(4)}$$

$$\Rightarrow \frac{l}{b_1c_2-b_2c_1}=\frac{m}{c_1a_2-a_1c_2}=\frac{n}{a_1b_2-a_2b_1}$$

Hence direction ratios of line of intersection AB are

$b_1c_2 - b_2c_1$, $c_1a_2 - a_1c_2$, $a_1b_2 - a_2b_1$

let $l' = b_1c_2 - b_2c_1$, $m' = c_1a_2 - a_1c_2$, $n' = a_1b_2 - a_2b_1$

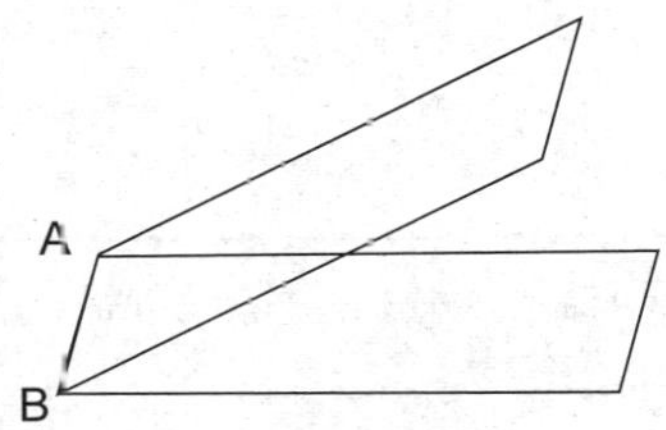

FIGURE 4.70

Direction ratios of x, y, z axes are 1, 0, 0 ; 0, 1, 0 and 0, 0, 1

If $n' = 0$, then $l'.0 + m'.0 + n'.1 = 0$ and line AB will be perpendicular to z-axis and parallel to xy-plane. Similarly, if $l' = 0$, then line AB is parallel to yz-plane and if $m' = 0$, then AB is parallel to zx-plane.

Let AB be not parallel to xy-plane

Let line AB cut xy-plane at $P(\alpha, \beta, 0)$

Then P lies on AB and hence it also lies in planes (1) and (2)

$$\Rightarrow a_1\alpha + b_1\beta + d_1 = 0 \quad \text{....(5)}$$

$$\text{and } a_2\alpha + b_2\beta + d_2 = 0 \quad \text{....(6)}$$

From (5) and (6), we have

$$\frac{\alpha}{b_1d_2-b_2d_1}=\frac{\beta}{d_1a_2-a_1d_2}=\frac{1}{a_1b_2-a_2b_1}$$

$$\Rightarrow \alpha=\frac{b_1d_2-b_2d_1}{a_1b_2-a_2b_1};\ \beta=\frac{d_1a_2-a_1d_2}{a_1b_2-a_2b_1}$$

Now direction ratios of AB are l, m, n and it passes through point $P(\alpha, \beta, 0)$, therefore its equation will be

$$\alpha = \frac{x-\dfrac{b_1d_2-b_2d_1}{a_1b_2-a_2b_1}}{b_1c_2-b_2c_1}=\frac{y-\dfrac{d_1a_2-a_1d_2}{a_1b_2-a_2b_1}}{c_1a_2-c_2a_1}=\frac{z-0}{a_1b_2-a_2b_1}$$

NOTES

(i) If $n' = 0$ and $l' \neq 0$, then point P may be taken as the point of intersection of line AB and yz-plane and if $m' \neq 0$, then P may be taken as the point where AB cuts zx-plane.

(ii) ***If one line is in symmetrical form and other in general form:*** *Let lines are* $\dfrac{x-x_1}{l}=\dfrac{y-y_1}{m}=\dfrac{z-z_1}{n}$ *and* $a_1x + b_1y + c_1z + d_1 = 0 = a_2x + b_2y + c_2z + d_2$

The condition for co-planarity is $\dfrac{a_1x_1+b_1y_1+c_1z_1+d_1}{a_2x_1+b_2y_1+c_2z_1+d_2}=\dfrac{a_1l+b_1m+c_1n}{a_2l+b_2m+c_2n}$

(iii) ***If both lines in general form:*** *Let lines are* $a_1x + b_1y + c_1z + d_1 = 0 = a_2x + b_2y + c_2z + d_2$ *and* $a_3x + b_3y + c_3z + d_3 = 0 = a_4x + b_4y + c_4z + d_4$

The condition that this pair of lines is co-planar is $\begin{vmatrix} a_1 & b_1 & c_1 & d_1 \\ a_2 & b_2 & c_2 & d_2 \\ a_3 & b_3 & c_3 & d_3 \\ a_4 & b_4 & c_4 & d_4 \end{vmatrix} = 0$

LLUSTRATION 54: Reduce in symmetrical form, the equation of the line represented by $x - y + 2z = 5$, $3x + z = 6$

SOLUTION: Let a, b, c be the direction ratios of the required line. Since the required line lies in both the given planes, we must have $a - b + 2c = 0$ and $3a + b + c = 0$

Solving these two equations by cross-multiplication, we get

$$\frac{a}{-1-2} = \frac{b}{6-1} = \frac{c}{1+3} \text{ or } \frac{a}{-3} = \frac{b}{5} = \frac{c}{4}$$

In order to find a point on the required line, we put $z = 0$ in the two given equations to obtain, $x - y = 5$, $3x + y = 6$

Solving these two equations, we obtain, $x = \frac{11}{4}$, $y = \frac{-9}{4}$

$\therefore$ Co-ordinates of point on the required line are $\left(\frac{11}{4}, \frac{-9}{4}, 0\right)$

Hence, the equation of the required line is; $\dfrac{x - \frac{11}{4}}{-3} = \dfrac{y - \left(-\frac{9}{4}\right)}{5} = \dfrac{z-0}{4}$

or $\dfrac{4x-11}{-3} = \dfrac{4y+9}{5} = \dfrac{z-0}{1}$

ILLUSTRATION 55: Reduce in symmetrical form, the equation of the line represent by $x = ay + b$, $z = cy + d$

SOLUTION: Let l, m, n be the direction ratios of the required line. Since the required line lies in both the given planes, we must have $l + m(-a) + n(0) = 0$ and $l.0 + m(-c) + n = 0$

Solving these two equations, we obtain $\dfrac{l}{-a} = \dfrac{m}{-1} = \dfrac{n}{-c}$ or $\dfrac{l}{a} = \dfrac{m}{1} = \dfrac{n}{c}$

To obtain the co-ordinates of a point on the required line, we put $y = 0$ in the two equations to obtain $x = b$, $z = d$ so, the co-ordinates of a point on the required lines are $(b, 0, d)$

$\therefore$ its equation is $\dfrac{x-b}{a} = \dfrac{y-0}{1} = \dfrac{z-d}{c}$

ILLUSTRATION 56: Find the angle between the line of intersection of the planes $\vec{r}.(\hat{i} + 2\hat{j} + 3\hat{k}) = 0$ & $\vec{r}.(3\hat{i} + 2\hat{j} + 3\hat{k}) = 0$ with the coordinate axes

SOLUTION: $d.r: \begin{vmatrix} \hat{i} & \hat{j} & \hat{k} \\ 1 & 2 & 3 \\ 3 & 2 & 3 \end{vmatrix} = \langle 0, 6, 4 \rangle$ or $\langle 0, 3, -2 \rangle$

Therefore angle with x-axis = $\pi/2$, with y-axis : $\cos^{-1}\left(\frac{3}{\sqrt{13}}\right)$, with z-axis: $\cos^{-1}\left(\frac{-2}{\sqrt{13}}\right)$

ILLUSTRATION 57: Prove that the line $x = ay + b$, $z = cy + d$ and $x = a'y + b'$, $z = c'y + d'$ are perpendicular if $aa' + cc' + 1 = 0$

SOLUTION: We can write the equations of straight line as

$$\frac{x-b'}{a'} = y, y = \frac{z-d'}{c'} \Rightarrow \frac{x-b'}{a'} = \frac{y-0}{1} = \frac{z-d'}{c'}$$

and $\frac{x-b}{a} = y, y = \frac{z-d}{c} \Rightarrow \frac{x-b}{a} = \frac{y-0}{1} = \frac{z-d}{c}$ ...(i)

we know $\frac{x-x_1}{a_1} = \frac{y-y_1}{b_1} = \frac{z-z_1}{c_1}$ and $\frac{x-x_2}{a_2} = \frac{y-y_2}{b_2} = \frac{z-z_2}{c_2}$

are perpendicular iff; $a_1a_2 + b_1b_2 + c_1c_2 = 0$

$\therefore$ (i) reduces to $aa' + 1 + cc' = 0$ (as the lines are perpendicular; given)

■ CONDITION OF INTERSECTION OF THREE PLANES

Given three planes

$P_1 = 0$ i.e. $a_1x + b_1y + c_1z = d_1$ ...(i)

$P_2 = 0$ i.e. $a_2x + b_2y + c_2z = d_2$ ...(ii) and

$P_3 = 0$ i.e. $a_3x + b_3y + c_3z = d_3$ ...(iii)

Solving the above three equations by Crammer's rule, we get

$\Delta.x = \Delta_1, \Delta.y = \Delta_2, \Delta.z = \Delta_3$

Case I: The given three planes cut at one point iff $\Delta \neq 0$. *i.e.* unique solution and the point of intersection is given by

(α, β, γ), where $\alpha = \frac{\Delta_1}{\Delta}, \beta = \frac{\Delta_2}{\Delta}, \gamma = \frac{\Delta_3}{\Delta}$

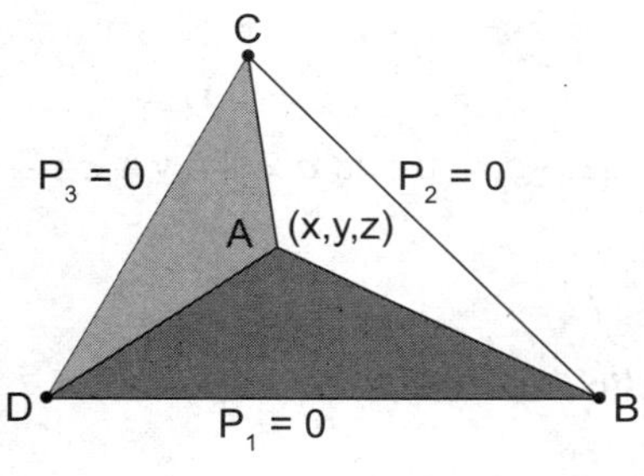

FIGURE 4.71

Case II: The given three planes does not have a common point iff set of equations have no solution.
i.e. $\Delta = 0$ and atleast one of $\Delta_1, \Delta_2, \Delta_3$ is non-zero.

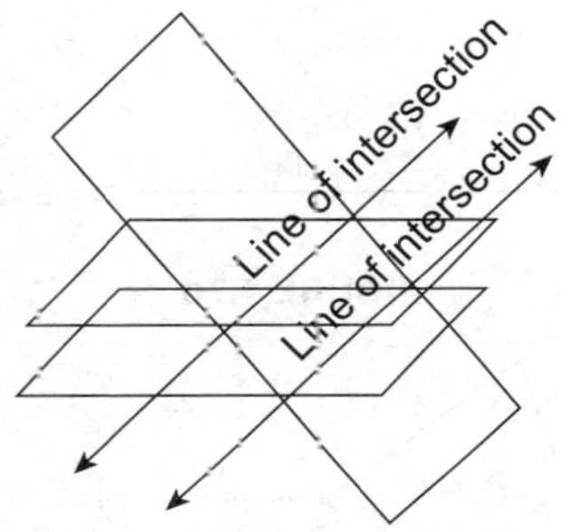

FIGURE 4.72

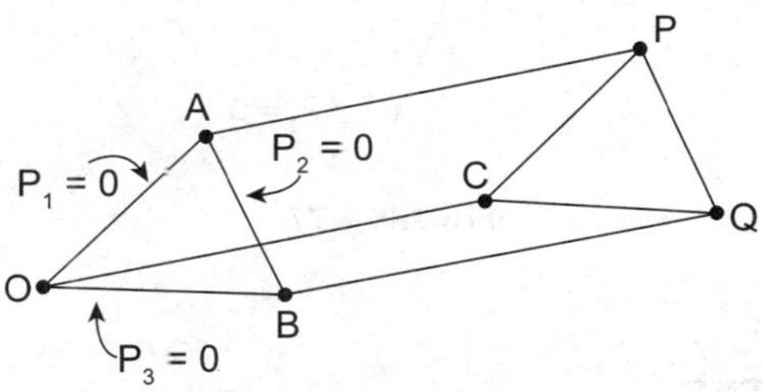

FIGURE 4.73

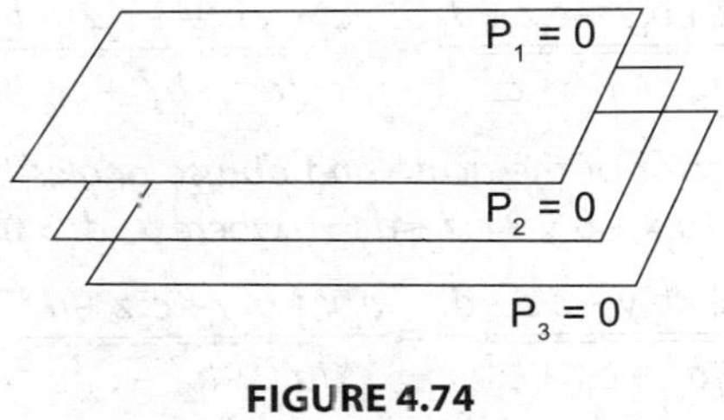

FIGURE 4.74

Case III: The given three planes have infinitely many solutions iff $\Delta = 0 = \Delta_1 = \Delta_2 = \Delta_3$.

All three row's of Δ are identical or two row's of Δ are identical

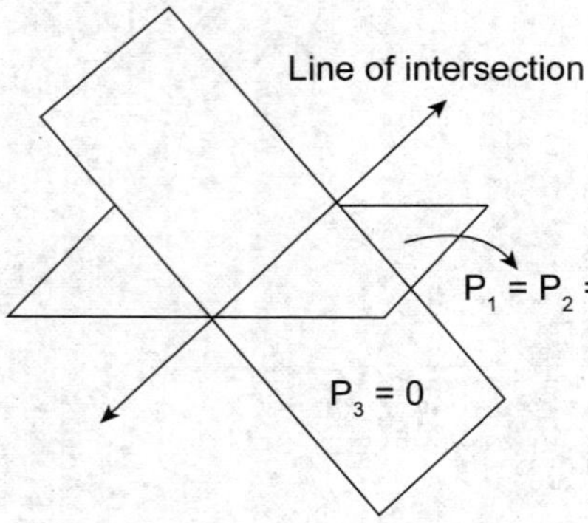

FIGURE 4.75

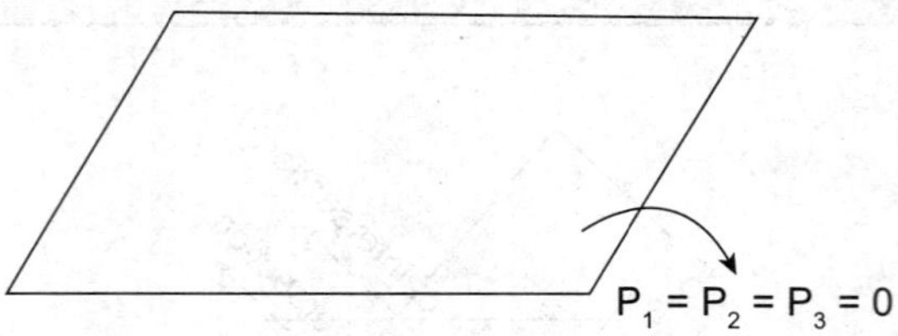

FIGURE 4.76

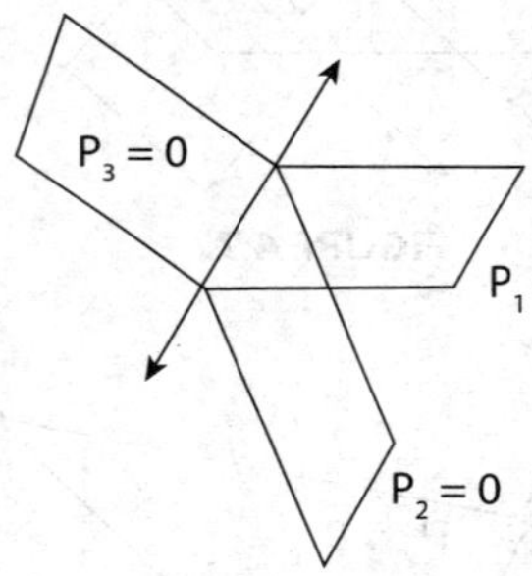

FIGURE 4.77

Equation of Bisectors of the Angle between two Planes

Equations of the bisectors of the planes

P_1: $ax + by + cz + d = 0$

P_2: $a_1x + b_1y + c_1z + d_1 = 0$

where $d > 0$ and $d_1 > 0$ are

$$\frac{|ax+by+cz+d|}{\sqrt{(a^2+b^2+c^2)}} = \frac{|a_1x+b_1y+c_1z+d|}{\sqrt{(a_1^2+b_1^2+c_1^2)}}$$

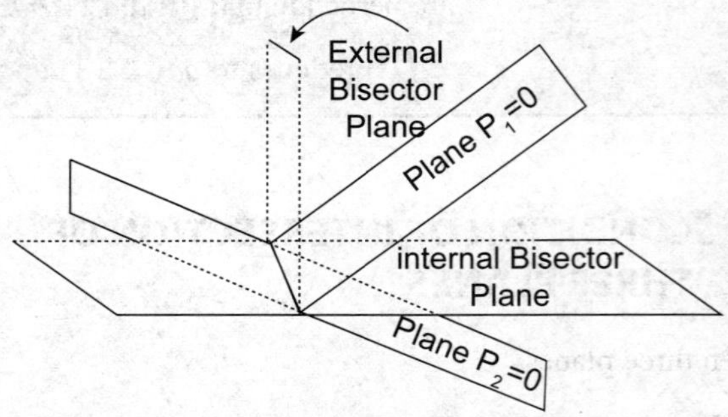

FIGURE 4.78

Conditions	Acute angle bisectors	obtuse angle bisectors
$aa_1 + bb_1 + cc_1 > 0$	–	+
$aa_1 + bb_1 + cc_1 < 0$	+	–

NOTES

(i) *Equation of bisector of the angle between the planes: $a_1x + b_1y + c_1z + d_1 = 0$ and $a_2x + b_2y + c_2z + d_2 = 0$ is*

$$\frac{a_1x+b_1y+c_1z+d_1}{\sqrt{a_1^2+b_1^2+c_1^2}} = \pm\frac{a_2x+b_2y+c_2z+d_2}{\sqrt{a_2^2+b_2^2+c_2^2}}$$

(ii) *Bisector of the acute and obtuse angles between two planes: Let the two planes be $a_1x + b_1y + c_1z + d_1 = 0$ and $a_2x+b_2y+c_2z+d_2=0$ where $d_1, d_2 > 0$*

$$\frac{a_1x+b_1y+c_1z+d_1}{\sqrt{a_1^2+b_1^2+c_1^2}} = \frac{a_2x+b_2y+c_2z+d_2}{\sqrt{a_2^2+b_2^2+c_2^2}}$$ *is the equation of acute and obtuse angle between the two planes according as $a_1a_2+b_1b_2+c_1c_2 < 0$ or > 0.*

Other bisector will be the bisector of the other angle between the two planes.

(iii) *To test whether origin lies in the acute or obtuse angle between two planes:Let the equation of two planes be $a_1x + b_1y + c_1z + d_1 = 0$ and $a_2x + b_2y + c_2z + d_2 = 0$ where Origin lies in the acute or obtuse angle between two planes according as $a_1a_2 + b_1b_2 + c_1c_2 < 0$ or > 0.*

ILLUSTRATION 58: Find the equation of the bisector planes of the angles between the planes $2x - y + 2z + 3 = 0$ and $3x - 2y + 6z + 8 = 0$ and specify the plane which bisects the acute angle and the plane which bisects the obtuse angle.

SOLUTION: The two given planes are $2x - y + 2z + 3 = 0$ and $3x - 2y + 6z + 8 = 0$, where $d_1, d_2 > 0$ and $a_1a_2 + b_1b_2 + c_1c_2 = 6 + 2 + 12 > 0$

$$\therefore \quad \frac{a_1x+b_1y+c_1z+d_1}{\sqrt{a_1^2+b_1^2+c_1^2}} = \frac{a_2x+b_2y+c_2z+d_2}{\sqrt{a_2^2+b_2^2+c_2^2}} \qquad \text{(obtuse angle bisector)}$$

$$\text{and } \frac{a_1x+b_1y+c_1z+d_1}{\sqrt{a_2^2+b_2^2+c_2^2}} = \frac{-(a_2x+b_2y+c_2z+d_2)}{\sqrt{a_2^2+b_2^2+c_2^2}} \qquad \text{(acute angle bisector)}$$

$$\text{i.e., } \frac{2x-y+2z+3}{\sqrt{4+1+4}} = \pm\frac{3x-2y+6z+8}{\sqrt{9+4+36}}$$

$\Rightarrow$ $(14x - 7y + 14z + 21) = \pm (9x - 6y + 18z + 24)$

Taking positive sign on the right hand side,

we get $5x - y - 4z - 3 = 0$ (obtuse angle bisector)

and taking negative sign on the right hand side,

we get $23x - 13y + 32z + 45 = 0$ (acute angle bisector)

ILLUSTRATION 59: Find the plane which bisects the obtuse angle between the planes $4x - 3y + 12z + 13 = 0$ and $x + 2y + 2z = 9$.

SOLUTION: Given planes are

$4x - 3y + 12z + 13 = 0$ .... (i)

and $x + 2y + 2z = 9$ .... (ii)

The equations of bisecting planes are $\dfrac{x+2y+2z-9}{\sqrt{1^2+2^2+2^2}} = \pm\dfrac{4x-3y+12z+13}{\sqrt{4^2+3^2+12^2}}$

$\Rightarrow$ $13(x + 2y + 2z - 9) = \pm 3(4x - 3y + 12z + 13)$

$\Rightarrow$ $13x + 26y + 26z - 117 = \pm 12x - 9y + 36z + 39)$

$\Rightarrow$ $x + 35y - 10z = 156$ [taking +ve sign] ....(iii)

and $25x + 17y + 62z = 78$ [taking –ve sign] ....(iv)

let θ be the angle between the planes (ii) and (iv), then

$$\cos\theta = \left(\frac{1}{3}\right)\left(\frac{25}{\sqrt{4758}}\right) + \left(\frac{2}{3}\right)\left(\frac{17}{\sqrt{4758}}\right) + \frac{2}{3}\left(\frac{62}{\sqrt{4578}}\right) = \frac{61}{\sqrt{4578}} > \frac{1}{\sqrt{2}} = \cos 45°$$

$\Rightarrow$ $\theta < 45°$

Hence (iv) is the bisector of the acute angle between the given planes.

$\Rightarrow$ plane (iii) *i.e.*, $x + 35y - 10z = 156$ is the bisector of obtuse angle between the planes.

TEXTUAL EXERCISE 9: (SUBJECTIVE)

1. Find the equation of the plane passing through the intersection of the planes $x + y + z = 6$ and $2x + 3y + 4z = 5$ and the point (1, 1, 1).

2. Find the reflection of the plane $2x - 3y + 4z - 3 = 0$ in the plane $x - y + z - 3 = 0$.

3. Find the equation of the plane, passing through the line of intersection of the planes $P \equiv ax + by + cz + d = 0$ and $P' \equiv a'x + b'y + c'z + d' = 0$ and parallel to x-axis.

Answer Key

1. $10x + 13y + 16z - 39 = 0$ 2. $4x - 3y + 2z - 15 = 0$ 3. $P/a = P'/a'$

TEXTUAL EXERCISE 6: (OBJECTIVE)

1. The plane $2x - (1 + \lambda)y + 3z = 0$ passes through the intersection of the planes
   (a) $2x - y = 0$ and $y - 3z = 0$
   (b) $2x + y = 0$ and $y + 3z = 0$
   (c) $2x - y = 0$ and $y + 3z = 0$
   (d) None of these

2. The equation of the plane passing through the intersection of the planes $2x - 3y + z - 4 = 0$ and $x - y + z + 1 = 0$ and perpendicular to the plane $x + 2y - 3z + 6 = 0$, is
   (a) $x + 5y + 3z + 23 = 0$
   (b) $x - 5y - 3z - 23 = 0$
   (c) $x - 5y + 3z - 23 = 0$
   (d) None of these

3. The equation of the plane through (1, 2, 3) and parallel to the plane $2x + 3y - 4z = 0$ is:
   (a) $2x + 3y - 4z + 4 = 0$
   (b) $2x - 3y - 4z + 4 = 0$
   (c) $2x + 3y + 4z + 4 = 0$
   (d) None of these

4. The equation of the plane passing through the line of intersection of the planes $x + y + z = 1$ and $2x + 3y - z + 4 = 0$ and parallel of x-axis is
   (a) $y + 3z + 6 = 0$ (b) $y - 3z - 6 = 0$
   (c) $y - 3z + 6 = 0$ (d) None of these

5. The equation of the plane which contains the line of intersection of the planes $x + 2y + 3z - 4 = 0$ and $2x + y - z + 5 = 0$ and which is perpendicular to the plane, $5x + 3y - 6z + 8 = 0$, is:
   (a) $45x - 45y + 50z - 41 = 0$
   (b) $33x + 45y + 50z - 41 = 0$
   (c) $45x + 45y - 50z - 41 = 0$
   (d) None of these

Answer Keys

1. (a) 2. (b) 3. (a) 4. (c) 5. (b)

MULTIPLE CHOICE QUESTIONS

SECTION–I

SUBJECTIVE SOLVED EXAMPLES

1. The equation of motion of a rocket are: $x = 2t$, $y = -4t$, $z = 4t$, where the time t is given in seconds and the co-ordinates of a moving point in kilometers. What is the path of the rocket? At what distance will the rocket be from the starting point $O(0, 0, 0)$ in 10 seconds?

Solution: Eliminating t from the given equations, we get the equation of the path $\frac{x}{2} = \frac{y}{-4} = \frac{z}{4} = t$

Thus the path of the rocket represents a straight line passing through the origin for $t = 10$ sec.

We have $x = 20$, $y = -40$, $z = 40$. Let $\vec{r} = x\hat{i} + y\hat{j} + z\hat{k}$

$\Rightarrow |\vec{r}| = \sqrt{x^2 + y^2 + z^2}$

$= \sqrt{400+1600+1600} = 60$ km

2. Find the locus of a point, the sum of squares of whose distances from the planes:
$x - z = 0$, $x - 2y + z = 0$ and $x + y + z = 0$ is 36

Solution: Given planes are $x - z = 0$, $x - 2y + z = 0$ and $x + y + z = 0$

Let the point whose locus is required be $P(\alpha, \beta, \gamma)$. According to the question,

$$\frac{|\alpha-\gamma|^2}{2} + \frac{|\alpha-2\beta+\gamma|^2}{6} + \frac{|\alpha+\beta+\gamma|^2}{3} = 36$$

$\Rightarrow 3(\alpha^2 + \gamma^2 - 2\alpha\gamma) + \alpha^2 + 4\beta^2 + \gamma^2 - 4\alpha\beta - 4\beta\gamma + 2\alpha\gamma + 2(\alpha^2 + \beta^2 + \gamma^2 + 2\alpha\beta + 2\beta\gamma + 2\alpha\gamma) = 36 \times 6$

$\Rightarrow 6\alpha^2 + 6\beta^2 + 6\gamma^2 = 36 \times 6$

$\Rightarrow \alpha^2 + \beta^2 + \gamma^2 = 36$

Hence the equation of required locus is $x^2 + y^2 + z^2 = 36$

3. If the planes $x - cy - bz = 0$, $cx - y + az = 0$ and $bx + ay - z = 0$ pass through a straight line, then the value of $a^2 + b^2 + c^2 + 2abc$.

Solution: Given planes are:

$x - cy - bz = 0$, ...(i)

$cx - y + az = 0$ ....(ii)

and $bx + ay - z = 0$ ....(iii)

Equation of plane passing through the line of intersection of planes (i) and (ii) may be taken as

$(x - cy - bz) + \lambda (cx - y + az) = 0$

or $x(1 + \lambda c) - y(c + \lambda) + z(-b + a\lambda) = 0$ ...(iv)

If planes (iii) and (iv) are same, then equation (iii) and (iv) will be identical

$\Rightarrow \frac{1+c\lambda}{b} = \frac{-(c+\lambda)}{a} = \frac{-b+a\lambda}{-1}$

$\Rightarrow \lambda = -\frac{(a+bc)}{(ac+b)}$ and $\lambda = -\frac{(ab+c)}{(1-a^2)}$

$\frac{-(a+bc)}{(ac+b)} = -\frac{(ab+c)}{(1-a^2)}$

$\Rightarrow a - a^3 + bc - a^2bc = a^2 bc + ac^2 + ab^2 + bc$

$\Rightarrow 2a^2bc + ac^2 + ab^2 + a^3 - a = 0$

$\Rightarrow a(2abc + c^2 + b^2 + a^2 - 1) = 0$

$\Rightarrow a^2 + b^2 + c^2 + 2abc = 1$

4. Find the angle between the two straight lines whose direction cosines ℓ, m, n are given by $2\ell + 2m - n = 0$ and $mn + n\ell + \ell m = 0$.

Solution: $2\ell + 2m - n = 0$ ...(i)

$mn + n\ell + \ell m = 0$ ...(ii)

put $n = 2\ell + 2m$ in (ii)

$\Rightarrow m(2\ell - 2m) + \ell(2\ell + 2m) + \ell m = 0$

$\Rightarrow 2\ell^2 + 5\ell m + 2m^2 = 0$

$\Rightarrow (\ell + 2m)(2\ell + m) = 0$

Case I: $\ell + 2m = 0 \Rightarrow \frac{\ell}{-2} = \frac{m}{1}$

$\therefore$ from (i), n = $\ell \Rightarrow \frac{\ell}{-2} = \frac{n}{-2} \Rightarrow \frac{\ell}{-2} = \frac{m}{1} = \frac{n}{-2}$

$\therefore \ell_1 = -2, m_1 = 1, n_1 = -2$

Case II: $2\ell + m = 0 \Rightarrow \frac{\ell}{1} = \frac{m}{-2}$

$\therefore$ from (i), $\frac{n}{-2} = \frac{m}{-2} \Rightarrow \frac{\ell}{1} = \frac{m}{-2} = \frac{n}{-2}$

$\Rightarrow \ell_2 = 1, \; m_2 = -2, \; n_2 = -2$

$\therefore \ell_1\ell_2 + m_1m_2 + n_1n_2 = 0 \Rightarrow \theta = 90°$

5. P is any point on the plane $\ell x + my + nz = p$. A point Q is taken on the line OP (where O is the origin) such that $OP.\ OQ = p^2$. Show that the locus of Q is $p(\ell x + my + nz) = x^2 + y^2 + z^2$.

Solution: Let the coordinates of P be (α, β, γ); Q be (x_1, x_2, x_3). Dr's of OP and OQ are (α, β, γ) and (x_1, x_2, x_3).

$\because$ O, P and Q are collinear,

$\Rightarrow \dfrac{\alpha}{x_1} = \dfrac{\beta}{y_1} = \dfrac{\gamma}{z_1} = k$ (say)

$\Rightarrow \alpha = kx_1, \beta = ky_1, \gamma = kz_1$

$\because$ $P(\alpha, \beta, \gamma)$ lie on $\ell x + my + nz = p$

$\Rightarrow \ell\alpha + m\beta + n\gamma = p$

$\Rightarrow k\ell x_1 + kmy_1 + knz_1 = p$ ...(i)

Also $OP.OQ = P^2$

$\Rightarrow \sqrt{\alpha^2+\beta^2+\gamma^2}\ \sqrt{x_1^2+y_1^2+z_1^2} = p^2$

$\Rightarrow \sqrt{k^2x_1^2+k^2y_1^2+k^2z_1^2}\ \sqrt{x_1^2+y_1^2+z_1^2} = p^2$

$\Rightarrow k(x_1^2+y_1^2+z_1^2) = p^2$ ...(ii)

$\Rightarrow$ (i) /(ii) $\Rightarrow \dfrac{\ell x_1+my_1+nz_1}{x_1^2+y_1^2+z_1^2} = \dfrac{1}{p}$

$\Rightarrow P(\ell x_1 + my_1 + nz_1) = x_1^2+y_1^2+z_1^2$

So locus of (x_1, y_1, z_1) is

$\Rightarrow P(\ell x + my + nz) = x^2 + y^2 + z^2$

6. The plane denoted by π_1: $4x + 7y + 4z + 81 = 0$ is rotated through a right angle about its line of intersection with the plane π_2 : $5x + 3y + 10z = 25$. If the plane in its new position be denoted by π, and the distance of this plane from the origin is $\sqrt{k}$, where $k \in \mathbb{N}$, then find k.

Solution: $4x + 7y + 4z + 81 = 0$ ...(i)

$5x + 3y + 10z = 25$ ...(ii)

Equation of plane passing through intersection of (i) and (ii) is given by $(4x + 7y + 4z + 81) + \lambda(5x + 3y + 10z - 25) = 0$

$\Rightarrow (4 + 5\lambda)x + (7 + 3\lambda)y + (4 + 10\lambda)z + 81 - 25\lambda = 0$ ...(iii)

plane (iii) is ⊥r to (i)

$\Rightarrow 4(4 + 5\lambda) + 7(7 + 3\lambda) + 4(4 + 10\lambda) = 0$

$\Rightarrow \lambda = -1$ putting $\lambda = -1$ in (iii), we get

$-x + 4y - 6z + 106 = 0$ ...(iv)

$\because$ distance of plane (iv) from (0, 0, 0) = $\sqrt{k}$ (given)

$\Rightarrow \dfrac{106}{\sqrt{1+16+36}} = \sqrt{k} \Rightarrow k = 212$

7. Find the equations of the straight line passing through the point (1, 2, 3) to intersect the straight line $x + 1 = 2(y - 2) = z + 4$ and parallel to the plane $x + 5y + 4z = 0$.

Solution: Let a, b, c are Dr's of required line, thus equation of line passing through (1, 2, 3)

$\dfrac{x-1}{a} = \dfrac{y-2}{b} = \dfrac{z-3}{c} = k$ (say) ....(i)

$\Rightarrow (ak + 1, bk + 2, ck + 3)$ is any general point on (i)

Also, given line, that intersect (i), is

$\dfrac{x-(-1)}{2} = \dfrac{y-2}{1} = \dfrac{z-(-4)}{2} = \lambda$ ... (ii)

$\Rightarrow (2\lambda - 1, \lambda + 2, 2\lambda - 4)$ is any general point on (ii)

$\because$ line (i) and (ii) are intersecting

$a = \dfrac{2\lambda-2}{k};\ b = \dfrac{\lambda}{k};\ c = \dfrac{2\lambda-7}{k}$

$\because$ (i) is ∥ to plane $x + 5y + 4z = 0$ i.e., perpendicular to normal vector.

$\Rightarrow$ so $a + 5b + 4c = 0$

$\Rightarrow \left(\dfrac{2\lambda-2}{k}\right) + 5\dfrac{\lambda}{k} + 4\left(\dfrac{2\lambda-7}{k}\right) = 0 \Rightarrow \lambda = 2$

$\Rightarrow a = \dfrac{2}{k};\ b = \dfrac{2}{k};\ c = -\dfrac{3}{k}$

$\therefore$ Required line is $\dfrac{x-1}{2} = \dfrac{y-2}{2} = \dfrac{z-3}{-3}$

8. Find the point where the line of intersection of the planes $x - 2y + z = 1$ and $x + 2y - 2z = 5$ intersects the plane $2x + 2y + z + 6 = 0$.

Solution: $\left.\begin{array}{l} P_1 \equiv x-2y+z=1 \\ P_2 \equiv x+2y-2z=5 \end{array}\right]$. Let Dr's of intersection of planes be a, b, c

$\Rightarrow a - 2b + c = 0$ and $a + 2b - 2c = 0$

$\Rightarrow \dfrac{a}{4-2} = \dfrac{b}{1+2} = \dfrac{c}{2+2} \Rightarrow \dfrac{a}{2} = \dfrac{b}{3} = \dfrac{c}{4}$

Calculating a point which lies on both plane P_1 and P_2, $x - 2y + z = 1 \Rightarrow 2y = x + z - 1$ and $x + 2y - 2z = 5 \Rightarrow 2y = -x + 2z + 5$

$\Rightarrow x + z - 1 = -x + 2z + 5 \Rightarrow 2x = z + 6$

Now, $z = 0 \Rightarrow x = 3 \Rightarrow y = 1$

$\therefore$ Equation of line passing through (3, 1, 0) and has dr's 2, 3, 4 is

$\therefore \dfrac{x-3}{2} = \dfrac{y-1}{3} = \dfrac{z}{4} = \lambda$(say)

$\therefore$ General point on it is $P(2\lambda + 3, 3\lambda + 1, 4\lambda)$

Now, solving with plane $2x + 2y + z + 6 = 0$

$\Rightarrow 2(2\lambda + 3) + 2(3\lambda + 1) + 4\lambda + 6 = 0$

$\Rightarrow 4\lambda + 6 + 6\lambda + 2 + 4\lambda + 6 = 0$

$\Rightarrow 14\lambda + 14 = 0 \Rightarrow \lambda = -1$

$\Rightarrow P(1, -2, -4)$ is the required point of intersection.

9. Feet of the perpendicular drawn from the point $P(2, 3, -5)$ on the axes of coordinates are A, B and C. Find the equation of the plane passing through their feet and the area of ΔABC.

Solution: Equation of plane through A, B and C is

$$\frac{x}{2}+\frac{y}{3}+\frac{z}{-5}=1$$

$\Rightarrow 15x + 10y - 6z = 30$

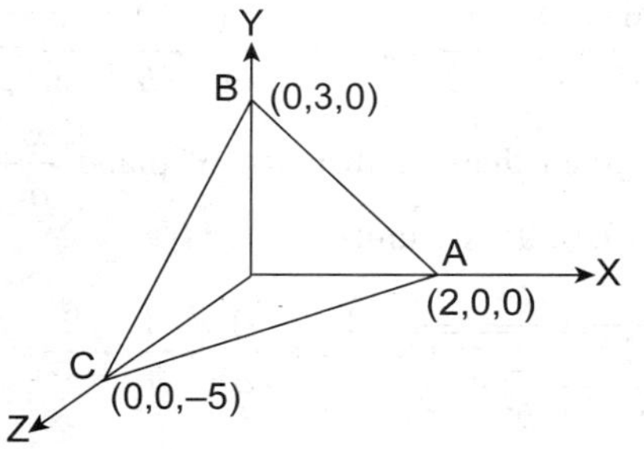

Now, $\overrightarrow{AB}=-2\hat{i}+3\hat{j}+0\hat{k}$; $\overrightarrow{AC}=-2\hat{i}+0\hat{j}-5\hat{k}$

$$\Rightarrow \overrightarrow{AB}\times\overrightarrow{AC}=\begin{vmatrix}\hat{i} & \hat{j} & \hat{k}\\ -2 & 3 & 0\\ -2 & 0 & -5\end{vmatrix}$$

$$=\hat{i}(-15)-\hat{j}(10)+\hat{k}(6)=-15\hat{i}-10\hat{j}+6\hat{k}$$

$$\Rightarrow \left|\overrightarrow{AB}\times\overrightarrow{AC}\right|=\sqrt{225+100+36}=19$$

$\therefore$ area of $\Delta ABC=\frac{1}{2}\left|\overrightarrow{AB}\times\overrightarrow{AC}\right|=\frac{19}{2}$ Square units.

10. Find the value of p so that the lines $\frac{x+1}{-3}=\frac{y-p}{2}=\frac{z+2}{1}$ and $\frac{x}{1}=\frac{y-7}{-3}=\frac{z+7}{2}$ are in the same plane. For this value of p, find the coordinates of their point of intersection and the equation of the plane containing them.

Solution: let the dr's of the required plane be a, b, c

$\Rightarrow -3a + 2b + c = 0$ and $a - 3b + 2c = 0$

$$\Rightarrow \frac{a}{4+3}=\frac{b}{1+6}=\frac{c}{9-2} \quad \Rightarrow \frac{a}{7}=\frac{b}{7}=\frac{c}{7}$$

$\Rightarrow a = b = c$

Equation of plane passing through $(0, 7, -7)$ and having dr's $(1, 1, 1)$ is $1(x - 0) + 1(y - 7) + 1(z + 7) = 0$

$\Rightarrow x + y + z = 0$; If also contains point $(-1, p, -2)$

$\Rightarrow -1 + p - 2 = 0 \quad \Rightarrow p = 3$

$\therefore$ Equation of the first line is

$$L_1 \equiv \frac{x+1}{-3}=\frac{y-3}{2}=\frac{z+2}{1}=\lambda \text{ (say)}$$

$\Rightarrow$ General point on line L_1 is $(-3\lambda - 1, 2\lambda + 3, \lambda - 2)$

and $L_2 \equiv \frac{x}{1}=\frac{y-7}{-3}=\frac{z+7}{2}=\mu$ (say)

$\Rightarrow$ General point on line L_2 is $(\mu, -3\mu + 7, 2\mu - 7)$

Now, Solving for point of intersection of line L_1 and L_1, we have $-3\lambda - 1 = \mu$,

$\Rightarrow 3\lambda + \mu + 1 = 0$; $\lambda - 2 = 2\mu - 7$

$\Rightarrow \lambda - 2\mu + 5 = 0$ and $2\lambda + 3 = -3\mu + 7$

$\Rightarrow$ On solving above equations, we get $\lambda = -1$, $\mu = 2$

$\therefore$ Point of intersection $\equiv (2, 1, -3)$

11. Find the equation of the line of greatest slope through the point $(7, 2, -1)$ in the plane $x - 2y + 3z = 0$ assuming that the axes are so placed that the plane $2x + 3y - 4z = 0$ is horizontal.

Solution: Let L be the Line of intersection of the planes

$P_1 : x - 2y + 3z = 0$ and

$P_2 : 2x + 3y - 4z = 0$

Further let a, bc are Dr's of L

$\Rightarrow a - 2b + 3c = 0$ and $2a + 3b - 4c = 0$

$$\Rightarrow \frac{a}{\begin{vmatrix}-2 & 3\\ 3 & -4\end{vmatrix}}=\frac{b}{-\begin{vmatrix}1 & 3\\ 2 & -4\end{vmatrix}}=\frac{c}{\begin{vmatrix}1 & -2\\ 2 & 3\end{vmatrix}} \Rightarrow \frac{a}{-1}=\frac{b}{10}=\frac{c}{7}$$

$\Rightarrow$ Required line L is $\frac{x-7}{\ell}=\frac{y-2}{m}=\frac{z+1}{n}$

Now $<\ell, m, n>$ are the dr's of the required line L

$\Rightarrow \ell - 2m + 3n = 0$ and $-\ell + 10m + 7n = 0$

$$\Rightarrow \frac{\ell}{\begin{vmatrix}-2 & 3\\ 10 & 7\end{vmatrix}}=\frac{m}{-\begin{vmatrix}1 & 3\\ -1 & 7\end{vmatrix}}=\frac{n}{\begin{vmatrix}1 & -2\\ -1 & 10\end{vmatrix}}$$

$$\Rightarrow \frac{\ell}{-44}=\frac{m}{-10}=\frac{n}{8} \quad \Rightarrow \frac{\ell}{22}=\frac{m}{5}=\frac{n}{-4}$$

$\Rightarrow$ required line: $\frac{x-7}{22}=\frac{y-2}{5}=\frac{z+1}{-4}$

12. The position vectors of the four angular points of a tetrahedron $OABC$ are $(0, 0, 0)$; $(0, 0, 2)$; $(0, 4, 0)$ and $(6, 0, 0)$ respectively. A point P inside the tetrahedron is at the same distance 'r' from the four plane faces of the tetrahedron. Find the value of 'r'.

Solution: $O(0, 0, 0)$; $A(0, 0, 2)$; $B(0, 4, 0)$; $C(6, 0, 0)$

$\therefore$ $OAB \rightarrow$ yz – plane

$\therefore$ OAC $\rightarrow$ zx – plane

$\therefore$ $OBC \rightarrow$ xy – plane

since point P is equidistant from zx, xy and yz plane. Hence, its co-ordinates are $P(r, r, r)$

Equation of plane ABC is $\begin{vmatrix} x & y & z-2 \\ 0 & 4 & -2 \\ 6 & 0 & -2 \end{vmatrix} = 0$

$\Rightarrow -8x - 12y - 24(z-2) = 0$

$\Rightarrow 2x + 3y + 6z = 12$

P is also at distance r from plane ABC.

$\frac{|2r+3r+6r-12|}{\sqrt{4+9+36}} = r \Rightarrow \frac{|11r-12|}{\sqrt{49}} = r$

$\Rightarrow |11r - 12| = 7r \Rightarrow 11r - 12 = \pm 7r$

$\Rightarrow r = \frac{12}{18}, \frac{12}{4}$ $(\because r < 2) \Rightarrow r = 2/3$

13. The line $\frac{x+6}{5} = \frac{y+10}{3} = \frac{z+14}{8}$ is the hypotenuse of an isosceles right angled triangle whose opposite vertex is (7, 2, 4). Find the equation of the remaining sides.

Solution: $\frac{x+6}{5} = \frac{y+10}{3} = \frac{z+14}{8} = \lambda$(say)

General point on above line is $(5\lambda - 6, 3\lambda - 10, 8\lambda - 14)$.

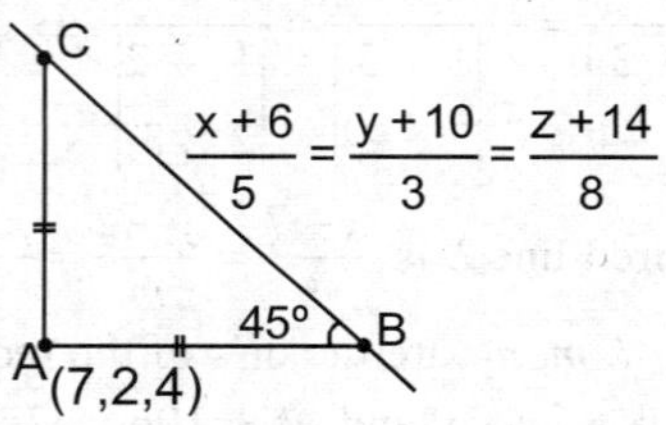

Let $B \equiv (5\lambda - 6, 3\lambda - 10, 8\lambda - 14)$

dr's of line AB are $<(5\lambda - 6 - 7), (3\lambda - 10 - 2), (8\lambda - 14 - 4)>$ i.e., $<5\lambda - 13, 3\lambda - 12, 8\lambda - 18>$

Also, dr's of line BC are <5, 3, 8>

Since angle between AB and BC is $\pi/4$

$$\Rightarrow \cos\frac{\pi}{4} = \frac{|(5\lambda-13)5+3(3\lambda-12)+8(8\lambda-18)|}{\sqrt{5^2+3^2+8^2}.\sqrt{(5\lambda-13)^2+(3\lambda-12)^2+(8\lambda-18)^2}}$$

$$\Rightarrow \frac{1}{\sqrt{2}} = \frac{|25\lambda+9\lambda+64\lambda-65-36-144|}{\sqrt{98}\sqrt{(5\lambda-13)^2+(3\lambda-12)^2+(8\lambda-18)^2}}$$

Solving above equation we get $\lambda = 3, 2$

Hence equation of line are

$\frac{x-7}{2} = \frac{y-2}{-3} = \frac{z-4}{6}$ and $\frac{x-7}{3} = \frac{y-2}{6} = \frac{z-4}{2}$

14. A variable plane at a distance of 1 unit from the origin cuts co-ordinate axes at A, B and C. If the centroid $D(x, y, z)$ of triangle ABC satisfies the relation $\frac{1}{x^2} + \frac{1}{y^2} + \frac{1}{z^2} = k$, then find the value of k.

Solution: Let the equation of variable plane be $\frac{x}{a} + \frac{y}{b} + \frac{z}{c} = 1$ which meets the axes at A(a, 0, 0); B(0, b, 0); and C(0, 0, c) respectively.

Centroid of ΔABC is $\left(\frac{a}{3}, \frac{b}{3}, \frac{c}{3}\right)$ and it satisfies the relation $\frac{1}{x^2} + \frac{1}{y^2} + \frac{1}{z^2} = k$

$\Rightarrow \frac{9}{a^2} + \frac{9}{b^2} + \frac{9}{c^2} = k \Rightarrow \frac{1}{a^2} + \frac{1}{b^2} + \frac{1}{c^2} = \frac{k}{9}$ ...(i)

Also given that the distance of plane $\frac{x}{a} + \frac{y}{b} + \frac{z}{c} = 1$ from (0, 0, 0) is 1 unit

$\Rightarrow \frac{1}{\sqrt{\frac{1}{a^2} + \frac{1}{b^2} + \frac{1}{c^2}}} = 1 \Rightarrow \frac{1}{a^2} + \frac{1}{b^2} + \frac{1}{c^2} = 1$ ... (ii)

From (i) and (ii) $k/9 = 1 \Rightarrow k = 9$

15. Find the equation of the plane containing the line $2x - y + z - 3 = 0$; $3x + y + z = 5$ and at a distance of $1/\sqrt{6}$ from the point (2, 1, –1).

Solution: The given line is the intersection of planes

$2x - y + z - 3 = 0$ ...(i)

and $3x + y + z - 5 = 0$ ...(ii)

Thus the plane containing given line is

$(2x - y + z - 3) + \lambda(3x + y + z - 5) = 0$

i.e., $(3\lambda + 2)x + (\lambda - 1)y + (\lambda + 1)z + (-5\lambda - 3) = 0$

As its distance from point (2, 1, –1) is $\frac{1}{\sqrt{6}}$

$$\Rightarrow \left|\frac{(3\lambda+2)2+(\lambda-1)1-(\lambda+1)+(-5\lambda-3)}{\sqrt{11\lambda^2+12\lambda+6}}\right| = \frac{1}{\sqrt{6}}$$

$\Rightarrow \lambda(5\lambda + 24) = 0$

$\Rightarrow \lambda = 0, -24/5$

$\therefore$ Required planes are $2x - y + z - 3 = 0$ and $62x + 29y + 19z - 105 = 0$

16. Let an incident ray is along the unit vector $\hat{v}$ and the reflected ray is along the unit vector $\hat{w}$. The normal is along unit vector $\hat{a}$ outwards. Express $\hat{w}$ in terms of $\hat{a}$ and $\hat{v}$

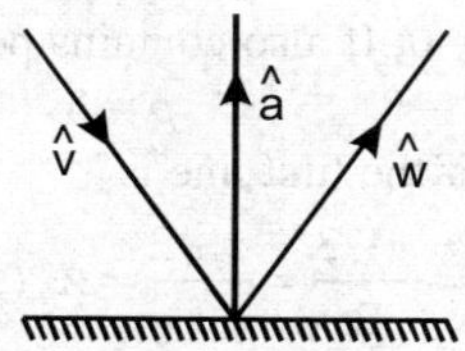

Solution: We know that the incident ray, reflected ray and normal lie in a plane and angle of incidence = angle of reflection.

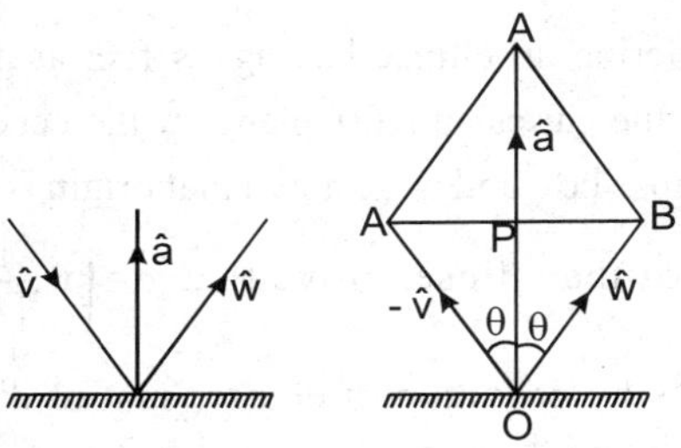

Thus $\hat{a}$ will be along the angle bisector of $\hat{w}$ & $-\hat{v}$

$$\therefore \quad \hat{a}=\frac{\hat{w}-\hat{v}}{|\hat{w}-\hat{v}|}$$

Now, $|\hat{w}-\hat{v}| = OC = 2OP = 2|\hat{w}|\cos\theta = 2\cos\theta$

$$\Rightarrow \hat{a}=\frac{\hat{w}-\hat{v}}{2\cos\theta} \qquad \Rightarrow \hat{w}=\hat{v}+2\cos\theta\,\hat{a}$$

$$\Rightarrow \hat{w}=\hat{v}-2(\hat{a}.\hat{v})\hat{a} \quad (\hat{a}.\hat{v}=-\cos\ )$$

17. The plane $ax + by = 0$ is rotated through an angle α about its line of intersection with the plane $z = 0$. Show that the equation to the plane in new position is

$$ax+by\pm z\sqrt{a^2+b^2}\tan\alpha=0$$

Solution: Given planes are $ax + by = 0$ ...(i)

and $z = 0$ ...(ii)

$\therefore$ Equation of any plane passing through the line of intersection of planes (i) and (ii) may be taken as;

$ax + by + kz = 0$ ...(iii)

The direction cosines of normal to the plane (iii) are:

$$\left\langle \frac{a}{\sqrt{a^2+b^2+k^2}}, \frac{b}{\sqrt{a^2+b^2+k^2}}, \frac{k}{\sqrt{a^2+b^2+k^2}} \right\rangle$$

The direction cosines of normal to the plane (i) are: $\left\langle \frac{a}{\sqrt{a^2+b^2}}, \frac{b}{\sqrt{a^2+b^2}}, 0 \right\rangle$

Since the angle between the planes (i) and (iii) is α,

$$\Rightarrow \cos\alpha=\frac{a.a+b.b+k.0}{\sqrt{a^2+b^2+k^2}\sqrt{a^2+b^2}}=\sqrt{\frac{a^2+b^2}{a^2+b^2+k^2}}$$

$$\Rightarrow k^2\cos^2\alpha = a^2(1-\cos^2\alpha)+b^2(1-\cos^2\alpha)$$

$$\Rightarrow k^2=\frac{(a^2+b^2)\sin^2\alpha}{\cos^2\alpha} \Rightarrow k=\pm\sqrt{a^2+b^2}\tan\alpha$$

putting in (iii) we get, equation of plane as;

$$ax+by\pm z\sqrt{a^2+b^2}\tan\alpha=0$$

18. Assuming the plane $4x - 3y + 7z = 0$ to be horizontal, find the equation of the line of greatest slope through the point (2, 1, 1) in the plane $2x + y - 5z = 0$.

Solution: The required line passing through the point $P(2, 1, 1)$ in the plane $2x + y - 5z = 0$ and is having greatest slope, so it must be perpendicular to the line of intersection of the planes.

$2x + y - 5z = 0$ ...(i)

and $4x - 3y + 7z = 0$ ..(ii)

Let the *d.r*'s of the line of intersection of (i) and (ii) are *a*, *b*, c

$\Rightarrow 2a + b - 5c = 0$ and $4a - 3b + 7c = 0$

[as *d.*r's of straight line (*a*, *b*, *c*) is perpendicular to *d.*r's of normal to both planes]

$$\Rightarrow \frac{a}{4}=\frac{b}{17}=\frac{c}{5}$$

Now let the direction ratios of required line be proportional to *l*, *m*, *n*, then its equation be

$$\frac{x-2}{l}=\frac{y-1}{m}=\frac{z-1}{n}$$

where $2l + m - 5n = 0$ and $4l + 17m + 5n = 0$

$$\text{so } \frac{l}{3}=\frac{m}{-1}=\frac{n}{1}$$

Thus the required line is $\frac{x-2}{3}=\frac{y-1}{-1}=\frac{z-1}{1}$

19. Find the equation of the plane which is equidistant from the line $\frac{x-1}{1}=\frac{y-2}{2}=\frac{z-3}{3}$ and $\frac{x-2}{3}=\frac{y-3}{1}=\frac{z-1}{2}$.

Solution: Equation of plane which contains the line $\frac{x-2}{3}=\frac{y-3}{1}=\frac{z-1}{2}$ is

$(x - 2 - 3(y - 3)) + \lambda (2(y - 3) - (z - 1)) = 0$

$\Rightarrow x+(2\lambda - 3)y - \lambda z + 7 - 5\lambda = 0$

If the plane is parallel to $\frac{x-1}{1}=\frac{y-2}{2}=\frac{z-3}{3}$

$\Rightarrow 1+(2\lambda - 3)2 - 3\lambda = 0 \Rightarrow \lambda = 5$

So equation of plane which contains second line and parallel to first is $x + 7y - 5z - 18 = 0$.

Similarly, equation of plane which contains first line and parallel to second is $(x - 1) + 7(y - 2) - 5(z - 3) = 0$

$\Rightarrow x + 7y - 5z = 0$. Hence equidistant plane is

$$\frac{(x+7y-5z-18)+(x+7y-5z)}{2}=0$$

$\Rightarrow x + 7y - 5z - 9 = 0$

20. If a variable plane forms a tetrahedron of constant volume 64 k^3 with the co-ordinate planes, find the locus of the centroid of the tetrahedron.

Solution: Let the variable plane intersects the co-ordinate axes at $A(a, 0, 0)$, $B(0, b, 0)$ and $C(0, 0, c)$.

Then the equation of the plane will be

$$\frac{x}{a}+\frac{y}{b}+\frac{z}{c}=1 \quad ....(i)$$

Let $P(\alpha, \beta, \gamma)$ be the centroid of tetrahedron $OABC$,

then $\alpha=\frac{a}{4}$, $\beta=\frac{b}{4}$, $\gamma=\frac{c}{4}$ or $a = 4\alpha$, $b = 4\beta$, $c = 4\gamma$.

$\Rightarrow$ Volume of tetrahedron $=\frac{1}{3}$(Area of ΔOAB). OC

$$\Rightarrow\ 64k^3=\frac{1}{3}\left(\frac{1}{2}ab\right)c=\frac{abc}{6}$$

$$\Rightarrow\ 64k^3=\frac{(4\alpha)(4\beta)(4\gamma)}{6}$$

$$\Rightarrow\ k^3=\frac{\alpha\beta\gamma}{6}$$

$\therefore$ Required locus of $P(\alpha, \beta, \gamma)$ is $xyz = 6k^3$.

21. A point P' moves on the plane $\frac{x}{p}+\frac{y}{q}+\frac{z}{r}=1$ which is fixed. The plane through P' which is perpendicular to OP' meets the axes at P, Q, R. The planes through P, Q, R parallel to YZ, ZX, XY planes intersect at B. Prove that if the axes be rectangular, the locus of B is $\frac{1}{x^2}+\frac{1}{y^2}+\frac{1}{z^2}=\frac{1}{px}+\frac{1}{qy}+\frac{1}{rz}$

Solution: Let the co-ordinates of point P' be (α, β, γ); then equation of the plane through P' and perpendicular to OP is $\alpha(x-\alpha)+\beta(y-\beta)+\gamma(z-\gamma)=0$

Let co-ordinates of point B are (x_1, y_1, z_1)

Now, since (x_1, y_1, z_1) satisfies the the given condition of plane

$$\Rightarrow\ x_1=\frac{\alpha^2+\beta^2+\gamma^2}{\alpha} \quad ...(i)$$

$$y_1=\frac{\alpha^2+\beta^2+\gamma^2}{\beta} \quad ...(ii)$$

$$z_1=\frac{\alpha^2+\beta^2+\gamma^2}{\gamma} \quad ..(iii)$$

and $\frac{\alpha}{p}+\frac{\beta}{q}+\frac{\gamma}{r}=1$ ....(iv)

$$\frac{1}{x_1^2}+\frac{1}{y_1^2}+\frac{1}{z_1^2}=\frac{\alpha^2+\beta^2+\gamma^2}{(\alpha^2+\beta^2+\gamma^2)^2}=\frac{1}{\alpha^2+\beta^2+\gamma^2} \quad ..(v)$$

Put the values of α, β, γ from (i), (ii) and (iii) in equation (iv), we get $(\alpha^2+\beta^2+\gamma^2)\left(\frac{1}{px_1}+\frac{1}{qy_1}+\frac{1}{rz_1}\right)=1$

By using equation (v) locus of point B is

$$\frac{1}{px}+\frac{1}{qy}+\frac{1}{rz}=\frac{1}{x^2}+\frac{1}{y^2}+\frac{1}{z^2}$$

22. Considering an ellipse having its foci at $A(\vec{r}_1)$ and $B(\vec{r}_2)$ in the cartesian XOY plane. If the eccentricity of the ellipse be e and it is known that origin is an interior point of the ellipse, prove that $e\in\left(0,\frac{|\vec{r}_1-\vec{r}_2|}{|\vec{r}_1|+|\vec{r}_2|}\right)$.

Solution: As by definition of ellipse, sum of distances on any point on the curve from foci is $2a$

$\Rightarrow PB + PA = 2a \Rightarrow |\vec{r}-\vec{r}_1|+|\vec{r}-\vec{r}_2|=2a$ ...(i)

and $AB = 2ae$ or $|\vec{r}_1-\vec{r}_2|=2ae$ ...(ii)

from (i) and (ii) $|\vec{r}-\vec{r}_1|+|\vec{r}-\vec{r}_2|=\frac{|\vec{r}_1-\vec{r}_2|}{e}$ ...(iii)

As origin lies inside the ellipse (using $S_1 < 0$)

$$\Rightarrow |\vec{0}-\vec{r}_1|+|\vec{0}-\vec{r}_2|-\frac{|\vec{r}_1-\vec{r}_2|}{e}<0$$

$$\Rightarrow |\vec{r}_1|+|\vec{r}_2|<\frac{|\vec{r}_1-\vec{r}_2|}{e} \quad \Rightarrow \quad e<\frac{|\vec{r}_1-\vec{r}_2|}{|\vec{r}_1|+|\vec{r}_2|}$$

$$\Rightarrow e\in\left(0,\frac{|\vec{r}_1-\vec{r}_2|}{|\vec{r}_1|+|\vec{r}_2|}\right).$$

23. Show that the straight lines whose direction cosines are given by the equations $al + bm + cn = 0$, $ul^2 + vm^2 + wn^2 = 0$ are parallel or perpendicular accordingly $\frac{a^2}{u}+\frac{b^2}{v}+\frac{c^2}{w}=0$ or $a^2(v + w) + b^2(w + u) + c^2(u + v) = 0$

Solution: Here $l=-\frac{(bm+cn)}{a}$ and $ul^2 + m^2v + wn^2 = 0$,

eliminating l, we get $\frac{u(bm+cn)^2}{a^2}+m^2v+wn^2=0$

$\Rightarrow u(b^2m^2 + 2bcmn + c^2n^2) + va^2m^2 + wa^2n^2 = 0$

$\Rightarrow (b^2u + a^2v)m^2 + 2bcu)mn + (c^2u + a^2w)n^2 = 0$

$$\Rightarrow (b^2u+a^2v)\left(\frac{m}{n}\right)^2+(2bcu)\left(\frac{m}{n}\right)+(c^2u+a^2w)=0$$

which is a quadratic in (m/n) having roots $\left(\frac{m_1}{n_1}\right)$ and $\left(\frac{m_2}{n_2}\right)$

(a) If the straight lines are parallel:

the quadratic in m/n has got equal roots

i.e., Discriminant = 0

$\Rightarrow (2bcu)^2 - 4(b^2u + a^2v)(c^2u + a^2w) = 0$

$\Rightarrow b^2c^2u^2 = (b^2u + a^2 v)(c^2u + a^2 w)$

$\Rightarrow a^2vw + b^2uw + c^2 uv = 0$ or $\frac{a^2}{u}+\frac{b^2}{v}+\frac{c^2}{w}=0$

(b) If straight lines are perpendicular:

$\Rightarrow \frac{m_1}{n_1}\cdot\frac{m_2}{n_2}=\frac{c^2u+a^2w}{b^2u+a^2v}$ (product of roots)

$\Rightarrow \frac{m_1m_2}{c^2u+a^2w}=\frac{n_1n_2}{b^2u+a^2v}$

Similarly, by eliminating n, we get

$\frac{l_1l_2}{b^2w+c^2v}=\frac{m_1m_2}{c^2u+a^2w}$ ...(ii)

From (i) and (ii)

$\frac{l_1l_2}{b^2w+c^2v}=\frac{m_1m_2}{c^2u+a^2w}=\frac{n_1n_2}{b^2u+a^2v}=\lambda$

Since they are perpendicular $l_1l_2 + m_1m_2 + n_1n_2 = 0$

$\Rightarrow \lambda(b^2w + c^2v) + \lambda(c^2u + a^2w) + \lambda(b^2u + a^2v) = 0$

$\Rightarrow a^2(v + w) + b^2 (w + u) + c^2(u + v) = 0$

Hence the lines are:

(a) parallel if: $\frac{a^2}{u}+\frac{b^2}{v}+\frac{c^2}{w}=0$ and

(b) perpendicular if:

$a^2(v + w) + b^2 (w + u) + c^2(u + v) = 0$

24. T is a parallelopiped in which A,B,C and D are vertices of one face. And the face just above it has corresponding vertices A', B', C' and D'. T is now compressed to S with face $ABCD$ remaining same and A', B', C' and D' shifting to A'', B'', C'' and D'' in S. The volume of parallelopiped S is reduced to 90 % of T. Prove that locus of A'' is a plane.

Solution: Let the equation of plane $ABCD$ be $ax + by + cz + d = 0$ .... (i)

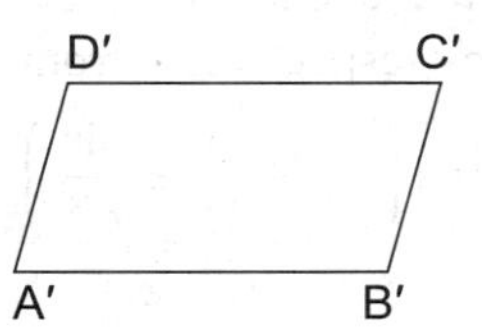

Given A'' is the new position of A' when the parallelopiped T is compressed

Let $A'' \equiv (\alpha, \beta, \gamma)$

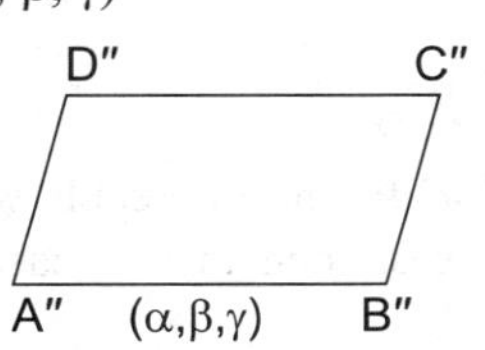

Given volume of the compressed parallelopiped S = 90 % of volume of T = (0.9) volume of T

But parallelopiped S and T have same base $ABCD$

$\therefore$ Height of parallelopiped S

= 0.9 height of parallelopiped T

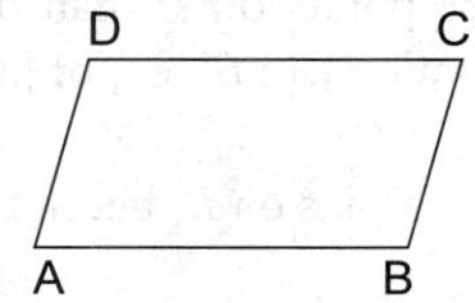

$\Rightarrow$ length of perpendicular from $A''(\alpha,\beta,\gamma)$ to plane $ABCD$ = 0.9 h

$\Rightarrow \left|\frac{a\alpha+b\beta+c\gamma+d}{\sqrt{a^2+b^2+c^2}}\right|=0.9h$

Where h is the height of parallelopiped T

Hence locus of A'' (α, β, γ) is $ax + by + cz + d = \pm 0.9\, h\, \sqrt{a^2+b^2+c^2}$

Clearly locus of A'' is a plane parallel to plane $ABCD$

25. A plane is parallel to two lines whose direction ratios are (1, 0, –1) and (–1, 1, 0) and it contains the point (1, 1, 1).If it cuts coordinate axes at A, B, C respectevily then find the volume of the tetrahedron $OABC$.

Solution: Let the equation of plane be

$ax + by + cz + d = 0$ ....(1)

Since plane (i) contains point (1,1,1)

$\therefore\ a + b + c + d = 0$ ....(2)

Since plane (i) is parallel to the lines having direction ratios (1,0,–1) and (–1,1,0)

$\therefore$ Normal to the plane is perpendicular to these lines

$\Rightarrow a + 0\,.\,b - c = 0$ ......(3)

and $-a + b + 0\,.\,c = 0$ $\therefore$ $a = b = c$

$\therefore$ From (2) , $3a + d = 0 \Rightarrow a = -\frac{d}{3} = b = c$ .....(4)

From (1), required plane is $-\frac{d}{3}(x + y + z) + d = 0$

Or $x + y + z = 3$ .....(5)

Since plane (5) cuts coordinates axes at A, B, C respectively, volume of tetrahedron $OABC$

magnitude of $\frac{1}{6}\begin{vmatrix}0&0&0&1\\3&0&0&1\\0&3&0&1\\0&0&3&1\end{vmatrix}$

$=\frac{1}{6}$magnitude of $\begin{vmatrix}3&0&0\\0&3&0\\0&0&3\end{vmatrix}=\frac{27}{6}=\frac{9}{2}$ cubic units.

26. Two planes P_1 and P_2 pass through origin. Two lines L_1 and L_2 also passing through origin are such that L_1 lies on P_1 but not on P_2, L_2 lies on P_2 but not on P_1. A,B,C are three points other than origin, then prove that the permutation $[A', B', C']$ of $[A,B,C]$ exists such that

(i) A lies on L_1, B lies on P_1 but not on L_1, C does not lie on P_1

(ii) A' lies on L_2, B' lies on P_2 but not on L_2, C' does not lie on P_2.

Solution: Given (i) A lies on L_1

(ii) B lies on P_1 but not L_1

(iii) C does not lie on P_1

(iv) A' lies on L_2

(v) B' lies on P_2 but not L_2

(vi) C' does not lies on P_2

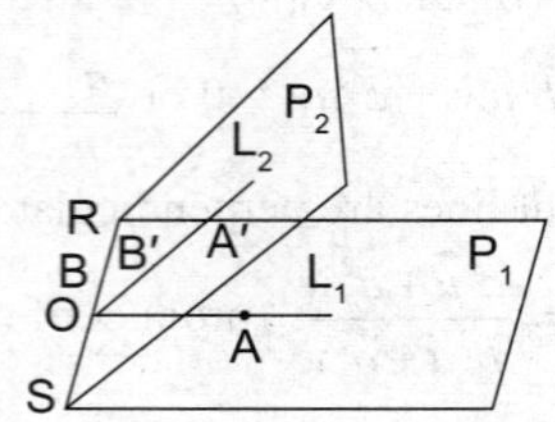

To prove $[A', B', C']$ is permutation of $[A, B, C]$ i.e., A' is one of A, B, C. B' is one of remaining two C' is the remaining third

If we take $A' = C$ and $C' = A$

$B' = B$ = a point on line of intersection RS of plane P_1 and P_2 other than point O.

Thus there exists a permutation $[A', B', C']$ of $[A, B, C]$ such that all the conditions from (i) to (vi) are satisfied.

SECTION–II

OBJECTIVE SOLVED EXAMPLES

1. The vertex A of the triangle ABC is on the line $\vec{r} = \hat{i} + \hat{j} + \lambda\hat{k}$ and the vertices B and C have respective position vectors $\hat{i}$ and $\hat{j}$. Let Δ be the area of the triangle and $\Delta \in \left[\frac{3}{2}, \frac{\sqrt{33}}{2}\right]$, then the range of values λ corresponding to 'A' is

(a) $[-8, -4] \cup [4, 8]$ (b) $[-4, 4]$

(c) $[-2, 2]$ (d) $[-4, -2] \cup [2, 4]$

Solution: (d) $\Delta = \frac{1}{2}\left|(\hat{j} + \lambda\hat{k}) \times (\hat{i} + \lambda\hat{k})\right|$

$$= \frac{1}{2}\left|-\hat{k} + \lambda\hat{i} + \lambda\hat{j}\right| = \frac{1}{2}\sqrt{2\lambda^2 + 1}$$

$$\Rightarrow \frac{9}{4} \le \frac{1}{4}(2\lambda^2 + 1) \le \frac{33}{4}$$

$$\Rightarrow 4 \le \lambda^2 \le 16 \Rightarrow 2 \le |\lambda| \le 4.$$

2. The line of intersection of planes $\vec{r}.(\hat{i} + \hat{j} + \hat{k}) = 3$ and $\vec{r}.(2\hat{i} + 3\hat{j} + \hat{k}) = 9$ is perpendicular to plane $\vec{r}.(a\hat{i} + b\hat{j} + 4\hat{k}) = 5$, then value of $a + b$ is equal to

(a) 8 (b) –4

(c) 4 (d) –8

Solution: (b) Line of intersection of given planes is along

$$\begin{vmatrix} \hat{i} & \hat{j} & \hat{k} \\ 1 & 1 & 1 \\ 2 & 3 & 1 \end{vmatrix} = \hat{i}(1-3) + \hat{j}(2-1) + \hat{k}(3-2) = -2\hat{i} + \hat{j} + \hat{k}$$

Now this is perpendicular to third plane so

$$\frac{a}{-2} = \frac{b}{1} = \frac{4}{1} \Rightarrow a = -8,\ b = 4 \Rightarrow a + b = -4$$

3. Two systems of rectangular axes have the same origin. If a plane cuts them at distances a, b, c and a', b', c' respectively from the origin, then $\frac{1}{a^2} + \frac{1}{b^2} + \frac{1}{c^2} = k\left(\frac{1}{a'^2} + \frac{1}{b'^2} + \frac{1}{c'^2}\right)$, where $k =$

(a) 1 (b) 2

(c) 4 (d) None of these

Solution: (a) Let a, b, c be the intercepts when Ox, Oy, Oz are taken as axes: then the equation of the plane is

$$\frac{x}{a} + \frac{y}{b} + \frac{z}{c} = 1 \quad ....(1)$$

Also let a', b', c' be the intercepts when OX, OY, OZ are taken as axes; then in this case equation of the same plane is

$$\frac{X}{a'} + \frac{Y}{b'} + \frac{Z}{c'} = 1 \quad ....(2)$$

Now (1) and (2) are equations of the same plane and in both the cases, the origin is the same. Hence length of the perpendicular drawn from the origin to the plane in both the case must be the same,

i.e., $\dfrac{1}{\sqrt{\dfrac{1}{a^2}+\dfrac{1}{b^2}+\dfrac{1}{c^2}}}=\dfrac{1}{\sqrt{\dfrac{1}{a'^2}+\dfrac{1}{b'^2}+\dfrac{1}{c'^2}}}$

or $\dfrac{1}{a^2}+\dfrac{1}{b^2}+\dfrac{1}{c^2}=\dfrac{1}{a'^2}+\dfrac{1}{b'^2}+\dfrac{1}{c'^2} \Rightarrow k=1$

4. The length of the perpendicular from the origin to the plane passing through three non-collinear points with position vector $\vec{a},\vec{b},\vec{c}$ is

(a) $\dfrac{[\vec{a}\ \vec{b}\ \vec{c}]}{|\vec{a}\times\vec{b}+\vec{c}\times\vec{a}+\vec{b}\times\vec{c}|}$

(b) $\dfrac{2[\vec{a}\ \vec{b}\ \vec{c}]}{|\vec{a}\times\vec{b}+\vec{b}\times\vec{c}+\vec{c}\times\vec{a}|}$

(c) $\left[\vec{a},\vec{b},\vec{c}\right]$

(d) None of these

Solution: (a) The vector equation of the plane passing through points with position vectors $\vec{a},\vec{b},$ and $\vec{c}$ is $\vec{r}.(\vec{a}\times\vec{b}+\vec{b}\times\vec{c}+\vec{c}\times\vec{d})=[\vec{a}\vec{b}\vec{c}]$

Therefore, the length of the $\perp r$ from the origin to this plane is given by $\dfrac{[\vec{a}\vec{b}\vec{c}]}{|\vec{a}\times\vec{b}+\vec{b}\times\vec{c}+\vec{c}\times\vec{a}|}$

5. The lines $\vec{r}=\vec{a}+\lambda(\vec{b}\times\vec{c})$ and $\vec{r}=\vec{b}+\mu(\vec{c}\times\vec{a})$ will intersect if ($\vec{a},\vec{b},\vec{c}$ are non-coplanar)

(a) $a\times c=b\times c$ (b) $a.\ c=b.\ c$

(c) $b\times a=c\times a$ (d) None of these

Solution: (b) The lines $\vec{r}=\lambda(\vec{b}\times\vec{c})$ and $\vec{r}=\vec{b}+\mu(\vec{c}\times\vec{a})$ pass through points $\vec{a}$ and $\vec{b}$ respectively and are parallel to vector $\vec{b}\times\vec{c}$ and $\vec{c}\times\vec{a}$ respectively. Therefore, they intersect if $\vec{a}-\vec{b},\vec{b}\times\vec{c}$ and $\vec{c}\times\vec{a}$ are co-planar and so $(\vec{a}-\vec{b}).\{(\vec{b}\times\vec{c})\times(\vec{c}\times\vec{d})\}=0$

$\Rightarrow\ (\vec{a}-\vec{b}).[(\vec{b}\ \vec{c}\ \vec{a})\vec{c}-[\vec{b}\ \vec{c}\ \vec{c}]\vec{a})=0$

$\Rightarrow\ ((\vec{a}-\vec{b}.\vec{c})[\vec{b}\ \vec{c}\ \vec{a}]=0$ $\left(\because \vec{a},\vec{b},\vec{c}\text{ are non-coplanar}\right)$

$\Rightarrow\ \vec{a}.\vec{c}=\vec{b}.\vec{c}$ $\quad\Rightarrow\ [\vec{b}\ \vec{c}\ \vec{a}]\neq 0$

6. A straight line $\vec{r}=\vec{a}+\lambda\vec{b}$ meets the plane $\vec{r}.\vec{n}=0$ in *P*. The position vector of *P* is

(a) $\vec{a}+\dfrac{\vec{a}.\vec{n}}{\vec{b}.\vec{n}}\vec{b}$ (b) $\vec{a}-\dfrac{\vec{a}.\vec{n}}{\vec{b}.\vec{n}}\vec{b}$

(c) $\dfrac{\vec{a}.\vec{n}}{\vec{b}.\vec{n}}\vec{b}$ (d) None of these

Solution: (c, *b*) A straight line $\vec{r}=\vec{a}+\lambda\vec{b}$ meets the plane $\vec{r}.\vec{n}=0$ at *P* for which λ is given by

$\left(\vec{a}+\lambda\vec{b}\right).\vec{n}=0\Rightarrow\lambda=-\dfrac{\vec{a}.\vec{n}}{\vec{b}.\vec{n}}$

Thus, the position vector of *P* is

$\vec{r}=\vec{a}-\dfrac{\vec{a}\vec{n}}{\vec{b}\vec{n}}\vec{b}$ [putting the value of λ in $\vec{r}=\vec{a}+\lambda\vec{b}$

7. The length of the perpendicular from the origin to the plane passing through the point $\vec{a}$ and containing the line $\vec{r}=\vec{a}+\lambda\vec{c}$ is

(a) $\dfrac{[\vec{a}\vec{b}\vec{c}]}{|\vec{a}\times\vec{b}+\vec{b}\times\vec{c}+\vec{c}\times\vec{a}|}$ (b) $\dfrac{[\vec{a}\vec{b}\vec{c}]}{|\vec{a}\times\vec{b}+\vec{b}\times\vec{c}|}$

(c) $\dfrac{[\vec{a}\vec{b}\vec{c}]}{|\vec{b}\times\vec{c}+\vec{c}\times\vec{a}|}$ (d) $\dfrac{[\vec{a}\vec{b}\vec{c}]}{|\vec{c}\times\vec{a}+\vec{a}\times\vec{b}|}$

Solution: (c) The given plane passes through $\vec{a}$ and parallel to the vectors $\vec{b}-\vec{a}$ and $\vec{c}$.

$\therefore$ it is normal to $(\vec{b}-\vec{a})\times\vec{c}$

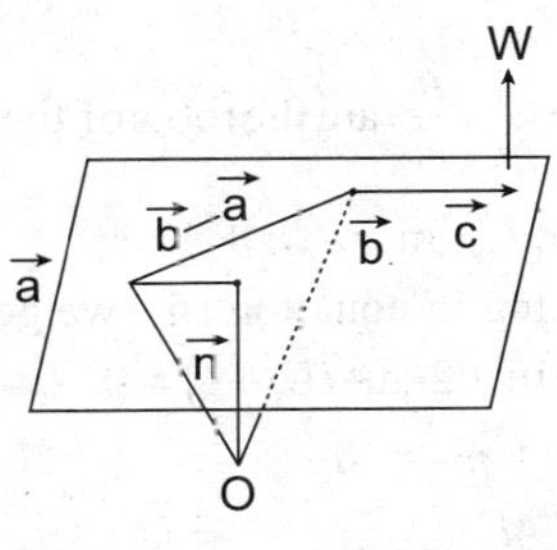

$\therefore$ Length of perpendicular from origin

$=\vec{d}.((\vec{b}-\vec{b})\times\vec{c})=\dfrac{\vec{a}.(\vec{b}\times\vec{c}-\vec{a}\times\vec{c})}{|\vec{b}\times\vec{c}-\vec{a}\times\vec{c}|}$

$=\dfrac{\left[\vec{a}\ \vec{b}\ \vec{c}\right]}{|\vec{b}\times\vec{c}-\vec{a}\times\vec{c}|}$

8. The line of intersection of the planes $\vec{r}.(3\hat{i}-\hat{j}+\hat{k})=1$ and $\vec{r}.(\hat{i}+4\hat{j}-2\hat{k})=2$ is parallel to the vector

(a) $2\hat{i}+7\hat{j}+13\hat{k}$ (b) $-2\hat{i}-7\hat{j}+13\hat{k}$

(c) $2\hat{i}+7\hat{j}+13\hat{k}$ (d) $-2\hat{i}+7\hat{j}+13\hat{k}$

Solution: (d) The line of intersection of the planes $\vec{r}.(3\hat{i}-\hat{j}+\hat{k})=1$ and $\vec{r}.(\hat{i}+4\hat{j}-2\hat{k}) = 2$ is $\perp r$ to each of the normal vectors $\vec{n}_1 = 3\hat{i}-\hat{j}+\hat{k}$ and $\vec{n}_2 = \hat{i}+4\hat{j}-2\hat{k}$

$\therefore$ It is parallel to the vector $\vec{n}_1 \times \vec{n}_2$

$= (3\hat{i}-\hat{j}+\hat{k})\times(\hat{i}+4\hat{j}-2\hat{k}) = 2\hat{i}+7\hat{j}+13\hat{k}$

9. If the direction ratios of two lines are given by $l + m + n = 0$, $mn - 2ln + lm = 0$, then the angle between the line is

(a) $\frac{\pi}{4}$ (b) $\frac{\pi}{3}$

(c) $\frac{\pi}{2}$ (d) 0

Solution: (c) Given lines are

$l + m + n = 0 \Rightarrow l = -(m + n)$ ....(i)

and $mn - 2ln + lm = 0$ ....(ii)

$\Rightarrow mn + 2(m+n)n - (m+n)m = 0$ (from eq (i))

$\Rightarrow mn + 2mn + 2n^2 - m^2 - nm = 0$

$\Rightarrow 2\left(\frac{n}{m}\right)^2 + \left(\frac{2n}{m}\right) - 1 = 0$

This is a quadratic equation in $\left(\frac{n}{m}\right)$

$\therefore \frac{n_1 n_2}{m_1 m_2} = \frac{-1}{2}$ ......(iii)

$\left[\text{where } \frac{n_1}{m_1}, \frac{n_2}{m_2} \text{ are the roots of the equation}\right]$

From eq (i), m = $-(n + 1)$

On putting in equation (ii), we get

$-(n+l)n - 2l\text{n} - l(n+l) = 0$

$\Rightarrow l^2 + 4ln + n^2 = 0$

$\Rightarrow \left(\frac{l}{n}\right)^2 + \frac{4l}{n} + 1 = 0 \Rightarrow \frac{l_1 l_2}{n_1 n_2} = 1$ ....(iv)

$\left[\text{where } \frac{l_1}{n_1}, \frac{l_2}{n_2} \text{ are the roots of the equation}\right]$

$\therefore$ From equation (iii) and (iv) $l_1 l_2 = -\frac{1}{2} m_1 m_2 = n_1 n_2$

$\Rightarrow \frac{l_1 l_2}{1} = \frac{m_1 m_2}{-2} = \frac{n_1 n_2}{1} = k$

Now $l_1 l_2 + m_1 m_2 + n_1 n_2 = k - 2k + k = 0$

$\therefore \cos\theta = 0 \Rightarrow \theta = 90°$, i.e., $\pi/2$.

10. If the direction ratios of two lines are given by $3lm - 4ln + mn = 0$ and $l + 2m + 3n = 0$, then the angle between the lines is

(a) $\frac{\pi}{6}$ (b) $\frac{\pi}{4}$

(c) $\frac{\pi}{3}$ (d) $\frac{\pi}{2}$

Solution: (d) Given $3lm - 4ln + mn = 0$ ....(i)

and $l + 2m + 3n = 0$ ....(ii)

From eq (ii), $l = -(2m + 3n)$, putting in eq (i), we get

$-3(2m + 3n)m + 4(2m + 3n)n + mn = 0$

$\Rightarrow -6m^2 + 12n^2 = 0 \Rightarrow m \pm \sqrt{2}n$

Now $m = \pm\sqrt{2}n$

$\Rightarrow l = -\left(2\sqrt{2}n + 3n\right) = -\left(2\sqrt{2}+3\right)n$

$\therefore l : m : n = -\left(3+2\sqrt{2}\right)n ; \sqrt{2}n : n$

$= -\left(3+2\sqrt{2}\right) : \sqrt{2} : 1$

Also, $m = -\sqrt{2}n \Rightarrow l = -\left(-2\sqrt{2}+3\right)n$

$\therefore l : m : n = -\left(3-2\sqrt{2}\right)n : -\sqrt{2}n : n$

$= -\left(3-2\sqrt{2}\right) : -\sqrt{2} : 1$

$\Rightarrow \cos\theta =$

$$\frac{\left(3+2\sqrt{2}\right)\left(3-2\sqrt{2}\right)+\left(\sqrt{2}\right)\left(-\sqrt{2}\right)+1.1}{\sqrt{\left(3+2\sqrt{2}\right)^2+\left(\sqrt{2}\right)^2+1^2}\sqrt{\left(3-2\sqrt{2}\right)^2+\left(-\sqrt{2}\right)^2+1^2}} = 0$$

$\Rightarrow \theta = \frac{\pi}{2}$

11. If l_1, m_1, n_1 and l_2, m_2, n_2 are DCs of the two lines inclined to each other at an angle θ, then the DCs of the internal bisector of the angle between these lines are

(a) $\frac{l_1+l_2}{2\sin\theta/2}, \frac{m_1+m_2}{2\sin\theta/2}, \frac{n_1+n_2}{2\sin\theta/2}$

(b) $\frac{l_1+l_2}{2\cos\theta/2}, \frac{m_1+m_2}{2\cos\theta/2}, \frac{n_1+n_2}{2\cos\theta/2}$

(c) $\frac{l_1-l_2}{2\sin\theta/2}, \frac{m_1-m_2}{2\sin\theta/2}, \frac{n_1-n_2}{2\sin\theta/2}$

(d) $\frac{l_1-l_2}{2\cos\theta/2}, \frac{m_1-m_2}{2\cos\theta/2}, \frac{n_1-n_2}{2\cos\theta/2}$

Solution: (b) Let OA and OB be two lines with $DC's$ l_1, m_1, n_1 and l_2, m_2, n_2. Let $OA = OB = 1$. Then co-ordinates of A and B are (l_1, m_1, n_1) and (l_2, m_2, n_2) respectively. Let $OC\ Z$ be the bisector of $\angle AOB$ such that C is the mid-point of AB and so its co-ordinates are $\left(\frac{l_1+l_2}{2}, \frac{m_1+m_2}{2}, \frac{n_1+n_2}{2}\right)$

$\therefore$ $DR's$ of OC are $\frac{l_1+l_2}{2}, \frac{m_1+m_2}{2}, \frac{n_1+n_2}{2}$

∴ We have

$$OC=\sqrt{\left(\frac{l_1+l_2}{2}\right)^2+\left(\frac{m_1+m_2}{2}\right)^2+\left(\frac{n_1+n_2}{2}\right)^2}$$

$$=\frac{1}{2}\sqrt{\begin{array}{l}(l_1^2+m_1^2+n_1^2)+(l_2^2+m_2^2+n_2^2)+\\2(l_1l_2+m_1m_2+n_1n_2)\end{array}}$$

$$=\frac{1}{2}\sqrt{2+2\cos\theta}\ [\therefore\ \cos\theta==l_1l_2+m_1m_2+n_1n_2]$$

$$=\frac{1}{2}\sqrt{2(1+\cos\theta)}=\cos\left(\frac{\theta}{2}\right).$$

$\therefore$ DCs of $\overrightarrow{OC}$ are $\frac{l_1+l_2}{2(OC)},\frac{m_1+m_2}{2(OC)},\frac{n_1+n_2}{2(OC)}$

i.e., $\frac{l_1+l_2}{2\cos\theta/2},\frac{m_1+m_2}{2\cos\theta/2},\frac{n_1+n_2}{2\cos\theta/2}$

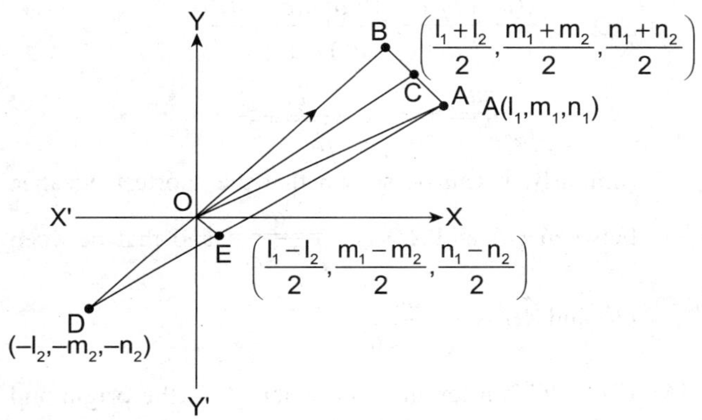

12. In above question, the DC's of the external bisector of the angle between the lines are

(a) $\frac{l_1+l_2}{2\sin\theta/2},\frac{m_1+m_2}{2\sin\theta/2},\frac{n_1+n_2}{2\sin\theta/2}$

(b) $\frac{l_1+l_2}{2\cos\theta/2},\frac{m_1+m_2}{2\cos\theta/2},\frac{n_1+n_2}{2\cos\theta/2}$

(c) $\frac{l_1-l_2}{2\sin\theta/2},\frac{m_1-m_2}{2\sin\theta/2},\frac{n_1-n_2}{2\sin\theta/2}$

(d) $\frac{l_1-l_2}{2\cos\theta/2},\frac{m_1-m_2}{2\cos\theta/2},\frac{n_1-n_2}{2\cos\theta/2}$

Solution: (c) In above figure OE is the external bisector. The co-ordinates of E are $\left(\frac{l_1-l_2}{2},\frac{m_1-m_2}{2},\frac{n_1-n_2}{2}\right)$.

Therefore DR's of OE are $\frac{l_1-l_2}{2\sin\theta/2},\frac{m_1-m_2}{2\sin\theta/2},\frac{n_1-n_2}{2\sin\theta/2}$

13. A mirror and a source of light are situated at the origin O and at a point on OX respectively. A ray of light from the source strikes the mirror and is reflected. If the DRs of the normal to the plane are 1, –1, 1, then DCs of the reflected ray are

(a) $\frac{1}{3},\frac{2}{3},\frac{2}{3}$ (b) $-\frac{1}{3},\frac{2}{3},\frac{2}{3}$

(c) $-\frac{1}{3},-\frac{2}{3},-\frac{2}{3}$ (d) $-\frac{1}{3},-\frac{2}{3},\frac{2}{3}$

Solution: (d) Let the source of light be situated at $A(a, 0, 0)$, where $a \neq 0$. Let OA be the incident ray and OB the reflected ray. ON is the normal to the mirrior at O.

$\therefore\quad \angle NOA=\angle NOB=\frac{6}{2}$

DR's of OA are $\langle a, 0, 0\rangle$ and so its DC'S are (1, 0, 0)

DC's of ON are $\frac{1}{\sqrt{3}},-\frac{1}{\sqrt{3}},\frac{1}{\sqrt{3}}\ \therefore\ \cos\frac{\theta}{2}=\frac{1}{\sqrt{3}}$

Let l, m, n be the DC's of the reflected ray OB. Then as in above question

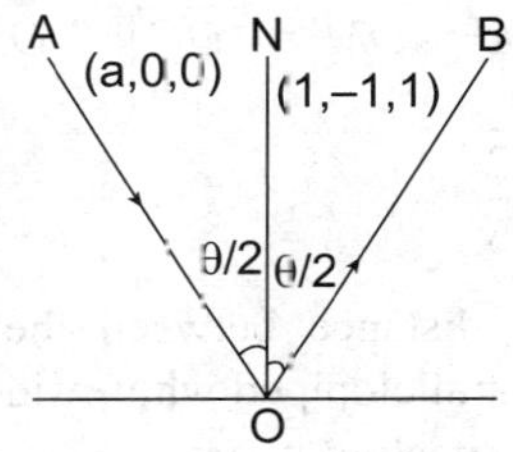

$$\frac{l+1}{2\cos\theta/2}=\frac{1}{\sqrt{3}},\frac{m-0}{2\cos\theta/2}=-\frac{1}{\sqrt{3}}$$

and $\frac{n+0}{2\cos\theta/2}=\frac{1}{\sqrt{3}}$

$\Rightarrow\ l=\frac{2}{3}-1,\ m=\frac{-2}{3},\ n=\frac{2}{3}$

$\Rightarrow\ l=-\frac{1}{3},\ m=-\frac{2}{3},\ n=\frac{2}{3}$

Hence, DC's of the reflected ray are $-\frac{1}{3},-\frac{2}{3},\frac{2}{3}$

14. The perpendicular distance of a corner of a unit cube from a diagonal not passing through it, is

(a) $\sqrt{\frac{2}{3}}$ (b) $\frac{2}{3}$

(c) $\frac{\sqrt{3}}{2}$ (d) $\frac{3}{2}$

Solution: (a) Let the edges OA, OB, OC of the unit cube, be along OX, OY and OZ respectively. Since $OA = OB = OC = 1$ unit. Therefore, $\overrightarrow{OA}=\hat{i},\overrightarrow{OB}=\hat{j}$ and $\overrightarrow{OC}=\hat{k}$

Let CM be the perpendicular from the corner C on the diagonal OP

The vector equation of $\overline{OP}$ is $\vec{r} = \lambda(\hat{i}+\hat{j}+\hat{k})$

$\therefore$ OM = Projection of $\overline{OC}$ on $\overline{OP}$

$$= \hat{k}.\frac{(\hat{i}+\hat{j}+\hat{k})}{\sqrt{3}} = \frac{1}{\sqrt{3}}.$$

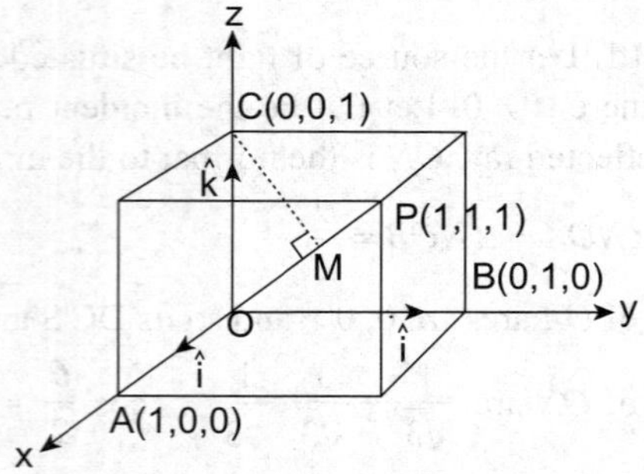

Now, $OC^2 = OM^2 + CM^2$

$\Rightarrow CM^2 = OC^2 - OM^2 = |\overline{OC}|^2 - OM^2 = 1 - \frac{1}{3} = \frac{2}{3}$

$\Rightarrow CM = \sqrt{\frac{2}{3}}$

15. The shortest distance between the diagonals of a rectangular parallelopiped whose sides are a, b, c and the edges not meeting it, are

(a) $\frac{bc}{\sqrt{b^2-c^2}}, \frac{ca}{\sqrt{c^2-a^2}}, \frac{ab}{\sqrt{a^2-b^2}}$

(b) $\frac{bc}{\sqrt{b^2+c^2}}, \frac{ca}{\sqrt{c^2+a^2}}, \frac{ab}{\sqrt{a^2+b^2}}$

(c) $\frac{2bc}{\sqrt{b^2-c^2}}, \frac{2ca}{\sqrt{c^2-a^2}}, \frac{2ab}{\sqrt{a^2-b^2}}$

(d) None of these

Solution: (b) Let one vertex of the parallelopiped be at the origin O and three co-terminus edges OA, OB, OC be along OX, OY and OZ respectively. The co-ordinates of the vertices of the parallelopiped are marked in figure.

The edges not meeting the diagonal OF are AH, AD, BD and their parallel edges i.e., BE, CE and CH respectively.

The vector equation of the diagonal OF is

$\vec{r} = \vec{0} + \lambda(a\hat{i} + b\hat{j} + c\hat{k})$ .....(1)

The vector equation of the edge BD is

$\vec{r} = b\hat{j} + \mu a\hat{i}$ .....(2)

We have,

$(a\hat{i} + b\hat{j} + c\hat{k}) \times a\hat{i} = ba(\hat{j}\times\hat{i}) + ca(\hat{k}\times\hat{i}) = -ba\hat{k} + ca\hat{j}$

$\therefore$ $|(a\hat{i}+b\hat{j}+c\hat{k})\times a\hat{i}| = \sqrt{b^2a^2+c^2a^2}$

and $\{(a\hat{i}+b\hat{j}+c\hat{k})\times a\hat{i}\}.(b\hat{j}-\vec{0}) = (-ba\hat{k}+ca\hat{j}).b\hat{j}$
$= abc$

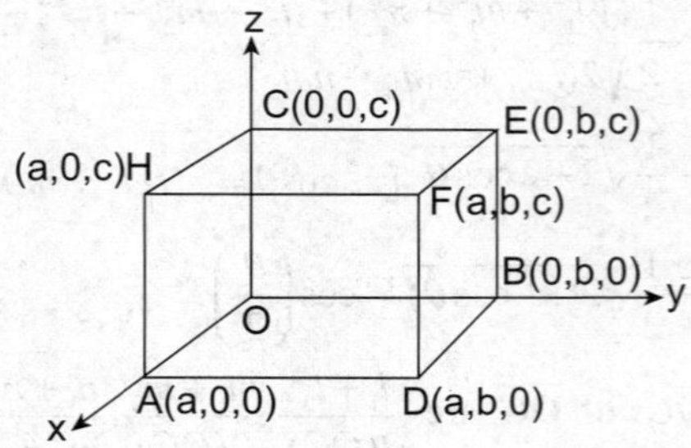

Thus, the shortest distance between and lines (1) and (2) is given by

$$S.D. = \frac{|\{(a\hat{i}+b\hat{j}+c\hat{k})\times a\hat{i}\}.(b\hat{j}-\vec{0})|}{|(a\hat{i}+b\hat{j}+c\hat{k})\times a\hat{i}|}$$

$$= \frac{abc}{\sqrt{b^2a^2+c^2a^2}} = \frac{bc}{\sqrt{b^2+c^2}}$$

Similarly, it can be shown that the shortest distance between OF and AD is $\frac{ca}{\sqrt{a^2+c^2}}$ and that between OF and AH is $\frac{ab}{\sqrt{a^2+b^2}}$.

16. If $OABC$ is a tetrahedron, where O is the origin and A, B, C are three other vertices with position vectors $\vec{a}, \vec{b}$ and $\vec{c}$ respectively, then the centre of sphere circumscribing the tetrahedron is given by the position vector

(a) $\frac{a^2(\vec{b}\times\vec{c})+b^2(\vec{c}\times\vec{a})+c^2(\vec{a}\times\vec{b})}{2[\vec{a}\ \vec{b}\ \vec{c}]}$

(b) $\frac{b^2(\vec{b}\times\vec{c})+a^2(\vec{c}\times\vec{a})+c^2(\vec{a}\times\vec{b})}{[\vec{a}\ \vec{b}\ \vec{c}]}$

(c) $\frac{b^2(\vec{b}\times\vec{c})+a^2(\vec{c}\times\vec{a})+c^2(\vec{a}\times\vec{b})}{2[\vec{a}\ \vec{b}\ \vec{c}]}$

(d) $\frac{a^2(\vec{a}\times\vec{b})+b^2(\vec{b}\times\vec{c})+c^2(\vec{c}\times\vec{a})}{2[\vec{a}\ \vec{b}\ \vec{c}]}$

Solution: **(a)** If the centre 'P' has position vector, $\vec{r}$ then $\vec{a}-\vec{r} = \overrightarrow{PA}$, $\vec{b}-\vec{r} = \overrightarrow{PB}$, $\vec{c}-r = \overrightarrow{PC}$

where $|\overrightarrow{PA}| = |\overrightarrow{PB}| = |\overrightarrow{PC}| = |\overrightarrow{OP}| = |\vec{r}|$

Consider $|\vec{a}-\vec{r}| = |\vec{r}|$

$\Rightarrow |\vec{a}-\vec{r}|.|\vec{a}-\vec{r}| = \vec{r}.\vec{r}$

$\Rightarrow a^2 - 2\vec{a}.\vec{r} + r^2 = r^2 \Rightarrow a^2 = 2\vec{a}.\vec{r}$

Similarly, $b^2 = 2\vec{b}\cdot\vec{r}$ and $c^2 = 2\vec{c}\cdot\vec{r}$

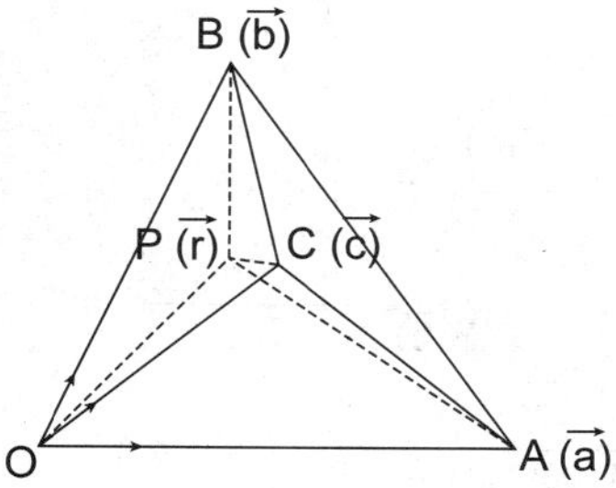

Since $(\vec{b}\times\vec{c}), (\vec{c}\times\vec{a})$ and $(\vec{a}\times\vec{b})$ are non-co-planar, then $\vec{r} = x(b\times c)+y(\vec{c}\times\vec{a})+z(\vec{a}\times\vec{b})$

$\Rightarrow \vec{a}\cdot\vec{r} = x\vec{a}.(b\times c)+y\,.\,0+z\,.\,0 = x[\vec{a}\,\vec{b}\,\vec{c}]$

$\Rightarrow x = \dfrac{\vec{a}.\vec{r}}{[\vec{a}\,\vec{b}\,\vec{c}]} = \dfrac{a^2}{2[\vec{a}\,\vec{b}\,\vec{c}]}$

Similarly, $y = \dfrac{b^2}{2[\vec{a}\;\vec{b}\;\vec{c}]}$ and $z = \dfrac{c^2}{2[\vec{a}\;\vec{b}\;\vec{c}]}$

Hence $\vec{r} = \dfrac{a^2(\vec{b}\times\vec{c})+b^2(\vec{c}\times\vec{a})+c^2(\vec{a}\times\vec{b})}{2[\vec{a}\vec{b}\vec{c}]}$

17. Let the area of a given triangle ABC be Δ. Points A_1, B_1, C_1 are the mid-points of the sides BC, CA and AB respectively. Point A_2 is the mid-point of CA_1. Lines C_1A_1 and AA_2 meet the median BB_1 at points E and D respectively. If Δ_1 be the area of the quadrilateral A_1A_2DE, then $\dfrac{\Delta_1}{\Delta}$ is equal to

(a) $\dfrac{14}{64}$ (b) $\dfrac{11}{56}$

(c) $\dfrac{12}{52}$ (d) $\dfrac{13}{48}$

Solution: (b) Let the position vectors of A, B and C be $\vec{0}$, $\vec{b}$ and $\vec{c}$ respectively. We have

$\overrightarrow{AC_1} = \dfrac{\vec{b}}{2}, \overrightarrow{AB_1} = \dfrac{\vec{c}}{2}, \overrightarrow{AA_1} = \dfrac{\vec{b}+\vec{c}}{2}, \overrightarrow{AA_2} = \dfrac{3\vec{c}+\vec{b}}{4}$

Equations of the lines BB_1, AA_2 and C_1A_1 are respectively $\vec{r} = \vec{b}+\lambda_1\left(\dfrac{\vec{c}}{2}-\vec{b}\right), \vec{r} = \lambda_2\dfrac{3\vec{c}+\vec{b}}{4}$ and

$\vec{r} = \dfrac{\vec{b}}{2}+\lambda_3\left(\dfrac{\vec{c}}{2}\right)$

For point D, we have $\vec{b}+\lambda_1\left(\dfrac{\vec{c}}{2}-\vec{b}\right) = \lambda_2\left(\dfrac{3\vec{c}+\vec{b}}{4}\right)$

$\Rightarrow \vec{b}\left(1-\lambda_1-\dfrac{\lambda_2}{4}\right)+\dfrac{\vec{c}}{4}(2\lambda_1-3\lambda_2) = \vec{0}$

$\Rightarrow 1-\lambda_1-\dfrac{\lambda_2}{4} = 0$ and $2\lambda_1-3\lambda_2 = 0$

$\therefore \overrightarrow{AD} = \dfrac{1}{7}(\vec{b}+3\vec{c})$

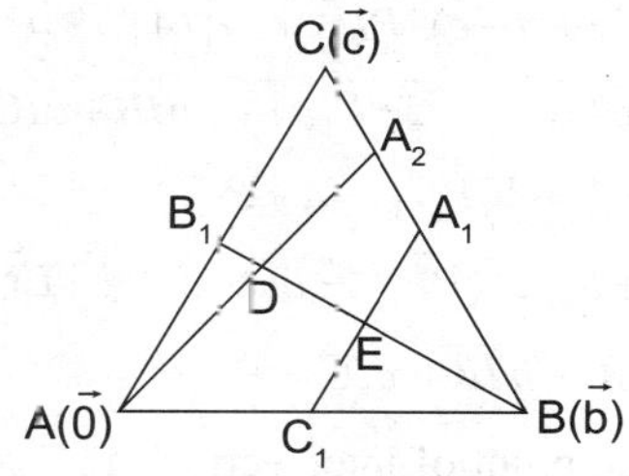

For point E we have

$\Rightarrow \vec{b}+\lambda_1\left(\dfrac{\vec{c}}{2}-\vec{b}\right) = \dfrac{\vec{b}}{2}+\dfrac{\lambda_3}{2}\vec{c}$

$\Rightarrow \vec{b}\left(\dfrac{1}{2}-\lambda_1\right)+\dfrac{\vec{c}}{2}(\lambda_1-\lambda_3) = \vec{0}$

$\Rightarrow \lambda_1 = \lambda_3 = \dfrac{1}{2} \Rightarrow \overrightarrow{AE} = \dfrac{2\vec{b}+\vec{c}}{4}$

Now $\overrightarrow{EA_2} = \dfrac{3\vec{c}+\vec{b}-2\vec{b}-\vec{c}}{4} = \dfrac{2\vec{c}-\vec{b}}{4}$,

$\overrightarrow{DA_1} = \dfrac{\vec{b}+\vec{c}}{2}-\dfrac{3\vec{c}+\vec{b}}{7} = \dfrac{5\vec{b}+\vec{c}}{14}$

Area of quadrilateral $EA_1A_2D = \dfrac{1}{2}\left|\overrightarrow{EA_2}\times\overrightarrow{DA_1}\right|$

$= \dfrac{1}{112}\left|(2\vec{c}-\vec{b})\times(5\vec{b}+\vec{c})\right| = \dfrac{1}{112}\left|10\vec{c}\times\vec{b}-\vec{b}\times\vec{c}\right|$

$= \dfrac{11}{112}\left|\vec{c}\times\vec{b}\right| = \dfrac{11}{56}\cdot\dfrac{1}{2}\left|\vec{c}\times\vec{b}\right| = \dfrac{11}{56}$ area of ΔABC

Thus required ratio is $\dfrac{11}{56}$

18. Let 'I' be the incentre of triangle ABC. Then using vector method for any point 'P', $a(PA)^2 + b(PB)^2 + c(PC)^2$ is equal to (where a, b and c have usual meanings)

(a) $a(IA)^2 + b(IB)^2 + c(IC)^2 + (a+b+c)(IP)^2$

(b) $b(IA)^2 + a(IB)^2 + c(IC)^2 + (a+b+c)(IP)^2$

(c) $b(IA)^2 + c(IB)^2 + a(IC)^2 + (a+b+c)(IP)^2$

(d) $c(IA)^2 + b(IB)^2 + a(IC)^2 + (a+b+c)(IP)^2$

Solution: (a) We have, $\overrightarrow{PI}+\overrightarrow{IA} = \overrightarrow{PA}$

$\Rightarrow |\overrightarrow{PA}|^2 = |\overrightarrow{PI}|^2+|\overrightarrow{IA}|^2+2\overrightarrow{PI}\cdot\overrightarrow{IA}$

$\Rightarrow a|\overrightarrow{PA}|^2 = a|\overrightarrow{PI}|^2+a|\overrightarrow{IA}|^2+2\overrightarrow{PI}\cdot(a\overrightarrow{IA})$ ......(1)

Similarly, $b|\overrightarrow{PB}|^2 = b|\overrightarrow{PI}|^2+b|\overrightarrow{IB}|^2+2\overrightarrow{PI}\cdot(b\overrightarrow{IB})$ .....(2)

and $c|\overrightarrow{PC}|^2 = c|\overrightarrow{PI}|^2 + c|\overrightarrow{IC}|^2 + 2\overrightarrow{PI}.(c\overrightarrow{IC})$ ....(3)

On adding equations(1), (2) and (3), we get

$$a|\overrightarrow{PA}|^2 + b|\overrightarrow{PB}|^2 + c|\overrightarrow{PC}|^2$$
$$= (a+b+c)|\overrightarrow{PI}|^2 + a|\overrightarrow{IA}|^2 + b|\overrightarrow{IB}|^2 + c|\overrightarrow{IC}|^2 + 2\overrightarrow{PI}.(a\overrightarrow{IA}+b\overrightarrow{IB}+c\overrightarrow{IC})$$
$$\Rightarrow a|\overrightarrow{PA}|^2 + b|\overrightarrow{PB}|^2 + c|\overrightarrow{PC}|^2 = (a+b+c)|\overrightarrow{PI}|^2 + a|\overrightarrow{IA}|^2 + b|\overrightarrow{IB}|^2 + c|\overrightarrow{IC}|^2$$

as $a\overrightarrow{IA} + b\overrightarrow{IB} + c\overrightarrow{IC} = 0$

(since D be point of intersection of AI with side BC) we have $BD: DC = c: b$ and $AI: ID = (a+c):a$

$$\Rightarrow \overrightarrow{ID} = \frac{c\overrightarrow{IC} + b\overrightarrow{IB}}{(b+c)} \text{ and } a\overrightarrow{AI} = (b+c)\overrightarrow{ID}$$

$$\Rightarrow a\overrightarrow{AI} = c\overrightarrow{IC} + b\overrightarrow{IB} \Rightarrow a\overrightarrow{IA} + b\overrightarrow{IB} + c\overrightarrow{IC} = \vec{0}$$

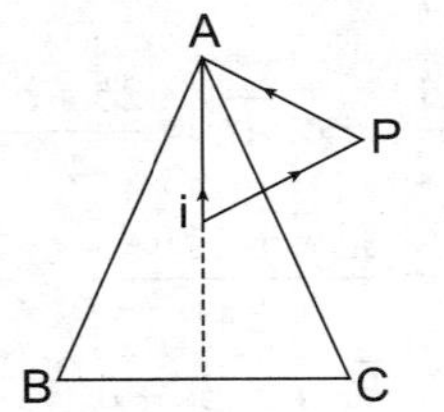

19. P is any point on the circumcircle of ΔABC other than the vertices. H is the orthocentre of ΔABC, M is the mid-point of PH and D is the mid-point of BC. Then

(a) AP is opposite side of DM
(b) DM is parallel to AP
(c) DM is perpendicular to AP
(d) None of the above

Solution: (c) Let S be the circumcentre of ΔABC.

Let $\vec{a}, \vec{b}, \vec{c}$ and $\vec{p}$ be the position vectors of A, B, C and P respectively with reference to origin S.

$\overrightarrow{SA} = \vec{a}, \overrightarrow{SB} = \vec{b}, \overrightarrow{SC} = \vec{c}, \overrightarrow{SP} = \vec{p}$

and $|\vec{p}| = |\vec{a}| = |\vec{b}| = |\vec{c}| = R$ = circumradius.

Now, $\vec{a}+\vec{b}+\vec{c} = \overrightarrow{SA}+\overrightarrow{SB}+\overrightarrow{SC}$

$= \overrightarrow{SA} + 2\overrightarrow{SD} = \overrightarrow{SA} + \overrightarrow{AH} = \overrightarrow{SH}$

($\because$ $HG : GS = 2:1$ where G is centroid)

Position vector of $H = \vec{a}+\vec{b}+\vec{c}$

So, position vector of $M = \dfrac{\vec{a}+\vec{b}+\vec{c}+\vec{p}}{2}$

$\overrightarrow{DM}$ = p.v of M – p.v. of D

$$= \frac{\vec{a}+\vec{b}+\vec{c}+\vec{p}}{2} - \frac{\vec{b}+\vec{c}}{2} = \frac{\vec{a}+\vec{p}}{2}$$

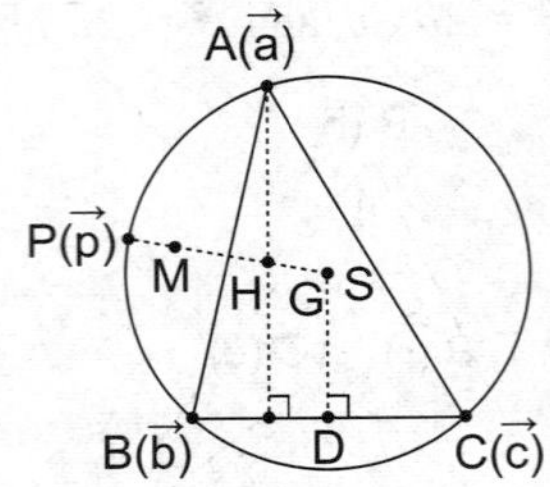

Now $\overrightarrow{DM}.\overrightarrow{PA} = \left(\dfrac{\vec{a}+\vec{p}}{2}\right).\left(\dfrac{\vec{a}-\vec{p}}{2}\right)$

$$= \frac{|\vec{a}|^2 - |\vec{p}|^2}{2} = 0 \Rightarrow \overrightarrow{DM} \perp \overrightarrow{AP}$$

20. A straight line 'L' cuts the sides AB, AC and AD of a parallelogram $ABCD$ at points B_1, C_1 and D_1 respectively.If $\overrightarrow{AB_1} = \lambda_1 \overrightarrow{AB}$, $\overrightarrow{AD_1} = \lambda_2 \overrightarrow{AD}$ and $\overrightarrow{AC_1} = \lambda_3 \overrightarrow{AC}$, then $\dfrac{1}{\lambda_3}$ is equal to

(a) $\dfrac{1}{\lambda_1}+\dfrac{1}{\lambda_2}$ (b) $\dfrac{1}{\lambda_1}-\dfrac{1}{\lambda_2}$

(c) $-\lambda_1 + \lambda_2$ (d) $\lambda_1 + \lambda_2$

Solution: (a) Let $\overrightarrow{AB} = \vec{a}$, $\overrightarrow{AD} = \vec{b}$,

then $\overrightarrow{AC} = \vec{a}+\vec{b}$

Given $\overrightarrow{AB_1} = \lambda_1\vec{a}, \overrightarrow{AD_1} = \lambda_2\vec{b}, \overrightarrow{AC_1} = \lambda_3(\vec{a}+\vec{b})$

$\overrightarrow{B_1D_1} = \overrightarrow{AD_1} - \overrightarrow{AB_1} = \lambda_2\vec{b} - \lambda_1\vec{a}$

Since vectors $\overrightarrow{D_1C_1}$ and $\overrightarrow{B_1D_1}$ are collinear, we have.

$\overrightarrow{D_1C_1} = k\,\overrightarrow{B_1D_1}$ for some $k \in \mathbb{R}$

$\Rightarrow \overrightarrow{AC_1} - \overrightarrow{AD_1} = k\,\overrightarrow{B_1D_1}$

$\Rightarrow \lambda_3(\vec{a}+\vec{b}) - \lambda_2\vec{b} = k.(\lambda_2\vec{b} - \lambda_1\vec{a})$

$\Rightarrow \lambda_3\vec{a} + (\lambda_3 - \lambda_2)\vec{b} = k.\lambda_2\vec{b} - k.\lambda_1\vec{a}$

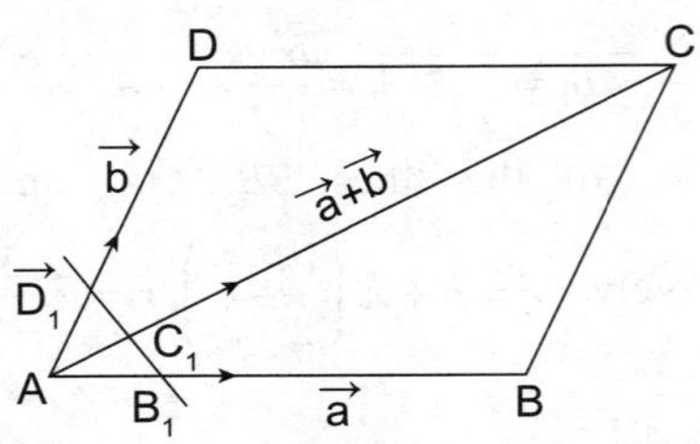

Hence, $\lambda_3 = -k\,\lambda_1$ and $\lambda_3 - \lambda_2 = k\,\lambda_2$

$$\Rightarrow k = -\frac{\lambda_3}{\lambda_1} = \frac{\lambda_3 - \lambda_2}{\lambda_2} \Rightarrow \lambda_1\lambda_2 = \lambda_1\lambda_3 + \lambda_2\lambda_3$$

$$\Rightarrow \frac{1}{\lambda_3} = \frac{1}{\lambda_1} + \frac{1}{\lambda_2}.$$

Assertion reason type

21. Consider three planes

$P_1 : x - y + z = 1$

$P_2 : x + y - z = -1$

$P_3 : x - 3y + 3z = 2$

Let L_1, L_2, L_3 be the lines of intersection of the planes P_2 and P_3, P_3 and P_1, P_1 and P_2, respectively.

Statement 1: At least two of the lines L_1, L_2 and L_3 are non-parallel. **and**

Statement 2: The three planes do not have a common point.

(a) Statement-1 is True, Statement-2 is True; statement-2 is a correct explanation for statement-1

(b) Statement-1 is True, Statement-2 is True; statement-2 is **NOT** a correct explanation for statement-1

(c) Statement-1 is True, Statement-2 is False

(d) Statement-1 is False, Statement-2 is True

Solution: (d) $P_1 :\ x - y + z = 1$ ...(1)

$P_2 : x + y - z = -1$ ...(2)

$P_3 : x - 3y + 3z = 2$ ...(3)

Line L_1 is intersection of P_2, P_3

$\therefore$ L_1 is || to vector

$$\begin{vmatrix} \hat{i} & \hat{j} & \hat{k} \\ 1 & 1 & -1 \\ 1 & -3 & 3 \end{vmatrix} = -4\hat{j} - 4\hat{k}$$

L_2 is intersection of P_3 and P_1

$$\therefore\ L_2 \text{ is } \| \text{ to vector } \begin{vmatrix} \hat{i} & \hat{j} & \hat{k} \\ 1 & -1 & 1 \\ 1 & -3 & 3 \end{vmatrix} = -2\hat{j} - 2\hat{k}$$

and line L_3 is intersection of P_1 and P_2

$$\therefore\ L_3 \text{ is } \| \text{ to vector } \begin{vmatrix} \hat{i} & \hat{j} & \hat{k} \\ 1 & -1 & 1 \\ 1 & 1 & -1 \end{vmatrix} = 2\hat{j} + 2\hat{k}$$

clearly lines L_1, L_2 and L_3 are || to each other

Also family of planes passing through the inter section of P_1 and P_2 is $P_1 + \lambda P_2 = 0$. If P_3 is represented by $P_1 + \lambda P_2 = 0$ for some value of λ, then the three planes pass through the same point $P_1 + \lambda P_2 = 0$

$x(1 + \lambda) + y(\lambda - 1) + z(1 - \lambda) + \lambda - 1 = 0$

This will be identical to P_3 if

$$\frac{1+\lambda}{1} = \frac{\lambda-1}{-3} = \frac{1-\lambda}{3} = \frac{1-\lambda}{2} \quad \dots (4)$$

taking $\frac{1+\lambda}{1} = \frac{1-\lambda}{2} \Rightarrow \lambda = -\frac{1}{3}$

taking $\frac{1+\lambda}{1} = \frac{1-\lambda}{3} \Rightarrow \lambda = -\frac{1}{2}$

$\therefore$ there is no value of λ which satisfies equation (4). The three planes do not have a common point

$\Rightarrow$ statement (2) is true therefore, (d) is correct

Passage

A: If A_{xy}, A_{yz}, A_{zx} be the area of projections of an area A on the xy, yz and zx planes respectively, then considering $\vec{A}$, a vector quantity whose direction is normal to surface A and its component along the co-ordinate axes be A_x, A_y, and A_z such that $\vec{A} = A_x\hat{i} + A_y\hat{j} + A_z\hat{k}$, therefore we can say $|A_x| = A_{zy}$, $|A_y| = A_{xz}$, $|A_z| = A_{xy}$ and hence the area $|\vec{A}| = \sqrt{A^2_x + A^2_y + A^2_z}$

$\Rightarrow A^2 = A^2_{xy} + A^2_{yz} + A^2_{zx}$

22. The area of Δ whose vertices are (1, 2, 3), (2, 4, 1), (3, 4, 5) respectively is

(a) 10 (b) 16

(c) $\sqrt{26}$ (d) 212

23. A plane makes intercepts a, b, c on x, y, z axes respectively, then twice the area of ΔABC including both its sides (a,b,c are +ve) is

(a) $\sqrt{a^2+b^2+c^2}$ (b) $\sqrt{a^2b^2+b^2c^2+c^2a^2}$

(c) $2(ab+bc+ca)$ (d) None of these

24. Through a point $P(h, k, l)$ a plane is drawn at right angle to OP to meet the co-ordinate axes in A,B,C and if $OP = p$, then the area of $\Delta\ ABC$ is

(a) $\frac{p^5}{3hkl}$ (b) $\frac{p^5}{hkl}$

(c) $\frac{p^5}{2hkl}$ (d) None of these

Solution:

22. (c) Let $A \equiv (1, 2, 3)$; $B = (2, 4, 1)$; $C \equiv (3, 4, 5)$

$\therefore$ Area of $\Delta ABC = \frac{1}{2}|\overrightarrow{AB} \times \overrightarrow{AC}|$

$$= \frac{1}{2}\begin{vmatrix} \hat{i} & \hat{j} & \hat{k} \\ 1 & 2 & -2 \\ 2 & 2 & 2 \end{vmatrix} = \sqrt{26} \text{ square units}$$

Aliter: $A_{xz} = 3;\ A_{xy} = 1;\ A_{yz} = 4 \Rightarrow A = \sqrt{9+1+16} = \sqrt{26}$

23. **(b)** Coordinates of points A, B, C are $(a, 0, 0)$; $(0, b, 0)$ and $(0, 0, c)$. Now A_x, A_y, A_z are projection area of ΔABC on plane $x = 0$, $y = 0$, $z = 0$ respectively

$$\therefore \quad A_x = A_{\Delta OBC} = \frac{1}{2}|\overline{OB}|.|\overline{OC}| = \frac{1}{2}bc$$

Similarly, $A_y = \frac{1}{2}ac; A_z = \frac{1}{2}ab$

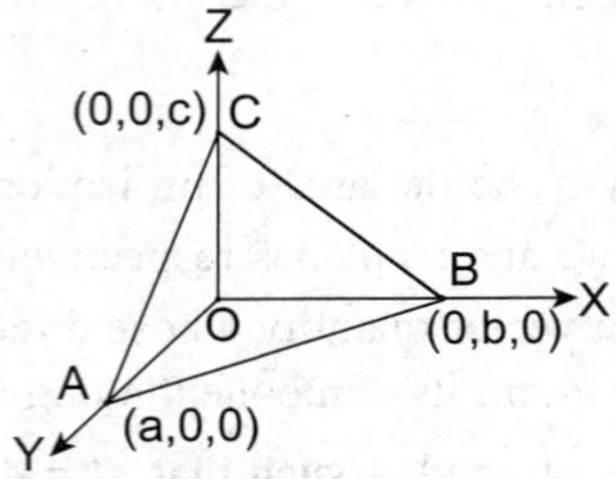

$$\Rightarrow A_{\Delta ABC} = \frac{1}{2}\sqrt{a^2b^2 + b^2c^2 + a^2c^2}$$

$$\Rightarrow 2A_{\Delta ABC} = \sqrt{a^2b^2 + b^2c^2 + c^2a^2}$$

24. (c) $OP = p = \sqrt{h^2 + k^2 + l^2}$

Direction cosines of OP are

$$\left\langle \frac{h}{\sqrt{h^2+k^2+l^2}}, \frac{k}{\sqrt{h^2+k^2+l^2}}, \frac{l}{\sqrt{h^2+k^2+l^2}} \right\rangle$$

$\because$ OP is normal to plane; equation will be

$$\left(\frac{h}{\sqrt{h^2+k^2+l^2}}\right)x + \left(\frac{k}{\sqrt{h^2+k^2+l^2}}\right)y + \left(\frac{l}{\sqrt{h^2+k^2+l^2}}\right)z = \sqrt{h^2+k^2+l^2}$$

$$\Rightarrow hx + ky + lz = h^2 + k^2 + l^2 = p^2$$

$$\therefore \quad A \equiv \left(\frac{p^2}{h}, 0, 0\right); B \equiv \left(0, \frac{p^2}{k}, 0\right); C \equiv \left(0, 0, \frac{p^2}{l}\right)$$

$$\Rightarrow A_{xy} = \frac{1}{2}\frac{p^4}{|hk|}, A_{yz} = \frac{1}{2}\frac{p^4}{|kl|}, A_{zx} = \frac{1}{2}\frac{p^4}{|hl|}$$

$$\Rightarrow \Delta = \sqrt{(A_{xy})^2 + (A_{yz})^2 + (A_{zx})^2}$$

$$= \sqrt{\frac{p^8}{4h^2k^2l^2}(h^2 + k^2 + l^2)} = \sqrt{\frac{p^8.p^2}{4h^2k^2l^2}} = \left(\frac{p^5}{2hkl}\right)$$

B: Consider the lines

$$L_1 = \frac{x+1}{3} = \frac{y+2}{1} = \frac{z+1}{2};$$

$$L_2 : \frac{x-2}{1} = \frac{y+2}{2} = \frac{z-3}{3}$$

25. The unit vector perpendicular to both L_1 and L_2 is

(a) $\dfrac{-\hat{i} + 7\hat{j} + 7\hat{k}}{\sqrt{99}}$ (b) $\dfrac{-\hat{i} - 7\hat{j} + 5\hat{k}}{5\sqrt{3}}$

(c) $\dfrac{-\hat{i} + 7\hat{j} + 5\hat{k}}{5\sqrt{3}}$ (d) $\dfrac{7\hat{i} - 7\hat{j} - \hat{k}}{\sqrt{99}}$

26. The shortest distance between L_1 and L_2 is

(a) 0 (b) $\dfrac{17}{\sqrt{3}}$

(c) $\dfrac{41}{5\sqrt{3}}$ (d) $\dfrac{17}{5\sqrt{3}}$

27. The distance of the point (1, 1, 1) from the plane passing through the point (–1, –2, –1) and whose normal is perpendicular to both lines L_1 and L_2 is

(a) $\dfrac{2}{\sqrt{75}}$ (b) $\dfrac{7}{\sqrt{75}}$

(c) $\dfrac{13}{\sqrt{75}}$ (d) $\dfrac{23}{\sqrt{75}}$

Solution:

25. **(b)** Vector in the direction of $L_1 = \vec{n}_1 = 3\hat{i} + \hat{j} + 2\hat{k}$

Vector in the direction of $L_2 = \vec{n}_2 = \hat{i} + 2\hat{j} + 3\hat{k}$

$\therefore$ Vector perpendicular to both L_1 and L_2

$$= \vec{n}_1 \times \vec{n}_2 = \begin{vmatrix} \hat{i} & \hat{j} & \hat{k} \\ 3 & 1 & 2 \\ 1 & 2 & 3 \end{vmatrix} = -\hat{i} - 7\hat{j} + 5\hat{k}$$

$\therefore$ Required unit vector

$$= \hat{n} = \frac{-\hat{i} - 7\hat{j} + 5\hat{k}}{\sqrt{1+49+25}} = \frac{-\hat{i} - 7\hat{j} + 5\hat{k}}{5\sqrt{3}}$$

26. (d) The shortest distance between L_1 and L_2 is

$$= \frac{|(\vec{a}_2 - \vec{a}_1).\vec{b}_1 \times \vec{b}_2|}{|\vec{b}_1 \times \vec{b}_2|} = |(\vec{a}_2 - \vec{a}_1).\hat{n}|$$

Where $\vec{a}_1 = -\hat{i} - 2\hat{j} - \hat{k}$; $\vec{a}_2 = 2\hat{i} - 2\hat{j} + 3\hat{k}$

$$\Rightarrow \vec{a}_2 - \vec{a}_1 = 3\hat{i} + 4\hat{k} \quad \Rightarrow \quad (\vec{a}_2 - \vec{a}_1).\hat{n}$$

$$\Rightarrow (3\hat{i} + 4\hat{k}).\left(\frac{-\hat{i} - 7\hat{j} + 5\hat{k}}{5\sqrt{3}}\right) = \frac{-3+20}{5\sqrt{3}} = \frac{17}{5\sqrt{3}}$$

27. (c) The plane passing through (–1, –2, –1) and having normal along is $-1(x + 1) - 7(y + 2) + 5(z + 1) = 0$

Or $x + 7y - 5z + 10 = 0$

$\therefore$ Distance of point (1,1,1) from the above plane is

$$= \frac{1 + 7\times1 - 5\times1 + 10}{\sqrt{1+49+25}} = \frac{13}{\sqrt{75}}$$

Matrix Match Type

28. Consider the following linear equation

$ax + by + cz = 0$

$bx + cy + az = 0$

$cx + ay + bz = 0$

Match the conditions/expressions in Column I with statements in Column II

Column I

(a) $a + b + c \neq 0$ and $a^2 + b^2 + c^2 = ab + bc + ca$

(b) $a + b + c = 0$ and $a^2 + b^2 + c^2 \neq ab + bc + ca$

(c) $a + b + c \neq 0$ and $a^2 + b^2 + c^2 \neq ab + bc + ca$

(d) $a + b + c = 0$ and $a^2 + b^2 + c^2 = ab + bc + ca$

Column II

(p) The equations represent planes meeting only at a single point

(q) The equations represent the line $x = y = z$.

(r) The equations represent identical planes

(s) The equations represent the whole of the three-dimensional space

Ans. (a) → r, (b) → q, (c) → p, (d) → s

Solution: Here we have, the determinant of the coefficient matrix of given equation as, $\Delta = \begin{vmatrix} a & b & c \\ b & c & a \\ c & a & b \end{vmatrix}$

$$= -(a+b+c)(a^2+b^2+c^2-ab-bc-ca)$$

$$= -\frac{1}{2}(a+b+c)\left[(a-b)^2+(b-c)^2+(c-a)^2\right]$$

(a) $a + b + c \neq 0$

and $a^2 + b^2 + c^2 - ab - bc - ca = 0$

$\Rightarrow (a - b)^2 + (b - c)^2 + (c - a)^2 = 0$

$\Rightarrow a = b = c$ (but $\neq 0$ as $a + b + c \neq 0$)

Thus equations represent identical planes.

(b) $a + b + c = 0$

and $a^2 + b^2 + c^2 - ab - bc - ca \neq 0$

$\Rightarrow \Delta = 0$ and a, b, c are not all equal

$\therefore$ All equations are not identical but have infinite many solutions

$\therefore$ $ax + by = (a + b) z$ (using $a + b + c = 0$)

and $bx + cy = (b + c)z$

$\Rightarrow (b^2 - ac) y = (b^2 - ac)z \Rightarrow y = z$

$\therefore$ $ax + by + cy = 0 \quad \Rightarrow ax = -(b + c)y$

$\Rightarrow ax = ay \quad (\because a + b + c = 0)$

$\Rightarrow x = y \quad \Rightarrow x = y = z$

$\therefore$ The equations represent the line $x = y = z$

(c) $a + b + c \neq 0$ and $a^2 + b^2 + c^2 - ab - bc - ca \neq 0$

$\Rightarrow \Delta \neq 0 \Rightarrow$ Equations have only trivial solution, i.e,, $x = y = z = 0$

$\therefore$ the equations represents the three planes meeting at a single point namely origin

(d) $a + b + c = 0$ and $a^2 + b^2 + c^2 - ab - bc - ca = 0$

$\Rightarrow a = b = c$ and $\Delta = 0$

$\Rightarrow a = b = c = 0$

$\Rightarrow$ All equations are satisfied by $\forall$ x, y and z

$\Rightarrow$ The equations represent the whole of the three dimensional space (all points in 3-D)

TUTORIAL EXERCISE

SECTION–III

SINGLE CORRECT ANSWERS

1. Direction cosines l, m, n of two lines which are connected by the relation $l + m + n = 0$; $2\,lm + 2ln - mn = 0$, then DC's of two lines are
(a) $\pm\frac{1}{\sqrt{6}}(1, -2, 1); \pm\frac{1}{\sqrt{6}}(1, 1, -2)$
(b) (1, 2, 3)(1, –1, 0)
(c) (1, 2, –3) and (1, –1, 0)
(d) $\left(\frac{1}{\sqrt{6}}, \frac{-2}{\sqrt{6}}, \frac{1}{\sqrt{6}}\right), \left(\frac{1}{\sqrt{6}}, \frac{1}{\sqrt{6}}, \frac{-2}{\sqrt{6}}\right)$

2. The vertices of a triangle ABC are the points (–1, 2, –3), (5, 0, –6), (0, 4, –1) respectively. Then DR's of bisector of the angle BAC are
(a) 25, 8, 5 (b) 20, 8, 5
(c) 25, – 8, 5 (d) None of these

3. Three vertices of a tetrahedron are (0, 0, 0) (6, –5, 1) and (–4, 1, 3) and centroid is (1, –2, 5) then fourth vertex is
(a) (2, –4, 16) (b) (2, –4, 18)
(c) (2, 4, 16) (d) None of these

4. If points A(4, 5, 10), B(2, 3, 4), C(1, 2, –1) are three vertices of a parallelogram $ABCD$, then coordinate of D and equation of AB are.
(a) $(3,4,5); \frac{x-4}{1} = \frac{y-5}{1} = \frac{z-10}{3}$
(b) $(3,-4,5); \frac{x-4}{1} = \frac{y+5}{1} = \frac{z-10}{3}$
(c) $(4,5,3); \frac{x-4}{1} = \frac{y-5}{1} = \frac{z-10}{3}$
(d) None of these

5. The condition for the line $\frac{x-\alpha}{l} = \frac{y-\beta}{m} = \frac{z-\gamma}{n}$ to intersect the locus of the equations $ax^2 + by^2 = 1$, $z = 0$ is
(a) $a(\alpha n - \gamma l)^2 + b(n\beta - m\gamma)^2 = n^2$
(b) $a(\alpha n + \gamma l)^2 + b(n\beta - m\gamma)^2 = n^2$
(c) $a(\alpha n - \gamma l)^2 - b(n\beta - m\gamma)^2 = n^2$
(d) $a(\alpha n - \gamma l)^2 + b(n\beta + m\gamma)^2 = n^2$

6. Intersection point of the line $\frac{x-1}{2} = \frac{y-2}{3} = \frac{z-3}{4}$ and $\frac{x-4}{5} = \frac{y-1}{2} = \frac{z}{1}$
(a) (1, 1, 1) (b) $(-1,-1,-1)$
(c) $(1,0,1)$ (d) None of these

7. Projection of line segment joining the points $(-1,0,3)$ and $(2,5,1)$ on the line whose direction ratios are $(6,2,3)$ is
(a) $\frac{22}{7}$ (b) $\frac{22}{17}$
(c) $\frac{23}{7}$ (d) None of these

8. Equation of plane through $P(a, b, c)$ and perpendicular to OP (O is origin) is
(a) $ax + by + cz = a^2 + b^2 + c^2$
(b) $ax + by + cz + a^2 + b^2 + c^2 = 0$
(c) $ax + by + cz = \pm(a^2 + b^2 + c^2)$
(d) None of these

9. Angle between planes $2x - y + z = 6, x + y + 2z = 7$ is
(a) $\pi/3$ (b) $\pi/6$
(c) 0 (d) $\pi/2$

10. Area of ΔABC whose vertices are (1,2,3); (–2,1,–4) and (3,4 – 2)
(a) $\frac{\sqrt{1220}}{2}$ (b) $\sqrt{\frac{1219}{2}}$
(c) $\frac{\sqrt{1218}}{2}$ (d) None of these

11. A tetrahedron has vertices at O(0, 0, 0), A(1, 2, 1), B (2, 1, 3) and C(–1, 1, 2). Then the angle between the faces OAB and ABC will be
(a) $\cos^{-1}\left(\frac{19}{35}\right)$ (b) $\cos^{-1}\left(\frac{17}{31}\right)$
(c) 30° (d) 90°

12. The line of intersection of planes $\vec{r}.\left(\hat{i} + \hat{j} + \hat{k}\right) = 3$ and $\vec{r}.\left(2\hat{i} + 3\hat{j} + \hat{k}\right) = 9$ is perpendicular to plane

$\vec{r}\cdot\left(a\hat{i}+b\hat{j}+4\hat{k}\right)=5$, then the value of $a + b$ is equal to

(a) 8 (b) –4

(c) 4 (d) –8

13. Image of the line $\dfrac{x-1}{9}=\dfrac{y-2}{-1}=\dfrac{z+3}{-3}$ in the plane $3x - 3y + 10z - 26 = 0$ is

(a) $\dfrac{x+4}{9}=\dfrac{y+1}{-1}=\dfrac{z-7}{-3}$

(b) $\dfrac{x-4}{9}=\dfrac{y-1}{-1}=\dfrac{z-7}{-3}$

(c) $\dfrac{x-4}{9}=\dfrac{y+1}{-1}=\dfrac{z-7}{-3}$

(d) None of these

14. If the plane $2x - 3y + 6z - 11 = 0$ makes an angle $\sin^{-1}(\lambda)$ with x-axis, then λ is equal to

(a) $\dfrac{2}{7}$ (b) $\dfrac{-2}{7}$

(c) $\dfrac{1}{7}$ (d) None of these

15. If the point $O(0,0,0)$; $A(a, 1, 1)$; $B(1, b,1)$; $C(1,1,c)$ are coplanar, then value of $\dfrac{1}{1-a}+\dfrac{1}{1-b}+\dfrac{1}{1-c}$ is equal to

(a) 1 (b) –1

(c) 0 (d) None of these

16. The equation of the plane which bisects the line joining (2, 3, 4) and (6, 7, 8) is :

(a) $x + y + z - 15 = 0$ (b) $x - y + z - 15 = 0$

(c) $x - y - z - 15 = 0$ (d) $x + y + z + 15 = 0$

17. The angle between the line $\dfrac{x-2}{a}=\dfrac{y-2}{b}=\dfrac{z-2}{c}$ and the plane $ax + by + cz + 6 = 0$ is

(a) $\sin^{-1}\left(\dfrac{1}{\sqrt{a^2+b^2+c^2}}\right)$

(b) 45°

(c) 60°

(d) 90°

18. The direction cosines of two mutually perpendicular lines are l_1, m_1, n_1, and l_2, m_2, n_2. The direction cosines of the line perpendicular to both the given lines will be

(a) $l_1 + l_2, m_1 + m_2, n_1 + n_2$

(b) $l_1 - l_2, m_1 - m_2, n_1 - n_2$

(c) $l_1 l_2, m_1m_2, n_1n_2$

(d) $m_1n_2 - m_2n_1, n_1l_2 - n_2l_1, l_1m_2 - l_2m_1$

19. The locus represented by $xy + yz = 0$ is

(a) A pair of perpendicular lines

(b) A pair of parallel lines

(c) A pair of parallel planes

(d) A pair of perpendicular planes

20. The planes $x + y = 0$, $y - z = 0$ and $x + z = 0$

(a) meet in a unique point

(b) meet in a unique line

(c) are mutually perpendicular

(d) None of these

21. Lines OA and OB are drawn from $O \equiv (0, 0, 0)$ with direction cosines proportional to (1, –2, –1) and (3, –2, 3) respectively. The direction ratios of the normal to the plane OAB are

(a) (4, 3, –2) (b) (-4, 3, –2)

(c) (4, –3, –2) (d) (4, 3, 2)

22. The direction ratios of the normal to the plane passing through (1, 0, 0), (0, 1, 0) and making an angle $\pi/4$ with the plane $x + y = 3$ are

(a) $(1, \sqrt{2}, 1)$ (b) $(1, 1, \sqrt{2})$

(c) (1, 1, 2) (d) $(\sqrt{2}, 1, 1)$

23. The equation of a plane passing through the line of intersection of the planes $x + y + z = 5$, $2x - y + 3z = 1$ and parallel to the line $y = z = 0$ is

(a) $3x - z = 9$ (b) $3y - z = 9$

(c) $x - 3z = 9$ (d) $y - 3z = 9$

24. Centroid of the tetrahedron $OABC$, where $A \equiv (a, 2, 3)$, $B \equiv (1, b, 2)$, $C \equiv (2, 1, c)$ and O is the origin is (1, 2, 3). The value of $a^2 + b^2 + c^2$ is equal to

(a) 75 (b) 80

(c) 121 (d) None of these

25. The distance of the point (1, –2, 3) from the plane $x - y + z - 5 = 0$, measured parallel to the line $\dfrac{x}{2}=\dfrac{y}{3}=\dfrac{z-1}{-6}$ is equal to

(a) 1 unit (b) 2 units

(c) 3 units (d) None of these

26. The length of projection of the line segment joining the points (1, –1, 0) and (–1, 0, 1), onto the plane $2x + y + 6z = 1$, is equal to

(a) $\sqrt{\dfrac{255}{41}}$ (b) $\sqrt{\dfrac{237}{41}}$

(c) $\sqrt{\dfrac{137}{41}}$ (d) $\sqrt{\dfrac{155}{41}}$

27. The direction cosines of the line which is perpendicular to the lines with direction cosines proportional to 6, 4, – 4 and – 6, 2, 1 is

(a) 2, 3, 6 (b) $\frac{2}{7}, \frac{3}{7}, \frac{6}{7}$

(c) $\frac{2}{3}$, 1, 2 (d) $\frac{1}{3}, \frac{3}{2}$, 3

28. The lines whose direction cosine are given by the relations $a^2l + b^2m + c^2n = 0$ and $mn + nl + lm = 0$ are parallel if

(a) $(a^2 - b^2 + c^2)^2 = 4a^2c^2$

(b) $(a^2 + b^2 + c^2)^2 = 4a^2c^2$

(c) $(a^2 - b^2 + c^2)^2 = a^2c^2$

(d) None of these

29. The coordinates of A, B, C are $A(-1, 2, -3)$, $B(5, 0, -6)$, $C(0, 4, -1)$. The direction cosines of the internal bisector of $\angle BAC$ are proportional to

(a) 6, – 2, 13 (b) 21, 2, 2

(c) 26, – 4, 6 (d) 25, 8, 5

30. Three lines with direction ratios <1, 1, 2> <√3–1, –√3 – 1, 4> and <–√3 – 1, √3 – 1, 4> form

(a) a right angled triangle

(b) an isosceles triangle

(c) an equilateral triangle

(d) None of these

31. The plane $x + y + z = 0$ is rotated through right angle about its line of intersection with the plane $2x + y + 4 = 0$, the equation of the plane in its new position is

(a) $x - z + 4 = 0$ (b) $x + z + 4 = 0$

(c) $x - z + y = 4$ (d) $x - y = 4$

32. The value of λ for which the planes $4x - 5y + 2z + \lambda = 0$, $3x - 3y + \lambda z = 3$ and $5x - y - \lambda z + 8 = 0$ forms a prism is

(a) λ = 1 (b) λ = – 1

(c) λ = 0 (d) no value of λ

33. The value of λ, k for which the line $\frac{x-1}{1} = \frac{y}{-1} = \frac{z+2}{2}$ lies in the plane $2x + 3y + \lambda z + k = 0$

(a) λ = 1/2, k = –1

(b) λ = 1/2, k = 1

(c) λ = –1/2, any value of k

(d) λ = –1/2, k = –3

34. The planes $2x - 3y - 7z = 0$, $3x - 14y - 13z = 0$, $8x - 31y - 33z = 0$

(a) forms a prism

(b) passes through one line

(c) intersects only at a point

(d) None of these

35. The three planes $2x - y + z = 4$, $5x + 7y + 2z = 0$ and $3x + 4y - 2z + 3 = 0$ intersect in

(a) a point (b) a line

(c) a prism (d) None of these

36. If points $(2 - x, 2, 2)$, $(2, 2 - y, 2)$, $(2, 2, 2 - z)$ and $(1, 1, 1)$ are coplanar, then

(a) $\frac{1}{x} + \frac{1}{y} + \frac{1}{z} = 1$ (b) $\frac{1}{1-x} + \frac{1}{1-y} + \frac{1}{1-z} = 1$

(c) $x + y + z = 1$ (d) None of these

37. The distance of the point (1, 1, 1) from the plane passing through the points (2, 1, 1), (1, 2, 1) and (1, 1, 2) is

(a) $\frac{1}{\sqrt{3}}$ (b) 1

(c) √3 (d) None of these

38. The reflection of the point (2, –1, 3) in the plane $3x - 2y - z = 9$ is

(a) $\left(\frac{26}{7}, \frac{15}{7}, \frac{17}{7}\right)$ (b) $\left(\frac{26}{7}, \frac{-15}{7}, \frac{17}{7}\right)$

(c) $\left(\frac{15}{7}, \frac{26}{7}, \frac{-17}{7}\right)$ (d) $\left(\frac{26}{7}, \frac{17}{7}, \frac{-15}{7}\right)$

39. The image of the point $P(\alpha, \beta, \gamma)$ in the plane $\ell x + my + nz = 0$ is $Q(\alpha', \beta', \gamma')$ then

(a) $\alpha^2 + \beta^2 + \gamma^2 = \ell^2 + m^2 + n^2$

(b) $\alpha^2 + \beta^2 + \gamma^2 = (\alpha')^2 + (\beta')^2 + (\gamma')^2$

(c) $\alpha\alpha' + \beta\beta' + \gamma\gamma' = 0$

(d) $\ell(\alpha - a') + m(\beta - \beta') + n(\gamma - \gamma') = 0$

40. Distance of the point $P(2, -3, 4)$ from plane $\vec{r}.(\hat{i} + \hat{j} + \hat{k}) = 5$ measured parallel to x-axis, is

(a) 1 (b) √2

(c) 2 (d) 4

41. The plane $ax + by + cz = d$, meets the coordinate axes at the points A, B and C respectively. Area of triangle ABC is equal to

(a) $\frac{d^2\sqrt{a^2 + b^2 + c^2}}{|abc|}$ (b) $\frac{d^2\sqrt{a^2 + b^2 + c^2}}{2|abc|}$

(c) $\frac{d^2\sqrt{a^2 + b^2 + c^2}}{4|abc|}$ (d) None of these

42. Equation of plane which passes through the point of intersection of lines $\frac{x-1}{3}=\frac{y-2}{1}=\frac{z-3}{2}$ and $\frac{x-3}{1}=\frac{y-1}{2}=\frac{z-2}{3}$ and at greatest distance from the point (0, 0, 0) is

(a) $4x + 3y + 5z = 25$ (b) $4x + 3y + 5z = 50$
(c) $3x + 4y + 5z = 49$ (d) $x + 7y - 5z = 2$

43. $\vec{A}$ is a vector with direction cosines cos α, cosβ and cos γ respectively. Assuming *yz* plane as a mirror the direction cosines of the reflected image of $\vec{A}$ in the *yz* plane is

(a) cosα, cosβ, cosγ (b) cosα, cosβ, cosγ
(c) –cosα, cosβ, cosγ (d) cosα, – cosβ, –cosγ

44. *P* is fixed point (*a*, *a*, *a*) on a line through the origin equally inclined to the axes, then any plane through *P* perpendicular to *OP* , makes intercepts on the axes, the sum of whose reciprocals is equal to

(a) *a* (b) 3/2*a*
(c) 3*a*/2 (d) 1/*a*

45. The projection of any line on co-ordinate axes be respectively 3, 4, 5, then its length is :

(a) 12 (b) 50
(c) $5\sqrt{2}$ (d) None of these

46. The length and foot of the perpendicular from the point (2, –1, 5) to the line $\frac{x-11}{10}=\frac{y+2}{-4}=\frac{z+8}{-11}$ are

(a) $\sqrt{14}, (1,2,-3)$ (b) $\sqrt{14}, (1,-2,3)$
(c) $\sqrt{14}, (1,2,3)$ (d) None of these

47. The point at which the line joining the points(2,–3, 1) and (3, – 4, – 5) intersects the plane, $2x + y + z = 7$ is

(a) (1, 2, 7) (b) (1, –2, 7)
(c) (–1, 2, 7) (d) (1, – 2, – 7)

48. The distance of the point (1, –2, 3) from the plane $x - y + z = 5$ measured parallel to the line $\frac{x}{2}=\frac{y}{3}=\frac{z}{-6}$ is:

(a) 1 (b) 6/7
(c) 1/7 (d) None of these

49. The angle between the lines $2x = 3y = -z$ and $6x = -y = -4z$ is:

(a) 0° (b) 30°
(c) 45° (d) 90°

50. The ratio in which the line joining the points(*a, b, c*) and (–*a*, – *c*, – *b*) is divided by the *xy*-plane is :

(a) *a* : *b* (b) *b* : *c*
(c) *c* : *a* (d) *c* : *b*

51. A tetrahedron has vertices at *O* (0, 0, 0), *A* (1, 2, 1), *B* (2, 1, 3) and *C* (–1, 1, 2) . Then the angle between the faces *OAB* and *ABC* will be

(a) $\cos^{-1}\left(\frac{19}{35}\right)$ (b) $\cos^{-1}\left(\frac{17}{31}\right)$
(c) 30° (d) 90°

52. Distance of the point (x_1, y_1, z_1) from the line $\frac{x-x_2}{l}=\frac{y-y_2}{m}=\frac{z-z_2}{n}$, where *l*, *m* and *n* are the direction consines of line is

(a) $\{(x_1-x_2)^2+(y_1-y_2)^2+(z_1-z_2)^2 - [l(x_1-x_2)+m(y_1-y_2)+n(z_1-z_2)]^2\}^{1/2}$
(b) $\sqrt{(x_1-x_2)^2+(y_2-y_1)^2+(z_2-z_1)^2}$
(c) $\sqrt{(x_2-x_1)l+(y_2-y_1)m+(z_2-z_1)n}$
(d) None of these

53. The co-ordinates of the points *A* and *B* are (2, 3, 4) and (–2, 5, –4) respectively. If a point *P* moves so that $PA^2 - PB^2 = k$, where *k* is a constant , then the locus of *P* is

(a) A line (b) A plane
(c) A sphere (d) None of these

54. The equation of plane through the line of intersection of planes $ax + by + cz + d = 0$, $a'x + b'y + c'z + d' = 0$ and parallel to the line $y = 0$, $z = 0$ is

(a) $(ab' - a'b)x + (bc' - b'c)y + (ad' - a'd) = 0$
(b) $(ab' - a'b)x + (bc' - b'c)y + (ad' - a'd)z = 0$
(c) $(ab' - a'b)y + (ac' - a'c)z + (ad' - a'd) = 0$
(d) None of these

55. A square *ABCD* of diagonal 2*a* is folded along the diagonal *AC* so that the planes *DAC* and *BAC* are at right angle. The shortest distance between *DC* and *AB* is

(a) $\sqrt{2}a$ (b) $2a/\sqrt{3}$
(c) $2a/\sqrt{5}$ (d) $\left(\sqrt{3}/2\right)a$

56. The planes $2x + 5y + 3z = 0$, $x - y + 4z = 2$ and $7y - 5z + 4 = 0$

(a) meet in a point
(b) meet in a line

(c) neither meet in a point nor in a line
(d) are equidistant from origin.

57. The shortest distance between the line $x = y = z$ and the line $2x + y + z - 1 = 0$, $3x + y + 2z - 2 = 0$ is

(a) $\frac{1}{\sqrt{2}}$ (b) $\sqrt{2}$
(c) $\frac{3}{\sqrt{2}}$ (d) $\frac{\sqrt{3}}{2}$

58. The line $x + 2y - z - 3 = 0$, $x + 3y - z - 4 = 0$ is parallel to
(a) *xy* plane (b) *yz* plane
(c) *zx* plane (d) z-axis.

59. If $\vec{a}$ and $\vec{b}$ are non -collinear vectors, then the point of intersection of the lines $\vec{r} = \vec{a} - 2\vec{b} + \lambda(\vec{b} + 2\vec{a})$ and $\vec{r} = 2\vec{a} - \vec{b} + \mu(\vec{a} + 2\vec{b})$ is $\frac{k}{3}(\vec{a} - \vec{b})$; then numerical quantity k must be
(a) 5 (b) 0
(c) 1 (d) 2

60. A variable plane is at a constant distance p from the origin and meets the axes in A, B and C. If the locus of centroid of the tetrahedron $OABC$ is $\frac{1}{x^2} + \frac{1}{y^2} + \frac{1}{z^2} = \frac{\lambda}{p^2}$, then the numerical quantity λ should be
(a) 16 (b) 15
(c) 11 (d) None of these

61. Equation of plane containing the two parallel lines. $\frac{x+1}{3} = \frac{y-2}{2} = \frac{z}{1}$ and $\frac{x-3}{3} = \frac{y+4}{2} = \frac{z-1}{1}$ is
(a) $8x - y - 26z + 6 = 0$
(b) $8x + y - 26z + 6 = 0$
(c) $8x + y + 26z + 6 = 0$
(d) None of these

62. A line with direction cosines proportionate to <2, 7, –5> is drawn to intersect straight lines $\frac{x-5}{3} = \frac{y-7}{-1} = \frac{z+2}{1}$ and $\frac{x+3}{-3} = \frac{y-3}{2} = \frac{z-6}{4}$, then equation of line and length intercepted on it is

(a) $\frac{x-2}{2} = \frac{y-8}{7} = \frac{z+3}{-5}, \sqrt{78}$

(b) $\frac{x-2}{-2} = \frac{y-8}{7} = \frac{-z+3}{5}, \sqrt{78}$

(c) $\frac{x+2}{2} = \frac{y-8}{7} = \frac{z+3}{-5}, \sqrt{76}$

(d) None of these

63. If $P_1 = 0$ and $P_2 = 0$ be two non parallel planes, then the equation $P_1 + \lambda P_2 = 0, \lambda \in \mathbb{R}$ represents the family of all planes through the line of intersection of the planes $P_1 = 0$ and $P_2 = 0$ except the plane:
(a) $P_1 = 0$ (b) $P_2 = 0$
(c) $P_1 + P_2 = 0$ (d) $P_1 - P_2 = 0$

64. A plane passes through (1, –2, 1) and is perpendicular to two planes $2x - 2y + z = 0$ and $x - y + 2z = 4$, then the distance of the plane from the point (1,2,2) is
(a) 0 (b) 1
(c) $\sqrt{2}$ (d) $2\sqrt{2}$

65. If the straight lines $x = 1 + s$, $y = -3 - \lambda s$, $z = 1 + \lambda s$ and $x = \frac{t}{2}$, $y = 1 + t$, $z = 2 - t$, with parameter s and t respectively are coplanar, then λ equals:
(a) –2 (b) –1
(c) –1/2 (d) 0

66. The direction consines l, m, n of two lines are connected by the relation $l + m + n = 0$, $lm = 0$, then the angles between them is
(a) $\pi/3$ (b) $\pi/4$
(c) $\pi/2$ (d) 0

67. The equation of a plane through the line of intersection of $2x + 3y + z - 1 = 0$ and $x + 5y - 2z + 7 = 0$ and parallel to the line $y = 0 = z$ is
(a) $7x + 5y + 15 = 0$ (b) $7y - 5z + 15 = 0$
(c) $13y - 3z + 13 = 0$ (d) $4x + 7y + 5z + 15 = 0$

68. The line $\frac{x}{k} = \frac{y}{k} = \frac{z}{-12}$ makes an isosceles triangle with the planes $2x + y + z - 1 = 0$ and $-x - 2y - 3z + 1 = 0$, then the value of k is
(a) 1 (b) 12
(c) 3 (d) 4

69. Direction consine of normal to the plane containing lines $x = y = z$ and $x - 1 = y - 1 = \frac{z-1}{d}$ (where $d \in \mathbb{R} - \{1\}$) are

(a) $\pm\left\{\frac{1}{\sqrt{2}}, -\frac{1}{\sqrt{2}}, 0\right\}$ (b) $\left\{\frac{1}{\sqrt{2}}, 0, \frac{1}{\sqrt{2}}\right\}$

(c) $\left\{0, \frac{1}{\sqrt{2}}, \frac{1}{\sqrt{2}}\right\}$ (d) None of these

SECTION–IV

MORE THAN ONE CORRECT ANSWERS

1. If a straight line makes an angle of 60° with each of the x and y-axes, the angle which it makes with the z-axis is.

(a) $\pi/3$ (b) $\pi/4$
(c) $\pi/2$ (d) $3\pi/4$

2. The lines $\frac{x-2}{1}=\frac{y-3}{1}=\frac{z-4}{-k}$ and $\frac{x-1}{k}=\frac{y-4}{2}=\frac{z-5}{1}$ are coplanar if

(a) $k = 0$ (b) $k = -1$
(c) $k = -3$ (d) $k = 3$

3. The plane $x - 2y + 7z + 21 = 0$

(a) Contains the line $\frac{x+1}{-3}=\frac{y-3}{2}=\frac{z+2}{1}$
(b) Contains the point (0, 7, –1)
(c) Perpendicular to the line $\frac{x}{1}=\frac{y}{-2}=\frac{z}{7}$
(d) Parallel to the plane $x - 2y + 7z = 0$

4. If p_1, p_2, p_3 denotes the distances of the plane $2x - 3y + 4z + 2 = 0$ from the planes $2x - 3y + 4z + 6 = 0$, $4x - 6y + 8z + 3 = 0$ and $2x - 3y + 4z - 6 = 0$ respectively, then

(a) $p_1 + 8p_2 - p_3 = 0$ (b) $p_3 = 16p_2$
(c) $8p_2 = p_1$ (d) $p_1 + 2p_2 + 3p_3 = \sqrt{29}$

5. In three dimensional geometry $ax + by + c = 0$ represents

(a) a striaght line on xy plane
(b) a plane parallel to z-axis
(c) a plane perpendicular to z-axis
(d) a plane perpendicular to xy plane

6. If $P(2, 3, 1)$ is a point and $L \equiv x - y - z - 2 = 0$ is a plane, then

(a) Origin and P lie on the same side of the plane
(b) Distance of P from the plane is $\frac{4}{\sqrt{3}}$
(c) Foot of perpendicular is $\left(\frac{10}{3},\frac{5}{3},-\frac{1}{3}\right)$
(d) Image of point P by the plane is $\left(\frac{10}{3},\frac{5}{3},-\frac{1}{3}\right)$

7. The distances of the point (1, 2, 3) from the coordinate axes is A, B and C respectively. Which of these hold(s) true?

(a) $A^2 = B^2 + C^2$ (b) $B^2 = 2C^2$
(c) $2A^2 C^2 = 13B^2$ (d) None of these

8. Which of the following conditions, such that the line $\frac{x-p}{l}=\frac{y-q}{m}=\frac{z-r}{n}$ lies on the plane $Ax + By + Cz + D = 0$ is/are correct?

(a) $lp + mq + nr + D = 0$
(b) $Ap + Bq + Cr + D = 0$
(c) $Al + Bm + Cn = 0$
(d) None of these

9. The plane containing the lines $\vec{r}=\vec{a}+t\vec{a}'$ and $\vec{r}=\vec{a}'+s\vec{a}$

(a) must be parallel to $\vec{a}\times\vec{a}'$
(b) must be the perpendicular to $\vec{a}\times\vec{a}'$
(c) must be $[\vec{r},\vec{a},\vec{a}']=0$
(d) $(\vec{r}-\vec{a}).(\vec{r}\times\vec{a}')=0$

10. Let $\vec{r}.\vec{n}_1 = p_1$ and $\vec{r}\,.\,\vec{n}_2 = p_2$ be two planes and $\vec{a}$ be a given point, then

(a) the line passing through $\vec{a}$ and parallel to the line of intersection of given planes must be perpendicular to $\vec{n}_1\times\vec{n}_2$
(b) The line passing through $\vec{a}$ and parallel to line of intersection of given planes must be parallel to $\vec{n}_1\times\vec{n}_2$
(c) The line passing through $\vec{a}$ and parallel to line of intersection of given planes must be $(\vec{r}-\vec{a}).(\vec{n}_1\times\vec{n}_2)=\vec{O}$
(d) The line passing through $\vec{a}$ and parallel to line of intersection of given planes must be $(\vec{r}-\vec{a})\times(\vec{n}_1\times\vec{n}_2)=\vec{O}$

11. Which of the following is (are) correct?

(a) The three coordinate planes divide the whole system in 8 octant
(b) The perpendicular distance of the point (3 cos θ, 3 sin θ, 4) from the z-axis is constant
(c) In a tetrahedron, each of four vertices is the intersection of four lines
(d) The yz plane divides the line joining the points (2, 4, 5), (3, 5, –4) in the ratio 2 : 3 (internally)

SECTION–V

ASSERTION AND REASON TYPE QUESTIONS

The questions given below consist of an assertion (A) and the reason (R). Use the following key to choose the appropriate answer.

(a) If both assertion and reason are correct and reason is the correct explanation of the assertion.

(b) If both assertion and reason are correct but reason is not correct explanation of the assertion.

(c) If assertion is correct, but reason is incorrect

(d) If assertion is incorrect, but reason is correct

Now consider the following statements:

1. **A:** Line $\frac{x-1}{3}=\frac{y-2}{11}=\frac{z+1}{11}$ lies in the plane $11x-3z-14=0$

   R: A straight line lies in plane if the line is parallel to the plane and a point of the line lies in the plane.

2. **A:** The lines $\frac{x-1}{3}=\frac{y-3}{4}=\frac{z-4}{5}$ and $\frac{x-1}{3}=\frac{y-3}{1}=\frac{z-4}{-2}$ are co-planar.

   R: If two lines are perpendicular to each other, then these are co-planar.

3. **A:** Two perpendicular non-intersecting lines are not co-planar.

   R: Two skew lines are not co-planar.

4. **A:** Let A $(\hat{i}+\hat{j}+\hat{k})$ and B $(\hat{i}-\hat{j}+\hat{k})$ be two points, then point P $(2\hat{i}+3\hat{j}+\hat{k})$ is exterior to the sphere with A and B as ends of its diameter.

   R: If A and B are any two points and P is a point in space such that $\overline{PA}\,.\,\overline{PB}>0$, then the point P lies exterior to the sphere with AB as one of its diameters.

5. **A:** The points (2, 1, 5) and (3, 4, 3) lie on opposite sides of the plane $2x + 2y - 2z - 1 = 0$.

   R: The algebraic perpendicular distance from the given points to line have opposite signs.

6. **A:** A homogeneous equation of second degree in x, y and z represents a pair of plane passing through origin.

   R: A homogeneous equation of second degree in x,y and z can be factorised into two linear factors.

7. **A:** The locus of a point which moves so that $|x| + |y| + |z| = k$ is an octahedron

   R: The equation of the type $x + y + z = k$ represents a plane

8. **A:** If distance between two points is defined as $d(p,q) = |(x_2-x_1)| + |y_2-y_1| + |z_2-z_1|$; then for a vector $\overline{OP}$ where $P = <l, m, n>$; the relation $|l| + |m| + |n| = 1$ holds true

   R: When distance is given by $d(p,q) = \sqrt{(x_1-x_2)^2+(y_1-y_2)^2+(z_1-z_2)^2}$, then $l^2 + m^2 + n^2 = 1$

9. **A:** Let g be the volume of the parallelopiped formed by the vector $\vec{a}=a_1\hat{i}+a_2\hat{j}+a_3\hat{k}$, $\vec{b}=b_1\hat{i}+b_2\hat{j}+b_3\hat{k}$, $\vec{c}=c_1\hat{i}+c_2\hat{j}+c_3\hat{k}$. If a_r, b_r, c_r where r = 1, 2, 3 are non-negative real numbers and $\sum_{r=1}^{3}(a_r+b_r+c_r)=3L$; then $V \le L^3$

   R: $x^3 + y^3 + z^3 \le (x + y + z)$

SECTION–VI

COMPREHENSION TYPE QUESTIONS

Passage 1:

A: Two space lines are said to be skew lines, if they are non-co-planar. A line which is perpendicular to two skew lines is called a line of shortest distance, we call it *LSD*. The distance intercepted by *LSD* between the two skew lines is called the length of shortest distance (*SD*) between the two skew lines. (Note that we are studying *SD* and *LSD* of skew lines only). For co-planar lines these are trivial for example *SD* of co-plannar non-parallel lines = 0).

(a) *SD* of two skew lines L_1 and L_2 is equal to projection of line joining a point on L_1 and a point on L_2 on *LSD*.

(b) *SD* of two skew lines L_1 and L_2 is also equal to perpendicular distance of the plane drawn through L_1 and parallel to L_2 for any point on L_2.

(c) Let $L_1: \frac{x-x_1}{l_1} = \frac{y-y_1}{m_1} = \frac{z-z_1}{n_1}$ and $L_2: \frac{x-x_2}{l_2} = \frac{y-y_2}{m_2} = \frac{z-z_2}{n_2}$ be two lines and let l, m, n be the direction ratios of *LSD*. Then l, m, n are easily determined by solving $ll_1 + mm_1 + mn_1 = 0$, $ll_2 + mm_2 + nn_2 = 0$. The equation of the plane containing L_1 and *LSD* is

$$\begin{vmatrix} x-x_1 & y-y_1 & z-z_1 \\ l_1 & m_1 & n_1 \\ l & m & n \end{vmatrix} = 0$$ and plane containing L_2 and *LSD* is $$\begin{vmatrix} x-x_2 & y-y_2 & z-z_2 \\ l_2 & m_2 & n_2 \\ l & m & n \end{vmatrix} = 0$$

These two planes together determine *LSD* in unsymmetrical form.

(d) The *SD* of two lines given in unsymmetrical form is found by the following procedure: Let lines be $u_1 = 0 = v_1$ and $u_2 = 0 = v_2$. Any plane through the first line is $u_1 + \lambda v_1 = 0$ and through the second line is $u_2 + \mu v_2 = 0$. If we choose λ, μ such that these two planes are parallel, then the distance between these parallel planes shall give us the *SD* between the two lines.

(e) The shortest distance between two lines $\vec{r} = \vec{a}_1 + \lambda \vec{b}_1$, $\vec{r} = \vec{a}_2 + \mu \vec{b}_2$ must be $\frac{|(\vec{a}_2 - \vec{a}_1).(\vec{b}_1 \times \vec{b}_2)|}{|\vec{b}_1 \times \vec{b}_2|}$

1. If $2d$ is the shortest distance between the lines $\frac{y}{b} + \frac{z}{c} = 1, x = 0$ and $\frac{x}{a} - \frac{z}{c} = 1, y = 0$, then
   (a) $d^2 = a^2 + b^2 + c^2$
   (b) $d^{-2} = a^{-2} + b^{-2}$
   (c) $4d^{-2} = a^{-2} + b^{-2} + c^{-2}$
   (d) None of these

2. In a rectangular parallelopiped of edges a, b, c the shortest distance between any edge and a body diagonal not intersecting it may be
   (a) $\frac{ac}{\sqrt{a^2+c^2}}$ (b) $\frac{2bc}{\sqrt{b^2+c^2}}$
   (c) $\frac{b+c}{2}$ (d) $\frac{abc}{a^2+b^2+c^2}$

3. The lines $\frac{x+4}{3} = \frac{y+6}{5} = \frac{z-1}{-2}$, $3x - 2y + z + 5 = 0 = 2x + 3y + 4z - k$ are co-planar for $k =$
   (a) 0 (b) 2
   (c) 3 (d) 4

Passage 2:

B: Let *AB* be the straight line $\frac{x}{2} = \frac{y}{-3} = \frac{z}{6}$. From the point $P(1, 2, 5)$ perpendicular *PN* is drawn to *AB*, where *N* is the foot of perpendicular. A straight line *PQ* is drawn parallel to the plane $3x + 4y + 5z = 0$ to meet *AB* in *Q*, then

4. Co-ordinates of *N* are
   (a) $\left(\frac{52}{49}, \frac{78}{49}, \frac{156}{49}\right)$ (b) $\left(-\frac{52}{49}, \frac{78}{49}, \frac{156}{49}\right)$
   (c) $\left(\frac{52}{49}, \frac{-78}{49}, \frac{156}{49}\right)$ (d) $\left(\frac{52}{49}, \frac{78}{49}, \frac{-156}{49}\right)$

5. Co-ordinates of *Q* are
   (a) $(3, -9/2, 9)$ (b) $(-3, 9/2, 9)$
   (c) $(3, 9/2, -9)$ (d) None of these

6. Equation of *PQ* is
   (a) $\frac{x-1}{4} = \frac{2-y}{13} = \frac{z-5}{8}$
   (b) $\frac{x-1}{4} = \frac{y-2}{13} = \frac{z-5}{8}$
   (c) $\frac{x-1}{4} = \frac{y-2}{13} = \frac{5-z}{8}$
   (d) $\frac{x-1}{-4} = \frac{y-2}{13} = \frac{z-5}{8}$

Passage 3:

C: $\left.\begin{matrix} x+y=2\lambda \\ x+\lambda^2 y = \mu \end{matrix}\right\}$ system has infinite solutions and the position vectors of two points *A* and *B* are given as $(1, \lambda, 2\mu)$ and $(1, \mu, \lambda^2)$ respectively. *AB* line segment is divided by *x-y* plane in the ratio n/m such that $\frac{n}{m} \in I$; where *m* and *n* are related by the quadratic equation $m^2x^2 + an^2x + mn = 0$

7. If roots of the quadratic equation are real $\forall\ a \in \mathbb{R}$, then points *A* and *B* are
   (a) on the same side of the *x-y* plane
   (b) on the opposite side of the $x - y$ plane
   (c) on the same side of the plane $x + y - z + 1 = 0$
   (d) on the opposite side of *y-z* plane

8. For every possible value of λ, the roots of the quadratic are real in all possible ways, then

(a) $a \in \mathbb{R}$ (b) $|a| \geq \frac{1}{4}$

(c) $|a| \leq \frac{1}{4}$ (d) $|a| \geq 4$

9. If both points are on the opposite sides of *x-y* plane, then the equation of a plane perpendicular to *AB* vector and passing through origin will be

(a) $y - 5z = 0$ (b) $y + 5z = 0$

(c) $5y - z = 0$ (d) $5y + z = 0$

10. Equation of a plane parallel to all possible *AB* vectors and passing through (a, a, a) where a is the value at which sum of the roots of quadratic becomes 16 is

(a) $y = -1$

(b) $2(x + 1) = 0$

(c) $2(x + 1) + (y + 1) + 3(z + 1) = 0$

(d) $y + z = -2$

11. If system of equation is inconsistent, then the point $(1, \lambda^2, 2\mu^2)$ may lie on the plane may

(a) $x + y + z = 10$ (b) $x - y + z = 8$

(c) $x + y + z = 3$ (d) $x - y - z + 8 = 0$

12. If the roots of the quadratic equation are always real. What are the possible values of 'a' such that both roots of the quadratic are positive?

(a) $a \in (0, \infty)$ (b) $a \in (-1/2, 1/2)$

(c) $a \in \mathbb{R}$ (d) None of these

13. If the system of equations has infinitely many solutions and both points are on the opposite sides of the *x-y* plane, then the number of terms in the binomial expansion of $(1 + x)^{n/m}$ is

(a) 3 (b) 4

(c) 5 (d) 8

Passage 4:

D: Given two straight lines $L_1 : \vec{r} = \vec{a} + \lambda\vec{b}$ passing through point A with position vector $\vec{a}$ and parallel to vector $\vec{b}$ and $L_2 : \vec{r} = \vec{c} + \mu\vec{d}$, passing through point $C(\vec{c})$ and parallel to vector $\vec{d}$, then these lines shall be

(i) parallel if $\vec{b} = \lambda\vec{d}$

(ii) perpendicular if $\vec{b}.\vec{d} = 0$

(iii) coincident if $(\vec{c} - \vec{a}) = k\vec{b} = \ell\vec{d}$

(iv) intersecting; when $(\vec{c} - \vec{a}) = k\vec{b} \neq \ell\vec{d}$ (then point of intersection must be *C*); when $(\vec{c} - \vec{a}) = \ell\vec{d} \neq k\vec{b}$ (then point of intersection must be *A*)

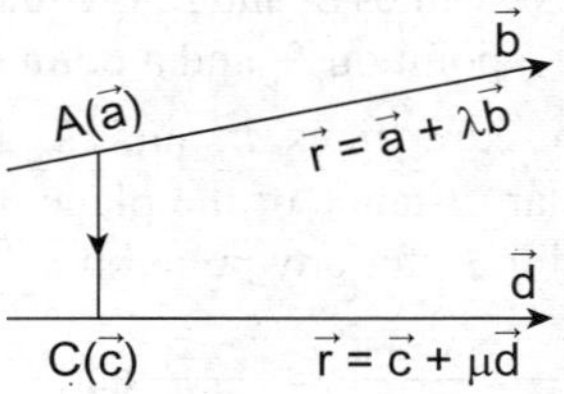

14. The angle between two lines $\frac{x-1}{2} = \frac{y-3}{3} = \frac{z-2}{1}$ and $\frac{x-2}{2} = \frac{y-1}{-2} = \frac{z-3}{2}$

(a) 0 (b) $\frac{\pi}{2}$

(c) $\frac{\pi}{3}$ (d) None of these

15. Given that $\vec{a} = -\hat{i} - 2\hat{j} - \hat{k}$; $\vec{b} = 2\hat{i} + 2\hat{j} + \hat{k}$; $\vec{c} = 2\hat{i} + 2\hat{j} + 4\hat{k}$ and $\vec{d} = 6\hat{i} + 8\hat{j} + 10\hat{k}$, then

(a) L_1 and L_2 are skew lines and ⊥ to each other

(b) L_1 and L_2 are skew lines with angle between them $\theta = \cos^{-1}\left(\frac{19}{15\sqrt{2}}\right)$

(c) L_1 and L_2 are non skew lines with angle of intersection $\theta = \cos^{-1}\left(\frac{19}{15\sqrt{2}}\right)$

(d) L_1 and L_2 are intersecting lines ⊥ to each other.

16. The point of intersection of L_1 and L_2

(a) does not exist (b) is (1, 2, 1)

(c) is (– 1, – 2, – 1) (d) none of these.

Passage 5:

E: To find the foot of perpendicular/image of a point (x_1, y_1, z_1) in a given plane $\pi : ax + by + cz + d = 0$. Consider a line through *P* perpendicular to plane π say *PP'* and any point *Q(x,y,z)* on it. DR's of *PP'* are $< x - x_1, y - y_1, z - z_1 >$, which must be proportionate to < a , b, c > i.e. *D.*R's of normal to the plane. Therefore equation of *PP'* will be $\frac{x - x_1}{a} = \frac{y - y_1}{b} = \frac{z - z_1}{c}$

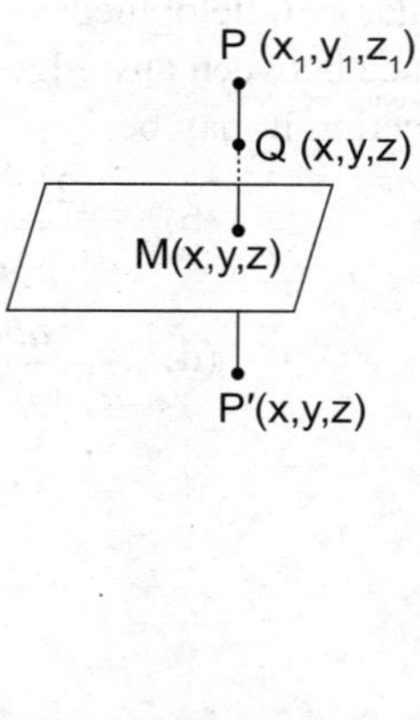

$$= \frac{a(x-x_1)+b(y-y_2)+c(z-z_1)}{a^2+b^2+c^2}$$

$$\Rightarrow \frac{x-x_1}{a} = \frac{y-y_1}{b} = \frac{z-z_1}{c}$$

$$= \frac{(ax+by+cz+d)-(ax_1+by_1+cz_1+d)}{a^2+b^2+c^2}$$

Now for Q to be foot of perpendicular: (x,y,z) must lie in the plane i.e. $ax + by + cz + d = 0$

$$\Rightarrow \frac{x-x_1}{a} = \frac{y-y_1}{b} = \frac{z-z_1}{c} = \frac{-(ax_1+by_1+cz_1+d)}{a^2+b^2+c^2}$$

Also for Q to be image of P': mid point of (x_1,y_1,z_1) and $P(x, y, z)$ must lie in the plane, i.e., $ax + by + cz + d = (ax_1 + by_1 + cz_1 + d)$

$$\Rightarrow \frac{x-x_1}{a} = \frac{y-y_1}{b} = \frac{z-z_1}{c} = \frac{-2(ax_1+by_1+cz_1+d)}{a^2+b^2+c^2}$$

17. If $(-9, 1, 1)$ is the image of any point $P(\alpha,\beta,\gamma)$ in the plane $2x + y + z = 0$ then $P(\alpha, \beta, \gamma)$ are

(a) $(-3, 5, 7)$ (b) $(3, -5, 7)$
(c) $(3,5,7)$ (d) None of these

18. Image of line $\frac{x+1}{1} = \frac{y+2}{2} = \frac{z+1}{-3}$ in the plane $x + 2y - 3z + 12 = 0$ is

(a) $\frac{x+1}{1} = \frac{y+2}{2} = \frac{z-7}{-3}$

(b) $\frac{x+1}{1} = \frac{y+2}{2} = \frac{z+1}{-3}$

(c) $\frac{x-1}{1} = \frac{y-2}{2} = \frac{z-1}{-3}$

(d) None of these

19. If $Q(2, 4, -4)$ be the foot of perpendicular of any point $P(x_1, y_1, z_1)$ in the plane $x + 3y - 2z - 22 = 0$, then point P is

(a) $(-1, -1, -2)$ (b) $(1, -1, -2)$
(c) $(1, 1, -2)$ (d) $(-1, 1, -2)$

20. In above question image of point $P(x_1, y_1, z_1)$ is

(a) $(3, 7, -6)$ (b) $(3, -7, -6)$
(c) $(-3,-7,-6)$ (d) None of these

21. Co-ordinates of point Q which is twice as much distance away as that of $F(3,2,-2)$with respect to plane $x - y - z = 9$ but on opposite side of plane is

(a) $(9,4,8)$ (b) $(9,-4,-8)$
(c) $(9,-4,8)$ (d) None of these

Passage 6:

F: If $P_1 \equiv a_1x + b_1y + c_1z - d_1 = 0$ and $P_2 \equiv a_2x + b_2y + c_2z = d_2 = 0$ be two planes, then linear equation $P_1 + \lambda P_2 = 0$ where λ is an arbitrary constant represents a family of plane passing through line of intersection of planes $P_1 = 0$ and $P_2 = 0$ because it is a linear equation so represents equation of plane and since consist of parameter λ therefore it is a family of plane and for each point (x_0, y_0, z_0) common to planes $P_1 = 0$ and $P_2 = 0$, the above equation is always satisfied for all values of λ. Above concept is widely used in solving various problems on plane.

22. The equation of plane passing through intersection of planes $x + 2y - z = 2$ and $2x - y + 2z - 5 = 0$ and containing origin is given by

(a) $x + y - 5z = 0$ (b) $2x + 3y - 5z = 0$
(c) $x + 12y - 9z = 0$ (d) all of the above

23. The equation of plane passing through intersection of $x + y + z = 4$ and $3x - y + 2z - 4 = 0$ and containing the point $(2, 2, 0)$ on it is

(a) $4x + 3z = 8$ (b) $2x - 2y + z = 0$
(c) $7x - y + 5z - 12 = 0$ (d) $5x - 3y + 3z - 4 = 0$

24. The equation of image of a plane $x + y + z = 3$ in the xy plane as a mirror is

(a) $x + y - z = 2$ (b) $x - y + z = 3$
(c) $x + y - z = 3$ (d) None of these

SECTION–VII

COLUMN MATCHING

1. Column I

(i) $\frac{x-1}{2} = \frac{y-2}{3} = \frac{z-3}{4}$ and $\frac{x-1}{3} = \frac{y-3}{4} = \frac{z-5}{5}$:

(ii) $\frac{x-1}{2} = \frac{y-2}{3} = \frac{z-3}{4}$ and $\frac{x-3}{2} = \frac{y-5}{3} = \frac{z-7}{4}$:

(iii) $\frac{x-2}{5} = \frac{y+3}{4} = \frac{5-z}{2}$ and $\frac{x-7}{5} = \frac{y+1}{4} = \frac{z-2}{-2}$:

(iv) $\frac{x-3}{2} = \frac{y+2}{4} = \frac{z-4}{5}$ and $\frac{x-3}{3} = \frac{y-2}{2} = \frac{z-7}{5}$:

Column II

(p) coincident

(q) parallel and different

(r) skew

(s) Intersecting in a point

2. **Column I**

(i) Foot of perpendicular drawn from point (1, 2, 3) to the line $\frac{x-2}{2}=\frac{y-1}{3}=\frac{z-2}{4}$ is

(ii) Image of point (1, 2, 3) in the line $\frac{x-2}{2}=\frac{y-1}{3}=\frac{z-2}{4}$ is

(iii) Foot of perpendicular from the point (2, 3, 6) to the plane $2x + 3y - 4z + 17 = 0$ is

(iv) Image of the point (2, 5, 1) in the plane $3x - 2y + 4z - 5 = 0$ is

Column - II

(p) $\left(\frac{107}{29},\frac{30}{29},\frac{69}{29}\right)$

(q) $\left(\frac{88}{29},\frac{125}{29},\frac{69}{29}\right)$

(r) $\left(\frac{68}{29},\frac{44}{29},\frac{78}{29}\right)$

(s) $\left(\frac{46}{29},\frac{69}{29},\frac{198}{29}\right)$

3. Column I contains some equations and column II some loci. Match the equations with their corresponding loci

Column I

(i) $|x| \le 0$ and $y^2 + z^2 \ge 0$

(ii) $|y - b| \le 0$ and $x^2 + z^2 \ge 0$

(iii) $x^2 + y^2 \le 0$

(iv) $x^2 + z^2 + a^2 + c^2 \le 2(ax + cz)$

Column II

(p) z-axis

(q) A straight line || to y-axis through $(a, 1, c)$

(r) A plane || to z-x plane passing through $(1, b, 2)$

(s) y-z plane

4. **Column I**

(i) $|x - a| \le 0$ and $|y - 2| \le 1$ and $|z - 1| \le 4$

(ii) $x = \alpha$ where $\alpha \in \mathbb{Z}$ such that $\sqrt{x-1}+\sqrt{3-x}$ is real and $[y] = [z + 2] = 0$; where $[x]$ denotes greatest integer function of $x, y \in [0,3]$ represents.

(iii) value of λ for which planes $2x - 3y + z = 1$ and $3x + 3y + \lambda z = 2$ are perpendicular is

(iv) $z^2 - 3z + 2 = 0$ represents

Column II

(p) pair of planes || to x-y plane

(q) 3 planes with total area 3 square unit

(r) plane surface(s) || to y-z, plane

(s) 3

SECTION–VIII

INTEGER TYPE QUESTIONS

1. Find the volume enclosed by the equations $|x| \le 8$, $|y| \le 8$, $|z| \le 8$ and $|x + y + z| \le 8$.

2. If the shortest distance between any two opposite edges of a tetrahedron formed by the planes $y + z = 0$, $x + z = 0$, $x + y = 0$, $x + y + z = \sqrt{3}a$ is equal to $\sqrt{k}a$, then find the value of k

3. If a line is passing through (a,b,c) and intersecting $y = 0$, $z^2 = 4\alpha x$ lies on the surface $(bz - cy)^2 = k\alpha (b - y)(bx - ay)$; then find the value of k

4. If the projections of $\overline{PQ}$ on OX, OY, OZ are respectively 1, 2, 3 and 4 ; then the magnitude of $\overline{PQ}$ is given by k; then find k.

5. If the locus of a point which moves such that the sum of its distances from points $A(0, 0, -a)$ and $B(0, 0, a)$ is constant (b) is given by $\frac{x^2+y^2}{\beta^2-a^2}+\frac{z^2}{\beta^2}=k$, then find the value of k.

6. Let f be a one-one function with domain $\{-2, 1, 0\}$ and range $\{1, 2, 3\}$ such that exactly one of the following statements is true : $f(-2) = 1$, $f(1) \ne 1$, $f(0) \ne 2$ and the remaining two are false. If the area of the triangle formed by $(-2,1,0)$ and $(f(-2), f(1), f(0))$ and the origin is given by $\frac{\sqrt{k}}{2}$; then find the value of k.

7. A triangle is so placed that the middle points of its sides are on the axes. If a,b,c be the lengths of its sides and the equation of its plane is given by $\frac{x}{x_1}+\frac{y}{y_1}+\frac{z}{z_1}=k$ where $2x_1^2 = b^2 + c^2 - a^2$; $2y_1^2 = a^2 + c^2 - b^2$; and $2z_1^2 = a^2 + b^2 - c^2$; then find the value of $1/|k|$

8. If the reflection of the plane $x + 2y + 3z + 4 = 0$ in the plane $x + y + z + 3 = 0$ is given by $x + 2y + 3z + 4 + \lambda(x + y + z + 3) = 0$, then find the value of 'λ'.

9. If the d.r's of 2 lines are given by $3\,lm - 4ln + mn = 0$ and $l + 2m + 3n = 0$ and the angle between them is given by π/k, then find the value of k

10. The three lines $\frac{x}{\alpha} = \frac{y}{\beta} = \frac{z}{\gamma}, \frac{x}{a\alpha} = \left(\frac{y}{b\beta}\right) = \frac{z}{c\gamma}; \frac{x}{l} = \frac{y}{m} = \frac{z}{n}$ all will lie on one plane if $\frac{l}{\alpha}\cdot(b - c) + \frac{m}{\beta}(c - a) + \frac{n}{\gamma}(a - b) = k$; then find the value of k.

11. The length of the edge of a regular tetrahedron $DABC$ is 'l' units. Points E and F are taken on the edges AD and BD respectively such that E divides $\overrightarrow{DA}$ and F divides $\overrightarrow{BD}$ in the ratio 2: 1 each. If $A(l)$ be the area of ΔCEF, then find $[A(6)]$. (where $[x]$ denotes integer part of number x).

12. Points X and Y are taken on the sides QR and RS, respectively of a parallelogram $PQRS$, so that $\overline{QX} = 4\overline{XR}$ and $\overline{RY} = 4\overline{YS}$. The line XY cuts the line PR at Z if $\overrightarrow{PR} = k\overrightarrow{PZ}$, where k is a scalar, then find the integer part of k.

13. If $\vec{a}$, $\vec{b}$, $\vec{c}$ be non-co-planar unit vectors, equally inclined to one another at an angle θ and $\vec{a}\times\vec{b}+\vec{b}\times\vec{c}= p\vec{a}+q\vec{b}+r\vec{c}$, then number of non-negative integer values of $\frac{pq}{r^2}$ is equal to.....

14. The internal angle bisectors of the ΔABC meet the opposite sides in D, E, F respectively (where $a = 2$, $b = 3$, $c = 4$ units), such that the area of $\Delta ABC = k$ (area of ΔDEF) then integer part of k is given as.

Answer Key

SECTION III

1. (a)	**2.** (a)	**3.** (a)	**4.** (a)	**5.** (a)	**6.** (b)	**7.** (a)	**8.** (a)	**9.** (a)	**10.** (c)
11. (a)	**12.** (b)	**13.** (c)	**14.** (a)	**15.** (a)	**16.** (a)	**17.** (d)	**18.** (d)	**19.** (d)	**20.** (a)
21. (a)	**22.** (b)	**23.** (b)	**24.** (a)	**25.** (a)	**26.** (b)	**27.** (b)	**28.** (a)	**29.** (d)	**30.** (b)
31. (a)	**32.** (a)	**33.** (a)	**34.** (b)	**35.** (a)	**36.** (a)	**37.** (a)	**38.** (b)	**39.** (b)	**40.** (c)
41. (b)	**42.** (b)	**43.** (c)	**44.** (d)	**45.** (c)	**46.** (c)	**47.** (b)	**48.** (c)	**49.** (d)	**50.** (d)
51. (a)	**52.** (a)	**53.** (b)	**54.** (c)	**55.** (b)	**56.** (b)	**57.** (a)	**58.** (c)	**59.** (a)	**60.** (a)
61. (b)	**62.** (a)	**63.** (b)	**64.** (d)	**65.** (a)	**66.** (d)	**67.** (b)	**68.** (b)	**69.** (a)	

SECTION–IV

1. (b,d) **2.** (a,c) **3.** (a,b,c,d) **4.** (a,b,c,d) **5.** (b,d) **6.** (a,b,c) **7.** (b,c) **8.** (b,c) **9.** (b,c,d)
10. (b,d) **11.** (a,b)

SECTION–V

1. (a) **2.** (c) **3.** (a) **4.** (a) **5.** (a) **6.** (a) **7.** (b) **8.** (b) **9.** (a)

SECTION–VI

1. (b)	**2.** (a)	**3.** (d)	**4.** (c)	**5.** (a)	**6.** (a)	**7.** (b)	**8.** (b)	**9.** (a)	**10.** (b)
11. (c)	**12.** (d)	**13.** (c)	**14.** (b)	**15.** (c)	**16.** (c)	**17.** (d)	**18.** (b)	**19.** (c)	**20.** (a)
21. (b)	**22.** (c)	**23.** (a,b)	**24.** (c)						

SECTION–VII

1. (i) → (s); (ii) → (p); (iii) → (q); (iv) → (r)
2. (i) → (r); (ii) → (p); (iii) → (s); (iv) → (q)
3. (i) → (s); (ii) → (r); (iii) → (p); (iv) → (q)
4. (i) → (r); (ii) → (q,r); (iii) → (s); (iv) → (p)

SECTION–VIII

1. 2048	**2.** 2	**3.** 4	**4.** 13	**5.** 1	**6.** 61	**7.** 2	**8.** –4	**9.** 2	**10.** 0
11. 9	**12.** 1	**13.** 3	**14.** 4						

HINTS AND SOLUTIONS

TEXTUAL EXERCISE 1:

1. Let $R(x, 0, 0)$ be the point on x-axis which is equidistant from $P(4, 3, 1)$ and $Q(-2, -6, -2)$
$\Rightarrow (x-4)^2 + (-3)^2 + (-1)^2 = (x+2)^2 + 6^2 + 2^2$
gives $-12x = 18$ so $x = -1.5$ hence $R \equiv (-3/2, 0, 0)$

2. $ABCD$ plane is parallel to xy plane
$B(1, -2, 1)$, $C(4, -2, 1)$, $D(4, 1, 1)$, $E(4, 1-2)$, $F(1, 1-2)$, $G(1, -2, -2)$, $H(4, -2, -2)$

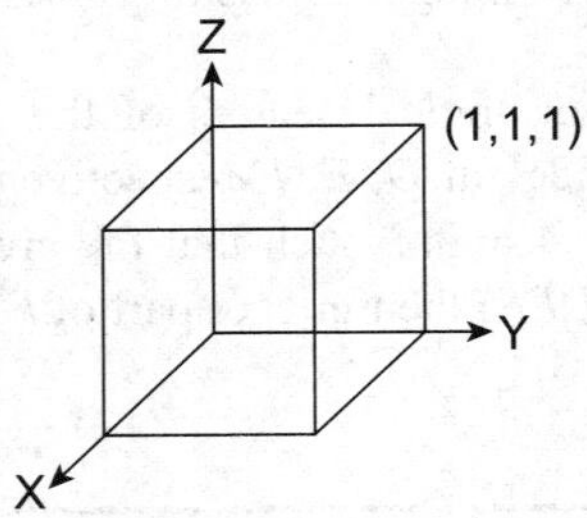

3. Let the line segment has a point R intersecting on the surface of the sphere)
$\Rightarrow R = \left(\frac{3\lambda}{1+\lambda} + \frac{4\lambda+1}{1+\lambda}, \frac{5\lambda+2}{1+\lambda}\right)$
So $9\lambda^2 + 16\lambda^2 + 1 + 8\lambda + 25\lambda^2 + 4 + 20\lambda - 25\ \{\lambda^2 + 1 + 2\lambda\} = 0$
$\Rightarrow 25\lambda^2 - 22\lambda - 20 = 0$
$\Rightarrow \lambda = \frac{22 \pm \sqrt{484+2000}}{50} = \frac{22 \pm \sqrt{2484}}{50} = \frac{11 \pm \sqrt{621}}{25}$

4. A point on the line through $P(3, 4, 1)$ and $Q(5, 1, 6)$ will have a general point $R\ (\vec{r}) = \left(\frac{5\lambda+3}{1+\lambda}, \frac{\lambda+4}{\lambda+1}, \frac{6\lambda+1}{\lambda+1}\right)$
This point will line on $x-y$ plane, when $\frac{6\lambda+1}{\lambda+1} = 0$
So $\lambda = -1/6 \Rightarrow R\left(\frac{13}{5}, \frac{23}{5}, 0\right)$

5. $P(2, 3, 4)$ and $Q(3, -4, 7)$ is divided internally in the ratio 5 : 3 by a point R, so $R = \left(\frac{21}{8}, \frac{-11}{8}, \frac{47}{8}\right)$

6. The reflection of a point $p(\alpha, \beta, \gamma)$ in $x-y$ plane will be $P'(\alpha, \beta, -\gamma)$

7. $(a, 0, 0)$ is the point on x-axis that is nearest to the point $P(a, b, c)$. The required minimum distance $= \sqrt{b^2+c^2}$ units

8. Let $A(0, 7, 10)$, $B(-1, 6, 6)$ and $C(-4, 9, 6)$, then $|AB|^2 = 1^2 + 1^2 + 4^2 = 18$, $|BC|^2 = 3^2 + (-3)^2 + 0^2 = 18$, $|AC|^2 = 4^2 + (-2)^2 + 4^2 = 36$. We observe that $|AB| = |BC|$ and $AC^2 = AB^2 + BC^2$

So ΔABC is isosceles and right angled. Hence triangle is right angled isosceles.

9. Consider mid points D and E respectively on OB and AC then $D(\vec{d}) = \frac{\vec{b}}{2}$ and $E(\vec{e}) = \frac{\vec{a}+\vec{c}}{2}$. Let a general point R_1 be on $\overline{DE}$, then $\frac{\frac{\vec{b}}{2} + \lambda\left(\frac{\vec{a}+\vec{c}}{2}\right)}{(1+\lambda)} = \frac{(\vec{a}+\vec{c})\lambda + \vec{b}}{2(1+\lambda)}$

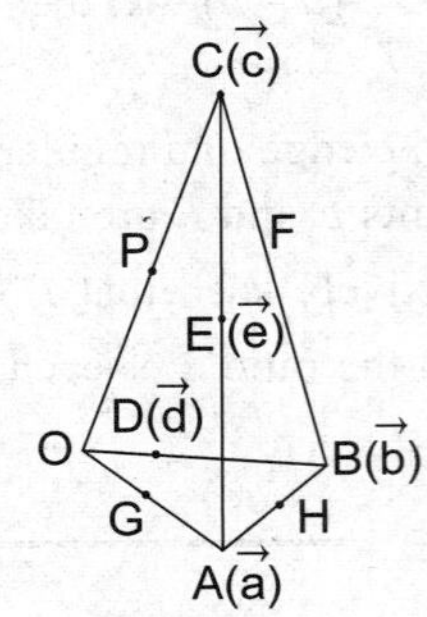

Similarly consider point $F(\vec{f})$ on BC and $G(\vec{g})$ on OA
so $G(\vec{g}) = \frac{\vec{a}}{2}, F(\vec{f}) = \frac{\vec{b}+\vec{c}}{2}$

Now $R_2 = \frac{\frac{\vec{a}}{2} + \left(\frac{b}{2}+c\right)\lambda}{1+\lambda} = \frac{\vec{a} + (\vec{b}+\vec{c})\lambda}{2(1+\lambda)}$

Observe that for $\lambda = 1$, $R_1 = R_2$

Similarly $H(\vec{h}) = \frac{\vec{a}+\vec{b}}{2}$ and $P(\vec{p}) = \frac{\vec{c}}{2}$

Mid point is $\frac{\vec{a}+\vec{b}+\vec{c}}{2(2)}$ which is true for $\lambda = 1$

$\therefore$ The points are concurrent

$\Rightarrow R_1 = R_2 = R_3 = \frac{\vec{a}+\vec{b}+\vec{c}}{4}$.

10. A general point $R(x, y, 0)$ will be on (x-y) plane so if it is on the line segment through $P(2, 4, 5)$ and $Q(3, 5, -4)$ then
$R = \left(\frac{3\lambda+2}{1+\lambda}, \frac{5\lambda+4}{1+\lambda}, \frac{-4\lambda+5}{1+\lambda}\right) = (x, y, 0)$
$\Rightarrow \lambda = 5/4$ then $R\left\{\frac{23}{9}, \frac{41}{9}, 0\right\}$ and $\lambda : 1 = 5 : 4$

11. Let point C divide line segment joining $A(2, 1, 5)$ and $(3, 4, 3)$ in the ratio $\lambda : 1$ and it lies on $2x + 2y - 2z = 1$
$\Rightarrow \lambda = \frac{5}{7}$ So $\lambda : 1 = 5 : 7$ and $C\left(\frac{29}{12}, \frac{27}{12}, \frac{50}{12}\right) = \left(\frac{29}{12}, \frac{9}{4}, \frac{25}{6}\right)$

12. Let $P(x, y, z)$ be the foot of perpendicular from $A(1, 2, 1)$ on the line joining points $B(1, 4, 6)$ and $C(5, 4, 4)$

then $\left(\frac{5\lambda+1}{1+\lambda}, \frac{4\lambda+4}{\lambda+1}, \frac{4\lambda+6}{\lambda+1}\right) = (x, y, z)$

Also $4\left\{\frac{4\lambda}{\lambda+1}\right\} - 2\left\{\frac{3\lambda+5}{\lambda+1}\right\} = 0$

so $16\lambda - 6\lambda = 10$ gives $\lambda = 1$

i.e., the mid point of AB so $P = (3, 4, 5)$

TEXTUAL EXERCISE 2: (SUBJECTIVE)

1. $A(-1, -3, 4)$; $B(5, -1, 1)$; $C(7, -4, 7)$; $D(1, -6, 10)$

$\Rightarrow |AB| = \sqrt{6^2+2^2+3^2} = 7$, $BC = \sqrt{2^2+3^2+6^2} = 7$,

$CD = \sqrt{6^2+2^2+3^2} = 7$, $AD = \sqrt{2^2+3^2+6^2} = 7$,

As sides are equal so it is a rhombus.

2. Given $\ell + m + n = 0$ and $mn - 2n\ell - 2\ell m = 0$

Put $\ell = -(m+n)$ so $mn + 2n(m+n) + 2m(m+n) = 0$

Gives $2m^2 + 2n^2 + 5mn = 0$, i.e., $(2m+n)(m+2n) = 0$

$\Rightarrow \quad m = -\frac{n}{2}$ or $-2n \Rightarrow \ell = -\frac{n}{2}$ or n respectively

i.e., D.C. s are $\left\langle -\frac{n}{2}, -\frac{n}{2}, n \right\rangle$ or $< n, -2n, n>$

Case (i): For $\left\langle -\frac{n}{2}, -\frac{n}{2}, n \right\rangle$

$\frac{n^2+n^2+4n^2}{4} = 1 \Rightarrow n = \pm\sqrt{\frac{2}{3}}$

Hence D.c's are $\left\langle \mp\frac{1}{\sqrt{6}}, \mp\frac{1}{\sqrt{6}}, \pm\sqrt{\frac{2}{3}} \right\rangle$

Case (ii): For $<n, -2n, n>$

$n^2 + 4n^2 + n^2 = 1 \Rightarrow n = \pm\frac{1}{\sqrt{6}}$

D.C.'s are $\left\langle \pm\frac{1}{\sqrt{6}}, \mp\frac{2}{\sqrt{6}}, \pm\frac{1}{\sqrt{6}} \right\rangle$

3. $\ell + m + n = 0$ so $\ell = -(m+n)$, then $n\ell - 2mn - 2m\ell = 0$ becomes $(-n)\{m+n\} - 2mn + 2m\{m+n\} = 0$

So $2m^2 - n^2 - nm = 0 \Rightarrow (2m+n)(m-n) = 0$

Given $m = n, \frac{-n}{2}$ so D.C. s are $<-2n, n, n>$

$\Rightarrow 4n^2 + n^2 + n^2 = 1 \quad \Rightarrow \quad n = \pm\frac{1}{\sqrt{6}}$

$\Rightarrow \langle \ell_1, m_1, n_1 \rangle \equiv \left\langle \mp\frac{2}{\sqrt{6}}, \pm\frac{1}{\sqrt{6}}, \pm\frac{1}{\sqrt{6}} \right\rangle$

and $\langle \ell_2, m_2, n_2 \rangle \equiv \left\langle \mp\frac{1}{\sqrt{6}}, \mp\frac{1}{\sqrt{6}}, \pm\sqrt{\frac{2}{3}} \right\rangle$

4. Let $ax + by + cz + d = 0$ be the plane, then $O(0, 0, 0)$; $A(1, -2, -1)$; $B(3, -2, 3)$

$\Rightarrow d = 0$ and $a - 2b - c = 0$ also $3a - 2b + 3c = 0$

Putting $c = (a - 2b)$, we get $6a = 8b$

or $\quad a = \frac{4}{3}b \therefore a = \frac{4}{3}b$, $b = b$ and $c = -\frac{2b}{3}$

And the plane is $b\left(\frac{4}{3}x + y - \frac{2}{3}z\right) = 0$

Or $4x + 3y - 2z = 0$

The normal $\pm(\vec{n} = 4\hat{i} + 3\hat{j} - 2\hat{k})$

or $\quad \hat{n} = \pm\left(\frac{4}{\sqrt{29}}\hat{i} + \frac{3}{\sqrt{29}}\hat{j} - \frac{2}{\sqrt{29}}\hat{k}\right)$

D.C's of normal vector $\left\langle \pm\frac{4}{\sqrt{29}}, \pm\frac{3}{\sqrt{29}}, \pm\frac{-2}{\sqrt{29}} \right\rangle$

5. Let ℓ, m, n be the direction cosines of such a line $\ell = m = n$

$\Rightarrow \quad \ell = m = n = \pm\frac{1}{\sqrt{3}}$, gives $\pm\frac{1}{\sqrt{3}}, \pm\frac{1}{\sqrt{3}}, \pm\frac{1}{\sqrt{3}}$

D.c's are $\left\langle \frac{1}{\sqrt{3}}, \frac{1}{\sqrt{3}}, \frac{1}{\sqrt{3}} \right\rangle$ or $\left\langle \frac{-1}{\sqrt{3}}, \frac{-1}{\sqrt{3}}, \frac{-1}{\sqrt{3}} \right\rangle$

6. Given $\alpha = 30°$, $\beta = 45°$ $\therefore \ell = \frac{\sqrt{3}}{2}$, $m = \frac{1}{\sqrt{2}}$

from $\ell^2 + m^2 + n^2 = 1$, we get $n^2 = 1 - \frac{3}{4} - \frac{1}{2} = -\frac{1}{4}$

such a line is not possible

7. $|\vec{r}| = 21$, $D.R'.s = <2, -3, 6>$

DC's $\left(\text{since} \frac{\pi}{2} < \alpha < \pi\right) = \left\langle -\frac{2}{7} \frac{3}{7} \frac{-6}{7} \right\rangle$

As result $\vec{r} = -6\hat{i} + 9\hat{j} - 18\hat{k}$

8. Since ℓ_1, m_1, n_1 are the D.C's of the line L_1 $\therefore$ Unit vector along L_1 is $\ell_1\hat{i} + m_1\hat{j} + n_1\hat{k}$

Similarly unit vector along L_2 is $\ell_2\hat{i} + m_2\hat{j} + n_2\hat{k}$

Vector along the $\angle$bisector is

$(\ell_1 + \ell_2)\hat{i} + (m_1 + m_2)\hat{j} + (n_1 + n_2)\hat{k}$

$\therefore$ D.C's of bisector are proportional to $(\ell_1 + \ell_2)$, $(m_1 + m_2)$, $(n_1 + n_2)$

9. **(i)** $\ell = -(m+n) \quad \Rightarrow 2\ell m + 2\ell n - mn = 0$

So $(-2)(m+n)(m+n) - mn = 0$ gives

$2m^2 - 5mn + 2n^2 = 0$ or $(2m+n)(m+2n) = 0$

Case i: $m = -2n \quad \Rightarrow$ D.R's $<n, -2n, n>$

$\therefore \quad D.c's \pm\left\langle \frac{1}{\sqrt{6}}, \frac{-2}{\sqrt{6}}, \frac{1}{\sqrt{6}} \right\rangle$

Case **ii:** m $= -\frac{n}{2}, \ell = -\frac{n}{2}$ gives D.R's $\left\langle -\frac{n}{2}, -\frac{n}{2}, n \right\rangle$

And D.C's are $\mp\left\langle \frac{1}{\sqrt{6}}, \frac{1}{\sqrt{6}}, \frac{-2}{\sqrt{6}} \right\rangle$

(ii) $\ell = 5m - 3n$ gives $7\ell^2 = 7(5m-3n)^2 = 3n^2 - 5m^2$
$\Rightarrow 7(25m^2 + 9n^2 - 30mn) + 5m^2 - 3n^2 = 0$
$\Rightarrow 30\{6m^2 + 2n^2 - 7mn\} = 0$
$\Rightarrow (3m - 2n)(2m - n) = 0$

Case (i): $m = \frac{n}{2}$ gives D.R.'s $\left\langle -\frac{n}{2}, \frac{n}{2}, n \right\rangle$

So D.C. s $\pm\left\langle -\frac{1}{\sqrt{6}}, \frac{1}{\sqrt{6}}, \frac{2}{\sqrt{6}} \right\rangle$

Case (ii): $m = \frac{2}{3}n$ gives D.R.s $\left\langle \frac{n}{3}, \frac{2n}{3}, n \right\rangle$

Hence D.C.'s are $\pm\left\langle \frac{1}{\sqrt{14}}, \frac{2}{\sqrt{14}}, \frac{3}{\sqrt{14}} \right\rangle$

10. $P(1, 3, 5)$, $O(0, 0, 0)$ and the plane is $x + y - z + 3 = 0$

$\lambda = \frac{-\{2\}}{\{3\}} < 0 \Rightarrow \frac{P_1}{P_2} > 0$ so points are on the same side

11. $A(-1, 2, -3)$, $B(5, 0, -6)$, $C(0, 4, -1)$

D.R.'s of AB = <6, –2, –3> so D.C.' s $\left\langle \frac{6}{7}, \frac{-2}{7}, \frac{-3}{7} \right\rangle$

Similarly DR's of AC <1, 2, 2> so D.C.s $\left\langle \frac{1}{3}, \frac{2}{3}, \frac{2}{3} \right\rangle$

D.R's of the bisector of angle BAC = <25, 8, 5>

TEXTUAL EXERCISE 3: (SUBJECTIVE)

1. $-\ell = (m + n)$ and $\ell^2 = m^2 - n^2$
$\Rightarrow \{-(m + n)\}^2 = m^2 + n^2 + 2mn = m^2 - n^2$
Gives $2n(n + m) = 0$

So (i) $n = 0$, then $m = -\ell$, so D.C's $\left\langle \frac{1}{\sqrt{2}}, \frac{-1}{\sqrt{2}}, 0 \right\rangle$

(ii) $n = -m$, then $\ell = 0$, so D.C's $\left\langle 0, \frac{1}{\sqrt{2}}, \frac{-1}{\sqrt{2}} \right\rangle$

Angle between the lines $|\cos\theta| = \left|\frac{1}{2}\right|$ gives $\theta = \frac{\pi}{3}$

2. D.R. of line $L_1 = \langle 6, 9, 18 \rangle = \left\langle \frac{2}{7}, \frac{3}{7}, \frac{6}{7} \right\rangle$

D.R of line $L_2 = \langle 1, 2, 2 \rangle = \left\langle \frac{1}{3}, \frac{2}{3}, \frac{2}{3} \right\rangle$

$\cos\theta = \frac{2 + 6 + 12}{(3)(7)} = \frac{20}{21}$. Hence $\theta = \cos^{-1}\left(\frac{20}{21}\right)$

3. Length of line vector = 63

D.R.'s = <3, –2, 6> $\Rightarrow \vec{r} = 27\hat{i} + 18\hat{j} + 54\hat{k}$

Components are $27, -18, 54$

4. Foot of perpendicular from origin is (11, 11, 11)
$\Rightarrow$ Normal vector $\vec{n} = \pm(11\hat{i} + 11\hat{j} + 11\hat{k})$

Normal vector $\vec{n} = \pm(\hat{i} + \hat{j} + \hat{k})$ and the plane is $P: x + y + z + d = 0$ since (11, 11, 11) lies on the plane so $d = -33$ and $P: x + y + z - 33 = 0$ i.e., x – intercept = y – intercept = z – intercept = 33
The required sum = $3 \times (33)^2 = 3267$

5. As shown DR's of = <1, 1, 1>
D.R's of DB = <1, 1, –1>
D.R's of AG = <–1, 1, 1>
DR.s of CE <1, –1, 1>

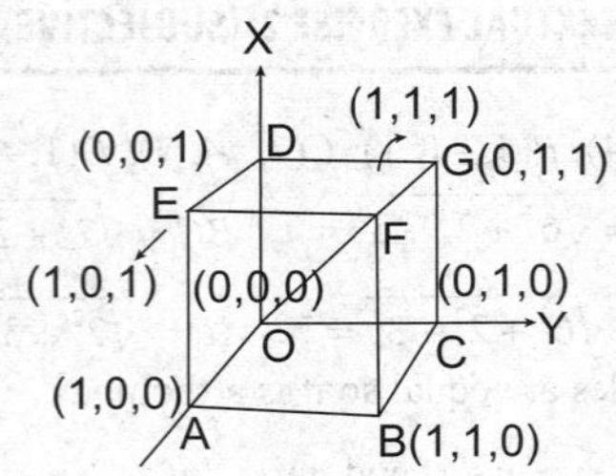

Let ℓ, m, n be the D.C.' s of the line and it makes $\angle$s $\alpha, \beta, \gamma, \phi$ with these four vectors (Diagonals)
$\cos^2\alpha + \cos^2\beta + \cos^2\gamma + \cos^2\phi$

$$= \frac{\ell^2 + m^2 + n^2}{3} + \frac{\ell^2 + m^2 + n^2}{3} + \frac{\ell^2 + m^2 + n^2}{3} + \frac{\ell^2 + m^2 + n^2}{3}$$

$$= \frac{4}{3}(\ell^2 + m^2 + n^2) = \frac{4}{3}$$

6. Let line vector be $\vec{r} = x\hat{i} + y\hat{j} + z\hat{k}$, then projection with coordinate axes will be x, y, z respectively
$\Rightarrow \vec{r} = 4\hat{i} + 12\hat{j} + 3\hat{k}$

$\Rightarrow |\vec{r}| = 13$ units $\Rightarrow$ D.C.'s are $\left\langle \frac{4}{13}, \frac{12}{13}, \frac{3}{13} \right\rangle$

7. $a^2\ell + b^2m + c^2n = 0$
$\Rightarrow \ell = \frac{-1}{a^2}\{b^2m + c^2n\}$ $nm + n\ell + \ell m = 0$

$\Rightarrow mn + (b^2m + c^2n)\left(\frac{-1}{a^2}\right)(m + n) = 0$

$\Rightarrow b^2m^2 + c^2n^2 + (b^2 + c^2 - a^2)mn = 0$

$\Rightarrow m = \{a^2 - (b^2 + c^2)\}n$
$\pm\sqrt{\{(b^2 + c^2) - a^2\}^2 n^2 - 4b^2c^2n^2}$

The lines will be parallel when there is only one value of m, i.e., $\{(b^2 + c^2) - a^2\}^2 = 4b^2c^2$
or $|(b^2 + c^2 - a^2)| = |\pm 2bc|$
$b^2 + c^2 + 2bc = a^2$ or $(b + c)^2 = a^2$
$b^2 + c^2 - 2bc = a^2$ or $(b - c)^2 = a^2$
$\Rightarrow$ so $|b \pm c| = |a| \Rightarrow$ one possibility is $a + b + c = 0$

8. *Observe* that distance of $A(3, 2, 2)$; $B(-1, 1, 3)$; $C(0, 5, 6)$; $D(2, 1, 6)$ from $P(1, 3, 4)$ is $|AP| = |BP| = |CP| = |DP| = \sqrt{1^2 + 2^2 + 2^2} = 3$ units. Hence the points lie on a sphere of radius 3 units

9. A general point on the line joining in (3, –1, 2) and (9 –3, 6) is $\left(\frac{9\lambda+3}{1+\lambda}, \frac{-3\lambda-1}{1+\lambda}, \frac{6\lambda+2}{1+\lambda}\right)$

The point will lie on the sphere $x^2 + y^2 + z^2 - 350 = 0$

If $(9\lambda + 3)^2 + (-3\lambda - 1)^2 + (6\lambda + 2)^2 - 350\ (\lambda + 1)^2 = 0$

$\Rightarrow\ (126 - 350)\lambda^2 + (72 - 700)\lambda + (14 - 350) = 0$

or $4(56\lambda^2 + 157\lambda + 84\} = 0$ gives $\lambda = \frac{-157 \pm \sqrt{5833}}{112}$

10. Let α, β, γ be the angles that a unit vector $\left(\hat{r} = \ell\hat{i} + m\hat{j} + n\hat{k}\right)$ makes with these three mutually perpendicular lines

$\Rightarrow\ \cos\alpha = \cos\beta = \cos\gamma = \frac{1}{\sqrt{3}}$

since $\cos^2\alpha + \cos^2\beta + \cos^2\gamma = 1$

$p = 1, 2, 3 \Rightarrow (\ell\ell_p + mm_p + nn_p)^2 = 1/3$ (Similarly other parts)

and $\ell_1\ell_2 + m_1m_2 + n_1n_2 = 0$ (Similarly other parts)

$\ell_1^2 + m_1^2 + n_1^2 = 1$ (Similarly other parts)

This will give $\ell^2\left(\ell_1^2 + m_1^2 + n_1^2\right) = \left(\frac{\ell_1 + \ell_2 + \ell_3}{\sqrt{3}}\right)^2$

i.e., $\ell = \frac{\ell_1 + \ell_2 + \ell_3}{\sqrt{3}}$. Similarly m and n

11. Let x-axis be along OA (and other axis similarly)

$\overline{OF} = a\hat{i} + b\hat{j} + c\hat{k}$

$\widehat{OF} = \frac{a\hat{i} + b\hat{j} + c\hat{k}}{\sqrt{a^2 + b^2 + c^2}}$

$\overline{CE} = a\hat{i} - b\hat{j} + c\hat{k}$

$\widehat{CE} = \frac{a\hat{i} - b\hat{j} + c\hat{k}}{\sqrt{a^2 + b^2 + c^2}}$, $\widehat{EC} = \frac{-a\hat{i} + b\hat{j} - c\hat{k}}{\sqrt{a^2 + b^2 + c^2}}$

Angle is given by

$$|\cos\theta| = \left|\frac{a^2 - b^2 + c^2}{a^2 + b^2 + c^2}\right|, \left|\frac{-a^2 + b^2 - c^2}{a^2 + b^2 + c^2}\right|$$

Similarly other possibilities $\Rightarrow \theta = \cos^{-1}\left(\frac{\pm a^2 \pm b^2 \pm c^2}{a^2 + b^2 + c^2}\right)$

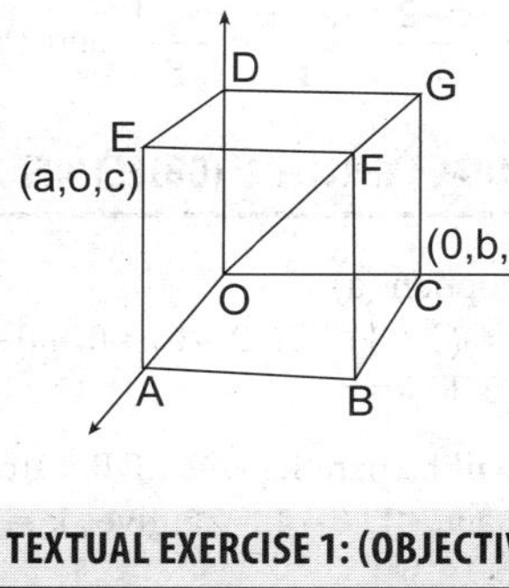

TEXTUAL EXERCISE 1: (OBJECTIVE)

1. (c) Distance between $A(1, 3, 2)$ and $B(2, 1, 3)$ is $|AB| = \sqrt{1^2 + (-2)^2 + 1^2} = \sqrt{6}$

2. (d) The D.C.'s of a normal to x-y plane will be <0, 0, 1>

3. (a) $y^2 + z^2 = 0 \Rightarrow y = 0$ and $z = 0$. Now only x can vary

$\Rightarrow$ This is possible for the points on x-axis

4. (a) $\left\langle \frac{1}{2}, \frac{1}{3}, n \right\rangle$ are the D.C.'s of a straight line

$\Rightarrow\ \frac{1}{4} + \frac{1}{9} + n^2 = 1$ so $n^2 = \frac{23}{36}$ i.e., $n = \pm\frac{\sqrt{23}}{6}$

5. (i) (a) Point (x, y, z) when y = 0 is xz plane

(ii) (b) $z = c \Rightarrow$ a plane parallel to xy plane

(iii) (a) $y = 0, z = 0 \Rightarrow$ x-axis

(iv) (b) $y = b, z = c$

$\Rightarrow$ A straight line parallel to x-axis and passing through (0, b, c)

6. **(a)** Projection of a line on coordinate axes are 2, 3, 6

$\Rightarrow$ Length of the line = $\sqrt{2^2 + 3^2 + 6^2} = 7$ units

7. **(b)** We know that $\cos^2\alpha + \cos^2\beta + \cos^2\gamma = 1$ and $\sin^2\alpha + \sin^2\beta + \sin^2\gamma = 2$

So $\cos 2\alpha + \cos 2\beta + \cos 2\gamma = (2\cos^2\alpha - 1) + (2\cos^2\beta - 1) + (2\cos^2\gamma - 1) = -1$

8. (b) $A(2, 4, 5)$ and $B(-4, 3, -2)$ will be divided by x-y plane in the ratio λ : 1, then $z = \frac{-2\lambda + 5}{\lambda + 1} = 0$

so λ = 5/2 i.e., λ : 1 = 5:2

9. **(b)** Distance of $A(1, 2, 3)$ from x-axis = $\sqrt{4+9} = \sqrt{13}$, from y-axis = $\sqrt{1+9} = \sqrt{10}$ and from z axis = $\sqrt{4+1} = \sqrt{5}$ respectively

$\Rightarrow\ \sqrt{13}, \sqrt{10}, \sqrt{5}$

10. (a) $\overline{AB} = \hat{i} + 2\hat{j} - 2\hat{k}$; $\overline{CD} = 2\hat{i} + 3\hat{j} + 4\hat{k} = \sqrt{29}$

D.R.'s of AB are <1, 2, –2> and D.R.'s of Δ CD are <2, 3, 4>

$\therefore$ Projection of AB on $CD = \frac{|2 + 6 - 8|}{\sqrt{29}} = 0 \Rightarrow AB \perp CD$

11. **(b)** Point $P(x, y, z)$ moves parallel to x-axis

So y and z values remain fixed.

12. **(a)** D.R.'s of AB = <3, 5, –2>

D.R.' s of CD <6, 2, 3>

Projection AB on $CD = \frac{18 + 10 - 6}{7} = \frac{22}{7}$

13. **(c)** *Observe* that (0, 0, 1) is the mid point of (1, –1, 1) and (–1, 1, 1), similarly (2, 2, 2) is the mid point of (1, 2, 3) and (3, 2, 1). Also $A(2, 0, -1)$; $B(3, 2, -2)$ and $C(5, 6, -4)$ are collinear as D.R.'s of AB = <1, 2, –1> and D.R.'s of AC = <3, 6, –3>. Points under option (c) are not collinear

As AB has D.R.'s <5, –7, 1> and DR's of AC = <–1, –6, 7>

14. **(a)** $A(-2, 4, 7)$, $B(3, -6, -8)$ C(1, –2, –2)

D.R.'s of AB = <5, –10, – 15> D.R.'s of BC = < –2, 4, 6>

observe that D.R.'s are proportionate so points are collinear

15. **(b)** Projection of AB line on a line CD where angle = θ will be $AB\cos\theta$.

16. **(b)** $A(1, 2, -1)$ and $B(-1, 0, 1)$. Now P divides externally in the ratio 1 : 2 i.e., 1 : –2 intersecting

$$\Rightarrow P\left(\frac{-3}{-1}, \frac{-4}{-1}, \frac{3}{-1}\right) = (3, 4, -3)$$

17. **(b)** The vertices of a Δ are $A(0, 1, 2)$; $B(2, -1, 3)$; $C(1, -3, 1)$

$$AB = \sqrt{2^2 + 2^2 + 1^2} = 3;\ BC = \sqrt{(-1)^2 + (-2)^2 + (-2)^2} = 3$$

$$AC = \sqrt{1^2 + (-4)^2 + (-1)^2} = 3\sqrt{2}$$

Observe that $AB = BC$ and $AB^2 + BC^2 = AC^2$

∴ Right ∠ed at B and isosceles

18. **(b)** Let (a, b, c) be a point in space, then sum of the squares of distances from the axes

$= (b^2 + c^2) + (c^2 + a^2) + (a^2 + b^2) = 36.$

so $a^2 + b^2 + c^2 = 18 \Rightarrow OP = \sqrt{18} = 3\sqrt{2}$ units

19. **(c)** Let $x - y$ plane divide the line joining $A(2, 4, 5)$ and $B(3, 5, -4)$ in the ratio λ : 1

$$\Rightarrow \frac{(-4\lambda + 5)}{\lambda + 1} = 0, \text{ i.e., } \lambda = 5/4 \text{ or } \lambda : 1 = 5 : 4$$

and the point on x-y plane $\left(\frac{23}{9}, \frac{41}{9}, 0\right)$

20. **(a)** Let mid points be $D(1, 5, -1)$; $E(0, 4, -2)$; $F(2, 3, 4)$

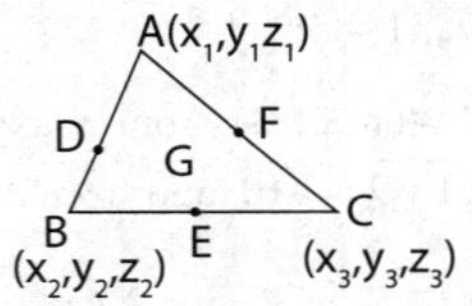

$$\Rightarrow \text{Centroid } G = \left(\frac{3}{3}, \frac{12}{3}, \frac{1}{3}\right)$$

$$\text{Since } G = \left(\frac{x_1 + x_2 + x_3}{3}, \frac{y_1 + y_2 + y_3}{3}, \frac{z_1 + z_2 + z_3}{3}\right)$$

$$\text{and } D = \left(\frac{x_1 + x_2}{2}, \frac{y_1 + y_2}{2}, \frac{z_1 + z_2}{2}\right)$$

So $C = 3G - 2D = (1, 2, 3)$
$B = 3G - 2F = (-1, 6, -7)$
$A = 3G - 2E = (3, 4, 5)$
Vertices are (3, 4, 5), (–1, 6, –7)

21. **(a)** $A(-1, 2, -3)$; $B(5, 0, -6)$; $C(0, 4, -1)$

$\overline{AB} = 6\hat{i} - 2\hat{j} - 3\hat{k} \Rightarrow$ D.C.'s of $\overline{AB} = \left\langle \frac{6}{7}, \frac{-2}{7}, \frac{-3}{7} \right\rangle$

and $\overline{AC} = \hat{i} + 2\hat{j} + 2\hat{k}$; so D.C.'s of $\overline{AC} = \left\langle \frac{1}{3}, \frac{2}{3}, \frac{2}{3} \right\rangle$

D.R's of ∠ bisector of ∠BAC = <25, 8, 5>

22. **(b)** Perpendicular distance of a point $P(x, y, z)$ is from x-axis $= \sqrt{y^2 + z^2}$; from y-axis $= \sqrt{x^2 + z^2}$; from z-axis $= \sqrt{x^2 + y^2}$

23. **(a)** Let $O(0, 0, 0)$; $A(a, 0, 0)$; $B(0, b, 0)$; $C(0, 0, c)$

Let $P(x, y, z)$ be equidistance from O, A, B, C then $x^2 + y^2 + z^2 = (x - a)^2 + y^2 + z^2 = x^2 + (y - b)^2 + z^2 = x^2 + y^2 + (z - c)^2$

Now $x^2 + y^2 + z^2 = (x - a)^2 + y^2 + z^2$

⇒ Either $a = 0$ or $x = a/2$

Similarly (b = 0) **or** $y = \frac{b}{2}$ and (c = 0) or $z = \frac{c}{2}$.Hence

$$P\left(\frac{a}{2}, \frac{b}{2}, \frac{c}{2}\right)$$

24. **(a)** $\ell + m + n = 0$ is satisfied by the values in option (a) and (b). Further $2\ell(m + n) = mn$ is satisfied only by the values under option (a)

TEXTUAL EXERCISE 4: (SUBJECTIVE)

1. $A(1, 2, -1)$, $B(2, 1, 1)$ gives $\vec{a} = \hat{i} + 2\hat{j} - \hat{k}$, $\overline{AB} = \vec{b} = \hat{i} - \hat{j} + 2\hat{k}$

⇒ The required vector equation of straight line is $\vec{r} = (\hat{i} + 2\hat{j} - \hat{k}) + \lambda(\hat{i} - \hat{j} + 2\hat{k})$

The Cartesian form is $\frac{x-1}{1} = \frac{y-2}{-1} = \frac{z+1}{2}$

2. $\vec{a} = \hat{i} + 2\hat{j} + 3\hat{k}$ and $\vec{b} = \hat{i} - 2\hat{j} + 3\hat{k}$

The vector equation is $\vec{r} = (\hat{i} + 2\hat{j} + 3\hat{k}) + \lambda(\hat{i} - 2\hat{j} + 3\hat{k})$

The Cartesian form is $\frac{x-1}{1} = \frac{y-2}{-2} = \frac{z-3}{3}$

3. $\vec{a} = \hat{i} - \hat{j} + 2\hat{k}, \vec{b} = \hat{i} + 2\hat{j} - 2\hat{k}$

The vector equation is $\vec{r} = (\hat{i} - \hat{j} + 2\hat{k}) + \lambda(\hat{i} + 2\hat{j} - 2\hat{k})$

The Cartesian equation is $\frac{x-1}{1} = \frac{y+1}{2} = \frac{z-2}{-2}$

4. $A(4, 5, 10)$, $B(2, 3, 4)$, $C(1, 2, -1)$ vector equation of AB is $\vec{r} = 4\hat{i} + 5\hat{j} + 10\hat{k} + \lambda(2\hat{i} + 2\hat{j} + 6\hat{k})$

The Cartesian equation is $\frac{x-4}{2} = \frac{y-5}{2} = \frac{z-10}{6}$

Vector equation of BC: $\vec{r} = 2\hat{i} + 3\hat{j} + 4\hat{k} + \lambda(\hat{i} + \hat{j} + 5\hat{k})$

Cartesian form $\frac{x-2}{1} = \frac{y-3}{1} = \frac{z-4}{5}$ and D:(3, 4, 5)

TEXTUAL EXERCISE 2: (OBJECTIVE)

1. **(a)** Observing option (a)
$(10)(4 - 1) + (-4)(3 + 1) + 7(-2 - 0) = 0$ and $10(2 - 1) + (-4)(1 - 2) + (7)(-3 + 1) = 0$

2. **(a)** The lines will be parallel when DR's are in proportion i.e., <1, 2, –2> and <1, k – 1, –2> gives k = 3

3. **(a)** The line $\frac{x-0}{k} = \frac{y-0}{k} = \frac{z-0}{k} = \lambda$; where k = direction cosine.

$\Rightarrow \quad 3k^2 = 1 = k = \dfrac{1}{\sqrt{3}} \text{ or} -\dfrac{1}{\sqrt{3}}$

One possible combination is $\left(\dfrac{1}{\sqrt{3}}, \dfrac{1}{\sqrt{3}}, \dfrac{1}{\sqrt{3}}\right)$

4. **(b)** There are eight possible combinations of D.C.'s $\left(\dfrac{\pm 1}{\sqrt{3}} \dfrac{\pm 1}{\sqrt{3}} \dfrac{\pm 1}{\sqrt{3}}\right)$ with four lines of support

   $\Rightarrow$ No. of lines = 4 {as these are not directed lines}

5. The equation of a line parallel to z-axis passing through (a, b, c) will have DR's <0, 0, 1>.

   Hence the equation is $\dfrac{x-a}{0} = \dfrac{y-b}{0} = \dfrac{z-c}{1}$

6. **(c)** The equation of x-axis $\dfrac{x-0}{1} = \dfrac{y-0}{0} = \dfrac{z-0}{0}$

7. **(d)** The given line has D.R.'s <3, 1, 0>. Now z-axis has D.R.'s = <0, 0, 1> and product of D.R.'s = 0 i.e., 3(0) + 1(0) + 0(1) = 0 $\Rightarrow$ line is perpendicular to z-axis

8. (b) Projection of vector $3\hat{i} + 5\hat{j} - 2\hat{k}$ on a line with D.R.'s <6, 2, 3> is $\dfrac{18+10-6}{7} = \dfrac{22}{7}$

9. **(a)** D.R.'s of the line <3, 2, 4>

   Normal to the plane $\vec{n} = 2\hat{i} + \hat{j} - 3\hat{k}$

   $\Rightarrow \quad \sin\theta = \dfrac{|6+2-12|}{\sqrt{29}\sqrt{14}} = \dfrac{4}{\sqrt{406}} \Rightarrow \theta = \sin^{-1}\left(\dfrac{4}{\sqrt{406}}\right)$

10. **(d)** The lines are $\dfrac{x}{1/2} = \dfrac{y}{1/3} = \dfrac{z}{-1}$ .....(i)

    $\Rightarrow$ DR's of (i) are <3, 2, –6>

    and $\dfrac{x}{1/6} = \dfrac{y}{-1} = \dfrac{z}{-1/4}$ ...(ii)

    $\Rightarrow$ DR's of (ii) are <2, –12, –3>

    $\Rightarrow \quad \cos\theta = \dfrac{|6-24+18|}{7\sqrt{157}} = 0 \Rightarrow \theta = 90°$

11. **(b)** If $\dfrac{x-x_1}{\ell} = \dfrac{y-y_1}{m} = \dfrac{z-z_1}{n}$ is parallel to $ax + by + cz + d = 0$, then normal to the plane $\vec{n} = a\hat{i} + b\hat{j} + c\hat{k}$ is perpendicular to this line with DR's $<\ell, m, n>$

    $\Rightarrow \quad a\ell + bm + cn = 0$

12. **(d)** DR's of the lines are <2, 2, –1> and <1, 2, 2>

    $\Rightarrow \quad \cos\theta = \dfrac{|2+4-2|}{(3)(3)} = \dfrac{4}{9} \Rightarrow \theta = \cos^{-1}\left(\dfrac{4}{9}\right)$

TEXTUAL EXERCISE 5: (SUBJECTIVE)

1. (i) Observe that $\vec{b}_1 = \dfrac{1}{2}\vec{b}_2$

   So lines are parallel $\Rightarrow \theta = 0^0$

   Aliter: Angle between L_1 and $L_2 \Rightarrow \cos\theta = \dfrac{\vec{b}_1.\vec{b}_2}{|\vec{b}_1||\vec{b}_2|}$

   $= \dfrac{(\hat{i}+2\hat{j}-2\hat{k}).(2\hat{i}+4\hat{j}-4\hat{k})}{(3)(6)} = 1 \Rightarrow \theta = 0^0$

   (ii) $\vec{r}_1 = \lambda(\hat{i}+\hat{j}+2\hat{k})$

   $\vec{r}_2 = 2\hat{j} + \mu\{(\sqrt{3}-1)\hat{i} - (\sqrt{3}+1)\hat{j} + 4\hat{k}\}$

   $\Rightarrow \quad \cos\theta = \dfrac{(\sqrt{3}-1)-(\sqrt{3}+1)+8}{\sqrt{6}\sqrt{24}} = \dfrac{6}{12} \Rightarrow \theta = \dfrac{\pi}{3}$

2. D.R.'s of lines <2, 2, 1> and <4, 1, 8>

   $\therefore \quad \cos\theta = \dfrac{8+2+8}{(3)(9)} = \dfrac{2}{3} \Rightarrow \theta = \cos^{-1}\left(\dfrac{2}{3}\right)$

3. D.R.'s of the line $\dfrac{x-3}{4} = \dfrac{y-5}{2} = \dfrac{z+1}{3}$ are <4, 2, 3>

   $\Rightarrow$ The required line through (1, 2, –4) will be $\dfrac{x-1}{4} = \dfrac{y-2}{2} = \dfrac{z+4}{3}$

4. A vector perpendicular to $\dfrac{x-1}{1} = \dfrac{y-2}{2} = \dfrac{z-3}{3}$ and $\dfrac{x}{-3} = \dfrac{y}{2} = \dfrac{z}{5}$ is $\vec{b}_1 \times \vec{b}_2$

   i.e., $\vec{n} = \pm\begin{vmatrix} \hat{i} & \hat{j} & \hat{k} \\ 1 & 2 & 3 \\ -3 & 2 & 5 \end{vmatrix} = \pm(4\hat{i} - 14\hat{j} + 8\hat{k})$

   The required line through (2, 1, 3) will be

   $\vec{r} = (2\hat{i}+\hat{j}+3\hat{k}) + \lambda(2\hat{i} - 7\hat{j} + 4\hat{k})$ in vector form and $\dfrac{x-2}{2} = \dfrac{y-1}{-7} = \dfrac{z-3}{4}$ in cartesian form.

5. Line passing through (2, –1, –1) and parallel to $6x - 2 = 3y + 1 = 2z - 2$ i.e., $\dfrac{x-1/3}{(1/6)} = \dfrac{y+\frac{1}{3}}{(1/3)} = \dfrac{z-1}{(1/2)}$ will be

   $\vec{r} = (2\hat{i} - \hat{j} - \hat{k}) + \lambda(\hat{i} + 2\hat{j} - 3\hat{k})$

6. The line will be perpendicular when $\{-9\lambda + 2\lambda - 10\} = 0$ or $\lambda = \dfrac{-10}{7}$

7. $d = \sqrt{(\vec{r}_1)^2 - (\vec{r}_1.\hat{r}_2)^2}$

   $r_1^2 = 0^2 + (+1)^2 + (+10)^2 = 101, \left(\vec{r}_1 = 0\hat{i} + \hat{j} + 10\hat{k}\right)$

   $\hat{r}_2 = \dfrac{2\hat{i} - 3\hat{j} + 8\hat{k}}{\sqrt{77}}$ **and** $\vec{r}_1.\hat{r}_2 = \dfrac{+77}{\sqrt{77}}$

   $d = \sqrt{101-77} = \sqrt{24} = 2\sqrt{6}$ units

   Foot of perpendicular $= (\hat{i} - \hat{j} - 10\hat{k}) + (\vec{r}_1.\hat{r}_2)\hat{r}_2$

   $= \left(\hat{i} - \hat{j} - 10\hat{k}\right) + (2\hat{i} - 3\hat{j} + 8\hat{k})$

   $= 3\hat{i} - 4\hat{j} - 2\hat{k} \therefore M(3, -4, -2)$

8. $P(2, 4, -1)$ and $(\lambda -5 -2) + 4\{4\lambda -3 -4\} + (-9)\ \{(-9\lambda) + 6 + 1\} = 0$
Gives $\lambda = 1$ and $(\lambda - 5, 4\lambda -3, -9\lambda + 6) = (-4, 1, -3)$
$\Rightarrow$ Equation of perpendicular $\dfrac{x-2}{-6} = \dfrac{y-4}{-3} = \dfrac{z+1}{-2}$

9. Point $P(5, 9, 3)$ and $2(2\lambda + 1 -5) + 3(3\lambda + 2 -9) + 4(4\lambda +3 -3) = 0$ gives $\lambda = 1$ and foot $M(2\lambda + 1, 3\lambda + 2, 4\lambda + 3) = (3, 5, 7)$ (from $Q = 2M - P$). Now the image $Q = (1, 1, 11)$

10. $P(2, -1, 5)$ and $10(10\lambda + 11 - 2) + (-4)\ \{-4\lambda - 2 + 1\} - 11\ \{-11\lambda - 8 - 5\} = 0$ gives $\lambda = -1$ and Foot $M(10\lambda + 11, -4\lambda - 2, -11\lambda - 8) = (1, 2, 3)$
The image $= 2M - P = (0, 5, 1)$

Vector Method: $P(\vec{p}) = 2\hat{i} - \hat{j} + 5\hat{k},\ \ \vec{r}_1 = -9\hat{i} + \hat{j} + 13\hat{k}$

and $\hat{r}_2 = \dfrac{10\hat{i} - 4\hat{j} - 11\hat{k}}{\sqrt{237}}$

Foot $M(\vec{m}) = (11\hat{i} - 2\hat{j} - 8\hat{k}) + (\vec{r}_1.\hat{r}_2)\hat{r}_2$

$= (11\hat{i} - 2\hat{j} - 8\hat{k}) + \dfrac{-237}{237}\{10\hat{i} - 4\hat{j} - 11\hat{k}\} = \hat{i} + 2\hat{j} + 3\hat{k}$

so $M = (1, 2, 3)$

Hence the image $Q(\vec{q}) = 2\vec{m} - \vec{p} = 0\hat{i} + 5\hat{j} + \hat{k}\ Q = (0,5,1)$

11. (a) $A(3, 4, 1)$ and $B(5, 1, 6)$
Line AB will meet xy plane for $z = 0$ and let $P(x, y, 0)$ divide AB in $\lambda : 1$ ratio

So $\dfrac{6\lambda + 1}{\lambda + 1} = 0 \Rightarrow \lambda = -\dfrac{1}{6} \Rightarrow P\left(\dfrac{3 - \frac{5}{6}}{5/6}, \dfrac{4 - \frac{1}{6}}{5/6}, 0\right)$

$\Rightarrow\ P \equiv \left(\dfrac{13}{5}, \dfrac{23}{5}, 0\right)$

(b) Let the line through $A(5, 1, 6)$ and $B(3, 4, 1)$ intersect YZ plane in $\lambda : 1$ ratio at $P(0, y, z)$

So $\dfrac{3\lambda + 5}{\lambda + 1} = 0$ gives $\lambda = -5/3$

Now $P\left(\dfrac{-5+5}{(-2/3)}, \dfrac{\frac{-17}{3}}{(-2/3)}, \dfrac{\frac{13}{3}}{(-2/3)}\right)$

So $P\left(0, \dfrac{17}{2}, -\dfrac{13}{2}\right)$

Let point P on $2x + y + z = 7$ divide the line joining $A(3, -4, -5)$ and $B(2, -3, 1)$ in $\lambda : 1$ ratio

$\Rightarrow\ \dfrac{2(2\lambda + 3) + (-3\lambda - 4) + (\lambda - 5)}{(1 + \lambda)} = 7$ gives $\lambda = -2$

and $P \equiv (1, -2, 7)$

12. Equation of line joining $A(4, 7, 8)$, and $B(-1, -2, 1)$ is $\vec{r}_1 = (4\hat{i} + 7\hat{j} + 8\hat{k}) + (-\lambda)(5\hat{i} + 9\hat{j} + 7\hat{k})$
Similarly, equation of line joining the points $C(2, 3, 4)$ and $D(1, 2, 5)$ is $\vec{r}_2 = (2\hat{i} + 3\hat{j} + 4\hat{k}) + (-\mu)(\hat{i} + \hat{j} - \hat{k})$
$\vec{r}_1 = \vec{r}_2$ gives $4 - 5\lambda = 2 - \mu;\ 7 - 9\lambda = 3 - \mu;\ 8 - 7\lambda = 4 + \mu$.

$\Rightarrow\ \lambda = 1/2,\ \mu = -2 + 5\lambda = 1/2$

$\therefore$ The point of intersection is $\left(\dfrac{3}{2}, \dfrac{5}{2}, \dfrac{9}{2}\right)$

13. (a) $(\lambda - 1) + 2(2\lambda + 1 - 6) + 3(3\lambda + 2 - 3) = 0$ gives $14\lambda - 14 = 0$ so $\lambda = 1$ where $P(1, 6, 3)$. The foot of perpendicular $M(1, 3, 5)$. The image $Q = 2M - P = (1, 0, 7)$.

(b) $P(\vec{p}) = \hat{i} + 2\hat{j} + 3\hat{k}$

$\vec{r} = (6\hat{i} + 7\hat{j} + 7\hat{k}) + \lambda(3\hat{i} + 2\hat{j} - 2\hat{k})$

Now $\vec{r}_1 = -5\hat{i} - 5\hat{j} - 4\hat{k}$

Foot of perpendicular $M(\vec{m}) = (6\hat{i} + 7\hat{j} + 7\hat{k}) + (\vec{r}_1.\hat{r}_2)\hat{r}_2$

$= (6\hat{i} + 7\hat{j} + 7\hat{k}) + \dfrac{(-17)}{17}(3\hat{i} + 2\hat{j} - 2\hat{k})$

$= \vec{m} = 3\hat{i} + 5\hat{j} + 9\hat{k}$

Image of P is $Q\ (\vec{q}) = 2\vec{m} - \vec{p}$

$= 5\hat{i} + 8\hat{j} + 15\hat{k}$, so $Q(5, 8, 15)$

14. $L_1 : \dfrac{x}{1} = \dfrac{y-2}{2} = \dfrac{z+3}{3} = \lambda \Rightarrow \vec{r}_1 = \lambda i + (2\lambda + 2)\hat{j} + (3\lambda - 3)\hat{k}$

$L_2 : \dfrac{x-2}{2} = \dfrac{y-6}{3} = \dfrac{z-3}{4} = \mu$

$\Rightarrow\ \vec{r}_2 = (2 + 2\mu)\hat{i} + (6 + 3\mu)\hat{j} + (3 + 4\mu)\hat{k}$

Equating $\lambda = 2 + 2\mu;\ 2 + 2\lambda = 6 + 3\mu$ given $6 + 4\mu = 6 + 3\mu$, so $\mu = 0$ and $\lambda = 2$ which also satisfies $3\lambda - 3 = 3 + 4\mu$
So the point of intersection is $(2, 6, 3)$ (i.e., point C)

15. $L_1 : \dfrac{x-1}{3} = \dfrac{y+1}{2} = \dfrac{z-1}{5} = \lambda$

$\Rightarrow\ \vec{r}_1 = (3\lambda + 1)\hat{i} + (2\lambda - 1)\hat{j} + (5\lambda + 1)\hat{k}$

And $L_2 : \dfrac{x+2}{4} = \dfrac{y-1}{3} = \dfrac{z+1}{-2} = \mu$

$\Rightarrow\ \vec{r}_2 = (4\mu - 2)\hat{i} + (3\mu + 1)\hat{j} + (-2\mu - 1)\hat{k}$

Equating $3\lambda + 1 = 4\mu - 2$ and $2\lambda - 1 = 3\mu + 1$ gives $\lambda = -17,\ \mu = -12$
Putting in $5\lambda + 1 = -2\mu - 1$, gives $-84 = 23$ which is not true
$\therefore$ lines do not cross each other

16. Line $L_1 : \vec{r}_1 = (\hat{i} + \hat{j} - \hat{k}) + \lambda(3\hat{i} - \hat{j})$
and $L_2 : \vec{r}_2 = (4\hat{i} - \hat{k}) + \mu(2\hat{i} + 3\hat{k})$

{Observe that $\vec{b} \neq p\vec{d}$ and $\vec{c} - \vec{a} = \vec{b}$ so $\vec{c}$ is the point of intersection}

$$\left[(\vec{c} - \vec{a})\ \vec{b}\ \vec{d}\right] = \begin{vmatrix} 3 & -1 & 0 \\ 3 & -1 & 0 \\ 2 & 0 & 3 \end{vmatrix} = 0$$

Lines intersect
So $3\lambda + 1 = 2\mu + 4$; $-\lambda + 1 = 0$; $-1 = 3\mu - 1$
(gives $\lambda = 1$); (gives $\mu = 0$)
The point of intersection is $\vec{c}$ i.e., $(4, 0, -1)$

TEXTUAL EXERVCISE 3: (OBJECTIVE)

1. (c) $A=(\vec{a})=(1,2,1), B(\vec{b})=(1,4,6), C(\vec{c})=(5,4,4)$,
$\vec{r}_1=\overrightarrow{BA}=-2\hat{j}-5\hat{k}$, $\vec{r}_2=\overrightarrow{BC}=4\hat{i}-2\hat{k}$
Foot of perpendicular $M(\vec{m})=\vec{b}+(\vec{r}_1.\hat{r}_2)\hat{r}_2$
$=(\hat{i}+4\hat{j}+6\hat{k})+\frac{10}{20}(4\hat{i}-2\hat{k})=3\hat{i}+4\hat{j}+5\hat{k}$

2. (a) Let the foot be $M(5\lambda-3, 2\lambda+1, 3\lambda-4\}$, then $5\{5\lambda-3-0\}+2\{2\lambda+1-2\}+3\{3\lambda-4-3\}=0$
Gives $38\lambda-38=0$ so $\lambda=1$ and $M(2, 3, -1)$ (distance)
Length of perpendicular $=\sqrt{2^2+1^2+4^2}=\sqrt{21}$ units

3. (a) Let $M(\lambda, 2\lambda+1, 3\lambda+2)$ be the foot perpendicular then $(\lambda-1)+2(2\lambda+1-6)+3(3\lambda+2-3)=0$
Gives $14\lambda-14=0$ so $\lambda=1$ and $M(1, 3, 5)$
The image $Q=2M-P=(1, 0, 7)$

4. **(a)** Let $M(\lambda, 2\lambda+1, 3\lambda+2)$ be the of foot of perpendicular from $P(1, 2, 3)$, then $(\lambda-1)+2(2\lambda+1-2)+3(3\lambda+2-3)=0$
$\Rightarrow$ $14\lambda-6=0$ gives $\lambda=3/7$,
so $M\left(\frac{3}{7},\frac{13}{7},\frac{23}{7}\right)$

5. **(a)** Let $M(\vec{m})=(2\lambda, 3\lambda+1, 3\lambda+1)$ be the foot of perpendicular from (1, 2, 3), then $2(2\lambda-1)+3(3\lambda+1-2)+3(3\lambda+1-3)=0$ gives $22\lambda-11=0$ so $\lambda=1/2$ and the foot
$M(\vec{m})=\left(1,\frac{5}{2},\frac{5}{2}\right)$

6. **(c)** $\vec{r}_1=(5\hat{i}-\hat{j}+4\hat{k})+\lambda(\hat{i}+2\hat{j}+2\hat{k})$
$\vec{r}_2=(7\hat{i}+2\hat{j}+2\hat{k})+\mu(3\hat{i}+2\hat{j}+6\hat{k})$
$\Rightarrow \cos\theta=\frac{\vec{b}_1.\vec{b}_2}{|\vec{b}_1||\vec{b}_2|}=\frac{|3+4+12|}{(3)(7)}$
$\Rightarrow \cos\theta=\frac{19}{21}$

7. **(a)** The angle between $\frac{x}{1}=\frac{y}{0}=\frac{z}{-1}$ and $\frac{x}{3}=\frac{y}{4}=\frac{z}{5}$
is given by $\cos\theta=\frac{|3+0-5|}{\sqrt{2}\sqrt{50}}=\frac{2}{5(2)}=\frac{1}{5}$
$\Rightarrow \theta=\cos^{-1}(1/5)$

8. (b, c) D.R.s of L_1: <a, b, c>
D.R.' s of $L_2:\left\langle\frac{1}{bc}\ \frac{1}{ca}\ \frac{1}{ab}\right\rangle=\left\langle\frac{a}{abc}\ \frac{b}{abc}\ \frac{c}{abc}\right\rangle\equiv\langle a,b,c\rangle$
$\Rightarrow$ lines are parallel or coincident.

9. (c) $P(1, 2, 3)$ and the line $L:\frac{x-6}{3}=\frac{y-7}{2}=\frac{z-7}{-2}$
Length of perpendicular $d=\sqrt{(\vec{r}_1)^2-(\vec{r}_1.\hat{r}_2)^2}$
where $\vec{r}_1=-5\hat{i}-5\hat{j}-4\hat{k}\Rightarrow(\vec{r}_1)^2=(\sqrt{66})^2=66$
and $\hat{r}_2=\frac{3\hat{i}+2\hat{j}-2\hat{k}}{\sqrt{17}}$
$\Rightarrow d=\sqrt{65-\left(\frac{17}{\sqrt{17}}\right)^2}=\sqrt{49}=7$ **units**

11. **(a, c)** Line $L_1:\vec{r}_1=(3\hat{i}+2\hat{j}+4\hat{k})+\lambda(\hat{i}+2\hat{j}+2\hat{k})$
Line $L_2:\vec{r}_2=(5\hat{i}-2\hat{j})+\mu(3\hat{i}+2\hat{j}+6\hat{k})$
$\cos\theta=\vec{b}_1.\vec{d}_1=\frac{|3+4+12|}{(3)(7)}=\frac{19}{21}$
$\sin\theta=\frac{\sqrt{80}}{21}=\frac{4\sqrt{5}}{21}$
$\Rightarrow \theta=\cos^{-1}\left(\frac{19}{21}\right)$

12. **(c)** $L_1:\vec{r}_1=(\hat{i}+\hat{j}-\hat{k})+\lambda(3\hat{i}-j)$
$L_2:\vec{r}_2=(4\hat{i}-\hat{k})+\mu(2\hat{i}+3\hat{k})$
Comparison gives $3\lambda+1=2\mu+4$, $1-\lambda=0$ gives $\lambda=1$ and $3\mu-1=-1\Rightarrow\mu=0$
$\lambda=1$, $\mu=0$ satisfies $\therefore$ $C(\vec{c})=4\hat{i}-k$ is the point of intersection $C(4, 0, -1)$

13. **(b)** $L_1:\vec{r}_1=(2\lambda+1)\hat{i}+(3\lambda-1)\hat{j}+(4\lambda+1)\hat{k}$
$L_2:\vec{r}_2=(\mu+3)\hat{i}+(\mu+k)\hat{j}+\mu\hat{k}$
i.e., $2\lambda+1=\mu+3$; $4\lambda+1=\mu$ gives $\mu=-5$, $\lambda=-3/2$
putting in $\mu+k=3\lambda-1\Rightarrow k-5=-9/2-1$
$\Rightarrow k=-1/2$

14. (a) $L_1:\vec{r}_1=(\lambda+3)\hat{i}+(\lambda+k)\hat{j}+\lambda\hat{k}$
$L_2:\vec{r}_2=(2\mu+1)\hat{i}+(3\mu+2)\hat{j}+(4\mu+3)\hat{k}$
gives $2\mu+l=\lambda+3$; $\lambda=4\mu+3$, gives $\mu=-5/2$, $\lambda=-7$
point of intersection $\equiv\left(-4,-\frac{11}{2},-7\right)$

15. (a) A general point P on the given line is
$\vec{r}=(2\lambda+1)i+(-3\lambda+2)\hat{j}+(4\lambda-3)\hat{k}$
If it meets the plane $2x+4y-z=1$,
then $4\lambda+2+8-12\lambda-4\lambda+3=1$ gives $\lambda=1$
$\therefore$ $P(3, -1, 1)$

16. **(c)** Let $M(10\lambda+11, -4\lambda-2, -11\lambda-8)$ be the foot of $\perp$ from $(2, -1, 5)$ then $10(10\lambda+11-2)-4(-4\lambda-2+1)-11(-11\lambda-8-5)=0$ or $237\lambda+237=0$ so $\lambda=-1$
$\therefore$ $M(1, 2, 3)$ and Length of perpendicular
$=\sqrt{1^2+(-3)^2+2^2}=\sqrt{14}$

17. **(d)** A general point P on the line will be $(3\lambda+2, 4\lambda-1, 12\lambda+2)$. If it also lies on the plane $x-y+z=5$, then
$(3\lambda+2)-(4\lambda-1)+(12\lambda+2)=5$ gives $\lambda=0$
$\Rightarrow$ $P(2, -1, 2)$ and its distance from $A(-1, -5, -10)$ is
$d=\sqrt{3^2+4^2+12^2}=13$ units

18. (c) $P(2, 4, -1), A = (-5, -3, 6)$

$\vec{r}_1 = \overline{AP} = 7\hat{i} + 7\hat{j} - 7\hat{k}$ and $\hat{r}_2 = \dfrac{\hat{i} + 4\hat{j} - 9\hat{k}}{\sqrt{98}}$

$d = \sqrt{(\vec{r}_1)^2 - (\vec{r}_1.\hat{r}_2)^2} = \sqrt{49 \times 3 - \dfrac{98 \times 98}{98}} = \sqrt{49} = 7$ units

19. (a) $L_1 : \vec{r}_1 = (5\lambda + 4)\hat{i} + (2\lambda + 1)\hat{j} + \lambda\hat{k}$

$L_2 : \vec{r}_2 = (2\mu + 1)\hat{i} + (3\mu + 2)\hat{j} + (4\mu + 3)\hat{k}$

$\Rightarrow 5\lambda + 4 = 2\mu + 1;\ 2\lambda + 1 = 3\mu + 2;$

$\Rightarrow \lambda = 4\mu + 3$ gives $\mu = -1$ and $\lambda = -1$

Which satisfies the other equation

$\therefore$ Point of intersection $P(-1, -1, -1)$

TEXTUAL EXERCISE 6: (SUBJECTIVE)

1. $\vec{r}_1 = (\hat{i} - 2\hat{j} + 3\hat{k}) + t(-\hat{i} + \hat{j} - \hat{k})$

$\vec{r}_2 = (-\hat{i} + \hat{j} - \hat{k}) + \lambda(\hat{i} + \hat{j} - \hat{k})$

$\vec{a}_2 - \vec{a}_1 = -2\hat{i} + 3\hat{j} - 4\hat{k}$ and

$$\vec{b}_1 \times \vec{b}_2 = \begin{vmatrix} \hat{i} & \hat{j} & \hat{k} \\ -1 & 1 & -1 \\ 1 & 1 & -1 \end{vmatrix} = 0\hat{i} - 2\hat{j} - 2\hat{k} \Rightarrow |\vec{b}_1 \times \vec{b}_2| = \sqrt{8} \text{ units}$$

$\therefore$ Shortest distance $d = \left| \dfrac{(\vec{a}_2 - \vec{a}_1).(\vec{b}_1 \times \vec{b}_2)}{\sqrt{8}} \right| = \dfrac{2}{\sqrt{8}} = \dfrac{1}{\sqrt{2}}$ units

2. (i) $\vec{r}_1 = (\hat{i} + 2\hat{j} + 3\hat{k}) + \lambda(2\hat{i} + 3\hat{j} + 4\hat{k})$

$\vec{r}_2 = (2\hat{i} + 3\hat{j} + 5\hat{k}) + t(3\hat{i} + 4\hat{j} + 5\hat{k})$

Now $\vec{a}_2 - \vec{a}_1 = \hat{i} + \hat{j} + 2\hat{k}$ **and**

$\vec{b}_1 \times \vec{b}_2 = \hat{i} + 2\hat{j} - \hat{k} \Rightarrow |\vec{b}_1 \times \vec{b}_2| = \sqrt{6}$

$\therefore$ shortest distance $d = \left| \dfrac{(\vec{a}_2 - \vec{a}_1).(\vec{b}_1 \times \vec{b}_2)}{|\vec{b}_1 \times \vec{b}_2|} \right| = \dfrac{1}{\sqrt{6}}$ **units**

(ii) $\vec{r}_1 = (\hat{i} - 2\hat{j} + 3\hat{k}) + t(-\hat{i} + \hat{j} - 2\hat{k})$

$\vec{r}_2 = (\hat{i} - \hat{j} - \hat{k}) + \lambda(\hat{i} + 2\hat{j} - 2\hat{k})$

Now $\vec{a}_2 - \vec{a}_1 = \hat{j} - 4\hat{k}$ and $\vec{b}_1 \times \vec{b}_2 = 2\hat{i} - 4\hat{j} - 3\hat{k} = \sqrt{29}$

$\therefore$ Shortest distance $d = \dfrac{|-4 + 12|}{\sqrt{29}} = \dfrac{8}{\sqrt{29}}$ **units.**

3. (i) $\vec{r}_1 = (\hat{i} + \hat{j} - \hat{k}) + \lambda(3\hat{i} - \hat{j})$,

$\vec{r}_2 = (4\hat{i} - \hat{k}) + \mu(2\hat{i} + 3\hat{k})$,

Now $\vec{a}_2 - \vec{a}_1 = 3\hat{i} - \hat{j}$ and $\vec{b}_1 \times \vec{b}_2 = \begin{vmatrix} \hat{i} & \hat{j} & \hat{k} \\ 3 & -1 & 0 \\ 2 & 0 & 3 \end{vmatrix}$

$\vec{b}_1 \times \vec{b}_2 = -3\hat{i} - 9\hat{j} + 2\hat{k} \Rightarrow |\vec{b}_1 \times \vec{b}_2| = \sqrt{94}$

$\therefore$ Shortest distance $d = \left| \dfrac{(\vec{a}_2 - \vec{a}_1).(\vec{b}_1 \times \vec{b}_2)}{|\vec{b}_1 \times \vec{b}_2|} \right| = 0$

Lines do intersect

(ii) $\vec{r}_1 = (\hat{i} - \hat{j}) + \lambda(2\hat{i} + 3\hat{j} + \hat{k})$,

$\vec{r}_2 = (-\hat{i} + 2\hat{j} + 2\hat{k}) + \mu(5\hat{i} + \hat{j} + 0\hat{k})$,

Now $\vec{a}_2 - \vec{a}_1 = -2\hat{i} + 3\hat{j} + 2\hat{k}$

$$b_1 \times b_2 = \begin{vmatrix} \hat{i} & \hat{j} & \hat{k} \\ 2 & 3 & 1 \\ 5 & 1 & 0 \end{vmatrix} = -\hat{i} + 5\hat{j} - 13\hat{k}$$

$\therefore$ S.D. $= \left| \dfrac{(\vec{a}_2 - \vec{a}_1).(\vec{b}_1 \times \vec{b}_2)}{|\vec{b}_1 \times \vec{b}_2|} \right| = \left| \dfrac{2 + 15 - 26}{\sqrt{195}} \right| = \dfrac{9}{\sqrt{195}} \neq 0$

Lines do not intersect

4. $\vec{r}_1 = (\hat{i} + \hat{j}) + \lambda(2\hat{i} - \hat{j} + \hat{k})$,

$\vec{r}_2 = (2\hat{i} + \hat{j} - \hat{k}) + t(4\hat{i} - 2\hat{j} + 2\hat{k})$,

Now $\vec{a}_2 - \vec{a}_1 = \hat{i} - \hat{k}, b_1 = 2\hat{i} - \hat{j} + \hat{k} = \sqrt{6}$

Shortest distance

$d = \dfrac{(\vec{a}_2 - \vec{a}_1) \times \vec{b}_1}{|\vec{b}_1|} = \dfrac{|\hat{i} + 3\hat{j} - \hat{k}|}{\sqrt{6}} = \dfrac{\sqrt{11}}{\sqrt{6}}$ units.

5. A point on the straight line

$L_1 : M(2\lambda + 1, 3\lambda + 2, 4\lambda + 3)$ and

$L_2 : N(3t + 2, 4t + 4, 5t + 5)$

D.R.'s of $MN = (1 + 3t - 2\lambda, 4t + 2 - 3\lambda, 5t + 2 - 4\lambda)$

Since $MN \perp L_1$

$\Rightarrow 2 + 6t - 4\lambda + 12t + 6 - 9\lambda + 20t + 8 - 16\lambda = 0$

i.e., $38t - 29\lambda + 16 = 0$ ....(i)

Similarly, $3 + 9t - 6\lambda + 16t + 8 - 12\lambda + 25t + 10 - 20\lambda = 0$

$50t - 38\lambda + 21 = 0$ ....(ii)

From (i) and (ii), we get $\lambda = 1/3$, $t = -1/6$

$\Rightarrow M\left(\dfrac{5}{3}, 3, \dfrac{13}{3}\right)$ and $N\left(\dfrac{3}{2}, \dfrac{10}{3}, \dfrac{25}{6}\right)$

So $MN = \sqrt{\left(\dfrac{1}{6}\right)^2 + \left(\dfrac{-2}{6}\right)^2 + \left(\dfrac{1}{6}\right)^2} = \dfrac{1}{\sqrt{6}}$ units.

Equation of $MN = \dfrac{3x - 5}{3} = \dfrac{y - 3}{-2} = \dfrac{3z - 13}{3}$.

6. A general point on straight lines L_1 and L_2 are given by $M(-6\lambda + 23, -4\lambda + 19, 3\lambda + 25)$ and $N(12 - 9t, 4t + 1, 2t + 5)$

$\Rightarrow$ D.R.'s of $MN = (6\lambda - 9t - 11, 4\lambda + 4t - 18, 2t - 3\lambda - 20)$

Since $MN \perp L_1$

$\Rightarrow 66 + 54t - 36\lambda + 72 - 16\lambda - 16t + 6t - 9\lambda - 60 = 0$

So $44t - 61\lambda + 78 = 0$

Similarly $MN \perp L_2 \Rightarrow 44t - 61\lambda + 78 = 0$ ....(i)

and $81t + 99 - 54\lambda + 16\lambda + 16t - 72 + 4t - 6\lambda - 40 = 0$

So $101t - 44\lambda - 13 = 0$ ...(ii)

From (i) and (ii), we get $\lambda = 2, t = 1$
So $M(11, 11, 31)$ and $N(3, 5, 7)$

7. $L_1: \vec{r}_1 = (\lambda-1)\hat{i} + (\lambda+1)\hat{j} - (\lambda+1)\hat{k}$,
$L_2: \vec{r}_2 = (1-\mu)\hat{i} + (2\mu-1)\hat{j} + (\mu+2)\hat{k}$,
$M = (\lambda - 1, \lambda + 1, -\lambda - 1)$ and $N(1 - \mu, 2\mu - 1, \mu + 2)$
D.R.'s of $MN = 2 - \mu - \lambda, 2\mu - \lambda - 2, \mu + \lambda + 3$
So $MN \perp L_1$ gives $(2 - \mu - \lambda) + (2\mu - \lambda - 2) - (\mu + \lambda + 3) = 0$
i.e., $-3\lambda - 3 = 0 \Rightarrow \lambda = -1$
$MN \perp L_2$ gives $\mu + \lambda - 2 + 4\mu - 2\lambda - 4 + \mu + \lambda + 3 = 0$
i.e., $6\mu - 3 = 0 \Rightarrow \mu = 1/2$ so $M(-2, 0, 0)$ and $N(1/2, 0, 5/2)$

and $d = \sqrt{\left(\frac{5}{2}\right)^2 + \left(\frac{5}{2}\right)^2} = \sqrt{\frac{50}{4}} = \frac{5}{\sqrt{2}}$

The equation of line MN; $\vec{r} = -2\hat{i} + \lambda\left(\frac{5}{2}\hat{i} + \frac{5}{2}\hat{k}\right)$

or $\vec{r} = -2\hat{i} + \lambda\left(\hat{i} + \hat{k}\right)$

8. Let L_1: $M(2\lambda, 2 - \lambda, -3)$ and L_2: $N(3\mu + 4, \mu, \mu + 3)$
D.R's of $MN = 3\mu + 4 - 2\lambda, \mu + \lambda - 2, \mu + 6$
$MN \perp L_1$ gives $6\mu + 8 - 4\lambda - \mu - \lambda + 2 = 0$
i.e., $5\mu - 5\lambda + 10 = 0$ ....(i)
Similarly $MN \perp L_2$ gives $9\mu - 6\lambda + 12 + \mu + \lambda - 2 + \mu + 6 = 0$
$\Rightarrow 11\mu - 5\lambda + 16 = 0$ ....(ii)
Gives $\mu = -1, \lambda = 1$, So $M(2, 1, -3)$ and $N(1, -1, 2)$

$d = \sqrt{(-1)^2 + (-2)^2 + (5)^2} = \sqrt{30}$ units

$\vec{r} = (2\hat{i} + \hat{j} - 3\hat{k}) + \lambda(-\hat{i} - 2\hat{j} + 5\hat{k})$

TEXTUAL EXERCISE 4: (OBJECTIVE)

1. **(d)** $\frac{x}{1} = \frac{y}{2} = \frac{z}{3}$ and $\frac{x+1}{1} = \frac{y+2}{2} = \frac{z+3}{3}$ are parallel as D.R's are equal, also point $\lambda - 1, 2\lambda - 2, 3\lambda - 3$ lie on first line.
$\Rightarrow$ Lines are coinciding.

2. **(d)** *Observe* that (1, 2, 3) is a common point both for L_1 and L_2 and $\cos\theta = \frac{|(1)(2)+(2)(2)+(3)(-2)|}{\sqrt{14}\sqrt{12}} = 0$

Gives $\theta = 90°$, i.e., lines intersect at $90°$

3. **(c)** $\vec{a}_1 = 2\hat{i} + 3\hat{j} + 4\hat{k}$ and $\vec{a}_2 = \hat{i} + 4\hat{j} + 5\hat{k}$

$\vec{a}_2 - \vec{a}_1 = -\hat{i} + \hat{j} + \hat{k}$

The lines will be coplanar when $\left[\vec{a_2} - \vec{a_1}\ \vec{b}\ \vec{d}\right] = 0$

i.e., $\begin{vmatrix} -1 & 1 & 1 \\ 1 & 1 & -k \\ k & 2 & 1 \end{vmatrix} = (-1)\{2 + 2k + k^2 + k - 2\} = 0$

$\Rightarrow k^2 + 3k = 0$, so $k = 0, -3$

4. **(a)** Three line passing through the origin will be coplanar when

$\begin{vmatrix} \ell_1 & n_1 & m_1 \\ \ell_2 & n_2 & m_2 \\ \ell_3 & n_3 & m_3 \end{vmatrix} = 0$ or $\begin{vmatrix} \ell_1 & m_1 & n_1 \\ \ell_2 & m_2 & n_2 \\ \ell_3 & m_3 & n_3 \end{vmatrix} = 0$

5. (d) $L_1: \frac{x-1}{1} = \frac{y+3}{-\lambda} = \frac{z-1}{\lambda} = s$

$L_2: \frac{x}{\left(\frac{1}{2}\right)} = \frac{y-1}{1} = \frac{z-2}{-1} = t$

Lines will be coplanar when $\left[(\vec{c} - \vec{a})\ \vec{b}\ \vec{d}\right] = 0$

i.e., $\begin{vmatrix} 1 & -4 & -1 \\ 1 & -\lambda & \lambda \\ 1 & 2 & -2 \end{vmatrix} = 0$ gives $-5\lambda - 10 = 0$, so $\lambda = -2$

6. **(b)** $L_1: \frac{x}{1} = \frac{y+a}{1} = \frac{z}{1} \Rightarrow M(\lambda, \lambda - a, \lambda)$

$L_2: \frac{x+a}{1} = \frac{y}{1/2} = \frac{z}{1/2} \Rightarrow N(2\mu - a, \mu, \mu)$

(By Hit and trial or guessing) on putting $\lambda = 3a$ and $\mu = a$, we get $M(3a, 2a, 3a)$ and $N(a, a, a)$.

7. **(d)** Line parallel to x-axis will have D.R.'s <0, 0, 1> if it passes through (a, b, c), then $\frac{x-a}{0} = \frac{y-b}{0} = \frac{z-c}{1}$

TEXTUAL EXERCISE 7: (SUBJECTIVE)

1. Intercepts formed by the plane $2x - 3y + 4z = 12$ on coordinate axis
x – intercept = a = 6 units
y – intercept = b = -4units
z – intercept = c = 3units
$\Rightarrow$ 6, –4, 3

2. D.R's of the line joining $A(4, -1, 2)$ and $B(-3, 2, 3)$ is <7, – 3, –1>
Since it is normal to the plane passing through (–10, 5, 4)
$\therefore$ The plane will be $7(x + 10) - 3(y - 5) - 1(z - 4) = 0$
or $7x - 3y - z + 89 = 0$

3. A plane parallel to x-axis will have a normal of the form $0\hat{i} + b\hat{j} + c\hat{k}$
Hence the plane (in general form), P: $by + cz + d = 0$
Now (2, 3, 1) and (4, –5, 3) lie on it
$\Rightarrow 3b + c + d = 0$ and $-5b + 3c + d = 0$
$\Rightarrow 4b = c \Rightarrow d = -7b$; Hence the plane will be $b\{y + 4z - 7\} = 0$, i.e., $y + 4z = 7$

4. Let the point be $A(a, 0, 0)$, $B(0, b, 0)$ and $C(0, 0, c)$. Since the centroid of ΔABC is $(1, 2, 3) \Rightarrow a = 3, b = 6, c = 9$

Hence the plane is $\frac{x}{3} + \frac{y}{6} + \frac{z}{9} = 1$ or $6x + 3y + 2z = 18$.

5. $A(1, 2, 3)$, $B(3, 4, 5)$ mid point $C(2, 3, 4)$ and D.R.'s of AB < 2, 2, 2> or <1, 1, 1>

Hence the plane $(x-2)+(y-3)+(z-4)=0$
or $x+y+z=9$

6. Let the intercepts be a, b, c, then $\frac{1}{a}+\frac{1}{b}+\frac{1}{c}=\frac{1}{2}$

$\Rightarrow \frac{2}{a}+\frac{2}{b}+\frac{2}{c}=1$

Since the equation of the plane with a, b, c as intercepts will be $\frac{x}{a}+\frac{y}{b}+\frac{z}{c}=1$

$\therefore$ (2, 2, 2) lies on the plane irrespective of the individual values of a, b, c.

Hence the plane always passes through (2, 2, 2).

7. $B(-2, 1, 4)$ and $A(3, 1, 2)$ D.R.'s of $BA = (5, 0, -2)$
So the plane is $5(x-3)+0(y-1)-2(z-2)=0$
or $5x-2z=11$

8. The plane passes through $P(2, -1, 3)$ also it is parallel to $\vec{a}(3,0,-1)$ and $\vec{b}(-3,2,2)$

$\Rightarrow$ The required plane is $P:\begin{vmatrix} x-2 & y+1 & z-3 \\ 3 & 0 & -1 \\ -3 & 2 & 2 \end{vmatrix}=0$

or $2(x-2)-3(y+1)+6(z-3)=0$
i.e., $2x-3y+6z-25=0$

9. A plane will be passing through $A(4, 5, 1)$; $B(0, -1, -1)$; $C(3, 9, 4)$; $D(-4, 4, 4)$

If $\overrightarrow{AB}, \overrightarrow{AC}, \overrightarrow{AD}$ vectors are coplanar i.e., $\overrightarrow{AB}.(\overrightarrow{AC}\times\overrightarrow{AD})=0$

so $\begin{vmatrix} -4 & -6 & -2 \\ -1 & 4 & 3 \\ -8 & -1 & 3 \end{vmatrix} = \begin{vmatrix} 0 & 0 & -2 \\ -7 & -5 & 3 \\ -14 & -10 & 3 \end{vmatrix}=0$

Hence these points are coplanar.

10. Since the plane π is parallel to y-axis

$\therefore$ The equation (in general) for $\pi: \frac{x}{a}+\frac{z}{c}=1$

Now $c=3$, $a=4$, so $\frac{x}{4}+\frac{z}{3}=1$ or $3x+4z=12$

11. Let $ax+by+cz+d=0$ be the plane ⊥cular to $2x-y+z+5=0$

$\Rightarrow$ $2\hat{i}-\hat{\mu}+\hat{k}$ is parallel to the required planes

$\therefore$ $2a-b+c=0$ ....(i)

Now (1, 1, 1) lies on the plane so $a+b+c=-d$
Also (1, –1, –1) lies on the plane so $a-b-c=-d$
we get $b=-c$ so $a=-d$
Putting in (i), we get $2a-b-b=0$ so $a=b$
The plane will be $ax+ay-az-a=0$
or $x+y-z=1$

12. The plane $\frac{x}{2}+\frac{y}{3}+\frac{z}{4}=1$

area of $\Delta ABC=\sqrt{(\Delta AOB)^2+(\Delta AOC)^2+(\Delta BOC)^2}$

$=\sqrt{9+16+36}=\sqrt{61}$ square units.

TEXTUAL EXERCISE 5: (OBJECTIVE)

1. **(b)** Given $a=b=c=1 \Rightarrow$ The plane is $0\frac{x}{1}+\frac{y}{1}+\frac{z}{1}=1$

2. **(c)** $P(1, 1, 0)$; $Q(1, 2, 1)$ and $R(-2, 2, -1)$ are on the plane

So $\begin{vmatrix} x-1 & y-1 & z \\ 0 & 1 & 1 \\ -3 & 0 & -2 \end{vmatrix}=0 \Rightarrow 2-2x+3-3y+3z=0$

or $2x+3y-3z-5=0$

3. **(a)** Let the plane make intercepts of length a, b, c on the coordinate axes

$\Rightarrow \left(\frac{a}{3},\frac{b}{3},\frac{c}{3}\right)=(p,q,r) \Rightarrow a=3p,\ b=3q$

$c=3r$ and the plane is

$\frac{x}{3p}+\frac{y}{3q}+\frac{z}{3r}=1$ **or** $\frac{x}{p}+\frac{y}{q}+\frac{z}{r}=3$

4. **(b)** Plane passes through $A(2, 2, 1)$ and $B(9, 3, 6)$ and it is ⊥ to $2x+6y+6z=9$

The required plane is $\begin{vmatrix} x-2 & y-2 & z-1 \\ 7 & 1 & 5 \\ 2 & 6 & 6 \end{vmatrix}=0$

$\Rightarrow$ $3x+4y-5z=9$

5. (c) $\overrightarrow{OP}=a\hat{i}+b\hat{j}+c\hat{k}$ where $P(a, b, c)$

So plane through P with $\overrightarrow{OP}$ as normal vector will be $a(x-a)+b(y-b)+c(z-c)=0$

or $ax+by+cz=(a^2+b^2+c^2)$

6. **(b)** $A(1, 2, 3)$, $B(-2, 1, -4)$ and $C(3, 4, -2)$ are the vertices of ΔABC

So area $\Delta ABC=\frac{1}{2}|(\overrightarrow{AC}\times\overrightarrow{BC})| = \frac{1}{2}\begin{vmatrix} \hat{i} & \hat{j} & \hat{k} \\ 2 & 2 & -5 \\ 5 & 3 & 2 \end{vmatrix}$

$=\frac{1}{2}|19\hat{i}-29\hat{j}-4\hat{k}|=\frac{\sqrt{1218}}{2}$ square units

7. **(d)** A general point on the line will be $(r, 2r+1, 3r-2)$. If it is also lies on the plane, then $2r+6r+3+3r-2=0$

gives $r=-\frac{1}{11}$. Hence the point is $\left(-\frac{1}{11},\frac{9}{11},\frac{-25}{11}\right)$

8. **(c)** If $4x+4y+kz=0$ contains the line $\frac{x-1}{2}=\frac{y+1}{3}=\frac{z}{4}$

then $4(2)+4(3)+k(4)=0$

$\Rightarrow$ $k=-5$

9. (c) A general point on the line is $(1-r, 2r+1, -r)$ putting these in the given planes

L.H.S gives $2x+3y+4z=2-2r+6r+3-4r=5$

$\Rightarrow$ Plane (c) contains this line

10. (b) The plane ⊥ cular to the line $\frac{x}{1}=\frac{y}{2}=\frac{z}{3}$ and passing through (2, 3, 4) will be $(x-2)+2(y-3)+3(z-4)=0$ i.e., $x+2y+3z=20$

11. **(d)** The given two lines are $L_1: \vec{r}_1=(\hat{i}+2\hat{j}+\hat{k})+\lambda(\hat{i}+\hat{j}+\hat{k})$

And $L_2: \vec{r}_2=(\hat{i}+2\hat{j}+\hat{k})+\mu(\hat{i}+2\hat{j}+2\hat{k})$

Observe that $(\hat{i}+2\hat{j}+\hat{k})$ is the point of intersection of these two lines.

So the plane can be written as

$\vec{r}=(\hat{i}+2\hat{j}+\hat{k})+\lambda(\hat{i}+\hat{j}+\hat{k})+\mu(\hat{i}+2\hat{j}+2\hat{k})$

12. **(c)** The plane will contain the line $\frac{x-x_1}{a_1}=\frac{y-y_1}{b_1}=\frac{z-z_1}{c_1}$

and parallel to line $\frac{x-x_2}{a_2}=\frac{y-y_2}{b_2}=\frac{z-z_2}{c_2}$

If (x_1, y_1, z_1) lies on the plane and

$(a_1\hat{i}+b_1\hat{j}+c_1\hat{k})\times(a_2\hat{i}+b_2\hat{j}+c_2\hat{k})$ is normal to it

The required plane is $\begin{vmatrix} x-x_1 & y-y_1 & z-z_1 \\ a_1 & b_1 & c_1 \\ a_2 & b_2 & c_2 \end{vmatrix}=0$

13. **(c)** According to the given $z+x=y$ or $x-y+z=0$

14. **(a)** The equation of the plane through (1, 1, 1), (1, –1, 1), (–7, –3, –5) is $\begin{vmatrix} (x-1) & (y-1) & (z-1) \\ 0 & -2 & 0 \\ -8 & -4 & -6 \end{vmatrix}=0$

$\Rightarrow$ $12(x-1)+(z-1)(-16)=0$ or $3x-4z+1=0$

15. **(b)** Normal to the plane $ax+by+cz+d=0$ is $a\hat{i}+b\hat{j}+c\hat{k}$. Equation of line passing through (α, β, γ) will be $\vec{r}=(\alpha\hat{i}+\beta\hat{j}+\gamma\hat{k})+\lambda(a\hat{i}+b\hat{j}+c\hat{k})$

or $\frac{x-\alpha}{a}=\frac{y-\beta}{b}=\frac{z-\gamma}{c}$

16. **(c)** Foot of perpendicular from origin to the plane is (2, 4, –3)

$\therefore$ $2\hat{i}+4\hat{j}-3\hat{k}$ is the normal vector and therefore the plane is $2(x-2)+4(y-4)-3(z+3)=0$ or $2x+4y-3z=29$.

17. **(a)** The plane $3y+4z=0$ is satisfied by a general point on x-axis is $(a, 0, 0)$

$\Rightarrow$ It contains x-axis

18. **(b)** $P(a, b, c)\Rightarrow$ Foot on *yz* plane and *zx* from *P* are points $A(0, b, c)$ and $B(a, 0, c)$ respectively. The plane through $O(0, 0, 0)$, *A* and *B* will be

$\begin{vmatrix} x & y & z \\ 0 & b & c \\ a & 0 & c \end{vmatrix}=0 \Rightarrow bcx+acy-abz=0$

$\frac{x}{a}+\frac{y}{b}-\frac{z}{c}=0$

19. **(c)** If a plane is parallel to x-axis then the normal to the plane will be perpendicular to x-axis.

$\Rightarrow$ $by+cz-d=0$.

20. **(a)** Normal to the plane $by+cz+d=0$ is $b\hat{j}+c\hat{k}$ which will be perpendicular to $a\hat{i}$. Now $a\hat{i}$ is normal to *YOZ* plane

21. (a) The line $\frac{x-2}{3}=\frac{y-3}{4}=\frac{z-4}{0}$ has D.R.'s <3, 4, 0> and $z=4$. So this line will be parallel to xy-plane

22. **(c)** The line $\frac{x-x_0}{\ell}=\frac{y-y_0}{m}=\frac{z-z_0}{n}$ will be parallel to *xy*-plane if $n=0$

23. **(a)** *Observe* that (3, 2, 0) and (3, 6, 4) lie on $x-y+z=1$ Also the product of D.R's <1, 5, 4> and <1, –1, 1> being zero so line lies in the plane

24. (b) A general point on the line is $(3r+1, 4r-2, 3-2r)$ If it lies on $2x-y+3z-1=0$, then $6r+2-4r+2+9-6r-1=0$ gives $4r=12$ or $r=3$

So $P(10, 10, -3)$

TEXTUAL EXERCISE 8: (SUBJECTIVE)

1. Plane π: $x+2y-2z-a=0$ and point $P(1, -2, 1)$ distance of *P*(from plane π) $d=\frac{|1-4-2-a|}{3}=5$, gives $a=10>0$

Further let *M* be the foot of perpendicular, then $M(r+1, 2r-2, -2r+1)$ satisfies π

so $r+1+4r-4+4r-2-10=0$

Gives $r=\frac{5}{3}$ so $M\left(\frac{8}{3},\frac{4}{3},\frac{-7}{3}\right)$

2. Volume of parallelopiped $=\begin{vmatrix} -1 & 1 & 1 \\ 0 & 0 & 2 \\ 0 & 1 & 1 \end{vmatrix}=(-2)(-1)=2$ cubic units

Equation of the plane passing through $P(-1, 1, 1)$, $Q(0, 1, 1)$ and $R(0, 0, 2)$ is $\begin{vmatrix} x+1 & y-1 & z-1 \\ 1 & 0 & 0 \\ 0 & -1 & 1 \end{vmatrix}=0$ gives $1-y+1-z=0\Rightarrow y+z-2=0$. Hence distance from $O(0, 0, 0)$ to plane $y+z-2=0$ is $\frac{|-2|}{\sqrt{2}}=\sqrt{2}$ units.

3. D.R.'s of the line of intersection of two planes

$=\begin{vmatrix} \hat{i} & \hat{j} & \hat{k} \\ 2 & 3 & 1 \\ 1 & 3 & 2 \end{vmatrix}=3\hat{i}-3\hat{j}+3\hat{k}$ or <1, –1, 1>

$\Rightarrow$ $\cos\alpha=\frac{1}{\sqrt{3}}$

4. D.R.'s of the normal to the required plane

$$\begin{vmatrix} \hat{i} & \hat{j} & \hat{k} \\ 2 & -2 & 1 \\ 1 & -1 & 2 \end{vmatrix} = -3\hat{i} - 3\hat{j} + 0\hat{k} \text{ or } <1, 1, 0>$$

$\therefore$ The required plane is $x + y + 1 = 0$

So distance from (1, 2, 2) is $d = \dfrac{|1+2+0+1|}{\sqrt{2}} = 2\sqrt{2}$

$\Rightarrow$ $d = 2\sqrt{2}$ units.

5. Under the given condition the plane $x + 2y + 3z - 6 = 0$ serves the purpose $as \dfrac{|-6+5|}{\sqrt{14}} = \dfrac{|-7+6|}{\sqrt{14}}$

$\Rightarrow$ π plane: $x + 2y + 3z - 6 = 0$

6. Angle between the plane $2x - y + z - 1 = 0$ and $x - 2y + z + 2 = 0$ is $\cos\theta = \dfrac{|2+2+1|}{\sqrt{6}\sqrt{6}} = \dfrac{5}{6}$, so $\cos\theta = (5/6)$

7. Given $a = 8$, $b = 4$, $c = 4$, so the plane is $\dfrac{x}{8} + \dfrac{y}{4} + \dfrac{z}{4} = 1$ or $x + 2y + 2z - 8 = 0$ and distance from origin $= \dfrac{|-8|}{3} = \dfrac{8}{3}$

8. Plane passing through (1, 2, 3) and parallel to $x + 2y + 5z = 0$ will be $(x - 1) + 2(y - 2) + 5(z - 3) = 0$ i.e., $x + 2y + 5z - 20 = 0$.

9. Let $M(2r + 1, -r + 3, r + 4)$ be the foot of perpendicular from $P(1, 3, 4)$ on the plane $2x - y + z + 3 = 0$, then $4r + 2 + r - 3 + r + 4 + 3 = 0$. So $r = -1$ and $M(-1, 4, 3)$

$\Rightarrow$ The image Q(of point P) will be $(-3, 5, 2)$.

10. Angle between the planes $2x - y + z = 6$ and $x + y + 2z = 3$ is given by $\cos\theta = \dfrac{|2-1+2|}{\sqrt{6}\sqrt{6}} = \dfrac{1}{2}$ $\quad \Rightarrow \theta = \dfrac{\pi}{3}$

11. The plane $3x - 6y - 2z = 7$ and $2x + y - kz = 5$ will be $\perp$ cular when $6 - 6 + 2k = 0 \Rightarrow k = 0$.

12. Distance of point(2, 3, 4) from the plane $3x - 6y + 2z + 11 = 0$ is $d = \dfrac{|6-18+8+11|}{7} = 1$; so $d = 1$ units.

13. $ax + by + cz + d = 0$ and $a'x + b'y + c'z + d' = 0$ will perpendicular if $aa' + bb' + cc' = 0$.

14. Angle between the planes $3x - 4y + 5z = 0$ and $2x - y - 2z = 5$ is given by $\cos\theta = \dfrac{|6+4-10|}{3\sqrt{50}} = 0$

$\Rightarrow$ $\theta = \dfrac{\pi}{2}$.

15. Angle between the plane $ax + by + cz + d = 0$ and a line with d.c's $<\ell, m, n>$ will be given by

$\sin\theta = \dfrac{|a\ell + bm + cn|}{\sqrt{a^2+b^2+c^2}}$, so $\theta = \sin^{-1}\left(\dfrac{|a\ell + bm + cn|}{\sqrt{a^2+b^2+c^2}}\right)$

16. Distance between the plane P_1: $2x - 2y + z + 3 = 0$ and P_2: $2x - 2y + z + 5/2 = 0$ is $d = \dfrac{|3-5/2|}{3} = \dfrac{1}{6}$ Units.

17. The line $\dfrac{x-x_1}{\ell} = \dfrac{y-y_1}{m} = \dfrac{z-z_1}{n}$ will be parallel to the plane $ax + by + cz + d = 0$ if $al + bm + cn = 0$

TEXTUAL EXERCISE 9: (SUBJECTIVE)

1. Let $\lambda(x + y + z - 6) + (2x + 3y + 4z - 5) = 0$ be the plane passing through the intersection.

Since it contains (1, 1, 1)

so $\lambda(-3) + 4 = 0$ gives $\lambda = 4/3$. Hence the required plane is $10x + 13y + 16z - 39 = 0$.

2. $4x - 3y + 2z - 15 = 0$ the equation of image plane is

$P_1 + \lambda p = 0$

$2x - 3y + 4z - 3 + \lambda(x - y + z - 3) = 0$

$P_2 : (2 + \lambda)x - (3 + \lambda)y + (4+\lambda)z - 3(1+\lambda) = 0$

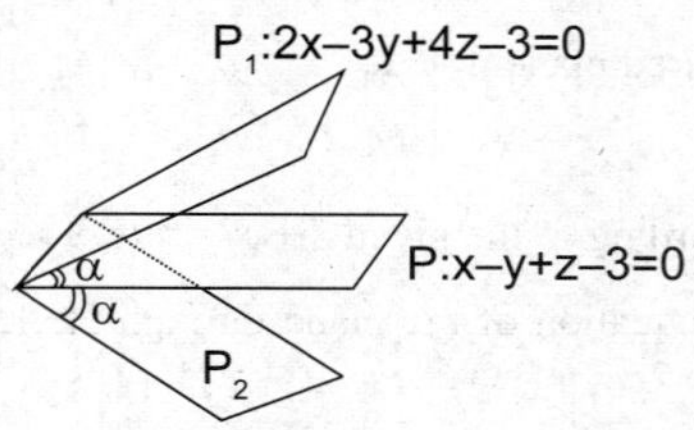

$\because$ Angle b/w p_1 and p must be same as angle b/w p_2 and p

thus $\dfrac{|2+3+4|}{\sqrt{29}\sqrt{3}} = \dfrac{|2+\lambda+3+\lambda+4+\lambda|}{\sqrt{3}\sqrt{(2+\lambda)^2+(3+\lambda)^2+(4+\lambda)^2}}$

$81(3\lambda^2 + 18\lambda + 29) = 29(3\lambda + 9)^2$

$9(3\lambda^2 + 18\lambda + 29) = 29(\lambda^2 + 6\lambda + 9)$

$\Rightarrow$ $2\lambda^2 + 12\lambda \geq 0$

$\Rightarrow$ $2\lambda(\lambda + 6) = 0$

$\Rightarrow$ $\lambda = 0, -6$

For $\lambda = -6$ we get the equation of image plane as $-4x + 3y - 2z + 15 = 0$ i.e. $4x - 3y + 2z - 15 = 0$

3. Let $P_3 = \lambda$; $P + P' = 0$ the required plane. Then D.R.'s of the normal to the plane are $<a\lambda + a', b\lambda + b', c\lambda + c'>$. Since the plane is parallel to x-axis

$\Rightarrow$ $1(a\lambda + a') = 0$ $\quad \Rightarrow \lambda = -\dfrac{a'}{a}$

$\therefore$ The equation of the plane P_3 will be given by $-\dfrac{a'}{a}P + P' = 0$ or $a'P = P'a$ i.e., $\dfrac{P}{a} = \dfrac{P'}{a'}$.

TEXTUAL EXERCISE 6: (OBJECTIVE)

1. (a) The plane $2x - (1 + \lambda)y + 3z = 0$ (for $\lambda = 1$) can be passing through intersection of $2x - y = 0$ and $y - 3z = 0$ as $(2x - y) + (-1)(y - 3z) = 0$ or $2x - 2y + 3z = 0$

2. **(b)** Let λ $(2x - 3y + z - 4) + (x - y + z + 1) = 0$ or $(2\lambda + 1)x + (-3\lambda - 1)y + (\lambda + 1)z + (1 - 4\lambda) = 0$
The plane will be perpendicular to the plane $x + 2y - 3z + 6 = 0$ when $(2\lambda + 1) - 6\lambda - 2 - 3\lambda - 3 = 0$
which gives $\lambda = -\frac{4}{7}$ and the plane is $x - 5y - 3z - 23 = 0$

3. **(a)** The plane passing through (1, 2, 3) and parallel to $2x + 3y - 4z = 0$ will be $2(x - 1) + 3(y - 2) - 4(z - 3) = 0$, i.e., $2x + 3y - 4z + 4 = 0$

4. **(c)** Let $P = \lambda (x + y + z - 1) + (2x + 3y - z + 4) = 0$ be the required plane with D.R.'s of the normal as $<(\lambda + 2), (\lambda + 3), (\lambda - 1)>$
Since this plane is parallel to x-axis
$\therefore$ $(\lambda + 2)(1) = 0 \Rightarrow \lambda = -2$
Hence $P = y - 3z + 6 = 0$

5. **(b)** Let $P = \lambda (x + 2y + 3z - 4) + (2x + y - z + 5) = 0$ be the required plane with D.R.'s of the normal as $< \lambda + 2, 2\lambda + 1, 3\lambda - 1>$
Since the plane is normal (perpendicular) to the plane $5x + 3y - 6z + 8 = 0$
$\Rightarrow$ $5\lambda + 10 + 6\lambda + 3 - 18\lambda + 6 = 0$ gives $\lambda = 19/7$ and the plane will be $33x + 45y + 50z - 41 = 0$

SECTION III:

1. (a) Given $\ell + m + n = 0$
$\Rightarrow$ $\ell = -(m + n)$ and $2\ell m + 2ln - mn = 0$
(also $\ell^2 + m^2 + n^2 = 1$), putting $\ell = -(m + n)$
we get $(-2)(m^2 + n^2 + 2mn) - mn = 0$
or $2m^2 + 2n^2 + 5mn = 0 \Rightarrow (2m + n)(m + 2n) = 0$
(i) when $m = -\frac{n}{2}$ then $\ell = -\frac{n}{2}$ so $d.c's\left(-\frac{n}{2}, -\frac{n}{2}, n\right)$
$$\equiv \left(\mp\frac{1}{\sqrt{6}}, \mp\frac{1}{\sqrt{6}}, \pm\frac{2}{\sqrt{6}}\right)$$
(ii) when $m = -2n$ then $\ell = n$, so D.R's $(n, -2n, n)$
$$\Rightarrow d.c's\left(\pm\frac{1}{\sqrt{6}}, \mp\frac{2}{\sqrt{6}}, \pm\frac{1}{\sqrt{6}}\right)$$

2. **(a)** $\overrightarrow{AC} = \hat{i} + 2\hat{j} + 2\hat{k}$
So $\widehat{AC} = \frac{(\hat{i} + 2\hat{j} + 2\hat{k})}{3}$ and $\overrightarrow{AB} = 6\hat{i} - 2\hat{j} - 3\hat{k}$ so
$$\Rightarrow \widehat{AB} = \frac{6i - 2\hat{j} - 3\hat{k}}{7}$$
Vector along angle bisector $= \widehat{AC} + \widehat{AB}$
$$= \frac{\hat{i} + 2\hat{j} + 2\hat{k}}{3} + \frac{6\hat{i} - 2\hat{j} - 3\hat{k}}{7} = \frac{25\hat{i} + 8\hat{j} + 5\hat{k}}{21}$$
So D.R's of the bisector are <25, 8, 5>

3. **(a)** Centroid is at $\frac{z_1 + z_2 + z_3 + z_4}{4} = (1, -2, 5)$
so $z_4 \equiv (2, -4, 16)$

4. (a) $A(4, 5, 10)$, $B(2, 3, 4)$, $C(1, 2, -1)$, $D = (3, 4, 5)$
Now $\overrightarrow{AB} = -2\hat{i} - 2\hat{j} - 6\hat{k} = (-2)\left\{\hat{i} + \hat{j} + 3\hat{k}\right\}$
Hence equation line AB is $\frac{x - 4}{1} = \frac{y - 5}{1} = \frac{z - 10}{3}$

5. **(a)** Line is $\frac{x - \alpha}{\ell} = \frac{y - \beta}{m} = \frac{z - \gamma}{n} = p$ (say)
$\Rightarrow$ $z = np + \gamma$ for $z = 0$, we get $p = -\frac{\gamma}{n}$
So $x = \frac{n\alpha - \ell\gamma}{n}$ and $y = \frac{n\beta - m\gamma}{n}$
Putting in $ax^2 + by^2 = 1$, we get
$a(n\alpha - \ell\gamma)^2 + b(n\beta - m\gamma)^2 = n^2$

6. **(b)** The point of intersection of $\frac{x - 1}{2} = \frac{y - 2}{3} = \frac{z - 3}{4} = \lambda$
and $\frac{x - 4}{5} = \frac{y - 1}{2} = \frac{z}{1} = \mu$ will be given by $2\lambda + 1 = 5\mu + 4$, $3\lambda + 2 = 2\mu + 1$, $4\lambda + 3 = \mu$
$\Rightarrow$ $\lambda = \mu = -1$ and then point is $(-1, -1, -1)$

7. **(a)** Let $A = (-1, 0, 3)$ and $B = (2, 5, 1) \Rightarrow \overrightarrow{AB} = 3\hat{i} + 5\hat{j} - 2\hat{k}$
Projection of $\overrightarrow{AB}$ on $6\hat{i} + 2\hat{j} + 3\hat{k}$ will be
$$P = \frac{18 + 10 - 6}{7} = \frac{22}{7}$$

8. (a) $\overrightarrow{OP} = a\hat{i} + b\hat{j} + c\hat{k}$
Plane $\perp$ to OP passing through (a, b, c) will be $(a)(x - a) + (b)(y - b) + (c)(z - c) = 0$ gives $ax + by + cz = a^2 + b^2 + c^2$

9. **(a)** Angle between plane P_1: $2x - y + z - 6 = 0$ and $P_2 = x + y + 2z - 7 = 0$ is $\cos\theta = \left(\frac{2 - 1 + 2}{\sqrt{6}\sqrt{6}}\right) \Rightarrow \theta = \frac{\pi}{3}$

10. **(c)** $A(1, 2, 3)$; $B(-2, 1, -4)$; $C(3, 4, -2)$; $\overrightarrow{AB} = -3\hat{i} - \hat{j} - 7\hat{k}$ and $\overrightarrow{AC} = 2\hat{i} + 2\hat{j} - 5\hat{k}$
$$\Rightarrow \text{Area of } \Delta ABC = \left|\frac{1}{2}\right|\overrightarrow{AB} \times \overrightarrow{AC}\left|\right| = \frac{1}{2}\left\|\begin{matrix} \hat{i} & \hat{j} & \hat{k} \\ 3 & 1 & 7 \\ 2 & 2 & -5 \end{matrix}\right\|$$
$$= \frac{1}{2}\left|-19\hat{i} + 29\hat{j} + 4\hat{k}\right| = \frac{1}{2}\sqrt{361 + 841 + 16} = \frac{1}{2}\sqrt{1218}$$

11. **(a)** Given $O(0, 0, 0)$, $A(1, 2, 1)$, $B(2, 1, 3)$, $C(-1, 1, 2)$ are the vertices of a tetrahedron. Vector normal to face
$$OAB = \begin{vmatrix} \hat{i} & \hat{j} & \hat{k} \\ 1 & 2 & 1 \\ 2 & 1 & 3 \end{vmatrix} = 5\hat{i} - \hat{j} - 3\hat{k}$$
Similarly vector normal to face
$$ABC = \begin{vmatrix} \hat{i} & \hat{j} & \hat{k} \\ 1 & -1 & 2 \\ -2 & -1 & 1 \end{vmatrix} = \hat{i} - 5\hat{j} - 3\hat{k}$$

Now $\cos\theta = \dfrac{(5\hat{i} - \hat{j} - 3\hat{i}).(\hat{i} - 5\hat{j} - 3\hat{k})}{\sqrt{35}\sqrt{35}}$

$= \dfrac{5+5+9}{35} = \dfrac{19}{35}$ so $\theta = \cos^{-1}\dfrac{19}{35}$

12. **(b)** The D.R.'s of the line of intersection of $P_1 : \vec{r}.(\hat{i} + \hat{j} + \hat{k}) = 3$ and $P_2 : \vec{r}.(2\hat{i} + 3\hat{j} + \hat{k}) = 9$ will be

$\begin{vmatrix} \hat{i} & \hat{j} & \hat{k} \\ 1 & 1 & 1 \\ 2 & 3 & 1 \end{vmatrix} = -2\hat{i} + \hat{j} + \hat{k}$ or $-8\hat{i} + 4\hat{j} + 4\hat{k}$

Since this vector is perpendicular to $\vec{r}.(a\hat{i} + b\hat{j} + 4\hat{k}) = 5$
So $a = -8$ and $b = 4 \Rightarrow a + b = -4$

13. **(c)** Observe that the product of D.R.'s viz. 9(3) + (–1) (–3) + (–3) (10) = 0

$\therefore$ Line is parallel to the plane and it is at a distance of $\dfrac{|+3-6-30-26|}{\sqrt{118}} = \sqrt{\dfrac{59}{2}}$ units

The image will also have same DR's and it will also be at the same distance

(c) Option satisfies as $\dfrac{|12+3+70-26|}{\sqrt{118}} = \sqrt{\dfrac{59}{2}}$ units

14. **(a)** D.R's of x-axis <1, 0, 0>; DR's of normal to plane are <2, –3, 9>; $\sin\theta = \dfrac{2}{7} = \lambda$ (given)

$\Rightarrow \lambda = \dfrac{2}{7}$

15. **(a)** {As (0, 0, 0} satisfies}. Let the plane be $\ell x + my + nz = 0$.
Now A(a, 1, 1) gives $\ell a + m + n = 0$ .....(i)
$B(1, b, 1)$ gives $\ell + mb + n = 0$ .....(ii)
And $C(1, 1, c)$ gives $\ell + m + nc = 0$ ......(iii)

Now from (I) we get $a = \dfrac{-(m+n)}{\ell}$

so $1 - a = \dfrac{\ell + m + n}{\ell}$

Similarly $1 - b = \dfrac{\ell + m + n}{m}$ and $1 - c = \dfrac{\ell + m + n}{n}$

$\Rightarrow \dfrac{1}{1-a} + \dfrac{1}{1-b} + \dfrac{1}{1-c} = \dfrac{\ell + m + n}{\ell + m + n} = 1$

16. **(a)** Mid point of (2, 3, 4) and (6, 7, 8) is (4, 5, 6) which satisfies $x + y + z - 15 = 0$

17. **(d)** The angle between the line $\dfrac{x-2}{a} = \dfrac{y-2}{b} = \dfrac{z-2}{c}$ and the plane $ax + by + cz + 6 = 0$ will be given by $\sin\theta = \dfrac{a^2 + b^2 + c^2}{a^2 + b^2 + c^2} = 1$

$\Rightarrow$ line is parallel to normal to the plane i.e., Line is perpendicular to the plane

18. (d) D.C.'s of the lines are $<\ell_1, m_1, n_1>$ and $<\ell_2, m_2, n_2>$ {(D.C.'s)

D.R's of the} line perpendicular to both will be $\begin{vmatrix} \hat{i} & \hat{j} & \hat{k} \\ \ell_1 & m_1 & n_1 \\ \ell_2 & m_2 & n_2 \end{vmatrix}$

$= (m_1 n_2 - m_2 n_1)\hat{i} + (\ell_2 n_1 - \ell_1 n_2)\hat{j} + (\ell_1 m_2 - \ell_2 m_1)\hat{k}$

19. (d) Given $y(x + z) = 0$
So either $y = 0$ which is xz-plane or $x + z = 0$ which is a plane containing y-axis and inclined to x-axis at $-\pi/4$ and inclined to z-axis at $\pi/4$.But these planes are mutually perpendicular.

20. (a) The planes $x + z = 0, x + y = 0, y + z = 0$ are intersecting in a unique point (0, 0, 0).

21. (a) $\overrightarrow{OA} = \hat{i} - 2\hat{j} - \hat{k}$ and $\overrightarrow{OB} = 3\hat{i} - 2\hat{j} + 3\hat{k}$

normal to the planes $OAB = \begin{vmatrix} \hat{i} & \hat{j} & \hat{k} \\ 1 & -2 & -1 \\ 3 & -2 & 3 \end{vmatrix} = -8\hat{i} - 6\hat{j} + 4\hat{k}$ or

<4, 3, –2>.

22. **(b)** Since we are to find the D.R's hence the products of D.R.'S will be $= \dfrac{1}{\sqrt{2}} = \cos\dfrac{\pi}{4}$

Which is satisfied as $\cos\theta = \dfrac{(1)(1)+(1)(1)}{\sqrt{1^2+1^2}\sqrt{1^2+1^2+\left(\sqrt{2}\right)^2}}$.

23. **(b)** The line $y = z = 0$ is x-axis which has D.R.'s <1, 0, 0>
Let the required plane which is parallel to x-axis be
$P{:}(\lambda + 2)x + (\lambda - 1)y + (\lambda + 3)z - (5\lambda + 1) = 0$
So the product of D.R.'s will be zero i.e., $\lambda + 2 = 0$ and the plane P will be $P{:}\ -3y + z + 9 = 0$ or $3y - z = 9$

24. (a) $A(a, 2, 3)$, $B(1, b, 2)$, $C(2, 1, c)$, $O(0, 0, 0)$

Given centroid at $G = (1,2,3) \equiv \left(\dfrac{a+3}{4}, \dfrac{b+3}{4}, \dfrac{c+5}{4}\right)$

$\Rightarrow a = 1, b = 5, c = 7$
Hence $a^2 + b^2 + c^2 = 75$

25. **(a)** Equation of line parallel to line $\dfrac{x}{2} = \dfrac{y}{3} = \dfrac{z-1}{-6}$ and through $P(1, -2, 3)$ is $\dfrac{x-1}{2} = \dfrac{y+2}{3} = \dfrac{z-3}{-6} = r$;

$\Rightarrow$ Any point of this line is $(2r + 1, 3r - 2, -6r + 3) \equiv Q$(say)

It is lies on plane $x - y + z - 5 = 0$,

$\Rightarrow r = \dfrac{1}{7} \Rightarrow Q \equiv \left(\dfrac{9}{7}, -\dfrac{11}{7}, \dfrac{15}{7}\right) \Rightarrow PQ = 1$

26. **(b)** Line segment joining (1, –1, 0) and (–1, 0, 1) is $\vec{r} = -2\hat{i} + \hat{j} + \hat{k} \Rightarrow |\vec{r}| = \sqrt{6}$

The given plane is $2x + y + 6z - 1 = 0$

The required length is $d=\sqrt{|\vec{r}|^2-(\vec{r}.\hat{n})^2}$

$=\sqrt{6-\frac{9}{41}}=\sqrt{\frac{237}{41}}$

27. (b) D.R.'s of line L_1 : <6, 4, –4>
D.R.'s of line L_2: <–6, 2, 1>
Vector perpendicular to both these lines is

$$\begin{vmatrix}\hat{i} & \hat{j} & \hat{k}\\ 6 & 4 & -4\\ -6 & 2 & 1\end{vmatrix}=12\hat{i}+18\hat{j}+36k = 6\{2\hat{i}+3\hat{j}+6\hat{k}\}$$

D.C's are $\left\langle\frac{2}{7},\frac{3}{7},\frac{6}{7}\right\rangle$

28. (a) Given: $mn + \ell m + n\ell = 0$

So $m(n+\ell)=-n\ell \quad\Rightarrow\quad m=-\frac{n\ell}{n+\ell}$

Putting in $a^2\ell + b^2m + c^2n = 0$, we get

$a^2\ell+\frac{b^2(-n\ell)}{n+\ell}+c^2n=0$ which gives

$a^2\ell^2 + a^2n\ell - b^2n\ell + c^2n\ell + c^2n^2 = 0$

or $a^2\ell^2 + (a^2 + c^2 - b^2)n\ell + c^2 n^2 = 0$

$$\Rightarrow\quad \ell=\frac{(b^2-a^2-c^2)\pm\sqrt{(a^2+c^2-b^2)^2n^2-4a^2c^2n^2}}{2a^2}$$

Since lines are parallel

$\therefore\quad n^2(a^2+c^2-b^2)^2-4a^2c^2n^2=0$

$\Rightarrow\quad (a^2+c^2-b^2)=4a^2c^2$

29. (d) $A(-1, 2, -3)$, $B(5, 0, -6)$, $C(0, 4, -1)$

gives $\overline{AB}=6\hat{i}-2\hat{j}-3\hat{k}$ so $\widehat{AB}=\frac{1}{7}\{6\hat{i}-2\hat{j}-3\hat{k}\}$

$\overline{AC}=\hat{i}+2\hat{j}+2\hat{k}\Rightarrow\widehat{AC}=\left\{\frac{\hat{i}+2\hat{j}+2\hat{k}}{3}\right\}$

Vector along internal bisectors of $\angle BAC$

$=\frac{6\hat{i}-2\hat{j}-3\hat{k}}{7}+\frac{\hat{i}+2\hat{j}+2\hat{k}}{3}$

$=\frac{25\hat{i}+8\hat{j}+5\hat{k}}{21}\Rightarrow$ D.R.'s <25, 8, 5>

30. (b, c) Let D.R.'s of $\overline{AB}=<1,1,2>$;

$\overline{AC}<\sqrt{3}-1,-\sqrt{3}-1,4>$;

$\overline{BC}=\left\langle-\sqrt{3}-1,\sqrt{3}-1,4\right\rangle$

So $\cos A=\frac{\sqrt{3}-1-\sqrt{3}-1+8}{\sqrt{6}\sqrt{24}}=\frac{1}{2}\Rightarrow A=60°$

and $\cos C=\frac{-3+1-3+1+16}{\sqrt{24}\sqrt{24}}=\frac{12}{24}\Rightarrow C=60°$

Obviously $B = 60°$

$\therefore$ Triangle will be an equilateral. Further an equilateral triangle is also isosceles

31. (a) D.R.'s of the line of intersection of $x + y + z = 0$ and

$2x+y+4=0$ will be $\begin{vmatrix}\hat{i} & \hat{j} & \hat{k}\\ 1 & 1 & 1\\ 2 & 1 & 0\end{vmatrix}=-\hat{i}+2\hat{j}-\hat{k}$

The required plane must be parallel to the vector obtained above. Also the sum of products of D.R's should vanish
This is fulfilled by $x - z + 4 = 0$
As (1) (1) + 0 (1) + (–1) (1) = 0
Also (–1)1 + 2 (0) + (–1) (–1) = 0
$\therefore\quad x - z + 4 = 0$ is the required plane

32. (a) The line $L:\frac{x-1}{1}=\frac{y}{-1}=\frac{z+2}{2}$
Will be parallel to the plane P: $2x + 3y + \lambda z + k = 0$
When (2) (1) + (3) (–1) + (λ) (2) = 0 $\Rightarrow \lambda = 1/2$
Now point (1, 0, –2) will lie on the plane when
$2 + 0 - 1 + k = 0 \Rightarrow k = -1$

33. (a) A prism will be formed when all the three lines of intersection (by two planes taken each time) are parallel.

Now $\begin{vmatrix}\hat{i} & \hat{j} & \hat{k}\\ 4 & -5 & 2\\ 3 & -3 & \lambda\end{vmatrix}=(6-5\lambda)\hat{i}+(6-4\lambda)\hat{j}+3\hat{k}$

$$\begin{vmatrix}\hat{i} & \hat{j} & \hat{k}\\ 4 & -5 & 2\\ 5 & -1 & -\lambda\end{vmatrix}=(5\lambda+2)\hat{i}+(4\lambda+10)\hat{j}+21\hat{k}$$

Comparing we get $\lambda = 1$ and D.R.'s = <1, 2, 3>
Using $\lambda = 1$ in the 3rd combination for checking

$\begin{vmatrix}\hat{i} & \hat{j} & \hat{k}\\ 3 & -3 & 1\\ 5 & -1 & -1\end{vmatrix}=4\hat{i}+8\hat{j}+12\hat{k}=4(\hat{i}+2\hat{j}+3\hat{k})$ which is true

34. (b) Observe that $2x - 3y - 7z = 0$, $3x - 14y - 13z = 0$ and $8x - 31y - 33z = 0$ intersect in (0, 0, 0) (which is obvious)
Let $\lambda\ (2x - 3y - 7z) + (3x - 14y - 13z) = 8x - 31y - 33z$
for some λ, gives $\frac{2\lambda+3}{8}=\frac{+(3\lambda+14)}{+31}=\frac{+(7\lambda+13)}{+33}$
First two equations give, $\lambda = 1/2$ which also satisfies the third equation
$\therefore$ The planes intersect in a line

35. (a) Solving $2x - y + z = 4$
$5x + 7y + 2z = 0$
$3x + 4y - 2z = -3$
By matrix / determinant method we get $\Delta = -61$, $\Delta_1 = -61$
$\Delta_2 = 61$, $\Delta_3 = -61$ so $x = 1$, $y = -1$, $z = 1$
So the three planes intersect in a point

36. (a) $\begin{vmatrix}(1-x) & 1 & 1\\ 1 & (1-y) & 1\\ 1 & 1 & (1-z)\end{vmatrix}=0$ gives

$(x-1)(y-1)(z-1)=(x+y+z)-1$

On simplification we get $x\,y\,z = xy + yz + zx$

$\Rightarrow \frac{1}{x}+\frac{1}{y}+\frac{1}{z}=1$

37. **(a)** Let $ax + by + cz + d = 0$ be the plane passing through $A(2, 1, 1)$, $B(1, 2, 1)$, $C(1, 1, 2)$

$2a + b + c + d = 0$ ...(i)

$a + 2b + c + d = 0$ ....(ii)

$a + b + 2c + d = 0$ ...(iii)

From (i) and (ii); $a = b$, from (ii) and (iii); $b = c$ and from (i) and (iii); $a = c$ so $a = b = c = 1$ (say)

$\Rightarrow x + y + z + d = 0$ and $d = -4$

The plane $P: x + y + z - 4 = 0$, distance of (1, 1, 1) from the plane P is $d=\frac{|-1|}{\sqrt{3}}=\frac{1}{\sqrt{3}}$

38. (b) Reflection of point (2, –1, 3) is given by

$$\frac{x-2}{3}=\frac{y+1}{-2}=\frac{z-3}{-1}=\frac{-2(6+2-3-9)}{9+4+1}$$

$$\Rightarrow x=\frac{26}{7}, y=-\frac{15}{7}, z=\frac{17}{7}$$

Aliter: A general point towards the foot of perpendicular from (2, –1, 3) will be $(2 + 3r, -1 - 2r, 3 - r)$ and if it lies on plane $3x - 2y - z - 9 = 0$

$\Rightarrow r=\frac{2}{7} \Rightarrow$ Image of point $\equiv\left(\frac{26}{7},\frac{-15}{7},\frac{17}{7}\right)$

39. **(b)** Image of $P(\alpha, \beta, \gamma)$ in the plane $P: \ell x + my + nz = 0$ is $Q(\alpha', \beta', \gamma')$, then $\frac{\ell\alpha+m\beta+n\gamma}{\sqrt{\ell^2+m^2+n^2}}=\frac{-(\ell\alpha'+m\beta'+n\gamma')}{\sqrt{\ell^2+m^2+n^2}}$

$\Rightarrow \ell(\alpha + \alpha') + m(\beta + \beta') + n(\gamma + \gamma') = 0$

Also $\frac{\alpha-\alpha'}{\ell}=\frac{\beta-\beta'}{m}=\frac{\gamma-\gamma'}{n}=p$ (say)

So $\ell=\frac{\alpha-\alpha'}{p}, m=\frac{\beta-\beta'}{p}, n=\frac{\gamma-\gamma'}{p}$

$$\Rightarrow \frac{\alpha^2-(\alpha')^2}{p}+\frac{\beta^2-(\beta')^2}{p}+\frac{\gamma^2-(\gamma')^2}{p}=0$$

i.e., $\alpha^2 + \beta^2 + \gamma^2 = (\alpha')^2 + (\beta')^2 + (\gamma')^2$

40. **(c)** Any point on the line {passing through $P(2, -3, 4)$} which is parallel to x-axis will be $(2 + r, -3, 4)$. This point will lie on $r.(\hat{i}+\hat{j}+\hat{k})-5=0$, when $(2 + r) + (-3) + 4 - 5 = 0$ which gives $r = 2$

41. **(b)** The plane $ax + by + cz - d = 0$ will meet the coordinates axes in $A\left(\frac{d}{a},0,0\right); B\left(0,\frac{d}{b},0\right)$ and $C\left(0,0,\frac{d}{c}\right)$

$\Rightarrow \overline{AB}=\left(-\frac{d}{a}\hat{i}+\frac{d}{b}\hat{j}+0\hat{k}\right)$

and $\overline{AC}\left(-\frac{d}{a}\hat{i}+0\hat{j}+\frac{d}{c}\hat{k}\right)$

$$\therefore \text{ Area of } \Delta ABC=\frac{1}{2}\left\|\begin{vmatrix}\hat{i} & \hat{j} & \hat{k}\\ -\frac{d}{a} & \frac{d}{b} & 0\\ -\frac{d}{a} & 0 & \frac{d}{c}\end{vmatrix}\right\|$$

$$=\frac{1}{2}\left|\left\{\frac{d^2}{bc}\hat{i}+\frac{d^2}{ac}\hat{j}+\frac{d^2}{ab}\hat{k}\right\}\right|=\frac{1}{2}(d^2)\sqrt{\frac{a^2+b^2+c^2}{a^2b^2c^2}}$$

$$=\frac{d^2\sqrt{a^2+b^2+c^2}}{2|abc|}$$

Aliter: The three points on the coordinates axes are $A\left(\frac{d}{a},0,0\right),\left(0,\frac{d}{b},0\right)$ and $C\left(0,0,\frac{d}{c}\right)$.Consider a tetrahedron with origin as the fourth point:

$$\text{Area}=\frac{\text{vol of ||piped}\times 3}{\text{distance of origin from the plane}}$$

$$\Rightarrow \text{Area}=\frac{\left(3\times\frac{1}{6}\right)}{\left(\frac{d}{\sqrt{a^2+b^2+c^2}}\right)}\begin{vmatrix}\frac{d}{a} & 0 & 0\\ 0 & \frac{d}{b} & 0\\ 0 & 0 & \frac{d}{c}\end{vmatrix}$$

$$=\frac{\sqrt{a^2+b^2+c^2}}{2d}\left|\frac{d^3}{abc}\right|=\frac{d^2\sqrt{a^2+b^2+c^2}}{2|abc|}$$

42. **(b)** A general point on the line

$L_1: \frac{x-1}{3}=\frac{y-2}{1}=\frac{z-3}{2}=\lambda$ ....(i)

will be $(3\lambda + 1, \lambda + 2, 2\lambda + 3)$ and similarly on

$L_2: \frac{x-3}{1}=\frac{y-1}{2}=\frac{x-2}{3}=\mu$ ....(ii)

will be $(\mu + 3, 2\mu + 1, 3\mu + 2)$

From (i) and (ii) we get $\lambda = \mu = 1$ and point of intersection is $P(4, 3, 5)$. The plane passing through $P(4, 3, 5)$ which is at maximum distance from origin will have normal along $\overline{OP}$ i.e., $\vec{n}=4\hat{i}+3\hat{j}+5\hat{k}$

Hence the plane will be $4(x - 4) + 3(y - 3) + 5(z - 5) = 0$ i.e., $4x + 3y + 5z = 50$

43. **(c)** Since yz-plane serves as a mirror

$\Rightarrow$ only angle with x-axis changes and it changes from α to $(180° - \alpha)$ so D.C's are $(-\cos\alpha, \cos\beta, \cos\gamma)$

44. **(d)** The normal to the plane has D.R.'s <1, 1, 1>

Hence the plane is $(x - a) + (y - a) + (z - a) = 0$ i.e., $x + y + z = 3a$ as a result the intercepts on the coordinates axes are $3a$ each

$\Rightarrow$ Sum of reciprocals $=\frac{1}{3a}\times 3=\frac{1}{a}$

45. **(c)** Let the line segment be joining $A(x_1, y_1, z_1)$ $B(x_2, y_2, z_2)$. So the projections on axes are $(|x_2 - x_1|;\ |y_2 - y_1|,\ |z_2 - z_1|)$

$\therefore$ Length of the line $= \sqrt{3^2+4^2+5^2} = 5\sqrt{2}$ units

46. (c) The line is $L: \dfrac{x-11}{10} = \dfrac{y+2}{-4} = \dfrac{z+8}{-11}$ and the point $P(2, -1, 5)$. Unit vector along the line L is $\widehat{AB} = \dfrac{10\hat{i} - 4\hat{j} - 11\hat{k}}{\sqrt{237}}$

and $\vec{r} = \overrightarrow{AP} = -9\hat{i} + \hat{j} + 13\hat{k}$

so Length of perpendicular $= \sqrt{\vec{r}^2 - (\vec{r}.\widehat{AB})^2}$

$= \sqrt{251 - 237} = \sqrt{14}$ units

Foot of perpendicular $B = (11\hat{i} - 2\hat{j} - 8\hat{k}) + (\vec{r}.\widehat{AB})\widehat{AB}$

$= 11\hat{i} - 2\hat{j} - 8\hat{k} + \dfrac{-237}{\sqrt{237}}\left(\dfrac{10\hat{i} - 4\hat{j} - 11\hat{k}}{\sqrt{237}}\right)$

$= \hat{i} + 2\hat{j} + 3\hat{k} = (1, 2, 3)$

47. **(b)** The line joining the point $A(2, -3, 1)$ and $B(3, -4, -5)$ is $L: \vec{r} = (2\hat{i} - 3\hat{j} + \hat{k}) + \lambda(\hat{i} - \hat{j} - 6\hat{k})$.

This will intersect the plane $2x + y + z - 7 = 0$

When $4 + 2\lambda - 3 - \lambda + 1 - 6\lambda - 7 = 0$

Gives $\lambda = -1$ then $\vec{r} = \hat{i} - 2\hat{j} + 7\hat{k} = (1, -2, 7)$

48. **(c)** A general point on the line from (1, –2, 3) with D.R.'s <2, 3 –6> is $(2d+1, 3d-2, -6d+3)$

This will lie on the plane $x - y + z - 5 = 0$

i.e., $2d + 1 - 3d + 2 - 6d + 3 - 5 = 0$ gives $d = \dfrac{1}{7}$ units.

49. **(d)** The line are $L_1: \dfrac{x}{\left(\frac{1}{2}\right)} = \dfrac{y}{(1/3)} = \dfrac{z}{-1}$

And $L_2: \dfrac{x}{(1/6)} = \dfrac{y}{-1} = \dfrac{2}{\left(-\frac{1}{4}\right)}$

Angle between the line is $\cos\theta = \dfrac{\frac{1}{12} - \frac{1}{3} + \frac{1}{4}}{\frac{7}{6} \cdot \frac{\sqrt{157}}{12}} = 0$

$\Rightarrow \theta = 90^o$

50. **(d)** The equation of xy-plane is $z = 0$. The points $P_1(a, b, c)$ and $P_2(-a, -c, -b)$. The required ratio is $\dfrac{-c}{(-b)} = c : b$

51. **(a)** Given $O(0,0,0); A(1,2,1); B(2,1,3); C(-1,1,2)$ $\overline{OA} \times \overline{OB}$ gives normal $\vec{n}_1$ to plane OAB

$\therefore \quad \vec{n}_1 = \begin{vmatrix} \hat{i} & \hat{j} & \hat{k} \\ 1 & 2 & 1 \\ 2 & 1 & 3 \end{vmatrix} = 5\hat{i} - \hat{j} - 3\hat{k}$

and normal to the plane ABC is $\vec{n}_2 = \begin{vmatrix} \hat{i} & \hat{j} & \hat{k} \\ 1 & -1 & 2 \\ -2 & -1 & 1 \end{vmatrix}$

$\Rightarrow \quad \vec{n}_2 = \hat{i} - 5\hat{j} - 3\hat{k}$

and angle between $\vec{n}_1$ and $\vec{n}_2$ is $\cos\theta = \dfrac{5+5+9}{\sqrt{35}\sqrt{35}}$

$\Rightarrow \quad \theta = \cos^{-1}\left(\dfrac{19}{35}\right)$

52. (a) Let $\vec{r} = \overrightarrow{AP}$ and $\overrightarrow{AM} = \hat{n} = \ell\hat{i} + m\hat{j} + n\hat{k}$

Now $PM = \sqrt{(\vec{r})^2 - (\vec{r}.\hat{n})^2}$

$= [(x_1 - x_2)^2 + (y_1 - y_2)^2 + (z_1 - z_2)^2 - \{(x_1 - x_2)\ell + (y_1 - y_2) m + (z_1 - z_2)n\}^2]^{1/2}$

53. **(b)** Given $PA^2 - PB^2 = k$

$\Rightarrow \{(x-2)^2 + (y-3)^2 + (z-4)^2\}$

$- \{(x+2)^2 + (y-5)^2 - (z+4)^2\} = k$

Gives $-8x - 16 + 4y - 16z = k$

Or $8x - 4y + 16z + k + 16 = 0$ which is a plane

54. (c) The line $y = 0,\ z = 0$ will be the line x-axis with D.R's = <1, 0, 0>

Now plane passing though the intersection is $(a\lambda + a')x + (b\lambda + b')y + (c\lambda + c') + (d\lambda + d') = 0$

Since the plane is parallel to x-axis $\Rightarrow a\lambda + a' = 0$, i.e., $\lambda = -a'/a$

Hence the plane is $(ab' - ab)y + (ac' - a'c)z + (ad' - a'd) = 0$

55. **(b)** Let $\overline{CD}$ be $\vec{r}_1$

$\vec{r}_1 = (-a\hat{i}) + \lambda(a\hat{i} + a\hat{k})$ Similarly

$\overline{AB} = \vec{r}_2 = (a\hat{i}) + u(-a\hat{i} + a\hat{j})$

So shortest distance $SD = \dfrac{|2a\hat{i}.(a\hat{i} + a\hat{k}) \times (-a\hat{i} + a\hat{j})|}{|(a\hat{i} + a\hat{k}) \times (-a\hat{i} + a\hat{j})|}$

$= \dfrac{|2a^3\hat{i}.(-\hat{i} - \hat{j} + \hat{k})|}{a^2|-\hat{i} - \hat{j} + \hat{k}|} = \dfrac{2a}{\sqrt{3}}$ units

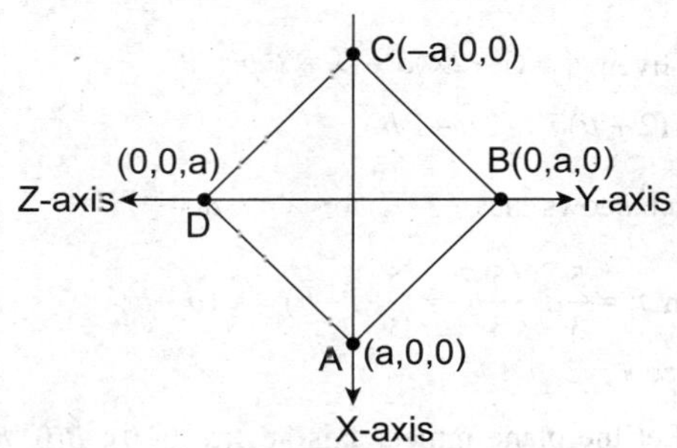

56. **(a)** Let $P_1 = 2x + 5y + 3z = 0$

$P_2 = x - y + 4z = 2$

$P_3 = 7y - 5z = -4$

Observe that only P_1 passes through origin so these planes can not be at equal distance from origin.

$$\Delta = \begin{vmatrix} 2 & -5 & 3 \\ 1 & -1 & 4 \\ 0 & 7 & 5 \end{vmatrix}$$

$$= \Delta_x = \begin{vmatrix} 0 & 5 & 3 \\ 2 & -1 & 4 \\ -4 & 7 & -5 \end{vmatrix} = 0; \Delta_y = \begin{vmatrix} 2 & 0 & 3 \\ 1 & 2 & 4 \\ 0 & -4 & -5 \end{vmatrix} = 0$$

$$\Delta_z = \begin{vmatrix} 2 & 5 & 0 \\ 1 & -1 & 2 \\ 0 & 7 & -4 \end{vmatrix} = 0 \text{ (As } R_1 - 2R_2 = R_3)$$

$\therefore$ planes meet in a line

Aliter: $P_1 - 2P_2 = P_3$

$\because$ $(2x + 5y + 3z) + (-2)(x - y + 4z - 2) = (7y - 5z + 4)$

$\Rightarrow$ plane pan thugh a line

57. (a) Let line $L_1 : \frac{x}{1} = \frac{y}{1} = \frac{z}{1}$ and it passes though (0, 0, 0)

Now solving $2x + y + z = 1$ and $3x + y + 2z = 2$

We get $x + z = 1$ put x = 0 then z = 1 and it gives y = 0 so the line of intersection is passing through (0, 0, 1) D.R. of line of intersection are $\begin{vmatrix} \hat{i} & \hat{j} & \hat{k} \\ 2 & 1 & 1 \\ 3 & 1 & 2 \end{vmatrix} = \hat{i} - \hat{j} - \hat{k}$

So the shortest distance $d = \left| \frac{k.(\hat{i} - \hat{j} - \hat{k}) \times (\hat{i} + \hat{j} + \hat{k})}{|(\hat{i} - \hat{j} - \hat{k}) \times (\hat{i} + \hat{j} + \hat{k})|} \right|$

$$= \left| \frac{k.(-2\hat{j} + 2\hat{k})}{|-2\hat{j} + 2k|} \right| = \frac{2}{2\sqrt{2}} = \frac{1}{\sqrt{2}} \text{ units}$$

58. (c) The line of intersection of $x + 2y - z - 3 = 0$ and $x + 3y - z - 4 = 0$ is given by $\begin{vmatrix} \hat{i} & \hat{j} & \hat{k} \\ 1 & 2 & -1 \\ 1 & 3 & -1 \end{vmatrix} = \hat{i} + \hat{k}$ which is parallel to $x - z$ planes

59. (a) Given $\vec{r}_1 = (1 + 2\lambda)\vec{a} + (\lambda - 2)\vec{b}$

$\vec{r}_2 = (2 + \mu)\vec{a} + (2\mu - 1)\vec{b}$

Which shows that $\vec{r}_1 = \vec{r}_2$ for $\lambda = -\mu = \frac{1}{3}$

Then $\vec{r}_1 = \frac{5}{3}\vec{a} - \frac{5}{3}\vec{b} = \frac{5}{3}(\vec{a} - \vec{b}) = \frac{k}{3}(\vec{a} - \vec{b})$

Hence $k = 5$

60. (a) Let the plane mmets axis at $A(a, 0, 0)$; $B(0, b, 0)$ and $C(0, 0, c)$

$\Rightarrow$ equation of plane is $\frac{x}{a} + \frac{y}{b} + \frac{z}{c} = 1$

Its distance form origin $= \frac{1}{\sqrt{\frac{1}{a^2} + \frac{1}{b^2} + \frac{1}{c^2}}} = p$ (given)

$\Rightarrow \frac{1}{a^2} + \frac{1}{b^2} + \frac{1}{c^2} = \frac{1}{b^2}$ ...... (i)

Also centroid $\equiv (x, y, z) \equiv \left(\frac{a}{4}, \frac{b}{4}, \frac{c}{4}\right)$

$\Rightarrow a = 4x, b = 4y, c = 4z$ .... (ii)

$\therefore$ from (i) and (ii) $\frac{1}{x^2} + \frac{1}{y^2} + \frac{1}{z^2} = \frac{16}{p^2} = \frac{\lambda}{p^2}$

Putting in the given relation

$\Rightarrow \lambda = 16 \Rightarrow$ (a) is correct

61. (b) The required plane passes through $A(-1, 2, 0)$, $B(3, -4, 1)$ and it contains a vector with D.R. < 3, 2, 1>

and henc it is give by $\begin{vmatrix} (x+1) & (y-2) & z \\ 4 & -6 & 1 \\ 3 & 2 & 1 \end{vmatrix} = 0$

Which gives $(-8)(x + 1) - (y - 2) + 26z = 0$

i.e., $8x + y - 26z + 6 = 0$

Fast method: Select that plane which gives sum of the product of D.R.'s (with D.R's of the line) as zero. This is $8x + y - 26z + 6 = 0$. It also contains A and B so Ans. (b) option

62. (a) A general point on L_1 is

$\vec{r}_1 = (3\lambda + 5, -\lambda + 7, \lambda - 2)$

and on L_2 is $\vec{r}_2 = (-3\mu - 3, 2\mu + 3, 4\mu + 6)$

Now $\vec{r}_1 - \vec{r}_2 = (2p, 7p, -5p)$

i.e., $3\lambda + 3\mu + 8 = 2p$ ....(i)

$-\lambda - 2\mu + 4 = 7p$ .... (ii)

$\lambda - 4\mu - 8 = -5p$ ....(iii)

Solving we get $\lambda = \mu = -1$, p = 1

So $\vec{r}_1 = (2, +8, -3)$ and $\vec{r}_2 = (0, 1, 2)$

So $|\vec{r}_1 - \vec{r}_2| = \sqrt{2^2 + 7^2 + 5^2} = \sqrt{78}$

Hence the equation is

$\frac{x-2}{2} = \frac{y-8}{7} = \frac{z+3}{-5}$ and length = $\sqrt{78}$

63. (b) $p_1 = 0$ and $p_2 = 0$

Now $p_1 + \lambda p_2 = 0$ for $\lambda \in R$ represents the family of planes (excepts plane $p_2 = 0$)

64. (d) D.R. of the normal to the plane that that is perpendicular to the plane $2x - 2y + z = 0$ and $x - y + 2z = 4$ is given

by $\begin{vmatrix} \hat{i} & \hat{j} & \hat{k} \\ 2 & -2 & 1 \\ 1 & -1 & 2 \end{vmatrix} = -3\hat{i} - 3\hat{j}$ or $\hat{i} + \hat{j}$

so the required plane passing through (1, –2, 1) is $(x - 1) + (y + 2) = 0$ or $x + y + 1 = 0$

Hence the distance of (1, 2, 2) form this plane is $d = \frac{4}{\sqrt{2}} = 2\sqrt{2}$ units

65. (a) $L_1 = \vec{r}_1 = (1+s, -3-\lambda s, 1+\lambda s)$

So $A(\vec{a}) = (1,-3,1)$ **and** $(\vec{b}) = \hat{i} - \lambda\hat{j} + \lambda\hat{k}$

and $L_2 = \vec{r}_2 = \left(0+\frac{t}{2}, 1+t, 2-t\right)$

so $C(\vec{c}) = (0,1,2)$ and $\vec{d} = \frac{\hat{i}}{2} + \hat{j} - \hat{k}$

Since L_1 and L_2 are coplanar

So $(\vec{a}-\vec{c}).(\vec{b}\times\vec{d}) = \begin{vmatrix} 1 & -4 & -1 \\ 1 & -\lambda & \lambda \\ \frac{1}{2} & 1 & -1 \end{vmatrix} = 0$

$\Rightarrow -\frac{5}{2}\lambda = 5$ so $\lambda = -2$

66. (d) $\ell + m + n = 0$ and $\ell m = 0$

Case (i): $\ell = 0$, ($m \neq 0$) {∵ if both $\ell = m = 0$, then n = 0 which is not possible}

then m = – n since $\ell^2 + m^2 + m^2 = 1$ so

$(\ell, m, n) = \left(0, \frac{-1}{\sqrt{2}}, -\frac{1}{\sqrt{2}}\right)$ or $\left(0, \frac{1}{\sqrt{2}}, \frac{1}{\sqrt{2}}\right)$

Similarly Case (ii) when m = 0 (but $\ell \neq 0$)

then $(\ell, m, n) = \left(\frac{1}{\sqrt{2}}, 0, -\frac{1}{\sqrt{2}}\right)$ or $\left(\frac{-1}{\sqrt{2}}, 0, \frac{1}{\sqrt{2}}\right)$

$\cos\theta = -1 \Rightarrow \theta = \pi$ (or 0)

67. (b) The line y = z = 0 is x – $axis$ with D.R.s. < 1, 0, 0 >. The plane through the intersection will be

$(2\lambda + 1)x + (3\lambda + 5)y + (\lambda - 2)z + (7 - \lambda) = 0$

Since it parallel to x-axis, $2\lambda + 1 = 0$, i.e., $\lambda = -1/2$

And hence the plane is $\frac{7}{2}y - \frac{5}{2}z + \frac{15}{2} = 0$

or $7y - 5z + 15 = 0$

68. (b) According to question $k.2 + k.1 - 36 = -k - 2k + 36$

$\Rightarrow 6k = 72 \Rightarrow k = 12$

69. (a) The line $L_1: \frac{x}{1} = \frac{y}{1} = \frac{z}{1}$ has D.R's < 1, 1, 1>

and the line $L_2: \frac{x-1}{1} = \frac{y-1}{1} = \frac{z-1}{d}$ has D.R.s < 1, 1, d >

Now D.R.s of the normal

$= \begin{vmatrix} \hat{i} & \hat{j} & -\hat{k} \\ 1 & 1 & 1 \\ 1 & 1 & d \end{vmatrix} = (d-1)\hat{i} + (1-d)\hat{j} \equiv$ <1, –1, 0> or <–1, 1, 0>

So D.C's the normal to the plane = $\pm\left(\frac{1}{\sqrt{2}}, \frac{-1}{\sqrt{2}}, 0\right)$

MORE THEN ONE CORRECT

1. (b, d) $\alpha = \beta = 60^0$; $\gamma = ?$

$\alpha = \beta = 60^0 \Rightarrow \ell = m = 1/2$. So $n^2 = \frac{1}{2}$ or $n = \pm\frac{1}{\sqrt{2}}$

$\Rightarrow \gamma = \frac{\pi}{4} \Rightarrow \frac{3\pi}{4}$

2. (a, b) The lines are

$L_1 = \vec{a} + \lambda\vec{b}$ where $\vec{a} = (2,3,4)$ and $\vec{b}(1,1,-k)$ and

$L_2 = \vec{c} + \mu\vec{d}$ where $\vec{c} = (1,4,5)$ and $\vec{d} = (k,2,1)$

The lines will be coplanar when $(\vec{a}-\vec{c}).(\vec{b}\times\vec{d}) = 0$

i.e., $\begin{vmatrix} 1 & -1 & -1 \\ 1 & 1 & -k \\ k & 2 & 1 \end{vmatrix} = 0$

i.e., $2k + 2 + k^2 + k - 2 = 0$ or k $(k + 3) = 0$ so k = 0, –3

3. (a,b,c,d) Since (1)(–3) + (–2)(2) + 7(1) = 0 and 1(–1) – 2(3) + 7(–2) + 21 = 0

So line is contained in plane.

Similarly (0, 7, –1) lies on the plane $x - 2y + 7z + 21 = 0$.

obviously other options are also true.

4. (a,b,c,d) $P(xyz) = 2x - 3y + 4z + 2$ and $P_1 : P + 4 = 0$;

$P_2 = P - \frac{1}{2} = 0$; $P_3 = P - 8 = 0$

p_1 = distance between $P(x, y, z) = 0$ and $P_1 = 0 \Rightarrow p_1 = \frac{4}{\sqrt{29}}$

$P_2 = \frac{\left(\frac{1}{2}\right)}{\sqrt{29}}$ and $p_3 = \frac{8}{\sqrt{29}}$ observe that $8p_2 = p_1$

and $16p_2 = p_3$ also $p_1 + 8p_2 - p_3 = 0$

Now $p_1 + 2p_2 + 3p_3 = \frac{4+1+24}{\sqrt{29}} = \sqrt{29}$

5. (b and d) $ax + by + c = 0$ represents a plane with normal's D.R'S <a, b, 0 >. Since the product with <0, 0, 1> is zero

∴ The plane is perpendicular to xy plane and parallel to z-axis

6. (a,b,c) P(2, 3, 1) and L ≡ $x - y - z - 2 = 0$

$\frac{L(P)}{L(O)} = \frac{-4}{-2} = 2 > 0$ so they are on the same side of plane

and distance of P from the plane $= \frac{|-4|}{\sqrt{3}} = \frac{4}{\sqrt{3}}$

P(2, 3, 1) and $M\left(\frac{10}{3}, \frac{5}{3}, \frac{-1}{3}\right)$ gives $\overline{PM} = \frac{4}{3}\hat{i} - \frac{4}{3}\hat{j} - \frac{4}{3}\hat{k}$

which is parallel to the normal

Also observe that $\left(\frac{10}{3}, \frac{5}{3}, \frac{1}{3}\right)$ lies on the plane so $\left(\frac{10}{3}, \frac{5}{3}, \frac{-1}{3}\right)$ is the foot of perpendicular from P.

7. (b and c) Point P (1, 2, 3) distance from x-axis is $A=\sqrt{2^2+3^2}=\sqrt{13}$,
Distance from y – axis is $B=\sqrt{1^2+3^2}=\sqrt{10}$,
Distance from z axis is $C=\sqrt{1^2+2^2}=\sqrt{5}$
Clearly $A^2 \neq B^2 + C^2$; $B^2 = 2C^2$
$2A^2 C^2 = 130 = 13B^2$

8. (b and c) If $\frac{x-p}{\ell}=\frac{y-q}{m}=\frac{z-r}{n}$ lies on the plane $Ax + By + Cz + D = 0$, then point (p, q, r) will satisfy $Ap + Bq + Cr + D = 0$. Also $Al + Bm + Cn = 0$

9. (b, c and d) $\vec{r}_1=\vec{a}+t\vec{a}'$ and $\vec{r}_2=\vec{a}'+s\vec{a}$
Since $\vec{a}\times\vec{a}'$ is perpendicular to both $\vec{a}$ and $\vec{a}'$, so it is perpendicular to the plane of $\vec{a}$ and $\vec{a}'$. Since.
$(\vec{r}-\vec{a}).\{\vec{a}\times\vec{a}'\}=0$ also $(\vec{r}-\vec{a}').\{\vec{a}\times\vec{a}'\}=0$
So $\vec{r}.\{\vec{a}\times\vec{a}'\}=[\vec{r}\ \vec{a}\ \vec{a}']=0(as\ \vec{a}.\{\vec{a}\times\vec{a}'\}=0]$
Also $(\vec{r}-\vec{a}).(\vec{r}\times\vec{a}')=\vec{r}.(\vec{r}\times\vec{a}')=\vec{a}.(\vec{r}\times\vec{a}')=0-0=0$

10. (b and d) $\vec{r}.\vec{n}_1=p_1$ and $\vec{r}.\vec{n}_2=p_2$ are the two planes and $\vec{a}$ is a given point
Now $\vec{n}_1\times\vec{n}_2$ is perpendicular to both the planes and it will be parallel to the line of intersection of planes. Since line passing through $\vec{a}$ and parallel to the line of intersection of plane will be $\vec{r}=\vec{a}+\lambda\ (\vec{n}_1\times\vec{n}_2)$ so $\vec{r}-\vec{a}=\lambda(\vec{n}_1\times\vec{n}_2)$
(since $\vec{u}\times\vec{u}=\vec{o}$) $\Rightarrow (\vec{r}-\vec{a})\times(\vec{n}_1\times\vec{n}_2)=\vec{0}$

11. (a, b) (a) statement is true
(b) distance of (3 cos θ, 3 sin θ, 4) from z-axis = $\sqrt{(3\cos\theta)^2+(3\sin\theta)^2}=3$ which is constant and independent of θ
(c) In a tetrahedron a vertex is formed by the intersection of three lines
(d) The line joining A(2, 4, 5) and B(3, 5–4) is dividing by yz plane in the ratio externally as $2 + 3\lambda = 0$ gives $\lambda = = -2/3$

ASSERTION REASON TYPE

1. **R:** The statement is true
A: The line is $L:\frac{x-1}{3}=\frac{y-2}{11}=\frac{z+1}{11}$ and the plane $P: 11x - 3z - 14 = 0$
Observe that (1, 2, –1) lies in the plane , Also (3)(11) + (11) (–3) = 0
⇒ The line lies in the plane
Statement 'A' is true and completely supported by R
Ans (a) option

2. **R:** The statement is false. The two lines will be coplanar if they intersect in a point. The perpendicular lines may or may not intersect.
A: The statement is true as these two lines intersect at (1, 3, 4)
Ans (c) option

3. **R:** Statement is true as the coplanar lines must intersect in some point (where as the skew lines never intersect)
A: The statement is true since the given lines are given to be non-intersecting
⇒ Assertion is true and it is fully supported by R.
Ans (a)

4. **R:** The statement is true consider a point P_3 on the sphere with AB as one of its diameters then $\overrightarrow{P_3A}.\overrightarrow{P_3B}=0$ and θ = 90: When point lies outside the sphere, then 0 < θ < π/2 so $\overrightarrow{P_1A}.\overrightarrow{P_1B}>0$

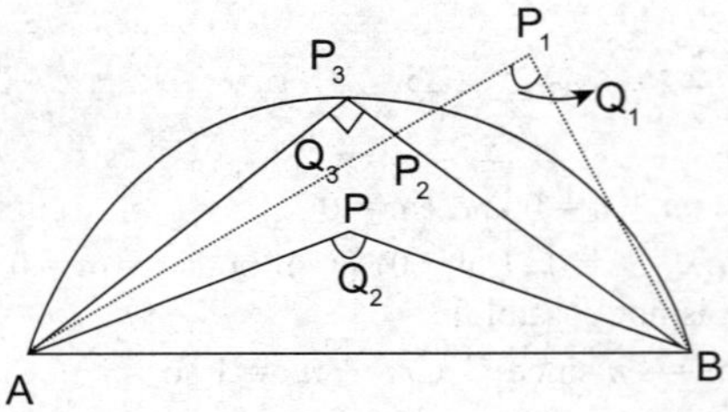

A: The statement is true : In this case $\overrightarrow{PA}=(-\hat{i}-2\hat{j})$ and $\overrightarrow{PB}=(-\hat{i}+4\hat{j})$ so $\overrightarrow{PA}.\overrightarrow{PB}=1+8=9>0$
The statement is true and it follows from R
Ans (a)

5. **R:** The statement is true when two points $A(x_1, y_1, z_1)$ and $B(x_2, y_2, z_2)$ lie on the opposite sides of a plane $P(x, y, z) = 0$, then $P(x_1, y_1, z_1)$. $P(x_2, y_2, z_2) < 0$
A: The statement is true. Points are $A(2, 1, 5)$ and $P(3, 4, 3)$
∴ P(2,1,5) . P(3,4,5) = (–5) (7) < 0
Ans (a) option

6. **R:** The statement is true
A: A homogenous equation of second degree in x, y, z when factorized will give two linear factors which will represent two planes both passing through origin. The statement is true and it is supported by R.
Ans (a) option

7. **R:** The statement is true as $x + y + z = k$ represents a plane
A: The statement is true as |x| + |y| + |z| = k will give 8 planes and it result into the formation of an *oct*ahedron. So 'A' is true but it is not fully supported by R as mere formation of planes does not ensure formation of an octahedron.
Ans (b) option

8. **R:** The statement is true for the given considerations
A: The statement is true for the given system. But the statement can not follow from R. In 'R' the square root of sum of squares is involved where as in 'A'. It is sum of moduli
Ans (b) option

9. $V = \left\|\begin{matrix} a_1 & a_2 & a_3 \\ b_1 & b_2 & b_3 \\ c_1 & c_2 & c_3 \end{matrix}\right\|$

$= |a_1b_2c_3 - a_1c_2b_3 - a_2b_1c_3 + a_2b_3c_1 + a_3b_1c_2 - a_3b_2c_1|$

$= \left|(a_1b_2c_3 + a_2b_3c_1 + a_3b_1c_2) - (a_1c_2b_3 + a_2b_1c_3 + a_3b_2c_1)\right|$

Without loss of generality let $a_1b_2c_3 + a_2b_3c_1 + a_3b_1c_2 \geq a_1c_2b_3 + a_2b_1c_3 + a_3b_2c_1$

$\therefore \quad V \leq (a_1b_2c_3 + a_2b_3c_1 + a_3b_1c_2)$ ....(i)

By A.M. ≤ G.M., $(a_1 + b_2 + c_3) \geq 3(a_1b_2c_3)^{1/3}$

Similarly $(a_2 + b_3 + c_1) \geq 3(a_2b_3c_1)^{1/3}$ and $(a_3 + b_1 + c_2) \geq 3(a_3b_1c_2)^{1/3}$

$\Rightarrow$ $(a_1 + b_2 + c_3)^3 \geq 27(a_1b_2c_3)$; $(a_2 + b_3 + c_1)^3 \geq 27(a_2b_3c_1)$ and $(a_3 + b_1 + c_2)^3 \geq 27(a_3b_1c_2)$

Adding we get,

$(a_1 + b_2 + c_3)^3 + (a_2 + b_3 + c_1)^3 + (a_3 + b_1 + c_2)^3 \geq 27(a_1b_2c_3 + a_2b_3c_1 + a_3b_1c_2)$ ....(ii)

$\therefore$ from (i) and (ii)

$$V \leq \frac{1}{27}\left[(a_1+b_2+c_3)^3 + (a_2+b_3+c_1)^3 + (a_3+b_1+c_2)^3\right]$$

$$\Rightarrow V \leq \frac{1}{27}\left[(a_1+b_1+c_1)+(a_2+b_2+c_2)+(a_3+b_3+c_3)\right]^3$$

$$\left[\because x^3+y^3+z^3 \leq (x+y+z)^3 \text{ for } x,y,z \geq 0\right]$$

$$\Rightarrow \quad V \leq \frac{1}{27}[3L]^3 = L^3 \quad \Rightarrow V \leq L^3$$

$\Rightarrow$ Assertion as well as reason both are correct and reason is the correct explanation of assertion

$\Rightarrow$ option (a) is correct.

SECTION VI COMPREHENSION TYPE

1. (b) x = 0, $cy + bz - bc = 0$ represents a line through $(0, b, 0)$ with D.R.s <0, b, $-c$> similarly $y = 0$, $\frac{x-a}{a} = \frac{z-0}{c}$ represents a line though (a, 0, 0) with D.R.s <a, 0, c> Hence

$$S.D. = \frac{|(\vec{a}-\vec{c}).(\vec{b}\times\vec{d})|}{|\vec{b}\times\vec{d}|} \text{ gives}$$

$$2d = \frac{|2abc|}{\sqrt{b^2c^2+a^2c^2+a^2b^2}}$$

$$= d^2 = \frac{a^2b^2c^2}{b^2c^2+a^2c^2+a^2b^2}$$

$$\Rightarrow \quad d^2 = \frac{1}{a^{-2}+b^{-2}+c^{-2}} \Rightarrow d^{-2} = a^{-2}+b^{-2}+c^{-2}$$

2. (a) Consider the body diagonal from O (0, 0, 0) to $C(a, b, c)$ so any point on the diagonal is $\vec{r}_1 = (a\hat{i} + b\hat{j} + c\hat{k})\lambda$

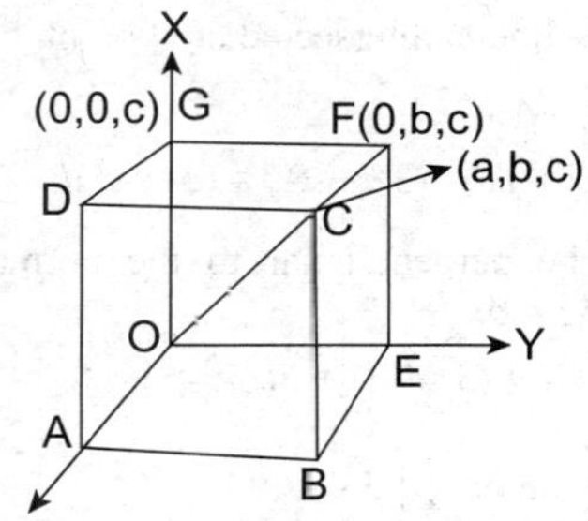

Consider the edge $\overrightarrow{GF}$ from G(0, 0, c) to F (0, b, c) any point on $\overrightarrow{GF}$ is $\vec{r}_2 = c\hat{k} + \mu b\hat{j}$

$$\text{Hence } S.D. = \frac{|c\hat{k}.\{(a\hat{i}+b\hat{j}+c\hat{k})\times b\hat{j}\}|}{|(a\hat{i}+b\hat{j}+c\hat{k})\times b\hat{j}|}$$

$$= \frac{|abc|}{\sqrt{a^2b^2+b^2c^2}} = \frac{ac}{\sqrt{a^2+c^2}} \quad \text{(a, c > 0 being edge lengtrs)}$$

3. (d) D.R.s of the line of intersection of the two planes

$$= \begin{vmatrix} \hat{i} & \hat{j} & \hat{k} \\ 3 & -2 & 1 \\ 2 & 3 & 4 \end{vmatrix} = -11\hat{i} - 10\hat{j} + 13\hat{k}$$

Now the given line is $L: \frac{x+4}{3} = \frac{y+6}{5} = \frac{z-1}{-2}$

observe that this line is not parallel to the line of intersection of planes. so both lines must intersect in order to be coplanar. The line intersects the plane $3x - 2y + z + 5 = 0$ for λ given by $3(3\lambda - 4) - 2(5\lambda - 6) + (-2\lambda + 1) + 5 = 0$

$\Rightarrow$ $-3\lambda + 6 = 0$ or $\lambda = 2$ and the point of intersection is (2, 4, –3). This point will also satisfy the equation of second plane so $4 + 12 - 12 - k = 0$ gives k = 4

Passage 2:

4. (c) $\overrightarrow{OP} = \hat{i} + 2\hat{j} + 5\hat{k}$

$$|\overrightarrow{ON}| \frac{\overrightarrow{OP}.\vec{n}}{|n|}\hat{n}$$

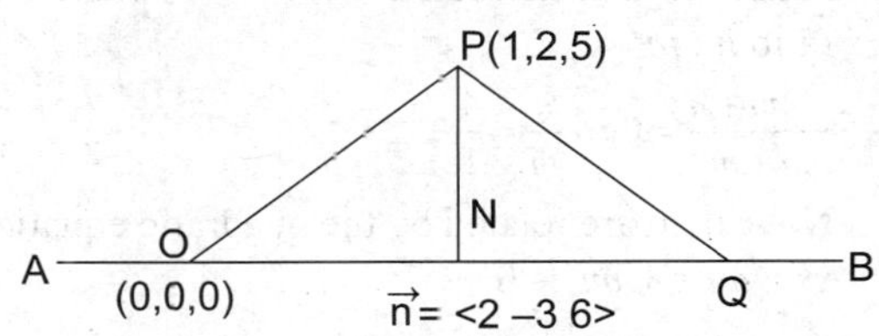

$$= \frac{(\hat{i}+2\hat{j}+5\hat{k}).(2\hat{i}-3\hat{j}+6\hat{k})}{7}\hat{n}$$

$$\Rightarrow \quad N = \frac{26(2\hat{i}-3\hat{j}+6\hat{k})}{49}$$

$$\text{so} \quad N\left(\frac{52}{49}, \frac{-78}{49}, \frac{156}{49}\right)$$

5. **(a)** Now AB line is intersected at Q point.
Let Q $(2\lambda, -3\lambda, 6\lambda)$
so $\overline{PQ} = (2\lambda - 1)\hat{i} - (3\lambda + 2)\hat{j} + (6\lambda - 5)\hat{k}$
This must be perpendicular to the normal to the plane $3x + 4y + 5z = 0$
so $3(2\lambda - 1) - 4(3\lambda + 2) + 5(6\lambda - 5) = 0$
gives $\lambda = \frac{3}{2}$, then $Q\left(3, -\frac{9}{2}, 9\right)$

6. (a) for $\lambda = 3/2$ the equation of $\overline{PQ}$ will be
$\overline{PQ} = 2\hat{i} - \frac{13}{2}\hat{j} + 4\hat{k}$ and
line PQ will be $\frac{x-1}{2} = \frac{y-2}{\frac{-13}{2}} = \frac{z-5}{4}$
or $\frac{x-1}{4} = \frac{2-y}{13} = \frac{z-5}{8}$

Paasage 3:

Given system of equations $x + y = 2\lambda$ .... (i)
and $x + \lambda y = 2\mu$ .... (ii)
infinitely many solutions
$\Rightarrow \frac{1}{1} = \frac{1}{\lambda^2} = \frac{2\lambda}{\mu} \Rightarrow \lambda^2 = 1; \mu = 2\lambda^3$
$\Rightarrow \lambda 2 = 1, \mu = 2\lambda$
$\Rightarrow \lambda = \pm 1; \mu = \pm 2$
For $\lambda = 1; \mu = 2$
$A(1, 1, 4)$; $B(1, 2, 1)$
Now AB is divided by $x - y$ plane in the ratio $n : m$
$\Rightarrow \frac{4m+n}{n+m} = 0 \Rightarrow \frac{n}{m} = \frac{-4}{1}$
For $\lambda = -1; \mu = -2;$
$A(1,-1,-4)$; $B(1,-2,1)$
Again it is intersected by $x - y$ plane in the ratio $n : m$
$\Rightarrow \frac{-4m+n}{n+m} = 0 \Rightarrow \frac{n}{m} = \frac{4}{1}$ .... (iv)
Now, n, m are related by the quadratic equation $m^2 x^2 + an^2x + mn = 0$

7. Roots of quadratic equation value are real $\forall a \in \mathbb{R}$
$\Rightarrow (an^2)^2 - 4m^2(mn) \geq 0 \; \forall a \in \mathbb{R}$
$\Rightarrow a^2n^4 - 4m^3n \geq 0 \; \forall a \in \mathbb{R}$
$\Rightarrow a^2\frac{n^4}{m^4} - 4.\frac{n}{m} \geq 0 \; \forall a \in \mathbb{R}$
Let $\frac{n}{m} = k \Rightarrow a^2k^4 - 4k \geq 0 \; \forall a \in \mathbb{R}$
which hold for $\forall a \in \mathbb{R}$ and $k < 0$
i.e., $k = -4$ and $\forall a \in \mathbb{R}$
$\Rightarrow \frac{n}{m} = -\frac{4}{1}$ xy plane divides extermally
$\Rightarrow$ points A, B lie on same side of xy plane.

8. (b) ponble value of λ are $\lambda = 1$ or -1
For $\lambda = 1$; quadrate equation has rediblwts
$\Rightarrow a^2(-4)^4 - 4(-4) \geq 0$
$\Rightarrow 16a^2 + 1 \geq 0$ which holds $\forall a \in \mathbb{R}$
For $\lambda = -1$; quadut equation have real lwts
$\Rightarrow a^2(4)^4 - 4(4) \geq 0$
$\Rightarrow 16a^2 - 1 \geq 0 \Rightarrow a^2 \geq \frac{1}{16}$
$\Rightarrow$ for, $1 = 1$, or -1, $|a| \geq \frac{1}{4}$ gives real loots

9. (a) When both the points are on opposite sides:
(for $\lambda = -1$) we get $A = (1, -1, -4)$ and $B(1, -2, 1)$ and $\overline{AB} = -\hat{j} + 5\hat{k}$ and the required plane perpendicular to AB is $y - 5z = 0$

10. (b) When sum of the roots of quadratic $\left(\frac{\lambda^2}{16}x^2 + ax + \frac{\lambda}{4}\right) = 0$ is 16, then $\frac{-a(16)}{\lambda^2} = 16$ which gives $a = -1$
Now $A(1, -1, -4)$ and $B(1, -2, 1) \Rightarrow \left(\overline{AB}\right)_1 = -\hat{j} + 5\hat{k}$
and $A(1, 1, 4)$ and $B(1, -2, 1)$ $(\overline{AB})_2 = \hat{j} - 3\hat{k}$
vector perpendicular to $\left(\overline{AB}\right)_1$ and $\left(\overline{AB}\right)_2$ is
$$\begin{vmatrix} \hat{i} & \hat{j} & \hat{k} \\ 0 & -1 & 5 \\ 0 & 1 & -3 \end{vmatrix} = -2\hat{i}$$
Hence the required parallel plane is $(-2)(x + 1) = 0$ or $2(x + 1) = 0$

11. (c) The system is consistent when $\lambda = \pm 1$ and $\mu = 2\lambda$ so $(1, \lambda^2, 2\mu^2)$ is $(1, 1, 8)$ this point $(1, 1, 8)$ lies on $x - y + z = 8$, so $x + y + z = 10$ and $x - y - z + 8 = 0$
Since we are considering inconsistent system so the point will not lie on these planes. It may lie on some other plane

12. (d) When roots of the quadratic equation are always real and +ve, then $\lambda = -1$ so that product is also positive so $x^2 + 16ax + 4 = 0$ has +ve roots $\Rightarrow a < 0$ and $(256a^2 - 16) \geq 0$
i.e., $a^2 \geq 1/16$ (i.e., $|a| \geq 1/4$) $a \in \left(-\infty, -\frac{1}{4}\right)$

13. (c) When the system is constant and the points are on opposite sides of $x - y$ plane, then — so $(1 + x)^{n/m} = (1 + x)^4$ which gives 5 terms

14. (b) Angle between $\frac{x-1}{2}=\frac{y-3}{3}=\frac{z-2}{1}$

and $\frac{x-2}{2}=\frac{y-1}{-2}=\frac{z-3}{2}$ is given by $\cos\theta=\frac{4-6+2}{\sqrt{14}\sqrt{12}}=0$

$\Rightarrow \theta = 90°$

15. (c) Observe that $\vec{c}-\vec{a}=3\hat{i}+4\hat{j}+5\hat{k}=\frac{1}{2}\vec{d}$

so lines intersect at $\vec{a}$

Now $\cos\theta=\frac{19}{(3)(5\sqrt{2})} \Rightarrow \cos\left(\frac{19}{15\sqrt{2}}\right)$

16. (c) As stated above lines intersect at $A(\vec{a})=(-1,-2,-1)$

Passage 5

17. (d) $\frac{-9-\alpha}{2}=\frac{1-\beta}{1}=\frac{1-\gamma}{1}=\frac{-2(2\alpha+\beta+\gamma)}{(4+1+1)}$

$\Rightarrow \alpha=\frac{5}{3};\beta=\frac{19}{3},\gamma=\frac{19}{3}\Rightarrow P\left(\frac{5}{3},\frac{19}{3},\frac{19}{3}\right)$

18. (b) The line is $\frac{x+1}{1}=\frac{y+2}{2}=\frac{z+1}{-3}$

and the plane is $x + 2y - 3z + 12 = 0$. Since D.R.s of the line and normal to the plane are the same

∴ Line is perpendicular to plane hence it itself is the image

19. (c) Q(2, 4, –4) is the foot of perpendicular of P (x_1, y_1, z_1)on $x + 3y + 2z - 22 = 0$ then $<x_1 - 2, y_1 - 4, z_1 + 4> : <1, 3, -2>$ when $(x_1, y_1, z_1) \equiv (1, 1, -2)$ the conditions are satisfied

20. (a) The image of P(1, 1, –2) will be (4 –1, 8 – 1, –8 + 2) = (3, 7, – 6)

21. (b) P(3, 2, –2) and the plane is $x - y - z - 9 = 0$

for the given requirements $\frac{(x-3)}{1}=\frac{y-2}{-1}$

$=\frac{z+2}{-1}=\frac{(-3)(-6)}{3}=6$

$\Rightarrow$ (x, y, z) = (9, –4, –8)

Passage E:

22. (c) $P_1 : x + 2y - z - 2 = 0$ and $P_2 : 2x - y + 2z - 5 = 0$
Let the equation of the plane through intersection of P_1 and P_2 be $P_1 + \lambda P_2 = 0$
$\Rightarrow x(1 + 2\lambda) + y(2 - \lambda) + z(2\lambda - 1) - (2 + 5\lambda) = 0$
if this plane is to pass through origin, then $\lambda = -2/5$ and the plane is $\frac{x}{5}+\frac{12y}{5}-\frac{9}{5}z=0$ or $x + 12y - 9z = 0$

23. (a and b) Let the plane through the intersection be $\lambda(x + y + z - 4) + 3x - y + 2z - 4 = 0$
i.e., $(\lambda + 3)x + (\lambda - 1)y + (\lambda + 2)z - 4(\lambda + 1) = 0$
Since (2, 2, 0) lies on the place
$2\lambda + 6 + 2\lambda - 2 - 4\lambda - 4 = 0$ (which is always true) $\Rightarrow \lambda \in \mathbb{R}$
It means the point (2, 2, 0) lies on the line of intersection
By puting l = 1 and l = –1 we get plane given in options (a) and (b)

24. (c) D.R.s of normal to plane = <1, 1, 1> D.R.s of the normal to the (image taken in xy plane) is < 1, 1, –1>
The intersection of plane $x + y + z = 3$ and xy plane (xy plane means z = 0) is $x - y = 3$, a line with D.R $\left\langle\frac{1}{\sqrt{2}},\frac{1}{\sqrt{2}},0\right\rangle$
Now image plane is $x - y - z + k = 0$ will contains the line of intersection i.e $x + y = 3$ and z = 0) so $3 - z + k = 0$ gives k = 3
Hence the requireD plane is $x + y - z - 3 = 0$

SECTION VII: COLUMN MATCHING

1. (i) $L_1 : \frac{x-1}{2}=\frac{y-2}{3}=\frac{z-3}{4}=\lambda$

so $A(\vec{a})=(1,2,3)$ and $\vec{b}=2\hat{i}+3\hat{j}+4\hat{k}$

and $L_2 : \frac{x-1}{3}=\frac{y-3}{4}=\frac{z-5}{5}=\mu$

so $C(\vec{c})=(1,3,5)$ and $\vec{d}=3\hat{i}+4\hat{j}+5\hat{k}$

we find $[\vec{c}-\vec{a}\ \vec{b}\ \vec{d}] = \begin{vmatrix}0 & 1 & 2\\ 2 & 3 & 4\\ 3 & 4 & 5\end{vmatrix}=0$

so the lines are intersecting in a point
Ans (i) → (s) verification for λ = 3, μ = 2
we get (x, y, z) = (7, 11, 15)

(ii) $L_1 : \frac{x-1}{2}=\frac{y-2}{3}=\frac{z-3}{4}=\lambda$

and $L_2 : \frac{x-3}{2}=\frac{y-5}{3}=\frac{z-7}{4}=\mu$

observe that D.R's are identical also for λ = 1 and μ = 0 we get (x, y, z) = (3, 5, 7) so lines are coincident (superimposition)
Ans (ii) → (p)

(iii) $L_1 : \frac{x-2}{5}=\frac{y+3}{4}=\frac{z-5}{-2}=\lambda$

and $L_2 : \frac{x-7}{5}=\frac{y+1}{4}=\frac{z-2}{-2}=\mu$

observe that D.R's are identical
If the lines are coincident then $5\lambda + 2 = 5\mu + 7$ ....(i),
$4\lambda - 3 = 4\mu - 1$ ....(ii)
and $-2\lambda + 5 = -2\mu + 2$ .....(iii)
Now from (i) and (ii) we get $\lambda - \mu = 3$
and form (i) and (ii) we get $3(\lambda - \mu) = 2$
so the lines do not intersect ⇒ lines are parallel and distinct
(iii) → (q)

(iv) $L_1 : \frac{x-3}{2}=\frac{y+2}{4}=\frac{z-4}{5}=\lambda$

and $L_2 : \frac{x-3}{3}=\frac{y-2}{2}=\frac{z-7}{5}=\mu$

so; $\vec{a}=(3,-2,4);\vec{b}=(2,4,5);\vec{c}=(3,2,7);\vec{d}=(3,2,5)$

Now $\left[\vec{c}-\vec{a}\ \ \vec{b}\ \ \vec{d}\right]=\begin{vmatrix}0&4&3\\2&4&5\\3&2&5\end{vmatrix}=20-24=-4$

since $[\vec{c}-\vec{a}\ \ \vec{b}\ \ \vec{d}]\neq 0$

(iv) → (r)

2. (i) Foot of ⊥r from $P(1,2,3)$ to given line $x = 2r + 2y = 3r + 1$; $z = 4r + 2$ is given by such that $2(2l + 2 - 1) + 3(3l + 1 - 2) + 4(4l + 2 - 3) = 0$

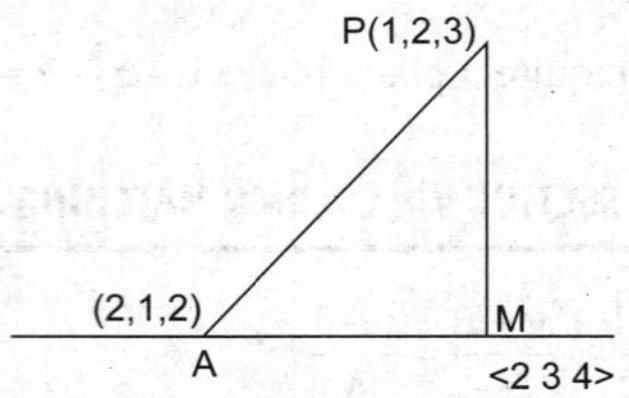

⇒ $l = 5/29$ ∴ foot of ⊥r $=\left(\frac{68}{29},\frac{44}{29},\frac{78}{29}\right)$

⇒ (i) → (r)

(ii) Image of ⊥r from P(1,2,3) is given by 2(foot of ⊥r) – point $P\equiv\left(\frac{107}{29},\frac{30}{29},\frac{69}{29}\right)$

∴ (ii) → (p)

(iii) Using given $\frac{x-2}{2}=\frac{y-3}{3}$

$=\frac{z-6}{-4}=\frac{-(4+9-24+17)}{29}=\frac{-6}{29}$

$x=\frac{58-12}{29}=\frac{46}{29};\ y=\frac{87-18}{29}=\frac{69}{29};z=\frac{198}{29}$

i.e., $\left(\frac{46}{29},\frac{69}{29},\frac{198}{29}\right)$

(iii) → (s)

(iv) image of point (2, 5, 1) in the plane $3x - 2y + 4z - 5 = 0$ is given by

$\frac{x-2}{3}=\frac{y-5}{-2}=\frac{z-1}{4}=\frac{(-2)(6-10+4-5)}{29}=\frac{10}{29}$

gives $x=\frac{88}{29},y=\frac{125}{29},z=\frac{69}{29}$ i.e., $\left(\frac{88}{29},\frac{125}{29},\frac{69}{29}\right)$

(iv) → (q)

3. (i) Given $y^2 + z^2 \geq 0$ which is always true and $|x| \leq 0$ gives $|x| = 0$ (as $|x| < 0$ is not true) ⇒ $x = 0, y, z \in \mathbb{R}$
This gives $y - z$ plane
Ans. (i) → (s)

(ii) Given $x^2 + y^2 \geq 0$ which is always true and $|y - b| \leq 0$ gives y = b from $|y - b| = 0 \Rightarrow x, z \in \mathbb{R}, y = b$
This is a plane parallel to $x - z$ plane passing through (0, b, 0), (i.e., at a distance of b units along y-axis) x, z can have any value like (1, b, 2)
(ii) → (r)

(iii) $x^2 + y^2 = \tilde{0}$ means $x^2 + y^2 = 0$, i.e., x = 0, y = 0
Now z can have any value. So it will be $z - axis$
(iii) → (p)

(iv) $x^2 + z^2 + a^2 + c^2 - 2ax - 2cz \leq 0$
gives $(x - a)^2 + (z - c)^2 \leq 0$ only possibility is $(x - a)^2 + (z - c)^2 = 0$ so $x = a, z = c$. Now y can have any value. it gives a line ||el to $y - axis$ passing through (a, 1, c)
(iv) → (q)

4. (i) $|x - a| \leq 0$ gives x = a ;
$|y - 2| \leq 1$ gives y ∈ [1, 3]; $|z - 1| \leq 4$ gives z ∈ [–3, 5]

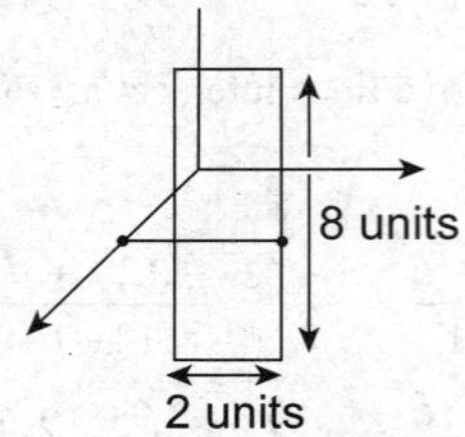

As shown it gives a plane surface parallel to yz plane (Area 16 square units)
(i) → (r)

(ii) x = α where $a \in \mathbb{Z}$ (integer set)
since $\sqrt{x-1}+\sqrt{3-x}$ is real ⇒ x ∈ [1, 2, 3]
Now [y] [z + 2] = 0 ⇒ either [y] = 0 or [z + 2] = 0

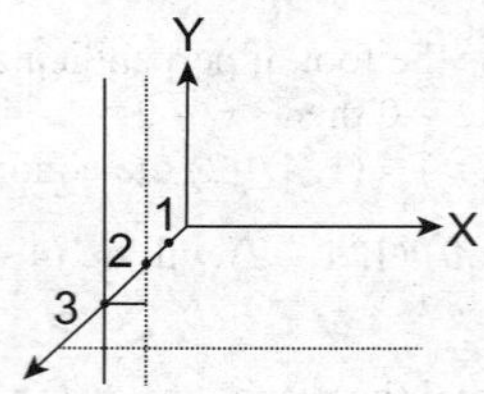

Case (i): [y] = 0 ⇒ y ∈ [0, 1)
Case (ii): [z + 2] = 0 ⇒ z ∈ [–2, –1)
gives three surface parallel to $y - z$ plane with total area 3 square units
(ii) → (q), (r)

(iii) $P_1 : 2x - 3y + z - 1 = 0$ and $P_2 : 3x + 3y + \lambda z - 2 = 0$ are perpendicular ⇒ 6 –9 + λ = 0 ⇒ λ = 3
(iii) → (s)

(iv) $z^2 - 3z + 2 = 0 \Rightarrow (z - 2)(z - 1) = 0$
gives z = 1, 2. Now x and y can have any real value. This gives two planes parallel to $x - y$ plane.
(iv) → (p)

SECTION VIII: (INTEGER TYPE)

1. $|x| \leq 8 \Rightarrow x \in [-8, 8]$ similarly for y and z. This represent a cube of side 16 units with centre at origin
Now $-8 \leq x + y + z \leq 8$ gives space between two panes namely

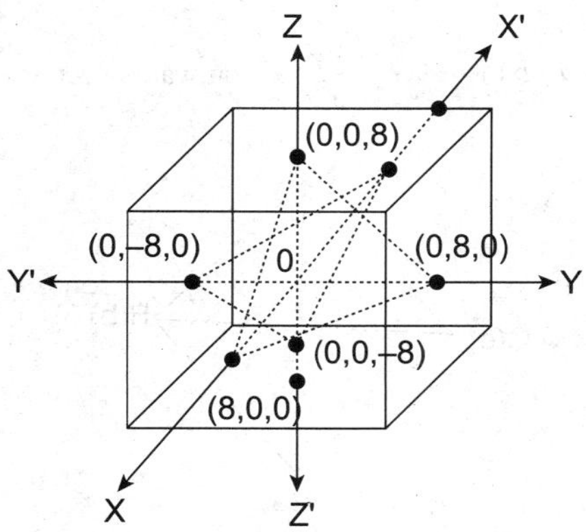

$x + y + z + 8 = 0$ and $x + y + z - 8 = 0$ subject to the limits of x, y, z $\in [-8, 8]$

This will take out $\left(\frac{1}{4}+\frac{1}{4}\right)$.volume of the cube

$\Rightarrow$ The required volume $= \frac{1}{2}\times(16)^3 = 2048$

Ans: 2048 Cubic units

2. $y + z = 0, x + z = 0, y + z = 0 \Rightarrow (0, 0, 0)$ is a vertex

$x + y = 0,\ x + y + z = \sqrt{3}a \Rightarrow z = \sqrt{3}a$

similarly for other parts

All this combined will give a regular tetrahedron of side $\ell = 2a$

shortest distance between any two opposite edges

$= \frac{\ell}{\sqrt{2}} = \sqrt{2}a$ (as $\ell = 2a$)

According to the given $\sqrt{2}a = \sqrt{k}\,a$ so k = 2 **Ans**

3. Any point on parabola $z^2 = 4ax$, $y = 0$ is given by $Q(\alpha t^2, 0, 2\alpha t)$

Now equation of line joining P(a,b,c) and Q(αt^2, 0, $2\alpha t$) is given by $\frac{x-a}{a-\alpha t^2} = \frac{y-b}{b-0} = \frac{z-c}{c-2\alpha t} = \lambda$ (say)

$\Rightarrow$ $x = a + \lambda(a - \alpha t^2)$; $y = b + b\lambda$; $z = c + \lambda$; $z = c + \lambda(c - \alpha t)$ by given condition point Q lies on $(bz - cy)^2 = k\alpha(b - y)(bx - ay)$

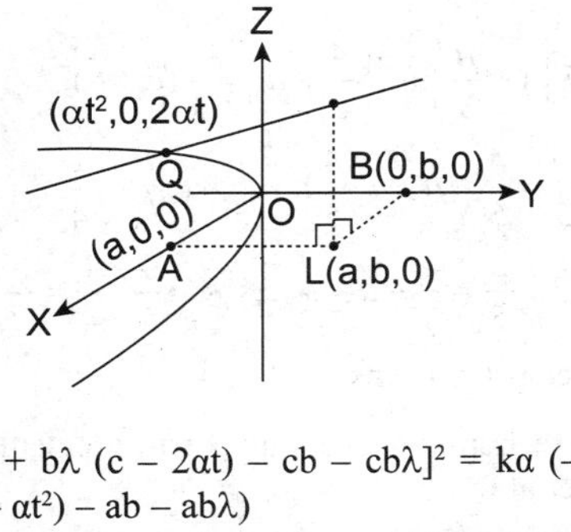

$\Rightarrow$ $[bc + b\lambda(c - 2\alpha t) - cb - cb\lambda]^2 = k\alpha(-b\lambda)(ba + b\lambda(a - \alpha t^2) - ab - ab\lambda)$

$\Rightarrow$ $[bc + b\lambda c - 2\alpha b\lambda t - cb - cb\lambda]^2 = -kb\alpha\lambda(ba + ab\lambda - \alpha b\lambda t^2 - ab - ab\lambda)$

$\Rightarrow$ $4\alpha^2 b^2 \lambda^2 t^2 = -kb\alpha\lambda(-\alpha b\lambda t^2)$

$\Rightarrow$ $4\alpha^2 b^2\lambda^2 t^2 = kb^2\alpha^2\lambda^2 t^2 \Rightarrow k = 4$

4. Projection of $\overrightarrow{PQ}$ on coordinates axes are 12, 3, 4 respectively so $\overrightarrow{PQ} = 12\hat{i} + 3\hat{j} + 4\hat{k}$

hence $\left|\overrightarrow{PQ}\right| = \sqrt{144+9+16} = 13$ units **Ans**

5. According to the given condition

$\sqrt{(x^2+y^2)+(z-a)^2} + \sqrt{(x^2+y^2)+(z+a)^2} = b$

gives $(x^2 + y^2) + (z + a)^2 = b^2 + (x^2 + y^2) + (z - a)^2 - 2b\sqrt{(x^2+y^2)+(z-a)^2}$

$\Rightarrow$ $4az - b^2 = -2b\sqrt{(x^2+y^2)+(z-a)^2}$

on squaring $(x^2 + y^2) + (z - a)^2 = \frac{16a^2z^2 + b^4 - 8azb^2}{4b^2}$

$\Rightarrow$ $(x^2 + y^2) + z^2 + a^2 - 2az = \frac{4a^2z^2}{b^2} + \frac{b^2}{4} - 2az$

i.e. $(x^2+y^2) + z^2\left(\frac{b^2-4a^2}{b^2}\right) = \frac{b^2-4a^2}{4}$

or $\frac{x^2+y^2}{b^2-4a^2} + \frac{z^2}{b^2} = \frac{1}{4}$ gives $\frac{x^2+y^2}{\left(\frac{b}{2}\right)^2 - a^2} + \frac{z^2}{\left(\frac{b}{2}\right)^2} = 1$

putting $\frac{b}{2} = \beta$ we get $\frac{x^2+y^2}{\beta^2 - a^2} + \frac{z^2}{\beta^2} = 1$

$\Rightarrow$ **Ans k = 1;** $\ell = -(m + n)$

6. Under the given conditions the possible situation is $f(-2) = 2$; $f(0) = 3$; $f(1) = 1$

{where $f(-2) = 1$ is false; $f(0) \neq 2$ is true and $f(1) \neq 1$ is false}. The triangle formed is with vertices A(–2, 1, 0), B(2, 1, 3) and O (0, 0, 0)

Area of $\Delta AOB = \frac{1}{2}\left\|\begin{matrix}\hat{i} & \hat{j} & \hat{k}\\ 2 & 1 & 3\\ -2 & 1 & 0\end{matrix}\right\|$

$= \frac{1}{2}\left|-3\hat{i} - 6\hat{j} + 4\hat{k}\right| = \frac{1}{2}\sqrt{61}$ square units $= \frac{\sqrt{k}}{2}$; so k = 61

7. Observe that mid-points also satisfy the equation of the plane so the mid points are

$L(x_1 k, 0, 0)$; M $(0, y_1 k, 0)$; N $(0, 0, z_1 k)$

Let $L(x_1$ k, 0, 0); M (0, y_1k, 0) be parallel to side a

so by mid point theorem $a = 2\sqrt{(x_1k)^2 + (y_1k)^2}$

i.e., $a^2 = 4k^2(x_1^2 + y_1^2)$, similarly $b^2 = 4k^2(y_1^2 + z_1^2)$

and $c^2 = 4k^2(x_1^2 + z_1^2)$ so on adding

$a^2 + b^2 + c^2 = 4k^2(x_1^2 + y_1^2 + z_2^2)\times 2$

but $2x_1^2 + 2y_1^2 + 2z_1^2 = a^2 + b^2 + c^2$ (given)

$\Rightarrow$ $a^2 + b^2 + c^2 = (a^2 + b^2 + c^2)4k^2 \Rightarrow 4k^2 = 1$ and **|k| = 1/2**

$\Rightarrow$ **so** $\frac{1}{k} = 2$

8. Consider a point (x_1, y_1, z_1) lying on $x + y + z + 3 = 0$, then $x_1 + y_1 + z_1 = -3$ distance of this point (x_1, y_1, z_1) from the two given planes will be equal in magnitude (opposite sign)

i.e., $\dfrac{(x_1+2y_1+3z_1+4)}{\sqrt{1^2+2^2+3^2}}$

$$= \frac{-(x_1+2y_1+3z_1+4)-\lambda(x_1+y_1+z_1+3)}{\sqrt{(1+\lambda)^2+(2+\lambda)^2+(3+\lambda)^2}}$$

on squaring and rearranging, we get

$\{(1+\lambda)^2+(2+\lambda)^2+(3+\lambda)^2\} = \{14\}$

or $\lambda^2 + 2\lambda + 1 + \lambda^2 + 4 + 4\lambda + \lambda^2 + 6\lambda + 9 = 14$

so $3\lambda^2 + 12\lambda = 0 \Rightarrow \lambda = 0, -4$ ($\lambda = 0$ is rejected)

$\Rightarrow \lambda = -4$ **Ans**

9. Given $\ell + 2m + 3n = 0$ so $\ell = -(2m + 3n)$ and $\ell(3m - 4n) + mn = 0$

putting $\ell = -(2m + 3n)$ we get

$mn - (2m + 3n)(3m - 4n) = 0$ i.e., $6m^2 = 12n^2$

so $m = \pm\sqrt{2}\,n$

Hence the D.R.'s of the two lines are

(i) $\ell = -(2\sqrt{2}+3)n;\ m = \sqrt{2}n;\ n$

(ii) $\ell = (2\sqrt{2}-3)n;\ m = -\sqrt{2}n;\ n$

angle θ between the lines is given by

$$\cos\theta = \frac{1-2+1}{\sqrt{17+12\sqrt{2}+2+1}\,\sqrt{17-12\sqrt{2}+2+1}}$$

Hence $\theta = 90^o = \dfrac{\pi}{2}$ (lines are perpendicular)

$\dfrac{\pi}{2} = \dfrac{\pi}{k}$ gives k = 2 **Ans**

10. Observe that (0, 0, 0) satisfies all the three given equation of the lines (so concurrent lines) and vector product of any two sets of D.R's will give the plane and the scalar triple product will be zero

$$\text{Hence} \begin{vmatrix} \alpha & \beta & \gamma \\ a\alpha & b\beta & c\gamma \\ \ell & m & n \end{vmatrix} = 0$$

(i.e., $(\alpha b\beta n - \alpha m c\gamma) + (\beta\ell c\gamma - \alpha\beta a n) + (\alpha\gamma a m - \gamma\ell b\beta) = 0$

rearrangement and then dividing by $\alpha\beta\gamma$ gives

$$-\left\{\frac{\ell}{\alpha}(b-c)+\frac{m}{\beta}(c-a)+\frac{n}{\gamma}(a-b)\right\} = 0 = k$$

so k = 0 Ans

11. Let P.V. of D (taken as origin) $= \vec{O}$ and $A(\vec{a}), B(\vec{b}), C(\vec{c})$ be the vertices

Now $\vec{E} = \dfrac{2\vec{a}}{3}$ similarly $F = \dfrac{1}{3}\vec{b}$

In ΔCEF we get $\overline{CE} = \left(\dfrac{2}{3}\vec{a}-\vec{c}\right)$ and $\overline{CF} = \left(\dfrac{\vec{b}}{3}-\vec{c}\right)$

$$\text{area } \Delta CEF = \left|\frac{1}{2}\left(\frac{2}{3}\vec{a}-\vec{c}\right)\times\left(\frac{\vec{b}}{3}-\vec{c}\right)\right|$$

$$= \left|\frac{1}{9}(\vec{a}\times\vec{b})+\frac{1}{3}\vec{c}\times\vec{a}+\frac{1}{6}\vec{b}\times\vec{c}\right| \text{ outwards vectors)}$$

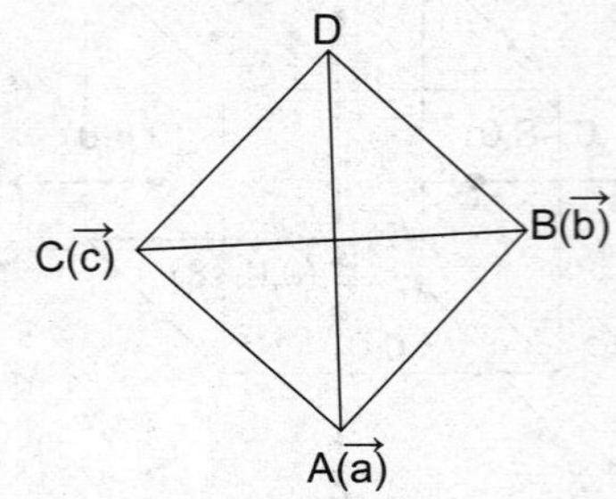

since $\vec{a}\times\vec{b} = \vec{c}\times\vec{a} = \vec{b}\times\vec{c}$ and area vectors are outwards

so area $\Delta CEF = \dfrac{22}{36}\left(\dfrac{\sqrt{3}}{4}\ell^2\right)$ and for $\ell = 6$

we get area $= \dfrac{11}{2}\sqrt{3}$

$\Rightarrow \left[\dfrac{11}{2}\sqrt{3}\right] = [9.526] = 9$ **Ans**

12. $\overline{OX} = 4\overline{XR}$ and $\overline{RY} = 4\overline{YS}$ also $k\overline{PZ} = \overline{PR}$

$\Rightarrow (k-1)\,\overline{PZ} = \overline{ZR}$

Let origin be at P and

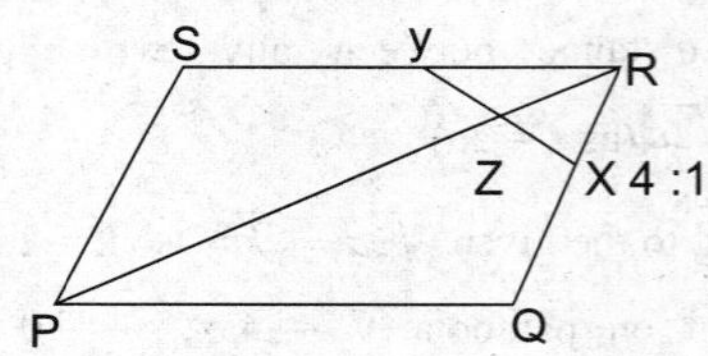

$\overline{PQ} = \vec{a}$ and $\overline{PS} = \vec{b}$

Then $\overline{PX} = \vec{a} + \dfrac{4}{5}\vec{b}$ and $\overline{PY} = \vec{b} + \dfrac{\vec{a}}{5}$

also $\overline{PR} = \vec{a}+\vec{b} \Rightarrow \overline{PZ} = \dfrac{1}{k}(\vec{a}+\vec{b})$

Now $\left(\vec{a}+\dfrac{4}{5}\vec{b}\right)+\mu\left(\vec{b}+\dfrac{\vec{a}}{5}\right) = \dfrac{1}{k}(\vec{a}+\vec{b})$

or $\vec{a}\left(1+\dfrac{\mu}{5}\right)+\vec{b}\left(\dfrac{4}{5}+\mu\right) = \dfrac{1}{k}(\vec{a}+\vec{b})$

$\Rightarrow 1+\dfrac{\mu}{5} = \dfrac{4}{5}+\mu \Rightarrow \dfrac{4}{5}\mu = \dfrac{1}{5}$ so $\mu = \dfrac{1}{4}$

and $1+\dfrac{\mu}{5} = \dfrac{4}{5}+\mu = k \Rightarrow k = \dfrac{4}{5}+\dfrac{1}{4} = \dfrac{16+5}{20} = \dfrac{21}{20}$

Hence [k] = 1 **Ans**

13. $\vec{a},\vec{b},\vec{c}$ are non-coplanar unit vectors equally inclined to each other at 0

$\Rightarrow \vec{a}.\vec{b} = \vec{b}.\vec{c} = \vec{c}.\vec{a} = \cos\theta$ .... (i)

$|\vec{a}| = |\vec{b}| = |\vec{c}| = 1$ .... (ii)

and $[\vec{a}\vec{b}\vec{c}] \neq 0$ .... (iii)

Now $\vec{a}\times\vec{b}+\vec{b}\times\vec{c} = p\vec{a}+q\vec{b}+r\vec{c}$

⇒ $\vec{a}.(\vec{a}\times\vec{b})+\vec{a}.(\vec{b}\times\vec{c}) = p+q\cos\theta+r\cos\theta$

(By taking dot product with $\vec{a}$)

⇒ $[\vec{a}\vec{b}\vec{c}] = p+q\cos\theta+r\cos\theta$ .... (iv)

⇒ O = p cos θ + q + r cos q .... (v)

(dot product with $\vec{b}$)

⇒ $[\vec{a}\vec{b}\vec{c}] = p\cos + q\cos\theta + r$ ...... (vi)

(dot product with $\vec{c}$)

∴ From (iv) and (vi); p + r cos θ = p cos θ + r

⇒ p(1 – cos θ) = r (1 – cos θ)

⇒ p = r ($\because \theta = 0° \Rightarrow \vec{a},\vec{b},\vec{c}$ and coplanar) .... (vii)

using p = r in (v) we get p cos θ + q + p cos θ = 0

⇒ 2 p cos θ = –q .... (viii)

∴ $\frac{pq}{r^2} = \frac{pq}{p^2} = \frac{q}{p} = -\cos\theta$ having integer

Values ∈ {–2, –1, 0, 1, 2}

But for –2cos θ = –2 ⇒ θ = 0 which is impossible as otherwise the vectors $\vec{a},\vec{b},\vec{c}$ will be coplanar.

Also –2cos θ = 2 ⇒ θ = π which is again impossible as otherwise $a,\vec{b},\vec{c}$ will be collinear and cannot be equally include to each other.

⇒ $\frac{pq}{r^2} \in \{-1,0,1\}$ for $\theta = \frac{\pi}{3}; \theta = \frac{\pi}{2}; \theta = \frac{2\pi}{3}$

∴ Total 3 integer values are possible.

14. Given area of ΔABC = k (area of ΔDEF) .... (i)

Let A be the origin then $\overrightarrow{AB} = \vec{c}$ (say); where $|\vec{c}| = 4$

$\overrightarrow{AC} = \vec{b}$; where $|\vec{b}| = 3$

then by angle biscctor theorem, point D divides BC in the ration $|\overrightarrow{AB}| : |\overrightarrow{AC}|$

and $\overrightarrow{AD} = \frac{4\vec{b}+3\vec{c}}{7}$ .... (ii);

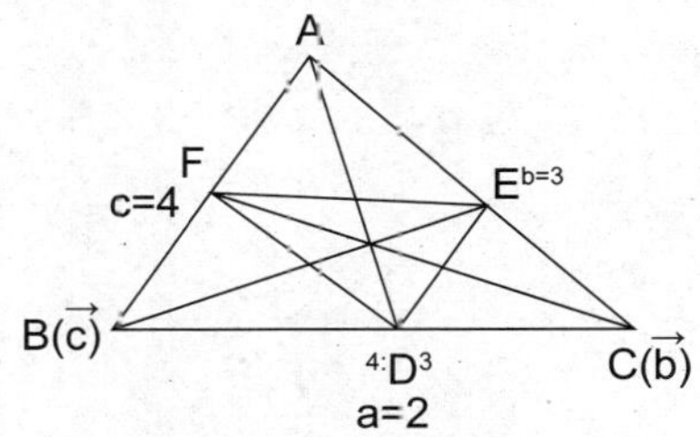

similarly; $\frac{\overrightarrow{AB}}{\overrightarrow{FB}} = \frac{3}{2} \Rightarrow \overrightarrow{AF} = \frac{3}{5}\vec{c}; \frac{\overrightarrow{AE}}{\overrightarrow{EC}} = \frac{4}{2} \Rightarrow \overrightarrow{AE} = \frac{2}{3}\vec{b}$

by (i) $\frac{1}{2}|\overrightarrow{AB}\times\overrightarrow{AC}| = k.\frac{1}{2}|\overrightarrow{DF}\times\overrightarrow{DE}|$

⇒ $|\vec{c}\times\vec{b}| = k|(\overrightarrow{AF}-\overrightarrow{AD})\times(\overrightarrow{AE}-\overrightarrow{AD})|$

⇒ $|\vec{c}\times\vec{b}| = k\left|\left(\frac{3}{5}\vec{c}-\left(\frac{4\vec{b}+3\vec{c}}{7}\right)\right)\times\left(\frac{2}{3}\vec{b}-\left(\frac{4\vec{b}+3\vec{c}}{7}\right)\right)\right|$

⇒ $|\vec{c}\times\vec{b}| = k\left|\left(\frac{6}{36}\vec{c}-\frac{4}{7}\vec{b}\right)\times\left(\frac{2}{21}\vec{b}-\frac{3}{7}\vec{c}\right)\right|$

⇒ $|\vec{c}\times\vec{b}| = k\left|\frac{4}{245}\vec{c}\times\vec{b}+\frac{12}{49}\vec{b}\times\vec{c}\right|$

⇒ $|\vec{c}\times\vec{b}| = k\left|\frac{4}{245}-\frac{12}{49}\right||\vec{c}\times\vec{b}|$

⇒ $245 = k|4-60| \Rightarrow k = \frac{245}{56} \Rightarrow [k] = \left[\frac{245}{56}\right] = 4$

5

Complex Numbers

■ INTRODUCTION

Till now we have been exposed to real numbers. Humans, by nature have always been attracted to the opposite of what prevails. Now you must be tempted to shoot a volley of questions like (1) Are there any non-real numbers? How can the numbers be non-real? Do the non-real numbers really exist or is it merely a mathematical jugglery? (2) If we have non-real numbers, what are they called? how are they represented?, and how do we visualize them? (3) What is the arithmetic of these numbers? And finally, (4) why did we need to define these numbers as such?, to what use we can put them into?

The answers to first three questions shall unfold as we progress but spare me the last one. It is just like asking me "of what use is a born baby?" I would say every baby is of some use depending on how carefully and meticulously we groom it. But the real use comes only after it is grown and matured. Similarly, the usefulness of studying complex numbers is to develop familiarity with its mathematics. At an appropriate time you can apply the learnt concepts to different branches of physics, like alternating current etc.

In fact greeks recognised that square root of negative real number does not exist in real number but th eindian mathematician Mahavire (580 AD) first of all stated that "negative numbers are not a square quantity thus have no square noot" in pair "Ganitarare Sangraha". After that Bookare (1150 AD) in his Bijaganita; candon in 1545 AD Albert Girard in 1625 AD accepted square root of negative numbers. Leonahrd Enler introduced sgribol of i($i = \sqrt{-1}$) and W.R. Hamilton (1830) regarded conplex numbers as numbers of the four axis as an ordered pair (a, b) of real number and thus astablished it difiritios mathamatically avoiding the name imaginary numbers.

■ REAL NUMBER SYSTEM

Natural Numbers ($\mathbb{N}$) The numbers which are used for counting are known as natural numbers (also known as set of positive integers) i.e., { 1, 2, 3, 4, 5, 6,....... }

Whole Numbers (W) If '0' is included in the set of natural numbers, then we get the set of Whole Numbers, i.e., $W = \{ 0, 1, 2, 3, 4, ... \} = \mathbb{N} \cup \{0\}$

Integer Numbers ($\mathbb{Z}$) If negative of natural numbers are included in the set of whole numbers, then we get set of integers i.e., {......., – 3, – 2, – 1, 0, 1, 2, 3,......}

Rational Numbers ($\mathbb{Q}$) The numbers which are in the form of $\frac{p}{q}$, where $p, q \in \mathbb{Z}$ and $q \neq 0$ are called rational numbers. e.g., 2/3, 3, 1/3, 0.76, 1.2322 etc.

Irrational Numbers ($\overline{\mathbb{Q}}$) The numbers which are not rationals, i.e., which can not be expressed in p/q form ($p, q \in \mathbb{Z}$ and $q \neq 0$) or whose decimal part is non-terminating and non repeating but which may represent magnitudes of physical quantities are known as irrational numbers. e.g., $\sqrt{2}$, $5^{1/3}$, π, e. etc.

Properties of Rational and Irrational Numbers

1. Terminating decimals are rationals.
2. Non-terminating recurring decimals are rationals, e.g., $1.\overline{25} = x \Rightarrow 100x = 125.\overline{25} \Rightarrow x = \frac{124}{99}$
3. Non-terminating and non-recurring decimals are irrationals.

Real Numbers ($\mathbb{R}$)

The set containing rational and irrational numbers is called set of Real Numbers. The set of real numbers is denoted by $\mathbb{R}$ i.e., $\mathbb{R} = \mathbb{Q} \cup \bar{\mathbb{Q}}$. Thus $\mathbb{N} \subset W \subset \mathbb{Z} \subset \mathbb{Q} \cup \bar{\mathbb{Q}} = \mathbb{R}$.

Another definition

A number whose square is non-negative is called a real number i.e., $x \in \mathbb{R}$ iff $x^2 \geq 0$

Properties of Real Numbers

1. Number zero is neither positive nor negative, but is an even number.
2. Real number field is an ordered field, i.e., $\forall\ a, b \in \mathbb{R}$ $a > b$ or $a < b$ or $a = b$ (law of trichotomy).
3. All real numbers can be represented by points on a straight line. This line is called real number line.
4. Even the smallest interval on real number line contains infinite rational and infinite irrational numbers.
5. Between any two unequal real numbers there lie infinitely many real numbers.
6. Square of every real number is non-negative, i.e., $x \in \mathbb{R} \Leftrightarrow x^2 \geq 0$
7. Number '0' is an additive identity, i.e., $a + 0 = a = 0 + a\ \forall\ a \in \mathbb{R}$
8. Number '1' is multiplicative identity. i.e., $a.1 = a = 1.\ a\ \forall\ a \in \mathbb{R}$
9. Infinity is the concept of the number greater than greatest one can imagine. It is not a number, it is just a concept, so we do not associate equality with it.
10. Division by zero is meaningless.
11. A positive integer p is called a prime number if it has exactly two positive integer divisors which are 1 and the number p itself. i.e., 2, 3, 5, 7, 11,....
12. The magnitude of a physical quantity may be expressed as a non negative real number times, a standard unit. e.g., 5 metre distance, 4 m/sec² acceleration etc.

Modulus of a Real Number

The modulus of a real number x is defined as follows:

$$|x| = \begin{cases} x; & x \geq 0 \\ -x; & x < 0 \end{cases} \Rightarrow |x - a| = \begin{cases} x - a & \text{if } x \geq a \\ -(x-a) & \text{if } x < a \end{cases}$$

e.g., $|3| = 3$ and $|-6| = -(-6) = 6$.

The graph of $y = |x|$ is as shown below: $|x|$ represents the distance of real number x on Number line from 0.

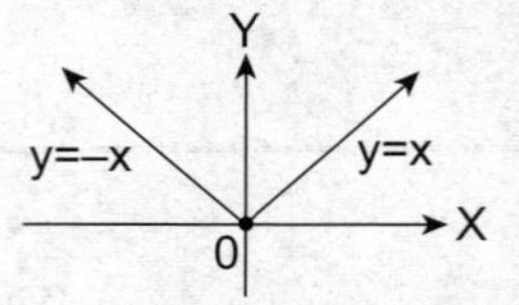

FIGURE 5.1

Properties of modulus of real numbers

1. $|x_1.x_2.x_3...x_n| = |x_1|.|x_2|.|x_3|...|x_n|\ \forall\ x_1, x_2,... x_n \in \mathbb{R}$
2. $\left|\dfrac{x_1}{x_2}\right| = \dfrac{|x_1|}{|x_2|}$ provided $x_2 \neq 0$ and $x_1, x_2 \in \mathbb{R}$
3. $|x^n| = |x|^n\ \forall\ x \in \mathbb{R}$ and $|x|^{2n} = x^{2n}\ \forall\ n \in \mathbb{Z}$ (when defined for $x \in \mathbb{R}$)
4. $|-x| = |x|\ \forall\ x \in \mathbb{R}$
5. Triangle inequality: $|x| - |y| \leq |x + y| \leq |x| + |y|\ \forall\ x, y \in \mathbb{R}$
6. $|x - a|$ = distance of x from a;
7. $|x - a| = \delta \Rightarrow x = a + \delta$ or $a - \delta$
8. $|x - a| < \delta \Rightarrow a - \delta < x < a + \delta$
9. $|x - a| > \delta \Rightarrow x > a + \delta$ or $x < a - \delta$

Intervals

Let a, x, b are real numbers so that

$x \in [a, b] \Rightarrow a \leq x \leq b$; $[a, b]$ is known as the closed interval a, b

$x \in (a, b) \Rightarrow a < x < b$; (a, b) is known as the open interval a, b

$x \in (a, b] \Rightarrow a < x \leq b$; $(a, b]$ is known as semi open, semi closed interval a, b

$x \in [a, b) \Rightarrow a \leq x < b$; $[a, b)$ is known as semi closed, semi open interval a, b

Imaginary numbers (Non real numbers)

A number whose square is not positive is termed as an imaginary number, e.g., $\sqrt{-2}$ or $(1 + \sqrt{-2})$. Therefore it can be said that the square root of a non positive real number is an imaginary number, for instance if $x^2 + 1 = 0$

$\Rightarrow x^2 = -1$

$\Rightarrow$ x is non-real number, i.e., imaginary number.

Euler introduced the symbol i for the number $\sqrt{-1}$ and is known as iota (a Greek word for 'imaginary')

Remark:

Imaginary numbers do not follow the property of order, i.e., for z_1 and z_2 imaginary numbers we cannot say which one is greater. Since i is neither positive nor negative nor zero (think why?)

Purely imaginary numbers (I)

The number z whose square is non positive real number (negative or zero) is termed as purely imaginary number. For example $z^2 + a^2 = 0$ where $a \in \mathbb{R} \sim \{0\}$.

$\Rightarrow z^2 = -a^2$ Clearly $z \notin \mathbb{R}$ as $z^2 < 0$.

$\Rightarrow z = \pm\sqrt{-a^2} \Rightarrow z = \pm a\sqrt{-1} \Rightarrow z = \pm ai \Rightarrow i = \sqrt{-1}$

Note that $z = 0$ is also taken as purely imaginary number as well as real number. Thus the set of imaginary number (I) is given by $\boldsymbol{I = \{z : z = ai}$, **where** $\boldsymbol{a} \in \mathbb{R}$ **and** $\boldsymbol{i} = \sqrt{-1}\}$

Geometrical Representation of Purely Imaginary Numbers

Since $x(i^2) = x\,(i \times i) = -x\ (\forall\, x \in \mathbb{R})$, hence $-x$ can also be obtained by rotating x geometrically in anti-clockwise direction through 180°. Hence twice multiplication by i is equivalent to geometrical rotation of the number by π radians in anti-clockwise direction and therefore single multiplication by i is equivalent to geometrical rotation of number by $\pi/2$ radians anti-clockwise. That is the reason why angle between real axis and imaginary axis is $\pi/2$ radians.

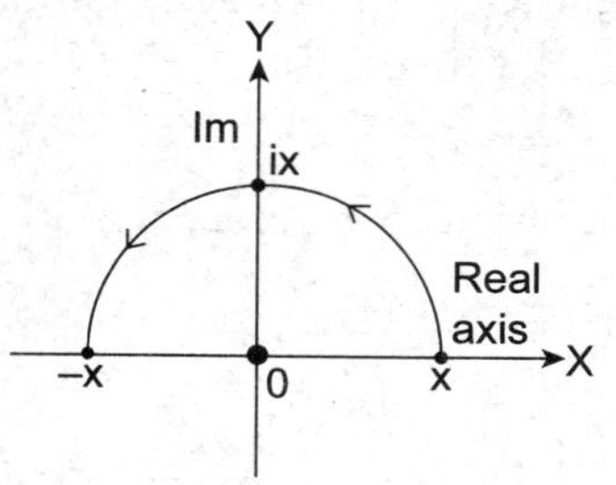

FIGURE 5.2

Therefore purely imaginary numbers are represented as points lying on y axis of Argand's Plane. For example, $z = ai$ is represented by point $(0, a)$ on y axis as shown below:

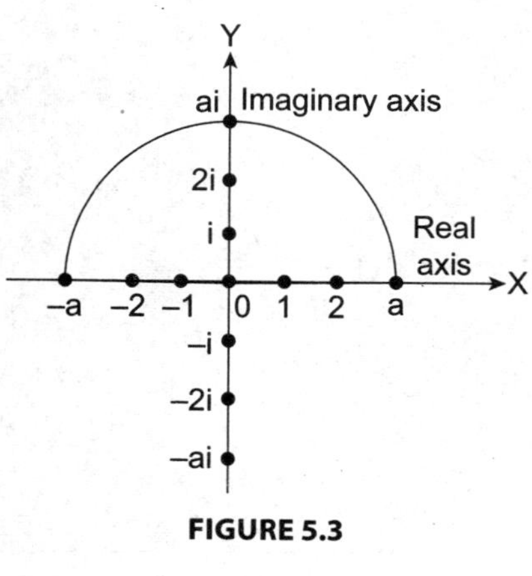

FIGURE 5.3

Algebra of Purely Imaginary Numbers

Let z_1 and z_2 be two purely imaginary numbers given as $z_1 = ai, z_2 = bi\ (a, b \in \mathbb{R})$

Addition : $z_1 + z_2 = (a + b)i$

Subtraction : $z_1 - z_2 = (a - b)i$

Multiplication : $z_1 \,.\, z_2 = -ab$

Division : $z_1/z_2 = a/b$. (provided $b \neq 0$)

Closure law: Holds for addition and subtraction but not for product and division. i.e. $z_1 \pm z_2$ are purely imaginary, where as $z_1.z_2$ and z_1/z_2 ($z_2 \neq 0$) are real; $z_1\, z_2 \in I$

Commutative law: Holds for Addition and Multiplication. i.e. $z_1 \,.\, z_2 = z_2 \,.\, z_1$ and $z_1 + z_2 = z_2 + z_1$. $\forall\, z_1\, z_2 \in I$

Associative law: Holds for both addition and multiplication of imaginary numbers. i.e., $z_1, z_2, z_3 \in$ I

$\Rightarrow z_1 + (z_2 + z_3) = (z_1 + z_2) + z_3$ and $z_1\,(z_2.z_3) = (z_1.z_2)z_3$

Distributive law: Multiplication distributes over addition and subtraction operations. i.e. $z_1(z_2 \pm z_3) = z_1z_2 \pm z_1z_3$

Existence of Identity: Zero is the identity element for addition and 1 is the identity element for multiplication. i.e., $z + 0 = z = 0 + z$ and $z.1 = z = 1.z\ \forall$ purely imaginary numbers z.

Conjugate Element: For each $z = ai$; $\bar{z} = -ai$ is called conjugate element of z.

Existence of Additive Inverse: Additive inverse of ai is $-ai$ as $ai + (-ai) = 0 = (-ai) + ai$.

Multiplicative Inverse of $\boldsymbol{z = ai}$**:** Multiplicative inverse of z is $z^{-1} = 1/ai$ as $zz^{-1} = 1$ provided $a \neq 0$.

Cancellation law: Holds for addition as well as multiplication. i.e. $z_1 + z_2 = z_1 + z_3$

$\Rightarrow z_2 = z_3$ and $z_1.z_2 = z_1.z_3 \Rightarrow z_2 = z_3$ (provided $z_1 \neq 0$)

Properties of Iota

1. $i^0 = 1, i^2 = -1, i^3 = -i, i^4 = 1$
2. Periodic properties of i
   $i^{4n} = 1, i^{4n+1} = i, i^{4n+2} = -1, i^{4n+3} = -i\ \forall\, n \in \mathbb{Z}$
3. $i^{-1} = -i$
4. Sum of four consecutive power terms of i is zero.
   i.e., $i^n + i^{n+1} + i^{n+2} - i^{n+3} = 0\ \forall\, n \in \mathbb{Z}$
5. For any two real numbers a and b, $\sqrt{a} \times \sqrt{b} = \sqrt{ab}$ is true only when atleast one of a and b is either 0 or +ve.

NoteS

1. *The plane formed by real and imaginary axes is called Argand/Gaussian/Complex Plane.*
2. *It should be kept in mind that any equation not having real roots does not necessarily posses imaginary roots. For example, the equation $x+5=x+7$ is neither satisfied by real numbers nor is satisfied by imaginary numbers.*

ILLUSTRATION 1: Find the value of $\dfrac{i^n+i^{n+1}+i^{n+2}+i^{n+3}}{1-i+i^3-i^5}$

SOLUTION: $i^n + i^{n+1} + i^{n+2} + i^{n+3} = i^n\,[1 + i + i^2 + i^3] = i^n\,[1 + i - 1 - i] = i^n\,[0] = 0$

$\Rightarrow$ the given number is zero as denominator is $1 - 3i \neq 0$

ILLUSTRATION 2: Find the sum of series $i^2 + i^4 + i^6 + \ldots.+(2n + 1)$ terms.

SOLUTION: Given series is a G.P. with first term i^2 and common ratio i^2. So sum of G.P. is

$$=\frac{i^2[1-(i^2)^{2n+1}]}{1-i^2}=\frac{(-1)(1-(i)^{4n+2}]}{1+1}=\frac{(-1)(1+1)}{2}=-1$$

ILLUSTRATION 3: Find the smallest positive integral value of n for which $\left(\dfrac{1-i}{1+i}\right)^n$ is purely imaginary with positive imaginary part.

SOLUTION: $\dfrac{1-i}{1+i}=\dfrac{(1-i)^2}{1-i^2}=\dfrac{-2i}{2}=-i \quad \therefore \quad \left(\dfrac{1-i}{1+i}\right)^n=(-i)^n$ to be imaginary $n = 1, 3, 5, \ldots..$

$\Rightarrow$ $(-i)^n$ has + *ve* imaginary part for $n = 3, 7, \ldots.$

$\therefore$ $n = 3$ is smallest positive integer.

ILLUSTRATION 4: Prove that $\dfrac{2^k}{(1+i)^{2k}}+\dfrac{(1+i)^{2k}}{2^k}$ is equal to 0 or 2 depending upon k, whether it is odd or even.

SOLUTION: Here $\dfrac{2^k}{(1+i)^{2k}}+\dfrac{(1+i)^{2k}}{2^k}=\dfrac{2^k}{(1+i^2+2i)^k}+\dfrac{(1+i^2+2i)^k}{2^k}$

$$=\frac{2^k}{(2i)^k}+\frac{(2i)^k}{2^k}=\frac{1}{i^k}+i^k=\frac{i^k}{i^{2k}}+i^k=\frac{i^k}{(-1)^k}+i^k$$

$$=i^k\left\{\frac{1}{(-1)^k}+1\right\} \text{ or } i^k\,\{(-1)^k+1\}=\begin{cases}0 & \textit{when k is odd}\\ 2 & \textit{when k is even}\end{cases}$$

ILLUSTRATION 5: If n is an odd integer and $i=\sqrt{-1}$, then evaluate $(1 + i)^{6n} + (1 - i)^{6n}$.

SOLUTION: Consider $(1 + i)^{6n} + (1 - i)^{6n} = (1 + i^2 + 2i)^{3n} + (1 + i^2 - 2i)^{3n}$

$= (2i)^{3n} + (-2i)^{3n}$

$= (2i)^{3n} + (-1)^{3n}\,(2i)^{3n}$

$= (2i)^{3n} - (2i)^{3n} = 0$ (as n is odd)

TEXTUAL EXERCISE 1: (SUBJECTIVE)

1. (a) Explain the fallacy $-1 = i \times i = \sqrt{-1} \times \sqrt{-1} = \sqrt{(-1)(-1)} = \sqrt{1} = 1$. Hence evaluate $\sqrt{-25} \times \sqrt{-49}$.

   (b) Show that

   (i) $i^{4n} = 1 \forall n \in Z$ (ii) $i^{4n+1} = i \forall n \in Z$

   (iii) $i^{4n+2} = -1 \forall n \in Z$ (iv) $i^{4n+3} = -i \forall n \in Z$

2. Show that $(i)^{-1} = (-i)$ and hence evaluate

   (a) i^{-47} (b) i^{-98}

   (c) i^{-1001} (d) i^{-10279}

3. Evaluate following:

   (i) i^{1998} (ii) i^{1999}

   (iii) i^{2000} (iv) i^{2001}

   (v) $\sum_{k=1}^{4n+7} i^k$ (vi) $[i^{457} + (1/i)^{25}]^2$

4. Evaluate

   (a) $(1 + i)^{22}$ (b) $\left(\frac{1-i}{1+i}\right)^{98}$

   (c) $(1 + i)^{3n}; n \in \mathbb{Z}$ (d) $\frac{1+2i}{1-(1-i)^2}$

   (e) $\frac{(1-i)^3}{1-i^3}$ (f) $(1 + i)^{3n}$; where n is an even integer

5. Show that $i^n + i^{n+1} + i^{n+2} + i^{n+3} = 0 \ \forall n \in Z$ and hence evaluate

   (a) $\sum_{1}^{1001} i^n$ (b) $\sum_{n=1}^{32} (i)^{3n}$

   (c) $\sum_{n=50}^{100} i^n$ (d) $\sum_{n=1}^{501} (1+i)^{2n}$

6. Evaluate $1 + i + i^2 + i^3 + ... + i^{n-1} - \frac{1}{2}(i^{n+2} + i^{n+3})$

7. Find the remainder obtained when

   (a) $(i)^{1112}$ is divided by 7

   (b) $(i)^{21122}$ is divided by 13

8. Find the following information for the series $\sum_{k=1}^{4n-1} i^k$

   (a) Number of real terms.

   (b) Number of imaginary terms

   (c) Number of positive real terms

   (d) Number of imaginary terms with positive imaginary part.

9. Find the sum of the following series

   (a) $\sum_{k=0}^{4n} i^{2k}$ (b) $\sum_{k=1}^{4n+11} i^k$

   (c) $\sum_{k=0}^{4n+1} i^{3k}$ (d) $\sum_{k=1}^{4n+6} i^k + \sum_{k=1}^{4n+7} i^k + \sum_{k=1}^{4n+5} i^k$

10. Evaluate $\left[i^{-53} + (i^n + i^{n+1} + i^{n+2} + i^{n+3} + 4)^{1/2} . i\right]$

Answer Key

1. (a) -35 **2.** (a) i (b) -1 (c) $-i$ (d) i **3.** (i) -1 (ii) $-i$ (iii) 1 (iv) i (v) -1 (vi) 0

4. (a) $-(2^{11})i$ (b) -1 (c) $2^n(i-1)^n$ or $\sqrt{2i}$ (d) 1 (e) -2 (f) $2^{3n/2}(-i)^{n/2}$

5. (a) i (b) 0 (c) $-i$ (d) $\frac{(2i)\left[2^{501}(i)-1\right]}{(2i-1)}$ **6.** $\frac{1+i}{2}$ **7.** (a) 1 (b) 12

8. (a) $2n-1$ (b) $2n$ (c) $n-1$ (d) n **9.** (a) 1 (b) -1 (c) $\frac{2}{1+i}$ (d) $2(i-1)$ **10.** $-3i$, i

TEXTUAL EXERCISE 1: (OBJECTIVE)

1. Who introduced the symbol i for $\sqrt{-1}$?

   (a) L.Euler (b) J.Bernaulei

   (c) Pascal (d) Cauchi

2. Which of the following statements are true?

   (a) For set of real numbers $\sqrt{16} = 4$ where as for set of complex numbers $\sqrt{16} = \pm 4$

(b) $\sqrt{ab} = \sqrt{a}\sqrt{b}$ iff both a and b are + ve

(c) $\sum_{k=1}^{n} i^{16k+5}$ is equal to – 1

(d) Both set of real and set of imaginary numbers are subset of set of complex numbers.

3. Select the true statement of the following:

(a) $\sqrt{-16} + 3\sqrt{-25} + \sqrt{-36} - \sqrt{-625} = 0$

(b) $1 + i^{14} + i^{18} + i^{22}$ is a real number

(c) $i^{3k} + i^{3k+1} + i^{3k+2} + i^{3k+3} = 0$

(d) $6i^{54} + 5i^{37} - i^{11} + 6i^{68} = 7i$

4. Which of the following is not true about the set of purely imaginary numbers?

(a) It is closed under addition operation.

(b) It is closed for multiplication operation.

(c) It posseses Additive identity.

(d) It is closed for division operation.

5. Which of the following is not true about the set of purely imaginary numbers?

(a) Imaginary numbers follow property of order.

(b) $i > 0$ is meaningless statement.

(c) Addition of Imaginary numbers are commutative in nature.

(d) Zero is purely imaginary but not imaginary

6. The value of $(i)^{222157}$ is

(a) i (b) $-i$

(c) 1 (d) –1

7. $(1 + i)^{8n+6}$ is; $n \in \mathbb{Z}$

(a) a real number

(b) a purely imaginary

(c) Imaginary but not purely

(d) depends on the value of n

8. The value of $(1 + i)^{6n+2}$; $n \in \mathbb{Z}$ is

(a) Real for is odd values of n.

(b) Real for is even values of n.

(c) Purely imaginary for is even n.

(d) purely Real $\forall n \in \mathbb{Z}$

9. The value of $\sum_{n=0}^{100} (i)^{2n}$ is

(a) 1 (b) –1

(c) 0 (d) i

10. The value of $\sum_{n=1}^{100} (1-i)^{2n}$ is

(a) $2^n i^n$ (b) $\frac{4-2i}{5}(2^{100}+1)$

(c) $\left(\frac{2i+4}{5}\right)(2^{100}-1)$ (d) None of these

11. The remainder obtained when $(i)^{2000010}$ is divided by 51 is

(a) –1 (b) 1

(c) 50 (d) 49

12. If 'r' denotes the remainder obtained when $(i)^{-202}$ is divided by 8, then the value of $(2)^r$ is

(a) 64 (b) 128

(c) 1/64 (d) 1/2

13. The value of $\frac{i^{592}+i^{590}+i^{588}+i^{586}+i^{584}}{i^{582}+i^{580}+i^{578}+i^{576}+i^{574}} - 1 =$

(a) –1 (b) –2

(c) –3 (d) –4

14. The value of sum $\sum_{n=1}^{13} (i^n + i^{n+1})$, where $i = \sqrt{(-1)}$ equals

(a) i (b) $i - 1$

(c) $-i$ (d) 0

15. The value of $\left(\sum_{m=1}^{2n+1} i^{2m}\right)^{\sum_{k=1}^{107} i^k}$ is

(a) i (b) $-i$

(c) –1 (d) 1

16. The value of $\sum_{k=1}^{k=4m+1} \left(i^k + i^{2k} + i^{3k} + i^{4k}\right)$ is

(a) $4m + 1$ (b) $4m$

(c) $4m - 1$ (d) None of these

Answer Key

1. (a) 2. (a, d) 3. (a, b, c) 4. (b, d) 5. (a) 6. (a) 7. (b) 8. (a, c) 9. (a)
10. (c) 11. (c) 12. (b) 13. (b) 14. (b) 15. (c) 16. (b)

■ COMPLEX NUMBER

A number z resulting as a sum of a purely real number x and a purely imaginary number iy is called a complex number i.e. a number of the form $z = x + iy$ where $x, y \in \mathbb{R}$ and $i = \sqrt{-1}$ is called a complex number. Here x is called real part and y is called imaginary part of the complex number and they are expressed as $Re(z) = x$, $Im(z) = y$. Here if $x = 0$ the complex number is purely imaginary and if $y = 0$ the complex number is purely real. A complex number may also be defined as an ordered pair of real numbers and may be denoted by the symbol (a, b). If we write $z = (a, b)$, then a is called the real part and b the imaginary part of the complex number z.

The set of complex numbers is denoted by $\mathbb{C}$ and is given by $\mathbb{C} = \{z : z = x + iy;$ where $x, y \in \mathbb{R}$ and $i = \sqrt{-1}\}$

Argand Plane

Any complex number $z = a + ib$ can be written as an ordered pair (a, b) which can be represented on a plane by the point $P(a, b)$ (known as affix of point P) as shown below in the figure. This plane is called Argand Plane, Complex plane or the Gaussian plane. The Argand plane is generated by real and imaginary axis. Conversely every point in this plane represents a complex number.

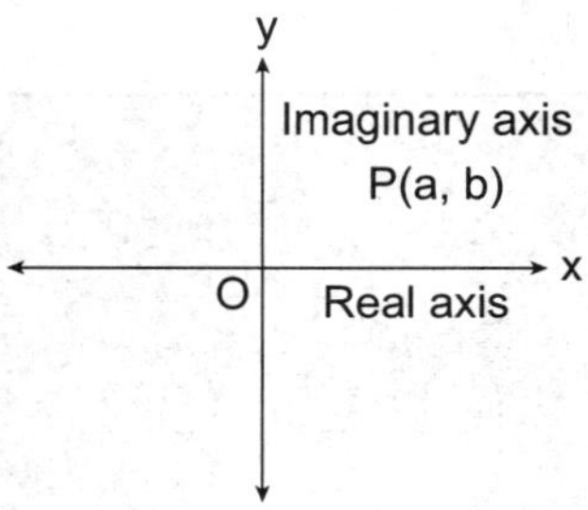

FIGURE 5.4

Representation of Complex Numbers

Complex numbers can be represented by following forms

1. **Cartesian form (rectangular form):** A complex number $z = x + iy$ can be represented by the point P having coordinate (x, y).
2. **Vector form (Algebraic form) :** Every complex number z is regarded as a position vector $(\overrightarrow{OP})$ which is sum of two position vectors : Purely real vector x $(\overrightarrow{OA})$ and purely imaginary vector iy $(\overrightarrow{OB})$

$$\because \overrightarrow{OP} = \overrightarrow{OA} + \overrightarrow{AP} = \overrightarrow{OA} + \overrightarrow{OB} \Rightarrow z = x + iy$$

Modulus of z: Distance of point P from the origin is called modulus of complex number z and is denoted by $|z|$. It represent the length of $(\overrightarrow{OP})$ or it is the distance of $P(z)$ from origin.

$$\therefore |z| = |\overrightarrow{OP}| = \sqrt{x^2 + y^2} = \sqrt{(R_e(z))^2 + (Im(z))^2}$$

Argument of z: argument of z is the angle made by $\overrightarrow{OP}$ with the positive direction of real axis. Also known as amplitude z and is denoted by $amp(z)$.

$\text{Arg}(z) = \theta$; where $\tan\theta = \dfrac{y}{x}$, θ lies in the quadrant in which complex number z lies.

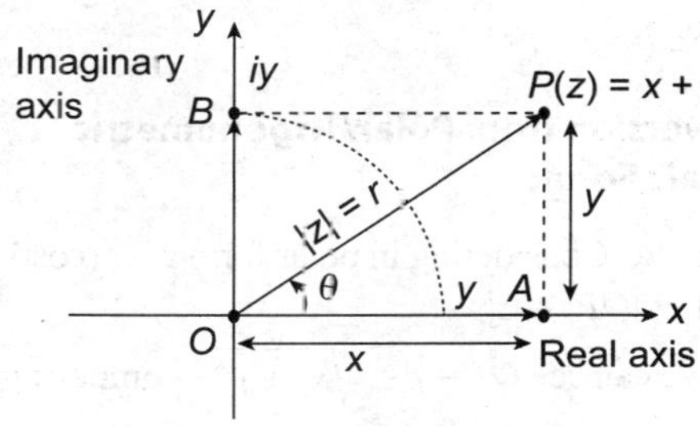

FIGURE 5.5

Note: The principal arguments $\theta \in (-\pi, \pi]$

3. **Polar form (amplitude modulus form) :** In ΔOAP : $OP = |z| = r$

$\Rightarrow OA = x = r\cos\theta$ and $AP = y = r\sin\theta$

$\Rightarrow z = x + iy = r(\cos\theta + i\sin\theta) = r\,\text{cis}\theta$

4. **Euler form (Exponential form):** Euler represented complex number z as an exponential function of its argument θ and described as below

As we know that using Taylor's series expansion $\cos\theta$ and $\sin\theta$ can be expanded in terms of polynomial in θ as given below:

$$\cos\theta = 1 - \frac{\theta^2}{2!} + \frac{\theta^4}{4!} - \frac{\theta^6}{6!} + \ldots\ldots\ldots \text{ and}$$

$$\sin\theta = \theta - \frac{\theta^3}{3!} + \frac{\theta^5}{5!} - \frac{\theta^7}{7!} + \ldots\ldots\ldots$$

$\therefore$ $(\cos\theta + i\sin\theta)$

$$= 1 + i\theta + \frac{(i\theta)^2}{2!} + \frac{(i\theta)^3}{3!} + \frac{(i\theta)^4}{4!} + \ldots\ldots to\,\infty = e^{i\theta}$$

$\Rightarrow z = x + iy = r(\cos\theta + i\sin\theta) = re^{i\theta}$

Advantages of Using Euler's Form

- Convenient for division and multiplication of complex numbers.
- Suitable for exponential, logarithmic and irrational functions involving complex numbers.

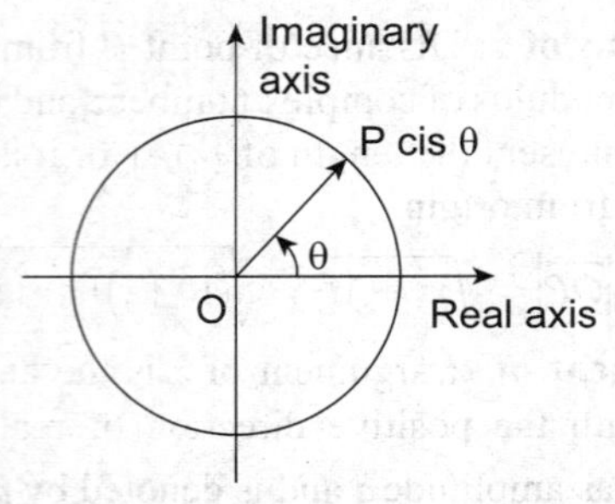

FIGURE 5.6

$$z = re^{i\theta} = r(\cos\theta + i\sin\theta) = r(cis\ \theta);$$

where r is the modulus of complex number z and θ is the argument of z.

Inter-conversion from Polar/Trigonometric to Algebraic Form:

Given $z = x + iy$. Considering in polar form $z = r(\cos\theta + i\sin\theta)$ In ΔOAP; Let $|OP| = |z| = r$

Now we can see $OP = r = \sqrt{x^2+y^2}$; comparing the real and imaginary parts, we have

$OA = x = r\cos\theta$ .....(i)

and $AP = y = r\sin\theta$ ....(ii)

$$\therefore \cos\theta = \frac{x}{r} = \frac{x}{\sqrt{x^2+y^2}} \ \&\ \sin\theta = \frac{y}{r} = \left(\frac{y}{\sqrt{x^2+y^2}}\right)$$

Using above equations we can convert complex number in one form to another form. i.e. Polar to Algebraic or Algebraic to Polar form.

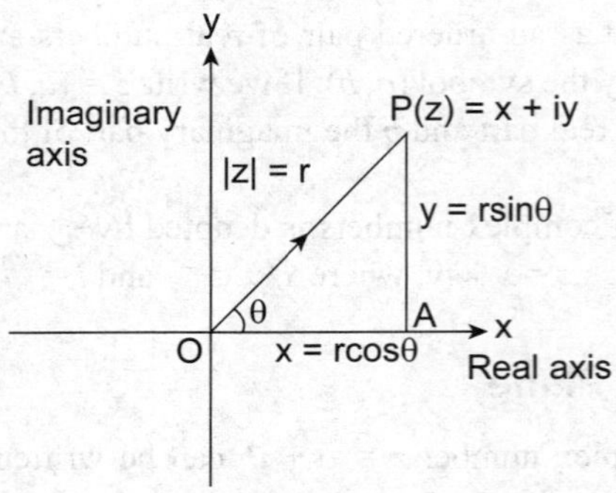

FIGURE 5.7

> ***Remark***
>
> *cis θ is unimodular complex number and acts as unit vector in the direction of θ where θ is arg z.*

ILLUSTRATION 6: Convert the complex number $z = -1 - i$ into polar form.

SOLUTION: Let $z = -1 - i$, here $r = |z| = \sqrt{2}$ and $\theta = \arg z = \frac{5\pi}{4}$ or $-\frac{3\pi}{4}$

$\therefore$ Polar form of z is $\sqrt{2}\left(\cos\frac{5\pi}{4} + i\sin\frac{5\pi}{4}\right)$ or $\sqrt{2}\left[\cos\left(-\frac{3\pi}{4}\right) + i\sin\left(-\frac{3\pi}{4}\right)\right]$

Hence, $\sqrt{2}\left[\cos\left(-\frac{3\pi}{4}\right) + i\sin\left(-\frac{3\pi}{4}\right)\right] = \sqrt{2}\left[\cos\frac{3\pi}{4} - \sin\frac{3\pi}{4}\right]$

But $\sqrt{2}\left(\cos\frac{3\pi}{4} - i\sin\frac{3\pi}{4}\right)$ is not the polar form of z

ILLUSTRATION 7: Express the following complex numbers in Euler form.

(a) $1 + i$ (b) $-2 + 2i$

(c) $-1 - i\sqrt{3}$

SOLUTION: (a) Let $z = 1 + i$, then $r = |z| = \sqrt{1^2+1^2} = \sqrt{2}$

and $\theta = \arg(z) = \frac{\pi}{4}$. So, Euler form of z is $\sqrt{2}e^{\frac{i\pi}{4}}$

(b) Let $z = -2 + 2i$. Then, $r = |z| = \sqrt{(-2)^2 + 2^2} = 2\sqrt{2}$

Let θ be the argument of z, then $\tan\theta = \frac{2}{-2} = -1 \Rightarrow \theta = \frac{3\pi}{4}$ ($\because$ Complex no. $(-2,2)$ is in second quadrant) So Euler form of z is $2\sqrt{2}\,e^{\frac{i3\pi}{4}}$

(c) Let $z = -1 - i\sqrt{3}$. Then $r = |z| = \sqrt{(-1)^2 + (-\sqrt{3})^2} = 2$

Let θ be the argument of z. Then $\tan\theta = \frac{-\sqrt{3}}{-1} = \sqrt{3} \Rightarrow \theta = \frac{4\pi}{3}$ or $-\frac{2\pi}{3}$

So Euler form of z is $e^{\frac{-i2\pi}{3}}$ or $e^{\frac{i4\pi}{3}}$

ILLUSTRATION 8: If $e^{i\theta} = \cos\theta + i\sin\theta$, then for the ΔABC evaluate $e^{iA}.e^{iB}.e^{iC}$.

SOLUTION: $e^{iA}.e^{iB}.e^{iC} = (\cos A + i\sin A)(\cos B + i\sin B)(\cos C + i\sin C)$

$= \cos(A + B + C) + i\sin(A + B + C)$

$= \cos\pi + i\sin\pi = -1$

TEXTUAL EXERCISE 2: (SUBJECTIVE)

1. Convert the following complex numbers to polar and Euler form

(a) $\frac{1}{2} + \frac{\sqrt{3}}{2}i$ (b) $\sqrt{3} - i$

2. Write the following numbers in Algebraic form:

(a) $2\sqrt{2}\left(\cos\frac{13\pi}{4} + i\sin\frac{13\pi}{4}\right)$

(b) $4\left(\cos\frac{13\pi}{3} - i\sin\frac{13\pi}{3}\right)$

(c) $6e^{10i\pi/3}$

3. Simplify the following complex numbers to $(x + iy)$ form and express them in, polar and Euler forms.

(a) $\left(\frac{1+i}{1-i}\right)^{200}$ (b) $\left(\frac{1}{1-i}\right)^{100}$

(c) $\frac{(\sqrt{3}+i)^{17}}{(1-i)^{50}}$ (d) $\frac{(x+i)^2}{(x-i)} - \frac{(x-i)^2}{(x+i)}, x \in \mathbb{R}$

(e) $(\sqrt{4+3\sqrt{-20}} + (\sqrt{4-3\sqrt{-20}}))^4$

Answer Key

1. (a) $\left(\cos\frac{\pi}{3} + i\sin\frac{\pi}{3}\right); e^{i\pi/3}$ (b) $2\left(\cos\left(\frac{-\pi}{6}\right) + i\sin\left(\frac{-\pi}{6}\right)\right); 2e^{-i\pi/6}$

2. (a) $-2-2i$ (b) $2-2\sqrt{3}i$ (c) $-3-3\sqrt{3}i$

3. (a) $1 + 0i$, $1(\cos 0 + i\sin 0)$, $1e^{0i}$ (b) $-(2)^{-50} + 0i$; $(2)^{-50}(\cos\pi + i\sin\pi)$; $(2)^{-50}e^{i\pi}$

(c) $-2^{-9} - 2^{-9}\sqrt{3}i; 2^{-8}\left(\cos\frac{4\pi}{3} + i\sin\frac{4\pi}{3}\right); 2^{-8}e^{i4\pi/3}$ (d) $0 + \left(\frac{6x^2-2}{x^2+1}\right)i; \left(\frac{6x^2-2}{x^2+1}\right)\left(\cos\frac{\pi}{2} + i\sin\frac{\pi}{2}\right); \left(\frac{6x^2-2}{x^2+1}\right)e^{i\pi/2}$

(e) $(6)^4 + 0i$; $(6)^4[\cos 0 + i\sin 0]$; $(6)^4e^{0i}$ or $25 + 0i; 25[\cos 0 + i\sin 0]; 25e^{0i}$

TEXTUAL EXERCISE 2: (OBJECTIVE)

1. Which of the following is/are value of i^i?
(a) –1 (b) $e^{\pi/2}$
(c) $e^{-\pi/2}$ (d) none of these

2. If $z = (1 + \cos\theta) + i(\sin\theta)$; $\theta \in [\pi, 3\pi]$, then $|z|$ is
(a) $2\cos\frac{\theta}{2}$ (b) $\cos\frac{\theta}{2}$
(c) $-2\cos\frac{\theta}{2}$ (d) $2\sin\frac{\theta}{2}$

3. Which of the following is/are value of $\sin \ln (i^i)^{i^2} + \cos \ln (i^i)^{i^2}$?
(a) –1 (b) 1
(c) 0 (d) none of these

4. The value of $e^{2ki\cot^{-1}m}\cdot\left(\frac{mi+1}{mi-1}\right)^k =$ is; $k \in \mathbb{Z}$; $m > 0$
(a) 0 (b) 1
(c) –1 (d) none of these

5. If z is any non-zero complex number having arg $(z) = \theta$, then $\left|\frac{z}{|z|} - 1\right|$ equals
(a) $2\sin\frac{\theta}{2}$ (b) $-2\sin\frac{\theta}{2}$
(c) $2\left|\sin\frac{\theta}{2}\right|$ (d) $2\sin\theta$

6. If z is a non-zero complex number with $\arg(z) = \theta$, then the maximum value of $\left|\frac{z}{|z|} - 1\right|$ is
(a) 1 (b) 2
(c) 3 (d) none of these

7. If $z_1 = (3 - 4i)\, e^{i\pi/4}$ and $z_2 = (4 + 3i)\, e^{i\pi/6}$; then
(a) $|z_1| > |z_2|$
(b) $|z_1| < |z_2|$
(c) $|z_1| = |z_2|$
(d) $|z_1|$ and $|z_2|$ can't be compared.

8. The expression $\tan\left\{i\,\ell n\left(\frac{a-ib}{a+ib}\right)\right\}$ equals
(a) $\frac{ab}{a^2+b^2}$ (b) $\frac{2ab}{a^2-b^2}$
(c) $\frac{ab}{a^2-b^2}$ (d) none of these

Answer Key

1. (c) 2. (c) 3. (b) 4. (b) 5. (c) 6. (b) 7. (c) 8. (b)

Properties of Complex Numbers

(i) **Equality:** Two complex numbers z_1 and z_2 are equal only when their real and imaginary parts are respectively equal.
i.e. $Re(z_1) = Re(z_2)$ and $I_m(z_1) = I_m(z_2)$ or $|z_1| = |z_2|$ and arg (z_1) = arg (z_2)

Proof: $z_1 = z_2 \Leftrightarrow Re(z_1) = Re(z_2)$ and $Im(z_1) = Im(z_2)$

Let $z_1 = a + ib$ and $z_2 = c + id$; $a, b, c, d \in \mathbb{R}, i = \sqrt{-1}$

Consider $z_1 = z_2$

$\therefore\ a + ib = c + id$

$\Rightarrow (a - c) + i\,(b - d) = 0$

$\Rightarrow a - c = 0$ and $b - d = 0$

$\Rightarrow a = c$ and $b = d$

$\Rightarrow Re(z_1) = Re(z_2)$ and $Im(z_1) = Im(z_2)$ ...(i)

Conversely: Consider $a = c$, $b = d$

$\therefore\ z_2 = c + id \Rightarrow z_2 = a + ib \Rightarrow z_2 = z_1$

$\therefore\ Re(z_1) = Re(z_2)$ and $Im(z_1) = Im(z_2)$

$\Rightarrow z_1 = z_2$ ....(ii)

From (i) and (ii) we get $z_1 = z_2 \Leftrightarrow Re(z_1) = Re(z_2)$ and $Im(z_1) = Im(z_2)$

☞ so if $z = 0 \Rightarrow x + iy = 0 \Rightarrow x = 0$ and $y = 0$
The students must note that $x, y \in \mathbb{R}$ and $x, y \neq 0$. Then if $x + y = 0 \Rightarrow x = -y$ is correct but $x + iy = 0 \Rightarrow x = -iy$ is incorrect (unless both x and y are zero)
Hence a real number cannot be equal to the imaginary number, unless both are zeros.

(ii) **Inequality:** Inequality in complex number is not defined because 'i' is neither non-negative nor negative so $4 + 3i > 1 + 2i$ or $i < 0$ or $i > 0$ is meaningless.

(iii) If $Re(z) = 0$, then z is **purely imaginary** and if $Im(z) = 0$, then z is **purely real.**

(iv) $z = 0 \Rightarrow Re(z) = Im(z) = 0$, therefore the complex number 0 is purely real and purely imaginary both.

Proof: Let $z = a + ib$, where $a, b \in \mathbb{R}$, $i = \sqrt{-1}$

Now consider $z = 0 \Rightarrow a + ib = 0$

$\Rightarrow a = -ib$

Squaring both sides, we get $a^2 = -b^2$

$\Rightarrow a^2 + b^2 = 0 \Rightarrow a = b = 0$

$\Rightarrow z = 0$ means $Re(z) = Im(z) = 0$ ...(i)

Conversely: Let $a = b = 0$

$\therefore z = 0 + 0i = 0$

therefore $Re(z) = Im(z) = 0 \Rightarrow z = 0$ ...(ii)

Now from (i) and (ii) we get, $z = 0$

$\Leftrightarrow Re(z) = Im(z) = 0$

(v) If $z = x + iy$, then $iz = -y + ix \Rightarrow Re(iz) = -Im(z)$ and $Im(iz) = Re(z)$

(vi) Conjugate of complex number: $z = x + iy$ is denoted as $\overline{z} = (x - iy)$ i.e., a complex number with same real part as that of z and negative imaginary part as that of z.

(vii) If z is purely real and positive $\Rightarrow Arg(z) = 0$

(viii) If z is purely real and negative $\Rightarrow Arg(z) = \pi$

(ix) If z is purely imaginary with positive imaginary part $\Rightarrow Arg(z) = \pi/2$

(x) If z is purely imaginary with negative imaginary part $\Rightarrow Arg(z) = -\pi/2$

(xi) $Arg(0)$ is not defined

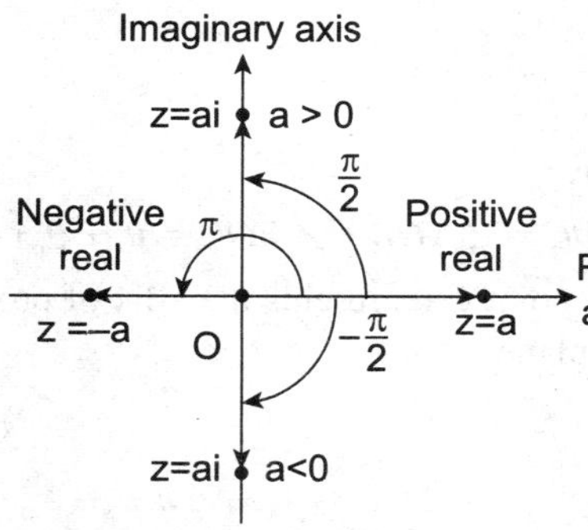

FIGURE 5.8

Binary Operations Defined on set of Complex Numbers

Binary operation on set of complex number is a function from $C \times C$; where C is set of complex numbers to itself. i.e., if $z_1, z_2 \in C$ and * is a binary operation on the set of complex numbers then $z_1 * z_2 \in C$. Following binary operations are defined on set of complex numbers.

(i) **Addition of two complex numbers**

Let $z_1 = x_1 + iy_1$ and $z_2 = x_2 + iy_2$

$\Rightarrow z_1 + z_2 = (x_1 + iy_1) + (x_2 + iy_2)$

$= (x_1 + x_2) + i(y_1 + y_2)$

i.e $z_1 + z_2 = [R(z_1) + R(z_2)] + i[I(z_1) + I(z_2)] \in C$

Geometric representation: Consider two complex numbers $z_1 = (x_1 + iy_1)$ and $z_2 = (x_2 + iy_2)$ represented by vector $z_1 = \overline{OA}$; $z_2 = \overline{OB}$ as shown in the figure given below.

Then by parallelogram law of vector addition,

$z_1 + z_2 = \overrightarrow{OA} + \overrightarrow{OB} = \overrightarrow{OC}$

Hence C represents the affix of $(z_1 + z_2)$

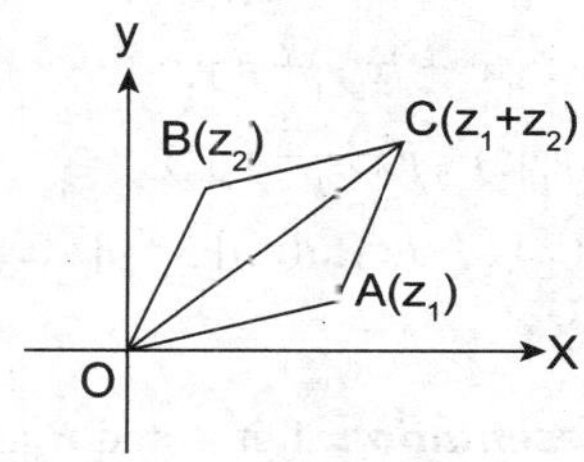

FIGURE 5.9

(ii) Subtraction of two complex numbers

Let $z_1 = x_1 + iy_1$ and $z_2 = x_2 + iy_2$,

then $z_1 - z_2 = (x_1 + iy_1) - (x_2 + iy_2)$

$= (x_1 - x_2) + i(y_1 - y_2)$

i.e., $z_1 - z_2 = [R(z_1) - R(z_2)] + i[I(z_1) - I(z_2)] \in C$

Geometric representation

Using again vector representation, we have

$\overline{BA} = \overline{OA} - \overline{OB} = z_1 - z_2 = \overline{OC}$

Hence, the other diagonal of the parallelogram represents the difference vector of z_1 and z_2

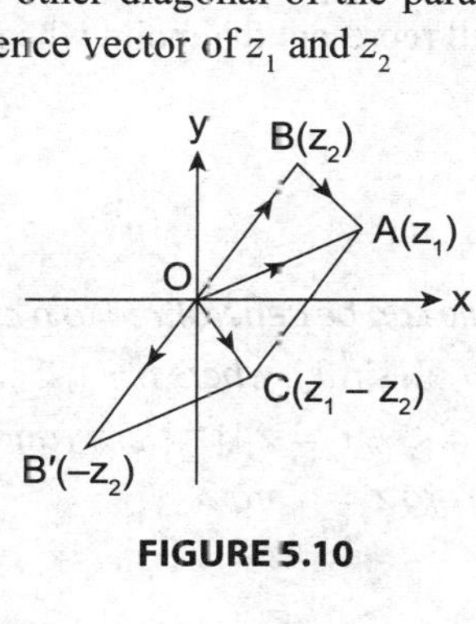

FIGURE 5.10

Notes

1. *In ΔOAC [Since sum of two sides of a Δ is always greater than the third side] $\because OA + AC \geq OC \Rightarrow |\overrightarrow{OA}| + |\overrightarrow{OB}| \geq |\overrightarrow{OC}|$*
   $\Rightarrow |z_1| + |z_2| \geq |z_1 + z_2|$ *This is called triangle inequality. Also considering ΔOAB; $OA + OB \geq AB$*
   $\Rightarrow |\overrightarrow{OA}| + |\overrightarrow{OB}| \geq |\overrightarrow{BA}| \Rightarrow |z_1| + |z_2| \geq |z_1 - z_2|$
2. *While $\overrightarrow{BA}$ represents the free vector corresponding to $z_1 - z_2$, $\overrightarrow{OC}$ represents the position vector of $z_1 - z_2$.*
   $\Rightarrow$ *C is affix of complex number $z_1 - z_2$*
3. *In a triangle, the difference of two sides is always less than the third side.*
   $\Rightarrow \left||\overrightarrow{OB}| - |\overrightarrow{OA}|\right| \leq |\overrightarrow{AB}| \Rightarrow ||z_2| - |z_1|| \leq |z_2 + z_1|$
4. *Triangle Inequality:* $||z_1| - |z_2|| \leq |z_1 \pm z_2| \leq |z_1| + |z_2|$

(iii) Multiplication of two complex numbers

Let $z_1 = x_1 + iy_1$, and $z_2 = x_2 + iy_2$

then $z_1.z_2 = (x_1 + iy_1).(x_2 + iy_2)$

$= (x_1.x_2) + ix_1y_2 + ix_2y_1 + i^2y_1y_2$

$= (x_1.x_2 - y_1y_2) + i(x_2y_1 + x_1y_2)$

$= [R(z_1).R(z_2) - I(z_1).I(z_2)] + i[R(z_2).I(z_1) + R(z_1).I(z_2)] \in C$

Geometric representation: Let A and B are two points in the complex plane whose affixes are z_1 and z_2 respectively, where

$z_1 = r_1(\cos\theta_1 + i\sin\theta_1)$ and $z_2 = r_2(\cos\theta_2 + i\sin\theta_2)$

Join OA and OB. Then, $|\overrightarrow{OA}| = r_1$ $\angle AOX = \theta_1$ and

$|\overrightarrow{OB}| = r_2$, $\angle BOX = \theta_2$ and $\angle BOX = \theta_2$

Then $z_1.z_2 = r_1r_2(\cos\theta_1 + i\sin\theta_1)(\cos\theta_2 + i\sin\theta_2)$

$= r_1r_2[(\cos\theta_1\cos\theta_2 - \sin\theta_1\sin\theta_2) + i(\sin\theta_1\cos\theta_2 + \sin\theta_2\cos\theta_1)]$

$= r_1r_2[(\cos(\theta_1 + \theta_2) + i\sin(\theta_1 + \theta_2)]$

This suggests that a point whose polar co-ordinates are $(r_1.r_2, \theta_1 + \theta_2)$ will represent that point whose affix is z_1z_2

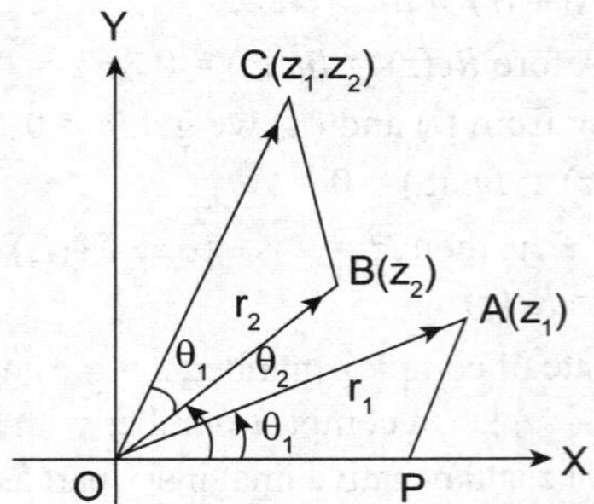

FIGURE 5.11

Take a point P on the real axis such that $OP = 1$. Join AP. Now construct the triangle BOC, similar to the triangle POA

From similar triangles POA and BOC, we have

$$\frac{OC}{OB} = \frac{OA}{OP} \text{ or } \frac{OC}{r_2} = \frac{r_1}{1}$$

$\Rightarrow OC = r_1r_2$

And $\angle XOC = \angle XOB + \angle BOC = \theta_2 + \theta_1$ i.e. $\theta_1 + \theta_2$

Hence the point C represents the affix of product $z_1.z_2$ in the Argand plane

Result

The product rule can be generalized to n complex numbers

Let $z_n = r_n(\cos\theta_n + i\sin\theta_n)$, where $n = 1, 2, ...$

Now $|z_1.z_2...z_n| = r_1r_2...r_n = |z_1||z_2|.....|z_n|$ and $\arg(z_1z_2...z_n) = \theta_1 + \theta_2 + ... + \theta_n = \arg z_1 + \arg z_2 + ... + \arg z_n$

As special case $\arg z^n = n\arg z$

(iv) **Division of two complex numbers**

Let $z_1 = x_1 + iy_1$ and $z_2 = x_2 + iy_2$

$\Rightarrow z_1/z_2 = (x_1 + iy_1)/(x_2 + iy_2)$

$= (x_1 + iy_1).(x_2 - iy_2)/(x_2 + iy_2).(x_2 - iy_2)$

$$= \frac{(x_1.x_2 + y_1.y_2) + i(x_2.y_1 - x_1.y_2)}{(x_2^2 + y_2^2)}$$

$$= \frac{(x_1.x_2 + y_1.y_2)}{(x_2^2 + y_2^2)} + \frac{i(x_2.y_1 - x_1.y_2)}{(x_2^2 + y_2^2)} \in C$$

Geometric Representation: Let A and B be two points in the complex plane whose affixes are z_1 and z_2 respectively, where $z_1 = r_1(\cos\theta_1 + i\sin\theta_1)$ and $z_2 = r_2(\cos\theta_2 + i\sin\theta_2)$. Take a point P on x-axis i.e $OP = 1$

$$\text{Now } \frac{z_2}{z_1} = \frac{r_2(\cos\theta_2 + i\sin\theta_2)}{r_1(\cos\theta_1 + i\sin\theta_1)}$$

$$= \frac{r_2(\cos\theta_2 + i\sin\theta_2)(\cos\theta_1 - i\sin\theta_1)}{r_1(\cos\theta_1 + i\sin\theta_1)(\cos\theta_1 - i\sin\theta_1)}$$

On simplification, we get

$$\frac{z_2}{z_1} = \frac{r_2}{r_1}[\cos(\theta_2 - \theta_1) + i\sin(\theta_2 - \theta_1)]$$

This suggests that a point whose polar co-ordinates are $\left(\frac{r_2}{r_1}, \theta_2 - \theta_1\right)$ will represent that point whose affix is $\frac{z_2}{z_1}$.

Join OA and OB

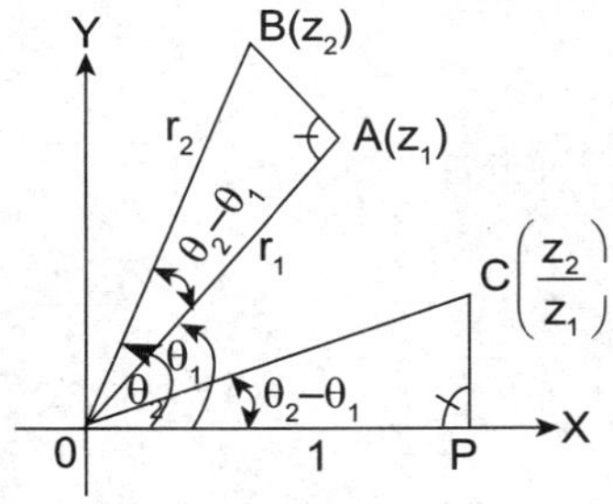

FIGURE 5.12

Then, $|\overrightarrow{OA}| = r_1$, $\angle AOX = \theta_1$ and $|\overrightarrow{OB}| = r_2$, $\angle BOX = \theta_2$, Draw a triangle OPC similar to triangle OAB.

From similar triangles OPC and OAB, we have

$$\frac{OC}{OB} = \frac{OP}{OA} \text{ or } \frac{OC}{r_2} = \frac{1}{r_1} \Rightarrow OC = \frac{r_2}{r_1}.$$

Also $\angle XOC = \angle AOB = \angle XOB - \angle XOA = \theta_2 - \theta_1$

Hence the point C represents the affix of $\frac{z_2}{z_1}$. Similarly

If we want to represent $\frac{z_1}{z_2}$ geometrically, then

$$\frac{z_1}{z_2} = \frac{r_1(\cos\theta_1 + i\sin\theta_1)}{r_2(\cos\theta_2 + i\sin\theta_2)}$$

$$= \frac{r_1(\cos\theta_1 + i\sin\theta_1)(\cos\theta_2 - i\sin\theta_2)}{r_2(\cos\theta_2 + i\sin\theta_2)(\cos\theta_2 - i\sin\theta_2)}$$

$$\frac{r_1\left[\begin{pmatrix}\cos\theta_1\cos\theta_2 + \sin\theta_1\sin\theta_2\end{pmatrix} + \\ i(\sin\theta_1\cos\theta_2 - \cos\theta_1\sin\theta_2\end{pmatrix}\right]}{r_2}$$

$-[\cos(\theta_1 - \theta_2) + \sin(\theta_1 - \theta_2)]$

Therefore this suggests that $\frac{z_1}{z_2}$ would represent the affix of the point whose arguments is $(\theta_1 - \theta_2)$ and at distance $= \frac{r_1}{r_2}$ from the origin, as shown below in the diagram.

Here triangle $\Delta OAB \sim \Delta OCP \Rightarrow \frac{OA}{OC} = \frac{OB}{OP}$

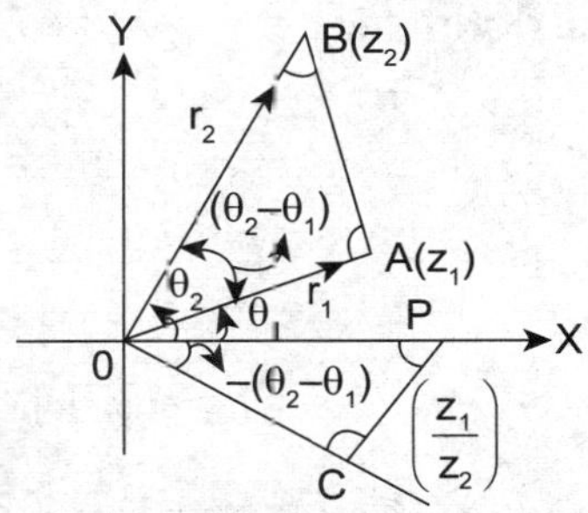

FIGURE 5.13

$$\Rightarrow \frac{r_1}{OC} = \frac{r_2}{1} \Rightarrow OC = \frac{r_1}{r_2} \text{ and } \Delta XOC = -(\theta_2 - \theta_1)$$

Notes

1. *If θ_1 and θ_2 are principal values of argument of z_1 and z_2, then $\theta_1 + \theta_2$ may not necessarily be the principal value of argument of $z_1.z_2$ and $\theta_1 - \theta_2$ may not necessarily be principal value of argument of z_1/z_2. To make this argument as principal value, add or subtract $2n\pi$, where n is such an integer, which makes the argument as principal value.*
2. *Note that angle α between two vectors $\overrightarrow{OA}$ and $\overrightarrow{OB}$ is $\alpha = \theta_2 - \theta_1$, $\alpha = \arg z_2 - \arg z_1$*

Algebraic Structure of set of Complex Numbers

(i) **Closure Law:** Complex numbers are closed under addition, subtraction and multiplication operation i.e., $z_1 + z_2 \in C$, $z_1z_2 \in C$ for all $z_1z_2 \in C$, $z_1/z_2 \in C$ for $z_2 \neq 0$ *i.e* closure law holds good for division on set of non-zero complex numbers.

(ii) **Commutative Law:** commutative law holds for addition and multiplication of complex numbers

i.e., $z_1 + z_2 = z_2 + z_1$ and $z_1z_2 = z_2z_1$

(iii) **Associative Law:** Associative Law holds for addition and multiplication of complex numbers
i.e., $z_1 + (z_2 + z_3) = (z_1 + z_2) + z_3$ and $(z_1.z_2).z_3 = z_1.(z_2.z_3)$ and $z_1(z_2.z_3) = (z_1.z_2)(z_3)$
Let $z_1 = a + ib$, $z_2 = c + id$, $z_3 = e + $ if, then
L.H.S $= z_1 + (z_2 + z_3)$
$= a + ib + (c + id + e + if)$
$= (a + c + e) + i(b + d + f)$
$= (a + c) + (b + d) + (e + if)$
$= (z_1 + z_2) + z_3 =$ R.H.S

(iv) **Existence of identity elements: 0** is the **additive identity** and **1** is the **multiplicative identity** because $z + 0 = z = 0 + z$ and $z.1 = z = 1.z \ \forall z \in C$

(v) **Existence of inverse element**: For any complex number z there exists another complex number $-z$ such that $z + (-z) = 0$ (**additive identity**) $= (-z) + z$, $-z$ is called **additive inverse** element of z. For any non-zero complex number z there exist another complex number $(1/z)$ such that $z.(1/z) = 1 =$ (**multiplicative identity**) called as **multiplicative inverse** element of z.

(vi) **Distributive law:** Multiplication of complex number is distributive over addition and subtraction
i.e $z_1.(z_2 + z_3) = z_1.z_2 + z_1.z_3$ (**left distributive law**)
and $(z_1 + z_2).z_3 = z_1.z_3 + z_2.z_3$ (**right distributive law**)

(vii) In context of real number every real number has a unique square root known as principal square root.e.g. $\sqrt{9} = 3$ (not ±3) and $\sqrt{16} = 4$ etc. But in case of complex number $\sqrt{4} = \pm2$, $\sqrt{9} = \pm3$, $\sqrt{-a^2} = \pm ai$ where a is a real number

(viii) **Existence of conjugate element:** Every complex number $z = x + iy$ has unique **conjugate** denoted as $x - iy$.

ILLUSTRATION 9: Find z so that $z(3 + 4i) = 2 + 3i$

SOLUTION: Let $z = x + iy$

$\Rightarrow (x + iy)(3 + 4i) = 2 + 3i$

$\Rightarrow (3x - 4y) + i(4x + 3y) = 2 + 3i$ Equating real and imaginary parts, we get

$3x - 4y = 2$ ....(i)

$4x + 3y = 3$ ....(ii)

Solving equations (i) and (ii), we get $x = \frac{18}{25}$ and $y = \frac{1}{25}$ $\therefore z = \frac{18+i}{25}$

ILLUSTRATION 10: Solve the following equations for x and y

(a) $2 + (x + yi) = (3 - i)$ (b) $x + 4i = y + xi + 3$

(c) $\left\{\frac{(1+i)x-2i}{3+i}\right\}+\left\{\frac{(2+3i)y+i}{3-i}\right\} = i$

SOLUTION: (a) $2 + (x + yi) = (3 - i)$

Equating real part and imaginary part, we get

$\Rightarrow 2 + x = 3$ and $y = -1 \Rightarrow x = 1$

(b) Given $x + 4i = y + xi + 3 \Rightarrow x + 4i = y + 3 + xi$

Equating real and imaginary parts, we get

$\Rightarrow y + 3 = x$ and $x = 4 \Rightarrow y = 1$ and $x = 4$

(c) Let $\left\{\frac{(1+i)x-2i}{3+i}\right\}+\left\{\frac{(2+3i)y+i}{3-i}\right\}=i$

$\Rightarrow \frac{x+xi-2i}{3+i}+\frac{2y+3iy+i}{3-i}=i \Rightarrow \frac{x+i(x-2)}{3+i}+\frac{2y+i(3y+1)}{3-i}=i$

$\Rightarrow \frac{(x+ix-2i)(3-i)+(2y+i+3yi)(3+i)}{10}=i$

$\Rightarrow 3x + 3ix - 6i - ix + x - 2 + 6y + 3i + 9yi + 2yi - 1 - 3y = 10i$

$\Rightarrow (4x + 3y - 3) + 2ix + 11iy - 3i = 10i$

$\Rightarrow (4x + 3y - 3) + i(2x + 11y - 3) = 10i$

$\Rightarrow 4x + 3y = 3$ and $2x + 11y = 13$

$\Rightarrow x = -3/19, y = 23/19$

ILLUSTRATION 11: Prove the following results

(a) $(1 + i^{14} + i^{18} + i^{22})$ is a real number.

(b) $\frac{\sqrt{7}+i\sqrt{3}}{\sqrt{7}-i\sqrt{3}}+\frac{\sqrt{7}-i\sqrt{3}}{\sqrt{7}+i\sqrt{3}}$ is a real number

SOLUTION: (a) $(1 + i^{14} + i^{18} + i^{22}) = (1 + i^{4\times3+2} + i^{4\times4+2} + i^{4\times5+2})$

$= 1 - 1 - 1 - 1$

$= -2$ is a real number

(b) Let $\frac{\sqrt{7}+i\sqrt{3}}{\sqrt{7}-i\sqrt{3}}+\frac{\sqrt{7}-i\sqrt{3}}{\sqrt{7}+i\sqrt{3}} \Rightarrow \left[\frac{\sqrt{7}+i\sqrt{3}}{\sqrt{7}-i\sqrt{3}}\times\frac{\sqrt{7}+i\sqrt{3}}{\sqrt{7}+i\sqrt{3}}\right]+\left[\frac{\sqrt{7}-i\sqrt{3}}{\sqrt{7}+i\sqrt{3}}\times\frac{\sqrt{7}-i\sqrt{3}}{\sqrt{7}-i\sqrt{3}}\right]$

$\Rightarrow \frac{4+2\sqrt{21}i}{10}+\frac{4-2\sqrt{21}i}{10}=\frac{4}{5}$

ILLUSTRATION 12: Given that $(x + iy)^{1/3} = (a + ib)$, then prove that $\frac{x}{a}+\frac{y}{b}=4(a^2-b^2)$

SOLUTION: $(x + iy)^{1/3} = (a + ib)$

Cubing both sides

$\Rightarrow x + iy = a^3 - ib^3 + 3a.ib(a + ib)$

$\Rightarrow x + iy = a^3 - ib^3 + 3a^2.ib - 3ab^2$

Equating real and imaginary parts we get, $x = a^3 - 3ab^2$ and $y = b(3a^2 - b^2)$

L.H.S $\frac{a^3-3ab^2}{a}+\frac{3a^2b-b^3}{b}=\frac{a^3b-3ab^3+3a^3b-ab^3}{ab}=\frac{3ab(a^2-b^2)+ab(a^2-b^2)}{ab}$

$=\frac{(a^2-b^2)(3ab+ab)}{ab}=\frac{4ab(a^2-b^2)}{ab}=4(a^2-b^2)=$ R.H.S

ILLUSTRATION 13: Given $a^2 + b^2 = 1$ then prove that $\frac{1+b+ia}{1+b-ia}=b+ia$.

SOLUTION: L.H.S. $=\frac{1+b+ia}{1+b-ia}=b+ia=\frac{(1+b+ia)(1+b+ia)}{(1+b-ia)(1+b+ia)}=b+ia$

$=\frac{1+b+ia+b^2+b+aib+ia+aib-a^2}{(1+b)^2+(a)^2}$

$$= \frac{2b+2ia+2aib+b^2-a^2+1}{1+b^2+a^2+2b} \qquad (\because\ (a^2+b^2=1)$$

$$= \frac{b+ia+aib+b^2}{1+b} = \frac{b(1+b)+ia(1+b)}{1+b} = b+ia = \text{R.H.S}$$

ILLUSTRATION 14: Solve the equation $\frac{(a+i)^2}{2a-i} = p+iq$, for p and q and hence prove that $p^2+q^2 = \frac{(a^2+1)^2}{4a^2+1}$.

SOLUTION: Given equation $\frac{(a^2-1+2ai)}{(2a-i)} \times \frac{(2a+i)}{(2a+i)} = p+iq$

$$\Rightarrow \frac{(2a^3-2a+4a^2i+a^2i-i-2a)}{(2a)^2+(1)^2} = p+iq$$

$$\Rightarrow \frac{(2a^3-4a+5a^2i-i)}{4a^2+1} = p+iq \Rightarrow \frac{2a(a^2-2)+i(5a^2-1)}{4a^2+1} = p+iq$$

$$\Rightarrow p = \frac{2a^3-4a}{4a^2+1},\ q = \frac{5a^2-1}{4a^2+1};\ \text{Now, } p^2+q^2 = \frac{4a^6+16a^2-16a^4+25a^4+1-10a^2}{16a^4+1+8a^2}$$

$$= \frac{a^4+1+2a^2+4a^2+8a^4+4a^6}{16a^4+8a^2+1} = \frac{(a^2+1)^2+4a^2(1+2a^2+a^4)}{16a^4+8a^2+1} = \frac{(a^2+1)^2+(1+4a^2)}{(4a^2+1)^2}$$

$$= \frac{(a^2+1)^2}{4a^2+1}, \text{ hence the result.}$$

ILLUSTRATION 15: Express $\frac{(2-5i)^3}{(3+2i)^2}$ in the form $A+iB$

SOLUTION: $\frac{(2-5i)^3}{(3+2i)^2} = \frac{8+125i-6(5i)(2-5i)}{9-4+12i} = \frac{8+125i-60i-150}{5+12i}$

$$= \frac{-142+65i}{5+12i} = \frac{(-142+65i)(5-12i)}{169} = \frac{-710+1704i+325i+780}{169} = \frac{70}{169}+\frac{2029i}{169}$$

ILLUSTRATION 16: Find the additive inverse of $\frac{2-3i}{4+5i}$ and express it in $x+iy$ form.

SOLUTION: Let $z = \frac{2-3i}{4+5i} = \frac{(2-3i)(4-5i)}{16+25} = \frac{8-10i-12i-15}{41} = \frac{-7}{41}-\frac{22}{41}i$

$\therefore$ Additive inverse of $z = \frac{7}{41}+\frac{22}{41}i$ **Ans.**

ILLUSTRATION 17: Find the multiplicative inverse of $\frac{2+5i}{3-7i}$ and express it in $x+iy$ form.

SOLUTION: Let $z = \frac{2+5i}{3-7i}$

M.I. of (z) is $\frac{1}{z} = \frac{3-7i}{2+5i} = \frac{3-7i}{2+5i} \times \frac{2-5i}{2-5i}$

$$= \frac{6-15i-14i-35}{4+25} = \frac{-29-29i}{29} = -1-i \ \textbf{Ans.}$$

TEXTUAL EXERCISE 3: (SUBJECTIVE)

1. Express the following in the form $A + iB$
   (i) $(3 + 2i)(3 - 2i)$ (ii) $(i - 2)^2$
   (iii) $\dfrac{2-i}{4+3i}$ (iv) $\dfrac{1+2i+3i^2}{1-2i+3i^2}$
   (v) $\left(\dfrac{1+i}{1-i}\right)^2$ (vi) $\left(\dfrac{1+2i}{2-i}\right)^2$
   (vii) $\dfrac{1}{(2+i)^2} - \dfrac{1}{(2-i)^2}$

2. Express the following in the form $A + iB$
   (a) $\dfrac{(a+i)^2}{(a-i)} - \dfrac{(a-i)^2}{(a+i)}$
   (b) $\left(\dfrac{1+\sin\alpha + i\cos\alpha}{1+\sin\alpha - i\cos\alpha}\right)^n$
   (c) $\left(\dfrac{1+2i}{1+i}\right)^n$ for $n = \pm 1, \pm 2, \ldots.$

3. Prove that $(1 + i)^{2n} + (1 - i)^{2n} = 0$ if n is an odd integer and $\dfrac{2^{n+1}}{(-1)^{n/2}}$ if n is an even integer.

4. Find the value of $a^6 + a^4 + a^2 + 1$ when $a = \dfrac{1+i}{\sqrt{2}}$.

5. Simplify $\left(\dfrac{1+i}{1-i}\right)^{200}$.

6. Evaluate $\left[i^{19} + \left(\dfrac{1}{i}\right)^{25}\right]^2$.

7. Express $\left(\dfrac{1}{1-2i} + \dfrac{3}{1+i}\right)\left(\dfrac{3+4i}{2-4i}\right)$ in the form $A + iB$.

8. Simplify $\dfrac{20}{\sqrt{3}-\sqrt{-2}} + \dfrac{30}{3\sqrt{-2}-2\sqrt{3}} - \dfrac{14}{2\sqrt{3}-\sqrt{-2}}$.

9. Find x and y if $(3x - 2iy)(2 + i)^2 = 10(1 + i)$

10. If $(x^4 + 2xi) - (3x^2 + yi) = (3 - 5i) + (1 + 2yi)$, then evaluate the values of x and y, where x and y are real numbers.

11. If $\dfrac{3}{2+\cos\theta + i\sin\theta} = a + ib$, then prove that $a^2 + b^2 = 4a - 3$

12. Find the multiplicative inverse of
    (a) $3 + 2i$ (b) $\dfrac{2-3i}{4+5i}$ (c) $\dfrac{(2-5i)^2}{(3-2i)}$

13. If $(x + iy)^5 = p + iq$, then express $(y + ix)^5$ in the form $A + iB$.

14. If x, y, z are three distinct complex numbers such that $\dfrac{x}{y-z} + \dfrac{y}{z-x} + \dfrac{z}{x-y} = 0$, then find the value of $\sum \dfrac{x^2}{(y-z)^2}$.

15. If $x = \dfrac{1}{2}(5 - \sqrt{3}\,i)$, then find the value of $x^4 - x^3 - 12x^2 + 23x + 12$.

16. If $f(x) = x^4 - 8x^3 + 4x^2 + 4x + 39$ and $f(3 + 2i) = a + ib$, then evaluate $a : b$.

Answer Key

1. (i) $13 + 0i$ (ii) $3 - 4i$ (iii) $\dfrac{1}{5} - \dfrac{2}{5}i$ (iv) $0 - i$ (v) -1 (vi) $-1 + 0i$ (vii) $0 - \dfrac{8}{25}i$

2. (a) $2i \times \dfrac{(3a^2-1)}{a^2+1}$ (b) $\cos(n\pi/2 - n\alpha) + i\sin(n\pi/2 - n\alpha)$ (c) $(5/2)^{n/2}[\cos(n\tan^{-1} 1/3) + i\sin(n\tan^{-1} 1/3)]$

4. 0 5. 1 6. –4 7. $\dfrac{1}{4} + \dfrac{9}{4}i$ 8. 0 9. $x = 14/15$, $y = 1/5$

10. $x = 2, y = 3$ or $x = -2, y = 1/3$ 12. (i) $\dfrac{3-2i}{13}$ (ii) $\dfrac{-7+22i}{13}$ (iii) $\dfrac{-23+102i}{841}$

13. $q + ip$ 14. 2 15. 5 16. $-\dfrac{1}{8}$

TEXTUAL EXERCISE 3: (OBJECTIVE)

1. $p + iq > r + it$ is meaningful only when:
(a) $p = 0, r = 0$ (b) $p = 0, t = 0$
(c) $q = 0, r = 0$ (d) $q = 0, t = 0$

2. The multiplicative inverse of a number is the number itself, then its value is
(a) i (b) -1
(c) 1 (d) $-i$

3. If $z_1 = (4,5)$ and $z_2 = (-3, 2)$, then $\frac{z_1}{z_2}$ equals
(a) $\left(-\frac{23}{12}, \frac{-2}{13}\right)$ (b) $\left(\frac{2}{13}, \frac{-23}{13}\right)$
(c) $\left(\frac{-2}{13}, \frac{23}{13}\right)$ (d) $\left(\frac{-2}{13}, \frac{-23}{13}\right)$

4. $[2i/(1 + i)]^2 =$
(a) i (b) $2i$
(c) $1 - i$ (d) $1 - 2i$

5. If $z = 1 + i$, then the multiplicative inverse of z^2 is (where $i = \sqrt{-1}$)
(a) $2i$ (b) $1 - i$
(c) $-i/2$ (d) None of these

6. If $a = \cos\theta + i\sin\theta$, then $\frac{1+a}{1-a}$ is equal to
(a) $\cot\theta$ (b) $\cot\frac{\theta}{2}$
(c) $i\cot\frac{\theta}{2}$ (d) $i\tan\frac{\theta}{2}$

7. The real part of $\frac{1}{1-\cos\theta + i\sin\theta}$ is equal to
(a) 1/4 (b) 1/2
(c) $\tan\theta/2$ (d) $1/(1 - \cos\theta)$

8. If $(x + iy)(p + iq) = (x^2 + y^2)i$, then
(a) $p = x, q = y$ (b) $p = x^2, q = y^2$
(c) $p = y, q = x$ (d) None of these

9. If $\frac{(1+i)x-2i}{3+i} + \frac{(2-3i)y+i}{3-i} = i$, then the real values of x and y are given y:
(a) $x = -3, y = -1$ (b) $x = 3, y = -1$
(c) $x = 3, y = 1$ (d) $x = 1, y = -3$

10. The least positive integer n which will reduce $\left(\frac{1+i}{1-i}\right)^n$ to unity is
(a) 2 (b) 4
(c) 8 (d) 12

11. The smallest positive integer 'n' for which $(1 + i)^{2n} = (1 - i)^{2n}$ is:
(a) 4 (b) 8
(c) 2 (d) 12

12. The least positive integer n which will reduce $\left(\frac{i-1}{i+1}\right)^n$ to a real number is
(a) 2 (b) 3
(c) 4 (d) 5

13. If $x = 2 + 5i$, then $x^3 - 5x^2 + 33x - 19 =$
(a) 12 (b) $25 + 6i$
(c) 10 (d) None of these

14. Let $f(z)$ be a polynomial in $z \in \mathbb{C}$, when $f(z)$ is divided by $z - i$ and $z + i$, the remainder is $\frac{1+i}{2}$ and $\frac{3i+1}{2}$ respectively. What is the remainder when $f(z)$ is divided by $z^2 + 1$?
(a) $\frac{1}{2}(1+2i-z)$ (b) $iz + i + 1$
(c) $\frac{1}{2}(2iz+2i+1)$ (d) None of these

15. Given that equation $z^2 + (p + iq)z + r + is = 0$, where p,q,r,s are non-zero reals, has real roots, then:
(a) $pqr = r^2 + p^2s$ (b) $prs = q^2 + r^2p$
(c) $prs = p^2 + s^2q$ (d) $pqs = s^2 + q^2r$.

16. Integral solutions of the equation $(1 - i)^x = 2^x$ is/are
(a) 0 (b) $4n, n \in \mathbb{N}$
(c) 0,1 (d) None of these

17. If n_1, n_2 are positive integers, then $(1+i)^{n_1} + (1+i^3)^{n_1} + (1+i^5)^{n_2} + (1+i^7)^{n_2}$ is real number if and only if:
(a) $n_1 = n_2 + 1$
(b) $n_1 + 1 = n_2$
(c) $n_1 = n_2$
(d) n_1, n_2 are any positive integers

18. a, b, c, a_1, b_1, c_1 are non-zero complex numbers satisfying $\frac{a}{a_1}+\frac{b}{b_1}+\frac{c}{c_1} = 1 + i$ and $\frac{a_1}{a}+\frac{b_1}{b}+\frac{c_1}{c} = 0$, then $\frac{a^2}{a_1^2}+\frac{b^2}{b_1^2}+\frac{c^2}{c_1^2}$ is equal to:

(a) $2i$ (b) $2 + 2i$
(c) 2 (d) None

19. If $\begin{vmatrix} 6i & -3i & 1 \\ 4 & 3i & -1 \\ 20 & 3 & i \end{vmatrix} = x - iy$, then

(a) $x = 3, y = 1$ (b) $x = 1, y = 3$
(c) $x = 0, y = 3$ (d) $x = 0, y = 0$

Answer Key

1. (d)	**2.** (b),(c)	**3.** (d)	**4.** (b)	**5.** (c)	**6.** (c)	**7.** (b)	**8.** (c)	**9.** (b)	**10.** (b)
11. (c)	**12.** (a)	**13.** (c)	**14.** (a)	**15.** (d)	**16.** (a)	**17.** (d)	**18.** (a)	**19.** (d)	

■ CONJUGATE OF A COMPLEX NUMBER

Conjugate of a complex no. $z = x + iy$ is defined as $\bar{z} = x - iy$ It is mirror image of z in real axis as mirror. as shown in the figure.

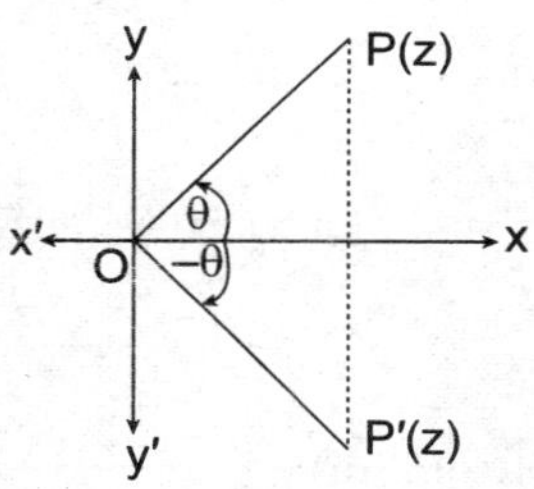

FIGURE 5.14

Let $z = r(\cos\theta + i\sin\theta)$

$\Rightarrow \bar{z} = r(\cos\theta - i\sin\theta) = r[\cos(-\theta) + i\sin(-\theta)]$

$\Rightarrow \bar{z}$ represents the affix of point having magnitude r and argument $-\theta$

■ PROPERTIES OF CONJUGATE OF COMPLEX NUMBERS

1. $R(\bar{z}) = R(z), I(\bar{z}) = -I(z)$

2. $z.\bar{z} = |\bar{z}|^2 = |z|^2 = (R(z))^2 + (I(z))^2$

3. $(\bar{\bar{z}}) = z, , (\bar{\bar{\bar{z}}}) = \bar{z}$

4. $|z| = |\bar{z}|$ and $-$ Agr z = Arg $\bar{z}$

5. If $z = \bar{z}$ i.e., $|z| = |\bar{z}|$ and arg z = arg $\bar{z} \Rightarrow z$ is purely real.

6. If $\bar{z} = -z$ i.e., $|-z| = |\bar{z}|$ and arg $z = -$ arg $\bar{z} \Rightarrow z$ is purely imaginary

7. $R(z) = \frac{z+\bar{z}}{2} = x = R(\bar{z})\,;\, I_m(z) = \frac{z-\bar{z}}{2i} = y = -\text{Im}(\bar{z})$

8. $\cos\theta = \left(\frac{e^{i\theta}+e^{-i\theta}}{2}\right)$; $\sin\theta = \left(\frac{e^{i\theta}-e^{-i\theta}}{2i}\right)$

9. $\overline{(z_1 + z_2 + z_3 + ... + z_n)} = \bar{z}_1 - \bar{z}_2 + \bar{z}_3 + ... + \bar{z}_n$

10. $\overline{(z_1 z_2 z_3 ... z_n)} = (\bar{z}_1)(\bar{z}_2)(\bar{z}_3)...(\bar{z}_n)$

11. $\overline{(z_1/z_2)} = \frac{(\bar{z}_1)}{(\bar{z}_2)}$

12. $\overline{(z^n)} = (\bar{z})^n$

13. If $\omega = f(z)$, then $\bar{\omega} = f(\bar{z})$, where $f(z)$ is algebraic polynomial

14. $z_1\bar{z}_2 + z_2\bar{z}_1 = 2R(\bar{z}_2 z_1)$

15. $|z_1 + z_2| = \sqrt{|z_1|^2 + |z_2|^2 + 2\text{Re}(z_1\bar{z}_2)}$

or $\sqrt{|z_1|^2 + |z_2|^2 + 2\text{Re}(\bar{z}_1.z_2)}$

Proof: $|z_1 + z_2|^2 = (z_1 + z_2).(\bar{z}_1 + \bar{z}_2)$

$= z_1\bar{z}_2 + z_2\bar{z}_1 + z_1\bar{z}_1 + z_2\bar{z}_2 = |z_1|^2 + |z_2|^2 + 2\text{Re}(z_1.\bar{z}_2)$

$\Rightarrow |z_1 + z_2| = \sqrt{|z_1|^2 + |z_2|^2 + 2\text{Re}(z_1.\bar{z}_2)}$

Paralelly $|z_1 + z_2| = \sqrt{|z_1|^2 + |z_2|^2 + 2\text{Re}(z_1.\bar{z}_2)}$

16. $|z_1 + z_2|^2 + |z - z_2|^2 = 2(|z_1|^2 + |z_2|^2)$

ILLUSTRATION 18: Show that $\left(\frac{\sqrt{3}+i}{\sqrt{3}-i}\right)^{3n}+1=0$ for all odd integral values of n.

SOLUTION: $\frac{\sqrt{3}+i}{\sqrt{3}-i}=\frac{(\sqrt{3}+i)(\sqrt{3}+i)}{(\sqrt{3}-i)(\sqrt{3}+i)}=\frac{2+2\sqrt{3}\,i}{4}=\frac{1+\sqrt{3}\,i}{2}=e^{i\pi/3}$

$\Rightarrow \left(\frac{\sqrt{3}+i}{\sqrt{3}-i}\right)^{3n}+1=(e^{i\pi/3})^{3n}+1=(e^{i\pi n})+1$

$\cos(n\pi) + i\sin(n\pi) + 1 = -1 + 0 + 1 = 0$ {where n is odd}

ILLUSTRATION 19: If $\sqrt{a+ib}=x+iy$, prove that $\sqrt{a-ib}=x-iy$

SOLUTION: $\sqrt{a+ib}=x+iy$

$\Rightarrow a + ib = (x + iy)^2 = (x^2 - y^2) + 2xyi$; Equating real and imaginary parts,

$\Rightarrow a = x^2 - y^2$ and $b = 2xy \Rightarrow a - ib = (x^2 - y^2) - 2xyi = (x - iy)^2$; Hence, $\sqrt{a-ib}=x-iy$

ILLUSTRATION 20: If equation $z^2 + \alpha z + \beta = 0$ has a real root, prove that $(\alpha\bar{\beta})(\bar{\alpha}-\alpha)=(\beta-\bar{\beta})^2$

SOLUTION Let x be a real root of equation $z^2 + \alpha z + b = 0$, then $x^2 + \alpha x + \beta = 0 \Rightarrow \beta = -x^2 - \alpha x$ ....(i)

$\therefore\ \bar{\beta}=-\overline{x^2}-\bar{\alpha}\bar{x}$ or $\bar{\beta}=-x^2-\bar{\alpha}x$ ....(ii)

(i) – (ii) $\Rightarrow \beta-\bar{\beta}=(\bar{\alpha}-\alpha)x$ ....(iii)

From (ii), $\alpha\bar{\beta}=-\alpha x^2-\alpha\bar{\alpha}x$ ....(iv)

From (i), $\bar{\alpha}\beta=\bar{\alpha}x^2-\bar{\alpha}\alpha x$ ....(v)

(iv) – (v) $\Rightarrow \alpha\bar{\beta}-\beta\bar{\alpha}=(\bar{\alpha}-\alpha)x^2$

Now $\left(\alpha\bar{\beta}-\beta\bar{\alpha}\right)(\bar{\alpha}-\alpha)=(\bar{\alpha}-\alpha)^2x^2=\left(\beta-\bar{\beta}\right)^2$ [from (iii)]

ILLUSTRATION 21: If $z_1 = a + ib$ and $z_2 = c + id$ are complex numbers such that $|z_1| = |z_2| = 1$ and $R(z_1.\bar{z}_2) = 0$, then show that the pair of complex numbers $\omega_1 = a + ic$ and $\omega_2 = b + id$ satisfy.

(i) $|\omega_1| = 1$ (ii) $|\omega_2| = 1$ (iii) $R(\omega_1\bar{\omega}_2) = 0$

SOLUTION: Given, $z_1 = a + ib$, $z_2 = c + id$, $\omega_1 = a + ic$, $\omega_2 = b + id$

$|z_1| = |z_2| = 1 \Rightarrow a^2 + b^2 = 1$ ....(i)

and $c^2 + d^2 = 1$ .....(ii)

Now, $z_1\,\bar{z}_2 = (a + ib)(c - id) = ac + bd + i(bc - ad)$

Again $R(z_1\bar{z}_2) = 0 \Rightarrow ac + bd = 0 \Rightarrow ac = -bd$

$\therefore\ \frac{a}{d}=\frac{b}{-c}=k(\text{say})$ ..(iii)

$\therefore\ a = kd$ and $b = -kc$; From (i) $a^2 + b^2 = 1 \Rightarrow k^2d^2 + k^2c^2 = 1$ or $k^2(c^2 + d^2) = 1$

or $k^2 = 1$ [$\because c^2 + d^2 = 1$] $\therefore$ $k = 1$ or -1

when $k = 1$, $a = d$, $b = -c$ and when $k = -1$, $a - d$, $b = c$ $\Rightarrow$ $|a| = |d|$; $|b| = |c|$

(i) $|\omega_1|=\sqrt{a^2+c^2}=\sqrt{a^2+b^2}=1$ [$\because |c| = |b|$]

(ii) $|\omega_2|=\sqrt{b^2+d^2}=\sqrt{b^2+a^2}=1$ [$\because |d| = |a|$]

(iii) $\omega_1\bar{\omega}_2=(a+ic)(b-id) \Rightarrow R(\omega_1\bar{\omega}_2)=ab+cd$

$= -dc + cd = 0$ [$\because a = d, b = -c$ or $a = -d, b = c$]

TEXTUAL EXERCISE 4: (SUBJECTIVE)

1. Find the conjugate and modulus for the following:

(i) $z = (3 - 2i)(3 + 2i)(1 + i)$

(ii) $\dfrac{2+i}{4i + (1+i)^2}$

2. Let z_1, z_2 be two complex numbers. Find the condition that both $(z_1 + z_2)$ and $z_1 z_2$ are real.

3. (a) If $|z| = 1$, then prove that $\dfrac{z-1}{z+1}$ is purely imaginary.

(b) Find real θ such that $\dfrac{3+2i\sin\theta}{1-2i\sin\theta}$ is

(i) real

(ii) purely imaginary

(c) Find the number of solutions of $Re(z^2) = 0$ and $|z| = a\sqrt{2}$, (where z is a complex number and $a > 0$)

4. For any three complex numbers z_1, z_2 and z_3 prove that $z_1 Im(\bar{z}_2 z_3) + z_2 Im(\bar{z}_3 z_1) + z_3 Im(\bar{z}_1 . z_2) = 0$

5. Let z_1 and z_2 be complex numbers such that $z_1 \neq z_2$ and $|z_1| = |z_2|$, If z_1 has positive real part and z_2 has negative imaginary part, then prove that $(z_1 + z_2)/(z_1 - z_2)$ is always purely imaginary.

Answer Key

1. (i) $13 - 13i$, $13\sqrt{2}$ (ii) $\dfrac{1+2i}{6}$, $\sqrt{5}/6$ **2.** $I(z_1) + I(z_2) = 0$, $R(z_1)I(z_2) + R(z_2)I(z_1) = 0$

3. (b) (i) $\theta \in n\pi$ (ii) $n\pi \pm \pi/3$ (c) 4

TEXTUAL EXERCISE 4: (OBJECTIVE)

1. The complex numbers $\sin x + i\cos^2 x$ and $\cos x - i\sin 2x$ are conjugate to each other for

(a) $x = n\pi$ (b) $x = \left(n+\dfrac{1}{2}\right)\pi$

(c) $x = 0$ (d) No value of x

2. The values of x and y for which the numbers $3 + ix^2y$ and $x^2 + y + 4i$ are conjugate complex numbers can be

(a) (–2, –1) or (2, –1)

(b) (–1, 2) or (–2, 1)

(c) (1, 2) or (–1, –2)

(d) None of these

3. If $y = \cos\theta + i\sin\theta$, then the value of $y + \dfrac{1}{y}$ is

(a) $2\cos\theta$ (b) $2\sin\theta$

(c) $2\text{cosec}\theta$ (d) $2\tan\theta$

4. If $x + \dfrac{1}{x} = \sqrt{3}$, then x is equal to

(a) $\cos\dfrac{\pi}{3} + i\sin\dfrac{\pi}{3}$ (b) $\cos\dfrac{\pi}{2} + i\sin\dfrac{\pi}{2}$

(c) $\sin\dfrac{\pi}{6} + i\cos\dfrac{\pi}{6}$ (d) $\cos\dfrac{\pi}{6} \pm i\sin\dfrac{\pi}{6}$

5. If $z = \dfrac{1+i\sqrt{3}}{\sqrt{3}+i}$, then $(\bar{z})^{100}$ lies in

(a) I quadrant

(b) II quadrant

(c) III qudarant

(d) IV quadrant

6. For the complex number z, the number $z + \bar{z}$ and $z\bar{z}$ is

(a) A real number

(b) An imaginary number

(c) Both are real numbers

(d) Both are imaginary numbers

7. $(z + a)(\bar{z} + a)$, where a is real, is equivalent to

(a) $|z - a|$ (b) $z^2 + a^2$

(c) $|z + a|^2$ (d) None of these

8. If $\dfrac{z-i}{z+i} (z \neq -i)$ is a purely imagainary number, then $z.\bar{z}$ is equal to

(a) 0 (b) 1

(c) 2 (d) None of these

9. If $\frac{c+i}{c-i} = a + ib$, where a,b, c are real, then $a^2 + b^2 =$
(a) 1 (b) –1
(c) c^2 (d) $-c^2$

10. If the conjugate of $(x + iy)(1 - 2i)$ be $1 + i$, then
(a) $x = \frac{1}{5}$ (b) $y = \frac{3}{5}$
(c) $x + iy = \frac{1-i}{1-2i}$ (d) $x - iy = \frac{1-i}{1+2i}$

11. The conjugate of $\frac{(2+i)^2}{3+i}$, in the form of $a + ib$, is
(a) $\frac{13}{2}+i\left(\frac{15}{2}\right)$ (b) $\frac{13}{10}+i\left(\frac{-15}{2}\right)$
(c) $\frac{13}{10}+i\left(\frac{-9}{10}\right)$ (d) $\frac{13}{10}+i\left(\frac{9}{10}\right)$

12. The conjugate of complex number $\frac{2-3i}{4-i}$, is
(a) $\frac{3i}{4}$ (b) $\frac{11+10i}{17}$
(c) $\frac{11-10i}{17}$ (d) $\frac{2+3i}{4i}$

13. If $\bar{z}$ be the conjugate of the complex number z, then which of the following relations is false?
(a) $|z| = |\bar{z}|$ (b) $z.\bar{z} = |\bar{z}|^2$
(c) $\overline{z_1 + z_2} = \bar{z}_1 + \bar{z}_2$ (d) arg z = arg $\bar{z}$

14. If $z_1 = 1 + 2i$ and $z_2 = 3 + 5i$, then $Re\left(\frac{\bar{z}_2 z_1}{z_2}\right)$ is equal to
(a) $\frac{-31}{71}$ (b) $\frac{17}{22}$
(c) $\frac{-17}{22}$ (d) $\frac{22}{17}$

15. If the complex number z satisfies the equation $(i - z)(1 + 2i) + (1 - iz)(3 - 4i) = 1 + 7i$, then $z + \bar{z} + z\bar{z}$ is equal to
(a) 0 (b) 1
(c) –1 (d) None of these

16. For $z_1, z_2, z_3 \in C$, $\sum z_1 I_m (\bar{z}_2 z_3) =$
(a) $z_1 + z_2 + z_3$ (b) 0
(c) $\frac{1}{2i}(z_1 + z_2 + z_3)$ (d) None of these

17. Let $z_1 = a + ib$, $z_2 = c + id$ be two complex numbers such $|z_1| = |z_2| = 1$ and $Re\ (z_1\bar{z}_2) = 0$. If $w_1 = a + ic$ and $w_2 = b + id$, then Re $(w_1\bar{w}_2)$ is
(a) 1 (b) 0
(c) –1 (d) None of these

Answer Key

1. (d)	**2.** (a)	**3.** (a)	**4.** (d)	**5.** (c)	**6.** (c)	**7.** (c)	**8.** (b)	**9.** (a)	**10.** (c)
11. (c)	**12.** (b)	**13.** (d)	**14.** (d)	**15.** (a)	**16.** (b)	**17.** (b)			

MODULUS OF COMPLEX NUMBERS

Modulus of a complex number $z = x + iy$ is denoted by $|z|$. If point $P(x,y)$ represents the complex number z on Argand's plane, then $|z| = OP = \sqrt{x^2 + y^2}$ = distance between origin and point $P = \sqrt{[R(z)]^2 + [I(z)]^2}$

Properties of Modulus of Complex Numbers

1. Modulus of a complex no. is distance of complex no. from origin.
$|z| \geq 0 \Rightarrow |z| = 0$ iff $z = 0$ and $|z| > 0$ iff $z \neq 0$
2. $-|z| \leq Re(z) \leq |z|$ and $-|z| \leq Im(z) \leq |z|$
3. $|z| = |\bar{z}| = |-z| = |-\bar{z}|$
4. $z\bar{z} = |z|^2$
5. $|z_1 z_2| = |z_1||z_2|$
In general $|z_1 z_2 z_3 \ldots\ldots z_n| = |z_1||z_2||z_3|\ldots\ldots|z_n|$
6. $\left|\frac{z_1}{z_2}\right| = \frac{|z_1|}{|z_2|}$ $(z_2 \neq 0)$
7. **Triangle inequality:** $|z_1 \pm z_2| \leq |z_1| + |z_2|$
In general $|z_1 \pm z_2 \pm z_3 \ldots\ldots \pm z_n| = |z_1| + |z_2| + |z_3| + \ldots\ldots + |z_n|$
Proof: $|z_1 + z_2| \leq |z_1| + |z_2|$

For this consider

$|z_1+z_2|^2 = |z_1|^2+|z_2|^2+z_1\bar{z}_2+z_2\bar{z}_1$

$= |z_1|^2+|z_2|^2+z_1\bar{z}_2+\overline{\bar{z}_2 z_1}$

$= (|z_1|^2+|z_2|^2)+2\text{Re}(z_1\bar{z}_2)$ $(\because z+\bar{z} = 2Re(z))$

$\le |z_1|^2+|z_2|^2+2|z_1.\bar{z}_2|$

$\le |z_1|^2+|z_2|^2+2|z_1|.|\bar{z}_2|$

$\le |z_1|^2+|z_2|^2+2|z_1|.|z_2|$ $(\because |\bar{z}|=|z|)$

$\le (|z_1|+|z_2|)^2 \Rightarrow |z_1+z_2|^2 \le (|z_1|+|z_2|)^2$

$\therefore \quad |z_1+z_2| \le |z_1|+|z_2|$

Now replacing z_2 by $-z_2$ in above inequality we get

$|z_1+(-z_2)| \le |z_1|+|-z_2|$ or $|z_1-z_2| \le |z_1|+|z_2|$

$(\because (|-z|=|z|)$

Now, $|z_1 \pm (z_2 \pm z_3)| \le |z_1|+|z_2 \pm z_3| \le |z_1|+|z_2|+|z_3|$

Similarly the result can be generalised for n complex numbers

8. Similarly $|z_1 \pm z_2| \ge |z_1|-|z_2|$.

9. $|z^n| = |z|^n$

10. $||z_1|-|z_2|| \le |z_1+z_2| \le |z_1|+|z_2|$

Thus $|z_1|+|z_2|$ is the greatest possible value of $|z_1+z_2|$ and $||z_1|-|z_2||$ is the least possible value of $|z_1+z_2|$.

11. $|z_1 \pm z_2|^2 = |z_1|^2+|z_2|^2 \pm (z_1\bar{z}_2+\bar{z}_1 z_2)$

$= |z_1|^2+|z_2|^2 \pm 2\text{Re}(z_1\bar{z}_2)$

$= |z_1|^2+|z_2|^2 \pm 2|z_1||z_2|\cos(\theta_1-\theta_2)$

13. $|z_1+z_2|^2 = |z_1|^2-|z_2|^2 \Leftrightarrow \dfrac{z_1}{z_2}$ is purely imaginary

15. $|az_1+bz_2|^2+|bz_1-az_2|^2 = (a^2+b^2)(|z_1|^2+|z_2|^2)$ where $a, b \in \mathbb{R}$

16. Unimodular: if z is unimodular, then $|z| = 1$. Now if $f(z)$ is a unimodular, then it can always be expressed as $f(z) = \cos\theta + i\sin\theta$, $\theta \in \mathbb{R}$

17. $|z_1+z_2|^2+|z_1-z_2|^2 = 2(|z_1|^2+|z_2|^2)$

Proof: For this consider $|z_1+z_2|^2 = (z_1+z_2)\overline{(z_1+z_2)}$

$(\because |z|^2 = z\bar{z})$

$= (z_1+z_2)(\bar{z}_1+\bar{z}_2)$ $(\because \overline{z_1+z_2} = \bar{z}_1+\bar{z}_2)$

$= z_1\bar{z}_1+z_1\bar{z}_2+z_2\bar{z}_1+z_2\bar{z}_2$

$= |z_1|^2+|z_2|^2+z_1\bar{z}_2+z_2\bar{z}_1$ ......(i)

$\Rightarrow |z_1-z_2|^2 = (z_1-z_2)(\bar{z}_1-\bar{z}_2)$

$= |z_1|^2+|z_2|^2-z_1\bar{z}_2-z_2\bar{z}_1$ ....(ii)

Adding (I) and (ii), we get

$|z_1+z_2|^2+|z_1-z_2|^2 = 2(|z_1|^2+|z_2|^2)$

ILLUSTRATION 22: If $z = x+iy$ and $w = \dfrac{1-iz}{z-i}$, show that z is purely real if $|w| = 1$

SOLUTION: $|w| = 1 \Rightarrow \left|\dfrac{1-iz}{z-i}\right| = 1$

$\Rightarrow |1-iz| = |z-i|$

$\Rightarrow |(1+y)-ix| = |x-(y-1)i|$

$\Rightarrow (1+y)^2+x^2 = x^2+(y-1)^2$

$\Rightarrow 2y = -2y \Rightarrow y = 0$

Hence, $z = x+i0 = x$ which is purely real

ILLUSTRATION 23: If $|z_1| = |z_2| = ... = |z_n| = 1$, prove that $|z_1+z_2+....+z_n| = \left|\dfrac{1}{z_1}+\dfrac{1}{z_2}+...+\dfrac{1}{z_n}\right|$

SOLUTION: Given, $|z_1| = |z_2| = ... = |z_n| = 1$

Now, R.H.S $= \left|\dfrac{1}{z_1}+\dfrac{1}{z_2}+...+\dfrac{1}{z_n}\right| = \left|\dfrac{\bar{z}}{z_1\bar{z}_1}+\dfrac{\bar{z}_2}{z_2\bar{z}_2}+...+\dfrac{\bar{z}_n}{|z_n|^2}\right|$

$= \left|\dfrac{\bar{z}_1}{|z_1|^2}+\dfrac{\bar{z}_2}{|z_2|^2}+...+\dfrac{\bar{z}_n}{|z_n|^2}\right| = |\bar{z}_1+\bar{z}_2+....+\bar{z}_n| = |\overline{z_1+z_2+z_3+...+z_r}|$

$= |z_1+z_2+....+z_n|$ $[\because |\bar{z}| = |z|]$

ILLUSTRATION 24: Prove that $\left|\dfrac{z_1 - z_2}{1-\bar{z}_1 z_2}\right| < 1$ if $|z_1| < 1$, $|z_2| < 1$.

SOLUTION: $\left|\dfrac{z_1 - z_2}{1-\bar{z}_1 z_2}\right| < 1 \Leftrightarrow \left|\dfrac{z_1 - z_2}{1-\bar{z}_1 z_2}\right|^2 < 1$

$\Leftrightarrow \dfrac{|z_1 - z_2|^2}{|1-\bar{z}_1 z_2|^2} < 1 \Leftrightarrow |z_1 - z_2|^2 < |1-\bar{z}_1 z_2|^2 \qquad \Leftrightarrow (z_1 - z_2)\overline{(z_1 - z_2)} < \overline{(1-\bar{z}_1 z_2)}(1-\bar{z}_1 z_2)$

$\Leftrightarrow (z_1 - z_2)(\bar{z}_1 - \bar{z}_2) < (1 - z_1\bar{z}_2)(1-\bar{z}_1 z_2)$

$\Leftrightarrow z_1\bar{z}_1 - z_1\bar{z}_2 - z_2\bar{z}_1 + z_2\bar{z}_2 < 1 - \bar{z}_1 z_2 + z_1\bar{z}_1 z_2\bar{z}_2 - z_1\bar{z}_2$

$\Leftrightarrow |z_1|^2 + |z_2|^2 < 1 + |z_1|^2|z_2|^2 \qquad \Leftrightarrow 1 - |z_1|^2 - |z_2|^2 + |z_1|^2|z_2|^2 > 0$

$\Leftrightarrow (1 - |z_1|^2) - |z_2|^2(1 - |z_1|^2) > 0 \Leftrightarrow (1 - |z_1|^2)(1 - |z_2|^2) > 0$

$\Leftrightarrow (1 + |z_1|)(1 - |z_1|)(1 + |z_2|)(1 - |z_2|) > 0$

$\Leftrightarrow (1 - |z_1|)(1 - |z_2|) > 0$ [$\because 1 + |z_1| > 0,\ 1 + |z_2| > 0$]

Which is true as $|z_1| < 1$ and $|z_2| < 1$; Hence $\left|\dfrac{z_1 - z_2}{1-\bar{z}_1 z_2}\right| < 1$

TEXTUAL EXERCISE 5: (SUBJECTIVE)

1. Find the modulus of the following:

(a) $\dfrac{1-i\sqrt{3}}{2+2i}$ (b) $\dfrac{2+i}{4i+(1+i)^2}$

2. If $z = 1 + i\tan\alpha$, where $\pi < \alpha < \dfrac{3\pi}{2}$, then prove that $|z| = -\sec\alpha$.

3. If $(\cos\theta - i\sin\theta)^2 = x - iy$, then prove that $x^2 + y^2 = 1$.

4. If $x + iy = \sqrt{\dfrac{a+ib}{c+id}}$, then prove that $(x^2 + y^2)^2 = \dfrac{a^2+b^2}{c^2+d^2}$.

5. If $(c + i)/(c - i) = (a + ib)$, $c \in \mathbb{R}$, then prove that $a^2 + b^2 = 1$, $b/a = 2c/(c^2 - 1)$.

6. Simplify $\left|\dfrac{z-3}{z+3}\right| = 2$ in terms of x, y, where $z = x + iy$.

7. If $|z+1| = \sqrt{2}\,|z-1|$, where $z = x + iy$, then prove that $x^2 + y^2 - 6x + 1 = 0$.

8. Find the complex number z such that $z^2 + |z| = 0$.

9. If $|z - i| < 1$, then show that $|z + 12 - 6i| < 14$.

10. If $a > 0$, $z|z| + az + 1 = 0$, show that z is a negative real number.

11. If $\left|z - \dfrac{4}{z}\right| = 2$, show that greatest value of $|z|$ is $\sqrt{5} + 1$.

12. If $|z + 4| \le 3$, find the least and greatest values of $|z + 1|$.

13. Prove that for a complex number z, minimum value of $|z| + |z - 2|$ is 2.

14. If α, β be two complex numbers, then prove that $|\alpha^2| + |\beta^2| = \dfrac{1}{2}(|\alpha+\beta|^2 + |\alpha-\beta|^2)$.

6. $x^2 + y^2 + 10x + 9 = 0$ **8.** $0, \pm i$ **12.** $0, 6$

TEXTUAL EXERCISE 5: (OBJECTIVE)

1. If $z = \dfrac{(1-i\sqrt{3})(\cos\theta + i\sin\theta)}{2(1-i)(\cos\theta - i\sin\theta)}$, then modulus of z is

(a) $\dfrac{1}{\sqrt{2}}$ (b) $\dfrac{1}{2\sqrt{2}}$

(c) $\dfrac{1}{\sqrt{3}}$ (d) None of these

2. If α and β are different complex numbers with $|\beta| = 1$, then $\left|\dfrac{\beta-\alpha}{1-\bar{\alpha}\beta}\right|$ is equal to

(a) 0 (b) 1/2

(c) 1 (d) 2

3. If a,b,c are complex numbers such that $a + b + c = 0$ and $|a| = |b| = |c| = 1$, then $1/a + 1/b + 1/c =$

(a) 0 (b) 3

(c) $\sqrt{3}$ (d) None of these

4. If $|z| \geq 3$, the least value of $\left|z+\dfrac{1}{z}\right|$ is

(a) 3/8 (b) 8/3

(c) 10/3 (d) None of these

5. If $\left|z-\dfrac{1}{z}\right| = 1$, then

(a) $|z|_{max} = \dfrac{1+\sqrt{5}}{2}$ (b) $|z|_{min} = \dfrac{1+\sqrt{5}}{2}$

(c) $|z|_{max} = \dfrac{-1+\sqrt{5}}{2}$ (d) None of these

6. The maximum distance from the origin to the point z satisfying $\left|z+\dfrac{1}{z}\right| = 2$ is

(a) $\dfrac{1}{2}(2+\sqrt{5})$ (b) $1+\sqrt{2}$

(c) $\sqrt{2}-1$ (d) None of these

7. If $\left|z-\dfrac{4}{z}\right| = 2$, then the maximum value of $|z|$ is equal to:

(a) $\sqrt{5}+1$ (b) 2

(c) $2+\sqrt{2}$ (d) $\sqrt{3}+1$

8. If $|z_1| = 2$, $|z_2| = 5$, $|z_1 + z_2| = 3$, then $|4z_2 + 25z_1| =$

(a) 29 (b) 30

(c) 10 (d) 15

9. For any two complex numbers z_1, z_2 we have $|z_1 + z_2|^2 = |z_1|^2 + |z_2|^2$, then

(a) $Re\left(\dfrac{z_1}{z_2}\right) = 0$ (b) $Im\left(\dfrac{z_1}{z_2}\right) = 0$

(c) $Re(z_1.\bar{z}_2) = 0$ (d) $Im(z_1z_2) = 0$

10. If z and ω are two non-zero complex numbers such that $|z\omega| = 1$ and $\arg(z) - \arg(\omega) = \dfrac{\pi}{2}$, then $\bar{z}\omega$ is equal to

(a) 1 (b) -1

(c) i (d) $-i$

11. If $\left|\dfrac{z_1 - 2z_2}{2 - z_1\bar{z}_2}\right| = 1$, $|z_2| \neq 1$, then $|z_1| =$

(a) 4 (b) 2

(c) 1 (d) None of these

12. If $|z| = 1$ and $\omega = \dfrac{z-1}{z+1}$ (where $z \neq -1$), then $Re(\omega)$ is:

(a) 0 (b) $-\dfrac{1}{|z+1|^2}$

(c) $\dfrac{\sqrt{2}}{|z+1|^2}$ (d) None of these

13. If $\omega = \alpha + i\beta$, $\beta \neq 0$ and $z \neq 1$ satisfies the condition $\dfrac{\omega - \bar{\omega}z}{1-z}$ is purely real, then the set of values of z is

(a) $\{z : |z| = 1\}$ (b) $\{z : z = 2\}$

(c) $\{z : |z| = 1, z \neq 1\}$ (d) $\{z : z \neq 1\}$

14. If $|z_1| < 1 < |z_2|$, $z_1, z_2 \in C$, then $\left|(1 - z_1\bar{z}_2)/(z_1 - z_2)\right|$ is

(a) <1 (b) >1

(c) = 1 (d) None of these

15. Maximum value of $\left|(z_1\bar{z}_2 + \bar{z}_1z_2)/|z_1 z_2|\right|$ is

(a) 1 (b) 2

(c) 4 (d) None of these

16. The number of points in the complex plane that satisfy the conditions $|z - 2| = 2$, $z(1 - i) + \bar{z}(1 + i) = 4$ is

(a) 0 (b) 1

(c) 2 (d) More than 2

17. The maximum value of $|z|$ satisfying the equations $\dfrac{1}{12}(z+\bar{z})^2 = 1 - \dfrac{1}{3}|z|^2$ is:

(a) $\sqrt{2}$ (b) $\sqrt{3}$
(c) 4 (d) 6

18. If $\frac{2z_1}{3z_2}$ is a purely imaginary number other than zero, then $\left|\frac{z_1 - z_2}{z_1 + z_2}\right| =$

(a) 3/2 (b) 1
(c) 2/3 (d) 4/9

19. If z_1 and z_2 are two complex numbers satisfying the equation $\left|\frac{z_1 + z_2}{z_1 - z_2}\right| = 1$, then $\frac{z_1}{z_2}$ is a number which is

(a) Positive real (b) Negative real
(c) Purely imaginary (d) None of these

20. If z_1 and z_2 be complex numbers such that $z_1 \neq z_2$ and $|z_1| = |z_2|$. If z_1 has positive real part and z_2 has negative imaginary part, then $\frac{(z_1 + z_2)}{(z_1 - z_2)}$ may be

(a) Purely imaginary (b) Real and positive
(c) Real and negative (d) None of these

21. $\left|\frac{1}{2}(z_1 + z_2) + \sqrt{z_1 z_2}\right| + \left|\frac{1}{2}(z_1 + z_2) - \sqrt{z_1 z_2}\right| =$

(a) $|z_1 + z_2|$ (b) $|z_1 - z_2|$
(c) $|z_1| + |z_2|$ (d) $|z_1| - |z_2|$

22. If $|z_1 + z_2| = |z_1| + |z_2|$ where z_1 and z_2 are different non-zero complex numbers, then

(a) $Re\ (z_1/z_2) = 0$ (b) $Im\ (z_1/z_2) = 0$
(c) $z_1 + z_2 = 0$ (d) None of these

23. If $|z - iRe(z)| = |z - Im(z)|$, then

(a) $Im(z) = 2$ (b) $Re(z) = 2$
(c) $Re(z) = Im(z) = 2$ (d) None of these

24. For any two complex numbers z_1, z_2 and any two real numbers a and b, $|az_1 - bz_2|^2 + |bz_1 + az_2|^2 =$

(a) $(a + b)(|z_1|^2 + |z_2|^2)$
(b) $(a^2 + b^2)\ (|z_1|^2 + |z_2|^2)$
(c) $(a^2 + b^2)\ (|z_1| + |z_2|)$
(d) None of these

25. If $|z| \leq 4$, then maximum value of $|iz + 3 - 4i|$ is equal to

(a) 2 (b) 4
(c) 3 (d) 9

26. If z_1 and z_2 are two non-zero complex numbers satisfying $\left|\frac{z_1 - iz_2}{z_1 + iz_2}\right| = 1$, then $\frac{z_1}{z_2}$ is

(a) Purely imaginary (b) Purely real
(c) Of unit modulus (d) None of these

27. If $|z - 3 + 2i| = 4$, then sum of max$|z|$ and min $|z|$ is

(a) $\sqrt{2} - 1$ (b) 4
(c) 8 (d) None of these

28. z_1 and z_2 are two non-zero complex number such that $|z_1| = |z_2| + |z_1 - z_2|$, then

(a) $Re(z_1/z_2) = 0$ (b) $Im(z_1/z_2) = 0$
(c) $Im(z_1 z_2) = 0$ (d) $Re(z_1 z_2) = 0$

29. For $z \in C$ minimum value of $|z - 4 + 3i| + |z + 3 - 4i|$ is

(a) 10 (b) 0
(c) $7\sqrt{2}$ (d) 2

30. Let C be the set of all complex numbers z such that $|z| = 1$ and define the relation R on C by $z_1 R z_2$ iff $|\arg z_1 - \arg z_2| = 2\pi/3$, then R is

(a) Reflexive (b) Symmetric
(c) Transitive (d) Anti-symmetric

Answer Key

1. (a)	**2.** (c)	**3.** (a)	**4.** (b)	**5.** (a)	**6.** (b)	**7.** (a)	**8.** (b)	**9.** (c)	**10.** (d)
11. (b)	**12.** (a)	**13.** (c)	**14.** (a)	**15.** (b)	**16.** (c)	**17.** (b)	**18.** (b)	**19.** (c)	**20.** (a)
21. (c)	**22.** (b)	**23.** (d)	**24.** (b)	**25.** (d)	**26.** (b)	**27.** (c)	**28.** (b)	**29.** (c)	**30.** (b)

ARGUMENT AND PRINCIPAL ARGUMENT OF COMPLEX NUMBERS

Argument of z (arg z) also known as amp(z) is angle which the radius vector $\overrightarrow{OP}$ makes with positive direction of real axis. **Principal Argument:** In general, argument of a complex number is not unique since if θ is the argument, then $2n\pi + \theta$ is also the argument of the complex number where $n = 0, \pm 1, \pm 2,.....$ Hence, we define principal value of argument θ, which satisfies the condition $-\pi < \theta \leq \pi$. Hence, Principal value of arg(z) is taken as an angle lying in $(-\pi, \pi]$ if $\arg z \notin (-\pi, \pi]$, then $P(\arg z) = \arg z \pm 2k\pi$.

A complex number z given as $(x + iy)$ lies in different quadrant depending upon the sign of x and y. Based on the quadrantal location of the complex number its principal argument is a shown below:

Sign of x and y	Location of z	Principle Argument
$x > 0, y > 0$,	Ist quadrant	$\theta = \alpha = \tan^{-1}\left\lvert\frac{y}{x}\right\rvert$
$x < 0, y > 0$	IInd quadrant	$\theta = (\pi - \alpha) = \pi - \tan^{-1}\left\lvert\frac{y}{x}\right\rvert$
$x < 0, y < 0$	IIIrd quadrant	$= -\pi + \tan^{-1}\left\lvert\frac{y}{x}\right\rvert$
$x > 0, y < 0$,	IVth quadrant	$\theta = -\alpha = -\tan^{-1}\left\lvert\frac{y}{x}\right\rvert$

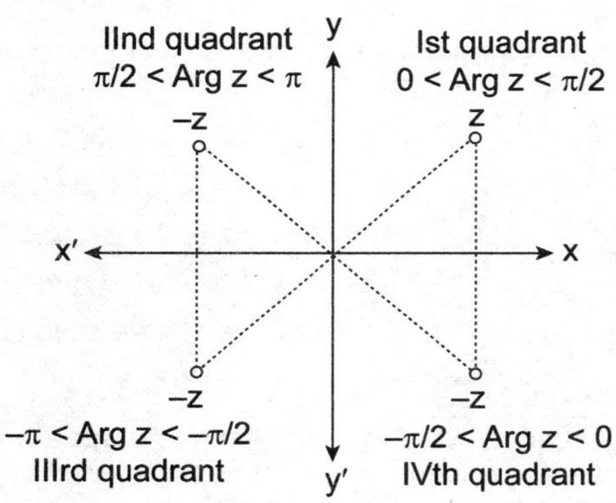

FIGURE 5.15

Caution:

A usual mistake is to take the argument of $z = x + iy$ as $\tan^{-1}(y/x)$ irrespective of the value of the x and y.

- remember that $\tan^{-1}(y/x)$ lies in the interval $\left(-\frac{\pi}{2}, \frac{\pi}{2}\right)$

  Whereas the principal value of argument of z (Arg(z)) lies in the interval $(-\pi, \pi]$.

  Thus, if $z = x + iy$, then

$$Arg(z) = \begin{cases} \tan^{-1}(y/x) & \text{if } x > 0 \\ \tan^{-1}(y/x) + \pi & \text{if } x < 0, y \geq 0 \\ \tan^{-1}(y/x) - \pi & \text{if } x < 0, y < 0 \\ \pi/2 & \text{if } x = 0, y > 0 \\ -\pi/2 & \text{if } x = 0, y < 0 \\ \text{not defined} & \text{for } x = 0, y = 0 \end{cases}$$

PROPERTIES OF ARGUMENT OF COMPLEX NUMBERS

1. $\arg(z_1 . z_2) = \arg z_1 + \arg z_2$
2. $\arg(z^n) = n(\arg z)$
3. $\arg\left(\frac{z_1}{z_2}\right) = \arg z_1 - \arg z_2$

Proof

1. Let $z_1 = r_1(\cos\theta_1 + i\sin\theta_1)$, $z_2 = r_2(\cos\theta_2 + i\sin\theta_2)$
   Now $z_1 z_2 = r_1 r_2 [(\cos\theta_1 \cos\theta_2 - \sin\theta_1 \sin\theta_2) + i(\sin\theta_1 \cos\theta_2 + \cos\theta_1 \sin\theta_2)]$
   $= r_1 r_2 [\cos(\theta_1 + \theta_2) + i\sin(\theta_1 + \theta_2)]$
   $= r(\cos\theta + i\sin\theta)$, where $r = r_1 . r_2$ and $\theta = \theta_1 + \theta_2$
   $\therefore \arg(z_1 . z_2) = \theta = \theta_1 + \theta_2 = \arg z_1 + \arg z_2$
2. $\arg(z_1 . z_2 . z_3 ...... z_n) = \arg z_1 + \arg z_2 + ... + \arg z_n$
   putting $z_1 = z_2 = ... z_n = z$, we get
   $\arg(z^n) = n(\arg z)$
3. $$\frac{z_1}{z_2} = \frac{r_1(\cos\theta_1 + i\sin\theta_1)}{r_2(\cos\theta_2 + i\sin\theta_2)}$$
   $$= \frac{r_1(\cos\theta_1 + i\sin\theta_1)(\cos\theta_2 - i\sin\theta_2)}{r_2(\cos\theta_2 + i\sin\theta_2)(\cos\theta_2 - i\sin\theta_2)}$$
   $$= \frac{r_1}{r_2}\frac{[(\cos\theta_1\cos\theta_2 + \sin\theta_1\sin\theta_2) + i(\sin\theta_1\cos\theta_2 - \cos\theta_1\sin\theta_2)]}{\cos^2\theta_2 + \sin^2\theta_2}$$
   $$= \frac{r_1}{r_2}[\cos(\theta_1 - \theta_2) + i\sin(\theta_1 - \theta_2)]$$
   $$\therefore \arg\left(\frac{z_1}{z_2}\right) = \theta_1 - \theta_2 = \arg z_1 - \arg z_2$$
4. $\arg(z) = 0$ (or $2n\pi$; $n \in \mathbb{Z}$)
   $\Rightarrow$ complex number z is purely real and positive
5. $\arg(z) = \pi$ (or $(2n + 1)\pi$; $n \in \mathbb{Z}$)
   $\Rightarrow$ complex number z is purely real and negative
6. $\arg(z) = \pi/2$ (or $(4n + 1)\pi/2$; $n \in \mathbb{Z}$)
   $\Rightarrow$ complex number z is purely imaginary with positive $Im(z)$
7. $\arg(z) = -\pi/2$ (or $(4n + 3)\pi/2$; $n \in \mathbb{Z}$)
   $\Rightarrow$ complex number z is purely imaginary with negative $Im(z)$
8. $\arg(z) =$ not defined $\Leftrightarrow z = 0$
9. $\arg(z) = \pi/4 \Rightarrow z = (1 + i)$ or $(x + xi)$ etc for $(x > 0)$.

PROPERTIES OF PRINCIPAL ARGUMENT: (PRINCIPAL ARGUMENT OF COMPLEX NUMBER IS DENOTED BY ARG. (Z))

1. If $z_k = r_k(\cos\theta_k + i\sin\theta_k) = r_k e^{i\theta_k}$, are number of complex numbers, then $Arg\left(\prod_{k=1}^{n} z_k\right) = \sum_{k=1}^{n} Arg\, z_k \pm 2k\pi$, where $k \in \mathbb{Z}$ for suitably choose value of k such that principal Arg of resultant no. lies in principal range i.e., $(-\pi, \pi)$.
2. $\text{Arg}\left(\frac{z}{\bar{z}}\right) = 2\text{Arg}(z) + 2n\pi$ for suitably chosen value of n.
3. $\text{Arg}(z^n) = n\,\text{Arg}\, z \pm 2k\pi$; for suitable integer k.
4. $\text{Arg}(-z) = -\pi + \text{Arg}\, z$ or $\pi + \text{Arg}\, z$ respectively when $\text{Arg}\, z > 0$ or < 0, respectively.
6. $\text{Arg}(1/z) = -\text{Arg}\, z$

ILLUSTRATION 25: Find the modulus and principal arguments of the following complex numbers.

(a) $\{i(1 + i\sqrt{3})\}(\sqrt{3} - i)$ (b) $\frac{1+2i}{(1-i)^2 - 2}$

SOLUTION: (a) The given number in the $a + ib$ form is $-2 + 2\sqrt{3}i$

$\Rightarrow$ The magnitude is $\sqrt{(-2)^2 + (2\sqrt{3})^2} = 4$ and the principal argument is

$$\pi - \tan^{-1}\frac{2\sqrt{3}}{2} = \pi - \tan^{-1}\sqrt{3} = \pi - \frac{\pi}{3} = \frac{2\pi}{3}$$

(b) The number in the $a + ib$ form is $-\frac{3}{4} - \frac{1}{4}i$

$\Rightarrow$ Magnitude is $\frac{\sqrt{10}}{4}$ and the argument is $-\pi + \tan^{-1}\frac{1}{3}$

ILLUSTRATION 26: If z_1, z_2 are the two non-zero complex numbers such that $|z_1 + z_2| = |z_1| + |z_2|$, then evaluate $amp\frac{z_1}{z_2}$.

SOLUTION: $|z_1 + z_2| = |z_1| + |z_2|$ can hold when $0, z_1, z_2$ are collinear with 0 at one end

$\therefore$ $\text{amp}\frac{z_1}{z_2} = \text{amp}\, z_1 - \text{amp}\, z_2 = 0$

ILLUSTRATION 27: If $z = x + iy$ and $\omega = \frac{1-iz}{z-i}$, then prove that $|w| = 1$ implies z is purely imaginary.

SOLUTION: $w = \frac{1-i(x+iy)}{(x+iy)-i} = \frac{(1+y)-ix}{x+i(y-1)}$

Now $|w| = 1$ $\Rightarrow (1 + y)^2 + x^2 = x^2 + (y - 1)^2$

$\Rightarrow 2y = -2y \Rightarrow y = 0$ $\Rightarrow z = x$ i.e, purely real

ILLUSTRATION 28: Let z be a complex number of constant modulus such that z^2 is purely imaginary then find all possible values of z.

SOLUTION: Let $|z| = \sqrt{2}k$ $\Rightarrow x^2 + y^2 = 2k^2$ ....(i)

$Re(x + iy)^2 = 0$, i.e., $x^2 - y^2 = 0$ ......(ii)

Solving (i) and (ii), we get $x = \pm k$, $y = \pm k$.

$\therefore$ $z = \pm k(1 \pm i)$; $k \in 0$ are the possible values z.

ILLUSTRATION 29: If $|z_1 - 1| < 1$, $|z_2 - 2| < 2$, $|z_3 - 3| < 3$, then prove that $|z_1 + z_2 + z_3| < 12$

SOLUTION: Let $|z_1 + z_2 + z_3| = |(z_1 - 1) + (z_2 - 2) + (z_3 - 3) + 6|$

$\le |z_1 - 1| + |z_2 - 2| + |z_3 - 3| + 6 < 1 + 2 + 3 + 6 = 12$

ILLUSTRATION 30: Find the complex number z satisfying the relation $|z + 1| = z + 2(1 + i)$.

SOLUTION: Let $z = x + iy$

$\therefore \ |x + iy + 1| = x + iy + 2(1 + i)$ $\Rightarrow \sqrt{(x+1)^2 + y^2} = (x+2) + i(y+2)$

$\Rightarrow \sqrt{(x+1)^2 + y^2} = (x+2)$ and $y + 2 = 0$ $\Rightarrow (x + 1)^2 + y^2 = (x + 2)^2$ and $y = -2$

$\Rightarrow 2x + 5 = 4x + 4$ and $y = -2$ $\Rightarrow x = 1/2; y = 2$

$\Rightarrow z = \frac{1}{2}(1 - 4i)$

ILLUSTRATION 31: If $\left|z^3 + \frac{1}{z^3}\right| \le 2$, then find the range of $\left|z + \frac{1}{z}\right|$.

SOLUTION: $\left(z + \frac{1}{z}\right)^3 = z^3 + \frac{1}{z^3} + 3\left(z + \frac{1}{z}\right)$; Put $\left|z + \frac{1}{z}\right| = a$

$\left|z + \frac{1}{z}\right|^3 = \left|\left(z + \frac{1}{z}\right)^3\right| = \left|z^3 + \frac{1}{z^3} + 3\left(z + \frac{1}{z}\right)\right|$ $(\because |z|^n = |z^n|)$

$\le \left|z^3 + \frac{1}{z^3}\right| + 3\left|z + \frac{1}{z}\right|$

$\Rightarrow a^3 \le 2 + 3a$ $\Rightarrow a^3 - 3a - 2 \le 0$

$\Rightarrow (a - 2)(a + 1)^2 \le 0$ $\Rightarrow a \le 2 \ \therefore \ a \in (-\infty, 2]$

But $a = \left|z + \frac{1}{z}\right| \ge 0$ $\Rightarrow$ Range of a is $[0,2]$ **Ans**

ILLUSTRATION 32: Evaluate the minimum value of $|z - 4i| + |z - 2i|$, for any complex number z.

SOLUTION: $2i = (z - 2i) - (z - 4i)$

$\therefore \ |2i| = |(z - 2i) - (z - 4i)| \le |z - 2i| + |z - 4i|$

$\therefore \ 2 \le |z - 2i| + |z - 4i|$

$\therefore$ Minimum value of $|z - 2i| + |z - 4i|$ is 2.

ILLUSTRATION 33: If $\left|z - \frac{6}{z}\right| = 4$, then find the greatest integral value of $|z|$

SOLUTION: $|z| = \left|\left(z - \frac{6}{z}\right) + \frac{6}{z}\right| \le \left|z - \frac{6}{z}\right| + \frac{6}{|z|}$

$\therefore \ |z| \le 4 + \frac{6}{|z|}$ $\Rightarrow |z|^2 - 4|z| \le 6$

$\Rightarrow |z|^2 - 4|z| + 4 \le 10$ $\Rightarrow (|z| - 2)^2 \le 10$

$\Rightarrow -\sqrt{10} \le | \ | - 2 \le \sqrt{10}$

$\therefore$ The greatest value of $= |z| \ 2 + \sqrt{10} \simeq 5.162$

$\therefore$ The greatest integral value of $|z|$ is 5.

ILLUSTRATION 34: If $a > 0$, $z\,|z| + az + 1 = 0$, show that z is a negative real number.

SOLUTION: $z\,|z| + az + 1 = 0 \Rightarrow z(|z| + a) = -1 \Rightarrow z = -\dfrac{1}{a+|z|} < 0\,[\because a > 0]$

Hence z is a negative real number

Second method: Let $z = x + iy$

Now $z\,|z| + az + 1 = 0 \quad \Rightarrow (x + iy)\sqrt{x^2+y^2} + a(x + iy) + 1 = 0$

$\Rightarrow x\sqrt{x^2+y^2} + ax + 1 + iy(\sqrt{x^2+y^2} + a) = 0 + i0$ ...(i)

Equating real and imaginary parts, we get $x\sqrt{x^2+y^2} + ax + 1 = 0$ .....(i)

and $y(\sqrt{x^2+y^2} + a) = 0 \Rightarrow y = 0\left[\because a > 0 \Rightarrow \sqrt{x^2+y^2} + a > 0\right]$

when $y = 0$, form (i), $x\sqrt{x^2} + ax + 1 = 0 \Rightarrow x|x| + ax + 1 = 0]$

$\Rightarrow x = \dfrac{-1}{a+|x|} < 0 \qquad \Rightarrow z = x < 0$, i.e., negative real number

ILLUSTRATION 35: Find the range of real number 'α' for which the equation $z + \alpha|z - 1| + 2i = 0$; $z = x + iy$ has a solution. Also find the solution.

SOLUTION: $z = x + iy$ where $x, y \in \mathbb{R}$

Given, $z + \alpha\,|z - 1| + 2i = 0$ or $x + iy + \alpha\,|x + iy - 1| + 2i = 0$

or $x + \alpha\sqrt{x^2+y^2-2x+1} + i(y+2) = 0$

Equating real and imaginary parts, we get $x + \alpha\sqrt{x^2+y^2-2x+1} = 0$ ....(i)

and $y + 2 = 0$ ....(ii)

From (ii), $y = -2$

Putting the value of y in (i), we ge $x + \alpha\sqrt{x^2-2x+5} = 0$ ....(iii)

or $\alpha\sqrt{x^2-2x+5} = -x$ or $\alpha^2(x^2 - 2x + 5) = x^2$ or $(\alpha^2 - 1)x^2 - 2\alpha^2 x + 5\alpha^2 = 0$ ....(iv)

For $\alpha^2 = 1$; $x = 5/2$; For $\alpha^2 \neq 1$; Equation (iv) represents a quadratic equation.

Now for $x \in \mathbb{R}$; Disc ≥ 0; $\qquad 4\alpha^4 - 4(\alpha^2 - 1)(5\alpha^2) \geq 0$

$\Rightarrow \alpha^4 - 5\alpha^2(\alpha^2 - 1) \geq 0$; $\qquad \alpha^2(\alpha^2 - 5\alpha^2 + 5) \geq 5$

$\Rightarrow \alpha^2(5 - 4\alpha^2) \geq 0 \qquad \Rightarrow \alpha^2 \leq \dfrac{5}{4} \Rightarrow \alpha \in \left[\dfrac{-\sqrt{5}}{2}, \dfrac{\sqrt{5}}{2}\right]$

From (iii); $\dfrac{x}{\alpha} = -\sqrt{x^2-2x+5} = -\sqrt{(x-1)^2+4} \Rightarrow \dfrac{x}{\alpha} < 0$ ...(v)

Again from (iv), $x = \dfrac{\alpha^2 \pm \alpha\sqrt{5-4\alpha^2}}{(\alpha^2-1)} \Rightarrow \dfrac{x}{\alpha} = \dfrac{\alpha \pm \sqrt{5-4\alpha^2}}{(\alpha^2-1)}$ ....(vi)

In view of (v) and (vi), we get $\dfrac{\alpha \pm \sqrt{5-4\alpha^2}}{\alpha^2-1} < 0$

Case (i): Now $\dfrac{\alpha + \sqrt{5-4\alpha^2}}{\alpha^2-1} < 0$

Clearly $\alpha^2 > 1$ and $\alpha > 0$ is rejected and $\alpha^2 > 1$; $\alpha < 0$

$\Rightarrow \alpha < -\sqrt{5-4\alpha^2} \qquad \Rightarrow \sqrt{5-4\alpha^2} < -\alpha$

$\Rightarrow 5 - 4\alpha^2 < \alpha^2 \qquad (\because -\alpha > 0)$

$\Rightarrow \alpha^2 > 1$ (which is true) $\quad \therefore \quad \alpha \in \left(-\frac{\sqrt{5}}{2}, -1\right)$

Again $\frac{\alpha+\sqrt{5-4\alpha^2}}{\alpha^2-1} < 0$; For $\alpha^2 < 1; \alpha+\sqrt{5-4\alpha^2} > 0$

$\Rightarrow \sqrt{5-4\alpha^2} > -\alpha$; Which holds for $\alpha \geq 0$ i.e., for $\alpha \in [0, 1)$ and for $\alpha < 0$

$\Rightarrow 5 - 4\alpha^2 > \alpha^2 \qquad \Rightarrow \alpha^2 < 1$

Which is true i.e., $\alpha \in (-1, 1)$

Thus $\frac{x}{\alpha} = \frac{\alpha+\sqrt{5-4\alpha^2}}{\alpha^2-1}$ for $\alpha \in \left[\frac{-\sqrt{5}}{2}, 1\right) \sim \{-1\}$

Case (ii): Next, $\frac{\alpha-\sqrt{5-4\alpha^2}}{\alpha^2-1} < 0$

Clearly, $\alpha^2 < 1$; $\alpha < 0$ is rejected

$\therefore \alpha^2 < 1; \alpha \geq 0; \qquad \Rightarrow \alpha \in [0, 1)$

$\Rightarrow \alpha > \sqrt{5-4\alpha^2} \qquad \Rightarrow \alpha^2 > 5-4\alpha^2 \ (\because \alpha \geq 0)$

$\Rightarrow \alpha^2 > 1$, Which is not true. Now, for $\alpha^2 > 1$; $\alpha - \sqrt{5-4\alpha^2} < 0$

$\Rightarrow \alpha < \sqrt{5-4\alpha^2}$, which holds for $\alpha \leq 0$, i.e., for $\alpha \in \left[-\frac{\sqrt{5}}{2}, -1\right)$ and for $\alpha > 0$; $\alpha^2 < 5 - 4\alpha^2$.

$\Rightarrow \alpha^2 < 1$; which is not true.

$\therefore \frac{x}{\alpha} = \frac{\alpha-\sqrt{5-4\alpha^2}}{\alpha^2-1}$ for $\alpha \in \left[-\frac{\sqrt{5}}{2}, 1\right)$

Thus the final solution are $z = \begin{cases} \frac{5}{2} - 2i & \text{for } \alpha = \pm 1 \\ \frac{\alpha^2 \pm \alpha\sqrt{5-4\alpha^2}}{\alpha^2-1} - 2i & \text{for } \alpha \in \left[-\frac{\sqrt{5}}{2}, -1\right) \\ \frac{\alpha^2 + \alpha\sqrt{5-4\alpha^2}}{\alpha^2-1} - 2i & \text{for } \alpha \in (-1, 1) \end{cases}$

ILLUSTRATION 36: For every real number $a \geq 0$, find all the complex numbers z satisfying the equation $2|z| - 4az + 1 + ia = 0$

SOLUTION: Let $z = x + iy$, where $x, y \in \mathbb{R}$

Given $2|z| - 4az + 1 + ia = 0; \alpha \geq 0$ ....(i)

$\therefore \ 2\sqrt{x^2+y^2} - 4a(x+iy) + 1 + ia = 0$ or $2\sqrt{x^2+y^2} - 4ax + 1 - i(4ay - a) = 0$

Equating real and imaginary parts, we get $2\sqrt{x^2+y^2} - 4ax + 1 = 0$ ....(ii)

and $4ay - a = 0 \Rightarrow y = 1/4$, [$\because$ from (i), $a \neq 0$]

Putting the value of y in (ii), we get $2\sqrt{x^2 + \frac{1}{16}} = 4ax - 1$ ...(iii)

or $4\left(x^2 + \frac{1}{16}\right) = 16a^2x^2 + 1 - 8ax \qquad$ or $(4 - 16a^2)x^2 + 8ax - \frac{3}{4} = 0$

$$\therefore \quad x=\frac{-8a\pm\sqrt{64a^2+4(4-16a^2)\frac{3}{4}}}{2(4-16a^2)}=\frac{-8a\pm\sqrt{16a^2+12}}{2(4-16a^2)}=\frac{4a\pm\sqrt{4a^2+3}}{4(4a^2-1)} \qquad \text{........(iv)}$$

From (ii), $4ax = 1 + 2\sqrt{x^2+\frac{1}{16}} \ge 1+2\sqrt{0^2+\frac{1}{16}}=\frac{3}{2} \Rightarrow x \ge \frac{3}{8a} \Rightarrow x>0 \text{ as } a>0$ ....(v)

Case-I: When $x=\dfrac{4a-\sqrt{4a^2+3}}{4(4a^2-1)}$; Now form (v), $\dfrac{4a-\sqrt{4a^2+3}}{4(4a^2-1)}-\dfrac{3}{8a}\ge 0$

$\Rightarrow \dfrac{2a(4a-\sqrt{4a^2+3})-3(4a^2-1)}{8a(4a^2-1)}\ge 0$ $\qquad\Rightarrow$ Now $3-4a^2-2a\sqrt{4a^2+3}=0$

$\Rightarrow (3-4a^2)^2 = 4a^2(4a^2+3)$ $\qquad\Rightarrow 9-36a^2=0 \Rightarrow a=\frac{1}{2}\,[\because a>0]$

Also $8a(4a^2-1)=0 \Rightarrow a = 1/2$ [$\because a>0$]; Sign scheme for $\dfrac{3-4a^2-2a\sqrt{4a^2+3}}{8a(4a^2-1)}$

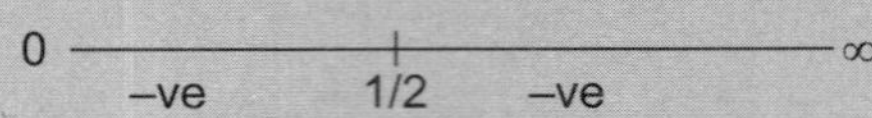

FIGURE 5.16

$\therefore \dfrac{3-4a^2-2a\sqrt{4a^2+3}}{8(4a^2-1)}\ge 0$ for no value of a (>0)

Case-II: When $x=\dfrac{4a+\sqrt{4a^2+3}}{4(4a^2-1)}$ From (v) $\dfrac{4a+\sqrt{4a^2+3}}{4(4a^2-1)}\ge\dfrac{3}{8a}$

$\Rightarrow \dfrac{3-4a^2+2a\sqrt{4a^2+3}}{8a(4a^2-1)}\ge 0$; Now $3-4a^2+2a\sqrt{4a^2+3}=0$ $\qquad(\because a>0)$

Now, sign scheme for $\dfrac{3-4a^2+2a\sqrt{4a^2+3}}{8a(4a^2-1)}$ is as follows

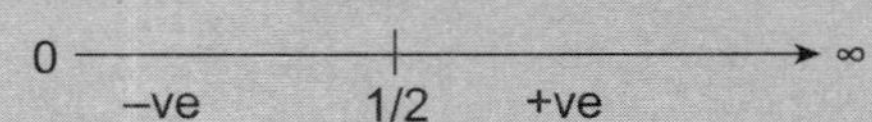

FIGURE 5.20

$\therefore \dfrac{3-4a^2+2a\sqrt{4a^2+3}}{8a(4a^2-1)}>0$ for $\frac{1}{2}<a<\infty$; Thus $z=x+iy=\dfrac{4a+\sqrt{4a^2+3}}{4(4a^2-1)}+\dfrac{1}{4}i$

when $\frac{1}{2}<a<\infty$; For $0\le a\le\frac{1}{2}$, no value of z is possible

ILLUSTRATION 37: If α and β are any two complex numbers, show that

$$\left|\alpha+\sqrt{\alpha^2-\beta^2}\right|+\left|\alpha-\sqrt{\alpha^2-\beta^2}\right|=|\alpha+\beta|+|\alpha-\beta|$$

SOLUTION: For any two complex numbers z_1 and z_2, we have

$$|z_1+z_2|^2+|z_1-z_2|^2=2|z_1|^2+2|z_2|^2 \qquad \text{.....(i)}$$

Let $z_1=\sqrt{\alpha^2-\beta^2}$ and $z_2=\alpha-\sqrt{\alpha^2-\beta^2}$

Then L.H.S $= |z_1| + |z_2|$

Now, $(|z_1| + |z_2|)^2 = |z_1|^2 + |z_2|^2 + 2|z_1|\,|z_2|$

$$= \frac{1}{2}\left[|z_1+z_2|^2 + |z_1-z_2|^2\right] + 2|z_1||z_2| = \frac{1}{2}\left[|2\alpha|^2 + \left|2\sqrt{\alpha^2-\beta^2}\right|^2\right] + 2|\beta^2|$$

$$= \frac{1}{2}\left[4|\alpha|^2 + 4|\alpha^2-\beta^2|\right] + 2|\beta|^2 = 2|\alpha|^2 + 2|\alpha^2-\beta^2| + 2|\beta|^2$$

$$= 2[|\alpha^2-\beta^2| + |\alpha^2| + |\beta^2|] = 2(|\alpha|^2 + |\beta|^2) + 2|\alpha-\beta||\alpha+\beta|$$

$$= |\alpha+\beta|^2 + |\alpha-\beta|^2 + 2|\alpha-\beta||\alpha+\beta| = (|\alpha+\beta| + |\alpha-\beta|)^2$$

$\therefore\ (|z_1| + |z_2|)^2 = (|\alpha+\beta| + |\alpha-\beta|)^2 \quad \Rightarrow |z_1| + |z_2| = |\alpha+\beta| + |\alpha-\beta|$

TEXTUAL EXERCISE 6: (SUBJECTIVE)

1. Find the modulus and amplitude of $\dfrac{1}{(1-i)^2} - \dfrac{1}{(1+i)^2}$
2. Find the argument of the following:

   (a) $-\sqrt{3}-i$ (b) $\dfrac{1+i}{1-\sqrt{3}i}$
3. If $z = \dfrac{(1+i)(1+\sqrt{3}\,i)^2}{(1-i)}$, then find $|z|$ and argz.
4. Find the principal argument of complex number

   (i) $-1-i$ (ii) $-1+\sqrt{3}i$
5. If $z_1 = 3i$ and $z_2 = -1-i$, find the value of $\arg\dfrac{z_1}{z_2}$
6. If $|z_1 + z_2| = |z_1 - z_2|$ prove that amp z_1 − amp $z_2 = \pm\dfrac{\pi}{2}$.
7. If $z + \sqrt{2}\,|z+1| + i = 0$, then express z in the form of $a + ib$ and find the principal value of the arg z.

Answer Key

1. $1, \pi/2$ **2.** (a) $7\pi/6$ (b) $-5\pi/12$ **3.** $4, 7\pi/6$ **4.** **(i)** $-3\pi/4$ (ii) $2\pi/3$
5. $-3\pi/4$ **7.** $z = -2-i$ and $\arg z = -(\pi/2 + \tan^{-1}2)$

TEXTUAL EXERCISE 6: (OBJECTIVE)

1. If Arg $(z) = \theta$, then Arg $(\bar{z})$ =

   (a) θ (b) $-\theta$
   (c) $\pi-\theta$ (d) $\theta-\pi$
2. The sum of amplitude of z and another complex number is π. The other complex number can be written as

   (a) $\bar{z}$ (b) $-\bar{z}$
   (c) z (d) $-z$
3. If $z_r = \cos(\pi/3^r) + i\sin(\pi/3^r)$, $r = 1, 2, 3,\ldots$, then $z_1 . z_2 . z_3 =$

   (a) 1 (b) $-i$
   (c) i (d) -1
4. If $a = \cos\alpha + i\sin\alpha$ and $b = \cos\beta + i\sin\beta$, then $\dfrac{1}{2}\left(ab + \dfrac{1}{ab}\right)$

   (a) $\cos(\alpha+\beta)$ (b) $\sin(\alpha+\beta)$
   (c) $\cos(\alpha-\beta)$ (d) $\sin(\alpha-\beta)$
5. If $z = C_1.C_2.C_3.C_4$ where $C_r = \cos\dfrac{r\pi}{10} + i\sin\dfrac{r\pi}{10}$, then arg z =

   (a) 0 (b) π
   (c) $-\pi/2$ (d) None of these
6. If $(\cos\alpha + i\sin\alpha)(\cos 2\alpha + i\sin 2\alpha)\ldots\ldots\ldots.(\cos n\alpha + i\sin n\alpha) = 1$, then the value of α is

(a) $4m\pi$ (b) $\frac{2m\pi}{n(n+1)}$

(c) $\frac{4m\pi}{n(n+1)}$ (d) $\frac{m\pi}{n(n+1)}$

7. For any integer n, the argument of $z = \frac{(\sqrt{3}+i)^{4n+1}}{(1-i\sqrt{3})}$ is:

(a) $\pi/6$ (b) $\pi/3$

(c) $\pi/2$ (d) $2\pi/3$

8. If $z = x + iy$, $|z + 1| = |z - 1|$ and $\arg\left(\frac{z-1}{z+1}\right) = \frac{\pi}{4}$ then $z =$

(a) $(\sqrt{2}+1)i$ (b) $(1-\sqrt{2})i$

(c) $\sqrt{2}-1$ (d) $(\sqrt{2}-1)i$

9. If $a = \cos\alpha + i\sin\alpha$, $b = \cos\beta + i\sin\beta$, $c = \cos\gamma + i\sin\gamma$ and $\frac{b}{c}+\frac{c}{a}+\frac{a}{b} = 1$, then $\cos(\beta - \gamma) + \cos(\gamma - \beta) + \cos(\alpha - \beta) =$

(a) 3/2 (b) –3/2

(c) 0 (d) 1

10. If $|z_1z_2| = |2\cos\pi/4 - 2i\sin\pi/4|$ and $\arg\left(\frac{z_1}{z_2}\right) = \frac{\pi}{3}$, then $z_1^2\bar{z}_2^2 =$

(a) $2 - (-1 - i\sqrt{3})$ (b) $2(-1+\sqrt{3})$

(c) $4(-1+\sqrt{3})$ (d) $4(1+i\sqrt{3})$

11. The solution of the equation $|z| - z = 1 + 2i$

(a) $2 - \frac{3}{2}i$ (b) $\frac{3}{2} + 2i$

(c) $\frac{3}{2} - 2i$ (d) $-2 + \frac{3}{2}i$

12. The amplitude of the complex number $z = \sin\alpha + i(1 - \cos\alpha)$is

(a) $2\sin\frac{\alpha}{2}$ (b) $\frac{\alpha}{2}$

(c) α (d) None of these

13. $\arg\left(\frac{3+i}{2-i}+\frac{3-i}{2+i}\right)$ is equal to

(a) $\pi/2$ (b) $-\pi/2$

(c) 0 (d) $\pi/4$

14. If $z_1 z_2 .... z_n = z_a$ then $\text{Arg}\, z_1 + \text{Arg}\, z_2 + ... + \text{Arg}\, z_n$ and arg z differ by

(a) Multiple of 2π (b) Multiple of $\pi/2$

(c) Greater than π (d) Less than π

15. If $|z| = 4$ and arg $z = -\pi/4$ then z is

(a) $2\sqrt{2}+i2\sqrt{2}$ (b) $-2\sqrt{2}+i\sqrt{2}$

(c) $2\sqrt{2}-i2\sqrt{2}$ (d) None of these

16. If z_1 and z_2 are two non-zero complex numbers such that $|z_1 + z_2| = |z_1| + |z_2|$ then $\text{Arg}\, z_1 - \text{Arg}\, z_2$ is equal to

(a) $-\pi$ (b) $\pi/2$

(c) $-\pi/2$ (d) 0

Answer Key

1. (b)	**2.** (b)	**3.** (c)	**4.** (a)	**5.** (b)	**6.** (c)	**7.** (c)	**8.** (a)	**9.** (d)	**10.** (b)
11. (c)	**12.** (b)	**13.** (c)	**14.** (a)	**15.** (c)	**16.** (d)				

SOLVING AN EQUATION CONSISTING OF COMPLEX VARIABLES

Let the given equation be $f(z) = g(z)$. To solve this equation we have following four methods.

Method 1: Put $z = x + iy$ in the given equation and equate the real and imaginary parts of both sides and solve to find x and y and hence $z = x + iy$.

ILLUSTRATION 38: Solve the equation $z^2 = 5 + 12i$ for complex number z

SOLUTION: Given equation is $z^2 = 5 + 12i$; putting $z = x + iy$, we get $x^2 - y^2 + 2ixy = 5 + 12i$.

comparing real and imaginary parts of LHS and RHS, we get $x^2 - y^2 = 5$ ....(1)

and $2xy = 12$ ....(2)

$\therefore y = \frac{6}{x}$, putting in equation (1), we get $x^2 - \frac{36}{x^2} = 5 \Rightarrow (x^2 - 9)(x^2 + 4) = 0$

$\Rightarrow x = -3$ and $y = -2$ or $x = 3$ and $y = 2$ $\Rightarrow$ (–3, –2) and (3 ,2) are solutions.

i.e., $z = (-3 - 2i), (3 + 2i)$ are the required solutions.

Method 2: Put $z = r(\cos\theta + i\sin\theta)$ and equate the real and imaginary parts of both sides and solve to get r and θ and hence z.

ILLUSTRATION 39: Solve the equation $2z^2 = 1 + \sqrt{3}i$

SOLUTION: Given equation is $2z^2 = 1 + \sqrt{3}i$; Put $z = r(\cos\theta + i\sin\theta)$

$\Rightarrow 2r^2(\cos\theta + i\sin\theta)^2 = 1 + \sqrt{3}i \Rightarrow 2r^2(\cos 2\theta + i\sin 2\theta) = 1 + \sqrt{3}i$

$\Rightarrow 2r^2\cos 2\theta + 2r^2 i\sin 2\theta = 1 + \sqrt{3}i \Rightarrow 2r^2\cos 2\theta = 1; 2r^2\sin 2\theta = \sqrt{3}$

$\Rightarrow \tan 2\theta = \sqrt{3}$ $\Rightarrow 2\theta = \frac{\pi}{3}$ (Taking Principal Argument)

$\Rightarrow \theta = \frac{\pi}{6} \Rightarrow 2r^2\sin\frac{\pi}{3} = \sqrt{3} \Rightarrow 2r^2.\frac{\sqrt{3}}{2} = \sqrt{3}$

$\Rightarrow r^2 = 1$ $\Rightarrow r = \pm 1$ $\Rightarrow z = \pm\left(\frac{\sqrt{3}}{2} - i\frac{1}{2}\right)$

Method 3: Take conjugate of both sides of given equations . Thus we get two equations. $f(z) = g(z)$ ...... (1)

and $f(\bar{z}) = g(\bar{z})$ ....(2)

Adding and Subtracting above two equations we get two new equations solving which we get z.

ILLUSTRATION 40: Solve the equation $z^2 - 1 = z + 5$

SOLUTION: $z^2 - 1 = z + 5$ . . . . (i)

Taking conjugate, we get $\left(\overline{z^2 - 1}\right) = \left(\overline{z + 5}\right) \Rightarrow (\bar{z})^2 - 1 = \bar{z} + 5$ ....(ii)

equation (i) + (ii) gives $z^2 + \bar{z}^2 - 2 = z + \bar{z} + 10$ ....(iii)

equation (i) – (ii) gives $z^2 - \bar{z}^2 = z - \bar{z}$ ....(iv)

From equation (iii), $(z + \bar{z})^2 - 2z\bar{z} - 2 = (z + \bar{z}) + 10$

$\Rightarrow (2x)^2 - 2(x^2 + y^2) - 2 = 2x + 10 \Rightarrow 4x^2 - 2x^2 - 2y^2 - 2 = 2x + 10$

$\Rightarrow 2x^2 - 2y^2 - 2x - 12 = 0 \Rightarrow x^2 - x - y^2 - 6 = 0 \Rightarrow x^2 - x - 6 = y^2$ ....(v)

Also from (iv) $(z - \bar{z})(z + \bar{z} - 1) = 0$ $\Rightarrow z = \bar{z}$ or $z + \bar{z} = 1$

$\Rightarrow y = 0$ or $x = \frac{1}{2}$; For $y = 0$; $x^2 - x - 6 = 0$ (from (v))

$\Rightarrow (x - 3)(x - 2) = 0 \Rightarrow x = 3$ or $x = 2$ for $x = 1/2$; $y^2 = \frac{1}{4} - \frac{1}{2} - 6 < 0$

$\Rightarrow y \notin \mathbb{R}$; (so rejected) $\therefore$ z = 2 or $z = 3$

Method 4: **Geometrical Solution:** From the given equation we follow the geometry of complex number z and find its locus.

ILLUSTRATION 41: If $|z| = 1$ and $z - 1 = ik(z + 1)$, then find range of k.

SOLUTION : $\because$ $|z| = 1$; z lies on a unit circle with centre at origin as shown below

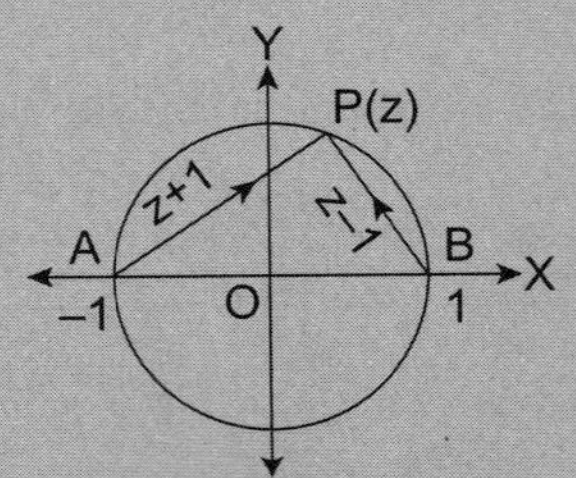

FIGURE 5.17

Now, $z - 1$ is $\overrightarrow{BP}$ and $z + 1$ is $\overrightarrow{AP}$;

Since $\angle APB = \dfrac{\pi}{2}$; P lies on upper or lower semi-circle

$$\therefore\ z - 1 = ik(z + 1) \Rightarrow |k| = \frac{|z-1|}{|z+1|} = \frac{BP}{AP}$$

$$\Rightarrow |k| \in [0, \infty) \Rightarrow k \in (-\infty, \infty) = \mathbb{R}$$

TEXTUAL EXERCISE 7: (SUBJECTIVE)

1. For every real number $c \geq 0$, find all complex numbers z which satisfy the equation $|z|^2 - 2iz + 2c(1 + i) = 0$.
2. Find all complex numbers satisfying the equation $2|z|^2 + z^2 - 5 + i\sqrt{3} = 0$
3. For every real number $a > 0$, find all complex numbers z satisfying the equation, $z|z| + az + i = 0$.
4. Solve the equation for z in complex number system
   (i) $z^3 = -\bar{z}$
   (ii) $z^2 = \bar{z}$
5. If $|z - 2| = 2|z - 1|$; where z is a complex number, then find $z\bar{z}$, where z lies on the line $x = 9$.
6. If $\sqrt[3]{a - ib} = x^2 + iy^2$, then show that $\dfrac{a}{x^2} + \dfrac{b}{y^2} = -2(x^4 + y^4)$.
7. If $\text{Arg}(z - 1) = \pi/4$ and $z - \bar{z} = 3i$, then find z
8. Find the solutions of the equations $2\sqrt{2}\,x^4 = (\sqrt{3} - 1) + i(\sqrt{3} - 1)$

Answer Key

1. $c \in \left[0, \sqrt{2} - 1\right]$

2. $z = \dfrac{1}{\sqrt{6}} - \dfrac{3}{\sqrt{2}}i,\ \dfrac{-1}{\sqrt{6}} + \dfrac{3}{\sqrt{2}}i,\ \sqrt{\dfrac{3}{2}} - \dfrac{1}{\sqrt{2}}i,\ -\sqrt{\dfrac{3}{2}} + \dfrac{1}{\sqrt{2}}i$

3. $z = \dfrac{a - \sqrt{a^2 + 4}}{2}i$

4. (i) $0, e^{\frac{\pi}{4}i}, e^{\frac{3\pi}{4}i}, e^{\frac{5\pi}{4}i}, e^{\frac{7\pi}{4}i}$ (ii) $0, 1 - \dfrac{1}{2} \pm i\dfrac{\sqrt{3}}{2}$

5. 12

7. $z = \dfrac{5}{2} + \dfrac{3}{2}i$

8. $\pm e^{5\pi/48}, \pm e^{19\pi/48}$

TEXTUAL EXERCISE 7: (OBJECTIVE)

1. If $iz^3 + z^2 - z + i = 0$, where $i = \sqrt{-1}$, then $|z|$ is equal to
(a) 1
(b) 1/2
(c) 1/4
(d) None of these

2. The solution of the equation $|z + 1| = z + 2 + 2i$ is
(a) $\frac{1}{2}(3 + 4i)$ (b) $\frac{1}{2}(1 + 6i)$
(c) $\frac{1}{2}(3 - 4i)$ (d) $\frac{1}{2}(1 - 4i)$

3. If z_n, $n = 1, 2, 3,..$ are solution of the system of equations $\left|\frac{z-12}{z-8i}\right| = \frac{5}{3}; \left|\frac{z-4}{z-8}\right| = 1$, then $\Sigma|z_n| =$
(a) 10 (b) 15
(c) 25 (d) None of these

4. Number of solutions of the equation $z^2 = z$ is
(a) 2 (b) 0
(c) 4 (d) ∞

5. If $iz^2 - \bar{z} = 0$, then $|z|$ is equal to
(a) 1 (b) 0
(c) 0 or 1 (d) None of these

6. If $|z - 3| = |z - 6|$ and $|z| = 5$, then z is
(a) $9 \pm \sqrt{19}i$ (b) $2 \pm 9i$
(c) $\frac{9}{2} \pm \frac{\sqrt{19}i}{2}$ (d) None of these

7. If $|z| = 1$ and $\frac{3}{2+z} = w$; where $w = a + ib$ and $|w| = \sqrt{la-3}$, then value of l is
(a) 5 (b) 3
(c) 6 (d) 4

8. If $\frac{1-ix}{1+ix} = a - ib$ for some $x \in \mathbb{R} \sim \{0\}$, then
(a) $(a - b)(a + b) = 1$ (b) $\left(\frac{a-b}{a+b}\right) = 1$
(c) $a^2 + b^2 = 1$ (d) None of these

9. If $z = x + iy$, then $|5z - 1| = 5|z - 2|$; then Re(z) is
(a) 1.2 (b) 1.1
(c) 2 (d) depends on z.

10. If $|z + 1| + |z - 3| = 6$ and $|z| = |z - 2|$, then z equals
(a) $1 \pm \sqrt{5}i$ (b) $2 \pm \sqrt{3}i$
(c) $-2 \pm \sqrt{5}i$ (d) None of these

Answer Key

1. (a) **2.** (d) **3.** (d) **4.** (a) **5.** (c) **6.** (c) **7.** (d) **8.** (c) **9.** (b) **10.** (a)

■ SQUARE ROOT OF A COMPLEX NUMBER

(1) Algebraic method:

If $z = a + ib$

Now square root of a complex number must be a complex number, therfore

Let $z^{1/2} = x + iy = (a + ib)^{1/2}$

Squaring both sides, we get $x^2 - y^2 + 2xyi = a + i\,b$

Equating R and I parts we get

$x^2 - y^2 = a$ ...(i)

$2xy = b$ ....(ii)

We have $(x^2 + y^2)^2 = (x^2 - y^2)^2 + 4x^2y^2 = a^2 + b^2$

$\Rightarrow x^2 + y^2 = \sqrt{a^2+b^2}$ [–ve root is rejected since $x^2 + y^2 \geq 0$]

$\therefore\ x^2 + y^2 = |z|$ ....(iii)

solving (i) and (iii) $x^2 = \frac{|z|+a}{2}$,

$y^2 = \pm\frac{|z|-a}{2}$

$\Rightarrow x = \pm\sqrt{\frac{|z|+a}{2}}, y = \sqrt{\frac{|z|-a}{2}}$

Where x, y have same sign for $b > 0$

$\Rightarrow z^{1/2} = \pm\left[\sqrt{\frac{|z|+a}{2}} + i\sqrt{\frac{|z|-a}{2}}\right]$

Further x, y have different signs for $b < 0$

$\Rightarrow z^{1/2} = \pm\left[\sqrt{\frac{|z|+a}{2}} - i\sqrt{\frac{|z|-a}{2}}\right]$

Hence square roots of $z = a + ib$ are given by

$$\pm\left[\sqrt{\frac{|z|+a}{2}}+i\sqrt{\frac{|z|-a}{2}}\right] \text{ for } b>0 \text{ and}$$

$$\pm\left[\sqrt{\frac{|z|+a}{2}}-i\sqrt{\frac{|z|-a}{2}}\right] \text{ for } b<0$$

2. *Trigonometric method*

If $z = r(\cos\theta + i\sin\theta)$

$$\text{Then } z^{1/2} = r^{1/2}\left(\cos\frac{2k\pi+\theta}{2}+i\sin\frac{2k\pi+\theta}{2}\right), k = 0, 1$$

$$= r^{1/2}\left(\cos\frac{\theta}{2}+i\sin\frac{\theta}{2}\right),$$

$$r^{1/2}\left(\cos\left(\pi+\frac{\theta}{2}\right)+i\sin\left(\pi+\frac{\theta}{2}\right)\right)$$

$$= \pm r^{1/2}\left(\cos\frac{\theta}{2}+i\sin\frac{\theta}{2}\right) = \pm r^{1/2}e^{i\theta/2}$$

Thus $z = re^{i\theta} = re^{i(\theta+2k\pi)} \Rightarrow z^{1/2} = r^{1/2}\, e^{i\left(\frac{2k\pi+\theta}{2}\right)}$
where $k = 0, 1$

3. Shortcut method

Let $z_0 = a + ib$ and let $\sqrt{a+ib} = x+iy$

Step 1: Consider $\frac{I_m(z_0)}{2} = \frac{b}{2}$

Step 2: Factorise $b/2$ into factors x.
$y{:}x^2 - y^2 = Re(z_0) = a$

Step 3: Therefore $a + ib = (x + iy)^2$
$\Rightarrow \sqrt{a+ib} = \pm(x+iy)$

Note

If $\sqrt{z} = \pm z_1$ then $\sqrt{\bar{z}} = \pm \bar{z}_1$

ILLUSTRATION 42: Find the square root of $8 - 15i$.

SOLUTION: **Algebraic method**:

Let $\sqrt{8-15i} = x+iy \quad \Rightarrow 8 - 15i = x^2 - y^2 + i(2xy)$

Equating Real and Imaginary parts, we get $x^2 - y^2 = 8$ ....(1)

and $2xy = -15$ ....(2)

Now, $(x^2 + y^2)^2 = (x^2 - y^2)^2 + 4x^2y^2 = (8)^2 + (15)^2 = 64 + 225 = 289$

$\Rightarrow x^2 + y^2 = 17$ ....(3)

(1) + (3) gives $2x^2 = 25$; $x^2 = 25/2$

$\Rightarrow x = \frac{\pm5}{\sqrt{2}}$ $\therefore$ (3) – (1) gives, $2y^2 = 9$; $y^2 = 9/2$; $y = \frac{\pm3}{\sqrt{2}}$ $\because 2xy = -15 < 0$

$\Rightarrow$ x and y are of opposite sign

$$\therefore \sqrt{8-5i} = \frac{5}{\sqrt{2}}-\frac{3}{\sqrt{2}}i \text{ or } \frac{-5}{\sqrt{2}}+\frac{3}{\sqrt{2}}i$$

$$\therefore \sqrt{8-5i} = \pm\left(\frac{5}{\sqrt{2}}-\frac{3}{\sqrt{2}}i\right) = \pm\frac{1}{\sqrt{2}}(5-3i)$$

Short-cut Method: $(8 - 15i) = a + ib \quad \Rightarrow a = 8, b = -15$

Now $30/2 = 15 = p \quad \therefore\ b/2 = -15/2 = x.y$ such that $x^2 - y^2 = a = 8$

$\Rightarrow x = \frac{-5}{\sqrt{2}}, y = \frac{3}{\sqrt{2}}$ or $x = \frac{5}{\sqrt{2}}, y = \frac{-3}{\sqrt{2}}$ $\quad \therefore\ (a + ib) = (x^2 - y^2) + i2xy = (x + iy)^2$

$\Rightarrow \sqrt{a+ib} = x+iy \quad \Rightarrow \sqrt{8-15i} = \pm\frac{1}{2}(5-3i)$

ILLUSTRATION 43: Find the square root of $7 - 30\sqrt{2}i$

SOLUTION: **Algebraic method:**

Let $\sqrt{7-30\sqrt{2}i} = x+iy \Rightarrow 7-30\sqrt{2}i = x^2 - y^2 + i(2xy)$

Equating real and imaginary parts, we get $x^2 - y^2 = 7$ ....(1)

and $2xy = -30\sqrt{2}$ ......(2)

Now, $(x^2 + y^2)^2 = (x^2 - y^2)^2 + (2xy)^2 = (7)^2 + (-30\sqrt{2})^2 = 49 + 1800 = 1849$

$\therefore\ x^2 + y^2 = \pm\sqrt{1849} = 43$ ......(3)

Now, (3) + (1) gives $2x^2 = 50$

$\Rightarrow x^2 = 25$ $\qquad \Rightarrow x = \pm 5$; (3) – (1) gives, $2y^2 = 36 \Rightarrow y^2 = 18$

$\Rightarrow y = \pm 3\sqrt{2}$ $\qquad \because\ 2xy = -30\sqrt{2} < 0$

$\Rightarrow$ x and y must be of opposite signs

$\therefore$ If $x = 5, y = -3\sqrt{2}$ and If $x = -5, y = 3\sqrt{2}$ $\therefore\ \sqrt{7-30\sqrt{-2}} = \pm(5-3\sqrt{2}i)$

Short-cut method: $7-30\sqrt{2}i$; Imaginary part = $-30\sqrt{2}i$ (divisible by 2)

Now $\frac{30\sqrt{2}}{2} = -15\sqrt{2} = \frac{}{2} = x.y$ such that $x^2 - y^2 = a = 7 > 0 \Rightarrow |x| > |y|$

$\Rightarrow$ factors of b are $-5\times 3\sqrt{2}$ or $-5\sqrt{2}\times 3$

or $-15\times\sqrt{2}$ or $-15\sqrt{2}\times 1$ and $(5)^2 - (3\sqrt{2})^2 = 25 - 18 = 7 \Rightarrow x = \pm 5, y = \pm 3\sqrt{2}$

$\because\ xy < 0 \Rightarrow x = 5, y = -3\sqrt{2}$ or $x = -5, y = 3\sqrt{2}$

$\therefore\ 7 - 30\sqrt{2}i = (5 - 3\sqrt{2}i)^2$ or $(-5 + 3\sqrt{2}i)^2$ $\qquad \therefore\ \sqrt{7-30\sqrt{2}i} = \pm(5-3\sqrt{2}i)$

ILLUSTRATION 44: Find the square root of $\sqrt{i}+\sqrt{-i}$

SOLUTION: $i = 0 + 1i = 1/2\,(0 + 2i)$. Imaginary part = 2

$\therefore\ \frac{b}{2} = \frac{2}{2} = 1 = x.y$ such that $x^2 - y^2 = a = 0 \quad \Rightarrow (x, y) = (1, 1)$ or $(-1, -1)$

$\therefore\ \sqrt{i} = \pm\frac{1}{\sqrt{2}}(1+i)$; Taking conjugate, $\sqrt{-i} = \pm\frac{1}{\sqrt{2}}(1-i)$

$\therefore\ \sqrt{i}+\sqrt{-i} = \pm\frac{1}{\sqrt{2}}(1+i)\pm\frac{1}{\sqrt{2}}(1-i)$

$= \frac{1}{\sqrt{2}}[\pm(1+i)\pm(1-i)] = \frac{1}{\sqrt{2}}[2]; \frac{1}{\sqrt{2}}(2i); \frac{1}{\sqrt{2}}(-2i); \frac{1}{\sqrt{2}}(-2) = \pm\sqrt{2}; \pm\sqrt{2}i$

ILLUSTRATION 45: Find the roots of $\sqrt[4]{-81}$.

SOLUTION: $(-81)^{1/4} = (81i^2)^{1/4} = (\pm 9i)^{1/2} = 3\sqrt{i}, 3\sqrt{-i}$

As found above, $\sqrt{i} = \pm\frac{1}{\sqrt{2}}(1+i)$ and $\sqrt{-i} = \pm\frac{1}{\sqrt{2}}(1-i)$

$\therefore\ \sqrt[4]{-81} = (3\sqrt{i}) = 3\left(\pm\frac{1}{\sqrt{2}}(1+i)\right)$ and $3\sqrt{-i} = 3\left(\pm\frac{1}{\sqrt{2}}(1-i)\right)$

$\therefore\ \sqrt[4]{-81} = \pm\frac{3}{\sqrt{2}}(1\pm i)$ **Ans**

■ CUBE ROOT OF UNITY

Let $\sqrt[3]{1}$ = cube root of unity

$\Rightarrow x^3 = 1 \Rightarrow (x-1)(x^2+x+1) = 0$

$\Rightarrow x = 1$ or $x = \dfrac{-1\pm\sqrt{1-4}}{2} = \dfrac{-1\pm\sqrt{3}i}{2} = \omega, \omega^2$

where $\omega = \dfrac{-1+\sqrt{3}i}{2}$ and $\omega^2 = \dfrac{-1-\sqrt{3}i}{2}$

$\therefore$ Cube roots of unity are 1, ω, ω^2 and ω, ω^2 are called the imaginary cube roots of unity

■ PROPERTIES OF CUBE ROOTS OF UNITY

P(1): $|\omega| = |\omega^2| = 1$

Proof: $\left|\dfrac{-1}{2}\pm\dfrac{\sqrt{3}i}{2}\right| = \sqrt{\left(\dfrac{-1}{2}\right)^2+\left(\dfrac{\pm\sqrt{3}}{2}\right)^2} = \sqrt{\dfrac{1}{4}+\dfrac{3}{4}} = 1$

P(2): $\bar{\omega} = \omega^2$

Proof: $\omega = \dfrac{-1}{2}+\dfrac{\sqrt{3}}{2}i \Rightarrow \bar{\omega} = \dfrac{-1}{2}-\dfrac{\sqrt{3}}{2}i = \omega^2$

P(3): $\omega^3 = 1$

Proof: $\omega^3 = \omega.\omega^2 = \left[\dfrac{-1+\sqrt{3}i}{2}\right]\left[\dfrac{-1-\sqrt{3}i}{2}\right]$

$= \left(\dfrac{-1}{2}\right)^2 - \left(\dfrac{\sqrt{3}}{2}i\right)^2 = \dfrac{1}{4}+\dfrac{3}{4} = 1$

P(4): $\omega^{3n} = 1$; $\omega^{3n+1} = \omega$ and $\omega^{3n+2} = \omega^2\ \forall n\in\mathbb{Z}$

Proof: $(\omega^{3n}) = (\omega^3)^n = (1)^n = 1$;

$\omega^{3n+1} = \omega^{3n}.\omega = 1.\omega = \omega$ and

$\omega^{3n+2} = \omega^{3n}.\omega^2 = 1.\omega^2 = \omega^2\ \forall n\in\mathbb{Z}$

P(5): Sum of cube roots of unity is 0

i.e., $1+\omega+\omega^2 = 0$

Proof: $1+\omega+\omega^2 = 1+\left(\dfrac{-1}{2}+\dfrac{\sqrt{3}}{2}i\right)+\left(\dfrac{-1}{2}-\dfrac{\sqrt{3}}{2}i\right) = 0$

Remarks

1. $\because\ \bar{\omega} = \omega^2$ and $1+\omega+\omega^2 = 0 \Rightarrow 1+\omega+\bar{\omega} = 0$
2. $\because\ \bar{\omega} = \omega^2$ and $\omega = \omega.1 = \omega.\omega^3 = \omega^4 = (\omega^2)^2 = (\bar{\omega})^2$ $\therefore\ 1+\omega+\omega^2 = 1+(\bar{\omega})^2+\bar{\omega} \Rightarrow 1+\bar{\omega}+(\bar{\omega})^2 = 0$

P(6): $1+\omega^n+\omega^{2n} = \begin{cases}3; \text{when } n \text{ is a multiple of } 3\\ 0; \text{when } n \text{ is not a multiple of } 3\end{cases}$

Proof: Case (i) When $n = 3k$; $k\in\mathbb{Z}$, then $1+\omega^n+\omega^{2n} = 1+\omega^{3k}+\omega^{6k} = 1+(\omega^3)^k+(\omega^3)^{2k} = 1+1+1 = 3$

Case (ii) When $n = 3k+1$; $k\in\mathbb{Z}$, then $1+\omega^n+\omega^{2n} = 1+\omega^{3k+1}+\omega^{6k+2} = 1+\omega+\omega^2 = 0$ $[\because \omega^{3k} = \omega^{6k} = 1]$

Case (iii) When $n = 3k+2$; $k\in\mathbb{Z}$, then $1+\omega^n+\omega^{2n} = 1+\omega^{3k+2}+\omega^{6k+4} = 1+\omega^2+\omega^4 = 1+\omega^2+\omega = 0$

P(7): 1, ω, ω^2 are the vertices of an equilateral Δ having each side $= \sqrt{3}$, as shown below

$\because\ AB = BC = AC = \sqrt{3}$

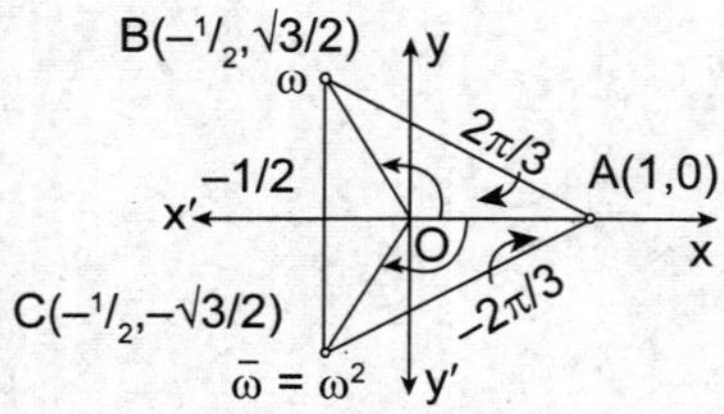

FIGURE 5.18

P(8): Circumcentre of ΔABC with vertices as cube roots of unity lies at origin and the radius of circumcircle is 1 unit

Clearly, $OA = OB = OC = 1$

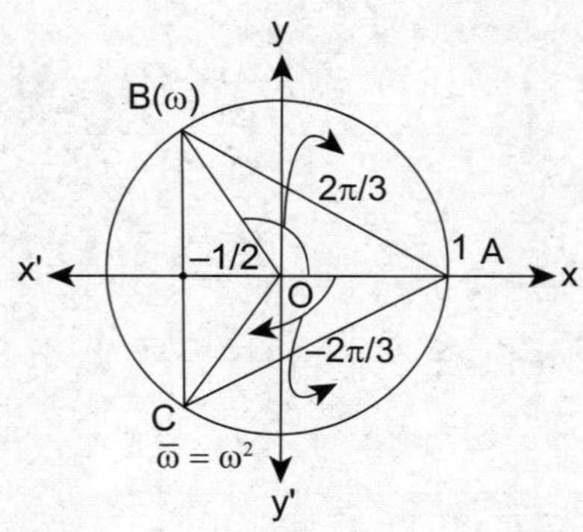

FIGURE 5.19

Remark

From above properties clearly cube roots of unity are the vertices of an equilateral Δ having each side = √3, and circumscribed by circle of unit radius and having its centre at origin.

P(9): $\arg(\omega) = \arg\left(-\frac{1}{2}+\frac{\sqrt{3}i}{2}\right) = \pi - \phi;$

$$\tan\phi = \left|\frac{\sqrt{3}/2}{-1/2}\right| = \sqrt{3} \text{ and } \phi \text{ is acute}$$

$\Rightarrow \phi = \pi/3$

$\Rightarrow \arg(\omega) = \pi - \pi/3 = 2\pi/3$

and $\arg(\omega^2) = \left(-\frac{1}{2}-\frac{\sqrt{3}}{2}i\right) = \pi + \phi;$

and $\tan\phi = \left|\frac{-\sqrt{3}/2}{-1/2}\right| = \sqrt{3}$; ϕ is acute

$\Rightarrow \phi = \pi/3$

$\therefore \arg(\omega^2) = \pi + \pi/3 = 4\pi/3$

P(10): Any complex number $a + ib$ for which $(a : b) = \frac{1}{\sqrt{3}}$ or $\sqrt{3} : 1$ can always be expressed in terms of i, w, w^2.

e.g.,: $1+i\sqrt{3} = -2\omega^2;$

$$\sqrt{3}+i = \frac{2i}{2}\left(1+\frac{\sqrt{3}}{i}\right) = \frac{2i}{2}\left(1-i\sqrt{3}\right)$$

$$= \frac{2}{i}\left(\frac{-1+i\sqrt{3}}{2}\right) = \frac{2\omega}{i}$$

IMPORTANT RELATIONS

(a) $x^2 + x + 1 = (x - \omega)(x - \omega^2)$

(b) $x^2 - x + 1 = (x + \omega)(x + \omega^2)$

(c) $x^2 + xy + y^2 = (x - y\omega)(x - y\omega^2)$

(d) $x^2 - xy + y^2 = (x + y\omega)(x + y\omega^2)$

(e) $x^2 + y^2 = (x + iy)(x - iy)$

(f) $x^3 + y^3 = (x + y)(x - y\omega)(x + y\omega^2)$

(g) $x^3 - y^3 = (x - y)(x - y\omega)(x - y\omega^2)$

(h) $x^2 + y^2 + z^2 - xy - yz - zx = (x + y\omega + z\omega^2)(x + y\omega^2 + z\omega)$

(i) $x^3 + y^3 + z^3 - 3xyz = (x + y + z)(x + y\omega + z\omega^2)(x + \omega^2 y + \omega z) = (x + y\omega^2 + z\omega)(x\omega + \omega^2 y + z)(x\omega^2 + y\omega + z)$

(j) Two points $P(z_1)$ and $Q(z_2)$ lie on the same side or opposite sides of the line $\bar{a}z + a\bar{z} + b$ accordingly as $\bar{a}z_1 + a\bar{z} + b$ and $\bar{a}z_2 + a\bar{z}_2 + b$ have same sign or opposite signs.

ILLUSTRATION 46: If ω is an imaginary cube root of unity, then evaluate $(1 + \omega - \omega^2)^7$

SOLUTION: We know that $1 + \omega + \omega^2 = 0$

$\therefore\ 1 + \omega - \omega^2 = -2\omega^2$ or $(1 + \omega - \omega^2)^7 = -128\omega^{14} = -128\omega^2$ $\quad\{\because \omega^3 = 1\}$

ILLUSTRATION 47: If α, β, γ be roots of $x^3 - 3x^2 + 3x + 26 = 0$, evaluate (a) $\sum\left(\frac{\alpha-1}{\beta-1}\right)$ (b) $\sum\left(\frac{\alpha-1}{\beta-1}\right)^2$

SOLUTION: $x^3 - 3x^2 + 3x + 26 = (x - 1)^3 + 27 = 0$

$\Rightarrow \left(\frac{x-1}{-3}\right) = 1^{1/3} = 1, \omega, \omega^2 \Rightarrow x - 1 = -3, -3\omega, -3\omega^2$

$\Rightarrow \alpha - 1 = -3, \beta - 1 = -3\omega, \gamma - 1 = -3\omega^2$

$$\Rightarrow \sum\left(\frac{\alpha-1}{\beta-1}\right) = \left(\frac{\alpha-1}{\beta-1}\right)+\left(\frac{\beta-1}{\gamma-1}\right)+\left(\frac{\gamma-1}{\alpha-1}\right) = \left(\frac{-3}{-3\omega}\right)+\left(\frac{-3\omega}{-3\omega^2}\right)+\left(\frac{-3\omega^2}{-3}\right) = 3\omega^2$$

$$\text{(b)} \sum\left(\frac{\alpha-1}{\beta-1}\right)^2 = \left(\sum\frac{\alpha-1}{\beta-1}\right)^2 - 2\sum\left(\frac{\alpha-1}{\beta-1}\right)\left(\frac{\beta-1}{\alpha-1}\right) = 9\omega - 2(\omega + \omega + \omega) = 3\omega.$$

ILLUSTRATION 48: If 1, ω, ω^2 are cube roots of unity, show that $(1 - \omega + \omega^2)(1 - \omega^2 + \omega^4)(1 - \omega^4 + \omega^8)$...$2n$ factors $= 2^{2n}$

SOLUTION: We know that $1 = \omega^3 = \omega^6 = \omega^9$.....................;

$\omega = \omega^4 = \omega^7 = \omega^{10} =$ ....; and $\omega^2 = \omega^5 = \omega^8 = \omega^{11} =$ ....

$\Rightarrow$ LHS $= (1 - \omega + \omega^2)(1 + \omega - \omega^2)(1 - \omega + \omega^2)$................$2n$ factors

$= (1 + \omega^2 - \omega)^n (1 + \omega - \omega^2)^n = (-\omega - \omega)^n (-\omega^2 - \omega^2)^n$

$= (-2\omega)^n (-2\omega^2)^n = (-2)^{2n} . (\omega^3)^n = 2^{2n}. 1 = 2^{2n} =$ RHS

ILLUSTRATION 49: If ω, ω^2 be the imaginary cube roots of unity, then prove that

(i) $(3 + 3\omega + 5\omega^2)^6 - (2 + 6\omega + 2\omega^2)^3 = 0$

(ii) $(2 - \omega)(2 - \omega^2)(2 - \omega^{10})(2 - \omega^{11}) = 49$

SOLUTION: (i) $(3 + 3\omega + 5\omega^2)^6 - (2 + 6\omega + 2\omega^2)^3$

$= (3 + 3\omega + 3\omega^2 + 2\omega^2)^6 - (2 + 2\omega + 2\omega^2 + 4\omega)^3$

$= \{3(1 + \omega + \omega^2) + 2\omega^2\}^6 - \{2(1 + \omega + \omega^2) + 4\omega\}^3$

$= (2\omega^2)^6 - (4\omega)^3$ [since $1 + \omega + \omega^2 = 0$]

$= 64\omega^{12} - 64\omega^3 = 64 - 64 = 0$

(ii) $(2 - \omega)(2 - \omega^2)(2 - \omega^{10})(2 - \omega^{11})$

$= (2 - \omega)(2 - \omega^2)(2 - \omega)(2 - \omega^2)$

$= (2 - \omega)^2 (2 - \omega^2)^2 = [(2 - \omega)(2 - \omega^2)]^2$

$= (4 - 2\omega - 2\omega^2 + \omega^3)^2 = [5 - 2(\omega + \omega^2)]^2$

$= (5 + 2)^2 = 49$

ILLUSTRATION 50: If ω is an imaginary cube root of unity, then show that

(i) $(1 - \omega)(1 - \omega^2)(1 - \omega^4)(1 - \omega^5) = 9$

(ii) $(1 - \omega + \omega^2)^5 + (1 + \omega - \omega^2)^5 = 32$

SOLUTION: $\because$ (i) $\omega^4 = \omega^3 . \omega = \omega$ and $\omega^5 = \omega^3 . \omega^2 = \omega^2$

$\therefore$ $(1 - \omega)(1 - \omega^2)(1 - \omega^4)(1 - \omega^2)$

$= (1 - \omega)(1 - \omega^2)(1 - \omega)(1 - \omega^2)$

$= (1 - \omega)^2 (1 - \omega^2)^2 = [(1 - \omega)(1 - \omega^2)]^2$

$= [1 - (\omega + \omega^2) + \omega^3]^2$

$= [1 - (-1) + 1]^2 = (3)^2 = 9$ $\quad$ [$\because 1 + \omega + \omega^2 = 0 \Rightarrow \omega + \omega^2 = -1$]

(ii) $(1 - \omega + \omega^2)^5 + (1 + \omega - \omega^2)^5$

$= (1 + \omega^2 - \omega)^5 + (1 + \omega - \omega^2)^5$

$= (-\omega - \omega)^5 + (-\omega^2 - \omega^2)^5$ [$\because$ $1 + \omega = -\omega^2$ and $1 + \omega^2 = -\omega$]

$= (-2\omega)^5 + (-2\omega^2)^5 = -32\omega^5 - 32\omega^{10} = -32\omega^2 - 32(\omega^3)^3 \cdot \omega$

$= -32\omega^2 - 32\omega = -32(\omega^2 + \omega) = (-32) \times (-1) = 32$

ILLUSTRATION 51: If ω is an imaginary cube root of unity, then evaluate $(1 + \omega)(1 + \omega^2)(1 + \omega^4)(1 + \omega^8)$.. to n factors .

SOLUTION: $(1 + \omega)(1 + \omega^2)(1 + \omega)(1 + \omega^2)$........ to n factors

$= (-\omega^2)(-\omega)(-\omega^2)(-\omega)$........ to n factors ...(i)

Case I: When $n = 2m$ (even)

L.H.S. $= (-\omega^2)(-\omega)(-\omega^2)(-\omega)$...... to $2m$ factors

$= [(-\omega^2)(-\omega)][(-\omega^2)(-\omega)]$...... to m factors $= \omega^3 . \omega^3 . \omega^3$...... to m factors $= 1$

Case II: When $n = 2m + 1$ (odd)

$= (-\omega^2)(-\omega)(-\omega^2)(-\omega)(-\omega^2)$..... to $(2m + 1)$ factors

$= [(-\omega^2)(-\omega)][(-\omega^2)(-\omega)]$...... to $2m$ factors$] (-\omega^2)$

$= (-\omega^2)(-\omega)^m(-\omega^2)^m = (-\omega^2)(\omega^3)^m = -\omega^2$

ILLUSTRATION 52: If 1, ω, ω^2 be the cube roots of unity, find the roots of the equation $(x-1)^3 + 8 = 0$

SOLUTION: Given equation is $(x-1)^3 + 8 = 0$ or $(x-1)^3 = -8 = (-2)^3$

$\therefore\ x - 1 = -2, -2\omega, -2\omega^2$ $\qquad \therefore\ x = -1, 1-2\omega, 1-2\omega^2$

Note

If one cube root of any real number is a, then its other two cube roots will $a\omega$ and $a\omega^2$

ILLUSTRATION 53: Show that $x^{3p} + x^{3q+1} + x^{3r+2}$, where p, q, r are positive integers is divisible by $x^2 + x + 1$

SOLUTION: **when $x^2 + x + 1 = 0$**

$\Rightarrow x = \omega$ or ω^2; When $x = \omega$,

$x^{3p} + x^{3q+1} + x^{3r+2} = \omega^{3p} + \omega^{3q+1} + \omega^{3r+2} = 1 + \omega + \omega^2 = 0$

When $x = \omega^2$,

$x^{3p} + x^{3q+1} + x^{3r+2} = \omega^{6p} + \omega^{6q+2} + \omega^{6r+4} = 1 + \omega^2 + \omega^4 = 1 + \omega^2 + \omega = 0$

Since all the roots of equation $x^2 + x + 1 = 0$ satisfy the equation

$x^{3p} + x^{3q+1} + x^{3r+2} = 0$

$\therefore\ x^{3p} + x^{3q+1} + x^{3r+2}$ is divisible by $x^2 + x + 1$

DEMOIVRE'S THEORM

It states that

(i) $(\cos\theta + i\sin\theta)^n = \cos n\theta + i\sin n\theta$ if n is an integer.

(ii) $(\cos\theta + i\sin\theta)^{p/q}$ has one of its values given by

$\cos\frac{p}{q}\theta + i\sin\frac{p}{q}\theta$ if $\frac{p}{q}$ is a rational number.

(iii) $(\cos\theta + i\sin\theta)^{1/n} = [\cos(\theta + 2k\pi) + i\sin(\theta + 2k\pi)]^{1/n}$

($\because$ period of $\sin\theta$ and $\cos\theta$ is 2π)

$$= \cos\frac{(2k\pi + \theta)}{n} + i\sin\frac{(2k\pi + \theta)}{n},\ k = 0,1,2,..,n-1.$$

n^{th} ROOTS OF UNITY

Let x be an nth root of unity, then

$$x = (1)^{\frac{1}{n}} = (\cos 0 + i\sin 0)^{\frac{1}{n}}$$

$$= \cos\left(\frac{2r\pi + 0}{n}\right) + i\sin\left(\frac{2r\pi + 0}{n}\right),\ r = 0; 1,2,.......,n-1.$$

$$= \cos\frac{2r\pi}{n} + i\sin\frac{2r\pi}{n};\ r = 0, 1, 2,....,n-1$$

$$= e^{\frac{i2r\pi}{n}};\ r = 0, 1,2,.....,n-1 = 1, e^{i\frac{2\pi}{n}} e^{i\frac{4\pi}{n}}, ...e^{i\frac{2(n-1)\pi}{n}}$$

$$= 1, \alpha, \alpha^2..... \alpha^{n-1}, \text{ where } \alpha = e^{i\frac{2\pi}{n}}$$

PROPERTIES OF nth ROOTS OF UNITY

P(1): n^{th} roots of unity form a G.P

P(2): $1 + \alpha + \alpha^2 + ... + \alpha^{n-1} = 0$

P(3): $1.\ \alpha.\alpha^2..\alpha^{n-1} = (-1)^{n-1}$

Proof: ***P(1):*** $\because$ n^{th} roots of unity are $1, \alpha, \alpha^2,...,\alpha^{n-1}$ where $\alpha = e^{i\frac{2\pi}{n}}$ which are clearly in *G.P* with common ratio α

P(2): $1+\alpha+\alpha^2+ \ldots + \alpha^{n-1} = \dfrac{1(1-\alpha^n)}{1-\alpha} = 0$

$$\left[\because \alpha^n = \left(e^{i\frac{2\pi}{n}}\right)^n = e^{i2\pi} = \cos 2\pi + i\sin 2\pi = 1\right]$$

P(3): $1.\ \alpha\ .\ \alpha^2 \ \ldots\ldots\ \alpha^{n-1} = \alpha^{1+2+\ldots+(n-1)}$

$$= \alpha^{\frac{(n-1)n}{2}} = \left(\alpha^{\frac{n}{2}}\right)^{n-1} = \left[\left(e^{i\frac{2\pi}{n}}\right)^{\frac{n}{2}}\right]^{n-1}$$

$$= (e^{i\pi})^{n-1} = (\cos\pi + i\sin\pi)^{n-1} = (-1)^{n-1}$$

P(4): n^{th} roots of unity are vertices of n sided regular polygon circumscribed by a unit circle having its centre at origin.

Case (i) When n is odd

Let $n = 2m + 1$, m is some positive integer, then only one root is real i.e., 1 and remaining $2m$ roots are non real complex conjugates. (shown in figure 5.24).

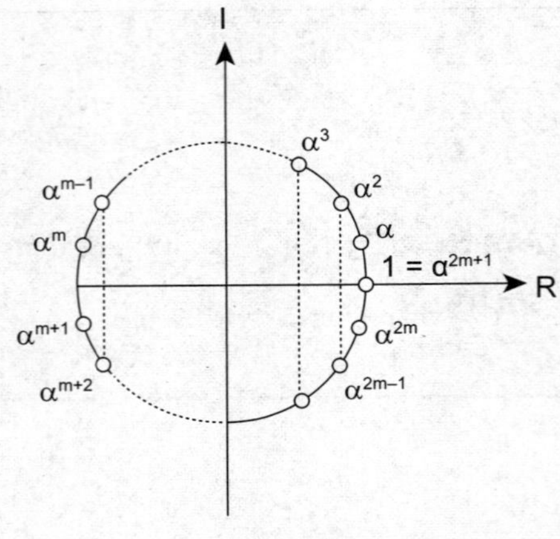

FIGURE 5.20

The $2m$ non-real roots are (α, α^{2m}), $(\alpha^2, \alpha^{2m-1})$, $(\alpha^3, \alpha^{2m-2})$ . . . . . (α^m, α^{m+1}) where the ordered pairs are $(z, \bar{z})$ i.e. non-real roots and their conjugates and $\alpha = e^{i\frac{2\pi}{n}}$.

Note

The nth roots given as ordered pairs are conjugate and reciprocal of each other.

$$\left\{\because \alpha^{-1} = \frac{1}{\alpha} = \frac{\alpha^{2m+1}}{\alpha} = \alpha^{2m} \text{ as } \alpha = \alpha^{2m+1} = 1; \overline{\alpha^m} = \left(\frac{1}{\alpha}\right)^m = \frac{1}{\alpha^m} = \frac{\alpha^{2m+1}}{\alpha^m} = \alpha^{m+1}\right\}$$

Case (ii) When n is even

Let $n = 2m$, $\alpha = cis\,\dfrac{2\pi}{n} = cis\left(\dfrac{\pi}{m}\right)$; except 1 and -1, other roots are non real complex conjugate pairs as shown in the (figure 5.25).

$$\alpha^m = cis\ \pi = -1 = \overline{\alpha^m} \text{ and}$$

$$\alpha^{m-1} = \alpha^m(\alpha^{-1}) = -1(\bar{\alpha}) = -\bar{\alpha}$$

$\alpha^{2m} = 1$	$\alpha,$	$\alpha^2,$	$\alpha^3,$	....,	α^{m-1}	$\alpha^m = -1$
	α^{2m-1}	α^{2m-2}	α^{2m-3}	....	α^{m+1}	

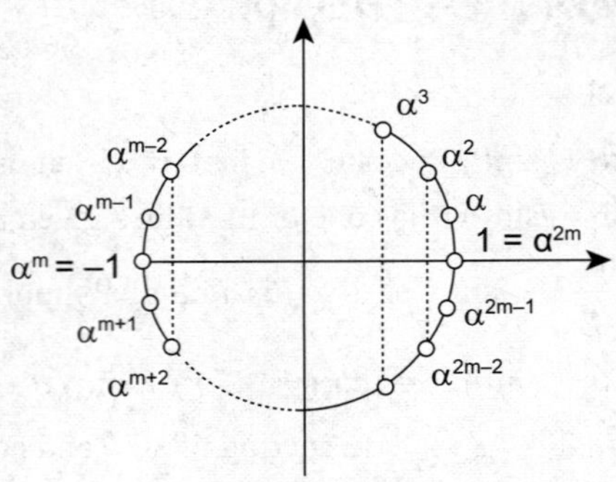

FIGURE 5.21

Note

The nth roots arranged vertically below are conjugate and reciprocal of each other and diagonally are negative of each other.

ILLUSTRATION 54: Show that $\left(\dfrac{\cos\theta + i\sin\theta}{\sin\theta + i\cos\theta}\right)^4 = \cos 8\theta + i\sin 8\theta$

SOLUTION: $(\cos\theta + i\sin\theta)^4 = \cos 4\theta + i\sin 4\theta$

$$(\sin\theta + i\cos\theta)^4 = \left[i\left(\cos\theta + \frac{1}{i}\sin\theta\right)\right]^4 = i^4(\cos\theta - i\sin\theta)^4 = \cos 4\theta - i\sin 4\theta$$

Now $\left(\dfrac{\cos\theta + i\sin\theta}{\sin\theta + i\cos\theta}\right)^4 = \dfrac{\cos 4\theta + i\sin 4\theta}{\cos 4\theta - i\sin 4\theta}$

$$= \frac{(\cos 4\theta + i\sin 4\theta)(\cos 4\theta + i\sin 4\theta)}{(\cos 4\theta - i\sin 4\theta)(\cos 4\theta + i\sin\theta)} = \frac{(\cos 4\theta + i\sin 4\theta)^2}{1} = \cos 8\theta + i\sin 8\theta$$

ILLUSTRATION 55: If $z^2 - 2z\cos\theta + 1 = 0$, show that $z^2 + z - 2 = 2\cos 2\theta$

SOLUTION: Given $z^2 - 2z\cos\theta + 1 = 0$

$$\therefore\ z = \frac{2\cos\theta \pm \sqrt{4\cos^2\theta - 4}}{2} = \cos\theta \pm \sqrt{\cos^2\theta - 1}$$

$$= \cos\theta \pm \sqrt{-\sin^2\theta} = \cos\theta \pm \sqrt{i^2\sin^2\theta} = \cos\theta \pm i\sin\theta$$

when $z = \cos\theta + i\sin\theta$

$z^2 + z^{-2} = \cos 2\theta + i\sin 2\theta + (\cos 2\theta - i\sin 2\theta) = 2\cos 2\theta$

when $z = \cos\theta - i\sin\theta$

$z^2 + z^{-2} = \cos 2\theta - i\sin 2\theta + \cos 2\theta + i\sin 2\theta = 2\cos 2\theta$

ILLUSTRATION 56: If $x_r = \cos\dfrac{\pi}{2^r} + i\sin\dfrac{\pi}{2^r}$, Prove that $x_1.x_2.x_3 \ldots$ to $\infty = -1$.

SOLUTION: $x_r = \cos\dfrac{\pi}{2^r} + i\sin\dfrac{\pi}{2^r} = e^{i\frac{\pi}{2^r}}$

Now $x_1 . x_2 . x_3 \ldots$ to $\infty = e^{i\frac{\pi}{2}} . e^{i\frac{\pi}{2^2}} . e^{i\frac{\pi}{2^3}} \ldots\ldots$

$$= e^{i\frac{\pi}{2}\left(1 + \frac{1}{2} + \frac{1}{2^2} + \ldots\ldots\infty\right)} = e^{i\frac{\pi}{2}\left(\frac{1}{1-\frac{1}{2}}\right)} = e^{i\frac{\pi}{2}} = \cos\pi + i\sin\pi = -1$$

ILLUSTRATION 57: Show that $\sin^4\alpha\cos^5\alpha = \dfrac{1}{256}(\cos 9\alpha + \cos 7\alpha - 4\cos 5\alpha - 4\cos 3\alpha + 6\cos\alpha)$.

SOLUTION: Let $z = \cos\alpha + i\sin\alpha$

$\Rightarrow z^n = \cos n\alpha + i\sin n\alpha$ and $z^{-n} = \cos n\alpha - i\sin n\alpha$

$\therefore\ z^n + \dfrac{1}{z^n} = 2\cos n\alpha$

For $n = 1$, $z + 1/z = 2\cos\alpha$

Again $z - \dfrac{1}{z} = \cos\alpha + i\sin\alpha - \cos\alpha + i\sin\alpha = 2i\sin\alpha$

Thus $(2i\sin\alpha)^4 \cdot (2\cos\alpha)^5$

$$= \left(z - \frac{1}{z}\right)^4 \left(z + \frac{1}{z}\right)^5 = \left(z^2 - \frac{1}{z^2}\right)^4 \left(z + \frac{1}{z}\right)$$

$$= \left(z^8 - 4z^4 + 6 - \frac{4}{z^4} + \frac{1}{z^8}\right)\left(z + \frac{1}{z}\right)$$

$$= \left(z^9 + \frac{1}{z^9}\right) + \left(z^7 + \frac{1}{z^7}\right) - 4\left(z^5 + \frac{1}{z^5}\right) - 4\left(z^3 + \frac{1}{z^3}\right) + 6\left(z + \frac{1}{z}\right)$$

$$= 2\cos 9\alpha + 2\cos 7\alpha - 8\cos 5\alpha - 8\cos 3\alpha + 12\cos\alpha$$

$$\therefore\ \sin^4\alpha\cos^5\alpha = \frac{1}{256}(\cos 9\alpha + \cos 7\alpha - 4\cos 5\alpha - 4\cos 3\alpha + 6\cos\alpha).$$

ILLUSTRATION 58: Find the sum of the series. $\cos\theta + \cos 2\theta + \cos 3\theta + \ldots + \cos n\theta$ for $0 < \theta < 2\pi$.

SOLUTION: **Method 1:** Consider the complex number $\cos\theta + i\sin\theta$. We have $(\cos\theta + i\sin\theta)^k = \cos k\theta + i\sin k\theta$, for any integer k. If we put $z = \cos\theta + i\sin\theta$, then $\cos k\theta =$ Real part of z^k

Hence we can write the given series in the form

$S_n = \cos\theta + \cos 2\theta + \ldots\ldots + \cos n\theta$

$= $ Real part of $(z + z^2 + \ldots\ldots + z^n)$

$= Re\,(1 + z + \ldots.z^n - 1)$

If $0 < \theta < 2\pi$, then $z \neq 1$. Hence, we get

$$S_n = Re\left(\frac{z^{n+1} - 1}{z - 1} - 1\right)$$

$$\text{Thus } S_n = Re\left\{\left[\frac{\cos(n+1)\theta + i\sin(n+1)\theta - 1}{\cos\theta + i\sin\theta - 1}\right] - 1\right\}$$

$$= \text{Re}\left[\frac{[(\cos\theta - 1) - i\sin\theta][\cos(n+1)\theta - 1 + i\sin(n+1)\theta]}{[(\cos\theta - 1) + i\sin\theta][(\cos\theta - 1) - i\sin\theta]}\right] - 1$$

$$= \frac{(\cos\theta - 1)(\cos(n+1)\theta - 1) + \sin\theta\sin(n+1)\theta}{(\cos\theta - 1)^2 + \sin^2\theta} - 1$$

$$= \frac{\cos n\theta - \cos(n+1) - \cos\theta + 1}{2(1 - \cos\theta)} - 1 = \frac{\cos n\theta - \cos(n+1)\theta}{2(1 - \cos\theta)} - \frac{1}{2}$$

This can be further simplified to give $S_n = \dfrac{2\sin\left(n + \frac{1}{2}\right)\theta\sin(\theta/2)}{4\sin^2\frac{\theta}{2}} - \dfrac{1}{2}$

$$= \frac{\sin\left(n + \frac{1}{2}\right)\theta}{2\sin(\theta/2)} - \frac{1}{2};\ \frac{\sin\left(n + \frac{1}{2}\right)\theta - \sin\frac{\theta}{2}}{2\sin(\theta/2)} = \frac{\sin\frac{n\theta}{2}\cos\left(\frac{n+1}{2}\right)\theta}{\sin(\theta/2)}$$

Method-2: From Euler's form $\cos\theta = \dfrac{e^{i\theta} + e^{-i\theta}}{2}$

So $S = \cos\theta + \cos 2\theta + \ldots. + \cos n\theta$

$$\Rightarrow\ S = \frac{e^{i\theta} + e^{-i\theta}}{2} + \frac{e^{i2\theta} + e^{-2i\theta}}{2} + \ldots. + \frac{e^{in\theta} + e^{-in\theta}}{2} = \frac{e^{i\theta} + e^{i2\theta} + \ldots. + e^{in\theta}}{2} + \frac{e^{-i\theta} + e^{-i2\theta} + \ldots. + e^{-in\theta}}{2}$$

$$= \frac{e^{i\theta}\left[e^{in\theta} - 1\right]}{2(e^{i\theta} - 1)} + \frac{e^{-i\theta}\left[e^{-in\theta} - 1\right]}{2(e^{-i\theta} - 1)} = \frac{e^{i\theta}\left[e^{in\theta} - 1\right]}{2(e^{i\theta} - 1)} + \frac{e^{-in\theta}\left[e^{in\theta} - 1\right]}{2(e^{i\theta} - 1)} = \frac{\left(e^{in\theta} - 1\right)}{(e^{i\theta} - 1)}\left[\frac{e^{i\theta} + e^{-in\theta}}{2}\right]$$

$$=\left(\frac{\cos n\theta+i\sin n\theta-1}{\cos\theta+i\sin\theta-1}\right)\left[\frac{\cos\theta+i\sin\theta+\cos n\theta-i\sin n\theta}{2}\right]$$

$$=\left[\frac{2\sin^2\left(\frac{n\theta}{2}\right)-i2\sin\left(\frac{n\theta}{2}\right)\cos\left(\frac{n\theta}{2}\right)}{2\sin^2\left(\frac{\theta}{2}\right)-i2\sin\left(\frac{\theta}{2}\right)\cos\left(\frac{\theta}{2}\right)}\right]$$

$$=\left(\frac{2\cos\left(\left(\frac{n+1}{2}\right)\theta\right).\cos\left(\left(\frac{n-1}{2}\right)\theta\right)-i\left(2\cos\left(\frac{n+1}{2}\right)\theta\sin\left(\frac{n-1}{2}\right)\theta\right)}{2}\right)$$

$$=\frac{2\sin\frac{n\theta}{2}}{2\sin\frac{\theta}{2}}\left(\frac{\sin\frac{n\theta}{2}-i\cos\frac{n\theta}{2}}{\sin\frac{\theta}{2}-i\cos\frac{\theta}{2}}\right)-\cos\left(\frac{n+1}{2}\right)\theta\left[\cos\left(\frac{n-1}{2}\right)\theta-i\sin\left(\frac{n-1}{2}\right)\theta\right]$$

$$=\frac{\sin\left(\frac{n\theta}{2}\right)}{\sin\frac{\theta}{2}}.\cos\left(\frac{n+1}{2}\right).\theta\left(\frac{(-i)\ e^{\frac{in\theta}{2}}}{(-i)\ e\frac{i\theta}{2}}\right)\left(e^{-i(n-1)\frac{\theta}{2}}\right)$$

$$\therefore\quad S=\frac{\sin\left(\frac{n\theta}{2}\right)}{\sin\frac{\theta}{2}}.\left(\cos\left(\frac{n+1}{2}\right)\theta\right)$$

ILLUSTRATION 59: Find the sum of infinite series $\sin\alpha+\frac{1}{2}\sin 2\alpha+\frac{1}{2^2}\sin 3\alpha+\frac{1}{2^3}\sin 4\alpha+.....\infty$

SOLUTION: Let $S=\sin\ \alpha+\frac{1}{2}\sin 2\alpha+...$

and $C=\cos\ \alpha+\ \frac{1}{2}\ \cos 2\alpha+\ ......$

Using sum of an infinite G.P., we get $C+iS=\frac{e^{i\alpha}}{1-\frac{1}{2}e^{i\alpha}}=\frac{2e^{i\alpha}}{2-e^{i\alpha}}$ $\left\{\because\ r=\left|\frac{1}{2}e^{i\alpha}\right|=\frac{1}{2}<1\right\}$

On simplifying we get, $C+iS=\frac{4\cos\alpha-2}{5-4\cos\alpha}+i\frac{4\sin\alpha}{5-4\cos\alpha}$

On separating the real and imaginary parts, we have $C=\frac{4\cos\alpha-2}{5-4\cos\alpha}$ and $S=\frac{4\sin\alpha}{5-4\cos\alpha}$

ILLUSTRATION 60: Use complex numbers to prove that the sum $\sum_{r=0}^{n-1}\cos^2\left(\alpha+\frac{r\pi}{n}\right)=\frac{n}{2}$ where $n\in\mathbb{N};\ n\geq 2$

SOLUTION: L.H.S $=\cos^2\alpha+\cos^2(\alpha+\theta)+\cos^2(\alpha+2\theta)+....+\cos^2(\alpha+(n-1)\theta)$, where $\theta=\frac{\pi}{n}$

$$=\frac{n}{2}+\frac{1}{2}\ [\cos 2\alpha+\cos 2(\alpha+\theta)+\cos 2(a+2\theta)+...+\cos 2\ (\alpha+(n-1)\theta)]\qquad...(i)$$

Consider, $C = \cos 2\alpha + \cos 2(\alpha + \theta) + ... + \cos 2\left[\alpha + (n-1)\theta\right]$ and

$S = \sin 2\alpha + \sin 2(\alpha + \theta) + ... + \sin 2\left[\alpha + \overline{n-1}\theta\right]$.

$$\Rightarrow C + iS = e^{i2\alpha}[1 + e^{i2\theta} + e^{i4\theta} + ... + e^{i2(\overline{n-1}\theta)}] = e^{i2\alpha}\frac{[e^{i2n\theta} - 1]}{e^{2i\theta} - 1} = \frac{e^{i2\alpha}.e^{in\theta}[e^{in\theta} - e^{-in\theta}]}{e^{i\theta}[e^{i\theta} - e^{-i\theta}]}$$

Thus $C + iS = e^{i(2\alpha + \overline{n-1}\theta)}\frac{[2i\sin n\theta]}{2i\sin\theta}$; Since $\theta = \frac{\pi}{n}$

$\therefore$ So $C + iS = 0 \quad \Rightarrow C = 0, S = 0$

From (1) we have L.H.S $= n/2$, hence proved

n^{th} ROOT OF A COMPLEX NUMBER ($\sqrt[n]{z}$)

Let, $z = r \text{ cis } \theta$, $z^{1/n} = (r^{1/n})\ (\text{cis}(2k\pi + \theta))^{1/n} = (r^{1/n})\ \text{cis}\left(\frac{2k\pi}{n} + \frac{\theta}{n}\right)$, where $r^{1/n}$ is positive n^{th} root of r.

$= (r^{1/n})\ cis\frac{2k\pi}{n}.cis\left(\frac{\theta}{n}\right)$ where $cis\frac{2k\pi}{n}$, is n^{th} root of unity, $k = 0, 1, 2, ..., n - 1$

ILLUSTRATION 61: If $n > 1$, show that the roots of the equation $z^n = (z + 1)^n$ are collinear.

SOLUTION: Given, $(z + 1)^n = z^n \Rightarrow \left(1 + \frac{1}{z}\right)^n = 1 \Rightarrow 1 + \frac{1}{z} = (1)^{\frac{1}{n}}$

$$\Rightarrow 1 + \frac{1}{z} = (\cos 0 + i\sin 0)^{\frac{1}{n}} \Rightarrow 1 + \frac{1}{z} = \cos\frac{2r\pi}{n} + i\sin\frac{2r\pi}{n}$$

where $r = 0, 1, 2, ...(n - 1)$.But $r = 0 \Rightarrow \frac{1}{z} = 0$ (not possible)

$$\therefore \quad z = \frac{1}{-1 + \cos\frac{2r\pi}{n} + i\sin\frac{2r\pi}{n}}, r = 1, 2, ..., (n-1).$$

$$= \frac{1}{2i^2\sin^2\frac{r\pi}{n} + 2i\sin\frac{r\pi}{n}\cos\frac{r\pi}{n}} = \frac{1}{2i\sin\frac{r\pi}{n}}.e^{-i\frac{r\pi}{n}} = \frac{1}{2i}\left(\cot\frac{r\pi}{n} - i\right)$$

$\therefore \quad z = -\frac{1}{2} - \frac{1}{2}i\cot\frac{r\pi}{n}$; where $r = 1, 2, 3 .... (n - 1)$

So, roots of given equation lies on a line $x = -1/2$ or $\text{Re}(z) = -1/2$

ILLUSTRATION 62: Solve the equation $x^7 + 1 = 0$ and deduce that $\cos\frac{\pi}{7}\cos\frac{3\pi}{7}\cos\frac{5\pi}{7} = -\frac{1}{8}$

SOLUTION: Given $x^7 + 1 = 0$ or $x^7 = -1 = \cos\pi + i\sin\pi$

$$\therefore \quad x = (\cos\pi + i\sin\pi)^{1/7} = \cos\frac{2r\pi + \pi}{7} + i\sin\frac{2r\pi + \pi}{7}, r = 0, 1, 2, ...6$$

$$= \cos\frac{\pi}{7} \pm i\sin\frac{\pi}{7}, \cos\frac{3\pi}{7} \pm i\sin\frac{3\pi}{7}, \cos\frac{5\pi}{7} \pm i\sin\frac{5\pi}{7}, \cos\pi + i\sin\frac{\pi}{7}(= -1)$$

Second part; $x^7 + 1 = (x+1)\left(x^2 - 2\cos\frac{\pi}{7}x + 1\right)\left(x^2 - 2\cos\frac{3\pi}{7}x + 1\right)\left(x^2 - 2\cos\frac{5\pi}{7}x + 1\right)$

Putting $x^2 + 1 = 0$ i.e, $x = i$, we get $i^7 + 1 = (1+i)\left(-2i\cos\frac{\pi}{7}\right)\left(-2i\cos\frac{3\pi}{7}\right)\left(-2i\cos\frac{5\pi}{7}\right)$

$\Rightarrow -i + 1 = (1+i)\left(8i\cos\frac{\pi}{7}\cos\frac{3\pi}{7}\cos\frac{5\pi}{7}\right)$

$= (-i-1)\left(8\cos\frac{\pi}{7}\cos\frac{3\pi}{7}\cos\frac{5\pi}{7}\right) = (-i+1)\left(-8\cos\frac{\pi}{7}\cos\frac{3\pi}{7}\cos\frac{5\pi}{7}\right)$

$\Rightarrow \cos\frac{\pi}{7}\cos\frac{3\pi}{7}\cos\frac{5\pi}{7} = -\frac{1}{8}$

TEXTUAL EXERCISE 8: (SUBJECTIVE)

1. Obtain the square root of the following complex numbers:
(a) $5 + 12i$ (b) $8 - 6i$
(c) $8 - 15i$ (d) i
(e) $-4 - 3i$ (f) $2xy - i(x^2 - y^2);\ x > y$
(g) $a^2 - 1 + 2ai;\ a > 0$

2. Find the square root of $-5 + 12i$.

3. Find the value of $\dfrac{\sqrt{5+12i}+\sqrt{5-12i}}{\sqrt{5+12i}-\sqrt{5-12i}}$.

4. Find the quadratic equations with real coefficients whose one root is a square root of $7 - 30\sqrt{-2}$.

5. Find the quadratic equations with real coefficients whose one root is a square root of $-47 + 8\sqrt{-3}$.

6. Evaluate $\sqrt{i} - \sqrt{-i}$.

7. Find the cube roots of following complex numbers:
(a) 64 (b) -27

8. If 1, ω, ω^2 be the cube roots of unity, then prove that
(a) $(1 + \omega - \omega^2)^6 = 64$
(b) $(1 + \omega - \omega^2)^3 = (1 - \omega + \omega^2)^3 = -8$
(c) $(2 + 5\omega + 2\omega^2)^6 = (2 + 5\omega^2 + 2\omega)^6 = 729$
(d) $(1 + \omega)^3 - (1 + \omega^2)^3 = 0$
(e) $(3 + 3\omega + 5\omega^2)^3 - (2 + 4\omega + 2\omega^2)^3 = 0$
(f) $(2 - \omega)(2 - \omega^2)(2 - \omega^{10})(2 - \omega^{11}) = 49$

9. Prove that $x^3 + x^2 + x$ is a factor of $(x + 1)^n - x^n - 1$ (*when n is an odd integer greater than* 3, *but not a multiple of* 3)

10. Prove that $\left(\dfrac{-1+\sqrt{-3}}{2}\right)^{29} + \left(\dfrac{-1-\sqrt{-3}}{2}\right)^{29} = -1.$

11. If α and β are non-real cube roots of unity,then prove that $(1 - \alpha)(1 - \beta)(1 - \alpha^2)(1 - \beta^2) = 9$

12. If 1, ω, ω^2 be the cube roots of unity, prove that.
(a) $(x - y)(x\omega - y)(x\omega^2 - y) = x^3 - y^3$
(b) $(a + b + c)(a + b\omega + c\omega^2)(a + b\omega^2 + c\omega) = a^3 + b^3 + c^3 - 3abc$

13. If $x = a + b$, $y = a\omega + b\omega^2$, $z = a\omega^2 + b\omega$, where ω is a cube root of unity, prove that....
(a) $x^2 + y^2 + z^2 = 6ab$ (b) $xyz = a^3 + b^3$

14. If α, β, γ are the cube roots of p, $p < 0$, then for any x, y and z, evaluate $\dfrac{x\alpha + y\beta + z\gamma}{x\beta + y\gamma + z\alpha}$

15. If α, β, γ are the roots of the equation $x^3 - 3x^2 + 3x + 7 = 0$, then evaluate $(\alpha - 1)(\beta - 1)(\gamma - 1)$

16. Find the common roots of the equation $z^3 + 2z^2 + 2z + 1 = 0$ and $z^{1985} + z^{100} + 1 = 0$.

17. Find all the six sixth roots of unity. Which of these are also cube roots of unity?

18. Prove that the product of any two of the ten, tenth roots of unity is again one of the ten roots.

19. (a) Find the n, n^{th} roots of unity and prove that the sum of their p^{th} power vanishes unless p be a multiple of n, p being an integer and if p is a multiple of n, the sum is n.

(b) Find the 7th roots of unity and prove that sum of their n^{th} power always vanishes unless n be a multiple of 7 (n be integer), otherwise the sum is 7.

20. If $1, \alpha_1, \alpha_2, ..., \alpha_{n-1}$ are n, n^{th} roots of unity, then evaluate following:

(a) $\prod_{k=1}^{n-1}(1-\alpha_k)$ (b) $\prod_{k=1}^{n-1}(2-\alpha_k)$

(c) $\prod_{k=1}^{n-1}(m-\alpha_k)$ (d) $\prod_{k=1}^{n-1}(1+\alpha_k)$

21. Simplify $\dfrac{(\cos 3\theta - i\sin 3\theta)^6(\sin\theta - i\cos\theta)^3}{(\cos 2\theta + i\sin 2\theta)^5}$

22. Prove $(cis\ m\theta)^n = (cis\ n\theta)^m = cis\ mn\theta = (cis\ \theta)^{mn}$ and hence simplify the expression

$$\frac{(\cos 3\theta + i\sin 3\theta)^4(\cos 4\theta - i\sin 4\theta)^5}{(\cos 4\theta + i\sin 4\theta)^3(\cos 5\theta + i\sin 5\theta)^{-4}}.$$

23. Prove that $(1+\cos\theta + i\sin\theta)^n + (1+\cos\theta - i\sin\theta)^n = 2^{n+1}\cos^n(\theta/2)\cos n\theta/2$.

24. Prove the following:

(a) $(a+ib)^{m/n} + (a-ib)^{m/n}$

$= 2(a^2+b^2)^{m/2n}\cdot\cos\left(\dfrac{m}{n}\tan^{-1}\dfrac{b}{a}\right).$

(b) $\left(\dfrac{1+\sin\alpha + i\cos\alpha}{1+\sin\alpha - i\cos\alpha}\right)^n =$

$\cos\left(\dfrac{n\pi}{2} - n\alpha\right) + i\sin\left(\dfrac{n\pi}{2} - n\alpha\right)$

25. If $2\cos\theta = x + 1/x$, $2\cos\phi = y + 1/y$, show that one of the values of

(a) $x^m y^n + 1/x^m y^n$ is $2\cos(m\theta + n\phi)$

(b) $x^m/y^n + y^n/x^m$ is $2\cos(m\theta - n\phi)$

26. If $\cos\theta = a$ and $\sin\theta = b$, then evaluate $\cos 3\theta$ and $\sin 3\theta$ using De-moivre's theorem.

Answer Key

1. (a) $3+2i, -3-2i$ (b) $3-i, -3+i$ (c) $\pm 1/\sqrt{2}(5-3i)$

(d) $1/\sqrt{2} + i/\sqrt{2}, -(1/\sqrt{2} + (i/\sqrt{2}))$ (e) $1/\sqrt{2} - 3/\sqrt{2}i, -1/\sqrt{2} + 3/\sqrt{2}i$ (f) $\dfrac{(x+y)+i(x-y)}{\sqrt{2}}, \dfrac{-(x+y)+i(x-y)}{\sqrt{2}}$

(g) $\pm(a+i)$ 2. $\pm(2+3i)$ 3. $-\dfrac{3i}{2}$ 4. $x^2 \pm 10x + 43 = 0$ 5. $x^2 - 2x + 49 = 0$

6. $\pm\sqrt{2}i$ 7. (a) $4, 4\omega, 4\omega^2$ (b) $-3, -3\omega, -3\omega^2$ 14. ω^2 15. -8 16. ω, ω^2

17. $e^{i\frac{2k\pi}{3}}$ where $k = 0, 1, 2, 3, 4, 5$ for $k = 0, 2, 4$ it is cube root of unity

19. (a) $e^{i\frac{2k\pi}{n}}$; $k = 0, 1, ...n-1$ (b) $e^{i\frac{2k\pi}{n}}$; $k = 0, 1, ..., 6$ 20. (a) n (b) $2^n - 1$ (c) $\dfrac{m^n - 1}{m-1}$

(d) $\begin{cases} 0 & \text{if } n \text{ is even} \\ -1 & \text{if } n \text{ is odd} \end{cases}$ 21. $\sin 25\theta + i\cos 25\theta$ 22. 1 26. $4a^3 - 3a, 3b - 4b^3$

TEXTUAL EXERCISE 8: (OBJECTIVE)

1. Square roots of $-7-24i$ are:

(a) $\pm(4-3i)$ (b) $\pm(3-4i)$

(c) $\pm(3+4i)$ (d) None of these

2. If α and β are imaginary cube roots of unity, then $\alpha^4 + \beta^4 + \dfrac{1}{\alpha\beta} =$

(a) 3 (b) 0

(c) 1 (d) 2

3. If $\omega\ (\neq 1)$ is a cube root of unity and $(1+\omega)^7 = A + B\omega$, then A and B are respectively, the numbers

(a) 0, 1 (b) 1, 0

(c) 1, 1 (d) -1, 1

4. If ω is an imaginary cube root of unity, then the value of $\sin\left[(\omega^{10} + \omega^{23})\pi - \dfrac{\pi}{4}\right]$ is

(a) $-\sqrt{3}/2$ (b) $-1/\sqrt{2}$

(c) $1/\sqrt{2}$ (d) $\sqrt{3}/2$

5. If ω is an imaginary cube root of unity, $(1+\omega-\omega^2)^7$ equals

(a) 128ω (b) -128ω
(c) $128\omega^2$ (c) $-128\omega^2$

6. If ω is a complex root of the equation $z^3 = 1$, then $\omega+\omega^{\left(\frac{1}{2}+\frac{3}{8}+\frac{9}{32}+\frac{27}{128}+\dots\dots\right)}$ is equal to
(a) -1 (b) 0
(c) 9 (d) i

7. The value of $(1 + 2\omega + \omega^2)^{3n} - (1 + \omega + 2\omega^2)^{3n}$ is equal to
(a) 0 (b) 1
(c) ω (d) ω^2

8. If ω is a non-real cube root of unity, then $(a + b)(a + b\omega)(a + b\omega^2)$ is
(a) $a^3 + b^3$ (b) $a^3 - b^3$
(c) $a^2 + b^2$ (d) $a^2 - b^2$

9. If ω is a complex cube root of unity, then $225 + (3\omega + 8\omega^2)^2 + (3\omega^2 + 8\omega)^2$ is equal to
(a) 72 (b) 192
(c) 200 (d) 248

10. If 1, ω, ω^2 are the cube root of unity, then $(1 - 2\omega + \omega^2)^6$ is equal to
(a) 729 (b) 246
(c) 243 (d) 81

11. If ω is a complex cube root of unity, then the value of $\omega^{99} + \omega^{100} + \omega^{101}$ is
(a) 1 (b) -1
(c) 3 (d) 0

12. If ω is a complex cube root of unity, then the value of
$$\frac{a+b\omega+c\omega^2}{c+a\omega+b\omega^2}+\frac{a+b\omega+c\omega^2}{b+c\omega+a\omega^2}$$ is
(a) 1 (b) 0
(c) 2 (d) -1

13. If ω is imaginary cube root of unity, then $\text{Arg}(i\omega) + \text{Arg}(i\omega^2) =$
(a) 0 (b) $\pi/2$
(c) π (d) None of these

14. If α and β are the roots of the equations $x^2 - x + 1 = 0$, then $\alpha^{2009} + \beta^{2009} =$
(a) 2 (b) -2
(c) -1 (d) 1

15. Sum of common roots of the equations $z^3 + 2z^2 + 2z + 1 = 0$ and $z^{100} + z^{32} + 1 = 0$ is equal to
(a) 0 (b) -1
(c) 1 (d) None of these

16. If $1,\omega,\omega^2,\dots\dots,\omega^{n-1}$ are n,n^{th} roots of unity, then $(2 - \omega)(2 - \omega^2)..(2 - \omega^{n-1})$ equals:
(a) $2^n - 1$
(b) $[{}^{2n}C_0 + {}^{2n+1}C_1 + {}^{2n+1}C_2 + \dots + {}^{2n+1}C_n]^{1/2} - 1$
(c) $2^n + 1$
(d) ${}^nC_1 + {}^nC_2 + .. + {}^nC_n$

17. If ω, ω^2 are imaginary cube roots of unity and
$$\frac{1}{a+\omega}+\frac{1}{b+\omega}+\frac{1}{c+\omega} = 2\omega^2 \text{ and}$$
$$\frac{1}{a+\omega^2}+\frac{1}{b+\omega^2}+\frac{1}{c+\omega^2} = 2\omega, \text{ then}$$
$$\frac{1}{a+1}+\frac{1}{b+1}+\frac{1}{c+1} \text{ equals}$$
(a) 1 (b) -1
(c) 3 (d) 2

18. Let z be a complex number satisfying $z^2 + z + 1 = 0$. If n is not a multiple of 3, then the value of $z^n + z^{2n}$ is
(a) 1 (b) -2
(c) 0 (d) -1

19. If ω ($\neq 1$) is a cube root of unity, then
$$\begin{vmatrix} 1 & 1+i+\omega^2 & \omega^2 \\ 1-i & -1 & \omega^2-1 \\ -i & -i+\omega-1 & -1 \end{vmatrix}$$ equals
(a) 0 (b) $-i$
(c) i (d) ω

20. If ω,ω^2 are the cube roots of unity, then the value of $(1 + \omega^2 - \omega)(1 - \omega^2 + \omega)^6$ is
(a) 128ω (b) -128ω
(c) $-128\omega^2$ (d) $128\omega^2$

21. If $i = \sqrt{(-1)}$, then $4 + 5\left(-\frac{1}{2}+\frac{i\sqrt{3}}{2}\right)^{334}+3\left(-\frac{1}{2}+\frac{i\sqrt{3}}{2}\right)^{365} =$
(a) $1-i\sqrt{3}$ (b) $-1+\sqrt{3}$
(c) $i\sqrt{3}$ (d) $-i\sqrt{3}$

22. Let z_1 and z_2 be nth roots of unity which subtend a right angle at origin. Then n must be of the form
(a) $4k + 1$ (b) $4k + 2$
(c) $4k + 3$ (d) $4k$

23. If ω is an imaginary cube root of unity, then $1(2 - \omega)(2 - \omega^2) + 2(3 - \omega)(3 - \omega^2) + \dots + \dots + (n - 1)(n - \omega)(n - \omega^2) =$

(a) $\frac{1}{4}[n(n+1)]^2$ (b) $\frac{1}{4}n^2(n+1)^2 - n$

(c) $\frac{1}{4}n^2(n-1)^2 - n$ (d) None of these

24. Let $\omega = \frac{1}{2} + i\frac{\sqrt{3}}{2}$, Then the value of the determinant

$$\begin{vmatrix} 1 & 1 & 1 \\ 1 & -1-\omega^2 & \omega^2 \\ 1 & \omega^2 & \omega^4 \end{vmatrix}$$ is:

(a) 3ω (b) $3\omega(\omega - 1)$

(c) $3\omega^2$ (d) $3\omega(1 - \omega)$

25. If ω is a cube root of unity ($\omega \neq 1$), then the least value of n, where n is positive integer such that $(1 + \omega^2)^n = (1 + \omega^4)^n$ is

(a) 2 (b) 3

(c) 5 (d) 6

26. If ω is a cube root of unity, ($\neq 1$), then the minimum value of $|a + b\omega + c\omega^2|$; ($a,b,c$ are integers not all equal) is

(a) 0 (b) $\sqrt{3}/2$

(c) 1 (d) 2

27. Product of the distinct $(2n)^{th}$ roots of $1+i\sqrt{3}$ is

(a) $-1+i\sqrt{3}$ (b) $-1-i\sqrt{3}$

(c) $1+i\sqrt{3}$ (d) 1

28. If $z^2 + z + 1 = 0$, $z \in C$, then $\left(z+\frac{1}{z}\right)^2+\left(z^2+\frac{1}{z^2}\right)^2+\left(z^3+\frac{1}{z^3}\right)^2+...+\left(z^6+\frac{1}{z^6}\right)^2 =$

(a) 18 (b) 54

(c) 6 (d) 12

29. What are the four values of $\left(\frac{1}{2}+\frac{1}{2}\sqrt{-3}\right)^{3/4}$?

(a) $\pm\frac{1}{\sqrt{2}}(1\pm i)$ (b) $\left(\pm\frac{1}{\sqrt{2}}\right)\pm i$

(c) $\pm 1 \pm \frac{i}{\sqrt{2}}$ (d) $\pm 1 \pm \sqrt{3}\,i$

30. Let $z = \cos\theta + i\sin\theta$. Then the value of $\sum_{m=1}^{15} \text{Im}(z^{2m-1})$ at $\theta = 2°$ is

(a) $\frac{1}{\sin 2°}$ (b) $\frac{1}{3\sin 2°}$

(c) $\frac{1}{2\sin 2°}$ (d) $\frac{1}{4\sin 2°}$

31. If α is non-real and $\alpha = \sqrt[5]{1}$, then the value of $2|1 + \alpha + \alpha^2 + \alpha^{-2} + \alpha^{-1}|$ is equal to

(a) 4 (b) 2

(c) 1 (d) None of these

32. The number of roots of equations $z^{15} = 1$ and $|\arg z| < \pi/2$ is

(a) 6 (b) 7

(c) 8 (d) None of these

33. If z_1, z_2, z_3, z_4 are the roots of the equation $z^4 = 1$, then $\sum_{i=1}^{4} z_i^3$ is equal to

(a) 4 (b) 0

(c) $1 + i$ (d) $-1 - i$

34. Let $z - \frac{1}{z} = i$ then

(a) $z^{98} + \frac{1}{z^{98}} = 1$ (b) $z^{100} + \frac{1}{z^{100}} = 1$

(c) $z^{99} + \frac{1}{z^{99}} = 0$ (d) $z^{100} + \frac{1}{z^{100}} = -1$

Answer Key

1. (b)	**2.** (b)	**3.** (c)	**4.** (c)	**5.** (d)	**6.** (a)	**7.** (a)	**8.** (a)	**9.** (d)	**10.** (a)
11. (d)	**12.** (d)	**13.** (d)	**14.** (d)	**15.** (b)	**16.** (a,b,d)	**17.** (d)	**18.** (d)	**19.** (a)	**20.** (b)
21. (c)	**22.** (d)	**23.** (b)	**24.** (b)	**25.** (b)	**26.** (c)	**27.** (b)	**28.** (d)	**29.** (a)	**30.** (d)
31. (d)	**32.** (b)	**33.** (b)	**34.** (a,c,d)						

■ LOGARITHM OF COMPLEX NUMBERS

Consider $z = x + iy$, {converting '$x + iy$' into Euler's form, such that θ = principal value of argument of z}

then, we get $\log_e(x + iy) = \log_e(|z|e^{i\theta})$

$\Rightarrow \log_e(x + iy) = \log_e|z| + \log_e e^{i\theta}$

$\Rightarrow \log_e(x + iy) = \log_e|z| + i\theta$

In general $\log_e(x + iy) = \log_e|z| + i(\theta + 2n\pi)$; $n \in \mathbb{Z}$

ILLUSTRATION 63: Find the value of i^i.

SOLUTION: Let $z = i^i$

$$\log_e z = \log_e i^i = i \log_e i = i \log_e e^{i\frac{\pi}{2}} = i^2 \frac{\pi}{2} \log_e e = -\frac{\pi}{2} \Rightarrow z = e^{-\pi/2}$$

ILLUSTRATION 64: If $z = i\log_e(2-\sqrt{3})$, then find the value of cosz.

SOLUTION: We know $\cos z = \dfrac{e^{iz}+e^{-iz}}{2} = \dfrac{e^{i^2 \log_e(2-\sqrt{3})}+e^{-i^2 \log_e(2-\sqrt{3})}}{2}$

$$= \frac{e^{\log_e(2-\sqrt{3})^{-1}}+e^{\log_e(2-\sqrt{3})}}{2} = \frac{(2-\sqrt{3})^{-1}+(2-\sqrt{3})}{2} = \frac{1}{2}\left[\frac{1}{2-\sqrt{3}}+(2-\sqrt{3})\right]$$

$$= \frac{1}{2}\left[\frac{2+\sqrt{3}}{4-3}+(2-\sqrt{3})\right] = \frac{1}{2}[2+\sqrt{3}+2-\sqrt{3}] = 2$$

ILLUSTRATION 65: Evaluate natural logarithm of $(1 + i \tan\alpha)$, when $\alpha \in \left(0, \frac{\pi}{2}\right)$.

SOLUTION: Let $ln(1 + i \tan \alpha) = a + ib$

$\Rightarrow 1 + i \tan \alpha = e^a . e^{ib} \Rightarrow 1 = e^a \cos b$ ....(i)

and $\tan\alpha = e^a \sin b$ ....(ii)

Squaring and adding (i) and (ii), $1 + \tan^2\alpha = e^{2a}$

$\Rightarrow 2a = \log_e(1 + \tan^2\alpha) \Rightarrow a = \frac{1}{2} ln(1+\tan^2\alpha)$ ....(iii)

Dividing equation (ii) by (i), we get $\tan \alpha = \tan b \Rightarrow b = n\pi + \alpha;\ n \in \mathbb{Z}$

$\Rightarrow a + ib = \frac{1}{2} ln(1+\tan^2\alpha) + i(n\pi+\alpha); n \in \mathbb{Z}$

Aliter: $z = 1 + i \tan \alpha = \sec \alpha (\cos \alpha + i \sin \alpha) = \sec\alpha\, e^{i\alpha}$

$\Rightarrow ln\, z = ln \sec\alpha + i\alpha = \frac{1}{2} ln(1+\tan^2\alpha) + i\alpha$

TEXTUAL EXERCISE 9: (SUBJECTIVE)

1. Prove that $\tan\left(i \ln\left(\dfrac{a-ib}{a+ib}\right)\right) = \dfrac{2ab}{a^2-b^2}$.
2. Find the principal and general value of $ln(-1 + i)$.
3. If $i^{i^{\cdots\infty}} = A + iB$, (principal values only being considered), prove that

   (a) $\tan \frac{1}{2}\pi A = \frac{B}{A}$ (b) $A^2 + B^2 = e^{-\pi B}$
4. Express $ln\,[ln(\cos\theta + i \sin \theta)]$ in the form $A + iB$.
5. Find the imaginary part of following complex numbers

   (i) $\log_e(-i)$ (ii) $\log_e(1-i)$
   (iii) $\log_e(1+i)$ (iv) $\log_e(4+3i)$
6. Prove that $i^{\alpha+i\beta} = e^x(\cos y + i \sin y)$ where $x = -\frac{1}{2}\pi\beta$, $y = \frac{1}{2}(4n+1)\pi\alpha$. Also deduce that if $i^{\alpha+i\beta} = \alpha + i\beta$, then $\alpha^2 + \beta^2 = e^{-(4n+1)\pi\beta}$.
7. If sin log (i^i) = $a + ib$, find a and b. Hence find cos (ln i^i).
8. If $(a + ib)^p = m^{x+iy}$, then prove that $\dfrac{y}{x} = \dfrac{2\tan^{-1}\frac{b}{a}}{\ln(a^2+b^2)}$ when only principal value is considered.
9. Show that $(1 + i)^{\ln(1-i)}$ is purely real.

Answer Key

2. $\ln\sqrt{2}+i\frac{3\pi}{4}, i\left(\frac{3\pi}{4}+2n\pi\right)+\ln\sqrt{2}$ **4.** $\log_e \theta + i\left(2n\pi+\frac{\pi}{2}\right)$ **5.** (i) $(4n-1)\pi/2$ (ii) $(8n-1)\pi/4$

(iii) $(8n+1)\pi/4$ (iv) $2n\pi+\tan^{-1}\frac{3}{4}$ **7.** $-1, 0$

TEXTUAL EXERCISE 9: (OBJECTIVE)

1. If $\ln(1 + i\tan\alpha) = A + iB$, then $A =$ (Consider only principal values)

(a) $\sec\alpha$ (b) $ln\,|\sec\alpha|$
(c) α (d) None of these

2. The principal value of $ln\,(-1+i) - ln\,(-1-i)$ is

(a) $\frac{3\pi}{2}i$ (b) $\frac{\pi}{2}i$
(c) $-\pi i$ (d) None of these

3. The complex number $\sin\left[i\,ln\,\frac{1+\sin\theta - i\cos\theta}{1+\sin\theta + i\cos\theta}\right]$ is

(a) Real
(b) purely imaginary
(c) neither real nor imaginary
(d) real or purely imaginary depending on value of θ

4. The value of i^i is

(a) Real
(b) purely imaginary
(c) neither real nor imaginary
(d) nothing can be said

5. The real part of $i^{ln(1+i)}$ is (Consider only principal values)

(a) $e^{\frac{-\pi^2}{8}}$ (b) $2e^{\frac{-\pi^2}{8}}$
(c) $\sqrt{2}e^{\frac{\pi^2}{8}}$ (d) $\sqrt{2}e^{-\frac{\pi^2}{8}}$

6. The value of i^{-i} is (Consider only principal values)

(a) $\pi/2$ (b) $e^{-\pi/2}$
(c) $e^{\pi/2}$ (d) None of these

7. The value of $(1+\sqrt{3}i)^i$ is (Consider only principal values)

(a) $2e^{-\pi/3}$ (b) $2^i e^{-\pi/3}$
(c) $2^i e^{\pi/3}$ (d) None of these

8. If $z = 2i\ln(\sqrt{3}-1)$, then the value of $\cos z$ is (Consider only principal values)

(a) $\frac{10-3\sqrt{3}}{4}$ (b) $\frac{10+3\sqrt{3}}{4}$
(c) $10-3\sqrt{3}$ (d) None of these

9. The imaginary part of $ln\,i^{ln(1+\sqrt{3}i)}$ is (Consider only principal values)

(a) $ln\,2$ (b) $\frac{\pi}{2}\ln 2$
(c) $-\frac{\pi}{2}\ln 2$ (d) None of these

Answer Key

1. (b) **2.** (a) **3.** (a) **4.** (a) **5.** (d) **6.** (c) **7.** (b) **8.** (a) **9.** (b)

■ GEOMETRY OF COMPLEX NUMBERS

Line Segment in Argand's Plane

Any line segment joining the complex numbers z_1 and z_2 (*directed towards* z_2) represents a complex number given by $z_2 - z_1$. Since every complex number has magnitude and direction therefore $z_2 - z_1$ also.

$|z_2 - z_1|$ represents the length of line segment AB i.e., distance between z_1 and z_2 and $\arg(z_2 - z_1)$ represents the angle which line segment AB (*on producing*) makes with positive direction of real axis.

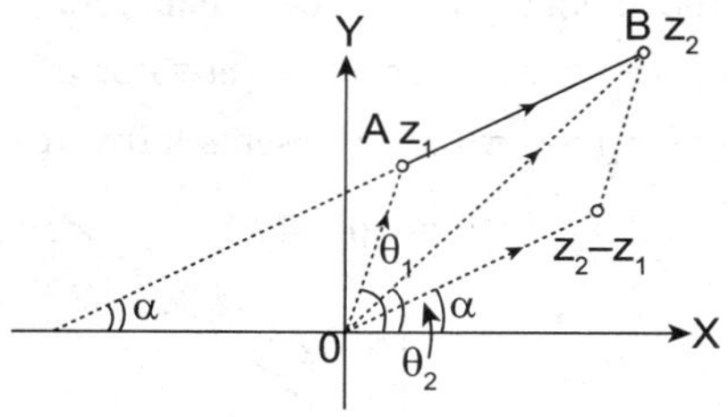

FIGURE 5.22

ANGLE BETWEEN TWO LINE SEGMENTS (ROTATION THEOREM OR CONI'S THEOREM)

Consider three complex numbers z_1, z_2 and z_3 such that angle between line segments joining z_1 to z_2 and z_3 to z_1 is equal to θ.

Then $\theta = \alpha - \beta = \arg(z_3 - z_1) - \arg(z_2 - z_1)$

$$= \arg\left(\frac{z_3 - z_1}{z_2 - z_1}\right) = \arg\left(\frac{\text{Post rotation vector}}{\text{Pre rotation vector}}\right)$$

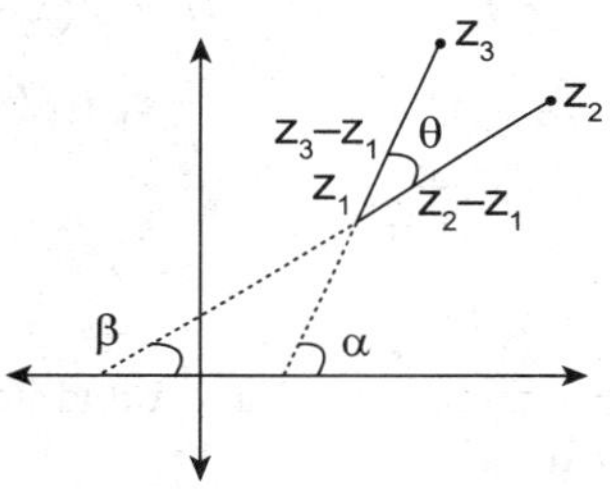

FIGURE 5.23

$$\Rightarrow \arg\left(\frac{z_3 - z_1}{z_2 - z_1}\right) = \theta = \arg(\rho e^{i\theta})$$

$$\Rightarrow (z_3 - z_1) = (z_2 - z_1)\,\rho\, e^{i\theta}, \text{ where } \rho = \left|\frac{z_3 - z_1}{z_2 - z_1}\right|. \text{ If } z_1 = 0.$$

$\Rightarrow$ $z_3 = \rho z_2\, e^{i\theta}$, $\arg(z_3/z_2)$ is an angle through which z_2 is to be rotated to coincide it with z_3.

That means if a complex number $(z_2 - z_1)$ is multiplied by another complex number $re^{i\theta}$, then the complex number. $z_2 - z_1$ gets rotated by the argument (θ) of multiplying complex number in anti-clockwise direction (It is called **Rotation Theorem or Coni's Theorem**)

APPLICATION OF ROTATION THEOREM

A(1) To find the conditions for perpendicularity of two straight lines:

Condition that $\angle A$ of $\Delta\, ABC$ where $A(z_1)$ $B(z_2)$ $C(z_3)$ is right angle and can be obtained by applying Rotation Theorem at A

$$Arg\left(\frac{z_3 - z_1}{z_2 - z_1}\right) = \frac{\pi}{2}, -\frac{\pi}{2} \quad .....(i)$$

$$\Rightarrow \left(\frac{z_3 - z_1}{z_2 - z_1}\right) = \rho e^{\pm\frac{i\pi}{2}} = \pm \rho i\,;\ \rho = \left|\frac{z_3 - z_1}{z_2 - z_1}\right|$$

$$\Rightarrow R\left(\frac{z_3 - z_1}{z_2 - z_1}\right) = 0 \Rightarrow \frac{z_3 - z_1}{z_2 - z_1} + \frac{\overline{z}_3 - \overline{z}_1}{\overline{z}_2 - \overline{z}_1} = 0$$

$$\Rightarrow |z_2 - z_3|^2 = |z_3 - z_1|^2 + |z_2 - z_1|^2$$

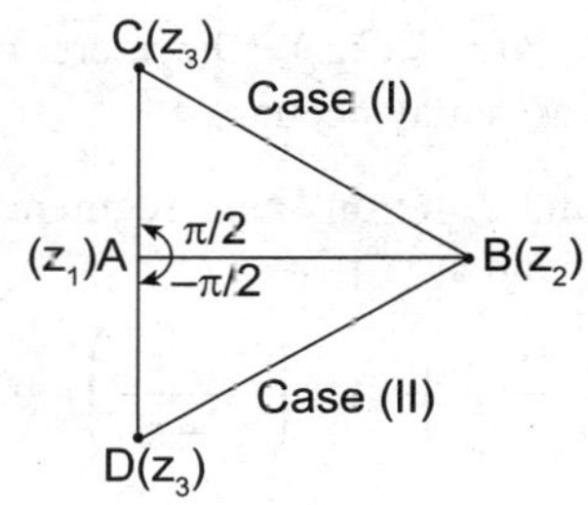

FIGURE 5.24

If ABC is **right angled isosceles triangle** with $AB = AC$. $\Rightarrow \rho = 1 \Rightarrow \dfrac{z_3 - z_1}{z_2 - z_1} = \pm i$

A(2): Conditions for ΔABC to be an equilateral triangle:

Let the ΔABC where $A(z_1)$ $B(z_2)$ $C(z_3)$ be an equilateral triangle

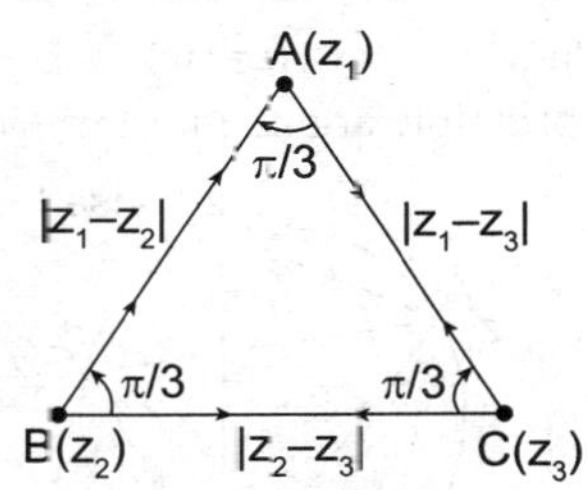

FIGURE 5.25

The following conditions hold

(i) $|z_1 - z_2| = |z_2 - z_3| = |z_3 - z_1|$

(ii) $\text{Arg}\left(\dfrac{z_3 - z_1}{z_2 - z_1}\right) = \pm\dfrac{\pi}{3}$ and $|z_3 - z_1| = |z_2 - z_1|$

(Aplying rotation theorem at A and knowing $CA = BA$)

(iii) $Arg\left(\dfrac{z_3 - z_1}{z_2 - z_1}\right) = Arg\left(\dfrac{z_1 - z_2}{z_3 - z_2}\right) = \dfrac{\pi}{3}$

(Aplying rotation theorem at A and B)

(iv) $z_1^2 + z_2^2 + z_3^2 = z_1 z_2 + z_2 z_3 - z_3 z_1$

Proof : $\because$ $AB = BC = CA$; both $\dfrac{z_3 - z_1}{z_2 - z_1}, \dfrac{z_1 - z_2}{z_3 - z_2}$, are unimodular and have same argument

$$\Rightarrow \frac{z_3 - z_1}{z_2 - z_1} = \frac{z_1 - z_2}{z_3 - z_2}$$

$$\Rightarrow z_3^2 - z_3 z_2 - z_1 z_3 + z_1 z_2 = z_1 z_2 - z_2^2 - z_1^2 + z_1 z_2$$

$$\Rightarrow z_1^2 + z_2^2 + z_3^2 = z_1 z_2 + z_2 z_3 + z_3 z_1$$

(v) $\dfrac{z_1 - z_2}{z_3 - z_2} = e^{i\frac{\pi}{3}} = \dfrac{1}{2} + i\dfrac{\sqrt{3}}{2}$

A(3): Conditions for four points to be concyclic:

If points $A(z_1)$, $B(z_2)$, $C(z_3)$, $D(z_4)$ are con-cyclic, then following two cases may occur

Case I: If z_3 and z_4 lie on same segment with respect to chord joining z_1 and z_2.

$$\Rightarrow \text{Arg}\left(\frac{z_2 - z_4}{z_1 - z_4}\right) - Arg\left(\frac{z_2 - z_3}{z_1 - z_3}\right) = 0$$

$$\Rightarrow \text{Arg}\underbrace{\left(\frac{z_2 - z_4}{z_1 - z_4} \cdot \frac{z_1 - z_3}{z_2 - z_3}\right)}_{w} = 0 \text{ (refer figure 5.30)}$$

$\Rightarrow$ w is real and positive or $I_m(w) = 0$

Case II: If z_3 and z_4 lie on opposite segment of circle.

$$\Rightarrow Arg\left(\frac{z_2 - z_3}{z_1 - z_3}\right) + Arg\left(\frac{z_1 - z_4}{z_2 - z_4}\right) = \pi$$

$\Rightarrow Arg\,(1/w) = \pi \quad \Rightarrow Arg\,(w) = -\pi$

So the principle argument of $w = \pi$

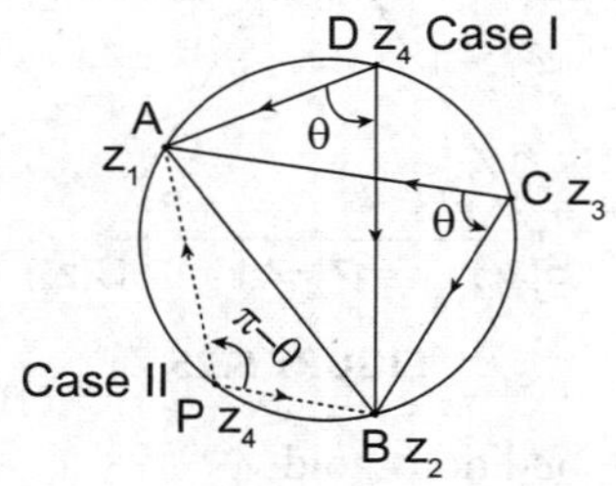

FIGURE 5.26

Conclusion! Four complex numbers z_1, z_2, z_3, z_4 to be concyclic $Arg\underbrace{\left(\dfrac{(z_1 - z_3)(z_2 - z_4)}{(z_2 - z_3)(z_1 - z_4)}\right)}_{w} = 0$ or π

$\Rightarrow$ w is purely real i.e., $I(w) = 0 \Rightarrow \overline{w} = w$

■ LOCI IN ARGAND PLANE

A(1): Straight line in Argand plane:

Line through z_0 making angle α with positive real axis.

$\text{Arg}(z - z_0) = \alpha$ or $-\pi + \alpha$

- The above equation excludes the point z_0.
- Arg $(z - z_0) = \alpha$ represents rightwards of z_0 ray.
- Arg $(z - z_0) = -\pi + \alpha$ represents leftwards of z_0 ray.

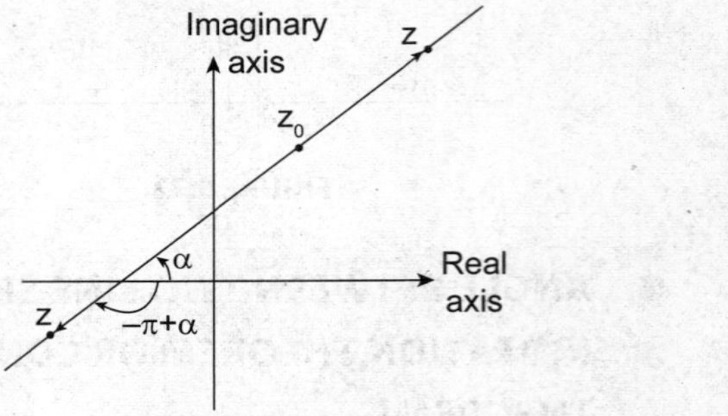

FIGURE 5.27

A(2): Line through points $A(z_1)$ and $B(z_2)$:

Consider a straight line passing through $A(z_1)$ and $B(z_2)$ taking a variable point $P(z)$ on it.

$\because$ for each position of P, $\overrightarrow{AP}$ is collinear with $\overrightarrow{AB}$

$\Rightarrow \overrightarrow{AP} = \lambda\overrightarrow{AB} \qquad \Rightarrow \overrightarrow{AP} = \lambda(z_2 - z_1)$

$\because \overrightarrow{OP} = \overrightarrow{OA} + \overrightarrow{AP} \qquad \Rightarrow z = z_1 + \lambda(z_2 - z_1)$

$\Rightarrow z = z_1(1 - \lambda) + \lambda z_2$

Conclusion:

1. If $z = xz_1 + yz_2$; $x + y = 1$ and x and $y \in \mathbb{R}$, then z, z_1, z_2 are collinear.
2. Equation represents line segment AB if $\lambda \in [0,1]$
3. Rightward ray through B if $\lambda \in (1, \infty)$
4. Leftward ray through A if $\lambda \in (-\infty, 0)$

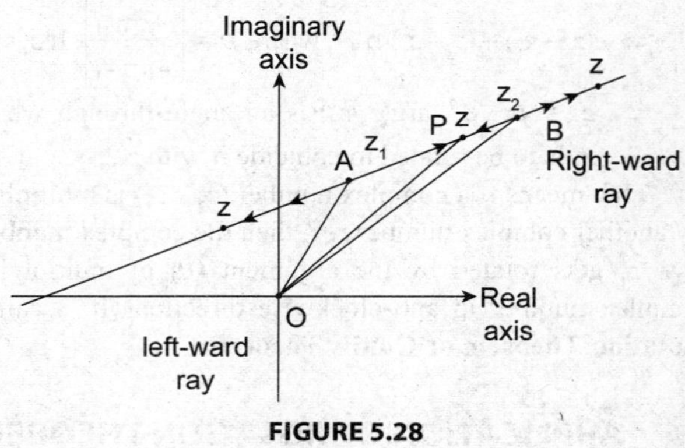

FIGURE 5.28

A(3): Line segment AB:

The equation of the line segment AB is given by

$$Arg\left(\frac{z - z_1}{z - z_2}\right) = \pi$$

A(4): Equation of two rays excluding the line segment AB:

$$Arg\left(\frac{z-z_1}{z-z_2}\right)=0$$

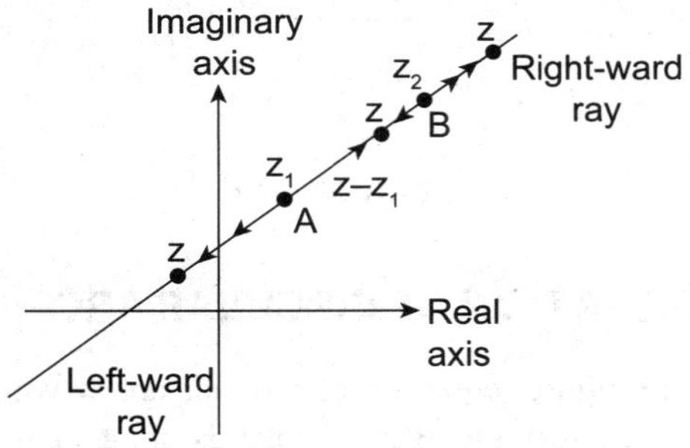

FIGURE 5.29

A(5): Complete line except z_1 and z_2:

The equation is given by

$$\text{Arg}\left(\frac{z-z_1}{z-z_2}\right)=0,\pi \text{ i.e., } I\left(\frac{z-z_1}{z-z_2}\right)=0$$

$$\Rightarrow \frac{z-z_1}{z-z_2}=\frac{\bar{z}-\bar{z}_1}{\bar{z}-\bar{z}_2}$$

$$\Rightarrow z\bar{z}-\bar{z}_2z-z_1\bar{z}+z_1\bar{z}_2$$

$$=z\bar{z}-\bar{z}_1z-z_2\bar{z}+z_2\bar{z}_1$$

$$\Rightarrow (\bar{z}_1-\bar{z}_2)z+(z_2-z_1)\bar{z}+z_1\bar{z}_2-z_2\bar{z}_1=0$$

$$\Rightarrow \frac{(\bar{z}_1-\bar{z}_2)}{2i}z+\frac{(z_2-z_1)}{2i}\bar{z}+I(z_1\bar{z}_2)=0$$

$$\Rightarrow a\bar{z}+\bar{a}z+b=0; \text{ where}$$

$$\Rightarrow \text{where } a=\frac{z_2-z_1}{2i} \text{ and } \bar{a}=\frac{\bar{z}_2-\bar{z}_1}{-2i}=\frac{\bar{z}_1-\bar{z}_2}{2i}$$

■ THEOREM

Perpendicular distance of $P(c)$ (where $c = c_1 + ic_2$) from the straight line is given by $p=\dfrac{|a\bar{c}+\bar{a}c+b|}{2|a|}$.

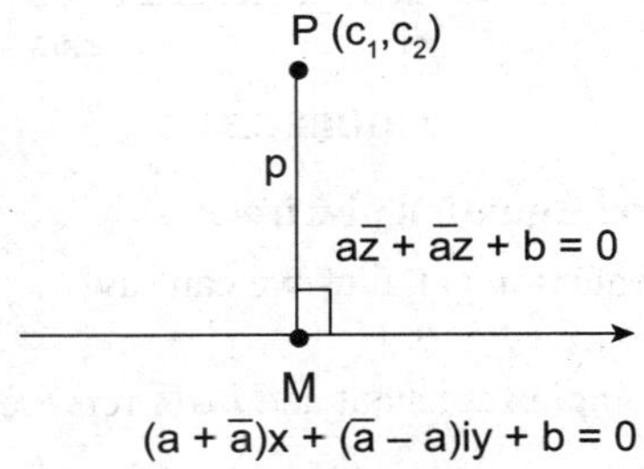

FIGURE 5.30

Proof: Equation of line $\bar{a}z+a\bar{z}+b=0$

$$\Rightarrow (a+\bar{a})x+(\bar{a}-a)iy+b=0$$

$$\Rightarrow PM=p=\frac{|(a+\bar{a})c_1+(\bar{a}-a)ic_2+b|}{\sqrt{(a+\bar{a})^2+(i(\bar{a}-a))^2}}$$

$$=\frac{|a(c_1-ic_2)+(c_1+ic_2)\bar{a}+b|}{\sqrt{a^2+\bar{a}^2+2a\bar{a}-(a^2+\bar{a}^2-2a\bar{a})}}$$

$$=\frac{|a\bar{c}+\bar{a}c+b|}{\sqrt{4a\bar{a}}}=\frac{|a\bar{c}+\bar{a}c+b|}{2|a|}$$

■ COMPLEX SLOPE OF THE LINE

If z_1 and z_2 are two unequal complex numbers represented by points P and Q, then $\dfrac{z_1-z_2}{\bar{z}_1-\bar{z}_2}$ is called the complex slope of the line joining z_1 and z_2

(i.e., line PQ) and is denoted by w; Thus $w=\dfrac{z_1-z_2}{\bar{z}_1-\bar{z}_2}$

Notes

1. *The equation of line PQ is $z-z_1=w\,(\bar{z}-\bar{z}_1)$; Clearly $|w|=\dfrac{|z_1-z_2|}{|\bar{z}_1-\bar{z}_2|}=\dfrac{|z_1-z_2|}{|z_1-z_2|}=1$*
2. *The two lines having complex slopes w_1 and w_2 are parallel if and only if $w_1=w_2$*

■ CIRCLE IN ARGAND PLANE

A(1): Centre radius form:

The equation of circle with z_0 as centre and a positive real number k as radius is given by $|z-z_0|=k$

$$\Rightarrow |z-z_0|^2=k^2$$

$$\Rightarrow (z-z_0)(\bar{z}-\bar{z}_0)=k^2$$

$$\Rightarrow z\bar{z}-z_0\bar{z}-\bar{z}_0z+|z_0|^2-k^2=0 \qquad \text{..........(1)}$$

If $z_0=0$, then $|z|=k$

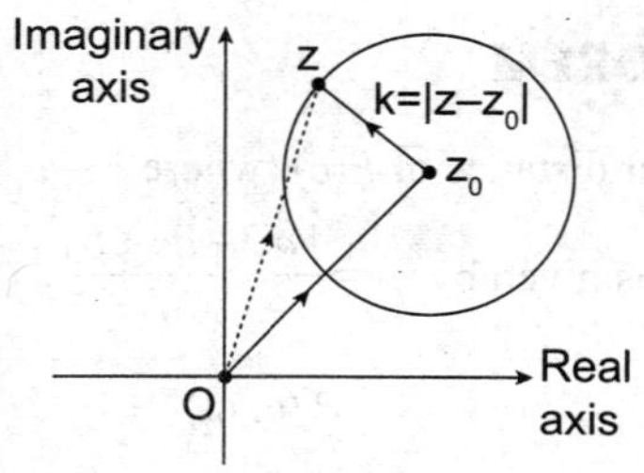

FIGURE 5.31

A(2): General Equation of Circle:

Refering to equation (1), thus we can say

$$z\bar{z} + \bar{a}z + a\bar{z} + b = 0 \qquad ....(2)$$

where a is complex constant and $b \in \mathbb{R}$ represents a general circle.

Compairing (2) with (1), we note that **centre = –*a* and radius =** $\sqrt{|a|^2 - b}$

A(3): Diametric form of circle:

As we know that diameter of any circle subtends right angle at any point on the circumference. Equation of circle with $A(z_1)$ and $B(z_2)$ as end points of diameter.

$$\text{Arg}\left(\frac{z-z_2}{z-z_1}\right) = \begin{cases} \dfrac{\pi}{2} & \text{Case I} \\ -\dfrac{\pi}{2} & \text{Case II} \end{cases} \quad \text{(See the figure 5.36)}$$

$$\Rightarrow \frac{z-z_2}{z-z_1} = \pm ki \text{ where } k = \left|\frac{z-z_2}{z-z_1}\right|$$

$$\Rightarrow \frac{z-z_2}{z-z_1} = -\frac{\bar{z}-\bar{z}_2}{\bar{z}-\bar{z}_1} \quad \Rightarrow \quad \frac{z-z_2}{z-z_1} + \frac{\bar{z}-\bar{z}_2}{\bar{z}-\bar{z}_1} = 0$$

$$\Rightarrow |z-z_1|^2 + |z-z_2|^2 = |z_1 - z_2|^2$$

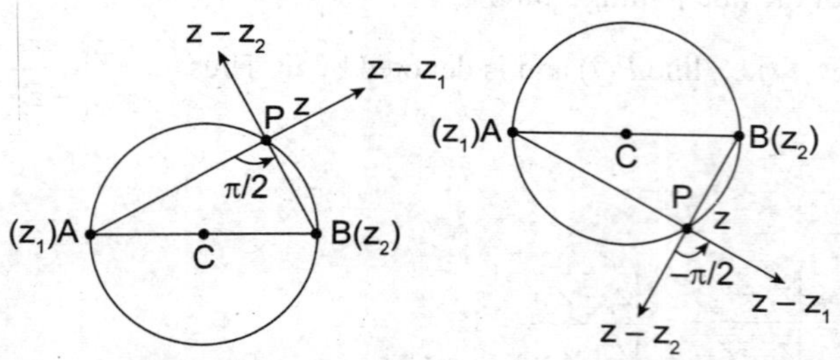

Case I Case II

FIGURE 5.32

■ APPOLONEOUS CIRCLE

If $\left|\frac{z-z_1}{z-z_2}\right| = k$ i.e., $|z - z_1| = k\,|z - z_2|$. Then equation represents apploloneous circle of $A\,(z_1)\,B(z_2)$ with respect to ratio k. When $k = 1$, this gives $|z - z_1| = |z - z_2|$ which is straight line i.e., perpendicular bisector of line segment joining z_1 to z_2.

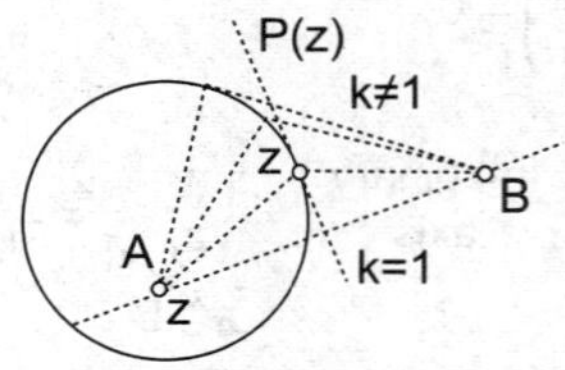

FIGURE 5.33

■ EQUATION OF CIRCULAR ARC

As per the figure; equation of circular arc at which chord AB, (where $A(z_1)$ and $B(z_2)$) subtends angle α is given as

$$Arg\left(\frac{z-z_2}{z-z_1}\right) = \alpha$$

Case I: If $0 < \alpha < \pi/2$ or $-\pi/2 < \alpha < 0$ **(major arc of circle)**

Case II: $\alpha = \pm\dfrac{\pi}{2}$ **(semicircular arc)**

Case III: $\alpha \in \left(-\pi, \dfrac{\pi}{2}\right) \cup \left(\dfrac{\pi}{2}, \pi\right)$ **(Minor arc of circle)**

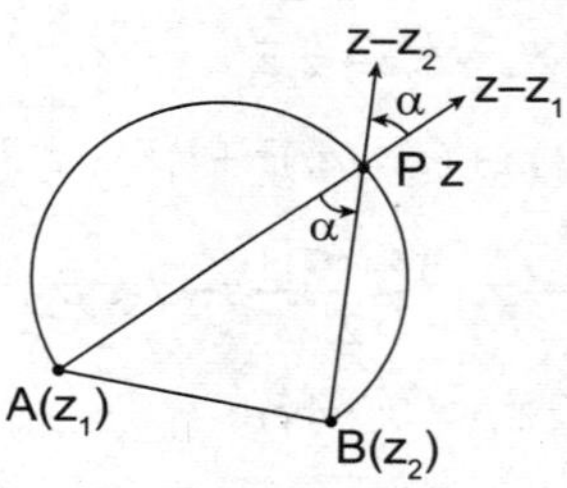

FIGURE 5.34

Case IV: $\alpha = 0$ **(Major arc of ∞ radius)**

Case V: $\alpha = \pi$ **(Minor arc of ∞ radius)**

■ EQUATION OF PARABOLA

Equation of parabola with directrix $a\bar{z} + \bar{a}z + b = 0$ and focus z_0 is given as

$$SP = PM$$

$$|z - z_0| = \frac{|a\bar{z} + \bar{a}z + b|}{2|a|}$$

$$\Rightarrow 4|z - z_0|^2 |a|^2 = |a\bar{z} + \bar{a}z + b|^2$$

$$\Rightarrow 4a\bar{a}(z - z_0)(\bar{z} - \bar{z}_0) = |a\bar{z} + \bar{a}z + b|^2$$

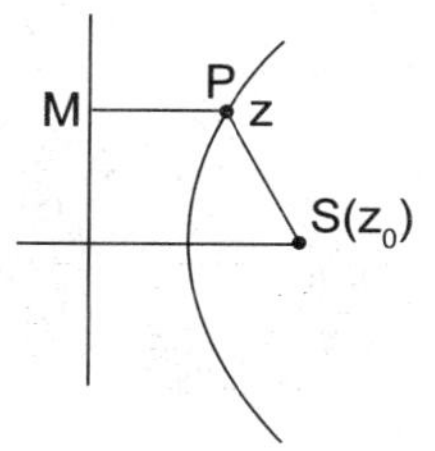

FIGURE 5.35

$$\Rightarrow \quad 4a\bar{a}(z\bar{z} - z\bar{z}_0 - z_0\bar{z} + z_0\bar{z}_0) = |a\bar{z} + \bar{a}z + b|^2$$

■ EQUATION OF ELLIPSE

Ellipse is locus of point $P(z)$ such that sum of its distances from two fixed points $A(z_1)$ and $B(z_2)$ (foci of ellipse) remains constant ($2a$).

$\Rightarrow$ $PA + PB = 2a$

$\Rightarrow$ $|z - z_1| + |z - z_2| = \mathbf{2a}$ where $2a$ is length of major axis

Case I: If $2a > |z_1 - z_2| = AB$ **(locus is ellipse)**

Case II: $2a = |z_1 - z_2|$ **(locus is segment *AB*)**

Case III: $2a < |z_1 - z_2|$ **(No locus)**

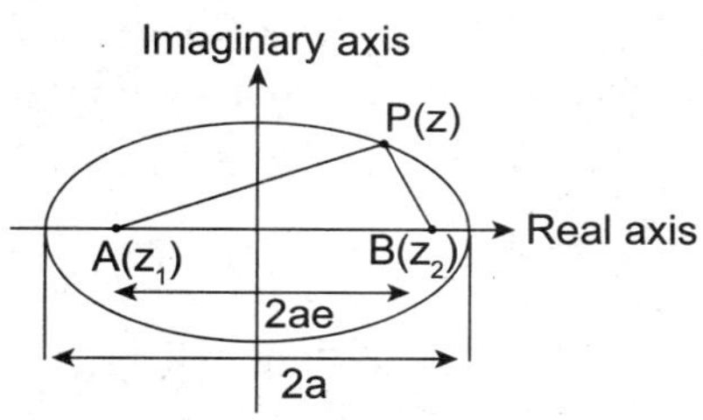

FIGURE 5.36

Case IV: If $|z - z_1| + |z - z_2| > 2a : 2a > |z_1 - z_2|$ **(exterior of ellipse)**

Case V: If $|z - z_1| + |z - z_2| < 2a : 2a > |z_1 - z_2|$ **(interior of ellipse)**

■ EQUATION OF HYPERBOLA

Hyperbola is locus of point $P(z)$ such that difference of its distances from two fixed points $A(z_1)$ and $B(z_2)$ (foci of hyperbola) remains constant ($2a$).

$\Rightarrow$ $PA - PB = 2a$

$\Rightarrow$ $||z - z_1| - |z - z_2|| = 2a$ where $2a$ is length of major axis.

Case I: If $2a < |z_1 - z_2| = AB$ **(locus is branch of hyperola).**

Case II: $2a = |z_1 - z_2|$ **(locus is union of two rays)**

Case III: $2a > |z_1 - z_2|$ **(No locus).**

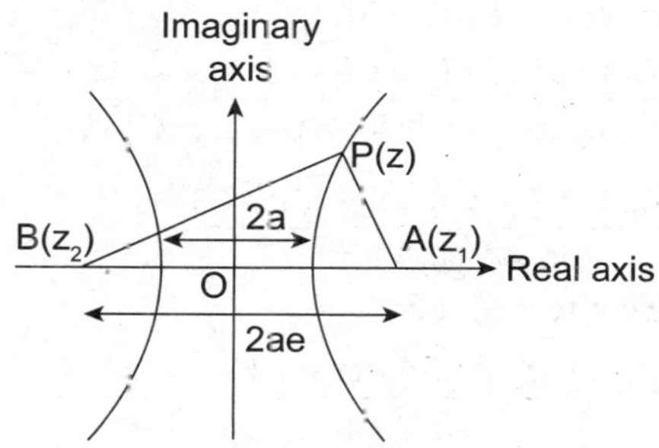

FIGURE 5.37

Case IV: If $||z - z_1| - |z - z_2|| > 2a : 2a < |z_1 - z_2|$ **(exterior of hyperbola)**

Case V: If $||z - z_1| - |z - z_2|| < 2a : 2a < |z_1 - z_2|$ **(interior of hyperbola).**

■ SOME IMPORTANT FACTS

A (1): If A, B, C are the vertices of a triangle represented by complex numbers z_1, z_2, z_3 respectively in anti-clockwise sense and $\angle BAC = \alpha$, then $\dfrac{z_3 - z_1}{|z_3 - z_1|} = \dfrac{z_2 - z_1}{|z_2 - z_1|}.e^{i\alpha}$

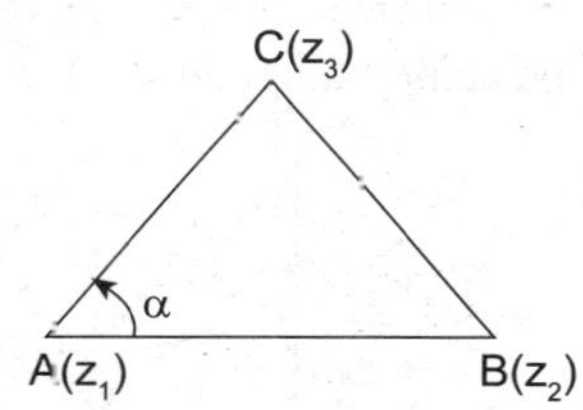

FIGURE 5.38

A(2): If z_1 and z_2 are two complex numbers representing the points A and B, then the point on AB which divides line segment AB in ratio m: n is given by $\dfrac{nz_1 + mz_2}{m+n}$.

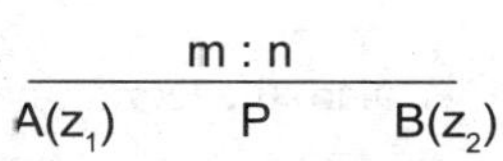

FIGURE 5.39

A(3): If a,b,c are three real numbers not all simultaneously zero such that $az_1 + bz_2 + cz_3 = 0$ and $a + b + c = 0$, then z_1, z_2, z_3 will be collinear.

A(4): If z_1, z_2, z_3 represent the vertices A,B,C of ΔABC, then

(i) **Centroid** of $\Delta ABC = \dfrac{z_1 + z_2 + z_3}{3}$

(ii) **In centre** of $\Delta ABC = \dfrac{az_1 - bz_2 + cz_3}{a+b+c}$

(iii) **Orthocentre** of ΔABC

$$= \frac{(a\sec A)z_1 + (b\sec B)z_2 + (c\sec C)z_3}{(a\sec A) + (b\sec B) + (c\sec C)}$$

$$= \frac{(z_1\tan A + z_2\tan B + z_3\tan C)}{\tan A + \tan B + \tan C}$$

(iv) **Circumcentre** of

$$\Delta ABC = \frac{z_1\sin 2A + z_2\sin 2B + z_3\sin 2C}{\sin 2A + \sin 2B + \sin C}$$

A(5): **amp(z) = θ** represents a ray emanating from origin and inclined at an angle θ with the positive direction of x-axis

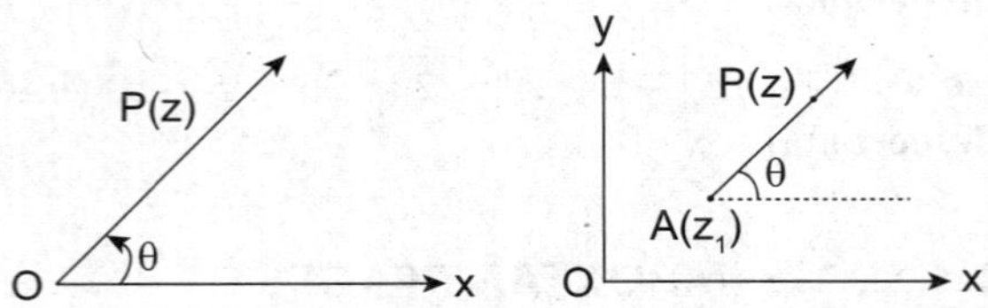

FIGURE 5.40

Also $\arg(z - z_1) = \theta$ represents the ray originating from $A(z_1)$ inclined at an angle θ with positive direction of x-axis as shown in the above diagram.

A(6): $|z - z_1| = |z - z_2|$ represents **perpendicular bisector** of line segment joining the points A(z_1) and $B(z_2)$ as shown below:

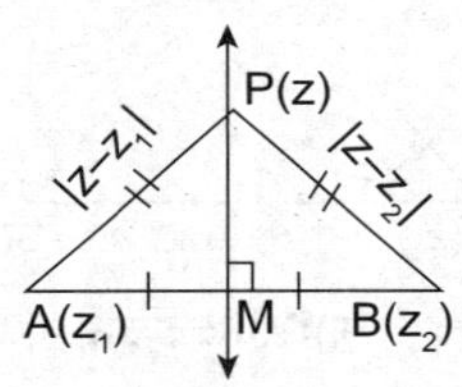

FIGURE 5.41

A(7): The equation of a line passing through the points $A(z_1)$ and $B(z_2)$ can be expressed in determinant form as $\begin{vmatrix} z & \bar{z} & 1 \\ z_1 & \bar{z}_1 & 1 \\ z_2 & \bar{z}_2 & 1 \end{vmatrix} = 0$, it is also the condition for three points z_1, z_2, z_3 (when z is replaced by z_3) to be collinear.

A(8): $|z - z_1| = a$ represents circle of radius a and having centre at z_1

$|z - z_1| < a$ represents **interior** of above circle.

$|z - z_1| > a$ represents **exterior** of above circle.

A(9): $a < |z| < b$ represents points lying inside the circular annulus bounded by circles having radii a and b and having their centres at origin as shown below:

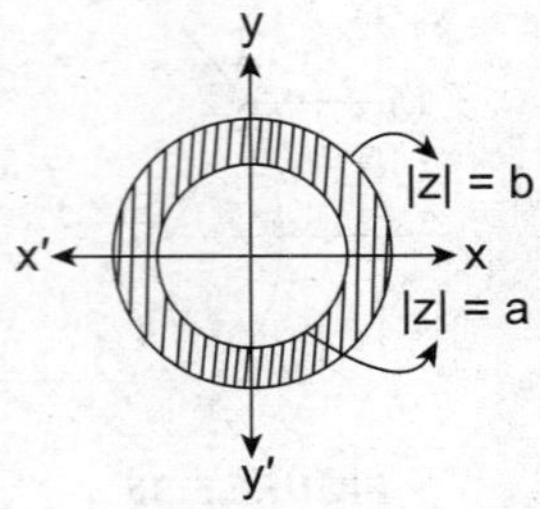

FIGURE 5.42

A(10): $|z + z_1| = |z| + |z_1|$ represents the ray originating from origin and passing through the point A (z_1) as shown below:

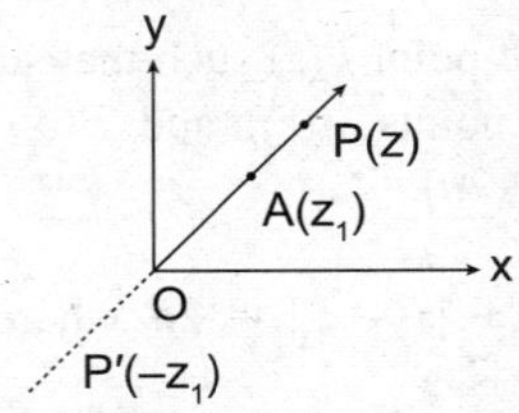

FIGURE 5.43

$$|z + z_1| = PP' = PO + OP' = |z| + OA = |z| + |z_1|$$
$$(\because OP' = OA)$$

A(11): $|z - z_1| = |z| - |z_1|$ represents a ray originating from A(z_1) but not passing through the origin as shown below:

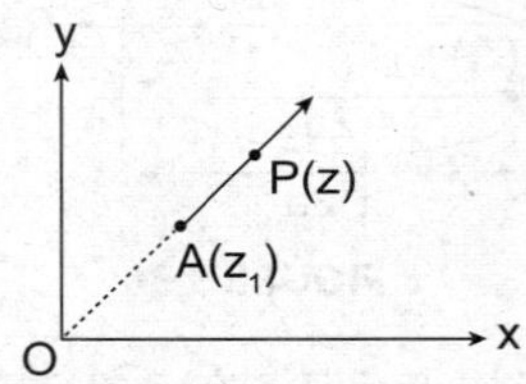

FIGURE 5.44

$$|z - z_1| = OP - OA = |z| - |z_1|$$

A(12): **Re(z) ≥ a** represents the half plane to the right of straight line $x = a$ including the line itself as shown below:

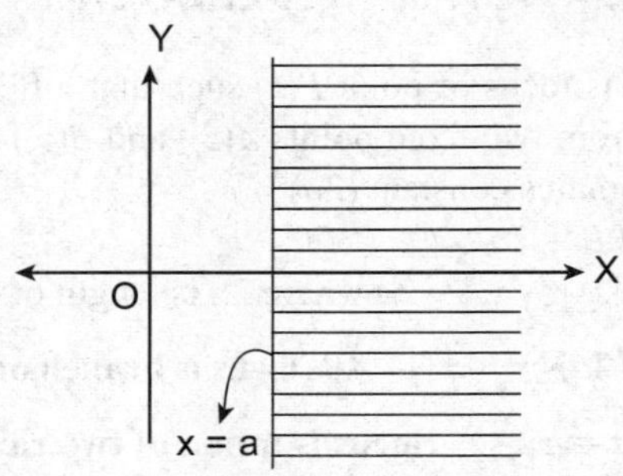

FIGURE 5.45

Re(z) ≤ a represents the half plane to the left of straight line $x = a$ including the line itself as shown below:

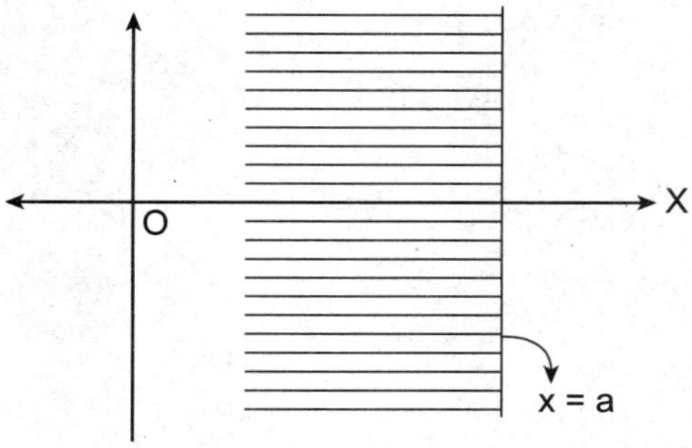

FIGURE 5.46

Im(z) ≤ a represents the half plane below the straight line $y = a$ including the line itself as shown below:

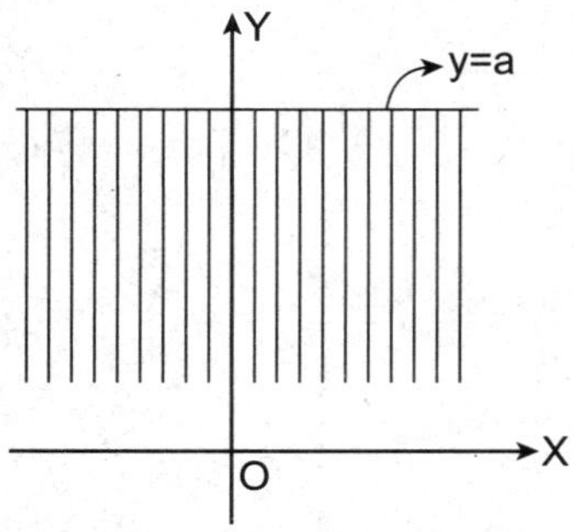

FIGURE 5.47

Im(z) ≥ a represents the half plane above the straight line $y = a$ including the line itself as shown below:

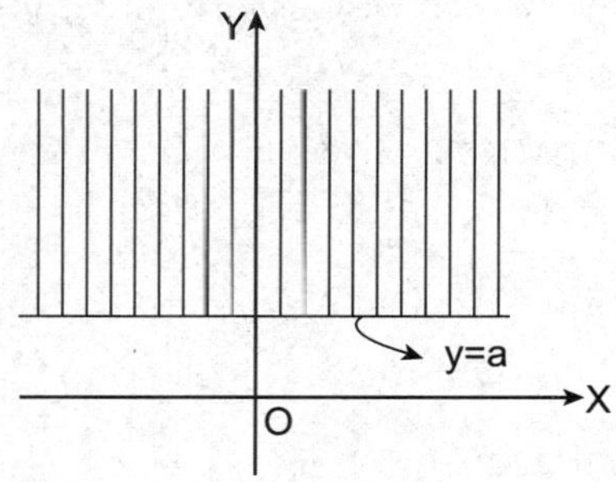

FIGURE 5.48

A(13): **Inverse points. w.r.t. a circle**

Two points A and B are said to be inverse *w.r.t* a circle with centre 'O' and radius a, if:

(i) The points O, A, B are collinear and on the same side of O and

(ii) $OA.OB = a^2$

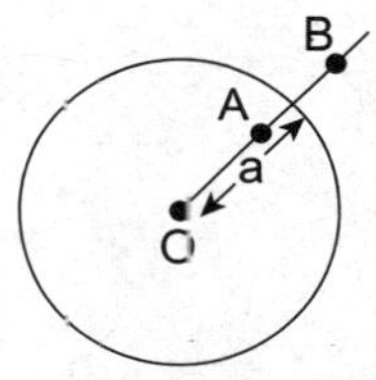

FIGURE 5.49

Remark

Two points z_1 and z_2 will be the inverse points w.r.t the circle $z\bar{z} + \bar{\beta}z + \beta\bar{z} + r = 0$, if and only if $z_1\bar{z}_2 + \bar{\beta}z_1 + \beta\bar{z}_2 + r = 0$.

A(14): If λ is a positive real constant, and z satisfies $\left|\dfrac{z - z_1}{z - z_2}\right| = \lambda$, then the point z decribes a circle of which A, B are inverse points; unless $\lambda = 1$, in which case z describes the perpendicular bisector of AB;

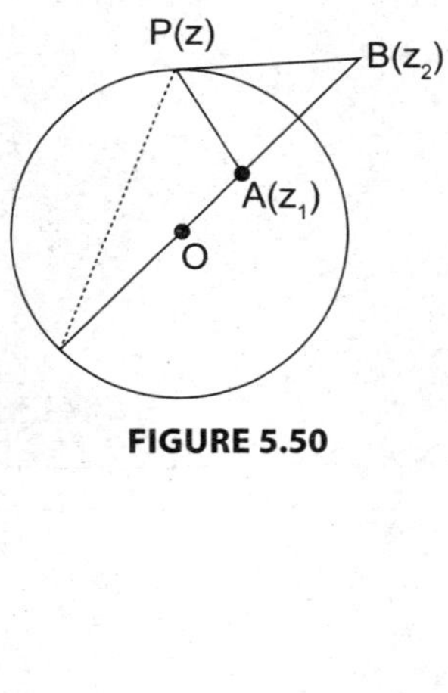

FIGURE 5.50

A(15): To convert an equation from cartesian to complex form put $x = \dfrac{z + \bar{z}}{2}$ and $y = \dfrac{z - \bar{z}}{2i}$ and to convert an equation in complex form to cartesian form put $z = x + iy$ and $\bar{z} = x - iy$.

ILLUSTRATION 66: Discuss locus of the inequation $\log_{1/2}\left\{\frac{|z-1|+4}{3|z-1|-2}\right\}>1.$

SOLUTION: Given inequality is $\log_{1/2}\left\{\frac{|z-1|+4}{3|z-1|-2}\right\}>1. \Rightarrow \frac{|z-1|+4}{3|z-1|-2}<\frac{1}{2}$

$\Rightarrow 2(|z-1|+4) < 3|z-1| - 2 \Rightarrow 10 < |z-1| \Rightarrow |z-1| > 10 \Rightarrow (x-1)^2 + y^2 > 100$

This represents the outside region of the circle $(x-1)^2 + y^2 = 100$.

ILLUSTRATION 67: If $|z| \le 1$. $|w| \le 1$ show that $|z-w|^2 \le (|z| - |w|^2) + (\arg z - \arg w)^2$

SOLUTION: Let, $z = r_1(\cos\alpha + i\sin\alpha)$ and $w = r_2(\cos\beta + i\sin\beta)$. Given, $|z| \le 1$ and $|w| \le 1$

$\Rightarrow r_1 \le 1,\ r_2 \le 1$

Now, L.H.S $= |z-w|^2$

$= |r_1(\cos\alpha + i\sin\alpha) - r_2(\cos\beta + i\sin\beta)|^2$

$= |(r_1\cos\alpha - r_2\cos\beta) + i(r_1\sin\alpha - r_2\sin\beta)|^2$

$= \left(\sqrt{(r_1\cos\alpha - r_2\cos\beta)^2 + (r_1\sin\alpha - r_2\sin\beta)^2}\right)^2$

$= r_1^2\cos^2\alpha + r_2^2\cos^2\beta - 2r_1r_2\cos\alpha\cos\beta + r_1^2\sin^2\alpha + r_2^2\sin^2\beta - 2r_1r_2\sin\alpha\sin\beta$

$= r_1^2 + r_2^2 - 2r_1r_2\cos(\alpha-\beta)$

$= (r_1-r_2)^2 + 2r_1r_2 2\left[\sin\left(\frac{\alpha-\beta}{2}\right)\right]^2 \le (r_1-r_2)^2 + 2.1.1.2\left(\frac{\alpha-\beta}{2}\right)^2$

$\Rightarrow |z-w|^2 \le (|z|-|w|)^2 + (\alpha-\beta)^2 \Rightarrow |z-w|^2 \le (|z|-|w|)^2 + (\arg z - \arg w)^2$

ILLUSTRATION 68: Let $z_1 = 10 + 6i$ and $z_2 = 4 + 6i$. If z is any complex number such that amplitude of $\frac{z-z_1}{z-z_2}$ is $\frac{\pi}{4}$, then prove that $|z - 7 - 9i| = 3\sqrt{2}$.

SOLUTION: Amp $\left(\frac{z-z_1}{z-z_2}\right) = \frac{\pi}{4}$; where $z_1 = (10+6i)$, $z_2 = (4+6i)$ represent a major arc of circle with chord joining z_1 and z_2 subtending angle $\frac{\pi}{4}$ on it. So at centre of the arc angle subtended by chord AB is $\frac{\pi}{2}$.

Clearly M (mid point of chord AB) is (7, 6)

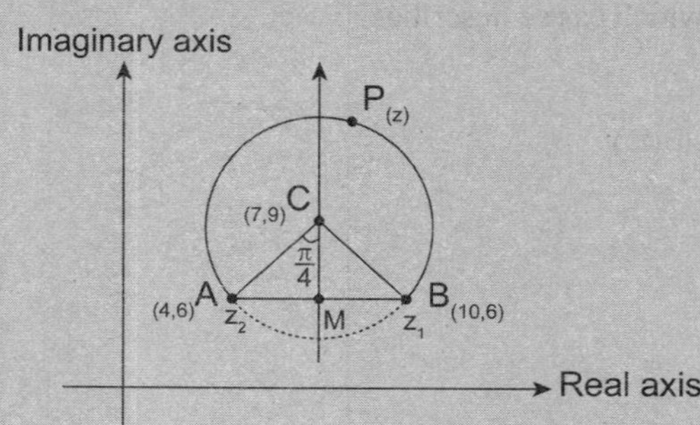

FIGURE 5.51

Now in ΔACM, $\angle ACM = \frac{\pi}{4} \Rightarrow AM = CM = 3$

$\Rightarrow$ Co-ordinate of centre C (7, 9) and radius $AC = \sqrt{3^2+3^2} = 3\sqrt{2}$

$\Rightarrow$ Equation of circular arc in centre radius form is $|z-7-9i| = 3\sqrt{2}$

Aliter: $z = x + iy$

$$\frac{z-z_1}{z-z_2} = \frac{x+iy-10-6i}{x+iy-4-6i} = \frac{(x-10)+i(y-6)}{(x-4)+i(y-6)} \times \frac{x-4-i(y-6)}{x-4-i(y-6)}$$

$$= \frac{(x-10)(x-4)+(y-6)^2+i[(x-4)(y-6)-(x-10)(y-6)]}{(x-4)^2+(y-6)^2}$$

$$= \frac{[(x-10))(x-4)+(y-6)^2]+i[6(y-6)]}{(x-4)^2+(y-6)^2}$$

Given, $amp\left(\frac{z-z_1}{z-z_2}\right) = \frac{\pi}{4} \Rightarrow \frac{6(y-6)}{(x-10)(x-4)+(y-6)^2} = 1$

$\Rightarrow x^2 - 14x + 40 + y^2 + 36 - 12y = 6y - 36 \Rightarrow x^2 + y^2 - 14x - 18y + 112 = 0$

L. H.S. $= |z-7-9i| = \sqrt{(x-7)^2+(y-9)^2} = \sqrt{x^2+y^2-14x-18y+130}$

$= \sqrt{(x^2+y^2-14x-18y+112+18}$ (from equation (i))

$= \sqrt{18} = 3\sqrt{2}$ = R.H.S.

ILLUSTRATION 69: Find all non-zero complex numbers z satisfying $\bar{z} = iz^2$.

SOLUTION: Let $z = x + iy$. Given $\bar{z}$ iz

$\Rightarrow x - iy = i(x+iy)^2 = i(x^2 - y^2 + i\,2xy) \Rightarrow x - iy = -2xy + i(x^2 - y^2)$

Equating real and imaginary parts, we get $x = -2xy$ ...(i)

and $-y = x^2 - y^2$ ...(ii)

$\Rightarrow x = 0$ or $y = -\frac{1}{2}$ ...(iii)

From equaiton (ii), $x^2 - y^2 + y = 0$; When, $x = 0$, $y - y^2 = 0$

$\Rightarrow y(y-1) = 0 \Rightarrow y = 0$ or 1

$\therefore$ $z = (0, 0)$ and $(0, 1)$ and when $y = -\frac{1}{2}; x = \pm\frac{\sqrt{3}}{2}$

Thus non-zero complex number are $z = i$ and $\pm\frac{\sqrt{3}}{2} - \frac{1}{2}i$

ILLUSTRATION 70: If α, β are complex numbers, then find the complex numbers z_1 and z_2 so that the points z_1, z_2 and α, β be the corners of the diagonals of a square.

SOLUTION: Here, $\alpha - z_1 = (\beta - z_1)e^{i\pi/2} = i(\beta - z_1)$

$\Rightarrow \alpha - i\beta = z_1(1-i) \qquad \Rightarrow z_1 = \frac{\alpha - i\beta}{1-i} = \frac{(\alpha - i\beta)(1+i)}{2}$

$\Rightarrow z_1 = \frac{(\alpha+\beta)+i(\alpha-\beta)}{2} = \frac{\alpha+\beta}{2} + i\left(\frac{\alpha-\beta}{2}\right)$

Similarly, $\beta - z_2 = (\alpha - z_2)e^{i\pi/2} \Rightarrow z_2 = \frac{\alpha+\beta}{2} - i\left(\frac{\alpha-\beta}{2}\right)$

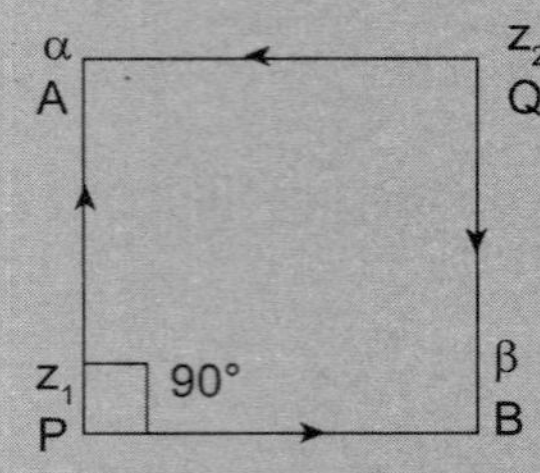

FIGURE 5.52

ILLUSTRATION 71: Let $|z| = 1$, then find the locus of points $2 + 4z$.

SOLUTION: The points z which satisfy the condition $|z| = 1$ lie on a circle of radius 1 with centre at the origin. All points $4z$, where $|z| = 1$, are located on a circle of radius 4 with centre at the origin. The point $4z + 2$ is obtained from point $4z$ by a rightward shift of 2 unit. And so the points $2 + 4z$, where $|z| = 1$, are located on the circle of radius 4 with centre at the point (2,0) as shown below:

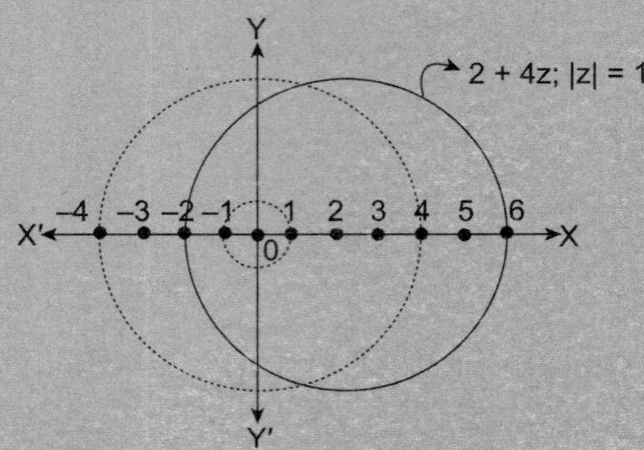

FIGURE 5.53

ILLUSTRATION 72: Locate the complex numbers $z = x + iy$ for which

(i) $\log_{1/4}|z - 4| > \log_{1/4}|z - 2|$ (ii) $\log_{1/4}|z - 4| < \log_{1/4}|z - 2|$

(iii) $\log_{1/4}|z - 4| = \log_{1/4}|z - 2|$

SOLUTION: For the validity of above inequalities and third equation $z \neq 2,4$.

Now $\log_{1/4}|z - 4| > \log_{1/4}|z - 2| \Rightarrow |z - 4| < |z - 2|$

Now $|z - 4| = |z - 2|$ represents the perpendicular bisector of line segment joining the point $z = 2$ and $z = 4$ i.e., $x = 3$. Now we want to locate the points on complex plane which are nearer to $z = 4$ as compared to $z = 2$. This will be the region of half plane to the right of straight line $x = 3$ excluding the line itself and point $z = 4$ as shown in the diagram given below. For the inequality $\log_{1/4}|z - 4| < \log_{1/4}|z - 2|$, the points on complex plane will be those nearest to $z = 2$ as compared to $z = 4$, this will be the region of half plane to the left of straight line $x = 3$ excluding the line itself and the point $z = 2$ as shown in the given below diagram.

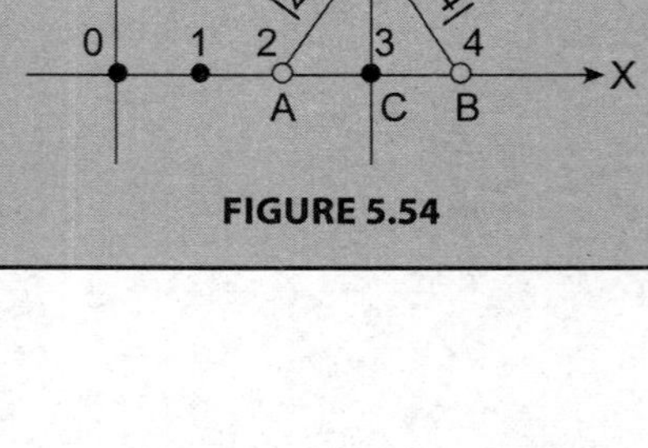

FIGURE 5.54

ILLUSTRATION 73: Find the locus of z satisfying the equation $\arg\left(\frac{z-2}{z+2}\right)=\frac{\pi}{4}$.

SOLUTION: Let $z = x + iy$

$$\therefore \quad \frac{z-2}{z+2}=\frac{(x-2)+iy}{(x+2)+iy}=\frac{(x^2+y^2-4)+i(4y)}{(x+2)^2+y^2}$$

Thus, we have $\tan\left[\arg\left(\frac{z-2}{z+2}\right)\right]=\frac{4y}{x^2+y^2-4}$

A.T.Q. $\frac{4y}{x^2+y^2-4}=\tan\left(\frac{\pi}{4}\right)=1$

$\Rightarrow x^2 + y^2 - 4y - 4 = 0$ which represents a circle having its centre at (0, 2) and radius = $2\sqrt{2}$ geometrically it would be the arc of circle above the x-axis as shown below:

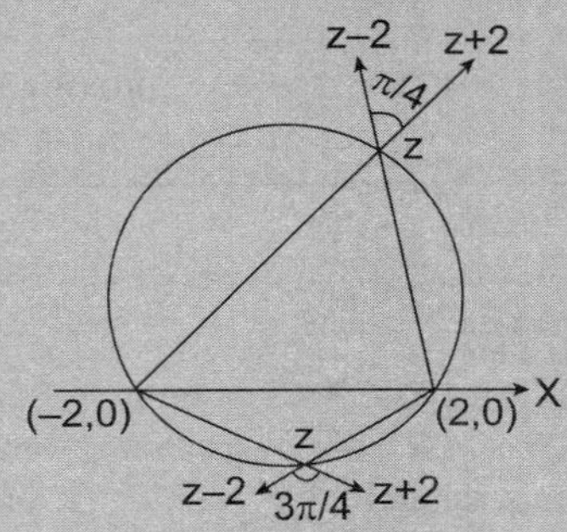

FIGURE 5.55

ILLUSTRATION 74: Find the locus of complex numbers satisfying the inequality $|z-1| + |z+1| \leq 4$.

SOLUTION: $|z-1| + |z+1| = 4$

As $|z_1 - z_2| = |1-(-1)| = 2 < 4 \Rightarrow |z-1| + |z+1| \leq 4$ represents ellipse and its interior region with foci at (–1, 0) and (1, 0) and with length of major axis = 2

Aliter: $|z-1| + |z+1| = 4$

$\Rightarrow |x-1+iy| + |x+1+iy| = 4$

$\Rightarrow \sqrt{(x-1)^2+y^2}+\sqrt{(x+1)^2+y^2}=4$

$\Rightarrow (x-1)^2+y^2=(x+1)^2+y^2-8\sqrt{(x+1)^2+y^2}+16$

$\Rightarrow x+4=2\sqrt{(x+1)^2+y^2}$

$\Rightarrow x^2+8x+16=4(x^2+y^2+2x+1)$

$\Rightarrow 3x^2+4y^2=12 \Rightarrow \frac{x^2}{4}+\frac{y^2}{3}=1$. It is an ellipse.

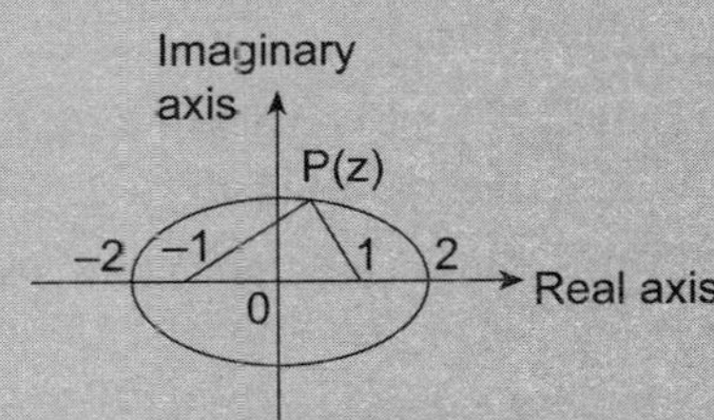

FIGURE 5.56

Hence the points z satisfying $|z-1| + |z+1| \leq 4$ lie in Argand plane on the boundary and in the interior of the ellipse $\frac{x^2}{4}+\frac{y^2}{3}=1$.

ILLUSTRATION 75: Show that the equation $|z-z_1|^2 + |z-z_2|^2 = k$.

(where k is a real number) will represent a circle if $k \geq \frac{1}{2}|z_1-z_2|^2$

SOLUTION: Given equation is $|z - z_1|^2 + |z - z_2|^2 = k$

$\Rightarrow |z|^2 + |z_1|^2 - 2R(z\bar{z}_1) + |z|^2 + |z_2|^2 - 2R(z\bar{z}_2) = k$

$\Rightarrow 2|z|^2 - 2R[z(\bar{z}_1 + \bar{z}_2)] = k - (|z_1|^2 + |z_2|^2)$

$$\Rightarrow |z|^2 - 2R\left[z\left(\overline{\frac{z_1+z_2}{2}}\right)\right] + \frac{1}{4}|z_1+z_2|^2 = \frac{k}{2} + \frac{1}{4}\left[|z_1+z_2|^2 - 2|z_1|^2 - 2|z_2|^2\right]$$

$$\Rightarrow \left|z - \frac{z_1+z_2}{2}\right|^2 = \frac{1}{2}\left[k - \frac{1}{2}\left\{|z_1|^2 + |z_2|^2 - 2R(z_1\bar{z}_2)\right\}\right]$$

$$\text{or} \quad \left|z - \frac{z_1+z_2}{2}\right|^2 = \frac{1}{2}\left[k - \frac{1}{2}|z_1 - z_2|^2\right] \qquad \text{....(1)}$$

Equation (1) represents a circle with centre at

$\frac{1}{2}(z_1 + z_2)$ and radius $\frac{1}{2}\sqrt{2k - |z_1 - z_2|^2}$, provided $k \geq \frac{1}{2}|z_1 - z_2|^2$

TEXTUAL EXERCISE 10: (SUBJECTIVE)

1. Let z_1, z_2, z_3, z_4 represent the vertices A, B, C, D respectively of a square on the Argand diagram taken in anti-clockwise direction, then prove that
   (i) $2z_2 = (1 + i)z_1 + (1 - i)z_3$.
   (ii) $2z_4 = (1 - i)z_1 + (1 + i)z_3$.

2. (a) Write equation of straight line which makes angle 60° and passing through point $z_0 = 2 + i$.
   (b) Write equation of line passing through $z_1(-2 - i)$ and $z_2(3 + i)$.

3. (a) If z_1, z_2, z_3 be vertices of an isosceles Δ right angled at z_2, then prove that $z_1^2 + 2z_2^2 + z_3^2 = 2z_2(z_1 + z_3)$.
   (b) If in above case right angle is at z_3, then show that $(z_1 - z_2)^2 = 2(z_1 - z_3)(z_3 - z_2)$.

4. If z_1, z_2, z_3 be three distinct complex numbers satisfying $|z_1 - 1| = |z_2 - 1| = |z_3 - 1|$. Let A, B and C be the points represented in the Argand plane corresponding to z_1, z_2 and z_3 respectively. Prove that $z_1 + z_2 + z_3 = 3$ if and only if ΔABC is an equilateral triangle.

5. (a) If z_1, z_2, z_3 represents vertices of an equilateral triangle, then prove that $z_1^2 + z_2^2 + z_3^2 = z_1 z_2 + z_2 z_3 + z_3 z_1$.
   (b) Let the complex numbers z_1, z_2, z_3 represents vertices of an equilateral triangle. If z_0 be the circumcentre of the triangle, then prove that $z_1^2 + z_2^2 + z_3^2 = 3z_0^2$.

6. Prove that the triangle whose vertices are the points z_1, z_2, z_3 on the Argand plane is an equilateral triangle if and only if $\frac{1}{z_2 - z_3} + \frac{1}{z_3 - z_1} + \frac{1}{z_1 - z_2} = 0$.

7. If $z_r (r = 1, 2, ...6)$ are the vertices of a regular hexagon, then prove that $\sum_{r=1}^{6} z_r^2 = 6z_0^2$, where z_0 is the circumcentre.

8. Find the number of complex numbers z for which $\text{Arg}\left(\frac{3z-6-3i}{2z-8-6i}\right) = \frac{\pi}{4}$ and $|2z - 3 + i| = 3$.

9. Let z_1 and z_2 be roots of the equation $z^2 + pz + q = 0$, where the coefficients p and q may be complex numbers. Let A and B represent z_1 and z_2 in the complex plane. If $\angle AOB = \alpha \neq 0$ and $OA = OB$, where O is the origin, prove that $|p|^2 = 4|q| \cos^2\alpha/2$.

10. Find the area bounded by the curves $\text{Arg } z = \pi/3$, $\text{Arg } z = 2\pi/3$ and $\text{Arg }(z - 2 - 2\sqrt{3}\, i) = \pi$ on the complex plane.

11. If the area of the triangle formed by z, iz and $z + iz$ is 8 sq. units, then find $|z|$.

12. Let z_1 and z_2 be two complex numbers represented by points on the circle $|z_1| = 1$ and $|z_2| = 2$ respectively, then prove that

(a) max. $|2z_1 + z_2| = 4$
(b) min. $|z_1 + z_2| = 1$
(c) $|z_2 + 1/z_1| \le 3$

13. (a) Find the centre and radius of circle given by equation, $z\bar{z}+(3+4i)\bar{z}+(3-4i)z+24=0$
(b) Find the equation of circle whose end points of diameter are given by $(2 - i)$ and $(3 + i)$
(c) Trace the locus represented by following relation;

$$\frac{\pi}{3} \le \arg\left(\frac{z-i}{z+i}\right) \le \frac{2\pi}{3}$$

14. If $|z| = 2$, then locate,
(a) $z + 2$ (b) $z + z_0$
(c) $z - 1 + i$

15. Obtain the complex numbers z satisfying $|z - 25i| \le 15$ and having:
(a) least positive arg (b) greatest positive arg
(c) least modulus (d) greatest modulus

16. If z is any complex number satisfying $|z - k| = k$, where k is + *ve* real number, then which of the following is correct?
(a) $2\arg z = \arg(z - k)$ (b) $\arg(z - k) = \arg(z + k)$
(c) $|z|_{max} = 2k$ (d) $|z|_{min} = 0$
(e) $(\arg z)_{max} \to \pi/2$ (f) $|z - i|_{max} = k + \sqrt{k^2+1}$
(g) $|z - i|_{min} = \sqrt{k^2+1} - k$

17. Determine locus of z given by the following equations:
(a) $1 < |z + 2i| \le 3$
(b) $Re(z) > 3$ and $|Im\, z| < 2$
(c) $\frac{\pi}{6} \le amp\,(z) \le \frac{\pi}{3}$
(d) $\arg z = \frac{\pi}{2}$ and $|z| < 5$
(e) $|z - 1|^2 - |z + 1|^2 = 4$
(f) $|z - i| = 1$ and $\arg z = \frac{\pi}{4}$
(g) $|z + i| = |z - 2|$
(h) $|z - 1| = |z - 3| = |z - i|$
(i) $|z| - 4 = |z - i| = |z + 5i|$
(j) $|\pi - \arg z| \le \pi/4$
(k) $|z - i| + |z + i| = 2$, $|z - i| + |z + i| > 2$, $|z - i| + |z + i| < 2$

18. Interpret the following equations geometrically on the Argand plane.
(a) $|z - 1| + |z + 1| = 4$
(b) $Arg\,(z - i) - Arg\,(z - i) = \pi/2$
(c) $1 < |z - 2 - 3i| < 4$
(d) $\pi/4 < Arg(z) < \pi/3$
(e) $\log_{\cos\pi/3}\left\{\frac{|z-1|+4}{3|z-1|-2}\right\} > 1$
(f) $\log_{1/2}|z - 2| > \log_{1/2}|z|$
(g) $\log_{1/\sqrt{3}}\frac{|z|^2 - |z| + 1}{2+|z|} > -2$

Answer Key

2. (a) $\arg(z - 2 - i) = \pi/3, -2\pi/3$ (b) $\frac{z-z_2}{z-z_1} = \frac{\bar{z}-\bar{z}_2}{\bar{z}-\bar{z}_1}$ where $z_1 = -2 - i$, $z_2 = 3 + i$ **8.** 2 **10.** $4\sqrt{3}$ **11.** 4

13. (a) $C: -(3 + 4i)$, $R: 1$ (b) $\arg\left(\frac{z-3-i}{z-2+i}\right) = \pm\pi/2$; $\left(\frac{z-3-i}{z-2+i}\right) = \pm ri$ (c)

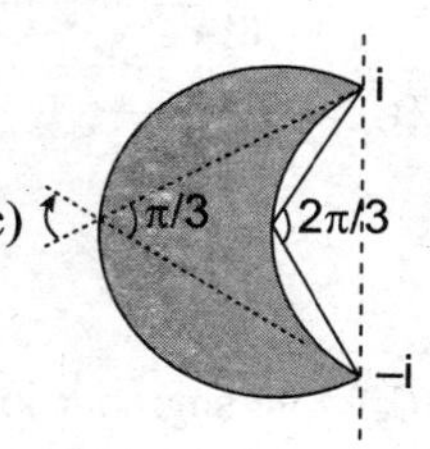

14. (a)

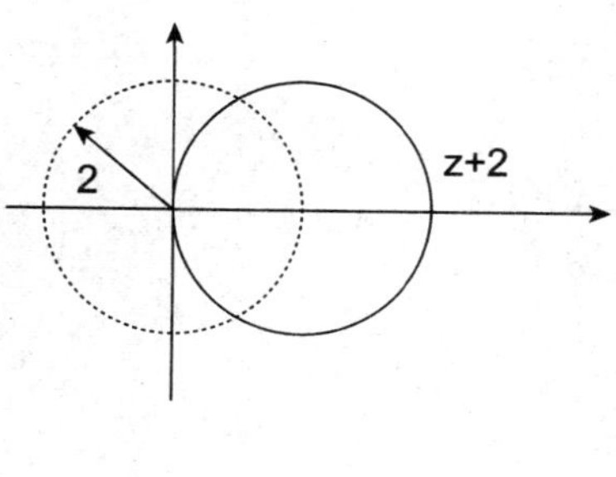

(b)

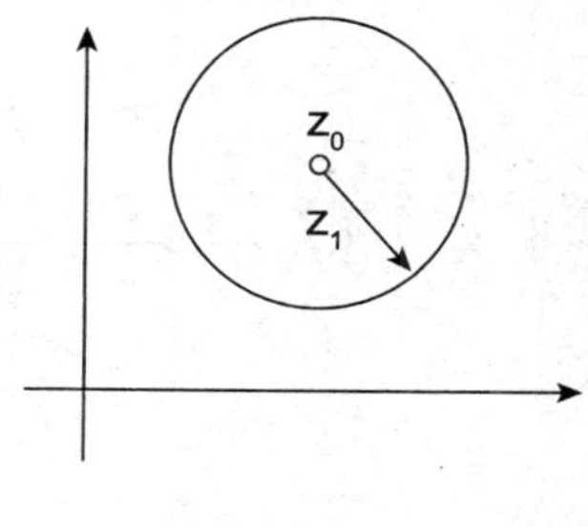

(c)

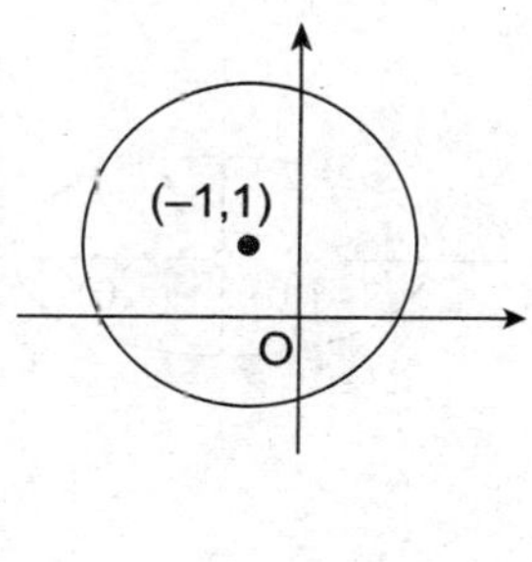

15. 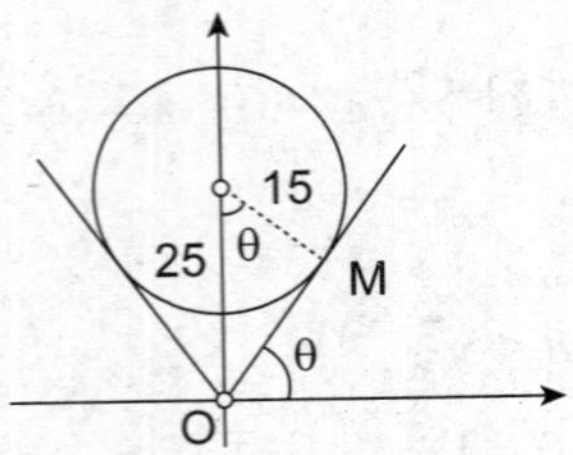

(a) $12 + 16i$ (b) $-12 + 16i$ (c) $10i$ (d) $40i$

16. (a) True (b) False (c) True (d) True (e) True (f) True (g) True

17. (a) 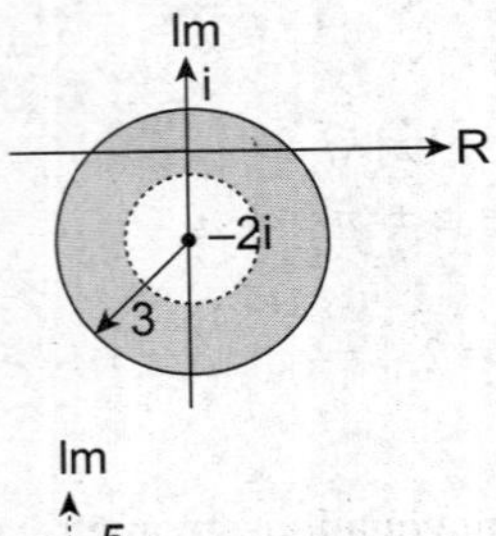

(b) 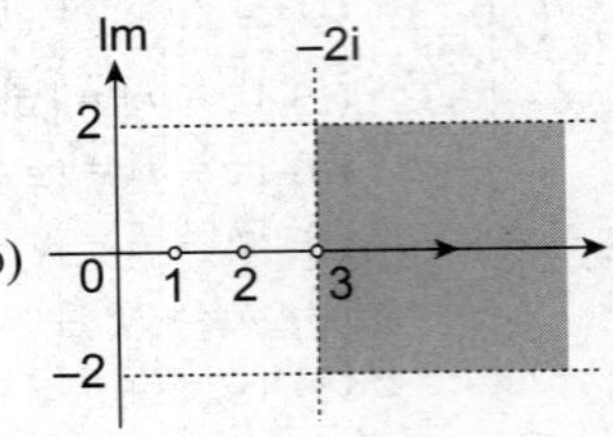

(c) 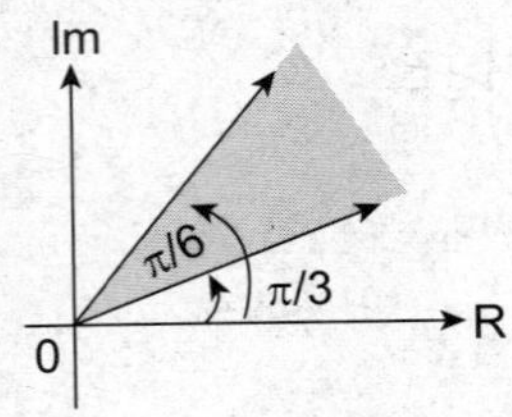

(d) 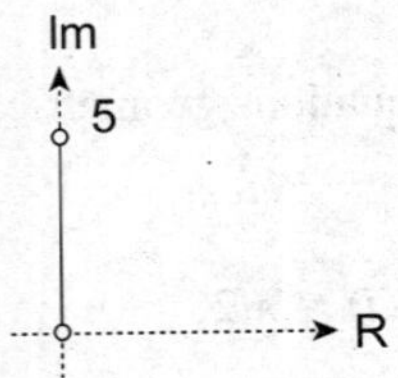

(e) 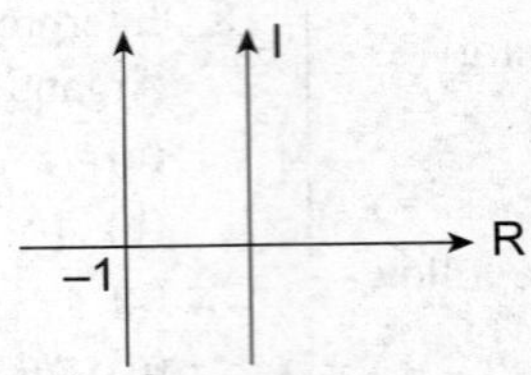

$x + 1 = 0$

(f) 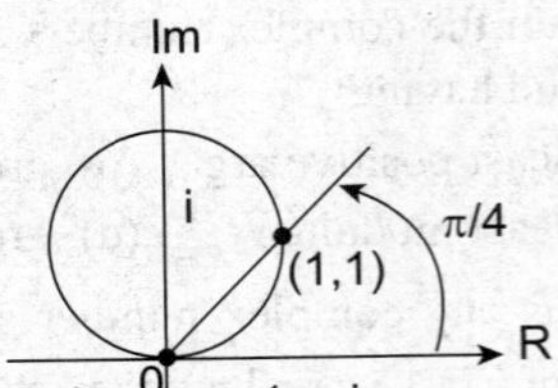

$z = \frac{1}{\sqrt{2}} + \frac{i}{\sqrt{2}}$

(g) 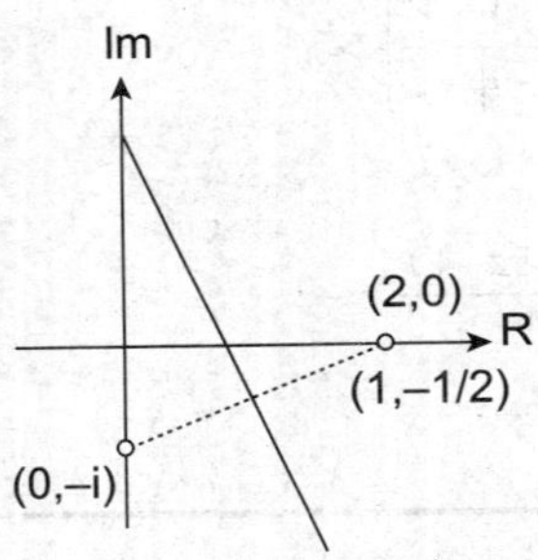

Locus is straight line $4x + 2y - 3 = 0$

(h) 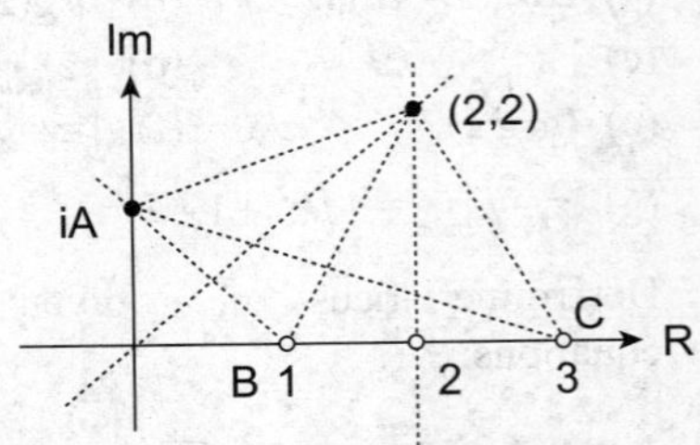

Circumcentre of ΔABC

(i) 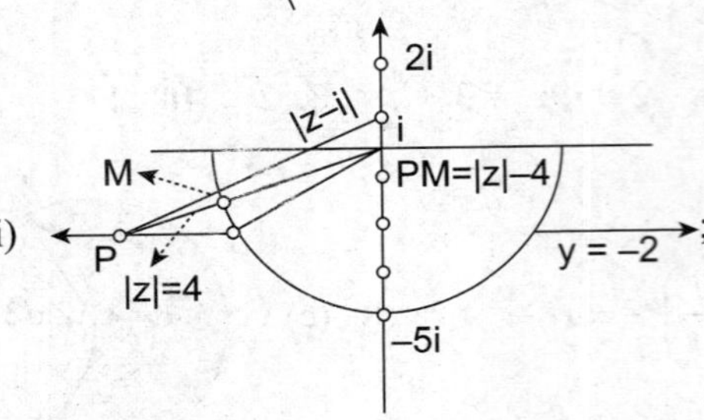

; no locus is obtained

(j) 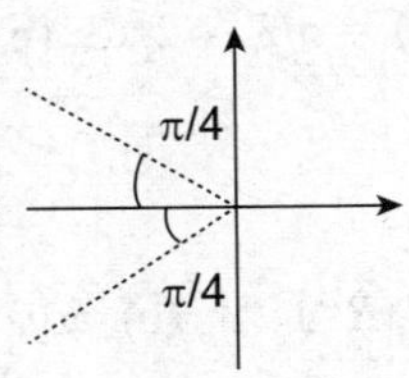

(k) line segment joining i and $-i$; complete argand plane except line segment joining i and $-i$; no locus

18. (a) 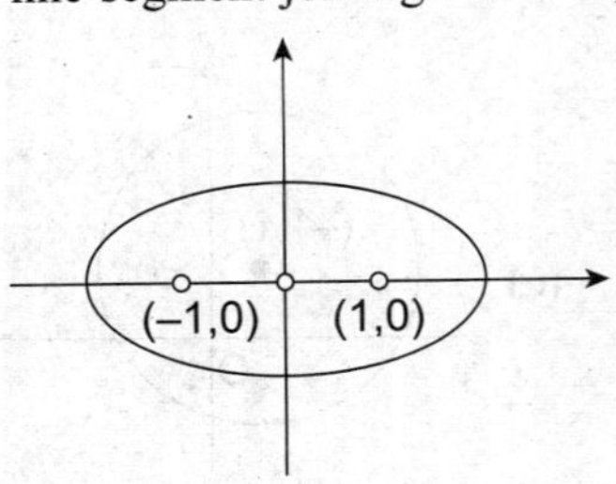

(b) 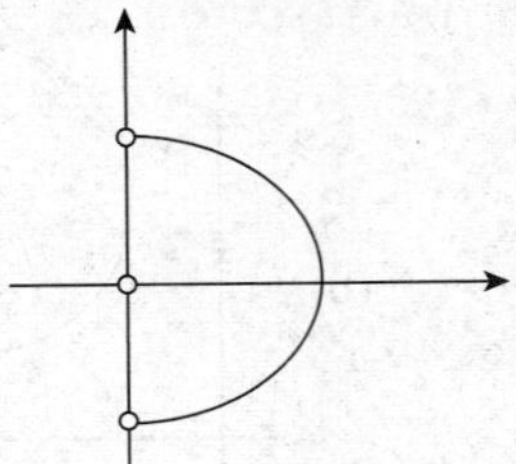

(c) 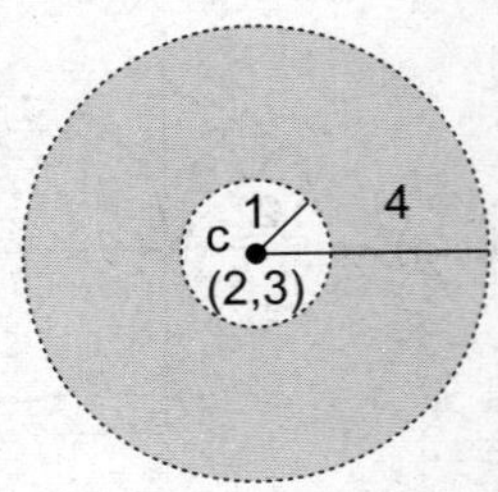

(d) 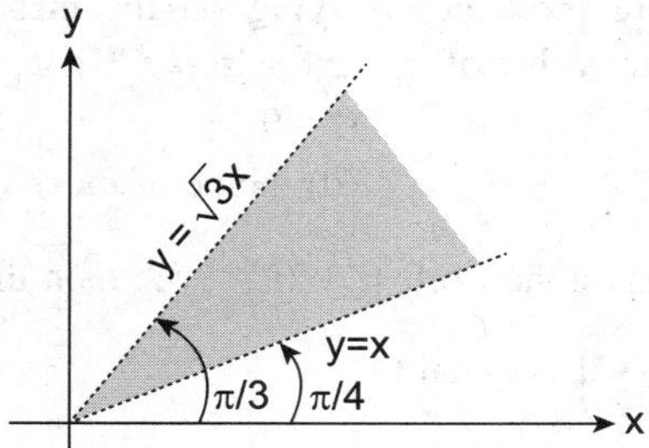

(e) 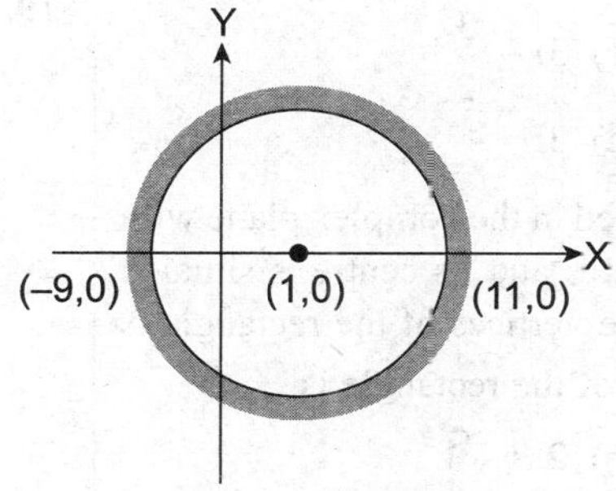

(f) All points towards the right of $x = 1$ except the point (2,0)

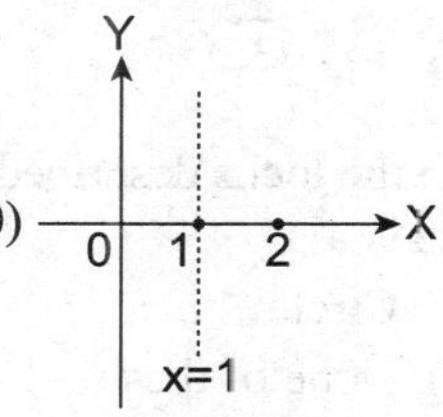

(g) All points inside the circle $|z| = 5$

TEXTUAL EXERCISE 10: (OBJECTIVE)

1. If z_1, z_2 are two complex numbers such that $\left|\dfrac{z_1 - z_2}{z_1 + z_2}\right| = 1$ and $iz_1 = kz_2$, where $k \in (\mathbb{R} - \{0\})$, then the angle between $z_1 - z_2$ and $z_1 + z_2$ is

(a) $\tan^{-1}\left(\dfrac{2k}{k^2+1}\right)$ (b) $\tan^{-1}\left(\dfrac{2k}{1-k^2}\right)$

(c) $-2\tan^{-1}\left(\dfrac{1}{k}\right)$ (d) $2\tan^{-1}\left(\dfrac{1}{k}\right)$

2. The points z_1, z_2, z_3, z_4, in the complex plane are the vertices of a parallelogram taken in order, if and only if

(a) $z_1 + z_4 = z_2 + z_3$ (b) $z_1 + z_3 = z_2 + z_4$

(c) $z_1 + z_2 = z_3 + z_4$ (d) None of these

3. The equation $z\bar{z} + a\bar{z} + \bar{z}z + b = 0$, $b \in \mathbb{R}$, represents a circle if

(a) $|a|^2 = b$ (b) $|a|^2 > b$

(c) $|a|^2 < b$ (d) None of these

4. Let the complex numbers z_1, z_2 and z_3 be the vertices of an equilateral triangle. Let z_0 be the circumcentre of the triangle, then $z_1^2 + z_2^2 + z_3^2$ is equal to

(a) z_0^2 (b) $-z_0^2$

(c) $3z_0^2$ (d) $-3z_0^2$

5. The equation $\bar{b}z + b\bar{z} = c$, where b is a non-zero complex constant and c is real, represents

(a) A circle (b) A straight line

(c) A parabola (d) None of these

6. If a and b are real numbers between 0 and 1 such that the points $z_1 = a + i$, $z_2 = 1 + bi$ and $z_3 = 0$ form an equilateral triangle, then

(a) $a = b = 2 + \sqrt{3}$

(b) $a = b = 2 - \sqrt{3}$

(c) $a = 2 - \sqrt{3}$, $b = 2 + \sqrt{3}$

(d) None of these

7. If $|z| = 2$, then the points representing the complex numbers $-1 + 5z$ will lie on a

(a) Circle (b) Straight line

(c) Parabola (d) None of these

8. If the vertices of a quadrilateral be $a = 1 + 2i$, $b = -3 + i$, $c = -2 - 3i$ and $d = 2 - 2i$, then the quadrilateral is a

(a) Parallelogram (b) Rectangle

(c) Square (d) Rhombus

9. POQ is a straight line through the origin O, P and Q represent the complex numbers $a + ib$ and $c + id$ respectively and $OP = OQ$, then

(a) $|a + ib| = |c + id|$

(b) $a + c = b + d$

(c) $arg\,(a + ib) = arg(c + id)$

(d) None of these

10. The vertices B and D of a parallelogram are $1 - 2i$ and $4 + 2i$. If the diagonals are at right angles and $AC = 2BD$, the complex number representing A is

(a) $\frac{5}{2}$ (b) $3i - \frac{3}{2}$

(c) $3i - 4$ (d) $3i + 4$

11. The rectangle is constructed in the complex plane with its sides parallel to the axes and its centre is situated at the origin. If one of the vertices of the rectangle is $a + ib\sqrt{3}$, then the area of the rectangle is

(a) $ab\sqrt{3}$ (b) $2ab\sqrt{3}$

(c) $3ab\sqrt{3}$ (d) $4ab\sqrt{3}$

12. If $|z + 1| = \sqrt{2}/|z + 1|$, then the locus described by the point z in the Argand plane is a

(a) Straight line (b) Circle

(c) Parabola (d) None of these

13. The region of the complex plane for which $\left|\frac{z-a}{z+\bar{a}}\right| = 1$ $[R(a) \neq 0]$ is

(a) x-axis (b) y-axis

(c) Straight line $x = a$ (d) None of these

14. If $\log_{\sqrt{3}}\left(\frac{|z^2|-|z|+1}{2+|z|}\right) < 2$, then the locus of z is

(a) $|z| = 5$ (b) $|z| < 5$

(c) $|z| > 5$ (d) None of these

15. If $z = x + iy$ is a complex number satisfying $\left|z+\frac{1}{2}\right|^2 = \left|z-\frac{1}{2}\right|^2$, then the locus of z is

(a) $2y = x$ (b) $y = x$

(c) y-axis (d) x-axis

16. Which of the following equations can represent a circumcentre of triangle?

(a) $|z - 1| = |z - 2|$ (b) $|z - 1| = |z - 2| = |z - i|$

(c) $|z - 1| - |z - 2| = 2a$ (d) $|z - 1|^2 + |z - 2|^2 = 4$

17. The number of solutions for the equations $|z - 1| = |z - 2| = |z - i|$ is

(a) One (b) Three

(c) Two (d) zero

18. The roots of the cubic equation $(z + \alpha\beta)^3 = \alpha^3\ (\alpha \neq 0)$, represent the vertices of a triangle of sides of length.

(a) $\frac{1}{\sqrt{3}}|\alpha\beta|$ (b) $\sqrt{3}\,|\alpha|$

(c) $\sqrt{3}\,|\beta|$ (d) $\frac{1}{\sqrt{3}}|\alpha|$

19. z_1, z_2, z_3 are three points lying on the circle $|z| = 1$. Maximum value of $|z_1 - z_2|^2 + |z_2 - z_3|^2 + |z_2 - z_1|^2$ is

(a) 6 (b) 9

(c) 12 (d) None of these

20. If 'z' lies on the circle $|z - 2i| = 2\sqrt{2}$, then the value of $\arg\left(\frac{z-2}{z+2}\right)$ is equal to

(a) $\pi/3$ (b) $\pi/4$

(c) $\pi/6$ (d) $\pi/2$

21. $A(z_1)$, $B(z_2)$, $C(z_3)$ are the vertices of an equilateral triangle ABC, value of $arg\left(\frac{z_2+z_3-2z_1}{z_3-z_2}\right)$ is equal to

(a) $\pi/4$ (b) $\pi/2$

(c) $\pi/3$ (d) $\pi/6$

22. If $|a_k| < 3$, $1 \leq k \leq n$, then all the complex numbers z satisfying the equation $1 + a_1z + a_2z^2 + \ldots + a_nz^n = 0$.

(a) lie outside the circle $|z| = 1/4$

(b) lie inside the circle $|z| = 1/4$

(c) lie on the circle $|z| = 1/4$

(d) lie in $1/3 < |z| < 1/2$

23. Let z_1 and z_2 be two complex numbers such that $\frac{z_1}{z_2} + \frac{z_2}{z_1} = 1$.

(a) z_1, z_2 and origin are collinear

(b) z_1, z_2 and origin form a right angled triangle

(c) z_1, z_2 and origin form an equilateral triangle

(d) None of these

24. z_1 and z_2 are the roots of $z^2 + az + b = 0$, where a,b are non-zero complex numbers. It is known that the line joining the point $A(z_1)$ and $B(z_2)$ passes, through the origin, then a^2/b is

(a) Real (b) Purely imaginary

(c) $\arg(a^2/b) = \pi/4$ (d) None of these

25. The points z of the complex plane satisfying $z + |z| = 0$, lie on:

(a) the x-axis, $x \leq 0$ (b) the x-axis, $x > 0$

(c) the y-axis (d) None of these

26. Consider a square $OABC$, where 'O' is the origin $A(z_0)$ and vertices are given in anti-clockwise order. The equation of the circle that can be inscribed in the square is:

(a) $|z - z_0(1 + i)| = |z_0|$

(b) $\left|z - \frac{z_0(1-i)}{2}\right| = |z_0|$

(c) $2\left|z - \frac{z_0(1+i)}{2}\right| = |z_0|$

(d) $2|z - z_0(1 + i)| = |z_0|$

27. If z_1 and $\bar{z}_1$ represent adjacent vertices of a regular polygon of n sides and if $\frac{\text{Im}(z_1)}{\text{Re}(z_1)} = \sqrt{2} - 1$, then n is equal to:

(a) 8 (b) 16
(c) 18 (d) 24

28. Let $z_1, z_2, \ldots, z_n$ be in G.P with first term as unity such that $z_1 + z_2 + \ldots + z_n = 0$. Now if $z_1, z_2, \ldots, z_n$ represent vertices of a polygon, then distance between the incentre and circumcentre of the polygon is:

(a) 2 (b) 1
(c) 0 (d) None of these

29. A regular hexagon is drawn with two of its vertices forming a shorter diagonal at $z = -2$ and $z = 1 - i\sqrt{3}$. The other four vertices are:

(a) $\pm 2\sqrt{3}, \pm i$
(b) $\pm\sqrt{3}, \pm i$
(c) $\sqrt{3}, \sqrt{3} \pm i, -1 - i\sqrt{3}$
(d) None of these

30. If one vertex of the triangle having maximum area that can be inscribed in the circle $|z - i| = 5$ is $3 - 3i$, then another vertex of the triangle can be:

(a) $\frac{1}{2}\left[-3+4\sqrt{3}+(3\sqrt{3}+6)i\right]$

(b) $\frac{1}{2}[3+4\sqrt{3}-(3\sqrt{3}-2)i]$

(c) $\frac{1}{2}[3-4\sqrt{3}+(3\sqrt{3}+4)i]$

(d) $-[3+4\sqrt{3}-(3\sqrt{3}+2)]$

31. Let A, B and C represent the complex numbers z_1, z_2, z_3 respectively on the complex plane. If the circumcentre of the triangle ABC lies at the origin, then the orthocentre is represented by the complex number.

(a) $z_1 + z_2 - z_3$ (b) $z_2 + z_3 - z_1$
(c) $z_3 + z_1 - z_2$ (d) $z_1 + z_2 + z_3$

32. A rectangle of maximum area is inscribed in the circle $|z - 3 - 4i| = 1$. If one vertex of the rectangle is $4 + 4i$, then another adjacent vertex of this rectangle can be:

(a) $3 + 4i$ or $4 - 3i$ (b) $3 + 5i$ or $3 + 3i$
(c) $3 - 5i$ or $3 + 3i$ (d) $3 - 4i$ or $4 + 3i$

33. If tangents drawn to circle $|z| = 2$ at $A(z_1)$ and $B(z_2)$ meet at $P(z_p)$ then:

(a) $z_p = \left(\frac{z_1 + z_2}{2}\right)$ (b) $z_p = \frac{2(z_1 + z_2)}{\sqrt{z_1 z_2}}$

(c) $z_p = \frac{2z_1 z_2}{z_1 + z_2}$ (d) $z_p^2 = z_2 z_1$

34. If A and B represent the complex numbers z_1 and z_2 such that $|z_1 + z_2| = |z_1 - z_2|$, then the circumcentre of the ΔOAB, where O is the origin is:

(a) $\frac{z_1 + z_2}{2}$ (b) $\frac{z_1 - z_2}{2}$

(c) $\frac{z_1 + z_2}{3}$ (d) None of these

35. Let z be such that is equidistant from three distinct points z_1, z_2, z_3 in the Argand plane. If z, z_1 and z_2 are collinar, then $\arg((z_3 - z_2)/(z_3 - z_1))$ will be (z_1, z_2, z_3 are in anti-clockwise sence):

(a) $\pi/2$ (b) $\pi/4$
(c) $2\pi/3$ (d) None of these

36. If the imaginary part of $(2z + 1)/(iz + 1)$ is -2, then the locus of the point representing z in the complex plane is

(a) A circle (b) A straight line
(c) A parabola (d) None of these

37. If z_1, z_2, z_3 are vertices of an equilateral triangle inscribed in the circle $|z| = 2$ and if $z_1 = 1 + \sqrt{3}i$, then

(a) $z_2 = -2, z_3 = 1 - i\sqrt{3}$
(b) $z_2 = 2, z_3 = 1 - i\sqrt{3}$
(c) $z_2 = -2, z_3 = -1 + i\sqrt{3}$
(d) None of these

38. Let $O, A(z_1), B(z_2)$ be an isosceles right angled triangle with right angle at O. Then $(z_1 - z_2)^2 =$

(a) $-2z_1 z_2$ (b) $2z_1 z_2$
(c) $(z_1 + z_2)^2$ (d) None of these

39. The complex number z_1, z_2 and z_3 satisfying $\frac{z_1 - z_3}{z_2 - z_3} = \frac{1 - i\sqrt{3}}{2}$ are the vertices of a triangle which is

(a) of area zero (b) right angled isosceles
(c) equilateral (d) obtuse angled isosceles

40. Complex equation of all circles which are orthogonal to $|z| = 1$ and $|z - 1| = 4$ is

(a) $|z + 7 - \alpha i| = \sqrt{48+\alpha^2}, \alpha \in \mathbb{R}$

(b) $|z - 7 + \alpha i| = \sqrt{48+\alpha^2}, \alpha \in \mathbb{R}$

(c) $|z - 7 - \alpha i| = \sqrt{48+\alpha^2}, \alpha \in \mathbb{R}$

(d) None of these

41. If $|z^2 - 1| = |z|^2 + 1$, then z lies on

(a) a circle (b) the imaginary axis

(c) the real axis (d) an ellipse

42. If $\omega = \dfrac{z}{z-(1/3)i}$ and $|\omega| = 1$, then z lies on

(a) circle (b) ellipse

(c) parabola (d) straight line

43. If one of the vertices of the square circumscribing the circle $|z - 1| = \sqrt{2}$ is $2 + \sqrt{3}i$, then centroid of the triangle formed by other vertices is:

(a) $1-\sqrt{3}i$ (b) $\dfrac{2}{3}-\dfrac{1}{\sqrt{3}}i$

(c) $\dfrac{2\sqrt{3}}{3}-i$ (d) None of these

44. PQ and PR are two infinite rays. QAR is an arc. Any point lying in the shaded region excluding the boundary satisfies.

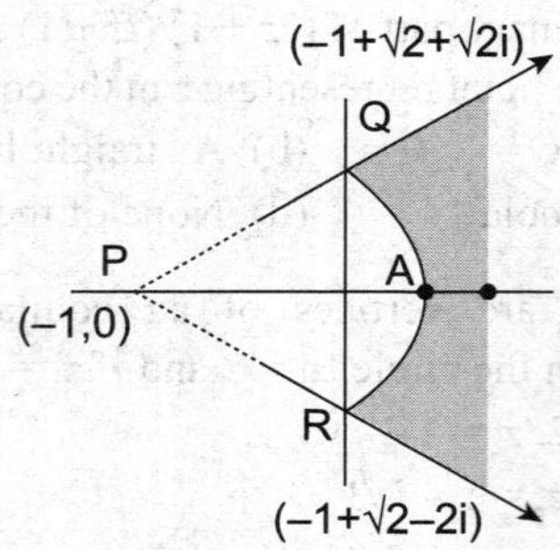

FIGURE 5.57

(a) $|z - 1| > 2$: $|\text{Arg}(z - 1)| < \pi/4$

(b) $|z - 1| > 2$: $|\text{Arg}(z - 1)| < \pi/2$

(c) $|z + 1| > 2$: $|\text{Arg}(z + 1)| < \pi/4$

(d) $|z + 1| > 2$: $|\text{Arg}(z + 1)| < \pi/2$

45. Let $A = 2 - 2i$, $B = -6 + 2i$ be two complex numbers. P is a variable point such that $\dfrac{PA}{PB} = 3$(P is not on AB)

Then locus of P is:

(a) a circle with centre (–7,5)

(b) circle with radius $2\sqrt{5}$

(c) circle with centre (–7,5/2)

(d) Circle with radius $\dfrac{3\sqrt{5}}{2}$

46. Let z_1, z_2, z_3 be three complex numbers such that $|z_1| = |z_2| = |z_3| = 1$ and $z_1 + z_2 + z_3 = 0$. If z_1, z_2, z_3 denote the vertices of a ΔABC, then

(a) origin is orthocentre

(b) $\arg\dfrac{z_3-z_2}{z_3-z_1} = \arg\dfrac{z_2}{z_1}$

(c) $z_1^2+z_2^2+z_3^2 = z_1z_2+z_2z_3+z_3z_1$

(d) area of $\Delta ABC = \dfrac{\sqrt{3}}{4}$

47. If the vertices of an equilateral triangle are $z = 0$, $z = z_1$, $z = z_2$ then

(a) $\dfrac{1}{z_1-z_2}+\dfrac{1}{z_2}=\dfrac{1}{z_1}$ (b) $z_1^2+z_2^2 = z_1z_2$

(c) $|z_1 - z_2| = |z_1| = |z_2|$ (d) $\arg z_1 \sim \arg z_2 = \pi/3$

48. If $z \in C$, then the equation $\left|\dfrac{3z+i}{z+2}\right| = \lambda \in \mathbb{R}$ represents a circle when

(a) $\lambda = 1$ (b) $\lambda = 3$

(c) $\lambda = 2$ (d) $\lambda = 5$

49. Let z be variable complex number and z_1,z_2 are fixed complex numbers (which may or may not be distinct) in the Argand plane. If $|z - z_1| + |z - z_2| = k$, $k \in \mathbb{R}$. Then locus of z may be

(a) ellipse (b) line segment

(c) circle (d) point

Answer Key

1. (b,c,d)	**2.** (b)	**3.** (b)	**4.** (c)	**5.** (b)	**6.** (a,b)	**7.** (a)	**8.** (a,b,c,d)	**9.** (a,c)	**10.** (b)
11. (d)	**12.** (b)	**13.** (b)	**14.** (b)	**15.** (c)	**16.** (b)	**17.** (a)	**18.** (b)	**19.** (b)	**20.** (b)
21. (b)	**22.** (a)	**23.** (c)	**24.** (a)	**25.** (a)	**26.** (c)	**27.** (a)	**28.** (c)	**29.** (d)	**30.** (a)
31. (d)	**32.** (b)	**33.** (c)	**34.** (a)	**35.** (a)	**36.** (b)	**37.** (a)	**38.** (a)	**39.** (c)	**40.** (a)
41. (b)	**42.** (d)	**43.** (b)	**44.** (c)	**45.** (c),(d)	**46.** (a,c,d)	**47.** (a,b,c,d)	**48.** (a,c,d)	**49.** (a,b,c,d)	

MULTIPLE CHOICE QUESTIONS

SECTION–I

SUBJECTIVE SOLVED EXAMPLES

1. Show that a unimodular complex number, not purely real can always be expressed as $\frac{c+i}{c-i}$ for some real c.

Solution: Let z be a unimodular complex number.

Let $z = \cos\theta + i\sin\theta$

If possible let $\cos\theta + i\sin\theta = \frac{c+i}{c-i}$, where c is real

then, $\cos\theta + i\sin\theta = \frac{c^2-1+2ci}{c^2+1}$

Equating real and imaginary parts, we get $\cos\theta = \frac{c^2-1}{c^2+1}$

and $\sin\theta = \frac{2c}{c^2+1} \Rightarrow (\sin\theta)c^2 - 2c + \sin\theta = 0$

$\Rightarrow (\sin\theta)c^2 - 2c + \sin\theta = 0$

$$\Rightarrow c = \frac{2\pm\sqrt{4-4\sin^2\theta}}{2\sin\theta} = \frac{1\pm\cos\theta}{\sin\theta}$$

$$= \frac{1+\cos\theta}{\sin\theta}, \frac{1-\cos\theta}{\sin\theta} = \cot\frac{\theta}{2}, \tan\frac{\theta}{2}$$

From above common value of $c = \cot\frac{\theta}{2}$

where $\theta \neq 2n\pi$ [$\because$ z is not purely real]

Thus $z = \frac{c+i}{c-i}$, where $c = = \cot\frac{\theta}{2}, \theta \neq 2n\pi$

2. If the expression $\frac{\sin\frac{x}{2}+\cos\frac{x}{2}-i\tan x}{1+2i\sin\frac{x}{2}}$ is real, then find the set of all possible values of x

Solution: Let the given expression be z, then

$$z = \frac{\left(\sin\frac{x}{2}+\cos\frac{x}{2}-i\tan x\right)\left(1-2i\sin\frac{x}{2}\right)}{\left(1+2i\sin\frac{x}{2}\right)\left(1-2i\sin\frac{x}{2}\right)}$$

Since z is real, $I_m(z) = 0$

$$\Rightarrow -2\sin\frac{x}{2}\left(\sin\frac{x}{2}+\cos\frac{x}{2}\right) - \tan x = 0$$

$$\Rightarrow 2\sin\frac{x}{2}\left(\sin\frac{x}{2}+\cos\frac{x}{2}\right) + \frac{2\sin\frac{x}{2}.\cos\frac{x}{2}}{\cos x} = 0$$

$$\Rightarrow \frac{2\sin\frac{x}{2}}{\cos x}\left[\left(\sin\frac{x}{2}+\cos\frac{x}{2}\right)\cos x + \cos\frac{x}{2}\right] = 0$$

$\Rightarrow$ either $\sin x/2 = 0 \Rightarrow x/2 = n\pi \Rightarrow x = 2n\pi$, $n = 0, \pm 1, \pm 2,.......$

or $\left(\sin\frac{x}{2}+\cos\frac{x}{2}\right)\cos x + \cos\frac{x}{2} = 0$

$$\Rightarrow \sin\frac{x}{2}\left(1-2\sin^2\frac{x}{2}\right) + \cos\frac{x}{2}\left(2\cos^2\frac{x}{2}-1\right) + \cos\frac{x}{2} = 0$$

$$\Rightarrow 2\sin^3\frac{x}{2} - 2\cos^3\frac{x}{2} - \sin\frac{x}{2} = 0$$

$$\Rightarrow 2\tan^3\frac{x}{2} - 2 - \tan\frac{x}{2}\sec^2\frac{x}{2} = 0$$

$\left[\text{Dividing by } \cos^3\frac{x}{2}\right]$

$$\Rightarrow 2\tan^3\frac{x}{2} - 2 - \tan\frac{x}{2}\left(1+\tan^2\frac{x}{2}\right) = 0$$

$$\Rightarrow \tan^3\frac{x}{2} - \tan\frac{x}{2} - 2 = 0$$

$\Rightarrow u^3 - u - 2 = 0$; where $u = \tan\frac{x}{2}$ ...(i)

let $f(u) = u^3 - u - 2$

Clearly, $f(0) = -2 < 0$ and $f(2) = 4 > 0$

Hence equation (i) has a real root between 0 and 2

Let α be a value of x which satisfies equation (i),

then, $u = \tan\frac{\alpha}{2}$

$\therefore \tan\frac{x}{2} = \tan\frac{\alpha}{2} \Rightarrow \frac{x}{2} = n\pi + \frac{\alpha}{2}$

or $x = 2n\pi + \alpha$ where $\tan^3\frac{\alpha}{2} - \tan\frac{\alpha}{2} - 2 = 0$

Thus $x = 2n\pi,\ 2n\pi + \alpha,\ n \in \mathbb{Z}$, where $\tan^3\frac{\alpha}{2} - \tan\frac{\alpha}{2} - 2 = 0$

3. If $\left|z+\frac{1}{z}\right| = a$, where z is a complex number and $a > 0$, find the greatest value of $|z|$

Solution: Let $|z| = r$ and arg $z = \theta$,
then $z = r(\cos\theta + i\sin\theta)$

and $\frac{1}{z} = \frac{1}{r(\cos\theta + i\sin\theta)} = \frac{1}{r}(\cos\theta - i\sin\theta)$

Given $\left|z+\frac{1}{z}\right| = a[\text{Here } z \neq 0 \Rightarrow r \neq 0]$

$\therefore \quad \left|\left(r+\frac{1}{r}\right)\cos\theta + i\left(r-\frac{1}{r}\right)\sin\theta\right| = a$

$\Rightarrow \left(r+\frac{1}{r}\right)^2\cos^2\theta + \left(r-\frac{1}{r}\right)^2\sin^2\theta = a^2$

$\Rightarrow r^2 + \frac{1}{r^2} + 2(\cos^2\theta - \sin^2\theta) = a^2$

$\Rightarrow \left(r-\frac{1}{r}\right)^2 + 2 + 2\cos 2\theta = a^2$

$\Rightarrow \left(r-\frac{1}{r}\right)^2 = a^2 - 4\cos^2\theta$ ....(ii)

Let $r > 1$ In this case $\frac{1}{r} < 1 \therefore r - \frac{1}{r} > 0$ and as r increases, $\frac{1}{r}$ decreases and $r - \frac{1}{r}$ increase

$\therefore$ r will be greatest $\Leftrightarrow r - \frac{1}{r}$ is greatest $\Leftrightarrow \left(r-\frac{1}{r}\right)^2$ is greatest

Now, $r - \frac{1}{r} = 0 \Rightarrow r^2 = 1 \Rightarrow r = 1\ [\because r > 0]$

Therefore, we will consider three cases as (i) $r > 1$ (ii) $r = 1$ (iii) $r < 1$

Since we have to find the greatest value of r (i.e., $|z|$), therefore,first of all we will consider the case $r > 1$. If no solution is obtained in this case, then we will consider the case $r = 1$. If no solution is obtained in this case also then we will lastly consider the case $r < 1$

But from (ii), $\left(r-\frac{1}{r}\right)^2$ will be greatest when $\cos^2\theta = 0$ i.e., $\theta = \frac{\pi}{2}$ or $\frac{3\pi}{2}$

$\therefore$ From (ii), incase of greatest value of r, $\left(r-\frac{1}{r}\right)^2 = a^2$

or $r - \frac{1}{r} = a\left[\because r - \frac{1}{r} > 0 \text{ and } a > 0\right]$

or $r^2 - ar - 1 = 0$

$\Rightarrow r = \frac{a \pm \sqrt{a^2+4}}{2} = \frac{a+\sqrt{a^2+4}}{2}\ [\because r > 0]$

$\therefore$ greatest value of $r = \frac{a+\sqrt{a^2+4}}{2}$

Thus $r = 1$ and $r < 1$ are rejected for greatest value.

Note: For greatest value $|z|$, $\cos^2\theta = 0$ or $\cos\theta = 0$

$\therefore$ $z = r(\cos\theta + i\sin\theta) = i\, r\sin\theta =$ a purely imaginary number

Second method: $a = \left|z+\frac{1}{z}\right| \Rightarrow a \geq |z| - \frac{1}{|z|}$

$[\because |z_1 + z_2| \geq |z_1| - |z_2|$ and $|z_1 + z_2| |z_1|]$ here we have

Taken $|z| - \frac{1}{|z|}$ since we have to find the greatest value of $|z|$ and hence we have taken the case when $|z| > 1]$

From (i), $|z|^2 - a|z| - 1 \leq 0$

$\Rightarrow \frac{a-\sqrt{a^2+4}}{2} \leq |z| \leq \frac{a+\sqrt{a^2+4}}{2}$

But $|z|$ cann't be negative $\therefore 0 < |z| \leq \frac{a+\sqrt{a^2+4}}{2}$

[$\because$ here $|z| \neq 0$ otherwise $z = 0$ and hence $\frac{1}{|z|}$ will not be defined]

$\therefore$ Greatest value of $|z| = \frac{a+\sqrt{a^2+4}}{2}$

4. If $\left|z+\frac{1}{z}\right| = a$, where z is a complex number and $a > 0$, find the least value of $|z|$

Solution: As in $\left(r-\frac{1}{r}\right)^2 = a^2 - 4\cos^2\theta$ ....(i)

or $\left(\frac{1}{r}-r\right)^2 = a^2 - 4\cos^2\theta$ ....(ii)

Since we have to find the least value of r, therefore we consider the case when $r < 1$

In this case $\frac{1}{r}$ increases, $\left(\frac{1}{r}-r\right)$ increases as r decreases

$\therefore$ r will be least $\Leftrightarrow \left(\frac{1}{r}-r\right)$ is greatest $\Leftrightarrow \left(\frac{1}{r}-r\right)^2$ is greatest.

From (ii) $\left(\frac{1}{r}-r\right)^2 = a^2 - 4\cos^2\theta$ ...(iii)

For least value of r, $\left(\frac{1}{r}-r\right)^2$ should be greatest which is possible only when $\cos^2\theta = 0$ i.e., $\theta = \frac{\pi}{2}$ or $\frac{3\pi}{2}$

$\therefore$ From (iii) in case of least value of r, $\frac{1}{r} - r = a$

or $r^2 + ar - 1 = 0 \Rightarrow r = \frac{-a \pm \sqrt{a^2+4}}{2}$

$\therefore$ least value of $r = \frac{-a+\sqrt{a^2+4}}{2}$

Note: For least value of $|z|$, $z = r(\cos\theta + i\sin\theta) = i\, r\sin\theta$ [$\because \cos\theta = 0$]

5. If $1, \alpha_1, \alpha_2, \ldots\ldots, \alpha_{n-1}$ be the n roots of unity, show that $(1-\alpha_1)(1-\alpha_2)\ldots\ldots(1-\alpha_{n-1}) = n$

Solution: Let x be a nth root of unity, then $x^n = 1$ or $x^n - 1 = 0$

But according to the problem $1, \alpha_1, \alpha_2, \ldots, \alpha_{n-1}$ are the n roots of unity

$\therefore$ $(x^n - 1) = (x-1)(x-\alpha_1)\ldots\ldots(x-\alpha_{n-1})$

or $(x-\alpha_1)(x-\alpha_2)\ldots\ldots(x-\alpha_{n-1}) = \frac{x^n-1}{x-1}$

$\Rightarrow (x-\alpha_1)(x-\alpha_2)\ldots\ldots(x-\alpha_{n-1})$
$= 1 + x + x^2 + \ldots\ldots + x^{n-1}$

Putting $x = 1$ in the above expression, we get
$(1-\alpha_1)(1-\alpha_2)\ldots\ldots(1-\alpha_{n-1}) = 1+1+1+\ldots\ldots +1$ (n times) $= n$

6. If z is any non-zero complex number, then show that

(a) $\left|\frac{z}{|z|}-1\right| \le |\arg z|$ (b) $|z-1| \le ||z|-1| + |z|\,|\arg z|$

Solution: (a) Let $|z| = r$ and $\arg z = \theta$

Given $|z| \ne 0 \Rightarrow r \ne 0$

Now $z = r(\cos\theta + i\sin\theta) \Rightarrow \frac{z}{|z|} = (\cos\theta + i\sin\theta)$

$\therefore \left|\frac{z}{|z|}-1\right| = |(\cos\theta - 1) + i\sin\theta| = \sqrt{(\cos\theta-1)^2+\sin^2\theta}$

$= \sqrt{2(1-\cos\theta)} = 2\sqrt{\sin^2(\theta/2)} = 2|\sin(\theta/2)|$

Now $2\left|\sin\frac{\theta}{2}\right| \le 2\left|\frac{\theta}{2}\right| = |\theta|$ since $|\sin\theta| \le |\theta|$

thus $\left|\frac{z}{|z|}-1\right| \le |\arg z|$

Aliter: **Geometrically:** $z = |z|\, e^{i\theta} \Rightarrow \frac{z}{|z|} = e^{i\theta}$

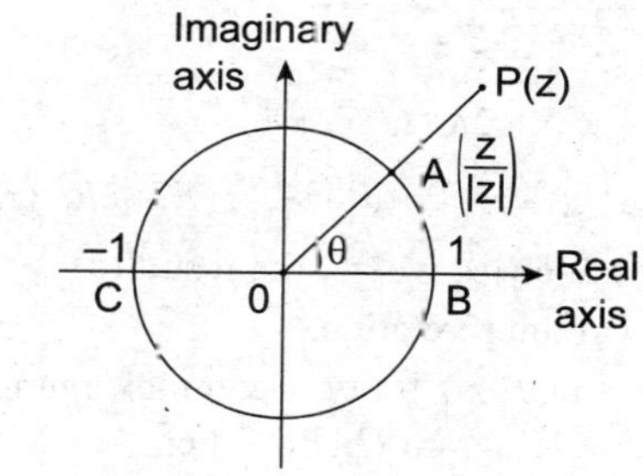

Now consider unit circle with centre origin and point $P(z)$. Such that OP makes angle θ with real axis and $OP = |z|$ referring to diagram.

$OB = OA = 1 \Rightarrow A$ denotes $\frac{z}{|z|}$ and B is real number 1.

$\because \quad AB = \left|\frac{z}{|z|}-1\right| < \widehat{AB} \quad \Rightarrow \quad \left|\frac{z}{|z|}-1\right| < |\theta|$

$\Rightarrow \left|\frac{z}{|z|}-1\right| < |\arg z|$

(b) from the diagram $BQ = ||z| - 1|$ and $BP = |z-1|$
$PQ = |z - |z||$

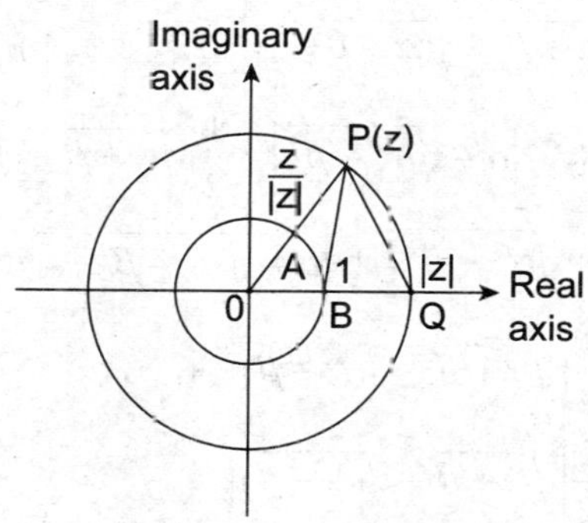

By triangle inequality $BQ + PQ \ge BP$

$||z|-1| + |z - |z|| \ge |z-1|$ .... (i)

from part (a) we know that $\left|\frac{z}{|z|}-1\right| \le |\arg z|$

$\Rightarrow |z - |z|| \le |z|\,|\arg z|$ ....(ii)

Combining the inequality (i) and (ii) using transition property $||z|-1| + |z|\,|\arg z| \ge |z-1|$.

7. Prove that

(a) $|z_1+z_2|^2+|z_1-z_2|^2=2|z_1|^2+2|z_2|^2$ and interpret the result geometrically and deduce that

(b) $\left|\alpha+\sqrt{\alpha^2-\beta^2}\right|+\left|\alpha-\sqrt{\alpha^2-\beta^2}\right|=|\alpha+\beta|+|\alpha-\beta|$

where α and β are complex numbers

Solution: Part (a)

Consider $|z_1+z_2|^2=(z_1+z_2)\overline{(z_1+z_2)}$ ...(i)

$=|z_1|^2+|z_2|^2+z_1\bar{z}_2+\bar{z}_1z_2$

$=|z_1|^2+|z_2|^2+2Re(z_1\bar{z}_2)$

Similarly, $|z_1-z_2|^2=|z_1|^2+|z_2|^2-2Re(z_1\bar{z}_2)$ ....(ii)

Adding (i) and (ii), we get the result (a)

Geomertical interpretation.

Let $A(z_1)$ and $B(z_2)$ be two complex numbers. Construct a parallelogram $OARB$. Then

$|OA|=|z_1|$, $|OB|=|z_2|$

$|OR|=|z_1+z_2|$ and $|AB|=|z_2-z_1|$

From part (a), we have

$OR^2+AB^2=2(OA^2+OB^2)$ i.e., the sum of the squares of the diagonals of the parallelogram is equal to the sum of the squares of its sides.

For part (*b*)

Consider $\left|\alpha+\sqrt{\alpha^2-\beta^2}\right|=\frac{1}{2}\left|2\alpha+2\sqrt{\alpha^2-\beta^2}\right|$

$=\frac{1}{2}\left|(\alpha+\beta)+(\alpha-\beta)+2\sqrt{(\alpha+\beta)(\alpha-\beta)}\right|$

$=\frac{1}{2}\left|(\sqrt{\alpha+\beta}+\sqrt{(\alpha-\beta)})^2\right|$

$=\frac{1}{2}\left|\sqrt{\alpha+\beta}+\sqrt{(\alpha-\beta)}\right|^2$ $(\because |z^2|=|z|^2)$

Similarly, $\left|\alpha-\sqrt{\alpha^2-\beta^2}\right|=\frac{1}{2}\left|\sqrt{\alpha+\beta}-\sqrt{(\alpha-\beta)}\right|^2$

$\therefore$ $\left|\alpha+\sqrt{\alpha^2-\beta^2}\right|+\left|\alpha-\sqrt{\alpha^2-\beta^2}\right|$

$=\frac{1}{2}\left|\sqrt{\alpha+\beta}+\sqrt{(\alpha-\beta)}\right|^2+$

$\frac{1}{2}\left|\sqrt{\alpha+\beta}-\sqrt{(\alpha-\beta)}\right|^2$

$=\left|\sqrt{\alpha+\beta}\right|^2+\left|\sqrt{(\alpha-\beta)}\right|^2$ [Using part (a)]

$=|\alpha+\beta|+|\alpha-\beta|$ $(\because |z^2|=|z|^2)$

8. Prove that the triangle ABC whose vertices are the point z_1, z_2 and z_3 on the Argand diagram is an equilateral triangle iff $\frac{1}{z_1-z_2}+\frac{1}{z_2-z_3}+\frac{1}{z_3-z_1}=0$

Solution: Let $z_1-z_2=\alpha$, $z_2-z_3=\beta$ and

$z_3-z_1=\gamma$; $\frac{1}{\alpha}+\frac{1}{\beta}+\frac{1}{\gamma}=0$ (Given)

$\Rightarrow \frac{1}{\alpha}=-\frac{(\beta+\gamma)}{\beta\gamma}=\frac{\alpha}{\beta\gamma}$ $(\because \alpha+\beta+\gamma=0)$

$\Rightarrow \alpha^2=\beta\gamma$ ....(i)

and $\bar{\alpha}^2=\overline{\beta\gamma}=\bar{\beta}\,\bar{\gamma}$ ...(ii)

multiplying (i) and (ii), we get $(\alpha\bar{\alpha})^2=\beta\bar{\beta}\,\gamma\bar{\gamma}$

$\Rightarrow |\alpha|^4=|\beta|^2|\gamma|^2$ $\Rightarrow |\alpha|^6=|\alpha|^2|\beta|^2|\gamma|^2$

By symmetry

$|\alpha|^6=|\beta|^6=|\gamma|^6 \Rightarrow |\alpha|=|\beta|=|\gamma|$

$\Rightarrow AB=BC=CA$

$\Rightarrow$ triangle ABC is an equilateral triangle

Conversely, let triangle $A(z_1)$, $B(z_2)$ and $C(z_3)$ be an equilateral triangle.

$\therefore$ $|z_1-z_2|=|z_2-z_3|=|z_3-z_1|=a$

consider, $\frac{1}{z_1-z_2}=\frac{\overline{z_1-z_2}}{(z_1-z_2)(\bar{z}_1-\bar{z}_2)}=\frac{\bar{z}_1-\bar{z}_2}{a^2}$

Similarly, $\frac{1}{z_2-z_3}=\frac{\bar{z}_2-\bar{z}_3}{a^2}$ and $\frac{1}{z_3-z_2}=\frac{\bar{z}_3-\bar{z}_2}{a^2}$

$\Rightarrow \frac{1}{z_1-z_2}+\frac{1}{z_2-z_3}+\frac{1}{z_3-z_1}=\frac{0}{a^2}=0$

9. If the vertices of a square $ABCD$ are z_1, z_2, z_3 and z_4 taken in anti-clockwise order, prove that $z_3=z_2-i(z_1-z_2)$.

Solution: $\frac{z_1-z_2}{z_3-z_2}=\left|\frac{z_1-z_2}{z_3-z_2}\right|e^{i\pi/2}$

$=\frac{|z_1-z_2|}{|z_3-z_2|}(\cos\pi/2+i\sin\pi/2)$

$=\frac{AB}{BC}.i=i$ $(\because AB=BC)$

$\Rightarrow (z_1-z_2)=(z_3-z_2)\,i$

$\Rightarrow i(z_1-z_2)=-z_3+z_2$ and $z_3=z_2-i(z_1-z_2)$

10. Find a complex number satisfying $|z-5i|=4$ and having least argument.

Solution: Let $z=x+iy$

$\therefore$ $|z-5i|=4$ ......(i)

$\Rightarrow |x+i(y-5)|=4$

$\Rightarrow x^2+(y-5)^2=16$ ....(ii)

which is the equation of a circle, having centre at (0, 5) and radius 4. Therefore, all points on this circle satisfy the equation (i). But we want a complex number having least argument. Let us observe the problem graphically. OP is tangent to the circle and point P represents the required complex number.

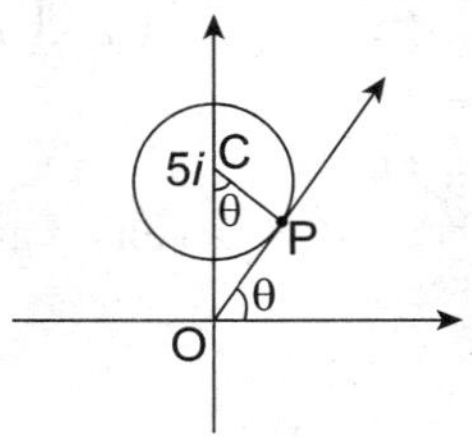

$\Rightarrow \angle PCO = \theta$, $\tan\theta = 3/4$

$\Rightarrow z_P = |z|\, e^{i\theta}$

$= 3(\cos\theta + i\sin\theta) = 3(4/5 + i\,3/5) = \frac{3}{5}(4+3i)$

11. Let $A_1, A_2, \ldots\ldots, A_n$ be the vertices of an n sided regular polygon such that $\frac{1}{A_1A_2} = \frac{1}{A_1A_3} + \frac{1}{A_1A_4}$.

Find the value of n.

Solution: Let O be the origin and complex number representing A_1 be z_1, A_2 be z_2, A_3 be z_3 and A_4 be z_4.

Now, $\frac{z_2 - 0}{z_1 - 0} = \frac{OA_2}{OA_1} e^{i\frac{2\pi}{n}}$

or, $z_2 = z_1 e^{i\frac{2\pi}{n}}$ [$\because$ $OA_1 = OA_2 = \ldots\ldots = OA_n$]

Similarly, $z_3 = z_1 e^{i\frac{4\pi}{n}}$ and $z_4 = z_1 e^{i\frac{6\pi}{n}}$

now $A_1A_2 = |z_2 - z_1|$

$$= \left| z_1 e^{i\frac{2\pi}{n}} - z_1 \right| = |z_1| \left| \cos\frac{2\pi}{n} + i\sin\frac{2\pi}{n} - 1 \right|$$

$$= |z_1| \left| \left(\cos\frac{2\pi}{n} - 1\right) + i\sin\frac{2\pi}{n} \right|$$

$$= |z_1| \sqrt{2 - 2\cos\frac{2\pi}{n}} = 2|z_1| \sin\frac{\pi}{n}$$

Similarly, $A_1A_3 = 2|z_1|\sin\frac{2\pi}{n}$ and

$A_1A_4 = 2|z_1|\sin\frac{3\pi}{n}$

From given condition

$$\frac{1}{2|z_1|\sin\frac{\pi}{n}} = \frac{1}{2|z_1|\sin\frac{2\pi}{n}} + \frac{1}{2|z_1|\sin\frac{3\pi}{n}}$$

$$\Rightarrow \frac{1}{\sin\frac{\pi}{n}} = \frac{1}{\sin\frac{2\pi}{n}} + \frac{1}{\sin\frac{3\pi}{n}}$$

$$\Rightarrow \sin\frac{2\pi}{n}\sin\frac{3\pi}{n} = \sin\frac{\pi}{n}\left(\sin\frac{2\pi}{n} + \sin\frac{3\pi}{n}\right)$$

$$\Rightarrow 2\sin\frac{\pi}{n}\cos\frac{\pi}{n}\sin\frac{3\pi}{n} = \sin\frac{\pi}{n}\left(\sin\frac{2\pi}{n} + \sin\frac{3\pi}{n}\right)$$

$$\Rightarrow \sin\frac{4\pi}{n} + \sin\frac{2\pi}{n} = \sin\frac{2\pi}{n} + \sin\frac{3\pi}{n}$$

$$\Rightarrow \sin\frac{3\pi}{n} = \sin\frac{4\pi}{n}$$

or, $\frac{3\pi}{n} = m\pi + (-1)^m \frac{4\pi}{n}$, $m = 0, \pm1, \pm2, \ldots\ldots$

when $m = 0$, $\frac{3\pi}{n} = \frac{4\pi}{n} \Rightarrow 3 = 4$ (not possible)

when $m = 1$, $\frac{3\pi}{n} = \pi - \frac{4\pi}{n}$

$\Rightarrow \frac{7\pi}{n} = \pi \quad \Rightarrow \therefore n = 7$

12. Prove that $1 + R\cos\theta + R^2\cos 2\theta + R^3\cos 3\theta + \ldots\ldots$

$= \frac{1 - R\cos\theta}{1 - 2R\cos\theta + R^2}$; where $|R| < 1$

Solution: Let $S = 1 + R\cos\theta + R^2\cos 2\theta + R^3\cos 3\theta + \ldots\ldots$ and $P = R\sin\theta - R^2\sin 2\theta + R^3\sin 3\theta + \ldots\ldots$,

$\therefore$ S = Real of $(S + iP)$

Consider $S + iP = 1 + R(\cos\theta + i\sin\theta) + R^2(\cos 2\theta + i\sin 2\theta) + R^3(\cos 3\theta + i\sin 3\theta) + \ldots = 1 + Re^{i\theta} + R^2e^{2i\theta} + R^3e^{i3\theta} + \ldots\ldots = \frac{1}{1 - Re^{i\theta}}$ (It is infinite G.P.)

$$= \frac{1}{1 - R(\cos\theta + i\sin\theta)}$$

$$= \frac{1}{(1 - R\cos\theta) - iR\sin\theta} \times \frac{(1 - R\cos\theta) + iR\sin\theta}{(1 - R\cos\theta) + iR\sin\theta}$$

$$= \frac{(1 - R\cos\theta) + iR\sin\theta}{(1 - R\cos\theta)^2 + (R\sin\theta)^2} = \frac{(1 - R\cos\theta) + iR\sin\theta}{1 + R^2 - 2R\cos\theta}$$

Therefore, $S = \frac{1 - R\cos\theta}{1 + R^2 - 2R\cos\theta}$

13. In the equation $z^2 + 2\lambda z + 1 = 0$, λ is parameter which can take any real value. Show that if $-1 < \lambda < 1$ the roots of this equation lie on a certain circle in the Argand diagram, but if $\lambda > 1$, one root lies inside the unit circle and one outside. Prove that for every large value of λ the roots are approximately -2λ, $-\frac{1}{2\lambda}$

Solution: $z^2 + 2\lambda z + 1 = 0$ (given)

$\Rightarrow z = -\lambda \pm \sqrt{\lambda^2 - 1}$ ....(i)

Case I. $-1 < \lambda < 1$

$\Rightarrow z = -\lambda \pm i\mu \ (\mu = \sqrt{1-\lambda^2})$

$\Rightarrow z + \lambda = \pm i\mu$ ......(ii)

$\Rightarrow \mu$ is a + ve real

$\Rightarrow \overline{z+\lambda} = \pm \overline{i\mu} = \mp i\mu$ ....(iii)

$\Rightarrow$ multiplying (ii) and (iii), we get $(z+\lambda)(\overline{z+\lambda}) = \mu^2$

$\Rightarrow |z+\lambda|^2 = \mu^2 \quad \Rightarrow |z+\lambda| = \mu$

this means that z lies on the circle having centre at $-\lambda$ and radius μ

Case II: $\lambda > 1$

$z = -\lambda \pm \sqrt{\lambda^2 - 1}$ (from (i))

$\Rightarrow z = -\lambda \pm \beta$ $(\lambda^2 - 1 = \beta^2$ (say))

Let z_1 and z_2 be roots of (i)

$\therefore z_1 = -\lambda + \sqrt{\lambda^2-1} \Rightarrow z_2 = -\lambda - \sqrt{\lambda^2-1}$

$z_1z_2 = (-\lambda)^2 - (\lambda^2 - 1) = 1$

$\Rightarrow |z_1||z_2| = 1 \quad \Rightarrow$ If $|z_1| < 1$ then $|z_2| > 1$

i.e., one root lies inside the unit circle and the other outside for large $\lambda > 1$

$z_2 = -\lambda - \sqrt{\lambda^2-1}$. Now if λ is very large $\sqrt{\lambda^2-1} \approx \lambda$. So $z_2 = \lambda - \lambda = -2\lambda$

and $z_1 = -\lambda + \sqrt{\lambda^2-1} = \dfrac{-1}{\lambda+\sqrt{\lambda^2-1}}$

$$\cong -\frac{1}{\lambda+\lambda} \text{ (for large } \lambda) = -\frac{1}{2\lambda}$$

14. Let $z_k = r_k(\cos\theta_k + i\sin\theta_k)$, $k = 1, 2, 3$ and $\sum_{k=1}^{3}\frac{r_k}{z_k} = 0$. Show that $\sum_{k=1}^{3}\cos 2.\theta_k = 0$

Solution: Given, $\sum_{k=1}^{3}\frac{r_k}{z_k} = 0$ .....(i)

$$\Rightarrow \sum_{k=1}^{3}\frac{1}{\cos\theta_k + i\sin\theta_k} = 0$$

$$\Rightarrow \sum_{k=1}^{3}(\cos\theta_k - i\sin\theta_k) = 0$$

$$\Rightarrow \sum_{k=1}^{3}\cos\theta_k = 0 \text{ and } \sum_{k=1}^{3}\sin\theta_k = 0$$

$$\Rightarrow \sum_{k=1}^{3}(\cos\theta_k + i\sin\theta_k) = 0$$

$$\Rightarrow \sum_{k=1}^{3}\left(\frac{z_k}{r_k}\right) = 0 \qquad \text{....(ii)}$$

Now, $(a + b + c)^2 = a^2 + b^2 + c^2 + 2(ab + bc + ca)$

$= a^2 + b^2 + c^2 + 2abc(1/a + 1/b + 1/c)$

Applying this we get:

$$\left(\sum_{k=1}^{3}\frac{z_k}{r_k}\right)^2 = \sum_{k=1}^{3}\left(\frac{z_k}{r_k}\right)^2 + 2\left(\frac{z_1}{r_1}\right)\left(\frac{z_2}{r_2}\right)\left(\frac{z_3}{r_3}\right)\sum_{k=1}^{3}\frac{r_k}{z_k}$$

.....(iii)

Since $\sum_{k=1}^{3}\frac{r_k}{z_k} = 0$ (given) and $\sum_{k=1}^{3}\left(\frac{z_k}{r_k}\right) = 0$ (From (i)))

$\therefore$ From (iii), $\sum_{k=1}^{3}\left(\frac{z_k}{r_k}\right)^2 = 0$

$\Rightarrow \sum_{k=1}^{3}(\cos\theta_k + i\sin\theta_k)^2 = 0$

[Applying De-Moivre's Theorem]

$\Rightarrow \sum_{k=1}^{3}\cos 2\theta_k = 0$ and $\sum_{k=1}^{3}\sin 2\theta_k = 0$ (Equating real and imaginary parts)

15. If z is any point on the circle $|z + 1| = 3$, then find the locus of $w = [4 + i - z]^{-1}$

Solution: $w = \dfrac{1}{4+i-z} \Rightarrow z = (4+i) - \dfrac{1}{w}$

$z + 1 = 5 + i - \dfrac{1}{w}$

Taking modules on both sides, we get $|5 + i - 1/w| = |z + 1| = 3$

$\Rightarrow |(5 + i)w - 1|^2 = 9|w|^2$

$\Rightarrow \{(5 + i)w - 1\}\{(5 - i)\bar{w} - 1\} = 9w\bar{w}$

$\Rightarrow 26w\bar{w} - (5 - i)\bar{w} - (5 + i)w + 1 = 9w\bar{w}$

$$\Rightarrow w\bar{w} - \frac{(5-i)\bar{w}}{17} - \frac{(5+i)w}{17} + \frac{1}{17} = 0$$

$$\Rightarrow \left(w - \frac{5-i}{17}\right)\left(\bar{w} - \frac{5+i}{17}\right) - \frac{26}{17^2} + \frac{1}{17} = 0$$

$$\Rightarrow \left|w - \frac{5-i}{17}\right|^2 = \frac{9}{17^2} \Rightarrow \left|w - \frac{5-i}{17}\right| = \left(\frac{3}{17}\right)^2$$

So locus of w is a circle having centre at $\dfrac{5-i}{17}$ and radius $\dfrac{3}{17}$

16. Find the greatest and the least values of the moduli of complex numbers z satisfying the equation $|z - 4/z| = 2$. Find also the corresponding complex numbers

Solution: We have $||z| - |4/z|| \le |z - 4/z| = 2$

$$\Rightarrow -2 \le |z| - \frac{4}{|z|} \le 2$$

$\Rightarrow |z|^2 + 2|z| - 4 \ge 0$ and $|z|^2 - 2|z| - 4 \le 0$

$\Rightarrow (|z|+1)^2 - 5 \ge 0$ and $(|z|-1)^2 \le 5$

$\Rightarrow (|z| + 1 + \sqrt{5})(|z| + 1 - \sqrt{5}) \ge 0$ and $(|z| - 1 + \sqrt{5})(|z| - 1 - \sqrt{5}) \le 0$

$\Rightarrow (|z| \le -\sqrt{5} - 1$ or $|z| \ge \sqrt{5} - 1$ and $\sqrt{5} - 1 \le |z| \le \sqrt{5} + 1$

$\Rightarrow \sqrt{5}-1 \le |z| \le \sqrt{5}+1$

$\Rightarrow$ Greatest value of $|z| = \sqrt{5} + 1$ and least value of $|z| = \sqrt{5} - 1$

$|z| = \sqrt{5} + 1 \Rightarrow \dfrac{4}{|z|} = \sqrt{5} - 1$

Now, $\dfrac{4}{z} = \dfrac{4\bar{z}}{|z|^2} \Rightarrow \dfrac{4}{z}$ lying in the direction of $\bar{z}$

$|z - 4/z| = PR = 2$ (given)

We have $OP = \sqrt{5} + 1$ and $OR = \sqrt{5} - 1$

$$\Rightarrow \cos 2\theta = \frac{OP^2 + OR^2 - PR^2}{2OP.OR}$$

$$= \frac{(\sqrt{5}+1)^2 + (\sqrt{5}-1)^2 - 4}{2(5-1)} = 1$$

$\Rightarrow 2\theta = 0, 2\pi \Rightarrow z = \pm(\sqrt{5} + 1)$

Similarly for $|z| = \sqrt{5} - 1$, we get $z = \pm(\sqrt{5} - 1)$

17. If $\alpha = \left|\dfrac{z-i}{z+i}\right|$, show that when z lies above the real axis, α will lie within the unit circle which has centre at the origin. Find the locus of α as z travels on the real axis from $-\infty$ to $+\infty$

Solution: From given condition, it is clear that $|z - i| < |z + i|$ (as z lies above the real axis)

$\Rightarrow |\alpha| = \left|\dfrac{z-i}{z+i}\right| < 1$

$\Rightarrow \alpha$ lies within the unit circle which has centre at the origin

Now if z is travelling on the real axis, then $Im(z) = 0$ and $Re(z)$varies from $-\infty$ to $+\infty$ Let $z = x + i0$

$\Rightarrow \alpha = \dfrac{x-i}{x+i}$

$\Rightarrow |\alpha| = \left|\dfrac{x-i}{x+i}\right| = 1$ (as $|x - i| = |x + i| \; \forall x \in \mathbb{R}$

$\Rightarrow \alpha$ moves on the unit circle which has centre at the origin.

18. Two different non – parallel lines cut the circle $|z| = r$ at points represented by complex number a, b, c and d respectively. Prove that these lines meet in the point z given by $z = \dfrac{a^{-1}+b^{-1}-c^{-1}-d^{-1}}{a^{-1}b^{-1}-c^{-1}d^{-1}}$

Solution: Since P, Q, R are collinear, $\begin{vmatrix} z & \bar{z} & 1 \\ c & \bar{c} & 1 \\ d & \bar{d} & 1 \end{vmatrix} = 0$

$\Rightarrow z(\bar{c}-\bar{d}) - \bar{z}(c-d) + (c\bar{d} - \bar{c}d) = 0$ ....(i)

Similarly, $z(\bar{a}-\bar{b}) - \bar{z}(a-b) + (a\bar{b} - \bar{a}b) = 0$ ......(ii)

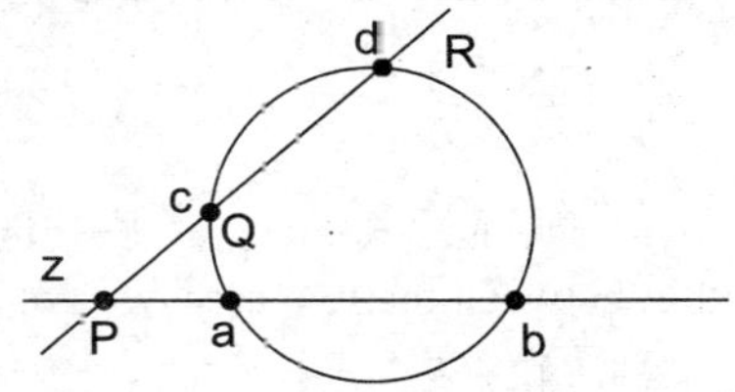

From { (i) × (a – b) } – {(ii) × (c – d)}

$\Rightarrow z[(\bar{c}-\bar{d})(a-b) - (\bar{a}-\bar{b})(c-d)]$

$= (a\bar{b} - b\bar{a})(c-d) - (c\bar{d} - \bar{c}d)(a-b)$ ....(iii)

now $a\bar{a} = r^2 \Rightarrow \bar{a} = \dfrac{r^2}{a}$

Similarly $\bar{b} = \dfrac{r^2}{b}, \bar{c} = \dfrac{r^2}{c}, \bar{d} = \dfrac{r^2}{d}$

$\therefore$From (iii), $z\left[\left(\dfrac{r^2}{c}-\dfrac{r^2}{d}\right)(a-b) - \left(\dfrac{r^2}{a}-\dfrac{r^2}{b}\right)(c-d)\right]$

$= \left(\dfrac{ar^2}{b} - \dfrac{br^2}{a}\right)(c-d) - \left(\dfrac{cr^2}{d} - \dfrac{r^2 d}{c}\right)(a-b)$

$\Rightarrow z\left[\dfrac{(d-c)(a-b)}{cd} - \dfrac{(b-a)(c-d)}{ab}\right]$

$= \dfrac{(a^2-b^2)(c-d)}{ab} - \dfrac{(c^2-d^2)(a-b)}{cd}$

$\Rightarrow z\left[-\dfrac{1}{cd} + \dfrac{1}{ab}\right] = \dfrac{(a+b)}{ab} - \dfrac{(c+d)}{cd}$

($\because$ a, b, c, d are different $\Rightarrow a - b \ne 0, c - d \ne 0$)

$\Rightarrow z = \dfrac{a^{-1}+b^{-1}-c^{-1}-d^{-1}}{a^{-1}b^{-1}-c^{-1}d^{-1}}$

19. Plot the region represented by $\dfrac{\pi}{3} \le \arg\left(\dfrac{z+1}{z-1}\right) \le \dfrac{2\pi}{3}$ in the Argand plane.

Solution: Let us take $\arg\left(\dfrac{z+1}{z-1}\right) = \dfrac{2\pi}{3}$. Clearly z lies on the minor arc of circle passing through (1,0) and (–1, 0). Similarly, $\arg\left(\dfrac{z+1}{z-1}\right) = \dfrac{\pi}{3}$ means that z is lying on the major arc of the circle passing through (1, 0) and (–1, 0).

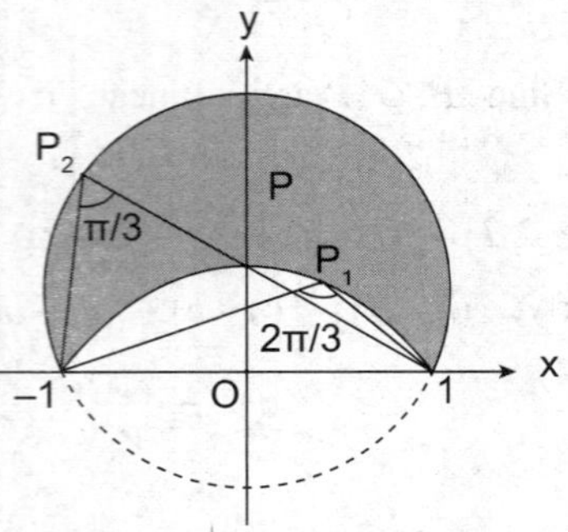

Now if we take any point say $P(z)$, in the region included in between the two arcs, we get,

$\frac{\pi}{3} \le \arg\left(\frac{z+1}{z-1}\right) \le \frac{2\pi}{3}$

Thus $\frac{\pi}{3} \le \arg\left(\frac{z+1}{z-1}\right) \le \frac{2\pi}{3}$ represents the shaded region (excluding the points (1, 0) and (–1, 0)).

20. Construct an equation whose roots are $\pm i$, $\sec(2\pi/5)$, $\sec(4\pi/5)$

Solution: Let $5\theta = 2n\pi$, $n \in \mathbb{Z} \Rightarrow 3\theta = 2n\pi - 2\theta$

$\Rightarrow \cos 3\theta = \cos 2\theta$

$\Rightarrow 4\cos^3\theta - 2\cos^2\theta - 3\cos\theta + 1 = 0$

Put $\cos\theta = x$, here note that θ may be 0 or $2\pi/5$ or $4\pi/5$ for $n = 0, 1, 2$ and also if we take $n = 3, 4, 5.....$, then the value of $\cos\theta$ will start repeating

$\Rightarrow 4x^3 - 2x^2 - 3x + 1 = 0 \Rightarrow (x - 1)(4x^2 + 2x - 1) = 0$

$\Rightarrow 4x^2 + 2x - 1 = 0$ where $x = \cos(2\pi/5), \cos(4\pi/5)$

Hence required equation is $(4/x^2 + 2/x - 1)(x^2 + 1) = 0$

$\Rightarrow (x^2 - 2x - 4)(x^2 + 1) = 0$

$\Rightarrow x^4 - 2x^3 - 3x^2 - 2x - 4 = 0$

21. If a is complex number such that $|a| = 1$. find the values of a, so that equation $az^2 + z + 1 = 0$ has one purely imaginary root.

Solution: $az^2 + z + 1 = 0$ ....(i)

Where z is purely imaginary.

Taking conjugate of both sides, $\overline{az^2 + z + 1} = \overline{0}$

$\Rightarrow \overline{a}(\overline{z})^2 + \overline{z} + \overline{1} = 0$

$\Rightarrow \overline{a}(z)^2 - z + 1 = 0$ (since $\overline{z} = -z$ as z is purely imaginary) ....(ii)

Eliminating z using the equations, (i) and (ii)

$\Rightarrow (\overline{a} - a)^2 + 2(a + \overline{a}) = 0$

Let $a = \cos\theta + i\sin\theta$ (since $|a| = 1$)

So $(-2i\sin\theta)^2 + 2(2\cos\theta) = 0$

$\Rightarrow -4\sin^2\theta + 4\cos\theta = 0 \quad \Rightarrow \cos^2\theta + \cos\theta - 1 = 0$

$\Rightarrow \cos\theta = \frac{-1 \pm \sqrt{1+4}}{2}$

Only feasible value of $\cos\theta$ is $\frac{\sqrt{5}-1}{2}$

$\Rightarrow \theta = 2n\pi \pm \cos^{-1}\left(\frac{\sqrt{5}-1}{2}\right)$

Hence $a = \cos\phi + i\sin\phi$,

where $\phi = 2n\pi \pm \cos^{-1}\left(\frac{\sqrt{5}-1}{2}\right); n \in \mathbb{Z}$

22. If $iz^3 + z^2 - z + i = 0$, then show that $|z| = 1$.

Solution: $iz^3 + z^2 - z + i = 0$

By substituting $z = i$ in the equation, we get $0 = 0$

Hence $z - i$ is a factor of $iz^3 + z^2 - z + i$

$\Rightarrow iz^2(z - i) - 1(z - i) = 0 \Rightarrow (iz^2 - 1)(z - i) = 0$

$\Rightarrow$ Either $iz^2 - 1 = 0$ or $z - i = 0$

when $z - i = 0$, $z = i$

$\therefore$ $|z| = |0 + i.1| = \sqrt{0^2 + 1^2} = 1$

when $iz^2 - 1 = 0$, $z^2 = 1/i = -i$

$\therefore$ $|z^2| = |0 - 1.i| = \sqrt{0^2 + (-1)^2} = 1$

$\therefore$ $|z^2| = 1$ or $|z| = 1$

$\therefore$ In any case we have $|z| = 1$

23. *ABCD* is a rhombus. Its diagonals *AC* and *BD* intersect at the point *M* and satisfy *BD* = 2*AC*. Its points *D* and *M* represent the complex numbers $1 + i$ and $2 - i$ repectively. Find the complex number represented by *A*.

Solution: Let *A* be $z = x + iy$

i.e., point (x, y)

It is given that $BD = 2AC$

$\Rightarrow MD = 2AM$

$\Rightarrow (1 - 2)^2 + (1 + 1)^2$

$= 4[(x - 2)^2 + (y + 1)^2]$ ....(i)

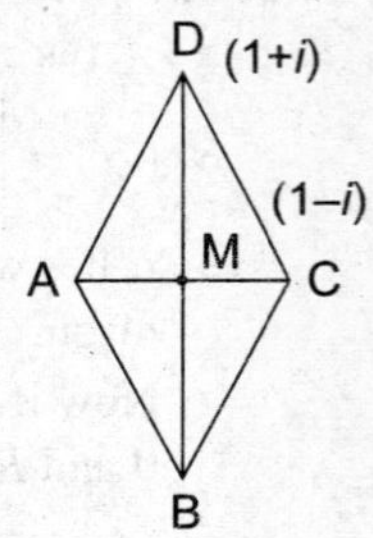

and $\frac{y+1}{x-2} \cdot \frac{1+1}{1-2} = -1$

$\Rightarrow 2(y + 1) = x - 2$

$\therefore$ (i) gives $(y + 1)^2 = 1/4 \Rightarrow y = -1/2, -3/2$

$\Rightarrow x = 3, 1 \Rightarrow$ A represents $z = 3 - i/2$ or $1 - 3i/2$

24. Find z such that $|z - 2 + 2i| \le 1$ and z has

(i) least absolute value

(ii) numerically least amplitude

Solution: (i) Given equation represents a circular disc with centre (2, – 2) and radius 1.

Distance of z from origin will be minimum if z is along the line which is normal to circle passing through origin, so it will pass through centre also.

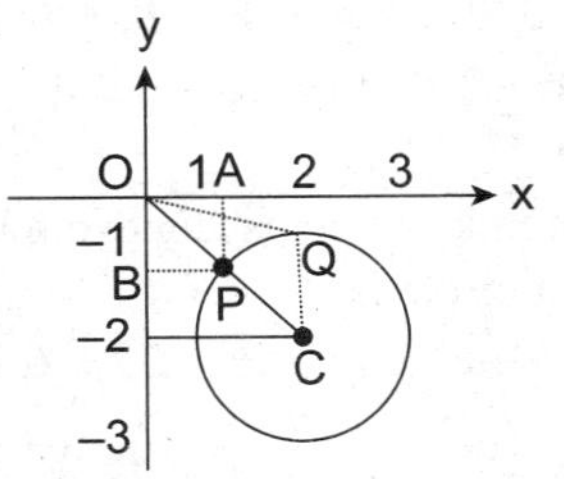

$OP = (2\sqrt{2} - 1)$ and $OA = OP \cos 45°$

And $OB = -OP \sin 45°$

So $z = \frac{(2\sqrt{2}-1)}{\sqrt{2}} - i\left(\frac{2\sqrt{2}-1}{\sqrt{2}}\right) = \frac{2\sqrt{2}-1}{\sqrt{2}}(1-i)$

(ii) We have to find the complex number z represented by Q

Now $OQ = \sqrt{OC^2 - CQ^2} = \sqrt{|2-2i|^2 - 1^2}$

$= \sqrt{2^2 + (-2)^2 - 1} = \sqrt{7} \Rightarrow |z| = \sqrt{7}$

Now, $\angle QOX = -|\angle COX - \angle COQ| = -\left|\frac{\pi}{4} - \sin^{-1}\frac{1}{OC}\right|$

$= \left|\frac{\pi}{4} - \sin^{-1}\frac{1}{|2-2i|}\right| = -\left(\frac{\pi}{4} - \sin^{-1}\frac{1}{2\sqrt{2}}\right)$

$\Rightarrow amp\ (z) = -\left(\frac{\pi}{4} - \sin^{-1}\frac{1}{2\sqrt{2}}\right)$

$\Rightarrow z = |z|\ \{\cos\ (amp(z)) + i \sin\ (amp(z))\}$

$$= \sqrt{7}\left[\cos\left\{-\left(\frac{\pi}{4} - \sin^{-1}\frac{1}{2\sqrt{2}}\right)\right\} + i\sin\left\{-\left(\frac{\pi}{4} - \sin^{-1}\frac{1}{2\sqrt{2}}\right)\right\}\right]$$

$$= \sqrt{7}\left[\cos\left(\frac{\pi}{4} - \sin^{-1}\frac{1}{2\sqrt{2}}\right) - i\sin\left(\frac{\pi}{4} - \sin^{-1}\frac{1}{2\sqrt{2}}\right)\right]$$

25. A cubic equation $f(x) = 0$ has one real root α and two complex roots $\beta \pm i\gamma$. Points A, B, C represents roots α, $\beta + i\gamma$ and $\beta - i\gamma$ respectively on the Argand plane. Show that the roots of the derived equation $f'(x) = 0$ are complex, if A falls inside one of the two equilateral triangles described on base BC.

Solution: Let $f(x) = k(x - \alpha)(x - \beta - i\gamma)(x - \beta + i\gamma)$

$= k(x - \alpha)[(x - \beta)^2 + \gamma^2]$

$\therefore f'(x) = k[\{(x - \beta)^2 + \gamma^2\} + 2(x - \alpha)(x - \beta)]$

Discriminant of equation $f'(x) = 0$ is given by

$D = 4[(\alpha + 2\beta)^2 - 3(\beta^2 + \gamma^2 + 2\alpha\beta)]$

$= 4(\alpha^2 + \beta^2 - 3\gamma^2 - 2\alpha\beta)]$

Now, $PL = \sqrt{3}\,|\gamma|$

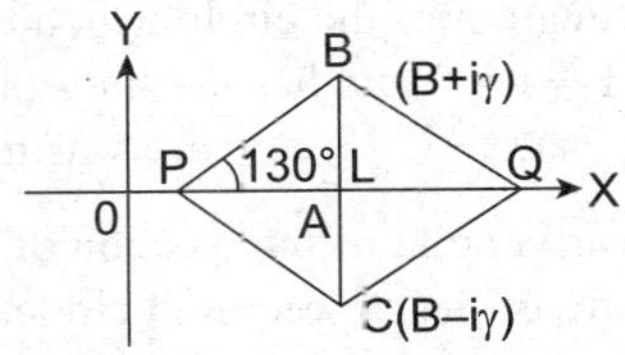

If A lies inside the equilateral triangles having BC as base, then $|\beta - \alpha| < \sqrt{3}|\gamma|$ or $(\beta - \alpha)^2 < 3\gamma^2$

or $\beta^2 + \alpha^2 - 3\gamma^2 - 2\alpha\beta < 0$

$\therefore$ From (1), $D < 0$ and hence roots of equation $f'(x) = 0$ are imaginary if A lies between P and Q on the line segment PQ.

26. For complex numbers z_1 and z_2, prove that $|z_1|^2 z_2 - |z_2|^2 z_1 = z_1 - z_2$ if and only if $z_1 = z_2$ or $z_1\bar{z}_2 = 1$

Solution: $|z_1|^2 z_2 - |z_2|^2 z_1 = z_1 - z_2$

$\Rightarrow z_1(1 + |z_2|^2) = z_2(1 - |z_1|^2)$

$\Rightarrow \frac{z_1}{z_2} = \frac{1+|z_1|^2}{1+|z_2|^2} \quad \Rightarrow \frac{z_1}{z_2}$ is purely real

$\Rightarrow \frac{z_1}{z_2} = \frac{\bar{z}_1}{\bar{z}_2} \quad \Rightarrow z_1\bar{z}_2 = \bar{z}_1 z_2$

Now $|z_1|^2 z_2 - |z_2|^2 z_1 = z_1 - z_2$

$\Rightarrow z_1\bar{z}_1 z_2 - z_2\bar{z}_2 z_1 = z_1 - z_2$

$\Rightarrow z_1(\bar{z}_1 z_2 - 1) - z_2(\bar{z}_2 z_1 - 1) = 0$

$\Rightarrow (z_1 - z_2)(z_1\bar{z}_2 - 1) = 0$ ($\because$ of (i))

$\Rightarrow z_1 = z_2$ or $z_1\bar{z}_2 = 1$

Conversely, if $z_1 = z_2$ or $z_1\bar{z}_2 - 1 = 0$

$\Rightarrow \overline{z_1 z_2} = 1 \Rightarrow z_1\bar{z}_2 = \bar{z}_1 z_2$

$\Rightarrow (z_1 - z_2)(z_1\bar{z}_2 - 1) = 0$

$\Rightarrow z_1(z_1\bar{z}_2 - 1) - z_2(z_1\bar{z}_2 - 1) = 0$

$\Rightarrow z_1(\bar{z}_1 z_2 - 1) - z_2(z_1\bar{z}_2 - 1) = 0$

$\Rightarrow z_1\bar{z}_1 z_2 - z_1 - z_2\bar{z}_2 z_1 + z_2 = 0$

$\Rightarrow |z_1|^2 z_2 - |z_2|^2 z_1 = z_1 - z_2$

27. If $z = x + iy$ is a complex number with $x, y \in Q$ and $|z| = 1$. Show that $|z^{2n} - 1|$ is a rational number for every $n \in \mathbb{N}$.

Solution: $|z = 1 \Rightarrow z = e^{i\theta} = x + iy$

$\Rightarrow x = \cos\theta, y = \sin\theta \Rightarrow \cos\theta$ and $\sin\theta \in Q$

now, $|z^{2n} - 1|^2 = (z^{2n} - 1)(\bar{z}^{2n} - 1)$

$(z\bar{z})^{2n} - z^{2n} - \bar{z}^{2n} + 1 = 2 - (z^{2n} + \bar{z}^{2n})$

$= 2 - (e^{2in\theta} + e^{-i2n\theta}) = 2(1 - \cos 2n\theta) = 4\sin^2 n\theta$

$\Rightarrow |z^{2n} - 1| = 2|\sin n\theta|$

Now, $\sin n\theta = {}^nC_1 \cos^{n-1}\theta \sin\theta - {}^nC_3 \cos^{n-3}\theta \sin^3\theta + \ldots\ldots$ Which is a rational number (as $\sin\theta$, $\cos\theta$ are rationals)

$\Rightarrow |z^{2n} - 1|$ is a rational number.

28. Find the equation of the circle which touches the line $iz + \bar{z} + 1 + i = 0$ and has the lines $(1 - i)z = (1 + i)\bar{z}$ and $(1 + i)z + (i - 1)\bar{z} = 4i$ as its normals.

Solution: Clearly, point of intersection of normals would be the centre of the the required circle.

$$(1 - i)\, z = (1 + i)\, \bar{z} \Rightarrow \bar{z} = \frac{1-i}{1+i}\, z \quad \text{...(i)}$$

$$(1 + i)z + (i - 1)\, \bar{z} = 4i \Rightarrow \bar{z} = \frac{4i-(1+i)z}{(i-1)} \quad \text{..(ii)}$$

$\therefore$ From (i) and (ii), we get $\dfrac{1-i}{1+i}\, z = \dfrac{4i-(1+i)z}{(i-1)}$

$\Rightarrow (1 - i)\,(i - 1)z = 4i\,(1 + i) - (1 + i)^2\, z$

$\Rightarrow z\,[(1 + i)^2 - (1 - i)^2] = 4i\,(1 + i)$

$\Rightarrow z\,(4i) = 4i(1 + i) \Rightarrow z = (1 + i)$, which is the centre of circle

Now equation of tangent can be rewritten as

$$\frac{1}{1+i}(iz + \bar{z}) + 1 = 0$$

$\Rightarrow i(1 - i)z + (1 - i)\bar{z} + 2 = 0$

$\Rightarrow (i + 1)z + (1 - i)\bar{z} + 2 = 0$

Now distance of $z = (1 + i)$ from this line

$$= \frac{|(1+i)(1+i)+(1-i)(1-i)+2|}{2|1+i|} = \frac{1}{\sqrt{2}}$$

Thus the equation of required circle is, $|z - (1 + i)| = \dfrac{1}{\sqrt{2}}$

29. Find $a \in \mathbb{R}$ if atleast one complex number z is to satisfy $|z + 3| = a^2 - 2a + 6$ and $|z - 3\sqrt{3}i| < a^2$ simultaneously.

Solution: $|z + 3| = a^2 - 2a + 6$

$\Rightarrow$ z lies on a circle whose centre is $(-3 + i.0)$ and radius is $a^2 - 2a + 6$. Here $a^2 - 2a + 6 > 0$, $\forall\, a \in \mathbb{R}$ (as the roots of the corresponding equation are imaginary)

and $|z - 3\sqrt{3}i| < a^2$ .....(ii)

$\Rightarrow$ z lies in the interior of a circle whose centre is $(0 + 3\sqrt{3}i)$ and radius is a^2.

Clearly atleast one complex number would satisfy both the equations if the two circles cut in two real and distinct points or first circle lies entirely inside the second circle.

We know that two circles with centres at C_1 and C_2 and radii being r_1 and r_2 respectively, will never intersect and are outside each other if $C_1C_2 \geq r_1 + r_2$

$\Rightarrow |-3 - 3\sqrt{3}i| \geq a^2 + a^2 - 2a + 6$

$\Rightarrow 6 \geq 2a^2 - 2a + 6 \Rightarrow a^2 - a \leq 0$

$\Rightarrow a \in [0, 1]$ ......(iii)

Now condition for second circle lies entirely in the first circle is

$|r_1 - r_2| \geq C_1\, C_2 \Rightarrow a^2 - 2a + 6 - a^2 \geq 6 \Rightarrow a \leq 0$ ....(iv)

From (iii) and (iv) $a \in (-\infty, 1]$ which is not required.

Hence desired values of $a \in \mathbb{R} - (-\infty\ 1] = (1, \infty)$

30. Consider a triangle formed by the points $A\left(\dfrac{2}{\sqrt{3}}e^{i\frac{\pi}{2}}\right)$; $B\left(\dfrac{2}{\sqrt{3}}e^{-i\frac{\pi}{6}}\right)$; $C\left(\dfrac{2}{\sqrt{3}}e^{-i\frac{5\pi}{6}}\right)$. Let $P(z)$ be any point on it's in-circle. Prove that $AP^2 + BP^2 + CP^2 = 5$.

Solution: Let $z_1 = \dfrac{2}{\sqrt{3}}e^{i\frac{\pi}{2}}$, $z_2 = \dfrac{2}{\sqrt{3}}e^{-i\frac{\pi}{6}}$, $z_3 = \dfrac{2}{\sqrt{3}}e^{-i\frac{5\pi}{6}}$

Clearly the points lie on the circle $|z| = \dfrac{2}{\sqrt{3}}$

If I be the length of side of the ΔABC, $AD = I \sin 60°$

$\Rightarrow AD = \dfrac{\sqrt{3}}{2}I$

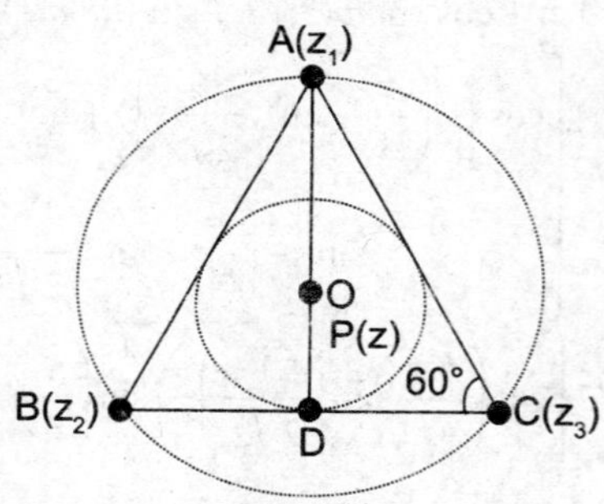

$\Rightarrow OD = \dfrac{1}{3}AD = \dfrac{\sqrt{3}}{6}I$

Now, $OA = \dfrac{2}{3}AD = \dfrac{2}{3}.\dfrac{\sqrt{3}}{2}I = \dfrac{2}{\sqrt{3}}$ (radius)

$\Rightarrow I = 2$ and $OD = \dfrac{2\sqrt{3}}{6} = \dfrac{1}{\sqrt{3}}$

$\Rightarrow$ Equation of incircle is $|z| = \dfrac{1}{\sqrt{3}}$

Let $P(z)$ be any point on the incircle,

$\Rightarrow z = \dfrac{1}{\sqrt{3}}e^{i\theta}$

Now, $(AP)^2 = |z - z_1|^2 = |z|^2 + |z_1|^2 - (z\,\overline{z}_1 + \overline{z}\,z_1)$
similarly, $(BP)^2 = |z|^2 + |z_2|^2 - (z\,\overline{z}_2 + \overline{z}\,z_2)$
and $(CP)^2 = |z|^2 + |z_3|^2 - (z\,\overline{z}_3 + \overline{z}\,z_3)$
$\therefore$ $(AP)^2 + (BP)^2 + (CP)^2 = 3|z|^2 + |z_1|^2 + |z_2|^2 + |z_3|^2 - z(\overline{z}_1 + \overline{z}_2 + \overline{z}_3) - \overline{z}(z_1 + z_2 + z_3) = 1 + 3.4/3 - z(0) - \overline{z}(0) = 5$

31. If $\alpha = e^{\frac{i2\pi}{7}}$ and $f(x) = a_0 + \sum_{k=1}^{20} a_k . x^k$. Then prove that the value of $f(x) + f(\alpha x) + ... + f(\alpha^6 x)$ is independent of α.

Solution: $f(x) + f(\alpha x) + ... + f(\alpha^6 x)$
$= 7a_0 + a_1 (x + \alpha x + ... + \alpha^6 x) + a_2(x^2 + \alpha^2 x^2 + ... + \alpha^{12} x^2) + ... + a_{20}(x^{20} + \alpha^{20} x^{20} + ... (\alpha^{120} x^{20})$
$= 7a_0 + xa_1 (1 + \alpha + ... + \alpha^6) + a_2 x^2 (1 + \alpha^2 + ... + \alpha^{12}) + ... + a_{20} x^{20} (1 + \alpha^{20} + ...\alpha^{120})$

$$= 7a_0 + a_1 x.\left(\frac{1-\alpha^7}{1-\alpha}\right) + a_2\left(\frac{1-\alpha^{14}}{1-\alpha^2}\right)x^2 + ...a_{20}x^{20}.$$

$\left(\frac{1-\alpha^{140}}{1-\alpha^{20}}\right)$ as $\alpha = e^{\frac{i2\pi}{7}} = \alpha^7 = 1$

$\Rightarrow \alpha^{14} = 1$ and so on
$\Rightarrow S = 7a_0 + a_1\, x.0 + ... + a_7 x^7(7) + ... a_{14} + ...$
$= 7(a_0 + a_7 x^7 + a_{14} x^{14})$

32. If α, β are the roots of equation $t^2 - 2t + 2 = 0$ and $\frac{(x+\alpha)^n - (x+\beta)^n}{(\alpha - \beta)} = \frac{\sin n\theta_1}{\sin^n \theta_1}$, $(x \in \mathbb{R})$ then prove that $x = \cot\theta_1 - 1$.

Solution: $t^2 - 2t + 2 = 0$

$$\Rightarrow t = \frac{2 \pm \sqrt{4-8}}{2} = \frac{2 \pm 2i}{2} = 1 \pm i$$

let, $\alpha = 1 + i$, $\beta = 1 - i \Rightarrow \alpha - \beta = 2i$
Now, $x + \alpha = x + 1 + i$, $x + \beta = x + 1 - i$
Let, $z = x + \alpha = (x + 1) + i = Re^{i\theta}$
$\Rightarrow \overline{z} = Re^{-i\theta} = (x + 1) - i = x + \beta$

where $R^2 = (x + 1)^2 + 1$, $\tan\theta = \frac{1}{(x+1)}$

$\Rightarrow x = \cot\theta - 1$
Now, $(x + \alpha)^n = R^n. e^{in\theta}$, $(x + \beta)^n = R^n. e^{-in\theta}$

$$\Rightarrow \frac{(x+\alpha)^n - (x+\beta)^n}{(\alpha-\beta)} = \frac{R^n(e^{in\theta} - e^{-in\theta})}{2i}$$

$= R^n.\sin n\theta = \sin n\theta. (\cot^2\theta + 1)^{n/2}$ (as $x + 1 = \cot\theta$)

$$= \frac{\sin n\theta}{\sin^n \theta} = \frac{\sin n\theta_1}{\sin^n \theta_1} \text{ (given)}$$

$\Rightarrow \theta = \theta_1 \Rightarrow x = \cot\theta_1 - 1$

33. If the complex number z lies on a circle with centre at $1 + i$ and unit radius, then find the locus of $\frac{3z-4}{5i}$

Solution: We have $|z - 1 - i| = 1$

Let $\omega = \frac{3z-4}{5i} \Rightarrow 5i\omega = 3z - 4 \Rightarrow \frac{5i\omega + 4}{3} = z$

$$\Rightarrow \frac{5i\omega+4}{3} - 1 - i = z - 1 - i$$

$$\Rightarrow \left|\frac{5i\omega + 4 - 3 - 3i}{3}\right| = |z - 1 - i|$$

$\Rightarrow |(5\omega - 3)i + 1| = 3 \Rightarrow |i|\,|5\omega - 3 + 1/i| = 3$

$$\Rightarrow |5\omega - 3 - i| = 3 \Rightarrow \left|\omega - \frac{3+i}{5}\right| = \frac{3}{5}$$

So locus of w is a circle with centre at (3/5, 1/5) and radius 3/5

34. Let $A(z_1)$, $B(z_2)$ and $C(z_3)$ be the vertices of an equilateral triangle and z_c be the circumcentre of the triangle, Prove
(a) $z_1^2 + z_2^2 + z_3^2 = z_1 z_2 - z_2 z_3 + z_1 z_3$
(b) $z_1^2 + z_2^2 + z_3^2 = 3z_0^2$

Solution: (a) $\frac{z_1 - z_2}{z_3 - z_2} = \left|\frac{z_1 - z_2}{z_3 - z_2}\right| e^{iB}$ $(\because z = |z|\, e^{i\theta})$

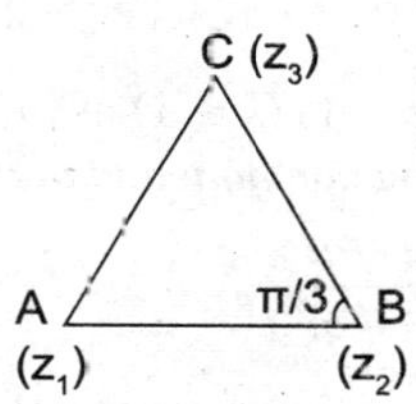

$$= \frac{|z_1 - z_2|}{|z_3 - z_2|} e^{i\pi/3} = \frac{AB}{BC} e^{i\pi/3} = e^{i\pi/3} \quad ....(i)$$

similarly, $\frac{z_2 - z_3}{z_1 - z_3} = \left|\frac{z_2 - z_3}{z_1 - z_3}\right| e^{iC} = e^{i\pi/3}$ ......(ii)

$\therefore$ From (i) and (ii), we have $\frac{z_1 - z_2}{z_3 - z_2} = \frac{z_2 - z_3}{z_1 - z_3}$

$\Rightarrow z_1^2 + z_2^2 + z_3^2 = z_1 z_2 + z_2 z_3 + z_1 z_3$

(b) $z_0 = \frac{z_1 + z_2 + z_3}{3}$

$\Rightarrow 9z_0^2 = (z_1 + z_2 + z_3)^2$
$= z_1^2 - z_2^2 + z_3^2 + 2(z_1 z_2 + z_2 z_3 + z_1 z_3)$
$= 3(z_1^2 + z_2^2 + z_3^2)$ [using part (a)]
$\Rightarrow 3z_0^2 = z_1^2 + z_2^2 + z_3^2$

35. Locate the complex number z such that $\log_{\cos\frac{\pi}{6}}\left(\frac{|z-2|+5}{4|z-2|-4}\right)<2$

Solution: Here $\log_{\frac{\sqrt{3}}{2}}\left(\frac{|z-2|+5}{4|z-2|-4}\right)<\log_{\frac{\sqrt{3}}{2}}\left(\frac{\sqrt{3}}{2}\right)^2$

$\Rightarrow \frac{|z-2|+5}{4|z-2|-4}>\frac{3}{4}$ $\left(\because \text{base}=\frac{\sqrt{3}}{2}<1\right)$

Also for the logarithm to be defined,
$4|z-2|-4>0$ i.e., $|z-2|>1$

When $|z-2|>1$, $\frac{|z-2|+5}{4|z-2|-4}>\frac{3}{4}$ gives

$(|z-2|+5)>3.\{(|z-2|-1)\}$
$\Rightarrow |z-2|+5>3|z-2|-3$

$\Rightarrow 8>2|z-2|$ $\quad\therefore |z-2|<4$

$\therefore$ z is such that $1<|z-2|<4$

Hence the region for x in the Argand plane is as shown below by the shaded area.

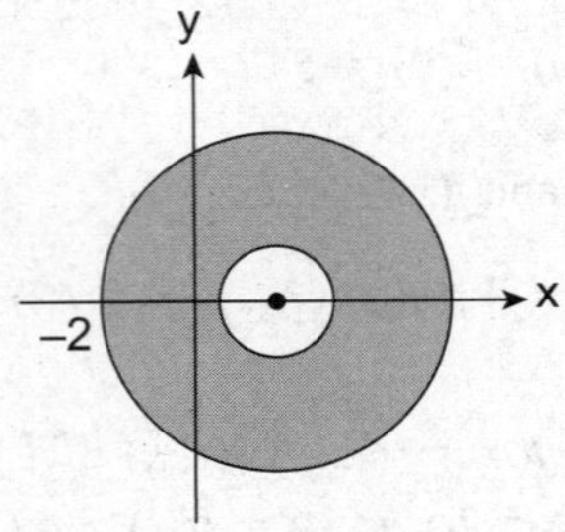

This is the area shaded between two circles with a common centre $z=2$ and radii 1 and 4.

SECTION–II

SOLVED OBJECTIVE EXAMPLES

1. If the number $(z-1)/(z+1)$ is purely imaginary, then
(a) $|z|=1$ (b) $|z|>1$
(c) $|z|<1$ (d) $|z|>2$

Solution: (a) Let $(z-1)/(z+1)=ai$, where a is a real number. Applying *componendo and dividendo*, we get

$$\frac{z+1+z-1}{z+1-(z-1)}=\frac{1+ai}{1-ai}$$

$$\Rightarrow z=\frac{1+ai}{1-ai} \qquad \Rightarrow |z|=\left|\frac{1+ai}{1-ai}\right|=1$$

3. The equation $|z-i|+|z+i|=k, a>0$, can represents an ellipse if k is
(a) 1 (b) 2
(c) 4 (d) None of these

Solution: (c) For ellipse $k>|i-(-i)|$
$(\because SP+S'P=2a\Rightarrow 2a>SS')$

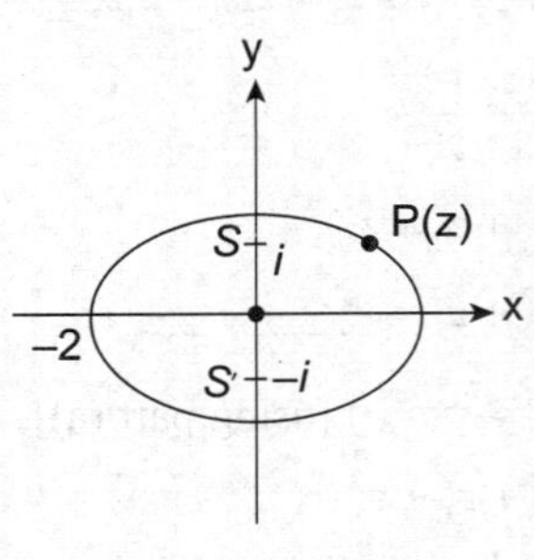

$\Rightarrow k>2$

Hence $k=4$

4. The number of solutions to the equation $z^2+\bar{z}=0$ is
(a) 1 (d) 2
(c) 3 (d) 4

Solution: (c) Let $z=x+iy$. Then $z^2+\bar{z}=0$ is equivalent to $(x^2-y^2+x)+i(2xy-y)=0$

Equating the real and imaginary parts, we get
$x^2-y^2+x=0$ and $2xy-y=0$
Now, from $2xy-y=0$, we get $y=0$ or $x=1/2$.
If $y=0$, then $x^2-y^2+x=0$
$\Rightarrow x^2+x=0$
$\Rightarrow x=0 \qquad \Rightarrow z=0+0i=0$
If $x=1/2$, then $x^2-y^2+x=0$

$$\Rightarrow y^2=\frac{1}{4}+\frac{1}{2}=\frac{3}{4}$$

$$\Rightarrow y=\pm\frac{\sqrt{3}}{2} \qquad \Rightarrow z=\frac{1}{2}\pm\frac{\sqrt{3}}{2}i$$

Thus, the given problem has three solutions.

5. If z_1, z_2, z_3, z_4, are the roots of the equation $z^4=1$, then $\sum_{i=1}^{4}z_i^3$ is equal to
(a) 4 (b) 0
(c) $1+i$ (d) $-1-i$

Solution: (b) Roots of the equation $z^4 = 1$ i.e., $(z^2 - 1)(z^2 + 1) = 0$ are $1, -1, i, -i$.

$\therefore \sum_{i=1}^{4} z_i^3 = 1^3 + (-1)^3 + i^3 + (-i)^3 = 1 - 1 - i + i = 0$

8. The real value of θ for which the expression, $\dfrac{1+i\cos\theta}{1-2i\cos\theta}$ is a real number is

(a) $2n\pi + \dfrac{\pi}{2}; n \in \mathbb{Z}$ (b) $2n\pi - \dfrac{\pi}{2}; n \in \mathbb{Z}$

(c) $2n\pi \pm \dfrac{\pi}{2}; n \in \mathbb{Z}$ (d) None of these

Solution: (a,b,c) $\dfrac{1+i\cos\theta}{1-2i\cos\theta} = \dfrac{(1+i\cos\theta)(1+2i\cos\theta)}{(1-2i\cos\theta)(1+2i\cos\theta)}$

$= \dfrac{(1+2i\cos\theta)+3i\cos\theta}{1+4\cos^2\theta}$

Thus $(1 + i\cos\theta)/(1 - 2i\cos\theta)$ is a real number if $\cos\theta = 0$

$\Rightarrow \theta = 2n\pi \pm \dfrac{\pi}{2}$, where n is an integer.

9. Let $z = 1 - t + i\sqrt{t^2+t+2}$, where t is a real parameter. The locus of z in the Argand plane is

(a) a hyperbola (b) an ellipse
(c) a straight line (d) None of these

Solution: (a) Let $z = x + iy$, then

$x+iy = 1-t+i\sqrt{t^2+t+2} \Rightarrow x = 1-t,\ y = \sqrt{t^2+t+2}$

Putting $t = 1 - x$ in the other relation, we get

$y^2 = t^2 + t + 2 = (1-x)^2 + 1 - x + 2 = \left(x - \dfrac{3}{2}\right)^2 + \dfrac{7}{4}$

or $y^2 - \left(x - \dfrac{3}{2}\right)^2 = \dfrac{7}{4}$, which is a hyperbola.

10. If $1, \omega, \omega^2, \ldots\ldots, \omega^{n-1}$ are the nth roots of unity, then $(2-\omega)(2-\omega^2)\ldots.(2-\omega^{n-1})$ equals

(a) $2^n - 1$
(b) ${}^nC_1 + {}^nC_2 + \ldots. + {}^nC_n$
(c) $[{}^{2n+1}C_1 + {}^{2n+1}C_2 + \ldots.. + {}^{2n+1}C_n]^{1/2} - 1$
(d) None of these

Solution: (a, b) Since $z^n - 1$

$\Rightarrow (z-1)(z-\omega)(z-\omega^2)\ldots..(z-\omega^{n-1})$

$\Rightarrow (z-\omega)(z-\omega^2)\ldots(z-\omega^{n-1}) = \dfrac{z^n-1}{z-1}$

Putting $z = 2$, we get

$(2-\omega)(2-\omega^2)\ldots.(2-\omega^{n-1}) = \dfrac{2^n-1}{2-1} = 2^n - 1$

Also, ${}^nC_1 + {}^nC_2 + \ldots.. + {}^nC_n = 2^n - 1$

Also ${}^{2n+1}C_1 + {}^{2n+1}C_2 + \ldots + {}^{2n+1}C_n = 2^{2n} - 1$

So (c) is wrong only option (a) and (b) are correct.

11. If $|z| = 1$, then point representing the complex number $-2 + 3z$ will lie on;

(a) a straight line (b) a circle
(c) the real axis (d) on imaginary axis

Solution: (b) Let $z' = -2 + 3z$

$\Rightarrow z' + 2 = 3z$ $\quad\Rightarrow |z' + 2| = 3|z|$

$\Rightarrow |z' + 2| = 3$ $\quad\Rightarrow z'$ lies on a circle.

12. If the roots of $z^3 + az^2 + bz + c = 0$, $a,b,c \in C$ acts as the vertices of an equilateral triangle in the Argand plane, then

(a) $a^2 + b = c$ (b) $a^2 = b$
(c) $a^2 + b = 0$ (d) None of these

Solution: (d) $(z_1 + z_2 + z_3)^2 = 3(z_1z_2 + z_2z_3 + z_3z_1)$

$\Rightarrow a^2 = 3b$

13. If $z = x + iy$ and $z^{1/3} = a - ib$ where $a, b \in \mathbb{R}$ and $b \neq 0, \pm1$, then $\dfrac{x}{a} - \dfrac{y}{b} = \lambda(a^2 - b^2)$, where λ is equal to

(a) 2 (b) 3
(c) 4 (d) 5

Solution: (c) $2^{1/3} = a - ib$

$\Rightarrow x + iy = (a - ib)^3 = a^3 + ib^3 - 3a^2bi - 3ab^2$

$= (a^2 - 3ab^2) + i(b^3 - 3a^2b)$

$\Rightarrow x = a^3 - 3ab^2$ and $y = b^3 - 3a^2b$

$\Rightarrow \dfrac{x}{a} - \dfrac{y}{b} = a^2 - 3b^2 - b^2 + 3a^2$

$= 4(a^2 - b^2)$ $\quad\Rightarrow \lambda = 4$

14. For a, b and $c \in \mathbb{R}$, if $ax^2 + bx + c$ is real for real values of x and imaginary for imaginary values of x, then

(a) $a > 0$ (b) $a < 0$
(c) $a = 0$ (d) $a \in \mathbb{Z}$

Solution: (c) Clearly, $ax^2 + bx + c \in \mathbb{R}$ whenever $x \in \mathbb{R}$ $\forall a, b, c \in \mathbb{R}$

Let $x = \alpha + i\beta$; $\beta \neq 0$, then $ax^2 + bx$

$= a(\alpha + i\beta)^2 + b(\alpha + i\beta) = a[\alpha^2 - \beta^2 + 2\alpha\beta i] + b\alpha + ib\beta$

$= a(\alpha^2 - \beta^2) + b\alpha + i[2a\alpha\beta + b\beta]$

Now $ax^2 + bx \in \mathbb{R}$ if $2a\alpha\beta + b\beta = 0$

$\Rightarrow \beta(2a\alpha + b) = 0.$

$\Rightarrow 2a\alpha + b = 0\ (\because \beta \neq 0) \quad \Rightarrow \quad \alpha = -\dfrac{b}{2a}$

$\therefore\ ax^2 + bx + c \in \mathbb{R}$ for $a \neq 0$ and $x = -\dfrac{b}{2a} + i\beta$;

$\beta \in \mathbb{R}; \beta \neq 0$

Thus for this complex value of x, $ax^2 + bx + c$ is not imaginary

$\therefore\ a = 0$ and in this case $ax^2 + bx + c \equiv bx + c$ which fulfils the given condition.

15. If one root of equation $z^2 + (p + iq)z + m + in = 0$ be real where $p, q, m, n \in \mathbb{R}$, then $n^2 + mq^2 - pqn$ will be equal to

(a) 0 (b) –1
(c) 1 (d) None of these

Solution: (a) Given equation is

$z^2 + (p + iq)z + m + in = 0$ ... (1)

Let α be real root of (1), then

$\alpha^2 + (p + iq)\alpha + m + in = 0$

$\Rightarrow (\alpha^2 + p\alpha + m) + i(q\alpha + n) = 0$

$\Rightarrow \alpha^2 + p\alpha + m = 0$ ...(2)

and $\alpha = -\dfrac{n}{q}$ ...(3)

from (2) and (3), $\dfrac{n^2}{q^2} - p.\dfrac{n}{q} + m = 0$

$\Rightarrow n^2 + mq^2 - pqn = 0$

16. If z lies on the circle centred at origin. If area of the triangle whose vertices are z, ωz and $z + \omega z$, where w is the cube root of unity, is $4\sqrt{3}$ sq. unit. Then radius of the circle is

(a) 1 unit (b) 2 units
(c) 3 units (d) 4 units

Solution: (d) $\angle AOB = 2\pi/3$

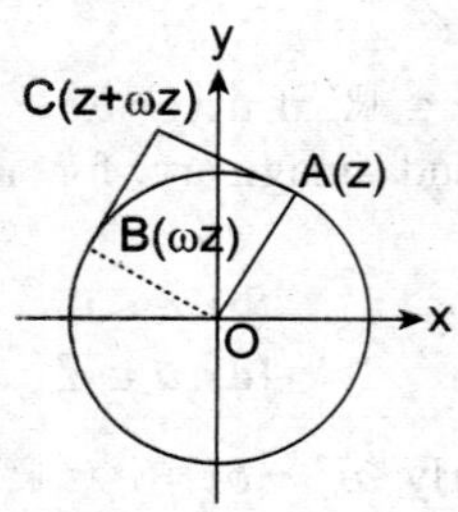

$\Delta OAB \cong \Delta ABC$

$\therefore$ Area of ΔABC = Area of ΔOAB

$= \dfrac{1}{2}\ |z|\ |wz| \sin\dfrac{2\pi}{3} = 4\sqrt{3}$

$\Rightarrow |z| = 4$ = radius of the circle

17. Let $OA.OB = 1$ and let O, A, B be three collinear points. If O and B represent the complex numbers 0 and z, then A represents

(a) $\dfrac{1}{z}$ (b) $\dfrac{1}{\bar{z}}$
(c) $\bar{z}$ (d) z^2

Solution: (a) Let O be the origin and $B = z = r_1 e^{i\alpha_1}$ and $A = z_1 = r_2 e^{i\alpha_2}$

$\therefore\ OA.\ OB = 1$ (given) $\Rightarrow r_1 r_1 e^{i(\alpha_1+\alpha_2)} = 1$

$\Rightarrow r_2 = \dfrac{1}{r_1}$ and $\alpha_2 = -\alpha_1 = \alpha$ (say)

$\Rightarrow z_1 = \dfrac{1}{r_1} e^{-i\alpha} = \dfrac{1}{\bar{z}}$

18. The point of intersection of the curves arg $(z - 3i) = \dfrac{3\pi}{4}$ and arg $(2z + 1 - 2i) = \dfrac{\pi}{4}$ is

(a) $\dfrac{3}{4}+\dfrac{9}{4}i$ (b) $\dfrac{9}{4}+\dfrac{3}{4}i$
(c) $1 + i$ (d) None of these

Solution: (a) Given arg $(z - 3i) = \dfrac{3\pi}{4}$

$\Rightarrow \arg[x + i(y - 3)] = \dfrac{3\pi}{4}$

$\Rightarrow \dfrac{y-3}{x} = \tan\dfrac{3\pi}{4} \Rightarrow y + x = 3$ ... (1)

Also $\arg[2x + 1 + i(2y - 2)] = \dfrac{\pi}{4}$

$\Rightarrow 2y - 2x = 3$

Solving (1) and (2) we get $x = \dfrac{3}{4}, y = \dfrac{9}{4}$

$\Rightarrow z = \dfrac{3}{4}+\dfrac{9}{4}i$

19. Let z be a complex number having the argument θ, $0 < \theta < \dfrac{\pi}{2}$ and satisfying the equation $|z - 3i| = 3$, then $\cot\theta - \dfrac{6}{z}$ is equal to

(a) 1 (b) i
(c) –1 (d) $-i$

Solution: (b) $|z - 3i| = 3$ is the equation of a circle with centre $C(0, 3)$ and radius = 3

$\Rightarrow z = 6 \sin\theta\ (\cos\theta + i \sin\theta)$

$\Rightarrow \dfrac{6}{z} = \dfrac{1}{\sin\theta(\cos\theta + i\sin\theta)} = \dfrac{\cos\theta - i\sin\theta}{\sin\theta} = \cot\theta - i$

$\Rightarrow \cot\theta - \frac{6}{z} = i$

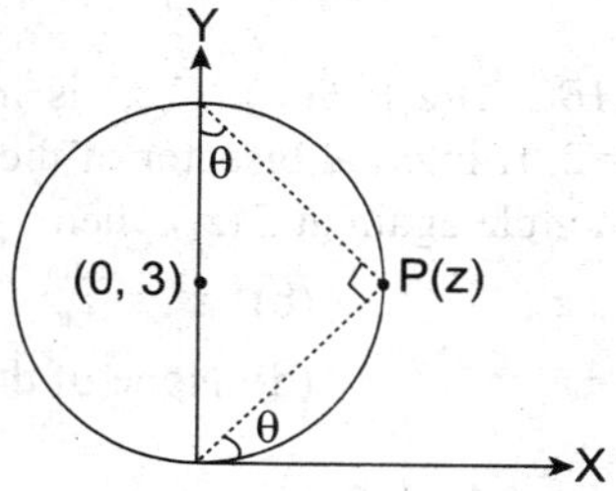

20. If $z_1 = \sqrt{3} + i\sqrt{3}$ and $z_2 = \sqrt{3} + i$, then the complex number $\left(\frac{z_1}{z_2}\right)^{50}$ lies in the

(a) first quadrant (b) second quadrant
(c) third quadrant (d) fourth quadrant

Solution: (d) $\left(\frac{z_1}{z_2}\right)^{50} = \left(\frac{\sqrt{3}+i\sqrt{3}}{\sqrt{3}+i}\right)^{50}$

$= \left\{\left[\frac{\sqrt{3}(1+i)}{\sqrt{3}+i}\right]^2\right\}^{25} = \left(\frac{3i}{1+\sqrt{3}i}\right)^{25}$

$= \frac{3^{25}.i^{25}}{(-2\omega^2)^{25}} = -\left(\frac{3}{2}\right)^{25}.\frac{1}{\omega^2} = -\left(\frac{3}{2}\right)^{25}.\omega$

$= \left(\frac{3}{2}\right)^{25}\left[\frac{1}{2} - \frac{\sqrt{3}}{2}i\right]$

21. If a, b, c are complex numbers such that $a + b + c = 0$ and $|a| = |b| = |c|$, then $\frac{1}{a}+\frac{1}{b}+\frac{1}{c}$ will be equal to

(a) 0 (b) 1
(c) –1 (d) None of these

Solution: (a) Let $a = re^{i\alpha_1}$, $b = re^{i\alpha_2}$, $c = re^{i\alpha_3}$

$\Rightarrow \frac{1}{a} = r^{-1}e^{-i\alpha_1}, \frac{1}{b} = r^{-1}e^{-i\alpha_2}, \frac{1}{c} = r^{-1}e^{-i\alpha_3}$

Now, $a + b + c = 0$

$\Rightarrow r(e^{i\alpha_1} + e^{i\alpha_2} + e^{i\alpha_3}) = 0$

$\Rightarrow (\cos\alpha_1 + \cos\alpha_2 + \cos\alpha_3) + i(\sin\alpha_1 + \sin\alpha_2 + \sin\alpha_3) = 0$

$\Rightarrow \cos\alpha_1 + \cos\alpha_2 + \cos\alpha_3 = 0$ and $\sin\alpha_1 + \sin\alpha_2 + \sin\alpha_3 = 0$

$\Rightarrow \frac{1}{a}+\frac{1}{b}+\frac{1}{c}$

$= (\cos\alpha_1 + \cos\alpha_2 + \cos\alpha_3) - i(\sin\alpha_1 + \sin\alpha_2 + \sin\alpha_3) = 0$

23. If $z = x + iy$ satisfies, $\arg(z - 1) = \arg(z + 3i)$, then the value of $(x - 1): y$ is equal to

(a) 2: 1 (b) 1: 3
(c) –1: 3 (d) None of these

Solution: (b) $\arg(x + iy - 1) = \arg(x + iy + 3i)$

$\Rightarrow \tan^{-1}\frac{y}{x-1} = \tan^{-1}\frac{3+y}{x}$

$\Rightarrow \frac{y}{x-1} = \frac{3+y}{x}$

$\Rightarrow xy = 3x + xy - 3 - y \quad \Rightarrow \frac{x-1}{y} = \frac{1}{3}$

24. If the number $\frac{z-1}{z+1}$ is purely imaginary, then

(a) $|z| = 1$ (b) $|z| > 1$
(c) $|z| < 1$ (d) $|z| > 2$

Solution: (a) Since $\frac{z-1}{z+1}$ is purely imaginary

$\Rightarrow \arg\left(\frac{z-1}{z+1}\right) = \pm\frac{\pi}{2}$

$\Rightarrow z$ lies on circle whose diameter has end points (1, 0) and (–1, 0)

$\Rightarrow z$ lies on unit circle with centre at the origin

$\Rightarrow |z| = 1$

25. If $|z^2 - 4| = 2|z|$, then maximum value of $|z|$ is

(a) $1 + \sqrt{5}$ (b) $\sqrt{5} - 1$
(c) 4 (d) None of these

Solution: (a) $|z^2 - 4| \ge ||z|^2 - 4| \Rightarrow 2|z| \ge ||z|^2 - 4|$

$\Rightarrow -2|z| \le |z|^2 - 4 \le 2|z|$

$\Rightarrow |z|^2 - 2|z| - 4 \le 0$ and $|z|^2 + 2|z| - 4 \ge 0$

$\Rightarrow \sqrt{5} - 1 \le |z| \le 1 + \sqrt{5}$

Thus maximum value of $|z|$ is $1 + \sqrt{5}$

26. If one root of the equation $z^2 + (a + i)z + b + ic = 0$ be real, where $a, b, c \in R$ then $c^2 + b - ac =$

(a) 0 (b) –1
(c) 1 (d) None of these

Solution: (a) Given equation is $z^2 + (a + i)z + b + ic = 0$

Let α be a real root, then $\alpha^2 - (a + i)\alpha + b + ic = 0$

$\Rightarrow \alpha^2 + a\alpha + b = 0$ .....(1)

and $\alpha + c = 0$

$\Rightarrow \alpha = -c$ ......(2)

Putting the value of α in (1), we get $c^2 - ac + b = 0$

27. If α is a non real complex number and $x^2 + \alpha x + \bar{\alpha} = 0$ has a real root γ, then

(a) $\gamma = \alpha + \bar{\alpha}$ (b) $\gamma = 2[\alpha + \bar{\alpha}]$
(c) $\gamma = 1$ (d) None of these

Solution: (c) $\gamma^2 + \alpha\gamma + \bar{\alpha} = 0$

$\gamma^2 + \bar{\alpha}\gamma + \alpha = 0$ (Taking conjugate of above equation)

$$\Rightarrow \frac{\gamma^2}{\alpha^2 - \bar{\alpha}^2} = \frac{\gamma}{\bar{\alpha} - \alpha} = \frac{1}{\bar{\alpha} - \alpha} \Rightarrow \gamma = 1$$

28. If $|z| = 2$ and $\frac{z_1 - z_2}{z_2 - z_3} = \frac{z-2}{z+2}$, then z_1, z_2, z_3 will be the vertices of
(a) equilateral triangle
(b) acute angled triangle
(c) right angled triangle
(d) None of these

Solution: (c) Clearly, $\arg\left(\frac{z-2}{z+2}\right) = \pm\frac{\pi}{2}$

$$\Rightarrow \arg\left(\frac{z_1 - z_2}{z_2 - z_3}\right) = \pm\frac{\pi}{2}$$

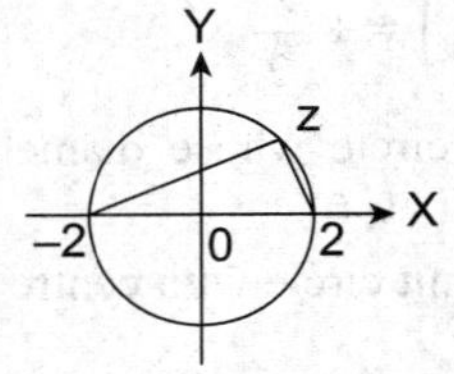

$\Rightarrow$ z_1, z_2, z_3 will be the vertices of a right angled triangle

29. If $|z + 2 - i| = 5$, then maximum value of $|2z + 7 - 6i|$ is;
(a) 10 (b) 15
(c) 20 (d) 25

Solution: (b) $|2z + 7 - 6i|$

$\Rightarrow |2(z + 2 - i) + 3 - 4i| \le 2|z + 2 - i| + |3 - 4i|$

$\Rightarrow 2(5) + 5 = 15$

Thus maximum value of $|z + 2 - i|$ is 15.

30. It z is a complex number and a_1, a_2, a_3, b_1, b_2, b_3 all are real, then $\begin{vmatrix} a_1 z + b_1\bar{z} & a_2 z + b_2\bar{z} & a_3 z + b_3\bar{z} \\ a_1\bar{z} + b_1 z & b_2 z + a_2\bar{z} & b_3 z + a_3\bar{z} \\ b_1 z + a_1 & b_2 z + a_2 & b_3 z + a_3 \end{vmatrix}$ is equal to
(a) $(a_1 a_2 a_3 + b_1 b_2 b_3)^2 |z|^2$
(b) $|z|^2$
(c) 3
(d) None of these

Solution: (d) $\Delta = \begin{vmatrix} z & \bar{z} & 1 \\ \bar{z} & z & 1 \\ 1 & z & \bar{z} \end{vmatrix} \times \begin{vmatrix} a_1 & b_1 & 0 \\ a_2 & b_2 & 0 \\ a_3 & b_3 & 0 \end{vmatrix} = 0$

31. Triangle ABC; $A(z_1)$, $B(z_2)$, $C(z_3)$ is inscribed in the circle $|z| = 2$. If internal bisector of the angle A meets it's circumcircle again at $D(z_d)$, then
(a) $z_d^2 = z_2 z_3$ (b) $z_d^2 = z_1 z_3$
(c) $z_d^2 = z_2 z_1$ (d) None of these

Solution: (a) $\Rightarrow Arg\left(\frac{z_d}{z_2}\right) = A \Rightarrow Arg\left(\frac{z_3}{z_2}\right) = 2A$

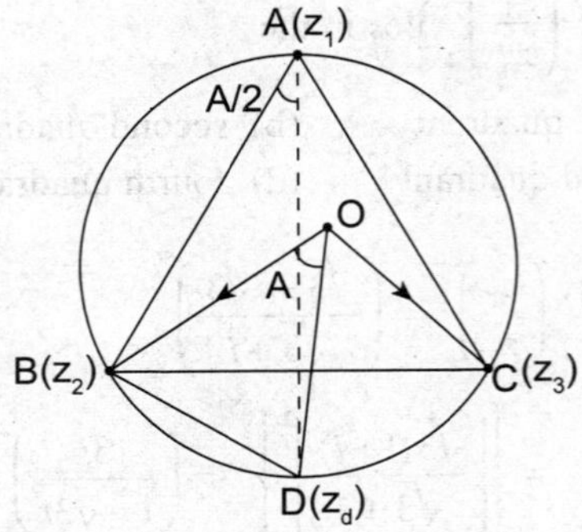

$$\Rightarrow \frac{z_d}{z_2} = e^{iA} \text{ and } \frac{z_3}{z_2} = e^{i2A} = \left(\frac{z_d}{z_2}\right)^2$$

$$\Rightarrow z_d^2 = z_2 z_3$$

LINKED COMPREHENSION PASSAGE

Let z_1, z_2, z_3 be three non-zero complex numbers in harmonic progression, i.e., $\frac{1}{z_1}, \frac{1}{z_2}, \frac{1}{z_3}$ are in arithmetic progression, i.e., $\frac{2}{z_2} = \frac{1}{z_1} + \frac{1}{z_3}$

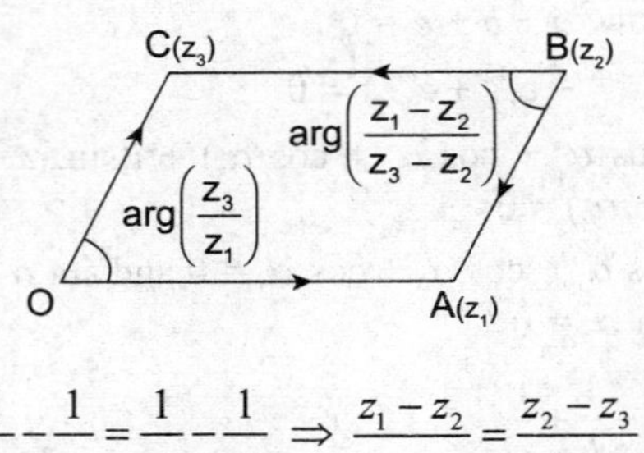

$$\Rightarrow \frac{1}{z_2} - \frac{1}{z_1} = \frac{1}{z_3} - \frac{1}{z_2} \Rightarrow \frac{z_1 - z_2}{z_2 z_1} = \frac{z_2 - z_3}{z_3 z_2}$$

$$\Rightarrow \frac{z_1 - z_2}{z_2 - z_3} = \frac{z_1}{z_3} \qquad \Rightarrow \frac{z_1 - z_2}{z_3 - z_2} = -\frac{z_1}{z_3}$$

$$\Rightarrow \arg\left(\frac{z_1 - z_2}{z_3 - z_2}\right) = \arg\left(\frac{-z_1}{z_3}\right) = \arg(-1) - \arg\left(\frac{z_3}{z_1}\right)$$

$$= \pi - \arg\left(\frac{z_3}{z_1}\right)$$

$$\Rightarrow \arg\left(\frac{z_1 - z_2}{z_3 - z_2}\right) + \arg\left(\frac{z_3}{z_1}\right) = \pi$$

$\Rightarrow$ *OABC* is a cyclic quadrilateral

$\Rightarrow$ origin, z_1, z_2, z_3 lie on a circle.

Thus, if z_1, z_2, z_3 are non-zero complex numbers in H.P., then z_1, z_2, z_3 lie on a circle passing through origin.

However the converse is not true, as for two non-zero complex numbers z_1 and z_3, their H.M. is unique and there are infinitely many z_2's such that z_1, z_2, z_3 lie on a circle passing through origin. Thus if z_1, z_2, z_3 lie on a circle passing through origin, then they may not be in H.P. Now answer the following questions.

36. If $z_1 = 2 + \sqrt{3}i$, z_2 & $z_3 = 2 - \sqrt{3}i$ lie on a circle passing through origin, then a possible value of z_2 is

(a) $2 + (1/\sqrt{3})i$ (b) $2 - (1/\sqrt{3})i$

(c) $7/2 + 0i$ (d) None of these

Solution: (c) $2 + \frac{1}{\sqrt{3}}i$, & $2 - \frac{1}{\sqrt{3}}i$ are collinear with z_1 and z_3 where as $\frac{7}{2} + 0i = \frac{2z_1z_3}{z_1 + z_3} \Rightarrow z_1, \frac{7}{2} + 0i, z_3$ are in H.P.

$\Rightarrow z_1, z_2, z_3$ lies on a circle passing through origin.

37. If the co-ordinate axes are rotated through an angle $\pi/3$ anticlockwise then, w.r.t. new co-ordinate system, z_2 (found in above question) becomes

(a) $\frac{7}{4} + \frac{7\sqrt{3}}{4}i$ (b) $\frac{7}{4} - \frac{7\sqrt{3}}{4}i$

(c) $\frac{3}{2} - \frac{5}{6}\sqrt{3}i$ (d) None of these

Solution: (b) When the co-ordinate axes are rotated through an angle $\pi/3$ anticlockwise, z_2 can be considered as rotated through an angle $\pi/3$ clockwise.

Thus new z_2 becomes $e^{-i\pi/3}z_2$

$$= \left[\cos\left(\frac{\pi}{3}\right) - i\sin\left(\frac{\pi}{3}\right)\right]z_2 = \left[\frac{1}{2} - \frac{\sqrt{3}}{2}i\right]\left(\frac{7}{2} + 0i\right)$$

$$= \frac{7}{4} - \frac{7\sqrt{3}}{4}i$$

38. If $4, \frac{24}{13}(3 + 2i), 6i$ lies on a circle, then the radius of circle is

(a) $\sqrt{13}$ units (b) $\sqrt{15}$ units

(c) 3 units (d) None of these

Solution: (a) Let $z_1 = 4$

$$z_2 = \frac{24}{13}(3 + 2i) \qquad z_3 = 6i$$

$$\text{Now } \frac{2z_1z_3}{z_1 + z_3} = \frac{2(4)(6i)}{4 + 6i} = \frac{24i}{2 + 3i} = \frac{24i}{2 + 3i} \times \frac{2 - 3i}{2 - 3i}$$

$$= \frac{48i - 72i^2}{4 + 9} = \frac{48i + 72}{13} = \frac{24(3 + 2i)}{13} = z_2$$

$$\therefore \frac{2z_1z_3}{z_1 + z_3} = z_2$$

$\Rightarrow z_1, z_2, z_3$ are in H.P.

$\Rightarrow z_1, z_2, z_3$ lies on a circle passing through origin as shown below in diagram

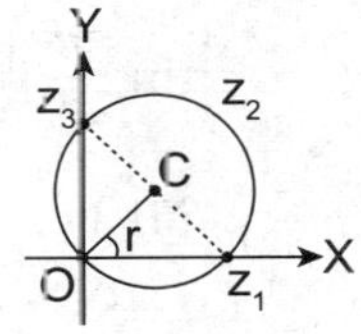

$\Rightarrow$ Centre of circle will be mid point of $z_1z_3 = (2 + 3i) \equiv C$ (say)

$\therefore$ Radius of circle $= |2 + 3i| = \sqrt{13}$ *units.*

TUTORIAL EXERCISE

SECTION–III

SINGLE CORRECT ANSWER

1. If z and ω are two non-zero complex numbers such that $|z\omega| = 1$ and Arg (z) – Arg $(\omega) = \frac{\pi}{2}$, then $\bar{z}\omega$ is equal to
(a) 1 (b) –1
(c) i (d) $-i$

2. The value of $(1 + 2\omega + \omega^2)^{3n} - (1 + \omega + 2\omega^2)^{3n}$ is equal to
(a) 0 (b) 1
(c) ω (d) ω^2

3. If ω is a complex cube root of unity, then $225 + (3\omega + 8\omega^2)^2 + (3\omega^2 + 8\omega)^2$ is equal to
(a) 72 (b) 192
(c) 200 (d) 248

4. If for complex numbers z_1 and z_2, arg $(z_1/z_2) = 0$, then $|z_1 - z_2|$ is equal to
(a) $|z_1| + |z_2|$ (b) $|z_1| - |z_2|$
(c) $||z_1| - |z_2||$ (d) 0

5. If $|z_1 + z_2| = |z_1 - z_2|$, then the difference in the amplitudes of z_1 and z_2 is
(a) $\frac{\pi}{4}$ (b) $\frac{\pi}{3}$
(c) $\frac{\pi}{2}$ (d) 0

6. If $|z_1| = |z_2|$ and arg $\left(\frac{z_1}{z_2}\right) = \pi$, then $z_1 + z_2$ is
(a) 0 (b) Purely imaginary
(c) Purely real (d) None of these

7. If $0 < Amp\ (z) < \pi$, then $Amp\ (z) - Amp\ (-z) =$
(a) 0 (b) 2 $Amp\ (z)$
(c) π (d) $-\pi$

8. If the number $(z - 1)/(z + 1)$ is purely imaginary, then
(a) $|z| = 1$ (b) $|z| > 1$
(c) $|z| < 1$ (d) $|z| > 2$

9. The region of the Argand's plane defined by $|z - 2| + |z + 2| \le 4$ is
(a) interior of an ellipse
(b) interior of circle
(c) boundary and interior of an ellipse
(d) a line segment

10. If $|z| \ne 1$ and $\left|\frac{z - z_1}{1 - \bar{z}\, z_1}\right| = 1$, then which of the following is true?
(a) $|z_1| = 0$ (b) $0 < |z_1| < 1$
(c) $|z_1| = 1$ (d) $|z_1| > 1$

11. If $|z| = 1$, $|a| \ne 1$, and $w = z/(\alpha - z)(z\bar{\alpha} - 1)$, then
(a) $w \ge 1$ (b) $0 < w < 1$
(c) $w < 0$ (d) $w > 0$

12. If $|a| = |b|$ and $\bar{a}c \ne b\bar{c}$, then the equation $az + b\bar{z} + c = 0$ has
(a) infinitely many solutions
(b) finitely many solutions
(c) no solution
(d) exactly one solution

13. If $|a| = |b| \ne 0$ and $\bar{a}c = b\bar{c}$, then $az + b\bar{z} + c = 0$ represents
(a) a point (b) a straight line
(c) an ellipse (d) a circle

14. The equation $\bar{z} = \bar{z}_0 + \frac{r^2}{z - z_0}, r > 0$ represents
(a) a parabola with focus z_0
(b) a straight line through point $\bar{z}_0$.
(c) an ellipse with foci at z_0 & $\bar{z}_0$
(d) a circle

15. A complex number z satisfies $|z - 2| = 2|z - 1|$, then $3|z|^2 - 4Re(z)$ equals
(a) 3 (b) 0
(c) –3 (d) None of these

16. If $k > 0$ and $z|z| + kz + 2k = 0$, then the complex number z must be
(a) a negative real number
(b) 0
(c) a positive real number
(d) purely imaginary

17. The number of complex numbers satisfying the equation $|z-1| = 3$ and $|z-i| = |z-1|$ is

(a) 1 (b) infinite
(c) 0 (d) 2

18. If the equation $z^2 + az + b = 0$ has all roots real, then which of the following represents the value of expression $(Im(b))^2 + (Im(a))$ is

(a) –4 (b) 4
(c) 0 (d) $2i$

19. If complex number z_1 satisfies the inequality $|z-5| < 7$ and z_2 lies on $|z-1| + |z+2| = 5$. A real number k is such that $k = |z_1 - z_2|$, then

(a) $0 \le k \le 15$ (b) $0 < k \le 17$
(c) $0 \le k \le 17$ (d) $0 \le k < 15$

20. If $a \neq 0$, then $Re(z/a) = 1$ represents

(a) a straight line
(b) rectangular hyperbola
(c) a hyperbola with eccentricity $\sqrt{2}$.
(d) part of circle with centre at a.

21. The value of $\sin(\ell n(i)^i) + \cos(\ell n(i)^i)$ is

(a) 1 (b) –1
(c) i (d) –i

22. Roots of equation $4x^2 - \pi^2 = 0$ are

(a) $\pm(i)^i$ (b) $(i)^i$ and $(i)^{-i}$
(c) $\ell n(i^i)$ and $\ell n(i^{-i})$ (d) None of these

23. If $|z| = 1$ and $z \neq \pm 1$, then all the values of $\frac{z}{1-z^2}$ lie on

(a) a line not passing through the origin
(b) $|z| = \sqrt{2}$
(c) the x-axis
(d) the y-axis

24. Let ω be a complex cube root unity with $\omega \neq 1$. A fair die is thrown three times. If r_1, r_2 and r_3 are the numbers obtained on the die, then the probability that $\omega^{r_1} + \omega^{r_2} + \omega^{r_3} = 0$ is

(a) $\frac{1}{18}$ (b) $\frac{1}{9}$
(c) $\frac{2}{9}$ (d) $\frac{1}{36}$

25. If ω is an imaginary cube root of unity, then the value of $\sin\{(\omega^{19} + \omega^{101})\pi - \pi/6\}$ is

(a) $-\frac{1}{2}$ (b) $-\sqrt{3}/2$
(c) $\frac{1}{2}$ (d) None of these

26. a,b,c are integers, not all simultaneously equal and ω is cube root of unity ($\omega \neq 1$), then minimum value of $|a\omega^{10} + b\omega^{20} + c|$ is

(a) 0 (b) 1
(c) $\frac{\sqrt{3}}{2}$ (d) $\frac{1}{2}$

27. If z_1 and z_2 be complex numbers such that $z_1 \neq z_2$ and $|z_1| = |z_2|$. If z_1 has positive real part and z_2 has negative imaginary part, then $\frac{(z_1+z_2)}{(z_1-z_2)}$ may be

(a) Purely imaginary (b) Real and positive
(c) Real and negative (d) None of these

28. If $|z-1| + |z-3| \le 8$, then the range of values of $|z-4|$ is

(a) (0, 8) (b) [0,8]
(c) [1, 9] (d) [0, 6]

29. If $z^2 + z|z| + |z|^2 = 0$, then the locus of z is

(a) a straight line (b) pair of straight lines
(c) pair of rays (d) a circle

30. A man walks a distance of 3 units form the origin towards the noth east ($N45°E$) direction. From there, he walk a distance of 4 units towads the north-west ($N\,45°\,W$) direction to reach a point P. then the position of P in the Argand plane is

(a) $3e^{i\pi/4} + 4i$ (b) $(3-4i)e^{i\pi/4}$
(c) $(4+3i)e^{i\pi/4}$ (d) $(3+4i)e^{i\pi/4}$

31. A particle P starts from the point $z_0 = 1 + 2i$ where $i = \sqrt{-1}$ It moves first horizontally away from origin by 5 units and then vertically away from origin by 3 units to reach a point z_1. From z_1 the particle moves $\sqrt{2}$ units in the direction of the vector $\hat{i} + \hat{j}$ and then it moves through an angle $\frac{\pi}{2}$ in anti-clockwise direction on a circle with centre at origin to reach a point z_2. The point z_2 is given by:

(a) $6 + 7i$ (b) $-7 + 6i$
(c) $7 + 6i$ (d) $-6 + 7i$

32. The complex number z satisfies the condition $\left|z - \frac{25}{z}\right| = 24$. Then the maximum distance from the origin to the point represented by z in the Argand plane is

(a) 25 (b) 24
(c) 30 (d) 32

33. If z_1 and z_2 are two complex numbers such that $\left|\frac{z_1 - z_2}{z_1 + z_2}\right| = 1$, and $i\sqrt{3}\, z_1 = z_2$, then the principal argument of $\frac{z_1 - z_2}{z_1 + z_2}$ is

(a) $\frac{2\pi}{3}$ (b) $-\frac{2\pi}{3}$

(c) $-\frac{\pi}{6}$ (d) $\frac{\pi}{6}$

34. If z_1 and z_2 are two complex numbers such that $iz_1 = k z_2$, where $0 < k < 1$, then the principal argument of $\frac{z_1 - z_2}{z_1 + z_2}$ is

(a) $-\pi + 2\tan^{-1} k$ (b) $\pi - 2\tan^{-1} k$

(c) $2\tan^{-1} k$ (d) $-2\tan^{-1} k$

35. If $z_1 = a + ib$ and $z_2 = c + id$ are two complex numbers lying on the circle $x^2 + y^2 = 1$ in the Argand's plane and $Re\ (-z_1\bar{z}_2) = 0$, then the complex numbers $w_1 = (a + ic)$ and $w_2 = b + id$ are such that

(a) only w_1 lies on the circle $x^2 + y^2 = 1$

(b) only w_2 lies on the circle $x^2 + y^2 = 1$

(c) $Re\ (\overline{w_1} w_2) = 0$

(d) None of these

36. Let z be a complex number satisfying $|z - 5i| \le 1$ such that ***amp*** z is minimum. Then z is equal to

(a) $\frac{2\sqrt{6}}{5} + \frac{24i}{5}$ (b) $\frac{24}{5} + \frac{2\sqrt{6}}{5}i$

(c) $\frac{2\sqrt{6}}{5} - \frac{24i}{5}$ (d) None of these

37. Let the affix of $2 - 4i$ be P. Then OP is rotated about O through an angle of 180° and is stretched 5/2 times. The complex number corresponding to the new position of P is

(a) $5 - 10i$ (b) $5 + 10i$

(c) $-5 + 10i$ (d) None of these

38. The triangle with the vertices at the points z_1, z_2 and $(1 - i)\, z_1 + iz_2$ is

(a) right angled but not isosceles

(b) isosceles but not right angled

(c) right angled and isosceles

(d) equilateral

SECTION–IV

OBJECTIVE TYPE (MORE THAN ONE CORRECT ANSWERS)

1. The equation, whose roots are nth power of the roots of the equation $x^2 - 2x\cos\theta + 1 = 0$ is given by

(a) $(x - \cos n\,\theta)^2 + \sin^2 n\theta = 0$

(b) $(x + \cos n\,\theta)^2 + \sin^2 n\,\theta = 0$

(c) $x^2 - 2x\cos n\,\theta + 1 = 0$

(d) $x^2 - \cos n\,\theta + 1 = 0$

2. Let z_1, z_2 be two complex numbers represented by points on the circle $|z| = 1$ and $|z| = 2$ respectively, then

(a) $\max|2z_1 + z_2| = 4$ (b) $\min|z_1 - z_2| = 1$

(c) $\left|z_2 + \frac{1}{z_1}\right| \le 3$ (d) None of these

3. Let $P(x)$ and $Q(x)$ be two polynomials. Suppose that $f(x) = P(x^3) + x\,Q(x^3)$ is divisible by $x^2 + x + 1$, then

(a) $P(x)$ is divisible by $(x - 1)$ but $Q(x)$ is not divisible by $x - 1$

(b) $Q(x)$ is divisible by $(x - 1)$ but $P(x)$ is not divisible by $x - 1$

(c) Both $P(x)$ and $Q(x)$ are divisible by $x - 1$

(d) $f(x)$ is divisible by $x - 1$

4. The equation not representing a circle (with $r > 0$) is given by

(a) $\text{Re}\left(\frac{1+z}{1-z}\right) = 0$ (b) $z\bar{z} + iz - i\bar{z} + 1 = 0$

(c) $\arg\left(\frac{z-1}{z+1}\right) = \frac{\pi}{2}$ (d) $\left|\frac{z-1}{z+1}\right| = 1$

5. If z_1 and z_2 are two complex numbers such that $\left|\frac{z_1 - z_2}{1 - \bar{z}_1 z_2}\right| = 1$, then

(a) $|z_1| = 1$

(b) $|z_2| = 1$

(c) $z_1 = e^{i\theta}$, $\theta \in \mathbb{R}$

(d) either $z_1 = e^{i\theta}$ or $z_2 = e^{i\theta}; \theta \in \mathbb{R}$

6. The complex number z satisfying the equations $\left|\frac{z - 12i}{z - 8i}\right| = 1$ and $\left|\frac{z-4}{z-8}\right| = 1$ is

(a) $10 + 6i$ (b) $10 - 6i$
(c) $6 - 10i$ (d) $6 + 10i$

7. If $\left(\frac{z-a}{z+a}\right) = \pm\frac{\pi}{2}$ where a is a fixed number, then the locus of z is a subset of
(a) a straight line
(b) a circle with the centre at the origin
(c) circle with the radius $|a|$
(d) None of these

8. If $|z_1| = |z_2| = |z_3| = 4$ and $z_1 + z_3 = 0$, then which of the following is true about $A(z_1)$, $B(z_2)$ and $C(z_3)$?
(a) ΔABC is obtuse angled
(b) ΔABC is equilateral
(c) z_1, z_2, z_3 are the vertices of a right angled triangle
(d) z_1 and z_3 are extremities of the diameter of circum-circle of ΔABC

9. If a complex number z has modulus 1 and argument $\pi/3$, then which of the following is true?
(a) $z^2 + z$ is purely imaginary
(b) $|z^2 + z| = \sqrt{3}$
(c) $z^2 - z$ is purely real
(d) None of these

10. A complex number z satisfies the inequality $|z - 1 - 2i| \le 1$, then which of the following is true about z?
(a) max. $(|z|) = \sqrt{5} + 1$
(b) min. $(|z|) = \sqrt{5} - 1$
(c) min. $(arg\ (z)) = \tan^{-1}\left(\frac{3}{4}\right)$
(d) max. $(arg\ (z)) = \pi/2$

11. Which of the following represent the subset of set of complex number z satisfying $\log_{1/3}(\log_{1/2}(|z|^2 + 4|z| + 3)) > 0$,
(a) $[-1,3]$ (b) $\{z : \text{Re}(z) \ge 1\}$
(c) $\{z : I(z) \le 2\}$ (d) None of these

12. If $\log_{|z-2i|}\left|1+\sqrt{3}i\right| > \log_{|z-2i|}\left|4-3i\right|$ and $z \in \mathbb{C}$, then $z \ne 2i$ lies
(a) outside the curve $z = -2i + 2e^{i\theta}$, $\theta \in \mathbb{R}$
(b) inside the curve $z = 2i + e^{i\theta}$, $\theta \in \mathbb{R}$
(c) inside the circular disc $|z - 2i| < 5$
(d) inside a circle passing through the origin

13. A complex number z is such that $|z| = 2$, then which of the following equals to $\frac{1+\bar{z}}{4+z}$?
(a) z (b) $\frac{\bar{z}}{4}$
(c) $\frac{1}{z}$ (d) $z - \bar{z}$

14. Given the equation of two circles as $C_1 : z\bar{z} + \bar{\alpha}z + \alpha\bar{z} + \gamma = 0$ and $C_2 : z\bar{z} + \bar{\beta}z + \beta\bar{z} + \delta = 0$ where $\alpha, \beta \in \mathbb{C}$ & $\gamma, \delta \in \mathbb{R}$
(a) C_1 and C_2 will touch externally if $|\alpha - \beta| = \sqrt{|\alpha|^2 - \gamma} + \sqrt{|\beta|^2 - \delta}$
(b) C_1 and C_2 will intersect orthogonally iff $\alpha\bar{\beta} + \bar{\alpha}\beta = \gamma + \delta$
(c) Radius of circle C_1 is $\sqrt{|\alpha|^2 - \gamma}$
(d) none of these

15. If k is positive, then which of the following is true for the ellipse $|z - ki| + |z + ki| = 3k$?
(a) minor axis is the real axis
(b) major axis is the imaginary axis
(c) Equation of directrix is $\text{Im}(z) = \pm\frac{9k}{4}$
(d) eccentricity is 2/3

16. ABC is an equilateral triangle whose circumcentre is at the origin. Let the point A be represented by $-1 + \sqrt{3}i$.
(a) length of side of ΔABC is $2\sqrt{3}$
(b) Centroid of ΔABC is $-1 + i$
(c) Orthocenter of ΔABC is O.
(d) inradius of ΔABC is 1.

17. Let z_1 and z_2 be two distinct complex numbers and let $z = (1 - t)\, z_1 + tz_2$ for some real number t with $0 < t < 1$. If $\text{Arg}(w)$ denotes the principal argument of a non-zero complex number w, then
(a) $|z - z_1| + |z - z_2| = |z_1 - z_2|$
(b) $\text{Arg}\ (z - z_1) = \text{Arg}\ (z - z_2)$
(c) $\begin{vmatrix} z - z_1 & \bar{z} - \bar{z}_1 \\ z_2 - z_1 & \bar{z}_2 - \bar{z}_1 \end{vmatrix} = 0$
(d) $\text{Arg}\ (z - z_1) = \text{Arg}\ (z_2 - z_1)$

18. The expression $\frac{\left[\sin\left(\frac{x}{2}\right) + \cos\left(\frac{x}{2}\right) + i\tan(x)\right]}{\left[1 + 2i\sin\left(\frac{x}{2}\right)\right]}$ is real, then possible values of x are

(a) $2n\pi;\ n \in \mathbb{Z}$
(b) $n\pi + \tan^{-1} 1;\ n \in \mathbb{Z}$
(c) $(2n + 1)\pi;\ n \in \mathbb{Z}$
(d) $2n\pi + \tan^{-1}k;\ n \in \mathbb{Z}$ and k is a real root of equation $t^3 + t - 2 = 0$

19. For complex number $z_1 = x_1 + iy_1$ and $z_2 = x_2 + iy_2$, we write $z_1 \cap z_2$, if $x_1 \le x_2$ and $y_1 \le y_2$. Then for all complex numbers z with $1 \cap z$. (ω, ω^2, non real cube roots of unity)

(a) $\omega^2 \cap z$
(b) $\omega \cap z$
(c) $\left(\frac{1-z}{1+z}\right) \cap 0$
(d) All of the above

SECTION–V

ASSERTION AND REASON TYPE

The questions given below consist of an assertion (A) and the reason (R). Use the following key to choose the appropriate answer.

(a) If both assertion and reason are correct and reason is the correct explanation of the assertion.
(b) If both assertion and reason are correct but reason is not correct explanation of the assertion.
(c) If assertion is correct but reason is incorrect
(d) If assertion is incorrect but reason is correct

Now consider the following statements:

1. A : The product of the real part of the roots ofthe equation $z^2 + 4z + 4i = 0$ is $2 - 2\sqrt{2}$.

R : The roots of equation is given as $2\left(-1 \pm \sqrt[4]{2}\, e^{-i\frac{\pi}{8}}\right)$ and then take the product of real part.

2. A: If z is a complex number ($z \neq 1$) then $\left|\frac{z}{|z|} - 1\right| \le |\arg z|$

R: In a unit radius circle chord (AP) $\le$ arc (AP)

3. A: If $|z| \ge 2$, then the least value of $\left|z + \frac{1}{2}\right|$ is $\frac{3}{2}$.

R: $|z_1 + z_2| \le |z_1| + |z_2|$

4. A : The minimum distance between the complex numbers of the set A to that of set B; where $A = \{z : |z + 2i| = 2;\ z \in \mathbb{C}\}$ and $B = \left\{z : Arg(z - 3i) = \frac{\pi}{4} \text{ or } -\frac{3\pi}{4}; z \in \mathbb{C}\right\}$ is $\frac{5\sqrt{2} - 4}{2}$

R : Shortest distance between the two smooth, continuous curves is always along the path which is normal to both the curves.

5. A: If $|z - 3 + 2i| \le 4$, then the sum of least and greatest value of $|z|$ is 8

R: $||z_1| - |z_2|| \le |z_1 + z_2| \le |z_1| + |z_2|$

6. A: Let z be a complex number satisfying $|z - 3| \le |z - 1|$, $|z - 3| \le |z - 5|$, $|z - i| \le |z + i|$ and $|z - i| \le |z - 5i|$. Then the area of region in which z lies is 12 sq unit.

R: Area of trapezium $= \frac{1}{2} \times$ (Sum of parallel sides) $\times$ (Distance between parallel sides)

7. A: If $z_1 = 9 + 5i$ and $z_2 = 3 + 5i$ and if $\arg\left(\frac{z - z_1}{z - z_2}\right) = \frac{\pi}{4}$, then the value of $|z - 6 - 8i| = 3\sqrt{2}$, where $i = \sqrt{-1}$.

R: If three points are non-collinear, then they must lie on a circle and the angle at centre by a chord is double the angle on circumference by that chord.

8. A: Centre of circle $\left|\frac{z+1}{z-1}\right| = 2$ is $\left(\frac{5}{3}, 0\right)$.

R: Radius of circle $\left|\frac{z-1}{z+1}\right| = 2$ is $\frac{4}{3}$.

9. A : Given $f(x) = \sum_{k=0}^{n} a_k x^k$ be a polynomial with real coefficients and with non-zero leading coefficients such that all the roots of $f(x) = 0$ are of unit magnitude, then $a_r = a_{n-r}$ for all coefficients holds good.

R : If α be root of a polynomial $f(x) = 0$, then $\bar{\alpha}$ is also root, as coefficients are real and if α is root, then $1/\alpha$ is also root of $f(x) = 0$ means $f(x) = 0$ is self reciprocal equation.

SECTION–VI

LINKED COMPREHENSION TYPE

A. Let $z = a + ib = re^{i\theta}$ where $a, b, \theta \in \mathbb{R}$ and $i = \sqrt{-1}$,

Then $r = \sqrt{(a^2 + b^2)} = |z|$ and $\theta = \tan^{-1}\left(\frac{b}{a}\right) = \arg(z)$

Now $|z|^2 = a^2 + b^2 = (a + ib)(a - ib) = z\bar{z}$

$\Rightarrow \frac{1}{z} = \frac{\bar{z}}{|z|^2}$ and $|z_1 z_2 z_3 \ldots\ldots z_n| = |z_1||z_2||z_3|\ldots|z_n|$

If $|f(z)| = 1$, then $f(z)$ is called unimodular. In this case $f(z)$ can always be expressed as $f(z) = e^{i\alpha}$, $\alpha \in \mathbb{R}$

Also $e^{i\alpha} + e^{i\beta} = e^{i\left(\frac{\alpha+\beta}{2}\right)}.2\cos\left(\frac{\alpha-\beta}{2}\right)$ and

$e^{i\alpha} - e^{i\beta} = e^{i\left(\frac{\alpha+\beta}{2}\right)}.2i\sin\left(\frac{\alpha-\beta}{2}\right)$ where $\alpha, \beta, \in \mathbb{R}$.

1. If z_1, z_2, z_3 are complex numbers such that $|z_1| = |z_2| = |z_3| = |z_1 + z_2 + z_3| = 1$, then $\left|\frac{1}{z_1} + \frac{1}{z_2} + \frac{1}{z_3}\right|$ is

(a) equal to 1 (b) less than 1
(c) greater than 3 (d) equal to 3

2. If $|z_1| = 1, |z_2| = 2, |z_3| = 3$ and $|z_1 + z_2 + z_3| = 1$, then $|9z_1z_2 + 4z_3z_1 + z_2z_3|$ is equal to

(a) 6 (b) 36
(c) 216 (d) 1296

3. The value of $\tan\left(i \ln\left(\frac{a - ib}{a + ib}\right)\right)$, (where $i = \sqrt{-1}$) is equal to

(a) $\frac{2ab}{b^2 - a^2}$ (b) $\frac{2ab}{a^2 - b^2}$
(c) $\frac{a^2 + b^2}{a^2 - b^2}$ (d) $\frac{a^2 - b^2}{a^2 + b^2}$

4. If z_1 and z_2 are complex numbers satisfying $\left|\frac{z_1 + z_2}{z_1 - z_2}\right| = 1$ and $\arg\left(\frac{z_1 - z_2}{z_1 + z_2}\right) \neq m\pi$ $(m \in \mathbb{Z})$, then $\frac{z_1}{z_2}$ is

(a) zero (b) a rational number
(c) a +ve real number (d) a purely imaginary

B. Let a quadratic equation $az^2 + bz + c = 0$ where $a, b, c \in \mathbb{R}$ and $a \neq 0$. If one root of this equation is $p + iq$, then other must be the conjugate $p - iq$ and vice-versa. $(p, q \in \mathbb{R}$ and $i = \sqrt{-1})$. But if a, b, c are non real, then roots of $az^2 + bz + c = 0$ are not conjugate to each other. i.e., if one root is real, then other may be non real. Now, combining both cases, we can say that $az^2 + bz + c = 0$ where $a, b, c \in C$ and $a \neq 0$.

5. If one root of the quadratic equation $(1 + i)x^2 - (7 + 3i)x + (6 + 8i) = 0$, where $i = \sqrt{-1}$ is $4 - 3i$, then the other root must be

(a) $4 + 3i$ (b) $1 - i$
(c) $1 + i$ (d) $i(i - 1)$

6. If equation $az^2 + bz + c = 0$ and $z^2 + 2z + 3 = 0$ have a common root where $a, b, c \in \mathbb{R}$, then $a: b: c$ is

(a) 2: 3: 1 (b) 1: 2: 3
(c) 3: 1: 2 (d) 3: 2: 1

7. If the quadratic equation $z^2 + (a + ib) + c + id = 0$ where a, b, c, d are non-zero real and $i = \sqrt{-1}$, has a real root, then

(a) $abd = b^2c + d^2$ (b) $abc = bc^2 + d^2$
(c) $abd = bc^2 + ad^2$ (d) $abc = bc^2 + ad^2$

C. Let $z_1 = a_1 + ib_1 \equiv (a_1, b_1)$ and $z_2 = a_2 + ib_2 \equiv (a_2, b_2)$ where $i = \sqrt{-1}$, be two complex numbers

If $\angle POQ = \theta$, From rotation theorem

$\frac{z_2 - 0}{z_1 - 0} = \frac{|z_2|}{|z_1|}e^{i\theta} \Rightarrow \frac{z_2\bar{z}_1}{z_1\bar{z}_1} = \frac{|z_2|}{|z_1|}e^{i\theta}$

$\Rightarrow \frac{z_2\bar{z}_1}{|z_1|^2} = \frac{|z_2|}{|z_1|}e^{i\theta} \Rightarrow z_2\bar{z}_1 = |z_1||z_2|\, e^{i\theta}$

$\Rightarrow z_2\bar{z}_1 = |z_1||z_2|(\cos\theta + i\sin\theta)$

$\therefore Re\ z_2\bar{z}_1 = |z_1||z_2|\cos\theta$ ..... (i)

and $Im\ (z_2\bar{z}_1) = |z_1||z_2|\sin\theta$ ...... (ii)

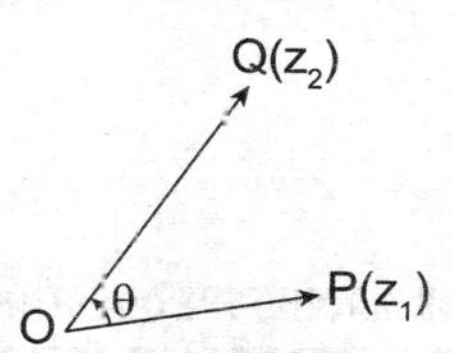

The dot product of z_1 and z_2 is defined by $z_1.z_2 = |z_1||z_2|\cos\theta = Re(z_2\bar{z}_1)$ [from (i)] and cross product of z_1 and z_2 is defined by $z_1 \times z_2 = |z_1||z_2|\sin\theta = Im(\bar{z}_1 z_2)$ [from Eq. (ii)]

8. If $z_1 = 2 + 5i$, $z_2 = 3 - i$, then the value of $\sqrt{(z_1.z_2 + z_2 \times z_1)}$ is equal to

(a) 2 (b) 3
(c) $2\sqrt{3}$ (d) $3\sqrt{2}$

9. If $z_1 = 3 + 4i$ and $z_2 = 4 + 3i$, then the value of $\sin\theta$ $\left(\pi < \theta < \frac{3\pi}{2}\right)$ is equal to

(a) $-\frac{1}{7}$ (b) $-\frac{7}{25}$

(c) $-\frac{24}{25}$ (d) $-\frac{1}{25}$

10. If $z_1 = 5 + 12i$ and $z_2 = 3 + 4i$, then (the projection of z_1 on z_2 + projection of z_2 on z_1) is equal to

(a) $\frac{4131}{65}$ (b) $\frac{3411}{65}$

(c) $\frac{1134}{65}$ (d) $\frac{1341}{65}$

11. Let $P(z_1)$ and $P(z_2)$ be roots of the equation $z^2 + z + 1 = 0$. If $\angle POQ = \alpha \neq 0$ $(0 < \alpha < \pi)$; where O is the origin, then α is equal to

(a) $\alpha/4$ (b) $\alpha/2$

(c) $\alpha/3$ (d) $2\alpha/3$

D. Let $A(z_1)$, $B(z_2)$, $C(z_3)$ be the vertices of an equilateral triangle ABC such that $|z_1| = |z_2| = |z_3| = 2$. A circle is inscribed in the triangle ABC which touches the sides AB, BC and CA at $D(z_4)$, $E(z_5)$ and $F(z_6)$ respectively. $P(z)$ be any point on its incircle other than D,E,F.

12. The value of $(AB)^2 + (BC)^2 + (CA)^2$ is equal to

(a) 9 (b) 18

(c) 27 (d) 36

13. The value of $(DE)^2 + (EF)^2 + (FD)^2$ is equal to

(a) 12 (b) 3

(c) $3\sqrt{3}$ (d) 9

14. The value of $Re\ (z_1\bar{z}_2 + z_2\bar{z}_3 + z_3\bar{z}_1)$ is equal to

(a) 0 (b) 6

(c) –6 (d) –3

15. If $z_1 = \sqrt{3} + i, i = \sqrt{-1}$, then the value of $\sqrt{|z_2 - z_3|^2 + |z_2 + z_3|^2}$ is equal to

(a) 0 (b) 2

(c) 4 (d) 6

16. $\frac{z_1}{z_3}$ is equal to

(a) $1 - i\sqrt{3}$ (b) $1 + i\sqrt{3}$

(c) $\frac{-1 + i\sqrt{3}}{2}$ (d) $\frac{1 + i\sqrt{3}}{2}$

E. Let A,B,C be three sets of complex numbers as defined below

$A = \{z : Imz \geq 1\}$

$B = \{z : |z - 2 - i| = 3\}$

$C = \{z : \text{Re}((1-i)z) = \sqrt{2}\}$

17. The number of elements in the set $A \cap B \cap C$ is

(a) 0 (b) 1

(c) 22 (d) ∞

18. Let z be any point in $A \cap B \cap C$. Then $|z + 1 - i|^2 + |z - 5 - i|^2$ lies between

(a) 25 and 29 (b) 30 and 34

(c) 35 and 39 (d) 40 and 44

19. Let z be any point in $A \cap B \cap C$ and let w be any point satisfying $|w - 2 - i| < 3$. Then, $|z - w| + 3$ lies between

(a) –6 and 3 (b) –3 and 6

(c) –6 and 6 (d) –3 and 9

SECTION–VII

MATRIX MATCH TYPE QUESTIONS

1. Column I:

(i) Locus of the point z satisfying the equation $\text{Re}(z^2) = (z + \bar{z})$

(ii) Locus of the point z satisfying the equation $|z - z_1| + |z - z_2| = \lambda$, $\lambda \in \mathbb{R}^+$ and $\lambda \not< |z_1 - z_2|$

(iii) Locus of the point z satisfying the equation $\left|\frac{2z - i}{z + 1}\right| = m$; where $i = \sqrt{-1}$ and $m \in \mathbb{R}^+$

Column II:

(a) A hyperbola with eccentricity $\sqrt{2}$

(b) A line segment or straight line

(c) An ellipse

(d) A rectangular hyperbola

(e) A circle

2. Column I:

(i) If z_1, z_2, z_3 are the vertices of an equilateral triangle with z_0 as its nine point centre, then $z_1^2 + z_2^2 + z_3^2$ is

(ii) If z_1, z_2, z_3 are the vertices A, B, C respectively of an isosceles right angled triangle with right angle at C, then

(iii) If z_1, z_2, z_3 are the vertices A, B, C respectively of an isosceles triangle and the angle at B and C are each equal to $\pi/6$, then

Column II:

(a) $|z_1 - z_2|^2 = 2|z_1 - z_3||z_3 - z_2|$

(b) $3z_0^2$

(c) $|(z_2 - z_3)^2| = |3(z_3 - z_1)(z_1 - z_2)|$

(d) $z_1z_2 + z_2z_3 + z_3z_1$

(e) $\dfrac{z_2 - z_3}{z_1 - z_3} = e^{i\pi/2}$

3. Column I:

(i) If $1, \omega, \omega^2, \ldots\ldots, \omega^{n-1}$ are the n, n^{th} roots of unity, then $(2 - \omega)(2 - \omega^2) \ldots. (2 - \omega^{n-1})$ equals

(ii) If $z_1, z_2, \ldots, z_n$ lie on a circle $|z| = 2$, then the value of $|z_1 + z_2 + \ldots\ldots + z_n| - 4\left|\dfrac{1}{z_1} + \dfrac{1}{z_2} + \ldots + \dfrac{1}{z_n}\right|$ is

(iii) If P is a multiple of n, then the sum of the pth power of nth roots of unity is

Column II:

(a) $2^n - 1$

(b) ${}^nC_0 - {}^nC_1 + {}^nC_2 - {}^nC_3 + \ldots.$

(c) ${}^nC_{n-1} + {}^nC_{n-2} + {}^nC_{n-3} + \ldots\ldots + {}^nC_0$

(d) ${}^nC_1$

(e) $\sqrt{({}^{(2n+1)}C_0 + {}^{(2n+1)}C_1 + \ldots. + {}^{(2n+1)}C_n)} - 1$

4. If $\alpha, \beta \in \mathbb{R}$ and $\alpha^2 - 4\beta \geq 0$, the equation $z^4 + \alpha z^2 + \beta = 0$ has

Column-I

(i) four imaginary roots if

(ii) four equal roots if

(iii) four real roots if

(iv) two real and two imaginary roots if

Column-II

(a) $\alpha > 0, \beta > 0$

(b) $\alpha = 0, \beta = 0$

(c) $\alpha \leq 0$

(d) $\alpha \leq 0, \beta < 0$

5. Column I:

(i) G is the greatest and L be the least value of $|z - 2|$ where z satisfies $|z + 2 + 3i| \leq 1$, then

(ii) G is the greatest and L is least value of $|z|$, when z satisfies $|z - 5i| \leq 1$, then

(iii) G and L are the roots of $t^2 - 10t + 25 = 0$, then

(iv) G is the sum of infinite geometric series $5 + \dfrac{5}{2} + \dfrac{5}{2^2} + \dfrac{5}{2^3} + \ldots$ and $L = G - 10$, then

Column II:

(a) $L + G = 10$

(b) $LG = 24$

(c) $G - L = 2$

(d) $\dfrac{G}{L} = \dfrac{3}{2}$.

6. Column I:

(i) The set of points z satisfying $|z - i|z|| = |z + i|z||$ is contained in or equal to

(ii) The set of points z satisfying $|z + 4| + |z - 4| = 10$ is contained in or equal to

(iii) If $|w| = 2$, then the set of points $z = w - 1/w$ is contained in or equal to

(iv) If $|w| = 1$, then the set of points $z = w + 1/w$ is contained in or equal to

Column II:

(a) an ellipse with eccentricity 4/5

(b) the set of points z satisfying $Im\ z = 0$

(c) the set of points z satisfying $|Im\ z| \leq 1$

(d) the set of points z satisfying $|Re\ (z)| \leq 2$

(e) the set of points z satisfying $|z| \leq 3$

SECTION–VIII

INTEGER TYPE QUESTIONS

1. If $|z - 1| = |z - 5|$ and $Re(z) = k$; then evaluate k

2. If $|z - 1| = |z - 5|$ and $|z| = \sqrt{13}$, then find $|Im(z)|$

3. If $|z - 2 - 3i| = 1$, then the greatest value of $|z|$ is $\sqrt{k} + m$, then evaluate $\sqrt{(k+m)+2}$

4. If $|z + 1 + 3i| = 1$, then the least value of $|z|$ is $\sqrt{k} - m$, then evaluate $\sqrt{k - m}$

5. If $|z - 2 + 3i| = 2$ and $z + 1 + 3i| = 1$, then evaluate $|z - 4|$

6. If z and w are two complex numbers having non-negative imaginary parts such that

$\arg\left(\frac{z-2}{z+2}\right) = \arg\left(\frac{w-1}{w+1}\right) = \pi/2$, then $|w - z| < k$; evaluate k. (Here k is least upper bond)

7. Find the least value of $|z|$ for which $\left|\frac{z+2}{z+i}\right| \le 2$.

8. If z lies on the locus $\left|\frac{z+2}{z+i}\right| = 2$ and by transformation $w \to z + \left(\frac{4}{3} + \sqrt{\frac{20}{9}}i\right)$ (say), a new locus is formed, then the greatest value of $|w|$ is $\frac{2}{3}\left(\sqrt{m} + \sqrt{n}\right)$; then evaluate $|m - n|$.

9. If (h, k) is centre and r is radius of circle represented by $Im\left(\frac{z}{z+4i}\right) = 2$, then evaluate $|h + k - r|$.

10. If $z = \cos\frac{\pi}{7} + i\sin\frac{\pi}{7}$; then evaluate $\left(z + z^3 + z^5\right) + \left(\frac{1}{z} + \frac{1}{z^3} + \frac{1}{z^5}\right)$.

11. If $|z - 2 + i| \le 2$ and L and G are least and greatest value of $|z|$, then evaluate $(G - L)$.

12. Find the value of square of semi-minor axis of ellipse represented by equation $|z - 2| + |z + 2| = 6$

13. If area of region represented by inequality $\log_{\sqrt{2}}\left(\frac{|z|^2 - |z| + 8}{|z| + 1}\right) < 4$ is $k\pi$, then evaluate $\sqrt{k+1}$

14. If $\text{Re}\left(\frac{1}{z}\right) \ge \frac{1}{4}$, then find the greatest value of $|z_1 - z_2|$; where z_1, z_2 satisfy the given inequality

15. If $2^7\cos^8\theta = \cos 8\theta + a\cos 6\theta + b\cos 4\theta + c\cos 2\theta + d$, then evaluate $\sqrt[3]{a+b+c+d-2}$

Answer Key

SECTION III

1. (d) 2. (a) 3. (d) 4. (c) 5. (c) 6. (a) 7. (c) 8. (a) 9. (c) 10. (c)
11. (d) 12. (c) 13. (b) 14. (d) 15. (b) 16. (a) 17. (d) 18. (c) 19. (a) 20. (a)
21. (b) 22. (c) 23. (d) 24. (c) 25. (c) 26. (b) 27. (a) 28. (d) 29. (b) 30. (d)
31. (d) 32. (a) 33. (b) 34. (a) 35. (c) 36. (a) 37. (c) 38. (c)

SECTION IV

1. (a,c) 2. (a,b,c) 3. (c,d) 4. (b,d) 5. (a,b,c,d) 6. (a,c) 7. (b,c) 8. (c,d) 9. (a,b,c)
10. (a,b,c,d) 11. (a,b,c) 12. (b,c) 13. (b,c) 14. (a,b,c) 15. (a,b,c,d) 16. (a,c,d) 17. (a,c,d) 18. (a,b) 19. (a,c)

SECTION V

1. (a) 2. (a) 3. (b) 4. (a) 5. (a) 6. (d) 7. (a) 8. (b) 9. (a)

SECTION VI

1. (a) 2. (a) 3. (b) 4. (d) 5. (c) 6. (b) 7. (a) 8. (d) 9. (b) 10. (c)
11. (d) 12. (d) 13. (d) 14. (c) 15. (c) 16. (c) 17. (b) 18. (c) 19. (d)

SECTION VII

1. (i)→(a,d) (ii)→(b,c) (iii)→(b,e) 2. (i)→(b,d) (ii)→(a,e) (iii)→(c)
3. (i)→(a,c,e) (ii)→(b) (iii)→(d) 4. (i)→(a) (ii)→(b) (iii)→(b,c,d) (iv)→(d)
5. (i) → (a,b,c,d) (ii) → (a,b,c,d) (iii) → (a) (iv) → (a)
6. (i) → (b,c) (ii) → (a) (iii) → (a,d,e) (iv) → (b,c,d,e)

SECTION VIII

1. 3 2. 2 3. 4 4. 3 5. 5 6. 3 7. 0 8. 1 9. 6 10. 1
11. 4 12. 5 13. 4 14. 4 15. 5

HINTS AND SOLUTIONS

TEXTUAL EXERCISE 1: (SUBJECTIVE)

1. (a) $\sqrt{a}\times\sqrt{b}=\sqrt{ab}$ iff at least one of a and b is non-negative real number

Now $\sqrt{-25}\times\sqrt{-49}=5i\times 7i=35i^2=-35$

(b) (i) $i^{4n}=(i^4)^n=1^n=1$ for all $n\in\mathbb{Z}$

(ii) $i^{4n+1}=i\,.i^{4n}=i.1=i$ for all $n\in\mathbb{Z}$

(iii) $i^{4n+2}=i^2.i^{4n}=(-1)(1)=-1$ for all $n\in\mathbb{Z}$

(iv) $i^{4n+3}=i^3.i^{4n}=(-i)(1)=-i$ for all $n\in\mathbb{Z}$

2. (a) $(i)^{-1}=\frac{1}{i^1}=\frac{i^4}{i}=i^3=-i$

So $i^{-47}=(-i)^{-47}=(-1)^{47}i^{44}.i^3=(-1)(1)(-i)=i$

(b) $i^{-98}=(-i)^{98}=(-1)^{98}.i^{98}=i^{96}.i^2=(1)(-1)=-1$

(c) $i^{-1001}=(-i)^{1001}=(-1)^{1001}.i^{1000}.i=(-1)(1)(i)=-i$

(d) $i^{-10279}=(-i)^{10279}=(-1)^{10279}i^{10276}.i^3=(-1)(1)(-i)=i$

3. (i) $i^{1998}=i^{1996}.i^2=(1)(-1)=-1$

(ii) $i^{1999}=i^{1996}.i^3=(1)(-i)=-i$

(iii) $i^{2000}=(i^4)^{500}=1$

(iv) $i^{2001}=i^{2000}\,i=1\,(i)=i$

(v) $\sum_{k=1}^{4n+7} i^k=i+i^2+i^3+...+i^{4n+7}$

Using $i^p+i^{p+1}+i^{p+2}+i^{p+3}=0$

We get L.H.S. $=(i+i^2+i^3+i^4)+(i^5+i^6+i^7+i^8)+....+(i^{4n+1}+i^{4n+2}+i^{4n+3}+i^{4n+4})+(i^{4n+5}+i^{4n+6}+i^{4n+7})=0+(i^5+i^6+i^7)=i+i^2+i^3=i-1-i=-1$

(vi) $\left\{i^{457}+\left(\frac{1}{i}\right)^{25}\right\}^2=(i-i)^2=0$

4. (a) $(1+i)^{22}=\{(1+i)^2\}^{11}=(2i)^{11}=2^{11}(-i)=-(2^{11})i$

(b) $\left(\frac{1-i}{1+i}\right)^{98}=\left\{\frac{(1-i)^2}{1-i^2}\right\}^{98}=\left(\frac{-2i}{2}\right)^{98}$

$=(-1)^{98}.i^{98}=i^{96}.i^2=-1$

(c) $(1+i)^{3n}=(1+i)^{2n}(1+i)^n=2^n i^n(1+i)^n=2^n(-1+i)^n$

$=2^n\{-2i\}^{n/2}=2^n.2^{n/2}.i^{n/2}(-1)^{n/2}=(\sqrt{2})^{3n}(i)^{\frac{3n}{2}}=(\sqrt{2i})^{3n}$

(d) $\frac{1+2i}{1-(1-i)^2}=\frac{1+2i}{1-(1-1-2i)}=\frac{1+2i}{1+2i}=1$

(e) $\frac{(1-i)^3}{1-i^3}=\frac{(1-i)(1-i)^2}{i(1-i)}=\frac{(-2i)}{i}=-2$

(f) Let $z=(1+i)^{3n}$ {where n is an even integer}

Put $n=2m$

$\Rightarrow z=(2i)^{3m}=2^{3m}.i^{3m}=2^{3n/2}.(-i)^m=2^{\frac{3n}{2}}.(-i)^{n/2}$

5. $i^n+i^{n+1}+i^{n+2}+i^{n+3}$

$=i^n\{1+i+i^2+i^3\}=i^n\{1+i-1-i\}=0$

(a) $\sum_{n=1}^{n=1001} i^n=(i+i^2+i^3+i^4)+(i^5+i^6+i^7+i^8)+....+(i^{997}+i^{998}+i^{999}+i^{1000})+i^{1001}$

$=0+0+...+0+i^{1000}.i=i$

(b) $\sum_{n=1}^{n=32} i^{3n}=i^3+i^6+i^9+i^{12}+......+i^{96}$

$=(-i)+(-i)^2+(-i)^3+(-i)^4+...+(-i)^{32}$

Which is a G.P. with first term $-i$ and common ratio $-i$

$\therefore$ sum $=\frac{(-i)\{1-(-i)^{32}\}}{1-(-i)}=\frac{(-i)\{1-1\}}{1+i}=0$

(c) $\sum_{n=50}^{n=100} i^n=i^{50}+i^{51}+i^{52}+......+i^{100}$

$=(i^{50}+i^{51}+i^{52})+(i^{53}+i^{54}+i^{55}+i^{56})+...+(i^{97}+i^{98}+i^{99}+i^{100})$

$=(i^2+i^3+i^4)+0+0+...+0$

$=(-1-i+1)+0=-i$

(d) $\sum_{n=1}^{n=501}(1+i)^{2n}=\sum_{n=1}^{n=501}(2i)^n=2i+(2i)^2+...+(2i)^{501}$

$=\frac{2i\{1-(2i)^{501}\}}{1-2i}=\frac{2i(1+2i)\{1-2^{501}.i\}}{5}$

$=\frac{(-4+2i)(1-2^{501}i)}{5}$

6. To evaluate $1+i+i^2-......+i^{n-1}-\frac{1}{2}\{i^{n+2}+i^{n+3}\}$

$=\frac{(1+i)\{1-i^n\}}{2}-\frac{-i^n-i^n.i}{2}$

$=\frac{1+i-i^n-i^{n+1}+i^n+i^{n+1}}{2}=\frac{1+i}{2}$

7. (a) $(i)^{1112}=(i^4)^{278}=1$

So remainder when $(i)^{1112}$ is divided by 7 is 1

(b) $(i)^{21122}=(i)^{21120}.i^2=(-1).(1)=-1$

So remainder when $(i)^{2112}$ is divided by 13

Will be 12 (as $-13+12=-1$) = 12

8. $\sum_{k=1}^{k=4n-1} i^k=i+i^2+...+i^{4n-1}+(i^{4n}-i^{4n})$

(a) Number of real terms = $2n-1$

(b) Number of imaginary terms = $2n$

(c) Number of positive real terms = $n-1$

(d) Number of imaginary terms with positive imaginary part = n

9. (a) $\sum_{k=0}^{4n} i^{2k}=1+i^2+i^4+....+i^{8n}$

$=\underbrace{1+(-1+1)+(-1+1)+....+(-1+1)}_{2n\text{-groups}}=1$

(b) $\sum_{k=1}^{4n+11} i^k = i + i^2 + i^3 + ... + i^{4n+11}$

$= \{i + i^2 + i^3 + i^4\} + \{i^5 + i^6 + i^7 + i^8\} + ...+ \{i^{4n+5} + i^{4n+6} + i^{4n+7} + i^{4n+8}\} + \{i^{4n+9} + i^{4n+10} + i^{4n+11}\} = 0 + 0 + 0 + ... + 0 + \{i + i^2 + i^3\} = (i - 1 - i) = -1$

(c) $\sum_{k=0}^{4n+1} i^{3k} = 1 + i^3 + i^6 + ... + i^{12n+3}$

$$= \frac{1\{1-(i^3)^{4n+2}\}}{1-i^3} = \frac{1-(-i)^{4n+2}}{1+i} = \frac{1-i^2}{1+i} = \frac{2}{1+i} = 1-i$$

(d) $\sum_{k=1}^{4n+5} i^k + \sum_{k=1}^{4n+6} i^k + \sum_{k=1}^{4n+7} i^k$

Observe that $\sum_{k=1}^{4n+5} i^k = i + i^2 + i^3 + ... + i^{4n+4} + i^{4n+5} = i$

So $\sum_{k=1}^{4n+6} i^k = i + i^{4n+6} = i + i^2 = i - 1$ and

$\sum_{k=1}^{4n+7} i^k = i - 1 - i = -1$

Hence $\sum_{k=1}^{4n+5} i^k + \sum_{k=1}^{4n+6} i^k + \sum_{k=1}^{4n+7} i^k = 2(i-1)$

10. To evaluate $i^{-53} + \{i^n + i^{n+1} + i^{n+2} + i^{n+3} + 4\}^{1/2} i$

$= \frac{1}{i^{53}} + (0+4)^{1/2} i = i^3 - 2i = \pm 2i - i = -3i, i$

TEXTUAL EXERCISE 1: OBJECTIVE

3. (a), (b), (c)

(a) $\sqrt{-16} + 3\sqrt{-25} + \sqrt{-36} - \sqrt{-625}$

$= 4i + 15i + 6i - 25i = 0;\ r_1 = $ R.H.S. (true)

(b) $1 + i^{14} + i^{18} + i^{22} = 1 + i^2 + i^2 + i^2 = 1 - 1 - 1 - 1 = -2$ is a real number. (true)

(c) $i^{3k}\{1 + i + i^2 + i^3\} = i^{3k}\{1 + i - 1 - i\} = 0 = $ R.H.S. (true)

(d) $6i^{54} + 5i^{37} - i^{11} + 6i^{68} = 6(-1) + 5i + i + 6 = 6i \neq 7i.$ (true)

6. (a) Value of $(i)^{222157} = i^{222156}\ .\ i = 1(i) = i$

7. (b) $(1+i)^{8n+6} = (2i)^{4n+3} = (-2)^{4n+3}.\ i$, which is purely imaginary

8. (a, c) $(1+i)^{6n+2} = (2i)^{3n+1} = 2^{3n+1}\ .\ (i^3)^n.i = 2^{3n+1}(-i)^n.\ i = (-1)^n.2^{3n+1}\ .\ i^{n+1}$

Which is real when n is odd and it is purely imaginary when n is even

9. (a) $\sum_{n=0}^{n=100} (i)^{2n} = 1 + i^2 + i^4 + i^6 + ... + i^{200} = 1$ (101 terms)

10. (c) $\sum_{n=1}^{n=100} (1-i)^{2n} = (-2i)^1 + (-2i)^2 + ... + ..(-2i)^{100}$

$$= \frac{(-2i)\{1-(-2i)^{100}\}}{1+2i} = \frac{2(i)\{2^{100}-1\}}{(1+2i)} = \frac{(2i+4)}{5}\{2^{100}-1\}$$

11. (a) $(i)^{2000010} = i^{2000008}\ .\ i^2 = 1(-1) = -1$

$\Rightarrow$ When $(i)^{2000010}$ is divided by 51, then remainder is 50 (as $-51 + 50 = -1$)

12. (b) $(i)^{-202} = \frac{i^{204}}{i^{202}} = i^2 = -1$

So remainder obtained when $(i)^{-202}$ is divided by 8 is $r = 7$ ($\because -8 + 7 = -1$)

Hence $2^r = 2^7 = 128$

13. (b) $\frac{i^{592} + i^{590} + i^{588} + i^{586} + i^{584}}{i^{582} + i^{580} + i^{578} + i^{576} + i^{574}} - 1 = i^{10} - 1 = i^2 - 1 = -2$

14. (b) $\sum_{n=1}^{n=13} (i^n + i^{n+1}) = (i + i^2) + (i^2 + i^3) + (i^3 + i^4) + ... + (i^{13} + i^{14})$

$= i + i^{14} + 2\{i^2 + i^3 + i^4 + ... + i^{13}\}$

$= i - 1 + 2\{(i^2 + i^3 + i^4 + i^5) + (i^6 + i^7 + i^8 + i^9) + (i^{10} + i^{11} + i^{12} + i^{13})\} = i - 1 + 2(0) = i - 1$

15. (c) $\left(\sum_{m=1}^{2n+1} i^{2m}\right)^{\sum_{k=1}^{k=107} i^k}$

$$= \left\{\begin{matrix}(-1) + (-1)^2 + (-1)^3 + ... + (-1)^{2n+1} \\ \text{(i.e., } 2n+1 \text{ terms)}\end{matrix}\right\}^{(i+i^2+i^3+.....+i^{107})}$$

$$= (-1)^{i-1-i} = (-1)^{-1} = \frac{1}{(-1)^1} = -1$$

16. (b) $\sum_{k=1}^{k=4m+1} (i^k + i^{2k} + i^{3k} + i^{4k})$

Observe that for $k = 1$;

$i^k + i^{2k} + i^{3k} + i^{4k} = i + i^2 + i^3 + i^4 = 0$

For $k = 2$; $i^2 + i^4 + i^6 + i^8 = -1 + 1 - 1 + 1 = 0$

For k = 3; $i^3 + i^6 + i^9 + i^{12} = -i - 1 + i + 1 = 0$

For k = 4; $i^4 + i^8 + i^{12} + i^{16} = 4$

Similarly upto 4 m for k = 4, 8, 12, ……,$4m$

We get 4 + 4 + 4+……+4 (m times) = $4m$

$\Rightarrow \sum_{k=1}^{k=4m+1} (i^k + i^{2k} + i^{3k} + i^{4k}) = 4m$

TEXTUAL EXERCISE 2: SUBJECTIVE

1 (a) Let $z = \frac{1}{2} + \frac{\sqrt{3}}{2} i = \left(\cos\frac{\pi}{3} + i\sin\frac{\pi}{3}\right) = e^{i\pi/3}$

(b) $z = \sqrt{3} - i = 2\left\{\frac{\sqrt{3}}{2} - \frac{i}{2}\right\} = 2\left\{\cos\left(\frac{\pi}{6}\right) - i\sin\left(\frac{\pi}{6}\right)\right\}$

$= 2e^{-i\pi/6}$

2 (a) $z = 2\sqrt{2}\left\{\cos\frac{13\pi}{4} + i\sin\frac{13\pi}{4}\right\}$

$\Rightarrow z = 2\sqrt{2}\left(-\frac{1}{\sqrt{2}}\right) + 2\sqrt{2}\left(-\frac{1}{\sqrt{2}}\right)i = -2 - 2i$

(b) $z = 4\left\{\cos\frac{13\pi}{3} - i\sin\frac{13\pi}{3}\right\}$

$\Rightarrow z = 4\left\{\left(\frac{1}{2}\right) - \frac{\sqrt{3}}{2} i\right\} = 2 - 2\sqrt{3}i$

(c) $z = 6.e^{\frac{10\pi i}{3}} = 6\left\{\cos\frac{10\pi}{3} + i\sin\frac{10\pi}{3}\right\}$

$= 6\left\{-\frac{1}{2} - \frac{\sqrt{3}}{2}i\right\} = -3 - 3\sqrt{3}i$

3. (a) $z = \left(\frac{1+i}{1-i}\right)^{200} = \left\{\frac{(1+i)^2}{(1-i)^2}\right\}^{100} = \left(\frac{2i}{-2i}\right)^{100} = (-1)^{100} = 1$

In vector form $z = 1 + 0i$

In polar form $z = 1$ (cos0 + i sin 0}

In Euler form z = 1 $\{e^{0i}\}$

(b) $z = \left(\frac{1}{1-i}\right)^{100} = \left(\frac{1}{-2i}\right)^{50} = \left(-\frac{1}{2}\right)^{50} \cdot \frac{1}{i^{50}} = z = \frac{1}{2^{50}}(-1)$

In vector from $z = \frac{-1}{2^{50}} + 0i$

In polar form $z = \frac{1}{2^{50}}\{\cos\pi + i\sin\pi\}$

In Euler form $z = \frac{1}{2^{50}}\{e^{\pi i}\}$

(c) $z = \left(\sqrt{4+3\sqrt{-20}} + \sqrt{4-3\sqrt{-20}}\right)^4$

Observe that $4 + 3.2.\sqrt{-5} = (3+\sqrt{-5})^2$

$\Rightarrow \sqrt{4+3\sqrt{-20}} = \pm(3+\sqrt{5}i)$

and $4 - 3.5\sqrt{-5} = (3-\sqrt{-5})^2$

$\Rightarrow \sqrt{4-3\sqrt{-20}} = \pm(3-\sqrt{5}i)$

So $z = \left\{3 + i\sqrt{5}i + 3 - \sqrt{5}\,i\right\}^4 = 6^4$

or $\{3+\sqrt{5}i - 3 + \sqrt{5}i\}^4 = 25$

$\therefore$ $z - 6^4 = 6^4$ (cos 0 + i sin 0) = $6^4\, e.^{i0}$

or $z = 25 = 25$ (cos 0 + i sin 0) = $25e^{i0}$

(d) $z = \frac{\left(\sqrt{3}+i\right)^{17}}{(1-i)^{50}} = \frac{\left(\sqrt{3}+i\right)^{17}}{(-2i)^{25}} = \frac{\left(\sqrt{3}+i\right)^{17}}{(-2)^{25}i} = \frac{\left(\sqrt{3}+i\right)^{17}}{2^{25}}i$

$= \frac{(2)^{17}}{2^{25}} \cdot \left\{\cos\frac{\pi}{6} + i\sin\frac{\pi}{6}\right\}^{17} i$

$= \frac{i}{2^8}\left\{\cos\frac{17\pi}{6} + i\sin\frac{17\pi}{6}\right\} = \left\{\frac{-\sqrt{3}}{2} + \frac{i}{2}\right\}\frac{i}{2^8}$

$= \frac{1}{2^8}\left\{-\frac{1}{2} - \frac{\sqrt{3}}{2}i\right\}$

In vector form $z = \frac{1}{2^9}\{-1 - \sqrt{3}i\}$

In polar form $= \frac{1}{2^8}\left\{\cos\left(-\frac{2\pi}{3}\right) + i\sin\left(\frac{-2\pi}{3}\right)\right\}$ or

$z = \frac{1}{2^8}\left\{\cos\frac{4\pi}{3} + i\sin\frac{4\pi}{3}\right\}$

In Euler form $z = \frac{1}{2^8}e^{-\frac{2\pi}{3}i}$ or $\frac{1}{2^8}e^{\frac{4\pi}{3}i}$

(e) $z = \frac{(x+i)^2}{(x-i)} - \frac{(x-i)^2}{(x+i)} = \frac{(x+i)^3}{x^2+1} - \frac{(x-i)^3}{x^2+1} = \frac{6x^2-2}{x^2+1}i$

In vector from $z = 0 + \frac{6x^2-2}{x^2+1}i$

In Polar form $z = \frac{6x^2-2}{x^2+1}\left\{\cos\frac{\pi}{2} + i\sin\frac{\pi}{2}\right\}$

In Euler form $z = \frac{6x^2-2}{x^2+1}e^{\frac{\pi}{2}i}$

TEXTUAL EXERCISE 2: (OBJECTIVE)

1. (c) $x = i^i = \left(e^{\frac{\pi}{2}i}\right)^i = e^{-\pi/2}$

2. (c) $z = 1 + \cos\theta + i\sin\theta$; where $\theta \in [\pi, 3\pi]$

$z = 2\cos^2\frac{\theta}{2} + 2\cos\frac{\theta}{2}\sin\frac{\theta}{2}i = 2\cos\frac{\theta}{2}\left\{\cos\frac{\theta}{2} + i\sin\frac{\theta}{2}\right\}$

$\Rightarrow \quad |z| = \left|2\cos\frac{\theta}{2}\right| = -2\cos\frac{\theta}{2}$ as $\frac{\theta}{2} \in \left[\frac{\pi}{2}, \frac{3\pi}{2}\right]$

3 (b) Let $z = \sin\ln(i^i)^{i^2} + \cos\ln(i^i)^{i^2}$

$= \sin\left\{\ln\left(e^{-\frac{\pi}{2}}\right)^{-1}\right\} + \cos\left\{\ln\left(e^{-\pi/2}\right)^{-1}\right\} = \sin\frac{\pi}{2} + \cos\frac{\pi}{2} = 1$

4. (b) $z = e^{2ki\cot^{-1}m} \cdot \left(\frac{mi+1}{mi-1}\right)^k$

$= [\cos(2k\cot^{-1}m) + i\sin(2k\cot^{-1}m)].\left(\frac{mi+1}{mi-1}\right)^k$

$= e^{i(2k\theta)}\left[\frac{(m-i)^2}{\left(\sqrt{m^2+1}\right)^2}\right]^k = e^{i(2k\theta)}.\left[\frac{m-i}{\sqrt{m^2+1}}\right]^{2k}$

$= e^{i(2k\theta)}[\cos\theta - i\sin\theta]^{2k} = e^{i(2k\theta)}.e^{-i(2k\theta)} = 1$

5. (c) Let $z = r(\cos\theta + i\sin\theta)$

Then $\frac{z}{|z|} = \cos\theta + i\sin\theta$

$\Rightarrow \quad \left|\frac{z}{|z|} - 1\right| = |(\cos\theta - 1) + i\sin\theta|$

$= \left|-2\sin^2\frac{\theta}{2} + 2i\sin\frac{\theta}{2}\cos\frac{\theta}{2}\right|$

$= \left|2\sin\frac{\theta}{2}i\right|\left|\cos\frac{\theta}{2} + i\sin\frac{\theta}{2}\right| = 2\left|\sin\frac{\theta}{2}\right|$

6. (b) Let $\left|\frac{z}{|z|} - 1\right| = \left|2\sin\frac{\theta}{2}i\right|\left|\cos\frac{\theta}{2} + i\sin\frac{\theta}{2}\right|$

Then the maximum value of $\left|\frac{z}{|z|} - 1\right| = 2$

7. (c) $z_1 = |3-4i|.|e^{i\pi/4}| = 5$ and $z_2 = |4+3i|\,.\,|e^{i\pi/6}| = 5$

$\therefore\ |z_1| = |z_2|$

8. (b) $z = \tan\left\{i\ell n\left(\dfrac{a-ib}{a+ib}\right)\right\}$

$$= \tan\left\{i\ell n\left(\frac{a}{\sqrt{a^2+b^2}} - \frac{ib}{\sqrt{a^2+b^2}}\right)^2\right\}. \text{ Let } \tan^{-1}\frac{b}{a} = \theta$$

$$\Rightarrow\ z = \tan\{i\,\ell n(\cos\theta + i\sin\theta)^2\} = \tan\{2i\ell ne^{i\theta}\} = \tan\{-2\theta\}$$

$$= \frac{-2\tan\theta}{1-\tan^2\theta} = \frac{2b/a}{1-b^2/a^2} = \frac{2ab}{a^2-b^2}$$

TEXTUAL EXERCISE 3: (SUBJECTIVE)

1. (i) $z = (3+2i)(3-2i) = 9+4 = 13$. So $z = 13 + 0i$

(ii) $z = (i-2)^2 = -1+4-4i = 3-4i$

(iii) $z = \dfrac{2-i}{4+3i} = \dfrac{(2-i)(4-3i)}{16+9} = \dfrac{5-10i}{25} = \dfrac{1}{5} - \dfrac{2i}{5}$

(iv) $z = \dfrac{1+2i+3i^2}{1-2i+3i^2} = \dfrac{1+2i-3}{1-2i-3} = \dfrac{-2i}{2} = 0-i$

(v) $z = \left(\dfrac{1+i}{1-i}\right)^2 = \dfrac{2i}{-2i} = -1+0i$

(vi) $z = \left(\dfrac{1+2i}{2-i}\right)^2 = \left\{\dfrac{(1+2i)(2+i)}{(2-i)(2+i)}\right\}^2 = \dfrac{-25}{25} = -1+0i$

(vii) $\dfrac{1}{(2+i)^2} - \dfrac{1}{(2-i)^2} = \dfrac{(2-i)^2}{25} - \dfrac{(2+i)^2}{25}$

$$= \frac{-4(2)(i)}{25} = 0 - \frac{8}{25}i$$

2. (a) $z = \dfrac{(a+i)^2}{(a-i)} - \dfrac{(a-i)^2}{(a+i)} = \dfrac{(a+i)^3-(a-i)^3}{(a^2+1)}$

$$= \frac{2(3a^2-1)i}{(a^2+1)}$$

(b) $z = \left(\dfrac{1+\sin\alpha + i\cos\alpha}{1+\sin\alpha - i\cos\alpha}\right)^n$

$$\Rightarrow\ z = \left\{\frac{\cos\left(\frac{\pi}{4}-\frac{\alpha}{2}\right) + i\sin\left(\frac{\pi}{4}-\frac{\alpha}{2}\right)}{\cos\left(\frac{\pi}{4}-\frac{\alpha}{2}\right) - i\sin\left(\frac{\pi}{4}-\frac{\alpha}{2}\right)}\right\}^n = \left\{\frac{e^{i\left(\frac{\pi}{4}-\frac{\alpha}{2}\right)}}{e^{i\left(-\frac{\pi}{4}+\frac{\alpha}{2}\right)}}\right\}^n$$

$$= \left\{e^{\left(\frac{\pi}{4}-\frac{\alpha}{2}\right)i}\right\}^{2n} = e^{\left(\frac{\pi}{2}-\alpha\right)ni}$$

$$= \cos\left(\frac{n\pi}{2} - n\alpha\right) + i\sin\left(\frac{n\pi}{2} - n\alpha\right)$$

(c) $z = \left(\dfrac{1+2i}{1+i}\right)^n$ for $n = \pm1, \pm2, \pm3, \ldots\ldots$

Now $\dfrac{1+2i}{1+i} = \dfrac{3+i}{2} = \sqrt{\dfrac{5}{2}}\left\{\dfrac{3}{\sqrt{10}} + \dfrac{i}{\sqrt{10}}\right\} = \sqrt{\dfrac{5}{2}}e^{i\theta}$

$$\Rightarrow\ z = \left(\frac{5}{2}\right)^{n/2}\left[\cos n\theta + i\left(\frac{5}{2}\right)^{n/2}.\sin n\theta\right];$$

Where $\cos\theta = \dfrac{3}{\sqrt{10}}$ and $\sin\theta = \dfrac{1}{\sqrt{10}}$

Or $z = \left(\dfrac{5}{2}\right)^{n/2} \text{cis}\left\{n\tan^{-1}\left(\dfrac{1}{3}\right)\right\}^n$

3. $z = (1+i)^{2n} + (1-i)^{2n} = (2i)^n + (-2i)^n = \{2^n + (-2)^n\}$

Case 1: When n is odd, $z = 0$

Case 2: When n is even, then

$z = i^n\{2^n + (-2)^n\} = 2.2^n\, i^n = 2^{n+1}.i^n$

$= 2^{n+1}.(-1)^{n/2}$ (as n is even) $\quad\Rightarrow\quad x = \dfrac{2^{n+1}}{(-1)^{n/2}}$

4. Given $a = \dfrac{1+i}{\sqrt{2}}$. To find the value of $z = a^6 + a^4 + a^2 + 1$

Observe that $a^2 = \dfrac{1-1+2i}{2} = i$

$\Rightarrow\ z = i^3 + i^2 + i + 1 = -i - 1 + i + 1 = 0$

5. $z = \left(\dfrac{1+i}{1-i}\right)^{200} = \left(\dfrac{2i}{-2i}\right)^{100} = \left(\dfrac{1}{-1}\right)^{100} = 1$

6. $z = \left\{i^{19} + \left(\dfrac{1}{i}\right)^{25}\right\}^2 \quad\Rightarrow\quad z = \left\{i^3 + \dfrac{1}{i}\right\}^2 = (-i-i)^2 = 4i^2 = -4$

7. $z = \left\{\dfrac{1}{1-2i} + \dfrac{3}{1+i}\right\}\left\{\dfrac{3+4i}{2-4i}\right\}$

$$= \left\{\frac{1+2i}{5} + \frac{3-3i}{2}\right\}\left\{\frac{(3+4i)(2+4i)}{20}\right\}$$

$$\left(\frac{2+4i+15-15i}{10}\right).\left(\frac{6-16+20i}{20}\right)$$

$$= \left(\frac{17-11i}{10}\right).\left(\frac{-10+20i}{20}\right) = \frac{(17-11i)(-1+2i)}{20} = \frac{1}{4} + \frac{9}{4}i$$

8. $z = \dfrac{20}{\sqrt{3}-\sqrt{-2}} + \dfrac{30}{3\sqrt{-2}-2\sqrt{3}} - \dfrac{14}{2\sqrt{3}-\sqrt{-2}}$

$$\Rightarrow\ z = \frac{20\left(\sqrt{3}+\sqrt{2}i\right)}{(3+2)} + \frac{30\{-2\sqrt{3}-3\sqrt{2}i\}}{(12+18)} - \frac{14\{2\sqrt{3}+\sqrt{2}i\}}{(12+2)}$$

$$\Rightarrow\ 4\sqrt{3} + 4\sqrt{2}i - 2\sqrt{3} - 3\sqrt{2}i - 2\sqrt{3} - \sqrt{2}i = 0$$

9. Given $(3x-2iy)(2+i)^2 = 10+10i$

L.H.S. $= (3x-2iy)\{3+4i\} = (9x+8y) + (12x-6y)i$

Gives $9x + 8y = 10$ and $12x - 6y = 10$

$\Rightarrow\ y = 1/5$ and $x = 14/15$

10. $(x^4 + 2xi) - (3x^2 + yi) = (3-5i) + (1+2yi)$

$\Rightarrow\ x^4 - 3x^2 = 4$ so $(x^2)^2 - 3(x^2) - 4 = 0$

So $(x^2-4)(x^2+1) = 0$ hence $x = \pm 2$

Also $2xi - yi = -5i + 2yi$; So $3yi = (5+2x)i$

When $x = 2$, $y = 3$ and for $x = -2$, $y = 1/3$ Ans

11. Given $a+ib=\dfrac{3}{(2+\cos\theta)+i\sin\theta}$

$\Rightarrow \quad a-ib=\dfrac{3}{2+\cos\theta-i\sin\theta}$

$\Rightarrow \quad a^2+b^2=\dfrac{9}{4+\cos^2\theta+\sin^2\theta+4\cos\theta}=\dfrac{9}{5+4\cos\theta}$

Now $a+ib=\dfrac{3(2+\cos\theta)-3i\sin\theta}{5+4\cos\theta}$

So $a^2+b^2=\dfrac{9}{5+4\cos\theta}=\dfrac{4.3(2+\cos\theta)-3(5+4\cos\theta)}{5+4cos\theta}$

$= a^2 + b^2 = 4a - 3$

12. (a) $z=3+2i \Rightarrow \quad \text{M.I}=\dfrac{\bar{z}}{z\bar{z}}=\dfrac{3-2i}{13}$

(b) $z=\dfrac{2-3i}{4+5i}=\dfrac{(2-3i)(4-5i)}{16+25}=\dfrac{8-15-22i}{41}=\dfrac{-7-22i}{41}$

$\Rightarrow$ Multiplicative inverse $\dfrac{(-7+22i)(41)}{(49+484)}=\dfrac{-7+22i}{13}$

(c) $z=\dfrac{(2-5i)^2}{(3-2i)}$; M.I. of z is

$\dfrac{1}{z}=\dfrac{3-2i}{(2-5i)^2}=\dfrac{(3-2i)(2+5i)^2}{29\times 29}=\dfrac{-23+102i}{841}$

13. $(x + iy)^5 = p + iq$

$\Rightarrow \; i^5 \{y - ix\}^5 = p + iq$ or $(y - ix)^5 = q \equiv ip$

Taking conjugate $(y + ix)^5 = q + ip$

14. Given $\dfrac{x}{y-z}+\dfrac{y}{z-x}+\dfrac{z}{x-y}=0$

Squaring we get,

$$\sum\frac{x^2}{(y-z)^2}=(-2)\sum\frac{xy}{(y-z)(z-x)} \quad \text{.......(i)}$$

Observe that $\dfrac{xy}{(y-z)(z-x)}+\dfrac{yz}{(z-x)(x-y)}+\dfrac{xz}{(y-z)(x-y)}$

$=\dfrac{xy(x-y)+yz(y-z)+zx(z-x)}{(x-y)(y-z)(z-x)}$

$=\dfrac{-(x-y)(y-z)(z-x)}{(x-y)(y-z)(z-x)}=-1 \quad \text{.......(ii)}$

$\therefore$ Using (i) and (ii), we get $\sum\dfrac{x^2}{(y-z)^2}=2$

15. Given $2x - 5 = -\sqrt{3}i$

Squaring $4x^2 + 25 - 20x = -3$

$\therefore \; 4x^2 - 20x = -28$ or $x^2 - 5x = -7$

Hence $x^4 - x^3 - 12x^2 + 23x + 12$

$= (5x - 7)^2 - x(5x - 7) - 12(5x - 7) + 23x + 12$

$= 20x^2 - 100x + 145 = 20(-7) + 145 = 5$

16. $f(x) = x^4 - 8x^3 + 4x^2 + 4x + 39$

When $x = 3 + 2i$ then $(x - 3)^2 = (2i)^2$

i.e., $x^2 + 9 - 6x = -4$

Hence $x^4 - 8x^3 + 4x^2 + 4x + 39$

$= (6x - 13)^2 - 8x(6x - 13) + 4(6x - 13) + 4x + 39$

Gives L.H.S. $= -12x^2 - 24x + 156 = (-12)(-13) + 156 - 96x$

$= 312 - 96(3 + 2i) = 24 - 192i = a + ib$

$\Rightarrow \quad \dfrac{a}{b}=\dfrac{24}{-192}=\dfrac{-1}{8}$

TEXTUAL EXERCISE 3: (OBJECTIVE)

1. (d) $p + iq > r + i$ is meaningful only when both sides are purely real, i.e., $q = 0$ and $t = 0$

2. (b, c) If the multiplicative inverse of a number is the number itself, then $z=\dfrac{1}{z}\Rightarrow z^2=1$ so $z=\pm1$

3. (d) $z_1 = (4, 5)$ and $z_2 = (-3, 2)$

So $z=\dfrac{z_1}{z_2}=\dfrac{4+5i}{-3+2i}=\dfrac{(4+5i)(-3-2i)}{13}=\dfrac{-2-23i}{13}$

So $z=\left(\dfrac{-2}{13},\dfrac{-23}{13}\right)$

4. (b) $z=\left(\dfrac{2i}{1+i}\right)^2=\dfrac{-4}{2i}=2i$

5. (c) $z = 1 + i \Rightarrow z^2 = 2i$

$\therefore$ Multiplicative inverse of z^2 is $\dfrac{1}{2i}=\dfrac{-i}{2}$

6. (c) $a = \cos\theta + i\sin\theta$

$\Rightarrow \quad z=\dfrac{1+a}{1-a}=\dfrac{1+\cos\theta+i\sin\theta}{1-\cos\theta-i\sin\theta}$

$\Rightarrow \quad z=\dfrac{2\cos^2\frac{\theta}{2}+2i\sin\frac{\theta}{2}.\cos\frac{\theta}{2}}{2\sin^2\frac{\theta}{2}-2i\sin\frac{\theta}{2}\cos\frac{\theta}{2}}$

$=\dfrac{2\cos\frac{\theta}{2}\left\{\cos\frac{9}{2}+i\sin\frac{\theta}{2}\right\}}{\left(-2i\sin\frac{\theta}{2}\right)\left\{\cos\frac{\theta}{2}+i\sin\frac{\theta}{2}\right\}}=i\cot\dfrac{\theta}{2}$

7. (b) Let $a+ib=\dfrac{1}{1-\cos\theta+i\sin\theta}$

$=\dfrac{1-\cos\theta-i\sin\theta}{1+\cos^2\theta-2\cos\theta+\sin^2\theta}$

$=\dfrac{1-\cos\theta}{2-2\cos\theta}-\dfrac{i\sin\theta}{2-2\cos\theta} \quad \Rightarrow \quad a=\dfrac{1}{2}$

8. (c) $(x + iy)(p + iq) = (x^2 + y^2)i$

$\Rightarrow xp - yq = 0$ and $xq + yp = x^2 + y^2$

Observe that when $x = q$ and $y = p$, then both equations are satisfied

9. (b) Given: $\dfrac{(1+i)x-2i}{3+i}+\dfrac{(2-3i)y+i}{3-i}=i$

L.H.S $=\dfrac{\{x+(x-2)i\}\{3-i\}+\{2y+(1-3y)i\}\{3+i\}}{10}$

L.H.S $= \dfrac{(4x-2)+(2x-6)i+(9y-1)+(3-7y)i}{10}$

Gives $4x + 9y - 3 = 0$ and $2x - 7y - 3 = 10$

$\Rightarrow y = -1, x = 3$

10. (b) $z = \left(\dfrac{1+i}{1-i}\right)^n = \left(\dfrac{2i}{2}\right)^n = i^n$

If $z = 1$ then, $n = 4, 8, 12 \ldots$

So minimum value of $n = 4$

11. (c) $(1 + i)^{2n} = (1 - i)^{2n}$ where $n \in \mathbb{N}$

$\Rightarrow (2i)^n = (-2i)^n$ or $(i)^n = (-i)^n$ gives $n = 2$

12. (a) $z = \left(\dfrac{i-1}{i+1}\right)^n = \left\{\dfrac{-(1-i)^2}{2}\right\}^n = \left(\dfrac{2i}{2}\right)^n = i^n$

z will be a real number when $n = 2$

13. (c) Given $x - 2 = 5i$ and $x^2 + 4 - 4x = -25$

Now, $x^3 - 5x^2 + 33x - 19 = x(x^2 - 4x) + 33x - 19 - x^2$

Gives L.H.S $= -29x - 4x + 29 + 33x - 19 = 10$

14. (a) $f(z) = (z-i).\, g_1(z) + \dfrac{1+i}{2}$ ......(i)

Also $f(z) = (z+i)\, g_2(z) + \dfrac{1+3i}{2}$ ......(ii)

Operate $(z + i)$ (i) – $(z - i)$ (ii), we get $2i\, f(z) = (z^2 + 1)$ $\{g_1(z) - g_2(z)\} + (i - zi - 2)$

So, $f(z) = (z^2 + 1)\{g_2(z) - g_1(z)\}i + \dfrac{(1-z)i}{2i} - \dfrac{2}{2i}$

$= (z^2 + 1)\{g_2(z) - g_1(z)\}i + \dfrac{1}{2}\{1 - z + 2i\}$

Hence remainder $= \dfrac{1}{2}(1 + 2i - z)$

15. (d) $z^2 + (p + iq)z + (r + is) = 0$ has real roots where (p, q, r, s are non-zero real numbers)

$\Rightarrow z^2 + pz + r = 0$ and $qz + s = 0$, hence $z = -\dfrac{s}{q}$

So putting in $z^2 + pz + r = 0$, we get

$\dfrac{s^2}{q^2} + p\left(\dfrac{-s}{q}\right) + r = 0$ gives $s^2 + rq^2 = pqs$

16. (d) $(1 - i)^x = 2^x$

Observe that $(1 - 1 - 2i)^{x/2} = 2^x$

$2^{x/2}(-i)^{x/2} = 2^x$ Only possibility is $x = 0$

Alternatively:

$(1 - i)^x = 2^x \quad \Rightarrow \quad (-2i)^{x/2} = 2^x$

This will hold only for $x = 0$

17. (d) Let $z = (1+i)^{n_1} + (1-i)^{n_1} + (1+i)^{n_2} + (1-i)^{n_2}$

Observe that $(1+i)^{n_1} + (1-i)^{n_1} = \left(\sqrt{2}\right)\left\{2\cos\dfrac{n_1\pi}{4}\right\}$,

always real $\forall\, n_1 \in \mathbb{N}$

Similarly $(1+i)^{n_2} + (1-i)^{n_2}$ is always real $\forall\, n_2 \in \mathbb{N}$

$\Rightarrow n_1, n_2$ may be any positive integers

18. (a) $\dfrac{a}{a_1} + \dfrac{b}{b_1} + \dfrac{c}{c_1} = 1 + i$ and $\dfrac{a_1}{a} + \dfrac{b_1}{b} + \dfrac{c_1}{c} = 0$

For easy working put $\dfrac{a}{a_1} = x; \dfrac{b}{b_1} = y; \dfrac{c}{c_1} = z$

Then $x + y + z = 1 + i$ and $\dfrac{1}{x} + \dfrac{1}{y} + \dfrac{1}{z} = 0$

Now, $\dfrac{1}{x} + \dfrac{1}{y} + \dfrac{1}{z} = \dfrac{xy + yz + zx}{xyz} = 0$

So $xy + yz + zx = 0$

$\Rightarrow x^2 + y^2 + z^2 = (x + y + z)^2 = (1 + i)^2 = 2i$

19. (d) $\Delta = \begin{vmatrix} 6i & -3i & 1 \\ 4 & 3i & -1 \\ 20 & 3 & i \end{vmatrix} = \begin{vmatrix} (4+6i) & 0 & 0 \\ 4 & 3i & -1 \\ 20 & 3 & i \end{vmatrix}$

$= (4 + 6i)\{3i^2 + 3\} = 0$ so $x = 0, y = 0$

TEXTUAL EXERCISE 4: (SUBJECTIVE)

1. (i) $z = (3 - 2i)(3 + 2i)(1 + i) = 13 + 13i$

So $\bar{z} = 13 - 13i$ and $|z| = 13\sqrt{2}$

(ii) $z = \dfrac{2+i}{6i} = \dfrac{1}{6} - \dfrac{1}{3}i = \dfrac{1-2i}{6}$

So $\bar{z} = \dfrac{1}{6} + \dfrac{1}{3}i$ and $|z| = \dfrac{\sqrt{5}}{6}$

2. $z_1 + z_2 =$ real and $z_1 z_2 =$ real

$\Rightarrow Im(z_1) + Im(z_2) = 0$ and $Re(z_1)\, Im(z_2) + Re(z_2)\, Im(z_1) = 0$

3. $|z| = 1 \quad \Rightarrow \quad z = \cos\theta + i\sin\theta$

$\Rightarrow \dfrac{z-1}{z+1} = \dfrac{(\cos\theta - 1) + i\sin\theta}{(1+\cos\theta) + i\sin\theta} = \dfrac{2i\sin\dfrac{\theta}{2}\left(\cos\dfrac{\theta}{2} + i\sin\dfrac{\theta}{2}\right)}{2\cos\dfrac{\theta}{2}\left(\cos\dfrac{\theta}{2} + i\sin\dfrac{\theta}{2}\right)}$

$= i.\tan\theta$; which is purely imaginary

Aliter: $|z| = 1$, then Arg $\left(\dfrac{z-1}{z+1}\right) = \dfrac{\pi}{2}$

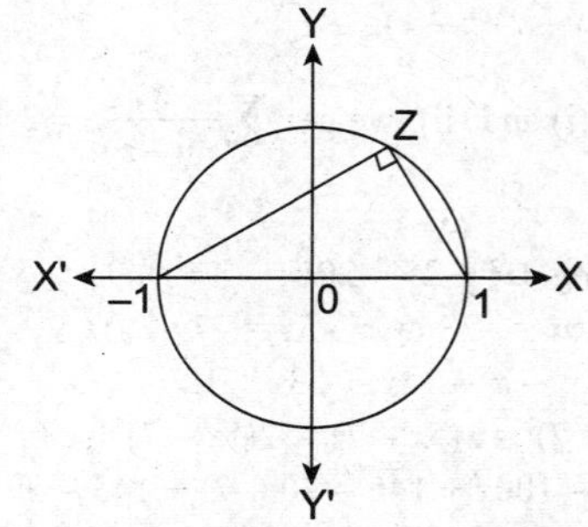

{Observe that $|z| = 1$, represents the circle $x^2 + y^2 = 1$}

Hence $\dfrac{z-1}{z+1}$ is purely imaginary

(b) $z = \dfrac{3+2i\sin\theta}{1-2i\sin\theta} = \dfrac{3-4\sin^2\theta+8i\sin\theta}{1+4\sin^2\theta}$

(i) z will be purely real when $\sin\theta = 0$
i.e., $\theta = n\pi$; $n \in \mathbb{Z}$

(ii) Similarly z will be purely imaginary, when $3 - 4\sin^2\theta = 0$

i.e., $\sin^2\theta = \dfrac{3}{4}$ or $\sin\theta = \pm\dfrac{\sqrt{3}}{2}$

$\Rightarrow$ $\theta = n\pi \pm \pi/3$; $n \in \mathbb{Z}$

(c) To solve $\text{Re}(z^2) = 0$ and $|z| = a\sqrt{2}$

Let $z = re^{i\theta}$

$\Rightarrow$ $|z| = r = a\sqrt{2}$ (where $a > 0$) and then $z^2 = 2a^2 e^{2i\theta}$

Now $\text{Re}(z^2) = 2a^2\cos 2\theta = 0$ gives $2\theta = n\pi \pm \dfrac{\pi}{2}$; $n \in \mathbb{Z}$

$\Rightarrow$ $\theta = \dfrac{n\pi}{2} \pm \dfrac{\pi}{4}; n \in \mathbb{Z}$

$\therefore$ In one revolution it gives, $\theta = \pm\dfrac{\pi}{4}, \pm\dfrac{3\pi}{4}$

Hence four solutions are possible namely

$z = \sqrt{2}a\,e^{\frac{\pi}{4}i}, \sqrt{2}ae^{-\frac{\pi}{4}i}, \sqrt{2}ae^{\frac{3\pi}{4}i}, \sqrt{2}ae^{-\frac{3\pi}{4}i}$

$\therefore$ 4 solutions

TEXTUAL EXERCISE 4: (OBJECTIVE)

1. (d) Given $z_1 = \sin x + i\cos^2 x$ and $z_2 = \cos x - i\sin 2x$

If $\overline{z}_1 = z_2$, then $\sin x = \cos x$ and $\cos^2 x = -2\sin x\cos x$. But both these conditions are never satisfied simultaneously.

2. (a) Let $z_1 = 3 + x^2yi$ and $z_2 = (x^2 + y) + 4i$

If $\overline{z}_1 = z_2$, then $x^2 + y = 3$ and $x^2y = -4$

Which is possible when $x^2 = 4$ and $y = -1$ or $x^2 = -1$, $y = 4$

$\Rightarrow$ $(x, y) \equiv (-2, -1)$ or $(2, -1)$; $(i, 4)$; $(-i, 4)$

3 (a) $y = \cos\theta + i\sin\theta$

$\Rightarrow$ $\dfrac{1}{y} = \dfrac{1}{\cos\theta + i\sin\theta} = \cos\theta - i\sin\theta$

Hence $y + \dfrac{1}{y} = 2\cos\theta$

4. (d) $x^2 - \sqrt{3}x + 1 = 0$ gives $x = \dfrac{\sqrt{3} \pm \sqrt{3-4}}{2} = \dfrac{\sqrt{3} \pm i}{2}$

$= \cos\dfrac{\pi}{6} \pm i\sin\dfrac{\pi}{6}$

5. (c) $z = \dfrac{i(\sqrt{3}-i)}{\sqrt{3}+i} = \dfrac{i\{3-1-2\sqrt{3}i\}}{4}$

$= \dfrac{\sqrt{3}}{2} + \dfrac{i}{2} = \cos\dfrac{\pi}{6} + i\sin\dfrac{\pi}{6}$

So $\overline{z} = \cos\left(-\dfrac{\pi}{6}\right) + i\sin\left(-\dfrac{\pi}{6}\right)$

Hence $(\overline{z})^{100} = \cos\left(-\dfrac{100}{6}\pi\right) + i\sin\left(\dfrac{-100\pi}{6}\right)$

$= \cos\left(-\dfrac{2\pi}{3}\right) + i\sin\left(-\dfrac{2\pi}{3}\right)$

$\therefore$ $(\overline{z})^{100}$ lies in IIIrd quadrant

6. (c) Let $z = a + ib$ then $\overline{z} = a - ib$

So $z + \overline{z} = 2a$ and $z\overline{z} = a^2 + b^2$. We observe that both are real numbers.

7. (c) $(z+a)(\overline{z}+a) = z\overline{z} + a^2 + a(z+\overline{z})$

$= |z|^2 + a^2 + 2a\text{Re}(z) = \{|z+a|\}^2$

Alternatively:

Let $z = x + iy$ $\Rightarrow$ $|z|^2 = x^2 + y^2$

So $z + a = (x + a) + iy$ $\Rightarrow$ $|z + a|^2 = (x + a)^2 + y^2$

$= x^2 + a^2 + 2ax + y^2 = |z|^2 + a^2 + 2a\,\text{Re}(z)$

8. (b) Given that $\dfrac{z-i}{z+i}$ is purely imaginary so $Arg\dfrac{z-i}{z+i} = \pm\dfrac{\pi}{2}$

$\Rightarrow$ z lies on the circle $x^2 + y^2 = 1$

$\Rightarrow$ $z\overline{z} = |z|^2 = 1$

9. (a) Given $\dfrac{c+i}{c-i} = a + ib \Rightarrow a - ib = \dfrac{c-i}{c+i}$.

Hence $a^2 + b^2 = 1$

10. (c) Given: $(x + iy)(1 - 2i) = 1 - i$

So $(x + 2y) + (y - 2x)i = 1 - i$

Gives $x = 3/5$ and $y = 1/5$

Also $x + iy = \dfrac{1-i}{1-2i}$; Further $x - iy = \dfrac{1+i}{1+2i}$

11. (c) Let $z = \dfrac{(2+i)^2}{3+i} = \dfrac{(3+4i)(3-i)}{10}$

So $z = \dfrac{13+9i}{10}$. Hence $\overline{z} = \dfrac{13}{10} + \left(\dfrac{-9}{10}\right)i$

12. (b) Let $z = \dfrac{2-3i}{4-i} = \dfrac{(2-3i)(4+i)}{17} = \dfrac{11-10i}{17}$

So $\overline{z} = \dfrac{11}{17} + \dfrac{10i}{17}$

13. (d) False statement is $Arg z = -Arg(\overline{z})$

14. (d) Given $z_1 = 1 + 2i$ and $z_2 = 3 + 5i$, then

$\text{Re}\left(\dfrac{z_1\overline{z}_2}{z_2}\right) = \text{Re}\left\{\dfrac{(1+2i)(3-5i)^2}{34}\right\} = \text{Re}\left(\dfrac{44-62i}{34}\right) = \dfrac{22}{17}$

15. (a) Given $(i - z)(1 + 2i) + (1 - iz)(3 - 4i) = 1 + 7i$

$\Rightarrow$ $(1 + 2i)(-z) + (3 - 4i)(-iz) = 1 + 7i - 3 + 4i - i + 2$

Gives $(-5)(1 + i)z = 10i$

Gives $z = \dfrac{2i(-1)}{1+i} = \dfrac{2(-1-i)}{2} = -1-i$

$\Rightarrow \quad z + \bar{z} + z\bar{z} = -2 + 2 = 0$

16. (b) Let $z_1 = r_1 e^{i\theta_1}$, $z_2 = r_2 e^{i\theta_2}$; $z_3 = r_3 e^{i\theta_3}$

$\Rightarrow \quad \text{Im}(\bar{z}_2 z_3) = r_2 r_3 \sin(\theta_3 - \theta_2)$

Hence Z_1 Im $(\bar{z}_2 z_3) = r_1.r_2.r_3 e^{i\theta_1} \sin(\theta_3 - \theta_2)$

$\Rightarrow \quad \Sigma z_1 \,\text{Im}(\bar{z}_2 z_3) = r_1 r_2 r_3$

$= \{e^{i\theta_1} \sin(\theta_3 - \theta_2)\; e^{i\theta_2} \sin(\theta_1 - \theta_3) + e^{i\theta_3} \sin(\theta_2 - \theta_1)\} = 0$

17. (b) $z_1 = a + ib$; $z_2 = c + id$

Since $|z_1| = |z_2| = 1 \quad \Rightarrow \quad a^2 + b^2 = c^2 + d^2 = 1$

$\text{Re}(z_1\bar{z}_2) = \text{Re}\,(ac + bd + ibc - iad) = ac + bd = 0$

Hence $ac = -bd \quad \Rightarrow \quad \dfrac{a}{d} = \dfrac{-b}{c} = k$ (say) ...(i)

Now $\text{Re}(w_1\bar{w}_2) = \text{Re}\,\{(a + ic)(b - id)\} = ab + cd$

From $\dfrac{a}{d} = \dfrac{-b}{c} = k$ (say) $\Rightarrow a = dk$ and $b = -ck$

$a^2 + b^2 = k^2(c^2 + d^2) = 1$ but $c^2 + d^2 = 1$

$k^2 = 1 \quad \Rightarrow \quad k = \pm 1$

Case 1: $k = 1$, then $a = d$ and $b = -c$

So $ab + cd = -cd + cd = 0$

Case 2: $k = -1$, then $a = -d$ and $b = c$,

then, $ab + cd = -cd + cd = 0$

Hence $\text{Re}(w_1\bar{w}_2) = 0$

TEXTUAL EXERCISE 5: (SUBJECTIVE)

1. (a) Let $|z| = \left|\dfrac{1-i\sqrt{3}}{2+2i}\right| = \dfrac{|1-i\sqrt{3}|}{|2+2i|} = \dfrac{\sqrt{4}}{\sqrt{8}} = \dfrac{1}{\sqrt{2}}$

(b) $|z| = \left|\dfrac{2+i}{4i+(1+i)^2}\right| = \dfrac{|2+i|}{|6i|} = \dfrac{\sqrt{5}}{6}$

2. $z = 1 + i\tan\alpha$ where $\alpha \in \left(\pi, \dfrac{3\pi}{2}\right)$

We know that in IIIrd quadrant $\tan\theta \geq 0$ and $\sec\theta \leq -1$

$\Rightarrow \quad |z| = \left(\sqrt{1+\tan^2\alpha}\right) = |\sec\alpha| = -\sec\alpha$

3. $(\cos\theta - i\sin\theta)^2 = x - iy$

$\Rightarrow \quad (\cos\theta + i\sin\theta)^2 = x + iy$

$\Rightarrow \quad x^2 + y^2 = (\cos^2\theta + \sin^2\theta)^2 = 1$

4. Given $x + iy = \sqrt{\dfrac{a+ib}{c+id}}$

$\Rightarrow \quad (x+iy)^2 = \dfrac{a+ib}{c+id}$ and $(x-iy)^2 = \dfrac{a-ib}{c-id}$

So $(x^2+y^2)^2 = \dfrac{(a+ib)}{(c+id)}\cdot\dfrac{(a-ib)}{(c=id)} = \dfrac{a^2+b^2}{c^2+d^2}$

5. Given $(c + i)/(c - i) = a + id$; When $c \in \mathbb{R}$

$\Rightarrow \quad \dfrac{c^2-1+2ci}{c^2+1} = a + ib \Rightarrow \dfrac{b}{a} = \dfrac{2c}{(c^2-1)}$

Now $(a + ib)(a - ib) = a^2 + b^2 = \dfrac{(c+i)}{(c-i)}\cdot\dfrac{(c-i)}{(c+i)}$

$\Rightarrow \quad a^2 + b^2 = 1$

6. $\left|\dfrac{z-3}{z+3}\right| = 2$; where $z = x + iy$

$\Rightarrow \quad |(x - 3) + iy)| = 2|(x + 3) + iy)|$

$\Rightarrow \quad (x - 3)^2 + y^2 = 4(x + 3)^2 + 4y^2$

Gives $3y^2 + 3x^2 + 30x + 27 = 0$ or $x^2 + y^2 + 10x + 9 = 0$

Rewriting $(x + 5)^2 + y^2 = 4^2$ which is circle of radius $= 4$ units and centre at $C(-5, 0)$

7. $|z+1| = \sqrt{2}|z-1| \Rightarrow (x + 1)^2 + y^2 = 2\{(x - 1)^2 + y^2\}$

$\Rightarrow \quad y^2 + x^2 - 6x + 1 = 0$

8. $z^2 + |z| = 0 \quad \Rightarrow \quad x^2 - y^2 + 2xyi + \sqrt{x^2+y^2} = 0$

$\Rightarrow \quad x^2 - y^2 = -\sqrt{x^2+y^2}$ and $2xy = 0$

Case 1: $x = 0, y = 0$, both equations are satisfied

$\Rightarrow \quad z = 0$

Case 2: $x = 0, y \neq 0 \quad \Rightarrow \quad -y^2 = -\sqrt{y^2}$

$\Rightarrow \quad y = \pm 1 \quad \Rightarrow \quad z = \pm i$

Case 3: $x \neq 0, y = 0 \quad \Rightarrow \quad x^2 = -\sqrt{x^2}$

Which is possible only if $x = 0$, so no solution.

Thus $z = 0, \pm i$

9. Given $|z - i| < 1$. Now

$|z + 12 - 6i| = |z - i + 12 - 5i| \leq |z - i| + |12 - 5i| < 1 + 13 = 14$

Thus $|z + 12 - 6i| < 14$

Aliter: Gives interior of a circle having radius 1 unit and centre at (0, 1) as shown below:

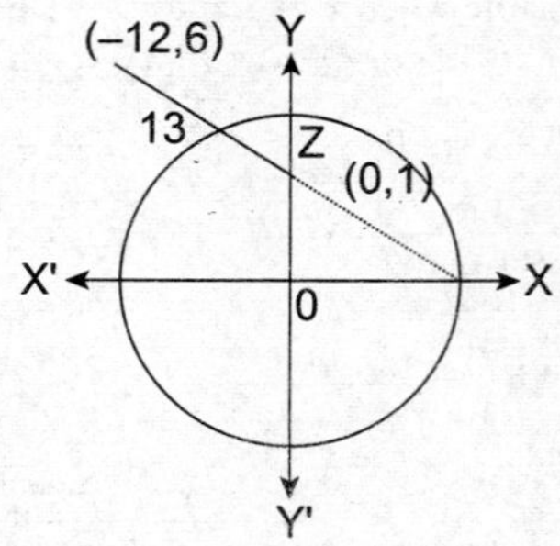

$|z + 12 - 6i| = |(z - i) + (12 - 5i)|$

Distance of (–12, 6) from (0, 1) is 13 units.

So $|13 - 1| < |z + 12 - 6i| < |13 + 1|$

Hence $|z + 12 - 6i| < 14$

10. For $a > 0$, $z\,|z| + az + 1 = 0$

Gives $z\,(|z| + a) = -1$

Since $a > 0$ and $|z| \geq 0$ so $(|z| + a) > 0$

$\Rightarrow \quad z$ is a negative real number

11. $\left||z| - \frac{4}{|z|}\right| < \left|z - \frac{4}{z}\right| = 2$ gives $|z| - \frac{4}{|z|} < 2$

So $|z|^2 - 2|z| - 4 < 0$

Now, $|z|^2 - 2|z| - 4 = 0$ has roots $|z| = 1 \pm \sqrt{5}$ however $|z| \geq 0$ so $|z|$ can have a maximum value of $1 + \sqrt{5}$

12. Given $|z + 4| \leq 3$

$\therefore$ $|z + 1| = |z + 4 - 3| \leq |z + 4| + |-3| \leq 6$

Now $|z + 1| = |z + 4 - 3|$

$= |3 - (z + 4)| \geq ||3| - |z + 4|| \geq |3 - 3| = 0$

Hence $0 \leq |z + 1| \leq 6$

The minimum $|z + 1| = 0$

The maximum $|z + 1| = 6$

13. $|z| + |z - 2| \geq 2$; we know that $|z| + |z - 2| \geq |z \pm (z - 2)|$

So, $|z| + |z - 2| \geq |z - (z - 2)| = 2$

14. Let $\alpha = a + ib$ and $\beta = c + id$

Then $|\alpha^2| + |\beta^2| = a^2 + b^2 + c^2 + d^2$

Now, $|(\alpha + \beta)|^2 + |\alpha - \beta|^2$

$= (a + c)^2 + (b + d)^2 + (a - c)^2 + (b - d)^2$

$= 2\,(a^2 + b^2 + c^2 + d^2)$

Hence $|\alpha^2| + |\beta^2| = \frac{1}{2}\,\{|\alpha + \beta|^2 + |\alpha - \beta|^2\}$

TEXTUAL EXERCISE 5: (OBJECTIVE)

1. (a) $|z| = \frac{|1 - i\sqrt{3}||\cos\theta + i\sin\theta|}{|2(1-i)||\cos\theta - i\sin\theta|} \Rightarrow |z| = \frac{\sqrt{4}(1)}{\sqrt{8}(1)} = \frac{1}{\sqrt{2}}$

2. (c) Given $|\beta| = 1 \Rightarrow \beta\bar{\beta} = 1$

Now $|z| = \left|\frac{\beta - \alpha}{1 - \bar{\alpha}\beta}\right| = \frac{|\beta - \alpha|}{|\beta\bar{\beta} - \bar{\alpha}\beta|} = \frac{|\beta - \alpha|}{|\beta||\bar{\beta} - \bar{\alpha}|} = 1$

Since $|\beta| = 1$ and $|z| = |\bar{z}|$

3. (a) Now $|a| = 1 \Rightarrow a\bar{a} \Rightarrow a = \frac{1}{\bar{a}}$

Similarly, $b = \frac{1}{\bar{b}}$ and $c = \frac{1}{\bar{c}}$

$\Rightarrow \frac{1}{a} + \frac{1}{b} + \frac{1}{c} = \bar{a} + \bar{b} + \bar{c} = 0 = \overline{(a + b + c)} = \bar{0} = 0$

4. (b) Given $|z| \geq 3$ so $\frac{1}{|z|} \leq \frac{1}{3}$ gives $|\ \ | \geq 3$ and $-\frac{1}{|\ \ |} \geq -\frac{1}{}$

Now $\left||z| - \frac{1}{|z|}\right| \leq \left|z + \frac{1}{z}\right| \Rightarrow \left|z + \frac{1}{z}\right| \geq \left|3 - \frac{1}{3}\right| = \frac{8}{3}$

5. (a) Given $\left|z - \frac{1}{z}\right| = 1$ and $\left|z - \frac{1}{z}\right| \geq \left|z - \frac{1}{|z|}\right| \geq |z| - \frac{1}{|z|}$

$\Rightarrow |z|^2 - |z| - 1 \leq 0$

Roots of $|z|^2 - |z| - 1 = 0$ are $|z| = \frac{1 \pm \sqrt{5}}{2}$ but $|z| > 0$

(otherwise for $|z| = 0$, $1/z$ is not defined)

Hence $|z| = \frac{\sqrt{5} + 1}{2}$; which is the maximum value.

6. (b) $|z| = \left|z + \frac{1}{z} - \frac{1}{z}\right| \leq \left|z + \frac{1}{z}\right| + \frac{1}{|z|} = 2 + \frac{1}{|z|}$

$\Rightarrow |z|^2 - 2|z| - 1 \leq 0$; roots are $|z| = \frac{2 \pm 2\sqrt{2}}{2} = 1 \pm \sqrt{2}$ but $|z| > 0$ so $|z| \leq \sqrt{2} + 1$

Hence maximum distance of z from origin $\sqrt{2} + 1$

7. (a) $\left|z - \frac{4}{z}\right| = 2 \Rightarrow |z| - \frac{4}{|z|} \leq \left|z - \frac{4}{z}\right| = 2$

$\Rightarrow |z|^2 - 2|z| - 4 \leq 0$

Roots of equation are $|z| = 1 \pm \sqrt{5}$; but $|z| > 0$

So maximum value of $|z| = \sqrt{5} + 1$

8. (b) Given that $|z_1| = 2$, $|z_2| = 5$ and $|z_1 + z_2| = 3$

Now, $|4z_2 + 25z_1| = |z_1\bar{z}_1 z_2 + z_2\bar{z}_2 z_1|$

$= |z_1 z_2|\{|\bar{z} + \bar{z}_2|\} = (2)(5)(3) = 30$

9. (c) Given $|z_1 + z_2|^2 = |z_1|^2 + |z_2|^2$

i.e., $|z_1|^2 + |z_2|^2 + 2\text{Re}(z_1\bar{z}_2) = |z_1|^2 + |z_2|^2$

So $\text{Re}(z_1\bar{z}_2) = 0$

10. (d) Given $|z\omega| = 1$ and $Arg(z) - Arg\omega = \frac{\pi}{2}$

Using $Arg(\bar{z}) = -Arg(z)$ {for $\text{Arg}(z) \neq \pi$}

we get $Arg(\bar{z}) = -\frac{\pi}{2} - Arg\omega$

So Arg $\bar{z} + Arg\omega = -\frac{\pi}{2}$ i.e., $Arg(\bar{z}w) = -\frac{\pi}{2}$

$\therefore \frac{\bar{z}w}{|\bar{z}\,w|} = e^{-\frac{\pi}{2}i} = -i$

11. (b) Given: $|z_1 - 2z_2| = |2 - z_1\bar{z}_2|$ and $(|z_2| \neq 1)$

$\Rightarrow (z_1 - 2z_2)(\bar{z}_1 - 2\bar{z}_2) = (2 - z_1\bar{z}_2)(2 - \bar{z}_1 z_2)$

$\Rightarrow |z_1|^2 + 4|z_2|^2 - 2(z_1\bar{z}_2 + \bar{z}_1 z_2)$

$= \{4 - 2(z_1\bar{z}_2 + \bar{z}_1 z_2) + |z_1|^2|z_2|^2\}$

Gives $|z_1|^2 + 4|z_2|^2 = 4 + |z_1|^2\,|z_2|^2$

$\Rightarrow (|z_1|^2 + 4|z_2|^2) - |z_1|^2\,|z_2|^2 = 4$

$\Rightarrow |z_1|^2\,|z_2|^2 + 4 - |z_1|^2 - 4|z_2|^2 = 0$

or $(|z_1|^2 - 4)\,(|z_2|^2 - 1) = 0$

Since $|z_2|^2 \neq 1$ so $|z_1|^2 = 4$ or $|z_1| = 2$

12. (a) $\omega = \dfrac{z-1}{z+1}$; $|z| = 1$;

$$\overline{\omega} = \frac{\overline{z}-1}{\overline{z}+1} = \frac{\frac{1}{z}-1}{\frac{1}{z}+1} = \frac{1-z}{1+z} = -\left(\frac{z-1}{z+1}\right) = -\omega$$

$\therefore\quad \overline{\omega} = -\omega \qquad \Rightarrow$ ω is purely imaginary

$\Rightarrow$ Re(ω) = 0

13. (c) Given: ω = α + iβ (where β ≠ 0 and z ≠ 1)

and $\dfrac{\omega - \overline{\omega}z}{1-z}$ is purely real = k (say)

$\therefore\quad \omega - \overline{\omega}z = k - kz$

$\Rightarrow\ (k-\overline{\omega})z = k - w \qquad \Rightarrow\ z = \dfrac{k-\omega}{k-\overline{\omega}}$

i.e., $z = \dfrac{(k-\alpha)-i\beta}{(k-\alpha)+i\beta}$; since β ≠ 0 so |z| = 1 and z ≠ 1

14. (a) Let $\left|\dfrac{(1-z_1\overline{z}_2)}{(z_1-z_2)}\right| \le 1(\text{or} \ge 1)$

Squaring, we get $(1-z_1\overline{z}_2)(1-\overline{z}_1z_2) \le (\text{or}\ge)(z_1-z_2)(\overline{z}_1-\overline{z}_2)$

$\Rightarrow\ 1 + |z_1|^2|z_2|^2 - z_1\overline{z}_2 - \overline{z}_1z_2 \le (\text{or}\ge)|z_1|^2 + |z_2|^2 - z_1\overline{z}_2 - \overline{z}_1z_2$

Gives $1 + |z_1|^2|z_2|^2 - |z_1|^2 - |z_2|^2 \le 0$ or ≥ 0 or $(1 - |z_1|^2)(1 - |z_2|^2) \le 0$ or ≥ 0

Since $|z_1|, |z_2| \ne 1$

$(1 - |z_1|^2)(1 - |z_2|^2) < 0$ or > 0

Since $|z_2| - 1 > 0$ and $|z_1| - 1 < 0$

$\Rightarrow\ (1 - |z_2|^2)(1 - |z_1|^2) < 0$

$\therefore\quad \left|\dfrac{1-z_1\overline{z}_2}{z_1-z_2}\right| < 1$

15. (b) Using $|z_1 + z_2| \le |z_1| + |z_2|$, we get

$$\left|\frac{z_1\overline{z}_2 + \overline{z}_1z_2}{|z_1z_2|}\right| \le \frac{|z_1\overline{z}_2|}{|z_1z_2|} + \frac{|\overline{z}_1z_2|}{|z_1z_2|} = 2$$

16. (c) $|z - 2| = 2 \Rightarrow |(x-2) + iy)| = 2$

$\Rightarrow\ (x-2)^2 + y^2 = 4$ ....(i)

and $z(1-i) + \overline{z}(1+i) = 4$

$\Rightarrow\ (z+\overline{z}) - i(z-\overline{z}) = 4 \Rightarrow 2x - i(2iy) = 4$

$\Rightarrow\ x + y = 2$ ....(ii)

From (i) and (2), we get $y = \pm\sqrt{2}$; $x = 2 \mp \sqrt{2}$

$\therefore$ These are two points of intersection $(2-\sqrt{2}, \sqrt{2})\ \&\ (2+\sqrt{2}, \sqrt{-2})$.

Aliter: $|z - 2| = 2$ gives the boundary of a circle with radius 2 units centered at (2, 0)

The equation $= z(1-i) + \overline{z}(1+i) = 4$

Represents the line x + y = 2 which happens to be passing through (2, 0) (i.e., the centre the circle)

$\therefore$ 2 Points of intersection

17. (b) Given $\dfrac{1}{12}(z+\overline{z})^2 = 1 - \dfrac{1}{3}\left(|\overline{z}|^2\right)$

$\Rightarrow\ |z|^2 - 3 = \dfrac{1}{4}(z+\overline{z})^2 = \{\text{Re}(z)\}^2$ or $|z|^2 = 3 - \{\text{Re}(z)\}^2 \le 3$

Hence maximum value of $|z| = \sqrt{3}$

18. (b) Given $\dfrac{2z_1}{3z_2} = mi$ where m is a non-zero real number

Now $\left|\dfrac{z_1-z_2}{z_1+z_2}\right| = \dfrac{|z_2|\left\{\left|\frac{z_1}{z_2}-1\right|\right\}}{|z_2|\left\{\left|\frac{z_1}{z_2}+1\right|\right\}} = \left|\dfrac{\frac{3}{2}mi-1}{\frac{3}{2}mi+1}\right|$ gives $\left|\dfrac{z_1-z_2}{z_1+z_2}\right| = 1$

19. (c) Given $|z_1 + z_2| = |z_1 - z_2|$

Squaring both sides, we get $|z_1|^2 + |z_2|^2 + z_1\overline{z}_2 + \overline{z}_1z_2$

$= |z_1|^2 + |z_2|^2 - z_1\overline{z}_2 - \overline{z}_1z_2$

So, $2(z_1\overline{z}_2 + \overline{z}_1z_2) = 0$ *i.e.* $z_1\overline{z}_2 = -\overline{z}_1z_2$

$\Rightarrow\ \dfrac{z_1}{z_2} = -\overline{\left(\dfrac{z_1}{z_2}\right)}$ gives $\dfrac{z_1}{z_2}$ is purely imaginary.

20. (a) $|z_1| = |z_2| \Rightarrow |z_1|^2 = |z_2|^2$

$\Rightarrow\ z_1\overline{z}_1 = z_2\overline{z}_2 \Rightarrow \dfrac{\overline{z}_1}{z_2} = \dfrac{\overline{z}_2}{z_1}$ ....(i)

Now $\overline{\left(\dfrac{z_1+z_2}{z_1-z_2}\right)} = \dfrac{\overline{z}_1+\overline{z}_2}{\overline{z}_1-\overline{z}_2} = \left(\dfrac{1+\frac{\overline{z}_2}{\overline{z}_1}}{1-\frac{\overline{z}_2}{\overline{z}_1}}\right)$

$= \left(\dfrac{1+\frac{z_1}{z_2}}{1-\frac{z_1}{z_2}}\right) = -\left(\dfrac{z_1+z_2}{z_1-z_2}\right)$

$\Rightarrow\ \dfrac{z_1+z_2}{z_1-z_2}$ is purely imaginary

21. (c) $\dfrac{1}{2}\left\{\left|z_1 + z_2 + 2\sqrt{z_1z_2}\right| + \left|z_1 + z_2 - 2\sqrt{z_1.z_2}\right|\right\}$

$= \dfrac{1}{2}\left\{\left|\sqrt{z_1}+\sqrt{z_2}\right|^2 + \left|\sqrt{z_1}-\sqrt{z_2}\right|^2\right\}$

$= \dfrac{1}{2}\left\{2\left|\sqrt{z_1}\right|^2 + 2\left|\sqrt{z_2}\right|^2\right\} = |z_1| + |z_2|$

22. (b) Given $|z_1 + z_2| = |z_1| + |z_2|$

$\Rightarrow\ |z_1|^2 + |z_2|^2 + 2\,\text{Re}\,(z_1.\overline{z}_2) = |z_1|^2 + |z_2|^2 + 2|z_1||z_2|\cos(\theta_1 - \theta_2) = |z_1|^2 + |z_2|^2 + 2|z_1||z_2|$

$\Rightarrow\ \cos(\theta_1 - \theta_2) = 1$

$\Rightarrow\ \theta_1 - \theta_2 = 2n\pi;\ n \in \mathbb{Z}$

$\therefore\quad I_m\dfrac{z_1}{z_2} = 0$

Aliter: $|z_1 + z_2|$ = distance of the resultant of $z_1 + z_2$ from origin $|z_1| + |z_2|$ = sum of individual distances $|z_1 + z_2| = |z_1| + |z_2|$

$\Rightarrow$ $z_1 = pz_2$ where p is a positive real number

$\Rightarrow$ $\frac{z_1}{z_2}$ is a real number $\Rightarrow \text{Im}\left(\frac{z_1}{z_2}\right) = 0$

23. (d) Let $z = x + iy$ then $|z - i\,\text{Re}(z)| = |z - \text{Im}(z)|$

$\Rightarrow |x + (y - x)i|^2 = |(x - y) + iy|^2$

$\Rightarrow x^2 + (y - x)^2 = (x - y)^2 + y^2 \Rightarrow n^2 = y^2$

$\Rightarrow |x| = |y| \quad \Rightarrow \quad |\text{Re}(z)| = |\text{Im}(z)|$

24. (b) $|az_1 - bz_2|^2 + |bz_1 + az_2|^2 = a^2|z_1|^2 + b^2|z_2|^2 - 2ab\,\text{Re}(z_1\bar{z}_2)$
$+ b^2|z_1|^2 + a^2|z_2|^2 + 2ab\text{Re}(z_1\bar{z}_2) = (b^2 + a^2)(|z_1|^2 + |z_2|^2|$

25. (d) $|iz| + 3 - 4i| \le |iz| + |3 - 4i| = |z| + 5 \le 4 + 5 = 9$

26. (b) Given $\left|\frac{z_1 - iz_2}{z_1 + iz_2}\right| = \frac{|z_2|\left|\frac{z_1}{z_2} - i\right|}{|z_2|\left|\frac{z_1}{z_2} + i\right|} = 1$

$\Rightarrow \left|\frac{z_1}{z_2} - i\right| = \left|\frac{z_1}{z_2} + i\right| \quad \left(\frac{z_1}{z_2} - i\right)\left(\frac{\bar{z}_1}{z_2} + i\right) = \left(\frac{z_1}{z_2} + i\right)\left(\frac{\bar{z}_1}{z_2} - i\right)$

$\Rightarrow \left(\frac{z_1}{z_2}\right) = \overline{\left(\frac{z_1}{z_2}\right)}$ is purely real

27. (c) Given $|z - (3 - 2i)| = 4$

$\Rightarrow ||z| - |3 - 2i|| \le |z - (3 - 2i)| = 4$

$\Rightarrow -4 \le |z| - \sqrt{13} \le 4 \quad \Rightarrow \quad 4 - \sqrt{13} \le |z| \le 4 + \sqrt{13}$

$\therefore$ Maximum, $|z| = 4 + \sqrt{13}$ and minimum, $|z| = 4 - \sqrt{13}$

$\Rightarrow$ Maximum $|z|$ + minimum $|z| = 8$

28. (b) Given: $|z_1| = |z_2| + |z_1 - z_2|$

Observe that $z_1 = z_2$ is a solution, so $\text{Im}\left(\frac{z_1}{z_2}\right) = 0$

Aliter: $|z_1| - |z_2| = |z_1 - z_2| \Rightarrow \left|\frac{z_1}{z_2}\right| - 1 = \left|\frac{z_1}{z_2} - 1\right|$

$\Rightarrow$ $\frac{z_1}{z_2}$ and 1 are collinear $\Rightarrow$ $\frac{z_1}{z_2}$ is purely real

$\Rightarrow \text{Im}\left(\frac{z_1}{z_2} = 0\right)$

29. (c) $\because |z_1| + |z_2| \ge |z_1 - z_2|$

$\Rightarrow |z - (4 - 3i) + |z - (3 + 4i)| \ge |z - 4 + 3i - z - 3 + 4i)|$
$= 7\sqrt{2}$

30. (b) $|z| = 1$ for $z \in \mathbb{C}$ and $z_1 R z_2$ iff $|\text{Arg } z_1 - \text{Arg } z_2| = 2\pi/3$

On checking we find that $z_1 R z_1$ gives

$|\text{Arg } z_1 - \text{Arg } z_1| = 0 \ne 2\pi/3$

So relation is not reflective

Relation is symmetric as shown below

Since $z_1 R z_2$ gives $|\text{Arg } z_1 - \text{Arg } z_2| = 2\pi/3$

Also $z_2 R z_1$ as $|(\text{Arg } z_2 - \text{Arg } z_1)| = \frac{2\pi}{3}$

Now, if $z_1 R z_2$ gives $|\text{Arg } z_1 - \text{Arg } z_2| = 2\pi/3$ and $z_2 R z_3$ gives $|\text{Arg } z_2 - \text{Arg } z_3| = 2\pi/3$;

Clearly $|\text{Arz } z_1 - \text{Arz}_3| = 2\pi/3$ is not necessarily true

$\therefore$ Relation is symmetric.

TEXTUAL EXERCISE 6: (SUBJECTIVE)

1. Let $z = \frac{1}{(1-i)^2} - \frac{1}{(1+i)^2} = \frac{1}{-2i} - \frac{1}{2i}$

So $z = -\frac{1}{i} = i \quad \Rightarrow \quad Amp(z) = \frac{\pi}{2}$ and $|z| = 1$

2. (a) $z = -\sqrt{3} - i = 2\left(\frac{-\sqrt{3}}{2} - \frac{i}{2}\right) = 2e^{\frac{7\pi}{6}i}$

Hence $Amp(z) = \frac{7\pi}{6}$

(b) $z = \frac{1+i}{1-i\sqrt{3}} = \frac{(1-\sqrt{3}) + (\sqrt{3}+1)i}{4}$

So $Arg(z) = \tan^{-1}\frac{\sqrt{3}+1}{(-\sqrt{3}+1)}$

$= -\tan^{-1}(2 + \sqrt{3}) = -\frac{5\pi}{12} = -75°$

3. $z = \frac{(1+i)(1+\sqrt{3}i)^2}{(1-i)} \quad \Rightarrow \quad |z| = \frac{|1+i|}{|1-i|}\left(|1+i\sqrt{3}|\right)^2 = 4$

and $Amp\ z = \frac{\pi}{4} + 2\frac{\pi}{3} - \left(-\frac{\pi}{4}\right) = \frac{7\pi}{6}$

4. (i) $z = -1 - i \Rightarrow$ Principal $Arg\ (z) = -\frac{3\pi}{4}$

(ii) $z = -1 + \sqrt{3}i = 2\left\{-\frac{1}{2} + \frac{\sqrt{3}}{2}i\right\}$

$\Rightarrow \quad Arg\ z = \frac{2\pi}{6}$

5. $z_1 = 3i,\ z_2 = -1 - i \Rightarrow Arg\left(\frac{z_1}{z_2}\right) = Arg\ z_1 - Arg\ z_2$

$= \frac{\pi}{2} - \left(-\frac{3\pi}{4}\right) \pm 2n\pi = \frac{-3\pi}{4}$

8. Given $|(z_1 + z_2)| = |z_1 - z_2|$

Squaring gives $|z_1|^2 + |z_2|^2 + 2|z_1z_2| \cos(\theta_1 - \theta_2)$
$= |z_1|^2 + |z_2|^2 - 2|z_1z_2| \cos(\theta_1 - \theta_2)$

$\Rightarrow \cos(\theta_1 - \theta_2) = 0$ so $\theta_1 = \theta_2 \pm \frac{\pi}{2}$

i.e., $\text{Amp}(z_1) - \text{Amp}(z_2) = \pm\pi/2$

$\Rightarrow |\text{Amp}(z_1 - \text{Amp}(z_2)| = \pi/2$

9. Given $z+\sqrt{2}|z+1|+i=0$

Let $z = x + iy$ then $x+iy+\sqrt{2}\,|((1+x)+iy)|+i=0$

or $x+\sqrt{2}\sqrt{(x+1)^2+y^2}+(y+1)i=0+0i$

Gives $y = -1$ and $\sqrt{2}\sqrt{(x+1)^2+y^2}=-x$

(So $x < 0$) squaring, we get

$2(x^2 + 1 + 2x + 1) = x^2 \Rightarrow x^2 + 4x + 4 = 0$

i.e., $x = -2$. Hence $z = -2 - i$

Principal $Arg(z)=-\pi+\tan^{-1}\left(\frac{1}{2}\right)$

$=-\frac{\pi}{2}-\left\{\frac{\pi}{2}-\tan^{-1}\left(\frac{1}{2}\right)\right\}=\frac{\pi}{2}-\tan^{-1}(2)=-\left\{\frac{\pi}{2}+\tan^{-1}(2)\right\}$

TEXTUAL EXERCISE 6: (OBJECTIVE)

1. (b) Given Arg(z) = θ, then $Arg(\bar{z})=-\theta$

2. (b) Let the other number be w and Amp (z) = θ

Then Amp (z) + Amp (w) = π ⇒ Amp w = π – θ

∴ If $z = |r_1|e^{i\theta}$, then $w=|r_1|e^{(\pi-\theta)i}=-|r_1|(\cos\theta-i\sin\theta)$

$=-|r_1|\{(\cos(-\theta)+i\sin(-\theta))\}=-\bar{z}$

3. (c) $z_1.z_2.z_3.......=e^{i\left(\frac{\pi}{3}+\frac{\pi}{3^2}+\frac{\pi}{3^3}+...\right)}=e^{i\left(\frac{\pi/3}{1-1/3}\right)}=e^{i\pi/2}=i$

4. (a) Given $a = \cos\alpha + i\sin\alpha = e^{\alpha i}$ and $b = \cos\beta + i\sin\beta = e^{\beta i}$

⇒ $ab=e^{i(\alpha+\beta)}$. Hence $\frac{1}{2}\left(ab+\frac{1}{ab}\right)=\cos(\alpha+\beta)$

5. Given $C_r=\cos\left(\frac{r\pi}{10}\right)+i\sin\left(\frac{r\pi}{10}\right)=e^{\frac{r\pi}{10}i}$

⇒ $C_1.C_2.C_3.C_4=e^{\left(\frac{\pi}{10}+\frac{2\pi}{10}+\frac{3\pi}{10}+\frac{4\pi}{10}\right)i}=e^{\pi i}$

So Arg (z) = π; where $z = C_1.C_2.C_3.C_4$

6. (c) L.H.S. = (cosα + isinα) (cos2α + isin2α) ….. (cos nα + isin nα)

= cos(α + 2α + 3α +…..+ nα) + isin (α + 2α + 3α + ……….+ nα)

$=\cos\left\{\frac{n(n+1)}{2}\alpha\right\}+i\sin\left\{\frac{n(n+1)}{2}\alpha\right\}=1$ (given)

∴ $\frac{n(n+1)\alpha}{2}=2m\pi$; where $m \in$ integer set

So, $\alpha=\frac{4m\pi}{n(n+1)}$

7. (c) $z=\frac{(\sqrt{3}+i)^{4n+1}}{(-i)(\sqrt{3}+i)}=i(\sqrt{3}+i)^{4n}=i2^{4n}\left\{e^{\frac{4n\pi}{6}i}\right\}$

⇒ $Arg\ z=\frac{\pi}{2}+\frac{4n\pi}{6}$; for $n = 0$, $Arg(z)=\frac{\pi}{2}$

For $n=1$; $Arg(z)=\frac{7\pi}{6}$

For $n=2$; $Arg(z)=\frac{11\pi}{6}$

For $n=3$; $Arg=2\pi+\frac{\pi}{2}=\frac{5\pi}{2}$

8. (a) $|z + 1| = |z - 1|$ is the line $x = 0$

Now $Arg\left(\frac{z-1}{z+1}\right)=\frac{\pi}{4}$

Gives the part of the circle with radius √2 units centered at (0, 1) so $z = 0 + (1 + \sqrt{2})i$

9. (d) Given $a = e^{\alpha i}$; $e^{\beta i} = b$ and $c = e^{\gamma i}$

Also $\frac{b}{c}+\frac{c}{a}+\frac{a}{b}=1$ i.e., $e^{i(\beta-\gamma)}+e^{i(\gamma-\alpha)}+e^{i(\alpha-\beta)}=1$

So, cos(β – γ) + cos (γ – α) + cos(α – β) = 1

10. (b) Given $|z_1z_2|=\left|2\cos\frac{\pi}{4}-2i\sin\frac{\pi}{4}\right|$

So $|z_1z_2|=|\sqrt{2}-\sqrt{2}i|=2=|z_1\bar{z}_2|$

Also $Arg\left(\frac{z_1}{z_2}\right)=\frac{\pi}{3}$ or $Arg\left(\frac{z_1\bar{z}_2}{|z_2|^2}\right)=\frac{\pi}{3}$

Now $z_1^2\bar{z}_2^2=(z_1\bar{z}_2)^2=|z_1\bar{z}_2|^2e^{\frac{2\pi}{3}i}$

$=2^2\left\{-\frac{1}{2}+\frac{\sqrt{3}}{2}i\right\}=2(-1+\sqrt{3}i)$

11. (c) Let $z = x + iy$, then $|z| - z = 1 + 2i$ gives

$\sqrt{x^2+y^2}-x-iy=1+2i$. So $y = -2$

∴ $\sqrt{x^2+4}=x+1$ gives $x = 3/2$

Hence $z=\frac{3}{2}-2i$

12. (b) $z = \sin\alpha + i(1 - \cos\alpha) = 2\sin\frac{\alpha}{2}\left\{\cos\frac{\alpha}{2}+i\sin\frac{\alpha}{2}\right\}$

∴ $Amp(z)=\frac{\alpha}{2}$

13. (c) Let $z=\frac{3+i}{2-i}+\frac{3-i}{2+i}=\frac{10}{5}=2$

Hence Arg z = 0.

14. (a) Given $z = z_1.z_2.z_3 \ldots z_n$

∴ Arg z = Arg(z_1) + $2m_1\pi$ + Arg(z_2) + $2m_2\pi$ + ….. + Arg(z_n) + $2m_n\pi$

So arguments will differ by a multiple of 2π

15. (c) $|z| = 4$ and Arg $(z) = -\pi/4$

∴ $z=|z|\left\{\cos\left(-\frac{\pi}{4}\right)+i\sin\left(-\frac{\pi}{4}\right)\right\}$ gives

$z=4\left\{\frac{1}{\sqrt{2}}-\frac{i}{\sqrt{2}}\right\}=2\sqrt{2}\{1-i\}$

16. (d) Given that $|z_1 + z_2| = |z_1| + |z_2|$

$\Rightarrow z_1, z_2$ are collinear

$\Rightarrow \frac{z_1}{z_2}$ is real $\Rightarrow Arg\left(\frac{z_1}{z_2}\right) = 0$

$\Rightarrow$ Arg $(z_1) -$ Arg$(z_2) = 0$

TEXTUAL EXERCISE 7: (SUBJECTIVE)

1. Let $z = x + iy$

Given $|z|^2 - 2iz + 2c + 2ci = 0$ and $c \geq 0$

i.e., $x^2 + y^2 + 2y + 2c + (2c - 2x)i = 0$

Equating real and imaginary parts, we get

$2c = 2x$ or $x = c$ (where $c \geq 0$) and $x^2 + y^2 + 2y + 2c = 0$

Gives $c^2 + 2c + y^2 + 2y = 0$

$y^2 + 2y + 1 = 1 - c^2 - 2c \Rightarrow (y + 1)^2 = 1 - c^2 - 2c$

$\Rightarrow y = -1 \pm \sqrt{1 - c^2 - 2c}$; $1 - c^2 - 2c \geq 0$; $c \geq 0$

$\Rightarrow c \in [0, \sqrt{2} - 1]$

$\therefore z + i(-1 \pm \sqrt{1 - c^2 - 2c})$; $c \in [0, \sqrt{2} - 1]$

2. Let $z = x + iy$

Then $2|z|^2 + z^2 = 5 - i\sqrt{3}$ gives

$2(x^2 + y^2) + (x^2 - y^2 + 2xyi) = 5 - \sqrt{3}i$

So $3x^2 + y^2 = 5$ and $2xy = -\sqrt{3}$ so $y = -\frac{\sqrt{3}}{2x}$

Thus $3x^2 + \frac{3}{4x^2} = 5$ gives $x^2 = \frac{3}{2}, \frac{1}{6}$

Case (i): $x = \sqrt{\frac{3}{2}}, y = -\frac{1}{\sqrt{2}} \Rightarrow z = \sqrt{\frac{3}{2}} - \frac{i}{\sqrt{2}}$

Case (ii): $x = -\sqrt{\frac{3}{2}}, y = \sqrt{\frac{1}{2}} \Rightarrow z = -\sqrt{\frac{3}{2}} + \frac{i}{\sqrt{2}}$

Case (iii): $x = \frac{1}{\sqrt{6}}, y = -\frac{3}{\sqrt{2}} \Rightarrow z = \frac{1}{\sqrt{6}} - \frac{3}{\sqrt{2}}i$

Case (iv): $x = \frac{-1}{\sqrt{6}}, y = \frac{3}{\sqrt{2}} \Rightarrow z = \frac{-1}{\sqrt{6}} + \frac{3}{\sqrt{2}}i$

3. Given $z\,|z| + az + i = 0$ where $a > 0$

$\Rightarrow z\,(|z| + a) = -i$ means z is purely imaginary (as $|z| + a > 0$) with negative imaginary part

So let $z = iy$ (for $y < 0$), then

$y(|y| + a) = -1$ gives $-y^2 + ay = -1$

So $y^2 - ay - 1 = 0$ gives $y = \frac{a \pm \sqrt{a^2 + 4}}{2}$; but $y < 0$

so $y = \frac{a - \sqrt{a^2 + 4}}{2}$ $\therefore z = \frac{a - \sqrt{a^2 + 4}}{2}i$

4. (i) Let $z = re^{i}$; Then $\bar{z} = (r)e^{-i\theta}$ and $z^3 = r^3e^{3\theta i}$

Now $z^3 = -\bar{z}$ $\Rightarrow r^3e^{3\theta i} = (-r)e^{-\theta i}$

Clearly $r = 0, 1$. When $r = 0$, then $z = 0$

For $r = 1$, we get $e^{3\theta i} = (-1)e^{-i\theta} \Rightarrow e^{4\theta i} = e^{\pi i}$

So $4\theta = \pi, 3\pi, 5\pi, 7\pi$, i.e., $\theta = \frac{\pi}{4}, \frac{3\pi}{4}, \frac{5\pi}{4}, \frac{7\pi}{4}$

Hence $z = 0, e^{\frac{\pi}{4}i}, e^{\frac{3\pi}{4}i}, e^{\frac{5\pi}{4}i}, e^{\frac{7\pi i}{4}}$

Aliter: Let $z = x + iy$, then $z^3 = (x^3 + 3xy^2) + (3x^2y - y^3)i$

So $z^3 = -\bar{z}$ gives $x(x^2 - 3y^2) = -x$ and $y(3x^2 - y^2) = y$

Clearly one solution is $x = 0$, $y = 0$ *i.e* $z = 0 + 0i$

Other possibilities:

(i) $x \neq 0, y = 0$, gives $x^2 = -1$ so no solution

(ii) $y \neq 0, x = 0$, gives $y^2 = -1$ so no solution

(iii) $x \neq 0, y \neq 0$ then $x^2 - 3y^2 = -1$ and $3x^2 - y^2 = 1$

Gives $x^2 = \frac{1}{2}$ and $y^2 = \frac{1}{2} \Rightarrow x = \pm\frac{1}{\sqrt{2}}, y = \pm\frac{1}{\sqrt{2}}$

$\Rightarrow z = e^{\frac{\pi}{4}i}, e^{\frac{3\pi}{4}i}, e^{\frac{5\pi}{4}i}, e^{\frac{7\pi}{4}i} \Rightarrow z = 0, e^{\frac{\pi}{4}i}, e^{\frac{3\pi}{4}i}, e^{\frac{5\pi}{4}i}, e^{\frac{7\pi}{4}i}$

4. (ii) $z^2 = \bar{z}$

Let $z = re^{i\theta}$ then $z^2 = r^2e^{2\theta i}$ and $\bar{z} = re^{-i\theta}$

So $z^2 = \bar{z}$ gives $r^2 e^{2i\theta} = re^{-i\theta}$

$\therefore$ $r = 0, 1$ when $r = 0$, then $z = 0 + 0i$

When $r = 1$, then $e^{2\theta i} = e^{-i\theta} \Rightarrow e^{3\theta i} = 1$

$\Rightarrow 3\theta = 0, 2\pi, 4\pi$ i.e., $\theta = 0, \frac{2\pi}{3}, \frac{4\pi}{3}$

So $z = e^0, e^{\frac{2\pi}{3}i}, e^{\frac{4\pi}{3}i}$ respectively

Finally $z = 0, 1, \left(-\frac{1}{2} + \frac{\sqrt{3}}{2}i\right), \left(-\frac{1}{2} - \frac{\sqrt{3}}{2}i\right)$

5. Let $z = x + iy$, then $|z - 2| = 2\,|z - 1|$

$\Rightarrow (x - 2)^2 + y^2 = 4\,(x - 1)^2 + 4y^2$

Thus $3x^2 + 3y^2 - 4x = 0 \Rightarrow x^2 + y^2 = \frac{4}{3}x$

$\Rightarrow z.\bar{z} = \frac{4}{3}x = 12$ at $x = 9 \Rightarrow z.\bar{z} = 12$

6. $(a - ib)^{1/3} = (x^2 + iy^2)$

$\Rightarrow a - ib = (x^2 + iy^2)^3 = x^6 + i^3 y^6 + 3x^2 y^2 i\,(x^2 + iy^2)$

$\Rightarrow a - ib = (x^2)^3 - 3x^2 y^4 + (3x^4 y^2 - y^6)i$

$\therefore \frac{a}{x^2} = x^4 - 3y^4$ and $\frac{b}{y^2} = y^4 - 3x^4$

Hence $\frac{a}{x^2} + \frac{b}{y^2} = -2x^4 - 2y^4 = (-2)\,(x^4 + y^4)$.

7. $Arg(z - 1) = \frac{\pi}{4}$ Now, $z - \bar{z} = 2yi = 3i$,

so $y = \frac{3}{2} \Rightarrow x = \frac{5}{2}$. Hence $z = \frac{5}{2} + \frac{3}{2}i$

8. Given $2^{3/2}x^4 = 2^{3/2}\left\{\frac{\sqrt{3} - 1}{2\sqrt{2}} - \frac{\sqrt{3} + 1}{2\sqrt{2}}i\right\}$

Let $x = re^{i\theta}$, so $r^4 e^{4i\theta} = (1)\left\{\frac{\sqrt{3} - 1}{2\sqrt{2}} + \frac{\sqrt{3} + 1}{2\sqrt{2}}i\right\}$

gives r = 1 and $4\theta = \frac{5\pi}{12} = 75^o$

$\Rightarrow e^{i\theta} = \left(\cos\frac{5\pi}{12} + i\sin\frac{5\pi}{12}\right)^{1/4} \Rightarrow z = \pm e^{\frac{5\pi}{48}i}, \pm e^{\frac{19}{48}\pi i}$

TEXTUAL EXERCISE 7: (OBJECTIVE)

1. (a) Given: $iz^3 + z^2 - z + i = 0$
$\Rightarrow iz(z^2 + i) + (z^2 + i) = 0$
So, $(z^2 + i)(iz + 1) = 0$
Either $z^2 = -i$ or $z = i$ (so $|z| = 1$)

2. Given: $|z + 1| = z + 2 + 2i$
$\Rightarrow |(x + 1) + iy| = (x + 2) + i(y + 2)$
$\Rightarrow (x + 1)^2 + y^2 = (x + 2)^2 - (y + 2)^2 + 2i(x + 2)(y + 2)$
$\Rightarrow x^2 + 1 + 2x + y^2$
$= x^2 + 4 + 4x - y^2 - 4 - 4y + 2i(x + 2)(y + 2) = 0$
$\Rightarrow 2y^2 + 4y - 2x + 1 = 0$ and $(x + 2)(y + 2) = 0$
For $x = -2$; $2y^2 + 4y + 5 = 0$
Disc. = 16 – 40 < 0
$\therefore x \neq -2 \quad \Rightarrow y = -2$
$\therefore 8 - 8 - 2x + 1 = 0 \quad \Rightarrow x = 1/2$
$\therefore z = 1/2 - 2i = 1/2(1 - 4i)$

3. (d) $\left|\frac{z-12}{z-8i}\right| = \frac{5}{3}$ and $\left|\frac{z-4}{z-8}\right| = 1$
Now $|z - 4| = |z - 8|$
$\Rightarrow$ On squaring, we get $(x - 4)^2 + y^2 = (x - 8)^2 + y^2$
$\therefore x = 6$ putting in $\left|\frac{z-12}{z-8i}\right| = \frac{5}{3}$, gives $\left|\frac{(6-12)+iy}{6+(y-8)i}\right| = \frac{5}{3}$
On squaring, we get
$9(36 + y^2) = 25\{(36) + y^2 + 64 - 16y\}$
$\Rightarrow 16y^2 - 400y + (16)(136) = 0$ or $y^2 - 25y + 136 = 0$ gives $(y - 17)(y - 8) = 0$, so $y = 8, 17$
$\therefore z = 6 + 8i$ or $6 + 17i$ gives $|z_1| = 10, |z_2| = \sqrt{325} = 5\sqrt{13}$
Hence $\Sigma|z_n| = 10 + 5\sqrt{13}$

4. (a) $z^2 - z = 0$ gives $z(z - 1) = 0$, so $z = 0, 1$
$\therefore$ Number of solutions = 2

5. (c) $iz^2 - \bar{z} = 0$ gives $i(x^2 - y^2 + 2xyi) = x - iy$
So $x^2 - y^2 = -y$ and $-2xy = x$ or $x^2 - y(y - 1) = 0$
and $x(2y + 1) = 0$
(i) $x = 0, y = 0$
(ii) $x = 0, y = -1/2$ from $2y + 1 = 0$
Then $x^2 - y^2 = -y$ is not satisfied
(iii) $x \neq 0, y = -1/2$ then $x^2 + \frac{1}{2}\left(\frac{-3}{2}\right) = 0$
So $x = \pm\frac{\sqrt{3}}{2}$ then $z = \frac{\sqrt{3}}{2} - \frac{i}{2}$ or $\frac{-\sqrt{3}}{2} - \frac{i}{2}$
(iv) $x = 0, y = 1$
$\therefore$ Solution are $0, 1, \frac{\sqrt{3}}{2} - \frac{i}{2}, \frac{-\sqrt{3}}{2} - \frac{i}{2} \Rightarrow |z| = 0, 1$

6. (c) $|z - 3| = |z - 6| \Rightarrow x = \frac{9}{2}$
$|z| = 5$ gives, $x = \frac{9}{2}, y \pm \sqrt{\frac{19}{2}}$; Hence $z = \frac{9}{2} \pm \frac{\sqrt{19}}{2}i$

7. (d) Let $z = x + iy$, now $|z| = 1 \Rightarrow x^2 + y^2 = 1$
So $w = \frac{3}{2+z} = \frac{3}{(x+2)+iy} = \frac{3\{(x+2)-iy\}}{x^2+4x+4+y^2}$
So $w = a + ib = \frac{3}{(x+2)+iy} = \frac{3\{(x+2)-iy\}}{x^2+4x+4+y^2}$
and $|w| = \sqrt{\ell a - 3}$ gives $|w|^2 = \ell a - 3$; $|z| = 1$
i,e., $3\ell\left[\frac{x+2}{5+4x}\right] - 3 = \frac{9}{5+4x}$
So $\frac{(x+2)\ell}{5+4x} = \frac{3}{5+4x} + 1 = \frac{4(x+2)}{5+4x}$. Hence $\ell = 4$

8. (c) Given $a - ib = \frac{1-ix}{1+ix} = \frac{1-x^2-2xi}{1+x^2}$
$\Rightarrow a + ib = \frac{(1-x^2)}{1+x^2} + \frac{2xi}{(1+x^2)}$
Clearly, $(a + ib)(a - ib) = a^2 + b^2 = \frac{1-ix}{1+ix} \times \frac{1+ix}{1-ix} = 1$
Now, $a^2 - b^2 = (a - b)(a + b) = \frac{(1-x^2)^2 - 4x^2}{(1+x^2)^2}$
$= \frac{x^4+1-6x^2}{(x^2+1)^2} \neq 1$ (only possible when $x = 0$)
and $\frac{a-b}{a+b} = \frac{1-x^2-2x}{1-x^2+2x} \neq 1$
$\Rightarrow \left(\frac{a-b}{a+b} = 1\right)$ (Only possible when $x = 0$)
(or $b = 0$ and $a \neq 0$)

9. (b) Given $|5z - 1| = 5|z - 1/5| = 5|z - 2|$. Gives $x = 1.1$

10. (a) $|z| = |z - 2|$ gives x = 1
Now $|z + 1| + |z - 3| = 6$
$\Rightarrow |2 + iy| + |-2 + iy| = 6 \Rightarrow \sqrt{4+y^2} + \sqrt{4+y^2} = 6$
$\Rightarrow 2\sqrt{4+y^2} = 6 \qquad \Rightarrow \sqrt{4+y^2} = 3$
$\Rightarrow 4 + y^2 = 9 \qquad \Rightarrow y^2 = 5$
$\Rightarrow y = \pm\sqrt{5} \qquad \therefore z = 1 \pm \sqrt{5}i$

TEXTUAL EXERCISE 8: (SUBJECTIVE)

1. (a) Let $z = a + ib = 5 + 12i$, so $|z| = 13$ and $z^{1/2} = \pm(x + iy)$,
Then $x = \sqrt{\frac{|z|+a}{2}} = \sqrt{\frac{13+5}{2}} = 3$ and $y = \sqrt{\frac{|z|-a}{2}} = \sqrt{\frac{8}{2}} = 2$
Hence $z^{1/2} = \pm(3 + 2i)$

(b) $z = 8 - 6i$, so $|z| = 10$ (here $a > 0$ and $b < 0$)

$\therefore \quad x = \sqrt{\frac{|z|+a}{2}} = 3$ and $y = -\sqrt{\frac{|z|-a}{2}} = -1$

Hence $z^{1/2} = \pm \{3 - i\}$

(c) $z = 8 - 15i$, so $|z| = 17$ (here $a > 0$ and $b < 0$)

$\therefore \quad x = \sqrt{\frac{|z|+a}{2}} = \frac{5}{\sqrt{2}}$ and $y = -\sqrt{\frac{|z|-a}{2}} = -\frac{3}{\sqrt{2}}$

So, $z^{1/2} = \pm\frac{1}{\sqrt{2}}\{5-3i\}$

(d) $z = i$ or $z = 0 + I$, here $|z| = 1$

So, $x = \sqrt{\frac{1+0}{2}} = \frac{1}{\sqrt{2}}$ and $y = \sqrt{\frac{1-0}{2}} = \frac{1}{\sqrt{2}}$

$\Rightarrow \quad z^{1/2} = \frac{\pm 1}{\sqrt{2}}(1+i)$

(e) $z = -4 - 3i \qquad \Rightarrow \quad |z| = 5$ {as $b < 0$}

So, $x = \sqrt{\frac{|z|+a}{2}} = \frac{1}{\sqrt{2}}$ and $y = -\sqrt{\frac{|z|-a}{2}} = \frac{-3}{\sqrt{2}}$

Hence $z^{1/2} = \pm\frac{1}{\sqrt{2}}\{1-3i\} = \pm\frac{1}{\sqrt{2}}\{1-3i\}$

(f) $z = 2xy - i(x^2 - y^2)$, so $|z| = x^2 + y^2$; $x > y$

Let $z^{1/2} = \pm(a + ib)$

So $a = \sqrt{\frac{x^2+y^2+2xy}{2}} = \frac{(x+y)}{\sqrt{2}}$ and

$b = -\sqrt{\frac{x^2+y^2-2xy}{2}} = -\frac{|x-y|}{\sqrt{2}} = -\frac{(x-y)}{\sqrt{2}}$ as $x > y$

Hence $z^{1/2} = \pm\frac{1}{\sqrt{2}}\{(x+y)-(x-y)i\}$

(g) $z = (a^2 - 1) + 2ai = (a + i)^2$

So $z^{1/2} = \pm (a + i)$

Aliter: Let $z^{1/2} = x + iy$ and $|z| = a^2 + 1$, so

$x = \sqrt{\frac{|z|+(a^2-1)}{2}}$

i.e., $x = \sqrt{\frac{2a^2}{2}} = |a| = a$ as $a > 0$ and

$y = \sqrt{\frac{|z|-(a^2-1)}{2}} = 1$. Hence $z^{1/2} = \pm (a + i)$

2. Let $z = a + ib = -5 + 12i$

So $|z| = 13$ {here a < 0 and b > 0}

So $x = \sqrt{\frac{|z|+a}{2}} = 2$ and $y = \sqrt{\frac{|z|-a}{2}} = 3$

Hence $z^{1/2} = \pm (2 + 3i)$

3. $z = \frac{\sqrt{5+12i}+\sqrt{5-12i}}{\sqrt{5+12i}-\sqrt{5-12i}} = \frac{(5+12i)+(5-12i)+2\sqrt{169}}{(5+12i-5+12i)}$

$= \frac{10+26}{24i} = \frac{3}{2i} = \frac{-3i}{2} = 0 - \frac{3}{2}i$

4. $z = 7 - 30\sqrt{2}i \Rightarrow \quad |z| = \sqrt{1849} = 43$ (here $a > 0$ and $b < 0$)

So $x = \sqrt{\frac{|z|+a}{2}} = \sqrt{\frac{43+7}{2}} = 5$ and $y = -\sqrt{\frac{43-7}{2}} = -\frac{6}{\sqrt{2}}$

Hence $z^{1/2} = \pm\{5 - 3\sqrt{2}i\}$

Case (i): Now a quadratic equation with one root as $5 - 3\sqrt{2}i$ will be $x^2 - (5 - 3\sqrt{2}i + 5 + 3\sqrt{2}i) + (25 + 9 \times 2) = 0$ that is $x^2 - 10x + 43 = 0$

Case (ii): One root as $-5 - 3\sqrt{2}i$ and other as $-5 - 3\sqrt{2}i$ will be $x^2 + 10x + 43 = 0$

Hence the required quadratic equation will be $x^2 \pm 10x + 43 = 0$

5 Proceeding similarly as in above question $z^{1/2} = \pm (1 + 4\sqrt{3}i)$ The quadratic equation is either $x^2 - 2x + 49 = 0$ or $x^2 + 2x + 49 = 0$

6. $z = \sqrt{i} - \sqrt{-i}$. We know that $(1 + i)^2 = 2i$

So $\sqrt{i} = \pm\frac{1}{\sqrt{2}}(1+i)$ and similarly $\sqrt{-i} = \pm\frac{1}{\sqrt{2}}(1-i)$

$\Rightarrow \quad z = \pm i\sqrt{2}, \pm\sqrt{2}i$

7. (a) $z^3 = 64$, then $z = (64)^{1/3} \Rightarrow z = 4, 4\omega, 4\omega^2$

(b) $z = -27 \qquad \Rightarrow \quad z = -3, -3\omega, -3\omega^2$

8. (a) $z = (1 + \omega + \omega^2 - 2\omega^2)^6 \Rightarrow z = (-2)^6\,\omega^{12} = 64$

(b) Rearrangement gives $z_1 = (-2\omega^2)^3$ and $z_2 = (-2\omega)^3$

So $z_1 = (-2)^3\,\omega^6 = -8$ and $z_2 = (-2)^3\,\omega^3 = -8$

Hence $(1 + \omega - \omega^2)^3 = (1 - \omega + \omega^2)^3 = -8$

(c) Let $z_1 = (2 + 5\omega + 2\omega^2)^6 = (2 + 2\omega + 2\omega^2 + 3\omega)^6 = 3^6\,\omega^6 = 729$

Similarly $z_2 = (2 + 5\omega^2 + 2\omega)^6 = (2 + 2\omega^2 + 2\omega + 3\omega^2)^6 = (3\omega^2)^6 = 3^6\omega^{12} = 729$

Hence $(2 + 5\omega + 2\omega^2) = (2 + 5\omega^2 + 2\omega)^6 = 729$

(d) Let $z = (1 + \omega)^3 - (1 + \omega^2)^3 = (-\omega^2)^3 - (-\omega)^3 = -\omega^6 + \omega^3 = -1 + 1 = 0$

(e) Let $z = (3 + 3\omega + 5\omega^2)^3 - (2 + 4\omega + 2\omega^2)^3 = (3 + 3\omega + 3\omega^2 + 2\omega^2)^3 - (2 + 2\omega + 2\omega^2 + 2\omega)^3$

$= (2\omega^2)^3 - (2\omega)^3 = 8\omega^6 - 8\omega^3 = 8 - 8 = 0$

(f) Let $z = (2 - \omega)(2 - \omega^2)(2 - \omega^{10})(2 - \omega^{11}) = \{(2 - \omega)(2 - \omega^2)\}^2 = (4 + 1 - 2\omega - 2\omega^2)^2$

$= (7 - 2 - 2\omega - 2\omega)^2 = 49$

9. Let $f(x) = (x - 1)^n - (x^n + 1)$

Observe that $f(0) = 1^n - 1 = 0$

Similarly $f(\omega) = (1 + \omega)^n - (\omega^n + 1) = (-\omega^2)^n - 1 - \omega^n = -\{1 + \omega^n + \omega^{2n}\}$

Since n is odd but not a multiple of 3

So $f(\omega) = 0$

Similarly $f(\omega^2) = (-\omega)^n - (\omega^{2n} + 1) = -\{1 + \omega^n + \omega^{2n}\}$

So $f(\omega^2) = 0$

It shows that x, $(x - \omega)$, $(x - \omega^2)$ are the factors of $(x + 1)^n - (x^n + 1)$

$\Rightarrow \quad x(x - \omega)(x - \omega)^2 = x^3 + x^2 + x$ divides $(x + 1)^n - (x^n + 1)$

10. To prove $z = \left(\frac{-1+\sqrt{3}i}{2}\right)^{29} + \left(\frac{-1-\sqrt{3}i}{2}\right)^{29} = -1$

Observe that $\frac{-1+\sqrt{3}i}{2} = e^{\frac{2\pi}{3}i}$ and

$\frac{-1-\sqrt{3}i}{2} = e^{-\frac{2\pi}{3}i} |z-(3-i)| = 3$

$\Rightarrow z = e^{\frac{58}{3}\pi i} + e^{-\frac{58}{3}\pi i} = e^{\left(20\pi - \frac{2\pi}{3}\right)i} + e^{\left(-20\pi + \frac{2\pi}{3}\right)i}$

$= e^{-\frac{2\pi}{3}i} + e^{\frac{2\pi}{3}i} = \frac{-1-\sqrt{3}i}{2} + \frac{-1+\sqrt{3}i}{2} = -1$

11. Let $\alpha = \omega$ and $\beta = \omega^2$ then $(1-\alpha)(1-\beta)(1-\alpha^2)(1-\beta^2)$
$= (1-\alpha)^2(1-\beta)^2\{(1+\alpha)(1+\beta))\} = (1-\omega)^2(1-\omega^2)^2\{(1+\omega)(1+\omega^2)\}$
$= (1-\omega)^2(1-\omega^2)^2(-\omega^2)(-\omega) = \{(1-\omega)(1-\omega^2)^2\}(1)$
$= \{1+\omega^3-\omega-\omega^2\}^2 = (1+1+1)^2 = 9$

12. (a) $x^3 - y^3 = (x-y)\{x^2+y^2+xy\} = (x-y)\{\omega^3x^2 - (\omega+\omega^2)(xy) + y^2\} = (x-y)\{(\omega x - y)(\omega^2 x - y)\}$

(b) $a^3 + b^3 + c^3 - 3abc = (a+b+c)\{a^2+b^2+c^2) - (ab+bc+ca)\}$
$= (a+b+c)\{a^2 + \omega^3 b^2 + \omega^3 c^2 + (\omega+\omega^2)(ab+bc+ca)\}$
$= (a+b+c)\{(a+b\omega+c\omega^2)(a+b\omega^2+c\omega)\}$

13. (a) Given $x = a+b$; $y = a\omega + b\omega^2$ and $z = a\omega^2 + b\omega$
$\Rightarrow x^2+y^2+z^2 = (a+b)^2 + \omega^2\{a^2 + b^2\omega^2 + 2ab\omega\} + \omega^2\{a^2\omega^2 + b^2 + 2ab\omega\}$
$= a^2+b^2+2ab + (\omega^2+\omega^4)(a^2+b^2) + 4ab\omega^3 = (a^2+b^2) - (a^2+b^2) + 6ab = 6ab$

(b) $xyz = (a+b)\{(a\omega + b\omega^2)(a\omega^2 + b\omega)\} = (a+b)\{a^2\omega^3 + b^2\omega^3 + ab(\omega^2+\omega^4)\}$
$= (a+b)\{a^2+b^2-ab\} = a^3+b^3$

14. Given α, β, γ are the cube roots of p(where $p<0$), so without loss of generality
We take $\alpha = p^{1/3}$, $\beta = p^{1/3}\omega$ and $\gamma = p^{1/3}\omega^2$,

then $\frac{x\alpha + y\beta + z\gamma}{x\beta + y\gamma + z\alpha} = \frac{p^{1/3}\{x + y\omega + z\omega^2\}}{p^{1/3}\omega\{x+y\omega+z\omega^2\}} = \frac{1}{\omega} = \omega^2$

Similarly we can put other values for α, β, γ but the result will be the same.

15. Given: $x^3 - 3x^2 + 3x + 7 = 0$
$\Rightarrow x^3 - 3x^2 + 3x - 1 = -8$
So $(x-1)^3 = (-2)^3$ {gives $x = -1, 1-2\omega, 1-2\omega^2$}
Or Let $x = \alpha, \beta, \gamma$ be its roots,
then $(\alpha-1)(\beta-1)(\gamma-1) = (-2)^3 = -8$

16. $z^3 + 1 + 2z(z+1) = 0$
So $(z+1)\{z^2 + 1 - z + 2z\} = 0$
Gives $z = -1, z = \omega, \omega^2$
Observe that $z = -1$ does not satisfy $z^{1985} + z^{100} + 1 = 0$, {as $(-1)^{1985} + (-1)^{100} + 1 = 1$}
Now $z = \omega$ gives $\omega^{1985} + \omega^{100} + 1 = \omega^2 + \omega + 1 = 0$
Similarly $z = \omega^2$ gives $\omega^{3970} + \omega^{200} + 1 = \omega + \omega^2 + 1 = 0$
Hence $z = \omega, \omega^2$ satisfy both the equations

17. Let $z^6 = 1 \quad \Rightarrow \quad z = e^{0i}, e^{\frac{\pi}{3}i}, e^{\frac{2\pi}{3}i}, e^{\pi i}, e^{\frac{4\pi}{3}i}, e^{\frac{5\pi}{3}i}$

Observe that $e^{\frac{2\pi}{3}i}$ and $e^{\frac{4\pi}{3}i}$ are also cube roots of unity.

18. Let $z^{10} = 1$, then $z = e^{\frac{2k\pi}{10}i}$
Where $k = 0, 1, 2, \ldots, 9$ (also $z^{10} = 1$)
We observe that the roots are in G.P., with common ratio $r = e^{\frac{\pi}{5}i}$

$\Rightarrow z_p z_q = e^{\frac{(p-1)\pi}{5}i} e^{\frac{(q-1)\pi}{5}i} = e^{\left(\frac{p+q-2}{5}\right)i}$

Now, $0 \le p, q \le 9 \quad \Rightarrow 0 \le p+q \le 18$
$\Rightarrow -2 \le p+q-2 \le 16$

Now, if $p+q-2 \in [0, 9]$, then $e^{\frac{(p+q-2)i}{5}}$ is a root of unity. So, Let $p+q-2 \in [10, 16]$
$\Rightarrow p+q-2 = 10+n$; where $0 \le n \le 6$,

then $e^{i\frac{(p+q-2)}{5}\pi} = e^{i\left(2+\frac{n}{5}\right)\pi} = e^{i2\pi}.e^{i\frac{n}{5}\pi} = e^{i\frac{n}{5}\pi}; n \in [0,6]$

Which is a tenth roots of unity.
If $p+q-2 \in [-2, 0]$ then $p+q-2 = -10+n$, where $n \in \{8, 9, 10\}$

$\therefore \quad e^{i\frac{(p+q-2)}{5}\pi} = e^{i\left(-2+\frac{n}{5}\right)\pi} = e^{-2\pi i}.e^{n/5\pi i} = 1.e^{\frac{n}{5}\pi i}; n \in \{8, 9, 10\}$

$\Rightarrow$ Tenth roots of unity

19. (a) Let $z^n = 1$, then $e^{\frac{2k\pi}{n}i}$; where $k = 0, 1, 2, 3, \ldots, (n-1)$
Let $z_1, z_2, z_3, \ldots, z_n$ the roots respectively when $k = 0, 1, 2, \ldots (n-1)$

$\Rightarrow z_1^p + z_2^p + z_3^p + \ldots z_n^p = \sum_{k=0}^{(n-1)} \frac{2kp\pi}{e^n} i,$

Which is a G.P. with C.R. $= e^{\frac{2p\pi}{n}i}$

$\therefore \quad \text{sum} = \left(\frac{1 - e^{2p\pi i}}{1 - e^{\frac{2p\pi}{n}i}}\right) = \frac{1-1}{(\ne 0)} = 0$

$\because$ P is not a multiple n. If p is a multiple of n the $z_i^p = z_i^{nk} = (z_i^n)^k = (1)^k = 1 \therefore \sum_{i=1}^{n} z_i^p = \sum_{i=1}^{n} 1 = n$

(b) Let $z = (1)^{1/7}$ or $z^7 = 1$

So $z = e^{\frac{2k\pi}{7}i}$ where $k = 0, 1, 2, 3, 4, 5, 6$ ..... (and $z^7 = 1$)

Let $z_1 = 1$, $z_2 = e^{\frac{2\pi}{7}i}, z_3 = e^{\frac{4\pi}{7}i}$ ....

When these roots are raised to power then $z_1^n + z_2^n + z_3^n + \ldots + z_7^n$

$= e^i + e^{\frac{2\pi n}{7}i} + e^{\frac{4\pi n}{7}i} + \ldots + e^{\frac{12\pi n}{7}i} = \frac{1 - e^{i2\pi n}}{1 - e^{\frac{i2\pi n}{7}}}$

Which shows that the sum will be zero when $n = 7m$, then $z_1^n = z_2^n = z_3^n \ldots = z_7^n$

$\Rightarrow z_1^n + z_2^n + z_3^n + \ldots z_1^n = 7$

20. (a) Given $1, \alpha_1, \alpha_2, \ldots, \alpha_{n-1}$ are the n, n^{th} roots of unity, then $z^n = 1$ or $z^n - 0.z^{n-1} + 0\, z^{n-2} + \ldots + 0z + 1\} = (z-1)(z-\alpha_1)(z-\alpha_2) \ldots (z-\alpha_{n-1}) = 0$

So $(z-\alpha_1)(z-\alpha_2) \ldots (z-\alpha_{n-1}) = z^{n-1} + z^{n-2} + \ldots + z + 1$

putting $z = 1$, we get $(1-\alpha_1)(1-\alpha_2)(1-\alpha_3) \ldots (1-\alpha_{n-1}) = n$

(b) Put $z = 2$ in $(z-\alpha_1)(z-\alpha_2)(z-\alpha_3) \ldots (z-\alpha_{n-1}) = 1 + z + z^2 + \ldots z^{n-1}$

$\Rightarrow (2-\alpha_1)(2-\alpha_2)(2-\alpha_3) \ldots (2-\alpha_{n-1}) = 1 + 2 + 2^2 + \ldots + 2^{n-1}$

So $\prod_{k=1}^{n-1}(2-\alpha_k) = \dfrac{1(2^n-1)}{(2-1)} = 2^n - 1$

(c) $\prod_{k=1}^{n-1}(m-\alpha_k) = \dfrac{1(m^n-1)}{m-1} = \dfrac{m^n-1}{m-1} \quad (m \neq 1)$

(d) Observe that $(-1-\alpha_1)(-1-\alpha_2)(-1-\alpha_3) \ldots (-1-\alpha_{n-1}) = 1 + (-1) + (-1)^2 + (-1)^3 + \ldots + (-1)^{n-1}$

Or $(-1)^{n-1} \prod_{k=1}^{n-1}(1+\alpha_k) = \dfrac{1\{(-1)^n - 1\}}{1-(-1)} = \dfrac{(-1)^n - 1}{2}$

$\Rightarrow \prod_{k=1}^{n-1}(1+\alpha_k) \begin{cases} = 0 \text{ if } n \text{ is even} \\ = 1 \text{ if } n \text{ is odd} \end{cases}$

21. Let $z = \dfrac{(\cos 3\theta - i\sin 3\theta)^6 (\sin\theta - i\cos\theta)^3}{(\cos 2\theta + i\sin 2\theta)^5}$

$= \dfrac{(e^{-18\theta i})(-i)^3(e^{3\theta i})}{e^{10\theta i}} = ie^{-25\theta i}$

$= i\{\cos 25\theta - i\sin 25\theta\} = \sin 25\theta + i\cos 25\theta$

22. By Demoiver's Theorem:

$(\text{cis } m\theta)^n = (\cos m\theta + i\sin m\theta)^n = (e^{m\theta i})^n = e^{imn\theta} = \text{cis}(mn\theta) = (\text{cis}n\theta)^m = (\text{cis}\theta)^{mn}$; Now let

$z = \dfrac{(\cos 3\theta + i\sin 3\theta)^4 (\cos 4\theta - i\sin 4\theta)^5}{(\cos 4\theta + i\sin 4\theta)^3 (\cos 5\theta + i\sin 5\theta)^{-4}} = \dfrac{(e^{12\theta i})(e^{-20\theta i})}{(e^{12\theta i})(e^{-20\theta i})} = 1$

23. Observe that $1 + \cos\theta + i\sin\theta = 2\cos^2\theta/2 + 2i\sin\theta/2\,.\cos\theta/2$

$= 2\cos\dfrac{\theta}{2}\left\{\cos\dfrac{\theta}{2} + i\sin\dfrac{\theta}{2}\right\} = 2\cos\dfrac{\theta}{2}.e^{\frac{\theta}{2}i}$

Similarly $1 + \cos\theta - i\sin\theta = 2\cos\dfrac{\theta}{2}.e^{-\frac{\theta}{2}i}$

Hence $(1 + \cos\theta + i\sin\theta)^n + (1 + \cos\theta - i\sin\theta)^n$

$= 2^n\cos^n\dfrac{\theta}{2}\left\{e^{\frac{n\theta}{2}i} + e^{-\frac{n\theta}{2}i}\right\} = 2^n.\cos^n\dfrac{\theta}{2}\left(2\cos\dfrac{n\theta}{2}\right)$

$= 2^{n+1}\cos^n\left(\dfrac{\theta}{2}\right).\cos\left(\dfrac{n\theta}{2}\right)$

24. (a) Let $z = a + ib = re^{\theta i}$ so $r = \sqrt{a^2+b^2}$ and $\theta = \tan^{-1}\left(\dfrac{b}{a}\right)$

Hence $(a+ib)^{m/n} + (a-ib)^{m/n} = r^{\frac{m}{n}}.e^{\frac{m\theta}{n}i} + r^{\frac{m}{n}}.e^{\frac{-m\theta}{n}i}$

$= r^{m/n}\left\{2\cos\dfrac{m\theta}{n}\right\} = 2(a^2+b^2)^{\frac{m}{2n}}\cos\left(\dfrac{m}{n}\tan^{-1}\dfrac{b}{a}\right)$

(b) $\left[\dfrac{1+\sin\alpha + \cos\alpha}{1+\sin\alpha - \cos\alpha}\right] \left[\dfrac{1+\cos\left(\frac{\pi}{2}-\alpha\right) + \sin\left(\frac{\pi}{2}-\alpha\right)}{1+\cos\left(\frac{\pi}{2}-\alpha\right) - \sin\left(\frac{\pi}{2}-\alpha\right)}\right]$

$= \left[\dfrac{2\cos^2\left(\frac{\pi}{4}-\frac{\alpha}{2}\right) + i2.\sin\left(\frac{\pi}{4}-\frac{\alpha}{2}\right)\cos\left(\frac{\pi}{4}-\frac{\alpha}{2}\right)}{2\cos^2\left(\frac{\pi}{4}-\frac{\alpha}{2}\right) - i2\sin\left(\frac{\pi}{4}-\frac{\alpha}{2}\right)\cos\left(\frac{\pi}{4}-\frac{\alpha}{2}\right)}\right]^n$

$= \left[\dfrac{e^{i\left(\frac{\pi}{4}-\frac{\alpha}{2}\right)}}{e^{-i\left(\frac{\pi}{4}-\frac{\alpha}{2}\right)}}\right]^n = e^{i\left(\frac{n\pi}{2}-\alpha\right)} = \cos\left(\dfrac{n\pi}{2}-\alpha\right) + i\sin\left(\dfrac{n\pi}{2}-\alpha\right)$

25. (a) Given $x + \dfrac{1}{x} = 2\cos\theta$

$\Rightarrow x^2 - 2\cos\theta\, x + \sin^2\theta + \cos^2\theta = 0$ or $(x - \cos\theta)^2 = (\pm\, i\sin\theta)^2$

$\Rightarrow x = e^{\theta i}$ or $e^{-\theta i}$

Similarly $y = e^{\phi i}$ or $e^{-\phi i}$; Taking $x = e^{i\theta}$ and $y = e^{i\phi}$

We have, $x^m y^n + \dfrac{1}{x^m y^n} = e^{m\theta i}.e^{n\phi i} + \dfrac{1}{e^{m\theta i}.e^{n\phi i}}$

So $x^m y^n + \dfrac{1}{x^m y^n} = e^{(m\theta + n\phi)i} + e^{-(m\theta + n\phi)i} = 2\cos(m\theta + n\phi)$

(b) Similarly $\dfrac{x^m}{y^n} + \dfrac{y^n}{x^m} = \dfrac{e^{m\theta i}}{e^{n\phi i}} + \dfrac{e^{n\phi i}}{e^{m\theta i}} = e^{(m\theta - n\phi)i} + e^{-(m\theta - n\phi)i}$

$= 2\cos(n\theta - n\phi)$

26. Given $\cos\theta = a$ and $\sin\theta = b$

$\Rightarrow a^2 + b^2 = 1$

$\Rightarrow z = a + ib = e^{i\theta}$ or $(a+ib)^3 = e^{3\theta i} = \cos 3\theta + i\sin 3\theta$

$\Rightarrow \cos 3\theta = a^3 - 3b^2 = a^3 - 3a(1-a^2) = 4a^3 - 3a$

Similarly $\sin 3\theta = 3a^2b - b^3 = 3(1-b^2)b - b^3 = 3b - 4b^3$

TEXTUAL EXERCISE 8: (SUBJECTIVE)

1. (b) Let $z = -7 - 24i$ and $z^{1/2} = \pm(a + ib)$

$\Rightarrow a^2 - b^2 = -7$ and $2ab = -24$

Hence $a = 3$, $b = -4 \Rightarrow z^{1/2} = \pm(3 - 4i)$

2. (b) Given α, β are the imaginary cube roots of unity so let $\alpha = \omega$ and $\beta = \omega^2$, then $\alpha^4 + \beta^4 + \dfrac{1}{\alpha\beta}$

$= \omega^4 + \omega^8 + \dfrac{1}{\omega^3} = 1 + \omega + \omega^2 = 0$

3. (c) Given: $\omega \neq 1$ and $A + B\omega = (1+\omega)^7$

$\Rightarrow A + B\omega = (1 + \omega + \omega^2 - \omega^2)^7 = (-1)^7\omega^{14} = -\omega^2$

So $A + B\omega = 1 + \omega$; Hence $A = 1$, $B = 1$

4. (c) Sin $\{(w^{10} + w^{23})\pi - \pi/4\}$

$= \sin\left\{(w + w^2)\pi - \dfrac{\pi}{4}\right\} = \sin\left(-\pi - \dfrac{\pi}{4}\right) = \dfrac{1}{\sqrt{2}}$

5. (d) $(1 + w - w^2)^7 = (1 + w + w^2 - 2w^2)^7 = (-2)^7 w^{14} = -128w^2$

6. (a) $\frac{1}{2}+\frac{3}{8}+\frac{9}{32}+\frac{27}{128}+ \ldots + = \left(\frac{1}{2}\right)\frac{1}{\left(1-\frac{3}{4}\right)}$

$\Rightarrow$ Given $= \omega + \omega^{\left(\frac{1}{2}\right)\frac{1}{\left(1-\frac{3}{4}\right)}} = \omega + \omega^2 = -1$

7. (a) $(1 + 2\omega + \omega^2)^{3n} - (1 + \omega + 2\omega^2)^{3n} = (1 + \omega + \omega^2 + \omega)^{3n} - (1 + \omega + \omega^2 + \omega^2)^{3n} = \omega^{3n} - (\omega^2)^{3n} = 1 - 1 = 0$

8. (a) $(a + b)(a + b\omega)(a + \omega^2 b) = (a + b)\{a^2 + ab(\omega + \omega^2) + b^2\omega^3\} = (a + b)(a^2 + b^2 - ab) = a^3 + b^3$

9. (d) $225 + (3\omega + 8\omega^2)^2 + (3\omega^2 + 8\omega)^2 = 225 + \omega^2\{(3 + 8\omega)^2 + (3\omega + 8)^2\}$
$= 225 + \omega^2\{73 + 73\omega^2 + 73\omega + 23\omega\} = 225 + 23 = 248$

10. (a) $(1 + w^2 + w - 3w)^6 = (-3)^6 w^6 = 729$

11. (d) $\omega^{99} + \omega^{100} + \omega^{101} = 1 + \omega + \omega^2 = 0$

12. (d) $\frac{a+b\omega+c\omega^2}{c+a\omega+b\omega^2}+\frac{a+b\omega+c\omega^2}{b+c\omega+a\omega^2}$

$= \frac{1}{\omega}\cdot\frac{a+b\omega+c\omega^2}{c\omega^2+a+b\omega}+\frac{1}{\omega^2}\cdot\frac{a+b\omega+c\omega^2}{b\omega+a+c\omega^2} = \omega^2(1)^2 + \omega(1) = -1$

13. (d) Arg $(i\omega)$ = Arg (i) + $Arg\ \omega = \frac{\pi}{2}+\frac{2\pi}{3}$

Similarly $Arg(i\omega^2) = \frac{\pi}{2}+\frac{4\pi}{3}$

$\Rightarrow$ Arg $(i\omega)$ + Arg $(i\omega^2) = \pi + 2\pi = 3\pi$

14. (d) Let β are the roots of $x^2 - x + 1 = 0$
So let $\alpha = -\omega$ and $\beta = -\omega^2$
Hence $\alpha^{2009} + \beta^{2009} = (-\omega)^{2009} + (-\omega^2)^{2009} = -\omega^2 - \omega = 1$

15. (b) $(z^3 + 1) + 2z(z + 1) = 0$
Gives $(z + 1)\{z^2 + 1 - z + 2z\} = (z + 1)(z^2 + 1 + z) = 0$
and the roots are $z = -1, \omega, \omega^2$
Observe that for $z = -1$, $z^{100} + z^{32} + 1 = 3$
For $z = \omega$, $z^{100} + z^{32} + 1 = \omega + \omega^2 + 1 = 0$ and similarly for $z = \omega^2$; $z^{100} + z^{32} + 1 = \omega^2 + \omega + 1 = 0$
Hence $z = \omega$ and ω^2 are the common roots
$\Rightarrow \omega + \omega^2 = -1$

16. (d) Given $1, \omega, \omega^2, \omega^3, \ldots, \omega^{n-1}$ are the n, n^{th} roots of unity
So $z^n - 1 = 0$ and $(z - \omega)(z - \omega^2)(z - \omega^3) \ldots (z - \omega^{n-1})$
$= z^{n-1} + z^{n-2} + z^{n-3} + \ldots + z + 1$
Hence $(2 - \omega)(2 - \omega^2)(2 - \omega^3) \ldots (2 - \omega^{n-1}) = 1 + 2 + 2^2 + 2^3 + \ldots + 2^{n-1}$

$= \frac{2^n - 1}{2 - 1} = 2^n - 1 = {}^nC_1 + {}^nC_1 + {}^nC_2 + {}^nC_3 + \ldots + {}^nC_n$

17. (d) Given: $\frac{1}{a+\omega}+\frac{1}{b+\omega}+\frac{1}{c+\omega} = 2\omega^2 = \frac{2}{\omega}$ and

$\frac{1}{a+\omega^2}+\frac{1}{b+\omega^2}+\frac{1}{c+\omega^2} = 2\omega = \frac{2}{\omega^2}$

From the equation $\frac{1}{a+x}+\frac{1}{b+x}+\frac{1}{c+x}=\frac{2}{x}$

We get, $x^3 - 0x^2 - (\Sigma ab)x - 2abc = 0$ and ω, ω^2 are its roots let the third root be α so $\alpha + \omega + \omega^2 = 0$

$\Rightarrow \alpha = 1 \quad \Rightarrow \frac{1}{1+a}+\frac{1}{1+b}+\frac{1}{1+c}=\frac{2}{1}=2$

18. (d) Given $z^2 + z + 1 = 0 \Rightarrow z = \omega, \omega^2$
As $n \neq 3m$ so $n = 3m + 1$ or $3m + 2$
Hence $z^n + z^{2n} = \omega^n + \omega^{2n} = \omega + \omega^2 = -1$

19. (a) Let $|A| = \begin{vmatrix} 1 & 1+i+\omega^2 & \omega^2 \\ 1-i & -1 & \omega^2-1 \\ -i & -i+\omega-1 & -1 \end{vmatrix}$

Observe that $R_1 + R_3 = R_2$ so $|A| = 0$ (By using $\omega + \omega^2 = -1$)

20. (b) Let $z = (1 + \omega^2 - \omega)(1 - \omega^2 + \omega)^6$
So $z = (-2\omega)(-2\omega^2)^6 = (-2)^7\omega^{13} = -128\omega$

21. (c) Let $z = 4+5\left(-\frac{1}{2}+\frac{\sqrt{3}}{2}i\right)^{334} + 3\left(-\frac{1}{2}+\frac{\sqrt{3}}{2}i\right)^{365}$

$= 4 + 5\omega + 3\omega^2 = 4 + 4\omega + 4\omega^2 + \omega - \omega^2 = \omega - \omega^2 = i\sqrt{3}$

22. (d) z_1 and z_2 are the nth roots of unity.
Since z_1 and z_2 subtend a right angle at origin.

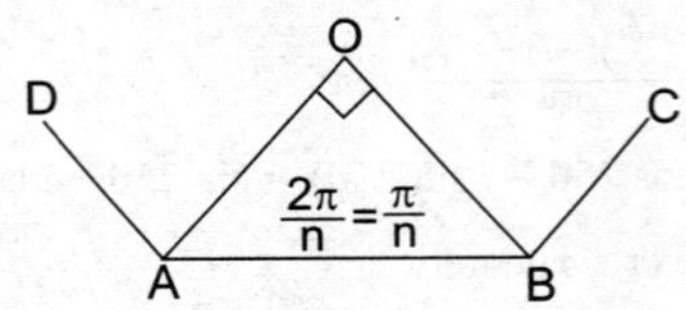

$\Rightarrow \frac{2\pi}{n}=\frac{\pi}{2}$, So $n = 4k$

23. (b) Let $z = \sum_{i=1}^{n}(i-1)(i-\omega)(i-\omega^2) = \sum_{i=1}^{n} i^3 - 1$

$= \frac{1}{4}n^2(n+1)^2 - n$

24. (b) Let $|A| = \begin{vmatrix} 1 & 1 & 1 \\ 1 & -1-\omega^2 & \omega^2 \\ 1 & \omega^2 & \omega \end{vmatrix}$ operate $R_1 \to R_1 + R_2 + R_3$

then $|A| = \begin{vmatrix} 3 & 0 & (1+\omega+\omega^2) \\ 1 & -1-\omega^2 & \omega^2 \\ 1 & \omega^2 & \omega \end{vmatrix}$

$= 3\{-\omega - \omega^3 - \omega^4\} = 3\{-\omega - 1 - \omega\}$
$= 3\{-1 - \omega - \omega^2 + \omega^2 - \omega\} = 3\{\omega^2 - \omega\} = 3\omega\{\omega - 1\}$

25. (b) Given $(1 + \omega^2)^n = (1 + \omega)^n$
So $(-\omega)^n = (-\omega^2)^n$ or $\omega^n = \omega^{2n}$
Which is true when $n = 3k$, so minimum positive value = 3.

26. (c) Consider $|a + b\omega + c\omega^2|^2 = (a + b\omega + c\omega^2)(a + b\bar{\omega} + c\bar{\omega}^2)$
$= a^2 + b^2 + c^2 + (\omega + \omega^2)(ab + bc + ca)$

$= a^2 + b^2 + c^2 - (ab + bc + ca)$

$= \frac{1}{2}\{(a-b)^2 + (b-c)^2 + (c-a)^2\}$

Since *a, b, c* are integers not all equal

$\therefore \quad \frac{1}{2}\{(a-b)^2 + (b-c)^2 + (c-a)^2\} \geq \frac{2}{2} = 1$

(**Note:** all equal means two numbers may be equal but not all the three are equal)

Hence $|a + b\omega + c\omega^2|^2 \geq 1$

$\Rightarrow$ Minimum value of $|a + b\omega + c\omega^2| = 1$

27. (b) $z^{2n} = 2\left\{\frac{1}{2} + \frac{\sqrt{3}}{2}i\right\} = 2e^{\frac{\pi}{3}i}$

Let $\alpha_1, \alpha_2, \alpha_3, \ldots\ldots, \alpha_{2n}$ be the roots, then $(z - \alpha_1)(z - \alpha_2)$

$(z - \alpha_3) \ldots\ldots (z - \alpha_{2n}) = z^{2n} - 2\left(\frac{1}{2} + \frac{\sqrt{3}}{2}i\right) = 0$

$\Rightarrow (-1)^{2n}\alpha_1 . \alpha_2 . \alpha_3 . \ldots . \alpha_{2n} = -2\left(\frac{1}{2} + \frac{\sqrt{3}}{2}i\right)$

So product of roots $= -1 - \sqrt{3}i$

28. (d) Given $z^2 + z + 1 = 0$

So $z = \omega, \omega^2$. Now for $z = \omega$

$\Rightarrow \quad z + \frac{1}{z} = \omega + \frac{1}{\omega} = \omega + \omega^2 = -1$

Similarly $z^2 + \frac{1}{z^2} = \omega^2 + \frac{1}{\omega^2} = \omega + \omega^2 = -1$

Now $z^3 + \frac{1}{z^3} = \omega^3 + \frac{1}{\omega^3} = 2$

$\Rightarrow \quad \left(z + \frac{1}{z}\right)^2 + \left(z^2 + \frac{1}{z^2}\right)^2 + \left(z^3 + \frac{1}{z^3}\right)^2 + \ldots + \left(z^6 + \frac{1}{z^6}\right)^2$

$= 1 + 1 + 4 + 1 + 1 + 4 = 12$

29. (a) Let $z = \frac{1}{2} + \frac{\sqrt{3}}{2}i = e^{\frac{\pi}{3}i}$

So $z^{3/4} = \left(e^{\frac{\pi}{3}i}\right)^{3/4} = \left(e^{\pi i}\right)^{1/4} = \left(\text{cis}\left(\frac{2k\pi + \pi}{4}\right)\right); k = 0,1,2,3$

So $z = \pm\left(\frac{1}{\sqrt{2}} \pm \frac{i}{\sqrt{2}}\right)$

30. (d) Let $z = \cos\theta + i\sin\theta = e^{\theta i}$

Now $\sum_{m=1}^{m=15} \text{Im}(z^{2m-1}) = \sin\theta + \sin 3\theta + \sin 5\theta + \ldots + \sin 29\theta$

$= \frac{2\sin\theta}{2\sin\theta}\{\sin\theta + \sin 3\theta + \sin 5\theta + \ldots + \sin 29\theta\}$

$= \frac{1 - \cos 30\theta}{2\sin\theta}$ putting $\theta = 2°$ we get $\frac{1 - (1/2)}{2\sin 2°} = \frac{1}{4\sin 2°}$

31. (d) Given $z^5 = 1$

$\Rightarrow \quad \frac{2|1 + \alpha + \alpha^2 + \alpha^3 + \alpha^4|}{|\alpha^2|} = \frac{2(0)}{|\alpha|} = 0$

32. (d) Given $z^{15} = 1$

Now $z = e^{\frac{2k\pi}{15}i}$ where $k = 0, 1, 2, \ldots, 14$

Since $|Arg\, z| < \frac{\pi}{2}$ and $\frac{2\pi}{15} = 24°$

We get $z = e^0, e^{\pm\frac{2\pi}{15}i}, e^{\pm\frac{4\pi}{15}i}, e^{\pm\frac{6\pi}{15}i}$; Seven possibilities

33. (b) z_1, z_2, z_3, z_4 are the roots of $z^4 = 1 \Rightarrow z = \pm 1, \pm i$

$\Rightarrow \quad \sum_{i=1}^{4} z_i^3 = 0$

34. (a,c,d) Given $z - \frac{1}{z} = i \Rightarrow z = e^{\frac{\pi}{6}i}, e^{\frac{5\pi}{6}i}$

For $z = e^{\frac{\pi}{6}i}$ we get $z^{98} + \frac{1}{z^{98}} = 2\cos\frac{98}{6}\pi = 1$

Similarly $z^{100} + \frac{1}{z^{100}} = 2\cos\frac{100\pi}{6} = -1$

and $z^{99} + \frac{1}{z^{99}} = 2\cos\frac{99\pi}{6} = 2\cos\frac{\pi}{2} = 0$

TEXTUAL EXERCISE 9: (SUBJECTIVE)

1. Let $z = \tan\left\{i\,\ell n\left(\frac{a - ib}{a + ib}\right)\right\}$

$= \tan\{i\,\ell n e^{-2\theta i}\}$ $\left(\text{where } \theta = \tan^{-1}\left(\frac{b}{a}\right)\right)$

So $z = \tan(+2\theta) = \frac{2\tan\theta}{1 - \tan^2\theta} = \frac{2(b/a)}{1 - \frac{b^2}{a^2}} = \frac{2ab}{a^2 - b^2}$

2 Let $z = ln(-1 + i) = \ln\left(\sqrt{2}e^{\frac{3\pi}{4}i}\right) = \ln\left(\sqrt{2}e^{\left(2n\pi + \frac{3\pi}{4}\right)i}\right)$

$= \frac{1}{2}\ln 2 + \left(\frac{3\pi}{4} + 2n\pi\right)i; n \in \mathbb{Z}$

3 Let $z = i^{i\ldots\infty} = A + iB$, then $z = \left(e^{\frac{\pi}{2}i}\right)^z = e^{\frac{\pi}{2}Ai - \frac{\pi}{2}B} = A + iB$

So $e^{-\frac{\pi}{2}B}\left\{\cos\frac{\pi}{2}A + i\sin\frac{\pi}{2}A\right\} = A + iB$

Hence $\tan\frac{\pi}{2}A = \frac{B}{A}$; Similarly $A^2 + B^2 = e^{-\pi B}$

4. Let $z = ln\{ln(e^{i\theta})\} = ln\, i\theta = ln\,\theta\,(0 + i)$

$= \ln\left\{|\theta|e^{\frac{\pi}{2}i}\right\} = \ln|\theta| + i\left(\frac{\pi}{2} + 2n\pi\right)$

5 (i) Let $z = \text{Log}_e(-i) = \text{Log}_e\left(e^{-\frac{\pi}{2}i}\right) = \left\{-\frac{\pi}{2} + 2n\pi\right\}i$

$\Rightarrow \quad \text{Im}(z) = (4n - 1)\frac{\pi}{2}; n \in \mathbb{Z}$

(ii) Let $z = \text{Log}_e(1-i) = \text{Log}_e\left\{\sqrt{2}\left(e^{-\frac{\pi}{4}i}\right)\right\}$

$= \frac{1}{2}\text{Log}_e 2 + \left(2n\pi - \frac{\pi}{4}\right)i; n \in \mathbb{Z}$

So Im(z) = $(8n - 1)\pi/4$

(iii) Let $z = \text{Log}_e(1+i) = \text{Log}_e\left\{\sqrt{2}\, e^{\frac{\pi}{4}i}\right\}$

$= \frac{1}{2}\text{Log}_e 2 + \left(\frac{\pi}{4} + 2n\pi\right)i; n \in \mathbb{Z}$

So Im (z) = $2n\pi + \pi/4 = (8n + 1)\pi/4$

(iv) Let $z = \text{Log}_e(4+3i) = \text{Log}_e\left\{5\left(\frac{4}{5} + \frac{3}{5}i\right)\right\}$

$= \text{Log}_e 5 + i(2n\pi + \theta)$ {where $\theta = \tan^{-1} 3/4$}

Hence $\text{Im}\, z = 2n\pi + \tan^{-1}\left(\frac{3}{4}\right)$

6 Given $i^{\alpha + i\beta} = e^{x\,(\cos y + i \sin y)}$

Putting $i = e^{\left(\frac{\pi}{2} + 2n\pi\right)i}$

$\therefore \quad i^{\alpha + i\beta} = \left[e^{\left(\frac{\pi}{2} + 2n\pi\right)i}\right]^{\alpha + i\beta}$

$= e^{-\beta\left(\frac{\pi}{2} + 2n\pi\right)} . e^{i\alpha\left(\frac{\pi}{2} + 2n\pi\right)} = e^x(\cos y + i \sin y)$

$\Rightarrow \quad x = -\frac{1}{2}(4n+1)\pi\beta; y = \frac{1}{2}(4n+1)\pi\alpha$

Also if $i^{\alpha + i\beta} = \alpha' + i\beta' \Rightarrow \alpha' = e^x \cos y; \beta' = e^x \sin y$

$\therefore \quad \alpha^2 + \beta^2 = e^{2x} = e^{-(4n+1)\pi\beta}$

7. We know that $i^i = \left(e^{\frac{\pi}{2}i}\right)^i = e^{-\frac{\pi}{2}}$

$\Rightarrow$ $\ln(i^i) = \ln(e^{-\pi/2}) = -\pi/2$

Hence $\sin \ln(i^i) = \sin(-\pi/2) = -1 = a + ib$ (given)

$\Rightarrow$ $a = -1, b = 0$

Also $\cos(\ln i^i) = \sqrt{1 - \sin(\ ni^i)} = \pm\sqrt{1-(1)} = 0$

8 Given $(a + ib)^p = m^{x + iy} \Rightarrow p \ln(a + ib) = (x + iy) \ln m$

Now $a + ib = \sqrt{a^2 + b^2}\left\{e^{i\tan^{-1}\left(\frac{b}{a}\right)}\right\}$

$\therefore \quad p\left\{\frac{1}{2}\ln(a^2 + b^2) + i\tan^{-1}\left(\frac{b}{a}\right)\right\} = (x + iy \ln m$

$\Rightarrow \quad x \ln m = \frac{p}{2}\ln(a^2 + b^2)$ and $y \ln m = p \tan^{-1}\left(\frac{b}{a}\right)$

Hence $\frac{y}{x} = \frac{2\tan^{-1}\left(\frac{b}{a}\right)}{\ln(a^2 + b^2)}$

9. Let $z = (1 + i)^{\ln(1 - i)}$

So $\ln z = \ln(1 - i) \ln(1 + i)$

$= \left\{\ln\sqrt{2} + i\left(-\frac{\pi}{4}\right)\right\} . \left\{\ln\sqrt{2} + i\frac{\pi}{4}\right\}$

$= \left(\ln\sqrt{2}\right)^2 - \frac{\pi^2}{16}i^2 = \left(\ln\sqrt{2}\right)^2 + \frac{\pi^2}{16}$

Which is purely real hence z is purely real.

TEXTUAL EXERCISE 9: (OBJECTIVE)

1. (b) Let $z = \ln(1 + i\tan\alpha) = \ln(\sec\alpha)\, e^{\alpha i}$

$\Rightarrow$ $z = \ln(\sec\alpha) + (\alpha + 2n\pi)i$

Hence real $z = \ln|(\sec\alpha)|$

2. (a) Let $z = \ln(-1 + i) - \ln(-1 - i)$

$= \left(\ln\sqrt{2} + \frac{3\pi}{4}i\right) - \left(\ln\sqrt{2} - \frac{3\pi}{4}i\right) = \frac{3\pi}{2}i$

3 (a) $z = i\ln\left(\frac{1 + \sin\theta - i\cos\theta}{1 + \sin\theta + i\cos\theta}\right)$

$= i\ln\left[\frac{\left(\cos\frac{\theta}{2} + \sin\frac{\theta}{2}\right)^2 - i\left(\cos^2\frac{\theta}{2} - \sin^2\frac{\theta}{2}\right)}{\left(\cos\frac{\theta}{2} + \sin\frac{\theta}{2}\right)^2 + i\left(\cos^2\frac{\theta}{2} - \sin^2\frac{\theta}{2}\right)}\right]$

$= i\ln\left[\frac{\left(\cos\frac{\theta}{2} + \sin\frac{\theta}{2}\right) - i\left(\cos\frac{\theta}{2} - \sin\frac{\theta}{2}\right)}{\left(\cos\frac{\theta}{2} + \sin\frac{\theta}{2}\right) + i\left(\cos\frac{\theta}{2} - \sin\frac{\theta}{2}\right)}\right]$

$= i\ln\left[\frac{\sin\left(\frac{\theta}{2} + \frac{\pi}{4}\right) - i\cos\left(\frac{\theta}{2} + \frac{\pi}{4}\right)}{\sin\left(\frac{\theta}{2} + \frac{\pi}{4}\right) + i\cos\left(\frac{\theta}{2} + \frac{\pi}{4}\right)}\right]$

$= i\ln\left[\frac{-\left(\cos\left(\frac{\theta}{2} + \frac{\pi}{4}\right) + i\sin\left(\frac{\theta}{2} + \frac{\pi}{4}\right)\right)}{\cos\left(\frac{\theta}{2} + \frac{\pi}{4}\right) - i\sin\left(\frac{\theta}{2} + \frac{\pi}{4}\right)}\right]$

$= i\ln\left[\frac{-e^{i\left(\frac{\theta}{2} + \frac{\pi}{4}\right)}}{e^{-i\left(\frac{\theta}{2} + \frac{\pi}{4}\right)}}\right]$

$= i\ln\left[-e^{i\left(\theta + \frac{\pi}{2}\right)}\right] = i\ln\left[-\cos\left(\theta + \frac{\pi}{2}\right) - i\sin\left(\theta + \frac{\pi}{2}\right)\right]$

$= i\ln\left[e^{-i\left(\theta + \frac{\pi}{2}\right)}\right] = \left(\theta + \frac{\pi}{2}\right)$

$\therefore$ $\sin z = \sin\left(\theta + \frac{\pi}{2}\right) = \cos\theta$

4 (a) Let $z = i^i = \left(e^{\frac{\pi}{2}i}\right)^i = e^{-\frac{\pi}{2}}$ which is purely real

5 (d) Let $z = i^{\ln(1+i)} = \left(e^{\frac{\pi}{2}i}\right)^{\ln(1+i)}$

So $\ln z = \{\ln(1+i)\}\left\{\frac{\pi}{2}i\right\}$

$$= \left(\ln\sqrt{2} + \frac{\pi}{4}i\right)\left(\frac{\pi}{2}i\right) = \frac{-\pi^2}{8} + i\frac{\pi}{2}\ln\sqrt{2}$$

$\Rightarrow\ z = e^{-\frac{\pi^2}{8}}.2.e^{\frac{i\pi}{4}} \quad \Rightarrow\ \text{Re}(z) = \sqrt{2}e^{-\frac{\pi^2}{8}}$

6 (c) Let $z = i^{-i} = \left(e^{\frac{\pi}{2}i}\right)^{-i} = e^{\frac{\pi}{2}}$

7 (b) Let $z = (1 + \sqrt{3}i)^i$, then $\ln z = i \ln(1 + \sqrt{3}i)$

$$= i\left\{\ln 2 + \frac{\pi}{3}i\right\} = -\frac{\pi}{3} + i\ln 2$$

Hence $z = e^{-\frac{\pi}{3}}.e^{\ln 2^i} = 2^i e^{-\frac{\pi}{3}}$

8 (a) Given $z = 2i\ln(\sqrt{3} - 1)$

$$\cos z = \frac{e^{iz} + e^{-iz}}{2} = \frac{e^{-2\ln(\sqrt{3}-1)} + e^{2\ln(\sqrt{3}-1)}}{2}$$

So $\cos z = \dfrac{(\sqrt{3}-1)^{-2} + (\sqrt{3}-1)^2}{2} = \dfrac{(\sqrt{3}+1)^2 + 4(\sqrt{3}-1)^2}{(4)(2)}$

$$= \frac{(3+1+2\sqrt{3}) + 4(3+1-2\sqrt{3})}{8} = \frac{20-6\sqrt{3}}{8} = \frac{10-3\sqrt{3}}{4}$$

9 (b) Let $z = i^{\ln(1+\sqrt{3}i)} = \left(e^{\frac{\pi}{2}i}\right)^{\ln(1+i\sqrt{3})}$

$\Rightarrow\ \ln z = \frac{\pi}{2}i\left\{\ln 2 + i\frac{\pi}{3}\right\} = -\frac{\pi^2}{6} + i\frac{\pi}{2}\ln 2$

Hence $\text{Im}(\ln z) = \frac{\pi}{2}\ln 2$

TEXTUAL EXERCISE 10 (SUBJECTIVE)

1. (i) $(z_1 - z_2) = i(z_3 - z_2)$
Also $z_2(i-1) = iz_3 - z_1$

$\Rightarrow\ z_2 = \dfrac{z_1 - iz_3}{1-i} = \dfrac{(1+i)z_1 - (1+i)iz_3}{2}$

or $2z_2 = (1+i)z_1 + (1-i)z_3$

(ii) Similarly $z_1 - z_4 = -i(z_3 - z_4)$
$\Rightarrow z_4(-i-1) = -iz_3 - z_1$ gives $2z_4 = (1-i)z_1 + (1+i)z_3$

2. (a) $Arg(z - z_1) = \frac{\pi}{3}$ or $-\frac{2\pi}{3}$

i.e., $Arg(z - 2 - i) = \frac{\pi}{3}$ or $-\frac{2\pi}{3}$

(b) Given $z_1 = (-2, -1)$ and $z_2 = (3, 1)$

$\Rightarrow\ a = \dfrac{z_2 - z_1}{2i} = \dfrac{3+i+2+i}{2i} = 1 + \dfrac{5}{2i} = 1 - \dfrac{5}{2}i$

and $\bar{a} = 1 + \frac{5}{2}i$; Now $b = \text{Im}(z_1\bar{z}_2) = \text{Im}\{6 + 1 + 2i + 3i\} = i$

Hence the equation of line through z_1 and z_2 is

$$\left(1 - \frac{5}{2}i\right)\bar{z} + \left(1 + \frac{5}{2}i\right)z - i = 0$$

3 (a) Given $z_1 - z_2 = i(z_3 - z_2)$ squaring both sides, we get
$z_1^2 + z_2^2 - 2z_1z_2 = -\left(z_3^2 + z_2^2 - 2z_2z_3\right)$
So $z_1^2 + 2z_2^2 + z_3^2 = 2z_2(z_1 + z_3)$

(b) When right angle is at z_3 then $z_1 - z_3 = -i(z_2 - z_3)$
So $(z_1 - z_3)^2 = -(z_2 - z_3)^2$ and $z_1 - z_2 = (z_3 - z_2) + (z_1 - z_3)$
Squaring both sides, we get $(z_1 - z_2)^2 = (z_3 - z_2)^2 + (z_1 - z_3)^2 + 2(z_3 - z_2)(z_1 - z_3)$
$= -(z_1 - z_3)^2 + (z_1 - z_3)^2 + 2(z_3 - z_2)(z_1 - z_3)$
So $(z_1 - z_2)^2 = 2(z_1 - z_3)(z_3 - z_2)$.

4. Since $|z_1 - 1| = |z_2 - 1| = |z_3 - 1| = r$ (say)
$\Rightarrow$ $A(z_1)$, $B(z_2)$, $C(z_3)$ lie on a circle with centre at (1, 0) with radius r.
$\Rightarrow$ (1, 0) is the Circumcentre of ΔABC

The centroid G of $\Delta ABC = \dfrac{z_1 + z_2 + z_3}{3}$

The centroid and Circumcentre will coincide only if ΔABC is equilateral in that case $z_1 + z_2 + z_3 = 3$

5 (a) ΔABC is equilateral so $z_1 - z_2 = (z_3 - z_2)e^{\frac{\pi}{3}i}$ and

$(z_2 - z_1)e^{i\frac{\pi}{3}} = (z_3 - z_1)$

Multiplication gives $-(z_1 - z_2)^2 = (z_3 - z_2)(z_3 - z_1)$
i.e., $-(z_1^2 + z_2^2) + 2z_1z_2 = z_3^2 - z_2z_3 + z_1z_2 - z_1z_3$
So $z_1z_2 + z_2z_3 + z_1z_3 = z_1^2 + z_2^2 + z_3^2$.

(b) ΔABC is an equilateral triangle. So circumcentre z_0 is the same as centroid

i.e., $\dfrac{z_1 + z_2 + z_3}{3} = z_0$; as proved in part (a)

$z_1^2 + z_2^2 + z_3^2 = z_1z_2 + z_2z_3 + z_1z_3$
$\Rightarrow\ (z_1 + z_2 + z_3)^2 = 9z_0^2$ or $z_1^2 + z_2^2 + z_3^2 + 2(z_1z_2 + z_2z_3 + z_1z_3) = 9z_0^2$
i.e., $3(z_1^2 + z_2^2 + z_3^2) = 9z_0^2$
So $z_1^2 + z_2^2 + z_3^2 = 3z_0^2$

6 Given $\dfrac{1}{z_1 - z_2} + \dfrac{1}{z_3 - z_1} + \dfrac{1}{z_2 - z_3} = 0$

$\Leftrightarrow\ z_1^2 + z_2^2 + z_3^2 = z_1z_2 + z_2z_3 + z_1z_3$
As proved in question 5. part (a) this is the condition for an equilateral triangle.

7 Clearly, Δ *ACE* and ΔBDF are equilateral Δ's with same centroid Z_0.

$\therefore\ \ z_1^2 + z_3^2 + z_5^2 = 3z_0^2$ ...(i)

and $z_2^2 + z_4^2 + z_6^2 = 3z_0^2$ ....(ii)

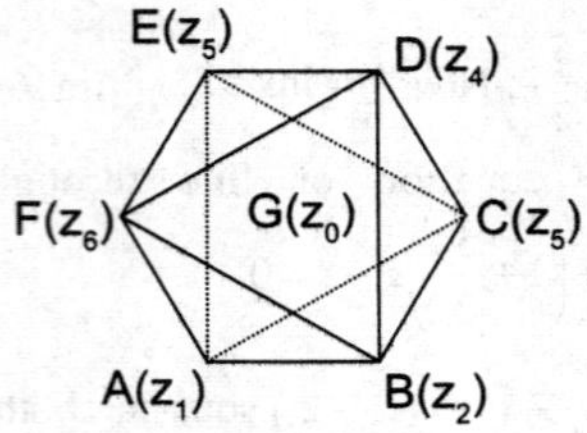

$\therefore$ (i) and (ii) gives $\sum_{r=1}^{6} zr^2 = 6z_0^2$.

8. $Arg\left(\frac{3z-6-3i}{2z-8-6i}\right) = \frac{\pi}{4}$ represents the major arc of circles with centre at $C_1(4, 1)$ and $C_2(2, 3)$ respectively and of radius 2 units as shown below

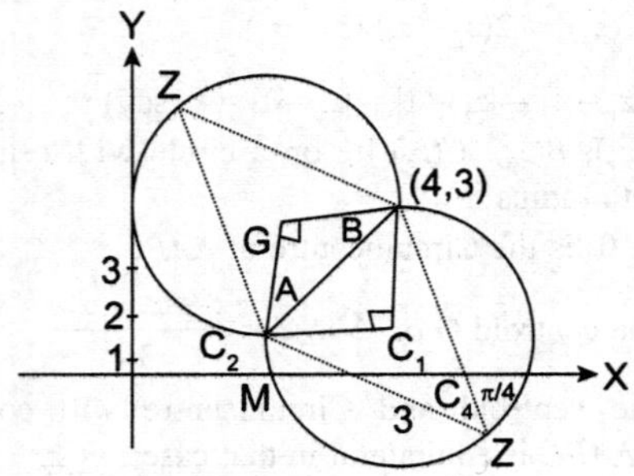

Also $|2z-3+i| = 3$ or $\left|z-\left(\frac{3}{2}-\frac{i}{2}\right)\right| = \frac{3}{2}$ represents a circle with centre at $M\left(\frac{3}{2}, \frac{-1}{2}\right)$ and radius = 3/2

Now, $MA = \sqrt{\left(\frac{3}{2}-2\right)^2 + \left(-\frac{1}{2}-1\right)^2} = \sqrt{\frac{1}{4}+\frac{9}{4}} = \frac{\sqrt{10}}{2} > \frac{3}{2}$

The circle $|2z-3+i| = 3$ will cut the lower circle possibly twice and will not cut the upper circle

Now $MC_1 = \sqrt{\left(4-\frac{3}{2}\right)^2 + \left(1+\frac{1}{2}\right)^2} = \sqrt{\frac{25}{4}+\frac{9}{4}} = \frac{\sqrt{34}}{2}$

$r_1 + r_2 = \frac{3}{2} + 2 = \frac{7}{2}$

$\therefore\ r_1 + r_2 > Mc_1$

$\Rightarrow$ Two circles one with centre at M and other with centre at C_1 will cut each other.

Clearly two complex number are possible.

9 $z^2 + pz + q = (z - z_1)(z - z_2) = 0$

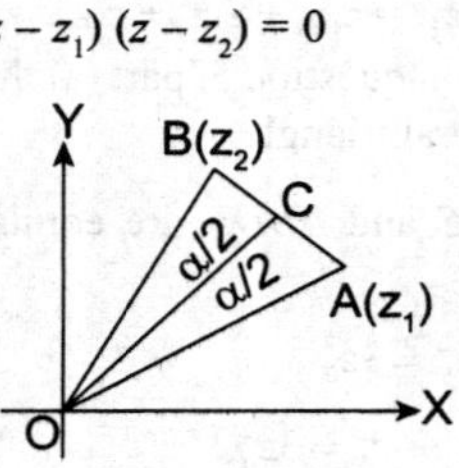

$\Rightarrow z_1 + z_2 = -p$ and $z_1 z_2 = q$

Let C be the mid - point of AB

So $OC = \left|\frac{z_1+z_2}{2}\right| = .\frac{|p|}{2} = OA\cos\frac{\alpha}{2} = OB\cos\frac{\alpha}{2}$

$\Rightarrow (OC)^2 = OA.OB\cos^2\frac{\alpha}{2}$

i.e., $\frac{|p|^2}{4} = |z_1 z_2|\cos^2\frac{\alpha}{2}$ or $|p|^2 = 4|q|\cos^2\frac{\alpha}{2}$

10 An equilateral triangle with height of $2\sqrt{3}$ units is formed with each side of the $\Delta ABC = 4$ units as shown below:

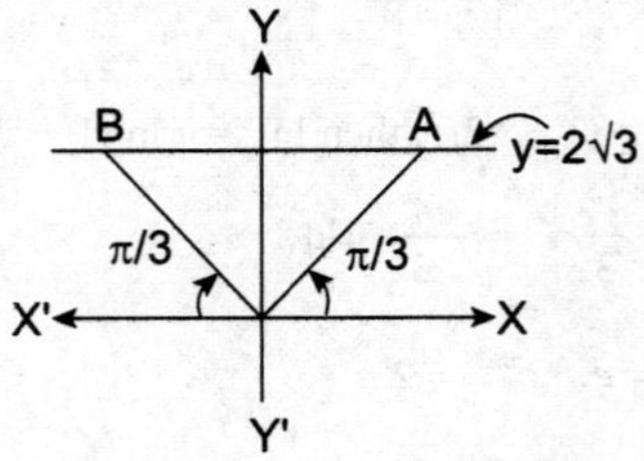

$\therefore$ Area of the $\Delta ABC = \frac{1}{2}\times 4\times 2\sqrt{3} = 4\sqrt{3}$ square units.

11 Area of the $\Delta ABC = \Delta ABC = \frac{1}{2}$ area of square $OABC$

$= \frac{1}{2}|z||iz| = 8 \quad \Rightarrow |z|^2 = 15 \Rightarrow |z| = 4$

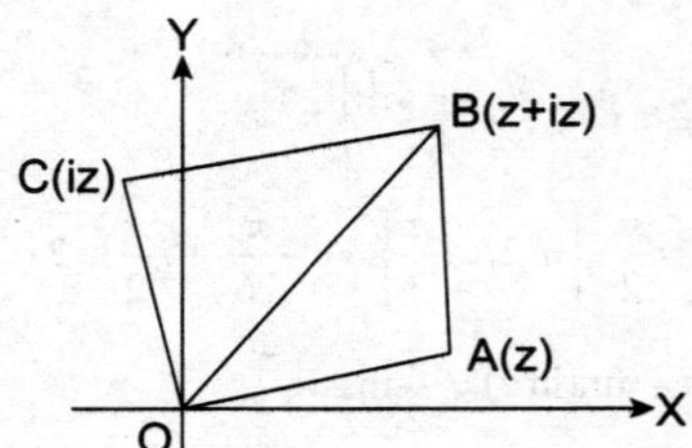

12 (a) Given $|z_1| = 1$ and $|z_2| = 2$

Now $|2z_1 + z_2| \le 2|z_1| + |z_2| = 4$

$\Rightarrow$ Max. $|2z_1 + z_2| = 4$

(b) $||z_2| - |z_1|| \le |z_1 + z_2| \le |z_1| + |z_2|$

So $1 \le |z_1 + z_2| \le 3 \quad \Rightarrow$ Min$|z_1 + z_2| = 1$

(c) $z_2 + \frac{1}{z_1} = z_2 + \overline{z}_1$ as $|z_1| = 1$

$\Rightarrow \left|z_2 + \frac{1}{z_1}\right| = |z_2 + \overline{z}_1| \le |z_2| + |\overline{z}_1| = 3$

$\Rightarrow \left|z_2 + \frac{1}{z_1}\right| \le 3$

13 (a) $z\overline{z} + (3+4i)\overline{z} + (3-4i)z + 24 = 0$

$\Rightarrow x^2 + y^2 + 3(z+\overline{z}) + 4i(\overline{z}-z) + 24 = 0$

So $x^2 + y^2 + 6x + 8y + 24 = 0$ which gives a circle with centre at $(-3, -4) = -3 - 4i$ and radius 1 units.

(b) Using the distance method $|z - 2 + i|^2 + |z - 3 - i|^2 = 1^2 + 2^2$.

So $2z\bar{z} - 5(z + \bar{z}) + 10 = 0$

Aliter: $Arg\left(\frac{z-(2-i)}{z-(3+i)}\right) = \pm\frac{\pi}{2}$ gives the required circle excepting points (3, 1) and (2, –1).

(c) $\frac{\pi}{3} \le Arg(z-i) - Arg(z+i) \le \frac{2\pi}{3}$; Using rotation theorem we get that the locus will represent the region enclosed between two circular arcs formed on the chord joining i and $-i$. The figure is shown in answer key.

14. (a) $|z| = 2$

$\Rightarrow$ $z + 2$ lies on the circle of radius 2 units centered at (2, 0). The figure is shown in answer key.

i.e., $|z - 2| = 2$

(b) $|z| = 2$.

$\Rightarrow$ $z + z_0$ lies on the circle with centre z_0 and radius 2 units. The figure is shown in answer key.

(c) $z - (1 - i) = z + (-1 + i)$ represents a circle of radius 2 units centered at (–1, 1). The figure is shown in answer key.

15 The figure is shown in answer key.

(a) z with least positive argument $OA = 20$ units as $\theta + \phi = 90°$

So point $A = (20\cos\phi + 20i\sin\phi)$

$$= 20\sin\theta + 20i\cos\theta = 20\left(\frac{3}{5}\right) + 20i\left(\frac{4}{5}\right) = 12 + 16i$$

(b) z with greatest positive argument by symmetry (about y-axis) is point $B = (-12 + 16i)$

(c) The point with smallest modulus in (0, 10) = $10i$

(d) The point with greatest modulus = $40i$

16 Given: k is a real positive number

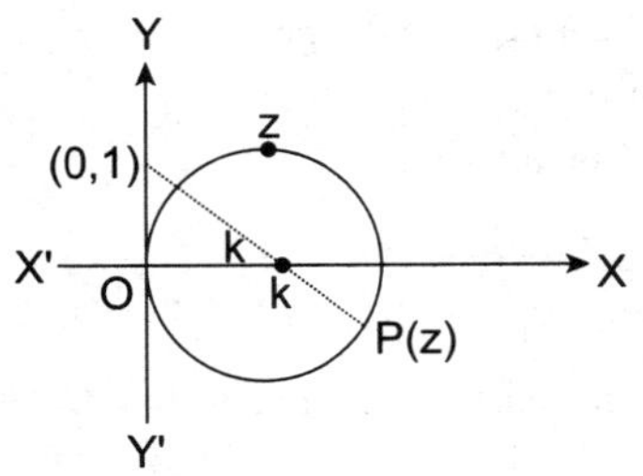

(a) $|z - k| = k$ gives a circle of radius k unit centered at $A(k, 0)$ observe that $2Arg(z) = Arg(z - k)$

$\Rightarrow$ True

(b) Observe that $Arg(z - k) \ne Arg(z + k)$

$\Rightarrow$ False

(c) $|z|_{max} = 2k$ is true and holds where $z = (2k, 0)$

$\Rightarrow$ True

(d) $|z|_{min.} = 0$ is true at (0, 0) i.e. origin.

$\Rightarrow$ True

(e) $(Arg\ z)_{max} \to \pi/2$ is true as (0, 0) is one end of the diameter OAB. This is the limiting value.

(i.e., approaching to) as $z \to$ origine from upwards side. $\Rightarrow$ True

(f) $|z - i|_{max} = k + \sqrt{k^2 + 1}$ $\Rightarrow$ True

(g) $|z - i|_{min} = \sqrt{k^2 + (-1)^2} - k = \sqrt{k^2 + 1} - k$ $\Rightarrow$ True

17 (a) $1 < |z + 2i| \le 3$ locus is the shaded portion between the circles $|(z - (-2i)| = 1$ and $|z - (-2i)| = 3$ boundary of larger circles is included but the boundary of smaller circle is excluded.

The figure is shown in answer key.

(b) $Re(z) > 3$ given R.H.S. of the line $x = 3$ and $|Im\ z| < 2$ gives the area between the lines $y = 2$, $y = -2$

The figure is shown in answer key.

(c) $\frac{\pi}{6} \le Amp(z) \le \frac{\pi}{3}$ is represented by the shaded area.

The figure is shown in answer key.

(d) $Arg(z) = \frac{\pi}{2}$ and $|z| < 5$ gives the line segment of y-axis where $y \in (0, 5)$.

The figure is shown in answer key.

(e) Given $|z - 1|^2 - |z + 1|^2 = 4$

Let $z = x + iy$

$\Rightarrow$ $(x - 1)^2 + y^2 - (x + 1)^2 - y^2 = 4$ gives $x = -1$ or $x + 1 = 0$

The figure is shown in answer key.

(f) $|z - i| = 1$ and $Arg(z) = \pi/4$ gives two points (0, 0) {which we can not include} and $(1 + i)$

The figure is shown in answer key.

(g) $|z + i| = |z - 2|$ gives the right bisector of the line segment passing through (0, –1) and (2, 0)

Locus of the straight line is $2y - x + 2 = 0$. The figure is shown in answer key.

(h) $|z - 1| = |z - 3| = |z - i|$ locus is the centre of the circle passing through these three points

Now $x = 2$ {right bisector of (1, 0) and (3, 0) line segment}

So $1^2 + y^2 = 1 + y^2 = 4 + (y - 1)^2$ gives $y = 2$

$\Rightarrow$ $z = 2 + 2i$

The figure is shown in answer key.

(i) Given $|z| - 4 = |z - i| = |z + 5i|$

Observe that $|z - i| = |z + 5i|$ givens $y = -2$

Now $|z| - 4 \ge 0$ gives the exterior of a circle centered at (0, 0) and radius 4 units. Consider a point $P(z)$ on the line $y = -2$

Now $|z| - 4 = PM$ (as shown) and $|z + 5i| = PB$ which can never be equal

Hence no solution is possible. The figure is shown in answer key.

(j) Given $|\pi - Arg\ z| < \frac{\pi}{4}$ gives $\frac{3\pi}{4} < Arg\ z < \frac{5\pi}{4}$. The figure is shown in answer key.

(k) $|z-i|+|z+i|=2$ gives the line segment joining $A(0, 1)$ and $B(0, -1)$

$|z-i|+|z+i|>2$ gives an ellipse with focus at (0, 1) and (0, –1). This will cover the whole argand plane except the line segment AB and $|z-i|+|z+i|<2$ gives no solution as distance between $A(0, 1)$ and $B(0, -1)$ is 2 units (the minimum required). So no locus is possible.

18 (a) $|z-1|+|z+1|<4$ gives as ellipse having focus at (1, 0) and (–1, 0)

The figure is shown in answer key.

(b) $\text{Arg}(z+i)-\text{Arg}(z-i)=\pi/2$

Means $Arg\left(\dfrac{z+i}{z-i}\right)=\dfrac{\pi}{2}$ gives the semi-circle on the RHS of y-axis.

The figure is shown in answer key.

(c) $1<|z-(2+3i)|<4$ gives (interior) the area between the circle of radius 1 and 4 both centered at (2, 3) both boundaries excluded.

The figure is shown in answer key.

(d) $\dfrac{\pi}{4}<Argz<\dfrac{\pi}{3}$ area between the line $y=x$ and $y=\sqrt{3}\,x$ (both boundary lines excluded)

The figure is shown in answer key.

(e) $\log_{\cos\frac{\pi}{3}}\left\{\dfrac{|z-1|+4}{3|z-1|-2}\right\}>1$ as $\cos\dfrac{\pi}{3}=\dfrac{1}{2}$

$\Rightarrow\ 0<\dfrac{|z-1|+4}{3|z-1|-2}<\dfrac{1}{2}$

Since $|z-1|+4>0$ so $3|z-1|>2$ in order to get $3|z-1|-2>0$

$\Rightarrow |z-1|>2/3$

Further $2|z-1|+8<3|z-1|-2$ {for $|z-1|>2/3$} gives $|z-1|>10$ i.e., $(x-1)^2+y^2>100$

i.e., exterior (excluding boundary) of a circle of radius 10 units centered at (1, 0)

The figure is shown in answer key.

(f) $\log_{1/2}|z-2|>\log_{1/2}|z|;\ z\neq(2, 0)$

$\Rightarrow |z|>|z-2|$

Consider $|z|=|z-2|$ which gives the line x = 1

So $|z|>|z-2|$ gives the R.H.S. of the line $x=1$ (excluding the line $x=1$)

i.e., $(x-1)>0$ except for the point (2, 0). The figure is shown in answer key.

(g) $\log_{1/\sqrt{3}}\dfrac{|z|^2-|z|+1}{|z|+2}>-2$ as $0<\dfrac{1}{\sqrt{3}}<1$

$\Rightarrow\ 0<\dfrac{|z|^2-|z|+1}{|z|+2}<\left(\dfrac{1}{\sqrt{3}}\right)^{-2}=3$

Since $|z|+2>0$

$\Rightarrow |z|^2-|z|+1>0$ (which is always true)

Hence $|z|^2-|z|+1<3|z|+6$, i.e., $|z|^2-4|z|-5<0$ gives $(|z|-5)(|z|+1)<0$

$\Rightarrow |z|<5$ also $|z|^2-|z|+1>0$ is always true

So $0\le|z|<5$ which is the interior of a circle of radius 5 units centered at (0, 0)

The figure is shown in answer key.

TEXTUAL EXERCISE 10: (OBJECTIVE)

1. (b, c, d) Given $|z_1-z_2|=|z_1+z_2|$ and $\dfrac{z_1}{z_2}=-ki\,(k\in\mathbb{R}, k\neq 0)$

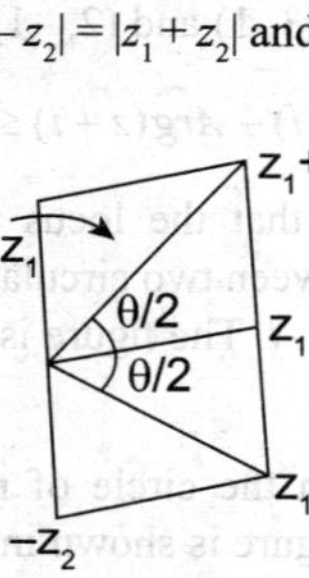

From the figure observe that $\tan\dfrac{\theta}{2}=\left|\dfrac{z_2}{z_1}\right|=\left|\dfrac{i}{k}\right|=\dfrac{1}{|k|}$

(so $\theta/2=\tan^{-1}(1/|k|)$)

$\Rightarrow\ |\tan\theta|=\left|\dfrac{\frac{2}{k}}{1-\frac{1}{k^2}}\right|=\left|\dfrac{2k}{k^2-1}\right|=\left|\dfrac{2k}{1-k^2}\right|$

2. (b) Observe that mid point of diagonals is O

$=\dfrac{z_1+z_3}{2}=\dfrac{z_2+z_4}{2}$

So $z_1+z_3=z_2+z_4$

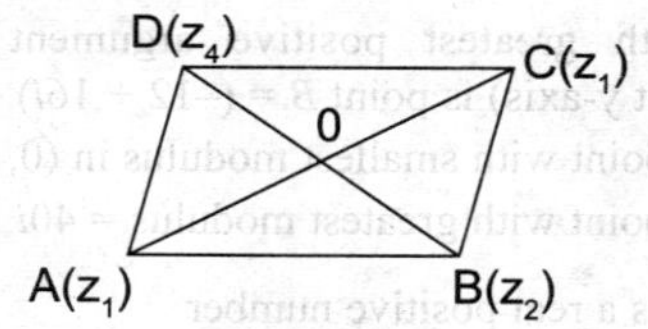

3. (b) $z\bar{z}+a\bar{z}+az+b=0$, gives $x^2+y^2+2ax+b=0$

or $(x+a)^2+y^2=a^2-b>0$

$\Rightarrow\ a^2>b$ or $|a^2|>b$

4. (c) $|z_1-z_2|=|z_2-z_3|=|z_3-z_1|$

Also $z_3-z_1=e^{\pi i/3}(z_2-z_1)$

In equilateral triangle circumcentre $C=\dfrac{z_1+z_2+z_3}{3}=z_0$

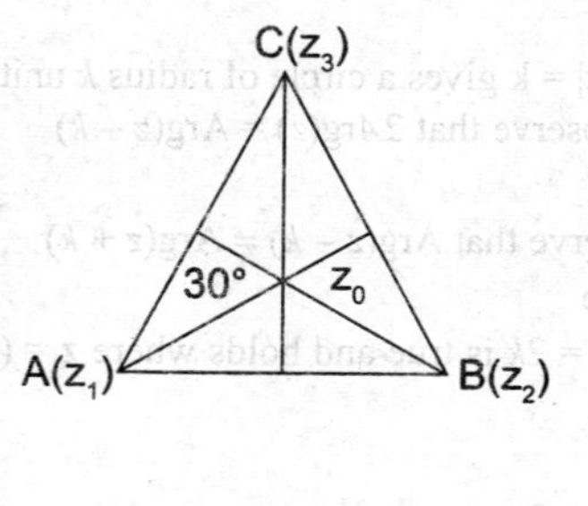

$\Rightarrow \quad z_1^2 + z_2^2 + z_3 + 2(z_1z_2 + z_2z_3 + z_3z_1) = 9z_0^2$

We know $\Sigma z_1 z_2 = \Sigma z_1^2 \quad \Rightarrow \quad 3(z_1^2 + z_2^2 + z_3^2) = 9z_0^2$

Hence $z_1^2 + z_2^2 + z_3^2 = 3z_0^2$

5. (b) $b\bar{z} + \bar{b}z - c = 0$

Represents a straight line (for $b \neq 0$), $c \in \mathbb{R}$

When b is a non-zero complex number

6. (a, b) According to the given $0 < a, b < 1$

$z_1 = a + i;\ z_2 = 1 + bi;\ z_3 = 0$

So $1 + b^2 = a^2 + 1 = (a-1)^2 + (1-b)^2$

Give $a = b \quad \Rightarrow \quad a^2 + 1 = 2(a^2 + 1 - 2a)$

i.e. $a^2 - 4a + 1 = 0 \quad \Rightarrow \quad a = \dfrac{4 \pm \sqrt{16-4}}{2} = 2 \pm \sqrt{3}$

Hence $a = b = (2 + \sqrt{3})$ or $(2 - \sqrt{3})$

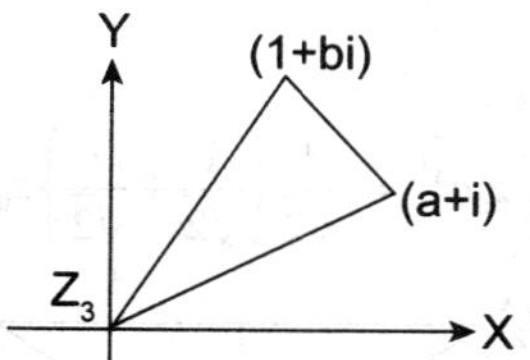

7. (a) $|z| = 2$

So $5z - 1$ will give a circle of radius 10 units centered at $(-1, 0)$

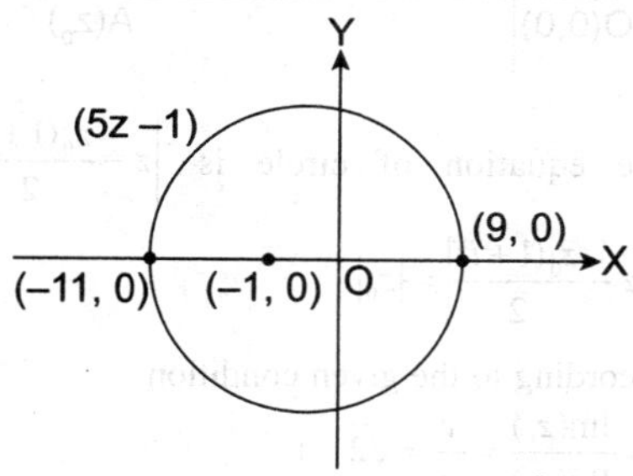

8. (a, b, c, d) Vertices of a quadrilateral are $a = 1 + 2i$, $b = -3 + i$; $c = -2 - 3i$; $d = 2 - 2i$

Observe that $a + c = -1 - i$ and $b + d = -1 - i$ and

$AB^2 = BC^2 = CD^2 = AD^2 = 17$ (as $4^2 + 1^2$)

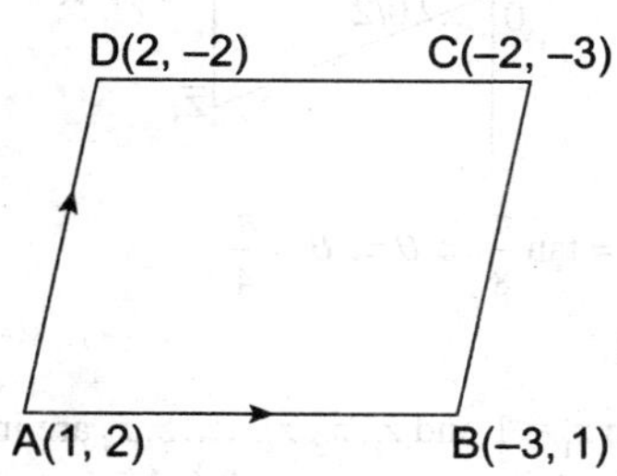

Now $\overrightarrow{AB} = -4 - i$ and $\overrightarrow{AD} = 1 - 4i$

Observe that $\overrightarrow{AB}.(-i) = 1 - 4i = \overrightarrow{AD}$

Hence sides are equal and at right angle to each other so the quadrilateral is a square. Since a square is also a rectangle as well as a rhombus as well as ||gm

9. (a, c) Given $OP = OQ$

Where $p = a + ib$ and $Q = c + id$

So $a + c = b + d = 0$; Also $|a + ib| = |c + id|$

Arg $(a + ib) = \pi +$ Arg $(c + id)$

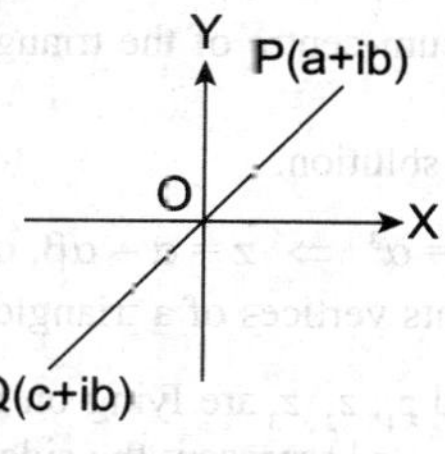

10. (b) $AC = 2BD$. We know that AC and BD bisect each other.

i.e., at $E\left(\dfrac{5}{2}, 0\right)$.

Hence $\overrightarrow{EA} = 2\,\overrightarrow{ED}(i) = (3 + 4i)i$ gives $\overrightarrow{EA} = -4 + 3i$

$\Rightarrow \quad A = -4 + \dfrac{5}{2} + 3i;\ A = -\dfrac{3}{2} + 3i$ or $3i - \dfrac{3}{2}$

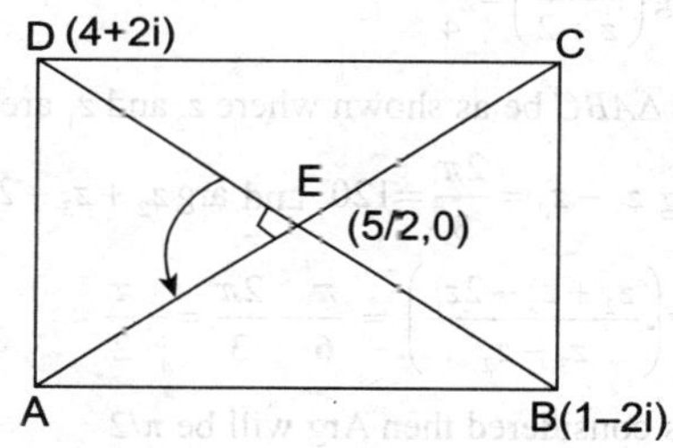

11. (d) Since the centre is at origin and sides are parallel to axes

$\therefore$ The vertices are as shown so the sides are $2a$ and $2\sqrt{3}b$

$\Rightarrow$ Area $= 4\sqrt{3}\,ab$ square units

12. (b) $|z + 1| = \dfrac{\sqrt{2}}{|z+1|} (z \neq -1)$

$\Rightarrow |z + 1|^2 = \sqrt{2}$ or $|z + 1| = 2^{1/4}$; which represents a circle

13. (b) Given $|z + \bar{a}| = |z - a|$ {where (real part) R(a) $\neq 0$}

Let $z = x + iy$ and $a = m + in$

So $(x + m)^2 + (y - n)^2 = (x - m)^2 + (y - n)^2$

$\Rightarrow 4mx = 0$; since $m =$ Real $(a) \neq 0$ so $x = 0$

(i.e. $z = 0 + iy$ where $y \in \mathbb{R}$) i.e. y – axis is the locus of z

14. (b) $\log_{\sqrt{3}}\left(\dfrac{|z|^2 - |z| + 1}{|z| + 2}\right) < 2$. Gives $0 < \dfrac{|z^2| - |z| + 1}{|z| + 2} < 3$

Since $|z| + 2 > 0$

$\therefore \quad |z|^2 - |z| + 1 > 0$ (which is always true)

Gives $|z|^2 - |z| + 1 < 3|z| + 6$

or $\quad |z|^2 - 4|z| - 5 < 0$, so $0 \leq |z| < 5$

15. (c) $\left|z+\frac{1}{2}\right|^2 = \left|z-\frac{1}{2}\right|^2 \Rightarrow \left|z+\frac{1}{2}\right| = \left|z-\frac{1}{2}\right|$

So the locus is $x = 0$ i.e. y – axis

16. (b) Observe that $|z-1| = |z-2| = |z-i|$

Represents the circum centre of triangle.

17. (a) $|z-1| = |z-2| = |z-i|$

Given the circum-centre of the triangle (as these points are not collinear)

∴ Only one solution.

18. (b) $(z+\alpha\beta)^3 = \alpha^3 \Rightarrow z = \alpha - \alpha\beta,\ \alpha\omega - \alpha\beta,\ \alpha\omega^2 - \alpha\beta$

z represents vertices of a triangle of side $\sqrt{3}|\alpha|$

19. (b) $|z| = 1$ and z_1, z_2, z_3 are lying on this circle and $|z_2 - z_3|$, $|z_1 - z_2|$ and $|z_1 - z_3|$ represent the sides of the triangle which gives a maximum sum when sides are equal

$\Rightarrow \sum|z_1 - z_2|^2 = 3|z_1 - z_2|^2 = 9$

20. (b) Given: $|z - 2i| = 2\sqrt{2}$

Observe that the angle formed by the chord joining (–2, 0) and (2, 0) subtends a right angle at the centre (0, 2)

$\Rightarrow Arg\left(\frac{z-2}{z+2}\right) = \frac{\pi}{4}$

21. (b) Let ΔABC be as shown where z_2 and z_1 are along x-axis

then $\text{Arg } z_3 - z_2 = \frac{2\pi}{3} = 120^\circ$ and $\arg z_2 + z_3 - 2z_1 = \frac{\pi}{6} = 30^0$

So $Arg\left(\frac{z_2 + z_3 - 2z_1}{z_3 - z_2}\right) = \frac{\pi}{6} - \frac{2\pi}{3} = -\frac{\pi}{2}$

If 'C' is considered then Arg will be $\pi/2$

22. (a) $a_1 z + a_2 z^2 + \ldots + a_n z^n = -1$

$\Rightarrow |a_1|\,|z| + |a_2||z|^2 + \ldots + |a_n|\,|z|^n = 1 \Rightarrow$ But $|a_i| < 3$

$\Rightarrow 1 < 3\,(|z| + |z|^2 + \ldots + |z|^n) < 3\,(|z| + |z|^2 + \ldots)$

$\Rightarrow 1 < 3\left[\frac{|z|}{1-|z|}\right]$ for $|z| < 1$ $\Rightarrow \frac{1}{3} < \frac{|z|}{1-|z|}$

$\Rightarrow 1 - |z| < 3|z| \qquad \Rightarrow 1 < 4|z| \Rightarrow 1/4 < |z| < 1$

∴ z lies outside the circle $|z| = 1/4$ even when $|z| \geq 1$.

23. (c) Given $\frac{z_1}{z_2} + \frac{z_2}{z_1} = 1$ then $z_1^2 + z_2^2 = z_1 z_2$

This will be possible when z_1, z_2 and origin are forming an equilateral triangle as proved $z_2 - 0 = (z_1 - 0)e^{i\pi/3}$

$\Rightarrow z_2^2 = z_1^2 e^{\frac{2\pi}{3}i}$ so $z_1^2 + z_2^2 = z_1^2\left\{1 + e^{\frac{2\pi}{3}i}\right\}$

$= z_1^2\left\{\frac{1}{2} + \frac{\sqrt{3}}{2}i\right\} = z_1^2 e^{i\pi/3} = z_1 z_2$

24. (a) Given $z_1 + z_2$ are the roots of $z^2 + az + b = 0$

$z_1 + z_2 = -a$ and $z_1 z_2 = b$

Since line joining $A(z_1)$ and $B(z_2)$ passes though origin

$\Rightarrow z_2 = kz_1$ $(k \in \mathbb{R};\ k \neq 0)$

{If $k = 0$ then $z_2 = 0 \Rightarrow b = 0$}

So $z_1 + z_2 = z_1(1 + k) = -a$ gives $z_1 = \frac{-a}{k+1}$ (for $k \neq -1$)

$\therefore\ z_1 z_2 = k\left(\frac{-a}{k+1}\right)^2 = b$

Hence $\frac{a^2}{b} = \frac{(k+1)^2}{k}$ which is real, when $k = -1$,

then $z_1 + z_2 = 0 \qquad \Rightarrow \frac{a^2}{b} = 0$ b is real

25. (a) Given $|z| = -z$

Since $|z| \geq 0$ is purely real

∴ z must be a purely real non-positive number i.e., $x \leq 0$ and $y = 0$

26. (c) Let D the centre of the square then radius of circle $= \frac{|z_0|}{2}$

$D = \frac{1}{\sqrt{2}} z_0 e^{\frac{\pi}{4}i} = \frac{1}{\sqrt{2}}\left\{\frac{1}{\sqrt{2}} + \frac{i}{\sqrt{2}}\right\} z_0 = \left(\frac{1}{2} + \frac{i}{2}\right) z_0$

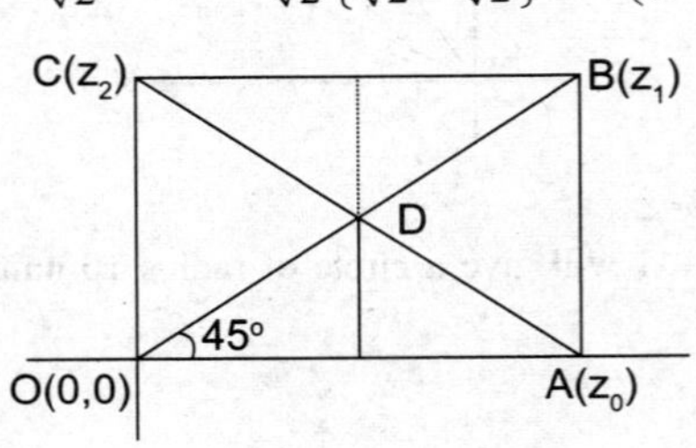

∴ The equation of circle is $\left|z - \frac{z_0(1+i)}{2}\right| = \frac{|z_0|}{2}$ or

$2\left|z - \frac{z_0(1+i)}{2}\right| = |z_0|$

27. (a) According to the given condition

$\tan\frac{\theta}{2} = \frac{\text{Im}(z_1)}{\text{Re}(z_1)} = \frac{y}{x} = \sqrt{2} - 1$

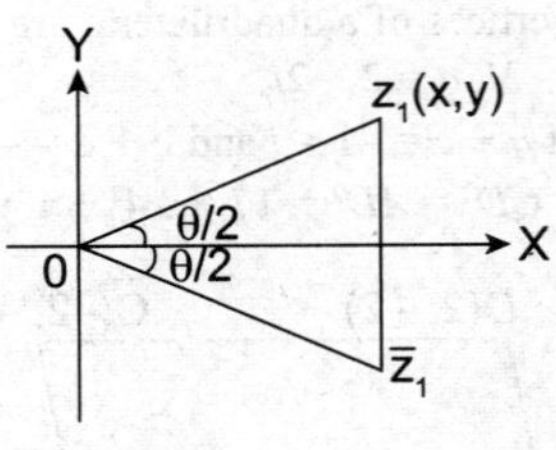

So $\tan\frac{\theta}{2} = \tan\frac{\pi}{8} \Rightarrow \theta \Rightarrow \theta = \frac{\pi}{4}$

∴ $n = 8$

28. (c) Given $z_1 = 1$ and $z_1, z_2, z_3, \ldots\ldots, z_n$ are in G.P.

Also $z_1 + z_2 + z_3 + \ldots\ldots + z_n = 0$ (where $z_1 = 1$)

The regular polygon will have 'n' sides. Hence Incentre and circum centre will coincide

⇒ Distance is zero

29. (d) As shown $(x-1)+i(y+\sqrt{3})=2e^{\frac{5\pi}{6}i}.e^{\frac{5\pi}{6}i}=-2,$

so $x=-1$ and $y=-\sqrt{3}$

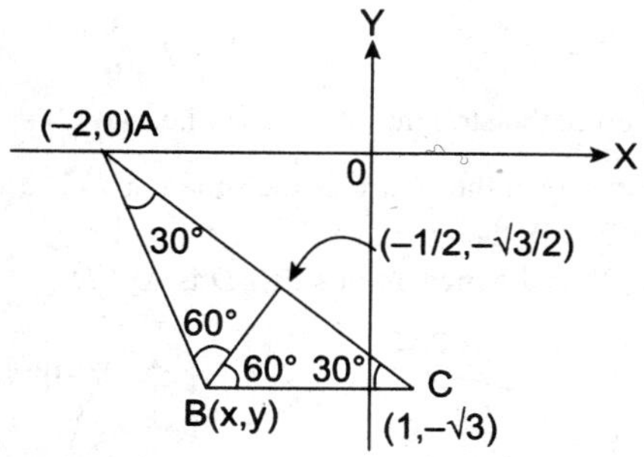

Hence $B=(-1,\sqrt{3})$ ∴ (Circum) centre of the hexagon (0, 0)
The other points (vertices) will be (2, 0), $(-1,\sqrt{3})$, $(1+\sqrt{3})$

30. **(a)** $z_2-i=(3-4i)e^{\frac{2\pi}{3}i}$ and $z_3-i=(3-4i)e^{-\frac{2\pi}{3}i}$

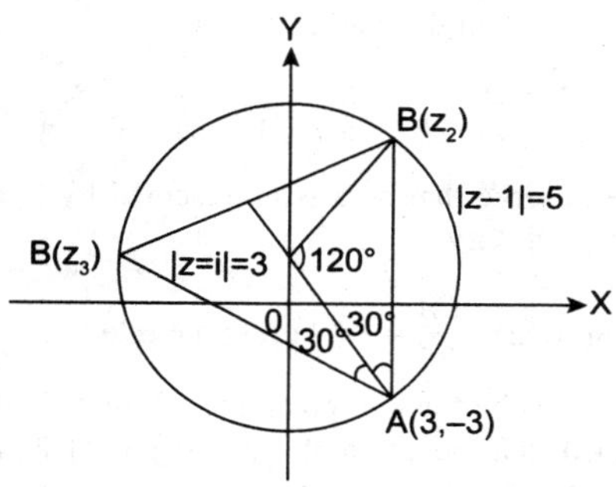

Gives $z_2=\frac{1}{2}\left\{-3+4\sqrt{3}+3\left(\sqrt{3}+2\right)i\right\}$ and

$$z_3=\left(-\frac{1}{2}\right)\left\{3+4\sqrt{3}+3\left(\sqrt{3}-2\right)i\right\}$$

Aliter: The triangle with maximum area will be an equilateral triangle

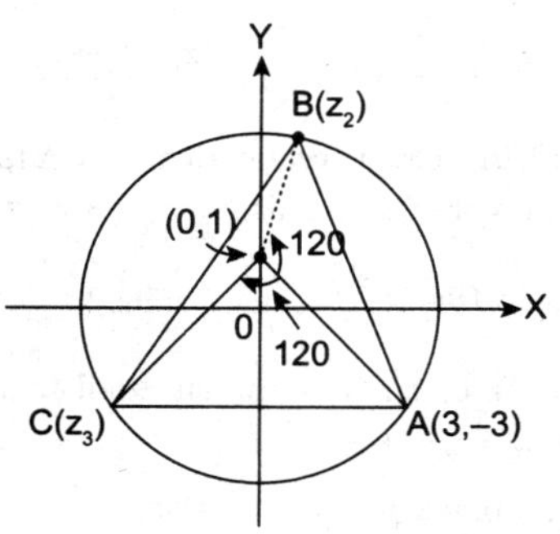

We know $R=\frac{2a}{3}\frac{\sqrt{3}}{2}=\frac{a}{\sqrt{3}}$. So $5\sqrt{3}$ units

$\sqrt{3}(-3+4i)e^{\pm\frac{\pi}{6}i}=z_p-3+3i$.

Where z_p is either z_3 or z_2 respectively.

$$\Rightarrow\quad z_p=\sqrt{3}\left(\frac{\sqrt{3}}{2}\pm\frac{i}{2}\right)(-3-4i)+3-3i$$

Gives $\frac{1}{2}\left\{-3+4\sqrt{3}+3\left(\sqrt{3}+2\right)i\right\}$

or $\left(\frac{-1}{2}\right)\left[3+4\sqrt{3}+3\left(\sqrt{3}-2\right)i\right]$

31. (d) From (Rule ONGC' we know that G divides OC' in the ratio 2 : 1 {C' is the circumcentre at (0, 0)}

Now C' = (0, 0) and $G=\frac{z_1+z_2+z_3}{3}$,

so orthocenter $O=z_1+z_2+z_3$

32. (b) Given rectangle with maximum area will be a square and the vertex is (3, 3) or (3, 5)

33. (c) Here $|DB|=|OA|$ and $|PA|=|PB|$

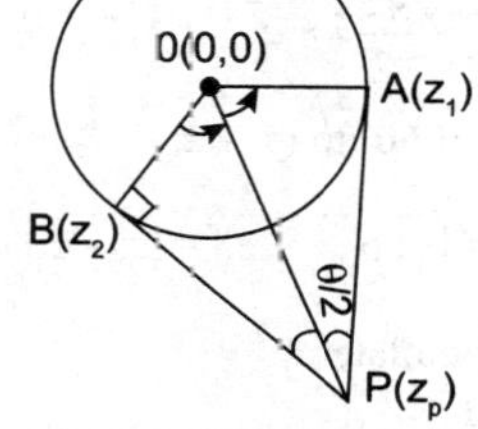

$(z_p-z_2)i=(0-z_2)\,k$; where $|k|=|\cot\theta/2|$
$(z_p-z_1)(-i)=(0-z_1)\,k$

So $\frac{z_p-z_2}{z_1-z_p}=\frac{z_2}{z_1}$ gives $\frac{z_1z_2}{z_1\quad z_2}$

34. (a) $|z_1+z_2|=|z_1-z_2|\Rightarrow z_2=\pm iz_1$
And as a result the circumcentre of ΔOAB is the mid point of AB, i.e., $\frac{z_1+z_2}{2}$

35. (a) Given z, z_1, z_2 are collinear also $|z_1-z|=|z_2-z|=|z_3-z|$

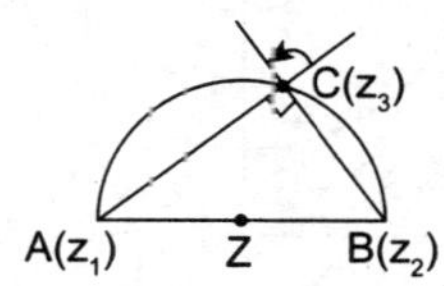

$$\Rightarrow\quad Arg\left(\frac{z_3-z_2}{z_3-z_1}\right)=\frac{\pi}{2}$$

36. (b) Let $\frac{2z+1}{1+iz}=p-2i$ (where $p\in\mathbb{R}$)

So $1+2z=p+2z-2i+p\,zi\ \Rightarrow\ pz=2+(p-1)i$

i.e., $z=x+iy=\frac{2}{p}+\left(1-\frac{1}{p}\right)i$ (for $p\neq 0$),

Eliminating p, $2/p=x$ and $\frac{1}{p}=1-y$ gives $2-2y=x$

i.e., $x+2y-2=0$ which is a straight line

37. (b) From the given condition, we conclude $z_2 = (-2, 0)$ and $z_3 = 1 - \sqrt{3}i$

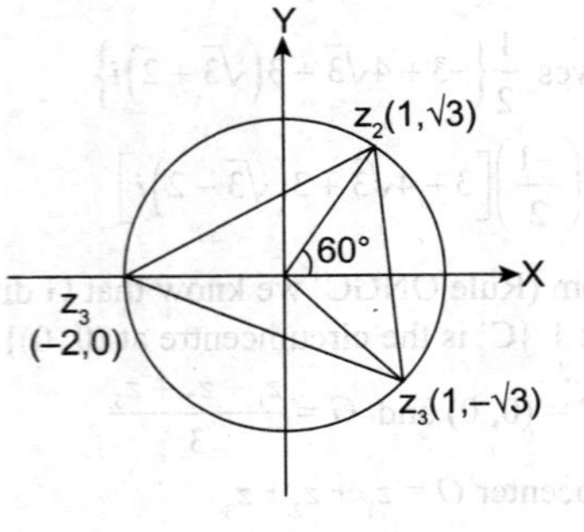

38. (a) $z_2 = iz_1$

$\therefore \quad (z_1 - z_2)^2 = z_1^2(1-i)^2$

$= z_1^2\{1-1-2i\} = (-2)\,(iz_1)(z_1) = -2z_1z_2$

39. (c) $\dfrac{z_1 - z_3}{z_2 - z_3} = \dfrac{1}{2} - \dfrac{\sqrt{3}}{2}i = e^{-\frac{\pi}{3}i}$

$\Rightarrow$ $(z_1 - z_3)$ is at 60° to $(z_2 - z_3)$

As $\left|e^{-\frac{\pi}{3}i}\right| = 1$, so $|z_1 - z_3| = |z_2 - z_3|$

$\therefore$ $\Delta\, ABC$ is equilateral

40. (a) Let z_3 be the point where a circle of radius r which is orthogonal to both given circles, then $|(z_3 - 0)|^2 = r^2 + 1$ and $|z_3 - 1|^2 = r^2 + 16$ gives real $(z_3) = -7$ as shown

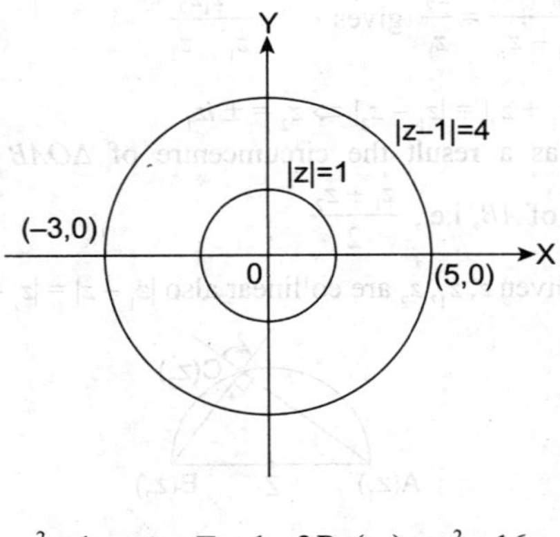

$$z_3\bar{z}_3 = r^2 + 1 \text{ and } z_3\bar{z}_3 + 1 - 2\,\text{Re}(z_3) = r^2 + 16$$

Putting $z_3\bar{z}_3 = r^2 + 1$, gives $-2Re\ (z_3) = 14$, so $\text{Re}(z_3) = -7$ then $z_3 = -7 + \alpha i$ (say)

$\Rightarrow \quad z_3\bar{z}_3 = r^2 + 1$

$\Rightarrow \quad (-7)^2 + \alpha^2 - 1 = 48 + \alpha^2$

$\Rightarrow \quad |z + 7 - \alpha i| = \sqrt{48 + \alpha^2}; \alpha \in \mathbb{R}$

41. **(b)** $|z^2 - 1| = |z|^2 + 1 \Rightarrow |x^2 - y^2 + 2ixy - 1| = x^2 + y^2 + 1$

$\Rightarrow$ $(x^2 - y^2 - 1)^2 + 4x^2y = (x^2 + y^2 + 1)^2$

Solving we get, $x = 0$

$\Rightarrow$ z lies on imaginary axes.

42. **(d)** Given $w = \dfrac{z}{z - \dfrac{i}{3}}$ and $|w| = 1$

So $|z| = \left|z - \dfrac{i}{3}\right| \quad \Rightarrow \quad \text{Im}(z) = \dfrac{1}{6}$

This gives the straight line y = 1/6 i.e., Im (z) = 1/6

43. **(b)** As shown the centre of the square is $E(1, 0)$.

Let $A(2, \sqrt{3})$, then $C(0, -\sqrt{3})$.

Now CE is the median of side BD is ΔBCD

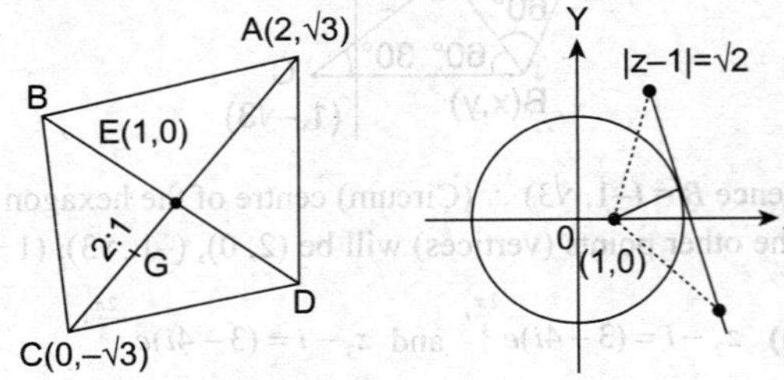

$\therefore$ $\quad G$ is 2/3rd on the way from C to E

$\Rightarrow \quad G = \dfrac{2 + 0 - \sqrt{3}i}{3} = \dfrac{2}{3} - \dfrac{i}{\sqrt{3}}$

44. **(c)** We observe that area is represented by $|z + 1| > 2$ and $|\text{Arg}\ (z + 1)| < \pi/4$.

45. **(c, d)** $B(-6, 2)$; $\dfrac{PA}{PB} = 3 \neq 1$ gives a circle.

Let C and D be the two positions of point P where line AB (extended) will be a line of symmetry (or Diameter)

$C = \dfrac{2 - 2i + 6i - 18}{4} = \dfrac{-16 + 4i}{4} = -4 + i$ and

$D = \dfrac{-2 + 2i + 6i - 18}{+2} = -10 + 4i$

So the circle will be having its centre at the mid point of C and $D = -7 + \dfrac{5i}{2}$ and it radius $r = \dfrac{3\sqrt{5}}{2}$

46. (a, c, d) $|z_1| = |z_2| = |z_3| = 1$ and $\dfrac{z_1 + z_2 + z_3}{3} = 0$

$\Rightarrow$ $G = (0, 0)$ = circum centre. Hence the ΔABC is equilateral.

$\Rightarrow$ Origin is orthocenter also $z_1^2 + z_2^2 + z_3^2 = \Sigma z_1z_2$ and area of the $\Delta ABC = \dfrac{\sqrt{3}}{4}$ square units.

47. **(a, b, c, d)** 0, z_1, z_2 form an equilateral triangle then $z_1^2 + z_2^2 + z_3^2 = z_1z_2 + z_2z_3 + z_1z_3$

Putting $z_3 = 0$, we get $z_1^2 + z_2^2 = z_1z_2$

$\text{Arg}(z_1) - \text{Arg}(z_2) = \pi/3$ also $|z_1 - z_2| = |z_1| = |z_2|$

Further using $z_1 = z_2e^{\frac{\pi}{3}i}$ we get $z_1 - z_2 = z_2e^{\frac{2\pi}{3}i}$

So $\dfrac{1}{z_1 - z_2} + \dfrac{1}{z_2} = \dfrac{1}{z_2}\left\{1 + e^{\frac{2\pi}{3}i}\right\} = \dfrac{1}{z_2}.e^{-\frac{\pi}{3}i} = \dfrac{1}{z_2e^{\frac{\pi}{3}i}} = \dfrac{1}{z_1}$

48. (a, c, d) $|3z + i| = \lambda|z + 2|$ will represent a circle when $\frac{\lambda}{3} \neq 1$

Hence $\lambda = 1, 2, 5$ will given circles.

49. (a, b, c, d) $|z - z_1| + |z - z_2| = k$, where $k \in \mathbb{R}$ when $k > |z_1 - z_2|$, then the locus is an ellipse

When $k = |z_1 - z_2|$, then it the line segment AB (joining z_1 and z_2)

When $k < |z_1 - z_2|$, then it gives no locus.

If $z_1 - z_2$ then $2|z_1 - z| = k$

If $k = 0$, then we get a point $z = z_1$

If $k > 0$ then $|z - z_1| = k/2$ which gives a circle.

SECTION III: (ONLY ONE CORRECT)

1. (d) Given $Arg(z) - Arg(\omega) = \frac{\pi}{2}$ and $|z\,\omega| = 1$

Using $\text{Arg}(\bar{z}) = -\text{Arg}(z)$ we get $-\text{Arg}(\bar{z}) - \text{Arg}\omega = \frac{\pi}{2}$

$\Rightarrow \text{Arg}(\bar{z}\omega) = -\frac{\pi}{2} \quad \Rightarrow \quad \bar{z}\omega = -i$

{Since $|z\omega| = 1$, so $|\bar{z}\omega| = 1$}

2. (a) Let $z = (1 + 2\omega + \omega^2)^{3n} - (1 + \omega + 2\omega^2)^{3n}$

So $z = (\omega^3)^n - (\omega^6)^n = 1^n - 1^n = 0$

3. (d) $225 + (3\omega + 8\omega^2)^2 + (3\omega^2 + 8\omega)^2 = 225 + 9\omega^2 + 64\omega + 48 + 9\omega + 64\omega^2 + 48$

$= 273 + 73\omega + 73\omega^2 + 48 = 248 + 73(1 + \omega + \omega^2) = 248$

4. (c) Given $\arg\left(\frac{z_1}{z_2}\right) = 0 \Rightarrow \frac{z_1}{z_2}$ is purely real

i.e., $z_1 = kz_2$ where $k > 0$; So $|z_1 - z_2| = ||z_1| - |z_2||$

5. (c) Given $|z_1 + z_2| = |z_1 - z_2| \quad \Rightarrow \quad \arg\left(\frac{z_1}{z_2}\right) = \pm\frac{\pi}{2}$

6. (a) Given $|z_1| = |z_2|$ and $\arg\left(\frac{z_1}{z_2}\right) = \pi$

$\Rightarrow z_1 = -z_2$, so $z_1 + z_2 = 0$

7. (c) Given $0 < \text{Amp}(z) < \pi$

$\Rightarrow \text{Amp}(-z) = -\pi + \text{Amp}(z) \Rightarrow \text{Amp}(z) - \text{Amp}(-z) = \pi$

8. (a) Let $z_1 = \frac{z-1}{z+1} = \frac{(z-1)(\bar{z}+1)}{(z+1)(\bar{z}+1)} = \frac{z\bar{z} - 1 + (z - \bar{z})}{(z+1)(\bar{z}+1)}$

Since z_1 is purely imaginary so $z\bar{z} - 1 = 0$ i.e., $|z| = 1$

9. (d) Given $|z - 2| + |z + 2| \leq 4$

For $|z - 2| + |z + 2| = 4$ we get the line segment joining $(-2, 0)$ and $(2, 0)$

We get no solution for $|z - 2| + |z + 2| < 4$

10. (c) Given $|z| \neq 1$ and $\left|\frac{z - z_1}{1 - \bar{z}z_1}\right| = 1$

$\Rightarrow \quad (z - z_1)(\bar{z} - \bar{z}_1) = (1 - \bar{z}z_1)(1 - z\bar{z}_1)$

gives $z\bar{z} + z_1\bar{z}_1 = 1 + z\bar{z}z_1\bar{z}_1$ or $z_1\bar{z}_1(1 - z\bar{z}) = (1 - z\bar{z})$

$\Rightarrow \quad |z_1|^2(1 - |z|^2) = (1 - |z|^2)$

Since $|z| \neq 1 \qquad \Rightarrow \quad |z_1| = 1$

11. (d) Given $\omega = \frac{z}{(\alpha - z)(z\bar{\alpha} - 1)}$; where $|z| = 1$ and $|\alpha| \neq 1$)

$\Rightarrow \quad \omega = \frac{z\bar{z}}{(\alpha - z)(\bar{\alpha}z\bar{z} - \bar{z})} = \frac{|z|^2}{(\alpha - z)(\bar{\alpha}|z|^2 - \bar{z})}$

$= \frac{1}{(\alpha - z)(\bar{\alpha} - \bar{z})} = \frac{1}{|\alpha - z|^2}$

Since $|\alpha| \neq 1$ and $z = 1 \Rightarrow \omega > 0$

12. (c) $az + b\bar{z} + c = 0 \qquad$ ...(i)

$\Rightarrow \quad \bar{a}\bar{z} + \bar{b}z + \bar{c} = 0 \qquad$ ....(ii)

Multiplying (i) by $\bar{a}$ and (ii) by b and subtracting, we get $a\bar{a}z - b\bar{b}z = b\bar{c} - \bar{a}c$

$\Rightarrow \quad (|a|^2 - |b|^2)z = b\bar{c} - \bar{a}c \qquad$ ....(iii)

$\because \quad |a| = |b|$ and $\bar{a}c \neq b\bar{c}$ (given)

$\Rightarrow$ LHS $= 0 \neq$ RHS

Equation (iii) is satisfied by no complex number z

$\Rightarrow$ There is no solution

13. (b) From above question $(|a|^2 - |b|^2)z = b\bar{c} - \bar{a}c \qquad$ ...(i)

Now, $|a| = |b| \neq 0$ and $\bar{a}c = b\bar{c}$ (given)

$\Rightarrow$ L.H.S. = R.H.S. $= 0\ \forall\ z$ lying on $az + b\bar{z} + c = 0 \qquad$ ....(ii)

Now multiplying (ii) by $\bar{a}$ we get $a\bar{a}z + \bar{a}b\bar{z} + \bar{a}c = 0$

$\Rightarrow \quad b\bar{b}z + \bar{a}b\bar{z} + b\bar{c} = 0$

$(\because\ a\bar{a} = |a|^2 = |b|^2 = b\bar{b}$ and $\bar{a}c = b\bar{c})$

$\Rightarrow \quad \bar{b}z + \bar{a}\bar{z} + \bar{c} = 0\ \ (|b| \neq 0 \Rightarrow b \neq 0) \qquad$ ....(iii)

Now (ii) + (iii) gives, $(a + \bar{b})z + (\bar{a} + b)\bar{z} + (c + \bar{c}) = 0$

or $\bar{\alpha}z + \alpha\bar{z} + \beta = 0$; where $\alpha = \bar{a} + b$ and $\beta = c + \bar{c}$

Which represents a straight line.

14. (d) Given $\bar{z} = \bar{z}_0 + \frac{r^2}{z - z_0}$, $r > 0$

$\Rightarrow \quad z\bar{z} - \bar{z}z_0 = z\bar{z}_0 - z_0\bar{z}_0 + r^2$

i.e., $|z - z_0|^2 = r^2$, so $|z - z_0| = r$ (as $r > 0$), the equation represents a circle with centre at z_0 and radius $= r$

15. (b) $|z - 2| = 2|z - 1|$

$\Rightarrow \quad (z - 2)(\bar{z} - 2) = 4(z - 1)(\bar{z} - 1)$

$\Rightarrow \quad z\bar{z} - 2z - 2\bar{z} + 4 = 4z\bar{z} - 4z - 4\bar{z} + 4$

$\Rightarrow \quad 3|z|^2 - 2(z + \bar{z}) = 0$

$\Rightarrow \quad 3|z|^2 - 4Re(z) = 0$

16. (a) Given $z|z| + kz + 2k = 0$ (where $k > 0$)

$\Rightarrow \quad z(|z| + k) = -2k$

Since $k > 0$ (so $|z| + k \geq k > 0$)

$\Rightarrow \quad z < 0$. i.e., z is a negative real number.

17. **(d)** Given $|z-1| = |z-i|$ which is the right bisector of line segment joining (1, 0) and (0, 1) and $|z-1| = 3$ will given two points on the right bisector.

18. **(c)** Given: $z^2 + az + b = 0$ has real roots z_1 and z_2 (say), then $z_1 + z_2 = -a$ and $z_1z_2 = b$
So $-a, b$ are purely real
$\Rightarrow$ Im(b) = Im$(a) = 0$ $\quad\Rightarrow$ $(\text{Im } b)^2 + (\text{Im } a) = 0$

19. **(d)** z_1 lies inside the circle $|z-5| = 7$ and z_2 lies on $|z+2| + |z-1| = 5$

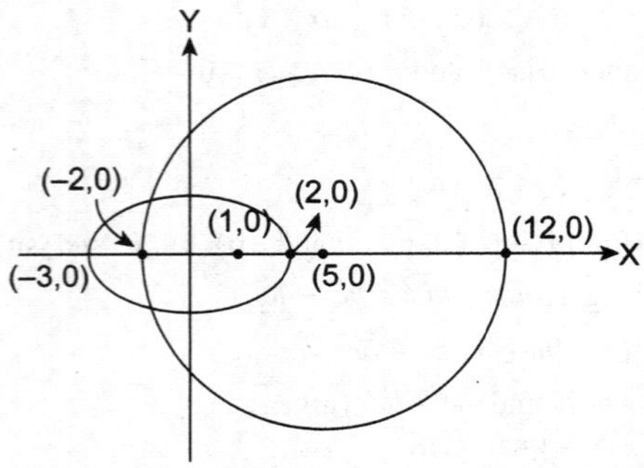

Observe that $k = |z_1 - z_2|$
Is maximum when $z_1(12, 0)$ and $z_2 = (-3, 0)$.
Minimum value of $k = 0$, as part of the ellipse lies in the circle
$\Rightarrow$ $0 \le k < 15$

20. **(a)** Given $a \ne 0$ and Re$(z/a) = 1$, which represent a straight line

21. **(b)** $\sin(\ln (i)^i) + \cos (\ln (i)^i) = \sin\left(-\frac{\pi}{2}\right) + \cos\left(-\frac{\pi}{2}\right) = -1$

22. **(c)** Given $4x^2 - \pi^2 = 0 \Rightarrow x = \pm\frac{\pi}{2} = \pm\ln i^i$

So roots are $\ln(i)^i$ and $\ln(i^{-i})$

23. **(d)** $|z| = 1$ and $z \ne \pm 1$
$\therefore$ $1 - z^2 \ne 0$

Now $\frac{z}{1-z^2} = \frac{z - z\bar{z}\bar{z}}{|1-z^2|^2} = \frac{z-\bar{z}}{|1-z^2|^2}$ which is purely imaginary (here $x \ne \pm 1, y \ne 0$)

$\Rightarrow$ $\frac{z}{1-z^2} = \frac{2yi}{|1-z^2|^2}$ represents a straight line y-axis (but excluding the origin)

So $\frac{z}{1-z^2}$ will lies on y-axis

24. **(c)** We know that $1 + \omega + \omega^2 = 0$
When a fair die is thrown three times then $n(S) = 216$
Let $r_1 = 1, 4$; $r_2 = 2, 5$; $r_3 = 3, 6$; where r_1, r_2, r_3 can be permutated in 3! ways.
Number of favourable case $n(E) = 2^3 \times 3! = 48$

Hence $P(E) = \frac{48}{216} = \frac{2}{9}$

25. **(c)** $\sin\{\omega^{19} + \omega^{101})\pi - \pi/6\} = \sin\left(-\pi - \frac{\pi}{6}\right)$

$= -\sin\left(\pi + \frac{\pi}{6}\right) = \frac{1}{2}$

26. **(b)** a, b, c are integers not simultaneously equal (but any two may be equal)
So $|a\omega + b\omega^2 + c|^2 = (a\omega + b\omega^2 + c)(a\omega^2 + b\omega + c) = a^2 + b^2 + c^2 - (ac + bc + ca)$

$= \frac{1}{2}\{(a-b)^2 + (b-c)^2 + (c-a)^2\}$

So $|a\omega + b\omega^2 + c|^2 \ge 1$ hence $|a\omega + b\omega^2 + c| \ge 1$
or $|a\omega^{10} + b\omega^{20} + c| \ge 1$

27. **(a)** Given $|z_1| = |z_2|$ but $z_1 \ne z_2$
Let $z_1 = x_1 + iy_1$ and $z_2 = x_2 + iy_2$; where $x_1 > 0$ and $y_2 < 0$;

Now $\frac{z_1 + z_2}{z_1 - z_2} = \frac{(z_1 + z_2)(\bar{z}_1 - \bar{z}_2)}{(z_1 - z_2)(\bar{z}_1 - \bar{z}_2)}$

$= \frac{2i\,\text{Im}(z_1\bar{z}_2)}{|z_1 - z_2|^2} = \frac{2i(x_1y_2 - x_2y_1)}{|z_1 - z_2|^2}$

Which is purely imaginary

28. **(d)** $|z-1| + |z-3| \le 8$ gives the boundary and interior of the ellipse.
The point (–2, 0) is at max distance from (4, 0)
$\Rightarrow$ $|z-4| \in [0, 6]$

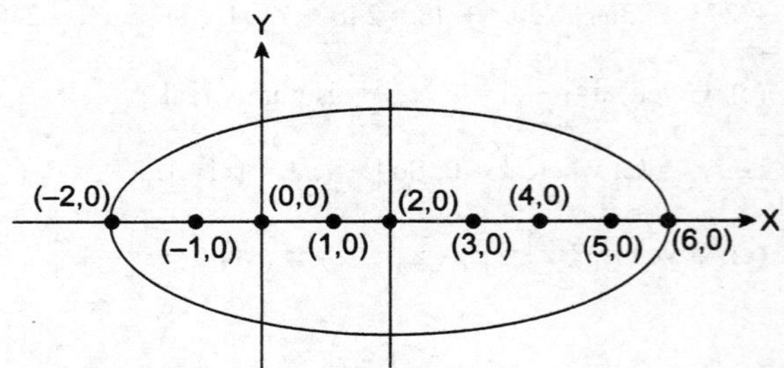

29. **(c)** $z^2 + z|z| + |z|^2 = 0$
Let $z = x + iy$, then
$x^2 - y^2 + 2xyi + (x + iy)\left(\sqrt{x^2 + y^2} + (x - iy)\right) = 0$

Gives $2x^2 + x\sqrt{x^2 + y^2} + \left(2xy + y\sqrt{x^2 + y^2}\right)i = 0$

Gives $(x + yi)\left\{2x + \sqrt{x^2 + y^2}\right\} = 0$

Either $x = 0, y = 0$ or $\left(2x + \sqrt{x^2 + y^2}\right) = 0$

So $\sqrt{x^2 + y^2} = -2x$
$\Rightarrow$ $x \le 0$; squaring we get $x^2 + y^2 = 4x^2$
So $y = \pm\sqrt{3}x$ for $x \le 0$ gives two says starting from (0, 0) as shown below.

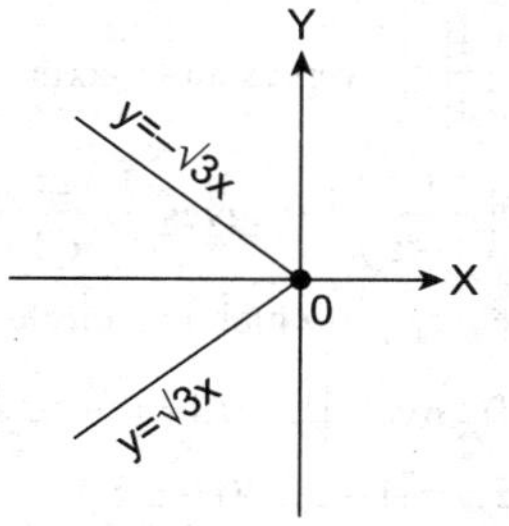

30. (d) $\overrightarrow{AP} = \frac{4}{3}\left(-\frac{3}{\sqrt{2}} - \frac{3}{2}i\right)e^{-\frac{\pi}{2}i} = -\frac{4}{3}i\left(-\frac{3}{\sqrt{2}} - \frac{3}{\sqrt{2}}i\right)$

$= -2\sqrt{2} + 2\sqrt{2}\, i$

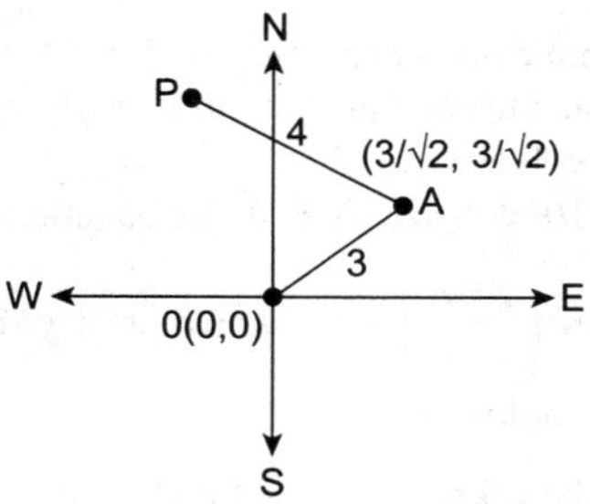

So $\overrightarrow{OP} = -2\sqrt{2} + i2\sqrt{2} + \frac{3}{\sqrt{2}} + \frac{3i}{\sqrt{2}}$

$= -\frac{1}{\sqrt{2}} + \frac{7}{\sqrt{2}}i = (3+4i)\left(\frac{1}{\sqrt{2}} + \frac{i}{\sqrt{2}}\right) = (3+4i)e^{i\frac{\pi}{4}}$

31. (d) $z_0 = 1 + 2i$
$A = 6 + 2i$
$z_1 = 6 + 5i$
$B = 7 + 6i$

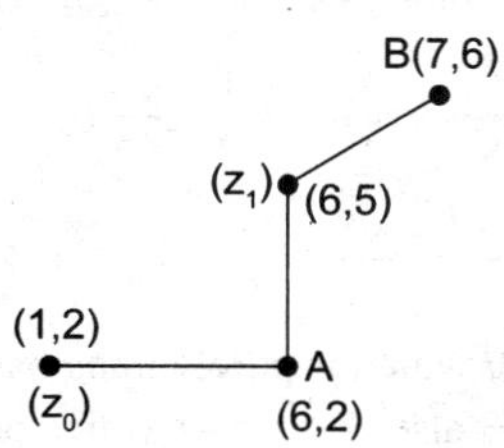

Vector $\overrightarrow{OB}$ moves about O by $\pi/2$ in anti-clockwise direction

$\Rightarrow z_2 = (7 + 6i)i = -6 + 7i$

32. (a) Given: $\frac{|z^2 - 25|}{|z|} = 24$ observe that $|z| = 25$ satisfies

33. (b) $|z_1 - z_2| = |z_1 + z_2|$ and $z_2 = \sqrt{3}i\, z_1$; $|\tan\theta| = \left|\frac{z_2}{z_1}\right| = \sqrt{3}$

$\Rightarrow |\theta| = 60°$. Hence the required angle is $-2|\theta| = \frac{-2\pi}{3}$.

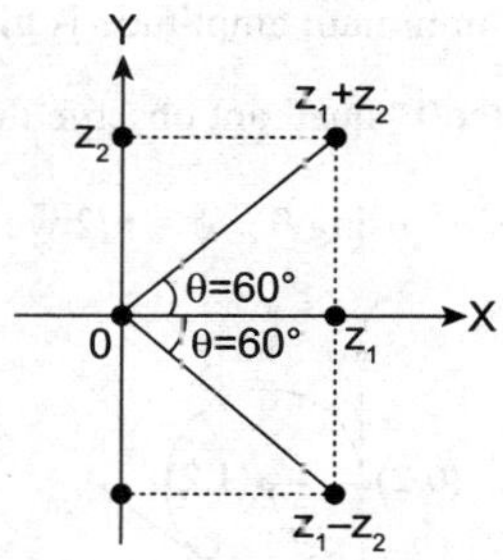

34. (a) Given $iz_1 = kz_2$ (where $0 < k < 1$)

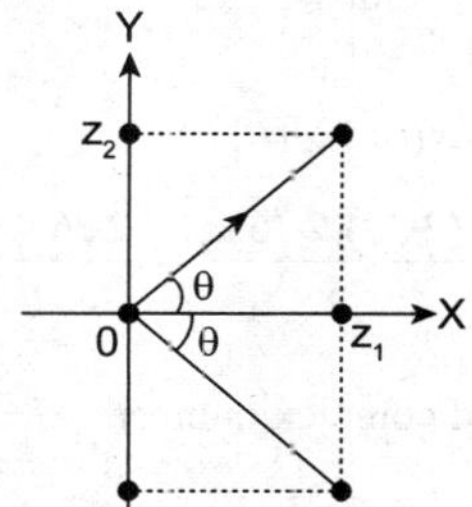

So $z_2 = \frac{i}{k}z_1$

$\Rightarrow |\tan\theta| = \left|\frac{z_2}{z_1}\right| = \frac{1}{k} > 1; \frac{\pi}{2} > |\theta| = \tan^{-1}\left(\frac{1}{k}\right) > \frac{\pi}{4}$

So $|2\theta| = 2\tan^{-1}\left(\frac{1}{k}\right)$ (where $2\theta > \pi/2$)

We observe that anticlockwise direction means the required angle $= -2|\theta| = -2\tan^{-1}\left(\frac{1}{k}\right)$

Now $\tan^{-1}\frac{1}{k} = \frac{\pi}{2} - \tan^{-1}k$ (as $0 < k < 1$)

$\Rightarrow -2\tan^{-1}\left(\frac{1}{k}\right) = -\pi + 2\tan^{-1}(k)$

35. (c) Given $z_1 = a + ib$ and $z_2 = c + id$

$\Rightarrow a^2 + b^2 = c^2 + d^2 = 1$

Now $\text{Re}(-z_1\bar{z}_2) = -ac - bd = 0$

$\Rightarrow \frac{a}{b} = \frac{-d}{c} = k$ (say)

$\Rightarrow b^2(1 + k^2) = a^2 + b^2 = 1$, so $b^2 = \frac{1}{k^2+1}$

Similarly $c^2(1 + k^2) = 1$

$\therefore b = \pm c$

Case (i): $b = c$, then $a = -d$

Case (ii): $b = -c$, then $a = d$

Using this result $\omega_1 = a + ic$

$\Rightarrow |\omega_1|^2 = a^2 + c^2 = a^2 + b^2 = 1$

Similarly $\omega_2 = b + id$

$\Rightarrow |\omega_2|^2 = 1$ and $\text{Re}(\bar{\omega}_1\omega_2) = ab + cd = 0$

36. **(a)** $|z - 5i| \le 1$ minimum amplitude is given by the tangent from origin in the 1st quadrant observe that $\sin\theta = \frac{1}{5}$ and $OP = \sqrt{24} = 2\sqrt{6}$; using $\theta + \phi = \pi/2$ we get

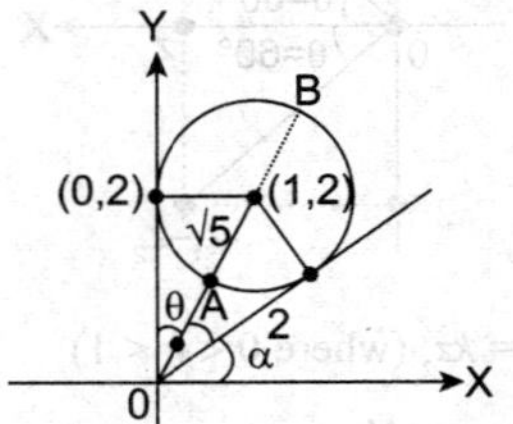

$$P = 2\sqrt{6}\{\cos\theta + i\sin\theta\}$$

$$= \frac{2\sqrt{6}}{5} + \frac{(2\sqrt{6})(2\sqrt{6})i}{5} = \frac{2\sqrt{6}}{5} + \frac{24}{5}i$$

37. **(c)** The required complex number $= -\frac{5}{2}\{2-4i\} = 5 + 10i$

38. **(c)** Let $z_3 = (1 - i)z_1 + iz_2$

$\Rightarrow z_3 = z_1 - iz_1 + iz_2 \qquad \Rightarrow z_3 - z_1 = i\,(z_2 - z_1)$

$\Rightarrow |z_3 - z_1| = |z_2 - z_1|$ and $Arg\left(\frac{z_3 - z_1}{z_2 - z_1}\right) = \frac{\pi}{2}$

$\Rightarrow z_1, z_2, z_3$ are vertices of a right angled isosceles Δ.

SECTION IV: (OBJECTIVE TYPE)

1. (a), (c) $x^2 - 2x\cos\theta + 1 = 0$ has roots $x = \frac{2\cos\theta \pm \sqrt{4\cos^2\theta - 4}}{2}$

$x = \cos\theta \pm i\sin\theta = e^{\pm i\theta}$; When the roots are $x^n = e^{\pm in\theta}$

then the equation will be $x^2 - 2x\cos n\theta + 1 = 0$

$\Rightarrow$ Which can also be written as $(x - \cos n\theta)^2 + \sin^2 n\theta = 0$

2. (a), (b), (c) $|z_1| = 1$ and $|z_2| = 2$

$|2z_1 + z_2| \le 2|z_1| + |z_2| = 4$, so max $|2z_1 + z_2| = 4$

Minimum $|z_1 - z_2| = ||z_1| - |z_2|| = 1$;

similarly $\left|z_2 + \frac{1}{z_1}\right| \le |z_2| + \frac{1}{|z_1|} = 2 + 1 = 3$

3. (c, d) Given $f(x) = P(x^3) + x\,Q(x^3)$

Now $f(x)$ is divisible by $x^2 + x + 1 = (x - \omega)(x - \omega^2)$

$\Rightarrow f(\omega) = P(1) + \omega\,Q(1) = 0$ also $f(\omega^2) = P(1) + \omega^2\,Q(1) = 0$

Which is possible only if $P(1) = 0$ and $Q(1) = 0$

i.e., both $P(x)$ and $Q(x)$ are divisible by $(x - 1)$, then as a result $f(x)$ is also divisible by $(x - 1)$

4. (b, d) Observe that option (b) gives $x^2 + y^2 + i(2yi) + 1 = 0$ which gives a point circle at $(0, -1)$

Option (c) $\arg\left(\frac{z-1}{z+1}\right) = \frac{\pi}{2}$ gives a circle at (0, 0) with radius r = 1 unit.

Option (d) $\left|\frac{z-1}{z+1}\right| = 1$ represents y-axis

Option (a) $\text{Re}\left(\frac{1+z}{1-z}\right) = 0$ gives $\frac{1 - z\bar{z} + (z - \bar{z})}{(|1-z|)^2} = 0$

$\therefore\ |z|^2 = 1$, i.e., $|z| = 1$ which is a circle.

5. (a), (b), (c), (d) Given $|z_1 - z_2| = |1 - \bar{z}_1 z_2|$ gives

$(z_1 - z_2)(\bar{z}_1 - \bar{z}_2) = (1 - \bar{z}_1 z_2)(1 - z_1\bar{z}_2)$

$\Rightarrow |z_1|^2 + |z_2|^2 - 2\text{Re}(z_1\bar{z}_2) = 1 + |z_1|^2|z_2|^2 - 2\text{Re}(z_1\bar{z}_2)$

gives $|z_1|^2 = 1$, $|z_2|^2 = 1$

Since $|z_1| = |z_2| = 1$, so these can be represented as $e^{\theta i}$; where $\theta \in \mathbb{R}$.

6. (a), (c) Complex number satisfying $|z - 12i| = |z - 8i|$ will be $z = x + 10i$ and the complex number satisfying $|z - 4| = |z - 8|$ will be $z = 6 + yi$

So $z = 6 + 10i$ will satisfy both the equations.

7. (b), (c) $Arg\left(\frac{z-a}{z+a}\right) = \frac{\pi}{2}$, which is a circle centered at origin with radius $|a|$.

8. (c), (d) Given $|z_1| = |z_2| = |z_3| = 4$ and $z_1 + z_3 = 0$

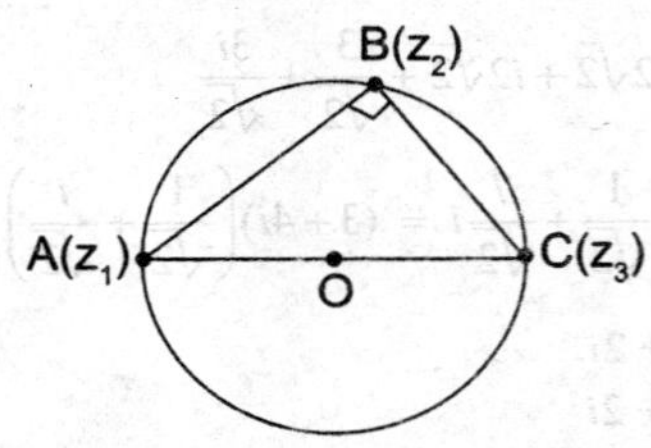

$\Rightarrow AC$ is the diameter (as $z_1 = -z_3$)

Hence the points will form a right angled triangle.

9. (a), (b), (c) Given $z = e^{\frac{\pi}{3}i} = \frac{1}{2} + \frac{\sqrt{3}}{2}i$

So $z^2 = e^{\frac{2\pi}{3}i} = -\frac{1}{2} + \frac{\sqrt{3}}{2}i$

$\Rightarrow z^2 + z = \sqrt{3}i$ which is purely imaginary

$\therefore\ |z^2 + z| = \sqrt{3}$ also $z^2 - z = -1$ which purely real

10. (a), (b), (c), (d) Max $|z| = \sqrt{5} + 1$ and Min $|z| = \sqrt{5} - 1$ for z at B and z at A respectively

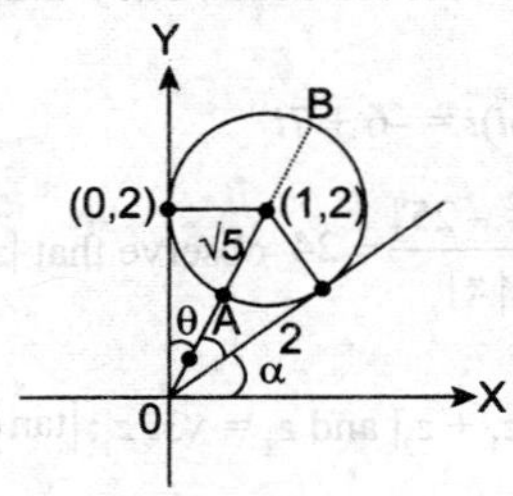

Max. Arg(z) = $\pi/2$ at (0, 2). Observe that $\sin\theta = \frac{1}{\sqrt{5}}$

or $\tan\theta = \frac{1}{2}$ $\Rightarrow$ $\tan 2\theta = \frac{1}{1-\frac{1}{4}} = \frac{4}{3}$

As $\alpha = \frac{\pi}{2} - 2\theta$, so $\tan\alpha = \frac{3}{4} \Rightarrow \alpha = \tan^{-1}\left(\frac{3}{4}\right)$

11. (a), (b), (c) $\log_{1/3}\{\log_{1/2}(|z|^2 + 4|z| + 3)\} > 0$
$\Rightarrow$ $0 < \log_{1/2}(|z|^2 + 4|z| + 3) < 1$
$\Rightarrow$ $|z|^2 + 4|z| + 3 > 1/2$
$\Rightarrow$ $2|z|^2 + 8|z| + 5 > 0$, which is always true
$\therefore$ All (a), (b), (c) represent subsets of set of complex numbers set.

12. (b), (c) Given $\log_{|z-2i|}|1 + \sqrt{3}i| > \log_{|z-2i|}|4 - 3i|$
Observe that $|z - 2i| \neq 0, 1$
Case (i): $0 < |z - 2i| = m < 1$, then $\log_m 2 > \log_m 5$
Which is true and meaningful. Obviously when
$|z - 2i| = n > 1$, then $\log_n 2 > \log_n 5$ is false
$\therefore$ $0 < |z - 2i| < 1$ is the solution
i.e., $(z - 2i)$ lies inside the curve $e^{i\theta}$ where $\theta \in \mathbb{R}$ except $z = 2i$
Since $|z - 2i| < 5$ forms a larger circle so the solution set of z also lies inside this curve.

13. (b), (c) Given $|z| = 2$, then $\frac{1+\bar{z}}{4+z} = \frac{1+\bar{z}}{z\bar{z}+z} = \frac{1}{z} = \frac{\bar{z}}{z\bar{z}} = \frac{\bar{z}}{4}$

14. (a), (b), (c) C_1: $z\bar{z} + \bar{\alpha}z + \alpha\bar{z} + \gamma = 0$ is $|z - (-\alpha)|^2 = |\alpha|^2 - \gamma$
$= \left(\sqrt{|\alpha|^2 - \gamma}\right)^2 = r_1^2$; where $(|\alpha|^2 - \gamma) \geq 0$

Similarly C_2 represents $|z - (-\beta)|^2 = (\sqrt{\beta^2 - \delta})^2 = r_2^2$
$\Rightarrow$ C_1 and C_2 will touch externally when
$|\alpha - \beta| = \sqrt{|\alpha|^2 - \gamma} + \sqrt{|\beta^2| - \delta}$
Also C_1 and C_2 will be orthogonal if
$|\alpha - \beta|^2 = |\alpha|^2 - \gamma + |\beta|^2 - \delta$
i.e., $|\alpha|^2 + |\beta|^2 - \alpha\bar{\beta} - \bar{\alpha}\beta = |\alpha|^2 + |\beta|^2 - \gamma - \delta$
$\Rightarrow$ $\alpha\bar{\beta} + \bar{\alpha}\beta = \gamma + \delta$

15. (a), (b), (c), (d) Given for $k > 0$ $|z - ki| + |z + ki| = 3k$
Which represents an ellipse with focus at $(0, k)$ and $(0, -k)$ and centre at $(0, 0)$
So major axis is along imaginary axis and minor axis is along real axis.

Now for $a = \frac{3}{2}k$ and $b = \frac{\sqrt{5}}{2}k$, the eccentricity $e = 2/3$

So the directrix is $\text{Im}(z) = \pm\frac{a}{e} = \pm\frac{9}{4}k$

16. (a), (c), (d) $A \equiv \{-1 + \sqrt{3}i\}$ and circumcentre is at origin.

Thus circum radius of ΔABC = R = 2 units.

In case of equilateral triangle. In-centre, centroid, orthocenter and circumcentre all are at the same point.

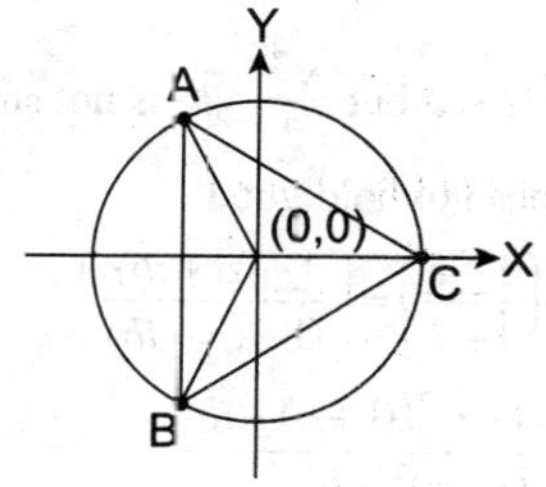

Also in equilateral Δ, $r = \frac{R}{2} = 1$ units. Further

$a = 2R\sin\frac{\pi}{3} = 2(2)\frac{\sqrt{3}}{2} = 2\sqrt{3}$ units.

17. (a), (c), (d) $z = (1 - t)z_1 + tz_2$ represent the line segment joining z_1 and z_2 for $t \in (0, 1)$
$\Rightarrow$ $|z - z_1| + |z - z_2| = |z_1 - z_2|$ and Arg z_1 = Arg $z_2 \pm \pi$
Observe that $z - z_1$ and $z_2 - z_1$ are collinear and are in the same direction.

Now $\begin{vmatrix} z - z_1 & \bar{z} - \bar{z}_1 \\ z_2 - z_1 & \bar{z}_2 - \bar{z}_1 \end{vmatrix} = 0$ gives $\frac{z - z_1}{\bar{z} - \bar{z}_1} = \frac{z_2 - z_1}{\bar{z}_2 - \bar{z}_1}$
Which is complex slope of the line and it is true

18. (a), (b) Given $z = \dfrac{\sin\left(\frac{x}{2}\right) + \cos\left(\frac{x}{2}\right) + i\tan(x)}{1 + 2i\sin\left(\frac{x}{2}\right)}$ be real

$$\Rightarrow \left(-2\sin\frac{x}{2}\right)\left\{\sin\frac{x}{2} + \cos\frac{x}{2}\right\} + \frac{\sin x}{\cos x} = 0$$

$$\Rightarrow \left(-2\sin\frac{x}{2}\right)\left\{\sin\frac{x}{2} - \cos\frac{x}{2} - \frac{\cos\frac{x}{2}}{\cos x}\right\} = 0$$

Now $\sin\frac{x}{2} = 0$ gives $x = 2n\pi$ (where $n \in$ integer)

Solving the other part $\sin\frac{x}{2} + \cos\frac{x}{2}\left(\frac{\cos x - 1}{\cos x}\right) = 0$

So $\cos\left(\frac{x}{2}\right)\left\{-2\sin^2\frac{x}{2}\right\} = \left(-\sin\frac{x}{2}\right)\cos x$

given $\sin x = \cos x$ or $\tan x = 1$
$\Rightarrow$ $x = n\pi + \pi/4$ or $n\pi + \tan^{-1}$; $n \in \mathbb{Z}$

19. (a), (c) $z_1 \cap z_2$
$\Rightarrow$ $x_1 \leq x_2$ and $y_1 \leq y_2$ for $z_1 = x_1 + iy_1$ and $z_2 = x_2 + iy_2$
Let $z = a + ib$ and $1 \cap z$ $\Rightarrow$ $1 \leq a$ and $0 \leq b$

Now $w^2 = \frac{-1}{2} - \frac{\sqrt{3}}{2}i$, clearly $-1/2 < 1 \leq a$

$\Rightarrow$ $-1/2 < a$ and $-\frac{\sqrt{3}}{2} < 0 \leq b \Rightarrow -\frac{\sqrt{3}}{2} < b$

$\Rightarrow$ $w^2 \cap z$ holds good $\Rightarrow$ (a) is true

Now $w = -\frac{1}{2} + \frac{\sqrt{3}}{2}i$

Here $-1/2 < a$ but $\frac{\sqrt{3}}{2} < b$ is not sure

$\Rightarrow$ $w \cap z$ does not hold good

Further $\left(\frac{1-z}{1+z}\right) = \left(\frac{1-(a+ib)}{(1+(a+ib)}\right)$

$$= \frac{[(1-a)-ib][(1+a)-ib]}{(1+a)^2+b^2}$$

$$= \left(\frac{1}{(1+a^2)}\right)[(1-a^2-b^2)+i(-b-ab-b+ab)]$$

$\Rightarrow$ $\text{Re}\left(\frac{1-z}{1+z}\right) = \frac{1-a^2-b^2}{(1+a)^2+b^2} = \frac{1-(a^2+b^2)}{(1+a)^2+b^2} < 0$ as $a \geq 1$

and $\text{Im}\left(\frac{1-z}{1+z}\right) = \frac{-2b}{(1+a)^2+b^2} \leq 0$ as $b \geq 0$

$\Rightarrow$ $\left(\frac{1-z}{1+z}\right) \cap 0$ holds good $\therefore$ (c) is also true

SECTION V: (ASSERTION AND REASON TYPE)

1. (a) **R:** Roots of equation $z^2 + 4z + 4i = 0$ is given by $(z+2)^2 = 4 - 4i = 4(1-i)$

$\Rightarrow$ $\{z-(-2)\}^2 = 4\sqrt{2}e^{-\frac{\pi}{4}i}$

$\Rightarrow$ $z = -2 \pm 2(2^{1/4})e^{-\frac{\pi}{8}i}$ and product of real parts is $(2 - 2\sqrt{2})$ which shows that the reason is true.

A: Statement is true as the product of real parts of roots

$$= (-2)^2\left\{1-\sqrt{2}\cos^2\frac{\pi}{8}\right\}$$

$$= 4\left\{1-\sqrt{2}\left(\frac{\sqrt{2}+1}{2\sqrt{2}}\right)^2\right\} = 2-2\sqrt{2}.$$

So Assertion is derived from reason.

2. (a) Reason is obviously true as straight line segment is the shortest distance between the end points of curve.

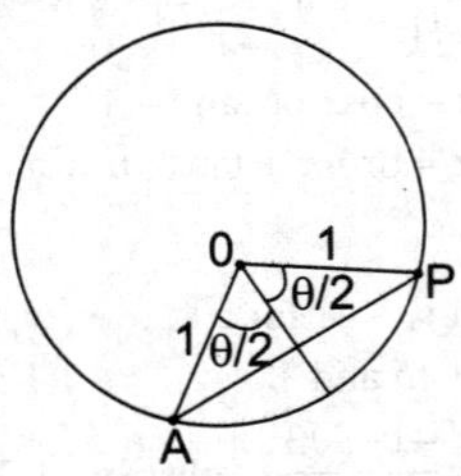

$\Rightarrow$ $AP \leq \widehat{AP}(\text{minor})$ $\Rightarrow$ $2OP\sin\frac{\theta}{2} \leq \theta.(OP)$

$\Rightarrow$ $2|z|\sin\frac{\theta}{2} \leq \theta.|z|$ $\Rightarrow$ $2\sin\frac{\theta}{2} \leq \theta$

$\Rightarrow$ $\left|\sin\frac{\theta}{2}\right| \leq \left|\frac{\theta}{2}\right|$

Let $\frac{z}{|z|} = \cos\theta + i\sin\theta$, then

$$\left|\frac{z}{|z|}-1\right| = |\cos\theta - 1 + i\sin\theta| = \left|2\sin\frac{\theta}{2}\right| \leq |\theta| = |\arg(z)|$$

Thus $\left|\frac{z}{|z|}-1\right| \leq \arg(z))$

$\Rightarrow$ Assertion is true and supported by Reason

3. (b) R: $|z_1 + z_2| \leq |z_1| + |z_2|$ is true

A: Assertion is true as $\left|z+\frac{1}{2}\right| = \frac{3}{2}$ when $z = -2$ and it is the least value of $\left|z+\frac{1}{2}\right|$

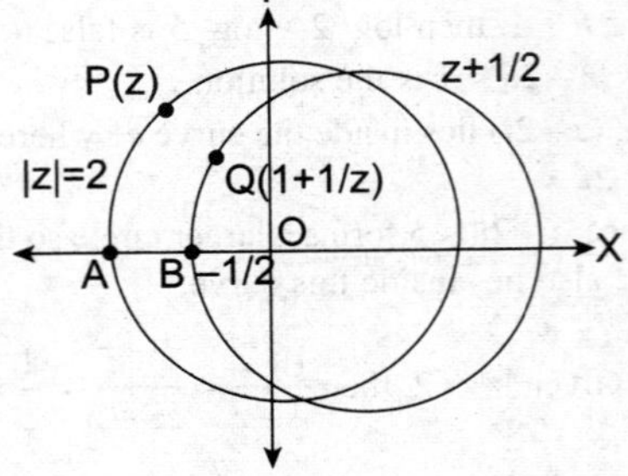

But it is not supported by $|z_1 + z_2| \leq |z_1| + |z_2|$

4. (a) **R:** Statement is true. Now set $A = \{z: |z + 2i| = 2; z \in \mathbb{C}\}$

$\Rightarrow$ z lies on circle of radius 2 and with centre at $(0, -2)$

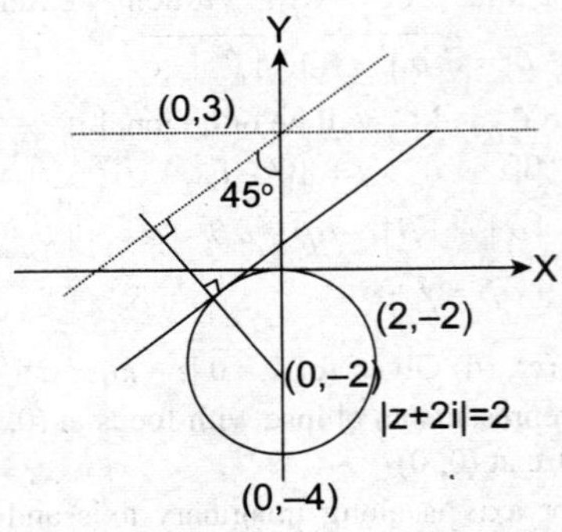

Set $B = \{z: \text{Arg}(z - 3i) = \pi/4 \text{ or } -3\pi/4\}$

$\therefore$ Shortest distance (from the centre) $= \frac{5}{\sqrt{2}}$

Shortest distance between the curves

$$= \frac{5}{\sqrt{2}} - 2 = \frac{5\sqrt{2}-4}{2}$$

Which is true and it follows from the reason.

5. (a) R: The statement is true

A: As $|z + (-3 + 2i)| \leq 4$ (given)

So from $||z_1| - |z_2|| \le |z_1 + z_2|$, we get
$||z| - |-3 + 2i|| \le |z + (-3 + 2i)| \le 4$

$\Rightarrow$ $||z| - |-3 + 2i|| \le 4$ or $|z| - \sqrt{13} \le 4$, i.e., $|z| \le 4 + \sqrt{13}$

$\Rightarrow$ Maximum value of $|z| = 4 + \sqrt{13}$

Similarly from $|z_1 + z_2| \le |z_1| + |z_2|$, we get

$|z + (-3 + 2i)| \le |z| + \sqrt{13}$ or $4 \le |z| + \sqrt{13}$

So $|z| \ge 4 - \sqrt{13}$

$\Rightarrow$ Minimum value of $|z| = 4 - \sqrt{13}$

$\therefore$ Sum of minimum and maximum value = 8

So assertion (A) is true and it follows from R.

6. (d) Clearly the reason is true.

The region represented by inequalities

$|z - 3| \le |z - 1|$ ....(i)

$|z - 3| \le |z - 5|$ ....(ii)

$|z - i| \le |z + i|$ ....(iii)

And $|z - i| \le |z - 5i|$ ....(iv)

is as shown below

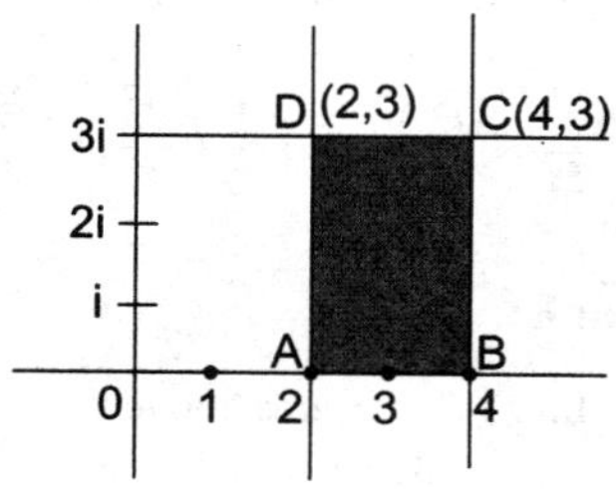

Thus the area of solution region solution is 6 square units as (2, 0), (4, 0), (2, 3) and (4, 3) are the vertices of the quadrilateral so formed. Hence "A" is false.

7. (a) Clearly, the reason is true. The centre of the circle will be at (6, 8)

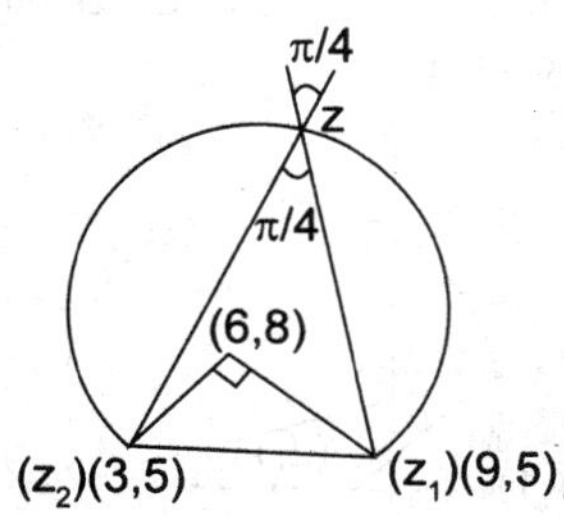

So $|z - 6 - 8i| = 3\sqrt{2}$ = radius of the circle

$\Rightarrow$ Assertion is true and it follows from R.

8. (b) **R:** Clearly, reason is true.

Given: $|z - 1| = 2|z + 1|$ observe that centre of the circle is at (–5/3, 0) and radius is 4/3.

A: $\dfrac{|z+1|}{|z-1|} = 2$ centre is at (5/3, 0) and radius is 4/3.

$\Rightarrow$ Assertion is true, Reason is true but Reason is not the correct explanation.

9. (a) **R:** The statement is true for the given conditions and requirements.

A: The statement is true and the polynomial will have the form $(x - 1)^{2p}$ (where $p \in \mathbb{N}$)

It is supported by Reason.

SECTION VI: (LINKED COMPREHENSION)

Comprehension A:

Given $|z_1| = |z_2| = |z_3| = 1$

1. (a) $z_1\bar{z}_1 = 1 \quad \Rightarrow \quad z_1 = \dfrac{1}{\bar{z}_1}$ or $|z_1| = \left|\dfrac{1}{z_1}\right|$

Now $|z_1 + z_2 + z_3| = 1$

So $\left|\dfrac{z_1\bar{z}_1}{\bar{z}_1} + \dfrac{z_2\bar{z}_2}{\bar{z}_2} + \dfrac{z_3\bar{z}_3}{\bar{z}_3}\right| = 1$

i.e., $\left|\dfrac{1}{\bar{z}_1} + \dfrac{1}{\bar{z}_2} + \dfrac{1}{\bar{z}_3}\right| = 1$ using $|z_1| = |\bar{z}_1|$ we get $\left|\dfrac{1}{z_1} + \dfrac{1}{z_2} + \dfrac{1}{z_3}\right| = 1$

2. (a) Given $|z_1| = 1$, $|z_2| = 2$, $|z_3| = 3$ and $|z_1 + z_2 + z_3| = 1$, then

$|9z_1z_2 + 4z_3z_1 + z_2z_3| = |z_3\bar{z}_3z_1z_2 + z_2\bar{z}_2z_1z_3 + z_1\bar{z}_1z_2z_3|$

$= (|z_1\, z_2\, z_3|)\ (|\bar{z}_1 + \bar{z}_2 + \bar{z}_3|) = |z_1|\ |z_2|\ |z_3|\ |\overline{(z_1 + z_2 + z_3)}|$

$= (1)\ (2)\ (3)\ (1) = 6$

3. (b) Let $a + ib = re^{i\theta}$ (where $\tan\theta = b/a$)

As $\dfrac{a - ib}{a + ib} = \dfrac{(a - ib)^2}{a^2 + b^2} = \dfrac{r^2e^{-2i\theta}}{r^2}$

$\Rightarrow \quad \ln\dfrac{a - ib}{a + ib} = \ln\left(e^{-2i\theta}\right) = -2\theta i$

So $\tan\left(i\tan\dfrac{a - ib}{a + ib}\right) = \tan 2\theta = \dfrac{2\tan\theta}{1 - \tan^2\theta} = \dfrac{2ab}{a^2 - b^2}$

4. (d) $|z_1 + z_2| = |z_1 - z_2|$

$\Rightarrow$ z_1, O, z_2 are forming a right angle at origin O

$\Rightarrow$ z_1/z_2 is a purely imaginary number.

Comprehension B:

5. (c) $(1 + i)x^2 - (7 + 3i)x + (6 + 8i) = 0$

Sum of the roots $= \dfrac{7 + 3i}{1 + i}$ where one root is $(4 - 3i) = 0$ then the other root is $1 + i$

6. (b) Since the coefficients are real

$\therefore$ α and $\bar{\alpha}$ are the roots $\quad \Rightarrow \quad \dfrac{a}{1} = \dfrac{b}{2} = \dfrac{c}{3}$

So $a : b : c = 1 : 2 : 3$.

7. (a) Given $z^2 + (a + ib)z + (c + id) = 0$ has one real root (say $z = p$) let the other root be

So $p + q = -a - ib$ and $pq = c + id$

$\Rightarrow$ $q = (-a - p) - ib$ and $q = \dfrac{c}{p} + \dfrac{id}{p}$

Equating, we get $-a-p=\dfrac{c}{p}$ and $-b=\dfrac{d}{p}$, so $p=\dfrac{-d}{b}$

Putting in the other equation we get $-a+\dfrac{d}{b}=\dfrac{-cb}{d}$

$\Rightarrow$ $d^2-abd=-cb^2$ or $abd=b^2c+d^2$

Comprehension C:

8. (d) Given $z_1=2+5i$ and $z_2=3-i$

$\Rightarrow$ Dot product $z_1.z_2=\text{Re}(z_2\bar{z}_1)=\text{Re}\,[(3-i)(2-5i)]=1$

and cross product $z_1\times z_2=\text{Im}(z_1\bar{z}_2)$

$=\text{Im}\,(2+5i)(3+i)=17$

Hence $\sqrt{z_1.z_2+z_2\times z_1}=\sqrt{18}=3\sqrt{2}$.

9. (b) $z_1=3+4i$ and $z_2=4+3i$, so $|z_1|=|z_2|=5$

Now $\text{Im}(z_2\bar{z}_1)=z_1\times z_2=|z_1|\,|z_2|\sin\theta$

$\Rightarrow$ $\sin\theta=\dfrac{\text{Im}[(4+3i)(3-4i)]}{25}=-\dfrac{7}{25}$

10. (c) $z_1=5+12i$ and $z_2=3+4i$

Projection of z_1 on $z_2=\dfrac{z_1.z_2}{|z_2|}=\dfrac{\text{Re}(z_2\bar{z}_1)}{5}$

$=\dfrac{\text{Re}(3+4i)(5-12i)}{5}=\dfrac{15+48}{5}=\dfrac{63}{5}$

Similarly projection of z_2 on z_1

$\dfrac{z_2.z_1}{|z_1|}=\dfrac{\text{Re}(z_1\bar{z}_2)}{13}=\dfrac{\text{Re}(5+12i)(3-4i)}{13}=\dfrac{63}{13}$

$\Rightarrow$ Required sum $=\dfrac{63}{5}+\dfrac{63}{13}=\dfrac{63\times18}{65}=\dfrac{1134}{65}$

11. (d) z_1 and z_2 are the roots of $z^2+z+1=0$

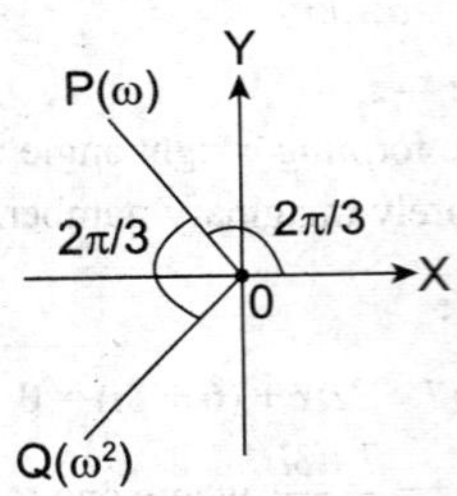

Let $z_1=\omega=e^{\frac{2\pi}{3}i}$,

then $z_2=\omega^2=e^{\frac{4\pi}{3}i}$ and $\angle POQ=\alpha\neq0$

$\Rightarrow$ $\alpha=\dfrac{2\pi}{3}$

Comprehension D:

12. (d) Given $R=\dfrac{a}{\sqrt{3}}\Rightarrow|AB|=|BC|=|CA|=2\sqrt{3}$

So $AB^2+AC^2+BC^2=36$

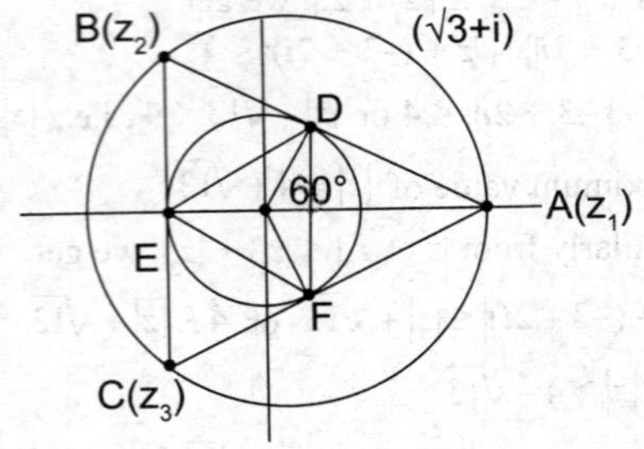

13. (d) Now $r=1\Rightarrow DE=\sqrt{3}$

$\Rightarrow$ $(DE)^2+(EF)^2+(FD)^2=3+3+3=9$

14. (c) Let $z_1=(2,0)$ then $z_2=2e^{\frac{2\pi}{3}i}$ and $z_3=2e^{\frac{4\pi}{3}i}$

$\Rightarrow$ $\text{Re}(z_1\bar{z}_2+z_2\bar{z}_3+z_3\bar{z}_1)=-2-2-2=-6$

15. (c) If $z_1=\sqrt{3}+i$ then $z_1=2e^{\frac{\pi}{6}i}$, $z_2=2e^{\frac{5\pi}{6}i}$ and $z_3=2e^{\frac{3\pi}{2}i}$

$\Rightarrow$ $\sqrt{|z_1-z_2|^2+|z_2+z_3|^2}=\sqrt{(2\sqrt{3})+4}=4$

(Here $z_2=-\sqrt{3}+i$ and $z_3=-2i$)

16. (c) $\dfrac{z_1}{z_3}=\dfrac{2e^{\frac{\pi}{6}i}}{2e^{\frac{3\pi}{2}i}}=\dfrac{\sqrt{3}+i}{-2i}=-\dfrac{1}{2}+\dfrac{\sqrt{3}}{2}i=e^{\frac{2\pi}{3}i}$

Comprehension E:

17. (b) $A=\{z\text{: Im }z\geq1\}\Rightarrow$ area above $y=1$

$B=\{z\text{: }|z-2-i|=3\}\Rightarrow$ circle

$C=\left\{z\text{:Re}(1-i)z=\sqrt{2}\right\}\Rightarrow\quad x+y=\sqrt{2}$

$\Rightarrow$ Straight Line

$A\cap B\cap C$ is value of z given by $x+y=\sqrt{2}$ and $(x-2)^2+(y-1)^2=9$ for $y\geq1$ we will get one value.

18. (c) Observe that $z=A\cap B\cap C$ lies on the part of circle above the line $y=1$

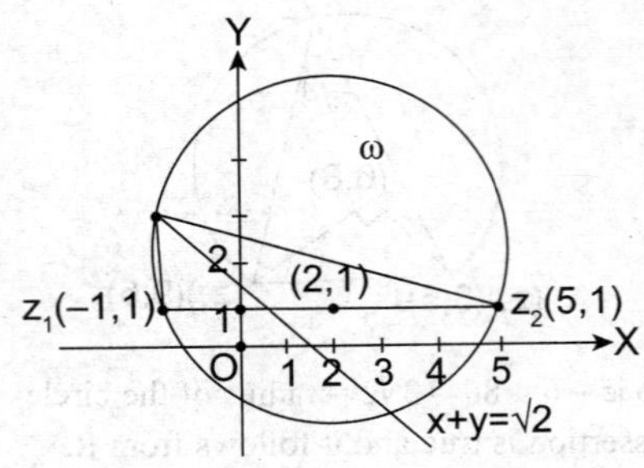

$z_1=-1+i$ and $z_2=5+i$ are the ends of the diameter

$\Rightarrow$ $|z-(-1+i)|^2+|z-(5+i)|^2=(\text{Diameter})^2=6^2=36$ which lies between 35 and 39

19. (d) Under the given conditions ω lies inside the circle and $|z-\omega|\in(0,6)$

Also $||z|-|\omega||\leq|z-\omega|<6$

$\Rightarrow$ $-6<|z|-|\omega|<6$ $\qquad\Rightarrow$ $-3<|z|-|\omega|+3<6$

SECTION VII: (MATRIX MATCHING)

1. (i) → (a, d); (ii) → (b, c); (iii) → (b, e)

(i) Let $z = x + iy$

$\therefore$ $\text{Re}(z^2) = z + \bar{z}$ gives $x^2 - y^2 = 2x$ or $(x-1)^2 - y^2 = 1$

Which is a rectangular hyperbola of eccentricity $e = \sqrt{2}$

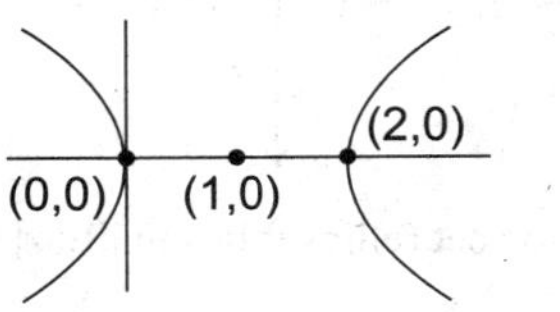

(ii) Locus of a point z such that $|z - z_1| + |z - z_2| = \lambda$, where $\lambda \in \mathbb{R}^+$ and $\lambda \not< |z_1 - z_2|$ gives line segment joining z_1 and z_2 for $\lambda = |z_1 - z_2|$ and it will give an ellipse when $|z_1 - z_2| < \lambda$.

(iii) $\dfrac{2\left|z - \frac{i}{2}\right|}{|z+1|} = m$ where $m \in \mathbb{R}^+$ for m = 2 it will give a straight line (the right bisector) and for $m \neq 2$ it will form a circle.

2 (i) → (b, d); (ii) → (a, e) ; (iii) → (c)

(i) We know that in equilateral triangle orthocenter, Nine point centre, centroid and Circumcentre are all at the same point (z_0) So $z_1^2 + z_2^2 + z_3^2 = 3z_0^2 = z_1z_2 + z_2z_3 + z_3z_1$

(ii) $\dfrac{z_2 - z_3}{z_1 - z_3} = e^{\frac{\pi}{2}i}$

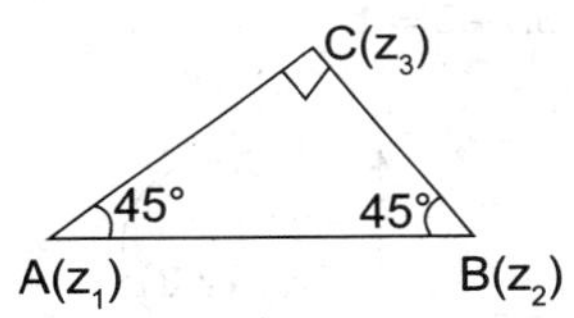

(As it is right angled isosceles)

Also $|z_1 - z_2|^2 = |AC|^2 + |BC|^2$, But $|AC| = |BC|$

$\Rightarrow$ $|z_1 - z_2|^2 = 2|(z_1 - z_3)|^2 = 2\,|z_1 - z_3|\,|z_3 - z_2|$

As $|AC| = |BC|$

(iii) $\overrightarrow{CD} = \dfrac{z_2 - z_3}{2} = \dfrac{z_1 - z_3}{|z_1 - z_3|}.e^{i\pi/6}.|z_1 - z_3|.\dfrac{\sqrt{3}}{2}$

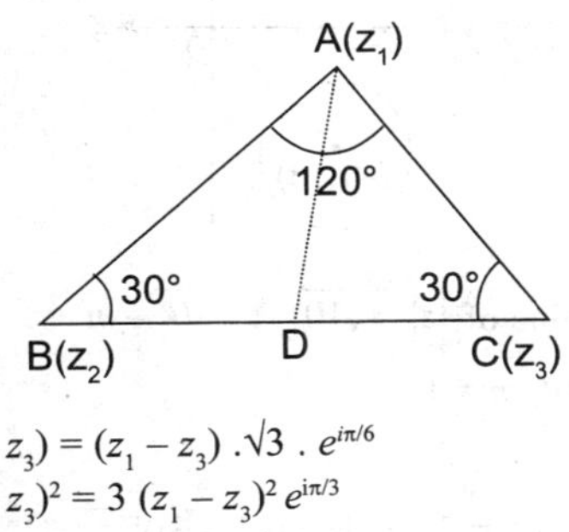

$\Rightarrow$ $(z_2 - z_3) = (z_1 - z_3).\sqrt{3}.\,e^{i\pi/6}$

$\Rightarrow$ $(z_2 - z_3)^2 = 3\,(z_1 - z_3)^2\, e^{i\pi/3}$

$= 3\,(z_1 - z_3)\,(z_1 - z_3)\, e^{i\pi/3} = 3(z_1 - z_3)(z_1 - z_3)\left[\dfrac{1}{2} + \dfrac{\sqrt{3}}{2}i\right]$

$= 3(z_3 - z_1)(z_1 - z_3)\left[-\dfrac{1}{2} - \dfrac{\sqrt{3}}{2}i\right]$

$= 3(z_3 - z_1)\,(z_1 - z_3)e^{-2\pi/3}$

$= -3\,(z_3 - z_1)\,(z_3 - z_1)e^{-2\pi/3} = -3(z_3 - z_1)(z_2 - z_1)$

$= 3\,(z_3 - z_1)\,(z_1 - z_2)$

3. (i) → (a, c, e); (ii) → (b); (iii) → (d)

(i) Let $1, \omega, \omega^2, \ldots\ldots, \omega^{n-1}$ are n, n^{th} roots of unity

So $(x-1)\,(x-\omega)\,(x-\omega^2)\ldots.\,(x-\omega^{n-1}) = x^n - 1$

or $(x-\omega)\,(x-\omega^2)(x-\omega^3)\,\ldots\ldots(x-\omega^{n-1})$

$= x^{n+1} + x^{n-2} + \ldots. + x + 1$

Hence $(2-\omega)\,(2-\omega^2)\,(2-\omega^3)\ldots..\,(2-\omega^{n-1})$

$= 2^{n-1} + 2^{n-2} + \ldots\ldots + 2 + 1 = \dfrac{2^n - 1}{2 - 1} = 2^n - 1 = \sqrt{2^{2n}} - 1$

$= {}^nC_0 + {}^nC_1 + {}^nC_2 + \ldots.. - {}^nC_{n-1} = \sqrt{2^{2n}} - 1$

$= \sqrt{{}^{2n+1}C_0 + {}^{2n+1}C_1 + \ldots. + {}^{2n+1}C_n} - 1$

(ii) $|z_1 + z_2 + z_3 + \ldots + z_n| - \left|\dfrac{4}{z_1} + \dfrac{4}{z_2} + \dfrac{4}{z_3} + \ldots. + \dfrac{4}{z_n}\right|$

Since $|z_i| = 2$ $\Rightarrow$ $z_i\bar{z}_i = 4$

So $|z_1 + z_2 + z_3 + \ldots\ldots + z_n| - \left|\dfrac{4}{z_1} + \dfrac{4}{z_2} + \dfrac{4}{z_3} + \ldots.. + \dfrac{4}{z_n}\right|$

$= |z_1 + z_2 + z_3 + \ldots.z_n| - |\bar{z}_1 + \bar{z}_2 + \bar{z}_3 + \ldots. + \bar{z}_n| = 0$

As $(1-1)^n = {}^nC_0 - {}^nC_1 + {}^nC_2 - {}^nC_3 + \ldots\ldots\ldots\ldots$

(iii) When p is a multiple of n then $p = mn$ (where $m, n \in \mathbb{N}$)

$\Rightarrow$ $(1)^{mn} = \omega^{mn} = (\omega^2)^{mn} = (\omega^3)^{mn} = \ldots\ldots\ldots\ldots.. = (\omega^{n-1})^{mn} = 1$

$\Rightarrow$ Sum of the pth power of roots

$= 1 + 1 + 1 \ldots\ldots.. + 1 = n = {}^nC_1$

4. (i) → (a); (ii) → (b); (iii) → (b, c, d); (iv) → (d)

(i) $\alpha, \beta \in \mathbb{R}$ and $\alpha^2 - 4\beta \geq 0$

$= z^4 + \alpha z^2 + \beta = 0$ $\Rightarrow$ $z^2 = \dfrac{-\alpha \pm \sqrt{\alpha^2 - 4\beta}}{2}$,

which is real. Now if $\alpha > 0$ and $\beta > 0$, then $\alpha^2 - 4\beta < \alpha^2$

$\Rightarrow$ $z^2 < 0$ so we will get all the four roots imaginary

(ii) When $\alpha = \beta = 0$, then $z^2 = 0$ so all the roots are real and equal to zero.

(iii) When $\alpha = \beta = 0$, then roots are real and equal to zero. When $\alpha \leq 0$ (β may be positive or negative) then again roots will be real

(iv) When $a \leq 0$ and $\beta < 0$, then $\alpha^2 - 4\beta > \alpha^2$

$\Rightarrow$ $\sqrt{\alpha^2 - 4\beta} > |\alpha| = -\alpha$; So $z^2 = -\alpha + \sqrt{\alpha^2 - 4\beta} > 0$ and

$z^2 = -\alpha - \sqrt{\alpha^2 - 4\beta} < 0$, we will get two real and two imaginary roots

5. (i) → (a, b, c, d); (ii) → (a, b, c, d); (iii) → (a); (iv) → (a)

(i) $|z - (-2 - 3i)| \leq 1$; $C(-2, -3)$;

$CP = 5$ units, so $G = 6$, $L = 4$

We get, $L + G = 10$; $LG = 24$; $G - L = 2$; $\dfrac{G}{L} = \dfrac{3}{2}$

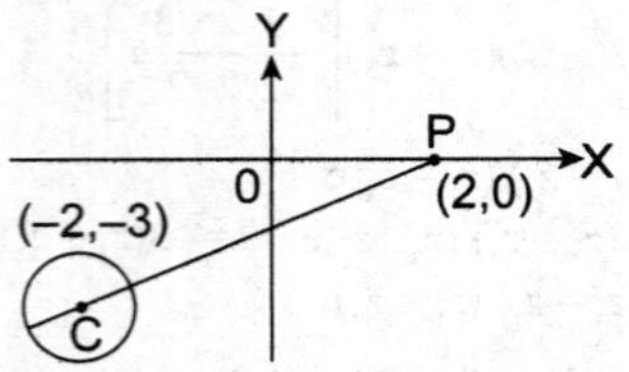

(ii) $|z - 5i| \leq 1 \Rightarrow G = 6, L = 4$ so same as (i)

$(\because G = |z_1| = 6$ and $L = |z_2| = 4)$

(iii) $t^2 - 10t + 25 = 0 \quad \Rightarrow t = 5$

$\Rightarrow G = L = 5$

$\Rightarrow G + L = 10; GL = 25, G - L = 0, G/L = 1.$

(iv) $G = 5 + \dfrac{5}{2} + \dfrac{5}{2^2} + ... = 5\{2\} = 10 \; ; L = G - 10 = 0$

$\Rightarrow G + L = 10; G - L = 10; GL = 0, G/L$ not defined.

6. (i) → (b, c); (ii) → (a); (iii) → (a, d, e); (iv) → (b, c, d, e)

(i) Let $z = x + iy$, then $|z - i\,|z|| = |z + i\,|z||$ gives

$$\left|x + iy - i\sqrt{x^2+y^2}\right| = \left|x + iy + i\sqrt{x^2+y^2}\right|$$

i.e., $\sqrt{x^2 + (y - \sqrt{x^2+y^2})^2} = \sqrt{x^2 + (y + \sqrt{x^2+y^2})^2}$

$\Rightarrow \left(y - \sqrt{x^2+y^2}\right) = \pm\left(y + \sqrt{x^2+y^2}\right)$

When $y - \sqrt{x^2+y^2} = y + \sqrt{x^2+y^2}$ we get $x^2 + y^2 = 0$, so $x = 0, y = 0$

When $y - \sqrt{x^2+y^2} = -y - \sqrt{x^2+y^2}$ then $y = 0$, which gives x-axis

This solution is contained in $\text{Im}\, z = 0$, $|\text{Im}\, z| \leq 1$

(ii) $|z + 4| + |z - 4| = 10$ is an ellipse with eccentricity $e = 4/5$

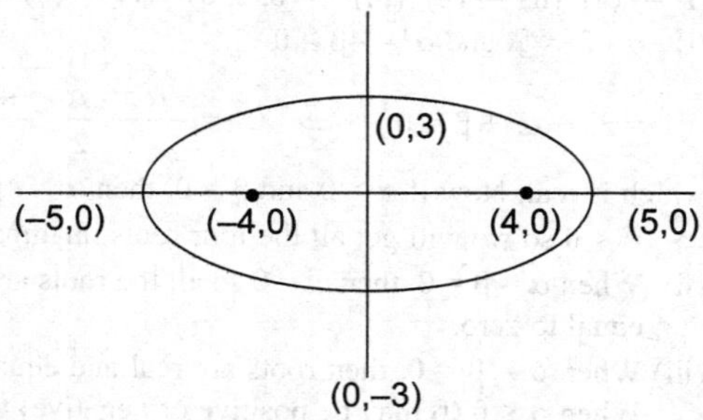

(iii) Given $|w| = 2$, now $z = w - \dfrac{1}{w} = w - \dfrac{\overline{w}}{w\overline{w}} = w - \dfrac{\overline{w}}{4}$

Let $w = x + iy$, then $z = \dfrac{3}{4}x + \dfrac{5}{4}yi$. Let $z = X + Yi$

$x^2 + y^2 = 1$ putting $(3/4)x = X$ and $(5/4)y = Y$,

$\left(\dfrac{4}{3}\right)^2 X^2 + \left(\dfrac{4}{5}\right)^2 Y^2 = 4$ i.e., $\dfrac{X^2}{\left(\dfrac{3}{2}\right)^2} + \dfrac{Y^2}{\left(\dfrac{5}{2}\right)^2} = 1$

Which gives an ellipse with major axis = 5 and minor axis = 3

The eccentricity work out to be e = 4 /5

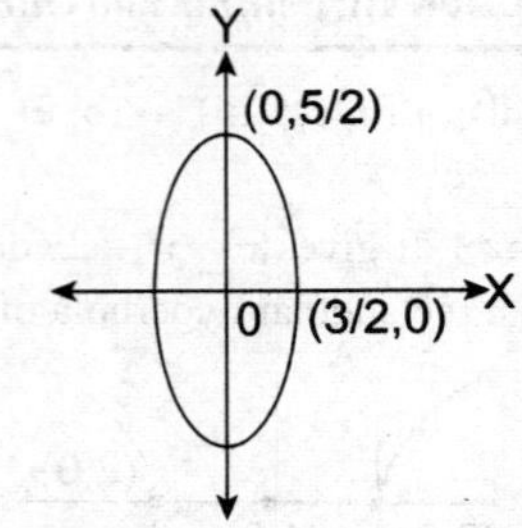

The solution set (ellipse) lies in $|\text{Re}\, z| \leq 2$ and also in $|z| \leq 3$

(iv) Given $|w| = 1$, Now $z = w + \dfrac{1}{w} = w + \dfrac{\overline{w}}{w\overline{w}} = w + \overline{w}$

Let $w = x + iy$, then $z = w + \overline{w} = 2x = X + iy$

$\Rightarrow X = 2x; Y = 0 \Rightarrow Z = 2x; -1 \leq x \leq 1$ as $x^2 + y^2 = 1$

This gives the line segment joining (–2, 0) and (2, 0) which is a subset of set represented by (a) (with major axis always x-axis.)

SECTION VIII: (INTEGER TYPE)

1. $|z - 1| = |z - 5|$ gives x = 3, i.e., Re(z) = 3 = k

$\Rightarrow$ **$k = 3$**

2. $|z - 1| = |z - 5|$ and $|z| = \sqrt{13}$ then Re(z) = 3, so Im (z) = $\pm\sqrt{4}$

$\Rightarrow |\text{Im}\,(z)| = 2$

3. $|z - 2 - 3i| = 1$; Max. $|z| = \sqrt{13} + 1 = \sqrt{k} + m$

So k = 13, m = 1

$\Rightarrow \sqrt{(k+m)+2} = 4$

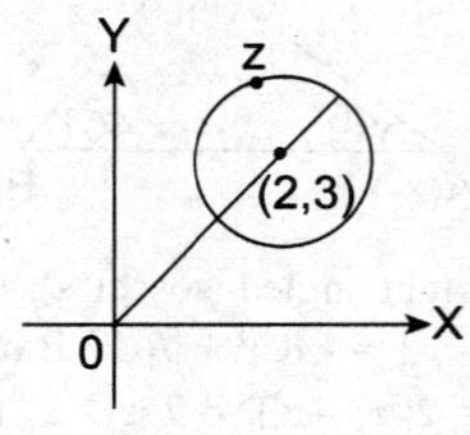

4. $|z - (1 - 3i)| = 1$

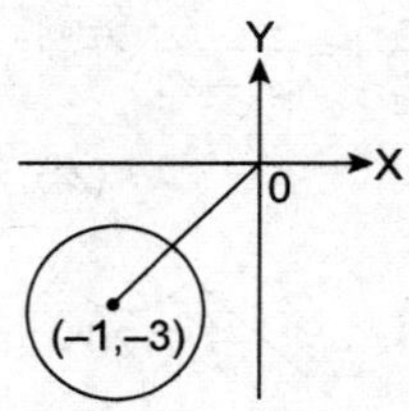

Least value of $|z| = \sqrt{10} - 1 = \sqrt{k} - m$

So $k = 10$, $m = 1$

$\Rightarrow \sqrt{k - m} = 3$

5. $|z - (2 - 3i)| = 2$ and $|z - (-1 - 3i)| = 1$

The circles will touch externally at (0, –3), i.e. $z = -3i$

$\Rightarrow |z - 4| = |-4 - 3i| = 5$

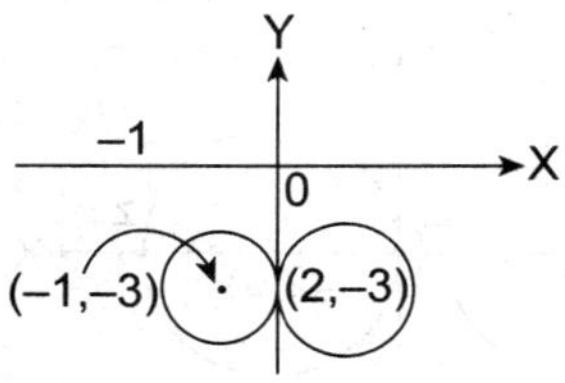

6. $Arg\left(\frac{z-2}{z+2}\right)=\frac{\pi}{2}$ gives semi– circle with radius r = 2

$Arg\left(\frac{w-1}{w+1}\right)=\frac{\pi}{2}$ gives semi circle with radius r = 1

Consider $z = 2^{-} + 0_i^{+}$ and w = $-1^{+} + 0^{+}i$

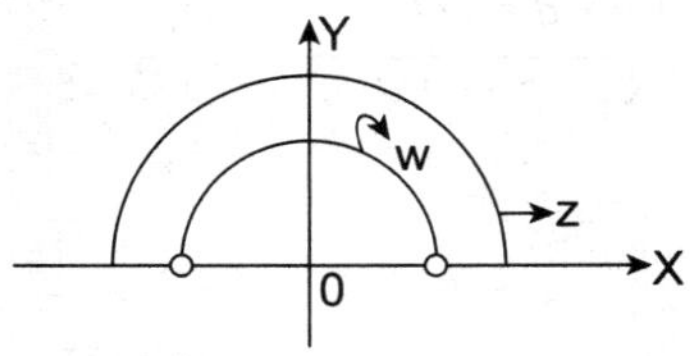

$\Rightarrow$ $|z - w| < 3$ so $k = 3$ (as $|z - w| < k$ and k is least upper bound)

7. Let $A = (-2, 0)$ and $B = (0, -1)$. Observe that $|z + 2| \le 2\,|z + i|$ is satisfied by (0, 0, 0) and $|z| = 0$ (minimum possible) $\{|z + 2| = 2\,|z + i|$ will form a circle$\}$

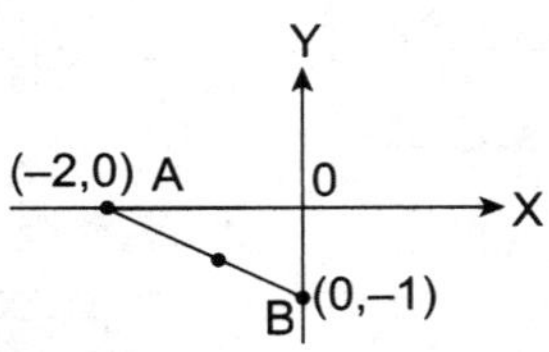

$\Rightarrow$ $x^2+y^2-\frac{4}{3}x+\frac{8}{3}y=0$, which passes through origin.

$\Rightarrow$ Least value of $|z| = 0$.

8. z lies on $\left|\frac{z+2}{z+1}\right|=2$

Which is represents a circle with at $\left(\frac{2}{3},\frac{-4}{3}\right)$ and radius

$=\frac{2\sqrt{5}}{3}$ i.e. $\left|z-\left(\frac{2}{3}-\frac{4}{3}i\right)\right|=\frac{2\sqrt{5}}{3}$

Now y transformation $w \to z+\left(\frac{4}{3}+\frac{2\sqrt{5}}{3}\right)i$

$\Rightarrow$ Thus new locus will be

$$\left|w-\left(\frac{2}{3}-\frac{4}{3}i\right)-\frac{4}{3}i-\frac{2\sqrt{5}}{3}i\right|=\frac{2\sqrt{5}}{3}$$

$$\Rightarrow \left|w-\left(\frac{2}{3}+\frac{2\sqrt{5}}{3}i\right)\right|=\frac{2}{3}\sqrt{5},$$

which is a circle with centre at $\left(\frac{2}{3},\frac{2\sqrt{5}}{3}\right)$ and radius $=\frac{2\sqrt{5}}{3}$

The maximum value of $|z|=\frac{2}{3}\sqrt{5}+\sqrt{\frac{4}{9}+\frac{20}{9}}$

$=\frac{2}{3}\sqrt{5}+\frac{2}{3}\sqrt{6}=\frac{2}{3}\left(\sqrt{m}+\sqrt{n}\right)$, so $m = 6, n = 5$

$\Rightarrow$ $|m - n| = 1$

9. Given $\text{Im}\left(\frac{z}{z+4i}\right)=2$.

Let $z = x + iy$, then $\text{Im}\left[\frac{(x+yi)\{(x)-(y+4)i\}}{\{x-(y+4)i\}\{x-(y+4)i\}}\right]=2$

$\Rightarrow$ $2\{x^2 + (y + 4)^2\} = xy - xy - 4x$, which gives
$2\{x^2 + 1 + 2x\} + 2\,(y + 4)^2 = 2$
i.e., $(x + 1)^2 + (y + 4)^2 = 1 \Rightarrow h = -1, k = -4, r = 1$
So $|h + k - r| = |-1 - 4 - 1| = 6$

10 Given $z=e^{\frac{\pi}{7}i}$ $\Rightarrow z^7 = -1$

Let $S=\left(z+z^3+z^5\right)+\left(\frac{1}{z}+\frac{1}{z^3}+\frac{1}{z^5}\right)$

$=\left(z+\frac{1}{z}\right)+\left(z^3+\frac{1}{z^3}\right)+\left(z^5+\frac{1}{z^5}\right)$

$=2\left\{\cos\frac{\pi}{7}+\cos\frac{3\pi}{7}+\cos\frac{5\pi}{7}\right\}$

Using $\cos\theta=\cos(2\pi-\theta)$, we get $S=\cos\frac{\pi}{7}+\cos\frac{3\pi}{7}+\cos\frac{5\pi}{7}$

$+\cos\frac{13\pi}{7}+\cos\frac{11\pi}{7}+\cos\frac{9\pi}{7}=0-\cos\frac{7\pi}{7}=1$

11. $|z - 2 + i| \le 2$, observe that $G = \sqrt{5} + 2$ and $L=\sqrt{5}-2$

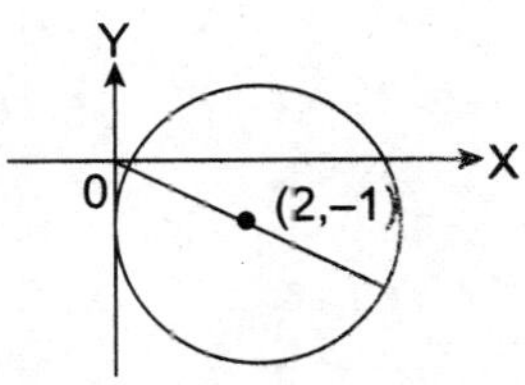

So $G - L = 4$

12. $|z - 2| + |z + 2| = 6$

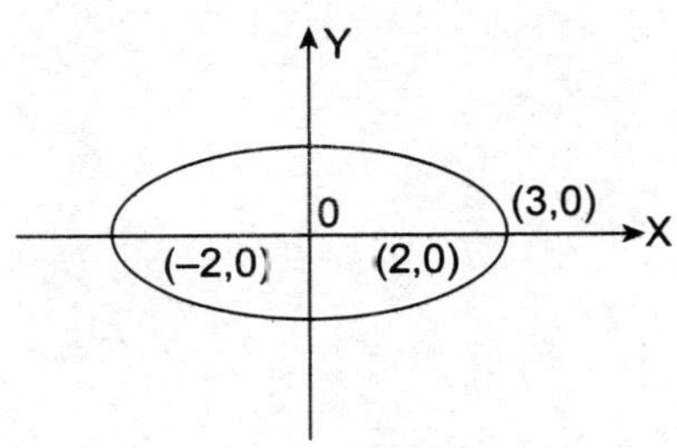

Semi-major axes $a = 3$, semi-minor axis $b = \sqrt{5}$, so $b^2 = 5$

13. Given $\log_{\sqrt{2}}\left(\dfrac{|z|^2-|z|+8}{|z|+1}\right)<4$

$\Rightarrow$ $|z|^2 - |z| + 8 < (|z| + 1) \Rightarrow |z|^2 - 5|z| + 4 < 0$
So $(|z| - 4|)(|z| - 1) < 0$
i.e., $1 < |z| < 4$
This gives the area $= 16\pi - \pi = 15\pi$
So $k = 15$ $\Rightarrow$ $\sqrt{k+1} = 4$

14. Given $\text{Re}(1/z) \geq 1/4$. Let $z = x + iy$

$$\text{Re}\left(\frac{\bar{z}}{|z|^2}\right)=\left(\frac{x}{x^2+y^2}\right)\geq\frac{1}{4}$$

$\Rightarrow$ $4x \geq x^2 + y^2$ i.e., $x^2 - 4x + 4 + y^2 \leq 4$
So $(x-2)^2 + y^2 \leq 2^2$ represents a circular disc with centre at (2, 0) and with radius $r = 2$

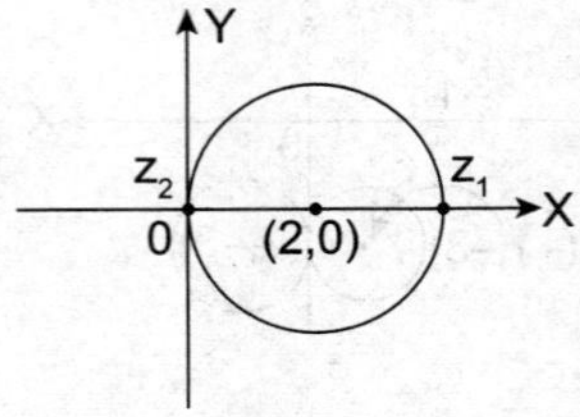

Now let $z_1 = 4$ and $z_2 = 0$
$\Rightarrow$ max. $|z_1 - z_2| = 4$

15. Given $2^7 \cos^8\theta = \cos 8\theta + a\cos 6\theta + b\cos 4\theta + c\cos 2\theta + d$
Put $\theta = 0$, so that $\cos n\theta = 1$.
$\Rightarrow$ $2^7 = 1 + a + b + c + d$
$\Rightarrow$ $a + b + c + d = 127$
Hence $\sqrt[3]{a+b+c+d-2} = \sqrt[3]{125} = 5$

6

Probability

■ INTRODUCTION

Human life is full of uncertainities, in our daily routine we make discussions about possibility of rain on a particular day, selection of a student in IIT-JEE, possibility of a party winning the election etc. Don't you think all the above are governed by chances?

Let us talk about one of hitechnological products 'The Telephone' wihout which mankind would have been crippled. While making a call to somebody a question always haunts one's mind whether the call will get through? Whether he will get the right person across the line? Similarily when telephone bell rings one always wonders about the possibility of one of his acquaintances on the line. So, the entire world is fraught with such instances where one can only weigh his chances. Sometimes finding one's chances is easier. On the other hand there are numerous cases where finding one's chances is pretty complicated.

The branch of mathematics which deals with such type of problems is known as *Probability* which defines how probable an event may be. Probability is measured on a scale of 0 to 1. Zero stands for an event with no chance of occurrance (impossible) while 1 stands for an event which is bound to occur (i.e., certain event).

While going long back into history one finds that Galileo (an italian mathematician) was the first man to attempt a quantitative measurement of probability, while dealing with some problem related with theory of dice in gambling. But the mathematical theory of probability was laid by two french mathematicians B.Pascal and P.Fermat and later enriched by "Treatise on probability: by J. Bernauli, N. Bernauli "Doctorine of chances" by De-moivre, "Inverse probability" by T. Bayes and "theoric analytique desprobability" by S.Laplace. In Present chapter we shall study the methodologies to compute the probability of an event (be it simple or complex). Human inquisitiveness had generated many tools to find out probability of complex events and by studying them we can prepare ourselves to handle with any problem based on probability (chances).

■ EXPERIMENTS

An experiment is a set of processes, which are carried out under stipulated conditions to study the phenomenon associated with it. It is defined as below:

"A mathematical operation which results in some well defined outcomes is known as experiment". Broadly there can be two types of experiments as given below:

Random Experiments

Random experiments are the experiments for which all possible outcomes are known in advance but prediction of any specific of them can not be done with certainty before the completion of the experiment. e.g., tossing of a coin rolling a die, drawing a card from a well shuffled pack of cards etc.

Non-Random Experiments

Non-random experiments are the experiments which are not random. i.e., the prediction of some of the outcomes can be done with certainty. e.g., Throwing a stone, tossing a two headed coin etc.

■ SAMPLE SPACE

The set of all possible outcomes of a random experiment is called **'Sample space'** denoted by S. Each element of S

denotes an outcome of the experiment and any performance of the experiment results in an outcome that corresponds to exactly one element of S.

Example:

(i) When a coin is tossed, then sample space $S = \{H, T\}$ $\Rightarrow n(S) = 2$

(ii) When two coins are tossed, then sample space (S_1) will be defined as cartesian product $S \times S = \{(H, H), (T, T), (H, T), (T, H)\} \Rightarrow n(S_1) = 4$

(iii) When a die is rolled, sample space $S = \{1, 2, 3, 4, 5, 6\} \Rightarrow n(S) = 6$

(iv) When two dice are rolled, sample space $S_2 = S \times S = \{(1, 1), (1, 2)........(6, 6)\} \Rightarrow n(S_2) = 36$

Sample spaces are classified as a finite or an infinite sample spaces as mentioned below:

Finite Sample Space

Sample space which has finite number of discrete elements are known as discrete sample spaces or finite sample spaces.

e.g., Sample spaces in the experiments: rolling a die, tossing a coin are finite sample spaces.

Infinite Sample Space

Sample spaces having infinite number of elements. These are of two types:

(i) **Discrete sample space:** Whose elements can be put into a one-to-one correspondence with the set of positive integers (i.e., countable sets). e.g., Suppose a coin is tossed till the first head appears. The sample space associated with the random experiment is $\{H, TH, TTH, TTTH, TTTTH, ...\}$

(ii) **Continuous Sample space:** Which has infinite number of elements distributed continuously. E.g., a computer hard disk manufactured by HCL is chosen randomly and its life is measured in hours, then the sample space in this case will be a continuous interval $[0, \infty)$. To understand the concept of continuous sample space, let us take following examples:

ILLUSTRATION 1: (a) A real number x is chosen randomly from the interval [0, 4] then find the probability that it satisfies the inequality

(i) $x^2 - 3x + 2 > 0$ (ii) $x^2 - 4x + 3 < 0$

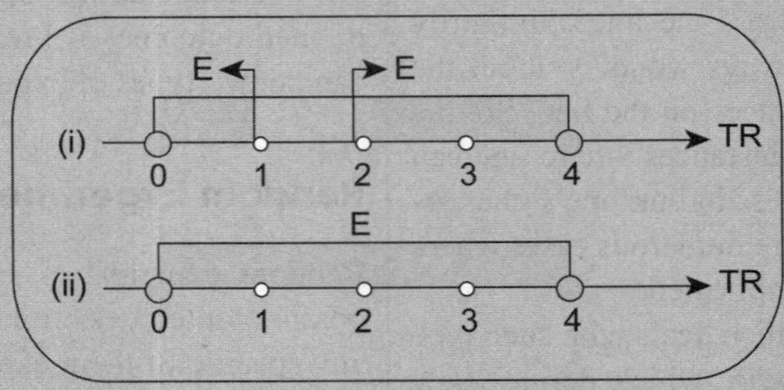

FIGURE 6.1

(b) A point is chosen randomly from the points on or within a circle. Find the probability that the point lies nearer to circumference than to the centre.

SOLUTION: Clearly, the number of real numbers belonging to [0, 4] as well as the number of points on or within a circle are infinite, therefore the sample spaces in above two cases will be continuous sample sapces.

NOTE

The problems related with continuous sample space are generally solved using geometrical equivalent of sample space and event space and they will be dealt in our final article under the heading of geometrical probability.

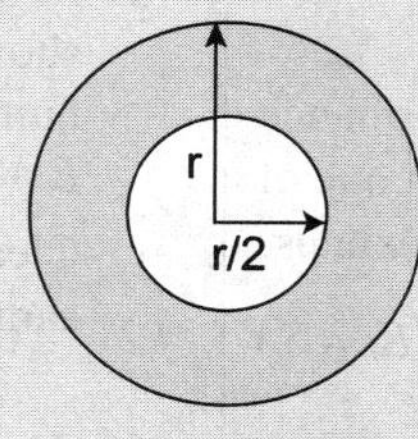

FIGURE 6.2

EVENTS AND THEIR CLASSIFICATION

The occurrence or non occurrence of a phenomenon is known as an event or outcome. It is defined as an outcome or a set of outcomes of the experiment. Therefore "an event is a subset of sample space". We say that an event $E(S)$ has occurred provided the outcome ω of the experiment is an element of E. e.g., if a die is tossed the outcomes are the occurrence of any one of the numbers 1, 2,..., 6, then any subset of sample space can be called as an 'Event', e.g., $E_1 = \{2, 4\}$, $E_2 = \{1, 3, 5\}$ etc.

Simple Events and Mixed/Compound Events

If an event is a set containing only one element of the sample space, then it is called a simple event (sample point).

A compound event is a set of sample points (*sample point is an individual element of sample space*). i.e., It is subset of S containing two or more than two elements.

e.g., occurrence of {1,3, 5} while rolling a die is a compound event.

The classification of an event as simple/compound events depends upon how we consider the sample space e.g., the event of drawing a heart E = {heart} from a deck of card is the subset of sample space S = {heart, spade, club, diamond}. Therefore A is a simple event while the event B of drawing a red card is a compound event since B = {heart ∪ diamond} = {heart, diamond}

Possible and Impossible Events

If event set lies out side of sample space or it is null set (ϕ), then event is known as impossible event. e.g., occurrence of 7 while rolling a die.

Therefore, If $E_1 \subseteq S \Rightarrow E_1$ is possible event. If $E_2 \cap S = \phi$, then E_2 is impossible event

NOTE

If $P(E_1)$ is the probability of occurrence of possible event E_1, then $(P(E_1)) \in (0, 1)$ while the probability of occurrence of impossible event E_2 is zero.

Certain Events

If the event set becomes equal to sample space ($E = S$), then the event is known as certain event. i.e., since S is also a subset of itself so it is also an event. S is known as sure event or certain event and therefore $P(S) = 1$

e.g., E = (occurrence of Head or tail while tossing a coin) is a certain event

Mutually Exclusive Events

A set of events is said to be *mutually exclusive* if occurrence of one of them precludes the occurrence of any of the remaining events. If a set of events $E_1, E_2, \ldots, E_n$ are mutually exclusive events. i.e., $E_i \cap E_j = \phi$ for all $i, j = 1, 2, \ldots, n$ and $i \neq j$, then $P(E_1 \cup E_2 \cup \ldots\ldots \cup E_n) = P(E_1) + P(E_2) + P(E_3) + \ldots\ldots + P(E_n)$

Example:

1. In rolling a die, event A is described as appearance of an even number and event B is described as appearance of an odd number. A = {2, 4, 6} and B = {1, 3, 5}. Clearly if one says that A has occured, then it instantly concludes that B cannot occur. So, $A \cap B = \phi$
2. When we throw a pair of dice, the events "a sum of 5 occurs", "a sum of 7 occurs" and "a sum of 9 occurs" are mutually exclusive.

Exhaustive Events

A set of events is said to be *exhaustive* if the performance of the experiment results in the occurrence of at least one of them. Therefore if a set of events $E_1, E_2,..., E_n$ are exhaustive events, then $P(E_1 \cup E_2 \cup .... \cup E_n) = 1$ $(\because \bigcup_{i=1}^{n} E_i = S)$

e.g., In rolling a dice three events are described as:
A_1: Appearance of the Even number
A_2: Appearance of number less than 4 and
A_3: Appearance of number greater than 4.
Hence A_1: {2, 4, 6}, A_2: {1, 2, 3}and A_3 = {5, 6}. Clearly $A_1 \cup A_2 \cup A_3 = \{1, 2, 3, 4, 5, 6\}$ which is the sample space for the experiment. So A_1, A_2 and A_3 are exhaustive events.

Equally Likely Events

The given events say $E_1, E_2,..., E_n$ are said to be equally likely, if taking into consideration all the factors, we have no reason to believe that anyone of these has better chances of occurrence than the other.

i.e., $P(E_1) = P(E_2) = ... = P(E_n)$

e.g.,

1. When an unbiased coin is tossed, then ocurrance of head or tail are equally likely cases and there is no reason to expect a head or a tail in preference to other
2. In rolling a die event A is described as number showing less than 4 and event B is described as number appearing greater than 3. A = {1, 2, 3} and B = {4, 5, 6}

   Clearly A and B have equal number of points in the sample space and hence are equally likely.

Disjoint Events

Events E_1 and E_2 are said to be disjoint when they have no common elements.

i.e., $E_1 \cap E_2 = \phi$

e.g., If events E_1 is occurence of odd numbers and E_2 is occurence of multiple of 4, when a die is rolled, then E_1 and E_2 are disjoint events.

Complementary Events

Let **S** be the sample space and E be the event. Then event complementary to E is a set of all those elements of the sample space which are not present in set E. Therefore the non-occurrence of $\bar{E}$ ensures the occurrence of E. It is denoted by $\bar{E}$ E' and E^c. e.g., in the experiment of throwing a die, S = {1, 2, 3, 4, 5, 6}.

If E = {1, 3, 5, 6}, then E' = {2, 4}

NOTE

$E \cup E^c = S$ and $E \cap E^c = \phi$

Independent and Dependent Events

Two events are said to be dependent if the occurence or non occurrence of one event decides and disturbs the occurrence or non-occurrence of the other. e.g., in the withdrawl of cards from a deck of cards without replacement, the outcomes will be dependent events but if the withdrawl is done with replacement the outcomes will be independent. If a set of events $E_1, E_2,..., E_n$ are independent events, then $P(E_1 \cap E_2 \cap E_3 \cap .... \cap E_n) = P(E_1).\ P(E_2)......P(E_n)$

Mutually Exclusive and Exhaustive Events

A set of events is said to be mutually exclusive as well as exhaustive if the conditions given below are satisfied.
$E_i \cap E_j = \phi \; \forall \; i, j$ such that $i \neq j$ and $E_1 \cup E_2 \cup .... \cup E_n = S$.

For mutually exclusive and exhaustive events $E_1, E_2,..., E_n$, probability of occurrence of atleast one of them
$= P(E_1 \cup E_2 \cup .... \cup E_n) = P(E_1) + P(E_2) + ... + P(E_n) = 1$

e.g., In rolling of a die, events E_1, E_2, E_3 and E_4 are described as below:

E_1 = occurrence of the number less than 2,
E_2 = occurrence of the odd number greater than 1
E_3 : occurrence of the number 2, E_4: occurrence of the even number greater than 2

Hence E_1 = {1}, E_2 = {3, 5}, E_3 = {2} and E_4 = {4, 6} Clearly, $\bigcup_{i=1}^{4} E_i$ = {1, 2, 3, 4, 5, 6} = S and

$E_1 \cap E_2 = E_1 \cap E_3 = E_1 \cap E_4 = E_2 \cap E_3 = E_2 \cap E_4 = E_3 \cap E_4 = \phi$

i.e., $E_i \cap E_j = \phi$, $\forall \; i, j$ such that $i \neq j$

■ TRIALS

When an experiment is repeated under similar conditions but does not provide same result instead may results in one of several possible outcomes, then we say that trials are being made and each of the experiment is known as trial. The number of times the experiment is repeated is known as number of trials. e.g., When a coin is tossed 6 times, then each toss of a coin is a trial and we say 6 trials are made.

NOTE

Generally the trials are made to check whether the possible outcomes they are equally likely or not and with the results of large number of trials performed the weight of different events in the sample space are decided.

TEXTUAL EXERCISE 1: (SUBJECTIVE)

1. (i) Which of the following statements are true?
   (a) mathematically experiment is defined as an operation which have well defined outcomes.
   (b) Stochastic (random/statistical) experiments are those whose outcomes depend on chances.
   (c) In random experiment all possible outcomes are known in advance.
   (d) weights of sample points are determined by experimental evidences performing large number of trials.
   (e) Concept of mutually exclusive events is set theoretic in nature but concept of independent events is probablistic in nature.
   (f) When two coins are tossed, let E_1 be occurrence of head on Ist coin and E_2 be occurrence of tail on 2nd coin, then E_1 and E_2 are mutually exclusive, therefore they are dependent events.

(ii) Which of the following is an example of random experiment?
   (a) tossing a fair coin
   (b) rolling a fair die
   (c) throwing a stone
   (d) drawing a card from a well shuffled pack of 52 cards.
   (e) opinion of voters regarding a new sale tax

2. State which of the following cases represent(s) problems of finite sample space?
   (a) tossing of two coins
   (b) rolling of three dice
   (c) choosing a real number from an interval (a, b); $a, b \in \mathbb{R}, a \neq b$
   (d) choosing a point (x, y) such that $x \in (-4, 4)$ and $y \in (-4, 4)$
   (e) choosing a point on or within a given circle of radius r, $(r \neq 0)$.

3. Which of the following events is/are possible?
   (a) occurrence of sum 13 when two dice are rolled
   (b) occurrence of 54 Sundays in a leap year
   (c) occurrence of 7 days in a randomly chosen week.
   (d) occurrence of 5 aces in a well shuffled pack of 52 cards.

4. Which of the following events is/are certain?
   (a) occurrence of a leap year in any four randomly chosen consecutive years, no year being a century year.
   (b) occurrence of a real number when a number is chosen from a set of complex numbers.
   (c) occurrence of a complex number when a number is chosen from a set of real numbers.

5. A die is rolled and following four events are defined:
   E_1 : occurrence of 2 or 4
   E_2 : occurrence of an even number.
   E_3 : occurrence of an odd digit.
   E_4 : occurrence of 3 or 5
   Which pair(s) of the pair of events is/are mutually exclusive?

6. A card is drawn from a well shuffled pack of 52 playing cards, then state which of the following events are mutually exclusive?
   E_1 : occurrence of a king.
   E_2 : occurrence of a queen.
   E_3 : occurrence of a club card.
   E_4 : occurrence of a court card.

7. Classify the pair of events A and B as mutually exclusive, non-exclusive dependent or independent events.
   (i) Two coins are tossed. Let A be the event that the first coin shows head and B be the event that the second coin shows a tail.
   (ii) A card is drawn from a pack of 52 cards. If A = card is of diamond, B = card is an ace and $A \cap B$ = card is ace of diamond.
   (iii) Two fair dice are tossed. Let A be the event that the first die shows an even number and B be the event that the second die shows an odd number.
8. If A and B be mutually exclusive events of same sample space, then prove that A and B are dependent events. Also show that $\bar{A}$ and $\bar{B}$ are dependent.
9. If A and B are two independent events, then prove that A and $\bar{B}$, $\bar{A}$ and B, $\bar{A}$ and $\bar{B}$ are independent.

Answer Key

1. (i) a, b, c, d, e (ii) a, b, d 2. a, b 3. c 4. a, c
5. E_2 and E_4, E_1 and E_4, E_2 and E_3, E_1 and E_4 6. E_1 and E_2 7. (i) non-mutually exclusive but independent
(ii) non-mutually exclusive and independent (iii) independent and non-mutually exclusive. 10. a, b

PROBABILITY OF OCCURRENCE OF AN EVENT

If an event can happen in x ways and fail to happen in y ways, and each of these ways is equally likely, then the probability or the chance, of its occurrence will be $\frac{x}{x+y}$ and that of its non-occurrence will be $\frac{y}{x+y}$.

So we can also assert that the chance of its occurrence is to the chance of its non-occurrence is x to y. Thus if the chance of its occurrence is represented by kx, where k is an undetermined constant, then the chance of its non-occurrence will be ky,

$$\left\{\frac{\text{chance of occurence}}{\text{chance of non-occurence}} = \frac{x}{y}\right\}$$

$\therefore$ chance of occurrence + chance of non-occurrence = $k(x + y)$

Since the event is certain to occur or not to occur; therefore the sum of the chances of occurrence and non-occurrence must represent certainty and therefore we agree to take certainty as our unit, we get $k(x + y) = 1$

or $k = \frac{1}{x+y}$; therefore the probability of the occurrence of event is $\frac{x}{x+y}$ and the probability that the event will not occur is $\frac{y}{x+y}$.

MATHEMATICAL OR CLASSICAL DEFINITION

For an experiment with continuous finite sample space S, the probability of occurrence of an event E is denoted by $P(E)$ and defined as $P(E) = \frac{n(E)}{n(S)}$

$$= \frac{\text{number of elements in } E}{\text{number of elements in space } S}$$

$$= \frac{\text{number of outcomes favourable to } E \text{ in sample space } S}{\text{total number of outcomes (elements) in } S}$$

e.g., In the experiment of throwing a die, the probability of getting 2 as outcome is 1/6

Properties

1. **Theorem:** The probability $P(E)$ of occurrence of any event E lies between 0 and 1
   Proof: Since $0 \le n(E) \le n(S)$; dividing both sides by $n(S)$, we get $0 \le \frac{n(E)}{n(S)} \le 1 \Rightarrow 0 \le P(E) \le 1$
2. **Theorem:** Complementary event of E is denoted as E^c or E' or $\bar{E}$ which literally means non-occurrence of E. Thus $\bar{E}$ occurs only when E does not occur. Therefore $P(E) + P(\bar{E}) = 1$
   Proof: Since $n(E) + n(\bar{E}) = n(S) \Rightarrow \frac{n(E)}{n(S)} + \frac{n(\bar{E})}{n(S)} = 1$
3. If E is impossible event, then $P(E) = 0$
4. If E is a possible event, then $0 < P(E) < 1$
5. If E is a certain event, then $P(E) = 1$

NOTE

1. *A die is a solid cube which has six faces and numbers 1, 2, 3, 4, 5 and 6 are marked on the faces respectively. In throwing or rolling a die, any one of the above numbers can appear on the uppermost face.*
2. *A pack of cards consists of 52 cards in 4 suits i.e., (a) spades ♠ (b) Clubs ♣, (c) Hearts ♥ (d) diamonds ♦. Each suit consists of 13 cards. Out of these spades and clubs are black faced cards, while hearts and diamonds are* ***red-faced cards.*** *The aces, kings, queens, jacks are called* **honour cards.** *Kings, queens and jacks are known as* ***court cards or face cards.***
3. *Game of Bridge: It is played by 4 players, each player is given 13 cards*
4. *Game of whist: It is played by two pairs of persons.*

ILLUSTRATION 2: Find the probability of showing odd numbers when a die is rolled.

SOLUTION: Event set $E = \{1, 3, 5\} \Rightarrow n(E) = 3$

Sample Space $S = \{1, 2, 3, 4, 5, 6\} \Rightarrow n(S) = 6$

So the required probability $P(E) = \dfrac{n(E)}{n(S)} = \dfrac{3}{6} = \dfrac{1}{2}$

ILLUSTRATION 3: If two coins are tossed find the probability that at least one head occurs.

SOLUTION: The sample space for the experiment $(S) = \{HH, HT, TH, TT\}$

$\Rightarrow n(S) = 4$

If E is the event representing the occurrence of atleast one head.

Then $E = \{HT, TH, HH\} \Rightarrow P(E) = \dfrac{n(E)}{n(S)} = \dfrac{3}{4}$

ILLUSTRATION 4: Two dice are thrown simultaneously. What is the probability of obtaining a total score of seven?

SOLUTION: There are six possible ways in which the first die can show a number on its top face and corresponding to each of these ways, there exist 6 possible ways outcomes on second dice. Hence total number of elements in sample space $n(S) = 6 \times 6 = 36$

The favourable ways to get the total score of 7 points are (1, 6), (6, 1), (2, 5), (5, 2), (3, 4), (4, 3). Thus $n(E) = 6$. Hence the required Probability $= \dfrac{6}{36} = \dfrac{1}{6}$

ILLUSTRATION 5: From a set of 27 cards 1,2,3,.......,26, 27 one is drawn at random. Find the probability that number on the drawn card would be divisible by 3 or 13.

SOLUTION: Number which are divisible by three are 3, 6, 9, 12, 15......27

Similarly numbers which are divisible by 13 are 13 and 26

$\Rightarrow$ Probability of the number written on the card to be divisible by 3 or 13 is = 11/27

ILLUSTRATION 6: From the bag containing 5 white, 7 red and 4 black balls a man draws 3 balls at random, find the probability of withdrawn balls being all white.

SOLUTION: Total number of balls in the bag = 5 + 7 + 4 = 16

The total number of ways in which 3 balls can be drawn is ${}^{16}C_3 = \dfrac{16 \times 15 \times 14}{3 \times 2 \times 1} = 560$

Thus the sample space S for this experiment has 560 outcomes i.e., $n(S) = 560$

Let E be the event of all the three balls being white and since total number of white balls is 5.

So the number of ways in which 3 white balls can be drawn $= {}^5C_3 = \dfrac{5\times4\times3}{3\times2\times1} = 10$ thus E has 10 elements of S, $\therefore\ n(E) = 10$

$\therefore$ The required probability of occurence $P(E) = \dfrac{n(E)}{n(S)} = \dfrac{10}{560} = \dfrac{1}{56}$

Note: In all such problems even the balls of same colour are considerd to be distinct.

ILLUSTRATION 7: From a pack of 52 playing cards, three cards are drawn at random. Find the probability of drawing a King and two knaves; where Queens, Jacks and cards with denomination 10 are defined to be knaves.

SOLUTION: Let S be the sample space and E be the event such that "out of the three cards drawn one is a king, two are knaves".

$\therefore\ n(S)$ = total number of ways of selecting 3 cards out of 52 cards $= {}^{52}C_3$

and $n(E)$ = number of ways of selecting 3 cards out of pack of 52 such that one is king and two are knaves $= {}^4C_1 \cdot {}^{12}C_2 = \dfrac{4\times12\times11}{2} = 264$

(Here 'and' symbolises multiplication rule)

$\therefore$ required probability $P(E) = \dfrac{n(E)}{n(S)} = \dfrac{264}{{}^{52}C_3} = \dfrac{264}{\frac{52.51.50}{1.2.3}} = \dfrac{66}{5525}$

■ STATISTICAL DEFINITION OF PROBABILITY

When a random experiment is repeated n times under similar conditions i.e., (n trials are made) and n is very large and an event E occurs r times out of the n trials, then the probability of occurrence of the event E is defined as

$$P(E) = \lim_{n\to\infty}\left(\frac{r}{n}\right)$$

■ ODDS IN FAVOUR AND ODDS AGAINST AN EVENT

If in an experiment, the number of outcomes favourable to an event E is x and number of outcomes not favourable to event E is y, then

(a) Odds in favour of

$$E = \frac{\text{number of outcomes favourable}\,(n(E))}{\text{number of outcomes unfavourable}\,(n(\bar{E}))} = \frac{P(E)}{P(\bar{E})} = \frac{x}{y}$$

(b) Odds against

$$E = \frac{\text{number of unfavourable outcomes}\,(n(\bar{E}))}{\text{number of favourable outcomes}\,(n(E))} = \frac{P(\bar{E})}{P(E)} = \frac{y}{x}$$

e.g., Odds in favour of getting a spade when a card is drawn from a well shuffled pack of 52 cards are $\dfrac{{}^{13}C_1}{{}^{39}C_1} = \dfrac{13}{39} = \dfrac{1}{3}$

NOTE

If odds in favour of an event are m: n, then the probability of the occurence of that event is $\dfrac{m}{m+n}$ and the probability of non occurence of that event is $\dfrac{n}{m+n}$

ILLUSTRATION 8: There are three events A, B and C one of which must, and only one can happen, the odds against A are 8 to 3 and 2 to 5 in favour of B. Find the odds, against C.

SOLUTION: $P(A) = 3/11$, $P(B) = 2/7$. Let us take $P(C) = x$

Since one must and only one can happen therefore A, B, C are mutually exclusive and exhaustive events.

So, $P(A) + P(B) + P(C) = 1 \Rightarrow 3/11 + 2/7 + x = 1$

$\Rightarrow x = \frac{77-21-22}{77} = \frac{34}{77}$ $\therefore$ Odds against $C = (77 - 34) : 34$ i.e., $43 : 34$

TEXTUAL EXCERISE 2: (SUBJECTIVE)

1. If two coins are tossed, find the probability that at least one head occurs.

2. If three coins are tossed, then find the number of elements in sample space and the event space of getting at least two heads.

3. If a pair of fair dice is rolled, then find the probability of getting the sum exactly 5.

4. Find the probability of getting the product a perfect square (square of a natural number), when two dice are thrown together.

5. Find the probability of getting the sum as a prime number when two dice are thrown together.

6. Find the probability that a leap year selected at random will contain 53 Sundays.

7. A four digit number is formed using the digits 1, 2, 3, 5 with no repetitions. Find the probability that the number is divisible by 5.

8. A five digit number is formed using the digits 1, 2, 3, 4, 5 without repetition. Find the probability that number is
   (i) even (ii) divisible by 4.
   (iii) divisible by 3. (iv) divisible by 6.
   (v) divisible by 12. (vi) divisible by 24.

9. A card is drawn from a well shuffled ordinary pack of 52 cards, then find the probability that it is
   (i) an honour card (ii) a court card
   (iii) king or queen (iv) heart

10. A fair die is thrown until a score of less than 5 points is obtained. Find the probability of obtaining not less than 2 points on the last throw.

11. From a pack of 52 cards two cards are drawn at random. Find the probability of the following events:
    (i) both cards are of spade.
    (ii) One card is of spade and of diamond.

12. Fifteen coupons are numbered 1, 2, 3,....,15. Seven coupons are selected at random one at a time with replacement. Find the probability that the largest number appearing on the selected coupon is 9.

13. Seven white balls and three black balls are randomly placed in a row. Find the probability that no two black balls are placed adjacently.

14. Six different balls are put in three different boxes, no box being empty. Find the probability of putting balls in the boxes in equal numbers.

15. There are m persons sitting in a row, two of them are selected at random. Find the probability that the two selected persons were not sitting together.

16. A party of ten take their seat at a round table. Find the odds against two specified persons (A, B) sitting together.

17. 5 boys and 5 girls are sitting together randomly in a row, find the probability that
    (i) all 5 girls sit together
    (ii) no two girls sit together
    (iii) neither two girls nor two boys sit together
    (iv) b_1 b_2 are together but g_1 g_2 are not together:

18. A die is made in such a way that even faces are twice as likely to occur as the odd faces. Find the probabililty of getting a prime number when die is thrown.

19. Only three students A, B and C appear at a competitive examination. The probability that A tops is 3 times

that of B and the probability that B tops three times that of C. Find the probability that A or B tops in the examination.

20. Seven accidents occured in a week. Find the proabability that they occured on the same day.

Answer Key

1. 3/4 **2.** 8, 4 **3.** 1/9 **4.** 2/9 **5.** 5/12 **6.** 2/7 **7.** 1/4 **8.** (i) 2/5 (ii) 1/5 (iii) 1 (iv) 2/5 (v) 1/5 (vi) 1/12 **9.** (i) 4/13 (ii) 3/13 (iii) 2/13 (iv) 1/4 **10.** 3/4 **11.** (i) 1/17 (ii) 13/102 **12.** $\frac{9^7-8^7}{15^7}$ **13.** 7/15 **14.** 1/6 **15.** $\frac{m-2}{m}$ **16.** 7/2 **17.** (i) $\frac{1}{42}$ (ii) $\frac{1}{42}$ (iii) $\frac{1}{126}$ (iv) $\frac{7}{45}$ **18.** 4/9 **19.** 12/13 **20.** $1/7^6$

TEXTUAL EXCERISE 1: (OBJECTIVE)

1. A determinants is chosen at random from the set of a determinants of order 2 with elements 0 or –1 only. The probability that the chosen determinant has value zero is.

(a) 3/16 (b) 5/8
(c) 1/4 (d) 1/8

2. A fair coin is tossed 100 times. The probability of getting tails an even number of times is

(a) 1/3 (b) 1/2
(c) 1/8 (d) 1/16

3. Ten identical balls are numbered 1, 2,.....9, 10 are put in a bag. A draws a ball and gets the number a. The ball is put back in the bag. Next B draws a ball and gets the number b. The probability that a and b satisfies the inequality $a - 3b + 12 \geq 0$ is

(a) $\frac{13}{20}$ (b) $\frac{17}{20}$
(c) $\frac{11}{20}$ (d) None of these

4. A and B pick two numbers (say) a and b respectively one after another without replacement from a bag containing numbers 10 to 15, the probability that the numbers satisfy the inequality $2a - b > 10$ is

(a) $\frac{11}{30}$ (b) $\frac{21}{30}$
(c) $\frac{19}{30}$ (d) None of these

5. An unbiased die with faces marked 1, 2, 3, 4, 5 and 6 is rolled.The probability that the minimum face value is not less than 2 and the maximum face value is not greater than 5 is,

(a) 1/3 (b) 2/3
(c) 5/3 (d) 4/3

6. If the papers of 3 students can be checked by any one of the 6 professors, then probability that all the 3 papers are checked by exactly 2 professors is.

(a) 5/12 (b) 7/12
(c) 1/12 (d) None of these

7. If m is an integer such that $-4 \leq m \leq 10$, then the probability that the roots of the quadratic equation $x^2 - mx + 2m + 3 = 0$ are real is

(a) 2/15 (b) 3/15
(c) 4/15 (d) None of these

8. Two letters are randomly picked from the word 'ABSCOND'. The probability that they are consecutive in dictionary order is.

(a) 2/21 (b) 4/21
(c) 5/21 (d) None of these

9. Ten white balls and five black balls are randomly placed in a row. The probability that no two black balls are placed adjacently equals

(a) 2/13 (b) 1/13
(c) 3/13 (d) None of these

10. There are 12 machines and it is known exactly three of them are faulty. They are tested one at a time and 3 in a day, till all the faulty machines are identified. Then the probability that only one day is needed day is

(a) 5/1236 (b) 3/1235
(c) 1/1320 (d) None of these

11. A group of $2n$ boys, $2n$ girls and $2n$ teachers randomly divided into two equal groups. The probability that each group contains the same number of boys, girls and teachers is.

(a) $\frac{\left({}^{6n}C_{2n}\right)^3}{{}^{6n}C_{3n}}$ (b) $\frac{\left({}^{2n}C_{n}\right)^3}{{}^{6n}C_{3n}}$

(c) $\frac{\left({}^{3n}C_{n}\right)^3}{{}^{6n}C_{3n}}$ (d) None of these

12. Four distinct numbers are selected from first 40 natural multiples of 5. The probability that all the four numbers are divisible by 3 as well as 5 is.

(a) $\frac{11}{1406}$ (b) $\frac{13}{1406}$

(c) $\frac{3}{1406}$ (d) None of these

13. A natural number x is chosen at random from the first one hundred natural numbers. The probability that $\frac{(x-10)(x-20)}{x-40} > 0$ is

(a) $\frac{69}{100}$ (b) $\frac{31}{50}$

(c) $\frac{71}{100}$ (d) None of these

14. A person writes 5 letters and 5 addresses on 5 envelopes. If the letters are placed in the envelopes at random, the probability that not all letters are placed in correct envelopes is

(a) $\frac{1}{120}$ (b) $\frac{11}{120}$

(c) $\frac{13}{60}$ (d) $\frac{119}{120}$

15. Three integers are chosen at random without replacement from the first 30 integers. The probability that their product is even is.

(a) $\frac{101}{116}$ (b) $\frac{105}{116}$

(c) $\frac{111}{116}$ (d) $\frac{103}{116}$

16. One of the two exclusive events must occur. If the chances of one is 2/3 of the other, then odds in favour of the other are:

(a) 1 : 3 (b) 3 : 1
(c) 2 : 3 (d) 3 : 2

17. For a post three persons A, B and C appear in the interview. The probability of A being selected is twice that of B and the probability of B being selected is thrice that of C. Then the odds in favour of B to be selected is:

(a) 3 : 7 (b) 7 : 3
(c) 1 : 4 (d) 4 : 1

18. A mapping is selected at random from set of all the mappings of the set $A = \{1,2...,n\}$ into itself. The probability that the mapping selected is an injection is:

(a) $1/n^n$ (b) $1/n!$

(c) $\frac{(n-1)!}{n^{n-1}}$ (d) $\frac{n!}{n^{n-1}}$

19. Twelve coupons are numbered from the 1 to 12. Six coupons are selected at random one at a time with replacement. The probability that the largest number appearing on a selected coupon is less than or equal to 8, is

(a) $(2/3))^6$ (b) $(7/12)^6$
(c) 1/33 (d) None of these

20. Three children are selected at random from a group of 6 boys and 4 girls. It is known that in this group exactly one girl and one boy belong to same parents. The probability that the selected group of chlidren have no blood relations, is equal to.

(a) 1/15 (b) 13/15
(c) 14/15 (d) 2/15

21. Let X be a universal set such that $n(X) = k$. The probability of selecting two subsets A and B of the set X such that $B = \overline{A}$ is:

(a) 1/2 (b) $1/(2^k - 1)$
(c) $1/2^k$ (d) $1/3^k$

22. The probability that the 13th day of a randomly chosen month is Friday is:

(a) 1/2 (b) 1/7
(c) 1/84 (d) None of these

23. The probability of three persons having the same date and month for the birthday in a non-leap year is

(a) 1/365 (b) $1/(365)^2$
(c) $1/(365)^3$ (d) None of these

24. A fair coin is tossed repeatedly until the outcomes of both types have been obtained. The probability that the coin will be tossed exactly 5 times, is equal to:

(a) 1/16 (b) 1/32
(c) 1/2 (d) 1/4

25. Let $x = 33^n$. The index n is given a positive integer value at random. The probability that the value of x will have 3 in the units place is:

(a) 1/4 (b) 1/2
(c) 1/3 (d) None of these

26. If n positive integers are taken at random and multiplied together, then the probability that the last digit of product is 2, 4, 6 or 8 is:

(a) $\left(\frac{4}{5}\right)^n$ (b) $\frac{3^n - 2^n}{5^n}$
(c) $\frac{4^n - 2^n}{5^n}$ (d) None of these

27. A box contains 2 fifty paise coins, 5 twenty five paise coins and 15 ten paise coins. Five coins are taken out of the box at random. Probability that the value of these five coins is less than one rupee and fifty paise is.

(a) $\frac{170}{^{22}C_5}$ (b) $1-\frac{150}{^{22}C_5}$
(c) $1-\frac{170}{^{22}C_5}$ (d) None of these

28. A car is parked among N cars standing in a row, but not at either end.On his return, the owner finds that exactly r of the N places are still occupied. The probability that both the places neighbouring his car are empty is.

(a) $\frac{^{N-3}C_{r-1}}{^{N-1}C_{r-1}}$ (b) $\frac{^{N}C_{r-1}}{^{N-1}C_{r-1}}$
(c) $\frac{^{N-1}C_{r}}{^{N-1}C_{r-1}}$ (d) None of these

29. A person while dialing a telephone number, forgets the last three digits of the number but remembers that exactly two of them are same. He dials the number randomly. The probability that he dialed the correct number, is equal to

(a) 1/35 (b) 1/27
(c) 1/54 (d) 1/270

30. A bag contains n tickets marked 1,2,3,....,n, If two tickets are drawn, then chance that the difference of the numbers on the tickets exceed $m < (n - 1)$ is:

(a) $\frac{(n-m)(n-m+1)}{n(n-1)}$ (b) $\frac{(n-m)(n-m+1)}{n(n-1)}$
(c) $\frac{(n-m)(n-m-1)}{n(n-1)}$ (d) None of these

31. Two numbers, x and y, are chosen at random (with replacement) from amongst the numbers 1, 2, 3,...,3n. The probability that $x^3 + y^3$ is divisible by 3 is

(a) 1/3 (b) 2/3
(c) $1/3n$ (d) $n/3n - 1$

32. Numbers 1, 2, 3, ...,100 are written down on each of the cards A, B and C. One number is selected at random from each of the cards. The probability that the numbers so selected can be the measured (in cm) of three sides of a right-angled is.

(a) $\frac{4}{100^3}$ (b) $\frac{3}{50^3}$
(c) $\frac{3!}{100^3}$ (d) $\frac{9}{2(50)^3}$

33. If the probability of choosing an integer 'n' out of $2m$ integers $\{1,2,3,...,2m-1, 2m\}$ is inversely proportional to n^4 $(1 \le n \le 2m)$, then the probability of the chosen number being odd is

(a) 1/2 (b) < 1/2
(c) > 1/2 (d) None of these

34. Two numbers b and c are chosen at random (with replacement from the numbers 1,2,3,4,5,6,7,8 and 9. The probability that $x^2 + bx + c > 0$ for all $x \in \mathbb{R}$, is given by:

(a) 32/81 (b) 49/81
(c) 16/81 (d) None of these

35. Five different balls are distributed in 10 different boxes, one each in a box. The probability that they will fill the 5 adjacent boxes is equal to:

(a) $\frac{27}{1250}$ (b) $\frac{9}{1250}$
(c) $\frac{3}{500}$ (d) None of these

36. If the integers m and n are chosen at random between 1 and 100, then the probability that a number of the form $7^n + 7^m$ is divisible by 5 equals

(a) 1/4 (b) 1/7
(c) 1/8 (d) 1/49

37. Each coefficient of the equation $ax^2 + bx + c = 0$ is determined by throwing an ordinary die. Then the probability that the equation has non-real complex roots is given by.

(a) 173/216 (b) 43/216
(c) 173/432 (d) None of these

38. A man takes a step forward with probability 0.4 and backward with probability 0.6. The probability that at the end of eleven steps he is one step away from the starting point is:

(a) $^{11}C_6(.4)^6(.6)^5$ (b) $^{11}C_6(.6)^6(.4)^5$
(c) $^{11}C_6(.24)^5$ (d) None of these

39. Three of the six vertices of a regular hexgon are chosen at random. The probability that the triangle formed with these vertices is equilateral, is equal to

(a) 1/2 (b) 1/5
(c) 1/10 (d) 1/20

40. Let ω be a complex cube root of unity with $\omega \neq 1$. A fair die is thrown three times. If r_1, r_2 and r_3 are the numbers obtained on the die, then the probability that $\omega^{r_1} + \omega^{r_2} + \omega^{r_3} = 0$ is

(a) 1/18 (b) 1/9
(c) 2/9 (d) 1/36

41. A fair coin is tossed 5 times. If k is the sum of probabilities of the events (a) at least 3 heads in succession and (b) at least three head, then 16 k is divisible by

(a) 4 (b) 3
(c) 6 (d) 9

Answer Key

1. (b)	**2.** (b)	**3.** (c)	**4.** (c)	**5.** (b)	**6.** (a)	**7.** (c)	**8.** (b)	**9.** (a)	**10.** (c)
11. (b)	**12.** (a)	**13.** (a)	**14.** (d)	**15.** (d)	**16.** (d)	**17.** (a)	**18.** (c)	**19.** (a)	**20.** (c)
21. (b)	**22.** (c)	**23.** (c)	**24.** (a)	**25.** (a)	**26.** (c)	**27.** (c)	**28.** (a)	**29.** (d)	**30.** (c)
31. (a)	**32.** (d)	**33.** (c)	**34.** (a)	**35.** (d)	**36.** (a)	**37.** (a)	**38.** (c)	**39.** (c)	**40.** (c)
41. (a, b, c)									

PROBABILITY OF COMPOUND EVENTS

If two or more events occur together, then their joint occurrence is called a compound event. We can combine E_1 and E_2 to form other new events which are called as compound events. Some typical cases are mentioned below:

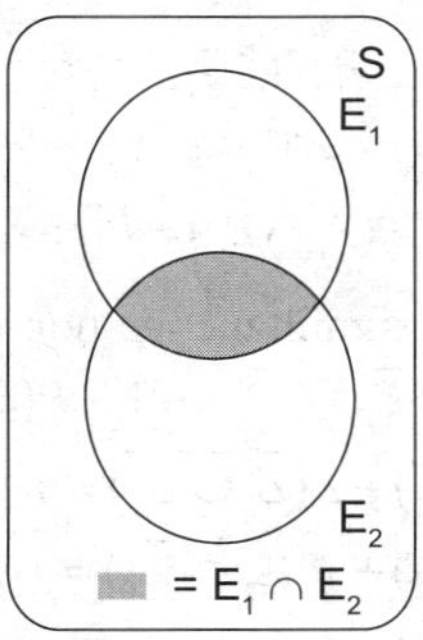

FIGURE 6.3

1. $E_1 \cap E_2$ is the event which occurs if both E_1 and E_2 occur $\Rightarrow P(E_1 \cap E_2) = \dfrac{n(E_1 \cap E_2)}{n(S)}$

2. $E_1 \cup E_2$ is the event which occurs if either E_1 or E_2 or both occur.
In other words, $E_1 \cup E_2$ occurs if at least one of E_1 and E_2 occurs.

$$\Rightarrow P(E_1 \cup E_2) = \frac{n(E_1 \cup E_2)}{n(S)}$$

$$= \frac{n(E_1) + n(E_2) - n(E_1 \cap E_2)}{n(S)}$$

$$\Rightarrow P(E_1 \cup E_2) = P(E_1) + P(E_2) - P(E_1 \cap E_2)$$

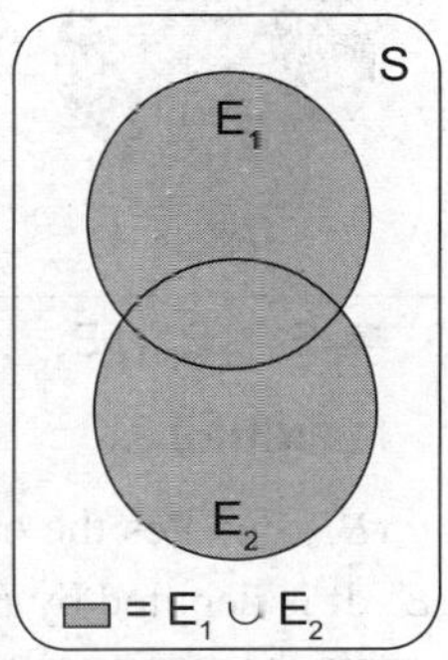

FIGURE 6.4

SET THEORETIC PRINCIPLE:

If E, E_1, E_2 and E_3 are four events, then

(a) $E_1 \cup E_2$ stands for occurrence of at least one of E_1 and E_2

(b) $E_1 \cap E_2$ stands for simultaneous occurrence of E_1 and E_2.

(c) E' or $\bar{E}$ or E^C stands for non occurrence of event E.

(d) $(\bar{E}_1 \cap \bar{E}_2) = \overline{E_1 \cup E_2}$ stands for non occurrence of both E_1 and E_2 i.e., the occurence of neither E_1 nor E_2.

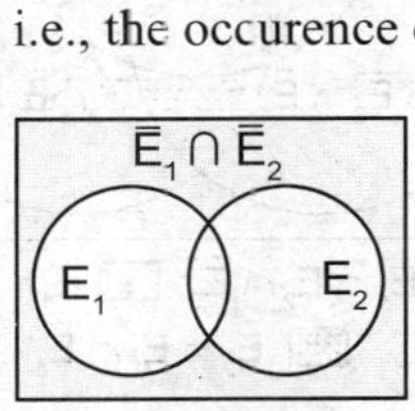

FIGURE 6.5

(e) $E_1 - E_2$ or $E_1 \cap \overline{E}_2$ denotes the occurence of event E_1 but not of E_2.

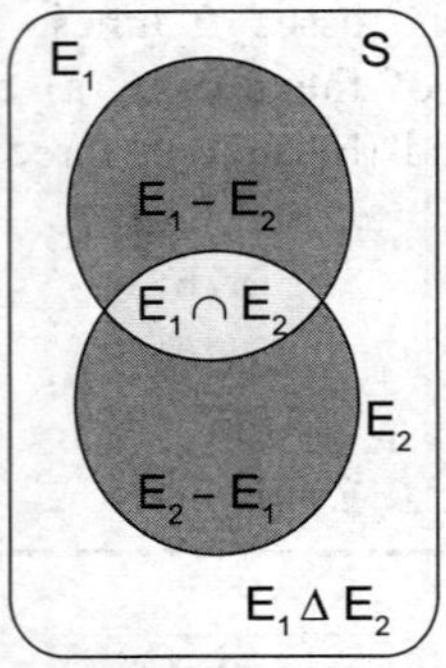

FIGURE 6.7

(f) $E_1 \cup E_2 \cup E_3$ denotes the occurence of at least one of the events E_1 or E_2 or E_3

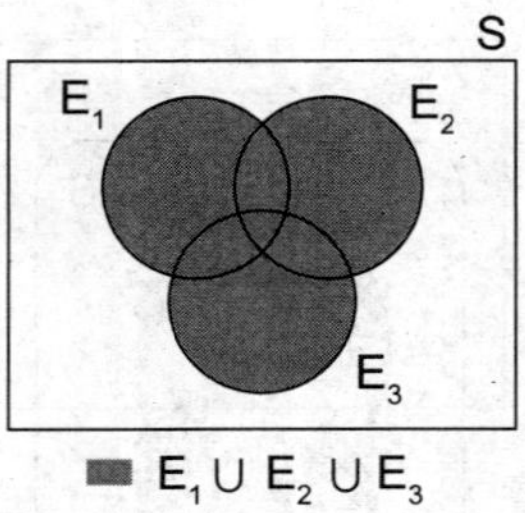

FIGURE 6.6

(g) $(E_1 \cap \overline{E}_2) \cup (\overline{E}_1 \cap E_2)$ denotes the occurence of exactly one of E_1 and E_2. It is denoted by $E_1 \, \Delta \, E_2$.
Where Δ represents the symmetric differecnce
It is represented by shaded region in the above Venn diagram.

(h) $E_1 \cap E_2 \cap E_3$ denotes the occurence of all the three events E_1, E_2 and E_3.

(i) $(E_1 \cap E_2 \cap \overline{E}_3) \cup (E_1 \cap \overline{E}_2 \cap E_3) \cup (\overline{E}_1 \cap E_2 \cap E_3)$
denotes the occurence of exactly two of E_1, E_2 and E_3.

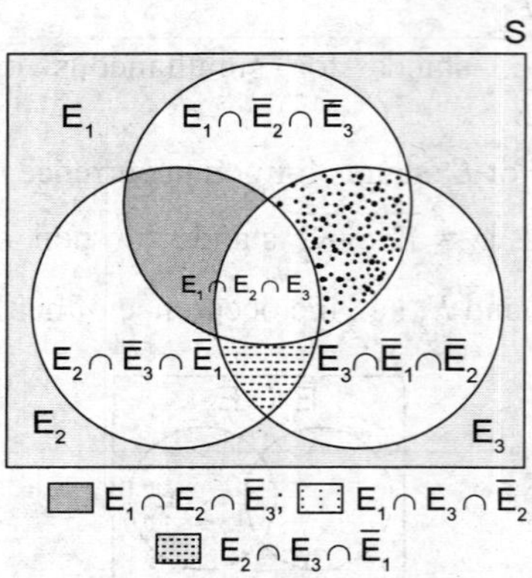

FIGURE 6.8

These concepts can be applied in different cases mentioned as below:

- Probability of non occurence of event $E_1 = P(\overline{E}_1) = 1 - P(E_1)$
As, $E_1 \cup \overline{E}_1 = S$ and E_1 and $\overline{E}_1$ are mutually exclusive events
$\Rightarrow P(E_1 \cup \overline{E}_1) = P(E_1) + P(\overline{E}_1) = P(S) = 1$
$\Rightarrow P(\overline{E}_1) = 1 - P(E_1)$

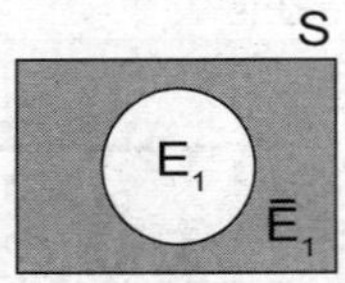

FIGURE 6.9

- $P(E_1 \cap \overline{E}_2) = P(E_1) - P(E_1 \cap E_2)$
As $E_1 \cap \overline{E}_2$ and $E_1 \cap E_2$ are mutually exclusive events and $(E_1 \cap \overline{E}_2) \cup (E_1 \cap E_2) = E_1$

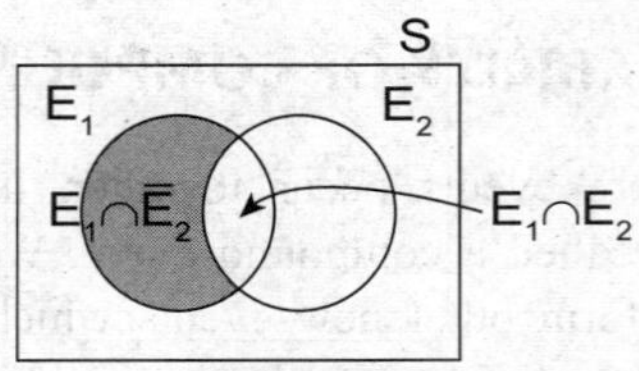

FIGURE 6.10

$\Rightarrow P(E_1 \cap \overline{E}_2) + P(E_1 \cap E_2) = P(E_1)$
$\Rightarrow P(E_1 \cap \overline{E}_2) = P(E_1) - P(E_1 \cap E_2)$
Similarly, $P(\overline{E}_1 \cap E_2) = P(E_2) - P(E_1 \cap E_2)$

- Probability of simultaneous non-occurence of events E_1 and $E_2 = P(\overline{E}_1 \cap \overline{E}_2) = 1 - P(E_1 \cup E_2)$.
As $P(E_1 \cup E_2) + P(\overline{E_1 \cup E_2}) = 1$
$\Rightarrow P(E_1 \cup E_2) + P(\overline{E}_1 \cap \overline{E}_2) = 1$
$\Rightarrow P(E_1 \cup E_2) = 1 - P(\overline{E}_1 \cap \overline{E}_2)$
$\Rightarrow P(\overline{E}_1 \cap \overline{E}_2) = 1 - P(E_1 \cup E_2)$

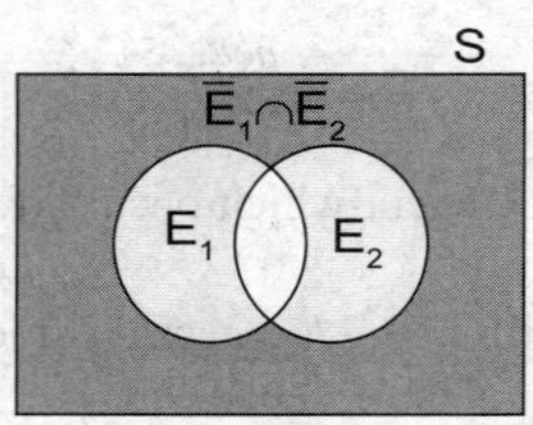

FIGURE 6.11

- Probability of occurence of exactly one of the events E_1 and E_2.
$= P(E_1 \cap \overline{E}_2) + P(\overline{E}_1 \cap E_2) = P(E_1) + P(E_2) - 2P(E_1 \cap E_2)$
$= P(E_1 \cup E_2) - P(E_1 \cap E_2) = P(\overline{E}_1 \cup \overline{E}_2) - P(\overline{E}_1 \cap \overline{E}_2)$

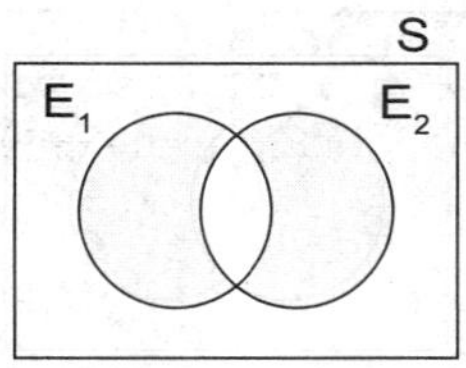

FIGURE 6.12

■ TYPES OF COMPOUND EVENTS

Independent Events

Two events are said to be independent if the occurence or non occurrence of one does not affect the occurrence or non-occurrence of the other. For independent events A and B, $P(A \cap B) = P(A).P(B)$

e.g., Consider the experiment of drawing a card from a pack of 52 cards.

P (E: card drawn is a diamond) = 13/52 = 1/4. P(F: card drawn is a king) = 4/52 = 1/13

P ($E \cap F$: card drawn is the King of Diamond) = 1/52

$P(EF)$ = 1/52 = 1/4 × 1/13 = $P(E)$. $P(F)$. So E and F are independent.

REMARKS

- *If $P(A) = 0 \Rightarrow$ for any event B, $0 \le P(A \cap B) \le P(A)$*
  $\Rightarrow P(A \cap B) = 0$, thus $P(A \cap B) = 0 = P(A). P(B)$.
  Hence "An impossible event would be independent of any other event".
- *Distinction between independent and mutually exclusive events must be carefully made, since independence is a property of probability whereas the mutual exclusion is a set theoretic concept. If A and B are two mutually exclusive and possible events of sample space S, then $P(A) > 0$, $P(B) > 0$ and $P(A \cap B) = 0 \ne P(A). P(B)$ so the event A and B can't be independent. In fact $P(A/B) = 0$ similarly $P(B/A) = 0$ and consequently, "mutually exclusive events are strongly dependent".*
- *Whenever there are two independent events there must be atleast one element common between them.*

Proof: Let A and B be the sets of the sample space corresponding to the events E and F, which are such that $P(EF) = P(E).P(F)$ with $P(E) \ne 0$, $P(F) \ne 0$. If $A \cap B = \phi$, then $P(E \cap F) = P(\phi) = 0$. So either $P(E)$ or $P(F)$ is zero.

This contradicts the hypothesis that neither of $P(E)$. $P(F)$ is zero. Hence $A \cap B \ne \phi$.

- Two events A and B are independent if and only if A and $\bar{B}$ are independent or $\bar{A}$ and B are independent or $\bar{A}$ and $\bar{B}$ are independent.

  We have $P(A \cap B) = P(A). P(B)$

Now $P(A \cap \bar{B}) = P(A) - P(A \cap B) = P(A) - P(A)\,P(B)$

$= P(A)\,(1 - P(B)) = P(A).\,P(\bar{B})$

Thus A and $\bar{\ }$ are independent

Similarly $P(\bar{A} \cap B) = P(B) - P(A \cap B) = P(B)\,P(\bar{A})$

Finally $P(\bar{A} \cap \bar{B}) = 1 - P(A \cup B)$

$= 1 - P(A) - P(B) + P(A \cap B) = 1 - P(A) - P(B) + P(A).\,P(B)$

$= (1 - P(A)) - P(B)\,(1 - P(A)) = (1 - P(A))\,(1 - P(B))$

$= P(\bar{A}).\,P(\bar{B})$

Thus $\bar{A}$ and B; $\bar{A}$ and $\bar{B}$ are also independent

ILLUSTRATION 9: An event A_1 can happen with probability p_1 and the event A_2 can happen with probability p_2. Then find the probability that

(i) exactly one of them happens

(ii) at least one of them happens (Given A_1 and A_2 are independent events)

SOLUTION: (i) The probability that A_1 happens is p_1, so the probability that A_1 fails is $1 - p_1$.

Also the probability that A_2 happens is p_2 and that of its failure is $(1 - p_2)$.

Now the chance that A_1 happens and A_2 fails is $p_1(1 - p_2)$ and the chance that A_1 fails and A_2 happens is $p_2\,(1 - p_1)$. The probability that one and only one of them happens is
$p_1\,(1 - p_2) + p_2(1 - p_1) = p_1 + p_2 - 2p_1\,p_2$

(ii) The probability that both of them fail to happen = $(1 - p_1)\,(1 - p_2)$. Probability that atleast one of the event happens = $1 - (1 - p_1)(1 - p_2) = p_1 + p_2 - p_1p_2$.

Mutual Independence and Pairwise Independence

- Three events E_1, E_2, E_3 are said to be mutually independent iff
$P(E_1 \cap E_2) = P(E_1)\,P(E_2)$; $P(E_1 \cap E_3) = P(E_1)\,P(E_3)$;
$P(E_2 \cap E_3) = P(E_2)\,P(E_3)$ and $P(E_1 \cap E_2 \cap E_3) = P(E_1)\,P(E_2)\,P(E_3)$

- These events would be called be pairwise independent when
$P(E_1 \cap E_2) = P(E_1)\,P(E_2)$; $P(E_2 \cap E_3) = P(E_2)\,P(E_3)$ and $P(E_1 \cap E_3) = P(E_1)\,P(E_3)$

Thus mutually independent events are always pairwise independent but the converse may not be true.

ILLUSTRATION 10: A person draws a card from a pack of 52, replaces it and shuffles it. He continuous to do so until he draws a spade. What is the chance that he has to make
(i) atleast 3 trials (ii) exactly 3 trials

SOLUTION: (i) For atleast 3 trials, he has to fail at the first 2 attempts and after that it doesn't make a difference if he fails or wins at the 3rd or the subsequent attempts Chance of success at any attempt = 1/4, chance of failure = 3/4, chance of failing in first two attempt = $(3/4)^2 = 9/16$
(ii) For exactly 3 trials he has to fail in the first two attempts and get success in the 3rd attempt .
$\therefore$ required probability = $(3/4)^2$. $1/4 = 9/64$

ILLUSTRATION11: Two candidates A and B appear for an interview. Their chances of getting selected are 1/3 and 1/5 respectively. Assuming that their selections are independent of each other, find
(a) the probability that both are selected
(b) the probability that exactly one of them is selected
(c) at least one of them is selected

SOLUTION: Let us denote the following events
E_1 : is event that A is selected
E_2 : is event that B is selected
$\Rightarrow$ $P(E_1) = 1/3$ and $P(E_2) = 1/5$
(a) P(both selected) = $P(E_1 \cap E_2) = P(E_1)\,P(E_2)$ (As E_1 and E_2 are independent) = (1/3) (1/5) = 1/15
(b) P (exactly one is selected) = P(only A is selected or only B is selected)
Now $E_1 \cap \bar{E}_2$ represents the event that only A is selected $\bar{E}_1 \cap E_2$ is the event that only B is selected $\Rightarrow$ P (Exactly one is selected) = $P(E_1 \cap \bar{E}_2) \cup (\bar{E}_1 \cap E_2)$

$$= P(E_1 \cap \bar{E}_2) + P(\bar{E}_1 \cap E_2) = P(E_1)P(\bar{E}_2) + P(\bar{E}_1)P(E_2) = \frac{1}{3}(1-1/5)+(1-1/3)\frac{1}{5} = \frac{6}{15} = \frac{2}{5}$$

(c) P (at least one is selected) = $P(E_1 \cup E_2) = P(E_1) + P(E_2) - P(E_1 \cap E_2)$
$= 1/3 + 1/5 - 1/3.1/5 = 8/15 - 1/15 = 7/15$

ILLUSTRATION12: Three identical dice are thrown
(a) What is the probability of getting a total score of 15
(b) What is the probability that an odd number is obtained on each die given that the sum obtained is 15?

SOLUTION: (a) Let A be the event that sum is 15. Then the favourable outcomes for A
= {(3,6,6); (4,5,6); (4,6,5); (5,4,6); (5,5,5); (5,6,4); (6,3,6);(6,4,5);(6,5,4); (6,6,3)}

and $n(S) = 6^3 = 216 \Rightarrow P(A) = \frac{10}{216} = \frac{5}{108}$

(b) Let B be the event that odd number appears on each die

$\Rightarrow P(B/A) = \frac{P(B \cap A)}{P(A)}$. We have $B \cap A = \{(5,5,5)\} \Rightarrow P(B/A) = \frac{1/216}{10/216} = \frac{1}{10}$

ILLUSTRATION 13: In a game, two persons A and B each draw a card from a pack of 52 cards one by one until an ace is obtained. The first one to draw an ace wins the game. If A starts the game and the cards are replaced after each drawing, then find the probability of A's win.

SOLUTION: Let A_i and B_i denote the event that A and B respectively draws ace in i^{th} attempt $P(A$ wins)
= $P(A$ wins in his Ist sttempt) + $P(A$ wins in his IInd attempt) +..

$$= \frac{4}{52} + \left(\frac{48}{52}\right)^2 \times \frac{4}{52} + \left(\frac{48}{52}\right)^4 \times \frac{4}{52} \ldots = \frac{4/52}{1-(48/52)^2} = \frac{4\times 52}{52^2 - 48^2} = \frac{13}{25}$$

ILLUSTRATION 14: A candidate has to appear in an examination in three subjects: English, Mathematics and Physics. His chances of passing in these subjects are 0.5, 0.7 and 0.9 respectively. Find the probability that

(a) he passes in at least one of the subjects

(b) he passes exactly in two subjects.

SOLUTION: Let us define three events A, B, C as : A : he passes in English

B : he passes in Mathematics $\quad C$: he passes in Physics

(a) P(he passes in at least one subject) = $P(A \cup B \cup C)$
$= P(A) + P(B) + P(C) - P(A \cap B) - P(A \cap C) - P(B \cap C) + P(A \cap B \cap C)$
$= 0.5 + 0.7 + 0.9 - (0.35 + 0.63 + 0.45) + 0.315 = 0.985$

(b) P (he passes exactly in two subjects)
$= P(A \cap B \cap \bar{C}) + P(A \cap \bar{B} \cap C) + P(\bar{A} \cap B \cap C)$
$= P(A)\, P(B)\, P(\bar{C}) + P(A)\, P(\bar{B})\, P(C) + P(\bar{A})\, P(B)\, P(C) = 0.485$

ILLUSTRATION 15: An urn contains four tickets having numbers 112, 121, 211, 222 written on them. If one ticket is drawn at random and A_i (i = 1, 2, 3) be the event that the ticket drawn has 1 as the ith digit from left in its number. Test whether the events A_1, A_2, A_3 are mutually independent or not.

SOLUTION: Let S be the sample space, then $n(S) = 4$ and given A_i = the event that the ith digit from left of the number on ticket drawn is 1.

$\Rightarrow A_1 = \{112, 121\}; A_2 = \{112, 211\}; A_3 = \{121, 211\}$

$\Rightarrow P(A_1) = \frac{2}{4} = \frac{1}{2}, P(A_2) = \frac{2}{4} = \frac{1}{2}, P(A_3) = \frac{2}{4} = \frac{1}{2}$

clearly, $A_1 \cap A_2 \cap A_3 = \phi$, $A_1 \cap A_2 = \{112\}$, $A_2 \cap A_3 = \{211\}$ and $A_3 \cap A_1 = \{121\}$

$\Rightarrow P(A_1 \cap A_2 \cap A_3) = 0$, $P(A_1 \cap A_2) = 1/4$, $P(A_2 \cap A_3) = 1/4$ and $P(A_3 \cap A_1) = 1/4$ and $P(A_1)$. $P(A_2)$. $P(A_3) = 1/2.\ 1/2.\ 1/2 = 1/8$

It is clear that $P(A_1 \cap A_2 \cap A_3) \neq P(A_1).\ P(A_2).\ P(A_3)$

$$\left.\begin{array}{ll} \text{But} & P(A_1 \cap A_2) = 1/4 = P(A_1).P(A_2) \\ & P(A_2 \cap A_3) = 1/4 = P(A_2)\ P(A_3) \\ \text{and} & P(A_3 \cap A_1) = 1/4 = P(A_3)\ P(A_1) \end{array}\right\}$$

Thus A_1, A_2, A_3 are pairwise independent but A_1, A_2, A_3 are not mutually independent events

ILLUSTRATION 16: Two dice are thrown such that the number 5 always occurs on the first die. Find the probability that the sum of the numbers on their faces be 9.

SOLUTION: Let S be the sample space, then $S = \{(a, b) : a \in \{1,2,3,4,5,6\}$ and $b \in \{1,2,3,4,5,6\}\}$

$\Rightarrow S = \{1,2,3,4,5,6\} \times \{1,2,3,4,5,6\} \Rightarrow n(S) = 36$

Let E_1 be the event that the sum of the numbers is 9 and E_2 be the event of occurence of 5 on the first die, therefore $E_1 = \{(3, 6), (6, 3), (4, 5), (5, 4)\}$

$\therefore$ $n(E_1) = 4$ and the event $E_2 = \{(5, 1), (5, 2), (5, 3), (5, 4), (5, 5), (5, 6)\}$

$\Rightarrow n(E_2) = 6$ and $E_1 \cap E_2 = \{(5, 4)\} \Rightarrow n(E_1 \cap E_2) = 1$

Now $P(E_1 \cap E_2) = \dfrac{n(E_1 \cap E_2)}{n(S)} = \dfrac{1}{36}$ and $P(E_2) = \dfrac{n(E_2)}{n(S)} = \dfrac{6}{36} = \dfrac{1}{6}$

$\therefore$ Required Probability $P\left(\dfrac{E_1}{E_2}\right) = \dfrac{P(E_1 \cap E_2)}{P(E_2)} = \dfrac{1/36}{1/6} = \dfrac{1}{6}$

Dependent Events

If the events are not independent, they are said to be dependent. Probabiity of dependent events are studied under the next article (conditional Probability). e.g., Consider the experiment of throwing two dice. Let E be the event of throwing the sum 10. Therfore the event will be E = (4, 6), (5, 5), (6, 4)} and so has the probability 3/36 = 1/12. Let F be the event that no die shows 5. The subset of the sample space corresponding to this event are $\{(x, y); x \neq 5, y \neq 5\}$. The probability of this event is 1 – 11/36 = 25/36. The simultaneous event $EF = E \cap F$ is $\{(4, 6), (6, 4)\}$ has probability 2/36 = 1/18. Clearly $P(EF) \neq P(E)\, P(F)$. So E and F are dependent events.

TEXTUAL EXERCISE 3: (SUBJECTIVE)

1. In a single throw of three dice, find the probability of getting a total of atleast 5.
2. Find the probability of drawing a card which is a spade or a king from a well shuffled pack of cards.
3. Two dice are thrown together. Find the probability that the sum of the numbers on the two faces is neither 9 nor 11.
4. From a set of 17 cards numbered 1, 2, 3,....16, 17, one is drawn at random. Find the probability of appearing a number divisible by 3 or 7.
5. A number is chosen at random from first two hundred naturals numbers. Find the probability that the number chosen is divisible by 6 or 8.
6. A bag contains 6 red and 4 black balls. Three balls are taken out randomly. Find the probability that
   (i) All are red
   (ii) Two are red and one is black
   (iii) All are of same colour.
   (iv) At least one is red.
   (v) At most two are red.
7. Bag A contains 4 red and 6 white balls, bag B contains 5 red and 7 white balls. One ball from each bag is taken out. Find the probability that this group contains
   (i) both red balls
   (ii) both balls of same colour
   (iii) both balls of different colours.
8. A drawer contains 50 bolts and 150 nuts. Half of the bolts and half of the nuts are rusted. If one item is chosen at random, find
   (i) the probability that it is either rusted or is a bolt.
   (ii) the probability that it is a rusted bolt
9. If two dice are rolled
   (a) Find the probability that the sum is either odd or divisible by 3
   (b) Find the probability that the sum is neither divisible by 3 nor is odd.
10. A can hit a target 3 times out of 7, B can 4 times out of 5, C can 2 times out of 3. They all fire together. What is the probability that at least two shots hit the target?

11. A police-man fires six bullets on a terrorist. The probability that the terrorist will be killed by one bullet is 0.6. Find the probability that terrorist is still alive.

12. The probability of a student getting I, II and III division in an examination is respectively 1/10, 3/5 and 1/4. Find the probability that the student fails in the examination.

13. Six married couples are standing in a room. If 2 persons are chosen at random, then find the probability that
 (i) they are a married couple.
 (ii) one is male and other is female.

14. Six married couples are standing in a room. If 4 persons are chosen at random, find the probability that:
 (i) 2 married couples are chosen.
 (ii) exactly one married couple is among the 4.
 (iii) no married couple is among the 4.

15. In a single cast of two fair dice, find the probability that digits appearing on them are two 4's, are a doublet, has sum 7, has same reading, sum = 10, sum > 10, sum ≥ 10, sum < 10, both odd, both even.

16. *A* has 3 shares in a lottery containing 3 prizes and 6 blanks. *B* has one share in a lottery containing one prize and 2 blanks. Compare their chances of success.

17. A number is chosen at random from the numbers 10 to 99. By seeing the number a man will laugh if product of the digits is 12. If he choose three numbers with replacement, then find the probability that he will laugh at least once.

18. A five-rupee coin, 3 two-rupee coins and 2 one rupee coins are stacked together in a column at random. Find the probability that the coins of the same denomination are consecutive.

19. There are 8 coloured balls and correspondingly 8 coloured (same as the balls) bags. The balls are placed in the bags, each one in one bag. Find the probability that 5 of the balls are placed in the respective coloured bags.

20. *A* can solve 75% of the problems in a book on mathematics and *B* can solve 70%. What is the probability that *A* or *B* can solve the problem chosen at random?

21. Let *A* be the set of four elements. From the set of all functions from *A* to *A*, a function is chosen at random. Find the chance that the selected function is an onto function.

22. If *A* and *B* are two independent events, such that $P(A \cap B) = \frac{8}{25}$ and $P(B') = \frac{13}{75}$, then find $P(A)$.

23. Let *E* and *F* be two independent events. The probability that both *E* and *F* happen is 1/12 and the probability that neither *E* nor *F* happens is 1/2, then find *P*(*E*) and *P*(*F*).

24. *A*, *B*, *C* are three mutually exclusive and exhaustive events associated with a random experiment. If $P(B) = \frac{3}{2}P(A)$ and $P(C) = \frac{1}{2}P(B)$, then find $P(A)$.

Answer Key

1. $\frac{53}{54}$ 2. $\frac{4}{13}$ 3. 5/6 4. $\frac{7}{17}$ 5. 1/4 6. (i) 1/6 (ii) 1/2 (iii) 1/5 (iv) 29/30 (v) 5/6

7. (i) 1/6 (ii) 31/60 (iii) 29/60 8. (i) 5/8 (ii) 1/8 9. (a) 2/3 (b) 1/3

10. 74/105 11. 0.004096 12. $\frac{1}{20}$ 13. (i) 1/11 (ii) 6/11

14. (i) 1/33 (ii) 16/33 (iii) 16/33 15. 1/36, 1/6, 1/6, 1/6, 1/12, 1/12, 1/6, 5/6, 1/4, 1/4

16. 16/7 17. $1-\left(\frac{43}{45}\right)^3$ 18. $\frac{1}{10}$ 19. 1/360

20. 37/40 21. $\frac{3}{32}$ 22. $\frac{12}{31}$

23. $P(E) = \frac{1}{3}$ and $P(F) = \frac{1}{4}$ or $P(E) = \frac{1}{4}$ and $P(F) = \frac{1}{3}$ 24. $\frac{4}{13}$

TEXTUAL EXERCISE 2: (OBJECTIVE)

1. There are 8 blue and 2 red balls in a bag. Each time one ball is drawn and replaced by a blue one. The probability of drawing the last red ball on the fourth draw is
(a) 0.0142 (b) 0.0434
(c) 0.0148 (d) None of these

2. There are n persons, 3 of them are selected at random. The probability that the 3 selected persons were not together is
(a) $\frac{6}{n(n-1)}$ (b) $1-\frac{1}{n(n-1)}$
(c) $1-\frac{6}{n(n-1)}$ (d) None of these

3. Two squares are chosen at random from upper half of a cheshboard. The probability that they have a side in common is
(a) 7/124 (b) 13/124
(c) 11/62 (d) None of these

4. A bag contains x white, y black balls. Two players, A and B alternately draw a ball from the bag, replacing the ball each time after the draw till one of them draws a white ball and wins the game. A begins the game. If the probability of winning the game by A is four times that by B, then ratio $x : y$ is
(a) 1:1 (b) 1:3
(c) 3:1 (d) None of these

5. A fair coin is tossed 200 times. The probability of getting head an even number of times is
(a) 1/12 (b) 1/8
(c) 3/8 (d) 1/2

6. For the three events A, B and C, P(exactly one of the events A or B occurs) = P(exactly one of the events B or C occurs) = P(exactly one of the events C or A occurs) = P(all the three events occur simultaneously) = p^2, where $0 < p < 1/2$. Then the probability of occuring at least one of three events A, B and C is
(a) $\frac{3p^2}{2}$ (b) p^2
(c) 2 (d) $\frac{5p^2}{2}$

7. A letter is taken at random from the letters of the word 'STATISTICS' and another from 'MATHEMATICS'. The probability that the selected letters are same is.
(a) $\frac{1}{55}$ (b) $\frac{3}{55}$
(c) $\frac{7}{55}$ (d) None of these

8. A pair of unbiased dice is rolled together till a sum of either 4 or 6 is obtained. The probability that the sum of the sum of 4 comes before 6 is
(a) $\frac{3}{8}$ (b) $\frac{5}{8}$
(c) $\frac{1}{8}$ (d) None of these

9. 20% bulbs in a set of 100 bulbs are defective, 5 bulbs are selected randomly from this set. The probability that the selected set has at least two and atmost 4 defective bulbs, is equal to
(a) $\frac{{}^{20}C_2 \cdot {}^{80}C_2 + {}^{20}C_4 \cdot {}^{80}C_1}{{}^{100}C_5}$
(b) $\frac{{}^{20}C_2 \cdot {}^{80}C_3 + {}^{20}C_3 \cdot {}^{80}C_2 + {}^{20}C_4 \cdot {}^{80}C_1}{{}^{100}C_5}$
(c) $\frac{{}^{20}C_2 \cdot {}^{80}C_3 + {}^{20}C_3 \cdot {}^{80}C_2}{{}^{100}C_5}$
(d) None of these

10. The probability that the persons P_1 and P_2 will die in a year are p and q respectively. The probability that at the end of the year only one of them will be alive, is equal to:
(a) $p + q - pq$ (b) $p + q - p^2 - q^2$
(c) $p + q - 2pq$ (d) $pq\,(p + q - pq)$

11. The numbers 1, 2, 3,...,n are arranged in a random order. The probability that the digits 1, 2, 3,....,k ($n > k$) occur together is:
(a) $\frac{(n-k)!}{n!}$ (b) $\frac{n-k+1}{{}^nC_k}$
(c) $\frac{n-k}{{}^nC_k}$ (d) $\frac{k!}{n!}$

12. It has been found that if A and B play a game 12 times. A wins 6 times, B wins 4 times and they draw twice. A and B take part in a series of 3 games. The probability that they will win alternately is
(a) 5/36 (b) 5/18
(c) 19/27 (d) None of these

13. A committee consists of 9 experts taken from three institution A, B and C, of which 2 are from A, 3 from B and 4 from C. If three experts resign from the commitee, then the probability of exactly two of the resigned experts being from the same institution, is equal to
(a) 4/7 (b) 25/84
(c) 55/84 (d) 37/84

14. In a non-leap year, probabiliy of getting 53 sundays or 53 Tuesdays or 53 Thursdays is
(a) 1/7 (b) 2/7
(c) 3/7 (d) 4/7

15. The probability of winning a test match by India-against Westindies is 1/2. Assuming independence from match to match the probability that in a match series India's second win occurs at the third test is:
(a) 1/8 (b) 1/4
(c) 1/2 (d) 2/3

16. A and B are two independent events. The probability that both A and B occur is 1/6 and the probability that neither of them occurs is 1/3. The probability of the occurrence of A is:
(a) 1/2 (b) 1/3
(c) (a) or (b) (d) None of these

17. Three houses are available in a locality. Three persons apply for the houses. Each applies for one house without consulting others. The probability that all the three apply for the same house is
(a) 1/9 (b) 2/9
(c) 7/9 (d) 8/9

18. An experiment has 10 equally likely outcomes. Let A and B be two non-empty events of the experiment. If A consists of 4 outcomes, the number of outcomes that B must have so that A and B are independent is :
(a) 2,4 or 8 (b) 3,6 or 9
(c) 4 or 8 (d) 5 or 10

19. If M and N are two events, the probability that exactly one of them occurs is:
(a) $P(M) + P(N) - 2P(M \cap N)$
(b) $P(M) + P(N) - P\overline{(M \cup N)}$
(c) $P(\bar{M}) - P(\bar{N}) - 2P(\bar{M} \cap \bar{N})$
(d) $P(M \cap \bar{N}) + P(\bar{M} \cap N)$

20. The Probabilities that a student passes in Mathematices, Physics and Chemistry are m, p and c respectively. The student has a 75% chance of passing in at least one, 50 % chance of passing in atleast two, and 40% chance of passing in exactly two. Which of the following relations are true:
(a) $p + m + c = 19/20$ (b) $p + m + c = 27/20$
(c) $pmc = 1/10$ (d) $pmc = 1/4$

21. An urn contains 5 red and 5 black balls. A ball is drawn at random, its colour is noted and is returned to the urn. Moreover, 2 additional balls of the colour drawn are put in the urn and then a ball is drawn at random. What is the probability that the second ball is red ?
(a) 1/3 (b) 1/2
(c) 1/4 (d) None of these

Answer Key

1. (b)	**2.** (c)	**3.** (b)	**4.** (c)	**5.** (d)	**6.** (d)	**7.** (c)	**8.** (a)	**9.** (b)	**10.** (c)
11. (b)	**12.** (a)	**13.** (c)	**14.** (c)	**15.** (b)	**16.** (c)	**17.** (a)	**18.** (d)	**19.** (a,c,d)	
20. (b, c)	**21.** (b)								

■ CONDITIONAL PROBABILITY

Probability of occurrence of event E_1 given that event E_2 has already occurred is known as conditional probability of E_1 w.r.t. E_2 and is denoted as $P\left(\frac{E_1}{E_2}\right)$. Since, event E_2 has already occurred, then the sample space reduces to E_2 i.e., outcomes favourable to E_2 become the total outcomes therefore the outcomes favourable to the event $\left(\frac{E_1}{E_2}\right)$ are actually the outcomes which are common to both E_1 and E_2.

$$\Rightarrow \quad P\left(\frac{E_1}{E_2}\right) = P(E_1 \text{ given } E_2 \text{ has occured})$$

$$= \frac{\text{Total number of favourable outcomes}}{\text{Total number of outcomes}}$$

$$= \frac{n(E_1 \cap E_2)}{n(E_2)} = \frac{P(E_1 \cap E_2)}{P(E_2)}, \; P(E_2) \neq 0$$

Similarly, $P(E_2$ given E_1 has occured)

$$= P\left(\frac{E_2}{E_1}\right) = \frac{P(E_1 \cap E_2)}{P(E_1)}, P(E_1) \neq 0$$

Properties

1. If E_1 and E_2 are independent events, then $P\left(\frac{E_2}{E_1}\right) = P(E_2)$
2. If $E_1, E_2, \ldots, E_n$ are independent events, then $P(E_1 \cup E_2 \cup .. \cup E_n) = 1 - P(E_1 \cup E_2 \cup .. \cup E_n)^c = 1 - P(E_1^c)P(E_2^c).....P(E_n^c)$
3. If E_1 and E_2 are two events such that $E_2 \neq \phi$, then $P\left(\frac{E_1}{E_2}\right) + P\left(\frac{\bar{E}_1}{E_2}\right) = 1$
4. If E_1 and E_2 are two events such that $E_1 \neq \phi$, then $P(E_2) = P(E_1).\ P\left(\frac{E_2}{E_1}\right) + P(\bar{E}_1).P\left(\frac{E_2}{\bar{E}_1}\right)$
5. If E_1 and E_2 and E_3 are three events such that $E_1 \neq \phi$, $E_1 \cap E_2 \neq \phi$, then $P(E_1 \cap E_2 \cap E_3) = P(E_1).$ $P\left(\frac{E_2}{E_1}\right).P\left(\frac{E_3}{E_1 \cap E_2}\right)$

Generalized Form

If $E_1, E_2, \ldots, E_n$ are n events such that $E_1 \neq \phi$, $E_1 \cap E_2 \neq \phi$, $E_1 \cap E_2 \cap E_3 \neq \phi, \ldots, E_1 \cap E_2 \cap E_3 \cap \ldots \cap E_{n-1} \neq \phi$, then $P(E_1 \cap E_2 \cap E_3 \ldots \cap E_n) = P(E_1).$ $P\left(\frac{E_2}{E_1}\right).P\left(\frac{E_3}{E_1 \cap E_2}\right)......P\left(\frac{E_n}{E_1 \cap E_2 \cap \ldots \cap E_{n-1}}\right)$

■ TOTAL PROBABILITY THEOREM (FOR DEPENDENT EVENTS)

Let A be an event of S and $A_1, A_2, A_3, \ldots, A_n$ be n mutually exclusive as well as exhaustive events and A depends upon them individually, then we can write $A = (A_1 \cap A) \cup (A_2 \cap A) \ldots \cup (A_n \cap A)$

As $A_1, A_2, \ldots A_n$ are mutually exclusive, $(A_1 \cap A)$, $(A_2 \cap A), \ldots\ldots, (A_n \cap A)$ would also be mutually exclusive. Therefore

$$\Rightarrow P(A) = P(A_1 \cap A) + P(A_2 \cap A) + \ldots\ldots + (A_n \cap A)$$

$$= P(A_1).\ P(A/A_1) + P(A_2)\ P(A/A_2) + \ldots + P(A_n).\ P(A/A_n)$$

$\therefore$ The total Probability of event A

$$= P(A) = \sum_{i=1}^{n} P(A_i).P(A/A_i)$$

NOTE

1. *We have already discussed that mutually exclusive set of events are strongly dependent because occurrence of one precludes the occurrence of the other.*
2. *Concept of mutual exclusive is set theoretic in nature while the concept of dependence/independence is probablistic in nature.*
3. *$P(A/A_i)$ represents the contribution of event A_i in the probability of occurrence of A.*

ILLUSTRATION17: In an experiment of throwing a die, what is the probability of getting 2, given that an even number has already occurred.

SOLUTION: Let the event A be occurrence of 2 and B be occurrence of an even number on the face of die.

Then, $P(A/B) = \dfrac{P(A \cap B)}{P(B)} = \dfrac{1/6}{3/6} = \dfrac{1}{3}$

ILLUSTRATION 18: Five cards are drawn from a pack of well-shuffled pack of 52 cards. The cards are drawn one by one without replacement

(a) what is the probability of getting 3 aces?

(b) what is the probability of obtaining aces on the first three cards only?

(c) what is the probability of getting exactly three but consecutive aces?

SOLUTION: (a) total number of ways to select 5 cards = ${}^{52}C_5$

number of ways to select three aces and two non-aces = ${}^{4}C_3\,{}^{48}C_2$

$$P\text{ (3 aces out of 5 cards)} = \frac{{}^{4}C_3\,{}^{48}C_2}{{}^{52}C_5} = \frac{4\times48\times47\times5!}{2\times52\times51\times50\times49\times48} = \frac{94}{13\times17\times5\times49} = \frac{94}{54145}$$

(b) Let A_i represents the event that ace is drawn on i^{th} card and N_i be the event that non-ace is drawn on i^{th} card, then probability of getting aces cn first three cards.

$= P(A_1 \cap A_2 \cap A_3 \cap N_4 \cap N_5) = P(A_1)$.

$$P\left(\frac{A_2}{A_1}\right)P\left(\frac{A_3}{A_1 \cap A_2}\right).P\left(\frac{N_4}{A_1A_2A_3}\right).P\left(\frac{N_5}{A_1A_2A_3N_4}\right) = \frac{4}{52}\times\frac{3}{51}\times\frac{2}{50}\times\frac{48}{49}\times\frac{47}{48} = \frac{47}{270725}$$

(c) P (three consecutive aces) = P (first three aces) + P (first non ace. 3 aces, last non-ace) + P (first two non-ace, last three aces)

$$= \frac{4}{52}\times\frac{3}{51}\times\frac{2}{50}\times\frac{48}{49}\times\frac{47}{48}+\frac{48}{52}\times\frac{4}{51}\times\frac{3}{50}\times\frac{2}{49}\times\frac{47}{48}+\frac{48}{52}\times\frac{47}{51}\times\frac{4}{50}\times\frac{3}{49}\times\frac{2}{48} = \frac{141}{270725}$$

ILLUSTRATION 19: Two cards are drawn one by one without replacement from a pack of 52 cards

(a) what is the probability of getting both aces?

(b) what is the probability that second card is an ace?

SOLUTION: Let A be the event when first withdrawl is an ace and B be the event when second withdrawl is an ace.

(a) P (both aces) = $P(A \cap B) = P(A)\,P(B/A) = \frac{4}{52}\times\frac{3}{51} = \frac{1}{221}$

(b) P(second is ace) = $P(B) = P(A \cap B \cup \bar{A} \cap B)$

$= P(A)\,P(B/A) + P(\bar{A})P(B/\bar{A}) = 4/52 \times 3/51 + 48/52\times 4/51 = 1/13$

ILLUSTRATION 20: A bag contains 3 red, 2 green and 4 yellow balls. A ball is drawn and if it is red or yellow it is replaced otherwise not. Find the probability that second drawn ball is a yellow ball.

SOLUTION: First of all, we should be very clear about the event of which probability is to be found and the events on which it depends

Let A_1 : First ball is either red or yellow; A_2 = First ball is green

A = second drawn ball is yellow

We have to calculate $P(A)$ which definitely depends on A_1 and A_2. Therefore

$P(A) = P(A_1)\,P(A/A_1) + P(A_2)\,P(A/A_2)$; where

$P(A/A_1)$ = Probability of A when A_1 has already happened = 4/9 (i.e., probability of A given A_1) and $P(A_1) = 7/9$, $P(A/A_2)$ = Probability of A when A_2 has already happened (Probability of A given A_2) = 4/8 and $P(A_2) = 2/9$. Hence total probability of occurrence of A. $P(A) = \frac{4}{9}\times\frac{7}{9}+\frac{4}{8}\times\frac{2}{9} = \frac{37}{81}$

ILLUSTRATION 21: The probability that certain electronic component fails in first use is 0.10. If it does not fail immediately, the probability that it lasts for one year is 0.99. What is the probability that a new component will last for one year?

SOLUTION: Given probability (electronic component fails in first use) = 0.10

i.e., $P(F) = 0.10 \therefore P(\bar{F}) = 1 - P(F) = 0.90$ $(\because P(F) + P(\bar{F}) = 1)$

and let $P(Y)$ = Probability of new component to last for one year

Obviously the two events F and $\bar{F}$ are mutually exclusive as well as exhaustive

$P(Y/F) = 0$ and $P(Y/\bar{F}) = 0.99$

$\therefore\ P(Y) = P(F).P(Y/F) + P(\bar{F}).P(Y/F)$

$= 0.10 \times 0 + 0.90 \times 0.99 = 0 + (0.9)(0.99) = 0.891$

ILLUSTRATION 22: In a class 30% students fail in English; 20% students fail in Hindi and 10% students fail in English and Hindi both. A student is chosen at random, then what is the probability that he is fail in English if he has failed in Hindi?

SOLUTION: Let S be the sample space. If $n(S) = 100$, then E_1 = The event that the chosen student is fail in English

$\therefore\ n(E_1) = 30$ and E_2 = The event that the chosen student is fails in Hindi

$\therefore\ n(E_2) = 20$ and $n(E_1 \cap E_2) = 10$

$\therefore\ P(E_2) = \dfrac{n(E_2)}{n(S)} = \dfrac{20}{100} = \dfrac{1}{5}$ and $P(E_1 \cap E_2) = \dfrac{n(E_1 \cap E_2)}{n(S)} = \dfrac{10}{100} = \dfrac{1}{10}$

$\therefore$ Required Probability $P\left(\dfrac{E_1}{E_2}\right) = \dfrac{P(E_1 \cap E_2)}{P(E_2)} = \dfrac{1/10}{1/5} = \dfrac{1}{2}$

ADDITION THEOREM (TOTAL PROBABILITY THEOREM)

(a) If A and B are two events in S, then $P(A \cup B) = P(A) + P(B) - P(A \cap B)$

If A and B are mutually exclusive, then $P(A \cap B) = 0$ and $P(A \cup B) = P(A) + P(B)$

(b) If A, B, C are any three events of the sample space, then

$P(A \cup B \cup C) = P(A) + P(B) + P(C) - P(A \cap B) - P(A \cap C) - P(B \cap C) + P(A \cap B \cap C)$

(c) If $A_1, A_2, \ldots A_n$ are n events, then $P(A_1 \cup A_2 \cup \ldots \cup A_n)$

$= \sum_{i=1}^{n} P(A_i) - \sum\sum_{1 \le r_1 < r_2 \le n} \left(P(A_{r_1} \cap A_{r_2})\right) + \sum\sum\sum_{1 \le r_1 < r_2 < r_3 \le n} \left(P(A_{r_1} \cap A_{r_2} \cap A_{r_3})\right) - \ldots\ldots$

(d) The probability that one of the several mutually exclusive events $A_1, A_2, \ldots\ldots A_n$ will occur is sum of the probabilities of the occurrence of separate events.i.e., $P(A_1 \cup A_2 \cup \ldots \cup A_n) = P(A_1) + P(A_2) + \ldots + P(A_n)$

(e) Probability that exactly one of A, B, C occurs:

$= P(A) + P(B) + P(C) - 2P(A \cap B) - 2P(B \cap C) - 2P(A \cap C) + 3P(A \cap B \cap C)$

(f) Probability that exactly two of A, B, C occurs:

$= P(A \cap B) + P(B \cap C) + P(A \cap C) - 3P(A \cap B \cap C)$

(g) Probability that at least two of A, B, C occurs:

$= P(A \cap B) + P(B \cap C) + P(A \cap C) - 2P(A \cap B \cap C)$

(h) If $A_1, A_2, \ldots, A_n$ are n events, then

(i) $P(A_1 \cup A_2 \cup \ldots \cup A_n) \le P(A_1) + P(A_2) + \ldots + P(A_n)$

(ii) $P(A_1 \cap A_2 \cap \ldots \cap A_n) \ge 1 - P(A'_1) - P(A'_2) - \ldots - P(A'_n)$

Proof: (i) For $n = 1$, the result is clearly true.

For $n = 2$ we have

$P(A_1 \cup A_2) = P(A_1) + P(A_2) - P(A_1 \cap A_2) \le P(A_1) + P(A_2)$ $[\because P(A_1 \cap A_2) \ge 0]$

Assume that the result is true for $n = m$,

i.e., $P(A_1 \cup A_2 \cup \ldots \cup A_m) \le P(A_1) + P(A_2) + \ldots + P(A_m)$

We now show that the result is true for $n = m + 1$.

Let $A_1 \cup A_2 \cup \ldots\ldots \cup A_m = B$

Then $P(A_1 \cup A_2 \cup \ldots \cup A_m \cup A_{m+1})$

$= P(B \cup A_{m+1}) \le P(B) + P(A_{m+1})$

[$\because$ the result is true for $n = 2$]

$= P(A_1 \cup A_2 \cup \ldots \cup A_m) \cup P(A_{m+1}) \le P(A_1) + P(A_2) + \ldots + P(A_m) + P(A_{m+1})$ [using the induction assumption]

Hence the result is true for all $n \in \mathbb{N}$.

(ii) For $n = 1$, we have $P(A_1) = 1 - (1 - P(A_1)) = 1 - P(A'_1)$ and for $n = 2$

$P(A_1 \cap A_2) = P(A_1) + P(A_2) - P(A_1 \cup A_2) \ge P(A_1) + P(A_2) - 1$ $(\because P(A_1 \cup A_2) \le 1)$

$= 1 - P(A'_1) + 1 - P(A'_2) - 1 = 1 - P(A'_1) - P(A'_2)$

Thus, the result is true for $n = 2$. Assume that the result is true for $n = m$ i.e.,

$P(A_1 \cap A_2 \cap .... \cap A_m) \geq 1 - P(A'_1) - P(A'_2) - ... - P(A'_m)$

We shall now show that the result is true for $n = m + 1$.

Let $(A_1 \cap A_2 \cap .... \cap A_m) = B$. Then $P(A_1 \cap A_2 \cap ... \cap A_m \cap A_{m+1}) \geq 1 - P(B') - P(A'_{m+1})$

Now $P(B') = P[(A_1 \cap A_2 \cap ... \cap A_m)'] = P[A'_1 \cup A'_2 \cup ... \cup A'_m]$

$\leq P(A'_1) + P(A'_2) + ... + P(A'_m)$ (by (i))

Thus $P(A_1 \cap A_2 \cap .... \cap A_n) \geq 1 - P(A'_1) - P(A'_2) - ... - P(A'_n)$

Hence by the principle of mathematical induction the result is true for all $n \in \mathbb{N}$

(i) If $A_1, A_2, ..., A_n$ are n events, then $P(A_1 \cap A_2 \cap .... \cap A_n) \geq P(A_1) + P(A_2) + ... + P(A_n) - (n - 1)$

(j) If A and B are two events such that $A \subseteq B$, then $P(A) \leq P(B)$

Proof: We have $B = A \cup (A' \cap B)$. Also A and $A' \cap B$ are mutually exclusive.

$\Rightarrow P(B) = P(A) + P(A' \cap B) \geq P(A)$

$\because \ (P(A' \cap B) \geq 0)$

(k) Max $[(P(A) + P(B) - 1, P(A), P(B)] \leq P(A \cup B) \leq P(A) + P(B)$

If $A \subseteq A \cup B \Rightarrow P(A) \leq P(A \cup B)$

Similarly if $B \subseteq A \cup B$

$\Rightarrow P(B) \leq P(A \cup B)$

$\Rightarrow P(A \cup B) \geq \text{Max}(P(A), P(B))$ ....(i)

Also $P(A \cup B) = P(A) + P(B) - P(A \cap B) \leq P(A) + P(B)$ ....(ii)

and $P(A) + P(B) - 1 \leq P(A \cup B)$

(As $0 \leq P(A \cap B) \leq 1$) .... (iii);

$\therefore$ from (i) and (iii), we have

Max $[(P(A) + P(B) - 1, P(A), P(B)] \leq P(A \cup B) \leq P(A) + P(B)$

ILLUSTRATION 23: For a post three persons A, B and C appear in the interview. The probability of A being selected is twice that of B and the probability of B being selected is thrice that of C, what are the individual probabilities of A, B, C being selected?

SOLUTION: Let E_1, E_2, E_3 be the events of selection of A, B and C respectively

Let $P(E_3) = x$ then $P(E_2) = 3P(E_3) = 3x$ and $P(E_1) = 2P(E_2) = 6x$

Since E_1, E_2, E_3 are mutually exclusive and exhaustive events

$\therefore \ P(E_1 \cup E_2 \cup E_3) = P(E_1) + P(E_2) + P(E_3) = 1$

$\Rightarrow 6x + 3x + x = 10x = 1 \quad \Rightarrow \quad x = 1/10$

Hence $P(E_1) = 6x = 3/5$ and $P(E_2) = 3x = 3/10$ and $P(E_3) = x = 1/10$.

ILLUSTRATION 24: A and B are two candidates seeking admission in I.I.T. The proabability that A is selected is 0.5 and the probability that both A and B are selected is at most 0.3. Is it possible that the probability of B getting selected is 0.9.

SOLUTION: Let E_1 and E_2 be the event of selection of A and B respectively.

Given $P(E_1 \cap E_2) \leq 0.3$ and $P(E_1) = 0.5$

Since $P(E_1 \cup E_2) = P(E_1) + P(E_2) - P(E_1 \cap E_2)$

and $P(E_1 \cup E_2) \leq 1 \Rightarrow P(E_1) + P(E_2) - P(E_1 \cap E_2) \leq 1$ or $P(E_1) + P(E_2) \leq 1 + P(E_1 \cap E_2)$

$\Rightarrow \ 0.5 + P(E_2) \leq 1 + 0.3 \Rightarrow P(E_2) \leq 0.8$. Hence $P(E_2) \neq 0.9$

ILLUSTRATION 25: Let A, B, C be three events. If the probability of occurrence of exactly one event out of A and B is $1 - a$, out of B and C is $1 - 2a$, out of C and A is $1 - a$ and that of occurrence of three events simultaneously is a^2, then prove that the probability that at least one out of A, B, C will occur is greater than 1/2.

SOLUTION: Given $P(A) + P(B) - 2P(A \cap B) = 1 - a$ .....(i)

$P(B) + P(C) - 2P(B \cap C) = 1 - 2a; \ \left(a \leq \frac{1}{2}\right)$ .....(ii)

$P(C) + P(A) - 2\,P(C \cap A) = 1 - a;$ ......(iii)

and $P(A \cap B \cap C) = a^2$ ....(iv)

$\therefore\ P(A \cup B \cup C) = P(A) + P(B) + P(C) - P(A \cap B) - P(B \cap C) - P(C \cap A) + P(A \cap B \cap C))$

$= \frac{1}{2}\ \{P(A) + P(B) - P(A \cap B) + P(B) + P(C) - P(B \cap C) + P(C) + P(A) - P(C \cap A)\ \}$

$+ P(A \cap B \cap C)$

$= \frac{1}{2}\ \{1 - a + 1 - 2a + 1 - a\} + a^2$ {from (i), (ii), (iii) and (iv)}

$= \frac{3}{2} - 2a + a^2 = (a-1)^2 + 1/2 \Rightarrow P(A \cup B \cup C) > 1/2\ \left(\text{as } a \le \frac{1}{2} \Rightarrow a \ne 1\right)$

ILLUSTRATION 26: If A, B, C are the three events such that $P(A) = 0.3$, $P(B) = 0.4$, $P(C) = 0.8$, $P(AB) = 0.08$, $P(AC) = 0.28$, $P(ABC) = 0.029$. If $P(A \cup B \cup C) \ge 0.75$, then show that $P(BC)$ lies in the interval [0.169, 0.419].

SOLUTION: Let $P(BC) = x$

Since $P(A \cup B \cup C) = P(A) + P(B) + P(C) - P(A\,B) - P(B\,C) - P(C\,A) + P(A\,B\,C)$

$= 0.3 + 0.4 + 0.8 - 0.08 - x - 0.28 + 0.029 = 1.169 - x$

But given $P(A \cup B \cup C) \ge 0.75$ and $P(A \cup B \cup C) \le 1$

$\Rightarrow 0.75 \le 1.169 - x \le 1 \quad \Rightarrow\ -0.75 \ge -1.169 + x \ge -1$ or $1.169 - 0.75 \ge x \ge 1.169 - 1$

$\Rightarrow 0.169 \le x \le 0.419$

TEXTUAL EXERCISE 4: (SUBJECTIVE)

1. Bag A contains 4 red and 5 black balls and bag B contains 5 red and 6 black balls. One ball is taken randomly from bag A and placed into bag B and then one ball is taken out randomly from bag B. Find the probability that ball drawn is red.

2. A, B, C, D are playing with a coin and the person who finds head first wins. A begins the game. Find the respective changes of winning.

3. A and B are playing with a pair of dice one after another. If A finds 6 before B finds 7, A wins. If B finds 7 before A finds 6, then B wins. Find the probability of wining of A (given that A begins the game).

4. A tosses 2 fair coins and B tosses 3 fair coins. The game is won by the person who throws greater number of heads. In case of a tie, the game is continued under identical rules until someone wins the game. Find the probability of A winning the game.

5. We are given two urns as follows; Urn A contains 3 red and 2 white marbles. Urn B contains 2 red and 5 white marbles. An urn is selected at random; a marble is drawn and put into the other urn; then a marble is drawn from the second urn. Find the probability that both the drawn marbles are of the same colour.

6. One of ten keys opens the door. If we try the keys one after another what are the chances that the door is opened on the (i) 1st attempt (ii) second attempt (iii) 10th attempt.

7. Consider a bag containing 10 balls of which a few are black. Probability that a bag contains exactly three black balls is 0.6 and probability that bag contains exactly one black ball is 0.4. Now balls drawn from the bag one at a time without replacement till all black balls have been drawn. Find the probability that this process would end at 6th draw.

8. A person draws a card from a pack of 52, replaces it and shuffles it. He continues doing it until he draws a spade. Find the chance that he has to make
   (i) atleast 3 trials (ii) exactly three trials

9. A draws a card from a pack of n cards marked 1, 2,... n, the card is replaced in the pack and B draws a card. Find the probability that A draws:
   (i) same card as B (ii) higher card than B.

10. Indian Airforce has 250 aircrafts, 150 mig-21, 50 Jaguar, 50 Sukhoi-31. The probability of aircrash for Jaguar is 1/3 while that of Mig-21 is 1/2 and Sukhoi-31 is 1/6 respectively. A pilot selects a plane

randomly and takes off. Find the chances that he will land safely.

11. A box contains three coins; one coin is fair, one is two-headed, and one is weighted so that the probability of appearin head is 1/3. A coin is selected at random and tossed. Find the probability that heads appears.

12. Find the least number of dice that must be thrown, so that there is a better than even chance of obtaining a six.

13. (a) A real estateman has eight master keys to open several new homes. If 25% of these homes are usually left unlocked, find the probability that the real estate man can get into a specific home if he selects three master keys at random before leaving the office (if all keys open equal number of locks).

(b) A non-century year is chosen randomly. Find the probability that it contains 53 sundays.

Answer Key

1. $\frac{49}{108}$ 2. 8/15,4/15, 2/15, 1/15 3. $\frac{30}{61}$ 4. 3/11 5. $\frac{901}{1680}$

6. (i) 1/10 (ii) 1/10 (iii) 1/10 7. 9/100 8. (i) 9/16 (ii) 9/64

9. (i) $1/n$ (ii) $\frac{n-1}{2n}$ 10. 3/5 11. 11/18 12. 4 13. (a) $\frac{17}{32}$ (b) $\frac{5}{28}$

TEXTUAL EXERCISE 3: (OBJECTIVE)

1. If two events A and B are such that $P(A') = 0.34$, $P(B) = 0.54$ and $P(A \cap B) = 0.32$, then $P[(A \cup B')]$ is

(a) $\frac{41}{50}$ (b) $\frac{39}{50}$

(c) $\frac{33}{50}$ (d) $\frac{16}{39}$

2. A bag contains some white and some black balls, all combinations of balls being equally likely. The total number of balls in the bag is 10. If three balls are drawn at random, then the probability that all of them are black is

(a) $\frac{1}{2}$ (b) $\frac{1}{3}$

(c) $\frac{1}{5}$ (d) $\frac{1}{4}$

3. There are three balls in an urn whose colours are not known (each ball can be either white or black). A black ball is put into the urn. A ball is drawn from the urn. The probability that it is black is

(a) $\frac{1}{8}$ (b) $\frac{1}{2}$

(c) $\frac{5}{8}$ (d) None of these

4. In a hurdle race, a runner has probability p of jumping over a specific hurdle.Given that in 7 trials, the runner succeeded 4 times, the conditional probability that the runner had suceeded in the first trial is

(a) $\frac{3}{7}$ (b) $\frac{4}{7}$

(c) $\frac{2}{7}$ (d) None of these

5. Three numbers are chosen at random without replacement from the set {1, 3, 5, 7.....29}. Let E_1 be the event that minimum of the chosen numbers is 7 and E_2 be that when their maximum is 19, then

(a) $P(E_1) = 44/91$ (b) $P(E_2) = 24/91$

(c) $P(E_1 \cap E_2) = 1/13$ (d) $P(E_1/E_2) = 7/24$

6. A box contains N coins, m of which are fair and rest are biased. The probability of getting a head when a fair coin is tosses is 1/2, while it is 2/3 when a biased coin is tossed. A coin is drawn from the box at random and is tossed twice. The probability that it shows a head first time and second time is

(a) $\frac{2}{9}+\frac{m}{36N}$ (b) $\frac{1}{9}+\frac{m}{36N}$

(c) $\frac{1}{3}+\frac{m}{36N}$ (d) None of these

7. Given that A, B and C are events such that $P(A) = P(B) = P(C) = 1/10$, $P(A \cap B) = P(B \cap C) = 0$ and $P(A \cap C) = 1/20$. The probability that at least one of the events A, B or C occurs is

(a) $\frac{1}{2}$ (b) $\frac{1}{3}$

(c) $\frac{1}{4}$ (d) None of these

8. Let A and B be two events such that $P(A \cap B') = 0.30$, $P(A' \cap B) = 0.20$, and $P(A \cap B) = 0.15$, then

(a) $P(A/B) = 3/7$ (b) $P(A) = 0.45$

(c) $P(A \cup B) = 0.65$ (d) $P(B/A) = 1/3$

9. A pair of dice are thrown. One die has 2 faces marked with 3, 2 faces marked with 2 and 2 faces marked with 4. Another die has 3 faces marked with 1,2 faces marked with 2 and 1 face marked with 3, then

(a) The most probable sum is 5

(b) The probability of most probable sum is 1/3

(c) The least probable sum is 7

(d) The probability of least probable sum is 1/18

10. A person has 4 digit pin code of A.T.M. card. He forgot his pin-code, but he knew that the sum of first two digits is same as that of last two digits. He tried a four digit number, then the probability that the tried code is correct is.

(a) $\frac{3}{2590}$ (b) $\frac{1}{(10)^4}$

(c) $\frac{1}{2(10)^4}$ (d) $\frac{1}{670}$

11. For possible events A and B, the expression $P(A|(A \cup B)$ is always equal to:

(a) $\frac{P(A\cup B)-P(B)}{P(A\cup B)}$ (b) $\frac{P(A\cup B)-P(A)}{P(A\cup B)}$

(c) $\frac{P(B)}{P(A\cup B)}$ (d) $\frac{P(A)}{P(A\cup B)}$

12. One ticket is selected randomly from the set of 100 tickets numbered as {00, 01, 02, 03, 04, 05,...., 92,99}. E_1 and E_2 be the evevnt that the sum and product of the digits of the number of the selected ticket is 9 and 0 respectively. The value of $P\left(\frac{E_1}{E_2}\right)$ is

(a) 1/9 (b) 2/19

(c) 3/19 (d) None of these

13. A factory A produces 10% defective valves and another factory B produces 20% defective. A bag contains 4 valves of factory A and 5 valves of factory B. If two valves are drawn at random from the bag, then the probability that atleast one valve is defective is equal to:

(a) $\frac{1283}{1800}$ (b) $\frac{26}{45}$

(c) $\frac{517}{1800}$ (d) None of these

14. A lot contains 20 articles. The probability that the lot contains exactly two defective articles is 0.4 and the probability that it contains exactly three defective articles is 0.6 Articles are drawn from the lot at random one by one without replacement and are tested till all the defective articles are found. The probability that the testing procedure ends at the 12th testing is equal to

(a) 99/1900 (b) 198/1900

(c) 99/3800 (d) None of these

15. Let E^c denotes the complement of an event E. Let E, F, G be pairwise independent events with $P(G) > 0$ and $P(E \cap F \cap G) = 0$. Then $P(E^c \cap F^c/G)$ equals

(a) $P(E^c) + P(F^c)$ (b) $P(E^c) - P(F^c)$

(c) $P(E^c) - P(F)$ (d) $P(E) - P(F^c)$

16. If A and B be two events such that $A \subset B$ and $P(B) \neq 0$, then which of the following is correct?

(a) $P(A|B) = \frac{P(B)}{P(A)}$ (b) $P(A|B) < P(A)$

(c) $P(A|B) \geq P(A)$ (d) None of these

Answer Key

1. (d) **2.** (d) **3.** (c) **4.** (b) **5.** (a, b, c, d) **6.** (a) **7.** (c)
8. (a, b, c, d) **9.** (a, b, c, d) **10.** (d) **11.** (d) **12.** (b) **13.** (c) **14.** (a)
15. (c) **16.** (c)

■ PARTITION OF SAMPLE SPACE

A family of non empty event sets E_1, E_2,...E_n is said to form a partition of set S (Sample space) if they are mutually exclusive as well as exhaustive. i.e., $E_i \cap E_j = \phi$ for all $i \neq j$ and $1 \leq i, j \leq n$ and $E_1 \cup E_2 \cup E_3 \cup .... \cup E_n = S$

BAYE'S THEOREM

Baye's theorem revises (reassigns) the probabilities of the events $A_1, A_2, ..., A_n$ related to a sample space, when there is an information about the outcome beforehand. The earlier probabilities of the events $P(A_i)$, $i = 1, 2, ..., n$ are called a priori probabilites and the probabilities of events calculated after the information is received i.e., (A_i/A) is called posteriori probabilites.

If $E_1, E_2, ..., E_n$ be n mutually exclusive and exhaustive events and E is an event which occurs together (in conjunction with) either of E_i i.e., If events $E_1, E_2, ...E_n$ form a partition of S and E be any event,

then $P\left(\frac{E}{E}\right) = \frac{P(E_i)P(E/E_i)}{\sum_{i=1}^{n} P(E_i)P(E/E_i)}$

Proof: Let $E_1, E_2, ...E_n$ be n mutually exclusive and exhaustive events and E be any event in sample space, then $E = (E \cap E_1) \cup (E \cap E_2) \cup .... \cup (E \cap E_n)$

$\Rightarrow P(E) = P(E \cap E_1) + P(E \cap E_2) + ... + (E \cap E_n)$

$= P(E_1).\ P(E/E_1) + P(E_2)\ P(E/E_2) + ... + P(E_n)\ P(E/E_n)$

Hence, $P\left(\frac{E_i}{E}\right) = \frac{P(E_i)P\left(\frac{E}{E_i}\right)}{\sum_{i=1}^{n} P(E_i)P\left(\frac{E}{E_i}\right)}$

NOTE

If in a problem some event has already happened and then the probability of another event is to be found, it is an application of Baye's theorem

ILLUSTRATION 27: A die is rolled and it is found that number turned up is an even number. Find the probability that it is 2.

SOLUTION: All possible events when we roll a die are

$A_1 = 1$ appears, $P(A_1) = 1/6$; $A_2 = 2$ appears, $P(A_2) = 1/6$;
$A_3 = 3$ appears, $P(A_3) = 1/6$; $A_4 = 4$ appears, $P(A_4) = 1/6$;
$A_5 = 5$ appears, $P(A_5) = 1/6$; $A_6 = 6$ appears, $P(A_6) = 1/6$;

We have the information that an even number is turned up. You should revise the probability of priori events A_i in the light of information received. (It will be totally foolish if we don't revise the probabilites. Since the information of even numbers is available, it makes the probabilities of 1, 3 and 5 equal to zero)

Let A: Even number has turned up

We have to calculate the probability of A_2 when A is given. Since $A_1, A_2, ...A_6$ are exhaustive and mutually exclusive, we can apply Baye's formula

$$\therefore\ P(A_2/A) = \frac{P(A_2)P(A/A_2)}{P(A_1)P(A/A_1) + P(A_2)P(A/A_2) + ... + P(A_6)P(A/A_6)}$$

$P(A/A_1)$ means probability of A when A_1 is given, i.e., the probability of getting an even number when 1 has appeared. Obviously it is zero. Hence $P(A/A_1) = 0$

Similarly, $P(A/A_2) = 1$, $P(A/A_3) = 0$, $P(A/A_4) = 1$, $P(A/A_5) = 0$, $P(A/A_6) = 1$

$$\text{Therefore } P(A_2/A) = \frac{1/6 \times 1}{1/6 \times 0 + 1/6 \times 1 + 1/6 \times 0 + 1/6 \times 1 + 1/6 \times 0 + 1/6 \times 1} = \frac{1}{3}$$

ILLUSTRATION 28: In a factory, machines A, B and C manufacture 15%, 25% and 60% of the total production of bolts respectively. Of the bolts manufactured by the machine A, B and C 4%, 2% and 3% are defective. A bolt is drawn at random and is found to be defective. What is the probability that it was produced by B?

SOLUTION: Let us take A = the event of bolt being defective

A_1 = the bolt is produced by B; A_2 = the bolt is produced by A

A_3 = the bolt is produced by C

$\therefore$ Required probability $= P(A_1/A) = \dfrac{P(A_1).P(A/A_1)}{\sum_{i=1}^{3} P(A_i)P(A/A_i)}$

$$= \frac{\frac{25}{100}\times\frac{2}{100}}{\left(\frac{15}{100}\times\frac{4}{100}\right)+\left(\frac{25}{100}\times\frac{2}{100}\right)+\left(\frac{60}{100}\times\frac{3}{100}\right)} = \frac{50}{60+50+180} = \frac{5}{29}$$

ILLUSTRATION 29: A bag contains 5 balls of unknown colours two balls are drawn at random and are found to be red. Find the probability that the bag contains exactly 4 red balls.

SOLUTION: First of all let's try to find out all the possibilites, which can happen w.r.t to given events. As two drawn balls are found to be red, So there are four possibilities. The bag contains only two red balls (say event A_2), bag contain 3 red balls (A_3), bag contains 4 red balls (A_4) or bag has all red balls (A_5). Let B be the event when two balls are drawn and found to be red. So it is obvious that we have to find the probability of A_4 given B, i.e., $P(A_4/B)$

Now, $P(A_4/B) = \dfrac{P(A_4)P(B/A_4)}{P(A_2)P(B/A_2)+P(A_3)P(B/A_3)+P(A_4)P(B/A_4)+P(A_5)P(B/A_5)}$

Now as all these four possible cases are equally likely, i.e., we cannot say that bag is more likely to contain 5 red balls, than 3 red balls, so priori probabilities of all these events will be equal, i.e., $P(A_2) = P(A_3) = P(A_4) = P(A_5)$. Since A_2, A_3, A_4 and A_5 are exhaustive

$\therefore$ $P(A_2) + P(A_3) + P(A_4) + P(A_5) = 1$

$\therefore$ $P(A_4) = 1/4$ (since A_2, A_3, A_4 and A_5 are equally likely also)

Now $P(B/A_4)$ means the probability of drawing two red balls when it contains 5 balls out of which 4 are red balls, which is obviously $\dfrac{{}^4C_2}{{}^5C_2}$

$$\therefore\quad P\left(\frac{A_4}{B}\right) = \frac{\frac{1}{4}\times\frac{{}^4C_2}{{}^5C_2}}{\frac{1}{4}\times\frac{{}^2C_2}{{}^5C_2}+\frac{1}{4}\times\frac{{}^3C_2}{{}^5C_2}+\frac{1}{4}\times\frac{{}^4C_2}{{}^5C_2}+\frac{1}{4}\times\frac{{}^5C_2}{{}^5C_2}} = \frac{6}{20} = \frac{3}{10}$$

TEXTUAL EXERCISE 5: (SUBJECTIVE)

1. Bag A contains 5 red and 6 white balls and bag B contains 6 red and 7 white balls. One bag is chosen at random and 1 ball is taken from it and it is found to be red. Find the probability that it cames from
   (i) bag A (ii) bag B

2. A and B are two factories producing 20% and 30% defective goods. From a sample one item is taken and it is found to be defective. Find the probability that it was produced by factory B.

3. A card from a pack of 52 cards is lost. From the remaining cards, two cards are drawn and are found to be spades. Find the probability that missing card is a spade.

4. In a test an examinee either guesses or copies or knows the answer to a multiple choice question with four choices out of which one is correct. The probability that he makes guess is 1/3 and copies is 1/6. The probability that answer is correct that he

copied is 1/8. Find the probability that he knows and the answer given that he answered correctly.

5. A person is known to speak the truth 4 times out of 5. He throws a die and reports that it is a six. Find the probability that it is actually six.

6. A person is known to speak the truth 4 times out of 5. He draws a card from a pack of 52 playing cards and reports that it is an ace. Find the probability that it is actually an ace.

7. I wrote a letter to my friend X and gave it to my son to post it. The probability that my son will forget to post the letter is 1/10 and the letter will be lost in post is 1/100. If my friend X did not receive the letter, then find the probability that
   (i) my son forgot to post the letter.
   (ii) the letter was lost in the post.

8. In a test an examine either guesses or copies or knowns the answer to a multiple choice question with m choice out of which exactly one is correct. The probability that he makes a guess is 1/3 and the probability that he copies the answer is 1/6. The probability that his answer is correct given that he copied it is 1/8. If the probability that he knew the answer to the question given that he correctly answered it is 120/141, find m.

9. A prisoner escapes from a jail and is equally likely to choose one of the four roads, I, II, III or IV to reach away from the hands of law. If he choose I road, he is successful with probability 1/6 and for II, III and IV this is 1/8, 1/10 and 1/12 respectively. If the prisoner is successful, the probability that he choose road.

(a) I	(p) 12/57
(b) II	(q) 15/57
(c) III	(r) 20/57
(d) IV	(s) 10/57

10. Shashi tosses a coin. If he gets a head he throws a fair cubical die and the number on it is noted. If he gets a tail he is asked to throw 5 coins and number of heads obtained is noted. If the number noted is 4. Find the probability that he threw a die.

11. A person goes to the office either by a car or by a scooter or by bus or by train.The probabilities of his using car, scooter, bus and train are respectively, 1/7, 2/7, 3/7 and 1/7. The probabilities of his reaching late in office by using these modes of transport are 2/9, 4/9, 1/9 and 1/9 respectively. If the person reach the office in time, find the probability that he used car to reach the office.

Answer Key

1. (i) 65/131 (ii) 66/131 **2.** 0.6 **3.** 11/50 **4.** 24/29 **5.** 4/9 **6.** 1/4
7. (i) 100/109 (ii) 9/109 **8.** 5 **9.** (a) → r, (b) → q, (c) → p, (d) → s **10.** 16/31 **11.** 1/7

TEXTUAL EXCERISE 4: (OBJECTIVE)

1. Each of the n urns contains 4 white and 6 black balls. The $(n + 1)$ th urn contains 5 white and 5 black balls. Out of $(n + 1)$ urns an urn is chosen at random and two balls are drawn from it without replacement. Both the balls are found to be black. If the probability that the $(n + 1)$ th urn was chosen to drawn the balls is 1/16, then value of n is

(a) 10	(b) 11
(c) 12	(d) 13

2. The chances of defective screws in three boxes A, B, and C are 1/5, 1/6, 1/7 respectively. A box is selected at random and a screw is drawn from it at random, is found to be defective. The probability that it came from the box A is:

(a) 16/29	(b) 1/15
(c) 27/59	(d) 42/107

3. In an entrance test there are multiple choice questions. There are four possible answers to each question, of which one is correct. The probability that a student knows the answer to a question is 90%. If he gets the correct answer to question, then the probability that he was guessing is:

(a) 37/40	(b) 1/37
(c) 36/37	(d) 1/9

4. The probability that an archer hits the target when it is breezy is equal to 2/5; when it is not breezy his probability of hitting the target is 7/10. On any shot the probability of gust of wind is 3/10. The probability

that there is no gust of wind on the occasion when he missed the target, is equal to:

(a) 5/13 (b) 19/39
(c) 7/13 (d) 23/29

5. In four schools B_1, B_2, B_3, B_4 the percentage of girls students is 12,20,13,17 respectively. From a school selected at random, one student is picked up at radom and it is found that the student is a girl. The probability that the selected school is B_2 is:

(a) 6/31 (b) 10/31
(c) 13/62 (d) 17/62

6. Three groups *A, B* and *C* are competing for positions on the Board of Directors of a company. The probabilities of their winning are 0.5, 0.3. 0.2 respectively. If the Group *A* wins, the probability of introducing a new product is 0.7 and the corresponding probabilities for groups *B* and *C* are 0.6 and 0.5 respectively.The probability that the new product will be introduced is given by

(a) 0.63 (b) 0.37
(c) 0.21 (d) None of these

7. A signal which can be green or red with probability 4/5 and 1/5 respectively, is received by station *A* and then transmited to station *B*. The probability of each station receiving the singal correctly is 3/4. If the signal received at station *B* is green, then the probability that the original signal was green is:

(a) 3/5 (b) 6/7
(c) 20/23 (d) 9/20

8. Of the students in a collage, it is known that 60% reside in hostel and 40 % are day scholars (not residing in hostel). Previous year results report that 30% of all students who reside in hostel attain *A* grade and 20% of day scholars attain *A* grade in their annual examination. At the end of the year, one student is chosen at random from the college and he has *A* grade, what is the probability that the student is a hostlier?

(a) 10/13 (b) 8/13
(c) 9/13 (d) None of these

9. A laboratory blood test is 99% effective in detecting a certain disease when it is in fact, present. However, the test also yields a false positive result for 0.5% of the healthy person tested (i.e., if a healthy person is tested, then with probability 0.005 the test will imply he has the disease). If 0.1 percent of the population actually has the disease, what is the probability that a person has the disease given that his test result is positive?

(a) $\frac{195}{1197}$ (b) $\frac{196}{1197}$
(c) $\frac{197}{1197}$ (d) $\frac{22}{133}$

10. There are three coins. One is a two headed coin (having head on both faces), another is a biased coin that comes up heads 75% of the time and third is an unbiased coin. One of the three coins is chosen at random and tossed. If it shows heads, what is the probability that it was the two headed coin?

(a) 2/9 (b) 3/9
(c) 4/9 (d) None of these

11. An insurance company insured 2000 scooter drivers, 4000 car drives and 6000 truck drivers. The probabilities of an accident of respective vehicle drivers are 0.01, 0.03 and 0.15. One of the insured persons meets with an accident. What is the probability that he is a scooter driver?

(a) 1/52 (b) 1/26
(c) 3/52 (d) None of these

12. A factory has two machines *A* and *B*. Past record shows that machine *A* produced 60 % of the items of output and machine *B* produced 40 % of the items. Further, 2% of the items produced by machine *A* and 1% produced by machine *B* were defective. All the items are put into one stockpile and then one item is chosen at random from this and is found to be defective. What is the probability that it was produced by machine *B*?

(a) 1/2 (b) 1/3
(c) 1/4 (d) 1/5

13. Suppose a girl throws a die. If she gets a 5 or 6, she tosses a coin three times and notes the number of heads. If she gets 1, 2, 3 or 4, she tosses a coin once and notes whether a head or tail obtained. If she obtained exactly one head, what is the probability that she threw 1, 2, 3 or 4 with the die?

(a) 8/11 (b) 9/11
(c) 10/11 (d) None of these

14. Probability that *A* speaks truth is 4/5. A coin is tossed. *A* reports that a head appears. The probability that actually there was head is

(a) $\frac{4}{5}$ (b) $\frac{1}{2}$
(c) $\frac{1}{5}$ (d) $\frac{2}{5}$

Answer Key

1. (a)	**2.** (d)	**3.** (b)	**4.** (c)	**5.** (b)	**6.** (a)	**7.** (c)	**8.** (c)	**9.** (d)	**10.** (c)
11. (a)	**12** (c)	**13.** (a)	**14.** (a)						

■ RANDOM VARIABLES AND THEIR PROBABILITY DISTRIBUTIONS

Definition

A random variable is a real valued function whose domain is the sample space of a random experiment. For example, let us consider the experiment of tossing a coin two times in succession. The sample space of the experiment is $S = \{HH, HT, TH, TT\}$. If X denotes the number of heads obtained, then X is a random variable and for each outcome, its value is as given below:

$X(HH) = 2, X(HT) = 1, X(TH) = 1, X(TT) = 0$

More than one random variables can be defined on the same sample space. For example, let Y denotes the number of heads minus the number of tails for each outcome of the above sample space S. Then $Y(HH) = 2$, $Y(HT) = 0$, $(TH) = 0$, $Y(TT) = -2$.

Thus X and Y are two different random variables defined on the same sample space S.

ILLUSTRATION 30: A person plays a game of tossing a coin thrice. For each head, he is given Rs 2 by the organiser of the game and for each tail, he has to give Rs 1 to the organiser. Let X denotes the amount gained or lost by the person. Show that X is a random variable and exhibit it as a function on the sample space of the experiment.

SOLUTION: X is a number whose values are defined on the outcomes of a random experiment. Therefore, X is a random variable.

Now, sample space of the experiment is

$S = \{HHH, HHT, HTH, THH, HTT, THT, TTH, TTT\}$

Then $X(HHH) = \text{Rs } (2 \times 3) = \text{Rs} = 6;$

$X(HHT) = X(HTH) = X(THH) = \text{Rs } (2 \times 2 - 1 \times 1) = \text{Rs } 3;$

$X(HTT) = X(THT) = (TTH) = \text{Rs } (1 \times 2) - (2 \times 1) = \text{Rs } 0$

and $X(TTT) = -\text{ Rs } (3 \times 1) = \text{Rs } (-3)$

Where, minus sign shows the loss to the player. Thus for each element of the sample space, X takes a unique value, hence, X is a function on the sample space whose range is $\{6,3,0,-3\}$.

■ PROBABILITY DISTRIBUTION OF A RANDOM VARIABLE

Definition

The probability distribution of a random variable X is the system of numbers

X	:	x	x_2	$\ldots\ldots x_n$
$P(X)$	:	p_1	p_2	$\ldots\ldots p_n$

Where, $p_i > 0, \sum_{i=1}^{n} p_i = 1, i = 1, 2 \ldots, n$

The real numbers $x_1, x_2, \ldots, x_n$ are possible values of the random variable X and $p_i (i = 1, 2, \ldots\ldots, n)$ is the probability of the random variable X taking the value x_i; i.e., $P(X = x_i) = p_i$

ILLUSTRATION 31: Two cards are drawn successively with replacement from a well shuffled deck of 52 cards. Find the probability distribution of the number of aces.

SOLUTION: The number of aces is a random variable. Let it be denoted by X. Clearly, X can take the values 0, 1 or 2.

Now, since the draws are done with replacement, therefore, the two draws form independent experiments.

Therefore, $P(X = 0) = P$ (non-ace and non-ace)

$$= P(\text{non-ace}) \times P(\text{non-ace}) = \frac{48}{52}\times\frac{48}{52} = \frac{144}{169}$$

Similarly, $P(X = 1) = P$(ace and non-ace or non-ace and ace)

$= P$(ace and non-ace)$+ P$(non-ace and ace)

$$= P(\text{ace}).\ P(\text{non-ace}) + P(\text{non-ace}).\ P(\text{ace}) = \frac{4}{52}\times\frac{48}{52}+\frac{48}{52}\times\frac{4}{52} = \frac{24}{169}$$

and $P(X = 2) = P(\text{ace and ace}) = P(\text{ace}).P(\text{ace}) = \frac{4}{52}\times\frac{4}{52} = \frac{1}{169}$

Thus, the required probability distribution is

X :	0	1	2
$P(X)$:	$\frac{144}{169}$	$\frac{24}{169}$	$\frac{1}{169}$

ILLUSTRATION 32: Let X denote the number of hours you study during a randomly selected school day. The probability that X can take the values x, has the following form, where k is some unkonwn constant

$$P(X = x) = \begin{cases} 0.1, \text{ if } x = 0 \\ kx, \text{ if } x = 1 \text{ or } 2 \\ k(5-x), \text{ if } x = 3 \text{ or } 4 \\ 0, \text{ otherwise} \end{cases}$$

(a) Find the value of k

(b) What is the probability that you study at least two hours? Exactly two hours? At most two hours?

SOLUTION: The probability of X is

x :	0	1	2	3	4
$P(X)$:	0.1	k	$2k$	$2k$	k

(a) We know that $\sum_{i=1}^{n} p_i = 1$

Therefore $0.1 + k + 2k + 2k + k = 1$, i.e., $k = 0.15$

(b) P(you study at least two hours) $= P(X \geq 2)$

$= P(X = 2) + P(X = 3) + P(X = 4) = 2k + 2k + k = 5k = 5 \times 0.15 = 0.75$

P(you study exactly two hours) $= P(X = 2) = 2k = 2 \times 0.15 = 0.3$

P (you study at most two hours) $= P(x \leq 2) = P(X = 0) + P(X = 1) + P(X = 2)$

$= 0.1 + k + 2k = 0.1 + 3k = 0.1 + 3 \times 0.15 = 0.55$

MEAN OF A RANDOM VARIABLE

Definition

Let X be a random variable whose possible values $x_1, x_2, x_3, \ldots, x_n$ occur with probabilities $p_1, p_2, p_3, \ldots, p_n$ respectively. The mean of X, denoted by μ is the number $\sum_{i=1}^{n} x_i p_i$ i.e., the mean of X is the weighted average of the possible values of X, each value being weighted by its probability with which it occurs.

The mean of a random variable X is also called the expectation of X, denoted by $E(X)$.

$$\text{Thus } E(x) = \mu = \sum_{i=1}^{n} x_i p_i = x_1 p_1 + x_2 p_2 + \ldots + x_n p_n$$

In other words, the mean or expectation of a random variable X is the sum of the products of all possible values of X by their repective probabilities.

ILLUSTRATION 33: Let a pair of dice be thrown and the random variable X be the sum of the numbers that appear on the two dice. Find the mean or expectation of X.

SOLUTION: The sample space of the experiment consists of 36 elementry events in the form of ordered pairs (x_i, y_i), where $x_i \in \{1,2,3,4,5,6\}$ and $y_i \in \{1,2,3,4,5,6\}$

The random variable X i.e., the sum of the numbers on the two dice takes the values 2,3,4,5,6,7,8,9,10,11 or 12.

Now, $P(X=2) = P(\{(1,1)\}) = 1/36$; $P(X=3) = P(\{(1,2), (2,1)\}) = 2/36$

$P(X=4) = P(\{(1,3), (2,2), (3,1)\}) = 3/36$; $P(X=5) = P(\{(1,4), (2,3), (3,2), (4,1)\}) = 4/36$

$P(X=6) = P(\{(1,5),(2,4), (3,3),(4,2), (5,1)\}) = 5/36$

$P(X=7) = P(\{(1,6), (2,5), (3,4), (4,3), (5,2),(6,1)\}) = 6/36$

$P(X=8) = P(\{(2,6), (3,5), (4,4), (5,3), (6,2)\}) = 5/36$

$P(X=9) = P(\{3,6), (4,5), (5,4), (6,3)\}) = 4/36$; $P(X=10) = P(\{4,6), (5,5), (6,4)\}) = 3/36$

$P(X=11) = P(\{(5,6), (6,5)\}) = 2/36$; $P(X=12) = P(\{(6,6)\} = 1/36$

The probability distribution of X is

X or x_i:	2	3	4	5	6	7	8	9	10	11	12
$P(X)$ or p_i:	1/36	2/36	3/36	4/36	5/36	6/36	5/36	4/36	3/36	2/36	1/36

Therefore, $\mu = E(X) = \sum_{i=1}^{n} x_i p_i = 2\times\frac{1}{36}+3\times\frac{2}{36}+4\times\frac{3}{36}+5\times\frac{4}{36}$

$+6\times\frac{5}{36}+7\times\frac{6}{36}+8\times\frac{5}{36}+9\times\frac{4}{36}+10\times\frac{3}{36}+11\times\frac{2}{36}+12\times\frac{1}{36}$

$=\frac{2+6+12+20+30+42+40+36+30+22+12}{36}=7$

Thus the mean of the sum of the numbers that appear on throwing two fair dice is 7.

VARIANCE OF A RANDOM VARIABLE

Definition

Let X be a random variable whose possible values $x_1, x_2, \ldots, x_n$ occur with probabilities $p(x_1), p(x_2), \ldots, p(x_n)$ respectively.

Let $\mu = E(X)$ be mean of X. The variance of X, denoted by Var (X) or σ_x^2 is defined as $\sigma_x^2 = \text{Var}(X) = \sum_{i=1}^{n}(x_i-\mu)^2 p(x_i)$

The non negative number

$\sigma_x = \sqrt{\text{Var}(X)} = \sqrt{\sum_{i=1}^{n}(x_i-\mu)^2 p(x_i)}$ is called the standard deviation of the random variable X.

ANOTHER FORMULA TO FIND THE VARIANCE OF A RANDOM VARIABLE

We know that, $\text{Var}(X) = \sum_{i=1}^{n}(x_i-\mu)^2 p(x_i)$

$= \sum_{i=1}^{n}(x_i^2+\mu^2-2\mu x_i)\,p(x_i)$

$= \sum_{i=1}^{n} x_i^2 p(x_i) + \sum_{i=1}^{n}\mu^2 p(x_i) - \sum_{i=1}^{n} 2\mu x_i\, p(x_i)$

$= \sum_{i=1}^{n} x_i^2 p(x_i) + \mu^2\sum_{i=1}^{n} p(x_i) - 2\mu\sum_{i=1}^{n} x_i\, p(x_i)$

$= \sum_{i=1}^{n} x_i^2 p(x_i) + \mu^2 - 2\mu^2$ $\left[\text{Since } \sum_{i=1}^{n} p(x_i) = 1 \text{ and } \mu = \sum_{i=1}^{n} x_i p(x_i)\right]$

$= \sum_{i=1}^{n} x_i^2 p(x_i) - \mu^2$

or $\text{Var}(X) = \sum_{i=1}^{n} x_i^2 p(x_i) - \left(\sum_{i=1}^{n} x_i\, p(x_i)\right)^2$

or $\text{Var}(X) = E(X^2) - [E(X)]^2$,

where $E(X^2) = \sum_{i=1}^{n} x_i^2 p(x_i)$

ILLUSTRATION 34: Two cards are drawn simultaneously (or successively without replacement) from a well shuffled pack of 52 cards. Fnd the mean, varance and standard deviation of the number of kings.

SOLUTION: Let X denotes the number of kings in a draw of two cards. X is a random variable which can assume the values 0, 1 or 2

Now $P(X=0) = P\text{ (no king)} = \dfrac{^{48}C_2}{^{52}C_2} = \dfrac{48\times 47}{52\times 51} = \dfrac{188}{221}$

$P(X=1) = P\text{ (one king and one non-king)} = \dfrac{^{4}C_1\,^{48}C_1}{^{52}C_2} = \dfrac{4\times 48\times 2}{52\times 51} = \dfrac{32}{221}$

and $P(X=2) = P\text{ (two kings)} = \dfrac{^{4}C_2}{^{52}C_2} = \dfrac{4\times 3}{52\times 51} = \dfrac{1}{221}$

Thus, the probability distribution of X is

X:	0	1	2
$P(X)$:	$\dfrac{188}{221}$	$\dfrac{32}{221}$	$\dfrac{1}{221}$

Now, Mean of $X = E(X) = \sum_{i=1}^{n} x_i\, p(x_i) = 0\times\dfrac{188}{221} + 1\times\dfrac{32}{221} + 2\times\dfrac{1}{221} = \dfrac{34}{221}$

Also $E(X^2) = \sum_{i=1}^{n} x_i^2\, p(x_i) = 0^2\times\dfrac{188}{221} + 1^2\times\dfrac{32}{221} + 2^2\times\dfrac{1}{221} = \dfrac{36}{221}$

Now $\text{Var}(X) = E(X^2) - [E(X)]^2 = \dfrac{36}{221} - \left(\dfrac{34}{221}\right)^2 = \dfrac{6800}{(221)^2}$

Therefore $\sigma_x = \sqrt{\text{Var}(X)} = \dfrac{\sqrt{6800}}{221} = 0.37$

■ BERNOULLI'S THEOREM OR BINOMIAL THEOREM OF PROBABILITY

Consider a random experiment with sample space S and an event E (a subset of S) associated with it. Then the event denoted by $\overline{E}$ signifies the non occurrence of E. Let $P(E) = p$ and $P(\overline{E}) = q$, so that $p, q > 0$ and $p + q = 1$. If the experiment results in the event E, we say a success (denoted by s), has occurred. If on the other hand, the event E does not occur (i.e., $\overline{E}$ occurs) the experiment is said to have resulted in a failure (denoted by f). The probability of a success is equal to p and that of a failure is $q = 1 - p$.

■ BINOMIAL THEOREM

Suppose a binomial experiment having constant probability of success p and that of failure q (such that $p + q = 1$) in any of its performance, is repeated n times under similar conditions (i.e., a series of n independent trials), then probability of exactly r successes is given by

$$P(x = r) = {}^nC_r p^r q^{n-r}, \text{ where } r = 0, 1, 2, 3, \ldots, n$$

Proof: Suppose the above experiment is carried out n times under identical conditions. If the success (occurrence of E) and failure (non-occurrence of E) are recorded successively as the experiment is repeated, we will get a result of the type $s\,f\,f\,s\,s\,f\,f\ldots\ldots f\,s\,f$

There are 2^n such outcomes, and they constitute the sample space of the combined experiment. Since the successive experiments are independent, the probability of the above outcome is $p\,q\,q\,p\,p\,q\,q\ldots\ldots q\,p\,q = p^r q^{n-r}$, where r is the number of successes in the outcome. If X denotes the random variable "number of successes", then the possible values of X are 0, 1, 2,......, n.

We shall now calculate the probability of the event $(X = r)$. Out of the 2^n outcomes, r successes and $(n - r)$ failures can occur in ${}^nC_r$ ways. Also, the probability of r success and $(n - r)$ failures is $p^r q^{n-r}$. Thus, $P(X = r) = {}^nC_r p^r q^{n-r}$.

REMARKS

(i) The probability of getting at least k successes is $P(r \geq k) = \sum_{r=k}^{n} {}^nC_r p^r q^{n-r}$

(ii) The probability of getting at most k successes is $P(0 \leq r \leq k) = \sum_{r=0}^{k} {}^nC_r . p^r . q^{n-r}$

ILLUSTRATION 35: (a) A biased coin (chances of getting head is the twice as that of getting tail) is tossed n times, find the probability that head appears odd number of times

(b) A coin is tossed 5 times. What is the probability of obtaining at most 3 heads?

SOLUTION: (a) Let success be getting head and failure be getting tail.

$\Rightarrow p + q = 1$ and $p = 2q$ $\Rightarrow p = 2/3$ and $q = 1/3$

P (odd number of heads) $= {}^nC_1\, p\, q^{n-1} + {}^nC_3\, p^3\, q^{n-3} + ..$

$$= \frac{(q+p)^n - (q-p)^n}{2} = \frac{1-(1/3-2/3)^n}{2} = \frac{3^n - (-1)^n}{2.3^n}$$

(b) Here $p = 1/2$ and $q = 1/2$

$\therefore$ P (at most 3 heads) $= P(r \leq 3) = P(r = 0) + P(r = 1) + P(r = 2) - P(r = 3)$

$= 1 - P(r = 4) - P(r = 5)$

$= 1 - {}^5C_4\, p^4\, q - {}^5C_5\, p^5 = 1 - \frac{5}{2^5} - \frac{1}{2^5} = \frac{13}{16}$

ILLUSTRATION 36: A man takes a step forward with probability 0.4 and backwards with probability 0.6. Find the probability that at the end of eleven steps he is one step away from the starting point.

SOLUTION: If the man is one step forward after eleven steps, he has taken six forward and five backward steps.

If the man is one step backward after eleven steps, he has taken five forward and six backward steps. There are only two possibilities

Let success : forward step and failure : backward step

$\Rightarrow p = 0.4$ and $q = 0.6$

P (one step away) $= P(6$ successes$) + P(5$ successes$)$

$\therefore$ P (one step away) $= {}^{11}C_6\, (0.4)^6\, (0.6)^5 + {}^{11}C_5\, (0.4)^5\, (0.6)^6$

$= {}^{11}C_6\, (0.4)^5\, (0.6)^5$

ILLUSTRATION 37: Six persons try to swim across a wide river. It is known that on an average, only three persons out of ten can successfully cross the river. What is the probability that atmost four of the six persons will cross the river safely?

SOLUTION: Let success be defined as crossing the river

$\Rightarrow$ probability of success (p) = 3/10 and that of failure (q) = 7/10

Since number of trials (n) = 6

$\therefore$ P (at most 4 success in 6 trials) $= 1 - {}^6C_5\, p^5 q - {}^6C_6\, p^5$

$$= 1-6\left(\frac{3}{10}\right)^5\left(\frac{7}{10}\right)-\left(\frac{3}{10}\right)^6 = 1-\left(\frac{3}{10}\right)^6(13) = 0.9905$$

ILLUSTRATION 38: In a rainy season, there is 60% chance that it will rain on a particular day. What is the probability that there will be exactly 5 rainy days in a week?

SOLUTION: Let the probability of raining on a particular day p (success) = 3/5

And probability that no rain on a particular day q (other possibilities) = 2/5

$\therefore$ Probability of exactly 5 rainy days is i.e., 5 successes out of 7 trials

$$= {}^7C_5(p)^5(q)^2 = \frac{7!}{5!.2!}\times\left(\frac{3}{5}\right)^5\times\left(\frac{2}{5}\right)^2 = \frac{21\times(6)^5}{5^7}.$$

Binomial Distribution

Since $(p + q)^n = C_0 q^n + C_1 q^{n-1}p + ... + C_r q^{n-r} p^r + ... + C_n p^n$

The probability distribution of the random variable X is as given below

X	0	1	2	...	r	...	n
$P(X)$	q^n	${}^nC_1pq^{n-1}$	${}^nC_2p^2q^{n-2}$		${}^nC_rp^rq^{n-r}$		p^n

Mean (or expectation): The mean of the random variable X is defined as $E(X) = \sum_{i=1}^{n} p_i x_i(r)$

Variance: The variance of X is defined as:

$$\text{Var}(X) = \sum_{i=1}^{n} p_i(x_i - E(X))^2$$

The mean, the variance and the standard deviation of binomial distribution are np, npq, $\sqrt{npq}$

Mode of Binomial Distribution: Mode of binomial distribution is the value of r when $P(X = r)$ is maximum

$$(n + 1)p - 1 \le r \le (n + 1)p$$

ILLUSTRATION 39: Write probability distribution of number of heads when three coins are tossed.

SOLUTION: Let X be the random variable denoting the number of heads occurred, then

$P(X = 0)$ = Probability of occurrence of zero head

$P(TTT)$ = 1/2. 1/2. 1/2 = 1/8, $P(X = 1)$ = Probability of occurrence of one head

$= P(HTT) + P(THT) + P(TTH)$ = (1/2. 1/2 1/2) + (1/2.1/2.1/2) + (1/2. 1/2.1/2) = 3/8

$P(X = 2)$ = Probability of occurrence of 2 heads = $P(HHT) + P(HTH) + P(THH)$

= (1/2.1/2.1/2) +(1/2.1/2 + 1/2) + (1/2. 1/2.12) = 3/8

$P(X = 3)$ = Probability of occurrence of 3 heads = $P(HHH)$ = 1/2. 1/2. 1/2 = 1/8

Thus the probability distribution when three coins are tossed is as given below

X	0	1	2	3
$P(X)$	1/8	3/8	3/8	1/8

ILLUSTRATION 40: The mean and variance of a binomial variable X are 2 and 1 respectively. Find the probability that X takes values greater than 1.

SOLUTION: Given mean $np = 2$ ..(i)

and variance $npq = 1$ ..(ii)

Dividing (ii) by (i), then $q = 1/2$

$\therefore$ $p = 1 - q = 1/2$ from (i) $n \times 1/2 = 2 \Rightarrow n = 4$. The binomial distribution is $\left(\frac{1}{2}+\frac{1}{2}\right)^4$

Now $P(X > 1) = P(X = 2) + P(X = 3) + P(X = 4)$

$$= {}^4C_2(1/2)^2(1/2)^2 + {}^4C_3(1/2)^1(1/2)^3 + {}^4C_4(1/2)^4 = \frac{6+4+1}{16} = \frac{11}{16}$$

Application of Multinomial Theorem

If a die has m faces marked 1, 2, 3,..., m and if such n dices are thrown. Then the probability that the sum of the numbers on the upper faces is equal to r is given by the coefficient of x^r in $(x + x^2 + x^3 + ... + x^m)^n$

ILLUSTRATION 41: A special die with numbers 1, –1, 2, –2, 0 and 3 is thrown thrice. What is the probability that the total is (i) zero (ii) 6 ?

SOLUTION: Let a, b and c be the numbers on the upper face of die in first, second and third throw respectively.

(i) Now number of favourable cases such that sum of upper faces is zero equals to number of integral solution of $a + b + c = 0$ subject to the condition $-2 \le a, b, c \le 3$ (i.e., equal to coefficient of t^0 in $(t^{-2} + t^{-1} + ... + t^3)^3$ = coefficient of t^6 in $(1 - t + ... + t^5)^3 = {}^8C_2 - 3 = 25$

Therefore, required probability $= \dfrac{25}{216}$

(ii) In this case number of favourable cases will be equal to number of integral solutions of $a + b + c = 6$ i.e., equal to coefficient of t^{12} in $(1 + t + ... + t^5)^3 = 10$ Therefore required probability $= \dfrac{10}{216} = \dfrac{5}{108}$

ILLUSTRATION 42: A person throws two dice, one the common cube, and the other a regular tetrahedron, the number on the lowest face being taken in the case of the tetrahedron, then find the probability that the sum of the numbers appearing on the dice is 6

SOLUTION: Let S be the sample space, then $S = \{1, 2, 3, 4\} \times \{1, 2, 3, 4, 5, 6\}$

$\therefore\ n(S) = 24$

If E be the event that the sum of numbers on dice is 6, then $n(E)$ = coefficient of x^6 in $(x^1 + x^2 + x^3 + x^4)(x^1 + x^2 + x^3 + x^4 + x^5 + x^6) = 1 + 1 + 1 + 1 = 4$

$\therefore$ Required probability $P(E) = \dfrac{n(E)}{n(S)} = \dfrac{4}{24} = \dfrac{1}{6}$

Expectations

If p be the probability of success of a person in any venture and M be the sum of money which he will receive in case of success, the sum of money denoted by pM is called his expectation.

ILLUSTRATION 43: A and B throw with one die for a stake of Rs. 11 which is to be won by the player who throw 6. If A has the first throw, what are their respective expectations?

SOLUTION: Since A can win the game at the Ist, 3rd, 5th,.....trials

If p be the probability of success and q be the probability of failure, then $p = 1/6$ and $q = 5/6$

$P(A$ wins at the first trial$) = 1/6$

$P(A$ wins at the 3 trial$) = 5/6.\ 5/6.1/6$

$P(A$ wins at the 5 trial$) = 5/6.\ 5/6.\ 5/6.5/6.1/6$ and so on. Therefore

$$P(A \text{ wins}) = \frac{1}{6} + \left(\frac{5}{6}\right)^2 \frac{1}{6} + \left(\frac{5}{6}\right)^4 . \frac{1}{6} + ...\infty = \frac{1/6}{1-(5/6)^2} = \frac{6}{11}$$

Similarly, $P(B \text{ wins}) = \frac{5}{6}.\frac{1}{6} + \left(\frac{5}{6}\right)^3 \frac{1}{6} + \left(\frac{5}{6}\right)^5 \frac{1}{6} + \ldots = \frac{5/6.1/6}{1-(5/6)^2} = \frac{5}{11}$

Hence expectations of A and B are Rs. $\frac{6}{11} \times 11$ and Rs $\frac{5}{11} \times 11$ respectively i.e. expectations of A and B are Rs. 6 and Rs. 5 respectively

■ GEOMETRICAL PROBABILITY

When the number of points in the sample space is infinite, it becomes difficult to apply classical definition of probability. For instance, if we are interested to find the probability that a point selected at random from the interval [1, 5] lies either in the interval [1, 2] or [4, 5], we cannot apply the classical definition of probability. In this case we define the probability as follows: $P\{x \in A\} = \frac{\text{Measure of region } A}{\text{Measure of the sample space } S}$

where measure stands for length, area or volume depending upon whether S is an one-dimensional, two dimensional or three dimensional region.

NOTE

The problems related to continuous (uncountable) uniform sample space is dealt geometrically as can be seen from following examples:

ILLUSTRATION 44: From each of two equal lines of length ℓ, a portion is cut off at random and removed. What is the chance that the sum of the remainders is less than ℓ ?

SOLUTION: Place the lines parallel to one another, and suppose that after cutting the right-hand portions are removed. Then the question is equivalent to asking what is the chance that the sum of the right hand portions is greater than the sum of the left-hand portions. It is clear that the first sum is equally likely to be greater or less than the second. thus the required probability is 1/2

ILLUSTRATION 45: Three tangents are drawn at random to a given circle: show that the odds are 3 to 1 against the circle being inscribed in the triangle formed by them.

SOLUTION: Draw three random lines P, Q R in the same plane in the circle, and draw to the circle the six tangents parallel to these lines. Then of the 8 triangles so formed it is evident that the circle will be escribed to 6 and inscribed in 2; and as this is true whatever be the original directions of P, Q, R the required result follows

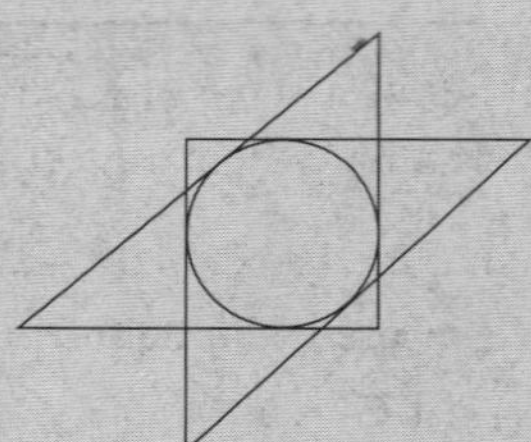

FIGURE 6.13

ILLUSTRATION 46: Consider the cartesian plane R^2, and let X denotes the subset of points for which both coordinates are integers. A coin of diameter 1/2 is tossed randomly on the plane, Find the probability p that the coin covers a point of X.

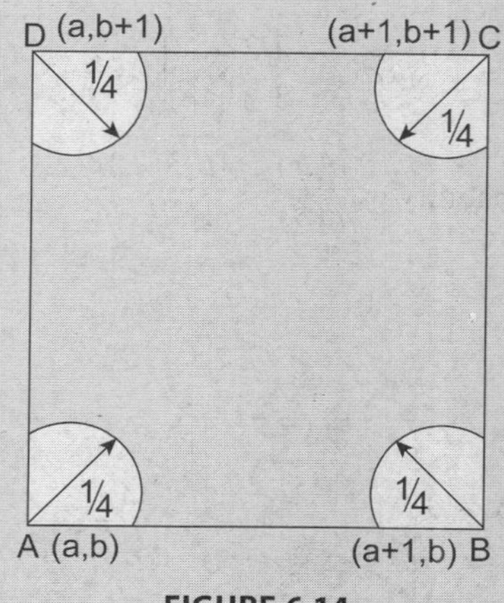

FIGURE 6.14

SOLUTION: Let S denotes the set of points inside a square with corners (a, b), $(a + 1, b)$, $(a + 1, b + 1)$, $(a, b + 1) \in X$

Let P denotes the set of points in S with distance less than 1/4 from any corner point. (Observe that the area of P is equal to the area inside a circle of radius 1/4). Thus a coin, whose centre falls in S, will cover a point of X if an only if its centre falls in a point of P. Hence

$$p = \frac{\text{area of } P}{\text{area of } S} = \frac{\pi (1/4)^2}{1} = \frac{\pi}{16}$$

ILLUSTRATION 47: If p is chosen at random in the closed interval [0, 5], what is the probability of the equation $x^2 + px + \frac{1}{4}(p + 2) = 0$ to have real roots.

SOLUTION: Here $n(S)$ is infinite because a real number p can be selected from the closed interval [0, 5] in infinite ways. so, we apply geometrical method.

Here $n(S)$ = length of the interval [0, 5] = 5

$n(E)$ = length of the interval $\subseteq$ [0, 5] to which p belongs such that the given equation has real roots Now, $x^2 + px + \frac{1}{4}(p + 2) = 0$ will have real roots if $D \geq 0$

$\Rightarrow p^2 - 4.1.\frac{1}{4}(p + 2) \geq 0$ or $p^2 - p - 2 \geq 0$ or $(p - 2)(p + 1) \geq 0$

So, by sign-scheme $p \leq -1$ or $p \geq 2$; But $p \in [0, 5]$. Hence $E = [2, 5]$

$\therefore$ $n(E)$ = length of the interval [2, 5] = 3

$\therefore$ the required probability $= \frac{n(E)}{n(S)} = \frac{3}{5}$

ILLUSTRATION 48: Two real numbers x and y are selected such that $x \in [0, 4]$ and $y \in [0, 4]$. Find the probability that the selected numbers satisfy the inequation $y^2 \leq x$.

SOLUTION: Corresponding to a pair of real numbers x, y where $x \in [0, 4]$ and $y \in [0, 4]$. we get a point (x, y) in the square bounded by the lines $x = 0$, $x = 4$, $y = 0$, $y = 4$

$\therefore$ $n(S)$ = area of the square = 4 × 4 = 16 square unit

The selected numbers x, y will satisfy $y^2 \leq x$ if the point (x, y) is an interior point of the parabola $y^2 = x$

$\therefore$ n (E) = area of that portion of the square which falls in the interior of the parabola

$$= \int_0^4 (y)_{parabola}\, dx = \int_0^4 \sqrt{x}\, dx = \left[\frac{2}{3} x^{3/2}\right]_0^4 = \frac{2}{3} \cdot 4^{3/2} = \frac{16}{3}$$

$$\therefore \text{ the required probability} = \frac{n(E)}{n(S)} = \frac{16/3}{16} = \frac{1}{3}$$

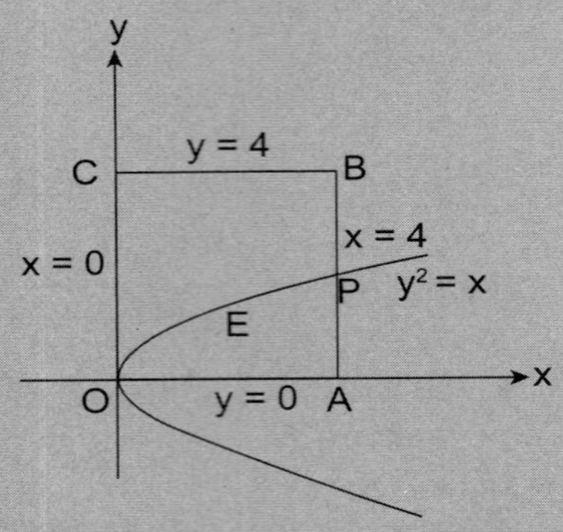

FIGURE 6.15

TEXTUAL EXERCISE 6: (SUBJECTIVE)

1. A coin is tossed 'n' times. Find the probability of getting head
   (i) 5 number of times
   (ii) odd number of times.

2. A coin is tossed $(2n + 1)$ times. Find the probability of getting head at most n times.

3. A fair coin is tossed a fixed number of times. If the probability of getting 7 heads is equal to that of getting 9 heads, find the probability of getting 2 heads.

4. A die is rolled n times. Find the probability that multiple of 3 will occur odd number of times.

5. If it is known that 25% ships get lost when travel in a particular weather, what is the probability that exactly 75 ships will return safely when 100 ships are sent to journey?

6. In a rainy season there is 60% chance that it will rain on a particular day. Find the probability that there will be exactly 4 rainy days in a week.

7. A fair dice is tossed eight times. Find the probability that on the eighth throw a third six is observed.

8. Any real number is chosen randomly from the interval [1, 5]. Find the chance that number satisfies the inequality $x^2 + 2x + 1 > 0$.

9. The variates a and b are uniformly distributed in the intervals $0 \le a \le 6$ and $0 \le b \le 9$. Find the probability that the equation $x^2 - ax + b = 0$ has two real roots.

10. A point is chosen from 1st quadrant randomly such that $x, y \in [0, 4]$, find the probability that it satisfies $[x] + [y] = 3$.

11. A point is selected at random inside a circle. Find the probability that the point is farther from the centre of the circle than to it's circumference.

12. The random variable k is uniformly distributed over the interval (0, 5), find the probability that the roots of the equation $4x^2 + 4xk + k + 2 = 0$ are real.

13. Let S be the rectangle $\{(x, y)\colon 0 \le x \le \pi, 0 \le y \le 1\}$ and C be the circle $\{(x, y)\colon x^2 + y^2 \le 1\}$. Find the probability that point $P \in S$ also belongs to C.

14. A natural number is selected at random from the set $X = \{x;\ 1 \le x \le 100\}$. Find the probability that the number satisfies the inequation $x^2 - 13x - 30 < 0$.

15. There are two circles in x - y plane whose equations are $x^2 + y^2 - 2y = 0$, $x^2 + y^2 - 3 = 0$. A point (x, y) is picked up at random inside the larger circle, find the probability that the point has been taken from the smaller circle.

16. Three points P, Q, R are selected at random from the circumference of a circle. Find the probability that the points lie on a semicircle.

17. Two persons A and B agree to meet at a place between 11 to 12 noon. The first one to arrive will wait for 20 minutes and then leave. If the time of their arrival be independent and at random, find the probability that A and B meet.

18. Two points are taken at random on the given line segment AB of length 'a'. Prove that the probability of their distance exceeding a given length c ($< a$) is equal to $\left(1-\frac{c}{a}\right)^2$.

19. Two dice are thrown simultaneously to get the co-ordinates of a point on $x-y$ plane. Find the probability that this point satisfies the inequality $|x| + |y| \le 3$; x, y $\in \mathbb{Z}$

20. If three line are chosen at random, prove that they are just as likely as not to denote the sides of a possible triangle.

21. The sides of a rectangle are chosen at random, each less than a given length 'a', all such lengths being equally likely. Show that the chance that the diagonal is less than a is $\pi/4$.

22. A point (x, y) is chosen randomly, such that $x \in [-4, 4]$, $y \in [-4, 4]$ (where x and y are real). Find the probability that it satisfies $|x| + |y| \le 4$.

23. A point is chosen such that $[x]\ [y] = 1$, find the probability that point lies below the line $y = x$.

24. A real number x is chosen from $0 < x < 10$, such that it satisfies the relation $f(x) = (\lambda - x^n)^{1/n}\ \forall\ \lambda > 0$ and 'n' being an odd natural number. Find the probability that x also satisfies the relation $f(f(x)) = x$.

25. Any point is chosen randomly from the interval $0 \le x < 2$ and $0 \le y < 2$. Find the probability that the point lies in the region enclosed by curve $y^2 = 4x$ and $x = 1$, $y = 0$ in 1st quadrant.

26. Find the probability distribution of
(i) number of heads in two tosses of a coin
(ii) number of tails in the simultaneous tosses of three coins
(iii) number of heads in four tosses of a coin

27. Find the probability distribution of the number of successes in two tosses of a die, where a success is defined as
(a) number greater than 4
(b) six appears on at least one die

28. The random variable X has a probability distribution $P(X)$ of the following form, where k is some number

$$P(X) = \begin{cases} k, \text{ if } X = 0 \\ 2k, \text{ if } X = 1 \\ 3k, \text{ if } X = 2 \\ 0, \text{ otherwise} \end{cases}$$

(a) Determine the value of k
(b) Find $P(X < 2)$, $P(X \le 2)$, $P(X \ge 2)$

29. A class has 15 students whose ages are 14, 17, 15, 14, 21, 17, 19, 20, 16, 18, 20, 17, 16, 19 and 20 years. One student is selected in such a manner that each has the same chance of being chosen and the age X of the selected student is recorded. What is the porobability distrbution of the random variable X? Find mean, variance and standard deviation of X.

Answer Key

1. (i) ${}^nC_5\ 1/2^n$ (ii) 1/2 **2.** 1/2 **3.** $\frac{15}{2^{13}}$ **4.** $\frac{1}{2}\{1-(1/3)^n\}$ **5.** ${}^{100}C_{75}\left(\frac{3}{4}\right)^{75}\left(\frac{1}{4}\right)^{25}$ **6.** $\frac{4536}{15625}$

7. ${}^7C_2\frac{5^5}{6^8}$ **8.** 1 **9.** 1/3 **10.** 1/4 **11.** 3/4 **12.** 3/5 **13.** $\frac{1}{4}$ **14.** 3/20

15. $\left(\frac{14\pi - 9\sqrt{3}}{36\pi}\right)$ **16.** $\frac{3}{4}$ **17.** $\frac{5}{9}$ **19.** 1/12 **22.** 1/2 **23.** 1/2 **24.** 1 **25.** 1/3

26. (i)

x	0	1	2
P(x)	$\frac{1}{4}$	$\frac{1}{2}$	$\frac{1}{4}$

(ii)

x	0	1	2	3
P(x)	$\frac{1}{8}$	$\frac{3}{8}$	$\frac{3}{8}$	$\frac{1}{8}$

(iii)

x	0	1	2	3	4
P(x)	$\frac{1}{16}$	$\frac{1}{4}$	$\frac{3}{8}$	$\frac{1}{4}$	$\frac{1}{16}$

27. (a)

x	0	1	2
$P(x)$	$\frac{4}{9}$	$\frac{4}{9}$	$\frac{1}{9}$

(b)

x	0	1
$P(x)$	$\frac{25}{36}$	$\frac{11}{36}$

28. (a) $k=\frac{1}{6}$ (b) $P(x<2)=\frac{1}{2}, P(x\le 2)=1; P(x\ge 2)=\frac{1}{2}$

29.

x	14	15	16	17	18	19	20	21
$P(x)$	$\frac{2}{15}$	$\frac{1}{15}$	$\frac{2}{15}$	$\frac{3}{15}$	$\frac{1}{15}$	$\frac{2}{15}$	$\frac{3}{15}$	$\frac{1}{15}$

Mean 17.53, var (x) = 4.78 and S.D (x) = 2.19

TEXTUAL EXERCISE 5: (OBJECTIVE)

1. If the mean and variance of binomial variate X are 6 and 2 respectively. then the probability that X takes a value at most 8 is

(a) $\frac{19015}{19683}$ (b) $\frac{19171}{19683}$

(c) $\frac{19257}{19683}$ (d) None of these

2. 90 identicial coins, each with probability p of showing heads are tossed once. If $0 < p < 1$ and the probability of heads showing on 45 coins is equal to that of heads showing on 46 coins, the value of p is.

(a) $\frac{1}{2}$ (b) $\frac{45}{91}$

(c) $\frac{44}{91}$ (d) $\frac{46}{91}$

3. Suppose X follows a binomial distribution with parameters n and p, where $0 < p < 1$. If $P(X = r)/P(X = n - r)$ is independent of n for every value of r, then

(a) $p = 1/4$ (b) $q = 3/4$

(c) $p = 1/2$ (d) $q = 1/2$

4. The least number of times a fair coin must be tossed so that the probability of getting at least one tail is at least 0.6 is.

(a) 3 (b) 5

(c) 4 (d) 2

5. If m is an integer such that $m^2 - 25 \le 0$, then the probability that the quadratic equation $2x^2 + 2mx + m + 1 = 0$ has real roots is

(a) $\frac{2}{11}$ (b) $\frac{3}{11}$

(c) $\frac{6}{11}$ (d) $\frac{8}{11}$

6. A fair coins is tossed 200 times.The probability of getting tails 1, 3, 5, 7...,99 times is.

(a) $\frac{1}{2}$ (b) $\frac{1}{8}$

(c) $\frac{1}{16}$ (d) $\frac{1}{4}$

7. Each of two persons A and B, toss five fair coins. The probability that both get the same number of heads is

(a) $\frac{61}{256}$ (b) $\frac{63}{256}$

(c) $\frac{65}{256}$ (d) None of these

8. The probability that a student is not a swimmer is 1/3. The probability that out of 10 students exactly 7 are swimmer is.

(a) $\left(\frac{2}{3}\right)^9$ (b) $10\left(\frac{1}{3}\right)^9$

(c) $10\left(\frac{2}{3}\right)^9$ (d) None of these

9. Two integers x and y are choosen with replacement out of the set {0, 1, 2, 3,........, 10}. Then the probability that $|x - y| > 5$ is

(a) $\frac{81}{121}$ (b) $\frac{30}{121}$

(c) $\frac{25}{121}$ (d) $\frac{20}{121}$

10. If the sum of the ordinate and abscissa of a point $P(x,y)$ is $2n$, where x and y are natural numbers, then probability that the point does not lie on $y = x$ is

(a) $\frac{n-1}{n+3}$ (b) $\frac{2n-2}{2n-1}$

(c) $\frac{2n+1}{2n+3}$ (d) None of these

11. The mean of the numbers obtained on throwing a die having 1 on three faces, 2 on two faces and 5 on one face is

(a) 1 (b) 2
(c) 5 (d) 8/3

12. Suppose that two cards are drawn at random from a deck of cards. Let X be the number of aces obtained. Then the value of $E(X)$ is

(a) $\frac{37}{221}$ (b) $\frac{5}{13}$
(c) $\frac{1}{13}$ (d) $\frac{2}{13}$

13. In a binomial distribution $B\left(n, p=\frac{1}{4}\right)$, if the probability of at least one success is greater than or equal to 9/10, then the least posible value of x is

(a) $\frac{1}{\log_{10} 4+\log_{10} 3}$ (b) $\frac{9}{\log_{10} 4+\log_{10} 3}$
(c) $\frac{9}{\log_{10} 4-\log_{10} 3}$ (d) $\frac{1}{\log_{10} 4-\log_{10} 3}$

14. Four six-faced fair dice are thrown together. The probability that the sum of the numbers appearing on the dice is k $(4 \le k \le 9)$ is

(a) $\frac{(k-1)(k-2)(k-3)}{6^5}$
(b) $\frac{(k-1)(k-2)(k-3)}{1296}$
(c) $\frac{k(k-1)(k-2)}{6^5}$
(d) None of these

15. There are 30% chances that it rains on any particular day. If there is at least one rainy day in a week, the probability that there are at least two rainy days, is equal to:

(a) ${}^7C_2(.7)^5(.3)^2$
(b) $1-{}^7C_1(.7)^6(.3)$
(c) $(.7)^6 \times 2.8$
(d) $\frac{1-(.7)^6\times(2.8)}{1-(0.7)^7}$

Answer Key

1. (b)	**2.** (d)	**3.** (c, d)	**4.** (d)	**5.** (d)	**6.** (d)	**7.** (b)	**8.** (c)	**9.** (b)	**10.** (b)
11. (b)	**12.** (d)	**13.** (d)	**14.** (a)	**15.** (d)					

MULTIPLE CHOICE QUESTIONS

SECTION–I

SUBJECTIVE SOLVED EXAMPLES

1. A determinant of the second order is made with the elements 0 and 1. What is the probability that the determinant made is non-negative ?

Solution: The number of determinants of the second order that can be made with 0,1

$= 2 \times 2 \times 2 \times 2 = 16$ ($\because$ each of the four places of elements can be filled in 2 ways i.e., by 0 or 1).

$\therefore\ n(S) = 16$

Let E = the event of getting non-negative determinants.

Then $\bar{E}$ = the event of getting negative determinants.

Clearly, negative determinants of the second order that can be made with 0,1 are

$$\begin{vmatrix} 0 & 1 \\ 1 & 0 \end{vmatrix}, \begin{vmatrix} 0 & 1 \\ 1 & 1 \end{vmatrix}, \begin{vmatrix} 1 & 1 \\ 1 & 0 \end{vmatrix}; P(\bar{E}) = \frac{n(\bar{E})}{n(S)} = \frac{3}{16}$$

$$\Rightarrow P(E) = 1 - P(\bar{E}) = 1 - \frac{3}{16} = \frac{13}{16}$$

Hence, the required probability $= \dfrac{13}{16}$

2. A is a set containing 'n' element. A subset P of A is chosen at random, and the set A is reconstructed by replacing the elements of P. Another subset Q of A is now chosen at random. Find the probability that $P \cup Q$ contains exactly r elements. (with $1 \le r \le n$)

Solution: Let $A = \{a_1, a_2, \ldots\ldots, a_n\}$

For each $a_i \in A$ $(1 \le i \le n)$, we have the following four choices.

1. $a_i \in P$ and $a_i \in Q$ **2.** $a_i \in P$ and $a_i \notin Q$

3. $a_i \notin P$ and $a_i \in Q$ **4.** $a_i \notin P$ and $a_i \notin Q$

Therefore, for one element a_i of A, total number of cases is 4. Let S be the sample space.

$\therefore\ n(S) = 4^n$ and number of cases in which $a_i \in P \cup Q$ is 3 since in case 4, $a_i \notin P \cup Q$ and let E be the event of favourable cases, then $n(E)$ = number of ways in which exactly r elements of A will belong to $P \cup Q = {}^nC_r (3)^r (1)^{n-r} = {}^nC_r 3^r$

$\therefore$ Required Probability, $P(E) = \dfrac{n(E)}{n(S)} = \dfrac{{}^nC_r 3^r}{4^n}$

3. If 'n' positive integers taken at random are multiplied together, show that the probability that the last digit of the product is 5 is $\dfrac{5^n - 4^n}{10^n}$ and that the probability of the last digit being 0 is $\dfrac{10^n - 8^n - 5^n + 4^n}{10^n}$

Solution: Let n positive integers be $x_1, x_2, \ldots\ldots, x_n$.

Let $a = x_1 . x_2 \ldots\ldots x_n$

Let S be the sample space. Since the last digit in each of the numbers $x_1, x_2, \ldots\ldots, x_n$ can be any one of the digits 0, 1, 2, 3,....., 9 (total 10)

$\therefore\ n(S) = 10^n$

First Part: Let E_1 and E_2 be the events when the last digit in a is 1, 3, 5, 7 or 9 and 1, 3, 7 or 9 respectively

$\therefore\ n(E_1) = 5^n$ and $n(E_2) = 4^n$

and let E be the event that the last digit in a is 5.

$n(E) = n(E_1) - n(E_2) = 5^n - 4^n$

Hence required probability $P(E) = \dfrac{n(E_4)}{n(S)} = \dfrac{5^n - 4^n}{10^n}$

Second part: Let E_3 be the event when the last digit in a is 1, 2, 3, 4, 6, 7, 8, or 9 and E_4 is the event that last digit is '0'. Then $n(E_4) = n(S) - n(E_3) - n(E)$

$= 10^n - 8^n - (5^n - 4^n) = 10^n - 8^n - 5^n + 4^n$

$\therefore$ Required probability $P(E_4) = \dfrac{n(E_4)}{n(S)}$

$= \dfrac{10^n - 8^n - 5^n + 4^n}{10^n}$

4. Two teams A and B play a tournament. The first one to win $(n + 1)$ games win the series. The probability that A wins a game is p and that B wins a game is q (no ties). Find the probability of A winning the series.

Hence or otherwise prove that $\sum_{r=0}^{n} {}^{(n+1)}C_r \dfrac{1}{2^{n+r}} = 1$

Solution: A wins the series say in $(n + r + 1)$ games

$\therefore$ He wins the $(n + r + 1)$th game and n out of the first $(n + r)$ games

$$\therefore\ P(A) = \left(\sum_{r=0}^{n} {}^{n+r}C_n p^n q^r\right) p\ ; (p + q = 1). \text{ Similarly,}$$

$$P(B) = \left(\sum_{r=0}^{n} \left({}^{n+r}C_n\right) q^n . p^r\right) . q$$

Now $P(A) + P(B) = 1$.

$\therefore \sum_{r=0}^{n} \left({}^{n+r}C_n\right) [p^{n+1}.\, q^r + q^{n+1}.p^r] = 1$

put $p = 1/2 = q \therefore \sum_{r=0}^{n} \left({}^{n+r}C_n\right) \left[\frac{1}{2^{n+r+1}} + \frac{1}{2^{n+r+1}}\right] = 1$

$\therefore \sum_{r=0}^{n} \left({}^{n+r}C_n\right) \frac{1}{2^{n+r}} = 1$

5. A die is rolled three times, find the probability of getting every time a number larger than the previous number.

Solution: Method 1: Let S be the sample space and E be the event space of getting a larger number larger than the previous number.

$\therefore\ n(S) = 6 \times 6 \times 6 = 216$

Now we count the number of favourable ways. Obviously, the second number has to be greater than 1st. If the second number is i $(i > 1)$, then the number of favourable ways $= (i - 1) \times (6 - i)$

$\therefore\ n(E) =$ Total number of favourable ways

$= \sum_{i=1}^{6} (i-1) \times (6-i)$

$= 0 + 1 \times 4 + 2 \times 3 + 3 \times 2 + 4 \times 1 + 5 \times 0$

$= 4 + 6 + 6 + 4 = 20$

Therefore, the required probability is,

$P(E) = \frac{n(E)}{n(S)} = \frac{20}{216} = \frac{5}{54}$

Method 2: Let q_1 = number on first throw

q_2 = number on second throw

q_3 = number on third throw

So, $q_1 < q_2 < q_3$

Out of 6 available numbers we have to select 3,

so $n(E) = {}^6C_3 \Rightarrow P(E) = \frac{{}^6C_3}{216} = \frac{20}{216} = \frac{5}{54}$

6. A bag contains 'a' number of white and 'b' number of black balls. Two players A and B alternately draw a ball from the bag, replacing the ball each time after the draw till one of them draws a whilte ball and wins the game. If A begins the game and the probability of A winning the game is three times that of B, show that $a : b = 2 : 1$.

Solution: Let E_1 denotes the event of drawing a white ball at any draw and E_2 that for a black ball, and let E be the event of winning the game by 'A'.

$\therefore\ P(E_1) = \frac{a}{a+b}$ and $P(E_2) = \frac{b}{a+b}$

$\therefore\ P(E) = P(E_1$ or $E_2E_2E_1$ or $E_2E_2E_2E_2E_1$ or.....)

$= P(E_1) + P(E_2E_2E_1) + P(E_2E_2E_2E_2E_1) + \ldots\ldots$

$= P(E_1) + P(E_2)\, P(E_2)\, P(E_1) + P(E_2)\, P(E_2)\, P(E_2)\, P(E_2)\, P(E_1) + \ldots..$

($\because E_1$ and E_2 are independent)

$= \frac{P(E_1)}{1 - \{P(E_2)\}^2}$ [Sum of infinite G.P.]

$= \frac{a/(a+b)}{1 - \left(\frac{b}{a+b}\right)^2} = \frac{a(a+b)}{a^2 + 2ab} \Rightarrow P(E) = \frac{a+b}{a+2b}$

Then $P(\bar{E})$ is the probability of B winning the game

$\therefore\ P(\bar{E}) = 1 - P(E) = 1 - \frac{a+b}{a+2b} = \frac{b}{a+2b}$

According to the problem, $P(E) = 3P(\bar{E})$

$\Rightarrow \frac{a+b}{a+2b} = \frac{3b}{a+2b} \Rightarrow a + b = 3b \Rightarrow a = 2b$

$\therefore\ \frac{a}{b} = \frac{2}{1} \Rightarrow a : b = 2 : 1$

7. A lot contains 50 defective and 50 non-defective bulbs. Two bulbs are drawn at random one at a time with replacement. The event A, B, C are defined as:

A : the first bulb is defective

B : the second bulb is non defective

C : both the bulbs are defective or both are non-defective.

Determine whether (i) A, B, C are pairwise independent? (ii) A, B, C are mutually independent

Solution: Let probability of defective bulb is denoted by P_d and non-defective bulb is denoted by P_n So, $P_d = P_n = 1/2$

Let D_1 : First bulb is defective, D_2 : Second bulb is defective

N_1 : First bulb is non-defective N_2 : Second bulb is non defective

Sample space $= \{D_1D_2, D_1N_2, N_1D_2, N_1N_2\}$

Now event A is either (first bulb is defective and second bulb is defective) or (first bulb is defective and second bulb is non-defective)

$\therefore\ A = \{D_1D_2, D_1N_2\} \Rightarrow P(A) = 2/4 = 1/2$

Similarly, $B = \{D_1N_2, N_1N_2\} \Rightarrow P(B) = 1/2$

and $C = \{D_1D_2, N_1N_2\} \Rightarrow P(C) = 1/2$

Again $A \cap B = \{D_1N_2\}$, $B \cap C = \{N_1N_2\}$, $C \cap A = \{D_1D_2\}$

$\therefore\ P(A \cap B) = P(B \cap C) = P(C \cap A) = 1/4$

$\therefore\ P(A \cap B) = P(A)\, P(B) = P(B \cap C) = P(B)\, P(C)$

$= P(C \cap A) = P(C)P(A) = \frac{1}{4}$

$\therefore$ Above equations show that A, B, C are pairwise independent

$A \cap B \cap C = \phi \therefore P(A \cap B \cap C) = 0 \neq 1/8$

$P(A) . P(B) . P(C)$

So, A, B, C are not mutually independent events.

8. A speaks truth 3 out of 4 times. He reported that Mohan Bagan has won the match. Find the probability that his report was correct.

Solution: Let T : A speaks the truth and B : Mohan Bagan won the match

Given, $P(T) = \frac{3}{4} \therefore P(\bar{T}) = 1 - \frac{3}{4} = \frac{1}{4}$

A match can be won, drawn or lost

$\therefore P(B/T) = \frac{1}{3};\ P(B/\bar{T}) = \frac{2}{3}$

Using Baye's theorem we get

$$P(T/B) = \frac{P(T).P(B/T)}{P(T).P(B/T) + P(\bar{T})P(B/\bar{T})}$$

$$= \frac{\frac{3}{4}\times\frac{1}{3}}{\frac{3}{4}\times\frac{1}{3}+\frac{1}{4}\times\frac{2}{3}} = \frac{\frac{1}{4}}{\frac{5}{12}} = \frac{3}{5}$$

9. An unbaised coin is tossed. If the result is head, a pair of unbiased dice is rolled and the number obtained by adding the numbers on the two dice is noted. If the result is a tail, a card from a well-shuffled pack of 11 cards numbered 2, 3, 4,......, 12 is picked and the number on the card is noted. What is the chance that the number noted is 7 or 8.

Solution: Let us define the events A, B, C as A : Head appears on the coin.

B : Tail appears on the coin.

C : number obtained in 7 or 8

We have to find the probability of C i.e., $P(C)$. Probability of occurence of C depends on two mutually exclusive and exhaustive events A and B. So by total theorem of probability.

$P(C) = P(A)\,P(C/A) + P(B) . P(C/B)$

$P(A)$ = probability of appearing head = 1/2

$P(C/A)$ = Probability that event C takes place i.e., 7 or 8 being noted when head has already appeared $= \frac{11}{36}$

Similarly, $P(B) = 1/2$

$P(B/C) = \frac{2}{11}$ (Two favourable cases 7 or 8 and total number of cases = 11).

Hence, $P(C) = \frac{1}{2}\times\frac{11}{36}+\frac{1}{2}\times\frac{2}{11} = \frac{193}{792}$

10. Four cards are drawn at random from a well-shuffled pack of 52 cards. Find the probability that there is exactly one pair.

Solution: Let H, C, D, S denotes heart, club, diamond and spade respectively. We have to draw 4 cards at random, so that it consists of exactly one pair. {A pair means two cards of same denomination} e.g., (5H, 5C)} or four-selected cards should look like. $2H, 2S, 3C, 5D$

Now we will find in how many ways, we can do this. We have a pack of cards like this.

$1H,\ 1C,\ 1D,\ 1S$ (Aces) .... (1)
$2H,\ 2C,\ 2D,\ 2S$ ....(2)
$3H,\ 3C,\ 3D,\ 3S$ ....(3)
⋮
$JH,\ JC,\ JD,\ JS$ .... (11)
$QH,\ QC,\ QD,\ QS$ ....(12)
$KH,\ KC,\ KD,\ KS$ ....(13)

We now select a pair. This can be done by firstly selecting a row and then from the selected row we select a pair out of it.

There are 13 rows. and a row is selected in ${}^{13}C_1$ ways. Each row contain 4 elements and a pair from the selected row is selected in ${}^{4}C_2$ ways.

Number of ways a pair is selected ${}^{13}C_1 \times {}^{4}C_2$.

Remaining two cards has to be selected so that it does not pair with any of other three cards. So the third card has to be selected from those cards which do not belong to the row we selected earlier, i.e., selection has to be made from remaining 48 cards Third card can be selected in ${}^{48}C_1$ ways.

For the fourth card we do not select that card which belongs to either the row we selected or the row to which third card belongs. So selection of fourth card is made from remaining 44 cards in ${}^{44}C_1$ ways.

$\therefore$ Number of ways of selecting four cards $= {}^{13}C_1 \times {}^{4}C_2 \times {}^{48}C_1 \times {}^{44}C_1$

Total number of ways $= {}^{52}C_4$

$\therefore$ required probability $= \frac{{}^{13}C_1 \times {}^{4}C_2 \times {}^{48}C_1 \times {}^{44}C_1}{{}^{52}C_4}$

11. A has $(n + 1)$ and B has 'n' fair coins, which they flip, now show that the probability that A gets more head than B is 1/2.

Solution: Method 1: Suppose that A and B each toss n coins then the probability that A gets 'i' heads and B gets 'j' heads is

$$P(E_{ij}) = \left({}^nC_i \frac{1}{2^n}\right)\left({}^nC_j \frac{1}{2^n}\right) = \frac{({}^nC_i)({}^nC_j)}{2^{2n}}$$

Let E_1 denotes the event that A gets more heads than B and E_2 denotes the event that A and B get the same number of heads then we have $E_1 = \bigcup_{i>j} E_{ij}$ and $E_2 = \bigcup_{i=j} E_{ij}$

$$P(E_1) = \sum_{i>j} P(E_{ij}) = \sum_{i>j} \frac{({}^nC_i)({}^nC_j)}{2^{2n}} \text{ and}$$

$$P(E_2) = \sum_{i=j} P(E_{ij}) = \sum_{i=0}^{n} \frac{({}^nC_i)^2}{(2)^{2n}}$$

Now, $({}^nC_0 + {}^nC_1 + ... + {}^nC_n)^2 = (2^n)^2 = 2^{2n}$

$$\Rightarrow \sum_{i=0}^{n} ({}^nC_i)^2 + 2\sum_{i>j} ({}^nC_i)({}^nC_j) = 2^{2n}$$

But $\sum_{i=0}^{n} ({}^nC_i)^2 = {}^{2n}C_n$. therefore,

$$\sum_{i>j}^{n} ({}^nC_i)({}^nC_j) = \frac{2^{2n} - {}^{2n}C_n}{2}$$

Thus $P(E_1) = \frac{2^{2n} - {}^{2n}C_n}{2^{2n+1}}$ and $P(E_2) = \frac{{}^{2n}C_n}{2^{2n}}$

Let E denote the event that A gets more heads than B when A tosses $(n + 1)$ coins and B tosses n coins. If E_1 has already occurred, then the outcome of the $(n + 1)^{\text{th}}$ toss is immaterial. If E_2 has already occurred, then the outcome of the $(n + 1)^{\text{th}}$ coin must be a head. Therefore, $P(E/E_1) = P(H \text{ or } T) = 1$

$P(E/E_2) = P(H) = 1/2$ [Because when within n tosses A and B have same number of heads, A must have a head in $(n + 1)^{\text{th}}$ toss]

$P(E) = P(E_1)\, P(E/E_1) + P(E_2)\, P(E/E_2)$

$$= \frac{2^{2n} - {}^{2n}C_n}{2^{2n+1}}.1 + \frac{{}^{2n}C_n}{2^{2n}}.\frac{1}{2}$$

$$= \frac{2^{2n} - {}^{2n}C_n + {}^{2n}C_n}{2^{2n+1}} = \frac{2^{2n}}{2^{2n+1}} = \frac{1}{2}$$

Method 2: Here A has $(n + 1)$ coins and B has n coins. n can be anything and there is no loss of generality if we assume n is very large.

Therefore, we can say that if A flip his n coins he will get $n/2$ heads and $n/2$ tails. Case is exactly same with B, if he will flip his n coins he will get $n/2$ heads and $n/2$ tails.

Now A is left with 1 coin. He has to get 1 head, so in this coin head must appear Hence the probability of appearing head = 1/2

Probability of getting one more head = 1/2

12. From an urn containing a white and b black balls, k ($<a, b$) balls are drawn and laid aside, their colours are noted. Then one more ball is drawn Find the probability that it is white.

Solution: Let E_i denotes the event that out of the first k balls drawn, i balls are white

Let A denotes the event that the $(k + 1)^{\text{th}}$ ball drawn is also white. Then occurrence of A depends on mutually exclusive and exhaustive events E_i $\forall$ i = $\in \{1, 2,..., n\}$. $P(E_i) = \frac{({}^aC_i)({}^bC_{k-i})}{{}^{a+b}C_k} (0 \le i \le k)$ and

$$P(A|E_i) = \left(\frac{a-i}{a+b-k}\right) (0 \le i \le k)$$

$\therefore$ By theorem of total probability,

$$P(A) = \sum_{j=0}^{k} P(E_j)P(A|E_j)$$

$$= \sum_{j=0}^{k} \frac{({}^aC_j)({}^bC_{k-j})}{{}^{a+b}C_k} . \frac{a-j}{a+b-k}$$

$$= \sum_{j=0}^{k} \frac{a({}^{a-1}C_j)({}^bC_{k-j})}{(a+b).{}^{a+b-1}C_k}$$

$$= \frac{a}{a+b} . \frac{1}{{}^{a+b-1}C_k} \sum_{j=0}^{k} ({}^{a-1}C_j)({}^bC_{k-j})$$

Also $(1 + x)^{a-1} (1 + x)^b = ({}^{a-1}C_0 + {}^{a-1}C_1\, x + {}^{a-1}C_2\, x^2 + ... + {}^{a-1}C_{a-1}\, x^{a-1}) \times ({}^bC_0 + {}^bC_1\, x + {}^bC_2\, x^2 + ... + {}^bC_b\, x^b)$ ....(1)

$\therefore$ $\sum_{j=0}^{k} ({}^{a-1}C_j)({}^bC_{k-j})$ = Coefficient of x^k on the RHS of (1)

= Coefficient of x^k in $(1 + x)^{a+b-1} = {}^{a+b-1}C_k$

Hence, $P(A) = a/(a + b)$.

13. There are 4 T.V and 4 repairmen in a town. 4 T.V sets of that town get damaged. Find the probability that

(i) Exactly 1 repairman is called

(ii) Exactly 2 repairmen are called

(iii) Exactly 3 repairmen are called

(iv) Exactly 4 repairmen are called

Solution: Method 1: Suppose 4 repairmen are 1, 2, 3 and 4 and four callers are A, B, C and D. First we will calculate the total number of ways.

Since every repairman can be called in 4 ways hence total number of ways = $4^4 = 256$ ways

(i) Exactly 1 repairman can be called in four ways

$A1, B1, C1, D1 \rightarrow$ i.e., all caller call repairman 1.

Similarly $A2, B2, C2, D2$

$A3, B3, C3, D3$

$A4, B4, C4, D4$

Hence Probability = $\frac{4}{256} = \frac{1}{64}$

(ii) There can be two cases in which exactly two repairmen can be called

(a) Three caller call same repairman (say 1) and one caller call different repairman. e.g.

$A1, B1, C1, D2$

$A1, B1, C1, D3$

$A1, B1, C1, D4$

There will be 3 such combination each, for three caller calling repairmen 2, 3 and 4

$\therefore$ Total number of combination = $4 \times 3 = 12$

Each such combination ($A1, B1, C1\ D2$) can be arranged in $4!/3! = 4$ ways

Hence total ways = $4 \times 12 = 48$

(b) Two callers call one repairman and two callers call other repairmen alike. e.g., $A1\ B1\ C2\ D2$

There will be ${}^4C_2$ such combinations and each combination can be arranged in $\frac{4!}{2!2!} = 6$ ways

Hence total ways = $6 \times 6 = 36$

Therefore total number of ways of calling exactly two repairmen

$= 48 + 36 = 84$ $\therefore$ required probability $= \frac{84}{256} = \frac{21}{64}$

(iii) Exactly three repairmen can be called in such a way

$A1\ B1\ C2\ D3$

$A1\ B1\ C2\ D4$

$A1\ B1\ C3\ D4$

There will be 3 such combination each for two caller calling repairmen 2, 3 and 4.

Total combination = $3 \times 4 = 12$

Number of arrangement for each combination = $4!/2! = 12$

Total number of ways = $12 \times 12 = 144$

Probability = $\frac{144}{256} = \frac{9}{16}$

(iv) Probability of calling exactly 4 repairmen will therefore be $1 - \left(\frac{1}{64} + \frac{21}{64} + \frac{36}{64}\right) = \frac{6}{64} = \frac{3}{32}$

Method 2: Exclusion/Inclusion method

Let four persons whose T.V is out of order be A, B, C and D

Let T.V repairmen be 1, 2, 3, 4

(i) Exactly one of the repairmen can be called in ${}^4C_1\,(1^4) = 4$ ways

(ii) For calling exactly two repairmen, we can select two repairmen from four in ${}^4C_2$ ways. Let us suppose repairmen 2 and 4 are the only called for.

Person A has two choices i.e., he can call either the repairman 2 or repairman 4.

Similarly B, C and D each has two choices.

$\Rightarrow$ they can call one of these two repairmen in 2^4 ways. But these also include the ways in which all of them (i.e., A, B, C and D) are calling the same repairman.

$\Rightarrow$ Total number of ways of calling repairmen 2 and 4 both is $2^4 - 2$ ways.

$\Rightarrow$ Total number of ways of calling exactly two repairmen = ${}^4C_2({}^2C_2\, 2^4 - {}^2C_1\,(1^4)) = 84$

(iii) Similarly exactly three of the repairmen can be called in

$3^4 - {}^3C_2\,(2^4 - 2) - {}^3C_1 = 3^4 - {}^3C_2 + 2.\,{}^3C_2 - {}^3C_1$

$= {}^4C_3[{}^3C_3\, 3^4 - {}^3C_2\, 2^4 - {}^3C_1\,(1)^4] = 144$

(iv) Similarly, exactly four of them can be called in ${}^4C_4\,[{}^4C_4\, 4^4 - {}^4C_3\,(3^4) + {}^4C_2\,(2^4) - {}^4C_1\,(1)^4]$ $= 24$

Thus total number of ways = 4 + 84 + 144 + 24 = 256

Hence the probability in four cases can be calculated very easily.

This method is used for finding number of onto functions from A to B.

14. Sixteen players S_1, S_2,......, S_{16} play in a tournament. They are divided into eight pairs at random. From each pair a winner is decided on the basis of a game played between the two players of the pair. Assume that all the players are of equal strength (skill)

(a) Find the probability that the player S_1 is among eight winners.

(b) Find the probability that exactly one of the two players S_1 and S_2 is among eight winners.

Solution: (a) Among 16 players S_1, S_2, S_3,......., S_{16}, 8 players will win, when they will play in knock out round forming eight pairs at random. Therefore among many combinations of eight winners one such combination may look like this

$S_1, S_2, S_3, S_4, S_{13}, S_{14}, S_{15}, S_{16}$

It is clearly an analogy of the problems like this:

$(S_1, S_2, \ldots\ldots S_{16})$ 16 persons and a committee is to be formed of 8 persons in which a particular person (S_1) should always present.

which can be solved by following manner:

We will select S_1, then we have to select 7 persons out of 15 persons, which we can do in

$= ({}^{15}C_7)$ ways. (This is the number of committees in which S_1 is always present)

Total number of ways $= {}^{16}C_8$

(Total number of committees with or without S_1)

Hence the probability that S_1 is always among 8 winner $= \dfrac{{}^{15}C_7}{{}^{16}C_8} = \dfrac{1}{2}$.

(b) Similarly, the second case is analogy of the problem like:

Form a committee of 8 players, in which S_1 is present but S_2 should not and if S_2 is present S_1 should not present.

Number of favourable ways can be calculated as, we will select S_1 in 1 way.

Now we are left with 15 players but S_2 should not be among them hence effectively we have 14 persons, out of which we have to select 7, which can be done in $({}^{14}C_7)$ ways.

Similarly calculation for the case

"S_2 should be among them but S_1 not" $= ({}^{14}C_7)$

Hence the probability

$$= P(S_1\bar{S}_2) + P(\bar{S}_1S_2) = \frac{2.{}^{14}C_7}{{}^{16}C_8}$$

15. Eight players $P_1, P_2, \ldots, P_8$ play a knock-out tournament. It is known that whenever the players P_i and P_j play, the players P_i will win if $i < j$. Assuming that the players are paired at random in each round, what is the probability that the player P_4 reaches to the final?

Solution: There are eight players $P_1, P_2, P_3, \ldots\ldots\ldots\ldots P_8$ and they are going to play a knock out round in which any one can play with any-one. The player P_i wins if $i < j$ and we have to find the probability of P_4 entering in the final round.

There will be 2 rounds before final. In the first round, 4 players will get eliminated and in next round 2 players will get eliminated, sending only two players to the final round.

First we will see and calculate in how many ways P_4 can enter into final. It is sure that it has to win first round and that is possible only when it plays with either of P_5, P_6, P_7, P_8. But finding the cases for the win in first round in isolation (i.e. without taking scenario of 2nd round into consideration) won't do. Suppose he faces a condition like this in second round, $(P_1 P_2 P_3 P_4)$, then P_4 can not win with either of P_1, P_2, P_3. So he won't be able to make into final. Therefore he had at least one less skilled player in 2nd round i.e., P_i $(i \geq 5)$. P_4 can play with P_i $(i \geq 5)$ in 4 ways $\{P_4 P_5, P_4, P_6, P_4 P_7$ and $P_4 P_8\}$ and will eliminate any one of them say P_6 now only three less skilled players left P_5, P_7, P_8 at least one has to win. The fact is only one out of these three can win which is possible only when out of these three, 2 players play with each other. Which can be done in 3 ways. $\{P_5 P_7, P_5 P_8, P_7 P_8\}$ by doing this out of these three, one will enter in second round say P_5 and one will get eliminated say P_7. Now P_8 can play with any of P_1, P_2, P_3 in three ways $\{P_1 P_8, P_2 P_8, P_3 P_8\}$ without effecting the outcome. Hence favourable ways for first round is $4 \times 3 \times 3 = 36$.

Now second round will look like this. $(P_1 P_3 P_4 P_5)$ and if P_4 has to enter in final and if it has to win, then only way is to play with P_5

So, total number of ways in which it can enter in final is (4) (3)(3) (1) = 36

Calculation of total number of ways: In how many ways you can arrange knock out among four players. (say $P_1, P_2, P_3 P_4$) probably ${}^4C_2$ ways? but the answer is definitely not becuase if you try to arrange

$P_1 P_2, P_3 P_4$ (1 Way)

$P_1 P_3, P_2 P_4$ (1 Way)

$P_1 P_4, P_2 P_3$ (1 Way).

You can see that only 3 ways are possible in which, you can arrange a knock out among 4 players.

So, how we will calculate? Try this any of the 4 players say P_1 can play with either of remaining three in 3 ways.

When he played with any one, only 2 players left which can play in only one possible way. Hence the total no. of ways are $3 \times 1 = 3$

Now, suppose we have 6 players $(P_1 P_2, P_3 P_4, P_5 P_6)$ i.e., 3 Ways

$P_1 P_3 (P_2 P_4 P_5 P_6)$ 3 Ways

$P_1 P_4 (P_2 P_3 P_5 P_6)$ 3 Ways

$P_1 P_5 (P_2 P_3 P_5 P_6)$ 3 Ways

$P_1 P_6 (P_2 P_3 P_4 P_5)$ 3 Ways = 15 Ways

Which can also be calculated as any of 6 players say P_1 can play with rest 5 in five ways, out of remaining 4, any one can play with.

Hence total ways are 5 × 3 × 1 = 15. So with the 8 players 7 × 5 × 3 × 1 = 105 ways in first round. There are 4 players in second round hence 3 × 1 = 3 ways in 2nd round.

Hence the probability $P=\frac{4\times3\times3}{105}\times\frac{1}{3}=\frac{4}{35}$

16. A player tosses a coin and scores one point for every head and two points for every tail that turns up. He plays on until his score reaches or passes n. If P_n denotes the probability of getting a score of exactly n, show that

$$P_n=\frac{1}{2}[P_{n-1}+P_{n-2}]\ \forall\, n\geq 3 \text{ and hence show that}$$

$$P_n=\frac{1}{3}\left[2+(-1)^n\frac{1}{2^n}\right] \text{ for } n\geq 1$$

Solution: The scores of n can be reached in the following two mutually exclusive ways: (i) by throwing a head when the score is $(n-1)$, and (ii) by throwing a tail when the score is $(n-2)$. Since $P(H) = P(T) = 1/2$, we get

$$P_n=\frac{1}{2}P_{n-1}+\frac{1}{2}P_{n-2}=\frac{1}{2}(P_{n-1}+P_{n-2})$$

$$\Rightarrow P_n+\frac{1}{2}P_{n-1}=P_{n-1}+\frac{1}{2}P_{n-2}=P_{n-2}+\frac{1}{2}P_{n-3}$$

$$=\ldots\ldots=P_2+\frac{1}{2}P_1$$

Now, a score of 1 can be obtained by throwing a head at a single toss, and a score of 2 can be obtained by throwing either a tail at single toss or a head at the first as well as the second toss. Thus, $P_1 = 1/2$ and $P_2 = 1/2 + (1/2)(1/2) = 3/4$. Therefore, $P_n+\frac{1}{2}P_{n-1}$

$$=\frac{3}{4}+\left(\frac{1}{2}\right)\left(\frac{1}{2}\right)=1$$

$$\Rightarrow P_n-\frac{2}{3}=-\frac{1}{2}\left(P_{n-1}-\frac{2}{3}\right)=\left(-\frac{1}{2}\right)^2\left(P_n-\frac{2}{3}\right)$$

$$=\left(-\frac{1}{2}\right)^3\left(P_{n-3}-\frac{2}{3}\right)$$

$$=\left(-\frac{1}{2}\right)^{n-1}\left(P_1-\frac{2}{3}\right)=\left(-\frac{1}{2}\right)^{n-1}\left(\frac{1}{2}-\frac{2}{3}\right)$$

$$=\left(-\frac{1}{2}\right)^{n-1}\left(-\frac{1}{6}\right)=\frac{1}{3}\left(\frac{1}{2}\right)^{n}$$

$$\Rightarrow P_n=\frac{2}{3}+(-1)^n.\frac{1}{3}.\frac{1}{2^n}=\frac{1}{3}\left(2+(-1)^n.\frac{1}{2^n}\right)$$

17. Two gamblers A and B bet on the outcomes of the successive toss of a coin. On each toss, if the coin shows a head A collects one unit from B, whereas if the coin shows a tail, A pays one unit to B. They continue to do this until one of them runs out of money. If it is assumed that the successive tosses of the coin are independent, what is the probability that A ends up with all the money if he starts with i units and B starts with $(N-i)$ units.

Solution: Let E denotes the event that A ends up with all the money. Let P_k denote the probability that A ends with all the money when A has k units and B has $(N-k)$ units. Note that $P(E) = P_i$. Let H denotes the event that the outcome of the first trial is a head. We have $P(E) = P(H)\,P(E/H) + P(H^c)\,P(E/H^c) = [P(E/H) + P(E/H^c)]$

But $P(E/H) = P_{i+1}$ as A begins with I units and collects one unit from B after the first toss. Similarly, $P(E/H) = P_{i-1}$

Thus, $P_i=\frac{1}{2}(P_{i+1}+P_{i-1})$ ....(i)

Also, $P_0 = 0$ as it is impossible for A to end up with all the money when he has nothing to begin with, and $P_N = 1$ as A ends up with all the money when he has N units to begin with.

Equation (1) show that $P_0, P_1, P_2, \ldots\ldots, P_N$ form an A.P., with $P_0 = 0$ and $P_N = 1$. Therefore, $P_i = i/N$.

18. There are two bags, each containing 5 red and 3 black balls. Two persons, A and B, are given one bag each. Each of them is to draw one ball at random from the bag till one of them gets a black ball. The balls are to be replaced after each draw. Find the probability that the maximum number of trials required is n.

Solution: Let X be the number of the trial in which A draws a black ball, and Y be the number of the trial in which B draws a black ball.

Now, $P(X=k)=P(Y=k)=\left(\frac{3}{8}\right)\left(\frac{5}{8}\right)^{k-1}$

(Since there must be failure at the first $(k-1)$ draws and a success at the kth draw.)

Let $Z = \max(X, Y)$. We are interested in $P(Z = n)$. We have

$$P(Z = n) = P(Z \le n) - P(Z \le n-1)$$
$$= P[\max(X,Y) \le n] - P[\max(X,Y) \le n-1]$$
$$= P[(X \le n) \cap (Y \le n)] - P[(X \le n-1) \cap (Y \le n-1)]$$
$$= P(X \le n)\,P(Y \le n) - P((X \le n-1)\,P(Y \le n-1)$$
[∵ X and Y are independent]

$$= \left[\sum_{k=1}^{n}\left(\frac{3}{8}\right)\left(\frac{5}{8}\right)^{k-1}\right]^2 - \left[\sum_{k=1}^{n-1}\left(\frac{3}{8}\right)\left(\frac{5}{8}\right)^{k-1}\right]^2$$

$$= \left[\frac{\left(\frac{3}{8}\right)\left[1-\left(\frac{5}{8}\right)^{n}\right]}{1-\frac{5}{8}}\right]^2 - \left[\frac{\frac{3}{8}\left[1-\left(\frac{5}{8}\right)^{n-1}\right]}{1-\frac{5}{8}}\right]^2$$

$$= \left[1-\left(\frac{5}{8}\right)^{n}\right]^2 - \left[1-\left(\frac{5}{8}\right)^{n-1}\right]^2$$

$$= \left[\left(\frac{5}{8}\right)^{n-1} - \left(\frac{5}{8}\right)^{n}\right]\left[2-\left(\frac{5}{8}\right)^{n-1} - \left(\frac{5}{8}\right)^{n}\right]$$

$$= \frac{3}{8}\left(\frac{5}{8}\right)^{n-1}\left[2-\left(\frac{5}{8}\right)^{n-1} - \left(\frac{5}{8}\right)^{n}\right]$$

19. Rachit and Rakshit make an appointment to meet on 15th October at Appu Ghar, but without fixing the time further so that it is between 2 pm and 3 pm. They decided to wait not longer than 10 minutes for each other. Assuming that each is independently equally likely to arrive at any time during the hour, find the probability that they meet.

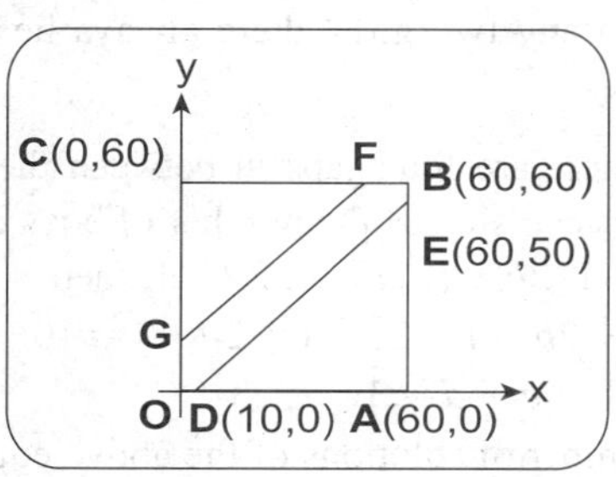

Solution: Suppose that Rachit (Rakshit) arrives at $x(y)$ minutes past 2 pm, where $0 \le x, y \le 60$. Rachit and Rakshit will meet provided $|x - y| \le 10$. Note that (x, y) lies on or inside the square with vertices $O(0,0)$, A (60,0), B(60, 60) and C(0, 60). if P (Rachit and Rakshit meet) $= p$, then p (they do not meet) $= 1 - p$, i.e., $(|x - y|) > 10$).

The region that lying inside the square $OABC$ and satisfying the inequality $|x - y| > 10$ consisting of two triangles DAE and GFC. Sum of areas of these two triangles is $\frac{1}{2}(50)^2 + \frac{1}{2}(50)^2 = 50^2$

Probability of the required event $= 1 - \frac{50^2}{60^2} = 1 - \frac{25}{36} = \frac{11}{36}$

20. A printing machine can print n letters say α_1, α_2, α_2,....., α_n. It is operated by electrical impulses, each letter being produced by a different impulse. Assume that there exists a constant probability P of prinit-ing the correct letter and also assume independence. One of the n impulses chosen at random was fed in the machine twice and both times the letter α_1, was printed. Compute the probability that the impulses chosen was meant to be α_1.

Solution: Let E = event that both times α_1 was printed.

A = event that impulse selected was meant to print α_1

$$P(A/E) = \frac{P(A \cap E)}{P(E)} = \frac{P(A)P(E/A)}{P(A)P(E/A) + P(\bar{A})P(E/\bar{A})}$$

$$= \frac{(1/n)P^2}{\frac{1}{n}P^2 + \left(1-\frac{1}{n}\right)\left(\frac{1-P}{n-1}\right)^2}$$

21. An even number of cards are drawn from a pack of 52. Find the probability that half of these cards will be red and the other half black.

Solution: No. of ways of drawing an even number of cards is $= {}^{52}C_2 + {}^{52}C_4 + {}^{52}C_6 + \ldots\ldots + {}^{52}C_{52} = 2^{52-1} - {}^{52}C_0 = 2^{51} - 1$

If half of them should be black and other half white, then number of favourable ways $= ({}^{26}C_1)({}^{26}C_1) + {}^{26}C_2 \times {}^{26}C_2 + \ldots + {}^{26}C_{26} \times {}^{26}C_{26}$

$= {}^{52}C_{26} - 1$(using $\sum_{r=0}^{n}({}^{n}C_r)^2 = {}^{2n}C_n$)

Required probability $= \frac{{}^{52}C_{26} - 1}{2^{51} - 1}$

22. Two integers x and y are chosen at random from the set $\{x : 0 \le x \le 10, x \text{ is an integer}\}$ then find the probability for $|x - y| \le 5$.

Solution: There are 11 ways to chose x and 11 ways to choose y. If S be the sample space, then number of elements in sample space

$n(S)$ = Total number of ways of choosing x and $y = 11 \times 11 = 121$

The number of different values of y for a given value of x can be determined as below:

when $x = 0$, we have $|0 - y| \le 5$

$\Rightarrow |y| \le 5 \Rightarrow -5 \le y \le 5 \Rightarrow 0 \le y \le 5$ [because $y \ge 0$]

gives six values of y, i.e., $\{0, 1, 2, 3, 4, 5\}$

when $x = 1$, we have $|1 - y| \le 5$

$\Rightarrow -5 \le 1 - y \le 5 \Rightarrow 5 \ge 1 - y \ge -5 \Rightarrow 6 \ge y \ge -4$

$\therefore\ 0 \le y \le 6$ [because $y \ge 0$]

gives seven values of y, i.e., $\{0, 1, 2, 3, 4, 5, 6\}$

When $x = 2$, we have $|2 - y| \le 5$

$\Rightarrow -5 \le 2 - y \le 5 \Rightarrow 5 \ge -2 + y \ge -5$

$\Rightarrow 7 \ge y \ge -3 \therefore 0 \le y \le 7$ (since $y \ge 0$)

gives 8 values of y, i.e., $\{0, 1, 2, 3, 4, 5, 6, 7\}$ similarly we can show that when x equals 3, 4, 5, 6, 7, 8, 9, 10 there are 9, 10, 11, 10, 9, 8, 7, 6; values of y respectively.

Let E be the event of favourable cases, then

$n(E) = 6 + 7 + 8 + 9 + 10 + 11 + 10 + 9 + 8 + 7 + 6 = 91$

Hence requried probability is, $P(E) = \dfrac{n(E)}{n(S)} = \dfrac{91}{121}$

23. If $a \in [-20, 0]$, then find the probability that the graph of the function $y = 16x^2 + 8(a + 5)x - 7a - 5$ is strictly above the x-axis.

Solution: Since the graph $y = 16x^2 + 8(a + 5)x - 7a - 5$ is strictly above the x-axis, therefore, $y > 0$ for all x

$\Rightarrow 16x^2 + 8(a + 5)x - 7a - 5 > 0\ \forall x$

$\therefore$ Discriminant < 0

$\Rightarrow 64(a + 5)^2 - 4.16(-7a - 5) < 0 \Rightarrow a^2 + 17a + 30 < 0$

$\Rightarrow (a + 15)(a + 2) < 0 \Rightarrow -15 < a < -2$

$\therefore$ required probability $= \dfrac{\int_{-15}^{-2} dx}{\int_{-20}^{0} dx} = \dfrac{13}{20}$,

or $= \dfrac{\text{Length of requaired interval}}{\text{Length of total interval}} = \dfrac{13}{20}$

24. Once upon a time there was a dictator. An astrologer forecast something bad for him; so the dictator awarded a death penalty to the astrologer. The latter pleaded for his life, so the dictator gave him a chance to save himself and decreed as follows: "I will allow you to put two white and two black balls in any manner you like in two urns without disclosing it to anybody". My executioner will choose one of the urns, dip his hand into it and take out a ball. If the ball is black, he will cut off your head. If the ball he picks is white, your life is saved. Try save yourself if you can.

What would you advise the astrolger to do, in order to give himself the maximum probability of saving his life? The different possibilities of distributions of the 4 balls into the two urns are pictorially depicted in given figure.

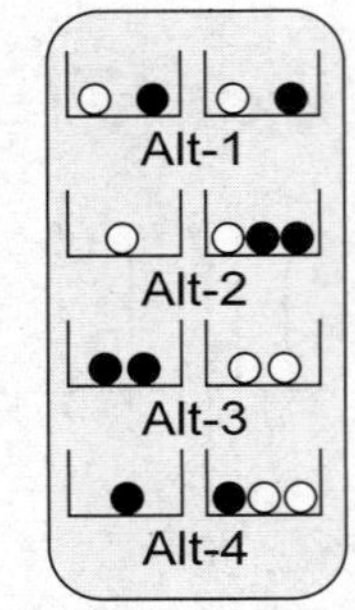

Solution: In Alt-1, Probability (white ball) = Probability (white withdrawl from urn-I) + Probability (white withdrawl from 2nd urn) = (Probability of selection of urn I) (Probability of white ball) + (Probability of selection urn II) × (Probability of white ball)

$= 1/2 \times 1/2 + 1/2 \times 1/2 = 1/2$

In Alt-2 $= 1/2 \times 1 + 1/2 \times 1/3 = 2/3$

In Alt-3 $= 1/2 \times 0 + 1/2 \times 1 = 1/2$

In Alt-4 $= 1/2 \times 0 + 1/2 \times 2/3 = 1/3$

Thus in order to maximize his probability of saving his life, the astrologer should be advised to go with Alt-2.

25. 5 girls and 10 boys sit at random in a row having 15 chairs numbered as 1 to 15. Find the probability that end seats are occupied by the girls and between any two girls, there always lie odd number of boys.

Solution: There are four gaps in between the girls where the boys can sit. Let the number of boys in these gaps be $2a + 1, 2b + 1, 2c + 1, 2d + 1$, then

$2a + 1 + 2b + 1 + 2c + 1 + 2d + 1 = 10$

or $a + b + c + d = 3$

The number of solutions of the above equation

= coefficient of x^3 in $(1 - x)^{-4} = {}^6C_3 = 20$

Thus boys and girls can sit in $20 \times 10! \times 5!$ ways.

Total ways $= 15!$

Hence the required probability $= \dfrac{20 \times 10! \times 5!}{15!}$

26. Two numbers x and y are chosen at random (without replacement) from amongst the numbers 1, 2, 3,....., $3n$. Then find the probability that $x^3 + y^3$ is divisible by 3.

Solution: Total number of ways of choosing x and y is ${}^{3n}C_2 = \dfrac{3n(3n-1)}{2}$

$\therefore$ If S be the sample space, then $n(S) = \dfrac{3n(3n-1)}{2}$

Now arrange the given numbers as below,

1, 4, 7,....., $3n - 2$

2, 5, 8,......, $3n - 1$

3, 6, 9,....., $3n$

We see that $x^3 + y^3$ will be divisible by 3 in the following cases:

Case I: One of the two numbers belongs to the first row and the other one (of the two numbers) belongs to the second row

Case II: Both numbers occur in third row. If E be the event for favourable cases, then

$$n(E) = (n)\,(n) + {}^nC_2 = n^2 + \frac{n(n-1)}{2} = \frac{n}{2}(3n-1)$$

$$\therefore\quad P(E) = \frac{\frac{n}{2}(3n-1)}{\frac{3n(3n-1)}{2}} = \frac{1}{3}$$

27. A car is parked among N parking slots in a row, but not at either end. On his return, the owner finds that exactly r of the N places are still occupied. What is the probability that both the places neighbouring his car are empty?

Solution: Finding r cars in N places, there are $(r - 1)$ cars other than his own in $(N - 1)$ places.

$\therefore$ total no. of ways $= {}^{n-1}C_{r-1} = \dfrac{(N-1)!}{(r-1)!(N-r)!}$

Now the $(r - 1)$ cars must be parked in $(N - 3)$ places (because neightbouring slots are empty).

$\therefore$ No. of favourable ways $= {}^{N-3}C_{r-1} = \dfrac{(N-3)!}{(r-1)!(N-r-2)!}$

$\therefore$ Required probability $= \dfrac{\text{Favourable ways}}{\text{Total ways}}$

$$= \frac{(N-3)!}{(r-1)!(N-r-2)!} \times \frac{(r-1)!(N-r)!}{(N-1)!}$$

$$= \frac{(N-r)(N-r-1)}{(N-1)(N-2)}$$

28. An artilery target may be either at point I with probability $\frac{8}{9}$ or at point II with probability $\frac{1}{9}$. We have 21 shells each of which can be fired at point I and II. Each shell may hit the target independently of the other shell with proabability $\frac{1}{2}$. How many shells must be fired at point I to hit the target with maximum probability ?

Solution: Let A denotes the event that the target is hit when x shells are fired at point I. Let E_1E_2 denote the event denoting the targets being point I and II respectively.

we have $P(E_1) = \frac{8}{9}$, $P(E_2) = \frac{1}{9}$

$$\Rightarrow P(A/E_1) = 1 - \left(\frac{1}{2}\right)^x \text{ and } P(A/E_2) = 1 - \left(\frac{1}{2}\right)^{21-x}$$

$$\text{Now } P(A) = \frac{8}{9}\left[1-\left(\frac{1}{2}\right)^x\right] + \frac{1}{9}\left[1-\left(\frac{1}{2}\right)^{21-x}\right]$$

$$\Rightarrow \frac{dP(A)}{dx} = \frac{8}{9}\left[\left(\frac{1}{2}\right)^x \log 2\right] + \frac{1}{9}\left[-\left(\frac{1}{2}\right)^{21-x} \log 2\right]$$

Now we must have $\dfrac{dP(A)}{dx} = 0$

$\Rightarrow x = 12$, also $\dfrac{d^2P(A)}{dx^2} < 0$

Hence $P(A)$ is maximum where $x = 12$.

29. Of three independent events, the chance that only the first occurs is a, the chance that only second occurs is b and the chance that only third occurs is c. Show that the chances of three events are respectively $\dfrac{a}{a+x}$, $\dfrac{b}{b+x}$, $\dfrac{c}{c+x}$, where x is root of the equation $(a + x)(b + x)(c + x) = x^2$.

Solution: Let A, B, C be three independent events having probabilities p, q and r respectively.

Then according to the question, we have

P (only the first occurs) $= P(A \cap \bar{B} \cap \bar{C})$

[$\because$ A, B, C are independent]

$= P(A)\,P(\bar{B})P(\bar{C}) = p(1 - q)\,(1 - r) = a$ ... (1)

P(only the second occurs) $= P(\bar{A} \cap B \cap \bar{C})$

$= P(\bar{A})\,P(B)\,P(\bar{C}) = (1 - p)\,q(1 - r) = b$ ... (2)

and P(only the third occurs) $= P(\bar{A} \cap \bar{B} \cap C) = P(\bar{A})\,P(\bar{B})\,P(C) = (1 - p)\,(1 - q)\,r = c$ ... (3)

Multiplying (1), (2) and (3), then $pqr[(1 - p)\,(1 - q)\,(1 - r)]^2 = abc$

or $\dfrac{abc}{pqr} = [(1 - p)\,(1 - q)\,(1 - r)]^2 = x^2$ (say) ... (4)

$\therefore\ (1 - p)\,(1 - q)\,(1 - r) = x$ ... (5)

Dividing (1) by (5), we get $\frac{p}{1-p} = \frac{a}{x}$ or $px = a - ap$

$\therefore\ p = \frac{a}{(a+x)}$

Similarly, $q = \frac{b}{(b+x)}$ and $r = \frac{c}{(c+x)}$

Replacing the values of p, q and r in (4),

$$\Rightarrow \left\{\left(1-\frac{a}{a+x}\right)\left(1-\frac{b}{b+x}\right)\left(1-\frac{c}{c+x}\right)\right\}^2 = x^2$$

$$\Rightarrow \frac{(x^3)^2}{(a+x)^2(b+x)^2(c+x)^2} = x^2$$

$$\Rightarrow \frac{x^3}{(a+x)(b+x)(c+x)} = x$$

or $(a + x)(b + x)(c + x) = x^2$

Hence x is a root of the equation $(a + x)(b + x)(c + x) = x^2$

30. Out of $(2n + 1)$ tickets consecutively numbered, three are drawn at random. Find the chance that the numbers on them are in A.P.

Solution: Let us consider first $(2n + 1)$ natural numbers as $(2n + 1)$ consecutive numbers,

Let S be the sample space and E be the required event.

$$n(S) = {}^{2n+1}C_3 = \frac{(2n+1)2n(2n-1)}{1.2.3} = \frac{n(4n^2-1)}{3}$$

Let the three number drawn be a, b, c where $a < b < c$.

Common difference d	Triplets (a, b, c)	Number of triplets
1	(1, 2, 3), (2, 3, 4),....., (2n – 1, 2n, 2n + 1)	2n – 1
2	(1, 3, 5), (2, 4, 6),....., (2n – 3, 2n – 1, 2n + 1)	2n – 3
3	(1, 4, 7), (2, 5, 8),....., (2n – 5, 2n – 2, 2n + 1)	2n – 5
.....	....	.....
.....	....	.....
.....	....	.....
n – 1	(1, n, 2n – 1), (2, n + 1, 2n), (3, n + 2, 2n + 1)	3
n	(1, n + 1, 2n + 1)	1

$\therefore\ n(E) = 1 + 3 + ... + (2n - 5) + (2n - 3) + (2n - 1)$

$= \frac{n}{2}\{1 + 2n - 1\} = n^2$

$\therefore$ Required Probability

$$P(E) = \frac{n(E)}{n(S)} = \frac{n^2}{\frac{n(4n^2-1)}{3}} = \frac{3n}{(4n^2-1)}$$

Aliter: Let S be the sample space and E be the event containing favourable cases.

$$\therefore\ n(S) = {}^{2n+1}C_3 = \frac{(2n+1)2n(2n-1)}{1.2.3} = \frac{n(4n^2-1)}{3}$$

Let the three numbers a, b, c are drawn where $a < b < c$ and given a, b, c are in A.P.

$\therefore\ b = \frac{a+c}{2}$ or $2b = a + c$ ... (1)

It is clear from (1) a and c are both odd or both even. Out of $(2n + 1)$ tickets consecutively numbered either $(n + 1)$ of them will be odd and n of them will be even (If the numbers begin with an odd number) or $(n + 1)$ of them will be even and n of them will be odd (If the number begin with an even number).

$$\therefore\ n(E) = {}^{n+1}C_2 + {}^{n}C_2 = \frac{(n+1)n}{2} + \frac{n(n-1)}{2} = n^2$$

$\therefore$ Required probability

$$P(E) = \frac{n(E)}{n(S)} = \frac{n^2}{\frac{n(4n^2-1)}{3}} = \frac{3n}{(4n^2-1)}$$

31. Seven digits from the numbers 1, 2, 3, 4, 5, 6, 7, 8 and 9 are written in random order. Find the probability that this seven-digit number is divisible by 9.

Solution: Let a_1, a_2, a_3, a_4, a_5, a_6, a_7 be the seven digits and the remaining two be a_8 and a_9.

Let $a_1 + a_2 + a_3 + a_4 + a_5 + a_6 + a_7 = 9k,\ k \in \mathbb{Z}$ ...(1)

Also $a_1 + a_2 + a_3 + a_4 + ... + a_9 = 1 + 2 + 3 + 4 + ... + 9 = \frac{9 \times 10}{2} = 45$ ...(2)

Subtracting (1) from (2), then $a_8 + a_9 = 45 - 9k$ ...(3)

Since $a_1 + a_2 + a_3 + ... + a_7$ are divisible by 9 if and only if $a_8 + a_9$ is divisible by 9. Let S be the sample space and E be the event that the sum of the digits a_8 and a_9 is divisible by 9.

$\because\ a_8 + a_9 = 45 - 9k$

Maximum value of $a_8 + a_9 = 17$ and minimum value of $a_8 + a_9 = 3$

$\therefore\ 3 \le 45 - 9k \le 17$

$\Rightarrow -42 \le -9k \le -28 \Rightarrow \frac{42}{9} \ge k \ge \frac{28}{9}$

or $\frac{28}{9} \le k \le \frac{42}{9}$

Hence $k = 4$ ($\because$ k is positive integer)

$\therefore$ from (3) $a_8 + a_9 = 45 - 9(4) \Rightarrow a_8 + a_9 = 9$

Now possible pair of (a_8, a_9) can be {(1, 8), (2, 7), (3, 6), (4, 5)}

$\therefore$ $E = \{(1, 8), (2, 7), (3, 6), (4, 5)\}$

$\therefore$ $n(E) = 4$ and $n(S) = {}^9C_2 = 36$

$\therefore$ Required probability $P(E) = \dfrac{n(E)}{n(S)} = \dfrac{4}{36} = \dfrac{1}{9}$.

32. I write a letter to my friend and do not recieve a reply. It is known that one out of m letters does not reach its destination. What is the probability that my friend recieved the letter?
(It is certain that my friend would have replied, if he did recieve my letter)

Solution: $A_1 \equiv$ letter written to friend reaches its destination

$A_2 \equiv$ letter does not reach its destination

$E \equiv$ I don't receive a reply.

$P(E) = P(A_1)\ P(E/A_1) + P(A_2)\ P(E/A_2) = (1 - 1/m)$

$1/m + 1/m \times 1 = \dfrac{2m-1}{m^2}$; $P(A_1/E) = \dfrac{P(A_1 \cap E)}{P(E)} =$

$\dfrac{P(A_1)P(E/A_1)}{P(E)} = \dfrac{(1-1/m)1/m}{(2m-1)/m^2} = \dfrac{m-1}{2m-1}$

33. Given that $x + y = 2a$ where a is constant and that all values of x between 0 and $2a$ are equally likely, show that the chance that $xy > \dfrac{3}{4}a^2$ is $\dfrac{1}{2}$

Solution: Let PQ be a diameter of a circle with centre) 'O' and radius a. Take a point A at random on PQ

Let $AP = x$, $AQ = y$, then $x + y = 2a$, and all values of x between 0 to $2a$ equally likely.

Draw the ordinate AB, then $AB^2 = AP.AQ = xy$

If P', Q' are the mid-points of OP and OQ represently.

The ordinates at these points are equal to $a\sqrt{\dfrac{3}{4}}$.

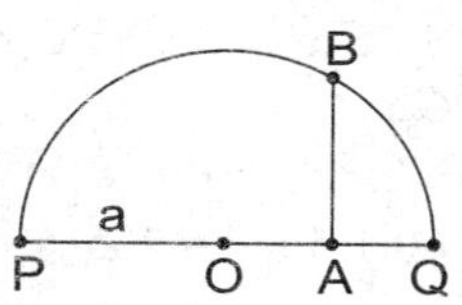

Hence $AB > a\sqrt{\dfrac{3}{4}}$ if and only if, A lies in " $P'Q'$ "

Hence the chance that $x\,y > \dfrac{3}{4}a^2$ is $\dfrac{PQ}{PQ}$ i.e., $\dfrac{1}{2}$

34. Suppose a sample consists of the integers 1, 2, 3,...., 2n. The probability of choosing an integer k is proportional to log k. Show that the conditional probability of choosing the integer 2, given that an even integer is chosen, is $\dfrac{\log 2}{[n \log 2 + \log(n!)]}$

Solution: Let E_i be the event that the integer $2i$ is drawn and A be the event that an even number is drawn, then (where $i = 1, 2, 3, \ldots, n$)

$A = E_1 \cup E_2 \cup \ldots\ldots \cup E_n$

$\therefore$ $P(A) = P(E_1 \cup E_2 \cup \ldots\ldots \cup E_n)$

$= P(E_1) + P(E_2) + \ldots + P(E_n)$ ... (1)

[$\because$ $E_1, E_2, \ldots\ldots, E_n$ are mutually exclusive]

But given $P(E_i) \propto \log 2i$

$\Rightarrow$ $P(E_i) = c \log 2i$, where c is a constant

$\therefore$ $P(A) = c \log 2 + c \log 4 + c \log 6 + \ldots + c \log 2n$ {from (1)}

$= c\,[\log 2 + \log 4 + \log 6 + \ldots\ldots + \log 2n]$

$= c \log (2.\,4.\,6, \ldots\ldots, 2n) = c \log\{2^n.\,(1.\,2.\,3, \ldots, n)\}$

$= c \log (2^n.\,n\,!) = c \log 2^n + c \log n!$

$= c\,(n \log 2 + \log n!)$

and let B be the event that integer 2 is chosen

Also $B = E_2$ $\therefore$ $A \cap B = E_2$ {$\because$ $E_2 \subseteq A$}

$\therefore$ $P(A \cap B) = P(E_2) = c \log 2$

$\therefore$ Required probability,

$P(B/A) = \dfrac{P(A \cap B)}{P(A)} = \dfrac{P(E_2)}{P(A)}$

$= \dfrac{c \log 2}{c\{n \log 2 + \log n!\}} = \dfrac{\log 2}{(n \log 2 + \log n!)}$

35. Out of $3n$ consective integers, three are selected at random. Find the chance that their sum is divisible by 3.

Solution: Let $3n$ consecutive integers (start with the integer m) are $m, m + 1, m + 2, \ldots, m + 3n - 1$

Now we write these $3n$ numbers in 3 rows as follows:

$m, m + 3, m + 6, \ldots\ m + 3n - 3$

$m + 1, m + 4, m + 7, \ldots\ m + 3n - 2$

$m + 2, m + 5, m + 8, \ldots\ m + 3n - 1$

The total number of ways of choosing 3 integers out of $3n$ is

$${}^{3n}C_3 = \frac{3n(3n-1)(3n-2)}{1.2.3} = \frac{n(3n-1)(3n-2)}{2}$$

The sum of the three numbers shall be divisible by 3 if and only if either all the three numbers are from the same row or all the three numbers are from different rows.

Therefore, the number of favourable ways is

$$3\,({}^nC_3) + ({}^nC_1)\,({}^nC_1)\,({}^nC_1) = \frac{3n(n-1)(n-2)}{1.2.3} + n^3$$

$$= \frac{3n^3 - 3n^2 + 2n}{2}$$

$\therefore$ The requried probability $= \dfrac{\text{Favourable ways}}{\text{Total ways}}$

$$= \frac{\dfrac{3n^3 - 3n^2 + 2n}{2}}{\dfrac{n(3n-1)(3n-2)}{2}} = \frac{3n^2 - 3n + 2}{(3n-1)(3n-2)}$$

36. In a test an examinee either guesses or copies or knows the answer to a multiple choice question which has 4 choices. The probability that he makes a guess is 1/3 and the probability that he copies is 1/6. The probability that his answer is correct (given that he copied it), is 1/8. Find the probability that he knew the answer to the question, given that he answered it correctly.

Solution: $P(g)$ = probability of guessing =1/3

$P(c)$ = probability of copying = 1/6

$P(k)$ = probability of knowing = 1 – 1/3 – 1/6 = 1/2

(Since the three-events g, c and k are mutually exclusive and exhaustive)

Let $P(w)$ = probability that answer is correct.

Then the probability that he answers correctly when he guesses is 1/4, i.e., $p\left(\dfrac{w}{g}\right) = \dfrac{1}{4}$

$P(w/c) = 1/8$, (given that he copied)

$P(w/k) = 1$ because it is certain that he answers correctly when he knows the answer.

$$P(k/w) = \frac{P(w/k).P(k)}{P(w/c)P(c) + P(w/k)P(k) + P(w/g)P(g)}$$

(using Baye' s theorem)

$$= \frac{1 \times \dfrac{1}{2}}{\left(\dfrac{1}{8}\cdot\dfrac{1}{6}\right) + \left(1 \times \dfrac{1}{2}\right) + \left(\dfrac{1}{4} \times \dfrac{1}{3}\right)} = \frac{24}{29}$$

37. Two squares are chosen at random from the small squares drawn on a chessboard. What is the chance that the two squares chosen have exactly one corner in common?

Solution: Total number of small squares on a chessboard = 64

$\therefore$ the total number of ways of selecting 2 squares $= n(S) = {}^{64}C_2$.

Two squares selected can have a corner common if they are selected from two consecutive rows (or columns). The number of ways to select two consecutive rows (or columns) = 7, because there are 8 rows (or columns) of small squares.

For each pair of two consecutive rows (or columns), the number of pairs of squares having exactly one common corner = 2 × 7 = 14.

$\therefore$ the number of favourable selections = $n(E) = 7 \times 14$.

$$= \frac{n(E)}{n(S)} = \frac{7 \times 14}{{}^{64}C_2} = \frac{7 \times 14 \times 2}{64 \times 63} = \frac{7}{144}$$

38. Five ordinary dies are rolled at random and the sum of the numbers shown on them is 16. What is the probability that the number shown on each is any one from 2, 3, 4 or 5?

Solution: If the number shown be integers x_1, x_2, x_3, x_4 and x_5, then $x_1 + x_2 + x_3 + x_4 + x_5 = 16$,

where $1 \le x_1 \le 6$; $1 \le x_2 \le 6$;......; $1 \le x_5 \le 6$.

The number of solutions of this equation

= coefficient of x^{16} in $(x + x^2 + x^3 + x^4 + x^5 + x^6)^5$

= coefficient of x^{11} in $(1 + x + x^2 + x^3 + x^4 + x^5)^5$

= coeffcient of x^{11} in $\left(\dfrac{1-x^6}{1-x}\right)^5$ = coeffcient of x^{11} in

$(1 - x^6)^5 . (1 - x)^{-5}$

= coefficient of x^{11} in $\{{}^5C_0 - {}^5C_1x^6 + {}^5C_2x^{12} - \ldots\ldots\} \times \{{}^4C_0 + {}^5C_1x + {}^6C_2x^2 + \ldots + {}^{15}C_{11}x^{11} + \ldots$ to $\infty\}$

$= {}^5C_0 . {}^{15}C_{11} - {}^5C_1 . {}^9C_5 = \dfrac{15.14.13.12}{24} - 5\dfrac{9.8.7.6}{24}$

= 15. 7. 13 – 10. 9. 7 = 1365 – 630 = 735

$\therefore\ n(S) = 735$

Now, $n(E)$ = the number of integral solutions of $x_1 + x_2 + \ldots\ldots + x_5 = 16$

where $2 \le x_1 \le 5$, $2 \le x_2 \le 5$,..........., $2 \le x_5 \le 5$

= coefficient of x^{16} in $(x^2 + x^3 + x^4 + x^5)^5$

= coefficient of x^6 in $(1 + x + x^2 + x^3)^5$ = coefficient of x^6 in $(1 + x)^5 . (1 + x^2)^5$ = coefficient of x^6 in $\{{}^5C_0 + {}^5C_1x + {}^5C_2x^2 + \ldots + {}^5C_5x^5\} \times \{{}^5C_0 + {}^5C_1x^2 + {}^5C_2x^4 + \ldots + {}^5C_5x^{10}\}$

$= {}^5C_0 . {}^5C_3 + {}^5C_2 . {}^5C_2 + {}^5C_4 . {}^5C_1$

= 10 + 10 × 10 + 5 × 5 = 135

$\therefore$ the required probability $= \dfrac{n(E)}{n(S)} = \dfrac{135}{735} = \dfrac{9}{49}$

39. Two non-negative integers are chosen at random from the set of non-negative integers with replacement. What is the probability that the sum of their squares is divisible by 10?

Solution: Let the two non-negative integers be x, y.

Now $x^2 + y^2$ will be divisible by 10 if the sum of digits in the units places of x and y is 0 or 10.

The units place of x as well as y can be filled in 10 ways any one of 0, 1, 2, 3,....., 9 can be used

$\therefore$ the number of ways for the number x, y to have a digit each in their units places = $10 \times 10 = 100$.

The digits in the units place of x^2 as well as y^2 can be from 0, 1, 4, 5, 6, 9 because the square of any number can have only one of these digits in the units place.

Sum of the digits in units places of x^2 and y^2 should be 0 or 10.

So, getting back to x and y, if x has 0 in units place, y must have 0 in units place

if x has 1 or 9 in units place, y must have 3 or 7 in units place.

if x has 2 or 8 in units place, y must have 4 or 6 in units place.

if x has 5 in units place, y must have 5 in units place.

if x has 4 or 6 in units place, y must have 2 or 8 in units place.

if x has 3 or 7 in units place, y must have 1 or 9 in units place.

$\therefore$ the number of ways for the numbers x, y to have a digit in their units places whose sum is 0 or 10

$= 1 \times 1 + 2 \times 2 + 2 \times 2 + 1 \times 1 + 2 \times 2 + 2 \times 2 = 18$

$\therefore$ the required probability $= \dfrac{18}{100} = \dfrac{9}{50}$

40. The sum of the digits of a seven-digit number is 59. Find the probability that this number is divisible by 11.

Solution: Since $7 \times 8 = 56$ and the sum of seven digits is 59, clearly at least three of the digits must be 9.

Obviously, the seven digits of the number will be as follows:

(a) 9, 9, 9, 8, 8, 8, 8 (b) 9, 9, 9, 9, 8, 8, 7

(c) 9, 9, 9, 9, 9, 7, 7 (d) 9, 9, 9, 9, 9, 8, 6

(e) 9, 9, 9, 9, 9, 9, 5

$\therefore$ the total number of ways to form a seven-digit number whose sum of digits is 59.

$$= \frac{7!}{3!4!} + \frac{7!}{4!2!} + \frac{7!}{5!2!} + \frac{7!}{5!} + \frac{7!}{6!}$$

$$= \frac{7.6.5}{3.2} + \frac{7.6.5}{2} + \frac{7.6}{2} + 7.6 + 7 = 210 \quad \text{... (1)}$$

A number is divisible by 11 if the difference of the sum of the digits in odd places and that of the digits in even places is divisible by 11.

As the number is of seven digits we must have (for favourable case), sum of four digits in odd places – sum of three digits in even places.

= 0, 11, 22, 33, 44, 55.

If the two sums are denoted by x and y respectively, then

$$\left.\begin{array}{l} x+y=59 \\ x-y=0 \end{array}\right\} \text{........(i) or } \left.\begin{array}{l} x+y=59 \\ x-y=11 \end{array}\right\} \text{........(ii)}$$

$$\text{or } \left.\begin{array}{l} x+y=59 \\ x-y=22 \end{array}\right\} \text{........(iii) or } \left.\begin{array}{l} x+y=59 \\ x-y=33 \end{array}\right\} \text{........(iv)}$$

$$\text{or } \left.\begin{array}{l} x+y=59 \\ x-y=44 \end{array}\right\} \text{......(v) or } \left.\begin{array}{l} x+y=59 \\ x-y=55 \end{array}\right\} \text{........(vi)}$$

Clearly, (i), (iii) and (v), do not give integral values of x and y.

(ii) $\Rightarrow x = 35, y = 24$; (iv) $\Rightarrow x = 46, y = 13$

(vi) $\Rightarrow x = 57, y = 2$.

Obviously, from (a),(b),(c),(d) and (e) we get, sum of three digits y cannot be 2 or 13.

Hence, only favourable case takes place when the sum of four digits in the odd places = 35 and the sum of the three digits in even places = 24.

$\therefore$ in the favourable numbers we will get,

9, 9, 9, 8 in odd places and 8, 8, 8 in even places

or 9, 9, 9, 8 in odd places and 9, 8, 7 in even places

or 9, 9, 9, 8 in odd places and 9, 9, 6 in even places

$\therefore$ the count of numbers divisible by 11

$$= \frac{4!}{3!} + \frac{4!}{3!} \times 3! + \frac{4!}{3!} \times \frac{3!}{2!} = 4 + 24 + 12 = 40 \quad \text{... (2)}$$

$\therefore$ from (1) and (2), we get the required probability

$$= \frac{40}{210} = \frac{4}{21}$$

41. Two numbers x and y are chosen at random from the set {1, 2, 3,....., 3n}. Find the probability that $x^2 - y^2$ is divisible by 3.

Solution: $x^2 - y^2 = (x + y)(x - y)$ and 3 is a prime number.

$\therefore$ $x^2 - y^2$ is divisible by 3 if $x + y$ or $x - y$ is divisible by 3.

Now, $\{1, 2, 3,....., 3n\} = \{3, 6, 9,......, 3n\} \cup \{1, 4, 7,....., 3n-2\} \cup \{2, 5, 8,......, 3n - 1\} = A \cup B \cup C$ (say).

Clearly, if x, y are selected from A, then both $x + y$ and $x - y$ are divisible by 3; and, if x, y are selected one from B and the other from C then $x + y$ is divisible by 3.

∴ the probability of $x^2 - y^2$ is divisible by 3
= probability of selecting x, y from A + probability of selecting x, y; one from B and the other from C

$$= \frac{^nC_2}{^{3n}C_2} + \frac{^nC_1 \times {}^nC_1}{^{3n}C_2} \times 2 = \frac{n-1}{3(3n-1)} + \frac{2n^2}{3n(3n-1)} \times 2$$

$$= \frac{n-1}{3(3n-1)} + \frac{4n}{3(3n-1)} = \frac{5n-1}{3(3n-1)}$$

42. For the three independent events A, B and C, the probability of exactly one of the events A or B occuring is equal to the probability of exactly one of the events B or C occuring is equal to the probability of exactly one of the events C or A occuring is equal to p. If the probability of all the events occuring simultaneously be p^2 where $0 < p < 0.5$, then find the probability of at least one of the events A, B and C occuring.

Solution: The probability of exactly one of the events A or B occuring
$= P(A \cap B') + P(A' \cap B) = P(A).\ P(B') + P(A').\ P(B)$
$= P(A).\ \{1 - P(B)\} + \{1 - P(A)\}.\ P(B)$
∴ $p = P(A) + P(B) - 2P(A).\ P(B)$ ... (1)
Similarly, $p = P(B) + P(C) - 2P(B).\ P(C)$ .... (2)
$p = P(C) + P(A) - 2P(C).\ P(A)$ ... (3)
$(1) - (2) \Rightarrow 0 = P(A) - P(C) - 2P(B).\{P(A) - P(C)\}$
∴ $\{P(A) - P(C)\}\ \{1 - 2P(B)\} = 0$
∴ $P(A) = P(C)$ or $P(B) = \frac{1}{2}$

If $P(B) = \frac{1}{2}$; $(1) \Rightarrow p = \frac{1}{2}$

But $0 < p < \frac{1}{2}$ (given) ∴ $P(A) = P(C)$;
similarly, $P(B) = P(C)$.
Therefore $P(A) = P(B) = P(C) = x$ (say)
Now, $P(A \cup B \cup C)$
$= \Sigma P(A) - \Sigma\{P(A).\ P(B)\} + P(A \cap B \cap C)$
$= 3x - 3x^2 + p^2$ (from question)
Also, from (1), $p = x + x - 2x.\ x = 2x - 2x^2$

$\Rightarrow x - x^2 = \frac{p}{2}$

∴ $P(A \cup B \cup C) = 3(x - x^2) + p^2$

$= \frac{3p}{2} + p^2 = \frac{1}{2}p(3 + 2p)$

43. The decimal parts of the logarithms of two numbers taken at random are found to six places of decimal. What is the chance that the second can be subtracted from the first without "borrowing"?

Solution: For each column of the two numbers,
$n(S)$ = number of ways to fill the two places by the digits 0,1,2,......,9 = 10 × 10 = 100
Let E be the event of subtracting in a column without borrowing. If the pair of digits be (x, y) in the column where x is in the first number and y is in the second number, then

E = {(0,0), (1,0), (2,0),.....,(9,0), (1,1), (2,1),..... (9,1), (2,2), (3,2),.........(9,2), (3,3), (4,3),.........(9,3), ... (8,8), (9,8), (9,9)}

$n(E) = 10 + 9 + 8 + \ldots + 2 + 1 = \frac{10.11}{2} = 55$

∴ the proability of subtracting without borrowing in each column $= \frac{55}{100}$

∴ the required probability $= \left(\frac{55}{100}\right)^6 = \left(\frac{11}{20}\right)^6$

44. In a multiple-choice question, there are four alternative answers of which one or more answers are correct. A candidate gets marks if he ticks all the correct answers. The candidate, being ignorant about the answers, decides to tick at random. How many attempts at least should he be allowed so that the probability of his getting marks in the question may exceed $\frac{1}{5}$?

Solution: Each answer may be marked or unmarked.
∴ the number of ways to tick answers = $2^4 - 1$.
(∵ the candidate cannot keep all answers unmarked)
As there is only one way of marking correctly, the probability of getting marks in one attempt

$= \frac{1}{2^4 - 1} = \frac{1}{15}$

∴ the probability of getting no marks in one attempt

$= 1 - \frac{1}{15} = \frac{14}{15}$

∴ the probability of getting no marks in n attempts

$= \left(\frac{14}{15}\right)^n$

∴ the probability of getting marks in n attempts

$= 1 - \left(\frac{14}{15}\right)^n$

Now, $1 - \left(\frac{14}{15}\right)^n > \frac{1}{5}$ or $\frac{4}{5} > \left(\frac{14}{15}\right)^n$ .....(1)

Clearly $\frac{4}{5} < \frac{14}{15}, \frac{4}{5} < \left(\frac{14}{15}\right)^2, \frac{4}{5} < \left(\frac{14}{15}\right)^3,$

$\frac{4}{5} > \left(\frac{14}{15}\right)^4, \frac{4}{5} > \left(\frac{14}{15}\right)^5, \ldots\ldots$

$\therefore$ from (1), $n = 4, 5, \ldots\ldots$, So the least value of $n = 4$,

$\therefore$ the candidate should be allowed at least 4 attempts.

45. Three critics review a book, odds in favour of the book are 5 : 2, 4 : 3 and 3 : 4 respectively for the three critics. Find the probability that majority are in favour of the book.

Solution: Let the critics be A, B and C. Let $P(A)$ denote the probability of the critic A to be in favour of the book, etc.

$\because$ the odds in favour of the book for the critic $A = 5 : 2$,

$P(A) = \frac{5}{5+2} = \frac{5}{7}$. Similarly,

$P(B) = \frac{4}{7}$ and $P(C) = \frac{3}{7}$

Clearly, the event of majority being in favour = the event of at least two critics being in favour $\therefore$ the required probability

$= P(ABC) + P(AB\bar{C}) + P(A\bar{B}C) + P(\bar{A}BC)$

$= P(A). P(B). P(C) + P(A). P(B). P(\bar{C}) + P(A). P(\bar{B}). P(C) + P(\bar{A}). P(B). P(C)$

$$= \frac{5}{7}.\frac{4}{7}.\frac{3}{7} + \frac{5}{7}.\frac{4}{7}\left(1-\frac{3}{7}\right) + \frac{5}{7}.\left(1-\frac{4}{7}\right).\frac{3}{7} + \left(1-\frac{5}{7}\right).\frac{4}{7}.\frac{3}{7}$$

$$= \frac{1}{7^3}(60 + 80 + 45 + 24) = \frac{209}{343}.$$

46. A and B play a game of tennis. The situation of the game is as follows:

If one scores two consecutive points after a deuce he wins; if loss of a point is followed or preceded by win of a point, it is deuce. The chance of a server to win a point is $\frac{2}{3}$. The game is at deuce and A is serving. What is the chance that A will win the game?

Solution: Let E = the event of A winning a point.

Here $P(E) = \frac{2}{3}$; $\therefore$ $P(\bar{E}) = 1 - \frac{2}{3} = \frac{1}{3}$.

The event of deuce $= D = (E \cap \bar{E}) \cup (\bar{E} \cap E)$

$\therefore$ The probability of a deuce

$= P(D) = P\{(E \cap \bar{E}) \cup (\bar{E} \cap E)\}$

$= P(E) . P(\bar{E}) + P(\bar{E}).P(E) = \frac{2}{3}.\frac{1}{3} + \frac{1}{3}.\frac{2}{3} = \frac{4}{9}$.

The event of A winning the game = the event of any number of deuce followed by two consecutive points won by A.

$\therefore$ The required probability

$$= \left(\frac{2}{3}\right)^2 + \frac{4}{9}\left(\frac{2}{3}\right)^2 + \left(\frac{4}{9}\right)^2\left(\frac{2}{3}\right)^2 + \left(\frac{4}{9}\right)^3\left(\frac{2}{3}\right)^2 \text{ to } \infty.$$

$$= \left(\frac{2}{3}\right)^2 \left\{1 + \frac{4}{9} + \left(\frac{4}{9}\right)^2 + \left(\frac{4}{9}\right)^3 + \ldots\ldots \text{ to } \infty\right\}$$

$$= \frac{4}{9}.\frac{1}{1-4/9} = \frac{4}{9}.\frac{9}{5} = \frac{4}{5}$$

47. There are $n + 3 (n > 1)$ seats numbered 1, 2, 3,......, $n + 3$. There are also $n + 3$ persons who are holding tickets numbered 1, 2, 3,...... $n + 3$. They take seats at random. Find the probability that exactly three persons take seats having the same numbers as that in their tickets.

Solution: The number of ways in which 3 persons can take seats having the same numbers as that in their tickets $= {}^{n+3}C_3$. Of these, let in one of the ways, persons having the tickets numbered $n + 1$, $n + 2$ and $n + 3$ take their corresponding seats.

The remaining n persons are to take n seats such that all of them are in the seats having number different from that of their ticket.

$$\therefore \quad P(E) = \frac{{}^{n+3}C_3\left(n!\left(1 - \frac{1}{1!} + \frac{1}{2!} - \frac{1}{3!} + \ldots + \right)(-1)^n.\frac{1}{n!}\right)}{(n+3!)}$$

$$= \frac{1}{3!}\left[1 - \frac{1}{1!} + \frac{1}{2!} + \frac{1}{3!} + \ldots + (-1)^n.\frac{1}{n!}\right]$$

48. A wire of length ℓ is cut into three pieces. Find the probability that the three pieces form a triangle.

Solution: Method 1: The elementary event w is characterized by two parameters x and y [since $z = \ell - (x + y)$]. We depict the event by a point on $x - y$ plane (as shown in figure). The conditions $x > 0$, $y > 0$, $x + y < l$ are imposed on the quantities x and y; the sample space is the intetrior of a right triangle with ℓ units legs i.e., $S_w = \ell^2/2$. The condition A requiring to the following two conditions

(i) The sum of any two sides is larger than the third side;

(ii) the difference between any two sides is smaller than the third side. This condition is associated with the triangular domain A. (as shown in figure) with area $S_A = (1/2)(\ell^2/4) = \ell^2/8$

$$P(A) = \frac{S_A}{S_w} = \frac{(\ell^2/8)}{(\ell^2/2)} = \frac{1}{4}.$$

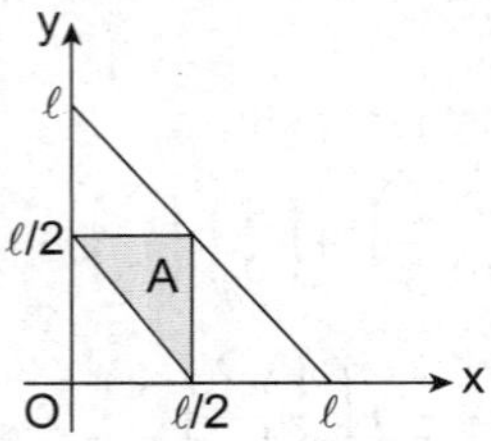

Method 2: Let the lengths of three parts of the wire be x, y and $\ell - (x + y)$. Then $x > 0, y > 0$ and $\ell - (x + y) > 0$ i.e., $x + y < \ell$ or $y < \ell - x$

Since a triangle, the sum of any two sides is greater than thirds side, so $x + y > \ell - (x + y) \Rightarrow y > \ell/2 - x$

and $x + \ell - (x + y) > y \Rightarrow y < \ell/2$

and $y + \ell - (x + y) > x \Rightarrow x < \ell/2$

$\Rightarrow \ell/2 - x < y < \ell/2$ and $0 < x < \ell/2$

So required Probability

$$= \frac{\int_0^{\ell/2}\int_{\ell/2-x}^{\ell/2} dy\,dx}{\int_0^{\ell}\int_0^{\ell-x} dy\,dx} = \frac{\int_0^{\ell/2}\{\ell/2 - (\ell/2 - x)\}dx}{\int_0^{\ell}(\ell - x)dx}$$

$$= \frac{\int_0^{\ell/2} x\,dx}{\int_0^{\ell}(\ell - x)dx} = \frac{\ell^2/8}{\ell^2/2} = \frac{1}{4}$$

SECTION–II

OBJECTIVE SOLVED EXAMPLES

1. A box contains 15 transistors, 5 of which are defective. An inspector takes out one transistor at random, examines it for defects, and replaces it. After it has been replaced another inspector does the same thing, and then so does a third inspector. The probability that at least one of the inspector finds a defective transistor, is equal to

(a) 1/27 (b) 8/27
(c) 19/27 (d) 26/27

Solution: (c) Let A_i be the event that i^{th} inspector finds a defective transistor. Hence required probability is

$P(A_1 \cup A_2 \cup A_3) = 1 - P((A_1 \cup A_2 \cup A_3)^c)$

$= 1 - P(A_1^c \cap A_2^c \cap A_3^c) = 1 - P(A_1^c).\, P(A_2^c).\, P(A_3^c)$

(As A_1, A_2, A_3 are mutually indepenent events.)

$$= 1 - \frac{10}{15}.\frac{10}{15}.\frac{10}{15} = 19/27 \;[\because\; P(\bar{A}_i) = 10/15 = 2/3]$$

2. The probability that a man aged x years will die in a year is 'p'. The probability that out of 'n' men M_1, M_2,.......M_n, each aged years x, M_1 will die and be the first to die is:

(a) $1/n^2$ (b) $1 - (1 - p)^n$
(c) $\frac{1}{n^2[1-(1-p)^n]}$ (c) $\frac{1}{n}[1-(1-p)^n]$

Solution: (d) Probability that a man aged x dies in a year $= p$. Therefore the proabability that at least one man dies in a year $= 1-(1-p)^n$ i.e., $1 - p$ (no man dies in a year). Probability that out of n men, M_1 is first to die $= 1/n$ since this event is independent. Hence, the probability that M_1 dies in the year and he is first to die $= \frac{1-(1-p)^n}{n}$

3. One ticket is selected at random from 100 tickets numbered 00, 01, 02,...., 99. Suppose X and Y are the sum and product of the digit found on the ticket $P(X = 7; Y = 0)$ is given by

(a) 2/3 (b) 2/19
(c) 1/50 (d) None of these

Solution: (c) We have $(X = 7) = \{07, 16, 25, 34, 43, 52, 61, 70\}$ and $(Y = 0) = \{00, 01, 02,....., 10, 20, 30,.... 90\}$

Thus $(X = 7) \cap (Y = 0) = \{07, 70\}$

$$\therefore\; P(X = 7; Y = 0) = \frac{2}{100} = \frac{1}{50}$$

4. If X and Y are independent binomial variates of binomial distribution $B(5, 1/2)$ and $B(7, 1/2)$ respectively, then $P(X + Y = 3)$ is

(a) 55/1024 (b) 55/4098
(c) 55/2048 (d) None of these

Solution: (a) $P(X + Y = 3) = P(X = 0, Y = 3) + P(X = 1, Y = 2) + P(X = 2, Y = 1) + P(X = 3, Y = 0)$
$= P(X = 0)\, P(Y = 3) + P(X = 1)\, P(Y = 2) + P(X = 2)\, P(Y = 1) + P(X = 3)\, P(Y = 0)$ (X and Y are independent)

$= {}^5C_0\ (1/2)^5\ {}^7C_3\ (1/2)^7 + {}^5C_1\ (1/2)^5\ {}^7C_2\ (1/2)^7 + {}^5C_2\ (1/2)^5;\ {}^7C_1\ (1/2)^7 + {}^5C_3\ (1/2)^5\ {}^7C_0\ (1/2)^7$

$= (1/2)^{12}\ \{(1)\ (35) + (5)\ (21) + (10)\ (7) + (10)\ (1)\}$

$= 220/2^{12} = 55/1024$

5. If $\frac{1+4p}{4}, \frac{1-p}{2}, \frac{1-2p}{2}$ are probabilities of three mutually exclusive events, then

(a) $1/3 \le p \le 1/2$ (b) $1/3 \le p \le 2/3$
(c) $1/6 \le p \le 1/2$ (d) None of these

Solution: (d) As $\frac{1+4p}{4}, \frac{1-p}{2}, \frac{1-2p}{2}$ are probabilities of three mutually exclusive events, we must have

$0 \le \frac{1+4p}{4} \le 1, 0 \le \frac{1-p}{2} \le 1, 0 \le \frac{1-2p}{2} \le 1$

and $0 \le \frac{1+4p}{4} + \frac{1-p}{2} + \frac{1-2p}{2} \le 1$

$\Rightarrow -1/4 \le p \le 3/4, -1 \le p \le 1, -1/2 \le p \le 1/2$ and $1/2 \le p \le 5/2$

$\Rightarrow$ max $\{-1/4, -1, -1/2, 1/2\} < p \le$ min $\{3/4, 1, 1/2, 5/2\}$

$\Rightarrow 1/2 \le p \le 1/2 \Rightarrow p = 1/2$

6. A man is known to speak the truth 3 out of 4 times. He throws a die and reports that it is a six. The probability that it is actually a six is

(a) $\frac{3}{8}$ (b) $\frac{1}{5}$
(c) $\frac{3}{4}$ (d) None of these

Solution: (a) Let E denotes the event that a six occurs and A the event that the man reports that it is a six.

We have $P(E) = \frac{1}{6}, P(E') = \frac{5}{6}, P(A/E) = \frac{3}{4}$

and $P(A/E') = \frac{1}{4}$

$\therefore$ By Baye's theorem

$$P(E/A) = \frac{P(E)\ P(A/E)}{P(E)P(A/E) + P(E')P(A/E')}$$

$$\Rightarrow \frac{1/6 \times 3/4}{1/6 \times 3/4 + 5/6 \times 1/4} = \frac{3}{8}$$

7. A die is thrown $(2n + 1)$ times, $n \in N$. The probability that faces with even numbers show odd number of times is

(a) $\frac{2n+1}{2n+3}$ (b) less that 1/2
(c) greater than 1/2 (d) None of these

Solution: (d) Probability of showing even number in a throw = 3/6 = 1/2

$\therefore$ Required probability

$= {}^{2n+1}C_1.\ 1/2.(1/2)^{2n} + {}^{2n+1}C_3.\ (1/2)^3.\ (1/2)^{2n-2} + ... + {}^{2n+1}C_{2n+1}(1/2)^{2n+1}$

$= (1/2)^{2n-1}\ \{{}^{2n+1}C_1 + {}^{2n+1}C_3 + ... + {}^{2n+1}C_{2n+1}\}$

$= \frac{1}{2^{2n+1}} \times 2^{2n+1-1} = 1/2$

8. A natural number x is chosen at random from the first one hundred natural numbers. The probability that $\frac{(x-20)(x-40)}{(x-30)} < 0$ is

(a) 1/50 (b) 3/50
(c) 7/25 (d) 9/50

Solution: (c) $x \in N$, Total ways $= {}^{100}C_1 = 100$

$\Rightarrow n(S) = 100$

20 30 40
– + – +

$\frac{(x-20)(x-40)}{(x-30)} < 0 \therefore x \in (-\infty, 20) \cup (30, 40)$

$\therefore E = \{1, 2, 3,....19, 31, 32, 33,......, 39\}$

$\Rightarrow n(E) = 28$

$\therefore$ Required probability = 28/100 = 7/25

9. A number of six digits is written down at random. Probability that sum of digits of the number be even is

(a) 1/2 (b) 3/8
(c) 3/7 (d) None of these

Solution: (a) Let $x_1\ x_2\ x_3\ x_4\ x_5\ x_6$ be the number then each of x_1, x_2, x_3, x_4, x_5 has 9, 10, 10, 10, 10 choices respectively. Now summing these five digits the sum is either odd or even. If it is odd, take $x_6 \in \{1, 3, 5, 7, 9\}$ and if it is even, take $x_6 \in \{0, 2, 4, 6, 8\}$ so that the sum of six digits becomes even. Thus number of desired type of numbers $= 9 \times 10^4 \times 5$.

Thus $P(E) = \frac{9 \times 10 \times 5}{9 \times 10} = \frac{1}{2}$

10. Two small squares on a chess board are chosen at random. Probability that they have a common side is

(a) 1/3 (b) 1/9
(c) 1/18 (d) None of these

Solution: (c) There are 64 small squares on a chess board.

$\Rightarrow$ Total number of ways to choose two squares $= {}^{64}C_2 = 32.63$

For favourable ways we must choose two consecutive small squares for any row or any columns

$\Rightarrow$ Number of favourable ways = (7. 8) 2

$\Rightarrow$ Required Probability $= \frac{7.8.2}{32.63} = \frac{1}{18}$

11. A bag contains 17 tickets numbered 1 to 17. A ticket is drawn and replaced, then one more ticket is drawn and replaced. Probability that first drawn number is even and second is odd, is

(a) $\frac{81}{289}$ (b) $\frac{72}{289}$

(c) $\frac{64}{289}$ (d) None of these

Solution: (b) Let A be the event that first drawn number is even and B be event that the second number drawn number is odd.

Total number of even numbers = [17/2] = 8

$\Rightarrow P(A) = \frac{8}{17}$ and $P(B) = \frac{9}{17} \Rightarrow P(A \cap B) = \frac{72}{289}$

12. A die is thrown three times and the sum of three numbers obtained is 15. The probability of first throw being four is

(a) 1/18 (b) 1/5

(c) 4/5 (d) 17/18

Solution: (b) If first throw is four then sum of numbers appearing on last two throws must be equal to eleven. That means last two throws are (6, 5) or (5, 6)

Now there are 10 ways to get the sum as 15.

i.e., {(4, 5, 6), (4, 6, 5),..., (3, 6, 6)}

$\Rightarrow$ Required Probability $= \frac{2}{10} = \frac{1}{5}$

13. Fifteen coupons are numbered 1, 2, 3,...., 15. Seven coupons are selected at random one at a time with replacement. The probability that the largest number appearing on the selected coupon is 9, is

(a) $\left(\frac{9}{16}\right)^5$ (b) $\left(\frac{8}{15}\right)^7$

(c) $\left(\frac{3}{5}\right)^7$ (d) None of these

Solution: (d) Total ways = $(15)^7$

For favorable ways, we must select 7 coupons numbered from 1 to 9 so that 9 is selected atleast once. Thus total number of favourable ways are $9^7 - 8^7$

$\Rightarrow$ Required probability $= \frac{9^7 - 8^7}{15^7}$

14. A fair die is thrown until a score of less than 5 points is obtained. The probability of obtaining not less than 2 points on the last thrown is

(a) 3/4 (b) 5/6

(c) 4/5 (d) 1/3

Solution: (a) Score less than 5 means the occurence of 1,2,3, or 4. now on the last throw we should not obtain a score less than 2 i.e., one. Clearly the favourable outcomes are 2,3 or 4. Thus the required probability = 3/4

15. A fair die is tossed eight times. Probability that on the eighth throw a third six is observed is

(a) ${}^8C_3 \frac{5^5}{6^8}$ (b) $\frac{{}^7C_2 5^5}{6^8}$

(c) $\frac{{}^7C_2 5^5}{6^7}$ (d) None of these

Solution: (b) Third six occurs on 8th trial. It means that in first 7 trials we must have exactly 2 sixes and 8th trial must result in a six

$\Rightarrow$ Required probability $= {}^7C_2\ (1/6)^2.\ (5/6)^5.\ (1/6)$

$= \frac{{}^7C_2 5^5}{6^8}$

16. If the papers of 4 students can be checked by any one of the 7 teachers, then the probability that all the 4 papers are checked by exactly 2 teachers is

(a) 2/7 (b) $\frac{32}{343}$

(c) $\frac{12}{49}$ (d) None of these

Solution: (d) Total number of ways in which 4 papers can be distributed among 7 teachers = 7^4 ways

Now exactly 2 teachers out of 7 can be chosen in ${}^7C_2$ ways. And total number of ways in which 4 papers can be given to these 2 teachers (each one getting atleast one) = $(2^4 - 2) = 14$

$\Rightarrow$ Total number of ways in which exactly 2 teachers check all four papers $= {}^7C_2.14 = 21.14$

$\Rightarrow$ Required probability $= \frac{21.14}{7^4} = \frac{3.2}{7^2} = \frac{6}{49}$

17. A number is chosen at random from the numbers 10 to 99. By seeing the number a man will laugh if product of the digits is 12. If he choose three numbers with replacement, then the probability that he will laugh at least once is

(a) $1-\left(\frac{3}{5}\right)^3$ (b) $\left(\frac{43}{45}\right)^3$

(c) $1-\left(\frac{4}{25}\right)^3$ (d) $1-\left(\frac{43}{45}\right)^3$

Solution: (d) There can be four such numbers, i.e., 43, 34, 62, 26

Whose product of digits is 12

$\Rightarrow$ Probability that the man will laugh by seeing the chosen numbers $= \frac{4}{90} = \frac{2}{45}$

$\Rightarrow$ Required Probability $= 1-\left(1-\frac{2}{45}\right)^3 = 1-\left(\frac{43}{45}\right)^3$

18. If head means one and tail means two, then coefficient of quadratic equation $ax^2 + bx + c = 0$ are chosen by tossing three fair coins. The probability that roots of the equations are imaginary is

(a) 5/8 (b) 3/8

(c) 7/8 (d) 1/8

Solution: (c) $b^2 - 4ac < 0$

For $b = 1$ any a and c which can be chosen in 4 ways

For $b = 2$ either $a = 1, c = 2$

or $a = 2, c = 1$ or $a = 2, c = 2$

$\Rightarrow$ Required Probability = 7/8

19. There are m persons sitting in a row. Two of them are selected at random. The probability that the two selected persons are not together is

(a) $\frac{2}{m}$ (b) $1-\frac{2}{m}$

(c) $\frac{m(m-1)}{(m+1)(m+2)}$ (d) None of these

Solution: (b) Total number of ways of selecting two persons out of m is $\frac{m(m\ \ 1)}{}$

Number of ways in which the two selected persons are together is $(m - 1)$

Therefore, number of ways in which the two selected persons are not together is

$${}^mC_2-(m-1)=\frac{(m-1)(m-2)}{2}$$

Thus the probability of the required event is

$$\frac{(m-1)(m-2)/2}{m(m-1)/2}=\frac{m-2}{m}=1-\frac{2}{m}$$

20. For two events A and B, if $p(A) = p(A/B) = 1/4$ and $p(B/A) = 1/2$, then

(a) A and B are dependent

(b) A and B are mutually exclusive

(c) $p(A'/B) = \frac{3}{4}$

(d) $p=\left(\frac{B'}{A'}\right)=\frac{1}{2}$

Solution: (c, d) We have $p(A) = p(A/B) = \frac{p(A\cap B)}{p(B)}$

$\Rightarrow p(A \cap B) = p(A)p(B)$

Therefore A and B are indepedent

Since $p(A \cap B) = p(A)\,p(B/A) = \left(\frac{1}{4}\right)\left(\frac{1}{2}\right)=\frac{1}{8}\neq 0$

A and B cannot be mutually exclusive

As A and B are independent $P\left(\frac{\bar{B}}{\bar{A}}\right)=P(\bar{B})$

$\Rightarrow P\left(\frac{\bar{B}}{\bar{A}}\right)=1-P(B)=1-\frac{1}{2}=\frac{1}{2}$;

Also $P\left(\frac{A'}{B}\right)=\frac{P(A'\cap B)}{P(B)}$

$$=\frac{P(B)-P(A\cap B)}{P(B)}1-P\left(\frac{A}{B}\right)=1-\frac{1}{4}=\frac{3}{4}$$

21. A student appears for tests, I, II and III. The student is sucessful if he passes either in tests I and II or tests I and III. The probabilities of the student passing in tests I, II, III are p, q and 1/2, respectively. If the probability that the student is successful is 1/2, then

(a) $p = 1, q = 0$

(b) $p = 2/3, q = 1/2$

(c) $p = 3/5, q = 2/3$

(d) there are infinitely many values of p and q

Solution: (a, b, c, d) Let A, B and C be the events that the student is successful in test I, II and III respectively. Then P (the student is successful)

$= P[(A \cap B \cap C') \cup (A \cap B' \cap C) \cup (A \cap B \cap C)]$

$= P(A \cap B \cap C') + P(A \cap B' \cap C) + P(A \cap B \cap C)$

$= P(A) . P(B) . P(C') + P(A) . P(B') . P(C) + P(A) . P(B) . P(C)$ [$\because A$, B and C are independent]

$$= pq\left(1-\frac{1}{2}\right)+p(1-q)\left(\frac{1}{2}\right)+(pq)\left(\frac{1}{2}\right)$$

$$=\frac{1}{2}[pq+p(1-q)+pq]=\frac{1}{2}p(1+q)$$

$\therefore \quad \frac{1}{2}=\frac{1}{2}p(1+q) \qquad \Rightarrow p(1+q)=1$

This equation is satisfied for all pairs of values in (a), (b) and (c). Also it is satisfied for infinitely many values of p and q.

For instance, when $p=\frac{n}{n+1}$ and $q=\frac{1}{n}$, where n is any positive integer.

22. Three six-faced fair dice are thrown together. The probability that sum of the numbers appearing on the dice is k $(3 \le k \le 8)$ is

(a) $\frac{(k-1)(k-2)}{432}$ (b) $\frac{k(k-1)}{432}$

(c) $\frac{k^2}{432}$ (d) None of these

Solution: (a) Total number of cases $= 6 \times 6 \times 6 = 6^3 = 216$

Number of favourable ways

$=$ coefficient of x^k in $(x + x^2 +... + x^6)^3$

$=$ coefficient of x^{k-3} in $(1-x^6)^3(1-x)^{-3}$

$=$ coefficient of x^{k-3} in $(1-x)^{-3}$ $(\because 0 \le k-3 \le 5)$

$=$ coefficient of x^{k-3} in $(1 + {}^3C_1x + {}^4C_2x^2 + {}^5C_3x^3 +...)$

$= {}^{k-3+2}C_{k-3} = {}^{k-1}C_2 = \frac{(k-1)(k-2)}{2}$

$\therefore$ Probability of the required event is $\frac{(k-1)(k-2)}{432}$

23. Given that $x \in [0, 1]$ and $y \in [0, 1]$. Let A be the event of (x, y) satisfying $y^2 \le x$ and B be the event of (x, y) satisfying $x^2 \le y$, then

(a) $P(A \cap B) = 1/3$ (b) A, B are exclusive

(c) $P(A) = P(B)$ (d) None of these

Solution: (a, c) $P(A) = \frac{\int_0^1 \sqrt{x}dx}{\int_0^1 dx} = \frac{2}{3}$;

$$P(A \cap B) = \frac{\int_0^1 \sqrt{x}\,dx - \int_0^1 x^2\,dx}{\int_0^1 dx} = \frac{2}{3}-\frac{1}{3}=\frac{1}{3};$$

So $P(A \cap B) = \frac{1}{3} \neq 0$ so A and B are not exclusive

$$\text{also } P(B) = \frac{1-\int_0^1 x^2 dx}{\int_0^1 dx} = \frac{2}{3}$$

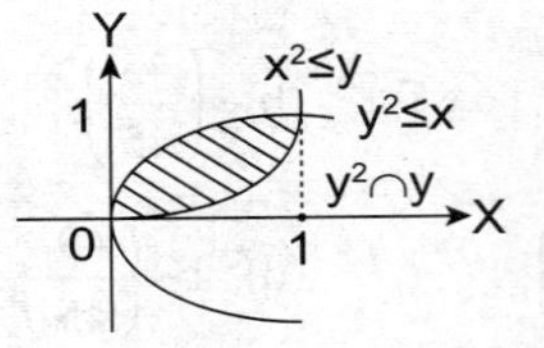

24. Suppose m boys and m girls take their seats randomly round a circle, The probability of their sitting is $\frac{1}{{}^{2m-1}C_m}$ when

(a) no two boys sit together

(b) no two girls sit together

(c) boys and girls sit alternatively

(d) all the boys sit together

Solution: (a, b, c) The number of ways in which m boys and m girls take their seats randomly round a circle is $(2m-1)!$

(a) We make the girls sit first around the circle. This can be done in $(m-1)!$ After this boys can take their seats in $m!$ (exactly one boy between two girls means m boys are to be adjusted at m places) Thus the number of ways in which no two boys sit together is $m!\,(m-1)!$

$\therefore$ Probability that no two boys sit together $= \frac{m!(m-1)!}{(2m-1)!} = \frac{1}{{}^{2m-1}C_m}$

(b) Similar to (*a*)

(c) Boys and girls sit alternatively if and only if no two boys (girls) together. Therefore, the probability of this event is also $({}^{2m-1}C_m)^{-1}$.

(d) We tie the boys together and treat them as a single boy. We can put $(m + 1)$ objects (m girls and one boy) around a circle in $m!$ ways. But the boys can be tied in $m!$ ways. Thus probability of this event is

$\frac{m!\,m!}{(2m-1)!} \neq \frac{1}{{}^{2m-1}C_m}$

25. There are two balls in an urn whose colours are not known (ball can be either white or black). A white ball is put into the urn. A ball is then drawn from the urn. The probability that it is white is

(a) $\frac{1}{4}$ (b) $\frac{1}{3}$

(c) $\frac{2}{3}$ (d) $\frac{1}{6}$

Solution: (c) Let E_i $(0 \le i \le 2)$ denotes the event that urn contains i white and $2-i$ black balls. Let A

denotes the event that a white ball is drawn from the urn.

We have $P(E_i) = \frac{1}{3}$ for i = 0, 1, 2 and $P(A/E_1) = \frac{1}{3}$,

$P(A/E_2) = \frac{2}{3}$, $P(A/E_3) = 1$

By the total probability rule,

$$P(A) = P(E_1)P\left(\frac{A}{E_1}\right) + P(E_2)P\left(\frac{A}{E_2}\right) + P(E_3)P\left(\frac{A}{E_3}\right)$$

$$= \frac{1}{3}\left[\frac{1}{3} + \frac{2}{3} + 1\right] = \frac{2}{3}$$

26. If E_1 and E_2 are two events such that $P(E_1)$ = 1/4, $P(E_2/E_1)$ =1/2 and $P(E_1/E_2)$ = 1/4

(a) then E_1 and E_2 are independent
(b) E_1 and E_2 are exhaustive
(c) E_2 is twice as likely to occur as E_1
(d) Probabilities of the events $E_1 \cap E_2$, E_1 and E_2 are in G.P.

Solution: (a, c, d) $P(E_2/E_1) = \frac{P(E_1 \cap E_2)}{P(E_1)}$

$\Rightarrow \frac{1}{2} = \frac{P(E_1 \cap E_2)}{1/4}$

$\Rightarrow P(E_1 \cap E_2) = \frac{1}{8} = P(E_2).\ P(E_1/E_2)$

$= P(E_2).\ \frac{1}{4} \Rightarrow P(E_2) = \frac{1}{2}$

Since $P(E_1 \cap E_2) = \frac{1}{8} = P(E_1).\ P(E_2)$

Therefore events are independent

Also $P(E_1 \cup E_2) = \frac{1}{2} + \frac{1}{4} - \frac{1}{8} = \frac{5}{8} \neq 1$

$\Rightarrow$ E_1 and E_2 are non exhaustive. Also, clearly $E_1 \cap E_2$, E_1, E_2 are in G.P.

27. A bag initially contains one red and two blue balls. An experiment consisting of selecting a ball at random, noting its colour and replacing it together with an additional ball of the same colour. If three such trials are made, then:

(a) probability that atleast one blue ball is drawn is 0.9
(b) probability that exactly one blue ball is drawn is 0.2
(c) probability that all the drawn balls are red given that all the drawn balls are of same colour is 0.2
(d) probability that atleast one red ball is drawn is 0.6.

Solution: (a, b, c, d) (a) Let E_1 = Event of drawing atleast one blue ball

E_2 = Event of drawing exactly one blue ball.
E_3 = Event of drawing all red balls
E_4 = Event of drawing atleast one red ball.

$$P(E_1) = 1 - P(R\ R\ R) = 1 - \left[\frac{1}{3}.\frac{2}{4}.\frac{3}{5}\right] = 0.9$$

(b) $P(E_2) = 3\ P(B\ R\ R) = 3.\ \frac{2}{3}.\frac{1}{4}.\frac{2}{5} = 0.2$

(c) $P(E_3) = P\left[\frac{RRR}{(RRR) \cup (BBB)}\right]$

$= \frac{P(RRR)}{P(RRR) + P(BBB)}$

but $P(B\ B\ B) = \frac{2}{3}.\frac{3}{4}.\frac{4}{5} = 0.4$

$\Rightarrow P(E_3) = \frac{0.1}{0.1 + 0.4} = 0.2$

(d) $P(E_4) = 1 - P(B\ B\ B) = 1 - \frac{2}{5} = 0.6$

TUTORIAL EXERCISE

SECTION–III

OBJECTIVE TYPE (ONLY ONE CORRECT ANSWER)

1. Exactly one of the two events must happen. Given that the chance of one is two-third of the other, the odds in favour of the other are
(a) 3 : 5 (b) 2 : 5
(c) 3 : 2 (d) None of these

2. The letters of word SOCIETY are placed at random in a row. The probability that the three vowels come together is
(a) 6/7 (b) 1/7
(c) 3/7 (d) None of these

3. The letters of the word ARTICLE are arranged at random. The probability that the vowels may occupy the even places, is
(a) 1/35 (b) 4/35
(c) 7/35 (d) None of these

4. Two unbiased six faced dice are thrown. The probability that the sum of the numbers on faces turned up is a prime number greater than 5 is
(a) 1/6 (b) 1/4
(c) 2/9 (d) 4/9

5. For independent events $A_1, A_2, \ldots\ldots, A_n$, $P(A_i) = \frac{1}{i+1}$, $i = 1,2,\ldots\ldots,n$. Then the probability that none of the events will occur, is
(a) $\frac{n}{n+1}$ (b) $\frac{n-1}{n+1}$
(c) $\frac{1}{n+1}$ (d) None of these

6. A fair coin is tossed repeatedly. If the tail appears on first four tosses, then the probability of head appearing on the fifth toss equals
(a) 1/2 (b) 1/32
(c) 31/32 (d) 1/5

7. A bag contains 4 tickets numbered 1,2,3,4 and another bag contains 6 tickets numbered 2, 4, 6, 7, 8, 9. One bag is chosen and a ticket is drawn. The probability that the ticket bears the number 4 is
(a) 1/48 (b) 1/8
(c) 5/24 (d) None of these

8. Two dice are thrown. The probability that the numbers appeared have a sum 8, if it is known that the second die always exhibit 4, is
(a) 5/6 (b) 1/6
(c) 2/3 (d) None of these

9. A fair coin is tossed 99 times. Let X be the number of times head occurs. Then $P(X = r)$ is maximum when r is
(a) 49 (b) 52
(c) 51 (d) None of these

10. 10 apples are distributed at random among 6 persons. The probability that at least one of them will receive none is
(a) $\frac{6}{143}$ (b) $\frac{^{14}C_4}{^{15}C_5}$
(c) $\frac{137}{143}$ (d) None of these

11. A fair die is thrown twenty times. The probability that on the tenth throw, the fourth six appears is
(a) $\frac{^{20}C_{10}5^6}{6^{20}}$ (b) $\frac{120 \times 5^7}{6^{10}}$
(c) $\frac{84 \times 5^6}{6^{20}}$ (d) None of these

12. From a group of 10 persons consisting of 5 lawyers, 3 doctors and 2 engineers, four persons are selected at random. The probability that the selection contains at least one of each category is
(a) 1/2 (b) 1/3
(c) 2/3 (d) None of these

13. A draws two cards at random from a pack of 52 cards. After returning them to the pack and shuffling it, B draws two cards at random. The probability that their draws contain exactly one common card is
(a) $\frac{25}{546}$ (b) $\frac{50}{663}$
(c) $\frac{25}{663}$ (d) None of these

14. The odds against a given event are 5 : 2 and the odds in favour of another independent event are 6 : 5. The probability that at least one of the events will happen is
(a) 22/77 (b) 52/77
(c) 12/77 (d) 65/77

15. If the letters of the word 'REGULATION' be arranged at random, the probability that there will be exactly 4 letters between ***R*** and ***E*** is
(a) 1/9 (b) 3/55
(c) 49/55 (d) None of these

16. Seven chits are numbered 1 to 7. Four chits are drawn one by one with replacement. The probability that the least number appearing on any selected chit is 5, is
(a) $(3/7)^4$ (b) $(6/7)^3$
(c) $60/(7)^3$ (d) $(3/4)^4$

17. Entries of a 2 × 2 determinant are chosen from the set $\{-1, 1\}$. The probability that determinant has zero value is
(a) 1/4 (b) 1/3
(c) 1/2 (d) None of these

18. Fifteen persons, among whom *A* and *B*, sit ramdomly around a round table. The probability that there are 4 persons between *A* and *B* is
(a) 3/7 (b) 4/7
(c) 2/7 (d) 1/7

19. A letter is taken at random out of each of the words CHOICE and CHANCE. The probability that they should be the same letter is
(a) 1/6 (b) 1/9
(c) 5/36 (d) 1/324

20. 4 letters are chosen at random from the letters of the word "INFINITE". The probability that there will be three like letters and one different is
(a) $\frac{2}{11}$ (b) $\frac{4}{21}$
(c) $\frac{7}{22}$ (d) $\frac{1}{14}$

21. A bag contains 2 white and 4 black balls. One ball is drawn 5 times, each being replaced before another is drawn. The probability that atleast 4 of the balls drawn are white is:
(a) $\frac{4}{81}$ (b) $\frac{10}{243}$
(c) $\frac{11}{243}$ (d) None of these

22. Two men, in turn draw balls (without replacement) from an urn containing 2 white and 6 black balls. The person who is the first to draw a white ball wins the game. The probability that the first person will be the vinner is:
(a) 3/4 (b) 4/7
(c) 5/12 (d) None of these

23. An unbiased cubic die marked with 1, 2, 2, 3, 3, 3 is rolled 3 times. The probability of getting a total score of 4 or 6 is
(a) $\frac{25}{104}$ (b) $\frac{25}{108}$
(c) $\frac{1}{104}$ (d) None of these

24. Three athletes *A*, *B* and *C* participate in a race. Both *A* and *B* have the same probability of winning the race and each is twice as likely to win as *C*. The probability that *B* or *C* wins the race is
(a) 2/3 (b) 3/5
(c) 3/4 (d) 13/25

25. If the mean and variance of a binomial variate *X* are 7/3 and 14/9 respectively. Then probability that *X* takes value 6 or 7 is equal to
(a) $\frac{1}{729}$ (b) $\frac{5}{729}$
(c) $\frac{7}{729}$ (d) $\frac{13}{729}$

26. A three digit number, which is multiple of 11, is chosen at random. Probability that the number so chosen is also a multiple of 9 is equal to
(a) 1/9 (b) 2/9
(c) 1/100 (d) 9/100

27. Seven digits from the digits 1, 2, 3, 4, 5, 6, 7, 8, 9 are written in a random order. The probability that this seven digit number is divisible by 9 is
(a) 2/9 (b) 1/5
(c) 1/3 (d) 1/9

28. If *A* and *B* are two events such that, $P(A) > 0$ and $P(B) \neq 0$, then $P\left(\frac{\bar{A}}{\bar{B}}\right)$ is equal to:
(a) $1 - P\left(\frac{A}{\bar{B}}\right)$ (b) $1 - P\left(\frac{\bar{A}}{B}\right)$
(c) $1 - \frac{P(AB)}{P(\bar{B})}$ (d) $\frac{P(\bar{A})}{P(\bar{B})}$

29. An elevator starts with m passengers and stops at n floors ($m \le n$). The probability that no two passengers alight at the same floor, is

(a) $\frac{^nP_m}{m^n}$ (b) $\frac{^nP_m}{n^m}$

(c) $\frac{^nC_m}{m^n}$ (d) $\frac{^nC_m}{n^m}$

30. Consider a set P containing n elements. A subset A of P is drawn and thereafter set P is reconstructed. Now one more subset B of P is drawn. Probability of drawing sets A and B so that $A \cap B$ has exactly one element is

(a) $\left(\frac{3}{4}\right)^n . n$ (b) $n.\left(\frac{3}{4}\right)^{n-1}$

(c) $n\left(\frac{1}{4}\right)^n$ (d) None of these

31. A box contains 100 tickets numbered 1,2,....., 100. Two tickets are chosen at random. It is given that the maximum number on the two chosen tickets is not more than 10. The minimum number on them is 5 with probability

(a) 1/9 (b) 2/9

(c) 3/9 (d) 4/9

32. A bag contains 6 red and 3 white balls. Four balls are drawn one by one and not replaced. The probability that they are alternatively of different colours is equal to

(a) 2/21 (b) 5/42

(c) 1/6 (d) None of these

33. If $\frac{1+4p}{4}, \frac{1-p}{4}, \frac{1-2p}{4}$ are probabilities of three mutually exclusive events, then the set of positive values of p is

(a) $\left(0, \frac{2}{3}\right)$ (b) $\left(0, \frac{1}{2}\right]$

(c) $\left(\frac{1}{2}, \frac{2}{3}\right)$ (d) None of these

34. If $\frac{2-3p}{3}, \frac{1+4p}{3}, \frac{1+p}{6}$ are the probabilities of three mutually exclusive and exhaustive events, then the set to which p belongs is

(a) (0, 1) (b) (1/4, 1/3)

(c) (0, 1/3) (d) None of these

35. An unbiased die with faces marked 1,2,3,4,5 and 6 is rolled four times. Out of four face values obtained, the probability that the minimum face value is not less than 2 and the maximum face value is not greater than 5 is

(a) $\frac{16}{81}$ (b) $\frac{1}{81}$

(c) $\frac{80}{81}$ (d) $\frac{65}{81}$

36. A is a set containing n elements. A subset P of A is chosen at random. The set A is reconstructred by replacing the elements of P. A subset Q of A is again chosen at random. The probability that P and Q have no common element is

(a) $\left(\frac{1}{4}\right)^n$ (b) $\left(\frac{3}{4}\right)^n$

(c) $\left(\frac{1}{2^n}\right)$ (d) $1-\left(\frac{3}{4}\right)^n$

37. Two subsets A and B of a set S consisting of 'n' elements are constructed randomly. The probability that $A \cap B = \phi$ and $A \cup B = S$ is equal to

(a) $1-\left(\frac{3}{4}\right)^n$ (b) $\left(\frac{3}{4}\right)^n$

(c) $\frac{1}{2}$ (d) $\frac{1}{3^n}$

38. If A and B are any two mutually exclusive events, then

(a) $P(A) \le P(\bar{B})$ (b) $P(A) > P(\bar{B})$

(c) $P(A) < P(\bar{B})$ (d) None of these

39. If three dice are thrown, then the probability that they show the numbers in A.P. is

(a) 1/36 (b) 1/18

(c) 5/18 (d) 2/9

40. Let A and B be two events such that

$P\left(\overline{A \cup B}\right) = \frac{1}{6}, P\left(A \cap B\right) = \frac{1}{4}$ and $P\left(\bar{A}\right) = \frac{1}{4}$, where $\bar{A}$ stands for complement of event A. Then events A and B are

(a) Independent but not equally likely

(b) Mutually exclusive and independent

(c) Equally likely and mutually exclusive

(d) Equally likely but not independent

41. Let A, B, C be three mutually independent events. Consider the two statements S_1 and S_2.

S_1 : A and $B \cup C$ are independent ;

S_2: A and $B \cap C$ are independent, then

(a) both S_1 and S_2 are true
(b) only S_1 is true
(c) only S_2 is true
(d) neither S_1 nor S_2 is true.

42. A die is thrown three times and the sum of three numbers obtained is 15. The probability of first throw being 4 is

(a) 1/18 (b) 1/5
(c) 4/5 (d) 17/18

43. The sum of two natural numbers n_1 and n_2 is equal to 100. The probability of their product being greater than 1600, is equal to

(a) $\frac{20}{33}$ (b) $\frac{58}{99}$
(c) $\frac{13}{33}$ (d) $\frac{59}{99}$

44. If A and B are two events such that $P(A \cup B) = 5/6$, $P(A \cap B) = 1/3$, $P(A) = 2/3$, then A and B are....

(a) dependent events
(b) independent events
(c) mutually exclusive events
(d) mutually exclusive and independent events

45. If two events A and B are such that $P(A^c) = 0.3$, $P(B) = 0.4$ and $P(AB^c) = 0.5$, then $P\left(\frac{B}{A \cup B^c}\right)$ is equal to

(a) 1/3 (b) 1/2
(c) 1/4 (d) can't be determined

46. There are four machines and it is known that exactly two of them are faulty. They are tested, one by one in a random order till both the faulty machines are identified. Then the probability that only two tests are needed is

(a) 1/3 (b) 1/6
(c) 1/2 (d) 1/4

47. An urn contains 2 white and 2 black balls. A ball is drawn at random. If it is white, it is not replaced into the urn. Otherwise it is replaced along with another ball of the same colour. The process is repeated. The probability that the third drawn ball is black is;

(a) 15/29 (b) 11/30
(c) 7/30 (d) 23/30

48. The probability that a teacher will give an unannounced test during any class meeting is 1/5. If a student is absent twice, then the probability that the student will miss at least one test is

(a) 4/5 (b) 2/5
(c) 7/5 (d) 9/25

49. 3 firemen X, Y and Z shoot at a common target. The probabilities that X and Y can hit the target are $\frac{2}{3}$ and $\frac{3}{4}$ respectively. If the probability that exactly two bullets are found on the target is $\frac{11}{24}$, then the proficiency of Z to hit the target is

(a) 1/3 (b) 1/4
(c) 1/2 (d) None of these

50. A fair coin is tossed a fixed number of times. If the probability of getting seven heads is equal to that of getting nine heads, the probability of getting two heads is

(a) $\frac{15}{2^8}$ (b) $\frac{2}{15}$
(c) $\frac{15}{2^{13}}$ (d) None of these

51. If A and B are events of an experiment with $P(A) = 0.2$, $P(B) = 0.5$, then maximum value of $P(A' \cap B)$ is

(a) 1/4 (b) 1/2
(c) 1/8 (d) 1/16

52. The probability that when 12 balls are distributed among three boxes, the first box will contain three balls is

(a) $\frac{2^9}{3^{12}}$ (b) $\frac{^{12}C_3.2^9}{3^{12}}$
(c) $\frac{^{12}C_3.2^{12}}{3^{12}}$ (d) None of these

53. 7 boys and 8 girls have to sit on 15 chairs arranged in a row numbered from 1 to 15. Then the probability that the end seats are occupied by the boys and between any two boys an even number of girls occupy seats is

(a) $\frac{\lfloor 7 \lfloor 8}{\lfloor 15}$ (b) $^9C_4 \frac{\lfloor 8 \lfloor 7}{\lfloor 15}$
(c) $\frac{\lfloor 8}{\lfloor 15}$ (d) $\frac{\lfloor 7}{\lfloor 15}$

54. If $P(A_1 \cup A_2) = 1 - P(A_1^c)P(A_2^c)$, where c stands for complement, then the events A_1 and A_2 are

(a) Mutually exclusive
(b) Independent
(c) Equally likely
(d) None of these

55. Six married couples are standing in a room. If the 12 people are divided into six pairs, then the probability that

(i) each pair is married is

(a) $\frac{1}{10395}$ (b) $\frac{16}{231}$

(c) $\frac{16}{10395}$ (d) None of these

(ii) each pair contains a male and a female is

(a) $\frac{1}{10395}$ (b) $\frac{16}{231}$

(c) $\frac{16}{10395}$ (d) None of these

56. If head means one and tail means two, then coefficient of quadratic equation $ax^2 + bx + c = 0$ are chosen by tossing three fair coins. The probability that roots of the equations are imaginary is

(a) 5/8 (b) 3/8

(c) 7/8 (d) 1/8

57. A sample space for the equally likely results from one fair die and another biased die with a six twice as likely as any other score, contains the following number of sample points.

(a) 36 (b) 30

(c) 42 (d) 18

58. Ten teams participate in a basket ball championship, out of which two groups (A and B) each consisting 5 teams are formed at random. Four teams are of first class. The probability that all the first class teams get into the same group is

(a) 1/42 (b) 1/21

(c) 1/7 (d) 2/5

59. If $P(A/B) = P(B/A)$, A and B are two non-mutually exclusive events, then

(a) A and B are necessarily same events

(b) $P(A) = P(B)$

(c) $P(A \cap B) = P(A)\,P(B)$

(d) all of the above

60. An urn contains $(2n + 1)$ coins of which n coins have a head on both sides and the remaining $(n + 1)$ coins are fair. A coin is taken out of the urn and tossed. If the probability of obtaining a head be $\frac{37}{50}$, then n is equal to

(a) 10 (b) 11

(c) 12 (d) 13

61. A person has a bunch of n keys, only one of which can open a lock. The person tries the keys at random rejecting those which do not open the lock, the probability that the lock is opened at the $k^{th}(\le n)$ trial is

(a) $\frac{1}{n}$ (b) $\frac{k}{n}$

(c) $\frac{k-1}{n}$ (d) $\left(1-\frac{1}{n}\right)^{k-1}\frac{1}{n}$

62. Assume that the chances of a patient having a heart attack is 40%. It is also assumed that a meditation and yoga course reduces the risk of heart attack by 30% and prescription of certain drug reduces its chances by 25%. At a time a patient can choose any one of the two options with equal probabilities. It is given that after going through any options the patient selected at random suffers a heart attack. Then the probability that the patient followed a course of meditation and yoga is

(a) 4/29 (b) 14/29

(c) 1/2 (d) None of these

63. A and B are two independent witnesses in a case, The probability that A will speak the truth is x. The probability that B will speak the truth is y. A and B agree in a certain statement, then the probability that the statement is true is

(a) $\frac{xy}{1+x+y-2xy}$ (b) $\frac{xy}{x+y+2xy}$

(c) $\frac{xy}{1-x-y+2xy}$ (d) None of these

64. Out of 10,000 families with 4 children each, the probable number of families all of whose children are daughters is

(a) 625 (b) 375

(c) 225 (d) None of these

65. The probability that the birthdays of six different persons will fall in exactly two calander months is

(a) 1/6 (b) $\frac{^{12}C_2 \times 2^6}{12^6}$

(c) $\frac{^{12}C_2 \times 2^6 - 1}{12^6}$ (d) $\frac{341}{12^5}$

66. The sum of two positive real numbers is $2a$. The probability that product of these two numbers is not less than (3/4) times the greatest possible product is

(a) 1/2 (b) 1/3

(c) 1/4 (d) 9/16

67. The numbers 1,2,3,...., n are arranged in random order. The probability that the digits 1, 2, 3,......., k ($k < n$) appear as neighbours in that order is

(a) $\frac{1}{n!}$ (b) $\frac{k!}{n!}$

(c) $\frac{(n-k)!}{n!}$ (d) None of these

68. A bag contains 24 balls of which 12 are black and 12 are white. The balls are drawn at random from the box one at a time with replacement. The probability that a white ball is drawn for the 4th time on the 7th draw is

(a) $\frac{5}{64}$ (b) $\frac{27}{32}$

(c) $\frac{5}{32}$ (d) $\frac{1}{2}$

69. n letters are written to n different persons and addresses on the n envelopes are written. If the letters are placed in the envelopes at random, the probability that atleast one letter is not placed in the right envelope, is

(a) $1-\frac{1}{n}$ (b) $1-\frac{1}{2n}$

(c) $1-\frac{1}{n^2}$ (d) $1-\frac{1}{n!}$

70. A die is rolled three times, the probability of getting a larger number than the previous number each time is

(a) 15/216 (b) 5/54

(c) 13/216 (d) 1/18

71. A wire of length l is cut into three pieces. Then the probability that the three pieces form a triangle is

(a) 1/2 (b) 1/4

(c) 2/3 (d) None of these

72. The adjoining figure gives the road plan of lines connecting two parallel roads AB and A_1B_1. A man walking on the road AB takes a turn at random to reach the road A_1B_1. It is known that he reaches the road A_1B_1 from O by taking a straight line path. The chance that he moves on a straight line from the road AB to A_1B_1 is

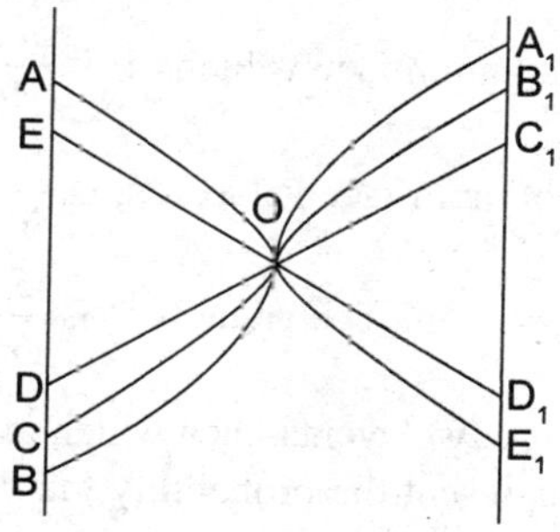

(a) 0.25 (b) 0.04

(c) 0.2 (d) None of these

73. If m rupee coins and n ten paise coins are placed in a line, then the probability that the extreme coins are ten paise coins is (coins are identical in their respectively category)

(a) ${}^{(m+n)}C_m$ (b) $\frac{n(n-1)}{(m+n)(m+n-1)}$

(c) ${}^{(m+n)}P_m$ (d) ${}^{(m+n)}P_n$

74. A child throws 2 fair dice. If the numbers showing are unequal, he adds them together to get his final score. On the other hand, if the numbers showing are equal, he throws 2 more dice and adds all 4 numbers showing to get his final score. The probability that his final score is 4 is:

(a) $\frac{1}{18}$ (b) $\frac{1}{12}$

(c) $\frac{1}{9}$ (d) $\frac{73}{1296}$

75. The probability that $\sin^{-1}(\sin x) - \cos^{-1}(\cos y)$ is an integer $x, y \in \{1, 2, 3, 4\}$ is

(a) $\frac{1}{16}$ (b) $\frac{3}{16}$

(c) $\frac{15}{16}$ (d) None of these

SECTION–IV

OBJECTIVE TYPE (MORE THAN ONE CORRECT ANSWERS)

1. For two given events A and B, $P(A \cap B)$ is

(a) not less than $P(A) + P(B) - 1$

(b) not greater than $P(A) + P(B)$

(c) equal to $P(A) + P(B) - P(A \cup B)$

(d) equal to $P(A) + P(B) + P(A \cup B)$

2. An unbiased die with faces marked 1,2,3,4,5 and 6 is rolled four times. Out of four face values obtained, the probability that

(a) The minimum face value is 2, is $\frac{5^4 - 4^4}{6^4}$

(b) The maximum face value is 5, is $\frac{5^4 - 4^4}{6^4}$

(c) The minimum face value is 2, is $\frac{5^4}{6^4}$

(d) The maximum face value is 5, is $\frac{5^4}{6^4}$

3. If A and B are two events, then which of the following does not represent the probability that exactly one of A, B occurs?
(a) $P(A) + P(B) - P(A \cap B)$
(b) $P(A \cap B') + P(A' \cap B)$
(c) $P(A') + P(B') - 2P(A' \cap B)$
(d) $P(A) + P(B) - 2P(A \cap B)$

4. A and B are two events. The probability that at most one of A, B occurs is
(a) $1 - P(A \cap B)$
(b) $P(A') + P(B') - P(A' \cap B')$
(c) $P(A') + P(B') - P(A \cup B) - 1$
(d) $P(A \cap B') + P(A' \cap B) + P(A' \cap B')$

5. If A and B are two events, then
(a) $P(A \cap B) \le \min. \{P(A), P(B)\}$
(b) $P(A \cap B) \ge \max. \{0, P(B) + P(A')\}$
(c) $P(A \cap B) \le P(A \cup B)$
(d) $P(A \cap B) \ge \max. \{0, P(A) + P(B) - 1\}$

6. Suppose A, B and C are three events with $P(C) = 0$. Then
(a) $P(A \cap C) = P(A)P(C)$
(b) $P(B \cup C) = P(B)$
(c) $P(A \cup C) = P(A) + P(C)$
(d) $P(A \cup B \cup C) = P(A) + P(B) - P(A \cap B)$

7. Which of the following statements is/are correct?
(a) $P(A/B) \ge \frac{P(A) + P(B) - 1}{P(B)}$, $P(B) \ne 0$ is always true
(b) $P(A \cap \overline{B}) = P(A) - P(A \cap B)$ does not hold
(c) $P(A \cup B) = 1 - P(\overline{A})P(\overline{B})$ if A and B are independent
(d) $P(A \cup B) = 1 - P(\overline{A})P(\overline{B})$, if A and B are disjoint

8. Identify the correct statements: If E and F are independent events such that $0 < P(E) < 1$ and $0 < P(F) < 1$, then
(a) E and F are mutually exclusive
(b) E and F^c are independent
(c) E^c and F^c are independent
(d) $P(E/F) + P(E^C/F) = 1$

9. Which of the following statements are true?
(a) $P(B/A) = \frac{P(A \cap B)}{P(A)}$ where $P(A) \ne \phi$.
(b) When two dice are thrown, the number of ways of getting a total r is $(r - 1)$ if $2 \le r \le 7$
(c) When two dice are thrown, the number of ways of getting a total r is $(13 - r)$ if $8 \le r \le 12$
(d) None of these

10. When three dice are thrown, the number of ways of getting a total r is:
(a) $\frac{(r-1)(r-2)}{2}$ if $3 \le r \le 18$
(b) $\frac{(19-r)(20-r)}{2}$ if $13 \le r \le 18$
(c) 25 if $r = 9$ or 12
(d) 27 if $r = 10$ or 11.

11. If A and B are two independent events such that $P(A' \cap B) = 2/15$ and $P(A \cap B') = 1/6$, then $P(B)$ is
(a) 1/5 (b) 1/6
(c) 4/5 (d) 5/6

SECTION–V

ASSERTION AND REASON TYPE

The questions given below consist of an assertion (A) and the reason (R). Use the following key to choose the appropriate answer.
(a) If both assertion and reason are correct and reason is the correct explanation of the assertion.
(b) If both assertion and reason are correct but reason is not correct explanation of the assertion.
(c) If assertion is correct, but reason is incorrect
(d) If assertion is incorrect, but reason is correct

Now consider the following statements:

1. A: Compound event is a subset of sample space.
R: Union of simple events produces a compound event

2. A: Weight of an event which is not likely to occur is very close to zero and weights of equally likely events are equal.

R: Weight of sample points signifies relative chances of occurences of events and sum of weights of all sample points in sample space = 1

3. A: If two events E_1 and E_2 are mutually exclusive, then they must be strongly dependent.

R: Occurrence of one precludes the occurrence of the other for mutually exclusive events.

4. A: Occurrence of war or non-occurrence of war between two neighbouring countries is an equally likely event

R: two events are called equally likely if there is no reason to say that one has better chance of occurrence than the other.

5. A: If A and B are two finite sets such that $n(A) = m$, $n(B) = n$ and for $n \geq m$ if a mapping is selected at random from the set of all mappings from A to B, then the probability that mapping is a many one function is $1 - \frac{{}^nP_m}{n^m}$

R: For $n(A) \leq n(B)$ the probability of the mapping from A into B is a one-one function is $\frac{{}^nP_m}{n^m}$ and

$P(E) + P(\bar{E}) = 1$

6. A: Mutually exclusive events of same experiment are strongly dependent.

R: Exclusion of events is set theoretic principle where as dependence of events is probabilistic in nature.

7. A: If the odds against an event is 2/3, then probability of occurring of that event is 3/5

R: For two events A and B, $P(A' \cap B') = 1 - P(A \cup B)$

8. A: If two events A and B are such that $P(\bar{A}) = 0.3$, $P(B) = 0.4$ and $P(A\bar{B}) = 0.5$, then $P\left(\frac{B}{A \cup \bar{B}}\right)$ is $\frac{1}{4}$

R: $P(A \cap B) = P(B)\,P(A/B) = P(B)P(A)$ if A and B are dependent events

9. A: A fair die is rolled. The probability that the first time 1 occurs at the even throw is 5/11

R: Sum of an infinite G.P. i.e., $S_\infty = \frac{a}{1-r}$ where $|r| < 1$ and $P\left(\frac{E_i}{E}\right) = \frac{P(E_i).P\left(\frac{E}{E_i}\right)}{\sum P(E_i)P\left(\frac{E}{E_i}\right)}$

10. A: If $\bar{E}$ and $\bar{F}$ are complement of events E and F respectively and $0 < P(F) < 1$, then $P\left(\frac{E}{F}\right) + P\left(\frac{\bar{E}}{F}\right) = 1$

R: $P(\bar{E}) = 1 - P(E)$ and $P\left(\frac{A}{B}\right) = \frac{P(A \cap B)}{P(B)}$

11. A: The probability of occurrence of a multiple of 2 on a die and a multiple of 3 on other die is $\frac{1}{3}$ if both are thrown together.

R: If A and B are independent events, then $P(A \cap B) = P(A).P(B)$ and if A and B are mutually exclusive events, then $P(A \cup B) = P(A) + P(B)$

12. A: Out of 7 tickets consecutively numbered. Three are drawn at random, the chance that the numbers on them are in A.P. is 9/35

R: Out of $(2n + 1)$ tickets consecutively numbered three are drawn at random, the chance that the numbers on them are in A.P. is $\frac{3n}{4n^2 - 1}$.

13. A: Two non-negative integers are chosen at random. The probability that the sum of their squares is divisible by 5 is 9/25.

R: If the unit place digit in any number is zero, then the number is divisible by 5 only.

SECTION–VI

LINKED COMPREHENSION TYPE

A: If any natural number n is chosen randomly from the 1st 100 natural number and let E be the event such that $n + \frac{100}{n} > 50$.

1. $P(E)$ is

(a) 55/100 (b) 17/55

(c) 55/90 (d) None of these

2. $P(n)$, if $(n < 5)$ is

(a) 3/55 (b) 2/55

(c) 1/11 (d) None of these

3. $P(E_2)$ where E_2 is the event of getting a prime no. which are less than 37, is

(a) 11/24 (b) 13/25

(c) 9/27 (d) None of these

B: Let $n = 10k + r$ where $k, r \in W, 0 \le r \le 9$. A number a is chosen at random from the set $\{1,2,......, n\}$ and let p_n denotes the probability that $a^2 - 1$ is divisible by 10.

4. If $r = 0$, p_n equals

(a) $2k/n$ (b) $(k + 1)/n$

(c) $(2k + 1)/n$ (d) k/n

5. If $r = 9$, p_n equals

(a) $2k/n$ (b) $2(k + 1)/n$

(c) $(2k + 1)/n$ (d) k/n

6. If $1 \le r \le 8$, p_n equals

(a) $(2k - 1)/n$ (b) $2k/n$

(c) $(2k + 1)/n$ (d) k/n

7. $\lim\limits_{n\to\infty} p_n$ equals

(a) 1/10 (b) 2/5

(c) 1/5 (d) 3/5

8. If q_n denotes the probability that $a^2 + 1$ is divisible by 10, then $\lim\limits_{n\to\infty} q_n$ equals

(a) 1/5 (b) 2/5

(c) 3/5 (d) None of these

C: It can be observed that the number of positive integers from 1 to N which are divisible by a fixed positive integer k, $(1 < k \le N)$ is $\left[\frac{N}{k}\right]$, where $[x]$ denotes greatest integer $\le x$. Several probability problems involving divisibility may require this notation. Thus if one number is selected from the set $\{1, 2, 3,....., N\}$, the probability p_N that the number is divisible by 5 must be given by $p_N = \dfrac{\left[\frac{N}{5}\right]}{N}$

If $N = 5k + r$, where $r = 0, 1, 2, 3, 4$, then $\left[\frac{N}{5}\right] = k$

$$\Rightarrow \lim_{N\to\infty} p_N = \lim_{k\to\infty} \frac{k}{5k + r} = \frac{1}{5}$$

9. If two numbers x and y are drawn with replacement from the set $S = \{1, 2, 3,.......,n\}$, then the probability p_2 that $x^2 - y^2$ is divisible by 2 is given by

(a) $p_2 = 1/2$

(b) $\left(\dfrac{\left[\frac{n}{2}\right]}{n}\right)^2$

(c) $p_2 = 1 - 2\dfrac{\left[\frac{n}{2}\right]}{n} + 2\left(\dfrac{\left[\frac{n}{2}\right]}{n}\right)^2$

(d) None of these

10. If two numbers x and y are drawn with replacement from the set $S = \{1, 2, 3,....., n\}$, then the probability p_3 that $x^2 - y^2$ is divisible by 3 is given by

(a) $\dfrac{\left[\frac{n}{3}\right]}{n}$

(b) $\left(\dfrac{\left[\frac{n}{3}\right]}{n}\right)^2$

(c) $1 - \dfrac{3 - \left[\frac{n}{3}\right]}{n} - 3\left(\dfrac{\left[\frac{n}{3}\right]}{n}\right)^2$

(d) $1 - 2\dfrac{\left[\frac{n}{3}\right]}{n} + 2\left(\dfrac{\left[\frac{n}{3}\right]}{n}\right)^2$

11. Which of the following is true?

(a) p_2 is always greater than p_3 if $n \ge 2$

(b) p_2 is always greater than p_3 if $n > 3$

(c) $p_2 + p_3 = 1$

(d) $p_2 = p_3$ for some $n > 6$

D: The game of chess is purely strategic. A strong player generally does not loose against weaker players. Most of the times the rules of the game become more important. Suppose you have to play with Anand, Botvinik and Casablanca (sequence in weeker to stronger). Once in a 3-game tournament, your chances of winning against these players are a,b,c. You win the tournament if you win two consecutive games other wise you loose, but you can choose in which order to play the three games.

12. If I play in the order ABC, the probability of winning is
(a) abc
(b) $a(1 - b)(1 - c) + b(1 - a)(1 - c) + c(1 - a)(1 - b)$
(c) $ab + (1 - a)bc$
(d) None of these

13. The probability that I win by playing A first must be equal to
(a) $ab(1 - c)$ (b) $a + b + c - abc$
(c) $ab + bc + ac - abc$ (d) $ab + 2bc + ac - 2abc$

14. If I want to maximize my chances of winning I must play
(a) Anand Ist (b) Anand IInd
(c) Anand IIIrd (d) None of these

E: If A is one of 6 horses entered for a race, and is to be ridden by one of two jockeys B and C. It is 2 to 1/9 that B rides A, in which case all the horses are equally likely to win. If C rides A, his chance of winning is 1/3. Now define the following events:
$E \to$ The event that horse A wins.
$E_1 \to$ the event that jockey B rides horse A.
$E_2 \to$ the event that jockey C rides horse A.
$A_1 = E_1 \cap E$ and $A_2 = E_2 \cap E$. Then

15. The value of $P(E/E_1)$ is:
(a) 1/3 (b) 1/6
(c) 1/2 (d) None of these

16. The value of $P\left(\frac{E}{E_2}\right)$ is:
(a) 1/3 (b) 1/6
(c) 1/2 (d) None of these

17. The vlaue of $P(A_1)$ is
(a) 1/3 (b) 1/9
(c) 1/2 (d) None of these

18. The vlaue of $P(A_2)$ is
(a) 1/3 (b) 1/6
(c) 1/2 (d) 2/9

19. The vlaue of $P(E)$ is
(a) 1/3 (b) 1/6
(c) 1/2 (d) None of these

20. The odds against winning of A is:
(a) 2: 1 (b) 7: 2
(c) 1: 1 (d) None of these

F: In a town with a population of n, a person sends two letters to two separate persons, each of whom is asked to repeat the procedure. Thus for each letter received, two letters are sent to separate persons chosen at random. (irrespective of what happened in past).

Let $P_1, P_2, \ldots\ldots, P_n$ be n persons in the town. It is given that the person who starts the chain letter sends two letters to two separate persons, each of whom is asked to repeat the procedure. This means that at the ith stage 2^i letters are sent. Then

21. The value of $P(A_2)$ (i.e., Probability that P_1 does not receive a letter at 2nd stage) is:
(a) $\frac{2^3}{2^n}$ (b) $\left(\frac{n-2}{n-1}\right)$
(c) $\left(\frac{n-2}{n-1}\right)^2$ (d) None of these

22. The probability that in the first m stages, the person who started the chain letter will not receive a letter is,
(a) $\frac{2(2^n - 1)}{2^n}$ (b) $\frac{2^m - 1}{2^n}$
(c) $\left(\frac{n-2}{n-1}\right)^{2^m - 2}$ (c) None of these

23. The value of $P(A_m / A_2 \cap A_3 \cap \ldots\ldots \cap A_{m-1})$ (i.e., Probability that P_1 does not receive a letter at m^{th} stage):
(a) $\frac{2^{m-1}}{2^n}$ (b) $\frac{2^m}{2^n}$
(c) $\left(\frac{n-2}{n-1}\right)$ (d) None of these

G: A key ring has 10 keys of a given house of which only one opens the main door of the house. A thief finds the key ring and trying the keys one after another (without replacement), then answer the following problems

24. The chances that the door is opened in the 1st attempt is
(a) 1/10 (b) 3/10
(c) 2/10 (d) None of these

25. Chances that door is opened in 6th attempt is
(a) 3/10 (b) 3/5
(c) 1/10 (d) None of these

26. Chances that the door is opened till 5th attempt is
(a) 1/2 (b) 1/3
(c) 2/5 (d) None of these

27. Probability that door will be opened up to 10th attempt is

(a) 1/10 (b) 3/10
(c) 1 (d) None of these

28. Probability that atleast 3 attempt are needed to open the door is
(a) 3/10 (b) 4/5
(c) 3/5 (d) None of these

H: Indian Airforce has 250 aircrafts Mig-21 (150 in numbers) jaguar (50 in number) sukhoi-31 (50 in numbers) The probability of aircrash for jaguar is 1/3, for Mig-21 is 1/2 and that of sukhoi-31 is 1/6. A pilot selects a plane randonly, then answer the following question:

29. Chances that he will land safely are
(a) 1/5 (b) 2/5
(c) 3/5 (d) None of these

30. If an aircrash is reported, Then the probability that the crashed plane was sukhoi is
(a) 1/12 (b) 2/11
(c) 1/11 (d) None of these

31. If he lands safely, then he again takes off and the process is continued. Then the probability that he dies due to aircrash (assuming that he does not surviv if crash happens) is
(a) 1/2 (b) 1/3
(c) 1 (d) None of these

I: The theory of probability is frequently used in genetics and sex distribution in families. We can assume that sex of a child is independent of sex of other children in the family. Suppose q is the probability of the child being a girl child. let there be a family with n children and let the probability of each child being a boy is a constant p, then $p + q = 1$.

32. The probability that first $k(k \le n)$ children are of the same sex and rest are of opposite sex, must be
(a) $p^k q^{n-k}$ (b) $p^k q^{n-k} + p^{n-k} q^k$
(c) $p^k + q^{n-k}$ (d) None of these

33. The probability that first s children are boys and in all there are $k(n \ge k > s)$ boys, is
(a) ${}^{n-k}C_{k-s}\, p^k q^{n-k}$ (b) ${}^{n}C_{k-s}\, p^k q^{n-k}$
(c) ${}^{n-s}C_{k-s}\, p^k q^{n-k}$ (b) None of these

34. The probability that first s children are boys and hence are atleast k boys $(n \ge k > s)$ boys, is
(a) $\sum_{r=0}^{r=n-k} {}^{n-r}C_{n-k-r} . p^{k-r} . q^{n-k-r}$
(b) $\sum_{r=0}^{r=n-k} {}^{n-s}C_{n-k-r} . p^{k-r} . q^{n-k+r}$
(c) $\sum_{r=0}^{r=n-k} {}^{n-s}C_{n-k-r} . p^{k+r} . q^{n-k-r}$
(d) None of these

J: A random point 'P' is randomely selected in a square of side length 1 unit. Then the probabilities of the event of

35. The distance of 'P' to a fixed side of the square does not exceed x, $(x < 1)$ is:
(a) x (b) $x/2$
(c) $x/3$ (d) $x/4$

36. The distance of 'P' to the nearest side does not exceed x, $\left(\text{as } \frac{1}{\sqrt{2}} > \frac{1}{2}\right)$ is:
(a) $(1 - x)$ (b) $4(1 - x)$
(c) $4x(1 - x)$ (d) $4x^2 (1 - x)$

37. The distance of 'P' to the centre does not exceed x, $\left(x < \frac{1}{\sqrt{2}}\right)$ is
(a) $\pi x^2 + \sqrt{4x^2 - 1} - 4x^2 \tan^{-1}\sqrt{4x^2 - 1}$ for $\frac{1}{2} \le x < \frac{1}{\sqrt{2}}$
(b) $\pi x^2 - \sqrt{4x^2 - 1} - 4x^2 . \tan^{-1}\sqrt{4x^2 - 1}$
(c) πx^2 for $0 \le x \le \frac{1}{2}$
(d) $\pi x^2 + \sqrt{4x^2 - 1}$

38. The distance of 'P' to the fixed vertex of the square does not exceed x, $(x < \sqrt{2})$ is
(a) $\frac{\pi x^2}{4} - x^2 \tan^{-1}\sqrt{x^2 - 1} + \sqrt{x^2 - 1}$ for $1 \le x < \sqrt{2}$
(b) $\frac{\pi x^2}{4} + x^2 \tan^{-1}\sqrt{x^2 - 1}$
(c) $\frac{\pi x^2}{4}$ for $0 \le x \le 1$
(d) 0

K: A player throws a fair cubical die and scores the number appearing on the die. If he throws 1, he gets a further throw. Let p_r denote the probability of getting a total score of exactly r, then

39. p_1 equals
(a) 1/6 (b) 1
(c) 0 (d) None of these

40. p_2 equal
(a) 1/6 (b) 1
(c) 0 (d) None of these

41. $2 \le r \le 6 \Rightarrow p_r$ equals

(a) $1-\left(\frac{1}{6}\right)^{r-1}$ (b) $\frac{1}{5}\left[1-\left(\frac{1}{6}\right)^{r-1}\right]$

(c) $5^r/6^r$ (d) None of these

42. If $r > 6 \Rightarrow p_r$ equals

(a) $1-\left(\frac{1}{6}\right)^{r-1}$

(b) $\frac{1}{5}\left[1-\left(\frac{1}{6}\right)^{r-1}\right]$

(c) $\frac{1}{5}\left[\left(\frac{1}{6}\right)^{r-6}-\left(\frac{1}{6}\right)^{r-1}\right]$

(d) None of these

43. Sum of the series $S = \sum_{r=1}^{\infty} p_r$ is

(a) 1 (b) 1/6

(c) 1/5 (d) 2/3

L: Given a set $A = \{x_1, x_2, x_3, x_4\}$ and set $B = \{y_1, y_2, y_3, y_4\}$ and a mapping is randomly selected out of all $f: A \to B$, then answer the following

44. The probability that selected map f is one-one is

(a) 29/32 (b) 3/32

(c) 9/256 (d) None of these

45. The probability that f is many one is

(a) 29/32 (b) 3/32

(c) 9/256 (d) None of these

46. The probability that f is onto is

(a) 29/32 (b) 3/32

(c) 9/256 (d) None of these

47. The probability that f is into is

(a) 29/32 (b) 3/32

(c) 9/256 (d) None of these

48. The probability that f is such that $f(x_i) \ne (y_i)$ and it is one-one is

(a) 29/32 (b) 3/32

(c) 9/256 (d) None of these

SECTION–VII

MATRIX MATCH TYPE

1. Three distinct numbers a, b, c are chosen at random from the numbers 1,2,......,100. The probability that

Column I

(i) a, b, c are in A.P.

(ii) a, b, c are in G.P.

(iii) $\frac{1}{a}, \frac{1}{b}, \frac{1}{c}$ are in G.P.

(iv) $a + b + c$ is divisible by 2

Column II

(a) $\frac{53}{161700}$

(b) $\frac{1}{66}$

(c) $\frac{1}{22}$

(d) 1/2

2. A bag contains some white and some black balls, all combinations being equally likely. The total number of balls in the bag is 12. Four balls are drawn at random from the bag at random without replacement. Now match the entries from the following two columns:

Column I

(i) Probability that all the four balls are black is equal to

(ii) If the bag contains 10 black and 2 white balls, then the probability that all four balls are black is equal to

(iii) If all the four balls are black, then the probability that the bag contains 10 black balls is equal to

(iv) Proability that two balls are black and two are white is equal to

Column II

(a) 14/33

(b) 1/5

(c) 70/429

(d) 13/165

3. n-natural numbers or numbers are randomly chosen and multiplied, then match the following

Column-I

(i) Probability that last digit is 1, 3, 7 or 9 is

(ii) Probability that last digit is 2, 4, 6 or 8 is

(iii) Probability that last digit is 5 is

Column II

(a) $\dfrac{8^n - 4^n}{10}$

(b) $\dfrac{5^n - 4^n}{10^n}$

(c) $\left(\dfrac{}{10}\right)$

4. **Column I**

(i) The number of five-digit numbers having the product of digits 20 is

(ii) A man took 5 space plays out of an engine to clean them.The number of ways in which he can place atleast two plays in the engine from where they came out is

(iii) The number of integers between 1 and 1000 inclusive in which atleast two consecutive digits are equal is

(iv) The value of $\dfrac{1}{15}\sum_{1\le i\le j\le 9}\sum i.j$ is

Column II

(a) 77

(b) 31

(c) 50

(d) 181

SECTION–VIII

INTEGER TYPE QUESTIONS

1. Six dice are thrown simultaneously. If the probability that all of them show different faces is p/q, where gcd $(p.q) = 1$, then find $p + q$

2. If the probability for A to fail in an examination is 0.2 and that for B is 0.3, then the probability that either A or B fails in the examination is $0\cdot\overline{ab}$, then find the value of $(a^2 + b^2)$.

3. If $P(A \cap B) = 1/4$, $P(A' \cap B') = 1/5$ and $P(A) = P(B) = p$, then find the value of 40p.

4. A fair die is tossed eight times. Then the probability that on the eight throw a third six observed is ${}^nC_r p^p/(p + 1)^{p+3}$ then find the value of $n + p + r$.

5. The sum of two numbers is an even number, the probability that their product is also an even number is p/q, then evaluate $p + q$, where gcd $(p, q) = 1$

6. A and B are two candidates seeking admission into IIT. The probability that A is selected is 0.5 and probability that both A and B are selected is at most 0.3. Find maximum possible probability of B's selection.

7. Urn A contains 4 white and 3 black balls. Urn B contains 3 white and 7 black balls. An urn is selected at random and a ball is drawn and is found to be white. If the chance that urn A was selected is p/q; HCF of $(p, q) = 1$, then find the value of q.

8. X and Y are two independent events. The probability that both X and Y occur is 1/6 and the probability neither of them occurs is 1/3. find the sum of reciprocals of probabilities of their separately occurence.

9. A box contains 100 tickets numbers 1, 2, 3,...., 100. Two tickets are chosen at random. It is given that the maximum number on chosen tickets is not more than 10. If the chance that minimum number on them is 5, is p/q, then evaluate $\dfrac{q+p}{q-p}$

10. Three fair special dice whose face numbers are –3, –2, –1, 0,1,2 are rolled. Probability that the sum of numbers on their faces is 3 is p/q, then evaluate $\dfrac{q-3}{p}$.

11. If a and b are chosen randomly from the set consisting of numbers 1,2,3,4,5,6 with replacement and the probability that $\lim\limits_{x\to 0}\left(\dfrac{a^x+b^x}{2}\right)^{1/x} = 6$ is p/q and $gcd(p, q) = 4$, then evaluate $\sqrt{q} - \sqrt{p}$

12. Suppose $f(x) = x^3 + ax^2 + bx + c$ (a, b, c are chosen respectively by throwing a die three times). Then the probability that

(i) $f(x)$ is an increasing function is p/q then evaluate $\sqrt{q} - \sqrt{p}$; where $gcd\ (p, q) = 1$

(ii) The probability that $f(x)$ is increasing function without any critical point is p/q, then evaluate $(q - p)$; *where* $gcd\ (p, q) = 1$

Answer Key

SECTION III

1. (c) 2. (b) 3. (a) 4. (c) 5. (c) 6. (a) 7. (c) 8. (b) 9. (a) 10. (c)
11. (c) 12. (a) 13. (b) 14. (b) 15. (a) 16. (a) 17. (c) 18. (d) 19. (a) 20. (d)
21. (c) 22. (b) 23. (b) 24. (b) 25. (b) 26. (a) 27. (d) 28. (a) 29. (b) 30. (c)
31. (a) 32. (b) 33. (b) 34. (d) 35. (a) 36. (b) 37. (c) 38. (a) 39. (b) 40. (a)
41. (a) 42. (b) 43. (d) 44. (b) 45. (c) 46. (b) 47. (d) 48. (d) 49. (c) 50. (c)
51. (b) 52. (b) 53. (b) 54. (b) 55. (i) (a) (ii) (b) 56. (c) 57. (c) 58. (b) 59. (b)
60. (c) 61. (a) 62. (b) 63. (c) 64. (a) 65. (d) 66. (c) 67. (d) 68. (c) 69. (d)
70. (b) 71. (b) 72. (c) 73. (b) 74. (d) 75. (b)

SECTION IV

1. (a, b, c) 2. (a, b) 3. (a, c) 4. (a, b, d) 5. (a, c, d) 6. (a, b, c, d) 7. (a, c) 8. (b, c, d) 9. (a, b, c)
10. (b, c, d) 11. (b, c)

SECTION V

1. (a) 2. (a) 3. (a) 4. (d) 5. (a) 6. (b) 7. (b) 8. (c) 9. (a) 10. (a)
11. (b) 12. (a) 13. (c)

SECTION VI

1. (a) 2. (b) 3. (d) 4. (a) 5. (b) 6. (c) 7. (c) 8. (a) 9. (c) 10. (d)
11. (b) 12. (c) 13. (d) 14. (b) 15. (b) 16. (a) 17. (d) 18. (b) 19. (d) 20. (b)
21. (c) 22. (c) 23. (d) 24. (a) 25. (c) 26. (a) 27. (a) 28. (b) 29. (c) 30. (a)
31. (c) 32. (b) 33. (c) 34. (c) 35. (a) 36. (c) 37. (a,c) 38. (a,c) 39. (c) 40. (a)
41. (b) 42. (c) 43. (a) 44. (b) 45. (a) 46. (b) 47. (a) 48. (c)

SECTION-VII

1. (i) → (b) (ii) → (a), (iii) → (a), (iv) → (d)
2. (i) → (b) (ii) → (a), (iii) → (c), (iv) → (b)
3. (i) → (c), (ii) → (a), (iii) → (b),
4. (i) → (c), (ii) → (b), (iii) → (d), (iv) → (a)

SECTION-VIII

1. 329 2. 32 3. 21 4. 14 5. 3 6. 0.6 7. 61 8. 5 9. 2 10. 21
11. 10 12. (i) 1, (ii) 7

HINTS AND SOLUTIONS

TEXTUAL EXERCISE 1: (SUBJECTIVE)

1 (i) (a), (b), (c), (d), (e)
(ii) (a), (b), (d); very clear from definition

2 (a) (b); as their sample spaces have 4 and 216 elements respectively.

3 (c)

4 (a), (c); as every four consective years (no year being century) has a leap year and every real number is complex.

5 E_1 and E_3, E_1 and E_4, E_2 and E_3, E_2 and E_4

6 E_1 and E_2

7 (i) non-mutually exclusive but independent
(ii) non-mutually exclusive and independent
(iii) non-mutually exclusive but independent

8 $\because$ A and B are mutually exclusive events, $P(A \cap B) = 0$
$\Rightarrow$ $P(A) = 0 \neq P(A) \cdot P(B)$ as each of $P(A)$ and $P(B)$ is non-zero.
$\Rightarrow$ A and B are dependent events
Now $P(\bar{A} \cap \bar{B}) = P(\overline{A \cup B}) = 1 - P(A \cup B)$
$= 1 - [P(A) + P(B)] \neq P(\bar{A}).P(\bar{B})$
$= [1 - P(A)]\, [1 - P(B)]$
$\Rightarrow$ $P(\bar{A}\bar{B}) \neq P(\bar{A}).P(\bar{B})$
$\Rightarrow$ $\bar{A}$ and $\bar{B}$ are dependent events
Aliter: $P(A \cap B) = 0$
$\Rightarrow$ Occurrence of any one (say A) rules out the possibility of occurrence of other i.e., A and B are dependent events.

9 $\because$ A and B are two independent events
$\Rightarrow$ $P(A \cap B) = P(AB) = P(A).P(B)$ ....(i)
Now $P(A \cap \bar{B}) = P(A) - P(A \cap B)$
$= P(A) - P(A) \cdot P(B) = P(A).[1 - P(B)]$
$= P(A).P(\bar{B})$
Similarly $P(\bar{A} \cap B) = P(\bar{A}).P(B)$
Now, $P(\bar{A} \cap \bar{B}) = P(\overline{A \cup B})$
$= 1 - [P(A) + P(B) - P(A \cap B)]$
$= 1 - P(A) - P(B) + P(A) \cdot P(B)$
$= [1 - P(A)] \cdot [1 - P(B)] = P(\bar{A}).P(\bar{B})$
Thus $\bar{A}, \bar{B}$ are independent events.

TEXTUAL EXERCISE 2: (SUBJECTIVE)

1 Two coins are tossed S = {HH, HT, TH, TT} at least one head occurs E = {HH, HT, TH}
P (at least one head) = 3/4

2 Three coins are tossed S = {HHH, HHT, HTH, THH, THT, TTH, HTT, TTT} $\Rightarrow n(S) = 8$
At least two heads occur means
E = {HHH, HHT, HTH, THH} $\therefore$ $n(E) = 4$

3 $n(S) = 36$ as two dice are rolled so getting a sum of 5 means
$E = \{(1, 4), (4, 1), (2, 3), (3, 2)\}$
$P(\text{sum of } 5) = \frac{4}{36} = \frac{1}{9}$

4 Two dice are rolled together so $n(S) = 36$
Getting the product a perfect square $1 = 1 \times 1$; $4 = 2 \times 2$
or 1×4 or (4×1);
$9 = 3 \times 3$; $16 = 4 \times 4$; $25 = 5 \times 5$; $36 = 6 \times 6$;
$\therefore$ $n(E) = 8$ so $P(E) = 2/9$

5 Two dice are rolled together $n(S) = 36$
Getting the sum a prime number
$2 = 1 + 1$; $3 = 2 + 1$; $1 + 2$
$5 = 1 + 4$; $4 + 1$, $2 + 3$; $3 + 2$;
$7 = 1 + 6$; $6 + 1$; $2 + 5$; $5 + 2$; $3 + 4$; $4 + 3$;
$11 = 5 + 6$; $6 + 5$ so $n(E) = 15$
$P(\text{sum is a prime number}) = 5/12$

6 A leap year has 366 days having 52 complete weeks and 2 days left. These two days will be two consecutive days like (S, M), (M, T), (T, W), (W, Th), (Th, F), (F, S), (S, S) out of these seven two are favorable $\Rightarrow$ P(53 Sundays) = 2/7

7 Count of four digit numbers formed with 1, 2, 3, 5 (without any repetition) = 4!
For a number to be divisible by 5 the unit place must have 0 or 5.
$\Rightarrow$ □ □ □ [5]
So 3! Numbers can be formed. Required probability
$= \frac{3!}{4!} = \frac{1}{4}$

8 Counts of five digit numbers formed without repetition using 1, 2, 3, 4, 5 $\Rightarrow n(S) = 5!$
(i) Even number will be formed when 2 or 4 is put at unit place $\Rightarrow n(E) = 2 \times 4!$
So $P(E) = \frac{2}{5}$
(ii) Divisible by 4 : So last two digits favorable to the requirements will be 12, 24, 32, 52
$n(E) = 3! \times 4 = 4!$ $\Rightarrow$ $P(E) = \frac{1}{5}$
(iii) Sum of digits = 15 divisible by 3 $\Rightarrow$ $n(E) = 5!$
$\Rightarrow$ P (E) = 1
(iv) Number must be even so unit place will have 2 or 4
$\Rightarrow n(E) = 2 \times 4! \Rightarrow P(E) = \frac{2 \times 4!}{5!} = \frac{2}{5}$

(v) Divisible by 12

$\Rightarrow$ Number must be divisible by 3 or 4 which are relatively prime (co-prime)

$P(E) = 4 \times 3!$ $\Rightarrow$ $P(E) = \dfrac{1}{5}$

(vi) Divisible by 24

$\Rightarrow$ Number must be divisible by 3 or 8 (last three digits divisibility for 8)

Gives 152, 312, 352, 432, 512 (as last 3 digits)

$N(E) = 5 \times 2!$

$\Rightarrow$ $P(E) = 1/12$

9. (i) Total number of cards $n(S) = 52$

Number of honours cards $n(E) = 16$

$\Rightarrow$ $P(E) = \dfrac{4}{13}$

(ii) Number of court cards $= 12 \Rightarrow P(E) = \dfrac{3}{13}$

(iii) Number of kings and queens $= 8 \Rightarrow P(E) = \dfrac{2}{13}$

(iv) Number of cards of hearts $= 13 \Rightarrow P(E) = \dfrac{1}{4}$

10 Let S be the event when a score less than 5 but not less than 2 is obtained i.e., score $\in \{2, 3, 4\}$ and F be the event when the score obtained is greater than or equal to 5.

$\therefore$ Required probability $= P(S \text{ or } FS \text{ or } FFS \text{ or } FAFS \ldots.)$

$$= \frac{3}{6} + \frac{2}{6} \times \frac{3}{6} + \frac{2}{6} \times \frac{2}{6} \times \frac{3}{6} \ldots. = \frac{3/6}{1-2/6} = \frac{3}{4}$$

11. Two cards are drawn in ${}^{52}C_2$ ways $\Rightarrow n(S) = {}^{52}C_2$

(i) Both cards are spade $n(E) = {}^{13}C_2$

$$\Rightarrow P(E) = \frac{{}^{13}C_2}{{}^{52}C_2} = \frac{13 \times 12 \times 2}{2 \times 52 \times 51} = \frac{1}{17}$$

(ii) One card is spade (${}^{13}C_1$ ways) and one card is diamond ${}^{13}C_1$ ways

$$\therefore P(E) = \frac{{}^{13}C_1 \times {}^{13}C_1}{{}^{52}C_2} = \frac{13 \times 13 \times 2}{52 \times 51} = \frac{13}{102}$$

12. Since coupons are to be selected by replacement, each trail has 15 choices

$\therefore$ In seven selections, no. of selection ways $= (15)^7$. Since we want to have largest number $= 9$, therefore we must reject those selection having numbers less than 9.

$\therefore$ Required number of desirable ways $= 9^7 - 8^7$

$$\therefore \text{Required probability } P(E) = \frac{9^7 - 8^7}{15^7}$$

13. 7 white and 3 black balls so $n(S) = 10$

$\times\, W \times W \times W \times W \times W \times W \times W \times$

The number of ways placing 3 black balls in 10 place $= {}^{10}C_3$. When no two black balls are together it means selecting three places out of spaces marked with $\times$. i.e., ${}^{8}C_3$ ways

$$\Rightarrow \text{Required probability} = \frac{{}^{8}C_3}{{}^{10}C_3} = \frac{8 \times 7 \times 6}{10 \times 9 \times 8} = \frac{7}{15}$$

14. Putting 6 different balls into three different boxes (where no box remains empty) is to find the number of onto functions

$$\sum_{r=1}^{m} {}^{n}C_r(-1)^{n-r} = 3 - 3.2^6 + 3^6 = 540$$

Number of groups (of (2 each) from 6 numbers can be in ${}^{6}C_2 = 15$ ways

So three groups are formed (in 15 possible ways).

The number of ways to put these into the boxes

$= 15 \times 3! = 90$ ways

$$\text{Required probability} = \frac{90}{540} = \frac{1}{6}$$

15. Two persons out of m can be selected in ${}^{m}C_2$ ways. When the two persons were sitting together so for m persons there are 2!.(m – 1)! ways

$$\therefore \text{ Required probability } P(E) = 1 - \frac{2(m-1)!}{m!} = \frac{m-2}{m}$$

16. Ten persons sitting on a round table in 9! Ways. When two particular persons (A, *B*) sitting together, then it is $2 \times 8!$ ways

$\therefore$ odds against the event $= (9! - 2 \times 8!) : (2 \times 8!) = 7 : 2$

17. (i) 5 girls and 5 boys sit together in 10! ways. All 5 girls together can arrange themselves in 5! ways

5 boys and (5 girls group) can sit in $6! \times 5!$ ways

$$\therefore P(E) = \frac{6! \times 5!}{10!} = \frac{1}{42}$$

(ii) No. two girls sit together $\times B \times B \times B \times B \times B \times$

Boys can sit in 5! ways, 5 girls must go to 5 places (out of total 6) marked $\times$ in ${}^{6}P_5 = 6!$ ways

$\Rightarrow$ Number of ways $n(E) = 6! \times 5!$

$$\Rightarrow P(E) = \frac{6! \times 5!}{10!} = \frac{1}{42}$$

(iii) No two boys and no two girls sit together. Now A row can start with a boy (boy and girl sitting alternate) or it can start with a girl (girl and boy sitting alternate)

So $n(E) = 2 \times 5! \times 5! \Rightarrow P(E) = \dfrac{2! \times 5! \times 5!}{10!} = \dfrac{1}{126}$

(iv) No. of ways when b_1b_2 are together $= 9! \times 2!$

No. of ways when b_1b_2 and g_1g_2 are together $= 8! \times 2! \times 2!$

$\therefore$ No. of ways when b_1b_2 are together but g_1g_2 are not together $= 9! \times 2! - 8! \times 2! \times 2!$

$$\therefore \text{Required probability} = \frac{8! \times 2! \times 7}{10!} = \frac{14}{90} = \frac{7}{45}$$

18. Let the probability of odd face(*s*) $= x$; then the probability of even face(*s*) $= 2x$

$\Rightarrow$ $3x + 3(2x) = 9x = 1$ $\Rightarrow$ $x = 1/9$

The set of prime numbers when a die in rolled is

$E = \{2, 3, 5\}$ and $P(E) = \dfrac{2}{9} + \dfrac{1}{9} + \dfrac{1}{9} = \dfrac{4}{9}$

19. Let $P(C) = k$

$\Rightarrow$ $P(B) = 3P(C) = 3k$ and $P(A) = 3P(B) = 9k$

$\Rightarrow$ $13k = 1$, so $k = 1/13$

$$P(A \cup B) = P(A) + P(B) = 3k + 9k = 12k = \frac{12}{13}$$

20. Any accident can happen on any day of the week = 7 ways

$\Rightarrow$ So 7 accidents in 7^7 ways. All the accidents can happen on one day of the week in 7 ways.

$\Rightarrow$ Required probability $P(E) = \frac{7}{7^7} = \frac{1}{7^6}$

TEXTUAL EXERCISE 1: (OBJECTIVE)

1. (b) $|A|_{2\times 2} = \begin{vmatrix} a_{11} & a_{12} \\ a_{21} & a_{22} \end{vmatrix}$ (using 0 or –1 as entries)

$|A|$ can be formed in $2^4 = 16$ ways

$|A| \neq 0$ can be formed in 6 ways as shown

$\begin{vmatrix} -1 & 0 \\ 0 & -1 \end{vmatrix}, \begin{vmatrix} 0 & -1 \\ -1 & 0 \end{vmatrix}, \begin{vmatrix} 0 & -1 \\ -1 & -1 \end{vmatrix},$

$\begin{vmatrix} -1 & -1 \\ 0 & -1 \end{vmatrix}, \begin{vmatrix} -1 & -1 \\ -1 & 0 \end{vmatrix}, \begin{vmatrix} -1 & 0 \\ -1 & -1 \end{vmatrix}$

$\therefore \quad P(|A| = 0) = \frac{10}{16} = \frac{5}{8}$

2. **(b)** Sample space $n(S) = 2^{100}$

Now $(1 + 1)^{100} = {}^{100}C_0 + {}^{100}C_1 + {}^{100}C_2 + \ldots + {}^{100}C_{100}$

$\Rightarrow$ 100 = Number of heads + Number of tails

Set of required number of tails = {0, 2, 4, 6, …., 100}

$\Rightarrow n(E) = {}^{100}C_0 + {}^{100}C_2 + {}^{100}C_4 + \ldots + {}^{100}C_{100} = \frac{1}{2}2^{100}$

$\Rightarrow \quad P(E) = \left(\frac{1}{2}\right)\frac{2^{100}}{2^{100}} = \frac{1}{2}$

3. (c) Number of balls = 10

Two persons drawing one ball each $\Rightarrow n(S) = 100$

$3b \le 12 + a$ or $b \le 4 + \frac{a}{3}$

$a = 1$;	$b = 1, 2, 3, 4$	$\Rightarrow$ 4 ways
$a = 2$;	$b = 1, 2, 3, 4$	$\Rightarrow$ 4 ways
$a = 3$;	$b = 1, 2, 3, 4, 5$	$\Rightarrow$ 5 ways
$a = 4$;	$b = 1, 2, 3, 4, 5$	$\Rightarrow$ 5 ways
$a = 5$;	$b = 1, 2, 3, 4, 5$	$\Rightarrow$ 5 ways
$a = 6$;	$b = 1, 2, 3, 4, 5, 6$	$\Rightarrow$ 6 ways
$a = 7$;	b = 1 to 6	$\Rightarrow$ 6 ways
$a = 8$;	b = 1 to 6	$\Rightarrow$ 6 ways
$a = 9$;	b = 1 to 7	$\Rightarrow$ 7 ways
$a = 10$;	b = 1 to 7	$\Rightarrow$ 7 ways

$n(E) = 8 + 15 + 18 + 14 = 55$ ways

$\Rightarrow \quad P(E) = \frac{11}{20}$

4. (c) Count of numbers (from 10 to 15) = 6

Two numbers can be arranged in ${}^6P_2$ ways = 30 ways.

From the given condition $2a > 10 + b$ and $a \neq b$

$a = 15$;	$b = 10, 11, 12, 13, 14$	$\Rightarrow$ 5 ways
$a = 14$;	$b = 10, 11, 12, 13, 15$	$\Rightarrow$ 5 ways
$a = 13$;	$b = 10, 11, 12, 14, 15$	$\Rightarrow$ 5 ways
$a = 12$;	$b = 10, 11, 13$	$\Rightarrow$ 3 ways
$a = 11$;	$b = 10$	$\Rightarrow$ 1 ways
$a = 10$;	b no solution	$\Rightarrow P(E) = \frac{19}{30}$

5. (b) A die has 6 faces $\Rightarrow n(S) = 6$

When the minimum face value is not less than 2 and the maximum value is not greater than 5, under these given conditions $E = \{2, 3, 4, 5\}$, so $n(E) = 4$

Required probability $= \frac{4}{6} = \frac{2}{3}$

6. (a) Any paper can be checked by any one of the six professors $\Rightarrow$ 6 ways

3 papers (of 3 students) will be possible in 6^3 ways. When 3 papers are checked by exactly two professors.

Out of 6 teachers, 2 persons can be selected in ${}^6C_2 = 15$ ways.

The 3 papers can be given to exactly 2 teachers in 8 – 2 = 6 ways

$\therefore$ Required probability $\frac{6\times 15}{6^3} = \frac{15}{36} = \frac{5}{12}$

7. (c) m is an integer and m $\in$ [–4, 10] = 15 integers. When roots of $x^2 - mx + (2m + 3) = 0$ are real, then $m^2 - 8m - 12 \ge 0$ i.e., $(m - 4)^2 \ge 28$ or $|m - 4| \ge 2\sqrt{7} \approx 5.28$

$m - 4 \ge 5.28$	$\Rightarrow m \ge 9.28$	$\Rightarrow m = 10$ (one value)
or $m - 4 \le -5.28$	$\Rightarrow m \le -1.28$	$\Rightarrow m = -4, -3, -2$ (three values)

Total $n(E) = 4 \quad \Rightarrow \quad P(E) = \frac{4}{15}$

8. (b) Two letters from the word ABSCOND (7 letters) can be pieked in ${}^7C_2 = 21$ ways $= n(S)$

AB, BC, CD and NO are in order $\therefore n(E) = 4$

Required probability = 4/21

9. (a) Ten white and five black balls can be placed in 15! ways in a row.

There will be 11 places generated (arround them marked ×) when 10 white balls are placed.

Since no two black balls are to be kept adjacently

$\Rightarrow$ Selecting 5 places from 11 places in ${}^{11}C_5$ ways

$\times W \times W \times W \times W \times W \times W \times W \times W \times W \times W \times$

$\Rightarrow$ Required probability $P(E) = \frac{{}^{11}C_5 \times 10! \times 5!}{15!}$

$= \frac{11!\,10!\,5!}{5!\,6!\,15!} = \frac{2}{13}$

10. (c) 1st m/c can be selected in 12 ways

2nd m/c can be selected in 11 ways

3rd m/c can be selected in 10 ways

If only one day is to be used, then the group where all the three faulty m/cs are taken together

$$\Rightarrow \quad P(E) = \frac{1}{1320}$$

11. (b) $n(S) = 6n$, Number of ways to selected $3n$ persons $= {}^{6n}C_{3n}$

When the groups contain exactly n teachers, n boys and n girls then $n(E) = {}^{2n}C_n \times {}^{2n}C_n \times {}^{2n}C_n$ ways

$$\Rightarrow \quad P(E) = \frac{\left({}^{2n}C_n\right)^3}{\left({}^{6n}C_{3n}\right)}$$

12 (a) First fourty multiplies of 5 are {5, 10, 15, 20, …., 200}

The numbers divisible by both 3 and 5 are {15, 30, 45, 60, …, 195}

$$P(E) = \frac{{}^{13}C_4}{{}^{40}C_4} = \frac{13!\,36!\,4!}{4!\,9!\,40!} = \frac{11}{1406}$$

13 (a) $n(S) = 100$

$$\frac{(x-10)(x-20)}{(x-40)} > 0 \ (x \neq 10, 20, 40)$$

either $x > 40$ or $10 < x < 20$

$\Rightarrow$ x ∈ {11,12,13,….19} ∪ {41,42,43,,,,,100}

$$N(E) = 69 \Rightarrow P(E) = \frac{69}{100}$$

14. (d) 5 letters can be put into 5 envelopes (one each) in 5! ways

There is only one way to put all the letters in correct envelopes

$$\therefore \quad P(E) = 1 - \frac{1}{120} = \frac{119}{120}$$

15. (d) There integers out of 30 integers can be chosen (without replacement) in ${}^{30}C_3$ ways. The 3 odd integers will form an odd product.

$\therefore$ P(Even product) = 1 – P(Odd product)

$$= 1 - \frac{{}^{15}C_3}{{}^{30}C_3} = 1 - \frac{13}{116} = \frac{103}{116}$$

16. (d) Let $p(B) = k$

Two mutually exclusive and exhaustive events; $P(A) = \frac{2}{3}k$

$$\text{Now, } P(A) + P(B) = \left(\frac{2}{3} + 1\right)k = 1$$

$$\Rightarrow \quad k = \frac{3}{5} = P(B) \text{ and } P(A) = 2/5$$

$\Rightarrow$ Odds in favor of B = 3 : (5 –3) = 3 : 2

17. (a) Let $P(C) = k \Rightarrow P(B) = 3k$ and $P(A) = 2P(B) = 6k$

Now $10k = 1$ so $k = \frac{1}{10}$ and $P(B) = 3/10$

Odds in favour of B = 3 : 7

18. (c) Total no of functions $= n^n = n(S)$

when the mapping is injective (i.e., one – one)

no. of functions $= n! = n(E)$

$$\Rightarrow \quad P(E) = \frac{n!}{n^n} = \frac{(n-1)!}{n^{n-1}}$$

19. (a) Twelve coupons are numbered as 1 to 12

$\therefore$ A coupon can be selected in 12 ways If the coupon has value $\leq 8 \Rightarrow 8$ ways

$\Rightarrow$ Probability in one trial = 2/3

No of trials = 6 $\therefore$ The required prob = $(2/3)^6$

20. (c) Three children form a group of 6 boys and 4 girls can be selected in ${}^{10}C_3$ ways. When the closed blood relation children are not to be included.

Number of ways of selection $= {}^8C_3 + {}^2C_1 \times {}^8C_2$

$\therefore$ Required probability

$$= \frac{{}^8C_3}{{}^{10}C_3} + \frac{{}^2C_1 \times {}^8C_2}{{}^{10}C_3} = \frac{8\times7\times6}{10\times9\times8} + \frac{2\times8\times7\times6}{2\times10\times9\times8} = \frac{14}{15}$$

21. (b) $n(X) = k$, Number of subsets of $X = 2^k$

The number of elements and the number of sets are given by the binomial expansion

$2^k = {}^kC_0 + {}^kC_1 + {}^kC_2 + \ldots\ldots\ldots + {}^kC_{k-2} + {}^kC_{k-1} + {}^kC_k$

${}^kC_0$ = null set (without any element) and ${}^kc_k$ (universal set) are complementary

Similarly there are k singletons (${}^kC_1$) which will have k sets with (k–1) elements each as their complementary sets.

$\therefore$ No of such combinations = 1/2 (2^k)

Now two subsets from 2^k subsets can be selected in ${}^{2^k}C_2$ ways

$$\therefore \quad \text{Required probability } P(E) = \frac{2^k}{2.{}^{2^k}C_2}$$

$$\text{Put } 2^k = m \text{ so } P(E) = \frac{m.2}{2.m(m-1)} = \frac{1}{m-1} = \frac{1}{(2^k - 1)}$$

22. (c) The probability that 13th of a month is Friday = 1/7

Since there are 12 month $\Rightarrow$ The required probability = 1/84

23. (c) The birthday of a person can be in 365 ways

$\Rightarrow$ Birth days of three persons can occur in $(365)^3$ ways

The birthday of all the three persons can be on any one day. As there are 365 days so 365 ways.

$$\text{The required probability } P(E) = \frac{1}{(365)^3}$$

24. (a) There are two ways HHHHT or TTTTH $\Rightarrow n(E) = 2$.

When the coin tossed 5 time $n(S) = 32$

$\Rightarrow$ Required probability $P(E) = 1/16$

25. (a) $x = 33^n$

If four consecutive values (natural numbers) are considered one value gives the desired result $P(E) = \frac{1}{4}$

26. (c) An integer can have unit place occupied by 0, 1, 2, 3,…., 9 ≡ 10 ways

For n integers we have 10^n ways.
Last digit if happens to be 0,5 then we will have 0 or 5 in the product. So exclude these.
If 1,3,5,7 are choosen at unit place then product will be odd

$$\Rightarrow P(E) = \frac{8^n - 4^n}{10^n} = \frac{4^n - 2^n}{5^n}$$

27. (c) **Value** 50*p*. 25*p*. 10*p*
No. 2 5 15

5 Coins out of 22 can be chosen in ${}^{22}C_5$ ways. Let x be the no. of 50*P* coins selected. y be the no. of 25*p*. coins selected and z be the no of 10 p. coins selected. We desire that $50x + 25y + 10z < 150$ or $10x + 5y + 2z < 30$ where $0 \le x \le 2$; or $0 \le y \le 5$, $0 \le z \le 14$ and $x + y + z = 5$. Thus following cases are impossible

Case (i): $x = 2, y = 2, z = 1$
No. of ways of such selections $= {}^2C_2 \times {}^5C_2 \times {}^{15}C_1 = 1 \times 10 \times 15 = 150$

Case (ii): $x = 1, y = 4, z = 0$
No of ways of such selections $= {}^2C_1 \times {}^5C_4 = 10$

Case (iii): $x = 2, y = 3, z = 0$. No of ways of such selection $= {}^2C_2 \times {}^5C_3 \times {}^{15}C_0 = 1 \times 10 = 10$

$\therefore$ Total $= 150 + 10 + 10 = 170$ ways are to be rejected

$\therefore$ Required probability $= \frac{170}{22}$

28. **(a)** The set of (N – 1) places are to be filled by (r –1) cars in ${}^{N-1}C_{r-1}$ ways
When two of the neighbouring positions are vacant (empty) $\Rightarrow$ (N – 3) places for (r – 1) cars, so ${}^{N-3}C_{r-1}$ ways are favourable

$$\Rightarrow P(E) = \frac{{}^{N-3}C_{r-1}}{{}^{N-1}C_{r-1}}$$

29. **(d)** The last three digits under the given conditions are possible in 10 × 9 × 3 ways
Probability of correct dialing (as only one combination is correct) = 1/270

30. **(c)** Two tickets from n marked tickets can be drawn in ${}^nC_2$ ways. Under the given conditions if $m < (n - 1)$
$n_1 = n$ then $n_2 = 1,2,3,\ldots,(n - m - 1)$
$n_1 = n-1$ then $n_2 = 1,2,3,\ldots,(n - m - 2)$
....
....
$n_1 = (m + 3)$; $n_2 = 1,2$
$n_1 = (m + 2)$; $n_2 = 1$
No of possible ways $= 1 + 2 + 3 + \ldots (n - m - 1)$

$$= \frac{(n-m-1)}{2}\{2 + (n-m-2)\} = \frac{(n-m)(n-m-1)}{2}$$

$$P(E) = \frac{(n-m)(n-m-1)}{2.{}^nC_2} = \frac{(n-m)(n-m-1)}{n(n-1)}$$

31. **(a)** Two numbers out of 3*n* numbers can be drawn in ${}^{3n}C_2$ ways. We get numbers in the form
$n_1 = 3k + 1 = \{1,4,7, \ldots, 3n-2\}$
$n_2 = 3k + 2 = \{2,5,8,\ldots,3n-1\}$
$n_3 = 3k + 3$ (or $3k$) $= \{3,6,9,\ldots,3n\}$
$x^3 + y^3 = (x + y)\{(x+y)^2 - 3(xy)\}$
divisibility by 3 gives $(x + y)$ is divisible by 3. Which is possible when $(n_1 + n_2)$ or $(n_3 + n_3)$ system is chosen

$$\Rightarrow P(E) = \frac{{}^nC_2 + {}^nC_1 \times {}^nC_1}{{}^{3n}C_2} = \frac{2n^2 + n(n-1)}{3n(3n-1)}$$

$$= \frac{3n^2 - n}{3n(3n-1)} = \frac{n(3n-1)}{3n(3n-1)} = \frac{1}{3}$$

32. **(d)** A number from each card (marked 1 to 100) can be selected in $({}^{100}C_1)^3$ ways
The right angled triangle can be formed in 36 ways
As $(3k, 4k, 5k)$ where $k \in \{1,2,3,\ldots\ldots.20\}$
$(12m, 5m, 13m)$ where $m \in \{1,2,3,\ldots.7\}$
$(15p, 8p, 17p)$ where $p \in \{1,2,3,4,5\}$
$(24r, 7r, 25r)$ where $r \in \{1,2,3,4\}$

$$\Rightarrow \text{required probability} = \frac{36}{(100)^3} = \frac{9}{2(50)^3}$$

33. **(c)** There are 2*m* integers $\{1,2,3,\ldots,2m - 1, 2m\}$ $n(S) = 2m$
As given $P(n) = \frac{1}{n^4}$ (where $1 \le n \le 2m$)
From the given

$$\left(\frac{1}{1^4} + \frac{1}{2^4}\right) + \left(\frac{1}{3^4} + \frac{1}{4^4}\right) + \ldots + \left\{\frac{1}{(2m-1)^4} + \frac{1}{(2m)^4}\right\} = 1 \quad \ldots\text{(i)}$$

(we know that) $k^4 < (k + 1)^4$ for $k \in \mathbb{N}$

$$\Rightarrow \frac{1}{k^4} > \frac{1}{(k+1)^4}$$

$$\frac{1}{1^4} > \frac{1}{2^4}; \frac{1}{3^4} > \frac{1}{4^4}; \ldots\ldots; \frac{1}{(2m-1)^4} > \frac{1}{(2m)^4}$$

$$\Rightarrow \frac{1}{1^4} + \frac{1}{3^4} + \frac{1}{5^4} + \ldots + \frac{1}{(2m-1)^4}$$

$$> \frac{1}{2^4} + \frac{1}{4^4} + \frac{1}{6^4} + \ldots + \frac{1}{(2m)^4}$$

$$\Rightarrow \sum_{p=1}^{m} \frac{1}{(2p-1)^4} > \sum_{p=1}^{m} \frac{1}{(2p)^4} \quad \ldots\text{(ii)}$$

$$\Rightarrow \sum \frac{1}{(2p-1)^4} > \frac{1}{2} \text{ (in view of (i) and (ii))}$$

34. **(a)** *b* and *c* both can be selected in ${}^9C_1 \times {}^9C_1 = 81$ ways
$x^2 + bx + c > 0 \Rightarrow b^2 - 4c < 0$ or $b^2 < 4c$
$b = 1$; $c = 1, 2, 3,\ldots, 9$ (9 ways)
$b = 2$; $c = 2, 3, 4,\ldots, 9$(8 ways)
$b = 3$; $c = 3, 4, 5, 6, 7, 8, 9$ (7 ways)
$b = 4$; $c = 5, 6, 7, 8, 9$ (5ways)
$b = 5$; $c = 7, 8, 9$ (3ways) (Total 32 ways)

Required probability $P(E) = \frac{32}{81}$

35. **(d)** Five different balls when put one each in ten boxes is equivalent to the number of injections from A to B

In $^{10}P_5$ ways

Five adjacent boxes out of ten can be selected in 6 ways i.e. (1 to 5), (2 to 6),...(6 to 10).

Balls can be arranged in 5! ways

$$\therefore \quad P(E) = \frac{6\times 5!}{^{10}P_5} = \frac{6\times 120}{10.9.8.7.6} = \frac{1}{42}$$

36. **(a)** Observe the unit places in $7^1 = \boxed{7}, 7^2 = 4\boxed{9}, 7^3 = 34\boxed{3}, 7^4 = 240\boxed{1}$;

The sum $7^m + 7^n$ will be divisible by 5 when m, n are odds belonging to $\{4k + 1, 4k + 3\}$ or are evens belonging to $\{4k + 1, 4k + 4\}$ are selected to get zero(0) at the unit place. Two integers can be selected (with replacement) out of 100 integers in $n(S) = (100)^2$ ways

$n(E) = 2\{25C_1 \times {}^{25}C_1 + {}^{25}C_1 \times {}^{25}C_1\}$

$$\Rightarrow \quad P(E) = \frac{2\{(25)^2 + (25)^2\}}{(100)^2} = \frac{1}{4}$$

37. **(a)** Die will be thrown 3 times $\therefore n(S) = 6^3$

For $ax^2 + bx + c = 0$, to have non-real complex roots $b^2 - 4ac < 0$ or $b^2 < 4ac$

$b = 1 \quad a = 1$ to 6, $c = 1$ to 6 $\Rightarrow$ 36 ways

$b = 2$ excluding ($a = 1, c = 1$) all other values 1 to 6 $\Rightarrow$ 35 ways

$b = 3$ excluding (a,c) = (1,1), (2,1), (1,2) $\Rightarrow$ 33 ways

$b = 4$ excluding (1,1), (2,1), (1,2), (1,3), (1,4), (3,1),(4,1), (2,2) $\Rightarrow$ 28 ways

$b = 5$ excluding product upto $ac = 6$ $\Rightarrow$ 22 ways

$b = 6$ Excluding product up to $ac = 9$ $\Rightarrow$ 19 ways

Total 173 ways

$$\therefore \quad P(E) = \frac{173}{216}$$

38. **(c)** There are two ways → 6 steps forward and 5 steps background or 5 steps forward and 6 steps backward treating forward step as success $p = 0.6$ and backward step as failure $q = 0.4$ we get

$P(E) = P(\text{one step away}) = P(6 \text{ success}) + P(5 \text{ success})$

$= {}^{11}C_6(0.6)^6(0.4)^5 + {}^{11}C_5(0.6)^5(0.4)^6$

$= {}^{11}C_6(0.6)^5(0.4)^5\{0.6 + 0.4\} = {}^{11}C_6(0.6)^5(0.4)^5 = {}^{11}C_6(0.24)^5$

39. **(c)** Three vertices are to be selected out of six. Only two triangles will be equilateral (Formed by selecting alternative vertices) $P(E) = \dfrac{2}{5.4} = \dfrac{1}{10}$

40. **(c)** $w^{r_1} + w^{r_2} + w^{r_3} = 0$

The desired result occure when $r_1 = (3k + 1)$ $(k = 0,1)$ $r_2 = 3k + 2$ and $r_3 = 3k + 3 \Rightarrow 8$ ways

r_1, r_2, r_3 can be permuted in 6 ways.

$n(E) = 48$; $n(S) = 216$

$$P(E) = \frac{48}{216} = \frac{2}{9}$$

41. **(a, b, c)** Fair coin is tossed 5 times $n(S) = 32$

(a) probability of getting at least 3 heads is succession $= 8/32 = 1/4$ as the event is E = {HHHTT, THHHT, TTHHH, HHHTH, HTHHH, HHHHT, THHHH, HHHHH} $\Rightarrow$ 8 ways of event E.

(b) At least three heads $= P(E) = \dfrac{^5C_5 + {}^5C_4 + {}^5C_3}{2^5} = \dfrac{1}{2}$

$\therefore$ Total probability $= \dfrac{1}{4} + \dfrac{1}{2} = \dfrac{3}{4} = k$

$\Rightarrow$ $16k = 12$, Now 12 is divisible by 3,4,6

TEXTUAL EXERCISE 3: (SUBJECTIVE)

1. Three dice thrown simultaneously $\Rightarrow n(S) = 216$

A sum upto 4 can be obtained by {(1, 1, 1), (2, 1, 1), (1, 2, 1), (1, 1, 2)} ≡ 4 ways

Required probability $P(A \text{ sum of at least } 5) = 1 - \dfrac{4}{216} = \dfrac{53}{54}$

2. Pack of cards $n(S) = 52$

A spade can be drawn 13 ways which will include the king of spade.

A king can be drawn in 4 ways (including the king of spade)

$$P(E) = \frac{13 + 4 - 1}{52} = \frac{16}{52} = \frac{4}{13}$$

3. Two dice are thrown $n(S) = 36$.

A sum of 9 can be obtained by {(3, 6), (6, 3), (4, 5), (5, 4)} and a sum of 11 can be obtained as {(5, 6), (6, 5)}

$P(\text{neither a sum of 9 nor 11}) = 1 - \dfrac{6}{36} = \dfrac{5}{6}$

4. Numbering on the card 1 to 17

$\Rightarrow$ $n(S) = 17$ a number divisible by 3 or 7 is {3, 6, 9, 12, 15, 7, 14}. Required probability = 7/17

5. First 200 numbers $\Rightarrow n(S) = 200$

Integers divisible by 6 = {6, 12, 18, ..., 198} = 33

Integers divisible by 8 = {8, 16, 24, ... 200} = 25

Integers divisible by both 6 and 8 (i.e. by 24)

= {24, 48, ..., 192} = 8

$\therefore$ required probability $= \dfrac{33 + 25 - 8}{200} = \dfrac{50}{200} = \dfrac{1}{4}$

6. 6 red and 4 black balls $\Rightarrow n(S) = {}^{10}C_3$

(i) $P(\text{All are red}) = \dfrac{^6C_3}{^{10}C_3} = \dfrac{20}{120} = \dfrac{1}{6}$

(ii) $P(\text{Two red and one black}) = \dfrac{^6C_2 \times {}^4C_1}{120} = \dfrac{6\times 5\times 4}{2\times 120} = \dfrac{1}{2}$

(iii) $P(\text{all are the same colour}) = \dfrac{^6C_3 + {}^4C_3}{^{10}C_3} = \dfrac{20 + 4}{120} = \dfrac{1}{5}$

(iv) $P(\text{At least one red}) = 1 - P(\text{no red ball})$

$$= 1 - \frac{^4C_3}{^{10}C_3} = 1 - \frac{4}{120} = \frac{29}{30}$$

(v) $P(\text{At most two are red}) = 1 - P(\text{All are red})$
$= 1 - \frac{1}{6} = \frac{5}{6}$

7 Bag A: 4 red and 6 white balls
Bag B: 5 red and 7 white balls

(i) $P(\text{both balls are red}) = \frac{4}{10} \times \frac{5}{12} = \frac{1}{6}$

(ii) $P(\text{both balls are of same colour}) = P(\text{both red}) + P(\text{both white}) = \frac{4}{10} \times \frac{5}{12} + \frac{6}{10} \times \frac{7}{12} = \frac{62}{120} = \frac{31}{60}$

(iii) $P(\text{both balls of different colour})$
$= P(\text{red from A and white from } B) + P(\text{white from A and red from } B) = \frac{4}{10} \times \frac{7}{12} + \frac{6}{10} \times \frac{5}{12} = \frac{58}{120} = \frac{29}{60}$

Alter: Required probability $= 1 - P(\text{both balls of same colour}) = 1 - \frac{31}{60} = \frac{29}{60}$.

8. 50 bolts and 150 nuts in a drawer $\Rightarrow n(S) = 200$;
Half (i.e., 25 bolts and 75 nuts) are rusted. One piece (item) is taken out (in 200 ways)

(i) $P(\text{item is either rusted or it is a bolt})$
$= P(\text{rusted item}) + P(\text{it is a bolt}) - P(\text{it is a rusted bolt})$
$= \frac{1}{2} + \frac{1}{4} - \frac{25}{200} = \frac{1}{2} + \frac{1}{8} = \frac{5}{8}$

(ii) $P(\text{it is a rusted bolt}) = \frac{25}{200} = \frac{1}{8}$

9. Two dice are rolled $\Rightarrow n(S) = 36$

(a) Sum is either odd or divisible by 3
$\Rightarrow E = \{3, 5, 6, 7, 9, 11, 12\}$ $(2 \le \text{sum} \le 12)$
Sum $= 3 \Rightarrow \{(2, 1), (1, 2)\} \Rightarrow 2$ ways
Sum $= 5 \Rightarrow \{(1, 4), (4, 1), (2, 3), (3, 2)\} \Rightarrow 4$ ways
Sum $= 6 \Rightarrow \{(1, 5), (5, 1), (2, 4), (4, 2), (3, 3)\} \Rightarrow 5$ ways
Sum $= 7 \Rightarrow \{(1, 6), (6, 1), (2, 5), (5, 2), (3, 4), (4, 3)\} \Rightarrow 6$ ways
Sum $= 9 \Rightarrow \{(3, 6), (6, 3), (4, 5), (5, 4)\} \Rightarrow 4$ ways
Sum $= 11 \Rightarrow \{(5, 6), (6, 5)\} \Rightarrow 2$ ways
Sum $= 12 \Rightarrow \{(6, 6)\} \Rightarrow 1$ ways

$\Rightarrow$ Total = 24 ways $\Rightarrow P(E) = \frac{24}{36} = \frac{2}{3}$

(b) $P(\text{sum is neither odd nor it is divisible by 3}) = 1 - P(\text{sum is divisible by 3 or it is odd}) = 1/3$ ways

10. $P(A) = \frac{3}{7}$, $P(B) = \frac{4}{5}$, $P(C) = \frac{2}{3}$;

$P(\text{at least two shots hit the target})$
$= P(AB\bar{C} + A\bar{B}C + \bar{A}BC + ABC)$
$= 1 - P$ (Not more than one shot hits the target)
$= \frac{3}{7} \times \frac{4}{5} \times \frac{1}{3} + \frac{3}{7} \times \frac{1}{5} \times \frac{2}{3} + \frac{4}{7} \times \frac{4}{5} \times \frac{2}{3} + \frac{3}{7} \times \frac{4}{5} \times \frac{2}{3} = \frac{74}{105}$

11. In one attempt $\{P(\text{successes})\} = p = 0.6$
$\Rightarrow P(\text{failure}) = q = 0.4$.

Probability that none of the 6 bullets have hit the terrorist
$= (0.4)^6 = (0.16)^3 = \frac{4096}{10^6} = 0.00406$

12. Let event A = Ist Division $\Rightarrow P(A) = \frac{1}{10}$;

Event B = IInd Division $\Rightarrow P(B) = \frac{3}{5}$

Event C = IIIrd division $\Rightarrow P(C) = \frac{1}{4}$; Event D = failure

These are mutually exclusive and exhaustive events

$\therefore P(D) = 1 - \left(\frac{1}{10} + \frac{1}{4} + \frac{3}{5}\right) = \frac{1}{20}$

13. (i) Six married couples = 6 males and 6 females
Two persons can be chosen in ${}^{12}C_2$ ways

$P(\text{they are a married couples}) = \frac{6}{{}^{12}C_2} = \frac{6 \times 2}{12 \times 11} = \frac{1}{11}$

(ii) $P(\text{one is male the other is female})$
$= \frac{{}^6C_1 \times {}^6C_1}{{}^{12}C_2} = \frac{6 \times 6 \times 2}{12 \times 11} = \frac{6}{11}$

14. Six married couples = 6 males and 6 females

(i) $P(\text{two married couples are chosen})$

$= \frac{}{12} = \frac{6 \times 5 \times 24}{2 \times 12 \times 11 \times 10 \times 9} = \frac{1}{33}$

(ii) $P(\text{Exactly one married couple among the four persons from the rest of 10 persons})$
$= P(\text{one married couple}) \,.\, P(\text{Not a married couple})$
$= \frac{{}^6C_1\{{}^{10}C_2 - {}^5C_1\}}{{}^{12}C_4} = \frac{6(40)}{495} = \frac{16}{33}$

(iii) $P(\text{No married couple}) = 1 - P(\text{2 married couples chosen}) - P(\text{exactly 1 married couple chosen among 4 persons}) = 1 - \frac{1}{33} - \frac{16}{33} = \frac{16}{33}$.

15. Two fair dice are thrown $n(S) = 36$

(i) (4, 4) appears $\Rightarrow P(4, 4) = \frac{1}{36}$

(ii) doublet appears $\Rightarrow P(k, k) = \frac{6}{36} = \frac{1}{6}$

(iii) A sum of 7 $\Rightarrow P(\text{sum} = 7) = \frac{1}{6}$
$E = \{(1, 6), (6, 1), (2, 5), (5, 2), (3, 4), (4, 3)\}$

(iv) has same reading means doublets, i.e., $P(k, k) = \frac{1}{6}$

(v) Sum $= 10 P(\text{sum} = 10) = \frac{3}{36} = \frac{1}{12}$

(vi) Sum$> 10; \Rightarrow E = \{(5,6), (6,5), (6,6)\}$; $P(\text{sum} > 10) = \frac{1}{12}$

(vii) $P(\text{sum} \ge 10) = \frac{6}{36} = \frac{1}{6}$

(viii) $P(\text{sum} < 10) = 1 - p(s \geq 10) = 1 - \frac{1}{6} = \frac{5}{6}$

(ix) $P(\text{both numbers are odd}) = \frac{9}{36} = \frac{1}{4}$

as $E = \{(1, 1), (1, 3), (1, 5), (3, 1), (3, 3), (3, 5), (5, 1), (5, 3), (5, 5)\}$

(x) $P(\text{Both numbers are even}) = \frac{9}{36} = \frac{1}{4}$

as $E = \{(2, 2), (2, 4), (2, 6), (4, 2), (4, 4), (4, 6), (6, 2), (6, 4), (6, 6)\}$

16. $P(B) = \frac{1}{3}$

Now $P(A) = 1 - \frac{{}^6C_3}{{}^9C_3} = 1 - \frac{5}{21} = \frac{16}{21}$

So $P(A) : P(B) = \frac{16}{21} : \frac{1}{3} = 16 : 7$

17. Numbers marked from 10 to 99 ≡ 90 numbers

These are two digit numbers. A product of 12 is obtained when (2, 6), (6, 2), (3, 4), (4, 3) are obtained

∴ In one attempt probability of success $= \frac{4}{90} = \frac{2}{45}$

Probability of at least one laughter (success) in three trials

= 1 – probability of failure in the three trials

$= 1 - \left(\frac{43}{45}\right)^3$

18. 1(5 Rs. coin) + 3 (2 Rs. Coins) + 2 (1 Rs. coins) can be arranged in $\frac{6!}{3!2!}$ ways. Now same denomination coins consecutive can be arranged in 3! ways

∴ Required probability $= \frac{3!}{\left(\frac{6!}{3!\,2!}\right)} = \frac{6 \times 6 \times 2}{720} = \frac{1}{10}$

19. 8 different coloured balls and 8 bags of respective colours. Balls can be put in the bags (one each) in 8! ways

When 5 balls are in their respective bags it is possible in ${}^8C_5$ ways.

Now 3 balls go into de-arrangement (in 2 ways)

$\Rightarrow P(E) = \frac{{}^8C_5 \times 2}{8!} = \frac{8!2}{5!3!8!} = \frac{2}{120 \times 6} = \frac{1}{360}$

20. $P(A) = 75\% = \frac{3}{4}$; $P(B) = 70\% = \frac{7}{10}$

Since these are independent events

∴ $P(A \cup B) = P(A) + P(B) - P(A) \,.\, P(B)$

so $P(A \cup B) = \frac{3}{4} + \frac{7}{10} - \frac{3}{4}.\frac{7}{10} = \frac{30 + 28 - 21}{40} = \frac{37}{40}$

21. Number of elements in set A = Number of elements in set B

So $n(A) = n(B) = 4$

⇒ Total number of functions $n(S) = 4^4 = 256$

Number of onto functions (Since it is one-one and onto) $n(E) = 4!$

$\Rightarrow P(E) = \frac{4!}{256} = \frac{3}{32}$

22. $P(\bar{B}) = \frac{13}{75} \Rightarrow P(B) = \frac{62}{75}$

$P(A)$ and $P(B)$ are independent events

So $P(A \cap B) = P(A) \,.\, P(B) = \frac{8}{25}$ (given)

$\Rightarrow P(A) = \frac{8}{25} \times \frac{75}{62} = \frac{12}{31}$

23. Given $P(E \cap F) = \frac{1}{12}$ and $P(\bar{E} \cap \bar{F}) = \frac{1}{2}$

$\Rightarrow P(E \cup F) = \frac{1}{2}$

Since these are independent events

∴ $P(E) + P(F) - P(E \cap F) = P(E \cup F) = \frac{1}{2}$

⇒ $P(E) + P(F) = 7/12$ and $P(E) \,.\, P(F) = 1/12$

So gives $\left\{P(E) = \frac{4}{12}, P(F) = \frac{3}{12}\right\}$

or $\left\{P(E) = \frac{3}{12}, P(F) = \frac{4}{12}\right\}$

24. Let $P(A) = m, \Rightarrow P(B) = \frac{3}{2}m$ and $P(C) = \frac{1}{2}P(B)$

$\Rightarrow P(C) = \frac{3}{4}m$

Since these are mutually exclusive and exhaustive events

$\Rightarrow m + \frac{3}{2}m + \frac{3}{4}m = 1$ or $\frac{(4+6+3)}{4}m = 1$

$\Rightarrow m = \frac{4}{13} = P(A)$

TEXTUAL EXERCISE 2: (OBJECTIVE)

1. (b) 8 blue balls and 2 red balls ⇒ $P(B) = 8/10$, $P(R) = 2/10$. Once the first red ball is drawn in (any of) the first three draws (and replacement by blue ball) after that we are to draw last red ball in fourth draw.

∴ $P(E) = P(RBBR \text{ or } BRBR \text{ or } BBRR)$

$= \frac{2}{10}.\frac{9}{10}.\frac{9}{10}.\frac{1}{10} + \frac{8}{10}.\frac{2}{10}.\frac{9}{10}.\frac{1}{10} + \frac{8}{10}.\frac{8}{10}.\frac{2}{10}.\frac{1}{10}$

$= \frac{162 + 144 + 128}{10^4} = \frac{434}{10000} = 0.0434$

2. (c) Out of n-persons three persons can be selected in ${}^nC_3$ ways. Out of n-person, 3 persons can be selected together in following (n – 2) ways (1, 2, 3), (2, 3, 4), (3, 4, 5), ..., (n – 2, n – 1, n)

$\therefore$ Required probability $P(E) = 1 - \dfrac{(n-2)(6)}{n(n-1)(n-2)}$

$= 1 - \dfrac{6}{n(n-1)}$

5. **(b)** wo squares having a common side can be selected by taking any two consecutive squares horizontally or vertically e.g. (A, B), (B, C) …..(G, H) or (I, J), (J, K)…. (K, L) etc.

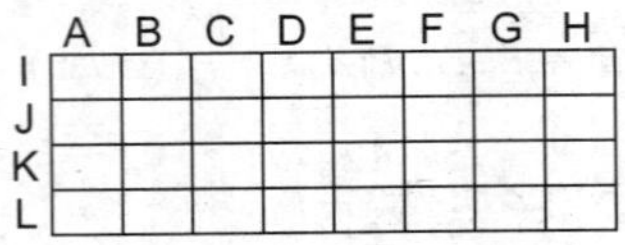

$\therefore$ Required no. of favorable ways $= 7 \times 4 + 3 \times 8 = 52$

$\therefore$ Required probability $= \dfrac{52}{{}^{32}C_2} = \dfrac{13}{124}$

6. (c) Bag has x white and y black balls

$P(\text{White}) = \dfrac{x}{x+y}, P(\text{Black}) = \dfrac{y}{x+y}$

$$P(A) = \frac{x}{(x+y)} + \left(\frac{y}{x+y}\right)^2\left(\frac{x}{x+y}\right) + \left(\frac{y}{x+y}\right)^4\left(\frac{x}{x+y}\right) + \ldots..$$

$$= \frac{x}{(x+y)}\left\{\frac{1}{1-\dfrac{y^2}{x^2+y^2+2xy}}\right\} = \frac{x(x+y)}{x(x+2y)} = \frac{x+y}{x+2y}$$

Similarly $P(B) = \left(\dfrac{y}{x+y}\right)\left(\dfrac{x}{x+y}\right) +$

$$\left(\frac{y}{x+y}\right)^3 \frac{x}{x+y} + \left(\frac{y}{x+y}\right)^5 \frac{x}{x+y} + \ldots.$$

$$= \frac{xy}{(x+y)^2}\left\{\frac{1}{1-\dfrac{y^2}{(x+y)^2}}\right\} = \frac{y}{x+2y}$$

$\Rightarrow \dfrac{P(A)}{P(B)} = \dfrac{4}{1} \qquad \Rightarrow \left(\dfrac{x+y}{x+2y}\right)\Big/\left(\dfrac{y}{x+2y}\right) = \dfrac{4}{1}$

So $x = 3y \qquad \Rightarrow x : y = 3 : 1$

7. (d) A fair coin is tossed 200 times $\Rightarrow n(S) = 2^{200}$.

$2^{200} = {}^{200}C_0 + {}^{200}C_1 + {}^{200}C_2 + \ldots.. + {}^{200}C_{200}$

$= \{{}^{200}C_0 + {}^{200}C_2 + {}^{200}C_4 + \ldots. + {}^{200}C_{200}\} + \{{}^{200}C_1 + {}^{200}C_3 + {}^{200}C_5$

$+ \ldots\ldots\ldots + {}^{200}C_{199}\}$

Sum of even indexed terms = sum of the odd indexed terms

$\Rightarrow n(E) = \left(\dfrac{1}{2}\right)2^{200} \qquad \Rightarrow P(E) = \dfrac{1}{2}$

8. (d) $P(A \Delta B) = P(A) + P(B) - 2P(A \cap B) = p^2$

$P(B \Delta C) = P(B) + P(C) - 2P(B \cap C) = p^2$

$P(C \Delta A) = P(C) + P(A) - 2P(A \cap C) = p^2$

Adding and dividing by 2 $\Rightarrow \Sigma P(A) - \Sigma P(A \cap B) = \dfrac{3}{2}p^2$

Also $P(A \cap B \cap C) = p^2$

Using $P(A \cup B \cup C)$

$= \sum P(A) - \sum P(A \cap B) + \sum P(A \cap B \cap C)$

$= \dfrac{3}{2}p^2 + p^2 = \dfrac{5}{2}p^2$

9. (c) Statistics has 10 letters such that

$P(S) = \dfrac{3}{10},\ P(T) = \dfrac{3}{10},\ P(A) = \dfrac{1}{10},$

$P(C) = \dfrac{1}{10},\ P(I) = \dfrac{2}{10}$

Mathematics has 11 letters such that

$P(S) = \dfrac{1}{11}, P(T) = \dfrac{2}{11}, P(A) = \dfrac{2}{11}, P(C) = \dfrac{1}{11},\ P(I) = \dfrac{1}{11};$

Now common letters $\in$ {T, A, I, S, C}

$P(\text{both letter same}) = \dfrac{3}{10}.\dfrac{1}{11} + \dfrac{3}{10}.\dfrac{2}{11} + \dfrac{1}{10}.\dfrac{2}{11} + \dfrac{1}{10}.\dfrac{1}{11} + \dfrac{2}{10}.\dfrac{1}{11}$

$= \dfrac{3+6+2+1+2}{110} = \dfrac{14}{110} = \dfrac{7}{55}$

10. (a) A pair of unbiased dice is rolled $\Rightarrow n(S) = 36$

To get *a* sum of 4 $\Rightarrow$ {(1, 3), (2, 1), (2, 2)} is desired set and to get a sum of 6 $\Rightarrow$ {(1, 5), (5, 1), (2, 4), (4, 2), (3, 3)}

$\therefore$ The probability that the sum of 4 is obtained before sum of 6

$$= \frac{\dfrac{3}{36} + \dfrac{28}{36}\times\dfrac{3}{36} + \dfrac{28}{36}\times\dfrac{28}{36}\times\dfrac{3}{36} + \ldots}{\dfrac{8}{36} + \dfrac{28}{36}\times\dfrac{8}{36} + \dfrac{28}{36}\times\dfrac{28}{36}\times\dfrac{8}{36} + \ldots} = \left[\frac{\dfrac{3}{36}\left(\dfrac{1}{1-\dfrac{28}{36}}\right)}{\dfrac{8}{36}\left(\dfrac{1}{1-\dfrac{28}{36}}\right)}\right] = \frac{3}{8}$$

11. (b) In a lot of 100 bulbs 20 are defective, so 80 are non-defective. No. of ways to select 5 bulbs $= {}^{100}C_5$

$P(\text{at least 2 bulbs and at the most 4 bulbs defective})$

$= \dfrac{{}^{20}C_2.{}^{80}C_3 + {}^{20}C_3.{}^{80}C_2 + {}^{20}C_4.{}^{80}C_1}{{}^{100}C_5}$

12. (c) Probability of P_1 to die in a year $= p$

Probability of P_2 to die in a year $= q$

Probability that at the end of the year only one is alive

$= P_1\bar{P}_2 + \bar{P}_1P_2 = p(1-q) + q(1-p) = p + q - 2pq$ or

$1 - (P_1P_2 \text{ or } \overline{P_1}\,\overline{P_2}) = 1 - (pq) - (1-p)(1-q) = p + q - 2pq$

13. (b) (1, 2, 3,…k), k + 1, k + 2, …,n can be arranged in (n – k + 1)! × k! ways (keeping 1 to k together)

But total no of ways of arranging = n!

$\therefore$ Required Probability $= P(E) = \dfrac{(n-k+1)!k!}{n!}$

$= \dfrac{(n-k+1)}{{}^nC_k}$

14 (a) $P(A)=\frac{1}{2};\ P(B)=\frac{1}{3};\ P(C)=\frac{1}{6}$

Where $P(A)$ = probability of 'A' as winner;
$P(B)$ = probability of 'B' as winner
$P(C)$ = probability of a draw
There are two ways to win alternatively A B A or B A B

$\therefore\ P(ABA)=\frac{1}{2}\times\frac{1}{3}.\frac{1}{2}=\frac{1}{12}$ and $P(BAB)=\frac{1}{3}.\frac{1}{2}.\frac{1}{3}=\frac{1}{18}$

$\therefore$ Total probability $=\left\{\frac{1}{12}+\frac{1}{18}\right\}=\frac{5}{36}$

17. (c) Experts from institution $A = 2, B = 3, C = 4$
Now 3 experts can resign in ${}^9C_3 = 84$ ways
If two experts are from the same institution then the number of ways
$n(E) = {}^2C_2({}^3C_1 + {}^4C_1) + {}^3C_2({}^2C_1 + {}^4C_1) + {}^4C_2({}^2C_1 + {}^3C_1)$
$= 7 + 3(6) + 6(5) = 55$

$\Rightarrow$ required probability $P(E)=\frac{55}{84}$

19. (c) In a non leap year, the number of days = 365 = 52 × 7 + 1
$\Rightarrow$ P(53 Sundays) = P(53 Tuesdays) = P(53 Thursdays) = 1/7 (each)
Since these are exclusive events
P(getting 53 Sundays or 53 Tuesdays or 53 Thursdays) = 3/7

20. (b) Probability of India winning $P(I)=\frac{1}{2}$

Probability of India not winning $P(\bar{I})=\frac{1}{2}$ (includes draw possibilities)
If India wins 2nd matches on 3rd chance (test), then it is possible as $I\bar{I}I$ or $\bar{I}II$

$\therefore$ Required probability $=\frac{1}{8}+\frac{1}{8}=\frac{1}{4}$

22 (c) From the given $P(A\cap B) = 1/6 = P(A).P(B)$
and $P(A\cup B)' = 1 - P(A\cup B) = 1/3 \Rightarrow P(A\cup B) = 2/3$

either $P(A)=\frac{1}{2}$ and $P(B)=\frac{1}{3}$ or $P(A)=\frac{1}{3}$ and $P(B)=\frac{1}{2}$

23 (a) Let the three persons be A, B, C and the three house be H_1, H_2, H_3.
for H_1 : Probability of 'A' Applying = probability of 'B' applying = Probability of 'C' applying = 1/3 each
Similarly for H_2 and H_3

Probability of all the three persons applying for $H_1=\frac{1}{27}$

for H_2 = for H_3
$\Rightarrow$ In general applying for the house (any one house)

$=3\times\frac{1}{27}=\frac{1}{9}$

24 (d) As there are ten equally likely outcomes
$\therefore$ P(any one outcome) = 1/10

Since event A has four outcomes $P(A) = 4/10$
Let event B has m outcomes; $1 \le m \le 10$

$\Rightarrow\ P(B)=\frac{m}{10}$

Since for independent events the number of common events must be some natural number

$\therefore\ P(A).P(B)=\frac{k}{10}$ where $k\in\mathbb{N}$ or $\frac{4}{10}.\frac{m}{10}=\frac{k}{10}\Rightarrow 2m=5k$

$\because\ 2m \in [2, 20] \Rightarrow k \in \{2, 4\}$
$\Rightarrow\ m = 5$ or 10

25 (a, c, d) If exactly one of M and N event occurs, then $P(M\,\Delta\, N) = P(M) + P(N) - 2P(M\cap N)$ ....((a) option)

Also $P(M\,\Delta\, N)=P(M\cap\bar{N})+P(\bar{M}\cap N)$ ....((c) option)

Also $P(\bar{M})+P(\bar{N})-2P(\bar{M}\cap\bar{N})$
$=P(S)-P(M)+P(S)-P(N)-2P(\overline{M\cup N})$
$=-P(M)-P(N)+2P(M\cup N)$
$=-P(M)-P(N)+2[P(M)+P(N)-P(M\cap N)]$
$=P(M)+P(N)-2P(M\cap N)$....((d) option)

26. (b, c) $P(\overline{\text{Math}})=1-m$; $P(\overline{\text{Physics}})=1-p$; $P(\overline{\text{Chemistry}})=1-c$
$\Rightarrow$ P(Math) = m and P(Physics) = p, P(Chemistry) = c
Probability (Passing in at least one subject) = 75% = 3/4 = $P(A\cup B\cup C)$
Probability (passing in exactly two subjects) = 40%
Probability (passing in at least two subjects) = 50%
$\therefore$ Probability of passing in all the three subjects $P(Math \cap Physics \cap Chemistry) = pmc = 10\% = 1/10$

Using $\frac{1}{2} = P(A\cap B) + P(B\cap C) + P(A\cap C) - 2P(A\cap B\cap C)$ = P (passing At least two subjects)

$P(\text{Exactly two subjects})=\frac{2}{5}=P(A\cap B)+P(B\cap C)+P(A\cap C)-3P(A\cap B\cap C)$

Now $P(A) + P(B) + P(C) = P(A\cup B\cup C) + \{P(A\cap B) + P(B\cap C) + P(A\cap C)\} - P(A\cap B\cap C)$

$=\frac{3}{4}+\frac{1}{2}+\frac{1}{10}=\frac{27}{20}$

27 **(b)** $P(R_1R_2 \text{ or } B_1R_2)=P(R_1).P\left(\frac{R_2}{R_1}\right)+P(B_1).P\left(\frac{R_2}{B_1}\right)$

$=\frac{1}{2}.\frac{7}{12}+\frac{1}{2}\frac{5}{12}=\frac{12}{24}=\frac{1}{2}$

TEXTUAL EXERCISE 4: (SUBJECTIVE)

1. P(Red from gab B)
$= P(R_A R_B$ or $B_A R_B)$; R_A = Red from bag A etc.

$=P(R_A).\left(\frac{R_B}{R_A}\right)+P(B_A).P\left(\frac{R_B}{B_A}\right)=\frac{4}{9}\times\frac{6}{12}+\frac{5}{9}\times\frac{5}{12}=\frac{49}{108}$

2. $P(H) = 1/2; P(T) = 1/2$
A can win in 1st, 5th, 9th turn etc.

$$\therefore \quad P(A) = \frac{1}{2} + \left(\frac{1}{2}\right)^5 + \left(\frac{1}{2}\right)^9 + \ldots = \frac{1}{2}\left\{\frac{1}{1-\frac{1}{16}}\right\} = \frac{8}{15}$$

$$\text{similarly, } P(B) = \left(\frac{1}{2}\right)^2 + \left(\frac{1}{2}\right)^6 + \left(\frac{1}{2}\right)^{10} + \ldots = \frac{1}{4}\cdot\frac{6}{15} = \frac{4}{15};$$

$$P(C) = \left(\frac{1}{2}\right)^3 + \left(\frac{1}{2}\right)^7 + \left(\frac{1}{2}\right)^{11} + \ldots = \frac{1}{8}\cdot\frac{16}{15} = \frac{2}{15};$$

$$\text{and } P(D) = \left(\frac{1}{2}\right)^4 + \left(\frac{1}{2}\right)^8 + \left(\frac{1}{2}\right)^{12} + \ldots = \frac{1}{16}\cdot\frac{16}{15} = \frac{1}{15}$$

$$\Rightarrow \quad P(A); P(B); P(C); P(D) = \frac{8}{15}; \frac{4}{15}; \frac{2}{15}; \frac{1}{15}$$

3. A pair of fair dice is thrown $\Rightarrow n(S) = 36$
A is to get a sum of 6. Sum of 6 = {(1, 5), (5, 1), (2, 4), (4, 2), (3, 3)}

$$\Rightarrow \quad P(A) = \frac{5}{36} \text{ and } P(\bar{A}) = \frac{31}{36}$$

Similarly B is to get a sum of 7. Sum of 7 = {(1, 6), (6, 1) (2, 5), (5, 2), (3, 4), (4, 3)}

$$\Rightarrow \quad P(B) = \frac{6}{36} \text{ and } P(\bar{B}) = \frac{30}{36} = \frac{5}{6} \text{ A beings the game}$$

P(A wins before B)

$$= \frac{5}{36} + \left(\frac{31}{36}\times\frac{5}{6}\right)\frac{5}{36} + \left(\frac{31}{36}\cdot\frac{5}{6}\right)^2\frac{5}{36} + \left(\frac{31}{36}\cdot\frac{5}{6}\right)^3\frac{5}{36} + \ldots$$

$$= \frac{5}{36}\left\{\frac{36\times 6}{36\times 6 - 31\times 5}\right\} = \frac{30}{61}$$

4. A can win the game at first throw 2 and 3 coins respectively and A wins in the following cases.
Case (i): A : 1 head, B : 0 head
Case (ii): A : 2 heads, B = 0 heads
Case (iii): A : 2 heads, B = 1 head
∴ P(A's win at first throw)

$$= \frac{2}{4}\times\frac{1}{8} + \frac{1}{4}\times\frac{1}{8} + \frac{1}{4}\times\frac{3}{8} = \lambda \text{ (say)}$$

Similarly, A can win the game at second throw, when game is tie at first throw i.e. both threw equal no of heads in the following cases
Case (iv): A : 0 head, B = 0 head
Case (v): A : 1 head, B : 1 head
Case (vi): A : 2 head; B : 2 head

$$\therefore \quad P(tie) = \frac{1}{4}\times\frac{1}{8} + \frac{2}{4}\times\frac{3}{8} + \frac{1}{4}\times\frac{3}{8} = \mu \text{ (say)}$$

∴ P(A' win the game)

$$= \underbrace{\left(\frac{2}{4}\times\frac{1}{8} + \frac{1}{4}\times\frac{1}{8} + \frac{1}{4}\times\frac{3}{8}\right)}_{\text{win at first threw}} + \underbrace{\left(\frac{1}{4}\times\frac{1}{8} + \frac{2}{4}\times\frac{3}{8} + \frac{1}{4}\times\frac{3}{8}\right)}_{\text{tie}}.$$

$$\left(\frac{2}{4}\times\frac{1}{8} + \frac{1}{4}\times\frac{1}{8} + \frac{1}{4}\times\frac{3}{8}\right) + \ldots$$

$$= \lambda + \mu\lambda + \mu\mu.\lambda + \mu\mu\mu\lambda + \ldots$$

$$= \lambda(1 + \mu + \mu^2 + \mu^3 + \ldots)$$

$$= \lambda\left[\frac{1}{1-\mu}\right] = \frac{\lambda}{1-\mu} = \frac{\frac{1}{4}\times\frac{1}{8}(2+1+3)}{1-\frac{1}{32}(1+6+3)} = \frac{6}{32-10} = \frac{6}{22} = \frac{3}{11}$$

5. Probability of selection of urn A = *probability of selection* of urn $B = 1/2$
Let event A = Urn A is selected and B = Urn B is selected
P(Both drawn marbles of same colors)
$= P(AR_A\, R_B \text{ or } AW_AW_B \text{ or } BR_BR_A \text{ or } BW_BW_A)$

$$= P(A).P\left(\frac{R_A}{A}\right).P\left(\frac{R_B}{ARA}\right) + \ldots$$

$$= \frac{1}{2}\left(\frac{3}{5}\right)\left(\frac{3}{8}\right) + \frac{1}{2}\left(\frac{2}{5}\right)\left(\frac{3}{4}\right) + \frac{1}{2}\left(\frac{2}{7}\right)\left(\frac{2}{3}\right) + \frac{1}{2}\left(\frac{5}{7}\right)\left(\frac{1}{2}\right)$$

$$= \frac{1}{2}\left\{\frac{9}{40} + \frac{6}{20} + \frac{4}{21} + \frac{5}{14}\right\} = \frac{901}{1680}$$

6. Probability of opening the lock on 1st attempt = 1/10
Probability of opening the lock on 2nd attempt = $\frac{9}{10}\times\frac{1}{9} = \frac{1}{10}$

Probability of opening the lock in 10th attempt

$$= \frac{9}{10}\times\frac{8}{9}\times\frac{7}{8}\times\ldots\times\frac{2}{3}\times\frac{1}{2}\times\frac{1}{1} = \frac{1}{10}$$

7. P(Exactly three black balls) = 0.6
P (exactly one black ball) = 0.4
⇒ These are two mutually exclusive and exhaustive events
Case (i): When the number of black balls = 1, then
It is drawn on 6th attempt P(Black ball on exactly 6th attempt) = $0.4\times\frac{9}{10}\times\frac{8}{9}\times\frac{7}{8}\times\frac{6}{7}\times\frac{5}{6}\times\frac{1}{5} = 0.04$ .....(i)

Case (ii): When Number of black balls is exactly:
Now 2 black balls will be drawn in the first five draws and the 3rd ball on 6th draw. Thus P(last black on 6th drawn)
$= {}^5C_2\times 0.6\times\frac{1}{120} = \frac{1}{20} = 0.05$ ....(ii)

Total prob. = 0.09 = 9/100

8. (i) To get a spade in at least three attempts
= 1 – (spade on 1st draw) – P(spade on the 2nd drawn)

$$= 1 - \frac{1}{4} - \frac{3}{4}\times\frac{1}{4} = \frac{9}{16}$$

(ii) To get a spade in exactly three attempts

$$= \frac{3}{4}\times\frac{3}{4}\times\frac{1}{4} = \frac{9}{64}$$

9 (i) Let A gets a card at value v then $p_A(v) = 1/n$
Similarly $P_B(v) = 1/n$
P(Both getting the same card) $=1/n^2$ and there are n such cases, as there are n cards

$$\Rightarrow \quad p = n\left(\frac{1}{n^2}\right) = \frac{1}{n}$$

(ii) **Case (i)** If B drawn 1, A can draw 2, 3, 4,….n

$\Rightarrow \quad P(A>B)=\frac{1}{n}.\frac{n-1}{n}$

If B draws 2, A can draw 3, 4, 5,….,n and so on Required Probabilities $=\left[\frac{(n-1)(n-2)+...+1}{n^2}\right]$

$=\frac{(n-1)}{2n^2}=\frac{(n-1)}{2n}$

10. Total no of Air crafts = 250, $P(\text{mig}-21)=\frac{150}{250}=\frac{3}{5}$

P(jaguar) = 1/5 and P(sukhoi) = 1/5

Prob of safe landing P(S.L.) = 1 – Prob (crash)

$=1-\left\{\frac{3}{5}\times\frac{1}{2}+\frac{1}{5}\times\frac{1}{3}+\frac{1}{5}\times\frac{1}{6}\right\}=1-\frac{2}{5}=\frac{3}{5}$

11. P(Fair coin) = 1/3, P(Double Headed) = 1/3; P(Weighed coin) = 1/3

Prob of getting a head $=\frac{1}{3}\times\frac{1}{2}+\frac{1}{3}\times1+\frac{1}{3}\times\frac{1}{3}=\frac{11}{18}$

12. Let n no. of dice be thrown at a time and consider that the number appears less than 6

So P(getting a six) $=1-\left(\frac{5}{6}\right)^n$

When the chance is better than even (i.e break even) $P>\frac{1}{2}$

So $1-\left(\frac{5}{6}\right)^n>\frac{1}{2}\Rightarrow\left(\frac{5}{6}\right)^n<\frac{1}{2}$

for $n=3,\left(\frac{5}{6}\right)^n>\frac{1}{2}\Rightarrow\left(\frac{5}{6}\right)^4=\frac{625}{1296}<\frac{1}{2}\Rightarrow n=4$

13. (a) P(Entering the specific house)

= P(unlocked and enter) + P(locked and enter)

$=P(\text{unlocked})\times P\left(\frac{Enter}{unlocked}\right)+P(L).P\left(\frac{E}{L}\right)$

$=\frac{1}{4}\times1+\frac{3}{4}\times\frac{3}{8}=\frac{17}{32}$

14. **(b)** Out of a slab of 4 years one year will be a leap year and 3 years will be non-leap years

$\therefore$ Required Prob. $P=\left(\frac{1}{7}\right)\frac{3}{4}+\frac{1}{4}\left(\frac{2}{7}\right)=\frac{5}{28}$

TEXTUAL EXERCISE 3 (OBJECTIVE)

1. **(d)** $P(A')=0.34;\ P(B)=0.54$

$P(A\cap B)=0.32$

$P(B/A\cup B')=\frac{P\{(B\cap(A\cup B')\}}{P(A\cup B')}$

$=\frac{P(A\cap B)}{1-P(B)+P(A\cap B)}=\frac{0.32}{0.78}=\frac{16}{39}$

2. **(d)** The possible combinations are

White 0 1.. ....9 10

Black 10 9..............1 0

(11 possible ways)

If three balls are drawn and are all black then

$P=\frac{1}{11}\left\{\frac{{}^{10}C_3+{}^{9}C_3+{}^{8}C_3+...+{}^{3}C_3}{{}^{10}C_3}\right\}$

$=\frac{1}{11}\left\{\frac{120+84+56+35+20+10+4+1}{120}\right\}=\frac{30}{120}=\frac{1}{4}$

3. **(c)** There are 4 possibilities

Original	after addition	Prob
0 black ball	$\Rightarrow$ 1 B	1/4
1 black ball	$\Rightarrow$ 2B	1/2
2 Black balls	$\Rightarrow$ 3B	3/4
3 Black balls	$\Rightarrow$ 4B	1

$So=P=\frac{1}{4}\left\{\frac{1}{4}+\frac{1}{2}+\frac{3}{4}+1\right\}=\frac{5}{8}$

4. **(b)** Let A = event of getting success in first trial

B = event of getting success 4 times put 7 trails

$\therefore \quad P\left(\frac{A}{B}\right)=\frac{P(A\cap B)}{P(B)}=\frac{p.{}^6C_3(p)^3(1-p)^3}{(p)^4.{}^7C_4(1-p)^3}$

$=\frac{{}^6C_3}{{}^7C_4}=\frac{6\times5\times4}{7\times6\times5}=\frac{4}{7}$

5. (a, b, c, d) $A=\{1,3,5……,29\}$ so $n(A)=15$ three number are chosen (without replacement) in ${}^{15}C_3$ ways

$E_1\ (n\geq7)=\{7,9,11,…29\}\Rightarrow n(E_1)=12$

And $E_2\ (n\leq19)=\{1,3,5,….,19\}\Rightarrow n(E_2)=10$

Further $E_1\cap E_2=\{7,9,11,..\ .,19\}\Rightarrow n(E_1\cap E_2)=7$

So $P(E_1)=\frac{{}^{12}C_3}{{}^{15}C_3}=\frac{12.11.10}{15.14.13}=\frac{44}{91}$

And $P(E_2)=\frac{{}^{10}C_3}{{}^{15}C_3}=\frac{10.9.8}{15.14.13}=\frac{24}{91}$

$P(E_1\cap E_2)=\frac{{}^{7}C_3}{{}^{15}C_3}=\frac{7.6.5}{15.14.13}=\frac{1}{3}$

$P(E_1/E_2)=\frac{P(E_1\cap E_2)}{P(E_2)}=\frac{1\times91}{13\times24}=\frac{7}{24}$

6. **(a)** **Case (i):** No of fair coins = m prob of getting head on 1st throw and tail of second throw

$\Rightarrow \quad P(I)=\frac{m}{N}\times\frac{1}{2}\times\frac{1}{2}=\frac{m}{4N}$

Case (ii) : No of biased coins = N – m

$\Rightarrow \quad P(II)=\frac{N-m}{N}.\frac{2}{3}.\frac{1}{3}=\frac{2(N-m)}{9N}$

Hence total prob . $P=\frac{m}{4N}+\frac{2N-2m}{9N}$

$=\frac{9m+8N-8m}{36N}=\frac{8N}{36N}+\frac{m}{36N}=\frac{2}{9}+\frac{m}{36N}$

7. **(c)** $P(A) = P(B) = P(C) = 1/10$;

$P(A \cap B) = P(B \cap C) = 0$ and $P(A \cap C) = \frac{1}{20}$

Obviously $P(A \cap B \cap C) = 0$

Hence $P(A \cup B \cup C) = P(A) + P(B) + P(C) - P(A \cap C) - P(A \cap B) - P(B \cap C) + P(A \cap B \cap C)$

$= \frac{3}{10} - \frac{1}{20} = \frac{5}{20} = \frac{1}{4}$

8. **(a, b, c, d)** $P(A \cap B') = 0.30$; $p(A' \cap B) = 0.20$ and $P(A \cap B) = 0.15$

Now $P(A \cap B') = P(A) - P(A \cap B)$

$\Rightarrow P(A) = 0.30 + 0.15 = 0.45$

Similarly $P(B) = 0.35$ so $P(A \cup B) = 0.65$

$\therefore \quad P(A/B) = \frac{P(A \cap B)}{P(B)} = \frac{0.15}{0.35} = \frac{3}{7}$

$P(B/A) = \frac{P(A \cap B)}{P(A)} = \frac{0.15}{0.45} = \frac{1}{3}$

9. **(a, b, c, d)** 1ST die has $P(3) = P(2) = P(4) = 1/3$

2nd die has $P(1) = 1/2$; $P(2) = 1/3$; $P(3) = 1/6$

The most probable sum $P(sum = 3 \text{ as } 2 + 1) = 1/6$;

$P(sum = 4 \text{ as } 3 + 1 \text{ or } 2 + 2) = \frac{1}{6} + \frac{1}{9} = \frac{5}{18}$

$P(sum = 5 \text{ as } 3 + 2 \text{ or } 2 + 3 \text{ or } 4 + 1) = \frac{1}{9} + \frac{1}{18} + \frac{1}{6} = \frac{1}{3}$

$P(Sum = 6 \text{ as } 4 + 2 \text{ or } 3 + 3) = \frac{1}{9} + \frac{1}{18} = \frac{1}{6}$

$P(sum\ 7 \text{ as } 4 + 3) = 1/18$

$\therefore$ Most probable sum is 5 with $P(sum = 5) = 1/3$

The least probable sum is 7 with $P(sum = 7) = 1/18$

10. **(d)** $A + B = C + D$ Observe that a sum of $A + B = n \in \{0,1,2,\ldots\ldots,9\}$ and can be obtained with $(n + 1)$ distinct (non negative) integers

Example: Numbers are 0,1,2,3,4,5,6,7,8,9 consider the combinations as (0,9), (1,8), (2,7), (3,6), (4,5)

The same is applicable to $C + D$

Similarly a sum of 10 to 18 can be obtained in a reversed manner i.e $10 \le n \le 18 \Rightarrow$ no of ways $= (18 - n) + 1$

$\therefore$ Number of ways $= 1^2 + 2^2 + 3^2 + \ldots\ldots + 9^2 + 10^2 + 9^2 + 8^2 + \ldots\ldots + 2^2 + 1^2$

$= 2\{1^2+2^2+3^2+\ldots+9^2\}+10^2 = 2\left(\frac{9\times10\times19}{6}\right)+100 = 670$

Since there is one correct way

$\Rightarrow$ Prob (P) = 1/670

11. **(d)** $P(A/A \cup B) = \frac{P\{A \cap (A \cup B)\}}{P(A \cup B)} = \frac{P(A)}{P(A \cup B)}$

12. **(b)** A ticket can be selected in 100 ways E_2 = Product of digits is zero, which is possible when number is {00,01, 02……,10,20,30,40,50,60,70,80,90}

$N(E_2) = 19 \Rightarrow P(E_2) = \frac{19}{100}$

E_1 = sum digits is $9 \Rightarrow E_1 \cap E_2 = \{09,90\}$ so $n(E_1 \cap E_2) = 2$

$\therefore \quad P(E_1 \cap E_2) = \frac{2}{100}$ Hence $P\left(\frac{E_1 = 9}{E_2 = 0}\right) = \frac{2}{19}$

13. **(c)** Factory A's contribution = 4 valves (10 % defective)

Factory B's contribution 5 valves (20 % defective)

Two valves can be selected in $^9C_2 = 36$ ways

Now Prob (At least one valve defective) = 1 – P(No defective valve)

The two selected valves may be

(a) both from factory A (b) both from factory B

(c) One from each

$\therefore$ Required Probability $= 1 - \frac{1}{^9C_2}$

$\left\{^4C_2\left(\frac{9}{10}\right)^2 + {^5C_2}\left(\frac{4}{5}\right)^2 + {^4C_1}{^5C_1}\frac{9.4}{10.5}\right\}$

$= 1 - \frac{1}{36}\left\{\frac{486}{100} + \frac{160}{25} + \frac{720}{50}\right\} = 1 - \frac{2566}{3600} = \frac{517}{1800}$

14. (a) Total number of articles = 20

P(exactly two defective articles) = 0.4

P(exactly three defective articles) = 0.6

These are mutually exclusive and exhaustive events.

Case (i): Exactly two defective articles: Since articles are drawn one by one without replacement

$\therefore$ Required prob $= (11)\left\{\frac{1}{190}\right\}(0.4) = \frac{11}{190} \times 0.4 = \frac{44}{1900}$

Case (ii): Exactly three defective articles

Required probability $= {^{11}C_2}(0.6)\frac{3.2.1}{20.19.18} = \frac{55}{1900}$

Total probability $= \frac{99}{1900}$

15. **(c)** $P\left\{\frac{E^c \cap F^c}{G}\right\} = \frac{P(G) - P(F \cap G) - P(E \cap G)}{P(G)}$

$= 1 - P(F) - P(E) = P(E^c) - P(F)$

16. **(c)** $P(A/B) = \frac{P(A \cap B)}{P(B)}$ Now $A \subset B$

$\Rightarrow P(A \cap B) = P(A)$

$\Rightarrow \quad P(A/B) = \frac{P(A)}{P(B)} \ge P(A)$

Since $P(A) \le P(B) \le 1$

$\therefore \quad P(A/B) \ge P(A)$

TEXTUAL EXERCISE 5: (SUBJECTIVE)

1. Let E be the event that the drawn ball is red. The probability of each bag being selected is 1/2

(a) E_1 = The ball is from bag A

E_2 = The ball is from bag B

So $P\left(\frac{E_1}{E}\right) = \frac{P(E_1).P(E/E_1)}{P(E_1).P(E/E_1) + P(E_2).P\left(\frac{E}{E_2}\right)}$

$$= \frac{\frac{1}{2}\left(\frac{5}{11}\right)}{\frac{1}{2}\left(\frac{5}{11}\right) + \frac{1}{2}\left(\frac{6}{13}\right)} = \frac{65}{131}$$

(b) Similarly $P\left(\frac{E_2}{E}\right) = \frac{\frac{1}{2}\left(\frac{6}{13}\right)}{\frac{1}{2}\left(\frac{6}{13}\right) + \frac{1}{2}\left(\frac{5}{11}\right)} = \frac{66}{131}$

2. Let E be the event that the item is defective. The item produced has equal changes of being manufactured (produced) by either factory
E_1 = *The* item is from factory A
E_2= *The* item is from factory B

$$P\left(\frac{E_2}{E}\right) = \frac{P(E_2).P(E/E_2)}{P(E_1)P\left(\frac{E}{E_1}\right) + P(E_2).P(E/E_2)}$$

$$= \frac{\frac{1}{2}\left(\frac{3}{10}\right)}{\frac{1}{2}\left(\frac{3}{10}\right) + \frac{1}{2}\left(\frac{2}{10}\right)} = \frac{3}{5} = 0.6$$

3. Let E be the event that two cards are drawn out of 51 cards (since one card is missing) and found to be spades
E_1 = *missing card is spade*
E_2= *missing card is non spade*

$$p(E_1/E) = \frac{P(E_1).P(E/E_1)}{P(E_1).P(E/E_1) + P(E_2).P\left(\frac{E}{E_2}\right)}$$

$$= \frac{\frac{1}{4}\left(\frac{^{12}C_2}{51C_2}\right)}{\frac{1}{4}\left(\frac{^{12}C_2}{^{51}C_2}\right) + \frac{3}{4}\left(\frac{^{13}C_2}{^{51}C_2}\right)} = \frac{12.11}{51.50\left\{\frac{12}{51}.\frac{11}{50} + \frac{3.13.12}{51.50}\right\}}$$

$$= \frac{12.11}{12.11 + .3.13.12} = \frac{11}{50}$$

4. Let A be the event that the given answer is correct
A_1 **:** He knows the answer $\Rightarrow P(A_1) = 1/2$
A_2 **:** He guesses it $\Rightarrow P(A_2)= 1/3$
A_3: He Copies it $\Rightarrow P(A_3) = 1/6$

$$P\left(\frac{A_1}{A}\right) = \frac{P(A_1).P\left(\frac{A}{A_1}\right)}{P(A_1).P\left(\frac{A}{A_1}\right) + P(A_2).P\left(\frac{A}{A_2}\right) + P(A_3)P\left(\frac{A}{A_3}\right)}$$

$$= \frac{\frac{1}{2}\times 1}{\frac{1}{2}\times 1 + \frac{1}{3}.\frac{1}{4} + \frac{1}{6}.\frac{1}{8}} = \frac{48}{2\{24+4+1\}} = \frac{24}{29}$$

5. Let E be the event that six is reported
E_1 : six appears on the die
E_2 : Six does not appear on the die

$$P\left(\frac{E_1}{E}\right) = \frac{P(E_1)P\left(\frac{E}{E_1}\right)}{P(E)P\left(\frac{E}{E_1}\right) - P(E_2).P\left(\frac{E}{E_2}\right)}$$

$$= \frac{\frac{1}{6}\times\frac{4}{5}}{\frac{1}{6}\times\frac{4}{5} + \frac{5}{6}\times\frac{1}{5}} = \frac{4}{4+5} = \frac{4}{9}$$

6. Let A be the event that ace is reported
A_1 : Ace is drawn
A_2 : Non –ace card appeared

$$P\left(\frac{A}{A_1}\right) = \frac{P(A_1).P\left(\frac{A}{A}\right)}{P(A_1).P\left(\frac{A}{A_1}\right) + P(A_2).P\left(\frac{A}{A_2}\right)}$$

$$P(A/A_1) = \frac{\frac{1}{13}\times\frac{4}{5}}{\frac{1}{13}\times\frac{4}{5} + \frac{12}{13}\times\frac{1}{5}} = \frac{4}{16} = \frac{1}{4}$$

7. Let E be the event that the letter is not received by the concerned friend
E_1 = *Letter was not posted (Forgotten by the son)*
E_2= *Letter was lost in transit*

(i) $P\left(\frac{E_1}{E}\right) = \frac{P(E_1).P\left(\frac{E}{E_1}\right)}{P(E_1)P\left(\frac{E}{E_1}\right) - P(E_2)P\left(\frac{E}{E_2}\right)}$

$$= \frac{\frac{1}{10}(1)}{\frac{1}{10}(1) + \frac{9}{10}\left(\frac{1}{100}\right)} = \frac{1}{10\left\{\frac{1}{10} + \frac{9}{1000}\right\}} = \frac{100}{109}$$

(ii) Similarly $P\left(\frac{E_2}{E}\right) = \frac{\frac{9}{10}.\frac{1}{100}}{\frac{109}{1000}} = \frac{9}{109}$

8. Let E be the event that the given answer is correct
E_1 = *He* knows the answer $\Rightarrow P(E_1) = 1/2$
E_2 = *He* copies it $\Rightarrow P(E_2) = 1/6$

Given : $P\left(\frac{E_1}{E}\right) = \frac{120}{141} = \frac{40}{47} \Rightarrow \frac{40}{47} = \frac{\frac{1}{2}\times 1}{\frac{1}{2}\times 1 + \frac{1}{3}\times\frac{1}{m} + \frac{1}{6}\frac{1}{8}}$

Or $\frac{80}{47} = \left\{\frac{48m}{25m+16}\right\}$ Gives $16m = 80$ so $m = 5$

9. Let A be the event that the prisoner is successful in running away

A_1 = *He selects road I*
A_2 = *He selects road II*
A_3 = *He selects road III*
A_4 = *He selects road IV*

$$\therefore \quad P\left(\frac{A_1}{A}\right) = \frac{P(A_1).P\left(\frac{A}{A_1}\right)}{\sum_{i=1}^{4} P(A_i)P\left(\frac{A}{A_i}\right)}$$

$$= \frac{\frac{1}{4}\times\frac{1}{6}}{\frac{1}{4}\left\{\frac{1}{6}+\frac{1}{8}+\frac{1}{10}+\frac{1}{12}\right\}} = \frac{1\{120\}}{6\{20+15+12+10\}} = \frac{20}{57}$$

Similarly $P\left(\frac{A_2}{A}\right) = \frac{\frac{1/8}{57}}{120} = \frac{15}{57} = \frac{5}{19}$;

$$P\left(\frac{A_3}{A}\right) = \frac{\left(\frac{1}{10}\right)}{\left(\frac{57}{120}\right)} = \frac{12}{57} = \frac{4}{19}$$

And $P\left(\frac{A_4}{A}\right) = \frac{(1/12)}{(57/120)} = \frac{10}{57}$

$\therefore$ (a) $\to$ r; (b) $\to$ q; (c) $\to$ p; (d) $\to$ s

10. Let $P(H)$= 1/2 and $P(T)$ = 1/2
Let E be the event that 4 is noted by the person
E_1 = *die* was thrown
E_2 = 5 coins were tossed

$$= P\left(\frac{E_1}{E}\right) = \frac{P(E_1).P\left(\frac{E}{E_1}\right)}{P(E_1),P\left(\frac{E}{E_1}\right) + P(E_2)P\left(\frac{E}{E_2}\right)}$$

$$= \frac{\frac{1}{2}\left(\frac{1}{6}\right)}{\frac{1}{2}\cdot\frac{1}{6}+\frac{1}{2}\cdot\frac{5}{32}} = \frac{1\ \ (96)}{6\ \{16+15\}} = \frac{16}{31}$$

11. Let A be the event that the person reached office in time
A_1= *He used the car* $\Rightarrow P(A_1) = 1/7$
A_2= *He used the scooter* $\Rightarrow P(A_2) = 2/7$
A_3= *He used the bus* $\Rightarrow P(A_3) = 3/7$
A_4= *He used the train* $\Rightarrow P(A_4) = 1/7$

$$\therefore \quad P\left(\frac{A_1}{A}\right) = \frac{P(A_1).P\left(\frac{A}{A_1}\right)}{\Sigma P(A_i).P(A/A_i)} = \frac{\frac{1}{7}\times\frac{7}{9}}{\frac{7+10+24+8}{63}} = \frac{1}{7}$$

TEXTUAL EXERCISE 4: (OBJECTIVE)

1. (a) Let E be the event that two balls drawn are of black colour $E_1, E_2, \ldots\ldots, E_n$ be the event that respective urn from similar 'n' urns

and E_{n+1} = $(n+1)^{th}$ urn is selected.

$$P\left(\frac{E_{n+1}}{E}\right) = \frac{P(E_{n+1}).P(E/E_{n+1})}{P(E_{n+1}).P(E/E_{n+1}) + \sum_{i=1}^{n} P(E_i)P\left(\frac{E}{E_i}\right)}$$

$$\frac{1}{16} = \frac{\left(\frac{1}{n+1}\right)\left({}^5C_2/{}^{10}C_2\right)}{\frac{1}{n+1}\left(\frac{5C_2}{{}^{10}C_2}\right) + \frac{n}{n+1}\cdot\frac{{}^6C_2}{{}^{10}C_2}}$$

$$\frac{1}{16} = \frac{10}{10+n(15)} \Rightarrow n = 10$$

2. (d) Let E be the event that the screw drawn is found to be defective
Let E_1 = *screw is from box A*
E_2 = *screw is from box B*
E_3 = *screw is from box C*

$$P(E_1/E) = \frac{P(E_1).P(E/E_1)}{\sum_{i=1}^{3} P(E_i).P\left(\frac{E}{E_i}\right)}$$

$$= \frac{\left(\frac{1}{3}\right)\left(\frac{1}{5}\right)}{\left(\frac{1}{3}\right)\left\{\frac{1}{5}+\frac{1}{6}+\frac{1}{7}\right\}} = \frac{42}{\{42+35+30\}} = \frac{42}{107}$$

3. (b) Let A be the event that the given answer is correct
A_1 = *the* students knows the answer $\Rightarrow P(A_1) = 90\ \%$
A_2 = *the* student makes a guess $\Rightarrow P(A_2) = 10\ \%$

$$P\left(\frac{A_2}{A}\right) = \frac{P(A_2).P(A/A_2)}{P(A_1).P\left(\frac{A}{A_1}\right) + P(A_2).P(A/A_2)}$$

$$= \frac{\frac{1}{4}\left(\frac{1}{10}\right)}{\frac{1}{4}\left(\frac{1}{10}\right)+\frac{9}{10}\times 1} = \frac{1}{1+9\times 4} = \frac{1}{37}$$

4. (c) Let E be the event that the target has been missed
E_1 = *day* is windy so $P(E_1) = 3/10$ Prob of Hitting the target

$= 2/5$; $P\left(\frac{E}{E_1}\right) = \frac{2}{5}$; $P\left(\frac{\bar{E}}{E_1}\right) = \frac{3}{5}$

E_2 = *day* is not windy so $P(E_2)$ = 7/10 and probality of hitting; the target = 7/10; $P\left(\frac{E}{E_2}\right) = \frac{7}{10}$; $P\left(\frac{\bar{E}}{E_2}\right) = \frac{3}{10}$

$$\text{Now } P(E_2/\bar{E}) = \frac{P(E_2)P\left(\frac{\bar{E}}{E_2}\right)}{P(E_1)P\left(\frac{\bar{E}}{E_1}\right) + P(E_2).P\left(\frac{\bar{E}}{E_2}\right)}$$

$$= \frac{\frac{7}{10}\cdot\frac{3}{10}}{\frac{7}{10}\cdot\frac{3}{10}+\frac{3}{10}\cdot\frac{3}{5}} = \frac{21}{21+18} = \frac{7}{13}$$

5. **(b)** Let E be the event that the selected students is a girl

E_{B_1} = girl is from school B_1

E_{B_2} = girl is from school B_2

E_{B_3} = girl is from school B_3

E_{B_4} = girl is from school B_4

Now $P\left(\frac{E_{B_2}}{E}\right) = \frac{P(E_{B_2}).P(E/E_{B_2})}{\sum_{i=4}^{4} P(E_{B_i})P\left(\frac{E}{E_{Bi}}\right)}$

$$= \frac{\frac{1}{4}\times\frac{20}{100}}{\frac{1}{100}\times\frac{1}{4}\{12+20+13+17\}} = \frac{20}{62} = \frac{10}{31}$$

6. **(a)** Probality of winning: $P(Group\ A) = 0.5$; $P(Group - B) = 0.3$; $P(Group - C) = 0.2$;

New product launch : $P(A) = 0.7$; $P(B) = 0.6$; $P(C)$; $= 0.5$

Total Probability $\Sigma P(Group - A)\ .\ P(A) = 0.5 \times 0.7 + 0.3 \times 0.6 + 0.2 \times 0.5 = 0.35 + 0.18 + 0.10 = 0.63$

7. **(c)** Let E be the event that the signal received at station B is green

E_1 = original signal is green $\Rightarrow P(E_1) = 4/5$

E_2 = Original signal is red $\Rightarrow P(E_2) = 1/5$

Transmission accuracy prob = ¾

Now $P\left(\frac{E_1}{E}\right) = \frac{P(E_1)P\left(\frac{E}{E_1}\right)}{P(E_1).P\left(\frac{E}{E_1}\right)+P(E_2)P\left(\frac{E}{E_2}\right)}$

$$= \frac{\left(\frac{36}{80}+\frac{4}{80}\right)}{\left(\frac{36}{80}+\frac{4}{80}\right)+\left(\frac{3}{80}+\frac{3}{80}\right)} = \frac{40}{46} = \frac{20}{23}$$

8. **(c)** Let E be the event that the selected student has attained 'A' grade

E_1 = student is a hostelier $P(E_1) = 60\ \%$

E_2 = student is a day scholar, so $P(E_2) = 40\%$

$$P\left(\frac{E_1}{E}\right) = \frac{P(E_1).P\left(\frac{E}{E_1}\right)}{P(E_1)P\left(\frac{E}{E_1}\right)+P(E_2)P\left(\frac{E}{E_2}\right)} = \frac{\frac{6}{10}\times\frac{3}{10}}{\frac{6}{10}\times\frac{3}{10}+\frac{4}{10}\times\frac{2}{10}}$$

$$= \frac{18}{26} = \frac{9}{13}$$

9. **(d)** Let E be the event that the test report is positive

E_1 = person really has the disease, $P(E_1) = \frac{1}{1000}$

E_2 = Person does not have the disease in reality, $P(E_2) = \frac{999}{1000}$

$$P(E_1/E) = \frac{P(E_1)P(E/E_1)}{P(E_1).P\left(\frac{E}{E_1}\right)+P(E_2)P\left(\frac{E}{E_2}\right)}$$

$$= \frac{\frac{1}{1000}\times\frac{99}{100}}{\frac{1}{1000}\times\frac{99}{100}+\frac{999}{1000}\times\frac{5}{1000}} = \frac{990}{990+4995} = \frac{198}{1197} = \frac{22}{133}$$

10. **(c)** Let E be the event that head appeared on the tossed coin

E_1 = Coin is double headed

E_2 = Coin is biased

E_3 = Coin is fair

$$P\left(\frac{E_1}{E}\right) = \frac{P(E_1).P\left(\frac{E}{E_1}\right)}{P(E_1).P\left(\frac{E}{E_1}\right)+P(E_2)P\left(\frac{E}{E_2}\right)+P(E_3)P\left(\frac{E}{E_3}\right)}$$

$$= \frac{\frac{1}{3}\times 1}{\frac{1}{3}\left\{1+\frac{3}{4}+\frac{1}{2}\right\}} = \frac{8}{(8+6+4)} = \frac{4}{9}$$

11 **(a)** Let E be the event that a driver has met with an accident

E_1 = He was scooter driver, $\Rightarrow P(E_1) = 1/6$

E_2 = He was a car driver , $\Rightarrow P(E_2) = 1/3$

E_3 = He was a truck driver, $\Rightarrow P(E_3) = 1/2$

Now $P\left(\frac{E_1}{E}\right) = \frac{P(E_1).P\left(\frac{E}{E}\right)}{\sum_{i=1}^{3} P(E_i).P\left(\frac{E}{E_i}\right)}$

$$\frac{\frac{1}{6}\times\frac{1}{100}}{\frac{1}{6}\times\frac{1}{100}+\frac{1}{3}\times\frac{3}{100}+\frac{1}{2}\times\frac{15}{100}} = \frac{1}{1+6+45} = \frac{1}{52}$$

12. **(c)** Let E be the event that the selected item is defective

E_1 = item is produced on machine A, $\Rightarrow P(E_1) = \frac{6}{10}$

E_2 = item is produced on machine B $\Rightarrow P(E_2) = 4/10$

Now $P(E\ /E)\ \ \frac{P(E_2).P(E/E_2)}{P(E_1),P\left(\frac{E}{E_1}\right)\ \ P(E_2)P\left(\frac{E}{E_2}\right)}$

$$= \frac{\frac{4}{10}\times\frac{1}{100}}{\frac{4}{10}\times\frac{1}{100}\times\frac{6}{10}\times\frac{2}{100}} = \frac{1}{4}$$

13. **(a)** Let E be the event that a head has been reported

E_1 = 5 or 6 appeared on the die $\Rightarrow$ $P(E_1) = \frac{2}{6} = \frac{1}{3}$

E_2 = 1,2,3, or 4 appeared on the die $\Rightarrow$ $P(E_2) = \frac{2}{3}$

$$P\left(\frac{E_2}{E}\right)=\frac{P(E_2).P\left(\frac{E}{E_2}\right)}{P(E_2).P\left(\frac{E}{E_2}\right)+P(E_1).P\left(\frac{E}{E_1}\right)}$$

$$=\frac{\frac{2}{3}\times\frac{1}{2}}{\frac{2}{3}\times\frac{1}{2}+\frac{1}{3}\times\frac{3}{8}}=\frac{8}{11}$$

14. (a) Let E be the event that a head has been reported

E_1 = *Head* appeared on the tossed coin

E_2 = *Tail* appears on the tossed coin

$$=P\left(\frac{E_1}{E_2}\right)=\frac{\frac{1}{2}\times\frac{4}{5}}{\frac{1}{2}\times\frac{4}{5}+\frac{1}{2}\times\frac{1}{5}}=\frac{4}{5}$$

TEXTUAL EXERCISE 6: (SUBJECTIVE)

1. (i) By Bernoulli's theorem $p(5)={}^nC_5\left(\frac{1}{2}\right)^5\left(\frac{1}{2}\right)^{n-5}=\frac{{}^nC_5}{2^n}$

(ii) P (1 or 3 or 5…) $={}^nC_1.\frac{1}{2^n}+{}^nC_3.\frac{1}{2^n}+{}^nC_5.\frac{1}{2^n}+..$

$$=\frac{1}{2^n}({}^nC_1+{}^nC_3+{}^nC_5+....)=\frac{1}{2^n}(2^{n-1})=\frac{1}{2}$$

2. $p(r\le n)\ ({}^{2n+1}C_0+{}^{2n+1}C_1+{}^{2n+1}C_2+....+{}^{2n+1}C_n)\left[\frac{1}{2n+1}\right]$

$$=\frac{1}{2}\left({}^{2n+1}C_0+{}^{2n+1}C_1+...+{}^{2n+1}C_{2n+1}\right)\times\frac{1}{2^{2n+1}}=\frac{(2)^{2n+1}}{2^{2n+2}}=\frac{1}{2}$$

3. If the fair coin be tossed n times, then total ways $= 2^n$

Now P(7 heads) $=\frac{{}^nC_7}{2^n}=P$ (9 heads) $=\frac{{}^nC_9}{2^n}$

$\Rightarrow n = 16$ so P (two heads) $=\frac{{}^{16}C_2}{2^{16}}=\frac{15}{2^{13}}$

4. A die is rolled 'n' times

Two outcomes (namely 3 or 6) are favourable. We want favourable outcomes to occur odd number of times

$P(3k, k=1, 2) = 1/3$

$\therefore$ *P*(*m*ultiple of 3 odd number of times)

$$={}^nC_1\left(\frac{1}{3}\right)^1\left(\frac{2}{3}\right)^{n-1}+{}^nC_3\left(\frac{1}{3}\right)^3\left(\frac{2}{3}\right)^{n-3}+{}^nC_5\left(\frac{1}{3}\right)^5\left(\frac{2}{3}\right)^{n-5}+.....$$

$$={}^nC_1xy^{n-1}+{}^nC_3x^3y^{n-3}+{}^nC_5x^5y^{n-5}+...;$$

Where $x = 1/3$, $y = 2/3$

$=\frac{1}{2}\left[(x+y)^n+(x-y)^n\right]$ for n = odd

And $=\frac{1}{2}\left[(x+y)^n-(x-y)^n\right]$ for n = even

$$\therefore\ P(E)=\frac{1}{2}\left[1-\frac{1}{3^n}\right]$$

5. Consider safe return as success with $p = 3/4$

Then failure $q = 1/4$

Probability that 75 out of 100 ships return safely

$$={}^{100}C_{75}\,p^{75}q^{25}={}^{100}C_{75}\left(\frac{3}{4}\right)^{75}\left(\frac{1}{4}\right)^{25}$$

6. Consider rainy day as success with probability $p = 3/5$

Then failure to rain $q = 2/5$

The probability that it will rain exactly 4 days in a weak $={}^7C_4\left(\frac{3}{5}\right)^4\left(\frac{2}{5}\right)^3=\frac{4536}{15625}$

7. Third time 6 (six) is obtained on the 8th throw, so six should appear twice in the first 7 throws

$\Rightarrow$ The required probability $={}^7C_2\left(\frac{1}{6}\right)^2\left(\frac{5}{6}\right)^5\left(\frac{1}{6}\right)$

$$={}^7C_2\left(\frac{5}{6}\right)^5\left(\frac{1}{6}\right)^3={}^7C_2\left(\frac{5^5}{6^8}\right)$$

8. Length of the interval [1,5] = 4 units

Now $x^3 + 2x + 1 > 0 \Rightarrow (x + 1)^2 > 0 \Rightarrow x \neq -1$

Now [1,5] is a subset of $(\mathbb{R} - \{-1\})$ $\therefore P = 1$

9. Given $0 \le a \le 6$ and $0 \le b \le 9$

The equation $x^2 - ax + b = 0$ has real roots

When $a^2 \ge 4b$

Or $a \ge 2\sqrt{b}$

The inequality will be satisfied when a point lies above the parabola {here $b = x$ and $a = y$}

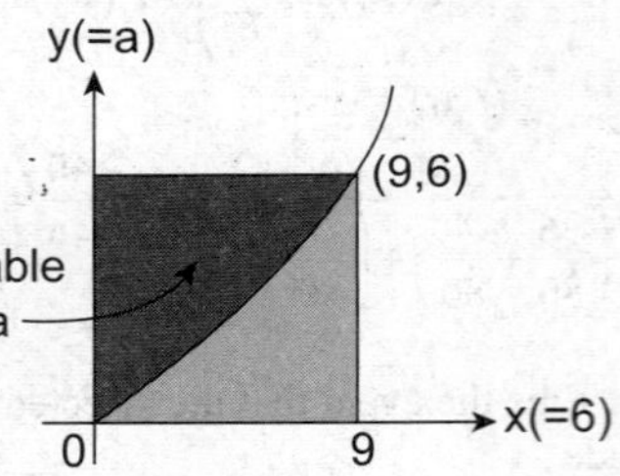

Total Area = 54 square units

Favorable area $= 54-\int_0^9 2\sqrt{x}\,dx$

$$=54-\frac{2\times2}{3}\left[x^{3/2}\right]_0^9=54-36=18 \text{ square units}$$

$$P(E)=\frac{18}{54}=\frac{1}{3}$$

10. $0 \le x,y \le 4 \Rightarrow n(S)$ 16 sq units

To find the solutions to [x] + [y] = 3

Is to find coefficient t^3 in

$\{t^0 + t^1 + t^2 + t^3\}\{t^0 + t^1 + t^2 + t^3\}$

= (1 + 1 + 1 + 1) = 4 ways i.e.,

(i) [x] = 0, [y] = 3 $\Rightarrow 0 \le x < 1; 3 \le y < 4$

(ii) [x] = 1, [y] = 2 $\Rightarrow 1 \le x < 2; 2 \le y < 3$

(iii) [x] = 2, [y] = 1 $\Rightarrow 2 \le x < 3; 1 \le y < 2$

(iv) [x] = 3, [y] = 0 $\Rightarrow 3 \le x < 4;\ 0 \le y < 1$

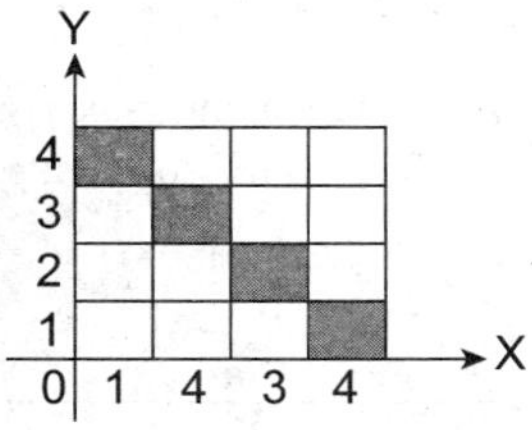

$\Rightarrow\ n(E) = 4$ sq units $\quad \Rightarrow\ P(E) = \dfrac{n(E)}{n(S)} = \dfrac{1}{4}$

11. Consider any point p on any diameter AOB. To check if $OP > PB$. Now $OP > PB$ (means $OP > r/2$) so $r/2 < OP < r$

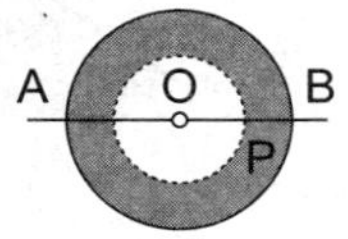

Total area of circle $= \pi r^2$ sq units

Favorable area $n(E) = \left\{\pi r^2 - \pi \dfrac{r^2}{4}\right\} = \dfrac{3\pi}{4} r^2$

$\Rightarrow\ P(E) = 3/4$

12. Given: $k \in (0,5) \Rightarrow$ length of interval = 5. Roots of $4x^2 + 4kx + (k+2) = 0$ will be real when $D \ge 0$ i.e., $(4k)^2 - 16(k+2) \ge 0$
Gives $16(k-2)(k+1) \ge 0$
So $k \ge 2$ gives $k \in [2,5)$ so length of favourable interval $= n(E) = 3$
$\therefore$ Required probability $P(E) = 3/5 = 0.6$

13. S : Rectangle of area $(\pi)(1) = \pi$ square units.
$C : x^2 + y^2 \le 1$
The common points will the boundary and interior of the quarter part of circle

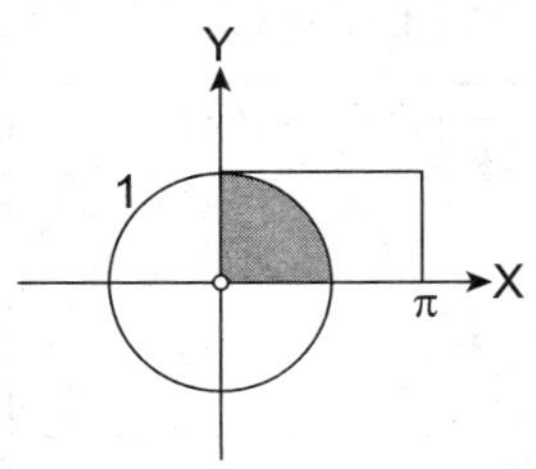

$\therefore\ n(S) = \pi$ sq.units and $n(E) = \dfrac{\pi}{4}$ square units

so P (E) = 1/4

14. A natural number is selected from $X = \{x : 1 \le x \le 100\}$
$\Rightarrow n(s) = 100$
Now $x^2 - 13x - 30 < 0 \Rightarrow (x-15)(x+2) < 0$
So $x \in (-2,15) \Rightarrow n(E) = 14$
{since we get $x = 1,2,3,\ldots,14$}
$\therefore$ The required probability $= \dfrac{14}{100} = \dfrac{7}{50} = 0.14$

15. Let $C_1 : x^2 + (y-1)^2 = 1$ and $C_2 : x^2 + y^2 = 3$

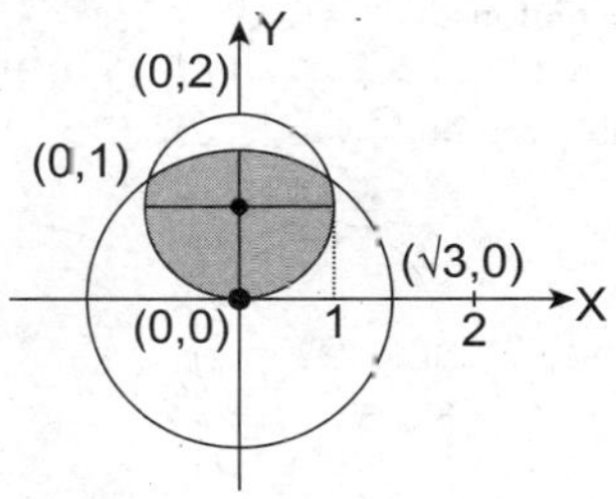

Solving C_1 and C_2 we get $x = \pm\dfrac{\sqrt{3}}{2},\ y = \dfrac{3}{2}$. Area of the smaller circle lying outside the larger circle (with $r = \sqrt{3}$)

$$= \int_{-\sqrt{3}/2}^{\sqrt{3}/2} (C_1 - C_2)\,dx = 2\int_0^{\sqrt{3}/2} 1 + \sqrt{1-x^2} - \sqrt{3-x^2}\,dx$$

Now $n(S) = 3\pi$ square units

$$n(E) = \pi - 2\int_0^{\sqrt{3}/2} \left\{1 + \sqrt{1-x^2} - \sqrt{3-x^2}\right\} dx$$

$$= \pi - 2\left\{x + \frac{x}{2}\sqrt{1-x^2} + \frac{1}{2}\sin^{-1} x - \frac{x}{2}\sqrt{3-x^2} - \frac{3}{2}\sin^{-1}\left(\frac{x}{\sqrt{3}}\right)\right\}_0^{\sqrt{3}/2}$$

$$n(E) = \pi - 2\left\{\frac{3\sqrt{3}}{8} - \frac{\pi}{12}\right\} = \frac{7\pi}{6} - \frac{3\sqrt{3}}{4}$$

$$P(E) = \frac{7\pi}{5.3\pi} - \frac{3\sqrt{3}}{4.3\pi} = \frac{7}{18} - \frac{\sqrt{3}}{4\pi} = \left(\frac{14\pi - 9\sqrt{3}}{36\pi}\right)$$

16. Let the arc length $(\widehat{PQ}) = x;\ \ell(\widehat{PR}) = y$ and let the length of circumference be $2s$.

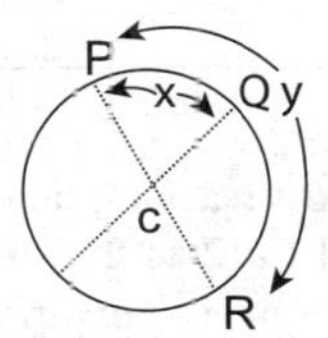

Clearly, $0 \le x \le 2s;\ 0 \le y \le 2s \Rightarrow$ Total region $= 2s \times 2s = 4s^2$
Now following four case arise which are favorable to event
Case (i): $x, y \le s$, then clearly, the three points lie in semicircle
$\therefore\ x, y \in [0, s]$ is favorable region

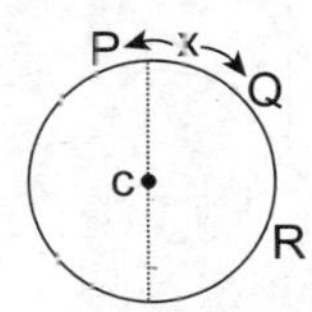

Case (ii): $x \le s,\ y \ge x + s$

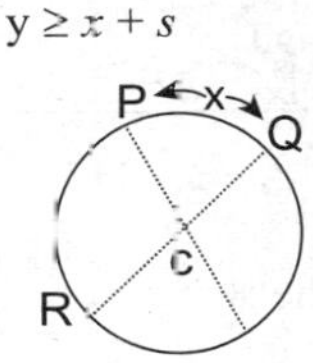

Clearly P, Q, R lie on semi-circle x ∈ [0, s]; y ∈ [$x + s$, 2s] is favorable region

Case (iii): x ≥ s, y ≥ s clearly P, Q, R lie on semi-circle with favorable region x, y ∈ [s, 2s]

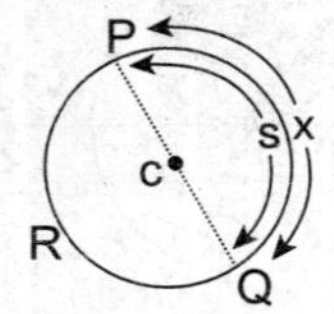

Case (iv): y ≤ s; x ≥ $y + s$

∴ Favorable region is y ∈ [0, s]; x ∈ [$y + s$, 2s]

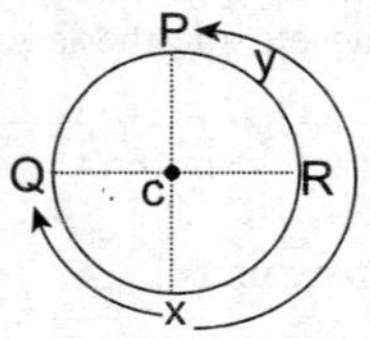

The favorable region is shown below

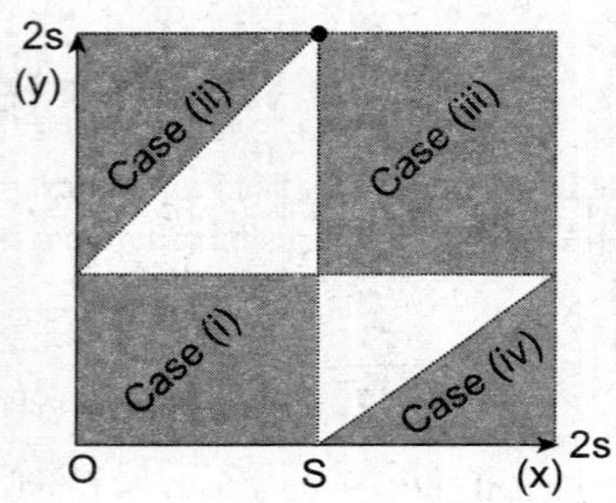

$$\therefore \quad P(\text{Event}) = \frac{s^2 + \frac{1}{2}s^2 + s^2 + \frac{1}{2}s^2}{4s^2} = \frac{3}{4}$$

17. Let x – $a$xis represent reaching time of A and y-axis as that of B (mark from 11 to 12 as shown in three parts)

According to the given conditions |y – x| < 1/3 **or** $x - \frac{1}{3} < y < x + \frac{1}{3}$

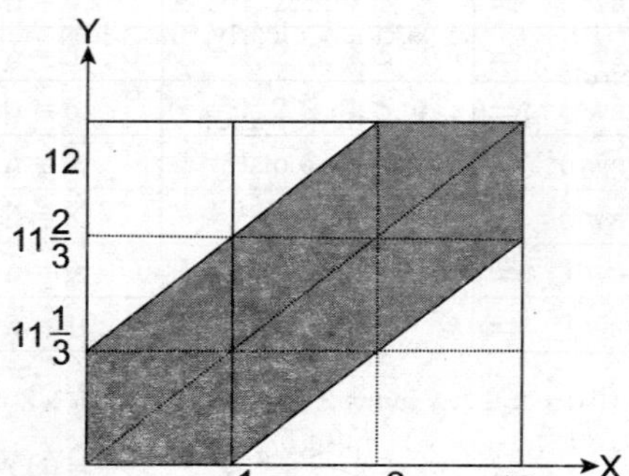

{as 11 ≤ x ≤ 12} The shaded area represents the favorable area (5 square units)

$n(E)$ = 5sq units; $n(s)$ = 9 sq units

so $P(E)$ = 5/9

18. Plot a along x-axis and b along y-axis. Now |b – a| > c

Total area $n(S)$ = a^2 sq units favorable area $n(E) = \frac{1}{2}(a-c)^2 \times 2 = (a-c)^2$

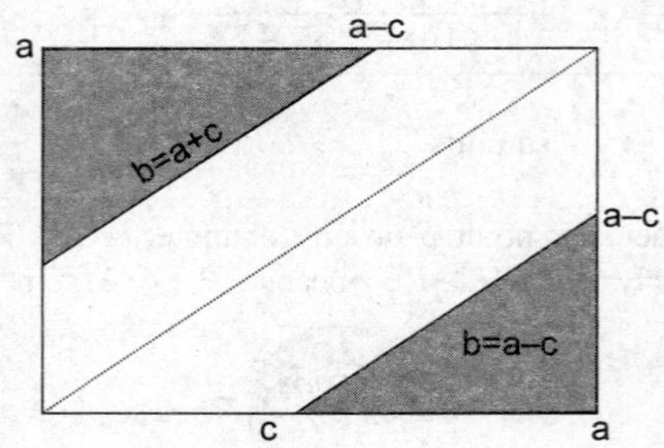

So $P(E) = \left(\frac{a-c}{a}\right)^2 = \left(1 - \frac{c}{a}\right)^2$

19. When two dice are rolled, then $n(S)$ = 36. For |x| + |y| ≤ 3 gives x = 1, y = 1, x = 1, y = 2; x = 2, y = 1

so three points are favourable to event.

$\Rightarrow \quad P(E) = \frac{3}{36} = \frac{1}{12}$

20. Let a, b, c be the lengths of three line segments. A triangle will be formed when the sum of any two sides is larger than the third one i.e $b + a > c$; $a + c > b$; $b + c > a$

All these inequalities have equal probability of being true

so $P(E) = \frac{1}{2}$

21. Let ℓ_1, $\ell_2 < a$ be the sides of the rectangle ⇒ $\sqrt{\ell_1^2 + \ell_2^2}$ = $l$ength of diagonal $\sqrt{2}a$. Favourable region is the interior 1/4 of a circle of radius 'a' units

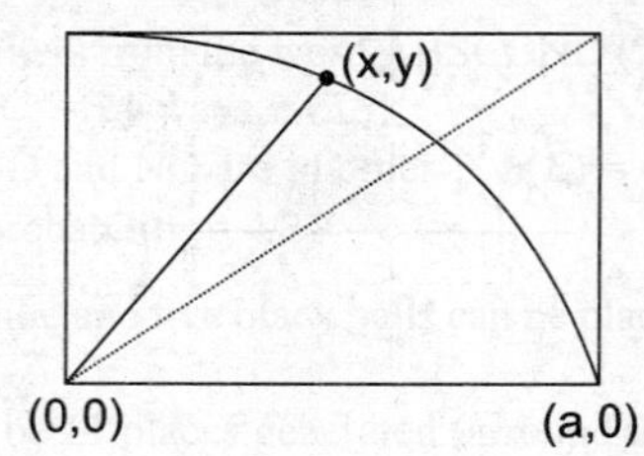

$\therefore \quad n(E) = \frac{\pi a^2}{4}$ square units

$n(S)$ = a^2 square units

$n(E) = \frac{\pi a^2}{4}$ sq units

$\therefore \quad P(E) = \frac{\pi}{4}$

22. x ∈ [–4, 4], y ∈ [–4, 4]

∴ $n(s)$ = 64 square units

Given condition : $|x| + |y| \le 4$
This is area bounded by the lines
$x + y = 4, x + y = -4, y - x = 4, x - y = 4$

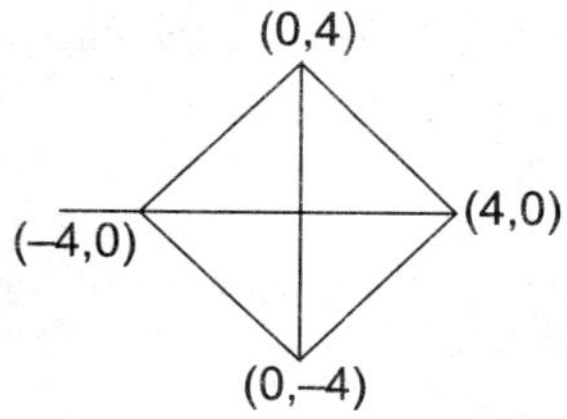

$\therefore \quad n(E) = 4.\frac{1}{2}(16) = 32$ square units. $\therefore P(E) = 1/2$

23. $[x]\,[y] = 1 \Rightarrow 1 \le x < 2;\ 1 \le y < 2$
or $-1 \le x < 0;\ -1 \le y < 0$

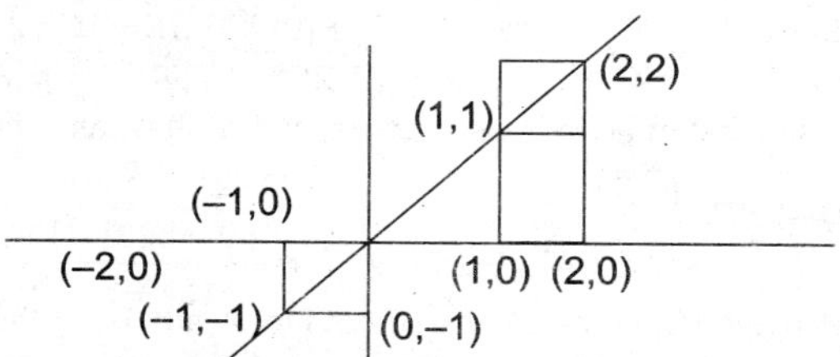

So $n(S) = 2$ square units
Area lying below the line ($y = x$)

$n(E) = \frac{1}{2} + \frac{1}{2} = 1$ sq units $\Rightarrow P(E) = \frac{1}{2}$

24. $f(x) = (\lambda - x^n)^{1/n}$ where $\lambda > 0$ and n is an odd natural number so $f(x)$ is real defined for all $0 < x < 10$
So $n(S) = 10$
Now $f\{f(x)\} = [\lambda - \{f(x)\}^n]^{1/n}$

$= \left[\lambda - \left(\lambda - x^n\right)\right]^{1/n} = \left[x^n\right]^{1/n} = x$

So $f\{f(x)]^{1/n} = [x^n]^{1/n} = x$ So $f\{f(x)\} = x$
for all x $\Rightarrow n(E) = 10 \quad \Rightarrow \quad P(E) = 1$

25. Total area $n(S) = 4$ square units, $y = 0$ means x – *axis*

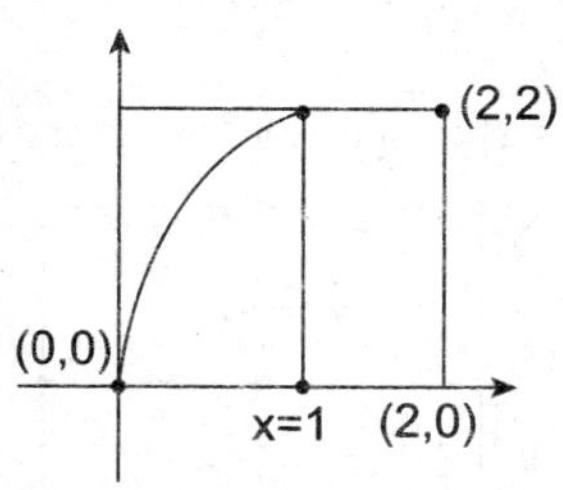

Area enclosed by $y^2 = 4x$, $y = 0$ and $x = 1$ is

$n(E) = \int_0^1 2\sqrt{x}\,dx = \frac{2}{(3/2)} x^{3/2}\Big|_0^1$

$= 4/3$ square units so $P(E) = \frac{1}{3}$

26. (i) A coin is tossed twice so $n(S) = 4$ viz {HH, HT, TH, TT}
These events are equally likely
Let x denote the number of heads
So $x = 0$, $P(x = 0) = 1/4$
$x = 1$, $P(x = 1) = 1/2$
$x = 2$, $P(x = 2) = 1/4$, then the probability distribution is

x:	0	1	2
$P(x)$:	1/4	1/2	1/4

(ii) Three coins are tossed all at a time $\Rightarrow n(S) = 8$ viz {HHH, HHT, HTH, THH, HTT, TTH, THT, TTT}
Let x denote the number of tails, then the probability distribution is

x	0	1	2	3
$P(x)$	1/8	3/8	3/8	1/8

(iv) Four coins are tossed all at a time $\Rightarrow n(S) = 16$ viz {HHHH, HHHT, HHTH, HTHH, THHH,……,TTTT}
Let x denote the number of heads, then the probability distribution is

x	0	1	2	3	4
$P(x)$	1/16	1/4	3/8	1/4	1/16

27. (a) A die tossed twice $\Rightarrow n(S) = 36$. Let x denote the case that more than 4 appears on a throw
(i) $x = 0$ (more than 4 does not appear), $n(E_{x=0}) = 16$ cases
(ii) $x = 1$ (more than 4 appears exactly on one throw), $n(E_{x=1}) = 16$ cases
(iii) $x = 2$ (more than 4 appears exactly on both the throws), $n(E_{x=2}) = 4$ cases, then the probability distribution is

x	0	1	2
$P(x)$	4/9	4/9	1/9

(b) Let x denote that six appears
$x = 0$, six does not appear , $n(E_{x=0}) = 25$ cases
$x = 1$ (Six appears on exactly one throw), $n(E_{x=1}) = 10$ cases
$x = 2$ (Six appear on both the throws), $n(E_{x=2}) = 1$, then the probability distribution is

x	0	1 or 2
$P(x)$	$\frac{25}{36}$	$\frac{11}{36}$

28. $P(X) = \begin{cases} k \text{ if } x = 0 \\ 2k \text{ if } x = 1 \\ 3k \text{ if } x = 2 \\ 0 \text{ otherwise} \end{cases}$

(a) Total Probability $= k + 2k + 3k + 0 = 6k = 1$ so $k = 1/6$
Hence, the probability distribution is

x	0	1	2	>2
P(x)	1/6	1/3	1/2	0

(b) So $P(x<2)=\frac{1}{6}+\frac{1}{3}=\frac{1}{2}$

$P(x\le 2)=\frac{1}{6}+\frac{1}{3}+\frac{1}{2}=1$

$P(x\ge 2)=\frac{1}{2}+0=\frac{1}{2}$

29.

x	14	15	16	17	18	19	20	21
p(x)	2/15	1/15	2/15	3/15	1/15	2/15	3/15	1/15
$x_i p_i$	28/15	15/15	32/15	51/15	18/15	38/15	60/15	21/15

$\therefore\quad E(X)=\frac{263}{15}=17.53$, $Var(x)=\sigma^2=\sum p_i x_i^2-\left(\sum p_i x_i\right)^2$

$=\frac{2}{15}(14)^2+\frac{1}{15}(15)^2+...+\frac{1}{15}(21)^2-(17.53)^2=4.78$

and $\sigma = S.D(x) = 2.19$

TEXTUAL EXERCISE 5: (OBJECTIVE)

1. **(b)** $E(X)=6$, $Var(X)=2\Rightarrow np=6$ and $npq=2$
Hence $q=1/3$, so $p=2/3$ and $n=9$

$\therefore\quad P(x\le 8)=1-P(X=9)=1-{}^9C_9\left(\frac{2}{3}\right)^9\left(\frac{1}{3}\right)^0$

$=1-\frac{512}{19683}=\frac{19171}{19683}$

2. **(d)** Probability of showing a head (success) $= p$ so $q = 1-p$
According to question ${}^{90}C_{45}\,q^{45}p^{45}={}^{90}C_{46}\,q^{44}p^{46}$

or $\frac{90!}{45!45!}(1-p)=\frac{90!}{44!\,46!}$ p gives $46-46p=45p$

so $p=\frac{46}{91}$

3. **(c, d)** Given: $\frac{P(X=r)}{P(X=n-r)}$ is independent of n for every value of r. This possible only if $p=q$ so $p=q=1/2$

4. **(d)** Let n be the minimum number of times a fair coin needs to be tossed.
Now P(Getting at least one tail) $= 1-P$(getting no tail)

$=1-\left(\frac{1}{2}\right)^n\ge 0.6$ or $\left(\frac{1}{2}\right)^n\le 0.4$ gives $n\ge 2$

5. **(d)** $m\in\mathbb{Z}$ and $m^2-25\le 0\Rightarrow m\in\{-5,-4,-3,......,4,5\}$
So $n(S)=11$
Now if $2x^2+2mx+(m+1)=0$, has real roots
Then $D\ge 0$ i.e., $4m^2-8(m+1)\ge 0$ so $m^2-2m-2\ge 0$
and roots are $m=(1-\sqrt{3}),(1+\sqrt{3})$

$\Rightarrow\quad m\in\left(-\infty,1-\sqrt{3}\right]\cup\left[1+\sqrt{3},\infty\right)$

$\Rightarrow$ $n(E)=8$ as $m\in\{-5,-4,-3,-2,-1,3,4,5\}$ are suitable values
So $P(E)=8/11$

6. **(d)** Since a fair coin is tossed 200 times

$\therefore\quad p=q=\frac{1}{2}$

$P(r=1,3,5,7,....,99)={}^{200}C_1\left(\frac{1}{2}\right)^{200}+{}^{200}C_3\left(\frac{1}{2}\right)^{200}$

$+.........+{}^{200}C_{99}\left(\frac{1}{2}\right)^{200}$ ....(i)

We know that sum of even index coefficients = sum of odd index coefficients

Hence ${}^{200}C_1+{}^{200}C_3+.....+{}^{200}C_{199}=\frac{1}{2}2^{200}=2^{199}$

Since ${}^nC_r={}^nC_{n-r}$ .Hence $2[{}^{200}C_1+{}^{200}C_3+.....+{}^{200}C_{99}\}=2^{199}$
So ${}^{200}C_1+{}^{200}C_3+{}^{200}C_5+{}^{200}C_{99}=2^{198}$ ....(ii)
Using binomial index properties, and from (i) and (ii)

$P=2^{198}\left(\frac{1}{2}\right)^{200}=\frac{1}{4}$

7. **(b)** five fair coins are tossed both by A and B, so the probabilities are identical for both. Let x denote the number of heads

$\Rightarrow$ $P(x=0)=1/32=P(x=5)$; $P(x=1)=5/32=P(x=4)$;

$P(x=2)=\frac{10}{32}=P(x=3)$

$\therefore$ P{Getting the same number of heads}

$=\frac{1}{(32)^2}\{2(1)^2+2(5)^2+2(10)^2\}=\frac{252}{32\times 32}=\frac{63}{256}$

8. **(c)** Probability that a student is a swimmer $p = 2/3$ so $q = 1/3$
Now $P(X = 7$ out of 10 students)

$={}^{10}C_7.(2/3)^7\left(\frac{1}{3}\right)^3=10\left(\frac{2}{3}\right)^9$

9. **(b)** Two integers x and y are chosen with replacement from {0, 1, 2, 3,……,10}
$\Rightarrow$ $n(S) = 121$
Now $|x-y|>5$ gives $y-x>5$ or $x-y>5$

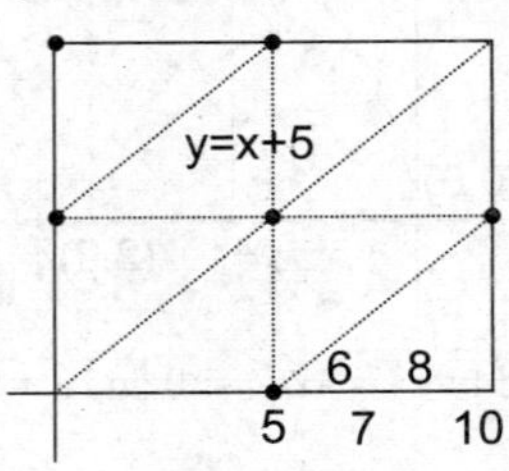

Number of favourable points $= 2\{5+4+3+2+1\}$ $= 30 = n(E)$

$\Rightarrow\quad P(E)=\frac{30}{121}$

10. (b) According to the given $P(x, y)$ is a point with $x + y = 2n$
Since x, y $\in \mathbb{N} \Rightarrow$ x , y, $\in$ {1, 2, 3,……,$2n - 1$}
Now $x + y = 2n \Rightarrow E = \{(1, 2n - 1), (2, 2n - 2), (3, 2n - 3),\ldots,(n, n),\ldots,(2n - 1, 1)\}$ and only (n,n) lies on $y = x$
$n(s) = 2n - 1$ and $n(E) = 2n - 2$

Hence $P(E) = \dfrac{2n-2}{2n-1}$

11. **(b)** According to given condition

No(x)	1	2	5
P(x)	3/6	2/6	1/6

$$E(x) = \sum x_i p_i = \frac{3}{6} + \frac{4}{6} + \frac{5}{6} = \frac{12}{6}$$

So $E(x) = 2$

12. (d) Two cards are drawn from a pack of cards randomly
$\therefore$ in ${}^{52}C_2 = 26 \times 51$ ways
Let x denote the number of aces obtained,
$x = 0$ i.e., No ace appears $\Rightarrow \dfrac{48\times 47}{2}$ ways
$x = 1$ i.e., one ace appears $\Rightarrow 48 \times 4$ ways
$x = 2$ Two aces appear $= {}^4C_2 = 6$ ways

$$E(x) = \frac{48\times 4}{26\times 51} + \frac{6}{26\times 51} = \frac{16\times 2}{13\times 17} + \frac{1}{13\times 17}$$

$$\Rightarrow E(x) = \frac{34}{221} = \frac{2}{13}$$

13. **(d)** P(at least one success) $= 1 - P$ (No success).
now $p = 1/4$ so $q = 3/4$
Further P(at least one success) $\geq \dfrac{9}{10}$

i.e. $1 - {}^nC_0\left(\dfrac{3}{4}\right)^n \geq \dfrac{9}{10}$ gives $\left(\dfrac{3}{4}\right)^n \leq \dfrac{1}{10}$

$\therefore$ $n\{\log_{10} 3 - \log_{10} 4\} \leq -1$

{As $\log_{10} 3 - \log_{10} 4 < 0$} so $n \geq \dfrac{1}{\log_{10} 4 - \log_{10} 3}$

14. (a) Four fair dice are thrown $\Rightarrow n(S) = 6^4$.
The sum of digits $S = \{4, 5, 6, \ldots, 24\}$
Required sum of numbers $= k$; where $4 \leq k \leq 9$
The number of ways to get a sum of k is given by the coefficient of x^k in the expansion $(x + x^2 + x^3 + x^4 + x^7 + x^6)^4$.

i.e., coefficient of x^k in $\dfrac{x^4(1-x^6)^4}{(1-x)^4}$

Coefficient of x^k in $\{1 - 4x^6 + 6x^{12} - 4x^{18} + x^{24}\}$ $\{x^4 + {}^4C_1x^5 + {}^5C_2x^6 + {}^6C_3x^7 + {}^7C_4x^8 + {}^8C_5x^9 + {}^9C_6\, x^{10} + \ldots\}$
Since $4 \leq k \leq 9$ $\Rightarrow n(E) = {}^{k-1}C_3$.
So required probability

$$P(E) = \frac{{}^{k-1}C_3}{6^4} = \frac{(k-1)(k-2)(k-3)}{6^5}$$

15. (d) Let A = event that there is at least one rainy day in a week. B = event that there are at least two rainy days in a week.

$$\therefore \quad P\left(\frac{B}{A}\right) = \frac{P(A\cap B)}{P(A)} = \frac{P(B)}{P(A)} \text{ as } B \subseteq A$$

$$= \frac{1 - P(\text{one rainy day or no rainy day})}{1 - P(\text{no rainy day})}$$

$$= \frac{1 - \left[{}^7C_1(0.3)^1(0.7)^6 + {}^7C_0(0.7)^7\right]}{1-(0.7)^7} = \frac{1-(2.8)(0.7)^6}{1-(0.7)^7}$$

SECTION III : (SINGLE CORRECT ANSWER)

1. **(c)** As per given $P(A) = 2/3\ P(B)$ {As $P(B)$ is the other case here}

So $P(A) + P(B) = \dfrac{5}{3}P(B) = 1$ {Mutually exclusive and exhaustive events)

So $P(B) = \dfrac{3}{5}$ and $P(A) = \dfrac{2}{5}$

$\Rightarrow$ Odds in favour of B is 3 : 2

2. **(b)** SOCIETY $\Rightarrow$ Number of words formed $= 7!$
Now the three vowels namely I,E,O can form one Packet $\Rightarrow$
No of ways to arrange $= 3!5!$

$\Rightarrow$ Required probability $= \dfrac{3!5!}{7!} = \dfrac{6}{7.6} = \dfrac{1}{7}$

3. **(a)** From letters of word **article** $\Rightarrow$ Number of words formed 7! Now there are three vowels A,I,E which will occupy even places
$\Rightarrow$ Number of ways to arrange $= 3!\ 4!$

$\therefore$ The required probability $= \dfrac{3!4!}{7!} = \dfrac{6}{7.6.5} = \dfrac{1}{35}$

4. **(c)** Two unbiased cubic dice are tossed $\Rightarrow n(S) = 36$
Sum = Prime number larger than 5, so it gives sum = 7 or 11
Sum = 7 $\Rightarrow$ {(1,6) , (2,5), (3,4), (4,3), (5,2), (6,1)}
Sum = 11 $\Rightarrow$ { (5,6), (6,5)}

So required probability $= \dfrac{8}{36} = \dfrac{2}{9}$

5. (c) $A_1, A_2, A_3, \ldots, A_n$ are n independent events .

Now $P(A_i) = \dfrac{1}{i+1}$

P (None of the events will occur)

$$= P\left(\bar{A}_1 \cap \bar{A}_2 \cap \bar{A}_3 \ldots\ldots\ldots \cap \bar{A}_n\right) = P(\bar{A}_1)P(\bar{A}_2)P(\bar{A}_3)\ldots..(\bar{A}_n)$$

$$= \left(1-\frac{1}{2}\right)\left(1-\frac{1}{3}\right)\left(1-\frac{1}{4}\right)\ldots..\left(1-\frac{1}{n+1}\right)$$

$$= \frac{1}{n+1}\ \frac{1}{2}.\frac{2}{3}.\frac{3}{4}\ldots\ldots\frac{n}{n+1} = \frac{1}{n+1}$$

$$= \frac{1}{2}\times\frac{2}{3}\times\frac{3}{4}\times\ldots\times\frac{n}{n+1} = \frac{1}{n+1}$$

6. **(a)** A fair coin is tossed repeatedly so the outcome of each toss is independent of any previous outcome
$\Rightarrow P$(Head on 5th toss) $= 1/2$

7. (c) Let Bag A contain four tickets numbered 1 to 4 and Bag B contain 6 tickets numbered 2,4,6,7,8,9
Probability of selection of each bag = 1/2
Probability of selected number being 4 is
$=\frac{1}{2}\times\frac{1}{4}+\frac{1}{2}\times\frac{1}{6}=\frac{3+2}{24}=\frac{5}{24}$

8. (b) Since it is known that second die always exhibits 4 so a sum of 8 will be achieved only if first die shows 4
$\Rightarrow \quad P(4,4)=P(4).P(4)=\frac{1}{6}\times 1=\frac{1}{6}$

9. (a) A fair coin is tossed 99 times $P(Head = success) = P(Tail\ failure) = 1/2$
$\Rightarrow$ The binomial distribution gives
$P(X = r \text{ i.e. r Head}) = {}^{99}C_r\left(\frac{1}{2}\right)^{99}$ which is maximum when $r = 49, 50$

10. (c) 10 apples are to be distributed among six(6) persons such that at least one person gets none.
Required probability
$= 1 - P(\text{every one gets at least one})$
$= 1-\left[\frac{\text{No.of sol.of } x_1+x_2+x_3+\ldots+x_6=4; x_i\geq 0}{\text{No.of sol.of } x_1+x_2+x_3+\ldots+x_6=10; x_i\geq 0}\right]$
$= 1-\left(\frac{{}^9C_4}{{}^{15}C_5}\right)=1-\left[\frac{9!}{4!5!}\times\frac{5!\times 10!}{15!}\right]$
$= 1-\left[\frac{9\times8\times7\times6\times5}{15\times14\times13\times12\times11}\right]=1-\left(\frac{6}{143}\right)=\frac{137}{143}$

11. (c) The fourth six appears on 10th throw where a fair die is thrown 20 times so $n(S) = 6^{20}$
Since the fourth six appears on 10th throw
$\Rightarrow$ six appears thrice in the first 9 throws
$\therefore \quad n(E)=\left\{{}^9C_3\left(\frac{1}{6}\right)^3\left(\frac{5}{6}\right)^6\frac{1}{6}\right\}.6^{10}$
Hence the required probability
$p(E)=\frac{9.8.7}{6}\frac{5^6}{6^{20}}=\frac{84\times 5^6}{6^{20}}$

12. (a) From a group of 10 persons, 4 persons can be selected in ${}^{10}C_4$ ways $\Rightarrow n(S) = {}^{10}C_4$
Since the group consists of 5 lawyers, 3 doctors and 2 engineers and at least one person is to selected from each category
$\Rightarrow n(E) = {}^5C_2{}^3C_1{}^2C_1 + {}^5C_1{}^3C_2{}^2C_1 + {}^5C_1{}^3C_1{}^2C_2$
So $P(E)=\frac{10.3.2+5.3.2+5.3}{210}=\frac{105}{210}=\frac{1}{2}$

13. (b) A can draw two cards in ${}^{52}C_2$ ways say (L, M). Now replacing these cards B has to draw either L or M, i.e. 2 choices. Corresponding to this single draw second draw should be any one from remaining 50 (excluding L and M), which can be done in ${}^{50}C_1$ ways
$\therefore$ Required probability $=\frac{{}^{52}C_2\times 2\left({}^{50}C_1\right)}{{}^{52}C_2\times{}^{52}C_2}$
$=\frac{100\times 2}{52\times 51}=\frac{50}{13\times 51}=\frac{50}{663}$

14. (b) Odds against a given event (A say) = 5 : 2
$\Rightarrow P(A) = 2/7$
Similarly odds in favour of another independent event (B say) = 6 : 5 $\Rightarrow P(B)=\frac{6}{11}$
Since these events are independent
$\therefore \quad P(A\cap B)=P(A).P(B)=\frac{2}{7}\times\frac{6}{11}=\frac{12}{77}$
so $P(\text{At least one event will happen}) = P(A\cup B)$
$= P(A)+P(B)-P(A\cap B)=\frac{2}{7}+\frac{6}{11}-\frac{12}{77}$
$=\frac{22+42-12}{77}=\frac{52}{77}$

15. (a) Regulation All letters are distinct
$\Rightarrow n(S) = 10!$
When there are exactly 4 letters between R and E, then R E
Required number of arrangements = ${}^8C_4 \times 4! \times 2 \times 5!$
$=\frac{8!}{4!4!}\times 4!\times 2!\times 5!$
$\Rightarrow \quad P(E)=\frac{2\times5\times8!}{10!}=\frac{1}{9}$

16. (a) Since chit is being replaced so every time the situation is the same
Four draws are made $\Rightarrow n(S) = 7^4$
Now if number drawn is at least 5 on every draw then, $n(E) = 3^4$ {as 5,6,7 will be appearing each time}
$\Rightarrow \quad P(E)=\frac{(3)^4}{(7)^4}=\left(\frac{3}{4}\right)^7$

17. (c) The number of determinants formed = 16. Observe that the determinant is non-zero when exactly once (–1) appears as shown $\begin{vmatrix}1 & 1\\-1 & 1\end{vmatrix}=2 \Rightarrow 4$ ways
Similarly the determinant is non-zero when (–1) is used exactly three times as shown $\begin{vmatrix}-1 & -1\\-1 & 1\end{vmatrix}=-2\Rightarrow 4$ ways
So non-zero determinant can be obtained in 8 ways. Similarly determinant will be zero in 8 determinants
$\Rightarrow P(E) = 1/2$

18. (d) Fifteen persons sit at a round table at random.
$\Rightarrow n(S) = 14!$
Four persons sit between A and B and A and B can switch/inter-change their positions.

$\Rightarrow$ $n(E) = {}^{13}C_4 \times 2 \times 4! \times 9!$

$\Rightarrow$ $P(E) = \frac{13!}{4! \times 9!} \times \frac{2 \times 4! \times 9!}{14!} = \frac{1}{7}$

19. **(a)** Let $P(C)$ denotes the probability of choosing (C)

CHOICE	**CHANCE**
(one letter is selected)	**(when one letter is selected)**
$P(C) = 2/6$	$P(C) = 2/6$
$P(H) = 1/6$	$P(H) = 1/6$
$P(I) = 1/6$	$P(A) = 1/6$
$P(O) = 1/6$	$P(N) = 1/6$
$P(E) = 1/6$	$P(E) = 1/6$

Observe that C,H,E are common so by law of total probability the required prob

$= \left(\frac{2}{6}\right)^2 + \left(\frac{1}{6}\right)^2 + \left(\frac{1}{6}\right)^2 = \frac{6}{36} = \frac{1}{6}$

20. **(d)** Infinite out of 8 letters 4 letters can be selected ${}^8C_4$ ways Since three like letters are to be selected so they are all I's. Now only one more letter is be selected form $2N$, $1T$, IE, $1F$ in 5 ways $\Rightarrow P(E) = \frac{5}{{}^8C_4} = \frac{5.24}{8.7.6.5} = \frac{1}{14}$

21. **(c)** The bag contains 2 white and 4 black balls since each time the ball is being replaced so each draw is independent of the previous results under the given conditions. For each draw $P(W) = \frac{1}{3}$ and $p(B) = 2/3$

P(getting at least 4 white balls in 5 draws) = P(exactly four white balls) + P(All five white balls)

$= 5.\left(\frac{1}{3}\right)^4\left(\frac{2}{3}\right)^1 + \left(\frac{1}{3}\right)^5 = \frac{10}{243} + \frac{1}{243} = \frac{11}{243}$

22. **(b)** There are 2 white and 6 black balls . Since the ball is not being replaced back and we want the first person to be a winner.

$\therefore$ $P(A) = P(W) + P(BBW) + P(BBBBW) + P(BBBBBBW)$ Winning

$P(A) = \frac{1}{4} + \frac{5}{28} + \frac{3}{28} + \frac{1}{28} = \frac{7+5+3+1}{28} = \frac{16}{28} = \frac{4}{7}$

23. (b) The cubic die is unbiased but making is different so P(1) = 1/6, P(2) = 1/3, P(3) = 1/2

Now in 3 throws a sum of 4 is possible as 1 + 1 + 2 which can happen in 3 ways

$\Rightarrow$ $P(\text{Total sum} = 4) = 3.\frac{1}{6}.\frac{1}{6}.\frac{1}{3} = \frac{1}{36}$

Similarly to get a total of 6 in three thrown is possible as 1 + 2 + 3 or 2 + 2 + 2

$\Rightarrow$ $P(\text{total sum} = 6) = 6\left(\frac{1}{6}\right)\left(\frac{1}{3}\right)\left(\frac{1}{2}\right) + \left(\frac{1}{3}\right)^3$

$= \frac{1}{6} + \frac{1}{27} = \frac{9+2}{54} = \frac{11}{54}$

So total prob .(Sum 4 or 6) = $\frac{1}{36} + \frac{11}{54} = \frac{3+22}{108} = \frac{25}{108}$

Aliter: For the given die it is $(x + 2x^2 + 3x^3)^3$ .We are to find the coefficient when index is 4 or 6

$\Rightarrow$ $x^3\{1 + 2x + 3x^2\}^3 = x^3(1 + 2x + 3x^2) \times \{1 + 4x^2 + 9x^4 + 4x + 12x^3 + 6x^2\}$

Now observe that x^4 is possible as

$x^3\{1 \times 4x + 1 \times 2x\} = 6x^4 \Rightarrow P(\text{sum} = 4) = \frac{6}{216}$

Similarly x^6 is possible as

$x^6\{12 + 8 + 12 + 12\} = 44x^6 \Rightarrow P(\text{sum}\,6) = \frac{44}{216}$

Hence total required probability $= \frac{50}{216} = \frac{25}{108}$

24. (b) $P(A) = P(B) = 2\,P(C)$

Since these are mutually exclusive and exhaustive events,

$\therefore$ $P(A) = P(B) = \frac{2}{5}$ and $P(C) = \frac{1}{5}$

So $P(B \cup C) = P(B) + P(C) = 3/5$

25. **(b)** Given $E(x) = np = 7/3$

$\text{Var}(X) = 14/9 = npq \Rightarrow q = \frac{2}{3}$

So $p = 1/3$ and $n = 7$

$\therefore$ $P(X = 6) = {}^7C_6\left(\frac{1}{3}\right)^6\left(\frac{2}{3}\right)$ and $P(X = 7) = \left(\frac{1}{3}\right)^7$

$\Rightarrow$ $P(X = 6 \text{ or } 7) = \frac{7.2}{3^7} + \frac{1}{3^7} = \frac{5}{3^6} = \frac{5}{729}$

26. (a) Three digit number divisible by 11 will belong to $\{10 \times 11, 11 \times 11, 12 \times 11, \ldots\ldots, 90 \times 11\}$ = 81 numbers The number that is also divisible by 9 will be $\{18 \times 11, 27 \times 11, 36 \times 11, \ldots., 90 \times 11\}$ = 9 numbers i.e., $n(S) = 81$ and $n(E) = 9 \Rightarrow P(E) = 1/9$

27. **(d)** Since 7 digits are choosen out of 9 so 2 digits are to be dropped from 1,2,3,.....9 (Total *sum* = 45)

The dropped digits must result in a sum of 9 (or its multiple) Which is possible only as (1,8), (2,7), (3,6) ,(4,5)

(i.e., 4 ways) $\Rightarrow n(E) = 4$

Now two digits out of nine can be dropped out in ${}^9C_2 = 36$ ways $= n(S)$

$\Rightarrow$ So required $P(E) = \frac{4}{36} = \frac{1}{9}$

Aliter: After withdrawing two digits remaining 7 can be arranged in 7! Ways.

$\therefore$ Required number of ways = 4 × 7!

But total number of ways $= {}^9P_7$

$\therefore$ $P(E) = \frac{4 \times 7! \times 2!}{9!} = \frac{4 \times 2}{9 \times 8} = \frac{1}{9}$

28. **(a)** $P\left(\frac{\bar{A}}{\bar{B}}\right) = \frac{P(\bar{A} \cap \bar{B})}{P(\bar{B})} = \frac{1 - P(A \cap B)}{P(\bar{B})}$

$= \frac{1 - P(A \cup B)}{P(\bar{B})} = \frac{P(\bar{B}) - P(A \cap \bar{B})}{P(\bar{B})} = 1 - P\left(\frac{A}{\bar{B}}\right)$

29. (b) Let us deal with functions with domain {1, 2, 3, ...,m} and co-domain = {1, 2, 3,.....,n}

∴ Total number of functions = n^m

Persons	Floors
1	1
2	2
3	3
⋮	⋮
m	n

= the number of ways all the m passengers can align = $n(S)$

Now the number of one-one functions= ^nP_m

= No two passengers align at the same floor = $n(E)$

Hence required probability $P(E) = \frac{^nP_m}{n^m}$

30. (c) Cardinal number of $P = n$

1. Let $a_i \in P$ $(1 \le i \le n)$ we have the following choices (1) $a_i \in A$ and $a_i \in B$
2. $a_i \in A$ and $a_i \notin B$
3. $a_i \notin A$ and $a_i \in B$ (4) $a_i \notin A$ and $a_i \notin B$

Out of these only (#1) i.e., $a_i \in A$ and $a_i \in B$ is the case where $a_i \in A \cap B$

So $n(S) = 4^n$ and $n(E)$ = number of ways in which exactly one element of P wil belong to $A \cap B = {}^nC_1(1)^n$

$\Rightarrow \quad P(E) = \frac{n}{4^n} = n\left(\frac{1}{4}\right)^n$

31. (a) Out of 100 tickets numbered 1 to 100, Two tickets are chosen at random. Largest number appearing on these two tickets = 10 ⇒ Number of ways $^{10}C_2 = 45$ ways

Let A be the event of drawing two tickets,

$\Rightarrow \quad n(A) = {}^{10}C_2 \qquad \Rightarrow \quad P(A) = \frac{^{10}C_2}{^{100}C_2}$

Let B be the event that minimum of these tickets is 5

$\Rightarrow \quad P(B) = \frac{^5C_1}{^{100}C_2}$

Hence $P(B/A) = \frac{P(B \cap A)}{P(A)} = \frac{^5C_1}{^{10}C_2} = \frac{5}{45} = \frac{1}{9}$

32. (b) 4 balls are drawn (without replacement) from a bag containing 6 red and 3 white balls of alternative colours can be drawn as RWRW or WRWR

Total probability = $\frac{6}{9}\cdot\frac{3}{8}\cdot\frac{5}{7}\cdot\frac{2}{6} + \frac{3}{9}\cdot\frac{6}{8}\cdot\frac{2}{7}\cdot\frac{5}{6} = \frac{5}{42}$

33. (b) Here $P(A), P(B), P(C) \in [0, 1]$

However if probability of any one of A, B or C is 1, then probability of other two events must be simultaneously zero, which is impossible as $\frac{1+4p}{4} = 0 \Rightarrow p = \frac{-1}{4}$

$\Rightarrow \quad P(B), P(C) \ne 0$

$\Rightarrow \quad P(A), P(B), P(C) \in [0,1)$. Further A, B and C are mutually exclusive events

$\Rightarrow \quad 0 < P(A) + P(B) + P(C) \le 1$

$\Rightarrow \quad 0 < \frac{1+4p}{4} + \frac{1-p}{4} + \frac{1-2p}{4} \le 1$

$\Rightarrow \quad 0 < 3 + p \le 4 \Rightarrow p \in (3, 1]$

Further $0 \le \frac{1+4p}{4} < 1, \frac{1-p}{4} < 1; 0 \le \frac{1-2p}{4} < 1$

$\Rightarrow \quad p \in \left[\frac{-1}{4}, \frac{3}{4}\right] \cap (-3,1] \cap \left[-\frac{3}{2}, \frac{1}{2}\right] \cap (0, \infty)$

$\Rightarrow \quad p \in \left(0, \frac{1}{2}\right]$

34. (d) For three mutually exclusive and exhaustive events $\frac{4-6p+2+8p+1+p}{6} = 1$; $7 + 3p = 6$ gives $p = -1/6$

35. (a) An unbiased die is tossed four times. Minimum face value obtained = 2 and Maximum face value obtained = 5

$n(S) = (6)^4$ and, $n(E) = (4)^4$

$\Rightarrow \quad P(E) = \left(\frac{4}{6}\right)^4 = \left(\frac{2}{3}\right)^4 = \frac{16}{81}$

36. (b) Cardinal number of set $A = n$

Let $a_i \in A$ $(1 \le i \le n)$

For a_i we have the following 4 possibilities

1. $a_i \in P$ and $a_i \in Q$ 2. $a_i \in P$ and $a_i \notin Q$
3. $a_i \notin P$ and $a_i \in Q$ 4. $a_i \notin P$ and $a_i \notin Q$

Now $P \cap Q = \phi$ is

Possible except when $a_i \in P$ and $a_i \in Q$

Hence the required probability $P(e) = \frac{3^n}{4^n} = \left(\frac{3}{4}\right)^n$

37. (c) ∵ For every element three are four choices $A \cap B^c$, $A^c \cap B$, $A \cap B$, $(A \cup B)^c$ out of which only two are favorable $A \cap B^c$ and $A^c \cap B$

∴ Required probability = $\left(\frac{2^n}{4^n}\right) = \frac{1}{2^n}$

38. (a) $P(A \cup B) = P(A) + P(B) \le 1$

$\Rightarrow P(A) \le 1 - P(B) = P(\bar{B})$. So $P(A) \le P(\bar{B})$

39. (b) Three fair dice are thrown, so $n(S) = 216$

The cases where numbers are in A.P.

$d = 1 \Rightarrow$ (1,2,3), (2,3,4), (3,4,5), (4,5,6)

$d = 2 \Rightarrow$ (1,3,5), (2,4,6) and their reversals

$d = 3,4,5$ not possible

$\Rightarrow \quad n(E) = 6 \times 2$

Hence $p(E) = \frac{6 \times 2}{216} = \frac{1}{18}$

40. (a) Given $P(\overline{A \cup B}) = \frac{1}{6}, P(A \cap B) = \frac{1}{4}$

And $P(\bar{A}) = \frac{1}{4}$

So $P(A) = \frac{3}{4}$ and $P(A \cup B) = 1 - \frac{1}{6} = \frac{5}{6}$

So from $P(A \cup B) = P(A) + P(B) - P(A \cap B)$

$P(B) = \frac{5}{6} + \frac{1}{4} - \frac{3}{4} = \frac{1}{3}$ (Now $P(A) \neq P(B)$)

Observe that $P(A).P(B) = \frac{3}{4}.\frac{1}{3} = \frac{1}{4} = P(A \cap B)$

$\Rightarrow$ A and B are mutually independents but not equally likely

41. (a) Since A,B,C are three mutually independent events

$\Rightarrow P(A \cap B) = P(A).P(B); P(A \cap C) = P(A).P(C)$

$P(B \cap C) = P(B).P(C)$ and $P(A \cap B \cap C) = P(A).P(B).P(C)$

$S_1 = A$ and $B \cup C$ are independent the statements is true if we prove that $P\{B \cup C) \cap A\} = P(A).P(B \cup C)$

Proof: $P(A \cap (B \cup C)\} = P(A \cap B) \cup (A \cap C)\}$

$= P(A \cap B) + P(A \cap C) - P\{(A \cap B) \cap (A \cap C)\}$

$= P(A).P(B) + P(A).P(C) - P(A).P(B).P(C)$

$= P(A)\{P(B) + P(C) - P(B).P(C)\}$

$= P(A)\{(P(B) + P(C) - P(B \cap C)\} = P(A).P(B \cap C)$

$\{ \text{as } P\{(A \cap B) \cap (A \cap C)\} = P(A \cap B \cap C) \}$

Hence S_1 is true

Similarly we can prove that

$P(A \cap (B \cap C) = P(A).P(B).P(C) = P(A \cap B \cap C)$

So S_2 is also true

42. (b) Let A be the event that the sum obtained is 15 when a die is thrown 3 times

A_1 = *first throw shows up 4*

A_2 = *first throw shows 3*

A_3 = *first throw shows 5*

A_4 = *first throw shows 6*

$$P\left(\frac{A_1}{A}\right) = \frac{P(A_1).P\left(\frac{A}{A_1}\right)}{P(A_1).P\left(\frac{A}{A_1}\right) + P(A_2).\left(\frac{A}{A_2}\right) + P(A_3)P\left(\frac{A}{A_3}\right) + P(A_4).P\left(\frac{A}{A_4}\right)}$$

$$= \frac{\frac{1}{6}.\frac{2}{216}}{\frac{1}{6}.\frac{2}{216} + \frac{1}{6}.\frac{1}{216} + \frac{1}{6}.\frac{3}{216} + \frac{1}{6}.\frac{4}{216}}$$

$$= \frac{2}{2+1+3+4} = \frac{2}{10} = \frac{1}{5}$$

43. (d) Given that $n_1, n_2 \in \mathbb{N}$ and $n_1 + n_2 = 100$, Let $n_1 = x$ then $n_2 = 100 - x$

$\Rightarrow n_1 \in \{1,2,3,.....98,99\}$

And $n_2 \in \{99,98,97......,2,1\}$

With respective matching $n(S) = 99$

When product is greater than 1600 then $100x - x^2 > 1600$ or $x^2 - 100x + 1600 < 0$

$\Rightarrow (x - 20)(x - 80) < 0 \Rightarrow x \in (20, 80)$

$\therefore n_1 \in \{21,22,23,...78,79\}$ and $n_2 \in \{79, 78, 79,... 22,21\}$

$\Rightarrow n(E) = 59$, Hence $P(E) = \frac{59}{99}$

44. (b) $P(A \cup B) = 5/6; P(A \cap B) = 1/3$ and $P(A) = 2/3$

$\Rightarrow \frac{5}{6} = \frac{2}{3} + P(B) - \frac{1}{3}$ gives $P(B) = \frac{1}{2}$

Observe that $P(A).P(B) = \frac{2}{3}.\frac{1}{2} = \frac{1}{3} = P(A \cap B)$

Hence events are independent events

45. (c) $P(A^C) = 0.3 \Rightarrow p(A) = 0.7$

$P(B) = 0.4$

$P(A \cap B^c) = 0.5 \Rightarrow P(A) - P(A \cap B) = 0.5$

So $P(A \cap B) = 0.2$

Further $P(A \cup B^C) = P(B^C) + P(A \cap B)$

{Since (B^C) and ($A \cap B$) are mutually exclusive or say disjoint events}

So $P(A \cup B^C) = 0.8$

Also $P(B \cap (A \cup B^C)) = P(A \cap B) = 0.2$

Hence $P\left(\frac{B}{A \cup B^C}\right) = \frac{0.2}{0.8} = \frac{1}{4}$

46. (b) Two machines out of four can be selected in 6 ways. If only two tests are needed then number of ways $= {}^2C_2 = 1$

$\Rightarrow$ Required prob $= 1/6$.

47. (d) Urn contains 2 white and 2 black balls.

Let w_i denotes white ball drawn in i^{th} draw, etc.

$\therefore P(W_1W_2B_3$ or $W_1B_2B_3$ or $B_1W_2B_3$ or $B_1B_2B_3)$

$$= P(w_1).P\left(\frac{w_2}{w_1}\right)P\left(\frac{B_3}{w_1w_2}\right) + P(w_1).P\left(\frac{B_2}{w_1}\right).P\left(\frac{B_3}{w_1B_2}\right) + ...$$

$$= \frac{1}{2}.\frac{1}{3}.1 + \frac{1}{2}.\frac{2}{3}.\frac{3}{4} + ... + \frac{1}{2}.\frac{2}{5}.\frac{3}{4} + \frac{1}{2}.\frac{3}{5}.\frac{2}{5} = \frac{23}{30}$$

48. (d) Probability that teacher will give a test $p = 1/5$ so $q = 4/5$

Since the student has missed two classes

$\therefore$ Probability (At least one test is missed) $= 1 - P$ (no. test missed)

$$= 1 - P(\text{No test was held}) = 1 - \left(\frac{4}{5}\right) \times \frac{4}{5} = \frac{9}{25}$$

49. (c) $P(X) = \frac{2}{3}; P(Y) = \frac{3}{4}; P(Z) = p$

P(exactly two bullets hit the target)

$$= P(XY\bar{Z}) + P(X\bar{Y}Z) + P(\bar{X}YZ) = \frac{11}{24}$$

Gives $\frac{2}{3}.\frac{3}{4}(1 - p) + \frac{2}{3}\frac{1}{4}.p + \frac{1}{3}.\frac{3}{4}p = \frac{11}{24}$

$6 - 6p + 2p + 3p = \frac{11}{2} \Rightarrow p = \frac{1}{2}$

$\therefore P(Z) = 1/2$

50. (c) Since a fair coin is tossed $\therefore p = q = 1/2$

Given ${}^nC_7 p^7.q^{n-7} = {}^nC_9 p^9 q^{n-9}$

$\Rightarrow {}^nC_7 = {}^nC_9$ so $n = 16$

Hence $p(r = 2) = {}^{16}C_2\left(\frac{1}{2}\right)^{16} = \frac{15}{2^{13}}$

51. **(b)** $P(A) = 0.2 \Rightarrow P(A') = 0.8$ and $P(B) = 0.5$; $P(A' \cap B) = P(B) - P(A \cap B) \le P(B)$

$\therefore$ Maximum value of $P(A' \cap B) = P(B) = 0.5$

52. **(b)** 12 balls can be put into three boxes in 3^{12} ways so $n(S) = 3^{12}$

When 3 balls are put in one box then the 3 balls can be selected in ${}^{12}C_3$ ways and the rest of 9 balls can be put into 2 boxes in 2^9 ways

Hence $P(E) = \dfrac{{}^{12}C_3 2^9}{3^{12}}$

53. (b) Number of ways in which 2 end seats are occupied by boys $= {}^7C_2.2!$

Now boys can occupy seats only after an even number of girls

i.e. 1 2 3 4 5 6 7 8 9 10 11 12 13 14 15

B B

Already 1 and 15 are occupied by boys

Hence after 1, a boy can occupy seat No 4, 6, 8, 10, 12, 14, $2 = {}^7C_5 . 5!$

Seats left to girls = 3,5,7,9,11,13

Total number of ways in which girls can sit $= {}^8P_4$

Total probability $= \dfrac{9.{}^7C_2.2!.{}^7C_5 5!.8!.8}{15!.4!} = \dfrac{{}^9C_4.7!8!}{15!}$

54. (b) $P(A_1 \cup A_2) = 1 - P(A_1^c).P(A_2^c)$

$= 1 - \{1 - P(A_1)\}\{1 - P(A_2)\} = 1 - 1 + P(A_1) + P(A_2) - P(A_1)P(A_2)$

$\Rightarrow P(A_1 \cup A_2) = P(A_1) + P(A_2) - P(A_1).P(A_2)$

But $P(A_1 \cup A_2) = P(A_1) + P(A_2) - P(A_1 \cap A_2)$

$\Rightarrow P(A_1 \cap A_2) = P(A_1)P(A_2)$ $\therefore$ independent events

55. 12 people can be divided

(i) (a) into six pairs in $\left(\dfrac{{}^{12}C_2 \times {}^{10}C_2 \times {}^8C_2 \times {}^6C_2 \times {}^4C_2 \times {}^2C_2}{6!}\right)$

$= 99 \times 105$

Number of ways to select six pairs of couples = 1

$\therefore$ $P(E) = \dfrac{1}{99 \times 105} = \dfrac{1}{10395}$

(ii) (b) Each pair contains a male and a female. Let each group contains a male, now six females can be distributed among these six groups in 6! ways.

$\therefore$ $P(\text{Required selections}) = \dfrac{6!}{99 \times 105} = \dfrac{720}{99 \times 105} = \dfrac{16}{231}$

56. (c) Let (a,b,c) forms the tripet of the outcomes of tossing three fair coins

$\Rightarrow n(S) = 8$ i.e {HHH, HHT, HTH, THH, HTT, THT, TTH,TTT} taken as ordered triplets.

The roots will be imaginary when $b^2 - 4ac < 0$

Further Head =1 and tail = 2 so from $4ac > b^2$, the equality $4ac = b^2$ is achieved only when a = Head, c = Head and b is tail which is HTH case. In all other cases $4ac > b^2$ will hold.

$\Rightarrow P(E) = 7/8$

57. **(c)** In case of fair die $P(I) = 1/6$ where $I \in \{1, 2, 3, 4, 5, 6\}$.

When the die is biased $P(1) = P(2) = P(3) = P(4)$

$= P(5) = \dfrac{1}{7}$ and $P(6) = \dfrac{2}{7}$

Construction of the biased die:

Now the biased die will be 7 faced having marked 6 on two faces

$\therefore$ Number of points = 42

58. **(b)** Out of ten teams two groups (A and B) of 5 teams each can be formed in ${}^{10}C_5$ ways.

Now all the four first class teams go into one group (in two ways all 4 in group A or in group B) then the 5th team can be selected in ${}^6C_1$ ways

$\therefore$ The required probability $= \dfrac{2 \times {}^6C_1}{{}^{10}C_5} = \dfrac{2 \times 6.5!}{10.9.8.7.6} = \dfrac{1}{21}$

59. **(b)** Given $P(A/B) = P(B/A)$

$\Rightarrow \dfrac{P(A \cap B)}{P(B)} = \dfrac{P(A \cap B)}{P(A)}$

Since A and B are non-mutually exclusive

$\therefore$ $P(A \cap B) \ne 0$ $\Rightarrow P(A) = P(B)$

60. **(c)** Urn contains : Number of coins with (double) head-on both the sides = n

Number of fair coins = $n + 1$

$P(\text{Head}) = \dfrac{n}{2n+1}(1) + \dfrac{n+1}{2n+1}\left(\dfrac{1}{2}\right) = \dfrac{(3n+1)}{2(2n+1)} = \dfrac{37}{50}$

$\Rightarrow 150n + 50 = 74(2n + 1)$, so $2n = 24$

Gives $n = 12$.

61. **(a)** There are n keys out of which only one is proper

Let the kth attempt (trial) opens the lock (success), then the required probability

$P = \dfrac{n-1}{n}.\dfrac{n-2}{n-1}.\dfrac{n-3}{n-2} \;.....\; \dfrac{(n-k+1)}{(n-k+2)}\left(\dfrac{1}{n-k+1}\right) = \dfrac{1}{n}$

62. **(b)** Let A be the event that the person suffered a heart attack

A_1 : He followed mediation and yoga

A_2 : He followed medicine

$\therefore$ $P(A_1/A) = \dfrac{P(A_1)P\left(\dfrac{A}{A_1}\right)}{p(A_1).p\left(\dfrac{A}{A_1}\right) + p(A_2)P\left(\dfrac{A}{A_2}\right)}$

$= \dfrac{\dfrac{1}{2} \times \dfrac{40}{100} \times \left(1 - \dfrac{30}{100}\right)}{\dfrac{1}{2} \times \dfrac{40}{100} \times \left(1 - \dfrac{30}{100}\right) + \dfrac{1}{2} \times \dfrac{40}{100} \times \left(1 - \dfrac{25}{100}\right)}$

$= \dfrac{\left(\dfrac{70}{100}\right)\left(\dfrac{1}{2}\right)}{\left(\dfrac{70}{100}\right)\left(\dfrac{1}{2}\right) + \left(\dfrac{75}{100}\right)\left(\dfrac{1}{2}\right)} = \dfrac{70}{70 + 75} = \dfrac{14}{29}$

63. **(c)** Let E be the event that the statement is true

E_1 : A says the truth

E_2 : B says the truth

Since these are independent witnesses

$\therefore$ $P(E_1 \cap E_2) = P(E_1).P(E_2)$ and $P(E_1' \cap E_2') = P(E_1').P(E_2')$

The required probability

$$P\left(\frac{E}{E_1 \cap E_2}\right) = \frac{P(E_1).P(E_2)}{P(E_1).P(E_2) + P(\overline{E_1}).P(\overline{E_2})}$$

$$= \frac{xy}{xy + (1-x)(1-y)} = \frac{xy}{1-x-y+2xy}$$

64. **(a)** For any family number of possible ways of having children $= (2)^4 = 16$, out of which one is favourable when both the children are girls.

$\therefore$ Probability of such a family $= 1/16$

$\therefore$ Probable number of such families out of

$$10{,}000 = \frac{1}{16} \times 10{,}000 = 625$$

65. **(d)** Two months out of 12 months can be selected in ${}^{12}C_2 = 66$ ways

Now birthdays of six different people falling in exactly two months is the number of onto function which is possible in $(2^6 - 2)$ ways

$$\Rightarrow P(E) = \frac{n(E)}{n(S)} = \frac{66 \times 62}{12^6} = \frac{11 \times 31}{12^5} = \frac{341}{12^5}$$

66. **(c)** Let the numbers be x, y.

Given the sum of two positive real numbers $= x + y = 2a$.

$\therefore$ Maximum product $= a^2$

Permissible product $\in \left[\frac{3a^2}{4}, a^2\right]$

Now $\frac{3a^2}{4} = a^2 - \frac{a^2}{4} = \left(a + \frac{a}{2}\right)\left(a - \frac{a}{2}\right)$

$\Rightarrow$ $x, y, \in \left[\frac{a}{2}, \frac{a}{2}\right]$; The required probability $= \frac{a^2}{4a^2} = \frac{1}{4}$

67. **(d)** n numbers can be arranged in n! ways

When (1, 2, 3,…,k) appear as a specific system (1,2,3,…), $k + 1$, …,n

This is possible in $(n + 1 - k)$ ways $= \frac{(n+1-k)!}{n!}$

68. **(c)** Given $p(W) = 1/2$ and $p(B) = 1/2$. Now 4th white ball appears on the 7th draw.

$\Rightarrow$ Three (3) white balls appear in the first 6 draws in ${}^6C_3$ ways

$\Rightarrow$ Required probability $= {}^6C_3\left(\frac{1}{2}\right)^7 = \frac{6.5.4}{6}\left(\frac{1}{2^7}\right) = \frac{5}{32}$

69. **(d)** n letters can be put into addressed envelopes in n! ways

Probability that at least one letter is not in the right envelope $= 1 - P$ (all letters in the right envelopes)

$= 1 - \frac{1}{n!}$

Important note:

Actually (practically) it will be never one letter but it will be at least two letters.

70. **(b)** A die is rolled three time $\Rightarrow n(S) = 216$. Let the middle number be k (of 2nd throw), then the lower numbers will be 1, 2, 3,…k – 1 and the higher numbers will be $k + 1$, $k + 2$,……, 6

So

(i) $k = 2 \Rightarrow$ small # is 1 and larger number will be 3, 4, 5, 6 $\Rightarrow$ 4 cases

(ii) $k = 3 \Rightarrow$ small # is 1,2 and larger is 4,5,6 $\Rightarrow$ 6 cases

(iii) $k = 4 \Rightarrow$ small # is 1,2,3 and larger is 5,6 $\Rightarrow$ 6 cases

(iv) $k = 5 \Rightarrow$ small # is 1,2,3,4 and larger is 6 $\Rightarrow$ 4 cases

Total favourable cases $n(E) = 20$

$\therefore$ $P(E) = \frac{20}{216} = \frac{5}{54}$

71. Let the sides be x, y, $\ell - (x + y)$

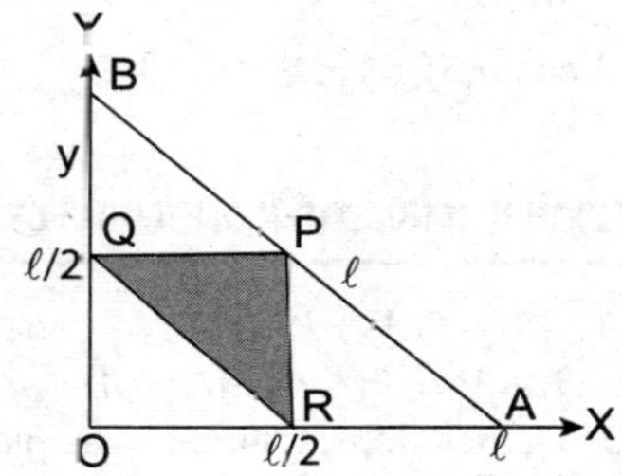

Since the triangle will be formed when sum of two sides is larger than the third

i.e. $\ell - y > y$, $\ell - x > x$ and $x + y > \ell - (x + y)$

$\Rightarrow$ $0 < y < \frac{\ell}{2}, 0 < x < \frac{\ell}{2}$ and $\frac{\ell}{2} < (x + y) < \ell$

Hence required probability $= \frac{\Delta PQR}{\Delta OAB} = \frac{1}{4}$

(as $OQ = 1/2$ OB)

72. **(c)** There are five ways to approach point O from road AB and there are two straight roads OC_1 and OD_1 from O to the road A_1B_1

$\Rightarrow$ $n(s) = 5 \times 2 = 10$

Only two roads *Viz.* DC_1 and ED_1 are straight $\Rightarrow n(E) = 2$

Hence $P(E) = \frac{2}{10} = 0.2$

73. **(b)** Since coins are identical so m coins (1 Rupee each) and n coins of 10 paise each can be placed in a line in

$n(S) = \frac{(m+n)!}{m!n!}$ ways

When two extreme positions are occupied by 10 paise coins,

then $n(E) = \frac{(m+n-2)!}{m!(n-2)!}$

$$\Rightarrow P(E) = \frac{(m+n-2)!m!n!}{m!(n-2)!(m+n)!} = \frac{n(n-1)}{(m+n)(m+n-1)}$$

74. **(d)** Let E_1 = event that unequal numbers appear, then favourable cases = {(1, 3), (3, 1)}

E2 = event that equal numbers appear, then favourable cases are {1, 1}, then {1, 1}

E = event that sum is 4.

$$\therefore \quad P(E) = P(E_1).P\left(\frac{E}{E_1}\right) + P(E_2).P\left(\frac{E}{E_2}\right)$$

$$= \frac{30}{36} \times \frac{2}{30} + \frac{6}{36} \times \frac{1}{6} \times \frac{1}{36} = \frac{5}{6} \times \frac{1}{15} + \frac{1}{1296} = \frac{1}{18} + \frac{1}{1296}$$

$$= \frac{72+1}{1296} = \frac{73}{1296}$$

75. **(b)** Given x, y, ∈ {1, 2, 3, 4} observe that $\sin^{-1}(\sin x) = x$ when $x = 1$, and $\sin^{-1}(\sin x) = \pi - x$ when $x = 2, 3, 4$

Further $\cos^{-1}(\cos y) = y$ when $y = 1,2,3$ and $\cos^{-1}(\cos y) = 2\pi - y$ for $y = 4$

Hence $\sin^{-1}(\sin x) - \cos^{-1}(\cos y)$ will be an integer when $x = 1$ and $y = 1,2,3$

$\Rightarrow$ $n(E) = 3$ and $n(S) = 16$; So $P(E) = \frac{3}{16}$

SECTION IV (MORETHEN ONE CORRECT)

1. **(a, b, c)** $P(A \cap B) = P(A) + P(B) - P(A \cup B) \leq P(A) + P(B)$

Since $P(A \cup B) \leq 1 \Rightarrow P(A \cap B) \geq P(A) + P(B) - 1$

Option (c) being inclution exclution principle is also true.

2. **(a, b)** An unbiased die is tossed four times so $n(S) = 6^4$.

When minimum face value is 2, then $n(E) = 5^4 - 4^4$

$$\Rightarrow \quad P(E_1) = \frac{5^4 - 4^4}{6^4}$$

Similarly when maximum face value is 5 then $n(E_2) = 5^4 - 4^4$

$$\Rightarrow \quad P(E_2) = \frac{5^4 - 4^4}{6^4}$$

3. (a, c) $P(A \Delta B) = P(A) + P(B) - 2P(A \cap B)$

Alternatively $P(A \Delta B) = P(A \cap B') + P(B \cap A')$

So (b) and (d) option are true

$\Rightarrow$ options which do not represent $P(A \Delta B)$ are (a) and (c)

4. (a, b, d) Probability of occurrence of at the most one event $= 1 - P(A \cap B)$

$= P(A \cap B') + P(A' \cap B) + P(A' \cap B')$ using $P(A') = 1 - P(A)$ and $P(A \cap B) = P(A) + P(B) - P(A \cup B)$

We get $P(at\ the\ most\ event) = 1 - [\{1 - p(A')\} + \{1 - P(B')\} - P(A \cup B)]$

$= P(A') + P(B') + P(A \cup B) - 1 = P(A') + P(B') - P(A' \cap B')$

5. (a, c, d) $P(A \cap B) \leq \min\{P(A), P(B)\}$ is true as $A \cap B \subseteq A, B \Rightarrow P(A \cap B) \leq P(A), P(B)$

$P(A \cap B) \geq \max\{0, P(B) + P(A')\}$ is false as $A \cap B \subseteq B \Rightarrow P(A \cap B) \leq P(B) \Rightarrow P(A \cap B) \leq P(B), P(A')$

$P(A \cap B) \leq P(A \cup B)$ is true as $(A \cap B) \subseteq (A \cup B)$

$P(A \cap B) \geq \max\{0, P(A) + P(B) - 1\}$ is true as $P(A \cap B) = P(A) + P(B) - P(A \cup B) \geq P(A) + P(B) - 1$

6. **(a, b, c, d)** Given $P(C) = 0$

$\Rightarrow$ $P(A \cap C) = 0 = P(A)\,P(C)$

Similarly $P(B \cup C) = P(B) + P(C) - P(B \cap C) = P(B) + 0 - P(B).P(C) = P(B)$

And also $P(A \cup C) = P(A) + P(C)$ (as $P(C) = 0$)

Further $P(A \cup B \cup C) = P(A \cup B) = P(A) + P(B) - P(A \cap B)$

7. **(a, c)** $P\left(\frac{A}{B}\right) = \frac{P(A \cap B)}{P(B)}$

$$= \frac{P(A) + P(B) - P(A \cup B)}{P(B)} \geq \frac{P(A) + P(B) - 1}{P(B)}$$

{as $P(A \cup B) \leq 1$}

Now $P(A \cap \bar{B}) = P(A) - P(B) = P(A) - P(A \cap B)$

Similarly $P(A \cup B) = P(A) + P(B) - P(A \cap B)$

If A and B are independent events, then $P(A \cap B) = P(A).\,P(B)$

So $P(A \cup B) = 1 - \{1 - P(A) - P(B) + P(A).P(B)\}$

$= 1 - \{1 - P(A)\}\{1 - P(B)\} = 1 - P(\bar{A})P(\bar{B})$

If A and B are disjoint, then $P(A \cap B) = 0$

$\Rightarrow$ $P(A \cup B) = P(A) + P(B) - P(A \cap B)$

$= P(A) + P(B) = 2 - [1 - P(A) + 1 - P(B)$

$= 2 - \left(P(\bar{A}) + P(\bar{B})\right) \neq 1 - P(\bar{A}).P(\bar{B})$

otherwise $P(A).P(B) = 0$ which is not true.

So (a) and (c) option hold good

8. **(b, c, d)** E and F are independent events with $0 < P(E) < 1$ and $0 < P(F) < 1$

$\Rightarrow$ $P(E).\,P(F) = P(E \cap F) \neq 0$

Hence these cannot be exclusive. E and F^c; E^c and F^c are independent similarly $P\left(\frac{E}{F}\right) + P\left(\frac{E^c}{F}\right)$

$$= \frac{P(E \cap F)}{P(F)} + \frac{P(E^c \cap F)}{P(F)} = \frac{P(E).P(F)}{P(F)} + \frac{P(E^c).P(F)}{P(F)}$$

$$= P(E) + P(E^c) = 1$$

9. **(a, b, c)** $P\left(\frac{B}{A}\right) = \frac{P(A \cap B)}{P(A)}$, when $P(A) \neq 0$

When two dice are throw the number of ways to get a total of r are (1, r – 1), (2, r – 2), (3, r – 3),....,(r – 1, 1) which are (r – 1) when $2 \leq r \leq 7$ and the number of ways to get $8 \leq r \leq 12$ is $(13 - r)$.

10. (b, c, d) When three dice are rolled, then (the number of ways) to get a sum of $3 \leq r \leq 18$ is given by coefficient of x^r in $(x^3 - 3x^9 + 3x^{15} - x^{21})\{1 + 3x + 6x^2 + 10x^3 + 15x^4 + 21x^5 + 28x^6 + \ldots\}$

When $r = 9$, then coefficient = 25 (as 28 – 3) (true)

When $r = 12$, then coefficient = 55 –30 = 25 (true)

When $r = 10$, then coefficient = 36 – 9 = 27 (true)

When $r = 11$, then coefficient = 45 – 18 = 27 (true)

where $r = 13$, then coefficient = 66 – 45 = 21

putting $r = 9$ in $\frac{(r-1)(r-2)}{2}$,we get 28 (Flase)

Putting $r = 13$ in $\frac{(19-r)\ (20-r)}{2}$ we get 21 (true)

11. **(b, c)** $P(A' \cap B) = 2/15$ and $P(A \cap B') = 1/6$

$\Rightarrow$ $P(B) - P(A \cap B) = 2/15$ and $P(A) - P(A \cap B) = 1/6$

$\therefore$ $P(A) - P(B) = 1/30$

Since A and B are independent events

So $P(A).P(B) = P(A \cap B)$

Gives $P(B) - P(B)\{P(B) + 1/30\} = 2/15$

$\Rightarrow$ $30\{P(B)\}^2 - 29P(B) + 4 = 0$ so $P(B) = \frac{4}{5}, \frac{1}{6}$

SECTION V (ASSERTION AND REASON TYPE)

1. R: The statement is true as compound event is proceduced by the simple events

A: The statement is true because simple events constitute the compound event. Since simple events belong to the sample space so a compound event is also a sub-set of sample space and it follows from R. **Ans (a) option**

2. R: The statement is true from definition

A: The statement is true from definition of R and it follows from R. Ans (a) option

3. R: Reason is true as the occurrence of one precludes the occurrence of the other for mutually exclusive events.

A: When events are mutually exclusive then occurrence of one will depend upon the non-occurrence of other. So they are strongly dependent and it follows from R $\Rightarrow$ **Ans (a)**

4. R: Statement is true by definition

A: The statement is not true as war probability between two neighboring countries is dependent upon happening of some particular events **Ans (d) option**

5. R: The statement is true as $P(E)+P(\bar{E})=1$. Also number of one-one functions from A to B where $n(A) = m$ and $n(B) = n(\text{when } n \geq m)$ is ${}^nP_m \Rightarrow P(\text{one} - \text{one}) = \frac{{}^nP_m}{n^m}$

A: The statement follows from R as $1 - P$ (one – one) gives P (not one – one) i.e., $P(\overline{\text{one}-\text{one}})$ which is the probability of many – one function. **Ans (a) option**

6. R: The given statements is true

A: The statement is true on its own but it no where follows form R. **Ans (b) option**

7. R: The statement is true by De morgan's law that $P(A' \cap B') = 1 - P(A \cup B)$

A: The statement is true *i.e.* if odds against an event is 2/3, then its probability of occurrence is $\frac{3}{5}$ but it in no way follows from R.

8. R: The statement is false as $P(A \cap B) = P(B).P(A/B) = P(A).P(B)$, only if A and B are independent.

A: The statement is true

$P(A) = 0.7$, $P(\bar{B}) = 0.6$

Now $P(A \cap \bar{B}) = P(A) - P(A \cap B) = 0.5$

$\Rightarrow$ $P(A \cap B) = 0.2$

Hence $P(A \cup \bar{B}) = P(A) + P(\bar{B}) - P(A \cap \bar{B})$

$= 0.7 + 0.6 - \{P(A) - P(A \cap B)\}$

$= 0.7 + 0.6 - 0.5 = 0.8$

Now $P\left(\frac{B}{A \cup \bar{B}}\right) = \frac{P(A \cap B)}{P(A \cup \bar{B})} = \frac{0.2}{0.8} = \frac{1}{4}$

Ans (c) option.

9. R: The statement is true since $S_\infty = a + ar + ar^2 + ar^3 + \ldots + \infty = \frac{a}{1-r}$ for $|r| < 1$ and $P\left(\frac{E_i}{E}\right) = \frac{P(E_i).P\left(\frac{E}{E_i}\right)}{\Sigma\ P(E_i).P\left(\frac{E}{E_i}\right)}$

(By Baye's theorem)

A: The statement is true as P(getting 1 on even throw)

$= \frac{5}{6}.\frac{1}{6} + \frac{5}{6}.\frac{5}{6}.\frac{5}{6}.\frac{1}{6} + \frac{5}{6}.\frac{5}{6}.\frac{5}{6}.\frac{5}{6}.\frac{5}{6}.\frac{1}{6} + \ldots$

$= \frac{5}{36}\left\{\frac{1}{1-\frac{25}{36}}\right\} = \frac{5}{11}$

so the statement follows from R $\Rightarrow$ **Ans (a) option**

10. R: The statement is true Since by definition $P(\bar{E}) = 1 - P(E)$ and $P\left(\frac{A}{B}\right) = \frac{P(A \cap B)}{P(B)}$

A: The statement is true, since

$P\left(\frac{E}{F}\right) = P\left(\frac{\bar{E}}{F}\right) = \frac{P(E \cap F) + P(\bar{E} \cap F)}{P(F)} = \frac{P(F)}{P(F)} = 1$

and it follows from R $\Rightarrow$ **Ans (a) option**

11. R: The statement is true since by the definition of independent events $P(A \cap B) = P(A).P(B)$ and form exclusive events $P(A \cup B) = P(A) + P(B)$

A: Statement is true. Two dice are thrown simultaneously we can get multiple of 2 on 1st die and multiple of 3 on the other with probability $2\left(\frac{1}{2} \times \frac{1}{3}\right) = \frac{1}{3}$

The statement is true on the basis of reasons. $\Rightarrow$ **Ans (b) option**

12. R: The statement is true as we can prove the statement by following the complete solution

A: The statement is true. For $n = 3$ we ge the required probability $= \frac{3n}{4n^2 - 1} = \frac{9}{35}$. So the statement follows from R $\Rightarrow$ **Ans (a) option**

13. R: The statement is false we know that if there is zero at unit place, then the number is divisible by 5 as well as 10.

A: The statement is true. Consider the square of unit place : $0^2 = 0$; $1^2 = 1$; $2^2 = 4$; $3^2 = 9$; $4^2 = 16$; $5^2 = \mathbf{25}$; $6^2 = 36$; $7^2 = \mathbf{49}$, $8^2 = \mathbf{64}$; $9^2 = 81$

We can combine 0 + 0; 0 + 5; 1 + 4; or 1 + 9 , 6 + 4, 9 + 6 which are given by the square of

(i) {(0,0) for (0+0)}
(ii) (0,5) for (0 + 5)
(iii) {(1,2), (1,8), (9,2), (9,8)} for (1 + 4)
(iv) {(1,3), (1,7), (9,3), (9,7)} for (1 + 9)
(v) {(2,4), (2,6), (8,4), (8,6)} for (6 + 4)
(vi) {(3,4), (3,6), (7,4), (7,6)} for (9 + 6)

$\Rightarrow$ Required prob. $= \dfrac{2\times 18}{10\times 10} = \dfrac{9}{25}$ **Ans (c) option**

SECTION IV: (LINKED COMPRESENSION TYPE)

Passage (a)

1. (a) Given $n \in \mathbb{N}$ and $n^2 - 50n + 100 > 0$

Roots are $\dfrac{50\pm\sqrt{2100}}{2} \cong \dfrac{50\pm 45.8}{2} \cong 2.1, 47.9$

Since $n \in \mathbb{N} \Rightarrow n \in \{1, 2\} \cup \{48, 49,\ldots,100\}$

So $P(E) = \dfrac{55}{100}$

2. (b) $P(n)$ {If $n < 5$} = 2/55

3. (d) E_2 = getting a prime number less than 37 {here only 2 is belonging to the solutions}
$P(E_2) = 1/55$

Passage B:

4. (a) Given $n = 10k + r$ where $k \in \mathbb{N}$ and $r \in W$ (Whole number set) also $0 \le r \le 9$
The number 'a' is chosen at random from the set {1,2,3……., n} observe that $a^2 - 1$ is divisible by 10 when the unit place of 'a' is occupied by 1 or 9
(so that 0 is obtained at unit place in $a^2 - 1$)
where $r = 0$ then $p_n = \dfrac{2k}{n}$

5. (b) If $r = 9$ then we get (count of favorable) numbers $= 2k + 2$

$\Rightarrow \; p_n = \dfrac{2(k+1)}{n}$

6. (c) If $r = 8$ then favorable number are $E = 2k + 1$

$\Rightarrow \; P_n = \dfrac{2k+1}{n}$

7. (c) $\lim\limits_{n\to\infty} P_n = \dfrac{2k}{10k} = \dfrac{1}{5}$

8. (a) Here $a^2 + 1$ is divisible by 10 so a^2 must have 9 at unit place $\Rightarrow a = 3, 7$. Hence $\lim\limits_{n\to\infty} q_n = \dfrac{1}{5}$

Passage C

9. (c) $x^2 - y^2$ will be divisible by 2 when x^2 and y^2 are either both even or both odd.

Observe that out of n natural number {1,2,3,…n} $\left[\dfrac{n}{2}\right]$ are even and $n - \left[\dfrac{n}{2}\right]$ are odd

$$\Rightarrow P_2(x^2 - y^2 \text{ divisible by 2}) = \left(\frac{\left[\frac{n}{2}\right]}{n}\right)^2 + \left(\frac{n-\left[\frac{n}{2}\right]}{n}\right)^2$$

$$= 1 + 2\left(\frac{\left[\frac{n}{2}\right]}{n}\right)^2 - \frac{2\left[\frac{n}{2}\right]}{n}$$

10. (d) Let E be the event that 3 divides $(x^2 - y^2)$

$\Rightarrow n(\bar{E}) = n(x = 3k$ and $y = 3k + 1$ or $3k + 2) + n(x = 3k + 1$ or $3k + 2$ and $y = 3k)$

$$= \left[\frac{n}{3}\right]\left(n-\left[\frac{n}{3}\right]\right) + \left(n-\left[\frac{n}{3}\right]\right)\left[\frac{n}{3}\right]$$

$$= 2n\left[\frac{n}{3}\right] - 2\left[\frac{n}{3}\right]^2$$

$$\therefore \; P(E) = 1 - \frac{n(\bar{E})}{n(S)} = 1 - 2\frac{\left[\frac{n}{3}\right]}{n} + 2\left(\frac{\left[\frac{n}{3}\right]}{n}\right)^2$$

11. (b) AS worked isabove two question

$$P_2 = 1 - 2\left(\frac{\left[\frac{n}{2}\right]}{n}\right) + 2\left(\frac{\left[\frac{n}{2}\right]}{n}\right)^2$$

and $P_3 = 1 - 2\left(\dfrac{\left[\frac{n}{3}\right]}{n}\right) + 2\left(\dfrac{\left[\frac{n}{3}\right]}{n}\right)^2$

When $n = 2$ then $P_2 = 1 - \dfrac{2}{2} + \dfrac{2}{4} = \dfrac{1}{2}$ and $p_3 = 1$ as $\left[\dfrac{n}{3}\right] = 0$

So $P_3 > P_2$ similarly when $n = 3$ then $\left[\dfrac{n}{2}\right] = \left[\dfrac{n}{3}\right]$

then $P_2 = P_3$ and For $n > 3$, $p_2 > P_3$

Passage (D)

12. (c) Since games are to be played in the order ABC so there are two possibilities of my winning
(i) I win against A and B $\Rightarrow$ Probability $= ab$ (then the game is over)

(ii) I lose against A but win against B and C

$\Rightarrow$ Probability = $(1 - a)bc$

So Total Probability = $ab + (1 - a)bc$

13. (d) According to the given: 1st game will be with A

Case i: If I win then the second game can be selected with B or C So probability = $ab + ac$

Case ii: If I lose then I must win B and C (in that order) or C and B

So probability = $(1 - a)bc + (1 - a)cb$

Hence total probability = $ab + 2bc + ac - 2abc$

14. (b) $P(\text{Anand } I) = ab + ac + (1 - a)bc + (1 - a)cb = ab + 2bc - 2abc + ac$

$P(\text{Anand II}) = ba + ca + (1 - b)ac + (1 - c)ab = 2ab + 2ca - 2abc$

$P(\text{Anand III}) = bc + cb + (1 - b)ca + (1 - c)ba = ab + ca + 2bc - 2abc$

$\Rightarrow P(\text{Anand } I) = P(\text{Anand III}) = ab + ca + 2b - 2abc$ and $P(\text{Anand II}) = 2ab + 2ca - 2abc$

Now $a > c, a > b \Rightarrow a - c > 0, a - b > 0$

$\Rightarrow b(a - c) > 0, c(a - b) > 0 \Rightarrow ba - bc + ca - cb > 0$

$\Rightarrow ba + ca > 2bc \Rightarrow 2ab + 2ca > ab + ac + 2bc$

$\Rightarrow P(\text{Anand II}) > P(\text{Anand I}), P(\text{Anand III})$

Passage E:

$P(B \text{ rides } A) = \dfrac{2}{3} \qquad \Rightarrow P(E_1) = \dfrac{2}{3}$

$P(C \text{ rides } A) = \dfrac{1}{3} \qquad \Rightarrow P(E_2) = \dfrac{1}{3}$

It is given that when B rides A, probability of wining of all the horses are equally likely

$$\Rightarrow P\left(\frac{E}{E_1}\right) = \frac{1}{6} \qquad \text{......(i)}$$

Also probability of winning of A when C rides A is given to be $\dfrac{1}{3}$

$$\text{i.e., } P\left(\frac{E}{E_2}\right) = \frac{1}{3} \qquad \text{.........(ii)}$$

$$\text{Further } P(E) = P(E_1).P\left(\frac{E}{E_1}\right) + P(E_2).P\left(\frac{E}{E_2}\right)$$

$$= \frac{2}{3} \times \frac{1}{6} + \frac{1}{3} \times \frac{1}{3} = \frac{2}{9} \qquad \text{.......(iii)}$$

$$\text{Now } P(A_1) = P(E_1 \cap E) = P(E_1).P\left(\frac{E}{E_1}\right) = \frac{2}{3} \times \frac{1}{6} = \frac{1}{9} \qquad \text{......(iv)}$$

$$P(A_2) = P(E_2 \cap E) = P(E_2).P\left(\frac{E}{E_2}\right) = \frac{1}{3} \times \frac{1}{3} = \frac{1}{9} \qquad \text{....(v)}$$

$$\text{The odds against the wining of A} = \frac{P(\bar{E})}{P(E)} = \frac{1 - 2/9}{2/9} = \frac{7}{2} \qquad \text{........(vi)}$$

15. (b) (from (i))

16. (a) (from (ii))

17. (d) (from (iv))

18. (b) (from (v))

19. (d) (from (iii))

20. (b) (from (vi))

Passage F:

21. (c) Let $a_1, a_2, a_3, \ldots, a_n$ be n people of the town

1st stage = ${}^nC_1 \cdot {}^{n-1}C_2$. 2nd stage = ${}^{n-1}C_2 \cdot {}^{n-1}C_2$.

When a_1 does not receive a letter, there are two possibilities

(1) if the chain started with a_1

$\Rightarrow {}^{n-1}C_2 \cdot {}^{n-2}C_2 \cdot {}^{n-2}C_2$

(2) if it did not start with $a_1 \Rightarrow {}^{n-1}C_1 \cdot {}^{n-2}C_2 \cdot {}^{n-2}C_2 \cdot {}^{n-2}C_2$.

P(after 2 stages) a_1 does not receives a letter

$$= \frac{{}^{n-1}C_2 \cdot {}^{n-2}C_2 \cdot {}^{n-2}C_2 + {}^{n-1}C_2 \cdot {}^{n-2}C_2 \cdot {}^{n-2}C_2}{{}^nC_1 \, {}^{n-1}C_2 \, {}^{n-1}C_2 \, {}^{n-1}C_2} = \left[\frac{n-2}{n-1}\right]^2$$

22. (c) Basically, the numerator of the above fraction will continue increasing to ${}^{n-1}C1 \cdot {}^{n-2}C_2 \cdot {}^{n-2}C_2$ ...... m stages hence, the probability that a_1 will not receive the after

$$\text{m stages} = \frac{\left[\frac{n-2}{n-1}\right]^{2m}}{\left[\frac{n-1}{n-1}\right]^2} = \left[\frac{n-2}{n-1}\right]^{2^m - 2}$$

23. (d) p_1 does not receive a letter at mth stage as done is **Q.21**

The numerator has to be multiplied by itself m times

$$\Rightarrow p = \frac{\left[\frac{n-2}{n-1}\right]^{2m}}{\left[\frac{n-2}{n-1}\right]^2}$$

Passage G:

24. (a) chances that the door is opened on 1st attempt = 1/10

25. (c) Chances the door is opened on 6th attempt

$$= \frac{9}{10} \times \frac{8}{9} \times \frac{7}{5} \times \frac{6}{7} \times \frac{5}{6} \times \frac{1}{5} = \frac{1}{10}$$

26. (a) Chances that the door is opened till 5th attempt

$$= \frac{1}{10} + \frac{1}{10} + \frac{1}{10} + \frac{1}{10} + \frac{1}{10} = \frac{1}{2}$$

27. (a) Probability that the door is opened upto 10th attempt

$$= \frac{1}{10}$$

28. **(b)** Probability that atleast three (3) attempts are needed

$= 1 - \frac{2}{10} = \frac{4}{5}$

Passage H:

29. **(c)** Mig(21) (150) ⇒ $P(MS) = 3/5$, $P(MC) = 1/2$

Jaguar (50) ⇒ $p(JS) = 1/5$, $P(JC) = 1/3$

Sukhoi (50) ⇒ $P(SS) = 1/5$, $P(SC) = 1/6$

Chance of safe landing

$= \frac{3}{5} \times \frac{1}{2} + \frac{1}{5} \times \frac{2}{3} + \frac{1}{5} \times \frac{5}{6} = \frac{9+4+5}{30} = \frac{3}{5}$

30. **(a)** $P\left(\frac{\text{sukhoi plane crashed}}{\text{crash reported}}\right)$

$= \frac{\frac{1}{5} \times \frac{1}{6}}{\frac{1}{5} \times \frac{1}{6} + \frac{1}{5} \times \frac{1}{3} + \frac{3}{5} \times \frac{1}{2}} = \frac{1}{12}$

31. **(c)** Ultimate crash probability $= P(um) + P(uj) + P(us)$

$= \frac{3}{5}\left\{\frac{1}{2} + \frac{1}{2}.\frac{1}{2} + \frac{1}{2}.\frac{1}{2}.\frac{1}{2} + ...\right\}$

$+ \frac{1}{5}\left\{\frac{1}{3} + \frac{2}{3}.\frac{1}{3} + \frac{2}{3}.\frac{2}{3}.\frac{1}{3} + \frac{2}{3}.\frac{2}{3}.\frac{2}{3}.\frac{1}{3} + ...\right\}$

$\frac{1}{5}\left\{\frac{1}{6} + \frac{5}{6}.\frac{1}{6} + \frac{5}{6}.\frac{5}{6}.\frac{1}{6} + ...\right\} = \frac{3}{10}(2) + \frac{1}{15}(3) + \frac{1}{30}(6) = 1$

Passage I:

32. (b) The probability the first k ($k \le n$) children are of same gender $= p^k q^{n-k} + p^{n-k} q^k$

33. **(c)** Out of total n children first 's' are boys and in all there are k ($s < k \le n$) boys.

⇒ Out of $(n - s)$ children there has to be $k - s$ boys.

Hence required probability $= p^s({}^{n-s}C_{k-s}\, p^{k-s}.\, q^{n-k}) = {}^{n-s}C_{k-s}\, p^k.\, q^{n-k}$

34. **(c)** Probability that the first 's' children are boys and there are at least k boys in all then required probability

$= p^s.\left[\sum_{r=0}^{n-k} {}^{n-s}C_{k-s+r}.p^{k-s+r}.q^{n-k-r}\right] = \sum_{r=0}^{n-k} {}^{n-s}C_{n-k-r}.p^{k+r}.q^{n-k-r}$

Passage J:

35. **(a)** Let AB be the fixed side. When distance is less than x then ABEF is the favorable area ⇒ Required prob $= \frac{1.x}{1^2} = x$

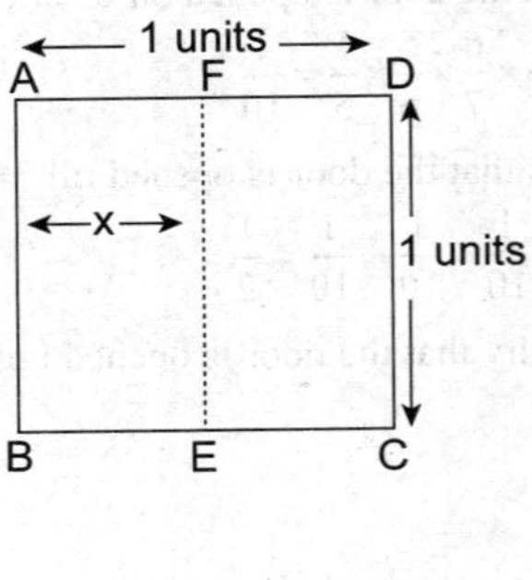

36. (c) When distance form the nearest side does not exceed x, then the favorable area $= 1 - (1 - 2x)^2 = 4x - 4x^2 = 4x(1 - x)$

⇒ Required probability $= 4x(1 - x)/1 = 4x(1 - x)$

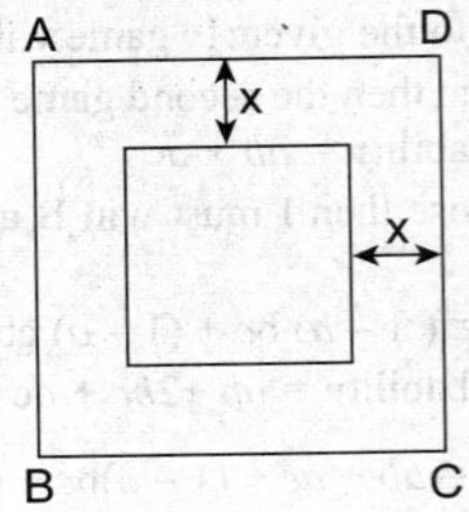

37. **(a,c)** *Case i:* when $0 \le x \le 1/2$

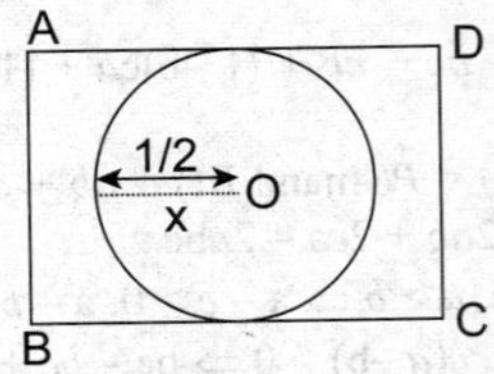

then, the favourable area $= \pi x^2$

Case ii: When $\frac{1}{2} \le x < \frac{1}{\sqrt{2}}$ then

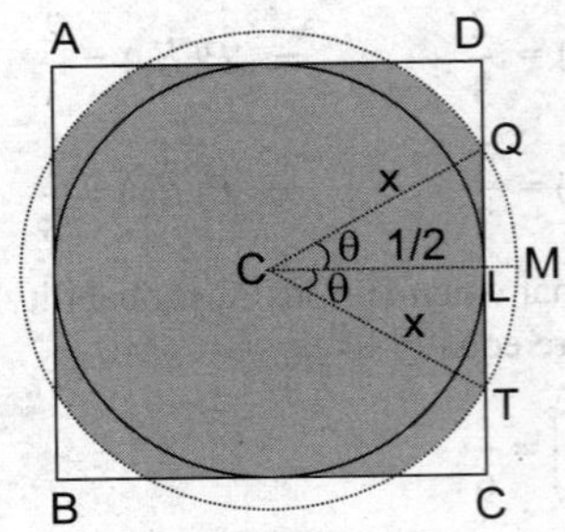

Favourable region = *shaded*

Now $QL = \sqrt{x^2 - \frac{1}{4}} = \frac{\sqrt{4x^2 - 1}}{2}$

⇒ $\tan\theta = \frac{\sqrt{4x^2 - 1}/2}{1/2} = \sqrt{4x^2 - 1}$

⇒ $\theta = \tan^{-1}\sqrt{4x^2 - 1}$

∴ Shaded area= $\pi x^2 - 4$ (area of segment QLTM)

$= \pi x^2 - 4\left[\frac{2\tan^{-1}\sqrt{4x^2-1}}{2\pi}.\pi x^2 - \frac{1}{2}\sqrt{4x^2-1} \times \frac{1}{2}\right]$

$= \pi x^2 - 4x^2 \tan^{-1}\sqrt{4x^2-1} + \sqrt{4x^2-1} = A_2(say)$

∴ Required Probability

$= \pi x^2 + \sqrt{4x^2-1} - 4x^2\tan^{-1}\sqrt{4x^2-1}$ (∵ total area = 1)

38. (a,c) *Case i:* when $0 \le x \le 1$, then the favorable area is as shown below $= \frac{\pi x^2}{4}$ ⇒ Probability $= \frac{\pi x^2}{4}$ for $0 \le x \le 1$

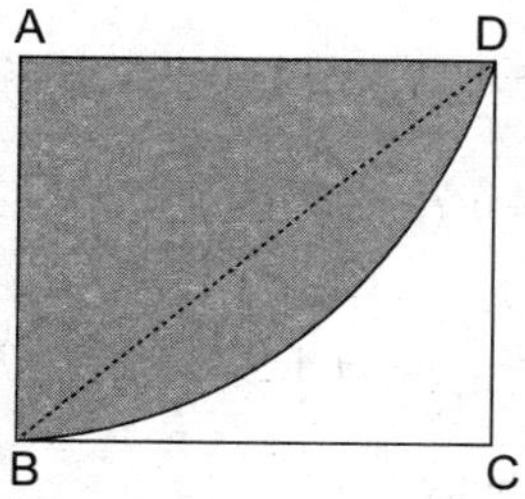

Case ii: $1 \le x \le \sqrt{2}$, the favorable area is an shown below

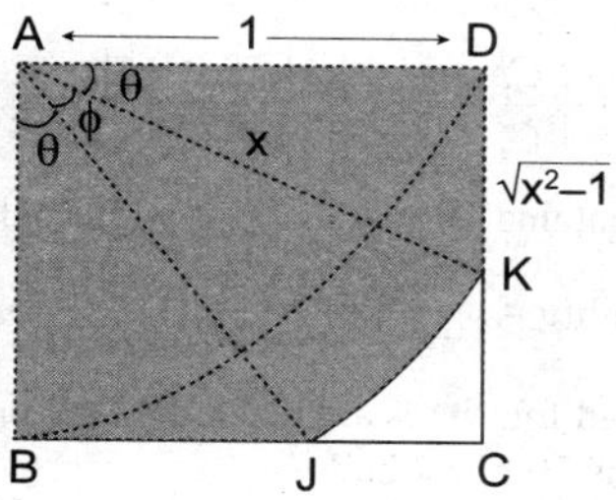

Thus the total favorable area is
ABJKDA = area of ΔAKD + area of ΔAJB + area of sector AJK .... (i)

Here $\theta = \tan^{-1}\sqrt{x^2-1}$

$$\Rightarrow \phi = \frac{\pi}{2} - 2\theta = \frac{\pi}{2} - 2\tan^{-1}\sqrt{x^2-1}$$

$\therefore$ Area of sector

$$\text{AJK} = \frac{\phi}{2\pi}.\pi x^2 = \frac{1}{2}x^2\left(\frac{\pi}{2} - 2\tan^{-1}\sqrt{x^2-1}\right)$$

$\therefore$ from (i) favorable area

$$\frac{1}{2}\sqrt{x^2-1} + \frac{\pi x^2}{4} - x^2\tan^{-1}\sqrt{x^2-1} + \frac{1}{2}\sqrt{x^2-1}$$

$$= \frac{\pi x^2}{4} - x^2\tan^{-1}\sqrt{x^2-1} + \sqrt{x^2-1}$$

$= P(E)$ as $n(S) = 1$

Passage K:

39. (c) If player gets one (1) on the first throw then he will throw the die again so total score $> 1 \Rightarrow P_1 = 0$

40. (a) $P_2 = \frac{1}{6}$ (as he can get 2 on the throw)

41. (b) Observe that when $r \ge 3$ then it can be obtained as r on first throw; or 1 on first throw and $(r-1) > 1$ on 2nd throw; or 1 on first and 2nd throw and $(r-2) > 1$ on the third throw …….. and so on.

$$\Rightarrow P(2) = \frac{1}{6};\ P(3) = P(3 \text{ or } 1,2) = \frac{1}{6} + \frac{1}{6}.\frac{1}{6};$$

$$P(4) = P(4 \text{ or } 1,3 \text{ or } 112) = \frac{1}{6} + \frac{1}{6^2} + \frac{1}{6^3}$$

i.e., $P_r = \frac{1}{6} + \frac{1}{6^2} + \ldots \frac{1}{6^{r-1}}$ for $3 \le r \le 6$

$\Rightarrow$ P_r for $2 \le r \le 6$ is given by $P_r = \frac{1}{5}\left\{1 - \left(\frac{1}{6}\right)^{r-1}\right\}$

42. (c) When $r > 6$; $P(r = 7) = P(1, 6$ or $1,1,5$ or $1,1,1,4$ or $1,1,1,1,3$ or $1,1,1,1,1,2)$ $\frac{1}{6}\times\frac{1}{6} + \frac{1}{6^3}\times\frac{1}{6^4} + \frac{1}{6^5}\times\frac{1}{6^6}$

$$= \frac{1}{6^2} + \frac{1}{6^3} + \frac{1}{6^4} + \frac{1}{6^5} + \frac{1}{6^6}$$

$P(r = 8) = P(1,1,6$ or $1,1,1,5$ or $1,1,1,1,4$ or $1,1,1,1,1,3$ or $1,1,1,1,1,1,2) = \frac{1}{6^3} + \frac{1}{6^4} + \frac{1}{6^5} + \frac{1}{6^6} + \frac{1}{6^7}$

$$= P(7 \le r) = \frac{1}{(6)^{r-5}} + \frac{1}{(6)^{r-4}} + \ldots + \frac{1}{(6)^{r-1}} = \frac{1}{(6)^{r-5}}\left[\frac{1-\left(\frac{1}{6}\right)^5}{1-\frac{1}{6}}\right]$$

$$= \frac{1}{6^{r-5}} \times \frac{6}{5}\left(\frac{6^5-1}{6^5}\right) = \frac{1}{5}\left[\left(\frac{1}{6}\right)^{r-6} - \left(\frac{1}{6}\right)^{r-1}\right]$$

43. (a) Sum of the series $\sum_{r=1}^{\infty} P_r$

$$= \sum_{r=1}^{6}\frac{1}{5}\left\{1-\left(\frac{1}{6}\right)^{r-1}\right\} + \sum_{r=7}^{\infty}\frac{1}{5}\left\{\left(\frac{1}{6}\right)^{r-6} - \left(\frac{1}{6}\right)^{r-1}\right\}$$

$$= \frac{1}{5}\left\{5 - \left(\frac{1}{6} + \frac{1}{6^2} + \frac{1}{6^3} + \frac{1}{6^4} - \frac{1}{6^5}\right)\right\}$$

$$+ \frac{1}{5}\left\{\frac{1}{6} + \frac{1}{6^2} + \frac{1}{6^3} + \frac{1}{6^4} + \frac{1}{6^5}\right\} = 1$$

Passage L:

$F : A \to B$ where Set $A = \{x_1, x_2, x_3, x_4\}$
and set $B = \{y_1, y_2, y_3, y_4\}$
Now total number of functions $= 4^4 = 256$
Number of one –one (and onto) functions $= 4! = 24$

44. (b) Since cardinal numbers of set A and set B are equal so number of onto functions and one-one functions is the same

$$\text{P(one –one function)} = \frac{24}{256} = \frac{3}{32}$$

45. (a) $P(\text{many one functions}) = 1 - \frac{3}{32} = \frac{29}{32}$

46. (b) $P(\text{on to function}) = \frac{3}{32}$

47. (a) Since into function will be many one

$$\Rightarrow P(\text{into function}) = \frac{29}{32}$$

48. (c) $P\{f(x_i) \neq y_i \text{ and f is one-one}\} = \dfrac{4!\left\{1-\frac{1}{1!}+\frac{1}{2!}-\frac{1}{3!}+\frac{1}{4!}\right\}}{256}$

$= \dfrac{12-4+1}{256} = \dfrac{9}{256}$

SECTION VII: (MATRIX MATCH TYPE)

1. (i) → (b); (ii) → (a); (iii) → (a); (iv) → (d)

(i) Three numbers a,b,c can be drawn out of 100 natural numbers in $^{100}C_3$ ways

When a,b,c are in AP then $2b = a + c$ so either a and c are both even or both are odd

⇒ E (number of favourable ways to select)

$= {}^{50}C_2 + {}^{50}C_2 = 50 \times 49$

So the required probability

$= \dfrac{50\times 49}{^{100}C_3} = \dfrac{50\times 49\times 6}{100\times 99\times 98} = \dfrac{1}{66}$

(ii) Taking the common ratio $r = 2,3,4, \ldots,10$

The number of favourable ways = 53

As (1,10,100), (1,9,81); (1,8,64), (1,7,49) (2,14, 98).....

(using) number of ways $= \sum \left[\dfrac{100}{r^2}\right]$

$= \left[\dfrac{100}{10^2}\right]+\left[\dfrac{100}{9^2}\right]+\left[\dfrac{100}{8^2}\right]+\left[\dfrac{100}{7^2}\right]+\left[\dfrac{100}{6^2}\right]+\ldots+\left[\dfrac{100}{2^2}\right]$

$= 1 + 1 + 1 + 2 + 2 + 4 + 6 + 11 + 25 = 53$

The required probability $= \dfrac{53\times 6}{100\times 99\times 98} = \dfrac{53}{161700}$

(iii) $\dfrac{1}{a},\dfrac{1}{b},\dfrac{1}{c}$ in G.P. ⇒ a,b,c are in G.P.

(iv) $(a + b + c)$ is divisible by 2 means $a + b + c$ is even which is possible as

(A) all a,b,c are even (B) Two odd and one even

$= \dfrac{^{50}C_3 + {}^{50}C_1 \times {}^{50}C_2}{^{100}C_3} = \dfrac{\frac{50\times 49\times 48}{6}+\frac{50\times 50\times 49\times 3}{6}}{\frac{100\times 99\times 98}{6}}$

$= \dfrac{50\times 49\times 48 + 50\times 50\times 49\times 3}{100\times 99\times 98} = \dfrac{50\times 49\{48+150\}}{100\times 99\times 98}$

$= \dfrac{198}{99\times 4} = \dfrac{1}{2}$

2. (i) → (b); (ii) → (a); (iii) → (c); (iv) → (b)

(i) Total number of balls = 12 balls

Possible combination:

White: 0 1 2.................12

Black: 12 11 10…….......0

Four balls are drawn at random without replacement. Let E_i denote the event that the bag contains i black balls and $(12 - i)$ white balls (where (i = 0, 1,2,3,…….,12). Let A denote the event that the four draw balls are black

$P(E_i) = \dfrac{1}{13}$ as there are 13 possible situations

Now $P\left(\dfrac{A}{E_i}\right) = 0$ (for i = 0,1,2,3)

And $P\left(\dfrac{A}{E_i}\right) = \dfrac{^iC_4}{^{12}C_4}$ for $4 \leq i \leq 12$

So total probability.

$P(A) = \dfrac{1}{13}\times\dfrac{1}{^{12}C_4}\left\{{}^4C_4 + {}^5C_4 + {}^6C_4 + \ldots + {}^{12}C_4\right\}$

$= \dfrac{1}{13}\times\dfrac{^{13}C_5}{^{12}C_4} = \dfrac{13.12.11.10.9\ (4!)}{13.12.11.10.9\ (5!)} = \dfrac{1}{5}$

(ii) Bag contains 10 black and 2 white balls then required probability $= \dfrac{^{10}C_4}{^{12}C_4} = \dfrac{10.9.8.7\ \ (4!)}{12.11.10.9(4!)} = \dfrac{14}{33}$

(iii) When all four balls are black then the probability of bag contains 10 black balls

$\dfrac{\frac{1}{13}\left\{({}^{10}C_4)/{}^{12}C_4\right\}}{\frac{1}{^{12}C_4}\times\frac{1}{13}\left\{{}^4C_4 + {}^5C_4 + {}^6C_4 + \ldots + {}^{12}C_4\right\}}$

$= \dfrac{^{10}C_4}{^{13}C_5} = \dfrac{10.9.8.7\ \ \ (5!)}{13.12.11.10.9(4!)} = \dfrac{70}{429}$

(iv) 2 balls are black & 2 are white probability

$= \dfrac{\frac{1}{13}\left\{{}^2C_2\times{}^{10}C_2 + {}^3C_2\times{}^9C_2 + {}^4C_2\times{}^8C_2 + \ldots + {}^{10}C_2\times{}^2C_2\right\}}{^{12}C_4}$

$= \dfrac{2\{5\times 9 + 3\times 36 + 6\times 28 + 10\times 21\} + 225}{13\left(\frac{12\times 11\times 10\times 9}{24}\right)}$

$= \dfrac{1287\times 24}{13\times 12\times 11\times 10\times 9} = \dfrac{1}{5}$

3. (i) → (c); (ii) → (a); (iii) → (b)

A natural number can end in 0,1,2,…,9 (i.e. unit place containing this number)

$\Rightarrow n(S) = 10^n$

(i) In the product if we want the last digit to be from 1,3,7,9 then only these numbers must be used

$\Rightarrow E = 4^n$ and $P(E) = \left(\dfrac{4}{10}\right)^n$

(ii) If we use any even number (other than zero) at least once in addition to 1,3,7,9 we will get an even product (not ending in zero or 5) $\Rightarrow E = 8^n - 4^n$

$\Rightarrow P(E) = \dfrac{8^n - 4^n}{10^n}$

(iii) The last digit will end in 5 if 5 is used at least once and only 1,3,7,9 are used $E = 5^n - 4^n$

$\Rightarrow P(E) = \dfrac{5^n - 4^n}{10^n}$